# How to Prepare for
# QUANTITATIVE
# APTITUDE
## for
# CAT

# How to Prepare for
# QUANTITATIVE APTITUDE
## for
# CAT

**Arun Sharma**

*Educational Consultant*

## McGraw Hill Education (India) Private Limited

Published by McGraw Hill Education (India) Private Limited
444/1, Sri Ekambara Naicker Industrial Estate, Alapakkam, Porur, Chennai 600 116, Tamil Nadu, India

**How to Prepare for Quantitative Aptitude for CAT, 8e**

McGraw-Hill Education (India) Private Limited

**ISBN-13: 978-93-5316-018-0**
**ISBN-10: 93-5316-018-9**

**07 08 09 10 11 RAJ 24 23 22 21 20**

Typeset at The Composers, 260, C.A. Apt., Paschim Vihar, New Delhi 110 063, and Printed and bound in India at Rajkamal Electric Press, Plot No. 2, Phase – IV, Kundli, Haryana.

Cover Design: Neeraj Dayal

Visit us at: www.mheducation.co.in; Phone (Toll free in India): **1800 103 5875**
Write to us at: info.india@mheducation.com

CIN: U80302TN2010PTC111532

*Dedicated to*

**My Father (Mr MK Sharma), Mother (Mrs Renu Sharma)
and Brother (Mr Ravi Sharma)
who have instilled in me the courage to have my convictions
and to stand by them**

# Preface to the Eighth Edition

With the evolution of CAT in its online avatar, I felt the need to create a comprehensive and updated book that caters to CAT aspirants. Any book on CAT QA should take into account the latest changes in the test pattern and nature. Hence, I have kept in mind the following facts while designing the book you now hold in your hands:

**1. Questions from this book:** Over the past decade, it has been noticed that a minimum of 10–20% questions in CAT and other major management entrance examinations have been directly taken from the questions provided in this book. Furthermore, it has been seen that between 2003 (when the book was first released) and 2018, 80–90% of the questions in CAT and other top management entrance tests were covered in this book.

CAT, having gone online, saw no change in this trend. Many questions in each of the test papers that CAT has administered in its online avatar since 2009 are covered in this book.

In fact, 2009 onwards, the onset of CAT online pattern has created a significant shift in terms of the CAT preparation process. This is because, 2009 was the first year when there were multiple CAT papers to study, analyse and base our writing and preparation process on. In subsequent years, with the increase of CAT window, the number of papers every year had gone up to around 30–40 papers. CAT in 2015, however, went back to a two-slot test and hence, had a total of only two test papers. CAT 2017, was also a significant shift point in this journey—as for the first time in the history of the Online CAT, the actual test paper was released for the students who took the exam. Thus, all said, overall I am richer by the experience of 150 plus test papers, when it comes to understanding what I need to provide to my readers for their preparation. It is on the basis of this rather rich insight that I have based the changes in this edition (Note: Similar changes have been incorporated in my other books *How to Prepare for Verbal Ability and Reading Comprehension for CAT, How to Prepare for Data Interpretation for CAT,* and *How to Prepare for Logical Reasoning for CAT)* as also in the *Previous Years' Solved* CAT Papers book.

**2. CAT 2015, a watershed year for CAT:** Looking rationally into the patterns of the 150 plus CAT papers, we have had the good fortune of being able to track and analyse, that while things have remained the same in a lot of ways, they have also drastically changed during this period. In this context, we found that the changes in the exam introduced in CAT 2015 are significant, as they drastically alter the process of preparation for this exam. The trend introduced in CAT 2015 was just carried on and continued in CAT 2016 and CAT 2017. Hence, there is a lot to learn for us—from the analysis of these tests.

So am I contradicting myself here by saying that the exam has remained the same and at the same time has changed drastically? Not at all! When I say that the exam has remained the same in the online avatar, what I mean to say is that there are no changes in the patterns, the quality, the difficulty and the portion of coverage of questions asked in Quantitative Aptitude in CAT.

However, some of the noticeable changes seen in CAT 2015 to CAT 2017 that significantly alter the way you should study are:

**(a) 3-section mode of the examination:** Quantitative Aptitude, Verbal Ability and Reading Comprehension, Data Interpretation and Logical Reasoning being the three separate sections, you would need to display competence in each of the three areas of the exam in order to get a good percentile. This was a departure from the previous two section exam pattern (as of CAT 2013-2014), with Section 1: Quantitative Aptitude and Data Interpretation and Section 2: Verbal

Ability/Reading Comprehension and Logical Reasoning. So this is a significant change in terms of preparation strategies; for instance, the two-section exam pattern which allowed the aspirant to take a strategy of doing well in the Logical Reasoning questions in Section 2 and hence get through that section without being too good at Verbal Ability/Reading Comprehension. Likewise, aspirants could get through Section 1, by being really good at DI and moderately skilled in Quantitative Aptitude. The three-section exam does not provide the aspirant with that luxury any longer. An aspirant has to develop his skills in each of the areas of the exam and can no longer work on a selective skills development approach.

(b) **Introduction of questions having no options:** CAT 2015, CAT 2016 and CAT 2017 have on average had as many as 30+ questions out of 100 with no options. The presence of such a large number of questions without options clearly meant that students were tested for the clarity of their concepts in each area — especially in the QA section. Since this trend is supposed to continue, it is quite clear that you would need to know the exact answer for every question that you are trying to solve — gone are the days where an 'educated' guess would take you through a few questions in the exam.

However, you need to understand an important point in this context that the QA section is not a test of your mathematical knowledge. A closer look at the kind of questions (in which no options are given) reveals that these are pretty much solvable using simple numeric logic rather than using hard-core mathematical process and formula. There was not a single question in this category that forced you to follow the hard-core mathematical way, of solving such questions.

3. **The need for greater variety in your preparation:** Prior to the CAT going online, preparing for QA used to be a battle for Blocks 1, 4, 5 and 6. Even out of these, if someone did Blocks I and V well, he stood a strong chance at the QA section, since over 60% of the questions asked in the papers were from these areas.

However, as explained below, the latest changes of this exam requires the aspirant to be much more balanced in the context of portion coverage.

As per the scheme followed in this book, the QA portion can be divided into six major parts (or blocks as I call them in this book).

The underlying constant that used to exist in the paper-and-pen version (through the entire decade prior to the first online CAT) was the prominence of Block I and Block V. (Block I comprising Number Systems and Progressions and Block V comprising the chapters on Functions, Inequalities, Quadratic and other Equations and Logarithms.)

In each of the years from 1999 to 2008, the QA section required you to get a net score of approximately 30 – 40% of the total marks in order to score a high 90 percentile in this section.

In the light of this fact, the importance of Block I and Block V can be gauged from the table below:

| Block | Weightage (as a % of total marks) |
| --- | --- |
| Block I | 30 – 50% |
| Block V | 15 – 50% |
| Combined weightage of Blocks I & V | 60 – 80% |

Add to this, the chapter on Time, Speed and Distance with a minimum weightage of 5–10% and you pretty much had the QA section well covered. In a nutshell, QA for CAT preparation had become "do 10 chapters well".

However, this scenario has changed in the context of the online version of the exam.

The balance of weightage of questions shifted and each of the six blocks have become important. The aspirant of CAT online version saw a weightage distribution of the kind illustrated below.

| Block | Total Out of 34 Questions |
| --- | --- |
| Block I | 6 – 8 questions |
| Blocks II & III | 6 – 9 questions |
| Block IV | 5 – 8 questions |
| Block V | 5 – 9 questions |
| Block VI | 2 – 5 questions |

4. **Qualifying scores and attempts required at various accuracy levels:** In the current context of the CAT, you need to be able to solve around 23–25 (out of 34) questions at 100 percent accuracy to reach a 99.8+ percentile in the exam. Naturally, at 90–95% accuracy, this number would be around 30+ attempts. The following table would give you a clear idea about your targets based on the percentile you are targeting in the QA section.

| To score | Number of attempts required at 100% accuracy | Number of attempts required at 90–95% accuracy |
|---|---|---|
| 99.8+ percentile | 23–25 | 30+ |
| 99 percentile | 20–22 | 28–30 |
| 98 percentile | 19–20 | 24–27 |
| 95 percentile | 17+ | 22–24 |
| 90 percentile | 14+ | 20–22 |
| 80 percentile | 12+ | 16–20 |

**5. Accuracy is more important than speed:**   This is a clear trend indication if you look at the scoring patterns at various percentiles. A student solving questions with 100% accuracy requires only 23–25 attempts to get a top 400 All India Rank in the test (99.8+ percentile). However, if your accuracy drops by just 5% to 95%, your attempts need to go up to 30+ to ensure the same score. What this means, is that if your accuracy is just 5% off the 100% accuracy level, you would almost completely lose the choice of skipping questions. A student solving between 23–25 questions at 100 percent accuracy, can skip 9–11 questions out of 34, while at 95% accuracy since the same percentile would require 30+ attempts, such a student would practically have no leeway to leave questions.

Hence, the key learning for you while preparing is to focus on improving your accuracy as well as the belief in your process of solving. This is especially true while preparing for the QA section. While solving a QA question, you should be able to know that if your process is correct then your answer would also be correct. The need to check the answer to a QA question is something that is only required for minds weak in Quantitative Aptitude. This is where an under-prepared aspirant loses out to the best—in the knowledge of whether what they are solving is correct or not.

Unfortunately, most students I see are more interested in seeing the answer to the question as soon as they solve the same.

This is a habit I would strongly discourage you from. The ideal preparation process for you should be:

(a)  solve the question,

(b)  review your process and tell yourself, "if your process is correct, so is your answer", and

(c)  only check your answer after you have reviewed your process.

This is important, because when you are solving a QA question inside CAT, you would not have the cushion to 'look' at the answer. The only thing you have is the question and the process you use in solving the same. Your mind should be able to tell you whether the answer you have got is correct or not. This is a key difference in solving questions in practise and solving them under exam pressure.

Hence, developing more confidence in your QA problem-solving processes becomes a key ingredient and objective of your preparation process for this section.

**6. Tougher level of CAT exam:**   As already stated above, the quality of questions asked in the CAT over the past couple of years has become extremely good—requiring an upgradation of your grasp of concepts and understanding of each particular topic to a level not required before. This shift has necessitated that we do more through this book.

**7.** I have also come to know that many readers use this book for their preparation of other important management entrance exams (like XAT, IIFT, CMAT, MAT, SNAP, etc.). So now, I have also included/modified the contents so that aspirants of the above exams need not look for any other resource beyond this book for strengthening their hold on the quantitative aptitude section.

Apart from management entrance examinations, the book also has relevance for aspirants of UPSC and state civil services, Bank PO exams, GATE, engineering placement exams, etc. In short, the scope of this book has considerably widened to cover the entire subject of quantitative aptitude that finds a resonance for all career aspirants.

The book you now hold in your hand has always been written keeping in mind the avowed objective of developing your quantitative intelligence to a point where you can quickly scale the height of preparation in each chapter of the portion.

*Key features:*

1. **Comprehensive solutions** (wherever relevant) to questions in all LODs of all chapters.
2. Based on an assessment of any logic I have missed in any chapter, I have introduced extra questions for readers in the form of **additional block-wise practice tests**. The questions in these tests have been carefully selected to ensure that I do not miss out on any probable question type.
3. In some chapters, where I felt that there is some deficiency in the number and variety of questions (due to the increased difficulty level of the CAT) based on the concepts of the chapter, I have **introduced new questions into the LODs** of the chapter.

4. At some places, the need was felt to introduce an entire additional exercise on concepts of a chapter. This too has been accomplished in this revision.

5. **The training ground**: Perhaps the biggest differentiator in this book is the introduction of the 'Training Ground'— which is an area through which I teach the readers real time higher-end problem solving. The training ground is a section where I tell you exactly how to think inside the examination hall when faced with questions of varying difficulty levels. Hence, a must read for all management aspirants.

**Logic of the Training Ground**

The quality of the questions in the Quantitative Aptitude section (especially in CAT and XAT) is of such a high quality level that even if you know the basics of each chapter within a particular block, it might not be enough to reach a point where you might be able to solve the questions from the chapter/block. In order to have a grip on any chapter/block and be able to handle application-based questions in the actual examination, you would need to raise your level of thinking and ideation in that chapter/block to the point where you are able to tackle any twists and turns that can be thrown up by it.

For this edition, the training ground has been introduced into four of the major blocks of chapters of this book — and you can expect a very extensive training ground section especially for Block V and Block VI. (Block V covers the chapters on Functions, Inequalities, Logs and Quadratic and Other Equations, while Block VI covers the chapters on Permutations and Combinations, Probability and Set Theory).

6. Introduction of a critical section within each block called 'Taste of the Exams' that covers the questions asked in the CAT, IIFT and XAT (the three major MBA entrance exams) for the last two decades. What's more, these sections are completely solved, with illustrative thought processes as well as thought short cuts that you would not find in any other book of this type.

7. Introduction of questions without options in each of the relevant chapters of the book. This is in keeping with the latest trends introduced in the last CAT examination.

8. Completely revamped question banks at Level of Difficulty 1 and Level of Difficulty 2 for many chapters. We felt the need to update the chapter LODs in various critical chapters, based on the latest trends in the exam.

The book is now totally in sync with the new trend and pattern of the examination.

Ultimately the endeavour is to provide a one-stop solution for CAT and MBA exam aspirants to tackle the QA section of all major management entrance exams—an endeavour I feel I have managed to do pretty well.

Through this book, I am confident of giving you—the reader—an invaluable resource for enhancing your QA section score drastically. Contained in this book is the very best advisory for each and every question type. Your job is simple—to ensure that you follow the process contained in this advisory.

## ◈ KEY POINTS FOR YOUR PREPARATION

### Outline and Strategy

The first aspect I would like to deal with here is to focus on helping you with the formulation of your strategy with respect to the portion to be covered for the Quantitative Aptitude section of the various management entrance exams including CAT, XAT, CMAT, IIFT, MHCET and other examinations.

Let us start by trying to understand some of the key areas in Quantitative Aptitude (QA).

### Tackling each portion

My experience shows that very often students look at the vast number of chapters and concepts to be studied for QA and get disheartened. This is especially true for students who do not have a strong traditional background in Mathematics. Indeed if you were to look at it with a chapter-wise approach, you can easily define the course to be studied by dividing it into 20+ chapters— preparation for which is such a long-drawn effort that it ends up draining the student's energy, enthusiasm and motivation.

It is in this context and for this precise reason that I have divided this book into six manageable blocks—the approach being rationalising the chapters and grouping them according to the amount of shared concepts these chapters have amongst each other.

The outline as defined in the contents to this book would divide your work into six major areas to prepare for. For your convenience and strategising I have put down the relative importance of each of these six blocks into perspective:

***Block I:*** Number Systems and Progressions

*Importance:*   **Very High** for CAT, XAT, IIFT, FMS and **High** for MAT, CMAT, SNAP, IRMA, etc.

**Block II:**   Averages and Alligations

*Importance:*   **Low** for QA in CAT, XAT, IIFT, but **High** for Data Interpretation as a lot of questions in DI are based on the concepts of averages and alligations. Also, **High** for MAT, CMAT, IRMA, NMIMS, etc.

**Block III:**   Percentages, Ratio, Proportion and Variation, Time and Work, Time, Speed and Distance. (Subsidiary but almost redundant chapters in this block — Interest and Profit & Loss)

*Importance:*   **Moderate to High** for QA in CAT, XAT, IIFT, and **Very High** for Data Interpretation (DI) as DI is almost entirely based on the concept of Percentages and Ratio and Proportions. **Very High** for MAT, CMAT, IRMA, NMIMS, etc.

---

**Note:**   *The chapter on "Time, Speed and Distance" is extremely important for these exams (especially for the CAT as this chapter has been a constant presence in the CAT for the last two decades.)*

---

**Block IV:**   Geometry, Mensuration and Coordinate Geometry

*Importance:*   **Very High** for CAT, XAT. **Average** for MAT, CMAT, SNAP, IRMA, IIFT, etc.

**Block V:**   Functions, Inequalities, Logs and Quadratic Equations

*Importance:*   **Very High** for CAT, XAT. **Low** for MAT, CMAT, IRMA, NMIMS, etc.

**Block VI:**   Permutations and Combinations, Probability and Set Theory

*Importance:*   **Very High** for CAT, XAT, IIFT, etc. **Average** for MAT, CMAT, IRMA, etc.

Based on the experience of the online CAT, the strategic preparation imperative for you should be to do at least four blocks and if possible up to six blocks really well.

What does it mean to prepare a block "really well"? This is something I feel needs emphasis here.

Well what I mean to say is that do not just focus on studying the theory in each of these areas but develop an intuitive knowledge of all problem scenarios which emerge out of each block.

Only then would you be able to reach a situation in the exam—that when the question presents itself to you in the exam—you would have had the logic for the same worked out before hand. This is something that can make a huge difference to your chances in CAT.

## Analysing Your Knowledge Level

The first thing you need to focus on is an analysis of your knowledge level in each of these seven parts. In each of the above areas, first analyse your level of knowledge/ability. In order to do so the typical question you should ask yourself is: For the next 100 questions I face in each of these areas, how many would I be able to handle comfortably?

Think of a number as an answer to this question for each of the six blocks.

Based on your answer, the following analysis would provide you a thumb rule which would tell you how much of a knowledge issue you have:

1. 90+: You know pretty much every question type and variant in the area. You should focus your energies on other aspects rather than knowledge improvement in the area.
2. 80+: Maybe you need to increase your exposure to questions a little bit; around 200–300 more questions in that area would be sufficient.
3. 60–80+: You have a significant knowledge issue in the area. You might need to go back to the basics, but it is less likely to be a theory issue but more of an exposure to questions issue.
4. <60: You need to work on both theory and exposure to questions.

Needless to say, the target and objective for preparations has to be to reach the 90+ range as explained above in any block you intend to do "really well".

## Looking beyond Ability (Quick Reflexes)

A common frustrating experience for test-takers while taking the test is to not being able to solve a known question/logic and subsequently, not being able to score marks in questions which they knew.

In order to handle this problem, you would need to work on your reactions and reflexes when faced with QA questions. Once you have solved your knowledge/ability issue in a particular block, your next step is to improve your reactions and reflexes while solving a question. Needless to say you would need to do this block wise.

So obviously the main issue is how to improve reflexes and reactions.

(a) For every block, once you have solved the LODs and the Pre-assessment/Review tests, the most crucial exercise in this context would be a comprehensive revision and review of each and every question you have solved in that block. Solve every question of every LOD and Pre-assessment/Review test again and review the logic/process of problem solving used. This need to be done to the point where you almost "recollect" the logic of the question and are able to recognise the same if it is used again in a different context/problem.

(b) A thorough revision on the theory of the block.

## 1. Improve your ability to select what you know and leave what you do not

In the context of an examination where the required scores for 99 percentile would be 60–70% attempts with 100% accuracy, it is easy to see that perfect knowledge is perhaps not needed in order to crack CAT. Hence, even if you have around 60–70% knowledge of the questions in an average test, you are perhaps good enough to crack the exam. A good way to test whether you have sufficient knowledge would be to pick up 10–20 test papers and divide your QA section into blocks of five questions each. Then test your knowledge by looking at the average number of questions you know. If on an average for every five QA test questions that you pick up, if you know more than three, then the prognosis would be that you have adequate knowledge for cracking CAT. Thus, while you may want to move towards knowing 5 out of 5 in this context, there are other things that you should focus on—developing your ability to decide on whether you are going to be able to solve a question while reading it for the first time. This would help you stop *fishing* during the test. (*Fishing* can be described as the activity of trying to solve a question without knowing whether you would actually complete the question.)

Your mind should give you a clear indication of whether you would be able to do the last step in a question, before you start doing it. In that sense you should be able to clearly define three types of outcomes when you finish reading a question for the first time:

(a) **I see a clear flowchart** and the steps are manageable—Obviously you need to go on and solve these questions.

(b) **I see a clear flowchart** but the steps are too lengthy—In this case, you need to see where you stand in your test-time and attempt-wise.

(c) **I do not see a clear flowchart but I can try as I see a starting point**—This is potentially the most dangerous situation for you in the duration of the test, as once you get sucked into a question, there is a strong tendency to lose track of the time you are using up while trying the question. My advice is that while taking the test, you should not even start doing such questions.

(d) **I see no flowchart and no starting point to the question**—Obviously you should leave such questions and in fact if these are limited to around 20–30% of the paper there is no problem and you need not worry about them.

## 2. Focus on thorough knowledge of 'problem scenarios' rather than theoretical learning

To illustrate this, I would like to start with a few examples.

Consider the following string of three questions. Before I come to my main point here, I would like you to start by solving these questions before looking at the explanations provided:

1. A boy starts adding consecutive natural numbers starting from 1. After some time, he reaches a total of 1000 when he realises that he has double counted a number. Find the number double counted.
2. A boy starts adding consecutive natural numbers starting from 1. He reaches a total of 575 when he realises that he has missed a number. What can be said about the number missed?
3. Find the 288th term of the series: ABBCCCDDDDEEEEEFFFFFFG....

*We can now start to look at each of these questions:*

1. Consider the fact that when you add numbers as stated above $(1 + 2 + 3 + 4 + ......)$ the result is known as a triangular number. Hence, numbers like $1, 1 + 2 = 3, 1 + 2 + 3 = 6$ and so on are triangular numbers. This question asks us to consider the possibility of making the mistake of double counting a number. So instead of $1 + 2 + 3 + 4$ if you were to do by error $1 + 2 + 3 + 3 + 4$, you would realise that the number you would get would be 13 which would be more than 10 (which should have been your correct addition) and less than 15 (the sum of 1 to 5) which is the next triangular number. The double counted value could be achieved by spotting 10 as the immediately lower value—and the difference between 10 and 13 would give you the required double counted number.

   To carry forward this logic into the given question, we should realise that we are just bothered about finding the last triangular number below 1000, and in trying to work this out is where we really apply our intelligence.

   Before one writes about that though, one fully realises that a lot of readers (especially aspirants with an engineering background) at this point are thinking about $n \times (n + 1)/2$. Knowing that process, one chooses to write about the alternate way to think about in this question.

$$1 + 2 + 3 + 4 ... + 10 = 55$$

Hence, we can easily see that $11 + 12 + 13 + 14 + 15 + ... + 20$ would equal 155 and the sum of 21 to 30 would equal 255 and so on.

Thus, in trying to find the last triangular number below 1000 we can just do: $55 + 155 + 255 + 355 = 820$ (which is the sum of the first 40 natural numbers) and since we have still not reached close to 1000, we start by adding more numbers as: $820 + 41 + 42 + 43 + 44 = 990$ and the difference between 990 and 1000 is 10 which is the required answer.

2. For this question, we would just need to carry the learning from the previous question forward and realise that when we miss a number, we actually get a total which is lower than the correct total. Hence, if we want to find the number missed, all we need to do is to find the first triangular number greater than 575. This can be got simply by, $55 + 155 + 255 + 31 + 32 + 33 + 34 = 595$, so the number missed has to be 20.

3. In this question all you would need to notice is that in the series ABBCCCDDDDEEEEEF... A ends after the first term; B ends after the third (1+2) term; C ends after the sixth (1+2+3) term and so on. So we can infer that what we are looking at is how many numbers need to be added before we get to a number just below 288. So $55 + 155 + 21 + 22 + 23$ gives us 276 which pretty much means that the 24th alphabet (i.e., $x$) would be running in this series when we reach the 288th term.

So looking at the three questions above and the solutions, one wants the reader to only answer one specific question:

How much does knowing the first question and developing your thought ability and your intelligence help you in solving the second and the third one? I hope you see the connection. For your information, the three questions presented above were asked in CAT 2001, CAT 2002 and CAT 2003!!! And such questions are pretty much standard in the years of the online CAT.

## CONCLUDING NOTE

You sit in front of your CAT question paper and the first question comes in front of you; if you have identified the logic of the question or seen the question itself earlier, your entire QA preparation is fructified. In fact, every question/logic (that you would face in your test) which you have seen earlier represents a triumph of your preparation process. It is for this very reaction that you prepare for an aptitude exam like CAT. Any other preparation is quite worthless.

Your battle for CAT would be won if you get a "YES I KNOW THIS PATTERN/LOGIC" reaction to 50–60% of the questions in your test.

Contained in this book is the finest collection of questions which you would hope to find anywhere. Remember, each question solved needs to be a learning experience—one that is to be kept in your mind for future problem solving. Adopt this approach with the problems contained in this book and I am quite confident that you would KNOW over 70% of your actual CAT test paper since you have already solved something like that before!!

**All The BEST !!!!!!**

**Arun Sharma**

# Preface to the First Edition

Over the last few years, as a trainer of CAT and other aptitude tests, I have felt the need for a comprehensive book on the subject. Students appearing for the CAT and other aptitude tests usually struggle for appropriate study material to prepare for this vital section of the examination.

This book comes as a humble attempt to fulfil this gap.

## Structure of the book

The book is divided into 19 chapters and five test papers. Each chapter is divided into three broad parts:

  (a) Theory
  (b) Solved examples
  (c) Chapter end exercises (LODs I, II & III), with answer key

The questions in the chapter end exercises have been categorised into three levels of difficulty, viz, Level of Difficulty I, Level of Difficulty II and Level of Difficulty III.

**Level of Difficulty I (LOD I):**   These are the basic types of questions pertaining to the chapter. A majority of the MBA entrance tests would test the student with LOD I questions. Tests which ask LOD I questions include MAT, IMT, IRMA, IIFT, NIFT, CET Maharashtra, Bank PO examinations, BBA, BCA, Law, and so on. Besides, there are about 10 questions of LOD I type in the CAT nowadays.

**Level of Difficulty II (LOD II):**   These are questions, which are more advanced than the LOD I questions. These questions test all basic as well as applied concepts in the chapter. *LOD II questions are closest to the difficulty levels of the CAT.* Hence, the objective of LOD II questions should be to:

  (a) Clearly understand the concept which underlies the question.
  (b) Create a judgment of time required for different mental processes.
  (c) Identify the time guzzlers.
  (d) Reinforce application of a method in mental processes through the question.
  (e) Learn to flowchart complex questions.

**Level of Difficulty III (LOD III):**   LOD III questions build on the previous questions and are a step beyond the LOD II questions. Although they are also normally more difficult than the average CAT question, approximately 5–10 LOD III questions could be asked in the CAT every year. Hence, the learning objectives at LOD III are to:

  (a) Learn applications of the basic concepts at the highest level.
  (b) Sharpen the flowcharting skills learnt at LOD II.
  (c) Use each question as a learning opportunity.

One should not be disheartened if he/she is unable to solve LOD III questions. These questions are extremely tough and uncommon in the CAT and other aptitude tests. Questions in actual tests will appear very simple and elementary if one can solve LOD III questions.

## Approach Taken in Writing This Book

In my experience, the 'math skill' of students appearing for CAT can be classified into three levels:

Level 1: Students who are weak at Mathematics
Level 2: Students who are average at Mathematics
Level 3: Students who are strong at Mathematics

This book has been written keeping in mind all the three kinds of students.

From my experience I have given below my perspective of what one should aim for (based on the category that he/she belongs to). It is important to clearly understand the starting level and accordingly define strategy for the QA section.

**Level 1: Students who are weak at mathematics:** Typically, these are students who were weak at mathematics in school and/or have left mathematics after their 10th or 12th class. They face a mental block in mathematics and have problems in writing equations. They also have severe problems in understanding mathematical language and are unable to convert the mathematical language into mathematical equations. They make mistakes even in interpretation of the most basic statements in mathematics (leave alone the complex statements). Besides, these students also have problems in solving equations. They suffer from the insecurity of knowing that they are unable to solve most problems which they face.

**Level 2: Students who are average at mathematics:** These students lie between the Level 1 and Level 3 students.

**Level 3: Students who are strong at mathematics:** These are the students who have got strong, structured and logical thinking ability. They not only understand the basic repetitive statements in mathematics but also complex statements. They are able to create their own flowcharts to arrive at solutions of these complex mathematical situations.

There are two alternative approaches that a student can take in solving this book.

**Approach 1:** "Start with basic concepts, solved examples then move on to LOD I, then LOD II in the chapter. Do not go into LOD III in the chapter in the first go. Complete all 19 chapters and then re-start with Chapter 1 — review the basic concepts, resolve LOD I and LOD II, then move on to LOD III. This approach is advocated for students who are weak to average in mathematics (i.e., students of Level 1 and Level 2).

After completing the theory and practice exercises of the book for a second time, go to the practice sets 1–5 provided at the end of book. Set a time limit of 40 minutes for each set and take the tests. The questions contained in the sets are questions which have appeared in the CAT over the last 5 years (based on memory)."

**Approach 2:** "Start with the basic concepts, solved examples and then go through the exercises of LOD I, LOD II and LOD III. This is recommended for students who have strong concepts in mathematics (Level 3 students)."

Then go to the 5 practice tests given at the end of the book and take them one by one (time limit of 40 minutes for each test)."

**An Important Point**
Each of the questions contained in the LOD I, LOD II and LOD III exercises in the chapters have immense learning value. Hence, the approach that one takes while solving the questions should be one of learning. The reader should try to clearly understand the interpretation of each sentence used in the construction of the questions.

In other words the learning in every chapter should not be restricted to the solved examples or the theory contained in the chapter, but should continue through each of the questions contained in the exercises.

In conclusion, this is a book which is unique in approach and coverage. Any CAT aspirant who goes through the questions contained in this book in the manner advised in this book would get a distinct advantage when he/she faces the CAT.

**Arun Sharma**

# Acknowledgements

The text and questions contained in this book are the manifestation of a learning process that began for me over 23 years ago. During the intervening period, I have come across some wonderful people in the form of relatives, friends or acquaintances from whom I have learnt immensely. While it is not possible to name them individually, I would like to express a deep sense of gratitude towards them.

I would also like to express my heartfelt thanks to my wonderful students due to whom I have had a wonderful opportunity to live a highly fulfilled life. This book would not have been possible in the absence of this opportunity. This work would not have been possible without the support and encouragement from McGraw Hill Education, India. My sincere thanks and words of appreciation to the team. I would like to make specific mention of Tanmoy Roychowdhury, Shukti Mukherjee and the entire team at McGraw-Hill Education. A special word of thanks to Atul Gupta, whose untiring work was a strong support in helping me bring out a higher quality product in the eighth edition.

I would also like to thank my colleagues who have supported me through thick and thin during the last few years. These include my colleagues at Mindworkzz - Mr Arun Chaturvedi, Lokesh Agarwal, Rajeshwar Tiwari, Saeed Khan, Abhinandan Kumar Sarkar, Tanisha Narang, Renu Rai, Mukul Garg, Sanjeeta Khattar, Yogita Kapoor, Priyanca Verma, Kavita Jindal, Aanchal Sharma, Jyoti Bisht, Shyam Kumar, Prakash Purti, Harhsit Chaudhary, Deendayal, Deepak Sahani, Sanjay, Rohit Singh Bundela, Suresh Singh and Manish Chauhan. Besides, a special mention of thanks to Sudhir Shrivastava who has worked as hard as me (if not harder) on this book. This book would not have been possible but for his technical inputs and unyielding efforts.

My mind also gets reminded of the multitude of people who have worked on the previous editions of this book – and I would like to mention a special word of thanks and appreciation to each of them.

No amount of thanks can ever repay the great debt that I owe to my wife, Meenakshi, who has provided me with the constant inspiration over the past few years. In fact, this book would not have been possible but for the direct and indirect support, inspiration and guidance from Meenakshi who has been a constant partner in all my efforts over the past years. Last but not the least, a special mention of my son, Shaurya, bringing whom up over the past few years has helped me transform myself as an individual and who has also now started to contribute significantly to my writing efforts.

**Arun Sharma**

# Contents

## First Things First  Developing Your Calculations    FTF.1–FTF.17

## Block I  Numbers    I.1–I.158

**Block III   Arithmetic and Word-based Problems          III.1–III.230**

## 11. GEOMETRY AND MENSURATION IV.7

## 12. COORDINATE GEOMETRY IV.105

## TASTE OF THE EXAMS—BLOCK IV IV.130

## Block V  Algebra V.1–V.158

## 13. FUNCTIONS V.9

---

## On Book's OLC (Online Learning Center)

**MOCK TEST PAPERS 1–3**
**MODEL TEST PAPER**
**SOLVED PAPERS**
   IIFT 2013
   SNAP 2011
   XAT 2014

# Developing Your Calculations

**FIRST THINGS FIRST**

Developing your ability to calculate well should be one of your major thrust areas for your preparation strategy for Quantitative Aptitude. In fact, most of the times (in most coaching programs and books) this area is totally bypassed leaving the student broadly to develop his/her own methods to calculate faster. Needless to say, your work in trying to develop your ability to calculate would always be greatly superior if you are guided properly with approaches that have been tested and have stood the test of time. The following advisory contained in this special section of the book not just aims to give you the best advice for each and every type of calculation, but also gives you a comprehensive plan to develop your calculation speed—for every conceivable type of calculation.

My focus throughout this special note on calculations is to help you to develop the relevant calculations only, viz., calculations that you are likely to encounter inside the CAT based on the experiences of the past CAT examinations. For this purpose this section has been divided into the following chapters:

**Chapter 1: ADDITIONS and SUBTRACTIONS** Ideas for developing your ability to add & subtract well;

**Chapter 2: MULTIPLICATIONS** Ideas for developing your ability to multiply well;

**Chapter 3: DIVISIONS, PERCENTAGE CALCULATIONS and RATIO COMPARISONS** Ideas for developing your ability to divide well as well as to compare ratios more efficiently;

**Chapter 4: SQUARES and CUBES of NUMBERS**

*Chapter 1* – **Additions and Subtractions (As an Extension of Additions)**

*Chapter 2* – **Multiplications**

*Chapter 3* – **Divisions, Percentage Calculations and Ratio Comparisons**

*Chapter 4* – **Squares and Cubes of Numbers**

This special section contains the best available approaches for all kind of calculations that you are likely to face in the CAT or any other aptitude examination...

# CHAPTER 1

# Additions and Subtractions (As an Extension of Additions)

## IDEAS FOR ADDING AND SUBTRACTING WELL

Addition is perhaps the most critical skill when it comes to developing your calculations. As you would see through the discussions in the remaining chapters of this section of the book, if you have the ability to add well you would be able to handle all the other kinds of calculations with consummate ease.

*Skill 1 for addition:* The ability to react with the addition of two numbers when you see them.

The first and foremost skill in the development of your addition abilities is the ability to react to 2 two digit numbers when you come across them. You simply have to develop the ability to react with their totals whenever you come across 2 two digit numbers.

For instance, suppose I were to give you two numbers at random—5, 7 and ask you to **STOP!! STOP YOUR MIND BEFORE IT GIVES YOU THE SUM OF THESE TWO NUMBERS!!** What happened? Were you able to stop your mind from saying 12? No! of course not you would say.

TRY AGAIN: 12 + 7 STOP YOUR MIND!! You could not do it again!!

TRY AGAIN: 15+12 STOP!! Could not?

TRY AGAIN: 88+ 73 = ?? STOP!! If you belong to the normal category of what I call "addition disabled aspirants" you did not even start, did you?

TRY AGAIN: 57 + 95 =??

TRY AGAIN: 78+88 =??

What went wrong? You are not used to such big numbers, you would say. Well, if you are serious about your ability to crack aptitude exams, you better make this start to happen in your mind. You would know what I mean if you just try to look at a 5 year old child who has just learnt to add, struggle with a calculation like 12 + 7 on his fingers or his abacus.

His struggle with something like 12 + 7 or even 15 + 12 would be akin to the average aspirant's ability to react

to 88+ 78. However, just as you know 15 + 12 is not a special skill so also 88+78 is not a special skill. It is just a function of how much you practice your calculations especially in the domain of 2 digit additions.

So what am I trying to tell you here?

All I am trying to communicate to you is to tell you to work on developing your ability to react to 2 two digit numbers with their addition as soon as these numbers hit your mind. What I am trying to tell you that the moment you make your mind adept at saying something like 74 + 87 = 161 just the way you would do 9 + 6 =15 you would have made a significant movement in your mind's ability to crack aptitude exams.

Why do I say that—you might be justified in asking me at this point of time? In order to answer your question I would like to present the following argument to you:

In numerical questions, a normal student/aspirant would be roughly calculating for approximately 50% of the time that he/she takes to solve a question. This means that half the total time that you would spend in solving questions of Quantitative Aptitude or data interpretation would essentially go into calculations.

Thus, in the current pattern of the CAT, where you solve QA for 60 minutes and DI for 30 minutes approximately, out of the total 90 minutes solving numerical questions, you would use close to 40-45 minutes calculating—if your calculating ability is similar to most average CAT aspirants.

So, the contention is this: If you can improve your calculation speed to 5 times your current calculation speed, the calculations you would be doing in 40 to 45 minutes currently, would get done in 8 to 9 minutes—giving you a whopping 32 to 36 minutes extra inside the exam. In an exam like the CAT (or for that matter any other parallel aptitude exam you might be preparing for), an extra 30 minutes converts straight to extra questions solved—and hence extra marks. On a conservative estimate, if you are in the category of students who are attempting 15-20 questions in one hour in the QA section, you are solving one question in 3-4 minutes. In this context, an extra 30 minutes available in the exam, would straight away convert to an extra

8-10 attempts—the difference between an 85 and a 95 percentile in the exam!

Addition being the mother of all calculations has the potential of giving you the extra edge you require to dominate this all important examination.

Over the next few chapters in this section of the book, all I am going to show you is how knowing additions well would have an impact on each and every calculation type that you might encounter in this exam and indeed for all aptitude tests. However, before we go that far you need to develop your ability to add well.

Let us look at the simple calculation of 78 + 88. For eternity you have been constrained to doing this as follows using the carry over method:

$$\begin{array}{r} 1\phantom{0} \\ 7\ 8 \\ +\ 8\ 6 \\ \hline 1\ 6\ 4 \end{array}$$

The problem with this thought is that no matter how many times you practice this process you would still be required to write it down. The other option of doing this same addition is to think on the number line as this:

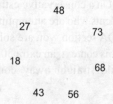

78 + 86 – how to think of this addition problem

As you can see, the above thinking in an addition situation requires no carry over and after some practice would require no writing at all. It is just an extension of how you are able to naturally react to 5+11 so also you can train your mind to react to 58+63 and react with a two step thought (as 61 → 121—with practice this can be done inside a fraction of a second. It is just a matter of how much you are willing to push your mind for this). Once you can do that your next target is to be able to add multiple 2 digit numbers written randomly on a single page:

**Try this: Add the following**

$$48$$
$$27 \qquad\qquad 73$$
$$18 \qquad\qquad\qquad 68$$
$$43 \qquad 56$$

In order to do this addition your thinking should go like this:

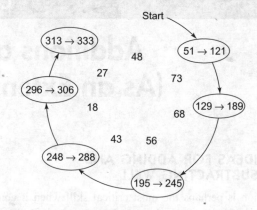

Alternately you may also do this the other way. The result would be quite the same:

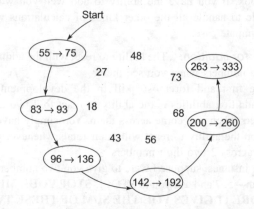

While you are trying to work on this addition you would realize the following about your abilities to add (if you belong to the normal category of aspirants')

1. Something like 121 + 68 would be easier than 189 + 56 because the latter requires you to shift hundreds—something that the former does not require you to do.
2. Something like 48 + 27 would be easier for you to do initially than 136 + 56; and 136 + 56 would be easier than 543 + 48 because your mind would be more comfortable with smaller numbers than you would be with larger numbers.

However as you start practicing your additions, these additions would become automatic for your mind—as they would then fall into the range where your mind can react with the answers. That is the point to which we would want you to target your skill levels for additions.

To put it in other terms, you would need to work on your additions in such a way that 10 numbers written around a circle (as shown above) should be done in around 10-12 seconds in your mind.

Till the time your addition skill levels reach that point, I would want you to work aggressively on your addition ability.

The following 10 × 10 table done at least once daily might be a good way to work on your additions:

| | 59 | 68 | 77 | 96 | 84 | 32 | 17 | 69 | 81 | 38 | TOTALS |
|---|---|---|---|---|---|---|---|---|---|---|---|
| 48 | | | | | | | | | | | |
| 54 | | | | = 96 + 54 = 150 | | | | | | | |
| 67 | | | | | | | | | | | |
| 89 | | | | | | | | | | | |
| 56 | | | | | | | | | | | |
| 73 | | | | | | 105 | | | | | |
| 88 | | | | | | | | | | | |
| 24 | | | | | | | | | | | |
| 47 | | | | | | | | | | | |
| 96 | | | | | | | | | | | |
| TOTALS | | | | | | | | | | | |

Inside the table you would broadly do two things:

(a) For each cell you would add the values in the corresponding row and the corresponding column in order to get the value inside the cell. Thus, the second row and 4th column intersection would give you 54+96=150, the sixth row and the sixth column would add to 73+32 = 105 as shown in the table.

(b) Add the total of the 10 numbers seen in each row after you finish doing the values inside the cells in the total. This would give you the final total of the row. Repeat the same process for the addition of the 10 numbers in the columns.

By this time, I guess you would have realized that we are targeting two broad addition skills—

(i) Your ability to react with the total when you see two 2 digit numbers (like 57+78=135)

(ii) Your ability to add multiple 2 digit numbers if they are given to you consecutively (like 57+78+43+65 +91+38+44+18+64+72=570 in 8–10 seconds)

You might require around 1–2 months of regular practice to get proficient at this. However once you acquire this skill, every conceivable calculation that any aptitude exam can throw at you (or indeed has thrown at you over the past 20 years) would be very much within your zone.

How do you do larger additions?

One you have the skills to handle two digit additions as specified above handling bigger additions should be a cakewalk.

Suppose you were adding:

57436 + 64123 + 44586 + 78304 + 84653 + 5836. In order to do this, first add the thousands. 57 + 64 (=121) + 44 (=165) + 78 (=243) + 84 (=327) + 5 (=332). Thus, you have an interim answer of 332 thousands. At this stage you know that your answer would be 332000 + a maximum of 6000 ( as there are 6 numbers whose last 3 digits you have neglected). If a range of 332000 to 338000 suffices for you in the addition based on the closeness of the options, you would be through with your calculation at this point. In the event that you need to get to a closer answer than this, the next step would involve taking the 100s digit into account.

Thus for the above calculation: 57436+ 64123 +44586+78304+84653 +5836 when you add the hundreds, you get 4+1+5+3+6+8 = 27 hundreds. Your answer gets refined to 334700 and at this point you also know that the upper limit of the addition has to be a maximum of 600 more than 334700 i.e. the answer lies between 334700 to 335300. In case this accuracy level is still not sufficient you may then look at the last 2 digits of the numbers. Our experience tells us that normally that would not be required.

However, in case you still need to add these digits-it would amount to 2 digit additions again. So you would need to add 57436+64123+44586+78304+84653 +5836 → 36+23 (=59) +86 (=145) + 4 (=149) + 53 (=202) +36 (=238).

**Thus, the correct total would be 334700 + 238 = 334938 and while doing this entire calculation we have not gone above 2 digit additions anywhere.**

Apart from that, the biggest advantage of the process explained above is that in this process, you could stop the moment you had an answer that was sufficient in the context of the provided options.

## SUBTRACTIONS—JUST AN EXTENSION OF ADDITIONS

The better your additions are, the better you would be able to implement the process explained for subtractions. So, a piece of advice from me—make sure that you have worked on your additions seriously for at least 15 days before you attempt to internalize the process for subtractions that is explained in this chapter.

Throughout school you have always used the conventional carry over method of subtracting. But, I am here to show you that you have an option—something that would be much faster and much more superior to the current process you are using. What is it you would ask me? Well what would you do in case you are trying to subtract 38 from 72?

The conventional process tells us to do this as:

|  | Carry over 1 |  |
|---|---|---|
|  | 7 | 2 |
| − | 3 | 8 |
|  | 3 | 4 |

Well, the alternative and much faster way of thinking about subtractions is shown on the number line below:

Difference between any 2 numbers is equal to the distance between the numbers on the number line

The principle used for doing subtractions this way is that the difference between any two numbers can be seen as the distance between them on the number line.

Thus, imagine you are standing on the number 38 on the number line and you are looking towards 72. To make your calculation easy, your first target has to be to reach a number ending with 2. When you start to move to the right from 38, the first number you see that ends in 2 is the number 42. To move from 38 to 42 you need to cover a distance of +4 (as shown in the figure).Once you are at 42, your next target is to move from 42 to 72. The distance between 42 to 72 is 30.

Thus, the subtraction's value for the numbers 72–38 would be 34.

Consider, the following examples:

**Illustration 1**  95 – 39

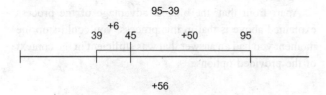

**Illustration 2**  177 – 83

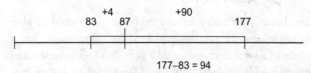

177–83 = 94

Alternately:

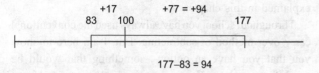

177–83 = 94

**Illustration 3**  738 – 211

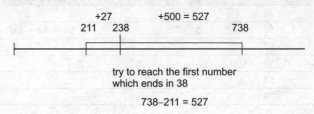

try to reach the first number which ends in 38

738–211 = 527

In this case the first objective is to reach the first number ending in 38 as you start moving to the right of 211. The first such number to the right of 211 being 238, first reach 238 (by adding 27 to 211) and then move from 238 to 738 (adding 500 to 238 to reach 738)

In case you need an intermediate number before reaching 238 you can also think of doing the following:

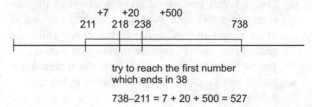

try to reach the first number which ends in 38

738–211 = 7 + 20 + 500 = 527

**Illustration 4**  813 – 478

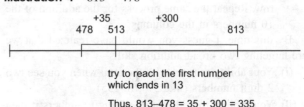

try to reach the first number which ends in 13

Thus, 813–478 = 35 + 300 = 335

Alternately, this thought can also be done as:

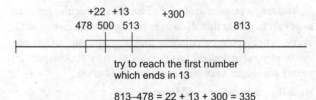

try to reach the first number which ends in 13

813–478 = 22 + 13 + 300 = 335

Also, you could have done it as follows:

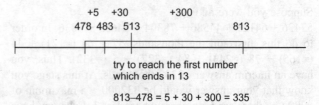

try to reach the first number which ends in 13

813–478 = 5 + 30 + 300 = 335

Even if we were to get 4 digit numbers, you would still be able to use this process quite easily.

# CHAPTER 2

# Multiplications

Multiplications are the next calculation which we need to look at—these are obviously crucial because most questions in Mathematics do involve multiplications.

The fundamental view of multiplication is essentially that when we need to add a certain number consecutively— say we want to add the number 17 seven times:

i.e. $17 + 17 + 17 + 17 + 17 + 17 + 17$ it can also be more conveniently done by using $17 \times 7$.

Normally in aptitude exams like the CAT, multiplications would be restricted to 2 digits multiplied by 2 digits, 2 digits multiplied by 3 digits and 3 digits multiplied by 3 digits.

So what are the short cuts that are available in Multiplications? Let us take a look at the various options you have in order to multiply.

## 1. The straight line method of multiplying two numbers (From Vedic Mathematics and also from the Trachtenberg System of Speed Mathematics)

Let us take an example to explain this process:

Suppose you were multiplying two 2 digit numbers like $43 \times 78$.

The multiplication would be done in the following manner:

$$\begin{array}{r} 4\ 3 \\ \times\ 7\ 8 \\ \hline \end{array}$$

### Step 1: Finding the Unit's digit

The first objective would be to get the unit's digit. In order to do this we just need to multiply the units' digit of both the numbers. Thus, $3 \times 8$ would give us 24. Hence, we would write 4 in the units' digit of the answer and carry over the digit 2 to the tens place as follows:

$$\begin{array}{r} 4\ 3 \\ \times\ 7\ 8 \\ \hline 4 \end{array}$$

2 carry over to the tens place

At this point we know that the units' digit is 4 and also that there is a carry over of 2 to the tens place of the answer.

### Step 2: Finding the tens' place digit

$$\begin{array}{r} 4\ 3 \\ \times\ 7\ 8 \\ \hline 5\ 4 \end{array}$$

5 carry over to
hundreds place

> **Thought Process:**
> $4 \times 8 + 3 \times 7 = 32 + 21 = 53$
> $53 + 2$ (from carry over) $= 55$
> Thus we write 5 in the tens place and carry over 5 to the hundreds place

In the above case, we have multiplied the units digit of the second number with the tens digit of the first number and added the multiplication of the units digit of the first number with the tens digit of the second number. Thus we would get:

8 (units digit of the second number) $\times$ 4 (tens digit of the first number) + 7 (tens digit of the second number) $\times$ 3 (units digit of the first number + 2 (carry over from the units' digit calculation)

$= 32 + 21 + 2 = 55.$

We write down 5 in the tens' digit of the answer and carry over 5 to the hundreds digit of the answer.

### Step 3: Finding the hundreds' place digit

$$\begin{array}{r} 4\ 3 \\ \times\ 7\ 8 \\ \hline 3\ 3\ 5\ 4 \end{array}$$

> **Thought Process:**
> $$4 \times 7 = 28$$
> $$28 + 5 = 33$$
> Since, 4 and 7 are the last digits on the left in both the numbers this is the last calculation in this problem and hence we can write 33 for the remaining 2 digits in the answer

Thus, the answer to the question is 3354.

With a little bit of practice you can do these kinds of calculations mentally without having to write the intermediate steps.

Let us consider another example where the number of digits is larger:

Suppose you were trying to find the product of 43578 $\times$ 6921

## Step 1: Finding the units digit

Units digit: $1 \times 8 = 8$

$$
\begin{array}{r}
4\ 3\ 5\ 7\ 8 \\
\times\ 6\ 9\ 2\ 1 \\
\hline
8
\end{array}
$$

## Step 2: Finding the tens digit

$$
\begin{array}{r}
4\ 3\ 5\ 7\ 8 \\
\times\ 6\ 9\ 2\ 1 \\
\hline
3\ 8
\end{array}
$$

Carry over 2

**Thought Process:**

Tens digit would come by multiplying tens with units and units with tens

$$7 \times 1 + 2 \times 8 = 7 + 16 = 23$$

In order to think about this, we can think of the first pair - by thinking about which number would multiply 1 (units digit of the second number) to make it into tens.

Once, you have spotted the first pair the next pair would get spotted by moving right on the upper number (43578) and moving left on the lower number (6921)

## Step 3: Finding the hundreds digit

Let us look at the broken down thought process for this step:

$$
\begin{array}{r}
4\ 3\ 5\ 7\ 8 \\
\times\ 6\ 9\ 2\ 1 \\
\hline
3\ 8
\end{array}
$$

Carry over 2

**Thought Process:**

Locate the first pair that would give you your hundreds digit.

For this first think of what you need to multiply the digit in the units place of the second number (digit 1) with to get the hundreds digit of the answer.

Since:

Units × Hundreds = Hundreds

We need to pair 1 with 5 in the upper number as shown in the figure.

Once you have identified $5 \times 1$ as the first pair of digits, to identify the next pair, move 1 to the right of the upper number and move 1 to the left of the lower number.

Thus, you should be able to get $7 \times 2$ as your next pair.

$$
\begin{array}{r}
4\ 3\ 5\ 7\ 8 \\
\times\ 6\ 9\ 2\ 1 \\
\hline
3\ 8
\end{array}
$$

Carry over 2

For the last pair, you can again repeat the above thought-move to the right in the upper number and move to the left in the lower number.

Thus, the final thought for this situation would look like:

$$
\begin{array}{r}
4\ 3\ 5\ 7\ 8 \\
\times\ 6\ 9\ 2\ 1 \\
\hline
3\ 3\ 8
\end{array}
$$

9 carry over to thousands place

**Thought Process:**

First pair: $5 \times 1$

Second pair: $7 \times 2$ (move right on upper number and move left on the lower number)

Third pair: $8 \times 9$ (move right on upper number and move left on the lower number)

Thus, $5 \times 1 + 7 \times 2 + 8 \times 9 = 91$

$91 + 2$ (carry over) $= 93$

Hundreds place digit would be 3 and carry over to the thousands place would be 9

## Step 4: Finding the thousands digit

We would follow the same process as above. For doing the same first identify the first pair as $3 \times 1$ (thousands from the first number multiplied by units from the second number) and then start moving right and moving left on both the numbers to find the other pairs.

$$
\begin{array}{r}
4\ 3\ 5\ 7\ 8 \\
\times\ 6\ 9\ 2\ 1 \\
\hline
3\ 3\ 1\ 8
\end{array}
$$

13 carry over to
ten thousands place

**Thought Process:**

$3 \times 1 + 5 \times 2 + 7 \times 9 + 8 \times 6 = 124$

thousands × units + hundreds × tens + tens × hundreds + units × thousands

$124 + 9$ (from the carry over) $= 133$

put down 3 as the thousands place digit and carry over 13 to the ten thousands place

## Step 5: Finding the ten thousands digit

$4 \times 1$ would be the first pair here followed by $3 \times 2$; $5 \times 9$ and $7 \times 6$ as shown below:

$$
\begin{array}{r}
4\ 3\ 5\ 7\ 8 \\
\times\ 6\ 9\ 2\ 1 \\
\hline
0\ 3\ 3\ 3\ 8
\end{array}
$$

11 carry over to
the lacs place

### Step 6: Finding the digit in the lakhs' place

$$\begin{array}{r} 4\ 3\ 5\ 7\ 8 \\ \times\ 6\ 9\ 2\ 1 \\ \hline 6\ 0\ 3\ 3\ 3\ 8 \end{array}$$

7 carry over to
the ten lakhs place

### Step 7: Finding the ten lakh's digit

$$\begin{array}{r} 4\ 3\ 5\ 7\ 8 \\ \times\ 6\ 9\ 2\ 1 \\ \hline 1\ 6\ 0\ 3\ 3\ 3\ 8 \end{array}$$

6 carry over to the next place

### Step 8: Finding the next digit

$$\begin{array}{r} 4\ 3\ 5\ 7\ 8 \\ \times\ 6\ 9\ 2\ 1 \\ \hline 3\ 0\ 1\ 6\ 0\ 3\ 3\ 3\ 8 \end{array}$$

The above process of multiplication- although it looks extremely attractive and magical – especially for larger numbers, it's actual usage in the examination context might actually be quite low. This is because there are better ways of doing multiplication of 2 to 3 digits and larger multiplications might not be required to be executed in an exam like the CAT.

However, in order to solve questions where you might be asked to find the hundreds or even the thousands' digit of a big multiplication like the one showed above, this might be your only option.

Let us look at a few more alternative approaches in order to calculate multiplication problems.

### 2. Using squares to multiply two numbers

In this approach the usage of the mathematical result $a^2 - b^2 = (a - b)(a + b)$ helps us to find the result of a multiplication.

For instance $18 \times 22$ can be done using $20^2 - 2^2 = 400 - 4 = 396$, taking $a = 20$ and $b = 2$

Similarly, $22 \times 28 = 25^2 - 3^2 = 625 - 9 = 616$
$$35 \times 47 = 41^2 - 6^2 = 1681 - 36 = 1645$$

In case the difference between the two numbers is not even, we can still use this process by modifying it thus:

$$24 \times 33 = 24 \times 32 + 24 = 28^2 - 4^2 + 24$$
$$= 784 - 16 + 24 = 792$$

However, obviously this process might be ineffective in the following cases:

(i) If the values of the squares required to calculate an multiplication are difficult to ascertain (For two digit numbers, we can bypass this by knowing the short cut to calculate the squares of 2 digit numbers- **You may want to look at the methods given in Chapter 4 of this part to find out the squares of 2 digit numbers in order to be more effective with these kinds of calculations.**)

(ii) When one is trying to multiply two numbers which are very far from each other, there might be other processes for multiplying them that might be better than this process. For instance, if you are trying to multiply $24 \times 92$ trying to do it as $58^2 - 34^2$ obviously would not be a very convenient process.

(iii) Also, in case one moves into trying to multiply larger numbers, obviously this process would fail. For instance $283 \times 305$ would definitely not be a convenient calculation if we use this process.

### 3. Multiplying numbers close to 100 and 1000

A specific method exists for multiplying two numbers which are both close to 100 or 1000 or 10000.

For us, the most important would be to multiply 2 numbers which are close to 100.

The following example will detail this process for you:

Let us say you are trying to multiply 94 × 96.

**Step 1:**   Calculate the difference from 100 for both numbers and write them down (or visualize them) as follows:

$$
\begin{array}{r}
\text{Difference} \\
\text{from 100} \\
9\ 4 \quad -6 \\
\times 9\ 6 \quad -4 \\
\hline
\end{array}
$$

**Step 2:**   The answer would be calculated in two steps–
 (a) The last two digits of the answer would be calculated by multiplying –6 × –4 to get 24.

$$
\begin{array}{r}
9\ 4 \quad -6 \\
\times \\
\times 9\ 6 \quad -4 \\
\hline
\end{array}
$$

| initial digits of the multiplication | last 2 digits would be got by multiplying –6 × –4 |
|---|---|

Note here that we divide the answer into two parts:

**Last 2 digits and Initial digits**

(In case the numbers were close to 1000 we would divide the calculation into the last three digits and the initial digits)

When we multiply –6 × –4 we get 24 and hence we would write that as our last 2 digits in the answer.

We would then reach the following stage of the multiplication:

$$
\begin{array}{r}
9\ 4 \quad -6 \\
\times \\
9\ 6 \quad -4 \\
\hline
\quad \big|\ 2\ 4 \\
\end{array}
$$

initial digits of the multiplication

The next task is to find the initial digits of the answer: This can be done by cross adding 94 + (–4) or 96 + (–6) to get the digits as 90 as shown in the figure below:

$$
\begin{array}{r}
\text{Difference} \\
\text{from 100} \\
9\ 4 \quad -6 \\
\times \\
\times 9\ 6 \quad -4 \\
\hline
9\ 0\ \big|\ 2\ 4 \\
\end{array}
$$

Let us take another example to illustrate a few more points which might arise in such a calculation:

Let us say, you were doing 102 × 103.

$$
\begin{array}{r}
1\ 0\ 2 \quad +2 \\
1\ 0\ 3 \quad +3 \\
\hline
1\ 0\ 5\ \big|\ 0\ 6 \\
\end{array}
$$

Initial digits | Last 2 digits

Consider: 84 × 88

$$
\begin{array}{r}
8\ 4 \quad -16 \\
8\ 8 \quad -12 \\
\hline
7\ 3 \ \big|\ 9\ 2 \\
\end{array}
$$

| Initial digits | Last 2 digits |
|---|---|

7392 is the answer

Now consider the situation where one number is above 100 and the other below 100.

For instance:

$$92 \times 104$$

The following figure would show you what to do in this case:

$$
\begin{array}{r}
1\ 0\ 4 \quad +4 \\
\times\ 9\ 2 \quad -8 \\
\hline
9\ 6\ 0\ 0 \\
-\ 3\ 2 \\
\hline
9\ 5\ 6\ 8
\end{array}
$$

| Initial | Last 2 |
|---------|--------|
| digits | digits |

### Thought Process:

The problem in this calculation is that $+4 \times (-8) = -32$ and hence cannot be directly written as the last two digits of the answer.

In this case, first leave the last 2 digits as 00 and find the initial digits of the answer.

Initial digits:

$104 + (-8) = 96 = 92 + 4$

When you write 96 having kept the last 2 digits of the number as 00, the meaning of the number's value would be 9600.

Now, from this subtract $= 4 \times (-8) = -32$ to get the answer as $9600 - 32 = 9568$.

For a multiplication like $994 \times 996$ the only adjustment you would need to do would be to look at the second part of the answer as a 3- digit number:

The following would make the process clear to you for such cases:

$$
\begin{array}{r}
9\ 9\ 4 \quad -6 \\
\times\ 9\ 9\ 6 \quad -4 \\
\hline
9\ 9\ 0 \quad 0\ 2\ 4
\end{array}
$$

| Initial | Last 3 |
|---------|--------|
| digits | digits |

### Thought Process:

Last 3 digits $= -6 \times -4 = 24 \rightarrow$ Hence, we write it as 024
Initial digits: Cross addition of $994 + (-4) = 990$
Alternately, $996 + (-6) = 990$
Thus, the answer would be 990024.

### Note:

(i) The above process for multiplication is extremely good in cases when the two numbers are close to any power of 10 (like 100,1000,10000 etc)

However, when the numbers are far away from a power of 10, the process becomes infeasible.

Thus, this process would not be effective at all in the case of $62 \times 34$.

(ii) For finding squares of numbers between 80 to 120, this process is extremely good and hence you should use

this whenever you are faced with the task of finding the square of a number in this range.

For instance, if you are multiplying $91 \times 91$ you can easily see the answer as 8281.

### 4. Using additions to multiply

Consider the following view of an option for multiplying
Let us say we are trying to multiply $83 \times 32$

**This can be converted most conveniently into $80 \times 30 + 3 \times 30 + 2 \times 83 = 2400 + 90 + 166 = 2656$**

**This could also have been done as: $83 \times 30 + 2 \times 83 = 2490 + 166 = 2656$**

**However in the case of $77 \times 48$ the second conversion shown above might not be so easy to execute- while the first one would be much easier:**

**$70 \times 40 + 7 \times 40 + 8 \times 77 = 70 \times 40 + 7 \times 40 + 8 \times 70 + 8 \times 7 = 2800 + 280 + 560 + 56 = 3696$.**

The advantage of this type of conversion is that at no point of time in the above calculation are you doing anything more than single digit $\times$ single digit multiplication.

### 5. Use of percentages to multiply

Another option that you have can be explained as below:
Let us say you are trying to find $43 \times 78$.

In order to calculate $43 \times 78$ first calculate 43% of 78 as follows:

43% of 78 = 10% of 78 + 10% of 78 +10% of 78 +10% of 78 + 1% of 78 + 1% of 78 + 1% of 78 = 7.8 + 7.8 + 7.8 + 7.8 + 0.78 + 0.78 + 0.78 = 33.34

This can be done using: $7 \times 4 = 28$ as the integer part.

For adding the decimals, consider all the decimals as two digit numbers. In the addition if your total is a 2 digit number, write that down in the decimals place of the answer. If the number is a 3 digit number, carry over the hundreds' digit to the integer part of the answer.

Thus, in this case you would get:

$80 + 80 + 80 + 80 + 78 + 78 + 78 = 554$. This 554 actually means 5.54 in the context that we have written down 0.80 as 80.

Thus, the total is 33.54.

We have found that 43% of 78 is 33.54 and our entire addition has been done in single and 2 digits. We of course realize that 43% of 78 being the same as $0.43 \times 78$ the digits for $43 \times 78$ would be the same as the digits for what we have calculated.

Now, the only thing that remains is to put the decimals back where they belong.

There are many ways to think about this- perhaps the easiest being that $43 \times 78$ should have 4 as it's units digit and hence the correct answer is 3354.

Of course, this could also have been done by calculating 78% of 43 as $21.5 + 10.75 + 0.43 + 0.43 + 0.43 = 31 + 2.54 = 33.54 \rightarrow$ Hence, the answer is 3354.

You can even handle 2 digit $\times$ 3 digit multiplication through the same process:

Suppose you were multiplying 324 × 82, instead of doing the multiplication as given, find 324 % of 82.

The question converts to: 3.24 × 82 = 82 × 3 + 8.2 + 8.2 + 0.82 + 0.82 + 0.82 + 0.82 = 246 + 16 + 3.68 = 265.68.

Hence, the answer is 26568.

We would encourage you to try to multiply 2 digits × 2 digits and 2 digits × 3 digits and 3 digits × 3 digits by the methods you find most suitable amongst those given above.

**In my view, the use of percentages to multiply is the most powerful tool for carrying out the kinds of multiplications you would come across in Aptitude exams.** Once you can master how to think about the decimals digits in these calculations, it has the potential to give you a significant time saving in your examination.

Obviously, when you convert a multiplication into an addition using any of the two processes given above, the speed and efficiency of your calculation would depend largely on your ability to add well. If your 2 digit additions are good (or if you have made your additions of 2 digit numbers good by using the process given in the chapter on additions) you would find the addition processes given here the best.

The simple reason is because this process has the advantage of being the most versatile- in the sense that it is not dependant on particular types of numbers.

Besides, after enough practice you would be able to do 2 digits × 2 digits and 2 digits × 3 digits and 3 digits × 3 digits orally.

---

# CHAPTER 3

# Divisions, Percentage Calculations and Ratio Comparisons

## CALCULATING DECIMAL VALUES FOR DIVISION QUESTIONS USING PERCENTAGE CALCULATIONS

I have chosen to club these two together because they are actually parallel to each other—in the sense that for any ratio we can calculate two values—the percentage value and the decimal value. The digits in the decimal value and the percentage value of any ratio would always be the same. Hence, calculating the percentage value of a ratio and the decimal value of the ratio would be the same thing.

How do you calculate the percentage value of a ratio?

## PERCENTAGE RULE FOR CALCULATING PERCENTAGE VALUES THROUGH ADDITIONS

Illustrated below is a powerful method of calculating percentages. In my opinion, the ability to calculate percentage through this method depends on your ability to handle 2 digit additions. Unless you develop the skill to add 2 digit additions in your mind, you are always likely to face problems in calculating percentage through the method illustrated below. In fact, trying this method without being strong at 2-digit additions/subtractions (including 2 digits after decimal point) would prove to be a disadvantage in your attempt at calculating percentages fast.

This process, essentially being a commonsense process, is best illustrated through a few examples:

**Example** What is the percentage value of the ratio: 53/81?

**Solution** The process involves removing all the 100%, 50%, 10%, 1%, 0.1% and so forth of the denominator from the numerator.

Thus, 53/81 can be rewritten as: (40.5 + 12.5)/81 = 40.5/81 + 12.5/81 = 50% + 12.5/81

$$= 50\% + (8.1 + 4.4)/81 = 50\% + 10\% + 4.4/81$$
$$= 60\% + 4.4/81$$

At this stage you know that the answer to the question lies between 60 – 70% (Since 4.4 is less than 10% of 81)

At this stage, you know that the answer to the calculation will be in the form: 6a.bcde ....

All you need to do is find out the value of the missing digits.

In order to do this, calculate the percentage value of 4.4/81 through the normal process of multiplying the numerator by 100.

Thus the % value of $\dfrac{4.4}{81} = \dfrac{4.4 \times 100}{81} = \dfrac{440}{81}$

[**Note:** Use the multiplication by 100, once you have the 10% range. This step reduces the decimal calculations.]

Thus $\dfrac{440}{81}$ = 5% with a remainder of 35

Our answer is now refined to 65.bcde. (1% Range)

Next, in order to find the next digit (first one after the decimal point) add a zero to the remainder;

Hence, the value of 'b' will be the quotient of

$b \rightarrow 350/81 = 4$ Remainder 26

Answer: 65.4*cde* (0.1% Range)

$c \rightarrow 260/81 = 3$ Remainder 17

Answer: 65.43 (0.01% Range)

and so forth.

The advantages of this process are two fold:

(1) You only calculate as long as you need to in order to eliminate the options. Thus, in case there was only a single option between 60–70% in the above question, you could have stopped your calculations right there.

(2) This process allows you to go through with the calculations as long as you need to.

However, remember what I had advised you right at the start: Strong Addition skills are a primary requirement for using this method properly.

**To illustrate another example:**

What is the percentage value of the ratio $\dfrac{223}{72}$?

$223/72 \rightarrow 300 - 310\%$ Remainder 7
$700/72 \rightarrow 9$. Hence $309 - 310\%$, Remainder 52
$520/72 \rightarrow 7$. Hence, 309.7, Remainder 16
$160/72 \rightarrow 2$. Hence, 309.72 Remainder 16

Hence, 309.7222 (2 recurs since we enter an infinite loop of 160/72 calculations).

In my view, percentage rule (as I call it) is one of the best ways to calculate percentages since it gives you the flexibility to calculate the percentage value up to as many digits after decimals as you are required to and at the same time allows you to stop the moment you attain the required accuracy range.

Of course I hope you realize that when you get 53/81 = 65.43 % the decimal value of the same would be 0.6543 and for 223/72, the decimal value would be 3.097222.

The kind of exam that the CAT is, I do not think you would not need to calculate ratios beyond 2 digits divided by 2 digits. In other words, if you are trying to calculate 5372/8164, you can take an approximation of this ratio as 53/81 and calculate the percentage value as shown in the process above. The accuracy in the calculation of 53/81 instead of 5372/8164 would be quite sufficient to answer questions on ratio values that the CAT may throw up in Quantitative Aptitude or even in Data Interpretation questions.

## ✎ RATIO COMPARISONS

## CALCULATION METHODS related to RATIOS

### (A) *Calculation methods for Ratio comparisons:*

There could be four broad cases when you might be required to do ratio comparisons:

The table below clearly illustrates these:

| | Numerator | Denominator | Ratio | Calculations |
|---|---|---|---|---|
| Case 1 | Increases | Decreases | Increase | Not required |
| Case 2 | Increases | Increases | May Increase or Decrease | Required |
| Case 3 | Decreases | Increases | Decreases | Not required |
| Case 4 | Decreases | Decreases | May Increase or Decrease | Required |

In cases 2 and 4 in the table, calculations will be necessitated. In such a situation, the following processes can be used for ratio comparisons.

### 1. The Cross Multiplication Method

Two ratios can be compared using the cross multiplication method as follows. Suppose you have to compare

12/17 with 15/19

Then, to test which ratio is higher cross multiply and compare $12 \times 19$ and $15 \times 17$.

If $12 \times 19$ is bigger the Ratio 12/17 will be bigger. If $15 \times 17$ is higher, the ratio 15/19 will be higher.

In this case, $15 \times 17$ being higher, the Ratio 15/19 is higher.

---

**Note:** In real time usage (esp. in D.I.) this method is highly impractical and calculating the product might be more cumbersome than calculating the percentage values.

---

Thus, this method will not be able to tell you the answer if you have to compare $\dfrac{3743}{5624}$ with $\dfrac{3821}{5783}$

### 2. Percentage Value Comparison Method

Suppose you have to compare: $\dfrac{173}{212}$ with $\dfrac{181}{241}$

In such a case just by estimating the 10% ranges for each ratio you can clearly see that —

the first ratio is $> 80\%$ while the second ratio is $< 80\%$

Hence, the first ratio is obviously greater.

This method is extremely convenient if the two ratios have their values in different 10% ranges.

However, this problem will become slightly more difficult, if the two ratios fall in the same 10% range. Thus, if you had to compare $^{173}/_{212}$ with $^{181}/_{225}$, both the values would give values between $80 - 90\%$. The next step would be to calculate the 1% range.

The first ratio here is $81 - 82\%$ while the second ratio lies between $80 - 81\%$

Hence the first ratio is the larger of the two.

---

**Note:** For this method to be effective for you, you will first need to master the percentage rule method for calculating the percentage value of a ratio. Hence if you cannot see that 169.6 is 80% of 212 or for that matter that 81% of 212 is 171.72 and 82% is 173.84 you will not be able to use this method effectively. (This is also true for the next method.)

However, once you can calculate percentage values of 3 digit ratios to 1% range, there is not much that can stop you in comparing ratios. The CAT and all other aptitude exams normally do not challenge you to calculate further than the 1% range when you are looking at ratio comparisons.

## 3. Numerator Denominator Percentage Change Method

There is another way in which you can compare close ratios like 173/212 and 181/225. For this method, you need to calculate the percentage changes in the numerator and the denominator.

Thus:

$173 \to 181$ is a % increase of $4 - 5\%$

While $212 \to 225$ is a % increase of $6 - 7\%$.

In this case, since the denominator is increasing more than the numerator, the second ratio is smaller.

This method is the most powerful method for comparing close ratios—provided you are good with your percentage rule calculations.

### (B) Method for calculating the value of a percentage change in the ratio:

PCG (Percentage Change Graphic) gives us a convenient method to calculate the value of the percentage change in a ratio.

Suppose, you have to calculate the percentage change between 2 ratios. This has to be done in two stages as:

$$\text{Original Ratio} \xrightarrow[\text{numerator}]{\text{Effect of}} \text{Intermediate Ratio}$$

$$\xrightarrow[\text{Denominator}]{\text{Effect of}} \text{Final Ratio}$$

Thus if 20/40 becomes 22/50

Effect of numerator = $20 \to 22$(10% increase)

Effect of denominator = $50 \to 40$(20% decrease) (reverse fashion)

Overall effect on the ratio:

$$100 \xrightarrow[\substack{\text{Numerator} \\ \text{Effect}}]{10\%\uparrow} 110 \xrightarrow[\substack{\text{Denominator} \\ \text{Effect}}]{20\%\downarrow} 88$$

Hence, overall effect = 12% decrease.

# CHAPTER 4

# Squares and Cubes of Numbers

## 🌀 SQUARES AND SQUARE ROOTS

When any number is multiplied by itself, it is called as the square of the number.

Thus, $3 \times 3 = 3^2 = 9$

Squares have a very important role to play in mathematics. In the context of preparing for CAT and other similar aptitude exams, it might be a good idea to be able to recollect the squares of 2 digit numbers.

Let us now go through the following table carefully:

**Table 4.1**

| Number | Square | Number | Square | Number | Square |
|--------|--------|--------|--------|--------|--------|
| 1 | 1 | 12 | 144 | 23 | 529 |
| 2 | 4 | 13 | 169 | 24 | 576 |
| 3 | 9 | 14 | 196 | 25 | 625 |
| 4 | 16 | 15 | 225 | 26 | 676 |
| 5 | 25 | 16 | 256 | 27 | 729 |
| 6 | 36 | 17 | 289 | 28 | 784 |
| 7 | 49 | 18 | 324 | 29 | 841 |
| 8 | 64 | 19 | 361 | 30 | 900 |
| 9 | 81 | 20 | 400 | 31 | 961 |
| 10 | 100 | 21 | 441 | 32 | 1024 |
| 11 | 121 | 22 | 484 | 33 | 1089 |

*Contd*

| Number | Square | Number | Square | Number | Square |
|--------|--------|--------|--------|--------|--------|
| 34 | 1156 | 57 | 3249 | 80 | 6400 |
| 35 | 1225 | 58 | 3364 | 81 | 6561 |
| 36 | 1296 | 59 | 3481 | 82 | 6724 |
| 37 | 1369 | 60 | 3600 | 83 | 6889 |
| 38 | 1444 | 61 | 3721 | 84 | 7056 |
| 39 | 1521 | 62 | 3844 | 85 | 7225 |
| 40 | 1600 | 63 | 3969 | 86 | 7396 |
| 41 | 1681 | 64 | 4096 | 87 | 7569 |
| 42 | 1764 | 65 | 4225 | 88 | 7744 |
| 43 | 1849 | 66 | 4356 | 89 | 7921 |
| 44 | 1936 | 67 | 4489 | 90 | 8100 |
| 45 | 2025 | 68 | 4624 | 91 | 8281 |
| 46 | 2116 | 69 | 4761 | 92 | 8464 |
| 47 | 2209 | 70 | 4900 | 93 | 8649 |
| 48 | 2304 | 71 | 5041 | 94 | 8836 |
| 49 | 2401 | 72 | 5184 | 95 | 9025 |
| 50 | 2500 | 73 | 5329 | 96 | 9216 |
| 51 | 2601 | 74 | 5476 | 97 | 9409 |
| 52 | 2704 | 75 | 5625 | 98 | 9604 |
| 53 | 2809 | 76 | 5776 | 99 | 9801 |
| 54 | 2916 | 77 | 5929 | 100 | 10000 |
| 55 | 3025 | 78 | 6084 | | |
| 56 | 3136 | 79 | 6241 | | |

So, how does one get these numbers onto one's finger tips? Does one memorize these values or is there a simpler way?

Yes indeed! There is a very convenient process when it comes to memorising the squares of the first 100 numbers.

First of all, you are expected to memorise the squares of the first 30 numbers. In my experience, I have normally seen that most students already know this. The problem arises with numbers after 30. You do not need to worry about that. Just follow the following processes and you will know all squares upto 100.

**Trick 1:** For squares from 51 to 80 – (**Note:** This method depends on your memory of the first thirty squares.)

The process is best explained through an example.

Suppose, you have to get an answer for the value of $67^2$. Look at 67 as $(50 + 17)$. The 4 digit answer will have two parts as follows:

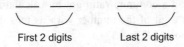

First 2 digits    Last 2 digits

The last two digits will be the same as the last two digits of the square of the number 17. (The value 17 is derived by looking at the difference of 67 with respect to 50.)

Since, $17^2 = 289$, you can say that the last two digits of $67^2$ will be 89. (i.e. the last 2 digits of 289.) Also, you will need to carry over the '2' in the hundreds place of 289 to the first part of the number.

The first two digits of the answer will be got by adding 17 (which is got from $67 - 50$) and adding the carry over (2 in this case) to the number 25. (Standard number to be used in all cases.) Hence, the first two digits of the answer will be given by $25 + 17 + 2 = 44$.

Hence, the answer is $67^2$ = 4489.

Similarly, suppose you have to find $76^2$.

**Step 1:** $76 = 50 + 26$.

**Step 2:** $26^2$ is 676. Hence, the last 2 digits of the answer will be 76 and we will carry over 6.

**Step 3:** The first two digits of the answer will be $25 + 26 + 6 = 57$.

Hence, the answer is 5776.

This technique will take care of squares from 51 to 80 (if you remember the squares from 1 to 30). You are advised to use this process and see the answers for yourself.

## SQUARES FOR NUMBERS FROM 31 TO 50

Such numbers can be treated in the form $(50 - x)$ and the above process modified to get the values of squares from 31 to 50. Again, to explain we will use an example. Suppose you have to find the square of 41.

**Step 1:** Look at 41 as $(50 - 9)$.

Again, similar to what we did above, realise that the answer has two parts—the first two and the last two digits.

**Step 2:** The last two digits are got by the last two digits in the value of $(- 9)^2 = 81$. Hence, 81 will represent the last two digits of $41^2$.

**Step 3:** The first two digits are derived by $25 - 9 = 16$ (where 25 is a standard number to be used in all cases and $- 9$ comes from the fact that $(50 - 9) = 41$).

Hence, the answer is 1681.

**Note**: In case there had been a carry over from the last two digits it would have been added to 16 to get the answer.

For example, in finding the value of $36^2$ we look at $36 = (50 - 14)$

Now, $(-14)^2 = 196$. Hence, the last 2 digits of the answer will be 96. The number '1' in the hundreds place will have to be carried over to the first 2 digits of the answer.

The, first two digits will be $25 - 14 + 1 = 12$

Hence, $36^2 = 1296$.

With this process, you are equipped to find the squares of numbers from 31 to 50.

## FINDING SQUARES OF NUMBERS BETWEEN 81 TO 100

Suppose you have to find the value of $82^2$. The following process will give you the answers.

**Step 1:** Look at 82 as $(100 - 18)$. The answer will have 4 digits whose values will be got by focusing on getting the value of the last two digits and that of the first two digits.

**Step 2:** The value of the last two digits will be equal to the last two digits of $( - 18)^2$.

Since, $( - 18)^2 = 324$, the last two digits of $82^2$ will be 24. The '3' in the hundreds place of $(- 18)^2$ will be carried over to the other part of the answer (i.e. the first two digits).

**Step 3:** The first two digits will be got by: $82 + (- 18) + 3$ Where 82 is the original number; $(- 18)$ is the number obtained by looking at 82 as $(100 - x)$; and 3 is the carry over from $(- 18)^2$. Thus, the answer is 6724.

Similarly, $87^2$ will give you the following thought process:

$87 = 100 - 13 \rightarrow (- 13)^2 = 169$. Hence, 69 are the last two digits of the answer $\rightarrow$ Carry over 1. Consequently, $87 + (-13) + 1 = 75$ will be the first 2 digits of the answer.

Hence, $87^2 = 7569$.

With these three processes you will be able to derive the square of any number up to 100.

**Properties of squares:**

1. When a perfect square is written as a product of its prime factors each prime factor will appear an even number of times.

2. The difference between the squares of two consecutive natural numbers is always equal to the sum of the natural numbers. Thus, $41^2 - 40^2 = (40 + 41) = 81$.

   This property is very useful when used in the opposite direction—i.e. Given that the difference between the squares of two consecutive integers is 81, you should immediately realise that the numbers should be 40 and 41.

3. The square of a number ending in 1, 5 or 6 also ends in 1, 5 or 6 respectively.

4. The square of any number ending in 5: The last two digits will always be 25. The digits before that in the answer will be got by multiplying the digits leading up to the digit 5 in the number by 1 more than itself.
   **Illustration:**
   $$85^2 = \underline{\quad}25.$$
   The missing digits in the above answer will be got by $8 \times (8 + 1) = 8 \times 9 = 72$. Hence, the square of 85 is given by 7225.
   Similarly, $135^2 = \underline{\quad}25$. The missing digits are $13 \times 14 = 182$. Hence, $135^2 = 18225$.

5. The value of a perfect square has to end in 1, 4, 5, 6, 9 or an even number of zeros. In other words, a perfect square cannot end in 2, 3, 7, or 8 or an odd number of zeros.

6. If the units digit of the square of a number is 1, then the number should end in 1 or 9.

7. If the units digit of the square of a number is 4, then the units digit of the number is 2 or 8.

8. If the units digit of the square of a number is 9, then the units digit of the number is 3 or 7.

9. If the units of the square of a number is 6, then the unit's digit of the number is 4 or 6.

10. The sum of the squares of the first '$n$' natural numbers is given by
    $$[(n)\ (n + 1)\ (2n + 1)]/6.$$

11. The square of a number is always non-negative.

12. Normally, by squaring any number we increase the value of the number. The only integers for which this is not true are 0 and 1. (In these cases squaring the number has no effect on the value of the number).

    Further, for values between 0 to 1, squaring the number reduces the value of the number. For example $0.5^2 < 0.5$.

## Say, you have to Find the Square Root of a Given Number

Say 7056

**Step 1:** Write down the number 7056 as a product of its Prime factors. $7056 = 2 \times 2 \times 2 \times 2 \times 21 \times 21$
$$= 2^4 \times 21^2$$

**Step 2:** The required square root is obtained by halving the values of the powers.

Hence, $\sqrt{7056} = 2^2 \times 21^1$

## CUBES AND CUBE ROOTS

When a number is multiplied with itself two times, we get the cube of the number.

Thus, $x \times x \times x = x^3$

**Method to find out the cubes of 2 digit numbers:** The answer has to consist of 4 parts, each of which has to be calculated separately.

The first part of the answer will be given by the cube of the ten's digit.

Suppose you have to find the cube of 28.

The first step is to find the cube of 2 and write it down.
$$2^3 = 8.$$

The next three parts of the number will be derived as follows.

Derive the values 32, 128 and 512.

(by creating a G. P. of 4 terms with the first term in this case as 8, and a common ratio got by calculating the ratio of the unit's digit of the number with its tens digit. In this case the ratio is 8/2 = 4.)

Now, write the 4 terms in a straight line as below. Also, to the middle two terms add double the value.

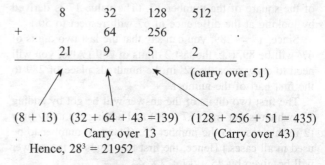

$$(8 + 13) \quad (32 + 64 + 43 = 139) \quad (128 + 256 + 51 = 435)$$
$$\text{Carry over 13} \qquad \text{(Carry over 43)}$$
Hence, $28^3 = 21952$

## Properties of Cubes

1. When a perfect cube is written in its standard form the values of the powers on each prime factor will be a multiple of 3.

2. In order to find the cube root of a number, first write it in its standard form and then divide all powers by 3.

   Thus, the cube root of $3^6 \times 5^9 \times 17^3 \times 2^6$ is given by $3^2 \times 5^3 \times 17 \times 2^2$

3. The cubes of all numbers (integers and decimals) greater than 1 are greater than the number itself.

4. $0^3 = 0$, $1^3 = 1$ and $-1^3 = -1$. These are the only three instances where the cube of the number is equal to the number itself.

5. The value of the cubes of a number between 0 and 1 is lower than the number itself. Thus, $0.5^3 < 0.5^2 < 0.5$.

6. The cube of a number between 0 and $-1$ is greater than the number itself. $(-0.2)^3 > -0.2$.

7. The cube of any number less than $-1$, is always lower than the number. Thus, $(-1.5)^3 < (-1.5)$.

# Numbers

**BLOCK**

**I**

As already mentioned in the introductory note, Block I constituted the most crucial aspect of the Quantitative Aptitude Section in the paper & pen version of the CAT. Throughout the decade 1999 to 2008, almost 30–50% of the total questions in every CAT paper came from the twochapters given in this block. However, the online CAT has shifted this weightage around, and consequently, the importance of Block I has been reduced to around 20–25% of the total marks in the section.

Thus, although Block I remains an important block for your preparations, it has lost its pre-eminence (as reflected in the strategy—"Do Block I well and you can qualify the QA section"). However, this does not change the need for you to go through this block in great depth.

Thus my advice to you is: Go through this block in depth and try to gain clarity of concepts as well as exposure to questions for honing your ability to do well in this area.

# ...BACK TO SCHOOL

- **Chapters in this Block: Number Systems and Progressions**
- **Block Importance–20–25%**

The importance of this block can be gauged from the table below:

| Year | % of Marks from Block 1 | Qualifying Score (approx. score for 96 percentile) |
|---|---|---|
| 2000 | 48% | 35% |
| 2001 | 36% | 35% |
| 2002 | 36% | 35% |
| 2003 (cancelled) | 30% | 32% |
| 2003 (retest) | 34% | 35% |
| 2004 | 32% | 35% |
| 2005 | 40% | 35% |
| 2006 | 32% | 40% |
| 2007 | 24% | 32% |
| 2008 | 40% | 35% |
| Online CAT 2009–2017 | 15–30% | 60% with no errors |

As you can see from the table above, doing well in this block alone could give you a definite edge and take you a long way to qualifying the QA section. Although the online CAT has significantly varied the relative importance to this block, the importance of this block remains high. Besides, there is a good chance that once the IIMs get their act together in the context of the online CAT and its question databases—the pre eminence of this block of chapters might return.

Hence, understanding the concepts involved in these chapters properly and strengthening your problem solving experience could go a long way towards a good score.

Before we move into the individual chapters of this block, let us first organise our thinking by looking at the core concepts that we had learnt in school with respect to these chapters.

## Pre-assessment Test

This test consists of 25 questions based on the chapters of BLOCK I (Number Systems and Progressions). Do your best in trying to solve each question.

The time limit to be followed for this test is 30 minutes. However, after the 30 minutes is over continue solving till you have spent enough time and paid sufficient attention to each question. After you finish thinking about each and every question of the test, check your scores. Then go through the SCORE INTERPRETATION ALGORITHM given at the end of the test to understand the way in which you need to approach the chapters inside this block.

1. The number of integers $n$ satisfying $-n+2 \geq 0$ and $2n \geq 4$ is
   (a) 0      (b) 1
   (c) 2      (d) 3

2. The sum of two integers is 10 and the sum of their reciprocals is 5/12. Then the larger of these integers is
   (a) 2      (b) 4
   (c) 6      (d) 8

3. If $x$ is a positive integer such that $2x + 12$ is perfectly divisible by $x$, then the number of possible values of $x$ is
   (a) 2      (b) 5
   (c) 6      (d) 12

4. Let K be a positive integer such that $k + 4$ is divisible by 7. Then the smallest positive integer $n$, greater than 2, such that $k + 2n$ is divisible by 7 equals.
   (a) 9      (b) 7
   (c) 5      (d) 3

5. $2^{73} - 2^{72} - 2^{71}$ is the same as
   (a) $2^{69}$      (b) $2^{70}$
   (c) $2^{71}$      (d) $2^{72}$

6. Three times the first of three consecutive odd integers is 3 more than twice the third. What is the third integer?
   (a) 15      (b) 9
   (c) 11      (d) 5

7. $x$, $y$ and $z$ are three positive integers such that $x > y > z$. Which of the following is closest to the product $xyz$?
   (a) $xy(z-1)$      (b) $(x-1)yz$
   (c) $(x-y)xy$      (d) $x(y+1)z$

8. A positive integer is said to be a prime number if it is not divisible by any positive integer other than itself and 1. Let $p$ be a prime number greater than 5, then $(p^2 - 1)$ is
   (a) never divisible by 6.
   (b) always divisible by 6, and may or may not be divisible by 12.
   (c) always divisible by 12, and may or may not be divisible by 24.
   (d) always divisible by 24.

9. Iqbal dealt some cards to Mushtaq and himself from a full pack of playing cards and laid the rest aside. Iqbal then said to Mushtaq "If you give me a certain number of your cards, I will have four times as many cards as you will have. If I give you the same number of cards, I will have thrice as many cards as you will have". Of the given choices, which could represent the number of cards with Iqbal?
   (a) 9      (b) 31
   (c) 12      (d) 35

10. In Sivakasi, each boy's quota of match sticks to fill into boxes is not more than 200 per session. If he reduces the number of sticks per box by 25, he can fill 3 more boxes with the total number of sticks assigned to him. Which of the following is the possible number of sticks assigned to each boy?
    (a) 200      (b) 150
    (c) 125      (d) 175

11. A lord got an order from a garment manufacturer for 480 Denim Shirts. He bought 12 sewing machines and appointed some expert tailors to do the job. However, many didn't report for duty. As a result, each of those who did, had to stitch 32 more shirts than originally planned by Alord, with equal distribution of work. How many tailors had been appointed earlier and how many had not reported for work?
    (a) 12, 4      (b) 10, 3
    (c) 10, 4      (d) None of these

12. How many 3-digit even numbers can you form such that if one of the digits is 5, the following digit must be 7?
    (a) 5      (b) 405
    (c) 365      (d) 495

13. To decide whether a number of $n$ digits is divisible by 7, we can define a process by which its magnitude is reduced as follows: ($i_1, i_2, i_3 \ldots i_n$ are the digits of the number, starting from the most significant digit).

$$i_1 i_2 \ldots i_n \Rightarrow i_1 \cdot 3^{n-1} + i_2 \cdot 3^{n-2} + \ldots + i_n 3^0.$$

e.g.    $259 \Rightarrow 2.3^2 + 5.3^1 + 9.3^0 = 18 + 15 + 9 = 42$

Ultimately the resulting number will be seven after repeating the above process a certain number of times.

After how many such stages, does the number 203 reduce to 7?

(a) 2                    (b) 3

(c) 4                    (d) 1

14. A teacher teaching students of third standard gave a simple multiplication exercise to the kids. But one kid reversed the digits of both the numbers and carried out the multiplication and found that the product was exactly the same as the one expected by the teacher. Only one of the following pairs of numbers will fit in the description of the exercise. Which one is that?

(a) 14, 22              (b) 13, 62

(c) 19, 33              (d) 42, 28

15. If $8 + 12 = 2$, $7 + 14 = 3$ then $10 + 18 = ?$

(a) 10                   (b) 4

(c) 6                    (d) 18

16. Find the minimum integral value of $n$ such that the division $55n/124$ leaves no remainder.

(a) 124                  (b) 123

(c) 31                   (d) 62

17. What is the value of $k$ for which the following system of equations has no solution:

$2x - 8y = 3$; and $kx + 4y = 10$.

(a) −2                   (b) 1

(c) −1                   (d) 2

18. A positive integer is said to be a prime if it is not divisible by any positive integer other than itself and one. Let $p$ be a prime number strictly greater than 3. Then, when $p^2 + 17$ is divided by 12, the remainder is

(a) 6                    (b) 1

(c) 0                    (d) 8

19. A man sells chocolates that come in boxes. Either full boxes or half a box of chocolates can be bought from him. A customer comes and buys half the number of boxes the seller has plus half a box. A second customer comes and buys half the remaining number of boxes plus half a box. After this, the seller is left with no chocolates box. How many chocolates boxes did the seller have before the first customer came?

(a) 2                    (b) 3

(c) 4                    (d) 3.5

20. X and Y are playing a game. There are eleven 50 paise coins on the table and each player must pick up at least one coin but not more than five. The person picking up the last coin loses. X starts. How many should he pick up at the start to ensure a win no matter what strategy Y employs?

(a) 4                    (b) 3

(c) 2                    (d) 5

21. If $a < b$, which of the following is always true?

(a) $a < (a + b) / 2 < b$

(b) $a < ab/2 < b$

(c) $a < b^2 - a^2 < b$

(d) $a < ab < b$

22. The money order commission is calculated as follows. From ₹ X to be sent by money order, subtract 0.01 and divide by 10. Get the quotient and add 1 to it, if the result is Y, the money order commission is ₹ 0.5Y. If a person sends two money orders to Aurangabad and Bhatinda for ₹ 71 and ₹ 48, respectively. The total commission will be

(a) ₹ 7.00              (b) ₹ 6.50

(c) ₹ 6.00              (d) ₹ 7.50

23. The auto fare in Ahmedabad has the following formula based upon the metre reading. The metre reading is rounded up to the next higher multiple of 4. For instance, if the metre reading is 37 paise, it is rounded up to 40 paise. The resultant is multiplied by 12. The final result is rounded off to nearest multiple of 25 paise. If 53 paise is the metre reading what will be the actual fare?

(a) ₹ 6.75              (b) ₹ 6.50

(c) ₹ 6.25              (d) ₹ 7.50

24. Juhi and Bhagyashree were playing simple mathematical puzzles. Juhi wrote a two digit number and asked Bhayashree to guess it. Juhi also indicated that the number is exactly thrice the product of its digits. What was the number that Juhi wrote?

(a) 36                   (b) 24

(c) 12                   (d) 48

25. It is desired to extract the maximum power of 3 from 24!, where $n! = n.(n - 1) . (n - 2) \ldots 3.2.1$. What will be the exponent of 3?

(a) 8                    (b) 9

(c) 11                   (d) 10

## ANSWER KEY

| | | | |
|---|---|---|---|
| 1. (b) | 2. (c) | 3. (c) | 4. (a) |
| 5. (c) | 6. (a) | 7. (b) | 8. (d) |
| 9. (b) | 10. (b) | 11. (c) | 12. (c) |
| 13. (a) | 14. (b) | 15. (a) | 16. (a) |
| 17. (c) | 18. (a) | 19. (b) | 20. (a) |
| 21. (a) | 22. (b) | 23. (a) | 24. (b) |
| 25. (d) | | | |

## Solutions

1. The only value that will satisfy will be 2.

2. ¼ + 1/6 will give you 5/12.

3. The possible values are 1, 2, 3, 4, 6 and 12. (i.e. the factors of 12).

4. $k$ will be a number of the form $7n + 3$. Hence, if you take the value of $n$ as 9, $k + 2n$ will become $7n + 3 + 18 = 7n + 21$. This number will be divisible by 7. The numbers 3, 5 and 7 do not provide us with this solution.

5. $2^{73} - 2^{72} - 2^{71} = 2^{71}(2^2 - 2 - 1) = 2^{71}(1)$. Hence option (c) is correct.

6. Solve through options.

7. The closest value will be option (b), since the percentage change will be lowest when the largest number is reduced by one.

8. This is a property of prime numbers greater than 5.

9. He could have dealt a total of 40 cards, in which case Mushtaq would get 9 cards. On getting one card from Mushtaq, the ratio would become 4:1, while on giving away one card to Mushtaq, the ratio would become 3:1.

10. Looking at the options you realise that the correct answer should be a multiple of 25 and 50 both. The option that satisfies the condition of increasing the number of boxes by 3 is 150. (This is found through trial and error.)

11. Trial and error gives you option 3 as the correct answer.

12. Given that the number must have a 57 in it and should be even at the same time, the only numbers possible are 570, 572, 574, 576 and 578. Also, if there is no 5 in the number, you will get 360 more numbers.

13. 203 becomes → $2.3^2 + 0 + 3.3^0 = 21$ → $2.3^1 + 1.3^0 = 7$. Hence, clearly two steps are required.

14. Trial and error will give option (b) as the correct answer, since $13 \times 62 = 26 \times 31$

15. The solutions are defined as the sum of digits of the answer. Hence, 10 is correct.

16. There are no common factors between 55 and 124. Hence the answer should be 124.

17. At $k = -1$, the two equations become inconsistent with respect to each other and there will then be no solution to the system of equations.

18. Try with 5, 7, 11. In each case the remainder is 6.

19. Trial and error gives you the answer as 3. Option (b) is correct.

20. Picking up 4 coins will ensure that he wins the game.

21. Option (a) is correct (since the average of any two numbers lies between the numbers.

22. $8/2 + 5/2 = 6.5$.

23. The answer will be $56 \times 12 = 672$ → 675. Hence, ₹ 6.75.

24. The given condition is satisfied only for 24.

25. The answer will be given by $8 + 2 = 10$.

(This logic is explained in the Number Systems chapter)

## 🔍 THE NUMBER LINE

## Core Concepts

I. The concept of the number line is one of the most crucial concepts in Basic Numeracy.

The number line is a line that starts from zero and goes towards positive infinity when it moves to the right and towards negative infinity when it moves to the left.

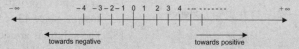

The difference between the values of any two points on the number line also gives the distance between the points.

Thus, for example if we look at the distance between the points $+3$ and $-2$, it will be given by their difference. $3 - (-2) = 3 + 2 = 5$.

II. Types of numbers—

We will be looking at the types of numbers in detail again when we go into the chapter of number systems. Let us first work out in our minds the various types of numbers. While doing so do not fail to notice that most of these number types occur in pairs (i.e. the definition of one of them, defines the other automatically).

Note here that the number line is one of the most critical concepts in understanding and grasping quantitative aptitude and indeed mathematics.

## Multiples on the Number Line

All tables and multiples of every number can be visualised on the number line. Thus, multiples of 7 on the number line would be seen as follows:

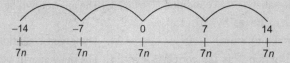

In order to visualize this you can imagine a frog jumping consistently 7 units every time. If it lands on $-14$, the next landing would be on $-7$, then on 0, then 7 and finally at 14. This is how you can visualise the table of 7 (in mathematical terms we can also refer to this as $7n$ – meaning the set of numbers which are multiples of 7 or in other words the set of numbers which are divisible by 7).

You can similarly visualise $5n$, $4n$, $8n$ and so on—practically all tables on the number line as above.

## What do We Understand by $7n + 1$ and Other such Notations & the Equivalence of $7n + 1$ and $7n - 6$

Look at the following figure closely:

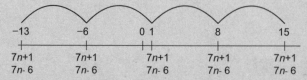

Our $7n$ frog is made to first land on $-13$ and then asked to keep doing it's stuff (jumping 7 to the right everytime). What is the result? It lands on $-6$, $+1$, 8, 15 and it's next landing would be on 22, 29 and so forth. These numbers cannot be described as $7n$, but rather they all have a single property which is constant for all numbers.

They can be described as: "One more than a multiple of 7" and in mathematical terms such numbers are also called as $7n + 1$. Alternately these numbers also have the property that they are "6 less than multiples of 7" and in mathematical terms such numbers can also be called as $7n - 6$.

That is why in mathematics, we say that the set of numbers represented by $7n + 1$ is the same as the set of numbers represented by $7n - 6$.

## The Implication in Terms of Remainders

This concept can also be talked about in the context of remainders.

When a number which can be described as $7n + 1$ or $7n - 6$ (like the numbers 8, 15, –6, –13, –20, –27, –34, –41...) is divided by 7, the remainder in every case is seen to be 1. For some people reconciling the fact that the remainder when –27 is divided by 7 the remainder is 1, seems difficult on the surface. Note that this needs to be done because about remainders we should know that remainders are always non-negative.

However, the following thinking would give you the remainder in every case:

27/7, remainder is 6.

–27/7, remainder is –6. In the context of dividing by 7, a remainder of –6 means a remainder of $7 - 6 = 1$.

Let us look at another example:

What is the remainder when –29 is divided by 8.

First reaction 29/8 $\rightarrow$ remainder 5, –29/8 $\rightarrow$ remainder –5, hence actual remainder is $8 - 5 = 3$.

The student is advised to practice more such situations and get comfortable in converting positive remainders to negative remainders and vice versa.

## Even and Odd Numbers

***The meaning of 2n and 2n + 1:***  $2n$ means a number which is a multiple of the number 2. Since, this can be visualised as a frog starting from the origin and jumping 2 units to the right in every jump, you can also say that this frog represents $2n$.

(**Note**: Multiples of 2, are even numbers. Hence, $2n$ is also used to denote even numbers.)

So, what does $2n + 1$ mean?

Well, simply put, if you place the above frog on the point represented by the number 1 on the number line then the frog will reach points such as 3, 5, 7, 9, 11 .....and so on. This essentially means that the points the frog now reaches are displaced by 1 unit to the right of the $2n$ frog. In mathematical terms, this is represented as $2n + 1$.

In other words, $2n + 1$ also represents numbers which leave a remainder of 1, when divided by 2. (**Note**: This is also the definition of an odd number. Hence, in Mathematics $(2n + 1)$ is used to denote an odd number. Also note that taken together $2n$ and $2n + 1$ denote the entire set of integers. i.e. all integers from $-\infty$ to $+\infty$ on the number line can be denoted by either $2n$ or $2n + 1$. This happens because when we divide any integer by 2, there are only two results possible with respect to the remainder obtained, viz: A remainder of zero $(2n)$ or a remainder of one $(2n + 1)$.

This concept can be expanded to represent integers with respect to any number. Thus, in terms of 3, we can only have three types of integers $3n$, $3n + 1$ or $3n + 2$ (depending on whether the integer leaves a remainder 0, 1 or 2 respectively when divided by 3.) Similarly, with respect to 4, we have 4 possibilities—$4n$, $4n + 1$, $4n + 2$ or $4n + 3$.

Needless to say, from these representations above, the representations $2n$ and $2n + 1$ (which can also be represented as $2n - 1$) have great significance in Mathematics as they represent even and odd numbers respectively. Similarly, we use the concept of $4n$ to check whether a year is a leap year or not.

These representations can be seen on the number line as follows:

**Representation of $2n$ and $2n + 1$:**

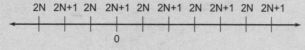

**Representation of $3n$, $3n + 1$ and $3n + 2$:**

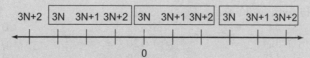

**Representation of $4n$, $4n + 1$, $4n + 2$ and $4n + 3$:**

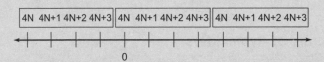

## One Particular Number can be a Multiple of more than 1 Number—The Concept of Common Multiples

Of course one of the things you should notice as you go through the above discussion is that individual numbers can indeed be multiples of more than 1 number—and actually often are.

Thus, for instance the number 14 is a multiple of both 7 and 2—hence 14 can be called as a common multiple of 2 and 7. Obviously, I think you can visualise more such numbers which can be classified as common multiples of 2 and 7?? 28,42,56 and in fact the list is infinite—i.e. the numbers never end. Thus, the common multiples of 2 and 7 can be represented by the infinite set:

$$\{14,28,42,56,70\ldots\ldots\ldots 1400\ldots\ldots 14000\ldots\ldots 140000\ldots\ldots\text{and so on}\}$$

## The LCM and It's Significance

From the above list, the number 14 (which is the lowest number in the set of Common multiples of 2 and 7) has a lot of significance in Mathematics. It represents what is commonly known as the **Least Common Multiple (LCM)** of 2 and 7. It is the first number which is a multiple of both 2 and 7 and there are a variety of questions in quantitative aptitude which you would come across—not only when you solve questions based on number systems (where the LCM has it's dedicated set of questions), but applications of the LCM are seen even in chapters like Time, Speed Distance, Time and Work, etc.

*So what did school teach us about the process of finding LCM?*
Before you start to review/ relearn that process you first need to know about prime factors of a number.

*I hope at this point you recognize the difference between finding factors of a number and prime factors of a number.*
Simply put, finding factors of a number means finding the divisors of the number. Thus, for instance the factors of the number 80 would be the numbers 1, 2, 4, 5, 8, 10, 16, 20, 40 and 80. On the other hand finding the prime factors of the same number would mean writing the number 80 as $2^4 \times 5^1$. This form of writing the number is also called the **STANDARD FORM** or the **CANONICAL FORM** of the number.

*The school process of writing down the standard form of a number:*
Now this is something I would think most of you would remember and recognize:

Finding the prime factors of the number 80

| | |
|---|---|
| 2 | 80 |
| 2 | 40 |
| 2 | 20 |
| 2 | 10 |
| 5 | 5 |
| | 1 |

The prime factors of the number 80 are: $2 \times 2 \times 2 \times 2 \times 5 = 2^4 \times 5^1$.

## Exercise for Self-practice

Write down the standard form of the following numbers.
(a) 20  (b) 44  (c) 142  (d) 200
(e) 24  (f) 324  (g) 120  (h) 84
(i) 371  (j) 143  (k) 339  (l) 147
(m) 1715

### Finding the LCM of two or more numbers: The school process

**Step 1:**   Write down the prime factor form of all the numbers;
Let us say that you have 3 numbers whose standard forms are:

$$2^4 \times 3^2 \times 5^3 \times 7^1$$

$$2^3 \times 3^1 \times 5^2 \times 11^2$$

$$2^4 \times 3^2 \times 5^1 \times 13^1$$

To write down the LCM of these numbers write down all the prime numbers and multiply them with their highest available powers. The resultant number would be the LCM of these numbers.
Thus, in the above case the LCM would be:

$$2^4 \times 3^2 \times 5^3 \times 7^1 \times 11^2 \times 13^1$$

**Note:**   Short cuts to a lot of these processes have been explained in the main chapters of the book.

### Divisors (Factors) of a number

As we already mentioned, finding the factors or divisors of a number are one and the same thing. In order to find factors of a number, the key is to spot the factors below the square root of the number. Once you have found them, the factors above the square root would be automatically seen. Consider this for factors of the number 80:

| **Factors below the square root** *of 80 (8.xxx)* Hence, factors up to and including 8 | |
| --- | --- |
| 1 | |
| 2 | |
| 4 | |
| 5 | |
| 8 | |

Once you can visualise the list on the left, the factors on the right would be seen automatically.

| **Factors below the square root** *of 80 (8.xxx)* Hence, factors up to and including 8 | *Factors above the square root* |
| --- | --- |
| 1 | 80 |
| 2 | 40 |
| 4 | 20 |
| 5 | 16 |
| 8 | 10 |

Note that these will be seen automatically the moment you have the list on the left.

## Common Divisors Between 2 Numbers

### List of Common Divisors

When we write down the factors of two numbers, we can look for the common elements within the two lists.
For instance, the factors of 80 are (1, 2, 4, 5, 8, 10, 16, 20, 40 and 80) while the factors of 144 are (1, 2, 3, 4, 6, 8, 9, 12, 16, 18, 24, 36, 48, 72 and 144)
If you observe the two lists closely you will get the following list of common factors or common divisors between the two:

### List of common factors of 80 and 144: *(1, 2, 4, 8, 16)*
The number 16 being the highest in this list of common factors (or divisors) is also called the Highest Common Factor or the Greatest Common Divisor. In short it is denoted as HCF or GCD. It has a lot of significance in terms

of quantitative thinking—as the HCF is used in a multitude of problems and hence being able to spot the HCF of two or more numbers is one of the critical operations in Mathematics. You would be continuously seeing applications of the HCF in problems in the chapter of Number systems and right through the chapters of arithmetic (defined as word based problems in this book).

### Rounding off and its use for approximation

One of the important things that we learnt in school was the use of approximation in order to calculate.

Thus, $72 \times 53$ can be approximated to $70 \times 50$ and hence seen as 3500.

Similarly, the addition of $48 + 53 + 61 + 89$ can be taken as $50 + 50 + 60 + 90 = 250$

## Number Types You Should Know

**Integers and Decimals:**   All numbers that do not have a decimal in them are called integers. Thus, –3, –17, + 4, + 13, + 1473, 0 etc are all integers.

Obviously, decimal numbers are numbers which have a decimal value attached to them. Thus, 1.3, 14.76, – 12.24, etc are all decimal numbers, since they have certain values after the decimal point.

Before we move ahead, let us pause a brief while, to further understand decimals. As you shall see, the concept of decimals is closely related to the concept of division and divisibility. Suppose, I have 4 pieces of bread which I want to divide equally between two people. It is easy for me to do this, since I can give two whole pieces to each of them.

However, if we alter the situation in such a way, that I now have 5 pieces of bread to distribute equally amongst 2 people. What do I do?

I give two whole pieces each, to each of them. The 5th piece has to be divided equally between the two. I can no longer do this, without in some way breaking the 5th piece into 2 parts. This is the elementary situation that gives rise to the need for decimals in mathematics.

Going back to the situation above, my only option is to divide the 5th piece into two equal parts (which in quants are called as halves).

This concept has huge implications for problem solving especially once you recognise that a half (i.e. a '.5' in the decimal) only comes when you divide a whole into two parts.

Thus, in fact, all standards decimals emerge out of certain fixed divisors.

Hence, for example, the divisor 2, gives rise to the decimal · 5.

Similarly the divisor 3 gives rise to the decimals ·33333 and ·66666, etc.

**Prime numbers and Composite numbers**   Amongst natural numbers, there are three broad divisions–

**Unity**   It is representative of the number 1.

**Prime numbers**   These are numbers which have no divisors/ factors apart from 1 and itself.

**Composite numbers**   On the other hand, are numbers, which have at least one more divisor apart from 1 and itself.

---

**Note:**   A brief word about factors/ division—A number X is said to divide Y (or is said to be a divisor or factor of Y) when the division of Y/X leaves no remainder.

---

All composite numbers have the property that they can be written as a product of their prime factors.

Thus, for instance, the number 40 can be represented as: $40 = 2 \times 2 \times 2 \times 5$     or,     $40 = 2^3 \times 5^1$

This form of writing is called as the **standard form** of the composite number.

**The difference between Rational and Irrational numbers:** This difference is one of the critical but unfortunately one of the less well understood differences in elementary Mathematics.

**The definition of Rational numbers:** Numbers which can be expressed in the form $p/q$ where $q \neq 0$ are called rational numbers.

Obviously, numbers which cannot be represented in the form $p/q$ are called as irrational numbers.

However, one of the less well understood issues in this regard is what does this mean?

The difference becomes clear when the values of decimals are examined in details:

Consider the following numbers.

(1)  4.2,

(2)  4.333….,

(3)  4.1472576345…….

What is the difference between the decimal values of the three numbers above?

To put it simply, the first number has what can be described as a finite decimal value. Such numbers can be expressed in the form $p/q$ easily. Since 4.2 can be first written as 42/10 and then converted to 21/5.

Similarly, numbers like 4.5732 can be represented as 45732/10000. Thus, numbers having a finite terminating decimal value are rational.

Now, let us consider the decimal value: 4.3333……..

Such decimal values will continue endlessly, i.e. they have no end. Hence, they are called **infinite decimals** (or non-terminating decimals).

But, we can easily see that the number 4.333…. can be represented as 13/3. Hence, this number is also rational. In fact, all numbers which have infinite decimal values, but have any recurring form within them can be represented in the $p/q$ form.

For example the value of the number: 1.14814814814…. is 93/81.

(What I mean to say is that whenever you have any recurring decimal number, even if the value of '$q$' might not be obvious, but it will always exist.)

Thus, we can conclude that all numbers whose decimal values are infinite (non-terminating) but which have a recurring pattern within them are rational numbers.

This leaves us with the third kind of decimal values, viz. **Infinite non-recurring decimal values**. These decimals neither have a recurring pattern, nor do they have an end—they go on endlessly. For such numbers it is not possible to find the value of a denominator '$q$' which can be used in order to represent them as $p/q$. Hence, such numbers are called as irrational numbers.

In day-to-day mathematics, we come across numbers like $\sqrt{3}$ , $\sqrt{5}$ , $\sqrt[3]{7}$ , $\pi$, $e$, etc. which are irrational numbers since they do not have a $p/q$ representation.

---

**Note:**  $\sqrt{3}$  can also be represented as $3^{1/2}$, just as $\sqrt[3]{7}$ can be represented as $7^{1/3}$.

---

## An Important Tip:

**Rational and Irrational numbers do not mix.:** This means that in case you get a situation where an irrational number has appeared while solving a question, it will remain till the end of the solution. It can only be removed from the solution if it is multiplied or divided by the same irrational number.

**Consider an example:** The area of an equilateral triangle is given by the formula $(\sqrt{3}/4) \times a^2$ (where $a$ is the side of the equilateral triangle). Since, $\sqrt{3}$ is an irrational number, it remains in the answer till the end. Hence, the area of an equilateral triangle will always have a $\sqrt{3}$ as part of the answer.

Before we move ahead we need to understand one final thing about recurring decimals.

As I have already mentioned, recurring decimals have the property of being able to be represented in the $p/q$ form. The question that arises is—Is there any process to convert a recurring decimal into a proper fraction?

Yes, there is. In fact, in order to understand how this operates, you first need to understand that there are two kinds of recurring decimals. The process for converting an infinite recurring decimal into a fraction basically varies for both of these types. Let's look at these one by one.

**Type 1—Pure recurring decimals:** These are recurring decimals where the recurrence starts immediately after the decimal point.

For example:          $0.5555… = 0.\overline{5}$

$3.242424… = 3.\overline{24}$

$5.362362… = 5.\overline{362}$

The process for converting these decimals to fractions can be illustrated as:

$0.5555 = 5/9$

$$3.242424 = 3 + (24/99)$$
$$5.362362 = 5 + (362/999)$$

A little bit of introspection will tell you that what we have done is nothing but to put down the recurring part of the decimal as it is and dividing it by a group of 9's. Also the number of 9's in this group equals the number of digits in the recurring part of the decimal.

Thus, in the second case, the fraction is derived by dividing 24 by 99. (24 being the recurring part of the decimal and 99 having 2 nines because the number of digits in 24 is 2.)

Similarly, $0.43576254357625.... = \dfrac{4357625}{9999999}$

**Type 2—Impure recurring decimals:** Unlike pure recurring decimals, in these decimals, the recurrence occurs after a certain number of digits in the decimal. The process to convert these into a fraction is also best illustrated by an example:

Consider the decimal 0.435424242

$$= 0.435\overline{42}$$

The fractional value of the same will be given by: $(43542 - 435)/99000$. This can be understood in two steps.

**Step 1:**   Subtract the non-recurring initial part of the decimal (in this case, it is 435) from the number formed by writing down the starting digits of the decimal value upto the digit where the recurring decimals are written for the first time;

Expanding the meaning—

**Note**: For 0.435424242, subtract 435 from 43542

**Step 2:**   The number thus obtained, has to be divided by a number formed as follows; Write down as many 9's as the number of digits in the recurring part of the decimal. (in this case, since the recurring part '42' has 2 digits, we write down 2 9's.) These nines have to be followed by as many zeroes as the number of digits in the non recurring part of the decimal value. (In this case, the non recurring part of the decimal value is '435'. Since, 435 has 3 digits, attach three zeroes to the two nines to get the number to divide the result of the first step.)

Hence divide $43542 - 435$ by 99000 to get the fraction.

Similarly, for 3.436213213 we get $\dfrac{436213 - 436}{999000}$.

## Mixed Fractions

A *mixed number* is a whole number plus a fraction. Here are a few mixed numbers:

$$1\frac{1}{2}, \quad 1\frac{1}{4}, \quad 2\frac{1}{3}, \quad 2\frac{2}{7}, \quad 5\frac{4}{5}$$

In order to convert a mixed fraction to a proper fraction you do the following conversion process.

$$1\frac{1}{2} = (1 \times 2 + 1)/2 = 3/2$$

$$2\frac{1}{3} = (2 \times 3 + 1)/3 = 7/3$$

Similarly,   $1\frac{1}{4} = 5/4$

$2\frac{2}{7} = 16/7$

$5\frac{4}{5} = 29/5$ and so on.

i.e. multiply the whole number part of the mixed number by the denominator of the fractional part and add the resultant to the numerator of the fractional part to get the numerator of the proper fraction. The denominator of the proper fraction would be the same as the denominator of the mixed fraction.

# ❻ OPERATIONS ON NUMBERS

## Exponents and Powers

**Exponents, or powers, are an important part of math as they are necessary to indicate that a number is multiplied by itself for a given number of times.**

When a number is multiplied by itself it gives the 'square of the number'.

Thus, $n \times n = n^2$ (for example $3 \times 3 = 3^2$)

If the same number is multiplied by itself twice we get the cube of the number.

Thus, $n \times n \times n = n^3$ (for example $3 \times 3 \times 3 = 3^3$)

$n \times n \times n \times n = n^4$ and so on.

With respect to powers of numbers, there are 5 basic rules which you should know:

For any number '$n$' the following rules would apply:

Rule 1: $n^a \times n^b = n^{(a+b)}$. Thus, $4^3 \times 4^5 = 4^8$.

Rule 2: $n^a / n^b = n^{a-b}$ . Thus, $3^9/3^4 = 3^5$.

Rule 3: $(n^a)^b = n^{ab}$. Thus, $(3^2)^4 = 3^8$.

Rule 4: $n^{(-a)} = 1/n^a$. Thus, $3^{-4} = 1/3^4$.

Rule 5: $n^0 = 1$. Thus, $5^0 = 1$.

These are also popularly known as the rules of indices.

## General Form of Writing 2-3 Digit Numbers

In mathematics many a time we have to use algebraic equations in order to solve questions. In such cases an important concept is the way we represent two or three digit numbers in equation form.

For instance, suppose we have a 2 digit number with the digits '$AB$'.

In order to write this in the form of an equation, we have to use:

$10A + B$. This is because in the number '$AB$' the digit $A$ is occupying the tens place. Hence, in order to represent the value of the number '$AB$' in the form of an equation — we can write $10A + B$.

Thus, the number $29 = 2 \times 10 + 9 \times 1$

Similarly, for a three digit number with the digits $A$, $B$ and $C$ respectively — the number '$ABC$' can be represented as below:

$$ABC = 100\,A + 10\,B + C.$$

Thus,  $243 = 2 \times 100 + 4 \times 10 + 3 \times 1$

**The BODMAS Rule:**  It is used for the ordering of mathematical operations in a mathematical situation:

In any mathematical situation, the first thing to be considered is Brackets followed by Division, Multiplication, Addition and Subtraction in that order.

Thus $3 \times 5 - 2 = 15 - 2 = 13$

Also,  $3 \times 5 - 6 \div 3$  $= 15 - 2 = 13$

Also,  $3 \times (5 - 6) \div 3$  $= 3 \times (-1) \div 3 = -1$.

*Operations on Odd and Even numbers*

*ODDS*

| | |
|---|---|
| Odd × odd | = Odd |
| Odd + odd | = Even |
| Odd − odd | = Even |
| Odd ÷ odd | = odd |

*EVENS*

| | |
|---|---|
| Even × Even | = Even |
| Even + Even | = Even |
| Even − even | = Even |
| Even ÷ even | = Even or odd |

*ODDS & EVENS*

| | |
|---|---|
| Odd × Even | = Even |
| Odd + Even | = Odd |
| Odd – Even | = Odd |
| Even ÷ odd | = Even |

Odd ÷ Even → Not divisible

## SERIES OF NUMBERS

In many instances in Mathematics we are presented with a series of numbers formed simply when a group of numbers is written together. The following are examples of series:

1. 3, 5, 8, 12, 17...
2. 3, 7, 11, 15, 19...(Such series where the next term is derived by adding a certain fixed value to the previous number are called as Arithmetic Progressions).
3. 5, 10, 20, 40 .....(Such series where the next term is derived by multiplying the previous term by a fixed value are called as Geometric Progressions).
   (**Note**: You will study AP and GP in details in the chapter of progressions which is chapter 2 of this block.)
4. 2, 7, 22, 67 ....
5. 1/3, 1/5, 1/7, 1/9, 1/11...
6. $1/1^2$, $1/2^2$, $1/3^2$, $1/4^2$, $1/5^2$...
7. $1/1^3$, $1/3^3$, $1/5^3$...

Remember the following points at this stage:

1. AP and GP are two specific instances of series. They are studied in details only because they have many applications and have defined rules.
2. Based on the behaviour of their sums, series can be classified as:

**Divergent:** These are series whose sum to '$n$' terms keeps increasing and reaches infinity for infinite terms.

**Convergent:** Convergent series have the property that their sum tends to approach an upper limit/lower limit as you include more terms in the series. They have the additional property that even when infinite terms of the series are included they will only reach that value and not cross it.

For example consider the series;

$1/1^2 + 1/3^2 + 1/5^2 + 1/7^2$ ...

It is evident that subsequent terms of this series keep getting smaller. Hence, their value becomes negligible after a few terms of the series are taken into account.

If taken to infinite terms, the sum of this series will reach a value which it will never cross. Such series are called convergent, because their sum converges to a limit and only reaches that limit for infinite terms.

**Note:** Questions on finding infinite sums of convergent series are very commonly asked in most aptitude exams including CAT and XAT.

NOTE TO THE READER: NOW THAT YOU ARE THROUGH WITH THE *BACK TO SCHOOL* SECTION, YOU ARE READY TO PROCEED INTO THE CHAPTERS OF THIS BLOCK. HAPPY SOLVING!!

# Number Systems

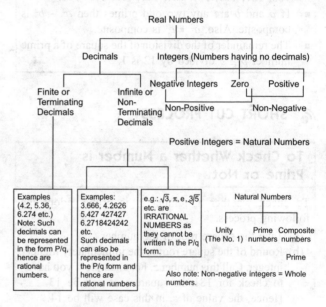

## INTRODUCTION

The chapter on Number Systems is amongst the most important chapters in the entire syllabus of Quantitative Aptitude for the CAT examination (and also for other parallel MBA entrance exams).Students are advised to go through this chapter with utmost care understanding each concept and question type on this topic. The CAT has consistently contained anything between 20–40% of the marks based on questions taken from this chapter. Naturally, this chapter becomes one of the most crucial as far as your quest to reach close to the qualification score in the section of Quantitative Aptitude is concerned.

Hence, going through this chapter and its concepts properly is imperative for you. It would be a good idea to first go through the basic definitions of all types of numbers. Also closely follow the solved examples based on various concepts discussed in the chapter. Also, the approach and attitude while solving questions on this chapter is to try to maximize your learning experience out of every question. Hence, do not just try to solve the questions but also try to think of alternative processes in order to solve the same question. Refer to hints or solutions only as a last resort.

To start off, the following pictorial representation of the types of numbers will help you improve your quality of comprehension of different types of numbers.

## DEFINITION

**Natural Numbers**   These are the numbers (1, 2, 3, etc.) that are used for counting. In other words, all positive integers are natural numbers.

There are infinite natural numbers and the number 1 is the least natural number.

Examples of natural numbers: 1, 2, 4, 8, 32, 23, 4321 and so on.

The following numbers are examples of numbers that are not natural: –2, –31, 2.38, 0 and so on.

Based on divisibility, there could be two types of natural numbers: *Prime* and *Composite*.

**Prime Numbers**   A natural number larger than unity is a prime number if it does not have other divisors except for itself and unity.

**Note:**   Unity (i.e. 1) is not a prime number.

## Some Properties of Prime Numbers

- The lowest prime number is 2.
- 2 is also the only even prime number.
- The lowest odd prime number is 3.

*Contd*

## Some Properties of Prime Numbers
(*Contd*)

- The remainder when a prime number $p \geq 5$ is divided by 6 is 1 or 5. However, if a number on being divided by 6 gives a remainder of 1 or 5 the number need not be prime. Thus, this can be referred to as a necessary but not sufficient condition.
- The remainder of the division of the square of a prime number $p \geq 5$ divided by 24 is 1.
- For prime numbers $p > 3$, $p^2 - 1$ is divisible by 24.
- Prime Numbers between 1 to 100 are: 2, 3, 5, 7, 11, 13, 17, 19, 23, 29, 31, 37, 41, 43, 47, 53, 59, 61, 67, 71, 73, 79, 83, 89, 97.
- Prime Numbers between 100 to 200 are: 101, 103, 107, 109, 113, 127, 131, 137, 139, 149, 151, 157, 163, 167, 173, 179, 181, 191, 193, 197, 199.
- If $a$ and $b$ are any two odd primes then $a^2 - b^2$ is composite. Also, $a^2 + b^2$ is composite.
- The remainder of the division of the square of a prime number $p \geq 5$ divided by 12 is 1.

## ⌕ SHORT CUT PROCESS

## To Check Whether a Number is Prime or Not

To check whether a number N is prime, adopt the following process.

(a) Take the square root of the number.

(b) Round of the square root to the immediately higher integer. Call this number $z$. For example if you have to check for 181, its square root will be 13.___ Hence, the value of $z$, in this case will be 14.

(c) Check for divisibility of the number $N$ by all prime numbers below $z$. If there is no prime number below the value of $z$ which divides $N$ then the number $N$ will be prime.

To illustrate :-
The value of $\sqrt{239}$ lies between 15 to 16. Hence, take the value of $z$ as 16.

Prime numbers less than or equal to 16 are 2, 3, 5, 7, 11 and 13, 239 is not divisible by any of these. Hence you can conclude that 239 is a prime number.

## A Brief Look into why this Works?

Suppose you are asked to find the factors of the number 40.

An untrained mind will find the factors as : 1, 2, 4, 5, 8, 10, 20 and 40.

The same task will be performed by a trained mind as follows:

$$
\begin{array}{ccc}
1 & \times & 40 \\
2 & \times & 20 \\
4 & \times & 10 \\
\text{and} \quad 5 & \times & 8
\end{array}
$$

i.e., The discovery of one factor will automatically yield the other factor. In other words, factors will appear in terms of what can be called as factor pairs. The locating of one factor, will automatically pinpoint the other one for you. Thus, in the example above, when you find 5 as a factor of 40, you will automatically get 8 too as a factor.

Now take a look again at the pairs in the example above. If you compare the values in each pair with the square root of 40 (i.e. 6.___) you will find that for each pair the number in the left column is lower than the square root of 40, while the number in the right column is higher than the square root of 40.

This is a property for all numbers and is always true.

Hence, we can now phrase this as: Whenever you have to find the factors of any number N, you will get the factors in pairs (i.e. factor pairs). Further, the factor pairs will be such that in each pair of factors, one of the factors will be lower than the square root of N while the other will be higher than the square root of N.

As a result of this fact one need not make any effort to find the factors of a number above the square root of the number. These come automatically. All you need to do is to find the factors below the square root of the number.

*Extending this logic, we can say that if we are not able to find a factor of a number upto the value of its square root, we will not be able to find any factor above the square root and the number under consideration will be a prime number.* This is the reason why when we need to check whether a number is prime, we have to check for factors only below the square root.

But, we have said that you need to check for divisibility only with the prime numbers below (and including) the square root of the number.

Let us look at an example to understand why you need to look only at prime numbers below the square root.

Uptil now, we have deduced that in order to check whether a number is prime, we just need to do a factor search below (and including) the square root.

Thus, for example, in order to find whether 181 is a prime number, we need to check with the numbers = 2, 3, 4, 5, 6, 7, 8, 9, 10, 11, 12, and 13.

The first thing you will realise, when you first look at the list above is that all even numbers will get eliminated automatically (since no even number can divide an odd number and of course you will check a number for being prime only if it is odd!)

This will leave you with the numbers 3, 5, 7, 9, 11 and 13 to check 181.

**Why do we not need to check with composite numbers below the square root?** This will again be understood best if explained in the context of the example above. The only composite number in the list above is 9. You do not need to check with 9, because when you checked $N$ for divisibility with 3 you would get either of two cases:

**Case I: If N is divisible by 3:** In such a case, $N$ will automatically become non-prime and you can stop your checking. Hence, you will not need to check for the divisibility of the number by 9.

**Case II: N is not divisible by 3**: If $N$ is not divisible by 3, it is obvious that it will not be divisible by 9. Hence, you will not need to check for the divisibility of the number by 9.

Thus, in either case, checking for divisibility by a composite number (9 in this case) will become useless. This will be true for all composite numbers.

Hence, when we have to check whether a number $N$ is prime or not, we need to only check for its divisibility by prime factors below the square root of $N$.

## Finding Prime Numbers: The Short Cut

Using the logic that we have to look at only the prime numbers below the square root in order to check whether a number is prime, we can actually cut short the time for finding whether a number is prime drastically.

Before I start to explain this, you should perhaps realise that in an examination like the CAT, or any other aptitude test for that matter whenever you would need to be checking for whether a number is prime or not, you would typically be checking 2 digit or maximum 3 digit numbers in the range of 100 to 200.

Also, one would never really need to check with the prime number 5, because divisibility by 5 would automatically be visible and thus, there is no danger of anyone ever declaring a number like 35 to be prime. Hence, in the list of prime numbers below the square root we would never include 5 as a number to check with.

## Checking Whether a Number is Prime (For Numbers below 49)

The only number you would need to check for divisibility with is the number 3. Thus, 47 is prime because it is not divisible by 3.

## Checking Whether a Number is Prime (For Numbers above 49 and below 121)

Naturally you would need to check this with 3 and 7. But if you remember that 77, 91 and 119 are not prime, you would be able to spot the prime numbers below 121 by just checking for divisibility with the number 3.

Why? Well, the odd numbers between 49 and 121 which are divisible by 7 are 63, 77, 91, 105 and 119. Out of these perhaps 91 and 119 are the only numbers that you can mistakenly declare as prime. 77 and 105 are so obviously

not-prime that you would never be in danger of declaring them prime.

Thus, for numbers between 49 and 121 you can find whether a number is prime or not by just dividing by 3 and checking for its divisibility.

For example:
61 is prime because it is not divisible by 3 and it is neither 91 nor 119.

## Checking Whether a Number is Prime (For Numbers above 121 and below 169)

Naturally you would need to check this with 3, 7 and 11. But if you remember that 133,143 and 161 are not prime, you would be able to spot the prime numbers between 121 to 169 by just checking for divisibility with the number 3.

Why? The same logic as explained above. The odd numbers between 121 and 169 which are divisible by either 7 or 11 are 133,143,147,161 and 165. Out of these 133,143 and 161 are the only numbers that you can mistakenly declare as prime if you do not check for 7 or 11. The number 147 would be found to be not prime when you check its divisibility by 3 while the number 165 you would never need to check for, for obvious reasons.

Thus, for numbers between 121 and 169 you can find whether a number is prime or not by just dividing by 3 and checking for its divisibility.

For example:
149, is prime because it is not divisible by 3 and it is neither 133,143 nor 161.

Thus, we have been able to go all the way till 169 with just checking for divisibility with the number 3.

This logic can be represented on the number line as follows:

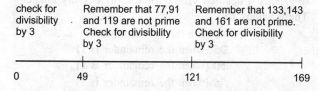

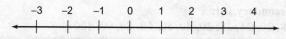

**Integers** A set which consists of natural numbers, negative integers $(-1, -2, -3 \ldots -n \ldots)$ and zero is known as the set of integers. The numbers belonging to this set are known as integers.

Integers can be visualised on the number line:

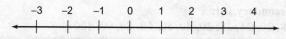

---

**Note:** Positive integers are the same thing as natural numbers.

---

The moment you define integers, you automatically define **decimals**.

## Decimals

A *decimal* number is a number with a *decimal point* in it, like these: 1.5, 3.21, 4.173, 5.1, etc.

The number to the left of the decimal is an ordinary whole number. The first number to the right of the decimal is the number of tenths (1/10's). The second is the number of hundredths (1/100's) and so on. So, for the number 5.1, this is a shorthand way of writing the mixed number $5\frac{1}{10}$. 3.27 is the same as $3 + 2/10 + 7/100$.

---

### A word on where decimals originate from

Consider the situation where there are 5 children and you have to distribute 10 chocolates between them in such a way that all the chocolates should be distributed and each child should get an equal number of chocolates? How would you do it? Well, simple—divide 10 by 5 to get 2 chocolates per child.

Now consider what if you had to do the same thing with 9 chocolates amongst 5 children? In such a case you would not be able to give an integral number of chocolates to each person. You would give 1 chocolate each to all the 5 and the 'remainder' 4 would have to be divided into 5 parts. 4 out of 5 would give rise to the decimal 0.8 and hence you would give 1.8 chocolates to each child. That is how the concept of decimals enters mathematics in the first place.

Taking this concept further, you can realize that the decimal value of any fraction essentially emerges out of the remainder when the numerator of the fraction is divided by the denominator. Also, since we know that each divisor has a few defined remainders possible, there would be a limited set of decimals that each denominator gives rise to.

Thus, for example the divisor 4 gives rise to only 4 remainders (viz. 0,1,2 and 3) and hence it would give rise to exactly 4 decimal values when it divides any integer. These values are:

0 (when the remainder is 0)
.25 (when the remainder is 1)
.50 (when the remainder is 2)
.75 (when the remainder is 3)

There would be similar connotations for all integral divisors—although the key is to know the decimals that the following divisors give you:

**Primary list:**
2, 3, 4, 5, 6, 7, 8, 9, 10, 11, 12, 15, 16

**Secondary list:**
18, 20, 24, 25, 30, 40, 50, 60, 80, 90, 120

---

**Composite Numbers** It is a natural number that has at least one divisor different from unity and itself.

Every composite number $n$ can be factored into its prime factors. (This is sometimes called the canonical form of a number.)

In mathematical terms: $n = p_1^{m} \cdot p_2^{n} \ldots p_k^{s}$, where $p_1, p_2 \ldots p_k$ are prime numbers called factors and $m, n \ldots k$ are natural numbers.

Thus, $24 = 2^3 \cdot 3$, $84 = 7 \cdot 3 \cdot 2^2$, etc.

This representation of a composite number is known as the standard form of a composite number. It is an extermely useful form of seeing a composite number as we shall see.

**Whole Numbers** The set of numbers that includes all natural numbers and the number zero are called whole numbers. Whole numbers are also called as non-negative integers.

**The Concept of the Number Line** The number line is a straight line between negative infinity on the left to positive infinity to the right.

The distance between any two points on the number line is got by subtracting the lower value from the higher value. Alternately, we can also start with the lower number and find the required addition to reach the higher number.

For example: The distance between the points 7 and –4 will be $7 - (-4) = 11$.

**Real Numbers** All numbers that can be represented on the number line are called real numbers. Every real number can be approximately replaced with a terminating decimal.

The following operations of addition, subtraction, multiplication and division are valid for both whole numbers and real numbers: [For any real or whole numbers $a$, $b$ and $c$].

(a) Commutative property of addition: $a + b = b + a$.
(b) Associative property of addition: $(a + b) + c = a + (b + c)$.
(c) Commutative property of multiplication: $a \cdot b = b \cdot a$.
(d) Associative property of multiplication: $(a \cdot b) \cdot c = a \cdot (b \cdot c)$.
(e) Distributive property of multiplication with respect to addition: $(a + b) c = ac + bc$.
(f) Subtraction and division are defined as the inverse operations to addition and multiplication respectively.

Thus if $a + b = c$, then $c - b = a$ and if $q = a/b$ then $b \cdot q = a$ (where $b \neq 0$).

Division by zero is not possible since there is no number $q$ for which $b \cdot q$ equals $a$ non zero number $a$ if $b$ is zero.

**Rational Numbers** A rational number is defined as a number of the form $a/b$ where $a$ and $b$ are integers and $b \neq 0$.

The set of rational numbers encloses the set of integers and fractions. The rules given above for addition, subtraction, multiplication and division also apply on rational numbers.

Rational numbers that are not integral will have decimal values. These values can be of two types:

(a) **Terminating (or finite) decimal fractions:** For example, 17/4 = 4.25, 21/5 = 4.2 and so forth.

(b) **Non-terminating decimal fractions:** Amongst non-terminating decimal fractions there are two types of decimal values:

(i) *Non-terminating periodic fractions*: These are non-terminating decimal fractions of the type $x \cdot a_1 a_2 a_3 a_4$ $\ldots a_n a_1 a_2 a_3 a_4 \ldots a_n a_1 a_2 a_3 a_4 \ldots a_n$. For example $\frac{16}{3} = 5.3333, 15.23232323, 14.287628762\ 876 \ldots$ and so on.

(ii) *Non-terminating non-periodic fractions*: These are of the form $x \cdot b_1 b_2 b_3 b_4 \ldots b_n c_1 c_2 c_3 \ldots c_n$. For example: 5.2731687143725186....

Of the above categories, terminating decimal and non-terminating periodic decimal fractions belong to the set of rational numbers.

*Irrational Numbers* Fractions, that are non-terminating, non-periodic fractions, are irrational numbers.

Some examples of irrational numbers are $\sqrt{2}$, $\sqrt{3}$, etc. In other words, all square and cube roots of natural numbers that are not squares and cubes of natural numbers are irrational. Other irrational numbers include $\pi$, $e$ and so on.

Every positive irrational number has a negative irrational number corresponding to it.

All operations of addition, subtraction, multiplication and division applicable to rational numbers are also applicable to irrational numbers.

As briefly stated in the Back to School section, whenever an expression contains a rational and an irrational number together, the two have to be carried together till the end. In other words, an irrational number once it appears in the solution of a question will continue to appear till the end of the question. This concept is particularly useful in Geometry For example: If you are asked to find the ratio of the area of a circle to that of an equilateral triangle, you can expect to see a $\pi / \sqrt{3}$ in the answer. This is because the area of a circle will always have a $\pi$ component in it, while that of an equilateral triangle will always have $\sqrt{3}$.

You should realise that once an irrational number appears in the solution of a question, it can only disappear if it is multiplied or divided by the same irrational number.

### THE CONCEPT OF GCD (GREATEST COMMON DIVISOR OR HIGHEST COMMON FACTOR)

Consider two natural numbers $n$, and $n_2$.

If the numbers $n_1$ and $n_2$ are exactly divisible by the same number $x$, then $x$ is a common divisor of $n_1$ and $n_2$.

The highest of all the common divisors of $n_1$ and $n_2$ is called as the GCD or the HCF. This is denoted as GCD $(n_1, n_2)$.

### Rules for Finding the GCD of Two Numbers $n_1$ and $n_2$

(a) Find the standard form of the numbers $n_1$ and $n_2$.

(b) Write out all prime factors that are common to the standard forms of the numbers $n_1$ and $n_2$.

(c) Raise each of the common prime factors listed above to the lesser of the powers in which it appears in the standard forms of the numbers $n_1$ and $n_2$.

(d) The product of the results of the previous step will be the GCD of $n_1$ and $n_2$.

**Illustration:** Find the GCD of 150, 210, 375.

*Step 1:* Writing down the standard form of numbers

$$150 = 5 \times 5 \times 3 \times 2$$
$$210 = 5 \times 2 \times 7 \times 3$$
$$375 = 5 \times 5 \times 5 \times 3$$

*Step 2:* Writing Prime factors common to all the three numbers is $5^1 \times 3^1$

*Step 3:* This will give the same result, i.e. $5^1 \times 3^1$

*Step 4:* Hence, the HCF will be $5 \times 3 = 15$

For practice, find the HCF of the following:

(a) 78, 39, 195
(b) 440, 140, 390
(c) 198, 121, 1331

### SHORTCUT FOR FINDING THE HCF

The above 'school' process of finding the HCF (or the GCD) of a set of numbers is however extremely cumbersome and time taking. Let us take a look at a much faster way of finding the HCF of a set of numbers.

Suppose you were required to find the HCF of 39,78 and 195

*Logic* The HCF of these numbers would necessarily have to be a factor (divisor) of the difference between any pair of numbers from the above 3. i.e. the HCF has to be a factor of $(78 - 39 = 39)$ as well as of $(195 - 39 = 156)$ and $(195 - 78 = 117)$. Why?

Well the logic is simple if you were to consider the tables of numbers on the number line.

For any two numbers on the number line, a common divisor would be one which divides both. However, for any number to be able to divide both the numbers, it can only do so if it is a factor of the difference between the two numbers. Got it??

Take an example:

Let us say we take the numbers 68 and 119. The difference between them being 51, it is not possible for any number outside the factor list of 51 to divide both 68 and 119. Thus, for example a number like 4, which divides 68 can never divide any number which is 51 away from 68- because 4 is not a factor of 51.

Only factors of 51, i.e. 51,17,3 and 1 *'could'* divide both these numbers simultaneously.

Hence, getting back to the HCF problem we were trying to tackle—take the difference between any two numbers of the set—of course if you want to reduce your calculations in the situation, take the difference between the two closest numbers. In this case that would be the difference between 78 and 39 =39.

'You can of course realise that in case you see a prime number difference between two of the numbers, you would prefer the prime number difference even if it is not the smallest difference—as in such a case, either the prime number itself would be the HCF of all the numbers or in case it does not divide even one of the numbers, 1 would become the HCF. For example: If you had to find the HCF of 122,144,203 & 253, the difference between 144 and 203 can be seen to be 59 & it is evident that 59 is not the HCF here & hence the HCF of the given numbers would be 1.'

**The HCF has then to be a factor of this number.** In order to find the factors quickly remember to use the fact we learnt in the back to school section of this part of the book—that whenever we have to find the list of factors/ divisors for any number we have to search the factors below the square root and the factors above the square root would be automatically visible)

A factor search of the number 39 yields the following factors:

$$1 \times 39$$
$$3 \times 13$$

Hence, one of these 4 numbers has to be the HCF of the numbers 39,78 and 195. Since we are trying to locate the **Highest** common factor—we would begin our search from the highest number (viz:39)

**Check for divisibility by 39** Any one number out of 39 and 78 and also check the number 195 for divisibility by 39. You would find all the three numbers are divisible by 39 and hence 39 can be safely taken to be the correct answer for the HCF of 39,78 and 195.

Suppose the numbers were:
**39, 78 and 182?**

The HCF would still be a factor of 78 – 39 = 39. The probable candidates for the HCF's value would still remain 1,3,13 and 39.

When you check for divisibility of all these numbers by 39, you would realize that 182 is not divisible and hence 39 would not be the HCF in this case.

The next check would be with the number 13. It can be seen that 13 divides 39 (hence would automatically divide 78—no need to check that) and also divides 182. Hence, 13 would be the required HCF of the three numbers.

## Typical questions where HCF is used directly

**Question 1:** The sides of a hexagonal field are 216, 423, 1215, 1422, 2169 and 2223 metres. Find the greatest length of tape that would be able to exactly measure each of these sides without having to use fractions/parts of the tape?

In this question we are required to identify the HCF of the numbers 216,423,1215, 1422, 2169 and 2223.

In order to do that, we first find the smallest difference between any two of these numbers. It can be seen that the difference between 2223-2169 = 54. Thus, the required HCF would be a factor of the number 54.

The factors of 54 are:

$$1 \times 54$$
$$2 \times 27$$
$$3 \times 18$$
$$6 \times 9$$

One of these 8 numbers has to be the HCF of the 6 numbers. 54 cannot be the HCF because the numbers 423 and 2223 being odd numbers would not be divisible by any even number. Thus, we do not need to check any even numbers in the list.

27 does not divide 423 and hence cannot be the HCF. 18 can be skipped as it is even.
Checking for 9:
9 divides 216,423,1215,1422 and 2169. Hence, it would become the HCF. (Note: we do not need to check 2223 once we know that 2169 is divisible by 9)

**Question 2:** A nursery has 363,429 and 693 plants respectively of 3 distinct varieties. It is desired to place these plants in straight rows of plants of 1 variety only so that the number of rows required is the minimum. What is the size of each row and how many rows would be required?

The size of each row would be the HCF of 363, 429 and 693. Difference between 363 and 429 = 66. Factors of 66 are 66, 33, 22, 11, 6, 3, 2, 1.

66 need not be checked as it is even and 363 is odd. 33 divides 363, hence would automatically divide 429 and also divides 693. Hence, 33 is the correct answer for the size of each row.

For how many rows would be required we need to follow the following process:

Minimum number of rows required = 363/33 + 429/33 + 693/33 = 11 + 13 + 21 = 45 rows.

## THE CONCEPT OF LCM (LEAST COMMON MULTIPLE)

Let $n_1$, and $n_2$ be two natural numbers distinct from each other. The smallest natural number $n$ that is exactly divisible by $n_1$ and $n_2$ is called the Least Common Multiple (LCM) of $n_1$ and $n_2$ and is designated as LCM ($n_1, n_2$).

## Rule for Finding the LCM of two Numbers $n_1$ and $n_2$

(a) Find the standard form of the numbers $n_1$ and $n_2$.

(b) Write out all the prime factors, which are contained in the standard forms of either of the numbers.

(c) Raise each of the prime factors listed above to the highest of the powers in which it appears in the standard forms of the numbers $n_1$ and $n_2$.

(d) The product of results of the previous step will be the LCM of $n_1$ and $n_2$.

**Illustration:** Find the LCM of 150, 210, 375.

**Step 1:** Writing down the standard form of numbers

$$150 = 5 \times 5 \times 3 \times 2$$
$$210 = 5 \times 2 \times 7 \times 3$$
$$375 = 5 \times 5 \times 5 \times 3$$

**Step 2:** Write down all the prime factors: that appear at least once in any of the numbers: 5, 3, 2, 7.

**Step 3:** Raise each of the prime factors to their highest available power (considering each to the numbers).

The LCM $= 2^1 \times 3^1 \times 5^3 \times 7^1 = 5250$.

**Important Rule:**

GCD $(n_1, n_2)$. LCM $(n_1, n_2) = n_1 \cdot n_2$

i.e. The product of the HCF and the LCM equals the product of the numbers.

**Note:** This rule is applicable only for two numbers

## 🔊 SHORT CUT FOR FINDING THE LCM

The LCM (least common multiple) again has a much faster way of doing it than what we learnt in school.

The process has to do with the use of co-prime numbers.

Before we look at the process, let us take a fresh look at what co-prime numbers are:

Co-prime numbers are any two numbers which have an HCF of 1, i.e. when two numbers have no common prime factor apart from the number 1, they are called co-prime or relatively prime to each other.

## Some Rules for Co-primes

### 2 Numbers being co-prime

(i) Two consecutive natural numbers are always co-prime (Example 5, 6; 82, 83; 749, 750 and so on)

(ii) Two consecutive odd numbers are always co-prime (Examples: 7, 9; 51, 53; 513, 515 and so on)

(iii) Two prime numbers are always co-prime (Examples: 13, 17; 53, 71 and so on)

(iv) One prime number and another composite number (such that the composite number is not a multiple of the prime number) are always co-prime (Examples:

17, 38; 23, 49 and so on, but note that 17 and 51 are not co-prime)

(v) Two odd numbers with a difference that is equal to any power of 2. (Examples: 17,21; 33,97; 21,85; 33,65)

(vi) Two numbers that have a difference of 3, but are themselves not multiples of 3 (Examples: 32,35; 43,46; 71,74 and so on)

3 or more numbers being co-prime with each other means that all possible pairs of the numbers would be co-prime with each other.

Thus, 47, 49, 51 and 52 are co-prime since each of the 6 pairs (47,49); (47,51); (47,52); (49,51); (49,52) and (51,52) are co-prime.

## Rules for Spotting three Co-prime Numbers

(i) Three consecutive odd numbers are always co-prime (Examples: 15, 17, 19; 51, 53, 55 and so on)

(ii) Three consecutive natural numbers with the first one being odd (Examples: 15, 16, 17; 21, 22, 23; 41, 42, 43 and so on). Note that 22, 23, 24 are not co-prime

(iii) Two consecutive natural numbers along-with the next odd number such that the first no. is even (Examples: 22, 23, 25; 52, 53, 55; 68, 69, 71 and so on). Please note that this would not be true in case the first and the last number would be a multiple of 3.

(iv) Three prime numbers (Examples: 17, 23, 29; 13, 31, 43 and so on)

(v) Two prime numbers and one composite number such that the composite number is not a multiple of either of the primes (Examples: 23,31 & 42; 17,23 & 28; 13,23 & 27 and so on)

(vi) Three odd numbers for which the pair wise difference for each of the three pairs of numbers taken two at a time is a power of 2. (Examples: 21,25,29; 55,63,71 and so on)

So what do co-prime numbers have to do with LCMs?

By using the logic of co-prime numbers, you can actually bypass the need to take out the prime factors of the set of numbers for which you are trying to find the LCM. How?

The following process will make it clear:

Let us say that you were trying to find the LCM of 9,10,12 and 15.

The LCM can be directly written as: $9 \times 10 \times 2$. The thinking that gives you the value of the LCM is as follows:

**Step 1:** If you can see a set of 2 or more co-prime numbers in the set of numbers for which you are finding the LCM- write them down by multiplying them.

So in the above situation, since we can see that 9 and 10 are co-prime to each other we can start off writing the LCM by writing $9 \times 10$ as the first step.

**Step 2:** For each of the other numbers, consider what part of them have already been taken into the answer and what part remains outside the answer. In case you see any part of the other numbers such that it is not a part of the value of the LCM you are writing—such a part would need to be taken into the answer of the LCM.

The process will be clear once you see what we do (and how we think) with the remaining 2 numbers in the above problem.

At this point when we have written down $9 \times 10$ we already have taken into account the numbers 9 and 10 leaving us to account for 12 and 15.

**Thought about 12:** 12 is $2 \times 2 \times 3$

$9 \times 10$ already has a 3 and 2 in its prime factors. However, the number 12 has two 2's. This means that one of the two 2's of the number 12 is still not accounted for in our answer. Hence, we need to modify the LCM by multiplying the existing $9 \times 10$ by a 2. With this change the LCM now becomes:

$$9 \times 10 \times 2$$

**Thought about 15:** 15 is $5 \times 3$

$9 \times 10 \times 2$ already has a 5 and a 3. Hence, there is no need to add anything to the existing answer.

Thus, $9 \times 10 \times 2$ would become the correct answer for the LCM of the numbers 9, 10, 12 and 15.

What if the numbers were: 9, 10, 12 and 25

Step 1: 9 and 10 are co-prime

Hence, the starting value is $9 \times 10$

**Thought about 12:** 12 is $2 \times 2 \times 3$

$9 \times 10$ already has a 3 and one 2 in it prime factors. However, the number 12 has two 2's. This means that one of the two 2's of the number 12 is still not accounted for in our answer. Hence, we need to modify the LCM by multiplying the existing $9 \times 10$ by a 2. With this change the LCM now becomes:

$$9 \times 10 \times 2$$

**Thought about 25:** 25 is $5 \times 5$

$9 \times 10 \times 2$ has only one 5. Hence, we need to add another 5 to the answer.

Thus, $9 \times 10 \times 2 \times 5$ would become the correct answer for the LCM of the numbers 9, 10, 12 and 25.

## Rule for Finding out HCF and LCM of Fractions

(A) HCF of two or more fractions is given by:

$$\frac{\text{HCF of Numerators}}{\text{LCM of Denominators}}$$

(B) LCM of two or more fractions is given by:

$$\frac{\text{LCM of Numerators}}{\text{HCF of Denominators}}$$

**Note:** Make sure that you reduce the fractions to their lowest forms before you use these formulae.

### Typical questions on LCMs

You would be able to see most of the standard questions on LCMs in the practice exercise on HCF and LCM given below.

## HCF and LCM

### PRACTICE EXERCISE

(Typical questions asked in Exams)

1. Find the common factors for the numbers.
   - (a) 24 and 64
   - (b) 42, 294 and 882
   - (c) 60, 120 and 220

2. Find the HCF of
   - (a) 420 and 1782
   - (b) 36 and 48
   - (c) 54, 72, 198 ·
   - (d) 62, 186 and 279

3. Find the LCM of
   - (a) 13, 23 and 48
   - (b) 24, 36, 44 and 62
   - (c) 22, 33, 45, and 72
   - (d) 13, 17, 21 and 33

4. Find the series of common multiples of
   - (a) 54 and 36
   - (b) 33, 45 and 60

   [*Hint*: Find the LCM and then create an Arithmetic progression with the first term as the LCM and the common difference also as the LCM.]

5. The LCM of two numbers is 936. If their HCF is 4 and one of the numbers is 72, the other is:
   - (a) 42
   - (b) 52
   - (c) 62
   - (d) None of these

   [Answer: (b). Use HCF × LCM = product of numbers.]

6. Two alarm clocks ring their alarms at regular intervals of 50 seconds and 48 seconds. If they first beep together at 12 noon, at what time will they beep again for the first time?
   - (a) 12:10 P.M.
   - (b) 12:12 P.M.
   - (c) 12:11 P.M.
   - (d) None of these

   [Answer: (d). The LCM of 50 and 48 being 1200, the two clocks will ring again after 1200 seconds.]

7. 4 Bells toll together at 9:00 A.M. They toll after 7, 8, 11 and 12 seconds respectively. How many times will they toll together again in the next 3 hours?
   - (a) 3
   - (b) 4
   - (c) 5
   - (d) 6

   [Answer: (c). The LCM of 7, 8, 11 and 12 is 1848. Hence, the answer will be got by the quotient of the ratio (10800)/(1848) → 5.]

8. On Ashok Marg three consecutive traffic lights change after 36, 42 and 72 seconds, respectively. If the lights are first switched on at 9:00 A.M. sharp, at what time will they change simultaneously?
   - (a) 9 : 08 : 04
   - (b) 9 : 08 : 24
   - (c) 9 : 08 : 44
   - (d) None of these

   [Answer (b). The LCM of 36, 42 and 72 is 504. Hence, the lights will change simultaneously after 8 minutes and 24 seconds.]

9. The HCF of 2472, 1284 and a third number 'N' is 12. If their LCM is $2^3 \times 3^2 \times 5^1 \times 103 \times 107$, then the number 'N' could be:

   (a) $2^2 \times 3^2 \times 7^1$      (b) $2^2 \times 3^3 \times 103$

   (c) $2^2 \times 3^2 \times 5^1$      (d) None of these

   [Answer: (c)]

10. Two equilateral triangles have the sides of lengths 34 and 85, respectively.

    (a) The greatest length of tape that can measure both of them exactly is:

    [Answer: HCF of 34 and 85 is 17.]

    (b) How many such equal parts can be measured?

    [Answer: $\frac{34}{17} \times 3 + \frac{85}{17} \times 3 = 2 \times 3 + 5 \times 3 = 21$]

11. Two numbers are in the ratio 17:13. If their HCF is 15, what are the numbers?

    (Answer: $17 \times 15$ and $13 \times 15$ i.e. 255 and 195 respectively.) [Note : This can be done when the numbers are co-prime.]

12. A forester wants to plant 44 apple trees, 66 banana trees and 110 mango trees in equal rows (in terms of number of trees). Also, he wants to make distinct rows of trees (i.e. only one type of tree in one row). The number of rows (minimum) that are required are:

    (a) 2      (b) 3

    (c) 10      (d) 11

    [Answer: (c) 44/22 + 66/22 + 110/22 (Since 22 is the HCF)]

13. Three runners running around a circular track can complete one revolution in 2, 4 and 5.5 hours, respectively. When will they meet at the starting point?

    (a) 22      (b) 33

    (c) 11      (d) 44

    (The answer will be the LCM of 2, 4 and 11/2. This will give you 44 as the answer).

14. The HCF and LCM of two numbers are 33 and 264, respectively. When the first number is divided by 2, the quotient is 33. The other number is?

    (a) 66      (b) 132

    (c) 198      (d) 99

    [Answer: $33 \times 264 = 66 \times n$. Hence, $n = 132$]

15. The greatest number which will divide: 4003, 4126 and 4249:

    (a) 43      (b) 41

    (c) 45      (d) None of these

    The answer will be the HCF of the three numbers. (1 in this case)

16. Which of the following represents the largest 4 digit number which can be added to 7249 in order to make the derived number divisible by each of 12, 14, 21, 33, and 54.

    (a) 9123      (b) 9383

    (c) 8727      (d) None of these

    [Answer: The LCM of the numbers 12, 14, 21, 33 and 54 is 8316. Hence, in order for the condition to be satisfied we need to get the number as:

    $$7249 + n = 8316 \times 2$$

    Hence,      $n = 9383$.]

17. Find the greatest number of 5 digits, that will give us a remainder of 5, when divided by 8 and 9, respectively.

    (a) 99931      (b) 99941

    (c) 99725      (d) None of these

    [Answer: The LCM of 8 and 9 is 72. The largest 5 digit multiple of 72 is 99936. Hence, the required answer is 99941.]

18. The least perfect square number which is divisible by 3, 4, 6, 8, 10 and 11 is:

    Solution: The number should have at least one 3, three 2's, one 5 and one 11 for it to be divisible by 3, 4, 6, 8, 10 and 11.

    Further, each of the prime factors should be having an even power in order to be a perfect square. Thus, the correct answer will be: $3 \times 3 \times 2 \times 2 \times 2 \times 2 \times 5 \times 5 \times 11 \times 11$

19. Find the greatest number of four digits which when divided by 10, 11, 15 and 22 leaves 3, 4, 8 and 15 as remainders, respectively.

    (a) 9907      (b) 9903

    (c) 9893      (d) None of these

    [Answer: First find the greatest 4 digit multiple of the LCM of 10, 11, 15 and 22. (In this case it is 9900). Then, subtract 7 from it to give the answer.]

20. Find the HCF of $(3^{125} - 1)$ and $(3^{35} - 1)$.

    [Answer: The solution of this question is based on the rule that:

    The HCF of $(a^m - 1)$ and $(a^n - 1)$ is given by $(a^{\text{HCF of } m, n} - 1)$

    Thus, in this question the answer is: $(3^5 - 1)$. Since 5 is the HCF of 35 and 125.]

21. What will be the least possible number of the planks, if three pieces of timber 42 m, 49 m and 63 m long have to be divided into planks of the same length?

    (a) 7      (b) 8

    (c) 22      (d) None of these

22. Find the greatest number, which will divide 215, 167 and 135 so as to leave the same remainder in each case.

    (a) 64      (b) 32

    (c) 24      (d) 16

23. Find the L.C.M of 2.5, 0.5 and 0.175.

    (a) 2.5      (b) 5

    (c) 7.5      (d) 17.5

24. The L.C.M of 4.5; 0.009; and 0.18 = ?

    (a) 4.5      (b) 45

    (c) 0.225      (d) 2.25

25. The L.C.M of two numbers is 1890 and their H.C.F is 30. If one of them is 270, the other will be
    (a) 210          (b) 220
    (c) 310          (d) 320

26. What is the smallest number which when increased by 6 is divisible by 36, 63 and 108?
    (a) 750          (b) 752
    (c) 754          (d) 756

27. The smallest square number, which is exactly divisible by 2, 3, 4, – 9, 6, 18, 30 and 60, is
    (a) 900          (b) 1600
    (c) 3600         (d) None of these

28. The H.C.F of two numbers is 11, and their L.C.M is 616. If one of the numbers is 88, find the other.
    (a) 77           (b) 87
    (c) 97           (d) None of these

29. What is the greatest possible rate at which a man can walk 51 km and 85 km in an exact number of minutes?
    (a) 11 km/min    (b) 13 km/min
    (c) 17 km/min    (d) None of these

30. The HCF and LCM of two numbers are 12 and 144 respectively. If one of the numbers is 36, the other number is
    (a) 4            (b) 48
    (c) 72           (d) 432

## ANSWER KEY

| | | | | |
|---|---|---|---|---|
| 21. (c) | 22. (d) | 23. (d) | 24. (a) | 25. (a) |
| 26. (a) | 27. (a) | 28. (a) | 29. (c) | 30. (b) |

**Solutions**

4. (a) The first common multiple is also the LCM. The LCM of 36 and 54 would be 108. The next common multiple would be 216, 324 and so on. Thus, the required series would be 108, 216, 324, 432, 540, 648….

   (b) The LCM of 33, 45 and 60 = 60 × 3 × 11 = 1980. Thus, the required series is: 1980, 3960, 5940…

5. LCM × HCF = 936 × 4 = $N_1 \times N_2 \to$ 936 × 4 = 72 × $N_2 \to N_2$ = 13 × 4 = 52. Option (b) is correct.

6. The first time the alarm clocks would ring together would be after a time that is equal to the LCM of 50 and 48. The LCM of 50 and 48 is 50 × 24 = 1200. Hence, the first time they would ring together after 12 noon would be exactly 1200 seconds or 20 minutes later. Option (d) is correct.

7. The LCM of 7, 8, 11 and 12 is given by 12 × 11 × 2 × 7 = 264 × 7 = 1848. 1848 seconds is 30 minutes 48 seconds. Hence, the 4 bells would toll together every 30 minutes 48 seconds.

   The number of times they would toll together in the next 3 hours would be given by the quotient of the division:

3 × 60 × 60 /1848 → 5 times

Alternately, by thinking of 1848 seconds as 30 minutes 48 seconds you can also solve the same question by thinking as follows:

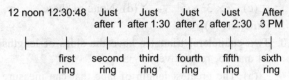

Since the sixth ring is after 3 PM, we can say that the bells would toll 5 times in the next 3 hours

9. $2472 = 2^3 \times 103 \times 3$; $1284 = 2^2 \times 107 \times 3$. Since the HCF is 12, the number must have a component of $2^2 \times 3^1$ at the very least in it. Also, since the LCM is $2^3 \times 3^2 \times 5^1 \times 103 \times 107$ we can see that the minimum requirement in the required number has to be $3^2 \times 5^1$. Combining these two requirements we get that the number should have $2^2 \times 3^2 \times 5^1$ at the minimum and the power of 2 could also be $2^3$ while we could also have either one of $103^1$ and/or $107^1$ as a part of the required number.

   Thus, for instance, the number could also be $2^3 \times 3^2 \times 5^1 \times 103^1 \times 107^1$. The question has asked us- what *'could'* the number be?

   Option (c) gives us a possible value of the number and is hence the correct answer.

21. The least possible number of planks would occur when we divide each plank into a length equal to the HCF of 42, 49 and 63. The HCF of these numbers is clearly 7- and this should be the size of each plank. Number of planks in this case would be: 42/7 + 49/7 + 63/7 = 6 + 7 + 9 = 22 planks. Hence, option (c) is correct.

22. The difference between 135 and 167 is 32, while the difference between 167 and 215 is 48. The answer to this question would be the HCF of these differences. Hence, HCF of 32 and 48 = 16. Hence, option (d) is correct.

23. The numbers are 5/2, ½ and 175/1000 = 7/40. The LCM of three fractions is given by the formula:
    LCM of numerators/HCF of denominators = (LCM of 5, 1 and 7)/(HCF of 2 and 40) = 35/2 = 17.5

24. Use the same process as for question 23 for the numbers 9/2; 9/1000 & 9/50.
    (LCM of 9,9,9)/(HCF of 2,1000 & 50) = 9/2= 4.5

25. 1890 × 30 = 270 × $N_2 \to N_2$ = 210. Hence, option (a) is correct.

26. The LCM of 36, 63 and 108 is 756. Hence, the required number is 750. Option (a) is correct.

27. The LCM of the given numbers is 180. Hence, all multiples of 180 would be divisible by all of these numbers. Checking the series 180, 360, 540, 720, 900 we can see that 900 is the first perfect square in the list. Option (a) is correct.

28. Using the property HCF × LCM = product of the numbers, we get:

    $616 \times 11 = 88 \times N_2 \to N_2 = 77$. Option (a) is correct.

29. The answer would be given by the HCF of 51 and 85 – which is 17. Hence, option (c) is correct.

30. Using the property HCF × LCM = product of the numbers, we get:

    $12 \times 144 = 36 \times N_2 \to N_2 = 48$. Option (b) is correct.

## DIVISIBILITY

A number $x$ is said to be divisible by another number '$y$' if it is completely divisible by $y$ (i.e., it should leave no remainder).

In general it can be said that any integer $I$, when divided by a natural number $N$, there exist a unique pair of numbers $Q$ and $R$ which are called the quotient and Remainder respectively.

Thus, $I = QN + R$.

Where $Q$ is an integer and $N$ is a natural number or zero and $0 \le R < N$ (i.e. remainder has to be a whole number less than $N$.)

If the remainder is zero we say that the number $I$ is divisible by $N$.

When $R \ne 0$, we say that the number $I$ is divisible by $N$ with a remainder.

Thus, 25/8 can be written as: $25 = 3 \times 8 + 1$ (3 is the quotient and 1 is the remainder)

While, –25/7 will be written as $-25 = 7 \times (-4) + 3$ (–4 is the quotient and 3 is the remainder)

**Note:** An integer $b \ne 0$ is said to divide an integer $a$ if there exists another integer $c$ such that:

$$a = bc$$

It is important to explain at this point a couple of concepts with respect to the situation, when we divide a negative number by a natural number $N$.

Suppose, we divide – 32 by 7. Contrary to what you might expect, the remainder in this case is + 3 (and not – 4). This is because the remainder is always non negative.

Thus, –32/7 gives quotient as – 5 and remainder as + 3.

**The relationship between the remainder and the decimal:**

1. Suppose we divide 42 by 5. The result has a quotient of 8 and remainder of 2.

   But 42/5 = 8.4. As you can see, the answer has an integer part and a decimal part. The integer part being 8 (equals the quotient), the decimal part is 0.4 (and is given by 2/5).

   Since, we have also seen that for any divisor $N$, the set of remainders obeys the inequality $0 \le R < N$, we should realise that any divisor $N$, will yield exactly $N$ possible remainders. (For example If the divisor is 3, we have 3 possible remainders 0, 1 and 2. Further,

when 3 is the divisor we can have only 3 possible decimal values .00, .333 & 0.666 corresponding to remainders of 0, 1 or 2. I would want you to remember this concept when you study the fraction to percentage conversion table in the chapter on percentages.)

2. In the case of –42 being divided by 5, the value is – 8.4. In this case the interpretation should be thus: The integer part is – 9 (which is also the quotient of this division) and the decimal part is 0.6 (corresponding to 3/5) Notice that since the remainder cannot be negative, the decimal too cannot be negative.

### Theorems of Divisibility

> (a) If $a$ is divisible by $b$ then $ac$ is also divisible by $b$.
>
> (b) If $a$ is divisible by $b$ and $b$ is divisible by $c$ then $a$ is divisible by $c$.
>
> (c) If $a$ and $b$ are natural numbers such that $a$ is divisible by $b$ and $b$ is divisible by $a$ then $a = b$.
>
> (d) If $n$ is divisible by $d$ and $m$ is divisible by $d$ then $(m + n)$ and $(m - n)$ are both divisible by $d$. This has an important implication. Suppose 28 and 742 are both divisible by 7. Then $(742 + 28)$ as well as $(742 - 28)$ are divisible by 7. (and in fact so is + 28 – 742).
>
> (e) If $a$ is divisible by $b$ and $c$ is divisible by $d$ then $ac$ is divisible by $bd$.
>
> (f) The highest power of a prime number $p$, which divides $n!$ exactly is given by
>
> $$[n/p] + [n/p^2] + [n/p^3] + \ldots$$
>
> where $[x]$ denotes the greatest integer less than or equal to $x$.

As we have already seen earlier—

Any composite number can be written down as a product of its prime factors. (Also called standard form)

Thus, for example the number 1240 can be written as $2^3 \times 31^1 \times 5^1$.

The standard form of any number has a huge amount of information stored in it. The best way to understand the information stored in the standard form of a number is to look at concrete examples. As a reader I want you to understand each of the processes defined below and use them to solve similar questions given in the exercise that follows and beyond:

1. **Using the standard form of a number to find the sum and the number of factors of the number:**

   (a) **Sum of factors of a number:**

   Suppose, we have to find the sum of factors and the number of factors of 240.

   $$240 = 2^4 \times 3^1 \times 5^1$$

   The sum of factors will be given by:

   $$(2^0 + 2^1 + 2^2 + 2^3 + 2^4)(3^0 + 3^1)(5^0 + 5^1)$$
   $$= 31 \times 4 \times 6 = 744$$

**Note**: This is a standard process, wherein you create the same number of brackets as the number of distinct prime factors the number contains and then each bracket is filled with the sum of all the powers of the respective prime number starting from 0 to the highest power of that prime number contained in the standard form.

Thus, for 240, we create 3 brackets—one each for 2, 3 and 5. Further in the bracket corresponding to 2 we write $(2^0 + 2^1 + 2^2 + 2^3 + 2^4)$.

Hence, for example for the number $40 = 2^3 \times 5^1$, the sum of factors will be given by: $(2^0 + 2^1 + 2^2 + 2^3)$ $(5^0 + 5^1)$ {2 brackets since 40 has 2 distinct prime factors 2 and 5}

(b) **Number of factors of the number:**

Let us explore the sum of factors of 40 in a different context.

$(2^0 + 2^1 + 2^2 + 2^3) (5^0 + 5^1)$

$= 2^0 \times 5^0 + 2^0 \times 5^1 + 2^1 \times 5^0 + 2^1 \times 5^1 + 2^2 \times 5^0 + 2^2 \times 5^1 + 2^3 \times 5^0 + 2^3 \times 5^1$

$= 1 + 5 + 2 + 10 + 4 + 20 + 8 + 40 = 90$

A clear look at the numbers above will make you realize that it is nothing but the addition of the factors of 40

Hence, we realise that the number of terms in the expansion of $(2^0 + 2^1 + 2^2 + 2^3) (5^0 + 5^1)$ will give us the number of factors of 40. Hence, 40 has $4 \times 2 = 8$ factors.

**Note:** The moment you realise that $40 = 2^3 \times 5^1$ the answer for the number of factors can be got by $(3 + 1) (1 + 1) = 8$

2. **Sum and Number of even and odd factors of a number.**

Suppose, you are trying to find out the number of factors of a number represented in the standard form by: $2^3 \times 3^4 \times 5^2 \times 7^3$

As you are already aware the answer to the question is $(3 + 1) (4 + 1) (2 + 1) (3 + 1)$ and is based on the logic that the number of terms will be the same as the number of terms in the expansion: $(2^0 + 2^1 + 2^2 + 2^3)$ $(3^0 + 3^1 + 3^2 + 3^3 + 3^4)(5^0 + 5^1 + 5^2) (7^0 + 7^1 + 7^2 + 7^3)$.

Now, suppose you have to find out the sum of the even factors of this number. The only change you need to do in this respect will be evident below. The answer will be given by:

$(2^1 + 2^2 + 2^3)(3^0 + 3^1 + 3^2 + 3^3 + 3^4) (5^0 + 5^1 + 5^2)$ $(7^0 + 7^1 + 7^2 + 7^3)$

**Note:** We have eliminated $2^0$ from the original answer. By eliminating $2^0$ from the expression for the sum of all factors you are ensuring that you have only even numbers in the expansion of the expression.

Consequently, the number of even factors will be given by: $(3) (4 + 1) (2 + 1) (3 + 1)$

i.e., since $2^0$ is eliminated, we do not add 1 in the bracket corresponding to 2.

Let us now try to expand our thinking to try to think about the number of odd factors for a number.

In this case, we just have to do the opposite of what we did for even numbers. The following step will make it clear:

Odd factors of the number whose standard form is : $2^3 \times 3^4 \times 5^2 \times 7^3$

Sum of odd factors $= (2^0) (3^0 + 3^1 + 3^2 + 3^3 + 3^4)$ $(5^0 + 5^1 + 5^2) (7^0 + 7^1 + 7^2 + 7^3)$

i.e.: Ignore all powers of 2. The result of the expansion of the above expression will be the complete set of odd factors of the number. Consequently, the number of odd factors for the number will be given by the number of terms in the expansion of the above expression.

Thus, the number of odd factors for the number $2^3 \times 3^4 \times 5^2 \times 7^3 = 1 \times (4 + 1) (2 + 1) (3 + 1)$.

3. **Sum and number of factors satisfying other conditions for any composite number**

These are best explained through examples:

(i) Find the sum and the number of factors of 1200 such that the factors are divisible by 15.

Solution : $1200 = 2^4 \times 5^2 \times 3^1$.

For a factor to be divisible by 15 it should compulsorily have $3^1$ and $5^1$ in it. Thus, sum of factors divisible by 15 $= (2^0 + 2^1 + 2^2 + 2^3 + 2^4) \times (5^1 + 5^2)$ $(3^1)$ and consequently the number of factors will be given by $5 \times 2 \times 1 = 10$.

(What we have done is ensure that in every individual term of the expansion, there is a minimum of $3^1 \times 5^1$. This is done by removing powers of 3 and 5 which are below 1.)

*Task for the student: Physically verify the answers to the question above and try to convert the logic into a mental algorithm.*

**NOTE FROM THE AUTHOR—The need for thought algorithms:**

I have often observed that the key difference between understanding a concept and actually applying it under examination pressure, is the presence or absence of a mental thought algorithm which clarifies the concept to you in your mind. The thought algorithm is a personal representation of a concept—and any concept that you read/understand in this book (or elsewhere) will remain an external concept till it remains in someone else's words. The moment the thought becomes internalised the concept becomes yours to apply and use.

## Practice Exercise on Factors

For the number 2450 find.

1. The sum and number of all factors.

2. The sum and number of even factors.

3. The sum and number of odd factors.

4. The sum and number of factors divisible by 5

5. The sum and number of factors divisible by 35.

6. The sum and number of factors divisible by 245.

For the number 7200 find.

7. The sum and number of all factors.

8. The sum and number of even factors.

9. The sum and number of odd factors.

10. The sum and number of factors divisible by 25.

11. The sum and number of factors divisible by 40.

12. The sum and number of factors divisible by 150.

13. The sum and number of factors not divisible by 75.

14. The sum and number of factors not divisible by 24.

15. Find the number of divisors of 1728.
    - (a) 18
    - (b) 30
    - (c) 28
    - (d) 20

16. Find the number of divisors of 1080 excluding the divisors, which are perfect squares.
    - (a) 28
    - (b) 29
    - (c) 30
    - (d) 31

17. Find the number of divisors of 544 excluding 1 and 544.
    - (a) 12
    - (b) 18
    - (c) 11
    - (d) 10

18. Find the number of divisors 544 which are greater than 3.
    - (a) 15
    - (b) 10
    - (c) 12
    - (d) None of these.

19. Find the sum of divisors of 544 excluding 1 and 544.
    - (a) 1089
    - (b) 545
    - (c) 589
    - (d) 1134

20. Find the sum of divisors of 544 which are perfect squares.
    - (a) 32
    - (b) 64
    - (c) 42
    - (d) 21

21. Find the sum of odd divisors of 544.
    - (a) 18
    - (b) 34
    - (c) 68
    - (d) 36

22. Find the sum of even divisors of 4096.
    - (a) 8192
    - (b) 6144
    - (c) 8190
    - (d) 6142

23. Find the sum the sums of divisors of 144 and 160.
    - (a) 589
    - (b) 781
    - (c) 735
    - (d) None of these

24. Find the sum of the sum of even divisors of 96 and the sum of odd divisors of 3600.
    - (a) 639
    - (b) 735
    - (c) 651
    - (d) 589

## ANSWER KEY

| | | | | |
|---|---|---|---|---|
| 15. (c) | 16. (a) | 17. (d) | 18. (b) | 19. (c) |
| 20. (d) | 21. (a) | 22. (c) | 23. (b) | 24. (c) |

### Solutions

***Solutions to Questions 1 to 6:***

$2450 = 50 \times 49 = 2^1 \times 5^2 \times 7^2$

1. Sum and number of all factors:

   Sum of factors $= (2^0 + 2^1)(5^0 + 5^1 + 5^2)(7^0 + 7^1 + 7^2)$

   Number of factors $= 2 \times 3 \times 3 = 18$

2. Sum of all even factors:

   $(2^1)(5^0 + 5^1 + 5^2)(7^0 + 7^1 + 7^2)$

   Number of even factors $= 1 \times 3 \times 3 = 9$

3. Sum of all odd factors:

   $(2^0)(5^0 + 5^1 + 5^2)(7^0 + 7^1 + 7^2)$

   Number of odd factors $= 1 \times 3 \times 3 = 9$

4. Sum of factors divisible by 5:

   $(2^0 + 2^1)(5^1 + 5^2)(7^0 + 7^1 + 7^2)$

   Number of factors divisible by $5 = 2 \times 2 \times 3 = 12$

5. Sum of factors divisible by 35:

   $(2^0 + 2^1)(5^1 + 5^2)(7^1 + 7^2)$

   Number of factors divisible by $35 = 2 \times 2 \times 2 = 8$

6. Sum of all factors divisible by 245:

   $(2^0 + 2^1)(5^1 + 5^2)(7^2)$

   Number of factors divisible by $245 = 2 \times 2 \times 1 = 4$

***Solutions to Questions 7 to 14:***

$7200 = 72 \times 100 = 12 \times 6 \times 100 = 2^5 \times 3^2 \times 5^2$

7. **Sum and number of all factors:**

   Sum of factors $= (2^0 + 2^1 + 2^2 + 2^3 + 2^4 + 2^5)(3^0 + 3^1 + 3^2)(5^0 + 5^1 + 5^2)$

   Number of factors $= 6 \times 3 \times 3 = 54$

8. **Sum and number of even factors:**

   Sum of even factors $= (2^1 + 2^2 + 2^3 + 2^4 + 2^5)(3^0 + 3^1 + 3^2)(5^0 + 5^1 + 5^2)$

   Number of even factors $= 5 \times 3 \times 3 = 45$

9. **Sum and number of odd factors:**

   Sum of odd factors $= (2^0)(3^0 + 3^1 + 3^2)(5^0 + 5^1 + 5^2)$

   Number of odd factors $= 1 \times 3 \times 3 = 9$

10. **Sum and number of factors divisible by 25:**

    Sum of factors divisible by $25 = (2^0 + 2^1 + 2^2 + 2^3 + 2^4 + 2^5)(3^0 + 3^1 + 3^2)(5^2)$

    Number of factors divisible by $25 = 6 \times 3 \times 1 = 18$

11. **Sum and number of factors divisible by 40:**

    Sum of factors divisible by $40 = (2^3 + 2^4 + 2^5)(3^0 + 3^1 + 3^2)(5^1 + 5^2)$

    Number of factors $= 3 \times 3 \times 2 = 18$

12. **Sum and number of factors divisible by 150:**

    Sum of factors divisible by 150 = $(2^1 + 2^2 + 2^3 + 2^4 + 2^5)$ $(3^1 + 3^2)$ $(5^2)$

    Number of factors divisible by 150 = $5 \times 2 \times 1 = 10$

13. **Sum and number of factors not divisible by 75:**

    Sum of factors not divisible by 75 = Sum of all factors – Sum of factors divisible by 75 =

    $(2^0 + 2^1 + 2^2 + 2^3 + 2^4 + 2^5)$ $(3^0 + 3^1 + 3^2)$ $(5^0 + 5^1 + 5^2)$ $-$ $(2^0 + 2^1 + 2^2 + 2^3 + 2^4 + 2^5)$ $(3^1 + 3^2)$ $(5^2)$

    Number of factors not divisible by 75 = Number of factors of 7200 – Number of factors of 7200 which are divisible by 75 = $6 \times 3 \times 3 - 6 \times 2 \times 1 = 54 - 12 = 42$

14. **Sum and number of factors not divisible by 24:**

    Sum of factors not divisible by 24 = Sum of all factors – Sum of factors divisible by 24 =

    $(2^0 + 2^1 + 2^2 + 2^3 + 2^4 + 2^5)$ $(3^0 + 3^1 + 3^2)$ $(5^0 + 5^1 + 5^2)$ $-$ $(2^3 + 2^4 + 2^5)$ $(3^1 + 3^2)$ $(5^0 + 5^1 + 5^2)$

    Number of factors not divisible by 24 = Number of factors of 7200 – Number of factors of 7200 which are divisible by 24 = $6 \times 3 \times 3 - 3 \times 2 \times 3 = 54 - 18 = 36$

15. **Number of divisors of 1728**

    $1728 = 4 \times 432 = 16 \times 108 = 64 \times 27 = 2^6 \times 3^3$

    Number of factors = $7 \times 4 = 28$. Option (c) is correct.

16. $1080 = 108 \times 10 = 27 \times 4 \times 10 = 3^3 \times 2^3 \times 5^1$

    Number of factors = $4 \times 4 \times 2 = 32$.

    In order to see the number of factors of 1080 which are perfect squares we need to visualize the structure for writing down the sum of perfect square factors of 1080.

    This would be given by:

    Sum of all perfect square factors of 1080 = $(2^0 + 2^2)$ $(3^0 + 3^2)$ $(5^0)$.

    From the above structure it is clear that the number of perfect square factors is going to be $2 \times 2 \times 1 = 4$

    Thus, the number of factors of 1080 which are not perfect squares are equal to $32 - 4 = 28$.

    Option (a) is correct.

17. $544 = 17^1 \times 2^5$. Hence, the total number of factors of 544 is $2 \times 6 = 12$. But we have to count factors excluding 1 and 544. Thus, we need to remove 2 factors from this. The required answer is $12 - 2 = 10$. Option (d) is correct.

18. Using the fact that 544 has a total of 12 factors and the numbers 1 and 2 are the two factors which are lower than 3, we would get a total of 10 factors greater than 3. Option (b) is correct.

19. The required answer would be given by: Sum of all factors of $544 - 1 - 544 = (2^0 + 2^1 + 2^2 + 2^3 + 2^4 + 2^5)$ $(17^0 + 17^1) - 545 = 63 \times 18 - 545 = 589$. Option (c) is correct.

20. Sum of divisors of 544 which are perfect square is: $(2^0 + 2^2 + 2^4)$ $(17^0) = 21$. Option (d) is correct.

21. Sum of odd divisors of 544 = $(2^0)$ $(17^0 + 17^1) = 18$. Option (a) is correct.

22. $4096 = 2^{12}$.

    Sum of even divisors = $(2^1 + 2^2 + 2^3 + 2^4 + 2^5 + 2^6 + 2^7 + 2^8 + 2^9 + 2^{10} + 2^{11} + 2^{12}) = 2^{13} - 2 = 8190$

23. $144 = 2^4 \times 3^2 \rightarrow$ Sum of divisors of 144 = $(2^0 + 2^1 + 2^2 + 2^3 + 2^4)$ $(3^0 + 3^1 + 3^2) = 31 \times 13 = 403$

    $160 = 2^5 \times 5^1 \rightarrow$ Sum of divisors of 160 = $(2^0 + 2^1 + 2^2 + 2^3 + 2^4 + 2^5)$ $(5^0 + 5^1) = 63 \times 6 = 378$.

    Sum of the two = $403 + 378 = 781$.

24. $96 = 2^5 \times 3^1$. Sum of even divisors of 96 = $(2^1 + 2^2 + 2^3 + 2^4 + 2^5)$ $(3^0 + 3^1) = 62 \times 4 = 248$

    $3600 = 2^4 \times 5^2 \times 3^2$. Sum of odd divisors of 3600 = $(2^0)$ $(3^0 + 3^1 + 3^2)$ $(5^0 + 5^1 + 5^2) = 13 \times 31 = 403$

    Sum of the two = $248 + 403 = 651$.

    Option (c) is correct.

## NUMBER OF ZEROES IN AN EXPRESSION

Suppose you have to find the number of zeroes in a product: $24 \times 32 \times 17 \times 23 \times 19 = (2^3 \times 3^1) \times (2^5) \times 17^1 \times 23 \times 19$.

As you can notice, this product will have no zeroes because it has no 5 in it.

However, if you have an expression like: $8 \times 15 \times 23 \times 17 \times 25 \times 22$

The above expression can be rewritten in the standard form as:

$$2^3 \times 3^1 \times 5^1 \times 23 \times 17 \times 5^2 \times 2^1 \times 11^1$$

Zeroes are formed by a combination of $2 \times 5$. Hence, the number of zeroes will depend on the number of pairs of 2's and 5's that can be formed.

In the above product, there are four twos and three fives. Hence, we shall be able to form only three pairs of $(2 \times 5)$. Hence, there will be 3 zeroes in the product.

### Finding the Number of Zeroes in a Factorial Value

Suppose you had to find the number of zeroes in 6!.

$6! = 6 \times 5 \times 4 \times 3 \times 2 \times 1 = (3 \times 2) \times (5) \times (2 \times 2) \times (3) \times (2) \times (1)$.

The above expression will have only one pair of $5 \times 2$, since there is only one 5 and an abundance of 2's.

It is clear that in any factorial value, the number of 5's will always be lesser than the number of 2's. Hence, all we need to do is to count the number of 5's. The process for this is explained in Solved Examples 1.1 to 1.3.

### Exercise for Self-practice

Find the number of zeroes in the following cases:

1. 47!
2. 58!
3. $13 \times 15 \times 22 \times 125 \times 44 \times 35 \times 11$
4. $12 \times 15 \times 5 \times 24 \times 13 \times 17$
5. 173!
6. $144! \times 5 \times 15 \times 22 \times 11 \times 44 \times 135$
7. 148!
8. 1093!
9. 1132!
10. $1142! \times 348! \times 17!$

## Solutions

1. $47/5 \rightarrow$ Quotient 9. $9/5 \rightarrow$ Quotient $\rightarrow 1$. $9 + 1$ = 10 zeroes.

2. $58/5 \rightarrow$ Quotient 11. $11/5 \rightarrow$ Quotient $\rightarrow 2$. $11 + 2$ = 13 zeroes.

3. The given expression has five 5's and three 2's. Thus, there would be three zeroes in the expression.

4. The given expression has two 5's and five 2's. Thus, there would be two zeroes in the expression.

5. $173/5 \rightarrow$ Quotient 34. $34/5 \rightarrow$ Quotient 6. $6/5 \rightarrow$ Quotient 1. $34 + 6 + 1 = 41$ zeroes.

6. 144! Would have $28 + 5 + 1 = 34$ zeroes and the remaining part of the expression would have three zeroes. A total of $34 + 3 = 37$ zeroes.

7. $148/5 \rightarrow$ Quotient 29. $29/5 \rightarrow$ Quotient 5. $5/5 \rightarrow$ Quotient 1. $29 + 5 + 1 = 35$ zeroes.

8. $1093/5 \rightarrow$ Quotient 218. $218/5 \rightarrow$ Quotient 43. $43/5 \rightarrow$ Quotient 8. $8/5 \rightarrow$ Quotient 1. $218 + 43 + 8 + 1$ = 270 zeroes.

9. $1132/5 \rightarrow$ Quotient 226. $226/5 \rightarrow$ Quotient 45. $45/5 \rightarrow$ Quotient 9. $9/5 \rightarrow$ Quotient 1. $226 + 45 + 9 + 1$ = 281 zeroes.

10. $1142/5 \rightarrow$ Quotient 228. $228/5 \rightarrow$ Quotient 45. $45/5 \rightarrow$ Quotient 9. $9/5 \rightarrow$ Quotient 1. $228 + 45 + 9 + 1$ = 283 zeroes.

    $348/5 \rightarrow$ Quotient 69. $69/5 \rightarrow$ Quotient 13. $13/5 \rightarrow$ Quotient 2. $69 + 13 + 2 = 84$ zeroes.

    $17/5 \rightarrow$ Quotient 3 $\rightarrow$ 3 zeroes.

    Thus, the total number of zeroes in the expression is: $283 + 84 + 3 = 370$ zeroes.

**A special implication:** Suppose you were to find the number of zeroes in the value of the following factorial values:

45!, 46!, 47!, 48!, 49!

What do you notice? The number of zeroes in each of the cases will be equal to 10. Why does this happen? It is not difficult to understand that the number of fives in any of these factorials is equal to 10. The number of zeroes will only change at 50! (It will become 12).

In fact, this will be true for all factorial values between two consecutive products of 5.

Thus, 50!, 51!, 52!, 53! And 54! will have 12 zeroes (since they all have 12 fives).

Similarly, 55!, 56!, 57!, 58! And 59! will each have 13 zeroes.

Apart from this fact, did you notice another thing? That while there are 10 zeroes in 49! there are directly 12 zeroes in 50!. This means that there is no value of a factorial which will give 11 zeroes. This occurs because to get 50! we multiply the value of 49! by 50. When you do so, the result is that we introduce two 5's in the product. Hence, the number of zeroes jumps by two (since we never had any paucity of twos.)

**Note:** at 124! you will get $24 + 4 \Rightarrow 28$ zeroes.

At 125! you will get $25 + 5 + 1 = 31$ zeroes. (A jump of 3 zeroes.)

## Exercise for Self-practice

1. $n!$ has 23 zeroes. What is the maximum possible value of $n$?

2. $n!$ has 13 zeroes. The highest and least values of $n$ are?

3. Find the number of zeroes in the product $1^1 \times 2^2 \times 3^3 \times 4^4 \times 5^5 \times 6^6 \times \dots \times 49^{49}$

4. Find the number of zeroes in:
   $100^1 \times 99^2 \times 98^3 \times 97^4 \times \dots \dots \times 1^{100}$

5. Find the number of zeroes in:
   $1^{1!} \times 2^{2!} \times 3^{3!} \times 4^{4!} \times 5^{5!} \times \dots \dots 10^{10!}$

6. Find the number of zeroes in the value of:
   $2^2 \times 5^4 \times 4^6 \times 10^8 \times 6^{10} \times 15^{12} \times 8^{14} \times 20^{16} \times 10^{18} \times 25^{20}$

7. What is the number of zeroes in the following:
   (a) $3200 + 1000 + 40000 + 32000 + 15000000$
   (b) $3200 \times 1000 \times 40000 \times 32000 \times 16000000$

## Solutions

1. This can never happen because at 99! number of zeroes is 22 and at 100! the number of zeroes is 24.

2. 59 and 55, respectively.

3. The fives will be less than the twos. Hence, we need to count only the fives.

   Thus : $5^5 \times 10^{10} \times 15^{15} \times 20^{20} \times 25^{25} \times 30^{30} \times 35^{35} \times 40^{40} \times 45^{45}$

   gives us: $5 + 10 + 15 + 20 + 25 + 25 + 30 + 35 + 40 + 45$ fives. Thus, the product has 250 zeroes.

4. Again the key here is to count the number of fives. This can get done by:
   $100^1 \times 95^6 \times 90^{11} \times 85^{16} \times 80^{21} \times 75^{26} \times \dots \dots 5^{96}$

   $(1 + 6 + 11 + 16 + 21 + 26 + 31 + 36 + 41 + 46 + \dots \dots + 96) + (1 + 26 + 51 + 76)$

   $= 20 \times 48.5 + 4 \times 38.5$    (Using sum of A.P. explained in the next chapter.)

   $= 970 + 154 = 1124.$

5. The answer will be the number of 5's. Hence, it will be 5! + 10!

6. The number of fives is again lesser than the number of twos.

The number of 5's will be given by the power of 5 in the product:

$$5^4 \times 10^8 \times 15^{12} \times 20^{16} \times 10^{18} \times 25^{20}$$
$$= 4 + 8 + 12 + 16 + 18 + 40 = 98.$$

7. A. The number of zeroes in the sum will be two, since:

$$
\begin{array}{r}
3200 \\
1000 \\
40000 \\
32000 \\
15000000 \\
\hline
15076200
\end{array}
$$

Thus, in such cases the number of zeroes will be the least number of zeroes amongst the numbers.

Exception: 3200 + 1800 = 5000 (three zeroes, not two).

B. The number of zeroes will be:
$$2 + 3 + 4 + 3 + 6 = 18.$$

**An extension of the process for finding the number of zeroes.**

Consider the following questions:

1. Find the highest power of 5 which is contained in the value of 127!
2. When 127! is divided by $5^n$ the result is an integer. Find the highest possible value for $n$.
3. Find the number of zeroes in 127!

In each of the above cases, the value of the answer will be given by:

$$[127/5] + [127/25] + [127/125]$$
$$= 25 + 5 + 1 = 31$$

This process can be extended to questions related to other prime numbers. For example:
Find the highest power of:

1. 3 which completely divides 38!
   Solution: $[38/3] + [38/3^2] + [38/3^3] = 12 + 4 + 1 = 17$
2. 7 which is contained in 57!
   $[57/7] + [57/7^2] = 8 + 1 = 9.$

This process changes when the divisor is not a prime number. You are first advised to go through worked out problems 1.4, 1.5, 1.6 and 1.19.

Now try to solve the following exercise:

1. Find the highest power of 7 which divides 81!
2. Find the highest power of 42 which divides 122!
3. Find the highest power of 84 which divides 342!
4. Find the highest power of 175 which divides 344!
5. Find the highest power of 360 which divides 520!

**Solutions**

1. $81/7 \rightarrow$ Quotient 11. $11/7 \rightarrow$ Quotient 1. Highest power of 7 in 81! = 11 + 1 = 12.

2. In order to check for the highest power of 42, we need to realize that 42 is $2 \times 3 \times 7$. In 122! the least power between 2,3 and 7 would obviously be for 7. Thus, we need to find the number of 7's in 122! (or in other words— the highest power of 7 in 122!). This can be done by:
   $122/7 \rightarrow$ Quotient 17. $17/7 \rightarrow$ Quotient 2. Highest power of 7 in 122! = 17 + 2 = 19.

3. $84 = 2 \times 2 \times 3 \times 7$. This means we need to think of which amongst $2^2$, 3 and 7 would appear the least number of times in 342! It is evident that there would be more $2^2$s and 3's than 7's in any factorial value (Because if you write any factorial $1 \times 2 \times 3 \times 4 \times 5 \times 6 \times 7 \times 8 \times 9 \times 10 \times 11 \times 12 \times 13 \times 14 \times 15...$ you can clearly see that before a 7 or it's multiple appears in the multiplication, there are at least two 2's and one 3 which appear beforehand.)

   Hence, in order to solve this question we just need to find the power of 7 in 342!

   This can be done as:
   $342/7 \rightarrow$ Quotient 48. $48/7 \rightarrow$ Quotient 6. $6/7 \rightarrow$ Quotient 0. Highest power of 7 in 342! = 48 + 6 = 54.

4. $175 = 5 \times 5 \times 7$. This means we need to think of which amongst $5^2$ and 7 would appear the least number of times in 175! In this case it is not immediately evident that whether there would be more $5^2$s or more 7's in any factorial value (Because if you write any factorial $1 \times 2 \times 3 \times 4 \times 5 \times 6 \times 7 \times 8 \times 9 \times 10 \times 11 \times 12 \times 13 \times 14 \times 15...$ you can clearly see that although the 5's appear more frequently than the 7's it is not evident that we would have at least two fives before the 7 appears.) Hence, in this question we would need to check for both the number of $5^2$s and the number of 7's.

   Number of 7's in 344!
   $344/7 \rightarrow$ Quotient 49. $49/7 \rightarrow$ Quotient 7. $7/7 \rightarrow$ Quotient 1. Highest power of 7 in 344! = 49 + 7 + 1 = 57.

   In order to find the number of $5^2$s in 344! we first need to find the number of 5's in 344!
   $344/5 \rightarrow$ Quotient 68. $68/5 \rightarrow$ Quotient 13. $13/5 \rightarrow$ Quotient 2. Number of 5's in 344! = 68 + 13 + 2 = 83.

   83 fives would obviously mean [83/2] = 41 $5^2$s

   Thus, there are 41 $5^2$s and 57 7's in 344!

   Since, the number of $5^2$s are lower, they would determine the highest power of 175 that would divide 344!

   The answer is 41.

5. $360 = 5 \times 2 \times 2 \times 2 \times 3 \times 3$. This means we need to think of which amongst $2^3, 3^2$ and 5 would appear the least number of times in 520! In this case it is not immediately evident which of these three would appear least number of times. Hence, in this question we would need to check for all three – $2^3$s, $3^2$s and 5s.

Number of 5's in 520!

$520/5 \to$ Quotient 104. $104/5 \to$ Quotient 20. $20/5 \to$ Quotient 4. Highest power of 5 in 520! $= 104 + 20 + 4 = 128$.

In order to find the number of $3^2$s in 520! we first need to find the number of 3's in 520!

$520/3 \to$ Quotient 173. $173/3 \to$ Quotient 57. $57/3 \to$ Quotient 19. $19/3 \to$ Quotient 6. $6/3 \to$ Quotient 2. $2/3 \to$ Quotient 0. Number of 3's in 520! $= 173 + 57 + 19 + 6 + 2 = 257$.

257 threes would obviously mean $[257/2] = 128$ $3^2$s. In order to find the number of $2^3$s in 520! we first need to find the number of 2's in 520!

$520/2 \to$ Quotient 260. $260/2 \to$ Quotient 130. $130/2 \to$ Quotient 65. $65/2 \to$ Quotient 32. $32/2 \to$ Quotient 16. $16/2 \to$ Quotient 8. $8/2 \to$ Quotient 4. $4/2 \to$ Quotient 2. $2/2 \to$ Quotient 1. $1/2 \to$ Quotient 0.

Number of 2's in 520! $= 260 + 130 + 65 + 32 + 16 + 8 + 4 + 2 + 1 = 518$. 518 twos would obviously mean $[518/3] = 172$ $2^3$s.

Thus, there are 128 $3^2$s, 128 5's and 172 $2^3$s in 520! The highest power of 360 that would divide 520! would be the least of 128, 128 and 172.

The answer is 128.

## Exercise for Self-practice

1. Find the maximum value of $n$ such that 157! is perfectly divisible by $10^n$.
   - (a) 37
   - (b) 38
   - (c) 16
   - (d) 31

2. Find the maximum value of n such that 157! is perfectly divisible by $12^n$.
   - (a) 77
   - (b) 76
   - (c) 75
   - (d) 78

3. Find the maximum value of n such that 157! is perfectly divisible by $18^n$.
   - (a) 37
   - (b) 38
   - (c) 39
   - (d) 40

4. Find the maximum value of n such that 50! is perfectly divisible by $2520^n$.
   - (a) 6
   - (b) 8
   - (c) 7
   - (d) None of these

5. Find the maximum value of n such that 50! is perfectly divisible by $12600^n$.

   - (a) 7
   - (b) 6
   - (c) 8
   - (d) None of these

6. Find the maximum value of n such that 77! is perfectly divisible by $720^n$.
   - (a) 35
   - (b) 18
   - (c) 17
   - (d) 36

7. Find the maximum value of n such that $42 \times 57 \times 92 \times 91 \times 52 \times 62 \times 63 \times 64 \times 65 \times 66 \times 67$ is perfectly divisible by $42^n$.
   - (a) 4
   - (b) 3
   - (c) 5
   - (d) 6

8. Find the maximum value of n such that $570 \times 60 \times 30 \times 90 \times 100 \times 500 \times 700 \times 343 \times 720 \times 81$ is perfectly divisible by $30^n$.
   - (a) 12
   - (b) 11
   - (c) 14
   - (d) 13

9. Find the maximum value of $n$ such that $77 \times 42 \times 37 \times 57 \times 30 \times 90 \times 70 \times 2400 \times 2402 \times 243 \times 343$ is perfectly divisible by $21^n$.
   - (a) 9
   - (b) 11
   - (c) 10
   - (d) 6

Find the number of consecutive zeroes at the end of the following numbers.

10. 72!
    - (a) 17
    - (b) 9
    - (c) 8
    - (d) 16

11. $77! \times 42!$
    - (a) 24
    - (b) 9
    - (c) 27
    - (d) 18

12. $100! + 200!$
    - (a) 73
    - (b) 24
    - (c) 11
    - (d) 22

13. $57 \times 60 \times 30 \times 15625 \times 4096 \times 625 \times 875 \times 975$
    - (a) 6
    - (b) 16
    - (c) 17
    - (d) 15

14. $1! \times 2! \times 3! \times 4! \times 5! \times \text{-------} \times 50!$
    - (a) 235
    - (b) 12
    - (c) 262
    - (d) 105

15. $1^1 \times 2^2 \times 3^3 \times 4^4 \times 5^5 \times 6^6 \times 7^7 \times 8^8 \times 9^9 \times 10^{10}$.
    - (a) 25
    - (b) 15
    - (c) 10
    - (d) 20

16. $100! \times 200!$
    - (a) 49
    - (b) 73
    - (c) 132
    - (d) 33

## ANSWER KEY

1. (b)    2. (c)    3. (a)    4. (b)    5. (b)
6. (c)    7. (b)    8. (b)    9. (d)    10. (d)
11. (c)    12. (b)    13. (d)    14. (c)    15. (b)
16. (b)

**Solutions**

1. [157/5] = 31. [31/5] = 6. [6/5] = 1. 31 + 6 + 1 = 38. Option (b) is correct.

2. No of 2's in 157! = [157/2] + [157/4] + [157/8]... + [157/128] = 78 + 39 + 19 + 9 + 4 + 2 + 1 = 152.
   Hence, the number of $2^2$s would be [152/2] = 76.
   Number of 3's in 157! = 52 + 17 + 5 + 1 = 75.
   The answer would be given by the lower of these values. Hence, 75 (Option c) is correct.

3. From the above solution:
   Number of 2's in 157! = 152
   Number of $3^2$s in 157! = [75/2] = 37.
   Hence, option (a) is correct.

4. 2520 = $7 \times 3^2 \times 2^3 \times 5$.
   The value of n would be given by the value of the number of 7s in 50!
   This value is equal to [50/7] + [50/49] = 7 + 1 = 8
   Option (b) is correct.

5. 12600 = $7 \times 3^2 \times 2^3 \times 5^2$
   The value of '*n*' would depend on which of number of 7s and number of $5^2$s is lower in 50!.
   Number of 7's in 50! = 8. Note here that if we check for 7's we do not need to check for $3^2$s as there would be at least two 3's before a 7 comes in every factorial's value. Similarly, there would always be at least three 2's before a 7 comes in any factorial's value. Thus, the number of $3^2$s and the number of $2^3$s can never be lower than the number of 7s in any factorial's value.
   Number of 5s in 50! = 10 + 2 = 12. Hence, the number of $5^2$s in 50! = [12/2] = 6.
   6 will be the answer as the number of $5^2$s is lower than the number of 7's.
   Option (b) is correct.

6. 720 = $2^4 \times 5^1 \times 3^2$
   In 77! there would be 38 + 19 + 9 + 4 + 2 + 1 = 73 twos → hence [73/4] = 18 $2^4$s
   In 77! there would be 25 + 8 + 2 = 35 threes → hence [35/2] = 17 $3^2$s
   In 77! there would be 15 + 3 = 18 fives
   Since 17 is the least of these values, option (c) is correct.

7. In the expression given, there are three 7's and more than three 2's and 3's. Thus, Option (b) is correct.

8. Checking for the number of 2's, 3's and 5's in the given expression you can see that the minimum is for the number of 3's (there are 11 of them while there are 12 5's and more than 11 2's) Hence, option (b) is correct.

9. The number of 7's in the number is 6, while there are more than six 3's. Hence, Option (d) is correct.

10. The number of zeroes would depend on the number of 5's in the value of the factorial.
    72! → 14 + 2 = 16. Option (d) is correct.

11. The number of zeroes would depend on the number of 5's in the value of the factorial.
    77! × 42! → 15 + 3 = 18 (for 77!) and 8 + 1 = 9 (for 42!).
    Thus, the total number of zeroes in the given expression would be 18 + 9 = 27. Option (c) is correct.

12. The number of zeroes would depend on the number of 5's in the value of the factorial.
    100! would end in 20 + 4 = 24 zeroes
    200! Would end in 40 + 8 + 1 = 49 zeroes.
    When you add the two numbers (one with 24 zeroes and the other with 49 zeroes at it's end), the resultant total would end in 24 zeroes. Option (b) is correct.

13. The given expression has fifteen 2's and seventeen 5's. The number of zeroes would be 15 as the number of 2's is lower in this case. Option (d) is correct.

14. 1! to 4! would have no zeroes while 5! to 9! All the values would have 1 zero. Thus, a total of 5 zeroes till 9!. Going further 10! to 14! would have two zeroes each — so a total of 10 zeroes would come out of the product of 10! × 11! × 12! × 13! × 14!.
    Continuing this line of thought further we get:
    Number of zeroes between 15! × 16!... × 19! = 3 + 3 + 3 + 3 + 3 = 3 × 5 = 15
    Number of zeroes between 20! × 21!... × 24! = 4 × 5 = 20
    Number of zeroes between 25! × 26!... × 29! = 6 × 5 = 30
    Number of zeroes between 30! × 31!... × 34! = 7 × 5 = 35
    Number of zeroes between 35! × 36!... × 39! = 8 × 5 = 40
    Number of zeroes between 40! × 41!... × 44! = 9 × 5 = 45
    Number of zeroes between 45! × 46!... × 49! = 10 × 5 = 50
    Number of zeroes for 50! = 12
    Thus, the total number of zeroes for the expression 1! × 2! × 3! .... × 50! = 5 + 10 + 15 + 20 + 30 + 35 + 40 + 45 + 50 + 12 = 262 zeroes. Option (c) is correct.

15. The number of 5's is `15 while the number of 2's is much more. Option (b) is correct.

16. The number of zeroes would depend on the number of 5's in the value of the factorial.
    100! would end in 20 + 4 = 24 zeroes
    200! Would end in 40 + 8 + 1 = 49 zeroes.
    When you multiply the two numbers (one with 24 zeroes and the other with 49 zeroes at it's end), the resultant total would end in 24 + 49 = 73 zeroes. Option (b) is correct.

*Co-Prime or Relatively Prime Numbers* Two or more numbers that do not have a common factor are known as co-prime or relatively prime. In other words, these numbers have a highest common factor of unity.

If two numbers $m$ and $n$ are relatively prime and the natural number $x$ is divisible by both $m$ and $n$ independently then the number $x$ is also divisible by $mn$.

*Key Concept 1:* The spotting of two numbers as co-prime has a very important implication in the context of the two numbers being in the denominators of fractions.

The concept is again best understood through an example:

Suppose, you are doing an operation of the following format — $M/8 + N/9$ where $M$ & $N$ are integers.

What are the chances of the result being an integer, if M is not divisible by 8 and N is not divisible by 9? A little bit of thought will make you realise that the chances are zero. The reason for this is that 8 and 9 are co-prime and the decimals of co-prime numbers never match each other. **Note:** this will not be the case in the case of:

$$M/3 + N/27.$$

In this case even if 3 and 27 are not dividing $M$ and $N$ respectively, there is a possibility of the values of $M$ and $N$ being such that you have an integral answer.

For instance: $5/3 + 36/27 = 81/27 = 3$

The result will never be integral if the two denominators are co-prime.

**Note:** This holds true even for expressions of the nature $A/7 - B/6$, etc.

This has huge implications for problem solving especially in the case of solving linear equations related to word based problems. Students are advised to try to use these throughout Blocks I, II and III of this book.

**Example:** Find all five-digit numbers of the form $34x5y$ that are divisible by 36.

**Solution:** 36 is a product of two co-primes 4 and 9. Hence, if $34x5y$ is divisible by 4 and 9, it will also be divisible by 36. Hence, for divisibility by 4, we have that the value of $y$ can be 2 or 6. Also, if $y$ is 2 the number becomes $34x52$. For this to be divisible by 9, the addition of $3 + 4 + x + 5 + 2$ should be divisible by 9. For this $x$ can be 4.

Hence the number 34452 is divisible by 36.

Also for $y = 6$, the number $34x56$ will be divisible by 36 when the addition of the digits is divisible by 9. This will happen when $x$ is 0 or 9. Hence, the numbers 34056 and 34956 will be divisible by 36.

### Exercise for Self-practice

Find all numbers of the form $56x3y$ that are divisible by 36.
Find all numbers of the form $72xy$ that are divisible by 45.
Find all numbers of the form $135xy$ that are divisible by 45.
Find all numbers of the form $517xy$ that are divisible by 89.

## Divisibility Rules

**Divisibility by 2 or 5:** A number is divisible by 2 or 5 if the last digit is divisible by 2 or 5.

**Divisibility by 3 (or 9):** All such numbers the sum of whose digits are divisible by 3 (or 9) are divisible by 3 (or 9).

**Divisibility by 4:** A number is divisible by 4 if the last 2 digits are divisible by 4.

**Divisibility by 6:** A number is divisible by 6 if it is simultaneously divisible by 2 and 3.

**Divisibility by 8:** A number is divisible by 8 if the last 3 digits of the number are divisible by 8.

**Divisibility by 11:** A number is divisible by 11 if the difference of the sum of the digits in the odd places and the sum of the digits in the even places is zero or is divisible by 11.

**Divisibility by 12:** All numbers divisible by 3 and 4 are divisible by 12.

**Divisibility by 7, 11 or 13:** The integer $n$ is divisible by 7, 11 or 13 if and only if the difference of the number of its thousands and the remainder of its division by 1000 is divisible by 7, 11 or 13.

For Example: 473312 is divisible by 7 since the difference between $473 - 312 = 161$ is divisible by 7.

**Even Numbers:** All integers that are divisible by 2 are even numbers. They are also denoted by $2n$.

**Example:** 2, 4, 6, 12, 122, –2, –4, –12.
Also note that zero is an even number.
2 is the lowest positive even number.

**Odd Numbers:** All integers that are not divisible by 2 are odd numbers. Odd numbers leave a remainder of 1 on being divided by 2. They are denoted by $2n + 1$ or $2n - 1$.

Lowest positive odd number is 1.

**Example:** –1, –3, –7, –35, 3, 11, etc.

**Complex Numbers:** The arithmetic combination of real numbers and imaginary numbers are called complex numbers.

**Alternately:** All numbers of the form $a + ib$, where $i = \sqrt{-1}$ are called complex number.

**Twin Primes:** A pair of prime numbers are said to be twin prime when they differ by 2.

**Example:** 3 and 5 are Twin Primes, so also are 11 and 13.

**Perfect Numbers:** A number $n$ is said to be a perfect number if the sum of all the divisors of $n$ (including $n$) is equal to $2n$.

**Example:** $6 = 1 \times 2 \times 3$ sum of the divisors $= 1 + 2 + 3 + 6 = 12 = 2 \times 6$

$$28 = 1, 2, 4, 7, 14, 28, = 56 = 2 \times 28$$

**Task for student:** Find all perfect numbers below 1000.

**Mixed Numbers:** A number that has both an integral and a fractional part is known as a mixed number.

**Triangular Numbers:** A number which can be represented as the sum of consecutive natural numbers starting with 1 are called as triangular numbers.

e.g.: $1 + 2 + 3 + 4 = 10$. So, 10 is a triangular number.

## Certain Rules

1. Of $n$ consecutive whole numbers $a, a + 1 \ldots a + n - 1$, one and only one is divisible by $n$.
2. *Mixed numbers:* A number that has both the integral and fractional part is known as mixed number.
3. If a number $n$ can be represented as the product of two numbers $p$ and $q$, that is, $n = p \cdot q$, then we say that the number $n$ is divisible by $p$ and by $q$ and each of the numbers $p$ and $q$ is a divisor of the number $n$. Also, each factor of $p$ and $q$ would be a divisor of $n$.
4. Any number $n$ can be represented in the decimal system of numbers as
   $N = a_k \times 10^k + a_{k-1} \times 10^{k-1} + \ldots + a_i \times 10 + a_0$
   **Example:** 2738 can be written as: $2 \times 10^3 + 7 \times 10^2 + 3 \times 10^1 + 8 \times 10^0$.
5. $3^n$ will always have an even number of tens. (Example: 2 in 27,8 in 81,24 in 243,72 in 729 and so on.)
6. A sum of 5 consecutive whole numbers will always be divisible by 5.
7. The difference between 2 two digit numbers:
   $(xy) - (yx)$ will be divisible by 9
8. The square of an odd number when divided by 8 will always leave a remainder of 1.
9. The product of 3 consecutive natural numbers is divisible by 6.
10. The product of 3 consecutive natural numbers the first of which is even is divisible by 24.
11. Products:
    Odd × odd = odd
    Odd × even = even
    Even × even = even
12. All numbers not divisible by 3 have the property that their square will have a remainder of 1 when divided by 3.
13. $(a^2 + b^2)/(b^2 + c^2) = (a^2/b^2)$ if $a/b = b/c$.
14. The product of any $r$ consecutive integers (numbers) is divisible by $r!$.
15. If $m$ and $n$ are two integers then $(m + n)!$ is divisible by $m!n!$
16. Difference between any number and the number obtained by writing the digits in reverse order is divisible by 9. (for any number of digits)

## Certain Rules *(Contd)*

17. Any number written in the form $10^n - 1$ is divisible by 3 and 9.
18. If a numerical expression contains no parentheses, first the operations of the third stage (involution or raising a number to a power) are performed, then the operations of the second stage (multiplication and division) and, finally, the operations of the first stage (addition and subtraction) are performed. In this case the operations of one and the same stage are performed in the sequence indicated by the notation. If an expression contains parentheses, then the operation indicated in the parentheses are to be performed first and then all the remaining operations. In this case operations of the numbers in parentheses as well as standing without parentheses are performed in the order indicated above.

    If a fractional expression is evaluated, then the operations indicated in the numerator and denominator of the function are performed and the first result is divided by the second.
19. $(a)^n/(a + 1)$ leaves a remainder of
    $a$ if $n$ is odd
    1 if $n$ is even
20. $(a + 1)^n/a$ will always give a remainder of 1.
21. For any natural number $n$, $n^5$ has the same units digit as $n$ has.
22. For any natural number: $n^3 - n$ is divisible by 6.
23. The expression $\dfrac{1 \times 2 \times 3 \times 4 \times \cdots (n-1)}{n}$ gives a remainder of $(n - 1)$ if $n$ is prime.

    In case $n$ is composite, the remainder would be 0.

## THE REMAINDER THEOREM

Consider the following question:

$$17 \times 23.$$

Suppose you have to find the remainder of this expression when divided by 12.

We can write this as:

$$17 \times 23 = (12 + 5) \times (12 + 11)$$

Which when expanded gives us:

$$12 \times 12 + 12 \times 11 + 5 \times 12 + 5 \times 11$$

You will realise that, when this expression is divided by 12, the remainder will only depend on the last term above:

Thus, $\dfrac{12 \times 12 + 12 \times 11 + 5 \times 12 + 5 \times 11}{12}$ gives the same

remainder as $\dfrac{5 \times 11}{12}$

*Contd*

Hence, 7.

This is the remainder when $17 \times 23$ is divided by 12.

**Learning Point:** In order to find the remainder of $17 \times 23$ when divided by 12, you need to look at the individual remainders of 17 and 23 when divided by 12. The respective remainders (5 and 11) will give you the remainder of the original expression when divided by 12.

Mathematically, this can be written as:

The remainder of the expression $[A \times B \times C + D \times E]/M$, will be the same as the remainder of the expression $[A_R \times B_R \times C_R + D_R \times E_R]/M$.

Where $A_R$ is the remainder when $A$ is divided by $M$,

$B_R$ is the remainder when $B$ is divided by $M$,

$C_R$ is the remainder when $C$ is divided by $M$

$D_R$ is the remainder when $D$ is divided by $M$ and

$E_R$ is the remainder when $E$ is divided by $M$,

We call this transformation as the remainder theorem transformation and denote it by the sign $\xrightarrow{R}$

Thus, the remainder of $1421 \times 1423 \times 1425$ when divided by 12 can be given as:

$$\frac{1421 \times 1423 \times 1425}{12} \xrightarrow{R} \frac{5 \times 7 \times 9}{12} = \frac{35 \times 9}{12}$$

$$\xrightarrow{R} \frac{11 \times 9}{12}.$$

$\xrightarrow{R}$ gives us a remainder of 3.

In the above question, we have used a series of remainder theorem transformations (denoted by $\xrightarrow{R}$) and equality transformations to transform a difficult looking expression into a simple expression.

Try to solve the following questions on Remainder theorem:

Find the remainder in each of the following cases:

1. $17 \times 23 \times 126 \times 38$ divided by 8.

2. $243 \times 245 \times 247 \times 249 \times 251$ divided by 12.

3. $\dfrac{173 \times 261}{13} + \dfrac{248 \times 249 \times 250}{15}$.

4. $\dfrac{1021 \times 2021 \times 3021}{14}$.

5. $\dfrac{37 \times 43 \times 51}{7} + \dfrac{137 \times 143 \times 151}{9}$.

## 🎧 USING NEGATIVE REMAINDERS

Consider the following question:

Find the remainder when: $14 \times 15$ is divided by 8.

The obvious approach in this case would be

$$\frac{14 \times 15}{8} \xrightarrow{R} \frac{6 \times 7}{8} = \frac{42}{8} \xrightarrow{R} 2 \text{ (Answer)}.$$

However there is another option by which you can solve the same question:

When 14 is divided by 8, the remainder is normally seen as $+ 6$. However, there might be times when using the negative value of the remainder might give us more convenience. Which is why you should know the following process:

**Concept Note:** Remainders by definition are always non-negative. Hence, even when we divide a number like $- 27$ by 5 we say that the remainder is 3 (and not $- 2$). However, looking at the negative value of the remainder—it has its own advantages in Mathematics as it results in reducing calculations.

Thus, when a number like 13 is divided by 8, the remainder being 5, the negative remainder is $- 3$.

***

**Note:** It is in this context that we mention numbers like 13, 21, 29, etc. as $8n + 5$ or $8n - 3$ numbers.

***

Thus $\dfrac{14 \times 15}{8}$ will give us $\dfrac{-2 \times -1}{8} R \to 2$.

Consider the advantage this process will give you in the following question:

$$\frac{51 \times 52}{53} \xrightarrow{R} \frac{-2 \times -1}{53} \xrightarrow{R} 2.$$

(The alternative will involve long calculations. Hence, the principle is that you should use negative remainders wherever you can. They can make life much simpler!!!)

## What if the Answer Comes Out Negative

For instance, $\dfrac{62 \times 63 \times 64}{66} \xrightarrow{R} \dfrac{-4 \times -3 \times -2}{66} R \to \dfrac{-24}{66}$.

But, we know that a remainder of $-24$, equals a remainder of 42 when divided by 66. Hence, the answer is 42.

Of course nothing stops you from using positive and negative remainders at the same time in order to solve the same question —

Thus $\dfrac{17 \times 19}{9} \xrightarrow{R} \dfrac{(-1) \times (1)}{9} R \to -1 R \to 8.$

**Dealing with large powers** There are two tools which are effective in order to deal with large powers —

(A) If you can express the expression in the form $\dfrac{(ax + 1)^n}{a}$, the remainder will become 1 directly. In such a case, no matter how large the value of the power $n$ is, the remainder is 1.

For instance, $\dfrac{\left(37^{12635}\right)}{9} \xrightarrow{R} \dfrac{\left(1^{12635}\right)}{9} \xrightarrow{R} 1.$

In such a case the value of the power does not matter.

(B) $\dfrac{(ax-1)^n}{a}$. In such a case using −1 as the remainder it will be evident that the remainder will be +1 if $n$ is even and it will be −1 (Hence $a-1$) when $n$ is odd.

e.g.: $\dfrac{31^{127}}{8} \xrightarrow{R} \dfrac{(-1)^{127}}{8} \xrightarrow{R} \dfrac{(-1)}{8} \xrightarrow{R} 7$

## 🔥 ANOTHER IMPORTANT POINT

Suppose you were asked to find the remainder of 14 divided by 4. It is clearly visible that the answer should be 2.

But consider the following process:

$14/4 = 7/2 \xrightarrow{R} 1$ (The answer has changed!!)

What has happened?

We have transformed 14/4 into 7/2 by dividing the numerator and the denominator by 2. The result is that the original remainder 2 is also divided by 2 giving us 1 as the remainder. In order to take care of this problem, we need to reverse the effect of the division of the remainder by 2. This is done by multiplying the final remainder by 2 to get the correct answer.

**Note:** In any question on remainder theorem, you should try to cancel out parts of the numerator and denominator as much as you can, since it directly reduces the calculations required.

## 🔥 AN APPLICATION OF REMAINDER THEOREM

Finding the last two digits of an expression:

Suppose you had to find the last 2 digits of the expression:

$22 \times 31 \times 44 \times 27 \times 37 \times 43$

The remainder the above expression will give when it is divided by 100 is the answer to the above question.

Hence, to answer the question above find the remainder of the expression when it is divided by 100.

**Solution:** $\dfrac{22 \times 31 \times 44 \times 27 \times 37 \times 43}{100}$

$= \dfrac{22 \times 31 \times 11 \times 27 \times 37 \times 43}{25}$ (on dividing by 4)

$\xrightarrow{R} \dfrac{22 \times 6 \times 11 \times 2 \times 12 \times 18}{25} = \dfrac{132 \times 22 \times 216}{25}$

$\xrightarrow{R} \dfrac{7 \times 22 \times 16}{25}$

$= \dfrac{154 \times 16}{25} \xrightarrow{R} \dfrac{4 \times 16}{25} \xrightarrow{R} 14$

Thus the remainder being 14, (after division by 4). The actual remainder should be 56.

[Don't forget to multiply by 4 !!]

Hence, the last 2 digits of the answer will be 56.

Using negative remainders here would have helped further.

**Note:** Similarly finding the last three digits of an expression means finding the remainder when the expression is divided by 1000.

THE PRIME NUMBER DIVISOR RULE:

This rule states that: If 'P' is a prime number then:

The remainder of the expression $\dfrac{A^{P-1}}{P}$ is 1. (Provided A is not a multiple of P)

For example: The remainder of $\dfrac{24^{82}}{83} = 1$

SPLITTING THE DENOMINATOR INTO CO-PRIME NUMBERS:

This is also sometime referred to as the 'Chinese Remainder Theorem'. It is useful when you have to find the remainder when there is a large denominator, and no other short cuts are working. It is best explained through an example.

Suppose you were trying to find the remainder of $\dfrac{107^{1444}}{136}$. You can split the denominator into two co-prime numbers as 17 & 8.

First find the remainder of $\dfrac{107^{1444}}{17} \rightarrow \dfrac{5^{1444}}{17} =$

$\dfrac{5^{16n} \times 5^4}{17} \rightarrow \dfrac{1 \times 5^4}{17} \rightarrow Remainder = 13$. This means that $107^{1444}$ is a $17n+13$ number.

Next, find the remainder of $\dfrac{107^{1444}}{8} \rightarrow \dfrac{3^{1444}}{8} =$ $\dfrac{3^{2n}}{8} \rightarrow Remainder = 1$. This means that $107^{1444}$ is a $8n + 1$ number.

The next step is to find a number below 136 that is both a $17n + 13$ as well as an $8n + 1$ number. That number would be the answer.

The list of $17n + 13$ numbers below 136 is: 13, 30, 47, 64, 81, 98, 115 and 132. 81 can be seen to be an $8n + 1$ number too.

Thus, the correct answer is 81.

## Exercise for Self-practice

1. Find the remainder when 73 + 75 + 78 + 57 + 197 is divided by 34.
   - (a) 32
   - (b) 4
   - (c) 15
   - (d) 28

2. Find the remainder when $73 \times 75 \times 78 \times 57 \times 197$ is divided by 34.

3. Find the remainder when $73 \times 75 \times 78 \times 57 \times 197 \times 37$ is divided by 34.

   (a) 22            (b) 30

   (c) 15            (d) 28

4. Find the remainder when $43^{197}$ is divided by 7.

   (a) 2             (b) 4

   (c) 6             (d) 1

5. Find the remainder when $51^{203}$ is divided by 7.

   (a) 4             (b) 2

   (c) 1             (d) 6

6. Find the remainder when $59^{28}$ is divided by 7.

   (a) 2             (b) 4

   (c) 6             (d) 1

7. Find the remainder when $67^{99}$ is divided by 7.

   (a) 2             (b) 4

   (c) 6             (d) 1

8. Find the remainder when $75^{80}$ is divided by 7.

   (a) 4             (b) 3

   (c) 2             (d) 6

9. Find the remainder when $41^{77}$ is divided by 7.

   (a) 2             (b) 1

   (c) 6             (d) 4

10. Find the remainder when $21^{875}$ is divided by 17.

   (a) 8             (b) 13

   (c) 16            (d) 9

11. Find the remainder when $54^{124}$ is divided by 17.

   (a) 4             (b) 5

   (c) 13            (d) 15

12. Find the remainder when $83^{261}$ is divided by 17.

   (a) 13           (b) 9

   (c) 8             (d) 2

13. Find the remainder when $25^{102}$ is divided by 17.

   (a) 13           (b) 15

   (c) 4             (d) 2

## ANSWER KEY

| | | | | |
|---|---|---|---|---|
| 1. (b) | 2. (a) | 3. (a) | 4. (d) | 5. (a) |
| 6. (b) | 7. (d) | 8. (a) | 9. (c) | 10. (b) |
| 11. (a) | 12. (d) | 13. (c) | | |

### Solutions

1. The remainder would be given by: $(5 + 7 + 10 + 23 + 27)/34 = 72/34 \to$ remainder = 4. Option (b) is correct.

2. The remainder would be given by: $(5 \times 7 \times 10 \times 23 \times 27)/34 \to 35 \times 230 \times 27/ 34 \to 1 \times 26 \times 27/34 = 702/34 \to$ remainder = 22. Option (a) is correct.

3. The remainder would be given by: $(5 \times 7 \times 10 \times 23 \times 27 \times 3)/34 \to 35 \times 230 \times 27 \times 3/34 \to 1 \times 26 \times$

$81/34 \to 26 \times 13/34 = 338/34 \to$ remainder = 32. Option (a) is correct.

4. $43^{197}/7 \to 1^{197}/7 \to$ remainder =1. Option (d) is correct.

5. $51^{203}/7 \to 2^{203}/7 = (2^3)^{67} \times 2^2/7 = 8^{67} \times 4/7 \to$ remainder = 4. Option (a) is correct.

6. $59^{28}/7 \to 3^{28}/7 = (3^6)^4 \times 3^4/7 = 729^6 \times 81/7 \to$ remainder = 4. Option (b) is correct.

7. $67^{99}/7 \to 4^{99}/7 = (4^3)^{33}/7 = 64^{33}/7 \to$ remainder = 1. Option (d) is correct.

8. $75^{80}/7 \to 5^{80}/7 = (5^6)^{13} \times 5^2/7 \to 1^{13} \times 25/7 \to$ remainder = 4. Option (a) is correct.

9. $41^{77}/7 \to 6^{77}/7 \to$ remainder = 6 (as the expression is in the form $a^n/(a + 1)$. Option (c) is correct.

10. $21^{875}/17 \to 4^{875}/17 = (4^4)^n \times 4^3/17 = 256^n \times 64/17 \to 1^n \times 13/17 \to$ remainder =13. Option (b) is correct.

11. $54^{124}/17 \to 3^{124}/17$. At this point, like in each of the other questions solved above, we need to plan the power of 3 which would give us a convenient remainder of either 1 or –1. As we start to look for remainders that powers of 3 would have when divided by 17, we get that at the power $3^6$ the remainder is 15. If we convert this to –2 we will get that at the fourth power of $3^6$, we should get a 16/17 situation (as $-2 \times -2 \times -2 \times -2 = 16$). This means that at a power of $3^{24}$ we are getting a remainder of 16 or –1. Naturally then if we double the power to $3^{48}$, the remainder would be 1.

With this thinking we can restart solving the problem: $3^{124}/17 = 3^{48} \times 3^{48} \times 3^{24} \times 3^4/17 \to 1 \times 1 \times 16 \times 81/17 \to 16 \times 13/17 = 208/17 \to$ remainder = 4. Option (a) is correct.

(Note that if we are dividing a number by 17 and if we see the remainder as 15, we can logically say that the remainder is –2 — even though negative remainders are not allowed in mathematics)

12. Using the logic developed in Question 11 above, we have $83^{261}/17 \to 15^{261}/17 \to (-2)^{261}/17 \to (-2^4)^{65} \times (-2)/17 \to 16^{65} \times (-2)/17 \to (-1) \times (-2)/17 \to$ remainder = 2. Option (d) is correct.

13. $25^{102}/17 \to 8^{102}/17 = 2^{306}/17 = (2^4)^{76} \times 2^2/17 \to 16^{76} \times 4/17 \to 1 \times 4/17 \to$ remainder = 4. Option (c) is correct.

## BASE SYSTEM

All the work that we carry out with numbers is called as the decimal system. In other words we work in the decimal system. Why is it called decimal? It is because there are 10 digits in the system 0–9.

However, depending on the number of digits contained in the base system other number systems are also possible. Thus a number system with base 2 is called the binary number system and will have only two digits 0 and 1. Some of the most commonly used systems are: Binary (base 2), Octal (base 8), Hexadecimal (base 16).

Binary system has 2 digits : 0, 1. Octal has 8 digits : – 0, 1, 2, 3, ... 7.

Hexadecimal has 16 digits – 0, 1, 2, ... 9, $A, B, C, D, E, F$. Where $A$ has a value 10, $B = 11$ and so on.

Before coming to the questions asked under this category, let us first look at a few issues with regard to converting numbers between different base systems.

**1. Conversion from any base system into decimal:**

Suppose you have to write the decimal equivalent of the base 8 number $146_8$.

In such a case, follow the following structure for conversion:

$$146_8 = 1 \times 8^2 + 4 \times 8^1 + 6 \times 8^0$$
$$= 64 + 32 + 6 = 102.$$

**Note:** If you remember the process, for writing the value of any random number, say 146, in our decimal system (base 10) we use: $1 \times 10^2 + 4 \times 10^1 + 6 \times 10^0$. All you need to change, in case you are trying to write the value of the number in base 8, is that you replace 10 with 8 in every power.

Try to write the decimal equivalents of the following numbers:

$143_5$, $143_6$, $143_7$, $143_8$, $143_9$

$1256_7$, $1256_8$, $1256_9$.

**2. Conversion of a number in decimals into any base:**

Suppose you have to find out the value of the decimal number 347 in base 6. The following process is to be adopted:

**Step 1:** Find the highest power of the base (6 in this case) that is contained in 347. In this case you will realise that the value of $6^3 = 216$ is contained in 347, while the value of $6^4 = 1296$ is not contained in 347. Hence, we realise that the highest power of 6 contained in 347 is 3. This should make you realise that the number has to be constructed by using the powers $6^0$, $6^1$, $6^2$, $6^3$ respectively. Hence, a 4-digit number.

Structure of number: – – – –

**Step 2:** We now need to investigate how many times each of the powers of 6 is contained in 347. For this we first start with the highest power as found above. Thus we can see that $6^3$ (216) is contained in 347 once. Hence our number now becomes:

1 – – –

That is, we now know that the first digit of the number is 1. Besides, when we have written the number 1 in this place, we have accounted for a value of 216 out of 347. This leaves us with 131 to account for.

We now need to look for the number of times $6^2$ is contained in 131. We can easily see that $6^2 = 36$ is contained in 131 three times. Thus, we write 3 as the next digit of our number which will now look like:

1 3 – –

In other words we now know that the first two digits of the number are 13. Besides, when we have written the number 3 in this place, we have accounted for a value of 108 out of 131 which was left to be accounted for. This leaves us with 131–108 = 23 to account for.

We now need to look for the number of times $6^1$ is contained in 23. We can easily see that $6^1 = 6$ is contained in 23 three times. Thus, we write 3 as the next digit of our number which will now look like:

1 3 3 –

In other words we now know that the first three digits of the number are 133. Besides, when we have written the number 3 in this place, we have accounted for a value of 18 out of the 23 which was left to be accounted for. This leaves us with 23 – 18 = 5 to account for.

The last digit of the number corresponds to $6^0 = 1$. In order to make a value of 5 in this place we will obviously need to use this power of 6, 5 times thus giving us the final digit as 5. Hence, our number is:

1 3 3 5.

A few points you should know about base systems:
(1) In single digits there is no difference between the value of the number—whichever base we take. For example, the equality $5_6 = 5_7 = 5_8 = 5_9 = 5_{10}$.
(2) Suppose you have a number in base $x$. When you convert this number into its decimal value, the value should be such that when it is divided by $x$, the remainder should be equal to the units digit of the number in base $x$.

In other words, $342_8$ will be a number of the form $8n + 2$ in base 10. You can use this principle for checking your conversion calculations.

The following table gives a list of decimal values and their binary, octal and hexadecimal equivalents:

| Decimal | Binary | Octal | Hexadecimal |
|---------|--------|-------|-------------|
| 0 | 0 | 0 | 0 |
| 1 | 1 | 1 | 1 |
| 2 | 10 | 2 | 2 |
| 3 | 11 | 3 | 3 |
| 4 | 100 | 4 | 4 |
| 5 | 101 | 5 | 5 |
| 6 | 110 | 6 | 6 |
| 7 | 111 | 7 | 7 |
| 8 | 1000 | 10 | 8 |
| 9 | 1001 | 11 | 9 |
| 10 | 1010 | 12 | A |
| 11 | 1011 | 13 | B |

## Illustrations

1. The number of $x$ digit numbers in $n$th base system will be
   (a) $n^x$        (b) $n^x - 1$
   (c) $n^x - n$      (d) $n^x - n^{(x-1)}$

**Solution** Base $\rightarrow n$, digit $\rightarrow x$

So, required number of numbers = $n^x - n^{(x-1)}$

2. The number of 2 digit numbers in binary system is

(a) 2                  (b) 90

(c) 10                (d) 4

**Solution** By using the formula, we get the required number of numbers = $2^2 - 2^1 = 2$

$\Rightarrow$ Option (a)

3. The number of 5 digit numbers in binary system is

(a) 48                (b) 16

(c) 32                (d) 20

**Solution** Required number of numbers = $2^5 - 2^4 = 32 - 16 = 16$

$\Rightarrow$ Option (b)

4. I celebrate my birthday on $12^{th}$ January on earth. On which date would I have to celebrate my birthday if I were on a planet where binary system is being used for counting. (The number of days, months and years are same on both the planets.)

(a) $11^{th}$ Jan          (b) $111^{th}$ Jan

(c) $110^{th}$ Jan         (d) $1100^{th}$ Jan

**Solution** On earth (decimal system is used). $12^{th}$ Jan

$\Rightarrow 12^{th}$ Jan

The $12^{th}$ day on the planet where binary system is being used will be called

$$(12)_{10} = (?)_2$$

$$= \frac{1}{2^3} \frac{1}{2^2} \frac{0}{2^1} \frac{0}{2^0}$$

i.e., $1100^{th}$ day on that planet

So, $12^{th}$ January on earth = $1100^{th}$ January on that planet

$\Rightarrow$ Option (d)

5. My year of birth is 1982. What would the year have been instead of 1982 if base 12 were used (for counting) instead of decimal system?

(a) 1182             (b) 1022

(c) 2082             (d) 1192

**Solution** The required answer will equal to $(1982)_{10}$ = $(?)_{12}$.

$$= \frac{1}{12^3} \frac{1}{12^2} \frac{9}{12^1} \frac{2}{12^0} \rightarrow$$

$1 \times 12^3 + 1 \times 12^2 + 9 \times 12^1 + 2 \times 9^0 = 1728 + 144 + 108 + 2 = 1982$

Hence, the number $(1192)_{12}$ represents 1982 in our base system.

$\Rightarrow$ Option (d)

6. 203 in base 5 when converted to base 8, becomes

(a) 61                (b) 53

(c) 145              (d) 65

**Solution** $(203)_5 = (?)_{10}$

$$= 2 \times 5^2 + 0 \times 5^1 + 3 \times 5^0$$

$$= 50 + 0 + 3 = 53$$

Now,

$$(53)_{10} = (?)8$$

$$= \frac{6}{8^1} \frac{5}{8^0}$$

$$= (203)_5 = (65)_8$$

$\Rightarrow$ Option (d)

7. $(52)_7 + 46_8 = (?)_{10}$

(a) $(75)_{10}$          (b) $(50)_{10}$

(c) $(39)_{39}$          (d) $(28)_{10}$

**Solution** $(52)_7 = (5 \times 7^1 + 2 \times 7^0)_{10} = (37)_{10}$

also, $(46)_8 = (4 \times 8^1 + 6 \times 8^0)_{10} = (38)_{10}$

sum = $(75)_{10}$

$\Rightarrow$ Option (a)

8. $(23)_5 + (47)_9 = (?)_8$

(a) 70                (b) 35

(c) 64                (d) 18

**Solution** $(23)_5 = (2 \times 5^1 + 3 \times 5^0)_{10} = (13)_{10} = (1 \times 8^1 + 5 \times 8^0)_8 = (15)_8$

also, $(47)_9 = (4 \times 9^1 + 7 \times 9^0)_{10} = (43)_{10}$

$= (5 \times 8^1 + 3 \times 8^0)_8 = (53)_8$

sum = $(13)_{10} + (43)_{10} = (56)_{10} \rightarrow (70)_8$

$\Rightarrow$ Option (a)

9. $(11)_2 + (22)_3 + (33)_4 + (44)_5 + (55)_6 + (66)_7 + (77)_8 + (88)_9 = (?)_{10}$

(a) 396             (b) 276

(c) 250             (d) 342

**Solution** $(11)_2 = (1 \times 2^1 + 1 \times 2^0)_{10} = (3)_{10}$

$(22)_3 = (2 \times 3^1 + 2 \times 3^0)_{10} = (8)_{10}$

$(33)_4 = (3 \times 4^1 + 3 \times 4^0)_{10} = (15)_{10}$

$(44)_5 = (4 \times 5^1 + 4 \times 5^0)_{10} = (24)_{10}$

$(55)_6 = (5 \times 6^1 + 5 \times 6^0)_{10} = (35)_{10}$

$(66)_7 = (6 \times 7^1 + 6 \times 7^0)_{10} = (48)_{10}$

$(77)_8 = (7 \times 8^1 + 7 \times 8^0)_{10} = (63)_{10}$

$(88)_9 = (8 \times 9^1 + 8 \times 9^0)_{10} = (80)_{10}$

sum = $(276)_{10}$

$\Rightarrow$ Option (b)

10. $(24)_5 \times (32)_5 = (?)_5$

(a) 1423             (b) 1422

(c) 1420             (d) 1323

**Solution** $(24)_5 = 14_{10}$ and $32_5 = 17_{10}$. Hence, the required answer can be got by $14 \times 17 = 238_{10} = 1 \times 5^3 + 4 \times 5^2 + 2 \times 5^1 + 3 \times 5^0 \rightarrow 1423$ as the correct answer.

Alternately, you could multiply directly in base 5 as follows:

$$\begin{array}{r} (2\ 4) \\ \times\ \underline{(3\ 2)} \\ \underline{(1\ 4\ 2\ 3)} \end{array}$$

Unit's digit of the answer would correspond to: $4 \times 2 = 8$

→ 13$_5$. Hence, we write 3 in the units place and carry over 1.

(Note that in this process when we are doing $4 \times 2$ we are effectively multiplying individual digits of one number with individual digits of the other number. In such a case we can write $4 \times 2 = 8$ by assuming that both the numbers are in decimal system as the value of a single digit in any base is equal.)

The tens digit will be got by: $2 \times 2 + 4 \times 3 = 16 + 1 = 17$ → 32$_5$

Hence, we write 2 in the tens place and carry over 3 to the hundreds place.

Where we get $3 \times 2 + 3 = 9 \to 14$

Hence, the answer is 14.

⇒ Option (a)

**11.** In base 8, the greatest four digit perfect square is

    (a) 9801           (b) 1024

    (c) 8701           (d) 7601

**Solution** In base 10, the greatest 4 digit perfect square = 9801

In base 9, the greatest 4 digits perfect square = 8701

In base 8, the greatest 4 digits perfect square = 7601

Alternately, multiply $(77)_8 \times (77)_8$ to get 7601 as the answer.

## Unit's Digit

(A) The unit's digit of an expression can be calculated by getting the remainder while the expression is divided by 10.

Thus for example if we have to find the units digit of the expression:

$$17 \times 22 \times 36 \times 54 \times 27 \times 31 \times 63$$

We try to find the remainder –

$$\frac{17 \times 22 \times 36 \times 54 \times 27 \times 31 \times 63}{10}$$

$$\xrightarrow{R} \frac{7 \times 2 \times 6 \times 4 \times 7 \times 3}{10}$$

$$= \frac{14 \times 24 \times 21}{10} \xrightarrow{R} \frac{4 \times 4 \times 1}{10} = \frac{16}{10} \xrightarrow{R} 6.$$

Hence, the required answer is 6.

This could have been directly got by multiplying: $7 \times 2 \times 6 \times 4 \times 7 \times 1 \times 3$ and only accounting for the units' digit.

(B) Unit's digits in the contexts of powers — Study the following table carefully.

### Unit's digit when 'N' is raised to a power

| Number Ending With | Value of power | | | | | | | | |
|---|---|---|---|---|---|---|---|---|---|
| | 1 | 2 | 3 | 4 | 5 | 6 | 7 | 8 | 9 |
| 1 | 1 | 1 | 1 | 1 | 1 | 1 | 1 | 1 | 1 |
| 2 | 2 | 4 | 8 | 6 | 2 | 4 | 8 | 6 | 2 |

*Contd*

| Number Ending With | Value of power | | | | | | | | |
|---|---|---|---|---|---|---|---|---|---|
| | 1 | 2 | 3 | 4 | 5 | 6 | 7 | 8 | 9 |
| 3 | 3 | 9 | 7 | 1 | 3 | 9 | 7 | 1 | 3 |
| 4 | 4 | 6 | 4 | 6 | 4 | 6 | 4 | 6 | 4 |
| 5 | 5 | 5 | 5 | 5 | 5 | 5 | 5 | 5 | 5 |
| 6 | 6 | 6 | 6 | 6 | 6 | 6 | 6 | 6 | 6 |
| 7 | 7 | 9 | 3 | 1 | 7 | 9 | 3 | 1 | 7 |
| 8 | 8 | 4 | 2 | 6 | 8 | 4 | 2 | 6 | 8 |
| 9 | 9 | 1 | 9 | 1 | 9 | 1 | 9 | 1 | 9 |
| 0 | 0 | 0 | 0 | 0 | 0 | 0 | 0 | 0 | 0 |

In the table above, if you look at the columns corresponding to the power 5 or 9 you will realize that the unit's digit for all numbers is repeated (i.e. it is 1 for 1, 2 for, 3 for 3….9 for 9.)

This means that whenever we have any number whose unit's digit is '$x$' and it is raised to a power of the form $4n + 1$, the value of the unit's digit of the answer will be the same as the original units digit.

**Illustrations:** $(1273)^{101}$ will give a unit's digit of 3. $(1547)^{25}$ will give a units digit of 7 and so forth.

Thus, the above table can be modified into the form –

### Value of Power

| Number ending in | If the value of the Power is | | | |
|---|---|---|---|---|
| | $4n + 1$ | $4n + 2$ | $4n + 3$ | $4n$ |
| 1 | 1 | 1 | 1 | 1 |
| 2 | 2 | 4 | 8 | 6 |
| 3 | 3 | 9 | 7 | 1 |
| 4 | 4 | 6 | 4 | 6 |
| 5 | 5 | 5 | 5 | 5 |
| 6 | 6 | 6 | 6 | 6 |
| 7 | 7 | 9 | 3 | 1 |
| 8 | 8 | 4 | 2 | 6 |
| 9 | 9 | 1 | 9 | 1 |

[Remember, at this point that we had said (in the Back to School section of Part 1) that all natural numbers can be expressed in the form $4n + x$. Hence, with the help of the logic that helps us build this table, we can easily derive the units digit of any number when it is raised to a power.)

**A special Case**

**Question:** What will be the unit's digit of $(1273)^{122!}$?

**Solution:** 122! is a number of the form $4n$. Hence, the answer should be 1. [**Note:** 1 here is derived by thinking of it as 3 (for $4n + 1$), 9 (for $4n + 2$), 7 (for $4n + 3$), 1(for $4n$)]

## Exercise for Self-practice

Find the Units digit in each of the following cases:

1. $2^2 \times 4^4 \times 6^6 \times 8^8$

2. $1^1 \times 2^2 \times 3^3 \times 4^4 \times 5^5 \times 6^6 \dots \times 100^{100}$

3. $17 \times 23 \times 51 \times 32 + 15 \times 17 \times 16 \times 22$

4. $13 \times 17 \times 22 \times 34 + 12 \times 6 \times 4 \times 3 - 13 \times 33$

5. $37^{123} \times 43^{144} \times 57^{226} \times 32^{127} \times 52^{5!}$

6. $67 \times 37 \times 43 \times 91 \times 42 \times 33 \times 42$

   (a) 2      (b) 6
   (c) 8      (d) 4

7. $67 \times 35 \times 43 \times 91 \times 47 \times 33 \times 49$

   (a) 1      (b) 9
   (c) 5      (d) 6

8. $67 \times 35 \times 45 \times 91 \times 42 \times 33 \times 81$

   (a) 2      (b) 4
   (c) 0      (d) 8

9. $67 \times 35 \times 45 + 91 \times 42 \times 33 \times 82$

   (a) 8      (b) 7
   (c) 0      (d) 5

10. $(52)^{97} \times (43)^{72}$

    (a) 2      (b) 6
    (c) 8      (d) 4

11. $(55)^{75} \times (93)^{175} \times (107)^{275}$

    (a) 7      (b) 3
    (c) 5      (d) 0

12. $(173)^{45} \times (152)^{77} \times (777)^{999}$

    (a) 2      (b) 4
    (c) 8      (d) 6

13. $81 \times 82 \times 83 \times 84 \times 86 \times 87 \times 88 \times 89$

    (a) 0      (b) 6
    (c) 2      (d) 4

14. $82^{43} \times 83^{44} \times 84^{97} \times 86^{98} \times 87^{105} \times 88^{94}$

    (a) 2      (b) 6
    (c) 4      (d) 8

15. $432 \times 532 + 532 \times 974 + 537 \times 531 + 947 \times 997$

    (a) 5      (b) 6
    (c) 9      (d) 8

## ANSWER KEY

| 6. (d) | 7. (c) | 8. (c) | 9. (b) | 10. (a) |
|--------|--------|--------|--------|---------|
| 11. (c) | 12. (c) | 13. (b) | 14. (b) | 15. (d) |

### Solutions

1. The units digit would be given by the units digit of the multiplication of $4 \times 6 \times 6 \times 6 = 4$

2. 0

3. $7 \times 3 \times 1 \times 2 + 0 \rightarrow 2 + 0 = 2$

4. $8 + 4 - 9 \rightarrow 3$

5. $3 \times 1 \times 9 \times 8 \times 6 = 6$

6. $7 \times 7 \times 3 \times 1 \times 2 \times 3 \times 2 = 4$

7. Since we have a 5 multiplied with odd numbers, the units digit would naturally be 5.

8. $5 \times 2 \rightarrow 0$

9. $5 + 2 \rightarrow 7$

10. $2 \times 1 \rightarrow 2$

11. $5 \times 7 \times 3 \rightarrow 5$

12. $3 \times 2 \times 3 \rightarrow 8$

13. $2 \times 3 \times 4 \times 6 \times 7 \times 8 \times 9 \rightarrow 6$

14. $8 \times 1 \times 4 \times 6 \times 7 \times 4 \rightarrow 6$

15. $4 + 8 + 7 + 9 \rightarrow 8$

*Space for Notes*

# 🎯 WORKED-OUT PROBLEMS

**Problem 1.1** Find the number of zeroes in the factorial of the number 18.

**Solution** 18! contains 15 and 5, which combined with one even number give zeroes. Also, 10 is also contained in 18!, which will give an additional zero. Hence, 18! contains 3 zeroes and the last digit will always be zero.

**Problem 1.2** Find the numbers of zeroes in 27!

**Solution** $27! = 27 \times 26 \times 25 \times ... \times 20 \times ... \times 15 \times ... \times 10 \times ... \times 5 \times ... \times 1$.

A zero can be formed by combining any number containing 5 multiplied by any even number. Similarly, everytime a number ending in zero is found in the product, it will add an additional zero. For this problem, note that $25 = 5 \times 5$ will give 2 zeroes and zeroes will also be got by 20, 15, 10 and 5. Hence 27! will have 6 zeroes.

*Short-cut method:* Number of zeroes is $27! \rightarrow [27/5] + [27/25]$ where $[x]$ indicates the integer just lower than the fraction Hence, $[27/5] = 5$ and $[27/5^2] = 1$, 6 zeroes

**Problem 1.3** Find the number of zeroes in 137!

**Solution** $[137/5] + [137/5^2] + [137/5^3]$
$$= 27 + 5 + 1 = 33 \text{ zeroes}$$
(since the restriction on the number of zeroes is due to the number of fives.)

## Exercise for Self-practice

Find the number of zeroes in

(a) 81!        (b) 100!        (c) 51!

**Answers**

(a) 19        (b) 24        (c) 12

**Problem 1.4** What exact power of 5 divides 87!?

**Solution** $[87/5] + [87/25] = 17 + 3 = 20$

**Problem 1.5** What power of 8 exactly divides 25!?

**Solution** If 8 were a prime number, the answer should be $[25/8] = 3$. But since 8 is not prime, use the following process.

The prime factors of 8 is $2 \times 2 \times 2$. For divisibility by 8, we need three twos. So, everytime we can find 3 twos, we add one to the power of 8 that divides 25! To count how we get 3 twos, we do the following. All even numbers will give one 'two' at least $[25/2] = 12$

Also, all numbers in 25! divisible by $2^2$ will give an additional two $[25/2^2] = 6$

Further, all numbers in 25! divisible by $2^3$ will give a third two. Hence $[25!/2^3] = 3$

And all numbers in 25! divisible by $2^4$ will give a fourth two. Hence $[25!/2^4] = 1$

Hence, total number of twos in 25! is 22. For a number to be divided by 8, we need three twos. Hence, since 25! has 22 twos, it will be divided by 8 seven times.

**Problem 1.6** What power of 15 divides 87! exactly?

**Solution** $15 = 5 \times 3$. Hence, everytime we can form a pair of one 5 and one 3, we will count one.
87! contains $- [87/5] + [87/5^2] = 17 + 3 = 20$ fives

Also 87! contains $- [87/3] + [87/3^2] + [87/3^3] + [87/3^4] = 29 + ...$ (more than 20 threes).

Hence, 15 will divide 87! twenty times since the restriction on the power is because of the number of 5s and not the number of 3s.

In fact, it is not very difficult to see that in the case of all factors being prime, we just have to look for the highest prime number to provide the restriction for the power of the denominator.

Hence, in this case we did not need to check for anything but the number of 5s.

## Exercise for Self-practice

(a) What power of 30 will exactly divide 128!

*Hint:* $[128/5] + [128/5^2] + [128/5^3]$

(b) What power of 210 will exactly divide 142!

**Problem 1.7** Find the last digit in the expression $(36472)^{123!} \times (34767)^{76!}$.

**Solution** If we try to formulate a pattern for 2 and its powers and their units digit, we see that the units digit for the powers of 2 goes as: 2, 4, 8, 6, 2, 4, 8, 6, 2, 4, 8, 6 and so on. The number 2 when raised to a power of $4n + 1$ will always give a units digit of 2. This also means that the units digit for $2^{4n}$ will always end in 6. The power of 36472 is 123! . 123! can be written in the form $4n$. Hence, $(36472)^{123!}$ will end in 6.

The second part of the expression is $(34767)^{76!}$. The units digit depends on the power of 7. If we try to formulate a pattern for 7 and its powers and their units digit, we see that the units digit for the powers of 7 go as: 7 9 3 1 7 9 3 1 and so on. This means that the units digit of the expression $7^{4n}$ will always be 1.

Since 76! can be written as a multiple of 4 as $4n$, we can conclude that the unit's digit in $(34767)^{76!}$ is 1.

Hence the units digit of $(36472)^{123!} \times (34767)^{76!}$ will be 6.

# Counting

**Problem 1.8** Find the number of numbers between 100 to 200 if

    (i) Both 100 and 200 are counted.

    (ii) Only one of 100 and 200 is counted.

    (iii) Neither 100 nor 200 is counted.

**Solution**

    (i) Both ends included-Solution: $200 - 100 + 1 = 101$

    (ii) One end included-Solution: $200 - 100 = 100$

    (iii) Both ends excluded-Solution: $200 - 100 - 1 = 99$.

**Problem 1.9** Find the number of even numbers between 122 and 242 if:

    (i) Both ends are included.

    (ii) Only one end is included.

    (iii) Neither end is included.

**Solution**

    (i) Both ends included—Solution: $(242 - 122)/2 = 60 + 1 = 61$

    (ii) One end included-Solution: $(242 - 122)/2 = 60$

    (iii) Both ends excluded-Solution: $(242 - 122)/2 - 1 = 59$

## Exercise for Self-practice

    (a) Find the number of numbers between 140 to 259, both included, which are divisible by 7.

    (b) Find the number of numbers between 100 to 200, that are divisible by 3.

**Problem 1.10** Find the number of numbers between 300 to 400 (both included), that are not divisible by 2, 3, 4, and 5.

**Solution** Total numbers: 101

**Step 1:** Not divisible by 2 = All even numbers rejected: 51 Numbers left: 50.

**Step 2:** Of which: divisible by 3 = first number 300, last number 399. But even numbers have already been removed, hence count out only odd numbers between 300 and 400 divisible by 3. This gives us that:

First number 303, last number 399, common difference 6

*So, remove:* $[(399 - 303)/6] + 1 = 17$.

∴ $50 - 17 = 33$ numbers left.

We do not need to remove additional terms for divisibility by 4 since this would eliminate only even numbers (which have already been eliminated)

**Step 3:** Remove from 33 numbers left all odd numbers that are divisible by 5 and not divisible by 3.

Between 300 to 400, the first odd number divisible by 5 is 305 and the last is 395 (since both ends are counted, we have 10 such numbers as: $[(395 - 305)/10 + 1 = 10]$.

However, some of these 10 numbers have already been removed to get to 33 numbers.

*Operation left:* Of these 10 numbers, 305, 315...395, reduce all numbers that are also divisible by 3. Quick perusal shows that the numbers start with 315 and have common difference 30.

Hence [(Last number − First number)/Difference + 1]
= $[(375 - 315)/30 + 1] = 3$

These 3 numbers were already removed from the original 100. Hence, for numbers divisible by 5, we need to remove only those numbers that are odd, divisible by 5 but not by 3. There are 7 such numbers between 300 and 400.

So numbers left are: $33 - 7 = 26$.

## Exercise for Self-practice

Find the number of numbers between 100 to 400 which are divisible by either 2, 3, 5 and 7.

**Problem 1.11** Find the number of zeroes in the following multiplication: $5 \times 10 \times 15 \times 20 \times 25 \times 30 \times 35 \times 40 \times 45 \times 50$.

**Solution** The number of zeroes depends on the number of fives and the number of twos. Here, close scrutiny shows that the number of twos is the constraint. The expression can be written as

$5 \times (5 \times 2) \times (5 \times 3) \times (5 \times 2 \times 2) \times (5 \times 5) \times (5 \times 2 \times 3) \times (5 \times 7) \times (5 \times 2 \times 2 \times 2) \times (5 \times 3 \times 3) \times (5 \times 5 \times 2)$

Number of 5s – 12, Number of 2s – 8.
Hence: 8 zeroes.

**Problem 1.12** Find the remainder for $[(73 \times 79 \times 81)/11]$.

**Solution** The remainder for the expression: $[(73 \times 79 \times 81)/11]$ will be the same as the remainder for $[(7 \times 2 \times 4)/11]$

That is, $56/11 \Rightarrow$ remainder $= 1$

**Problem 1.13** Find the remainder for $(3^{560}/8)$.

**Solution** $(3^{560}/8) = [(3^2)^{280}/8] = (9^{280}/8)$

$= [9.9.9...(280 \text{ times})]/8$

remainder for above expression = remainder for $[1.1.1...(280 \text{ times})]/8 \Rightarrow$ remainder $= 1$.

**Problem 1.14** Find the remainder when $(2222^{5555} + 5555^{2222})/7$.

**Solution** This is of the form: $[(2222^{5555})/7 + (5555^{2222})/7]$

We now proceed to find the individual remainder of : $(2222^{5555})/7$. Let the remainder be $R_1$.

When 2222 is divided by 7, it leaves a remainder of 3.

Hence, for remainder purpose $(2222^{5555})/7 \xrightarrow{R} (3^{5555}/7)$
$= (3.3^{5554})/7 = [3(3^2)^{2777}]/7 = [3.(7+2)^{2777}]/7 \xrightarrow{R} (3.2^{2777})/7$
$= (3.2^2 \cdot 2^{2775})/7 = [3.2^2 \cdot (2^3)^{925}]/7$
$= [3.2^2 \cdot (8)^{925}] /7 \xrightarrow{R} (12/7)$ Remainder $= 5$.

Similarly, $(5555^{2222})/7 \xrightarrow{R} (4^{2222})/7 = [(2^2)^{2222}]/7 = (2)^{4444}/7 = (2.2^{4443})/7 = [2.(2^3)^{1481}]/7 = [2.(8)^{1481}]/7 \xrightarrow{R} [2.(1)^{1481}]/7 \rightarrow 2$ (remainder).

Hence, $(2222^{5555})/7 + (5555^{2222})/7 \xrightarrow{R} (5+2)/7 \Rightarrow$ Remainder $= 0$.

**Problem 1.15**  Find the GCD and the LCM of the numbers 126, 540 and 630.

**Solution**  The standard forms of the numbers are:
$$126 \rightarrow 3 \times 3 \times 7 \times 2 \rightarrow 3^2 \times 7 \times 2$$
$$540 \rightarrow 3 \times 3 \times 3 \times 2 \times 2 \times 5 \rightarrow 2^2 \times 3^3 \times 5$$
$$630 \rightarrow 3 \times 3 \times 5 \times 2 \times 7 \rightarrow 2 \times 3^2 \times 5 \times 7$$

For GCD we use Intersection of prime factors and the lowest power of all factors that appear in all three numbers.
$2 \times 3^2 = 18$.

For LCM → Union of prime factors and highest power of all factors that appear in any one of the three numbers
$\Rightarrow 2^2 \times 3^3 \times 5 \times 7 = 3780$.

## Exercise for Self-practice

Find the GCD and the LCM of the following numbers:
  (i) 360, 8400
  (ii) 120, 144
  (iii) 275, 180, 372, 156
  (iv) 70, 112
  (v) 75, 114
  (vi) 544, 720

**Problem 1.16**  The ratio of the factorial of a number $x$ to the square of the factorial of another number, which when increased by 50% gives the required number, is 1.25. Find the number $x$.
  (a) 6
  (b) 5
  (c) 9
  (d) None of these

**Solution**  Solve through options: Check for the conditions mentioned. When we check for option (a) we get $6! = 720$ and $(4!)^2 = 576$ and we have $6!/(4!)^2 = 1.25$, which is the required ratio.

Hence the answer is **(a)**

**Problem 1.17**  Three numbers $A$, $B$ and $C$ are such that the difference between the highest and the second highest two-digit numbers formed by using two of $A$, $B$ and $C$ is 5. Also, the smallest two two-digit numbers differ by 2. If $B > A > C$ then what is the value of $B$?
  (a) 1
  (b) 6
  (c) 7
  (d) 8

**Solution**  Since $B$ is the largest digit, option (a) is rejected. Check for option (b).

If $B$ is 6, then the two largest two-digit numbers are 65 and 60 (Since, their difference is 5) and we have $B = 6$, $A = 5$ and $C = 0$.

But with this solution we are unable to meet the second condition. Hence (b) is not the answer. We also realise here that $C$ cannot be 0.

Check for option (c).

$B$ is 7, then the nos. are 76 and 71 or 75 and 70. In both these cases, the smallest two two-digit numbers do not differ by 2.

Hence, the answer is not (c).

Hence, option **(d)** is the answer

[To confirm, put $B = 8$, then the solution $A = 6$ and $C = 1$ satisfies the 2nd condition.]

**Problem 1.18**  Find the remainder when $2851 \times (2862)^2 \times (2873)^3$ is divided by 23.

**Solution**  We use the remainder theorem to solve the problem. Using the theorem, we see that the following expressions have the same remainder.

$$\Rightarrow \frac{2851 \times (2862)^2 \times (2873)^3}{23}$$

$$\Rightarrow \frac{22 \times 10 \times 10 \times 21 \times 21 \times 21}{23}$$

$$\Rightarrow \frac{22 \times 8 \times 441 \times 21}{23} \quad \Rightarrow \quad \frac{22 \times 21 \times 8 \times 4}{23}$$

$$\Rightarrow \frac{462 \times 32}{23} \quad \Rightarrow \quad \frac{2 \times 9}{23} \quad \Rightarrow \text{ Remainder is } \mathbf{18}.$$

**Problem 1.19**  For what maximum value of $n$ will the expression $\dfrac{10200!}{504^n}$ be an integer?

**Solution**  For $\dfrac{10200!}{504^n}$ to be a integer, we need to look at the prime factors of $504 \rightarrow$
$$504 = 3^2 \times 7 \times 8 = 2^3 \times 3^2 \times 7$$

We thus have to look for the number of 7s, the number of $2^3$s and the number of $3^2$s that are contained in 10200!. The lowest of these will be the constraint value for $n$.

To find the number of $2^3$s we need to find the number of 2s as

$$\left[\frac{10200}{2}\right] + \left[\frac{10200}{4}\right] + \left[\frac{10200}{8}\right] + \left[\frac{10200}{16}\right] + \left[\frac{10200}{32}\right]$$

$$+ \left[\frac{10200}{64}\right] + \left[\frac{10200}{128}\right] + \left[\frac{10200}{256}\right] + \left[\frac{10200}{512}\right] + \left[\frac{10200}{1024}\right]$$

$$+ \left[\frac{10200}{2048}\right] + \left[\frac{10200}{4096}\right] + \left[\frac{10200}{8192}\right]$$

where [ ] is the greatest integer function.

$= 5100 + 2550 + 1275 + 637 + 318 + 159 + 79 + 39 + 19 + 9 + 4 + 2 + 1$

Number of twos $= 10192$

Hence, number of $2^3 = 3397$

Similarly, we find the number of 3s as

$$\text{Number of threes} = \left[\frac{10200}{3}\right] + \left[\frac{10200}{9}\right] + \left[\frac{10200}{27}\right]$$

$$\left[\frac{10200}{81}\right] + \left[\frac{10200}{243}\right] + \left[\frac{10200}{729}\right] + \left[\frac{10200}{2187}\right]$$

$$+ \left[\frac{10200}{6561}\right]$$

$= 3400 + 1133 + 377 + 125 + 41 + 13 + 4 + 1$

Number of threes $= 5094$

∴ Number of $3^2 = 2547$

Similarly we find the number of 7s as

$$\left[\frac{10200}{7}\right] + \left[\frac{10200}{49}\right] + \left[\frac{10200}{343}\right] + \left[\frac{10200}{2401}\right]$$

$$= 1457 + 208 + 29 + 4 = 1698.$$

Thus, we have, 1698 sevens, 2547 nines and 3397 eights contained in 10200!.

The required value of $n$ will be given by the lowest of these three [The student is expected to explore why this happens]

Hence, answer $= \textbf{1698}$.

**Short Cut** We will look only for the number of 7s in this case. *Reason*: $7 > 3 \times 2$. So, the number of 7s must always be less than the number of $2^3$.

And $7 > 2 \times 3$, so the number of 7s must be less than the number of $3^2$.

Recollect that earlier we had talked about the finding of powers when the divisor only had prime factors. There we had seen that we needed to check only for the highest prime as the restriction had to lie there.

In cases of the divisors having composite factors, we have to be slightly careful in estimating the factor that will reflect the restriction. In the above example, we saw a case where even though 7 was the lowest factor (in relation to 8 and 9), the restriction was still placed by 7 rather than by 9 (as would be expected based on the previous process of taking the highest number).

**Problem 1.20** Find the units digit of the expression: $78^{5562} \times 56^{256} \times 97^{1250}$.

**Solution** We can get the units digits in the expression by looking at the patterns followed by 78, 56 and 97 when they are raised to high powers.

In fact, for the last digit we just need to consider the units digit of each part of the product.

A number (like 78) having 8 as the units digit will yield units digit as

| | | |
|---|---|---|
| $78^1 \to 8$ | $78^5 \to 8$ | |
| $78^2 \to 4$ | $78^6 \to 4$ | |
| $78^3 \to 2$ | $78^7 \to 2$ | |
| $78^4 \to 6$ | $78^8 \to 6$ | |

$$\boxed{\begin{array}{l} 8^{4n+1} \to 8 \\ 8^{4n+2} \to 4 \\ \text{Hence } 78^{5562} \text{ will yield} \\ \text{four as the units digit} \end{array}}$$

Similarly, 
$56^1 \to 6$     $\to 56^{256}$ will yield 6 as
$56^2 \to 6$     the units digit.
$56^3 \to 6$

Similarly,

$97^1 \to 7$     $\boxed{\begin{array}{l} 7^{4n+1} \to 7 \\ 7^{4n+2} \to 9 \\ \text{Hence, } 97^{1250} \text{ will yield a units digit of 9.} \end{array}}$
$97^2 \to 9$
$97^3 \to 3$
$97^4 \to 1$

Hence, the required units digit is given by $4 \times 6 \times 9 \to$ **6** (answer).

**Problem 1.21** Find the GCD and the LCM of the numbers $P$ and $Q$ where $P = 2^3 \times 5^3 \times 7^2$ and $Q = 3^3 \times 5^4$.

**Solution** GCD or HCF is given by the lowest powers of the common factors.

Thus, GCD $= 5^3$.

LCM is given by the highest powers of all factors available.

Thus, LCM $= 2^3 \times 3^3 \times 5^4 \times 7^2$

**Problem 1.22** A school has 378 girl students and 675 boy students. The school is divided into strictly boys or strictly girls sections. All sections in the school have the same number of students. Given this information, what are the minimum number of sections in the school.

**Solution** The answer will be given by the HCF of 378 and 675.

$$378 = 2 \times 3^3 \times 7$$
$$675 = 3^3 \times 5^2$$

Hence, HCF of the two is $3^3 = 27$.

Hence, the number of sections is given by: $\frac{378}{27} + \frac{675}{27} = 14 + 25 = \textbf{39 sections}$.

**Problem 1.23** The difference between the number of numbers from 2 to 100 which are not divisible by any other number except 1 and itself and the numbers which are divisible by at least one more number along with 1 and itself.

   (a) 25               (b) 50

   (c) 49               (d) can't be determine

**Solution** From 2 to 100.

The number of numbers which are divisible by 1 and itself only $= 25$

Also, the number of numbers which are divisible by at least one more number except 1 and itself (i.e., composite numbers) $99 - 25 = 74$

So, required difference = 74 – 25 = 49
⇒ **Option (c)**

**Problem 1.24** If the sum of $(2n +1)$ prime numbers where $n \in N$ is an even number, then one of the prime numbers must be

(a) 2           (b) 3

(c) 5           (d) 7

**Solution** For any $n \in N$, $2n + 1$ is odd.

Also, it is given in the problem that the sum of an odd number of prime numbers = even. Since all prime numbers except 2 are odd, the above condition will only be fulfilled if we have an (odd + odd + even) structure of addition. Since, the sum of the three prime numbers is said to be even, we have to include one even prime number. Hence 2 being the only even prime number must be included.

If we add odd number of prime numbers, not including 2 (two), we will always get an odd number, because

$$\frac{\text{odd} + \text{odd} + \text{odd} + \text{-----} + \text{odd}}{\text{(an odd number of times)}} = \text{odd number}$$

⇒ **Option (a)**

**Problem 1.25** What will be the difference between the largest and smallest four digit number made by using distinct single digit prime numbers?

(a) 1800          (b) 4499

(c) 4495          (d) 5175

**Solution** Required largest number → 7532
Required smallest number → 2357
     Difference → 5175
⇒ **Option (d)**

**Problem 1.26** The difference between the two three-digit numbers $XYZ$ and $ZYX$ will be equal to

(a) difference between $X$ and $Z$ i.e. $|x - z|$

(b) sum of $X$ and z i.e $(X + Z)$

(c) $9 \times$ difference between $X$ and $Z$

(d) $99 \times$ difference between $X$ and $Z$

**Solution** From the property of numbers, it is known that on reversing a three digit number, the difference (of both the numbers) will be divisible by 99. Also, it is known that this difference will be equal to 99 × difference between the units and hundreds digits of the three digit number.
⇒ Option (d)

**Problem 1.27** When the difference between the number 842 and its reverse is divided by 99, the remainder will be

(a) 0           (b) 1

(c) 74          (d) 17

**Solution** From the property (used in the above question) we can say that the difference will be divisible by 99

⇒ Remainder = 0 (zero)
⇒ Option (a)

**Problem 1.28** When the difference between the number 783 and its reverse is divided by 99, the quotient will be

(a) 1           (b) 10

(c) 3           (d) 4

**Solution** The quotient will be the difference between extreme digits of 783, i.e. 7 – 3 = 4 (This again is a property which you should know.)
⇒ Option (d)

**Problem 1.29** A long Part of wood of same length when cut into equal pieces each of 242 cms, leaves a small piece of length 98 cms. If this Part were cut into equal pieces each of 22 cms, the length of the leftover wood would be

(a) 76 cm         (b) 12 cm

(c) 11 cm         (d) 10 cm

**Solution** As 242 is divisible by 22, so the required length of left wood will be equal to the remainder when 98 is divided by 22:
Hence, 10 [98/22; remainder 10]
⇒ Option (d)

**Problem 1.30** Find the number of numbers from 1 to 100 which are not divisible by 2.

(a) 51           (b) 50

(c) 49           (d) 48

**Solution** The 1st number from 1 to 100, not divisible by 2 is 1 and the last number from 1 to 100, not divisible by 2 is 99.

Every alternate number (i.e, at the gap of 2) will not be divisible by 2 from 1 to 99. (1, 2, 3, - - - - , 95, 97, 99)

So, the required number of nos $= \dfrac{\text{last no.} - \text{first no.}}{\text{gap (or step)}} + 1$

$$= \frac{99 - 1}{2} + 1 = 50$$

⇒ Option (b)

**Alternate method**

Total number of nos from 1 to 100 = 100       (i)

Now, if we count number of numbers from 1 to 100 which are divisible by 2 and subtract that from the total number of numbers from 1 to 100, as a result we will find the number of numbers from 1 to 100 which are not divisible by 2.

To count the number of nos from 1 to 100 which are divisible by 2:

The 1st number which is divisible by 2 = 2

The last number which is divisible by 2 = 100

            (2, 4, 6, - - - - , 96, 98, 100)

Gap/step between two consecutive numbers = 2

So, the number of numbers which are divisible by 2 =

$$\frac{\text{last no.} - \text{first no.}}{\text{gap (or step)}} + 1 = \frac{100 - 2}{2} + 1 = 50 \qquad \text{(ii)}$$

So, from (i) & (ii)

Required number of numbers = 100 − 50 = 50

⇒ Option (b)

**Problem 1.31** Find the number of numbers from 1 to 100 which are not divisible by any one of 2 & 3.

    (a) 16         (b) 17

    (c) 18         (d) 33

**Solution** From 1 to 100

Number of numbers not divisible by 2 & 3 = Total number of numbers–number of numbers divisible by either 2 or 3.

Now, total number of numbers = 100     (ii)

For number of numbers divisible by either 2 or 3:

Number of numbers divisible by 2 = $\dfrac{\text{last no.} - \text{first no.}}{\text{gap (or step)}} + 1$

$$= \frac{100 - 2}{2} + 1 = 50$$

Now, the number of numbers divisible by 3 (but not by 2, as it has already been counted)

1st such no. = 3 and the gap will be 6. Hence 2nd such no. will be 9, 3rd no. would be 15 and the last number would be 99. Hence this series is 3, 9, 15, ..., 93, 99

So, the number of numbers divisible by 3 (but not by 2) =

$$\frac{\text{last such no.} - \text{first such no.}}{\text{gap/step}} + 1 = \frac{99 - 3}{6} + 1 = 17$$

Hence, the number of numbers divisible by either 2 or 3 = 50 + 17 = 67

So, from (i), (ii) & (iii) required number of numbers = 100 − 67 = 33

⇒ Option (d)

**Problem 1.32** Find the number of numbers from 1 to 100 which are not divisible by any one of 2, 3, and 5.

    (a) 26         (b) 27

    (c) 29         (d) 32

**Solution** From the above question, we have found out that From 1 to 100, number of numbers divisible by 2 = 50

    (i)

Number of numbers divisible by 3 ( but not by 2) = 17

    (ii)

Now, we have to find out the number of numbers which are divisible by 5 (but not by 2 and 3). Numbers which are divisible by 5

(5) 10 15 20 (25) 30 (35) 40 45 50 (55) 60 (65) 70 75 80 (85) 90 (95) 100

That is, there are 7 such numbers     (iii)

Another way to find out the number of numbers that are divisible by 5 but not 2 and 3 is to first only consider odd multiples of 5.

You will get the series of 10 numbers: 5, 15, 25, 35, 45, 55, 65, 75, 85 and 95

From amongst these we need to exclude multiples of 3. In other words, we need to find the number of common elements between the above series and the series of odd multiples of 3, viz, 3, 9, 15, 21 …. 99.

This situation is the same as finding the number of common elements between the two series for which we need to first observe that the first such number is 15. Then the common terms between these two series will themselves form an arithmetic series and this series will have a common difference which is the LCM of the common differences of the two series. (In this case the common difference of the two series are 10 and 6 respectively and their LCM being 30, the series of common terms between the two series will be 15, 45 and 75.) Thus, there will be 3 terms out of the 10 terms of the series 5, 15, 25…95 which will be divisible by 3 and hence need to be excluded from the count of numbers which are divisible by 5 but not 2 or 3.

Hence, the required answer would be: 100 − 50 − 17 − 7 = 26

⇒ Option (a)

**Problem 1.33** Find the number of numbers from 1 to 100 which are not divisible by any one of 2, 3, 5 & 7.

    (a) 22         (b) 24

    (c) 23         (d) 27

**Solution** From the above question we have seen that from 1 to 100.

number of numbers divisible by 2 = 50     (i)

number of numbers divisible by 3 but not by 2 = 17     (ii)

number of numbers divisible by 5 but not by 2 and 3 = 7     (iii)

number of numbers divisible by 7 but not by 2, 3 & 5; such numbers are 7, 49, 77, 91 = 4 numbers     (iv)

Required number of numbers = Total number of numbers from 1 to 100 − {(i) + (ii) + (iii) + (iv)}

$$= 100 - (50 + 17 + 7 + 4)$$

$$= 22$$

⇒ Option (a)

**Problem 1.34** What will be the remainder when − 34 is divided by 5?

    (a) 1         (b) 4

    (c) 2         (d) − 4

**Solution** $-34 = 5 \times (-6) + (-4)$

Remainder = −4, but it is wrong because remainder cannot be negative.

So,         $-34 = 5 \times (-7) + 1$

⇒ Option (a)

Alternately, when you see a remainder of −4 when the number is divided by 5, the required remainder will be equal to 5 − 4 = 1.

**Problem 1.35**  What will be the remainder when −24.8 is divided by 6?

    (a) 0.8          (b) 5.2
    (c) −0.8        (d) −5.2

**Solution**  −24.8 = 6 × (−4) + (−0.8)

Negative remainder, so not correct −24.8 = 6 × (−5) + 5.2

Positive value of remainder, so correct

⇒ Option (b)

**Problem 1.36**  If $p$ is divided by $q$, then the maximum possible difference between the minimum possible and maximum possible remainder can be?

    (a) $p − q$      (b) $p − 1$
    (c) $q − 1$      (d) None of these

**Solution**  $\frac{p}{q}$ minimum possible remainder = 0 (when $q$ exactly divides $P$)

Maximum possible remainder = $q − 1$

So, required maximum possible difference = $(q − 1) − 0$ = $(q − 1)$

⇒ Option (c)

**Problem 1.37**  Find the remainder when $2^{256}$ is divided by 17.

    (a) 0          (b) 1
    (c) 3          (d) 5

**Solution**  $\frac{2^{256}}{17} = \frac{(2^4)^{64}}{17} = \frac{16^{64}}{17} \Rightarrow R = 1$

∵ $\frac{a^n}{a+1}$ ; $R = 1$

when $n \to$ even

⇒ Option (b)

***Space for Rough Work***

**Problem 1.38**  Find the difference between the remainders when $7^{84}$ is divided by 342 & 344.

    (a) 0          (b) 1
    (c) 3          (d) 5

**Solution**  $\frac{7^{84}}{342} = \frac{(7^3)^{28}}{342} = \frac{343^{28}}{342} \Rightarrow R = 1$

also, $\frac{7^{84}}{344} = \frac{(7^3)^{28}}{344} = \frac{343^{28}}{344} \Rightarrow R = 1$

The required difference between the remainders = 1 − 1 = 0

⇒ Option (a)

**Problem 1.39**  What will be the value of $x$ for $\frac{(100^{17} − 1) + (10^{34} + x)}{9}$ ; the remainder = 0

    (a) 3          (b) 6
    (c) 9          (d) 8

**Solution**  $\frac{(100^{17} − 1) + (10^{34} + x)}{9}$

$100^{17} − 1 = \frac{1000...00 − 1}{17\ zeroes} = \frac{9999...99}{16\ nines} \Rightarrow$ divisible by 9 $\Rightarrow R = 0$

Since the first part of the expression is giving a remainder of 0, the second part should also give 0 as a remainder if the entire remainder of the expression has to be 0. Hence, we now evaluate the second part of the numerator.

$10^{34} + x = \frac{1000...00 + x}{34\ zeroes} = \frac{1000...00x}{33\ zeroes}$

with $x$ at the right most place. In order for this number to be divisible by 9, the sum of digits should be divisible by 9.

⇒ $1 + 0 + 0 \cdots + 0 + x$ should be divisible by 9.

⇒ $1 + x$ should be divisible by 9 ⇒ $x = 8$

⇒ Option (d)

# LEVEL OF DIFFICULTY (I)

1. The last digit of the number obtained by multiplying the numbers $81 \times 82 \times 83 \times 84 \times 85 \times 86 \times 87 \times 88 \times 89$ will be
   (a) 0
   (b) 9
   (c) 7
   (d) 2

2. The sum of the digits of a two-digit number is 10, while when the digits are reversed, the number decreases by 54. Find the changed number.
   (a) 28
   (b) 19
   (c) 37
   (d) 46

3. When we multiply a certain two-digit number by the sum of its digits, 405 is achieved. If you multiply the number written in reverse order of the same digits by the sum of the digits, we get 486. Find the number.
   (a) 81
   (b) 45
   (c) 36
   (d) 54

4. The sum of two numbers is 15 and their geometric mean is 20% lower than their arithmetic mean. Find the numbers.
   (a) 11, 4
   (b) 12, 3
   (c) 13, 2
   (d) 10, 5

5. The difference between two numbers is 48 and the difference between the arithmetic mean and the geometric mean is two more than half of 1/3 of 96. Find the numbers.
   (a) 49, 1
   (b) 12, 60
   (c) 50, 2
   (d) 36, 84

6. If $A381$ is divisible by 11, find the value of the smallest natural number $A$.
   (a) 5
   (b) 6
   (c) 7
   (d) 9

7. If $381A$ is divisible by 9, find the value of smallest natural number $A$.
   (a) 5
   (b) 5
   (c) 7
   (d) 6

8. What will be the remainder obtained when $(9^6 + 1)$ will be divided by 8?
   (a) 0
   (b) 3
   (c) 7
   (d) 2

9. Find the ratio between the LCM and HCF of 5, 15 and 20.
   (a) 8 : 1
   (b) 14 : 3
   (c) 12 : 2
   (d) 12 : 1

10. Find the LCM of 5/2, 8/9, 11/14.
    (a) 280
    (b) 360
    (c) 420
    (d) None of these

11. If the number A is even, which of the following will be true?
    (a) 3A will always be divisible by 6
    (b) 3A + 5 will always be divisible by 11
    (c) $(A^2 + 3)/4$ will be divisible by 7
    (d) All of these

12. A five-digit number is taken. Sum of the first four digits (excluding the number at the units digit) equals sum of all the five digits. Which of the following will not divide this number necessarily?
    (a) 10
    (b) 2
    (c) 4
    (d) 5

13. A number $15B$ is divisible by 6. Which of these will be true about the positive integer $B$?
    (a) $B$ will be even
    (b) $B$ will be odd
    (c) $B$ will be divisble by 6
    (d) Both (a) and (c)

14. Two numbers $P = 2^3.3^{10}.5$ and $Q = 2^5.3^1.7^1$ are given. Find the GCD of $P$ and $Q$.
    (a) $2.3.5.7$
    (b) $3.2^2$
    (c) $2^2.3^2$
    (d) $2^3.3$

15. Find the units digit of the expression $25^{6251} + 36^{528} + 73^{54}$.
    (a) 4
    (b) 0
    (c) 6
    (d) 5

16. Find the units digit of the expression $55^{725} + 73^{5810} + 22^{853}$.
    (a) 4
    (b) 0
    (c) 6
    (d) 5

17. Find the units digit of the expression $11^1 + 12^2 + 13^3 + 14^4 + 15^5 + 16^6$.
    (a) 1
    (b) 9
    (c) 7
    (d) 0

18. Find the units digit of the expression $11^1.12^2.13^3.14^4.15^5.16^6$.
    (a) 4
    (b) 3
    (c) 7
    (d) 0

19. Find the number of zeroes at the end of 1090!
    (a) 270
    (b) 268
    (c) 269
    (d) 271

20. If 146! is divisible by $5^n$, then find the maximum value of $n$.
    (a) 34
    (b) 35
    (c) 36
    (d) 37

21. Find the number of divisors of 1420.
    (a) 14
    (b) 15
    (c) 13
    (d) 12

22. Find the HCF and LCM of the polynomials $(x^2 - 5x + 6)$ and $(x^2 - 7x + 10)$.
    (a) $(x - 2), (x - 2)(x - 3)(x - 5)$
    (b) $(x - 2), (x - 2)(x - 3)$
    (c) $(x - 3), (x - 2)(x - 3)(x - 5)$
    (d) $(x - 2), (x - 2)(x - 3)(x - 5)^2$

**Directions for Questions 23 to 25:** Given two different prime numbers $P$ and $Q$, find the number of divisors of the following:

23. $P.Q$
    (a) 2        (b) 4
    (c) 6        (d) 8

24. $P^2Q$
    (a) 2        (b) 4
    (c) 6        (d) 8

25. $P^3Q^2$
    (a) 2        (b) 4
    (c) 6        (d) 12

26. The sides of a pentagonal field (not regular) are 1737 metres, 2160 metres, 2358 metres, 1422 metres and 2214 metres respectively. Find the greatest length of the tape by which the five sides may be measured completely.
    (a) 7        (b) 13
    (c) 11       (d) 9

27. There are 576 boys and 448 girls in a school that are to be divided into equal sections of either boys or girls alone. Find the minimum total number of sections thus formed.
    (a) 24       (b) 32
    (c) 16       (d) 20

28. A milkman has three different qualities of milk. 403 gallons of 1st quality, 465 gallons of 2nd quality and 496 gallons of 3rd quality. Find the least possible number of bottles of equal size in which different milk of different qualities can be filled without mixing.
    (a) 34       (b) 46
    (c) 26       (d) 44

29. What is the greatest number of 4 digits that when divided by any of the numbers 6, 9, 12, 17 leaves a remainder of 1?
    (a) 9997     (b) 9793
    (c) 9895     (d) 9487

30. Find the least number that when divided by 16, 18 and 20 leaves a remainder 4 in each case, but is completely divisible by 7.
    (a) 364      (b) 2254
    (c) 2964     (d) 2884

31. Four bells ring at the intervals of 6, 8, 12 and 18 seconds. They start ringing together at 12'O' clock. After how many seconds will they ring together again?
    (a) 72       (b) 84
    (c) 60       (d) 48

32. For Question 31, find how many times will they ring together during the next 12 minutes. (including the 12 minute mark)
    (a) 9        (b) 10
    (c) 11       (d) 12

33. The units digit of the expression $125^{813} \times 553^{3703} \times 4532^{828}$ is
    (a) 4        (b) 2
    (c) 0        (d) 5

34. Which of the following is not a perfect square?
    (a) 1,00,856     (b) 3,25,137
    (c) 9,45,729     (d) All of these

35. Which of the following can never be in the ending of a perfect square?
    (a) 6        (b) 00
    (c) $x$ 000 where $x$ is a natural number
    (d) 1

36. The LCM of 5, 8,12, 20 will not be a multiple of
    (a) 3        (b) 9
    (c) 8        (d) 5

37. Find the number of divisors of 720 (including 1 and 720).
    (a) 25       (b) 28
    (c) 29       (d) 30

38. The LCM of $(16 - x^2)$ and $(x^2 + x - 6)$ is
    (a) $(x - 3)(x + 3)(4 - x^2)$
    (b) $4(4 - x^2)(x + 3)$
    (c) $(4 - x^2)(x - 3)$
    (d) None of these

39. GCD of $x^2 - 4$ and $x^2 + x - 6$ is
    (a) $x + 2$      (b) $x - 2$
    (c) $x^2 - 2$    (d) $x^2 + 2$

40. The number $A$ is not divisible by 3. Which of the following will not be divisible by 3?
    (a) $9 \times A$     (b) $2 \times A$
    (c) $18 \times A$    (d) $24 \times A$

41. Find the remainder when the number $9^{100}$ is divided by 8.
    (a) 1        (b) 2
    (c) 0        (d) 4

42. Find the remainder of $2^{1000}$ when divided by 3.
    (a) 1        (b) 2
    (c) 4        (d) 6

43. Decompose the number 20 into two terms such that their product is the greatest.
    (a) $x_1 = x_2 = 10$       (b) $x_1 = 5, x_2 = 15$
    (c) $x_1 = 16, x_2 = 4$    (d) $x_1 = 8, x_2 = 12$

44. Find the number of zeroes at the end of 50!
    (a) 13       (b) 11
    (c) 5        (d) 12

45. Which of the following can be a number divisible by 24?
    (a) 4,32,15,604          (b) 25,61,284
    (c) 13,62,480            (d) All of these

46. For a number to be divisible by 88, it should be
    (a) Divisible by 22 and 8
    (b) Divisible by 11 and 8
    (c) Divisible by 11 and thrice by 2
    (d) All of these

47. Find the number of divisors of 10800.
    (a) 57          (b) 60
    (c) 72          (d) 64

48. Find the GCD of the polynomials $(x + 3)^2(x - 2)(x + 1)^2$ and $(x + 1)^3(x + 3)(x + 4)$.
    (a) $(x + 3)^3 (x + 1)^2 (x - 2) (x + 4)$
    (b) $(x + 3)(x - 2)(x + 1)(x + 4)$
    (c) $(x + 3)(x + 1)^2$
    (d) $(x + 1)(x + 3)^2$

49. Find the LCM of $(x + 3)(6x^2 + 5x + 4)$ and $(2x^2 + 7x + 3)(x + 3)$
    (a) $(2x + 1)(x + 3)(3x + 4)$
    (b) $(4x^2 - 1)(x + 3)^2(3x + 4)$
    (c) $2(x + 3)^2(6x^2 + 5x + 4)(x + 1/2)$
    (d) $(2x - 1)(x + 3)(3x + 4)$

50. The product of three consecutive natural numbers, the first of which is an even number, is always divisible by
    (a) 12          (b) 24
    (c) 6           (d) All of these

51. Some birds settled on the branches of a tree. First, they sat one to a branch and there was one bird too many. Next they sat two to a branch and there was one branch too many. How many branches were there?
    (a) 3           (b) 4
    (c) 5           (d) 6

52. The square of a number greater than 1000 that is not divisible by three, when divided by three, leaves a remainder of
    (a) 1 always    (b) 2 always
    (c) 0           (d) either 1 or 2

53. The value of the expression $(15^3 \cdot 21^2)/(35^2 \cdot 3^4)$ is
    (a) 3           (b) 15
    (c) 21          (d) 12

54. If $A = \left(\dfrac{-3}{4}\right)^3$, $B = \left(\dfrac{-2}{5}\right)^2$, $C = (0.3)^2$, $D = (-1.2)^2$
    then
    (a) $A > B > C > D$          (b) $D > A > B > C$
    (c) $D > B > C > A$          (d) $D > C > A > B$

55. If $2 < x < 4$ and $1 < y < 3$, then find the ratio of the upper limit for $x + y$ and the lower limit of $x - y$.

    (a) 6           (b) 7
    (c) 8           (d) None of these

56. The sum of the squares of the digits constituting a positive two-digit number is 13. If we subtract 9 from that number, we shall get a number written by the same digits in the reverse order. Find the number.
    (a) 12          (b) 32
    (c) 42          (d) 52

57. The product of a natural number by the number written by the same digits in the reverse order is 2430. Find the numbers.
    (a) 54 and 45   (b) 56 and 65
    (c) 53 and 35   (d) 85 and 58

58. Find two natural numbers whose difference is 66 and the least common multiple is 360.
    (a) 120 and 54  (b) 90 and 24
    (c) 180 and 114 (d) 130 and 64

59. Find the pairs of natural numbers whose least common multiple is 78 and the greatest common divisor is 13.
    (a) 58 and 13 or 16 and 29
    (b) 68 and 23 or 36 and 49
    (c) 18 and 73 or 56 and 93
    (d) 78 and 13 or 26 and 39

60. Find two natural numbers whose sum is 85 and the least common multiple is 102.
    (a) 30 and 55   (b) 17 and 68
    (c) 35 and 55   (d) 51 and 34

61. Find the pairs of natural numbers the difference of whose squares is 55.
    (a) 28 and 27 or 8 and 3
    (b) 18 and 17 or 18 and 13
    (c) 8 and 27 or 8 and 33
    (d) 9 and 18 or 8 and 27

62. Which of these is greater?
    (a) $54^4$ or $21^{12}$          (b) $(0.4)^4$ or $(0.8)^3$

63. Is it possible for a common fraction whose numerator is less than the denominator to be equal to a fraction whose numerator is greater than the denominator?
    (a) Yes          (b) No

64. What digits should be put in place of $c$ in $38c$ to make it divisible by
    (1) 2           (2) 3
    (3) 4           (4) 5
    (5) 6           (6) 9
    (7) 10

65. Find the LCM and HCF of the following numbers: (54, 81, 135 and 189), (156, 195) and (1950, 5670 and 3900)

66. The last digit in the expansions of the three digit number $(34x)^{43}$ and $(34x)^{44}$ are 7 and 1, respectively. What can be said about the value of $x$?

(a) $x = 5$　　　　(b) $x = 3$

(c) $x = 6$　　　　(d) $x = 2$

**Directions for Questions 67 and 68:** Amitesh buys a pen, a pencil and an eraser for ₹ 41. If the least cost of any of the three items is ₹ 12 and it is known that a pen costs less than a pencil and an eraser costs more than a pencil, answer the following questions:

67. What is the cost of the pen?

(a) 12　　　　(b) 13

(c) 14　　　　(d) 15

68. If it is known that the eraser's cost is not divisible by 4, the cost of the pencil could be:

(a) 12　　　　(b) 13

(c) 14　　　　(d) 15

69. A naughty boy Amrit watches an innings of Sachin Tendulkar and acts according to the number of runs he sees Sachin scoring. The details of these are given below.

1 run　　Place an orange in the basket

2 runs　Place a mango in the basket

3 runs　Place a pear in the basket

4 runs　Remove a pear and a mango from the basket

One fine day, at the start of the match, the basket is empty. The sequence of runs scored by Sachin in that innings are given as 1123241123423232341121314. At the end of the above innings, how many more oranges were there compared to mangoes inside the basket? (The Basket was empty initially).

(a) 4　　　　(b) 5

(c) 6　　　　(d) 7

70. In the famous Bel Air Apartments in Ranchi, there are three watchmen meant to protect the precious fruits in the campus. However, one day a thief got in without being noticed and stole some precious mangoes. On the way out however, he was confronted by the three watchmen, the first two of whom asked him to part with 1/3rd of the fruits and one more. The last asked him to part with 1/5th of the mangoes and 4 more. As a result he had no mangoes left. What was the number of mangoes he had stolen?

(a) 12　　　　(b) 13

(c) 15　　　　(d) None of these

71. A hundred and twenty digit number is formed by writing the first x natural numbers in front of each other as 12345678910111213... Find the remainder when this number is divided by 8.

(a) 6　　　　(b) 7

(c) 2　　　　(d) 0

72. A test has 80 questions. There is one mark for a correct answer, while there is a negative penalty of $-1/2$ for a wrong answer and $-1/4$ for an unattempted question. What is the number of questions answered correctly, if the student has scored a net total of 34.5 marks?

(a) 45　　　　(b) 48

(c) 54　　　　(d) Cannot be determined

73. For Question 72, if it is known that he has left 10 questions unanswered, the number of correct answers are:

(a) 45　　　　(b) 48

(c) 54　　　　(d) Cannot be determined

74. Three mangoes, four guavas and five watermelons cost ₹750. Ten watermelons, six mangoes and 9 guavas cost ₹1580. What is the cost of six mangoes, ten watermelons and 4 guavas?

(a) 1280　　　　(b) 1180

(c) 1080　　　　(d) Cannot be determined

75. From a number $M$ subtract 1. Take the reciprocal of the result to get the value of '$N$'. Then which of the following is necessarily true?

(a) $0 \le M^N \le 2$　　　　(b) $M^N > 3$

(c) $1 < M^N < 3$　　　　(d) $1 < M^N < 5$

76. The cost of four mangoes, six guavas and sixteen watermelons is ₹ 500, while the cost of seven mangoes, nine guavas and nineteen watermelons is ₹ 620. What is the cost of one mango, one guava and one watermelon?

(a) 120　　　　(b) 40

(c) 150　　　　(d) Cannot be determined

77. For the question above, what is the cost of a mango?

(a) 20　　　　(b) 14

(c) 15　　　　(d) Cannot be determined

78. The following is known about three real numbers, $x$, $y$ and $z$.

$-4 \le x \le 4$, $-8 \le y \le 2$ and $-8 \le z \le 2$. Then the range of values that $M = xz/y$ can take is best represented by:

(a) $-\infty < x < \infty$　　　　(b) $-16 \le x \le 8$

(c) $-8 \le x \le 8$　　　　(d) $-16 \le x \le 16$

79. A man sold 38 pieces of clothing (combined in the form of shirts, trousers and ties). If he sold at least 11 pieces of each item and he sold more shirts than trousers and more trousers than ties, then the number of ties that he must have sold is:

(a) Exactly 11　　　　(b) At least 11

(c) At least 12　　　　(d) Cannot be determined

80. For Question 79, find the number of shirts he must have sold.

(a) At least 13　　　　(b) At least 14

(c) At least 15　　　　(d) At most 16.

81. Find the least number which when divided by 12, 15, 18 or 20 leaves in each case a remainder 4.

(a) 124　　　　(b) 364

(c) 184　　　　(d) None of these

82. What is the least number by which 2800 should be multiplied so that the product may be a perfect square?
    (a) 2              (b) 7
    (c) 14             (d) None of these

83. The least number of 4 digits which is a perfect square is:
    (a) 1064           (b) 1040
    (c) 1024           (d) 1012

84. The least multiple of 7 which leaves a remainder of 4 when divided by 6, 9, 15 and 18 is
    (a) 94             (b) 184
    (c) 364            (d) 74

85. What is the least 3 digit number that when divided by 2, 3, 4, 5 or 6 leaves a remainder of 1?
    (a) 131            (b) 161
    (c) 121            (d) None of these

86. The highest common factor of 70 and 245 is equal to
    (a) 35             (b) 45
    (c) 55             (d) 65

87. Find the least number, which must be subtracted from 7147 to make it a perfect square.
    (a) 86             (b) 89
    (c) 91             (d) 93

88. Find the least square number which is divisible by 6, 8 and 15
    (a) 2500           (b) 3600
    (c) 4900           (d) 4500

89. Find the least number by which 30492 must be multiplied or divided so as to make it a perfect square.
    (a) 11             (b) 7
    (c) 3              (d) 2

90. The greatest 4-digit number exactly divisible by 88 is
    (a) 8888           (b) 9768
    (c) 9944           (d) 9988

91. By how much is three fourth of 116 greater than four fifth of 45?
    (a) 31             (b) 41
    (c) 46             (d) None of these

92. If 5625 plants are to be arranged in such a way that there are as many rows as there are plants in a row, the number of rows will be:
    (a) 95             (b) 85
    (c) 65             (d) None of these

93. A boy took a seven digit number ending in 9 and raised it to an even power greater than 2000. He then took the number 17 and raised it to a power which leaves the remainder 1 when divided by 4. If he now multiples both the numbers, what will be the unit's digit of the number he so obtains?

(a) 7              (b) 9
(c) 3              (d) Cannot be determined

94. Two friends were discussing their marks in an examination. While doing so they realized that both the numbers had the same prime factors, although Raveesh got a score which had two more factors than Harish. If their marks are represented by one of the options as given below, which of the following options would correctly represent the number of marks they got?
    (a) 30,60          (b) 20,80
    (c) 40,80          (d) 20,60

95. A number is such that when divided by 3, 5, 6, or 7 it leaves the remainder 1, 3, 4, or 5 respectively. Which is the largest number below 4000 that satisfies this property?
    (a) 3358           (b) 3988
    (c) 3778           (d) 2938

96. A number when divided by 2,3 and 4 leaves a remainder of 1. Find the least number (after 1) that satisfies this requirement.
    (a) 25             (b) 13
    (c) 37             (d) 17

97. A number when divided by 2, 3 and 4 leaves a remainder of 1. Find the second lowest number (not counting 1) that satisfies this requirement.
    (a) 25             (b) 13
    (c) 37             (d) 17

98. A number when divided by 2, 3 and 4 leaves a remainder of 1. Find the highest 2 digit number that satisfies this requirement.
    (a) 91             (b) 93
    (c) 97             (d) 95

99. A number when divided by 2,3 and 4 leaves a remainder of 1. Find the highest 3 digit number that satisfies this requirement.
    (a) 991            (b) 993
    (c) 997            (d) 995

100. A frog is sitting on vertex A of a square ABCD. It starts jumping to the immediately adjacent vertex on either side in random fashion and stops when it reaches point C. In how many ways can it reach point C if it makes exactly 7 jumps?
    (a) 1              (b) 3
    (c) 5              (d) 0

101. Three bells ring at intervals of 5 seconds, 6 seconds and 7 seconds respectively. If they toll together for the first time at 9 AM in the morning, after what interval of time will they together ring again for the first time?
    (a) After 30 seconds    (b) After 42 seconds
    (c) After 35 seconds    (d) After 210 seconds

102. For the question above, how many times would they ring, together in the next 1 hour?

(a) 17　　　　　　　(b) 18
(c) 19　　　　　　　(d) None of these

103. A garrison has three kinds of soldiers. There are 66 soldiers of the first kind, 110 soldiers of the second kind and 242 soldiers of the third kind. It is desired to be arranging these soldiers in equal rows such that each row contains the same number of soldiers and there is only 1 kind of soldier in each row. What is the maximum number of soldiers who can be placed in each row?

(a) 11　　　　　　　(b) 1
(c) 22　　　　　　　(d) 33

104. For the question above, what are the minimum number of rows that would be required to be formed?

(a) 11　　　　　　　(b) 19
(c) 18　　　　　　　(d) None of these

105. A milkman produces three kinds of milk. On a particular day, he has 170 litres, 102 litres and 374 litres of the three kinds of milk. He wants to bottle them in bottles of equal sizes- so that each of the three varieties of milk would be completed bottled. How many bottle sizes are possible such that the bottle size in terms of litres is an integer?

(a) 1　　　　　　　(b) 2
(c) 4　　　　　　　(d) 34

106. For the above question, what is the size of the largest bottle which can be used?

(a) 1　　　　　　　(b) 2
(c) 17　　　　　　　(d) 34

107. For Question 105, what are the minimum number of bottles that would be required?

(a) 11　　　　　　　(b) 19
(c) 18　　　　　　　(d) None of these

108. Find the number of zeroes at the end of 100!

(a) 20　　　　　　　(b) 23
(c) 24　　　　　　　(d) 25

109. Find the number of zeroes at the end of 122!

(a) 20　　　　　　　(b) 23
(c) 24　　　　　　　(d) 28

110. Find the number of zeroes at the end of 1400!

(a) 347　　　　　　(b) 336
(c) 349　　　　　　(d) 348

111. Find the number of zeroes at the end of 380!

(a) 90　　　　　　　(b) 91
(c) 94　　　　　　　(d) 95

112. Find the number of zeroes at the end of 72!

(a) 14　　　　　　　(b) 15
(c) 16　　　　　　　(d) 17

113. The highest power of 3 that completely divides 40! is

(a) 18　　　　　　　(b) 15
(c) 16　　　　　　　(d) 17

114. $53!/3^n$ is an integer. Find the highest possible value of $n$ for this to be true.

(a) 19　　　　　　　(b) 21
(c) 23　　　　　　　(d) 24

115. The highest power of 7 that completely divides 80! is:

(a) 12　　　　　　　(b) 13
(c) 14　　　　　　　(d) 15

116. $115!/7^n$ is an integer. Find the highest possible value of $n$ for this to be true.

(a) 15　　　　　　　(b) 17
(c) 16　　　　　　　(d) 18

117. The highest power of 12 that completely divides 122! is:

(a) 54　　　　　　　(b) 56
(c) 57　　　　　　　(d) 58

118. $155!/20^n$ is an integer. Find the highest possible value of $n$ for this to be true.

(a) 77　　　　　　　(b) 38
(c) 75　　　　　　　(d) 37

119. The minimum value of $x$ so that $x^2/1024$ is an integer is

(a) 4　　　　　　　(b) 32
(c) 16　　　　　　　(d) 64

120. Find the sum of all 2 digit natural numbers which leave a remainder of 3 when divided by 7.

(a) 650　　　　　　(b) 663
(c) 676　　　　　　(d) 702

121. How many numbers between 1 and 200 are exactly divisible by exactly two of 3, 9 and 27?

(a) 14　　　　　　　(b) 15
(c) 16　　　　　　　(d) 17

122. A number $N$ is squared to give a value of $S$. The minimum value of $N + S$ would happen when $N$ is

(a) −0.3　　　　　　(b) −0.5
(c) −0.7　　　　　　(d) None of these

123. $L = x + y$ where $x$ and $y$ are prime numbers. Which of the following statement/s is/are true?

(i) The unit's digit of $L$ cannot be 5
(ii) The units digit of $L$ cannot be 0.
(iii) $L$ cannot be odd.

(a) All three　　　　(b) Only iii
(c) only ii　　　　　(d) None

124. $XYZ$ is a 3 digit number such that when we calculate the difference between the two three digit numbers $XYZ − YXZ$ the difference is exactly 90. How many possible values exist for the digits $X$ and $Y$?

(a) 9　　　　　　　(b) 8
(c) 7　　　　　　　(d) 6

125. What is the sum of all even numbers between 1 and 100 (both included)?

(a) 2450        (b) 2500

(c) 2600        (d) 2550

126. The least number which can be added to 763 so that it is completely divisible by 57 is

(a) 35        (b) 22

(c) 15        (d) 25

127. The least number which can be subtracted from 763 so that it is completely divisible by 57 is

(a) 35        (b) 22

(c) 15        (d) 25

128. The least number which can be added to 8441 so that it is completely divisible by 57 is

(a) 42        (b) 15

(c) 5        (d) 52

129. The least number which can be subtracted from 8441 so that it is completely divisible by 57 is

(a) 3        (b) 4

(c) 5        (d) 6

130. Find the least number of 5 digits that is exactly divisible by 79

(a) 10003        (b) 10033

(c) 10043        (d) None of these

131. Find the maximum number of 5 digits that is exactly divisible by 79.

(a) 99925        (b) 99935

(c) 99945        (d) 99955

132. The nearest integer to 773 which is exactly divisible by 12 is:

(a) 768        (b) 772

(c) 776        (d) None of these

133. A number when divided by 84 leaves a remainder of 57. What is the remainder when the same number is divided by 12?

(a) 7        (b) 8

(c) 9        (d) Cannot be determined

134. A number when divided by 84 leaves a remainder of 57. What is the remainder when the same number is divided by 11?

(a) 2        (b) 7

(c) 8        (d) Cannot be determined

135. 511 and 667 when divided by the same number, leave the same remainder. How many numbers can be used as the divisor in order to make this occur?

(a) 14        (b) 12

(c) 10        (d) 8

136. How many numbers between 200 and 400 are divisible by 13?

(a) 14        (b) 15

(c) 16        (d) 17

137. A boy was trying to find 5/8th of a number. Unfortunately, he found out 8/5th of the number and realized that the difference between the answer he got and the correct answer is 39. What was the number?

(a) 38        (b) 39

(c) 40        (d) 52

138. The sum of two numbers is equal to thrice their difference. If the smaller of the numbers is 10 find the other number.

(a) 15        (b) 20

(c) 40        (d) None of these

139. $4^{11} + 4^{12} + 4^{13} + 4^{14} + 4^{15}$ is divisible by which of the following?

(a) 11        (b) 31

(c) 341        (d) All of the above

140. The product of two numbers is 7168 and their HCF is 16. How many pairs of numbers are possible such that the above conditions are satisfied?

(a) 2        (b) 3

(c) 4        (d) 6

141. When 876 is added to another 3-digit number 2P3, we get a four digit number 10Q9 & 10Q9 is divisible by 11 then the value of P- Q is

142. There is a 22- digit number which consists of only one digit – from 1, 2, 3, 4, 5 or 6, e.g. 11111111…..11, 2222222….22, …..6666…..66. Such a number is always divisible by

143. The Product of the factors of 72 is

144. The number of ways of expressing 72 as a product of 2 factors is

145. In how many ways can 144 be expressed as a product of two distinct factors?

146. How many numbers lie between 100 and 1000 which when divided by 7 leaves remainder 3 and when divided by 11 leaves remainder 4?

147. HCF of $3^{15} - 1$ & $3^{25} - 1$ is

148. The HCF of two natural numbers $a$, $b$ is 10 & LCM of these numbers is 45. If $a = 15$ then $b = ?$

149. LCM and HCF of 10! and 15! are respectively

(a) 5! & 25!        (b) 5! & 30!

(c) 10! & 30!        (d) 15! & 10!

150. The remainder of $\dfrac{18^{116!}}{19}$ is

151. Given that $7x + y$ is a prime number for natural numbers $x$ & $y$, then what is the minimum value of $(x + y)$?

152. If n is an odd digit then unit's digit of the product $171n \times 1414 \times 729 \times 2015$ will be

153. If unit's digit of the product $171n \times 1413 \times 729 \times 2015$ is 0 then the maximum number of values that '$n$' may take?

154. The first two, 2 digit numbers that divide $(21^{12346} - 1)$ are?

155. What is the unit's digit of 1! + 2! + 3! + 4!+ 5! + 6! + 7! + …..+ 1000!.

156. Find the unit's digit of $(35!)^{35!}$

157. How many zeroes are there at the end of $(34!)^{6!}$

158. The unit's digit of $7^{51!^{31!}}$ is

159. If $N^2 = 1234567654321$, then $N = ?$

160. The LCM of two numbers is 421. What is the HCF of these two numbers?

161. Which of the following is greatest
$$3^{50}, 4^{40}, 5^{30}, 6^{20}$$

162. What is the value of $M*N$ if $M39048458N$ is divisible by 8 and 11, where $M$ and $N$ are single digit integers?

163. How many times does the digit 4 appear when we count from 21 to 500?

164. Find the remainder when the sum of 15 consecutive natural numbers starting from 3671 is divided by 3670.

165. $X$ is a number formed by writing 9 for 99 times. What will be the remainder of this number when divided by 7?

166. Find the remainder of $\dfrac{2^{41}}{41}$.

167. Find the remainder when 40! is divided by 41.

168. Find the remainder when $x^4 + 3x^3 + 4$ is divided by $x + 3$.

169. If $X$ is a prime number then for how many values of $X$, $X^2 + 7$ is also a prime number.

170. If $X = 99^3 - 63^3 - 36^3$ then the number of factors of $X$ is

171. If $x$ is a natural number & $4 < x < 50$, then the largest $n$, such that $n!$ would always divide: $x(x^2 - 1)(x^2 - 4)(x^2 - 9)(x + 4)$ is?

172. If $X$ is a natural number and $X!$ ends with $Y$ zeros then number of zeros at the end of $(5X)$ is

173. There are 90 questions in a test. Each correct answer fetches 1 mark, each wrong answer & unanswered question attract a penalty of ¼ marks & 1/8 marks respectively. Bilbo scored 23 marks in the test. What is the minimum possible number of the questions wrongly answered by him?

174. If $A = n^{2n^n}$, $B = n^{n^{2n}}$, $C = (n^{2n})^n$, $D = (n^n)^{n^2}$ when $n$ is a natural number & $n \neq 1$.
Then arrange them in terms of their values.

175. How many numbers in the form of $2^n - 1$, which are less than 5000 are prime?

*Space for Rough Work*

## LEVEL OF DIFFICULTY (II)

1. The arithmetic mean of two numbers is smaller by 24 than the larger of the two numbers and the GM of the same numbers exceeds by 12 the smaller of the numbers. Find the numbers.
   (a) 6 and 54
   (b) 8 and 56
   (c) 12 and 60
   (d) 7 and 55

2. Find the number of numbers between 200 and 300, both included, which are not divisible by 2, 3, 4 and 5.
   (a) 27
   (b) 26
   (c) 25
   (d) 28

3. Given $x$ and $n$ are integers, $(15n^3 + 6n^2 + 5n + x)/n$ is not an integer for what condition?
   (a) $n$ is positive
   (b) $x$ is divisible by $n$
   (c) $x$ is not divisible by $n$
   (d) (a) and (c)

4. The unit digit in the expression $36^{234}*33^{512}*39^{180} - 54^{29}*25^{123}*31^{512}$ will be
   (a) 8
   (b) 0
   (c) 6
   (d) 5

5. The difference of $10^{25} - 7$ and $10^{24} + x$ is divisible by 3 for $x = ?$
   (a) 3
   (b) 2
   (c) 4
   (d) 6

6. Find the value of $x$ in $\sqrt{x + 2\sqrt{x + 2\sqrt{x + 2\sqrt{3x}}}} = x$.
   (a) 1
   (b) 3
   (c) 6
   (d) 12
   (e) 9

7. If a number is multiplied by 22 and the same number is added to it, then we get a number that is half the square of that number. Find the number
   (a) 45
   (b) 46
   (c) 47
   (d) data insufficient

8. $12^{55}/3^{11} + 8^{48}/16^{18}$ will give the digit at units place as
   (a) 4
   (b) 6
   (c) 8
   (d) 0

9. The mean of $1, 2, 2^2 \ldots 2^{31}$ lies in between
   (a) $2^{24}$ to $2^{25}$
   (b) $2^{25}$ to $2^{26}$
   (c) $2^{26}$ to $2^{27}$
   (d) $2^{29}$ to $2^{30}$

10. $xy$ is a number that is divided by $ab$ where $xy < ab$ and gives a result $0.xyxyxy\ldots$ then $ab$ equals
    (a) 11
    (b) 33
    (c) 99
    (d) 66

11. A number $xy$ is multiplied by another number $ab$ and the result comes as $pqr$, where $r = 2y$, $q = 2(x + y)$ and $p = 2x$ where $x, y < 5$, $q \neq 0$. The value of $ab$ may be
    (a) 11
    (b) 13
    (c) 31
    (d) 22

12. $[x]$ denotes the greatest integer value just below $x$ and $\{x\}$ its fractional value. The sum of $[x]^3$ and $\{x\}^2$ is $-7.91$. Find $x$.
    (a) $-2.03$
    (b) $-1.97$
    (c) $-2.97$
    (d) $-1.7$

13. $16^5 + 2^{15}$ is divisible by
    (a) 31
    (b) 13
    (c) 27
    (d) 33

14. If $AB + XY = 1XP$, where $A \neq 0$ and all the letters signify different digits from 0 to 9, then the value of $A$ is
    (a) 6
    (b) 7
    (c) 9
    (d) 8

**Directions for Questions 15 and 16:** Find the possible integral values of $x$.

15. $|x - 3| + 2|x + 1| = 4$
    (a) 1
    (b) $-1$
    (c) 3
    (d) 2

16. $x^2 + |x - 1| = 1$
    (a) 1
    (b) $-1$
    (c) 0
    (d) 1 or 0

17. If $4^{n+1} + x$ and $4^{2n} - x$ are divisible by 5, $n$ being an even integer, find the least value of $x$.
    (a) 1
    (b) 2
    (c) 3
    (d) 0

18. If the sum of the numbers $(a25)^2$ and $a^3$ is divisible by 9, then which of the following may be a value for $a$?
    (a) 1
    (b) 7
    (c) 9
    (d) There is no value

19. If $|x - 4| + |y - 4| = 4$, then how many integer values can the set $(x, y)$ have?
    (a) Infinite
    (b) 5
    (c) 16
    (d) 9

20. $[3^{32}/50]$ gives a remainder and $\{.\}$ denotes the fractional part of that. The fractional part is of the form $(0 \cdot bx)$. The value of $x$ could be
    (a) 2
    (b) 4
    (c) 6
    (d) 8

21. The sum of two numbers is 20 and their geometric mean is 20% lower than their arithmetic mean. Find the ratio of the numbers.
    (a) 4 : 1          (b) 9 : 1
    (c) 1 : 1          (d) 17 : 3

22. The highest power on 990 that will exactly divide 1090! is
    (a) 101          (b) 100
    (c) 108          (d) 109

23. If 146! is divisible by $6^n$, then find the maximum value of $n$.
    (a) 74          (b) 70
    (c) 76          (d) 75

24. The last two digits in the multiplication of $35 \cdot 34 \cdot 33 \cdot 32 \cdot 31 \cdot 30 \cdot 29 \cdot 28 \cdot 27 \cdot 26$ is
    (a) 00          (b) 40
    (c) 30          (d) 10

25. The expression $333^{555} + 555^{333}$ is divisible by
    (a) 2          (b) 3
    (c) 37          (d) All of these

26. $[x]$ denotes the greatest integer value just below $x$ and $\{x\}$ its fractional value. The sum of $[x]^2$ and $\{x\}^1$ is 25.16. Find $x$.
    (a) 5.16          (b) −4.84
    (c) Both (a) and (b)          (d) 4.84

27. If we add the square of the digit in the tens place of a positive two-digit number to the product of the digits of that number, we shall get 52, and if we add the square of the digit in the units place to the same product of the digits, we shall get 117. Find the two-digit number.
    (a) 18          (b) 39
    (c) 49          (d) 28

28. Find two numbers such that their sum, their product and the differences of their squares are equal.
    (a) $\left(\dfrac{3+\sqrt{3}}{2}\right)$ and $\left(\dfrac{1+\sqrt{2}}{2}\right)$ or $\left(\dfrac{3+\sqrt{2}}{2}\right)$ and $\left(\dfrac{1+\sqrt{2}}{2}\right)$

    (b) $\left(\dfrac{3+\sqrt{7}}{2}\right)$ and $\left(\dfrac{1+\sqrt{7}}{2}\right)$ or $\left(\dfrac{3+\sqrt{6}}{2}\right)$ and $\left(\dfrac{1-\sqrt{6}}{2}\right)$

    (c) $\left(\dfrac{3-\sqrt{5}}{2}\right)$ and $\left(\dfrac{1-\sqrt{5}}{2}\right)$ or $\left(\dfrac{3+\sqrt{5}}{2}\right)$ and $\left(\dfrac{1+\sqrt{5}}{2}\right)$

    (d) None of these

29. The sum of the digits of a three-digit number is 17, and the sum of the squares of its digits is 109. If we subtract 495 from that number, we shall get a number consisting of the same digits written in the reverse order. Find the number.
    (a) 773          (b) 863
    (c) 683          (d) 944

30. Find the number of zeros in the product: $1^1 \times 2^2 \times 3^3 \times 4^4 \times \ldots\ldots\ 98^{98} \times 99^{99} \times 100^{100}$
    (a) 1200          (b) 1300
    (c) 1050          (d) 1225

31. Find the pairs of natural numbers whose greatest common divisor is 5 and the least common multiple is 105.
    (a) 5 and 105 or 15 and 35
    (b) 6 and 105 or 16 and 35
    (c) 5 and 15 or 15 and 135
    (d) 5 and 20 or 15 and 35

32. The denominator of an irreducible fraction is greater than the numerator by 2. If we reduce the numerator of the reciprocal fraction by 3 and subtract the given fraction from the resulting one, we get 1/15. Find the given fraction.
    (a) $\dfrac{2}{4}$          (b) $\dfrac{3}{5}$
    (c) $\dfrac{5}{7}$          (d) $\dfrac{7}{9}$

33. A two-digit number exceeds by 19 the sum of the squares of its digits and by 44 the double product of its digits. Find the number.
    (a) 72          (b) 62
    (c) 22          (d) 12

34. The sum of the squares of the digits constituting a two-digit positive number is 2.5 times as large as the sum of its digits and is larger by unity than the trebled product of its digits. Find the number.
    (a) 13 and 31          (b) 12 and 21
    (c) 22 and 33          (d) 14 and 41

35. The units digit of a two-digit number is greater than its tens digit by 2, and the product of that number by the sum of its digits is 144. Find the number.
    (a) 14          (b) 24
    (c) 46          (d) 35

36. Find the number of zeroes in the product $5 \times 10 \times 25 \times 40 \times 50 \times 55 \times 65 \times 125 \times 80$.
    (a) 8          (b) 9
    (c) 12          (d) 13

37. The highest power of 45 that will exactly divide 123! is
    (a) 28          (b) 30
    (c) 31          (d) 59

38. Three numbers are such that the second is as much lesser than the third as the first is lesser than the second. If the product of the two smaller numbers

is 85 and the product of two larger numbers is 115 find the middle number.

(a) 9
(b) 8
(c) 12
(d) 10

39. Find the smallest natural number $n$ such that $n!$ is divisible by 990.

(a) 3
(b) 5
(c) 11
(d) 12

40. $\sqrt{x}\sqrt{y} = \sqrt{xy}$ is true only when

(a) $x > 0, y > 0$
(b) $x > 0$ and $y < 0$
(c) $x < 0$ and $y > 0$
(d) All of these

**Directions for Questions 41 to 60:** Read the instructions below and solve the questions based on this.

In an examination situation, always solve the following type of questions by substituting the given options, to arrive at the solution.

However, as you can see, there are no options given in the questions here since these are meant to be an exercise in equation writing (which I believe is a primary skill required to do well in aptitude exams testing mathematical aptitude). Indeed, if these questions had options for them, they would be rated as LOD 1 questions. But since the option-based solution technique is removed here, I have placed these in the LOD 2 category.

41. Find the two-digit number that meets the following criteria. If the number in the units place exceeds, the number in its tens by 2 and the product of the required number with the sum of its digits is equal to 144.

42. The product of the digits of a two-digit number is twice as large as the sum of its digits. If we subtract 27 from the required number, we get a number consisting of the same digits written in the reverse order. Find the number?

43. The product of the digits of a two-digit number is one-third that number. If we add 18 to the required number, we get a number consisting of the same digits written in the reverse order. Find the number?

44. The sum of the squares of the digits of a two-digit number is 13. If we subtract 9 from that number, we get a number consisting of the same digits written in the reverse order. Find the number?

45. A two-digit number is thrice as large as the sum of its digits, and the square of that sum is equal to the trebled required number. Find the number?

46. Find a two-digit number that exceeds by 12 the sum of the squares of its digits and by 16 the doubled product of its digits.

47. The sum of the squares of the digits constituting a two-digit number is 10, and the product of the required number by the number consisting of the same digits written in the reverse order is 403. Find the 2 numbers that satisfy these conditions?

48. If we divide a two-digit number by the sum of its digits, we get 4 as a quotient and 3 as a remainder. Now, if we divide that two-digit number by the product of its digits, we get 3 as a quotient and 5 as a remainder. Find the two-digit number.

49. There is a natural number that becomes equal to the square of a natural number when 100 is added to it, and to the square of another natural number when 169 is added to it. Find the number.

50. Find two natural numbers whose sum is 85 and whose least common multiple is 102.

51. Find two- three -digit numbers whose sum is a multiple of 504 and the quotient is a multiple of 6.

52. The difference between the digits in a two-digit number is equal to 2, and the sum of the squares of the same digits is 52. Find all the possible numbers?

53. If we divide a given two-digit number by the product of its digits, we obtain 3 as a quotient and 9 as a remainder. If we subtract the product of the digits constituting the number, from the square of the sum of its digits, we obtain the given number. Find the number.

54. Find the three-digit number if it is known that the sum of its digits is 17 and the sum of the squares of its digits is 109. If we subtract 495 from this number, we obtain a number consisting of the same digits written in reverse order.

55. The sum of the cubes of the digits constituting a two-digit number is 243 and the product of the sum of its digits by the product of its digits is 162. Find the two two-digit numbers?

56. The difference between two numbers is 16. What can be said about the total numbers divisible by 7 that can lie in between these two numbers.

57. Arrange the following in descending order:

$111^4$, 110.109.108.107, 109.110.112.113

58. If $3 \le x \le 5$ and $4 \le y \le 7$. Find the greatest value of $xy$ and the least value of $x/y$.

59. Which of these is greater?

(a) $200^{300}$ or $300^{200}$ or $400^{150}$

(b) $5^{100}$ and $2^{200}$

(c) $10^{20}$ and $40^{10}$

60. The sum of the two numbers is equal to 15 and their arithmetic mean is 25 per cent greater than their geometric mean. Find the numbers.

61. Define a number $K$ such that it is the sum of the squares of the first $M$ natural numbers.(i.e. $K = 1^2 + 2^2 + \ldots + M^2$) where $M < 55$. How many values of $M$ exist such that $K$ is divisible by 4?

(a) 10
(b) 11
(c) 12
(d) None of these

62. $M$ is a two digit number which has the property that: the product of factorials of its digits > sum of factorials of its digits
    How many values of $M$ exist?
    (a) 56
    (b) 64
    (c) 63
    (d) None of these

63. A natural number when increased by 50% has its number of factors unchanged. However, when the value of the number is reduced by 75%, the number of factors is reduced by 66.66%. One such number could be:
    (a) 32
    (b) 84
    (c) 126
    (d) None of these

64. Find the 28383$^{rd}$ term of the series: 123456789101112....
    (a) 3
    (b) 4
    (c) 9
    (d) 7

65. If you form a subset of integers chosen from between 1 to 3000, such that no two integers add up to a multiple of nine, what can be the maximum number of elements in the subset. (Include both 1 and 3000.)
    (a) 1668
    (b) 1332
    (c) 1333
    (d) 1336

66. The series of numbers $(1,1/2,1/3,1/4$ ...............1/1972) is taken. Now two numbers are taken from this series (the first two) say $x$, $y$. Then the operation $x + y + x.y$ is performed to get a consolidated number. The process is repeated. What will be the value of the set after all the numbers are consolidated into one number?
    (a) 1970
    (b) 1971
    (c) 1972
    (d) None of these

67. $K$ is a three digit number such that the ratio of the number to the sum of its digits is least. What is the difference between the hundreds and the tens digits of $K$?
    (a) 9
    (b) 8
    (c) 7
    (d) None of these

68. In Question 67, what can be said about the difference between the tens and the units digit?
    (a) 0
    (b) 1
    (c) 2
    (d) None of these

69. For the above question, for how many values of $K$ will the ratio be the highest?
    (a) 9
    (b) 8
    (c) 7
    (d) None of these

70. A triangular number is defined as a number which has the property of being expressed as a sum of consecutive natural numbers starting with 1. How many triangular numbers less than 1000, have the property that they are the difference of squares of two consecutive natural numbers?
    (a) 20
    (b) 21
    (c) 22
    (d) 23

71. $x$ and $y$ are two positive integers. Then what will be the sum of the coefficients of the expansion of the expression $(x + y)^{44}$?
    (a) $2^{43}$
    (b) $2^{43} + 1$
    (c) $2^{44}$
    (d) $2^{44} - 1$

72. What is the remainder when $9 + 9^2 + 9^3 + ....9^{2n+1}$ is divided by 6?
    (a) 1
    (b) 2
    (c) 3
    (d) 4

73. The remainder when the number 123456789101112 ......484950 is divided by 16 is?
    (a) 3
    (b) 4
    (c) 5
    (d) 6

74. What is the highest power of 3 available in the expression 58!-38!?
    (a) 17
    (b) 18
    (c) 19
    (d) None of these

75. Find the remainder when the number represented by 22334 raised to the power $(1^2 + 2^2 + ..+ 66^2)$ is divided by 5?
    (a) 2
    (b) 4
    (c) 1
    (d) None of these

76. What is the total number of divisors of the number $12^{33} \times 34^{23} \times 2^{70}$ ?
    (a) 4658.
    (b) 9316
    (c) 2744
    (d) None of these

77. For Question 76, which of the following will represent the sum of factors of the number (such that only odd factors are counted)?
    (a) $\dfrac{(3^{34} - 1)}{2} \times \dfrac{(17^{24} - 1)}{16}$
    (b) $(3^{34}-1) \times (17^{24} - 1)$
    (c) $\dfrac{(3^{34} - 1)}{33}$
    (d) None of these

78. What is the remainder when $(1!)^3 + (2!)^3 + (3!)^3 + (4!)^3 +.....(1152!)^3$ is divided by 1152?
    (a) 125
    (b) 225
    (c) 325
    (d) 205

79. A set $S$ is formed by including some of the first one thousand natural numbers. $S$ contains the maximum number of numbers such that they satisfy the following conditions:
    1. No number of the set $S$ is prime.
    2. When the numbers of the set $S$ are selected two at a time, we always see co prime numbers.
    What is the number of elements in the set S?
    (a) 11
    (b) 12
    (c) 13
    (d) 7

*Find the last two digits of the following numbers*

80. $101 \times 102 \times 103 \times 197 \times 198 \times 199$
    (a) 54
    (b) 74
    (c) 64
    (d) 84

81. $65 \times 29 \times 37 \times 63 \times 71 \times 87$
   - (a) 05
   - (b) 95
   - (c) 15
   - (d) 25

82. $65 \times 29 \times 37 \times 63 \times 71 \times 87 \times 85$
   - (a) 25
   - (b) 35
   - (c) 75
   - (d) 85

83. $65 \times 29 \times 37 \times 63 \times 71 \times 87 \times 62$
   - (a) 70
   - (b) 30
   - (c) 10
   - (d) 90

84. $75 \times 35 \times 47 \times 63 \times 71 \times 87 \times 82$
   - (a) 50
   - (b) 70
   - (c) 30
   - (d) 90

85. $(201 \times 202 \times 203 \times 204 \times 246 \times 247 \times 248 \times 249)^2$
   - (a) 36
   - (b) 56
   - (c) 76
   - (d) 16

86. Find the remainder when $7^{99}$ is divided by 2400.
   - (a) 1
   - (b) 343
   - (c) 49
   - (d) 7

87. Find the remainder when $(10^3 + 9^3)^{752}$ is divided by $12^3$.
   - (a) 729
   - (b) 1000
   - (c) 752
   - (d) 1

88. Arun, Bikas and Chetakar have a total of 80 coins among them. Arun triples the number of coins with the others by giving them some coins from his own collection. Next, Bikas repeats the same process. After this Bikas now has 20 coins. Find the number of coins he had at the beginning.
   - (a) 22
   - (b) 20
   - (c) 18
   - (d) 24

89. The super computer at Ram Mohan Roy Seminary takes an input of a number $N$ and a $X$ where $X$ is a factor of the number $N$. In a particular case $N$ is equal to $83p796161q$ and $X$ is equal to 11 where $0 < p < q$. Find the sum of remainders when $N$ is divided by $(p + q)$ and $p$ successively.
   - (a) 6
   - (b) 3
   - (c) 2
   - (d) 9

90. On March 1st 2016, Sherry saved Re.1. Everyday starting from March 2nd 2016, he saved Re.1 more than the previous day. Find the first date after March 1st 2016 at the end of which his total savings will be a perfect square.
   - (a) 17th March 2016
   - (b) 18th April 2016
   - (c) 26th March 2016
   - (d) None of these

91. What is the rightmost digit preceding the zeroes in the value of $20^{53}$?
   - (a) 2
   - (b) 8
   - (c) 1
   - (d) 4

92. What is the remainder when $2(8!) - 21(6!)$ divides $14(7!) + 14(13!)$?

93. How many integer values of $x$ and $y$ are there such that $4x + 7y = 3$, while $|x| < 500$ and $|y| < 500$?
   - (a) 144
   - (b) 141
   - (c) 143
   - (d) 142

94. If $n = 1 + m$, where $m$ is the product of four consecutive positive integers, then which of the following is/are true?
   - (A) $n$ is odd
   - (B) $n$ is not a multiple of 3
   - (C) $n$ is a perfect square
   - (a) All three
   - (b) $A$ and $B$ only
   - (c) A and C only
   - (d) None of these

95. How many two-digit numbers less than or equal to 50, have the product of the factorials of their digits less than or equal to the sum of the factorials of their digits?
   - (a) 18
   - (b) 16
   - (c) 15
   - (d) None of these

96. A candidate takes a test and attempts all the 100 questions in it. While any correct answer fetches 1 mark, wrong answers are penalised as follows; one-tenth of the questions carry 1/10 negative mark each, one-fifth of the questions carry 1/5 negative marks each and the rest of the questions carry ½ negative mark each. Unattempted questions carry no marks. What is the difference between the maximum and the minimum marks that he can score?
   - (a) 100
   - (b) 120
   - (c) 140
   - (d) None of these

**Directions for Questions 97 to 99:** A mock test is taken at Mindworkzz. The test paper comprises of questions in three levels of difficulty—LOD1, LOD2 and LOD 3.

The following table gives the details of the positive and negative marks attached to each question type:

| Difficulty level | Positive marks for answering the question correctly | Negative marks for answering the question wrongly |
| --- | --- | --- |
| LOD 1 | 4 | 2 |
| LOD 2 | 3 | 1.5 |
| LOD 3 | 2 | 1 |

The test had 200 questions with 80 on LOD 1 and 60 each on LOD 2 and LOD 3.

97. If a student has solved 100 questions exactly and scored 120 marks, the maximum number of incorrect questions that he/she might have marked is
   - (a) 44
   - (b) 56
   - (c) 60
   - (d) None of these

93. (a) 1 (b) 7!
   (c) 8! (d) 9!

98. If Amit attempted the least number of questions and got a total of 130 marks, and if it is known that he attempted at least one of every type, then the number of questions he must have attempted is
    (a) 34
    (b) 35
    (c) 36
    (d) None of these

99. In the above question, what is the least number of questions he might have got incorrect?
    (a) 0
    (b) 1
    (c) 2
    (d) None of these

100. Amitabh has a certain number of toffees, such that if he distributes them amongst ten children he has nine left, if he distributes amongst 9 children he would have 8 left, if he distributes amongst 8 children he would have 7 left … and so on until if he distributes amongst 5 children he should have 4 left. What is the second lowest number of toffees he could have with him?
    (a) 2519
    (b) 7559
    (c) 8249
    (d) 5039

101. If a positive integer '$n$' is subtracted from the squares of three consecutive terms of an Arithmetic Progression, the numbers obtained are 108, 220 and 364 respectively. What is the sum of the digits of '$n$'?

102. How many integers exist such that not only are they multiples of $904^{2008}$ but also are factors of $904^{2015}$?

103. What is the remainder when $1^5 + 2^5 + 3^5 + \ldots\ldots+ 96^5$ is divided by 194?

104. If $\left[\dfrac{s}{2}\right]+\left[\dfrac{s}{3}\right]+\left[\dfrac{s}{7}\right]=\dfrac{41}{42}s$ where $[s]$ is the greatest integer less than or equal to '$s$' and $0 < s < 1000$, then find the number of possible values of '$s$'.

**Directions for questions 105 to 107:**
In a zoo with 100 rabbits, there are three kinds of rabbits, weight-wise viz. 1 kg rabbits, 2 kg rabbits and 5 kg rabbits. There are a minimum of 10 and a maximum of 60 of each kind of rabbit. On a particular day, the zoo director transfers 40 rabbits from his stock and sends them off to the neighbouring zoo. On weighing these rabbits, it was found that the total weight of these 40 rabbits, was 148 kgs. It was also found that the weight of the remaining rabbits was 212 kgs.

105. What is the minimum number of 1 kg rabbits that were transferred?

106. What is the maximum possible number of 5 kg rabbits that remain?

107. If, a total of 26 5 kg rabbits were transferred, then what is the maximum possible numbers of 1 kg rabbits that remain in the zoo?

108. Let $A$ be a two-digit number. The sum of the number $A$, the number formed by reversing the digits of $A$ and the value of the product of the digits of $A$ is found to equal 117. Then what is the sum of the digits of $A$?

109. Let $M$ be the product of all natural numbers between 35 and 250 that have an odd number of factors. Find the highest power of 12 in $M$.

110. $x$ and $y$ are natural numbers such that they satisfy the equation $x + y + 21 = 3xy$. Find the maximum possible integral power of 6 in $(xy)!.[n!$ is the product of the first '$n$' natural numbers.]

111. Let $X$ is the set of all the natural numbers each of which is equal to the number of its factors & $Y$ is the set of all natural numbers from 1 to 100, each of which differ from the sum of its factors 1. Also, let $x$ & $y$ represent the number of elements in the sets respectively. Then find the value of $[y/x]$, where $[]$ represents the greatest integer function:

112. A four digit number $X$ has 15 factors. What is the number of factors of $X^2$?

113. How many four- digit odd numbers are possible such that the hundreds digit is two more than the tens digit?

114. Three natural numbers $X$, $Y$, $Z$ are prime numbers less than 20 are in arithmetic progression. If $X > Y > Z$, then how many possible values can we get for $X + Y + Z$?

115. A 100- digit number is multiplied by a 200- digit number and the product is multiplied with a 300 digit number and this product is again multiplied with a 400 digits number. What is the least number of digits in the product?

116. What are the last two digits of the number $3^{400}$?

117. The unit digit in $1^7 \times 2^7 \times 3^7 \times \ldots\ldots\times 9^7 \times 11^7 \times 12^7\ldots..19^7 \times 21^7\ldots\ldots99^7$ is

118. How many two digit numbers have their squares as 1 more than a multiple of 24?

119. There are 80 questions in a test. Each correct answer fetches 1 mark, each wrong answer & unanswered question attract a penalty of 1/4 mark & 1/8 mark respectively each. Frodo scored 23 marks in the test. What is the minimum possible number of the question wrongly answered by him?

120. 1777 has exactly 5 digits when converted to base '$x$' from the decimal system what is the minimum possible value of $x$?
    (a) 3
    (b) 4
    (c) 6
    (d) None of these

121. What will be the sum of all natural numbers between 101 and 1000 which on division by 2, 4, 6, 8, 10 leave remainders 1, 3, 5, 7, 9, respectively?

122. Units digit of which of the following is the same as the units digits of $a^{17} + b^{17}$ for any positive integer value of $a$, $b$?
    (a) $a^2 + b^2$
    (b) $a^{12} + b^{12}$
    (c) $a^{13} + b^{13}$
    (d) $a^{10} + b^{10}$

123. How many 4-digit numbers are there in the decimal system, which have exactly 4 digits when expressed in Base 6, Base 7 and Base 8?
    (a) 158          (b) 248
    (c) 296          (d) 368

124. What is the difference between the highest and the least 4-digit natural numbers that have exactly 4 digits when expressed in Base 6 and Base 7.

125. If n is a natural number, then what is the sum of all the possible distinct remainders when $9^n + 6^n + 4^n + 11^n$ is divided by 10?

126. If $x$, $y$, $z$ and $w$ are natural numbers, then what is the sum of all the possible remainders when $9^x + 6^y + 4^z + 11^z$ is divided by 10?

127. What is the maximum possible sum of the number of Mondays and Thursdays in two consecutive years?

128. In the previous question find the minimum possible sum of the number of Mondays and Thursdays.

129. What will be the value of remainder when (111111111..........64terms)*(22222222..........55terms) is divided by 18?
    (a) 0          (b) 1
    (c) 2          (d) 17

130. Find the number of solutions of the equation: $x^2 - y^2$ = 777314:

    Directions for questions 131 and 132:

    There was a table in a room & there were 100 coins (coin 1 to coin 100) in a row on the table. All the coins were heads up initially. You entered the room and turned all the coins, the second time you entered the room and turned every $2^{nd}$ coin (coin 2, coin 4, .....), the $3^{rd}$ time you entered the room and turned every 3rd coin ( coin 3, coin 6, coin 9, .....) and so on, if you visited the room 100 times and continued this sequence every time. Then answer the following questions.

131. What were the states of $54^{th}$ & $91^{st}$ coin after the $100^{th}$ visit? Type 1 if both are heads; Type 2 if the first one is head and the other is tail; Type 3 if the first one is tail and the second is tail; Type 4 if both are tails.

132. After your $100^{th}$ visit how many coins were in the heads-up position?

133. What is the digit at the hundredths place of the number $(225)^{40}$?
    (a) 2          (b) 4
    (c) 6          (d) 8

134. Consider the set of the first 14 natural numbers. Three numbers $a$, $b$, $c$ are selected from this set such that $a > 3b > 4c$. How many such distinct triplets $(a, b, c)$ are possible?
    (a) 32          (b) 26
    (c) 22          (d) 18

135. How many four-digit numbers having distinct digits using the first five natural numbers (1 to 5) can be formed such that the numbers formed are divisible by each of the digits used in the number?
    (a) 0          (b) 1
    (c) 2          (d) 3

*Space for Rough Work*

## LEVEL OF DIFFICULTY (III)

1. What two-digit number is less than the sum of the square of its digits by 11 and exceeds their doubled product by 5?
   - (a) 15, 95
   - (b) 95
   - (c) Both (a) and (b)
   - (d) 15, 95 and 12345

2. Find the lower of the two successive natural numbers if the square of the sum of those numbers exceeds the sum of their squares by 112.
   - (a) 6
   - (b) 7
   - (c) 8
   - (d) 9

3. First we increased the denominator of a positive fraction by 3 and then we decreased it by 5. The sum of the resulting fractions proves to be equal to 19/42. Find the denominator of the fraction if its numerator is 2.
   - (a) 7
   - (b) 8
   - (c) 12
   - (d) 9

4. Find the last two digits of: $15 \times 37 \times 63 \times 51 \times 97 \times 17$.
   - (a) 35
   - (b) 45
   - (c) 55
   - (d) 85

5. Let us consider a fraction whose denominator is smaller than the square of the numerator by unity. If we add 2 to the numerator and the denominator, the fraction will exceed 1/3. If we subtract 3 from the numerator and the denominator, the fraction will be positive but smaller than 1/10. Find the value.
   - (a) $\dfrac{3}{8}$
   - (b) $\dfrac{4}{15}$
   - (c) $\dfrac{5}{24}$
   - (d) $\dfrac{6}{35}$

6. Find the sum of all three-digit numbers that give a remainder of 4 when they are divided by 5.
   - (a) 98,270
   - (b) 99,270
   - (c) 1,02,090
   - (d) 90,270

7. Find the sum of all two-digit numbers that give a remainder of 3 when they are divided by 7.
   - (a) 686
   - (b) 676
   - (c) 666
   - (d) 656

8. Find the sum of all odd three-digit numbers that are divisible by 5.
   - (a) 50,500
   - (b) 50,250
   - (c) 50,000
   - (d) 49,500

9. The product of a two-digit number by a number consisting of the same digits written in the reverse order is equal to 2430. Find the lower number.
   - (a) 54
   - (b) 52
   - (c) 63
   - (d) 45

10. Find the lowest of three numbers as described: If the cube of the first number exceeds their product by 2, the cube of the second number is smaller than their product by 3, and the cube of the third number exceeds their product by 3.
    - (a) $3^{1/3}$
    - (b) $9^{1/3}$
    - (c) 2
    - (d) Any of these
    - (e) None of these

11. How many pairs of natural numbers are there the difference of whose squares is 45?
    - (a) 1
    - (b) 2
    - (c) 3
    - (d) 4

12. Find all two-digit numbers such that the sum of the digits constituting the number is not less than 7; the sum of the squares of the digits is not greater than 30; the number consisting of the same digits written in the reverse order is not larger than half the given number.
    - (a) 52
    - (b) 51
    - (c) 49
    - (d) 53

13. In a four-digit number, the sum of the digits in the thousands, hundreds and tens is equal to 14, and the sum of the digits in the units, tens and hundreds is equal to 15. Among all the numbers satisfying these conditions, find the number the sum of the squares of whose digits is the greatest.
    - (a) 2572
    - (b) 1863
    - (c) 2573
    - (d) None of these

14. In a four-digit number, the sum of the digits in the thousands and tens is equal to 4, the sum of the digits in the hundreds and the units is 15, and the digit of the units exceeds by 7 the digit of the thousands. Among all the numbers satisfying these conditions, find the number the sum of the product of whose digit of the thousands by the digit of the units and the product of the digit of the hundreds by that of the tens assumes the least value.
    - (a) 4708
    - (b) 1738
    - (c) 2629
    - (d) 1812

15. If we divide a two-digit number by a number consisting of the same digits written in the reverse order, we get 4 as a quotient and 15 as a remainder. If we subtract 9 from the given number, we get the sum of the squares of the digits constituting that number. Find the number.
    - (a) 71
    - (b) 83
    - (c) 99
    - (d) None of these

16. Find the two-digit number the quotient of whose division by the product of its digits is equal to 8/3, and the difference between the required number and the number consisting of the same digits written in the reverse order is 18?

(a) 86      (b) 42

(c) 75      (d) None of these

17. Find the two-digit number if it is known that the ratio of the required number and the sum of its digits is 8 as also the quotient of the product of its digits and that of the sum is 14/9.

(a) 54      (b) 72

(c) 27      (d) 45

18. If we divide the unknown two-digit number by the number consisting of the same digits written in the reverse order, we get 4 as a quotient and 3 as a remainder. If we divide the required number by the sum of its digits, we get 8 as a quotient and 7 as a remainder. Find the number.

(a) 81      (b) 91

(c) 71      (d) 72

19. The last two-digits in the multiplication $122 \times 123 \times 125 \times 127 \times 129$ will be

(a) 20      (b) 50

(c) 30      (d) 40

20. The remainder obtained when $43^{101} + 23^{101}$ is divided by 66 is

(a) 2      (b) 10

(c) 5      (d) 0

21. The last three-digits of the multiplication $12345 \times 54321$ will be

(a) 865      (b) 745

(c) 845      (d) 945

22. The sum of the digits of a three-digit number is 12. If we subtract 495 from the number consisting of the same digits written in reverse order, we shall get the required number. Find that three-digit number if the sum of all pairwise products of the digits constituting that number is 41.

(a) 156      (b) 237

(c) 197      (d) Both (a) and (b)

23. A three-digit positive integer abc is such that $a^2 + b^2 + c^2 = 74$. a is equal to the doubled sum of the digits in the tens and units places. Find the number if it is known that the difference between that number and the number written by the same digits in the reverse order is 495.

(a) 813      (b) 831

(c) 613      (d) 713

24. Represent the number 1.25 as a product of three positive factors so that the product of the first factor by the square of the second is equal to 5 if we have to get the lowest possible sum of the three factors.

(a) $x_1 = 2.25, x_2 = 5, x_3 = 0.2$

(b) $x_1 = 1.25, x_2 = 4, x_3 = 4.5$

(c) $x_1 = 1.25, x_2 = 2, x_3 = 0.5$

(d) $x_1 = 1.25, x_2 = 4, x_3 = 2$

25. Find a number x such that the sum of that number and its square is the least.

(a) −0.5      (b) 0.5

(c) −1.5      (d) 1.5

26. When $2222^{5555} + 5555^{2222}$ is divided by 7, the remainder is

(a) 0      (b) 2

(c) 4      (d) 5

27. If x is a number of five-digits which when divided by 8, 12, 15 and 20 leaves respectively 5, 9, 12 and 17 as remainders, then find x such that it is the lowest such number.

(a) 10017      (b) 10057

(c) 10097      (d) 10077

28. $3^{2n} - 1$ is divisible by $2^{n+3}$ for n =

(a) 1      (b) 2

(c) 3      (d) None of these

29. $10^n - \left(5 + \sqrt{17}\right)^n$ is divisible by $2^{n+2}$ for what whole number value of n?

(a) 2      (b) 3

(c) 7      (d) None of these

30. $\dfrac{32^{32^{32}}}{9}$ will leave a remainder

(a) 4      (b) 7

(c) 1      (d) 2

31. Find the remainder that the number $1989 \cdot 1990 \cdot 1992^3$ gives when divided by 7.

(a) 0      (b) 1

(c) 5      (d) 2

32. Find the remainder of $2^{100}$ when divided by 3.

(a) 3      (b) 0

(c) 1      (d) 2

33. Find the remainder when the number $3^{1989}$ is divided by 7.

(a) 1      (b) 5

(c) 6      (d) 4

34. Find the last digit of the number $1^2 + 2^2 + ... + 99^2$.

(a) 0      (b) 1

(c) 2      (d) 3

35. Find gcd $(2^{100} - 1, 2^{120} - 1)$.

(a) $2^{20} - 1$      (b) $2^{40} - 1$

(c) $2^{60} - 1$      (d) $2^{10} - 1$

36. Find the gcd (111...11 hundred ones ; 11...11 sixty ones).

(a) 111...forty ones      (b) 111...twenty five ones

(c) 111...twenty ones      (d) 111...sixty ones

37. Find the last digit of the number $1^3 + 2^3 + 3^3 + 4^3 ... + 99^3$.

(a) 0      (b) 1

(c) 2      (d) 5

38. Find the GCD of the numbers $2n + 13$ and $n + 7$.
    (a) 1      (b) 2
    (c) 3      (d) 4

39. $\dfrac{32^{32^{32}}}{7}$
    (a) 4      (b) 2
    (c) 1      (d) 3

40. The remainder when $10^{10} + 10^{100} + 10^{1000} + \ldots + 10^{10000000000}$ is divided by 7 is
    (a) 0      (b) 1
    (c) 2      (d) 5

41. $n$ is a number, such that $2n$ has 28 factors and $3n$ has 30 factors. $6n$ has
    (a) 35      (b) 32
    (c) 28      (d) None of these

42. Suppose the sum of $n$ consecutive integers is $x + (x + 1) + (x + 2) + (x + 3) + \ldots + (x + (n - 1)) = 1000$, then which of the following cannot be true about the number of terms $n$
    (a) The number of terms can be 16
    (b) The number of terms can be 5
    (c) The number of terms can be 25
    (d) The number of terms can be 20

43. The remainder when $2^2 + 22^2 + 222^2 + 2222^2 + \ldots(222\ldots.49\ \text{twos})^2$ is divided by 9 is
    (a) 2      (b) 5
    (c) 6      (d) 7

44. $N = 202 \times 20002 \times 200000002 \times 20000000000000002 \times 200000000\ldots.2$ (31 zeroes) The sum of digits in this multiplication will be:
    (a) 112      (b) 160
    (c) 144      (d) Cannot be determined

45. Twenty five sets of problems on Data Interpretation– one each for the DI sections of 25 CATALYST tests were prepared by the AMS research team. The DI section of each CATALYST contained 50 questions of which exactly 35 questions were unique, i.e. they had not been used in the DI section of any of the other 24 CATALYSTs. What could be the maximum possible number of questions prepared for the DI sections of all the 25 CATALYSTs put together?
    (a) 1100      (b) 975
    (c) 1070      (d) 1055

46. In the above question, what could be the minimum possible number of questions prepared?
    (a) 890      (b) 875
    (c) 975      (d) None of these

**Directions for Questions 47 to 49:** At a particular time in the twenty first century there were seven bowlers in the Indian cricket team's list of 16 players short listed to play the next world cup. Statisticians discovered that that if you looked at the number of wickets taken by any of the 7 bowlers of the current Indian cricket team, the number of wickets taken by them had a strange property. The numbers were such that for any team selection of 11 players (having 1 to 7 bowlers) by using the number of wickets taken by each bowler and attaching coefficients of +1, 0, or −1 to each value available and adding the resultant values, any number from 1 to 1093, both included could be formed. If we denote $W_1$, $W_2$, $W_3$, $W_4$, $W_5$, $W_6$ and $W_7$ as the 7 values in the ascending order what could be the answer to the following questions:

47. Find the value of $W_1 + 2W_2 + 3W_3 + 4W_4 + 5W_5 + 6W_6$.
    (a) 2005      (b) 1995
    (c) 1985      (d) None of these

48. Find the index of the largest power of 3 contained in the product $W_1 W_2 W_3 W_4 W_5 W_6 W_7$.
    (a) 15      (b) 10
    (c) 21      (d) 6

49. If the sum of the seven coefficients is 0, find the smallest number that can be obtained.
    (a) − 1067      (b) − 729
    (c) − 1040      (d) − 1053

**Directions for Questions 50 and 51:** Answer these questions on the basis of the information given below.

In the ancient game of Honololo the task involves solving a puzzle asked by the chief of the tribe. Anybody answering the puzzle correctly is given the hand of the most beautiful maiden of the tribe. Unfortunately, for the youth of the tribe, solving the puzzle is not a cakewalk since the chief is the greatest mathematician of the tribe.

In one such competition the chief called everyone to attention and announced openly:

"A three-digit number '$mnp$' is a perfect square and the number of factors it has is also a perfect square. It is also known that the digits $m$, $n$ and $p$ are all distinct. Now answer my questions and win the maiden's hand."

50. If $(m + n + p)$ is also a perfect square, what is the number of factors of the six-digit number $mnpmnp$?
    (a) 36      (b) 72
    (c) 48      (d) Cannot be determined

51. If the fourth power of the product of the digits of the number $mnp$ is not divisible by 5, what is the number of factors of the nine-digit number, $mnpmnpmnp$?
    (a) 32      (b) 72
    (c) 48      (d) Cannot be determined

52. In a cricket tournament organised by the ICC, a total of 15 teams participated. Australia, as usual won the tournament by scoring the maximum number of points. The tournament is organised as a single round robin tournament—where each team plays with every other team exactly once. 3 points are awarded for a win, 2 points are awarded for a tie/washed out match and 1 point is awarded for a loss. Zimbabwe

had the lowest score (in terms of points) at the end of the tournament. Zimbabwe scored a total of 21 points. All the 15 national teams got a distinct score (in terms of points scored). It is also known that at least one match played by the Australian team was tied/washed out. Which of the following is always true for the Australian team?

(a) It had at least two ties/washouts.

(b) It had a maximum of 3 losses.

(c) It had a maximum of 9 wins.

(d) All of the above.

53. What is the remainder when $128^{1000}$ is divided by 153?

(a) 103        (b) 145

(c) 118        (d) 52

54. Find the remainder when $50^{51^{52}}$ is divided by 11.

(a) 6        (b) 4

(c) 7        (d) 3

55. Find the remainder when $32^{33^{34}}$ is divided by 11.

(a) 5        (b) 4

(c) 10        (d) 1

56. Find the remainder when $30^{72^{87}}$ is divided by 11.

(a) 5        (b) 9

(c) 6        (d) 3

57. Find the remainder when $50^{56^{52}}$ is divided by 11.

(a) 7        (b) 5

(c) 9        (d) 10

58. Find the remainder when $33^{34^{35}}$ is divided by 7.

(a) 5        (b) 4

(c) 6        (d) 2

59. Let $S_m$ denote the sum of the squares of the first $m$ natural numbers. For how many values of $m < 100$, is $S_m$ a multiple of 4?

(a) 50        (b) 25

(c) 36        (d) 24

60. For the above question, for how many values will the sum of cubes of the first $m$ natural numbers be a multiple of 5 (if $m < 50$)?

(a) 20        (b) 21

(c) 22        (d) None of these

61. How many integer values of $x$ and $y$ satisfy the expression $4x + 7y = 3$ where $|x| < 1000$ and $|y| < 1000$?

(a) 284        (b) 285

(c) 286        (d) None of these

62. $N = 7777.................7777$, where the digit 7 repeats itself 603 times. What is the remainder left when $N$ is divided by 1144?

63. How many factors of 19! are there, whose unit digit is 5?

64. $N = 1! - 2! + 3! - 4! +.....+ 47! - 48! + 49!, - 50! + 51!$ Then what is the unit digit of $N^N$?

65. How many numbers less than 100 have exactly four factors?

66. Two odd numbers have 36 factors each and the HCF of these two numbers is 225. What is the minimum possible LCM of these two numbers if the power of any prime factor in these two numbers is not more than 3?

67. Find the remainder when $[(7!)^{6!}]^{17777}$ is divided by 17?

68. A four digit number $wxyz$ is such that $x + y = 2w$ & $y + 6z = 2(w + x)$ & $w + 5z = 2y$. Find the sum of such four digit numbers which satisfy the given conditions.

69. Find the remainder when $(17)(9!)+2 (18!)$ is divided by $(9!)17408$.

70. $X$ is a number formed by writing the first 1002 natural numbers one after another from left to right then find the remainder when $X$ is divided by 9 is

71. $X$ is a number formed by writing the first 1002 whole numbers one after another from left to right then a vertical line is drawn which divides the number such that the number of digits on either side of line is the same. Find the remainder when the number formed by the digits on the left of the vertical line, is divided by 625.

72. Amongst all the four digit natural numbers divisible by 24, how many have the number 24 in them?

73. If $X$ is a natural number & $X < 100$ then the number of values of $X$ for which $18X + 2$ & $12X + 1$ are relatively prime?

74. $P$ is a natural number of at least 6 digits and its leftmost digit is 7. When this leftmost digit is removed from $P$, the number thus obtained is found to be 1/21 times of $P$. What is the product of the all the nonzero digits of $P$.

(a) 126        (b) 105

(c) 60        (d) 72

75. $X!$ is completely divisible by $11^{51}$ but not by $11^{52}$. What is the sum of digits of largest such number $X$?

76. If '$a$' is a natural number and HCF of $a, a + 5$ is 5. If the LCM of the two numbers is a three-digit number, then what is the difference between the maximum & minimum possible values of the smaller number?

(a) 25        (b) 35

(c) 40        (d) 45

77. How many times would 1 be used while writing all the natural numbers from 8 to 127 in the Binary number system?

(a) 212        (b) 218

(c) 424        (d) 436

78. What is the maximum number of elements that one can pick from the set of natural numbers from 1 to 20 such that the product of no two of them results in a perfect square or perfect cube?

79. *abcdefghij* is a ten digit number with distinct digits such that $a > b > c$, $d > e > f$, $g > h > i > j$. $a$, $b$, $c$ are consecutive even digits and $g$, $h$, $i$, $j$ are consecutive odd digits. If $d + e + f = 9$, then what is the value of $\left[ \dfrac{a \times b \times c \times d}{i} \right]$ (where [] denotes greatest integer function)?

(a) 42        (b) 0

(c) 54        (d) 66

80. $N = abc$ is a three digit number, the sum of whose digits is $1/7^{th}$ of the product of its digits. Then how many possible sets of $(a, b, c)$ are possible?

81. $(3132!)_{10} = (x)_{34}$, then what will be the number of consecutive zeroes at the end of '$x$'?

(a) 124        (b) 167

(c) 194        (d) None of these.

*Space for Rough Work*

# ANSWER KEY

## Level of Difficulty (I)

| | | | |
|---|---|---|---|
| 1. (a) | 2. (a) | 3. (b) | 4. (b) |
| 5. (a) | 6. (c) | 7. (d) | 8. (d) |
| 9. (d) | 10. (d) | 11. (a) | 12. (c) |
| 13. (d) | 14. (d) | 15. (b) | 16. (c) |
| 17. (b) | 18. (d) | 19. (a) | 20. (b) |
| 21. (d) | 22. (a) | 23. (b) | 24. (c) |
| 25. (d) | 26. (d) | 27. (c) | 28. (d) |
| 29. (b) | 30. (d) | 31. (a) | 32. (b) |
| 33. (c) | 34. (d) | 35. (c) | 36. (b) |
| 37. (d) | 38. (d) | 39. (b) | 40. (b) |
| 41. (a) | 42. (a) | 43. (a) | 44. (d) |
| 45. (c) | 46. (d) | 47. (b) | 48. (c) |
| 49. (c) | 50. (d) | 51. (a) | 52. (a) |
| 53. (b) | 54. (c) | 55. (d) | 56. (b) |
| 57. (a) | 58. (b) | 59. (d) | 60. (d) |
| 61. (a) | 62. (a) $\rightarrow (21)^{12}$ | (b) $\rightarrow (0.8)^3$ | |
| 63. (b) | | | |

64. 1. $\rightarrow$ 0, 2, 4, 6, 8
   2. $\rightarrow$ 1, 4, 7
   3. $\rightarrow$ 0, 4, 8
   4. $\rightarrow$ 0, 5
   5. $\rightarrow$ 4
   6. $\rightarrow$ 7
   7. $\rightarrow$ 0

65. LCM $\rightarrow$ 5670
   HCF $\rightarrow$ 27
   LCM $\rightarrow$ 780
   HCF $\rightarrow$ 39
   LCM $\rightarrow$ 737100
   HCF $\rightarrow$ 30

| | | | |
|---|---|---|---|
| 66. (b) | 67. (a) | 68. (c) | 69. (c) |
| 70. (c) | 71. (a) | 72. (d) | 73. (b) |
| 74. (b) | 75. (a) | 76. (b) | 77. (d) |
| 78. (a) | 79. (a) | 80. (b) | 81. (c) |
| 82. (b) | 83. (c) | 84. (c) | 85. (c) |
| 86. (a) | 87. (c) | 88. (b) | 89. (b) |
| 90. (c) | 91. (d) | 92. (d) | 93. (a) |
| 94. (c) | 95. (b) | 96. (b) | 97. (a) |
| 98. (c) | 99. (c) | 100. (d) | 101. (d) |
| 102. (a) | 103. (c) | 104. (b) | 105. (c) |
| 106. (d) | 107. (b) | 108. (c) | 109. (d) |
| 110. (c) | 111. (c) | 112. (c) | 113. (a) |
| 114. (c) | 115. (a) | 116. (d) | 117. (d) |
| 118. (b) | 119. (b) | 120. (c) | 121. (b) |
| 122. (b) | 123. (d) | 124. (b) | 125. (d) |
| 126. (a) | 127. (b) | 128. (d) | 129. (c) |
| 130. (b) | 131. (b) | 132. (a) | 133. (c) |
| 134. (d) | 135. (b) | 136. (b) | 137. (c) |
| 138. (b) | 139. (d) | 140. (b) | 141. 7 |

| | | | |
|---|---|---|---|
| 142. 11 | 143. $72^6$ | 144. 6 | 145. 7 |
| 146. 12 | 147. 242 | 148. Cannot be determined | |
| 149. d | 150. 1 | 151. 5 | 152. 0 |
| 153. 5 | 154. 10 and 11 | 155. 3 | 156. 0 |
| 157. 5040 | 158. 1 | 159. 1111111 | 160. 1 |
| 161. $4^{40}$ | 162. 24 | 163. 198 | 164. 120 |
| 165. 5 | 166. 2 | 167. 40 | 168. 4 |
| 169. 1 | 170. 96 | 171. 8 | 172. X + Y |
| 173. 5 | 174. $B \geq A > D \geq C$ | | 175. 4 |

## Level of Difficulty (II)

| | | | |
|---|---|---|---|
| 1. (a) | 2. (b) | 3. (c) | 4. (c) |
| 5. (b) | 6. (b) | 7. (b) | 8. (d) |
| 9. (c) | 10. (c) | 11. (d) | 12. (b) |
| 13. (d) | 14. (c) | 15. (b) | 16. (d) |
| 17. (a) | 18. (d) | 19. (c) | 20. (a) |
| 21. (a) | 22. (c) | 23. (b) | 24. (a) |
| 25. (d) | 26. (d) | 27. (c) | 28. (d) |
| 29. (b) | 30. (b) | 31. (a) | 32. (b) |
| 33. (a) | 34. (a) | 35. (b) | 36. (b) |
| 37. (a) | 38. (d) | 39. (c) | 40. (a) |
| 41. (24) | 42. (63) | 43. (24) | 44. (32) |
| 45. (27) | 46. (64) | 47. (13, 31) | 48. (23) |
| 49. (1056) | 50. (51, 34) | 51. (144, 864) | 52. (46,64) |
| 53. (63) | 54. (863) | 55. (36, 63) | |

56. may be 2 or 3 depending upon the numbers
57. $111^4 > 109.110.112.113 > 110.109.108.107$
58. greatest $\rightarrow$ 35 least 3/7
59. (a) $200^{300}$ (b) $5^{100}$ (c) $10^{20}$    60. (12, 3)

| | | | |
|---|---|---|---|
| 61. (c) | 62. (c) | 63. (b) | 64. (a) |
| 65. (d) | 66. (c) | 67. (b) | 68. (a) |
| 69. (a) | 70. (b) | 71. (c) | 72. (c) |
| 73. (d) | 74. (a) | 75. (b) | 76. (d) |
| 77. (a) | 78. (b) | 79. (b) | 80. (c) |
| 81. (b) | 82. (c) | 83. (d) | 84. (a) |
| 85. (c) | 86. (b) | 87. (d) | 88. (b) |
| 89. (d) | 90. (d) | 91. (a) | 92. (b) |
| 93. (c) | 94. (a) | 95. (a) | 96. (c) |
| 97. (b) | 98. (a) | 99. (a) | 100. (d) |
| 101. 9 | 102. 176 | 103. 0 | 104. 23 |
| 105. 1 | 106. 37 | 107. 10 | 108. 9 |
| 109. 8 | 110. 4 | 111. 12 | 112. 45 |
| 113. .360 | 114. 4 | 115. 997 | 116. 01 |
| 117. 0 | 118. 30 | 119. 6 | 120. (d) |
| 121. 4312 | 122. (c) | 123. 296 | 124. 295 |
| 125. 4 | 126. 8 | 127. 209 | 128. 208 |
| 129. (c) | 130. 0 | 131. 1 | 132. 90 |
| 133. (c) | 134. (c) | 135. (a) | |

## Level of Difficulty (III)

| | | | |
|---|---|---|---|
| 1. (a) | 2. (b) | 3. (b) | 4. (a) |
| 5. (b) | 6. (b) | 7. (b) | 8. (d) |
| 9. (d) | 10. (a) | 11. (c) | 12. (a) |
| 13. (d) | 14. (b) | 15. (d) | 16. (d) |
| 17. (b) | 18. (b) | 19. (b) | 20. (d) |

| | | | |
|---|---|---|---|
| 21. (b) | 22. (d) | 23. (a) | 24. (c) |
| 25. (a) | 26. (a) | 27. (d) | 28. (d) |
| 29. (d) | 30. (a) | 31. (d) | 32. (c) |
| 33. (c) | 34. (a) | 35. (a) | 36. (c) |
| 37. (a) | 38. (a) | 39. (a) | 40. (d) |
| 41. (a) | 42. (d) | 43. (c) | 44. (b) |
| 45. (d) | 46. (a) | 47. (a) | 48. (c) |
| 49. (c) | 50. (c) | 51. (a) | 52. (b) |
| 53. (d) | 54. (a) | 55. (c) | 56. (a) |
| 57. (b) | 58. (d) | 59. (d) | 60. (d) |
| 61. (b) | 62. 777 | 63. 1296 | 64. 1 |
| 65. 34 | 66. $3^3 \times 5^2 \times 7^2 \times 11 \times 13$ | 67. 1 | |
| 68. 9723 | 69. 17.9! | 70. 6 | 71. 601 |
| 72. 25 | 73. 99 | 74. (b) | 75. 14 |
| 76. (d) | 77. 436 | 78. 14 | 79. (c) |
| 80. 2 | 81. (c) | | |

## Solutions and Shortcuts

### Level of Difficulty (I)

1. The units digit in this case would obviously be '0' because the given expression has a pair of 2 and 5 in it's prime factors.

2. When you read the sentence "when the digits are reversed, the number decreases by 54, you should automatically get two reactions going in your mind.
   (i) The difference between the digits would be $54/9 = 6$.
   (ii) Since the number 'decreases'- the tens digit of the number would be larger than the units digit.
   Also, since we know that the sum of the digits is 10, we get that the digits must be 8 and 2 and the number must be 82. Thus, the changed number is 28.

3. The two numbers should be factors of 405. A factor search will yield the factors. (look only for 2 digit factors of 405 with sum of digits between 1 to 19).
   Also $405 = 5 \times 3^4$. Hence: $15 \times 27$
   $45 \times 9$ are the only two options.
   From these factors pairs only the second pair gives us the desired result.
   i.e. Number × sum of digits = 405.
   Hence, the answer is 45.

4. You can solve this question by using options. It can be seen that Option (b) 12,3 fits the situation perfectly as their Arithmetic mean = 7.5 and their geometric mean = 6 and the geometric mean is 20% less than the arithmetic mean

5. Two more than half of $1/3^{rd}$ of 96 = 18. Also since we are given that the difference between the AM and GM is 18, it means that the GM must be an integer. From amongst the options, only option (a) gives us a GM which is an integer. Thus, checking for option 1, we get the GM = 7 and AM = 25.

6. For the number A381 to be divisible by 11, the sum of the even placed digits and the odds placed digits should be either 0 or a multiple of 11. This means that $(A + 8) - (3 + 1)$ should be a multiple of 11 – as it is not possible to make it zero. Thus, the smallest value that $A$ can take (and in fact the only value it can take) is 7. Option (c) is correct.

7. For 381A to be divisible by 9, the sum of the digits $3 + 8 + 1 + A$ should be divisible by 9. For that to happen $A$ should be 6. Option (d) is correct.

8. $9^6$ when divided by 8, would give a remainder of 1. Hence, the required answer would be 2.

9. LCM of 5, 15 and 20 = 60. HCF of 5, 15 and 20 = 5. The required ratio is 60:5 = 12:1

10. LCM of 5/2, 8/9 and 11/14 would be given by: (LCM of numerators)/(HCF of denominators)
    = 440/1 = 440

11. Only the first option can be verified to be true in this case. If $A$ is even, 3A would always be divisible by 6 as it would be divisible by both 2 and 3. Options b and c can be seen to be incorrect by assuming the value of $A$ as 4.

12. The essence of this question is in the fact that the last digit of the number is 0. Naturally, the number is necessarily divisible by 2,5 and 10. Only 4 does not necessarily divide it.

13. $B$ would necessarily be even- as the possible values of $B$ for the three digit number 15B to be divisible by 6 are 0 and 6. Also, the condition stated in option (c) is also seen to be true in this case — as both 0 and 6 are divisible by 6. Thus, option (d) is correct.

14. For the GCD take the least powers of all common prime factors.
    Thus, the required answer would be $2^3 \times 3$

15. The units digit would be given by $5 + 6 + 9$ (numbers ending in 5 and 6 would always end in 5 and 6 irrespective of the power and $3^{54}$ will give a units digit equivalent to $3^{4n+2}$ which would give us a unit digit of $3^2$ i.e.9).

16. The respective units digits for the three parts of the expression would be:
    $5 + 9 + 2 = 16 \rightarrow$ required answer is 6. Option (c) is correct.

17. The respective units digits for the six parts of the expression would be:
    $1 + 4 + 7 + 6 + 5 + 6 = 29 \rightarrow$ required answer is 9. Option (b) is correct.

18. The respective units digits for the six parts of the expression would be:
    $1 \times 4 \times 7 \times 6 \times 5 \times 6 \rightarrow$ required answer is 0. Option (d) is correct.

19. The number of zeroes would be given by adding the quotients when we successively divide 1090 by 5:

1090/5 + 218/5 + 43/5 + 8/5 = 218 + 43 + 8 + 1 = 270. Option (a) is correct.

20. The number of 5's in 146! can be got by [146/5] + [29/5] + [5/5]= 29+5+1 = 35

21. $1420 = 142 \times 10 = 2^2 \times 71^1 \times 5^1$.

    Thus, the number of factors of the number would be $(2 + 1)(1 + 1)(1 + 1) = 3 \times 2 \times 2 = 12$.

    Option (d) is correct.

22. $(x^2 - 5x + 6) = (x - 2)(x - 3)$

    & $(x^2 - 7x + 10) = (x - 5)(x - 2)$

    Required HCF = $(x - 2)$; required LCM = $(x - 2)(x - 3)(x - 5)$.

    Option (a) is correct.

23. Since both $P$ and $Q$ are prime numbers, the number of factors would be $(1 + 1)(1 + 1) = 4$.

24. Since both $P$ and $Q$ are prime numbers, the number of factors would be $(2 + 1)(1 + 1) = 6$.

25. Since both $P$ and $Q$ are prime numbers, the number of factors would be $(3 + 1)(2 + 1) = 12$.

26. The sides of the pentagon being 1422, 1737, 2160, 2214 and 2358, the least difference between any two numbers is 54. Hence, the correct answer will be a factor of 54.

    Further, since there are some odd numbers in the list, the answer should be an odd factor of 54.

    Hence, check with 27, 9 and 3 in that order. You will get 9 as the HCF.

27. The HCF of 576 and 448 is 64. Hence, each section should have 64 children. The number of sections would be given by: 576/64 + 448/64= 9 + 7 = 16. Option (c) is correct.

28. The HCF of the given numbers is 31 and hence the number of bottles required would be

    403/31 + 465/31 + 496/31 = 13 + 15 + 16 = 44. Option (d) is correct.

29. The LCM of the 4 numbers is 612. The highest 4 digit number which would be a common multiple of all these 4 numbers is 9792. Hence, the correct answer is 9793.

30. The LCM of 16, 18 and 20 is 720. The numbers which would give a remainder of 4, when divided by 16, 18 and 20 would be given by the series:

    724, 1444, 2164, 2884 and so on. Checking each of these numbers for divisibility by 7, it can be seen that 2884 is the least number in the series that is divisible by 7 and hence is the correct answer. Option (d) is correct.

31. They will ring together again after a time which would be the LCM of 6, 8, 12 and 18. The required LCM = 72. Hence, they would ring together after 72 seconds. Option (a) is correct.

32. 720/72 = 10 times. Option (b) is correct.

33. $5 \times 7 \times 6 = 0$. Option (c) is correct.

34. All these numbers can be verified to not be perfect squares. Option (d) is correct.

35. A perfect square can never end in an odd number of zeroes. Option (c) is correct.

36. It is obvious that the LCM of 5,8,12 and 20 would never be a multiple of 9. At the same time it has to be a multiple of each of 3, 8 and 5. Option (b) is correct.

37. $720 = 2^4 \times 3^2 \times 5^1$. Number of factors = $5 \times 3 \times 2$ = 30. Option (d) is correct.

38. $16 - x^2 = (4 - x)(4 + x)$ and $x^2 + x - 6 = (x + 3)(x - 2)$

    The required LCM = $(4 - x)(4 + x)(x + 3)(x - 2)$. Option (d) is correct.

39. $x^2 - 4 = (x - 2)(x + 2)$ and $x^2 + x - 6 = (x + 3)(x - 2)$

    GCD or HCF of these expressions = $(x - 2)$.

    Option (b) is correct.

40. If A is not divisible by 3, it is obvious that 2A would also not be divisible by 3, as 2A would have no '3' in it.

41. $9^{100}/8 = (8 + 1)^{100}/8 \rightarrow$ Since this is of the form $(a + 1)^n/a$, the Remainder = 1. Option (a) is correct.

42. $2^{1000}/3$ is of the form $(a)^{EVEN\ POWER}/(a + 1)$. The remainder = 1 in this case as the power is even. Option (a) is correct.

43. The condition for the product to be the greatest is if the two terms are equal. Thus, the break up in option (a) would give us the highest product of the two parts. Option (a) is correct.

44. 50/5 =10, 10/5 =2.

    Thus, the required answer would be 10 + 2 = 12. Option (d) is correct.

45. Checking each of the options it can be seen that the value in option (c)[viz: 1362480]is divisible by 24.

46. Any number divisible by 88, has to be necessarily divisible by 11, 2, 4, 8, 44 and 22. Thus, each of the first three options is correct.

47. $10800 = 108 \times 100 = 3^3 \times 2^4 \times 5^2$.

    The number of divisors would be: $(3 + 1)(4 + 1)(2 + 1) = 4 \times 5 \times 3 = 60$ divisors. Option (b) is correct.

48. The GCD (also known as HCF) would be got by multiplying the least powers of all common factors of the two polynomials. The common factors are $(x + 3)$ – least power 1, and $(x + 1)$ – least power 2. Thus, the answer would be $(x + 3)(x + 1)^2$. Option (c) is correct.

49. For the LCM of polynomials write down the highest powers of all available factors of all the polynomials. The correct answer would be $2(x + 3)^2(6x^2 + 5x + 4)(x + 1/2)$.

50. Three consecutive natural numbers, starting with an even number would always have at least three 2's as their prime factors and also would have at least

one multiple of 3 in them. Thus, 6, 12 and 24 would each divide the product.

51. When the birds sat one on a branch, there was one extra bird. When they sat 2 to a branch one branch was extra.

    To find the number of branches, go through options. Checking option (a), if there were 3 branches, there would be 4 birds. (this would leave one bird without branch as per the question.)

    When 4 birds would sit 2 to a branch there would be 1 branch free (as per the question). Hence, the answer (a) is correct.

52. The number would either be $(3n + 1)^2$ or $(3n + 2)^2$. In the expansion of each of these the only term which would not be divisible by 3 would be the square of 1 and 2 respectively. When divided by 3, both of these give 1 as remainder.

53. The given expression can be written as:
    $5^3 \times 3^3 \times 3^2 \times 7^2/5^2 \times 7^2 \times 3^4 = 5^3 \times 3^5 \times 7^2/5^2 \times 7^2 \times 3^4 = 15$. Option (b) is correct.

54. $D = 1.44$, $C = 0.09$, $B = 0.16$, while the value of $A$ is negative.

    Thus, $D > B > C > A$ is the required order. Option (c) is correct.

55. The upper limit for $x + y = 4 + 3 = 7$. The lower limit of $x - y = 2 - 3 = -1$. Required ratio = 7/–1 = –7.

    Option (d) is correct.

56. For the sum of squares of digits to be 13, it is obvious that the digits should be 2 and 3. So the number can only be 23 or 32. Further, the number being referred to has to be 32 since the reduction of 9, reverses the digits.

57. trying the value in the options you get that the product of $54 \times 45 = 2430$. Option (a) is correct.

58. Option (b) can be verified to be true as the LCM of 90 and 24 is indeed 360.

59. The pairs given in option (d) 78 and 13 and 26 and 39 meet both the conditions of LCM of 78 and HCF of 13. Option (d) is correct.

60. Solve using options. Option (d) 51 and 34 satisfies the required conditions.

61. $28^2 - 27^2 = 55$ and so also $8^2 - 3^2 = 55$. Option (a) is correct.

62. (a) $21^{12} = (21^3)^4$
    Since $21^3 > 54$, $21^{12} > 54^4$.
    (b) $(0.4)^4 = (4/10)^4 = 1024/10000 = 0.1024$.
    $(0.8)^3 = (8/10)^3 = 512/1000 = 0.512$.
    Hence, $(0.8)^3 > (0.4)^4$.

63. This is never possible.

64. 1. $c = 0, 2, 4, 6$ or 8 would make $38c$ as even and hence divisible by 2.
    2. $c = 1, 4$ or 7 are possible values to make $38c$ divisible by 3.

3. $c = 0, 4$ or 8 would make the number end in 80, 84 or 88 and would hence be divisible by 4.

4. $c = 0$ or 5 would make the number 380 or 385 – in which case it would be divisible by 5.

5. For the number to become divisible by 6, it should be even and divisible by 3. From the values 1, 4 and 7 which make the number divisible by 3, we only have $c = 4$ making it even. Thus, $c = 4$.

6. For the number to be divisible by 9, $3 + 8 + c$ should be a multiple of 9. $c = 7$ is the only value of $c$ which can make the number divisible by 9.

7. Obviously $c = 0$ is the correct answer.

65. Use the standard process to solve for LCM and HCF.

66. For $34x^{43}$ to be ending in 7, $x$ has to be 3 (as $43 = 4n + 3$). Option (b) is correct.

**Solutions for 67 & 68:**

The given condition says that Pen<Pencil<Eraser.

Also, since the least cost of the three is ₹12, if we allocate a minimum of 12 to each we use up 36 out of the 41 available. The remaining 5 can be distributed as 0,1,4 or 0,2 and 3 giving possible values of Case 1: 12,13 and 16 or Case 2: 12,14 and 15.

67. In both cases, the cost of the pen is 12.

68. If the cost of the eraser is not divisible by 4, it means that Case 2 holds true. For this case, the cost of the pencil is 14.

69. Amrit would place eight oranges in the basket (as there are eight 1's).

    For the mangoes, he would place six mangoes (number of 2's) and remove four mangoes (number of 4's) from the basket. Thus, there would be 2 mangoes and 8 oranges in the basket.

    A total of $8 - 2 = 6$ extra oranges in the basket. Option (c) is correct.

70. Solve using trial and error – Option (c) fits the situation as if we start with 15 mangoes, the following structure would take place:

    Start with 15 mangoes → First watchman takes 1/3rd + 1 more = 5 + 1 = 6 mangoes → 9 mangoes left.
    Second watchman takes → 1/3rd + 1 more = 3 + 1 = 4 mangoes → 5 mangoes left.
    Third watchman takes → 1/5th + 4 more = 1 + 4 = 5 mangoes → 0 mangoes left.

71. The last 3 digits of the number would determine the remainder when it is divided by 8. The number upto the 120th digit would be 1234567891011… 646. 646 divided by 8 gives us a remainder of 6.

72. There would be multiple ways of scoring 34.5 marks. Think about this as follows:

    If he solves 80 and gets all 80 correct, he would end up scoring 80 marks.

With every question that would go wrong his score would fall down by: 1.5 marks (he would lose the 1 mark he is gaining and further attract a penalty of 0.5 marks).

Also, for every question he does not attempt his score would fall down by: 1.25 marks (he would lose the 1 mark he is gaining and further attract a penalty of 0.25 marks).

Thus, his score would drop @ 1.5 and @1.25 marks for every wrong and every unattempted question respectively.

Also, to get a total of 34.5 marks overall he has to lose 45.5 marks.

There are many possible combinations of non attempts and wrongs through which he can possibly lose 45.5 marks—for example:

17 wrongs (loses 25.5 marks) and 16 non-attempts (loses 20 marks)

12 wrongs (loses 18 marks) and 22 non attempts (loses 27.5 marks)

Hence, we cannot answer this question uniquely and the answer is Option (d).

73. Continuing the thought process for the previous question our thinking would go as follows:

10 questions unanswered → loses 12.5 marks

To lose another 33 marks he needs to get 22 incorrects.

Thus, the number of corrects would be $80 - 10 - 22 = 48$. Option (b) is correct.

74. $3M + 4G + 5W = 750$       (i)

$6M + 9G + 10W = 1580$     (ii)

Adding the two equations we get:

$9M + 13G + 15W = 2330$    (iii)

Dividing this expression by 3 we get:

$3M + 4.33G + 5W = 776.666$   (iv)

(iv) - (i) → $0.33 G = 26.666$ → $G = 80$

Now, if we look at the equation (i) and multiply it by 2, we get: $6M + 8G + 10W = 1500$. If we subtract the cost of 4 guavas from this we would get:

$6M + 4G + 10W = 1500 - 320 = 1180$

Option (b) is correct.

75. If you try a value of $M$ as 5, $N$ would become ¼. It can be seen that $5^{1/4}$ (which would be the value of $M^N$) would be around 1.4 and hence, less than 2.

If you try for possible values of $M^N$ by increasing the value of $M$, you would get $6^{1/5}$, $7^{1/6}$, $8^{1/7}$, $9^{1/8}$ and so on. In each of these cases you can clearly see that the value of $M^N$ would always be getting consecutively smaller than the previous value.

If you tried to go for values of $M$ such that they are lower than 5, you would get the following values for $M^N$:

$4^{1/3}$, $3^{1/2}$ and the last value would be $2^{1/1}$. In this case, we can clearly see that the value of the expression

$M^N$ is increasing. However, it ends at the value of 2 (for $2^{1/1}$) and hence that is the maximum value that $M^N$ can take. Option (a) is correct.

76. $(7M + 9G + 19W) - (4M + 6G + 16W) = 120$. Hence, $1M + 1G + 1W = 40$

77. The cost of a mango cannot be uniquely determined here because we have only 2 equations between 3 variables, and there is no way to eliminate one variable.

78. Since the value of $y$ varies between –8 to 2, it is evident that if we take a very small value for $y$, say 0.00000000000000000000001, and we take normal integral values for $x$ and $z$, the expression $xz/y$ would become either positive or negative infinity (depending on how you manage the signs of the numbers $x$, $y$ and $z$).

79. Ties < Trousers < Shirts. Since each of the three is minimum 11, the total would be a minimum of 33 (for all 3). The remaining 5 need to be distributed amongst ties, trousers and shirts so that they can maintain the inequality Ties < Trousers < Shirts

This can be achieved with 11 ties, and the remaining 27 pieces of clothing distributed between trousers and shirts such that the shirts are greater than the trousers.

This can be done in at least 2 ways: 12 trousers and 15 shirts; 13 trousers and 14 shirts.

If you try to go for 12 ties, the remaining 26 pieces of clothing need to be distributed amongst shirts and trousers such that the shirts are greater than the trousers and both are greater than 12.

With only 26 pieces of clothing to be distributed between shirts and trousers this is not possible. Hence, the number of ties has to be exactly 11. Option (a) is correct.

80. The number of shirts would be at least 14 as the two distributions possible are: 11, 12, 15 and 11, 13, 14. Option (b) is correct.

81. The LCM of 12, 15, 18 and 20 is 180. Thus, the least number would be 184.

Option (c) is correct.

82. $2800 = 20 \times 20 \times 7$. Thus, we need to multiply or divide with 7 in order to make it a perfect square.

83. The answer is given by $\sqrt{1024} = 32$.

This can be experimentally verified as $30^2 = 900$, $31^2 = 961$ and $32^2 = 1024$. Hence, 1024 is the required answer. Option (c) is correct.

84. First find the LCM of 6, 9, 15 and 18. Their LCM $= 18 \times 5 = 90$.

The series of numbers which would leave a remainder of 4 when divided by 6, 9, 15 and 18 would be given by:

LCM + 4; 2 × LCM + 4; 3 × LCM + 4; 4 × LCM + 4; 5 × LCM + 4 and so on .

Thus, this series would be:

94, 184, 274, 364, 454....

The other constraint in the problem is to find a number which also has the property of being divisible by 7. Checking each of the numbers in the series above for their divisibility by 7, we see that 364 is the least value which is also divisible by 7. Option (c) is correct.

85. LCM of 2, 3, 4, 5 and $6 = 6 \times 5 \times 2 = 60$ (Refer to the shortcut process for LCM given in the chapter notes).

Thus, the series 61, 121, 181 etc would give us a remainder 1 when divided by 2, 3, 4, 5 and 6.

The least 3 digit number in this series is 121. Option (c) is correct.

86. $70 = 2 \times 5 \times 7$; $245 = 5 \times 7 \times 7$.

HCF $= 5 \times 7 = 35$. Option (a) is correct.

87. 7056 is the closest perfect square below 7147. Hence, $7147 - 7056 = 91$ is the required answer. Option (c) is correct.

88. The LCM of 6, 8 and 15 is $120 = 2^3 \times 3 \times 5$. For a number to be a perfect square, all the prime factors should have even powers. Thus, if we multiply the above number by $2 \times 3 \times 5 = 30$, we will get the required smallest perfect square. Thus, the correct answer is $120 \times 30 = 3600$.

89. $30492 = 2^2 \times 3^2 \times 7^1 \times 11^2$.

For a number to be a perfect square each of the prime factors in the standard form of the number needs to be raised to an even power. Thus, we need to multiply or divide the number by 7 so that we either make it: $2^2 \times 3^2 \times 7^2 \times 11^2$ (if we multiply the number by 7) or

We make it: $2^2 \times 3^2 \times 11^2$. (if we divide the number by 7).

Option (b) is correct.

90. $88 \times 113 = 9944$ is the greatest 4 digit number exactly divisible by 88. Option (c) is correct.

91. $3/4^{th}$ of $116 = \frac{3}{4} \times 116 = 87$

$4/5^{th}$ of $45 = 4/5 \times 45 = 36$.

Required difference $= 51$.

Option (d) is correct.

92. The correct arrangement would be 75 plants in a row and 75 rows since 5625 is the square of 75.

93. $9^{EVEN POWER} \times 7^{4n+1} \to 1 \times 7 = 7$ as the units digit of the multiplication.

Option (a) is correct.

94. It can be seen that for 40 and 80 the number of factors are 8 and 10 respectively. Thus option (c) satisfies the condition.

95. In order to solve this question you need to realize that remainders of 1, 3, 4 and 5 in the case of 3, 5, 6 and 7, respectively, means remainders of –2 in each case.

In order to find the number which leaves remainder –2 when divided by these numbers you need to first find the LCM of 3, 5, 6 and 7 and subtract 2 from them. Since the LCM is 210, the first such number which satisfies this condition is 208. However, the question has asked us to find the largest such number below 4000. So you need to look at multiples of the LCM and subtract 2. The required number is 3990 $- 2 = 3988$

96. The number would be given by the (LCM of 2, 3 and 4) $+1 \to$ which is $12 + 1 = 13$. Option (b) is correct.

97. The number would be given by the $2 \times$ (LCM of 2, 3 and 4) $+1 \to$ which is $24 + 1 = 25$. Option (a) is correct.

98. In order to solve this you need to find the last 2 digit number in the series got by the logic:

(LCM of 2, 3, 4) + 1; $2 \times$ (LCM of 2, 3, 4) + 1; $3 \times$ (LCM of 2, 3, 4) + 1 ...

i.e. you need to find the last 2 digit number in the series:

13, 25, 37, 49....

In order to do so, you can do one of the following:

(a) Complete the series by writing the next numbers as:

61, 73, 85, 97 to see that 97 is the required answer.

(b) Complete the series by adding a larger multiple of 12 so that you reach closer to 100 faster.

Thus, if you have seen 13, 25, 37,,,,,, you can straightaway add any multiple of 12 to get a number close to 100 in the series in one jump.

Thus, if you were to add $12 \times 4 = 48$ to 37 you would reach a value of 85 (and because you have added a multiple of 12 to 37 you can be sure that 85 would also be on the same series.)

Thus, the thinking in this case would go as follows: 13, 25, 37, ..., 85, 97. Hence, the number is 97.

If you look at the two processes above- it would seem that there is not much difference between the two, but the real difference would be seen and felt if you would try to solve a question which might have asked you to find the last 3 digit number in the series. (as you would see in the next question). In such a case, getting to the number would be much faster if you use a multiple of 12 to jump ahead on the series rather than writing each number one by one.

(c) For the third way of solving this, you can see that all the numbers in the series:

13, 25, 37... are of the form $12n + 1$. Thus, you are required to find a number which is of the form $12n + 1$ and is just below 100.

For this purpose, you can try to first see what is the remainder when 100 is divided by 12.

Since the remainder is 4, you can realize that the number 100 is a number of the form $12n + 4$.

Obviously then, if 100 is of the form $12n + 4$, the largest $12n + 1$ number just below 100 would occur at a value which would be 3 less than 100. (This occurs because the distance between $12n + 4$ and $12n + 1$ on the number line is 3.)

Thus the answer is $100 - 3 = 97$.

Hence, Option (c) is correct.

99. In order to solve this you need to find the last 3 digit number in the series got by the logic:

(LCM of 2, 3, 4) +1; $2 \times$ (LCM of 2, 3, 4) +1; $3 \times$ (LCM of 2, 3, 4) + 1 …

i.e., you need to find the last 3 digit number in the series:

13, 25, 37, 49….

In order to do so, you can do one of the following:

(a) Try to complete the series by writing the next numbers as:

61, 73, 85, 97, 109… However, you can easily see that this process would be unnecessarily too long and hence infeasible to solve this question.

(b) Complete the series by adding a larger multiple of 12 so that you reach closer to 1000 faster.

This is what we were hinting at in the previous question. If we use a multiple of 12 to write a number which will come later in the series, then we can reach close to 1000 in a few steps. Some of the ways of doing this are shown below:

(i) 13, 25, 37, …….. 997 (we add $12 \times 80 = 960$ to 37 to get to $37 + 960 = 997$ which can be seen as the last 3 digit number as the next number would cross 1000).

(ii) 13, 25, 37, …… (add 600)….637, …(add 120)… 757,,,,, (add 120),,,, 877, ….(add 120)….**997**. This is the required answer.

(iii) 13, 25, 37, ……(add 120)….157, …(add 120)…277……(add 120)…..397….(add 120)……517…. (add 120)…637……(add 120)…757,,,,, (add 120),,,, 877, ….(add 120)….**997**. This is the required answer.

What you need to notice is that all the processes shown above are correct. So while one of them might be more efficient than the other, as far as you ensure that you add a number which is a multiple of 12(the common difference) you would always be correct.

(c) Of course you can also do this by using remainders. For this, you can see that all the numbers in the series:

13, 25, 37….are of the form $12n + 1$. Thus, you are required to find a number which is of the form $12n + 1$ and is just below 1000.

For this purpose, you can try to first see what is the remainder when 1000 is divided by 12.

Since the remainder is 4, you can realize that the number 1000 is a number of the form $12n + 4$.

Obviously then, if 1000 is of the form $12n + 4$, the largest $12n + 1$ number just below 1000 would occur at a value which would be 3 less than 1000. (This occurs because the distance between $12n + 4$ and $12n + 1$ on the number line is 3.)

Thus the answer is $1000 - 3 = 997$.

Hence, Option (c) is correct.

100. The logic of this question is that the frog can never reach point $C$ if it makes an odd number of jumps. Since, the question has asked us to find out in how many ways can the frog reach point $C$ in exactly 7 jumps, the answer would naturally be 0. Option (d) is correct.

101. They would ring together again after a time interval which would be the LCM of 5, 6 and 7. Since the LCM is 210, option (d) is the correct answer.

102. Since they would ring together every 210 seconds, their ringing together would happen at time intervals denoted by the following series- 210, 420, 630, 840, 1050, 1260, 1470, 1680, 1890, 2100, 2310, 2520, 2730, 2940, 3150, 3360, 3570 – a total of 17 times. This answer can also be calculated by taking the quotient of $3600/210 = 17$. Option (a) is correct.

103. The maximum number of soldiers would be given by the HCF of 66, 110 and 242. The HCF of these numbers can be found to be 22 and hence, option (c) is correct.

104. The minimum number of rows would happen when the number of soldiers in each row is the maximum. Since, the HCF is 22 the number of soldiers in each row is 22. Then the total number of rows would be given by:

$66/22 + 110/22 + 242/22 = 3 + 5 + 11 = 19$ rows. Option (b) is correct.

105. The Number of bottle sizes possible would be given by the number of factors of the HCF of 170, 102 and 374. Since, the HCF of these numbers is 34, the bottle sizes that are possible would be the divisors of 34 which are 1 litre, 2 litres, 17 litres and 34 litres, respectively. Thus, a total of 4 bottle sizes are possible. Option (c) is correct.

106. The size of the largest bottle that can be used is obviously 34 litres (HCF of 170, 102 and 374). Option (d) is correct.

107. The minimum number of bottles required would be: $170/34 + 102/34 + 374/34 = 5 + 3 + 11 = 19$. Option (b) is correct.

108. The answer would be given by the quotients of $100/5 + 100/25 = 20 + 4 = 24$. Option (c) is correct.

The logic of how to think about Questions 108 to 118 has been given in the theory in the chapter. Please have a relook at that in case you have doubts about any of the solutions till Question 118.

109. $24 + 4 = 28$. Option (d) is correct.

110. $280 + 56 + 11 + 2 = 349$. Option (c) is correct.

111. $76 + 15 + 3 = 94$. Option (c) is correct.

112. $14 + 2 = 16$. Option (c) is correct.

113. $13 + 4 + 1 = 18$. Option (a) is correct.

114. $17 + 5 + 1 = 23$. Option (c) is correct.

115. $11 + 1 = 12$. Option (a) is correct.

116. $16 + 2 = 18$. Option (d) is correct.

117. The number of 3's in $122! = 40 + 13 + 4 + 1 = 58$. The number of 2's in $122! = 61 + 30 + 15 + 7 + 3 + 1 = 117$. The number of $2^2$s is hence equal to the quotient of $117/2 = 58$. We have to choose the lower one between 58 and 58. Since both are equal, 58 would be the correct answer. Hence, Option (d) is correct.

118. The power of 20 which would divide 155! would be given by the power of 5's which would divide 155! since $20 = 2^2 \times 5$ and the number of $2^2$s in any factorial would always be greater than the number of 5s in the factorial. $31 + 6 + 1 = 38$. Option (b) is correct.

119. $1024 = 2^{10}$. Hence, $x$ has to be a number with power of 2 greater than or equal to 5. Since, we are asked for the minimum value, it must be 5. Thus, option (b) is correct.

120. The two digit numbers that would leave a remainder of 3 when divided by 7 would be the numbers 10, 17, 24, 31, 38, 45, ...94. The sum of these numbers would be given by the formula (number of numbers × average of the numbers) = There are 13 numbers in the series and their average is 52. Thus, the required answer is $13 \times 52 = 676$. Option (c) is correct.

(Note the logic used here is that of sum of an Arithmetic Progression and is explained in details in the next chapter).

121. All numbers divisible by 27 would also be divisible by 3 and 9. Numbers divisible by 9 but not by 27 would be divisible by 3 and 9 only and need to be counted to give us our answer.

The numbers which satisfy the given condition are: 9, 18, 36, 45, 63, 72, 90, 99, 117, 126, 144, 153, 171, 180 and 198. There are 15 such numbers.

Alternately, you could also think of this as:

Between 1 to 200 there are 22 multiples of 9. But not all these 22 have to be counted as multiples of 27 need to be excluded from the count. There are 7 multiples of 27 between 1 and 200. Thus, the answer would be given by $22 - 7 = 15$. Option (b) is correct.

122. The required minimum happens when we use (–0.5) as the value of $N$. $(-0.5)^2 + (-0.5) = 0.25 - 0.5 = -0.25$ is the least possible value for the sum of any number and it's square. Option (b) is correct.

123. Each of the statements are false as we can have the sum of 2 prime numbers ending in 5, 0 and the sum can also be odd. Option (d) is correct.

124. This occurs for values such as: $213 - 123$; $324 - 234$ etc where it can be seen that the value of $X$ is 1 more than $Y$. The possible pairs of $X$ and $Y$ are: 2,1;3,2...9,8 – a total of eight pairs of values. Option (b) is correct.

125. The required sum would be given by the formula $n(n + 1)$ for the first $n$ even numbers. In this case it would be $50 \times 51 = 2550$. Option (d) is correct.

126. 763/57 leaves a remainder of 22 when it is divided by 57. Thus, if we were to add 35 to this number the number we obtain would be completely divisible by 57. Option (a) is correct.

127. Since, 763/57 leaves a remainder of 22, we would need to subtract 22 from 763 in order to get a number divisible by 57. Option (b) is correct.

128. 8441/57 leaves a remainder of 5. Thus, if we were to add 52 to this number the number we obtain would be completely divisible by 57. Option (d) is correct.

129. Since, 8441/57 leaves a remainder of 5. We would need to subtract 5 from 8441 in order to get a number divisible by 57. Option (c) is correct.

130. 10000 divided by 79 leaves a remainder of 46. Hence, if we were to add 33 to 10000 we would get a number divisible by 79. The correct answer is 10033. Option (b) is correct.

131. 100000 divided by 79 leaves a remainder of 65. Hence, if we were to subtract 65 from 100000 we would get a number divisible by 79. The correct answer is 99935. Option (b) is correct.

132. It can be seen that in the multiples of 12, the number closest to 773 is 768. Option (a) is correct.

133. Since 12 is a divisor of 84, the required remainder would be got by dividing 57 by 12. The required answer is 9. Option (c) is correct.

134. Since 11 does not divide 84, there are many possible answers for this question and hence we cannot determine one unique value for the answer. Option (d) is thus correct.

135. The numbers that can do so are going to be factors of the difference between 511 and 667 i.e. 156. The factors of 156 are 1,2,3,4,6, 12,13, 26, 39, 52,78,156. There are 12 such numbers. Option (b) is correct.

136. The multiples of 13 between 200 and 400 would be represented by the series:

208, 221, 234, 247, 260, 273, 286, 299, 312, 325, 338, 351, 364, 377 and 390

There are a total of 15 numbers in the above series. Option (b) is correct.

*Note:* The above series is an Arithmetic Progression. The process of finding the number of terms in an Arithmetic Progression are defined in the chapter on Progressions.

137. $8n/5 - 5n/8 = 39n/40 = 39$. Solve for $n$ to get the value of $n = 40$. Option (c) is correct.

138. $x + y = 3(x - y) \rightarrow 2x = 4y$. If we take $y$ as 10, we would get the value of $x$ as 20. Option (b) is correct.

139. $4^{11} + 4^{12} + 4^{13} + 4^{14} + 4^{15} = 4^{11} (1 + 4^1 + 4^2 + 4^3 + 4^4) = 4^{11} \times 341$. The factors of 341 are:

1, 11, 31 and 341. Thus, we can see that the values in each of the three options would divide the expression. $4^{11} + 4^{12} + 4^{13} + 4^{14} + 4^{15}$. Thus, option (d) is correct.

140. Since the numbers have their HCF as 16, both the numbers have to be multiples of 16 (i.e. $2^4$).

$$7168 = 2^{10} \times 7^1$$

In order to visualise the required possible pairs of numbers we need to look at the prime factors of 7168 in the following fashion:

$7168 = 2^{10} \times 7^1 = (2^4 \times 2^4) \times 2^2 \times 7^1 = (16 \times 16) \times 2 \times 2 \times 7$ It is then a matter of distributing the 2 extra twos and the 1 extra seven in $2^2 \times 7^1$ between the two numbers given by 16 and 16 inside the bracket. The possible pairs are:

$32 \times 224$; $64 \times 112$; $16 \times 448$. Thus there are 3 distinct pairs of numbers which are multiples of 16 and whose product is 7168. However, out of these the pair $32 \times 224$ has it's HCF as 32 and hence does not satisfy the given conditions. Thus there are two pairs of numbers that would satisfy the condition that their HCF is 16 and their product is 7168. Option (a) is correct.

141. $876 + 2P3 = 10Q9$,

It is clear that there is no carry over obtained in the addition of the unit's digit, while the sum of hundredth digit of the numbers is same as the hundredths digit of the sum. It means $7 + P = Q$.

$10Q9$ is divisible by 11, so $(9 + 0) - (1 + Q) = 11n$, where $n = 0, 1, 2, 3, 4, \ldots$

$$Q = 8 \ \& \ P = Q - 7 = 1.$$

Therefore, $P - Q = 7$.

142. Since a number is divisible by 11 if the difference of the sum of digits in the odd places and sum of digits in the even places is 0 or divisible by 11. In the 22 digit number as described above, it is evident that there are 11 digits in the even place and 11 digits in the odd place. Since all the digits are equal, it means that the difference between these digits would be 0. Hence, the given numbers would be always divisible by 11.

143. $72 = 2^3 \times 3^2$

Total number of factors = $(3 + 1)(2 + 1) = 12$. This would mean that there are 6 pairs of factors, each of which pair would have a product of 72.

So the product of all the factors = $(72)^{\frac{12}{2}} = (72)^6$

144. $72 = 2^3 \times 3^2$

Total number of factors of 72 = $(3 + 1)(2 + 1) = 12$

Total number of ways of expressing 72 as a product of two factors = $\dfrac{12}{2} = 6$

145. $144 = 2^4 \times 3^2$

Total number of factors = $(4 + 1)(2 + 1) = 15$

Number of ways of expressing 144 as a product of two factors $= \dfrac{15+1}{2} = 8$

But the factors must be distinct so we exclude the $12 \times 12$ case.

So the correct answer = $8 - 1 = 7$

146. Let the number be $N$. According to the question:

$N = 7k + 3 = 11n + 4$ (where $k, l = 0, 1, 2, 3, 4, 5, \ldots$)

$$k = \frac{11n+1}{7}$$

Now put the minimum possible value of $n$ for which $k$ is an integer.

For $n = 5$, $k = 8$. So minimum possible value of $N = 7 \times 8 + 3 = 59$

Adding the LCM of 11 & 7 to 59 would get the next number. Thus, the next number would be $59 + 77 = 136$. Further numbers would be numbers belonging to the Arithmetic Progression, 136, 213, 290, .... 829, 906, 983. There are a total of 12 numbers which fulfill the given condition.

147. The HCF of $a^m - 1$, $a^n - 1 = a^{\text{HCF of } m,n} - 1$

The required HCF = $3^{\text{HCF of } 15,25} - 1 = 3^5 - 1 = 242$

148. The LCM must always be a multiple of the HCF. But here the LCM is not a multiple of the HCF, which is not possible. Hence, the correct answer would be that such a situation is not possible.

149. 10! Is contained in 15!, so the LCM of 10! & 15! is 15!. By the same logic their HCF is 10!.

150. $\dfrac{a^n}{a+1}$ leaves a remainder of 1, when n is even. Since 116! is an even number, so $\dfrac{18^{116!}}{19}$ leaves a remainder 1.

151. For $x = 1$, $y = 4$, $7x + y = 11$, which is a prime number. $x + y = 1 + 4 = 5$.

152. 1414 has 2 as a factor & 2015 has 5 as a factor so the unit's digit of the product must 0.

153. The Unit's digit of the product $1413 \times 729 \times 2015$ is 5. So if the product has 0 as its unit's digit then n must be either 0 or even. So 'n' may take maximum 5 values.

154. The given number is divisible by 10, 11.

    Remainder when we divide the number by 10 = $1^{12346} - 1 = 0$

    Remainder when we divide the number by 11 = $(-1)^{12346} - 1 = 1 - 1 = 0$

155. In the given expression, after 5! all the values would have a units' digit of 0. Thus, the units digit of the given expression just depends on the units' digit of $1! + 2! + 3! + 4!$

    $1! + 2! + 3! + 4! = 1 + 2 + 6 + 24 = 33$

    So unit's digit of $1! + 2! + 3! + 4! + 5! + \ldots + 1000! = 3$

156. 35! is perfectly divisible by 10. Then $(35!)^{35!}$ should also be divisible by 10. So unit's digit must be 0.

157. Number of zeroes at the end of $34! = [34/5] + [34/25] = 6 + 1 = 7$

    So number of zeroes at the end of $(34!)^{6!} = 7 \times 6! = 5040$.

158. $51!^{3^{11}}$ is divisible by 4 & unit's digit of $7^{4k}$ is 1. So unit's digit of $7^{51!^{3^{11}}}$ is 1.

159. $11^2 = 121$

    $111^2 = 12321$

    $1111^2 = 1234321$

    $11111^2 = 123454321$

    So $1234567654321 = (1111111)^2$

160. 421 is a prime number so $421 = 1 \times 421$. So HCF of the numbers is 1.

161. $3^{50} = (243)^{10}$, $4^{40} = (256)^{10}$, $5^{30} = (125)^{10}$, $6^{20} = (36)^{10}$,

    So $4^{40}$ is greatest of all.

162. A number is divisible by 8, if the number formed by the last three digits is divisible by 8. i.e 58N is divisible by $8 \Rightarrow N = 4$.

    Again a number is divisible by 11, if the difference between the sum of digits at even places and sum of digits at the odd places is either 0 or divisible by 11. i.e, $(M + 9 + 4 + 4 + 8) - (3 + 0 + 8 + 5 + N) = M - N + 9 = M + 5$ (since $N = 4$) It cannot be zero hence, $M + 5 = 11 \Rightarrow M = 6$.

    Hence $M*N = 24$.

163. We can check for the appearance of 4 in the units place, the tens place and the hundreds place separately. So, 4 in the units place would occur once in each number of the arithmetic series: 24,34,44,54,…494 → A total of 48 times. Further, 4 would appear once in each number of the series': 40,41,42,…49 (Thus, 10 times); Similarly, it would appear 10 times in the tens place in the 140s, the 240s, the 340s and the

440s. Thus a total of 50 appearances of 4, in the tens place. Also, 4 would appear in the hundreds' place exactly 100 times from 400 to 499. Thus, the correct answer would be: $48 + 50 + 100 = 198$.

164. Here, we want the remainder of $\dfrac{3671 + 3672 + 3673 + \ldots + 3685}{3670} \Rightarrow 1 + 2 + 3 + \ldots + 15 = 120$

165. 999999 is divisible by 7. It means 999999……99 ($6 \times 16$) times is divisible by 7.

    So the required remainder = Remainder of $\dfrac{999}{7} \Rightarrow 5$

166. We know that $A^{p-1} \div p$, leaves a remainder of 1, when $p$ is a prime number.

    Here 41 is a prime number. Hence, $\dfrac{2^{40}}{41}$ leaves a remainder 1. Thus, the remainder of $2^{41} \div 41$ would be equal to the remainder of $2^1 \div 41 \to 2$ (required remainder).

167. According to the Wilson theorem if $p$ is a prime number then $(p - 1)! + 1$ is a multiple of $p$.

    Here 41 is a prime number so $40! + 1$ is completely divisible by 41. This means that 40! leaves a remainder $-1$ when we divide it by 41 or it leaves a remainder $41 - 1 = 40$.

168. $x + 3 = 0$ for $x = -3$

    So the required remainder = $(-3)^4 + 3(-3)^3 + 4 = 4$

169. For any odd $X$, $X^2 + 7$ will be an even number. So for any odd $X$, $X^2 + 7$ cannot be a prime number. Only even prime number is 2 for which $2^2 + 7 = 11$ is also a prime number.

    So required number of values = 1.

170. $X = 99^3 - 63^3 - 36^3$ or $99^3 + (-63)^3 + (-36)^3$

    As we know that $a^3 + b^3 + c^3 = 3abc$ (if $a + b + c = 0$)

    So $X = 3(99)(-63)(-36) = 2^2 \times 3^7 \times 7^1 \times 11^1$

    Number of factors of $X = (2 + 1)(7 + 1)(1 + 1)(1 + 1) = 3 \times 8 \times 2 \times 2 = 96$

171. The given expression can be written as $x(x^2 - 1)(x^2 - 4)(x^2 - 9)(x + 4) = (x - 3)(x - 2)(x - 1)x(x + 1)(x + 2)(x + 3)(x + 4)$

    It is the product of eight consecutive natural numbers so this product should be divisible by 8!. Hence, the largest $n$, would be $n = 8$.

172. Number of zeros at the end of $$X! = \left[\frac{X}{5}\right] + \left[\frac{X}{25}\right] + \left[\frac{X}{125}\right] + \ldots = Y$$

    Number of zeros at the end of $$5X! = \left[\frac{5X}{5}\right] + \left[\frac{5X}{25}\right] + \left[\frac{5X}{125}\right] + \ldots \text{ or }$$

    $$[X] + \left[\frac{X}{5}\right] + \left[\frac{X}{25}\right] + \ldots$$

    So the number of zeros at the end of $5X!$ is $X + Y$. Alternately, you could also solve this question through trial and error. Suppose, you take $X$ as 10 and $5X$ as 50: You can see that in this case $Y = 2$ and the number of zeroes in $5X!$ is 12 which is also equal to $X + Y$. The relationship is maintained if you were to take $X = 20$ and $5X = 100$. Thus, 20! has 4 zeroes and 100! has 24 zeroes (again equal to $X + Y$).

173. He is losing a total of 67 marks in the test (from the all correct situation). Further, we know that if he answers a question wrongly, his score would drop by 1.25 marks from the maximum possible. The only other way for him to lose marks is if he leaves a question unanswered. In such a case, he is losing 1.125 marks (when he leaves a question unanswered, he gets a negative score of −0.125 marks instead of getting +1). Once we realise this, we need to check whether 0 wrong answers are possible. In such a case, we can think of the following table to find the correct answer to the question.

| Marks lost by wrong questions | Marks required to be lost by unanswered questions | Is that possible? |
| --- | --- | --- |
| 0 (0 wrong answers) | 67 | 67/1.125 is not an integer. Hence, No. |
| 1.25 (1 wrong answers) | 65.75 | 65.75/1.125 is not an integer. Hence, No. |
| 2.5 (2 wrong answers) | 64.5 | 64.5/1.125 is not an integer. Hence, No. |
| 3.75 (3 wrong answers) | 63.25 | 63.25/1.125 is not an integer. Hence, No. |
| 5 (4 wrong answers) | 62 | 62/1.125 is not an integer. Hence, No. |
| 6.25 (5 wrong answers) | 60.75 | 60.75/1.125 is an integer. Hence, Yes. |

Thus, the minimum number of wrong answers is 5.

174. For $n = 2$, $A = 2^{4^2} = 2^{16}$, $B = 2^{2^4} = 2^{16}$ So $A = B$ in this case. Also, For $n = 2$, $C = 2^8$ & $D$ is $2^8$.

However, if we go for values of n greater than 2, (3 for instance) we see that $B = 3^{729}$, $A = 3^{216}$, $D = 3^{27}$ and $C = 3^{18}$. We notice that this relationship continues for $n = 4$ too.

We can thus conclude that $B \geq A > D \geq C$

175. The numbers we need to check for are: 1,3,7,15,31,63,127,255, 511, 1023, 2047 and 4095. Out of these, the prime numbers are: 3,7,31 & 127. Hence, 4 numbers.

## Level of Difficulty (II)

1. If a and b are two numbers, then their Arithmetic mean is given by $(a + b)/2$ while their geometric mean is given by $(ab)^{0.5}$. Using the options to meet the conditions we can see that for the numbers in the first option (6 and 54) the AM being 30, is 24 less than the larger number while the GM being 18, is 12 more than the smaller number. Option (a) is correct.

2. Use the principal of counting given in the theory of the chapter. Start with 101 numbers (i.e. all numbers between 200 and 300 both included) and subtract the number of numbers which are divisible by 2 (viz. $[(300 - 200)/2] + 1 = 51$ numbers), the number of numbers which are divisible by 3 but not by 2 (Note: This would be given by the number of terms in the series 201, 207, ... 297. This series has 17 terms) and the number of numbers which are divisible by 5 but not by 2 and 3. (The numbers are 205, 215, 235, 245, 265, 275, 295. A total of 7 numbers) Thus, the required answer is given by $101 - 51 - 17 - 7 = 26$. Option (b) is correct.

3. Since $15n^3$, $6n^2$ and $5n$ would all be divisible by $n$, the condition for the expression to not be divisible by $n$ would be if $x$ is not divisible by n. Option (c) is correct.

4. It can be seen that the first expression is larger than the second one. Hence, the required answer would be given by the (units digit of the first expression – units digit of the second expression) = $6 - 0 = 6$. Option (c) is correct.

5. Suppose you were to solve the same question for $10^3 - 7$ and $10^2 + x$.

$10^3 - 7 = 993$ and $10^2 + x = 100 + x$.

Difference = $893 - x$

For $10^4 - 7$ and $10^3 + x$

The difference would be $9993 - (1000 + x)$

$$= (8993 - x)$$

For $10^5 - 7$ and $10^4 + x$

Difference: $99993 - (10000 + x) = 89993 - x$

You should realize that the difference for the given question would be $8999 \ldots \ldots 9\ 3 - x$. For this difference to be divisible by 3, $x$ must be 2 (since that is the only option which will give you a sum of digits divisible by 3).

6. The value of $x$ should be such that the left hand side after completely removing the square root signs should be an integer. For this to happen, first of all the square root of $3x$ should be an integer. Only 3 and 12 from the options satisfy this requirement. If we try to put $x$ as 12, we get the square root of $3x$ as 6. Then the next point at which we need to remove the square root sign would be $12 + 2(6) = 24$ whose square root would be an irrational number. This leaves us with only 1 possible value $(x = 3)$. Checking for this value of $x$ we can see that the expression is satisfied as LHS = RHS.

7. If the number is $n$, we will get that $22n + n = 23n$ is half the square of the number n. Thus, we have

$n^2 = 46\,n \rightarrow n = 46$

8. $12^{55}/3^{11} = 3^{44}.4^{55} \rightarrow 4$ as units place.

   Similarly, $8^{48}/16^{18} = 2^{72} \rightarrow 6$ as the units place.

   Hence, 0 is the answer.

9. $1 + 2 + 2^2 + \ldots + 2^{31} = 2^{32} - 1$

   Hence, the average will be: $\dfrac{2^{32} - 1}{32} = 2^{27} - 1/2^5$

   which lies between $2^{26}$ and $2^{27}$.

   Hence the answer will be (c).

10. The denominator 99 has the property that the decimals it gives rise to are of the form $0.xyxyxy$. This question is based on this property of 99. Option $c$ is correct.

11. The value of $b$ has to be 2 since, $r = 2y$. Hence, option $d$ is the only choice.

12. For $[x]^3 + \{x\}^2$ to give $-7.91$,

    $[x]^3$ should give $-8$ (hence, $[x]$ should be $-2$]

    Further, $\{x\}^2$ should be $+0.09$.

    Both these conditions are satisfied by $-1.7$.

    Hence option (d) is correct.

13. $16^5 + 2^{15} = 2^{20} + 2^{15} = 2^{15}(2^5 + 1) \rightarrow$ Hence, is divisible by 33.

14. The interpretation of the situation $AB + XY = 1XP$ is that the tens digit in $XY$ is repeated in the value of the solution (i.e. $1XP$). Thus for instance if $X$ was 2, it would mean we are adding a 2 digit number $AB$ to a number in the 20's to get a number in the 120's. This can only happen if $AB$ is in the 90's which means that $A$ is 9.

15. $|x - 3| + 2|x + 1| = 4$ can happen under three broad conditions.
    (a) When $2|x + 1| = 0$, then $|x - 3|$ should be equal to 4.
       Putting $x = -1$, both these conditions are satisfied.
    (b) When $2|x + 1| = 2$, $x$ should be 0, then $|x - 3|$ should also be 2. This does not happen.
    (c) When $2|x + 1| = 4$, $x$ should be $+1$ or $-3$, in either case $|x - 3|$ which should be zero does not give the desired value.

16. At a value of $x = 0$ we can see that the expression $x^2 + |x - 1| = 1 \rightarrow 0 + 1 = 1$. Hence, $x = 0$ satisfies the given expression. Also at $x = 1$, we get $1 + 0 = 1$. Option (d) is correct.

17. $4^{n+1}$ represents an odd power of 4 (and hence would end in 4). Similarly, $4^{2n}$ represents an even power of 4 (and hence would end in 6). Thus, the least number '$x$' that would make both $4^{n+1} + x$ and $4^{2n} - x$ divisible by 5 would be for $x = 1$.

18. Check for each value of the options to see that the expression does not become divisible by 9 for any of the initial options. Thus, there is no value that satisfies the divisibility by 9 case.

19. The expression would have solutions based on a structure of:

4 + 0; 3 + 1; 2 + 2; 1 + 3 or 0 + 4.

There will be $2*1 = 2$ solutions for 4 + 0 as in this case x can take the values of 8 and 0, while y can take a value of 4;

Similarly there would be $2*2 = 4$ solutions for 3 + 1 as in this case $x$ can take the values of 7 or 1, while $y$ can take a value of 5 or 3;

Thus, the total number of solutions can be visualised as:

2 (for 4 + 0) + 4 (for 3 + 1) + 4 (for 2 + 2) + 4 (for 1 + 3) + 2 (for (0 + 2) = 16 solutions for the set $(x, y)$ where both $x$ and $y$ are integers.

20. The numerator of $3^{32}/50$ would be a number that would end in 1. Consequently, the decimal of the form $.bx$ would always give us a value of $x$ as 2.

21. If we assume the numbers as 16 and 4 based on 4:1 (in option a), the AM would be 10 and the $GM = 8$ a difference of 20% as stipulated in the question. Option (a) is correct.

22. $990 = 11 \times 3^2 \times 2 \times 5$. The highest power of 990 which would divide 1090! would be the power of 11 available in 1090. This is given by $[1090/11] + [1090/121] = 99 + 9 = 108$

23. For finding the highest power of 6 that divides 146!, we need to get the number of 3's that would divide 146!. The same can be got by: $[146/3] + [48/3] + [16/3] + [5/3] = 70$.

24. There would be two fives and more than two twos in the prime factors of the numbers in the multiplication. Thus, we would get a total of 2 zeroes.

25. Both $333^{555}$ and $555^{333}$ are divisible by 3,37 and 111. Further, the sum of the two would be an even number and hence divisible by 2. Thus, all the four options divide the given number.

26. Both the values of options a and b satisfy the given expression. As for 5.16, the value of $[x]^2 = 25$ and the value of $\{x\} = 0.16$. Thus, $[x]^2 + \{x\}^1 = 25.16$

    Similarly for a value of $x = -4.84$, the value of $[x] = -5$ and hence $[x]^2 = 25$ and the value of $\{x\} = 0.16$. Thus, $[x]^2 + \{x\}^1 = 25.16$

27. The given conditions can be seen to be true for the number 49. Option (c) is correct.

28. Solve this question through options. Also realize that $a \times b = a + b$ only occurs for the situation $2 \times 2 = 2 + 2$. Hence, clearly the answer has to be none of these.

29. 863 satisfies each of the conditions and can be spotted through checking of the options.

30. The number of zeroes would be given by counting the number of 5's. The relevant numbers for counting the number of 5's in the product would be given by: $5^5; 10^{10}, 15^{15}, 20^{20}, 25^{25}\ldots$ and so on till $100^{100}$

    The number of 5's in these values would be given by: $(5 + 10 + 15 + 20 + 50 + 30 + 35 + 40 + 45 + 100 + 55 + 60 + 65 + 70 + 150 + 80 + 85 + 90 + 95 + 200)$

This can also be written as:

$(5 + 10 + 15 + 20 + 25 + 30 + 35 + 40 + 45 + 50 + 55 + 60 + 65 + 70 + 75 + 80 + 85 + 90 + 95 + 100) + (25 + 50 + 75 + 100)$

$= 1050 + 250 = 1300$

31. Option (a) is correct as the LCM of 5 and 105 is 105 and their HCF is 5. Also for the pair of values, 15 and 35 the HCF is 5 and the LCM is 105.

32. Solve using options. Using option b = 3/5 and performing the given operation we get:

    2/3 – 3/5 = (10 – 9)/15 = 1/15. Option (b) is hence correct.

33. Both the conditions are satisfied for option (a) = 72 as the number 72 exceeds the sum of squares of the digits by 19 and also 72 exceeds the doubled product of it's digits by 44.

34. Solve by checking the given options. 31 and 13 are possible values of the number as defined by the problem.

35. The given conditions are satisfied for the number 24.

36. The number of 2's in the given expression is lower than the number of 5's. The number of 2's in the product is 9 and hence that is the number of zeroes.

37. $45 = 3^2 \times 5$. Hence, we need to count the number of $3^2$'s and 5's that can be made out of 123!.

    Number of 3's = 41 + 13 + 4 + 1 = 59 → Number of $3^2$'s = 29

    Number of 5's = 24 + 4 = 28.

    The required answer is the lower of the two (viz. 28 and 29). Hence, option (a) 28 is correct.

38. The first sentence means that the numbers are in an arithmetic progression. From the statements and a little bit of visualization, you can see that 8.5, 10 and 11.5 can be the three values we are looking for – and hence the middle value is 10.

39. $990 = 11 \times 3^2 \times 5 \times 2$. For $n!$ to be divisible by 990, the value of $n!$ should have an 11 in it. Since, 11 itself is a prime number, hence the value of $n$ should be at least 11.

40. For the expression to hold true, $x$ and $y$ should both be positive.

41. Since, we are not given options here we should go ahead by looking within the factors of 144 (especially the two digit ones).

    The relevant factors are 72, 48, 36, 24, 18 and 12. Thinking this way creates an option for you where there is none available and from this list of numbers you can easily identify 24 as the required answer.

**42–46.** Write simple equations for each of the questions and solve.

47. Since the sum of squares of the digits of the two digit number is 10, the only possibility of the numbers are 31 and 13.

48. If the number is '$ab$' we have the following equations:

    $(10a + b) = 4(a + b) + 3 \rightarrow 6a - 3b = 3$

    $(10a + b) = 3(a \times b) + 5$.

    Obviously we would need to solve these two equations in order to get the values of the digits a and b respectively. However, it might not be a very prudent decision to try to follow this process- as it might turn out to be too cumbersome.

    A better approach to think here is:

    From the first statement we know that the number is of the form $4n + 3$. Thus, the number has to be a term in the series 11, 15, 19, 23, 27…

    Also from the second statement we know that the number must be a $3n + 5$ number.

    Thus, the numbers could be 11, 14, 17, 20, 23….

    Common terms of the above two series would be probable values of the number.

    It can be seen that the common terms in the two series are: 11, 23, 35, 47, 59, 71, 83 and 95. One of these numbers has to be the number we are looking for.

    If we try these values one by one, we can easily see that the value of the two digit number should be 23 since → 23/ (2 + 3) → Quotient as 4 and remainder = 3.

    Similarly, if we look at the other condition given in the problem we would get the following-

    23/6 → quotient as 3 and remainder = 5.

    Thus, the value of the missing number would be 23.

49. We can see from the description that the number (say $X$) must be such that $X + 100$ and $X + 169$ both must be perfect squares. Thus we are looking for two perfect squares which are 69 apart from each other. This would happen for $34^2$ and $35^2$ since their difference would be $(35 - 34)(35 + 34) = 69$.

50. Since their least common multiple is 102, we need to look for two factors of 102 such that they add up to 85. 51 and 34 can be easily spotted as the numbers.

51. If one number is $x$, the other should be $6x$ or $12x$ or $18x$ or $24x$ and so on. Also, their sum should be either 504 or 1008 or 1512. (Note: the next multiple of 504 = 2016 cannot be the sum of two three digit numbers.)

52. Obviously 46 and 64 are the possible numbers.

53. The key here is to look for numbers which are more than three times but less than four times the product of their digits. Also, the product of the digits should be greater than 9 so as to leave a remainder of 9 when the number is divided by the product of it's digits.

    In the 10s, 20s and 30s, the numbers 14,15,23 and 33 give us a quotient of 3, when divided by the product of their digits, but do not give us the required remainder. In the 40s, 43 is the only number which has a quotient of 3 when divided by 12 (product of it's digits). But 43/12 does not give us a remainder of 9 as required.

In the 50s the number 53 divided by 15 leaves a remainder of 8, while in the 60s, 63 divided by 18 gives us a remainder of 9 as required.

54. The first thing to use while solving this question is to look at the information that the sum of squares of the three digits is 109. A little bit of trial and error shows us that this can only occur if the digits are 8, 6 and 3. Using the other information we get that the number must be 863 since, 863 − 495 = 368.

55. It is obvious that the only condition where the cubes of 3 numbers add up to 243 is when we add the cubes of 3 and 6. Hence, the numbers possible are 36 and 63.

56. There would definitely be two numbers and in case we take the first number as $7n - 1$, there would be three numbers – (as can be seen when we take the first number as 27 and the other number is 43).

57. Between $111^4$, $110 \times 109 \times 108 \times 107$, $109 \times 110 \times 112 \times 113$.

It can be easily seen that

$111 \times 111 \times 111 \times 111 > 110 \times 109 \times 108 \times 107$

also $109 \times 110 \times 112 \times 113 > 109 \times 110 \times 108 \times 107$

Further the product $111 \times 111 \times 111 \times 111 > 109 \times 110 \times 112 \times 113$ ( since, the sum of the parts of the product are equal on the LHS and the RHS and the numbers on the LHS are closer to each other than the numbers on the RHS).

58. Both $x$ and $y$ should be highest for $xy$ to be maximum. Similarly $x$ should be minimum and $y$ should be maximum for $x/y$ to be minimum.

59. $200^{300} = (200^6)^{50}$
$300^{200} = (300^4)^{50}$
$400^{150} = (400^3)^{50}$
Hence $200^{300}$ is greater.

61. The sum of squares of the first n natural numbers is given by $n(n + 1)(2n + 1)/6$.

For this number to be divisible by 4, the product of $n(n + 1)(2n + 1)$ should be a multiple of 8. Out of $n$, $(n + 1)$ and $(2n + 1)$ only one of $n$ or $(n + 1)$ can be even and $(2n + 1)$ would always be odd.

Thus, either $n$ or $(n + 1)$ should be a multiple of 8. This happens if we use $n = 7, 8, 15, 16, 23, 24, 31, 32, 39, 40, 47, 48$. Hence, 12 such numbers.

62. In the 20s the numbers are: 23 to 29
In the 30s the numbers are: 32 to 39
Subsequently the numbers are 42 to 49, 52 to 59, 62 to 69, 72 to 79, 82 to 89 and 92 to 99.

A total of 63 numbers.

63. You need to solve this question using trial and error. For 32 (option 1):

$32 = 2^5$. Hence 6 factors. On increasing by 50%, $48 = 2^4 \times 3^1$ has 10 factors. Thus the number of factors is increasing when the number is increased by 50% which is not what the question is defining for the number. Hence, 32 is not the correct answer. Checking for option (b) 84.

$84 = 2^2 \times 3^1 \times 7^1 \rightarrow (2 + 1)(1 + 1)(1 + 1) = 12$ factors

On increasing by 50% $\rightarrow 126 = 2^1 \times 3^2 \times 7^1 \rightarrow (1 + 1)(2 + 1)(1 + 1) = 12$ factors. (no change in number of factors).

Second Condition: When the value of the number is reduced by 75% $\rightarrow 84$ would become 21 $(3^1 \times 7^1)$ and the number of factors would be $2 \times 2 = 4$ – a reduction of 66.66% in the number of factors.

64. There will be 9 single digit numbers using 9 digits, 90 two digit numbers using 180 digits, 900 three digit numbers using 2700 digits. Thus, when the number 999 would be written, a total of 2889 digits would have been used up. Thus, we would need to look for the 25494th digit when we write all 4 digit numbers. Since, 25494/4 = 6373.5 we can conclude that the first 6373 four digit numbers would be used up for writing the first 25492 digits. The second digit of the 6374th four digit number would be the required answer. Since, the 6374th four digit number is 7373, the required digit is 3.

65. In order to solve this question, think of the numbers grouped in groups of 9 as:
{1, 2, 3, 4, 5, 6, 7, 8, 9} {10, 11, 12.....18} and so on till {2989, 2990...2997} – A total of 333 complete sets. From each set we can take 4 numbers giving us a total of 333 × 4 = 1332 numbers.

Apart from this, we can also take exactly 1 multiple of 9 (any one) and also the last 3 numbers viz 2998, 2999 and 3000. Thus, there would be a total of 1332 + 4 = 1336 numbers.

66. It can be seen that for only 2 numbers (1 and ½) the consolidated number would be 1 + ½ + ½ = 2

For 3 numbers, (1, ½ , 1/3) the number would be 3. Thus, for the given series the consolidated number would be 1972.

67. The value of $K$ would be 199 and hence, the required difference is 9 − 1 = 8

68. 9 − 9 = 0 would be the difference between the units and the tens digits.

69. The highest ratio would be a ratio of 100 in the numbers, 100, 200, 300, 400, 500, 600, 700, 800 and 900. Thus a total of 9 numbers.

70. Basically every odd triangular number would have this property, that it is the difference of squares of two consecutive natural numbers. Thus, we need to find the number of triangular numbers that are odd.

    3, 15, 21, 45, 55, 91, 105, 153, 171, 231, 253, 325, 351, 435, 465, 561, 595, 703, 741, 861, 903 – A total of 21 numbers.

71. The coefficients would be $^{44}C_0$, $^{44}C_1$, $^{44}C_2$ and so on till $^{44}C_{44}$. The sum of these coefficients would be $2^{44}$ (since the value of $^nC_0 + {}^nC_1 + {}^nC_2 + \ldots {}^nC_n = 2^n$)

72. The remainder of each power of 9 when divided by 6 would be 3. Thus, for $(2n+1)$ powers of 9, there would be an odd number of 3's. Hence, the remainder would be 3.

73. The remainder when a number is divided by 16 is given by the remainder of the last 4 digits divided by 16 (because 10000 is a multiple of 16. This principle is very similar in logic to why we look at last 2 digits for divisibility by 4 and the last 3 digits for divisibility by 8). Thus, the required answer would be the remainder of 4950/16 which is 6.

74. $58! - 38! = 38! (58 \times 57 \times 56 \times 55 \times \ldots \times 39 - 1) \rightarrow 38!$. $(3n - 1)$ since the expression inside the bracket would be a $3n - 1$ kind of number. Thus, the number of 3's would depend only on the number of 3's in $38! \rightarrow 12 + 4 + 1 = 17$.

75. The given expression can be seen as $(22334^{\text{ODD POWER}})/5$, since the sum of $1^2 + 2^2 + 3^2 + 4^2 + \ldots + 66^2$ can be seen to be an odd number. The remainder would always be 4 in such a case.

76. $12^{33} \times 34^{23} \times 2^{70} = 2^{159} \times 3^{33} \times 17^{23}$. The number of factors would be $160 \times 34 \times 24 = 130560$. Thus, option (d) is correct.

77. Option (a) is correct.

78. $1152 = 2 \times 2 \times 2 \times 2 \times 2 \times 2 \times 2 \times 3 \times 3 = 2^7 \times 3^2$. Essentially every number starting from $4!^3$ would be divisible perfectly by 1152 since each number after that would have at least 7 twos and 2 threes.

    Thus, the required remainder is got by the first three terms:

    $(1 + 8 + 216)/1152 = 225/1152$ gives us 225 as the required remainder.

79. We can take only perfect squares of prime numbers and the number 1. Thus, for instance we can take numbers like 1, 4, 9, 25, 49, 121, 169, 289, 361, 529, 841 and 961. A total of 12 such numbers can be taken.

80. $(101 \times 102 \times 103 \times 197 \times 198 \times 199)/100 \rightarrow [1 \times 2 \times 3 \times (-3) \times (-2) \times (-1)]/100 \rightarrow -36$ as remainder $\rightarrow$ remainder is 64.

81. $[65 \times 29 \times 37 \times 63 \times 71 \times 87]/100 \rightarrow [-35 \times 29 \times 37 \times -37 \times -29 \times -13]/100 \rightarrow [35 \times 29 \times 37 \times 37 \times 29 \times 13]/100 = [1015 \times 1369 \times 377]/100 \rightarrow 15 \times 69 \times 77/100 \rightarrow$ remainder as 95.

82. $[65 \times 29 \times 37 \times 63 \times 71 \times 87 \times 85]/100 \rightarrow [-35 \times 29 \times 37 \times -37 \times -29 \times -13 \times -15]/100 \rightarrow [35 \times 29 \times 37 \times 37 \times 29 \times 13 \times -15]/100 = [1015 \times 1369 \times 377 \times -15]/100 \rightarrow [15 \times 69 \times 77 \times -15]/100 \rightarrow$ remainder as 75.

83. $[65 \times 29 \times 37 \times 63 \times 71 \times 87 \times 62]/100 \rightarrow [-35 \times 29 \times 37 \times -37 \times -29 \times -13 \times 62]/100 \rightarrow [35 \times 29 \times 37 \times 37 \times 29 \times 13 \times 62]/100 = [1015 \times 1369 \times 377 \times 62]/100 \rightarrow [15 \times 69 \times 77 \times 62]/100 \rightarrow [1035 \times 4774]/100 \rightarrow 35 \times 74/100 \rightarrow$ remainder as 90.

84. $[75 \times 35 \times 47 \times 63 \times 71 \times 87 \times 82]/100 = [3 \times 35 \times 47 \times 63 \times 71 \times 87 \times 41]/2 \rightarrow$ remainder $= 1$.

    Hence, required remainder $= 1 \times 50 = 50$.

85. For this question we need to find the remainder of:

    $(201 \times 202 \times 203 \times 204 \times 246 \times 247 \times 248 \times 249) \times (201 \times 202 \times 203 \times 204 \times 246 \times 247 \times 248 \times 249)$ divided by 100.

    $(201 \times 202 \times 203 \times 204 \times 246 \times 247 \times 248 \times 249) \times (201 \times 202 \times 203 \times 204 \times 246 \times 247 \times 248 \times 249)/100 = (201 \times 101 \times 203 \times 102 \times 246 \times 247 \times 248 \times 249) \times (201 \times 202 \times 203 \times 204 \times 246 \times 247 \times 248 \times 249)/25$

    $\rightarrow (1 \times 1 \times 3 \times 2 \times -4 \times -3 \times -2 \times -1) \times (1 \times 2 \times 3 \times 4 \times -4 \times -3 \times -2 \times -1)/25 = 144 \times 576/25 \rightarrow (19 \times 1)/25 = $ remainder 19.

    $19 \times 4 = 76$ is the actual remainder (since we divided by 4 during the process of finding the remainder).

86. $7^4/2400$ gives us a remainder of 1. Thus, the remainder of $7^{99}/2400$ would depend on the remainder of $7^3/2400 \rightarrow$ remainder $= 343$.

87. The numerator can be written as $(1729)^{752}/1728 \rightarrow$ remainder as 1.

88. Bikas's movement in terms of the number of coins would be:

    $B \rightarrow 3B$ (when Arun triples everyone's coins) $\rightarrow B$.

    Think of this as: When Bikas triples everyone's coins, and is left with 20 it means that the other 3 have 60 coins after their coins are tripled. This means that before the tripling by Bikas, the other three must have had 20 coins—meaning Bikas must have had 60 coins.

    But $60 = 3B \rightarrow B = 20$.

89. For $83p796161q$ to be a multiple of 11 (here $X$ is 11) we should have the difference between the sum of odd placed digits and even placed digits should be 0 or a multiple of 11.

    $(8 + p + 9 + 1 + 1) - (3 + 7 + 6 + 6 + q) = (19 + p) - (22 + q)$. For this difference to be 0, $p$ should be 3 more than $q$ which cannot occur since $0 < p < q$.

    The only way in which $(19 + p) - (22 + q)$ can be a multiple of 11 is if we target a value of $-11$ for the expression. One such possibility is if we take $p$ as 1 and $q$ as 9.

The number would be 8317961619. On successive division by $(p + q) = 10$ and 1 the sum of remainders would be 9.

90. $n(n + 1)/2$ should be a perfect square. The first value of $n$ when this occurs would be for $n = 8$. Thus, on the 8th of March the required condition would come true.

91. We have to find the unit's digit of $2^{53} \rightarrow 2^{4n+1} \rightarrow 2$ as the units digit.

92. $[7! (14 + 14 \times 13 \times 12 \times 11 \times 10 \times 9 \times 8)]/[7! (16 - 3)] = [(14 + 14 \times 13 \times 12 \times 11 \times 10 \times 9 \times 8)]/[(13)] \rightarrow$ remainder 1.

   Hence, the original remainder must be 7! (because for the sake of simplification of the numbers in the question we have cut the 7! from the numerator and the denominator in the first step).

93. $x = 6$ and $y = -3$ is one pair of values where the given condition is met.

   After that you should be able to spot that if you were to increase $x$ by 7, $y$ would decrease by 4. The number of such pairs would depend on how many terms are there in the series –498, –491, ..... –1, 6, 13, 20, ... 489, 496. The series has $994/7 + 1 = 143$ terms and hence there would be 143 pairs of values for $(x, y)$ which would satisfy the equation.

94. All three conditions can be seen to be true.

95. Product of factorials < Sum of factorials would occur for any number that has either 0 or 1 in it.

   The required numbers uptil and including 50 are: 10 to 19, 20, 21, 30, 31, 40, 41, 50. Besides for the number 22, the product of factorials of the digits would be equal to the sum of factorials of the digits. Thus a total of 18 numbers.

96. The maximum marks he can score is: 100 (if he gets all correct).

   The minimum marks he can score would be given by: $10 \times (-0.1) + 20 \times (-0.2) + 70 \times (-0.5) = -40$.

   The difference between the two values would be $100 - (-40) = 140$ marks.

**Logic for Questions 97 to 99:**

If a student solved 200 questions and got everything correct he would score a total of 620 marks. By getting a LOD 1 question wrong he would lose 4+2=6 marks, while by not solving an LOD 1 question he would lose 4 marks.

   Similarly for LOD 2 questions, Loss of marks = 4.5 (for wrong answers) and loss of marks= 3 (for not solved)

   Similarly for LOD 3 questions, Loss of marks = 3 (for wrong answers) and loss of marks = 2 (for not solved)

   Since, he has got 120 marks from 100 questions solved he has to lose 500 marks (from the maximum possible total

of 620) by combining to lose marks through 100 questions not solved and some questions wrong.

97. It can be seen through a little bit of trial and error with the options, that if he got 44 questions of LOD 1 correct and 56 questions of LOD 3 wrong he would end up scoring $44 \times 4 - 56 \times 1 = 176 - 56 = 120$. In such a case he would have got the maximum possible incorrects with the given score.

98. $32 \times 4 + 1 \times 3 - 1 \times 1 = 130$ (in this case he has solved 32 corrects from LOD 1, 1 correct from LOD 2 and 1 incorrect from LOD 3). Thus, a total of 34 attempts.

99. In the above case he gets 1 question incorrect. However, he can also get 130 marks by $30 \times 4 + 2 \times 3 + 2 \times 2$ where he gets 30 LOD 1 questions correct, and 2 questions correct each from LOD 2 and LOD 3). The least number of incorrects would be 0.

100. The least number would be (LCM of 10, 9, 8, 7, 6 and $5 - 1) = 2519$. The second least number = $2520 \times 2 - 1 = 5039$.

101. A quick scan of squares above the given numbers tells us that the required perfect squares are: 144, 256 and 400, which would be the squares of the numbers 12, 16 and 20 respectively. Hence, $n$ would be $144 - 108 = 36$. The sum of digits of $n$ is $3 + 6 = 9$.

102. The number $904 = 8 \times 113 = 2^3 \times 113$. This means that $904^{2008} = 2^{6024} \times 113^{2008}$. Also, $904^{2015} = 2^{6045} \times 113^{2015}$. Multiples of $904^{2008}$ would be numbers that would have $2^{6024 \text{ or more}}$ & $113^{2008 \text{ or more}}$. Also, factors of $904^{2015}$ would have $2^{6045 \text{ or less}}$ & $113^{2015 \text{ or less}}$. This means that the number of numbers that would be multiples of the first number and simultaneously be factors of the other number would be $22 \times 8 = 176$.

103. The expression $1^5 + 2^5 + 3^5 + ........ + 96^5$ can be written as $(1 + 2 + ... + 96)(1^4 + ........)$. The first bracket in this expression would have a value of $96 \times 97 \div 2 = 48 \times 97$. (Using the formula for the sum of the first n natural numbers.) Since, $48 \times 97$ is a multiple of 194, the required remainder would be 0.

104. Since, the LHS of the above expression would always be an integer, the RHS too needs to be an integer. This condition is satisfied when s is a multiple of 42. Also, on checking for values of $s$ as 42, 84 etc. we realise that for all values of $s$, the RHS gives a value that is equal to the LHS. So, in order to answer the question, we need to find out the number of multiples of 42 below 1000. We start from $42 \times 1$ and end at $42 \times 23$. Hence, there are 23 such numbers

**Solutions for 105 to 107:** The list of possible number of rabbits that were transferred for each weight category would be:

| 1 kg rabbits | 2 kg rabbits | 5 kg rabbits |
|---|---|---|
| 1 | 16 | 23 |
| 4 | 12 | 24 |
| 7 | 8 | 25 |
| 10 | 4 | 26 |
| 13 | 0 | 27 |

Possible number of rabbits remaining in the zoo:

| 1 kg rabbits | 2 kg rabbits | 5 kg rabbits |
|---|---|---|
| 1 | 28 | 31 |
| 4 | 24 | 32 |
| 7 | 20 | 33 |
| 10 | 16 | 34 |
| 13 | 12 | 35 |
| 16 | 8 | 36 |
| 19 | 4 | 37 |
| 22 | 0 | 38 |

The answers can be read off the tables:

105. The minimum number of 1 kg rabbits that were transferred was 1.

106. The maximum possible numbers of 5 kg rabbits that remain were 37. (Note: 38 is not possible, since the minimum number of 5 kg rabbits transferred out was 23 – and 23 + 38 would cross 60, which is not allowed in the question)

107. If 26, 5 kg rabbits were transferred, it means that there can be a maximum of 34, 5 kg rabbits that remain in the zoo. In such a case, we would get the highest numbers of 1 kg rabbits that remain in the zoo as 10. Hence, the correct answer for this question is '10'.

108. The best way to solve such questions is to do a selective trial and error. Scanning numbers, the first thing that becomes clear is that we cannot have both the digits of the number as even, in this context. This means that we need to scan only odd numbers. Scanning through the odd numbers, we find 36 & its' reverse 63 giving us the required value as 36 + 63 + 3 × 6 = 117. Also, we can see that even 63 + 36 +18 gives us the same value. In both cases, the sum of the digits turns out to be 9.

109. The numbers that have an odd number of factors are the perfect squares. Thus, $M = 36 × 49 × 64 × 81 × 100 × 121 × 144 × 169 × 196 × 225 = 2^{16} × 3^8 × 5^4 × 7^4 × 11^2 × 13^2$. 12 is a number consisted only of 2's and 3's. Also, $12 = 2^2 × 3^1 \rightarrow$ In the number M, we have 8 $2^2$s and 8 $3^1$s. Hence, the highest power of 12 in M is 8.

110. First through trial and error identify the two values of x & y that satisfy this. The first one that satisfies are the values 3 & 3, the next pair is 11 & 1. (This will also be the last pair!! Think why??)

Further, since we are looking for the maximum possible integral power of 6, we will use the pair 11 & 1. We need to find the highest power of 6 in 11! which is given by [11/3] + [11/9] = 3 + 1 = 4.

111. X has only 2 elements 1, 2 (so x = 2) & Y consists all the prime numbers. The prime numbers below 100 are 2,3,5,7,11,13,17,19,23,29,31,37,41,43,47, 53,59,61,67,71,73,79,83,89 and 97 → Y = 25. So the value of [y/x] = [25/2] = 12

112. If X has 15 factors, then it should either be of the form $a^{14}$ or $b^2 × c^4$ where a, b, c are prime numbers.
Case 1: When the number is of the form $a^{14}$ in this case the smallest possible number is $2^{14} = 16384$ which is a five digit number so this case is not possible.
Case 2: When the number is of the form $b^2 × c^4$.
The minimum possible number $3^2 × 2^4 = 144$

$$X^2 = b^4 × c^8$$

So the square of the number has (4 + 1).(8 + 1) = 5 × 9 = 45 factors.

113. If wxyz is the four digit number then according to the question:
x = y+ 2 therefore y can take any value from 0 to 7 for which x can take the respective values from 2 to 9. Since the number is odd, z can take five values (1, 3, 5, 7, 9). Now we have total 8 possibilities for x, y and five possibilities for z. For w, we have a total of 9 possibilities(from 1 to 9). So, the total possible numbers = 9 × 8 × 5 = 360.

114. X, Y, Z are in A.P. Let the common difference between them is d then following cases are possible.
Case 1: When d = 1, no triplet possible.
Case 2: When d = 2, possible triplet is (3, 5, 7). Sum = 15
Case 3: When d = 3, no triplet possible.
Case 4: When d = 4, possible triplet is (3, 7, 11). Sum = 21
Case 5: When d = 5, no triplet possible.
Case 6: When d = 6, possible triplet is (5, 11, 17), (7, 13, 19). Sum = 33, 39
Case 7: When d = 7, no triplet possible.
Case 8: When d = 8, possible triplet is (3, 11, 19). Sum = 33
For d > 8 no triplet possible. Hence, we see that the possible sums for X, Y and Z are 15, 21, 33 & 39 respectively. Hence, a total of 4 possibilities.

115. When a 'x' digit number is multiplied by a 'y' digit number, the product would have either 'x + y' or 'x + y – 1' digits.
So when we multiply a 100- digits number by a 200- digits number then the product will have 100 + 200 or 100+ 200 – 1 = 300 or 299 digits. Further, when this number is again multiplied by a 300 digit

number, we get a 598 to 600 digit number. Finally, when this number is further multiplied by a 400 digit number, the answer would have a minimum of 997 digits to a maximum of 1000 digits. Hence, the correct answer is 997.

116. $3^{400} \Rightarrow (3^4)^{100} \Rightarrow (81)^{100}$
$\Rightarrow (1 + 80)^{100} \Rightarrow 1^{100} + 80^{100}$

Now we can easily see that in $80^{100}$ last two digits will always be 00.

Hence $1 + 00 = 01$. **Answer**

117. This problem can be easily solved through Cyclicity principle. The units digits of all numbers starting from $1^7$ upto $9^7$ will be repeated ten times each for every range of ten numbers. Hence, we have to check out the units digit of $1^7 \times 2^7 \times \dots 9^7$ i.e.

$1^7$ end in 1

$2^7$ end in 8

$3^7$ end in 7

$4^7$ end in 4

$5^7$ ends in 5…. Hence, $1^7 \times 2^7 \times \dots 9^7$ would end in 0. Hence, the units digits would be 0 for the entire expression.

118. On division by 24, the square of a natural number, would leave a remainder of 1, only if the number is of the form $6n \pm 1$, where $n \in N$ (since $n$ must not be divisible by 2 or 3.)

In the two digit numbers, we have 15 numbers of the form $6n$ ($6 \times 2$, $6 \times 3$ till $6 \times 16$). Hence, there are a total of 30 two digit numbers of the form ($6n \pm 1$) [15 of the form $6n + 1$, 15 of the form of $6n - 1$].

119. Logical Solution: The maximum total marks, in the exam are 80 (if he gets all questions correct). From this number, he has two mechanisms for losing marks – For a wrong answer, he loses 1.25 marks for each wrong answer. For an unanswered question, he loses 1.125 marks per question. Since he has scored a total of only 23 marks, he has lost 57 marks (from the maximum possible total of 80). Since, we are trying to look for the minimum possible wrong answers, we can start trying to put the number of wrong answers as 0. In that case, we would need to lose the entire 57 marks due to not attempting questions. However, $57 \div 1.125$ is not an integer, hence 0 wrong answers is not possible. Going for 1 wrong answer, marks lost due to wrong answers = 1.25. Marks to be lost due to un-attempted questions = $57 - 1.25 = 55.75$. Going further in this direction, we realise that if we put 6 incorrect questions, we would need 49.5 marks to be lost due to un-attempted questions. $49.5 \div 1.125$ = 44. Hence, we get 6 as the required answer.

120. In base-3 the decimal value of a five digit number must lie from 81 to 242

$$[(10000)_3 = 81 \ \& \ (22222)_3 = 242]$$

Similarly in the base-4 the decimal value of a five-digit number must lie from 256 to 1023.

In base 5 the decimal value of the five-digit number must lie from 625 to 3124. Hence $x = 5$

Option (d) is correct.

121. Difference between the divisor and the remainder is 1 in each division. $[2 - 1 = 4 - 3 = 6 - 5 = 8 - 7 = 10 - 9 = 1]$

So the general form of the number will be LCM of $[2, 4, 6, 8, 10] - 1 = 120k - 1$ where '$k$' is a natural number.

There are 8 such numbers between 101 to 1000: 119, 239, 359, 479, 599, 719, 839, 959.

So the required sum = $119 + 239 + 359 + 479 + 599 + 719 + 839 + 959 = 4312$.

122. Any digit (from 0 to 9) raised to the power of the type $4k + 1$ ($k \in N$) will always end in the same digit. It means for all possible values of $x$, $x^{4k+1}$ has same unit digit as unit digit of $x$. So $a$ has same unit digit as unit digit of $a^5, a^9, a^{13}, a^{17}, a^{21}, \dots$ similarly $b$ has same unit digit as $b^5, b^9, b^{13}, b^{17}, b^{21}, \dots$ So $a^{13} + b^{13}$ has same unit digit as $a^{17} + b^{17}$.

123. The number of 4-digit numbers in decimal system will be from $10^3 = 1000$ to $10^4 - 1 = 9999$, i.e., 9000 numbers.

The number of 4-digit numbers in Base 8 will be from $8^3 = 512$ to $8^4 - 1 = 4095$. i.e. 3584 numbers.

The number of 4-digit numbers in Base 7 will be from $7^3 = 343$ to $7^4 - 1 = 2400$. i.e. 2058 numbers.

The number of 4-digit numbers in Base 6 will be from $6^3 = 216$ to $6^4 - 1 = 1295$. i.e. 1080 numbers.

So the numbers from 1000 to 1295, would have 4 digits in each of base 6, 7 and 8. So, there are a total of 296 numbers possible.

124. The number of 4-digit numbers in decimal system will be from $10^3 = 1000$ to $10^4 - 1 = 9999$.

The number of 4-digit numbers in Base 7 will be from $7^3 = 343$ to $7^4 - 1 = 2400$.

The number of 4-digit numbers in Base 6 will be from $6^3 = 216$ to $6^4 - 1 = 1295$.

So the common numbers are from 1000 to 1295. So, the required difference = $1295 - 1000 = 295$.

125. $9^n + 11^n$ is divisible by 10 when n is odd but when $n$ is even then it would leave a remainder of 2. (last digit of $9^2 + 11^2$.)

$6^n + 4^n$ is divisible by 10 when n is odd but when n is even then it would leave a remainder of 2. (Last digit of $6^2 + 4^2$). Hence, whenever n is odd there would be no remainder when 10 divides the expression.

When n is even, then the remainder would be $2 + 2 = 4$.

So the sum of all possible remainders in this case will be 4.

126. There are four possible scenarios for the units' digit combination of the four numbers. These essentially arise from the even/odd combinations taking x and z:

Scenario 1: Both even: $1 + 6 + 6 + 1 \rightarrow$ Remainder = 4;

Scenario 2: Both odd: $9 + 6 + 4 + 1 \rightarrow$ Remainder = 0

Scenario 3: x odd, z even: $9 + 6 + 6 + 1 \rightarrow$ Remainder = 2

Scenario 4: x even, y odd: $1 + 6 + 4 + 1 \rightarrow$ Remainder = 2

Thus, the sum of all remainders = $4 + 0 + 2 + 2$ = 8.

127. In order to think of the maximum possible Mondays and Thursdays we will need to consider one of the two years to be a leap year. In such a case, there are 104 weeks and 3 extra days in 2 years.

But these three extra days must be consecutive so if Monday is one of these three days then Thursday cannot be one of three days and vice-versa.

So maximum possible number of Mondays and Thursdays = $104 \times 2 + 1 = 209$.

128. In order to think of the minimum possible Mondays and Thursdays we will need to consider none of the two years to be a leap year. In such a case, there are 104 weeks and 2 extra days in 2 years.

So minimum possible number of Mondays and Thursdays = $104 \times 2 = 208$. (In the event that neither of these extra days is a Monday or a Thursday).

129. Remainder of
$$\frac{[(111111111\ldots\ldots64\,terms)*(22222222\ldots\ldots55\,terms)]}{18}$$
= 2 × Remainder of
$$\frac{[(111111111\ldots\ldots64\,terms)*(111111\ldots\ldots55\,terms)]}{9}$$
$\rightarrow$ Remainder = 1

So required remainder = $2 \times 1 = 2$

130. We can see from the expression that $(x - y)(x + y)$ is an even number. Both $x - y$ and $x + y$ are even numbers, so product of $(x - y)(x + y)$ must be divisible by 4. But 777314 is not divisible by 4. So it has no solution. The correct answer would be 0.

**Solutions for 131 & 132:**

Coin 1 was turned only once, coin 2 was turned twice, coin 3 was turned twice, coin 4 was turned thrice, coin 5 was turned twice, coin 6 was turned 4 times, coin 7 was turned twice, coin 8 was turned 4 times, while coin 9 was turned 3 times as so on.

We can easily see that each of the coins would be turned a number of times that would be equal to the number of factors the number on the coin has. Thus, it would be the coins having perfect square numbers that would be turned an odd number of times (hence

show tails) and the rest of the coins were turned an even number of times (Hence would be showing heads). There are a total 10 coins having perfect square numbers and these would be showing tails.

131. After the 100th visit coin numbers 54 and 91 were in Heads-up state.

132. After the 100th visit there were $100 - 10 = 90$ coins in Heads-up state.

133. The last three digits of any number are the same as the remainder when we divide the number by 1000.

$$\frac{(225)^{40}}{1000} = \frac{5^{80} \cdot 9^{40}}{1000} = \frac{5^{77} \cdot 9^{40}}{8}$$

$9^{40} = (8 + 1)^{40}$ gives remainder 1 when we divide it by 8.

$$\frac{5^{77}}{8} = \frac{5 \cdot (24+1)^{38}}{8}$$ leaves a remainder 5.

So last three digits of $(225)^{40} = 125 \times 5 = 625$.

So the value of 100th digit is 6.

134. 'c' cannot be greater than 3 because if $c \geq 4$ then 'a' should be greater than or equal to 16 which is not possible. Similarly 'b' cannot be greater than 4.

| c | b | a | Number of triplets |
|---|---|---|---|
| 3 | No possible values as 3b can be 13 or 14 only, but that gives us no value for b (as neither of these numbers is a multiple of 3) | No. values possible | 0 |
| 2 | 4 | 13, 14 | 2 |
| 2 | 3 | 10-14 | 5 |
| 1 | 2 | 7-14 | 8 |
| 1 | 3 | 10-14 | 5 |
| 1 | 4 | 13, 14 | 2 |
| | | | |

Total possible triplets = $0 + 2 + 5 + 8 + 5 + 2 = 22$.

135. There are two cases in this situation:

**If we include 5:** If this number consists of the digit 5 then we would need to use at least one of the even digits between 2 & 4. In this case, the number would need to be even and also divisible by 5. For this to occur, the number should end in 0 – which is not a possibility in the given case. So 5 cannot be one of these four digits.

**If we do not include 5:** In this case the number, would be consisting of the digits 1,2,3 and 4. In such a case, we can easily realise that such a number cannot be a multiple of 3, since the sum of digits of the number is 10.

**Hints**

### Level of Difficulty (III)

1. Of course with the options here you can check the values directly to see that the required condition fits for the numbers 15 and 95, respectively. However, in case you were solving this without options, and you were required to find the two digit numbers that satisfied the given condition, you would need a completely different process to solve this.

   In such a case, the following thought process would help you identify the number:

   The various squares of single digits are 1,4,9,16,25,36,49,64 and 81. If the first digit of the number was 1, the number would look like: 1x. In such a case, 11 more than this number would mean that $1^2 + x^2$ should be equal to a number in the 20s. The only possibility that exists for $1^2 + x^2$ to be in the 20s is if we take $x$ as 5. In such a case our number is 15 and $1^2 + 5^2 = 26 \rightarrow$ satisfies our condition.

   If the number is 2x, $2^2 + x^2$ needs to be in the 30s. The only relevant value to check is 26 compared to $2^2 + 6^2 = 40$, which does not satisfy the given condition.

   If the number is 3x, $3^2 + x^2$ needs to be in the 40s. The only relevant value to check is 36 compared to $3^2 + 6^2 = 45$, which does not satisfy the given condition.

   If the number is 4x, $4^2 + x^2$ needs to be in the 50s. The only relevant value to check is 46 compared to $4^2 + 6^2 = 52$, which does not satisfy the given condition.

   If the number is 5x, $5^2 + x^2$ needs to be in the 60s. The only relevant value to check is 56 compared to $5^2 + 6^2 = 61$, which does not satisfy the given condition.

   If the number is 6x, $6^2 + x^2$ needs to be in the 70s. There is no value that gives us $6^2 + x^2$ in the 70s.

   If the number is 7x, $7^2 + x^2$ needs to be in the 80s. The only relevant value to check is 76 compared to $7^2 + 6^2 = 85$, which does not satisfy the given condition.

   If the number is 8x, $8^2 + x^2$ needs to be in the 90s. There is no value that gives us $8^2 + x^2$ in the 90s.

   If the number is 9x, $9^2 + x^2$ needs to be between 100 and 110. The only relevant value to check is 95 compared to $9^2 + 5^2 = 106$. Here again we can see that the required difference of 11 is maintained.

   Author's note: Solving the same question without options takes a much longer time than solving it with the presence of options. The non-option based

questions were introduced for the first time in the CAT in CAT 2015. It led to a significant drop in the number of attempts that most students were able to make in the exam — results showing at least a 15-20% drop in the number of questions that the toppers were able to do in the test in order to get the same percentile. In that context, learning how to solve questions without options is one of the key changes you would need to make to your CAT prep process going forward.

2. Again, spotting this with options is quite easy as we can see that $7^2 + 8^2 = 113$ and that is 112 less than the value of $(7 + 8)^2 = 225$. Without options here you can think of $a^2 + b^2 + 112 = (a + b)^2 \rightarrow 2ab = 112$ or $ab = 56$. Since, the numbers are consecutive, sifting through the factor pairs of 56 we can see the numbers as 7 & 8, respectively.

3. Solving through options, you can see that if you were to take the required denominator as 9, you get

   $$\frac{2}{12} + \frac{2}{7} = \frac{38}{84} = \frac{19}{42}.$$

4. $15 \times 37 \times 63 \times 51 \times 97 \times 17$ on division by 100 would give us a remainder that would be equal to its' last 2 digits. First we can divide the numerator and the denominator by 5 to get the expression:

   $$\frac{3 \times 37 \times 63 \times 51 \times 97 \times 17}{20}$$ using remainder theo-

   rem $\rightarrow \dfrac{3 \times 17 \times 3 \times 11 \times 17 \times 17}{20} = \dfrac{51 \times 33 \times 289}{20}$

   using remainder theorem $\rightarrow \dfrac{11 \times 13 \times 9}{20} = \dfrac{143 \times 9}{20}$

   $\rightarrow \dfrac{3 \times 9}{20} = \dfrac{27}{20} \rightarrow$ Remainder = 7. Hence, the required remainder = $7 \times 5 = 35$, which would also be the last two digits of the given number.

5. You can do this directly by checking the options and select the one that matches the conditions.

6. The required numbers would be numbers in the Arithmetic Progression 104,109,114,119,....999. The sum of this series would be given as $n \times$ Average =

   $$180 \times \frac{1103}{2} = 99270$$

7. The required numbers would be numbers in the Arithmetic Progression 10,17,24...94. The sum of this series would be given as $n \times$ Average = $13 \times \dfrac{104}{2} = 676$

8. The required numbers would be numbers in the Arithmetic Progression 105,115,125,....995. The sum of this series would be given as $n \times$ Average =

   $$90 \times \frac{1100}{2} = 49500$$

9. A factor pair search of 2430 would give you the answer as $45 \times 54$. Hence, 45 is the correct answer.

10. Let the product of the numbers be $p$. Then the cubes of the numbers are: $p - 3$, $p + 2$ and $p + 3$. The numbers (using the options) can be found to be $3^{1/3}$; $9^{1/3}$ & 2.

11. $(x - y)(x + y) = 45$. Working through factor pairs of 45, we get $15 \times 3$; $45 \times 1$ & $9 \times 5$ as the three factor pairs here. The numbers are 9 & 6; 22 & 23; 7 & 2.

12. 52 is the only such number as in the numbers before the 50s, we see that if we try to keep the sum of the digits as 7 or more, we would not be able to satisfy the last condition (of the reverse not being larger than half the number). Also, in the numbers in the 60s and above, the sum of squares of the digits would exceed 30. Hence, the correct answer is 52.

13. The required number can be formed by making the hundreds and the tens digits as small as possible. You would also need to make the middle digits equal to each other (or as equal to each other as possible) 8339 would be the number required.

14. Since this question has close-ended options, it is fine if you were to solve it by just checking the options. However, I would encourage you to solve this in a no option scenario too.

15. The number would obviously need to have 1 as its' unit digit (as otherwise the quotient of 4 would not be possible to achieve). Hence, the only relevant numbers to check would be 71, 81 and 91 (for a quotient of 4). Out of these, the number 91 also meets the remainder of 15 requirements. Hence, the correct answer is 91.

16. The second condition requires the number to be one of 31, 42, 53, 64, 75, 86 or 97. 64 is the only number amongst these that meets the requirement of the quotient of the number divided by its' product of digits is 8/3. However, it is not given in the options. Hence, the correct answer is none of these.

17. Check through the options to see that 72 is the number that fits the required conditions.

18. Check through the options to see that 71 fits the required conditions.

19. Divide the given expression by 100 and find the remainder to get the answer. 50 would be the last two digits here.

20. $43^{101} + 23^{101}$ is of the form $a^n + b^n$ with $n$ odd. Such a number can be written to be a multiple of $(a + b)$. Thus, the given expression is a multiple of $(43 + 23) = 66$. Hence, the required remainder would be 0.

21. Divide the given expression by 1000 and find the remainder to get the answer. $12345 \times 54321 \div 1000$ $= 2469 \times 54321 \div 200$ —gives a remainder of $69 \times 121 \div 200 = 8349 \div 200 \rightarrow$ gives us a remainder of 149. Thus, the remainder would be $149 \times 5 = 745$. Hence, the last three digits would be 745.

22. Checking the options for the conditions, you would realise that both the values 156 and 237 satisfy the conditions of the problem. Note: Learning point from this question- The difference between a 3 digit number '$abc$' and the 3 digit number '$cba$' got by reversing the digits of $abc$, would be $99 \times |a - c|$.

23. This can be easily checked through the options. However, if the options were not present, you could still do this by working out the sum of squares of the digits to be 74 (the only possible combination for three squares to add up to 74 would be $8^2 + 1^2 + 3^2$ & $7^2 + 4^2 + 3^2$.) Amongst these, we can select 8,1,3 as the digits since we also need the reversal of the digits to give us a difference of 495.

24. Solving through the options is the best approach here.

25. This is a property of the number $-0.5$. The sum of the number and its' square $= -0.25$, which is the least possible value that can be created.

26. $2222^{5555} \div 7 \rightarrow 3^{5555} \div 7 \rightarrow 3^5 \div 7 \rightarrow$ Remainder = 5; $5555^{2222} \div 7 \rightarrow 4^{2222} \div 7 \rightarrow 4^2 \div 7 \rightarrow$ Remainder = 2. Hence, the required remainder would be $(5 + 2) \div 7 = 0$.

27. Since the LCM of 20,15,12 and 8 is 120 we need the smallest $120n - 3$ number in 5 digits. $120 \times 84 = 10080$. Thus, the required number is $10080 - 3 = 10077$.

28. Check the options to see that none of these match the required condition.

29. Check the options to see that none of these match the required condition.

30. $32^{32^{32}} \div 9 \rightarrow 5^{32^{32}} \div 9 = 5^{6n+x} \div 9$. We write this in the form of $5^{6n+x}$ because $5^6$ leaves a remainder of 1 when divided by 9. When we try to see $32^{32}$ as $6n + x$, we can find the value of x as the remainder of $2^{32}$ when divided by 6. The following thought process would help us find this value: $2^{32} \div 6 = 2^{31} \div 3 \rightarrow$ Remainder = 2 (by the $a^n \div (a + 1)$ rule). Thus, $2^{32} \div 6$ would have a remainder of $2 \times 2 = 4$. Hence, the required remainder would be $5^4 \div 9$, which is 4.

31. The required remainder would be $1 \times 2 \times 4 \times 4 \times 4 \div 7 \rightarrow 2$.

32. Since the power on 2 is even, the remainder would be 1.

33. $3^6 \div 7$ leaves a remainder of 1. If we look at the power 1989 as $6n + x$, we will get $x$ as 3. Hence, the remainder of $3^{1989} \div 7$ would be the same as the remainder of $3^3 \div 7$, i.e., 6.

34. The required units digit would be given by the series: $(1 + 4 + 9 + 6 + 5 + 6 + 9 + 4 + 1 + 0)$ repeated 10 times (since the units digit of $11^2 + 12^2 + \ldots + 19^2$

$+ 20^2$ would be the same as the unit digit of $1^2 + 2^2 + \ldots 9^2 + 10^2$). Hence, the required unit digit would be 0.

35. The GCD of $A^x - 1$ & $A^y - 1$ is given by $A^{(GCD \text{ of } x,y)} - 1$. Hence, the required answer would be $2^{20} - 1$

36. The required GCD would be 1111…111 twenty ones.

37. Approaching this again as the question number 34, we realise that the last digit of the expression would be the same pattern repeated 10 times. Hence, the last digit of the given expression would be 0.

38. You can experimentally verify that for all values of n, the required GCD would be 1 as the numbers would be co-prime to each other.

39. $32^{32^{32}} \div 7 \to 4^{32^{32}} \div 7 = 4^{3n+x} \div 7$. We write this in the form of $4^{3n+x}$ because $4^3$ leaves a remainder of 1 when divided by 7. When we try to see $32^{32}$ as $3n + x$, we can find the value of x as the remainder of $2^{32}$ when divided by 3. The following thought process would help us find this value:
$2^{32} \div 3 = 1$. (remainder)
Hence, the required remainder would be $4^1 \div 7$, which is 4.

40. The remainder of $(10^{10} + 10^{100} + 10^{1000} + \ldots + 10^{100\,000\,00000}) \div 7 \to (3^{10} + 3^{100} + 3^{1000} + \ldots + 3^{10000000000}) \div 7 \to (3^4 + 3^4 + 3^4 + 3^4 + 3^4 + 3^4 + 3^4 + 3^4 + 3^4 + 3^4) \div 7 = $ Remainder of $40 \div 7 \to 5$.

41. If we visualise the number as $2^p \times 3^q$, the number of factors would be $(p + 1)(q + 1)$; For $2n$, we realise that $2n = 2^{p+1} \times 3^q$ and its number of factors would be $(p + 2)(q + 1) = 28$. This has multiple possibilities based on the factors of 28. These are: $1 \times 28$; $2 \times 14$ and $4 \times 7$. Also, $3n = 2^p \times 3^{q+1}$ would have $(p + 1)(q + 2) = 30$ factors. Looking through the factor pairs of 30, we see $1 \times 30$, $2 \times 15$, $3 \times 10$ and $5 \times 6$. Considering both these lists, we can see that if we take p as 5 and q as 3, we get both the conditions fulfilled. Thus, $6n = 2^{p+1} \times 3^{q+1} = 2^6 \times 3^4$ would give us $7 \times 5 = 35$ factors.

42. Solve this question through the options. For n terms being 16 (option 1), we would need an AP with 16 terms and common difference 1, that would add up to 1000. Since, the average value of a term of this AP turns out to be $1000 \div 16 = 62.5$, we can create a 16 term AP as 55,56,57….62,63,64…70 that adds up to 1000. Hence, 16 terms is possible. Likewise, 5 terms gives the average as 200 & the 5 terms can be taken as 198,199,200,201,202. It is similarly possible for 25 terms with an average of 40, but is not possible for 20 terms with an average of 50. Hence, option (d) is correct.

43. The first remainder would be 4, the second one would be given by $4 \times 4 = 16/9 \to 7$, the third one $6 \times 6 = 36/9 \to 0$. The fourth one, $8 \times 8 = 64/9 \to 1$. Subsequent, remainders would be 1, 0, 7, 4, 0. This cycle would repeat for the next 9 numbers each time. Thus, the remainder for the first 45 numbers =

$(4 + 7 + 0 + 1 + 1 + 0 + 7 + 4 + 0)$ repeated 5 times $\to 120/9 \to$ remainder = 3. The last 4 terms would then add $4 + 7 + 0 + 1$ to the remainder. Thus the final remainder = $15/9 \to 6$.

44. The product would be 32323232…repeated 32 times. Hence, the sum of digits would be 160.

45. For the maximum number of questions, we would need to keep the 15 questions that are not unique, to be shared between the least number of tests (i.e., 2 each). This would give us 12 sets of 15 questions each that are not unique. Also, the number of unique questions would be $35 \times 25 = 875$. Thus, the required maximum number of questions would be $875 + 180 = 1055$.

46. For the minimum number of questions, we would need to share the 15 non-unique questions amongst the entire 25 sets. The number of questions in this case would be: $35 \times 25 + 15 = 875 + 15 = 890$.

**Solutions for 47 to 49:**
The given condition in the problem is a property of the numbers in the geometric series of the powers of 3.
The numbers from $W_1$ to $W_7$ would be 1,3,9,27,81,243 and 729. The answers can be got according to these values.

47. $1 + 2 \times 3 + 3 \times 9 + 4 \times 27 + 5 \times 81 + 6 \times 243 = 1 + 6 + 27 + 108 + 405 + 1458 = 2005$.

48. $3^0 \times 3^1 \times 3^2 \times 3^3 \times 3^4 \times 3^5 \times 3^6 = 3^{21}$.

49. We would need to use the coefficients as 1,1,1,0, −1, −1 & −1 to $W_1$ to $W_7$ in that order to get:
$1 + 3 + 9 + 0 - 81 - 243 - 729 = -1040$. (Note: In this question we have to take the coefficients as defined in the problem as +1, 0 or −1 only).

50&51. There are two 3 digit perfect square numbers that obey the factors are perfect squares rule - viz. 196 and 256. However, questions 50 and 51, both rule out the use of 256. Hence, for question 50, we are looking for the number of factors of $196196 = 2 \times 2 \times 7 \times 7 \times 7 \times 13 \times 11$. This number would have $3 \times 4 \times 2 \times 2 = 48$ factors. Hence, option (c) is correct. For question 51, we need the number of factors of $196196196 = 2 \times 2 \times 3 \times 7 \times 7 \times 333667$. This number gives us $3 \times 2 \times 3 \times 2 = 36$ factors.
*Note:* The number 333667 is a prime number.

52. Since each team scored a different number of points, it follows that the points scored by the 15 teams would be 21,22,23,24,…till 35. This is because, the total number of matches in the tournament is $^{15}C_2 = 105$ & there are 4 points for each match (either 3 + 1 or 2 + 2). Thus, the total number of points in the tournament is $105 \times 4 = 420$. The only way to fit in 420 points amongst 15 teams with each team getting different number of points & the least value for any team being 21 points would be to use the Arithmetic Progression 21,22,23,24…till 35. Once, we realise this, we know that Australia scored 35 points out of a maximum possible $14 \times 3 = 42$ (14 wins). This

means that Australia is dropping 7 points. Each loss makes you drop 2 points as instead of 3 for a win, you receive only 1 point for a loss. Hence, it is not possible for Australia to lose 4 matches. The maximum losses Australia could have had is 3.

53. We can solve this by splitting the denominator into two co-prime numbers 9 & 17. First find the remainder of $128^{1000}$ on division by 9.
$128^{1000} \div 9 \rightarrow 2^{1000} \div 9 = (2^6)^{166} \times 2^4 \div 9 \rightarrow$ Remainder $= 7$. This means that $128^{1000}$ is a $9n + 7$ number.
Next find the remainder of $128^{1000}$ on division by 17.
$128^{1000} \div 17 \rightarrow 9^{1000} \div 17 = [(9^{16})^{62} \times 9^8] \div 17 \rightarrow$ Remainder $= 1$. This means that $128^{1000}$ is a $17n + 1$ number. If we try to look for a number below 153, that is both $17n + 1$ as well as $9n + 7$, we would see that the number 52 fulfills this requirement. Hence, 52 is the required remainder of $128^{1000} \div 153$.

54. $\dfrac{50^{51^{52}}}{11} \rightarrow \dfrac{6^{51^{52}}}{11} = \dfrac{6^{10x} \times 6^1}{11} \rightarrow$ Remainder $= 6$.

55. Use the $-1$ remainder rule for even powers. Thus:
$\dfrac{32^{33^{34}}}{11} \rightarrow \dfrac{10^{\text{Odd Power}}}{11} - \rightarrow$ Remainder $= 10$.

56. $\dfrac{30^{72^{87}}}{11} \rightarrow \dfrac{8^{72^{87}}}{11} = \dfrac{8^{10x} \times 8^{2^{87}}}{11} \rightarrow \dfrac{1 \times 8^{2^{87}}}{11} \rightarrow \dfrac{8^{10x} \times 8^8}{11} \rightarrow$
Remainder $= 5$

57. $\dfrac{50^{56^{62}}}{11} \rightarrow \dfrac{6^{56^{62}}}{11} = \dfrac{6^{10x} \times 6^6}{11} \rightarrow$ Remainder $= 5$.

58. $\dfrac{33^{34^{35}}}{7} \rightarrow \dfrac{5^{34^{35}}}{7} = \dfrac{5^{6x} \times 5^4}{7} \rightarrow$ Remainder $= 2$.

59. We need the expression $\dfrac{n(n+1)(2n+1)}{6}$ to be a multiple of 4. For this to occur, the numerator of the above expression should be a multiple of 8. In the expression $n(n + 1)(2n + 1)$, $2n + 1$ would always be an odd number. Also, amongst $n$ and $(n + 1)$ one number would be odd and the other would be even. Since, we need $n(n + 1)(2n + 1)$ to be a multiple of 8, we would need either $n$ or $(n + 1)$ to be a multiple of 8 (while at the same time it should be below 100). Thus, we get the number series $n = 7,8,15,16,23,24,...95,96$. Since there are 12 multiples of 8 below 100, the required answer is $12 \times 2 = 24$.

60. We need the expression $\dfrac{[n(n+1)]^2}{2^2}$ to be a multiple of 5. For this to occur, the numerator of the above expression should be a multiple of 5. Either $n$ or $n + 1$ should be a multiple of 5. Below 50, there are 19 such instances. Hence, the correct answer is 19.

61. The first solution easily visible here would be at $x = -1$, and $y = 1$. In such equations, we should know that the value of $x$ would change with the coefficient

of $y$, while the value of y would change with the coefficient of x (& the two values would move in the opposite directions since there is a 'plus' sign in the middle). Thus, the series of values of x from its highest positive value below 1000 to the lower limit of being just above $-1000$ would be 993,986,......13,6, $-1,-8, -15,...$ $-995$. The number of terms in this series $= \dfrac{1988}{7} + 1 = 285$.

62. 1144 can be written as a product of 3 co-prime numbers – viz: $13 \times 8 \times 11$. Further, the given number when divided by 11, leaves a remainder of 7, when divided by 13 leaves a remainder of 10 (because, if you divide 777777 by 13, there is no remainder. Hence, when you divide the given number by 13, the remainder would only depend on the remainder of the last three 7's. i.e. $777 \div 13$.). Also, the given number when divided by 8, leaves a remainder of 1. Hence, the given number is a number that is simultaneously $13n + 10$, $8n + 1$ and $11n + 7$. If we create a series of $13n + 10$, we can see that the series would be: 10, 23, 36, 49, 62... At 62, the number is $13n + 10$ as well as an $11n + 7$ number. The next such number would be $62 + 143$ (because 143 is the LCM of 13 and 11). Thus, writing down the series of numbers that belong to $13n + 10$ and $11n + 7$ and checking when it also simultaneously becomes $8n + 1$, we can see that the series would be:
62, 205, 348, 491, 634, 777. The number 777 is also an $8n + 1$ number. Hence, the correct remainder is 777.

63. In order to solve this question, you would need to find the odd factors of 19! that are also multiples of 5.
$19! = 2^{16} \times 3^8 \times 5^3 \times 7^2 \times 11^1 \times 13^1 \times 17^1 \times 19^1$.
The required answer would be $1 \times 9 \times 3 \times 3 \times 2 \times 2 \times 2 \times 2 = 81 \times 16 = 1296$.

64. From 5! onwards, each of the numbers would have a units digit of 0. Hence, the units digit of the given number would depend on the units digit of $1! - 2! + 3! - 4!$, which would be $1 (1 - 2 + 6 - 4)$. Since N is a number that has a unit's digit of 1, when it is raised to any power, the units digit would not change. Hence, the correct answer would be 1.

65. Exactly 4 factors would occur for numbers that can be represented by a single prime factor as $p^3$. Also, any number that can be represented by a product of two prime factors $p^1 \times q^1$ would also have 4 factors. There are four perfect cubes below 100. Besides, numbers like $2^1 \times 3^1$; $2^1 \times 5^1$; ....$2^1 \times 47^1$ (a total of 14 numbers). Next we consider numbers with the lower prime factor as 3. These would be $3^1 \times 5^1$; $3^1 \times 7^1$; ...$3^1 \times 31^1$ (a total of 9 numbers). Next, we consider numbers with their lower prime factors as 5. These would be $5^1 \times 7^1$; $5^1 \times 11^1$; ...$5^1 \times 19^1$ (a total of 5 numbers). For numbers starting with

7, we would get $7^1 \times 11^1$; $7^1 \times 13^1$; (a total of 2 numbers). But, out of the 4 perfect cubes, 1 and 64 do not have 4 factors. Hence, there are a total of 32 such numbers, below 100 that would have exactly 4 factors.

66. Since both the numbers are odd, there are no 2's in their prime factors. Since, their HCF is 225, both these numbers would necessarily have $3^2 \times 5^2$ inside them. From the information, that both these numbers have 36 factors, we can realize that 36 factors can only occur in cases where the prime factors of the numbers look as follows: $p^8 \times q^3$; $p^{11} \times q^2$; $p^2 \times q^3 \times r^2$ & $p^2 \times q^2 \times r \times s$. Amongst these, the best strategy to make smaller numbers satisfying the criteria would obviously be to use the structures: $p^2 \times q^3 \times r^2$ and $p^2 \times q^2 \times r \times s$. Since, the third prime factor of the two numbers cannot be the same (else it would change the HCF), we would need to introduce 7 and 11. Also, we would not try to increase the powers of 7 and 11 as they are comparatively larger as compared to 3 and 5. Thus, we can visualize the numbers: $3^2 \times 5^2 \times 11 \times 13$, $3^3 \times 5^2 \times 7^2$. The required smallest LCM would be $3^3 \times 5^2 \times 7^2 \times 11 \times 13$.

67. $7! = 5040$. When we divide 7! by 17 it leaves a remainder 8. When $[(7!)^{61}]^{17777}$ is divided by 17 it leaves a remainder that is the same as when we divide $[(8)^{61}]^{17777}$ or $[(8)^{720}]^{17777}$ or $[(16)^{540}]^{17777}$ by 17.The remainder when $[(16)^{540}]^{17777}$ or $[(17-1)^{540}]^{17777}$ divided by 17 is 1 (since the power on 16 is even).

68. $x + y = 2w$ ......1
$y + 6z = 2(w + x)$ .......2
$w + 5z = 2y$ .....3
From equation 2 – equation 1 we get: $6z - x = 2x$ or $x = 2z$
Substituting $x = 2z$ in equation 1, we get : $2w - y = 2z$ .....(4)
Solving equation 3 and 4 we get $w = 3z$ & $y = 4z$
$z: y: x: w = 1: 4: 2: 3$
So 3241 & 6482 are two possible values of $wxyz$.
So the required sum = 3241+ 6482 = 9723.
Alternately, once you have the relationship $x = 2z$, you can think of values and try to fit in the conditions of the other equations. $z$ and $x$ can take only 4 feasible values: viz 1,2; 2,4;3,6 & 4,8.
This gives us four possibilities for the numbers: _2_1; _4_2; _6_3; _8_4. The fourth of these, with $z$ = 4 can be eliminated by looking at the third equation ($w + 5z = 2y$) as it would need $y$ to be greater than 10.
For $z = 3$ & $x = 6$; we get $w = 1$ & $y = 8$ or $w = 3$ and $y = 9$ from the third equation. Both these values do not match the second equation.
For $z = 2$ & $x = 4$; we get $w = 2$ & $y = 6$ or $w = 4$ and $y = 7$ or $w = 6$ and $y = 8$ or $w = 8$ and $y = 9$. Checking for the second equation, only the values of $w = 6$ & $y = 8$ matches. Hence, we get the number 6482.

69. Likewise, when you check for $z = 1$ & $x = 2$, you would be able to find the number 3241.

$$\frac{[17(9!) + 2(18!)]}{9!.17408} = \frac{17.9!}{9!17.2^{10}} + \frac{2.18!}{9!.17.2^{10}}$$

$$\frac{17.9!}{9!17.2^{10}} = \frac{1}{2^{10}} \quad \& \quad \text{remainder of } \frac{1}{2^{10}} = 1$$

Hence, the Remainder of $\left(\dfrac{17.9!}{9!17.2^{10}}\right) = 17.9!$

$2.18! = 2.18.17.16.15.14.13.12.11.10.9!$
In 18, 16, 14, 12, 10 the number of 2s are 1, 4, 1, 2 & 1, respectively.
So $2.18! = 2.18.17.16.15.14.13.12.11.10.9! = 2^{10}.17k.9! = $ Where $k$ is an integer.
Remainder $\left(\dfrac{2^{10}.17k.9!}{9!(17)2^{10}}\right) = 0$
So the required remainder is $17.9! + 0 = 17.9!$.

70. Remainder when $X$ is divided by 9, is same as remainder when sum of digits of $X$ is divided by 9.
Sum of digit of first 999 natural numbers is 13500, which is divisible by 9.
Now sum of digits of 1000, 1001, 1002 are 1, 2 and 3, respectively.
Sum of digits of $X$ is $9n + (1 + 2 + 3) = 9n + 6$. So the required remainder is 6.

71. $X = 0123456789..........1001$
$X$ has a total of $10 + 2 \times 90 + 3 \times 900 + 2 \times 4 = 2898$ digits.
So there are total 1449 digits are on the left of the vertical line out of these 1449 numbers there are total $1449 - (10 + 180) = 1259$ digits are digits of 3-digit number.

$$1259 = 419 \times 3 + 2$$

On the left side of the vertical line there are 419 3-digit numbers and 2 more digits.
419th 3-digit number = 518 and next two digits are 5, 1. Hence last four digits are 1851.
The remainder of any number divided by 625 is the remainder when last 4-digits of the number is divided by 625.
Required remainder = Remainder of (1851/625) = 601

72. If the 4- digit number is $abcd$ then three cases are possible for the number to have 24 in it:
Case a: If $cd$ = 24 then the numbers are of the form $ab24$

$$ab24 = 100ab + 24$$

24 is divisible by 24 and $100 \times ab$ must be divisible by 24. 100 is divisible so 4 then $ab$ must be divisible by 6. Possible values of $ab$ = 12, 18, 24, ...., 96. So there are 15 such numbers possible.
Case b: If $bc$ = 24 then the number is of the form $a24b$

$a24b$ must be divisible by 3 and 8. If $a24b$ is divisible by 8 then $24b$ is divisible by 8. Possible values of $b = 0, 8$.

Similarly $a + 2 + 4 + b = (a + b) + 6$ must be divisible by 3.

When $b = 0$ then $a = 3, 6, 9$ (3 possible cases)

When $b = 8$ then $a = 1, 4, 7$ (3 possible cases)

So there are total 6 possible cases.

Case c: $ab = 24$ so the number should be of the form $24cd$.

$$24cd = 2400 + cd$$

2400 is divisible by 24, $cd$ divisible by 24 when $cd = 00, 24, 48, 72, 96$ (5 possible cases).

However, the number 2424 occurred in cases $a$ & $c$ both. So the total possible numbers = $5 + 6 + 15 - 1 = 25$.

73. If $N$ divides both $18X + 2$, $12X + 1$ then their difference $6X + 1$ will also be divisible by $N$ & difference of $12X + 1$ & $6X + 1$ i.e. $6X$ will also be divisible by $N$. If $6X$ is divisible by $N$ then $N$ can also divide $12X$. It means $N$ divides both $12X$, $12X + 1$. Since $12X$ and $12X + 1$ both are consecutive numbers so $N = 1$. So the given numbers are relatively prime for all values of $X$ i.e. $X$ would have 99 values.

74. Let $P = 7 \times 10^{5+n} + k$ where $n, k$ are whole numbers. After removal of the leftmost digit the new number will be $k$.

According to the question:
$$7 \times 10^5 \times 10^n + k = 21k$$
$$7 \times 10^5 \times 10^n = 20k$$
$$\frac{7 \times 10^5 \times 10^n}{20} = k$$

$k = 35000 \times 10^n$

$P = 735000 \times 10^n$

The required product = $7 \times 3 \times 5 = 105$

75. $X!$ is completely divisible by $11^{51}$. So the value of $X$ should be less than $11 \times 51 = 561$

Highest power of 11 in 561! $\left[\frac{561}{11}\right] + \left[\frac{561}{11^2}\right] + \dots = 51 + 4 = 55$

If we subtract $11 \times 3 = 33$ from 561 we get $561 - 33 = 528$. Highest power of 11 in 528! is $\left[\frac{528}{11}\right] + \left[\frac{528}{11^2}\right] = 52$

Highest power of 11 in $528 - 1 = 527!$ is $= \left[\frac{527}{11}\right] + \left[\frac{527}{11^2}\right] = 47 + 4 = 51$

So the required number is 527.

Sum of the digits = $5 + 2 + 7 = 14$.

76. Let $a = 5k$ then $a + 5 = 5(k + 1)$. Both $k, k + 1$ are co-prime.

LCM of $a, a + 5 = 5.k.(k + 1)$

For $k = 4$, $5k(k + 1) = 100$.

So minimum possible value of smaller number is 20.

Maximum value of $k$ for which the LCM is a three-digit number is 13.

Maximum possible value of the smaller number = 65

So the required difference = $65 - 20 = 45$.

77. We need to look at writing the binary number system from $8 = (1000)_2$ to $127 = (1111111)_2$

There are 64 7-digit numbers in Binary system are from 1000000 to 1111111. There are six digits after the leftmost 1. Each of these 6 digits can be filled by either 0 or 1 and both are equally probable in any position. So the number of 1 from 1000000 to

$1111111 = 64 + 64 \times \dfrac{1}{2} \times 6 = 64 + 192 = 256$.

There are 32 6-digit numbers in Binary system are from 100000 to 111111. There are five digits after the leftmost 1. Each of these 5 digits can be filled by either 0 or 1 and both are equally probable in any position. So the number of 1 from 100000 to 111111

$= 32 + 32 \times \dfrac{1}{2} \times 5 = 32 + 80 = 112$.

Similarly, from 10000 to 11111 there are $16 + \dfrac{16}{2} \times 4 = 16 + 32 = 48$.

Similarly, from 1000 to 1111 there are $8 + 8 \times \dfrac{1}{2} \times 3 = 20$

So total 1's = $20 + 48 + 112 + 256 = 436$.

78. First of all pick all the prime number i.e. {2, 3, 5, 7, 11, 13, 17, 19}. We cannot pick perfect square numbers i.e. 4, 9, 16 & perfect cube numbers i.e. 8. Now we are left with the numbers 6, 10, 12, 14, 15, 18, 20 out of which 12 & 18 will give perfect square numbers when we multiplied them with 3 and 2, respectively. Also, we would need to take 1 into this list. So we have a total 14 such numbers {1, 2, 3, 5, 6, 7, 10, 11, 13, 14, 15, 17, 19, 20}. Note: If you try to improve this solution, by taking the perfect squares and the perfect cubes in, you would first need to get rid of 1, in the list. Also, you can take only one perfect square number (as if you were to take two perfect squares, their product would be a perfect square too). With respect to the perfect cube 8, we can see that $8 \times 2 = 16$ is a perfect square. Hence, if we try to take in 8, we would need to remove 2 from our list. Thus, you can see that you can take this list to a maximum of 14 numbers.

79. It is given that $d + e + f = 9$, now two cases are possible.

Case 1: When all three of them are odd. This case is not possible because if all three of them are odd then $g, h, i, j$ cannot be odd digits.

Case 2: When only one number is odd. This case is possible and the digit which is odd among $d, e, f$

can be 1 only. So the sum of rest of the two digits is 8 which is possible as 0 + 8 only.

$g = 9$, $h = 7$, $i = 5$ and $j = 3$ & $d = 8$, $f = 0$. So $e = 1$.

$a = 6$, $b = 4$ and $c = 2$

$$\left[\frac{a \times b \times c \times d}{i}\right] = \left[\frac{2 \times 4 \times 6 \times 8}{7}\right] = 54$$

80. If $N = abc$, then $a + b + c = abc/7$

As the product is divisible by 7 so one of the digits must be 7.

$a + b + 7 = ab.7/7$

$a + b + 7 = ab$

$ab - a - b = 7$

$ab - a - b + 1 = 8$

$a(b - 1) - (b - 1) = 8$

$(a - 1) (b - 1) = 8$. There are two possible ways to get 8 as a product of 2 digits. These are: $4 \times 2$ & $1 \times 8$

This gives us: $a = 5$, $b = 3$ & $a = 2$, $b = 9$

Possible sets of digits used in the numbers are (2, 9, 7), (3, 5, 7). Hence, the correct answer is 2 (i.e. 2 sets are possible)

81. In base 34, 10 means 34. In base 10, 10 is obtained by multiplying 2 and 5. In base 34, it is obtained by multiplying 2 and 17. Number of consecutive zeroes in base 34 at the end of the number is same as the number of 2's and 17's in 3132!. Since the number of 2's is much more than number of 17's, so we count number of 17's in 3132!

Maximum power of 17 in 3132! = $\left[\frac{3132}{17}\right] + \left[\frac{3132}{17^2}\right]$ = 184 + 10 = 194.

# Progressions

The chapter on progressions essentially yields common-sense based questions in examinations.

Questions in the CAT and other aptitude exams mostly appear from either Arithmetic Progressions (more common) or from Geometric Progressions.

The chapter of progressions is a logical and natural extension of the chapter on Number Systems, since there is such a lot of commonality of logic between the problems associated with these two chapters.

## ARITHMETIC PROGRESSIONS

Quantities are said to be in arithmetic progression when they increase or decrease by a common difference.

Thus each of the following series forms an arithmetic progression:

$$3, 7, 11, 15,\ldots$$

$$8, 2, -4, -10,\ldots$$

$$a, a + d, a + 2d, a + 3d,\ldots$$

*The common difference is found by subtracting any term of the series from the next term.*

That is, common difference of an A.P. $= (t_N - t_{N-1})$.

In the first of the above examples the common difference is 4; in the second it is $-6$; in the third it is $d$.

If we examine the series $a, a + d, a + 2d, a + 3d,\ldots$ we notice that *in any term the coefficient of d is always less by one than the position of that term in the series.*

Thus the $r$th term of an arithmetic progression is given by $T_r = a + (r - 1)d$.

If $n$ be the number of terms, and if $L$ denotes the last term or the $n$th term, we have

$$L = a + (n - 1)d$$

## To Find the Sum of the given Number of Terms in an Arithmetic Progression

Let $a$ denote the first term $d$, the common difference, and $n$ the total number of terms. Also, let $L$ denote the last term, and $S$ the required sum; then

$$S = \frac{n(a + L)}{2} \tag{1}$$
$$L = a + (n - 1)d \tag{2}$$
$$S = \frac{n}{2} \times [2a + (n - 1)d] \tag{3}$$

If any two terms of an arithmetical progression be given, the series can be completely determined; for this data results in two simultaneous equations, the solution of which will give the first term and the common difference.

When three quantities are in arithmetic progression, the middle one is said to be the **arithmetic mean** of the other two.

Thus $a$ is the arithmetic mean between $a - d$ and $a + d$. So, when it is required to arbitrarily consider three numbers in A.P. take $a - d$, $a$ and $a + d$ as the three numbers as this reduces one unknown thereby making the solution easier.

## To Find the Arithmetic Mean between any Two given Quantities

Let $a$ and $b$ be two quantities and $A$ be their arithmetic mean. Then since $a, A, b$, are in A.P. We must have

$$b - A = A - a$$

Each being equal to the common difference;

This gives us $\quad A = \dfrac{(a + b)}{2}$

Between two given quantities it is always possible to insert any number of terms such that the whole series thus formed shall be in A.P. The terms thus inserted are called the **arithmetic means**.

## To Insert a given Number of Arithmetic Means between Two given Quantities

Let $a$ and $b$ be the given quantities and $n$ be the number of means.

Including the extremes, the number of terms will then be $n + 2$ so that we have to find a series of $n + 2$ terms in A.P., of which $a$ is the first, and $b$ is the last term.

Let $d$ be the common difference;

then         $b =$ the $(n + 2)$th term

$$= a + (n + 1)d$$

Hence,     $d = \dfrac{(b - a)}{(n + 1)}$

and the required means are

$$a + \frac{(b - a)}{n - 1}, a + \frac{2(b - a)}{n + 1}, \cdots a + \frac{n(b - a)}{n + 1}$$

Till now we have studied A.P.s in their mathematical context. This was important for you to understand the basic mathematical construct of A.P.s. However, you need to understand that questions on A.P. are seldom solved on a mathematical basis, (Especially under the time pressure that you are likely to face in the CAT and other aptitude exams). In such situations the mathematical processes for solving progressions based questions are likely to fail or at the very least, be very tedious. Hence, understanding the following logical aspects about Arithmetic Progressions is likely to help you solve questions based on APs in the context of an aptitude exam.

Let us look at these issues one by one:

**1. Process for finding the nth term of an A.P.**

Suppose you have to find the 17th term of the
A.P. 3, 7, 11…….

The conventional mathematical process for this question would involve using the formula.

$$T_n = a + (n - 1)\, d$$

Thus, for the 17th term we would do

$$T_{17} = 3 + (17 - 1) \times 4 = 3 + 16 \times 4 = 67$$

Most students would mechanically insert the values for $a$, $n$ and $d$ and get this answer.

However, if you replace the above process with a thought algorithm, you will get the answer much faster. The algorithm goes like this:

In order to find the 17th term of the above sequence add the common difference to the first term, sixteen times. (**Note:** Sixteen, since it is one less than 17).

Similarly, in order to find the 37th term of the A.P. 3, 11 …, all you need to do is add the common difference (8 in this case), 36 times.

Thus, the answer is $288 + 3 = 291$.

(**Note:** You ultimately end up doing the same thing, but you are at an advantage since the entire solution process is reactionary.)

**2. Average of an A.P. and Corresponding terms of the A.P.**

Consider the A.P., 2, 6, 10, 14, 18, 22. If you try to find the average of these six numbers you will get: Average = $(2 + 6 + 10 + 14 + 18 + 22)/6 = 12$

Notice that 12 is also the average of the first and the last terms of the A.P. In fact, it is also the average of 6 and 18 (which correspond to the second and 5th terms of the A.P.). Further, 12 is also the average of the 3rd and 4th terms of the A.P.

(**Note:** In this A.P. of six terms, the average was the same as the average of the 1st and 6th terms. It was also given by the average of the 2nd and the 5th terms, as well as that of the 3rd and 4th terms. )

We can call each of these pairs as "CORRESPONDING TERMS" in an A.P.

**What you need to understand is that every A.P. has an average.**

**And for any A.P., the average of any pair of corresponding terms will also be the average of the A.P.**

If you try to notice the sum of the term numbers of the pair of corresponding terms given above:

1st and 6th (so that $1 + 6 = 7$)
2nd and 5th (hence, $2 + 5 = 7$)
3rd and 4th (hence, $3 + 4 = 7$)

---

**Note:** In each of these cases, the sum of the term numbers for the terms in a corresponding pair is one greater than the number of terms of the A.P.

---

This rule will hold true for all A.P.s.

For example, if an A.P. has 23 terms then for instance, you can predict that the 7th term will have the 17th term as its corresponding term, or for that matter the 9th term will have the 15th term as its corresponding term. (Since 24 is one more than 23 and $7 + 17 = 9 + 15 = 24$.)

**3. Process for finding the sum of an A.P.**

Once you can find a pair of corresponding terms for any A.P., you can easily find the sum of the A.P. by using the property of averages:

i.e.,         Sum = Number of terms × Average.

In fact, this is the best process for finding the sum of an A.P. It is much more superior than the process of finding the sum of an A.P. using the expression $\frac{n}{2}(2a+(n-1)d)$.

### 4. Finding the common difference of an A.P., given 2 terms of an A.P.

Suppose you were given that an A.P. had its 3rd term as 8 and its 8th term as 28. You should visualise this A.P. as
$$-, -, 8, -, -, -, -, 28.$$

From the above figure, you can easily visualise that to move from the third term to the eighth term, (8 to 28) you need to add the common difference five times. The net addition being 20, the common difference should be 4.

*Illustration*: Find the sum of an A.P. of 17 terms, whose 3rd term is 8 and 8th term is 28.

*Solution*: Since we know the third term and the eighth term, we can find the common difference as 4 by the process illustrated above.

The total = 17 × Average of the A.P.

Our objective now shifts into the finding of the average of the A.P. In order to do so, we need to identify either the 10th term (which will be the corresponding term for the 8th term) or the 15th term (which will be the corresponding term for the 3rd term.)

Again: Since the 8th term is 28 and $d = 4$, the 10th term becomes $28 + 4 + 4 = 36$.

Thus, the average of the A.P.
$$= \text{Average of 8th and 10th terms}$$
$$= (28 + 36)/2 = 32.$$

Hence, the required answer is sum of the A.P. $= 17 \times 32 = 544$.

The logic that has applied here is that the difference in the term numbers will give you the number of times the common difference is used to get from one to the other term.

For instance, if you know that the difference between the 7th term and 12th term of an AP is –30, you should realise that 5 times the common difference will be equal to –30. (Since $12 – 7 = 5$).

Hence, $d = -6$.

**Note:** Replace this algorithmic thinking in lieu of the mathematical thinking of:
$$12^{th} \text{ term} = a + 11d$$
$$7^{th} \text{ term} = a + 6d$$
Hence, difference $= -30 = (a + 11d) - (a + 6d)$
$$-30 = 5d$$
∴                               $d = -6$.

### 5. Types of A.P.s: Increasing and Decreasing A.P.s.

Depending on whether '$d$' is positive or negative, an A.P. can be increasing or decreasing.

Let us explore these two types of A.P.s further:

### (A) Increasing A.P.s:

Every term of an increasing A.P. is greater than the previous term.

Depending on the value of the first term, we can construct two graphs for sum of an increasing A.P.

*Case 1:* When the first term of the increasing A.P. is positive. In such a case the sum of the A.P. will show a continuously increasing graph which will look like the one shown in the figure below:

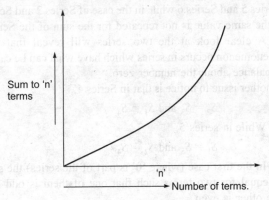

*Case 2:* When the first term of the increasing A.P. is negative. In such a case, the Sum of the A.P. plotted against the number of terms will give the following figure:

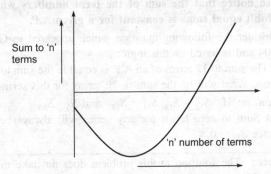

### The specific case of the sum to $n_1$ terms being equal to the sum to $n_2$ terms.

In the series case 2 above, there is a possibility of the sum to '$n$' terms being repeated for 2 values of '$n$'. However, this will not necessarily occur.

This issue will get clear through the following example:

Consider the following series:

**Series 1:** –12, –8, –4, 0, 4, 8, 12

As is evident the sum to 2 terms and the sum to 5 terms in this case is the same. Similarly, the sum to 3 terms is the same as the sum to 4 terms. This can be written as:

$$S_2 = S_5 \text{ and } S_3 = S_4.$$

In other words the sum to $n_1$ terms is the same as the sum to $n_2$ terms.

Such situations arise for increasing A.P.s where the first term is negative. But as we have already stated that this does not happen for all such cases.

Consider the following A.P.s.

Series 2 : –8, –3, +2, + 7, + 12...
Series 3 : –13, –7, –1, + 5, + 11...
Series 4 : –12, –6, 0, 6, 12 ...
Series 5 : –15, –9, –3, + 3, 9, 15 ...
Series 6 : –20, –12, –4, 4 , 12, ...

If you check the series listed above, you will realise that this occurrence happens in the case of Series 1, Series 4, Series 5 and Series 6 while in the case of Series 2 and Series 3 the same value is not repeated for the sum of the Series.

A clear look at the two series will reveal that this phenomenon occurs in series which have what can be called a balance about the number zero.

Another issue to notice is that in Series 4,

$$S_2 = S_3 \text{ and } S_1 = S_4$$

While in series 5,

$$S_1 = S_5 \text{ and } S_2 = S_4.$$

In the first case (where '0' is part of the series) the sum is equal for two terms such that one of them is odd and the other is even.

In the second case on the other hand (when '0' is not part of the series) the sum is equal for two terms such that both are odd or both are even.

**Also notice that the sum of the term numbers which exhibit equal sums is constant for a given A.P.**

Consider the following question which appeared in CAT 2004 and is based on this logic:

The sum to 12 terms of an A.P. is equal to the sum to 18 terms. What will be the sum to 30 terms for this series?

*Solution:* If $S_{12} = S_{18}$, $S_{11} = S_{19}$... and $S_0 = S_{30}$

But Sum to zero terms for any series will always be 0. Hence $S_{30} = 0$.

---

**Note:** The solution to this problem does not take more than 10 seconds if you know this logic

---

**(B) Decreasing A.P.s.**

Similar to the cases of the increasing A.P.s, we can have two cases for decreasing APs —

Case 1— Decreasing A.P. with first term negative.
Case 2— Decreasing A.P. with first term positive.

I leave it to the reader to understand these cases and deduce that whatever was true for increasing A.P.s with first term negative will also be true for decreasing A.P.s with first term positive.

## GEOMETRIC PROGRESSION

*Quantities are said to be in Geometric Progression when they increase or decrease by a constant factor.*

The constant factor is also called the *common ratio* and it is found by dividing any term by the term immediately preceding it.

If we examine the series $a$, $ar$, $ar^2$, $ar^3$, $ar^4$,...

*we notice that in any term the index of r is always less by one than the number of the term in the series.*

If $n$ be the number of terms and if $l$ denote the last, or $n$th term, we have

$$l = ar^{n-1}$$

*When three quantities are in geometrical progression, the middle one is called the geometric mean between the other two. While arbitrarily choosing three numbers in GP, we take a/r, a and ar. This makes it easier since we come down to two variables for the three terms.*

### To Find the Geometric Mean between Two Given Quantities

Let $a$ and $b$ be the two quantities; $G$ the geometric mean. Then since $a$, $G$, $b$ are in G.P.,

$$b/G = G/a$$

Each being equal to the common ratio

$$G^2 = ab$$

Hence $$G = \sqrt{ab}$$

### To Insert a given Number of Geometric Means between Two Given Quantities

Let $a$ and $b$ be the given quantities and $n$ the required number of means to be inserted. In all there will be $n + 2$ terms so that we have to find a series of $n + 2$ terms in G.P. of which $a$ is the first and $b$ the last.

Let $r$ be the common ratio;

Then $$b = \text{the } (n + 2)\text{th term} = ar^{n+1};$$

$$\therefore \quad r^{(n+1)} = \frac{b}{a}$$

$$\therefore \quad r = \left(\frac{b}{a}\right)^{\frac{1}{n+1}} \quad (1)$$

Hence the required number of means are $ar$, $ar^2$, ... $ar^n$, where $r$ has the value found in (1).

### To Find the Sum of a Number of Terms in a Geometric Progression

Let $a$ be the first term, $r$ the common ratio, $n$ the number of terms, and $S_n$ be the sum to $n$ terms.

If $r > 1$, then

$$S_n = \frac{a(r^n - 1)}{(r - 1)} \quad (1)$$

If $r < 1$, then

$$S_n = \frac{a(r^n - 1)}{(r-1)} \qquad (2)$$

**Note:** It will be convenient to remember both forms given above for $S$. Number (2) will be used in all cases except when $r$ is positive and greater than **one**.

Sum of an infinite geometric progression when $r < 1$

$$S_\infty = \frac{a}{(1-r)}$$

Obviously, this formula is used only when the common ratio of the G.P. is less than one.

Similar to A.P.s, G.P.s can also be logically viewed. Based on the value of the common ratio and its first term a G.P. might have one of the following structures:

### (1) Increasing G.P.s type 1:

A G.P. with first term positive and common ratio greater than 1. This is the most common type of G.P.,

e.g: 3, 6, 12, 24…(A G.P. with first term 3 and common ratio 2)

The plot of the sum of the series with respect to the number of terms in such a case will appear as follows:

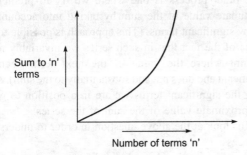

### (2) Increasing G.P.s type 2:

A G.P. with first term negative and common ratio less than 1.

e.g: –8, –4, –2, –1, – ……

As you can see in this G.P. all terms are greater than their previous terms.

[The following figure will illustrate the relationship between the number of terms and the sum to '$n$' terms in this case]

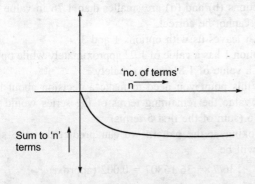

### (3) Decreasing G.P.s type 1:

These G.P.s have their first term positive and common ratio less than 1.

e.g: 12, 6, 3, 1.5, 0.75 …..

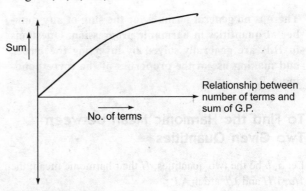

Relationship between number of terms and sum of G.P.

### (4) Decreasing G.P.s type 2:

First term negative and common ratio greater than 1.

e.g: –2, –6, –18 ….

In this case the relationship looks like.

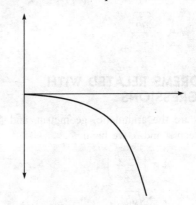

## HARMONIC PROGRESSION

Three quantities $a$, $b$, $c$ are said to be in Harmonic Progression when $a/c = \dfrac{(a-b)}{(b-c)}$.

In general, if $a$, $b$, $c$, $d$ are in A.P. then $1/a$, $1/b$, $1/c$ and $1/d$ are all in H.P.

Any number of quantities are said to be in harmonic progression when every three consecutive terms are in harmonic progression.

The reciprocals of quantities in harmonic progression are in arithmetic progression. This can be proved as:

By definition, if $a$, $b$, $c$ are in harmonic progression,

$$\frac{a}{c} = \frac{(a-b)}{(b-c)}$$

$$\therefore \quad a(b-c) = c(a-b),$$

dividing every term by $abc$, we get

$$\left[\frac{1}{c} - \frac{1}{b} = \frac{1}{b} - \frac{1}{a}\right]$$

which proves the proposition.

> There is no general formula for the sum of any number of quantities in harmonic progression. Questions in H.P. are generally solved by inverting the terms, and making use of the properties of the corresponding A.P.

## To Find the Harmonic Mean between Two Given Quantities

Let $a$, $b$ be the two quantities, $H$ their harmonic mean; then $1/a$, $1/H$ and $1/b$ are in A.P.;

$$\therefore \quad \frac{1}{H} - \frac{1}{a} = \frac{1}{b} - \frac{1}{H}$$

$$\frac{2}{H} = \frac{1}{a} + \frac{1}{b}$$

i.e. $\quad H = \dfrac{2ab}{(a+b)}$

## THEOREMS RELATED WITH PROGRESSIONS

If $A$, $G$, $H$ are the arithmetic, geometric, and harmonic means between $a$ and $b$, we have

$$A = \left(\frac{a+b}{2}\right) \tag{1}$$

$$G = \sqrt{ab} \tag{2}$$

$$H = \frac{2ab}{(a+b)} \tag{3}$$

Therefore, $A \times H = \dfrac{(a+b)}{2} \times \dfrac{2ab}{(a+b)} = ab = G^2$

that is, $G$ is the geometric mean between $A$ and $H$.
From these results we see that

$$A - G = \frac{a+b}{2} - \sqrt{ab} = \frac{(a+b-2\sqrt{ab})}{2}$$

$$= \left[\frac{(\sqrt{a} - \sqrt{b})}{\sqrt{2}}\right]^2$$

which is positive if $a$ and $b$ are positive. Therefore, the arithmetic mean of any two positive quantities is greater than their geometric mean.

Also from the equation $G^2 = AH$, we see that $G$ is intermediate in value between $A$ and $H$; and it has been proved that $A > G$, therefore $G > H$ and $A > G > H$.

**The arithmetic, geometric, and harmonic means between any two positive quantities are in descending order of magnitude**.

As we have already seen in the Back to school section of this block there are some number series which have a continuously decreasing value from one term to the next — and such series have the property that they have what can be defined as the sum of infinite terms. Questions on such series are very common in most aptitude exams. Even though they cannot be strictly said to be under the domain of progressions, we choose to deal with them here.

Consider the following question which appeared in CAT 2003.

Find the infinite sum of the series:

$$1 + \frac{4}{7} + \frac{9}{7^2} + \frac{16}{7^3} + \frac{25}{7^4} + \dots$$

    (a) 27/14              (b) 21/13
    (c) 49/27              (d) 256/147

*Solution:* Such questions have two alternative widely divergent processes to solve them.

The first relies on mathematics using algebraic solving. Unfortunately, this process being overly mathematical requires a lot of writing and hence is not advisable to be used in an aptitude exam.

The other process is one where we try to predict the approximate value of the sum by taking into account the first few significant terms. (This approach is possible to use because of the fact that in such series we invariably reach the point where the value of the next term becomes insignificant and does not add substantially to the sum). After adding the significant terms we are in a position to guess the approximate value of the sum of the series.

Let us look at the above question in order to understand the process.

In the given series the values of the terms are:

    First term = 1
    Second term = 4/7 = 0.57
    Third term = 9/63 = 0.14
    Fourth term = 16/343 = 0.04
    Fifth term = 25/2401 = 0.01

Addition upto the fifth term is approximately 1.76.

Options (b) and (d) are smaller than 1.76 in value and hence cannot be correct.

That leaves us with options 1 and 3.

Option 1 has a value of 1.92 approximately while option 3 has a value of 1.81 approximately.

At this point you need to make a decision about how much value the remaining terms of the series would add to 1.76 (sum of the first 5 terms)

Looking at the pattern we can predict that the sixth term will be

$$36/7^5 = 36/16807 = 0.002 \text{ (approx.)}$$

And the seventh term would be $49/7^6 = 49/117649 = 0.0004$ (approx.).

The eighth term will obviously become much smaller.

It can be clearly visualised that the residual terms in the series are highly insignificant. Based on this judgement you realise that the answer will not reach 1.92 and will be restricted to 1.81. Hence the answer will be option 3.

Try using this process to solve other questions of this nature whenever you come across them. (There are a few such questions inserted in the LOD exercises of this chapter)

## Useful Results

1. If the same quantity be added to, or subtracted from, all the terms of an A.P., the resulting terms will form an A.P., but with the same common difference as before.

2. If all the terms of an A.P. be multiplied or divided by the same quantity, the resulting terms will form an A.P., but with a new common difference, which will be the multiplication/division of the old common difference. (as the case may be)

3. If all the terms of a G.P. be multiplied or divided by the same quantity, the resulting terms will form a G.P. with the same common ratio as before.

4. If $a, b, c, d, ....$ are in G.P., they are also in continued proportion, since, by definition,
$$a/b = b/c = c/d = ... = 1/r$$
Conversely, a series of quantities in continued proportion may be represented by $x, xr, xr^2, ...$

5. If you have to assume 3 terms in A.P., assume them as
$$a - d, a, a + d \quad \text{or} \quad \text{as } a, a + d \text{ and } a + 2d$$
For assuming 4 terms of an A.P. we use: $a - 3d$, $a - d, a + d$ and $a + 3d$
For assuming 5 terms of an A.P., take them as:
$$a - 2d, a - d, a, a + d, a + 2d.$$
These are the most convenient in terms of problem solving.

6. For assuming three terms of a G.P. assume them as
$$a, ar \quad \text{and} \quad ar^2 \quad \text{or} \quad \text{as } a/r, a \text{ and } ar$$

7. To find the sum of the first $n$ natural numbers
Let the sum be denoted by $S$; then
$$S = 1 + 2 + 3 + ..... + n, \text{ is given by}$$
$$S = \frac{n(n+1)}{2}$$

8. To find the sum of the squares of the first $n$ natural numbers
Let the sum be denoted by $S$; then
$$S = 1^2 + 2^2 + 3^2 + ..... + n^2$$

This is given by : $S = \left\{ \dfrac{n(n+1)(2n+1)}{6} \right\}$

9. To find the sum of the cubes of the first $n$ natural numbers.
Let the sum be denoted by $S$; then
$$S = 1^3 + 2^3 + 3^3 + ... + n^3$$
$$S = \left[ \frac{n(n+1)}{2} \right]^2$$
Thus, the sum of the cubes of the first $n$ natural numbers is equal to the square of the sum of these numbers.

10. To find the sum of the first $n$ odd natural numbers.
$$S = 1 + 3 + 5 + ... + (2n - 1) \rightarrow n^2$$

11. To find the sum of the first $n$ even natural numbers.
$$S = 2 + 4 + 6 + ... + 2n \rightarrow n(n + 1)$$
$$= n^2 + n$$

12. To find the sum of odd numbers $\leq n$ where $n$ is a natural number:

*Case A:* If $n$ is odd $\rightarrow [(n + 1)/2]^2$
*Case B:* If $n$ is even $\rightarrow [n/2]^2$

13. To find the sum of even numbers $\leq n$ where $n$ is a natural number:

*Case A:* If $n$ is even $\rightarrow \{(n/2)[(n/2) + 1]\}$
*Case B:* If $n$ is odd $\rightarrow [(n-1)/2][(n + 1)/2]$

14. Number of terms in a count:
   - If we are counting in steps of 1 from $n_1$ to $n_2$ including both the end points, we get $(n_2 - n_1) + 1$ numbers.
   - If we are counting in steps of 1 from $n_1$ to $n_2$ including only one end, we get $(n_2 - n_1)$ numbers.
   - If we are counting in steps of 1 from $n_1$ to $n_2$ excluding both ends, we get $(n_2 - n_1) - 1$ numbers.

*Example:* Between 16 and 25 both included there are $9 + 1 = 10$ numbers.
Between 100 and 200 both excluded there are $100 - 1 = 99$ numbers.

   - If we are counting in steps of 2 from $n_1$ to $n_2$ including both the end points, we get $[(n_2 - n_1)/2] + 1$ numbers.
   - If we are counting in steps of 2 from $n_1$ to $n_2$ including only one end, we get $[(n_2 - n_1)/2]$ numbers.
   - If we are counting in steps of 2 from $n_1$ to $n_2$ excluding both ends, we get $[(n_2 - n_1)/2] - 1$ numbers.

*Contd*

*Contd*

## Useful Results (*Contd*)

- If we are counting in steps of 3 from $n_1$ to $n_2$ including both the end points, we get $[(n_2 - n_1)/3] + 1$ numbers.
- If we are counting in steps of 3 from $n_1$ to $n_2$ including only one end, we get $[(n_2 - n_1)/3]$ numbers.
- If we are counting in steps of 3 from $n_1$ to $n_2$, excluding both ends, we get $[(n_2 - n_1)/3] - 1$ numbers.

*Example:* Number of numbers between 100 and 200 divisible by three.

*Solution:* The first number is 102 and the last number is 198. Hence, answer = (96/3) + 1 = 33 (since both 102 and 198 are included).

Alternately, highest number below 100 that is divisible by 3 is 99, and the lowest number above 200 which is divisible by 3 is 201.

Hence, 201 − 99 = 102 → 102/3 = 34 → Answer = 34 − 1 = 33 (Since both ends are not included.)

### In General

- If we are counting in steps of $x$ from $n_1$ to $n_2$ including both the end points, we get $[(n_2 - n_1)/x] + 1$ numbers.

*Contd*

## Useful Results (*Contd*)

- If we are counting in steps of "$x$" from $n_1$ to $n_2$ including only one end, we get $(n_2 - n_1)/x$ numbers.
- If we are counting in steps of "$x$" from $n_1$ to $n_2$ excluding both ends, we get $[(n_2 - n_1)/x] - 1$ numbers.

For instance, if we have to find how many terms are there in the series 107, 114, 121, 128 ... 254, then we have

(254 − 107)/7 + 1 = 147/7 + 1 = 21 + 1 = 22 terms in the series

*Of course, an appropriate adjustment will have to be made when $n_2$ does not fall into the series. This will be done as follows:*

For instance, if we have to find how many terms of the series 107, 114, 121, 128 ... are below 258, then we have by the formula:

(258 − 107)/7 + 1 = 151/7 + 1 = 21.57 + 1. = 22.57. This will be adjusted by taking the lower integral value = 22. → The number of terms in the series below 258.

The student is advised to try and experiment on these principles to get a clear picture.

*Space for Notes*

## 🎯 WORKED-OUT PROBLEMS

**Problem 2.1** Two persons—Ramu Dhobi and Kalu Mochi have joined Donkey-work Associates. Ramu Dhobi and Kalu Mochi started with an initial salary of ₹ 500 and ₹ 640, respectively with annual increments of ₹ 25 and ₹ 20 each respectively. In which year will Ramu Dhobi start earning more salary than Kalu Mochi?

**Solution** The current difference between the salaries of the two is ₹ 140. The annual rate of reduction of this dfference is ₹ 5 per year. At this rate, it will take Ramu Dhobi 28 years to equalise his salary with Kalu Dhobi's salary.

Thus, in the 29th year he will earn more.

This problem should be solved while reading and the thought process should be 140/5 = 28. Hence, answer is 29th year.

**Problem 2.2** Find the value of the expression

$1 - 6 + 2 - 7 + 3 - 8 + \ldots\ldots$ to 100 terms

    (a) −250            (b) −500
    (c) −450            (d) −300

**Solution** The series $(1 - 6 + 2 - 7 + 3 - 8 + \ldots\ldots$ to 100 terms) can be rewritten as:

$\Rightarrow$ $(1 + 2 + 3 + \ldots$ to 50 terms$) - (6 + 7 + 8 + \ldots$ to 50 terms$)$

Both these are *AP*'s with values of $a$ and $d$ as →
$a = 1$, $n = 50$ and $d = 1$ and $a = 6$, $n = 50$ and $d = 1$, respectively.

Using the formula for sum of an A.P. we get:

→ $25(2 + 49) - 25(12 + 49)$

→ $25(51 - 61) = -250$

Alternatively, we can do this faster by considering $(1 - 6)$, $(2 - 7)$, and so on as one unit or one term.

$1 - 6 = 2 - 7 = \ldots = -5$. Thus the above series is equivalent to a series of fifty −5's added to each other.

So, $(1 - 6) + (2 - 7) + (3 - 8) + \ldots$ 50 terms $= -5 \times 50 = \mathbf{-250}$

**Problem 2.3** Find the sum of all numbers divisible by 6 in between 100 to 400.

**Solution** Here 1st term = $a$ = 102 (which is the 1st term greater than 100 that is divisible by 6.)

The last term less than 400, which is divisible by 6 is 396.

The number of terms in the *AP;* 102, 108, 114…396 is given by $[(396 - 102)/6] + 1 = 50$ numbers.

Common difference = $d = 6$

So,      $S = 25 (204 + 294) = 12450$

**Problem 2.4** If $x$, $y$, $z$ are in G.P., then $1/(1 + \log_{10}x)$, $1/(1 + \log_{10}y)$ and $1/(1 + \log_{10}z)$ will be in:

    (a) A.P.            (b) G.P.
    (c) H.P.            (d) Cannot be said

**Solution** Go through the options.

Checking option (a), the three will be in A.P. if the 2nd expression is the average of the 1st and 3rd expressions. This can be mathematically written as

$$2/(1 + \log_{10}y) = [1/(1 + \log_{10}x)] + [1/(1 + \log_{10}z)]$$

$$= \frac{[1 + (1 + \log_{10} x) + 1 + (1 + \log_{10} z)]}{[(1 + \log_{10} x)(1 + \log_{10} z)]}$$

$$= \frac{[2 + \log_{10} xz]}{(1 + \log_{10} x)(1 + \log_{10} z)}$$

Applying our judgement, there seems to be no indication that we are going to get a solution.

Checking option (b),

$$[1/(1 + \log_{10}y)]^2 = [1/(1 + \log_{10}x)] [1/(1 + \log_{10}z)]$$

$$= [1/(1 + \log_{10}(x + z) + \log_{10}xz)]$$

Again we are trapped and any solution is not in sight. Checking option (c),

$1/(1 + \log_{10}x )$, $1/(1 + \log_{10}y)$ and $1/(1 + \log_{10}z)$ are in *HP* then $1 + \log_{10}x$, $1 + \log_{10}y$ and $1 + \log_{10}z$ will be in A.P.

So, $\log_{10}x$, $\log_{10}y$ and $\log_{10}z$ will also be in A.P.

Hence,    $2 \log_{10}y = \log_{10}x + \log_{10}z$

$\Rightarrow$           $y^2 = xz$ which is given.

So, **(c)** is the correct option.

Alternatively, you could have solved through the following process.

$x$, $y$ and $z$ are given as logarithmic functions.

Assume  $x = 1$, $y = 10$ and $z = 100$ as $x$, $y$, $z$ are in G.P.

So,    $1 + \log_{10}x = 1$, $1 + \log_{10}y = 2$ and $1 + \log_{10}z = 3$

$\Rightarrow$ Thus we find that since 1, 2 and 3 are in A.P., we can assume that

    $1 + \log_{10}x$, $1 + \log_{10}y$  and  $1 + \log_{10}z$ are in A.P.

$\Rightarrow$ Hence, by definition of an H.P. we have that $1/(1 + \log_{10}x)$, $1/(1 + \log_{10}y )$ and $1/(1 + \log_{10}z)$ are in H.P. Hence, option (c) is the required answer.

*Author's Note:* In my experience I have always found that the toughest equations and factorisations get solved very easily when there are options, by assuming values in place of the variables in the equation. The values of the variables should be taken in such a manner that the basic restrictions put on the variables should be respected. For example, if an expression in three variables *a*, *b* and *c* is given and it is mentioned that $a + b + c = 0$ then the values that you assume for *a*, *b* and *c* should satisfy this restriction. Hence, you should look at values like 1, 2 and –3 or 2, –1, –1, etc.

This process is especially useful in the case where the question as well as the options both contain expressions. Factorisation and advanced techniques of maths are then not required. This process will be very beneficial for students who are weak at Mathematics.

**Problem 2.5**  Find $t_{10}$ and $S_{10}$ for the following series:

$$1, 8, 15, \ldots$$

**Solution**  This is an A.P. with first term 1 and common difference 7.

$$t_{10} = a + (n - 1)\, d = 1 + 9 \times 7 = 64$$

$$S_{10} = \frac{n[2a + (n-1)d]}{2}$$

$$= \frac{10[2(1) + (10-1)7]}{2} = 325$$

Alternatively, if the number of terms is small, you can count it directly.

**Problem 2.6**  Find $t_{18}$ and $S_{18}$ for the following series:

$$2, 8, 32, \ldots$$

**Solution**  This is a G.P. with first term 2 and common ratio 4.

$$t_{18} = ar^{n-1} = 2 \cdot 4^{17}$$

$$S_{18} = \frac{a(r^n - 1)}{r - 1} = \frac{2(4^{18} - 1)}{(4 - 1)}$$

**Problem 2.7**  Is the series 1, 4,… to *n* terms an A.P., or a GP, or an HP, or a series which cannot be determined?

**Solution**  *To determine any progression, we should have at least three terms.*

If the series is an A.P. then the next term of this series will be 7

Again, if the next term is 16, then this will be a GP series (1, 4, 16 …)

So, *we cannot determine* the nature of the progression of this series.

**Problem 2.8**  Find the sum to 200 terms of the series $1 + 4 + 6 + 5 + 11 + 6 + \ldots$

(a)  30,200          (b)  29,800

(c)  30,200          (d)  None of these

**Solution**  Spot that the above series is a combination of two A.P.s.

The 1st A.P. is $(1 + 6 + 11 + \ldots)$ and the 2nd A.P. is $(4 + 5 + 6 + \ldots)$

Since the terms of the two series alternate, $S = (1 + 6 + 11 + \ldots$ to 100 terms$) + (4 + 5 + 6 + \ldots$ to 100 terms$)$

$$= \frac{100[2 \times 1 + 99 \times 5]}{2} + \frac{100[2 \times 4 + 99 \times 1]}{2} \rightarrow \text{(Using the}$$

formula for the sum of an *AP*)

$$= 50[497 + 107] = 50[604] = 30200$$

Alternatively, we can treat every two consecutive terms as one.

So we will have a total of 100 terms of the nature:

$$(1 + 4) + (6 + 5) + (11 + 6) \ldots \rightarrow 5, 11, 17\ldots$$

Now, $a = 5$, $d = 6$ and $n = 100$

Hence the sum of the given series is

$$S = \frac{100}{2} \times [2 \times 5 + 99 \times 6]$$

$$= 50[604] = 30200$$

**Problem 2.9**  How many terms of the series –12, –9, –6,… must be taken that the sum may be 54?

**Solution**  Here $S = 54$, $a = -12$, $d = 3$, *n* is unknown and has to be calculated. To do so we use the formula for the sum of an *AP* and get.

$$54 = \frac{[2(-12) + (n-1)3]n}{2}$$

or      $108 = -24n - 3n + 3n^2$ or $3n^2 - 27n - 108 = 0$

or      $n^2 - 9n - 36 = 0$, or $n^2 - 12n + 3n - 36 = 0$

$$n(n - 12) + 3(n - 12) = 0 \Rightarrow (n + 3)(n - 12) = 0$$

The value of *n* (the number of terms) cannot be negative. Hence –3 is rejected.

So we have $n = 12$

Alternatively, we can directly add up individual terms and keep adding manually till we get a sum of 54. We will observe that this will occur after adding 12 terms. (In this case, as also in all cases where the number of terms is mentally manageable, mentally adding the terms till we get the required sum will turn out to be much faster than the equation based process.

**Problem 2.10**  Find the sum of n terms of the series 1.2.4 + 2.3.5 + 3.4.6 + …

(a)  $n(n + 1)(n + 2)$

(b)  $(n(n + 1)/12)(3n^2 + 19n + 26)$

(c)  $((n + 1)(n + 2)(n + 3))/4$

(d)  $(n^2(n + 1)(n + 2)(n + 3))/3$

**Solution**  In order to solve such problems in the examination, the option-based approach is the best. Even if you can find out the required expression mathematically, it is advisable to solve through the options as this will end up saving a lot of time for you. Use the options as follows:

If we put $n = 1$, we should get the sum as $1.2.4 = 8$. By substituting $n = 1$ in each of the four options we will get the following values for the sum to 1 term:

Option (a) gives a value of: 6

Option (b) gives a value of: 8

Option (c) gives a value of: 6

Option (d) gives a value of: 8

From this check we can reject the options (a) and (c).

Now put $n = 2$. You can see that up to 2 terms, the expression is $1.2.4 + 2.3.5 = 38$.

The correct option should also give 38 if we put $n = 2$ in the expression. Since, (a) and (c) have already been rejected, we only need to check for options (b) and (d).

Option (b) gives a value of 38.

Option (d) gives a value of 80.

Hence, we can reject option (d) and get (b) as the answer.

> **Note:** The above process is very effective for solving questions having options. The student should try to keep an eye open for the possibility of solving questions through options. In my opinion, approximately 50–75% of the questions asked in CAT in the QA section can be solved with options (at least partially).

*Space for Rough Work*

## LEVEL OF DIFFICULTY (I)

1. There is an AP 11, 13, 15.... Which term of this AP is 65?
   (a) 25th          (b) 26th
   (c) 27th          (d) 28th

2. Find the 25th term of the sequence 50, 45, 40, ...
   (a) −55           (b) −65
   (c) −70           (d) −75

3. If Ajit saves Rs. 400 more each year than he did the year before and if he saves Rs. 2000 in the first year, after how many years will his savings be more than Rs.100000 altogether?
   (a) 19 years      (b) 20 years
   (c) 21 years      (d) 18 years

4. The 6th and 20th terms of an AP are 8 and −20 respectively. Find the 30th term.
   (a) −34           (b) −40
   (c) −32           (d) −30

5. How many terms are there in the AP 10, 15, 20, 25,... 120?
   (a) 21            (b) 22
   (c) 23            (d) 24

6. Find the number of terms of the series 1/27, 1/9, 1/3,... 729.
   (a) 10            (b) 11
   (c) 12            (d) 13

7. If the fifth term of a G.P. is 80 and first term is 5, what will be the 4th term of the G.P.?
   (a) 20            (b) 15
   (c) 40            (d) 25

8. Binay was appointed to Mindworkzz in the pay scale of 12000–1500–22,500. Find how many years he will take to reach the maximum of the scale.
   (a) 7 years       (b) 8 years
   (c) 9 years       (d) 10 years

9. How many natural numbers between 100 to 500 are multiples of 9?
   (a) 44            (b) 48
   (c) 47            (d) 50

10. The sum of the first 20 terms of an AP whose first term and third term are 25 and 35, respectively is
    (a) 1200         (b) 1250
    (c) 1400         (d) 1450

11. A number 39 is divided into three parts which are in A.P. and the sum of their squares is 515. Find the largest number.
    (a) 17           (b) 15
    (c) 13           (d) 11

12. Sushil agrees to work at the rate of 10 rupee on the first day, 20 rupees on the second day, 40 rupees on the third day and so on. How much will Sushil get if he starts working on the 1st of April and finishes on the 20th of April?
    (a) $10.2^{20}$          (b) $10.2^{20} - 10$
    (c) $10.2^{20} - 1$      (d) $2^{19}$

13. Find the sum of all numbers in between 1–100 excluding all those numbers which are divisible by 7. (Include 1 and 100 for counting.)
    (a) 4315         (b) 4245
    (c) 4320         (d) 4160

14. The 3rd and 8th term of a GP are 1/3 and 81, respectively. Find the 2nd term.
    (a) 3            (b) 1
    (c) 1/27         (d) 1/9

15. The sum of 5 numbers in AP is 35 and the sum of their squares is 285. Which of the following is the third term?
    (a) 5            (b) 7
    (c) 6            (d) 8

16. The number of terms of the series 26 + 24 + 22 +... such that the sum is 182 is
    (a) 13           (b) 14
    (c) Both a and b (d) 15

17. Find the lowest number in an AP such that the sum of all the terms is 105 and greatest term is 6 times the least.
    (a) 5            (b) 10
    (c) 15           (d) (a), (b) & (c)

18. Find the general term of the GP with the third term 1 and the seventh term 8.
    (a) $(2^{3/4})^{n-3}$     (b) $(2^{3/2})^{n-3}$
    (c) $(2^{3/4})^{3-n}$     (d) $(2^{3/4})^{2-n}$

19. The sum of the first and the third term of a geometric progression is 15 and the sum of its first three terms is 21. Find the progression.
    (a) 3,6,12...     (b) 12, 6, 3...
    (c) Both of these (d) None of these

20. Ishita's salary is Rs.5000 per month in the first year. She has joined in the scale of 5000-500-10000. After how many years will her expenses be 64,800?
    (a) 8 years      (b) 7 years
    (c) 6 years      (d) Cannot be determined

21. A sum of money kept in a bank amounts to Rs. 1500 in 5 years and Rs. 2000 in 10 years at simple interest. Find the sum.
    (a) Rs. 1250     (b) Rs. 1200
    (c) Rs. 1150     (d) Rs. 1000

22. The sum of three numbers in a G.P. is 13 and the sum of their squares is 91. Find the smallest number.
    (a) 1            (b) 3
    (c) 4            (d) 12

23. Find the 1st term of an AP whose 8th and 12th terms are respectively 60 and 80.
    (a) 15          (b) 20
    (c) 25          (d) 30

24. The first term of an arithmetic progression is 13 and the common difference is 4. Which of the following will be a term of this AP?
    (a) 4003        (b) 10091
    (c) 7881        (d) 13631

25. Anuj receives Rs. 600 for the first week and Rs. 30 more each week than the preceding week. How much does he earn by the 30th week?
    (a) 31050       (b) 32320
    (c) 32890       (d) 32900

26. A number of squares are described whose areas are in G.P. Then their sides will be in
    (a) A.P.         (b) G.P.
    (c) H.P.         (d) Nothing can be said

27. How many terms are there in the G.P. 5, 10, 20, 40,... 1280?
    (a) 6           (b) 8
    (c) 9           (d) 10

28. The least value of $n$ for which the sum of the series $5 + 10 + 15...$ $n$ terms is not less than 765 is
    (a) 17          (b) 18
    (c) 19          (d) 20

29. Four geometric means are inserted between 5 and 160. Find the $2^{nd}$ geometric mean.
    (a) 80          (b) 40
    (c) 10          (d) 20

30. The seventh term of a GP is 4 times the 5th term. What will be the first term when its 4th term is 40?
    (a) 4           (b) 5
    (c) 3           (d) 2

31. How many terms are identical in the two A.P.s 21, 23, 25,... up to 120 terms and 23, 26, 29,... up to 80 terms?
    (a) 39          (b) 40
    (c) 41          (d) None of these.

32. The sum of the first four terms of an A.P. is 56 and sum of the first eight terms of the same A.P. is 176. Find the sum of the first 16 terms of the A.P.?
    (a) 646        (b) 640
    (c) 608        (d) 536

33. $X$ and $Y$ are two numbers whose A.M. is 41 and G.M. is 9. Which of the following may be a value of $X$?
    (a) 125        (b) 49
    (c) 81         (d) 25

34. Two numbers $A$ and $B$ are such that $A > B$ and their G.M. is 40% lower than their A.M. Find the ratio between the numbers.
    (a) 4 : 3       (b) 9 : 1
    (c)  : 1        (d) 3 : 1

35. A man saves Rs. 1000 in January 2015 and increases his saving by Rs. 500 every month over the previous month. What is the annual saving for the man in the year 2015?
    (a) Rs. 40000     (b) Rs .45000
    (c) Rs. 42000     (d) Rs. 41000

36. Find the 23rd term of the sequence: 1, 4, 5, 8, 9, 12, 13, 16, 17, .....
    (a) 33          (b) 39
    (c) 45          (d) 43

37. If $\log a$, $\log b$, $\log c$ are in A.P., then the GM of $a$ & $c$ is
    (a) $b$          (b) $b^2$
    (c) $b^4$         (d) None of these.

38. Each of the series $1 + 3 + 5 + 7 +....$ and $4 + 7 + 10 +...$ is continued to 1000 terms. Find how many terms are identical between the two series.
    (a) 335        (b) 334
    (c) 332        (d) 333

39. Find the sum of the series till 23rd terms for the series: 1, 4, 5, 8, 9, 12, 13, 16, 17; ......
    (a) 585        (b) 560
    (c) 540        (d) 520

40. What is the maximum sum of the terms in the arithmetic progression 25, 24, 23, 22......?
    (a) 325        (b) 345
    (c) 332.5      (d) 350

41. If $8^{th}$ term of an A.P. is the geometric mean of the $1^{st}$ and $22^{nd}$ terms of the same A.P. Find the common difference of the A.P., given that the sum of the first twenty-two terms of the A.P. is 770.
    (a) Either 1 or 1/2    (b) 2
    (c) 1           (d) Either 1 or 2

42. How many terms of the series $1 + 3 + 5 + 7 + ....$ amount to 1234567654321?
    (a) 1110111     (b) 1111011
    (c) 1011111     (d) 1111111

43. Tom and Jerry were playing mathematical puzzles with each other. Jerry drew a square of sides 32 cm and then kept on drawing squares inside the squares by joining the mid points of the squares. She continued this process indefinitely. Jerry asked Tom to determine the sum of the areas of all the squares that she drew. If Tom answered correctly then what would be his answer?
    (a) 2048       (b) 1024
    (c) 512        (d) 4096

44. The sum of the first two terms of an infinite geometric series is 36. Also, each term of the series is equal to the sum of all the terms that follow. Find the sum of the series
    (a) 48          (b) 54
    (c) 72          (d) 96

45. An equilateral triangle is drawn by joining the midpoints of the sides of another equilateral triangle. A third equilateral triangle is drawn inside the second one joining the midpoints of the sides of the second equilateral triangle, and the process continues infinitely. Find the sum of the areas of all the equilateral triangles, if the side of the largest equilateral triangle is 8 units.
    (a) $32\sqrt{3}$ units
    (b) $64\sqrt{3}$ units
    (c) 64 units
    (d) $64/\sqrt{3}$ units

46. After striking a floor a rubber ball rebounds (5/6)th of the height from which it has fallen. Find the total distance (in metres) that it travels before coming to rest, if it is gently dropped from a height of 210 metres.
    (a) 2960
    (b) 2310
    (c) 2080
    (d) 2360

    **For questions 47 to 57, there are no options. Kindly solve these and put down your answer to the question asked.**

47. In an infinite geometric progression, each term is equal to 3 times the sum of the terms that follow. If the first term of the series is 4, find the product of first three terms of the series?

48. A student takes a test consisting of 100 questions with differential marking is told that each question after the first is worth 5 marks more than the preceding question. If the 5$^{th}$ question of the test is worth 25 marks, What is the maximum score that the student can obtain by attempting 90 questions?

49. In Narora nuclear power plant a technician is allowed an interval of maximum 100 minutes. A timer with a bell rings at specific intervals of time such that the minutes when the timer rings are not divisible by 2, 3, 5 and 7. The last alarm rings with a buzzer to give time for decontamination of the technician. How many times will the bell ring within these 100 minutes and what is the value of the last minute when the bell rings for the last time in a 100 minute shift?

50. The internal angles of a plane polygon are in AP. The smallest angle is 100° and the common difference is 10°. Find the number of sides of the polygon.

51. If $\dfrac{a^{n+1}+b^{n+1}}{a^n+b^n}$ is the arithmetic mean of $a$ and $b$ then find the value of $n$.

52. If $\dfrac{a^{n+1}+b^{n+1}}{a^n+b^n}$ is the harmonic mean of a and b then find the value of n.
    (a) −1
    (b) 0
    (c) 1
    (d) None of these.

53. If $a$, $b$ are two numbers such that $a$, $b > 0$. If harmonic mean of $a$, $b$ is equals to geometric mean of $a$, $b$ then what can be said about the relationship between $a$ and $b$.

54. Product of 36 positive integers is 1. Their sum is ≥

55. If we have two numbers $a$, $b$. A.M. of $a$, $b$ is 12 and H.M. is 3. Find the value of $ab$

56. If $x+\dfrac{1}{yz}, y+\dfrac{1}{zx}, z+\dfrac{1}{xy}$ are in A.P. then $x, y, z$ are in:

***Space for Rough Work***

# LEVEL OF DIFFICULTY (II)

1. If $a$ times the $a^{th}$ term of an A.P. is equal to b times the $b^{th}$ term, find the $(a + b)^{th}$ term.
   (a) 0
   (b) $a^2 - b^2$
   (c) $a - b$
   (d) 1

2. A number 28 is divided into four parts that are in AP such that the product of the first and fourth is to the product of the second and third is 5: 6. Find the smallest part.
   (a) 2
   (b) 4
   (c) 8
   (d) 6

3. Find the value of the expression: $1 - 3 + 5 - 7...$ to 100 terms.
   (a) −150
   (b) −100
   (c) −50
   (d) 75

4. If a clock strikes once at 12 A.M., twice at 1 A.M., thrice at 2 A.M. and so on, how many times will the clock be struck in the course of 3 days? (Assume a 24 hour clock)
   (a) 756
   (b) 828
   (c) 678
   (d) 1288

5. What will be the maximum sum of 54, 52, 50, ... ?
   (a) 702
   (b) 704
   (c) 756
   (d) 700

6. Find the sum of the integers between 100 and 300 that are multiples of 7.
   (a) 10512
   (b) 5586
   (c) 10646
   (d) 10546

7. If $x > 1$, $y > 1$, $z > 1$ are in G.P., then $\dfrac{1}{1+ \log x}$, $\dfrac{1}{1+ \log y}$, $\dfrac{1}{1+ \log z}$ are in
   (a) A.P.
   (b) H.P.
   (c) G.P.
   (d) None of the above

8. Find the sum of all odd numbers lying between 1000 and 2000.
   (a) 7,50,000
   (b) 7,45,000
   (c) 7,55,000
   (d) 7,65,000

9. Find the sum of all integers of 3 digits that are divisible by 11.
   (a) 49,335
   (b) 41,338
   (c) 44,550
   (d) 47,300

10. The first and the last terms of an A.P. are 113 and 253. If there are six terms in this sequence, find the sum of sequence.
    (a) 980
    (b) 910
    (c) 1098
    (d) 920

11. Find the value of $1 - 2 - 3 + 2 - 3 - 4 +... +$ upto 100 terms.
    (a) −694
    (b) −626
    (c) −624
    (d) −660

12. What will be the sum to n terms of the series $7 + 77 + 777 +...$?

    (a) $7(10^n - 9n)/81$
    (b) $7(10^{n+1} - 10 - 9n)/81$
    (c) $7(10^{n-1} - 10)$
    (d) $7(10^{n+1} - 10)$

13. If log $a$, log $b$, log $c$ are in A.P., then $a$, $b$, $c$ are in
    (a) A.P.
    (b) G.P.
    (c) H.P.
    (d) None of these

14. After striking the floor, a rubber ball rebounds to 3/5th of the height from which it has fallen. Find the total distance that it travels before coming to rest if it has been gently dropped from a height of 20 metres.
    (a) 40 metres
    (b) 60 metres
    (c) 80 metres
    (d) 120 metres

15. If $x$ be the first term, $y$ be the nth term and $p$ be the product of n terms of a G.P., then the value of $p^2$ will be
    (a) $(xy)^{n-1}$
    (b) $(xy)^n$
    (c) $(xy)^{1-n}$
    (d) $(xy)^{n/2}$

16. The sum of an infinite G.P. whose common ratio is positive and is numerically less than 1 is 36 and the sum of the first two terms is 32. What will be the third term?
    (a) 1/3
    (b) 4/3
    (c) 8/3
    (d) 2

17. What will be the value of $2^{1/3}.2^{1/6}.2^{1/12}...$ to infinity.
    (a) $2^2$
    (b) $2^{2/3}$
    (c) $2^{3/2}$
    (d) 8

18. In an infinite G.P. the first term is A and the infinite sum 5, then A belongs to
    (a) $A < -10$
    (b) $0 < A < 10$
    (c) $0 < A \le 10$
    (d) None of these

19. Determine the fourth term of the geometric progression, the sum of whose first term and third term is 50 and the sum of the second term and fourth term is 150.
    (a) 120
    (b) 125
    (c) 135
    (d) 45

20. What is the $13^{th}$ term of 2/9, 1/4, 2/7, 1/3 ...........?
    (a) −2
    (b) 1
    (c) −3/13
    (d) −2/3

21. The sum of the third and the fourth term of an A.P. is 19 and that of the first and the seventh term is 22. Find the $9^{th}$ term.
    (a) 26
    (b) 17
    (c) 15
    (d) 16

22. How many terms of an A.P. must be taken for their sum to be equal to 200 if its third term is 16 and the difference between the 6th and the $1^{st}$ term is 30?
    (a) 6
    (b) 9
    (c) 7
    (d) 8

23. Four numbers are inserted between the numbers 4 and 34 such that an A.P. results. Find the smallest of these four numbers.

(a) 11.5      (b) 11
(c) 12      (d) 10

24. Find the sum of all three-digit natural numbers, which on being divided by 7, leave a remainder equal to 6.
(a) 70,208      (b) 70,780
(c) 70,680      (d) 71,270

25. The sum of the first three terms of the arithmetic progression is 24 and the sum of the squares of the first term and the second term of the same progression is 80. Find the $8^{th}$ term of the progression if its fifth term is known to be exactly divisible by 10.
(a) 32      (b) 36
(c) 40      (d) 42

26. Anita and Babita set out to meet each other from two places 200 km apart. Anita travels 20 km the first day, 19 km the second day, 18 km the third day and so on. Babita travels 8 km the first day, 10 km the second day, 12 km the third day and so on. After how many days will they meet?
(a) 9 days      (b) 8 days
(c) 7 days      (d) 6 days

27. If a man saves Rs. 1000 each year and invests at the end of the year at 5% compound interest, how much will the amount be at the end of 15 years?
(a) Rs 21,478      (b) Rs 21,578
(c) Rs 22,578      (d) Rs 22,478

28. If sum to n terms of a series is given by $(2n + 7)$ then its second term will be given by
(a) 10      (b) 9
(c) 8      (d) 2

29. If $A$ is the sum of the n terms of the series $2 + 1/2 + 1/8 + ...$ and $B$ is the sum of $2n$ terms of the series $2 + 1 + 1/2 + ...$, then find the value of $B/A$.
(a) 1/3      (b) 2
(c) 2/3      (d) 3/2

30. Aman receives a pension starting with Rs.1000 for the first year. Each year he receives 80% of what he received the previous year. Find the maximum total amount he can receive even if he lives forever.
(a) 4000      (b) 5000
(c) 1500      (d) 4900

31. The sum of the series $\dfrac{1}{1\times 5} + \dfrac{1}{5\times 9} + \dfrac{1}{9\times 13} ..... + \dfrac{1}{221\times 225}$ is
(a) 28/221      (b) 56/221
(c) 56/225      (d) None of these

32. The sum of the series $\dfrac{1}{\sqrt{3}+\sqrt{4}} + \dfrac{1}{\sqrt{4}+\sqrt{5}} +...+ \dfrac{1}{\sqrt{224}+\sqrt{225}}$ is:

(a) $15-\sqrt{3}$      (b) $\sqrt{15}-2$
(c) 12      (d) None of these

33. Find the infinite sum of the series $1/1 + 1/3 + 1/6 + 1/10 + 1/15 ....$
(a) 2      (b) 2.25
(c) 3      (d) 4

34. The sum of the series $3 \times 5 + 5 \times 7 + 7 \times 9 +....$ upto n terms will be:
(a) $\dfrac{n\left(4n^2+18n+23\right)}{3}$    (b) $\dfrac{n\left(4n^2+18n+23\right)}{6}$
(c) $n\left(4n^2+18n+23\right)$    (d) None of these.

35. The sum of the series: $1/3 + 4/15 + 4/35 + 4/63 + ...$ upto 6 terms is:
(a) 12/13      (b) 13/14
(c) 14/13      (d) None of these

36. For the above question 35, what is the sum of the series if taken to infinite terms:
(a) 1.1      (b) 1
(c) 14/13      (d) None of these

**Directions for Questions 37 to 39:** Answer these questions based on the following information. There are 250 integers $a_1, a_2, ... a_{250}$, not all of them necessarily different. Let the greatest integer of these 250 integers be referred to as Max, and the smallest integer be referred to as Min. The integers $a_1$ through $a_{124}$ form sequence $A$ and the rest form sequence $B$. Each member of $A$ is less than or equal to each member of $B$.

37. All values in $A$ are changed in sign, while those in $B$ remain unchanged. Which of the following statements is true?
(a) Every member of $A$ is greater than or equal to every member of $B$.
(b) Max is in $A$.
(c) If all numbers originally in $A$ and $B$ had the same sign, then after the change of sign, the largest number of $A$ and $B$ is in $A$.
(d) None of these

38. Elements of $A$ are in ascending order, and those of $B$ are in descending order. $a_{124}$ and $a_{125}$ are interchanged. Then which of the following statements is true?
(a) $A$ continues to be in ascending order.
(b) $B$ continues to be in descending order.
(c) $A$ continues to be in ascending order and $B$ in descending order.
(d) None of the above

39. Every element of $A$ is made greater than or equal to every clement of $B$ by adding to each element of $A$ an integer $x$. Then, $x$ cannot be less than:
(a) $2^{10}$      (b) the smallest value of $B$
(c) the largest value of $B$
(d) (Maximm-Minimum)

40. Rahul drew a rectangular grid of 625 cells, arranged in 25 Rows and 25 columns, and filled each cell with a number. The numbers with which he filled each cell were such that the numbers of each row taken from left to right formed an arithmetic series and the numbers of each column taken from top to bottom also formed an arithmetic series. The 6th and the 20th numbers of the fifth row were 37 and 73 respectively, while the 6th and the 20th numbers of the 25th row were 63 and 87, respectively. What is the sum of all the numbers in the grid?
    (a) 32798          (b) 65596
    (c) 52900          (d) None of these

41. How many four digit numbers have the property that their digits taken from left to right form an Arithmetic or a Geometric Progression?
    (a) 15          (b) 21
    (c) 20          (d) 23

**Directions for Questions 42 and 43:** These questions are based on the following data. At Goli - Vadapav—a famous fast food centre in Andheri in Mumbai, vadapavs are made only on an automatic vadapav making machine. The machine continuously makes different sorts of vadapavs by adding different sorts of fillings on a common bread. The machine makes the vadapavs at the rate of 1 vadapav per half a minute. The various fillings are added to the vadapavs in the following manner. The 1st, 3rd, 5th, 7th,...vadapavs are filled with a chicken patty; the 1st, 5th, 9th, .....vadapavs with vegetable patty; the 1st, 8th, 17th, .....vadapavs with mushroom patty; and the rest with plain cheese and tomato fillings. The machine makes exactly 500 vadapavs per day.

42. How many vadapavs per day are made with cheese and tomato as fillings?

43. How many vadapavs are made with all three fillings Chicken, vegetable and mushroom?

44. An arithmetic progression $P$ consists of terms. From the progression three different progressions $P_1$, $P_2$ and $P_3$ are created such that $P_1$ is obtained by the 1st, 4th, 7th terms of $P$, $P_2$ has the 2nd, 5th, 8th, terms of $P$ and $P_3$ has the 3rd, 6th, 9th, terms of $P$. It is found that of $P_1$, $P_2$ and $P_1$ two progressions have the property that their average is itself a term of the original Progression $P$. Which of the following can be a possible value of $n$?
    (a) 20          (b) 26
    (c) 36          (d) Both (a) and (b)

45. For the above question, if the Common Difference between the terms of $P_1$ is 6, what is the common difference of $P$?
    (a) 2          (b) 3
    (c) 6          (d) Cannot be determined

**Direction for question number 46 to 48:**
    If $S = a, b, b, c, c, c, d, d, d, d, .....z,z,z.$

46. Find the number of terms in the above series:

47. Find 144th term of the above series:

48. If $a = 1$, $b = 3$, $c = 5$, $d = 7$, .....,$z = 51$ then find the sum of all terms of $S$:

49. If $f(4x) = 8x + 1$. Then for how many positive real values of $x$, $f(2x)$ will be G.M. of $f(x)$ and $f(4x)$ :

50. If $x$, $y$, $z$, $w$ are positive real numbers such that $x$, $y$, $z$, $w$ form an increasing A.P. and $x$, $y$, $w$ form an increasing G.P. then $w/x =$?
    (a) 1          (b) 2
    (c) 3          (d) 4

51. If $x$, $y$, $z$ are the $m$th, $n$th and $p$th terms, respectively of a G.P. then $(n - p) \log x + (p - m) \log y + (m - n) \log z =$?

52. Find the sum of first $n$ groups of $1 + (1 + 2) + (1 + 2 + 3) + .....$
    (a) $\dfrac{n(n+1)(n+2)}{6}$
    (b) $\dfrac{n(n+1)(n+2)}{12}$
    (c) $\dfrac{n(n+1)(n+2)(n+3)}{6}$
    (d) None of these.

53. If $A = 1 + x + x^2 + x^3 + .....$ & $B = 1 + y + y^2 + y^3 + .....$ and $0 < x, y < 1$, then the value of $1 + xy + x^2y^2 + x^3y^3 + .....$is:
    (a) $AB/(A + B)$          (b) $AB/(A + B - 1)$
    (c) $(AB - 1)/(A + B)$          (d) $AB$

54. If all the angles of a quadrilateral are in G.P. and all the angles and the common ratio are natural numbers. Exactly two angles are acute and two are obtuse then find the largest angle.

55. The sum to 16 groups of the series $(1) + (1 + 3) + (1 + 3 + 5) + (1 + 3 + 5 + 7) + .....$

56. Sum of 16 terms of the series $1 + 1 + 3 + 1 + 3 + 5 + 1 + 3 + 5 + 7 + .....$

57. If the sum of $n$ terms of a progression is $2n^2 + 3$. Then which term is equals to 78?

58. Sum of 17 terms of the series $1^2 - 2^2 + 3^2 - 4^2 + 5^2 - 6^2 + .....$

59. Find the sum of 20 terms of the series $3 + 6 + 10 + 15 + .....$

60. If $1^n + 2^n + 3^n + ... + x^n$ is always divisible by $1 + 2 + 3 + ....+ x$ then $n$ is
    (a) Even          (b) odd
    (c) Multiple of 2          (d) None of these.

61. Find the 12th term of the series 3, 14, 61, 252, .....

## LEVEL OF DIFFICULTY (III)

1. If in any decreasing arithmetic progression, sum of all its terms, except for the first term, is equal to $-36$, the sum of all its terms, except for the last term, is zero, and the difference of the tenth and the sixth term is equal to $-16$, then what will be first term of this series?
   (a) 16      (b) 20
   (b) $-16$      (d) $-20$

2. The sum of all terms of the arithmetic progression having ten terms except for the first term, is 99, and except for the sixth term, 89. Find the third term of the progression if the sum of the first and the fifth term is equal to 10.
   (a) 15      (b) 5
   (c) 8      (d) 10

3. Product of the fourth term and the fifth term of an arithmetic progression is 456. Division of the ninth term by the fourth term of the progression gives quotient as 11 and the remainder as 10. Find the first term of the progression.
   (a) $-52$      (b) $-42$
   (c) $-56$      (d) $-66$

4. A number of saplings are lying at a place by the side of a straight road. These are to be planted in a straight line at a distance interval of 10 metres between two consecutive saplings. Mithilesh, the country's greatest forester, can carry only one sapling at a time and has to move back to the original point to get the next sapling. In this manner he covers a total distance of 1.32 kms. How many saplings does he plant in the process if he ends at the starting point?
   (a) 15      (b) 14
   (c) 13      (d) 12

5. A geometric progression consists of 500 terms. Sum of the terms occupying the odd places is $P_1$ and the sum of the terms occupying the even places is $P_2$. Find the common ratio.
   (a) $P_2/P_1$      (b) $P_1/P_2$
   (c) $P_2 + P_1/P_1$      (d) $P_2 + P_1/P_2$

6. The sum of the first ten terms of the geometric progression is $S_1$ and the sum of the next ten terms (11th through 20th) is $S_2$. Find the common ratio.
   (a) $(S_1/S_2)^{1/10}$      (b) $-(S_1/S_2)^{1/10}$
   (c) $\pm \sqrt[10]{S_2/S_1}$      (d) $(S_1/S_2)^{1/5}$

7. The first and the third terms of an arithmetic progression are equal, respectively, to the first and the third term of a geometric progression, and the second term of the arithmetic progression exceeds the second term of the geometric progression by

8. 0.25. Calculate the sum of the first five terms of the arithmetic progression if its first term is equal to 2.
   (a) 2.25 or 25      (b) 2.5
   (c) 1.5      (d) 3.25

8. If $(2 + 4 + 6 +\ldots 50 \text{ terms})/(1 + 3 + 5 +\ldots n \text{ terms}) = 51/2$, then find the value of $n$.
   (a) 12      (b) 13
   (c) 9      (d) 10

9. $(666\ldots n \text{ digits})^2 + (888\ldots n \text{ digits})$ is equal to
   (a) $(10^n - 1) \times \dfrac{4}{9}$      (b) $(10^{2n} - 1) \times \dfrac{4}{9}$
   (c) $\dfrac{4(10^n - 10^{n-1} - 1)}{9}$      (d) $\dfrac{4(10^n + 1)}{9}$

10. The interior angles of a polygon are in $AP$. The smallest angle is $120°$ and the common difference is $5°$. Find the number of sides of the polygon.
    (a) 7      (b) 8
    (c) 9      (d) 10

11. Find the sum to $n$ terms of the series $11 + 103 + 1005 + \ldots$
    (a) $\dfrac{10(10^n - 1)}{9} + 1$      (b) $\dfrac{10(10^n - 1)}{9} + n$
    (c) $\dfrac{10(10^n - 1)}{9} + n^2$      (d) $\dfrac{10(10^n + 1)}{11} + n^2$

12. The sum of the first term and the fifth term of an $AP$ is 26 and the product of the second term by the fourth term is 160. Find the sum of the first seven terms of this $AP$.
    (a) 110      (b) 114
    (c) 112      (d) 116

13. The sum of the third and the ninth term of an $AP$ is 10. Find a possible sum of the first 11 terms of this $AP$.
    (a) 55      (b) 44
    (c) 66      (d) 48

14. The sum of the squares of the fifth and the eleventh term of an $AP$ is 3 and the product of the second and the fourteenth term is equal it $P$. Find the product of the first and the fifteenth term of the $AP$.
    (a) $(58P - 39)/45$      (b) $(98P + 39)/72$
    (c) $(116P - 39)/90$      (d) $(98P + 39)/90$

15. If the ratio of harmonic mean of two numbers to their geometric mean is 12 : 13, find the ratio of the numbers.
    (a) 4/9 or 9/4      (b) 2/3 or 3/2
    (c) 2/5 or 5/2      (d) None of these

16. Find the sum of the series $1.2 + 2.2^2 + 3.2^3 + \ldots + 100.2^{100}$.

(a) $100.2^{101} + 2$     (b) $99.2^{100} + 2$

(c) $99.2^{101} + 2$     (d) None of these

17. The sequence $[x_n]$ is a *GP* with $x_2/x_4 = 1/4$ and $x_1 + x_4 = 108$. What will be the value of $x_3$?

(a) 42     (b) 48

(c) 44     (d) 56

18. If $x, y, z$ are in GP and $a^x$, $b^y$ and $c^z$ are equal, then $a$, $b$, $c$ are in

(a) *AP*     (b) *GP*

(c) *HP*     (d) None of these

19. Find the sum of all possible whole number divisors of 720.

(a) 2012     (b) 2624

(c) 2210     (d) 2418

20. Sum to $n$ terms of the series $\log m + \log m^2/n + \log m^3/n^2 + \log m^4/n^3 \ldots$ is

(a) $\log \left( \dfrac{m^{n+1}}{n^{n-1}} \right)^{\frac{n}{2}}$     (b) $\log \left( \dfrac{n^{n-1}}{m^{n+1}} \right)^{\frac{n}{2}}$

(c) $\log \left( \dfrac{m^n}{n^n} \right)^{\frac{n}{2}}$     (d) $\log \left( \dfrac{m^{1-n}}{n^{1-m}} \right)^{\frac{n}{2}}$

21. The sum of first 20 and first 50 terms of an *AP* is 420 and 2550. Find the eleventh term of a *GP* whose first term is the same as the *AP* and the common ratio of the *GP* is equal to the common difference of the *AP*.

(a) 560     (b) 512

(c) 1024     (d) 2048

22. If three positive real numbers $x, y, z$ are in *AP* such that $xyz = 4$, then what will be the minimum value of $y$?

(a) $2^{1/3}$     (b) $2^{2/3}$

(c) $2^{1/4}$     (d) $2^{3/4}$

23. If $a_n$ be the $n$th term of an *AP* and if $a_7 = 15$, then the value of the common difference that would make $a_2 a_7 a_{12}$ greatest is

(a) 3     (b) 3/2

(c) 7     (d) 0

24. If $a_1, a_2, a_3 \ldots a_n$ are in *AP*, where $a_i > 0$, then what will be the value of the expression

$1/(\sqrt{a_1} + \sqrt{a_2}) + 1/(\sqrt{a_2} + \sqrt{a_3}) + 1/(\sqrt{a_3} + \sqrt{a_4}) + \ldots$ to $n$ terms?

(a) $(1 - n)/(\sqrt{a_1} + \sqrt{a_n})$

(b) $(n - 1)/(\sqrt{a_1} + \sqrt{a_n})$

(c) $(n - 1)/(\sqrt{a_1} - \sqrt{a_n})$

(d) $(1 - n)/(\sqrt{a_1} + \sqrt{a_n})$

25. If the first two terms of a *HP* are 2/5 and 12/13, respectively, which of the following terms is the largest term?

(a) 4th term     (b) 5th term

(c) 6th term     (d) 2nd term

26. One side of a staircase is to be closed in by rectangular planks from the floor to each step. The width of each plank is 9 inches and their height are successively 6 inches, 12 inches, 18 inches and so on. There are 24 planks required in total. Find the area in square feet.

(a) 112.5     (b) 107

(c) 118.5     (d) 105

27. The middle points of the sides of a triangle are joined forming a second triangle. Again a third triangle is formed by joining the middle points of this second triangle and this process is repeated infinitely. If the perimeter and area of the outer triangle are $P$ and $A$ respectively, what will be the sum of perimeters of triangles thus formed?

(a) $2P$     (b) $P^2$

(c) $3P$     (d) $p^2/2$

28. In Problem 27, find the sum of areas of all the triangles.

(a) $\dfrac{4}{5}A$     (b) $\dfrac{4}{3}A$

(c) $\dfrac{3}{4}A$     (d) $\dfrac{5}{4}A$

29. A square has a side of 40 cm. Another square is formed by joining the mid-points of the sides of the given square and this process is repeated infinitely. Find the perimeter of all the squares thus formed.

(a) $160(1 + \sqrt{2})$     (b) $160(2 + \sqrt{2})$

(c) $160(2 - \sqrt{2})$     (d) $160(1 - \sqrt{2})$

30. In problem 29, find the area of all the squares thus formed.

(a) 1600     (b) 2400

(c) 2800     (d) 3200

31. The sum of the first $n$ terms of the arithmetic progression is equal to half the sum of the next $n$ terms of the same progression. Find the ratio of the sum of the first $3n$ terms of the progression to the sum of its first $n$ terms.

(a) 5     (b) 6

(c) 7     (d) 8

32. In a certain colony of cancerous cells, each cell breaks into two new cells every hour. If there is a single productive cell at the start and this process continues for 9 hours, how many cells will the colony have at the end of 9 hours? It is known that the life of an individual cell is 20 hours.

(a) $2^9 - 1$     (b) $2^{10}$

(c) $2^9$     (d) $2^{10} - 1$

33. Find the sum of all three-digit whole numbers less than 500 that leave a remainder of 2 when they are divided by 3.

(a) 49637      (b) 39767
(c) 49634      (d) 39770

34. If $a$ be the arithmetic mean and $b$, $c$ be the two geometric means between any two positive numbers, then $(b^3 + c^3)/abc$ equals
    (a) $(ab)^{1/2}/c$      (b) 1
    (c) $a^2c/b$      (d) None of these

35. If $p$, $q$, $r$ are three consecutive distinct natural numbers then the expression $(q + r - p)(p + r - q)(p + q - r)$ is
    (a) Positive      (b) Negative
    (c) Non-positive      (d) Non-negative

36. If $S = \left[1 + \left(-\frac{1}{3}\right)\right]\left[1 + \left(-\frac{1}{3}\right)^2\right]\left[1 + \left(-\frac{1}{3}\right)^4\right]\left[1 + \left(-\frac{1}{3}\right)^8\right]\dots$
    till $n$ terms. Then $S = ?$
    (a) $4(10^{2n} - 1)$      (b) $4/3(10^n - 1)$
    (c) $2/3(10^n - 1)$      (d) None of these

37. The number 7777....77 (total 133 digits) is:
    (a) divisible by 3
    (b) a composite number
    (c) None of these

38. $1^{st}$ term of an A.P. of consecutive integers is $n^2 + 1$ ($n$ is a positive integer). Sum of $1^{st}$ $2n$ terms of the series will be.
    (a) $n(2n^2 + 2n + 1)$      (b) $(2n^2 + 2n + 3)$
    (c) $n(2n^2 + 2n + 3)$      (d) None of these.

39. $S = \dfrac{1}{1! + 2!} + \dfrac{1}{2! + 3!} + \dfrac{1}{3! + 4!} + \dots + \dfrac{1}{19! + 20!}$ Then $S = ?$
    (a) $\dfrac{1}{2!} - \dfrac{1}{21!}$      (b) $\dfrac{1}{2!} - \dfrac{1}{20!}$
    (c) None of these.

40. $a$, $b$, $c$ are in H.P. and $n > 1$ then $a^n + c^n$ is:
    (a) Less than $2b^n$      (b) Less than or equals to $2b^n$
    (c) More than $2b^n$      (d) More than or equals to $2b^n$

41. The sum to 17 terms of the series
    $\dfrac{3}{1^2.2^2} + \dfrac{5}{2^2.3^2} + \dfrac{7}{3^2.4^2} + \dots$ is:

42. Find the value of $S$ if
    $S = \dfrac{4}{11} + \dfrac{44}{11^2} + \dfrac{444}{11^3} + \dfrac{4444}{11^4} + \dots\infty$

43. Find the value of $S$ if $S = \dfrac{1}{2.5} + \dfrac{1}{5.8} + \dfrac{1}{8.11} + \dots + \infty$
    (a) 1/3      (b) 1/2
    (c) 1/6      (d) None of these.

44. $A = a + A_1 + A_2 + \dots + A_N + b$
    $B = a + G_1 + G_2 + \dots + G_N + b$
    $A$ is the sum of $n + 2$ terms of an A.P. with first term $a$ & last term $b$.
    $B$ is the sum of $n + 2$ terms of a G.P. with first term $a$ & last term $b$.

Then, what can be said about the relative values of $A$ & $B$?

45. $\dfrac{9}{2} + \dfrac{25}{6} + \dfrac{49}{12} + \dots + \dfrac{9801}{2450} = ?$

46. Two series $X$ ($x_1$, $x_2$, $x_3$, $x_4$, ....$x_n$) and $Y$ ($y_1$, $y_2$, $y_3$, $y_4$, ....., $y_n$) are in A.P., such that $x_n - y_n = n - 2$. It is also known that $x_3 = b_5$. Find the value of $x_{99} - y_{197}$.
    (a) 47      (b) 48
    (c) 49      (d) 50

47. From the $1^{st}$ 12 natural numbers how many Arithmetic Progressions of 4 terms can be formed such that the common difference is a factor of the $4^{th}$ term?

48. The product of $1^{st}$ five terms of an increasing A.P. is 3840. If the $1^{st}$, $2^{nd}$ and $4^{th}$ terms of the A.P. are in G.P. Find $10^{th}$ term of the series.

49. If
    $$S = \left[1 + \left(-\frac{1}{3}\right)\right]\left[1 + \left(-\frac{1}{3}\right)^2\right]\left[1 + \left(-\frac{1}{3}\right)^4\right]\left[1 + \left(-\frac{1}{3}\right)^8\dots\right]$$
    then $S =$

50. Let the positive numbers $a$, $b$, $c$, $d$ be in A.P. Then the type of progression for the numbers $abc$, $abd$, $acd$, $bcd$ is:

51. Sum of the series $\dfrac{1^3}{1} + \dfrac{1^3 + 2^3}{1 + 3} + \dfrac{1^3 + 2^3 + 3^3}{1 + 3 + 5} + \dots$ to 10 terms:

---

## ANSWER KEY

**Level of Difficulty (I)**

| | | | |
|---|---|---|---|
| 1. (d) | 2. (c) | 3. (a) | 4. (b) |
| 5. (c) | 6. (a) | 7. (c) | 8. (a) |
| 9. (a) | 10. (d) | 11. (b) | 12. (b) |
| 13. (a) | 14. (d) | 15. (b) | 16. (c) |
| 17. (d) | 18. (a) | 19. (c) | 20. (d) |
| 21. (d) | 22. (a) | 23. (c) | 24. (c) |
| 25. (a) | 26. (b) | 27. (c) | 28. (a) |
| 29. (d) | 30. (b) | 31. (b) | 32. (c) |
| 33. (c) | 34. (b) | 35. (b) | 36. (c) |
| 37. (a) | 38. (d) | 39. (c) | 40. (a) |
| 41. (b) | 42. (d) | 43. (a) | 44. (a) |
| 45. (d) | 46. (b) | 47. 1 | 48. (d) |
| 49. 22,97 | 50. 8 | 51. 0 | 52. −1 |
| 53. a = b | 54. 36 | 55. 36 | 56. A.P. |

**Level of Difficulty (II)**

| | | | |
|---|---|---|---|
| 1. (a) | 2. (b) | 3. (b) | 4. (b) |
| 5. (c) | 6. (b) | 7. (b) | 8. (a) |
| 9. (c) | 10. (c) | 11. (b) | 12. (b) |
| 13. (b) | 14. (c) | 15. (b) | 16. (c) |
| 17. (b) | 18. (b) | 19. (c) | 20. (d) |
| 21. (a) | 22. (d) | 23. (d) | 24. (a) |

| | | | |
|---|---|---|---|
| 25. (a) | 26. (c) | 27. (b) | 28. (d) |
| 29. (d) | 30. (b) | 31. (c) | 32. (a) |
| 33. (a) | 34. (a) | 35. (d) | 36. (b) |
| 37. (d) | 38. (a) | 39. (d) | 40. (d) |
| 41. (d) | 42. 214 | 43. 18 | 44. (d) |
| 45. (a) | 46. 351 | 47. q | 48. 12051 |
| 49. 0 | 50. (d) | 51. 0 | 52. (a) |
| 53. (b) | 54. 1920 | 55. 1496 | 56. 56 |
| 57. 20 | 58. 153 | 59. 1770 | 60. (b) |
| 61. $4^{12}$-12 | | | |

### Level of Difficulty (III)

| | | | |
|---|---|---|---|
| 1. (a) | 2. (b) | 3. (d) | 4. (d) |
| 5. (a) | 6. (c) | 7. (b) | 8. (d) |

| | | | |
|---|---|---|---|
| 9. (b) | 10. (c) | 11. (c) | 12. (c) |
| 13. (a) | 14. (c) | 15. (a) | 16. (c) |
| 17. (b) | 18. (b) | 19. (d) | 20. (a) |
| 21. (d) | 22. (b) | 23. (d) | 24. (b) |
| 25. (d) | 26. (a) | 27. (a) | 28. (b) |
| 29. (b) | 30. (d) | 31. (b) | 32. (c) |
| 33. (b) | 34. (d) | 35. (d) | 36. (d) |
| 37. (c) | 38. (a) | 39. (a) | 40. (c) |
| 41. $\dfrac{323}{324}$ | 42. 22/5 | 43. (c) | 44. A > B |
| 45. 9849/50 | 46. (b) | 47. 13 | 48. 24 |
| 49. ¾ | 50. reciprocals are in H.P | | 51. 126.5 |

*Space for Rough Work*

**Solutions and Shortcuts**

*Level of Difficulty (I)*

1. The number of terms in a series are found by:

   $$\frac{\text{Difference between first and last terms}}{\text{Common Difference}} + 1 =$$

   $\frac{65-11}{2} + 1 = 27 + 1 = 28^{th}$ term. Option (d) is correct.

2. The first term is 50 and the common difference is −5, thus the 25th term is: $50 + 24 \times (-5) = -70$. Option (c) is correct.

3. We need the sum of the series 2000 + 2400 + 2800 to cross 100000. Trying out the options, we can see that in 20 years the sum of his savings would be: 2000 + 2400 + 2800 +...+ 9600. The sum of the series would be $20 \times 5800 = 116000$. If we remove the 20th year we will get the saving for 19 years. The series would be 2000 + 2400 + 2800 + ... + 9200. Sum of the series would be 116000 − 9600 = 106400. If we remove the 19th year's savings the savings would be 106400 − 9200 which would go below 100000. Thus, after 19 years his savings would cross 100000. Option (a) is correct.

4. $a + 5d = 8$ and $a + 19d = -20$. Solving we get $14d = -28 \rightarrow d = -2$. 30th term = 20th term + $10d = -20 + 10 \times (-2) = -40$. Option (b) is correct.

5. In order to count the number of terms in the AP, use the shortcut:
   [(last term − first term)/ common difference] + 1. In this case it would become:
   [(120 − 10)/5] + 1 = 23. Option (c) is correct.

6. $r = 3$. $729 = \frac{1}{27}(3)^{n-1}$, $n - 1 = 9$ or $n = 10$ option (a) is correct.

7. $5r^4 = 80 \rightarrow r^4 = 80/5 \rightarrow r = 2$. Thus, $4^{th}$ term = $ar^3 = 5 \times (2)^3 = 40$. Option (c) is correct.

8. 12000 − 1500 − 22500 means that the starting scale is 12000 and there is an increment of 1500 every year. Since, the total increment required to reach the top of his scale is 10500, the number of years required would be 10500/1500 = 7. Option (a) is correct.

9. The series will be 108, 117, 126,.... 495.

   Hence, Answer = $\frac{495-108}{9} + 1$ = 44. Option (a) is correct.

10. $a = 25$, $a + 2d = 35$ means $d = 5$. The 20th term would be $a + 19d = 25 + 95 = 120$. The sum of the series would be given by: $[20/2] \times [25 + 120] = 1450$. Option (d) is correct.

11. The three parts are 11, 13 and 15 since $11^2 + 13^2 + 15^2 = 515$. Since, we want the largest number, the answer would be 15. Option (b) is correct.

12. Sum of a G.P. with first term 10 and common ratio 2 and no. of terms 20. $\frac{10 \times (2^{20} - 1)}{2 - 1} = 10(2^{20} - 1)$. Option (b) is correct.

13. The answer will be given by:
    [1 + 2 + 3 +...+ 100]— [7 + 14 + 21 +... + 98]
    = 50 × 101 − 7 × 105
    = 5050 − 735 = 4315. Option (a) is correct.

14. 3rd term $ar^2 = 1/3$, 8th term $ar^7 = 81$
    $r^5 = 243$ Gives us: $r = 3$.
    Hence, the second term will be given by ($3^{rd}$ term/$r$) = 1/3  1/3 = 1/9. Option (d) is correct.
    [Note: To go forward in a G.P. you multiply by the common ratio, to go backward in a G.P. you divide by the common ratio.]

15. Since the sum of 5 numbers in AP is 35, their average would be 7. The average of 5 terms in an AP is also equal to the value of the 3rd term (logic of the middle term of an AP). Hence, the third term's value would be 7. Option (b) is correct.

16. Use trial and error by using various values from the options.
    If you find the sum of the series till 13 terms the value is 182. The $14^{th}$ term of the given series is 0, so also for 14 terms the value of the sum would be 182. Option (c) is correct.

17. Trying Option (a),
    We get least term 5 and largest term 30 (since the largest term is 6 times the least term).
    The average of the A.P becomes (5 + 30)/2 = 17.5
    Thus, 17.5 × n = 105 gives us:
    to get a total of 105 we need $n = 6$ i.e. 6 terms in this A.P. That means the A.P. should look like: 5, _, _, _, _, 30.
    It can be easily seen that the common difference should be 5. The A.P, 5, 10, 15, 20, 25, 30 fits the situation.
    The same process used for option (b) gives us the A.P. 10, 35, 60. (10 + 35 + 60 = 105) and in the third option 15, 90 (15 + 90 = 105).
    Hence, all the three options are correct.

18. Go through the options. The correct option should give value as 1, when $n = 3$ and as 8 when $n = 7$. Only option (a) satisfies both conditions.

19. The answer to this question can be seen from the options. Both 3, 6, 12 and 12, 6, 3 satisfy the required conditions— viz, GP with sum of first and third terms as 15. Thus, option (c) is correct.

20. The answer to this question cannot be determined because the question is talking about income and asking about expenses. You cannot solve this unless you know the value of the expenditure she incurs over the years. Thus, "Cannot be Determined" is the correct answer.

21. The difference between the amounts at the end of 5 years and 10 years will be the simple interest on the initial capital for 5 years.

    Hence, $(2000 - 1500)/5 = 100$ (simple interest.)

    Also, the Simple Interest for 5 years when added to the sum gives 1500 as the amount.

    Hence, the original sum must be 1000. Option (d) is correct.

22. Visualising the squares below 91, we can see that the only way to get the sum of 3 squares as 91 is: $1^2 + 3^2 + 9^2 = 1 + 9 + 81 = 91$. The smallest number is 1. Option (a) is correct.

23. Since the 8th and the 12th terms of the AP are given as 60 and 80, respectively, the difference between the two terms would equal 4 times the common difference. Thus we get $4d = 80 - 60 = 20$. This gives us $d = 5$. Also, the 8th term in the AP is represented by $a + 7d$, we get:

    $a + 7d = 60 \rightarrow a + 7 \times 5 = 60 \rightarrow a = 25$. Option (c) is correct.

24. The series would be given by: 13, 17, 21... which essentially means that all the numbers in the series are of the form $4n + 13$ or $4k + 1$ ( Where $k = n + 3$). Only the value in option (c) is a $4k + 1$ number and is hence the correct answer.

25. His total earnings would be $600 + 630 + 660 + ... + 1470 = $ Rs 31050. Option (a) is correct.

26. If we take the square of the side we get the area of the squares. Thus, if the side of the respective squares are $a_1, a_2, a_3, a_4...$ their areas would be $a_1^2$ $a_2^2$, $a_3^2$, $a_4^2$. Since the areas are in GP, the sides would also be in GP.

27. $1280 = 5. 2^{n-1}$ or $n - 1 = 8$ or $n = 9$. Thus, there are total of 9 terms in the series. Option (c) is correct.

28. Solve this question through trial and error by using values of $n$ from the options:

    For 16 terms, the series would be $5 + 10 + 15 + ... + 80$ which would give us a sum for the series as $8 \times 85 = 680$. The next term (17th term of the series) would be 85. Thus, $680 + 85 = 765$ would be the sum to 17 terms. It can thus be concluded that for 17 terms the value of the sum of the series is not less than 765. Option (a) is correct.

29. $5 \times r^5 = 160 \rightarrow r^5 = 32 \Rightarrow r = 2$.

    Thus, the series would be 5, 10, 20, 40, 80, 160. The second geometric mean between 5 and 160 in this case would be 20. Option (d) is correct.

30. In the case of a G.P. the 7th term is derived by multiplying the 5th term twice by the common ratio. (Note: this is very similar to what we had seen in the case of an A.P.) Since, the seventh term is derived by multiplying the 5th term by 4, the relationship.

$r^2 = 4$ must be true.

Hence, $r = 2$

If the 4th term is 40, the series in reverse from the 4th to the first term will look like:

40, 20, 10, 5. Hence, option (b) is correct.

31. The first common term is 23, the next will be 29 (Notice that the second common term is exactly 6 away from the first common term. 6 is also the LCM of 2 and 3 which are the respective common differences of the two series.)

    Thus, the common terms will be given by the A.P 23, 29, 35 ....., last term. To find the answer you need to find the last term that will be common to the two series.

    The first series is 23, 25, 27 ... 259

    While the second series is 23, 26, 29 ..... 260.

    Hence, the last common term is 257.

    Thus our answer becomes $\frac{257 - 23}{6} + 1 = 40$. Option (b) is correct.

32. Think like this:

    The average of the first 4 terms is 14, while the average of the first 8 terms must be 22.

    Now visualise this:

    1st $\underbrace{\text{2nd} \quad \text{3rd}}_{\text{average}=14}$ $\underbrace{\text{4th} \quad \text{5th}}_{\text{average}=22}$ 6th 7th 8th

    Hence, $d = 8/2 = 4$ [Note: understand this as a property of an A.P.]

    Hence, the average of the 8th and 9th term $= 22 + 4.4 = 38$ But this 38 also represents the average of the 16 term A.P.

    Hence, required answer $= 16 \times 38 = 608$. Option (c) is correct.

33. AM $= 41$ means that their sum is 82 and GM $= 9$ means their product is 81. The numbers can only be 81 and 1. Option (c) is correct.

34. Trial and error gives us that for option (b):

    With the ratio 9:1, the numbers can be taken as $9x$ and $1x$. Their AM would be $5x$ and their GM would be $3x$. The GM can be seen to be 40% lower than the AM. Option (b) is thus the correct answer.

35. The total savings would be given by the sum of the series: $1000 + 1500 + 2000 + ..... + 6500 = 12 \times 3750 = 45000$. Option (b) is correct.

36. The 23rd term of the sequence would be the 12th term of the sequence 1, 5, 9, 13, ....

    The 12th term of the sequence would be $1 + 4 \times 11 = 45$. Option (c) is correct.

37. $\log a, \log b, \log c$ are in A.P then $2\log b = \log a + \log c$ or $\log b^2 = \log ac$ or $b^2 = ac$

    So G.M. of $a$ and $c$ is $b$.

    Option (a) is correct.

38. The two series till their 1000th terms are 1, 3, 5, 7....1999 and 4, 7, 10...3001. The common terms of the series would be given by the series 7, 13, 19,...1999. The number of terms in this series of 333. Option (d) is correct.

39. The sum to 23 terms of the sequence would be:
The sum to 12 terms of the sequence 1, 5, 9, 13, ..... + The sum to 11 terms of the sequence 4, 8, 12, 16,....
The required sum would be
$\frac{12}{2}(2.1+(12-1)4)+\frac{11}{2}[2.4+(11-1)4]$ = 6 × 46 + 11 × 24 = 276 + 264 = 540. Option (c) is correct.

40. The maximum sum would occur when we take the sum of all the positive terms of the series. The series 25, 24, 23,... 1, 0 has 26 terms. The sum of the series would be given by:
$n \times$ average = 26 × 12.5 = 325
Option (a) is correct.

41. Since the sum of 22 terms of the AP is 770, the average of the numbers in the AP would be 770/22 = 35. This means that the sum of the first and last terms of the AP would be 2 × 35= 70. Trial and error gives us the terms of the required GP as 14, 28, 56. Thus, the common difference of the $AP = \frac{28-14}{7} = 2$.

42. It can be seen that for the series the average of first two terms is 2, for first 3 terms the average is 3 and so on. Thus, the sum of first 2 terms is $2^2$, of first 3 terms it is $3^2$ and so on. For 1111111 terms it would be $1111111^2 = 1234567654321$. Option (d) is correct.

43. The area of the first square would be 1024 sq cm. the second square would give 512, the third one 256 and so on. The infinite sum of the geometric progression 1024 + 512 + 256 + 128... = 2048. Option (a) is correct.

44. $a = \frac{ar}{1-r}$ or $1 - r = r$ or $r = 1/2$ $a + ar = 36$ or $a = 24$
Required sum $= \frac{24}{1-\frac{1}{2}} = 48$. Option (a) is correct.

45. The side of the first equilateral triangle being 8 units, the first area is $16\sqrt{3}$ square units. The second area would be 1/4 of area of largest triangle and so on.
$16\sqrt{3}$, $4\sqrt{3}$, $\sqrt{3}$, $\frac{\sqrt{3}}{4}$, $\frac{\sqrt{3}}{16}$,.....
The infinite sum of this series — $16\sqrt{3}/(1 - 1/4) =$ $64/\sqrt{3}$ square units.
Option (d) is correct.

46. The sum of the total distance it travels would be given by the infinite sum of the series:

$210+2\left[210\times\left(\frac{5}{6}\right)+210\times\left(\frac{5}{6}\right)^2+210\times\left(\frac{5}{6}\right)^3+.....\right]$

$210+ 2\cdot210\cdot\left(\frac{5}{6}\right)\left[1+\frac{5}{6}+\left(\frac{5}{6}\right)^2+.....\right]$

$210 + 350\left[\frac{1}{1-\frac{5}{6}}\right] = 210 + 350 \times 6 = -210 + 2100$
= 2310 metres.
Option (b) is correct.

47. Let the series be $a$, $ar$, $ar^2$, $ar^3$,....
According to the question $a= 3ar/(1 - r)$ or $r = 1/4$. The series would be 4, 4/4, 4/16,..... and so on. The product of first three terms of the series would be $4\cdot1\cdot\frac{1}{4}=1$.

48. $5^{th}$ term= 25. $1^{st}$ term = 25 − (4 × 5) = 5, $11^{th}$ term = 5 + 10 × 5 = 55, $100^{th}$ term = 5 + 99 × 5 = 500 Student will score maximum marks if he attempts question 11 to 100. The maximum score would be the sum of the series 55 + 60 + ... + 495 + 500 = (90 × 555)/2 = 24975.

49. In order to find how many times the alarm rings we need to find the number of numbers below 100, which are not divisible by 2, 3, 5 or 7. This can be found by:
**100 — (numbers divisible by 2) – (numbers divisible by 3 but not by 2) — (numbers divisible by 5 but not by 2 or 3) — (numbers divisible by 7 but not by 2 or 3 or 5).**
**Numbers divisible by 2** up to 100 would be represented by the series 2, 4, 6, 8, 10...100 → A total of 50 numbers.
**Numbers divisible by 3 but not by 2** up to 100 would be represented by the series 3, 9, 15, 21...99 → A total of 17 numbers. Note use short cut for finding the number of number in this series :
[(last term — first term)/ common difference] + 1 = [(99 — 3)/6] + 1 = 16 + 1 = 17.
**Numbers divisible by 5 but not by 2 or 3:** Numbers divisible by 5 but not by 2 up to 100 would be represented by the series 5, 15, 25, 35...95 → A total of 10 numbers. But from these numbers, the numbers 15, 45 and 75 are also divisible by 3. Thus, we are left with 10 — 3 = 7 new numbers which are Divisible by 5 but not by 2 and 3.
**Numbers divisible by 7, but not by 2, 3 or 5:** numbers divisible by 7 but not by 2 upto 100 would be represented by the series 7, 21, 35, 49, 63, 77, 91 → A total of 7 numbers. But from these numbers we should not count 21, 35 and 63 as they are divisible by either 3 or 5. Thus a total of 7 — 3 = 4 numbers are divisible by 7 but not by 2, 3 or 5.

Thus we get a total of 100 − 78 = 22 times. Also, the last time the bell would ring would be in the 97th minute (as 98, 99 and 100 are divisible by at least one of the numbers).

50. Smallest interior angle = 100, largest exterior angle= 180 − 100 =80

Similarly other exterior angles are 70, 60, 50, ....

Sum of all the exterior angles = 360

So $\dfrac{n(2.80+(n-1)(-10))}{2} = 360$ or $n(17 - n) = 72$

We can see that the above equation is true for both n = 8, 9. But for n = 9, the 9th exterior angle must be 0 which is not possible so only 8 is possible.

51. $\dfrac{a^{n+1}+b^{n+1}}{a^n+b^n} = \dfrac{a+b}{2}$

For n =0 the above equality is true. So n must be 0.

52. $\dfrac{a^{n+1}+b^{n+1}}{a^n+b^n} = \dfrac{2ab}{a+b}$

For n = −1 the above equality is true so n = −1.

53. According to the question $\dfrac{2ab}{a+b} = \sqrt{ab}$, this equality will be true only for a = b. Hence, a = b.

54. A.M. of n positive integers is always greater than or equals to G.M. of the numbers. Then according to the question,

Sum of the numbers ≥ n (product of n positive integers) $^{1/n}$

Sum of the numbers ≥ n

55. G.M.$^2$ = A.M. × H.M. = 12 × 3 =36.

56. We can solve this problem by checking for values. If we assume that x, y, z are in A.P. & x = 1, y = 2, z = 3.

$x+\dfrac{1}{yz} = 1+\dfrac{1}{6} = \dfrac{7}{6}$

$y+\dfrac{1}{zx} = 2+\dfrac{1}{3} = \dfrac{7}{3}$

$z+\dfrac{1}{xy} = 3+\dfrac{1}{2} = \dfrac{7}{2}$

We can see if x, y, z are in A. P. then

$x+\dfrac{1}{yz}, y+\dfrac{1}{zx}, z+\dfrac{1}{xy}$ are also in A.P.

**Level of Difficulty (II)**

1. Identify an AP which satisfies the given condition. Suppose we are talking about the second and third terms of the AP.

Then an AP with second term 3 and third term 2 satisfies the condition.

A times the $a^{th}$ term = b times the $b^{th}$ term.

In this case the value of a = 2 and b = 3.

Hence, for the $(a + b)^{th}$ term, we have to find the 5th term.

It is clear that the 5th term of the AP must be zero. Check the other three options to see whether any option gives 0 when a = 2 and b = 3.

Since none of the options b, c or d gives zero for this particular value, option (a) is correct.

2. Since the four parts of the number are in AP and their sum is 28, the average of the four parts must be 7. Looking at the options for the smallest part, only the value of 4 fits in, as it leads us to think of the AP 4, 6, 8, 10. In this case, the ratio of the product of the first and fourth (4 × 10) to the product of the first and second (6 × 8) are in 5: 6 ratio.

3. View: 1 − 3 + 5 − 7 + 9 − 11 ..... 100 terms as (1 − 3) + (5 − 7) + (9 − 11) ...... 50 terms. Hence, −2 + −2 + −2 ... 50 terms = 50 × −2 = −100. Option (b) is correct.

4. In a period of 1 day or 24 hours the clock would strike 1 + 2 + 3 + ....+ 23 = 276 times. In the course of 3 days the clock would strike 276 × 3 = 828 times. Option (b) is correct.

5. Since this is a decreasing A.P. with first term positive, the maximum sum will occur upto the point where the progression remains non-negative. 54, 52, 50, ..... 0 Hence, 28 terms × 27 = 756. Option (c) is correct.

6. The sum of the required series of integers would be given by 105 + 112 + 119 + ....294 = 28 × 199.5 = 5586. Option (b) is correct.

7. $y^2 = xz$, 1 + log x, 1 + log y, 1 + log z are in A.P. if 2 log y= log x + log z or $y^2 = xz$, Option (b) is right.

8. 1001 + 1003 + 1005 + ... 1999 = 1500 × 500 = 750000.

9. The required sum would be given by the sum of the series 110, 121, 132, .... 990. The number of terms in this series = (990 − 110)/11 + 1 = 80 + 1 = 81. The sum of the series = 81 × 550 (average of 110 and 990) = 44550. Option (c) is correct.

10. 6 × average of 113 and 253 = 6 × 183 = 1098. Option (c) is correct.

11. The first 100 terms of this (1 − 2 − 3) + (2 − 3 − 4) + ... + (33 − 34 − 35) + 34

The first 33 terms of the above series (indicated inside the brackets) will give an AP.:

−4, −5, −6.... −36 = 33 × −20 = −660 (sum of this A.P.). The required answer would be

−660 + 34 = −626.

12. Solve this one through trial and error. For n = 2 terms the sum upto 2 terms is equal to 84. Putting n in the options it can be seen that for option (b) the sum to two terms would be given by

7 × (1000 − 10 − 18)/81 = 7 × 972/81 = 7 × 12 = 84.

13. 2log b = log a+ log c or log $b^2$ = log ac or $b^2$ = ac, so a, b, c are in GP. Option (b) is correct.

14. The path of the rubber ball is:

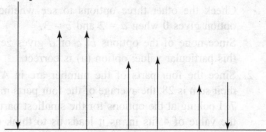

In the figure above, every bounce is 3/5th of the previous drop.

In the above movement, there are two infinite G.Ps (The GP representing the falling distances and the GP representing the rising distances.)

The required answer: (Using $a/(1 - r)$ formula)

$$\frac{20}{2/5} + \frac{12}{2/5} = 80$$ metres. Option (c) is correct.

15. Solve this for a sample GP. Let us say we take the GP as 2, 6, 18, 54. $x$, the first term is 2, let $n = 3$ then the 3rd term $y = 18$ and the product of 3 terms $p = 2 \times 6 \times 18 = 216 = 6^3$. The value of $p^2 = 216 \times 216 = 6^6$.

Putting these values in the options we have:

Option (a) gives us $(xy)^{n-1} = 36^2$ which is not equal to the value of $p^2$ we have from the options

Option (b) gives us $(xy)^n = 36^3 = 6^6$ which is equal to the value of $p^2$ we have from the options.

It can be experimentally verified that the other options yield values of $p^2$ which are different from $6^6$ and hence we can conclude that option (b) is correct.

16. Trying to plug in values we can see that the infinite sum of the GP 24, 8, 8/3... is 36. Hence the third term is 8/3.

17. The expression can be written as $2^{1/3+1/6+1/12+....} = 2^{\text{INFINITE SUM OF THE GP}} = 2^{2/3}$. Option (b) is correct.

18. $\dfrac{A}{1-r} = 5$ then $r = 1 - \dfrac{A}{5}$

Now since it is an infinite G.P. $|r| < 1$, implies

$-1 < 1 - \dfrac{A}{5} < 1$ or $0 < A < 10$

19. From the facts given in the question it is self evident that the common ratio of the GP must be 3 (as the sum of the 2nd and 4th term is thrice the sum of the first and third term).

$a + ar^2 = 50$ or $a = 50/(1 + 9) = 5$

Largest term $= 5.(3)^3 = 135$. Option (c) is correct.

20. 2/9, 1/4, 2/7, 1/3 ...........................

This is an HP series. The corresponding AP will be: 9/2, 4/1, 7/2, 3/1, .......................

or 4.5, 4, 3.5, 3 ...........................

i.e., this is an AP with first term 4.5 and common difference –0.5.

Hence $T_{13} = 4.5 + 12\,(-0.5) = -1.5$

The corresponding $T_{13}$ HP is $1/-1.5 = 1 \times -2/3 = -2/3$

21. Third term $= a + 2d$, Fourth term $= a + 3d$; 1st term $= a$, seventh term $= a + 6d$.

Thus $2a + 5d = 19$ and $2a + 6d = 22 \rightarrow d = 3$ and $a = 2$.

The 9th term $= a + 8d = 2 + 24 = 26$. Thus, option (a) is correct.

22. If the difference between the 6th and the 1st term is 30, it means that the common difference is equal to 6. Since, the third term is 16, the AP would be 4, 10, 16, 22, 28, 34, 40, 46 and the sum to 8 terms for this AP would be 200. Thus, option (d) is correct.

23. $5d = 30 \rightarrow d = 6$. Thus, the numbers are 4, 10, 16, 22, 28, 34. The smallest number is 10. Option (d) is correct.

24. Find sum of the series: 104, 111, 118,...993

Average $\times n = \dfrac{104 + 993}{2} \times 128 = 70208$. Option (a) is correct.

25. Since the sum of the first three terms of the AP is 24, the average of the AP till 3 terms would he 24/3 = 8. Value of the second term would be equal to this average and hence the second term is 8. Using the information about the sum of squares of the first and second terms being 80, we have that the first term must be 4. Thus, the AP has a first term of 4 and a common difference of 4. The seventh term would be 32. Thus option (a) is correct.

26. The combined travel would be 28 on the first day, 29 on the second day, 30 on the third day, 31 on the fourth day, 32 on the fifth day and 33 on the sixth day, 34 on 7th day. They meet after 7 days. Option (c) is correct.

27. This is an intensive calculation, problem and you are not supposed to know how to do the calculations in this question mentally. The problem has been put here to test your concepts about whether you recognize how this is a question of GPs. If you feel like, you can use a calculator/computer spreadsheet to get the answer to this question.

The logic of the question would hinge on the fact that the value of the investment of the fifteenth year would be 1000. At the end of the 15th year, the investment of the 14th year would be equal to $1000 \times 1.05$, the 13th year's investment would amount to $1000 \times 1.05^2$ and so on till the first year's investment which would amount to $1000 \times 1.05^{14}$ after 15 years. Thus, you need to calculate the sum of the GP: 1000, $1000 \times 1.05$, $1000 \times 1.05^2$, $1000 \times 1.05^3$ for 15 terms.

28. Since, sum to $n$ terms is given by $(2n + 7)$,

Sum to 1 terms $= 9$

Sum to 2 terms $= 11$

Thus, the 2nd term must be 2,

29. Solve this question by looking at hypothetical values for $n$ and $2n$ terms. Suppose, we take the sum to 1 ($n$ = 1) term of the first series and the sum to 2 terms ($2n$ = 2) of the second series we would get B/A as 3/2

    For $n$ = 2 and $2n$ = 4 we get $A$ = 5/2 and $B$ = 15/4 and $B/A$ = 15/4/5/2 = 3/2

    Thus, we can conclude that the required ratio is always constant at 3/2 and hence the correct option is (d).

30. We need to find the infinite sum of the GP: 1000, 800, 640….. (first term = 1000 and common ratio = 0.8) We get: infinite sum of the series as 1000/ (1 − 0.8) = 5000, Thus option (b) is correct.

31. Questions such as these have to be solved on the basis of a reading of the pattern of the question. The sum upto the first term is: 1/5. Upto the second term it is 2/9 and upto the third term it is 3/12. It can be easily seen that for the first term, second term and third term the numerators are 1, 2 and 3 respectively. Also, for 1/5 — the 5 is the second value in the denominator of $1/1 \times 5$ (the first term); for 2/9 also the same pattern is followed— as 9 comes out of the denominator of the second term of series and tar 3/13 the 13 comes out of the denominator of the third term of the series and so on. The given series has 56 terms and hence the correct answer would be 56/225.

32. Solve this on the same pattern as Question 31 and you can easily see that for the first term sum of the series is $2 - \sqrt{3}$, for 2 terms we have the sum as $\sqrt{5} - \sqrt{3}$ and so on. For the given series of 120 terms the sum would be $\sqrt{225} - \sqrt{3} = 15 - \sqrt{3}$. Option (a) is correct.

33. If you look for a few more terms in the series, the series is: 1, 1/3, 1/6, 1/10, 1/15, 1/21, 1/28, 1/36, 1/45, 1/55, 1/66, 1/78, 1/91, 1/105, 1/120, 1/136. 1/153 and so on. If you estimate the values of the individual terms it can be seen that the sum would tend to 2 and would not be good enough to reach even 2.25. Thus, option (a) is correct.

34. Solve this using trial and error. For 1 term the sum should be 15 and we get 15 only from the first option when we put is $n$ = 1. Thus, option (a) is correct.

35. For this question too you would need to read the pattern of the values being followed. The given sum has 6 terms.

    It can be seen that the sum to 1 term = 1/3

    Sum to 2 terms = 3/5

    Sum to 3 terms = 5/7

    Hence, the sum to 6 terms would be 11/13.

36. The sum to infinite terms would tend to 1 because we would get (infinity)/(infinity + 2).

37. All members of $A$ are smaller than all members of $B$. In order to visualise the effect of the change in sign in $k$ assume that $A$ is {1, 2, 3...124} and $B$ is {126, 12.7...250}. It can be seen that for this assumption of values neither options (a), (b) or (c) is correct.

38. If elements of $A$ are in ascending order $a_{124}$ would be the largest value in $A$. Also $a_{125}$ would be the largest value in $B$. On interchanging $a_{124}$ and $a_{125}$, $A$ continues to be in ascending order, but $B$ would lose its descending order arrangement since $a_{124}$ would be the least value in $B$. Hence, option (a) is correct.

39. Since the minimum is in $A$ and the maximum is in $B$, the value of $x$ cannot be less than Maximum − Minimum.

40. It is evident that the whole question is built around Arithmetic progressions. The 5th row has an average of 55, while the 25th row has an average of 75. Since even column wise each column is arranged in an AP we can conclude the following:

    1st row - average 51 - total = $25 \times 51$

    2nd row - average 52 - total $25 \times 52$.....

    25th row - average 75 - total $25 \times 75$

    The overall total can be got by using averages as: 25 (51 + 52 + 53 + …..+ 75)= 25.1575 = 39375

41. The numbers forming an AP would be:

    1234, 1357, 2345, 2468, 3210, 3456, 3579, 4321, 4567, 5432, 5678, 6543, 6420, 6789, 7654, 7531, 8765, 8642, 9876, 9753, 9630.

    A total of 21 numbers.

    If we count the GPs we get: 1248, 8421-a total of 2 numbers.

    Hence, we have a total of 23, 4-digit numbers why the digits are either APs or GPs.

    Thus, option (d) is correct.

42. Total vadapavs made = 500

    Vadapavs with chicken and mushroom patty =250 (Number of terms in the series 1,3, 5, 7, 9...499) out of which half of the vadapavs also have vegetable petty.

    Vadapavs with only mushroom patty = 36 (Number of terms of the series 8, 22, 36, ….)

    Vadapavs with chicken, mushroom and vegetable patty = 18 (Number of terms in the series 1, 29, 57... .

    Required answer = 500 − 250 − 36 = 214.

43. From the above question, we have 18 such vadapavs.

44. The key to this question is what you understand from the statement— 'for two progressions out of $P_1$, $P_2$ and $P_3$ the average is itself a term of the original progression P.' For option (a) which tells us that the Progression $P$ has 20 terms, we can see that $P_1$ would have 7 terms, $P_2$ would have 7 terms and $P_3$ would have 6 terms. Since, both $P_1$ and $P_2$ have an odd number of terms we can see that for $P_1$ and $P_2$ their 4th terms (being the middle terms for an AP with 7 terms) would be equal to their average. Since, all the terms of $P_1$, $P_2$ and $P_3$ have been taken out of the original AP

$P$, we can see that for $P_1$ and $P_2$ their average itself would be a term of the original progression $P$. This would not occur for $P_3$ as $P_3$, has an even number of terms. Thus, 20 is a correct value for $n$.

Similarly, if we go for $n = 26$ from the second option we get:

$P_1$, $P_2$ and $P_3$ would have 9, 9 and 8 terms, respectively and the same condition would be met here too.

For $n = 36$ from the third option, the three progressions would have 12 terms each and none of them would have an odd number of terms.

Thus, option (d) is correct as both options (a) and (b) satisfy the conditions given in the problem.

45. Since, $P_1$ is formed out of every third term of $P$, the common difference of $P_1$ would be three times the common difference of $P$. Thus, the common difference of $P$ would be 2.

46. $S$ consists one $a$, two $b$'s, three $c$'s and so on. So total number of terms $= 1 + 2 + 3 + \ldots + 26 =$
$\dfrac{26}{2}(1+26) = 13 \times 27 = 351.$

47. For $16^{\text{th}}$ alphabet total number of terms of $S = 136$. So $144^{\text{th}}$ term of $S$ will be $17^{\text{th}}$ alphabet, which is $q$.

48. Let $S'$ be the sum of all terms of the series $S$ then according to the question:
$S' = 1a + 2b + 3c + 4d + 5e + \ldots + 26z = 1.1 +$
$2.3 + 3.5 + 4.7 + \ldots + 26. 51 = \sum_{n=26} n(2n-1) =$
$\sum_{n=26} 2n^2 - n = 12051$

49. If $f(4x) = 8x + 1$ then $f(x) = 2x + 1$ & $f(2x) = 4x + 1$
$(4x + 1)^2 = (8x + 1)(2x + 1)$
$x = 0$

So for no positive value of $x$, $f(2x)$ is the G.M. of $f(x)$, $f(4x)$.

50. If $y = x + d$, $z = x + 2d$, $w = x + 3d$ then
$(x + d)^2 = x(x + 3d)$ or $d = x$
$w/x = 4x/x = 4$

51. Let the G.P. be 1, 3, 9, 27, 81,...
Let $m = 2$, $n = 3$, $p = 5$ then $(n - p) \log x + (p - m) \log y + (m - n) \log z = (3 - 5)\log 3 + (5 - 2)\log 9 + (2 - 3)\log 81 = -2\log 3 + 6 \log 3 - 4\log 3 = 0$

52. Go through options.
Option (a) $\dfrac{n(n+1)(n+2)}{6}$ for $n = 1$, sum = 1
For $n = 2$, Sum = 4
So option (a) is correct.

53. $A = 1/(1 - x)$ & $B = 1/(1 - y)$
$x = (A - 1)/A$ & $y = (B - 1)/B$
$1 + xy + x^2y^2 + x^3y^3 + \ldots =$
$\dfrac{1}{1-xy} = \dfrac{1}{1 - \dfrac{A-1}{A} \cdot \dfrac{B-1}{B}} = \dfrac{AB}{A+B-1}$

54. Let the angles are $x$, $xr$, $xr^2$, $xr^3$
$x + xr + xr^2 + xr^3 = 360^0$.
The angles are $24^0$, $48^0$, $96^0$, $192^0$. Largest angle = $192^0$

55. $\qquad S = 1 + 4 + 9 + 16 + \ldots$
$S_n = \sum n^2 = \dfrac{1}{6} n(n+1)(2n+1)$
$S_{16} = \dfrac{1}{6} \cdot 16.17.33 = 1496$

56. $S_{16} = 1 + (1 + 3) + (1 + 3 + 5) + (1 + 3 + 5 + 7) + (1 + 3 + 5 + 7 + 9) + 1$
$S_{16} = \dfrac{1}{6} 5(5+1)(2.5+1) + 1 = 56$

57. Going through the trial and error $= 2(20)^2 + 3 - 2(19)^2 - 3 = 78$

58. $1^2 - 2^2 + 3^2 - 4^2 + 5^2 - 6^2 + \ldots = (1 - 2) (1 + 2) + (3 - 4) (3 + 4) + \ldots + (15 - 16) (15 + 16) + 17^2$
$= -(1 + 2 + 3 + 4 + \ldots + 16) + 17^2 = 289 - 136 = 153$

59. $3 + 6 + 10 + 15 + \ldots$
$(1 + 2) + (1 + 2 + 3) + (1 + 2 + 3 + 4) + \ldots = 1 + (1 + 2) + (1 + 2 + 3) + (1 + 2 + 3 + 4) + \ldots - 1$
Required sum = Sum of 21 terms of series $1 + (1 + 2) + (1 + 2 + 3) + \ldots - 1 = \sum_{n=21} \dfrac{(n+1)n}{2} - 1 = 1771 - 1 = 1770$

60. If we take $x = 4$ and $n = 1$ then $1^1 + 2^1 + 3^1 = 6$ is divisible by $1 + 2 + 3 = 6$. But for $n = 2$ $1^2 + 2^2 + 3^2 = 14$ is not divisible by 6 again for $n = 3$, $1^n + 2^n + 3^n$ divisible by 6 and so on. So for every odd value of $n$, $1^n + 2^n + 3^n + \ldots + x^n$ is always divisible by $1 + 2 + 3 + \ldots + x$.

61. $3 = 4^1 - 1$
$14 = 4^2 - 2$
$61 = 4^3 - 3$
$252 = 4^4 - 4$
So $12^{\text{th}}$ term $= 4^{12} - 12$

## Level of Difficulty (III)

1. Since the difference between the tenth and the sixth terms is $-16$, the common difference would be $-4$. Using a trial and error approach with the options, we can see that if we take the first term as 16, we will get the series 16,12,8,4,0,−4,−8,−12,−16,−20. We can see that both the conditions given in the question are met by this series. Hence, the first term would be 16.

2. Any sub-part of an AP is also an AP. Thus, the third term would be the average of the first and the fifth term. Hence, the third term would be 5.

3. A factor search for factor pairs of 456 give us the following possibilities. 1,456; 2,228; 3,152; 4,114; 6,76; 8,57; 12,38 & 19,24. A check of the conditions given in the problem, tells us that if we take

12 as the 4$^{th}$ term and 38 as the 5$^{th}$ term, we would get the series till 9 terms as: −66,−40,−14,12,38,64, 90,116,142. In this series we can see that the division of the 9$^{th}$ term by the 4$^{th}$ term gives us a quotient of 11 and a remainder of 10. Hence, the required first term is −66.

4. The distances covered by him (to and fro) would be 20, 40, 60,80,100, 120, 140, 160,180, 200 &220 to get a total distance of 1.32 kms. There are 11 terms in this AP. However, he must also have planted one sapling at the starting point & hence the number of saplings planted would be 12.

5. The answer would directly be $P_2/P_1$. Assume a series having a few number of terms e.g. 1,2,4,8,16,32. The value of $P_2$ here = 42, while $P_1$ = 21. The common ratio can be seen to be $P_2/P_1$ = 2.

6. Solve on the same pattern as above. The correct answer is option (c).

7. Solve this question using options. The average of the sum of the first 5 terms of the AP can be used to get the value of the third term of the AP. If we try to use the options, in option 2, if the sum of the first 5 terms is 2.5, the third term must be 2.5/5 = 0.5. This means our AP is 2,1.25,0.5,−0.25,−1. The corresponding GP with the same 1$^{st}$ and 3$^{rd}$ terms is 2,1,0.5,0.25… The condition for the second term is also matched here.

8. Use the options to get the answer. For n=10, we get the required ratio as 51/2.

9. For 1 digit the sum would be 6$^2$ + 8, for 2 digits the sum would be 66$^2$ + 88 and so on. Checking the options gives us option (b) as the correct answer.

10. The sum of the interior angles of any polygon of n sides is given by
$(n - 2) \times 180$. This needs to match the sum of the AP 120 + 125 + 130 +…n terms. For n = 9, we get the two sums equal and hence option (c) is correct.

11. Solve this one using options to check the correct answer.

12. Tracing the second and fourth terms through factor pairs of 160, we get the numbers that fit in the requirements of the problem as: 7, 10, 13, 16, 19, 22, 25. The sum of the series is 112.

13. The third and ninth terms of an 11 term AP are a pair of corresponding terms of the AP. Hence, their average would be the average of the AP. This gives us the required sum of the AP as $11 \times 5 = 55$.

14. $(a + 4d)^2 + (a + 10d)^2 = 3 \rightarrow a^2 + 14ad + 58d^2 = 1.5$. Also, $(a + d)(a + 13d) = P \rightarrow a^2 + 14ad + 13d^2 = P$. Further, we need to find the value of $a^2 + 14ad$ (product of the first and fifteenth terms of the AP). From the above two equations, we get that $45d^2 = \frac{3}{2} - P \rightarrow 13d^2 = \frac{(39 - 26P)}{90}$

Thus, $a^2 + 14ad = P - \frac{(39 - 26P)}{90} = (116P - 39)/90$. Option (c) is correct.

15. Solve using options. The values in option (a) gives you the required 12:13 ratio between the HM and the GM. Hence, option (d) is correct.

16. Solve this based on pattern of the options. The given series has 100 terms. For $n = 100$, the options can be converted as:
Option (a) = $n \times 2^{(n + 1)} + 2$. This means that for 1 term, the sum should be $1 \times 2^2 + 2 = 6$. But we can see that for 1 term, the series has a sum of only $1 \times 2 = 2$. Hence, this option can be rejected. Option (c) satisfies the conditions.
Option (b) = $(n - 1) \times 2^n + 2$. For 1 term, this gives us a value of 2. For 2 terms, this gives us a value of 6, which does not match the actual value in the question.Hence, this option can be rejected.

17. Since the ratio of the 2$^{nd}$ to the fourth term is given as ¼, we can conclude that the common ratio of the GP is 2. Also, $a+ 8a= 108 \rightarrow 9a = 108 \rightarrow a = 12$. Thus, $x_3 = 48$.

18. You can try to fit in values to get the correct answer. $a,b,c$ would be in GP. If we take $x$, $y$ and $z$ as 1,2,4 we get $a,b,c$ as 4,2 and 1, respectively to keep $a^x$, $b^y$ & $c^z$ equal.

19. The prime factors of 720 are: $2^4 \times 3^2 \times 5^1$. The required sum of factors would be: $(1 + 2 + 2^2 + 2^3 + 2^4)(1 + 3 + 3^2)(1 + 5) = 31 \times 13 \times 6 = 2418$.

20. Check the options to get option (a) as the correct answer.

21. The first term of the given AP is 2 and the common difference is also 2. Thus, the 11$^{th}$ term of the GP = $2 \times 2^{10} = 2048$.

22. The minimum value of y would occur when all the three values are equal. Thus, $y^3 =4 \rightarrow y = 2^{2/3}$.

23. For the product to be the maximum, since the sum of $a_2$, $a_7$ and $a_{12}$ would be fixed; we would need to keep each of the three numbers as equal. Thus, the value of the common difference would be 0.

24. Solve based on patterns and options as discussed for question 16 above.

25. The corresponding AP would be 2.5, 1.0833,… This gives us a common difference of −1.4166. From the third term onwards, the AP and its reciprocal HP would both become negative. Hence, the largest term of the HP is the second term itself.

26. The series of plank sizes would be: $0.75 \times 0.5$, $0.75 \times 1$, $0.75 \times 1.5….0.75 \times 12$. The sum of this AP is 112.5.

27. Each subsequent triangle would have the sum of sides halved from the previous triangle. Thus, the sum of the perimeters would be given by $P + P/2 + P/4 + P/8 +….$ till infinite terms. Hence, the sum of all the perimeters of the infinite triangles would be $2P$.

28. The areas would be $A + A/4 + A/16 + \ldots$ till infinite terms. The infinite sum of all the perimeters would be $4A/3$.

29. The first perimeter is 160, the second one is $\dfrac{160}{\sqrt{2}}$, the third one would be 80 and so on till infinite terms.

    The infinite sum would be equal to $160(2 + \sqrt{2})$.

30. The areas would consecutively get halved. So, the first area being 1600, the next one would be 800, then 400 and so on till infinite terms. Thus, the infinite sum would be 3200.

31. If the sum of the first n terms is '$x$', the sum of the next $n$ terms is given as '$2x$' (as defined in the problem). Naturally, the sum of the next n terms would be '$3x$' (When you add the same number of terms of an AP consecutively, you get another AP). Thus, the required ratio is $6x/x = 6$.

32. Since, the problem says that the cell breaks into two new cells, it means that the original cell no longer exists. Hence, after 1 hour there would be $2^1$ cells, after 2 hours there would be $2^2$ cells and so on. After 9 hours there would be $2^9$ cells. Hence, option (c) is correct.

33. We need the sum of the AP: 101, 104,107,...497 = $133 \times 299 = 39767$.

34. Solve by taking values and checking with the options. If we take the numbers as 1 and 8, we would get $a = 4.5$ and $b$ and $c$ as 2 and 4 respectively. Then $(b^3 + c^3)/abc = 2$. None of the first three options gives us a value equal to 2. Hence, the correct answer is option (d).

35. This can be checked using any values of $p, q, r$. If we try with 1,2,3 we get the value as 0. If we try values of $p, q , r$ as 2,3,4 we get the expression as positive. Hence, we conclude that the expression's value would always be non-negative.

36. For $n = 1$ sum = 2/3
    For $n = 2$ sum = 20/27
    For $n = 3$ sum = 1640/2187
    None of the options matches these numbers and hence option (d) is correct.

37. $77777\ldots7777 = 7(10^{132} + \ldots + 10^2 + 10^1 + 1) = $
    $\dfrac{7(10^{133} - 1)}{10 - 1} = \dfrac{7(10^{133} - 1)}{9}$
    $10^{133} - 1$ is divisible by 9. Hence the given number is a composite number. Option (c) is correct.

38. $S = n^2 + 1 + n^2 + 2 + \ldots + n^2 + 2n = 2n^3 + n(2n + 1) = n(2n^2 + 2n + 1)$
    Option (a) is correct.
    Alternative Method: Suppose $n = 2$ then $1^{st}$ term of the series will be $2^2 + 1 = 5$. Now we want to find the sum of first $2n = 4$ terms. First 4 terms of the series will be 5, 6, 7, 8. Sum = 26.

If we put $n = 2$ in the above options then only option (a) satisfies.

39. $m$th term of the series $= \dfrac{1}{m!+ (m+1)!} = \dfrac{1}{m!(m+2)!}$

    $= \dfrac{1}{(m+1)!} = \dfrac{1}{(m+2)!}$

    $S = \dfrac{1}{2!} - \dfrac{1}{3!} + \dfrac{1}{3!} - \dfrac{1}{4!} + \ldots + \dfrac{1}{20!} - \dfrac{1}{21!} = \dfrac{1}{2!} - \dfrac{1}{21!}.$

    Option (a) is correct.

40. $\dfrac{a^n + c^n}{2} > \left(\dfrac{a+c}{2}\right)^n$, if $n$ does not lie between 0 and 1.

    But we know that A.M. > H.M.
    $b$ is the H.M. of $a$ and $c$.

    $\dfrac{a+c}{2} > b$

    As $n > 1$ $\left(\dfrac{a+c}{2}\right)^n > b^n$

    $\dfrac{a^n + c^n}{2} > \left(\dfrac{a+c}{2}\right)^n > b^n$

    $a^n + c^n > 2b^n$ Option (c) is correct.

41. $S = \dfrac{3}{1^2.2^2} + \dfrac{5}{2^2.3^2} + \dfrac{7}{3^2.4^2} + \ldots$

    $= \left(1 - \dfrac{1}{2^2}\right) + \left(\dfrac{1}{2^2} - \dfrac{1}{3^2}\right) + \left(\dfrac{1}{3^2} - \dfrac{1}{4^2}\right) + \ldots + \left(\dfrac{1}{17^2} - \dfrac{1}{18^2}\right)$

    $= 1 - \dfrac{1}{18^2} = \dfrac{323}{324}$

42. $S = \dfrac{4}{11} + \dfrac{44}{11^2} + \dfrac{444}{11^3} + \dfrac{4444}{11^4} + \ldots$

    $\dfrac{S}{11} = \dfrac{4}{11^2} + \dfrac{44}{11^3} + \dfrac{444}{11^4} + \ldots$

    $S - \dfrac{S}{11} = \dfrac{4}{11} + \dfrac{40}{11^2} + \dfrac{400}{11^3} + \ldots$

    $\dfrac{10S}{11} = \dfrac{4}{11}\left(1 + \dfrac{10}{11} + \dfrac{100}{11^2} + \ldots\right)$

    $\dfrac{10S}{11} = \dfrac{4}{11}\left(\dfrac{1}{1 - \dfrac{10}{11}}\right) = 4$

    $S = 44/10 = 22/5$

43. $S = \dfrac{1}{2.5} + \dfrac{1}{5.8} + \dfrac{1}{8.11} + \ldots + \infty$

    $S = \dfrac{1}{3}\left(\dfrac{1}{2} - \dfrac{1}{5} + \dfrac{1}{5} - \dfrac{1}{8} + \dfrac{1}{8} - \dfrac{1}{11} + \ldots - \dfrac{1}{\infty}\right)$

    $= \dfrac{1}{3} \times \dfrac{1}{2} = \dfrac{1}{6}$

44. We can easily solve these problems by considering suitable values.

Let G.P. be 1, 2, 4, 8, 16, 32 and A.P. be 1, 7.2, 13.4, 19.6, 25.8, 32.

$A = 99, B = 63$. So $A > B$

45.

$$4 + \frac{1}{2} + 4 + \frac{1}{6} + 4 + \frac{1}{12} + \dots.4 + \frac{1}{2450}$$

$$= 4 + \left(1 - \frac{1}{2}\right) + 4 + \left(\frac{1}{2} - \frac{1}{3}\right) + 4 + \left(\frac{1}{3} - \frac{1}{4}\right) + \dots.$$

$$+ 4 + \left(\frac{1}{49} - \frac{1}{50}\right)$$

$$= 49 \times 4 + \left(1 - \frac{1}{2} + \frac{1}{2} - \frac{1}{3} + \frac{1}{3} - \dots.. + \frac{1}{49} - \frac{1}{50}\right)$$

$$= 196 + \frac{49}{50} = \frac{9849}{50}$$

46. Let the common difference of the series $X$ be $d_1$ and that of $Y$ be $d_2$.

Since $x_n - y_n = n - 2$, $x_1 - y_1 = -1$ or $y_1 = x_1 + 1$

$x_3 = y_5$

$x_1 + 2d_1 = y_1 + 4d_2$

$x_1 + 2d_1 = x_1 + 1 + 4d_2$

$2d_1 - 4d_2 = 1$

$x_{99} - y_{197} = x_1 + 98d_1 - y_1 - 196d_2 = -1 + 49(2d_1 - 4d_2)$

$= -1 + 49 = 48$. Option (b) is correct.

47. If $a$ be the 1st term and d be the common difference of the A.P. the 4th term of the series will be $a + 3d$. If $a + 3d$ is divisible by $d$ then $a$ should be divisible by $d$. hence the cases are:

$d = 1, a = 1, 2, 3, 4, 5, 6, 7, 8, 9$

$d = 2, a = 2, 4, 6$

$d = 3, a = 3$

So the required answer is $9 + 3 + 1 = 13$

48. If $a - 2d$ be the first term and d be the common difference of A.P. then according to the question:

$(a - 2d)(a - d)a(a + d)(a + 2d) = 3840$     (1)

$$\frac{a-d}{a-2d} = \frac{a+d}{a-d}$$

$$d(3d - a) = 0$$

$$a = 3d$$

By putting $a = 3d$ in equation 1 we get:

$d \times 2d \times 3d \times 4d \times 5d = 3840$

By solving we get $d = 2$ & $a = 6$

10th term $= 6 + 9.2 = 24$.

49. Let $x = -1/3$

$S = (1 + x)(1 + x^2)(1 + x^4)\dots.$

$(1 - x)S = (1 - x)(1 + x)(1 + x^2)(1 + x^4)\dots$

$(1 - x)S = (1 - x^2)(1 + x^2)(1 + x^4)(1 + x^8)\dots..$

$(1 - x)S = (1 - x^4)(1 + x^4)(1 + x^8)\dots..$

Since $x < 0$ & $|x| < 1$ so the value of RHS would be equals to 1.

$(1 - x) S = 1$ or $S = 1/(1 - x)$ or $1/(1 - (-1/3)) = \frac{3}{4}$.

50. $a, b, c, d$ are in A.P.

$\dfrac{a}{abcd}, \dfrac{b}{abcd}, \dfrac{c}{abcd}, \dfrac{d}{abcd}$ are also in A.P.

$\dfrac{1}{bcd}, \dfrac{1}{acd}, \dfrac{1}{abd}, \dfrac{1}{abc}$ are also in A.P.

Hence their reciprocals are in H.P.

51. $n$th term $= \dfrac{\sum n^3}{\sum (2n-1)} = \dfrac{1}{4}(n^2 + 2n + 1)$

Sum of $n$ terms of the given series =

$$\frac{1}{4}\left(\frac{1}{6}n(n+1)(2n+1) + n(n+1) + n\right)$$

For $n = 10$ the required sum $= \dfrac{1}{4}[505] = 126.5$

**Space for Rough Work**

## TRAINING GROUND FOR BLOCK I

### 🎧 HOW TO THINK IN PROBLEMS ON BLOCK I

**1.** A number $x$ is such that it can be expressed as $a + b + c = x$ where $a$, $b$, and $c$ are factors of $x$. How many numbers below 200 have this property?

    (a) 31            (b) 32

    (c) 33            (d) 5

**Solution:** In order to think about this question you need to think about whether the number can be divided by the initial numbers below the square root like 2, 3, 4, 5... and so on.

Let us say, if we think of a number that is not divisible by 2, in such a case if we take the number to be divisible by 3, 5 and 7, then the largest factors of $x$ that we will get would be $\dfrac{x}{3}, \dfrac{x}{5}$ and $\dfrac{x}{7}$.

Even in this situation, the percentage value of these factors as a percentage of $x$ would only be: for $\dfrac{x}{3} = 33.33\%$, $\dfrac{x}{5} = 20\%$ and $\dfrac{x}{7} = 14.28\%$

Hence, if we try to think of a situation where $a = \dfrac{x}{3}$, $b = \dfrac{x}{5}$, and $c = \dfrac{x}{7}$ the value of $a + b + c$ would give us only $(33.33\% + 20\% + 14.28\%) = 67.61\%$ of $x$, which is not equal to 100%.

Since the problem states that $a + b + c = x$, the value of $a + b + c$ should have added up to 100% of $x$.

The only situation, for this to occur would be if

$a = \dfrac{x}{2} = 50\%$ of $x$      $b = \dfrac{x}{3} = 33.33\%$ of $x$ and

$c = \dfrac{x}{6} = 16.66\%$ of $x$.

This means that 2, 3 and 6 should divide $x$ necessarily. In other words $x$ should be a multiple of 6. The multiples of 6 below 200 are 6, 12, 18 … 198, a total of 33 numbers.

Hence the correct answer is c.

**2.** Find the sum of all 3 digit numbers that leave a remainder of 3 when divided by 7.

    (a) 70821            (b) 60821

    (c) 50521            (d) 80821

**Solution:** In order to solve this question you need to visualise the series of numbers, which satisfy this condition of the remainder 3 when divided by 7.

The first number in 3 digits for this condition is 101 and the next will be 108, followed by 115, 122 …

This series would have its highest value in 3 digits as 997.

The number of terms in this series would be 129 (using the logic that for any AP, the number of terms is given by $\dfrac{D}{d} + 1$).

Also the average value of this series is the average of the first and the last term i.e., the average of 101 and 997. Hence the required sum = $549 \times 129 = 70821$.

Hence the correct Option is (a).

**3.** How many times would the digit 6 be used in numbering a book of 639 pages?

    (a) 100            (b) 124

    (c) 150            (d) 164

**Solution:** In order to solve this question you should count the digit 6 appearing in units digit, separately from the instances of the digit 6 appearing in the tens place and appearing in the hundreds place.

When you want to find out the number of times 6 appears in the unit digit, you will have to make a series as follows: 6, 16, 26, 36 … 636.

It should be evident to you that the above series has 64 terms because it starts from 06, 16, 26 … and continues till 636. The digit 6 will appear once in the unit digit for each of these 64 numbers.

Next you need to look at how many times the digit 6 appears in the ten's place.

In order to do this we will need to look at instances when 6 appears in the tens place. These will be in 6 different ranges 60s, 160s, 260s, 360s, 460s, 560s and in each of these ranges there are 10 numbers each with exactly one instance of the digit 6 in the tens place, a total of 60 times.

Lastly, we need to look at the number of instances where 6 appears in the hundreds place. For this we need to form the series 600, 601, 602, 603 … 639. This series will have 40 numbers each with exactly one instance of the digit 6 appearing in the hundreds place.

Therefore, the required answer would be $64 + 60 + 40 = 164$.

Hence, Option (d) is correct.

**4.** A number written in base 3 is 100100100100100100. What will be the value of this number in base 27?

    (a) 999999            (b) 900000

    (c) 989999            (d) 888888

The number can be visualised as:

| 1 | 0 | 0 | 1 | 0 | 0 | 1 | 0 | 0 | 1 | 0 | 0 | 1 | 0 | 0 | 1 | 0 | 0 |
|---|---|---|---|---|---|---|---|---|---|---|---|---|---|---|---|---|---|
| $3^{17}$ | $3^{16}$ | $3^{15}$ | $3^{14}$ | $3^{13}$ | $3^{12}$ | $3^{11}$ | $3^{10}$ | $3^9$ | $3^8$ | $3^7$ | $3^6$ | $3^5$ | $3^4$ | $3^3$ | $3^2$ | $3^1$ | $3^0$ |

Now in the base 27, we can visualise this number as:

| — | — | — | — | — | — |
|---|---|---|---|---|---|
| $27^5$ | $27^4$ | $27^3$ | $27^2$ | $27^1$ | $27^0$ |

When you want to write this number in Base 27 the unit digit of the number will have to account for the value of $3^2$ in the above number. Since the unit digit of the number in Base 27 will correspond to $27^0$ we would have to use $27^0$, 9 times to make a value $3^2$. The number would now become:

| — | — | — | — | — | 9 |
|---|---|---|---|---|---|
| $27^5$ | $27^4$ | $27^3$ | $27^2$ | $27^1$ | $27^0$ |

Similarly, the number of times that we will have to use $27^1$ in order to make the value of $3^5$ (or 243) will be $\frac{243}{27}$ = 9. Hence the second last digit of the number will also be 9.

Similarly, to make a value of $3^8$ using $27^2$ the number of times we will have to use $27^2$ will be given by $\frac{3^8}{27^2} = \frac{3^8}{3^6}$ = 9. The number would now look as:

| — | — | — | 9 | 9 | 9 |
|---|---|---|---|---|---|
| $27^5$ | $27^4$ | $27^3$ | $27^2$ | $27^1$ | $27^0$ |

It can be further predicted that each of subsequent 1's in the original number will equal 9 in the number, which is being written in Base 27. Since the original number in Base 3 has 18 digits, the left most '1' in that number will be covered by a number corresponding to $27^5$ in the new number (i.e., $3^{15}$). Hence the required number will be a 6-digit number 999999. Hence, Option (a) is correct.

**5.** Let $x = 1640$, $y = 1728$ and $z = 448$. How many natural numbers are there that divide at least one amongst $x, y, z$.

    (a) 47                (b) 48
    (c) 49                (d) 50

**Solution:** 1640 can be prime factorised as $2^3 \times 5^1 \times 41^1$. This number would have a total of 16 factors.

Similarly, 1728 can be prime factorised as $2^6 \times 3^3$. Hence, it would have 28 factors. While $448 = 2^6 \times 7^1$ would have 14 factors. Thus there are a total of $(16 + 28 + 14) = 58$ factors amongst $x$, $y$ and $z$.

However, some of these factors must be common between $x, y, z$. Hence, in order to find the number of natural numbers that would divide at least one amongst $x, y, z$, we will need to account for double and triple counted numbers amongst these 58 numbers (by reducing the count by 2 for each triple counted number and by reducing the count by 1 for each double counted number).

The number of cases of triple counting would be for all the common factors of $(x, y, z)$. This number can be estimated by finding the HCF of $x$, $y$ and $z$ and counting the number of factors of the HCF. The HCF of 1640, 1728 and 448 is 8 and hence the factors of 8, i.e., 1, 2, 4 and 8 itself must have got counted in each of the 3 counts done above. Thus each of these 4 numbers should get subtracted twice to remove the triple count. This leaves us with $58 - 4 \times 2 = 50$ numbers.

We still need to eliminate numbers that have been counted twice, i.e., numbers, which belong to the factors of any two of these numbers (while counting this we need to ensure that we do not count the triple counted numbers again). This can be visualised in the following way:

Number of common factors that are common to only 1640 and 1728 and not to 448 ($x$ and $y$ but not $z$):
$$1640 = 2^3 \times 5^1 \times 41^1$$
$$1728 = 2^6 \times 3^3$$

It can be seen from these 2 standard forms of the numbers that the highest common factors of these 2 numbers is 8. Hence there is no new number to be subtracted for double counting in this case.

The case of 1640 and 448 is similar because $1640 = 2^3 \times 5^1 \times 41^1$ while $448 = 2^6 \times 7^1$ and HCF = $2^3$ and hence they will not give any more numbers as common factors apart from 1, 2, 4 and 8.

Thus there is no need of adjustment for the pair 1640 and 448.

Finally when we look for 1728 and 448, we realise that the HCF = $2^6$ = 64 and hence the common factors between 448 and 1728 are 1, 2, 4, 8, 16, 32, 64. But we are looking for factors which are common for 1728 and 448 but not common to 1640 to estimate the double counting error for this case.

Hence we can eliminate the number 1, 2, 4, 8 from this list and conclude that there are only 3 numbers 16, 32 and 64 that divide both 1728 and 448 but do not divide 1640.

If we subtract these numbers once each, from the 50 numbers we will end up with $50 - 3 \times 1 = 47$.

The complete answer can be visualised as $16 + 28 + 14 - 4 \times 2 - 3 \times 1 = 47$.

Hence, Option (a) is correct.

**6.** How many times will the digit 6 be used when we write all the six digit numbers?

    (a) 5,50,000          (b) 5,00,000
    (c) 4,50,000          (d) 4,00,000

**Solution:** When we write all 6-digit numbers we will have to write all the numbers from 100000 to 999999, a total of 9 lac numbers in 6 digits without omitting a single number. There will be a complete symmetry and balance in the use of all the digits. However, the digit 0 is not going to be used in the leftmost place.

Using this logic we can visualise that when we write 9 lakh, 6-digit numbers, the units place, tens place, hundreds place, thousands place, ten thousands place and lakh place — Each of these places will be written 9 lakh times. Thinking about the units place, we can think as follows: In writing the units place 9 lakh times (once for every number) we will be using the digit 0, 1, 2, 3 … 9 an equal number of times. Hence any particular digit like 6 would get used in the units digit a total number of 90000 times (9 lakh/10). The same logic will continue for tens, hundreds, thousands and ten thousands, i.e., the digit 6 will be used (9 lakh/10) = 90000 times in each of these places. (Note here that we are dividing by 10 because we have to equally distribute 9 lakh digits amongst the ten digits 0, 1, 2, 3,4, 5, 6, 7, 8, 9.)

Finally for the lakh place since "0" is not be used in the lakh place as it is the leftmost digit of the number, the number of times the digit 6 will be used would be 9 lakh/9 = 1 lakh. Hence the next time you are solving the problem of this type, you should solve directly using $\frac{9\,\text{lakh}}{9} + \frac{9\,\text{lakh}}{10} \times 5$ = 5,50,000.

Hence, Option (a) is the correct answer.

## 🎯 BLOCK REVIEW TESTS

## REVIEW TEST 1

1. In 1936, I was as old as the number formed by the last two digits of my year of birth. Find the date of birth of my father who is 25 years older to me.
   (a) 1868          (b) 1893
   (c) 1902          (d) 1900
   (e) Can't be determined

2. Find the total number of integral solutions of the equation $(407)x - (ddd)y = 2589$, where '$ddd$' is a three-digit number.
   (a) 0          (b) 1
   (c) 2          (d) 3
   (e) Can't be determined

3. Find the digit at the ten's place of the number $N = 7^{281} \times 3^{264}$.
   (a) 0          (b) 1
   (c) 6          (d) 5
   (e) None of these

4. Raju went to a shop to buy a certain number of pens and pencils. Raju calculated the amount payable to the shopkeeper and offered that amount to him. Raju was surprised when the shopkeeper returned him ₹ 24 as balance. When he came back home, he realised that the shopkeeper had actually transposed the number of pens with the number of pencils. Which of the following is certainly an invalid statement?
   (a) The number of pencils that Raju wanted to buy was 8 more than the number of pens.
   (b) The number of pens that Raju wanted to buy was 6 less than the number of pencils.
   (c) A pen cost ₹ 4 more than a pencil.
   (d) None of the above.

5. HCF of 384 and $a^5b^2$ is 16ab. What is the correct relation between $a$ and $b$?
   (a) $a = 2b$          (b) $a + b = 3$
   (c) $a - b = 3$          (d) $a + b = 5$

6. In ancient India, 0 to 25 years of age was called Brahmawastha and 25 to 50 was called Grahastha. I am in Grahastha and my younger brother is also in Grahastha such as the difference in our ages is 6 years and both of our ages are prime numbers. Also twice my brother's age is 31 more than my age. Find the sum of our ages.
   (a) 80          (b) 68
   (c) 70          (d) 71

7. Volume of a cube with integral sides is the same as the area of a square with integral sides. Which of these can be the volume of the cube formed by using the square and its replicas as the 6 faces?

8. Let A be a two-digit number and B be another two-digit number formed by reversing the digits of A. If A + B + (Product of digits of the number A) = 145, then what is the sum of the digits of A?
   (a) 9          (b) 10
   (c) 11          (d) 12

9. When a two-digit number N is divided by the sum of its digits, the result is Q. Find the minimum possible value of Q.
   (a) 10          (b) 2
   (c) 5.5          (d) 1.9

10. A one-digit number, which is the ten's digit of a two digit number $X$, is subtracted from $X$ to give $Y$ which is the quotient of the division of 999 by the cube of a number. Find the sum of the digits of $X$.
    (a) 5          (b) 7
    (c) 6          (d) 8

11. After Yuvraj hit 6 sixes in an over, Geoffery Boycott commented that Yuvraj just made 210 runs in the over. Harsha Bhogle was shocked and he asked Geoffery which base system was he using? What must have been Geoffery's answer?
    (a) 9          (b) 2
    (c) 5          (d) 4

12. Find the ten's digit of the number $7^{2010}$.
    (a) 0          (b) 1
    (c) 2          (d) 4

13. Find the HCF of 481 and the number '$aaa$' where '$a$' is a number between 1 and 9 (both included).
    (a) 73          (b) 1
    (c) 27          (d) 37

14. The number of positive integer valued pairs $(x, y)$, satisfying $4x - 17y = 1$ and $x < 1000$ is:
    (a) 59          (b) 57
    (c) 55          (d) 58

15. Let $a$, $b$, $c$ be distinct digits. Consider a two digit number '$ab$' and a three digit number '$ccb$' both defined under the usual decimal number system. If $(ab)^2 = ccb$ and $ccb > 300$ then the value of b is:
    (a) 1          (b) 0
    (c) 5          (d) 6

16. The remainder $7^{84}$ is divided by 342 is:
    (a) 0          (b) 1
    (c) 49          (d) 341

17. Let $x$, $y$ and $z$ be distinct integers, $x$ and $y$ are odd and positive, and $z$ is even and positive. Which one of the following statements can't be true?

(a) 19683          (b) 512
(c) 256          (d) Both (a) and (b)

(a) $(x-z)^2 y$ is even    (b) $(x-z)y^2$ is odd

(c) $(x-y)y$ is even    (d) $(x-y)^2 z$ is even

18. A boy starts adding consecutive natural numbers starting with 1. After some time he reaches a total of 1000 when he realises that he has made the mistake of double counting 1 number. Find the number double counted.

    (a) 44             (b) 45

    (c) 10             (d) 12

19. In a number system the product of 44 and 11 is 1034. The number 3111 of this system, when converted to decimal number system, becomes:

    (a) 406           (b) 1086

    (c) 213           (d) 691

20. Ashish is given ₹ 158 in one rupee denominations. He has been asked to allocate them into a number of bags such that any amount required between Re 1 and ₹ 158 can be given by handing out a certain number of bags without opening them. What is the minimum number of bags required?

    (a) 11             (b) 12

    (c) 13             (d) None of these

*Space for Rough Work*

## REVIEW TEST 2

1. Find the number of 6-digit numbers that can be formed using the digits 1, 2, 3, 4, 5, 6 once such that the 6-digit number is divisible by its unit digit.
   (a) 648　　　　　　　　(b) 528
   (c) 728　　　　　　　　(d) 128

2. Which is the highest 3-digit number that divides the number 11111....1(27 times) perfectly without leaving any remainder?
   (a) 111　　　　　　　　(b) 333
   (c) 666　　　　　　　　(d) 999

3. W1, W2, ... , W7 are 7 positive integral values such that by attaching the coefficients of +1, 0 and −1 to each value available and adding the resultant values, any number from 1 to 1093 (both included) could be formed. If W1, W2, ... , W7 are in ascending order, then what is the value of W3?
   (a) 10　　　　　　　　(b) 9
   (c) 0　　　　　　　　(d) 1

4. What is the unit digit of the number $63^{25} + 25^{63}$?
   (a) 3　　　　　　　　(b) 5
   (c) 8　　　　　　　　(d) 2

5. Find the remainder when $(2222^{5555} + 5555^{2222})$ is divided by 7.
   (a) 1　　　　　　　　(b) 0
   (c) 2　　　　　　　　(d) 5

6. What is the number of nines used in numbering a 453 page book?
   (a) 86　　　　　　　　(b) 87
   (c) 84　　　　　　　　(d) 85

7. How many four digit numbers are divisible by 5 but not by 25?
   (a) 2000　　　　　　　(b) 8000
   (c) 1440　　　　　　　(d) 9999

8. The sum of two integers is 10 and the sum of their reciprocals is 5/12. What is the value of larger of these integers?
   (a) 7　　　　　　　　(b) 5
   (c) 6　　　　　　　　(d) 4

9. Saurabh was born in 1989. His elder brother Siddhartha was also born in the 1980's such that the last two digits of his year of birth form a prime number P. Find the remainder when $(P^2 + 11)$ is divided by 5.
   (a) 0　　　　　　　　(b) 1
   (c) 2　　　　　　　　(d) 3

10. The HCF of $x$ and $y$ is H. Find the HCF of $(x − y)$ and $(x^3 + y^3)/(x^2 − xy + y^2)$.
    (a) H − 1　　　　　　(b) $H^2$
    (c) H　　　　　　　　(d) H + 1

11. 4 bells toll together at 9:00 A.M. They toll after 7, 8, 11 and 12 seconds, respectively. How many times will they toll together again in the next 3 hours?
    (a) 3　　　　　　　　(b) 5
    (c) 6　　　　　　　　(d) 9

12. What power of 210 will exactly divide 142!
    (a) 22　　　　　　　　(b) 11
    (c) 34　　　　　　　　(d) 33

13. Find the total numbers between 122 and 442 that are divisible by 3 but not by 9.
    (a) 70　　　　　　　　(b) 71
    (c) 72　　　　　　　　(d) 73

14. If 146! is divisible by $6^n$, then find the maximum value of n.
    (a) 74　　　　　　　　(b) 75
    (c) 76　　　　　　　　(d) 70

15. If we add the square of the digit in the tens place of a positive two-digit number to the product of the digits of that number, we shall get 52, and if we add the square of the digit in the units place to the same product of the digits, we shall get 117. Find the two-digit number.
    (a) 18　　　　　　　　(b) 39
    (c) 49　　　　　　　　(d) 28

16. Find the smallest natural number n such that $(n + 1)$ $n[(n − 1)!]$ is divisible by 990.
    (a) 2　　　　　　　　(b) 4
    (c) 10　　　　　　　　(d) 11

17. If $x, y$ and $z$ are odd, even and odd, respectively, then $(x^2 − yz^2 + y^3)$ and $(x^2 + y^2 + z^2)$ are respectively:
    (a) Odd & Odd　　　　(b) Even & Odd
    (c) Odd & Even　　　　(d) Odd & Odd

18. A two digit number N has its digits reversed to form another two digit number M. What could be the unit digit of M if product of M and N is 574?
    (a) 1　　　　　　　　(b) 3
    (c) 6　　　　　　　　(d) 9

19. For what relation between $b$ and $c$ is the number abcacb divisible by 7, if $b > c$?
    (a) $b + c = 7$　　　　(b) $b = c + 7$
    (c) $2bc = 7$　　　　　(d) $c = 7b$

20. What is the remainder when $a^6$ is divided by $(a + 1)$?
    (a) $a + 1$　　　　　　(b) $a$
    (c) 0　　　　　　　　(d) 1

*Space for Rough Work*

# REVIEW TEST 3

1. What is the last digit of 62^43^54^65^76^87?
   - (a) 2
   - (b) 4
   - (c) 6
   - (d) 8

2. $N = 99^3 - 36^3 - 63^3$, how many factors does N have?
   - (a) 51
   - (b) 96
   - (c) 128
   - (d) 192

3. Find the highest power of 2 in 1! + 2! + 3! + 4!.............600!
   - (a) 1
   - (b) 494
   - (c) 0
   - (d) 256

4. 100! is divisible by $160^n$...what is the maximum integral value of $n$?
   - (a) 19
   - (b) 24
   - (c) 26
   - (d) 28

5. What is the sum of the digits of the decimal form of the product $2^{999} * 5^{1001}$?
   - (a) 2
   - (b) 4
   - (c) 5
   - (d) 7

6. What is the remainder when 1*1 + 11*11 + 111*111 + 1111*1111 +......+ (2001 times 1)*(2001 times 1) is divided by 100 ?
   - (a) 99
   - (b) 22
   - (c) 01
   - (d) 21

7. What is the remainder when 789456123 is divided by 999?
   - (a) 123
   - (b) 369
   - (c) 963
   - (d) 189

8. What is the total number of the factors of 16!
   - (a) 2016
   - (b) 1024
   - (c) 3780
   - (d) 5376

9. Find the sum of the first 125 terms of the sequence 1, 2, 1, 3, 2, 1, 4, 3, 2, 1, 5, 4, 3, 2....
   - (a) 616
   - (b) 460
   - (c) 750
   - (d) 720

10. Umesh purchased a Tata Nano recently, but the faulty car odometre of Tata Nano proceeds from digit 4 to digit 6, always skipping the digit 5, regardless of position. If the odometre now reads 003008 (starting with 000000), how many km has the Nano actually travelled?

    - (a) 2100
    - (b) 1999
    - (c) 2194
    - (d) 2195

11. What is the number of consecutive zeroes in the end of 1000!?
    - (a) 248
    - (b) 249
    - (c) 250
    - (d) 251

12. Mr. Ramlal lived his entire life during the 1800s. In the last year of his life, Ramlal stated: Once I was $x$ years old in the year $x^2$. He was born in the year
    - (a) 1822
    - (b) 1851
    - (c) 1853
    - (d) 1806

13. Find the unit's digit of LCM of $13^{501} - 1$ and $13^{501} + 1$.
    - (a) 2
    - (b) 4
    - (c) 5
    - (d) 8

14. If you were to add all odd numbers between 1 and 2007 (both inclusive), the result would be
    - (a) A perfect square
    - (b) Divisible by 2008
    - (c) Multiple of 251
    - (d) All of the above

15. Find the remainder when $971(30^{99} + 61^{100}) * (1148)^{56}$ is divided by 31
    - (a) 25
    - (b) 0
    - (c) 11
    - (d) 21

16. What is the remainder when $2^{100}$ is divided by 101?
    - (a) 1
    - (b) 100
    - (c) 0
    - (d) 99

17. Find the last two digits of $2^{134.}$
    - (a) 04
    - (b) 84
    - (c) 24
    - (d) 64

18. Find the remainder when $(10^3 + 9^3)^{1000}$ is divided by $12^3$.
    - (a) 01
    - (b) 11
    - (c) 1001
    - (d) 1727

19. The number of factors of the number 3000 are
    - (a) 16
    - (b) 32
    - (c) 24
    - (d) 28

20. If N! has 73 zeroes at the end then find the value of N?
    - (a) 295
    - (b) 300
    - (c) 290
    - (d) Not possible

*Space for Rough Work*

# ANSWER KEY

## Review Test 1

| | | | |
|---|---|---|---|
| 1. (b) | 2. (a) | 3. (c) | 4. (d) |
| 5. (d) | 6. (a) | 7. (d) | 8. (c) |
| 9. (d) | 10. (a) | 11. (d) | 12. (d) |
| 13. (d) | 14. (a) | 15. (a) | 16. (b) |
| 17. (a) | 18. (c) | 19. (a) | 20. (d) |

## Review Test 2

| | | | |
|---|---|---|---|
| 1. (a) | 2. (a) | 3. (b) | 4. (c) |
| 5. (b) | 6. (d) | 7. (c) | 8. (c) |

| | | | |
|---|---|---|---|
| 9. (a) | 10. (c) | 11. (b) | 12. (a) |
| 13. (b) | 14. (d) | 15. (c) | 16. (c) |
| 17. (c) | 18. (a) | 19. (b) | 20. (d) |

## Review Test 3

| | | | |
|---|---|---|---|
| 1. (a) | 2. (b) | 3. (c) | 4. (a) |
| 5. (d) | 6. (c) | 7. (b) | 8. (d) |
| 9. (c) | 10. (c) | 11. (b) | 12. (d) |
| 13. (b) | 14. (d) | 15. (b) | 16. (a) |
| 17. (b) | 18. (a) | 19. (b) | 20. (d) |

# TASTE OF THE EXAMS—BLOCK I

## CAT

1. Let a, b, c be distinct digits. Consider a two digit number 'ab' and a three digit number 'ccb', both defined under the usual decimal number system. If $(ab)^2 = ccb$ and ccb > 300, then the value of b is:
   (a) 1    (b) 0
   (c) 5    (d) 6
   **(CAT 1999)**

2. The remainder when $7^{84}$ is divided by 342 is:
   (a) 0    (b) 1
   (c) 49    (d) 341
   **(CAT 1999)**

3. If $n = 1 + x$, where $x$ is the product of four consecutive positive integers, then which of the following is/are true?
   A. $n$ is odd        B. $n$ is prime
   C. $n$ is a perfect square
   (a) A and C only    (b) A and B only
   (c) A only    (d) None of the above.
   **(CAT 1999)**

4. For two positive integers a and b, define the function h(a, b) as the greatest common factor (gcf) of a, b. Let A be a set of n positive integers. G(A), the gcf of the elements of set A is computed by repeatedly using the function h. The minimum number of times h is required to be used to compute G is:
   (a) $12n$    (b) $(n-1)$
   (c) $n$    (d) None of the above
   **(CAT 1999)**

5. If $n^2 = 123456787654321$, what is n?
   (a) 12344321    (b) 1235789
   (c) 11111111    (d) 1111111
   **(CAT 1999)**

**Directions for Questions 6 to 8:** These questions are based on the situation given below.

There are 50 integers $a_1, a_2, ..., a_{50}$, not all of them are necessarily different. Let the greatest integer of these 50 integers be referred to as G and the smallest integer be referred to as L. The integers $a_1-a_{24}$ form sequence $S_1$, and the rest form sequence $S_2$. Each member of $S_1$ is less than or equal to each member of $S_2$.

6. If we change the sign of all values in $S_1$, while those in $S_2$ remain unchanged, which of the following statements is true?
   (a) Every member of $S_1$ is greater than or equal to every member of $S_2$.
   (b) G is in $S_1$

   (c) If all numbers originally in $S_1$ and $S_2$ had the same sign, then after the change of sign, the largest number of $S_1$ and $S_2$ will be in $S_1$.
   (d) None of the above.
   **(CAT 1999)**

7. Elements of $S_1$ are in ascending order, and those of $S_2$ are in descending order, $a_{24}$ and $a_{25}$ are interchanged. Then, which of the following statements is true?
   (a) $S_1$ continues to be in ascending order.
   (b) $S_2$ continues to be in descending order.
   (c) $S_1$ continues to be in ascending order and $S_2$ in descending order.
   (d) None of these.
   **(CAT 1999)**

8. Every element of $S_1$ is made greater than or equal to every element of $S_2$ by adding to each element of $S_1$ an integer x. Then, x cannot be less than
   (a) 210
   (b) The smallest value of $S_2$
   (c) The largest value of $S_2$
   (d) $(G-L)$
   **(CAT 1999)**

9. Let D be a recurring decimal of the form, D = 0. $a_1 a_2 a_1 a_2 a_1 a_2$ ............., where digits $a_1$ and $a_2$ lie between 0 and 9. Further, at most one of them is zero. Then which of the following numbers necessarily produces an integer, when multiplied by D.
   (a) 18    (b) 108
   (c) 198    (d) 288
   **(CAT 2000)**

10. Let S be the set of integers $x$ such that:
    (i) $100 \leq x \leq 200$
    (ii) $x$ is odd
    (iii) $x$ is divisible by 3 but not by 7
    How many elements does S contain?
    (a) 16    (b) 12
    (c) 11    (d) 13
    **(CAT 2000)**

11. Let $x$, y and z be distinct integers, that are odd and positive. Which one of the following statements cannot be true?
    (a) $xyz^2$ is odd.
    (b) $(x-y)^2 z$ is even.
    (c) $(x+y-z)^2 (x+y)$ is even.
    (d) $(x-y)(y+z)(x+y-z)$ is odd.
    **(CAT 2000)**

12. Let S be the set of prime numbers greater than or equal to 2 and less than 100. [Multiply all elements of S. With how many consecutive zeros will the product end?]

(a) 1                         (b) 4
(c) 5                         (d) 10

**(CAT 2000)**

13. Let $N = 1421 \times 1423/1425$, what is the remainder when $N$ is divided by 12?
    (a) 0                     (b) 9
    (c) 3                     (d) 6

**(CAT 2000)**

14. The integers 34041 and 32506 when divided by a three-digit integer $n$ leave the same remainder. What is $n$?
    (a) 289                   (b) 367
    (c) 453                   (d) 307

**(CAT 2000)**

15. Let $N = 55^3 + 17^3 - 72^3$, $N$ is divisible by:
    (a) both 7 and 13         (b) both 3 and 13
    (c) both 17 and 7         (d) both 3 and 17

**(CAT 2000)**

16. ABCDEFGH is a regular octagon. A and E are opposite vertices of the octagon. A frog starts jumping from vertex to vertex, beginning from A. From any vertex of the octagon except E, it may jump to either of the two adjacent vertices. When it reaches E, the frog stops and stays there. Let $a_n$ be the number of distinct paths of exactly n jumps ending in E. Then, what is the value of $a_{2n-1}$?
    (a) Zero
    (b) Four
    (c) 2n – 1
    (d) Cannot be determined

**(CAT 2000)**

17. Convert the number 1982 from base 10 to base 12. The result is:
    (a) 1182                  (b) 1912
    (c) 1192                  (d) 1292

**(CAT 2000)**

18. Let $x$, $y$ and $z$ be distinct integers, $x$ and $y$ are odd and positive, and $z$ is even and positive. Which one of the following statements can not be true?
    (a) $(x-z)^2 y$ is even
    (b) $(x-z)y^2$ is odd.
    (c) $(x-y)y$ or $x$ is odd
    (d) $(x-y)^2 z$ is even.

**(CAT 2001)**

19. A boy starts adding consecutive natural numbers starting with one. After reaching a total of 1000, he realises that he has made the mistake of double counting one number. Find the number double counted.
    (a) 44                    (b) 45
    (c) 10                    (d) 12

**(CAT 2001)**

20. $x$ and $y$ are real numbers satisfying the conditions $2 < x < 3$ and $-7 < y < -1$. Which of the following expressions will have the least value?

(a) $x^2y$                    (b) $xy^2$
(c) $5xy$                     (d) None of these

**(CAT 2001)**

21. In a number system the product of 44 and 11 is 1034. The number 3111 of this system, when converted to the decimal number system, becomes
    (a) 406                   (b) 1086
    (c) 213                   (d) 691

**(CAT 2001)**

22. Raju has 128 boxes with him. He can put a minimum of 120 oranges and a maximum of 144 in a box. Then the least number of boxes which will have the same number of oranges is:
    (a) 5                     (b) 103
    (c) 3                     (d) 6

**(CAT 2001)**

23. Three friends, returning from a movie, stopped to eat at a restaurant. After dinner, they paid their bill and noticed a bowl of mints at the front counter. Sita took one-third of the mints, but returned four because she had a momentary pang of guilt. Fatima then took one-fourth of what was left but returned three for similar reasons. Eswari then took half of the remainder but threw two back into the bowl. The bowl had only 17 mints left when the raid was over. How many mints were originally in the bowl?
    (a) 38                    (b) 31
    (c) 41                    (d) None of these

**(CAT 2001)**

24. Anita had to do a multiplication. Instead of taking 35 as one of the multipliers, she took 53. As a result, the product went up by 540. What is the new product?
    (a) 1050                  (b) 540
    (c) 1440                  (d) 1590

**(CAT 2001)**

25. In a four-digit number, the sum of the first two digits is equal to that of the last two digits. The sum of the first and last digits is equal to the third digit. Finally, the sum of the second and fourth digits is twice the sum of the other two digits. What is the third digit of the number?
    (a) 5                     (b) 8
    (c) 1                     (d) 4

**(CAT 2001)**

26. A red light flashes three times per minute and a green light flashes five times in two minutes at regular intervals. If both lights start flashing at the same time, how many times do they flash together in each hour?
    (a) 30                    (b) 24
    (c) 20                    (d) 60

**(CAT 2001)**

27. Ashish is given ₹158 in one rupee denominations. He has been asked to allocate them into a number of bags such that any amount required between Re.1 and

₹ 158 can be given by handing out a certain number of bags without opening them. What is the minimum number of bags required?

(a) 11        (b) 12

(c) 13        (d) None of these

**(CAT 2001)**

28. For a Fibonacci sequence, from the third term onwards, each term in the sequence is the sum of the previous two terms in that sequence. If the difference of squares of seventh and sixth terms of this sequence is 517, what is the tenth term of this sequence?

(a) 147

(b) 76

(c) 123

(d) Cannot be determined

**(CAT 2001)**

29. In some code, letters a, b, c, d and e represent numbers 2, 4, 5, 6 and 10. We don't know which letter represents which number. Consider the following relationships:

  (i) $a + c = e$      (ii) $b - d = d$

(iii) $e + a = b$

Which statement below is true?

(a) $b = 4, d = 2$      (b) $a = 4, e = 6$

(c) $b = 6, e = 2$      (d) $a = 4, c = 6$

**(CAT 2001)**

30. $m$ is the largest positive integer such that $n > m$. Also, it is known that $n^3 - 7n^2 + 11n - 5$ is positive. Then, the possible value for $m$ is:

(a) 4        (b) 5

(c) 8        (d) None of these.

**(CAT 2001)**

31. Let $b$ be a positive integer and $a = b^2 - b$. If $b \geq 4$, then $a^2 - 2a$ is divisible by

(a) 15        (b) 20

(c) 24        (d) None of these

**(CAT 2001)**

32. A change making machine contains 1 rupee, 2 rupee and 5 rupee coins. The total number of coins is 300. The amount is ₹ 960. If the number of 1 rupee coins and the number of 2 rupee coins are interchanged, the value comes down by ₹ 40. The total number of 5 rupee coins is:

(a) 100        (b) 140

(c) 60        (d) 150

**(CAT 2001)**

33. $7^{6n} - 6^{6n}$, where n is an integer > 0, is divisible by

(a) 13        (b) 127

(c) 559        (d) none of these

**(CAT 2002)**

**Directions for Questions 35 and 37:** Answer the questions independently of each other.

34. After the division of a number successively by 3, 4 and 7, the remainders obtained are 2, 1 and 4 respectively. What will be the remainder if 84 divides the number?

(a) 80        (b) 76

(c) 41        (d) 53

**(CAT 2002)**

35. Three pieces of cakes weighing 4 1/2 lbs, 6 3/4 lbs and 7 1/5 lbs respectively are to be divided into parts of equal weights. Further, each part must be as heavy as possible. If one such part is served to each guest, then what is the maximum number of guests that could be entertained?

(a) 54        (b) 72

(c) 20        (d) none of these

**(CAT 2002)**

36. At a bookstore, "MODERN BOOK STORE" is flashed using neon lights. The words are individually flashed at intervals of 2 1/2, 4 1/4, 5 1/8 seconds respectively and each word is put off after a second. The least time after which the full name of the bookstore can be read again is:

(a) 49.5 seconds      (b) 73.5 seconds

(c) 1744.5 seconds      (d) 855 seconds

**(CAT 2002)**

37. When $2^{256}$ is divided by 17, the remainder would be

(a) 1        (b) 16

(c) 14        (d) none of these

**(CAT 2002)**

38. A child was asked to add first few natural numbers (that is, $1 + 2 + 3 \ldots$) as long as his patience permitted. As he stopped, he gave the sum as 575. When the teacher declared the result wrong the child discovered he had missed one number in the sequence during addition. The number he missed was:

(a) less than 10      (b) 10

(c) 15        (d) more than 15

**(CAT 2002)**

39. A car rental agency has the following terms. If a car is rented for 5 hours or less, the charge is 60 per hour or ₹ 12 per kilometre, whichever is more. On the other hand, if the car is rented for more than 5 hours, the charge is ₹ 50 per hour or ₹ 7.50 per kilometre whichever is more. Akil rented a car from this agency, drove it for 30 kilometres and ended up paying ₹ 300. For how many hours did he rent the car?

(a) 4        (b) 5

(c) 6        (d) none of these

**(CAT 2002)**

40. Shyam visited Ram on vacation. In the mornings, they both would go for yoga. In the evenings they would play tennis. To have more fun, they indulge, only in one activity per day, i.e., either they went for yoga or played tennis each day. There were days

when they were lazy and stayed home all day long. There were 24 mornings when they did nothing, 14 evenings when they stayed at home, and a total of 22 days when they did yoga or played tennis. For how many days did Shyam stay with Ram?

(a) 32
(b) 24
(c) 30
(d) none of these

**(CAT 2002)**

**Directions for Questions 41 and 42:** Answer these questions based on the information given below.

A boy is asked to put in a basket one mango when ordered 'One', one orange when ordered 'Two', one apple when ordered 'Three' and is asked to take out from the basket one mango and an orange when ordered 'Four'. A sequence of orders is given as:

1 2 3 3 2 1 4 2 3 1 4 2 2 3 3 1 4 1 1 3 2 3 4

41. How many total oranges were in the basket at the end of the above sequence?

(a) 1
(b) 4
(c) 3
(d) 2

**(CAT 2002)**

42. How many total fruits will be in the basket at the end of the above order sequence?

(a) 9
(b) 8
(c) 11
(d) 10

**(CAT 2002)**

**Directions for Questions 43 to 44:** Answer the questions independently of each other.

43. A rich merchant had collected many gold coins. He did not want anybody to know about them. One day, his wife asked, "How many gold coins do we have?" After pausing a moment, he replied, "Well! If I divide the coins into two unequal numbers, then 48 times the difference between the two numbers equals the difference between the squares of the two numbers." The wife looked puzzled. Can you help the merchant's wife by finding out how many coins the merchant has?

(a) 96
(b) 53
(c) 43
(d) none of these

**(CAT 2002)**

44. On a straight road XY, 100 metres long, five heavy stones are placed two metres a part, beginning at the end X. A worker, starting at X, has to transport all the stones to Y, by carrying only one stone at a time. The minimum distance he has to travel (in metres) is:

(a) 860
(b) 422
(c) 744
(d) 844

**(CAT 2002)**

45. If there are 10 positive real numbers $n_1 < n_2 < n_3 \ldots < n_{10}$. How many triplets of these numbers $(n_1, n_2, n_3), (n_2, n_3, n_4), \ldots$ can be generated such that in each triplet the first number is always less than the second number, and the second number is always less than the third number?

(a) 45
(b) 90
(c) 120
(d) 180

**(CAT 2002)**

46. Davji Shop sells samosas in boxes of different sizes. The samosas are priced at ₹2 per samosa up to 200 samosas. For every additional 20 samosas, the price of the whole lot goes down by 10 paise per samosa. What should be the maximum size of the box that would maximise the revenue?

(a) 240
(b) 300
(c) 400
(d) none of these

**(CAT 2002)**

47. Three travellers are sitting around a fire, and are about to eat a meal. One of them has five small loaves of bread; the second has three small loaves of bread. The third has no food, but has eight coins. He offers to pay for some bread. They agree to share the eight loaves equally among themselves and the third traveller will pay eight coins for his share of the eight loaves. All loaves were the same size. The second traveller (who had three loaves) suggests that he be paid three coins and that the first traveller be paid five coins. The first traveller says that he should get more than five coins. How much should the first traveller get?

(a) 5
(b) 7
(c) 1
(d) none of these

**(CAT 2002)**

48. A piece of string is 40 centimetres long. It is cut into three pieces. The longest piece is 3 times as long as the middle-sized piece and the shortest piece is 23 centimeters shorter than the longest piece. Find the length of the shortest piece.

(a) 27
(b) 5
(c) 4
(d) 9

**(CAT 2002)**

49. Mayank, Mirza, Little and Jaspal bought a motorbike for $60.00. Mayank paid one half of the sum of the amounts paid by the other boys. Mirza paid one third of the sum of the amounts paid by the other boys; and Little paid one fourth of the sum of the amounts paid by the other boys. How much did Jaspal have to pay?

(a) 15
(b) 13
(c) 17
(d) none of these

**(CAT 2002)**

50. The owner of a local jewellery store hired three watchmen to guard his diamonds, but a thief still got in and stole some diamonds. On the way out, the thief met each watchman, one at a time. To each he gave half of the diamonds he had then, and two more besides that. He escaped with one diamond. How many did he steal originally?

(a) 40
(b) 36
(c) 25
(d) none of these

**(CAT 2002)**

51. If $x$, $y$ and $z$ are real numbers such that: $x + y + z = 5$ and $xy + yz + zx = 3$, what is the largest value that x can have?
    (a) 5/3
    (b) $\sqrt{19}$
    (c) 13/3
    (d) none of these
    **(CAT 2002)**

52. Number S is obtained by squaring the sum of digits of a two digit number D. If difference between S and D is 27, then the two digit number D is:
    (a) 24
    (b) 54
    (c) 34
    (d) 45
    **(CAT 2002)**

53. If three positive real numbers $x$, $y$, $z$ satisfy $y - x = z - y$ and $xyz = 4$, then what is the minimum possible value of $y$?
    (a) $2^{1/3}$
    (b) $2^{2/3}$
    (c) $2^{1/4}$
    (d) $2^{3/4}$
    **(CAT 2003)**

54. An intelligence agency forms a code of two distinct digits selected from 0,1,2,......9, such that the first digit of the code is not zero. The code, handwritten on a slip, can however potentially create confusion when read upside down—for example, the code 91 may appear as 16. How many codes are there for which no such confusion can arise?
    (a) 80
    (b) 78
    (c) 71
    (d) 69
    **(CAT 2003)**

55. Consider the sets Tn = {n, n + 1, n + 2, n + 3, n + 4}, where n = 1, 2, 3, ......, 96. How many of these sets contain 6 or any integral multiple thereof (i.e., any one of the numbers 6, 12, 18,...)?
    (a) 80
    (b) 81
    (c) 82
    (d) 83
    **(CAT 2003)**

56. What is the sum of all two-digit numbers that give a remainder of 3 when they are divided by 7?
    (a) 666
    (b) 676
    (c) 683
    (d) 777
    **(CAT 2003)**

57. Let $x$ and $y$ be positive integers such that $x$ is prime and y is composite. Then,
    (a) $y - x$ cannot be an even integer
    (b) $xy$ cannot be an even integer.
    (c) $(x + y)/x$ cannot be an even integer
    (d) None of the above statements is true.
    **(CAT 2003)**

58. Let $n > 1$ be a composite integer such that $\sqrt{n}$ is not an integer. Consider the following statements:
    A: $n$ has a perfect integer-valued divisor, which is greater than 1 and less than $\sqrt{n}$
    B: $n$ has a perfect integer-valued divisor, which is greater than $\sqrt{n}$ but less than $n$

Then,
    (a) Both A and B are false
    (b) A is true but B is false
    (c) A is false but B is true
    (d) Both A and B are true
    **(CAT 2003)**

59. Let $a$, $b$, $c$, $d$, and $e$ be integers such that $a = 6b = 12c$, and $2b = 9d = 12e$. Then which of the following pairs contain a number that is not an integer?
    (a) $(a/27, b/e)$
    (b) $(a/36, c/e)$
    (c) $(a/12, bd/18)$
    (d) $(a/6, c/d)$
    **(CAT 2003)**

60. If $a$, $a + 2$, and $a + 4$ are prime numbers, then the number of possible solutions for a is:
    (a) 1
    (b) 2
    (c) 3
    (d) more than 3
    **(CAT 2003)**

61. What is the remainder when $4^{96}$ is divided by 6?
    (a) 0
    (b) 2
    (c) 3
    (d) 4
    **(CAT 2003)**

62. Using only 2, 5, 10, 25 and 50 paise coins, what will be the minimum number of coins required to pay exactly 78 paise, 69 paise, and Re. 1.01 to three different persons?
    (a) 19
    (b) 20
    (c) 17
    (d) 18
    **(CAT 2003)**

63. Each family in a locality has at most two adults, and no family has fewer than 3 children. Considering all the families together, there are more adults than boys, more boys than girls, and more girls than families. Then, the minimum possible number of families in the locality is:
    (a) 4
    (b) 1
    (c) 2
    (d) 3
    **(CAT 2004)**

64. If the sum of the first 11 terms of an arithmetic progression equals that of the first 19 terms, then what is the sum of the first 30 terms?
    (a) 0
    (b) −1
    (c) 1
    (d) Not unique
    **(CAT 2004)**

65. On January 1, 2004 two new societies, $S_1$ and $S_2$ are formed, each with n members. On the first day of each subsequent month, $S_1$ adds b members while $S_2$ multiplies its current number of members by a constant factor r. Both the societies have the same number of members on July 2, 2004. If $b=10.5n$, what is the value of r?
    (a) 2.0
    (b) 1.9
    (c) 1.8
    (d) 1.7
    **(CAT 2004)**

66. Suppose n is an integer such that the sum of the digits of n is 2, and $10^{10} < n < 10^{11}$. The number of different values for n is

(a) 11 (b) 10
(c) 9 (d) 8

**(CAT 2004)**

67. The remainder, when $(15^{23} + 23^{23})$ is divided by 19, is
(a) 4 (b) 15
(c) 0 (d) 18

**(CAT 2004)**

68. Consider the sequence of numbers $a_1, a_2, a_3, \ldots$ to infinity where $a_1 = 81.33$ and $a_2 = -19$ and $a_j = a_{j-1} - a_{j-2}$ for $j \geq 3$. What is the sum of the first 6002 terms of this sequence?
(a) −100.33 (b) −30.00
(c) 62.33 (d) 119.33

**(CAT 2005)**

69. If $x = (16^3 + 17^3 + 18^3 + 19^3)$, then $x$ divided by 70. This leaves a remainder of:
(a) 0 (b) 1
(c) 69 (d) 35

**(CAT 2005)**

70. If $R = (30^{65} - 29^{65})/(30^{64} + 29^{64})$, then
(a) $0 < R \leq 0.1$ (b) $0.1 < R \leq 0.5$
(c) $0.5 < R \leq 1.0$ (d) $R > 1.0$

**(CAT 2005)**

71. Let $n! = 1 \times 2 \times 3 \times \ldots \times n$ for integer $n > 1$. If $p = (1 \times 1!) + (2 \times 2!) + (3 \times 3!) + \ldots + (10 \times 10!)$, then $p+2$ when divided by 11! leaves a remainder of:
(a) 10 (b) 0
(c) 7 (d) 1

**(CAT 2005)**

72. The digits of a three-digit number A are written in the reverse order to form another three-digit number B. If $B > A$ and $B-A$ is perfectly divisible by 7, then which of the following is necessarily true?
(a) $100 < A < 299$ (b) $106 < A < 305$
(c) $112 < A < 311$ (d) $118 < A < 317$

**(CAT 2005)**

73. The rightmost non-zero digit of the number $30^{2720}$ is:
(a) 1 (b) 3
(c) 7 (d) 9

**(CAT 2005)**

74. For a positive integer n, let pn denote the product of the digits of n, and sn denote the sum of the digits of n. The number of integers between 10 and 1000 for which $p_n + s_n = n$ is:
(a) 81 (b) 16
(c) 18 (d) 9

**(CAT 2005)**

75. Let S be a set of positive integers such that every element, n, of S satisfies the conditions
a) $1000 \leq n \leq 1200$
b) Every digit in n is odd
Then, how many elements of S are divisible by 3?

(a) 9 (b) 10
(c) 11 (d) 12

**(CAT 2006)**

76. If x = −0.5, then which of the following has the smallest value?
(a) $2^{1/x}$ (b) $1/x$
(c) $1/x^2$ (d) $2^x$
(e) $1/\sqrt{-x}$

**(CAT 2006)**

77. Which among $2^{1/2}, 3^{1/3}, 4^{1/4}, 6^{1/6}$ and $12^{1/12}$ is the largest?
(a) $2^{1/2}$ (b) $3^{1/3}$
(c) $4^{1/4}$ (d) $6^{1/6}$
(e) $12^{1/12}$

**(CAT 2006)**

78. A group of 630 children is arranged in rows for a group photograph session. Each row contains three fewer children than the row in front of it. What number of rows is not possible?
(a) 3 (b) 4
(c) 5 (d) 6
(e) 7

**(CAT 2006)**

79. The sum of four consecutive two-digit odd numbers, when divided by 10, becomes a perfect square. Which of the following can possibly be one of these four numbers?
(a) 21 (b) 25
(c) 41 (d) 67
(e) 73

**(CAT 2006)**

80. Consider the set S = 1, 2, 3, ; .., 10001. How many arithmetic progressions can be formed from the elements of S that start with 1 and end with 1000 and have at least 3 elements?
(a) 3 (b) 4
(c) 6 (d) 7
(e) 8

**(CAT 2006)**

**Directions for Questions 81 to 82:** Answer questions 81 and 82 on the basis of the information given below:

An airline has a certain free luggage allowance and charges for excess luggage at a fixed rate per kgs. Two passengers, Raja and Praja have 60 kgs of luggage between them, and are charged ₹ 1200 and ₹ 2400 respectively for excess luggage. Had the entire luggage belonged to one of them, the excess luggage charge would have been ₹ 5400.

81. What is the weight of Praja's luggage?
(a) 20 kgs (b) 25 kgs
(c) 30 kgs (d) 35 kgs
(e) 40 kgs

**(CAT 2006)**

82. What is the free luggage allowance?
    (a) 10 kgs
    (b) 15 kg
    (c) 20 kg
    (d) 25kg
    (e) 30kg

    **(CAT 2006)**

**Directions for Questions 83 to 104:** Answer each question independently

83. When you reverse the digits of the number 13, the number increases by 18. How many other two-digit numbers increase by 18 when their digits are reversed?
    (a) 5
    (b) 6
    (c) 7
    (d) 8
    (e) 10

    **(CAT 2006)**

84. The number of employees in Obelix Menhir Co. is a prime number and is less than 300. The ratio of the number of employees who are graduates and above, to that of employees who are not, can possibly be:
    (a) 101:88
    (b) 87:100
    (c) 10:111
    (d) 85:98
    (e) 97:84

    **(CAT 2006)**

85. Consider the set S = {1, 2, 3, 4, ...., 2n+1 }, where n is a positive integer larger than 2007. Define X as the average of the odd integers in S and Y as the average of the even integers in S. What is the value of X–Y?
    (a) 0
    (b) 1
    (c) (1/2)n
    (d) (n+1)/2n
    (e) 2008

    **(CAT 2007)**

86. Suppose you have a currency, named Miso, in three denominations: 1 Miso, 10 Misos and 50 Misos. In how many ways can you pay a bill of 107 Misos?
    (a) 17
    (b) 16
    (c) 18
    (d) 15
    (e) 19

    **(CAT 2007)**

87. A confused bank teller transposed the rupees and paise when he cashed a cheque for Shailaja, giving her rupees instead of paise and paise instead of rupees. After buying a toffee for 50 paise, Shailaja noticed that she was left with exactly three times as much as the amount on the cheque. Which of the following is a valid statement about the cheque amount?
    (a) Over ₹13 but less than ₹14
    (b) Over ₹7 but less than ₹8
    (c) Over ₹22 but less than ₹23
    (d) Over ₹18 but less than ₹19
    (e) Over ₹4 but less than ₹5

    **(CAT 2007)**

88. What are the last two digits of $7^{2008}$?
    (a) 21
    (b) 61
    (c) 01
    (d) 41
    (e) 81

    **(CAT 2008)**

89. A shop stores $x$ kg of rice. The first customer buys half this quantity plus half a kg of rice. The second customer buys half the remaining quantity plus half a kg of rice. The third customer also buys half the remaining quantity plus half a kg of rice. Thereafter, no rice is left in the shop. Which of the following best describes the value of $x$?
    (a) $2 \leq x \leq 6$
    (b) $5 \leq x \leq 8$
    (c) $9 \leq x \leq 12$
    (d) $11 \leq x \leq 14$
    (e) $13 \leq x \leq 18$

    **(CAT 2008)**

90. The number of common terms in the two sequences 17, 21, 25,……,417 and 16, 21, 26,….,466 is
    (a) 78
    (b) 19
    (c) 20
    (d) 77
    (e) 22

    **(CAT 2008)**

91. The integers 1, 2,…….., 40 are written on a blackboard. The following operation is then repeated 39 times: in each repetition, any two numbers say $a$ and $b$, currently on the blackboard are erased and a new number $a+b–1$ is written. What will be the number left on the board at the end?
    (a) 820
    (b) 821
    (c) 781
    (d) 819
    (e) 780

    **(CAT 2008)**

92. Three consecutive positive integers are raised to the first, second and third powers respectively and then added. The sum so obtained is a perfect square, whose square root equals the total of the three original integers. Which of the following best describes the minimum, say m, of these three integers?
    (a) $1 \leq m \leq 3$
    (b) $4 \leq m \leq 6$
    (c) $7 \leq m \leq 9$
    (d) $10 \leq m \leq 12$
    (e) $13 \leq m \leq 15$

    **(CAT 2008)**

93. The seed of any positive integer $n$ is defined as follows:
    Seed $(n) = n$, if $n < 10$
    $= \text{seed}(s(n))$, otherwise,
    where $s(n)$ indicates the sum of digits of n. For example,
    seed (7)=7, seed (248)= seed(2+4+8)= seed (14)=seed (1+4)=seed (5)=5, etc. How many positive integers $n$, such that $n < 500$, will have seed $(n) =9$?
    (a) 39
    (b) 72
    (c) 81
    (d) 108
    (e) 55

    **(CAT 2008)**

94. If a and b are integers of opposite signs such that $(a + 3)^2 : b^2 = 9:1$ and $(a – 1)^2 : (b – 1)^2 = 4:1$, then the ratio $a^2 : b^2$ is **(CAT 2017)**
    (a) 9:4
    (b) 81:4
    (c) 1:4
    (d) 25:4

95. If $x + 1 = x^2$ and $x > 0$, then $2x^4$ is **(CAT 2017)**
    (a) $6 + 4\sqrt{5}$
    (b) $3 + 5\sqrt{5}$
    (c) $5 + 3\sqrt{5}$
    (d) $7 + 3\sqrt{5}$

96. The number of solutions (x, y, z) to the equation x – y – z = 25, where x, y, and z are positive integers such that $x \leq 40$, $y \leq 12$, and $z \leq 12$ is **(CAT 2017)**
    (a) 101
    (b) 99
    (c) 87
    (d) 105

97. For how many integers n, will the inequality $(n – 5)(n – 10) – 3(n – 2) \leq 0$ be satisfied? **(CAT 2017)**

98. If the square of the 7th term of an arithmetic progression with positive common difference equals the product of the 3rd and 17th terms, then the ratio of the first term to the common difference is **(CAT 2017)**
    (a) 2:3
    (b) 3:2
    (c) 3:4
    (d) 4:3

99. Let $a_1, a_2, ........ a_{3n}$ be an arithmetic progression with $a_1 = 3$ and $a_2 = 7$. If $a_1 + a_2 + .... + a_{3n} = 1830$, then what is the smallest positive integer 'm' such that m $\times (a_1 + a_2 + .... + a_n) > 1830$? **(CAT 2017)**
    (a) 8
    (b) 9
    (c) 10
    (d) 11

100. If the product of three consecutive positive integers is 15600 then the sum of the squares of these integers is **(CAT 2017)**
    (a) 1777
    (b) 1785
    (c) 1875
    (d) 1877

101. Let $a_1, a_2, a_3, a_4, a_5$ be a sequence of five consecutive odd numbers. Consider a new sequence of five consecutive even numbers ending with $2a_3$. If the sum of the numbers in the new sequence is 450, then $a_5$ is **(CAT 2017)**

102. How many different pairs (a, b) of positive integers are there such that $a \leq b$ and $\frac{1}{a} + \frac{1}{b} = \frac{1}{9}$? **(CAT 2017)**

103. An infinite geometric progression $a_1, a_2, a_3 ...$ has the property that $a_n = 3(a_{n+1} + a_{n+2} + ....)$ for every n $\geq 1$. If the sum $a_1 + a_2 + a_3 + ..... = 32$, then $a_5$ is **(CAT 2017)**
    (a) 1/32
    (b) 2/32
    (c) 3/32
    (d) 4/32

104. If $a_1 = 1/2 \times 5$, $a_2 = 1/5 \times 8$, $a_3 = 1/8 \times 11$, ......, then $a_1 + a_2 + a_3 + .......... a_{100}$ is **(CAT 2017)**
    (a) 25/151
    (b) 1/2
    (c) 1/4
    (d) 111/55

## ANSWER KEY

| | | | |
|---|---|---|---|
| 1. (a) | 2. (b) | 3. (a) | 4. (b) |
| 5. (c) | 6. (d) | 7. (a) | 8. (d) |
| 9. (c) | 10. (d) | 11. (d) | 12. (a) |
| 13. (c) | 14. (d) | 15. (d) | 16. (a) |
| 17. (c) | 18. (a) | 19. (c) | 20. (c) |
| 21. (a) | 22. (d) | 23. (d) | 24. (d) |
| 25. (a) | 26. (a) | 27. (d) | 28. (c) |
| 29. (b) | 30. (b) | 31. (d) | 32. (b) |
| 33. (a) | 34. (d) | 35. (d) | 36. (b) |
| 37. (a) | 38. (d) | 39. (c) | 40. (c) |
| 41. (d) | 42. (c) | 43. (d) | 44. (a) |
| 45. (c) | 46. (b) | 47. (b) | 48. (c) |
| 49. (b) | 50. (b) | 51. (b) | 52. (b) |
| 53. (b) | 54. (b) | 55. (a) | 56. (b) |
| 57. (d) | 58. (d) | 59. (d) | 60. (a) |
| 61. (d) | 62. (a) | 63. (d) | 64. (a) |
| 65. (a) | 66. (a) | 67. (c) | 68. (c) |
| 69. (a) | 70. (d) | 71. (d) | 72. (b) |
| 73. (a) | 74. (d) | 75. (a) | 76. (b) |
| 77. (b) | 78. (d) | 79. (c) | 80. (d) |
| 81. (d) | 82. (b) | 83. (b) | 84. (e) |
| 85. (a) | 86. (c) | 87. (d) | 88. (c) |
| 89. (b) | 90. (c) | 91. (c) | 92. (a) |
| 93. (e) | 94. (d) | 95. (d) | 96. (b) |
| 97. 11 | 98. (a) | 99. (b) | 100. (d) |
| 101. 51 | 102. 3 | 103. (c) | 104. (a) |

## Solutions

1. It is self evident that the value of b can only be 1, 5 or 6 for $(ab)^2 = ccb$

   Given that ccb> 300, we need to start from squares of numbers greater than 17.

   $21^2 = 441$ will satisfy the given conditions.

2. $7^{84}/342 = (7^3)^{28}/342 = 343^{28}/342$  remainder 1. Option (a).

3. If x is the product of 4 consecutive positive integers, it must be even. Thus, $(x + 1)$ has to be odd. Also, by trial and error, it can be seen that $(x + 1)$ need not be prime, but it is always a perfect square. Thus, option (a) is correct.

4. The function h(a,b) is such that it takes two values as it's input and returns one value (the GCF of the two given values). Thus, there is a reduction of one number when we use the function 'h' once. Hence, if we have to reduce the set A containing 'n' elements into one element (as defined by G(A)) we would need to use the function 'h' n–1 times.

5. The squares of numbers containing only ones have a pattern which can be judged from the following:

$11^2 = 121$

$111^2 = 12321$

$1111^2 = 1234321$

Thus, 123456787654321 would be the square of 11111111. Hence, we mark option (c) as the correct answer.

6. In order to get to the correct option in this question, you need to try to disprove each of the options by thinking of possible values for the elements in $S_1$ and $S_2$.

   Options 1, 2 and 3, all would not be true in case we were to take the elements in $S_1$ to be 1–24, while the elements in $S_2$ as 25–50. Then, if we change the signs of each element of $S_1$, we will get these values as –1,–2,…–24. It can be seen that neither of the first three option statements would be true i.e., we would not have every member of $S_1$ greater than every member of $S_2$ (as stated in option 1), we would not have G in $S_1$ (as stated in option 2), and we would not have the largest number between $S_1$ and $S_2$ in $S_1$ (as stated in option 3). Thus, option (d) is correct.

7. Let the elements in $S_1$ be 1, 2, 3…24 and the elements in $S_2$ be 50, 49, 48…27, 26, 25. Then after interchanging $a_{24}$ and $a_{25}$, $S_1$ would have (1, 2, 3, 4….22, 23 and 50), while $S_2$ would have (24, 49, 48, 47…28, 27, 26, 25). It is obvious that $S_1$ would continue to be in ascending order, while $S_2$ would not continue to be in the descending order. Thus, option (a) is correct.

8. It is obvious that since every element of $S_1$ has to be made equal to or greater than every element of $S_2$, L would have to be made greater than or equal to G. For this the value of x cannot be less than, G-L. Thus, option (d) is correct.

9. Numbers which have 2 digits recurring after the decimal are related to denominators which have 99 as a factor. From the options only 198 is related to 99 and is hence the correct answer.

10. We first need to find odd numbers between 100 and 200 such that they are divisible by 3. This is given by the set: 105, 111, 117…195 ( a total of 16 such numbers). However, we do not have to count all these numbers as some of these would be divisible by 7 and we need to remove those before we can conclude our count. From the above list 105, 147 and 189 are three such numbers which are divisible by 7. Hence, the required answer is 16–3=13.

11. Let the numbers be 3, 5, 7. We can see easily that $xyz^2$ is odd as it is an Odd × Odd × odd situation. Thus, option (a) is necessarily true.

    Also $(x–y)^2 \times z$ = Even × Odd = Even. Thus option (b) is also true.

    $(x+y–z)^2 (x+y)$ = Odd × Even = Even. Thus option (c) is also true.

The last option represents Even × Even × Odd situation and hence should always give us an even value. Thus, the fourth option need not be true always.

12. The set of prime numbers would have only 1 multiple of 2 (2 itself) and one five (in 5 itself). Thus, the product would have only 1 zero.

13. $1421 \times 1423 \times 1425 /12 \rightarrow 5 \times 7 \times 9 /12 = 315/12 \rightarrow$ remainder 3.

14. The difference between 32506 and 34041 is 1535. The number which would leave the same remainder with both these numbers must necessarily be a factor of 1535. From the given options only 307 is a factor of 1535.

15. N would be divisible by 3 because it can be rewritten as:

    $(55+17)(55^2+….+17^2) - 72^3 = 72m – 72^3$ which would be divisible by 3. [Using $a^3+b^3 = (a+b)(a^2+….+b^2)$]

    N would be divisible by 17 because it can be rewritten as:

    $17^3 + (55 – 72)(55^2+…..+72^2) = 17^3 –17y$ which would be divisible by 17.

16. The point E is at an even number of steps away from point A. Thus, $a_{2n–1} = 0$.

17. The highest power of 12 in 1982 is $12^3 = 1728$. Thus, the number would be a 4 digit number.

| 1728 | 144 | 12 | 1 |
|------|-----|----|----|
| 1 | 1 | 9 | 2 |

Thus the number is 1192.

18. To solve this question, go through the options.

    Option (a) gives us: Odd x Odd ≠ even. Hence cannot be true and is the correct answer.

    The other options need not be checked since we have reached the correct option already.

19. The sum of the first 10 natural numbers are 55, that of the 11th to 20th natural numbers are 155 and so on. In order to find the number added twice, we need to reach the last triangular number below 1000. This can be got by adding 55+155+255+255+41+42+43+44= 990. Hence, the number added twice must be 10, i.e., option (c).

20. $x^2y$ and $5xy$ are both negative. Amongst them $5xy$ will be the smaller value. Hence, option (c) is correct.

21. The base can only be 5, 6, 7, 8 or 9. Testing for base 5, we can see that this is true in base 5. Thus, we need the value of 3111 in base 5. The value would be $3\times125 + 1\times25 + 1\times5 + 1\times1 = 406$.

22. He has to have at least six boxes with the same number of oranges in it. The logic of this question comes from the pigeon hole principle—where we take the ratio 128/25 and take the least integer value greater than this ratio. Note, 25 comes from the different values of oranges that you can put in the boxes. Hence, we would get six as the answer.

23. Such questions have to be solved using reverse thinking. So start thinking about the last person, Eswari must have seen 30 mints (only in such a case would you get 17 mints left after taking half and then returning 2 to the bowl.) For Eswari to see 30 mints, it must be the case that after Fatima took one-fourth of what she saw, there must have been 27 mints left and when she put 3 back, Eswari would have seen 30 mints.

    Further, for Fatima to see 36 mints, Sita must have seen 48 mints to start with—as to leave 36 after taking one-third of the mints she sees and then giving back 4 the only starting point possible is 48.

24. Since she increases one part of the product by 18 and the result in the answer is an increase of 540, she must have been multiplying the number by 30. Hence, the new product would be given by $53 \times 30 = 1590$.

25. If the number is abcd, then a+b=c+d, a+d=c and b+d= 2(a+c). Thus, b+d should be even. Thus either both b and d are even or both are odd. From the first expression, since both b and d are of the same nature—a and c should also have the same nature (both even or both odd).

    From this point it is best to move through informed trial and error solution. Try to take c as 5 and fit in the remaining values. Note the following while doing this thinking. If c= 5 then, b+d should be a minimum of 12. All we need to do is find 1 value which satisfies all conditions.

    So if we take b+d as 12, a+c should be 6. The number would be 1b5d. Trying to fit in value in this case we would get 1854 satisfying all conditions. Hence, (e) is correct.

26. The red light would flash every 20 seconds, the green light every 24 seconds. They would flash together every 2 minutes and hence 30 times in an hour.

27. In order to do this he should allocate an independent power of 2 in every bag. Thus, the first bag should contain Re, 1 the second, ₹2 the third 4 ₹8, 16, 32, 64. Using these he can form any value from 1 — 127. The last bag should contain the remaining ₹31 as we can add any combination of the above to 31 to get all values between 128 to 158.

28. Since 517 is a prime number, the two consecutive terms of the sequence (say $a$ and $b$) should be such that their values should obey the relationship (a–b)(a+b) = 517. 517 can be written as 11x47. Thus we need two numbers whose difference is 11 and sum is 47. 18 and 29 satisfy this condition. Thus, the series can be written from the sixth term onwards as:18, 29, 47, 76, 123

29. If b–d=d, it must be the case that b is 10 and d is 5. Then we get e=6 and using the other equations we would get that a= 4 as follows:

    A+c=e means either 2+4=6 or 4+2= 6 (in order). Since e+a=b it must follow that 6+4=10 and hence a=4 and e = 6. Option (b) satisfies.

30. The expression becomes positive when n>5. Hence, the largest possible value of $m$ is 5.

31. Using trial and error all the options can get eliminated. At b=11, the resultant value of the expression is not divisible by any of the three numbers.

32. The second statement means that there are 40 one rupee coins less than two rupee coins. Using this information the question can be easily solved through the options. The given conditions are satisfied at 140 five-rupee coins.

33. Suppose we take the value of $n$ as 1, we would get $(7^6-6^6) = (7^3-6^3)(7^3+6^3)$

    $(7–6)(7^2..) \times (7+6)(7^2....)$. It can be clearly seen that this is divisible by 13.

    You can easily visualise that even if we were to take the value of n as 2, there would always be a (7+6) component in the simplification.

    In general:
    $(7^{6n} – 6^{6n}) = (7^{3n} – 6^{3n})(7^{3n} + 6^{3n}) = (7 – 6)(7^{3n-1}..) \times (7 + 6)(7^{3n-1}....)$

34. From the options, the only number which gives successive remainders as 2,1 and 4 when divided successively by 3,4 and 7 respectively is 53. Hence, the correct answer is 53.

35. We need to find the HCF of 4.5, 6.75 and 7.2. Or 9/2, 27/4 and 36/5.

    HCF of Numerators/ LCM of denominators = 9/20 = 0.45.

    Dividing the cakes into these sizes, the number of pieces we would get would be:

    10+15+16=41 pieces—and hence 41 guests.

    The answer would be—None of these.

36. To solve this question, you would need to find the LCM of 7/2, 21/4, 49/8.

    LCM of Numerators/ HCF of denominators = 147/2 = 73.5.

37. $2^{256} = (2^4)^{64} = 16^{64}$. $16^{64}/17$ would give us a remainder of 1 (since 16/17 leaves a remainder -1, and when the power is even the remainder becomes +1).

38. In order to find the number missed, we need to find the least triangular number above 575. This can be done by 55(sum of the first 10 natural numbers)+155 (sum of the next ten natural numbers) + 255 (Sum of natural numbers from 21 to 30) + 31+32+33+34 =595.

39. He can only pay ₹ 300 if the car is rented for 6 hours @ ₹ 50 per hour.

40. The answer would be given by 22+8 and is quite easy to work out. We need to understand that since there are 22 days when they play tennis or do yoga, in each

of these 22 days there would be either a free morning or evening. This would account for a total of 22 free mornings/evenings. Also, the total number of free morning/evenings is 24+14=38. This means that 16 free mornings/evenings are still available—which would mean 8 days when they did nothing.

41. There are 6 twos and 4 fours. Hence, there would be 2 oranges in the basket.

42. $19-4 \times 2 = 11$

43. This question requires us to use the principle of difference of squares:

We know that $x^2 - y^2 = (x-y)(x+y)$. Hence, x+y should be 48.

44. 100+196+192+188+184 = 860

45. In this type of question, the key is to look at a systematic way of counting the number of instances. So with 1 & 2 as the first 2 numbers, we can get 8 sets (by varying the third value from 3 to 10), Similarly, with 1 & 3, we will get 7 pairs, with 1 & 4 six pairs, and so on till 1 & 9, we would get 1 pair. (A total of 1+2+3+4+5+6+7+8=36). Similarly for the first number to be starting with 2, we would get 1+2+3+...+7= 28 sets. Similarly, for sets starting with 3, there would be 21 sets, for 4, 15 sets, for sets starting with 5, 10 sets, for sets starting with 6, 6 sets, for sets starting with 7, 3 sets and for those starting with 8, 1 set. Thus, there would be a total of 36+28+21+15+10+6+3+1= 120.

46. It can be easily seen that the revenues at different values would be:

200×2, 220×1.9, 240×1.8, 260×1.7, 280×1.6, 300×1.5 and 320×1.4. The value goes up till 300×1.5 and then reduces. Hence, option (b) is correct.

47. The price per piece of bread would be 3 coins as the third traveller is paying 8 coins for his 2.66 loaves. Also the contribution of the first traveller is 2.33 loaves, while that of the second is only 0.33 loaves. Hence, the first traveller should get 2.33x3 = 7.

48. Solve using options. The required conditions are met by 4, 27 and 9. Hence, option (c) is correct.

49. From the statements, Mayank paid 20, Mirza paid 15, and Little paid 12. Thus Jaspal paid 13.

50. Since he is left with one diamond at the end, to the third watchman he must have reached with six diamonds, given him half (3) and two more (total 5) and be left with one diamond. With the same thought pattern you can solve the remaining part of the question. The thought process would go as this:

$1 \to 6 \to 16 \to 36$.

51. $(x+y+z)^2 = x^2 + y^2 + z^2 + 2xy + 2xz + 2yz = 25 \to x^2 + y^2 + z^2 = 19 \to$ maximum value of x can be the square root of 19 if we take $y^2$ and $z^2$ both to be 0.

52. Solve using options. The conditions are met for 54.

53. The expression y–x = z–y means that x,y and z are in arithmetic progression, y being the arithmetic mean between x and z. This also means that for y to have the minimum value given that xyz is equal to 4, x, y and z should be equal. Thus, the minimum value of y is $4^{1/3} = 2^{2/3}$.

54. The codes which will create a confusion would be:

16 and 91, 18 and 81, 19 and 61, 66 and 99, 68 and 89, 86 and 98: A total of 12 codes which will have confusion. Hence out of 90 two-digit codes, 78 would have no confusion.

55. Tn = {n, n + 1, n + 2, n + 3, n + 4} where n = 1, 2, ……96. So we have, T1 = { 1 to 5}, T2 = {2 to 6} ..T6 = {6 to 10 }, T7= {7 to 11} and so on. Clearly, only the sets T1,T7,T13,.....T91 would not have 6 in it. These are 16 sets out of 96. The other 80 would have no 6 in them. Thus, the correct answer would be option (a).

56. We need to find the sum of the arithmetic series: 10,17,24,31.....94.

The sum would be given by: number of terms x average = 13x52 = 676.

57. It can be seen clearly that y-x would be even, if we take both of them as odd, so the first option can be rejected. Similarly, if we take x as 2, we would get the product as even—thus, option (b) can also be rejected. Considering the (c) option we can see that (x+y)/x = 1 +y/x should be even. For this y/x should be odd. We can see this occurring at values like y=9 and x=3. Hence, even this option can be rejected. This leaves us only with the fourth option as the correct answer.

58. If N is a composite integer and is not a perfect square, it would mean that n would have at least one pair of factors (apart from $1 \times N$) such that one of this pair of factors would be user than the square root of N, while the other would be greter than the square root of N. This means that both statements A and B have to be true. Thus, option (d) is correct.

59. A sample set of numbers that satisfy the situation is: a=216, b= 36, c= 18,d=8, e= 6

It can be seen that each of a/27, b/e, a/36, c/e, a/12, bd/18 and a/6 are integers. The only expression which is not an integer is c/d. Thus, option (d) is correct.

60. The only possible solution is for the set of numbers 3,5,7. Option (a) is correct.

61. $4^{96}/6 = 2 \times 4^{95}/3 \to$ remainder of this expression would be 2. But, we would need to multiply this by 2 to get the actual remainder. Thus, the answer would be 4—option (d) is correct.

62. 78 = 50+10+10+2+2+2+2   7 coins

69 = 50+10+5+2+2   5 coins

Re 1.01 = 50+25+10+10+2+2+2   7 coins

Thus, a total 19 coins would be required (option a).

63. Two families can have 4 adults, 3 boys and 2 girls, however, the number of girls has to be greater than the number of families. Hence, the given constraints are not met at 2 families. With 3 families, we can have 6 adults, 5 boys and 4 girls. Hence, option (d) is correct.

64. Since $S_{11} = S_{19}$, it means that the sum of the 12th to 19th term of the AP would be zero. These terms represent an AP with an average of 0. It can also be seen that the average of the $12^{th}$ to $19^{th}$ terms can be derived out of the average of the middle terms ($15^{th}$ and 16th terms). So, the average of the $15^{th}$ and $16^{th}$ term of the AP would be equal to the average of the $12^{th}$ to $19^{th}$ terms of the AP = 0.

    Also, the $15^{th}$ and $16^{th}$ terms of the AP are also the middle terms of the AP with 30 terms. Hence, the average of the AP with 30 terms would also be equal to 0 thus their sum would be zero (option a).

65. Since the value of $b$ is given as 10.5$n$, the Society $S_1$ would have 64$n$ members on July 2, 2004. At the same time, $S_2$ also has 64$n$ members (as given in the question). Hence,

    $n \times r^6 = 64 n \rightarrow n = 2$

    Thus, option 2 is the correct answer.

66. $n$ is an integer greater than $10^{10} = 10000000000$ but less than $10^{11}$. (So, it is an 11 digit number). The sum of digits of $n$ can be equal to 2 only if,

    (a) the number starts with 1 and contains 9 zeroes and one 1 in the remaining $10^{th}$ places (This can occur in 10 ways as 11000000000, 10100000000... 10000000001) OR

    (b) the number starts with 2 and has 10 zeroes—which is the case in only 1 number, 20000000000. Hence, a total of 11 such numbers are possible (option a).

67. $(15^{23} + 23^{23}) = (15+23)(15^{22} + \ldots + 23^{22})$. This number would be divisible by 19. Hence, the remainder would be 0 (option c).

68. $a_3 = a_2 - a_1$ ---- gives $a_3 = -100.33$; $a_4 = a_3 - a_2 = -81.33$, $a_5 = a_4 - a_3 = 19$, $a_6 = a_5 - a_4 = 100.33$, $a_7 = 81.33$, $a_8 = -19$, $a_9 = -100.33$. We can see that there is a cyclicity of 6 in the value of the terms and the addition of the first six terms equals 0. $81.33 - 19 - 100.33 - 81.33 + 19 + 100.33 = 0$.

    So, the sum of the first 6000 terms would also be 0. Thus, the sum to 6002 terms would be the sum of the $6001^{st}$ and the $6002^{nd}$ terms, which would be the same as the sum of the first two terms of the sequence. Thus, the answer would be $81.33 - 19 = 62.33$ (option c).

69. The value can be written as: $(16+17+18+19)(\ldots) = 70x$. Hence, the number would be divisible by 70 and the remainder would be 0 (option a).

70. The numerator would be of the form: (30-29) $(30^{64} + \ldots + 29^{64})$. Hence, the value of R would definitely be greater than 1. Hence, R>1 is the correct answer (option d).

71. The value of p= $1 \times 1!$ $+2 \times 2!$ $+3 \times 3!$ $+ \ldots + 10 \times 10!$ = 11!-1. Hence, p+2 = 11!+1.

    When divided by 11!, the remainder would be 1. (option d)

72. When we reverse a three digit number, the new number formed differs from the original number by a multiple of 99. Also, the value of the multiple of 99 that we have, is decided by the difference between the hundred digit and the units digit. This would be easier to understand and explain using an example—321 becomes 123, and the difference of 198 is arrived at by 99×2 (where 2 comes out of the difference between 3 and 1—the hundreds digit and the units digit).

    Thus, in this question, when we see that the difference between B and A is given as a multiple of 7, we realise that the units digit of A must be 7 more than the hundreds digit. Thus, the first number possible is 108 (reversed 801) and the last number possible would be 299 (reversed 992). Only option (b) contains both these values.

73. The rightmost non zero digit of $30^{2720}$ would be given by the units digit of $3^{2720}$ = units digit of $3^{4n}$ = Units digit of $3^4$ = 1 (option a).

74. The only numbers for which this would be true would be 19, 29, 39, 49, 59, 69, 79, 89 and 99. It would not be true for any three digit number. Hence, the right answer is 9 (option d).

75. The numbers 1113,1119,1131,1137,1155,1173,1179, 1191 and 1197 would satisfy the given conditions. Option (a) is correct.

76. The first, third, fourth and fifth options are all positive. Obviously, it has to be option (b), as it is the only negative value in the (e) options.

    **Solving time is nearly 5–15 seconds.**

77. Solve by taking approximate values:

    We know that $2^{1/2} = 1.41$

    $3^{1/3}$ will be greater than 1.41 as $1.41 \times 1.41 \times 1.41 = 2 \times 1.41$ which would be lower than 3.

    $4^{1/4} = 1.41$ again as $1.41 \times 1.41 \times 1.41 \times 1.41 = 2 \times 2 = 4$.

    $6^{1/6}$ will definitely be lower than 1.4 as it can be seen that $1.4 \times 1.4 = 1.96$

    So, $1.4 \times 1.4 \times 1.4 \times 1.4 \times 1.4 \times 1.4$ would be closer to 8 than 6. Similarly, we can see that $12^{1/12}$ would also be lower than 1.4. So, option (b) is the largest value.

78. **Thought Process:**

    The number of people in the respective rows will form an AP with a common difference of –3.

In this case, we have to find which number of rows is not possible. For this, take it option by option.

Use the principle that for an AP the sum is given by n × average.

For 3 rows—the average of the AP would be 210. And, this would also be the value of the middle term (when there are 3 rows, the average of the AP is given by the middle term). We can thus form an AP of 3 terms with middle term 210 and common difference–3. Thus, it is possible to arrange the children in 3 rows.

For 4 rows—the average would be 630/4= 157.5. Since, there will be two middle terms in this case, the AP can be easily formed with the middle terms as 159 and 156 (so that they average 157.5 with a common difference of –3). Thus, it is possible to arrange the children in 4 rows.

For 5 rows—the average of the AP would be 630/5 = 126. And, this would also be the value of the middle term (as when there are 5 rows, the average of the AP is given by the middle term). We can thus form an AP of 5 terms with middle term 126 and common difference –3. Thus it is possible to arrange the children in 5 rows.

For 6 rows—The average would be 630/6= 105. Since, there will be two middle terms in this case, the AP would have to be formed with the two middle terms as 106.5 and 103.5 (so that they average 105 with a common difference of –3). Thus, it is not possible to arrange the children in 6 rows as the value of the terms in the AP would not be in integers.

Hence, we will mark option (d).

Maximum solution time: 45–60 seconds in case you know the principle of middle terms of an AP.

79. Thought process: The sum has to be divisible by 10. This would occur only if the numbers end in 7, 9, 1 and 3.

Option (a): if 21 has to be one of the numbers, the sum would have to be 17+19+21+23= 20×4(treating the series as an AP) =80. When divided by 10, this does not leave a perfect square.

Option (b): 25 is not possible as a value which would be part of the 4 numbers, as the sum would never end in 0.

Option (c): The numbers would be 37, 39, 41 and 43. 40×4= 160. When divided by 10, we get 16 as the value—giving us a perfect square as required. Hence, this is correct.

80. We need to find arithmetic progressions with first term 1 and last term 1000.

In order to do this, we would need to find the number of factors of 999—which is $37×3^3 \rightarrow 2 × 4 = 8$ factors. However, the factor 999 cannot be used. Thus, there will be 7 factors (option d).

81. What is the weight of Praja's luggage?
    (a)  20 kg                    (b)  25 kg
    (c)  30 kg                    (d)  35 kg
    (e)  40 kg

82. What is the free luggage allowance?
    (a)  10 kg                    (b)  5 kg
    (c)  20 kg                    (d)  25 kg
    (e)  30kg

**Note:** These were the options in the original CAT paper. The correct answer of 15 kg was missing from the options.

Start from the second question. From the given information, it is pretty clear that the extra luggage for Praja is twice the extra luggage for Raja. This means that, when the two of them take their luggage separately, after reducing the free luggage from 60 kgs, whatever remains has to be divided into three parts and two of them have to be carried by Praja and one by Raja.

This is because, if Raja and Praja were to both carry their luggage separately, the total free luggage would be twice the free luggage allowance of one of them.

Also, when only one person carried the luggage—the amount of extra luggage would be 50% higher than the extra luggage, when both are carrying their luggage separately.

From the options, it is clear that:

Option (a) is not possible as when both carry their luggage separately, extra luggage= 40 kgs. However, when only 1 carries all the luggage, the extra luggage would be 50 kgs. But from 40 to 50, we do not have a 50% increase. Hence, the option can be rejected.

Repeat the same thought process for Option (b). 50 to 55 not a 50% increase.

Option 3:  20 to 40 not a 50% increase.

Option 4:  10 to 35 not a 50% increase.

Option 5:  0 to 30 not a 50% increase.

Obviously the question is wrong. If you were to try to solve this through an equation:

$1.5(60–2x) = 60–x \rightarrow 2x=30$ and thus x=15. But the options did not contain this. A lot of students got stuck to this question, but the fact of the matter is that you should have been able to exit this question within a maximum of 1-2 minutes.

With a free luggage allowance of 15 kgs, Raja should have had 15+y and Praja 15+2y giving a total of the two as 60. Thus, 30+3y = 60 gives us y=10. Hence, Praja=35 kgs. Hence, option (d) is correct.

83. The numbers would be 24,35,46,57,68 and 79. Hence, 6 numbers. Option (b) is the correct answer.

84. It is obvious that only option 5 (97+84=181) gives us a prime number. Hence, option 5 is correct.

85. How did you react to this question? The ideal solution pattern in this question is on the basis of pattern recognition. Refer to the solution of question 24 of the CAT 2008 paper for this. Based on that solution pattern, we can try to get this done with a value of n as say 2. So, we have the series {1,2,3,4,5}.

   Then, X= 9/3=3 and Y= 3. Thus, X–Y = 0. Converting the options for n>2007, we get the options changing to:

   (a) 0                (b) 1
   (c) 1                (d) ¾
   (e) 2

   The first and second options obviously have nothing to do with the value of n. Note that the third and fourth options created above, have been created on the basis of n as 2. For the fifth option, 2008 is equivalent to the lowest value of n we can take. So for n=2008, if we get the value as 2008, for n=2, we should get a value of 2.

   If you want to be sure, you can also take the value of n as 3, in which case the numbers would be:

   {1,2,3,4,5,6,7}. In this case also, the values of X and Y will be equal to 4 and X–Y =0.

   A little bit of logical quantitative thinking here can also tell you that there will be no difference between, the values of X and Y ever. Thus, option (a) is correct.

86. Thought Process:

   **Deduction 1:** If you were to use 2, 50 miso notes, you can only pay the remaining 7 misos through 1 miso notes.

   **Deduction 2:** If you were to use only 1, 50 miso note, you could use 10 miso notes in 6 different ways (from 0 to 5).

   **Deduction 3:** If you want to avoid 50 miso notes, you could use 10 miso notes in 11 different ways (from 0 to 10).

   Hence, the required answer is 1+6+11=18 (option c).

   Maximum solution time: 45 seconds.

87. **Thought Process: for this question**

   **Deduction 1:** Question Interpretation: The solution language for this question requires you to think about what possible amount could be such that when it's rupees and paise value are interchanged, the resultant value is 50 paise more than thrice the original amount.

   **Deduction 2:** Option checking process:

   Armed with this logic, suppose we were to check for option 1 i.e., The value is above ₹22 but below ₹23.

This essentially means that the amount must be approximately between ₹22.66 to ₹22.69. (We get the paise amount to be between 66 to 69 based on the fact that the relationship between the Actual Amount, x and the transposed amount y is: y–50 paise = 3x. Hence, values below 22.66 and values above 22.70 are not possible.

→ From this point onwards, we just have to check whether this relationship is satisfied by any of the values between ₹22.66 to ₹22.69.

   Also, realise the fact that in each of these cases, the paise value in the value of the transposed amount y would be 22. Thus, 3x should give us the paise value as 72 (since we have to subtract 50 paise from the value of 'y' in order to get the value of 3x).

→ This also means that the unit digit of the paise value of 3x should be 2.

→ It can be clearly seen that none of the numbers 66, 67,68 or 69 when multiplied by 3 give us a units digit of 2. Hence, this is not a possible answer.

Checking for option (b) in the same fashion:

You should realise that the outer limit for the range of values when the amount is between 18 and 19 is: 18.54 to 18.57. Also, the number of paise in the value of the transposed sum 'y' would be 18. Hence, the value of 3x should give us a paise value as 68 paise. Again, using the units digit principle, it is clear that the only value where the units digit would be 8 would be for a value of 18.56.

Hence, we check for the check amount to be 18.56. Transposition of the Rupee and paise value would give us 56.18. When you subtract 50 paise from this you would get 55.68, which also happens to be thrice 18.56. Hence, the correct answer is Option (d).

Notice here that if you can work out this logic in your reactions, the time required to check each option would be not more than 30 seconds. Hence, the net problem solving time to get the second option as correct would not be more than 1 minute. Add the reading time and this problem should still not require more than 2 minutes.

88. Well, the solution depends on the fact that $7^4 = 2401$ gives the last two digits as 01. Thus, for every 4n power of 7, the last two digits would always be 01.

   Hence, the required answer would be 01 (option (c)).

   Solving time: If you knew this logic: 5–10 seconds

   If you had to discover this logic: 30-40 seconds (by looking at the pattern of the powers of 7)

89. This question is based on odd numbers as only with an odd value of x would you keep getting integers if you halved the value of rice and took out another half a kg from the shop store.

From the options, let us start from the second option. (**Note:** In such questions, one should make it a rule to start from one of the middle options as the normal realisation we would get from checking one option would have been that more than one option gets removed if we have not picked up the correct option- as we would normally know whether the correct answer needs to be increased from the value we just checked or it should be decreased.)

Thus, trying for x = 7 according to the second option, you would get

7 → 3 → 1 → 0 (after three customers).

This means that $5 \le x \le 8$ is a valid option for this question. Also, since the question is definitive about the correct range, there cannot be two ranges. Hence, we can conclude that option (b) is correct.

**Note:** The total solving time for this question should not be more than 30 seconds. Even, if you are not such an experienced solver through options, and you had to check (b)–(c) options in order to reach the correct option, you would still need a maximum of 90 seconds.

90. 7,21,25...417 and 16,21,26,...466 would have common terms as:

21, 41,61,.....401. The number of such terms would be 20 given by [(401–21)/20]+1 =20. Hence, option (c) is correct.

Note: This question should not have taken more than 20 seconds.

91. Well what are we doing? Every time we combine two numbers in the set, we replace it by adding the two and subtracting 1 from it. So, if there are 4 numbers say 1, 2, 3 and 4, our answer would be:

1  2  3  4
2  3  4  (After combining 1 & 2 in the row above)
4  4  (After combining 2 & 3 in the row above)
7  (After combining 4 & 4 in the row above)

Notice that what we are doing here is adding the numbers and subtracting 1 for every iteration. So for numbers from 1 to 40, we would get the sum of 1 to 40 → 55+155+255+355=820 and subtract 39 from that (as there would be 39 iterations that would leave us with only 1 number if we start with 40 numbers). Hence, 820 – 39 = 781 is the correct answer (option (c).

92. Trial and error gives us the feasibility of $3^1 + 4^2 + 5^3$ =144 which is the required perfect square. Note that at m=1 and m = 2, we do not get a perfect square as the value of the addition. Hence, Option (a) which contains the value of m=3 is the correct answer.

93. The first number to have a seed of 9 would be number 9 itself.

The next number whose seed would be 9 would be 18, then 27 and you should recognise that we are talking about numbers which are multiples of 9. Hence, the number of such numbers would be the number of numbers in the Arithmetic Progression: 9,18,27,36,45,....495 = [(495-9)/9] +1 = 55 such numbers. Hence, we will mark option (e).

94. $(a+3)^2 : b^2 = 9 : 1$ and $(a-1)^2 : (b-1)^2 = 4 : 1$

$(a+3) : b = \pm 3, \dfrac{a-1}{b-1} = \pm 2$

Four cases are possible:
a + 3 = 3b, a – 1 = 2b – 2; (a, b) = (3, 2) (Rejected, since the integers a, b are of opposite signs )
a + 3 = 3b, a – 1 = –2b + 2; a, b are non integers. (Rejected)
a + 3 = –3b, a – 1 = 2b – 2; a, b are non integers. (Rejected)
a + 3 = –3b, a – 1 = –2b + 2 ; a = 15, b = –6.

$a^2 : b^2 = \left(\dfrac{15}{6}\right)^2 = 25{:}4$

95. $x^2 - x - 1 = 0$ on solving we get: $x = \dfrac{1+\sqrt{5}}{2}$

$2x^4 + 2(x+1)^2 = 2x^2 + 4x + 2 = 2x + 2 + 4x + 2 = 6x$

$+ 4 = 6 \times \dfrac{1+\sqrt{5}}{2} + 4 = 7 + 3\sqrt{5}$

96. x – y – z = 25
x = 25 + y + z

Maximum possible value of y + z = 12 + 12 = 24, Minimum possible value of y + z = 1 + 1 = 2.

For y + z = 2, x = 25 + 2 = 27. (x, y, z) = (27, 1, 1) one value.

For y + z = 3, x = 25 + 3 = 28, (x, y, z) = (28, 1, 2), (25, 2, 1). Two possible values.

For y + z = 4, x = 25 + 4 = 29, (x, y, z) = (29, 1, 3), (29, 3, 1), (29, 2, 2). Three possible values.

Similarly for y + z = 5, Four possible values.

For y + z = 6, five possible values.

⋮
⋮

For y + z = 13, twelve possible values.

For y + z = 14, x = 39, eleven possible values.

For y + z = 14, x = 40, ten possible values.

The number of solutions = 1 + 2 + 3 + 4 + 5 + ..... + 12 + 11 + 10 = 99.

97. (n – 5) (n – 10) – 3(n – 2) ≤ 0
$n^2 - 15n + 50 - 3n + 6 \le 0$
$n^2 - 18n + 56 \le 0$
$n^2 - 14n - 4n + 56 \le 0$
n ∈ [4, 14]

Total 11 values are possible.

98. Let 'a' and 'd' are the first term and the common difference of the A.P.

$[a + 6d]^2 = (a + 2d)(a + 16d)$

$a^2 + 3d^2 + 12ad = a^2 + 18ad + 32d^2$

$4d^2 = 6ad, a : d = 2 : 3$

99. Common difference = $7 - 3 = 4$.

$a_1 + a_2 + \cdots + a_{3n} = 1830$,

$3 + 7 + 11 + \dots 3n$ terms = 1830.

$\frac{3n}{2}[2.3 + (3n - 1)4] = 1830$

$\frac{3n}{2}[2 + 12n] = 1830$

$3n(1 + 6n) = 1830 = 30 \times 61$

$3n = 30$ or $n = 10$.

$a_1 + a_2 + \dots + a_n = 3 + 7 + 11 + \dots 10$ terms = 210

$210m > 1830$

$m > 8.7$. Hence, the smallest integer value of $m = 9$.

100. $15600 = 24 \times 25 \times 26$

Sum of squares = $24^2 + 25^2 + 26^2 = 1877$

101. Five consecutive even numbers ending with $2a_3$. Hence, the numbers are $2a_3 - 8$, $2a_3 - 6$, $2a_3 - 4$, $2a_3 - 2$, $2a_3$.

Required sum = $2a_3 - 8 + 2a_3 - 6 + 2a_3 - 4 + 2a_3 - 2 + 2a_3 = 450$

$10a_3 - 20 = 450$ or $a_3 = 47$. Since, we are looking for 5 consecutive odd integers, we get $a_5 = 51$

102. You can experimentally verify that there would be only three pairs of values that would satisfy this- viz: (18, 18) ; (12, 36) and (10, 90). No other pair would satisfy this condition.

103. Let the first term be 'a' and the common ratio be 'r'.

$a_n = 3(a_{n+1} + a_{n+2} + \dots.)$

$ar^{n-1} = 3(ar^n + ar^{n+1} + \dots.)$

$ar^{n-1} = 3\left(\frac{ar^n}{1-r}\right)$ or $3r = 1 - r$ or $r = \frac{1}{4}$

$a_1 + a_2 + a_3 + \dots = 32$

$a + ar + ar^2 + \dots = 32$

$\frac{a}{1-r} = 32$

$a = 24$

$a_5 = ar^4 = 24 \cdot (1/4)^4 = 3/32$

104. $a_1 = \frac{1}{2 \times 5} = \frac{1}{3}\left(\frac{1}{2} - \frac{1}{5}\right)$

$a_2 = \frac{1}{5 \times 8} = \frac{1}{3}\left(\frac{1}{5} - \frac{1}{8}\right)$

$\vdots$

$\vdots$

$a_{100} = \frac{1}{299 \times 302} = \frac{1}{3}\left(\frac{1}{299} - \frac{1}{302}\right)$

The required sum = $a_1 + a_2 + a_3 + a_4 + a_5 \dots + a_{100}$ =

$\frac{1}{3}\left(\frac{1}{2} - \frac{1}{5}\right) + \frac{1}{3}\left(\frac{1}{5} - \frac{1}{8}\right) + \dots + \frac{1}{3}\left(\frac{1}{299} - \frac{1}{302}\right)$

$= \frac{1}{3}\left(\frac{1}{2} - \frac{1}{302}\right) = \frac{1}{3} \times \frac{300}{604} = \frac{100}{604} = \frac{25}{151}$

## IIFT

1. The sum of the series is: $\frac{1}{1.2.3} + \frac{1}{3.4.5} + \frac{1}{5.6.7} + \dots.$

**(IIFT 2009)**

(a) $e^2 - 1$  (b) $\log 2 - 1$

(c) $2 \log 2 - 1$  (d) None of these.

2. Find the sum of the following series: $\frac{2}{1!} + \frac{3}{2!} + \frac{6}{3!} + \frac{11}{4!} + \frac{18}{5!} +$

**(IIFT 2010)**

(a) $3e - 1$  (b) $3(e - 1)$

(c) $3(e + 1)$  (d) $3e + 1$

3. A small confectioner bought a certain number of pastries flavoured pineapple, mango and black-forest from the bakery, giving for each pastry as many rupees as there were pastry of that kind; altogether he bought 23 pastries and spent ₹211; find the number of each kind of pastry that he bought, if mango pastry are cheaper than pineapple pastry and dearer than black-forest pastry. **(IIFT 2010)**

(a) (10, 9, 4)  (b) (11, 9, 3)

(c) (10, 8, 5)  (d) (11, 8, 4)

4. The smallest perfect square that is divisible by 7!

**(IIFT 2010)**

(a) 44100  (b) 176400

(c) 705600  (d) 19600

5. There are four prime numbers written in ascending order of magnitude. The product of the first three is 7429 and last three is 12673. Find the first number.

**(IIFT 2011)**

(a) 19  (b) 17

(c) 13  (d) None of these.

6. Mr. and Mrs. Gupta have three children - Pratik, Writtik and Kajol, all of whom were born in different cities. Pratik is 2 years elder to Writtik. Mr. Gupta was 30 years of age when Kajol was born in Hyderabad, while Mrs. Gupta was 28 years of age when Writtik was born in Bangalore. If Kajol was 5 years of age when Pratik was born in Mumbai, then what were the ages of Mr. and Mrs. Gupta respectively at the time of Pratik's birth?

**(IIFT 2011)**

(a) 35 years, 26 years  (b) 30 years, 21 years
(c) 37 years, 28 years  (d) None of these.

7. $\left(\sqrt{\dfrac{225}{729}} - \sqrt{\dfrac{25}{144}}\right) \div \sqrt{\dfrac{16}{81}} = ?$  **(IIFT 2011)**

(a) $\dfrac{5}{16}$  (b) $\dfrac{7}{12}$

(c) $\dfrac{3}{8}$  (d) None of these

8. While preparing for a management entrance exami-nation Romit attempted to solve three papers, namely Mathematics, Verbal English and Logical Analysis, each of which have the full marks of 100. It is ob-served that one-third of the marks obtained by Romit in Logical Analysis is greater than half of his marks obtained in Verbal English by 5. He has obtained a total of 210 marks in the examination and 70 marks in Mathematics. What is the difference between the marks obtained by him in Mathematics and Verbal English?  **(IIFT 2011)**

(a) 40  (b) 10
(c) 20  (d) 30

9. If $\dfrac{x}{y} = \dfrac{7}{4}$. find the value of $\dfrac{x^2 - y^2}{x^2 + y^2}$  **(IIFT 2011)**

(a) 27/49  (b) 43/72
(c) 33/65  (d) None of the above

10. If 2, a, b, c, d, e, f and 65 form an arithmetic pro-gression, find out the value of 'e'  **(IIFT 2011)**

(a) 48  (b) 47
(c) 41  (d) None of the above

11. If k is an integer and $0.0010101 \times 10^k$ is greater than 1000, what is the least possible value of k?

(a) 4  (b) 5
(c) 6  (d) 7  **(IIFT 2012)**

12. The unit digit in the product of $(8267)^{153} \times (341)^{72}$ is  **(IIFT 2012)**

(a) 1  (b) 2
(c) 7  (d) 9

13. Z is the product of first 31 natural numbers If X = Z + 1, then the numbers of primes among X + 1, X + 2, ... X + 29, X + 30 is  **(IIFT 2012)**

(a) 30  (b) 2
(c) Cannot be determined  (d) None of these

14. Mrs. Sonia buys ₹249.00 worth of candies for the children of a school. For each girl she gets a straw-berry flavoured candy priced at ₹3.30 per candy; each boy receives a chocolate flavored candy priced at ₹2.90 per candy. How many candies of each type did she buy?  **(IIFT 2013)**

(a) 21, 57  (b) 57, 21
(c) 37, 51  (d) 27, 51

15. If the product of the integers a, b, c and d is 3094 and if 1 < a < b < c < d, what is the product of b and c?  **(IIFT 2013)**

(a) 26  (b) 91
(c) 133  (d) 221

16. If the product of n positive integers is $n^n$, then their sum is  **(IIFT 2013)**

(a) a negative integer  (b) equal to n
(c) equal to $n + \dfrac{1}{n}$  (d) never less than $n^2$

17. A tennis ball is initially dropped from a height of 180 m. After striking the ground, it rebounds (3/5) th of the height from which it has fallen. The total distance that the ball travels before it comes to rest is  **(IIFT 2013)**

(a) 540 m  (b) 600 m
(c) 720 m  (d) 900 m

18. In at school, students were called for the Flag Hoist-ing ceremony on August 15. After the ceremony, small boxes of sweets were distributed among the students. In each class, the student with roll no. 1 got one box of sweets, student with roll number 2 got 2 boxes of sweets. student with roll no. 3 got 3 boxes of sweets and so on. In class III, a total of 1200 boxes of sweets were distributed. By mistake one of the students of class III got double the sweets he was entitled to get, Identify the roll number of the student who got twice as many boxes of sweets as compared to his entitlement.  **(IIFT 2014)**

(a) 22  (b) 24
(c) 28  (d) 3

19. The sum of $1 - \dfrac{1}{6} + \dfrac{1}{6} \times \dfrac{1}{4} - \dfrac{1}{6} \times \dfrac{1}{4} \times \dfrac{5}{18} + \ldots$ is:

(a) $\dfrac{2}{3}$  (b) $\dfrac{2}{\sqrt{3}}$

(c) $\sqrt{\dfrac{2}{3}}$  (d) $\dfrac{\sqrt{3}}{2}$  **(IIFT 2014)**

20. In 2004, Rohini was thrice as old as her brother Arvind. In 2014, Rohini was only six years older than her brother. In which year was Rohini born?  **(IIFT 2015)**

(a) 1984  (b) 1986
(c) 1995  (d) 2000

21. If p, q and r are three unequal numbers such that p, q and r are in A.P. and p, r-q and q-p are in G.P. then p : q : r is equal to  **(IIFT 2015)**

(a) 1: 2: 3  (b) 2: 3: 4
(c) 3: 2: 1  (d) 1: 3: 4

22. A child, playing at the balcony of his multi-storied apartment, drops a ball from a height of 350 m. Each time the ball rebounds, it rises 4/5th of the height it has fallen through. The total distance travelled by the ball before it comes to rest is  **(IIFT 2016)**

(a) 2530 m  (b) 2800 m
(c) 3150 m  (d) 3500 m

23. What is the sum of integers 54 through 196 inclusive? **(IIFT 2016)**
    (a) 28,820    (b) 24,535
    (c) 20,250    (d) 17,875

24. In a certain sequence the term $x_n$ is given by formula

    $X_n = 5X_{n-1} - \dfrac{3}{4}X_{n-2}$ for $n \geq 2$. What is the value

    of $x_3$, if $x_0 = 4$ and $x_1 = 2$?    **(IIFT 2017)**
    (a) 67/2    (b) 37/2
    (c) 123/4    (d) None

25. If $10^{67} - 87$ is written as an integer in base 10 notation, what is the sum of digits in that integer?    **(IIFT 2017)**
    (a) 683    (b) 489
    (c) 583    (d) 589

## ANSWER KEY

| | | | |
|---|---|---|---|
| 1. (b) | 2. (c) | 3. (b) | 4. (b) |
| 5. (b) | 6. (a) | 7. (a) | 8. (c) |
| 9. (c) | 10. (b) | 11. (c) | 12. (c) |
| 13. (d) | 14. (b) | 15. (b) | 16. (d) |
| 17. (c) | 18. (b) | 19. (d) | 20. (c) |
| 21. (a) | 22. (c) | 23. (d) | 24. (a) |
| 25. (d) | | | |

## Solutions

1. $\dfrac{1}{1.2.3} + \dfrac{1}{3.4.5} + \dfrac{1}{5.6.7} + ....$

   $\dfrac{1}{1.2.3} = \dfrac{1}{2}\left(\dfrac{1}{1} - \dfrac{2}{2} + \dfrac{1}{3}\right)$

   $\dfrac{1}{3.4.5} = \dfrac{1}{2}\left(\dfrac{1}{3} - \dfrac{2}{4} + \dfrac{1}{5}\right)$

   $\dfrac{1}{5.6.7} = \dfrac{1}{2}\left(\dfrac{1}{5} - \dfrac{2}{6} + \dfrac{1}{7}\right)$

   nth term $= \dfrac{1}{2}\left(\dfrac{1}{2n-1} - \dfrac{2}{2n} + \dfrac{1}{2n+1}\right)$

   Required sum

   $= \dfrac{1}{2}\left[\left(\dfrac{1}{1} - \dfrac{2}{2} + \dfrac{1}{3}\right) + \left(\dfrac{1}{3} - \dfrac{2}{4} + \dfrac{1}{5}\right) + \right.$

   $\left(\dfrac{1}{5} - \dfrac{2}{6} + \dfrac{1}{7}\right) + ..... \left.\left(\dfrac{1}{2n-1} - \dfrac{2}{2n} + \dfrac{1}{2n+1}\right)\right]$

   $= \dfrac{1}{2}\left[2\left(\dfrac{1}{3} - \dfrac{1}{4} + \dfrac{1}{5} - \dfrac{1}{6} + \dfrac{1}{7} - \dfrac{1}{8} + .....\right)\right]$

   $= \dfrac{1}{3} - \dfrac{1}{4} + \dfrac{1}{5} - \dfrac{1}{6} + .....$

   $= 1 - \dfrac{1}{2} + \left(\dfrac{1}{3} - \dfrac{1}{4} + \dfrac{1}{5} - \dfrac{1}{6} + .....\right) - \dfrac{1}{2}$

   $= \log 2 - \dfrac{1}{2}$

2. In this series, you can simply try to take the values of the individual terms, till the value of the next term becomes insignificant – and then match the answer that is coming out with the given options.

   $S = \dfrac{2}{1!} + \dfrac{3}{2!} + \dfrac{6}{3!} + \dfrac{11}{4!} + \dfrac{18}{5!} + ..... = 2 + 1.5 + 1 + 0.5 + 0.1 + .... = 5.1 +$ a very small value.

   Option (b) $= 3(e - 1) = 5.1$. Hence, this option is correct.

3. Let the number of pastries of pineapple, mango and blackforest be x, y, z respectively and it is given that for each pastry as many rupees were given as there were pastry of that kind. Then according to the question:

   $x^2 + y^2 + z^2 = 211$    (1)
   $x + y + z = 23$    (2)

   Now, by inserting the values from the options, we can see that only option (b) satisfies equation (1) and equation (2). So option (b) is correct.

4. $7! = 7 \times 6 \times 5 \times 4 \times 3 \times 2 \times 1$
   $7! = 2^4 \times 3^2 \times 5 \times 7$

   So the smallest perfect square divisible by 7! Is: $2^4 \times 3^2 \times 5^2 \times 7^2 = 176400$

5. You can do a trial and error starting with the options. When you pick up option (b), which says that the smallest number is 17, the numbers would be 17, 19, 23 and 29. In that case, the product of the first three numbers: $7429 = 17 \times 19 \times 23$

   Product of the last three numbers: $12673 = 19 \times 23 \times 29$.

   The numbers are 17, 19, 23, 29.

   First number = 17

6. Pratik is 2 years elder to Writtik and Kajol is 5 years elder than Pratik.

   Mr. Gupta's age when Kajol born = 30 years

   So Mr. Gupta's age when Pratik born = 30 + 5 = 35 years

   Mrs. Gupta's age when Writtik was born = 28 years

   Mrs. Gupta's age when Pratik born = 28 – 2 = 26 years

7. $\left(\sqrt{\dfrac{225}{729}} - \sqrt{\dfrac{25}{144}}\right) \div \sqrt{\dfrac{16}{81}} = \left(\dfrac{15}{27} - \dfrac{5}{12}\right) \div \dfrac{4}{9}$

   $= \dfrac{5}{36} \times \dfrac{9}{4} = \dfrac{5}{16}$

8. Let the scores be M, V and L marks in Mathematics, Verbal and Logical reasoning respectively. According to the question:

   $L/3 - V/2 = 5$    ....(1)
   $L + V = 210 - 70 = 140$ OR $L/2 + V/2 = 70$ ....(2)
   $L/3 + L/2 = 75$ OR $L = 90, V = 140 - 90 = 50$.

Required difference = 70 − 50 = 20.

9. $\dfrac{x^2 - y^2}{x^2 + y^2} = \dfrac{7^2 - 4^2}{7^2 + 4^2} = \dfrac{33}{65}$

10. This A.P. has eight terms. Hence, the common difference = $\dfrac{65 - 2}{7} = 9$.

   $e = 2 + (6 - 1)9 = 47$.

11. Check the options:

   Option a: k = 4, the value becomes 0.0010101 × 10⁴. In this case the decimal point would shift by 4 places and give us a value of 10.101 for the expression.

   Option b: k = 5, the value becomes 0.0010101 × 10⁵. In this case the decimal point would shift by 5 places and give us a value of 101.01 for the expression.

   Option c: k = 6, it can be seen that the expression would give us the required value greater than 1000 for the first time.

   Hence, option (c) is correct.

12. The unit digit of $8267^{153}$ = the unit digit of $7^1 = 7$

   The unit digit $341^{72} = 1$

   Hence, the unit digit of $(8267)^{153} \times (341)^{72} = 7 \times 1 = 7$.

   Hence, option (c) is correct.

13. Z = 31! Hence, Z would be divisible by all numbers till 31.

   The number X + 1 = Z + 2 would be divisible by 2;

   X + 2 = Z + 3 would be divisible by 3

   X + 3 = Z + 4 would be divisible by 4

   X + 4 = Z + 5 would be divisible by 5 and so on.

   Finally, X + 30 = Z + 31 would be divisible by 31.

   Hence, there would be no prime numbers between X + 1 to X + 30. Hence, Option (d) is correct.

14. Solve this one through options. If you use Option (a) you get:

   21 × 3.3 + 57 × 2.9 = 234.6 ≠ 249.

   Option (b) gives us: 57 × 3.3 + 21 × 2.9 = 249.

   Hence, Option (b) is correct.

15. a × b × c × d = 3094 = 2 × 7 × 13 × 17

   b × c = 7 × 13 = 91.

16. Sum of n positive integers ≥ n × (product of n positive integers)$^{1/n}$

   Sum of n positive integers ≥ n × $(n^n)^{1/n}$

   Sum of n positive integers ≥ $n^2$

   Option (d).

17. Total distance travelled = 180 + 2 × [180(3/5) + 180(3/5)² + 180(3/5)³ + .....]

   $= 180 + 360 \dfrac{3/5}{1 - \dfrac{3}{5}} = 180 + \dfrac{360.3}{2} = 720$ m.

18. Let there be n students in the class. The number of boxes distributed in the class would be: 1 + 2 + 3 + ..... + n = n(n + 1)/2

   Let the student with roll no. 'a' got twice as many boxes as compared to his entitlement.

   $\dfrac{n(n + 1)}{2} + a = 1200$

   n(n + 1) + 2a = 2400

   We can identify, that n should be 48, since 48 × 49 = 2352, is the last product of two consecutive integers below 2400.

   2a + 2352 = 2400 or 2a = 48 or a = 24.

   Alternately, you can think of this question as one in which the sum of the first 'n' natural numbers has been added, with one number double counted to give us a total of 1200. Since, the sum of 1 to 10 is 55, the sum of 11 to 20 is 155 and so on, we can add:

   55 + 155 + 255 + 255 + 41 + 42 + 43 + 44 + 45 + 46 + 47 + 48 = 1176. Hence, the double counted number must be 24.

19. $1 - \dfrac{1}{6} + \dfrac{1}{6} \times \dfrac{1}{4} - \dfrac{1}{6} \times \dfrac{1}{4} \times \dfrac{5}{18} + ...$

   $= \left(1 - \dfrac{1}{6}\right) + \dfrac{1}{24}\left(1 - \dfrac{5}{18}\right) + ...$

   $\dfrac{5}{6} + \dfrac{1}{24} \times \dfrac{13}{18} = 0.833 + 0.03 = 0.863$

   Further terms would be less than 0.03 and these terms can be neglected.

   $\dfrac{\sqrt{3}}{2} = 0.866$

   Hence, option (d) is correct.

20. Let the age of Rohini and her brother in 2004 be R and A respectively. According to the question:

   R = 3A          (1)

   R = A + 6          (2)

   On solving we get, R = 9, A = 3.

   Hence, Rohini was born in 2004 − 9 = 1995.

21. Check the options, only option (a) satisfies the given conditions hence, this option is correct.

22. Total distance travelled $= 350 + 350 \times \dfrac{4}{5} + 350 \times \dfrac{4}{5}$

   $+ 350 \times \left(\dfrac{4}{5}\right)^2 + 350 \times \left(\dfrac{4}{5}\right)^2 + ....$

   $= 450 + 700\left[\dfrac{4}{5} + \left(\dfrac{4}{5}\right)^2 + .....\right]$

   $= 350 + 700 / \left(1 - \left(\dfrac{4}{5}\right)\right) = 350 + 700 \times 4 = 3150$ m.

23. Required sum = 54 + 55 + 56 + 57 + ..... + 196 =

$$\frac{[(196 - 54) + 1]}{2}(196 + 54) = \frac{143}{2} \times 250 = 17{,}875$$

24. $X_n = 5x_{n-1} - \frac{3}{4}x_{n-2}; n \geq 2$

$X_0 = 4, x_1 = 2$

Put n = 2 in the above equation

$X_2 = 5x_1 - \frac{3}{4}x_0$

$= 10 - \frac{3}{4} \times 4 = 7.$

Put x = 3

$X_3 = 5x_2 - \frac{3}{4}x_1 = 5 \times 7 - \frac{3}{4} \times 2 = 35 - 1.5 = 33.5.$

Option (a) is correct.

25. $10^{67} - 87 = 1000\ldots$ (67 zeros)... $0 - 87 = 9999\ldots$(65 times)...913

Sum of digits = $65 \times 9 + 1 + 3 = 589$. Option (d).

# XAT

1. In a cricket match, Team A scored 232 runs without losing a wicket. The score consisted of byes, wides and runs scored by two opening batsmen: Ram and Shyam. The runs scored by the two batsmen are 26 times wides. There are 8 more byes than wides. If the ratio of the runs scored by Ram and Shyam is 6 : 7, then the runs scored by Ram is  **(XAT 2008)**
   (a) 88                     (b) 96
   (c) 102                    (d) 112
   (e) None of these

**Directions for Questions 2-4:**  A, B, C, D, E and F are six positive integers such that:  **(XAT 2008)**

   B + C + D + E = 4A
   C + F = 3A
   C + D + E = 2F
   F = 2D
   E + F = 2C + 1

If A is a prime number between 12 and 20, then

2. The value of C is:
   (a) 13                     (b) 17
   (c) 23                     (d) 19
   (e) 21

3. The value of F is:
   (a) 14                     (b) 16
   (c) 20                     (d) 24
   (e) 28

4. Which of the following must be true?
   (a) B is the lowest integer and B = 12
   (b) D is the lowest integer and D = 14

   (c) C is the greatest integer and C = 23
   (d) F is the greatest integer and F = 24
   (e) A is the lowest integer and A = 13

5. In the following question, one statement is followed by three conclusions. Select the appropriate answer from the options given below.     **(XAT 2008)**
   (a) Using the given statement, only conclusion I can be derived.
   (b) Using the given statement, only conclusion II can be derived.
   (c) Using the given statement, only conclusion III can be derived.
   (d) Using the given statement, conclusion I, II, III can be derived.
   (e) Using the given statement, none of three conclusions I, II, III can be derived.

   $A_0, A_1, A_2, \ldots$ is a sequence of numbers with $A_0 = 1$, $A_1 = 3$, and $A_t = (t + 1) A_{t-1} - t A_{t-2} = 2, 3, 4,$ ...

   Conclusion 1: $A_8 = 77$
   Conclusion 2: $A_{10} = 121$
   Conclusion 3: $A_{12} = 145$

6. Let X be a four-digit number with exactly three consecutive digits being same and is a multiple of 9. How many such X's are possible?  **(XAT 2009)**
   (a) 12                     (b) 16
   (c) 19                     (d) 21
   (e) None of above.

**Directions for Questions 7-8:**  In the diagram below, the seven letters correspond to seven unique digits chosen from 0 to 9. The relationship among the digits is such that:

$$P \times Q \times R = X \times Y \times Z = Q \times A \times Y \quad \textbf{(XAT 2009)}$$

| P | | X |
|---|---|---|
| Q | A | Y |
| R | | Z |

7. The value of A is:
   (a) 0                      (b) 2
   (c) 3                      (d) 6
   (e) None of above.

8. The sum of digits which are not used is:
   (a) 8                      (b) 10
   (c) 14                     (d) 15
   (e) None of above

9. a, b, c d and e are integers such that $1 \leq a < b < c < d < e$. If a, b, c, d and e are in geometric progression and lcm (m, n) is the least common multiple of m and n, then the maximum value of

$$\frac{1}{\text{lcm}(a, b)} + \frac{1}{\text{lcm}(b, c)} + \frac{1}{\text{lcm}(c, d)} + \frac{1}{\text{lcm}(d, e)}$$ is:

   **(XAT 2010)**
   (a) 1                      (b) 15/16
   (c) 79/81                  (d) 7/8
   (e) None of these.

10. Let $a_n$ = 1111111.....1, where 1 occurs n number of time. Then, **(XAT 2011)**
    (i) $a_{741}$ is not a prime.
    (ii) $a_{534}$ is not a prime
    (iii) $a_{123}$ is not a prime
    (iv) $a_{77}$ is not a prime
    (a) (i) is correct.
    (b) (i) and (ii) are correct.
    (c) (ii) and (iii) are correct.
    (d) All of them are correct.
    (e) None of them is correct.

11. Three truck drivers, Amar, Akbar and Anthony stop at a road side eating joint. Amar orders 10 rotis, 4 plates of tadka, and a cup of tea. Akbar orders 7 rotis, 3 plates of tadka, and a cup of tea. Amar pays ₹80 for the meal and Akbar pays ₹60. Meanwhile, Anthony orders 5 rotis, 5 plates of tadka and 5 cups of tea. How much (in ₹) will Anthony pay?
    **(XAT 2012)**
    (a) 75      (b) 80
    (c) 95      (d) 100
    (e) None of above.

12. Consider the expression **(XAT 2013)**
    $$\frac{(a^2+a+1)(b^2+b+1)(c^2+c+1)}{abcde}$$
    $$\frac{(d^2+d+1)(e^2+e+1)}{abcde}$$
    Where a, b, c, d and e are positive numbers. The minimum value of the expression is
    (a) 3      (b) 1
    (c) 10      (d) 100
    (e) 243

13. How many whole numbers between 100 and 800 contain the digit 2? **(XAT 2013)**
    (a) 200      (b) 214
    (c) 220      (d) 240
    (e) 248

14. p, q and r are three non-negative integers such that p + q + r = 10. The maximum value of pq + qr + pr + pqr is **(XAT 2013)**
    (a) 40 and <50      (b) 50 and <60
    (c) 60 and <70      (d) 70 and <80
    (e) 80 and <90

15. A number is interesting if on adding the sum of the digits of the number, the product of the digits of the number, the result is equal to the number. What fraction of numbers between 10 and 100 (both 10 and 100 included) is interesting? **(XAT 2013)**
    (a) 0.1      (b) 0.11
    (c) 0.16      (d) 0.2
    (e) None of these

16. Consider the expression. $(xxx)_b = x^3$, where b is the base, and x is any digit of base b. find the value of b. **(XAT 2013)**

(a) 5      (b) 6
(c) 7      (d) 8
(e) None of these

17. Please read the following sentences carefully:
    **(XAT 2013)**
    I. 103 and 7 are the only prime factors of 100027
    II. $\sqrt[6]{6!} > \sqrt[7]{7!}$
    III. If I travel one half of my journey at an average speed of x km/h, it will be impossible for me to attain an average speed of 2x km/h for the entire journey.
    (a) All the statements are correct.
    (b) Only statement II is correct.
    (c) Only the statements III is correct.
    (d) Both the statements I and II are correct.
    (e) Both the statements I and III are correct.

18. p and q are positive numbers such that $p^q = q^p$. And q = 9p. The value of p is **(XAT 2013)**
    (a) $\sqrt{9}$      (b) $\sqrt[6]{9}$
    (c) $\sqrt[9]{9}$      (d) $\sqrt[8]{9}$
    (e) $\sqrt[3]{9}$

19. Two numbers, $297_B$ and $792_B$ belong to base B number system. If the first number is a factor of the second number then the value of B is: **(XAT 2014)**
    (a) 11      (b) 17
    (c) 15      (d) 17
    (e) 19

20. Read the following instruction carefully and answer the question that follows: Expression $\sum_{n=1}^{13} \frac{1}{n}$ can also be written as x/13!. What would be the remainder if x is divided by 11? **(XAT 2014)**
    (a) 2 28      (b) 4
    (c) 7      (d) 9
    (e) None of the above

21. Amitabh picks a random integer between 1 and 999, doubles it and gives the result to Sashi. Each time Sashi gets a number from Amitabh, he adds 50 to the number, and gives the result back to Amitabh, who doubles the number again. The first person, whose result is more than 1000, loses the game. Let 'x' be the smallest number that results in a win for Amitabh. The sum of the digits of 'x' is:
    **(XAT 2014)**
    (a) 3      (b) 5
    (c) 7      (d) 9
    (e) None of these

22. Consider four natural numbers: x, y, x + y, and xy. Two statements are provided below
    I. All four numbers are prime numbers.
    II. The arithmetic mean of the numbers is greater than 4.

Which of the following statements would be sufficient to determine the sum of the four numbers?

A. Statement I.
B. Statement II.
C. Statement I and Statement II.
D. Neither Statement I nor Statement II.
E. Either Statement I or Statement II. **(XAT 2014)**

23. What is the sum of the following series?

$-64, -66, -68, \ldots\ldots\ldots, -100$ **(XAT 2015)**

(a) $-1458$
(b) $-1558$
(c) $-1568$
(d) $-1664$
(e) None of these.

24. If a, b, c, d are four different positive integers selected from 1 to 25 then the highest possible value of $[(a + b) + (c + d)]/[(a + b) + (c - d)]$ would be:
**(XAT 2015)**

(a) 47
(b) 49
(c) 51
(d) 96
(e) None of these.

25. An ascending series of numbers satisfies the following conditions:

(i) When divided by 3, 4, 5, 6 the numbers leave a remainder of 2.
(ii) When divided by 11, the number leaves no remainder. **(XAT 2015)**

The sixth number of this series will be:

(a) 242
(b) 2882
(c) 3542
(d) 4202
(e) None of these.

26. Consider the set of numbers $(1, 3, 3^2, 3^3, \ldots\ldots, 3^{100})$. The ratio of the last number and the sum of the remaining numbers is closest to: **(XAT 2016)**

(a) 1
(b) 2
(c) 3
(d) 50
(e) 99

27. Two numbers in the base system B are $2061_B$ and $601_B$. The sum of these two numbers in decimal system is 432. Find the value of $1010_B$ in the decimal system. **(XAT 2016)**

(a) 110
(b) 120
(c) 130
(d) 140
(e) 150

28. For two positive integers a and b, if $(a + b)^{(a + b)}$ is divisible by 500, then the least possible value of $a \times b$ is: **(XAT 2016)**

(a) 8
(b) 9
(c) 10
(d) 12
(e) None of the above

29. a, b, c are integers, $|a| \neq |b| \neq |c|$ and $-10 \leq a, b, c \leq 10$. What will be the maximum possible value of $[abc - (a + b + c)]$? **(XAT 2016)**

(a) 524
(b) 693
(c) 731
(d) 970
(e) None of the above

30. If a, b and c are 3 consecutive integers between $-10$ to $+10$ (both inclusive), how many integer values are possible for the expression $(a^3 + b^3 + c^3 + 3abc)/(a + b + c)^2$? **(XAT 2016)**

(a) 0
(b) 1
(c) 2
(d) 3
(e) 4

31. The sum of series, $(-100) + (-95) + (-90) + \ldots\ldots\ldots + 110 + 115 + 120$, is: **(XAT 2017)**

(a) 0
(b) 220
(c) 340
(d) 450
(e) None of the above

32. If $N = (11^{p + 7})(7^{q - 2})(5^{r + 1})(3^s)$ is a perfect cube, where p, q, r and s are positive integers, then the smallest value of $p + q + r + s$ is: **(XAT 2017)**

(a) 5
(b) 6
(c) 7
(d) 8
(e) 9

33. Hari's family consisted of his younger brother (Chari), younger sister (Gouri), and their father and mother. When Chari was born, the sum of the ages of Hari, his father and mother was 70 years. The sum of the ages of four family members, at the time of Gouri's birth, was twice the sum of ages of Hari's father and mother at the time of Hari's birth. If Chari is 4 years older than Gouri, then find the difference in age between Hari and Chari. **(XAT 2017)**

(a) 5 years
(b) 6 years
(c) 7 years
(d) 8 years
(e) 9 years

---

## ANSWER KEY

| | | | |
|---|---|---|---|
| 1. (b) | 2. (c) | 3. (e) | 4. (a) |
| 5. (e) | 6. (e) | 7. (b) | 8. (e) |
| 9. (b) | 10. (d) | 11. (d) | 12. (e) |
| 13. (b) | 14. (c) | 15. (a) | 16. (e) |
| 17. (c) | 18. (d) | 19. (e) | 20. (d) |
| 21. (c) | 22. (a) | 23. (b) | 24. (c) |
| 25. (c) | 26. (b) | 27. (c) | 28. (b) |
| 29. (c) | 30. (b) | 31. (d) | 32. (e) |
| 33. (e) | | | |

**Solutions**

1. Let runs scored by Ram and Shyam be 6r and 7r respectively. Let us denote byes by b and wides by w.

According to the question:

$6r + 7r = 26w$ or $13r = 26w$ or $r = 2w$    (1)

$w + 8 = b$    (2)

$13r + w + b = 232$    (3)

By solving equation 1, 2, 3 we get:

$r = 16$

Runs scored by Ram $= 6r = 6 \times 16 = 96$

2. From the equations, we can make the following deductions:

   F must be even. C must be odd (since C + F = 3A and A must be an odd prime number - A = 13 or 17 or 19). D + E is even as (C + D + E = 2F), so D and E must both be even or both odd. Since, F is even, E must be odd (since E + F = 2C + 1). Thus, D and E must both be odd.

   Thus, we have: A odd; F even, C odd; D, E odd; B odd. With this information, we would need to start looking at the various possibilities, and also consider them from the options to questions 2 and 3:

   Assuming A = 17: The following thought process takes us to the values of the other variables:

   C + F = 3A = 51. Checking the option combinations for questions 2 and 3, the only way for C + F to be 51 would be C = 23, F = 28. Then: D = 14; C + D + E = 2F → E = 19; B + C + D + E = 4A → B = 12. With these values, the last equation E + F = 2C + 1 matches as we get 19 + 28 = 2 × 23 + 1. Hence, this option pair and this set of values work.

   If you take A = 13, 3A = 39, gives two possible option pairs for C + F = 39. Viz: 23 + 16 or 19 + 20. The 23, 16 combination gives, D = 8, E = 1 and B = 20. The last condition E + F = 2C + 1 does not match these numbers as 1 + 16 ≠ 2 × 23 + 1.

   With, A = 13, C = 19, F = 20, we get D = 10, E = 22 and B = 12. E + F = 2C + 1 condition is not satisfied here too.

   If you take A = 19, there is no option combination to match C + F = 3A.

   Hence, the correct solution is based on A = 17, C = 23, F = 28, D = 14, E = 19 and B = 12.

   The answers are: 2. Option (c) is correct.; 3. Option (e) is correct; 4. Option (a) is correct.

5. $A_2 = 3A_1 - 2A_0 = 7$

   $\quad A_3 = 4A_2 - 3A_1 = 19$

   $\quad A_4 = 5 \times 19 - 4 \times 7 = 67$

   $\quad A_5 = 6 \times 67 - 5 \times 19 = 307$

   $\quad A_6 = 7 \times 307 - 6 \times 67 = 1747$

   Similarly $A_7 > A_6$, $A_8 > A_7$.

   Hence, none of the conclusions are true. Option (e) is correct.

6. Let X = xxxy or yxxx. Since X is a multiple of 9 it means 3x + y should be either 9, 18, 27. (3x + y cannot be 36 because in this case x = y = 9. But x ≠ y according to the question).

   When 3x + y = 9

   Possible cases are: (1116, 6111, 2223, 3222, 3330, 9000)

   When 3x + y = 18

   Possible cases are: (3339, 9333, 4446, 6444, 5553, 3555, 6660)

   When 3x + y = 27

   Possible cases are: (6669, 9666, 8883, 3888, 7776, 6777, 9990)

   Hence, total number of cases is 20.

7. P, Q, R, A, X, Y and Z are distinct. Any of these numbers can never be either 0, 5 and 7 as it would lead to one of these three products to be different to the others. Hence, these seven digits are 1, 2, 3, 4, 6, 8 and 9.

   $P \times Q \times R \times A \times X \times Y \times Z = 1 \times 2 \times 3 \times 4 \times 6 \times 8 \times 9 = 2^7 \times 3^4$

   This gives us two scenarios: $PQR = XYZ = 2^2 \times 3^2$ OR $PQR = XYZ = 2^3 \times 3^2$

   In the first case: A = 2; In the second case A = $2^3$

   If A = 8, then QAY cannot be $2^2 \times 3^2$.

   So A must be 2, and the value of A is uniquely determinable.

   Option (b) is correct.

8. Required sum = 0 + 5 + 7 = 12. Option (e).

9. Since they are in G.P. Let the terms $a$, $ar$, $ar^2$, $ar^3$, $ar^4$ with $r > 1$ as the given numbers are integers in increasing order. Let the required sum be S.

   $$S = \frac{1}{1\,cm(a, ar)} + \frac{1}{1\,cm(ar, ar^2)} + \frac{1}{1\,cm(ar^2, ar^3)}$$
   $$+ \frac{1}{1\,cm(ar^3, ar^4)}$$
   $$= \frac{1}{ar} + \frac{1}{ar^2} + \frac{1}{ar^3} + \frac{1}{ar^4} = \frac{1}{ar}\left(1 + \frac{1}{r} + \frac{1}{r^2} + \frac{1}{r^3}\right)$$
   $$= \frac{(r^2 + 1)(r + 1)}{ar^4}$$

   Now for S to be the maximum value, Taking a = 1

   $$S = \frac{(r^2 + 1)(r + 1)}{r^4}$$

   Since a < b < c < d < e. So r ≠ 1

   For r = 2, $S = 5 \times \dfrac{3}{2^4} = \dfrac{15}{16}$

   For r = 3, $S = 10 \times \dfrac{4}{3^4} = \dfrac{40}{81}$

   For r = 4, $S = 17 \times \dfrac{5}{4^4} = \dfrac{85}{256}$. We can clearly see that the value of S is decreasing as we increase r.

   Hence the maximum value = 15/16. (Note: Since a, b, c, d and e are integers, r has to be an integer too).

10. Sum of digits of $a_{741}$ is 7 + 4 + 1 = 12. (Multiple of 3)

    Sum of digits of $a_{534}$ is 5 + 3 + 4 = 12. (Multiple of 3)

    Sum of digits of $a_{123}$ is 1 + 2 + 3 = 6. (Multiple of 3)

So statements i, ii, iii are correct. Only option (d) is correct.

11. Let cost of a roti, a tadka and a cup of tea be a, b, c respectively.

According to the question: $10a + 4b + c = 80$  (1)

$7a + 3b + c = 60$  (2)

By equation $2 \times 3 -$ equation $1 \times 2$, we get:

$a + b + c = 20$

Amount paid by Anthony $= 5a + 5b + 5c = 5(a + b + c) = 5 \times 20 = 100$.

12. As $\dfrac{a^2 + a + 1}{a} = a + 1 + \dfrac{1}{a}$

If $a > 0$, $a + \dfrac{1}{a} \geq 2$

$\therefore \quad a + 1 + \dfrac{1}{a} \geq 3$

$\therefore$ Minimum value of $\dfrac{a^2 + a + 1}{a} = 3$

Hence, the minimum value of

$$\dfrac{(a^2 + a + 1)(b^2 + b + 1)(c^2 + c + 1)(d^2 + d + 1)(e^2 + e + 1)}{abcde} = 3^5 = 243.$$

13. The total number of numbers from 100 to 799 $=$ $799 - 100 + 1 = 700$.

The number of numbers from 100 to 799 which do not have 2 as one of three digits $= 6 \times 9 \times 9 = 486$

Hence, the required number of numbers $= 700 - 486 = 214$.

14. $p + q + r = 10$

The product of p, q and r will be maximum if p, q and r are as symmetrical as possible.

Therefore, (p, q, r) must be (4, 3, 3 ).

Hence, maximum value of $pq + qr + pr + pqr = 4 \times 3 + 4 \times 3 + 3 \times 3 + 4 \times 3 \times 3 = 69$.

15. Let the number be 'ab'

According to the question: $10a + b = a + b + ab$

$\Rightarrow \quad 9a - ab = 0$

$\Rightarrow \quad b = 9$ (since $a \neq 0$)

Therefore, the required number is of the form 'a9'. 9 such numbers are possible from 10 to 100.

$\therefore$ The fraction $= 9/91 = 0.0989$. The closest option is option (a).

16. $(xxx)_b = x^3$

$\Rightarrow (x \times b^2 + x \times b + x) = x^3$

$\Rightarrow (b^2 + b + 1) = x^2$

This equation tells us that: $\Rightarrow x \geq b$

But x is a digit in base b, therefore $x < b$

Hence, option (e) is correct.

17. **Statement I:** $1000027 = 7 \times 19 \times 73 \times 103$

Hence, this statement is not true.

**Statements II:** Let $\sqrt[6]{6!} > \sqrt[7]{7!}$

$\Rightarrow \quad (6!)^7 > (7!)^6$

$\Rightarrow \quad 6! > 7^6$, which is not true.

The third statement is true since the value of the average speed is weighted by the time spent. For instance, if I am traveling 200 kms, and if I travel the first 100 km at 10 kmph, then I would take 10 hours to do it. To get an average speed of 20 kmph for the journey I would need to cover the whole journey in 10 hours, which is not possible.

Hence, only statement III is true. Option (c) is correct.

18. $p^q = q^p$

$\left(p^q\right)^{\frac{1}{p}} = \left(q^p\right)^{\frac{1}{p}}$

As, $\dfrac{p}{q} = 9$, the above equation transforms to:

$p^9 = q = 9p$ or $p^8 = 9$ or $p = 9^{\frac{1}{8}}$. Option (d) is correct.

19. Check the options one by one.

Option e: $297_{19} = 900$, $792_{19} = 2700$. 2700 is a multiple of 900. Option (e) is correct.

20. $\sum_{n=1}^{13} \dfrac{1}{n} = x/13!$

$\dfrac{1}{1} + \dfrac{1}{2} + \dfrac{1}{3} + \dfrac{1}{4} + \ldots + \dfrac{1}{13} = \dfrac{x}{13!}$

$x = 13! + \dfrac{13!}{2} + \dfrac{13!}{3} + \ldots + \dfrac{13!}{11} + \dfrac{13!}{12} + \dfrac{13!}{13}$

Except 13!/11 all the other terms are divisible by 11. So, we need to find the remainder of (13!/11)/11.

$\text{Rem}(13!/11)/11 = \dfrac{13.12.10!}{11} = 2.1.(-1) = -2 \rightarrow$

9. [According to Wilson theorem the remainder of $(p - 1)!/p = -1$]

21. Let Amitabh picks a random integer 'x'.

| Amitabh | Sakshi |
|---|---|
| 2x | 2x + 50 |
| 4x + 100 | 4x + 150 |
| 8x + 300 | 8x + 350 |
| 16x + 700 | 16x + 750 |
| 32x + 1500 (not possible) | 32x + 1550 (not possible) |

Thus, for Amitabh to win, the value of $16x + 750 > 1000 \rightarrow x > 15.66$

Hence, the smallest possible value of x would be 16.

Sum of digits $= 1 + 6 = 7$. Option c.

22. If we take only statement 1, for all four numbers to be prime one of them must be even and hence equal to 2. Only in such an event do we get x + y and x − y as odd numbers and only if they are odd can

all the four numbers be prime. A little bit of trial and error then gives us $x = 5$ and $y = 2$, $x + y = 7$ and $x – y = 3$. There is no other case of $x – y$, $x$ and $x + y$ being prime as if we take y as 2, these numbers become $x – 2$, $x$ and $x + 2$ and hence represent three consecutive odd numbers. (After 3, 5, 7 there is no situation where three consecutive odd numbers are all prime.)

Hence, statement 1 is sufficient.

Statement 2 can be easily rejected as all it is giving us is that the sum of all four numbers is greater than 16. As we can easily imagine there are infinite sets of four such numbers, which have a sum greater than 16.

Hence, option (a) is correct.

23. The conventional Arithmetic Progression route of solving this question would go as follows: $-100 = -64 + (n – 1)(-2) \to n = 19$.

$$S = \frac{19}{2}(2 \times -64 + (19 – 1)(-2)) = -1558.$$

Alternately, you can think of this as:

The average of the numbers is -82 and there are 19 numbers. Hence the sum is $-82 \times 19 = -1558$. (Note: 19 numbers can be seen using the logic:

$$\frac{\text{Difference between first and last number}}{\text{Common Difference}} + 1.$$

24. $\dfrac{[(a+b)+(c+d)]}{[(a+b)+(c-d)]} = \dfrac{[a+b+c-d+2d]}{[(a+b)+(c-d)]}$

$$= 1 + \frac{2d}{a+b+c-d}$$

So we need to maximize $\dfrac{2d}{a+b+c-d}$

$\dfrac{2d}{a+b+c-d}$ is maximum if $d = 25$ and $a + b + c – d = 1$

So maximum value of $\dfrac{2d}{a+b+c-d} = 2 \times 25 = 50$

So maximum value of $\dfrac{[(a+b)+(c+d)]}{[(a+b)+(c-d)]} = 1 + 50 = 51$.

25. When the numbers are divided by 3, 4, 5, 6 the numbers leave a remainder of 2.

So the number must be of the form: LCM of (3, 4, 5, 6) $\times a + 2 = 60a + 2$ (where $a = 1, 2, 3, .....$)

Numbers are divisible by 11 so it means $60a + 2 = 11b$

or $b = \dfrac{60a+2}{11}$ & b should be a positive integer.

This is possible only for $a = 4, 15, 26, 37, 48, 59$.

So the $6^{th}$ term of the series = $60 \times 59 + 2 = 3542$.

26. The last number = $3^{100}$. The sum of the remaining numbers = Sum of remaining numbers = $1 + 3 + 3^2 + 3^3 + ... \, 3^{99} = \dfrac{1(3^{100} – 1)}{3 – 1}$

$$\text{Required ratio} = \frac{\text{Last Number}}{\text{Sum of remaining numbers}}$$

$$= \frac{3^{100}}{\left[\dfrac{3^{100} - 1}{3 - 1}\right]} = \frac{2 . 3^{100}}{3^{100} - 1} \approx 2.$$

27. $2 \times B^3 + 6B + 1 + 6B^2 + 1 = 432$

$2B^3 + 6B^2 + 6B + 2 = 432 \to B^3 + 3B^2 + 3B + 1 = 432$

$(B + 1)^3 = 216$

$B + 1 = 6$ or $B = 5$

$1010_B = 1010_5 = 5^3 + 5 = 130$

28. $500 = 5 \times 5 \times 5 \times 2 \times 2$.

As the number is divisible by 500, $(a + b)$ should be divisible by 10.

The least possible value of $a + b = 10$.

Hence, the least possible value of $ab = 9 \times 1 = 9$.

29. To maximize the value of abc, two of a, b and c should be negative. Maximum value occur at, $a = -10$, $b = -9$, $c = 8$.

Then, $abc = (-10)(-9)8 = 720$.

$abc – (a + b + c) = 720 – (-10 – 9 + 8) = 731$.

Option (c) is correct.

30. To solve this question we would need to use the identity:

$$(a^3 + b^3 + c^3 – 3abc) = \frac{a+b+c}{2}[(a – b)^2 + (b – c)^2 + (c – a)^2]$$

Let the values of a, b and c are $p – 1$, p, $p + 1$. Then, $(a – b)^2 + (b – c)^2 + (c – a)^2 = [(p – 1 – p)^2 + (p – p – 1)^2 + (p + 1 – p + 1)^2] = 6$

Similarly we can see that $abc = p^3 – p$ and $a + b + c = p – 1 + p + p + 1 = 3p$.

$$\frac{a^3 + b^3 + c^3 + 3abc}{(a+b+c)^2} = \frac{a^3 + b^3 + c^3 - 3abc + 6abc}{(a+b+c)^2}$$

$$= \frac{a^3 + b^3 + c^3 - 3abc}{(a+b+c)^2} + \frac{6abc}{(a+b+c)^2} \frac{a+b+c}{2(a+b+c)^2}$$

$$[(a-b)^2 + (b-c)^2 + (c-a)^2]$$

$$+ \frac{6abc}{(a+b+c)^2} \frac{1}{6p} 6 + \frac{6(p^3 - p)}{9p^2}$$

$$= \frac{1}{p} + \frac{2p}{3} - \frac{2}{3p} = \frac{1}{3p} + \frac{2p}{3}$$

The above expression will have an integer value only when $p = 1$.

At $p = 1$, we get: $\dfrac{1}{3p} + \dfrac{2p}{3} = 1$

31. The number of terms in the series can be got using:

$$\frac{\text{Difference between first and last number}}{\text{Common Difference}} + 1$$

$$= \frac{220}{5} + 1 + 1 = 45.$$

Required sum $= \frac{45}{2} \times (-100 + 120) = 450.$

32. As 11, 7, 5 and 3 are prime numbers, so N is a perfect cube when each of the individual terms $11^{p+7}$, $7^{q-2}$, $5^{r+1}$ and $3^s$ are perfect cubes. It is possible for the minimum values of $p = 2$, $q = 2$, $r = 2$, $s = 3$.

Hence, $p + q + r + s = 2 + 2 + 2 + 3 = 9.$

33. When Hari was born: Let the age of Hari's father (when Hari was born) was F and his. Let it be the case that Chari was born after x years of Hari.

The age of Hari at the time when Chari born = x years

According to the question: $x + (F + x) + (M + x) = 70.$       (1)

When Gouri was born (after 4 more years), then the ages of the 4 family members $= 2 \times$ (Ages of father & mother at Hari's birth) $= (x + 4) + 4 + (F + x + 4) + (M + x + 4) = 2 \; 3x + 16 = F + M$    (2)

Putting value of $(F + M)$ from eqn. (2) to eqn (1), we get $3x + 3x + 16 = 70 \Rightarrow x = 9.$

Thus the required difference in age between Hari and Chari is 9 years.

# Averages and Mixtures

# ...BACK TO SCHOOL

- **The Relevance of Average**

Average is one of the most important mathematical concepts that we use in our day-to-day life. In fact, even the most non-mathematical individuals regularly utilize the concept of averages on a day-to-day basis.

So, we use averages in all the following and many more instances.

- How a class of students fared in an exam is assessed by looking at the average score.
- What is the average price of items purchased by an individual.
- A person might be interested in knowing his average telephone expenditure, electricity expenditure, petrol expenditure, etc.
- A manager might be interested in finding out the average sales per territory or even the average growth rate month to month.
- Clearly there can be immense application of averages that you might be able to visualise on your own.

- **The Meaning of an Average**

An average is best seen as a representative value which can be used to represent the value of the general term in a group of values.

For instance, suppose that a cricket team had 10 partnerships as follows:

| | |
|---|---|
| 1st wicket 28 | 2nd wicket 42 |
| 3rd wicket 112 | 4th wicket 52 |
| 5th wicket 0 | 6th wicket 23 |
| 7th wicket 41 | 8th wicket 18 |
| 9th wicket 9 | 10th wicket 15 |

On adding the ten values above, we get a total of 340—which gives an average of 34 runs per wicket, i.e., the average partnership of the team was 34 runs.

In other words, if we were to replace the value of all the ten partnerships by 34 runs, we would get the same total score. Hence, 34 represents the average partnership value for the team.

Suppose, in a cricket series of 5 matches between 2 countries, you are given that Team A had an average partnership of 58 Runs per wicket while Team B had an average partnership of 34 runs per wicket. What conclusion can you draw about the performance of the two teams, given that both the teams played 5 complete test matches?

Obviously, Team B would have performed much worse than Team A: For that matter, if I tell you that the average daytime high temperature of Lucknow was 18° C for a particular month, you can easily draw some kind of conclusion in your mind about the month we could possibly be talking about.

Thus, you should realize that the beauty of averages lies in the fact that it is one single number that tells you a lot about the group of numbers—hence, it is one number that represents an entire group of numbers.

But one of the key concepts that you need to understand before you move into the chapters of this block is the concept of WEIGHTED AVERAGES.

As always, the concept is best explained through a concrete example.

Suppose I had to buy a shirt and a trousers and let us say that the average cost of a shirt was ₹ 1200 while that of a trousers was ₹ 900.

*Contd*

In such a case, the average cost of a shirt and a trousers would be given by (1200 + 900)/2 = 1050.

This can be visualised on the number line as:

(midpoint) = answer

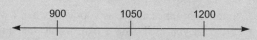

As you can easily see in the figure, the average occurs at the midpoint of the two numbers.

Now, let us try to modify the situation:

Suppose, I were to buy 2 trousers and 1 shirt. In such a case I would end up spending (900 + 900 + 1200) = ₹ 3000 in buying a total of 3 items. What would be my average in this case?

Obviously, 3000/3 = ₹ 1000!!

Clearly, the average has shifted!!

On the number line we could visualise this as follows:

(Answer)          (midpoint)

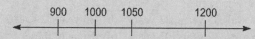

It is clearly visible that the average has shifted towards 900 (which was the cost price of the trousers—the larger purchased item.)

In a way, this shift is similar to the way a two pan weighing balance shifts on weights being put on it. The balance shifts towards the pan containing the larger weight.

Similarly, in this case, the correct average (1000) is closer to 900 than it is to 1200. This has happened because the number of elements in the group of average 900 is greater than the number of elements in the group having average 1200. Since, this is very similar to the system of weights, we call this as a weighted average situation.

At this stage, you should realise that weighted averages are not solely restricted to two groups. We can also come up with a weighted average situation for three groups (although in such a case the representation of the weighted average on the number line might not be so easily possible.) In fact, it is the number line representation of a weighted average situation that is defined as alligation (when 2 groups are involved).

## Pre-assessment Test

1. X's age is $1/10^{th}$ of Y's present age. Y's age will be thrice of Z's age after 10 years. If Z's eighth birthday was celebrated two years ago, then the present age of X must be
   (a) 5 years         (b) 10 years
   (c) 15 years        (d) 20 years

2. Dravid was twice as old as Rahul 10 years back. How old is Rahul today if Dravid will be 45 years old 15 years hence?
   (a) 20 years        (b) 10 years
   (c) 30 years        (d) None of these

3. A demographic survey of 100 families in which two parents were present revealed that the average age A, of the oldest child, is 15 years less than ½ the sum of the ages of the two parents. If X represents the age of one parent and Y the age of the other parent, then which of the following is equivalent to A?
   (a) $\dfrac{X+Y}{2} - 15$        (b) $\dfrac{X+Y}{2} + 15$

   (c) $\dfrac{X+Y}{2} - 15$        (d) $X + Y - 7.5$

4. If 10 years are subtracted from the present age of Randy and the remainder divided by 12, then you would get the present age of his grandson Sandy. If Sandy is 19 years younger to Sundy whose age is 24, then what is the present age of Randy?
   (a) 80 years        (b) 70 years
   (c) 60 years        (d) None of these

5. Two groups of students, whose average ages are 15 years and 25 years, combine to form a third group whose average age is 23 years. What is the ratio of the number of students in the first group to the number of students in the second group?
   (a) 8 : 2           (b) 2 : 8
   (c) 4 : 6           (d) None of these

6. A year ago, Mohit was four times his son's age. In six years, his age will be 9 more than twice his son's age. What is the present age of the son?
   (a) 10 years        (b) 9 years
   (c) 20 years        (d) None of these

7. In 1952, I was as old as the number formed by the last two digits of my birth year. When I mentioned this interesting coincidence to my grandfather, he surprised me by saying that the same applied to him also.
   The difference in our ages is:
   (a) 40 years        (b) 50 years
   (c) 60 years        (d) None of these

8. The average age of three boys is 18 years. If their ages are in the ratio 4:5:9, then the age of the youngest boy is
   (a) 8 years         (b) 9 years
   (c) 12 years        (d) 16 years

9. "I am eight times as old as you were when I was as old as you are", said a man to his son. Find out their present ages if the sum of their ages is 75 years.
   (a) 40 years and 35 years
   (b) 56 years and 19 years
   (c) 48 years and 27 years
   (d) None of these

10. My brother was 3 years of age when my sister was born, while my mother was 26 years of age when I was born. If my sister was 4 years of age when I was born, then what was the age of my father and mother respectively when my brother was born?
    (a) 35 years, 33 years   (b) 35 years, 29 years
    (c) 32 years, 23 years   (d) None of these

11. Namrata's father is now four times her age. In five years, he will be three times her age. In how many years, will he be twice her age?
    (a) 5               (b) 20
    (c) 25              (d) 15

12. A father is twice as old as his daughter. 20 years back, he was seven times as old as the daughter. What are their present ages?
    (a) 24, 12          (b) 44, 22
    (c) 48, 24          (d) none of these

13. The present ages of three persons are in the proportion of 5:8:7. Eight years ago, the sum of their ages was 76. Find the present age of the youngest person.
    (a) 20              (b) 25
    (c) 30              (d) None of these

14. The average age of a class is 14.8 years. The average age of the boys in the class is 15.4 years and that of girls is 14.4 years. What is the ratio of boys to girls in the class?
    (a) 1 : 2           (b) 3 : 2
    (c) 2 : 3           (d) None of these

15. In an organisation, the daily average wages of 20 illiterate employees is decreased from ₹ 25 to ₹ 10, thus the average salary of all the literate (educated) and illiterate employees is decreased by ₹ 10 per day. The number of educated employees working in the organisation are:
    (a) 15              (b) 20
    (c) 10              (d) 25

16. Mr. Akhilesh Bajpai while going from Lucknow to Jamshedpur covered half the distance by train at the speed of 96 km/hr, half the rest of the distance by his scooter at the speed of 60 km/hr and the remaining distance at the speed of 40 km/hr by car. The average speed at which he completed his journey is:
    (a) 64 km/hr      (b) 56 km/hr
    (c) 60 km/hr      (d) 36 km/hr

17. There are four types of candidates in MINDWORKZZ preparing for the CAT. The number of students of Engineering, Science, Commerce and Humanities is 400, 600, 500 and 300 respectively and the respective percentage of students who qualified the CAT is 80%, 75%, 60% and 50%, respectively the overall percentage of successful candidates in our institute is:
    (a) 67.77%      (b) 66.66%
    (c) 68.5%      (d) None of these

18. Mr. Jagmohan calculated the average of 10 'Three digit numbers'. But due to mistake he reversed the digits of a number and thus his average increased by 29.7. The difference between the unit digit and hundreds digit of that number is:
    (a) 4      (b) 3
    (c) 2      (d) can't be determined

**Directions for Questions 19 and 20:** Answer the questions based on the following Information.

Production pattern for number of units (in cubic feet) per day.

| Days | 1 | 2 | 3 | 4 | 5 | 6 | 7 |
|---|---|---|---|---|---|---|---|
| **Numbers of units** | 150 | 180 | 120 | 250 | 160 | 120 | 150 |

For a truck that can carry 2,000 cubic feet, hiring cost per day is ₹1,000. Storing cost per cubic feet is ₹5 per day. Any residual material left at the end of the seventh day has to be transferred.

19. If all the units should be sent to the market, then on which days should the trucks be hired to minimize the cost:
    (a) $2^{nd}$, $4^{th}$, $6^{th}$, $7^{th}$      (b) $7^{th}$
    (c) $2^{nd}$, $4^{th}$, $5^{th}$, $7^{th}$      (d) None of these

20. If the storage cost is reduced to ₹ 0.9 per cubic feet per day, then on which day/days, should the truck be hired?
    (a) $4^{th}$      (b) $7^{th}$
    (c) $4^{th}$ and $7^{th}$      (d) None of these

## ANSWER KEY

| | | | |
|---|---|---|---|
| 1. (a) | 2. (a) | 3. (a) | 4. (b) |
| 5. (b) | 6. (b) | 7. (b) | 8. (c) |
| 9. (c) | 10. (d) | 11. (b) | 12. (c) |
| 13. (b) | 14. (c) | 15. (c) | 16. (a) |
| 17. (a) | 18. (b) | 19. (a) | 20. (b) |

# Averages

## THEORY

The average of a number is a measure of the central tendency of a set of numbers. In other words, it is an estimate of where the center point of a set of numbers lies.

The basic formula for the average of $n$ numbers $x_1$, $x_2$, $x_3$, ... $x_n$ is

$A_n = (x_1 + x_2 + x_3 + ... + x_n)/n$ = (Total of set of $n$ numbers)/$n$

This also means $A_n \times n$ = total of the set of numbers.

The average is always calculated for a set of numbers.

**Concept of Weighted Average:** When we have two or more groups whose individual averages are known, then to find the combined average of all the elements of all the groups we use weighted average. Thus, if we have $k$ groups with averages $A_1$, $A_2$ ... $A_k$ and having $n_1$, $n_2$ ... $n_k$ elements then the weighted average is given by the formula:

$$A_w = \frac{n_1 A_1 + n_2 A_2 + n_3 A_3 + ... + n_k A_k}{n_1 + n_2 + n_3 + ... + n_k}$$

**Another Meaning of Average** The average [also known as *arithmetic mean* (AM)] of a set of numbers can also be defined as the number by which we can replace each and every number of the set without changing the total of the set of numbers.

**Properties of Average (AM)** The properties of averages [arithmetic mean] can be elucidated by the following examples:

**Example 1:** The average of 4 numbers 12, 13, 17 and 18 is:

**Solution:** Required average = (12 + 13 + 17 + 18)/4 = 60/4 = 15

This means that if each of the 4 numbers of the set were replaced by 15 each, there would be no change in the total.

This is an important way to look at averages. In fact, whenever you come across any situation where the average of a group of '$n$' numbers is given, you should visualise that there are '$n$' numbers, each of whose value is the average of the group. This view is a very important way to visualise averages.

This can be visualised as

$$12 \rightarrow +3 \rightarrow 15$$
$$13 \rightarrow +2 \rightarrow 15$$
$$17 \rightarrow -2 \rightarrow 15$$
$$\underline{18 \rightarrow -3 \rightarrow 15}$$
$$\overline{60 \rightarrow +0 \rightarrow 60}$$

**Example 2:** In Example 1, visualise addition of a fifth number, which increases the average by 1.

$$15 + 1 = 16$$
$$15 + 1 = 16$$
$$15 + 1 = 16$$
$$15 + 1 = 16$$

The +1 appearing 4 times is due to the fifth number, which is able to maintain the average of 16 first and then 'give one' to each of the first 4.

Hence, the fifth number in this case is 20.

**Example 3:** The average always lies above the lowest number of the set and below the highest number of the set.

**Example 4:** The net deficit due to the numbers below the average always equals the net surplus due to the numbers above the average.

**Example 5:** *Ages and averages:* If the average age of a group of persons is $x$ years today then after $n$ years their average age will be $(x + n)$.

Also, $n$ years ago their average age would have been $(x - n)$. This happens due to the fact that for a group of people, 1 year is added to each person's age every year.

**Example 6:** A man travels at 60 kmph on the journey from $A$ to $B$ and returns at 100 kmph. Find his average speed for the journey.

**Solution:**

> Average speed = (total distance)/(total time)

If we assume distance between 2 points to be $d$
Then

Average speed = $2d/[(d/60) + (d/100)] = (2 \times 60 \times 100)/(60 + 100) = (2 \times 60 \times 100)/160 = 75$

> Average speed = $(2S_1 \cdot S_2)/(S_1 + S_2)$
> [$S_1$ and $S_2$ are speeds]

of going and coming back, respectively.

**Short Cut** The average speed will always come out by the following process:
The ratio of speeds is $60 : 100 = 3 : 5$ (say $r_1 : r_2$)

*Space for Notes*

Then, divide the difference of speeds (40 in this case) by $r_1 + r_2$ ($3 + 5 = 8$, in this case) to get one part. (40/8 = 5, in this case)

The required answer will be three parts away (i.e. $r_1$ parts away) from the lower speed.

Check out how this works with the following speeds:

$$S_1 = 20 \quad \text{and} \quad S_2 = 40$$

**Step 1:** Ratio of speeds = $20 : 40 = 1 : 2$

**Step 2:** Divide difference of 20 into 3 parts ($r_1 + r_2$) → = $20/3 = 6.66$

Required average speed = $20 + 1 \times 6.66$

**Note:** This process is essentially based on alligations and we shall see it again in the next chapter.

## Exercise for Self-practice

Find the average speed for the above problem if

| | |
|---|---|
| (1) $S_1 = 20$ | $S_2 = 200$ |
| (2) $S_1 = 60$ | $S_2 = 120$ |
| (3) $S_1 = 100$ | $S_2 = 50$ |
| (4) $S_1 = 60$ | $S_2 = 180$ |

## WORKED-OUT PROBLEMS

**Problem 3.1** The average of a batsman after 25 innings was 56 runs per innings. If after the 26th inning his average increased by 2 runs, then what was his score in the 26th inning?

**Solution** *Normal process:*

Runs in 26th inning = Runs total after 26 innings – Runs total after 25 innings

$$= 26 \times 58 - 25 \times 56$$

For mental calculation use:

$$(56 + 2) \times 26 - 56 \times 25$$

$$= 2 \times 26 + (56 \times 26 - 56 \times 25)$$

$$= 52 + 56 = 108$$

**Short Cut** Since the average increases by 2 runs per innings it is equivalent to 2 runs being added to each score in the first 25 innings. Now, since these runs can only be added by the runs scored in the 26th inning, the score in the 26th inning must be $25 \times 2 = 50$ runs higher than the average after 26 innings (i.e. new average = 58).

Hence, runs scored in 26th inning = New Average + Old innings × Change in average

$$= 58 + 25 \times 2 = 108$$

Visualise this as

| Average in first 25 innings | Average after 26 innings |
|---|---|
| 56 | 58 |
| 56 | 58 |
| 56 | 58 |
| … | … |
| … | … |
| 25 times… | 26 times… |

Difference in total is two, 25 times and 58 once, that is, 58 $+ 25 \times 2$.

**Problem 3.2** The average age of a class of 30 students and a teacher reduces by 0.5 years if we exclude the teacher. If the initial average is 14 years, find the age of the class teacher.

**Solution** *Normal process:*

Age of teacher = Total age of (students + teacher)

– Total age of students

$$= 31 \times 14 - 30 \times 13.5$$

$$= 434 - 405$$

$$= 29 \text{ years}$$

**Short Cut** The teacher after fulfilling the average of 14 (for the group to which he belonged) is also able to give 0.5 years to the age of each of the 30 students. Hence, he has $30 \times 0.5 \rightarrow 15$ years to give over and above maintaining his own average age of 14 years.

Age of teacher = $14 + 30 \times 0.5 = 29$ years

(*Note:* This problem should be viewed as change of average from 13.5 to 14 when teacher is included.)

**Problem 3.3** The average marks of a group of 20 students on a test is reduced by 4 when the topper who scored 90 marks is replaced by a new student. How many marks did the new student have?

**Solution** *Normal process:*

Let initial average be $x$.

Then the initial total is $20x$

New average will be $(x - 4)$ and the new total will be $20 (x - 4) = 20x - 80$.

The reduction of 80 is created by the replacement.

Hence, the new student has 80 marks less than the student he replaces. Hence, he must have scored 10 marks.

**Short Cut** The replacement has the effect of reducing the average marks for each of the 20 students by 4. Hence, the replacement must be $20 \times 4 = 80$ marks below the original.

Hence, answer = 10 marks.

**Problem 3.4** The average marks of 3 students $A$, $B$ and $C$ is 48 marks. Another student $D$ joins the group and the new average becomes 44 marks. If another student $E$, who has 3 marks more than $D$, joins the group, the average of the 4 students $B$, $C$, $D$ and $E$ becomes 43 marks. Find how many marks $A$ got in the exam.

**Solution** Solve while reading. The first sentence gives you a total of 144 for $A$, $B$ and $C$'s marks. *Second sentence*: When $D$ joins the group, the total becomes $44 \times 4 = 176$. Hence $D$ must get 32 marks.

Alternatively, you can reach this point by considering the first 2 statements together as:

$D$'s joining the group reduces the average from 48 to 44 marks (i.e., 4 marks).

This means that to maintain the average of 44 marks, $D$ has to take 4 marks from $A$, 4 from $B$ and 4 from $C \rightarrow$ $A$ total of 12 marks. Hence, he must have got 32 marks.

From here:

The first part of the third sentence gives us information about $E$ getting 3 marks more than 32 → Hence, $E$ gets 35 marks.

Now, it is further stated that when $A$ is replaced by $E$, the average marks of the students reduces by 1 to 43.

Mathematically this can be shown as

$A + B + C + D = 44 \times 4 = 176$ while, $B + C + D + E$

$$= 43 \times 4 = 172$$

Subtracting the two equations, we get $A - E = 4$ marks. Hence, $A$ would have got 39 marks.

Alternatively, you can think of this as:

The replacement of $A$ with $E$ results in the reduction of 1 mark from each of the 4 people who belong to the group. Hence, the difference is 4 marks. Hence, $A$ would get 4 marks more than $E$ i.e., A gets 39 marks.

**Problem 3.5**  The mean temperature of Monday to Wednesday was 27 °C and of Tuesday to Thursday was 24 °C. If the temperature on Thursday was 2/3rd of the temperature on Monday, what was the temperature on Thursday?

**Solution**  From the first sentence, we get that the total from Monday to Wednesday was 81 while from Tuesday to Thursday was 72. The difference is arising out of the replacement of Monday by Thursday.

This can be mathematically written as

$$\text{Mon} + \text{Tue} + \text{Wed} = 81 \qquad (1)$$

$$\text{Tue} + \text{Wed} + \text{Thu} = 72 \qquad (2)$$

Hence,            $\text{Mon} - \text{Thu} = 9$

We have two unknown variables in the above equation. To solve for 2 unknowns, we need a new equation. Looking back at the problem we get the equation:

$$\text{Thu} = (2/3) \times \text{Mon}$$

Solving the two equations we get: Thursday = 18 °C.

However, in the exam, you should avoid using equation-solving as much as possible. You should, ideally, be able to reach half way through the solution during the first reading of the question, and then meet the gap through the use of options.

The answer to this problem should be got by the time you finish reading the question for the first time.

Thus suppose we have the equations:
$M - T = 9$ and $T = 2M/3$ or $T/M = 2/3$ and have the options for $T$ as

(a)  12            (b)  15

(c)  18            (d)  27

To check which of these options is the appropriate value, we need to check one by one.

Option (a) gives $T = 12$, then we have $M = 21$. But $12/21 \neq 2/3$. Hence, this is not the correct option.

Option (b) gives $T = 15$, then $M = 24$. But again $15/24 \neq 2/3$. Hence, this is not the correct option.

Option (c) gives $T = 18$, then $M = 27$. Now $18/27 = 2/3$. Hence, this is the correct option.

So we no longer need to check for option (d).

However, if we had checked for option (d) then $T = 27$, so $M = 36$. But again $27/36 \neq 2/3$. Hence, this is not the correct option.

In the above, we used 'solving-while-reading' and 'option-based' approaches.

These two approaches are very important and by combining the two, you can reach amazing speeds in solving the question.

You are advised to practice both these approaches while solving questions, which will surely improve your efficiency and speed. You will see that, with practice, you will be able to arrive at the solution to most of the LOD I problems (given later in this chapter) even as you finish reading the questions. And since it is the LOD I level problems that appear in most examinations (like IIFT, SNAP, NMAT, CLAT, CET, BANK PO, SSC, BBA/BMS entrance etc) you will gain a significant advantage in solving these problems.

On LOD II, LOD III and CAT type problems, you will find that using solving-while-reading and option-based approaches together would take you through anywhere between 30 and 70% of the question by the time you finish reading the question for the first time.

This will give you a tremendous time advantage over the other students appearing in the examination.

**Problem 3.6**  A person covers half his journey by train at 60 kmph, the remainder half by bus at 30 kmph and the rest by cycle at 10 kmph. Find his average speed during the entire journey.

**Solution**  Recognise that the journey by bus and that by cycle are of equal distance. Hence, we can use the short cut illustrated earlier to solve this part of the problem.

Using the process explained above, we get average speed of the second half of the journey as

$$10 + 1 \times 5 = 15 \text{ kmph}$$

Then we employ the same technique for the first part and get

$$15 + 1 \times 9 = 24 \text{ kmph (Answer)}$$

**Problem 3.7**  A school has only 3 classes that contain 10, 20 and 30 students, respectively. The pass percentage of these classes are 20%, 30% and 40% respectively. Find the pass percentage of the entire school.

## Solution

Using weighted average: $\dfrac{10 \times 0.2 + 20 \times 0.3 + 30 \times 0.4}{10 + 20 + 30}$

$= \dfrac{20}{60} = 33.33\%$

Alternatively, we can also use solving-while-reading as

*Space for Rough Work*

Recognise that the pass percentage would be given by

$$\dfrac{\text{Passed students}}{\text{Total students}}$$

As soon as you get into the second line of the question get back to the first sentence and get the total number of passed students = 2 + 6 + 12 and you are through with the problem.

## LEVEL OF DIFFICULTY (I)

1. The average of the first fifteen natural numbers is
   (a) 8.5      (b) 7.5
   (c) 6.5      (d) 8

2. The average of the first ten whole numbers is
   (a) 4.5      (b) 5
   (c) 5.5      (d) 4

3. The average of the first ten even numbers is
   (a) 18      (b) 22
   (c) 9      (d) 11

4. The average of the first ten odd numbers is
   (a) 11      (b) 10
   (c) 17      (d) 9

5. The average of the first ten prime numbers is
   (a) 15.5      (b) 12.5
   (c) 10      (d) 12.9

6. The average of the first ten composite numbers is
   (a) 12.9      (b) 11
   (c) 11.2      (d) 10

7. The average of the first ten prime numbers, which are odd, is
   (a) 12.9      (b) 13.8
   (c) 17      (d) 15.8

8. The average age of 13 boys and the principal is 10 years. When the principal's age is excluded, the average age decreases by 2 year. What is the age of the principal?
   (a) 34      (b) 36
   (c) 38      (d) 40

9. The average weight of 3 boys $A$, $B$ and $C$ is 74 kg. Another boy $D$ joins the group and the average now becomes 70 kg. If another boy $E$, whose weight is 3 kg more than that of $D$, replaces $A$ then the average weight of $B$, $C$, $D$ and $E$ becomes 75 kg. The weight of $A$ is
   (a) 40 kg      (b) 42 kg
   (c) 49 kg      (d) 41 kg

10. The mean temperature of Monday to Wednesday was 35 °C and of Tuesday to Thursday was 30 °C. If the temperature on Thursday was ½ that of Monday, the temperature on Thursday was
    (a) 30 °C      (b) 15 °C
    (c) 20 °C      (d) 25 °C

11. Five years ago, the average age of $A$, $B$ and $C$ was 25 years and that of $B$ and $C$ 10 years ago was 20 years. $A$'s present age is
    (a) 30 years      (b) 35 years
    (c) 40 years      (d) 48 years

12. Ganguly has a certain average for 4 innings. In the 5th inning, he scores 40 runs thereby increasing his average by 4 runs. His new average is
    (a) 20      (b) 24
    (c) 28      (d) 32

13. The average of the first six multiples of 5 is
    (a) 18.50      (b) 21
    (c) 28      (d) 17.50

14. There are three fractions $A$, $B$ and $C$. If $A = 1/5$ and $B = 1/8$ and the average of $A$, $B$ and $C$ is $1/10$. What is the value of $C$?
    (a) $-1/20$      (b) $-1/60$
    (c) $-1/30$      (d) $-1/40$

15. The marks obtained by Alan in Mathematics, English and Biology are respectively 90 out of 100, 70 out of 150 and 150 out of 200. Find his average score in percent.
    (a) 87.83      (b) 68.88
    (c) 76.33      (d) 77.33

16. The average monthly expenditure of a family was 2250 for the first 3 months, ₹2150 for the next three months and ₹ 5750 for the next three months. Find the average income of the family for the 9 months, if they save ₹500 per month.
    (a) ₹3866.66      (b) ₹3883.33
    (c) ₹3666.66      (d) ₹3222.66

17. The average age of a family of 5 members is 20 years. If the age of the youngest member be 5 years, what was the average age of the family at the birth of the youngest member?
    (a) 15.25      (b) 18.75
    (c) 21.25      (d) 12.50

18. The average age of 5 persons in a group is increased by 10 years when two men aged 30 years and 40 years are substituted by two women. Find the average age (in years) of the two women.
    (a) 60      (b) 65
    (c) 51      (d) 62

19. The average temperature for Wednesday, Thursday and Friday was 20 °C. The average for Thursday, Friday and Saturday was 21 °C. If the temperature on Saturday was 22 °C, what was the temperature on Wednesday?
    (a) 19 °C      (b) 24 °C
    (c) 18 °C      (d) 21 °C

20. The speed of the train in going from Kanpur to Lucknow is 60 km/hr while when coming back from Lucknow to Kanpur, its speed is 40 km/hr. Find the average speed (in km/hr) during the whole journey.
    (a) 45      (b) 48
    (c) 50      (d) 46

21. The average weight of a class of 19 students is 20 kg. If the weight of the teacher be included, the average rises by 1 kg. What is the weight of the teacher?
    (a) 40 kg          (b) 50 kg
    (c) 45 kg          (d) 55 kg

22. The average of 3 numbers is 20 and that of the first two is 25. Find the third number.
    (a) 15             (b) 10
    (c) 20             (d) 12

23. The average weight of 29 men in a ship is increased by 5 kg when one of the men, who weighs 120 kg, is replaced by a new man. Find the weight of the new man (In kg)
    (a) 265            (b) 205
    (c) 245            (d) 240

24. The age of A and B is in the ratio 1: 3. After 10 years, the ratio of their ages will become 1:2. Find the average of their ages after 20 years.
    (a) 22             (b) 40
    (c) 37             (d) 30

25. Find the average of the first 100 natural numbers.
    (a) 50.50          (b) 52.50
    (c) 51.50          (d) 49

26. Find the average of all prime numbers between 20 and 50.
    (a) 35.8           (b) 34.65
    (c) 35.85          (d) 31.8

27. If we take four numbers, the average of the first three is 20 and that of the last three is 25. If the last number is 30, the first number is
    (a) 20             (b) 21
    (c) 23             (d) 15

28. The average of 15 results is 40 and that of 25 more results is 48. For all the results taken together, the average is
    (a) 45             (b) 42
    (c) 46             (d) 44

29. The average of 7 consecutive numbers is 21. The highest of these numbers will be
    (a) 20             (b) 23
    (c) 24             (d) 22

30. The average age of 8 students is 11 years. If 2 more students of age 15 and 17 years join, their average will become
    (a) 13 years       (b) 12 years
    (c) 14 years       (d) 15 years

31. The average of 9 numbers is 14. If each number is increased by 4, the new average will be
    (a) 16             (b) 15
    (c) 18             (d) 17

32. The average of 11 consecutive numbers is $n$. If the next two numbers are also included, the average will.
    (a) increase by 1  (b) remain the same
    (c) increase by 1.4 (d) increase by 2

33. The average of 40 numbers is 45. If two numbers, namely, 65 and 25 are discarded, the average of the remaining numbers is
    (a) 35             (b) 45
    (c) 40             (d) 43

34. The average of 15 numbers is 18. If each number is multiplied by 9, then the average of the new set of numbers is
    (a) 162            (b) 152
    (c) 144            (d) 164

35. In a family of 5 males and a few ladies, the average monthly consumption of grain per head is 9 kg. If the average monthly consumption per head be 12 kg in the case of males and 8 kg in the case of females, find the number of females in the family.
    (a) 18             (b) 12
    (c) 9              (d) 15

36. Average marks obtained by a student in 3 papers is 63 and in the fourth paper he obtains 67 marks. Find his new average.
    (a) 54             (b) 62
    (c) 64             (d) 65

37. The average earning of Srikanth for the initial three months of the calendar year 2012 is ₹2100. If his average earning (in ₹) for the second and third month is ₹2250 find his earning in the first month?
    (a) 1950           (b) 1500
    (c) 1700           (d) 1800

38. In a hotel where rooms are numbered from 201 to 230, each room gives an earning of ₹2000 for the first fifteen days of a month and for the latter half, ₹1000 per room. Find the average earning per room per day (in ₹) over the month. (Assume 30 day month)
    (a) 1450           (b) 1500
    (c) 1750           (d) 1666.66

39. The average weight of 10 men is decreased by 2 kg when, one of them weighing 140 kg is replaced by another person. Find the weight of the new person.
    (a) 142 kg         (b) 130 kg
    (c) 138 kg         (d) 120 kg

40. The average age of a group of men is increased by 6 years when a person aged 26 years is replaced by a new person of aged 56 years. How many men are there in the group?
    (a) 3              (b) 4
    (c) 5              (d) 6

41. The average score of a cricketer in three matches is 33 runs and in two other matches, it is 23 runs. Find the average in all the five matches.
    (a) 31             (b) 26
    (c) 29             (d) 28

42. The average of 15 papers is 50. The average of the first 8 papers is 48 and of the last eight papers is 54. Find the marks obtained in the 8th paper.

(a) 66      (b) 64
(c) 58      (d) 56

43. The average age of the Indian cricket team playing the Coimbatore test is 28. The average age of 5 of the players is 26 and that of another set of 5 players, totally different from the first five, is 29. If it is the captain who was not included in either of these two groups, then find the age of the captain.
   (a) 35      (b) 30
   (c) 33      (d) 28

44. Siddhartha has earned an average of 3200 dollars for the first eleven months of the year. If he justifies his staying on in the US on the basis of his ability to earn at least 4000 dollars per month for the entire year, how much should he earn (in dollars) in the last month to achieve his required average for the whole year?
   (a) 11,800      (b) 12,800
   (c) 10,800      (d) 13,800

45. A bus goes to Ranchi from Patna at the rate of 80 km per hour. Another bus leaves Ranchi for Patna at the same time as the first bus at the rate of 90 km per hour. Find the average speed for the journeys of the two buses combined if it is known that the distance from Ranchi to Patna is 720 kilometres.
   (a) 84.705 kmph      (b) 84 kmph
   (c) 81.63 kmph      (d) 82.82 kmph

46. A train travels 12 km in the first quarter of an hour, 15 km in the second quarter and 30 km in the third quarter. Find the average speed of the train per hour over the entire journey.
   (a) 76 km/h      (b) 72 km/h
   (c) 77 km/h      (d) 73 km/h

47. The average weight of 6 men is 58.5 kg. If it is known that Ram and Tram weigh 65 kg each, find the average weight of the others.
   (a) 55 kg      (b) 54.25 kg
   (c) 54 kg      (d) 55.25 kg

48. The average score of a class of 30 students is 56. What will be the average score of the rest of the students if the average score of 10 of the students is 59.
   (a) 52.5      (b) 54.5
   (c) 52      (d) 53

49. The average age of 60 students of IIM, Bangalore of the 2005 batch is 23 years. What will be the new average if we include the 40 faculty members whose average age is 35 years?
   (a) 27 years      (b) 26.5 years
   (c) 27.8 years      (d) 28 years

50. Out of three numbers, the first is twice the second and three times the third. The average of the three numbers is 132. The smallest number is
   (a) 36      (b) 72
   (c) 42      (d) 48

51. The sum of three numbers is 147. If the ratio between the first and second is $2:3$ and that between the second and the third is $5:8$, then the second number is
   (a) 30      (b) 45
   (c) 72      (d) 48

52. The average height of 40 girls out of a class of 50 is 150 cm and that of the remaining girls is 155 cm. The average height of the whole class is
   (a) 151 cm      (b) 152 cm
   (c) 156 cm      (d) 153 cm

53. The average weight of 6 persons is increased by 1.5 kg when one of them, whose weight is 60 kg is replaced by a new man. The weight of the new man is
   (a) 71 kg      (b) 72 kg
   (c) 68 kg      (d) 69 kg

54. The average age of three boys is 24 years. If their ages are in the ratio 2:5:5, the age of the youngest boy is
   (a) 16 years      (b) 11 years
   (c) 21 years      (d) 12 years

55. The average age of $P$, $Q$, $R$ and $S$ four years ago was 46 years. By including $M$, the present average age of all the five is 51 years. The present age of $M$ is
   (a) 52 years      (b) 49 years
   (c) 55 years      (d) 58 years

56. The average salary of 30 workers in an office is ₹ 1800 per month. If the manager's salary is added, the average salary becomes ₹ 1900 per month. What is the manager's annual salary?
   (a) ₹ 48000      (b) ₹ 58,800
   (c) ₹ 46,800      (d) None of these

57. If $p$, $q$, $r$, $s$ and $t$ are five consecutive even numbers, then their average is
   (a) $(p+q+r+s+t)$      (b) $(p\,q\,r\,s\,t)/5$
   (c) $5(p+q+r+s+t)$      (d) None of these

58. The average of first five multiples of 7 is
   (a) 21      (b) 28
   (c) 14      (d) 18

59. The average weight of a class of 30 students is 50 kg. If the weight of the teacher be included, the average weight increases by 500 gm. The weight of the teacher is
   (a) 50.5 kg      (b) 65.5 kg
   (c) 62.5 kg      (d) 60.5 kg

60. In a management entrance test, a student scores 3 marks for every correct answer and loses 1 mark for every wrong answer. A student attempts all the 100 questions and scores 160 marks. The number of questions he answered correctly was
   (a) 62      (b) 64
   (c) 65      (d) 68

61. The average age of five children is 7 years, which is increased by 5 years when the age of the father is included. Find the age of the father.
    (a) 32  (b) 37
    (c) 39  (d) 35

62. The average weight of a class of 20 students is 50 kg. If, however, the weight of the teacher is included, the average becomes 51 kg. The weight of the teacher is
    (a) 69 kg  (b) 72 kg
    (c) 70 kg  (d) 71 kg

63. Ram bought 2 toys for ₹ 5.50 each, 3 toys for ₹ 3.66 each and 6 toys for ₹ 1.833 each. The average price per toy is (in ₹)
    (a) 3  (b) 10
    (c) 5  (d) 9

64. 40 oranges and 65 apples were purchased for ₹ 480. If the price per apple was ₹ 4, then the average price of oranges was (in ₹)
    (a) 5.5  (b) 6.5
    (c) 6  (d) 7

65. The average income of Aditya and Vikas is ₹ 4,000 and that of Sudhir and Raunak is ₹ 2500. What is the average income of Aditya, Vikas, Sudhir and Raunak (in ₹)?
    (a) 3150  (b) 3250
    (c) 3350  (d) 3550

66. A batsman made an average of 55 runs in 4 innings, but in the fifth inning, he was out on zero. What is the average after the fifth inning?
    (a) 54  (b) 64
    (c) 44  (d) 49

67. The average weight of 50 teachers of a school is 70 kg. If, however, the weight of the principal be included, the average decreases by 0.5 kg. What is the weight of the principal?
    (a) 44.5 kg  (b) 45 kg
    (c) 43.5 kg  (d) None of these

68. The average temperature of 4th, 5th and 6th December was 25.6 °C. The average temperature of the first two days was 27 °C. The temperature on the 6th of December was:
    (a) 22.2 °C  (b) 22.8 °C
    (c) 26.4 °C  (d) None of these

69. The average age of Gita and Sita is 30 years. Their average age 4 years hence will be
    (a) 30 years  (b) 26 years
    (c) 28 years  (d) 34 years

70. Three years ago, the average age of a family of 6 members was 18 years. A baby having been born, the average of the family is the same today. What is the age of the baby?
    (a) 1 year  (b) 2 years
    (c) 3 years  (d) 0 years

71. Ramu's average daily expenditure is ₹ 21 during July, ₹24 during August and ₹11 during September. His approximate daily expenditure for the 3 months is
    (a) ₹18  (b) ₹18.75
    (c) ₹17  (d) ₹18.25

72. A ship sails out to a mark at the rate of 25 km per hour and sails back at the rate of 30 km/h. What is its average rate of sailing?
    (a) 27.27 km  (b) 23.24 km
    (c) 25.85 km  (d) 28.45 km

73. The average temperature on Monday, Tuesday and Wednesday was 52 °C and on Tuesday, Wednesday and Thursday it was 50 °C. If on Thursday it was exactly 49 °C, then on Monday, the temperature was
    (a) 55°C  (b) 56 °C
    (c) 53 °C  (d) 51°C

74. The average of 15 results is 20 out of which the first 5 results are having an average of 10. The average of the rest 10 results is
    (a) 50  (b) 40
    (c) 20  (d) 25

75. A man had ten children. When their average age was 15 years a child aged 6 years died. The average age of the remaining 9 children is
    (a) 16 years  (b) 13 years
    (c) 17 years  (d) 15 years

76. The average income of Hari and Prasad is ₹200. The average income of Rahul and Ravi is ₹ 250. The average income of Hari, Prasad, Rahul and Ravi is
    (a) ₹275  (b) ₹ 225
    (c) ₹450  (d) ₹250

77. The average weight of 40 students is 40 kg. If the teacher of weight 122 kg is also included, then the average weight will become:
    (a) 41 kg  (b) 42 kg
    (c) 40 kg  (d) 45 kg

78. The average of $a$, $b$ and c is 25. $a$ is as much more than the average as $b$ is less than the average. Find the value of $c$.
    (a) 45  (b) 25
    (c) 35  (d) 15

79. Find the average of four numbers $2\frac{3}{4}, 4\frac{4}{5} \cdot 5\frac{1}{5}, 3\frac{3}{4}$
    (a) 4.125  (b) 3.20
    (c) 1.60  (d) None of these.

80. The average salary per head of all the workers in a company is ₹9000. The average salary of 15 officers is ₹5000 and the average salary per head of the rest is ₹10,000. Find the total number of workers in the company.
    (a) 75  (b) 80
    (c) 50  (d) 40

81. The average age of 10 men is increased by 3 years when one of them, whose age is 54 years is replaced by a woman. What is the age of the woman?
    (a) 68 years          (b) 82 years
    (c) 72 years          (d) 84 years

82. The average monthly expenditure of Aman was ₹ 100 during the first 3 months, ₹ 200 during the next 4 months and ₹ 400 during the subsequent five months of the year. If the total saving during the year was ₹3000, find Aman's average monthly income (to the closest rupee)
    (a) 508          (b) 515
    (c) 1033          (d) 425

83. Ram bought 2 articles for ₹5.50 each, and 3 articles for ₹3.50 each, and 3 articles for ₹5.50 and 5 articles for ₹ 1.50 each. The average price for one article is
    (a) ₹3          (b) ₹ 8.50
    (c) ₹3.50          (d) None of these.

84. In a bag, there are 150 coins of ₹1, 50 p and 25 p denominations. If the total value of coins is ₹150, then find how many rupees can be constituted by 50 p coins.
    (a) 16          (b) 20
    (c) 28          (d) None of these

85. What is the average of the first seven natural number multiples of 11?

86. The age of two friends Aman and Baman is in the ratio 1:2. After 5 years, the ratio of their ages will become 3:5. Find the average of their ages after 10 years.

87. If we take four numbers, the average of the first three is 20 and that of the last three is 10. If the first number is 20, the last number is:

88. Sachin has a batting average of 40 runs per innings in 15 ODIs. It was found that in the 2 ODI match series against South Africa (which were part of his first 15 ODIs), his average score was 40 and not 80. His correct average is:

89. The average of temperatures at noontime from Monday to Friday is 40; the lowest one is 35. What is the possible maximum temperature at noontime on any of these days?

90. The average age of a family of 3 members is 30 years. If the age of the youngest member is 5 years, then what was the average age of the family immediately prior to the birth of the youngest member?

91. The average of 50 numbers is zero. Of them, at the most, how many may be greater than zero?

92. The average of 40 numbers is 25. If two numbers namely 40 and 50 are discarded, the average of the remaining numbers is:

93. The average of ten numbers is 60. The average of the first five numbers is 50 and that of last four numbers is 30. Then the 6th number is:

94. The average of 10 integers is found to be 10. But after the calculation, it was detected that, by mistake, the integer 20 was copied as 30, while calculating the average. After the due correction is made, the new average will be:

*Space for Rough Work*

# LEVEL OF DIFFICULTY (II)

1. A bus travels with a speed of 10 km/h in the first 15 minutes, goes 5 km in the next 15 minutes, 15 km in the next 15, 10 km in the next 15. What is the average speed of the bus in kilometre per hour for the journey described?
   (a) 45 kmph      (b) 32.50 kmph
   (c) 50.50 kmph   (d) 40 kmph

2. With an average speed of 25 km/h, a train reaches its destination in time. If it goes with an average speed of 20 km/h, it is late by 1 hour. The length of the total journey is
   (a) 90 km        (b) 100 km
   (c) 120 km       (d) 80 km

3. In the month of January of a certain year, the average daily expenditure of an organisation was ₹60. For the first 15 days of the month, the average daily expenditure was ₹ 80 and for the last 17 days, ₹50. Find the amount spent by the organisation on the 15th of the month.
   (a) 190          (b) 160
   (c) 180          (d) 130

4. One-fifth of a certain journey is covered at the rate of 20 km/h, one-fourth at the rate of 50 km/h and the rest at 55 km/h. Find the average speed for the whole journey.
   (a) 53 km/h      (b) 40 km/h
   (c) 35 km/h      (d) 38 km/h

5. A batsman makes a score of 40 runs in the $5^{th}$ inning and thus increases his average by 4. Find the possible value of the new average.
   (a) 28           (b) 24
   (c) 12           (d) 20

6. Aman can type a sheet in 10 minutes, Baman in 20 minutes and Chaman in 30 minutes. The average number of sheets typed per hour per typist for all three typists is
   (a) 11/3         (b) 30/7
   (c) 55/9         (d) 32/11

7. Find the average increase rate (per annum) if increase in the population in the first year is 10% and that in the second year is 20%.
   (a) 11           (b) 16
   (c) 20           (d) 18

8. The average income of a person for the first 5 days of a month is ₹20, for the next 10 days it is ₹24, for the next 10 days it is ₹ 30 and for the remaining days of the month it is ₹ 10. Find the average income (in ₹) per day.

9. In hotel Clarks, the rooms are numbered from 101 to 150 on the first floor, 201 to 240 on the second floor and 316 to 355 on the third floor. In the month of May 2018, the room occupancy was 50% on the first floor, 50% on the second floor and 30% on the third floor. If it is also known that the room charges are ₹ 2000, ₹1000 and ₹1500 on each of the floors, then find the average income per room (in ₹) for the month of May 2017.
   (a) 676.92       (b) 880.18
   (c) 783.3        (d) 650.7

10. A salesman gets a bonus according to the following structure: If he sells articles worth ₹x then he gets a bonus of ₹(x/10 – 1000). In the month of January, his sales value was ₹10000, in February it was ₹12000, from March to November it was ₹30000 for every month and in December it was ₹12000. Apart from this, he also receives a basic salary of ₹3000 per month from his employer. Find his average income per month (in ₹) during the year.
    (a) 4533        (b) 4517
    (c) 4532        (d) 4668

11. The average of 61 results is 43. If the average of the first 48 results is 36 and that of the last 12 is 49. Find the 49th result.
    (a) 302         (b) 307
    (c) 304         (d) 328

12. A man covers half of his journey by train at 50 km/hr, half of the remainder by bus at 25 km/h and the rest by cycle at 5 km/h. Find his average speed during the entire journey.
    (a) 100/7 kmph  (b) 25/3 kmph
    (c) 14 kmph     (d) 18 kmph

13. In 2010, Sachin Tendulkar, the Indian cricketer, scored 900 runs for his county at an average of 30, in 2011, he scored 950 runs at an average of 30.65; in 2012, 1300 runs at an average of 32.50 and in 2013, 1100 runs at an average of 35.49. What was his county average for the four years?
    (a) 34.23       (b) 32.19
    (c) 33.88       (d) 30.98

14. The average weight of 10 men is decreased by 5 kg when, one of them weighing 100 kg is replaced by another person. This new person is again replaced by another person, whose weight is 10 kg lower than the person he replaced. What is the overall change in the average due to this dual change?

(a) 30           (b) 35
(c) 25           (d) Cannot be determined

(a) 5 kg      (b) 6 kg
(c) 12 kg      (d) 15 kg

15. Find the average weight of four packets, if it is known that the weight of the first packet is 20 kg and the weights of the second, third and fourth packets' each is defined by $f(x) = x^2 - \dfrac{2}{5} \times (x^2)$ where $x = 10$.

(a) 50 kg      (b) 90 kg
(c) 70 kg      (d) 40 kg

16. There are five boxes in a box hold. The weight of the first box is 40 kg and the weight of the second box is 50% higher than the weight of the third box, whose weight is 25% higher than the first boxes' weight. The fourth box at 150 kg is 50% heavier than the fifth box. Find the difference in the average weight of the four heaviest boxes and the four lightest boxes.

(a) 21.5 kg      (b) 25 kg
(c) 27.5 kg      (d) 22.5 kg

17. For Question 16, find the difference in the average weight of the heaviest three and the lightest three.

(a) 66.66 kg      (b) 25 kg
(c) 50 kg      (d) 53.33 kg

18. 20 persons went to a hotel for a combined dinner party. 15 of them spent ₹ 90 each on their dinner and the rest spent ₹ 30 more than the average expenditure of all the 20. What was the total money spent (in ₹) by them?

(a) 1700      (b) 2000
(c) 2200      (d) None of these

19. There were 30 students in a hostel. Due to the admission of 20 new students, the expenses of the mess increase by ₹1600 per day while the average expenditure per head diminished by ₹8. What was the original expenditure of the mess?

(a) 3000      (b) 1600
(c) 2000      (d) 1200

20. The average price of 3 precious diamond studded platinum thrones is ₹ 97610498312. If their prices are in the ratio 4:7:9. The price of the cheapest is

(a) 5, 65, 66, 298.972    (b) 5, 85, 66, 29, 8987.2
(c) 58, 56, 62, 889.72    (d) None of these

21. The average weight of 23boxes is 3kg. If the weight of the container (in which the boxes are kept) is included, the calculated average weight per box increases by 1 kg. What is the weight of the container?

(a) 26 kg      (b) 4 kg
(c) 5 kg      (d) None of these

22. A man covers 1/4th of his journey by cycle at 40 km/h, the ½ of the remaining by car at 20 km/h, and the rest by walking at 10 km/h. Find his average speed during the whole journey.

(a) 16 kmph      (b) 15 kmph
(c) 18 kmph      (d) 17 kmph

23. The average age of a group of 15 persons is 25 years and 5 months. Two persons, each 40 years old, left the group. What will be the average age of the remaining persons in the group?

(a) 23.17 years      (b) 24.25 years
(c) 25.35 years      (d) 25 years

24. The average salary of the entire staff in an department is ₹2000 per month. The average salary of officers is ₹ 3000 and that of non-officers is ₹ 1500. If the number of officers is 10, then find the number of non-officers in the office?

(a) 20      (b) 25
(c) 15      (d) 10

25. $\sum_{r=1}^{n}(n+1)r$, where $r = n$.

(a) $\dfrac{[(n-1)n(n+1)]}{2}$      (b) $\dfrac{[n(n+1)^2]}{2}$

(c) $\dfrac{n(n-1)^2}{2}$      (d) $\dfrac{n^2}{2}$

26. The average of '$n$' numbers is $z$. If the number $x$ is replaced by the number $x^1$, then the average becomes $z^1$. Find the relation between $n$, $z$, $z^1$, $x$ and $x^1$.

(a) $\left[\dfrac{z^1-2}{x^1-x}=\dfrac{1}{n}\right]$      (b) $\left[\dfrac{x^1-x}{z^1}=\dfrac{1}{n}\right]$

(c) $\left[\dfrac{z-z^1}{x-x^1}=\dfrac{1}{n}\right]$      (d) $\left[\dfrac{x-x^1}{z-z^1}=\dfrac{1}{n}\right]$

27. A person travels three equal distances at a speed of $x$ km/h, $y$ km/h and $z$ km/h respectively. What will be the average speed during the whole journey?

(a) $xyz/(xy + yz + zx)$    (b) $(xy + yz + zx)/xyz$
(c) $3xyz/(xy + yz + xz)$    (d) None of these

**Directions for questions 28 to 30:** Read the following passage and answer the questions that follow.

Aman, Binod, Charan, Dharam and Ehsaan are the members of the same family. Each and everyone loves one another very much. Their birthdays are in different months and on different dates. *Aman* remembers that his birthday is between 25th and 30th, of *Binod* it is between 20th and 25th, of *Charan* it is between 10th and 20th, of *Dharam* it is between 5th and 10th and of *Ehsaan* it is between 1st to 5th of the month. The sum of the date of birth is defined as the addition of the date and the month, for example 12th January will be written as 12/1 and will add to a sum of the date of 13. (Between 25th and 30th includes both 25 and 30).

28. What may be the maximum average of their sum of the dates of birth?

(a) 24.6      (b) 15.2
(c) 28      (d) 32

29. What may be the minimum average of their sum of the dates of births?

(a) 24.6      (b) 15.2

(c) 28      (d) 32

30. If it is known that the dates of birth of three of them are even numbers then find maximum average of their sum of the dates of birth.

(a) 24.6      (b) 15.2

(c) 27.6      (d) 28

31. If the dates of birth, of four of them are prime numbers, then find the maximum average of the sum of their dates of birth.

(a) 27.2      (b) 26.4

(c) 28      (d) None of these

32. The average age of a group of persons going for a movie is 20 years. 10 new persons with an average age of 10 years join the group on the spot due to which the average of the group becomes 18 years. Find the number of persons initially going for the movie.

(a) 20      (b) 40

(c) 50      (d) 30

33. An engineering college has only four batches that contain 20, 40, 60 and 80 students respectively. The pass percentage of these classes, are 10%, 20%, 30% and 40% respectively. Find the pass percentage of the entire college.

(a) 50%      (b) 70%

(c) 30%      (d) 60%

34. Find the average of $f(x)$, $g(x)$, $h(x)$, $d(x)$ at $x = 1$. $f(x)$ is equal to $x^3 + 12$, $g(x) = 15x^3 - 10$, $h(x) = \log 10x^2$ and $d(x) = x^2$

(a) 5      (b) 10

(c) 4      (d) 7

35. In question 34 find the average of $f(x) - g(x)$, $g(x) - h(x)$, $h(x) - d(x)$, $d(x) - f(x)$ at $x = 1$

(a) 0      (b) −2

(c) 5      (d) None of these.

36. The average salary of employees in TCP is ₹20,000, the average salary of managers being ₹40,000 and the management trainees being ₹5000. The total number of workers could be

(a) 350      (b) 300

(c) 100      (d) 500

**Directions for questions 37 to 40:** Read the following and answer the questions that follows.

During the final match of ICC championship 2000, India playing against Australia scored in the following manner:

| Partnership | Runs scored |
| --- | --- |
| 1st wicket | 62 |
| 2nd wicket | 48 |
| 3rd wicket | 32 |
| 4th wicket | 62 |
| 5th wicket | 26 |
| 6th wicket | 13 |

37. Find the average runs scored by the first four batsmen.

(a) 83.5      (b) 60.5

(c) 66.8      (d) Cannot be determined

38. The maximum average runs scored by the first five batsmen could be

(a) 48.6      (b) 36.8

(c) 46      (d) Cannot be determined.

39. The minimum average runs scored by the last five batsmen to get out could be

(a) 13.6      (b) 24.4

(c) 36.8      (d) 0

40. If the fifth down batsman gets out for a duck, then find the average runs scored by the first six batsmen.

(a) 27.1      (b) 33.3

(c) 28.5      (d) Cannot be determined

41. The weight of a metal piece as calculated by the average of 7 different experiments is 53.735 gm. The average of the first three experiments is 54.005 gm, of the fourth is 0.004 gm greater than the fifth, while the average of the sixth and seventh experiment was 0.010 gm less than the average of the first three. Find the weight of the body obtained by the fourth experiment.

(a) 49.353 gm      (b) 51.712 gm

(c) 53.072 gm      (d) 54.512 gm

42. Sumer's average expenditure for the first 4 months of the year was ₹251.25. For the next 5 months the average monthly expenditure was ₹26.27 more than what it was during the first 4 months. If the person spent ₹760 in all during the remaining 3 months of the year, find what percentage of his annual income of ₹3000 he saved in the year.

(a) 13.667%      (b) −5.0866%

(c) 12.333%      (d) None of these

43. A certain number of tankers were required to transport 60 lakh liters of oil from the IOCL factory in Mathura. However, it was found that since each tanker could take 50,000 liters of oil less, another 4 tankers were needed. How many tankers were initially, planned to be used?

(a) 10      (b) 15

(c) 20      (d) 25

44. One collective farm got an average harvest of 21 tons of wheat per hectare and another collective farm that had 12 acres of land less given to wheat, got 25 tons from a hectare. As a result, the second farm harvested 300 tons of wheat more than the first. How many tons of wheat did each farm harvest?

(a) 3150, 3450      (b) 3250, 3550

(c) 2150, 2450      (d) None of these

45. If the product of $n$ positive integers is $n^n$, then what is the minimum value of their average for $n = 6$?

**(IIFT 2013)**

46. The average of 7 consecutive numbers is P. If the next three numbers are also added, the average increases by **(IIFT 2013)**

**Directions for question number 47-48:** In 2001 there were 6 members in Binod's family and their average age was 28 years. He got married between 2001 and 2004 and in 2004 there was an addition of a child in his family. In 2006, the average age of his family is 32 years.

47. What is the present age (in 2006) of Binod's wife (in years) is:

48. If Binod's age is greater than his wife and in 2001 his age was a prime number then what is the minimum possible value of Binod's present age? (in 2006) (in years)

49. If the average of 21, 23, $x$, 24, 27 lies in between 25, 28 (including both). Find the number of possible integral values of $x$.

50. Rozer a great tennis player has 10 boxes with him, which have an average of 25 tennis balls per box. If each box has at least 8 balls and no two boxes have an equal number of balls, then what is the maximum possible number of balls in any box?

51. If the average of five different numbers is 6, and if all the numbers are positive integers then what is the largest possible value of the average of the 2 biggest numbers?

**Directions for question number 52–53:** In CMS, Delhi students of two different sections appeared for a test. The average score of students of Class $9^{th}$ is 80 and the average score of class $10^{th}$ is 73. Average scores of girls and boys of class $9^{th}$ are 70 and 85, respectively and that of class $10^{th}$ are 70 and 74, respectively. The number of boys of class $10^{th}$ is 3 times the number of girls of class $9^{th}$

52. What is the ratio of girls and boys of class $9^{th}$?

53. What is the average score of all the students of class $9^{th}$ and $10^{th}$ together?

54. There are four numbers $w$, $x$, $y$, $z$. If the sum of all possible distinct groups, each having two numbers from amongst $w$, $x$, $y$, $z$ is 1440, then what is the average of these four numbers?

***Space for Rough Work***

## LEVEL OF DIFFICULTY (III)

**Directions for Questions 1 to 8:** Read the following:

There are 3 classes having 20, 25 and 30 students respectively having average marks in an examination as 20, 25 and 30, respectively. If the three classes are represented by $A$, $B$ and $C$ and you have the following information about the three classes, answer the questions that follow:

$$A \rightarrow \text{Highest score 22, Lowest score 18}$$
$$B \rightarrow \text{Highest score 31, Lowest score 23}$$
$$C \rightarrow \text{Highest score 33, Lowest score 26}$$

If five students are transferred from $A$ to $B$.

1. What will happen to the average score of $B$?
   (a) Definitely increase   (b) Definitely decrease
   (c) Remain constant   (d) Cannot say
2. What will happen to the average score of $A$?
   (a) Definitely increase   (b) Definitely decrease
   (c) Remain constant   (d) Cannot say

In a transfer of 5 students from $A$ to $C$

3. What will happen to the average score of $C$?
   (a) Definitely increase   (b) Definitely decrease
   (c) Remain constant   (d) Cannot say
4. What will happen to the average score of $A$?
   (a) Definitely increase   (b) Definitely decrease
   (c) Remain constant   (d) Cannot say

In a transfer of 5 students from $B$ to $C$ (Questions 5–6)

5. What will happen to the average score of $C$?
   (a) Definitely increase   (b) Definitely decrease
   (c) Remain constant   (d) Cannot say
6. Which of these can be said about the average score of $B$?
   (a) Increases if $C$ decreases
   (b) Decreases if $C$ increases
   (c) Increases if $C$ decreases
   (d) Decreases if $C$ decreases
7. In a transfer of 5 students from $A$ to $B$, the maximum possible average achievable for group $B$ is
   (a) 25   (b) 24.5
   (c) 25.5   (d) 24
8. For the above case, the maximum possible average achieved for group $A$ will be
   (a) 20.66   (b) 21.5
   (c) 20.75   (d) 20.5
9. What will be the minimum possible average of Group $A$ if 5 students are transferred from $A$ to $B$?

   (a) 19.55   (b) 21.5
   (c) 19.33   (d) 20.5
10. If 5 students are transferred from $B$ to $A$, what will be the minimum possible average of $A$?
    (a) 20.69   (b) 21
    (c) 20.75   (d) 20.6
11. For question 10, what will be the maximum average of $A$?
    (a) 23.2   (b) 22.2
    (c) 18.75   (d) 19

**Directions for Questions 12 to 17:** Read the following and answer the questions that follow.

If 5 people are transferred from $A$ to $B$ and another independent set of 5 people are transferred back from $B$ to $A$, then after this operation (Assume that the set transferred from $B$ to $A$ contains none from the set of students that came to $B$ from $A$)

12. What will happen to $B$'s average?
    (a) Increase if $A$'s average decreases
    (b) Decrease always
    (c) Cannot be said
    (d) Decrease if $A$'s average decreases
13. What can be said about $A$'s average?
    (a) Will decrease
    (b) Will always increase if $B$'s average changes
    (c) May increase or decrease
    (d) Will increase only if $B$'s average decreases
14. At the end of the 2 steps mentioned above (in the *direction*)  what could be the maximum value of the average of class $B$?
    (a) 25.4   (b) 25
    (c) 24.8   (d) 24.6
15. For question 14, what could be the minimum value of the average of class $B$?
    (a) 22.4   (b) 24.2
    (c) 25   (d) 23
16. What could be the maximum possible average achieved by class $A$ at the end of the operation?
    (a) 25.2   (b) 26
    (c) 23.25   (d) 23.75
17. What could be the minimum possible average of class $A$ at the end of the operation?
    (a) 21.4   (b) 19.2
    (c) 28.5   (d) 20.25

**Directions for Questions 18 to 23:** Read the following and answer the questions that follow.

If 5 people are transferred from $C$ to $B$, further, 5 more people are transferred from $B$ to $A$, then 5 are transferred from *A* to *B* and finally, 5 more are transferred from *B* to *C*.

18. What is the maximum possible average achieved by class *C*?
    (a) 30.833    (b) 30
    (c) 29.66     (d) 30.66

19. What is the maximum possible average of class *B*?
    (a) 26    (b) 27
    (c) 25    (d) 28

20. What is the maximum possible average value attained by class *A*?
    (a) 22.75    (b) 23.75
    (c) 23.5     (d) 24

21. The minimum possible value of the average of group *C* is
    (a) 26.3    (b) 27.5
    (c) 29.6    (d) 28

22. The minimum possible average of group *B* after this set of operation is
    (a) 21.6    (b) 22.2
    (c) 21.8    (d) 21.4

23. The minimum possible average of group *A* after the set of 3 operation is
    (a) 20     (b) 20.3
    (c) 20.4   (d) 19.8

24. Which of these will definitely not constitute an operation for getting the minimum possible average value for group *A*?
    (a) Transfer of five 31s from *B* to *A*
    (b) Transfer of five 26s from *C* to *B*
    (c) Transfer of five 22s from *A* to *B*
    (d) Transfer of five 33s from *C* to *B*

25. For getting the lowest possible value of *C*'s average, the sequence of operations could be
    (a) Transfer five 33s from *C* to *B*, five 23s from *B* to *A*, five 18s from *A* to *B*, five 18s from *B* to *C*
    (b) Transfer five 33s from *C* to *B*, 31s from *B* to *A*,
    (c) Both a and b
    (d) None of the above

26. If we set the highest possible average of class *C* as the primary objective and want to achieve the highest possible value for class *B* as the secondary objective, what is the maximum value of class *B*'s average that is attainable?
    (a) 27    (b) 26
    (c) 25    (d) 24

27. For Question 26, if the secondary objective is changed to achieving the minimum possible average value of class *B*'s average, the lowest value of class *B*'s average that could be attained is

(a) 22.6    (b) 23
(c) 22.2    (d) 22

28. For question 27, what can be said about class *A*'s average?
    (a) Will be determined automatically at 22.25
    (b) Will have a maximum possible value of 22.25
    (c) Will have a minimum possible value of 22.25
    (d) Will be determined automatically at 22.5

29. A team of miners planned to mine 1800 tons of ore during a certain number of days. Due to technical difficulties in one-third of the planned number of days, the team was able to achieve an output of 20 tons of ore less than the planned output. To make up for this, the team overachieved for the rest of the days by 20 tons. The end result was that the team completed the task one day ahead of time. How many tons of ore did the team initially plan to ore per day?
    (a) 50 tons    (b) 100 tons
    (c) 150 tons   (d) 200 tons

30. According to a plan, a team of woodcutters decided to harvest 216 m³ of wheat in several days. In the first three days, the team fulfilled the daily assignment, and then it harvested 8 m³ of wheat over and above the plan everyday. Therefore, a day before the planned date, they had already harvested 232 m³ of wheat. How many cubic metres of wheat a day did the team have to cut according to the plan?
    (a) 12    (b) 13
    (c) 24    (d) 25

31. On an average, two litres of milk and one litre of water are needed to be mixed to make 1 kg of sudha shrikhand of type *A*, and 3 litres of milk and 2 litres of water are needed to be mixed to make 1 kg of sudha shrikhand of type *B*. How many kilograms of each type of shrikhand was manufactured if it is known that 130 litres of milk and 80 litres of water were used?
    (a) 20 of type *A* and 30 of type *B*
    (b) 30 of type *A* and 20 of type *B*
    (c) 15 of type *A* and 30 of type *B*
    (d) 30 of type *A* and 15 of type *B*

32. There are 500 seats in Minerva Cinema, Mumbai, placed in similar rows. After the reconstruction of the hall, the total number of seats became 10% less. The number of rows was reduced by 5 but each row contained 5 seats more than before. How many rows and how many seats in a row were there initially in the hall?
    (a) 20 rows and 25 seats
    (b) 20 rows and 20 seats
    (c) 10 rows and 50 seats
    (d) 50 rows and 10 seats

33. One fashion house has to make 810 dresses and another one 900 dresses during the same period of time. In the first house, the order was ready 3 days ahead of time and in the second house, 6 days ahead of time. How many dresses did each fashion house make a day if the second house made 21 dresses more a day than the first?

    (a) 54 and 75          (b) 24 and 48
    (c) 44 and 68          (d) 04 and 25

34. A shop sold 64 kettles of two different capacities. The smaller kettle cost a rupee less than the larger one. The shop made 100 rupees from the sale of large kettles and 36 rupees from the sale of small ones. How many kettles of either capacity did the shop sell and what was the price of each kettle?

    (a) 20 kettles for 2.5 rupees each and 14 kettles for 1.5 rupees each
    (b) 40 kettles for 4.5 rupees each and 24 kettles for 2.5 rupees each
    (c) 40 kettles for 2.5 rupees each and 24 kettles for 1.5 rupees each
    (d) either a or b

35. An enterprise got a bonus and decided to share it in equal parts between the exemplary workers. It turned out, however, that there were 3 more exemplary workers than it had been assumed. In that case, each of them would have got 4 rupees less. The administration had found the possibility to increase the total sum of the bonus by 90 rupees and as a result each exemplary worker got 25 rupees. How many people got the bonus?

    (a) 9          (b) 18
    (c) 8          (d) 16

**Directions for Questions 36 to 39:** Read the following and answer the questions that follows.

In the island of Hoola Boola Moola, the inhabitants have a strange process of calculating their average incomes and expenditures. According to an old legend prevalent on that island, the average monthly income had to be calculated on the basis of 14 months in a calendar year while the average monthly expenditure was to be calculated on the basis of 9 months per year. This would lead to people having an underestimation of their savings since there would be an underestimation of the income and an overestimation of the expenditure per month.

36. If the minister for economic affairs decided to reverse the process of calculation of average income and average expenditure, what will happen to the estimated savings of a person living on Hoola Boola Moola island?

    (a) It will increase
    (b) It will decrease

    (c) It will remain constant
    (d) Will depend on the value

37. If it is known that Mr. Magoo Hoola Boola estimates his savings at 10 Moolahs and if it is further known that his actual expenditure is 288 Moolahs in an year (Moolahs, for those who are not aware, is the official currency of Hoola Boola Moola), then what will happen to his estimated savings if he suddenly calculates on the basis of a 12 month calendar year?

    (a) Will increase by 5   (b) Will increase by 15
    (c) Will increase by 10  (d) Will triple

38. Mr. Boogie Woogie comes back from the USA to Hoola Boola Moola and convinces his community comprising 546 families to start calculating the average income and average expenditure on the basis of 12 months per calendar year. Now if it is known that the average estimated income on the island is (according to the old system) 87 Moolahs per month, then what will be the change in the average estimated savings for the island of Hoola Boola Moola. (Assume that there is no other change).

    (a) 251.60 Moolahs     (b) 565.5 Moolahs
    (c) 625.5 Moolahs      (d) Cannot be determined

39. Mr. Boogle Woogle comes back from the USSR and convinces his community comprising 273 families to start calculating the average income on the basis of 12 months per calendar year. Now if it is known that the average estimated income in his community is (according to the old system) 87 Moolahs per month, then what will be the change in the average estimated savings for the island of Hoola Boola Moola. (Assume that there is no other change).

    (a) 251.60 Moolahs     (b) 282.75 Moolahs
    (c) 312.75 Moolahs     (d) Cannot be determined

**Directions for Questions 40 to 44:** Read the following and answer the questions that follows.

The Indian cricket team has to score 360 runs on the last day of a test match in 90 overs, to win the test match. This is the target set by the opposing captain Brian Lara after he declared his innings closed at the overnight score of 411 for 7.

The Indian team coach has the following information about the batting rates (in terms of runs per over) of the different batsmen:

Assume that the run rate of a partnership is the weighted average of the individual batting rates of the batsmen involved in the partnership (on the basis of the ratio of the strike each batsman gets, i.e., the run rate of a partnership is defined as the weighted average of the run rates of the two batsmen involved weighted by the ratio of the number of balls faced by each batsman).

Since decimal fractions of runs are not possible for any batsman, assume that the estimated runs scored by a batsman in an inning (on the basis of his run rate and the number of overs faced by him) is rounded off to the next higher integer immediately above the estimated value of the runs scored during the innings.

For example, if a batsman scores at an average of 3 runs per over for 2.1666 overs, then he will be estimated to have scored 2.1666 × 3 = 6.5 runs in his innings, but since this is not possible, the actual number of runs scored by the batsman will be taken as 7 (the next higher integer above 6.5).

### Runs scored per over in different batting styles

| Name of Batsman | Defensive | Normal | Aggressive |
|---|---|---|---|
| Das | 3 | 4 | 5 |
| Dasgupta | 2 | 3 | 4 |
| Dravid | 2 | 3 | 4 |
| Tendulkar | 4 | 6 | 8 |
| Laxman | 4 | 5 | 6 |
| Sehwag | 4 | 5 | 6 |
| Ganguly | 3 | 4 | 5 |
| Kumble | 2 | 3 | 4 |
| Harbhajan | 3 | 4 | 5 |
| Srinath | 3 | 4 | 5 |
| Yohannan | 2 | 3 | 4 |

Also, this rounding off can take place only once for one innings of a batsman.

Assume no extras unless otherwise stated.

Assume that the strike is equally shared unless otherwise stated.

40. If the first wicket pair of Das and Dasgupta bats for 22 overs and during this partnership Das has started batting normally and turned aggressive after 15 overs while Dasgupta started off defensively but shifted gears to bat normally after batting for 20 overs, find the expected score after 22 overs.
    (a) 65                    (b) 71
    (c) 82                    (d) 58

41. Of the first-wicket partnership between Das and Dasgupta as per the previous question, the ratio of the number of runs scored by Das to those scored by Dasgupta is:
    (a) 46:25                 (b) 96:46
    (c) 41:32                 (d) Cannot be determined

42. The latest time by which Tendulkar can come to bat and still win the game, assuming that the run rate at the time of his walking the wicket is into 2.5 runs per over, is (assuming he shares strike equally with his partner and that he gets the maximum possible support at the other end from his batting partner and both play till the last ball).

(a) After 50 overs           (b) After 55 overs
(c) After 60 overs           (d) Cannot be determined

43. For question 42, where Tendulkar batted aggressively and assuming that it is the Tendulkar–Laxman pair that wins the game for India (after Tendulkar walks into bat with the current run rate at 2.5 per over, and at the latest possible time for him to win the game with maximum possible support from the opposite end), what will be Tendulkar's score for the innings (assume equal strike)?
    (a) 105                   (b) 120
    (c) 135                   (d) None of these

44. For questions 42 and 43, if it was Laxman who batted with Tendulkar for his entire innings, then how many runs would Laxman score in the innings?
    (a) 105                   (b) 75
    (c) 90                    (d) Cannot be determined

**Directions for Questions 45 to 49:** Read the following and answer the questions that follow (with reference to the data provided in the table for questions 40 to 44).

If Sachin Tendulkar walks into bat after the fall of the fifth wicket and has to share partnerships with Ganguly, Kumble, Harbhajan, Srinath and Yohannan, who have batted normally, defensively, defensively, defensively and defensively, respectively while Tendulkar has batted normally, aggressively, aggressively, aggressively and aggressively, respectively in each of the five partnerships that lasted for 12, 10, 8, 5 and 10 overs, respectively, sharing strike equally with Ganguly and keeping two-thirds of the strike in his other four partnerships, then answer the following questions:

45. How many runs did Sachin score during his innings?
    (a) 128                   (b) 212
    (c) 176                   (d) None of these

46. The highest partnership that Tendulkar shared in was worth
    (a) 60                    (b) 61
    (c) 62                    (d) 58

47. The above partnership was shared with:
    (a) Ganguly               (b) Yohannan
    (c) Kumble                (d) All three

48. If India proceeded to win the match based on the runs scored by these last five partnerships (assuming the last wicket pair remained unbeaten), what could be the maximum score at which Tendulkar could have come into bat?
    (a) 103 for 5             (b) 97 for 5
    (c) 100 for 5            (d) 104 for 5

49. For Question 48, what could be the minimum score at which Tendulkar could have come to bat?
    (a) 103 for 5             (b) 97 for 5
    (c) 104 for 5            (d) 98 for 5

| | | | |
|---|---|---|---|
| 41. (b) | 42. (c) | 43. (b) | 44. (d) |
| 45. (b) | 46. (b) | 47. (b) | 48. (d) |
| 49. (b) | | | |

# ANSWER KEY

## Level of Difficulty (I)

| | | | |
|---|---|---|---|
| 1. (d) | 2. (a) | 3. (d) | 4. (b) |
| 5. (d) | 6. (c) | 7. (d) | 8. (b) |
| 9. (d) | 10. (b) | 11. (a) | 12. (b) |
| 13. (d) | 14. (d) | 15. (b) | 16. (b) |
| 17. (b) | 18. (a) | 19. (a) | 20. (b) |
| 21. (a) | 22. (b) | 23. (a) | 24. (b) |
| 25. (a) | 26. (c) | 27. (d) | 28. (a) |
| 29. (c) | 30. (b) | 31. (c) | 32. (a) |
| 33. (b) | 34. (a) | 35. (d) | 36. (c) |
| 37. (d) | 38. (b) | 39. (d) | 40. (c) |
| 41. (c) | 42. (a) | 43. (c) | 44. (b) |
| 45. (a) | 46. (d) | 47. (d) | 48. (b) |
| 49. (c) | 50. (b) | 51. (b) | 52. (a) |
| 53. (d) | 54. (d) | 55. (c) | 56. (b) |
| 57. (d) | 58. (a) | 59. (b) | 60. (c) |
| 61. (b) | 62. (d) | 63. (a) | 64. (a) |
| 65. (b) | 66. (c) | 67. (a) | 68. (b) |
| 69. (d) | 70. (d) | 71. (b) | 72. (a) |
| 73. (a) | 74. (d) | 75. (a) | 76. (b) |
| 77. (b) | 78. (b) | 79. (a) | 80. (a) |
| 81. (d) | 82. (a) | 83. (c) | 84. (d) |
| 85. 44 | 86. 25 | 87. -10 | 88. 34.66 |
| 89. 60 | 90. 37.50 | 91. 49 | 92. 39.56 |
| 93. 230 | 94. 9 | | |

## Level of Difficulty (II)

| | | | |
|---|---|---|---|
| 1. (b) | 2. (b) | 3. (a) | 4. (b) |
| 5. (b) | 6. (a) | 7. (b) | 8. (d) |
| 9. (a) | 10. (a) | 11. (b) | 12. (a) |
| 13. (b) | 14. (b) | 15. (a) | 16. (c) |
| 17. (d) | 18. (b) | 19. (a) | 20. (b) |
| 21. (d) | 22. (a) | 23. (a) | 24. (a) |
| 25. (b) | 26. (c) | 27. (c) | 28. (c) |
| 29. (b) | 30. (d) | 31. (a) | 32. (b) |
| 33. (c) | 34. (a) | 35. (a) | 36. (a) |
| 37. (d) | 38. (a) | 39. (d) | 40. (d) |
| 41. (c) | 42. (b) | 43. (c) | 44. (a) |
| 45. 6 | 46. 1.5 | 47. 56 | 48. 58 |
| 49. 16 | 50. 142 | 51. 12 | 52. 2 |
| 53. 76 | 54. 120 | | |

## Level of Difficulty (III)

| | | | |
|---|---|---|---|
| 1. (b) | 2. (d) | 3. (b) | 4. (d) |
| 5. (d) | 6. (b) | 7. (b) | 8. (a) |
| 9. (c) | 10. (d) | 11. (b) | 12. (b) |
| 13. (b) | 14. (c) | 15. (a) | 16. (c) |
| 17. (d) | 18. (a) | 19. (b) | 20. (b) |
| 21. (b) | 22. (b) | 23. (a) | 24. (c) |
| 25. (a) | 26. (d) | 27. (c) | 28. (a) |
| 29. (b) | 30. (c) | 31. (a) | 32. (a) |
| 33. (a) | 34. (c) | 35. (b) | 36. (a) |
| 37. (b) | 38. (d) | 39. (b) | 40. (b) |

## Solutions and Shortcuts

### Level of Difficulty (I)

1. Required average = $(1 + 2 + 3 + \ldots + 15)/15 = 120/15 = 8$. Alternately you could use the formula for sum of the first $n$ natural numbers as $n(n+1)/2$ with $n$ as 15. Then average = Sum/15 = $(15 \times 16/2)/15 = 8$

2. Required average = $(0 + 1 + 2 + \ldots + 9)/10 = 45/10 = 4.5$

3. Required average = $(2 + 4 + 6 + 8 + 10 + 12 + 14 + 16 + 18 + 20)/10 = 110/10 = 11$. Alternately you could use the formula for sum of the first n even natural numbers as $n(n+1)$ with $n$ as 10. Then average = Sum/10 = $10 \times 11/10 = 11$.

4. The sum of the first $n$ odd numbers = $n^2$. In this case $n = 10 \to$ Sum = $10^2 = 100$. Required average = $100/10 = 10$.

5. Required average = $(2 + 3 + 5 + 7 + 11 + 13 + 17 + 19 + 23 + 29)/10 = 129/10 = 12.9$.

6. Required average = $(4 + 6 + 8 + 9 + 10 + 12 + 14 + 15 + 16 + 18)/10 = 112/10 = 11.2$.

7. Required average = $(3 + 5 + 7 + 11 + 13 + 17 + 19 + 23 + 29 + 31)/10 = 158/10 = 15.8$.

8. $P = 14 \times 10 - 13 \times 8 = 140 - 104 = 36$

9. D's weight = $4 \times 70 - 3 \times 74 = 280 - 222 = 58$. E's weight = $58 + 3 = 61$.
   Now, we know that $A + B + C + D = 4 \times 70 = 280$ and $B + C + D + E = 75 \times 4 = 300$. Hence, A's weight is 20 kg less than E's weight. $A = 61 - 20 = 41$ kg.

10. Monday + Tuesday + Wednesday = $3 \times 35 = 105$; Tuesday + Wednesday + Thursday = $3 \times 30 = 90$. Thus, Monday – Thursday = 15 and
    Thursday = Monday/2 $\to$ Monday = 30 and Thursday = 15

11. Total present age of $A$, $B$ and $C = 25 \times 3 + 15 = 75 + 15 = 90$.
    Total present age of $B$ and $C = 20 \times 2 + 20 = 60$.
    $A$'s age = $90 - 60 = 30$.

12. $4x + 40 = 5(x + 4) \to x = 20$ (average after 4 innings). Hence, new average = $20 + 4 = 24$.

13. $(5+10+15+20+25+30)/6 = 105/6 = 17.5$

14. $1/5 + 1/8 + C = 3 \times 1/10 \to C = -1/40$.

15. His total score is $90 + 70 + 150 = 310$ out of 450. This works out to a percentage score of = 68.88%

16. Average income over 9 months = $[3 \times (2250 + 500) + 3 \times (2150 + 500) + 3 \times (5750+500)]/9 = 3883.33$

17. Total age (at present) = $5 \times 20 = 100$ years. Total age of the family excluding the youngest member (for

the remaining 5 people) = 100 –5 = 95. Average age of the other 4 people in the family = 95/4 years.

5 years ago their average age = 95/4 – 5 = 75/4 = 18.75 years.

18. If the average age of 5 persons has gone up by 10 years it means the total age has gone up by 50 years. Thus the total age of the two women would be: 30 + 40 + 50 = 120. Hence, their average age = 60 years.

19. $W + T + F = 60$; $T + F + S = 63 \rightarrow S - W = 3$. Hence temperature on Wednesday = 22 – 3 = 19.

20. Average speed = $\dfrac{2 \times 60 \times 40}{60 + 40} = 48$ km/hr.

21. Teacher's weight = $21 \times 20 - 20 \times 19 = 420- 380 = 40$.

22. $3 \times 20 - 2 \times 25 = 60 - 50 = 10$.

23. The weight of the new man would be $29 \times 5$ kgs more than the weight of the man he replaces. New man's weight = $120 + 29 \times 5 = 265$ kgs.

24. Let their current ages be $x$ and $3x$. Then their ages after 10 years would be $x + 10$ and $3x + 10$. Now it is given that $(x + 10)/(3x + 10) = 1/2 \rightarrow x = 10$ and hence their current ages are 10 years and 30 years, respectively. So their current average age is 20 years. After 20 years their average age would be 20+20 = 40 years.

25. The average would be given by the average of the first and last numbers (since the series 1, 2, 3, 4…100 is an Arithmetic Progression).

Hence, the average = (1 + 100)/2 = 50.50

26. We need the average of the numbers: 23, 29, 31, 37, 41, 43 and 47

Average = Total/number of numbers $\rightarrow$ 251/7 = 35.85

27. Let the numbers be $a$, $b$, $c$ and $d$, respectively. $a + b + c = 20 \times 3 = 60$ and $b + c + d = 25 \times 3 = 75$. Also, since $d-a = 15$, we have 30- a = 15 or a = 15.

28. Required average = $(15 \times 40 + 25 \times 48)/40 = 1800/40 = 45$.

29. The numbers would form an $AP$ with common difference 1 and the middle term (also the $4^{th}$ term) as 21. Thus, the numbers would be 18, 19, 20, 21, 22, 23 and 24. The highest of these numbers would be 24.

30. Required average = $(8 \times 11 + 15 + 17)/10 = 120/10 = 12$.

31. The new average would also go up by 4. Hence, 14 + 4 = 18.

32. If the numbers are $a + 1$, $a + 2$, $a + 3$, $a + 4$, $a + 5$….$a+11$ the average would be $a + 6$. If we take 13 numbers as:

$a + 1$, $a + 2$, $a + 3$, $a + 4$, $a + 5$, $a + 6$…. and $a + 13$ their average would be a+7. Hence, the average increases by 1. You can also experimentally verify this by taking any 11 consecutive numbers and find-

ing their average, then adding the next two numbers and finding the average of the 13 numbers.

33. Total of 38 numbers = $40 \times 45 - 65 - 25 = 1710$. Average of 38 numbers = 1710/38 = 45.

34. When we multiply each number by 9, the average would also get multiplied by 9. Hence, the new average = $18 \times 9 = 162$.

35. Let the number of ladies be $n$. Then we have $5 \times 12 + n \times 8 = (5 + n) \times (9) \rightarrow 60 + 8n = 45 + 9n \rightarrow n = 15$.

36. $(3 \times 63 + 67)/4 = 256/4 = 64$.

37. $2100 \times 3 - 2250 \times 2 = 1800$.

38. $(2000 \times 15 + 1000 \times 15)/30 = (2000 + 1000)/2 = 1500$.

39. The decrease in weight would be 20 kgs (10 people's average weight drops by 2 kgs). Hence, the new person's weight = 140 - 20 = 120.

40. When a person aged 26 years, is replaced by a person aged 56 years, the total age of the group goes up by 30 years. Since this leads to an increase in the average by 6 years, it means that there are 30/6 = 5 persons in the group.

41. $(33 \times 3 + 23 \times 2)/5 = 145/5 = 29$.

42. Let the number of marks in the $8^{th}$ paper be $M$. Then the total of the first eight papers = $8 \times 48$ while the total of the last 8 (i.e., $8^{th}$ to $15^{th}$ papers) would be $8 \times 54$.

Total of $1^{st}$ 8 + total of $8^{th}$ to $15^{th}$ = total of all 15 + marks in the $8^{th}$ paper $\rightarrow$

$8 \times 48 + 8 \times 54 = 15 \times 50 + M$

$816 = 750 + M \rightarrow M = 66$

(Note: We write this equation since marks in the eighth paper is counted in both the first 8 and the last 8)

43. Let the captain's age by $C$. Then: $11 \times 28 = 26 \times 5 + 29 \times 5 + C \rightarrow 308 = 130 + 145 + C \rightarrow C = 33$.

44. His earning in the $12^{th}$ month should be: $4000 \times 12 - 3200 \times 11 = 48000 - 35200 = 12800$.

45. Total distance divided by total time = 1440/17 = 84.705.

46. In three quarters of an hour the train has traveled 57 km. Thus, in a full hour the train would have traveled $1/3^{rd}$ more (as it gets $1/3^{rd}$ time more). Thus, the speed of the train = $57+ 1 \times 57/3 = 57 + 19 = 76$.

47. Total weight of all 6 = $58.5 \times 6$. Total weight of Ram and Tram = $65 \times 2 = 130$. Average weight of the 4 people excluding Ram and Tram = $(58.5 \times 6 - 130)/4 = 55.25$ kg.

48. $10 \times 59 + 20 \times A = 30 \times 56 \rightarrow A = (1680 - 590)/20 = 1090/20 = 54.5$

49. $(60 \times 23 + 40 \times 35)/100 = 2780/100 = 27.8$

50. If we take the first number as 6n, the second number would be 3n and the third would be 2n. Sum of the three numbers = $6n + 3n + 2n = 11n = 132 \times 3 \rightarrow n = 36$. The smallest number would be 2n = 72.

51. The ratio between the first, second and third would be: 10:15:24. Since their total is 147, the numbers would be 30, 45 and 72 respectively. The second number is 45.

52. $(40 \times 150 + 10 \times 155)/50 = 151$. (Note: this question can also be solved using the alligation method explained in the next chapter.

53. The total weight of the six people goes up by 9 kgs (when the average for 6 persons goes up by 1.5 kg). Thus, the new person must be 9 kgs more than the person who he replaces. Hence, the new person's weight = 60 +9 = 69

54. Total age = $3 \times 24 = 72$. Individual ages being in the ratio 2:5:5 their ages would be 12, 30 and 30 years respectively. The youngest boy would be 12 years.

55. $50 \times 4 + M = 51 \times 5 \rightarrow M = 55$.

56. $(30 \times 1800 + M) = 31 \times 1900 \rightarrow M = 4900$. Hence, the salary is 4900 per month which also means ₹ 58,800 per year.

57. Five consecutive even numbers would always be in an Arithmetic progression and their average would be the middle number. The average would be 'r' in this case.

58. The average of 7, 14, 21, 28 and 35 would be 21.

59. $30 \times 50 + T = 31 \times 50.5 \rightarrow T = 1565.5 - 1500 = 65.5$ kgs.

60. If the number of questions correct is $N$, then the number of wrong answers is $100 - N$. Using this we get: $N \times 3 - (100 - N) \times 1 = 160 \rightarrow 4N = 260 \rightarrow N = 65$.

61. Required age of the father will be given by the equation: $6 \times 12 = 5 \times 7 + F \rightarrow F = 37$.

62. Teacher's weight = $21 \times 51 - 20 \times 50 = 1071 - 1000 = 71$.

63. Required average = $(2 \times 5.5 + 3 \times 3.666 + 6 \times 1.8333)/11 = (11 + 11 + 11)/11 = 3$.

64. $40 \times m + 65 \times 4 = 480 \rightarrow P = (480 - 260)/40 = 5.5$.

65. Required average = $(2 \times 4000 + 2 \times 2500)/4 = 13000/4 = 3250$.

66. Required average = Total runs/ total innings = $(55 \times 4 + 0)/5 = 220/5 = 44$.

67. Principal's weight = $51 \times 69.5 - 50 \times 70 = 3544.5 - 3500 = 44.5$

68. Temperature on 6th December = $25.6 \times 3 - 27 \times 2 = 76.8 - 54 = 22.8$

69. Average age 4 years hence would be 4 years more than the current average age. Hence, 30 + 4 = 34.

70. Total age 3 years ago for 6 people = $18 \times 6 = 108$. Today, the family's total age = $18 \times 7 = 126$. The age of the 6 older people would be $108 + 3 \times 6 = 126$. Hence, the baby's age is 0 years.

71. Required average = $(21 \times 31 + 24 \times 31 + 11 \times 30)/92 = (651 + 744 + 330)/92 = 1725/92 = 18.75$

72. Assume a distance of 150 km. In such a case, the Required average = Total distance/Total time = (150 + 150)/(6 + 5) = 300/11 = 27.27

73. (Mon + Tue + wed) = $52 \times 3 = 156$. (Tue + Wed + Thu) = $50 \times 3 = 150$.
    Mon – Thu = 156 – 150 = 6. Since Thursday's temperature is given as 49, Monday's temperature would be 49 + 6 = 55.

74. Required average = $(15 \times 20 - 5 \times 10)/10 = 250/10 = 25$.

75. Total age of 10 children = $15 \times 10 = 150$ years. When the 6 year old child dies, the total age of the remaining 9 children would be 150 – 6 = 144. Required average = 144/9 = 16 years

76. Required average = $(2 \times 200 + 2 \times 250)/4 = 900/4 = 225$.

77. Average weight including Teacher's weight = $(40 \times 40 + 122)/41 = (1600 + 122)/41 = 1722/41 = 42$kgs.

78. The statement 'a' is as much more than the average as 'b' is less than the average signifies that the numbers a, b, c form an Arithmetic Progression with c as the middle term. c's value would then be equal to the average of the three numbers. This average is given as 25. Hence, the correct answer is c = 25.

79. The sum of the given 4 numbers is 16.50. The required average = 16.50/4 = 4.125. Option (a) is correct.

80. Let the number of non officer workers in the company be $W$. Then we will have the following equation: $(15 \times 5000 + W \times 10000) = (15 + W) \times 9000 \rightarrow W = 60$. Thus, the total number of workers in the company would be 60 + 15 = 75.

81. The woman's age would be $10 \times 3 = 30$ years more than the age of the man she replaces. Age of the woman = $54 + 3 \times 10 = 84$ years.

82. Required average income = (Total expenditure + total savings]/12
    = $[(100 \times 3 + 200 \times 4 + 400 \times 5) + 3000]/12 = 6100/12 \approx 508$.

83. Required average = $(2 \times 5.5 + 3 \times 3.5 + 3 \times 5.5 + 5 \times 1.5)/13 = 45.5/13 = 3.5$.

84. For 150 coins to be of a value of ₹ 150, using only 25 paise, 50 paise and 1 Rupee coins, we cannot have any coins lower than the value of ₹1. Thus, the number of 50 paise coins would be 0. Option (d) is correct.

85. Since you can see that this is an Arithmetic Progression, the average of the six numbers is simply the average of the first and the last numbers in the series i.e., the average of 11 and 77 (which is 44).

86. Let the present ages of Aman and Baman be $x$ and $2x$ respectively.
$$\frac{x+5}{2x+5} = \frac{3}{5}$$

$$5x + 25 = 6x + 15$$

$x = 10$. Hence their present ages are 10 and 20. In 10 years time their ages would be 20 and 30 years respectively. The average age would be 25 years.

87. Let the numbers be $a$, $b$, $c$, $d$

$$a + b + c = 3 \times 20 \quad \ldots..(1)$$
$$b + c + d = 3 \times 10 \quad \ldots..(2)$$

Equation (1) – Equation (2)

$$a - d = 30$$
$$d = a - 30$$
$$d = 20 - 30 = -10.$$

88. Correct average

$$= \frac{15 \times 40 - 2(80 - 40)}{15} = \frac{520}{15} = 34.66$$

89. $M + T + W + Th + Fr = 40 \times 5 = 200$

If four of these were equal to the lowest possible, i.e. 35 each, the maximum possible temperature for the fifth day is $200 - 35 \times 4 = 60$.

90. Present sum of ages of the family $= 3 \times 30 = 90$

Sum of ages (5 years ago) $= 90 - 3 \times 5 = 75$.

Required average $= 75/2 = 37.50$ years

91. If the Average of 50 numbers is 0, then at most 49 of them can be greater than 0 and $50^{th}$ number can be such that its' negative value equals to the positive value of the first 49 numbers.

92. Required average $= \dfrac{40.25 - 50 - 40}{23} = \dfrac{910}{23} = 39.56$.

93. $6^{th}$ number $= (10 \times 60 - 5 \times 50 - 4 \times 30) = 230$

94. New average $= \dfrac{10 \times 10 - 30 + 20}{10} = 9$.

## Level of Difficulty (II)

1. Find the total distance covered in each segment of 15 minutes. You will get total distance = 32.50 kilometres in 60 minutes.

2. The train needs to travel 60 minutes extra @ 20 kmph. Hence, it is behind by 20 kms. The rate of losing distance is 5 kmph. Hence, the train must have travelled for $20/5 = 4$ hours@ 25 kmph $\rightarrow$ 100 km. Alternatively, you can also see that 20% drop in speed results in 25% increase in time. Hence, total time required is 4 hours @ 25 kmph $\rightarrow$ 100 kilometres.

Alternatively, solve through options.

3. Standard question requiring good calculation speed. Obviously, the 15th day is being double counted. Calculations can be reduced by thinking as:

Surplus in first 15 days – Deficit in last 17 days = $15 \times 20 - 17 \times 10 = 300 - 170 \rightarrow$ Net surplus of 130. This means that the sum is advancing by 130 due to the double counting of the 15th day. This can only mean that the 15th day's expenditure is 60 + 130 = 190.

(Lengthy calculations would have yielded the following calculations: $80 \times 15 + 50 \times 17 - 60 \times 31 = 190$).

4. Assume that the distance is 100 km. Hence, 20 km is covered @ 20 kmph, 25 @ 50 kmph and 55 km @ 55 kmph.

Then average speed is total distance/total time = $100/(1+0.5+1) = 40$ kmph.

5. $4x + 40 = (x + 4) \times 5$ (where x is the average of first four innings.)

On solving we get, $x = 20$. x is the old average here. Hence, the new average $= x + 4 = 20 + 4 = 24$.

6. In one hour the total number of sheets typed will be: $60/10 + 60/20 + 60/30 = 11$

Hence the number of sheets/hour per typist is 11/3.

7. $100 \rightarrow 110 \rightarrow 132$. Hence, $32/2 = 16$.

8. You do not know the number of days in the month. Hence, the question cannot be answered.

9. The number of rooms is $50 + 40 + 40 = 130$ on the three floors respectively.

Total revenues are: $25 \times 2000 + 20 \times 1000 + 12 \times 1500 = 88000$. Hence the required average = $88000/130 = 676.92$

10. Replace $x$ with the sales value to calculate the bonus in a month.

Bonus = 0 in January, 200 in February, 2000 each from March to November and 200 in December. Hence, his Total bonus = $0 + 200 + 2000 \times 9 + 200 = 18400$. Salary for the year = $3000 \times 12$. Total annual income = $36000 + 18400 = 54400$. Hence, the average monthly income = 4533.33. Option (a) is closest and hence is the correct answer.

11. $61 \times 43 = 48 \times 36 + x + 12 \times 49 \rightarrow x = 307$.

12. Use the same process as Q. No. 4 above. Let the journey be 100 km. The average speed is given by: Total Distance/Total time = $100/(1+1+5) = 100/7$ kmph.

13. Find out the number of innings in each year. Then the answer will be given by:

$$\frac{\text{Total runs in 4 years}}{\text{Total innings in 4 years}} = (4250/132 = 32.19)$$

14. The weight of the second man is 50 kg and that of the third is 40 kg. Hence, net result is a drop of 60 for 10 people. Hence, 6 kg is the drop in the average.

15. Put $x = 10$ to get the weight of the last three packets. These packets would weigh 60 kgs each. Thus the total of the four packets would be $60 \times 3 + 20 = 200$. Their average weight 200/4 = 50 kg.

16. The weight of the boxes are 1st box $\rightarrow$ 40, 3rd box $\rightarrow$ 50 kg, 2nd box $\rightarrow$ 75 kg, 4th box $\rightarrow$ 150 and 5th box $\rightarrow$ 100 kg. Hence difference between the heaviest 4 and the lightest 4 is 110 kg. Hence, difference in the averages is 27.5 kg.

17. Difference between heaviest three and lightest three totals is: $(150 + 100) − (40 + 50) = 160$
    Difference in average weights is $160/3 = 53.33$ kg.

18. Assume $x$ is the average expenditure of 20 people. Then, $20x = 15 \times 90 + 5(x + 30)$. On solving we get $x = 100$
    Total expenditure $= 20 \times 100 = ₹ 2000$.

19. $30 \times A + 1600 = 50 \times (A − 8) \rightarrow 20 \times A = 2000 \rightarrow A = 100$. Total expenditure original $= 100 \times 30 = ₹ 3000$.

20. The total price of the three stones would be $97610498312 \times 3 = 292831494936$. Since, this price is divided into the three stones in the ratio of 4: 7: 9, the price of the cheapest one would be $= (4 \times 2928314936/20) = 58566298987.2$.

21. The average weight per box is asked. Hence, the container does not have to be counted as the 5th item. Also, since the average for 23 boxes goes up by 1 kg, the total weight must have gone up by 23 kgs. That weight is the actual weight of the container. Hence, option (d) is correct.

22. Solve through the same process as the Q. No. 4 of this chapter. Assume the distance to be 160. Then the journey would get broken up into: 40 kms @ 40kmph, 60 kms @20kmph and 60 kms @10kmph. The average speed = Total distance/ total time = 160/ $(1 + 3 + 6) = 16$ kmph.

23. $(15 \times 305 − 2 \times 480)/13 = 278.07$ months or 23.17 years.

24. Use alligation to solve.

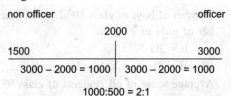

non officer                                officer

2000

1500                                        3000

$3000 − 2000 = 1000$  |  $3000 − 2000 = 1000$

$1000:500 = 2:1$

Non-officers = 20.

25. Solve through options by assuming the value of n and checking the value of the summation – and experimentally verifying it with the given options. At $n = 1$, we get the value of the summation as 2. Only option (b) gives the same summation for $n = 1$. Hence, the other options get rejected and option (b) stands as the correct answer.

26. $nz − x + x^1 = nz^1 \rightarrow$ Simplify to get Option (c) correct.

27. Let the equal distances be '$d$' each. Then using the formula for the average speed as: Total distance/ total time we get: Average speed $= 3d/(d/x + d/y + d/z) = 3xyz/(yx + yz + xz)$.

28–30. You have to take between 25th and 30th to mean that both these dates are also included.

28. The maximum average will occur when the maximum possible values are used. Thus:

*Aman* should have been born on 30th, *Binod* on 25th, *Charan* on 20th, *Dharam* on 10th and *Ehsaan* on 5th. Further, the months of births in random order will have to be between August to December to maximize the average.
Hence the maximum total will be $30 + 25 + 20 + 10 + 5 + 12 + 11 + 10 + 9 + 8 = 140$. Hence, the maximum average is 28.

29. The minimum average will be when we have $1 + 5 + 10 + 20 + 25 + 1 + 2 + 3 + 4 + 5 = 76$. Hence, average is $= 76/5 = 15.2$.

30. This does not change anything. Hence the answer is the same as Q. 28.

31. The prime dates must be 29th, 23rd, 19th and 5th. This represents a reduction in the totals from $30+25+20+5$ to $29+23+19+5$ – a drop of 4. Hence, the maximum possible average will reduce by $4/5 = 0.8$. Hence, the answer will be 27.2.

32.

            18
    20       |        10
    $18 − 10 = 8$  |  $20 − 18 = 2$
            8:2
            4:1

Number of person initially going to movie = 40

33. The number of pass candidates are $= 2 + 8 + 18 + 32 = 60$ out of a total of 200. Hence, 30%.

34. Put $x = 1$ in the given equations and find the average of the resultant values. You will get the respective values of $f(x) = 13$; $g(x) = 5$; $h(x) = 1$ and $d(x) = 1$. Hence, the required average $= 20/4 = 5$.

35. The values are: $f(x) − g(x) = 8$; $g(x) − h(x) = 4$; $h(x) − d(x) = 0$ and $d(x) − f(x) = −12$. The average of these four values $= \dfrac{8+4+0-12}{4} = 0$.

36. By alligation the ratio is 4: 3.

| Management trainee | | Manager |
|---|---|---|
| | 20,000 | |
| 5000 | | 40000 |
| $40000 − 20000$ | | $20000 − 5000 = 15000$ |
| | $20000:15000$ | |
| | $4:3$ | |

Hence, only 350 (multiple of $4+ 3 = 7$) is a possible value for the number of people.

37-40.

37. You don't know who got out when. Hence, cannot be determined.

38. Since possibilities are asked about, you will have to consider all possibilities. Assume, the sixth and seventh batsmen have scored zero. Only then will the possibility of the first 5 batsmen scoring the highest possible average arise. In this case the maximum possible average for the first 5 batsmen could be $243/5 = 48.6$

39. Again it is possible that only the first batsman has scored runs. Hence, the minimum average would be 0.

40. We cannot find out the number of runs scored by the 7th batsman. Hence the answer is (d).

41. You can take 53 as the base to reduce your calculations. Otherwise the question will become highly calculation intensive. Let the fifth experiments measurement be 'x' above 53. Then you get: $0.735 \times 7 = 1.005 \times 3 + (x + 0.004) + x + 0.995 \times 2 \rightarrow 5.145 = 3.015 + 2x + 0.004 + 1.99$. On solving this you get $x = 0.068$. Hence, the weight of the fifth body is 53.068 and the weight of the fourth body is 53.072. Hence, option (c) is correct.

42. $251.25 \times 4 + 277.52 \times 5 + 760 = 3152.6$
    Required percentage
    $$= \frac{3000 - 3152.6}{3000} = -5.087\%$$

43. Solve using options. 20 is the only possible value.

44. Check through options to solve. Option (a) is correct since if the first farm harvested 3150 tons of wheat, with an average harvest of 21 tons per hectare – the number of hectares would be $3150/21 = 150$. The second farm would then harvest 12 hectares less (as given in the question) - thus would harvest 138 hectares with an average output of 25 tons per hectare. The total harvest would be in this case $138 \times 3450$ – and is 300 tons more than the first farm as required. Hence, this answer is correct.

45. Let the numbers be $n_1, n_2, n_3, n_4, \ldots\ldots n_n$.
    $(n_1+n_2+n_3+n_4, \ldots\ldots +n_n)/n \geq (n_1, n_2, n_3, n_4, \ldots\ldots n_n)^{(1/n)}$
    $(n_1+n_2+n_3+n_4, \ldots\ldots +n_n)/n \geq n$
    For $n = 6$, the minimum value of $(n_1+ n_2+ n_3+ n_4, \ldots\ldots +n_n) = 6$
    Therefore, the minimum value of the average of these numbers = 6

46. If the numbers are 1, 2, 3, 4, 5, 6, 7 and we add 8, 9,10.
    Initial average $= (1 + 2 + 3 + 4 + 5 + 6 + 7)/7 = 4$
    Final average $= (1 + 2 + 3 + 4 + \text{-----}10)/10 = 5.5$
    Therefore, the average increases by 1.5.

47. If present age of Binod's wife is $x$ years.
    Then according to the question:
    $$\frac{33 \times 6 + x + 2}{8} = 32$$
    $x + 2 + 198 = 256$
    $x + 2 = 58$
    $x = 56$
    $x = 56$ years

48. Binod's wife's age in 2001 was 51 years. Therefore Binod's age in 2001 was greater than 51 and minimum possible prime number above 51 is 53.

Therefore minimum possible present age of Binod = 53 + 5 = 58 years.

49. $25 \leq \dfrac{21 + 23 + x + 24 + 27}{5} \leq 28$
    $125 \leq 95 + x \leq 140$
    $30 \leq x \leq 45$
    Number of possible values of $x$ = 16.

50. Total number of balls in all 10 boxes $= 10 \times 25 = 250$.
    Minimum possible number of balls in 9 of these 10 boxes $= 8 + 9 + 10 + 11 + 12 + 13 + 14 + 15 + 16 = 108$.
    Maximum possible number of balls in any box $= 250 - 108 = 142$.

51. Sum of these five numbers $= 6 \times 5 = 30$.
    Maximum average of the largest two numbers would occur when the three smaller numbers are as small as possible (i.e., when they are 1, 2 and 3, respectively) $\rightarrow$ Max. Average $= (30 - 1 - 2 - 3)/2 = 24/2 = 12$.

52. Let there be B number of boys, G number of girls in class 9th.
    $$\frac{B}{G} = \frac{80 - 70}{85 - 80} = \frac{10}{5} = 2{:}1$$

53. Let the number of girls and boys in class 10TH are g and b respectively.
    $$\frac{b}{g} = \frac{73 - 70}{74 - 73} = 3{:}1, b = 3g$$

    Number of boys of class 10th is three times the number of girls in 9th
    $b = 3G$
    let $B = 2k$, $G = k$, $b = 3k$, $g = k$
    Average score of all students of class 9th and 10th
    $$\frac{2k.85 + k.70 + 3k.74 + k.70}{2k + k + 3k + k} = \frac{532}{7} = 76$$

54. Total possible groups $= (w, x), (w, y), (w, z), (x, y), (x, z), (y, z)$
    According to the question $= w + x + w + y + w + z + x + y + x + z + y + z = 1440$
    $3 (w + x + y + z) = 1440$. Hence, $(w + x + y + z) = 480$.
    Required average $= 480/4 = 120$.

### Level of Difficulty (III)

1. Definitely decrease, since the highest marks in Class *A* is less than the lowest marks in Class *B*.

2. Cannot say since there is no indication of the values of the numbers which are transferred.

3. It will definitely decrease since the highest possible transfer is lower than the lowest value in *C*.

4. The effect on *A* will depend on the profile of the people who are transferred. Hence, anything can happen.

5. Cannot say since there is a possibility that the numbers transferred are such that the average can either increase, decrease or remain constant.

6. If *C* increases, then the average of *C* goes up from 30. For this to happen it is definite that the average of *B* should drop.

7. The maximum possible average for *B* will occur if all the 5 transferees from *A* have 22 marks.

8. The average of Group *A* after the transfer in Q. 7 above is:

   $(400 - 18*5)/15 = 310/15 = 20.66$

9. $(400 - 22*5)/15 = 19.33$

10. $400 + 23*5 = 515$. Average $= 515/25 = 20.6$

11. $400 + 31*5 = 555$. Average $= 555/25 = 22.2$

12. Will always decrease since the net value transferred from *B* to *A* will be higher than the net value transferred from *A* to *B*.

13. Since the lowest score in Class *B* is 23 which is more than the highest score of any student in Class *A*. Hence, *A*'s average will always increase.

14. The maximum possible value for *B* will happen when the *A* to *B* transfer has the maximum possible value and the reverse transfer has the minimum possible value.

15. For the minimum possible value of *B* we will need the *A* to *B* transfer to be the lowest possible value while the *B* to *A* transfer must have the highest possible value. Thus, *A* to *B* transfer → 18* 5 while *B* to *A* transfer will be 31*5. Hence answer is 22.4.

16. The maximum value for *A* will happen in the case of Q. 15. Then the increment for group *A* is:

    $31*5 - 18*5 = 5*(31 - 18) = 65$.

    Thus maximum possible value is $465/20 = 23.25$.

17. Minimum possible average will happen for the transfer we saw in Q. 14. Thus the answer will be $405/20 = 20.25$.

18. The maximum possible value for *C* will be achieved when the transfer from *C* is of five 26's and the transfer back from *B* is of five 31's. Hence, difference is totals will be +25. Hence, max. average = $(900 + 25)/30 = 30.833$.

    [Note here that 900 has come by 30*30]

19. For the maximum possible value of Class *B* the following set of operations will have to hold:

    Five 33's are transferred from *C* to *B*, whatever goes from *B* to *A* comes back from *A* to *B*, then five 23's are transferred from *B* to *C*. This leaves us with:

Increase of 50 marks → average increases by 2 to 27.

20. *A* will attain maximum value if five 33's come to *A* from *C* through *B* and five 18's leave *A*. In such a case the net result is going to be a change of +75. Thus the average will go up by $75/20 = 3.75$ to 23.75.

21–23. Will be solved by the same pattern as the above questions.

   *Note:* For question 22, you need to realise that there are only a maximum of six 31's in group B.

24. Option (c) is correct, since you need to transfer out whatever you got into *A*, in order to keep the value of *A*'s average at the minimum.

25–28. Will be solved by the same pattern as above questions.

29–35. These are standard questions using the concept of averages. Hence, analyse each and every sentence by itself and link the interpretations. If you are getting stuck, the only reason is that you have not used the information in the questions fully.

36. Monthly estimates of income is reduced as the denominator is increased from 12 to 14 at the same time the monthly estimate of expenditure is increased as the denominator is reduced from 12 to 9. Hence, the savings will be underestimated.

37–39. Use the averages formulae and common sense to answer.

40–49. The questions are commonsensical with a lot of calculations and assumptions involved. You have to solve these using all the information provided.

40. Das's score = $15*2 + 7*2.5 = 47.5 → 48$.

    Dasgupta's score = $20*1 + 2*1.5 = 23$.

41. From the above the answer is $48:23 = 96:46$.

42–44. By maximum possible support from the other end, you have to assume that he has Laxman or Sehwag batting aggressively for the entire tenure at the crease. Strike has to be shared equally.

42. Through options, After 60 overs, score would be 150. Then Tendulkar can score @ 4 runs per over (sharing the strike and batting aggressively) and get maximum support @ 3 runs per over. Thus in 30 overs left the target will be achieved.

43. Tendulkar's score for the innings will be $30*4 = 120$.

44. We do not know when Laxman would have come into bat. Hence this cannot be determined.

45–49. Build in each of the conditions in the problem to form a table like:

| Partnership | Partner | Overs faced | Tendulkar's score |
| --- | --- | --- | --- |
| | | Partner's score | |
| 6th wicket | Ganguly | 12 6 overs × 6 | 6 overs × 4 |
| 7th wicket | and so on | | |
| 8th wicket | | | |
| 9th wicket | | | |
| 10th wicket | | | |

# Alligations

**4**

## INTRODUCTION

The chapter of alligation is nothing but a faster technique of solving problems based on the weighted average situation as applied to the case of two groups being mixed together. I have often seen students having a lot of difficulty in solving questions on alligation. Please remember that all problems on alligation can be solved through the weighted average method. Hence, the student is advised to revert to the weighted average formula in case of any confusion.

The use of the techniques of this chapter for solving weighted average problems will help you in saving valuable time wherever a direct question based on the mixing of two groups is asked. Besides, in the case of questions that use the concept of the weighted average as a part of the problem, you will gain a significant edge if you are able to use the techniques illustrated here.

## THEORY

In the chapter on Averages, we had seen the use of the weighted average formula. To recollect, the weighted average is used when a number of smaller groups are mixed together to form one larger group.

If the average of the measured quantity was

| | | | | | |
|---|---|---|---|---|---|
| $A_1$ for group | 1 | containing | $n_1$ | elements |
| $A_2$ for group | 2 | containing | $n_2$ | elements |
| $A_3$ for group | 3 | containing | $n_3$ | elements |
| $A_k$ for group | k | containing | $n_k$ | elements |

We say that the weighted average, $Aw$ is given by:

$$Aw = (n_1A_1 + n_2A_2 + n_3A_3 + \ldots\ldots + n_kA_k)/(n_1 + n_2 + n_3 \ldots + n_k)$$

That is, the weighted average

$$= \frac{\text{Sum total of all groups}}{\text{Total number of elements in all groups together}}$$

In the case of the situation where just two groups are being mixed, we can write this as:

$$Aw = (n_1A_1 + n_2A_2)/(n_1 + n_2)$$

Rewriting this equation we get: $(n_1 + n_2)\,Aw = n_1A_1 + n_2A_2$

$$n_1(Aw - A_1) = n_2(A_2 - Aw)$$

or $n_1/n_2 = (A_2 - Aw)/(Aw - A_1) \rightarrow$ The alligation equation.

## The Alligation Situation

Two groups of elements are mixed together to form a third group containing the elements of both the groups.

If the average of the first group is $A_1$ and the number of elements is $n_1$ and the average of the second group is $A_2$ and the number of elements is $n_2$, then to find the average of the new group formed, we can use either the weighted average equation or the alligation equation.

As a convenient convention, we take $A_1 < A_2$. Then, by the principal of averages, we get $A_1 < Aw < A_2$.

## Illustration 1

Two varieties of rice at ₹ 10 per kg and ₹ 12 per kg are mixed together in the ratio 1 : 2. Find the average price of the resulting mixture.

**Solution** $1/2 = (12 - Aw)/(Aw - 10) \rightarrow Aw - 10 = 24 - 2Aw$

$\Rightarrow 3Aw = 34 \qquad \Rightarrow Aw = 11.33$ ₹/kg.

## Illustration 2

On combining two groups of students having 30 and 40 marks respectively in an exam, the resultant group has an average score of 34. Find the ratio of the number of students in the first group to the number of students in the second group.

**Solution** $n_1/n_2 = (40 - 34)/(34 - 30) = 6/4 = 3/2$

## Graphical Representation of Alligation

The formula illustrated above can be represented by the following cross diagram:

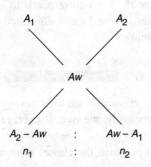

[Note that the cross method yields nothing but the alligation equation. Hence, the cross method is nothing but a graphical representation of the alligation equation.]

As we have seen, there are five variables embedded inside the alligation equation. These being:

the three averages $\rightarrow A_1$, $A_2$ and $Aw$

and the two weights $\rightarrow n_1$ and $n_2$

Based on the problem situation, one of the following cases may occur with respect to the knowns and the unknown, in the problem.

| Case | Known | Unknown |
|------|-------|---------|
| I | (a) $A_1$, $A_2$, $Aw$ | (a) $n_1 : n_2$ |
| | (b) $A_1$, $A_2$, $Aw$, $n_1$ | (b) $n_2$ and $n_1 : n_2$ |
| II | $A_1$, $A_2$, $n_1$, $n_2$ | $Aw$ |
| III | $A_1$, $Aw$, $n_1$, $n_2$ | $A_2$ |

Now, let us try to evaluate the effectiveness of the cross method for each of the three cases illustrated above:

**Case 1:** $A_1$, $A_2$, $Aw$ are known; may be one of $n_1$ or $n_2$ is known.

To find: $n_1 : n_2$ and $n_2$ if $n_1$ is known OR $n_1$ if $n_2$ is known.

Let us illustrate through an example:

## Illustration 3

On mixing two classes of students having average marks 25 and 40 respectively, the overall average obtained is 30 marks. Find

(a) The ratio of students in the classes
(b) The number of students in the first class if the second class had 30 students.

**Solution**

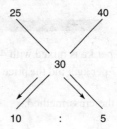

(a) Hence, solution is 2 : 1.
(b) If the ratio is 2 : 1 and the second class has 30 students, then the first class has 60 students.

---

**Note:** The cross method becomes pretty effective in this situation when all the three averages are known and the ratio is to be found out.

---

**Case 2:** $A_1$, $A_2$, $n_1$ and $n_2$ are known, $Aw$ is unknown.

## Illustration 4

4 kg of rice at ₹ 5 per kg is mixed with 8 kg of rice at ₹ 6 per kg. Find the average price of the mixture.

**Solution**

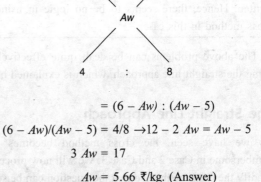

$$= (6 - Aw) : (Aw - 5)$$

$$\Rightarrow \quad (6 - Aw)/(Aw - 5) = 4/8 \rightarrow 12 - 2\,Aw = Aw - 5$$

$$3\,Aw = 17$$

$$\therefore \qquad Aw = 5.66 \text{ ₹/kg. (Answer)}$$

**Task for student:** Solve through the alligation formula approach and through the weighted average approach to get the solution. Notice, the amount of time required in doing the same.

**Note:** The cross method becomes quite cumbersome in this case, as this method results in the formula being written. Hence, there seems to be no logic in using the cross method in this case.

**Case 3:** $A_1$, $Aw$, $n_1$ and $n_2$ are known; $A_2$ is unknown.

## Illustration 5

5 kg of rice at ₹ 6 per kg is mixed with 4 kg of rice to get a mixture costing ₹ 7 per kg. Find the price of the costlier rice.

**Solution**   Using the cross method:

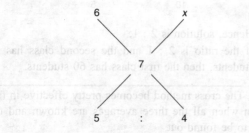

$$= (x - 7) : 1$$
$$\therefore \quad (x - 7)/1 = 5/4 \rightarrow 4x - 28 = 5$$
$$\therefore \quad x = ₹ 8.25.$$

**Task for student:** Solve through the alligation formula approach and through the weighted average approach to get the solution. Notice the amount of time required in doing the same.

**Note:** The cross method becomes quite cumbersome in this case since this method results in the formula being written. Hence, there seems to be no logic in using the cross method in this case.

The above problems can be dealt quite effectively by using the straight line approach, which is explained below.

## The Straight Line Approach

As we have seen, the cross method becomes quite cumbersome in Case 2 and Case 3. We will now proceed to modify the cross method so that the question can be solved graphically in all the three cases.

Consider the following diagram, which results from closing the cross like a pair of scissors. Then the positions of $A_1$, $A_2$, $Aw$, $n_1$ and $n_2$ are as shown.

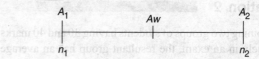

Visualise this as a fragment of the number line with points $A_1$, $Aw$ and $A_2$ in that order from left to right. Then,

(a) $n_2$ is responsible for the distance between $A_1$ and $Aw$ or $n_2$ corresponds to $Aw - A_1$

(b) $n_1$ is responsible for the distance between $Aw$ and $A_2$. or $n_1$ corresponds to $A_2 - Aw$

(c) $(n_1 + n_2)$ is responsible for the distance between $A_1$ and $A_2$. or $(n_1 + n_2)$ corresponds to $A_2 - A_1$.

The processes for the 3 cases illustrated above can then be illustrated below:

## Illustration 6

On mixing two classes of students having average marks 25 and 40 respectively, the overall average obtained is 30 marks. Find

(a) the ratio in which the classes were mixed.

(b) the number of students in the first class if the second class had 30 students.

**Solution**

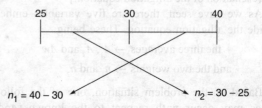

Hence, ratio is 2 : 1, and the second class has 60 students.

**Case 2**   $A_1$, $A_2$, $n_1$ and $n_2$ are known; $Aw$ is unknown.

## Illustration 7

4 kg of rice at ₹ 5 per kg is mixed with 8 kg of rice at ₹ 6 per kg. Find the average price of the mixture.

**Solution**

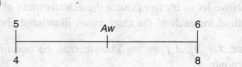

is the same as

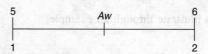

Then, by unitary method:

$$n_1 + n_2 \text{ corresponds to } A_2 - A_1$$
$$\rightarrow 1 + 2 \text{ corresponds to } 6 - 5$$

That is, 3 corresponds to 1

$$\therefore \quad n_2 \text{ will correspond to } \frac{(A_2 - A_1) \times n_2}{(n_1 + n_2)}$$

In this case $(1/3) \times 2 = 0.66$.

Hence, the required answer is 5.66.

---

**Note:** In this case, the problem associated with the cross method is overcome and the solution becomes graphical.

---

**Case 3:** $A_1$, $Aw$, $n_1$ and $n_2$ are known; $A_2$ is unknown.

## Illustration 8

5 kg of rice at ₹ 6 per kg is mixed with 4 kg of rice to get a mixture costing ₹ 7 per kg. Find the price of the costlier rice.

Using straight line method:

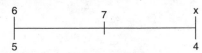

4 corresponds to $7 - 6$ and 5 corresponds to $x - 7$.

The thought process should go like:

$$4 \rightarrow 1$$
$$\therefore \qquad 5 \rightarrow 1.25$$

Hence, $x - 7 = 1.25$

and $\qquad x = 8.25$

## ⌕ SOME TYPICAL SITUATIONS WHERE ALLIGATIONS CAN BE USED

Given below are typical alligation situations, which students should be able to recognize. This will help them improve upon the time required in solving questions. Although in this chapter we have illustrated problems based on alligation at level 1 only, alligation is used in more complex problems where the weighted average is an intermediate step in the solution process.

The following situations should help the student identify alligation problems better as well as spot the way $A_1$, $A_2$, $n_1$ and $n_2$ and $Aw$ are mentioned in a problem.

In each of the following problems the following magnitudes represent these variables:

$$A_1 = 20, \quad A_2 = 30, \quad n_1 = 40, \quad n_2 = 60$$

Each of these problems will yield an answer of 26 as the value of $Aw$.

1. A man buys 40 kg of rice at ₹ 20/kg and 60 kg of rice at ₹ 30/kg. Find his average price. (26/kg)
2. Pradeep mixes two mixtures of milk and water. He mixes 40 litres of the first containing 20% water and 60 litres of the second containing 30% water. Find the percentage of water in the final mixture. (26%)
3. Two classes are combined to form a larger class. The first class having 40 students scored an average of 20 marks on a test while the second having 60 students scored an average of 30 marks on the same test. What was the average score of the combined class on the test. (26 marks)
4. A trader earns a profit of 20% on 40% of his goods sold, while he earns a profit of 30% on 60% of his goods sold. Find his percentage profit on the whole. (26%)
5. A car travels at 20 km/h for 40 minutes and at 30 km/h for 60 minutes. Find the average speed of the car for the journey. (26 km/hr)
6. 40% of the revenues of a school came from the junior classes while 60% of the revenues of the school came from the senior classes. If the school raises its fees by 20% for the junior classes and by 30% for the senior classes, find the percentage increase in the revenues of the school. (26%)

---

### Some Keys to spot $A_1$, $A_2$ and $Aw$ and differentiate these from $n_1$ and $n_2$

1. Normally, there are 3 averages mentioned in the problem, while there are only 2 quantities. This isn't foolproof though, since at times the question might confuse the student by giving 3 values for quantities representing $n_1$, $n_2$ and $n_1 + n_2$ respectively.
2. $A_1$, $A_2$ and $Aw$ are always rate units, while $n_1$ and $n_2$ are quantity units.
3. The denominator of the average unit corresponds to the quantity unit (i.e. unit for $n_1$ and $n_2$).
4. All percentage values represent the average values.

---

## A Typical Problem

A typical problem related to the topic of alligation goes as follows:

4 litres of wine are drawn from a cask containing 40 litres of wine. It is replaced by water. The process is repeated 3 times

(a) What is the final quantity of wine left in the cask.

(b) What is the ratio of wine to water finally.

If we try to chart out the process, we get: Out of 40 litres of wine, 4 are drawn out.

This leaves 36 litres wine and 4 litres water. (Ratio of 9 : 1)

Now, when 4 litres are drawn out of this mixture, we will get 3.6 litres of wine and 0.4 litres of water (as the ratio is 9 : 1). Thus at the end of the second step we get: 32.4 litres of wine and 7.6 litres of water. Further, the process is repeated, drawing out 3.24 litres wine and 0.76 litres water leaving 29.16 litres of wine and 10.84 litres of water.

This gives the final values and the ratio required.

A closer look at the process will yield that we can get the amount of wine left by:

$$40 \times 36/40 \times 36/40 \times 36/40 = 40 \times (36/40)^3$$
$$\Rightarrow 40 \times (1 - 4/40)^3$$

*Space for Notes*

This yields the formula:

Wine left : Capacity $\times$ (1 − fraction of wine withdrawn)$^n$ for $n$ operations.

Thus, you could have multiplied:

$$40 \times (0.9)^3 \text{ to get the answer}$$

That is, reduce 40 by 10% successively thrice to get the required answer.

Thus, the thought process could be:

$$40 - 10\% \rightarrow 36 - 10\% \rightarrow 32.4 - 10\% \rightarrow 29.16$$

## LEVEL OF DIFFICULTY (I)

1. A mixture of 160 gallons of wine and water contains 25% water. How much water must be added to the mixture in order to increase the percentage of water to 40% of the new mixture?
   - (a) 40 gals
   - (b) 50 gals
   - (c) 80 gals
   - (d) 33 gals

2. 800 students took the CAT exam in Delhi. 50% of the boys and 90% of the girls cleared the cut off in the examination. If the total percentage of qualifying students is 60%, how many girls appeared in the examination?
   - (a) 100
   - (b) 120
   - (c) 150
   - (d) 200

3. If 10 kg of sugar costing ₹15/kg and 20 kg of salt costing ₹10/kg are mixed, find the average cost of the mixture in ₹ per kilogram.
   - (a) 11.67
   - (b) 12.33
   - (c) 12.67
   - (d) 11.33

4. The average salary per head of all workers (Grade A and Grade B) of a company is ₹ 400. The average salary of 100 grade A workers is ₹ 1000. If the average salary per head of the rest of the Grade B workers is ₹ 300, find the total number of workers in the company.
   - (a) 1000
   - (b) 800
   - (c) 500
   - (d) 700

5. Ashok purchased two qualities of grains at the rate of ₹ 100 per quintal and ₹ 160 per quintal. In 50 quintals of the second quality, how much grain of the first quality should be mixed so that by selling the resulting mixture at ₹ 195 per quintal, he gains a profit of 30%?
   - (a) 10 quintals
   - (b) 14 quintals
   - (c) 20 quintals
   - (d) None of these

6. Two types of milk having the rates of ₹8/kg and ₹10/kg respectively are mixed in order to produce a mixture having the rate of ₹9.20/kg. What should be the amount of the second type of milk if the amount of the first type of milk in the mixture is 20 kg?
   - (a) 25 kg
   - (b) 30 kg
   - (c) 40 kg
   - (d) 20 kg

7. How many kilograms of salt worth ₹ 360 per kg should be mixed with 10 kg of salt worth ₹420 per kg, such that by selling the mixture at ₹ 480 per kg, there may be a gain of 20%?
   - (a) 5 kg
   - (b) 3 kg
   - (c) 2 kg
   - (d) 4 kg

8. Kiran lends ₹ 1000 on simple interest to Harsh for a period of 5 years. She lends a part of the amount at 2% interest and the rest at 8% and receives ₹ 300 as the amount of interest. How much money (in ₹) did she lend on 2% interest rate?
   - (a) 333.33
   - (b) 666.67
   - (c) 400
   - (d) 500

9. A tank contains 500 liters of wine. 50 liters of wine is taken out of it and replaced by water. The process is repeated again. Find the proportion of water and wine in the resulting mixture.
   - (a) 1 : 4
   - (b) 41 : 50
   - (c) 19 : 81
   - (d) 81 : 19

10. A man purchased a table and a chair for ₹2000. He sold the table at a profit of 20% and the chair at a profit of 40%. In this way, his total profit was 25%. Find the cost price (in ₹) of the table.
    - (a) 1500
    - (b) 900
    - (c) 1000
    - (d) 800

11. A dishonest shopkeeper purchased milk at ₹100 per litre and mixed 10 liters of water in it. By selling the mixture at the rate of ₹ 100 per litre he earns a profit of 25%. The quantity of the amount of the mixture that he had was:
    - (a) 50 liters
    - (b) 40 liters
    - (c) 25 liters
    - (d) 60 liters

12. A tank has a capacity of 10 gallons and is full of alcohol. 2 gallons of alcohol are drawn out and the tank is again filled with water. This process is repeated 5 times. Find out how much alcohol is left in the resulting mixture finally?
    - (a) 2048/625 gallons
    - (b) 3346/625 gallons
    - (c) 2048/3125 gallons
    - (d) 625 gallons

13. A vessel is full of milk 1/4 of the milk is taken out and the vessel is filled with water. If the process is repeated 4 times and 100 liters of milk is finally left in the vessel, what is the capacity of the vessel?
    - (a) 25600/243 liters
    - (b) $\frac{2461}{81}$ liters
    - (c) 25600/81 liters
    - (d) 30 liters

14. In what ratio should two qualities of tea having the rates of ₹ 40 per kg and ₹ 30 per kg be mixed in order to get a mixture that would have a rate ofRs 35per kg?
    - (a) 1 : 2
    - (b) 1 : 1
    - (c) 1 : 3
    - (d) 3 : 1

15. Raman steals four gallons of liquid soap kept in a train compartment's bathroom from a container that is full of liquid soap. He then fills it with water to avoid detection. Unable to resist the temptation he

steals 4 gallons of the mixture again, and fills it with water. When the liquid soap is checked at a station it is found that the ratio of the liquid soap now left in the container to that of the water in it is 36: 13. What was the initial amount of the liquid soap in the container if it is known that the liquid soap is neither used nor augmented by anybody else during the entire period?

(a)  7 gallons          (b)  14 gallons
(c)  21 gallons         (d)  28 gallons

16. In what ratio should water be mixed with soda costing ₹12 per litre so as to make a profit of 50% by selling the diluted liquid at ₹15 per litre?

(a)  10 : 1             (b)  5 : 1
(c)  1: 5              (d)  6 : 1

17. A sum of ₹ 4 is made up of 20 coins that are either 10 paise coins or 60 paise coins. Find out how many 20 paise coins are there in the total amount.

(a)  10                (b)  13
(c)  16                (d)  15

18. Pinku a dishonest grocer professes to sell pure butter at cost price, but he mixes it with adulterated fat and thereby gains 25%. Find the percentage of adulterated fat in the mixture assuming that adulterated fat is freely available.

(a)  20%               (b)  25%
(c)  33.33%            (d)  40%

19. A mixture of 75 liters of alcohol and water contains 20% of water. How much water must be added to the above mixture to make the water 25% of the resulting mixture?

(a)  5 liters          (b)  1.5 litre
(c)  2 liters          (d)  2.5 liters

20. A mixture of 40 liters of milk and water contains 10% water. How much water should be added to it to increase the percentage of water to 25%?

(a)  5 liters          (b)  6 liters
(c)  2.5 liters        (d)  8 liters

21. Two vessels contain a mixture of spirit and water. In the first vessel the ratio of spirit to water is 8 : 3 and in the second vessel the ratio is 5 : 1. A 35 litre cask is filled from these vessels so as to contain a mixture of spirit and water in the ratio of 4 :1. How many liters are taken from the first vessel?

(a)  11 liters         (b)  22 liters
(c)  16.5 liters       (d)  17.5 liters

22. There are two mixtures of milk and water, the quantity of milk in them being 20% and 80% of the mixture. If 2 liters of the first are mixed with three liters of the second, what will be the ratio of milk to water in the new mixture?

(a)  11 : 12           (b)  11 : 9
(c)  19 : 11           (d)  14 : 11

23. There are two kinds of alloys of silver and copper. The first alloy contains silver and copper such that 93.33% of it is silver. In the second alloy there is 86.66% silver. What weight of the first alloy should be mixed with some weight of the second alloy so as to make a 100 kg mass containing 90% of silver?

(a)  55 kg             (b)  50 kg
(c)  70 kg             (d)  25 kg

24. Two buckets of equal capacity are full of a mixture of milk and water. In the first, the ratio of milk to water is 1 : 7 and in the second it is 3 : 8. Now both the mixtures are mixed in a bigger container. What is the resulting ratio of milk to water?

(a)  35 : 141          (b)  42 : 49
(c)  43 : 41           (d)  41 : 53

25. A bag contains a total of 105 coins of ₹1, 50 p and 25 p denominations. Find the total number of coins of ₹ 1 if there are a total of 50.5 rupees in the bag and it is known that the number of 25 paise coins are 133.33% more than the number of 1 rupee coins.

(a)  56                (b)  25
(c)  24                (d)  None of these

26. Two vessels contain spirit and water mixed respectively in the ratio of 1: 4 and 4 : 1 Find the ratio in which these are to be mixed to get a new mixture in which the ratio of spirit to water is 1: 3.

(a)  11 : 1            (b)  13 : 1
(c)  11 : 2            (d)  11 : 3

27. The price of a table and a chair is ₹3000. The table was sold at a 20% profit and the chair at a 10% loss. If in the transaction a man gains ₹ 300, how much is cost price (in ₹) of the table?

(a)  1000             (b)  2500
(c)  2000             (d)  None of these

28. A person purchased a pen and a pencil for ₹ 15. He sold the pen at a profit of 20% and the pencil at a profit of 30%. If his total profit was 24%, find the cost price of the pen.

(a)  ₹10.50           (b)  ₹ 12
(c)  ₹ 9              (d)  ₹ 10

29. A container is full of a mixture of kerosene and petrol in which there is 18% kerosene. Eight liters are drawn off and then the vessel is filled with petrol. If the kerosene is now 15%, how much does the container hold?

(a)  40 liters         (b)  32 liters
(c)  36 liters         (d)  48 liters

30. Two solutions of 80% and 87% purity are mixed resulting in 35 liters of mixture of 84% purity. How much is the quantity of the first solution in the resulting mixture?

(a)  15 liters         (b)  12 liters
(c)  9 liters          (d)  6 liters

31. In the Delhi zoo, there are lions and there are hens. If the heads are counted, there are 180, while the legs are 448. What will be the number of lions in the zoo?
    (a) 36
    (b) 88
    (c) 44
    (d) 136

32. A bonus of ₹ 1,00,000 was divided among 500 workers of a factory. Each male worker gets 500 rupees and each female worker gets 100 rupees. Find the number of male workers in the factory.
    (a) 250
    (b) 375
    (c) 290
    (d) 125

33. What will be the ratio of honey and water in the final solution formed by mixing honey and water that are present in three vessels of equal capacity in the ratios 4:1, 5:2 and 6:1 respectively?
    (a) 166 : 22
    (b) 83 : 22
    (c) 83 : 44
    (d) None of these

34. A mixture worth ₹ 80 a kg is formed by mixing two types of flour, one costing 50 per kg while the other 110 per kg. In what proportion must they have been mixed?
    (a) 1 : 1
    (b) 1 : 2
    (c) 2 : 1
    (d) 1 : 3

35. A 10 percent gain is made by selling the mixture of two types of milk at ₹ 48 per kg. If the type costing ₹ 61 per kg was mixed with 100 kg of the other, how many kilograms of the former was mixed?
    (a) 38 kg
    (b) 30.5 kg
    (c) 19 kg
    (d) Cannot be determined

36. A man buys milk at ₹ 85 per liter and dilutes it with water. He sells the mixture at the same rate and thus gains 11.11%. Find the quantity of water mixed by him in every liter of milk.
    (a) 0.111 liters
    (b) 0.909 liters
    (c) 0.1 litre
    (d) 0.125 liters

37. In what proportion must water be mixed with honey so as to gain 10% by selling the mixture at the cost price of the honey? (Assume that water is freely available)
    (a) 1 : 4
    (b) 1 : 5
    (c) 1 : 6
    (d) 1 : 10

38. A milkman stole milk from a can that contained 50% of milk and he replaced what he had stolen with milk having 20% milk. The bottle then contained only 25% milk. How much of the bottle did he steal?
    (a) 80%
    (b) 83.33%
    (c) 85.71%
    (d) 88.88%

39. Shruti possessing ₹ 10,000, lent a part of it at 5% simple interest and the remaining at 20% simple interest. Her total income after 5 years was ₹7500. Find the sum lent at 20% rate.
    (a) ₹1666.67
    (b) ₹6666.67
    (c) ₹3333.33
    (d) None of these

40. Sharman decides to travel 100 kilometres in 8 hours partly by foot and partly on a bicycle, his speed on foot being 10 km/h and that on bicycle being 20 km/h, what distance would he travel on foot?
    (a) 20 km
    (b) 30 km
    (c) 50 km
    (d) 60 km

*Space for Rough Work*

# ANSWER KEY

## Level of Difficulty (I)

| | | | |
|---|---|---|---|
| 1. (a) | 2. (d) | 3. (a) | 4. (d) |
| 5. (a) | 6. (b) | 7. (a) | 8. (a) |
| 9. (c) | 10. (a) | 11. (a) | 12. (a) |
| 13. (c) | 14. (b) | 15. (d) | 16. (c) |
| 17. (c) | 18. (a) | 19. (a) | 20. (d) |
| 21. (a) | 22. (d) | 23. (b) | 24. (a) |
| 25. (c) | 26. (a) | 27. (c) | 28. (c) |
| 29. (d) | 30. (a) | 31. (c) | 32. (d) |
| 33. (b) | 34. (a) | 35. (d) | 36. (a) |
| 37. (d) | 38. (b) | 39. (b) | 40. (d) |

## Solutions and Shortcuts

### Level of Difficulty (I)

1. There are multiple ways of solving this question. In 160 gallons since we have 25% water, the composition would be 120 gallons of wine and 40 gallons of water. After adding more water to this, the water would become 40 + w, while the wine would remain at 120 gallons. This 120 gallons of wine would correspond to 60% wine in the final mixture. Since, 120 = 60%, 200 = 100%. So we need to add, 40 gallons of water. Alternately, you can solve this using options to check, the case when the wine to water becomes 60% to 40%. In 120 gallons of wine + 40 gallons of water, if you add 40 gallons of water, you will end up with 60% wine and 40% water. Hence, option (a) is correct.

2. The ratio of boys and girls appearing for the exam can be seen to be 3:1 using the following alligation figure.

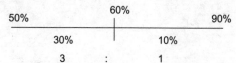

This means that out of 800 students, there must have been 200 girls who appeared in the exam.

3. Solving the following alligation figure:

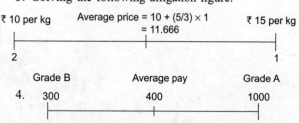

4.

From the figure we can see that the ratio of Grade A and Grade B workers is 1: 6. Since, there are 100 grade A workers, there would be 600 Grade B workers. Hence, total number of grade B workers = 600

Total workers in the company = 100 + 600 = 700.

5. By selling at 195 if we need to get a profit of 30% it means that the cost price would be 195/1.30 = 150.

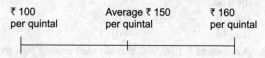

From the alligation figure, you can see that the ratio of the quantities of the two pulses would be 1:5. Since, we have 50 quintals of the second quality, we must have 10 quintals of the first. Hence, option (a) is correct.

6. Mixing ₹ 8/kg and ₹ 10/kg to get ₹ 9.20 per kg we get that the ratio of mixing is (10 − 9.2): (9.2 − 8) = 2:3. If the first milk is 20 kg, the second would be 30 kg.

7. Since by selling at ₹ 480 we want a profit of 20%, it means that the average cost required is ₹ 400 per kg. Mixing salt worth ₹ 360/kg and ₹ 420/kg to get ₹ 400/kg means a mixture ratio of 1:2. Thus, to 10 kg of the second variety we need to add 5 kg of the first variety to get the required cost price.

8. Since Kiran earns ₹ 300 in 5 years, it means that she earns an interest of 300/5 = ₹ 60 per year. On an investment of 1000, an annual interest of 60 represents an average interest rate of 6%.

Then using the alligation figure below:

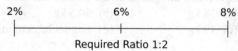

We get the ratio of investments as 1:2. Hence, she lent one third of the amount i.e. 1 × 1000/3 = 333.33 at 2% per annum.

9. Amount of wine left = 500 × 9/10 × 9/10 = 405 liters. Hence, water = 95 liters. Ratio of water and wine = 19:81. Option (c) is correct.

10. The ratio of the cost of the table and the chair would be (40 − 25):(25 − 20) or 3:1 as can be seen from the following alligation figure:

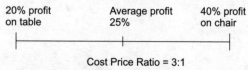

Thus, the cost of the table would be ₹ 1500.

11. Cost price of the mixture = ₹ 80 per liter

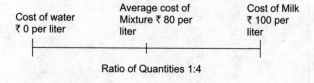

Since, water = 10 liters, Pure milk = 40 liters
Total quantity of the mixture = 40+ 10 = 50 liters.

12. The amount of alcohol left = $10 \times 4/5 \times 4/5 \times 4/5 \times 4/5 \times 4/5 = 10240/3125 = 2048/625$

13. Let the quantity of milk initially be $Q$. Then we have $Q \times \frac{3}{4} \times \frac{3}{4} \times \frac{3}{4} \times \frac{3}{4} = 100 \rightarrow Q = 25600/81$ liters.

14. The ratio would be 1:1 as seen from the figure:

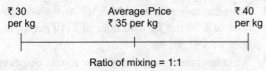

15. It can be seen from the ratio 36:13 that the proportion of liquid soap to water is 36/49 after two mixings. This means that $6/7^{th}$ of the liquid soap must have been allowed to remain in the container and hence $1/7^{th}$ of the container's original liquid soap, would have been drawn out by the thief. Since he takes out 4 gallons every time, there must have been 28 gallons in the container. (as 4 is $1/7^{th}$ of 28).

16. In order to sell at a 50% profit by selling at ₹15 the cost price should be 10. Also since water is freely available, we can say that the ratio of water and soda must be 1:5 as can be seen from the alligation figure.

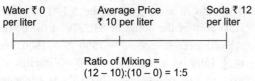

Hence, option (c) is correct.

17. The average value of a coin is 20 paise and there are only 10 paise and 60 paise coins in the sum. Hence, the ratio of the number of 10 paise coins to 60 paise coins would be 4: 1.

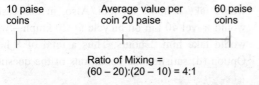

Since there are a total of 20 coins, the number of 10 paise coins would be $4 \times 20/5 = 16$ coins.

18. The ratio of mixing would be 1:4 which means that the percentage of adulterated fat would be 20%.

19.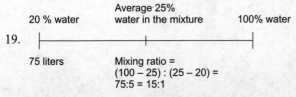

In the 15:1 ratio since, 15 corresponds to 75 liters, 1 would correspond to 5 liters. We should mix 5 liters of water.

20. In 40 liters there is 4 liters water and 36 liters milk. If we mix 8 liters of water to this (from option d); we would get a mixture containing 36 liters milk and 12 liters water – giving us the required 75% milk in the mixture. Hence, option (d) is correct.

21. Solving through options is the best way to tackle this question. Option (a) fits the conditions of the problem as if there are 11 liters in the first vessel, there would be 8 liters of spirit. Also it means that we would be taking 24 liters from the second vessel out of which there would be 20 liters of spirit. Thus, total spirit would be 28 out of 35 liters giving us 7 liters of water. This matches our requirement of a final ratio of 4:1 of spirit and water in the cask.

22. The percentage of milk in the new mixture would be:
$(2 \times 20 + 3 \times 80)/5 = 280/5 = 56\%$. The ratio of milk to water in the new mixture would be 56:44 = 14:11.

23. In order to mix two tin alloys containing 86.66% silver and 93.33% silver to get 90% silver, the ratio of mixing should be 1:1. Thus, each variety should be 50 kgs each.

24. Assume the capacity of the two containers is 88 liters each. When we mix 88 liters of the first and 88 liters of the second, the amount of milk would be: $88 \times 1/8 + 88 \times 3/11 = 11 + 24 = 35$ liters.
Consequently the amount of water would be $2 \times 88 - 35 = 176 - 35 = 141$ liters. Required ratio = 35: 141. Option (a) is correct.

25. $O + F + T = 105$
$O + 0.5F + 0.25T = 50.5$
$T = 2.333 \ O$.
Solving we get: 24 coins of ₹1.

26. The first vessel contains 20% spirit while the second vessel contains 80% spirit. To get a 1:3 ratio we need 25% spirit in the mixture. The ratio of mixing can be seen using the following alligation figure:

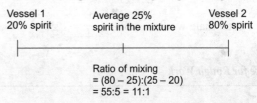

27. Solve using options as that would be the best way to tackle this question. Option (c) fits the situation perfectly as if we take the price of the table as ₹ 2000, the cost of the chair would be ₹ 1000. The profit in selling the table would be ₹ 400 while the loss in selling the chair would be ₹ 100. The total profit would be ₹ 300 as stipulated by the problem.

28. The following alligation visualization would help us solve the problem:

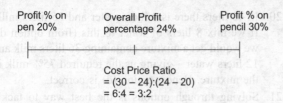

Cost of pen = 3/5 of the total cost price = $\frac{3}{5} \times 15$ = ₹ 9.

29. The following visualization would help:

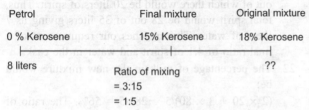

From the figure we can see that the original mixture would be 40 liters and the petrol being mixed is 8 liters. Thus, the container capacity is 48 liters.

30. 80% and 87% mixed to form 84% means that the mixing ratio is 3:4. The first solution would be $\frac{3}{7}$ × 35 = 15 liters.

31. If all the animals were hens we would have 180 heads and 360 legs. If we reduce the number of hens by 1 to 179 and increase the number of lions by 1 to 1, we would get an incremental 2 legs.
Since, the number of legs we need to increment is 88 i.e. (448 – 360 = 88), we need to have 44 lions and 136 hens.

32. Average bonus per worker = 100000/500 = 200.

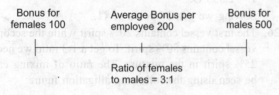

Total male workers = 500 × $\frac{1}{4}$ = 125.

33. In order to solve this we need to assume a value for the amounts in the vessels. If we assume 35 liters (LCM of 5, 7 and 7) as the quantities in all the three vessels we will get:
28 liters + 25 liters + 30 liters = 83 liters of honey and 22 liters of water in 105 liters of the mixture. The required ratio is 83:22.

34. The required ratio would be 1:1 as we are mixing flour of ₹ 50 per kg with flour of ₹110 per kg to get flour of ₹80 per kg.

35. We cannot determine the answer to this question as we do not know the price per kg of the other type of milk. Hence, we cannot find the ratio of mixing which would be required in order to move further in this question.

36. The requisite 11.11% profit can be got by mixing 0.111 liters of water in 1 liter of milk. In such a case the total milk quantity would be 1.111 liters and the price would be for 1 liter only. The profit would be 0.111/1 = 11.11%.

37. To gain 10% by selling at cost price, water should comprise 10 out of a total of 110. The ratio of mixing that achieves this is 1:10.

38. 20% milk is mixed with 50% milk to get 25% milk. The ratio of mixing would be 5:1. This means he stole 5/6th of the bottle or 83.33% of the bottle.

39. Annual interest income = 7500 /5 = 1500. Interest of ₹ 1500 on a lending of ₹10000 implies a 15% average rate of interest. This 15% is generated by mixing the two loans @ 5% and 20% respectively. The ratio in which the two loans should be allocated would be 1:2. The amount lent at 20% would be 2 × 10000/3 = 6666.67.

40. Solve using options. If he travels 60 km on foot he would take 6 hours on foot. Also, in this case he would travel 40 km on bicycle @ 20 kmph – which would take him 2 hours. Thus a total of 8 hours. Option (d) satisfies the conditions of the question.

*Space for Rough Work*

## 🎯 BLOCK REVIEW TEST

## REVIEW TEST

1. Rakshit bought 19 erasers for ₹ 10. He paid 20 paise more for each white eraser than for each brown eraser. What could be the price of a white eraser and how many white erasers could he have bought?
   - (a) 60 paise, 8
   - (b) 60 paise, 12
   - (c) 50 paise, 8
   - (d) 50 paise, 10

2. After paying all your bills, you find that you have ₹7.20 in your pocket. You have equal number of 50 paise and 10 paise coins; but no other coins nor any other currency notes. How many coins do you have?
   - (a) 8
   - (b) 24
   - (c) 27
   - (d) 30

3. Suresh Kumar went to the market with ₹ 100. If he buys three pens and six pencils he uses up all his money. On the other hand if he buys three pencils and six pens he would fall short by 20%. If he wants to buy equal number of pens & pencils, how many pencils can he buy?
   - (a) 4
   - (b) 5
   - (c) 6
   - (d) 7

4. For the above question, what is the amount of money he would save if he were to buy 3 pens and 3 pencils?
   - (a) ₹ 50
   - (b) ₹25
   - (c) ₹75
   - (d) ₹40

5. Abdul goes to the market to buy bananas. If he can bargain and reduce the price per dozen by ₹ 2, he can buy 3 dozen bananas instead of 2 dozen with the money he has. How much money does he have?
   - (a) ₹ 6
   - (b) ₹ 12
   - (c) ₹ 18
   - (d) ₹ 24

6. Two oranges, three bananas and four apples cost ₹15. Three oranges, two bananas and one apple cost ₹10. I bought 3 oranges, 3 bananas and 3 apples. How much did I pay?
   - (a) ₹10
   - (b) ₹8
   - (c) ₹15
   - (d) cannot be determined

7. John bought five mangoes and ten oranges together for forty rupees. Subsequently, he returned one mango and got two oranges in exchange. The price of an orange would be
   - (a) ₹ 1
   - (b) ₹ 2
   - (c) ₹ 3
   - (d) ₹ 4

8. Two towns A and B are 100 km apart. A school is to be built for 100 students of Town B and 30 students of Town A. The Expenditure on transport is ₹1.20 per km per person. If the total expenditure on transport by all 130 students is to be as small as possible, then the school should be built at
   - (a) 33 km from Town A
   - (b) 33 km from Town B
   - (c) Town A
   - (d) Town B

9. A person who has a certain amount with him goes to the market. He can buy 50 oranges or 40 mangoes. He retains 10% of the amount for taxi fare and buys 20 mangoes and of the balance he purchases oranges. Number of oranges he can purchase is
   - (a) 36
   - (b) 40
   - (c) 15
   - (d) 20

10. 72 hens costs ₹ _96.7_. Then what does each hen cost, where numbers at "_" are not visible or are written in illegible hand?
    - (a) ₹3.43
    - (b) ₹5.31
    - (c) ₹5.51
    - (d) ₹6.22

*Directions for Questions 10 to 12:* There are 60 students in a class. These students are divided into three groups A, B and C of 15, 20 and 25 students each. The groups A and C are combined to form group D

11. What is the average weight of the students in group D?
    - (a) more than the average weight of A.
    - (b) more than the average weight of C.
    - (c) less than the average weight of C.
    - (d) Cannot be determined.

12. If one student from Group A is shifted to group B, which of the following will be true?
    - (a) The average weight of both groups increases
    - (b) The average weight of both groups decreases
    - (c) The average weight of the class remains the same.
    - (d) Cannot be determined.

13. If all the students of the class have the same weight then which of the following is false?
    - (a) The average weight of all the four groups is the same.
    - (b) The total weight of A and C is twice the total weight of B.
    - (c) The average weight of D is greater than the average weight of A.
    - (d) The average weight of all the groups remains the same even if a number of students are shifted from one group to another.

14. The average marks of a student in ten papers are 80. If the highest and the lowest score are not considered

the average is 81. If his highest score is 92 find the lowest.

(a) 55
(b) 60
(c) 62
(d) Cannot be determined

15. A shipping clerk has five boxes of different but unknown weights each weighing less than 100 kg. The clerk weighs the boxes in pairs. The weights obtained are 110, 112, 113, 114, 115, 116, 117,118, 120 and 121 kg. What is the weight of the heaviest box?

(a) 60 kg
(b) 62 kg
(c) 64 kg
(d) Cannot be determined

16. The total expenses of a boarding house are partly fixed and partly varying linearly with the number of boarders. The average expense per boarder is ₹ 700 when there are 25 boarders and ₹ 600 when there are 50 boarders. What is the average expense per boarder when there are 100 boarders?

(a) 550
(b) 580
(c) 540
(d) 570

17. A yearly payment to a servant is ₹ 90 plus one turban. The servant leaves the job after 9 months and receives ₹65 and a turban, then find the price of the turban.

(a) ₹10
(b) ₹15
(c) ₹7.50
(d) Cannot be determined

18. A leather factory produces two kinds of bags, standard and deluxe. The profit margin is ₹20 on a standard bag and ₹30 on a deluxe bag. Every bag must be processed on machine A and on Machine B. The processing times per bag on the two machines are as follows:

Time required (Hours/bag)

| | Machine A | Machine B |
|---|---|---|
| Standard Bag | 4 | 6 |
| Deluxe Bag | 5 | 10 |

The total time available on machine A is 700 hours and on machine B is 1250 hours. Among the following production plans, which one meets the machine availability constraints and maximizes the profit?

(a) Standard 75 bags, Deluxe 80 bags
(b) Standard 100 bags, Deluxe 60 bags
(c) Standard 50 bags, Deluxe 100 bags
(d) Standard 60 bags, Deluxe 90 bags

19. Three math classes: X, Y, and Z, take an algebra test.

The average score of class X is 83.
The average score of class Y is 76.
The average score of class Z is 85.
What is the average score of classes X, Y, Z ?

(a) 81.5
(b) 80.5
(c) 83
(d) Cannot be determined

20. Prabhat ordered 4 Arrow shirts and some additional Park Avenue shirts. The price of one Arrow shirt was twice that of one Park Avenue shirt. When the order was executed it was found that the number of the two brands had been interchanged. This increased the bill by 40%. The ratio of the number of Arrow shirts to the number of Park Avenue shirts in the original order was:

(a) 1:3
(b) 1:4
(c) 1:2
(d) 1:5

21. Three groups of companies: Tata, Birla and Reliance announced the average of the annual profit for all years since their establishment.

The average profit of Tata is ₹ 75,000 lakh
The average profit of Birla is ₹ 64000 lakh
The average profit of Reliance is ₹ 73000 lakh
The average profit of all results of Tata and Birla together is ₹ 70000 lakh.
The average profit of all results of Birla and Reliance together is ₹ 69000 lakh.
Approximately what is the average profit for all the three group of companies?

(a) ₹ 70800 lakh
(b) ₹ 71086 lakh
(c) ₹ 70666 lakh
(d) Cannot be determined

## ANSWER KEY

### Review Test

| | | | |
|---|---|---|---|
| 1. (b) | 2. (b) | 3. (a) | 4. (b) |
| 5. (b) | 6. (c) | 7. (b) | 8. (d) |
| 9. (d) | 10. (c) | 11. (d) | 12. (c) |
| 13. (c) | 14. (b) | 15. (b) | 16. (a) |
| 17. (a) | 18. (a) | 19. (d) | 20. (a) |
| 21. (b) | | | |

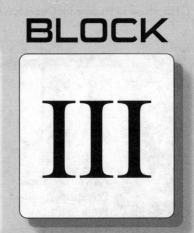

# BLOCK III

# Arithmetic and Word-based Problems

# ...BACK TO SCHOOL

As you are already aware, this block consists of the following chapters:

Percentages,

Profit and Loss,

Interest,

Ratio, Proportion and Variation,

Time and Work,

Time, Speed and Distance

To put it very simply, the reason for these seemingly diverse chapters to be under one block of chapters is: **Linear Equations**

Yes, the solving of linear equations is the common thread that binds all the chapters in this block.

But before we start going through what a linear equation is, let us first understand the concept of a variable and it's need in the context of solving mathematical expressions.

**Let us start off with a small exercise first:**

Think of a number.

Add 2 to it.

Double the number to get a new number.

Add half of this new number to itself.

Divide the no. by 3.

Take away the original number from it.

The number you now have is......... 2!!

How do I know this result?

The answer is pretty simple. Take a look. I am assuming that you had taken the initial number as 5 to show you what has happened in this entire process.

| Instruction | You | Me |
|---|---|---|
| Think of a number. | 5 | X |
| Add 2 to it. | 5 + 2 = 7 | X + 2 |
| Double the number to get a new number. | 7 × 2 = 14 | 2X + 4 |
| Add half of this new number to itself. | 14 + 7 = 21 | 3X + 6 |
| Divide the result by 3. | 21/3 = 7 | X + 2 |
| Take away the original number from it. | 7 − 5 = 2 | X + 2 − X = 2 |
| The number you now have is..... 2 and is independent of the value again. | The number you now have is..... 2! | The number you now have is..... 2! |

The above is a perfect illustration of what a variable is and how it operates.

In this entire process, it does not matter to me as to what number you have assumed. All I set up is a kind of a parallel world wherein the number in your mind is represented by the variable X in my mind.

By ensuring that the final value does not have an X in it, I have ensured that the answer is independent of the value you would have assumed. Thus, even if someone had assumed 7 as the original value, his values would go as: 7, 9, 18, 27, 9, 2.

*Contd*

What you need to understand is that in Mathematics, whenever we have to solve for the value of an unknown we represent that unknown by using some letter (like $x$, $y$, $a$ etc.) These letters are then called as the variable representations of the unknown quantity.

Thus, for instance, if you come across a situation where a question says: The temperature of a city increases by 1°C on Tuesday from its value on Monday, you assume that if Monday's temperature was $t$, then Tuesday's temperature will be $t + 1$.

The opposite of a variable is a constant. Thus if it is said in the same problem that the temperature on Wednesday is 34° C, then 34 becomes a constant value in the context of the problem.

Thus although you do not have the actual value in your mind, you can still move ahead in the question by assuming a variable to represent the value of the unknowns. All problems in Mathematics ultimately take you to a point which will give the value of the unknown—which then becomes the answer to the question.

Hence, in case you are stuck in a problem in this block of chapters, it could be due to any one of the following three reasons:

**Reason 1:** You are stuck because you have either not used all the information given in the problem or have used them in the incorrect order.

In such a case go back to the problem and try to identify each statement and see whether you have utilized it or not. If you have already used all the information, you might be interested in knowing whether you have used the information given in the problem in the correct order. If you have tried both these options, you might want to explore the next reason for getting stuck.

**Reason 2:** You are stuck because even though you might have used all the information given in the problem, you have not utilized some of the information completely.

In such a case, you need to review each of the parts of the information given in the question and look at whether any additional details can be derived out of the same information. Very often, in Quants, you have situations wherein one sentence might have more than one connotation. If you have used that sentence only in one perspective, then using it in the other perspective will solve the question.

**Reason 3:** You are stuck because the problem does not have a solution.

In such a case, check the question once and if it is correct go back to Reasons 1 and 2. Your solution has to lie there.

My experience in training students tells me that the 1st case is the most common reason for not being able to solve questions correctly. (more than 90% of the times) Hence, if you consider yourself to be weak at Maths, concentrate on the following process in this block of chapters.

## THE LOGIC OF THE STANDARD STATEMENT

What I have been trying to tell the students is that most of the times, you will get stuck in a problem only when you are not able to interpret a statement in the problem. Hence, my advise to students (especially those who are weak in these chapters)—concentrate on developing your ability to decode the mathematical meaning of a sentence in a problem.

To do this, even in problems that you are able to solve (easily or with difficulty) go back into the language of the question and work out the mathematical reaction that you should have with each statement.

It might not be a bad idea to make a list of standard statements along with their mathematical reactions for each chapter in this block of chapters. You will realise that in almost no time, you will come to a situation where you will only rarely encounter new language.

Coming back to the issue of **linear equations**:

Linear equations are expressions about variables that might help us get the value of the variable if we can solve the equation.

Depending upon the number of variables in a problem, a linear equation might have one variable, two variables or even three or more variables. The only thing you should know is that in order to get the value of a variable, the number of equations needed is always equal to the number of variables. In other words, if you have more variables in a system of equations than the number of equations, you cannot solve for the individual values of the variables.

The basic mathematical principle goes like this:

**For a system of equations to be solvable, the number of equations should be equal to the number of variables in the equations.**

Thus for instance, if you have two variables, you need two equations to get the values of the two variables, while if you have three variables you will need three equations.

This situation is best exemplified by the situation where you might have the following equation. $x + y = 7$. If it is known that both $x$ and $y$ are natural numbers, it yields a set of possibilities for the values of x & y as follows: (1, 6), (2, 5), (3, 4), (4, 3), (5, 2), (6, 1). One of these possibilities has to be the answer.

In fact, it might be a good idea to think of all linear equation situations in this fashion. Hence, before you go ahead to read about the next equation, you should set up this set of possibilities based on the first equation.

Consider the following situation where a question yields a set of possibilities:

Four enemies $A$, $B$, $C$ and $D$ gather together for a picnic in a park with their wives. $A$'s wife consumes 5 times as many glasses of juice as $A$. $B$'s wife consumes 4 times as many glasses of juice as $B$. $C$'s wife consumes 3 times as many glasses of juice as $C$ and $D$'s wife consumes 2 times as many glasses of juice as $D$. In total, the wives of the four enemies consume a total of 44 glasses of juice. If $A$ consumes at least 5 glasses of juice while each of the other men have at least one glass, find the least number of drinks that could have been consumed by the 4 enemies together.

    (1) 9            (2) 12

    (3) 11           (4) 10

In the question above, we have 8 variables—$A$, $B$, $C$, $D$ and $a$, $b$, $c$, $d$ — the number of glasses consumed by the four men and the number of glasses consumed by the four wives.

Also, the question gives us five informations which can be summarised into 5 equations as follows.

$a = 5A$

$b = 4B$

$c = 3C$

$d = 2D$

and $a + b + c + d = 44$

Also, $A > 5$.

Under this condition, you do not have enough information to get all values and hence you will get a set of possibilities.

Since the minimal value of $A$ is 5, $a$ can take the values 25, 30, 35 and 40 when $A$ takes the values 5, 6, 7 and 8, respectively. Based on these, and on the

realisation that $b$ has to be a multiple of 4, $c$ a multiple of 3 and $d$ a multiple of 2, the following possibilities emerge:

At $A = 5$

| $a$ | (multiple of 5) | 25 | 25 | 25 | 25 | 25 |
|-----|-----------------|----|----|----|----|----|
| $b$ | (multiple of 4) | 12 | 8 | 8 | 4 | 4 |
| $c$ | (multiple of 3) | 3 | 9 | 3 | 3 | 9 |
| $d$ | (multiple of 2) | 4 | 2 | 8 | 12 | 6 |
| $a+b+c+d$ | | 44 | 44 | 44 | 44 | 44 |

| $a$ | | $A=6,$ $a=30$ | $A=7,$ $a=35$ | $A=8,\ a=40$ |
|-----|-----------------|------|------|-------------|
| $b$ | (multiple of 4) | 4 | 4 | No solution |
| $c$ | (multiple of 3) | 6 | 3 | |
| $d$ | (multiple of 2) | 4 | 2 | |
| $a+b+c+d$ | | 44 | 44 | |

In this case the answer will be 10, since in the case of $a=35$, $b=4$, $c=3$ and $d=2$, the values for $A,B,C$ and $D$ will be respectively 7,1,1 and 1. This solution is the least number of drinks consumed by the 4 enemies together as in all the other possibilities the number of glasses is greater than 10.

**Such utilisations of linear equations are very common in CAT and top level aptitude examinations.**

*The relationship between the decimal value and the percentage value of a ratio:*

Every ratio has a percentage value and a decimal value and the difference between the two is just in the positioning of the decimal point.

Thus 2/4 can be represented as 0.5 in terms of its decimal value and can be represented by 50% in terms of its percentage value.

# Pre-assessment Test

1. Three runners A, B and C run a race, with runner A finishing 24 metres ahead of runner B and 36 metres ahead of runner C, while runner B finishes 16 metres ahead of runner C. Each runner travels the entire distance at a constant speed. .What was the length of the race?
   - (a) 72 metres
   - (b) 96 metres
   - (c) 120 metres
   - (d) 144 metres

2. A dealer buys dry fruits at ₹100, ₹ 80 and ₹ 60 per kilogram. He mixes them in the ratio 4:5:6 by weight, and sells at a profit of 50%. At what price per kilogram does he sell the dry fruit?
   - (a) ₹116
   - (b) ₹106
   - (c) ₹115
   - (d) None of these

3. There are two containers: the first contains 500 ml of alcohol, while the second contains 500 ml of water. Five cups of alcohol from the first container is taken out and is mixed well in the second container. Then, five cups of this mixture is taken out from the second container and put back into the first container. Let X and Y denote the proportion of alcohol in the first and the proportion of water in the second container. Then what is the relationship between X & Y? (Assume the size of the cups to be identical)
   - (a) X>Y
   - (b) X<Y
   - (c) X=Y
   - (d) Cannot be determined

4. Akhilesh took five papers in an examination, where each paper was of 200 marks. His marks in these' papers were in the proportion of 7: 8: 9 :10 : 11. In all papers together, the candidate obtained 60% of the total marks. Then, the number of papers in which he got more than 50% marks is:
   - (a) 1
   - (b) 3
   - (c) 4
   - (d) 5

5. A and B walk up an escalator (moving stairway). The escalator moves at a constant speed, A takes six steps for every four of B's steps. A gets to the top of the escalator after having taken 50 steps, while B (because his slower pace lets the escalator do a little more of the work) takes only 40 steps to reach the top. If the escalator were turned off, how many steps would they have to take to walk up?
   - (a) 80
   - (b) 100
   - (c) 120
   - (d) 160

6. Fifty per cent of the employees of a certain company are men, and 80% of the men earn more than ₹ 2.5 lacs per year. If 60% of the company's employees earn more than ₹ 2.5 lacs per year, then what fraction of the women employed by the company earn more than ₹ 2.5 lacs per year?
   - (a) 2/5
   - (b) 1/4
   - (c) 1/3
   - (d) 3/4

7. A piece of string is 80 centimetres long. It is cut into three pieces. The longest piece is 3 times as long as the middle-sized and the shortest piece is 46 centimetres shorter than the longest piece. Find the length of the shortest piece (in cm).
   - (a) 14
   - (b) 10
   - (c) 8
   - (d) 18

8. Three members of a family A, B, and C, work together to get all household chores done. The time it takes them to do the work together is six hours less than A would have taken working alone, one hour less than B would have taken alone, and half the time C would have taken working alone. How long did it take them to do these chores working together?
   - (a) 20 minutes
   - (b) 30 minutes
   - (c) 40 minutes
   - (d) 50 minutes

9. Fresh grapes contain 90% water by weight while dried grapes contain 20% water by weight. What is the weight of dry grapes available from 20 kg of fresh grapes?
   - (a) 2kg
   - (b) 2.4kg
   - (c) 2.5kg
   - (d) None of these

10. At the end of the year 2008, a shepherd bought twelve dozen goats. Henceforth, every year he added p% of the goats at the beginning of the year and sold q% of the goats at the end of the year where p> 0 and q >0. If the shepherd had twelve dozen goats at the end of the year 2012, (after making the sales for that year), which of the following is true?
    - (a) p = q
    - (b) p<q
    - (c) p>q
    - (d) p = q/2

**Directions for Questions 11 and 12:** Answer the questions based on the following information.

An Indian company purchases components X and Y from UK and Germany, respectively. X and Y form 40% and 30% of the total production cost. Current gain is 25%. Due to change in the international exchange rate scenario, the cost of the German mark increased by 50% and that of UK pound increased by 25%. Due to tough competitive market conditions, the selling price cannot be increased beyond 10%.

11. What is the maximum current gain possible?
    - (a) 10%
    - (b) 12.5%
    - (c) 0%
    - (d) 7.5%

12. If the UK pound becomes cheap by 15% over its original cost and the cost of German mark increased by 20%, what will be the gain if the selling price is not altered.
    (a) 10%                  (b) 20%
    (c) 25%                  (d) 7.5%

13. A college has raised 80% of the amount it needs for a new building by receiving an average donation of ₹ 800 from the people already solicited. The people already solicited represent 50% of the people, the college will ask for donations. If the college is to raise exactly the amount needed for the new building, what should be the average donation from the remaining people to be solicited?
    (a) 300                  (b) 200
    (c) 400                  (d) 500

14. A student gets an aggregate of 60%marks in five subjects in the ratio 10: 9: 8: 7: 6. If the passing marks are 45% of the maximum marks and each subject has the same maximum marks, in how many subjects did he pass the examination?
    (a) 2                    (b) 3
    (c) 4                    (d) 5

15. After allowing a discount of 12.5 % a trader still makes a gain of 40%. At what per cent above the cost price does he mark on his goods?
    (a) 45%                  (b) 60%
    (c) 25%                  (d) None of these

16. The owner of an art shop conducts his business in the following manner. Every once in a while he raises his prices by X%, then a while later he reduces all the new prices by X%. After one such up-down cycle, the price of a painting decreased by ₹ 441. After a second up-down cycle, the painting was sold for ₹ 1944.81. What was the original price of the painting (in ₹)?
    (a) 2756.25              (b) 2256.25
    (c) 2500                 (d) 2000

17. Manas, Mirza, Shorty and Jaipal bought a motorbike for $60,000. Manas paid 50% of the amounts paid by the other three boys, Mirza paid one third of the sum of the amounts paid by the other boys; and Shorty paid one fourth of the sum of the amounts paid by the other boys. How much did Jaipal have to pay?
    (a) $15000               (b) $13000
    (c) $17000               (d) None of these

18. A train X departs from station A at 11.00 a.m. for station B, which is 180 km away. Another train Y departs from station B at 11.00 a.m. for station A. Train X travels at an average speed of 70 kms/hr and does not stop anywhere until it arrives at sta-

tion B. Train Y travels at an average speed of 50 km/hr, but has to stop for 10 minutes at station C, which is 60 kms away from station B enroute to station A. Ignoring the lengths of the trains, what is the distance, to the nearest km, from station A to the point where the trains cross each other?
    (a) 110                  (b) 112
    (c) 116                  (d) None of these

19. In a survey of political preferences, 81% of those asked were in favour of at least one of the three budgetary proposals A, B and C. 50% of those asked favoured proposal A,30% favoured proposal B and 20% favoured proposal C. If 5% of those asked favoured all the three proposals, what percentage of those asked favoured more than one of the three proposals?
    (a) 10%                  (b) 12%
    (c) 9%                   (d) 14%

**Directions for Questions 20 and 21:** The petrol consumption rate of a new model car 'Palto' depends on its speed and may be described by the graph below:

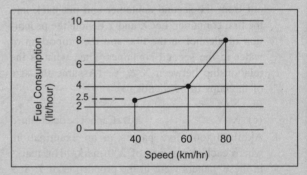

20. Manasa makes the 240 km trip from Mumbai to Pune at a steady speed of 60 km per hour. What is the amount of petrol consumed for the journey?
    (a) 12.5 litres          (b) 16 litres
    (c) 15 litres            (d) 19.75 litres

21. Manasa would like to minimise the fuel consumption for the trip by driving at the appropriate speed. How should she change the speed?
    (a) Increase the speed
    (b) Decrease the speed
    (c) Maintain the speed at 60 km/hour
    (d) Cannot be determined

**Directions for Questions 22 and 23:** Answer the questions based on the following information:

There are five machines—A, B, C, D, and E situated on a straight line at distances of 10 m, 20 m, 30 m, 40 m and 50 m, respectively from the origin of the line. A robot is stationed at the origin of the line. The robot serves the machines with raw material whenever a machine becomes idle. All the raw materials are located at the origin. The robot is in an idle state at the origin at the beginning of a day. As soon as one or more machines become idle, they send messages to the robot-station and the robot starts and serves all the machines from which it received messages. If a message is received at the station while the robot is away from it, the robot takes notice of the message only when it returns to the station. While moving, it serves the machines in the sequence in which they are encountered, and then returns to the origin. If any messages are pending at the station when it returns, it repeats the process again. Otherwise, it remains idle at the origin till the next message(s) is (are) received.

22. Suppose on a certain day, machines A and D have sent the first two messages to the origin at the beginning of the first second, C has sent a message at the beginning of the 7th second, B at the beginning of the 8th second and E at the beginning of the 10th second. How much distance has the robot traveled since the beginning of the day, when it notices the message of E? Assume that the speed of movement of the robot is 10m/s.
    (a) 140 m            (b) 80 m
    (c) 340 m            (d) 360 m

23. Suppose there is a second station with raw material for the robot at the other extreme of the line which is 60 m from the origin, i.e., 10 m from E. After finishing the services in a trip, the robot returns to the nearest station. If both stations are equidistant, it chooses the origin as the station to return to. Assuming that both stations receive the

messages sent by the machines and that all the other data remains the same, what would be the answer to the above question?
    (a) 120              (b) 160
    (c) 140              (d) 170

24. One bacteria splits into eight bacteria of the next generation. But due to environment, only 50% of a generation survive. If the eighth generation number is 8192 million, what is the number in the first generation?
    (a) I million        (b) 2 million
    (c) 4 million        (d) 8 million

25. I bought 10 pens, 14 pencils and 4 erasers. Ravi bought 12 pens, 8 erasers and 28 pencils for an amount which was half more what I had paid. What percent of the total amount paid by me was paid for the pens?
    (a) 37.5%            (b) 62.5%
    (c) 50%              (d) None of these

| ANSWER KEY | | | |
|---|---|---|---|
| 1. (b) | 2. (a) | 3. (c) | 4. (c) |
| 5. (b) | 6. (a) | 7. (c) | 8. (c) |
| 9. (c) | 10. (c) | 11. (a) | 12. (c) |
| 13. (b) | 14. (d) | 15. (b) | 16. (a) |
| 17. (b) | 18. (a) | 19. (d) | 20. (b) |
| 21. (b) | 22. (a) | 23. (a) | 24. (b) |
| 25. (b) | | | |

# Percentages

## INTRODUCTION

In my opinion, the chapter on Percentages forms the most important chapter (apart from Number Systems) in the syllabus of the CAT and the XLRI examination. The importance of 'percentages' is accentuated by the fact that there are a lot of questions related to the use of percentage in all chapters of commercial arithmetic (especially Profit and Loss, Ratio and Proportion, Time and Work, Time, Speed and Distance).

Besides, the calculation skills that you can develop while going through the chapter on percentages will help you in handling Data Interpretation (DI) calculations. A closer look at that topic will yield that at least 80% of the total calculations in any DI paper is constituted of calculations on additions and percentage.

## BASIC DEFINITION AND UTILITY OF PERCENTAGE

Percent literally, means 'for every 100' and is derived from the French word 'cent', which is French for 100.

The basic utility of Percentage arises from the fact that it is one of the most powerful tools for comparison of numerical data and information. It is also one of the simplest tools for comparison of data.

In the context of business and economic performance, it is specifically useful for comparing data such as profits, growth rates, performance, magnitudes and so on.

**Mathematical Definition of Percentage** The concept of percentage mainly applies to ratios, and the percentage value of a ratio is arrived at by multiplying by 100 the decimal value of the ratio.

For example, a student scores 20 marks out of a maximum possible 30 marks. His marks can then be denoted as 20 out of 30 = (20/30) or (20/30) × 100% = 66.66%.

The process for getting this is perfectly illustrated through the unitary method:

$$\begin{array}{cc} \textit{Marks scored} & \textit{Out of} \\ 20 \xrightarrow{\text{out of}} 30 \\ x \xrightarrow{\text{out of}} 100 \end{array}$$

then,

Then the value of $x \times 30 = 20 \times 100$

$x = (20/30) \times 100 \rightarrow$ the percentage equivalent of a ratio.

Now, let us consider a classic example of the application of percentage:

**Example:** Student $A$ scores 20 marks in an examination out of 30 while another student $B$ scores 40 marks out of 70. Who has performed better?

**Solution:** Just by considering the marks as 20 and 40, we do not a get clear picture of the actual performance of the two students. In order to get a clearer picture, we consider the percentage of marks.

Thus, $A$ gets $(20/30) \times 100 = 66.66\%$
While $B$ gets $(40/70) \times 100 = 57.14\%$

Now, it is clear that the performance of $A$ is better. Consider another example:

**Example:** Company $A$ increases its sales by 1 crore rupees while company $B$ increases its sales by 10 crore rupees. Which company has grown more?

**Solution:** Apparently, the answer to the question seems to be company $B$. The question cannot be answered since we don't know the previous year's sales figure (although on the face of it Company $B$ seems to have grown more).

If we had further information saying that company $A$ had a sales turnover of ₹ 1 crore in the previous year and company $B$ had a sales turnover of ₹ 100 crore in the previous year, we can compare growth rates and say that it is company $A$ that has grown by 100%. Hence, company

*A* has a higher growth rate, even though in terms of absolute value increase of sales, company *B* has grown much more.

## IMPORTANCE OF BASE/DENOMINATOR FOR PERCENTAGE CALCULATIONS

Mathematically, the percentage value can only be calculated for ratios that, by definition, must have a denominator. Hence, one of the most critical aspects of the percentage is the denominator, which in other words is also called the base value of the percentage. No percentage calculation is possible without knowing the base to which the percentage is to be calculated.

Hence, whenever faced with the question 'What is the percentage …?' always try first to find out the answer to the question 'Percentage to what base?'

## CONCEPT OF PERCENTAGE CHANGE

Whenever the value of a measured quantity changes, the change can be captured through
(a) Absolute value change  or
(b) Percentage change.

Both these measurements have their own advantages and disadvantages.

**Absolute value change:** It is the actual change in the measured quantity. For instance, if sales in year 1 is ₹ 2500 crore and the sales in year 2 is ₹ 2600 crore, then the absolute value of the change is ₹ 100 crore.

**Percentage change:** It is the percentage change got by the formula

$$\text{Percentage change} = \frac{\text{Absolute value change}}{\text{Original quantity}} \times 100$$

$$= \frac{100}{2500} \times 100 = 4\%$$

As seen earlier, this often gives us a better picture of the effect of the change.

---

**Note:** The base used for the sake of percentage change calculations is always the original quantity unless otherwise stated.

---

**Example:** The population of a city grew from 20 lakh to 22 lakh. Find the
(a) percentage change
(b) percentage change based on the final value of population

**Solution:** (a) percentage change = $(2/20) \times 100 = 10\%$
(b) percentage change on the final value = $(2/22) \times 100 = 9.09\%$

## Difference between the Percentage Point Change and the Percentage Change

The difference between the percentage point change and the percentage change is best illustrated through an example. Consider this:

The savings rate as a percentage of the GDP was 25% in the first year and 30% in the second year. Assume that there is no change in the GDP between the two years. Then:

Percentage point change in savings rate = 30%−25% = 5 percentage points.

Percentage change in savings rate = $\frac{30-25}{25} \times 100$ = 25%.

## PERCENTAGE RULE FOR CALCULATING PERCENTAGE VALUES THROUGH ADDITIONS

Illustrated below is a powerful method of calculating percentages. In my opinion, the ability to calculate percentage through this method depends on your ability to handle 2 digit additions. Unless you develop the skill to add 2 digit additions in your mind, you are always likely to face problems in calculating percentage through the method illus- trated below. In fact, trying this method without being strong at 2-digit additions/subtractions (including 2 digits after decimal point) would prove to be a disadvantage in your attempt at calculating percentages fast.

This process, essentially being a commonsense process, is best illustrated through a few examples:

**Example:** What is the percentage value of the ratio: 53/81?

**Solution:** The process involves removing all the 100%, 50%, 10%, 1%, 0.1% and so forth of the denominator from the numerator.

Thus, 53/81 can be rewritten as: (40.5 + 12.5)/81 = 40.5/81 + 12.5/81 = 50% + 12.5/81

= 50% + (8.1 + 4.4)/81 = 50% + 10% + 4.4/81
= 60% + 4.4/81

At this stage you know that the answer to the question lies between 60 and 70% (Since 4.4 is less than 10% of 81)

At this stage, you know that the answer to the calculation will be in the form: 6*a.bcde* ….

All you need to do is find out the value of the missing digits.

In order to do this, calculate the percentage value of 4.4/81 through the normal process of multiplying the numerator by 100.

Thus the % value of $\frac{4.4}{81} = \frac{4.4 \times 100}{81} = \frac{440}{81}$

[**Note**: Use the multiplication by 100, once you have the 10% range. This step reduces the decimal calculations.]

Thus $\dfrac{440}{81}$ = 5% with a remainder of 35

Our answer is now refined to 65.*bcde*. (1% Range)

Next, in order to find the next digit (first one after the decimal add a zero to the remainder;

Hence, the value of '*b*' will be the quotient of

$b \rightarrow 350/81$ = 4 Remainder 26

Answer: 65.4cde (0.1% Range)

$c \rightarrow 260/81$ = 3 Remainder 17

Answer: 65.43 (0.01% Range)

and so forth.

The advantages of this process are two fold:

(1) You only calculate as long as you need to in order to eliminate the options. Thus, in case there was only a single option between 60 and 70% in the above question, you could have stopped your calculations right there.

(2) This process allows you to go through with the calculations as long as you need to.

However, remember what I had advised you right at the start: Strong Addition skills are a primary requirement for using this method properly.

**To illustrate another example:**

What is the percentage value of the ratio $\dfrac{223}{72}$ ?

223/72 $\rightarrow$ 300 – 310% Remainder 7

700/72 $\rightarrow$ 9. Hence 309 – 310%, Remainder 52

520/72 $\rightarrow$ 7. Hence, 309.7, Remainder 16

160/72 $\rightarrow$ 2. Hence, 309.72 Remainder 16

Hence, 309.7222 (2 recurs since we enter an infinite loop of 160/72 calculations).

In my view, percentage rule (as *I* call it) is one of the best ways to calculate percentages since it gives you the flexibility to calculate the percentage value up to as many digits after decimals as you are required to and at the same time allows you to stop the moment you attain the required accuracy range.

## Effect of a Percent Change in the Numerator on a Ratio's Value

The numerator has a direct relationship with the ratio, that is, if the numerator increases the ratio increases. The percentage increase in the ratio is the same as the percentage increase in the numerator, if the denominator is constant.

Thus, $\dfrac{22}{40}$ is exactly 10% more than $\dfrac{20}{40}$. (in terms of percentage change)

## Percentage Change Graphic and its Applications

In mathematics there are many situations where one is required to work with percentage changes. In such situations

the following thought structure (Something I call Percentage Change Graphic) is a very useful tool:

What I call Percentage Change Graphic (PCG) is best illustrated through an example:

Suppose you have to increase the number 20 by 20%. Visualise this as follows:

$$20 \xrightarrow[=+4]{20\%\uparrow} 24$$

The PCG has 6 major applications listed and explained below: PCG applied to:

1. Successive changes
2. Product change application
3. Product constancy application
4. A $\rightarrow$ B$\rightarrow$A application
5. Denominator change to Ratio Change application
6. Use of PCG to calculate Ratio Changes

**Application 1: PCG Applied to Successive Changes**

This is a very common situation in most questions. Suppose you have to solve a question in which a number 30 has two successive percentage increases (20% and 10% respectively).

The situation is handled in the following way using PCG:

$$30 \xrightarrow[+6]{20\% \text{ increase}} 36 \xrightarrow[+3.6]{10\% \text{ increase}} 39.6$$

## Illustration

*A*'s salary increases by 20% and then decreases by 20%. What is the net percentage change in *A*'s salary?

*Solution:*

$$100 \xrightarrow[+20]{20\% \text{ inc.}} 120 \xrightarrow[-24]{20\% \text{ decrease}} 96$$

Hence, *A*'s salary has gone down by 4%

## Illustration

A trader gives successive discounts of 10%, 20% and 10% respectively. The percentage of the original cost price he will recover is:

*Solution:*

$$100 \xrightarrow[-10]{10\% \text{ decrease}} 90 \xrightarrow[-18]{20\% \text{ decrease}} 72 \xrightarrow[-7.2]{10\% \text{ decrease}} 64.8$$

Hence the overall discount is 35.2% and the answer is 64.8%.

## Illustration

A trader marks up the price of his goods by 20%, but to a particularly haggling customer he ends up giving a discount of 10% on the marked price. What is the percentage profit he makes?

*Solution:*

$$100 \xrightarrow[+20]{20\% \text{ increase}} 120 \xrightarrow[-12]{10\% \text{ decrease}} 108$$

Hence, the percentage profit is 8%.

## Application 2: PCG applied to Product Change

Suppose you have a product of two variables say 10 × 10.

If the first variable changes to 11 and the second variable changes to 12, what will be the percentage change in the product? [Note there is a 10% increase in one part of the product and a 20% increase in the other part.]

The formula given for this situation goes as: $(a + b + ab/100)$

Hence, Required % change = $10 + 20 + \dfrac{10 \times 20}{100}$

(Where 10 and 20 are the respective percentage changes in the two parts of the product) (This is being taught as a shortcut at most institutes across the country currently.)

However, a much easier solution for this case can be visualised as:

$$100 \xrightarrow[+20]{20\% \uparrow} 120 \xrightarrow[+12]{10\% \uparrow} 132 .$$ Hence, the final product shows a 32% increase.

Similarly suppose 10 × 10 × 10 becomes 11 × 12 × 13
In such a case the following PCG will be used:

$$100 \xrightarrow[+30]{30\% \uparrow} 130 \xrightarrow[+26]{20\% \uparrow} 156 \xrightarrow[+15.6]{10\% \uparrow} 171.6$$

Hence, the final product sees a 71.6 percent increase (Since, the product changes from 100 to 171.6)

**Note:** You will get the same result irrespective of the order in which you use the respective percentage changes.

Also note that this process is very similar to the one used for calculating successive percentage change.

## Application for DI:

Suppose you have two pie charts as follows:

Scooters: 23.47%

Total sales year 1: 17342.34 crores

Scooters: 26.55%

Total sales Year 2: 19443.56 crores

If you are asked to calculate the percentage change in the sales revenue of scooters for the company from year one to year two, what would you do?

The formula for percentage change would give us:

$$\frac{(0.2655 \times 19443.56) - (0.2347 \times 17342.34) \times 100}{(0.2347 \times 17342.34)}$$

i.e., $\dfrac{\text{New Sales Revenue} - \text{Original Sales Revenue}}{\text{Original Sales Revenue}} \times 100$

Obviously this calculation is easier said than done.

However, the Product change application of PCG allows us to execute this calculation with a lot of ease comparatively. Consider the following solution:

Product for year one is: 0.2347 × 17342.34
Product for year two is: 0.2655 × 19443.56

These can be approximated into:
234 × 173 and 265 × 194 respectively (Note that by moving into three digits we do not end up losing any accuracy. We have elaborated this point in the chapter on Ratio and Proportions.)

The overall percentage change depends on two individual percentage changes:
234 increases to 265: A % change of 31/234 = 13.2 % approx. This calculation has to be done using the percentage rule for calculating the percentage value of the ratio

173 increases to 194 — A percentage change of approximately 12%.

Thus PCG will give the answer as follows:

$$100 \xrightarrow[+13.2]{13.2\% \uparrow} 113.2 \xrightarrow[+13.56]{12\% \uparrow} 126.76$$

Hence, 26.76 % increase in the product's value. (Note that the value on the calculator for the full calculation sans any approximations is 26.82 %, and given the fact that we have come extremely close to the answer—the method is good enough to solve the question with a reasonable degree of accuracy.)

## Application 3 of PCG: Product Constancy Application (Inverse proportionality)

Suppose you have a situation wherein the price of a commodity has gone up by 25%. In case you are required to keep the total expenditure on the commodity constant, you would obviously need to cut down on the consumption. By what percentage? Well, PCG gives you the answer as follows:

$$100 \xrightarrow[\substack{+25 \\ \text{Price effect}}]{25\% \uparrow} 125 \xrightarrow[\substack{-25 \\ \text{Consumption Effect}}]{} 100$$

Hence, the percentage drop in consumption to offset the price increase is 20%.

I leave it to the student to discover the percentage drop required in the second part of the product if one part increases by 50 percent.

**Note:** Product constancy is just another name for Inverse proportionality.

Table 5.1 gives you some standard values for this kind of a situation.

### Application 4 of PCG: A→B→A.

Very often we are faced with a situation where we compare two numbers say $A$ and $B$. In such cases, if we are given a relationship from $A$ to $B$, then the reverse relationship can be determined by using PCG in much the same way as the product constancy use shown above.

## Illustration

$B$'s salary is 25% more than $A$'s salary. By what percent is $A$'s salary less than $B$'s salary?

$$100(A) \xrightarrow[+25]{25\%\uparrow} 125(B) \xrightarrow{-25} 100(A)$$

A drop of 25 on 125 gives a 20% drop.
Hence $A$'s salary is 20% less than $B$'s.

**Note:** The values which applied for Product Constancy also apply here. Hence Table 4.1 is useful for this situation also.

### Application 5 of PCG → Effect of change in Denominator on the Value of the Ratio

The denominator has an inverse relationship with the value of a ratio.

Hence the process used for product constancy (and explained above) can be used for calculating percentage change in the denominator.

For instance, suppose you have to evaluate the difference between two ratios:

Ratio 1    : 10/20
Ratio 2    : 10/25

As is evident the denominator is increasing from 20 to 25 by 25%.
If we calculate the value of the two ratios we will get:
Ratio 1 = 0.5, Ratio 2 = 0.4.

% change between the two ratios = $\dfrac{0.1}{0.5} \times 100 = 20\%$ Drop

This value can be got through PCG as:

$100 \longrightarrow 125 \longrightarrow 100$ Hence, 20% drop.

**Note:** This is exactly the same as Product constancy and works here because the numerator is constant.

Hence, $R_1 = N/D_1$ and $R_2 = N/D_2$
i.e. $R_1 \times D_1 = N$ and $R_2 \times D_2 = N$, which is the product constancy situation.

*Direct process for calculation*

To find out the percentage change in the ratio due to a change in the denominator follow the following process:

In order to find the percentage change from 10/20 to 10/25, calculate the percentage change in the denominator in the reverse fashion.

i.e., The required percentage change from $R_1$ to $R_2$ will be given by calculating the percentage change in the

denominators from 25 to 20 (i.e., in a reverse fashion) and not from 20 to 25.

**Table 5.1**    **Product Constancy Table, Inverse Proportionality Table, A → B → A table, Ratio Change to Denominator table**

| Product XY is Constant | X increases (%) | Y Decreases (%) |
|---|---|---|
| A→B→A | A → B % increase | B → A% decrease |
| X is inversely proportional to Y | X increases (%) | Y decreases (%) |
| Ratio change effect of Denominator change | Denominator increases (%) | (Ratio decreases (%) |
| Denominator change effect of Ratio change | Ratio increases (%) | As Denominator decreases (%) |
| Standard Value 1 | 9.09 | 8.33 |
| Standard Value 2 | 10 | 9.09 |
| Standard Value 3 | 11.11 | 10 |
| Standard Value 4 | 12.5 | 11.11 |
| Standard Value 5 | 14.28 | 12.5 |
| Standard Value 6 | 16.66 | 14.28 |
| Standard Value 7 | 20 | 16.66 |
| Standard Value 8 | 25 | 20 |
| Standard Value 9 | 33.33 | 25 |
| Standard Value 10 | 50 | 33.33 |
| Standard Value 11 | 60 | 37.5 |
| Standard Value 12 | 66.66 | 40 |
| Standard Value 13 | 75 | 42.85 |
| Standard Value 14 | 100 | 50 |

### Application 6: Use of PCG to Calculate Ratio Changes:

Under normal situations, you will be faced with ratios where both numerator and denominator change. The process to handle and calculate such changes is also quite convenient if you go through PCG.

## Illustration

Calculate the percentage change between the Ratios.
Ratio 1 = 10/20 Ratio 2 = 15/25

The answer in this case is 0.5 → 0.6 (20% increase). However, in most cases calculating the values of the ratio will not be easy. The following PCG process can be used to get the answer:

When 10/20 changes to 15/25, the change occurs primarily due to two reasons:

(A) Change in the numerator (Numerator effect)
(B) Change in the denominator (Denominator effect)

By segregating the two effects and calculating the effect due to each separately, we can get the answer easily as follows:

**Numerator Effect** The numerator effect on the value of the ratio is the same as the change in the numerator.

Hence, to calculate the numerator effect, just calculate the percentage change in the numerator:

In this case the numerator is clearly changing from 10 to 15 (i.e., a 50% increase.) This signifies that the numerator effect is also 50%.

**Denominator Effect** As we have just seen above, the effect of a percentage change in the denominator on the value of the ratio is seen by calculating the denominator's percentage change in the reverse order.

In this case, the denominator is changing from 20 to 25. Hence the denominator effect will be seen by going reverse from 25 to 20, i.e., 20% drop.

With these two values, the overall percentage change in the Ratio is seen by:

$$100 \xrightarrow[\substack{+50 \\ \text{Numerator} \\ \text{Effect}}]{50\% \uparrow} 150 \xrightarrow[\substack{-30 \\ \text{Denominator} \\ \text{Effect}}]{20\% \downarrow} 120$$

This means that the ratio has increased by 20%.
I leave it to the student to practice such calculations with more complicated values for the ratios.

## Implications for Data Interpretation

Percentage is perhaps one of the most critical links between QA and Data Interpretation.

In the chapter theory mentioned above, the Percentage Rule for Percentage Calculations and the PCG applied to product change and ratio change are the most critical.

As already shown, the use of PCG to calculate the percentage change in a product (as exhibited through the pie chart example above) as well as the use of PCG to calculate ratio changes are two extremely useful applications of the concepts of percentages into DI.

**Applying Percentages for the special case of comparing two ratios to find the larger one.**

Suppose you have two ratios to compare. Say $R_1 = N_1/D_1$ and $R_2 = N_2/D_2$

The first step is to find the ten percent ranges for each of these ratios. In case, they belong to different ranges of 10% (say R1 lies between 50 and 60 while R2 lies between 70 and 80), it becomes pretty simple to say which one will be higher.

In case, both of these values for percentage of the ratios belong to the same ten percent range, then we can use the following process

**Step 1:** Calculate the percentage change in the numerator

**Step 2:** Calculate the percentage change in the denominator.

There could be four cases in this situation, when we move from Ratio$_1$ to Ratio$_2$:

**Case 1:** Numerator is increasing while denominator is decreasing → obviously the net effect of the two changes will be an increase in the ratio. Hence, $R_2$ will be greater.

**Case 2:** Numerator is decreasing while denominator is increasing → obviously the net effect of the two changes will be a decrease in the ratio. Hence, $R_1$ will be greater.

It is only in the following cases that we need to look at the respective changes in the Numerator and denominator.

**Case 3:** Numerator and denominator are both increasing Calculate the percentage value of the respective increases. If the numerator is increasing more than the denominator the ratio will go up. On the other hand, if the denominator is increasing more than the numerator, Ratio$_2$ will be smaller than Ratio$_1$. (Note: Compare in percentage values)

**Case 4:** Numerator and denominator are both decreasing → Calculate the percentage value of the respective decreases. If the numerator is decreasing more than the denominator the ratio will go down. On the other hand, if the denominator is decreasing more than the numerator, Ratio$_2$ will be greater than Ratio$_1$.

## FRACTION TO PERCENTAGE CONVERSION TABLE

The following percentage values appear repeatedly over the entire area where questions can be framed on the topic of percentage. Further, it would be of great help to you if you are able to recognise these values separately from values that do not appear in the Table 5.2.

## Some Utilisations of the Table

- The values that appear in the table are all percentage values. These can be converted into decimals by just shifting the decimal point by two places to the left. Thus, 83.33% = 0.8333 in decimal value.

- A second learning from this table is in the process of division by any of the numbers such as 2, 3, 4, 5, 6, 7, 8, 9, 11, 12, 15, 16, 24 and so on, students normally face problems in calculating the decimal values of these divisions. However, if one gets used to the decimal values that appear in the Table 5.2, calculation of decimals in divisions will become very simple. For instance, when an integer is divided by 7, the decimal values can only be .14, .28, .42, .57, .71, .85 or .00. (There are approximate values)

- This also means that the difference between two ratios like $\dfrac{x}{6} - \dfrac{x}{7}$ can be integral if and only if $x$ is divisible by both 6 and 7.

This principle is very useful as an advanced short cut for option based solution of some questions. I leave it to the student to discover applications of this principle.

## Calculation of Multiplication by Numbers like 1.21, 0.83 and so on

In my opinion, the calculation of multiplication of any number by a number of the form 0.*xy* or of the form 1.*ab*

### Table 5.2   Percentage Conversion Table

| | 1 | 2 | 3 | 4 | 5 | 6 | 7 | 8 | 9 | 10 | 11 | 12 |
|---|---|---|---|---|---|---|---|---|---|---|---|---|
| 1 | 100 | | | | | | | | | | | |
| 2 | 50 | 100 | | | | | | | | | | |
| 3 | 33.33 | 66.66 | 100 | | | | | | | | | |
| 4 | 25 | 50 | 75 | 100 | | | | | | | | |
| 5 | 20 | 40 | 60 | 80 | 100 | | | | | | | |
| 6 | 16.66 | 33.33 | 50 | 66.66 | 83.33 | 100 | | | | | | |
| 7 | 14.28 | 28.57 | 42.85 | 57.14 | 71.42 | 85.71 | 100 | | | | | |
| 8 | 12.5 | 25 | 37.5 | 50 | 62.5 | 75 | 87.5 | 100 | | | | |
| 9 | 11.11 | 22.22 | 33.33 | 44.44 | 55.55 | 66.66 | 77.77 | 88.88 | 100 | | | |
| 10 | 10 | 20 | 30 | 40 | 50 | 60 | 70 | 80 | 90 | 100 | | |
| 11 | 9.09 | 18.18 | 27.27 | 36.36 | 45.45 | 54.54 | 63.63 | 72.72 | 81.81 | 90.09 | 100 | |
| 12 | 8.33 | 16.66 | 25 | 33.33 | 41.66 | 50 | 58.33 | 66.66 | 75 | 83.33 | 91.66 | 100 |
| 15 | 6.66 | 13.33 | 20 | 26.66 | 33.33 | 40 | | | | | | |
| 16 | 6.25 | 12.5 | 18.75 | 25 | | | | | | | | |
| 20 | 5 | 10 | 15 | 20 | 25 | | | | | | | |
| 24 | 4.166 | 8.33 | 12.5 | 16.66 | 20.83 | 25 | | | | | | |
| 25 | 4 | 8 | 12 | 16 | 20 | 24 | 28 | 32 | 26 | 40 | | |
| 30 | 3.33 | 6.66 | 10 | 13.33 | 16.66 | 20 | | | | | | |
| 40 | 2.5 | 5 | 7.5 | 10 | 12.5 | 15 | 17.5 | 20 | | | | |
| 60 | 1.66 | 3.33 | 5 | 6.66 | 8.33 | 10 | | | | | | |

**Formula for any cell = Column value × 100/Row value**

should be viewed as a subtraction/addition situation and not as a multiplication situation. This can be explained as follows.

***Example:***   Calculate 1.23 × 473.

*Solution:*   If we try to calculate this by multiplying, we will end up going through a very time taking process, which will yield the final value at the end but nothing before that (i.e. you will have no clue about the answer's range till you reach the end of the calculation).

Instead, one should view this multiplication as an addition of 23% to the original number. This means, the answer can be got by adding 23% of the number to itself.

Thus $473 \times 1.23 = 473 + 23\%$ of $473 = 473 + 94.6 + 3\%$ of $473 = 567.6 + 14.19 = 581.79$.

(The percentage rule can be used to calculate the addition and get the answer.)

The similar process can be utilised for the calculation of multiplication by a number such as 0.87

(Answer can be got by subtracting 13% of the number from itself and this calculation can again be done by percentage rule.)

Hence, the student is advised to become thorough with the percentage rules. Percentage calculation and additions of 2 and 3 digit numbers.

***Space for Notes***

## WORKED-OUT PROBLEMS

**Problem 5.1** *A* sells his goods 30% cheaper than *B* and 30% dearer than *C*. By what percentage is the cost of *C*'s goods cheaper than *B*'s goods.

**Solution** There are two alternative processes for solving this question:

**1. Assume the price of *C*'s goods as *p*.:** Then *A*'s goods are at 1.3 p and *B*'s goods are such that *A*'s goods are 30% cheaper than *B*'s goods, i.e., *A*'s goods are priced at 70% of *B*'s goods.

$$\text{Hence, } 1.3\,p \rightarrow 70$$
$$B\text{'s price} \rightarrow 100$$
$$B\text{'s price} = 130\,p/70 = 1.8571\,p$$

Then, the percentage by which *C*'s price is cheaper than *B*'s price =

$$(1.8571\,p - p) \times 100/(1.8571\,p) = 600/13 = \textbf{46.15\%}$$

**Learning task for student** Could you answer the question: Why did we assume *C*'s price as a variable *p* and then work out the problem on its basis. What would happen if we assumed *B*'s price as *p* or if we assumed *A*'s price as *p*?

**2. Instead of assuming the price of one of the three as p, assume the price as 100.**
Let *B* = 100. Then *A* = 70, which is 30% more than *C*. Hence *C* = 23.07% less than *A* (from Table 4.1) = approx. 53.84. Hence answer is 46.15% approximately.

(This calculation can be done mentally if you are able to work through the calculations by the use of percentage rule. The students are advised to try to assume the value of 100 for each of the variables *A*, *B* and *C* and see what happens to the calculations involved in the problem. Since the value of 100 is assumed for a variable to minimise the requirements of calculations to solve the problems, we should ensure that the variable assumed as 100 should have the maximum calculations associated with it.)

**Note:** In fact this question and the ones that follow contain some of the most basic operations in the chapter of percentages. The questions at the first level of difficulty would appear in examinations like CET Maharashtra, Bank P.O., MAT, NMAT, CLAT, NLS and most other aptitude exams. Hence, if you are able to do the operations illustrated here mentally, you would be able to solve LOD 1 questions easily and gain a significant time advantage over your competitors.

However, for the serious CAT aspirant, the logic used for LOD I questions would normally be used as a part of the entire logic. You would be able to see this in the questions of

the second and the third level of difficulties in the exercises later in the chapter. Hence, developing the process for solving questions of the LOD 1 level mentally would help you gain an improved speed for the CAT level questions.

Also remember that since percentages are the basis for most of the commercial mathematics as well as for calcula-tion and the Data Interpretation section, developing skills for calculation and problem solving illustrated here would go a long way towards helping you clear aptitude exams.

**Problem 5.2** The length and the breadth of a rectangle are changed by +20% and by –10%, respectively. What is the percentage change in the area of the rectangle.

**Solution** The area of a rectangle is given by: length × breadth. If we represent these by:

Area = $L \times B = LB \rightarrow$ then we will get the changed area as

$$\text{Area}_{(\text{NEW})} = 1.2\,L \times 0.9\,B = 1.08\,LB$$

Hence, the change in area is 8% increase.

**Note:** You can solve (and in fact, finish the problem) during your first reading by using percentage change graphic as follows:

$100 \xrightarrow{+20\%} 120 \xrightarrow{-10\%} 108$. Hence, the percentage change is **8%**.

**Problem 5.3** Due to a 25% price hike in the price of rice, a person is able to purchase 20 kg less of rice for ₹ 400. Find the initial price.

**Solution** Since price is rising by 25%, consumption has to decrease by 20%. But there is an actual reduction in the consumption by 20 kg. Thus, 20% decrease in consumption is equal to a 20 kg drop in consumption.

Hence, original consumption is: 100 kg of rice.

Money spent being ₹ 400, the original price of rice is ₹ 4 per kg.

(There, you see the benefit of internalising the product constancy table! It is left to the student to analyse why and how the product constancy table applies here.)

**Problem 5.4** *A*'s salary is 20% lower than *B*'s salary, which is 15% lower than *C*'s salary. By how much percent is *C*'s salary more than *A*'s salary?

**Solution** The equation approach here would be

$$A = 0.8\,B$$
$$B = 0.85\,C$$
Then $\qquad\qquad A = 0.8 \times 0.85\,C$

$A = 0.68\ C$ (Use percentage change graphic to calculate the value of 0.68)

Thus, $A$'s salary is 68 % of $C$'s salary.

If $A$'s salary is 68, $B$'s salary is 100.

Using percentage change graphic

$$68 \xrightarrow[\;+32\;]{(3200/68)\%} 100$$

Students are advised to refrain from using equations to solve questions of this nature. In fact, you can adopt the following process, which can be used while you are reading the problem, to get the result faster.

Assume one of the values as 100. (Remember, selection of the right variable that has to take the value of 100 may make a major difference to your solving time and effort required. The thumb rule for selecting the variable whose value is to be taken as 100 is based on three principal considerations:

Select as 100, the variable

1. With the maximum number of percentage calculations associated with it.

2. Select as 100 the variable with the most difficult calculation associated with it.

3. Select as 100 the variable at the start of the problem solving chain.

The student will have to develop his own judgment in applying these principles in specific cases.

Here I would take $C$ as 100, getting $B$ as 85 and $A$ as 68. Hence, the answer is $(32 \times 100/68)$.

**Problem 5.5** The cost of manufacture of an article is made up of four components $A$, $B$, $C$ and $D$ which have a ratio of 3 : 4 : 5 : 6 respectively. If there are respective changes in the cost of +10%, –20%, –30% and +40%, then what would be the percentage change in the cost?

**Solution** Assume the cost components to be valued at 30, 40, 50 and 60 as you read the question. Then we can get changed costs by effecting the appropriate changes in each of the four components.

Thus we get the new cost as 33, 32, 35 and 84 respectively.

The original total cost was 180 the new one is 184. The percent change is 4/180 = 2.22%.

**Problem 5.6** Harsh receives an inheritance of a certain amount from his grandfather. Of this he loses 32.5% in his effort to produce a film. From the balance, a taxi driver stole the sum of ₹ 1,00,000 that he used to keep in his pocket. Of the rest, he donated 20% to a charity. Further he purchases a flat in Ganga Apartment for ₹ 7.5 lakh. He then realises that he is left with only ₹ 2.5 lakh cash of his inheritance. What was the value of his inheritance?

**Solution** These sort of problems should either be solved through the reverse process or through options.

***Reverse process for this problem*** He is left with ₹ 2.5 lakh after spending ₹ 7.5 lakh on the apartment.

Therefore, before the apartment purchase he has ₹ 10 lakh. But this is after the 20% reduction in his net value due to his donation to charity. Hence, he must have given ₹ 2.5 lakh to charity (20% decrease corresponds to a 25% increase). As such, he had 12.5 lakh before the charity. Further, he must have had ₹ 13.5 lakh before the taxi driver stole the sum. From 13.5 lakh you can reach the answer by trial and error trying whole number values. You will get that if he had 20 lakh and lost 32.5% of it he would be left with the required 13.5 lakh.

Hence, the answer is ₹ 20 lakh.

This process can be done mentally by: 2.5 + 7.5 = 10 lakh → +25% → 12.5 lakh → + 1 lakh → 13.5 lakh.

From this point move by trial and error. You should try to find the value of the inheritance, which on reduction by 32.5%, would leave 13.5 lakh. A little experience with numbers leaves you with ₹ 20 lakh as the answer. This process should be started as soon as you finish reading the first time.

***Through options*** Suppose the options were:

(a) 25 lakh      (b) 22.5 lakh

(c) 20 lakh      (d) 18 lakh

Start with any of the middle options. Then keep performing the mathematical operation in the order given in the problem. The final value that he is left with should be ₹ 2.5 lakh. The option that gives this, will be the answer. If the final value yielded is higher than ₹ 2.5 lakh in this case, start with a value lower than the option checked. In case it is the opposite, start with the option higher than the one used.

As a thumb rule, start with the most convenient option— the middle one. This would lead us to start with ₹ 20 lakh here.

However, if we had started with ₹ 25 lakh the following would have occurred.

25 lakh –32.5% → 16.875 lakh –1 lakh → 15.875 lakh –20% – 7.5 lakh, should equal 2.5 lakh → (Prior to doing this calculation, you should see that there is no way the answer will yield a nice whole number like 2.5 lakh. Hence, you can abandon the process here and move to the next option)

Trying with 20 lakh, 20 –32.5% → 13.5 lakh –1ac. → 12.5 lakh –20% → 10 lakh – 7.5 lakh = **2.5 lakh** → Required answer.

## LEVEL OF DIFFICULTY (I)

1. If we express 12(4/15)% as a fraction, then it is equal to
   (a) 46/375            (b) 46/125
   (c) 23/250            (d) None of these.

2. What is 10% of 20% of 25% of 100?
   (a) 0.5               (b) 0.75
   (c) 0.25              (d) 1.0

3. Which of the following is the largest number?
   (a) 40% of 400        (b) 5% of 800
   (c) 1000% of 4        (d) 200% of 9

4. If 30% of a number is 300, then 50% of that number is:
   (a) 400               (b) 125
   (c) 150               (d) 500

5. If 25% of $x$ = 30% of $y$, then find the value of $x$ if $y$ = 5000.
   (a) 2000              (b) 3000
   (c) 4000              (d) 6000

6. 30% of $a$% of $b$ is 25% of $b$% of $c$. Which of the following is $c$?
   (a) 1.5$a$            (b) 0.667$a$
   (c) 0.5$a$            (d) 1.20a

7. 20% of a number when subtracted from 108, gives the number itself. Find the number.
   (a) 50                (b) 80
   (c) 70                (d) 90

8. When 40% of a number $A$ is added to another number $B$, $B$ becomes 125% of its previous value. Then which of the following is true regarding the values of $A$ and $B$?
   (a) $A > B$
   (b) $B > A$
   (c) $B = A$
   (d) Either (a) or (b) can be true depending upon the values of $A$ and $B$

9. Two students appeared at an examination. One of them secured 10 marks more than the other and his marks was 60% of the sum of their marks. The marks obtained by the better student are:

10. Two numbers A and B are such that the sum of 5% of A and 10% of B is 1/2 of the sum of 20% of A and 10% of B. Find the ratio of A:B?

11. Mr. Ram is worried about the balance of his monthly budget. The price of petrol has increased by 50%. By what percent should he reduce the consumption of petrol so that he is able to balance his budget?
    (a) 33.33            (b) 28.56
    (c) 25               (d) 14.28

12. In Question 11, if Mr. Ram wanted to limit the increase in his expenditure to 20% on his basic expenditure on petrol then what should be the corresponding decrease in consumption?
    (a) 33.33            (b) 12.50
    (c) 25               (d) 20

13. Ashok sells his goods 50% dearer than Shankar and 20% dearer than Bishnu. How much percentage is Bishnu's goods dearer than Shankar's?
    (a) 33.33%           (b) 25%
    (c) 66.66%           (d) 40%

14. In an election between 2 candidates, Chaman gets 80% of the total valid votes. If the total votes were 12000, what is the number of valid votes that the other candidate Dhande gets if 15% of the total votes were declared invalid?
    (a) 1645             (b) 1545
    (c) 1675             (d) 2040

15. In a physical measurement, by mistake Shyam gave his height as 25% more than normal. In the interview panel, he clarified that his height was 5 feet 5 inches. Find the percentage correction made by the candidate from his stated height to his actual height.
    (a) 20               (b) 28.56
    (c) 25               (d) 16.66

16. Raunak generally wears his father's coat. Unfortunately, his cousin Vikas told him one day that he was wearing a coat of length more than his height by 15%. If the length of Raunak's father's coat is 345 cm then find the actual length (in cm) of his coat.
    (a) 110              (b) 345
    (c) 300              (d) 105

17. A number is mistakenly divided by 2 instead of being multiplied by 2. Find the percentage change in the result due to this mistake.
    (a) 100%             (b) 125%
    (c) 200%             (d) 75%

18. Sachin wanted to subtract 10 from a number. Unfortunately, he added 10 instead of subtracting. Find the percentage change in the result.
    (a) 300%             (b) 66.66%
    (c) 50%              (d) Cannot be determined

19. In a mixture of 100 litres of milk and water, 25% of the mixture is milk. How much water should be added to the mixture so that milk becomes 20% of the mixture?
    (a) 25 litres        (b) 15 litres
    (c) 20 litres        (d) 24 litres

20. A landowner increased the length and the breadth of a rectangular plot by 20% and 30% respectively. Find the percentage change in the cost of the plot assuming land prices are uniform throughout his plot.
    (a) 23%                (b) 52%
    (c) 56%                (d) None of these

21. The height of a triangle is increased by 30%. What can be the maximum percentage increase in length of the base so that the increase in area is restricted to a maximum of 90%?
    (a) 33.33%             (b) 20.67%
    (c) 46.15%             (d) 25.34%

22. The length, breadth and height of a room in the shape of a cuboid are increased by 10%, 20% and 50%, respectively. Find the percentage change in the volume of the cuboid.
    (a) 47.20%             (b) 55.33%
    (c) 48%                (d) 98%

23. The salary of Ajay is 10% more than that of Vivek. Find by what percentage is the salary of Vivek less than that of Ajay?
    (a) 16.12%             (b) 13.07%
    (c) 11.23%             (d) 9.09%

24. The price of salt is reduced by 50% but, inspite of the decrease, Aayush ends up increasing his expenditure on salt by 50%. What is the percentage change in his monthly consumption of sugar?
    (a) +60%               (b) −100%
    (c) +25%               (d) 200%

25. The price of wheat falls by 20%. How much wheat can be bought now with the money that was sufficient to buy 100 kg of rice previously?
    (a) 105 kg             (b) 115 kg
    (c) 125 kg             (d) 130 kg

26. At an election, the candidate who got 60% of the votes cast won by 200 votes. Find the total number of voters on the voting list if 66.67% people cast their vote and there were no invalid votes.
    (a) 3000               (b) 2400
    (c) 1800               (d) 1500

27. The population of a town is 5,00,000. The rate of increase is 20% per annum. Find the population at the start of the third year.
    (a) 6,20,000           (b) 7,20,000
    (c) 8,30,000           (d) None of these.

28. The population of the city of Gotham is 50,000 at this moment. It increases by 20% in the first year. However, in the second year, due to immigration, the population drops by 10%. Find the population at the end of the third year if in the third year the population increases by 30%.
    (a) 82,340             (b) 70,200
    (c) 62,540             (d) 52,340

29. Shyam invests ₹ 40,000 in some shares in the ratio 1 : 4 : 5 which pay dividends of 10%, 15% and 25% (on his investment) for that year respectively. Find his dividend income.
    (a) 5900               (b) 2000
    (c) 8800               (d) 7800

30. In an examination, Madan obtained 20% more than Sahir but 40% less than Ravi. If the marks obtained by Sahir is 80, find the percentage marks obtained by Ravi if the full marks is 200.
    (a) 80%                (b) 70%
    (c) 78.33%             (d) 71.11%

31. In a class, 20% of the students were absent for an exam. 10% failed by 10 marks and 20% just passed because of grace marks of 5. Find the average score of the class if the remaining students scored an average of 50 marks and the pass marks are 30 (counting the final scores of the candidates).
    (a) 41.25              (b) 37
    (c) 38                 (d) 33

32. Sharad spends 20% of his monthly income on his household expenditure, 30% of the rest on food, 10% of the rest on clothes and saves the rest. On counting, he comes to know that he has finally saved ₹10080. Find his monthly income (in ₹).
    (a) 10000              (b) 15000
    (c) 20000              (d) 12000

33. Harish and Bhuvan have salaries that jointly amount to ₹ 10,000 per month. They spend the same amount monthly and then it is found that the ratio of their savings is 6: 1. Which of the following can be Harish's salary?
    (a) ₹ 6000             (b) ₹ 5000
    (c) ₹ 4000             (d) ₹ 3000

34. The population of a town is 6000. If the number of males increases by 10% and the number of females increases by 20%, then the population becomes 6800. Find the population of females in the town.
    (a) 2500               (b) 3000
    (c) 2000               (d) 3500

35. Raju sells his goods 20% cheaper than Bharat and 20% dearer than Charan. How much percentage Charan's goods cheaper/dearer than Bharat's?
    (a) 33.33% cheaper     (b) 50% dearer
    (c) 42.85% dearer      (d) None of these

36. In an election contested by two parties, Party SJP secured 12 percentage points of the total votes more than Party SJD. If party SJD got 132,000 votes and there are no invalid votes, by how many votes did it lose the election?
    (a) 18,000             (b) 25,000
    (c) 24,000             (d) 36,000

37. During winters, an athlete can run 'x' metres on one bottle of energy drink. But in the summer, he can only run 0.2 x metres on one bottle of energy drink. How many bottles of energy drink are required to run 1000 metres during summer?
    (a) 1000/x          (b) 5000/x
    (c) 2000/x          (d) 4500/x

38. Vinay's salary is 75% more than Ashok's. Vinay got a raise of 40% on his salary while Ashok got a raise of 25% on his salary. By what percent is Vinay's salary more than Ashok's?
    (a) 96%            (b) 51.1%
    (c) 90%            (d) 52.1%

39. On a morning prayer all the students of a school stand in three rows, the first row has 20% more students than the second row and the third row contains 20% less students than the second row. If the total number of students in all the rows is 300, then find the number of students in the first row.
    (a) 120            (b) 125
    (c) 100            (d) None of these.

40. An ore contains 20% of an alloy that has 50% copper. Other than this, in the remaining 80% of the ore, there is no copper. How many kilograms of the ore are needed to obtain 10 kg of pure copper?
    (a) 100 kg          (b) 125 kg
    (c) 80 kg          (d) 75 kg

41. Last year, the Australian Football team played 80 football matches out of which they managed to win only 20%. This year, so far it has played some matches, which has made it mandatory for it to win 80% of the remaining matches to maintain its existing winning percentage. Find the number of matches played by Australia so far this year.
    (a) 30            (b) 25
    (c) 28            (d) Insufficient Information

42. The population of a village is 4,00,000. Increase rate per annum is 20%. Find the population at the starting of the 4$^{th}$ year.
    (a) 691400          (b) 591200
    (c) 691200          (d) None of these

43. In a conference, out of 200 men, 100 women, 400 children present inside the building premises, 10% of the men, 20% of the women and 30% of the children were Indians. Find the percentage of people who were not Indian.
    (a) 73%            (b) 77%
    (c) 79%            (d) 83%

44. A table and a chair are priced at ₹3000 and ₹1000 respectively. If the price of the table and that of the chair is increased by 10% and 20% respectively, then the price of 10 tables and 20 chairs is:
    (a) 52,000          (b) 57,000
    (c) 54,000          (d) None of these

45. Out of the total production of Aluminum from Bauxite, an ore of Aluminum, 30% of the ore gets wasted, and out of the remaining ore, only 30% is pure Aluminum. If the pure Aluminum obtained in a year from a mine of Bauxite was 42,000 kg, then the quantity of Bauxite mined from that mine in the year is
    (a) 3,00,000 kg        (b) 2,00,000 kg
    (c) 2,50,000 kg        (d) None of these

46. Ramesh buys a house for ₹ 2,00,000. The annual repair cost comes to 6.0% of the price of purchase. Besides, he has to pay an annual tax of ₹ 12000. At what monthly rent must he rent out the house to get a return of 20% on his net investment (in ₹) of the first year?
    (a) ₹ 3867.67        (b) ₹ 3733.33
    (c) ₹ 3000          (d) ₹ 3212.50

47. Recently, while shopping in Meena Market in Lucknow, I came across two new trousers selling at a discount. I decided to buy one of them for my little boy Sherry. The shopkeeper offered me the first trouser for ₹ 42 and said that it usually sold for 8/7 of that price. He then offered me the other trouser for ₹ 36 and said that it usually sold for 7/6th of that price. Of the two trousers which one do you think is a better bargain and what is the percentage discount on it?
    (a) first trouser, 12.5% (b) second trouser, 14.28%
    (c) Both are same      (d) None of these

48. 4/5 th of the voters in Kanpur promised to vote for Modi and the rest promised to vote for Advani. Of these voters, 10% of the voters who had promised to vote for Modi, did not vote on the election day, while 20% of the voters who had promised to vote for Advani did not vote on the election day. What is the total number of votes polled if Modi got 216000 votes?
    (a) 200000          (b) 300000
    (c) 264000          (d) 100000

49. In an examination, 80% students passed in Physics, 70% in Chemistry while 15% failed in both the subjects. If 3250 students passed in both the subjects. Find the total number of students who appeared in the examination.
    (a) 7500            (b) 8,000
    (c) 3000            (d) 5,000

50. Sudhir spends 25% of his salary on house rent, 20% of the rest he spends on his children's education and 10% of the total salary he spends on clothes. After his expenditure, he is left with ₹ 20,000. What is Sudhir's salary?
    (a) ₹ 40,000        (b) ₹ 20,000
    (c) ₹ 25,000        (d) ₹ 35,000

51. The entrance ticket at the Imagica in Mumbai is worth ₹ 1000. When the price of the ticket was lowered, the sale of tickets increased by 25% while the collections recorded a decrease of 20%. Find the deduction in the ticket price.
    (a) ₹ 240
    (b) ₹ 360
    (c) ₹ 105
    (d) ₹ 120

52. Raman's monthly salary is $A$ rupees. Of this, he spends $X$ rupees. The next month he has an increase of $C$% in his salary and $D$% in his expenditure. The new amount saved is:
    (a) $A(1 + C/100) - X(1 + D/100)$
    (b) $(A/100)(C - (D) X (1 + D/100)$
    (c) $X(C - (D)/100$
    (d) $X(C + D)/100$

53. In the year 2010, the luxury bike industry had two bike manufacturers—Splendor and Passion with market shares of 30% and 70%, respectively. In 2011, the overall market for the product increased by 20% and a new player Yamaha also entered the market and captured 10% of the market share. If we know that the market share of Splendor increased to 40% in the second year, the share of Passion in that year was:

54. Ranjan buys goods worth ₹ 10,000. He gets a rebate of 20% on it. After getting the rebate, he pays sales tax @ 10%. Find the amount he will have to pay for the goods.

55. A number is mistakenly divided by 5 instead of being multiplied by 5. What is the percentage error in the result?

56. The salary of Anuj is 20% lower than Bhuwan's salary and the salary of Chauhan is 56.25% greater than Anuj's salary. By how much percent the salary of Bhuwan is less than the salary of Chauhan.
    (a) 20%
    (b) 25%
    (c) 40%
    (d) 15%

57. The length and breadth of a rectangle are changed by +20% and −50%. What is the percentage change in area of rectangle?

58. I recently got a promotion accompanied by 23% hike in salary but due to recession my company reduced my salary by 32%. What was the net change in my salary?

59. A number when reversed becomes 45% greater than the original. By how much percentage is the units place digit greater than the tens' place digit?

60. A batsman scored 100 runs which included 4 boundaries and 6 sixes. What percent of his total score did he make by running between the wickets?

***Space for Rough Work***

## LEVEL OF DIFFICULTY (II)

1. Due to a 25% hike in the price of rice per kilogram, a person is able to purchase 5 kg less for ₹200. Find the increased price of rice per kilogram.
   (a) ₹ 5          (b) ₹ 6
   (c) ₹ 10        (d) ₹ 4

2. A fraction is such that if the double of the numerator and the triple of the denominator is changed by +10% and –30% respectively then we get 33% of 16/21. Find the fraction.
   (a) $\dfrac{4}{25}$        (b) $\dfrac{8}{11}$
   (c) $\dfrac{3}{25}$        (d) None of these

3. After receiving two successive hikes, Karun's salary became equal to 15/8 times of his initial salary. By how much percent was the salary raised the first time if the second raise was twice as high (in percent) as the first?
   (a) 15%        (b) 20%
   (c) 25%        (d) 30%

4. After three successive equal percentage rise in the salary the sum of 1000 rupees turned into 1331 rupees. Find the percentage rise in the salary.
   (a) 10%        (b) 22%
   (c) 66%        (d) 82%

5. Sudhir, a very clever businessman, started off a business with very little capital. In the first year, he earned a profit of 50% and donated 50% of the total capital (initial capital + profit) to a charitable organisation. The same course was followed in the 2nd and 3rd years also. If at the end of three years, he is left with ₹ 33,750, then find the amount donated by him at the end of the 2nd year.
   (a) ₹ 90,000        (b) ₹ 25,000
   (c) ₹ 45,000        (d) ₹ 40,000

6. In an examination, 48% students failed in Physics and 32% students in Chemistry, 20% students failed in both the subjects. If the number of students who passed the examination was 880 (by passing both the subjects), how many students appeared in the examination if the examination consisted only of these two subjects?
   (a) 2000        (b) 2200
   (c) 2500        (d) 1800

7. A machine depreciates in value each year at the rate of 10% of its previous value. However, every second year there is some maintenance work so that in that particular year, depreciation is only 5% of its previous value. If at the end of the fourth year, the value of the machine stands at ₹ 1,46,205, then find the value of machine at the start of the first year.
   (a) ₹ 1,90,000        (b) ₹ 2,00,000
   (c) ₹ 1,95,000        (d) ₹ 2,10,000

8. Kaku's project report consists of 25 pages each of 60 lines with 75 characters on each line. In case the number of lines is reduced to 55 but the number of characters is increased to 90 per lines, what is the percentage change in the number of pages. (Assume the number of pages to be a whole number.)
   (a) +10%        (b) +5%
   (c) –8%        (d) –10%

9. The price of soap is collectively decided by five factors: raw materials, research, labour, advertisements and transportation. Assume that the functional relationship is
   Price of soap = ($k'$ × Raw material costs × Research costs × Labour costs × Advertising cost × Transportation cost).
   If there are respective changes of 20%, 20%, –20%, 25% and 10% in the five factors, then find the percentage change in the price of soap.
   (a) +58.40%        (b) 54.40%
   (c) 48.50%        (d) 56%

10. The ratio of Jim's salary for October to his salary for November was 9: 8 and the ratio of the salary for November to that for December was 3: 4. The worker got 40 rupees more for December than for October and received a bonus constituting 40 per cent of the salary for three months. Find the bonus. (Assume that the number of workdays is the same in every month.)

11. Praveen goes to a shop to buy a sofa set costing ₹ 13,080. The rate of sales tax is 10%. She tells the shopkeeper to reduce the price of the sofa set to such an extent that she has to pay ₹13080 inclusive of sales tax. Find the percentage reduction needed in the price of the sofa set to just satisfy her requirement.
    (a) 8.33%        (b) 9.09%
    (c) 9%        (d) 8.5%

12. The price of a certain product was raised by 20% in India. The consumption of the same article was increased from 400 tons to 440 tons. By how much percent will the expenditure on the article rise in the Indian economy?
    (a) 32%        (b) 25%
    (c) 27%        (d) 26%

13. In the university examination last year, Samanyu scored 65% in English and 82% in History. What is the minimum percent he should score in Sociology, which is out of 50 marks (if English and History were for 100 marks each), if he aims at getting 78% overall?
    (a) 94%
    (b) 92%
    (c) 98%
    (d) 96%

14. King Dashratha, at his eleventh hour, called his three queens and distributed his gold in the following way: He gave 50% of his wealth to his first wife, 50% of the rest to his second wife and again 50% of the rest to his third wife. If their combined share is worth 1,30,900 kilograms of gold, find the quantity of gold King Dashratha was having initially?
    (a) 1,50,000 kg
    (b) 1,49,600 kg
    (c) 1,51,600 kg
    (d) 1,52,600 kg

15. The population of Swansea increases with a uniform rate of 8% per annum, but due to immigration, there is a further increase of population by 1% (however, this 1% increase in population is to be calculated on the population after the 8% increase and not on the previous years population). Find what will be the percentage increase in population after 2 years.
    (a) 18.984
    (b) 18.081
    (c) 18.24
    (d) 17.91

16. 10% of Mexico's population migrated to South Asia, 10% of the remaining migrated to America and 10% of the rest migrated to Australia. If the female population, which was left in Mexico, remained only 3,64,500, find the population of Mexico City before the migration and its effects if it is given that before the migration the female population was half the male population and this ratio did not change after the migration?
    (a) 10,00,000
    (b) 12,00,000
    (c) 15,00,000
    (d) 16,00,000

17. Malti has ₹$M$ with her and her friend Chinki has ₹$C$ with her. Malti spends 12% of her money and Chinki also spends the same amount as Malti did. What percentage of her money did Chinki spend?
    (a) $\dfrac{18M}{C}$
    (b) $\dfrac{18C}{M}$
    (c) $\dfrac{12M}{C}$
    (d) $\dfrac{12C}{M}$

18. In a village consisting of $p$ persons, $x$% can read and write. Of the males alone $y$%, and of the females alone $z$% can read and write. Find the number of males in the village in terms of $p$, $x$, $y$ and $z$ if $z < y$.
    (a) $\dfrac{[p(x-z)]}{[y+x-z]}$
    (b) $\dfrac{[p(x-z)]}{[y+x-2z]}$
    (c) $\dfrac{[p(x-z)]}{[x-z]}$
    (d) $\dfrac{[p(x-z)]}{[y-z]}$

19. According to a recent survey report issued by the Commerce Ministry, Government of India, 30% of the total FDI goes to Gujarat and 20% of this goes to rural areas. If the FDI in Gujarat, which goes to urban areas, is \$72 m, then find the size of FDI in rural Andhra Pradesh, which attracts 50% of the FDI that comes to Andhra Pradesh, which accounts for 20% of the total FDI?
    (a) \$30 m
    (b) \$9 m
    (c) \$60 m
    (d) \$40 m

20. If in the previous question, the growth in the size of FDI for the next year with respect to the previous year is 20%, then find the share of urban Maharashtra next year if 12% of the total FDI going to Maharashtra went to urban areas (provided Maharashtra attracted only 10% of the total share for both years).
    (a) \$36 m
    (b) \$4.32 m
    (c) \$3 m
    (d) \$5 m

21. The cost of food accounted for 25% of the income of a particular family. If the income gets raised by 20%, then what should be the percentage point decrease in the food expenditure as a percentage of the total income to keep the food expenditure unchanged between the two years?
    (a) 3.5
    (b) 8.33
    (c) 4.16
    (d) 5

22. If the length, breadth and height of a cube are decreased, decreased and increased by 5%, 5% and 20%, respectively, then what will be the impact on the surface area of the cube (in percentage terms)?
    (a) 7.25%
    (b) 5%
    (c) 8.33%
    (d) 6.0833%

23. *Aman*'s salary is first increased by 25% and then decreased by 20%. The result is the same as *Baman*'s salary increased by 20% and then reduced by 25%. Find the ratio of *Baman*'s initial salary to that of *Aman*'s initial salary.
    (a) 4 : 3
    (b) 11 : 10
    (c) 10 : 9
    (d) 12 : 11

24. The minimum quantity of Kerosene in liters (in whole number) that should be mixed in a mixture of 60 liters in which the initial ratio of Kerosene to water is 1:4, so that the resulting mixture has 15% Kerosene is
    (a) 3
    (b) 4
    (c) 5
    (d) This is not possible

25. A person saves 5% of his income. Two years later, his income shoots up by 20% but his savings remain the same. Find the hike in his expenditure.
    (a) 25.95%
    (b) 24.07%
    (c) 21.05%.
    (d) 15.5%

26. $P$ is 50% more than $Q$, $R$ is 2/3 of $P$ and $S$ is 60% more than $R$. Now, each of $P$, $Q$, $R$ and $S$ is increased by 10%. Find what per cent of $Q$ is $S$(after the increase)?

(a) 150%                  (b) 160%

(c) 175%                  (d) 176%

27. *Alok* and *Bimal* have, between them, ₹ 12000. *Alok* spends 12% of his money while *Bimal* spends 20% of his money. They are then left with a sum that constitutes 85% of the whole sum. Find what amount is left with *Alok*.

    (a) ₹ 7500              (b) ₹ 8000

    (c) ₹ 7000              (d) ₹ 6600

28. In order to maximise his gain, a theatre owner decides to reduce the price of tickets by 20% and as a result of this, the sales of tickets increase by 40%. If, as a result of these changes, he is able to increase his weekly collection by 1,68,000, find by what value did the gross collection increase per day.

    (a) 14,000             (b) 18,000

    (c) 24,000             (d) 20,000

29. In a town consisting of three localities *A*, *B* and *C*, the population of the three localities *A*, *B* and *C* are in the ratio 9:8:3. In locality *A*, 80% of the people are literate, in locality *B*, 30% of the people are illiterate. If 90% people in locality *C* are literate, find the percentage literacy in that town.

    (a) 61.5%              (b) 78%

    (c) 75%                (d) None of these

30. To pass an examination, 30% marks are essential. *A* obtains 20% marks less than the pass marks and *B* obtains 50% marks less than *A*. What percent less than the sum of *A*'s and *B*'s marks should *C* obtain to pass the exam?

    (a) 40%                (b) 41(3/17)%

    (c) 28%                (d) None of these

**Directions for Questions 31 to 33:**   Read the following passage and answer the questions.

In a recent youth fete organised by Mindworkzz, the entry tickets were sold out according to the following scheme:

| Tickets bought in one lot | 6 | 12 | 18 |
|---|---|---|---|
| Percentage discount | 10% | 20% | 25% |

Original price per ticket: ₹40

   This offer could have been availed only when tickets were bought in a fixed lot according to the scheme and any additional ticket was available at its original price.

31. If a person has to buy 25 tickets, then what will be the minimum price per ticket?

    (a) Equal to ₹32       (b) ₹32.32

    (c) ₹31.84             (d) Cannot be determined.

32. In the above question, what will be the approximate possible maximum price per ticket (if discounts have been availed for 24 tickets)?

    (a) ₹30                (b) ₹32

    (c) ₹36                (d) ₹36.16

33. On the last day of the fete, with the objective of maximising participation, the number of tickets sold in a lot was halved with the same discount offer. Mr.

*X* is in a fix regarding the number of tickets he can buy with ₹ 532. The maximum number of tickets he can purchase with this money is

    (a) 14                 (b) 15

    (c) 16                 (d) 17

34. 800 people were supposed to vote on a resolution, but 1/3rd of the people who had decided to vote for the motion were abducted. However, the opponents of the motion, through some means managed to increase their strength by 100%. The motion was then rejected by a majority, which was 50% of that by which it would have been passed if none of these changes would have occurred. How many people finally voted for the motion and against the motion?

    (a) 200 (for), 400 (against)

    (b) 100 (for) and 200 (against)

    (c) 150 (for), 300 (against)

    (d) 200 (for) and 300 (against)

35. At IIM Bangalore, 60% of the students are boys and the rest are girls. Further 15% of the boys and 7.5% of the girls are getting a fee waiver. If the number of those getting a fee waiver is 90, find the total number of students getting 50% concession if it is given that 50% of those not getting a fee waiver are eligible to get half fee concession?

36. A watch gains by 2% per hour when the temperature is in the range of 40°C–50°C and it loses at the same rate when the temperature is in the range of 20°C–30°C. However, the watch owner is fortunate since it runs on time in all other temperature ranges. On a sunny day, the temperature started soaring up from 8 a.m. in the morning at the uniform rate of 2°C per hour and sometime during the afternoon it started coming down at the same rate. Find what time will it be by the watch at 7 pm, if at 8 am the temperature was 32°C and at 4 pm, it was 40°C.

    (a) 6 : 55 p.m.        (b) 6 : 55 : 12 p.m.

    (c) 6 : 55 : 24 p.m.   (d) None of these

37. There were '*a*' 10 ₹ Notes and '*b*' 100 ₹ Notes. If there had been '*a*' ₹ 100 notes and '*b*' ₹ 10 notes the amount would have been 200% more.

    Find the minimum possible value of *a* If $1 \leq b \leq 20$

38. In a garment shop there are four types of shirts namely *w*, *x*, *y*, *z*. There are 20% more shirts of type '*x*' than type '*w*'. 20% less shirts of type '*x*' than type '*y*' and there are 30% more shirts of type '*z*' than type '*x*'. If there are 156 shirts of type '*z*', then find the total number of shirts.

39. Of the adult population in Nagpur, 45% of men and 25% of women are married. What percentage of the total population of adults is married (assume that no man marries more than one woman and vice versa)?

40. The weight of a bucket increases by 33.33% when filled with water to 50% of its capacity. Which of

these may be 50% of the weight of the bucket when it is filled with water (assume the weight of bucket and its capacity in kg to be integers)?

(a) 7 kg       (b) 6 kg

(c) 5 kg       (d) 8 kg

41. Pakistan scored a total of $x$ runs in 20 overs. India tied the scores in 10% less overs. If India's average run-rate had been 50% higher the scores would have been tied 5 overs earlier. Find how many runs were scored by Pakistan.

(a) 60       (b) 20

(c) 80       (d) Cannot be determined

42. Ashish, a salesman is appointed on the basic salary of ₹ 1200 per month and the condition that for every sales of ₹ 10,000 above ₹ 10,000, he will get 50% of basic salary and 10% of the sales as a reward. This incentive scheme does not operate for the first ₹10000 of sales. What should be the value of sales if he wants to earn ₹7600 in a particular month?

(a) ₹ 60,000       (b) ₹ 50,000

(c) ₹ 40,000       (d) None of these

43. In the previous question, which of the following income cannot be achieved in a month?

(a) ₹6000

(b) ₹ 9000

(c) Both a and b

(d) Any income can be achieved

44. An organization gives its' sales staff incentives based on the value of their sales. In a particular year, despite a 5 percentage point increment on the commission from 20%, the total commission for a sales organization remained unaltered. Find the change in the volume of the sales.

(a) –10%       (b) –16%

(c) –25%       (d) –20%

45. In a Local election at Kanpur, the total turnout was 80% out of which 16% of the total voters on the voting list were declared invalid. Find which of the following can be the percentage votes got by the winner of the election if the candidate who came second got 20% of the total voters on the voting list. (There were only three contestants, only one winner and the total number of voters on the voters list was 20000.)

(a) 44.8%       (b) 46.6%

(c) 48%       (d) None of these

46. The hourly wages of Rahim are increased by 10%, whereas the weekly working hours are reduced by 10%. Find the percentage change in the weekly wages if she was getting ₹ 1000 per week for 50 hours previously.

(a) 1%       (b) 4%

(c) 2%       (d) None of these

47. Two numbers $A$ and $B$ are 20% and 28% less than a third number $C$. Find by what percentage is the number $B$ less than the number $A$.

(a) 8%       (b) 12%

(c) 10%       (d) 9%

48. Price of a commodity is first increased by $x$% and then decreased by $x$%. If the new price is $K/100$, find the original price.

(a) $(x-100)100/K$    (b) $(x^2-100^2)100/K$

(c) $(100-x)100/K$    (d) $100K/(100^2-x^2)$

49. The salary of Sahir is increased by ₹ 4800 and the rate of tax is decreased by 2% from 12% to 10%. The effect is such that he is now paying the same tax as before. If in both the cases, the standard tax deduction is fixed at 20% of the total income, find the increased salary?

(a) ₹ 32,800       (b) ₹ 36,800

(c) ₹ 28,000       (d) None of these

50. Seema goes to a shop to buy a radio costing ₹ 2568. The rate of sales tax is 7% and the final value is rounded off to the next higher integer. She tells the shopkeeper to reduce the price of the radio so that she has to pay ₹2568 inclusive of sales tax. Find the reduction needed in the price of the radio.

(a) ₹ 180       (b) ₹ 210

(c) ₹ 168       (d) None of these

**Questions 51 and 52:** Study the following table and answer the questions that follow.

| Beverages | % of Vitamin | % of Minerals | % of Micronutrients | Cost per 250 gram (In ₹) |
|-----------|--------------|---------------|---------------------|--------------------------|
| 7up | 12 | 18 | 30 | 8 |
| Dew | 15 | 20 | 10 | 10 |
| Sprite | 20 | 10 | 40 | 7 |

51. Which of the following beverages contains the maximum amount of vitamins?

(a) 7up worth ₹ 16

(b) Dew worth ₹ 15

(c) Sprite worth ₹ 8

(d) All the three worth ₹ 12.5 (125 grams of each)

52. Which of these is the cheapest?

(a) 200 grams of 7up + 200 grams of Dew

(b) 300 grams of Dew +100 grams of 7up

(c) 100 grams of Dew + 100 grams of 7up + 100 grams of Sprite

(d) 300 grams of Dew +100 grams of Sprite

**Directions for questions 53 to 54:** Three great gamblers Ajay, Biru, Chetan were playing a game of Teen-Patti (3 card flush). At the beginning of the game Ajay and Biru together had as much money as Chetan had and Ajay and Chetan together had 100% more money than Biru. At the end of the game Ajay and Biru together had 100% more money than Chetan. Also, Ajay and Chetan together had 200% more money than Biru. If at the end of the game Biru had ₹1500 then answer the following questions.

53. How many persons have suffered a loss?

54. The percentage change of money for Ajay is:

**Directions for questions 55 to 57:** Mindworkzz has two offices, one in Delhi and the other in Lucknow. This year the number of employees in the Lucknow office remained the same as the previous year but the ratio of male to female employees has changed. In the Delhi office, this year the number of employees grew by 25% to 2500. Last year the ratio of male to female employees in the Delhi office was 3:1. The number of female employees in the Delhi office grew by 20% from the last year to this. The number of male employees in the Lucknow office last year equals the number of female employees in Delhi this year. The total number of employees in both the company offices grew to 3500 this year. The number of female employees in Lucknow grew up by 25% from last year to this year. Based on this information, answer the following questions.

55. What is the number of females in the Delhi office this year?

56. The percentage growth of the number of men from last year to this year in the Delhi office is

57. The difference between number of male employees and number of female employees in Lucknow and Delhi office together this year.

58. A company has 'n' employees in 2011. In 2012, 20% of the employees left the company while no one was hired. In 2013 and 2014, the number of employees again grew by 50% and 15% respectively. In 2015 the company fired 280 employees and at the end of 2015 the percentage increase in the number of employees from 2011 was found to be 10%. Find the number of employees at the end of the year 2015:

(a) 1200        (b) 1300

(c) 1100        (d) None of these.

**Directions for Questions 59 to 60:** The Food and Beverage unit of Pepsi-co India produces 1,00,000 chips packets per annum. If each packet is being sold at ₹10 and the cost of raw material is ₹ 1 per packet, the cost of manufacturing and labour is ₹ 2 per packet. The maintenance and marketing cost is ₹ 1 per packet. 10% taxes are being paid on selling price of the packet. Based on this information, answer the following questions.

59. What is the percentage profit of the company at the end of the year?

(a) 25%        (b) 50%

(c) 33%        (d) None of these.

60. If government increased taxes from 10% to 20% and cost of raw material also increased by 100%, then the percentage increase in selling price per packet of chips to maintain the same profit would be.

*Space for Rough Work*

## LEVEL OF DIFFICULTY (III)

1. The price of raw materials has gone up by 15%, labour cost has also increased from 25% of the cost of raw material to 30% of the cost of raw material. By how much percentage should there be a reduction in the usage of raw materials so as to keep the cost same?

   (a) 17%          (b) 24%
   (c) 28%          (d) 25%

2. Mr. *A* is a computer programmer. He is assigned three jobs for which time allotted is in the ratio of 5 : 4 : 2 (jobs are needed to be done individually). But due to some technical snag, 10% of the time allotted for each job gets wasted. Thereafter, owing to the lack of interest, he invests only 40%, 30% and 20% of the hours of what was actually allotted. to do the three jobs individually. Find how much percentage of the total time allotted is the time invested by *A*.

   (a) 38.33%        (b) 39.4545%
   (c) 32.72%        (d) 36.66%

3. In the Mock CAT paper at Mindworkzz, questions were asked in five sections. Out of the total students, 5% candidates cleared the cut-off in all the sections and 5% cleared none. Of the rest, 25% cleared only one section and 20% cleared four sections. If 24.5% of the entire candidates cleared two sections and 300 candidates cleared three sections, find out how many candidates appeared at the Mock CAT at Mindworkzz?

   (a) 1000          (b) 1200
   (c) 1500          (d) 2000

4. There are three galleries in a coal mine. On the first day, two galleries are operative and after some time, the third gallery is made operative. With this, the output of the mine became half as large again. What is the capacity of the second gallery as a percentage of the first, if it is given that a four-month output of the first and the third galleries was the same as the annual output of the second gallery?

   (a) 70%          (b) 64%
   (c) 60%          (d) 65%

5. 10% of salty sea water contained in a flask was poured out into a beaker. After this, a part of the water contained in the beaker was vapourised by heating and due to this, the percentage of salt in the beaker increased *M* times. If it is known that after the content of the beaker was poured into the flask, the percentage of salt in the flask increased by *x*%.

Find the original quantity of sea water in the flask.

   (a) $\dfrac{9M + 1\%}{M - 1}$   (b) $\dfrac{(9M + 1)x\%}{M - 1}$

   (c) $\dfrac{9M - 1x\%}{M + 1}$   (d) $\dfrac{9M + x\%}{M + 1}$

6. In an election of 3 candidates *A*, *B* and *C*, *A* gets 50% more votes than *B*. *A* also beats *C* by 1,80,00 votes. If it is known that *B* gets 5 percentage point more votes than *C*, find the number of voters on the voting list (given 90% of the voters on the voting list voted and no votes were illegal)

   (a) 72,000        (b) 81,000
   (c) 90,000        (d) 1,00,000

7. A clock is set right at 12 noon on Monday. It loses 1/2% on the correct time in the first week but gains 1/4% on the true time during the second week. The time shown on Monday after two weeks will be

   (a) 12 : 25 : 12    (b) 11 : 34 : 48
   (c) 12 : 50 : 24    (d) 12 : 24 : 16

8. The petrol prices shot up by 7% as a result of the hike in the price of crudes. The price of petrol before the hike was ₹ 28 per litre. Vawal travels 2400 kilometres every month and his car gives a mileage of 18 kilometres to a litre. Find the increase in the expenditure that Vawal has to incur due to the increase in the price of petrol (to the nearest rupee)?

   (a) ₹ 270         (b) ₹ 262
   (c) ₹ 276         (d) ₹ 272

9. For Question 8, by how many kilometres should Vawal reduce his travel if he wants to maintain his expenditure at the previous level (prior to the price increase)?

   (a) 157 km        (b) 137 km
   (c) 168 km        (d) 180 km

10. In Question 8, if Vawal wants to limit the increase in expenditure to ₹ 200, what strategy should he adopt with respect to his travel?

    (a) Reduce travel to 2350 kilometres
    (b) Reduce travel to 2340 kilometres
    (c) Reduce travel to 2360 kilometres
    (d) None of these

11. A shopkeeper announces a discount scheme as follows: for every purchase of ₹ 3000 to ₹ 6000, the customer gets a 15% discount or a ticket that entitles him to get a 7% discount on a further purchase of goods costing more than ₹ 6000. The customer, how-

ever, would have the option of reselling his right to the shopkeeper at 4% of his initial purchase value (as per the right refers to the 7% discount ticket). In an enthusiastic response to the scheme, 10 people purchase goods worth ₹ 4000 each. Find the maximum. Possible revenue for the shopkeeper.

   (a) ₹ 38,400       (b) ₹ 38,000

   (c) ₹ 39,400       (d) ₹ 39,000

12. For question 11, find the maximum possible discount that the shopkeeper would have to offer to the customer.

   (a) ₹ 1600       (b) ₹ 2000

   (c) ₹ 6000       (d) ₹ 4000

**Directions for Questions 13 to 16:** Read the following and answer the questions that follow.

Two friends Shayam and Kailash own two versions of a car. Shayam owns the diesel version of the car, while Kailash owns the petrol version.

Kailash's car gives an average that is 20% higher than Shayam's (in terms of litres per kilometre). It is known that petrol costs 60% of its price higher than diesel.

13. The ratio of the cost per kilometre of Kailash's car to Shayam's car is

   (a) 3 : 1       (b) 1 : 3

   (c) 1.92 : 1       (d) 2 : 1

14. If Shayam's car gives an average of 20 km per litre, then the difference in the cost of travel per kilometre between the two cars is

   (a) ₹ 4.3       (b) ₹ 3.5

   (c) ₹ 2.5       (d) Cannot be determined

15. For Question 14, the ratio of the cost per kilometre of Shayam's travel to Kailash's travel is

   (a) 3 : 1       (b) 1 : 3

   (c) 1 : 1.92       (d) 2 : 1

16. If diesel costs ₹ 12.5 per litre, then the difference in the cost of travel per kilometre between Kailash's and Shayam's is (assume an average of 20 km per litre for Shayam's car and also assume that petrol is 50% of its own price higher than diesel)

   (a) ₹ 1.75       (b) ₹ 0.875

   (c) ₹ 1.25       (d) ₹ 1.125

**Directions for Questions 17 to 23:** Read the following and answer the questions that follow.

In the island of Hoola Boola Moola, the inhabitants have a strange process of calculating their average incomes and expenditures. According to an old legend prevalent on that island, the average monthly income had to be calculated on the basis of 14 months in a calendar year while the average monthly expenditure was to be calculated on the basis of 9 months per year. This would lead to people having an underestimation of their savings since there would be an underestimation of the income and an overestimation of the expenditure per month.

17. Mr. Boogle Woogle comes back from the USSR and convinces his community comprising 273 families to start calculating the average income and the average expenditure on the basis of 12 months per calendars year. Now if it is known that the average estimated income in his community is (according to the old system) 87 moolahs per month, then what will be the percentage change in the savings of the community of Mr. Boogle Woogle (assume that there is no other change)?

   (a) 12.33%       (b) 22.22%

   (c) 31.31%       (d) Cannot be determined

18. For Question 17, if it is known that the average estimated monthly expenditure is 19 moolahs per month for the island of Hoola Boola Moola, then what will be the percentage change in the estimated savings of the community?

   (a) 32.42%       (b) 38.05%

   (c) 25.23%       (d) Cannot be determined

19. For Question 18, if it is known that the average estimated monthly expenditure was 22 moolahs per month for the community of Boogle Woogle (having 273 families), then what will be the percentage change in the estimated savings of the community?

   (a) 30.77%       (b) 28.18%

   (c) 25.23%       (d) 25.73%

20. For Question 19, what will be the percentage change in the estimated average income of the community (calculated on the basis of the new estimated average)?

   (a) 14.28% increase       (b) 14.28% decrease

   (c) 16.66% increase       (d) 16.66% decrease

21. If the finance minister of the island Mr. Bhola Ram declares that henceforth the average monthly income has to be estimated on the basis of 12 months per year while the average monthly expenditure is to be estimated on the basis of 11 months to the year, what will happen to the savings in the economy of Hoola Boola Moola?

   (a) Increase       (b) Decrease

   (c) Remain constant       (d) Either (b) or (c)

22. For Question 21, what will be the percentage change in savings?

   (a) 3.1%       (b) 1.52%

   (c) 2.5%       (d) Cannot be determined

23. For Question 22, what will be the percentage change in the estimated monthly expenditure?

   (a) 22.22% decrease       (b) 22.22% increase

   (c) 18.18% decrease       (d) 18.18% increase

24. Abhimanyu Banerjee has 72% vision in his left eye and 68% vision in his right eye. On corrective therapy, he starts wearing contact lenses, which augment his vision by 15% in the left eye and 11% in the right eye. Find out the percentage of normal vision that he possesses after corrective therapy. (Assume that a person's eyesight is a multiplicative construct of the eyesight's of his left and right eyes)

    (a) 52.5%                    (b) 62.5%

    (c) 72.5%                    (d) 68.6%

25. A shopkeeper gives 3 consecutive discounts of 10%, 15% and 15% after which he sells his goods at a percentage profit of 30.05% on the C.P. Find the value of the percentage profit that the shopkeeper would have earned if he had given discounts of 10% and 15% only.

    (a) 53%                      (b) 62.5%

    (c) 72.5%                    (d) 68.6%

26. If the third discount in Question 25 was ₹ 2,29,50, then find the original marked price of the item.

    (a) ₹ 1,00,000              (b) ₹ 1,25,000

    (c) ₹ 2,00,000              (d) ₹ 2,50,000

27. Krishna Iyer, a motorist uses 24% of his fuel in covering the first 20% of his total journey (in city driving conditions). If he knows that he has to cover another 25% of his total journey in city driving conditions, what should be the minimum percentage increase in the fuel efficiency for non-city driving over the city driving fuel efficiency, so that he is just able to cover his entire journey without having to refuel? (Approximately)

    (a) 39.2%                    (b) 43.5%

    (c) 45.6%                    (d) 41.2%

**Directions for Questions 28 to 30:** Read the following and answer the questions that follow the BSNL announced a cut in the STD rates on 27 December 2011. The new rates and slabs are given in the table below and are to be implemented from 14 January 2012.

### Slab Details

| Distance | Rates (₹/min) | | | |
|---|---|---|---|---|
| | Peak Rates | | Off Peak | |
| | Old | New | Old | New |
| 50–200 | 4.8 | 2.4 | 1.2 | 1.2 |
| 200–500 | 11.6 | 4.8 | 3.0 | 2.4 |
| 500–1000 | 17.56 | 9.00 | 4.5 | 4.5 |
| 1000+ | 17.56 | 9.00 | 6.0 | 4.5 |

28. The maximum percentage reduction in costs will be experienced for calls over which of the following distances?

    (a) 50–200                   (b) 500–1000

    (c) 1000+                     (d) 200–500

29. The percentage difference in the cost of a set of telephone calls made on the 13th and 14th January having durations of 4 minutes over a distance of 350 km, 3 minutes for a distance of 700 km and 3 minutes for a distance of 1050 km is (if all the three calls are made in peak times)

    (a) 51.2%                     (b) 51.76%

    (c) 59.8 %                    (d) cannot be determined

30. If one of the three calls in Question 29 were made in an off peak time on both days, then the percentage reduction in the total cost of the calls between 13th and 14th January will

    (a) definitely reduce

    (b) definitely increase

    (c) will depend on which particular call was made in an off peak time

    (d) cannot be determined

**Directions for Questions 31 to 35:** Read the following caselet and answer the questions that follow.

The circulation of the *Deccan Emerald* newspaper is 3,73,000 copies, while its closest competitors are *The Times of Hindustan* and *India's Times,* which sell 2,47,000 and 20% more than that respectively (rounded off to the higher thousand). All the newspapers cost ₹ 2 each. The hawker's commissions offered by the three papers are 20%, 25% and 30%, respectively (these commissions are calculated on the sale price of the newspaper). Also, it is known that newspapers earn primarily through sales and advertising.

31. Taking the base as the net revenue of *Deccan Emerald*, the percentage difference of the net revenue (revenues — commission disbursed to hawkers) between *Deccan Emerald* and *India's Times* is

    (a) 24.62%                    (b) 30.32%

    (c) 26.28%                    (d) None of these

32. The ratio of the percentage difference in the total net revenue between *Deccan Emerald* and *India's Times* to the percentage difference in the total revenue between *Deccan Emerald* and *India's Times* is

    (a) 1.488                     (b) 0.3727

    (c) 0.6720                    (d) Cannot be determined

33. If the cost of printing the newspaper is ₹ 8, 7.5 and 7, respectively per day for *Deccan Emerald, Times of Hindustan* and *India's Times* respectively and on any day the available advertising space in the *Deccan Emerald* newspaper is 800 cc (column centimetres) and the advertising rate for *Deccan Emerald* is ₹ 3000 per cc then the percentage of the advertising space that must be utilised to ensure the full recovery of the day's cost for *Deccan Emerald* is

(a) 95.83%          (b) 99.46%

(c) 97.28%          (d) Cannot be determined

34. Based on the data in the previous question and the additional information that the space availability in *India's Times* is 1000 cc and that in the *Times of Hindustan* is 1100 cc, find the percentage point difference in the percentage of advertising space to be utilised in *India's Times* and that which must be utilised in *Times of Hindustan* so that both newspapers just break even.

(a) 4.5          (b) 5.2

(c) 10          (d) Cannot be determined

35. For the data in Questions 33 and 34 if it is known that the advertising rate in *Times of Hindustan* is ₹ 1800 per cc and that in the *India's Times* is ₹ 2100 per cc, then what is the percentage point difference in the percentage of advertising space to be utilised by *Times of Hindustan* and *India's Times* so that both of them are just able to break even?

(a) 4.18          (b) 5.6

(c) 4.09          (d) Cannot be determined

36. On a train journey, there are 5 kinds of tickets AC I, AC II, AC III, 3-tier, and general. The relationship between the rates of the tickets for the Eurail is:

AC II is 20% higher than AC III and AC I is 70% of AC III's value higher than the AC II ticket's value. The 3-tier ticket is 25% of the AC I's ticket cost and the general ticket is 1/3 the price of the AC II ticket. The AC II ticket costs 780 euros between London and Paris. The difference in the rates of 3 tier and general ticket is

(a) 41.25 euros          (b) 55.8 euros

(c) 48.75 euros          (d) 52.75 euros

37. For the above question, the total cost of one ticket of each class will be

(a) 3233.75          (b) 3533.75

(c) 4233.75          (d) 3733.75

**Directions for Questions 38 to 40:**  Read the following and answer the questions that follow.

A Eurailexpress train has 2 AC I bogeys having 24 berths each, 3 AC II bogeys having 45 berths each, 2 AC III bogeys having 64 berths each and 12 3-tier bogeys having 64 berths each. There are no general bogeys in the train. If 200 euros is the cost of an AC 3-tier berth from London to Glasgow, answer the following questions:

38. The value of the maximum revenues possible from the Eurailexpress between Glasgow to London and back is

(a) 3,15,600          (b) 2,44,800

(c) 2,98,400          (d) 2,96,760

39. For a Eurailexpress journey from London to Glasgow, 80% of the train was uniformly booked across class-

es. What percentage of the total revenues came out of the sales of 3-tier tickets?

(a) 44.23%          (b) 52.18%

(c) 39.23%          (d) 48.9%

40. If bookings for the above question was 40% in AC I, 70% in AC II, 60% in AC III and 55% in 3-tier, then what will happen to the percentage contribution of 3-tier to the total revenues on the train journey?

(a) Decrease          (b) Increase

(c) Remain constant          (d) Cannot be determined

41. A 14.4 kg gas cylinder runs for 104 hours when the smaller burner on the gas stove is fully opened while it runs for 80 hours when the larger burner on the gas stove is fully opened. Which of these values are the closest to the percentage difference in the usage of gas per hour, between the smaller and the larger burner?

(a) 26.23%          (b) 30%

(c) 32.23%          (d) 23.07%

42. For Question 41, assume that the rate of gas dispersal is directly proportional to the degree of opening of the aperture of the gas. If we are given that the smaller burner is open to 60% of its maximum and the larger burner is open to 50% of its maximum, the percentage decrease in the percentage difference between the smaller burner and the larger burner (in terms of hours per kg) is

(a) 72.22%          (b) 73.33%

(c) 66.66%          (d) None of these

43. Hursh Sarma has a salary of ₹10,800 per month. In the first month of the year, he spends 40% of his income on food, 50% on clothing and saves 11.11% of what he has spent. In the next two months, he saves 9.09% of what he has spent (spending 38.33% of his income on food). In the fourth month, he gets an increment of 11.11% on his salary and spends every single paise on celebrating his raise. But from the fifth month onwards good sense prevails on him and he saves 12.5%, 15%, 20%, 10%, 8.33%, 12.5%, 15% and 20% on his new income per month. The ratio between the sum of the savings for the two months having the highest savings to the sum of the savings for the two months having the lowest savings is

(a) 2.6666          (b) 5.3333

(c) 8          (d) None of these

44. In an economy, the rate of savings has a relation to the investment in industry for that year and the following three years. The relation is such that a percentage point change in investment in industry for that year has a relation to the total production output in the next 4 years. A 2 percentage point increase in the savings rate in a year, increases the

investment in the industry of the economy by 1%. Further, the rate of investment also goes up by 0.5% in the next year, by 0.25% in the second year and again by 0.25% in the third year. Also assume that the investment in an economy is only dependent on the patterns of savings in the previous 3 years in the economy. Also, the percentage change in the investment in a particular year is got by adding the effect of the previous three years savings pattern.

In fiscal 2008–09, the rate of savings in the Indian economy is 25% while that in the Pakistani economy, is 20%. This has remained constant since 2003. In 2009–10 the savings rate in the Indian economy suddenly rises by 5 percentage points to 30% while that in the Pakistani economy rises by 2 percentage points to 22%. It is further known that the value of the investment in the industry in the 2 countries was 2 million dollars and 1.8 million dollars respectively (for the previous year). The percentage difference between the investment in the Pakistani economy to the investment in the Indian economy in 2010–11 will be (if it is known that there is no change in the savings rate in 2010–11):

(a) 13.6%         (b) 15.12%

(c) 11.18%        (d) 12.2%

**Directions for Questions 45 to 48:** In an economy the rate of savings has a relation to the investment in industry for that year and for the following three years and the investment in industry for that year has a relation to the total production output in the next 4 years.

45. For Question 44, if there is no additional change in the savings rate until 2011–12, then the percentage difference in the value of the investment in India to the investment in Pakistan in 2011–12 (as a percentage of the investment in India) is

(a) 11.28%        (b) 14.18%

(c) 14.02%        (d) None of these

46. If the change in production is directly related to the change in investment in the previous year, and if the data of the savings rate change for the previous 2 questions are to be assumed true, then for which year did the difference between the production in the Indian economy and the production in the Pakistani economy show the maximum percentage change?

(a) 2010–11       (b) 2011–12

(c) 2012–13       (d) Cannot be determined

47. For Question 44, it is known that the percentage change in investment in a year leads to a corresponding equal percentage increase in the manufacturing production in the next year. Further, if the growth rate of manufacturing production is 27% of the GDP

growth rate of the country, then what is the GDP growth rate of India in 2010–11?

(a) 8.52%         (b) 7.28%

(c) 9.26%         (d) None of these

48. The Euro was ushered in on the Ist January 2002 and the old currencies of the European economies were exchanged into Euros. In France, 4 Francs were exchanged for 1 Euro while in Germany 5 Deutsche Marks were exchanged for 1 Euro and in Italy 3 Liras were exchanged for 1 Euro. The exchange rate for Moolahs, the official currency of Hoola Boola Moola, was set at 185 Moolahs per Euro. Dr. Krishna Iyer, an NRI doctor based in Europe, had a practice across each of these three countries and he sends back money orders to his native island of Hoola Boola Moola. The existing exchange rate of Moolahs with the above-mentioned currencies was 51 moolahs per Franc, 36 Moolahs per Deutsche Mark and 70 moolahs per Lira. If Dr. Iyer has this information, then what should he do with his currency holdings in these three currencies on the 31st December 2001 so that he maximises his moolah value on the Ist of January 2002. (Assume no arbitrage possibilities between the three currencies)

(a) Change to Francs

(b) Change to Deutsche Marks

(c) Change to Liras

(d) Remain indifferent

49. For the above questions, the exchange rates for the three currencies with respect to a dollar was: 2$ per Lira, 1.5$ per Franc and 1.4 dollar per Deutshce Mark. If Dr. Iyer has 100 liras, 100 Deutsche Marks and 100 Francs on 31st December 2001, the maximum percentage change he can achieve in his net holding in terms of dollars due to the arbitrage created by the Euro conversion could be

(a) 17.23%        (b) 7.33%

(c) 11.2%         (d) Cannot be determined

50. For Question 48, which one of the following will allow the calculation of all possibilities of percentage change in terms of moolah value of Dr. Iyer's portfolio? (That is possible through currency conversions.)

(a) Dr. Iyer's money holding in all three currencies

(b) Dr. Iyer's monthly earnings in all three currencies

(c) The inter-currency conversion rates between Liras, Deutsche Mark and Francs

(d) Both (a) and (c)

# ANSWER KEY

## Level of Difficulty (I)

| | | | |
|---|---|---|---|
| 1. (a) | 2. (a) | 3. (a) | 4. (d) |
| 5. (d) | 6. (d) | 7. (d) | 8. (d) |
| 9. 30 | 10. 1: 1 | 11. (a) | 12. (d) |
| 13. (b) | 14. (d) | 15. (a) | 16. (c) |
| 17. (d) | 18. (d) | 19. (a) | 20. (c) |
| 21. (c) | 22. (d) | 23. (d) | 24. (d) |
| 25. (c) | 26. (d) | 27. (b) | 28. (b) |
| 29. (d) | 30. (a) | 31. (a) | 32. (c) |
| 33. (a) | 34. (c) | 35. (a) | 36. (d) |
| 37. (b) | 38. (a) | 39. (a) | 40. (a) |
| 41. (d) | 42. (c) | 43. (b) | 44. (b) |
| 45. (b) | 46. (b) | 47. (b) | 48. (c) |
| 49. (d) | 50. (a) | 51. (b) | 52. (a) |
| 53. 50% | 54. 8800 | 55. 96% | 56. (a) |
| 57. –40% | 58. –16.36% | 59. 57.89% | 60. 48% |

## Level of Difficulty (II)

| | | | |
|---|---|---|---|
| 1. (c) | 2. (b) | 3. (c) | 4. (a) |
| 5. (c) | 6. (b) | 7. (b) | 8. (c) |
| 9. (a) | 10. 265.6 | 11. (b) | 12. (a) |
| 13. (d) | 14. (b) | 15. (a) | 16. (c) |
| 17. (c) | 18. (d) | 19. (a) | 20. (b) |
| 21. (c) | 22. (d) | 23. (c) | 24. (d) |
| 25. (c) | 26. (b) | 27. (d) | 28. (c) |
| 29. (d) | 30. (d) | 31. (c) | 32. (d) |
| 33. (c) | 34. (a) | 35. 330 | 36. (d) |
| 37. 29 | 38. 526 | 39. 32.14 | 40. (c) |
| 41. (d) | 42. (b) | 43. (b) | 44. (d) |
| 45. (d) | 46. (a) | 47. (c) | 48. (d) |
| 49. (d) | 50. (a) | 51. (a) | 52. (c) |
| 53. 2 | 54. 150 | 55. 600 | |
| 56. 26.67% | 57. 1300 | 58. (c) | 59. (b) |
| 60. 25% | | | |

## Level of Difficulty (III)

| | | | |
|---|---|---|---|
| 1. (a) | 2. (c) | 3. (b) | 4. (c) |
| 5. (b) | 6. (d) | 7. (a) | 8. (b) |
| 9. (a) | 10. (d) | 11. (a) | 12. (c) |
| 13. (a) | 14. (d) | 15. (a) | 16. (b) |
| 17. (d) | 18. (d) | 19. (a) | 20. (c) |
| 21. (a) | 22. (d) | 23. (c) | 24. (b) |
| 25. (a) | 26. (c) | 27. (b) | 28. (d) |
| 29. (b) | 30. (a) | 31. (b) | 32. (a) |
| 33. (b) | 34. (c) | 35. (b) | 36. (c) |
| 37. (a) | 38. (c) | 39. (a) | 40. (a) |
| 41. (b) | 42. (a) | 43. (b) | 44. (a) |
| 45. (c) | 46. (d) | 47. (c) | 48. (b) |
| 49. (d) | 50. (d) | | |

**Hints**

### Level of Difficulty (III)

1. Assume initial raw material price to be 100. This means that the initial labour cost is 25. Hence the net cost is 125. Now, since there is a 15% increment in raw material cost and the labour cost has gone up to 30% of the raw material cost, it is clear that the new total expenditure is 115*1.3 = 149.5. Reduce the cost to 125 by reducing the usage of raw materials used.

2. Assume that 50, 40 and 20 hours are available. There is no need to use 10% waste of time in this question.

4. Half as large again means 1.5 times (or an addition of 50%).

5. Assume values for $M$ and $x$ and solve through options.

6. $A = 1.5\ B$, $A - C = 180000$ and $B = 1.05\ C$. Solve to get $A$, $B$ and $C$. Also, $A + B + C = 90\%$ of total voters on voting list. This will give you the answer. Ideally solve this question through options.

7. Clock loses 0.5% of 168 hours in the first week and gains 0.25% of 168 hours in the second week. Hence, net loss is 0.25% of 168 hours.

8. Vawal uses 133.33 litres of petrol every month, while the price of petrol has gone up by ₹ 1.96. Hence, the increase in expenditure = 133.33 * 1.96 = ₹ 261 approximately.

11. Maximum revenue for the shopkeeper will occur when the minimum discount offer is used by the customer. This level is 4%.

12. This is the case of maximum discounts.

Hints for Questions 13–16

| | Diesel Shyam | Petrol Kailash |
|---|---|---|
| Average (in litre per km) | $x$ | $1.2x$ |
| Cost of Fuel (in ₹/litre) | $0.4\ p$ | $p$ |

13. Average in litre per kilometre multiplied by the Cost of fuel in ₹/litre will give the required cost per kilometre.

14. Shyam's car gives 20 km/litre means 0.05 litres per kilometre then Kailash's car gives 0.06 litre/km. However, since we do not know the price of petrol or diesel we cannot find out the difference in the cost of travel.

15. This question is the opposite of question 13.

16. Cost of petrol is ₹ 25 per litre. Cost per kilometre for Shyam = 12.5 × 0.05

Also, cost per kilometre for Kailash = 25 × 0.06

### Hints for Questions 17–23

Estimated average savings

$$= \frac{\text{Annual Income}}{14} - \frac{\text{Annual Expenditure}}{9}$$

17. The value will depend on the values of annual expenditure which is not available.

18. Average estimated monthly expenditure is given for the island of Hoola Boola Moola and not for Mr. Boogle Woogle's community.

19. Original estimated savings = 87 − 22 = 65 Moolahs.
New estimated savings = 1218/12 − 198/12 = 85.

24. $0.72 \times 1.15 \times 0.68 \times 1.11$.

25. Solve through options: A 15% reduction on the correct answer will give a profit of 30.05%.
Option (a) is correct.

26. The last discount being 22,950, it means that the value prior to this 15% discount must have been 1,53,000 checking with options:

$$200,000 \xrightarrow{15\%\downarrow} 17,000 \xrightarrow{10\%\downarrow} 1,53,000.$$

Hence option (c) is correct.

27. For 45% of the journey in city driving conditions, 54% of the fuel is consumed.
Hence, for the remaining 55% journey, 46% fuel is left.
Required increase in fuel efficiency

$$= \frac{\dfrac{55}{46} - \dfrac{45}{54}}{\dfrac{45}{54}} \times 100.$$

28. The maximum percentage reduction in peak rates is for the 200 − 500 category.

29. $\dfrac{(4\times11.6+3\times17.56+3\times17.56)-(4\times4.8+3\times9+3\times9)}{4\times11.6+3\times17.56+3\times17.56}$

33. Loss to be made up everyday = 373000(8 − 1.60)
= 6.4 × 373000.

No. of cc required to be sold = $\dfrac{373000 \times 6.4}{3000}$

34. Advertising rates have not been mentioned. Hence, we cannot solve the question.

36–40. The ticket cost are:
AC III → 100 (assume), AC – II → 120,
AC I → 190, 3 Tier → 47.5, General → 40.
Also, AC – II = 780 Euros for a London – Paris journey

36. (47.5 − 40) × 6.5 = 48.75

37. (100 + 120 + 190 + 47.5 + 40) × 6.5.

38. Maximum revenues on a return journey means 100% bookings both ways.

39. $\dfrac{\text{Revenues from 3-Tier}}{\text{Total Revenues}} \times 100$

41. $\dfrac{\dfrac{14.4}{80} - \dfrac{14.4}{104}}{\dfrac{14.4}{104}} = \dfrac{104-80}{80} = 30\%$

42. Original percentage difference = 30%

At 60% aperture opening the smaller gas will last $\dfrac{104}{0.6} = 173.33$ hours.

Similarly, the larger gas will last $\dfrac{80}{0.5} = 160$ hours.

Thus, the smaller gas lasts $\dfrac{173.33-160}{173.33} \times 100 = 8.33\%$ more than the larger gas.

Then, required answer = $\dfrac{30-8.33}{30} \times 100 = 72.22\%$

44. The 5% point increase in savings rate will account for a 2.5% increase in investment in 2005–06 and a further 1.25% increase in investment in 2006–07.
Thus, Indian investment is 2006–07 = 2 million × 1.025 × 1.0125 similarly, calculate for Pakistan.

45. Use the same process as for the previous question.

46. Cannot be determined since we do not know the initial values of the production output.

47. Since there is a 2.5% increase in investment in 2005–06, there will be a 2.5% increase in manufacturing production is 2006–07.
Then, GDP growth rate = $\dfrac{2.5}{0.27} = 9.26\%$.

### Solutions and Shortcuts

*Level of Difficulty (I)*

1. $12(4/15)\% = 184/15\%$. As a fraction, the value = $184/(15 \times 100) = 46/375$

2. 10% of 20% of 25% of 100 = $\dfrac{10}{100} \times \dfrac{20}{100} \times \dfrac{25}{100} \times 100 = 0.50$

3. It can be clearly seen that 40% of 400 = 160 is the highest number.

4. $0.30N = 300 => > 1000$. Thus, $0.50 \times 1000 = 500$.

5. 25% of $x$ = 30% of 5000 or $0.25x = 1500 = 6000$

6. (30/100) × (a/100) × (b) = (25/100) × (b/100) × (c)
= 30a = 25c, c = 1.2a

7. Check the options. If you check with Option d = 90, you get → 108 − 20% of 90 = 108 − 18 = 90. This matches the given requirement and hence Option (d) is the correct answer.

8. B + 40% of A = 125% of B
40% of A = 25% of B.
i.e. 0.4A = 0.25B
A/B = 5/8
Apparently it seems that B is bigger, but if you consider A and B to be negative the opposite would be true.
Hence, option (d) is correct.

9. Let their marks be ($x$ + 10) and $x$.
Then $\dfrac{x+10}{2x+10} \times 100 = 60$

$x = 20$

Hence $(x + 10) = 30$.

10. $0.05A + 0.1B = \dfrac{1}{2}(0.2A + 0.1B)$

$0.05A = 0.05B$

$A:B = 1:1$

11. The following PCG will give the answer:

$$100 \xrightarrow{50\%} 150 \xrightarrow{33.33\%} 100$$

Hence, the percentage reduction required is 33.33% (50/150).

12. $100 \text{------} \to 150 \text{-------} \to 120$.

The reduction from 150 to 120 is 20% and hence, it means that he needs to reduce his consumption by 20%.

13. Shankar $\xrightarrow{50\% \text{ more}}$ Ashok $\xleftarrow{20\% \text{ more}}$ Bishnu
    (100)                    (150)                  (125)

Required percentage $= \dfrac{25}{100} \times 100 = 25\%$

14. Total votes = 12000. Valid votes = 85% of 12000 = 10200. Chaman gets 80% of 10200 votes = 8160 votes and Dhande would get 10200 – 8160 = 2040 Votes.

15. If Shyam has inadvertently increased his height by 25% the correction he would need to make to go back to his original height would be to reduce the stated height by 20%.

16. Let Raunak's height be $H$. Then, $H \times 1.15 = 345$, $H = 345/1.15 = 300$.

17. Let the number be *100*. Then, 200 should be the correct outcome. But instead the value got is 50. Change in value = 200 – 50 = 150. The percentage change in the value = 150 × 100/200 = 75%. Alternately, you could think of this as the number being 'x' and the required result being 2x and the derived result being 0.5x. Hence, the percentage change in the result is 1.5x × 100/2x. Clearly, the value would be 75%. (Note: In this case, the percentage change in the answer does not depend on the value of 'x').

18. The percentage difference would be given by thinking of the percentage change between two numbers: $(x – 10)$ to $(x + 10)$ ['What he wanted to get' to 'what he got by mistake'].

The value of the percentage difference in this case depends on the value of $x$. Hence, this cannot be answered. Option (d) is correct.

19. From the first statement we get that out of 100 litres of the mixture, 25 litres must be milk. Since, we are adding water to this and keeping the milk constant, it is quite evident that 25 litres of milk should correspond to 20% of the total mixture. Thus, the amount in the total mixture must be 125, which means we need to add 25 litres of water to make 100 litres of the mixture.

20. Let the area of the land is 100 square units. On increasing the length of the land by 20% the area will get increased by 20%. Similarly on increasing the breadth by 30% the area would get increased by 30%. The answer can be thought on the following percentage change graphic (PCG):

$$100 \xrightarrow[\substack{+20 \\ \text{Effect of length} \\ \text{increase}}]{20\% \text{ increases}} 120 \xrightarrow[\substack{+36 \\ \text{Effect of breadth} \\ \text{increase}}]{30\% \text{ increases}} 156$$

Hence, the required answer is 56%

21. The area of a triangle depends on the product: base × height.

Since, the height increases by 30% and the area has to increase by 90% overall, the following PCG will give the answer. Let 100 be the original area.

$$100 \xrightarrow[\substack{+30 \\ \text{Effect of increase} \\ \text{in base}}]{30\% \text{ increase}} 130 \xrightarrow[\substack{\text{Effect of increase} \\ \text{in height}}]{} 190$$

The required answer will be $\dfrac{60}{130} \times 100 = 46.15\%$

22. The volume goes up by:

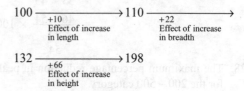

Hence, 98%.

23. Let the salary of Vivek and Ajay be ₹ 100 and ₹ 110 respectively.

Required percentage $= \dfrac{110 - 100}{110} \times 100 = 9.09\%$

24. $100 \xrightarrow[\text{Effect of price}]{50\% \text{ drop}} 50 \xrightarrow[\text{+100 Effect of consumption}]{} 150$

We have assumed initial expenditure to be 100, in the above figure. Then the final expenditure is 150. The percentage change in consumption can be seen to be $\dfrac{150 - 50}{50} \times 100 = 200\%$

25. If the price of wheat has fallen by 20% the quantity would be increased by 25% (if we keep the expenditure constant.)

This means that 100 kgs would increase by 25% to 125 kgs.

26. The winning candidate gets 60% of the votes cast and the losing candidate gets 40% of the votes cast. Thus, the gap between the two is 20% of the votes cast = 200 votes. Thus, the votes cast = 1000. Since, this is 66.67% of the number of voters on the voting list, the number of people on the voting list = 1500.

27. $500000 \xrightarrow{20\% \text{ increase}} 600000 \xrightarrow{20\% \text{ increase}} 720000$

28. $50{,}000 \xrightarrow{\text{20\% increase}} 60{,}000 \xrightarrow{\text{10\% decrease}} 54{,}000$

    $\xrightarrow{\text{30\% increase}} 70{,}200$

29. His investments are 4000, 16,000 and 20,000 respectively. His dividends are: 400, 2400 and 5000, which means that his total dividend = ₹7800.

30. Sahir obtained 80 marks, hence Madan obtained = $80 \times 1.2 = 96$. Ravi = $96/0.6 = 160$. 160 out of 200 means a percentage of 80%.

31. 10% students got a final score of 20. 20% students got a final score of 30 (inclusive of grace marks.) 50 % students got a final score of 50.

    Hence, average score of the class (Note: For the class average, we would not take into account the students who were absent)

    $$= \frac{10 \times 20 + 20 \times 30 + 50 \times 50}{80} = 41.25$$

32. If his income is 100, his household expenditure is 20, expenditure on food is 24, on clothes it is 5.6. Thus he saves: $100 - 20 - 24 - 5.6 = 50.4\%$ of his income. Since, this is given to us as 10080, the total income would be: $\dfrac{100}{50.4} \times 10080 = 20000$

33. The only logic for this question is that Harish's salary would be more than Bhuvan's salary. Thus, only option (a) is possible for Harish's salary.

34. By using options, you can easily see that option (c) satisfies.

    2000 females and 4000 males.

    Increase = $2000 \times 0.2 + 4000 \times 0.1 = 800$

35. If we take Raju as 100, we will get Bharat as 125 and Charan as 83.33. This means Charan's goods are priced at 2/3$^{rd}$ Bharat's and hence he sells his goods 33.33% cheaper than Bharat.

36. Let the percentage of the total votes secured by Party SJP be $x\%$ Then the percentage of total votes secured by Party SJD = $(x - 12)\%$ As there are only two parties contesting in the election, the sum total of the votes secured by the two parties should total up to 100%, i.e., $x + x - 12 = 100 \rightarrow 2x - 12 = 100$ or $2x = 112$ or $x = 56\%$. If Party SJP got 56% of the votes, then Party SJD got $(56 - 12) = 44\%$ of the total votes. 44% of the total votes = 132,000, i.e.,

    $$\frac{44}{100} \times T = 132{,}000$$

    $$T = \frac{132{,}000}{44} \times 100 = 300{,}000$$

    The margin by which Party SJD lost the election = 12% of the total votes = 12% of 300,000 = 36,000.

37. 1 Bottle = $0.2x$ metres

    ? Bottles = 1000 metres

Using unitary method, we get the number of bottles = $1000/0.2x = 5000/x$ Bottles.

38. If Ashok's salary = 100, then Vinay's salary = 175. Ashok's new salary = 125, Vinay's new salary = 175 $\times 1.4 = 245$. Percentage difference between Vinay's salary and Ashok's salary now = $120 \times 100/125 = 96\%$.

39. Let the second row has 100 students. Then, the first row would contain 120 students and the third row would contain 80 students. The total number of students would be $100 + 120 + 80 = 300$. But this number is given as 300. Thus, the first row would contain 120 students.

40. Since the only copper contained in the ore is 50% of 20%, the net copper percentage would be 10%. Thus, 10 kg should be 10% of the ore = $10/0.1 = 100$ kg.

41. The data is insufficient since the number of matches to be played by Australia this year is not given. (You cannot assume that they will play 80 matches.)

42. Start of the 4$^{th}$ year, means end of the third year too. The following PCG diagram gives us the answer:

    $400000 \xrightarrow{\text{20\% increase}} 480000 \xrightarrow{\text{20\% increase}}$

    $576000 \xrightarrow{\text{20\% increase}} 691200$

43. Total people present = $200 + 100 + 400 = 700$. Indians = $0.1 \times 200 + 0.2 \times 100 + 0.3 \times 400 = 160$ = 22.85% of the population. Thus, 77.15 % or 77% of the people were not Indians.

44. Price of a table after increase 10% = $3000 + 300 = 3300$. Price of a chair after 20% increase = $1000 + 20\%$ of 1000 = 1200. Cost of 10 tables and 20 chairs = $10 \times 3300 + 20 \times 1200 = ₹57000$.

45. $(100 \times 0.7 \times 0.3)\% = 42{,}000$ kg

    21% = 42,000 kg. Thus, the total quantity of hematite mined = 2,00,000 kg.

46. The total cost for a year = $2{,}00{,}000 + 6\%$ of 2,00,000 $+ 12000 = 2{,}00{,}000 + 24000 = 2{,}24{,}000$

    To get a return of 20% he must earn: $2{,}24{,}000 \times 0.20 = 44{,}800$ in twelve months.

    Hence, the monthly rent should be 44800/12 = 3733.33.

47. The sales price of the first trousers is $\dfrac{8}{7} \times 42 = ₹48$.

    Hence, I am being offered a discount of ₹ 6 on a price of ₹ 48 → a 12.5% discount.

    The sales price of the second trousers is $7/6 \times 36 = ₹ 42$.

    Hence, I am being offered a discount of ₹ 6 on ₹ 42 → a 14.28% discount. Hence, the second trouser is a better bargain.

48. 72% must have voted for Modi and 16% for Advani. Since, Modi got 216000 votes, 72% = 216000.1%

= 3000. Hence, total number of votes 88 × 3000 = 264000.

49. The following Venn diagram would solve this problem:

20% failed in Physics, 30% failed in Chemistry and 15% failed in both.

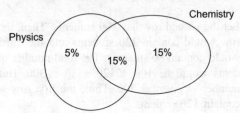

We can clearly see from the above figure that 35% of the people failed in at least one subject or 65% passed in both subjects. Since this value is given as 3250, we get that the total number of students who appeared for the exam is 5,000.

50. Out of 100, he spends 25 on house rent, 15 on children's education and 10 on clothes. Thus, he is left with 100 − 25 − 15 − 10 = 50% of his income. Since, he is left with ₹ 20000, his income must be ₹40000.

51. $100 \xrightarrow[\substack{\text{Effect of increases} \\ \text{in sales of tickets}}]{25\% \text{ increase}} 125 \xrightarrow[\substack{\text{Effect of reduction} \\ \text{in ticket price}}]{} 80$

From the PCG figure, we get that the deduction in

the ticket price = $\dfrac{125-80}{125} \times 100 = \dfrac{45}{125} \times 100 = 36\%$

Thus there is a drop of 36% of 1000 = ₹ 360

52. A C% increase in income means the new income is A (1 + C/100) while a D% increase in expenditure means that the new expenditure would be X(1 + D/100). Thus, the new savings = A(1 + C/100) − X(1 + D/100)

53. In 2001, YAHAMA = 10%, Spendor = 40% and hence Passion = 50%

54. Rebate = 20% of 10,000 = 2000;
Sales tax = 10% of (10000 − 2000) = 800;
Amount to be paid = 8000 + 800 = 8800.

55. The actual number should be 5x but it is x/5. So the

percentage error $\dfrac{5x - \dfrac{x}{5}}{5x} \times 100 = 96\%$

56. Let the salary of Bhuwan = ₹ 100
Salary of Anuj = ₹ 80

Salary of Chauhan = $\dfrac{80 \times 156.25}{100} = 125$

So the required percentage = $\dfrac{125 - 100}{125} \times 100 =$

20%

57. $100 \xrightarrow[\substack{\text{Effect of increase} \\ \text{in length}}]{20\% \text{ increase}} 120 \xrightarrow[\substack{\text{Effect of decrease} \\ \text{in breadth}}]{50\% \text{ decrease}} 60$

From the PCG we can make out that there must have been a 40% decrease.

58. $100 \xrightarrow[\substack{+23 \\ \text{Effect of increase}}]{23\% \text{ increase}} 123 \xrightarrow[\substack{39.36 \\ \text{Effect of decrease}}]{32\% \text{ decrease}} 83.64$

16.36% decrease or −16.36%.

59. Let the units place digit be x and the tens place digit be y. In that case the number is (10y + x). The reversed number is (10x + y). According to the question, we know that:

(10x + y) = 1.45(10y + x)

x = 1.5789y

This means that x is 57.89% greater than y.

60. Number of runs made by running

= 100 − (4 ×4 + 6 × 6)

= 100 − (52)

= 48

Required percentage = 48%.

### Level of Difficulty (II)

1. The expenditure is constant. Thus, the drop of 5 kg, in what he can buy, is equivalent to 20% of the original consumption. Hence, the original consumption should be 25 kg and the new consumption should be 20 kg. The increased price of rice would be 200/20 = ₹ 10.

Income of the salesman = 1200 + (1600x)

2. Solve using options. 8/11 fits the requirement.

3. The total raise of salary is 87.5% (That is what 15/8 means here).

Using the options and PCG, you get option (c) as the correct answer. You will see the following PCG if you try with 25% being the first raise.

$100 \xrightarrow[+25]{25\% \text{ increase}} 125 \xrightarrow[+62.5]{50\% \text{ increase}} 187.5$

4. Solve through trial and error using the options. 10% (option a) is the only value that fits the situation.

5. You can make the following table to see the flow of his capital:

| Year | Capital at the beginning | Capital after profit | Capital after donation |
|------|--------------------------|----------------------|------------------------|
| 1 | 100 | 150 | 75 |
| 2 | 75 | 112.5 | 56.25 |
| 3 | 56.25 | 84.375 | 42.1875 |

Since, this value is given to us as: 33750, we get 42.1875% = 33750 → 1% = 800. Hence, donation at the end of the 2nd year = 56.25 × 800 = 45000.

6. The following figure shows the percentage of failures:

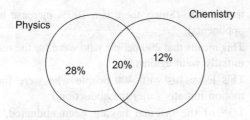

From the figure it is clear that 60% of the people have failed in at least one subject, which means that 40% of the students would have passed in both subjects. This value is given as 880 people. Hence, there would be 880/0.4 = 2200 students who would appear in the examination.

7. Solve using options. Checking for option (b), gives us:

200000 → 180000 → 171000 → 153900 → 146205 (by consecutively decreasing 200000 by 10% and 5% alternately)

8. Total characters in her report = $25 \times 60 \times 75$.
Let the new number of pages be $n$.
Then:

$$n \times 55 \times 90 = 25 \times 60 \times 75$$
$$n = 22.72$$

This means that her report would require 23 pages. A drop of 8% in terms of the pages.

9. The following percentage change thinking would give us the value of the percentage increase as 58.4%

$$100 \xrightarrow{+20\%} 120 \xrightarrow{+20\%} 144 \xrightarrow{-20\%}$$
$$115.2 \xrightarrow{+25\%} 144 \xrightarrow{+10\%} 158.4$$

10. October: November: December = 9:8:10.666 since, he got ₹40 more in December than October, we can conclude that 1.666 = 40 → 1 = 24.
Thus, total Bonus for the three months is:
$0.4 \times 27.666 \times 24 = 265.6$

11. 10% increase is offset by 9.09% decrease. Hence, option (b) is correct.

12. The expenditure increase can be calculated using PCG as:

$$100 \xrightarrow{+20\%} 120 \xrightarrow{+20\%} 132$$

A 32% increase.

13. Samanyu's scores in each area is 65 and 82 respectively out of 100 each. Since, the exam is of a total of 250 marks (100 + 100 + 50) he needs a total of 195 marks in order to get his target of 78% overall. Thus, he should score $195 - 65 - 82 = 195 - 147 = 48$ marks in Sociology, which would mean 96%.

14. The total wealth given would be 50% + 25% (which is got by 50% of the remaining 50%) + 12.5% (which is got by 50% of the remaining 25%). Thus, the total wealth given by him would be equivalent to 87.5%

of the total. Since, this is equal to 130900 kilograms of gold, the total gold would be:

$130900 \times 8/7 = 149600.$

15. Population at the start = 100.
Population after 2 years = $100 \times 1.08 \times 1.01 \times 1.08 \times 1.01 = 118.984$
Thus, the required percentage increase = 18.984%

16. After the migrations, 72.9% of the people would remain in the country. This would comprise females and males in the ratio of 1:2 (as given) and hence, the women's population left would be 1/3$^{rd}$ of 72.9% = 24.3% which is given as being equal to 364500.
Thus, the total population would be
$364500 \times 100/24.3 = 1500000$

17. Chinki would have spent 12% of Malti.
Thus, her percentage of expenditure would be 0.12 M $\times$ 100/C = 12 M/C

18. Option (d) is correct and can be verified experimentally by using values for $x, y, z$ and $p$.

19. 24% of the total goes to urban Gujarat = $72 m
1% = $ 3 million.
The required value for Rural AP
= 50% of 20% = 10%
Hence, required answer = $ 30 mn

20. In the previous question, the total FDI was $ 300 mn.
A growth of 20% this year means a total FDI of $360 mn.
The required answer is 12% of 10% of 360 mn
= 1.2% of 360 = $4.32 mn.

21. The income goes to 120. Food expenditure has to be maintained at 25. (i.e. 20.833%)
Hence, percentage point drop from 25 to 20.833 is 4.16%

22. Assume the initial surface area as 100 on each side. A total of 6 such surfaces would give a total surface area of 600. Two surface areas would be impacted by the combined effect of length and breadth, two would be affected by length and height and two would be affected by breadth and height. Thus, the respective surface areas would be (90.25 twice, 114 twice and 114 twice) Thus, new surface area = 180.5 + 456 = 636.5. A percentage increase of 6.0833%. Option (d) is correct.

23. Option (c) fits the situation as if the ratio is 10:9, the value of Baman's salary would first go up from 10 to 12 and then come down from 12 to 9 (after a 25% decrease). On the other hand, the value of Aman's salary would go up from 9 to 11.25 and then come back to 9 (Note that a 25% increase followed by a 20% decrease gets one back to the starting value.)

24. Initial quantity of Kerosene and water = 12 and 48 litres respectively. Since, this is already containing

20% Kerosene, adding more Kerosene to the mixture cannot make the mixture reach 15% Kerosene. Hence, it is not possible.

25. On 100 he saves ₹ 5. On 120 he still saves 5. Thus, his expenditure goes up from 95 to 115- a percentage increase of 20 on 95 = 21.05%.

26. Q = 100, P = 150, R = 100, S = 160. S is 160% of Q. Note that this does not change if all the values are incremented by the same percentage value.

27. Think about this problem through alligation. Since, A*lok* spends 12% of his money and *Bimal* spends 20% of his money and together they spend 15% of their money- we can conclude that the ratio of the money Alok had to the money Bimal had would be 5:3. Hence, Total money with *Alok* = 5/8 of 12000 = 5 × 12000/8 = 7500.

Money spent by *Alok* = 12% of 7500 = 900.

Money left with *Alok* = 7500 − 900 = 6600.

28. The weekly change is equal to ₹ 1,68,000. Hence, the daily collection will go up by 1,68,000/7 = 24,000.

29. The total population of the town can be taken as 9 + 8 + 3 = 20.

The number of literates would be:

80% of 9 + 70% of 8 + 90% of 3 = 7.2 + 5.6 + 2.7 = 15.5

15.5 out of 20 represents a 77.5% literacy rate.

30. Let the exam be of 100 marks. *A* obtains 24 marks while *B* obtains 12 marks (50% less than *A*). The sum of *A* and *B*'s marks are 24+ 12 = 36. To pass *C* can obtain 6 marks less than 36. This is a percentage of 16.67%. Thus, option (d) is correct.

31. The minimum price occurs at:

$$18 \times 30 + 6 \times 36 + 1 \times 40$$

Hence, the average price = 796/25 = 31.84

32. For the maximum price, discounts should be availed only at the minimum rate of discount. Thus, if one buys 4 lots of six tickets each at a discount of 10%, the condition required would be fulfilled. The total cost of 25 tickets = 36 × 24 + 40 × 1 = 904

Required average price per ticket = 904/25 = 36.16.

33. If the ticket lots are halved, the maximum discount will be available for 9 tickets (25%). A maximum number of 16 tickets can be bought in ₹532 as: 9 tickets for ₹30 each, 6 tickets for ₹32 each and 1 ticket for ₹40 would use up ₹502 of the amount available. The remaining ₹30 cannot be used to purchase another ticket since the price of the ticket is greater than that.

34. Solve using options.

Checking for option (a) will go as: According to this option 400 people have voted against the motion. Hence, originally 200 people must have favoured

the motion. (Since, there is a 100% increase in the opponents)

This means that 200 people who were for the motion initially went against it.

This leaves us with 400 people who were for the motion initially (after the abduction.)

1/3ʳᵈ of the original having been abducted, they should amount to half what is left.

This means that 600 (for) and 200 (against) were the original distribution of 800.

This option fits perfectly (given all the constraints) and hence is the correct answer.

35. The thought process would go like:

If we assume 100 students

Total            : 60 boys and 40 girls.

Fee waiver    : 9 boys and 3 girls.

This means that a total of 12 people are getting a fee waiver. (But this figure is given as 90.)

Hence, 1 corresponds to 7.5.

Now, number of students not getting a fee waiver

= 51 boys and 37 girls

Students getting a 50% concession = 25.5 boys and 18.5 girls (i.e. a total of 44.)

Hence, the required answer = 44 × 7.5 = 330.

36. At 12 noon, the watch would show the correct time (since till then the temperature range was below 40°C). The watch would gain 2% every hour between 12 and 4. An hour having 3600 seconds, it would gain 72 seconds in each of these hours. Thus, at 7 pm it would be 72 × 4 = 288 seconds ahead. The time exhibited would be 7: 04: 48.

37. 3 × (10a + 100b) = 100a + 10b

$$290b = 70a \rightarrow a = 29b/7$$

a will be an integer when b = 7 → a = 29.

38. According to the last statement

1.3x = z = 156 → x = 120.

1.2w = x = 120 → w = 100

0.8y = x = 120 → y = 150.

Therefore total number of shirts = 156 + 120 + 100 + 150 = 526

39. 1 man is married to 1 woman.

Hence, 45% of men = 25% of women.

i.e. 0.45 *M* = 0.25 *W*

Hence   $\dfrac{0.45}{0.25} = \dfrac{M}{W}$

Women to men ratio of 9:5

Using alligation, the required answer is 32.14

40. The required weight of the bucket to the water when full is 3:2. (Note: This is the interpretation of the first statement of the question – 'The weight of a bucket increases by 33.33% when filled with water to 50% of its capacity.')

If both the weights (bucket and water) are integers, then the total weight must be a multiple of 5.

Only option (c) shows this characteristic.

41. We do not have sufficient information to solve the question.

42. For every ₹10000 increase in sales, his income would increment by 600+1000 = ₹1600.

   If $x$ is the number of ₹10000 sales he achieves over the initial ₹10000, we would have:

   $$1200 + 1600 x = 7600$$

   We get $x = 4$.

   This means that the sales value must be ₹50000.

43. A sales value of ₹ 9000 cannot be achieved, since his basic salary is 1200 and his increments are only in quantum of 1600 for every 10000 rupees of sales. 9000 would not be a term of the arithmetic progression 1200, 2800, 4400, 6000, 7600, 9200…. Hence, option (b) is the correct answer.

44. This question is based on a product constancy situation. A 25% increment in the commission (How?? Note: When the commission goes up by 5 percentage points from 20 to 25, there is a 25% increment in the commission) would get offset by a 20% drop in the volume of the transaction. Option (d) is correct.

45. Out of a total of 100% votes; 80% voted. 16% were invalid and 20% went to the second placed candidate. This means that the maximum the winner can get is 44%. Options a, b and c are greater them 44% and hence cannot be correct. Hence, none of these.

46. Let the old wage = 1000 ₹ per week for 50 hours. The wages per hour would increase by 10% and the number of hours would decrease by 10%. Using PCG you can see that there would be a 1% decrease in the weekly wages.

47. If $C = 100$, $A = 80$ and $B = 72$.

   Thus, $B$ is less then $A$ by 10%

48. Assume values of $x$% = 10% and the original price as 100, then the final price = $K/100 = 99 \rightarrow K = 9900$.

   (Note: After an increase of 10% followed by a decrease of 10% a price of 100 would become 99).

   Put these values of $x$, and $K$ in the options. The option that gives a value of 100 for the original price should be the correct answer.

   Option (d) is correct.

49. The correct answer should satisfy the following condition: If '$x$' is the increased salary

$$x \times 0.8 \times 0.1 = (x - 4800) \times 0.8 \times 0.12.$$

None of the first 3 options satisfies this.

In fact, solving for $x$ we get $x = 28800$.

Option (d) is correct.

50. A sales tax of 7% on a price of 2568 would amount to a tax amount of 179.76. Since, the price is rounded off to the next higher integer, the tax would be rounded off to ₹180. This would also be the amount of discount (or reduction in price) that Seema is asking for.

51. 7up worth ₹ 16 would be containing 60 grams of vitamins would contain the maximum vitamin amongst the three.

52. Option (a) would cost: 6.4 + 8 = 14.8

   Option (b) would cost: 12 + 3.2 = 15.2

   Option (c) would cost: 4 + 3.2 + 2.8 = 10

   Option (d) would cost: 12 + 2.8 = 14.8

   Option (c) is the cheapest.

**Solutions to questions 53 and 54:** Let initially Ajay, Biru. Chetan had $A$, $B$ and $C$ rupees, respectively.

$$A + B = C \tag{1}$$
$$A + C = 2B \tag{2}$$

By solving equation (1) and (2) we get

   $A : B = 1 : 2$, $B:C = 2:3$

   $A : B : C = 1 : 2 : 3$

At the end of the game If they have $a$, $b$ and $c$ rupees respectively then:

$$a + b = 2c \tag{3}$$
$$a + c = 3b \tag{4}$$

By solving equation (3), (4) we get

   $a : b = 5 : 3$, $b : c = 3 : 4$

   $a : b : c = 5 : 3 : 4$

$b = 1500$. So $a = 2500$ and $c = 2000$. So, $a + b + c = 6000$.

Since the total amount of money at the start and at the end is equal we can say that: $A + B + C = 6000$. With a ratio of 1:2:3, the respective values of $A$, $B$ and C would be $A = 1000$, $B = 2000$, $C = 3000$.

53. Chetan and Biru had suffered a loss. So two people had suffered a loss.

54. Percentage change in money of Ajay = 150% (since the value for A has gone from 1000 to 2500).

   **Solution 55 to 57:** You will get the following table by using the information in the question

| | DELHI OFFICE | | | LUCKNOW OFFICE | | |
|---|---|---|---|---|---|---|
| | MALES | FEMALES | TOTAL | MALES | FEMALES | TOTAL |
| LAST YEAR | 1500 | 500 | 2000 | 600 | 400 | 1000 |
| THIS YEAR | 1900 | 600 | 2500 | 500 | 500 | 1000 |

Logic for the table:

Statement: In the Delhi office, this year the number of employees grew by 25% to 2500 → last years total employees in Delhi = 2000 and this years total number of employees in Delhi is 2500.

Statements: Last year the ratio of male to female employees in the Delhi office was 3:1. The number of female employees in the Delhi office grew by 20% from the last year to this. → Delhi Male employees last year = 1500; Delhi female employees last year = 500; Delhi Female employees this year = 600. Hence, Delhi male employees this year = 2500 − 600 = 1900.

Statement: The total number of employees in both the company offices grew to 3500 this year and this year the number of employees in the Lucknow office remained the same as the previous year → Lucknow total employees in each of the two years is equal to 1000 each.

Consequently, we can complete the number of employees (male and female) for Lucknow for both the years.

The answers are:

55. 600

56. % of growth = $\dfrac{1900-1500}{1500} \times 100 = 26.67\%$

57. Required difference = $(1900 + 500) - (600 + 500)$ = 1300

58. As per the question →

$$\left(1-\frac{20}{100}\right)\left(1+\frac{50}{100}\right)\left(1+\frac{15}{100}\right)n - 280 = 1.1n$$

$n \times 0.8 \times 1.5 \times 1.15 - 1.1\,n = 280$
$n = 1000$
$1.1n = 1100$

59. Per packet cost = $1 + 2 + 1 + 10 \times \dfrac{10}{100} = ₹\,5$

Per packet profit = $10 - 5 = ₹\,5$

% profit per packet = $\dfrac{5}{10} \times 100 = 50\%$

This will be the percentage profit of the company at the end of the year.

60. New cost per packet = $\left[1+\dfrac{100}{100}\right] + 2 + 1 + x\left(\dfrac{20}{100}\right)$
$= 5 + 0.2\,x$

(where $x$ is the new selling price)

$x - (5 + 0.2x) = 5$ (Note: The profit needs to be maintained at ₹ 5 per packet, in order to maintain the same profit)

$0.8x = 10$ or $x = 12.5$.

Required percentage increase in selling price = $\dfrac{2.5}{10} \times 100 = 25\%$

## Level of Difficulty (III)

1. Let the initial price of raw materials be 100. The new cost of the same raw material would be 115.

The initial cost of labour would be 25 and the new cost would be 30% of 115 = 34.5

The total cost initially would be ₹125.

The total cost for the same usage of raw material would now be: 115 + 34.5 = 149.5

This cost has to be reduced to 125. The percentage reduction will be given by 24.5/149.5 = 17 % approx.

2. Let the initial times allotted be: 50, 40 and 20 hours. Then, the time used in each activity is 20, 12 and 4 hours. Thus, 36 hours out of 110 are used in all.

Hence, the answer is 36/110 = 32.72 %

3. The following structure would follow:
Passed all: 5%
Passed 4: 20% of 90% =18%
Passed 1: 25% of 90% = 22.5%
Passed 2: 24.5%
Passed None: 5%
Passed 3: Rest $(100 - 5 - 18 - 22.5 - 24.5 - 5 = 25\%)$
But it is given that 300 people passed 3. Hence, 25% = 300.

Hence, 1200 students must have appeared in the test.

4. The third gallery making the capacity 'half as large again' means: an increase of 50%.

Further, it is given that : 4(first + third) = 12 (second)
In order to get to the correct answer, try to fit in the options into this situation.

(Note here that the question is asking you to find the capacity of the second gallery as a percentage of the first.)

If we assume option (a) as correct – 70% the following solution follows:

If second is 70, then first is 100 and first + second is 170. Then third will be 85 (50% of first + second). Then the equation:
$4 \times (100 + 85)$ should be equal to $12 \times 70$
But this is not true.

Through trial and error, you can see that the third option fits correctly.
$4 \times (100 + 80) = 12 \times 60$.

Hence, it is the correct answer.

5. Let the initial percentage of salt be 10% in 100 litres of sea water in the flask.

10% of this is poured out (i.e.,10 litres are poured out) and the water heated so as to increase the percentage of salt in the beaker 5 times (we have assumed M as 5 here.)

This means that there will be 30% salt in the beaker. Since, the salt concentration is increased by only evaporating water, the amount of salt remains the same.

Initially the salt was 10% of 10 litres (= worth 1 litre). Hence, the water must have been worth 9 litres.

Now, since this amount of salt becomes worth 50% of the total solution, the amount of water left after evaporation would have been 1 litre and the total would be 2 litres.

When the 2 litres are mixed back again: The new concentration of salt in sea water would go up. In this specific case by alligation we would get the following alligation situation:

Mix 90 litres of 10% salted sea water with 2 litres of 50% salted sea water.

The result using alligation will be: [10 + 40/46] % concentration of salted sea water. The value of the increase percentage will be 400/46. (this will be the value of $x$)

Now, try to use the given options in order to match the fact that originally the flask contained 100 litres of sea water.

Use $M = 5$, $x = 400/46$,

Only option (b) matches the situation.

$$\frac{(9 \times 5 + 1)\,400/46}{(5 - 1)} = 100$$

6. The only values that fit this situation are $C$ 25%, $B$ 30%, and $A$ 45%. These are the percentage of votes polled. (*Note*: these values can be got either through trial and error or through solving $c + c + 5 + 1.5$ $(c + 5) = 100\%$

   Then, 20% is 18000 (the difference between $A$ & $C$.) Hence, 90000 people must have voted and 100000 people must have been on the voter's list.

7. The net time lost over two weeks would be 0.25% of a week's time (since in the first week the clock loses 1/2% and in the second week the clock gains 1/4% on the true time.)

   A week contains 168 hours. Hence, the clock loses 0.42 hours.i.e. 25.2 minutes or 25 minutes 12 seconds. Hence, the correct time would be 12:25:12.

8. Traveling for 2400 kms at 18 kmph, Vawal will use 133.33 litres of petrol every month. The increase in expenditure for Vawal will be $133.33 \times 0.7 \times 28 = ₹$ 262 (approx).

9. The required answer will be given by: $(7/107) \times 2400$ = 157 km

10. The original expenditure is $28 * 133.333 = ₹ 3733.333$

    The new expenditure will be given by $28 \times 1.07 \times n/18$ where $n$ = the no. of kilometres to travel.

    Since the new expenditure should increase by ₹ 200, its value has to be equal to ₹ 3933.333

    This gives us $n = 2363.15$

    Hence, the answer is e.

11. The shopkeeper would get the maximum revenue when everybody opts for a 4% resale of the right. In such a case, the revenue for the shopkeeper from each customer would be: 96% of 4000 = 4000 – 160 = 3840. hence, total revenue is 38400.

12. Similarly, the highest discount would be if everybody opts for the 15% discount. In such a case, the total discount would be: $600 \times 10 = 6000$.

**13-16.** Detailed solutions for 13–16 are given in the hints of LOD III.

**17–23.** The average income estimated would be: Annual Income/14 (Underestimated savings).

The average monthly expenditure would be: Annual expenditure/9 (Overestimated expenditure)

**17–19** are explained in the hints of LOD III.

20. $x/14 = 87$. Hence, annual income = 1218.

    New income = 1218/12 = 101.5

    Change in estimated income due to the change in process of average calculation = 14.5/87 → 16.66% increase.

21. Estimated monthly income would go up, while the estimated monthly expenditure would go down. Hence, Savings (estimated) would increase.

22. Cannot be determined since the percentage change would depend on the actual values which are not available for this question.

23. The estimated monthly expenditure would change from: $x/9$ to $x/11$. Hence, percentage drop in the ratio will be 2/11 → 18.18%

    **24 to 29** are explained in the hints to LOD III.

**31-34.** The following table will give a clearer picture of the situation:

| Newspaper | Circulation (in 000) | Revenues | Commission | Net Revenues |
|---|---|---|---|---|
| Deccan Emerald | 373 | 746 | 20% | 596.8 |
| Times of Hindustan | 247 | 494 | 25% | 395.2 |
| India's Times | 297 | 594 | 30% | 415.8 |

31. Reduction of $\dfrac{181 * 100}{596.8} = 30.32\%$

32. The percentage difference between the revenues is: $(746 – 594) \times 100/746 = 20.37$

    Hence, the required value is 30.32/20.37 = 1.488

33. The day's cost of printing 373000 copies of Deccan Emerald is: $373000 \times 8 = 2984000$

    Out of this, the paper recovers 596800. The remaining cost to be recovered would be: 2387200.

    At ₹ 3000 per cc, 795.733 cc will have to be booked on any given day in order to obtain the cost. This represents 99.46% of the total value.

35. Times of Hindustan:
    Total cost = 2,47,000 × 7.5 = 18,52,500
    Net revenues from newspaper sales is 3,95,200
    Cost to be covered through advertising = 18,52,500 – 3,95,200 = 14,57,300.
    At an ad rate of ₹1800 per cc, they would have to sell 809.61 cc i.e.73.6%
    Similar calculations for India's Times will give 79.2%.
    Hence, the percentage point difference = 5.6

36. If Ac 3$^{rd}$ costs 100, Ac 2$^{nd}$ would cost 120 and AC 1$^{st}$ would cost 190. 3 Tier ticket would cost : 47.5 and general ticket would cost 40.
    $$AC\ 2^{nd} \rightarrow 780 = 120$$
    Then the difference between 3 Tier and general ticket would be: 7.5 × 780 = 48.75

37. Total cost → 100 + 120 + 190 + 47.5 + 40 = 497.5
    This gives (497.5/120) × 780 = 3233.75.

43. Hursh Sarma's savings:

| Month | Salary | Savings |
|-------|--------|---------|
| 1 | 10800 | 1080 |
| 2 | 10800 | 900 |
| 3 | 10800 | 900 |
| 4 | 10800 | 0 |
| 5 | 12000 | 1500 |
| 6 | 12000 | 1800 |
| 7 | 12000 | 2400 |
| 8 | 12000 | 1200 |
| 9 | 12000 | 1000 |
| 10 | 12000 | 1500 |
| 11 | 12000 | 1800 |
| 12 | 12000 | 2400 |

Required Ratio = 4800/900 = 5.333

48. Assume he has 1200 francs, 1200 DM and 1200 Liras. If he converts everything to francs, the result will be: 1200 DM will convert to 240 Euros which will convert to 960 francs. But 51 Moolas = 1 Franc. Thus the value of 1200 DM in terms of Moolas goes up from 1200 × 36 = 43200 to 960 × 51 = 48960. This increase in value has occurred only because of the change of currency. Hence, he should convert all his DM into Francs. However, before concluding on this you also will need to consider the effect of Liras.
    It is evident that 1200 DM will yield 240 Euros, which would yield 720 Liras (since 1 euro is 3 lira), which in turn would yield 720 × 70 = 5040 Moolas. Thus, it is evident that by converting DM into Liras the increase in value is higher than that achieved by converting DM into Francs.
    Similarly, converting Francs to Liras also increases the value of the Francs.
    1200 × 51 becomes equivalent to 900 × 70.
    *Note:* The thought process goes like this: 1200 Francs = 300 Euros (since 1 euro = 4 francs). Further 300 Euros equals 900 liras which equal 900 × 70 Moolas.

49. Cannot be determined since the conversion from dollar to Euro is not given, neither is the inter currency exchange rate between Lira, Francs and DMs.

50. Obviously, both a and c are required in order to answer this question.

# Profit & Loss

**6**

## INTRODUCTION

Traditionally, Profit & Loss has always been an important chapter for CAT. Besides, all other Management entrance exams like SNAP, CMAT, MAT, ATMA as well as Bank P.O. exams extensively use questions from this chapter. From the point of view of CAT, the relevance of this chapter has been gradually reducing. However, CAT being a highly unpredictable exam, my advice to students and readers would be to go through this chapter and solve it at least up to LOD II, so that they are ready for any changes in patterns.

Further, the Level of Difficulties at which questions are set in the various exams can be set as under:

LOD I: CAT, XLRI, IRMA, IIFT, CMAT, Bank PO aspirants, MAT, NIFT, NMAT, and SNAP and all other management exams.

LOD II: CAT, XLRI, IRMA (partially), etc.

LOD III: CAT, XLRI (students aiming for 60% plus in Maths in CAT).

## THEORY

Profit & Loss are part and parcel of every commercial transaction. In fact, the entire economy and the concept of capitalism is based on the so called "Profit Motive".

## Profit & Loss in Case of Individual Transactions

*We will first investigate the concept of Profit & Loss in the case of individual transactions. Certain concepts are important in such transactions. They are:*

The price at which a person buys a product is the cost price of the product for that person. In other words, the amount paid or expended in either purchasing or producing an object is known as its Cost Price (also written as CP).

The price at which a person sells a product is the sales price of the product for that person. In other words, the amount got when an object is sold is called as the *Selling Price* (*SP*) of the object from the seller's point of view.

When a person is able to sell a product at a price higher than its cost price, we say that he has earned a profit. That is,

If SP > CP, the difference, SP – CP is known as the profit or gain.

Similarly, if a person sells an item for a price lower than its cost price, we say that a loss has been incurred.

The basic concept of profit and loss is as simple as this.

If, however, SP < CP, then the difference, CP – SP is called the loss.

It must be noted here that the Selling Price of the seller is the Cost Price of the buyer.

Thus we can say that in the case of profit the following formulae hold true:

1. Profit = SP – CP
2. SP = Profit + CP
3. CP = SP – Profit
4. Percentage Profit = $\dfrac{\text{Profit} \times 100}{\text{CP}}$

**Percentage Profit is always calculated on CP unless otherwise stated.**

Notice that SP = CP + Gain
= CP + (Gain on ₹1) × CP
= CP + (Gain%/100) × CP

*Example:* A man purchases an item for ₹ 120. If he sells it at a 20 per cent profit find his selling price.

*Solution:* The selling price is given by $120 + 120 \times 0.2 = 144$

$$= CP + (Gain\%/100) \times CP = CP\left[1 + \frac{\%Gain}{100}\right]$$

For the above problem, the selling price is given by this method as: Selling Price = $1.2 \times 120 = 144$.

Hence, we also have the following:

1. $SP = \left[1 + \dfrac{\%Gain}{100}\right] \times C.P = \dfrac{(100 + Gain\%) \times CP}{100}$

2. $CP = \dfrac{100 \times SP}{(100 \times Gain\%)}$

**In case of loss**
1. Loss = CP – SP
2. SP = CP – Loss
3. CP = SP + Loss
4. Loss% = Loss on ₹ 100 = $\dfrac{Loss \times 100}{CP}$

**Precentage Loss is always calculated on CP unless otherwise stated.**

The above situation (although it is the basic building block of Profit and Loss) is not the normal situation where we face Profit and Loss problems. In fact, there is a wide application of profit and loss in day-to-day business and economic transactions. It is in these situations that we normally have to work out profit and loss problems.

Having investigated the basic concept of profit and loss for an individual transaction of selling and buying one unit of a product, let us now look at the concept of profit and loss applied to day-to-day business and commercial transactions.

## Profit & Loss as Applied to Business and Commercial Transactions

*Profit & Loss when Multiple Units of a Product are Being Bought and Sold* The basic concept of profit and loss remains unchanged for this situation. However, a common mistake in this type of problem can be avoided if the following basic principle is adopted:

**Profit or Loss in terms of money can only be calculated when the number of items bought and sold are equal.**

That is, Profit or Loss in money terms cannot be calculated unless we equate the number of products bought and sold.

This is normally achieved by equating the number of items bought and sold at 1 or 100 or some other convenient figure as per the problem asked.

Overlooking of this basic fact is one of the most common mistakes that students are prone to making in the solving of profit and loss problems.

*Types of Costs* In any business dealing, there is a situation of selling and buying of products and services. From the sellers point of view, his principle interest, apart from maximising the sales price of a product/service, is to minimise the costs associated with the selling of that product/service. The costs that a businessman/trader faces in the process of day-to-day business transaction can be subdivided into three basic categories:

1. **Direct Costs or Variable Costs** This is the cost associated with direct selling of product/service. In other words, this is the cost that varies with every unit of the product sold. Hence, if the variable cost in selling a pen for ₹ 20 is ₹ 5, then the variable cost for selling 10 units of the same pen is $10 \times 5 = ₹ 50$.

   As is clear from the above example, that part of the cost that varies directly for every additional unit of the product sold is called as direct or variable cost. *Typical examples of direct costs are:* Raw material used in producing one unit of the product, wages to labour in producing one unit of the product when the wages are given on a piece rate basis, and so on. In the case of traders, the cost price per unit bought is also a direct cost (i.e. every such expense that can be tied down to every additional unit of the product sold is a direct cost).

2. **Indirect Costs (Overhead Costs) or Fixed Costs** There are some types of costs that have to be incurred irrespective of the number of items sold and are called as fixed or indirect costs. For example, irrespective of the number of units of a product sold, the rent of the corporate office is fixed. Now, whether the company sells 10 units or 100 units, this rent is fixed and is hence a fixed cost.

   Other examples of indirect or fixed costs: Salary to executives and managers, rent for office, office telephone charges, office electricity charges.

   *Apportionment of indirect (or fixed) costs:* Fixed Costs are apportioned equally among each unit of the product sold. Thus, if *n* units of a product is sold, then the fixed cost to be apportioned to each unit sold is given by

   $$\frac{Fixed\ costs}{n}$$

3. **Semi-Variable Costs** Some costs are such that they behave as fixed costs under normal circumstances but have to be increased when a certain level of sales figure is reached. For instance, if the sales increase to such an extent that the company needs to take up additional office space to accommodate the increase in work

due to the increase in sales then the rent for the office space becomes a part of the semi-variable cost.

**The Concept of Margin or Contribution Per Unit** The difference between the value of the selling price and the variable cost for a product is known as the margin or the contribution of the product. This margin goes towards the recovery of the fixed costs incurred in selling the product/service.

**The Concept of the Break-even Point** The break-even point is defined as the volume of sale at which there is no profit or no loss. In other words, the sales value in terms of the number of units sold at which the company breaks even is called the break-even point. This point is also called the break-even sales.

Since for every unit of the product the contribution goes towards recovering the fixed costs, as soon as a company sells more than the break-even sales, the company starts earning a profit. Conversely, when the sales value in terms of the number of units is below the break-even sales, the company makes losses.

The entire scenario is best described through the following example.

Let us suppose that a *paan* shop has to pay a rent of ₹ 1000 per month and salaries of ₹ 4000 to the assistants.

Also suppose that this *paan* shop sells only one variety of *paan* for ₹ 5 each. Further, the direct cost (variable cost) in making one *paan* is ₹ 2.50 per *paan*, then the margin is ₹ (5 – 2.50) = ₹ 2.50 per *paan*.

Now, break-even sales will be given by:

Break-even-sales = Fixed costs/Margin per unit = 5000/2.5 = 2000 *paans*.

Hence, the *paan* shop breaks-even on a monthly basis by selling 2000 *paans*.

Selling every additional *paan* after the 2000th *paan* goes towards increasing the profit of the shop. Also, in the case of the shop incurring a loss, the number of *paans* that are left to be sold to break-even will determine the quantum of the loss.

Note the following formulae:

Profit = (Actual sales – Break-even sales) × Contribution per unit

Also in the case of a loss:

Loss = (Break-even sales – Actual sales) × Contribution per unit

Also, if the break-even sales equals the actual sales, then we reach the point of no profit no loss, which is also the technical definition of the break-even point.

Note that the break-even point can be calculated on the basis of any time period (but is normally done annually or monthly).

## Profit Calculation on the Basis of Equating the Amount Spent and the Amount Earned

We have already seen that profit can only be calculated in the case of the number of items being bought and sold being equal. In such a case, we take the difference of the money got and the money given to get the calculation of the profit or the loss in the transaction.

There is another possibility, however, of calculating the profit. This is done by equating the money got and the money spent. In such a case, the profit can be represented by the amount of goods left. This is so because in terms of money the person going through the transaction has got back all the money that he has spent, but has ended up with some amount of goods left over after the transaction. These left over items can then be viewed as the profit or gain for the individual in consideration.

Hence, profit when money is equated is given by Goods left. Also, cost in this case is represented by Goods sold and hence percentage profit = $\dfrac{\text{Goods left}}{\text{Goods sold}} \times 100$.

**Example:** A fruit vendor recovers the cost of 25 mangoes by selling 20 mangoes. Find his percentage profit.

*Solution:* Since the money spent is equal to the money earned the percentage profit is given by:

$$\% \text{ Profit} = \frac{\text{Goods left}}{\text{Goods sold}} \times 100 = 5 \times 100/20 = 25\%$$

## Concept of Mark Up

Traders/businessmen, while selling goods, add a certain percentage on the cost price. This addition is called percentage mark up (if it is in money terms), and the price thus obtained is called as the marked price (this is also the price printed on the product in the shop).
The operative relationship is

|  | CP + Mark up = Marked price |
|---|---|
| or | CP + % Mark up on CP = Marked Price |

The product is normally sold at the marked price in which case the marked price = the selling price

If the trader/shopkeeper gives a discount, he does so on the marked price and after the discount the product is sold at its discounted price.

Hence, the following relationship operates:

CP + % Mark up (Calculated on CP) = Marked Price
Marked price – % Discount = Selling price

### Use of PCG in Profit and Loss

1. The relationship between CP and SP is typically defined through a percentage relationship. As we have seen earlier, this percentage value is called as

the percentage mark up. (And is also equal to the percentage profit if there is no discount).

Consider the following situation —

Suppose the SP is 25% greater than the CP. This relationship can be seen in the following diagram.

$$CP \xrightarrow{\ 25\%\uparrow\ } SP$$

In such a case the reverse relationship will be got by the A→B→A application of PCG and will be seen as follows:

If the profit is 25% :

*Space for Notes*

*Example*:  $CP \xrightarrow{\ 25\%\uparrow\ } SP \xrightarrow{\ 20\%\downarrow\ } CP$

Suppose you know that by selling an item at 25%, profit the Sales price of a bottle of wine is ₹ 1600. With this information, you can easily calculate the cost price by reducing the sales price by 20%. Thus, the CP is

$$1600 \xrightarrow[\ -320\ ]{\ 20\%\downarrow\ } 1280$$

## WORKED-OUT PROBLEMS

Before we go into problems based on profit and loss, the reader should realize that there are essentially four phases of a profit and loss problem. These are connected together to get higher degrees of difficulty.

These are clues for (a) Cost calculations (b) Marked price calculations (c) Selling price calculations (d) Over-heads/fixed costs calculations.

It is left to the reader to understand the interrelationships between *a*, *b*, *c* and *d* above. (These have already been stated in the earlier part of this chapter.)

**Problem 6.1** A shopkeeper sold goods for ₹ 2000 at a profit of 50%. Find the cost price for the shopkeeper.

**Solution** The shopkeeper sells his items at a profit of 50%. This means that the selling price is 150% of cost price (Since CP + % Profit = SP)

For short you should view this as SP = 1.5 CP.

The problem with this calculation is that we know what 150% of the cost price is but we do not know what the cost price itself is. Hence, we have difficulty in directly working out this problem. The calculation will become easier if we know the percentage calculation to be done on the basis of the selling price of the goods.

Hence look at the equation from the angle → CP = SP/1.5.

Considering the SP as SP/1, we have to find CP as SP/1.5. This means that the denominator is increasing by 50%. But from the table of denominator change to ratio change of the chapter of percentages, we can see that when the denominator increases by 50% the ratio decreases by 33.33%.

Interpret this as the CP can be got from the SP by reducing the SP by 33.33%. Hence, the answer is 2000 − (1/3) × 2000 = ₹ 1333.33

Also, this question can also be solved through options by going from CP (assumed from the value of the option) to the SP by increasing the assumed CP by 50% to check whether the SP comes out to 2000. If a 50% increase in the assumed CP does not make the SP equal 2000 it means that the assumed CP is incorrect. Hence, you should move to the next option. Use logic to understand whether you go for the higher options or the lower options based on your rejection of the assumed option.

**Note:** The above question will never appear as a full question in the examination but might appear as a part of a more complex question. If you are able to interpret this statement through the denominator change to ratio change table, the time requirement will reduce significantly and you will gain a significant time advantage over this statement.

**Problem 6.2** A man buys a shirt and a trousers for ₹ 371. If the trouser costs 12% more than the shirt, find the cost of the shirt.

**Solution** Here, we can write the equation:
$s + 1.12s = 371 \rightarrow s = 371/2.12$ (however, this calculation is not very easily done)

An alternate approach will be to go through options. Suppose the options are

(a) ₹ 125      (b) ₹ 150
(c) ₹ 175      (d) ₹ 200

Checking for, say, ₹ 150, the thought process should go like:

Let *s* = cost of a shirt

If *s* = 150, 1.12*s* will be got by increasing s by 12% i.e. 12% of 150 = 18. Hence the value of 1.12*s* = 150 + 18 =168 and *s* + 1.12*s* = 318 is not equal to 371. Hence check the next higher option.

If *s* = 175, 1.12*s* = *s* + 12% of *s* = 175 + 21 = 196. i.e. 2.12 *s* = 371.

Hence, Option (c) is correct.

**Problem 6.3** A shopkeeper sells two items at the same price. If he sells one of them at a profit of 10% and the other at a loss of 10%, find the percentage profit/loss.

*Generic question:* A shopkeeper sells two items at the same price. If he sells one of them at a profit of *x*% and the other at a loss of *x*%, find the percentage profit/loss.

**Solution** The result will always be a loss of $[x/10]^2$%. Hence, the answer here is $[10/10]^2$% = 1% loss.

**Problem 6.4** For Problem 6.3, find the value of the loss incurred by the shopkeeper if the price of selling each item is ₹ 160.

**Solution** When there is a loss of 10% → 160 = 90% of $CP_1$. ∴ $CP_1$ = 177.77

When there is a profit of 10% → 160 = 110% of $CP_2$ ∴ $CP_2$ = 145.45

Hence total cost price = 177.77 + 145.45 = 323.23 while the net realisation is ₹ 320.

Hence loss is ₹ 3.23.

*Short cut for calculation:* Since by selling the two items for ₹ 320 the shopkeeper gets a loss of 1% (from the previous problem), we can say that ₹ 320 is 99% of the value of the cost price of the two items. Hence, the total cost is given by 320/0.99 (solution of this calculation can be approximately done on the percentage change graphic).

**Problem 6.5** If by selling 2 items for ₹ 180 each the shopkeeper gains 20% on one and loses 20% on the other, find the value of the loss.

**Solution** The percentage loss in this case will always be $(20/10)^2 = 4\%$ loss.

We can see this directly as $360 \rightarrow 96\%$ of the CP $\rightarrow$ CP = 360/0.96. Hence, by percentage change graphic 360 has to be increased by 4.166 per cent = $360 + 4.166\%$ of $360 = 360 + 14.4 + 0.6 = ₹ 375$.

Hence, the loss is ₹ 15.

**Problem 6.6** By selling 15 mangoes, a fruit vendor recovers the cost price of 20 mangoes. Find the profit percentage.

**Solution** Here since the expenditure and the revenue are equated, we can use percentage profit = (goods left × 100)/goods sold = 5 × 100/15 = 33.33%.

**Problem 6.7** A dishonest shopkeeper uses a 900 gram weight instead of 1 kilogram weight. Find his profit percent if he sells per kilogram at the same price as he buys a kilogram.

**Solution** Here again the money spent and the money got are equal. Hence, the percentage profit is got by goods left × 100/goods sold.

This gives us 11.11%.

**Problem 6.8** A manufacturer makes a profit of 15% by selling a colour TV for ₹ 6900. If the cost of manufacturing increases by 30% and the price paid by the retailer is increased by 20%, find the profit percent made by the manufacturer.

**Solution** For this problem, the first line gives us that the cost price of the TV for the manufacturer is ₹ 6000.

(By question stem analysis you should be able to solve this part of the problem in the first reading and reach at the figure of 6000 as cost, before you read further. This can be achieved advantageously if your percentage rule calculations are strong. Hence, work on it. The better you can get at it the more it will benefit you. In fact, one of the principal reasons I get through the CAT every year is the strength in percentage calculation. Besides, percentage calculation will also go a long way in improving your scores in data Interpretation.)

Further, if you have got to the 6000 figure by the end of the first line, reading further you can increase this advantage by calculating while reading as follows:

Manufacturing cost increase by 30% $\rightarrow$ New manufacturing cost = 7800 and new selling price is 6900 + 20% of 6900 = 6900 + 1380 = 8280.

Hence, profit = 8280 − 7800 = 480 and profit percent = 480 × 100/7800 = 6.15%.

**Problem 6.9** Find a single discount to equal three consecutive discounts of 10%, 12% and 5%.

**Solution** Using percentage change graphic starting from 100: we get 100 $\rightarrow$ 88 $\rightarrow$ 83.6 $\rightarrow$ 75.24 (Note we can change percentages in any order).

Hence, the single discount is 24.76%.

**Problem 6.10** A reduction in the price of petrol by 10% enables a motorist to buy 5 gallons more for $180. Find the original price of petrol.

**Solution** 10% reduction in price $\rightarrow$ 11.11% increase in consumption.

But 11.11% increase in consumption is equal to 5 gallons. Hence, original consumption is equal to 45 gallons for $180. Hence, original price = 4$ per gallon.

**Problem 6.11** Ashok bought an article and spent ₹ 110 on its repairs. He then sold it to Bhushan at a profit of 20%. Bhushan sold it to Charan at a loss of 10%. Charan finally sold it for ₹ 1188 at a profit of 10%. How much did Ashok pay for the article.

(a) ₹ 890        (b) ₹ 1000
(c) ₹ 780        (d) ₹ 840

**Solution** Solve through options using percentage rule and keep checking options as you read. Try to finish the first option-check before you finish reading the question for the first time. Also, as a thumb rule always start with the middle most convenient option. This way you are likely to be required lesser number of options, on an average.

Also note that LOD II and LOD III questions will always essentially use the same sentences as used in LOD I questions. The only requirement that you need to have to handle LOD II and III questions is the ability to string together a set of statements and interconnect them.

**Problem 6.12** A dishonest businessman professes to sell his articles at cost price but he uses false weights with which he cheats by 10% while buying and by 10% while selling. Find his percentage profit.

**Solution** Assume that the businessman buys and sells 1 kg of items. While buying he cheats by 10%, which means that when he buys 1 kg he actually takes 1100 grams. Similarly, he cheats by 10% while selling, that is, he gives only 900 grams when he sells a kilogram. Also, it must be understood that since he purportedly buys and sells the same amount of goods and he is trading at the same price while buying and selling, money is already equated in this case. Hence, we can directly use: % Profit = (Goods left × 100/Goods sold) = 200 × 100/900 = 22.22% (Note that you should not need to do this calculation since this value comes from the fraction to percentage conversion table).

If you are looking at 70% plus net score in quantitative ability you should be able to come to the solution in about 25 seconds inclusive of problem reading time. And the calculation should go like this:

Money is equated $\rightarrow$ % profit = 2/9 = 22.22%

The longer process of calculation in this case would be involving the use of equating the amount of goods bought and sold and the money value of the profit. However, if you try to do this you will easily see that it requires a much higher degree of calculations and the process will tend to get messy.

The options for doing this problem by equating goods would point to comparing the price per gram bought or sold. Alternatively, we could use the price per kilogram bought and sold (which would be preferable to equating on a per gram basis for this problem).

Here the thought process would be:

Assume price per kilogram = ₹ 1000. Therefore, he buys 1100 grams while purchasing and sells 900 grams while selling.

To equate the two, use the following process:

|  | Money paid |  | Amount of goods |
| --- | --- | --- | --- |
| **Buying** | ₹ 1000 | 1100 | grams (Reduce this by 10%) |
| After reduction | ₹ 900 | 990 | grams |
| **Selling** | ₹ 1000 | 900 | grams (Increase this by 10%) |
| After increase | ₹ 1100 | 990 | |

**Problem 6.13** RFO Tripathi bought some oranges in Nagpur for ₹ 32. He has to sell it off in Yeotmal. He is able to sell off all the oranges in Yeotmal and on reflection finds that he has made a profit equal to the cost price of 40 oranges. How many oranges did RFO Tripathi buy?

**Solution** Suppose we take the number of oranges bought as $x$. Then, the cost price per orange would be ₹ $32/x$, and his profit would by $40 \times 32/x = 1280/x$.

To solve for $x$, we need to equate this value with some value on the other side of the equation. But, we have no information provided here to find out the value of the variable $x$. Hence, we cannot solve this equation.

**Problem 6.14** By selling 5 articles for ₹ 15, a man makes a profit of 20%. Find his gain or loss percentage if he sells 8 articles for ₹ 18.4?

Questions of this type normally appear as part of a more complex problem in an exam like the CAT.

Remember, such a question should be solved by you as soon as you finish reading the question by solving-while-reading process, as follows.

By selling 5 articles for ₹ 15, a man makes a profit of 20% → SP = 3. Hence, CP = 2.5, if he sells 8 articles for ₹ 18.4 → SP = 2.3. Hence percentage loss = 8%. For solving this question through this method with speed you need to develop the skill and ability to calculate percentage changes through the percentage change graphic. For this purpose, you should not be required to use a pencil and a paper.

**Problem 6.15** Oranges are bought at 12 for a rupee and are sold at 10 for a rupee. Find the percentage profit or loss.

**Solution** Since money spent and got are equated, use the formula for profit calculation in terms of goods left/goods sold.

This will give you percentage profit = 2/10 = 20%.

Alternatively, you can also equate the goods and calculate the percentage profit on the basis of money as

CP of 1 orange = 8.33 paise

SP of 1 orange = 10 paise

8.33 paise → 10 paise (corresponds to a percentage increase of 20% on CP)

**Problem 6.16** In order to maximise its profits, AMS Corporate defines a function. Its unit sales price is ₹ 700 and the function representing the cost of production = 300 + $2p^2$, where $p$ is the total units produced or sold. Find the most profitable production level. Assume that everything produced is necessarily sold.

**Solution** The function for profit is a combination of revenue and costs. It is given by Profit = Revenue – Costs = $700 p - (300 + 2p^2) = -2p^2 + 700p - 300$.

In order to find the maxima or minima of any quadratic function, we differentiate it and equate the differentiated equation to zero.

Thus, the differentiated profit function is $-4p + 700 = 0 \rightarrow p = 175$. This value of production will yield the maximum profits in this case.

**Note:** Whether a quadratic function is maximum or minimum is decided by redifferentiating the differentiated equation. We then look at the sign of the constant term to determine whether the value got by equating the differentiated equation to zero corresponds to the maximum or the minimum. In the case of the constant term, left being negative, we say that the function is a maxima function and hence the solution point got would be a maximum point. In the event that the final constant term is positive, it is a minimum function.

**Short cut** Just look at the coefficient of $x^2$ in the function. If it is positive, equating the first differentiation to zero would yield the minimum point, and if the coefficient of $x^2$ is negative, the function is a maximum function.

**Problem 6.17** For Problem 6.16, what is the value of the maximum profits for AMS Corporate?

**Solution** For this, continuing from the previous question's solution, we just put the value of $p = 175$ in the equation for profit. Thus, substitute $p = 175$ in the equation. Profit = $-2p^2 + 700p - 300$ and get the answer.

**Problem 6.18** A shopkeeper allows a rebate of 25% to the buyer. He sells only smuggled goods and as a bribe, he pays 10% of the cost of the article. If his cost price is ₹ 2500, then find what should be the marked price if he desires to make a profit of 9.09%.

**Solution** Use solving-while-reading as follows: Cost price (= 2500) + Bribe (= 10% of cost of article = 250) = Total cost to the shopkeeper (2500 + 250 = 2750).

He wants a profit of 9.09 percent on this value → Using fraction to percentage change table we get 2750 + 9.09% of 2750 = 2750 + 250 = ₹ 3000.

But this ₹ 3000 is got after a rebate of 25%. Since we do not have the value of the marked price on which 25% rebate is to be calculated, it would be a good idea to work reverse through the percentage change graphic:

Going from the marked price to ₹ 3000 requires a 25% rebate. Hence the reverse process will be got by increasing ₹ 3000 by 33.33% and getting ₹ 4000.

[Notice the use of percentage change graphic in general and the product constancy table in particular in the solving of this question]

**Problem 6.19**  A man sells three articles, one at a loss of 10%, another at a profit of 20% and the third one at a loss of 25%. If the selling price of all the three is the same, find by how much percent is their average CP lower than or higher than their SP.

**Solution**

**Note:**  It is always convenient to solve questions involving percentages by using the number 100. The reason for this is that it reduces the amount of effort required in calculating the solution. Hence, it goes without saying that the variable to be fixed at 100 should be the one with the highest

*Space for Rough Work*

number of calculations associated with it. Another thumb rule for this is that the variable to be fixed at 100 should be the one with which the most difficult calculation set is associated.

We have to calculate: (average CP – average SP)/average SP.

Here, the selling price is equal in all three cases. Since the maximum number of calculations are associated with the SP, we assume it to be 100. This gives us an average SP of 100 for the three articles. Then, the first article will be sold at 111.11, the second at 83.33 and the third at 133.33. (The student is advised to be fluent at these calculations) Further, the CP of the three articles is 111.11 + 83.33 + 133.33 = 327.77.

The average CP of the three articles is 327.77/3 = 109.2566.

Hence, (average CP – average SP)/average SP = 9.2566%. higher

Any other process adopted for this problem is likely to require much more effort and time.

**Note:**  This process will be feasible if you have worked well with the percentage calculation techniques of the previous chapter.

## LEVEL OF DIFFICULTY (I)

1. By selling a watch for ₹ 560, a shopkeeper incurs a loss of 20%. Find the cost price of the watch for the shopkeeper.
   (a) ₹ 600          (b) ₹ 700
   (c) ₹ 610          (d) ₹ 640

2. By selling a cap for ₹ 29.75, a man gains 6.25%. What will be the CP of the cap?
   (a) ₹ 26           (b) ₹ 27.5
   (c) ₹ 28           (d) ₹ 27.80

3. A cellular phone when sold for ₹ 3808 fetches a profit of 12%. Find the cost price of the cellular phone.
   (a) ₹ 3190         (b) ₹ 3400
   (c) ₹3260          (d) ₹ 3560

4. A machine costs ₹ 1025. If it is sold at a loss of 25%, what will be its cost price as a percentage of its selling price?
   (a) 125%           (b) 116.67%
   (c) 120%           (d) 133.33%

5. A shopkeeper sold goods for ₹1800 and made a profit of 20% in the process. Find his profit per cent if he had sold his goods for ₹ 1687.5.
   (a) 11.5%          (b) 10.5%
   (c) 12.5%          (d) 6.25%

6. A tablet is sold for ₹6612.5 at a profit of 15%. What would have been the actual profit or loss on it, if it had been sold for ₹ 5380?
   (a) ₹ 370          (b) ₹ 410
   (c) ₹ 480          (d) ₹ 340

7. A marble table when sold for ₹ 6400 gives a loss of 11.11% to the merchant who sells it. Calculate his loss or gain per cent, if he sells it for ₹ 7812.
   (a) Loss of 8.625%   (b) Profit of 8.5%
   (c) Loss of 8%       (d) Profit of 7.5%

8. By selling bouquets for ₹ 69, a florist gains 15%. At what price should he sell the bouquets to gain 20% on the cost price?
   (a) ₹ 72           (b) ₹ 75
   (c) ₹ 66           (d) ₹ 78

9. A shopkeeper bought 480 chocolates at ₹ 6 per dozen. If he sold all of them at ₹ 0.75 each, what was his profit per cent?
   (a) 50%            (b) 33(1/3)%
   (c) 75%            (d) 20%

10. A feeding bottle is sold for ₹ 150. Sales tax accounts for one-fifth of this and profit one-third of the remainder. Find the cost price of the feeding bottle.
    (a) ₹ 72          (b) ₹ 80
    (c) ₹ 90          (d) ₹ 76

11. An iron merchant makes a profit of 30% by selling iron at ₹ 26 per quintal. If he sells the iron at ₹ 22.50 per quintal, what is his profit per cent on the whole investment?
    (a) 12.5%         (b) 6.66%
    (c) 7.5%          (d) 8%

12. The cost price of a shirt and a pair of trousers is ₹ 473. If the shirt costs 15% more than the trousers, find the cost price of the trouser.
    (a) ₹ 243         (b) ₹ 253
    (c) ₹ 210         (d) ₹ 220

13. A pet shop owner sells two puppies at the same price. On one he makes a profit of 25% and on the other he suffers a loss of 25%. Find his loss or gain per cent on the whole transaction.
    (a) Gain of 6.25%   (b) No profit no loss
    (c) Loss of 12.5%   (d) Loss of 6.25%

14. The marked price of a table is ₹1200, which is 20% above the cost price. It is sold at a discount of 10% on the marked price. Find the profit per cent.
    (a) 10%           (b) 8%
    (c) 7.5%          (d) 6%

15. 125 toffees cost ₹ 75. Find the cost of one million toffees if there is a discount of 40% on the selling price for this quantity.
    (a) ₹ 3,00,000    (b) ₹ 3,20,000
    (c) ₹ 3,60,000    (d) ₹ 4,00,000

16. A shopkeeper marks the price of an article at ₹ 250. Find the cost price if after allowing a discount of 20% he still gains 25% on the cost price.
    (a) 210           (b) 160
    (c) 200           (d) 180

17. In Question 16, what will be the selling price of the article if he allows two successive discounts of 10% each?
    (a) 202.5         (b) 225
    (c) 200           (d) 197.5

18. A dozen pairs of gloves quoted at ₹120 are available at a discount of 20%. Find how many pairs of gloves can be bought for ₹ 16.
    (a) 2             (b) 3
    (c) 4             (d) 6

19. Find a single discount equivalent to the discount series of 25%, 20%, 10%.
    (a) 66%           (b) 46%
    (c) 54%           (d) 34%

20. The printed price of a calculator is ₹ 225. A retailer pays ₹ 148.5 for it by getting successive discounts of 20% and another rate which is illegible. What is the second discount rate?

(a) 17%    (b) 18.5%
(c) 16%    (d) 17.5%

21. How much percent more than the cost price should a shopkeeper mark his goods, so that after allowing a discount of 6.25% he should have a gain of 25% on his outlay?
    (a) 33.33%    (b) 16.66%
    (c) 25%     (d) 20%

22. In order to maintain the price line, a trader allows a discount of 20% on the marked price of goods in his shop. However, he still makes a gross profit of 12% on the cost price. Find the profit per cent he would have made on the selling price had he sold at the marked price.
    (a) 35.67%    (b) 40.67%
    (c) 40%     (d) 35%

23. A whole-seller allows a discount of 25% on the list price to a retailer. The retailer sells at 10% discount on the list price. If the customer paid ₹ 54 for an article, what is the profit by the retailer?
    (a) 12     (b) 9
    (c) 5      (d) 8

24. In Question 23, also find the retailer's percentage profit on his cost giving your answer correct to two decimal places.
    (a) 33.33%    (b) 16.66%
    (c) 20%     (d) 25%

25. The cost of production of a cordless phone set in 2016 is ₹ 1100, divided between material, labour and overheads in the ratio 4 : 5 : 2. If the cordless phone set is marked at a price that gives a 10% profit on the component of price accounted for by labour, what is the marked price of the set?
    (a) ₹ 1140    (b) ₹ 1210
    (c) ₹ 1120    (d) ₹ 1150

26. For Question 25, if subsequently in 2017, the cost of material, labour and overheads increased by 20%, 30% and 10% respectively, calculate the cost of manufacturing in 2017.
    (a) ₹ 1350    (b) ₹ 1150
    (c) ₹ 1250    (d) ₹ 1450

27. What should be the new marked price if the criteria for profit is to remain the same as for Question 25 above?
    (a) ₹ 1420    (b) ₹ 1405
    (c) ₹ 1415    (d) None of these

28. By selling a casserole for ₹ 820, a man incurs a loss of 18%. At what price should he sell the casserole to gain 28%?
    (a) ₹ 1180    (b) ₹ 1280
    (c) ₹ 1220    (d) None of these

29. A man sells 5 articles for ₹ 15 and makes a profit of 20%. Find his gain or loss percent if he sells 8 such articles for ₹ 18.40.

30. (a) 2.22% profit    (b) 2.22% loss
    (c) 8% loss    (d) 8% profit

30. The cost price of 40 Oranges is equal to the selling price of 30 Oranges. Find the percentage profit.
    (a) 20%    (b) 25%
    (c) 33.33%    (d) None of these

31. P owns a house worth ₹ 20,000. He sells it to Q at a profit of 25%. After some time, Q sells it back to P at 25% loss. Find P's loss or gain percent.
    (a) 25% gain    (b) 6.25% gain
    (c) 31.56% gain   (d) 31.25% gain

32. A shopkeeper bought locks at the rate of 8 locks for ₹ 34 and sold them at the rate of 12 locks for ₹ 57. Calculate his gain percent.
    (a) 9.33%    (b) 12.5%
    (c) 11.11%    (d) 11.76%

33. Vikas bought an article at ₹ 150 and sold it at a profit of 20%. What would have been the increase in the profit percent if it was sold for ₹ 195?
    (a) 10%    (b) 5%
    (c) 15%    (d) None of these

34. A makes an article for ₹ 250 and sells it to B at a profit of 20%. B sells it to C who sells it for ₹ 386.4, making a profit of 15%. What profit percent did B make?
    (a) 20%    (b) 12%
    (c) 16.66%    (d) 33.33%

35. A reduction of 20% in the price of sugar enables a housewife to buy 5.4 kg. more for ₹ 432. Find the reduced price per kilogram
    (a) ₹ 20    (b) ₹16
    (c) ₹ 18    (d) None of these

36. A man buys 50 kg of oil at ₹10 per kilogram and another 40 kg of oil at ₹12 kilogram and mixes them. He sells the mixture at the rate of ₹11 per kilogram. What will be his gain percent if he is able to sell the whole lot?
    (a) 100/98%    (b) 100(10/49)%
    (c) 10(1/49)%    (d) None of these

37. If the cost price of 25 articles is equal to the selling price of 15 articles, find the profit percent.
    (a) 33.33%    (b) 20%
    (c) 66.67%    (d) 50%

38. A shopkeeper sells sugar in such a way that the selling price of 850 gm is the same as the cost price of one kilogram. Find his gain percent.
    (a) 150/17%    (b) 100/17%
    (c) 17(11/17)%   (d) 1/17%

39. A dealer buys eggs at ₹ 72 per gross. He sells the eggs at a profit of 6.25% on the cost price. What is the selling price per egg (approximately)?
    (a) 53 paise    (b) 50 paise
    (c) 49 paise    (d) 52 paise

40. *P* sold a table to *Q* at a profit of 25%. *Q* sold the same table to *R* for ₹ 90 thereby making a profit of 20%. Find the price at which *P* bought the table from *Z* if it is known that *Z* gained 25% in the transaction.
    (a) ₹ 80
    (b) ₹ 75
    (c) ₹ 90
    (d) ₹ 60

41. *A* sold a table to *B* at a profit of 15%. Later on, *B* sold it back to *A* at a profit of 20%, thereby gaining ₹ 69. How much did *A* pay for the table originally?
    (a) ₹ 300
    (b) ₹ 320
    (c) ₹ 345
    (d) ₹ 350

42. A dealer sold two TV sets for ₹ 9600 each, gaining 20% on one and losing 20% on the other set. Find his net gain or net loss.
    (a) ₹ 400 loss
    (b) ₹ 800 loss
    (c) ₹ 400 gain
    (d) ₹ 800 gain

43. On selling tea at ₹ 20 per kg a loss of 10% is incurred. Calculate the amount of tea (in kg) sold if the total loss incurred is ₹60.
    (a) 27 kg
    (b) 21 kg
    (c) 15 kg
    (d) 30 kg

44. A colour TV and a VCP were sold for ₹ 19,800 each. The TV was sold at a loss of 10% whereas the VCP was sold at a gain of 10%. Find gain or loss in the whole transaction.
    (a) ₹ 400 loss
    (b) ₹ 1000 loss
    (c) ₹ 960 loss
    (d) ₹ 1040 loss
    (*Note:* In this case there will always be a loss)

45. A man sells a TV set for ₹ 33000 and makes a profit of 10%. He sells another TV at a loss of 20%. If on the whole, he neither gains nor loses, find the selling price of the second TV set.
    (a) ₹ 15,000
    (b) ₹ 12,000
    (c) ₹ 30,000
    (d) ₹ 27,000

46. A man sells an article at 10% above its cost price. If he had bought it at 15% less than what he paid for it and sold it for ₹ 33 less, he would have gained 10%. Find the cost price of the article.
    (a) ₹ 400
    (b) ₹ 260
    (c) ₹ 325
    (d) ₹ 200

47. A briefcase was sold at a profit of 5%. If its cost price was 5% less and it was sold for ₹ 63 more, the gain would have been 20%. Find the cost price of the briefcase.
    (a) ₹ 800
    (b) ₹ 900
    (c) ₹700
    (d) ₹ 960

48. A man sells a plot of land at 8% profit. If he had sold it at 15% profit, he would have received ₹ 630 more. What is the selling price of the land?
    (a) ₹ 9320
    (b) ₹ 9600
    (c) ₹ 9820
    (d) ₹ 9720

49. Ashok bought an article and spent ₹ 110 on its repairs. He then sold it to Bhushan at a profit of 20%. Bhushan sold it to Charan at a loss of 10%. Charan finally sold it for ₹ 1188 at a profit of 10%. How much did Ashok pay for the article?
    (a) ₹ 890
    (b) ₹ 1000
    (c) ₹ 780
    (d) ₹ 840

50. A man buys two cycles for a total cost of ₹ 900. By selling one for 4/5 of its cost and other for 5/4 of its cost, he makes a profit of ₹ 90 on the whole transaction. Find the cost price of lower priced cycle.
    (a) ₹ 360
    (b) ₹ 250
    (c) ₹ 300
    (d) ₹ 420

51. A merchant bought two transistors, which together cost him ₹ 480. He sold one of them at a loss of 15% and other at a gain of 19%. If the selling price of both the transistors are equal, find the cost of the lower priced transistor.
    (a) ₹ 300
    (b) ₹ 180
    (c) ₹ 200
    (d) ₹ 280

52. A manufacturer makes a profit of 15% by selling a colour TV for ₹ 5750. If the cost of manufacturing increases by 30% and the price paid by the retailer is increased by 20%, find the profit percent made by the manufacturer.
    (a) 6(2/13)%
    (b) 4 (8/13)%
    (c) 6(1/13)%
    (d) 7(4/13)%

53. The cost of manufacturing an article is made up of materials, labour and overheads in the ratio 6 : 7 : 2. If the cost of labour is ₹ 350, find the profit percent if the article is sold for ₹ 900.
    (a) 30%
    (b) 33.33%
    (c) 20%
    (d) 25%

54. Two dealers *P* and *Q* selling the same model of TV set mark them under the same selling prices. *P* gives successive discounts of 20% and 15% and *Q* gives successive discounts of 18% and 17%. From whom is it more profitable to purchase the TV set?
    (a) From *P*
    (b) From *Q*
    (c) Indifferent between the two
    (d) Cannot be determined

55. *A* sells a car priced at ₹ 1,80,000. He gives a discount of 5% on the first ₹ 1,00,000 and 12.5% on the remaining ₹ 80,000. His competitor *B* sells a car on the same marked priced at ₹ 1,80,000. If he wants to be competitive what percent discount should *B* offer on the marked price.
    (a) 3.33%
    (b) 15.67%
    (c) 8.33%
    (d) 6.67%

56. An article costs ₹ 1400 to a manufacturer who lists its price at ₹ 1600. He sells it to a trader at a discount of 5%. The trader gets a further discount of 5% on his net payment for paying in cash. Calculate the amount that the trader pays to the manufacturer.
    (a) ₹ 1444
    (b) ₹ 1420
    (c) ₹ 1434
    (d) None of these

57. In Question 56, find the profit percent that the manufacturer makes on the sale.
    (a) 20/7%
    (b) 22/7%
    (c) 15/7%
    (d) None of these

58. A firm dealing in furniture allows 5% discount on the marked price of each item. What price must be marked on a dining table that cost ₹2000 to assemble, so as to make a profit of 14%?
    (a) ₹ 3800
    (b) ₹ 2700
    (c) ₹ 2500
    (d) ₹ 2400

59. A shopkeeper allows a discount of 10% on the marked price of a certain article and makes a profit of 12.5%. If the article cost the shopkeeper ₹ 360, what price must be marked on the article?
    (a) ₹ 410
    (b) ₹ 450
    (c) ₹ 480
    (d) None of these

60. A Camera shop allows a discount of 15% on the advertised price of a camera. What price must be marked on the camera, that costs him ₹ 600, so that he makes a profit of 19%?
    (a) ₹ 840
    (b) ₹ 820
    (c) ₹ 750
    (d) ₹ 880

61. A watch dealer pays 20% custom duty on a watch that costs ₹ 450 abroad. For how much should he mark it, if he desires to make a profit of 25% after giving a discount of 20% to the buyer?
    (a) ₹ 800
    (b) ₹ 843.75
    (c) ₹ 810
    (d) ₹ 840.75

62. A shopkeeper buys an article for ₹ 1200 and marks it for sale at a price that gives him 60% profit on his cost. He, however, gives a 35% discount on the marked price to his customer. Calculate the actual percentage profit made by the shopkeeper.
    (a) 2%
    (b) 4%
    (c) 3%
    (d) 56%

63. In the land of the famous milkman Merghese Durian, a milkman sells his buffalo for ₹15400 at some profit. Had he sold his buffalo at ₹ 8200, the quantum of the loss incurred would have been double that of the profit earned. What is the cost price?
    (a) ₹ 13200
    (b) ₹ 12900
    (c) ₹ 13500
    (d) None of these

64. A trader purchases apples at ₹ 70 per hundred. He spends 10% on the transportation. What should be the selling price per 100 to earn a profit of 30%?
    (a) ₹ 101.1
    (b) ₹ 100.1
    (c) ₹ 90.1
    (d) ₹ 99.1

65. A dishonest dealer professes to sell at cost price but uses a 800 gram weight instead of a 1 kilogram weight. Find the percent profit to the dealer.
    (a) 25%
    (b) 20%
    (c) 12.5%
    (d) None of these

*Space for Rough Work*

1. Mithilesh makes 750 articles at a cost of 60 paise per article. He fixes the selling price such that if only 600 articles are sold, he would have made a profit of 40% on the outlay. However, 120 articles got spoilt and he was able to sell 630 articles at this price. Find his actual profit percent as the percentage of total outlay assuming that the unsold articles are useless.

   (a) 42%        (b) 53%

   (c) 47%        (d) 46%

2. A manufacturer estimates that on inspection 12% of the articles he produces will be rejected. He accepts an order to supply 22,000 articles at ₹ 7.50 each. He estimates the profit on his outlay including the manufacturing of rejected articles, to be 20%. Find the cost of manufacturing each article.

   (a) ₹ 6        (b) ₹ 5.50

   (c) ₹ 5        (d) ₹ 4.50

3. The cost of setting up the type of a magazine is ₹ 1000. The cost of running the printing machine is ₹ 120 per 100 copies. The cost of paper, ink and so on is 60 paise per copy. The magazines are sold at ₹ 2.75 each. 900 copies are printed, but only 784 copies are sold. What is the sum to be obtained from advertisements to give a profit of 10% on the cost?

   (a) ₹ 730       (b) ₹ 720

   (c) ₹ 726       (d) ₹ 736

4. A tradesman fixed his selling price of goods at 30% above the cost price. He sells half the stock at this price, one-quarter of his stock at a discount of 15% on the original selling price and rest at a discount of 30% on the original selling price. Find the gain percent altogether.

   (a) 14.875%     (b) 15.375%

   (c) 15.575%     (d) 16.375%

5. A tradesman marks an article at ₹ 205 more than the cost price. He allows a discount of 10% on the marked price. Find the profit percent if the cost price is ₹ x.

   (a) $\dfrac{\left[\dfrac{x}{(18450)}-10\right]}{x}$     (b) $\dfrac{[(18450)]-10x}{x}$

   (c) $\dfrac{\left[\dfrac{x}{(18450)}-100\right]}{x}$     (d) $\dfrac{\left[\dfrac{18450}{x}-100\right]}{x}$

6. Dolly goes to a shop to purchase a doll priced at ₹ 400. She is offered 4 discount options by the shop-keeper. Which of these options should she opt for to gain maximum advantage of the discount offered?

   (a) Single discount of 30%

   (b) 2 successive discounts of 15% each

   (c) 2 successive discounts of 20% and 10%

   (d) 2 successive discounts of 20% and 12%

7. A dishonest dealer marks up the price of his goods by 20% and gives a discount of 10% to the customer. He also uses a 900 gram weight instead of a 1 kilogram weight. Find his percentage profit due to these maneuvers.

   (a) 8%         (b) 12%

   (c) 20%        (d) 16%

8. A dishonest dealer marks up the price of his goods by 20% and gives a discount of 10% to the customer. Besides, he also cheats both his supplier and his buyer by 100 grams while buying or selling 1 kilogram. Find the percentage profit earned by the shopkeeper.

   (a) 20%        (b) 25%

   (c) 32%        (d) 27.5%

9. For Question 8, if it is known that the shopkeeper takes a discount of 10% from his supplier and he disregards this discount while marking up (i.e. he marks up at the undiscounted price), find the percentage profit for the shopkeeper if there is no other change from the previous problem.

   (a) 32%        (b) 36.66%

   (c) 40.33%     (d) 46.66%

10. Cheap and Best, a *kirana* shop bought some apples at 4 per rupee and an equal number at 5 per rupee. He then sold the entire quantity at 9 for 2 rupees. What is his percentage profit or loss?

    (a) 1.23% loss    (b) 6.66%

    (c) 8.888%        (d) No profit no loss

11. A watch dealer sells watches at ₹ 600 per watch. However, he is forced to give two successive discounts of 10% and 5% respectively. However, he recovers the sales tax on the net sale price from the customer at 5% of the net price. What price does a customer have to pay him to buy the watch?

    (a) ₹ 539.75     (b) ₹ 539.65

    (c) ₹ 538.75     (d) ₹ 538.65

12. Deb bought 100 kg of rice for ₹ 1100 and sold it at a loss of as much money as he received for 20 kg rice. At what price did he sell the rice?

    (a) ₹ 9 per kg      (b) ₹ 9.1666 per kg

    (c) ₹ 9.5 per kg    (d) ₹ 10.33 per kg

13. A carpenter wants to sell 40 chairs. If he sells them at ₹ 156 per chair, he would be able to sell all the chairs. But for every ₹ 6 increase in price, he will be left with one additional unsold chair. At what selling price would he be able to maximise his profits (assuming unsold chairs remain with him)?
    (a) 198
    (b) 192
    (c) 204
    (d) 210

**Directions for Questions 14 and 15:** Read the following and answer the questions that follow.

Doctors have advised Renu, a chocolate freak, not to take more than 20 chocolates in one day. When she went to the market to buy her daily quota, she found that if she buys chocolates from the market complex she would have to pay ₹ 3 more for the same number of chocolates than she would have spent had she bought them from her uncle Scrooge's shop, getting two sweets less per rupee. She finally decided to get them from Uncle Scrooge's shop paying only in one rupee coins.

14. How many chocolates did she buy?
    (a) 12
    (b) 9
    (c) 18
    (d) 15

15. How much would she have spent at the market complex?
    (a) ₹ 6
    (b) ₹ 12
    (c) ₹ 9
    (d) ₹ 5

16. A shopkeeper makes a profit of $Q$% by selling an object for ₹ 24. Had the cost price and selling price been interchanged, it would have led to a loss of $62.5Q$%. With the latter cost price, what should be the new selling price to get a profit of $Q$%?
    (a) ₹ 34.40
    (b) ₹ 32.50
    (c) ₹ 25.60
    (d) ₹ 38.4

17. Find the change in the percentage profit for a fruit vendor who, after finding 20% of the fruits rotten, increased his selling price by 10% over and above 15% that he was already charging?
    (a) −15
    (b) +11.5
    (c) −13.8
    (d) −11.5

**Directions for Questions 18 and 19:** Read the following and answer the questions that follow.

Ramu and Shyamu decided to sell their cars each at ₹ 36,000. While Ramu decided to give a discount of 8% on the first ₹ 8000, 5% on next ₹ 12,000 and 3% on the rest to buyer Sashi, Shyamu decided to give a discount of 7% on the first 12,000, 6% on the next 8,000 and 5% on the rest to buyer Rajesh. These discounts were, however, subject to the buyers making the payment on time failing which the discount gets reduced by 1% for every delay of a week. In each case, the selling price of 36,000 was arrived at by increasing the cost price by 25%.

18. If each of them got the payments on time, what is the approximate percentage profit of the person getting the higher profit?
    (a) 19%
    (b) 21%
    (c) 25%
    (d) 17%

19. If Sashi defaults by 1 and 2 weeks in the second and third payments respectively, what would be the profit of Ramu in the sale of the car?
    (a) ₹ 5920
    (b) ₹ 6240
    (c) ₹ 5860
    (d) ₹ 5980

20. What would be the difference in the profits if both the buyers default in each payment by a week?
    (a) ₹ 200
    (b) ₹ 300
    (c) ₹ 400
    (d) ₹ 500

21. Find the selling price of goods if two salesmen claim to make 25% profit each, one calculating it on cost price while another on the selling price, the difference in the profits earned being ₹ 100 and selling price being the same in both the cases.
    (a) ₹ 2000
    (b) ₹ 1600
    (c) ₹ 2400
    (d) ₹ 2500

22. A shopkeeper calculates percentage profit on the buying price and another on the selling price. What will be their difference in profits if both claim a profit of 20% on goods sold for ₹ 3000?
    (a) ₹ 200
    (b) ₹ 100
    (c) ₹ 400
    (d) ₹ 150

23. A pharmaceutical company made 3000 strips of tablets at a cost of ₹ 4800. The company gave away 1000 strips of tablets to doctors as free samples. A discount of 25% was allowed on the printed price. Find the ratio of profit if the price is raised from ₹ 3.25 to ₹ 4.25 per strip and if at the latter price, samples to doctors were done away with. (New profit/old profit)
    (a) 55.5
    (b) 63.5
    (c) 75
    (d) 99.25

24. A merchant makes a profit of 20% by selling an article. What would be the percentage change in the profit percent had he paid 10% less for it and the customer paid 10% more for it?
    (a) 120%
    (b) 125%
    (c) 133.33%
    (d) 150%

25. An article costing ₹ 20 was marked 25% above the cost price. After two successive discounts of the same percentage, the customer now pays ₹ 20.25. What would be the percentage change in profit had the price been increased by the same percentage twice successively instead of reducing it?
    (a) 3600%
    (b) 3200%
    (c) 2800%
    (d) 4000%

26. Divya goes to buy fruits and after a lot of bargaining is able to get the price of a dozen apples reduced

by ₹ 1 from the initial price, thereby enabling her to get 1 apple extra for every rupee saved. (Getting no discount on the extra apple). What is the initial price of a dozen apples?

(a) ₹ 10        (b) ₹ 13

(c) ₹ 12        (d) ₹ 15

27. The accounts of a company show sales of ₹ 12,600. The primary cost is 35% of sales and trading cost accounts for 25% of the gross profit. Gross profit is arrived at by excluding the primary cost plus the cost of advertising expenses of ₹ 1400, director's salary of ₹ 650 per annum plus 2% of annual sales as miscellaneous costs. Find the percentage profit (approx) on a capital investment of ₹ 14,000?

(a) 35%        (b) 31%

(c) 28%        (d) Cannot be determined

28. Jonny has two cycles and one rickshaw. The rickshaw is worth ₹ 96. If he sells the rickshaw along with the first cycle, he has an amount double that of the value of the second cycle. But if he decides to sell the rickshaw along with the second cycle, the amount received would be less than the value of first cycle by ₹ 306. What is the value of first cycle?

(a) ₹ 900        (b) ₹ 600

(c) ₹ 498        (d) None of these

29. David sells his Laptop to Goliath at a loss of 20% who subsequently sells it to Hercules at a profit of 25%. Hercules, after finding some defect in the laptop, returns it to Goliath but could recover only ₹ 4.50 for every ₹ 5 he had paid. Find the amount of Hercules' loss if David had paid ₹ 1.75 lakh for the laptop.

(a) ₹ 3500        (b) ₹ 2500

(c) ₹ 17,500        (d) None of these

30. A dishonest shopkeeper, at the time of selling and purchasing, weighs 10% less and 20% more per kilogram respectively. Find the percentage profit earned by treachery. (Assuming he sells at Cost Price)

(a) 30%        (b) 20%

(c) 25%        (d) 33.33%

31. A dealer marks articles at a price that gives him a profit of 30%. 6% of the consignment of goods was lost in a fire in his premises, 24% was soiled and had to be sold at half the cost price. If the remainder was sold at the marked price, what percentage profit or loss did the dealer make on that consignment?

(a) 2%        (b) 2.5%

(c) 3%        (d) 6.2%

32. A book was sold for a certain sum and there was a loss of 20%. Had it been sold for ₹ 12 more, there would have been a gain of 30%. What would be the profit if the book were sold for ₹ 4.8 more than what it was sold for?

(a) No profit, no loss        (b) 20%

(c) 10%        (d) 25%

**For Questions 33 to 36 use the following data:**

33. Two thousand people lived in Business Village of which 55% were male and the rest were female. The male population earned a profit of 5% and the female population earned 8% on an investment of ₹ 50 each. Find the change in the percentage profit of the village if the ratio of male to female gets reversed the next year, population remaining the same.

(a) Drop of 0.3        (b) Increase of 0.3

(c) Increase of 0.45        (d) Drop of 0.45

34. In Question 33, find the change in the percentage profit of the village, if population increases by 10%. (Assume the ratio remains the same)

(a) Increase of 10%        (b) Increase of 11.11%

(c) No change        (d) Cannot be determined

35. For Question 34, find the percentage change in the profit.

(a) Increase of 10%        (b) Increase of 11.11%

(c) No change        (d) Cannot be determined

36. For Question 33, what would be the change in the percentage profit, if alongwith the reversal of the ratio of males to females, the profit also increases by 1% for both males and females?

(a) Drop of 1.3        (b) Increase of 1.3

(c) Increase of 0.8        (d) None of these

37. A rickshaw dealer buys 30 rickshaws for ₹ 4725. Of these, 8 are four-seaters and the rest are two-seaters. At what price must he sell the four-seaters so that if he sells the two-seaters at 3/4th of this price, he makes a profit of 40% on his outlay?

(a) ₹ 180        (b) ₹ 270

(c) ₹ 360        (d) ₹ 450

38. A flat and a piece of land were bought by two friends Raghav and Sita respectively at prices of ₹ 2 lakh and ₹ 2.2 lakh. The price of the flat rises by 20 percent every year and that of land by 10% every year. After two years, they decide to exchange their possessions. What is percentage gain of the gainer?

(a) 7.56%        (b) 6.36%

(c) 4.39%        (d) None of these

39. A, B and C form a company. A invests half of C expecting a return of 10%. B invests three-fourths of C, expecting a return of 15% on it. C invests ₹ 3000 and the profit of the firm is 25%. How much would B's share of profit be more than that of A's share if B gets an additional 8% for managing the business? (Assume that their expectations with respect to returns on capital invested are met before profit is divided in the ratio of capitals invested).

(a) 20%        (b) 18%

(c) 15%        (d) Cannot be determined

40. A driver of a autorickshaw makes a profit of 20% on every trip when he carries 3 passengers and the price of petrol is ₹ 30 a litre. Find the percentage profit for the same journey if he goes for four passengers per trip and the price of petrol reduces to ₹ 24 litre. (Assume that revenue per passenger is the same in both the cases.)
    - (a) 33.33%
    - (b) 65.66
    - (c) 100%
    - (d) Data inadequate

41. Raghav bought 25 washing machines and microwave ovens for ₹ 2,05,000. He sold 80% of the washing machines and 12 microwave ovens for a profit of ₹ 40,000. Each washing machine was marked up by 20% over cost and each microwave oven was sold at a profit of ₹ 2,000. The remaining washing machines and 3 microwave ovens could not be sold. What is Raghav's overall profit/loss?
    - (a) ₹ 1000 profit
    - (b) ₹ 2500 loss
    - (c) ₹ 1000 loss
    - (d) Cannot be determined

42. After selling a watch, Shyam found that he had made a loss of 10%. He also found that had he sold it for ₹ 27 more, he would have made a profit of 5%. The actual initial loss was what percentage of the profit earned, had he sold the watch for a 5% profit?
    - (a) 23%
    - (b) 150%
    - (c) 200%
    - (b) 180%

43. Sambhu buys rice at ₹ 10/kg and puts a price tag on it so as to earn a profit of 20%. However, his faulty balance shows 1000 gm when it is actually 800 gm. What is his actual gain percentage?
    - (a) 50%
    - (b) 40%
    - (c) 18%
    - (d) 10%

44. The profit earned when an article is sold for ₹ 800 is 20 times the loss incurred when it is sold for ₹ 275. At what price should the article be sold if it is desired to make a profit of 25%.
    - (a) ₹ 300
    - (b) ₹ 350
    - (c) ₹ 375
    - (d) ₹ 400

45. *A* sells to *B* goods at five-thirds the rate of profit at which *B* has decided to sell it to *C*. *C*, on other hand, sells it to *D* at one-third the rate of profit at which *B* sold it to *C*. If *D* gives ₹ 2145 to *C* at 10% profit, how much did *A* buy it for?
    - (a) ₹ 1000
    - (b) ₹ 2000
    - (c) ₹ 1500
    - (d) ₹ 1800

46. In the town of Andher Nagari Chaupat Raja, shopkeepers have to buy and sell goods in the range of ₹ 500 to ₹ 999. A shopkeeper in such a town decides not to buy or sell goods for amounts that contain the digit 9 or for amounts that add up to 13 or are a multiple of 13. What is the maximum possible profit he can earn?
    - (a) ₹ 388
    - (b) ₹ 389
    - (c) ₹ 488
    - (d) None of these

47. Manish bought a combined total of 25 monitors and printers. He marked up the monitors by 20% on the cost price, while each printer was marked up by ₹ 2000. He was able to sell 75% of the monitors and 2 printers and make a profit of ₹ 49,000. The remaining monitors and 3 printers could not be sold by him. Find his overall profit or loss if he gets no return on unsold items and it is known that a printer costs 50% of a monitor.
    - (a) Loss of ₹ 48,500
    - (b) Loss of 21,000
    - (c) Loss of ₹ 41,000
    - (d) Inadequate data

48. For Question 47, Manish's approximate percentage profit or loss is
    - (a) 14.37% loss
    - (b) 16.5% loss
    - (c) 12.14% loss
    - (d) Insufficient information

49. An orange vendor makes a profit of 20% by selling oranges at a certain price. If he charges ₹ 1.2 higher per orange he would gain 40%. Find the original price at which he sold an orange.
    - (a) ₹ 5
    - (b) ₹ 4.8
    - (c) ₹ 6
    - (d) None of these

50. The Mindworkzz prints 5000 copies of a magazine for ₹ 5,00,000 every month. In the July issue of the magazine, Mindworkzz distributed 500 copies free. Besides, it was able to sell 2/3 of the remaining magazines at 20% discount. Besides, the remaining magazines were sold at the printed price of the magazine (which was ₹ 200). Find the percentage profit of Mindworkzz in the magazine venture in the month of July (assume a uniform 20% of the sale price as the vendor's discount and also assume that Mindworkzz earns no income from advertising for the issue).
    - (a) 56%
    - (b) 24.8%
    - (c) 28.5%
    - (d) 22.6%

*Space for Rough Work*

## LEVEL OF DIFFICULTY (III)

The charges of a taxi journey are decided on the basis of the distance covered and the amount of the waiting time during a journey. Distance wise, for the first 2 kilometres (or any part thereof) of a journey, the metre reading is fixed at ₹ 10 (if there is no waiting). Also, if a taxi is boarded and it does not move, then the metre reading is again fixed at ₹ 10 for the first ten minutes of waiting. For every additional kilometre the metre reading changes by ₹ 5 (with changes in the metre reading being in multiples of ₹ 1 for every 200 metres travelled). For every additional minute of waiting, the metre reading changes by ₹ 1. (no account is taken of a fraction of a minute waited for or of a distance less than 200 metres travelled). The net metre reading is a function of the amount of time waited for and the distance travelled.

The cost of running a taxi depends on the fuel efficiency (in terms of mileage/litre), depreciation (straight line over 10 years) and the driver's salary (not taken into account if the taxi is self owned).

Depreciation is ₹ 100 per day everyday of the first 10 years. This depreciation has to be added equally to the cost for every customer while calculating the profit for a particular trip. Similarly, the driver's daily salary is also apportioned equally across the customers of the particular day. Assume, for simplicity, that there are 50 customers every day (unless otherwise mentioned). The cost of fuel is ₹ 15 per litre (unless otherwise stated).

The customer has to pay 20% over the metre reading while settling his bill. Also assume that there is no fuel cost for waiting time (unless otherwise stated).

Based on the above facts, answer the following:

1. If Sardar Preetpal Singh's taxi is 14 years old and has a fuel efficiency of 12 km/litre of fuel, find his profit in a run from Howrah Station to Park Street (a distance of 7 km) if the stoppage time is 8 minutes. (Assume he owns the taxi)
   (a) ₹ 32.25          (b) ₹ 40.85
   (c) ₹ 34.25          (d) ₹ 42.85

2. For question 2, Sardar Preetpal Singh's percentage profit is
   (a) 391.42%          (b) 380%
   (c) 489.71%          (d) 438.23%

3. For the same journey as in question 1 if on another day, with heavier traffic, the waiting time increases to 13 minutes, find the percentage change in the profit.
   (a) 12%              (b) 14%
   (c) 13%              (d) 16%

4. For Question 3, if Sardar Preetpal Singh idled his taxi for 7 minutes and if the fuel consumption dur-

ing idling is 50 ml per minute, find the percentage decrease in the profits.
   (a) 10.74%           (b) 11.21%
   (c) 10.87%           (d) 9.94%

**Directions for Questions 5 to 10:** Answer questions based on this additional information:

Mr. Vikas Verma owns a fleet of 3 taxis, where he pays his driver ₹ 3000 per month. He also insists on keeping an attendant for ₹ 1500 per month in each of his taxis. Idling requires 50 ml of fuel for every minute of idling. For a moving taxi, the fuel consumption is given by 12 km/per litre. On a particular day, he received the following reports about the three taxis.

| Taxi code | Total kilometres | Waiting time | Waiting time with idling | Waiting time without idling |
|-----------|------------------|--------------|--------------------------|-----------------------------|
| A | 260 | | 190 min | 30 min |
| B | 264 | | 170 min | 80 min |
| C | 275 | | 180 min | 60 min |

5. The maximum revenue has been generated by which taxi?
   (a) A                (b) B
   (c) C                (d) Cannot be determined

If it is to be assumed that every customer travelled at least 2 kilometres:

6. Which of the three taxis generated the maximum revenue?
   (a) A                (b) B
   (c) C                (d) Both A & B
   (e) Cannot be determined

7. What percentage of the total revenue was generated by taxi B?
   (a) 32.30            (b) 33.36
   (c) 34.32            (d) 34.36

8. The highest profit was yielded by which taxi?
   (a) A                (b) B
   (c) C                (d) Both A & B

9. The taxi which had the highest percentage profit for the day was
   (a) A                (b) B
   (c) C                (d) B & C

10. The profit as a percentage of costs for the day was:
   (a) 179.46%          (b) 150.76%
   (c) 163.28%          (d) 173.48%

**Directions for Questions 11 to 15:** Read the following and answer the questions that follow.

The Coca-Cola Company is setting up a plant for manufacture and sale of the soft drink.

The investment for the plant is ₹ 10 crore (to be invested in plant, machinery, advertising, infrastructure, etc.).

The following information is available about the different bottle sizes planned:

| Bottle size | Bottling cost | Cost of liquid | Transportation cost | Sale price | Dealer margin |
|---|---|---|---|---|---|
| 300 ml | ₹ 2 | ₹ 0.6 | 10 paise per bottle | ₹ 10 | ₹ 3 |
| 500 ml | ₹ 5 | ₹ 1 | 15 paise per bottle | ₹ 18 | ₹ 6 |
| 1.5 litre | ₹ 10 | ₹ 3 | 20 paise per bottle | ₹ 40 | ₹ 12 |

Based on this information answer the questions given below:

11. For which bottle should Coca-Cola try to maximise sales to maximise its profits? (Assume that the total number of litres of Coca-Cola sold is constant irrespective of the break up of the sales in terms of the bottle sizes)
    (a) 300 ml
    (b) 500 ml
    (c) 1.5 litres
    (d) Indifferent between the three sizes

12. If the company sells only 300 ml bottles in the first year, how many bottles should it sell to recover the investment made in the first year only?
    (a) 23,255,814
    (b) 232,558,140
    (c) 32,255,814
    (d) 322,558,140

13. If sales of 300 ml bottles to 500 ml bottles is 4:1, and there is no sale of 1500 ml bottles how many 300 ml bottles will be required to recover the investment?
    (a) 1,73,53,580
    (b) 2,93,25,512
    (c) 16,25,848
    (d) 16,25,774

14. For Question 13, the total number of both the types to be sold in India in order to recover the whole investment is
    (a) 3665890
    (b) 2032310
    (c) 21691975
    (d) 21723165

15. If we add administrative costs @ ₹ 1 per litre, which bottle size will have the maximum profitability?
    (a) 300 ml
    (b) 500 ml
    (c) 1.5 litres
    (d) Indifferent between the three sizes

16. Hotel Chanakya in Chankyapuri has a fixed monthly cost of ₹ 1,000,00. The advertising cost is ₹ 10,000 per month. It has 5 A/C rooms, which cost ₹ 600 per day and 10 non-A/C rooms, which cost ₹ 350 per day. Direct costs are ₹ 100 per day for an A/C room, and ₹ 50 for a non-A/C room. In the month of April 2020, the occupancy rate of A/C rooms is 50% while that of non-A/C rooms is 45%. Find the profit of the hotel in rupee terms for the month of April 2020.
    (a) 33,600
    (b) 28,800
    (c) (32,000) Loss
    (d) (17,750) Loss

17. For the above question, keeping the A/C occupancy constant at 50%, what should be the minimum occupancy rate for non-A/C rooms for incurring no loss for the month?
    (a) 75.66%
    (b) 80.66%
    (c) 83.33%
    (d) 86.66%

18. For Questions 15 and 16: ₹ 25,000 worth of advertising a sales promotion of 20% off on the bill doubles the occupancy rate. If this is done, what is the change in the profit or loss?
    (a) Reduction of loss by ₹ 5,900
    (b) Reduction of loss to ₹ 5,900
    (c) Reduction of loss by ₹ 26,100
    (d) Both b and c

19. Advertising worth ₹ 50,000 is done for the sales promotion of A/C rooms (advertising a 20% reduction in the bill for A/C rooms). This leads to a doubling of the occupancy rate of A/C rooms. Besides, it also has an effect of increasing non-A/C room occupancy by 20%. Is this advised?
    (a) Yes
    (b) No
    (c) Indifferent
    (d) Cannot be determined

A restaurant has a pricing policy that allows for the following mark-ups:

| | | |
|---|---|---|
| Soups | Mark-up of | 40% |
| Starters | Mark-up of | 50% |
| Meals | Mark-up of | 25% |
| Breads | Mark-up of | 75% |
| Sweets | Mark-up of | 75% |

20. Mr. Amarnath and his family of 4 went to the restaurant and got a bill for: Soups (₹ 126), Starters (₹ 180), Meals (₹ 300), Breads (₹ 245) and Sweets (₹ 210). Find the profit for the restaurant.
    (a) ₹ 341
    (b) ₹ 351
    (c) ₹ 361
    (d) ₹ 371

21. The approximate percentage profit for the restaurant on the bill is
    (a) 40%
    (b) 45%
    (c) 50%
    (d) 55%

22. Which of these are true:
    (i) Profit increases if a part of the money spent on starters was spent on breads and another part of the starters was spent on snacks.
    (ii) Profit increases if a part of the money spent on meal items was spent on starters and another part spent on soups was spent on breads.
    (iii) Profit decreases if a certain amount (say $x$) of the spending on soups was spent on starters and the same amount (₹ $x$) of the spending on soups is spent on meal items.
    (a) (ii) only
    (b) (iii) only
    (c) (ii) and (iii)
    (d) All the three

**Directions for Questions 23 to 28:** Read the following and answer the questions that follow.

Prabhat Ranjan inaugurates his internet cafe on the 1st of January 2003. He invests in 10 computers @ ₹ 30,000 per computer. Besides, he also invests in the other infrastructure of the centre, a sum of ₹ 1 lakh only. He charges his customers on the time spent on the internet a flat rate of ₹ 50 per hour. His initial investment on computers has to be written off equally in 3 years (1 lakh per year) and the infrastructure has to be written off in 5 years (@ ₹ 20,000 per year).

He has to pay a fixed rental of ₹ 8000 per month for the space and also hires an assistant at ₹ 2000 per month.

For every hour that he is connected to the internet, he has to bear a telephone charge of ₹ 20 irrespective of the number of machines operational on the internet at that time. On top of this, he also has to pay an electricity charge of ₹ 5 per computer per hour. Assume that there are no other costs involved unless otherwise mentioned. The internet cafe is open 12 hours a day and is open on all 7 days of the week. (Assume that if a machine is not occupied, it is put off and hence consumes no electricity).

23. Assuming a uniform 80% occupancy rate for the month of April 2003, find his profit or loss for the month.
    (a) ₹ 1,02,400
    (b) ₹ 1,22,400
    (c) ₹ 1,23,600
    (d) ₹ 1,20,733.33

24. If the occupancy rate drops to 60% in the month of June, what is the value of the profit for the month?
    (a) ₹ 90,000
    (b) ₹ 70,000
    (c) ₹ 1,23,600
    (d) ₹ 90,633.33

25. If Prabhat estimates a fixed occupancy rate of 80% during the peak hours of 2 to 8 pm and 40% in the off peak hours of 8 am to 2 pm find the expected profit for him in the month of July 2006.
    (a) ₹ 73,000
    (b) ₹ 93,000
    (c) ₹ 96,000
    (d) ₹ 1,27,500

26. The percentage margin is defined as the margin as a percentage of the variable cost for an hour of opera-

tion. Find the percentage margin of the cyber cafe Prabhat runs.
    (a) 600 %
    (b) 533.33%
    (c) 525%
    (d) Cannot be determined

27. For Question 25 above, how many 30-day months will be required for Prabhat to recover back the investment?
    (a) 3.58 months
    (b) 3.72 months
    (c) 5.71 months
    (d) Cannot be determined

28. If the internet rates per hour have to be dropped drastically to ₹ 20 per hour in the fourth year of operation, what is Prabhat's expected profit for the calendar year 2010 assuming an average of 60% occupancy rate for the year?
    (a) ₹ 2,66,600
    (b) ₹ 1,66,600
    (c) ₹ 88,500
    (d) ₹ 91,500

**Directions for Questions 29 to 33:** Read the following and answer the questions that follow.

A train journey from Patna to Delhi by the Magadh Express has 4 classes:
The fares of the 4 classes are as follows:

| 3 tier: ₹ 330 | No. of berths per bogey: 72 | No. of bogeys: 8 |
|---|---|---|
| AC 3 tier: ₹ 898 | No. of berths per bogey: 64 | No. of bogeys: 2 |
| AC 2 tier: ₹ 1388 | No. of berths per bogey: 45 | No. of bogeys: 2 |
| AC first: ₹ 2691 | No. of berths per bogey: 26 | No. of bogeys: 1 |

Patna to Delhi distance: 1100 kilometres. Assume the train does not stop at any station unless otherwise indicated. Running cost per kilometre: AC bogey → ₹ 25, non AC bogey → ₹ 10.

29. Assuming full occupancy, a bogey of which class exhibits the highest profit margin?
    (a) AC 3 tier
    (b) AC 2 tier
    (c) AC first class
    (d) 3 tier

30. Assuming full occupancy in all the classes, for a journey between Patna to Delhi, the profit margin (as a percentage of the running costs) of the class showing the lowest profit is approximately.
    (a) 116%
    (b) 127%
    (c) 109%
    (d) None of these

31. What is the approximate profit for the railways in rupees if the Magadh Express runs at full occupancy on a particular day?
    (a) ₹ 250,000
    (b) ₹ 275,000
    (c) ₹ 300,000
    (d) Cannot be determined

32. For Question 31, the percentage of the total profit that comes out of AC bogeys is (approximately)

(a) 50%     (b) 60%

(c) 70%     (d) 80%

33. The highest revenue for a journey from Patna to Delhi will always be generated by

(a) 3 tier     (b) AC 3 tier

(c) AC 2 tier     (d) Cannot be determined

34. A newspaper vendor sells three kinds of periodicals-dailies, weeklies and monthlies.

The weeklies sell for ₹ 12 at a profit of 20%, the monthlies sell for ₹ 50 at a profit of 25%, while the dailies sell at ₹ 3 at a profit of 50%. If there is a government restriction on the total number of periodicals that one particular news vendor, can sell, and Kalu a newspaper vendor, has sufficient demand for all the three types of periodicals, what should he do to maximise profits?

(a) Sell maximum weeklies

(b) Sell maximum monthlies

(c) Sell maximum dailies

(d) Cannot be determined

35. Without the restriction mentioned in the problem above, what should the newspaper vendor do to maximise his profits if his capital is limited?

(a) Sell maximum weeklies

(b) Sell maximum monthlies

(c) Sell maximum dailies

(d) Cannot be determined

36. A fruit vendor buys fruits from the fruit market at wholesale prices and sells them at his shop at retail prices. He operates his shop 30 days a month, as a rule. He buys in multiples of 100 fruits and sells them in multiples of a dozen fruits. He purchases mangoes for ₹ 425 per hundred and sells at ₹ 65 per dozen, he buys apples at ₹ 150 per hundred and sells at ₹ 30 per dozen, he buys watermelons (always of equal size) at ₹ 1800 per hundred and sells at ₹ 360 per dozen. Which of the three fruits yields him the maximum percentage profit?

(a) Mangoes     (b) Apples

(c) Watermelons     (d) Both (b) and (c)

37. For Question 36, if he adds oranges, which he buys at ₹ 180 per hundred and sells at ₹ 33 per dozen, what can be his maximum profit on a particular day if he invests ₹ 1800 in purchasing fruits everyday and he sells everything that he buys?

(a) ₹ 1200     (b) ₹ 1180

(c) ₹ 1260     (d) ₹ 1320

38. For Questions 36 and 37, if the fruit vendor hires you as a consultant and pays you 20% of his profit in the month of July 2006 as a service charge, what can be the maximum fees that you will get for your consultancy charges?

(a) ₹ 7200     (b) ₹ 14,400

(c) ₹ 7440     (d) Cannot be determined

39. A newspaper costs ₹ 11 to print on a daily basis. Its sale price (printed) is ₹ 3. The newspaper gives a sales incentive of 40% on the printed price, to the newspaper vendors. The newspaper makes up for the loss through advertisements, which are charged on the basis of per column centimetre rates. The advertisement rates of the newspaper are ₹ 300 per cc (column centimetre). It has to give an incentive of 15% on the advertising bill to the advertising agency. If the newspaper has a circulation of 12,000 copies, what is the approximate minimum advertising booking required if the newspaper has to break-even on a particular day. (Assume there is no wastage)

(a) 300 cc     (b) 350 cc

(c) 435 cc     (d) 450 cc

40. For Question 39, if it is known that the newspaper house is unable to recover 20% of its dues, what would be the approximate advertising booking target on a particular day in order to ensure the break-even point?

(a) 375 cc     (b) 438 cc

(c) 544 cc     (d) 562.5 cc

*Space for Rough Work*

# ANSWER KEY

## Level of Difficulty (I)

| | | | |
|---|---|---|---|
| 1. (b) | 2. (c) | 3. (b) | 4. (d) |
| 5. (c) | 6. (a) | 7. (b) | 8. (a) |
| 9. (a) | 10. (b) | 11. (a) | 12. (d) |
| 13. (d) | 14. (b) | 15. (c) | 16. (b) |
| 17. (a) | 18. (a) | 19. (b) | 20. (d) |
| 21. (a) | 22. (c) | 23. (b) | 24. (c) |
| 25. (d) | 26. (a) | 27. (c) | 28. (b) |
| 29. (c) | 30. (c) | 31. (d) | 32. (d) |
| 33. (a) | 34. (b) | 35. (b) | 36. (a) |
| 37. (c) | 38. (c) | 39. (a) | 40. (d) |
| 41. (a) | 42. (b) | 43. (a) | 44. (a) |
| 45. (b) | 46. (d) | 47. (c) | 48. (d) |
| 49. (a) | 50. (c) | 51. (c) | 52. (a) |
| 53. (c) | 54. (a) | 55. (c) | 56. (a) |
| 57. (b) | 58. (d) | 59. (b) | 60. (a) |
| 61. (b) | 62. (b) | 63. (d) | 64. (b) |
| 65. (a) | | | |

## Level of Difficulty (II)

| | | | |
|---|---|---|---|
| 1. (c) | 2. (b) | 3. (c) | 4. (b) |
| 5. (b) | 6. (a) | 7. (c) | 8. (c) |
| 9. (d) | 10. (a) | 11. (d) | 12. (b) |
| 13. (a) | 14. (a) | 15. (a) | 16. (d) |
| 17. (c) | 18. (a) | 19. (a) | 20. (c) |
| 21. (a) | 22. (b) | 23. (b) | 24. (c) |
| 25. (d) | 26. (c) | 27. (b) | 28. (a) |
| 29. (c) | 30. (d) | 31. (c) | 32. (a) |
| 33. (b) | 34. (c) | 35. (a) | 36. (b) |
| 37. (b) | 38. (d) | 39. (d) | 40. (c) |
| 41. (c) | 42. (c) | 43. (a) | 44. (c) |
| 45. (a) | 46. (a) | 47. (a) | 48. (a) |
| 49. (d) | 50. (b) | | |

## Level of Difficulty (III)

| | | | |
|---|---|---|---|
| 1. (d) | 2. (c) | 3. (b) | 4. (a) |
| 5. (d) | 6. (c) | 7. (b) | 8. (c) |
| 9. (a) | 10. (b) | 11. (a) | 12. (a) |
| 13. (a) | 14. (c) | 15. (a) | 16. (c) |
| 17. (b) | 18. (d) | 19. (b) | 20. (b) |
| 21. (c) | 22. (c) | 23. (a) | 24. (b) |
| 25. (a) | 26. (d) | 27. (d) | 28. (b) |
| 29. (c) | 30. (c) | 31. (b) | 32. (b) |
| 33. (d) | 34. (b) | 35. (c) | 36. (d) |
| 37. (a) | 38. (a) | 39. (c) | 40. (c) |

## Hints

### Level of Difficulty (III)

1-10. Concentrate on creation of the revenue equation and the cost equations separately. Revenue from a journey will depend on
  (a) length of journey (over 2 kilometres)
  (b) time of waiting.

Besides, the fixed metre reading of ₹ 10 at the start is used up at the rate of 1 ₹ per 200 metres and/or 1 ₹/minute of waiting.

11. Coca-Cola earns $(10 - 3) - (2 + 0.6 + 0.1) = ₹ 4.3$ per 300 ml bottle.
Similarly, for 500 ml bottle, the profit is
$$12 - 6.15 = ₹ 5.85.$$
and for 1500 ml bottle, $28 - 13.2 = 14.8$ for 1500 ml bottle.
The profit per ml sold has to be maximised.

12. $\dfrac{₹ 10 \text{ crore}}{4.3} = 2,32,55,814.$

13-14. The earning for one set of 5 bottles $= 4.3 \times 4 + 5.85 = ₹ 23.05.$

15. Maximum profitability $= \dfrac{\text{Margin per bottle}}{\text{Cost per bottle}}.$

16-19. Profit = Revenue – Expenses.

20-22. Observe the profitability rates for each type of item.

23. Revenues = 8 computers $\times$ ₹ 50/hr $\times$ 12 hours $\times$ 30 days
Costs = monthly cost $+ \dfrac{\text{Depreciation}}{12} +$ Hourly cost $\times$ 12 hours $\times$ 30 days.

24-28. Will be solved on the same principle as question 23.

29-33. Revenues = occupancy $\times$ cost/ticket.
$\dfrac{\text{Cost}}{\text{Kilometer}} \times$ no. of kilometres.

## Solutions and Shortcuts

### Level of Difficulty (I)

1. $0.8 \times \text{Price} = 560 \rightarrow$ Price 700.

2. The SP $= 106.25\%$ of the CP. Thus, CP $= 29.75/1.0625 = ₹ 28.$

3. $1.12 \times \text{Price} = 3808 \rightarrow$ Price = 3400.

4. A loss of 25% means a cost price of 100 corresponding to a selling price of 75. CP as a percentage of the SP would then be 133.33%

5. $1800 = 1.2 \times \text{cost price} \rightarrow$ Cost price = 1500
Profit at $1687.5 = ₹ 187.5$
Percentage profit $= (187.5/1500) \times 100 = 12.5\%$

6. CP $= 6612.5/1.15 = 5750.$ Selling this at 5380 would mean a loss of ₹370 on a CP of ₹ 5750.

7. The CP will be ₹ 7200 (got by $6400 \times 1.125$). Hence at an S.P. of 7812 the percentage profit will be 8.5%

8. CP $= 69/1.15 = 60.$ Thus, the required SP for 20% profit is $1.2 \times 60 = 72.$

9. The buying price is ₹ 6 per dozen, while the sales price is ₹ $0.75 \times 12 = 9$ per dozen – a profit of 50%

10. Sales tax $= 150/5 = 30.$ Thus, the SP contains ₹ 30 component of sales tax. Of the remainder ($150 - 30 = 120$) $1/3^{rd}$ is the profit. Thus, the profit $= 120/3 = 40.$ Cost price $= 120 - 40 = 80.$

11. C.P × 1.3 = 26 → CP = 20
    At a selling price of ₹ 22.5, the profit percent 2.5/20 = 12.5%

12. Solve using options. Option (d) gives you ₹220 as the cost of the trouser. Hence, the shirt will cost 15% more i.e. 220 + 22 + 11 = 253.
    This satisfies the total cost requirement of ₹ 473.

13. The formula that satisfies this condition is:
    Loss of $a^2/100\%$ (Where $a$ is the common profit and loss percentage). Hence, in this case 625/100 = 6.25% loss.

14. Cost price = ₹ 1000, selling price = 0.9 of 1200 = 1080.
    Hence, 8% is the correct answer.

15. The cost per toffee = 75/125 = ₹ 0.6 = 60 paise. Cost of 1 million toffees = 600000. But there is a discount of 40% offered on this quantity. Thus, the total cost for 1 million toffees is 60% of 600000 = 360000.

16. On a marked price of ₹ 250, a discount of 20% would mean a selling price of ₹ 200. Since this represents a 25% profit we get:
    1.25 × CP = 200 → CP = 160.

17. The thought process in this question would go as follows:
    250 − 10% of 250 = 225 (after the first discount).
    225 − 10% of 225 = 225 − 22.5 = 202.5 (after the second discount). You could do this on the PCG.

18. For ₹ 96, we can buy a dozen pair of gloves. Hence, for ₹ 16 we can buy 2 pairs of gloves.

19. 100 → 75 (after 25% discount) → 60 (after 20% discount) → 54 (after 10% discount).
    Thus, the single discount which would be equivalent would be 46%.

20. 225 × 0.8 × x = 148.5 → x = 0.825
    Which means a 17.5% discount.

21. If you assume the cost price to be 100 and we check from the options, we will see that for Option (a) the marked price will be 133.33 and giving a discount of 6.25% would leave the shopkeeper with a 25% profit.

22. Solve by trial and error using the options. If he marks his goods 40% above the cost price he would be able to generate a 12% profit inspite of giving a 20% discount.

23. The customer pays ₹54 after a discount of 10%. Hence, the list price must be ₹ 60.
    This also means that at a 25% discount, the retailer buys the item at ₹45.
    Hence, the profit for the retailer will be ₹9 (54 − 45).

24. The profit would be given by the percentage value of the ratio 9/45 = 20%.

25. The labour price accounts for ₹ 500. Since the profit percentage gives a 10% profit on this component i.e. 50.
    Hence, the marked price is 1150.

26. The costs in 2016 were 400, 500 and 200 respectively. An increase of 20% in material → increase of 80. An increase of 30% in labor → increase of 150. Increase of 10% in overheads → increase of 20. Total increase = 80 + 150 + 20 = 250. New cost = 1100 + 250 = 1350

27. For a 10% profit on labour cost, he should mark his goods at 1350 + 10% of 650 = 1415. Note, 650 is the new cost of labour after a 30% increase as described in Question 26.

28. SP = 820 = 0.82 × CP → CP = 1000. To gain a profit of 28%, the marked price should be 128% of 1000 = 1280.

29. The SP per article = ₹ 3. This represents a profit of 20%. Thus, CP = 3/1.2 = 2.5. 8 articles would cost ₹ 20 and hence selling at 18.40 would represent a loss of ₹1.6, which would mean an 8% loss on ₹20.

30. The percentage profit = $\dfrac{\text{Goods left}}{\text{Goods Sold}} \times 100.$
    $$= 10/30 \times 100 = 33.33\%$$
    (Note: This formula can be used if the money got and money spent is equated.)

31. In the question, $P$'s investment has to be considered as ₹ 20,000 (the house he puts up for sale).
    He sells at ₹25000 and buys back at ₹ 18750. Hence his profit is ₹ 6250.
    Required answer = (6250 × 100/20000) = 31.25%

32. For 12 locks, he would have paid ₹51, and sold them at ₹ 57. This would mean a profit percentage of 11.76%

33. 195/150 = 1.3 → the profit percentage would be 30% if sold at 195. Thus, the increase in profit percent = 30% − 20% = 10%.

34. A's selling price = 1.2 × 250 = 300. C's Cost price = B's selling price = 386.4/1.15 = 336. Thus, B's profit = ₹36 and his profit percent = 36 × 100/300 = 12%.

35. A 20% reduction in price increases the consumption by 25% (Refer Table 4.1). But the increase in consumption is 5.4 kg.
    Hence, the consumption (original) will be 5.4 × 4 = 21.6 kg.
    Hence, original price = 432/21.6 = ₹ 20.
    Hence, reduced price = ₹ 16

36. Total cost = 50 × 10 + 40 × 12 = 980. Total revenue = 90 × 11 = 990. Gain percent = (10 × 100)/980 = 100/98 %.

37. Percentage profit = $\dfrac{\text{Goods left}}{\text{Goods Sold}} \times 100$
    $$= 10/15 \times 100 = 66.67\%$$

38. The profit percent would be equal to 150 × 100 /850 = 15000/850 = 300/17% = 17 (11/17)%

39. A gross means 144 eggs. Thus, the cost price per egg = 50 paise and the selling price after a 6.25% profit = 53 paise (approximately).

40. Q sold the table at 20% profit at ₹ 90. Thus cost price would be given by: $CP_Q \times 1.2 = 90$

   Q's Cost price = ₹ 75.

   We also know that P sold it to Q at 25% profit. Thus,

   P's Cost price × 1.25 = 75

   → P's cost price = 60.

41. From the options, checking option (a): 300 (*A* buys at this value) → 345 (sells it to *B* at a profit of 15%) → 414 (*B* sells it back to *A* at a profit of 20% gaining ₹69 in the process). Thus, *A*'s original cost = ₹ 300.

42. Net loss = $(20/10)^2 = 4\%$ of cost price. Thus, 19200 (total money realized) represents 96% of the value. Thus, the cost price would be ₹ 20,000 and the loss would be ₹800.

43. CP × 0.9 = 20 → CP = ₹22.222, Loss per kg = ₹2.222. To incur a loss of ₹ 60, we need to sell 60/2.22 = 27 kgs of tea.

44. The CP of the TV → $CP_{TV} \times 0.9 = 19,800 \to CP_{TV} = 22,000$

   The CP of the VCP → $CP_{VCP} \times 1.1 = 19,800 \to CP_{VCP} = 18,000$.

   Total sales value = 19,800 × 2 = 39,600.

   Total cost price = 22000 + 18000 = 40,000. Loss = 40,000 − 39,600 = 400.

45. The profit of 10% amounts to ₹3000. This should also be the actual loss on the second TV.

   Thus, the actual loss = ₹3000 (20% of C.P.)

   Hence, the CP of the second set = ₹15000. SP of the second TV set = 15000 − 3000 = 12000.

46. Solve using options. The correct option (d) would work as follows: If CP = 200, the man sells at 220 (after 10% profit). If he bought for 15% less, he would have bought it at 0.85 × 200 = 170. Also, selling for ₹33 less than 220, means he would have sold at 220 − 33 = 187. This represents the required profit of 10% on his new cost price of 170. Hence, this option is correct. (Note: For the wrong options, the last percentage profit would not match the required 10% profit).

47. Let the cost price be *P*. Then, $P \times 0.95 \times 1.2 = P \times 1.05 + 63 \to P = 700$. Alternately, you could have solved this using options, as shown in the previous question.

48. 7% of the cost price = ₹ 630.

   Thus, cost price = ₹ 9000

   and selling price @ 8% profit = ₹ 9720.

49. From the last statement we have: Charan's cost price = 1188/1.1 = 1080 = Bhushan's selling price. Then,

Bhushan's CP would be given by the equation: CP × 0.9 = 1080 → CP for Bhushan = 1200 = SP for Ashok.

   Also, Ashok gains 20%. Hence, CP for Ashok → CP × 1.2 = 1200 → CP for Ashok = 1000.

   This includes ₹ 110 component of repairs. Thus, the purchase price for Ashok would be 1000 − 110 = 890.

50. Solve through the values given in the options. Option (c) is correct because at 4/5 × 300 + 5/4 × 600 we see that the profit earned = ₹90.

51. Solve this question using the options. The first thing you should realize is that the cost of the lower priced item should be less than 240. Thus, we can reject options (a) and (d). Checking option (c) we can see that if the lower priced item is priced at 200, the higher priced item would be priced at ₹ 280. Then: 1.19 × 200 = 238 and 0.85 × 280 = 238. It can be seen that in this condition the values of the selling price of both the items would be equal (as required by the conditions given in the problem). Thus, option (c) is the correct answer.

52. Original Cost Price = ₹ 5000

   New Cost Price = 1.3 × 5000 = ₹ 6500

   Price paid by retailer = 1.2 × 5750 = ₹ 6900

   Profit percentage = (400/6500) × 100 = 6 (2/13)%

53. The total manufacturing cost of the article = 300 + 350 + 100 = 750. SP = 900. Thus, profit = ₹ 150.

   Profit Percent = 150 × 100/750 = 20%

54. Assume marked price for both to be 100.

   *P*'s selling price = 100 × 0.8 × 0.85 = 68

   *Q*'s selling price = 100 × 0.82 × 0.83 = 68.06.

   Buying from '*P*' is more profitable.

55. The total discount offered by *A* = 5% on 1,00,000 + 12.5% on 80,000 = 5,000 + 10,000 = 15,000.

   If *B* wants to be as competitive, he should also offer a discount of ₹ 15,000 on 1,80,000. Discount percentage = 15000 × 100/1,80,000 = 8.33% discount.

56. The trader pays 1600 × 0.95 × 0.95 = ₹ 1444

57. Manufacturer's profit percentage = (44/1400) × 100 = (22/7)%

58. For a cost price of ₹2000, he needs a selling price of 2280 for a 14% profit. This selling price is arrived at after a discount of 5% on the marked price. Hence, the marked price MP = 2280/0.95 = 2400.

59. Solve using options. Option (b) fits the situation as a 10% discount on 450 would mean a discount of 45. This would leave us with a selling price of 405, which represents a profit percent of 12.5% on ₹ 360.

60. If he marks the camera at 840, a 15% discount would still allow him to sell at 714 – a profit of 19%. Alternately: Marked Price × 0.85 = 600 × 1.19 → Marked Price = 840

61. Cost price to the watch dealer
= 450 + 20% of 450 = ₹ 540
Desired selling price for 25% profit
= 1.25 × 540 = 675
But 675 is the price after 20% discount on the marked price.
Thus,
Marked price × 0.8 = 675 → MP = 843.75
Hence, he should mark the item at ₹843.75.

62. If the cost price is 100, a mark up of 60% means a marked price of 160. Further a 35% discount on the marked price would be given by:
160 − 35% of 160 = 160 − 56 = 104. Thus, the percentage profit is 4%.

63. A cost price of ₹13000 would meet the conditions in the problem as it would give us a loss of 4800 (if sold at 8200) and a profit of 2400 (when sold at 15400). You can think of this as: If you take the loss as 2x, the profit is x. Then, 3x = 15400 − 8200 = 7200 x = 2400. Thus, the profit is 2400 when he sells at 15400. Hence, the cost price must be 15400 − 2400 = 13000.

64. Cost per 100 apples = 70 + 10% of 70 = ₹77.
Selling price @ 30% profit = 1.3 × 77 = ₹100.1

65. Profit percent = (200/800) × 100 = 25%

## Level of Difficulty (II)

1. Total outlay (initial investment) = 750 × 0.6 = ₹ 450.
By selling 600, he should make a 40% profit on the outlay. This means that the selling price for 600 should be 1.4 × 450 → ₹ 630
Thus, selling price per article = 630/600 = 1.05. Since, he sells only 630 articles at this price, his total recovery = 1.05 × 630 = 661.5
Profit percent (actual) = (211.5/450) × 100 = 47%

2. In order to solve this problem, first assume that the cost of manufacturing 1 article is ₹1. Then 100 articles would get manufactured for ₹100. For a 20% profit on this cost, he should be able to sell the entire stock for ₹120. However since he would be able to sell only 88 articles (given that 12% of his manufactured articles would be rejected) he needs to recover ₹120 from selling 88 articles only. Thus, the profit he would need would be given by the ratio 32/88.
Now it is given to us that his selling price is ₹7.5. The same ratio of profitability i.e.32/88 is achieved if his cost per article is ₹ 5.5.

3. The total cost to print 900 copies would be given by:
Cost for setting up the type + cost of running the printing machine + cost of paper/ink etc

= 1000 + 120 × 9 + 900 × 0.6 = 1000 +1080 + 540 = 2620.
A 10% profit on this cost amounts to ₹ 262. Hence, the total amount to be recovered is ₹ 2882.
Out of this, 784 copies are sold for ₹ 2.75 each to recover ₹ 2156.
The remaining money has to be recovered through advertising.
Hence, The money to be recovered through advertising = 2882 − 2156 = ₹ 726. Option (c) is correct.

4. Total cost (assume) = 100.
Recovered amount = 65 + 0.85 × 32.5 + 0.7 × 32.5
= 65 + 27.625 + 22.75 = 115.375
Hence, profit percent = 15.375%

5. Cost price = x
Marked Price = x + 205
Selling Price = 0.9x + 184.5
Percentage Profit = [(−0.1x + 184.5)/x] × 100.
$$= \frac{18450 - 10x}{x}$$

6. She should opt for a straight discount of 30% as that gives her the maximum benefit.

7. If you assume that his cost price is ₹ 1 per gram, his cost for 1000 grams would be ₹ 1000. For supposed 1 kg sale he would charge a price of 1080 (after an increase of 20% followed by a decrease of 10%).
But, since he gives away only 900 grams the cost for him would be ₹ 900.
Thus he is buying at 900 and selling at 1080 − a profit percentage of 20%

8. While buying
He buys 1100 gram instead of 1000 grams (due to his cheating).
Suppose he bought 1100 grams for ₹ 1000
While selling:
He sells only 900 grams when he takes the money for 1 kg.
Now according to the problems he sells at a 8% profit (20% mark up and 10% discount).
Hence his selling price is ₹ 1080 for 900 grams.
To calculate profit percentage, we either equate the goods or the money.
In this case, let us equate the money as follows:
Buying;
1100 grams for ₹ 1000
Hence    1188 grams for ₹ 1080
Selling:   900 grams for ₹ 1080
Hence, profit% = 288/900 = 32%
(using goods left by goods sold formula)

9. The new situation is
Buying:
1100 grams for ₹ 900

Hence, 1320 grams for ₹ 1080

Selling: 900 grams for ₹ 1080

Profit % = $\frac{420}{900} \times 100 = 46.66\%$

10. Assume he bought 20 apples each. Net investment ⇒ ₹ 5 + ₹ 4 = ₹ 9 for 40 apples. He would sell 40 apples @ (40 × 2)/9 = ₹ 8.888 → Loss of ₹ 0.111 on ₹ 9 investment

Loss percentage = 1.23%

11. 600 – 10% of 600 = 540. 540 – 5% of 540 = 513. 513 + 5% of 513 = 538.65

12. The problem is structured in such a way that you should be able to interpret that if he had sold 120 kg of rice he would recover the investment on 100 kg of rice.

$$\% \text{ Loss/Profit} = \frac{\text{Goods left}}{\text{Goods sold}} \times 100$$

(−20/120) × 100 = 16.66% loss.

Since, cost price for Deb is ₹ 11; selling price per kg would be ₹ 9.166.

13. Comparisons have to be made between:

192 × 34, 198 × 33, 204 × 32 and 210 × 31 for the highest product amongst them.

The highest value of revenue is seen at a price of ₹ 198.

14 & 15: Using options from question 15. Suppose she had spent ₹ 6 at the market complex, she would spend ₹ 3 at her uncle's shop. The other condition (that she gets 2 sweets less per rupee at the market complex) gets satisfied in this scenario if she had bought 12 chocolates overall. In such a case, her buying would have been 2 per Rupee at the market and 4 per rupee at Uncle Scrooge's shop.

Trial and error will show that this condition is not satisfied for any other option combination.

16. The given situation fits if we take $Q$ as 60% profit and then the loss would be 37.5% (which is 62.5%) of $Q$. Thus, if ₹ 24 is the cost price, the selling price should be 24 × 1.6 = ₹ 38.4

17. Assume the price of 1 kg as 100. He initially sells the kg at 115. His original profit is 15%. When he is able to sell only 80% of his items: his new revenue would be given by 80 × 1.265 = 101.2 on a cost of 100. Profit percentage = 1.2%

Change in profit percent = −13.8 (It drops from 15 to 1.2)

18. Ramu's total discount:

8% on 8000 = ₹ 640
5% on 12000 = ₹ 600
3% on 16000 = ₹ 480

Total = ₹ 1720 on ₹ 36000.

Hence, Realised value = 34280.

Shyamu's Discounts:

7% on 12000 = 840
6% on 8000 = 480
5% on 16000 = 800

₹ 2120 on ₹ 36000

Hence, Realised value = 33880.

The higher profit is for Ramu.

Also, the CP has a mark up of 25% for the Marked price. Thus the CP must have been 28800 (This is got by 36000 – 20% of 36000 – PCG thinking)

Thus, the profit % for Ramu would be: (5480*100)/28800 → 19% approx.

19. In the case of the given defaults, the discount for Ramu would have gone down to:

4% on 12000 (the second payment) and the second discount would thus have been ₹480 meaning that the sale price would have risen by ₹120 (since there is a ₹120 drop in the discount)

1% on 16000 → A reduction of 2% of 16000 in the discount → a reduction of ₹ 320.

Hence, Ramu's profit would have gone up by ₹440 in all & would yield his new profit as:

5480 + 440 = ₹ 5920

20. The following working would show the answer:

Ramu's Discounts

7% on 8000 = ₹ 560
4% on 12000 = ₹ 480
2% on 16000 = ₹ 320

Total = ₹ 1360 on ₹ 36,000.

Shyamu's discounts:

6% on 12000 = 720
5% on 8000 = 400
4% on 16000 = 640

₹ 1760 on ₹ 36000

Thus, their profits would vary by ₹ 400 (since their cost price is the same)

21. Solve using options. Option (a) fits as if we take SP as 2000, we get CP$_1$ as 1500 and CP$_2$ as 1600 which gives us the required difference of ₹ 100.

22. The first one would get a profit of ₹ 500 (because his cost would be 2500 for him to get a 20% profit on cost price by selling at 3000).

The second one would earn a profit of 600 (20% of 3000).

Difference in profits = ₹100

23. Find out the total revenue realization for both the cases:

Case 1: (Old) Total sales revenue = 2000 × 3.25 × 0.75.

Profit$_{old}$ = Total sales revenue − 4800

Case 2: (New) Total sales revenue = 3000 × 4.25 × 0.75

Profit$_{new}$ = Total sales revenue – 4800

The ratio of profit will be given by Profit$_{new}$/Profit$_{old}$

24. Profit in original situation = 20%.

In new situation, the purchase price of 90 (buys at 10% less) would give a selling price of 132 (sells at 10% above 120).

The new profit percent = [(132 – 90) × 100]/90 = 46.66

Change in profit percent = [(46.66 – 20) × 100]/20 = 133.33%

25. The successive discounts must have been of 10% each. The required price will be got by reducing 25 by 10% twice consecutively. (use PCG application for successive change)

26. From the options you can work out that if the original price was ₹ 12 per dozen, the cost per apple would be ₹1.

If she is able to get a dozen apples at a reduced price (reduction of ₹ 1 per dozen), she would be able to purchase 1 extra apple for the 1 Rupee she saved. Thus, option (c) is correct.

27. The following calculations will show the respective costs:

Primary Cost: 35% of 12600 = 4410

Miscellaneous costs = 2% of 12600 = 252

Gross Profit = 12600 – 4410 – 1400 – 650 – 252 = 5888

Trading cost = 0.25 × 5888 = 1472

Hence, Net profit = 4416.

Percentage profit = 4416/14000 = 31.54%

28. If we assume the value of the first cycle as ₹ 900. Then 900 + 96 = 996 should be equal to twice the value of the second cycle. Hence, the value of the second cycle works out to be: 498.

Also 498 + 96 = 594 which is ₹306 less than 900.

Hence, Option (a) fits the situation perfectly and will be the correct answer.

Note here that if you had tried to solve this through equations, you would have got stuck for a very long time.

29. David (100) → Goliath (80) → Hercules (100) → Goliath (90)

Hercules loss corresponds to 10 when David buys the laptop for 100.

Hence, Hercules's loss would be ₹17500 when David buys the laptop for 1,75,000.

30. While purchasing he would take 1200 grams for the price of 1000 grams.

While selling he would sell 900 grams for the price of 1000 grams. Since CP = SP, the profit earned is through the weight manipulations. It will be given by:

Goods left/goods sold = 300 × 100/900 = 33.33%

31. Assume that for 100 items the cost price is ₹ 100, then the selling price is ₹ 130. Since 24 is sold at half the price, he would recover 24 × 1/2 = ₹12 (since it is sold at half the cost price)

The remaining 70 would be sold at 70 × 1.3 = ₹91. Total revenue = 91 + 12 = 103 → a profit of 3% (on a cost of 100).

32. An increase in the price by ₹12 will correspond to 50% of the CP.

Hence, The CP is ₹24 and initially the book was being sold at ₹19.2. Hence, if there is an increment of ₹ 4.8 in the selling price, there would be no profit or loss.

33. In the first year, the profit percentage would be:

$$\text{Old Profit Percentage} = \frac{0.55 \times 5 + 0.45 \times 8}{1} = 6.35\%$$

$$\text{New Profit Percentage} = \frac{0.55 \times 8 + 0.45 \times 5}{1} = 6.65$$

34. Since the ratio remains unchanged the percentage profit of the village will remain unchanged too.

35. The profit would increase by 10% as there is no change in the percentage profit.

36. Since the answer to question 33 is 0.3, if we increase the percentage profit for both men and women by 1 % the overall percentage profit would also go up by 1% - thus 0.3 + 1 = 1.3%

37. $x \times 8 + 0.75x \times 22 = 1.4 \times 4725 \rightarrow x = 270$.

On an investment of ₹ 4725, a profit of 40% means a profit of 1890.

Hence, the targeted sales realization is ₹ 6615.

The required equation would be:

$8p + 22 (3p)/4 = 6615$

$\rightarrow 8p + 33p/2 = 6615$

In this expression for LHS to be equal to RHS, we need $33p/2$ to be an odd number. This can only happen when $p$ is not a multiple of 4 (why?? Apply your mind). Hence, options a & c get eliminated automatically.

38. After 2 years, the flat would be worth ₹ 288000, while the land would be worth ₹ 266200. The profit percentage of the gainer would be given by:

$$(21800/266200) \times 100 = 8.189\%$$

Hence (d).

39. The total investment will be $A + B + C$.

$C$ being 3000, $B$ will be 2250 and $A$ will be 1500. The total investment is: 6750.

Returns to be given on their expectations:

$A$ = 150, $B$ = 337.5 and $C$ = 0.

From this point calculate the total profit, subtract $A$'s and $B$'s expected returns and $B$'s share of the profits for managing the business before dividing the profits in the ratio of capital invested. However, most of this information is unknown. Hence option (d) is correct.

40. The cost of the trip would be proportional to the price of petrol. So, if initially the cost is 100, the new cost would be 80. Also, initially since his profit is 20%, his revenue would be 120. When he takes 4 passengers instead of 3 his revenue would go up to 160 – and his profit would become 100% (cost 80 and revenue 160).

41. Total number of microwave ovens = 15
Hence, washing machines        = 10
Thus, He sells 80% of both at a profit of ₹ 40,000.
Cost of 80% of the goods = 0.8 × 2,05,000 = 1,64,000.
Total amount recovered = 1,64,000 + 40,000 = 2,04,000
Hence, loss = ₹ 1000

42. Since the actual initial loss was 10% and it is to be compared to a profit of 5%, it is 200% of the profit. Option (c) is correct.

43. He would be selling 800 grams for ₹12. Since a kg costs ₹10 800 grams would cost ₹ 8.
Hence, his profit percentage is 50%.

44. The interpretation of the first statement is that if the loss at 275 is L, the profit at 800 is 20L.
Thus, 21L = 800 – 275 = 525 → L = 25.
Thus, the cost price of the item is ₹300.
To get a profit of 25%, the selling price should be 1.25 × 300 = 375.

45. C's purchase price = 2145 × 10/11 =1950
B's rate of profit is 3 times C's rate of profit. Hence, B sells to C at 30% profit.
B's price + 30% profit = 1950 (C's price).

Hence, B's Price = 1500.
Further, since A's profit rate is 5/3$^{rd}$ the rate of profit of B, A's profit percent would be 30 × 5/3 = 50%.
Thus, A's Price + 50% profit = 1500 (B's price)
Thus, A's price = 1000

46. He would buy at 500 and sell at 888 to get a profit of 388

47. There were 5 printers (2 + 3) and 20 monitors. He sells 2 printers for a profit of ₹ 2000 each. Hence, profit from printer sales = ₹ 4000.
Then, profit from monitor sales = ₹ 45000
Thus, profit per monitor $= \dfrac{45000}{15} = ₹\,3000$
(Since, 15 monitors were sold in all.)
Hence, C.P. of monitor    = ₹ 15000
And C.P. of Printer       = ₹ 7500
Total cost = 15000 × 20 + 7500 × 5 = 3,37,500
Total Revenues = 18000 × 15 + 9500 × 2 = 28,900
Hence, loss of ₹ 48,500

48. Loss% $= \dfrac{48,500}{3,37,500} \times 100 = 14.37\%$

49. By charging ₹ 1.2 more his profit should double to 40%. This means that his profit of 40% should be equal to ₹ 2.4. Thus, his cost price must be ₹6 and his original selling price should be 7.2. Hence, option (d) is correct.

50. Total cost = 5 lacs
Total revenue = 3000 × 160 + 1500 × 200 – vendors discount of 20% of revenues
= 7.8 lacs – 1.56 lacs = 6.24 lacs.
Profit percent = (1.24 × 100)/5 = 24.8%

*Space for Notes*

# Interest

## INTRODUCTION

The chapter on Interest forms another important topic from the CAT's point of view. Questions from this chapter are a regular feature of QA section of the Online CAT. Besides, this chapter also has the additional importance of being a core chapter for Data Interpretation.

Prior to studying this chapter however, you are required to ensure that a clear understanding of percentages and percentage calculation is a must. The faster you are at percentage calculation, the faster you will be in solving questions of interests.

However, questions on interest are still important for exams like MAT, SNAP, ATMA, CMAT, IRMA and Bank P.O. exams. Hence, if you are planning to go for the entire spectrum of management exams—this chapter retains its importance in terms of mathematics too.

Questions from LOD I and LOD II of the chapter regularly appear in exams like the Bank PO or others management exams.

## CONCEPT OF TIME VALUE OF MONEY

The value of money is not constant. This is one of the principal facts on which the entire economic world is based. A rupee today will not be equal to a rupee tomorrow. Hence, a rupee borrowed today cannot be repaid by a rupee tomorrow. This is the basic need for the concept of interest. The rate of interest is used to determine the difference between what is borrowed and what is repaid.

There are two basis on which interests are calculated:

**Simple Interest** It is calculated on the basis of a basic amount borrowed for the entire period at a particular rate

of interest. The amount borrowed is the principal for the entire period of borrowing.

**Compound Interest** The interest of the previous year/s is/are added to the principal for the calculation of the compound interest.

This difference will be clear from the following illustration:

A sum of ₹ 1000 at 10% per annum will have

| Simple interest | | Compound interest |
|---|---|---|
| ₹ 100 | First year | ₹ 100 |
| ₹ 100 | Second year | ₹ 110 |
| ₹ 100 | Third year | ₹ 121 |
| ₹ 100 | Fourth year | ₹ 133.1 |

Note that the previous years' interests are added to the original sum of ₹ 1000 to calculate the interest to be paid in the case of compound interest.

## Terminology Pertaining to Interest

The man who lends money is the **Creditor** and the man who borrows money is the **Debtor**.

The amount of money that is initially borrowed is called the **Capital** or **Principal** money.

The period for which money is deposited or borrowed is called **Time**.

The extra money, that will be paid or received for the use of the principal after a certain period is called the **Total interest** on the capital.

The sum of the principal and the interest at the end of any time is called the **Amount**.

So,  **Amount = Principal + Total Interest**.

**Rate of Interest** is the rate at which the interest is calculated and is always specified in percentage terms.

## SIMPLE INTEREST

The interest of 1 year for every ₹ 100 is called the **Interest rate** per annum. If we say "the rate of interest per annum is $r\%$", we mean that ₹ $r$ is the interest on a principal of ₹ 100 for 1 year.

### Relation Among Principal, Time, Rate Percent of Interest Per Annum and Total Interest

Suppose, Principal = ₹ $P$, Time = $t$ years, Rate of interest per annum = $r\%$ and Total interest = ₹ $I$

Then
$$I = \frac{P \times t \times r}{100}$$

i.e. Total interest

$$= \frac{\text{Principal} \times \text{Time} \times \text{Rate of interest per annum}}{100}$$

Since the Amount = Principal + Total interest, we can write

$$\therefore \quad \text{Amount } (A) = P + \frac{P \times t \times r}{100}$$

$$\text{Time} = \left(\frac{\text{Total interest}}{\text{Interest on the Principal for one year}}\right) \text{years}$$

Thus, if we have the total interest as ₹ 300 and the interest per year is ₹ 50, then we can say that the number of years is 300/50 = 6 years.

**Note:** The rate of interest is normally specified in terms of annual rate of interest. In such a case we take the time $t$ in years.

However, if the rate of interest is specified in terms of 6-monthly rate, we take time in terms of 6 months.

Also, the half-yearly rate of interest is half the annual rate of interest. That is if the interest is 10% per annum to be charged six-monthly, we have to add interest every six months @ 5%.

## COMPOUND INTEREST

In monetary transactions, often, the borrower and the lender, in order to settle an account, agree on a certain amount of interest to be paid to the lender on the basis of specified unit of time. This may be yearly or half-yearly or quarterly, with the condition that the interest accrued to the principal at a certain interval of time be added to the principal so that the total amount at the end of an interval becomes the principal for the next interval. Thus, it is different from simple interest.

In such cases, the interest for the first interval is added to the principal and this amount becomes the principal for the second interval, and so on.

The difference between the amount and the money borrowed is called the *compound interest* for the given interval.

### Formula

**Case 1:** Let principal = $P$, time = $n$ years and rate = $r\%$ per annum and let $A$ be the total amount at the end of $n$ years, then

$$A = P\left[1 + \frac{r}{100}\right]^n$$

**Case 2:** When compound interest is reckoned half-yearly.

If the annual rate is $r\%$ per annum and is to be calculated for $n$ years.

Then in this case, rate = $(r/2)\%$ half-yearly and time = $(2n)$ half-years.

$\therefore$ From the above we get

$$A = P\left[1 + \frac{r/2}{100}\right]^{2n}$$

**Case 3:** When compound interest is reckoned quarterly. In this case, rate = $(r/4)\%$ quarterly and time = $(4n)$ quarter years.

$\therefore$ As before,

$$A = P\left[1 + \frac{r/4}{100}\right]^{4n}$$

**Note:** The difference between the compound interest and the simple interest over two years is given by

$$Pr^2/100^2 \quad \text{or} \quad P\left(\frac{r}{100}\right)^2$$

## DEPRECIATION OF VALUE

The value of a machine or any other article subject to wear and tear, decreases with time.

This decrease is called its *depreciation*.

Thus if $V_0$ is the value at a certain time and $r\%$ per annum is the rate of depreciation per year, then the value $V_1$ at the end of $t$ years is

$$V_1 = V_0\left[1 - \frac{r}{100}\right]^t$$

## ☞ POPULATION

The problems on Population change are similar to the problems on Compound Interest. The formulae applicable to the problems on compound interest also apply to those on population. The only difference is that in the application of formulae, the annual rate of change of population replaces the rate of compound interest.

However, unlike in compound interest where the rate is always positive, the population can decrease. In such a case, we have to treat population change as we treated depreciation of value illustrated above.

The students should see the chapter on interests essentially as an extension of the concept of percentages. All the rules of percentage calculation, which were elucidated in the chapter of percentages, will apply to the chapter on interests. Specifically, in the case of compound interests, the percentage rule for calculation of percentage values will be highly beneficial for the student.

Besides, while solving the questions on interests the student should be aware of the possibility of using the given options to arrive at the solution. In fact, I feel that the formulae on Compound Interest (CI) unnecessarily make a very simple topic overly mathematical. Besides, the CI formulae are the most unusable formulae available in this level of mathematics since it is virtually impossible for the student to calculate a number like 1.08 raised to the power 3, 4, 5 or more.

Instead, in my opinion, you should view CI problems simply as an extension of the concept of successive percentage increases and tackle the calculations required through approximations and through the use of the percentage rule of calculations.

Thus, a calculation: 4 years increase at 6% pa CI on ₹ 120 would yield an expression: $120 \times 1.06^4$. It would be impossible for an average student to attempt such a question and even if one uses advanced techniques of calculations, one will end up using more time than one has. Instead, if you have to solve this problem, you should look at it from the following percentage change graphic perspective:

$$120 \xrightarrow[= 7.2]{+6\%} 127.2 \xrightarrow[6+1.62]{+6\%}$$

$$134.82 \xrightarrow[6+2.1]{+6\%} 142.92 \xrightarrow[6+2.58]{+6\%} 15.15 \text{ (approx.)}$$

If you try to check the answer on a calculator, you will discover that you have a very close approximation. Besides, given the fact that you would be working with options and given sufficiently comfortable options, you need not calculate so closely; instead, save time through the use of approximations.

## ☞ APPLICATIONS OF INTEREST IN D.I.

**The difference between Simple Annual Growth Rate and Compound Annual Growth Rate:**

The Measurement of Growth Rates is a prime concern in business and Economics. While a manager might be interested in calculating the growth rates in the sales of his product, an economist might be interested in finding out the rate of growth of the GDP of an economy.

In mathematical terms, there are basically two ways in which growth rates are calculated. To familiarize yourself with this, consider the following example.

The sales of a brand of scooters increase from 100 to 120 units in a particular city. What does this mean to you? Simply that there is a percentage increase of 20% in the sales of the scooters. Now read further:

What if the sales moves from 120 to 140 in the next year and 140 to 160 in the third year? Obviously, there is a constant and uniform growth from 100 to 120 to 160 – i.e. a growth of exactly 20 units per year. In terms of the overall growth in the value of the sales over there years, it can be easily seen that the sale has grown by 60 on 100 i.e. 60% growth.

In this case, what does 20% represent? If you look at this situation as a plain problem of interests 20% represents the simple interest that will make 100 grow to 160.

In the context of D.I., this value of 20% interest is also called the Simple Annual Growth Rate. (SAGR)

The process for calculating SAGR is simply the same as that for calculating Simple Interest.

Suppose a value grows from 100 to 200 in 10 years – the SAGR is got by the simple calculation 100%/10 = 10%

**What is Compound Annual Growth Rate (CAGR)?**

Let us consider a simple situation. Let us go back to the scooter company.

Suppose, the company increases it's sales by 20% in the first year and then again increases its' sales by 20% in the second year and also the third year. In such a situation, the sales (taking 100 as a starting value) trend can be easily tracked as below:

$$100 \xrightarrow[+ 20]{20\% \uparrow} 120 \xrightarrow[+ 24]{20\% \uparrow} 144 \xrightarrow[+ 28.8]{20\% \uparrow} 172.8$$

As you must have realised, this calculation is pretty similar to the calculation of Compound interests. In the above case, 20% is the rate of compound interest which will change 100 to 172.8 in three years.

This 20% is also called as the Compound Annual Growth Rate (CAGR) in the context of Data interpretation.

Obviously, the calculation of the CAGR is much more difficult than the calculation of the SAGR and the Compound Interest formula is essentially a waste of time for anything more than 3 years.

(upto three years, if you know your squares and the methods for the cubes you can still feasibly work things out

– but beyond three years it becomes pretty much infeasible to calculate the compound interest).

So is there an alternative? Yes there is and the alternative largely depends on your ability to add well. Hence, before trying out what I am about to tell you, I would recommend you should strengthen yourself at addition.

Suppose you have to calculate the C.I. on ₹ 100 at the rate of 10% per annum for a period of 10 years.

You can combine a mixture of PCG used for successive changes with guesstimation to get a pretty accurate value.

In this case, since the percentage increase is exactly 10% (Which is perhaps the easiest percentage to calculate), we can use PCG all the way as follows:

$$100 \xrightarrow[+10]{10\%\uparrow} 110 \xrightarrow[+11]{10\%\uparrow} 121 \xrightarrow[+12.1]{10\%\uparrow} 133.1$$

$$\xrightarrow[+13.31]{10\%\uparrow} 146.4$$

$$\xrightarrow[14.64]{10\%\uparrow} 161.04 \xrightarrow[16.10]{10\%\uparrow} 177.14 \xrightarrow[17.71]{10\%\uparrow} 194.8$$

$$\xrightarrow[19.48]{10\%\uparrow} \dots$$

$$214.3 \xrightarrow[21.43]{10\%\uparrow} 235.7 \xrightarrow[23.57]{10\%\uparrow} 259.2$$

Thus, the percentage increase after 10 years @ 10% will be 159.2 (approx).

However, this was the easy part. What would you do if you had to calculate 12% CI for 10 years. The percentage calculations would obviously become much more difficult and infeasible. How can we tackle this situation?

$$100 \xrightarrow[+12]{12\%\uparrow} 112 \xrightarrow[?]{12\%\uparrow} ?$$

In order to understand how to tackle the second percentage increase in the above PCG, let's try to evaluate where we are in the question.

We have to calculate 12% of 112, which is the same as 12% of 100 + 12% of 12.

But we have already calculated 12% of 100 as 12 for the first arrow of the PCG. Hence, we now have to calculate 12% of 12 and add it to 12% of 100.

Hence the addition has to be:

$$12 + 1.44 = 13.44$$

Take note of the addition of 1.44 in this step. It will be significant later. The PCG will now look like:

$$100 \longrightarrow 112 \longrightarrow 125.44 \xrightarrow[?]{12\%\uparrow} ?$$

We are now faced with a situation of calculating 12% of 125.44. Obviously, if you try to do this directly, you will have great difficulty in calculations. We can sidestep this as follows:

12% of 125.44 = 12% of 112 + 12% of 13.44.

But we have already calculated 12% of 112 as 13.44 in the previous step.

Hence, our calculation changes to:

12% of 112 + 12% of 13.44 = 13.44 + 12% of 13.44

But 12% of 13.44 = 12% of 12 + 12% of 1.44. We have already calculated 12% of 12 as 1.44 in the previous step.

Hence 12% of 13.44 = 1.44 + 12% of 1.44

$$= 1.44 + 0.17 = 1.61 \text{ (approx)}$$

Hence, the overall addition is

$$13.44 + 1.61 = 15.05$$

Now, your PCG looks like:

$$100 \xrightarrow{+12} 112 \xrightarrow{+13.44} 125.44 \xrightarrow{+15.05} 140.49$$

$$\xrightarrow{+?} ?$$

You are again at the same point—faced with calculating the rather intimidating looking 12% of 140.49

12% of 140.49 = 12% of 125.44 + 12% of 15.05

**already calculated**

Compare this to the previous calculation:

12% of 125.44 = 12% of 112 + 12% of 13.44

**already calculated**

The only calculation that has changed is that you have to calculate 12% of 15.05 instead of 12% of 13.44. (which was approx 1.61). In this case it will be approximately 1.8. Hence you shall now add 16.85 and the PCG will look as:

$$100 \xrightarrow{+12} 112 \xrightarrow{+13.44} 125.44 \xrightarrow{+15.05} 140.49$$

$$\xrightarrow{+16.85} 166.34$$

If you evaluate the change in the value added at every arrow in the PCG above, you will see a trend—

The additions were:

+12, +13.44 (change in addition = 1.44), +15.05(change in addition = 1.61), +16.85 (change in addition = 1.8)

If you now evaluate the change in the change in addition, you will realize that the values are 0.17, 0.19. This will be a slightly increasing series (And can be easily approximated).

Thus, the following table (on the next page) shows the approximate calculation of 12% CI for 10 years with an initial value of 100.

Thus, 100 becomes 309.78

(a percentage increase of 209.78%)

Similarly, in the case of every other compound interest calculation, you can simply find the trend that the first 2 – 3 years interest is going to follow and continue that trend to get a close approximate value of the overall percentage increase.

Thus for instance 7% growth for 7 years at C.I. would mean:

$$100 \xrightarrow{+7} 107 \xrightarrow{+7.49} 114.49 \xrightarrow{+8.01} 122.5$$

$$\xrightarrow{+8.55} 131.05$$

$$\xrightarrow{+9.11} 140.16 \xrightarrow{+9.75} 149.91 \xrightarrow{+10.35} 160.24$$

| At the end of | Principal (approx.) | Interest for the year | Change in Addition | Change in change in Addition |
|---|---|---|---|---|
| year 0 | 100 | +12 | | |
| | | | 1.44 | |
| year 1 | 112 | +13.44 | | 0.17 |
| | | | 1.61 | |
| year 2 | 125.44 | +15.05 | | 0.19 |
| | | | 1.8 | |
| year 3 | 140.49 | +16.85 | | 0.21 |
| | | | 2.01 | |
| year 4 | 157.36 | +18.86 | | 0.24 |
| | | | 2.25 | |
| year 5 | 176.2 | 21.11 | | 0.28 |
| | | | 2.51 | |
| year 6 | 197.3 | 23.62 | | 0.31 |
| | | | 2.79 | |
| year 7 | 220.92 | 26.41 | | |
| | | | 3.1 | 0.35 |
| year 8 | 247.33 | 29.5 | | |
| | | | 3.45 | |
| year 9 | 276.83 | 32.95 | | |
| year 10 | 309.78 | | | |

This series is approximated giving all values in this table.

An approximate growth of 60.24%

The actual value (on a calculation) is around 60.57% – Hence as you can see we have a pretty decent approximation for the answer.

*Note:* The increase in the addition will need to be increased at a greater rate than as an A.P. Thus, in this case if we had considered the increase to be an A.P. the respective addition would have been:

+7, +7.49, +8.01, +8.55, +9.11, +9.69, +10.29.

However +7, +7.49, +8.01, +8.55, +9.11, +9.75, +10.35 are the actual addition used. Notice that using 9.75 instead of 9.69 is a deliberate adjustment, since while using C.I. the impact on the addition due to the interest on the interest shows an ever increasing behaviour.

**Space for Notes**

## ⊚ WORKED-OUT PROBLEMS

**Problem 7.1** The SI on a sum of money is 25% of the principal, and the rate per annum is equal to the number of years. Find the rate percent.

(a) 4.5%  (b) 6%
(c) 5%  (d) 8%

**Solution**

Let principal = $x$, time = $t$ years
Then interest = $x/4$, rate = $t$%
Now, using the SI formula, we get
Interest = (Principal × Rate × Time)/100

$\Rightarrow$ $x/4 = (x \times t \times t)/100$
$\Rightarrow$ $t^2 = 25$
$\Rightarrow$ $t = 5\%$

Alternatively, you can also solve this by using the options, wherein you should check that when you divide 25 by the value of the option, you get the option's value as the answer.

Thus, 25/4.5 ≠ 4.5. Hence, option (a) is incorrect.

Also, 25/6 ≠ 6. Hence option (b) is incorrect.

Checking for option (c) we get, 25/5 = 5. Hence, (c) is the answer.

**Problem 7.2** The rate of interest for first 3 years is 6% per annum, for the next 4 years, 7 per cent per annum and for the period beyond 7 years, 7.5 percentages per annum. If a man lent out ₹ 1200 for 11 years, find the total interest earned by him?

(a) ₹ 1002  (b) ₹ 912
(c) ₹ 864  (d) ₹ 948

**Solution**

> Whenever it is not mentioned whether we have to assume SI or CI we should assume SI.

For any amount, interest for the 1st three years @ 6% SI will be equal to 6 × 3 = 18%

Again, interest for next 4 years will be equal to 7 × 4 = 28%.

And interest for next 4 years (till 11 years) – 7.5 × 4 = 30%

So, total interest = 18 + 28 + 30 = 76%

So, total interest earned by him = 76% of the amount

$$= \frac{(76 \times 1200)}{100} = ₹912$$

This calculation can be done very conveniently using the percentage rule as 75% + 1% = 900 + 12 = 912.

**Problem 7.3** A sum of money doubles itself in 12 years. Find the rate percentage per annum.

(a) 12.5%  (b) 8.33%
(c) 10%  (d) 7.51%

**Solution** Let principal = $x$, then interest = $x$, time = 12 years.

Using the formula, Rate = (Interest × 100)/Principal × Time

$= (x \times 100)/(x \times 12) = 8.33\%$

*Alternatively:* It is obvious that in 12 years, 100% of the amount is added as interest.

So, in 1 year = (100/12)% of the amount is added.

Hence, every year there is an addition of 8.33% (which is the rate of simple interest required).

Alternatively, you can also use the formula.

If a sum of money gets doubled in $x$ years, then rate of interest = $(100/x)\%$.

**Problem 7.4** A certain sum of money amounts to ₹ 704 in 2 years and ₹ 800 in 5 years. Find the principal.

(a) ₹ 580  (b) ₹ 600
(c) ₹ 660  (d) ₹ 640

**Solution** Let the principal be ₹ $x$ and rate = $r\%$.

Then, difference in between the interest of 5 years and of 2 years equals to

₹ 800 – ₹ 704 = ₹ 96
So, interest for 3 years = ₹ 96
Hence, interest/year = ₹ 96/3 = ₹ 32
So, interest for 2 years → 2 × ₹ 32 = ₹ 64
So, the principal = ₹ 704 – ₹ 64 = ₹ 640

Thought process here should be
₹ 96 interest in 3 years → ₹ 32 interest every year.
Hence, principal = 704 – 64 = 640

**Problems 7.5** A sum of money was invested at SI at a certain rate for 3 years. Had it been invested at a 4% higher rate, it would have fetched ₹ 480 more. Find the principal.

(a) ₹ 4000  (b) ₹ 4400
(c) ₹ 5000  (d) ₹ 3500

**Solution** Let the rate be $y\%$ and principal be ₹ $x$ and the time be 3 years.

Then according to the question = $(x(y + 4) \times 3)/100 - (xy \times 3)/100 = 480$

$\Rightarrow$ $xy + 4x - xy = 160 \times 100$
$\Rightarrow$ $x = (160 \times 100)/4 = ₹ 4000$

*Alternatively:* Excess money obtained = 3 years @ 4% per annum

$= 12\%$ of whole money

So, according to the question, 12% = ₹ 480

So, 100% = ₹ 4000 (answer arrived at by using unitary method.)

**Problem 7.6** A certain sum of money trebles itself in 8 years. In how many years it will be five times?

(a) 22 years      (b) 16 years
(c) 20 years      (d) 24 years

**Solution** It trebles itself in 8 years, which makes interest equal to 200% of principal.

So, 200% is added in 8 years.

Hence, 400%, which makes the whole amount equal to five times of the principal, which will be added in 16 years.

**Problem 7.7** If CI is charged on a certain sum for 2 years at 10% the amount becomes 605. Find the principal?

(a) ₹ 550      (b) ₹ 450
(c) ₹ 480      (d) ₹ 500

**Solution** Using the formula, amount = Principal $(1 + \text{rate}/100)^{\text{time}}$

$$605 = p(1 + 10/100)^2 = p(11/10)^2$$
$$p = 605(100/121) = ₹\ 500$$

*Alternatively:* Checking the options,

**Option (a) ₹ 550**

First year interest = ₹ 55, which gives the total amount ₹ 605 at the end of first year. So not a valid option.

**Option (b) ₹ 450**

First year interest = ₹ 45
Second year interest = ₹ 45 + 10% of ₹ 45 = 49.5
So, amount at the end of 2 years = 450 + 94.5 = 544.5
So, not valid.

Hence answer has to lie between 450 and 550 (since 450 yields a shortfall on ₹ 605 while 550 yields an excess.)

**Option (c) ₹ 480**

First year interest = ₹ 48
Second year interest = ₹ 48 + 10% of ₹ 48 = 52.8
So, amount at the end of 2 years = 580.8 ≠ 605

**Option (d) ₹ 500**

First year's interest = ₹ 50
Second year's interest = ₹ 50 + 10% of ₹ 50
                 = ₹ 55.
∴               Amount = 605.

**Note:** In general, while solving through options, the student should use the principal of starting with the middle (in terms of value), more convenient option. This will often reduce the number of options to be checked by the student, thus reducing the time required for problem solving drastically. In fact, this thumb rule should be used not only for the chapter of interests but for all other chapters in maths.

Furthermore, a look at the past question papers of exams like Lower level MBA exams and bank PO exams will yield that by solving through options and starting with the middle more convenient option, there will be significant time savings for these exams where the questions are essentially asked from the LOD I level.

**Problem 7.8** If the difference between the CI and SI on a certain sum of money is ₹ 72 at 12 per cent per annum for 2 years, then find the amount.

(a) ₹ 6000      (b) ₹ 5000
(c) ₹ 5500      (d) ₹ 6500

**Solution** Let the principal = $x$

Simple interest = $(x \times 12 \times 2)/100$
Compound interest = $x[1 + 12/100]^2 - x$
So, $x[112/100]^2 - x - 24x/100 = 72$
$x[112^2/100^2 - 1 - 24/100] = 72 \Rightarrow x[12544/10000 - 1 - 24/100] = 72$
$\Rightarrow x = 72 \times 10000/144 = ₹\ 5000$

*Alternatively:* Simple interest and compound interest for the first year on any amount is the same.

Difference in the second year's interest is due to the fact that compound interest is calculated over the first year's interest also.

Hence, we can say that ₹ 72 = Interest on first year's interest → 12% on first year's interest = ₹ 72.

Hence, first year's interest = ₹ 600 which should be 12% of the original capital. Hence, original capital = ₹ 5000 (this whole process can be done mentally).

You can also try to solve the question through the use of options as follows.

**Option (a) ₹ 6000**

First year's CI/SI = ₹ 720
Difference between second year's CI and SI = 12% of ₹ 720 ≠ ₹ 72
Hence, not correct.

**Option (b) ₹ 5000**

First year's CI/SI = 12% of ₹ 5000 = ₹ 600
Difference between second year's CI and SI = 12% of 600 = 72 year's CI and SI = 12% of 600 = ₹ 72
Hence option (b) is the correct answer.
Therefore we need not check any other options.

**Problem 7.9** The population of Jhumri Tilaiya increases by 10% in the first year, it increases by 20% in the second year and due to mass exodus, it decreases by 5% in the third year. What will be its population after 3 years, if today it is 10,000?

(a) 11,540      (b) 13,860
(c) 12,860      (d) 12,540

**Solution** Population at the end of 1 year will be → 10,000 + 10% of 10,000 = 11,000

At the end of second year it will be 11,000 + 20% of 11,000 = 13,200

At the end of third year it will be 13,200-5% of 13,200 = 12,540.

**Problem 7.10** Seth Ankoosh Gawdekar borrows a sum of ₹ 1200 at the beginning of a year. After 4 months, ₹ 1800 more is borrowed at a rate of interest double the previous one. At the end of the year, the sum of interest on both the loans is ₹ 216. What is the first rate of interest per annum?

    (a) 9%        (b) 6%
    (c) 8%        (d) 12%

**Solution** Let the rate of interest be = $r$%

Then, interest earned from ₹ 1200 at the end of year = $(1200r)/100 = ₹ 12r$

Again, interest earned from ₹ 1800 at the end of year = $(1800/100) \times (8/12) \times 2r = ₹ 24r$

So, total interest earned = $36r$, which equals 216
$\Rightarrow r = 216/36 = 6\%$

*Alternatively:* Checking the options.

**Option (a) 9%**

Interest from ₹ 1200 = 9% of 1200 = 108

Interest from ₹ 1800 = two-thirds of 18% on ₹ 1800 = 12% on ₹ 1800 = ₹ 216

Total interest = ₹ 324

**Option (b) 6%**

Interest earned from ₹ 1200 = 6% on 1200 = ₹ 72

Interest earned from ₹ 1800 = two-thirds of 12% on ₹ 1800 = ₹ 144

(We were able to calculate the interest over second part very easily after observing in option (a) that interest earned over second part is double the interest earned over first part).

Total interest = ₹ 216

We need not check any other option now.

**Problem 7.11** Rajiv lend out ₹ 9 to Anni on condition that the amount is payable in 10 months by 10 equal instal-ments of ₹ 1 each payable at the start of every month. What is the rate of interest per annum if the first instalment has to be paid one month from the date the loan is availed.

**Solution** Money coming in : ₹ 9 today
Money going out:

₹ 1 one month later + ₹ 1, 2 months later ... + ₹ 1, 10 months later.

The value of the money coming in should equal the value of the money going out for the loan to be completely paid off.

In the present case, for this to happen, the following equation has to hold:

₹ 9 + Interest on ₹ 9 for 10 months = (₹ 1 + Interest on ₹ 1 for 9 months) + (₹ 1 + interest on ₹ 1 for 8 months)

+ (₹ 1 + interest on ₹ 1 for 7 months) + (₹ 1 + interest on ₹ 1 for 6 months)

+ (₹ 1 + interest on ₹ 1 for 5 months) + (₹ 1 + interest on ₹ 1 for 4 months)

+ (₹ 1 + interest on ₹ 1 for 3 months) + (₹ 1 + interest on ₹ 1 for 2 months)

+ (₹ 1 + interest on ₹ 1 for 1 months) + (₹ 1)

₹ 9 + Interest on ₹ 1 for 90 months = ₹ 10 + Interest on ₹ 10 for 45 months.

→ Interest on ₹ 1 for 90 months – Interest on ₹ 1 for 45 months = ₹ 10 – ₹ 9

→ Interest on ₹ 1 for 45 months = ₹ 1 (i.e. money would double in 45 months.)

Hence the rate of interest = $\dfrac{100\%}{45}$ = 2.222% per month.

So, the annual rate of interest = 26.66% per annum.

**Note:** The starting equation used to solve this problem comes from crediting the borrower with the interest due to early payment for each of his first nine instalments.

*Space for Rough Work*

## LEVEL OF DIFFICULTY (I)

1. ₹ 1200 is lent out at 5% per annum simple interest for 3 years. Find the amount after 3 years.
   - (a) ₹ 1380
   - (b) ₹ 1290
   - (c) ₹ 1470
   - (d) ₹ 1200

2. Interest obtained on a sum of ₹ 5000 for 3 years is ₹ 1500. Find the rate percent.
   - (a) 8%
   - (b) 9%
   - (c) 10%
   - (d) 11%

3. ₹ 2100 is lent at compound interest of 5% per annum for 2 years. Find the amount after two years.
   - (a) ₹ 2300
   - (b) ₹ 2315.25
   - (c) ₹ 2310
   - (d) ₹ 2320

4. ₹ 1694 is repaid after two years at compound interest. Which of the following is the value of the principal and the rate?
   - (a) ₹ 1200, 20%
   - (b) ₹ 1300, 15%
   - (c) ₹ 1400, 10%
   - (d) ₹ 1500, 12%

5. Find the difference between the simple and the compound interest at 5% per annum for 2 years on a principal of ₹ 2000.
   - (a) 5
   - (b) 105
   - (c) 4.5
   - (d) 5.5

6. Find the rate of interest if the amount after 2 years of simple interest on a capital of ₹ 1200 is ₹ 1440.
   - (a) 8%
   - (b) 9%
   - (c) 10%
   - (d) 11%

7. After how many years will a sum of ₹ 12,500 become ₹ 17,500 at the rate of 10% per annum?
   - (a) 2 years
   - (b) 3 years
   - (c) 4 years
   - (d) 5 years

8. What is the difference between the simple interest on a principal of ₹ 500 being calculated at 5% per annum for 3 years and 4% per annum for 4 years?
   - (a) ₹ 5
   - (b) ₹ 10
   - (c) ₹ 20
   - (d) ₹ 40

9. What is the simple interest on a sum of ₹700 if the rate of interest for the first 3 years is 8% per annum and for the last 2 years is 7.5% per annum?
   - (a) ₹ 269.5
   - (b) ₹ 283
   - (c) ₹ 273
   - (d) ₹ 280

10. What is the simple interest for 9 years on a sum of ₹ 800 if the rate of interest for the first 4 years is 8% per annum and for the last 4 years is 6% per annum?

    - (a) 400
    - (b) 392
    - (c) 352
    - (d) Cannot be determined

11. What is the difference between compound interest and simple interest for the sum of ₹ 20,000 over a 2 year period if the compound interest is calculated at 20% and simple interest is calculated at 23%?
    - (a) ₹ 400
    - (b) ₹ 460
    - (c) ₹ 440
    - (d) ₹ 450

12. Find the compound interest on ₹ 1000 at the rate of 20% per annum for 18 months when interest is compounded half-yearly.
    - (a) ₹ 331
    - (b) ₹ 1331
    - (c) ₹ 320
    - (d) ₹ 325

13. Find the principal if the interest compounded at the rate of 10% per annum for two years is ₹ 420.
    - (a) ₹ 2000
    - (b) ₹ 2200
    - (c) ₹ 1000
    - (d) ₹ 1100

14. Find the principal if compound interest is charged on the principal at the rate of $16\frac{2}{3}\%$ per annum for two years and the sum becomes ₹ 196.
    - (a) ₹ 140
    - (b) ₹ 154
    - (c) ₹ 150
    - (d) ₹ 144

15. The SBI lent ₹ 1331 to the Tata group at a compound interest and got ₹ 1728 after three years. What is the rate of interest charged if the interest is compounded annually?
    - (a) 11%
    - (b) 9.09%
    - (c) 12%
    - (d) 8.33%

16. In what time will ₹ 3300 become ₹ 3399 at 6% per annum interest compounded half-yearly?
    - (a) 6 months
    - (b) 1 year
    - (c) $1\frac{1}{2}$ year
    - (d) 3 months

17. Ranjan purchased a Maruti van for ₹ 1,96,000 and the rate of depreciation is $14\frac{2}{7}\%$ per annum. Find the value of the van after two years.
    - (a) ₹ 1,40,000
    - (b) ₹ 1,44,000
    - (c) ₹ 1,50,000
    - (d) ₹ 1,60,000

18. At what percentage per annum, will ₹ 10,000 amount to 17,280 in three years? (Compound Interest being reckoned)
    - (a) 20%
    - (b) 14%
    - (c) 24%
    - (d) 11%

19. Vinay deposited ₹ 8000 in ICICI Bank, which pays him 12% interest per annum compounded

quarterly. What is the amount that he receives after 15 months?

(a) ₹ 9274.2     (b) ₹ 9228.8

(c) ₹ 9314.3     (d) ₹ 9338.8

20. What is the rate of simple interest for the first 4 years if the sum of ₹ 360 becomes ₹ 540 in 9 years and the rate of interest for the last 5 years is 6%?

(a) 4%     (b) 5%

(c) 3%     (d) 6%

21. Harsh makes a fixed deposit of ₹ 20,000 with the Bank of India for a period of 3 years. If the rate of interest be 13% SI per annum charged half-yearly, what amount will he get after 42 months?

(a) 27,800     (b) 28,100

(c) 29,100     (d) 28,500

22. Ranjeet makes a deposit of ₹ 50,000 in the Punjab National Bank for a period of $2\frac{1}{2}$ years. If the rate of interest is 12% per annum compounded half-yearly, find the maturity value of the money deposited by him.

(a) 66,911.27     (b) 66,123.34

(c) 67,925.95     (d) 65,550.8

23. Vinod makes a deposit of ₹ 100,000 in Syndicate Bank for a period of 2 years. If the rate of interest be 12% per annum compounded half-yearly, what amount will he get after 2 years?

(a) 122,247.89     (b) 125,436.79

(c) 126,247.69     (d) 122436.89

24. What will be the simple interest on ₹ 700 at 9% per annum for the period from February 5, 1994 to April 18, 1994?

(a) ₹ 12.60     (b) ₹ 11.30

(c) ₹ 15     (d) ₹ 13

25. Ajay borrows ₹ 1500 from two moneylenders. He pays interest at the rate of 12% per annum for one loan and at the rate of 14% per annum for the other. The total interest he pays for the entire year is ₹ 186. How much does he borrow at the rate of 12%?

(a) ₹ 1200     (b) ₹ 1300

(c) ₹ 1400     (d) ₹ 300

26. A sum was invested at simple interest at a certain interest for 2 years. It would have fetched ₹ 60 more had it been invested at 2% higher rate. What was the sum?

(a) ₹ 1500     (b) ₹ 1300

(c) ₹ 2500     (d) ₹ 1000

27. The difference between simple and compound interest on a sum of money at 5% per annum is ₹ 25. What is the sum?

(a) ₹ 5000     (b) ₹ 10,000

(c) ₹ 4000     (d) Data insufficient

28. A sum of money is borrowed and paid back in two equal annual instalments of ₹ 882, allowing 5% compound interest. The sum borrowed was

(a) ₹ 1640     (b) ₹ 1680

(c) ₹ 1620     (d) ₹ 1700

29. Two equal sums were borrowed at 8% simple interest per annum for 2 years and 3 years respectively. The difference in the interest was ₹ 56. The sum borrowed were

(a) ₹ 690     (b) ₹ 700

(c) ₹ 740     (d) ₹ 780

30. In what time will the simple interest on ₹ 1750 at 9% per annum be the same as that on ₹ 2500 at 10.5% per annum in 4 years?

(a) 6 years and 8 months

(b) 7 years and 3 months

(c) 6 years

(d) 7 years and 6 months

31. In what time will ₹ 500 give ₹ 50 as interest at the rate of 5% per annum simple interest?

(a) 2 years     (b) 5 years

(c) 3 years     (d) 4 years

32. Shashikant derives an annual income of ₹ 688.25 from ₹ 10,000 invested partly at 8% p.a. and partly at 5% p.a. simple interest. How much of his money is invested at 5% ?

(a) ₹ 5000     (b) ₹ 4225

(c) ₹ 4800     (d) ₹ 3725

33. If the difference between the simple interest and compound interest on some principal amount at 20% per annum for 3 years is ₹ 48, then the principle amount must be

(a) ₹ 550     (b) ₹ 500

(c) ₹ 375     (d) ₹ 400

34. Raju lent ₹ 400 to Ajay for 2 years, and ₹ 100 to Manoj for 4 years and received together from both ₹ 60 as interest. Find the rate of interest, simple interest being calculated..

(a) 5%     (b) 6%

(c) 8%     (d) 9%

35. In what time will ₹ 8000 amount to 40,000 at 4% per annum? (simple interest being reckoned)

(a) 100 years     (b) 50 years

(c) 110 years     (d) 160 years

36. What annual payment will discharge a debt of ₹ 808 due in 2 years at 2% per annum?

(a) ₹ 200     (b) ₹ 300

(c) ₹ 400     (d) ₹ 350

37. A sum of money becomes 4 times at simple interest in 10 years. What is the rate of interest?

(a) 10%                    (b) 20%

(c) 30%                    (d) 40%

38. A sum of money doubles itself in 5 years. In how many years will it become four fold (if interest is compounded)?

    (a) 15                    (b) 10

    (c) 20                    (d) 12

39. A difference between the interest received from two different banks on ₹ 400 for 2 years is ₹ 4. What is the difference between their rates?

    (a) 0.5%                  (b) 0.2%

    (c) 0.23%                 (d) 0.52%

40. A sum of money placed at compound interest doubles itself in 3 years. In how many years will it amount to 8 times itself?

    (a) 9 years               (b) 8 years

    (c) 27 years              (d) 7 years

41. If the compound interest on a certain sum for 2 years is ₹ 21. What could be the simple interest?

    (a) ₹ 20                  (b) ₹ 16

    (c) ₹ 18                  (d) ₹ 20.5

42. Divide ₹ 6000 into two parts so that simple interest on the first part for 2 years at 6% p.a. may be equal to the simple interest on the second part for 3 years at 8% p.a.

    (a) ₹ 4000, ₹ 2000        (b) ₹ 5000, ₹ 1000

    (c) ₹ 3000, ₹ 3000        (d) None of these

43. Divide ₹ 3903 between Amar and Akbar such that Amar's share at the end of 7 years is equal to Akbar's share at the end of 9 years at 4% p.a. rate of compound interest.

    (a) Amar = ₹ 2028, Akbar = ₹ 1875

    (b) Amar = ₹ 2008, Akbar = ₹ 1000

    (c) Amar = ₹ 2902, Akbar = ₹ 1001

    (d) Amar = ₹ 2600, Akbar = ₹ 1303

44. A sum of money becomes 7/4 of itself in 6 years at a certain rate of simple interest. Find the rate of interest.

(a) 12%                    (b) 12.5%

(c) 8%                     (d) 14%

45. Sanjay borrowed ₹ 900 at 4% p.a. and ₹ 1100 at 5% p.a. for the same duration. He had to pay ₹ 364 in all as interest. What is the time period in years?

    (a) 5 years              (b) 3 years

    (c) 2 years              (d) 4 years

46. If the difference between compound and simple interest on a certain sum of money for 3 years at 2% p.a. is ₹ 604, what is the sum?

    (a) 5,00,000             (b) 4,50,000

    (c) 5,10,000             (d) None of these

47. If a certain sum of money becomes double at simple interest in 12 years, what would be the rate of interest per annum?

    (a) 8.33                 (b) 10

    (c) 12                   (d) 14

48. Three persons Amar, Akbar and Anthony invested different amounts in a fixed deposit scheme for one year at the rate of 12% per annum and earned a total interest of ₹ 3,240 at the end of the year. If the amount invested by Akbar is ₹ 5000 more than the amount invested by Amar and the amount invested by Anthony is ₹ 2000 more than the amount invested by Akbar, what is the amount invested by Akbar?

    (a) ₹ 12,000             (b) ₹ 10,000

    (c) ₹ 7000               (d) ₹ 5000

49. A sum of ₹ 600 amounts to ₹ 720 in 4 years at Simple Interest. What will it amount to if the rate of interest is increased by 2%?

    (a) ₹ 648                (b) ₹ 768

    (c) ₹ 726                (d) ₹ 792

50. What is the amount of equal instalment, if a sum of ₹1428 due 2 years hence has to be completely repaid in 2 equal annual instalments starting next year.

    (a) 700                  (b) 800

    (c) 650                  (d) Cannot be determined

***Space for Rough Work***

# LEVEL OF DIFFICULTY (II)

1. A sum of money invested at simple interest triples itself in 8 years at simple interest. Find in how many years will it become 8 times itself at the same rate?
   - (a) 24 years
   - (b) 28 years
   - (c) 30 years
   - (d) 21 years

2. A sum of money invested at simple interest triples itself in 8 years. How many times will it become in 20 years time?
   - (a) 8 times
   - (b) 7 times
   - (c) 6 times
   - (d) 9 times

3. If ₹ 1100 is obtained after lending out ₹ $x$ at 5% per annum for 2 years and ₹ 1800 is obtained after lending out ₹ $y$ at 10% per annum for 2 years, find $x + y$.
   - (a) ₹ 2500
   - (b) ₹ 3000
   - (c) ₹ 2000
   - (d) ₹ 2200

**Directions for Questions 4 to 6:** Read the following and answer the questions that follow.

4. A certain sum of money was lent under the following repayment scheme based on Simple Interest:
   8% per annum for the initial 2 years
   9.5% per annum for the next 4 years
   11% per annum for the next 2 years
   12% per annum after the first 8 years
   Find the amount which a sum of ₹ 9000 taken for 12 years becomes at the end of 12 years.
   - (a) 20,200
   - (b) 19,800
   - (c) 20,000
   - (d) 20,160

5. If a person repaid ₹ 22,500 after 10 years of borrowing a loan, at 10% per annum simple interest find out what amount did he take as a loan?
   - (a) 11,225
   - (b) 11,250
   - (c) 10,000
   - (d) 7500

6. Mr. $X$, a very industrious person, wants to establish his own unit. For this he needs an instant loan of ₹ 5,00,000 and, every five years he requires an additional loan of ₹100,000. If he had to clear all his outstandings in 20 years, and he repays the principal of the first loan equally over the 20 years, find what amount he would have to pay as interest on his initial borrowing if the rate of interest is 10% p.a. Simple Interest.
   - (a) ₹ 560,000
   - (b) ₹ 540,000
   - (c) ₹ 525,000
   - (d) ₹ 500,000

7. The population of a city is 200,000. If the annual birth rate and the annual death rate are 6% and 3% respectively, then calculate the population of the city after 2 years.
   - (a) 212,090
   - (b) 206,090
   - (c) 212,000
   - (d) 212,180

8. A part of ₹ 38,800 is lent out at 6% per six months. The rest of the amount is lent out at 5% per annum after one year. The ratio of interest after 3 years from the time when first amount was lent out is 5 : 4. Find the second part that was lent out at 5%.
   - (a) ₹ 26,600
   - (b) ₹ 28,800
   - (c) ₹ 27,500
   - (d) ₹ 28,000

9. If the simple interest is 10.5% annual and compound interest is 10% annual, find the difference between the interests after 3 years on a sum of ₹ 1000.
   - (a) ₹ 15
   - (b) ₹ 12
   - (c) ₹ 16
   - (d) ₹ 11

10. A sum of ₹ 1000 after 3 years at compound interest becomes a certain amount that is equal to the amount that is the result of a 3 year depreciation from ₹ 1728. Find the difference between the rates of CI and depreciation. (Given CI is 10% p.a.). (Approximately)
    - (a) 3.33%
    - (b) 0.66%
    - (c) 3%
    - (d) 2%

11. The RBI lends a certain amount to the SBI on simple interest for two years at 20%. The SBI gives this entire amount to Bharti Telecom on compound interest for two years at the same rate annually. Find the percentage earning of the SBI at the end of two years on the entire amount.
    - (a) 4%
    - (b) 3(1/7)%
    - (c) 3(2/7)%
    - (d) 3(6/7)%

12. Find the compound interest on ₹ 64,000 for 1 year at the rate of 10% per annum compounded quarterly (to the nearest integer).
    - (a) ₹ 8215
    - (b) ₹ 8205
    - (c) ₹ 8185
    - (d) None of these

13. If a principal $P$ becomes $Q$ in 2 years when interest $R$% is compounded half-yearly. And if the same principal $P$ becomes $Q$ in 2 years when interest $S$% is compound annually, then which of the following is true?
    - (a) $R > S$
    - (b) $R = S$
    - (c) $R < S$
    - (d) $R \le S$

14. Find the compound interest at the rate of 10% for 3 years on that principal which in 3 years at the rate of 10% per annum gives ₹ 300 as simple interest.

(a) ₹ 331       (b) ₹ 310

(c) ₹ 330       (d) ₹ 333

15. The difference between CI and SI on a certain sum of money at 10% per annum for 3 years is ₹ 620. Find the principal if it is known that the interest is compounded annually.

    (a) ₹ 200,000       (b) ₹ 20,000

    (c) ₹ 10,000       (d) ₹ 100,000

16. The population of Mangalore was 1283575 on 1 January 2011 and the growth rate of population was 10% in the last year and 5% in the years prior to it, the only exception being 2009 when because of a huge exodus there was a decline of 20% in population. What was the population on January 1, 2005?

    (a) 1,000,000       (b) 1,200,000

    (c) 1,250,000       (d) 1,500,000

17. According to the 2011 census, the population growth rate of Lucknow is going to be an increasing AP with first year's rate as 5% and common difference as 5%, but simultaneously the migration, rate is an increasing GP with first term as 1% and common ratio of 2. If the population on 31 December 2010 is 1 million, then find in which year will Lucknow witness its first fall in population?

    (a) 2015       (b) 2016

    (c) 2017       (d) 2018

18. Mohit Anand borrows a certain sum of money from the Mindworkzz Bank at 10% per annum at compound interest. The entire debt is discharged in full by Mohit Anand on payment of two equal amounts of ₹ 1000 each, one at the end of the first year and the other at the end of the second year. What is the approximate value of the amount borrowed by him?

    (a) ₹ 1852       (b) ₹ 1736

    (c) ₹ 1694       (d) ₹ 1792

19. In order to buy a car, a man borrowed ₹ 180,000 on the condition that he had to pay 7.5% interest every year. He also agreed to repay the principal in equal annual instalments over 21 years. After a certain number of years, however, the rate of interest has been reduced to 7%. It is also known that at the end of the agreed period, he will have paid in all ₹ 270,900 in interest. For how many years does he pay at the reduced interest rate?

    (a) 7 years       (b) 12 years

    (c) 14 years       (d) 16 years

20. A sum of ₹ 8000 is borrowed at 5% p.a. compound interest and paid back in 3 equal annual instalments. What is the amount of each instalment?

    (a) ₹ 2937.67       (b) ₹ 3000

    (c) ₹ 2037.67       (d) ₹ 2739.76

21. Three amounts $x$, $y$ and $z$ are such that $y$ is the simple interest on $x$ and $z$ is the simple interest on $y$. If in all the three cases, rate of interest per annum and the time for which interest is calculated is the same, then find the relation between $x$, $y$ and $z$.

    (a) $xyz = 1$       (b) $x^2 = yz$

    (c) $z = x^2y$       (d) $y^2 = xz$

22. A person lent out some money for 1 year at 6% per annum simple interest and after 18 months, he again lent out the same money at a simple interest of 24% per annum. In both the cases, he got ₹ 4704. Which of these could be the amount that was lent out in each case if interest is paid half-yearly?

    (a) ₹ 4000       (b) ₹ 4400

    (c) ₹ 4200       (d) ₹ 3600

23. A person bought a motorbike under the following scheme: Down payment of ₹ 15,000 and the rest amount at 8% per annum for 2 years. In this way, he paid ₹ 28,920 in total. Find the actual price of the motorbike. (Assume simple interest).

    (a) ₹ 26,000       (b) ₹ 27,000

    (c) ₹ 27,200       (d) ₹ 26,500

24. Hans Kumar borrows ₹ 7000 at simple interest from the village moneylender. At the end of 3 years, he again borrows ₹ 3000 and closes his account after paying ₹ 4615 as interest after 8 years from the time he made the first borrowing. Find the rate of interest.

    (a) 3.5%       (b) 4.5%

    (c) 5.5%       (d) 6.5%

25. Some amount was lent at 6% per annum simple interest. After one year, ₹ 6800 is repaid and the rest of the amount is repaid at 5% per annum. If the second year's interest is half of the first year's interest, find what amount of money was lent out.

    (a) ₹ 17,000       (b) ₹ 16,800

    (c) ₹ 16,500       (d) ₹ 17,500

26. An amount of ₹ 12820 due 3 years hence, is fully repaid in three annual instalments starting after 1 year. The first instalment is 1/2 the second instalment and the second instalment is 2/3 of the third instalment. If the rate of interest is 10% per annum, find the first instalment.

    (a) ₹ 2400       (b) ₹ 1800

    (c) ₹ 2000       (d) ₹ 2500

**Directions for Questions 27 and 28:** Read the following and answer the questions that follow.

The leading Indian bank ISBI, in the aftermath of the Kargil episode, announced a loan scheme for the Indian Army. Under this scheme; the following options were available.

| | Loans upto | Soft loan | Interest (Normal) |
|---|---|---|---|
| Scheme 1 | ₹ 50,000 | 50% of total | 8% |
| Scheme 2 | ₹ 75,000 | 40% of total | 10% |
| Scheme 3 | ₹ 100,000 | 30% of total | 12% |
| Scheme 4 | ₹ 200,000 | 20% of total | 14% |

Soft loan is a part of the total loan and the interest on this loan is half the normal rate of interest charged.

27. Soldier *A* took some loan under scheme 1, soldier *B* under scheme 2, soldier *C* under scheme 3 and soldier *D* under scheme 4. If they get the maximum loan under their respective schemes for one year, find which loan is MUL (MUL—Maximum Utility Loan, is defined as the ratio of the total loan to interest paid over the time. Lower this ratio the better the MUL).
    (a) *A*　　　　　　(b) *B*
    (c) *C*　　　　　　(d) *D*

28. Extending this plan, ISBI further announced that widows of all the martyrs can get the loans in which the proportion of soft loan will be double. This increase in the proportion of the soft loan component is only applicable for the first year. For all subsequent years, the soft loan component applicable on the loan, follows the values provided in the table. The widow of a soldier takes ₹ 40,000 under scheme 1 in one account for 1 year and ₹ 60,000 under scheme 2 for 2 years. Find the total interest paid by her over the 2 year period.
    (a) ₹ 11,600　　　　(b) ₹ 10,000
    (c) ₹ 8800　　　　　(d) None of these

29. A sum is divided between *A* and *B* in the ratio of 1 : 2. *A* purchased a car from his part, which depreciates $14\frac{2}{7}\%$ per annum and *B* deposited his amount in a bank, which pays him 20% interest per annum compounded annually. By what percentage will the total sum of money increase after two years due to this investment pattern (approximately)?
    (a) 20%　　　　　　(b) 26.66%
    (c) 30%　　　　　　(d) 25%

30. Michael Bolton has $90,000 with him. He purchases a car, a laptop and a flat for $15,000, $13,000 and $35,000 respectively and puts the remaining money in a bank deposit that pays compound interest @15% per annum. After 2 years, he sells off the three items at 80% of their original price and also withdraws his entire money from the bank by closing the account. What is the total change in his asset?
    (a) −4.5%　　　　　(b) +3.5%
    (c) −4.32%　　　　(d) +5.5%

*Space for Rough Work*

# ANSWER KEY

### Level of Difficulty (I)

| | | | |
|---|---|---|---|
| 1. (a) | 2. (c) | 3. (b) | 4. (c) |
| 5. (a) | 6. (c) | 7. (c) | 8. (a) |
| 9. (c) | 10. (d) | 11. (a) | 12. (a) |
| 13. (a) | 14. (d) | 15. (b) | 16. (a) |
| 17. (b) | 18. (a) | 19. (a) | 20. (b) |
| 21. (c) | 22. (a) | 23. (c) | 24. (a) |
| 25. (a) | 26. (a) | 27. (d) | 28. (a) |
| 29. (b) | 30. (a) | 31. (a) | 32. (d) |
| 33. (c) | 34. (a) | 35. (a) | 36. (c) |
| 37. (c) | 38. (b) | 39. (a) | 40. (a) |
| 41. (a) | 42. (a) | 43. (a) | 44. (b) |
| 45. (d) | 46. (a) | 47. (a) | 48. (b) |
| 49. (b) | 50. (d) | | |

### Level of Difficulty (II)

| | | | |
|---|---|---|---|
| 1. (b) | 2. (c) | 3. (a) | 4. (d) |
| 5. (b) | 6. (c) | 7. (d) | 8. (b) |
| 9. (c) | 10. (d) | 11. (a) | 12. (d) |
| 13. (c) | 14. (a) | 15. (b) | 16. (b) |
| 17. (b) | 18. (b) | 19. (c) | 20. (a) |
| 21. (d) | 22. (c) | 23. (b) | 24. (d) |
| 25. (a) | 26. (c) | 27. (a) | 28. (b) |
| 29. (a) | 30. (c) | | |

## Solutions and Shortcuts

### Level of Difficulty (I)

1. The annual interest would be ₹ 60. After 3 years the total value would be $1200 + 60 \times 3 = 1380$

2. The interest earned per year would be $1500/3 = 500$. This represents a 10% rate of interest.

3. $2100 + 5\%$ of $2100 = 2100 + 105 = 2205$ (after 1 year). Next year it would become:
$2205 + 5\%$ of $2205 = 2205 + 110.25 = 2315.25$

4. $1400 \xrightarrow{10\%\uparrow} 1540 \xrightarrow{10\%\uparrow} 1694$.

5. Simple Interest for 2 years $= 100 + 100 = 200$.
Compound interest for 2 years: Year 1 = 5% of 2000 = 100.
Year 2: 5% of 2100 = 105 → Total compound interest = ₹ 205.
Difference between the Simple and Compound interest = $205 - 200 = ₹ 5$

6. Interest in 2 years = ₹ 240.
Interest per year = ₹ 120
Rate of interest = 10%

7. 12500 @ 10% simple interest would give an interest of ₹ 1250 per annum. For a total interest of ₹ 5000, it would take 4 years.

8. 5% for 3 years (SI) = 15% of the amount; At the same time 4% SI for 4 years means 16% of the amount. The difference between the two is 1% of the amount. 1% of 500 = ₹ 5

9. 8% @ 700 = ₹ 56 per year for 3 years
7.5% @ 700 = ₹ 52.5 per year for 2 years
Total interest = $56 \times 3 + 52.5 \times 2 = 273$.

10. 8% of 800 for 4 years + 6% of 800 for 4 years = $64 \times 4 + 48 \times 4 = 256 + 192 = 448$. However, we do not know the rate of interest applicable in the 5th year and hence cannot determine the exact simple interest for 9 years.

11. Simple interest @ 23% = $4600 \times 2 = 9200$
Compound interest @ 20%
$$20000 \xrightarrow{20\%\uparrow} 24000 \xrightarrow{20\%\uparrow} 28800$$
→ ₹ 8800 compound interest.
Difference = $9200 - 8800 = ₹ 400$.

12. $1000 \xrightarrow{10\%\uparrow} 1100 \xrightarrow{10\%\uparrow} 1210 \xrightarrow{10\%\uparrow} 1331$.
Compound interest = $1331 - 1000 = ₹ 331$

13. Solve using options. Thinking about option (a):
$2000 \to 2200$ (after 1 year) $\to 2420$ (after 2 years) which gives us an interest of ₹420 as required in the problem. Hence, this is the correct answer.

14. $P \times 7/6 \times 7/6 = 196 \to P = (196 \times 6 \times 6)/7 \times 7 = 144$.

15. $1331 \times 1.090909 \times 1.090909 \times 1.090909 = 1331 \times 12/11 \times 12/11 \times 12/11 = 1728$. Hence, the rate of compound interest is 9.09%.

16. Since compounding is half yearly, it is clear that the rate of interest charged for 6 months would be 3%
$3300 \xrightarrow{3\%\uparrow} 3399$.

17. The value of the van would be $196000 \times 6/7 \times 6/7 = 144000$

18. Solve through options:
$10000 \xrightarrow{20\%\uparrow} 12000 \xrightarrow{20\%\uparrow} 14400 \xrightarrow{20\%\uparrow} 17280$.

19. 12% per annum compounded quarterly means that the amount would grow by 3% every 3 months.
Thus, $8000 \to 8000 + 3\%$ of $8000 = 8240$ after 3 months $\to 8240 + 3\%$ of $8240 = 8487.2$ after 6 months and so on till five 3 month time periods get over. It can be seen that the value would turn out to be 9274.2.

20. For the last 5 years, the interest earned would be: 30% of 360 = 108. Thus, interest earned in the first 4 years would be ₹ 72 → ₹ 18 every year on an amount of ₹ 360- which means that the rate of interest is 5%

21. He will get $20000 + 45.5\%$ of $20000 = 29100$.
[Note: In this case we can take 13% simple interest

compounded half yearly to mean 6.5% interest getting added every 6 months. Thus, in 42 months it would amount to 6.5 × 7 = 45.5%]

22. $50000 \xrightarrow{6\%\uparrow} 53000 \xrightarrow{6\%\uparrow} 56180 \xrightarrow{6\%\uparrow}$
    $59550.8 \xrightarrow{6\%\uparrow} 63123.84 \xrightarrow{6\%\uparrow} 66911.27$

23. 100000 + 6% of 100000 (after the first 6 months) = 106000.

    After 1 year: 106000 + 6% of 106000 = 112360

    After 1 ½ years: 112360 + 6% of 112360 = 119101.6

    After 2 years: 119101.6 + 6% of 119101.6 = 126247.69

24. $(73/365) \times 0.09 \times 700 = ₹ 12.6$.

    (Since the time period is 73 days)

25. The average rate of interest he pays is 186 × 100/1500 = 12.4%.

    The average rate of interest being 12.4%, it means that the ratio in which the two amounts would be distributed would be 4:1 (using alligation). Thus, the borrowing at 12% would be ₹ 1200.

26. Based on the information we have, we can say that there would have been ₹ 30 extra interest per year. For 2% of the principal to be equal to ₹ 30, the principal amount should be ₹ 1500

27. The data is insufficient as we do not know the time period involved.

28. $882 \times (1.05) + 882 = P \times (1.05)^2$

    Solve for $P$ to get $P = 1640$

29. The difference would amount to 8% of the value borrowed. Thus 56 = 0.08 × sum borrowed in each case → Sum borrowed = ₹ 700.

30. 42% on 2500 = ₹ 1050. The required answer would be: 1050/157.5 = 6 years and 8 months.

31. Interest per year = ₹ 25. Thus, an interest of ₹ 50 would be earned in 2 years.

32. The average Rate of interest is 6.8825%. The ratio of investments would be 1.1175: 1.8825 (@5% is to 8%). The required answer = 10000 × 1.1175/3 = 3725.

33. Solve using options. If we try 500 (option b) for convenience, we can see that the difference between the two is ₹ 64 (as the SI would amount to 300 and CI would amount to 100 + 120 + 144 = 364).

    Since, we need a difference of only ₹ 48 we can realize that the value should be 3/4ᵗʰ of 500. Hence, 375 is correct.

34. Total effective amount lent for 1 year
    $$= ₹ 400 \times 2 + ₹ 100 \times 4 = ₹ 1200$$
    Interest being ₹ 60, Rate of interest 5%

35. The value would increase by 4% per year. To go to 5 times it's original value, it would require an increment of 400%. At 4% SI it would take 100 years.

36. $A \times (1.02) + A = 808 \times (1.02)^2 \rightarrow A = ₹ 400$

37. The sum becomes 4 times → the interest earned is 300% of the original amount. In 10 years the interest is 300% means that the yearly interest must be 30%.

38. It would take another 5 years to double again. Thus, a total of 10 years to become four fold.

39. The difference in Simple interest represents 1% of the amount invested. Since this difference has occurred in 2 years, annually the difference would be 0.5%.

40. If it doubles in 3 years, it would become 4 times in 6 year and 8 times in 9 years.

41. If we take the principal as 100, the CI @ 10% Rate of interest would be ₹ 21. In such a case, the SI would be ₹ 20.

42. 12% of x = 24% of (600 − x) → x = 4000

    Thus, the two parts should be ₹ 4000 and ₹ 2000.

43. Akbars' share should be such that at 4% p.a. compound interest it should become equal to Amar's share in 2 years. Checking thorugh the options it is clear that option (a) fits perfectly as 1875 would become 2028 in 2 years @4% p.a. compound interest.

44. The total interest in 6 years = 75%

    Thus per year = SI = 12.5%

45. The interest he pays per year would be 36 + 55 = 91. Thus, in 4 years the interest would amount to ₹ 364.

46. Solve through trial and error using the values of the options. Option (a) 500000 fits the situation perfectly as the SI = ₹ 30000 while the CI = 30604.

47. 100/12 = 8.33%

48. 12% Rate of interest on the amount invested gives an interest of ₹ 3240. This means that 0.12 A = 3240 → A = ₹ 27000. The sum of the investments should be ₹ 27000. If Akbar invests x, Amar invests x − 5000 and Anthony invests x + 2000. Thus:

    x + x − 5000 + x + 2000 = 27000 → x = 10000.

49. 600 becomes 720 in 4 years SI → SI per year = ₹ 30 and hence the SI rate is 5%.

    At 7% rate of interest the value of 600 would become 768 in 4 years. (600 + 28% of 600)

50. The rate of interest is not defined.

    Hence, option (d) is correct.

### Level of Difficulty (II)

1. In 8 years, the interest earned = 200%

    Thus, per year interest rate = 200/8 = 25%

    To become 8 times we need a 700% increase
    $$700/25 = 28 \text{ years.}$$

2. Tripling in 8 years means that the interest earned in 8 years is equal to 200% of the capital value. Thus, interest per year (simple interest) is 25% of the capital. In 20 years, total interest earned = 500%

of the capital and hence the capital would become 6 times it's original value.

3. $x = ₹ 1000$ (As 1000 @ 5% for 2 years = 1100).
   Similarly $y = ₹ 1500$.
   $$x + y = 2500.$$

4. $9000 + 720 + 720 + 855 + 855 + 855 + 855 + 990 + 990 + 1080 + 1080 + 1080 + 1080$
   $= 9000 + 720 \times 2 + 855 \times 4 + 990 \times 2 + 1080 \times 4$
   $= 20160$

5. At 10% simple interest per year, the amount would double in 10 years. Thus, the original borrowin would be 22500/2 = 11250.

6. The simple interest would be defined on the basis of the sum of the AP.
   $50000 + 47500 + 45000 + \ldots + 2500 = 525000$.

7. The yearly increase in the population is 3%. Thus, the population would increase by 3% each year. 200000 would become 206000 while 206000 would become 212180.

8. $$\frac{F \times (0.06) \times 6}{(38800 - F) \times 0.05 \times 2} = 5/4$$
   where $F$ is the first part.
   $$1.44F = 19400 - 0.5F$$
   $$F = 19400/1.94 = 10000.$$
   Thus, the second part = 38800 − 10000 = 28800

9. At 10% compound interest the interest in 3 years would be 33.1% = ₹331
   At 10.5% simple interest the interest in 3 years would be 31.5% = ₹315
   Difference = ₹16

10. The amount @ 10% CI could become ₹ 1331. Also, ₹ 1728 depreciated at $R$% has to become ₹1331.
    Thus,
    $$1728 \times [(100-R)/100]^3 = 1331 \text{ (approximately)}.$$
    The closest value of $R = 8$%
    Thus, the difference is 2%.

11. SBI would be paying 40% on the capital as interest over two years and it would be getting 44% of the capital as interest from Bharti Telecom. Hence, it earns 4%.

12. $64000 \times (1.025)^4 = 70644.025$.
    Interest 6644.025
    Option (d). None of these is correct.

13. Since the interest is compounded half yearly at $R$% per annum, the value of R would be lesser than the value of S. (Remember, half yearly compounding is always profitable for the depositor).

14. At 10% per annum simple interest, the interest earned over 3 years would be 30% of the capital. Thus, 300 is 30% of the capital which means that the capital is 1000. In 3 years, the compound interest on the same amount would be 331.

15. Go through trial and error of the options. You will get:
    $$20000 \times (1.3) = 26000 \text{ (@ simple interest)}$$
    $$20000 \times 1.1 \times 1.1 \times 1.1 = 26620 \text{ @ compound interest.}$$
    Thus 20000 is the correct answer.

16. Solve through options to see that the value of 1200000 fits the given situation.

17. Population growth rate according to the problem:
    Year 1 = 5%, year 2 = 10%, year 3 = 15%
    Year 4 = 20%, year 5 = 25%, year 6 = 30%.
    Population decrease due to migration:
    Year 1 = 1%, year 2 = 2%, year 3 = 4%
    Year 4 = 8%, year 5 = 16%, year 6 = 32%.
    Thus, the first fall would happen in 2016.

18. P + 2 years interest on P = 1000 + 1 years interest on 1000 + 1000
    $\rightarrow 1.21P = 2100 \rightarrow P = 1736$ (approx).

19. Solve this one through options. Option (c) reduced rate for 14 years fits the conditions.

20. Let the repayment annually be X. Then:
    8000 + 3 years interest on 8000 (on compound interest of 5%) = X + 2 years interest on X + X + 1 years interest on X + X → X = 2937.67

21. You can think about this situation by taking some values. Let $x = 100$, $y = 10$ and $z = 1$ (at an interest rate of 10%). We can see that $10^2 = 100 \rightarrow y^2 = xz$

22. 4200 + (4 % of 4200) 3 times = 4200 + 0.04 × 3 × 4200 = 4704.

23. Solve using options. If the price is 27000, the interest on 12000 (after subtracting the down payment) would be 16% of 12000 = 1920. Hence, the total amount paid would be 28920.

24. The interest would be paid on
    7000 for 3 years + 10000 for 5 years.
    @ 6.5% the total interest for 8 years
    $$= 1365 + 3250$$
    $$= ₹ 4615$$

25. It can be seen that for 17000, the first year interest would be 1020, while the second year interest after a repayment of 6800 would be on 10200 @ 5% per annum. The interest in the second year would thus be ₹510 which is exactly half the interest of the first year. Thus, option (a) is correct.

26. Solve using options. Option (c) fits the situation as:
    12820 = 2000 + 2 years interest on 2000 + 4000 + 1 years interest on 4000 + 6000 (use 10% compound interest for calculation of interest) →
    12820 = 2000 + 420 + 4000 + 400 + 6000.
    Thus, option (c) fits the situation perfectly.

27. Interest for $A$ = 6% of 50000.
    Interest for $B$, $C$ and $D$ the interest is more than 6%.
    Thus $A$'s loan is MUL.

28. Interest she would pay under scheme 1:

Year 1 the entire loan would be @ 4% – hence interest on 40000 = ₹1600.

Total interest = 1600

Interest on loan 2:

In year 1: 80% of the loan (I.e 48000) would be on 5%, 12000 would be @10% – hence total interest = 3600

Year 2: 40% of the loan (24000) would be on 5%, while the remaining loan would be on 10% – hence total interest = 4800

Thus, total interest on the two loans would be 1600 + 3600 + 4800 = 10000.

29. Let the amounts be ₹100 and ₹200 respectively. The value of the 100 would become $100 \times 6/7 \times 6/7 = 3600/49 = 73.46$

The other person's investment of 200 would become $200 \times 1.2 \times 1.2 = 288$

The total value would become 288 + 73.46 = 361.46

This represents approximately a 20% increase in the value of the amount after 2 year. Hence, option (a) is correct.

30. The final value would be:

$0.8 \times 63000 + 27000 \times 1.15 \times 1.15 = 86107.5.$

→ Drop in value = 4.32%

# Ratio, Proportion and Variation

## INTRODUCTION

The concept of ratio, proportion and variation is an important one for the aptitude examinations. Questions based on this chapter have been regularly asked in the CAT exam (direct or application based). In fact, questions based on this concept regularly appear in all aptitude tests (XLRI, CMAT, NMIMS, SNAP, NIFT, IRMA, Bank PO, etc.).

Besides, this concept is very important in the area of Data Interpretation, where ratio change and ratio comparisons are very popular question types.

## RATIO

When comparing any two numbers, sometimes, it is necessary to find out how many times one number is greater (or less) than the other. In other words, we often need to express one number as a fraction of the other.

In general, the ratio of a number $x$ to a number $y$ is defined as the quotient of the numbers $x$ and $y$.

The numbers that form the ratio are called the terms of the ratio. The numerator of the ratio is called the *antecedent* and the denominator is called the *consequent* of the ratio.

The ratio may be taken for homogenous quantities or for heterogeneous quantities. In the first case, the ratio has no unit (or is unitless), while in the second case, the unit of the ratio is based on the units of the numerator and that of the denominator.

Ratios can be expressed as percentages. To express the value of a ratio as a percentage, we multiply the ratio by 100.

Thus, $4/5 = 0.8 = 80\%$

### The Calculation of a ratio:
### Percentage and decimal values

The calculation of ratio is principally on the same lines as the calculation of a percentage value.

Hence, you should see it as:

The ratio 2/4 has a percentage value of 50% and it has a decimal value of 0.5.

It should be pretty obvious to you that in order to find out the decimal value of any ratio, calculate the percentage value using the percentage rule method illustrated in the chapter of percentage and then shift the decimal point 2 places to the left.

Thus a ratio which has a percentage value of 62.47% will have a decimal value of 0.6247.

---

### Some Important Properties of Ratios

1. If we multiply the numerator and the denominator of a ratio by the same number, the ratio remains unchanged.

   That is, $\dfrac{a}{b} = \dfrac{ma}{mb}$

2. If we divide the numerator and the denominator of a ratio by the same number, the ratio remains unchanged. Thus

   $$a/b = \dfrac{(a/d)}{(b/d)}$$

3. Denominator equation method:
   The magnitudes of two ratios can be compared by equating the denominators of the two ratios and then checking for the value of the numerator.

*Contd*

## Some Important Properties of Ratios
*(Contd)*

Thus, if we have to check for

$$8/3 \quad \text{vs} \quad 11/4$$

We can compare $\dfrac{(8 \times 1.33)}{(3 \times 1.33)}$ vs $\dfrac{11}{4}$

That is, $\dfrac{10.66}{4} < \dfrac{11}{4}$

In fact, the value of a ratio has a direct relationship with the value of the numerator of the ratio. At the same time, it has an inverse relationship with the denominator of the ratio. Since the denominator has an inverse relationship with the ratio's value, it involves an unnecessary inversion in the minds of the reader. Hence, in my opinion, we should look at maintaining constancy in the denominator and work all the requisite calculations on the numerator's basis.

The reader should recall here the Product Constancy Table (or the denominator change to ratio change table) explained in the chapter of percentages to understand the mechanics of how a change in the denominator affects the value of the ratio. A clear understanding of these dynamics will help the student become much faster in solving the problems based on ratios.

4. The ratio of two fractions can be expressed as a ratio of two integers. Thus the ratio:

$$a/b : c/d = \frac{(a/b)}{(c/d)} = \frac{ad}{bc}$$

5. If either or both the terms of a ratio are a surd quantity, then the ratio will never evolve into integral numbers unless the surd quantities are equal. Use this principle to spot options in questions having surds.

***Example:*** $\dfrac{\sqrt{3}}{\sqrt{2}}$ can never be represented by integers.

This principle can also be understood in other words as follows:

Suppose while solving a question, you come across a situation where $\sqrt{3}$ appears as a part of the process. In such a case, it would be safe to assume that $\sqrt{3}$ will also be part of the answer. Since the only way the $\sqrt{3}$ can be removed from the answer is by multiplying or dividing the expression by $\sqrt{3}$. Thus for instance, the formula for the area of an equilateral triangle is $(\sqrt{3}/4)a^2$.

## Some Important Properties of Ratios
*(Contd)*

Hence, you can safely assume that the area of any equilateral triangle will have $\sqrt{3}$ in its answer. The only case when this gets negated would be when the value of the side has a component which has the fourth root of three.

6. The multiplication of the ratios $\dfrac{a}{b}$ and $\dfrac{c}{d}$ yields:

$$a/b \times c/d = \frac{ac}{bd}$$

7. When the ratio $a/b$ is compounded with itself, the resulting ratio is $a^2/b^2$ and is called the duplicate ratio. Similarly, $a^3/b^3$ is the triplicate ratio and $a^{0.5}/b^{0.5}$ is the sub-duplicate ratio of $a/b$.

8. If $a/b = c/d = e/f = g/h = k$ then

$$k = \frac{(a + c + e + g)}{(b + d + f + h)}$$

9. If $a_1/b_1, a_2/b_2, a_3/b_3 \dots a_n/b_n$ are unequal fractions Then the ratio:

$$\frac{(a_1 + a_2 + a_3 + \dots + a_n)}{(b_1 + b_2 + b_3 + \dots b_n)}$$

lies between the lowest and the highest of these fractions.

10. If we have two equations containing three unknowns as

$$a_1x + b_1y + c_1z = 0 \qquad (1)$$

and
$$a_2x + b_2y + c_2z = 0 \qquad (2)$$

Then, the value of $x$, $y$ and $z$ cannot be resolved without having a third equation.

However, in the absence of a third equation, we can find the proportion $x : y : z$. This will be given by $b_1c_2 - b_2c_1 : c_1a_2 - c_2a_1 : a_1b_2 - a_2b_1$.

This can be remembered by writing as follows:

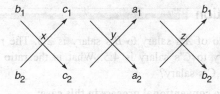

**Fig. 8.1**

Multiply the coefficients across the arrow indicated always taking a multiplication as positive if the arrow points downwards and taking it as negative if the arrow points upwards.

Thus $x$ corresponds to $b_1c_2 - b_2c_1$ and so on.

## Some Important Properties of Ratios
*(Contd)*

11. If the ratio $a/b > 1$ (called a ratio of greater inequality) and if $k$ is a positive number:

    $(a + k)/(b + k) < a/b$ and $(a - k)/(b - k) > a/b$

    Similarly if $a/b < 1$ then

    $(a + k)/(b + k) > a/b$ and $(a - k)/(b - k) < a/b$

    [The student should try assuming certain values and check the results]

12. Maintenance of equality when numbers are added in both the numerator and the denominators.

    This if best illustrated through an example:

    $$20/30 = (20 + 2)/(30 + 3)$$

    i.e., $a/b = (a + c)/(b + d)$ if and only if $c/d = a/b$. In other words, the ratio of the additions should be equal to the original ratio to maintain equality of ratios when two different numbers are added in the numerator and denominator.

    Consequently, if $c/d > a/b$ then $(a + c)/(b + d) > a/b$ and if $c/d < a/b$ then $(a + c)/(b + d) < a/b$

    The practical applications of (11) and (12) is of immense importance for all aptitude exams.

## 🔎 MATHEMATICAL USES OF RATIOS

### Use 1

#### As a bridge between 3 or more quantities:

Suppose you have a ratio relationship given between the salaries of two individuals $A$ and $B$. Further, if there is another ratio relationship between $B$ and $C$. Then, by combining the two ratios, you can come up with a single consolidated ratio between $A$, $B$ and $C$. This ratio will give you the relationship between $A$ and $C$.

### Illustration

The Ratio of $A$'s salary to $B$'s salary is 2:3. The ratio of $B$'s salary to $C$'s salary is 4:5. What is the ratio of $A$'s salary to $C$'s salary?

#### Using the conventional process in this case:

Take the LCM of 3 and 4 (the two values representing B's amount). The LCM is 12.

Then, convert $B$'s value in each ratio to 12.

Thus, Ratio 1 = 8/12 and Ratio 2 = 12/15

Thus, $A:B:C$ = 8:12:15

Hence, $A:C$ = 8:15

Further, if it were given that $A$'s salary was 800, you could derive the values of $C$'s salary (as 1500).

**SHORTCUT** for this process:

The LCM process gets very cumbersome especially if you are trying to create a bridge between more than 3 quantities.

Suppose, you have the ratio train as follows:

$A:B$ = 2:3
$B:C$ = 4:5
$C:D$ = 6:11
$D:E$ = 12:17

In order to create one consolidated ratio for this situation using the LCM process becomes too long.

The short cut goes as follows:

$A:B:C:D:E$ can be written directly as:

$2 \times 4 \times 6 \times 12 : 3 \times 4 \times 6 \times 12 : 3 \times 5 \times 6 \times 12 : 3 \times 5 \times 11 \times 12 : 3 \times 5 \times 11 \times 17$

#### The thought algorithm for this case goes as:

To get the consolidated ratio $A:B:C:D:E$, A will correspond to the product of all numerators ($2 \times 4 \times 6 \times 12$) while $B$ will take the first denominator and the last 3 numerators ($3 \times 4 \times 6 \times 12$). $C$ on the other hand takes the first two denominators and the last 2 numerators ($3 \times 5 \times 6 \times 12$), $D$ takes the first 3 denominators and the last numerator ($3 \times 5 \times 11 \times 12$) and $E$ takes all the four denominators ($3 \times 5 \times 11 \times 17$).

In mathematical terms this can be written as:

If $a/b = N_1/D_1$, $b/c = N_2/D_2$, $c/d = N_3/D_3$ and $d/e = N_4/D_4$ then $a : b : c : d : e = N_1N_2N_3N_4 : D_1N_2N_3N_4 : D_1D_2N_3N_4 : D_1D_2D_3N_4 : D_1D_2D_3D_4$

### Use 2

#### Ratio as a Multiplier

This is the most common use of Ratios:

If $A:B$ is 3:1, then the value of $B$ has to be multiplied by 3 to get the value of $A$.

#### CALCULATION METHODS related to RATIOS

#### (A) Calculation methods for Ratio comparisons:

There could be four broad cases when you might be required to do ratio comparisons:

The table below clearly illustrates these:

| | Numerator | Denominator | Ratio | Calculations |
|---|---|---|---|---|
| Case 1 | Increases | Decreases | Increase | Not required |
| Case 2 | Increases | Increases | May Increase or Decrease | Required |
| Case 3 | Decreases | Increases | Decreases | Not required |
| Case 4 | Decreases | Decreases | May Increase or Decrease | Required |

In case 2 and 4 in the table, calculations will be necessitated. In such a situation, the following process can be used for ratio comparisons.

#### 1. The Cross Multiplication Method

Two ratios can be compared using the cross multiplication method as follows. Suppose you have to compare 12/17 with 15/19

Then, to test which ratio is higher cross multiply and compare $12 \times 19$ and $15 \times 17$.

If $12 \times 19$ is bigger the Ratio 12/17 will be bigger. If $15 \times 17$ is higher, the ratio 15/19 will be higher.

In this case, $15 \times 17$ being higher, the Ratio 15/19 is higher.

---

**Note:** In real time usage (esp. in D.I.) this method is highly impractical and calculating the product might be more cumbersome than calculating the percentage values.

---

Thus, this method will not be able to tell you the answer if you have to compare $\dfrac{3743}{5624}$ with $\dfrac{3821}{5783}$

## 2. Percentage value comparison method:

Suppose you have to compare: $\dfrac{173}{212}$ with $\dfrac{181}{241}$

In such a case just by estimating the 10% ranges for each ratio you can clearly see that —
the first ratio is > 80% while the second ratio is < 80%

Hence, the first ratio is obviously greater.

This method is extremely convenient if the two ratios have their values in different 10% ranges.

However, this problem will become slightly more difficult, if the two ratios fall in the same 10% range. Thus, if you had to compare $^{173}/_{212}$ with $^{181}/_{225}$, both the values would give values between 80 and 90%. The next step would be to calculate the 1% range.

The first ratio here is 81 – 82% while the second ratio lies between 80 and 81%

Hence the first ratio is the larger of the two.

---

**Note:** For this method to be effective for you, you'll first need to master the percentage rule method for calculating the percentage value of a ratio. Hence if you cannot see that 169.6 is 80% of 212 or for that matter that 81% of 212 is 171.72 and 82% is 172.84 you will not be able to use this method effectively. (This is also true for the next method.) However, once you can calculate percentage values of 3 digit ratios to 1% range, there is not much that can stop you in comparing ratios. The CAT and all other aptitude exams normally do not challenge you to calculate further than the 1% range when you are looking at ratio comparisons.

---

## 3. Numerator denominator percentage change method:

There is another way in which you can compare close ratios like 173/212 and 181/225. For this method, you need to calculate the percentage changes in the numerator and the denominator.

Thus:

$173 \to 181$ is a % increase of 4 – 5%.
While $212 \to 225$ is a % increase of 6 – 7%.

In this case, since the denominator is increasing more than the numerator, the second ratio is smaller.

This method is the most powerful method for comparing close ratios—provided you are good with your percentage rule calculations.

## (B) Method for calculating the value of a percentage change in the ratio:

PCG (Percentage Change Graphic) gives us a convenient method to calculate the value of the percentage change in a ratio.

Suppose, you have to calculate the percentage change between 2 ratios. This has to be done in two stages as:

Original Ratio $\xrightarrow[\text{numerator}]{\text{Effect of}}$ Intermediate Ratio

$\xrightarrow[\text{Denominator}]{\text{Effect of}}$ Final Ratio

Thus if 20/40 becomes 22/50
Effect of numerator = $20 \to 22$(10% increase)
Effect of denominator = $50 \to 40$(20% decrease) (reverse fashion)
Overall effect on the ratio:

$$100 \xrightarrow[\substack{\text{Numerator} \\ \text{Effect}}]{10\%\uparrow} 110 \xrightarrow[\substack{\text{Denominator} \\ \text{Effect}}]{20\%\downarrow} 88$$

Hence, overall effect = 12% decrease.

## 📶 PROPORTION

When two ratios are equal, the four quantities composing them are said to be proportionals. Thus if $a/b = c/d$, then $a$, $b$, $c$, $d$ are proportionals. This is expressed by saying that $a$ is to $b$ as $c$ is to $d$, and the proportion is written as

$$a:b::c:d$$
$$\text{or}$$
$$a:b = c:d$$

• The terms $a$ and $d$ are called the extremes while the terms $b$ and $c$ are called the means.
• **If four quantities are in proportion, the product of the extremes is equal to the product of the means.**

Let $a$, $b$, $c$, $d$ be the proportionals.
Then by definition $a/b = c/d$

$\therefore \qquad\qquad ad = bc$

Hence if any three terms of proportion are given, the fourth may be found. Thus if $a$, $c$, $d$ are given, then $b = ad/c$.
• **If three quantities $a$, $b$ and $c$ are in continued proportion, then $a:b = b:c$**

$\therefore \qquad\qquad ac = b^2$

In this case, $b$ is said to be a *mean proportional* between $a$ and $c$; and $c$ is said to be a *third proportional* to $a$ and $b$.
• **If three quantities are proportionals the first is to the third is the duplicate ratio of the first to the second.**

That is: for $a:b::b:c$

$$a:c = a^2:b^2$$

• If four quantities *a*, *b*, *c* and *d* form a proportion, many other proportions may be deduced by the properties of fractions. The results of these operations are very useful. These results are

1. **Invertendo:** If $a/b = c/d$ then $b/a = d/c$
2. **Alternando:** If $a/b = c/d$, then $a/c = b/d$
3. **Componendo:** If $a/b = c/d$, then $\left(\dfrac{a + b}{b}\right) = \left(\dfrac{c + d}{d}\right)$
4. **Dividendo:** If $a/b = c/d$, then $\left(\dfrac{a - b}{b}\right) = \left(\dfrac{c - d}{d}\right)$
5. **Componendo and Dividendo:** If $a/b = c/d$, then $(a + b)/(a - b) = (c + d)/(c - d)$

## VARIATION

Essentially there are two kinds of proportions that two variables can be related by:

### (1) Direct Proportion

When it is said that *A* varies directly as *B*, you should understand the following implications:

(a) **Logical implication:** When *A* increases *B* increases
(b) **Calculation implication:** If *A* increases by 10%, *B* will also increase by 10%
(c) **Graphical implications:** The following graph is representative of this situation.

(d) **Equation implication:** The ratio *A/B* is constant.

### (2) Inverse Proportion:

When *A* varies inversely as *B*, the following implication arise.

*Space for Notes*

(a) **Logical implication:** When *A* increases *B* decreases
(b) **Calculation implication:** If *A* decreases by 9.09%, *B* will increase by 10%.
(c) **Graphical implications:** The following graph is representative of this situation.

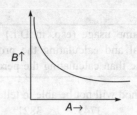

(d) **Equation implication:** The product $A \times B$ is constant.

A quantity '*A*' is said to vary directly as another '*B*' when the two quantities depend upon each other in such a manner that if *B* is changed, *A* is changed in the same ratio.

*Note:* The word directly is often omitted, and *A* is said to vary as *B*.

*The symbol $\propto$ is used to denote variation. Thus, $A \propto B$ is read "A varies as B".*

If $A \propto B$ then, $A = KB$ where *K* is any constant.

Thus to find $K = A/B$, we need one value of *A* and a corresponding value of *B*.

where $K = 3/12 = 1/4 \Rightarrow A = B \times (1/4)$.

**A quantity *A* is said to vary inversely as another *B* when *A* varies directly as the reciprocal of *B*. Thus if *A* varies inversely as *B*, $A = m/B$, where *m* is constant.**

**A quantity is said to vary jointly as a number of others when it varies directly as their product. Thus *A* varies jointly as *B* and *C*, when $A = mBC$.**

**If *A* varies as *B* when *C* is constant, and *A* varies as *C* when *B* is constant, then *A* will vary as *BC* when both *B* and *C* vary.**

The variation of *A* depends partly on that of *B* and partly on that of *C*. Assume that each letter variation takes place separately, each in its turn producing its own effect on *A*.

# WORKED-OUT PROBLEMS

**Problem 8.1** ₹ 5783 is divided among Sherry, Berry, and Cherry in such a way that if ₹ 28, ₹ 37 and ₹ 18 be deducted from their respective shares, they have money in the ratio 4:6:9. Find Sherry's share.

    (a) ₹ 1256          (b) ₹ 1228

    (c) ₹ 1456          (d) ₹ 1084

**Solution** The problem clearly states that when we reduce 28, 37 and 18 rupees, respectively from Sherry's, Berry's and Cherry's shares, the resultant ratio is: 4:6:9.

Thus, if we assume the reduced values as

$$4x, 6x \text{ and } 9x, \text{ we will have} \rightarrow$$

Sherry's share → $4x + 28$, Berry's share → $6x + 37$ and Cherry's share → $9x + 18$ and thus we have

$(4x + 28) + (6x + 37) + (9x + 18) = 5783$

→ $19x = 5783 - 83 = 5700$

Hence, $x = 300$.

Hence, Sherry's share is ₹ 1228.

---

**Note:** For problems based on this chapter we are always confronted with ratios and proportions between different number of variables. For the above problem we had three variables which were in the ratio of 4:6:9. When we have such a situation we normally assume the values in the same proportion, using one unknown '$x$' only (in this example we could take the three values as $4x$, $6x$ and $9x$, respectively).

Then, the total value is represented by the addition of the three giving rise to a linear equation, which on solution, will result in the answer to the value of the unknown '$x$'.

However, the student should realise that most of the time this unknown '$x$' is not needed to solve the problem. This is illustrated through the following alternate approach to solving the above problem:

Assume the three values as 4, 6 and 9

Then we have

$(4 + 28) + (6 + 37) + (9 + 18) = 5783$

→ $19 = 5783 - 83 = 5700 \rightarrow 1 = 300$

Hence, $4 + 28 = 1228$.

While adopting this approach the student should be careful in being able to distinguish the numbers in bold as pointing out the unknown variable.

---

**Problem 8.2** Two numbers are in the ratio $P : Q$. When 1 is added to both the numerator and the denominator, the ratio gets changed to $R/S$. Again, when 1 is added to both the numerator and the denominator, it becomes 1/2. Find the sum of $P$ and $Q$.

    (a) 3          (b) 4

    (c) 5          (d) 6

**Solution** The normal process of solving this problem would be through the writing of equations.

**Approach 1:** We have: Final ratio is $x/2x$.

Then, $\dfrac{x-2}{2x-2} = P/Q$

Then, $Qx - 2Q = 2Px - 2P$

$2(P - Q) = x(2P - Q)$ (At this stage we see that the solution is a complex one)

**Approach 2:** $\dfrac{R+1}{S+1} = \dfrac{1}{2}$

$$2R + 2 = S + 1 \rightarrow R = \dfrac{S-1}{2}$$

Now, $\dfrac{P+1}{Q+1} = \dfrac{R}{S} = \dfrac{S-1}{2S}$ (At this time we realise that we are getting stuck)

Start from front:

$\dfrac{P+2}{Q+2} = 1/2 \rightarrow 2P + 4 = Q + 2$ (Again the solution is not visible and we are likely to get stuck)

---

**Note:** Such problems should never be attempted by writing the equations since this process takes more time than is necessary to solve the problem and is impractical in the exam situation due to the amount of time required in writing.

Besides, in complex problems where the final solution is not visible to the student while starting off, many a times the student has to finally abort the problem midway. This results in an unnecessary wastage of time if the student has attempted to write equations.

In fact, the student should realise that selecting the correct questions to solve in aptitude exams like the CAT is more important than being aware of how all the problems are solved.

---

The following process will illustrate the option based solution process.

**Option A:** It has $P + Q = 3$. The possible values of $P/Q$ are 1/2 or 2/1.

Using 1/2, we see that on adding 2 to both the numerator and the denominator we get 3/4 (Not the required value.)

Similarly, we see that 2/1 will also not give the answer. We should also realise that the numerator has to be lower than the denominator to have the final value of 1/2.

Next we try **Option B**, where we have 1/3 as the only possible ratio.

Then we get the final value as 3/5 (Not equal to 1/2) Hence, we reject option B.

Next we try **Option C**, where we have 1/4 or 2/3

Checking for 1/4 we get 3/6 = 1/2. Hence, the option is correct.

**Problem 8.3** If 10 persons can clean 10 floors by 10 mops in 10 days, in how many days can 8 persons clean 8 floors by 8 mops?

(a) 12 ½ days      (b) 8 days
(c) 10 days      (d) 8 ⅓ days

**Solution** Do not get confused by the distractions given in the problem. 10 men and 10 days means 100 man-days are required to clean 10 floors.

That is, 1 floor requires 10 man-days to get cleaned. Hence, 8 floors will require 80 man-days to clean.

Therefore, 10 days are required to clean 8 floors.

**Problem 8.4** Three quantities $A$, $B$, $C$ are such that $AB = KC$, where $K$ is a constant. When $A$ is kept constant, $B$ varies directly as $C$; when $B$ is kept constant, $A$ varies directly $C$ and when $C$ is kept constant, $A$ varies inversely as $B$.

Initially, $A$ was at 5 and $A:B:C$ was $1:3:5$. Find the value of $A$ when $B$ equals 9 at constant $C$.

(a) 8      (b) 8.33
(c) 9      (d) 9.5

**Solution** Initial values are 5, 15 and 25.

Thus we have $5 \times 15 = K \times 25$.
Hence, $K = 3$.

Thus, the equation is $AB = 3C$.

For the problem, keep $C$ constant at 25. Then, $A \times 9 = 3 \times 25$.
i.e., $A = 75/9 = 8.33$

**Problem 8.5** If $x/y = 3/4$, then find the value of the expression, $(5x - 3y)/(7x + 2y)$.

(a) 3/21      (b) 5/29
(c) 3/29      (d) 5/33

**Solution** Assume the values as $x = 3$ and $y = 4$.
Then we have

$$\frac{(15-12)}{(21+8)} = 3/29$$

**Problem 8.6** ₹ 3650 is divided among 4 engineers, 3 MBAs and 5 CAs such that 3 CAs get as much as 2 MBAs and 3 Engineers as much as 2 CAs. Find the share of an MBA.

(a) 300      (b) 450
(c) 475      (d) None of these

**Solution**

$$4E + 3M + 5C = 3650$$

Also, $3C = 2M$, that is, $M = 1.5\,C$
and $3E = 2C$ that is, $E = 0.66C$
Thus, $4 \times 0.66C + 3 \times 1.5\,C + 5C = 3650$
$$C = 3650/12.166$$
That is, $C = 300$
Hence, $M = 1.5\,C = 450$

**Problem 8.7** The ratio of water and milk in a 30 litre mixture is $7:3$. Find the quantity of water to be added to the mixture in order to make this ratio $6:1$.

(a) 30      (b) 32
(c) 33      (d) 35

**Solution** Solve while reading → As you read the first sentence, you should have 21 litres of water and 9 litres of milk in your mind.

In order to get the final result, we keep the milk constant at 9 litres.

Then, we have 9 litres, which corresponds to 1
Hence, '?' corresponds to 6.
Solving by using unitary method we have
54 litres of water to 9 litres of milk.

Hence, we need to add 33 litres of water to the original mixture.

Alternatively, we can solve this by using options. The student should try to do the same.

**Problem 8.8** Three containers $A$, $B$ and $C$ are having mixtures of milk and water in the ratio of $1:5$, $3:5$ and $5:7$, respectively. If the capacities of the containers are in the ratio $5:4:5$, find the ratio of milk to water, if the mixtures of all the three containers are mixed together.

**Solution** Assume that there are 500, 400 and 500 litres respectively in the 3 containers.

Then we have, 83.33,150 and 208.33 litres of milk in each of the three containers.

Thus, the total milk is 441.66 litres. Hence, the amount of water in the mixture is

$$1400 - 441.66 = 958.33 \text{ litres.}$$

Hence, the ratio of milk to water is

$441.66:958.33 \rightarrow 53:115$ (Using division by 0.33333)

The calculation thought process should be:

$(441 \times 3 + 2) : (958 \times 3 + 1) = 1325 : 2875$.
Dividing by 25 → 53 : 115.

## LEVEL OF DIFFICULTY (I)

1. If $p, q, r, s$ are proportional, then $(p - q)(p - r)/p =$
   (a) $p + r + s$
   (b) $p + s - q - r$
   (c) $p + q + r + s$
   (d) $p + r - q - s$

2. What number must be added in each term of the fraction 7/31 so that it may become 5 : 17?
   (a) 9
   (b) 10
   (c) 11
   (d) 3

3. If $x$ varies inversely as $y^3 - 1$ and is equal to 3 when $y = 2$, find $x$ when $y = 4$.
   (a) 1/4
   (b) 1/3
   (c) 1/9
   (d) 1

4. If $x$ varies as $y$, and $y = 4$ when $x = 12$, find $x$ when $y = 15$.
   (a) 45
   (b) 54
   (c) 70
   (d) 15

5. $X$ varies jointly as $Y$ and $Z$; and $X = 6$ when $Y = 3$, $Z = 2$; find $X$ when $Y = 5$, $Z = 7$.
   (a) 8.75
   (b) 35
   (c) 7
   (d) 15

6. If $x$ varies as $y$ directly, and as $z$ inversely, and $x = 12$ when $y = 3$; find $z$ when $x = 4$, $y = 5$.
   (a) 25/4
   (b) 10
   (c) 12/7
   (d) Cannot be determined

7. Divide ₹1400 into three parts in such a way that half of the first part, one-fourth of the second part and one-eighth of the third part are equal.
   (a) 300, 600, 500
   (b) 200, 400, 800
   (c) 100, 400, 1000
   (d) None of these

8. Divide ₹5000 among $A$, $B$, $C$ and $D$ so that $A$ and $B$ together get $3/7^{th}$ of what $C$ and $D$ get together, $C$ gets 1.5 times of what $B$ gets and D gets 4/3 times as much as $C$. Now the value of what $B$ gets is
   (a) 500
   (b) 1000
   (c) 2000
   (d) 1500

9. If $\dfrac{p}{q + r} = \dfrac{q}{p + r} = \dfrac{r}{p + q}$ each fraction is equal to
   (a) $(p + q + r)^2$
   (b) 1/2
   (c) 1/3
   (d) None of these

10. If $3x^2 + 3y^2 = 10xy$, what is the ratio of $x$ to $y$?
    (a) 1:4
    (b) 3:2
    (c) 1:3
    (d) 1:2
    (Hint: Use options to solve fast)

11. If $p:q = r:s$, then the value of $(p^2 + q^2)/(r^2 + s^2)$ is
    (a) 1/2
    (b) $\dfrac{p + q}{r + s}$
    (c) $\dfrac{p - q}{r - s}$
    (d) $\dfrac{pq}{rs}$

12. If $p, q, r, s$ are in continued proportion then $\dfrac{(p - s)}{q - r} \geq x$. What is the value of $x$?
    (a) 5
    (b) 3
    (c) 7
    (d) 9

13. If 3 examiners can examine a certain number of answer books in 10 days by working 4 hours a day, for how many hours a day would 4 examiners have to work in order to examine thrice the number of answer books in 30 days?
    (a) 3
    (b) 1
    (c) 8
    (d) 6

14. In a mixture of 60 litres, the ratio of milk and water is 2 : 3. How much water must be added to this mixture so that the ratio of milk and water becomes 1 : 2?
    (a) 10 litres
    (b) 12 litres
    (c) 15 litres
    (d) 20 litres

15. If $P$ varies as $R$, and $Q$ varies as $R$, then which of the following is false:
    (a) $(P + Q) \propto R$
    (b) $(P - Q) \propto 1/R$
    (c) $\sqrt{PQ} \propto R$
    (d) $PQ \propto R^2$

16. If three numbers are in the ratio of $1 : 3 : 5$ and half the sum is 9, then the ratio of cubes of the numbers is:
    (a) $6 : 12 : 13$
    (b) $1 : 3 : 25$
    (c) $1 : 27 : 125$
    (d) $3 : 5 : 7$

17. The ratio between two numbers is $7 : 11$ and their LCM is 154. The first number is:
    (a) 14
    (b) 7
    (c) 22
    (d) 32

18. $P$ and $Q$ are two alloys of aluminum and brass prepared by mixing metals in proportions 7 : 2 and 7 : 11, respectively. If equal quantities of the two alloys are melted to form a third alloy $R$, the proportion of aluminum and brass in $R$ will be:
    (a) $5 : 9$
    (b) $5 : 7$
    (c) $7 : 5$
    (d) $9 : 5$

19. If 10 men working 6 hours a day can do a piece of work in 15 days, in how many days will 20 men working 14 hours a day do the same work?
    (a) 3.21 days
    (b) 3.5 days
    (c) 3 days
    (d) 4.5 days

20. The incomes of $P$ and $Q$ are in the ratio 1 : 2 and their expenditures are in the ratio 1 : 3. If each saves ₹500, then, $P$'s income can be:
    (a) ₹1000
    (b) ₹1500
    (c) ₹3000
    (d) ₹2000

21. If the ratio of sines of angles of a triangle is $1:1:\sqrt{2}$ then the ratio of square of the greatest side to sum of the squares of other two sides is
    (a) 3:4
    (b) 2:1
    (c) 1:1
    (d) 1:2

22. Divide ₹1360 among $p$, $q$ and $r$ such that $p$ gets 2/3 of what $q$ gets and $q$ gets 1/4th of what $r$ gets. Now the share of $r$ is:
    (a) ₹960
    (b) ₹600
    (c) ₹840
    (d) ₹720

23. $p$, $q$, $r$ enter into a partnership. p contributes one-third of the whole capital while $q$ contributes as much as $p$ and $r$ together contribute. If the profit at the end of the year is ₹1,68,000, how much would each receive?
    (a) 48,000, 40,000, 80,000
    (b) 56,000, 84,000, 28,000
    (c) 56,000, 84,000, 20,000
    (d) 56,000, 28,000, 84,000

24. The students in three batches at Mindworkzz are in the ratio 2:3:5. If 20 students are increased in each batch, the ratio changes to 4:5:7. The total number of students in the three batches before the increases were
    (a) 10
    (b) 90
    (c) 100
    (d) 150

25. The speeds of three bikes are in the ratio 1 : 2 : 3. The ratio between the times taken by these bikes to travel the same distance is
    (a) 2:3:4
    (b) 6:2:3
    (c) 4:3:6
    (d) 6:3:2

26. If $p$, $q$, $r$ and $s$ are proportional then the mean proportion between $p^2 + r^2$ and $q^2 + s^2$ is
    (a) $pr/qs$
    (b) $pq + rs$
    (c) $p/q + s/r$
    (d) $p^2/q^2 + r^2/s^2$

27. A number $z$ lies between 0 and 1. Which of the following is true?
    (a) $z > \sqrt{z}$
    (b) $z > 1/z$
    (c) $z^3 > z^2$
    (d) $1/z > \sqrt{z}$

28. ₹1200 is divided among three friends Amit, Bineet and Chaman in such a way that 1/3rd of Amit's share, 1/4th of Bineet's share and 1/5th of Chaman's share are equal. Find Amit's share.
    (a) ₹300
    (b) ₹500
    (c) ₹400
    (d) ₹200

29. After an increment of 5 in both the numerator and denominator, a fraction changes to 6/7. Find the original fraction.
    (a) 5/12
    (b) 7/9
    (c) 2/5
    (d) 3/8

30. The difference between two positive numbers is 11 and the ratio between them is 2:1. Find the product of the two numbers.
    (a) 242
    (b) 225
    (c) 272
    (d) 152

31. If 10 tractors can plough 1/6th of a field in 12 days, how many days 20 tractors will take to do the remaining work?
    (a) 30 days
    (b) 20 days
    (c) 15 days
    (d) 18 days

32. A cow takes 5 leaps for every 4 leaps of a goat, but 3 leaps of the goat are equal to 4 leaps of the cow. What is the ratio of the speed of the cow to that of the goat?
    (a) 11:15
    (b) 15:11
    (c) 16:15
    (d) 15:16

33. The present ratio of ages of $P$ and $Q$ is 3:5. 10 years ago, this ratio was 1:2. Find the sum total of their present ages.
    (a) 80 years
    (b) 100 years
    (c) 70 years
    (d) 90 years

34. Four numbers in the ratio 1:2:4:8 add up to give a sum of 120. Find the value of the biggest number.
    (a) 40
    (b) 30
    (c) 64
    (d) 60

35. Three men rent a farm for ₹14000 per annum. $A$ puts 220 cows in the farm for 3 months, $B$ puts 220 cows for 6 months and $C$ puts 880 cows for 3 months. What percentage of the total expenditure should $C$ pay?
    (a) 20%
    (b) 14.28%
    (c) 16.66%
    (d) 57.14%

36. 25 students can do a job in 12 days, but on the starting day, five of them informed that they are not coming. By what fraction will the number of days required for doing the whole work get increased?
    (a) 3/5
    (b) 3/7
    (c) 3/4
    (d) 1/4

37. A dishonest shopkeeper mixed 1 litre of water for every 3 litres of petrol and thus made up 36 litres of petrol. If he now adds 15 litres of petrol to the mixture, find the ratio of petrol and water in the new mixture.
    (a) 12:5
    (b) 14:3
    (c) 7:2
    (d) 9:4

38. ₹3000 is distributed among $p$, $q$ and $r$ such that $p$ gets 2/3rd of what $q$ and $r$ together get and $r$ gets ½ of what $p$ and $q$ together get. Find r's share.
    (a) ₹750
    (b) ₹1000
    (c) ₹800
    (d) ₹1200

39. If the ratio of the ages of A and B is 2:5 at present, and fifteen years from now, the ratio will get changed to 7:13, then find A's present age.
    (a) 20 years
    (b) 30 years
    (c) 15 years
    (d) 25 years

40. At constant temperature, pressure of a definite mass of gas is inversely proportional to the volume. If the pressure is reduced by 20%, find the respective change in volume.
    - (a) −16.66%
    - (b) +25%
    - (c) −25%
    - (d) +16.66%

41. If ₹232 is divided among 150 children such that each girl and each boy gets ₹ 1 and ₹2 respectively. Then how many girls are there?
    - (a) 52
    - (b) 54
    - (c) 68
    - (d) 62

42. If 620 bananas were distributed among three monkeys in the ratio $1/3 : 1/2 : 1/5$, how many bananas did the first monkey get?
    - (a) 200
    - (b) 180
    - (c) 102
    - (d) 104

43. A mixture contains milk and water in the ratio 3 : 1. On adding 5 litres of water, the ratio of milk to water becomes 2 : 1. The quantity of milk in the mixture is:
    - (a) 15 litres
    - (b) 25 litres
    - (c) 32.5 litres
    - (d) 30 litres

44. A beggar had one rupee, two rupees and five rupees coins in the ratio 5 : 15 : 12 respectively at the end of day. If that day he earned a total of ₹95, how many one rupee coins did he have?
    - (a) 1
    - (b) 10
    - (c) 5
    - (d) 15

45. Sudhir has coins of the denomination of ₹. 1, 50 p and 25 p in the ratio of 12 : 10 : 7. The total worth of the coins he has is ₹112.5. Find the number of 25 p coins that Sudhir has
    - (a) 48
    - (b) 72
    - (c) 60
    - (d) 42

46. If two numbers are in the ratio of 1 : 5 and if 10 be added to each, the ratio becomes 1 : 3. Now find the lower number.
    - (a) 5
    - (b) 10
    - (c) 15
    - (d) None of these

47. A Flask contains a mixture of 98 litres of alcohol and water in the proportion 5 : 2. How much water (in liters) must be added to it so that the ratio of alcohol to water may be 7 : 5?
    - (a) 14
    - (b) 22
    - (c) 7
    - (d) None of these

48. A cask contains 15 gallons of mixture of wine and water in the ratio 2 : 1. How much of the water must be drawn off, so the ratio of wine and water in the cask may become 4 : 1.
    - (a) 3.0 litres
    - (b) 2.5 litres
    - (c) 5 litres
    - (d) None of these

49. The total number of pupils in three classes of a school is 700. The number of pupils in classes I and II are in the ratio 1 : 4 and those in classes II and III are in the ratio 3 : 5. Find the number of pupils in the class that had the highest number of pupils.
    - (a) 60
    - (b) 125
    - (c) 105
    - (d) 400

50. Sahil can row a certain course up the stream in 84 minutes; they can row the same course down stream in 9 minutes less than they can row it in still water. How long would they take to row down with the stream.
    - (a) 45 or 23 minutes
    - (b) 63 or 12 minutes
    - (c) 60 minutes
    - (d) 19 minutes

51. If $(P + Q) : (Q + R) : (R + P) = 3 : 9 : 8$ & $P + Q + R = 20$. What is the value of $R$?

52. $x$ varies directly as $(y^2 + z^2)$. At $y = 2$ and $z = 3$, the value of $x$ is 26. Find the value of $x$, when $z = 1$, and $y = 5$.

53. The wages of laborers in a factory has increased in the ratio 22 : 25 and their number is decreased in the ratio 3 : 2. What was the original wage bill of the factory if the present bill is ₹5000?

54. The monthly salaries of two persons are in the ratio of 1 : 7. If each receives an increase of ₹2500 in the salary, the ratio is altered to 4 : 13. Find their respective salaries.

55. The ratio of boys to girls in a class is 5 : 3. The class has 16 more boys than girls. How many girls are there in the class?

56. $X$, $Y$ and $Z$ play cricket. $X$'s runs are to $Y$'s runs and $Y$'s runs are to $Z$'s as 3 : 2. They score a total of 342 runs. How many runs did Z make?

57. In a school, 5% of the number of girls is equal to $1/10$th of number of boys. The Ratio between the number of boys to the number of girls is

58. 2 men and 4 boys can do a piece of work in 10 days, while 4 men and 5 boys can do it in 6 days. Men and boys are paid wages according to their output. If the daily wage of man is ₹ 40, then the daily wages of a boy (in Rupees) will be

59. The ratio of the economy and business class fares between two airports is 4:1 and that of the number of passengers travelling by economy and business classes is 1:40. If on a day ₹1100 are collected as total fare, the amount collected from the business class passengers is

60. In an innings of a cricket match, three players X, Y and Z scored a total of 580 runs. If the ratio of the number of runs scored by X to that scored by Y was 3 : 2 and number of runs scored by Y to that scored by Z was 5 : 2, the number of runs scored by X was?

## LEVEL OF DIFFICULTY (II)

1. If the work done by $p$ men in $(p + 2)$ days is to the work done by $(p + 4)$ men in $(p - 1)$ days is in the ratio 1: 1, then the value of $p$ is
   (a) 2             (b) 4
   (c) 6             (d) 5

2. The duration of a railway journey varies as the distance and inversely as the velocity; the velocity varies directly as the square root of the quantity of coal used, and inversely as the number carriages in the train. In a journey of 50 km in half an hour with 18 carriages, 100 kg of coal is required. How much coal will be consumed in a journey of 42 km in 28 minutes with 16 carriages.
   (a) 64 kg        (b) 49 kg
   (c) 25 kg        (d) 36 kg

3. The mass of a circular disc varies as the squares of the radius when the thickness remains the same; it also varies as the thickness when the radius remains the same. Two discs have their thicknesses in the ratio of 16:3; find the ratio of the radii if the mass of the first is thrice that of the second.
   (a) 3 : 4        (b) 5 : 2
   (c) 2 : 1        (d) 1 : 2

4. If $p$ and $q$ are positive integers then $\sqrt{2}$ always lies between:
   (a) $(p + q)/(p - q)$ and $pq$
   (b) $p/q$ and $(p + 2q)/(p + q)$
   (c) $p$ and $q$
   (d) $pq/(p + q)$ and $(p - q)/pq$

5. The cost of digging a pit was ₹2,694. How much will it cost (approximately) if the wages of workmen per day had been increased by 1/8 of the former wages and length of the working day increased by 1/20 of the former period?
   (a) ₹2886        (b) ₹2468
   (c) ₹2878        (d) ₹2000

6. A vessel contains $p$ litres of wine, and another vessel contains q litres of water. r litres are taken out of each vessel and transferred to the other. If $r \times (p + q) = pq$. If $A$ and $B$ are the respective values of the amount of wine contained in the respective containers after this operation, then what can be said about the relationship between $A$ and $B$.

   (a) $A = B$        (b) $\dfrac{A - C}{B - C} > 2$

   (c) $A - B = 4c$      (d) None of these

7. If sum of the roots and the product of the roots of a quadratic equation $S$ are in the ratio of 3 : 1, then which of the following is true?

   (a) $f(S) < 0$
   (b) $(b^2 - 4ac) < 0$
   (c) $S$ is a perfect square
   (d) None of these

8. The incomes of Rahul, Saurav, and Sachin are in the ratio of 4: 5: 6 respectively and their spending are in the ratio of 6: 7: 8 respectively. If Rahul saves one fourth his income, then the savings of Rahul, Saurav, and Sachin are in the ratio:
   (a) 2 : 3 : 4       (b) 5 : 6 : 9
   (c) 5 : 9 : 6       (d) 9 : 5 : 6
   (e) None of these

9. If $a : b = c : d$, and $e : f = g : h$, then $(ae + bf) : (ae - bf) = ?$

   (a) $\dfrac{(e + f)}{(e - f)}$       (b) $\dfrac{(cg + dh)}{(cg - dh)}$

   (c) $\dfrac{(ce + df)}{(cg - dh)}$       (d) $\dfrac{e - f}{e + f}$

10. X is an alloy of A and B. Y is an alloy containing 80% of A, 4 % of B and 16% of C. A fused mass of X and Y is found to contain 74% of A, 16% of B, and 10% of C. The ratio of A to B in X is:
    (a) 9:16       (b) 12:17
    (c) 16:9       (d) None of these

11. Shatabdi Express without its rake can go 36 km in an hour, and the speed is diminished by a quantity that varies as the square root of the number of wagons attached. If it is known that with four wagons its speed is 24 km/h, the greatest number of wagons with which the engine can just move is
    (a) 35       (b) 40
    (c) 36       (d) 42

12. If $p$ varies as $q$ then $p^2 + q^2$ varies as
    (a) $p + q$       (b) $p - q$
    (c) $p^2 - q^2$       (d) None of these

13. If $f(x) = \dfrac{x + 1}{x - 1}$, then the ratio of $x$ to $f(y)$ where $y = f(x)$ is
    (a) $x : y$       (b) $x^2 : y^2$
    (c) $1 : 1$       (d) $y : x$

14. Sahil employs 200 men to build a bund. They finish 5/6 of the work in 10 weeks. Because of some natural calamity not only does the work remain suspended for 4 weeks but also half of the work already done is washed away. After the calamity, when the work is resumed, only 140 men turn up. The total time in which the contractor is able to complete the work assuming that there are no further disruptions in the schedule is

(a) 25 weeks     (b) 26 weeks
(c) 24 weeks     (d) 20 weeks

15. Rahim covers a distance of 48 km performed by train, bike and car in that order, the distance covered by the three ways in that order are in the ratio of $8:1:3$ and charges per kilometer in that order are in the ratio of $8:1:4$. If the train charges being 24 ₹ per kilometer, the total cost of the journey is
    (a) ₹ 924     (b) ₹ 1000
    (c) ₹ 1200     (d) None of these

16. A bag contains 25 paise, 50 paise and 1 Rupee coins. There are 220 coins in all and the total amount in the bag is ₹160. If there are thrice as many 1 Rupee coins as there are 25 paise coins, then what is the number of 50 paise coins?
    (a) 60     (b) 40
    (c) 120     (d) 80

**Directions for Questions 17 to 19:** Read the following and answer the questions that follow.

Sahir runs in a triathlon consisting of three phases in the following manner. Running 12 km, cycling 24 km and swimming 5 km. His speeds in the three phases are in the ratio $2:6:1$. He completes the race in $n$ minutes. Later, he changes his strategy so that the distances he covers in each phase are constant but his speeds are now in the ratio $3:8:1$. The end result is that he completes the race taking 20 minutes more than the earlier speed. It is also known that he has not changed his running speed when he changes his strategy.

17. What is his initial speed while swimming?
    (a) 1/2 km/min     (b) 0.05 km/min
    (c) 0.15 km/min     (d) None of these

18. If his speeds are in the ratio 1:3:1, with the running time remaining unchanged, what is his finishing time?
    (a) 500/3 min     (b) 250/3 min
    (c) 200/3 min     (d) 350/3 min

19. What is Sahir's original speed of running?
    (a) 9 kmph     (b) 18 kmph
    (c) 54 kmph     (d) 12 kmph

20. Concentrations of three type of milks $X$, $Y$ and $Z$ are 10%, 20% and 30%, respectively. They are mixed in the ratio $2:3:P$ resulting in a 23% concentration solution. Find $P$.
    (a) 7     (b) 6
    (c) 5     (d) 4

21. The cost of an article (which is composed of raw materials and wages) was 3 times the value of the raw materials used. The cost of raw materials increased in the ratio $3:7$ and wages increased in the ratio $4:9$. Find the present cost of the article if its original cost was ₹ 18.
    (a) ₹ 41     (b) ₹ 30
    (c) ₹ 40     (d) ₹ 46

22. In a co-educational school there are 15 more girls than boys. If the number of girls is increased by 10% and the number of boys is also increased by 16%, there would be 9 more girls than boys. What is the number of students in the school?
    (a) 140     (b) 125
    (c) 265     (d) 255

23. At IIM Bangalore class of 1995, Sonali, a first year student has taken 10 courses, earning grades $A$ (worth 4 points each), $B$ (worth 3 points each) and $C$ (worth 2 points each). Her grade point average is 3.2, and if the course in which she get $C$'s were deleted, her GPA in the remaining courses would be 3.333. How many $A$'s, $B$'s and $C$'s did she get?
    (a) 3, 1 and 6     (b) 1, 3 and 6
    (c) 3, 6 and 1     (d) 1, 6 and 3

24. Total expenses of running the hostel at Harvard Business School are partly fixed and partly varying linearly with the number of boarders. The average expense per boarder is $70 when there are 25 boarders and $60 when there are 50 boarders. What is the average expense per boarder when there are 100 boarders?
    (a) 55     (b) 56
    (c) 54     (d) 50

25. The speed of the engine of Gondwana Express is 42 km/h when no compartment is attached, and the reduction in speed is directly proportional to the square root of the number of compartments attached. If the speed of the train carried by this engine is 24 km/h when 9 compartments are attached, the maximum number of compartments that can be carried by the engine is
    (a) 49     (b) 48
    (c) 46     (d) 47

Three drunkards agree to pool their vodka and decided to share it with a fourth drunkard (who had no vodka) at a price equal to 5 roubles a litre. The first drunkard contributed 1 litre more than the second and the second contributed a litre more than the third. Then all four of them divided the vodka equally and drank it. The fourth drunkard paid money, which was divided in the ratio of each drunkard's contribution towards his portion. It was found that the first drunkard should get twice as much money as the second. Based on this information answer the questions 26–28. (Assume that all shares are integral).

26. How much money did the second drunkard get (in roubles)?
    (a) 8     (b) 10
    (c) 5     (d) Data insufficient

27. How many litres of vodka was consumed in all by the four of them?
    (a) 12
    (b) 16
    (c) 10
    (d) None of these

28. What proportion of the fourth drunkard's drink did the second drunkard contribute?
    (a) 1/3
    (b) 2/3
    (c) 1/2
    (d) None of these

29. In Ramnagar Colony, the ratio of school going children to non-school going children is 5:4. If in the next year, the number of non-school going children is increased by 20%, making it 35,400, what is the new ratio of school going children to non-school going children?
    (a) 4:5
    (b) 3:2
    (c) 25:24
    (d) None of these

30. A precious stone weighing 35 grams worth ₹ 12,250 is accidentally dropped and gets broken into two pieces having weights in the ratio of 2:5. If the price varies as the square of the weight then find the loss incurred.
    (a) ₹ 5750
    (b) ₹ 6000
    (c) ₹ 5500
    (d) ₹ 5000

31. On his deathbed, Mr. Kalu called upon his three sons and told them to distribute all his assets worth ₹ 5,25,000 in the ratio of 1/15 : 1/21 : 1/35 amongst themselves. Find the biggest share amongst the three portions.
    (a) 17,500
    (b) 2,45,000
    (c) 10,500
    (d) 13,250

32. Three jackals—Paar, Maar and Taar together have 675 loaves of bread. Paar has got three times as much as Maar but 25 loaves more than Taar. How many does Taar have?
    (a) 175
    (b) 275
    (c) 375
    (d) None of these

33. King Sheru had ordered the distribution of apples according to the following plan: for every 20 apples the elephant gets, the zebra should get 13 apples and the deer should get 8 apples. Now his servant Shambha jackal is in a fix. Can you help him by telling how much should he give to the elephant if there were 820 apples in total?
    (a) 140
    (b) 160
    (c) 200
    (d) 400

34. In the famous Bhojpur island, there are four men for every three women and five children for every three men. How many children are there in the island if it has 531 women?
    (a) 454
    (b) 1180
    (c) 1070
    (d) 389

35. Which of the following will have the maximum change in their values if 5 is added to both the numerator and denominator of all the fractions?
    (a) 3/4
    (b) 2/3
    (c) 4/7
    (d) 5/7

36. 40 men could have finished the whole project in 28 days but due to the inclusion of a few more men, work got done in 3/4 of the time. Find out how many more men were included (in whole numbers).
    (a) 12
    (b) 13
    (c) 14
    (d) None of these

37. Mr *AM*, the magnanimous cashier at *XYZ* Ltd., while distributing salary, adds whatever money is needed to make the sum a multiple of 50. He adds ₹ 10 and ₹ 40 to *A*'s and *B*'s salary respectively and then he realises that the salaries of *A*, *B* and *C* are now in the ratio 4:5:7. The salary of *C* could be
    (a) ₹ 2300
    (b) ₹ 2150
    (c) ₹ 1800
    (d) ₹ 2100

38. A mother divided an amount of ₹ 61,000 between her two daughters aged 18 years and 16 years respectively and deposited their shares in a bond. If the interest rate is 20% compounded annually and if each received the same amount as the other when she attained the age of 20 years, their shares are
    (a) ₹ 35,600 and ₹ 25,400
    (b) ₹ 30500 each
    (c) ₹ 24,000 and ₹ 37000
    (d) None of these

**Directions for Questions 39 to 41:** Read the passage below and answer the questions that follow:

Anshu gave Bobby and Chandana as many pens as each one of them already had. Then Chandana gave Anshu and Bobby as many pens as each already had. Now each had an equal number of pens. The total number of pens is 72.

39. How many pens did Bobby have initially?
    (a) 24
    (b) 18
    (c) 12
    (d) 6

40. How many pens did Chandana have initially?
    (a) 24
    (b) 18
    (c) 12
    (d) 6

41. How many pens did Anshu have initially?
    (a) 30
    (b) 36
    (c) 42
    (d) 48

42. The volume of a pyramid varies jointly as its height and the area of its base; and when the area of the base is 60 square dm and the height 14 dm, the volume is 280 cubic dm. What is the area of the base of a pyramid whose volume is 390 cubic dm and whose height is 26 dm?
    (a) 40
    (b) 45
    (c) 50
    (d) None of these

43. The expenses of an all boys' institute are partly constant and partly vary as the number of boys. The expenses were ₹ 10,000 for 150 boys and ₹ 8400 for 120 boys. What will the expenses be when there are 330 boys?
   (a) 18,000
   (b) 19,600
   (c) 22,400
   (d) None of these

44. The distance of the horizon at sea varies as the square root of the height of the eye above sea-level. When the distance is 14.4 km, the height of the eye is 18 metres. Find, in kilometres, the distance when the height of the eye is 8 metres.
   (a) 4.8 km
   (b) 7.2 km
   (c) 9.6 km
   (d) 12 km

45. A mixture of cement, sand and gravel in the ratio of $1:2:4$ by volume is required. A person wishes to measure out quantities by weight. He finds that the weight of one cubic foot of cement is 94 kg, of sand 100 kg and gravel 110 kg. What should be the ratio of cement, sand and gravel by weight in order to give a proper mixture?
   (a) $47:100:220$
   (b) $94:100:220$
   (c) $47:200:440$
   (d) None of these

### Direction for question number 46 to 47:
The sum of three numbers $x, y, z$ is 5000. If we reduce the first number by 50, the second number by 100, and the third number by 150, then the new ratio of $x$ & $y$ = 4: 5 & the new ratio of $y$ & $z$ =3: 4. Answer the following questions

46. $x + y = ?$

47. If we reduce $x$ by $a$ and $y$ by $b$ such that the new ratio of x and y is 1: 1 if $b = 2.4a$ then find the value of $|(a - b)|$.

### Direction for question number 48 to 49:
There are three containers $x, y, z$. In container $x$, the ratio of Milk and Water is 2: 1, in container y the ratio of water and milk is 2: a. If container x and y are mixed in the ratio of 2: 3, to get 100 litres of a mixture having Milk and Water in the ratio 3: 1.

48. Then a= ?

49. If after inspection, it was found that the milk we are using in container x, is actually a mixture of milk and water in the 1: 1 ratio, then the ratio of milk and water in the final mixture is?

### Direction for question number 50-52:
The temperature of Delhi and Lucknow were in the ratio 3:5 in July and 2: 3 in August. The percentage increase in temperature from August to September is twice as from July to August for Delhi and same as for July to August for Lucknow. If the ratio of the sum of the temperatures of these two cities in August and July was 5: 4, then answer the following questions.

50. What was the percentage increase in temperature of Lucknow from July to August?

51. What was the value of the ratio (Temperature of Lucknow in September/Temperature of Delhi in September)?

52. If temperature of Delhi in August was 20°C then what was the sum of the temperatures of these two cities in September?

53. In 2006, Raveendra was allotted 650 shares of Sun Systems Ltd in the initial public offer, at the face value of ₹10 per share. In 2007, Sun Systems declared a bonus at the rate of 3:13. In 2008, the company again declared a bonus at the rate of 2:4. In 2009, the company declared a dividend of 12.5%. What is the ratio of the dividend and the initial investment of Raveendra in 2009?        (IIFT 2010)

54. The ratio of 'metal 1' and 'metal 2' in Alloy 'A' is 3: 4. In Alloy 'B' same metals are mixed in the ratio 5: 8. If 26 kg of Alloy 'B' and 14 kg of Alloy 'A' are mixed then find out the ratio of 'metal 1' and 'metal 2' in the new Alloy =?        (IIFT 2011)

55. Karam Purchased four varieties of paint at the rate of 0.10 litres per ₹, 0.20 litres per ₹, 0.30 litres per ₹ and 0.40 litre per ₹. If he mixes all the four varieties of paints in the ratio of 1: 2: 3: 4 in the given order, then find the price (in ₹/litre) at which Karam should sell the mixture to make a profit of 10% on his entire stock.

### Space for Rough Work

## LEVEL OF DIFFICULTY (III)

1. An alloy of gold and silver is taken in the ratio of 1:2, and another alloy of the same metals is taken in the ratio of 2:3. How many parts of the two alloys must be taken to obtain a new alloy consisting of gold and silver that are in the ratio 3:5?

   (a) 3 and 5          (b) 2 and 9
   (c) 2 and 5          (d) 1 and 5

2. There are two quantities of oil, with the masses differing by 2 kg. The same quantity of heat, equal to 96 kcal, was imparted to each mass, and the larger mass of oil was found to be 4 degrees cooler than the smaller mass. Find the mass of oil in each of the two quantities.

   (a) 6 and 8          (b) 4 and 6
   (c) 2 and 9          (d) 4 and 9

3. There are two alloys of gold and silver. In the first alloy, there is twice as much gold as silver, and in the second alloy there is 5 times less gold than silver. How many times more must we take of the second alloy than the first in order to obtain a new alloy in which there would be twice as much silver as gold?

   (a) Two times        (b) Three times
   (c) Four times       (d) Ten times

4. Calculate the weight and the percentage of zinc in the zinc–copper alloy being given that the latter's alloy with 3 kg of pure zinc contains 90 per cent of zinc and with 2 kg of 90% zinc alloy contains 84% of zinc.

   (a) 2.4 kg or 80%    (b) 1.4 kg or 88%
   (c) 3.4 kg or 60%    (d) 7.4 kg or 18%

5. Two solutions, the first of which contains 0.8 kg and the second 0.6 kg of salt, were poured together and 10 kg of a new salt solution were obtained. Find the weight of the first and of the second solution in the mixture if the first solution is known to contain 10 per cent more of salt than the second.

   (a) 4 kg, 6 kg       (b) 3 kg, 7 kg
   (c) 4 kg, 9 kg       (d) 5 kg, 9 kg

6. From a full barrel containing 729 litres of honey we pour off '$a$' litre and add water to fill up the barrel. After stirring the solution thoroughly, we pour off '$a$' litre of the solution and again add water to fill up the barrel. After the procedure is repeated 6 times, the solution in the barrel contains 64 litres of honey. Find $a$.

   (a) 243 litres       (b) 81 litres
   (c) 2.7 litres       (d) 3 litres

7. In two alloys, the ratios of nickel to tin are 5:2 and 3:4 (by weight). How many kilogram of the first alloy and of the second alloy should be alloyed together to obtain 28 kg of a new alloy with equal contents of nickel and tin?

   (a) 9 kg of the first alloy and 22 kg of the second
   (b) 17 kg of the first alloy and 11 kg of the second
   (c) 7 kg of the first alloy and 21 kg of the second
   (d) 8 kg and 20 kg respectively

8. In two alloys, aluminium and iron are in the ratios of 4:1 and 1:3. After alloying together 10 kg of the first alloy, 16 kg of the second and several kilograms of pure aluminium, an alloy was obtained in which the ratio of aluminium to iron was 3:2. Find the weight of the new alloy.

   (a) 15               (b) 35
   (c) 65               (d) 95

9. There are two alloys of gold, silver and platinum. The first alloy is known to contain 40 per cent of platinum and the second alloy 26 per cent of silver. The percentage of gold is the same in both alloys. Having alloyed 150 kg of the first alloy and 250 kg of the second, we get a new alloy that contains 30 per cent of gold. How many kilogram of platinum is there in the new alloy?

   (a) 170 kg           (b) 175 kg
   (c) 160 kg           (d) 165 kg

10. Two alloys of iron have different percentage of iron in them. The first one weighs 6 kg and second one weighs 12 kg. One piece each of equal weight was cut off from both the alloys and the first piece was alloyed with the second alloy and the second piece alloyed with the first one. As a result, the percentage of iron became the same in the resulting two new alloys. What was the weight of each cut-off piece?

    (a) 4 kg            (b) 2 kg
    (c) 3 kg            (d) 5 kg

11. Two litres of a mixture of wine and water contain 12% water. They are added to 3 litres of another mixture containing 7% water, and half a litre of water is then added to whole. What is the percentage of water in resulting concoction?

    (a) 17(2/7)%        (b) 15 (7/11)%
    (c) 17(3/11)%       (d) 16 (2/3)%

12. Three vessels having volumes in the ratio of 1:2:3 are full of a mixture of coke and soda. In the first vessel, ratio of coke and soda is 2:3, in second, 3:7

and in third, 1 : 4. If the liquid in all the three vessels were mixed in a bigger container, what is the resulting ratio of coke and soda?

(a) 4:11      (b) 5:7

(c) 7:11      (d) 7:5

13. Two types of tea are mixed in the ratio of 3 : 5 to produce the first quality and if they are mixed in the ratio of 2 : 3, the second quality is obtained. How many kilograms of the first quality has to be mixed with 10 kg of the second quality so that a third quality having the two varieties in the ratio of 7 : 11 may be produced?

(a) 5 kg      (b) 10 kg

(c) 8 kg      (d) 9 kg

14. A toy weighing 24 grams of an alloy of two metals is worth ₹ 174, but if the weights of metals in alloy be interchanged, the toy would be worth ₹ 162. If the price of one metal be ₹ 8 per gram, find the price of the other metal in the alloy used to make the toy.

(a) ₹ 10 per gram      (b) ₹ 6 per gram

(c) ₹ 4 per gram      (d) ₹ 5 per gram

15. The weight of three heaps of gold are in the ratio 5 : 6 : 7. By what fractions of themselves must the first two be increased so that the ratio of the weights may be changed to 7 : 6 : 5?

(a) $\dfrac{24}{25}, \dfrac{2}{5}$      (b) $\dfrac{48}{50}, \dfrac{4}{5}$

(c) $\dfrac{48}{50}, \dfrac{3}{5}$      (d) $\dfrac{24}{25}, \dfrac{3}{7}$

16. An alloy of gold, silver and bronze contains 90% bronze, 7% gold and 3% silver. A second alloy of bronze and silver only is melted with the first and the mixture contains 85% of bronze, 5% of gold and 10% of silver. Find the percentage of bronze in the second alloy.

(a) 75%      (b) 72.5%

(c) 70%      (d) 67.5%

17. Gunpowder can be prepared by saltpetre and nitrous oxide. Price of saltpetre is thrice the price of nitrous oxide. Notorious gangster Kallu Bhai sells the gunpowder at ₹ 2160 per 10 g, thereby making a profit of 20%. If the ratio of saltpetre and nitrous oxide in the mixture be 2 : 3, find the cost price of saltpetre.

(a) ₹ 210/gm      (b) ₹ 300/gm

(c) ₹ 120/gm      (d) None of these

18. Two boxes A and B were filled with a mixture of rice and dal—in A in the ratio of 5 : 3, and in B in the ratio of 7 : 3. What quantity must be taken from the first to form a mixture that shall contain 8 kg of rice and 3 kg of dal?

(a) 4 kg

(b) 5 kg

(c) 6 kg

(d) This cannot be achieved

19. A person buys 18 local tickets for ₹ 110. Each first class ticket costs ₹ 10 and each second class ticket costs ₹ 3. What will another lot of 18 tickets in which the number of first class and second class tickets are interchanged cost?

(a) 112      (b) 118

(c) 121      (d) 124

20. Two jars having a capacity of 3 and 5 litres respectively are filled with mixtures of milk and water. In the smaller jar 25% of the mixture is milk and in the larger 25% of the mixture is water. The jars are emptied into a 10 litre cask whose remaining capacity is filled up with water. Find the percentage of milk in the cask.

(a) 55%      (b) 50%

(c) 45%      (d) None of these

21. Two cubes of bronze have their total weight equivalent to 60 kg. The first piece contains 10 kg of pure zinc and the second piece contains 8 kg of pure zinc. What is the percentage of zinc in the first piece of bronze if the second piece contains 15 per cent more zinc than the first?

(a) 15%      (b) 25%

(c) 55%      (d) 24%

22. Sonu gets a jewellery made of an alloy of copper and silver. The alloy with a weight of 8 kg contains $p$ per cent of copper. What piece of a copper–silver alloy containing 40 per cent of silver must be alloyed with the first piece in order to obtain a new alloy with the minimum percentage of copper if the weight of the second piece is 2 kg?

(a) 2 kg for $p > 60$, $a$ kg, where $a \in [0, 2]$, for $p = 60$, 0 kg for $0 < p < 60$

(b) 0 kg for $p > 60$, $a$ kg, where $a \in [0, 2]$, for $p = 60$, 2 kg for $0 < p < 60$

(c) 0 kg for $p > 60$, $a$ kg, where $a \in [0, 3]$, for $p = 70$, 0 kg for $0 < p < 70$

(d) None of these

23. From a vessel filled up with pure spirit to the brim, two litres of spirit was removed and 2 litres of water were added. After the solution was mixed, 2 litres of the mixture was poured off and again 2 litres of water was added. The solution was stirred again and 2 litres of the mixture was removed and 2 litres of water was added. As a result of the above operations, the volume of water in the vessel increased by 3 litres than the volume of spirit remaining in it. How many litres of spirit and water were there in the vessel after the above procedure was carried out?

(a) 0.7 litre of spirit and 3.7 litres of water

(b) 1.5 litres of spirit and 4.5 litres of water

(c) 8.5 litre of spirit and 11.5 litres of water

(d) 0.5 litre of spirit and 3.5 litres of water

24. There are two qualities of milk—Amul and Sudha having different prices per litre, their volumes being 130 litres and 180 litres respectively. After equal amounts of milk was removed from both, the milk removed from Amul was added to Sudha and vice-versa. The resulting two types of milk now have the same price. Find the amount of milk drawn out from each type of milk.

(a) 58.66                (b) 75.48

(c) 81.23                (d) None of these

25. Assume that the rate of consumption of coal by a locomotive varies as the square of the speed and is 1000 kg per hour when the speed is 60 km per hour. If the coal costs the railway company ₹ 15 per 100 kg and if the other expenses of the train be ₹ 12 per hour, find a formula for the cost in paise per kilometre when the speed is $S$ km per hour.

(a) $1200 + \dfrac{5S^2}{18}$          (b) $1200 + \dfrac{75S^2}{18}$

(c) $\dfrac{1200}{S} + \dfrac{75S}{18}$          (d) None of these

*Space for Rough Work*

## ANSWER KEY

### Level of Difficulty (I)

| | | | |
|---|---|---|---|
| 1. (b) | 2. (d) | 3. (b) | 4. (a) |
| 5. (b) | 6. (d) | 7. (b) | 8. (b) |
| 9. (b) | 10. (c) | 11. (d) | 12. (b) |
| 13. (a) | 14. b | 15. (b) | 16. (c) |
| 17. (a) | 18. (c) | 19. (a) | 20. (a) |
| 21. (c) | 22. (a) | 23. (b) | 24. (c) |
| 25. (d) | 26. (b) | 27. (d) | 28. (a) |
| 29. (b) | 30. (a) | 31. (a) | 32. (d) |
| 33. (a) | 34. (c) | 35. (d) | 36. (d) |
| 37. (b) | 38. (b) | 39. (a) | 40. (b) |
| 41. (c) | 42. (a) | 43. (d) | 44. (c) |
| 45. (d) | 46. (b) | 47. (b) | 48. (b) |
| 49. (d) | 50. (b) | 51. 14 | 52. 52 |
| 53. 6600 | | 54. ₹1500, 10500 | |
| 55. 24 | 56. 72 | 57. 1:2 | 58. 16 |
| 59. 1000 | 60. 300 | | |

### Level of Difficulty (II)

| | | | |
|---|---|---|---|
| 1. (b) | 2. (a) | 3. (a) | 4. (b) |
| 5. (a) | 6. (d) | 7. (d) | 8. (a) |
| 9. (b) | 10. (c) | 11. (a) | 12. (d) |
| 13. (c) | 14. (c) | 15. (a) | 16. (a) |
| 17. (c) | 18. (b) | 19. (b) | 20. (c) |
| 21. (a) | 22. (c) | 23. (c) | 24. (a) |
| 25. (b) | 26. (c) | 27. (a) | 28. (a) |
| 29. (c) | 30. (d) | 31. (b) | 32. (b) |
| 33. (d) | 34. (b) | 35. (b) | 36. (c) |
| 37. (d) | 38. (d) | 39. (d) | 40. (a) |
| 41. (c) | 42. (b) | 43. (b) | 44. (c) |
| 45. (a) | 46. 2850 | 47. 350 | 48. 8.3 |
| 49. 37:23 | 50. 20 | 51. 1.08 | 52. 69.33 |
| 53. 0.23 | 54. 0.67 | 55. 4.4 | |

### Level of Difficulty (III)

| | | | |
|---|---|---|---|
| 1. (a) | 2. (a) | 3. (a) | 4. (a) |
| 5. (a) | 6. (a) | 7. (c) | 8. (b) |
| 9. (a) | 10. (a) | 11. (c) | 12. (a) |
| 13. (c) | 14. (b) | 15. (a) | 16. (b) |
| 17. (b) | 18. (d) | 19. (d) | 20. (c) |
| 21. (b) | 22. (a) | 23. (d) | 24. (b) |
| 25. (c) | | | |

### Hints

### Level of Difficulty (III)

1. One alloy contains 33.33% gold, the other contains 40% gold. The mixture must contain 37.5% gold. Solve using alligation.

2. $\dfrac{96}{x} - \dfrac{96}{(x+2)} = 4$ (Required difference). Check using options.

3.
gives 1 : 2

4. Check using options whether the given conditions of mixing are met.
Option (a) gives : 2.4 kg of zinc @ 80% concentration. i.e., 3 kg alloy of 80% zinc concentration is mixed with 3 kg of pure zinc. Satisfies the given condition.

5. Solve using options the following equation $\dfrac{0.8}{x} - \dfrac{0.6}{10-x} = 0.1$

7. Check the options.

8. 80% aluminium (4:1) and 25% aluminium (1:3) have to be mixed with pure aluminium to obtain an alloy with 60% aluminium.
$$\therefore \quad \dfrac{10 \times 0.8 + 16 \times 0.25 + x}{10 + 16 + x} = 0.6$$

9. Since the percentage of gold in both alloys is the same, any mixture of the two will contain the same percentage concentration of gold.
Hence, we get

First alloy :          Gold :    Silver :   Platinum
                       30 :       30 :      40

AND Second alloy:   Gold :    Silver :   Platinum
                       30 :      26 :      44

10. Let 'w' be the weight of the cut off piece.
Then, $\dfrac{6-w}{w} = \dfrac{w}{12-w}$

13. First alloy has 37.5% of the first tea type. Similarly, the second alloy has 40% of the first tea type. The mixture should contain 42.85% of the first tea type. This is not possible.

16. When one alloy having 7% gold is mixed with another alloy having no gold, the result is a new alloy with 5% gold. Hence, ratio of mixing is 2 : 5.

19. $10x + (18 - x) \times 3 = 110$

20. Out of 8 litres milk and water mixture poured into the 10 litre cask, the milk is $0.25 \times 3 + 0.75 \times 5 = 4.5$.

21. $\dfrac{8}{x} - \dfrac{10}{60-x} = 0.15$.

22. Since the second alloy contains 60% copper, the requirement for the minimisation of copper will be fulfilled by option 2. Note, that the values of the number of kgs required of the second alloy will depend on the value of p.

24. Solve through options.

25. Total cost = Other expenses (paise/km) + Coal cost (paise/km).
Coal Consumption = $k \times s^2$
$\therefore \quad 1000 = k \times 60^2$

$k = \dfrac{5}{18}$ and Coal consumption $= \dfrac{5}{18} \times s^2$

$\therefore$ Required expression is

Total cost $= \dfrac{1200}{s} + \dfrac{5}{18} \, s \times 15.$

## Solutions and Shortcuts

### Level of Difficulty (I)

1. Assume a set of values for $p$, $q$, $r$, $s$ such that they are proportional i.e. $p/q = r/s$. Suppose we take $p:q$, as 1:4 and $r:s$ as 3:12 we get the given expression: $(p - q)(p - r)/p = -3 \times -2/1 = 6$. This value is also given by $p + s - q - r$ and hence option (b) is correct.

2. $\dfrac{7 + 3}{31 + 3} = \dfrac{10}{34} = \dfrac{5}{17}$

   Thus option (d) is correct.

3. $x = k/(y^3 - 1)$. This gives $k = 3 \times 7 = 21$.
   When, $y = 4$, the equation becomes $x = 21/(4^3 - 1)$ $= 21/63 = 1/3$.

4. $x = ky \to 12 = 4k \to k = 3$
   Hence, $x = 3 \times y$
   When, $y = 15$, $x = 3 \times 15 = 45$.

5. $X = K \times Y \times Z \to$ It is known that when $X = 6$, $Y = 3$ and $Z = 2$. Thus we get $6 = 6K \to K = 1$.
   Thus, our relationship between $X$, $Y$ and $Z$ becomes $X = Y \times Z$. Thus, when $Y = 5$ and $Z = 7$ we get $X = 35$.

6. $x = ky/z$
   We cannot determine the value of $k$ from the given information and hence cannot answer the question.

7. Solve this question using options. 1/2 of the first part should equal 1/4th of the second part and 1/8th of the third part. Only, option (b) satisfies these conditions thus this option is correct.

8. Check the options, B = 1000 and C = $1.5 \times 1000 =$
   1500, D $= \dfrac{4}{3} \times 1500 = 2000$
   A $= 5000 - 1000 - 1500 - 2000 = 500$.
   Now A + B $= 500 + 1000 = 1500$, C + D $= 1500 + 2000 = 3500$.
   As $1500 = \dfrac{3}{7} \times 1500$. So this option is correct.

9. The given condition has $p$, $q$ and $r$ symmetrically placed. Thus, if we use $p = q = r = 1$ (say) we get each fraction as 1/2.

10. Solve using options. It is clear that a ratio of $x:y$ as 1: 3 fits the equation.

11. Let p = 1, q = 2, r = 3, s = 6
    1 : 2 = 3 : 6 So, $(p^2 + q^2)/(r^2 + s^2) = 5/45 = 1/9$

From the given options, only $pq/rs$ gives us this value.

12. Experimentally if you were to take the value of $p$, q, r, and s as 1 : 2 : 4 : 8, you get the value of the expression as 3.5. If you try other values for p, q, r and $s$ experimentally you can see that while you can approach 3, you cannot get below that.
    For instance,
       1 : 1.1 : : 1.21 : 1.331
    Gives us: $- 0.331/ - 0.11$ which is slightly greater than 3.

13. $3 \times 10 \times 4 = 120$ man-hours are required for '$x$' no. of answer sheets. So, for '$3x$' answer sheets we would require 360 man-hours $= 4 \times 30 \times n \to n =$ 3 Hours a day.

14. In 60 liters, milk = 24 and water = 36. We want to create 1 : 2 milk to water mixture, for this we would need: 24 liters milk and 48 liters water. (Since milk is not increasing). Thus, we need to add 12 liters of water.

15. Option (b) is not true.

16. $1 : 3 : 5 \to x$, $3x$ and $5x$ add up to 18.
    So the numbers are: 2, 6 and 10.
    Ratio of cubes $= 8 : 216 : 1000 = 1: 27: 125$.

17. The numbers would be $7x$ and $11x$ and their LCM would be $77x$. This gives us the values as 14 and 22. The first number is 14.

18. Since equal quantities are being mixed, assume that both alloys have 18 kgs (18 being a number which is the LCM of 9 and 18).
    The third alloy will get, 14 kg of aluminum from the first alloy and 7 kg of aluminum from the second alloy. Hence, the required ratio: $21:15 = 7:5$

19. The total number of man-days-hours required $= 10 \times 6 \times 15 = 900$
    $20 \times 14 \times$ number of days $= 900 \to$ number of days $= 900/280 = 3.21$ days

20. Solve using options. Option (a) fits the situation as if you take $P$'s income as ₹1000, $Q$'s income will become ₹2,000 and if they each save ₹500, their expenditures would be ₹500 and ₹1500 respectively. This gives the required 1:3 ratio.

21. The given ratio for sines would only be true for a 45-45-90 triangle. The sides of such a triangle are in the ratio $1:1:\sqrt{2}$. The square of the longest side is 2 while the sum of the squares of the other two sides is also 2. Hence, the required ratio is 1:1.

22. $p$ gets 2/3 of what $q$ gets and $q$ gets 1/4th of what $r$ gets' means a ratio of 2:3:12 for p:q:r. Hence, r's share $= \dfrac{12}{17} \times 1360 = 960$. Alternately, you could also solve by using options. Option (a) r = 960 fits perfectly because if r = 960, $q = 240$ and p = 160.

23. $P$'s contribution = 33.33%

   $Q$'s contribution = 50%

   $R$'s contribution = 16.66%

   Ratio of profit sharing = Ratio of contribution

   $\qquad\qquad = 2 : 3 : 1$

   Thus, profit would be shared as : 56000 : 84000 : 28000.

24. $2x + 20 : 3x + 20 : 5x + 20 = 4 : 5 : 7 \rightarrow x = 10$ and initially the number of students would be 20, 30 and 50 → a total of 100.

25. The ratio of time would be such that speed × time would be constant for all three. Thus if you take the speeds as $x$, $2x$ and $3x$ respectively, the times would be $6y$, $3y$ and $2y$, respectively.

26. Again in order to solve this question, try to assume values for p, $q$, r and s such that $p : q = r : s$ (i.e. p, q, r and $s$ are proportional). Let us say we assume p = 1, q = 4, r = 3 and s = 12 we get:

   $p^2 + r^2 = 10$ and $q^2 + s^2 = 160$. The mean proportional between 10 and 160 is 40. $pq + rs$ gives us this value and can be checked by taking another set of values to see that it still works. It can also be verified that none of the other options yields this answer and hence option (b) is correct.

27. Option (d) is true since $1/z$ will be greater than 1 and $\sqrt{z}$ would be less then 1.

28. Amit's share should be divisible by 3. Option (d) gets rejected by this logic.

   Further: $A + B + C = 1200$. If Amit's share is 300 (according to option (a)). Bineet's share should be 400 & Chaman's share should be 500. (Gives us a total of 300 + 400 + 500 = 1200).

   Hence, option a is correct.

29. Check the options. Option b is correct.

30. Their ratio being 2: 1, the difference according to the ratio is 11 so the numbers must be 22 and 11 respectively. Hence, the product is 242.

31. 120 tractors days = 1/6 of the field → 720 tractors days are required to plough the field. Thus, the remaining work would be $720 \times \dfrac{5}{6} = 600$ tractors days. With 20 tractors, it would take 30 days.

32. Assume that 1 cow leap is equal to 3 metres and 1 goat leap is equal to 4 metres.

   Then the speed of the cow in one unit time = 3 × 5 = 15 meters.

   Also, the speed of the goat in one unit time = 4 × 4 = 16 meters.

   The required ratio is 15:16.

33. $3x$, and $5x$ are their current ages. According to the problem, $3x - 10 : 5x - 10 = 1:2 \rightarrow x = 10$ and hence the sum total of their present ages is 80 years (30 + 50 = 80).

34. $x + 2x + 4x + 8x = 120 \rightarrow x = 8$

   Thus, $8x = 64$.

35. The share of the rent is on the basis of the ratio of the number of cow months. $A$ uses 660 cow months (220 × 3), $B$ uses 1320(220 × 6) and $C$ uses 2640 cow months (880 × 3)

   Hence, the required ratio is: 660:1320:2640 = 1:2:4

   Required percentage = $\dfrac{4}{7} \times 100 = \dfrac{400}{7} = 57.14\%$

36. 25 × 12 = 300 man-days is required for the job. If only 20 students turn up, they would require 15 days to complete the task. The number of days is increasing by 1/4.

37. The initial amount of water is 9 litres and petrol is 27 litres. By adding 15 litres of petrol the mixture becomes 42 petrol and 9 water → 14:3 the required ratio.

38. From the first statement $p = 1200$ and $q + r = 1800$. From the second statement $r = 1000$ and $p + q = 2000$.

39. $2x + 15: 5x + 15 = 7:13$

   $\qquad \rightarrow 26x + 195 = 35x + 105$

   $\qquad 9x = 90 \rightarrow x = 10$

   A's present age = $2x = 20$ years

40. Since pressure and volume are inversely proportional, we get that if one is reduced by 20% the other would grow by 25%. Option (b) is correct.

41. Solve using options.

   For option (c), 68 girls. Hence, 82 boys

   $\qquad$ Amount with Girls = 68 × 1 = 68

   $\qquad$ Amount with Boys = 82 × 2 = 164.

   $\qquad$ Total of 68 + 164 = 232.

   Thus, option (c) fits the conditions.

42. The ratio : 1/3 : ½ : 1/5 = 10 : 15 : 6

   Thus, the first monkey would get $\left(620 \times \dfrac{10}{31}\right) = 200$ bananas.

43. Check the options. Only option (d) satisfies all the given conditions.

44. The ratio of the values of the three coins are:

   $\qquad 1 \times 5 : 15 \times 2 : 12 \times 5 = 5:30:60$

   Thus, one rupee coins correspond to ₹5. Hence, there will be 5 coins.

45. Ratio of number of coins = 12:10:7

   Ratio of individual values of coins = 1:0.5: 0.25

   Ratio of gross value of coins = 12 : 5 : 1.75

   $\qquad\qquad\qquad\qquad\qquad = 48 : 20 : 7 \rightarrow 112.5$

   Thus, he has ₹10.5 in 25 paisa coins. Which means that he would have 42 such coins.

46. Solve using options. 10/50 becomes 20/60 = 1/3

47. Initial alcohol = 70 liters

   Initial water = 28 litres

Since, we want to create 7: 5 mixture of alcohol and water by adding only water, it mean that the amount of alcohol is constant at 70 litres. Thus 7 : 5 = 70 : 50. So, we need 22 litres of water.

48. Initially the cask has 10 liters wine and 5 liters of water. If we were to draw out 2.5 litres of water, the ratio of wine to water would become 4:1. Hence, option (b) is correct.

49. The overall ratio is: 3: 12: 20. Dividing 700 in 3: 12: 20, we get number of students in class III (AS Class III has highest number of students) = $\frac{20}{35} \times 700 = 400$

50. If you try to solve this question through equations, the process becomes too long and almost inconclusive. The best way to approach this question is by trying to use options.

The question asks us to find the time in which the boat can move downstream.

The basic situation in this question is:

Percentage increase over still water speed while going downstream = Percentage decrease over still water speed while going upstream.

(Since: $S_{downstream} = S_{boat} + S_{stream}$ and $S_{upstream} = S_{boat} - S_{stream}$)

Hence, the percentage increase in time while going upstream should match the percentage decrease in time while going downstream in such a way that the percentage change in the speed is same in both the cases).

Testing for option (a):

$Time_{upstream}$ = 84 minutes (given)

$Time_{downstream}$ = 45 minutes (first value from the option)

$Time_{Stillwater}$ = 54 minutes (45 + 9)

% increase in time when going upstream = 30/54

[*Note:* The percentage increase should be written as $30 \times 100/54$. However, as I have repeatedly pointed out right from the chapter of percentages, you need to be able to look at % values of ratios directly by using the Percentage rule for calculations)

% decrease in time when going downstream = 9/54 = 16.66%

Since, the % decrease is 16.66%, this should correspond to a % increase in speed by 20% (Since, product speed × time is constant).

This means that the speed should drop by 20% while going upstream and hence the time should increase by 25% while going upstream. But, 30/54 does not give us a value of 25% increase. Hence this option is incorrect.

Testing for option (b):

$Time_{upstream}$ = 84 minutes (given)

$Time_{downstream}$ = 63 minutes (first value from the option)

$Time_{Stillwater}$ = 72 minutes (63 + 9)

% increase in time when going upstream = 12/72 = 16.66%

% decrease in time when going downstream = 9/72 = 12.5%

Since, the % decrease is 12.5%, this should correspond to a % increase in speed by 14.28% (Since, product speed × time is constant).

This means that the speed should drop by 14.28% while going upstream and hence the time should increase by 16.66% while going upstream. This is actually occurring. Hence, this option is correct.

Options (c) and (d) can be seen to be incorrect in this context.

51. If $P + Q = 3K$, $Q + R = 9K$, $R + P = 8K$
$2(P + Q + R) = 20K$
$P + Q + R = 10K = 20$, K = 2.
$P = 2$, $Q = 4$, $R = 14$.

52. $x \propto (y^2 + z^2)$
$x = k(y^2 + z^2)$
$26 = k(2^2 + 3^2)$
$k = 2$
Thus, $x = 2(y^2 + z^2)$
At z = 1, y = 5: x = 2(25 + 1)
x = 52

53. Let initial wage = $22x$
Final wage = $25x$
Let the initial laborers = $3y$
Final laborers = $2y$
Final bill = $25x \times 2y = 5000$
$xy = 100$
Hence, the Original wage bill = $22x \times 3y = 66 xy = 6600$.

54. If their salaries are $k$, $7k$
$$\frac{k + 2500}{7k + 2500} = \frac{4}{13}$$
On solving, we get $k = ₹1500$.
Their salaries are ₹1500, 10500.

55. $5k - 3k = 16$
$k = 8$
Total number of girls = $3k = 24$

56. $X: Y = 3 : 2$
$Y : Z = 3 : 2$
$X: Y: Z = 9: 6:4$
$9k + 6k + 4k = 342$
$$k = \frac{342}{19} = 18$$
Runs made by $Z = 4 \times 18 = 72$.

Ratio, Proportion and Variation   **III.109**

57. 5% of girls = $\frac{1}{10th}$ of boys

G/20 = B/10 (Where G and B are the number of girls and number of boys respectively.)

B: G = 1: 2

58. $(2m + 4b) \times 10 = (4m + 5b) \times 6$

$20m + 40b = 24m + 30b$

$4m = 10b$

$2m = 5b$

$b = \frac{2}{5}m = 0.4 \ m = 0.4 \times 40 = ₹16.$

59. Let the prices of economy and business class be $4x$ and $x$ respectively & the number of passengers be $y$ and $40y$ respectively.

$4x \times y + x \times 40y = 1100$

$44xy = 1100$

$4xy = 100$

Amount collected from business class passengers = $40xy = ₹1000.$

60. X: Y = 3: 2, Y: Z = 5: 2

X: Y: Z = 15: 10: 4

$15k + 10k + 4k = 580$

$k = 20$

Runs scored by X = 15k = 15 × 20 = 300.

## Level of Difficulty (II)

1. By taking the value of $p = 4$ from Option (b), the required ratio of 1: 1 is achieved.

2. $T = KD/V$. Also $V = (K_1 \sqrt{Q})/N$ where $K$ and $K_1$ are constants, $T$ is the time duration of the journey, $Q$ is the quantity of coal used and $N$ is the number of carriages.

Thus, $T = (KDN)/(K_1 \sqrt{Q})$ or $T = (K_2DN)/(\sqrt{Q}) \rightarrow$ if we take $K/K_1$ as $K_2$.

From the information provided in the question: 30 = $(K_2 \times 50 \times 18)/10 \rightarrow K_2 = 1/3$

Thus, the equation becomes: $T = (DN)/(3\sqrt{Q})$. Then, when $D = 42$, $T = 28$, and $N = 16$ we get:

$28 = 42 \times 16/(3\sqrt{Q}) \rightarrow Q = 64$

3. $3w/w = 16r_1^2/3r_2^2$

Thus, $r_1/r_2 = 3:4$

4. Suppose you take $p = 3$ and $q = 2$. It can be clearly seen that the square root of 2 does not lie between 2 and 3. Hence, option (c) is incorrect.

Further with these values for p and q option (a) also can be ruled out since it means that the value should lie between 5 and 6 which it obviously does not.

Also, Option (d) gives 6/5 and 1/6. This means that the value should lie between 0.1666 and 1.2 (which it obviously does not). Hence, option (b) is correct.

5. Since there is a 12.5% increase in the wages, the cost of digging the pit would get increase by 12.5%

- due to the increase in wages. However, since now the workers are working for 5% longer time, you can divide the increased wages by 1.05 to get the required answer. Thus, the answer would be: New cost = $2694 \times \frac{1.125}{1.05} = 2886$ (approximately)

6. The constraint given to us for the values of p, q, and r is $r \times (p + q) = pq$

So, if we take $p = 6$, $q = 3$ and $r = 2$, we have 18 = 18 and a feasible set of values for $p$, $q$ and $r$ respectively. With this set of values, we can complete the operation as defined and see what happens.

Wine left in the vessel A = 4 = (6 − 2)

Wine in the vessel B = 2

With these values none of the first 3 options matches. Thus, option (d) is correct.

7. The only information available here is that − $b/c$ should be equal to 9/1. This is not sufficient to make any of the first three options as conclusions. Hence, option (d) is correct.

8. Let the incomes be 4x, 5x, 6x

And the spending be 6y, 7y, 8y

And savings are (4x − 6y), (5x − 7y) & (6x − 8y)

Rahul saves 1/4th of his income.

Therefore 4x − 6y = 4x/4

4x − 6y = x

3x = 6y

x/y = 2 Therefore y = x/2

Ratio of Rahul's Saurav's & Sachin's savings = 4x − 6y : 5x − 7y : 6x − 8y

= x: 5x − 7y: 6x − 8y

= x: 5x − 7x/2: 6x − 8x/2

= x: 3x/2: 2x

= 2:3:4

9. Solve by taking values of $a$, $b$, $c$, $d$ and $e$, $f$, $g$, and $h$ independently of each other

$a = 1$, $b = 2$, $c = 3$, $d = 6$

and $e = 3$, $f = 9$, $g = 4$

and $h = 12$

gives $(ae + bf) : (ae − bf) = 21: − 15 = − 7/5$

Option (b) $(cg + dh)/(cg − dh) = 84/ − 60 = − 7/5.$ This would be the answer, since no other option gives us the same value.

10. Since X has 0% C and Y has 16% C, the ratio of mixing in the fused mass must be 3:5. Using alligation as follows:

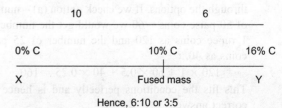

Hence, 6:10 or 3:5

Then, percentage of A in X can be got as follows:

```
        x           74              80
        |————————————|———————————————|
        X       Fused mass           Y
        3                             5
```
$$x = 64\%$$

Required ratio = $64 : (100 - 64) = 64 : 36 = 16 : 9$

11. Speed = $36 - k\sqrt{N}$.

    Putting value of $N = 4$ we get:

    $24 = 36 - 2k$. Hence, $k = 6$.

    Thus the equation is: $S = 36 - 6\sqrt{N}$

    This means that when $N = 36$, the speed will become zero. Hence, the train can just move when 35 wagons are attached.

12. $p$ varies as $q$, means $p = kq$. This does not have any relation to the variance of $p^2 + q^2$.

13. Let $x = 5$

    Then    $y = f(x) = 6/4 = 1.5$

    And    $f(y) = 2.5/0.5 = 5$.

    Thus, the ratio of $x : f(y) = 1 : 1$

    *Note:* Even if you take some other value of $y$, you would still get the same answer.

14. In 2000 man weeks before the calamity, $5/6^{th}$ of the work is completed. Hence, 2400 men weeks will be the total amount of work. However, due to the calamity half the work gets washed off → This means that 1000 man weeks worth of work must have got washed off. This leaves 1400 men weeks of work to be completed by the 140 men. They will take 10 more weeks and hence the total time required is 24 weeks.

15. Total distances covered under each mode = 32, 4 and 12 km respectively.

    Total charges = $32 \times 24 + 4 \times 3 + 12 \times 12 = ₹924$.

16. Let the number of coins of ₹ 1, 50 p, 25 p be A, B and C respectively.

    $$A + B + C = 220 \qquad (1)$$
    $$A = 3C \qquad (2)$$
    $$A + 0.5B + 0.25C = 160 \qquad (3)$$

    We have a situation with 3 equations and 3 unknowns. We can solve for

    A (no. of 1 rupee coins),

    B (no. of 50 paise coins)

    and  C (no. of 25 paise coins)

    However, a much smarter approach would be to go through the options. If we check option (a) – number of 50 paise coins = 60 we would get the number of 1 rupee coins as 120 and the number of 25 paise coins as 40.

    $$120 \times 1 + 60 \times 0.5 + 40 \times 0.25 = 160$$

    This fits the conditions perfectly and is hence the correct answer.

17 – 19.  In order to solve this question, if you try going through equation and expressions, it would lead you in to a very long drawn solution.

Thus:    $12/2x + 24/6x + 5/x = n/60$

and    $12/3y + 24/8y + 5/y = n + 20/60$

We also know that $3y = 2x$.

In order to handle this expression, you can try be substituting the values of the speeds. Also, we know that his running speed (initially) is twice his swimming speed.

Question 17 is asking us his swimming speed, while 19 is asking us his running speed. So the answer of the two questions should be in the ratio 1 : 2. However, a scrutiny of the options shows us that only the third option (values) in question 17 has a value which is half the values provided for in 19. (you would need to check for this after converting the values into kmph – you would see that for 18 kmph in question 19, you have a corresponding swimming speed of 9 kmph in question 17's option (c)).

So, we can start by checking the option (b) from question 19.

Checking for it we have:

Scenario 1: $12/18 + 24/54 + 5/9 = 40$ minutes + 1 hour = 1 hour 40 minutes.

Scenario 2: $12/18 + 24/48 + 5/6 = 40$ minutes + 30 minutes + 50 minutes = 2 hours.

This matches the condition of 20 minutes extra, and hence is the correct answer pair. His running speed is 18 kmph and swimming speed is 9 kmph or 0.15 km/minute.

**Answers are:**

17. (c)

18. (b) ($12/18 + 24/54 + 5/18 = \dfrac{36 + 24 + 15}{54} = \dfrac{75}{54}$ hours

    = 83.33 minutes. Note: Here we took the running speed as 18 kmph because that was the answer for the speed of running that we got when we solved question 19 and question 17 as a pair).

19. (b)

20. $(20 + 60 + 30P)/(2 + 3 + P) = 23 \rightarrow 80 + 30P = 115 + 23P$ or $P = 5$

21. Assume raw materials cost as 150 and total cost as 450. (Thus, wages cost is 300).

    Since, the cost of raw materials goes up in the ratio of 3:7 the new raw material cost would become 350 and the new wages cost would become in the ratio 4:9 as 675.

    The new cost would become, 1025.

    Since 450 become 1025 (change in total cost), unitary method calculation would give us that 18 would become ₹ 41.

22. Solve using options. For option (c), we will get that initially there are 125 boys and 140 girls. After the given increases, the number of boys would be 145 and the number of girls would become 154 which gives a difference of 9 as required.

23. From the question, it is evident that after leaving out the $C$ courses, Sonali's GPA goes to 3.33. This means that the number of subjects she must have had after leaving out the $C$'s must be a multiple of 3. This only occurs in Option c. Hence, that is the answer.

24. When there are 25 boarders, the total expenses are $1750. When there are 50 boarders, the total expenses are $3000. The change in expense due to the coming in of 25 boarders is $1250. Hence, expense per boarder is equal to $50. This also means that when there are 25 boarders, the variable cost would be $25 \times 50 = \$1250$. Hence, $500 must be the fixed expenses.

So for 100 boarders, the total cost would be: $500 (fixed) + $5000 = $5500

25. $S = 42 - k\sqrt{n}$

$$24 = 42 - k \times 3 \rightarrow k = 6$$

So, $\qquad S = 42 - 6\sqrt{n}$

For 49 compartments the train would not move. Hence it would move for 48 compartments.

26-28:

Let the third drunkard get in $x$ litres. Then the second will contribute $x + 1$ and the first will contribute $x + 2$ litres. Thus in all they have $3x + 3$ litres of the drink. Using option a in question 27, this value is 12, giving $x$ as 3.

Also, each drunkard will drink 3 litres.

Thus, the first drunkard brings 5 litres and the second 4 litres. Their contribution to the fourth drunkard will be in the ratio 2:1 and hence their share of money would be also in the ratio 2:1. Hence, this option is correct for question 27.

Hence, for question 26, the second drunkard will get 5 roubles (for his contribution of 1 litre to the fourth) and for question 28, the answer would be 1:3

29. $5 : 4 \rightarrow 5 : 4.8 \rightarrow 25 : 24$.

Option (c) is correct.

30. $P = K \times W^2 \rightarrow 12250 = K \times 35^2 \rightarrow K = 10$.

Thus our price and weight relationship is: $P = 10W^2$.

When the two pieces are in the ratio 2:5 (weight wise) then we know that their weights must be 10 grams and 25 grams respectively. Their values would be:

10 gram piece: $10 \times 10^2 = ₹ 1000$;

25 gram piece: $10 \times 25^2 = ₹ 6250$.

Total Price = 1000 + 62450 = 7250. From an initial value of 12250, this represents a loss of ₹ 5000.

31. The ratio of distribution should be:

$21 \times 35 : 15 \times 35 : 15 \times 21 \rightarrow 147 : 105{:}63 \rightarrow 7{:}5{:}3$

The biggest share will be worth: $7 \times 525000/15 = 245000$.

32. $P + M + T = 675 \rightarrow 3M + M + 3M - 25 = 675 \rightarrow 7M = 700$. Hence, $M = 100$. $P = 300$ and $T = 275$.

33. Ratio of distribution = 20 : 13 : 8

So the elephant should get $(20/41) \times 820 = 400$.

34. Women : Men = 3 : 4

Men : Children = 3 : 5

$\rightarrow$ Women : Men : children = 9 : 12 : 20

In the ratio, $9 \rightarrow 531$ Women

Thus, $\qquad 20 \rightarrow 1180$ children.

35. 2/3 becomes 7/8 a change from 0.666 to 0.875 while the other changes are smaller than this. For instance 4/7 becomes 9/12 a change from 0.5714 to 0.75 which is smaller than the change in 2/3. Similarly, the other options can be checked and rejected.

36. Since, the work gets done in 25% less time there must have been an addition of 33.33% men.

This would mean 13.33 men extra $\rightarrow$ which would mean 14 extra men (in whole numbers)

37. From the given options, we just need to look for a multiple of 7. 2100 is the only option which is a multiple of 7 and is hence the correct answer.

38. This is a simple question if you can catch hold of the logic of the question, i.e., the younger daughter's share must be such after adding a CI of 20% for two years, she should get the same value as her elder sister.

None of the options meets this requirement. Hence, None of these is correct.

39-41. You should realise that when Anshu gives her pens to Bobby & Chandana, the number of pens for both Bobby & Chandana should double. Also, the number of pens for Anshu & Bobby should also double when Chandana gives off her pens. Further the final condition is that each of them has 24 pens. The following table will emerge on the basis of this logic.

|              | Anshu | Bobby | Chandana |
| ------------ | ----- | ----- | -------- |
| Final        | 24    | 24    | 24       |
| Second round | 12    | 12    | 48       |
| Initial      | 42    | 6     | 24       |

42. $V = k\,AH \rightarrow 280 = k \times 60 \times 14 \rightarrow 280 = 840k$. Thus, $k = 1/3$ and the equation becomes:

$V = AH/3$ and $390 = 26A/3 \rightarrow A = 45$.

43. Expenses for 120 boys = 8400

Expenses for 150 boys = 10000.

Thus, variable expenses are ₹ 1600 for 30 boys.

If we add 180 more boys to make it 330 boys,

we will get an additional expense of $1600 \times 6 =$ ₹ 9600.

Total expenses are ₹ 19600.

44. Let the distance be $d$. Then, $d/14.4 = \sqrt{8}/\sqrt{18} \to d = 9.6$

45. $47 : 100 : 220$ would give: 0.5 cubic feet of Cement, 1cubic feet of sand and 2 cubic feet of gravel. Required ratio $1 : 2 : 4$ is satisfied.

46. If new values of $x, y, z$ are $x', y'$ and $z'$, and respectively then $x' : y' = 4:5$, $y' : z' = 3:4$
$x' : y' : z' = 12:15:20$
$x + y + z = 5000$
$x' + 50 + y' + 100 + z' + 150 = 5000$
$x' + y' + z' = 4700$
$12k + 15k + 20k = 4700$
$k = 100$
$x = 1200 + 50 = 1250$
$y = 1500 + 100 = 1600$
$z = 2000 + 150 = 2150$
$x + y = 1250 + 1600 = 2850$

47. $\dfrac{x-a}{y-2.4a} = 1$
$x - a = y - 2.4a$
$x - y = -1.4a$
$1.4a = y - x = 1600 - 1250 = 350$. Hence:
$a = \dfrac{3500}{14} = 250$

The required value of $|a-b|$ would be given by $|250 - 2.4 \times 250| = 350$

48. Quantity of $x$ in the container of100 litres = 40 litres
Quantity of $y$ in the container of 100 litres = 60 litres
Quantity of milk in final mixture = $100 \times \dfrac{3}{4} = 75$ litres
Quantity of water in final mixture = $100 - 75 = 25$ litres.
Quantity of milk and water in 40 litres of the mixture
$x = 40 \times \dfrac{2}{3}, 40 \times \dfrac{1}{3} = \dfrac{80}{3}, \dfrac{40}{3}$ (in litres)

Quantity of milk and water in 60 litres of mixture
$y = \dfrac{60 \times a}{(a+2)}, \dfrac{60 \times 2}{(a+2)} = \dfrac{60 \times a}{(a+2)}, \dfrac{120}{(a+2)}$

$\dfrac{80}{3} + \dfrac{60a}{a+2} = 75$

$\dfrac{60a}{a+2} = \dfrac{225-80}{3} = \dfrac{145}{3}$

$180a = 145a + 290$

$\to a = \dfrac{290}{35} = 8.28$

49. In container $x$ if milk is actually a mixture of milk and water in the 1:1, then the ratio of milk and water

in the container would be 1:2.

Thus, the quantity of milk in 40 litres of the mixture $x$ would be $= \dfrac{40}{3}$ litres.

Therefore, in the final mixture the quantity of milk will get reduced by $\dfrac{40}{3}$ litres and quantity of water will be increased by $\dfrac{40}{3}$ litres. This would mean that the required ratios would be:

$\dfrac{75 - \dfrac{40}{3}}{25 + \dfrac{40}{3}} = \dfrac{185}{115} = \dfrac{37}{23}$

**Solution for 50 to 52:**

Let the temperatures of Delhi and Lucknow in July be $3x$ and $5x$ respectively.

Let the temperatures of Delhi and Lucknow in August be $2y$ and $3y$ respectively.

It is given to us that (the ratio of the sum of the temperatures of these two cities in August and July was 5: 4) which essentially means that:

$\dfrac{5y}{8x} = \dfrac{5}{4}$

i.e. $y = 2x \to$ Temperature in Delhi and Lucknow in August would be $4x$ and $6x$ respectively.

50. The percentage increase in temperature of Lucknow from July to August $= \dfrac{3 \times 2x - 5x}{5x} \times 100 = 20\%$

51. The percentage increase in temperature of Delhi from July to August $= \dfrac{4x - 3x}{3x} \times 100 = 33.33\%$

Hence, the percentage increase in temperature of Delhi from August to September $= 2 \times 33.33\% = 66.66\%$

Temperature of Lucknow in September $=$
$3y\left(1 + \dfrac{20}{100}\right) = 3.6y$

Temperature of Delhi in September $=$
$2y\left(1 + \dfrac{66.66}{100}\right) = \dfrac{10y}{3}$

Required Ratio $= \dfrac{3.6y}{\dfrac{10}{3}y} = \dfrac{10.8}{10} = 1.08$

52. $2y = 20°C$
$y = 10°C$
Required Sum $(x) = 3.6y + \dfrac{10}{3}y$
$= 36 + 33.33$
$= 69.33°C$

53. In 2007 total number of shares $= 650 + 650 \times \dfrac{3}{13}$

= 800

In 2008, total number of shares $= 800 + 800 \times \dfrac{2}{4}$

= 1200.

The dividend being 12.5%, he would get ₹ 1.25 per share as the dividend (calculated as 12.5% of the face value of the share). Hence, his total dividend in 2009, would be ₹ 1500. Also, his total initial investment is ₹ 6500 (650 shares at ₹ 10 per share).

Hence, the required ratio = 1500/6500 = 3/13 = 0.23

$$\frac{\text{Dividend}}{\text{Initial investment}} = \frac{12.5}{100} \times \frac{1200}{650}$$

$$= 0.23$$

54. Quantity of Metal 1 in mixture $= 14 \times \dfrac{3}{7} + 26 \times \dfrac{5}{13}$

=16 kg.

$$\therefore \text{Required ratio} = \frac{16}{40-16} = \frac{16}{24} = 0.67$$

55. Price of all four varieties =10 ₹/litre, 5 ₹/litre.

$\dfrac{10}{3}$ ₹/litre, $\dfrac{10}{4}$ ₹/litre.

Let the cost price of mixture be $X$ then using the concept of weighted averages, we get that:

$$X = \frac{1}{(1+2+3+4)}\left(10 \times 1 + 5 \times 2 + \frac{10}{3} \times 3 + \frac{10}{4} \times 4\right) = \frac{₹40}{10}.$$

$\to X = 4$ ₹/litre.

Hence, the selling price to make a 10% Profit would need an increment of 10% on ₹ 4 per litre. Thus, the required selling price would be ₹ 4.4 per litre.

### Level of Difficulty (III)

1. You can use alligation between 33.33% and 40% to get 37.5%. Hence the ratio of mixing must be 2.5:4.16 → 3:5.

6. Check each of the options as follows:

Suppose you are checking option b which gives the value of $a$ as 81 litres.

Then, it is clear that when you are pouring out 81 litres, you are leaving 8/9 of the honey in the barrel. Thus the amount of honey contained after 6 such operations will be given by:

$729 \times (8/9)^6$. If this answer has to be correct this value must be equal to 64 (which it clearly is not since the value will be in the form of a fraction.)

Hence, this is not the correct option. You can similarly rule out the other options.

7. It is clear that if 7 kg of the first is mixed with 21 kg of the second you will get 5 + 9 = 14 kg of nickel and 14 kg of tin. You do not need to check the other options since they will go into fractions.

10. The piece that is cut off should be such that the fraction of the first to the second alloy in each of the two new alloys formed should be equal.

If you cut off 4 kg, the respective ratios will be:

First alloy: 2 kg of first alloy and 4 kg of second alloy

Second alloy: 4 kg of first alloy and 8 kg of the second alloy. It can easily be seen that the ratios are equal to 1:2 in each case.

13. This is again the typical alligation situation.

The required ratio will be given by (7/18 – 3/8) : (2/5 – 7/18)

Alternately, you can also look at it through options. It can be easily seen that if you take 8 kg of the first with 10 kg of the second you will get the required 7:11 ratio.

17. The cost of making one gram of gun powder would be ₹ 180. This will contain 0.4 gm of saltpetre and 0.6 gm of nitrous oxide. Check through options.

At the rate of saltpetre of 300/gm, the nitrous oxide will cost ₹100/gm. The total cost of 0.4 grams of saltpetre will be 120 and 0.6 grams of nitrous oxide will be ₹ 60 giving the total cost as 180.

20. There will be a total of 4.5 litres of milk (25% of 3 + 75% of 5) giving a total of 4.5. Hence, 45%.

23. Go through the options as follows:

According to option d, if the initial quantity of spirit is 4 litres, half the spirit is taken out when 2 litres are drawn out. Thus the spirit after three times of the operation would be:

$4 \times (1/2)^2 = 0.5$ litres. This matches the option. You can check for yourself that the first three options will not work.

# 9

# Time and Work

## INTRODUCTION

The concept of time and work is another important topic for the aptitude exams. Questions on this chapter have been appearing regularly over the past decade in all aptitude exams. Questions on Time and Work have regularly appeared in the CAT especially in its online format.

## Theory

In the context of the CAT, you have to understand the following basic concepts of this chapter:

If $A$ does a work in $a$ days, then in one day $A$ does

$\rightarrow \dfrac{1}{a}$ of the work.

If $B$ does a work in $b$ days, then in one day $B$ does

$\rightarrow \dfrac{1}{b}$ of the work.

Then, in one day, if $A$ and $B$ work together, then their combined work is $\dfrac{1}{a} + \dfrac{1}{b}$.

or $\dfrac{a+b}{ab}$

In the above case, we take the total work to be done as "1 unit of work". Hence, the work will be completed when 1 unit of work is completed.

For example, if $A$ can do a work in 10 days and $B$ can do the same work in 12 days, then the work will be completed in how many days.

One day's work = 1/10 + 1/12 = (12 + 10)/120

[Taking LCM of the denominators]

= 22/120

Then the number of days required to complete the work is 120/22.

Note that this is a reciprocal of the fraction of work done in one day. This is a benefit associated with solving time and work through fractions. It can be stated as—the number of time periods required to complete the full work will be the reciprocal of the fraction of the work done in one time period.

## ALTERNATIVE APPROACH

Instead of taking the value of the total work as 1 unit of work, we can also look at the total work as 100 per cent work. In such a case, the following rule applies:

If $A$ does a work in $a$ days, then in one day $A$ does

$\rightarrow \dfrac{100}{a}$ % of the work.

If $B$ does a work in $b$ days, then in one day $B$ does

$\rightarrow \dfrac{100}{b}$ % of the work.

Then, in one day, if $A$ and $B$ work together, then their combined work is

$$\dfrac{100}{a} + \dfrac{100}{b}$$

This is often a very useful approach to look at the concept of time and work because thinking in terms of percentages gives a direct and clear picture of the actual quantum of work done.

What I mean to say is that even though we can think in either a percentage or a fractional value to solve the problem, there will be a thought process difference between the two.

Thinking about work done as a percentage value gives us a linear picture of the quantum of the work that has been done and the quantum of the work that is to be done. On the other hand, if we think of the work done as a fractional value, the thought process will have to be slightly longer to get a full understanding of the work done.

For instance, we can think of work done as 7/9 or 77.77%. The percentage value makes it clear as to how much quantum is left. The percentage value can be visualised on the number line, while the fractional value requires a mental inversion to fully understand the quantum.

An additional advantage of the percentage method of solving time and work problems would be the elimination of the need to perform cumbersome fraction additions involving LCMs of denominators.

However, you should realise that this would work only if you are able to handle basic percentage calculations involving standard decimal values. If you have really internalised the techniques of percentage calculations given in the chapter of percentages, then you can reap the benefits for this chapter.

The benefit of using this concept will become abundantly clear by solving through percentages the same example that was solved above using fractions.

**Example:** If $A$ can do a work in 10 days and $B$ can do the same work in 12 days, then the work will be completed in how many days.

One day's work = 10% + 8.33% = 18.33% (Note, no LCMs required here)

Hence, to do 100% work, it will require: 100/18.33.

This can be solved by adding 18.33 mentally to get between 5–6 days. Then on you can go through options and mark the closest answer.

The process of solving through percentages will yield rich dividends if and only if you have adequate practice on adding standard percentage values. Thus, $18.33 \times 5 = 91.66$ should not give you any headaches and should be done while reading for the first time.

Thus a thought process chart for this question should look like this.

If $A$ can do a work in 10 days ($\rightarrow$ means 10% work) and $B$ can do the same work in 12 days ($\rightarrow$ 8.33% work $\rightarrow$ 18.33% work in a day in 5 days 91.66% work $\rightarrow$ leaves 8.33% work to be done $\rightarrow$ which can be done in 8.33/18.33 of a day = 5/11 of a day (since both the numerator and the denominator are divisible by 1.66), then the work will be completed in $5\dfrac{5}{11}$ days.

The entire process can be done mentally.

## The Concept of Negative Work

Suppose, that $A$ and $B$ are working to build a wall while $C$ is working to break the wall. In such a case, the wall is being built by $A$ and $B$ while it is being broken by $C$. Here, if we consider the work as the building of the wall, we can say that $C$ is doing negative work.

**Example:** $A$ can build a wall in 10 days and $B$ can build it in 5 days, while $C$ can completely destroy the wall in 20 days. If they start working at the same time, in how many days will the work be completed.

**Solution:** The net combined work per day here is:

$A$'s work + $B$'s work – $C$'s work = 10% + 20% – 5% = 25% work in one day.

Hence, the work will get completed (100% work) in 4 days.

The concept of negative work commonly appears as a problem based on pipes and cisterns, where there are inlet pipes and outlet pipes/leaks which are working against each other.

If we consider the work to be filling a tank, the inlet pipe does positive work while the outlet pipe/leak does negative work.

## Application of Product Constancy Table to Time and Work

The equation that applies to Time and Work problems is

Work Rate × Time = Work done

This equation means that if the work done is constant, then →

Work rate is inversely proportional to time. Hence, the Product Constancy Table will be directly applicable to time and work questions.

[Notice the parallelism between this formula and the formula of time speed and distance, where again there is product constancy between speed and time if the distance is constant.]

Time is usually in days or hours although any standard unit of time can be used. The unit of time that has to be used in a question is usually decided by the denominator of the unit of work rate.

Here, there are two ways of defining the Work rate.

(a) In the context of situations where individual working efficiencies or individual time requirements are given in the problem, the work rate is defined by the unit: Work done per unit time.

In this case, the total work to be done is normally considered to be 1 (if we solve through fractions) or 100% (if we solve through percentages).

Thus, in the solved problem above, when we calculated that $A$ and $B$ together do 18.33% work in a day, this was essentially a statement of the rate of work of $A$ and $B$ together.

Then the solution proceeded as:

18.33% work per day × No. of days required = 100% work

Giving us: the no. of days required = $100/18.33 = 5\dfrac{5}{11}$

(b) In certain types of problems (typically those involving projects that are to be completed), where a certain category of worker has the same rate of working, the Work rate will be defined as the number of workers of a particular category working on the project.

For instance, questions where all men work at a certain rate, the work rate when 2 men are working together will be double the work rate when 1 man is working alone. Similarly, the work rate when 10 men are working together will be 10 times the work rate when 1 man is working alone.

In such cases, the work to be done is taken as the number of man-days required to finish the work.

Note, for future reference, that the *work to be done can also be measured in terms of the volume of work defined in the context of day-to-day life.*

For example, the volume of a wall to be built, the number of people to be interviewed, the number of *chapattis* to be made and so on.

## WORK EQUIVALENCE METHOD (To Solve Time and Work Problems)

The work equivalence method is nothing but an application of the formula:

Work rate × Time = Work done (or work to be done)

Thus, if the work to be done is doubled, the product of *work rate × time* also has to be doubled. Similarly, if the work to be done increases by 20%, the product of *work rate × time* also has to be increased by 20% and so on.

This method is best explained by an example:

A contractor estimates that he will finish the road construction project in 100 days by employing 50 men.

However, at the end of the 50th day, when as per his estimation half the work should have been completed, he finds that only 40% of his work is done.

(a) How many more days will be required to complete the work?

(b) How many more men should he employ in order to complete the work in time?

**Solution:**

(a) The contactor has completed 40% of the work in 50 days.

If the number of men working on the project remains constant, the rate of work also remains constant. Hence, to complete 100% work, he will have to complete the remaining 60% of the work.

For this he would require **75** more days. (This calculation is done using the unitary method.)

(b) In order to complete the work on time, it is obvious that he will have to increase the number of men working on the project.

This can be solved as:

50 men working for 50 days → $50 \times 50 = 2500$ man-days.

2500 man-days has resulted in 40% work completion. Hence, the total work to be done in terms of the number of man-days is got by using unitary method:

Work left = 60% = $2500 \times 1.5 = 3750$ man-days

This has to be completed in 50 days. Hence, the number of men required per day is $3750/50 = 75$ men.

Since, 50 men are already working on the project, the contractor needs to hire 25 more men.

[Note, this can be done using the percentage change graphic for product change. Since, the number of days is constant at 50, the 50% increase in work from 40% to 60% is solely to be met by increasing the number of men. Hence, the number of men to be increased is 50% of the original number of men = 25 men.]

## The Specific Case of Building a Wall (Work as Volume of Work)

As already mentioned, in certain cases, the unit of work can also be considered to be in terms of the volume of work. For example, building of a wall of a certain length, breadth and height.

In such cases, the following formula applies:

$$\frac{L_1 B_1 H_1}{L_2 B_2 H_2} = \frac{m_1 t_1 d_1}{m_2 t_2 d_2}$$

where $L$, $B$ and $H$ are respectively the length, breadth and height of the wall to be built, while $m$, $t$ and $d$ are respectively the number of men, the amount of time per day and the number of days. Further, the suffix 1 is for the first work situation, while the suffix 2 is for the second work situation.

Consider the following problem:

**Example:** 20 men working 8 hours a day can completely build a wall of length 200 metres, breadth 10 metres and height 20 metres in 10 days. How many days will 25 men working 12 hours a day require to build a wall of length 400 metres, breadth 10 metres and height of 15 metres.

This question can be solved directly by using the formula above

$$\frac{L_1 B_1 H_1}{L_2 B_2 H_2} = \frac{m_1 t_1 d_1}{m_2 t_2 d_2}$$

| Here, | $L_1$ is 200 metres | $L_2$ is 400 metres |
|---|---|---|
| | $B_1$ is 10 metres | $B_2$ is 10 metres |
| | $H_1$ is 20 metres | $H_2$ is 15 metres |
| while | $m_1$ is 20 men | $m_2$ is 25 men |
| | $d_1$ is 10 days | $d_2$ is unknown |
| and | $t_1$ is 8 hours a day | $t_2$ is 12 hours a day |

Then we get $(200 \times 10 \times 20)/(400 \times 10 \times 15) = (20 \times 8 \times 10)/(25 \times 12 \times d_2)$

∴         $d_2 = 5.333/0.6666 = 8$ days

Alternatively, you can also directly write the equation as follows:

$d_2 = 10 \times (400/200) \times (10/10) \times (20/15) \times (20/25) \times (8/12)$

This can be done by thinking of the problem as follows:

The number of days have to be found out in the second case. Hence, on the LHS of the equation write down the unknown and on the RHS of the equation write down the corresponding knowns.

$$d_2 = 10 \times \ldots.$$

Then, the length of the wall has to be factored in. There are only two options for doing so, viz.

Multiplying by 200/400 (< 1, which will reduce the number of days) or multiplying by 400/200 (>1, which will increase the number of days).

The decision of which one of these is to be done is made on the basis of the fact that when the length of the wall is increasing, the number of days required will also increase.

Hence, we take the value of the fraction greater than 1 to get

$$d_2 = 10 \times (400/200)$$

We continue in the same way to get

No change in the breadth of the wall → hence, multiply by 10/10 (no change in $d_2$)

Height of the wall is decreasing → hence, multiply by 15/20 (< 1 to reduce $d_2$)

Number of men working is increasing → hence, multiply by 20/25 (< 1 to reduce $d_2$)

Number of hours per day is increasing → hence, multiply by 8/12 (< 1 to reduce the number of days)

*Space for Notes*

## The Concept of Efficiency

The concept of efficiency is closely related to the concept of work rate.

When we make a statement saying $A$ is twice as efficient as $B$, we mean to say that $A$ does twice the work as $B$ in the same time. In other words, we can also understand this as $A$ will require half the time required by $B$ to do the same work.

In the context of efficiency, another statement that you might come across is $A$ is two times more efficient than $B$. This is the same as $A$ is thrice as efficient as $B$ or $A$ does the same work as $B$ in 1/3rd of the time.

*Equating Men, Women and Children* This is directly derived from the concept of efficiencies.

**Example:** 8 men can do a work in 12 days while 20 women can do it in 10 days. In how many days can 12 men and 15 women complete the same work.

**Solution:** Total work to be done = $8 \times 12 = 96$ man-days.

or total work to be done = $20 \times 10 = 200$ woman-days.

Since, the work is the same, we can equate 96 man-days = 200 woman-days.

Hence, 1 man-day = 2.08333 woman-days.

Now, if 12 men and 15 women are working on the work we get

12 men are equal to $12 \times 2.08333 = 25$ women

Hence, the work done per day is equivalent to 25 + 15 women working per day.

That is, 40 women working per day.

Hence, $40 \times$ no. of days = 200 woman days

Number of days = 5 days.

## WORKED-OUT PROBLEMS

**Problem 9.1** *A* can do a piece of work in 10 days and *B* in 12 days. Find how much time they will take to complete the work under the following conditions:

(a) Working together
(b) Working alternately starting with *A*.
(c) Working alternately starting with *B*.
(d) If *B* leaves 2 days before the actual completion of the work.
(e) If *B* leaves 2 days before the scheduled completion of the work.
(f) If another person *C* who does negative work (i.e., works against *A* and *B* and can completely destroy the work in 20 days) joins them and they work together all the time.

**Solution**

(a) 1 day's work for *A* is 1/10 and 1 day's work for *B* is 1/12.

Then, working together, the work in one day is equal to:

$\frac{1}{10} + \frac{1}{12} = \frac{11}{60}$ of the work. Thus working together they

need 60/11 days to complete the work → 5.45 days.

Alternately, you can use percentage values to solve the above question:

*A*'s work =10%, *B*'s work = 8.33%. Hence, *A* + *B* = 18.33% of the work in one day.

Hence, to complete 100% work, we get the number of days required = 100/18.33 → 5.55 days.

This can be calculated as

@ 18.33% per day in 5 days, they will cover 18.33 × 5 = 91.66%. (The decimal value 0.33 is not difficult to handle if you have internalised the fraction to percentage conversion table of the chapter of percentages).

Work left on the sixth day is: 8.33%, which will require: 8.33/18.33 of the sixth day.

Since, both these numbers are divisible by 1.66 we get 5/11 of the sixth day will be used → 0.45 of the sixth day is used.

Hence, 5.45 days are required to finish the work.

*Note:* Although the explanation to the question through percentages seems longer, the student should realise that if the values in the fraction-to-percentage table is internalised by the student, the process of solution through percentage will take much lesser time because we are able to eliminate the need for the calculation of LCMs, which are often cumbersome. (if the numbers in the problem are those that are covered in the fraction

to percentage conversion table). In fact, the percentage method allows for solving while reading.

(b) Working alternately: When two people are working alternately the question has to be solved by taking 2 days as a unit of time instead of 1 day.

So in (a) above, the work done in 1 day will be covered in 2 days here.

Thus, in 2 days the work done will be 18.33%. In 10 days it will be 91.66%. On the 11th day *A* works by himself.

But *A*'s work in 1 day is 10%. Therefore, he will require 4/5 of the 11th day to finish the work.

(c) Working alternately starting with *B*: Here, there will be no difference in work completed by the 10th day. On the 11th day, *B* works alone and does 8.33% of the work (which was required to complete the work). Hence, the whole of the 11th day will get used.

(d) If *B* leaves 2 days before the actual completion of the work: In this case, the actual completion of the work is after 2 days of *B*'s leaving. This means, that *A* has worked alone for the last 2 days to complete the work. But *A* does, 10% work in a day. Hence, *A* and *B* must have done 80% of the work together (@18.33% per day). Then, the answer can be found by

80/18.33 + 20/10 days.

*Note:* For calculation of 80/18.33, we can use the fact that the decimal value is a convenient one. If they worked together they would complete 73.33% of the work in 4 days and the work that they would have done on the 5th day would be 6.66%.

At the rate of 18.33% work per day while working together, they would work together for 6.66/18.33 of the 5th day. Since both the numerator and denominator are divisible by 1.66 the above ratio is converted into 4/11 = 0.3636.

Hence, they work together for 4.3636 days after which *B* leaves and then *A* completes the work in 2 more days. Hence, the time required to finish the work would be = 6.3636 days.

(e) If *B* leaves 2 days before the scheduled completion of the work: Completion of the work would have been scheduled assuming that *A* and *B* both worked together for completing the work (say, this is *x* days). Then, the problem has to be viewed as *x* − 2 days was the time for which *A* and *B* worked together. The residual amount of work left (which will be got by 2 days work of *A* and *B* together) would be done by *A* alone at his own pace of work.

Thus we can get the solution by:

Number of days required to complete the work =
$$[(100/18.33) - 2] + \frac{36.66}{10}$$

(f) If $C$ joins the group and does negative work, we can see that one day's work of the three together would be

$A$'s work + $B$'s work − $C$'s work = 10% + 8.33% − 5% = 13.33%

Hence, the work will be completed in (100/13.33) days.
[*Note:* This can be calculated by $13.33 \times 7 = 13 \times 7 + 0.33 \times 7 = 93.33$.

Then, work left = 6.66, which will require half a day more at the rate of 13.33% per day.

***Advantage of Solving Problems on Time and Work through Percentages*** Students should understand here, that most of the times the values given for the number of days in which the work is completed by a worker will be convenient values like: 60 days, 40 days, 30 days, 25 days, 24 days, 20 days, 16 days, 15 days, 12 days, 11 days, 10 days, 9 days, 8 days, 7 days, 6 days, 5 days, 4 days, 3 days and 2 days. All these values for the number of days will yield convenient decimal values. If your fraction to percentage table is internalised, you can use the process of solving while reading by taking the percentage of work done per day process rather than getting delayed by the need to find LCM's while solving through the process of the fraction of work done per day.]

**Problem 9.2** A contractor undertakes to build a wall in 50 days. He employs 50 people for the same. However, after 25 days he finds that the work is only 40% complete. How many more men need to be employed to:

(a) complete the work in time?

**Solution** In order to complete the work in time, the contractor has to finish the remaining 60% of the work in 25 days.

Now, in the first 25 days the work done = $50 \times 25$ =1250 man-days → 40% of the work.

Hence, work left = 60% of the work = 1875 man-days.

Since, 25 days are left to complete the task, the number of people required is 1875/25 = 75 men.

Since, 50 men are already working, 25 more men are needed to complete the work.

Thought process should go like: 1250 → 40% of work. Hence, 1875 man-days required to complete the work.

Since there are only 25 days left, we need 1875/25 = 75 men to complete the work.

(b) Complete the work 10 days before time?

For this purpose, we have to do 1875 man-days of work in 15 days. Hence, men = 1875/15 = 125 men.

Hence, he would need to hire 75 more men.

**Problem 9.3** For the previous problem, if the contractor continues with the same workforce:

(a) how many days behind schedule will the work be finished?

**Solution** He has completed 40% work in 25 days. Hence, to complete the remaining 60% of the work, he would require 50% more days (i.e. 37.5 days) (Since, 60% is 1.5 times of 40%)

Hence, the work would be done 12.5 days behind schedule.

(b) how much increase in efficiency is required from the work force to complete the work in time?

**Solution** If the number of men working is kept constant, the only way to finish the work in time is by increasing the efficiency so that more work is done every man-day. This should be mathematically looked at as follows:

Suppose, that 1 man-day takes care of 1 unit of work. Then, in the first 25 days, work done = 25 (days) × 50 (men) × 1 (work unit per man-day) = 1250 units of work. Now, this 1250 units of work is just 40% of the work. Hence, work left = 1875 units of work.

Then, 25 (days) × 50 (men) × $z$ (work units per man-day) = 1875 → $z$ = 1.5

Thus, the work done per man-day has to rise from 1 to 1.5, that is, by 50%. Hence, the efficiency of work has to rise by **50%**.

**Problem 9.4** $A$ is twice as efficient as $B$. If they complete a work in 30 days find the times required by each to complete the work individually.

**Solution** When we say that $A$ is twice as efficient as $B$, it means that $A$ takes half the time that $B$ takes to complete the same work.

Thus, if we denote $A$'s 1 day's work as $A$ and $B$'s one day's work as $B$, we have

$$A = 2B$$

Then, using the information in the problem, we have: $30 A + 30 B = 100\%$ work

That is, $90 B = 100\%$ work → $B = 1.11$ % (is the work done by $B$ in 1 day) → $B$ requires **90 days** to complete the work alone.

Since, $A = 2B$ → we have $A = 2.22$ % → $A$ requires 45 days to do the work alone.

You should be able to solve this mentally with the following thought process while reading for the first time:
$\frac{100}{30} = 3.33\%$. $\frac{3.33}{3} = 1.11\%$. Hence, work done is 1.11% per day and 2.22% per day → 90 and 45 days.

**Problem 9.5** $A$ is two times more efficient than $B$. If they complete a work in 30 days, then find the times required by each to complete the work individually.

**Solution** Interpret the first sentence as $A = 3B$ and solve according to the process of the previous problem to get the answers. (You should get $A$ takes 40 days and $B$ takes 120 days.)

## LEVEL OF DIFFICULTY (I)

1. Raju can do 25% of a piece of work in 5 days. How many days will he take to complete the work ten times?
   (a) 150 days      (b) 250 days
   (c) 200 days      (d) 180 days

2. 6 men can do a piece of work in 12 days. How many men are needed to do the work in 18 days.
   (a) 3 men      (b) 6 men
   (c) 4 men      (d) 2 men

3. A can do a piece of work in 20 days and B can do it in 15 days. How long will they take if both work together?
   (a) $8\left(\dfrac{6}{7}\right)$ days      (b) $8\left(\dfrac{4}{7}\right)$ days
   (c) $9\left(\dfrac{3}{7}\right)$ days      (d) $9\left(\dfrac{4}{7}\right)$ days

4. In question 3 if C, who can finish the same work in 25 days, joins them, then how long will they take to complete the work?
   (a) $6\left(\dfrac{18}{47}\right)$ days      (b) 12 days
   (c) $2\left(\dfrac{8}{11}\right)$ days      (d) $47\left(\dfrac{6}{18}\right)$ days

5. Nishu and Archana can do a piece of work in 10 days and Nishu alone can do it in 12 days. In how many days can Archana do it alone?
   (a) 60 days      (b) 30 days
   (c) 50 days      (d) 45 days

6. Baba alone can do a piece of work in 10 days. Anshu alone can do it in 15 days. If the total wages for the work is ₹ 50. How much should Baba be paid if they work together for the entire duration of the work?
   (a) ₹ 30      (b) ₹ 20
   (c) ₹ 50      (d) ₹ 40

7. 4 men and 3 women finish a job in 6 days, and 5 men and 7 women can do the same job in 4 days. How long will 1 man and 1 woman take to do the work?
   (a) $22\left(\dfrac{2}{7}\right)$ days      (b) $25\left(\dfrac{1}{2}\right)$ days
   (c) $5\left(\dfrac{1}{7}\right)$ days      (d) $12\left(\dfrac{7}{22}\right)$ days

8. If 8 boys and 12 women can do a piece of work in 25 days, in how many days can the work be done by 6 boys and 11 women working together?
   (a) 15 days      (b) 10 days
   (c) 12 days      (d) Cannot be determined

9. A can do a piece of work in 10 days and B can do the same work in 20 days. With the help of C, they finish the work in 5 days. How long will it take for C alone to finish the work?
   (a) 20 days      (b) 10 days
   (c) 35 days      (d) 15 days

10. A can do a piece of work in 20 days. He works at it for 5 days and then B finishes it in 10 more days. In how many days will A and B together finish the work?
    (a) 8 days      (b) 10 days
    (c) 12 days      (d) 6 days

11. A and B undertake to do a piece of work for ₹ 100. A can do it in 5 days and B can do it in 10 days. With the help of C, they finish it in 2 days. How much should C be paid for his contribution?
    (a) ₹ 40      (b) ₹ 20
    (c) ₹ 60      (d) ₹ 30

12. Twenty workers can finish a piece of work in 30 days. After how many days should 5 workers leave the job so that the work is completed in 35 days?
    (a) 5 days      (b) 10 days
    (c) 15 days      (d) 20 days

13. Arun and Vinay together can do a piece of work in 7 days. If Arun does twice as much work as Vinay in a given time, how long will Arun alone take to do the work.
    (a) 6.33 days      (b) 10.5 days
    (c) 11 days      (d) 72 days

14. Subhash can copy 50 pages in 10 hours; Subhash and Prakash together can copy 300 pages in 40 hours. In how much time can Prakash copy 30 pages?
    (a) 13 h      (b) 12 h
    (c) 11 h      (d) 9 h

15. X number of men can finish a piece of work in 30 days. If there were 6 men more, the work could be finished in 10 days less. What is the original number of men?
    (a) 10      (b) 11
    (c) 12      (d) 15

16. Sashi can do a piece of work in 25 days and Rishi can do it in 20 days. They work for 5 days and then

Sashi goes away. In how many more days will Rishi finish the work?

(a) 10 days      (b) 12 days

(c) 14 days      (d) None of these

17. Raju can do a piece of work in 10 days, Vicky in 12 days and Tinku in 15 days. They all start the work together, but Raju leaves after 2 days and Vicky leaves 3 days before the work is completed. In how many days is the work completed?

(a) 5 days      (b) 6 days

(c) 7 days      (d) 8 days

18. Sambhu can do 1/2 of the work in 8 days while Kalu can do 1/3 of the work in 6 days. How long will it take for both of them to finish the work?

(a) $\dfrac{88}{17}$ days      (b) $\dfrac{144}{17}$ days

(c) $\dfrac{72}{17}$ days      (d) 8 days

19. Manoj takes twice as much time as Anjay and thrice as much as Vijay to finish a piece of work. Together they finish the work in 1 day. What is the time taken by Manoj to finish the work?

(a) 6 days      (b) 3 days

(c) 2 days      (d) 4 days

20. An engineer undertakes a project to build a road 15 km long in 300 days and employs 45 men for the purpose. After 100 days, he finds only 2.5 km of the road has been completed. Find the (approx.) number of extra men he must employ to finish the work in time.

(a) 43      (b) 45

(c) 55      (d) 68

21. Apurva can do a piece of work in 12 days. Apurva and Amit complete the work together and were paid ₹ 54 and ₹ 81 respectively. How many days must they have taken to complete the work together?

(a) 4 days      (b) 4.5 days

(c) 4.8 days      (d) 5 days

22. Raju is twice as good as Vijay. Together, they finish the work in 14 days. In how many days can Vijay alone do the same work?

(a) 16 days      (b) 21 days

(c) 32 days      (d) 42 days

23. In a company XYZ Ltd. a certain number of engineers can develop a design in 40 days. If there were 5 more engineers, it could be finished in 10 days less. How many engineers were there in the beginning?

(a) 18      (b) 20

(c) 25      (d) 15

24. If 12 men and 16 boys can do a piece of work in 5 days and 13 men and 24 boys can do it in 4 days, compare the daily work done by a man with that done by a boy?

(a) 1 : 2      (b) 1 : 3

(c) 2 : 1      (d) 3 : 1

25. A can do a work in 10 days and B can do the same work in 20 days. They work together for 5 days and then A goes away. In how many more days will B finish the work?

(a) 5 days      (b) 6.5 days

(c) 10 days      (d) $8\dfrac{1}{3}$ days

26. 30 men working 5 h a day can do a work in 16 days. In how many days will 20 men working 6 h a day do the same work?

(a) $22\dfrac{1}{2}$ days      (b) 20 days

(c) 21 days      (d) None of these

27. Ajay and Vijay undertake to do a piece of work for ₹ 200. Ajay alone can do it in 24 days while Vijay alone can do it in 30 days. With the help of Pradeep, they finish the work in 12 days. How much should Pradeep get for his work?

(a) ₹ 20      (b) ₹ 100

(c) ₹ 180      (d) ₹ 50

28. 15 men could finish a piece of work in 210 days. But at the end of 100 days, 15 additional men are employed. In how many more days will the work be complete?

(a) 80 days      (b) 60 days

(c) 55 days      (d) 50 days

29. Ajay, Vijay and Sanjay are employed to do a piece of work for ₹ 529. Ajay and Vijay together are supposed to do 19/23 of the work and Vijay and Sanjay together 8/23 of the work. How much should Ajay be paid?

(a) ₹ 245      (b) ₹ 295

(c) ₹ 300      (d) ₹ 345

30. Anmol is thrice as good a workman as Vinay and therefore is able to finish the job in 60 days less than Vinay. In how many days will they finish the job working together?

(a) $22\left(\dfrac{1}{2}\right)$ days      (b) $11\left(\dfrac{3}{2}\right)$ days

(c) 15 days      (d) 20 days

31. In a fort there was sufficient food for 200 soldiers for 31 days. After 27 days 120 soldiers left the fort. For how many extra days will the rest of the food last for the remaining soldiers?

(a) 12 days      (b) 10 days

(c) 8 days      (d) 6 days

32. Anju, Manju and Sanju together can reap a field in 6 days. If Anju can do it alone in 10 days and Manju

in 24 days. In how many days will Sanju alone be able to reap the field?

(a) 40 days     (b) 36 days

(c) 35 days     (d) 32 days

33. Ajay and Vijay can do a piece of work in 28 days. With the help of Manoj, they can finish it in 21 days. How long will Manoj take to finish the work all alone?

(a) 84 days     (b) 80 days

(c) 75 days     (d) 70 days

34. Ashok and Mohan can do a piece of work in 12 days. Mohan and Binod together do it in 15 days. If Ashok is twice as good a workman as Binod. In how much time will Mohan alone can do the work?

(a) 15 days     (b) 20 days

(c) 25 days     (d) 35 days

35. Ajay and Vijay together can do a piece of work in 6 days. Ajay alone does it in 10 days. What time does Vijay require to do it alone?

(a) 20 days     (b) 15 days

(c) 25 days     (d) 30 days

36. A cistern is normally filled in 5 hours. However, it takes 6 hours when there is leak in its bottom. If the cistern is full, in what time shall the leak empty it?

(a) 6 h     (b) 5 h

(c) 30 h     (d) 15 h

37. Pipe $A$ and $B$ running together can fill a cistern in 6 minutes. If $B$ takes 5 minutes more than $A$ to fill the cistern, then the time in $A$ and $B$ will fill the cistern separately what time?

(a) 15 min, 20 min     (b) 15 min, 10 min

(c) 10 min, 15 min     (d) 25 min, 20 min

38. $A$ can do a work in 18 days, $B$ in 9 days and $C$ in 6 days. $A$ and $B$ start working together and after 2 days $C$ joins them. In how many days will the job be completed?

(a) 4.33 days     (b) 4 days

(c) 4.66 days     (d) 5 days

39. 24 men working 8 h a day can finish a work in 10 days. Working at a rate of 10 h a day, the number of men required to finish the work in 6 days is

(a) 30     (b) 32

(c) 34     (d) 36

40. A certain job was assigned to a group of men to do it in 20 days. But 12 men did not turn up for the job and the remaining men did the job in 32 days. The original number of men in group was

(a) 32     (b) 34

(c) 36     (d) 40

41. 12 men complete a work in 18 days. 6 days after they had started working, 4 men join them. How

many more days will all of them take to complete the remaining work?

(a) 10 days     (b) 12 days

(c) 15 days     (d) 9 days

42. $A$ takes 5 days more than $B$ to do a certain job and 9 days more than $C$; $A$ and $B$ together can do the job in the same time as $C$. How many days $A$ would take to do it?

(a) 16 days     (b) 10 days

(c) 15 days     (d) 20 days

43. A cistern is normally filled in 6 h but takes 4 h longer to fill because of a leak in its bottom. If the cistern is full, the leak will empty it in how much time?

(a) 15 h     (b) 16 h

(c) 20 h     (d) None of these

44. If three taps are open together, a tank is filled in 10 h. One of the taps can fill in 5 h and another in 10 h. At what rate does the 3rd pipe work?

(a) Waste pipe emptying the tank is 10 h

(b) Waste pipe emptying the tank is 20 h

(c) Waste pipe emptying the tank is 5 h

(d) Fills the tank in 10 h

45. There are two pipes in a tank. Pipe $A$ is for filling the tank and Pipe $B$ is for emptying the tank. If $A$ can fill the tank in 10 hours and $B$ can empty the tank in 15 hours then find how many hours will it take to completely fill a half empty tank?

(a) 30 hours     (b) 15 hours

(c) 20 hours     (d) 33.33 hours

46. Abbot can do some work in 10 days, Bill can do it in 20 days and Clinton can do it in 40 days. They start working in turns with Abbot starting to work on the first day followed by Bill on the second day and by Clinton on the third day and again by Abbot on the fourth day and so on till the work is completed fully. Find the time taken to complete the work fully?

(a) 16 days     (b) 15 days

(c) 17 days     (d) 16.5 days

47. $A$, $B$ and $C$ can do some work in 36 days. $A$ and $B$ together do twice as much work as $C$ alone and $A$ and $C$ together can do thrice as much work as $B$ alone. Find the time taken by $C$ to do the whole work.

(a) 72 days     (b) 96 days

(c) 108 days     (d) 120 days

48. There are three Taps $A$, $B$ and $C$ in a tank. They can fill the tank in 10 hrs, 20 hrs and 25 hrs, respectively. At first, all of them are opened simultaneously. Then after 2 hours, tap $C$ is closed and $A$ and $B$ are kept running. After the 4th hour, tap $B$ is also closed. The remaining work is done by Tap $A$ alone. Find the percentage of the work done by Tap $A$ by itself.

(a) 32%      (b) 52%

(c) 75%      (d) None of these

49. Two taps are running continuously to fill a tank. The 1st tap could have filled it in 5 hours by itself and the second one by itself could have filled it in 20 hours. But the operator failed to realise that there was a leak in the tank from the beginning which caused a delay of one hour in the filling of the tank. Find the time in which the leak would empty a filled tank.

   (a) 15 hours      (b) 20 hours

   (c) 25 hours      (d) 40 hours

50. A can do some work in 24 days, B can do it in 32 days and C can do it in 60 days. They start working together. A left after 6 days and B left after working for 8 days. How many more days are required to complete the whole work?

   (a) 30      (b) 25

   (c) 22      (d) 20

51. A alone can complete a job in 4 days. He is twice as fast as B while B is twice as fast as C. If all of them work together, in how many days would the job get completed?

52. 36 men take 18 days to complete a piece of work. They worked for a period of 8 days. After that, they were joined by 4 more men. How many more days will be taken by them to complete the remaining work?

53. Tap M alone can fill a tank completely in 8 hrs. Another tap N alone can empty the same tank in 12 hrs. If both the taps are opened simultaneously in what time (in hours) would the tank get full?

54. A 50 × 35 m fishing pond was dug by 250 workers in 18 days. The number of days in which a 70 m × 40 m pond having the same depth can be dug by 300 workers is?

55. The wages of 8 men and 4 women amount to ₹ 3500 per week and the wages of 5 men and 3 women to ₹ 2275 per week . Find the daily wages of a man (in rupees, assuming that the wages for a week are paid on the basis of 7 day weeks):

56. 5 women can paint a building in 30 working hours. After 16 hours of work, 2 women decided to leave. How many hours will it take for the work to be finished?

57. A certain number of men complete a piece of work in 60 days. If there were 8 men more the work could be finished in 10 days less. How many men were originally there?

58. In a garrison, there was food for 1000 soldiers for one month. After 10 days, 1000 more soldiers joined the garrison. How many days would the soldiers be able to carry on with the remaining food?

59. The tank-full petrol in Ajay's motor-cycle lasts for 10 days. If he starts using 25% more every day, how many days will the tank-full petrol last?

60. A cistern has two pipes. One can fill it with water in 8 hours and other can empty it in 5 hours. In how many hours will the cistern be emptied if both the pipes are opened together when ¾ of the cistern is already full of water?

*Space for Notes*

## LEVEL OF DIFFICULTY (II)

1. Two forest officials in their respective divisions were involved in the harvesting of *tendu* leaves. One division had an average output of 21 tons from a hectare and the other division, which had 12 hectares of land less, dedicated to *tendu* leaves, got 25 tons of *tendu* from a hectare. As a result, the second division harvested 300 tons of *tendu* leaves more than the first. How many tons of *tendu* leaves did the first division harvest?

   (a) 3150        (b) 3450
   (c) 3500        (d) 3600

2. According to a plan, a drilling team had to drill to a depth of 270 metres below the ground level. For the first three days the team drilled as per the plan. However, subsequently finding that their resources were getting underutilised according to the plan, it started to drill 8 metres more than the plan every day. Therefore, a day before the planned date they had drilled to a depth of 280 metres. How many metres of drilling was the plan for each day.

   (a) 38 metres        (b) 30 metres
   (c) 27 metres  .      (d) 28 metres

3. A pipe can fill a tank in $x$ hours and another can empty it in $y$ hours. If the tank is 1/3rd full then the number of hours in which they will together fill it in is

   (a) $\dfrac{(3xy)}{2(y-x)}$        (b) $\dfrac{(3xy)}{(y-x)}$

   (c) $\dfrac{xy}{3(y-x)}$        (d) $\dfrac{2xy}{3(y-x)}$

4. Dev and Tukku can do a piece of work in 45 and 40 days respectively. They began the work together, but Dev leaves after some days and Tukku finished the remaining work in 23 days. After how many days did Dev leave

   (a) 7 days        (b) 8 days
   (c) 9 days        (d) 11 days

5. A finishes 6/7th of the work in $2z$ hours, $B$ works twice as fast and finishes the remaining work. For how long did $B$ work?

   (a) $\left(\dfrac{2}{3}\right)z$        (b) $\left(\dfrac{6}{7}\right)z$

   (c) $\left(\dfrac{6}{49}\right)z$        (d) $\left(\dfrac{3}{18}\right)z$

**Directions for Questions 6 to 10:** Read the following and answer the questions that follow.

A set of 10 pipes (set $X$) can fill 70% of a tank in 7 minutes. Another set of 5 pipes (set $Y$) fills 3/8 of the tank in 3 minutes. A third set of 8 pipes (set $Z$) can empty 5/10 of the tank in 10 minutes.

6. How many minutes will it take to fill the tank if all the 23 pipes are opened at the same time?

   (a) 5 minutes        (b) $5\dfrac{5}{7}$ minutes

   (c) 6 minutes        (d) $6\dfrac{5}{7}$ minutes

7. If only half the pipes of set $X$ are closed and only half the pipes of set $Y$ are open and all other pipes are open, how long will it take to fill 49% of the tank?
   (a) 16 minutes        (b) 13 minutes
   (c) 7 minutes        (d) None of these

8. If 4 pipes are closed in set $Z$, and all others remain open, how long will it take to fill the tank?
   (a) 5 minutes        (b) 6 minutes
   (c) 7 minutes        (d) 7.5 minutes

9. If the tank is half full and set $X$ and set $Y$ are closed, how many minutes will it take for set $Z$ to empty the tank if alternate taps of set $Z$ are closed.
   (a) 12 minutes        (b) 20 minutes
   (c) 40 minutes        (d) 16 minutes

10. If one pipe is added for set $X$ and set $Y$ and set $Z$'s capacity is increased by 20% on its original value and all the taps are opened at 2.58 p.m., then at what time does the tank get filled? (If it is initially empty.)
    (a) 3.05 p.m.        (b) 3.04 p.m.
    (c) 3.10 p.m.        (d) 3.03 p.m.

11. Ajit can do as much work in 2 days as Baljit can do in 3 days and Baljit can do as much in 4 days as Diljit in 5 days. A piece of work takes 20 days if all work together. How long would Baljit take to do all the work by himself?
    (a) 82 days        (b) 44 days
    (c) 66 days        (d) 50 days

12. Two pipes can fill a cistern in 14 and 16 hours respectively. The pipes are opened simultaneously and it is found that due to leakage in the bottom of the cistern, it takes 32 minutes extra for the cistern to be filled

up. When the cistern is full, in what time will the leak empty it?

(a) 114 h      (b) 112 h

(c) 100 h      (d) 80 h

13. A tank holds 100 gallons of water. Its inlet is 7 inches in diametre and fills the tank at 5 gallons/min. The outlet of the tank is twice the diametre of the inlet. How many minutes will it take to empty the tank if the inlet is shut off, when the tank is full and the outlet is opened? (*Hint:* Rate of filling or emptying is directly proportional to the diametre)

(a) 7.14 min      (b) 10.0 min

(c) 0.7 min      (d) 5.0 min

14. A tank of capacity 25 litres has an inlet and an outlet tap. If both are opened simultaneously, the tank is filled in 5 minutes. But if the outlet flow rate is doubled and taps opened the tank never gets filled up. Which of the following can be outlet flow rate in litres/min?

(a) 2      (b) 6

(c) 4      (d) 3

15. $X$ takes 4 days to complete one-third of a job, $Y$ takes 3 days to complete one-sixth of the same work and $Z$ takes 5 days to complete half the job. If all of them work together for 3 days and $X$ and $Z$ quit, how long will it take for $Y$ to complete the remaining work done.

(a) 6 days      (b) 8.1 days

(c) 5.1 days      (d) 7 days

16. A completes 2/3 of a certain job in 6 days. $B$ can complete 1/3 of the same job in 8 days and $C$ can complete 3/4 of the work in 12 days. All of them work together for 4 days and then $A$ and $C$ quit. How long will it take for $B$ to complete the remaining work alone?

(a) 3.8 days      (b) 3.33 days

(c) 2.22 days      (d) 4.3 days

17. Three diggers dug a ditch of 324 m deep in six days working simultaneously. During one shift, the third digger digs as many metres more than the second as the second digs more than the first. The third digger's work in 10 days is equal to the first digger's work in 14 days. How many metres does the first digger dig per shift?

(a) 15 m      (b) 18 m

(c) 21 m      (d) 27 m

18. $A$, $B$ and $C$ working together completed a job in 10 days. However, $C$ only worked for the first three days when 37/100 of the job was done. Also, the work done by $A$ in 5 days is equal to the work done by $B$ in 4 days. How many days would be required by the fastest worker to complete the entire work?

(a) 20 days      (b) 25 days

(c) 30 days      (d) 40 days

19. $A$ and $B$ completed a work together in 5 days. Had $A$ worked at twice the speed and $B$ at half the speed, it would have taken them four days to complete the job. How much time would it take for $A$ alone to do the work?

(a) 10 days      (b) 20 days

(c) 25 days      (d) 15 days

20. Two typists of varying skills can do a job in 6 minutes if they work together. If the first typist typed alone for 4 minutes and then the second typist typed alone for 6 minutes, they would be left with 1/5 of the whole work. How many minutes would it take the slower typist to complete the typing job working alone?

(a) 10 minutes      (b) 15 minutes

(c) 12 minutes      (d) 20 minutes

21. Three cooks have to make 80 idlis. They are known to make 20 pieces every minute working together. The first cook began working alone and made 20 pieces having worked for sometime more than three minutes. The remaining part of the work was done by the second and the third cook working together. It took a total of 8 minutes to complete the 80 idlis. How many minutes would it take the first cook alone to cook 160 idlis for a marriage party the next day?

(a) 16 minutes      (b) 24 minutes

(c) 32 minutes      (d) 40 minutes

22. It takes six days for three women and two men working together to complete a work. Three men would do the same work five days sooner than nine women. How many times does the output of a man exceed that of a woman?

(a) 3 times      (b) 4 times

(c) 5 times      (d) 6 times

23. Each of $A$, $B$ and $C$ need a certain unique time to do a certain work. $C$ needs 1 hour less than $A$ to complete the work. Working together, they require 30 minutes to complete 50% of the job. The work also gets completed if $A$ and $B$ start working together and $A$ leaves after 1 hour and $B$ works for a further 3 hours. How much work does $C$ do per hour?

(a) 16.66%      (b) 33.33%

(c) 50%      (d) 66.66%

24. Two women Renu and Ushi are working on an embroidery design. If Ushi worked alone, she would need eight hours more to complete the design than if they both worked together. Now if Renu worked alone, it would need 4.5 hours more to complete the design than they both working together. What time would it take Renu alone to complete the design?

(a)  10.5 hours      (b)  12.5 hours

(c)  14.5 hours      (d)  18.5 hours

25. Mini and Vinay are quiz masters preparing for a quiz. In $x$ minutes, Mini makes $y$ questions more than Vinay. If it were possible to reduce the time needed by each to make a question by two minutes, then in $x$ minutes Mini would make $2y$ questions more than Vinay. How many questions does Mini make in $x$ minutes?

(a)  $1/4[2(x+y) - \sqrt{(2x^2 + 4y^2)}\,]$

(b)  $1/4[2(x-y) - \sqrt{(2x^2 + 4y^2)}\,]$

(c)  Either a or b

(d)  $1/4\,[2(x-y) - \sqrt{(2x^2 - 4y^2)}\,]$

26. A tank of 3600 cu m capacity is being filled with water. The delivery of the pump discharging the tank is 20% more than the delivery of the pump filling the same tank. As a result, twelve minutes more time is needed to fill the tank than to discharge it. Determine the delivery of the pump discharging the tank.

(a)  40 m³/min      (b)  50 m³/min

(c)  60 m³/min      (d)  80 m³/min

27. Two pipes $A$ and $B$ can fill up a half full tank in 1.2 hours. The tank was initially empty. Pipe $B$ was kept open for half the time required by pipe $A$ to fill the tank by itself. Then, pipe $A$ was kept open for as much time as was required by pipe $B$ to fill up 1/3 of the tank by itself. It was then found that the tank was 5/6 full. The least time in which any of the pipes can fill the tank fully is

(a)  4.8 hours      (b)  4 hours

(c)  3.6 hours      (d)  6 hours

28. A tank of 425 litres capacity has been filled with water through two pipes, the first pipe having been opened five hours longer than the second. If the first pipe were open as long as the second, and the second pipe was open as long as the first pipe was open, then the first pipe would deliver half the amount of water delivered by the second pipe; if the two pipes were open simultaneously, the tank would be filled up in 17 hours. How long was the second pipe open?

(a)  10 hours      (b)  12 hours

(c)  15 hours      (d)  18 hours

29. Two men and a woman are entrusted with a task. The second man needs three hours more to cope with the job than the first man and the woman would need working together. The first man, working alone, would need as much time as the second man and the woman working together. The first man, working alone, would spend eight hours less than the double period of time the second man would spend working alone. How much time would the two men

and the woman need to complete the task if they all worked together?

(a)  2 hours      (b)  3 hours

(c)  4 hours      (d)  5 hours

30. The Bubna dam has four inlets. Through the first three inlets, the dam can be filled in 12 minutes; through the second, the third and the fourth inlet, it can be filled in 15 minutes; and through the first and the fourth inlet, in 20 minutes. How much time will it take all the four inets to fill up the dam?

(a)  8 min      (b)  10 min

(c)  12 min      (d)  None of these

**Directions for question number 31 & 32:**

Dipen Loomba builds an overhead tank in his house, which has three taps attached to it. While the first tap can fill the tank in 12 hours, the second one takes one and a half times the first one to fill it completely. A third tap is attached to the tank, which empties it in 36 hours. Now, one day, in order to fill the tank, Dipen opens the first tap and after an hour opens the second tap as well. However, at the end of the fourth hour, he realises that the third tap has been kept open right from the beginning and promptly closes it.

31. What is the ratio of volume occupied by water to volume of remaining part of the tank after 6 hours?

32. What will be the total time required to fill the tank (in minutes)?

**Directions for question number 33 & 34:**

33. In the ancient city of Portheus, the emperor has installed an overhead tank that is filled by two pumps — X and Y. X can fill the tank in 12 hours while Y can fill the tank in 15 hours. There is a pipe Z which can empty the tank in 10 hours. Both the pumps are opened simultaneously. The supervisor of the tank, before going out on a work, asks his assistant to open Z when the tank is exactly 40% filled so that tank is exactly filled up by the time he is back. If he starts X and Y at exactly 11:00 AM and he comes back at A:B. Then find the value of A+ B.

34. Due to a miscalculation by the assistant, he opens Z when the tank is one fourth filled. If the supervisor comes back as per the plan what percent of the tank is still empty?

35. Three students A,B and C were working on a project. A is 40% more efficient than B, who is 40% more efficient than C. A takes 10 days less than B to complete the project. A starts the project and works for 10 days and then B takes over. B works on the project for the next 14 days and then stops the work, handing it over to C to complete it. In how many days, would C complete the remaining project?

**Directions for questions 36 and 37:**

Three water pipes, A, B and C are all used to full a container. These pipes can fill the container individually in 6 minutes,

12 minutes and 18 minutes, respectively. All the three pipes were opened simultaneously. However, it was observed that pipes A and B were supplying water at 2/3rd of their normal rates for the first minute after which they supplied water at the normal rate. Pipe C supplied water at half of its normal rate for first 3 minutes, after which it supplied water at its normal rate. Now answer the following questions:

36. What fraction of the tank is empty after 2 hours?

37. In how much time (in minutes and to the closest second), would the container be filled?

38. A contract is to be completed in 72 days and 104 men are set to work, each working 8 hours a day. After 30 days, only 1/5th of the work is finished. How many additional men need to be employed so that the work may be completed on time. (If each man is now working 9 hours per day)?

39. X, Y, Z can complete a work in 4, 6 and 8 hours, respectively. At the most only one person can work in each hour and nobody can work for two consecutive hours. Find the minimum number of hours that they will take to finish the work?

40. The rate at which tap M fills a tank is 60% more than that of tap N. If both the taps are opened simultaneously, they take 50 hours to fill the rank. The time taken by N alone to fill the tank is (in hours).

# LEVEL OF DIFFICULTY (III)

**Directions for Questions 1 to 10:** Study the following tables and answers the questions that follow.

Darbar Toy Company has to go through the following stages for the launch of a new toy:

| | | Expert man-days required | Non-expert man-days required |
|---|---|---|---|
| 1. | Design and development | 30 | 60 |
| 2. | Prototype creation | 15 | 20 |
| 3. | Market survey | 30 | 40 |
| 4. | Manufacturing setup | 15 | 30 |
| 5. | Marketing and launch | 15 | 20 |

The profile of the company's manpower is

| Worker name | Expert at | Non-Expert at | Refusal to work on |
|---|---|---|---|
| A | Design and development | All others | Market survey |
| B | Prototype creation | All others | Market survey |
| C | Market survey and marketing and launch | All others | Design and development |
| D | Manufacturing | All others | Market survey |
| E | Market survey | All others | Manufacturing |

1. Given this situation, the minimum number of days in which the company can launch a new toy going through all the stages is
   (a) 40 days        (b) 40.5 days
   (c) 45 days        (d) 44 days

2. If A and C refuse to have anything to do with the manufacturing set up. The number of days by which the project will get delayed will be
   (a) 5 days        (b) 4 days
   (c) 3 days        (d) 6 days

3. If each of the five works is equally valued at ₹10,000, the maximum amount will be received by
   (a) A        (b) C        (c) D        (d) E

4. For question 3, the second highest amount will be received by
   (a) A        (b) C        (c) D        (d) E

5. If C works at 90.909% of his efficiency during marketing and launch, who will be highest paid amongst the five of them?
   (a) A        (b) C        (c) D        (d) E

6. If the company decides that the first 4 works can be started simultaneously and the experts will be allocated to their respective work areas only and a work will be done by a non-expert only if the work in his area of expertise is completed, then the expert who will first be assisted in his work will be (assume that marketing and launch can only be done after the first four are fully completed)
   (a) A        (b) B        (c) C        (d) D

7. For the question above, the minimum number of days in which the whole project will get completed (assume everything is utilised efficiently all the time, and nobody is utilised in a work that he refuses to work upon)
   (a) 22.5 days        (b) 15 days
   (c) 24.75 days        (d) 25.25 days

8. For the situation in question 6, the highest earning will be for
   (a) A        (b) Both B and D
   (c) C        (d) Cannot be determined

9. If each work has an equal payment of ₹10,000, the lowest earning for the above situation will be for
   (a) A        (b) E        (c) C        (d) B

10. The value of the earning for the highest earning person, (if the data for questions 6–9 are accurate) will be
    (a) 19,312.5        (b) 13,250
    (c) 12,875        (d) B

**Directions for Questions 11 to 20:** Read the following and answer the questions that follow.

A fort contains a granary, that has 1000 tons of grain. The fort is under a siege from an enemy army that has blocked off all the supply routes.

The army in the fort has three kinds of soldiers:
Sepoys → 2,00,000.
Mantris → 1,00,000
Footies → 1,00,000
100 Sepoys can hold 5% of the enemy for one month.
100 Mantris can hold 10% of the enemy for 15 days.
50 Footies can hold 5% of the enemy for one month.
A sepoy eats 1 kg of food per month, a Mantri eats 0.5 kg of food per month and a footie eats 3 kg of food. (Assume 1 ton = 1000 kg).

The king has to make some decisions based on the longest possible resistance that can be offered to the enemy.

If a king selects a soldier, he will have to feed him for the entire period of the resistance. The king is not obliged to feed a soldier not selected for the resistance.

(Assume that the entire food allocated to a particular soldier for the estimated length of the resistance is redistributed into the king's palace in case a soldier dies and is not available for the other soldiers.)

11. If the king wants to maximise the time for which his resistance holds up, he should
    (a) Select all mantris    (b) Select all footies
    (c) Select all sepoys    (d) None of these

12. Based on existing resources, the maximum number of months for which the fort's resistance can last is
    (a) 5 months    (b) 20 months
    (c) 7.5 months    (d) Cannot be determined

13. If the king makes a decision error, the maximum reduction in the time of resistance could be
    (a) 15 months    (b) 12.5 months
    (c) 16.66 months    (d) Cannot be determined

14. If the king estimates that the attackers can last for only 50 months, what should the king do to ensure victory?
    (a) Select all mantris
    (b) Select the mantris and the sepoys
    (c) Select the footies
    (d) The king cannot achieve this

15. If a reduction in the ration allocation by 10% reduces the capacity of any soldier to hold off the enemy by 10%, the number of whole months by which the king can increase the life of the resistance by reducing the ration allocation by 10% is
    (a) 4 months    (b) 2 months
    (c) No change    (d) This will reduce the time

16. The minimum amount of grain that should be available in the granary to ensure that the fort is not lost (assuming the estimate of the king of 50 months being the duration for which the enemy can last is correct) is
    (a) 2000 tons    (b) 2500 tons
    (c) 5000 tons    (d) Cannot be determined

17. If the king made the worst possible selection of his soldiers to offer the resistance, the percentage increase in the minimum amount of grain that should be available in the granary to ensure that the fort is not lost is
    (a) 100%    (b) 500%
    (c) 600%    (d) Cannot be determined

18. The difference in the minimum grain required for the second worst choice and the worst choice to ensure that the resistance lasts for 50 months is
    (a) 5000 tons    (b) 7500 tons
    (c) 10000 tons    (d) Cannot be determined

19. If the king strategically attacks the feeder line on the first day of the resistance so that the grain is no longer a constraint, the maximum time for which the resistance can last is
    (a) 100 months    (b) 150 months
    (c) 250 months    (d) Cannot be determined

20. If the feeder line is opened after 6 months and prior to that the king had made decisions based on food availability being a constraint then the number of months (maximum) for which the resistance could last is
    (a) 100 months    (b) 150 months
    (c) 5 months    (d) Cannot be determined

**Directions for Questions 21 to 25:** Study the following and answer the questions that follow.

A gas cylinder can discharge gas at the rate of 1 cc/minute from burner $A$ and at the rate of 2 cc/minute from burner $B$ (maximum rates of discharge). The capacity of the gas cylinder is 1000 cc of gas.

The amount of heat generated is equal to 1 kcal per cc of gas.

However, there is wastage of the heat as per follows:

| Gas discharge@ | Loss of heat |
| --- | --- |
| 0–0.5 cc/minute | 10% |
| 0.5–1 cc/minute | 20% |
| 1–1.5 cc/minute | 25% |
| 1.5 + cc/minute | 30% |

@(Include higher extremes)

21. If both burners are opened simultaneously such that the first is opened to 90% of its capacity and the second is opened to 80% of its capacity, the amount of time in which the gas cylinder will be empty (if it was half full at the start) will be:
    (a) 250 minutes    (b) 400 minutes
    (c) 200 minutes    (d) None of these

22. The maximum amount of heat with the fastest speed of cooking that can be utilised for cooking will be when:
    (a) The first burner is opened upto 50% of it's aperture
    (b) The second burner is opened upto 25% of it's aperture
    (c) Either (a) or (b)
    (d) None of these

23. The amount of heat utilised for cooking if a full gas cylinder is burnt by opening the aperture of burner $A$ 100% and that of burner $B$ 50% is
    (a) 900 kcal    (b) 800 kcal
    (c) 750 kcal    (d) Cannot be determined

24. For Question 23, if burner $A$ had been opened only 25% and burner $B$ had been opened 50%, the amount of heat available for cooking would be
    (a) 820 kcal    (b) 800 kcal
    (c) 750 kcal    (d) Cannot be determined

25. For Question 24, the amount of time required to finish a full gas cylinder will be
    (a) 900 minutes    (b) 833.33 minutes
    (c) 800 minutes    (d) None of these

# ANSWER KEY

## Level of Difficulty (I)

| | | | |
|---|---|---|---|
| 1. (c) | 2. (c) | 3. (b) | 4. (a) |
| 5. (a) | 6. (a) | 7. (a) | 8. (d) |
| 9. (a) | 10. (a) | 11. (a) | 12. (c) |
| 13. (b) | 14. (b) | 15. (c) | 16. (d) |
| 17. (c) | 18. (b) | 19. (a) | 20. (d) |
| 21. (c) | 22. (d) | 23. (d) | 24. (c) |
| 25. (a) | 26. (b) | 27. (a) | 28. (c) |
| 29. (d) | 30. (a) | 31. (d) | 32. (a) |
| 33. (a) | 34. (b) | 35. (b) | 36. (c) |
| 37. (c) | 38. (b) | 39. (b) | 40. (a) |
| 41. (d) | 42. (c) | 43. (a) | 44. (c) |
| 45. (b) | 46. (d) | 47. (c) | 48. (d) |
| 49. (b) | 50. (c) | 51. 2.29 | 52. 9 |
| 53. 24 | 54. 24 | 55. 50 | 56. 39.33 |
| 57. 40 | 58. 10 | 59. 8 | 60. 10 |

## Level of Difficulty (II)

| | | | |
|---|---|---|---|
| 1. (a) | 2. (b) | 3. (d) | 4. (c) |
| 5. (d) | 6. (b) | 7. (d) | 8. (a) |
| 9. (b) | 10. (d) | 11. (c) | 12. (b) |
| 13. (b) | 14. (b) | 15. (c) | 16. (b) |
| 17. (a) | 18. (a) | 19. (a) | 20. (b) |
| 21. (c) | 22. (d) | 23. (c) | 24. (a) |
| 25. (a) | 26. (c) | 27. (b) | 28. (c) |
| 29. (a) | 30. (b) | 31. 2:1 | 32. 504 |
| 33. 41 | 34. 10 | 35. 9.8 | 36. 19/36 |
| 37. 3 minutes 49 seconds | 38. 161 | 39. 5.33 |
| 40. 130 | | | |

## Level of Difficulty (III)

| | | | |
|---|---|---|---|
| 1. (b) | 2. (b) | 3. (b) | 4. (d) |
| 5. (b) | 6. (a) | 7. (c) | 8. (d) |
| 9. (c) | 10. (c) | 11. (a) | 12. (b) |
| 13. (c) | 14. (d) | 15. (c) | 16. (b) |
| 17. (b) | 18. (a) | 19. (c) | 20. (c) |
| 21. (c) | 22. (c) | 23. (b) | 24. (a) |
| 25. (c) | | | |

## Hints

### Level of Difficulty (III)

**1–10.** Interpretation of the first row of the first table in the question:

Design and Development requires 30 expert man-days or 60 non-expert man-days.

Hence, work done in 1 expert man-day = 3.33% and work done in 1 non-expert man-day = 1.66%. Further, from the second table, it can be interpreted that: A is an expert at design and development. Hence, his work rate is 3.33% per day and B, D and E are ready to work as non-experts on design and

development, hence their work rate is 1.66% per day each.

Thus, in 1 day the total work will be

$A + B + D + E = 3.33 + 1.66 + 1.66 + 1.66 = 8.33\%$ work.

Thus, 12 days will be required to finish the design and development phase.

1. $\dfrac{100}{8.33} + \dfrac{100}{26.66} + \dfrac{100}{6.66} + \dfrac{100}{16.66} + \dfrac{100}{26.66} = 40.5$

2. Increase of number of days $\rightarrow \dfrac{100}{10} - \dfrac{100}{16.66} = 4$ days.

   [This happens since the work rate will drop from 16.66% to 10% due to A and C's refusal to work.]

**3–4.** Find out the work done by each of the 5 workers.

**11–20.** The resistance offered is equal for 100 numbers of all types of soldiers.

**11–13.** If all sepoys are chosen, the food requirement will be 200 tons/month. The resistance will last for 5 months.

If footies are chosen, the food will last for $\dfrac{1000}{100 \times 3}$ = 3.33 months.

If mantris are chosen, the food will last for $\dfrac{1000}{100 \times 0.5}$ = 20 months.

Hence, all mantris must be chosen.

**19–20.** For these questions, since food is no longer a constraint, the constraint then becomes the number of lives. Then, the assumption will be that the resistance lasts for one month with a loss of either 2000 sepoys, 2000 mantris or 1000 footies.

19. Length of resistance = $\dfrac{200000}{2000} + \dfrac{100000}{2000} + \dfrac{100000}{1000}$ = 250 months.

20. In 6 months, the resistance will have lost 12000 mantris. He would also have lost all other soldiers since he has not fed them.

21. $\dfrac{500}{0.9 + 1.6} = 200.$

23. At 1 cc/minute, the loss of heat is 20%. Hence, when 1000 cc of the gas is used, out of the 1000 kcal of heat generated 200 kcal will be lost.

## Solutions and Shortcuts

### Level of Difficulty (I)

1. He will complete the work in 20 days. Hence, he will complete ten times the work in 200 days.

2. 6 men for 12 days means 72 mandays. This would be equal to 4 men for 18 days.

3. A's one day work will be 5%, while B will do 6.66 % of the work in one day. Hence, their total work will be 11.66% in a day.

   In 8 days they will complete $\rightarrow 11.66 \times 8 = 93.33\%$

This will leave 6.66% of the work. This will correspond to 4/7 of the ninth day since in 6.66/11.66 both the numerator and the denominator are divisible by 1.66.

4. $A$'s work = 5% per day

   $B$'s work = 6.66% per day

   $C$'s work = 4% per day.

   Total no. of days = 100/15.66 = 300/47 = 6(18/47)

5. $N + A = 10\%$

   $N = 8.33\%$

   Hence $A = 1.66\% \rightarrow 60$ days.

6. The ratio of the wages will be the inverse of the ratio of the number of days required by each to do the work. Hence, the correct answer will be 3:2 $\rightarrow$ ₹ 30

7. 24 man days + 18 women days = 20 man days + 28 woman days

   $\rightarrow$ 4 man days = 10 woman days.

   $\rightarrow$ 1 man day = 2.5 woman days

   Total work = 24 man days + 18 woman days = 60 woman days + 18 woman days = 78 woman days.

   Hence, 1 man + 1 woman = 3.5 women can do it in 78/3.5 = 156/7 = 22(2/7) days.

8. The data is insufficient, since we only know that the work gets completed in 200 boy days and 300 women days.

9. $A = 10\%$, $B = 5\%$ and Combined work is 20%. Hence, $C$'s work is 5% and will require 20 days.

10. In 5 days, $A$ would do 25% of the work. Since, $B$ finishes the remaining 75% work in 10 days, we can conclude that $B$'s work in a day = 7.5%

    Thus, $(A + B) = 12.5\%$ per day.

    Together they would take 100/12.5 = 8 days.

11. $A = 20\%$, $B = 10\%$ and $A + B + C = 50\%$. Hence, $C = 20\%$. Thus, in two days, $C$ contributes 40% of the total work and should be paid 40% of the total amount.

12. Total man days required = 600 man -days. If 5 workers leave the job after '$n$' days, the total work would be done in 35 days. We have to find the value of '$n$' to satisfy:

    $$20 \times n + (35 - n) \times 15 = 600.$$

    Solving for $n$, we get

    $$20n - 15n + 35 \times 15 = 600$$
    $$5n = 75$$
    $$n = 15.$$

13. Let the time taken by Arun be '$t$' days. Then, time taken by Vinay = $2t$ days.

    $1/t + 1/2t = 1/7 \rightarrow t = 10.5$

14. Subhash can copy 200 pages in 40 hours (reaction to the first sentence). Hence, Prakash can copy 100 pages in 40 hours. Thus, he can copy 30 pages in 30% of the time, i.e., 12 hours.

15. $30X = 20 (X + 6) \rightarrow 10X = 120 \rightarrow X = 12.$

16. Sashi = 4%, Rishi = 5%. In five days, they do a total of 45% work. Rishi will finish the remaining 55% work in 11 more days.

17. Raju = 10%, Vicky = 8.33% and Tinku = 6.66%. Hence, total work for a day if all three work = 25%. In 2 days they will complete, 50% work. On the third day onwards Raju doesn't work. The rate of work will become 15%. Also, since Vicky leaves 3 days before the actual completion of the work, Tinku works alone for the last 3 days (and must have done the last 6.66 × 3 = 20% work alone). This would mean that Vicky leaves after 80% work is done. Thus, Vicky and Tinku must be doing 30% work together over two days.

    Hence, total time required = 2 days (all three) + 2 days (Vicky and Tinku) + 3 days (Tinku alone)

18. Sambhu requires 16 days to do the work while Kalu requires 18 days to do the work.

    $$(1/16 + 1/18) \times n = 1$$
    $$\rightarrow n = 288/34 = 144/17$$

19. Let Anjay take $3t$ days, Vijay take $2t$ days and Manoj take $6t$ days in order to complete the work. Then we get:

    $1/3t + 1/2t + 1/6t = 1 \rightarrow t = 1$. Thus, Manoj would take $6t = 6$ days to complete the work.

20. After 100 days and 4500 man days, only 1/6th of the work has been completed. You can use the product change algorithm of PCG to solve this question.

    $100 \times 45 = 16.66\%$ of the work. After this you have 200 days (i.e., 100% increase in the time available) while the product 200 × number of men should correspond to five times times the original product.

    $$100 \xrightarrow[+100]{\substack{\text{TIME} \\ \text{100\% increase}}} 200 \xrightarrow[+300\ \text{required}]{?} 500$$

    This will be got by increasing the no. of men by 150% (300/200).

21. Since the ratio of money given to Apurva and Amit is 2:3, their work done would also be in the same ratio. Thus, their time ratio would be 3:2 (inverse of 2:3). So, if Apurva takes 12 days, Amit would take 8 days and the total number of days required ($t$) would be given by the equation:

    $(1/12 + 1/8)t = 1 \rightarrow t = 24/5 = 4.8$ days

22. Raju being twice as good a workman as Vijay, you can solve the following equation to get the required answer:

    $1/R + 1/2R = 1/14.$

    Solving will give you that Vijay takes 42 days.

23. $40n = 30 (n + 5) \rightarrow n = 15$

24. $12 \times 5$ man days $+ 16 \times 5$ Boy days

$= 13 \times 4$ man days $+ 24 \times 4$ Boy days

$\rightarrow 8$ man days $= 16$ Boy days

$1$ man day $= 2$ Boy days.

Required ratio of man's work to boy's work = 2 : 1.

25. $A$'s rate of working is 10 per cent per day while $B$'s rate of working is 5 per cent per day. In 5 days they will complete 75 per cent work. Thus the last 25 per cent would be done by $B$ alone. Working at the rate of 5 per cent per day, $B$ would do the work in 5 days.

26. Work equivalence method:

$30 \times 5 \times 16 = 20 \times 6 \times n$

Gives the value of $n$ as 20 days

27. Ajay's daily work = 4.1666%, Vijay's daily work = 3.33% and the daily work of all the three together is 8.33%. Hence, Pradeep's daily work will be 0.8333%. Hence, he will end up doing 10% of the total work in 12 days. This will mean that he will be paid ₹ 20.

28. Total work = $15 \times 210 = 3150$ mandays.

After 100 days, work done = $15 \times 100 = 1500$ mandays.

Work left = $3150 - 1500 = 1650$ mandays.

This work has to be done with 30 men working each day.

The number of days (more) required = 1650/30 = 55 days.

29.              $A + V + S = 1$                    (1)

$A + V = 19/23$

$V + S = 8/23$

$\rightarrow A + 2V + S = 27/23$          (2)

(2)–(1) gives us: $V = 4/23$.

30. Interpret the starting statement as: Anmol takes 30 days and Vinay takes 90 days. Hence, the answer will be got by:

$(1/30 + 1/90) * n = 1$

Alternatively, you can also solve using percentages as: $3.33 + 1.11 = 4.44\%$ is the daily work. Hence, the no. of days required is $100/4.44 = 22.5$ days.

31. After 27 days, food left = $4 \times 200 = 800$ soldier days worth of food. Since, now there are only 80 soldiers, this food would last for $800/80 = 10$ days. Number of extra days for which the food lasts = $10 - 4 = 6$ days.

32. Total work of Anju, Manju and Sanju = 16.66%

Anju's work = 10%

Manju's work = 4.166%

Sanju's work = 2.5%

So Sanju can reap the field in 40 days.

33. Ajay + Vijay = 1/28 and Ajay + Vijay + Manoj = 1/21.

Hence, Manoj = $1/21 - 1/28 = 1/84$.

Hence, Manoj will take 84 days to do the work.

34. $A + M = 8.33$, $M + B = 6.66$ and $A = 2B \rightarrow A$'s 1 days work = 3.33%, $M$'s = 5% and $B$'s = 1.66%. Thus, Mohan would require $100/5 = 20$ days to complete the work if he works alone.

35. $A + V = 16.66\%$ and $A = 10\% \rightarrow V = 6.66\%$. Consequently Vijay would require $100/6.66 = 15$ days to do it alone.

36. The rate of filling will be 20% and the net rate of filling (including the leak) is 16.66%. Hence, the leak accounts for 3.33% per hour, i.e., it will take 30 hours to empty the tank.

37. $A + B = 16.66\%$. From here solve this one using the options. Option (c) fits the situation as it gives us $A$'s work = 10%, $B$'s work = 6.66% as also that $B$ takes 5 minutes more than $A$ (as stipulated in the problem).

38. $A + B = 5.55 + 11.11 = 16.66$. In two days, 33.33% of the work will be done. $C$ adds 16.66% of work to that of $A$ and $B$. Hence, the rate of working will go to 33.33%. At this rate it would take 2 more days to complete the work.

Hence, in total it will take 4 days to complete the entire work.

39. $24 \times 8 \times 10 = N \times 10 \times 6 \rightarrow N = 32$

40. $n \times 20 = (n - 12) \times 32 \rightarrow n = 32$.

41. $12 \times 18 = 12 \times 6 + 16 \times t \rightarrow t = 9$

42. $(A + B)$'s work = $C$'s work.

Also if $A$ takes '$a$' days

$B$ would take '$a - 5$' days

and $C$ would take '$a - 9$' days.

Solving through options, option '$c$' fits.

$A$ (15 days) $\rightarrow A$'s work = 6.66%

$B$ (10 days) $\rightarrow B$'s work = 10%

$C$ (6 days) $\rightarrow C$'s work = 16.66%

43. The cistern fills in 6 hours normally, means that the rate of filling is 16.66% per hour. With the leak in the bottom, the rate of filling becomes 10% per hour (as it takes 10 hours to fill with the leak).

This means that the leak drains out water at the rate of 6.66% per hour. This in turn means that the leak would take $100/6.66 = 15$ hours to drain out the entire cistern.

44. Since the net work of the three taps is 10% and the first and second do 20% + 10% = 30%. Hence, the third pipe must be a waste pipe emptying at the rate of 20% per hour. Hence, the waste pipe will take a total of 5 hours to empty the tank.

45. $A$'s work = 10%

$B$'s negative work = 6.66%

$(A + B)$'s work = 3.33%

To fill a half empty tank, they would take 50/3.33 = 15 hours.

46. The work rate would be 10% on the first day, 5% on the second day and 2.5% on the third day. For every block of 3 days there would be 17.5% work done. In 15 days, the work completed would be $17.5 \times 5 = 87.5\%$. On the sixteenth day, work done = 10% → 2.5% work would be left after 16 days. On the 17th day the rate of work would be 5% and hence it would take half of the 17th day to complete the work. Thus, it would take 16.5 days to finish the work in this fashion.

47. $(A + B) = 2C$.
Also, $(A + C) = 3B$
$36(A + B + C) = 1$
Solving for $C$, we get:
$36 (2C + C) = 1 \rightarrow 108C = 1$
$C = 1/108$
Hence, $C$ takes 108 days.

48. $A + B + C = 19\%$. In the first two hours they will do 38 % of the work. Further, for the next two hours work will be done at the rate of 15% per hour. Hence, after 4 hours 68% of the work will be completed, when tap $B$ is also closed. The last 32% of the work will be done by $A$ alone. Hence, $A$ does 40% (first 4 days) + 32% = 72% of the work.

49. Without the leak:
Rate of work = 20% + 5% = 25%. Thus, it would have taken 4 hours to complete the work.
Due to the leak the filling gets delayed by 1 hour. Thus, the tank gets filled in 5 hours. This means that the effective rate of filling would be 20% per hour. This means that the rate at which the leak empties the tank is 5% per hour and hence it would have taken 20 hours to empty a filled tank.

50. In 6 days $A$ would do 25% of the work and in 8 days $B$ would do 25% of the work himself. So, $C$ has to complete 50% of the work by himself.
In all $C$ would require 30 days to do 50% of the work. So, he would require 22 more days.

51. $A$ is twice fast as $B$ therefore $B$ can complete the job in 8 days. Similarly $C$ can complete the job in 16 days. Therefore, together they can complete the job in
$$\frac{1}{\frac{1}{4}+\frac{1}{8}+\frac{1}{16}}=\frac{16}{7}=2.29 \text{ days.}$$
Alternately, you could have solved this using percentages. A's work for 1 day = 25%, B's work for 1 day = 12.5%, while C's work for 1 day would be = 6.25%. Thus, the total work of A,B and C for 1 day would be = (25 + 12.5 + 6.25)% = 43.75%. Hence, they would complete the work in 100/43.75 = 400/175 = 16/7 days = 2.29 days.

52. If they take '$x$' more days to complete the work then:
$36 \times 18 - (36 \times 8) = (36 + 4)x$
By solving we get $x = 9$ days

53. Required time = $\dfrac{1}{\dfrac{1}{8}-\dfrac{1}{12}}=\dfrac{96}{4}=24$ hours. (Note: This too can be solved using percentages as: Work of Tap M = 12.5%, Work of Tap N = –8.33%. Net work if both the taps are opened together = (12.5-8.33)% = 4.16%. To do 100% of the work, the time required would be 100/4.16 = 24 days.

54. $\dfrac{50\times35}{70\times40}=\dfrac{250\times18}{300\times x}$
$x=\dfrac{250\times18}{300}\times\dfrac{70\times40}{50\times35}=24 \text{ days.}$

55. $8m + 4w = 3500$       (1)
$5m + 3w = 2275$       (2)
By solving equations 1 and 2 we get :
$m = ₹ 350$/week or ₹ 50/day.

56. Let the work will be finishing in $x$ hours.
$5 \times 30 - 5 \times 16 = 3 \times (x - 16)$
By solving we get $x=\dfrac{118}{3}=39.33$ hours.

57. If there were '$x$' men originally then according to the question :
$x \times 60 = (x + 8)(60 - 10)$
$60x = 50x + 400$
$x = 40$

58. Let soldiers would be able to carry on the remaining food for $x$ more days.
$1000 \times 30 - 1000 \times 10 = (1000 + 1000)x$
$x=\dfrac{1000\times20}{2000}=10 \text{ days.}$

59. Mathematical approach: If initially he uses $x$ litres every day and now he is using $1.25x$ litre petrol every day then tank full petrol will last in
$\dfrac{x\times10}{1.25x}=8$

**Short cut approach using Percentage change graphic:** You can solve this by using the logic that if we increase the consumption by 25%, the number of days would drop by 20% (since the product of daily consumption and the number of days would be constant). Thus, the tank-full petrol would last for 20% less than 10 days = 8 days.

60. Required time to empty the tank (in hours) =
$$\frac{3/4}{\frac{1}{5}-\frac{1}{8}}=\frac{3/4}{3/40}=10 \text{ hours.}$$

**Short cut approach using percentage:** You can again solve this by interpreting that $3/4^{th}$ of the tank to be emptied means 75% of the tank needs to be emptied – a net work of –75. Also, the work of the inlet pipe is 12.5% per hour, while the work of the outlet pipe is –20% per hour. Net work when both the inlet and the outlet pipes are opened would be –7.5% per hour. This would mean that to empty 75% of the tank, it would take $75/7.5 = 10$ hours.

## Level of Difficulty (II)

1. $25\,(n - 12) = 21\,n + 300$. Solving this equation, $n = 150$. Hence, the first division harvest 3150 tons.

2. Let n be the number of metres planned per day. Start from the options to find the number of planned days. In the options the 2 feasible values are 30 metres and 27 metres (as these divide 270). Suppose we check for 30 metres per day, the work would have got completed in 9 days as per the original plan. In the new scenario:

   $3n + 5(n + 8) = 280 \rightarrow n = 30$ too. Hence, this option is correct.

   Note that if we tried with 27 metres per day the final equation would not match as we would get:

   $3n + 6(n + 8) = 280 \rightarrow$ which does not give us the value of $n$ as 27 and hence this option is rejected.

3. To solve this question first assume the values of $x$ and $y$ (such that $x < y$). If you take $x$ as 10 hours and $y$ as 15 hours, you will get a net work of 3.33% per hour. At this rate it will take 20 hours to fill the tank from one third full. Using this condition try to put these values of $x$ and $y$ into the options to check the values.

   For instance option (a) gives the value as $3 \times 10 \times 15/10 = 45$ which is not equal to 20.

4. $n(1/45 + 1/40) + 23/40 = 1 \rightarrow n = 9$.

5. Since $A$ finishes $6/7^{th}$ of the work in $2z$ hours.

   $B$ would finish $12/7$ of the work in $2z$ hours.

   Thus, to do $1/7^{th}$ of the work (which represents the remaining work), $B$ would require $2z/12 = z/6$ hours. Option (d) is correct.

### 6–10.

Set $X$ can fill 10% in a minute. Hence, every Pipe of set $X$ can do 1% work per minute. Set $Y$ has a filling capacity of 12.5% per minute (or 2.5% per minute for each tap in set $Y$). Set $Z$ has a capacity of emptying the tank at the rate of 5% per minute and each tap of set $Z$ can empty at the rate of 0.625% per minute.

6. If all the 23 pipes are opened the per minute rate will be:

   $10 + 12.5 – 5 = 17.5\% \rightarrow$ Option (b) is correct.

7. Set $X$ will do 5 % per minute and Set $Y$ will do 6.25% per minute, while set $Z$ will do 5% per minute

(negative work). Hence, Net work will be 6.25% per minute. To fill 49% it will take slightly less than eight minutes and the value will be a fraction. None of the first three options matches this requirement. Hence, the answer will be (d).

8. If 4 of the taps of set $Z$ are closed, the net work done by Set $Z$ would be –2.5% while the work done by Sets $X$ and $Y$ would remain 10% and 12.5% respectively. Thus, the total work per minute would be 20% and hence the tank would take 5 minutes to fill up.

9. Again if we close 4 taps of set $Z$, the rate of emptying by set $Z$ would be 2.5% per minute. A half filled tank would contain 50% of the capacity and hence would take $50/2.5 = 20$ minutes to empty.

10. The rate per minute with the given changes (in percentage terms) would be:

    Set $X = 11\%$, Set $Y = 15\%$ and Set $Z = –6\%$.

    Hence, the net rate $= 11 + 15 – 6 = 20\%$ per minute and it would take 5 minutes for the tank to fill. If all pipes are opened at 7:58, the tank would get filled at 3:03.

11. Let Ajit's rate of work be $100/2 = 50$ work units per day. Baljit would do $100/3 = 33.33$ work units per day and Diljit does $133.33/5 = 26.66$ units of work per day. Their 1 days work $= 50 + 33.33 + 26.66 = 110$ units of work per day. In 20 days, the total work done would be 2200 units of work and hence for Baljit to do it alone it would take: $2200/33.33 = 66$ days to complete the same work.

12. The 32 minutes extra represents the extra time taken by the pipes due to the leak.

    Normal time for the pipes $\rightarrow n \times (1/14 + 1/16) = 1$
    $\rightarrow n = 112/15 = 7$ hrs 28 minutes.

    Thus, with 32 minutes extra, the pipes would take 8 hours to fill the tank.

    Thus, $\quad 8(1/14 + 1/16) – 8 \times (1/L) = 1 \rightarrow 8/L$
    $= 8(15/112) – 1$
    $1/L = 15/112 – 1/8$
    $= 1/112$

    Thus, $L = 112$ hours.

13. The outlet pipe will empty the tank at a rate which is double the rate of filling (Hence, 10 gallons per minute). If the inlet is shut off, the tank will get emptied of 100 gallons of water in ten minutes.

14. The net inflow when both pipes are opened is 5 litres a minute.

    The outlet flow should be such that if its rate is doubled the net inflow rate should be negative or 0. Only an option greater than or equal to '5' would satisfy this condition.

    Option (b) is the only possible value.

15. $X \rightarrow 12$ days $\rightarrow 8.33\%$ of the work per day.
    $Y \rightarrow 18$ days $\rightarrow 5.55\%$ of the work per day

$Z \rightarrow 10$ days $\rightarrow 10\%$ of the work per day.

In three days, the work done will be $25 + 16.66 + 30 = 71.66\%$. The remaining work will get done by $Y$ in $28.33/5.55 = 5.1$ days.

[*Note:* You need to be fluent with your fraction to percentage conversions in order to do well at these kinds of calculations.]

16. $A$ takes 9 days to complete the work

    $B$ takes 24 days to complete the work

    $C$ takes 16 days to complete the work

    In 4e days, work done by all three would be:

    $4 \times (1/9 + 1/24 + 1/16)$

    $$= 4 \times \frac{(16 + 6 + 9)}{144} = 124/144$$

    $= 31/36$ of the work.

    Work left for $B$ would be 5/36 of the work.

    $B$ would require: $(5/36) \times 24 = 3.33$ days.

17. The per day digging of all three combined is 54 metres. Hence, their average should be 18. This means that the first should be $18 - x$, the second, 18 & the third $18 + x$.

    The required conditions are met if we take the values as 15, 18 and 21 metres for the first, second and third diggers, respectively. Hence, (a) is the correct answer.

18. The equations are:

    $3(A + B + C) = 37/100 = 37\%$ of the work.

    $7(A + B) = 63/10 \rightarrow A + B = 9/100 = 9\%$

    (Where $A$, $B$ and $C$ are 1 day's work of the three respectively).

    Further, $5A = 4B$ gives us

    $A = 4\%$ and $B = 5\%$ work per day.

    In 3 days $(A + B + C)$ do 37% of the work.

    Out of this $A$ and $B$ would do 27% ($= 3 \times 9\%$) of the work. So, $C$ would do 3.33% of the work per day.

    $$\frac{37 - 27}{3}$$

    Thus, $B$ is the fastest and he would require 20 days to complete the work.

19. $A + B = 20\%$ of the work. Use trial and error with the options to get the answer.

    Checking for option (a), $A = 10\%$ and $B = 10\%$. If $A$ doubles his work and $B$ halves his work rate, the total work in a day would become $A = 20$, $B = 5$. This would mean that the total work would get completed in 4 days which is the required condition that needs to be matched if the option is to be correct. Hence, this option is correct.

20. Since the first typist types for 4 minutes and the second typist types for exactly 6 minutes, the work left (which is given as 1/5 of the total work) would be the work the first typist can do in 2 minutes. Thus, the time taken by the first typist to do the work would be 10 minutes and his rate of work would be 10% per minute. Also, since both the typists can do the work together in 6 minutes, their combined rate of work would be $100/6 = 16.66\%$ per minute.

    Thus, the second typist's rate of work would be $16.66 - 10 = 6.66\%$ per minute.

    He would take $100/6.66 = 15$ minutes to complete the task alone.

21. From the condition of the problem and a little bit of trial and error we can see that the first cook worked for 4 minutes and the 2nd and 3rd cooks also worked for 4 minutes. As $4(A) + 4(B + C) = 4(A + B + C)$ and we know that $A + B + C = 20$ idlis per minute.

    Thus, the first cook make 20 idlis in 4 minutes. To make 160 idlis he would take 32 minutes.

22. Solve this using options. If we check for option (c), i.e., the work of a man exceeds the work of a woman by 5 times, we would get the following thought process:

    Total work = 6 days $\times$ (3 women + 2 men) = 18 woman days + 12 man days = 18 woman days + 60 woman days = 78 woman days.

    Thus, 9 women would take $78/9$ days = 8.66 days and hence 3 men should do the same work in 3.66 days. This translates to $3 \times 3.66 = 10$ man days or 50 woman days which is incorrect as the number of woman days should have been 78.

    Thus, we can reject this option.

    If we check for option (d), i.e., the work of a man exceeds the work of a woman by 6 times, we would get the following thought process:

    Total work = 6 days $\times$ (3 women + 2 men) = 18 woman days + 12 man days = 18 woman days + 72 woman days = 90 woman days.

    Thus, 9 women would take $90/9$ days = 10 days and hence 3 men should do the same work in 5 days. This translates to $3 \times 5 = 15$ man days or 90 woman days which is correct as the number of woman days should be 90.

    Thus, we select this option.

23. $0.5(A + B + C) = 50\%$ of the work.

    Means $\rightarrow A$, $B$ and $C$ can do the full work in 1 hour.

    Thus, $(A + B + C) = 100\%$

    From this point it is better to solve through options. Option (c) gives the correct answer based on the following thought process.

    If $c = 50\%$ work per hour, it means $C$ takes 2 hours to complete the work.

Consequently, A would take 3 hours and hence do 33.33% work per hour.

Since, $A + B + C = 100\%$, this gives us B's hourly work rate = 16.66%.

For this option to be correct these nos. should match the second instance and the information given there.

According to the second condition:

$A + 4B$ should be equal to 100%. Putting $A = 33.33\%$ and $B = 16.66\%$ we see that the condition is satisfied. Hence, this option is correct.

24. Option (a) is correct because: $1/10.5 + 1/14 = 1/6$ which matches all the conditions of the problem.

25. Solve by trial and error by putting values for $x$ and $y$ in the options.

26. Use options for this question as follows:

If discharging delivery is 40, filling delivery will be 16.66% less (this will give a decimal value right at the start and is unlikely to be the answer. Hence, put this option aside for the time being.)

Option (c) gives good values. If discharging delivery is 60, filling delivery will be 50. Also, time taken for discharge of 3600 cu m will be 60 minutes and the time taken for delivery will be 72 minutes (12 minutes more — which is the basic condition of the problem).

27. The interpretation of the first statement is that (a) and (b) do 41.66 percent of the work per hour. From this point if we go through the options, option (b) fits the situation as 4 hours per one person means 25 percent work per hour per person. Consequently this means 16.66 percent per work per hour per other person.

28. From the last statement we know that since both the pipes would require 17 hours to fill the tank together, they would discharge $425/17 = 25$ litres per hour together.

From this point try to fit the values from the options in order to see which one satisfies all the conditions.

In the case of option (a): Second pipe open for 10 hours, first pipe open for 15 hours.

When the interchange occurs: Second pipe open for 15 hours, first pipe open for 10 hours → gives us that the respective rates of the two pipes would be 3:4 (as the first pipe delivers half the amount of the second pipe— if it delivers 3 litres per minute the second pipe would need to deliver 4 litres per minute).

Thus, if the delivery of the first pipe is 3n litres per minute, the delivery of the second pipe would be 4n litres per minute. Then, in 10 hours of the second pipe and 15 hours of the first pipe, the total water would be 85n, which should be equal to the total water of the two pipes in 17 hours each. But in 17 hours each, the two pipes would discharge $17 \times 7n = 119n$. Thus, we reject this option.

In the case of option (c): Second pipe open for 15 hours, first pipe open for 20 hours.

When the interchange occurs: Second pipe open for 20 hours, first pipe open for 15 hours → gives us that the respective rates of the two pipes would be 2:3 (as the first pipe delivers half the amount of the second pipe- if it delivers 2 litre per minute the second pipe would need to deliver 3 litres per minute).

Thus, if the delivery of the first pipe is 2n litres per minute, the delivery of the second pipe would be 3n litres per minute. Then, in 15 hours of the second pipe and 20 hours of the first pipe, the total water would be 85n, which should be equal to the total water of the two pipes in 17 hours each. In 17 hours each, the two pipes would discharge $17 \times 5n = 85n$. Thus, we realize that this is the correct option.

29. In order to solve this question, if we look at the first statement, we could think of the following scenarios:

If the time taken by the first man and the woman is 1 hour (100% work per hour), the time taken by the second man would be 4 hours (25% work per hour). In such a case, the total time taken by all three to complete the task would be $100/125 = 0.8$ hours. But this value is not there in the options. Hence, we reject this set of values.

If the time taken by the first man and the woman is 2 hours (50% work per hour), the time taken by the second man would be 5 hours (20% work per hour). In such a case, the total time taken by all three to complete the task would be $100/70 = 10/7$ hours. But this value is not there in the options. Hence, we reject this set of values.

If the time taken by the first man and the woman is 3 hours (33.33% work per hour), the time taken by the second man would be 6 hours (16.66% work per hour). In such a case, the total time taken by all three to complete the task would be $100/50 = 2$ hours. Since this value is there in the options we should try to see whether this set of values meets the other conditions in the question.

In this case, it is given that the first man working alone takes as much time as the second man and the woman. Since, the work of all three is 50%, this means that the work of the first man is 25%. Consequently the work of the woman is 8.33%.

Looking at the third condition given in the problem – the time taken by the first man to do the work alone (@ 25% per hour he would take 4 hours) should be 8 hours less than double the time taken by the second man. This condition can be seen to be fulfilled here because the second man would take 6 hours to complete his work (@ 16.66% per hour) and hence, double his time would be 12 hours— which satisfies the difference of 8 hours.

Thus, the total time taken is 2 hours.

30. Let the inlets be $A$, $B$, $C$ and $D$.
$$A + B + C = 8.33\%$$
$$B + C + D = 6.66\%$$
$$A + D = 5\%$$
Thus, $\quad 2A + 2B + 2C + 2D = 20\%$
and $\quad\quad\quad A + B + C + D = 10\%$
→ 10 minutes would be required to fill the tank completely.

31. Short cut Solution: The best way to think in this situation is to assume the tank to have a capacity of 36 litres (LCM of 12,18 and 36). In such a case, the first tap would be filling the tank at the rate of 3 litres per hour, the second one would be filling at the rate of 2 litres per hour while the third one would be emptying the tank at the rate of 1 litre per hour. In 6 hours, the total quantity of water in the tank would be $6 \times 3 + 5 \times 2 - 4 \times 1 = 24$. Hence, the ratio of volume occupied by water to the volume that is not occupied by water is 24 : 12 = 2 : 1.

32. Based on the previous solution, we have seen that after 6 hours 24 litres of the tank are filled. To fill the remaining 12 litres, when both the inlet taps are open, we would need 12 ÷ 5 = 2.4 hours = 2 hours 24 minutes. Thus, it would take a total of 6 hours + 2 hours 24 minutes to fill the tank, i.e., 8 hours 24 minutes = 504 minutes.

33. Let the total capacity of the tank be 180 litres:
Efficiency of X = 15 l/hr.
Efficiency of Y = 12 l/hr.
Efficiency of Z = –18 l/hr.
Time taken to fill the tank to 40% of it's capacity (i.e., 72 litres) = 72/27 = 2 hours 40 minutes.
After 2 hours 40 minutes, Z starts working.
The rate at which the tank would be filled after this would be: 15 + 12 – 18 = 9 litres per hour.
The total quantity to be filled in order to fill up the tank = 180 – 72 = 108 litres.
This will take 108/9=12 hours to complete. Hence, the supervisor comes back after: 12 hours + 2 hours 40 minutes = 14 hours 40 minutes.
Hence, he is supposed to come back at: 1:40 AM (the next day).
The value of A + B = 41.

34. Z opens when the tank is filled with 45 litres of water. This means that Z opened after 45/27 = 1 hour 40 minutes. In the next 13 hours, 13 × 9 = 117 litres of water will get added to the tank. Thus, 10% of the tank would be empty when the supervisor comes back.

35. According to the situation provided in the question, A can do the work in 25 days, B in 35 days. The thought process that gives us these numbers is: Since it is given than A is 40% more efficient than B, it means that A would take 5/7th of the time that B

takes. Since it is given to us that A takes, 10 days less than B, the number of days can be worked out as 25 and 35 for A and B respectively. If you notice, when it is given that A is 40% more efficient than B, then B's number of days can be worked out by increasing A's number of days by 40% directly. This can be thought of as: If A is 40% more efficient than B, then B would take 40% more time to complete the work.
Consequently, C's time required would be 40% more than 35 days = 49 days.
Given the time frames for which they have worked we can get:
Work done by A and B = 80% of the total work.
C would complete the remaining 20% of the work in 49/5 = 9.8 days.

36. Let the total capacity of the container be 108 litres. The pipes A,B and C would respectively fill the container at the rates of 18 litre per minute, 9 litres per hour and 6 litres per hour. Thus, in the first two minutes, the container would get 12 + 6 + 3 + 18 + 9 + 3 = 51 litres of water. The fraction of the tank that would be empty would be 57/108 = 19/36.

37. To fill the remaining 57 litres of the container, in the third minute: Rate of filling =18 + 9 + 3 = 30 litres. This means that at the start of the fourth minute, the container would have 27 litres unfilled. The rate of filling in the fourth minute would be 18 + 9 + 6 = 33 litres. Thus, 27/33 or 9/11 of the 4th minute would be used. Thus, the container gets filled in 3(9/11) minutes = 3 minutes 49 seconds.

38. Using the work equivalence method we know that 1/5th of the work = 104 × 30 × 8 man hours.
Thus, the remaining work = 4 × 104 × 30 × 8. Since, this work has to be done in the remaining 42 days by working at 9 hours per day, the number of men required would be given by: (4 × 104 × 30 × 8) ÷ (42 × 9) = 264.12 = 265 men. This means that we would need to hire 161 additional men.

39. Let the total work be 24, therefore efficiencies of $X$, $Y$, $Z$ are 6, 4 and 3, respectively. To complete the work in minimum time the most efficient should start the work.
After 5 hours total work done =
Remaining work =
Z will complete the remaining work in 1/3 hours.
Total time required to complete the work =
hours.

40. If the rate at which Tap N fills the tank is 10 units per hour, the rate of Tap M would be 16 units per hour.
Hence, the capacity of the tank would be 26 × 50 = 1300.
Time taken by Tap N alone would be 1300/10 = 130 hours.

# 10

# Time, Speed and Distance

## INTRODUCTION

The concepts underlying the chapter of Time, Speed and Distance (TSD) are amongst the most important for the purpose of the Maths section in aptitude exams. The basic concepts of TSD are used in solving questions based on motion in a straight line, relative motion, circular motion, problems based on trains, problem based on boats, clocks, races, etc. Besides, these concepts can also be used for the creation of new types of problems. Your ability to solve these problems will depend only on the depth of your understanding.

Due to this diversity in the possibilities for question setting, this chapter is very important for CAT aspirants. Besides, all other exams based on Aptitude (CMAT, XLRI, FMS, IIFT, Bank PO) also require the use of TSD.

This chapter is one of the most important chapters in the entire portion of quantitative aptitude. The students are therefore advised to closely understand the concepts contained in this chapter to be comfortable with the problems related to this topic in the examination.

## THEORY OF TSD

### Concept of Motion and Mathematical Representation of Motion

Motion/movement occurs when a body of any shape or size changes its position with respect to any external stationary point. Thus, when a person travels from city $A$ to city $B$, we say that he has moved from city $A$ to city $B$. In general, whenever a body moves with respect to a stationary point, we say that the body has undergone a displacement/

motion with respect to the starting point. Thus, for motion to have occurred, there must have been some displacement with respect to a stationary point on the ground.

The mathematical model that describes motion has three variables, namely: Speed, Time and Distance. The interrelationship between these three is also the most important formula for this chapter, namely:

Speed × Time = Distance (Equation for the description of one motion of one body)

The above equation is the mathematical description of the movement of a body. In complex problems, students tend to get confused regarding the usage of this equation and often end up mixing up the speed, time and distance of different motions of different bodies.

It must be mentioned here that this formula is the cornerstone of the chapter Time, Speed and Distance.

Besides, this formula is also the source of the various formulae applied to the problems on the applications of time, speed and distance—to trains, boats and streams, clocks and races, circular motion and straight line motion.

In the equation above, *speed* can be defined as the rate at which distance is covered during the motion. It is measured in terms of *distance* per unit time and may have any combination of units of distance and time in the numerator and the denominator respectively. (m/s, km/hour, m/min, km/min, km/day, etc.)

When we say that the speed of a body is $S$ kmph, we mean to say that the body moves with $S$ kmph towards or away from a stationary point (as the case may be).

Time ($t$) is the time duration over which the movement/ motion occurs/has occurred. The unit used for measuring time is synchronous with the denominator of the unit used for measuring speed. Thus, if the speed is measured in terms of km/h then time is measured in hours.

Distance ($d$) is the displacement of the body during the motion.

The above equation, as is self-evident, is such that the interrelationship between the three parameters defines the value of the third parameter if two of the three are known. Hence we can safely say that if we know two of the three variables describing the motion, then the motion is fully described and every aspect of it is known.

## The Proportionalities Implicit in the Equation $S \times T = D$

The above equation has three implicit proportionality dimensions each of which has its own critical bearing on the solving of time, speed and distance problems.

### 1. Direct proportionality between time and distance (when the speed is constant) time $\propto$ distance

### Illustration

A car moves for 2 hours at a speed of 25 kmph and another car moves for 3 hours at the same speed. Find the ratio of distances covered by the two cars.

**Solution:** Since, the speed is constant, we can directly conclude that time $\propto$ distance.

Hence
$$\frac{t_A}{t_B} = \frac{d_A}{d_B}$$

Since, the times of travel are 2 and 3 hours respectively, the ratio of distances covered is also 2/3.

**Note:** This can be verified by looking at the actual distances travelled—being 50 km and 75 km in this case.

### 2. Direct Proportionality between speed and distance (when the time is constant) speed $\propto$ distance

(a) *A body travels at $S_1$ kmph for the first 2 hours and then travels at $S_2$ kmph for the next two hours. Here two motions of one body are being described and between these two motions the time is constant hence speed will be proportional to the distance travelled.*

(b) *Two cars start simultaneously from A and B respectively towards each other with speeds of $S_1$ kmph and $S_2$ kmph. They meet at a point C....* Here again, the speed is directly proportional to the distance since two motions are described where the time of both the motions is the same, that is, it is evident here that the first and the second car travel for the same time.

In such a case the following ratios will be valid:
$$S_1/S_2 = d_1/d_2$$

### Illustrations

(i) A car travels at 30 km/h for the first 2 hours of a journey and then travels at 40 km/h for the next 2 hours of the journey. Find the ratio of the distances travelled at the two speeds.

**Solution:** Since time is constant between the two motions described, we can use the proportionality between speed and distance.

Hence, $d_1/d_2 = s_1/s_2 = 3/4$

Alternatively, you can also think in terms of percentage as $d_2$ will be 33.33% higher than $d_1$ since $S_2$ is 33.33% higher than $S_1$ and time is constant.

(ii) Two cars leave simultaneously from points *A* and *B* on a straight line towards each other. The distance between *A* and *B* is 100 km. They meet at a point 40 km from *A*. Find the ratio of their speeds.

**Solution:** Since time is the same for both the motions described, we have ratio of speed = ratio of distance.

$$S_A/S_B = 40/60 = 2/3$$

(iii) Two cars move simultaneously from points *A* and *B* towards each other. The speeds of the two cars are 20 m/s and 25 m/s respectively. Find the meeting point if $d(AB) = 900$ km.

**Solution:** For the bodies to meet, the time of travel is constant (since the two cars have moved simultaneously).

Hence, speed ratio = distance ratio
$$\rightarrow 4/5 = \text{distance ratio}$$

Hence, the meeting point will be 400 km from *A* and 500 km from *B*.

### 3. Inverse proportionality between speed and time (when the distance is constant) Speed $\propto$ 1/time

(a) *A body travels at $S_1$ kmph for the first half of the journey and then travels at $S_2$ kmph for the second half of the journey. Here two motions of one body are being described and between these two motions the distance travelled is constant. Hence the speed will be inversely proportional to the time travelled for.*

(b) Two cars start simultaneously from *A* and *B* respectively towards each other. They meet at a point *C* and reach their respective destinations *B* and *A* in $t_1$ and $t_2$ hours respectively... Here again, the speed is inversely proportional to the time since two motions are described where the distance of both the motions is the same, that is, it is evident here that the first and the second car travel for the distance, viz., *AB*. In such a case, the following ratio will be valid:

$$S_1/S_2 = t_2/t_1 \quad \text{i.e.} \quad S_1 t_1 = S_2 t_2 = S_3 t_3 = K$$

### Illustrations

(i) A train meets with an accident and moves at 3/4 its original speed. Due to this, it is 20 minutes late. Find the original time for the journey beyond the point of accident.

**Solution:** Speed becomes 3/4 (Time becomes 4/3)
Extra time = 1/3 of normal time = 20 minutes
Normal time = 60 minutes

Alternatively, from the table on product constancy in the chapter of percentages, we get that a 25% reduction in speed leads to a 33.33% increase in time.

But, 33.33% increase in time is equal to 20 minutes increase in time.

Hence, total time (original) = 60 minutes.

(ii) A body travels half the journey at 20 kmph and the other half at 30 kmph. Find the average speed.

**Solution:** The short-cut process is elucidated in the chapter on 'averages'. Answer = 24 kmph.

(iii) A man travels from his house to his office at 5 km/h and reaches his office 20 minutes late. If his speed had been 7.5 km/h, he would have reached his office 12 minutes early. Find the distance from his house to his office.

**Solution:** Notice that here the distance is constant. Hence, speed is inversely proportional to time.
Solving mathematically

$$S_1/S_2 = t_2/(t_2 + 32)$$
$$5/7.5 = t_2/(t_2 + 32)$$
$$5t_2 + 160 = 7.5\ t_2$$
$$t_2 = 160/2.5 = 64 \text{ minutes}$$

Hence, the distance is given by $7.5 \times 64/60 = 8$ km.

Alternatively, using the Product Constancy Table from the chapter of percentages. If speed increases by 50%, then time will decrease by 33.33%.

But the decrease is equal to 32 minutes.

Hence, original time = 96 minutes and new time is 64 minutes.

Hence, the required distance = $5 \times 96/60$ km = 8 km.
or distance = $7.5 \times 64/60$ km = 8 km

[*Note:* The entire process can be worked out mentally while reading the problem.]

## CONVERSION BETWEEN kmph to m/s

1 km/h = 1000 m/h = 1000/3600 m/s = 5/18 m/s.

Hence, to convert $y$ km/h into m/s multiply by 5/18.

Thus, $y$ km/h = $\dfrac{5y}{18}$ m/s.

And vice versa : $y$ m/s = 18 $y$/5 km/h. To convert from m/s to kmph, multiply by 18/5.

## Relative Speed : Same Direction and Opposite Direction

Normally, when we talk about the movement of a body, we mean the movement of the body with respect to a stationary point. However, there are times when we need to determine the movement and its relationships with respect to a moving point/body. In such instances, we have to take into account the movement of the body/point with respect to which we are trying to determine relative motion.

**Relative movement, therefore, can be viewed as the movement of one body relative to another moving body.**

The following formulae apply for the relative speed of two **independent** bodies with respect to each other:

**Case I:** Two bodies are moving in *opposite* directions at speeds $S_1$ and $S_2$ respectively.
The relative speed is defined as $S_1 + S_2$

**Case II:** Two bodies are moving in the *same direction*.

The relative speed is defined as

(a) $S_1 - S_2$ when $S_1$ is greater than $S_2$.
(b) $S_2 - S_1$ when $S_1$ is lesser than $S_2$.

In other words, the relative speed can also be defined as the positive value of the difference between the two speeds, that is, $|S_1 - S_2|$.

## Motion in a Straight Line

Problems on situations of motion in a straight line are one of the most commonly asked questions in the CAT and other aptitude exams. Hence a proper understanding of the following concepts and their application to problem solving will be extremely important for the student.

*Motion in a straight line is governed by the rules of relative speed enumerated above.*

**A. Two or more bodies starting from the same point and moving in the same direction: Their relative speed is $S_1 - S_2$.**

(a) *In the case of the bodies moving to and fro between two points A and B:* The faster body will reach the end first and will meet the second body on its way back. The relative speed $S_1 - S_2$ will apply till the point of reversal of the faster body and after that the two bodies will start to move in the opposite directions at a relative speed of $S_1 + S_2$. The relative speed governing the movement of the two bodies will alternate between $S_1 - S_2$ and $S_1 + S_2$ everytime any one of the bodies reverses directions. However, if both the bodies reverse their direction at the same instant, there will be no change in the relative speed equation.

In this case, the description of the motion of the two bodies between two consecutive meetings will also be governed by the proportionality between speed and distance (since the time of movement between any two meetings will be constant).

*Distances covered in this case:* For every meeting, the total distance covered by the two bodies will be 2*D* (where $D$ is the distance between the extreme points). However, notice that the value of $2D$ would be applicable only if both the bodies reverse the direction between two meetings. In case only one body has reversed direction, the total distance would need to be calculated on a case-by-case basis. The respective coverage of the distance is in the ratio of the individual speeds.

Thus, for the 9th meeting (if both bodies have reversed direction between every 2 meetings) the total distance covered will be $9 \times 2D = 18D$.

This will be useful for solving problems that require the calculation of a meeting point.

(b) *In the case of the bodies continuing to move in the same direction without coming to an end point and reversing directions*: The faster body will take a lead and will keep increasing the lead and the movement of the two bodies will be governed by the relative speed equation: $S_1 - S_2$.

Here again, if the two bodies start simultaneously, their movement will be governed by the direct proportionality between speed and distance.

**B. Moving in the opposite direction:** Their relative speed will be initially given by $S_1 + S_2$.

(a) *In the case of the bodies moving to and fro between two points A and B starting from opposite ends of the path*: The two bodies will move towards each other, meet at a point in between $A$ and $B$, then move apart away from each other. The faster body will reach its extreme point first followed by the slower body reaching its extreme point next. Relative speed will change every time; one of the bodies reverses direction.

The position of the meeting point will be determined by the ratio of the speeds of the bodies (since the 2 movements can be described as having the time constant between them).

*Distances covered in the above case:* For the first meeting, the total distance covered by the two bodies will be $D$ (the distance between the extreme points). The coverage of the distance is in the ratio of the individual speeds.

Thereafter, as the bodies separate and start coming together, the combined distance to be covered is $2D$. Note that if only one body is reversing direction between two meetings, this would not be the case and you will have to work it out.

Thus, for the 10th meeting (if both bodies have reverse direction between every 2 meetings) the total distance covered will be $D + 9 \times 2D = 19D$.

This will be useful for solving of problems that require the calculation of a meeting point.

## Illustrations

(i) Two bodies $A$ and $B$ start from opposite ends $P$ and $Q$ of a straight road. They meet at a point $0.6D$ from $P$. Find the point of their fourth meeting.

**Solution:** Since time is constant, we have ratio of speeds as 3 : 2.

Also, total distance to be covered by the two together for the fourth meeting is $7D$. This distance is divided in a ratio of 3 : 2 and thus we have that $A$ will cover $4.2D$ and $B$ will cover $2.8D$.

The fourth meeting point can then be found out by tracking either $A$ or $B$'s movement. $A$, having moved a distance of $4.2D$, will be at a point $0.2D$ from $P$. This is the required answer.

(ii) $A$ starts walking from a place at a uniform speed of 2 km/h in a particular direction. After half an hour, $B$ starts from the same place and walks in the same direction as $A$ at a uniform speed and overtakes $A$ after 1 hour 48 minutes. Calculate the speed of $B$.

**Solution:** Start solving as you read the question. From the first two sentences you see that $A$ is 1 km ahead of $B$ when $B$ starts moving.

This distance of 1 km is covered by $B$ in 9/5 hours [1 hour 48 minutes = $1(4/5) = 9/5$ hours].

The equation operational here $(S_B - S_A) \times T$ = initial distance
$$(S_B - 2) \times 9/5 = 1$$

Solving, we get $S_B = 23/9$ km/h.

(b) *In the case of the bodies continuing to move in the same direction without coming to an end point and reversing directions*: The bodies will meet and following their meeting they will start separating and going away from each other. The relative speed will be given by $S_1 + S_2$ initially while approaching each other and, thereafter, it will be $S_1 + S_2$ while moving away from each other.

*Important:* The student is advised to take a closer look and get a closer understanding of these concepts by taking a few examples with absolute values of speed, time and distance. Try to visualise how two bodies separate and then come together. Also, clearly understand the three proportionalities in the equation $s \times t = d$, since these are very important tools for problem solving.

## Concept of Acceleration

Acceleration is defined as the rate of change of speed.

Acceleration can be positive (speed increases) or negative (speed decreases → also known as deceleration)

The unit of acceleration is speed per unit time (e.g. m/s²)

For instance, if a body has an initial speed of 5 m/s and a deceleration of 0.1 m/s² it will take 50 seconds to come to rest.

**Final speed = Initial speed + Acceleration × Time**

**Some more examples:**

(i) Water flows into a cylindrical beaker at a constant rate. The base area of the beaker is 24 cm². The water level rises by 10 cm every second. How quickly will the water level rise in a beaker with a base area of 30 cm².

**Solution:** The flow of water in the beaker is 24 cm² × 10 cm/s = 240 cm³/s.

If the base area is 30 cm² then the rate of water level rise will be 240/30 = 8 cm/s.

*Note:* In case of confusion in such questions the student is advised to use dimensional analysis to understand what to multiply and what to divide.

(ii) A 2 kilowatt heater can boil a given amount of water in 10 minutes. How long will it take for
   (a) a less powerful heater of 1.2 kilowatts to boil the same amount of water?
   (b) a less powerful heater of 1.2 kilowatts to boil double the amount of water?

**Solution:**

(a) The heating required to boil the amount of water is $2 \times 10 = 20$ kilowatt minutes. At the rate of 1.2 kilowatt, this heat will be generated in 20/1.2 minutes = 16.66 minutes.

(b) When the water is doubled, the heating required is also doubled. Hence, heating required = 40 kilowatt minutes. At the rate of 1.2 kilowatt, this heat will be generated in 40/1.2 = 33.33 minutes.

## AN APPLICATION OF ALLIGATION IN TIME, SPEED AND DISTANCE

**Consider the following situation:**
Suppose a car goes from A to B at an average speed of $S_1$ and then comes back from B to A at an average speed of $S_2$. If you had to find out the average speed of the whole journey, what would you do?

The normal short cut given for this situation gives the average speed as:

$$\frac{2S_1 S_2}{S_1 + S_2}$$

However, this situation can be solved very conveniently using the process of alligation as explained below:

Since, the two speeds are known to us, we will also know their ratio. The ratio of times for the two parts of the journey will then be the inverse ratio of the ratio of speeds. (Since the distance for the two journeys are equal). The answer will be the weighted average of the two speeds (weighted on the basis of the time travelled at each speed)

**The process will become clear through an example:**
A car travels at 60 km/h from Mumbai to Poona and at 120 km/h from Poona to Mumbai. What is the average speed of the car for the entire journey.

**Solution**

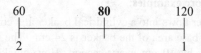

```
     60          80          120
     |_____|_____|
     2                       1
```

The process of alligation, will be used here to give the answer as 80. (*Note:* For the process of alligation; refer to the chapter of Alligations.)

Note here, that since the speed ratio is 1:2, the value of the time ratio used for calculating the weighted average will be 2:1.

What will happen in case the distances are not constant?

For instance, if the car goes 100 km at a speed of 66 kmph and 200 km at a speed of 110 kmph, what will be the average speed?

In this case the speed ratio being 6:10 i.e. 3:5 the inverse of the speed ratio will be 5:3. This would have been the ratio to be used for the time ratio in case the distances were the same (for both the speeds). But since the distances are different, we cannot use this ratio in this form. The problem is overcome by multiplying this ratio (5:3) by the distance ratio (in this case it is 1:2) to get a value of 5:6. This is the ratio which has to be applied for the respective weights. Hence, the alligation will look like:

**Solution**

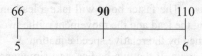

```
     66          90          110
     |_____|_____|
     5                       6
```

Thus the required answer is 90 kmph. (The student is advised to check this value through normal mathematical processes.)

## APPLICATIONS OF TIME, SPEED AND DISTANCE

**Trains**
Trains are a special case in questions related to time, speed and distance because they have their own theory and distinct situations.

**The basic relation for trains problems is the same: Speed × Time = Distance.**

*The following things need to be kept in mind before solving questions on trains:*

(a) When the train is crossing a moving object, the speed has to be taken as the **relative speed** of the train with respect to the object. All the rules for relative speed will apply for calculating the relative speed.

(b) The distance to be covered when crossing an object whenever a train crosses an object will be equal to: **Length of train + Length of object**

Thus, the following cases will yield separate equations, which will govern the crossing of the object by the train:

For each of the following situations the following notations have been used:

$S_T$ = Speed of train    $S_O$ = Speed of object    $t$ = time
$L_T$ = Length of train    $L_O$ = Length of object

**Case I:**  Train crossing a stationary object without length:

$$S_T \times t = L_T$$

**Case II:**  Train crossing a stationary object with length:

$$S_T \times t = (L_T + L_O)$$

**Case III:** Train crossing a moving object without length:

- In opposite direction: $(S_T + S_O) \times t = L_T$
- In same direction: $(S_T - S_O) \times t = L_T$

**Case IV:** Train crossing a moving object with length:

- In opposite direction: $(S_T + S_O) \times t = (L_T + L_O)$
- In same direction: $(S_T - S_O) \times t = (L_T + L_O)$

[*Note:* In order for a train to completely cross a stationary point on the ground, the train has to traverse a distance that is equal to its entire length.

This can be visualised by remembering yourself stationary on a railway platform and being crossed by a train. You would say that the train starts crossing you when the engine of the train comes in line with you. Also, you would say that you have been crossed by the train when the end of the guard's compartment comes in line with you. Thus, the train would have travelled its own length in crossing you].

## Illustrations

(i) A train crosses a pole in 8 seconds. If the length of the train is 200 metres, find the speed of the train.

**Solution:** In this case, it is evident that the situation is one of the train crossing a stationary object without length. Hence, Case I is applicable here.

Thus, $S_T = 200/8 = 25$ m/s $\rightarrow 25 \times \dfrac{18}{5} = 90$ kmph.

(ii) A train crosses a man travelling in another train in the opposite direction in 8 seconds. However, the train requires 25 seconds to cross the same man if the trains are travelling in the same direction. If the length of the first train is 200 metres and that of the train in which the man is sitting is 160 metres, find the speed of the first train.

**Solution:** Here, the student should understand that the situation is one of the train crossing a moving object without length. Thus the length of the man's train is useless or redundant data.

Then applying the relevant formulae after considering the directions of the movements we get the equations:

$$S_T + S_M = 25$$
$$S_T - S_M = 8$$

$$S_T = \frac{33}{2} = \frac{33 \times 18}{2 \times 5} = 59.4 \text{ kmph}$$

## Boats and Streams

The problems of boats and streams are also dependent on the basic equation of time, speed and distance : Speed × Time = Distance.

However, as in the case of trains the adjustments to be made for solving questions on boats and streams are:

The boat has a speed of its own, which is also called the *speed of the boat in still water* ($S_B$).

Another variable that is used in boats and streams problems is the *speed of the stream* ($S_S$).

The speed of the movement of the boat is dependent on whether the boat is moving:

(a) In still water the speed of movement is given by $\rightarrow S_B$.

(b) While *moving upstream* (or against the flow of the water), the speed of movement is given by $\rightarrow S_U = S_B - S_S$.

(c) While *moving downstream* (or with the flow of the water), the speed of movement is given by $\rightarrow S_D = S_B + S_S$

The time of movement and the distance to be covered are to be judged by the content of the problem.

**Circular motion:** A special case of movement is when two or more bodies are moving around a circular track.

*The relative speed of two bodies moving around a circle in the same direction is taken as $S_1 - S_2$.*

Also, *when two bodies are moving around a circle in the opposite direction, the speed of the two bodies is taken to be $S_1 + S_2$.*

The peculiarity inherent in moving around a circle in the same direction is that when the faster body overtakes the slower body it goes ahead of it. And for every unit time that elapses, the faster body keeps increasing the distance by which the slower body is behind the faster body. However, when the distance by which the faster body is in front of the slower body becomes equal to the circumference of the circle around which the two bodies are moving, the faster body again comes in line with the slower body. This event is called as overlapping or lapping of the slower body by the faster body. We say that the slower body has been lapped or overlapped by the faster body.

*First meeting:* Three or more bodies start moving simultaneously from the same point on the circumference of the circle, in the same direction around the circle. They will first meet again in the LCM of the times that the fastest runner takes in totally overlapping each of the slower runners.

For instance, if A, B, C and D start clockwise from a point X on the circle such that A is the fastest runner then we can define $T_{AB}$ as the time in which A completely overlaps B, $T_{AC}$ as the time in which A completely overlaps C and $T_{AD}$ as the time in which A completely overlaps D. Then the LCM of $T_{AB}$, $T_{AC}$ and $T_{AD}$ will be the time in which A, B, C and D will be together again for the first time.

*First meeting at starting point:* Three or more bodies start moving simultaneously from the same point on the circumference of a circle, in the same direction around the circle. Their first meeting at the starting point will occur after a time that is got by the LCM of the times that each of the bodies takes to complete one full round.

For instance, if A, B and C start from a point X on the circle such that $T_A$, $T_B$ and $T_C$ are the times in which A, B and C respectively cover one complete round around the circle, then they will all meet together at the starting point in the LCM of $T_A$, $T_B$ and $T_C$.

## Clocks

Problems on clocks are based on the movement of the minute hand and that of the hour hand as well as on the relative movement between the two. In my opinion, it is best to solve problems on clocks by considering a clock to be a circular track having a circumference of 60 km and each kilometre being represented by one minute on the dial of the clock. Then, we can look at the minute hand as a runner running at the speed of 60 kmph while we can also look at the hour hand as a runner running at an average speed of 5 kmph.

Since, the minute hand and the hour hand are both moving in the same direction, the relative speed of the minute hand with respect to the hour hand is 55 kmph, that is, for every hour elapsed, the minute hand goes 55 km (minute) more than the hour hand.

(Beyond this slight adjustment, the problems of clocks require a good understanding of unitary method. This will be well illustrated through the solved example below.)

---

### Important Information

*Number of right angles formed by a clock:* A clock makes 2 right angles between any 2 hours. Thus, for instance, there are 2 right angles formed between 12 to 1 or between 1 and 2 or between 2 and 3 or between 3 and 4 and so on.

However, contrary to expectations, the clock does not make 48 right angles in a day. This happens because whenever the clock passes between the time period 2–4 or between the time period 8–10 there are not 4 but only 3 right angles.

This happens because the second right angle between 2–3 (or 8–9) and the first right angle between 3–4 (or 9–10) are one and the same, occurring at 3 or 9.

*Contd*

---

### Important Information (*Contd*)

*Right angles are formed when the distance between the minute hand and the hour hand is equal to 15 minutes.*

Exactly the same situation holds true for the formation of straight lines. There are 2 straight lines in every hour. However, the second straight line between 5–6 (or 11–12) and the first straight line between 6–7 (or 12–1) coincide with each other and are represented by the straight line formed at 6 (or 12).

Straight lines are formed when the distance between the minute hand and the hour hand is equal to either 0 minutes or 30 minutes.

---

### Illustration

At what time between 2–3 p.m. is the first right angle in that time formed by the hands of the clock?

**Solution:** At 2 p.m. the minute hand can be visualised as being 10 kilometres behind the hour hand. (considering the clock dial to be a race track of circumference 60 km such that each minute represents a kilometre).

Also, the first right angle between 2–3 is formed when the minute hand is 15 kilometres ahead of the hour hand.

Thus, the minute hand has to cover 25 kilometres over the hour hand.

This can be written using the unitary method:

Distance covered by the minute hand over the hour hand.

55 kilometres _____ in 1 hour
25 kilometres _____ in what time?
→ 5/11 of an hour.

Thus, the first right angle between 2–3 is formed at 5/11 hours past 2 o'clock.

This can be converted into minutes and seconds using unitary method again as:

1 hour _____ 60 minutes
5/11 hours _____ ? minutes
→ 300/11 minutes = 27 (3/11) minutes
1 minute _____ 60 seconds
3/11 minutes _____ ? seconds → 180/11 seconds = 16.3636 seconds.

Hence, the required answer is: **2 : 27 : 16.36 seconds**.

---

*Space for Notes*

# LEVEL OF DIFFICULTY (I)

1. The Sinhagad Express left Pune at noon sharp. Two hours later, the Deccan Queen started from Pune in the same direction. The Deccan Queen overtook the Sinhagad Express at 8 p.m. Find the average speed of the two trains over this journey if the sum of their average speeds is 70 km/h.
   - (a) 34.28 km/h
   - (b) 35 km/h
   - (c) 50 km/h
   - (d) 12 km/h

2. Walking at 3/4 of his normal speed, Abhishek is 16 minutes late in reaching his office. The usual time taken by him to cover the distance between his home and his office is
   - (a) 48 minutes
   - (b) 60 minutes
   - (c) 42 minutes
   - (d) 62 minutes

3. Ram and Bharat travel the same distance at the rate of 6 km per hour and 10 km per hour respectively. If Ram takes 30 minutes longer than Bharat, the distance travelled by each is
   - (a) 6 km
   - (b) 10 km
   - (c) 7.5 km
   - (d) 20 km

4. Two trains for Mumbai leave Delhi at 6:00 a.m. and 6:45 a.m. and travel at 100 kmph and 136 kmph respectively. How many kilometres from Delhi will the two trains be together?
   - (a) 262.4 km
   - (b) 260 km
   - (c) 283.33 km
   - (d) 275 km

5. Two trains, Calcutta Mail and Bombay Mail, start at the same time from stations Kolkata and Mumbai respectively towards each other. After passing each other, they take 12 hours and 3 hours to reach Mumbai and Kolkata respectively. If the Calcutta Mail is moving at the speed of 48 km/h, the speed of the Bombay Mail is
   - (a) 24 km/h
   - (b) 22 km/h
   - (c) 21 km/h
   - (d) 96 km/h

6. Shyam's house, his office and his gym are all equidistant from each other. The distance between any 2 of them is 4 km. Shyam starts walking from his gym in a direction parallel to the road connecting his office and his house and stops when he reaches a point directly east of his office. He then reverses direction and walks till he reaches a point directly south of his office. The total distance walked by Shyam is
   - (a) 6 km
   - (b) 9 km
   - (c) 16 km
   - (d) 12 km

7. Lonavala and Khandala are two stations 600 km apart. A train starts from Lonavala and moves towards Khandala at the rate of 25 km/h. After two hours, another train starts from Khandala at the rate of 35 km/h. How far from Lonavala will they will cross each other?
   - (a) 250 km
   - (b) 300 km
   - (c) 279.166 km
   - (d) 475 km

8. Walking at 3/4 of his normal speed, a man takes 2(1/2) hours more than the normal time. Find the normal time.
   - (a) 7.5 h
   - (b) 6 h
   - (c) 8 h
   - (d) 12 h

9. Alok walks to a viewpoint and returns to the starting point by his car and thus takes a total time of 6 hours 45 minutes. He would have gained 2 hours by driving both ways. How long would it have taken for him to walk both ways?
   - (a) 8 h 45 min
   - (b) 7 h 45 min
   - (c) 5 h 30 min
   - (d) 6 h 45 min

10. Sambhu beats Kalu by 30 metres or 10 seconds. How much time was taken by Sambhu to complete a race 1200 meters.
    - (a) 6 min 30 s
    - (b) 3 min 15 s
    - (c) 12 min 10 s
    - (d) 2 min 5 s

11. What is the time taken by Chandu to cover a distance of 360 km by a motorcycle moving at a speed of 10 m/s?
    - (a) 10 h
    - (b) 5 h
    - (c) 8 h
    - (d) 6 h

12. Without stoppage, a train travels a certain distance with an average speed of 60 km/h, and with stoppage, it covers the same distance with an average speed of 40 km/h. On an average, how many minutes per hour does the train stop during the journey?
    - (a) 20 min/h
    - (b) 15 min/h
    - (c) 10 min/h
    - (d) 10 min/h

13. Rajdhani Express travels 650 km in 5 h and another 940 km in 10 h. What is the average speed of train?
    - (a) 1590 km/h
    - (b) 168 km/h
    - (c) 106 km/h
    - (d) 126 km/h

14. Rishikant, during his journey, travels for 20 minutes at a speed of 30 km/h, another 30 minutes at a speed of 50 km/h, and 1 hour at a speed of 50 km/h and 1 hour at a speed of 60 km/h. What is the average velocity?
    - (a) 51.18 km/h
    - (b) 63 km/h
    - (c) 39 km/h
    - (d) 48 km/h

15. A car travels from $A$ to $B$ at $V_1$ km/h, travels back from $B$ to $A$ at $V_2$ km/h and again goes back from $A$ to $B$ at $V_2$ km/h. The average speed of the car is:

    (a) $\dfrac{2V_1 V_2}{V_1 + 2V_2}$      (b) $\dfrac{2V_1 V_2}{V_2 + 2V_1}$

    (c) $\dfrac{3V_1 V_2}{V_2 + 2V_1}$      (d) $\dfrac{3V_1 V_2}{V_1 + 2V_2}$

16. Narayan Murthy walking at a speed of 20 km/h reaches his college 10 minutes late. Next time he increases his speed by 5 km/h, but finds that he is still late by 4 minutes. What is the distance of his college from his house?

    (a) 20 km          (b) 6 km
    (c) 12 km          (d) None of these

17. Jayshree goes to office at a speed of 6 km/h and returns to her home at a speed of 4 km/h. If she takes 10 hours in all, what is the distance between her office and her home?

    (a) 24 km          (b) 12 km
    (c) 10 km          (d) 30 km

18. A motor car does a journey in 17.5 hours, covering the first half at 30 km/h and the second half at 40 km/h. Find the distance of the journey.

    (a) 684 km         (b) 600 km
    (c) 120 km         (d) 540 km

19. Sujit covers a distance in 40 minutes if he drives at a speed of 60 kilometer per hour on an average. Find the speed at which he must drive at to reduce the time of the journey by 25%?

    (a) 60 km/h        (b) 70 km/h
    (c) 75 km/h        (d) 80 km/h

20. Manish travels a certain distance by car at the rate of 12 km/h and walks back at the rate of 3 km/h. The whole journey took 5 hours. What is the distance he covered on the car?

    (a) 12 km          (b) 30 km
    (c) 15 km          (d) 6 km

21. A railway passenger counts the telegraph poles on the rail road as he passes them. The telegraph poles are at a distance of 50 metres. What will be his count in 4 hours, if the speed of the train is 45 km per hour?

    (a) 600            (b) 2500
    (c) 3600           (d) 5000

22. Two trains $A$ and $B$ start simultaneously in the opposite direction from two points $A$ and $B$ and arrive at their destinations 9 and 4 hours respectively after their meeting each other. At what rate does the second train $B$ travel if the first train travels at 80 km per hour.

    (a) 60 km/h        (b) 100 km/h
    (c) 120 km/h       (d) 80 km/h

23. Vinay fires two bullets from the same place at an interval of 12 minutes but Raju sitting in a train approaching the place hears the second report 11 minutes 30 seconds after the first. What is the approximate speed of train (if sound travels at the speed of 330 metre per second)?

    (a) 660/23 m/s     (b) 220/7 m/s
    (c) 330/23 m/s     (d) 110/23 m/s

24. A car driver, driving in a fog, passes a pedestrian who was walking at the rate of 2 km/h in the same direction. The pedestrian could see the car for 6 minutes and it was visible to him up to a distance of 0.6 km. What was the speed of the car?

    (a) 30 km/h        (b) 15 km/h
    (c) 20 km/h        (d) 8 km/h

25. Harsh and Vijay move towards Hosur starting from IIM, Bangalore, at a speed of 40 km/h and 60 km/h respectively. If Vijay reaches Hosur 200 minutes earlier then Harsh, what is the distance between IIM, Bangalore, and Hosur?

    (a) 600 km         (b) 400 km
    (c) 900 km         (d) 200 km

26. A journey of 192 km takes 2 hours less by a fast train than by a slow train. If the average speed of the slow train be 16 kmph less than that of fast train, what is the average speed of the faster train?

    (a) 32 kmph        (b) 16 kmph
    (c) 12 kmph        (d) 48 kmph

27. A passenger train takes 2 h less for a journey of 300 kilometres if its speed is increased by 5 kmph over its usual speed. Find the usual speed.

    (a) 10 kmph        (b) 12 kmph
    (c) 20 kmph        (d) 25 kmph

28. If Arun had walked 1 km/h faster, he would have taken 10 minutes less to walk 2 kilometre. What is Arun's speed of walking?

    (a) 1 kmph         (b) 2 kmph
    (c) 3 kmph         (d) 6 kmph

29. A plane left half an hour later than the scheduled time and in order to reach its destination 1500 kilometre away in time, it had to increase its speed by 33.33 per cent over its usual speed. Find its increased speed.

    (a) 250 kmph       (b) 500 kmph
    (c) 750 kmph       (d) 1000 kmph

30. A train moves at a constant speed of 120 km/h for one kilometre and at 40 kmph for the next one kilometre. What is the average speed of the train?

    (a) 48 kmph        (b) 50 kmph
    (c) 80 kmph        (d) 60 kmph

31. A cyclist moving on a circular track of radius 100 metres completes one revolution in 2 minutes. What is the average speed of cyclist (approximately)?

(a) 314 m/minute    (b) 200 m/minute

(c) 300 m/minute    (d) 900 m/minute

32. A person travelled a distance of 200 kilometre between two cities by a car covering the first quarter of the journey at a constant speed of 40 km/h and the remaining three quarters at a constant speed of $x$ km/h. If the average speed of the person for the entire journey was 53.33 km/h what is the value of $x$?

(a) 55 km/h    (b) 60 km/h

(c) 70 km/h    (d) 80 km/h

33. A car travels 1/3 of the distance on a straight road with a velocity of 10 km/h, the next 1/3 with a velocity of 20 km/h and the last 1/3 with a velocity of 60 km/h. What is the average velocity of the car for the whole journey?

(a) 18 km/h    (b) 10 km/h

(c) 20 km/h    (d) 15 km/h

34. Two cars started simultaneously toward each other from town $A$ and $B$, that are 480 km apart. It took the first car travelling from $A$ to $B$ 8 hours to cover the distance and the second car travelling from $B$ to $A$ 12 hours. Determine at what distance from $A$ the two cars meet.

(a) 288 km    (b) 200 km

(c) 300 km    (d) 196 km

35. Walking at 3/4 of his usual speed, a man is 16 minutes late for his office. The usual time taken by him to cover that distance is

(a) 48 minutes    (b) 60 minutes

(c) 42 minutes    (d) 62 minutes

36. $A$ and $B$ travel the same distance at the rate of 8 kilometre and 10 kilometre an hour respectively. If $A$ takes 30 minutes longer than $B$, the distance travelled by $B$ is

(a) 6 km    (b) 10 km

(c) 16 km    (d) 20 km

37. Two trains for Patna leave Delhi at 6 a.m. and 6:45 a.m. and travel at 98 kmph and 136 kmph respectively. How many kilometres from Delhi will the two trains meet?

(a) 262.4 km    (b) 260 km

(c) 200 km    (d) None of these

38. Two trains $A$ and $B$ start from station $X$ to $Y$, $Y$ to $X$ respectively. After passing each other, they take 12 hours and 3 hours to reach $Y$ and $X$ respectively. If train $A$ is moving at the speed of 48 km/h, the speed of train $B$ is

(a) 24 km/h    (b) 96 km/h

(c) 21 km/h    (d) 20 km/h

39. $X$ and $Y$ are two stations 600 km apart. A train starts from $X$ and moves towards $Y$ at the rate of 25 km/h.

Another train starts from $Y$ at the rate of 35 km/h. How far from $X$ they will cross each other?

(a) 250 km    (b) 300 km

(c) 450 km    (d) 475 km

40. $A$ starts from a point that is on the circumference of a circle, moves 600 metre in the North direction and then again moves 800 metre East and reaches a point diametrically opposite the starting point. Find the diameter of the circle?

(a) 1000 m    (b) 500 m

(c) 800 m    (d) 900 m

41. Ram and Shyam run a race of 2000 m. First, Ram gives Shyam a start of 200 m and beats him by 30 s. Next, Ram gives Shyam a start of 3 min and is beaten by 1000 metres. Find the time in minutes in which Ram and Shyam can run the race separately.

(a) 8, 10    (b) 4, 5

(c) 5, 9    (d) 6, 9

42. A motorboat went downstream for 28 km and immediately returned. It took the boat twice as long to make the return trip. If the speed of the river flow were twice as high, the trip downstream and back would take 672 minutes. Find the speed of the boat in still water and the speed of the river flow.

(a) 9 km/h, 3 km/h    (b) 9 km/h, 6 km/h

(c) 8 km/h, 2 km/h    (d) 12 km/h, 3 km/h

43. A train requires 7 seconds to pass a pole while it requires 25 seconds to cross a stationary train which is 378 metres long. Find the speed of the train.

(a) 75.6 km/h    (b) 75.4 km/h

(c) 76.2 km/h    (d) 21 km/h

44. A boat sails downstream from point $A$ to point $B$, which is 10 km away from $A$, and then returns to $A$. If the actual speed of the boat (in still water) is 3 km/h, the trip from $A$ to $B$ takes 8 hours less than that from B to $A$. What must the actual speed of the boat for the trip from $A$ to $B$ to take exactly 100 minutes?

(a) 1 km/h    (b) 2 km/h

(c) 3 km/h    (d) 4 km/h

45. A boat sails down the river for 10 km and then up the river for 6 km. The speed of the river flow is 1 km/h. What should be the minimum speed of the boat for the trip to take a maximum of 4 hours?

(a) 2 kmph    (b) 3 kmph

(c) 4 kmph    (d) 5 kmph

46. A man rows 6 km/h in still water. If the river is running at 3 km per hour, it takes him 45 minutes to row to a place and back. How far is the place?

(a) 1.12 km    (b) 1.25 km

(c) 1.6875 km    (d) 2.5 km

47. A boat goes 40 km upstream in 8 h and a distance of 49 km downstream in 7 h. The speed of the boat in still water is
    (a) 5 km/h  (b) 5.5 km/h
    (c) 6 km/h  (d) 6.5 km/h

48. Two trains are running on parallel lines in the same direction at speeds of 40 kmph and 20 kmph respectively. The faster train crosses a man in the second train in 36 seconds. The length of the faster train is
    (a) 200 metres  (b) 185 metres
    (c) 225 metres  (d) 210 metres

49. The speed of the boat in still water is 12 km/h and the speed of the stream is 2 km/h. A distance of 8 km, going upstream, is covered in
    (a) 1 h  (b) 1 h 15 min
    (c) 1 h 12 min  (d) None of these

50. A boat goes 15 km upstream in 80 minutes. The speed of the stream is 5 km/h. The speed of the boat in still water is
    (a) 16.25 km/h  (b) 16 km/h
    (c) 15 km/h  (d) 17 km/h

51. In a stream, B lies in between A and C such that it is equidistant from both A and C. A boat can go from A to B and back in 6 h 30 minutes while it goes from A to C in 9 h. How long would it take to go from C to A?
    (a) 3.75 h  (b) 4 h
    (c) 4.25 h  (d) 4.5 h

52. Two trains pass each other on parallel lines. Each train is 100 metres long. When they are going in the same direction, the faster one takes 60 seconds to pass the other completely. If they are going in opposite directions they pass each other completely in 10 seconds. Find the speed of the slower train in km/h.
    (a) 30 km/h  (b) 42 km/h
    (c) 48 km/h  (d) 60 km/h

53. Vinay runs 100 metres in 20 seconds and Ajay runs the same distance in 25 seconds. By what distance will Vinay beat Ajay in a hundred metre race?
    (a) 10 m  (b) 20 m
    (c) 25 m  (d) 12 m

54. In a 100 m race, Shyam runs at 1.66 m/s. If Shyam gives Sujit a start of 4 m and still beats him by 12 seconds, what is Sujit's speed?
    (a) 1.11 m/s  (b) 0.75 m/s
    (c) 1.33 m/s  (d) 1 km/h

55. At a game of billiards, A can give B 15 points in 60 and A can give C 20 in 60. How many points can B give C in a game of 90?
    (a) 11  (b) 13
    (c) 10  (d) 14

56. In a 500 m race, the ratio of speed of two runners Vinay and Shyam is 3 : 4. If Vinay has a start of 140 m then Vinay wins by
    (a) 15 m  (b) 20 m
    (c) 25 m  (d) 30 m

57. How many seconds will a caravan 120 metres long running at the rate 10 m/s take to pass a standing boy.
    (a) 10 s  (b) 12 s
    (c) 11 s  (d) 14 s

58. Two trains are travelling in the same direction at 50 km/h and 30 km/h respectively. The faster train crosses a man in the slower train in 18 seconds. Find the length of the faster train.
    (a) 0.1 km  (b) 1 km
    (c) 1.5 km  (d) 1.4 km

59. Two trains for Howrah leave Muzaffarpur at 8:30 a.m. and 9:00 a.m. respectively and travel at 60 km/h and 70 km/h respectively. How many kilometres from Muzaffarpur will the two trains meet?
    (a) 210 km  (b) 180 km
    (c) 150 km  (d) 120 km

60. Without stoppage, a train travels at an average speed of 75 km/h and with stoppages it covers the same distance at an average speed of 60 km/h. How many minutes per hour does the train stop?
    (a) 10 minutes  (b) 12 minutes
    (c) 14 minutes  (d) 18 minutes

61. A boat rows 16 km up the stream and 30 km downstream taking 5 h each time. The velocity of the current
    (a) 1.1 km/h  (b) 1.2 km/h
    (c) 1.4 km/h  (d) 1.5 km/h

62. Vijay can row a certain distance downstream in 6 h and return the same distance in 9 h. If the stream flows at the rate of 3 km/h, find the speed of Vijay in still water.
    (a) 12 km/h  (b) 13 km/h
    (c) 14 km/h  (d) 15 km/h

63. Subbu can row 6 km/h in still water. When the river is running at 1.2 km/h, it takes him 1 hour to row to a place and back. How far in the place?
    (a) 2.88 km  (b) 2.00 km
    (c) 3.12 km  (d) 2.76 km

64. A dog is passed by a train in 8 seconds. Find the length of the train if its speed is 36 kmph.
    (a) 70 m  (b) 80 m
    (c) 85 m  (d) 90 m

65. A lazy man can row upstream at 16 km/h and downstream at 22 km/h. Find the man's rate in still water (in kmph).

(a) 19        (b) 14

(c) 17        (d) 18

66. A man can row 30 km upstream and 44 km downstream in 10 hours. It is also known that he can row 40 km upstream and 55 km downstream in 13 hours. Find the speed of the man in still water.

(a) 4 km/h        (b) 6 km/h

(c) 8 km/h        (d) 12 km/h

67. In a stream that is running at 2 km/h, a man goes 10 km upstream and comes back to the starting point in 55 minutes. Find the speed of the man in still water.

(a) 20 km/h        (b) 22 km/h

(c) 24 km/h        (d) 28 km/h

68. A man goes down stream at $x$ km/h and upstream at $y$ km/h. The speed of the boat in still water is

(a) $0.5(x+y)$        (b) $0.5(x-y)$

(c) $x+y$        (d) $x-y$

69. The length of the minutes hand of a clock is 8 cm. Find the distance travelled by its outer end in 15 minutes.

(a) $4\pi$ cm        (b) $8\pi$ cm

(c) $12\pi$ cm        (d) $16\pi$ cm

70. Between 5 a.m. and 5 p.m. of a particular day for how many times are the minute and the hour hands together?

(a) 11        (b) 22

(c) 33        (d) 44

71. At what time are the hands of clock together between 2 and 3 p.m.?

(a) 2/11 hours past 2 p.m.

(b) 2/9 hours past 2 p.m.

(c) 2:10 p.m.

(d) None of these

72. A motorboat went down the river for 14 km and then up the river for 9 km. It took a total of 5 hours for the entire journey. Find the speed of the river flow if the speed of the boat in still water is 5 km/h.

(a) 1 kmph        (b) 1.5 kmph

(c) 2 kmph        (d) 3 kmph

73. A motorboat whose speed in still water is 10 km/h went 91 km downstream and then returned to its starting point. Calculate the speed of the river flow if the round trip took a total of 20 hours.

(a) 3 km/h        (b) 4 km/h

(c) 6 km/h        (d) 8 km/h

74. In a race of 600 meters, Ajay beats Vijay by 60 metres and in a race of 500 meters Vijay beats Anjay by 25 meters. By how many meters will Ajay beat Anjay in a 400 meter race?

(a) 48 m        (b) 52 m

(c) 56 m        (d) 58 m

75. A motorboat whose speed in still water is 15 kmph goes 30 km downstream and comes back in a total 4 hours 30 min. Determine the speed of the stream.

(a) 2 kmph        (b) 3 kmph

(c) 4 kmph        (d) 5 kmph

76. In a 100 meters race $X$ can give $Y$ a 10 meters start and in a 18 km race $Y$ can give $Z$ a 2 km start. If the speed of $X$ is 20 m/s then the speed of $Z$ (in m/s) is?

77. In a 5 Km race Mohan wins by 500 meters over Sohan, while Sohan can give a start of 200 meters to Chotan in a 1 km race. In a 5 km race how much start (in meters) can Mohan give Chotan, so that both reach the destination simultaneously?

78. If the ratio of speeds of $A$ and $B$ is 5 : 4, then what start can $A$ give to $B$ so that in a 1 km race, $B$ must cover 10% less distance than $A$?

79. If the ratio of speeds of $X$ and $Y$ is 4 : 5 and $X$ loses the race by 250 m. then what is the length of the race track (in km)?

## Directions for questions 80 and 81:

Three persons $X, Y, Z$ run on a circular track of length 1 Km. at speeds of 20 m/s, 40 m/s and 60 m/s respectively in the same direction.

80. If they start running simultaneously, after how much time (in seconds) will they meet again ?

81. After how much time will they meet at the starting point ?

82. $X, Y, Z$ run on a circular track at speeds of 10 m/s, 20 m/s, 25 m/s respectively. If they start from the same point in the same direction at the same time and X covers 1 km when they meet again for the first time at the starting point, then the total distance covered by $Y$ (in Km) is ?

## Directions for questions 83 and 84:

John's office is 80 km from his house. One day he started from home, an hour later than his usual time of leaving for his office. In order to cover up the delay, he increased his speed by 4 kmph and thus reached the office on time. Now answer the following questions:

83. What is the final speed of John?

84. What is the percentage increase in John's speed?

85. The distance between two cities A and B is 100 km and the speed of Ram and Rahim are 50 km/h and 30 km/h respectively. Initially Ram is at A and Rahim is at B. If they move between A and B to and fro, then the distance (in kms) covered by Ram by the time they meet for the 3$^{rd}$ time would be?

*Space for Rough Work*

## LEVEL OF DIFFICULTY (II)

1. The J&K Express from Delhi to Srinagar was delayed by snowfall for 16 minutes and made up for the delay on a section of 80 km travelling with a speed 10 km per hour higher than its normal speed. Find the original speed of the J&K Express (according to the schedule)

   (a) 60 km/h       (b) 66.66 km/h
   (c) 50 km/h       (d) 40 km/h

2. Ayrton Senna had to cover a distance of 60 km. However, he started 6 minutes later than his scheduled time and raced at a speed 1 km/h higher than his originally planned speed and reached the finish at the time he would reach it if he began to race strictly at the appointed time and raced with the assumed speed. Find the speed at which he travelled during the journey described.

   (a) 25 km/h       (b) 15 km/h
   (c) 10 km/h       (d) 6 km/h

3. Amitabh covered a distance of 96 km two hours faster than he had planned to. This he achieved by travelling 1 km more every hour than he intended to cover every 1 hour 15 minutes. What was the speed at which Amitabh travelled during the journey?

   (a) 16 km/h       (b) 26 km/h
   (c) 36 km/h       (d) 30 km/h

4. An urgent message had to be delivered from the house of the Peshwas in Pune to Shivaji who was camping in Bangalore. A horse rider travels on horse back from Pune to Bangalore at a constant speed. If the horse increased its speed by 6 km/h, it would take the rider 4 hours less to cover that distance. And travelling with a speed 6 km/h lower than the initial speed, it would take him 10 hours more than the time he would have taken had he travelled at a speed 6 kmph higher than the initial speed. Find the distance between Pune and Bangalore.

   (a) 120 km        (b) 600 km
   (c) 720 km        (d) 750 km

5. A pedestrian and a cyclist start simultaneously towards each other from Aurangabad and Paithan which are 40 km apart and meet 2 hours after the start. Then they resumed their trips and the cyclist arrives at Aurangabad 7 hours 30 minutes earlier than the pedestrian arrives at Paithan. Which of these could be the speed of the pedestrian?

   (a) 4 km/h        (b) 5 km/h
   (c) 3 km/h        (d) 6 km/h

6. Two motorists met at 10 a.m. at the Dadar railway station. After their meeting, one of them proceeded in the East direction while the other proceeded in the North direction. Exactly at noon, they were 60 km apart. Find the speed of the slower motorist if the difference of their speeds is 6 km/h.

   (a) 28 km/h       (b) 18 km/h
   (c) 9 km/h        (d) 19 km/h

7. Two cyclists start simultaneously towards each other from Aurangabad and Ellora, which are 28 km apart. An hour later they meet and keep pedalling with the same speed without stopping. The second cyclist arrives at Ellora 35 minutes later than the first arrives at Aurangabad. Find the speed of the cyclist who started from Ellora.

   (a) 12 km/h       (b) 16 km/h
   (c) 15 km/h       (d) 10 km/h

8. Two ants start simultaneously from two ant holes towards each other. The first ant coveres 8% of the distance between the two ant holes in 3 hours, the second ant covered $\frac{7}{120}$ of the distance in 2 hours 30 minutes. Find the speed (feet/h) of the second ant if the first ant travelled 800 feet to the meeting point.

   (a) 15 feet/h     (b) 25 feet/h
   (c) 45 feet/h     (d) 35 feet/h

9. A bus left point $X$ for point $Y$. Two hours later a car left point $X$ for $Y$ and arrived at $Y$ at the same time as the bus. If the car and the bus left simultaneously from the opposite ends $X$ and $Y$ towards each other, they would meet 1.33 hours after the start. How much time did it take the bus to travel from $X$ to $Y$?

   (a) 2 h           (b) 4 h
   (c) 6 h           (d) 8 h

10. A racetrack is in the form of a right triangle. The longer of the legs of the track is 2 km more than the shorter of the legs (both these legs being on a highway). The start and end points are also connected to each other through a side road. The escort vehicle for the race took the side road and rode with a speed of 30 km/h and then covered the two intervals along the highway during the same time with a speed of 42 km/h. Find the length of the racetrack.

    (a) 14 km        (b) 10 km
    (c) 24 km        (d) 36 km

11. Two planes move along a circle of circumference 1.2 km with constant speeds. When they move in

different directions, they meet every 15 seconds and when they move in the same direction, one plane overtakes the other every 60 seconds. Find the speed of the slower plane.

(a) 0.04 km/s      (b) 0.03 km/s

(c) 0.05 km/s      (d) 0.02 km/s

12. Karim, a tourist leaves Ellora on a bicycle. Having travelled for 1.5 h at 16 km/h, he makes a stop for 1.5 h and then pedals on with the same speed. Four hours after Karim started, his friend and local guide Rahim leaves Ellora on a motorcycle and rides with a speed of 28 km/h in the same direction as Karim had gone. What distance will they cover before Rahim overtakes Karim?

(a) 88 km      (b) 90.33 km

(c) 93.33 km      (d) 96.66 km

13. A tourist covered a journey partly by foot and partly by tonga. He walked for 90 km and rode the tonga for 10 km. He spent 4 h less on the tonga than on walking. If the tourist had reversed the times he travelled by foot and on tonga, the distances travelled on each part of the journey would be equal. How long did he ride the tonga?

(a) He rode for 6 hours    (b) He rode for 4 hours

(c) He rode for 2 hours    (d) He rode for 5 hours

14. Two Indian tourists in the US cycled towards each other, one from point $A$ and the other from point $B$. The first tourist left point $A$ 6 hrs later than the second left point $B$, and it turned out on their meeting that he had travelled 12 km less than the second tourist. After their meeting, they kept cycling with the same speed, and the first tourist arrived at $B$ 8 hours later and the second arrived at $A$ 9 hours later. Find the speed of the faster tourist.

(a) 4 km/h      (b) 6 km/h

(c) 9 km/h      (d) 2 km/h

15. Two joggers left Delhi for Noida simultaneously. The first jogger stopped 42 min later when he was 1 km short of Noida and the other one stopped 52 min later when he was 2 km short of Noida. If the first jogger jogged as many kilometres as the second and the second as many kilometres as the first, the first one would need 17 min less than the second. Find the distance between Delhi and Noida.

(a) 5 km      (b) 15 km

(c) 25 km      (d) 35 km

16. A tank of 4800 m³ capacity is full of water. The discharging capacity of the pump is 10 m³/min higher than its filling capacity. As a result the pump needs 16 min less to discharge the fuel than to fill up the tank. Find the filling capacity of the pump.

(a) 50 m³/min      (b) 25 m³/min

(c) 55 m³/min      (d) 24 m³/min

17. An ant climbing up a vertical pole ascends 12 meters and slips down 5 meters in every alternate hour. If the pole is 63 meters high how long will it take it to reach the top?

(a) 18 hours

(b) 17 hours

(c) 16 hours 35 minutes

(d) 16 hours 40 minutes

18. Two ports $A$ and $B$ are 300 km apart. Two ships leave $A$ for $B$ such that the second leaves 8 hours after the first. The ships arrive at $B$ simultaneously. Find the time the slower ship spent on the trip if the speed of one of them is 10 km/h higher than that of the other.

(a) 25 hours      (b) 15 hours

(c) 10 hours      (d) 20 hours

19. An ant moved for several seconds and covered 3 mm in the first second and 4 mm more in each successive second than in its predecessor. If the ant had covered 1 mm in the first second and 8 mm more in each successive second, then the difference between the path it would cover during the same time and the actual path would be more than 6 mm but less than 30 mm. Find the time for which the ant moved (in seconds).

(a) 5 s      (b) 4 s

(c) 6 s      (d) 2 s

20. The Sabarmati Express left Ahmedabad for Mumbai. Having travelled 300 km, which constitutes 66.666 per cent of the distance between Ahmedabad and Mumbai, the train was stopped by a red signal. Half an hour later, the track was cleared and the engine-driver, having increased the speed by 15 km per hour, arrived at Mumbai on time. Find the initial speed of the Sabarmati Express.

(a) 50 kmph      (b) 60 kmph

(c) 75 kmph      (d) 40 kmph

21. Two swimmers started simultaneously from the beach, one to the south and the other to the east. Two hours later, the distance between them turned out to be 100 km. Find the speed of the faster swimmer, knowing that the speed of one of them was 75% of the speed of the other.

(a) 30 kmph      (b) 40 kmph

(c) 45 kmph      (d) 60 kmph

22. A motorcyclist left point $A$ for point $B$. Two hours later, another motorcyclist left $A$ for $B$ and arrived at $B$ at the same time as the first motorcyclist. Had both the motorcyclists started simultaneously from $A$ and $B$ travelling towards each other, they would have met in 80 minutes. How much time did it take the faster motorcyclist to travel from $A$ to $B$?

(a) 6 hours      (b) 3 hours

(c) 2 hours      (d) 4 hours

23. Two horses started simultaneously towards each other and meet each other 3 h 20 min later. How much time will it take the slower horse to cover the whole distance if the first arrived at the place of departure of the second 5 hours later than the second arrived at the point of departure of the first?
    (a) 10 hours       (b) 5 hours
    (c) 15 hours       (d) 6 hours

24. The difference between the times taken by two buses to travel a distance of 350 km is 2 hours 20 minutes. If the difference between their speeds is 5 kmph, find the slower speed.
    (a) 35 kmph        (b) 30 kmph
    (c) 25 kmph        (d) 20 kmph

25. One bad day, at 7 a.m. I started on my bike at the speed of 36 kmph to meet one of my relatives. After I had travelled some distance, my bike went out of order and I had to stop. After resting for 35 minutes, I returned home on foot at a speed of 14 kmph and reached home at 1 p.m. Find the distance from my house at which my bike broke down.
    (a) 54 km          (b) 63 km
    (c) 72 km          (d) None of these

**Direction for Questions 26 to 30:** Read the following data and answer the questions that follow.

Three brothers, Ram, Shyam and Mohan, travelled by road. They all left the college at the same time—12 noon. The description of the motions of the three are detailed below:

| Name | Ram | Shyam | Mohan |
|---|---|---|---|
| Phase I | Bus for 2 hours @ 10 mph | Bike for @ 1 hours 30 mph | Foot for 3 hours @ 3.33 mph |
| Phase II | Bike for 1.5 hours @ 40 mph | Foot for 3 hours @ 3.33 mph | Bus for 3 hours @ 10 mph |
| Phase III | Foot for 3 hours @ 3.33 mph | Bus for 4 hours @ 10 mph | Bike for 2 hours @ 30 mph |

26. When did Ram overtake Shyam?
    (a) 3:15 p.m.      (b) 2:22 p.m.
    (c) 2:30 p.m.      (d) 2:20 p.m.

27. At what distance from the start does Mohan overtake Shyam?
    (a) 40 miles       (b) 57 miles
    (c) 70 miles       (d) 80 miles

28. If Ram travelled by bike instead of foot in the last leg of his journey (for the same distance as he had covered by foot), what is the difference in the times of Ram and Mohan to cover 90 miles?
    (a) 6 h 50 minutes    (b) 10 h 40 minutes
    (c) 3 hrs 55 minutes  (d) 4 hrs 10 minutes

29. If all of them travelled a distance of 100 miles, who reached first and at what time (assume the last leg time increases to cover 100 miles)?
    (a) Mohan at 6 p.m.   (b) Ram at 8 p.m.
    (c) Shyam at 6 p.m.   (d) Mohan at 8 p.m.

30. In the above question, who reached last and at what time?
    (a) Ram at 9:30 p.m.  (b) Ram at 10 p.m.
    (c) Shyam at 9:30 p.m. (d) Shyam at 10 p.m.

31. A motorcyclist rode the first half of his way at a constant speed. Then he was delayed for 5 minutes and, therefore, to make up for the lost time he increased his speed by 10 km/h. Find the initial speed of the motorcyclist if the total path covered by him is equal to 50 km.
    (a) 36 km/h        (b) 48 km/h
    (c) 50 km/h        (d) 62 km/h

32. Ram Singh and Priyadarshan start together from the same point on a circular path and walk around, each at his own pace, until both arrive together at the starting point. If Ram Singh performs the circuit in 3 minutes 44 seconds and Priyadarshan in 6 minutes 4 seconds, how many times does Ram Singh go around the path?
    (a) 8              (b) 13
    (c) 15             (d) Cannot be determined

33. Ravi, who lives in the countryside, caught a train for home earlier than usual yesterday. His wife normally drives to the station to meet him. But yesterday he set out on foot from the station to meet his wife on the way. He reached home 12 minutes earlier than he would have done had he waited at the station for his wife. The car travels at a uniform speed, which is 5 times Ravi's speed on foot. Ravi reached home at exactly 6 O'clock. At what time would he have reached home if his wife, forewarned of his plan, had met him at the station?
    (a) 5 : 48         (b) 5 : 24
    (c) 5 : 00         (d) 5 : 36

34. Hemant and Ajay start a two-length swimming race at the same moment but from opposite ends of the pool. They swim in lane and at uniform speeds, but Hemant is faster than Ajay. They first pass at a point 18.5 m from the deep end and having completed one length, each one is allowed to rest on the edge for exactly 45 seconds. After setting off on the return length, the swimmers pass for the second time just 10.5 m from the shallow end. How long is the pool?
    (a) 55.5 m         (b) 45 m
    (c) 66 m           (d) 49 m

35. Rahim sets out to cross a forest. On the first day, he completes 1/10th of the journey. On the second day, he covers 2/3rd of the distance travelled the first day.

He continues in this manner, alternating the days in which he travels 1/10th of the distance still to be covered, with days on which he travels 2/3 of the total distance already covered. At the end of seventh day, he finds that $22\frac{1}{2}$ km more will see the end of his journey. How wide is the forest?

(a) $66\frac{2}{3}$ km     (b) 100 km

(c) 120 km     (d) 150 km

36. The metro service has a train going from Mumbai to Pune and Pune to Mumbai every hour, the first one at 6 a.m. The trip from one city to other takes $4\frac{1}{2}$ hours, and all trains travel at the same speed. How many trains will you pass while going from Mumbai to Pune if you start at 12 noon?

(a) 8     (b) 10

(c) 9     (d) 13

37. The distance between two towns is $x$ km. A car travelling between the towns covers the first $k$ km at an average speed of $y$ km/h and the remaining distance at $z$ km/h. The time taken for the journey is

(a) $\dfrac{k}{y} + \dfrac{(x-k)}{z}$     (b) $ky + \dfrac{(k-x)}{z}$

(c) $\dfrac{k}{y} + \dfrac{(k-x)}{z}$     (d) $ky + z(x-k)$

38. Two rifles are fired from the same place at a difference of 11 minutes 45 seconds. But a man who is coming towards the place in a train hears the second sound after 11 minutes. Find the speed of train.

(a) 72 km/h     (b) 36 km/h

(c) 81 km/h     (d) 108 km/h

**Directions for Questions 39 and 40:** Read the following and answer the questions that follow.

The Kalinga Express started from Patna to Tata at 7 p.m. at a speed of 60 km/h. Another train, Rajdhani Express, started from Tata to Patna at 4 a.m. next morning at a speed of 90 km/h. The distance between Patna to Tata is 800 km.

39. How far from Tata will the two trains meet?

(a) 164 km     (b) 156 km

(c) 132 km     (d) 128 km

40. At what time will the two trains meet?

(a) 5 : 32 a.m.     (b) 5 : 28 a.m.

(c) 5 : 36 a.m.     (d) 5 : 44 a.m.

**Directions for Questions 41 to 43:** Read the following and answer the question that follow.

A naughty bird is sitting on top of a car. It sees another car approaching it at a distance of 12 km. The speed of the two cars is 60 kmph each. The bird starts flying from the first car and moves towards the second car, reaches the second car and comes back to the first car and so on. If the speed at which the bird flies is 120 kmph then answer the following questions. Assume that the two cars have a crash.

41. The total distance travelled by the bird before the crash is

(a) 6 km     (b) 12 km

(c) 18 km     (d) None of these

42. The total distance travelled by the bird before it reaches the second car for the second time is

(a) 10.55 km     (b) 11.55 km

(c) 12.33 km     (d) None of these

43. The total number of times that the bird reaches the bonnet of the second car is (theoretically):

(a) 12 times     (b) 18 times

(c) Infinite times     (d) Cannot be determined

44. A dog sees a cat. It estimates that the cat is 25 leaps away. The cat sees the dog and starts running with the dog in hot pursuit. If in every minute, the dog makes 5 leaps and the cat makes 6 leaps and one leap of the dog is equal to 2 leaps of the cat. Find the time in which the cat is caught by the dog (assume an open field with no trees)

(a) 12 minutes     (b) 15 minutes

(c) 12.5 minutes     (d) None of these

45. Two people $A$ and $B$ start from $P$ and $Q$ (distance = $D$) at the same time towards each other. They meet at a point $R$, which is at a distance $0.4D$ from $P$. They continue to move to and fro between the two points. Find the distance from point $P$ at which the fourth meeting takes place.

(a) $0.8D$     (b) $0.6D$

(c) $0.3D$     (d) $0.4D$

46. A wall clock gains 2 minutes in 12 hours, while a table clock loses 2 minutes in 36 hours; both are set right at noon on Tuesday. The correct time when they both show the same time next would be

(a) 12:30 night     (b) 12 noon

(c) 1:30 night     (d) 12 night

47. Two points $A$ and $B$ are located 48 km apart on the riverfront. A motorboat must go from $A$ to $B$ and return to $A$ as soon as possible. The river flows at 6 km/h. What must be the least speed of the motorboat in still water for the trip from $A$ to $B$ and back again to be completed in not more than six hours (assume that the motorboat does not stop at $B$)?

(a) 18 km/h     (b) 16 km/h

(c) 25 km/h     (d) 46 km/h

48. Two *ghats* are located on a riverbank and are 21 km apart. Leaving one of the ghats for the other, a motorboat returns to the first *ghat* in 270 minutes, spending 40 min of that time in taking the passengers at the second *ghat*. Find the speed of the boat in still water if the speed of the river flow is 2.5 km/h?

(a) 10.4 km/h     (b) 12.5 km/h

(c) 22.5 km/h     (d) 11.5 km/h

49. A train leaves Muzaffarpur for Hazipur at 2:15 p.m. and travels at the rate of 50 kmph. Another train leaves Hazipur for Muzaffarpur at 1:35 p.m. and travels at the rate of 60 kmph. If the distance between Hazipur and Muzaffarpur is 590 km at what distance from Muzaffarpur will the two trains meet?
    (a) 200 km (b) 300 km
    (c) 250 km (d) 225 km

50. A dog after travelling 50 km meets a *swami* who counsels him to go slower. He then proceeds at 3/4 of his former speed and arrives at his destination 35 minutes late. Had the meeting occurred 24 km further the dog would have reached its destination 25 minutes late. The speed of the dog is
    (a) 48 km/h (b) 36 km/h
    (c) 54 km/h (d) 58 km/h

51. Ajay and Vijay start running simultaneously from the same point on a circular track in the same direction. If Ajay is running with a uniform speed of 'a' kmph and Vijay is running with 'b' kmph, they meet for the first time when Ajay is in his 4th round and Vijay is in his 3rd round. Which of the following can be value of $a : b$ (If $a > b$)?
    (a) 1.4 (b) 1.46
    (c) 1.35

    Type (1) If only one option is correct.
    Type (2) If two options are correct.
    Type (3) If all the options are correct.
    Type (4) If no option is correct.

52. Ozair starts for Pune from Mumbai at 2 PM, after reaching Pune he takes 2 hours to finish his work. After finishing his work he starts his return journey at 4/5th of his previous speed. He reached Mumbai at 8:30 PM on the same day. If the distance between Pune and Mumbai is 100 kilometers, then find the speed (in km/hr) with which he returns back to Mumbai?

**Directions for questions 53 and 54:**
Dhoni and Kohli start running simultaneously from opposite ends on a race-track of length 100 m with speeds of 10 m/s and 4 m/s respectively. If both of them keep running continuously from one end to the other end (to and fro) then answer the following questions.

53. After how much time (in seconds) would they meet for the third time?

54. When they meet for the third time what will be the distance of Dhoni (in meters) from his starting point?

**Directions for Questions 55 and 56:**
Two places A and B are 120 feet apart. Ramesh starts travelling from A to B and at the same time Akhilesh starts travelling from B to A. Ramesh travels 1/3rd of the total journey at a speed of 8 feet/minute, half of the remaining distance at 10 feet/minute and the rest at 16 feet/minute. Akhilesh completes the whole journey by travelling at 8 feet/minute, 10 feet/minute and 12 feet/minute, respectively, for equal intervals of time. Based on the above information answer questions 55 and 56:

55. The distance between Ramesh and Akhilesh after 5 minutes of the start of the journey was found to be '$x$' meters. Find the value of $x$.

56. After how much time (in seconds) of the starting of the journey will they cross each other?

57. Bhola and Vijay start running simultaneously on a circular track from the same points in the same direction. How many times Bhola meets Vijay before they meet at the starting point for the first time (Ratio of speeds of Bhola and Vijay is 6:1)?

**Directions for Questions 58 and 59:**
Two trains — *A* and *B* simultaneously started from Delhi to Agra and Agra to Delhi respectively. After reaching their respective destinations, they turned back towards their starting points and finished their journeys after reaching their starting stations. They met for the first time at a distance of 80 km away from the Delhi station and they met for the second time 40 km away from the Agra station. It is further known that during both the meetings they were travelling in the opposite direction. Answer the following questions:

58. What is the distance (in km) between Delhi and Agra?

59. What is the ratio of the speeds of trains B and A?

60. Anand Pagare entered a bar between 12 AM to 1 AM when the angle between the minute hand and the hour hand of the clock was at 30°. If he spent exactly 1 hour 20 minutes in the bar and came out, and he came out at a time represented by A:B:C where A represents hours, B represents minutes and C represents seconds. Then, find the value of A+B+C.
    *Note:* Take C as a whole number only.

## LEVEL OF DIFFICULTY (III)

1. Two people started simultaneously towards each other from Siliguri and Darjeeling, which are 60 km apart. They met 5 hours later. After their meeting, the first person, who travelled from Siliguri to Darjeeling, decreased his speed by 1.5 km/h and the other person, who travelled from Darjeeling to Siliguri, increased his speed by 1.5 km/h. The first person is known to arrive at Darjeeling 2.5 hours earlier than the second person arrived at Siliguri. Find the initial speed of the first person.
   (a) 4.5 km/h          (b) 6 km/h
   (c) 7.5 km/h          (d) 9 km/h

2. Two friends Arun and Nishit, on their last day in college, decided to meet after 20 years on a river. Arun had to sail 42 km to the meeting place and Nishit had to sail $35\frac{5}{7}$ per cent less. To arrive at the meeting place at the same time as his friend Nishit, Arun started at the same time as Nishit and sailed with the speed exceeding by 5 km/h the speed of Nishit. Find the speed of Arun.
   (a) 10 kmph          (b) 14 km/h
   (c) 9 kmph           (d) Both b and c

3. Three cars leave Patna for Ranchi after equal time intervals. They reach Ranchi simultaneously and then leave for Vizag, which is 120 km from Ranchi. The first car arrives there an hour after the second car, and the third car, having reached Vizag, immediately reverses the direction and 40 km from Vizag meets the first car. Find the speed of the first car.
   (a) 30 km/h          (b) 19 km/h
   (c) 32 km/h          (d) 22 km/h

4. Two sea trawlers left a sea port simultaneously in two mutually perpendicular directions. Half an hour later, the shortest distance between them was 17 km, and another 15 min later, one sea trawler was 10.5 km farther from the origin than the other. Find the speed of each sea trawler.
   (a) 16 km/h, 30 km/h   (b) 18 km/h, 24 km/h
   (c) 20 km/h, 22 km/h   (d) 18 km/h, 36 km/h

5. Shaurya and Arjit take a straight route to the same terminal point and travel with constant speeds. At the initial moment, the positions of the two and the terminal point form an equilateral triangle. When Arjit covered a distance of 80 km, the triangle becomes right- angled. When Arjit was at a distance of 120 km from the terminal point, the Shaurya arrived at the point. Find the distance between them at the initial moment assuming that there are integral distances throughout the movements described.

6. Mrinalini and Neha travel to Connaught Place along two straight roads with constant speeds. At the initial moment, the positions of Mrinalini, Neha, and Connaught Place form a right triangle. After Mrinalini travelled 30 km, the triangle between the points became equilateral. Find the distance between Mrinalini and Neha at the initial moment if at the time Mrinalini arrived at Connaught Place, Neha had to cover 6.66 km to reach Connaught Place.
   (a) $10\sqrt{3}$ km          (b) $12\sqrt{3}$ km
   (c) $30\sqrt{5}$ km          (d) None of these

7. Three cars started simultaneously from Ajmer to Benaras along the same highway. The second car travelled with a speed that was 10 km/h higher than the first car's speed and arrived at Benaras 1 hour earlier than the first car. The third car arrived at Benaras 33.33 minutes earlier than the first car, travelling half the time at the speed of the first car and the other half at the speed of the second car. Find the total distance covered by these three cars during their journey between Ajmer and Benaras.
   (a) 360 km          (b) 600 km
   (c) 540 km          (d) 840 km

8. Three sprinters $A$, $B$, and $C$ had to sprint from points $P$ to $Q$ and back again (starting in that order). The time interval between the starting times of the three sprinters $A$, $B$ and $C$ was 5 seconds each. Thus $C$ started 10 seconds after $A$, while $B$ started 5 seconds after $A$. The three sprinters passed a certain point $R$, which is somewhere between $P$ and $Q$, simultaneously (none of them having reached point $Q$ yet). Having reached $Q$ and reversed the direction, the third sprinter met the second one 9 m short of $Q$ and met the first sprinter 15 m short of $Q$. Find the speed of the first sprinter if the distance between $PQ$ is equal to 55 m.
   (a) 4 m/s          (b) 3 m/s
   (c) 2 m/s          (d) 1 m/s

9. Two trains start from the same point simultaneously and in the same direction. The first train travels at 40 km/h, and the speed of the second train is 25 per cent more than the speed of the first train. Thirty minutes later, a third train starts from the same point and in the same direction. It overtakes the second train 90 minutes later than it overtook the first train. What is the speed of the third train?

(a) 20 km/h     (b) 40 km/h

(c) 60 km/h     (d) 80 km/h

10. A passenger train left town Alpha for town Beta. At the same time, a goods train left Beta for Alpha. The speed of each train is constant throughout the whole trip. Two hours after the trains met, they were 450 km apart. The passenger train arrived at the place of destination 16 hours after their meeting and the goods train, 25 hours after the meeting. How long did it take the passenger train to make the whole trip?

(a) 21 hours     (b) 28 hours

(c) 14 hours     (d) None of these

11. Two ducks move along the circumference of a circular pond in the same direction and come alongside each other every 54 minutes. If they moved with the same speeds in the opposite directions, they would meet every 9 minutes. It is known that when the ducks moved along the cicumference in opposite directions, the distance between them decreased from 54 to 14 feet every 48 seconds. What is the speed of the slower duck?

(a) 20 feet/min     (b) 15 feet/min

(c) 30 feet/min     (d) 20.83 feet/min

12. Dev and Nishit started simultaneously from opposite points $X$ and $Y$ on a straight road, at constant speeds. When Dev had covered 40% of the distance from $X$ to $Y$, Nishit was 4 km away from Dev after having crossed Dev. When Nishit had covered half the way, Dev was 10 km short of the mid point. Find a possible of the time it took Dev to cover the distance from $X$ to $Y$ to the time it took Nishit to cover the same distance.

(a) $\left[\dfrac{1+\sqrt{3}}{2}\right]$     (b) $\dfrac{3\sqrt{2}+4}{2\sqrt{2}+1}$

(c) Either a or b     (d) None of these

13. For Question 12 which of these is a possible value of the distance between the points $X$ and $Y$:

(a) $20(2+\sqrt{3})$     (b) $20(1+\sqrt{2})$

(c) 60 km     (d) Both (a) and (b)

14. Two ships sail in a fog towards each other with the same speed. When they are 4 km apart, the captains decelerate the engines for 4 minutes with a deceleration rate of 0.1 m/s², and then the ships continue sailing with the speeds attained. For what range of values of the initial speed $V_0$ will the ships avoid collision?

(a) $0 < V_0 < 10$ m/s     (b) $0 < V_0 < 20$ m/s

(c) $0 < V_0 < 30$ m/s     (d) None of these

15. Three points $A$, $B$ and $C$ are located at the vertices of an equilateral triangle with sides equal to 168 metres. A donkey called Dinky starts from $A$ to $B$

at 60 metres/hour and at the same time a cow called Moo starts from $B$ to $C$ at 30 metres/hour. In what time after their departure will the distance between the donkey and the cow be the least?

(a) 2 h     (b) 3 h

(c) 0.5 h     (d) 8 h

16. A train has to travel the distance between Aurangabad and Daulatabad, equal to 20 km, at a constant speed. It travelled half the way with the specified speed and stopped for three minutes, to arrive at Daulatabad on time, it had to increase its speed by 10 km/h for the rest of the way. Next time the train stopped half-way for five minutes. By what speed must it increase its speed for the remaining half of the distance to arrive at Daulatabad as per the schedule?

(a) 10 kmph     (b) 20 kmph

(c) 15 kmph     (d) 16 kmph

17. Nishit travels from Patna to Kolkata, a distance of 200 km at the speed of 40 km/h. At the same time, Ravi starts from Kolkata at a speed of 20 kmph along a road, which is perpendicular to the road on which Nishit is travelling. When will Nishit and Ravi be closest to each other?

(a) In 1.5 hours     (b) In 4 hours

(c) In 3.33 hours     (d) In 5 hours

18. Two towns are at a distance of 240 km from each other. A motorist takes 8 hours to cover the distance if he travels at a speed of $V_0$ km/h from town $A$ to an intermediate town $C$, and then continues on his way with an acceleration of $x$ km/hr². He needs the same time to cover the whole distance if he travels from $A$ to $C$ at $V_0$ km/h and from $C$ to $B$ at $V_1$ km/h or from $A$ to $C$ at $V_1$ km/h and from $C$ to $B$ at $V_0$ km/h. Find $V_0$ if the acceleration '$x$' is double $V_0$ in magnitude and $V_0 \neq V_1$.

(a) 15 km/h     (b) 10 km/h

(c) 20 km/h     (d) 8 km/h

19. Jaideep travels from Alaska, which is on a highway, to Burgen, which is 16 km from the highway. The distance between Alaska and Burgen along a straight line is 34 km. At what point should Jaideep turn from the highway to reach Burgen in the shortest possible time, if his speed along the highway is 10 km/h and 6 km/h otherwise.

(a) 30 km away from $A$

(b) 20 km away from $A$

(c) 18 km away from $A$

(d) 15 km away from $A$

20. An object begins moving at time moment $t = 0$ and 4 s after the beginning of the motion, attains the acceleration of 3 m/s². Find the speed of the object 6 s after the beginning of motion if it is known that the speed of the body varies accordingly to the law $v(t) =$

$(t^2 + 2b.t + 4)$ m/s and the object moves along a straight line.

(a) 22 m/s          (b) 10 m/s

(c) 30 m/s          (d) 15 m/s

21. For problem 20, find the distance covered by the object in the first 7 seconds if we assume that the speed of the object in a particular second is the speed it attains at the start of the second.

(a) 15 metres       (b) 14 metres

(c) 10 metres       (d) 5 metres

22. Three *ghats* X, Y and Z on the Yamuna in Delhi are located on the river bank. The speed of the river flow is 8 km/h in the direction of its flow, *Ghat Y* being located midway between X and Z. A raft and a launch leave Y at the same time, the raft travelling down the river to Z and the launch travelling to X. The speed of the launch in still water is 5 km/h. Having reached X, the launch reverses its direction and starts to Z. Find the range of values of V for which the launch arrives at Z later than the raft.

(a) $8 < V < 24$ km/h     (b) $8 < V < 16$ km/h

(c) $8 < V < 20$ km/h     (d) $12 < V < 24$ km/h

23. A pedestrian left point A for a walk, going with the speed of 5 km/h. When the pedestrian was at a distance of 6 km from A, a cyclist followed him, starting from A and cycling at a speed 9 km/h higher than that of the pedestrian. When the cyclist overtook the pedestrian, they turned back and returned to A together, at the speed of 4 km/h. At what v will the time spent by the pedestrian on his total journey from A to A be the least?

(a) 5 km/h          (b) 6 km/h

(c) 6.1 kmph        (d) 5.5 km/h

24. A cyclist left point A for point B and travelled at the constant speed of 25 km/h. When he covered the distance of 8.33 km, he was overtaken by a car that left point A twelve minutes after the cyclist and travelled at a constant speed too. When the cyclist travelled another 30 km, he encountered the car returning from B. Assume that the car did not stop at point B. Find the distance between A and B.

(a) 39.5833 km      (b) 41.0833 km

(c) 60.833 km       (d) 43.33 km

25. A robot began moving from point A in a straight line at 6 p.m. with an initial speed of 3 m/s. One second later, the speed of the robot became equal to 4 m/s. Find the acceleration of the robot at the end of the 2nd second if its speed changes by the law $s(t) = (at^2 + 2t + (b))$

(a) 1 m/s²          (b) −2 m/s²

(c) 0 m/s²          (d) 2 m/s²

26. For Question 25, the distance of the robot from point A after 6 seconds will be (assuming that for every

second the robot travels at a constant speed equal to its starting speed for that second and any acceleration occurs at the start of the next second)

(a) 45 m            (b) 36 m

(c) 10 m            (d) 17 m

27. Two friends Amit and Akshay began moving simultaneously from point A along a straight line in the same direction: Amit started moving at the speed of 5 m/s and moved with an uniform acceleration of 4 m/s², while his friend Akshay moved at a uniform speed. The limits for Akshay's speed (S) so that he should first leave Amit behind and then get overtaken by Amit at a distance of 18 m from A are

(a) $5 < S < 9$      (b) $3 < S < 5$

(c) $4 < S < 8$      (d) None of these

28. On the banks of the river Ganges there are two bathing points in Varanasi and Patna. A *diya* left in the river at Varanasi reaches Patna in 24 hours. However, a motorboat covers the whole way to and fro in exactly 10 hours. If the speed of the motorboat in still water is increased by 40%, then it takes the motorboat 7 hours to cover the same way (from Varanasi to Patna and back again). Find the time necessary for the motorboat to sail from Varanasi to Patna when its speed in still water is not increased.

(a) 3 hours         (b) 4 hours

(c) 4.8 hours       (d) None of these

29. Two friends started walking simultaneously from points A and B towards each other. 144 minutes later the distance between them was 20% of the original distance. How many hours does it take the faster walker to cover the distance AB if he needs eight hours less to travel the distance than his friend (assume all times to be in whole numbers and in hours)?

(a) 3 hours         (b) 6 hours

(c) 12 hours        (d) 4 hours

30. Two cars left points A and B simultaneously, travelling towards each other. 9 hours after their meeting, the car travelling from A arrived at B, and 16 hours after their meeting, the car travelling from B arrived at A. How many hours did it take the slower car to cover the whole distance?

(a) 36 hours        (b) 21 hours

(c) 25 hours        (d) 28 hours

31. A pedestrian and a cyclist left Nagpur for Buti Bori at the same time. Having reached Buti Bori, the cyclist turned back and met the pedestrian an hour after the start. After their meeting, the pedestrian continued his trip to Buti Bori and the cyclist turned back and also headed for Buti Bori. Having reached Buti Bori, the cyclist turned back again and met the pedestrian 30 mins after their first meeting. Determine what time it takes the pedestrian to cover the distance between Nagpur and Buti Bori.

(a) 1 hour      (b) 2 hours
(c) 2.5 hours      (d) 3 hours

32. Points $A$, $B$ and $C$ are at the distances of 120, 104.66 and 112 km from point $M$ respectively. Three people left these points for point $M$ simultaneously: the first person started from point $A$, the second from $B$ and the third from $C$. The first person covered the whole way at a constant speed and arrived at $M$ an hour before the second and the third persons (who arrived simultaneously). The third person covered the whole way at a constant speed. The second person, having travelled 72 km at the same speed as the first, stopped for 2 hours. The rest of the way he travelled at a speed that is less than the speed of the third person by the same amount as the speed of the third is less than that of the first. Determine the speed of the first person.

(a) 6 kmph      (b) 5 kmph
(c) 4 kmph      (d) 3 kmph

33. Two people started simultaneously from points $A$ and $B$ towards each other. At the moment the person who started from $A$ had covered two-thirds of the way, the other person had covered 2 km less than half the total distance. If it is known that when the person who started from $B$ had covered 1/4 of the way, the other person was 3 km short of the mid point. Find the distance between $A$ and $B$. The speeds of the two people were constant.

(a) $(15 - 3\sqrt{17})$ km      (b) $(15 + 3\sqrt{17})$ km
(c) Both a and b      (d) $3\sqrt{17} - 5$ km

34. Sohan and Lallan left their house simultaneously. Thirty six minutes later, Sohan met his uncle travelling to their house, while Lallan met the uncle twelve minutes after Sohan. Twenty four minutes after his meeting with Lallan, the uncle rang the door bell at Sohan and Lallan's house. Assume each person travels at a constant speed. Find the ratio of the speeds of Sohan to Lallan to the uncle.

(a) 1 : 2 : 2      (b) 1 : 3 : 2
(c) 3 : 1 : 3      (d) 2 : 1 : 2

35. The distance between two towns—Aurangabad and Jalna is 80 km. A bus left Aurangabad and travelled at a constant speed towards Jalna. Thirty minutes later, Deepak Jhunjhunwala left Aurangabad in his car towards Jalna. He overtook the bus in thirty minutes and continued on his way to Jalna. Without stopping at Jalna, he turned back and again encountered the bus 80 minutes after he had left Aurangabad. Determine the speed of the bus.

(a) 40 kmph      (b) 45 kmph
(c) 50 kmph      (d) None of these

36. Rohit left Mahabaleshwar for Nashik at 6 a.m. An hour and a half later Vimal, whose speed was 5 km/h higher than that of Rohit left Mahabaleshwar. At 10 : 30 p.m. of the same day the distance between the two friends was 21 km. Find the speed of Vimal.

(a) 40 kmph      (b) 41 kmph
(c) 69 kmph      (d) Either b or c

37. Aurangzeb and Babar with their troops left from Delhi and Daulatabad towards each other simultaneously. Each of them marched at a constant speed and, having arrived at their respective points of destination, went back at once. Their first meeting was 14 km from Daulatabad, and the second meeting, eight hours after the first meeting was at a distance of 2 km from Delhi. Find the distance between the Delhi and Daulatabad.

(a) 30 km      (b) 25 km
(c) 35 km      (d) None of these

38. Two tourists left simultaneously point $A$ for point $B$, the first tourist covers each kilometre 2 minutes faster than the second. After travelling 30 per cent of the way, the first tourist returned to $A$, stopped there for 102 minutes and again started for $B$. The two tourists arrived at $B$ simultaneously. What is the distance between $A$ and $B$ if the second tourist covered it in 2.5 hours?

(a) 60 km      (b) 70 km
(c) 45 km      (d) None of these

39. Amar and Akbar left Bhubaneshwar simultaneously and travelled towards Cuttack. Amar's speed was 15 km/h and that of Akbar was 12 km/h. Half an hour later, Anthony left Bhubaneshwar and travelled in the same direction. Some time later, he overtook Akbar and 90 minutes further on he overtook Amar. Find Anthony's speed.

(a) 18 kmph      (b) 24 kmph
(c) 20 kmph      (d) 16 kmph

40. Two bodies, moving along a circle in the same direction, meet every 49 minutes. Had they moved at the same speeds in the opposite directions, they would meet every 7 minutes. If, moving in the opposite directions, the bodies are at the distance of 40 m from each other along the arc at time $t = 0$, then at $t = 24$ seconds, their distance will be 26 metres (the bodies do not meet during those 24 seconds). Find the speed of the faster body in metres per minute.

(a) 15      (b) 20
(c) 25      (d) None of these

41. The distance between Varanasi and Lucknow is 220 km. Two buses start from these towns towards each other. They can meet halfway if the first bus leaves 2 hours earlier than the second. If they start simultaneously, they will meet in 4 hours. Find the speeds of the buses.

(a) $17.5(3 + \sqrt{5})$ km/h, $17.5(1 + \sqrt{5})$ km/h

(b) $27.5(3 + \sqrt{5})$ km/h, $27.5(1 + \sqrt{5})$ km/h

(c) $27.5(3 - \sqrt{5})$ km/h, $27.5(\sqrt{5} - 1)$ km/h

(d) None of these

42. A road passes through the towns Sangamner and Yeotmal. A cyclist started from Sangamner in the direction of Yeotmal. At the same time, two pedestrians started from Yeotmal travelling at the same speed, the first of them towards Sangamner and the other in the opposite direction. The cyclist covered the distance between the towns in half an hour and, continued ahead in the same direction. He overtook the second pedestrian, 1.2 hours after he met the first pedestrian. Determine the time the cyclist spent travelling from Sangamner to the point of the meeting with the first pedestrian (assuming the speeds of the cyclist and the pedestrians to be constant).

(a) 24 min      (b) 18 min

(c) 30 min      (d) Cannot be determined

43. Two people A and B start moving from P and Q that are 200 km apart, towards each other A is on a moped and B on foot. They meet at a point R when A gives B a lift to P and returns to his original path to reach Q. On reaching Q he finds that he has taken 2.6 times his normal time. B on the other hand realises that he has saved 40 minutes over his normal travel time. Find the ratio of their speeds.

(a) 3 : 2      (b) 4 : 3

(c) 3 : 1      (d) None of these

44. For Question 43, find the speed of the moped.

(a) 160 kmph      (b) 180 kmph

(c) 200 kmph      (d) None of these

45. Three friends A, B and C start from P to Q that are 100 km apart. A is on a moped while B is riding pillion and C walks on. A takes B to a point R and returns to pick up C on the way and takes him to point Q. B, on the other hand, walks to Q from point R (R is the mid-point between P and Q).

If the ratio of speeds of the three people is 5 : 2 : 2, find where will the last person be when the first person reaches Q.

(a) 12.85 km from Q    (b) 12.75 km from Q

(c) 16.66 km from Q    (d) 83.33 km from P

46. A motorboat moves from point A to point B and back again, both points being located on the river-bank. If the speed of the boat in still water is doubled, then the trip from A to B and back again would take 20% of the time that the motorboat usually spends in the journey. How many times is the actual speed of the launch higher than the speed of the river flow?

(a) $\sqrt{\dfrac{3}{2}}$      (b) $\dfrac{\sqrt{3}}{3}$

(c) $\dfrac{2}{3}$      (d) $\dfrac{3}{2}$

47. A watch loses 2/3% time during the 1st week and gains 1/3% time during the next week. If on a Sunday noon, it showed the right time, what time will it show at noon on the Sunday after the next.

(a) 11 : 26 : 24 a.m.    (b) 10 : 52 : 18 a.m.

(c) 10 : 52 : 48 a.m.    (d) 11 : 36 : 24 a.m.

48. Clocks A, B and C strikes every hour. B slows down and takes 2 min longer than A per hour while C become faster and takes 2 min less than A per hour. If they strike together at 12 midnight, when will they strike together again

(a) 10 a.m.      (b) 11 a.m.

(c) 9 p.m.      (d) 8 p.m.

49. A boat went down the river for a distance of 20 km. It then turned back and returned to its starting point, having travelled a total of 7 hours. On its return trip, at a distance of 12 km from the starting point, it encountered a log, which had passed the starting point at the moment at which the boat had started downstream. The downstream speed of the boat is

(a) 7 kmph      (b) 13 kmph

(c) 16 kmph      (d) 10 kmph

50. Two boats go downstream from point X to point Y. The faster boat covers the distance from X to Y 1.5 times as fast as the slower boat. It is known that for every hour the slower boat lags behind the faster boat by 8 km. However, if they go upstream, then the faster boat covers the distance from Y to X in half the time as the slower boat. Find the speed of the faster boat in still water.

(a) 12 kmph      (b) 20 kmph

(c) 24 kmph      (d) 25 kmph

*Space for Rough Work*

# ANSWER KEY

## Level of Difficulty (I)

| | | | |
|---|---|---|---|
| 1. (a) | 2. (a) | 3. (c) | 4. (c) |
| 5. (d) | 6. (d) | 7. (c) | 8. (a) |
| 9. (a) | 10. (a) | 11. (a) | 12. (a) |
| 13. (c) | 14. (a) | 15. (c) | 16. (d) |
| 17. (a) | 18. (b) | 19. (d) | 20. (a) |
| 21. (c) | 22. (c) | 23. (c) | 24. (d) |
| 25. (b) | 26. (d) | 27. (d) | 28. (c) |
| 29. (d) | 30. (d) | 31. (a) | 32. (b) |
| 33. (a) | 34. (a) | 35. (a) | 36. (d) |
| 37. (d) | 38. (b) | 39. (d) | 40. (a) |
| 41. (b) | 42. (a) | 43. (a) | 44. (d) |
| 45. (c) | 46. (c) | 47. (a) | 48. (a) |
| 49. (d) | 50. (a) | 51. (b) | 52. (a) |
| 53. (b) | 54. (c) | 55. (c) | 56. (b) |
| 57. (b) | 58. (a) | 59. (a) | 60. (b) |
| 61. (c) | 62. (d) | 63. (a) | 64. (b) |
| 65. (a) | 66. (c) | 67. (b) | 68. (a) |
| 69. (a) | 70. (a) | 71. (a) | 72. (c) |
| 73. (a) | 74. (d) | 75. (d) | 76. 16 |
| 77. 1400 | 78. 100 | 79. 1250 | 80. 50 |
| 81. 50 | 82. 2 | 83. 20 | 84. 25 |
| 85. 312.5 | | | |

## Level of Difficulty (II)

| | | | |
|---|---|---|---|
| 1. (c) | 2. (a) | 3. (a) | 4. (c) |
| 5. (a) | 6. (b) | 7. (b) | 8. (d) |
| 9. (b) | 10. (a) | 11. (b) | 12. (c) |
| 13. (c) | 14. (b) | 15. (b) | 16. (a) |
| 17. (c) | 18. (d) | 19. (b) | 20. (b) |
| 21. (b) | 22. (c) | 23. (a) | 24. (c) |
| 25. (d) | 26. (b) | 27. (c) | 28. (c) |
| 29. (d) | 30. (d) | 31. (c) | 32. (b) |
| 33. (d) | 34. (b) | 35. (c) | 36. (c) |
| 37. (a) | 38. (c) | 39. (b) | 40. (d) |
| 41. (b) | 42. (b) | 43. (c) | 44. (c) |
| 45. (a) | 46. (b) | 47. (a) | 48. (d) |
| 49. (c) | 50. (a) | 51. 3 | 52. 40 |
| 53. 21.42 | 54. 14.28 | 55. 38 | 56. 414 |
| 57. 5 | 58. 200 | 59. 1.5 | 60. 53 |

## Level of Difficulty (III)

| | | | |
|---|---|---|---|
| 1. (c) | 2. (b) | 3. (a) | 4. (a) |
| 5. (b) | 6. (d) | 7. (b) | 8. (d) |
| 9. (c) | 10. (d) | 11. (d) | 12. (b) |
| 13. (b) | 14. (b) | 15. (a) | 16. (d) |
| 17. (b) | 18. (c) | 19. (c) | 20. (b) |
| 21. (b) | 22. (a) | 23. (b) | 24. (c) |
| 25. (b) | 26. (d) | 27. (a) | 28. (b) |
| 29. (d) | 30. (d) | 31. (b) | 32. (a) |

| | | | |
|---|---|---|---|
| 33. (c) | 34. (d) | 35. (a) | 36. (d) |
| 37. (d) | 38. (a) | 39. (a) | 40. (b) |
| 41. (d) | 42. (b) | 43. (d) | 44. (d) |
| 45. (a) | 46. (a) | 47. (c) | 48. (d) |
| 49. (d) | 50. (b) | | |

### Hints

## Level of Difficulty (III)

1. The first person who travels from Siliguri to Darjeeling is obviously faster than the second. Hence, reject Options (a) and (b). Then, check all the conditions with Options (c) and (d) and select the one which satisfies the conditions.

2. Since distance to be travelled by Nishit is $35\frac{5}{7}\%$ less, his speed will also be $35\frac{5}{7}\%$ less than Arun's speed. Check the options with the conditions that Arun's speed is 5 kmph higher than that of Nishit.

3. Let $S_1$, $S_2$ and $S_3$ be the speeds of the three cars.

   Then: $\dfrac{120}{S_1} - \dfrac{120}{S_2} = 1$ hour        (1)

   It is also known that the speed of the third car is double the speed of the first car.

   With these realisations, check for factors of 120 which can satisfy the equation above.

   [Note that in equations like (1) above, normally the respective values of $S_1$ and $S_2$ will be factors of 120.]

5. If the side of the initial equilateral triangle is $S$, then when Arjit covers $(S - 120)$ kms, Shaurya covers $S$ kilometres. Also, when Arjit covers a distance of 80 kilometres, Shaurya covers a distance such that the resultant triangle is right angled.

   Check these conditions through options.

6. Solve through a process similar to the previous question.

7. If $S_1$ is the speed of the first car, then $(S_1 + 10)$ will be the second car's speed. If $t_1$ hours is the time required for the first car, then $(t_1 - 1)$ hours is the time required for the second car in covering the same distance, while that of the third car is $\left(t_1 - \dfrac{33.33}{60}\right)$ hours.

   Check these conditions through options.

10. The relative speed is 225 km/hr.

11. The sum of the speeds of the ducks is 50 feet/min Hence, circumference = $9 \times 50 = 450$ feet and difference of speeds = $\dfrac{450}{54} = 8.33$.

15. Use options to solve.

16. Through trial and error try to find the initial speed of the train, so that the first condition is met.

17. Use options to solve.

18. Let the distance $AC = d$

Then, $\dfrac{d}{V_0} + \dfrac{240 - d}{V_1} = \dfrac{d}{V_1} + \dfrac{240 - d}{V_0}$

If $V_0 \neq V_1$, then the above condition will be satisfied only if $d = 120$ km.

19. The time required will be represented by

$$\dfrac{\text{Distance travelled on highway}}{10}$$

$$+ \dfrac{\text{Distance travelled on side roads}}{10}.$$

This has to be minimised, check the options.

20-21. Acceleration is $\dfrac{dv}{dt} = 2t + 2b$

At $t = 4$, the acceleration is given to be 3.

Hence, $b = \dfrac{-5}{2}$

Hence, the velocity equation becomes $V_{(t)} = t_2 - 5t + 4$

29. Total time taken to cover the entire distance together $= 144 \times \dfrac{5}{4} = 180$ minutes $= 3$ hours.

Hence, distance covered per hour = 33.33% of the total by both of them combined.

Check this condition for all the options.

31. Suppose $A$ and $B$ are the points where the first and the second meetings took place.

The total distance covered by the pedestrian and the cyclist before the first meeting = Twice the distance between Nagpur and Buti Bori.

Total time taken is 1 hour.

Total distance covered by the pedestrian and the cyclist between the two meetings = Twice the distance between $A$ and Buti Bori.

and time taken is half an hour.

Hence, $A$ is the mid-point. This will result in a GP.

32. Solve through options by checking all the conditions given in the question.

33. If $2d$ is the distance between $A$ and $B$, then

$$\dfrac{\frac{2}{3} \times 2d}{d - 2} = \dfrac{d - 3}{2d \times \frac{1}{4}}$$

34. In 24 minutes, the uncle covers the distance for which Lallan requires 48 minutes.

35. Check the options for all the conditions.

36. Vimal could either be 21 km behind Rohit or 21 km ahead of Rohit.

37. If $d$ is the distance between Delhi and Daulatabad, then you will get the following equation.

$$\dfrac{d - 14}{14} = \dfrac{28 + (d - 16)}{(d - 14) + 2}$$

38. Check the conditions through the options.

47. The net time loss is 1/3% of 168 hours.

49. In the time taken by the boat in traveling $d + (d - 12)$ kms, the log travels 12 km. Let, $S_B$ be the speed of the boat is still water and, $S_S$ be the speed of the stream.

Then

$$\dfrac{12}{S_S} = \dfrac{20}{(S_S + S_B)} + \dfrac{8}{(S_B - S_S)} \qquad (1)$$

It is also known that,

$$\dfrac{20}{(S_S + S_B)} + \dfrac{20}{(S_B - S_S)} = 7 \text{ hours} \qquad (2)$$

Solve through options.

## Solutions and Shortcuts

### Level of Difficulty (I)

1. The ratio of time for the travel is 4:3 (Sinhagad to Deccan Queen). Hence, the ratio of speeds would be 3:4. Since, the sum of their average speeds is 70 kmph, their respective speeds would be 30 and 40 kmph respectively. Use alligation to get the answer as 34.28 kmph.

2. When speed goes down to three fourth (i.e. 75%) time will go up to 4/3rd (or 133.33%) of the original time. Since, the extra time required is 16 minutes, it should be equated to 1/3rd of the normal time. Hence, the usual time required will be 48 minutes.

3. Since, the ratio of speeds is 3:5, the ratio of times would be 5:3. The difference in the times would be 2 (if looked at in the 5:3 ratio context.) Further, since Ram takes 30 minutes longer, 2 corresponds to 30. Hence, using unitary method, 5 will correspond to 75 and 3 will correspond to 45 minutes. Hence at 10 kmph, Bharat would travel 7.5 km.

4. The train that leaves at 6 am would be 75 km ahead of the other train when it starts. Also, the relative speed being 36 kmph, the distance from Mumbai would be:

$$(75/36) \times 136 = 283.33 \text{ km}$$

5. If you assume that the initial stretch of track is covered by the two trains in time $t$ each, the following figure will give you a clearer picture.

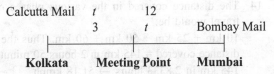

From the above figure, we can deduce that,

$t/3 = 12/t$.

Hence, $t^2 = 36$, gives us $t = 6$.

Hence, the distance between Kolkata to the starting point is covered by the Calcutta Mail in 6 hours, while the same distance is covered by the Bombay Mail in 3 hours.

Hence, the ratio of their speeds would be 1:2. Hence, the Bombay Mail would travel at 96 kmph.

6.

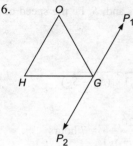

From the figure above we see that Shyam would have walked a distance of $4 + 4 + 4 = 12$ km. ($G$ to $P_1$, $P_1$ to $G$ and $G$ to $P_2$).

7. When the train from Khandala starts off, the train from Lonavala will already have covered 50 kms. Hence, 550 km at a relative speed of 60 kmph will take 550/60 hrs. From this, you can get the answer as:

$$50 + (550/60) * 25 = 279.166 \text{ km}.$$

8. When his speed becomes 3/4th, his time would increase by 1/3rd. Thus, the normal time = 7.5 hrs. (since increased time = 2.5 hrs).

9. Since he gains 2 hours by driving both ways (instead of walking one way) the time taken for driving would be 2 hours less than the time taken for walking. Hence, he stands to lose another two hours by walking both ways. Hence his total time should be 8 hrs 45 minutes.

10. Kalu's speed = 3 m/s.

For 1200 m, Kalu would take 400 seconds and Sambhu would take 10 seconds less. Hence, 390 seconds.

11. Since Chandu is moving at a speed of 10 m/s and he has to cover 360 km or 360000 meters, the time taken would be given by 360000/10 seconds = 36000 seconds = 36000/60 minutes = 600 minutes = 10 hours.

12. Since the train travels at 60 kmph, it's speed per minute is 1 km per minute. Hence, if it's speed with stoppages is 40 kmph, it will travel 40 minutes per hour.

13. Total distance/Total time = 1590/15 = 106 kmph.

14. The distance covered in the various phases of his travel would be:

10 km + 25 km + 50 km + 60 km. Thus the total distance covered = 145 km in 2 hours 50 minutes → 145 km in 2.8333 hours → 51.18 kmph

15. The average speed would be given by:

$$\frac{3d}{\dfrac{d}{v_1} + \dfrac{d}{v_2} + \dfrac{d}{v_2}} = \frac{3v_1v_2}{2v_1 + v_2}$$

16. By increasing his speed by 25%, he will reduce his time by 20%. (This corresponds to a 6 minute drop in his time for travel—since he goes from being 10 minutes late to only 4 minutes late.) Hence, his time originally must have been 30 minutes. Hence, the required distance is 20 kmph × 0.5 hours = 10 km.

17. $d/6 + d/4 = 10 → d = 24$ km.

18. If the car does half the journey @ 30 kmph and the other half at 40 kmph it's average speed can be estimated using weighted averages.

Since, the distance traveled in each part of the journey is equal, the ratio of time for which the car would travel would be inverse to the ratio of speeds. Since, the speed ratio is 3:4, the time ratio for the two halves of the journey would be 4:3. The average speed of the car would be:

$(30 × 4 + 40 × 3)/7 = 240/7$ kmph.

It is further known that the car traveled for 17.5 hours (which is also equal to 35/2 hours).

Thus, total distance = average speed × total time = $(240 × 35)/(2 × 7) = 120 × 5 = 600$ km

19. To reduce the time of the journey by 25%, he should increase his speed by 33.33% or 1/3rd. Thus, required speed = 80 kmph.

20. You can solve this question using the options. Option (a) fits the given situation best as if we take the distance as 12 km he would have taken 1 hour to go by car and 4 hours to come back walking—a total of 5 hours as given in the problem.

21. In four hours, the train will travel 180 km (180,000 metres). The number of poles would be 180,000/50 = 3600.

22. Is the same question as Question No. 5.

23.

| G | B | A |
|---|---|---|

In the above figure, the train travels from $A$ to $B$ in 11:30 minutes.

Suppose, you denote the time at which the first gunshot is heard as $t = 0$. Also, if you consider the travel of the sound of the second the gunshot is heard at point $B$ at $t = 11:30$ minutes. Also, the second gunshot should reach point $B$ at $t = 12$ minutes. Hence, the sound of the 2nd gunshot would take 30 seconds to travel from $B$ to $A$.

Thus, $\dfrac{S_{\text{train}}}{S_{\text{sound}}} = \dfrac{t_{\text{sound}}}{t_{\text{train}}}$

$S_{train} = 330 \times \dfrac{30}{690} = \dfrac{330}{23}$ m/s.

24. In 6 minutes, the car goes ahead by 0.6 km. Hence, the relative speed of the car with respect to the pedestrian is equal to 6 kmph, since, the pedestrian is walking at 2 kmph, hence, the net speed is 8 kmph.

25. At 40 kmph, Harsh would cover $(200/60) \times 40$ km. $= 400/3$ km. $= 133.33$ km.

    This represents the distance by which Vijay would be ahead of Harsh, when Vijay reaches the endpoint means in essence that Vijay must have travelled for 133.33/20 hours → 6.66 hours

    Hence, the distance is $60 \times 6.66 = 400$ km.

26. Solve this question using the values given in the options. Option (d) can be seen to fit the situation given by the problem as it gives us the following chain of thought:

    If the average speed of the faster train is 48 kmph, the average speed of the slower train would be 32 kmph. In this case, the time taken by the faster train $(192/48 = 4$ hours$)$ is 2 hours lesser than the time taken by the slower train $(192/32 = 6$ hours$)$. This satisfies the condition given in the problem and hence option (d) is correct.

27. The required speed $s$ would be satisfying the equation:

    $$300/s - 300/(s + 5) = 2$$

    Solving for $s$ from the options it is clear that $s = 25$.

28. Solve through options using trial and error. For usual speed 3 kmph we have:

    Normal time → 2/3 hours = 40 minutes.

    At 4 kmph the time would be 2/4 hrs, this gives us a distance of 10 minutes. Hence option (c) is correct.

29. By increasing the speed by 33.33%, it would be able to reduce the time taken for travel by 25%. But since this is just able to overcome a time delay of 30 minutes, 30 minutes must be equivalent to 25% of the time originally taken. Hence, the original time must have been 2 hours and the original speed would be 750 kmph. Hence, the new speed would be 1000 kmph.

30. The average speed would be given by:

    $$\frac{(120 \times 1 + 40 \times 3)}{4} = 60 \text{ kmph.}$$

31. The length of the circular track would be equal to the circumference of the circle. In 2 minutes thus, the cyclist covers $3.14 \times 200 = 628$ meters (using the formula for the circumference of a circle).

    Thus, the cyclist's speed would be $628/2 = 314$ meters/minute.

32. The total time taken by the motorist would be $200/53.333 = 200 \times 3/160 = 3.75$ hours $= 3$ hours 45 minutes. In the first half of the journey the motorist covers $1/4^{th}$ the distance @ 40kmph. This means

that he takes $50/40 = 1.25$ hours $= 1$ hour 15 minutes in covering the first 50 kms. This also means that he covers the remaining distance of 150 km in 2 hours 30 minutes → a speed of 60 kmph. Hence, option (b) is correct.

33. Assume a distance of 60 km in each stretch. Get the average speed by the formula. Total distance/ Total time $= 180/10 = 18$ kmph.

34. The speed of the first car would be 60 kmph while the speed of the second car would be 40 kmph. The relative speed of the two cars would be 100 kmph. To cover 480 km they would take $480/100 = 4.8$ hours → In 4.8 hours, the car traveling from $A$ to $B$ would have traveled $4.8 \times 60 = 288$ kms.

35. At $3/4^{th}$ speed, extra time $= 1/3^{rd}$ of time $= 16$ minutes. Normal time $= 48$ minutes.

36. Solve using options. The value in option (d) fits the situation as $20/8 - 20/10 = 2.5 - 2 = 0.5$ hours $= 30$ minutes.

37. $[73.5 \times 136]/38$. Same logic as for Question 4.

38. The time taken before their meeting would be given by $t^2 = 12 \times 3 = 36 \to t = 6$ hours. This means that their ratio of speeds is 1:2. Since train $A$ is traveling slower, the speed of train $B$ would be double the speed of train $A$. Required answer $= 48 \times 2 = 96$. (Please take a look at the solution of question number 5).

39. The distance would get divided in the ratio of speeds (since time is constant). Thus, the distance ratio would be 5 : 7 and required distance $= 5/12 \times 600 = 250$ km.

40. The diameter of the circle would be given by the hypotenuse of the right triangle with legs 600 and 800 respectively. Hence, the required diameter $= 1000$ meters.

41. When Ram runs 2000 m, Shyam runs $(1800 - 30s)$
    When Ram runs 1000 m, Shyam runs $(2000 - 180s)$.
    Then:

    $$2000/1000 = \frac{1800 - 30s}{2000 - 180s}$$

    Solving, we get $s = 6.66$ m/s

    Thus, Shyam's speed $= 400$ m/minute and he would take 5 minutes to cover the distance. Option (b) fits.

42. From the situation described in the first condition itself we can see that the speed of coming back has to be double the speed of going downstream. Checking the options, only option (a) fits this condition i.e. Downstream speed $= 2 \times$ Upstream speed.
    Hence, option (a) is correct.

43. $7 \times S_t = L_t$             (1)
    $25 \times S_t = L_t + 378$     (2)
    Solving, $S_t = 21$ m/sec.
              $= 21 \times 18/5 = 75.6$ kmph.

44. In order to solve this, you first need to think of the speed of the river flow (if the speed of the boat in

still water is 3 kmph). If we take the speed of the river flow as $s$, we get downstream speed as $3 + s$ and upstream speed as $3 - s$.

$10/(3 - s) - 10/(3 + s) = 8$ hours $\rightarrow s = 2$ kmph.

**Note:** It is obvious that since the difference between the downstream time and the upstream time is 8 hours, the upstream and downstream speeds would both be factors of 10. The only value of $s$ such that both $3 + s$ and $3 - s$ are factors of 10 is $s = 2$.

If the boat needs to reach 10 km downstream in 100 minutes (1.66 hours) it means: $10/1.66 = 6$ kmph is the downstream speed.

Since, the speed of the stream is 2 kmph, the required speed of the boat = 4 kmph

45. Solve through options. For option (c) at 4 kmph, the boat would take exactly 4 hours to cover the distance.

46. $x/9 + x/3 = 3/4 \rightarrow 4x/9 = 3/4 \rightarrow x = 27/16$ kms = 1.6875 kms.

47. Upstream speed = 40/8 = 5 kmph.
Downstream speed = 49/7 = 7 kmph.
Speed in still water = average of upstream and downstream speed = 6 kmph.

48. $(20 \times 5/18) \times 36 = L_t \rightarrow L_t = 200$ m.

49. $8/(12 - 2) = 8/10 = 0.8$ hours

50. 15 km upstream in 80 minutes $\rightarrow 15/1.33 = 11.25$ kmph. (upstream speed of the boat).
Thus, still water speed of the boat
$= 11.25 + 5 = 16.25$ kmph

51. Since $A$ to $C$ is double the distance of $A$ to $B$, it is evident that the time taken for $A$ to $C$ and back would be double the time taken from $A$ to $B$ and back (i.e. double of 6.5 hours = 13 hours). Since going from $A$ to $C$ takes 9 hours, coming back from $C$ to $A$ would take 4 hours (Since $9 + 4 = 13$).

52. $(S_f - S_s) \times 60 = 200$
Where $S_f$ and $S_s$ are speeds of the faster and slower train respectively
$\rightarrow S_f - S_s = 3.33$
Also, $(S_f + S_s) \times 10 = 200$.
$\rightarrow S_f + S_s = 20$.
Solving we get $S_s = 8.33$ m/s
$= 8.33 \times 18/5 = 30$ kmph.

53. Speed of Vinay = 5 m/s, Speed of Ajay = 4m/s. In a hundred meter race, Vinay would take 20 seconds to complete and in this time Ajay would only cover 80 meters. Thus, Vinay beats Ajay by 20 meters in a hundred meter race.

54. Solve using options 1.33 m/s fits perfectly.

55. When $A$ scores 60 points $B$ scores 45, and $C$ scores 40.
Thus, when $B$ scores 90, $C$ would score 80. So, $B$ can give $C$ 10 points in 90.

56. When Shyam does 500, Vinay does 375. Since Vinay has a start of 140 m, it means that Vinay only needs to cover 360 m to reach the destination.
When Vinay does 360, Shyam would cover 480 m and lose by 20 m. (Since the ratio of their speeds is 3:4)

57. Distance to be covered = 120 meters. Speed = 10m/s $\rightarrow$ Time required = 120/10 =12 seconds.

58. $20 \times (5/18) \times 18 = 100$ m = 0.1 km.

59. When the second train leaves Muzaffarpur, the first train would have already traveled 30 km. Now, after 9 AM, the relative speed of the two trains would be 10 kmph (i.e. the rate at which the faster train would catch the slower train).
Since the faster train has to catch up a relative distance of 30 km in order for the trains to meet, it would take $30/10 = 3$ hours to catch up.
Distance from Muzaffarpur = $70 \times 3 = 210$ km

60. Speed of running of the train = 1.25 km/hr.
With stoppage, an effective speed of 60 kmph means that the time of travel per hour would be $60/1.25 = 48$ minutes.
Thus, the train stops for 12 minutes per hour.

61. Upstream speed = 3.2 kmph
Downstream speed = 6 kmph.
Thus, speed of stream = 1.4 kmph.

62. Vijay takes 9 hours to return upstream after going for 6 hours downstream. Solve using options. Option (d) fits as we get Downstream speed = 18 kmph $\rightarrow$ distance = $18 \times 6$ =108 km
Also, upstream speed = 12 kmph $\rightarrow$ distance = $12 \times 9$ = 108 km

63. Upstream speed = 4.8 kmph
Downstream speed = 7.2 kmph.
$d/4.8 + d/7.2 = 1$
Solving we get $d = 2.88$ km.

64. The length of the train would be given by: $36 \times 5/18 \times 8 = 80$ meters.

65. Rate in still water = (16 + 22)/2 = 19 kmph

66. The given situations are satisfied with the speed of the boat as 8 kmph and the speed of the stream as 3 kmph. Option (c) is correct.

67. $10/(x - 2) + 10/(x + 2) = 55/60 = 11/12$ hours.
$x = 22$ fits the expression.

68. The speed of the boat in still water is the average of the upstream and downstream speeds. $(x + y)/2$.

69. $(1/4) \times 2\pi r = 4\pi$ (Since $r = 8$ cm).

70. The hands would be together once in each hour. However, the 12 noon time would be counted in both 11 to 12 and 12 to 1. Hence, the no. of times = $12 - 1 = 11$.

71. If we consider the clock to be a circle with circumference 60 km, the speed of the Minute hand = 60 kmph, while the speed of the hour hand = 5 kmph.

The relative speed = 55 kmph. At 2 PM, the distance between the two would be seen as 10 km. This would get covered in 10/55 = 2/11 hours. Option (a) is correct.

72. $14/(5 + x) + 9/(5 - x) = 5$

$x = 2$, fits this equation.

73. Look for the solution by thinking of the factors of 91. It can be seen that 91/13 + 91/7 = 7 + 13 = 20 hours. This means that the speed of the boat in still water is 10 kmph and the speed of the water flow would be 3 kmph. Option (a) is correct.

74. When Ajay does 600 metres, Vijay does 540 m.
When Vijay does 500 metres, Anjay does 475 m
Thus, Ajay : Vijay : Anjay = 600 : 540 : 513.
Thus, Ajay would beat Anjay by (87 × 2/3) = 58 m in a 400 m race.

75. $30/(15 + x) + 30/(15 - x) = 4$ hrs 30 minutes.
At $x = 5$, the equation is satisfied.

76. Ratio of $X$ and $Y$ = 100 : (100 − 10)
= 100 : 90
= 10 : 9
Ratio of speed of $Y$ and $Z$ = 9 : (9 − 1)
= 9 : 8
Ratio of speed of $X : Y : Z$ = 10 : 9 : 8

If speed of $X$ is 20 m/s, then speed of $Z = \dfrac{20}{10} \times 8 = 16$ m/s.

77. Ratio of speed of Mohan and Sohan =
5 : (5 − 0.5) = 5 : 4.5 = 10 : 9
Ratio of Sohan and Chotan= 1 : (1 − 0.2) = 5 : 4
Ratio of speeds of Mohan, Sohan and Chotan = 50 : 45 : 36
Therefore in a 5 Km race if Mohan runs 5000 meters then Chotan runs 3600 meters. Thus, he can give a start of 1400 meters.

78. Let the length of the race track be 1 Km. When $A$ moves 1 Km, $B$ moves 800 m. But 'B' must cover 900 m (according to the question).
∴ $B$ must be given a 100 meter start.

79. The ratio of distances would be equal to the ratio of the speeds (since they run for the same time). Thus, 4:5 = ratio of distance traveled. Since, the dfference in the distance = 250 meters, the race would be 250×5 = 1250 meters.

### Solution: 80 – 81:

80. $Z$ meets $X$ after every $= \dfrac{1000}{(60 \quad 20)} = \dfrac{1000}{40} = 25$ sec.

$Z$ meets $Y$ after every $= \dfrac{1000}{(60 - 40)} = \dfrac{1000}{20} = 50$ sec.

LCM of 25, 50 = 50 seconds
Therefore $X, Y, Z$ meet after every 50 seconds.

81. $X$ completes one round in $\dfrac{1000}{20} = 50$ sec.

$Y$ completes one round in $\dfrac{1000}{40} = 25$ sec.

$Z$ completes one round in $\dfrac{1000}{60} = \dfrac{100}{6} \dfrac{50}{3}$ sec.

LCM of $\left(50, 25, \dfrac{50}{3}\right) = \dfrac{50}{1} = 50$ seconds

Therefore $X, Y, Z$ would meet for the first time at the starting point after 50 seconds.

82. Ratio of distance covered by them =
Ratio of speeds of $X, Y, Z$ = 10 : 20 : 25 = 2 : 4 : 5
If $X$ covers 1 Km, then $Y$ covers 2 Km.

83. Let's assume the initial speed of John is $x$ kmph.
Now after increasing his speed by 4 kmph his final speed= $x$+ 4 kmph.
According to the question:
$\dfrac{80}{x} - \dfrac{80}{x + 4} = 1$
$x^2 + 4x - 320 = 0$
$(x - 16)(x + 20) = 0$
So $x = 16$ kmph.
Final speed of John = 16+ 4= 20 kmph.

84. Percentage change in speed $= \dfrac{20 - 16}{16} \times 100 = 25\%$

85. Distance covered by Ram and Rahim together till the 1st meeting = 100 km
Distance covered by Ram and Rahim together till the 3rd meeting =
100 km + 2 × 200 km = 500 km.
Distance covered by Ram and Rahim is always in the ratio of 5:3.
Distance covered by
Ram $= 500 \times \dfrac{5}{3 + 5} = \dfrac{2500}{8} = 312.5$ km.

### Level of Difficulty (II)

1. By travelling at 10 kmph higher than the original speed, the train is able to make up 16 minutes while traveling 80 km.
This condition is only satisfied at an initial speed of 50 (and a new speed of 60 kmph).

2. Solve this question through options. For instance, if he travelled at 25 kmph, his original speed would have been 24 kmph.
The time difference can be seen to be 6 minutes in this case:
60/24 − 60/25 = 0.1 hrs = 6 mins. Thus, this is the correct answer.

3. In 1 hours 15 minutes an individual will be able to cover 25% more than his speed per hour. The relationship between the original speed and the new speed is best represented as below:

Original speed $\xrightarrow{\text{25\% increase}}$ speed per 75 minutes $\xrightarrow{\text{+1 increase}}$ New speed.

Thus, to go from the new speed to the original speed the process would be:

New speed $\xrightarrow{-1}$ Speed per 75 minutes $\xrightarrow{20\%\downarrow}$ Original speed.

We need to use this process to check the option. Only the first option satisfies this condition. (at 16 kmph it would take 6 hours while at 12 kmph it would take 8 hours).

4. The question's structure (and solving) have to be done on the basis of integers. The following equations emerge:

$$\frac{d}{s} - \frac{d}{(s+6)} = 4 \text{ and } \frac{d}{(S-6)} - \frac{d}{(S+6)} = 10$$

Solving these expressions through normal solving methods is close to impossible (at the very least it would take a huge amount of time.) Instead this question has to be solved using the logic that integral difference in ratios in such a situation can only occur in all the three ratios ($d/s$), $d/(s+6)$ and $d/(s-6)$) are integers.

Hence, $d$ should have three divisors which are 6 units apart from each other.

5. The relative speed is 20 kmph. Also, the pedestrian should take 7:30 hours more than the cyclist. Using option (a) the speeds of the two people are 4km/hr and 16 km/hr respectively. At this speed, the respective times would be 10 hrs and 2:30 hours, giving the required answer.

6.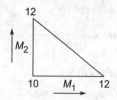

The distance between the motorists will be shown on the hypotenuse. Using the 3,4,5 Pythagoras triplet and the condition that the two speeds are 6 kmph different from each other, you will get the triplet as: 18,24,30. Hence, the slower motorist travelled at 18 kmph.

7. Since the two motorists meet after an hour, their relative speed is 28 kmph. Use options to check out the values. Since the speed of the faster cyclist is asked for it has to be greater than 14 kmph. Hence only check options > 14 kmph.

8. Since the second ant covers 7/120 of the distance in 2 hours 30 minutes, we can infer that is covers 8.4/120 = 7% of the distance in 3 hours. Thus, in 3 hours both ants together cover 15% of the distance

→ 5% per hour → they will meet in 20 hours. Also, ratio of speeds = 8 : 7.

So, the second ant would cover 700 ft to the meeting point in 20 hours and its speed would be 35 feet/hr.

9. In this question consider the total distance as 100%. Hence the sum of their speeds will be 75% per hour. Checking option (c).

If the bus took 6 hours, it would cover 16.66% distance per hour and the car would cover 25% distance per hour. (as it takes 2 hours less than the bus.)

This gives an addition of only 41.66%. Hence, the answer is not correct.

Option (b) is the correct answer.

10. The requisite conditions are met on a Pythagoras triplet 6,8,10. Since the racetrack only consists of the legs of the right triangle the length must be 6 + 8 = 14 km.

11. The sum of speeds would be 0.08 m/s (relative speed in opposite direction). Also if we go by option (b), the speeds will be 0.03 and 0.05 m/s respectively. At this speed the overlapping would occur every 60 seconds.

12. When Rahim starts, Karim would have covered 40 km. Also, their relative speed is 12 kmph and the distance between the two would get to 0 in 40/12 = 3.33 hours.

Distance covered = 28 × 3.33 = 93.33 km.

13. Solve this question through options.

For option (c), the conditions match since: If he rode for 2 hours (speed = 5 kmph), he would have walked for 6 hours (4 hours more) and his walking speed would be 15 kmph.

If we interchange the times, we get 15 × 2 = 5 × 6.

14. This is a complex trial and error based question and the way you would have to think in this is:

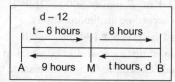

From the figure above, it is clear that $A$ is faster as he takes only $t + 2$ hours while $B$ has taken $t + 9$ hours to complete the journey.

Then, we get: $(t - 6)/9 = 8/t$

Solving for $t$, we get $t = -6$ (not possible)

Or $t = 12$. Putting this value of $t$ in the figure it changes to:

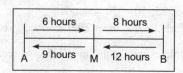

We also get ratio of speeds = 3 : 2 (inverse of ratio of times)

The next part of the puzzle is to think of the 12 km less traveled by the first person till the meeting point. If the speed of the faster person is 3s, that of the slower person = 2s.

Further

$$12 \times 2s - 6 \times 3s = 12 \text{ km}$$
$$s = 2 \text{ kmph}.$$

The speed of the faster tourist is $3 \times 2 = 6$ kmph

15. Solve using options. The first option you would check for (given the values in the questions) would be option (b). This would give that the first jogger would run at 3 min per km, while the second jogger would run at 4 min per km. In the new condition, the first jogger would jog for 13 km while the second jogger would jog for 14 km and their respective times would be 39 mins and 56 minutes. This is consistent with the condition in the question which talks about a difference of 17 minutes in their respective times.

16. Solve this through options as: For option (a)
$$4800/60 - 4800/50 = 16 \text{ minutes}$$

17. The ant would cover $7 \times 8 = 56$ meters in 16 hours. Further, it would require 7/12 of the 17th hour to reach the top. Thus time required = 16 hours 35 minutes

18. If the slower ship took 20 hours (option d) the faster ship would take 12 hours and their respective speeds would be 15 and 25 kmph. This satisfies the basic condition in the question.

19. The movement of the ant in the two cases would be 3, 7, 11, 15, 19, 23 and 1, 9, 17, 25, 33, 41. It can be seen that after 3 seconds the difference is 6mm, after 4 seconds, the difference is 16mm and after 5 seconds the difference is 30 mm. Thus, it is clearly seen that the ant moved for 4 seconds.

20. When the signal happened distance left was 150 km.
$$150/(s) - 150/(s + 15) = 1/2 \text{ hours} \rightarrow s = 60.$$

21. The following figure gives us the movement of the two swimmers:

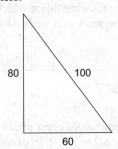

The faster swimmer must have traveled 80 km in 2 hours and hence his speed is 40 kmph.

22. Since they cover the distance in 80 minutes traveling in opposite directions we infer 100% distance is covered in 80 minutes → 1.25% per minute → 75% per hour.

i.e. their combined distance coverage is 75% per hour. Since we are asked for the time the faster motorcyclist takes, we can pick up this time from the options.

| Options | Time for faster motorcyclist | Faster's % coverage per hour | Slower's % coverage per hour |
|---|---|---|---|
| a | 6 hours | 16.66 | 58.33 |
| b | 3 hours | 33.33 | 41.66 |
| c | 2 hours | 50 | 25 |
| d | 4 hours | 25 | 50 |

It is clear that options a, b, d and e are not feasible as it is making the faster motorcyclist slower.

Thus option (c) has to be correct.

Note: You can use the values in option (c) to check the other condition in problem and see that it works.

23. Since the two horses meet after 200 minutes, they cover 0.5% of the distance per minute (combined) or 30% per hour. This condition is satisfied only if the slower rider takes 10 hours (thereby covering 10% per hour) and the faster rider takes 5 hours (thereby covering 20% per hour).

24. Solve through options the equation: $350/s - 350/(s + 5) = 2.33$ hours.
$$\rightarrow s = 25.$$

25. Solve this question through options. The total travel time should be 5 hours 25 minutes.

or   $5(5/12)$ hours = 65/12 hours
$$d/36 + d/14 = 65/12 \rightarrow d = 54.6 \text{ km}.$$

Thus, option (d) none of these is correct.

26–28. You can make the following table to chart out the motions of the three.

| Hour | Ram | Shyam | Mohan |
|---|---|---|---|
| 1 | 10 | 30 | 3.33 |
| 2 | 20 | 33.33 | 6.66 |
| 3 | 60 | 36.66 | 10 |
| 4 | 81.66 | 40 | 20 |
| 5 | 85 | 50 | 30 |
| 6 | 88.33 | 60 | 40 |
| | 90(6.5) | 70(7) | 70(7) |
| | | 80(8) | 100(8) |

26. It is evident that Ram would overtake Shyam between 2 and 3. At x, Shyam is ahead by 13.33 km.
Relative speed between 2 – 3 = 36.66 kmph.

Time required = 13.33/36.66 of the hour

= 4/11 of the hour

= 2 : 22. (approx)

27. Mohan would overtake Shyam after 70 miles.

28. Ram would cover 90 miles in 3 hours 45 minutes.

Mohan would cover 90 miles in 7 hours 40 minutes.

Time difference = 3 hours 55 minutes.

29. Mohan at 8 pm (each of the others would reach later).

30. Ram would reach at 9:30 p.m., while Shyam would reach at 10:00 p.m.

31. $25/s - 25/(s + 10) = 1/12$

$S = 50$ km/hr.

32. The respective times are 224 seconds and 364 seconds. They will meet at the starting point in the LCM of these times, i.e., $224 \times 13$. Hence, Ram Singh will cover the circle 13 times.

33. The wife drives for 12 minutes less than her driving on normal days.

Thus, she would have saved 6 minutes each way. Hence, Ravi would have walked for 30 minutes (since his speed is 1/5th of the car's speed).

In effect, Ravi spends 24 minutes extra on the walking (rather than if he had traveled the same distance by car).

Thus, if Ravi had got the car at the station only, he would have saved 24 minutes more and reached at 5:36.

34. The following figure represents the travel of the two:

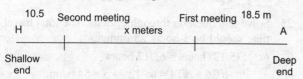

Once, you can visualise this figure, try to extract the value of $x$ by taking the length as given in the options. For option (a) length of pool is 55.5 meters, the ratio of speeds of Ajay to Hemant on the basis of the first meeting = 18.5/37. The ratio of speeds on the basis of the second meeting = Ajay's travel to Hemant's travel = 47.5/ 63.5. The two ratios are not the same- which they should have been as both these ratios represent the speed ratio between Ajay and Hemant.

For option (b), length of pool is 45 meters, the ratio of speeds of Ajay to Hemant on the basis of the first meeting = 18.5/26.5. The ratio of speeds on the basis of the second meeting = Ajay's travel to Hemant's travel = 37/ 53. The two ratios are the same — which they should have been as both these ratios represent the speed ratio between Ajay and Hemant. Hence, this is the correct answer.

35. The distances covered in percentage would be, 10% + 6.66% + 8.33% + 16.66% + 5.833% + 31.666 + 2.0833 = 81.25%

$(22.5/18.75) \times 100 = 120$ km

36. If you start at 12 noon, you would reach at 4:30 PM. You would be able to meet the train which left Mumbai at 8 AM, 9 AM, 10 AM, 11 AM, 12 Noon, 1 PM, 2 PM, 3 PM and 4 PM – a total of 9 trains.

37. The total time = time in the first part of the journey + time for the second part of the journey= $k/y + (x - k)/z$. Option (a) is correct.

38. If we assume the speed of the sound as 330 m/s, we can see that the distance traveled by the sound in 45 seconds is the distance traveled by the train in 11 minutes.

$330 \times 45 = 660 \times s \rightarrow s = 22.5$ m/s = 81 kmph

39–40. In 9 hours, (7 pm to 4 pm) the Kalinga Express would cover 540 kms.

Remaining distance = 260 kms

Relative speed = 150 kmph.

Time required = 260/150 =1.733 hours

= 104 minutes.

39. $1.733 \times 90 = 156$ km.

40. 4 A.M. + 1 hr 44 minutes = 5 : 44 A.M.

41. The total distance the bird would travel would be dependent on the time that the cars crash with each other. Also, the speed of the bird is the same as the relative speed of the cars. Hence, the answer to question 41 will be 12 km.

42. The bird would travel at 120 kmph for 4 + 4/3 + 4/9 minutes, i.e., 5.77 minutes. Hence, the answer is $(5.77/60) \times 120 = 11.55$ km.

43. The bird would be able to theoretically reach the bonnet of the second car an infinite number of times.

44. Initial distance = 25 dog leaps.

Per minute → dog makes 5 dog leaps

Per minute → Cat makes 6 cat leaps = 3 dog leaps.

Relative speed = 2 dog leaps/minutes.

An initial distance of 25 dog leaps would get covered in 12.5 minutes.

45. Refer to the following figure which helps us understand that the ratio of speeds of $A$ to $B$ would be 2:3.

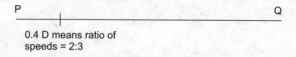

0.4 D means ratio of speeds = 2:3

The 4th meeting would occur after a combined movement of $D + 6D = 7D$. 2/5th of this distance would be covered by $A$ and 3/5th of this distance would be the distance covered by $B$. Thus, distance covered by $A$ would be 2/5$^{th}$ of 7$D$, i.e., distance covered by $A = 2.8D$ – which means that the 4$^{th}$ meeting occurs at a distance of 0.8$D$ from $P$.

46. In 36 hours, there would be a gap of 8 minutes. The two watches would show the same time when the gap would be exactly 12 hours or 720 minutes.

    The no. of 36 hour time frames required to create this gap = 720/8 = 90.

    Total time = 90 × 36 = 3240 hours. Since this is divisible by 24, the watches would show 12 noon.

47. Solve through options. At 18 kmph the motorboat would take exactly 6 hours.

48. Check through options. Option (d) will give us 14 kmph and 9 kmph as the down stream and up stream speeds. This would mean that the total travel time would be 1.5 hours and 2.33 hours down stream and up stream respectively.

49. At 2:15 PM the distance between the two trains would be 550 km as the train from Hazipur to Muzaffarpur would already have travelled for 40 minutes. After that they would take 550/110 = 5 hours to meet. Thus, the train from Muzaffarpur would have traveled 250 kms before meeting. Option (c) is correct.

50. The dog loses 1/3$^{rd}$ of his normal time from the meeting point. (Thus normal time = 35 × 3 = 105 minutes)

    If the meeting occurred 24 km further, the dog loses 25 minutes.

    This means that the normal time for the new distance would be 75 minutes. Thus, normally the dog would cover this distance of 24 km in 30 minutes. Thus, normal speed = 48 km/hr.

51. Let the length of circular track be '$x$' meters. If they met at '$y$' meters away from the starting point.

    $$\frac{a}{b} = \frac{3x+y}{2x+y} = 1 + \frac{x}{2x+y}$$

    Here '$y$' must be greater than 0 but less than '$x$'. This gives us that the lower limit of the answer would be 1.33 (if you take the higher extreme value of y as 1) and the upper limit would be 1.5 (If we take the lower extreme value of y as 0).

    All the given options lie within this range, hence the correct answer is 3.

52. Since he reduces his speed to 4/5$^{th}$ his going out speed, his time would increase to 5/4$^{th}$ of his normal time. Thus, the total travel time (if we assume that the time going out is t, the time coming back would be 1.25t) Thus, the total time would be 2.25t, which is also equal to 4 hours 30 minutes. This gives us t = 2 hours and the returning time = 2 hours 30 minutes. The return speed would be 100/2.5 =40 kmph.

53.

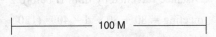

Dhoni will cover two laps in 20 seconds (as he runs at a speed of 10 m/s and the track is 100 meters). In the same time: Kohli will cover 4 × 20 = 80 meters.

Therefore, during the first 20 seconds they would meet twice.

Also, after covering the track twice, Dhoni would be back to his original position. At that time, the distance between them would be 20 meters (distance left for Kohli to finish his first lap). Also, they would be moving in opposite directions and hence their relative speed would be 14 m/s.

Therefore, they will meet after $\frac{20}{(10+4)} = \frac{10}{7}$ seconds.

So total time taken will be = 10 + 10 + $\frac{10}{7} = \frac{150}{7}$ = 21.42 seconds

54. At their third meeting, Dhoni will be at $10 \times \frac{10}{7} = \frac{100}{7}$ =14.28 meters from his starting point.

55. If Akhilesh travels at 8 feet/minute, 10 feet /minute and 12 feet/minute for '$t$' minutes then

    according to the conditions in the problem: 8t + 10t + 12t = 120 → t =4 minutes

    Distance travelled by Akhilesh in 5 minutes = 8 × 4 + 10 × 1 =42 meters.

    Time taken by Ramesh to travel 1/3$^{rd}$ of the distance = $\frac{120}{3 \times 8}$ = 5 minutes.

    Therefore, distance between Ramesh and Akhilesh after 5 minutes = 120 – (42 + 40) = 38 meters

56. Time after which Ramesh and Akhilesh meet = 5 minutes + $\frac{38}{10+10}$ = 6.9 minutes or 414 seconds

57. Since their ratio of speeds is 6:1, they will meet for the first time at the starting point when Vijay completes his first round. At that time, since Bhola too would have been running for the entire time, Bhola would have covered six times the distance which would mean that Bhola would have covered the track for the sixth time — thus it would be their sixth meeting. Hence, he would have met Vijay 5 times before they meet at the starting point.

58. Let the distance travelled by train $B$ before the first meeting be '$d$' km.

Distance travelled by train $A$ before 2$^{nd}$ and after first meeting = $(40 + d)$ km.

Distance travelled by train B before 2$^{nd}$ and after 1$^{st}$ meeting = $80 + 80 + d - 40 = (120 + d)$ km.

Since, their speeds are constant, the ratio of distances covered would be constant too (for both the time periods). This gives us the equation:

$$\frac{80}{d} = \frac{40 + d}{120 + d} \rightarrow d = 120.$$

Hence, the distance between Agra and Delhi = 80 + 120 = 200 km.

59. Required ratio $= \frac{120}{80} = \frac{3}{2} = 1.5$

60. Let Anand entered the bar at '$x$' minutes past 12 A.M.

Speed of minute hand $= \dfrac{360}{60}$ degree/minute

Speed of hour hand $= \dfrac{30}{60}$ degree/minute

$$\therefore (360° - 30°)\frac{x}{60} = 30°$$

$x = \dfrac{30 \times 60}{330} = \dfrac{60}{11} = 5\dfrac{5}{11}$ or 5.455 minutes or 5 minutes 27.27 seconds

Therefore, Anand entered the bar at 00:05:27 AM
He came out the bar at 00:05: 27 AM + 1:20:00
= 1:25:27 AM.

$\therefore$ A = 1; B =25 and C = 27. Sum of the three = 53.

# EXERCISE ON APPLICATIONS OF TIME, SPEED AND DISTANCE

1. At the ancient Athens Olympic games, in a duel between two runners, Portheus and Morpheus, they were made to start running in opposite direction from diametrically opposite ends of a circular race track of length (circumference) 2 kms. The first time they met was after 24 minutes. If the distance between them exactly '$n$' minutes after they start is equal to a quarter of the length of the track, which of the following is a possible value of '$n$'?
   - (a) 124
   - (b) 184
   - (c) 160
   - (d) 204

2. Aman and Biman started a walkathon around a circular track starting from the same point on the track in opposite directions. They met for the first after time '$t$'. Had they walked in the same direction with their speeds intact, they would have met after a time '$7t$'. It was also observed that Aman was slower than Biman, and Aman's speed was measured at 12 kmph. Find the speed of Biman.
   - (a) 4 m/s
   - (b) 5 m/s
   - (c) 6 m/s
   - (d) None of these

3. Abhishek and Aiswarya start from two opposite ends of a tunnel AB, which is 182 meters in length. Abhishek starts from A and Aiswarya starts from B. After they meet, they continue moving in their respective directions, till one of them reaches his end point and immediately reverses direction and starts walking back towards the other end. The ratio of their speeds is 7:6. At what distance (in metres) from A will they meet when Abhishek is in his 8th round?
   - (a) 105
   - (b) 130
   - (c) 125
   - (d) They would not meet.

4. For the above question, at what distance (in metres) from A will they meet when Abhishek is in his 12th round?
   - (a) 126
   - (b) 118
   - (c) 91
   - (d) They would not meet.

5. Two runners Portheus and Zeus, are running around a circular track at different speeds such that they meet after regular time intervals. The length of the track (circumference) is 1600 meters. If they run in opposite directions, they meet at eight different points while if they run in the same direction it is observed that they meet at 2 distinct points on the circular track. If they meet at intervals of 1.33 minutes when they run in the same direction, how much time does the faster runner (Portheus) take to complete one round?

6. At the Vijayantkhand Mini Stadium there are two circular race tracks— A with radii 40m and B 80 m respectively such that they touch each other at a point X. The coach Vijay Sir has a particular ritual with his best athletes Mridul and Odeon. Mridul runs at a speed of $80\pi$ m/min on Race Track A and Odeon runs at a speed of $40\pi$ m/min along the Race Track B. Both of them start from the point X and run multiple rounds. If Mridul gives Odeon a start of 4 mins exactly before he starts running himself, after how much time (in minutes) will the straight line distance between the two be exactly 240 m?
   - (a) 6
   - (b) 10
   - (c) 12.5
   - (d) Never

   - (a) 80 secs
   - (b) 32 secs
   - (c) 120 secs
   - (d) None of these

7. Bolt and Milkha, start running around a race track simultaneously. Bolt runs at a speed of '$s$' kmph, while Milkha runs at a speed of '$m$' kmph. They meet for the first time when Bolt is in his third round. Which of the following can be the value of $s:m$?
   - (a) 11 : 6
   - (b) 11 : 5
   - (c) 17 : 8
   - (d) 9 : 4

8. Amar, Abhijit and Arun start running on a circular race track (from the same point). Amar and Abhijit run in a clockwise fashion while Arun runs anticlockwise. When Amar and Arun meet for the first time, Arun is at a distance which is equal to a quarter of the circumference of the circular race track. It is also known that Amar runs faster than Arun. The ratio of speeds of Amar, Arun and Abhijit cannot be...?
   - (a) 5 : 1 : 2
   - (b) 3 : 1 : 1
   - (c) 4 : 2 : 1
   - (d) 3 : 2 : 1

9. At what time between 6 and 7 o'clock is the miniute hand of a clock 4 minutes ahead of the hour hand?
   - (a) $34\frac{1}{11}$ minutes past 6
   - (b) $36\frac{5}{11}$ minutes past 6
   - (c) $37\frac{1}{11}$ minutes past 6
   - (d) None of these

10. The minute hand of a clock overtakes the hour hand at intervals of 66 minutes of the correct time. How much time does the clock gain or lose in 4 hours?
    - (a) $1\frac{119}{121}$ minutes
    - (b) $1\frac{114}{121}$ minutes
    - (c) 2 minutes
    - (d) None of these

11. Robin Varkey's watch always runs faster than the actual time — and gains time unifromly. He sets the watch to be 10 minutes behind time at 12 noon on a Sunday. He observes that the watch is 5 minutes 48 seconds faster the following Sunday at 12 noon. At what exact time would the watch be correct?

    (a) $\frac{26}{79}$ hours past 10 PM on Thursday

    (b) $\frac{13}{79}$ hours past 8 PM on Thursday

    (c) $\frac{26}{79}$ hours past 6 PM on Thursday

    (d) None of these

12. Prawin Tiwari sets his clock right at 10 AM on Monday morning. However, being a defective piece (the clock), it loses 32 minutes every day. He has to get up on Friday at exactly 4 AM to catch his flight to Lebuana. At what time on Friday morning should he set the alarm on his watch in order for the watch to ring at exactly 4 AM?

    (a) 3 AM          (b) 2 AM
    (c) 5 AM          (d) None of these

13. At what time, in minutes , between 4 o'clock and 5 o'clock, would both the hands of a clock coincide with each other?

    (a) $22\frac{1}{11}$          (b) $21\frac{9}{11}$

    (c) $22\frac{4}{11}$          (d) $21\frac{7}{11}$

14. At what time between 8 PM to 9 PM will the hands of a clock be in the same straight line pointing away from each other?

    (a) $10\frac{8}{11}$ minutes past 8

    (b) $10\frac{10}{11}$ minutes past 8

    (c) $10\frac{3}{11}$ minutes past 8

    (d) $9\frac{10}{11}$ minutes past 8

15. A watch which gains 5 seconds in 3 minutes was set right at 7 am. In the afternoon of the same day, when it indicated quarter past 4 o'clock, the true time is:

    (a) $59\frac{7}{12}$ min. past 3    (b) 4 p.m

    (c) $58\frac{7}{11}$ min. past 3    (d) $2\frac{3}{11}$ min. past 4

16. In a 2000 m race between Portheus and Cassius, Portheus gives Cassius a head start of a minute but still beats him by 200 m. When, he increases the head start to 80 seconds, the race ends in a dead heat. Find the speed of Portheus.

    (a) 25 m/s          (b) 18 m/s
    (c) 13.33 m/s       (d) 16.66 m/s

17. How many right angles would be formed between the minute and the hour hand of a watch in a day?

    (a) 48          (b) 46
    (c) 45          (d) 44

18. How many times between 2 PM and 4 PM does the minutes hand coincide with the seconds hand?

    (a) 118          (b) 119
    (c) 120          (d) 121

19. A man enters his house at some time between 6 to 7 PM. When he leaves his house sometime between 7 to 8, he observes that the minute hand and the hour hand have interchanged positions. At what exact time did the man enter the house?

    (A) $38\frac{82}{121}$ minutes past 6

    (b) $37\frac{42}{121}$ minutes past 6

    (c) $37\frac{82}{121}$ minutes past 6

    (d) $37\frac{62}{121}$ minutes past 6

20. How many straight lines would be formed between the minute and the hour hand of a watch in a day?

    (a) 48          (b) 46
    (c) 45          (d) 44

21. Two friends started simultaneously from Kanpur towards Lucknow in the same direction along a straight road. The faster friend Raveesh was on a bike while Prakash was in an auto. The ratio of their speeds was 1 : 5 respectively. Two hours later, Raveesh parked his bike and started running back towards Prakash's auto. His speed dropped by 80% as a result of this. They meet at a point which is 15 km from Kanpur. What was the speed of the auto?

    (a) 2 km/hr          (b) 2.5 km/hr
    (c) 3 km/hr          (d) None of these.

22. Two brothers came to know about their sister's wedding at the last minute. The wedding was to be held at a location which was 800 kms away from Mumbai where both of them lived. The elder brother Kanhaiya came to know about the wedding at 6 PM and left immediately in his car. His younger brother Ramaiyya came to know about the wedding at 9:30 PM and left in his car immediately at a speed which was 15 kmph higher than the speed of his elder brother. At 4:30 AM it was found that the two cars were 70 km apart. If the cars had travelled continuously without taking any rest, find the speed (in km/hr) of Kanhaiya's car.

    (a) 40          (b) 50
    (c) 60          (d) Cannot be determined

23. Ranatunga once challenged Bolt to a race. The distance of the race was set at 2 km. They start at the same time and the ratio of their speeds is seen to be 4:1 (obviously Bolt would be faster). After some time passes, Bolt realises that he is far ahead and calculates that even if he stops for a snack and a nap for 'n' minutes, he would still reach his destination and beat Ranatunga by 13 minutes. Hence, he plans to take a break of 'n' minutes. Ranatunga keeps walking during this whole time. However, when Bolt wakes up, he realises that he has stopped for a total of (n+15) minutes. He redoubles his efforts by increasing his speed to double his original speed. The race eventually ended in a dead heat. If it is known that Bolt overstayed his stop by 6n/5 mins, how long did Ranatunga take to complete the race?
    (a) 32 mins        (b) 34 mins
    (c) 25 mins        (d) None of these

24. A and B run a 300 m race where the initial speed of B is double the speed of A. After some time, going on these speeds, A realising that he would be losing the race redoubled his effort and increased his speed to four times his initial speed. As a result, they reached the end point at the same time and the race resulted in a dead heat. What was the distance travelled by B, when A quadrupled his speed?
    (a) 100 m          (b) 200 m
    (c) 150 m          (d) None of these

25. Amit and Bimal start running around a circular track of circumference 4200 metres. Their respective speeds are 15m/s and 3 m/s. Their 14th meeting occurs at point P and their 22nd meeting occurs at the point Q. Find the longer distance (along the circumference) between Points P and Q.
    (a) 2800           (b) 1400
    (c) 3500           (d) 3150

26. In a 2 km race, Ravi beats Sandeep by 45 seconds and Sandeep beats Tarun by a further 75 seconds. In the same race, Ravi beats Tarun by 400 m. Find the time in which Ravi can run the race (in seconds).
    (a) 240            (b) 300
    (c) 360            (d) 480

## ANSWER KEY

| | | | |
|---|---|---|---|
| 1. (d) | 2. (d) | 3. (d) | 4. (a) |
| 5. (b) | 6. (d) | 7. (a) | 8. (d) |
| 9. (c) | 10. (a) | 11. (a) | 12. (b) |
| 13. (b) | 14. (b) | 15. (b) | 16. (d) |
| 17. (d) | 18. (d) | 19. (a) | 20. (c) |
| 21. (b) | 22. (b) | 23. (b) | 24. (b) |
| 25. (a) | 26. (d) | | |

**Solutions**

1. They would first meet after 24 minutes (after covering 50% of the distance represented by the circumference of the circle). The next time they would meet would be at 72 minutes, then 120 minutes, then 168 minutes, 216 minutes and so on.
   Every time they meet they would be together and after the meeting point they continue running in opposite directions till they meet again. Between two meeting points, the distance between them would be 25% of the length of the circle's circumference in two cases: first when they are going away from each other after meeeting (this would occur at a time of 12 minutes after the meeting point) and second when they are approaching each other before their next meeting (this would occur at a time of 12 minutes before the next meeting point.
   The meeting times 24, 72, 120, 168, 216, 264 etc, the times at which the distance would be 25% of the circumference:
   (24 −12 = 12); (24 + 12 = 36); (72 − 12 = 60); (72 + 12 = 84); (120 − 12 = 108); (120 + 12 = 132); (168 − 12 = 156); (168 + 12 = 180); (216 − 12 = 204).
   Only Option (d) is possible and hence is the correct answer.

2. The ratio of their speeds can be worked out to be 4:3. Hence, Biman's speed (b) would be 16 kmph.
   $b = 16$ kmph $= 16 \times 5 \div 18 = 80 \div 18$ m/s $= 4.44$ m/s. Option (d) is the correct answer.

3. When Abhishek would complete 7 rounds, Aiswarya would have completed: $7 \times 6 \div 7 = 6$ rounds.
   This means that both of them would be at the point B at this time. Since Abhishek is faster than Aiswarya, during his eighth round there would be no meeting with Aiswarya. Hence, Option (d) is correct.

4. When Abhishek would complete 11 rounds, Aiswarya would have completed: $11 \times 6 \div 7$ rounds $= 9\frac{3}{7}$ rounds.
   This means that Aiswarya would be at a distance of 3/7 from A, while Abhishek would be at B at this point of time. The distance between them would be 4/7 of the total distance between A and B. Aiswarya would further cover a distance of $4/7 \times 6/13$ in order to meet Abhishek. Thus the total distance from A is $(3/7 + 24/91) \times 182 = 63 \times 182 \div 91 = 126$ meters from A and 56 meters from B. Option (a) is correct.

5. Let the ratio of speeds be P:Z (where P>Z).
   Since they meet at 8 distinct points on the circle when they move in opposite directions, it automatically means that the sum of P+Z = 8. (I would like to encourage you to discover this piece of logic through trial and error.)

Similar logic gives us that P − Z = 2 (since they meet at two distinct points when travelling in the same direction.

Using these two equations, we can determine that if P = 5, Z=3. Let the speeds of P be 5x and Z be 3x (in m/s). Then we have: $1600/2x = 80$ secs → $x = 10$ and hence the speeds are P = 50 m/s and Z = 30 m/s.

P would take 1600 ÷ 50 = 32 seconds to complete one round.

Option (b) would be the correct answer.

6. Since the radii of the circles are 40m and 80m respectively, the circumference would be $80\pi$ and $160\pi$ meters respectively. Since Odeon's speed is $40\pi$ m/min, he would take 4 minutes to cover a round. This also means that when Mridul starts running, they would both be at point X, since Odeon would have covered 1 round exactly in 4 minutes. Also, for the straight line distance to be 240 m they should be at the diametrically opposite ends from the point X (of their respective circles). Mridul reaches the diametrically opposite end (from X) of his circle for the first time in 30 seconds and after that he would reach the same point every 1 minute at 1:30, 2:30 and so on. Odeon on the other hand would reach the diametrically opposite end at 2 minutes, 6 minutes, 10 minutes and so on. They would never be exactly 240 m apart. Option (d) is correct.

7. Check using the options. You can see that only in the case of Option (a) do they meet when Bolt is in his third round. For all other options, Bolt would cross Milkha when Bolt is in his second round.

8. Checking the options, it can be seen that the condition of diametrically opposite is satisfied in each of the first three options. It is only in Option (d) that it is not satisfied. Hence, Option (d) is correct.

9. At 6 o'clock, the minute hand is 30 minutes behind the hour hand.

From this position, we need to reach a position, where the minute hand is 4 minutes ahead of the hour hand. For this to occur, the minute hand has to gain (30 + 4) = 34 minute spaces on the hour hand. In one hour, the minute hand moves 60 mintues while the hour hand moves 5 minute spaces on the clock. Hence, the minute hand gains 55 minutes on the hour hand in an hour.

Hence, to gain, 34 minutes, the minute hand would take $\left(\frac{60}{55} \times 34\right) = 37\frac{1}{11}$ min.

The required answer would be $37\frac{1}{11}$ minutes past 6. Option (c) is correct.

10. Assume the clock to be a circular race track of 60 kms with each minute denoting 1 km. Also imagine two runners Mr. Minute and Mr. Hour running on

this track. Normally, in a correct clock, Mr. Minute would cover 55 kms more than Mr. Hour every hour. This means that they would be together (meaning Mr. Minute would overtake Mr. Hour) every $\left(\frac{60}{55} \times 60\right)$ min. $= 65\frac{5}{11}$ minutes. If they meet at longer time intervals than this, it means that the clock is slow. If the time intervals are shorter it would mean that the clock is fast.

In this problem they are together after 66 minutes. Thus, the clock loses time.

Loss in 66 minutes = $\left(66 - 65\frac{5}{11}\right) = \frac{6}{11}$ minutes.

Using unitary method we get loss in 4 hours = $\left(\frac{6}{11} \times \frac{60 \times 4}{66}\right)$ min. $= 1\frac{119}{121}$ minutes.

11. In one week the time elapsed is exaclty 168 hours. Robin's watch gains 15 minutes 48 seconds in 168 hours. In other words it gains $\left(10 + 5\frac{4}{5}\right)$ min. or $\frac{79}{5}$ minutes in 168 hrs.

To be showing the exact time, the watch should have gained exactly 10 minutes.

Using Unitary method it can be seen that 10 minutes would be gained by the watch in: $\left(168 \times \frac{5}{79} \times 10\right)$ hrs. $= 106\frac{26}{79}$ hours.

∴ Watch is correct at $\frac{26}{79}$ hours past 10 PM on Thursday. Option (a) is the correct answer.

12. Time from 10 AM on Monday to 2 AM on Friday = 88 hours.

Now 23 hrs 28 minutes of this clock = 24 hours of correct clock.

∴ $\frac{352}{15}$ hrs of this clock = 24 hours of correct clock

88 hrs of this clock = $\left(24 \times \frac{15}{352} \times 88\right)$ hrs of correct clock.

= 90 hrs of correct clock. This means that at 4 AM on Friday his clock would show 2 AM. Hence, if he needs to wake up at 4 AM, he should set his clock's alarm at 2 AM.

Hence, Option (b) is the correct answer.

13. Assume the clock to be a circular race track of 60 kms with each minute denoting 1 km. Also imagine two runners Mr. Minute and Mr. Hour running on this track. Normally, in a correct clock, Mr. Minute would cover 55 kms more than Mr. Hour every hour. At 4 o'clock, the minute hand is 20 kms behind the hour hand.

It would hence, need to gain 20 kms to coincide with the hour hand.

In 60 minutes, it gains 55 kms.

In t minutes, it gains 20 kms.

$$t = \left(\frac{60}{55} \times 20\right) \text{min.} = 21\frac{9}{11} \text{ minutes.}$$

14. Thinking as in the previous question, we can think that at 8 PM the minute hand is 40 kms behind the hour hand. For it to become 30 kms behind the hour hand, we would need it to cover 10 kms over the hour hand.

In 60 minutes, it gains 55 kms.

In t minutes, it gains 10 kms.

$$t = \left(\frac{60}{55} \times 10\right) \text{min.} = 10\frac{10}{11} \text{ minutes.}$$

Option (b) is correct.

15. Time from 7 am to 4:15 pm = 9 hrs 15min = $\frac{37}{4}$ hrs

3 min 5 sec of this clock = 3 min of the correct clock.

$$\Rightarrow \frac{37}{720} \text{ hrs of this clock} = \frac{1}{20} \text{ hrs of the clock.}$$

$$\Rightarrow \frac{37}{4} \text{ hrs of this clock} = \left(\frac{1}{20} \times \frac{720}{37} \times \frac{37}{4}\right) \text{ hrs of the correct clock}$$

= 9 hrs of the correct clock

The correct time is 9 hrs after 7 AM, i.e., 4 PM.

16. Since Cassius is able to get a dead heat when he gets a head start of 80 seconds, it means that he would cover 200 meters in 20 seconds. Hence, his speed is 10m/s.

Let the time taken by Portheus to finish the race be t seconds. Then tracking the movement of Cassius we get:

t ×10 + 60 × 10 = 2000 − 200.

So t = 120 seconds.

Hence, the speed of Portheus would be = 2000/120 = 250/15 = 50/3 = 16.666 m/s. Option (d) is correct.

17. There are 2 right angles that are formed every hour between the hands of a watch. Hence, in 24 hours, we would expect 48 right angles. However, between 2 to 4 AM and 2 to 4 PM the number of right angles formed is only 3, because the right angle formed at 3 O'Clock (both AM and PM) is the second right angle for the hour between 2 O'Clock and 3 O'Clock. It is also the first right angle between 3 O'Clock and 4 O'Clock. This makes the clock lose two of its 48 expected right angles. Similarly, two right angles are lost when the clock passes through 8 O'Clock to 10 O'Clock. Hence, there would be a total of 44 right angles formed. Option (d) is correct.

18. In two hours, the minute hand completes 2 rounds around the circumference of the clock's dial. In the same time, the seconds hand covers 120 rounds. If we count 2 PM coincidence as the first one, the 4 pm coincidence would be the last one. There would be a total of 121 coincidences in 2 hours. Option (d) is correct.

19. Assume the clock to be a circular race track of 60 kms with each minute denoting 1 km. Also imagine two runners Mr. Minute and Mr. Hour running on this track. Normally, in a correct clock, Mr. Minute would cover 55 kms more than Mr. Hour every hour. For the conditions given in the problem, when the man enters the house, the time would be somewhere between 6:35 to 6:40 while when he leaves the time would be somewhere between 7:30 to 7:35.

Let, the distance between the two be equal to x kms. When the hands interchange positions, the hour hand would have traveled x kms and the minute hand would have traveled (60 − x) kms.

Using unitary method we get:

When the minute hand travels 60 kms, the hour hand travels 5 kms.

When the minute hand travels '60 − x' kms, the hour hand travels 'x' kms.

$$60x = 300 - 5x \rightarrow x = \frac{300}{55} = 5\frac{5}{11} \text{ minutes.}$$

This means that when he comes home, the minute hand is $5\frac{5}{11}$ minutes ahead of the hour hand.

In order to find the exact time at which this happens between 6 to 7, we know that at 6, the minute hand is 30 kms behind the hour hand. For the minute hand to move $5\frac{5}{11}$ minutes ahead of the hour hand we would need the minute hand to cover $35\frac{5}{11}$ kms.

In 60 minutes, the minute hand covers 55 kms.

In t minutes, the minute hand covers $35\frac{5}{11}$ minutes.

$$t = 60 \times 35\frac{5}{11} \div 55 = \frac{12}{11} \times \frac{390}{11} \text{ minutes} = 4680 \div$$

$$121 = 38\frac{82}{121} \text{ minutes.}$$

He comes home at $38\frac{82}{121}$ minutes past 6.

20. There are 2 times that the hands of a watch form straight lines every hour. Hence, in 24 hours, we would expect 48 straight lines. However, between 11 to 1 and between 5 to 7 we would 'lose' one straight line as the 12 o'clock straight line and the 6 o'clock straight lines are double counted. Hence, the number of straight lines = 48 − 1 (for 5 AM to 7AM) − 1 (for 11 AM to 1 PM) − 1 (for 5 PM to 7 PM). Hence, there would be a total of 45 straight lines formed in a day. Option (c) is correct.

21. Solve this through options. Option (b) matches the conditions of the problem and is hence the correct answer.

The thought process for this goes as follows:
If the auto's speed is 2.5, the bike's speed would be 12.5. Naturally 2 hours later, Raveesh would be at 25 kms. while Prakash would be at 5 kms. A distance of 20 kms. When Raveesh starts back his speed would be 2.5 kmph and hence the total speed at which they would approach each other would be 5 kmph. They would meet 6 hours after starting — and in this time Prakash would have covered 15 km and hence they would meet at 15 km from Kanpur. (This last bit would not match for the other options.)
For example if we check Option (a):
The thought process for this goes as follows:
If the auto's speed is 2, the bike's speed would be 10. Naturally 2 hours later, Raveesh would be at 20 kms while Prakash would be at 4 kms. A distance of 16 kms. When Raveesh starts back his speed would be 2 kmph and hence the total speed at which they would approach each other would be 4 kmph. They would meet 6 hours after starting — and in this time Prakash would have covered 12 km and hence they would meet at 12 km from Kanpur which does not match the information in the problem.

22. Solve using options. For option (b), at 4:30 AM the elder brother has travelled for 10:30 hours and hence must have covered 525 kms. The younger brother has traveled only for 7 hours and at a speed of 65 kmph, the distance traveled would be 455 km. This would mean that the distance between them would be 70 km (as given). Hence, this option works correctly. The other options do not work and can be tested in a similar way. For instance for option (a), 40 kmph does not work because $10.5 \times 40 - 7 \times 55 \neq 70$.
Similarly, Option (c) can be rejected because $10.5 \times 60 - 7 \times 75 \neq 70$

23. Since Bolt outstretched his time by $6n/5$ mins and this is also equal to 15 mins. Solving we get: $n = 12.5$ mins.

**Space for Rough Work**

Let their original speeds be '$4s$' and '$s$' kmph respectively.
Had Bolt not overstretched his nap, he would have beaten Ranatunga by 13 min.

$$\therefore \frac{2000}{4s} + 12.5 + 13 = \frac{2000}{s} \Rightarrow s = 1000/17$$

Hence, the time taken by Ranatunga to complete the race = $2000 \times 17 \div 1000 = 34$ minutes.
Hence, Option (b) is correct.

24. The distance traveled by B in the initial phase of the race would be double the distance traveled by A during the same time. Likewise, in the second phase of the race, the distance travelled by A would be double the distance traveled by B. Also the total distance traveled by A and B would be 300 m. The only value which creates this symmetrical situation is if the initial phase is such that B travels 200 m and A travels 100 m. Hence, Option (b) is correct.

25. Imagine the circle to be a clock with 12 divisions on the circumference — each division equal to a distance of $4200 \div 12 = 350$ metres. (Imagine these are representing 1 o'Clock to 12 o'Clock for ease of understanding). Since they travel at a ratio of speed as 5:1, imagine Amit travels clockwise and Bimal travels anti clockwise. Their first meeting would occur at the point representing 10 o'Clock, the next at 8 o'clock, then 6 o'clock and so on. It can be seen that the 14th meeting would occur at 8 o'Clock and the 22nd meeting at 4 o'Clock. The longer distance between them would be equal to 8 markings on the clock. This distance would be $8 \times 350 = 2800$ metres. Option (a) is correct.

26. Ravi beats Tarun by 120 seconds or 400 meters. Hence, Tarun's speed is $400 \div 2 = 200$ m/minute. Also, when Ravi does 2000 meters, Tarun does 1600 meters — which he would do in 8 minutes. Thus Ravi takes 8 minutes = 480 seconds to complete the race. Option (d) is correct

## 🎯 BLOCK REVIEW TESTS

## REVIEW TEST 1

1. A man earns $x\%$ on the first ₹ 5,000 of his investment and $y\%$ on the rest of his investment. If he earns ₹ 1250 from ₹ 7,000 and ₹ 1750 from ₹ 9,000 invested, find the value of $x$.
   (a) 20%  (b) 15%
   (c) 25%  (d) None of these

2. The price of a telelvision set drops by 30% while the sales of the set goes up by 50% What is the percentage change in the total revenue from the sales of the set?
   (a) –4%  (b) –2%
   (c) +5%  (d) +2%

3. A person who has a certain amount with him goes to the market. He can buy 100 oranges or 80 mangoes. He retains 20% of the amount for petrol expenses and buys 40 mangoes and of the balance, he purchases oranges. The number of oranges he can purchase is:
   (a) 30  (b) 40
   (c) 15  (d) 20

4. A cloth merchant cheats his supplier and his customer to the tune of 20% while buying and selling cloth respectively. He professes to sell at the cost price but also offers a discount of 20% on cash payment, what is his overall profit percentage?
   (a) 20%  (b) 25%
   (c) 40%  (d) 15%

5. I sold two horses for ₹ 50000 each, one at the loss of 20% and the other at the profit of 20%. What is the percentage of loss (–) or profit (+) that resulted from the transaction?
   (a) (+) 20  (b) (–) 4
   (c) (+) 4  (d) (–) 20

6. The cost of a diamond varies directly as the square of its weight. A diamond fell and broke into four pieces whose weights were in the ratio 1:2:3:4. As a result the merchant had a loss of ₹ 700000. Find the original price of the diamond.
   (a) ₹ 14 lacs  (b) ₹ 20 lacs
   (c) ₹ 10 lacs  (d) ₹ 25 lacs

7. Two oranges, three bananas and four apples cost ₹ 25. Three oranges, two bananas and one apple cost ₹ 20. I brought 3 oranges, 3 bananas and 3 apples. How much did I pay ?
   (a) ₹ 22.5  (b) ₹ 27
   (c) ₹ 30  (d) Cannot be determined

8. From each of two given numbers, half the smaller number is subtracted. Of the resulting numbers the larger one is five times as large as the smaller one. What is the ratio of the two numbers?
   (a) 2: 1  (b) 3: 1
   (c) 3: 2  (d) None of these

**Directions for Questions 9 and 10:** Answer these questions based on the following information.

A watch dealer incurs an expense of ₹ 150 for producing every watch. He also incurs an additional expenditure of ₹ 30,000, which is independent of the number of watches produced. If he is able to sell a watch during the season, he sells it for ₹ 250. If he fails to do so, he has to sell each watch for ₹ 100.

9. If he is able to sell only 1,000 out of 1,500 watches he has made in the season, then he has made a profit of:
   (a) ₹ 90,000  (b) ₹ 75,000
   (c) ₹ 45,000  (d) ₹ 60, 000

10. If he produces 2000 watches, what is the number of watches that he must sell during the season (to the nearest 100) in order to break-even, given that he is able to sell all the watches produced?
    (a) 700  (b) 800
    (c) 900  (d) 1,000

11. A stockist wants to make some profit by selling oil. He contemplates about various methods. Which of the following would maximise his profit?
    I. Sell oil at 20% profit.
    II. Use 800 g of weight instead of 1 kg
    III. Mix 20% impurities in oil and selling it at cost price.
    IV. Increase the price by 10% and reduce weights by 10%.
    (a) I or III  (b) II
    (c) II and IV  (d) Profits are same

12. A dealer offers a cash discount of 20% and still makes a profit of 20%, when he further allows 160 articles when the customer buys 120. How much percent above the cost price were his wares listed?
    (a) 100%  (b) 80%
    (c) 75%  (d) 66(2/3)%

13. A man buys spirit at ₹ 600 per litre, adds water to it and then sells it at ₹ 750 per litre. What is the ratio of the spirit's weight to the weight of the water if his profit in the deal is 37.5%?

(a) 9:1          (b) 10:1

(c) 11:1         (d) None of these

**Directions for Questions 14 to 16:** Answer these questions based on the following information.

Aamir, on his death bed, keeps half his property for his wife and divides the rest equally among his three sons: Bimar, Cumar and Danger. Some years later, Bimar dies, leaving half his property to his widow and half to his brothers, Cumar and Danger together, sharing equally. When Cumar makes his will, he keeps half his property for his widow and the rest he bequeaths to his younger brother Danger. When Danger dies some years later, he keeps half his property for his widow and the remaining for his mother. The mother now has ₹ 15,75,0000

14. What was the worth of the total property?

    (a) ₹ 3 crore        (b) ₹ 0.8 crore

    (c) ₹ 1.8 crore       (d) ₹ 2.4 crore

15. What was Cumar's original share ?

    (a) ₹ 40 lakh        (b) ₹ 120 lakh

    (c) ₹ 60 lakh        (d) ₹ 50 lakh

16. What was the ratio of the property owned by the widows of the three sons, in the end?

    (a) 7:9:13         (b) 8:10:17

    (c) 5:7:9          (d) 9:12:13

17. At a bookstore, "MODERN BOOK STORE" is flashed using neon lights. The words are individually flashed at long intervals of $2\frac{1}{2}$, $4\frac{1}{4}$, $5\frac{1}{8}$ seconds respectively, and each word is put off after a second. The least time after which the full name of the bookstore can be read again, is:

    (a) 49.5 seconds      (b) 73.5 seconds

    (c) 1744.5 seconds    (d) 855 seconds

18. A train approaches a tunnel AB. Inside the tunnel a cat is located at a point that is $2/5^{th}$ the distance AB measured from the entrance A. When the train whistles, the cat runs. If the cat moves to the entrance of the tunnel, A, the train catches the cat exactly at the entrance. If the cat moves to the exit B, the train catches the cat at exactly the exit. The speed of the train is greater than the speed of the cat by what order?

    (a) 3 : 1          (b) 4: 1

    (c) 5: 1          (d) None of these

19. Six technicians working at the same rate complete the work of one server in 2.5 hrs. If one of them starts at 11:00 a.m. and one additional technician per hour is added beginning at 5:00 p.m., at what time the server will be complete?

    (a) 6:40 p.m,        (b) 7 p.m.

    (c) 7:20 p.m.        (d) 8:00 p.m.

**Directions for Questions 20 and 21:** Answer the questions based on the following information.

A thief, after committing the burglary, started fleeing at 12 noon, at a speed of 60 km/hr. He was then chased by a policeman X. X started the chase, 15 min after the thief had started, at a speed of 65 km/hr.

20. At what time did X catch the thief?

    (a) 3.30 p.m.        (b) 3 p.m.

    (c) 3.15 p.m.        (d) None of these

21. If another policeman had started the same chase along with X, but at a speed of 60 km/hr, then how far behind was he when X caught the thief?

    (a) 18.75 km       (b) 15 km

    (c) 21 km         (d) 37.5km

22. Two typists undertake to do a job. The second typist begins working one hour after the first. Three hours after the first typist has begun working, there is still 9/20 of the work to be done. When the assignment is completed, it turns out that each typist has done half the work. How many hours would it take each one to do the whole job individually?

    (a) 12 hr and 8 hr     (b) 8 hr and 5.6 hr

    (c) 10 hr and 8hr      (d) 5 hr and 4 hr

23. A man can walk up a moving 'up' escalator in 30 s. The same man can walk down this moving 'up' escalator in 90s. Assume that his walking speed is same upwards and downwards. How much time will he take to walk up the escalator, when it is not moving?

    (a) 30s           (b) 45s

    (c) 60s           (d) 90s

**Directions for Questions 24 and 26:** Answer the questions based on the following information.

Boston is 4 hr ahead of Frankfurt and 2 hrs behind India. X leaves Frankfurt at 6 p.m. on Friday and reaches Boston the next day. After waiting there for 2 hrs, he leaves exactly at noon and reaches India at 1 a.m. On his return journey, he takes the same route as before, but halts at Boston for 1 hr less than his previous halt there. He then proceeds to Frankfurt.

24. If his journey, including stoppage, is covered at an average speed of 180 mph, what is the distance between Frankfurt and India?

    (a) 3,600 miles      (b) 4,500 miles

    (c) 5580 miles       (d) Data insufficient

25. If X had started the return journey from India at 2.55 a.m. on the same day that he reached there, after how much time would he reach Frankfurt?

    (a) 24 hrs         (b) 25 hrs

    (c) 26 hrs         (d) Data insufficient

26. What is X's average speed for the entire journey (to and fro)?

    (a) 176 mph        (b) 180 mph

    (c) 165 mph        (d) Data insufficient

# REVIEW TEST 2

1. A car after traveling 18 km from a point A developed some problem in the engine and the speed became 4/5th of its original speed. As a result, the car reached point B 45 minutes late. If the engine had developed the same problem after travelling 30 km from A, then it would have reached B only 36 minutes late. The original speed of the car (in km per hour) and the distance between the points A and B (in km) are
   - (a) 25,130
   - (b) 30,150
   - (c) 20,190
   - (d) None of these

2. A, B and C individually can finish a work in 6,8 and 15 hours respectively. They started the work together and after completing the work got ₹ 94.60. when they divide the money among themselves. A, B and C will get respectively (in ₹)
   - (a) 44,33,17.60
   - (b) 43,27,24.60
   - (c) 45,30,19.60
   - (d) 42,28,24.60

3. Two trains are traveling in opposite direction at uniform speed 60 and 50 km per hour respectively. They take 5 seconds to cross each other. If the two trains had traveled in the same direction, then a passenger sitting in the faster moving train would have overtaken the other train in 18 seconds. The length of the trains in metres are
   - (a) 112, 78.40
   - (b) 97.78, 55
   - (c) 102.78, 50
   - (d) 102.78, 55

4. Assume that an equal number of people are born on each day. Find approximately the percentage of the people whose birthday will fall on 29th February.
   - (a) 0.374
   - (b) 0.5732
   - (c) 0.0684
   - (d) None of these.

5. A sum of money compounded annually becomes ₹ 625 in two years and ₹ 675 in three years. The rate of interest per annum is
   - (a) 7%
   - (b) 8%
   - (c) 6%
   - (d) 5%

6. Every day Asha's husband meets her at the city railway station at 6:00 p.m. and drives her to their residence. One day she left early from the office and reached the railway station at 5:00 p.m. She started walking towards her home, met her husband coming from their residence on the way and they reached home 10 minutes earlier than the usual time. For how long did she walk?
   - (a) 1 hour
   - (b) 50 minutes
   - (c) ½ hour
   - (d) 55 minutes

7. Three machines, A, B and C can be used to produce a product. Machine A will take 60 hours to produce a million units. Machine B is twice as fast as Machine A. Machine C will take the same amount of time to produce a million units as A and B running together.

How much time will be required to produce a million units if all the three machines are used simultaneously?
   - (a) 12 hours
   - (b) 10 hours
   - (c) 8 hours
   - (d) 6 hours

8. Mr. and Mrs. Shah travel from City A to City B and break journey at City C in between. Somewhere between City A and City C, Mrs. Shah asks "How far have we travelled?" Mr. Shah replies, "Half as far as the distance from here to city C". Somewhere between City C and City B, exactly 200 km from the point where she asked the first question, Mrs. Shah asks "How far do we have to go?" Mr. Shah replies "Half as far as the distance from City C to here." The distance between Cities A and B in km. is
   - (a) 200
   - (b) 100
   - (c) 400
   - (d) 300

9. A shop sells ball point pens and refills. It used to sell refills for 50 paise each, but there were hardly any takers. When he reduced the price, the remaining refills were sold out enabling the shopkeeper to realize ₹ 35.89. How many refills were sold at the reduced price?
   - (a) 37
   - (b) 71
   - (c) 89
   - (d) 97

10. Anand and Bharat can cut 5 kg of wood in 20 min, Bharat and Chandra can cut 5 kg of wood in 40 min. Chandra and Anand can cut 5 kg. of wood in 30 min. How much time Chandra will take to cut 5 kg of wood alone?
    - (a) 120 minutes
    - (b) 48 minutes
    - (c) 240 minutes
    - (d) (240/7) minutes

11. If 200 soldiers eat 10 tons of food in 200 days, how much will 20 soldiers eat in 20 days?(1ton = 1000 kgs)
    - (a) 1 ton
    - (b) 10 kg
    - (c) 100 kg
    - (d) 50 kg

12. A servant is paid ₹ 100 plus one shirt for a full year of work. He works for 6 months and gets ₹ 30 plus the shirt. What is the cost of the shirt? (in Rupees)?
    - (a) 20
    - (b) 30
    - (c) 40
    - (d) 50

13. A train without stopping travels at 60 km per hour and with stoppages at 40 km per hour. What is the time taken for stoppages on a route of 300 km?
    - (a) 11 hours
    - (b) 22 hours
    - (c) 5 hours
    - (d) 2.5 hours

14. A contractor receives a certain sum every week for paying wages. His own capital together with the weekly sum enables him to pay 45 men for 52 weeks. If he had 60 men and the same wages his capital and

weekly sum would suffice for 13 weeks, how many men can be maintained for 26 weeks?

(a) 60      (b) 52

(c) 50      (d) 65

15. A supply of water lasts for 150 days if 12 gallons leak off every day, but only for 100 days if 15 gallons leak off daily. What is the total quantity of water in the supply?

(a) 900      (b) 1125

(c) 3350      (d) 1250

16. If a dealer were to diminish the selling price of his wares by 10% he would double his sale making the same profit as before. In what ratio would his profit diminish if he were to increase his selling price by 10% and thereby halve his sale?

(a) 2:1.5      (b) 5:4

(c) 1:1.5      (d) 9:7

17. A can is full of paint. Out of this 5 litres are removed and a thinning liquid substituted. The process is repeated. Now the ratio of paint to thinner is 49:15. What is the full capacity of the can?

(a) 20 litres      (b) 60 litres

(c) 40 litres      (d) 50 litres

**Directions for Questions 18 to 20:** Use the following information.

Kachua Bhaiya started to move from point B towards point A exactly an hour after Jiggly Pup started from A in the opposite direction. Kachua Bhaiyas's speed was twice that of Jiggly Pup. When Jiggly Pup had covered one-sixth of the distance between the points A and B, Kachua Bhaiya had also covered the same distance.

18. The point where the two would meet is

(a) Closer to A

(b) Exactly between A and B

(c) Closer to B

(d) P and Q will not meet at all

19. How many hours would Jiggly Pup take to reach B?

(a) 2      (b) 5

(c) 6      (d) 12

**Space for Rough Work**

20. How many more hours would Jiggly Pup (compared to Kachua Bhaiya) take to complete his journey?

(a) 4      (b) 5

(c) 6      (d) 7

21. A group of workers was put on a publishing job. From the second day onwards one worker was withdrawn each day. The job was finished when the last worker was withdrawn. Had no worker been withdrawn at any stage, the group would have finished the job in two-thirds the time. How many workers were there in the group?

(a) 2      (b) 3

(c) 5      (d) 10

22. A ship leaves on a long voyage. When it is 18 miles from the shore, a seaplane, whose speed is ten times that of the ship, is sent to deliver mail. How far from the shore does the seaplane catch up with the ship?

(a) 24 miles      (b) 25 miles

(c) 22 miles      (d) 20 miles

23. One man can do as a woman can do in 2 days. A child does one-third the work in a day as a woman. If an estate-owner hires 39 pairs of hands, men, women and children in the ratio 6:5:2 and pays them in all ₹ 1113 at the end of days work, what must the daily wages of a child be, if the wages are proportional to the amount of work done?

(a) ₹ 14      (b) ₹ 5

(c) ₹ 20      (d) ₹ 7

24. A water tank has three taps A, B and C. A fills four buckets in 24 mins, B fills 8 buckets in 1 hour and C fills 2 buckets in 20 minutes. If all the taps are opened together a full tank is emptied in 2 hours. If a bucket can hold 5 litres of water, what is the capacity of the tank?

(a) 120 litres      (b) 240 litres

(c) 180 litres      (d) 60 litres

25. A man buys spirit at ₹ 60 per litre, adds water to it and then sells it at ₹ 75 per litre. What is the ratio of spirit to water if his profit in the deal is 37.5%?

(a) 9:1      (b) 10:1

(c) 11:1      (d) None of these

# REVIEW TEST 3

1. There is a leak in the bottom of a tank. This leak can empty a full tank in 8 hours. When the tank is full, a tap is opened into the tank which admits 6 litres per hour and the tank is now emptied in 12 hours. What is the capacity of the tank?

   (a) 28.8 litres        (b) 36 litres

   (c) 144 litres         (d) cannot be determined

2. The winning relay team in a high school sports competition clocked 48 minutes for a distance of 13.2 km. Its runners A, B, C and D maintained speeds of 15 kmph, 16, 17 kmph and 18 kmph respectively. What is the ratio of the time taken by B to that taken by D?

   (a) 5:16               (b) 5:17

   (c) 9:8                (d) 8:9

3. Three bells chime at intervals of 18,24 and 32 minutes respectively. At a certain time they begin to chime together. What length of time will elapse before they chime together again?

   (a) 2 hours 24 minutes  (b) 4 hours 48 minutes

   (c) 1 hours 36 minutes  (d) 5 hours

4. In a race of 200 meters run, Ashish beats Sunil by 20 metres and Nalin by 40 metres. If Sunil and Nalin are running a race of 100 metres with exactly the same speeds as before, then by how many metres will Sunil beat Nalin?

   (a) 11.11 metres       (b) 10 metres

   (c) 12 metres          (d) 25 metres

5. A man invests ₹ 3000 at a rate of 5% per annum. How much more should he invest at a rate of 8%, so that he can earn a total of 6% per annum?

   (a) ₹ 1200             (b) ₹ 1300

   (c) ₹ 1500             (d) ₹ 2000

*Use the following data for Questions 6 to 9:* Helitabh and Ruk Ruk are running along a circular course of radius 14 km in opposite directions such that when they meet they reverse their directions as well as they interchange their speeds i.e. after they meet Helitabh will run at the speed of Ruk Ruk and vice-versa. However, this interchange occurs only when they meet outside the starting point. They do not interchange directions or speeds when they meet at the starting point. Initially, the speed of Helitabh is thrice the speed of Ruk Ruk. Assume that they start from $M_0$ and they first meet at $M_1$, then at $M_2$, next $M_3$, and finally at $M_4$.

6. What is the shortest distance between $M_1$ and $M_2$?

   (a) 22 km.             (b) $14\sqrt{2}$ km

   (c) 14 km              (d) 28 km

7. What is the shortest distance between $M_1$ and $M_3$ along the course?

8. Which is the point that coincides with $M_0$?

   (a) $M_1$              (b) $M_2$

   (c) $M_3$              (d) $M_4$

9. What is the distance travelled by Helitabh when they meet at $M_3$?

   (a) 154 km.            (b) 132 km

   (c) 198 km             (d) 176 km

   (a) 44 km              (b) $28\sqrt{2}$ km

   (c) $44\sqrt{2}$ km    (d) 28 km

*Directions for Questions 10 to 12:* A certain race is made up of three stretches A, B and C, each 4 km long, and to be covered by a certain mode of transport. The following table gives these modes of transport for the stretches, and the minimum and maximum possible speeds (in kmph) over these stretches. The speed over a particular stretch is assumed to be constant. The previous record for the race is ten minutes.

| Stretch | Mode of transport | Min. Speed | Max Speed |
|---------|-------------------|------------|-----------|
| A | Car | 80 | 120 |
| B | Motor-cycle | 60 | 100 |
| C | Bicycle | 20 | 40 |

10. Anshuman travels at minimum speed by car over A and completes stretch B at the fastest possible speed. At what speed should he cover stretch C in order to break the previous record?

    (a) Max. speed for C

    (b) Min. speed for C

    (c) This is not possible

    (d) None of these

11. Mr. Hare completes the first stretch at the minimum speed and takes the same time for stretch B. He takes 50% more time than the previous record to complete the race. What is Mr. Hare's speed for the stretch C?

    (a) 21.8 kmph         (b) 26.66 kmph

    (c) 34.2 kmph         (d) None of these

12. Mr. Tortoise completes the race at an average speed of 40 kmph. His average speed for the first two stretches is 4 times that for the last stretch. Find his speed over stretch C.

    (a) 30 kmph           (b) 24 kmph

    (c) 20 kmph           (d) This is not possible

13. After allowing a discount of 11.11% a trader still makes a gain of 20%. At what percent above the cost price does he mark his goods?

    (a) 28.56%            (b) 35%

    (c) 22.22%            (d) None of these

14. A dealer buys oil at ₹ 100, ₹ 80 and ₹ 60 per litre. He mixes them in the ratio 5:6:7 by weight and sells them at a profit of 50%. At what price does he sell oil?

(a) ₹ 80/litre      (b) ₹ 116.666/ litre

(c) ₹ 95/litre      (d) None of these

15. An express train travelling at 80 kmph overtakes a goods train twice as long and going at 40 kmph on a parallel track, in 54 seconds. How long will the express train take to cross a station 400 m long?

     (a) 36 sec      (b) 45 sec

     (c) 27 sec      (d) none of these

16. A man earns x% on the first 2000 rupees and y% on the rest of his income. If he earns ₹ 700 from ₹ 4000 and ₹ 900 from ₹ 5000 of income. Find x.

     (a) 20      (b) 15

     (c) 25      (d) None of these

17. In the famous Harrods museum, the value of each of a set of gold coins varies as the square of its diameter, if its thickness remains constant and it varies as the thickness, if the diameter remains constant. If the diameters of the two coins are in the ratio 4:3, what should the ratio of their thickness be if the value of the first is 4 times that of the second?

     (a) 16:9      (b) 9:4

     (c) 9:16      (d) 4:9

A thief after committing a burglary, started fleeing at 12:00 noon at the speed of 60 kmph. He was then chased by a policeman X. X started the chase 15 minutes after the thief had started at a speed of 65 kmph.

18. At what time did X catch the thief?

     (a) 3:30 p.m.      (b) 3:00 p.m.

     (c) 3:15 p.m.      (d) None of these

19. If another policeman has started the same chase along with X, but at a speed of 60 kmph, then how far behind was he when X caught the thief?

     (a) 18.75 km      (b) 15 km

     (c) 21 km      (d) 47.5 km

20. A and B walk from X to Y, a distance of 27 km at 5 kmph and 7 kmph, respectively. B reaches Y and immediately turns back meeting A at Z. What is the distance from Y to Z?

     (a) 2 km      (b) 4.5 km

     (c) 3 km      (d) 7 km

21. A motorist leaves the post office to go to the airport to collect mail. The plane arrives early, and the mail is sent on a horse-cart. After half an hour, the motorist meets the horse-cart, collects the mail and returns to the post office, thus saving 20 minutes. How many minutes early did the plane arrive?

     (a) 20      (b) 25

     (c) 30      (c) 40

22. In his book on Leonardo da Vinci, Sigmund Freud, after a detailed psychoanalysis concluded that Goethe could complete the masterpiece in nine days as he could channelize overly but was more possessed as a result of which he could generate 50% more efficiency than Goethe. The number of days it takes Leonardo da Vinci to do the same piece of work that Goethe completes in nine days is:

     (a) 4 (1/2) days      (b) 6 days

     (c) 13 (1/2) days      (d) None of these

23. The North South Express is a pair of trains between the cities Jammu & Chennai. A train leaves Jammu for Chennai exactly at 12 noon every day of the week. Similarly, there is a train that leaves from Chennai to Jammu on every day of the week at exactly 12 noon. The time required by a train to cover the distance between Chennai & Jammu is exactly 7 days and 1 minute. Find the number of trains from Chennai to Jammu which a train from Jammu to Chennai will encounter in completing its journey. (Assume all trains run exactly on time).

     (a) 7      (b) 8

     (c) 14      (d) 15

24. For the question above, the minimum number of rakes that the Indian Railways will have to devote for running this daily service will be:

     (a) 16      (b) 32

     (c) 30      (d) None of these

25. There are two candles each of the same initial length. The first candle can burn for 24 hours, while the second candle can burn for 16 hours. Both of them are lit at the same time. After sometime, it was found that one of the candles was twice as long as the second. For how long had the candle been burning?

     (a) 6 hours      (b) 8 hours

     (c) 10 hours      (d) 12 hours

*Space for Rough Work*

# ANSWER KEY

## Review Test 1

| | | | |
|---|---|---|---|
| 1. (b) | 2. (c) | 3. (a) | 4. (a) |
| 5. (b) | 6. (c) | 7. (b) | 8. (b) |
| 9. (c) | 10. (c) | 11. (b) | 12. (a) |
| 13. (b) | 14. (d) | 15. (a) | 16. (b) |
| 17. (b) | 18. (c) | 19. (d) | 20. (c) |
| 21. (b) | 22. (c) | 23. (b) | 24. (b) |
| 25. (a) | 26. (a) | | |

## Review Test 2

| | | | |
|---|---|---|---|
| 1. (d) | 2. (a) | 3. (c) | 4. (c) |
| 5. (b) | 6. (d) | 7. (b) | 8. (d) |
| 9. (d) | 10. (c) | 11. (c) | 12. (c) |
| 13. (d) | 14. (c) | 15. (a) | 16. (a) |
| 17. (c) | 18. (a) | 19. (d) | 20. (c) |
| 21. (b) | 22. (d) | 23. (d) | 24. (b) |
| 25. (b) | | | |

## Review Test 3

| | | | |
|---|---|---|---|
| 1. (c) | 2. (c) | 3. (b) | 4. (a) |
| 5. (c) | 6. (b) | 7. (a) | 8. (d) |
| 9. (a) | 10. (c) | 11. (b) | 12. (c) |
| 13. (b) | 14. (b) | 15. (b) | 16. (b) |
| 17. (b) | 18. (c) | 19. (b) | 20. (b) |
| 21. (d) | 22. (b) | 23. (d) | 24. (a) |
| 25. (d) | | | |

# TASTE OF THE EXAMS—BLOCK II & III

## CAT (1999–2008, 2017)

1. The speed of a railway engine is 42 kmph when no compartment is attached, and the reduction in speed is directly proportional to the square root of the number of compartments attached. If the speed of the train carried by this engine is 24 kmph when 9 compartments are attached, the maximum number of compartments that can be carried by the engine is **(CAT 1999)**
   (a) 49          (b) 48
   (c) 46          (d) 47

2. Total expenses of a boarding house are partly fixed and partly varying linearly with the number of boarders. The average expense per boarder is ₹700 when there are 25 boarders and ₹600 when there are 50 boarders. What is the average expense per boarder when there are 100 boarders? **(CAT 1999)**
   (a) 550          (b) 580
   (c) 540          (d) 570

3. Forty per cent of the employees of a certain company are men, and 75% of the men earn more than ₹25,000 per year. If 45% of the company's employees earn more than ₹25,000 per year, what fraction of the women employed by the company earn less than or equal to ₹25,000 per year? **(CAT 1999)**
   (a) 2/11          (b) 1/4
   (c) 1/3          (d) 3/4

4. Navjivan Express from Ahmedabad to Chennai leaves Ahmedabad at 6.30 a.m. and travels at 50kmph towards Baroda situated 100 km away. At 7.00 a.m. Howrah-Ahmedabad Express leaves Baroda towards Ahmedabad and travels at 40 kmph. At 7.30 a.m. Mr Shah, the traffic controller at Baroda realizes that both the trains are running on the same track. How much time does he have to avert a head-on collision between the two trains? **(CAT 1999)**
   (a) 15 min          (b) 20 min
   (c) 25 min          (d) 30 min

**Directions for question 5 to 6:** The following table presents the sweetness of different forms relative to sucrose, whose sweetness is taken to be 1.00. **(CAT 1999)**

Lactose 0.16
Maltose 0.32
Glucose 0.74
Sucrose 1.00
Fructose 1.70
Saccharin 675.00

5. What is the minimum amount of sucrose (to the nearest gram) that must be added to one-gram of saccharin to make a mixture that will be at least 100 times as sweet as glucose?
   (a) 7          (b) 8
   (c) 9          (d) 100

6. Approximately how many times sweeter than sucrose is a mixture consisting of glucose, sucrose and fructose in the ratio of 1: 2: 3?
   (a) 1.3          (b) 1
   (c) 0.6          (d) 2.3

**Directions for question 7 to 9:** These questions are based on the situation given below.
A road network (shown in the figure below) connects cities A, B, C and D. All road segments are straight lines. D is the midpoint on the road connecting A and C. Roads AB and BC are at right angles to each other with BC shorter than AB. The segment AB is 100 km long. **(CAT 1999)**

Mr. X and Mr. Y leave A at 8: 00 am take different routes to city C and reach at the same time. X takes the highway from A to B to C and travels at an average speed of 61.875 km per hour. Y takes the direct route AC and travels at 45 km per hour on segment AD. Y's speed on segment DC is 55 km per hour. **(CAT 1999)**

7. What is the average speed of Y in km per hour?
   (a) 47. 5          (b) 49.5
   (c) 50          (d) 52

8. The total distance traveled by Y during the journey is approximately
   (a) 105 km          (b) 150 km
   (c) 130 km          (d) Cannot be determined

9. What is the length of the road segment BD?
   (a) 50 km          (b) 52.5 km
   (c) 55 km          (d) Cannot be determined

**Directions for question 10 to 11:** These questions are based on the situation given below.
Rajiv reaches city B from city A in 4 hours, driving at the speed of 35 km per hour for the first 2 hours and at 45 km per hour for the next two hours. Aditi follows the same route, but drives at three different speeds 30, 40 and 50 km per hour,

covering an equal distance in each speed segment. The two cars are similar with petrol consumption characteristics (km per liter) shown in the figure below.  **(CAT 1999)**

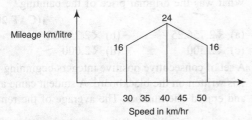

10. The amount of petrol consumed by Aditi for the journey is
    (a) 8.3 liters          (b) 8.6 liters
    (c) 8.9 liters          (d) 9.2 liters

11. Zoheb would like to drive Aditi's car over the same route from A to B and minimize the petrol consumption for the trip. The amount of petrol required by him is  **(CAT 1999)**
    (a) 6.67 liters          (b) 7 liters
    (c) 6.33 liters          (d) None of these.

12. A truck travelling at 70 km/hr uses 30% more diesel to travel a certain distance than it does when it travels at a speed of 50 km/hr. If the truck can travel 19.5 km/L of diesel at 50 km/hr, how far can the truck travel on 10 L of diesel at a speed of 70 km/hr?
    **(CAT 2000)**
    (a) 130 km          (b) 140 km
    (c) 150 km          (d) 175 km

13. Consider a sequence of seven consecutive integers. The average of the first five integers is n. The average of all the seven integers is  **(CAT 2000)**
    (a) n
    (b) n + 1
    (c) k × n, where k is a function of n
    (d) $n + \left(\dfrac{2}{7}\right)$

14. A shipping clerk has five boxes of different but unknown weights each weighing less than 100 kg. The clerk weighs the boxes in pairs. The weights obtained are 110, 112, 113, 114, 115, 116, 117, 118, 120 and 121 kg. What is the weight of the heaviest box?
    **(CAT 2000)**
    (a) 60 kg          (b) 62 kg
    (c) 64 kg          (d) Cannot be determined

15. The table below shows the age-wise distribution of the population of Reposia. The number of people aged below 35 years is 400 million.  **(CAT 2000)**

| Age group | Percentages |
|---|---|
| Below 15 years | 30.00 |
| 15 - 24 | 17.75 |
| 25 - 34 | 17.00 |
| 35 - 44 | 14.50 |
| 45 - 54 | 12.50 |
| 55 - 64 | 7.10 |
| 65 and above | 1.15 |

If the ratio of females to males in the 'below 15 years' age group is 0.96, then what is the number of females (in millions) in that age group?
(a) 82.8          (b) 90.8
(c) 80.0          (d) 90.0

**Directions for questions 16 and 17:** Answer the questions based on the following information.

There are five machines — A, B, C, D, and E — situated on a straight line at distances of 10 m, 20 m, 30 m, 40 m and 50 m respectively from the origin of the line. A robot is stationed at the origin of the line. The robot serves the machines with raw material whenever a machine becomes idle. All the raw materials are located at the origin. The robot is in an idle state at the origin at the beginning of a day. As soon as one or more machines become idle, they send messages to the robot-station and the robot starts and serves all the machines from which it received messages. If a message is received at the station while the robot is away from it, the robot takes notice of the message only when it returns to the station. While moving, it serves the machines in the sequence in which they are encountered, and then returns to the origin. If any messages are pending at the station when it returns, it repeats the process again. Otherwise, it remains idle at the origin till the next message(s) is(are) received.  **(CAT 2000)**

16. Suppose on a certain day, machines A and D have sent the first two messages to the origin at the beginning of the first second, and C has sent a message at the beginning of the 5th second and B at the beginning of the 6th second, and E at the beginning of the 10th second. How much distance has the robot travelled since the beginning of the day, when it notices the message of E? Assume that the speed of movement of the robot is 10 m/s.
    (a) 140 m          (b) 80 m
    (c) 340 m          (d) 360 m

17. Suppose there is a second station with raw material for the robot at the other extreme of the line which is 60 m from the origin, i.e. 10 m from E. After finishing the services in a trip, the robot returns to the nearest station. If both stations are equidistant, it chooses the origin as the station to return to. Assuming that both stations receive the messages

sent by the machines and that all the other data remains the same, what would be the answer to the above question?

(a) 120              (b) 140
(c) 340              (d) 70

**Directions for questions 18 and 19:** The petrol consumption rate of a new model car 'Palto' depends on its speed and may be described by the graph below

**(CAT 2001)**

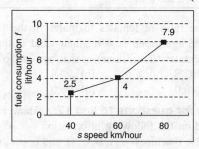

18. Manisha makes the 200 km trip from Mumbai in Pune at a steady speed of 60 km per hour. What is the amount of petrol consumed for the journey?
    (a) 12.5 liters       (b) 13.33 liters
    (c) 16 liters         (d) 19.75 liters

19. Manisha would like to minimize the fuel consumption for the trip by driving at the appropriate speed. How should she change the speed?
    (a) Increase the speed
    (b) Decrease the Speed
    (c) Maintain the speed at 60 km/hour
    (d) Cannot be determined

20. Three runners A, B and C run a race, with runner A finishing 12 meters ahead of runner B and 18 meters ahead of runner C, while runner B finishes 8 meters ahead of runner C. Each runner travels the entire distance at a constant speed. What was the length of the race?                                        **(CAT 2001)**
    (a) 36 meter          (b) 48 meters
    (c) 60 meters         (d) 72 meters

21. A train X departs from station A at 11.00 a.m. for station B, which is 180 km away. Another train Y departs from station B at the same time. Train X travels at an average speed of 70 km/hr and does not stop anywhere until it arrives at station B. Train Y travels at an average speed of 50 km/hr, but has to stop for 15 minutes at station C, which is 60 km away from station B enroute to station A. At what distance (to the closest kilometer) from A would they meet?                                        **(CAT 2001)**
    (a) 112               (b) 118
    (c) 120               (d) 113

22. The owner of an art shop conducts his business in the following manner: every once in a while he raises his prices by X%, then a while later he reduces all the

new prices by X%. After one such updown cycle, the price of a painting decreased by ₹441. After a second up-down cycle the painting was sold for ₹1,944.81. What was the original price of the painting?

**(CAT 2001)**

(a) ₹2,756.25         (b) ₹2,256.25
(c) ₹2,500            (d) ₹2,000

23. A set of consecutive positive integers beginning with 1 is written on the blackboard. A student came along and erased one number. The average of the remaining numbers is $35\frac{7}{17}$. What was the number erased?

**(CAT 2001)**

(a) 7                 (b) 8
(c) 9                 (d) None of these

24. Three math classes: X, Y and Z take an algebra test.

**(CAT 2001)**

The average score in class X is 83.
The average score in class Y is 76.
The average score in class Z is 85.
The average score of all students in classes X and Y together is 79.
The average score of all students in classes Y and Z together is 81.
What is the average for all the three classes?
(a) 81                (b) 81.5
(c) 82                (d) 84.5

25. A can complete a piece of work in 4 days. B takes double the time taken by A, C takes double that of B, and D takes double that of C to complete the same task. They are paired in groups of two each. One pair takes two-thirds the time needed by the second pair to complete the work. Which is the first pair?

**(CAT 2001)**

(a) A and B           (b) A and C
(c) B and C           (d) A and D

26. A college has raised 75% of the amount it needs for a new building by receiving an average donation of ₹600 from the people already solicited. The people already solicited represent 60% of the people the college will ask for donations. If the college is to raise exactly the amount needed for the new building, what should be the average donation from the remaining people to be solicited?   **(CAT 2001)**
    (a) ₹300             (b) ₹250
    (c) ₹400             (d) ₹500

27. At his usual rowing rate, Rahul can travel 12 miles downstream in a certain river in 6 hr less than it takes him to travel the same distance upstream. But if he could double his usual rowing rate for this 24 miles round trip, the downstream 12 miles would then take only 1 hr less than the upstream 12 miles. What is the speed of the current in miles per hour?

**(CAT 2001)**

(a)  7/3      (b)  4/3
(c)  5/3      (d)  8/3

28. Fresh grapes contain 90% water by weight while dried grapes contain 20% water by weight. What is the weight of dry grapes available from 20 kg of fresh grapes? **(CAT 2001)**
(a)  2 kg      (b)  2.4 kg
(c)  2.5 kg      (d)  None of these

**Directions for questions 29 and 30:** Answer the questions based on the following information.

The batting average (BA) of a Test batsman is computed from runs scored and innings played — completed innings and incomplete innings (not out) in the following manner:

$r_1$ = Number of runs scored in completed innings
$n_1$ = Number of completed innings
$r_2$ = Number of runs scored in incomplete innings
$n_2$ = Number of incomplete innings
$BA = (r_1 + r_2)/n_1$

To better assess a batsman's accomplishments, the ICC is considering two other measures $MBA_1$ and $MBA_2$ defined as follows:

$$MBA_1 = \frac{r_1}{n_1} + \frac{n_2}{n_1} \max\left[0, \left(\frac{r_2}{n_2} - \frac{r_1}{n_1}\right)\right]$$

$$MBA_2 = \frac{r_1 + r_2}{n_1 + n_2} \qquad \textbf{(CAT 2001)}$$

29. Based on the above information which of the following is true?
(a)  $MBA_1 \leq BA \leq MBA_2$
(b)  $BA \leq MBA_2 \leq MBA_1$
(c)  $MBA_2 \leq BA \leq MBA_1$
(d)  None of these

30. An experienced cricketer with no incomplete innings has BA of 50. The next time he bats, the innings is incomplete and he scores 45 runs. It can be inferred that
(a)  BA and $MBA_1$ will both increase
(b)  BA will increase and $MBA_2$ will decrease
(c)  BA will increase and not enough data is available to assess change in $MBA_1$ and $MBA_2$
(d)  None of these

31. A train approaches a tunnel AB. Inside the tunnel is a cat located at a point that is 3/8 of the distance AB measured from the entrance A. When the train whistles the cat runs. If the cat moves to the entrance of the tunnel A, the train catches the cat exactly at the entrance. If the cat moves to the exit B, the train catches the cat at exactly the exit. The speed of the train is greater than the speed of the cat by what order? **(CAT 2002)**
(a)  3 : 1      (b)  4 : 1
(c)  5 : 1      (d)  None of these

32. Three small pumps and a large pump are filling a tank. Each of the three small pumps works at 2/3rd the rate of the large pump. If all four pumps work at the same time, they should fill the tank in what fraction of the time that it would have taken the large pump alone? **(CAT 2002)**
(a)  4/7      (b)  1/3
(c)  2/3      (d)  3/4

33. On a 20 km tunnel, connecting two cities A and B, there are three gutters (1, 2 and 3). The distance between gutters 1 and 2 is half the distance between gutters 2 and 3. The distance from city A to its nearest gutter, gutter 1, is equal to the distance of city B from gutter 3. On a particular day, the hospital in city A receives information that an accident has happened at gutter 3. The victim can be saved only if an operation is started within 40 min. An ambulance started from city A at 30 km/hr and crossed gutter 1 after 5 min. If the driver had doubled the speed after that, what is the maximum amount of time would the doctor get to attend the patient at the hospital. Assume 1 min is elapsed for taking the patient into and out of the ambulance? **(CAT 2002)**
(a)  4 min
(b)  2.5 min
(c)  1.5 min
(d)  The patient died before reaching the hospital

34. Only a single rail track exists between stations A and B on a railway line. One hour after the northbound super fast train N leaves station A for station B, a south-bound passenger train S reaches station A from station B. The speed of the super fast train is twice that of a normal express train E, while the speed of a passenger train S is half that of E. On a particular day, N leaves for B from A, 20 min behind the normal schedule. In order to maintain the schedule, both N and S increased their speeds. If the super fast train doubles its speed, what should be the ratio (approximately) of the speeds of passenger train to that of the super fast train so that the passenger train S reaches exactly at the scheduled time at A on that day? **(CAT 2002)**
(a)  1 : 3      (b)  1 : 4
(c)  1 : 5      (d)  1 : 6

35. A milkman mixes 20 liters of water with 80 liters of milk. After selling one-fourth of this mixture, he adds water to replenish the quantity that he had sold. What is the current proportion of water to milk? **(CAT 2004)**
(a)  2 : 3      (b)  1 : 2
(c)  1 : 3      (d)  3 : 4

36. If a man cycles at 10 km/hr, then he arrives at a certain place at 1 p.m. If he cycles at 15 km/hr, he will arrive at the same place at 11 a.m. At what speed must he cycle to get there at noon? **(CAT 2004)**

(a) 11 km/hr      (b) 12 km/hr
(c) 13 km/hr      (d) 14 km/hr

37. Two boats, traveling at 5 and 10 kms per hour, head directly towards each other. They begin at a distance of 20 kms from each other. How far apart are they (in kms) one minute before they collide.

**(CAT 2004)**

(a) 1/12      (b) 1/6
(c) 1/4      (d) 1/3

38. Karan and Arjun run a 100-meter race, where Karan beats Arjun by10 meters. To do a favour to Arjun, Karan starts 10 meters behind the starting line in a second 100 meter race. They both run at their earlier speeds. Which of the following is true in connection with the second race? **(CAT 2004)**

(a) Karan and Arjun reach the finishing line simultaneously.

(b) Arjun beats Karan by 1 meter

(c) Arjun beats Karan by 11 meters.

(d) Karan beats Arjun by 1 meter.

**Directions for Questions 38 and 39:** Answer the questions on the basis of the information given below.

In an examination, there are 100 questions divided into three groups A, B and C such that each group contains at least one question. Each question in group A carries 1 mark, each question in group B carries 2 marks and each question in group C carries 3 marks. It is known that the questions in group A together carry at least 60% of the total marks.

**(CAT 2004)**

39. If group B contains 23 questions, then how many questions are there in Group C?

(a) 1      (b) 2
(c) 3      (d) Cannot be determined

40. If group C contains 8 questions and group B carries at least 20% of the total marks, which of the following best describes the number of questions in group B?

(a) 11 or 12      (b) 12 or 13
(c) 13 or 14      (d) 14 or 15

41. A sprinter starts running on a circular path of radius $r$ meters. Her average speed (in meters/minute) is $\pi r$ during the first 30 seconds, $\dfrac{\pi r}{2}$ during next one minute, $\dfrac{\pi r}{4}$ during next 2 minutes, $\dfrac{\pi r}{8}$ during the next 4 minutes, and so on. What is the ratio of the time taken for the nth round to that for the previous round? **(CAT 2004)**

(a) 4      (b) 8
(c) 16      (d) 32

42. A chemical plant has four tanks (A, B, C and D), each containing 1000 liters of a chemical. The chemical is being pumped from one tank to another as follows.

**(CAT 2005)**

From A to B @ 20 liters/minute
From C to A @ 90 liters/minute
From A to D @ 10 liters/minute
From C to D @ 50 liters/minute
From B to C @ 100 liters/minute
From D to B @ 110 liters/minute

Which tank gets emptied first, and how long does it take (in minutes) to get empty after pumping starts?

(a) A, 16.66      (b) C, 20
(c) D, 20      (d) D, 25

**Directions for questions 43 and 44:** Answer the questions on the basis of the information given below.

Ram and Shyam run a race between points A and B, 5 km apart, Ram starts at 9 a.m from A at a speed of 5 km/hr, reaches B, and returns to A at the same speed, Shyam starts at 9:45 a.m. from A at a speed of 10 km/hr, reaches B and comes back to A at the same speed. **(CAT 2005)**

43. At what time do Ram and Shyam first meet each other?

(a) 10 a.m      (b) 10:10 a.m
(c) 10:20 a.m      (d) 10:30 a.m.

44. At what time does Shyam over take Ram?

(a) 10:20 a.m      (b) 10:30 a.m
(c) 10:40 a.m      (d) 10:50 a.m

45. A telecom service provider engages male and female operators for answering 1000 calls per day. A male operator can handle 40 calls per day whereas a female operator can handle 50 calls per day.

The male and the female operators get a fixed wage of ₹250 and ₹300 per day respectively. In addition, a male operator gets ₹15 per call he answers and female operator gets ₹10 per call she answers. To minimize the total cost, how many male operators should the service provider employ assuming he has to employ more than 7 of the 12 female operators available for the job? **(CAT 2005)**

(a) 15      (b) 14
(c) 12      (d) 10

46. Arun, Barun and Kiranmala start from the same place and travel in the same direction at speeds of 30, 40 and 60 km per hour respectively. Barun starts two hours after Arun. If Barun and Kiranmala overtake Arun at the same instant, how many hours after Arun did Kiranmala start? **(CAT 2006)**

(a) 3      (b) 3.5
(c) 4      (d) 4.5
(e) 5

**Directions for questions 47 and 48:** Answer questions on the basis of the information given below:

An airline has a certain free luggage allowance and charges for excess luggage at a fixed rate per kg. Two passengers, Raja and Praja have 60 kg of luggage between them, and are charged ₹1200 and ₹2400 respectively for excess luggage.

Had the entire luggage belonged to one of them, the excess luggage charge would have been ₹5400.   **(CAT 2006)**

47. What is the weight of Praja's luggage?
    (a) 20kg               (b) 25 kg
    (c) 30 kg              (d) 35 kg
    (e) 40 kg

48. What is the free luggage allowance?
    (a) 10 kg              (b) 15 kg
    (c) 20 kg              (d) 25 kg
    (e) 30 kg

**Directions for Question 49:**   Each question is followed by two statements A and B. Indicate your response based on the following directives.   **(CAT 2007)**

Mark (a) if the question can be answered using A alone but not using B alone.

Mark (b) if the question can be answered using B alone but not using A alone.

Mark (c) if the question can be answered using A and B together, but not using either A or B alone.

Mark (d) if the question cannot be answered even using A and B together.

49. The average weight of a class of 100 students is 45 kg. The class consists of two sections, I and II, each with 50 students. The average weight, $W_I$, of Section I is smaller than the average weight $W_{II}$, of the Section II. If the heaviest student say Deepak, of section II is moved to Section I, and the lightest student, say Poonam, of Section I is moved to Section II, then the average weights of the two sections are switched, i.e., the average weight of Section I becomes $W_{II}$ and that of Section II becomes $W_I$. What is the weight of Poonam?

    A: $W_{II} - W_I = 1.0$.

    B: Moving Deepak from Section II to I (without any move I to II) makes the average weights of the two sections equal.

**Directions for Questions 50 and 51:**   Answer the following questions based on the information given below: Cities A and B are in different time zones. A is located 3000 km east of B. The table below describes the schedule of an airline operating non-stop flights between A and B. All the times indicated are local and on the same day.

| Departure | | Arrival | |
|---|---|---|---|
| City | Time | City | Time |
| B | 8:00 am | A | 3:00 pm |
| A | 4:00 pm | B | 8:00 pm |

Assume that planes cruise at the same speed in both directions. However, the effective speed is influenced by a steady wind blowing from east to west at 50 km per hour.   **(CAT 2007)**

50. What is the time difference between A and B?

(a) 1 hour and 30 minutes
(b) 2 hours
(c) 2 hours and 30 minutes
(d) 1 hour
(e) Cannot be determined

51. What is the plane's cruising speed in km per hour?
    (a) 700               (b) 550
    (c) 600               (d) 500
    (e) Cannot be determined.

**Directions for Questions 52 and 53:**   Answer the following questions based on the information given below: Mr. David manufactures and sells a single product at a fixed price in a niche market. The selling price of each unit is ₹30. On the other hand the cost, in rupees, of producing 'x' units is $240 + bx + cx^2$, where 'b' and 'c' are some constants. Mr. David noticed that doubling the daily production from 20 to 40 units increases the daily production cost by 66.66%. However, an increase in daily production from 40 to 60 units results in an increase of only 50% in the daily production cost. Assume that demand is unlimited and that Mr. David can sell as much as he can produce. His objective is to maximize the profit.   **(CAT 2007)**

52. How many units should Mr. David produce daily?
    (a) 130               (b) 100
    (c) 70                (d) 150
    (e) Cannot be determined

53. What is the maximum daily profit, in rupees, that Mr. David can realize from his business?
    (a) 620               (b) 920
    (c) 840               (d) 760
    (e) Cannot be determined

54. A shop stores x kg of rice. The first customer buys half this amount plus half a kg of rice. The second customer buys half the remaining amount plus half a kg of rice. Then the third customer also buys half the remaining amount plus half a kg of rice. Thereafter, no rice is left in the shop. Which of the following best describes the value of x?   **(CAT 2008)**
    (a) $2 \leq x \leq 6$        (b) $5 \leq x \leq 8$
    (c) $9 \leq x \leq 12$       (d) $11 \leq x \leq 14$
    (e) $13 \leq x \leq 18$

55. In a survey of political preferences, 78 per cent of those asked, were in favour of at least one of the proposals I, II and III. 50 per cent of those asked favoured proposal I, 30 per cent favoured proposal II and 20 per cent favoured proposal III. If 5 per cent of those asked favoured all the three proposals, what percentage of those asked favoured more than one?   **(CAT 1999)**

    (a) 10                (b) 12
    (c) 32                (d) 22

56. A student took five papers in an examination, where the full marks were the same for each paper. His marks in these papers were in the proportion of

6:7:8:9:10. In all papers together, the candidate obtained 60 per cent of the total marks. Then the number of papers in which he got more than 50 per cent marks is: **(CAT 2001)**

(a) 2          (b) 3
(c) 4          (d) 5

57. Every 10 years the Indian government counts all the people living in the country. Suppose that the director of the census has reported the following data on two neighbouring villages—ChotaHazri and MotaHazri. ChotaHazri has 4,522 fewer males than MotaHazri. MotaHazri has 4,020 more females than males. ChotaHazri has twice as many females as males. ChotaHazri has 2,910 fewer females than MotaHazri. What is the total number of males in ChotaHazri?
**(CAT 2001)**

(a) 11264        (b) 14174
(c) 5632         (d) 10154

58. Shyama and Vyom walk up an escalator (moving stairway). The escalator moves at a constant speed. Shyama takes three steps for every two of Vyom's steps. Shyama gets to the top of the escalator after having taken 25 steps, while Vyom (because her slower pace lets the escalator do a little more of the work) takes only 20 steps to reach the top. If the escalator were turned off, how many steps would they have to take to walk up? **(CAT 2001)**

(a) 40         (b) 50
(c) 60         (d) 80

59. A can complete a piece of work in 4 days. B takes double the time taken by A. C takes double that of B, and D takes double that of C to complete the same task. They are paired in groups of two each. One pair takes two-thirds the time needed by the second pair to complete the work. Which is the first pair? **(CAT 2001)**

(a) A, B        (b) A, C
(c) B, C        (d) A, D

60. A lot of work remains while preparing a birthday dinner. Even after the turkey is in the oven, there are still the potatoes and gravy, yams, salad, and cranberries, not to mention setting the table. Three friends, Asit, Arnold and Afzal work together to get all of these chores done. The time it takes them to do the work together is six hours less than Asit would have taken working alone, one hour less than Arnold would have taken alone, and half the time Afzal would have taken working alone. How long did it take them to do these chores working together? **(CAT 2001)**

(a) 20 minutes      (b) 30 minutes
(c) 40 minutes      (d) 50 minutes

61. Two men X and Y started working for a certain company at similar jobs on 1 January 1950. X asked for an initial salary of ₹300 with an annual increment of ₹30. Y asked for an initial salary of ₹200 with a raise of ₹15 every six months. Assume that the arrangements remained unaltered till 31 December 1959. Salary is paid on the last day of the month. What is the total amount paid to them as salary during the period? **(CAT 2001)**

(a) ₹93,300      (b) ₹93,200
(c) ₹93,100      (d) None of these

62. 9 December 2001 is Sunday. What was the day on 9 December 2001, 1971? **(CAT 2001)**

(a) Thursday      (b) Wednesday
(c) Saturday      (d) Sunday

63. Amol was asked to calculate the arithmetic mean of ten positive integers each of which had two digits. By mistake, he interchanged the two digits, say a and b, with one of these ten integers. As a result, his answer for the arithmetic mean was 1.8 more than what it should have been. Then, b – a equals
**(CAT 2002)**

(a) 1         (b) 2
(c) 3         (d) none of these

64. It takes six technicians a total of ten hours to build a new server from Direct Computer, with each working at the same rate. If six technicians start to build the server at 11.00 am, and one technician per hour is added beginning at 5.00 pm, at what time will the server be complete? **(CAT 2002)**

(a) 6:40 pm      (b) 7:00 pm
(c) 7:20 pm      (d) 8 pm

**Answer the questions 65 to 67 on the basis of the information given below.** Consider three circular parks of equal size with centers at $A_1$, $A_2$ and $A_3$ respectively. The parks touch each other at the edge as shown in the figure (not drawn to scale). There are three paths formed by the triangles $A_1A_2A_3$, $B_1B_2B_3$ and $C_1C_2C_3$, as shown. Three sprinters A, B and C begin running from points $A_1$, $B_2$ and $C_1$ respectively. Each sprinter traverses her triangular path clockwise and returns to her starting point.

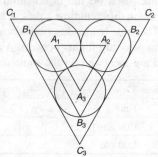

65. Let the radius of each circular park be r, and the distances to be traversed by the sprinters A, B and C be a, b and c, respectively. Which of the following is true? **(CAT 2003)**

(a) $b - a = c - b = 3\sqrt{3}\,r$
(b) $b - a = c - b = \sqrt{3}\,r$
(c) $b = (a+c)/2 = 2(1+\sqrt{3})\,r$
(d) $c = 2b - a = (2+\sqrt{3})\,r$

66. Sprinter A traverses distances $A_1A_2$, $A_2A_3$, and $A_3A_1$ at average speeds of 20, 30 and 15, respectively. B traverses her entire path at a uniform speed of $(10\,3 + 20)$. C traverses distances $C_1C_2$, $C_2C_3$, and $C_3C_1$ at average speeds of $(40/3)(\sqrt{3}+1)$, $(40/3)\sqrt{3}+1)$, and 120, respectively. All speeds are in the same unit. Where would B and C respectively be, when A finishes her sprint? **(CAT 2003)**
(a) $B_1, C_1$
(b) $B_3, C_3$
(c) $B_1, C_3$
(d) $B_1$, Somewhere between $C_3$ and $C_1$

67. Sprinters A, B and C traverse their respective paths at uniform speeds of u, v and w respectively. It is known that $u^2 : v^2 : w^2$ is equal to Area A: Area B: Area C, where Area A, Area B and Area C are the areas of triangles $A_1A_2A_3$, $B_1B_2B_3$, and $C_1C_2C_3$, respectively. Where would A and C be when B reaches point $B_3$? **(CAT 2003)**
(a) $A_2, C_3$
(b) $A_3, C_3$
(c) $A_3, C_2$
(d) Somewhere between $A_2$ and $A_3$, Somewhere between $C_3$ and $C_1$.

68. In a coastal village, every year floods destroy exactly half of the huts. After the flood water recedes, twice the number of huts destroyed are rebuilt. The floods occurred consecutively in the last three years namely 2001, 2002 and 2003. If floods are again expected in 2004, the number of huts expected to be destroyed is: **(CAT 2003)**
(a) Less than the number of huts existing at the beginning of 2001.
(b) Less than the total number of huts destroyed by floods in 2001 and 2003.
(c) Less than the total number of huts destroyed by floods in 2002 and 2003.
(d) More than the total number of huts built in 2001 and 2002.

69. Two straight rods R1 and R2 diverge from a point A at an angle of 120°. Ram starts walking from point A along R1 at a uniform speed of 3 km/hr. Shyam starts walking at the same time from A along R2 at a uniform speed of 2 km/h. They continue walking for 4 hours along their respective roads and reach points B and C on R1 and R2, respectively. There is a straight line path connecting B and C. Then, Ram returns to point A after walking along the line segments BC and CA. Shyam also returns to A after walking along line segments CB and BA. Their speeds remain unchanged. The time interval (in

hours) between Ram's and Shyam's return to point A is: **(CAT 2003)**
(a) $(10\sqrt{19}+26)/3$ (b) $(2\sqrt{19}+10)/3$
(c) $(\sqrt{19}+26)/3$ (d) $(\sqrt{19}+10)/3$

70. In a nuts and bolts factory, one machine produces only nuts at the rate of 100 nuts per minute and needs to be cleaned for 5 minutes after production of every 1000 units. Another machine produces only bolts at the rate of 75 bolts per minute and needs to be cleaned for 10 minutes after production of every 1500 bolts. If both the machines start production at the same time, what is the minimum duration required for producing 9000 pairs of nuts and bolts? **(CAT 2004)**
(a) 130 minutes (b) 135 minutes
(c) 170 minutes (d) 180 minutes

71. If $a/b = 1/3$, $b/c = 2$, $c/d = 1/2$, $d/e = 3$ and $e/f = 1/4$, then what is the value of $abc/def$? **(CAT 2006)**
(a) 3/8 (b) 27/8
(c) 3/4 (d) 27/4
(e) 1/4

72. Ten years ago, the ages of the members of a joint family of eight people added up to 231 years. Three years later, one member died at the age of 60 years and a child was born during the same year. After another three years, one more member died, again at 60, and a child was born during the same year. The current average age of this eight-member joint family is nearest to: **(CAT 2007)**
(a) 23 years (b) 22 years
(c) 21 years (d) 25 years
(e) 24 years

**Directions for Questions 73 and 74:** Shabnam is considering three alternatives to invest her surplus cash for a week. She wishes to guarantee maximum returns on her investment. She has three options, each of which can be utilised fully or partially in conjunction with others.

*Option A:* Invest in a public sector bank. It promises a return of + 0.10%.

*Option B:* Invest in mutual funds of ABC Ltd. A rise in the stock market will result in a return of + 5%, while a fall will entail a return of –3%.

*Option C:* Invest in mutual funds of CBA Ltd. A rise in the stock market will result in a return of –2.5%, while a fall will entail a return of + 2%.

73. The maximum guaranteed return to Shabnam is: **(CAT 2007)**
(a) 0.25% (b) 0.10%
(c) 0.20% (d) 0.15%
(e) 0.30%

74. Which strategy will maximise the guaranteed return to Shabnam? **(CAT 2007)**

(a) 100% in option A

(b) 36% in option B and 64% in option C

(c) 64% in option B and 36% in option C

(d) 1/3 in each of the three options

(e) 30% in option A, 32% in option B and 38% in option

75. Rahim plans to drive from city A to station C, at the speed of 70 km per hour, to catch a train arriving there from B. He must reach C at least 15 minutes before the arrival of the train. The train leaves B, located 500 km south of A, at 8:00 am and travels at a speed of 50 km per hour. It is known that C is located between west and northwest of B, with BC at 60° to AB. Also, C is located between south and south west of A with AC at 30° to AB. The latest time by which Rahim must leave A and still catch the train is closest to **(CAT 2008)**

(a) 6:15 am      (b) 6:30 am

(c) 6:45 am      (d) 7:00 am

(e) 7:15 am

76. In Coorg, the production of tea is three times the production of coffee. If a percent more tea and b percent more coffee were produced, the aggregate amount would be 5c percent more. But if b percent more tea and a percent more coffee were produced, the aggregate amount produced would be 3c percent more. What is the ratio a : b ? **(CAT 2009)**

(a) 1 : 3      (b) 1 : 2

(c) 2 : 1      (d) 3 : 1

77. A group of men was employed to shift 545 crates. Every day after the first, 6 more men than the previous day were put on the job. Also, every day after the first, each man working, shifted 5 fewer crates than the number of crates moved by each man the previous day. The result was that during the latter part of the period, the number of crates shifted per day began to go down. 5 days were required to finish the work. What was the number of crates shifted on the third day? **(CAT 2009)**

(a) 137      (b) 169

(c) 26      (d) 152

78. The velocity of a motorboat in still water is 20 km/hr. The current of the river is 6 km/hr. The boat must land at a point directly opposite on the other bank. Taking due care of the current of the river, the required resultant velocity of the boat is nearest to **(CAT 2010)**

(a) 18.5 km/h      (b) 19 km/h

(c) 19.5 Km/h      (d) 18 Km/h

79. The average of N numbers is X. If one of the numbers A is replaced by another number B, the new average is Y. The new number B equals: **(CAT 2010)**

(a) $NY - NX - A$      (b) $N(Y - x)$

(c) $N(Y - X) + A$      (d) $(X - Y)N - A$

80. A person bought some horses at ₹500 each, Sheep at ₹400 each, goats at ₹250 each and dogs at ₹100 each. The average price of animals per head worked out to be ₹300. Which of the following is not a possible value for the number of animals he bought? **(CAT 2010)**

(a) 24      (b) 15

(c) 21      (d) 32

81. At the end of year 1998, Shepard bought nine dozen goats. Henceforth, every year he added p per cent of the goats at the beginning of the year and sold q per cent of the goats at the end of the year where p > 0 and q > 0. If Shepard had nine dozen goats at the end of year 2002, after making the sales for that year, which of the following is true? **(CAT 2011)**

(a) p = q      (b) p < q

(c) p > q      (d) p = q/2

82. A leather factory produces two kinds of bags, standard and deluxe. The profit margin is ₹20 on a standard bag and ₹30 on a deluxe bag. Every bag must be processed on machine A and B. The processing time per bag on the two machines are as follows: Time required (Hours/bag) Machine A Machine B Standard Bag 4 6 Deluxe Bag 5 10 The total time available on machine A is 700 hours and on machine B is 1250 hours. Among the following production plans, which one meets the machine availability constraints and maximises the profit? **(CAT 2003)**

(a) Standard 75 bags, Deluxe 80 bags

(b) Standard 100 bags Deluxe 60 bags

(c) Standard 50 bags, Deluxe 100 bags

(d) Standard 60 bags, Deluxe 90 bags

**Directions for Questions 83 to 85:** Answer the questions on the basis of the information given below. A city has two perfectly circular and concentric ring roads, the outer ring road (OR) being twice as long as the inner ring road (IR). There are also four (straight line) chord roads from E1, the east end point of OR to N2, the north end point of IR; from N1, the north end point of OR to W2, the west end point of IR; from W1, the west end point of OR, to S2, the south end point of IR and from S1, the south end point of OR to E2, the east end point of IR.; Traffic moves at a constant speed of $30\pi$ km/hr on the IR road, and the OR road; $15\sqrt{5}$ km/hr on all the chord roads.

83. The ratio of the sum of the lengths of all chord roads to the length of the outer ring road is **(CAT 2003)**

(a) $\sqrt{5} : 2$      (b) $\sqrt{5} : 2\pi$

(c) $\sqrt{5} : \pi$      (d) None of the above

84. Amit wants to reach N2 from S1. It would take him 90 minutes if he goes on minor arc S1-E1 on OR, and then on the chord road E1-N2. What is the radius of the outer ring road in kms? **(CAT 2003)**

(a) 60      (b) 40

(c) 30      (d) 20

85. Amit wants to reach E2 from N1 using first the chord N1-W2 and then the inner ring road. What will be his travel time in minutes on the basis of information given in the above question? **(CAT 2003)**
   - (a) 60
   - (b) 45
   - (c) 90
   - (d) 105

**Directions for Questions 86 & 87:** Answer the questions on the basis of the information given below. A certain perfume is available at a duty-free shop at the Bangkok International Airport. It is priced in Thai currency–Baht, but other currencies are also acceptable. In particular, the shop accepts Euro and US Dollar at the following rates of exchange:

US Dollar 1 = 41 Bahts; Euro 1 = 46 Bahts.

The perfume is priced at 520 Bahts per bottle. After one bottle is purchased, subsequent bottles are available at a discount of 30 per cent. Three friends S, R and M together purchase three bottles of the perfume, agreeing to share the cost equally. R pays 2 Euros, M pays 4 Euros and 27 Thai Bahts and S pays the remaining amount in US Dollars.

86. How much does R owe to S in Thai Baht? **(CAT 2003)**
   - (a) 428
   - (b) 416
   - (c) 334
   - (d) 324

87. How much does M owe to S in US Dollars? **(CAT 2003)**
   - (a) 3
   - (b) 4
   - (c) 5
   - (d) 6

88. In a 10 km race, A, B, and C, each running at uniform speed, get the gold, silver, and bronze medals, respectively. If A beats B by 1 km and B beats C by 1 km, then by how many metres does A beat C? **(CAT 2017)**

89. Bottle 1 contains a mixture of milk and water in 7 : 2 ratio and Bottle 2 contains a mixture of milk and water in 9 : 4 ratio. In what ratio of volumes should the liquids in Bottle 1 and Bottle 2 be combined to obtain a mixture of milk and water in 3 : 1 ratio? **(CAT 2017)**
   - (a) 27 : 14
   - (b) 27 : 13
   - (c) 27 : 16
   - (d) 27 : 18

90. Arun drove from home to his hostel at 60 miles per hour. While returning home he drove half way along the same route at a speed of 25 miles per hour and then took a bypass road which increased his driving distance by 5 miles, but allowed him to drive at 50 miles per hour along this bypass road. If his return journey took 30 minutes more than his onward journey, then the total distance traveled by him is: **(CAT 2017)**
   - (a) 55 miles
   - (b) 60 miles
   - (c) 65 miles
   - (d) 70 miles

91. Out of the shirts produced in a factory, 15% are defective, while 20% of the rest are sold in the domestic market. If the remaining 8840 shirts are left for export, then the number of shirts produced in the factory is **(CAT 2017)**
   - (a) 13600
   - (b) 13000
   - (c) 13400
   - (d) 14000

92. The average height of 22 toddlers increases by 2 inches when two of them leave this group. If the average height of these two toddlers is one-third the average height of the original 22, then the average height, in inches, of the remaining 20 toddlers is **(CAT 2017)**
   - (a) 30
   - (b) 28
   - (c) 32
   - (d) 26

93. The manufacturer of a table sells it to a wholesale dealer at a profit of 10%. The wholesale dealer sells the table to a retailer at a profit of 30%. Finally, the retailer sells it to a customer at a profit of 50%. If the customer pays ₹4290 for the table, then its manufacturing cost (in ₹) is **(CAT 2017)**
   - (a) 1500
   - (b) 2000
   - (c) 2500
   - (d) 3000

94. A tank has an inlet pipe and an outlet pipe. If the outlet pipe is closed then the inlet pipe fills the empty tank in 8 hours. If the outlet pipe is open then the inlet pipe fills the empty tank in 10 hours. If only the outlet pipe is open then in how many hours the full tank becomes half-full? **(CAT 2017)**
   - (a) 20
   - (b) 30
   - (c) 40
   - (d) 45

95. Mayank buys some candies for ₹15 a dozen and an equal number of different candies for ₹12 a dozen. He sells all for ₹16.50 a dozen and makes a profit of ₹150. How many dozens of candies did he buy altogether? **(CAT 2017)**
   - (a) 50
   - (b) 30
   - (c) 25
   - (d) 45

96. In a village, the production of food grains increased by 40% and the per capita production of food grains increased by 27% during a certain period. The percentage by which the population of the village increased during the same period is nearest to **(CAT 2017)**
   - (a) 16
   - (b) 13
   - (c) 10
   - (d) 7

97. If a, b, c are three positive integers such that a and b are in the ratio 3:4 while b and c are in the ratio 2: 1, then which one of the following is a possible value of (a + b + c)? **(CAT 2017)**
   - (a) 201
   - (b) 205
   - (c) 207
   - (d) 210

98. A motorbike leaves point A at 1 pm and moves towards point B at a uniform speed. A car leaves point B at 2 pm and moves towards point A at a uniform

speed, which is double that of the motorbike. They meet at 3:40 pm at a point, which is 168 km away from A. What is the distance, in km, between A and B? **(CAT 2017)**

(a) 364      (b) 378

(c) 380      (d) 388

99. Amal can complete a job in 10 days and Bimal can complete it in 8 days. Amal, Bimal and Kamal together complete the job in 4 days and are paid a total amount of ₹1000 as remuneration. If this amount is shared by them in proportion to their work, then Kamal's share, in rupees, is **(CAT 2017)**

(a) 100      (b) 200

(c) 300      (d) None of these

100. Consider three mixtures - the first having water and liquid A in the ratio 1 : 2, the second having water and liquid B in the ratio 1 : 3, and the third having water and liquid C in the ratio 1 : 4. These three mixtures of A, B, and C, respectively, are further mixed in the proportion 4 : 3 : 2. Then the resulting mixture has **(CAT 2017)**

(a) The same amount of water and liquid B

(b) The same amount of liquids B and C

(c) More water than liquid B

(d) More water than liquid A

101. Arun's present age in years is 40% of Barun's. In another few years, Arun's age will be half of Barun's. By what percentage will Barun's age increase during this period? **(CAT 2017)**

102. A person can complete a job in 120 days. He works alone on Day 1. On Day 2, he is joined by another person who also can complete the job in exactly 120 days. On Day 3, they are joined by another person of equal efficiency. Like this, everyday a new person with the same efficiency joins the work. How many days are required to complete the job? **(CAT 2017)**

103. An elevator has a weight limit of 630 kg. It is carrying a group of people of whom the heaviest weighs 57 kg and the lightest weighs 53 kg. What is the maximum possible number of people in the group? **(CAT 2017)**

104. A man leaves his home and walks at a speed of 12 km per hour, reaching the railway station 10 minutes after the train had departed. If instead he had walked at a speed of 15 km per hour, he would have reached the station 10 minutes before the train's departure. The distance (in km) from his home to the railway station is **(CAT 2017)**

105. Ravi invests 50% of his monthly savings in fixed deposits. Thirty percent of the rest of his savings is invested in stocks and the rest goes into Ravi's savings bank account. If the total amount deposited by him in the bank (for savings account and fixed deposits) is ₹59500, then Ravi's total monthly savings (in ₹) is? **(CAT 2017)**

106. If a seller gives a discount of 15% on retail price, she still makes a profit of 2%. Which of the following ensures that she makes a profit of 20%? **(CAT 2017)**

(a) Give a discount of 5% on retail price

(b) Give a discount of 2% on retail price

(c) Increase the retail price by 2%

(d) Sell at retail price

107. A man travels by a motor boat down a river to his office and back. With the speed of the river unchanged, if he doubles the speed of his motor boat, then his total travel time gets reduced by 75%. The ratio of the original speed of the motor boat to the speed of the river is? **(CAT 2017)**

(a) $\sqrt{6} : \sqrt{2}$      (b) $\sqrt{7} : 2$

(c) $2\sqrt{5} : 3$      (d) $3 : 2$

108. Suppose C1, C2, C3, C4, and C5 are five companies. The profits made by C1, C2, and C3 are in the ratio 9 : 10 : 8 while the profits made by C2, C4, and C5 are in the ratio 18 : 19 : 20. If C5 has made a profit of ₹19 crore more than C1, then the total profit (in ₹) made by all five companies is: **(CAT 2017)**

(a) 438 crore      (b) 435 crore

(c) 348 crore      (d) 345 crore

109. The number of girls appearing for an admission test is twice the number of boys. If 30% of the girls and 45% of the boys get admission, the percentage of candidates who do not get admission is: **(CAT 2017)**

(a) 35      (b) 50

(c) 60      (d) 65

110. A stall sells popcorn and chips in packets of three sizes: large, super, and jumbo. The numbers of large, super, and jumbo packets in its stock are in the ratio 7 : 17 : 16 for popcorn and 6 : 15 : 14 for chips. If the total number of popcorn packets in its stock is the same as that of chips packets, then the numbers of jumbo popcorn packets and jumbo chips packets are in the ratio **(CAT 2017)**

(a) 1 : 1      (b) 8 : 7

(c) 4 : 3      (d) 6 : 5

111. In a market, the price of medium quality mangoes is half that of good mangoes. A shopkeeper buys 80 kg good mangoes and 40 kg medium quality mangoes from the market and then sells all these at a common price which is 10% less than the price at which he bought the good ones. His overall profit is: **(CAT 2017)**

(a) 6%      (b) 8%

(c) 10%      (d) 12%

112. If Fatima sells 60 identical toys at a 40% discount on the printed price, then she makes 20% profit. Ten of these toys are destroyed in fire. While selling the

rest, how much discount should be given on the printed price so that she can make the same amount of profit? **(CAT 2017)**

(a) 30%     (b) 25%
(c) 24%     (d) 28%

## ANSWER KEY

| | | | |
|---|---|---|---|
| 1. (b) | 2. (a) | 3. (d) | 4. (b) |
| 5. (b) | 6. (a) | 7. (b) | 8. (a) |
| 9. (b) | 10. (c) | 11. (a) | 12. (c) |
| 13. (b) | 14. (b) | 15. (b) | 16. (a) |
| 17. (a) | 18. (b) | 19. (b) | 20. (b) |
| 21. (a) | 22. (a) | 23. (a) | 24. (b) |
| 25. (d) | 26. (a) | 27. (b) | 28. (c) |
| 29. (d) | 30. (b) | 31. (b) | 32. (b) |
| 33. (c) | 34. (d) | 35. (a) | 36. (b) |
| 37. (c) | 38. (d) | 39. (a) | 40. (c) |
| 41. (c) | 42. (c) | 43. (b) | 44. (b) |
| 45. (d) | 46. (c) | 47. (d) | 48. (b) |
| 49. (c) | 50. (d) | 51. (b) | 52. (b) |
| 53. (d) | 54. (b) | 55. (c) | 56. (c) |
| 57. (c) | 58. (b) | 59. (d) | 60. (c) |
| 61. (a) | 62. (a) | 63. (b) | 64. (d) |
| 65. (a) | 66. (c) | 67. (b) | 68. (c) |
| 69. (b) | 70. (c) | 71. (a) | 72. (e) |
| 73. (c) | 74. (b) | 75. (b) | 76. (d) |
| 77. (b) | 78. (b) | 79. (c) | 80. (a) |
| 81. (c) | 82. (a) | 83. (c) | 84. (c) |
| 85. (c) | 86. (d) | 87. (c) | 88. 1900 |
| 89. (b) | 90. (c) | 91. (b) | 92. (c) |
| 93. (b) | 94. (a) | 95. (a) | 96. (c) |
| 97. (c) | 98. (b) | 99. (a) | 100. (c) |
| 101. 20 | 102. 15 | 103. 11 | 104. 20 |
| 105. 70,000 | 106. (d) | 107. (b) | 108. (a) |
| 109. (d) | 110. (a) | 111. (b) | 112. (d) |

### Solutions

1. The equation that will fit the situation is: $S = 42 - K\sqrt{n}$. At n = 9, S = 24. Thus, putting these values in the equation we get: 24 = 42-3K. Hence, K = 6. So the equation becomes $42 - 6\sqrt{n}$. At n = 49, the value of S would become equal to 0, thus, the railway engine can carry a maximum of 48 compartments (option (b)).

2. For 25 boarders, the total cost is ₹17,500 and for 50 boarders, the total cost is 30000. Thus, the cost is increasing by ₹12,500 when 25 new boarders are added to the boarding house. Thus, the variable cost is ₹500 per boarder (12500/25). So for 100 boarders, the total cost would be ₹30000 + ₹25000 = ₹55000. The required average is 55000/100 = ₹550

Alternately, you can solve this through equations as follows:

Let 'a' be the fixed cost and 'b' the variable cost

According to the question:

$$700 \times 25 = a + 25b \qquad (1)$$
$$600 \times 50 = a + 50b \qquad (2)$$

Solving the equation (1) and (2), we get

a = 5000, b = 500

Let the average expense of 100 boarders be 'X'. Then

$$100 \times X = 5000 + (500 \times 100)$$
$$\therefore \quad X = 550$$

3. Forty per cent are men and 60 per cent are women. Out of the men category, 75 per cent earn more than 25000 per year. Thus, a total of 30 per cent of the total employees of the company are males who earn more than 25000 per year. Since, there are a total of 45 per cent of the employees who earn more than 25000 per year, it means that out of the 60 per cent who are women 15 per cent earn more than 25000 and 45 per cent earn ₹25000 or less than that per year. Thus, the required ratio is 3/4 (option (d)).

4. The distance between Ahmedabad and Baroda being 100 kms, it is evident that by 7:30 am, Navjivan Express would have covered 50 kms (travelling @ 50kmph for 1hour), while the Howrah-Ahmedabad Express would have covered 20 kms (travelling 40 kmph for 30 minutes). Thus, the distance between the two trains would be 30 kms at 7:30 am. Since their relative speed is 90 kmph, the remaining distance of 30 kms would be covered in 1/3rd of an hour - or 20 minutes. Option (b)is correct.

5. If we mix 8 grams of sucrose to 1 gram of saccharine, we would have 9 grams with a sweetness quotient of 683. The average sweetness would be 683/9 = 75.88 which is greater than 100 times the sweetness of sucrose. If we mix 9 grams of sucrose to 1 gram of saccharine, the average would be below 74. Hence, option (b) is the required answer.

6. The average sweetness of the mixture as defined would be: (1x0.74 + 2x1 + 3x 1.7)/6 = 7.84/6 = 1.306. Thus, option (a) is correct.

7. As D is the midpoint of AC. So AD = DC

Y covers two equal distances AD and CD with speeds 45 kmph and 55 kmph respectively. Therefore the average speed of y must be $\dfrac{2 \times 45 \times 55}{45 + 55} = 49.5$ kmph.

Alternately, you could also think of this as:

The average speed for Y would be the weighted average of 45 and 55 in the ratio 55:45 (as the distance on both the segments AD and DC are equal). The value would be 49.5 (option (b)).

8. According to the question X and Y reach C at the same time therefore:

$$\frac{100 + BC}{61.875} = \frac{AC}{49.5}$$

$$BC = \sqrt{AC^2 - 100^2}$$

$$\frac{100 + \sqrt{AC^2 - 100^2}}{61.875} = \frac{AC}{49.5}$$

Now put the value of AC from the option and check. We get that for AC = 105, LHS = RHS.

Alternately, you could think as follows.

Since ABC is a right triangle, and D is the midpoint of the hypotenuse BD, it would be half the length of the hypotenuse. Question 8 is asking for the length of AC, while question 9 is asking for the length of BD. Looking at the information contained in the question, it is evident that these distances would not come under the cannot be determined category. Thus, we can solve questions 8 and 9simultaneously by looking at a value for the answer to 9, which should be half the answer to question 8. Thus, the answer to question 8 is :105 km (as that is the only value that fits).

9. AC = 105 km and D is the midpoint of AC. So, AD = DC = BD = 105/2 = 52.5 km

10. The distance between City A and City B would be $45 \times 2 + 35 \times 2 = 160$ kms (as per Rajiv's movement plan). Aditi would cover this distance in three equal parts of 53.33 kms @ of 30 kmph, 40 kmph and 50 kmph respectively.

Petrol consumed by Aditi = 53.33/16 + 53.33/24 + 53.33/16 = 160/48 + 160/72 + 160/48 = 640/72 = 8.9 liters (option (c)).

11. The distance between City A and City B would be $45 \times 2 + 35 \times 2 = 160$ kms (as per Rajiv's movement plan). Aditi would cover this distance in three equal parts of 53.33 kms @ of 30 kmph, 40 kmph and 50 kmph respectively.

In order to minimise the amount of petrol consumed, the journey should be traversed at 40 kmph (since the Highest mileage for the car is at that speed). Thus, the amount of fuel required would be 160/24 = 6.67 liters (option (a)).

12. If the fuel efficiency at 50 kmphis 19.5 km per liter, then at 70 kmph, the fuel efficiency would be 15 km per liter (since it uses 30% more fuel when it travels at 70 kmph as compared to traveling at 50 kmph). @ 15 km/liter, the truck would travel 150 kms in 10 liters of fuel.

13. The average of the 5 consecutive integers is the middle integer which is third integer, and the average of the 7 consecutive integers is the middle integer which is the fourth integer. Hence, it is one more than the average of five consecutive integers.

This can be verified experimentally by taking any 7 consecutive integers and checking for the averages of the first five and all 7 respectively. You can easily see that the average of all 7 would always be 1 more than the average of the first five of these integers.

14. We can solve this problem by taking the weight of the heaviest box from the options.

Option (a): If the weight of the heaviest box is 60 kg then to arrive at 121 kg, the other box will have to weigh 61 kg so this option can never be true.

Option (c): If the weight of the heaviest box is 64 then to get a total of 121 kg, the other weight will have to be 57 and to get a total 120 kg, the next box shall have a weight 63 kg. In this case the maximum possible total weight of the two boxes would be 64 + 63 = 127, which is again not possible.

Option (b): If the weight of the heaviest box is 62 kg then second heaviest box = 121- 62 = 59 kg.

Other possible combinations are 120 = 62 + 58, 118 = 62 + 56, 117 = 59 + 58, 116 = 62 + 54, 115 = 59 + 56, 113 = 59 + 54, 112 = 58 + 54, 110 = 56 + 54.

Thus, the weights of five boxes are 62, 59, 58, 56, 54kg.

Hence, option b is correct.

15. Number of people below 35 years = 30 + 17.75 + 17 = 64.75% of total population = 400 million

Total population = 617.76 million

Population below 15 years = 30% of 617.76 million = 185.32 million

Number of females in the below 15 age group = $\frac{0.96}{1.96}$ × 185.32 = 90.8 million

16. 

$OA = AB = BC = CD = DE = 10$ m

After receiving the message from A and D the robot begins to move to give material to machine A and then to machine D, it thus covers 10 + 30 = 40. It will take 4 seconds to reach D.

Then it returns back to the origin and covers 40 m again. When it arrives at the origin (after 8 seconds from beginning), the messages of B and C are already there, thus it moves to give the material to B and C and returns back to origin, for which it covers 30 + 30 = 60 m in total.

Hence, the total distance travelled by the robot (when it notices the message of E) will be 40 m + 40 m + 60 m = 140 m.

17. The roboting travelling would be from A to D to second raw material station (as that would be closer), a distance of 60 meters covered by the end of the sixth second. It would see the messages from C and B when it reaches the second station and move towards C and

then B and then go on to the origin. A total of 120 meters would be traversed before it sees the message from E.

18. At 60 kmph she consumes 4 liters per hour or goes 15 km per liter. Hence, she would use 200/15 = 13.33 liters of petrol for the journey.

19. The fuel consumption at 40 kmph = $\frac{200}{40} \times 2.5 = 12.5$ L

The fuel consumption at 60 kmph = $\frac{200}{60} \times 4 = 13.33$ L

The fuel consumption at 80 kmph = $\frac{200}{80} \times 7.9 = 19.75$ L

So Manisha has to decrease the speed.

The fuel efficiency per liter can be seen to be 15 kmpl at speeds of 15 kmpl – This has to be interpreted as: In one hour she travels 60 km (@60 kmph) and consumes 4 liters of fuel. Hence, her fuel consumption is 15 kmpl. If she increases her speed from 60 kmph, the graph clearly shows that her fuel consumption goes down. However, if she reduces her speed, her fuel efficiency goes up to 16 kmpl. Hence, she should reduce her speed.

20. Solve through options using unitary method. If the race was 36 meters long, the ratio of distances would be 36:24:18. This would not translate to a winning distance of 8 meters for B over C. For the second option, if the race was 48 meters, the ratio would be 48:36:30. This would translate into a ratio of B:C as 48:40 giving B a win by 8 meters as required in the problem. Hence, this answer is correct.

21. It can be seen that in effect the train Y is starting at 11:15 AM. In the 15 minutes that Y is stopping, only X would be covering some distance. That distance would be equal to 17.5 km. Hence, the remaining distance of 162.5 km would have to be covered by them together at a relative speed of 120 kmph. This would take 162.5/120 hours. The distance from A would then be given by: 17.5 + (162.5/120) × 70 = 112 km approx.

22. In both the cases, the price of the painting would reduce by the same percentage value. Going through the options, it is evident that options (b) and (d) would not be correct since, if we start with those options, we would find that a drop of 441 itself would take the value lower than 1944.81 (which we need after 2 such drops). Even on trying to reduce 2500 consecutively in such a manner that it reduces by 441 the first time and replicating the same percentage change the second time too—our end value would be much lower than the required 1944.81. Hence, the only possible answer, which fits the situation is 2756.25, which is the correct answer.

23. As the value of average of remaining numbers has 17 in the denominator so the value of the number of the remaining numbers must be an integer multiple of 17 and the average of these numbers must be greater than 35.

So the original number of numbers must be 17k + 1 (18, 35, 52, 69…..)

Average of $n$ consecutive numbers = $\frac{n+1}{2}$

For n = 18, 35, 52 the average would be 9.5, 18 and 26.5 respectively. So we can rule out these possibilities.

Now check for n = 69 the sum of total 69 numbers = $\frac{69(69+1)}{2} = 2415$.

Sum of remaining 68 numbers = $35\frac{7}{17} \times 68 = 2408$

This gives us that the number to be erased must be 7.

24. Given that the average of X and Y is 79, the ratio of the number of students in the two classes would be 3:4. (Using Alligation) Also, the ratio of number of students in Y and Z would be 4:5. Hence, the overall average would be 3:4:5.

Using weighted average the required average = $\frac{3 \times 83 + 4 \times 76 + 5 \times 85}{3+4+5} = 81.5$

25. Efficiency is inversely proportional to the time taken to complete the work. So if B takes double the time taken by A, his efficiency is half that of A. Let the efficiencies of D, C, B and A are X, 2X, 4X and 8X respectively.

According to the question, one pair takes two-thirds the time needed by the second pair to complete the work. It means, one pair has $\frac{1}{\frac{2}{3}} = \frac{3}{2}$ times the efficiency of the second pair.

The combined efficiency of A and D = X + 8X = 9X.
The combined efficiency of B and C = 2X + 4X = 6X.
Hence, A and D is the first pair.

Alternate solution:

A's work is 25 per cent, B's work is 12.5 per cent, C's works 6.25 per cent and D's works 3.125 per cent. It is evident that if we take A and D together, they would take two-thirds the time of the other pair since the work ratio would be 3:2.

26. Let there be a total of n people the college will ask for donations.

Amount raised from the people solicited = 600 × 0.6n = 360n

Let the total amount be x then 360n = 75% of x.

Hence 25% of x = 120n.

$\therefore$ Average donation from remaining people $= \dfrac{120\,n}{0.4n}$

$= 300$

Alternative approach: According to the question 60% of the people have contributed 75% of the amount. Thus, each person has contributed 1.25% of the total amount.

Rest of the 40% of the people have to contribute 25% of the amount. Thus, each person has contributed 0.625 % of the total amount (against 1.25% of first 60% people). Hence, the average contribution per person = 600/2 = ₹300.

27. Let x be the speed of Rahul, and v be the rate of current (in mph.)

$$\dfrac{12}{x-v} - \dfrac{12}{(x+v)} = 6 \Rightarrow \dfrac{v}{x^2 - v^2} = \dfrac{1}{4} \qquad (1)$$

$$\dfrac{12}{2x-v} - \dfrac{12}{(2x+v)} = 1.2 \Rightarrow \dfrac{v}{4x^2 - v^2} = \dfrac{1}{20} \qquad (2)$$

By solving equations (1) and (2) we get speed of current = 1.33 or 4/3 mph.

28. In 20 kg of fresh grapes –water = 18 kg and grape = 2 kg. The grape becomes 80 per cent of the total in the dried grape. Hence, the required weight is 2.5 kg.

29. BA is lower than MBA2, but we can't set a relation in between BA and MBA1. Hence, the correct answer is option (d).

30. Since only runs are getting added without any addition of innings, the value of BA will definitely increase. However, for MBA2 in a ratio of 50, we are adding a ratio of 45 (less than 50) it definitely decreases. This will definitely reduce the value of MBA2. Hence, option (b) is the correct.

31. Let the initial distance between train and point A be x and speed of train and cat be t & c respectively.

Now according to the question: $\dfrac{x}{t} = \dfrac{\frac{3d}{8}}{c}$ or

$$x = \dfrac{\left(\frac{3d}{8}\right) t}{c} \cdots \qquad (1)$$

and $\dfrac{x+d}{t} = \dfrac{\frac{5d}{8}}{c}$ or $x + d = \dfrac{\left(\frac{5d}{8}\right) t}{c} \qquad (2)$

By subtracting equation 2 from equation 1 we get d =

$\dfrac{\left(\frac{2d}{8}\right) t}{c}$ or $\dfrac{t}{c} = \dfrac{4}{1}$. Option b.

Alternate solution: Assume the distance of the tunnel to be 8x. Initially the cat is at 3x from A and 5x from B. Now if you were to use the options, to check which

option fits the situation, you would realize the following with option (b) – speed ratio is 4:1:

For the meeting at A: cat travels 3x, train travels 12x.

For the meeting at B: cat travels 5x, train travels 12x + 8x = 20x. This matches the given 4:1 ratio and hence is the correct answer.

Note: If you try this with the other options, the meeting at B would not match the given ratio.

32. Efficiency of three small pumps = Efficiency of two large pumps

Efficiency of (Three small + One large pumps) = Efficiency of three large pumps

$\therefore$ 1/3$^{rd}$ of the total time is taken by the large pump alone.

Alternately, you could think of this as follows:

Efficiency of the small pump = 2, Efficiency of the large pump = 3.

Efficiency of 3 small pumps and 1 large pump = 9 (is three times the efficiency of a large pump alone). Hence, the time taken would be 1/3$^{rd}$ of the time.

33. 

$$A \mathrel{\vert\!\!\underset{2.5\,km}{\vert}} \overset{\text{15 km}}{\underset{X\quad\ Y\quad\ Z}{\vert\quad\vert\quad\vert}} \underset{2.5\,km}{\vert\!\!\vert} B$$

Let X, Y and Z be the three gutters let XY be x/2 km and YZ be x km.

According to the question $\dfrac{AX}{30} = \dfrac{5}{60}$ or AX = 2.5 km

AX + x/2 + x + BX = 20 km

2.5 + 3x/2 + 2.5 = 20 km

3x/2 = 15 km

After crossing the gutter 1 he doubled his speed so final speed was 60 kmph.

Time taken to cover distance XZ and ZA =

$$\dfrac{(15+17.5)\ km}{2 \times 30\ km/hr} = \dfrac{32.5}{60} \times 60 = 32.5 \text{ minutes}$$

The patient reaches the hospital in a total of (32.5 + 5) = 37.5 minutes

Maximum time that the doctor gets to attend the patient = 40 – 37.5 – 1 = 1.5 minutes.

34. Check the options

Option b: Speed ratio is 4: 1. If the north bound train takes 12 min then the south bound train would take 48 minutes. As per the questions on that particular day the north bound train is late by 20 minutes, there are only 40 minutes left to complete the journey for both the trains. If the super fast doubles the speed then it would take only 6 minutes to complete the journey. So, the second train would take 40 – 6 = 34 minutes. Hence the required ratio of the speed is 6: 34 ≈ 1 : 6.

35. If he sells 25 liters of the mixture of milk and water, he would be left with 15 and 60 liters respectively.

When 25 liters of water of is mixed in this, the quantities would become 40 and 60. Thus the required ratio = 40: 60 = 2:3

36. The given situation can be interpreted as: When he increases his speed by 50 per cent, the time taken reduces by 33.33 per cent. So, the time reduction of 2 hours (Reaching the destination at 11 a.m. instead of 1 p.m.) represents a 33.33 per cent reduction from the original time required. Hence the original time was 6 hours. Now if the man wants to reach at noon he wants a reduction of 1 hour, which would mean a drop of 16.66 per cent in the time required. This can be achieved by increasing the speed by 20 per cent. Hence, the required speed to reach at noon would be 12 km/hr (option b).

37. Relative speed of the boats = 5 + 10 = 15 kmph

Distance between boats 1 minute before collision =

$\dfrac{1}{60} \times 15 = \dfrac{1}{4}$ km .

38. Since Karan beats Arjun by 10 meters in a 100 meter race, it means that their ratio of speeds is 10:9. Hence, when Karan has to move 110 meters to move, Arjun would do 99 meters. Hence, Karan would still beat Arjun by 100 meter (option d).

39. It can be seen that if Group C has 2 questions, then at least 60 per cent marks criteria for Group A cannot be fulfilled. The scenario works out as:

Group B = 23 questions, 46 marks, Group C = 2 questions, 6 marks, Group A = 75 questions, 75 marks. Percentage of marks in Group A = 75/127 < 60.

However, if we take C = 1 question, the condition is fulfilled.

Group B = 23 questions, 46 marks, Group C = 1 question, 3 marks, Group A = 76 questions, 76 marks. Percentage of marks Group A = 76/125 > 60.

Hence, we will mark option (a).

40. The following scenarios can get worked out. First test for 12 questions in group B.

| | Number of Questions | Number of marks | % of marks |
|---|---|---|---|
| Group A | 80 | 80 > 60 | |
| Group B | 12 | 24 | < 20 |
| Group C | 8 | 24 | |
| Total | 100 | 128 | |

Conditions not satisfied, hence reject both options (a) and (b).

Now test for 13 questions in Group B.

| | Number of questions | Number of marks | % of marks |
|---|---|---|---|
| Group A | 79 | 79 > 60 | |
| Group B | 13 | 26 | > 20 |

| | | |
|---|---|---|
| Group C | 8 | 24 |
| Total | 100 | 129 |

Hence, the third option is correct.

It can be reasoned that for 15 questions in Group B, the Group A marks condition (at least 60 per cent marks in group A) is rejected.

41. In every time segment, the sprinter would run $\pi r/2$ meters. Hence, the sprinter would take 4 time segments to run one round. So, if for one round he takes 1 + 2 + 4 + 8 = 15 minutes, for the next he would take 16 + 32 + 64 + 128 = 240 minutes. Hence, the required ratio of time would be 1:16 (option c).

42.

| Tank | Net inflow/ outflow (In Liter/ minute) |
|---|---|
| A | Inflow (60) |
| B | Inflow (30) |
| C | Outflow (40) |
| D | Outflow (50) |

So, tank D would get emptied first and it would take 1000/50 = 20 minutes.

43. At 10 AM, Ram is at point B and Shyam is 2.5 km away from A.

Distance between Ram and Shyam at 10 AM = 2.5 km

Now Ram starts running toward A and Shyam continues his movement towards B.

So, they are running in opposite direction with relative speed = 5 + 10 = 15 kmph.

Hence, they meet each other after 10 minutes or at 10:10 AM.

44. When Ram turns around at 10AM, Shyam is still moving towards B. Shyam reaches B at 10:15 and then turns back to start catching up on Ram. At 10:15, Ram would be 1.25 kilometers into his return journey – and there on their relative speed would be 5 kmph.

The time at which Shyam overtake Ram = 1.25/5 = 0.25 hours OR 15 minutes (after 10:15 AM).

Hence, Shyam overtakes Ram at 10:30 AM.

45. It is obvious that the female operators are cheaper—₹300 + ₹10 × 50 = ₹800 for 50 calls (per call cost of ₹16). For male operators, this cost = ₹250 + 15 × 40 = ₹850 for 40 calls. Hence, the service provider should employ as many female operators as possible—and consequently,he should hire all the 12 female operators available for the job. These operators would take care of 12 × 50 = 600 calls, which means that the remaining calls have to be handled by the male operators. Since there are residual 400 calls left, there should be 400/40 = 10 male operators (option d).

46. If Arun started at 12 noon, Barun starts at 2 pm and will catch up at 8 pm. So, we need to see which of the options will give us an exact 8 pm meeting point for Arun and Kiranmala.

    If Kiranmala starts at 4 pm, then the gap with Arun would be 120 km and would be covered in exactly 4 hours so that Kiranmala would overtake Arun at 8 pm. Hence, option (c) is correct.

47. Let the free allowed luggage be X. As Praja is charged exactly double than that of Raja. It means if Raja carries Y kg of excess luggage (OR X + Y kg of total luggage) then Praja carries 2Y kg (or X + 2y kg of total luggage).

    Total luggage = X + Y + X + 2Y = 2X + 3Y. The excess luggage charges are 1200 and 2400, which means that for Y kgs of extra luggage we are charged ₹1200 extra. Thus, if only one person traveled, the excess luggage would be 5400/1200 = 4.5Y.

    Thus, 2X + 3Y = X + 4.5Y → X = 1.5Y. Also, the total luggage is 2X + 3Y = 6Y = 60 (given). Hence, Y = 10 and X = 1.5Y = 15.

    Hence, Praja's luggage would be X + 2Y = 15 + 20 = 35.

48. The free luggage allowance is X = 15 kg. Option (c).

49. From statement 1: $W_I$ = 44.5kg, $W_{II}$ = 45.5 kg

    After using statement B we get the weight of Deepak = 70 kg. So, this is sufficient to get the weight of Poonam using the given statements. Option (c) is correct.

**Solution to questions 50 and 51:** Experience tells us that most students got stuck in this problem because they got stuck in equation creation and the infeasible thought processes. The correct thought process would give you the solution to this question in less than 45 seconds after reading the question fully. For this process, you need to get the following reactions:

Deduction 1: Since the plane flies at 8 am from City B and lands back at 8 pm the same day, the round trip takes 12 hours, out of which 1 hour is spent at City A (where it lands at 3 pm local time and takes off at 4 pm local time). Hence, the total flying time is 11 hours.

Deduction 2: Go into the options for question 51. Since the distance is 3000 and the speed of the wind is 50 kmph, options (a), (c) and (d) cannot give you an answer. WHY?? Simply because for option (a) to work we would need 3000/650 + 3000/750 to be equal to 11 hours. Leave alone 11, this will not even give us an integral answer hence we do not need to check this option' Similarly options (d) and (c) will not work as they would not give integral values for the above expression. Checking option (b), we get 3000/500 + 3000/600 = 11 hours. Hence, the cruising speed of the plane would be 550.

Deduction 3: Since we are now equipped with the answer to question 51, we can easily go back to question 50 and realise that the plane would take six hours to reach City A from City B. Thus, the time difference would be 1 hour (option d).

52. According to the question when we increase the production from 20 to 40 then daily production cost increases by 66.66%. It means

$$\frac{(240 + 40b + 40^2 c) - (240 + 20b + 20^2 c)}{240 + 20b + 20^2 c} = \frac{2}{3} \quad (1)$$

It is also given that when we increase the production from 40 to 60 then daily production cost increases by 50 %.

$$\frac{(240 + 60b + 60^2 c) - (240 + 40b + 40^2 c)}{240 + 40b + 40^2 c} = \frac{1}{2} \quad (2)$$

By solving equation 1 and equation 2 we get $c = \frac{1}{10}$ and b = 10

Cost for production of x units $= 240 + 10x + \frac{x^2}{10}$

Profit earned from x units $= \left(30x - 240 - 10x - \frac{x^2}{10}\right)$

$= 760 - \frac{1}{10}(x - 100)^2$

To maximize the profit, x – 100 should be equal to 0.

⇒   x = 100

53. Maximum profit = 760. Option (d)

54. The value of x must be odd because only with an odd value of x would you keep getting integers if you halved the value of rice and took out the another half of 1 kg from the shop store.

    Now let's start checking the options:

    Option (b): x = 7 kg

    $7 \rightarrow 3 \rightarrow 1 \rightarrow 0$

    It means x = 7 kg satisfies the given conditions. So this option is correct.

    Similarly, we can check the other options as well and see only option (b) is correct.

55. We can use the principle of set theory here directly.

    78 = 50% + 30% + 20% – (I intersection II)–(I intersection III) – (II intersection III) + 5% = 27 %

    Hence, the percentage of those who favored more than one of the three proposals was 32 per cent (option c).

56. Since his marks are in the ratio 6:7:8:9:10, we can assume the values of the numbers to be 6x, 7x, 8x, 9x and 10x. The average would be 8x and since the average is 60%, x = 7.5%. Hence, he would get over 50 per cent marks in four subjects.

57. The following table can be constructed for solving this question:

| Town | Males | Females |
|------|-------|---------|
| ChotaHazri | x | 2x |
| MotaHazri | x + 4522 | x + 4522 + 4020 = x + 8542 |

We also know that x + 8542 – 2x = 2910. Solving for x, we get x = 5632. Hence, option (c) is correct

58. This question has to be seen from the perspective of the work done by the escalator. Since the ratio of speeds of walking of Shyama and Vyom is 3:2, when Shyama take 25 steps, Vyom would take 16.66 steps. Let us say that the escalator would do x steps of work in this time. The value of x would be such that 25 + x would be equal to the total number of steps. We also know that when Vyom walks up the escalator he does 20 steps. Hence, in the time Vyom does 20 steps, the escalator should do 1.2x steps. So 20 + 1.2x should also give us the same value for the total number of steps. This means that the work done by the escalator should be 20 per cent higher when Vyom reaches the top than the work that was done when Shyama reached the top. From this point you can go in two ways:

(i) By equating 25 + x = 20 + 1.2x → x = 25. Hence, the escalator has 50 steps.

(ii) By going through options, we can easily see that if the escalator had 50 steps, then there would be a coverage of 25 steps for Shyama and 30 for Vyom which represents the required increase of 20 per cent.

59. A's work is 25 per cent, B's work is 12.5 per cent, C's work is 6.25 per cent and D's work is 3.125 per cent. It is evident that if we take A and D together, they would take two-thirds the time of the other pair since the work ratio would be 3:2.

60. Solving through options, the most convenient option to check is option (c). Since we are going to do percentage calculations— the vision you need to see this comes from the first information itself, which says that Asit takes 6 hours more than all the three take working together. If you were to take 40 minutes as the value, Asit would be 400 giving convenient percentage values of the work done by each person. You should realise that no other value gives as convenient values as this—hence at least this should be the first option to check for. Testing this option we get—Work done by all three per minute = 2.5% of the work.

Time taken by Asit = 400 minutes. Hence, work done per minute = 0.25%

Time taken by Arnold = 100 minutes.

Hence, work done per minute = 1%

Time taken by Afzal = 80 minutes. Hence, work done per minute = 1.25%

We can see that 2.5 = 0.25 + 1 + 1.25. Hence, this is the correct option.

It is a moot point that the first option we tried itself worked!! Were we lucky?? Not really. Try changing the other incorrect options forcefully and putting in whatever option you might want to insert. Can you create an option within a reasonable range of values where all the three times for Asit, Arnold and Afzal would be a convenient number so that the percentage values fit in?? Chances are you might not be able to find another single value which creates such 'convenient' decimals!!

61. Solve using sum of APs to get 93,300.

62. In a normal year, for the same, date the day of the week is advanced by 1, while for leap years the same is advanced by 2 days. Calculating backwards, we get 30 + 8 = 38. Gives 38/7 = + 3 giving us a Thursday.

63. The result of increasing the average by 1.8 is that the sum goes up by 18. This would happen because the one number which is tampered with would go up by 18. This can only happen if b–a = 2. (Interpret this as: the number is such that it increases by 18 when the digits are interchanged.)

64. Sixty man-hours are required. At 5 pm, 24 man-hours would be left which would be provided as 7 + 8 + 9 between 5–6, 6–7 and 7–8 respectively. The server gets completed at 8 pm.

65. a = 6r.

b = (2 + √3) × 3r

c = ((√3) + 1) × 6r

Hence, b – a = c – b = 3 × (√3) × r Option (a) is the correct answer.

66. Let time taken by A be t and r = 10. So, t = 2 × ((1/20) + (1/30) + (1/15)) × 10 = 3

Distance travelled by B = 3 × (10 (√3) + 20) = b

Time taken by C for to be written as C1C2 = 1.5

Hence C travels 2C/3 in time t. So, B reaches B1 and C reaches C3 (Option c).

67. As per the question, u = a/(2 × √3 ), v = b/(2 × √3 ), w = c/(2 × √3 )

Now, time taken by B = 4/( √3 ) So, Distance traveled by A = 2 × a/3 and, Distance traveled by C = 2 × c/3 Hence, they reach A3, C3 respectively. (Option b).

68. The following thought structure would give us the answer—

100(2001 start) → 50 → 150 (2002 start) → 75 → 225(2003 start) → 112.5 → 337.5(2004 start).

Thus, in this context, we can see that we expect a destruction of 168.75 huts, which is less than the total number of huts destroyed in 2002 and 2003. Option (c) is correct.

69. Draw triangle ABC with angle BAC = 120°, AB = 12, AC = 8.

By cosine formula, BC = root(304).

Time difference = [(CB + BA)/2] – [(BC + CA)/3]

This gives the answer as option (b).

70. The first machine would make 1000 nuts in 10 minutes and then be cleaned for 5 minutes (a gross block of 15 minutes), while the other machine would make 1500 bolts in 20 minutes and would be cleaned for 10 minutes (a gross block of 30 minutes). For 9000 nuts you would require 8 blocks of 15 minutes and 10 minutes more of production – a total of 130 minutes while for 9000 bolts you would require 5 blocks of 30 minutes and 20 minutes more – a total of 170 minutes. Hence, 170 minutes would be required to make the required 9000 pairs of nuts and bolts (option c).

71. $a = 1 \times 2 \times 1 \times 3 \times 1 = 6$.

$b = 3 \times 2 \times 1 \times 3 \times 1 = 18$

$c = 3 \times 1 \times 1 \times 3 \times 1 = 9$

$d = 3 \times 1 \times 2 \times 3 \times 1 = 18$

$e = 3 \times 1 \times 2 \times 1 \times 1 = 6$

$f = 3 \times 1 \times 2 \times 1 \times 4 = 24$

Thus abc/def = $6 \times 18 \times 9/18 \times 6 \times 24 = 3/8$ (option a). Estimated time for solution 55–65 seconds.

72. Solve this question while reading the statements (and react as you read). Ten years ago, the ages of the members of a joint family of eight people added up to 231 years. Reaction: 10 years ago, total age is 231. Three years later, one member died at the age of 60 years and a child was born during the same year.

Reaction: 7 years ago, total age would be 231 + 24-60 = 195

After another three years, one more member died, again at 60, and a child was born during the same year.

Reaction: 4 years ago, total age would be 195 + 24 – 60 = 159

The current average age of this eight member joint family is nearest to

Reaction: Total age today is 159 + 32 = 191.

Hence, the average age is 191/8 = 24 (approx) (a) 23 years (b) 22 years (c) 21 years (d) 25 years (e) 24 years Thus, option (e) is correct.

**Solution to questions 73 and 74:** To solve this question, proceed from Question 74. Note: This is a very common structure used in the CAT, where you have a set of two questions and starting from the second has a lot of advantages. Question 74 asks us to identify the investment scheme that would give us the maximum value of the minimum guaranteed return. For this purpose we need to see the minimum return which each investment ratio will give us, and compare this across different options. Note: The minimum guaranteed return would be the least return to be expected in the worst case scenario for a particular investment ratio. Although the amount of working in this question might seem to be high, you should realise that the value of the minimum guaranteed return which we would discover through this question would also answer the previous question for us. Thus, we are playing for 8 marks when we are solving this question. The following thought process ensues:

(a) 100% in option A – Return 0.1%

(b) 36% in option B and 64% in option C – If stock market rises:
Return = $0.05 \times 36 – 0.025 \times 64 = 36/20 – 64/40 = 1.8–1.6 = 0.2\%$ If stock market falls:
Return = $–0.03 \times 36 + 0.02 \times 64 = 1.28–1.08 = 0.2\%$ Thus, in both cases the minimum guaranteed return is 0.2% for this option (the lower value has to be taken).

(c) 64% in option B and 36% in option C If stock market rises:
Return = $0.05 \times 64 – 0.025 \times 36 = 64/20 – 36/40 = 3.2–0.9 = 2.3\%$ If stock market falls:
Return = $–0.03 \times 64 + 0.02 \times 36 = 0.72– 1.92 = –1.2\%$ Thus, for this case, the minimum guaranteed return is negative at –1.2%

(d) 1/3 in each of the three options If stock market rises:
Return = $0.05 \times 33.33 + 0.001 \times 33.33 – 0.025 \times 33.33 =$ The return is less than 0.2% (Can be seen without calculating—with a little bit of weighted average thinking. Since this value is less than 0.2% even if the next value is higher than 0.2%, it would not raise the minimum guaranteed return in this case to over 0.2%.
Hence, this option will not give the maximum value of the minimum guaranteed return.)

(e) 30% in option A, 32% in option B and 38% in option C If stock market rises: Return = $0.001 \times 30 + 0.05 \times 32 – 0.025 \times 38 = 0.03 + 1.6 – 0.95 = 0.68$ If stock market falls:
Return = $0.001 \times 30 – 0.03 \times 32 + 0.02 \times 38 = 0.03 + 0.76 – 0.96 =$ negative return

Thus, option (b) is the correct answer for 74. From Question 74 we also get the answer to question 73 as the value of the minimum guaranteed return is 0.2% (as seen in option (b) of Question 74). Thus, option (c) is the right answer for question 73.

75. The following figure will emerge for the triangle ABC. The triangle is a 30-60-90 triangle. Thus, BC would be 250 and AC would be $250\sqrt{3} = 432.5$ (approx). Since the train leaves B at 8 am, it would reach C at 1 pm and hence Rahim has to reach C by 12:45 pm—and he has to cover approximately 432.5 kms

@ 70 kmph. This would take him around 6 hours 10 minutes + . In order to reach at 12:45pm he should leave A at approximately 6:30 (option (b)).

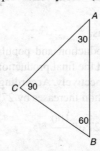

76. Let x be the production of tea and y be the production of coffee.

It is given that x = 3y.

Also, $x(100 + a) + y(100 + b) = (x + y)(100 + 5c)$

$\Rightarrow$ x (a – 5c) = y (5c – b) i.e. 3a – 15c = 5c – b i.e. 3a + b = 20c

Also, $x(100 + b) + y(100 + a) = (x + y)(100 + 3c)$

$\Rightarrow$ x(b – 3c) = y(3c – a)i.e. 3b – 9c = 3c – a i.e. a + 3b = 12c (ii) Eqn. (i) – 3 × Eqn. (ii) given, 3a + b = 20c a + 3b = 12c

– 8b = –16c i.e. b = 2c

3a = 18c $\Rightarrow$ a = 6c

a/b = 6c/2c = 3/1

Hence, Option (d) is correct.

77. Solve through trial and error. Option (b) is correct.

78. The following figure would give us the resultant velocity.

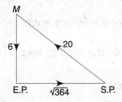

In the figure SP = Starting point of the boat, EP = Ending point of the boat and M is a random point in whose direction the boat needs to start when it starts rowing from the Starting point. Hence, Option (b) is correct.

79. The equation to represent this situation would be:

NX – A + B = NY → B = NY – NX + A or N(Y – X) + A. Thus, option (c) is correct.

80. Option (a): It is possible to get an average of 300, by using the following combinations of horses, sheep, goats and dogs: (1:1:2:1); (1:2:4:1); (2:1:6:1); (2:1:2:2).

From this logic it is possible to see that we can get an average of 300, using any multiple of 5, 7, 8, 10 (redundant). However, we cannot get an average of

300 using a multiple of 6. Thus, 24 is not a possible value for the number of animals. Hence, Option (a) is correct.

81. Since the number of goats at the end is the same as the number of goats at the start, the value of p would be greater than q (since the percentage increase is always greater in value than the percentage decrease.) For instance 100 is increased by 25% to go to 125, it needs to be dropped by 20% to get back to 100 (the increase is always greater than the decrease percentage) (option c).

82. The third and fourth options do not match the production constraints on machine B. Option (a) gives a profit of 75 × 20 + 80 × 30 = 3900, while option (b) gives a profit of 100 × 20 + 60 × 30 = 3800. Hence, option (a) is correct.

**Solutions for 83 to 85:** The given figure would show the road network described in the question.

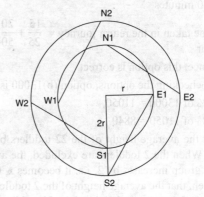

83. From the figure it is clear that the length of the chord road is $r\sqrt{5}$, which means that the length of the four chord roads is $4r\sqrt{5}$, while the length of OR is $4\pi r$. Hence, the required ratio would be $\sqrt{5}/\pi$ (Option c).

84. The total distance on the chord road would be $r\sqrt{5}$, while on the OR it would be $\pi r$. If we take the value of the radius of the outer ring road as 30 (from the options, we would see that he would require 1 hour on the chord road and 30 minutes on the outer ring road—to give 90 minutes. Hence, option c is correct.

85. Since the value of r is 15 for the previous question, the distance covered on the chord road will be $15\sqrt{5}$ while the distance of the inner ring road would be $15\pi$. The total time taken would be 1 hour + 30 minutes = 90 minutes (option c).

86. Since R has paid only 2 Euros (an equivalent of 92 bahts), he would have to further pay 324 Bahts more. Option (d) is correct.

87. The total cost of the three perfumes would be 520 + 364 + 364 = 1248. Thus, each person would have to pay 1248/3 = 416 bahts. M has paid 4 Euros + 27

bahts which adds up to 211 bahts. So he has to pay 205 Bahts to S. This would convert to 5 US Dollars (option c).

88. Ratio of speeds of A and B = 10 : 9

Ratio of speeds of B and C = 10 : 9

Ratio of speeds of A, B and C = 100 : 90 : 81

In 100 meters race A beats C by $100 - 81 = 19$ m. Therefore, in a 10 km race A beats C by 1900 m.

89.

$3/52 : 1/36 = 108 : 52 = 27 : 13$

90. Check the options: If he travels total 65 miles then he travelled 30 miles in his onward journey and 35 miles in his return journey.

For option (c) time taken in onward journey = 30/60 = 30 minutes

Time taken in the return journey = $\dfrac{15}{25} + \dfrac{20}{50} = \dfrac{50}{50} = 1$ hour

Hence, this option is correct.

91. On checking the options, option (b)13000 is correct.

85% of 13000 = 11050,

80% of 11050 = 8840.

92. Let the average height of the 22 toddlers be x inches. When the 2 toddlers are excluded, the average of the group increases by 2, i.e. it becomes x + 2. Also, given, that the average height of the 2 toddlers is one-third of the average height of the 22 toddlers or x/3.

$$\frac{\left[20(x+2) + 2 \cdot \dfrac{x}{3}\right]}{22} = x$$

$$22x = 20x + 40 + \frac{2x}{3}$$

$$\frac{4x}{3} = 40$$

Upon solving, x = 30 inches.

Average height of remaining 20 toddlers = x + 2 = 30 + 2 = 32 inches.

93. $100\text{---------}110\text{---------}143\text{---------}143 + 71.5 = 214.50\% = 4290$

100% = 2000

94. Let the capacity of the tank be 40 liters. Efficiency of the inlet pipe = 40/8 = 5 l/hr.

Efficiency of the outlet + inlet = 40/10 = 4 l/hr

Efficiency of the outlet pipe = 5 − 4 = 1 l/hr

Required time = (40/2)/1 = 20 hours.

95. Let him buy 'x' dozens of each type of candies. Then according to the question:

$$16.50 \times 2x - 15x - 12x = 150$$

$$x = 25$$

2x = 50 dozens.

96. Let initial production and population be 100, x respectively and the final production and population be 140 and y respectively. According to the question per capita production increases by 27%. Hence,

$$\frac{140}{y} = 1.27 \text{ of } \frac{100}{x}$$

$$\frac{y}{x} = \frac{140}{127} \approx 1.10$$

Required percentage = 10%.

97. a : b : c = $3 \times 2 : 4 \times 2 : 4 \times 1 = 6 : 8 : 4 = 3 : 4 : 2$

$3x + 4x + 2x = 9x$. Hence, the sum must be multiple of 9. Only option (c) is a multiple of 9. Hence, this option is correct.

98. Let the speeds of the motorbike at A and car at B be 'v' and '2v' respectively and the distance between A and B is 'd'. In the first hour between 1 to 2, the bike would cover 'v' km.

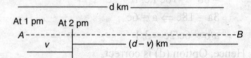

After 2 PM, Relative speed = v + 2v = 3v kmph.

Total time required to meet = $\dfrac{d-v}{3v} = 1\dfrac{2}{3} = \dfrac{5}{3}$

$$\frac{d-v}{v} = 5 \text{ or } d = 6v \text{ or } v = d/6.$$

Total distance travelled by bike = $\left(1\dfrac{2}{3} + 1\right) \times v = \dfrac{8v}{3} = 168$

v = 63 kmph

Total distance travelled by car = $1\dfrac{2}{3} \times 2v = \dfrac{10v}{3} = 210$ KM

Total distance between A and B = 168 + 210 = 378 km.

99. Let the total work be 40 units. Let the efficiencies of Amal, Bimal and Kamal be a, b and c respectively. Then, a = 40/10 = 4, b = 40/8 = 5, a + b + c = 40/4 = 10

On solving we get, c = 1.

Kamal's share = $\dfrac{1}{1+4+5} \times 1000 = ₹100$

100. 4 liters of mixture A would have $\dfrac{4}{3}$ liters of water and $\dfrac{8}{3}$ liters of liquid A.

3 liters of mixture B would have $\frac{3}{4}$ liters of water and $\frac{9}{4}$ liters of liquid B.

2 liters of mixture C would have $\frac{2}{5}$ liters of water and $\frac{8}{5}$ liters of liquid C.

Total amount of water $= \frac{4}{3} + \frac{3}{4} + \frac{2}{5} = \frac{149}{60}$ Liters.

Only option (c) is correct.

101. Let the ages of Arun and Barun be 4 and 10 years respectively. After 2 years Arun age will be half of the Barun's age. The required percentage $= \frac{2}{10} \times 100 = 20\%$.

102. Let the total work = 120 units

Efficiency of each person = 120/120 = 1unit per day

Total work done on day 1 = 1

Total work done on day 2 = 1 + 1 = 2

Total work done on day n = 1 + 1 + 1....n times = n

(Let the total work is finished in 'n' days)

$1 + 2 + 3 + .... + n = 120$

$\frac{n(n+1)}{2} = 120$

n(n + 1) = 240 or n = 15 days.

103. Let the maximum possible number of people is 'n'.

To maximize the value of n we assume that only one person weighs 57 kg and rest of the persons weigh 53 kg.

$57 + (n-1)53 = 630$ or $(n-1)$

$= \frac{630 - 57}{53} = \frac{573}{53} = 10.81$

Therefore maximum possible value of n-1 = 10 or n = 11 persons.

104. Let's assume if the man travels at a speed of 'v' kmph and reaches station in time (in t minutes). Let the distance between station and home is 'd' km.

According to the question:

$$\frac{d}{12} = \frac{d}{v} + \frac{10}{60} \qquad (1)$$

$$\frac{d}{15} = \frac{d}{v} - \frac{10}{60} \qquad (2)$$

$$\frac{d}{12} - \frac{d}{15} = \frac{10}{60} + \frac{10}{60} = \frac{20}{60}$$

On solving we get: d = 20 km

Alternate method: The speed of walking is increasing by 25%, hence the time reduction would be 20% (as the distance is constant). This time reduction is 20 minutes and hence, the original time would be 100 minutes. The distance would be $12 \times \frac{100}{60} = 20$ km.

105. Of every 100 saving, Ravi would deposit 50 in an FD, 15 in stocks and 35 in his bank account. Hence, the total savings deposited in bank would be 85%, which is given to us as 59500.

Total monthly savings $= \frac{59500}{85} \times 100 = 70,000$

106. Using the PCG logic, it is quite clear that if the cost price is 100 and the retail price is 120, giving a discount of 15% would mean selling at 102 – and this would give a profit of 2%.

Thus, to get a profit of 20%, he must sell at retail price.

107. Let the speed of the river be v and the speed of the boat be u and the distance between the home of the man and his office be 'd' km and 't' is the initial time taken.

$$t = \frac{d}{u-v} + \frac{d}{u+v} \qquad (1)$$

$$\frac{t}{4} = \frac{d}{2u-v} + \frac{d}{2u+v} \qquad (2)$$

From equations (1) and (2) we get:

$$\frac{2u}{u^2 - v^2} = \frac{16u}{4u^2 - v^2}$$

$$4u^2 - v^2 = 8u^2 - 8v^2$$

$$4u^2 = 7v^2$$

$$\frac{u^2}{v^2} = \frac{7}{4} \text{ or } \frac{u}{v} = \sqrt{7}:2$$

108. C1: C2: C3 = 9: 10: 8 = 162: 180: 144

C2: C4: C5 = 18: 19: 20 = 180: 190: 200

C1: C2: C3: C4: C5 = 162: 180: 144: 190: 200

If 200-162 = 38 → 19 CRORE

Then, $(162 + 180 + 144 + 190 + 200 = 876) \to \frac{19}{38} \times 876 = 438$ crore.

109. Let 200 girls and 100 boys be appearing for the admission test. 60 girls and 45 boys get admission.

Total candidates who do not get admission = 200 + 100 – 60 – 45 = 195.

Required percentage $= \frac{195}{300} \times 100 = 65\%$.

110. Let the number of large, super, and jumbo packets of popcorn in its stock are 7x, 17x, 16x and the number of large, super, and jumbo packets of chips in its stock are 6y, 15y, 14y.

$7x + 17x + 16x = 6y + 15y + 14y$

$40x = 35y$

$x : y = 7 : 8$

Required ratio = 16x: 14y $= \frac{16}{14} \times \frac{7}{8} = 1 : 1$.

111. Let the price of good mangoes be ₹100 per kg.

Cost price = $80 \times 100 + 40 \times \dfrac{100}{2} = 10{,}000$

Selling price = $120 \times 90 = 10800$

Percentage profit = $\dfrac{800}{10{,}000} \times 100 = 8\%$.

112. If we take the Cost price of the 60 toys as 100, the marked price should be such that after a 40% discount on the marked price, the selling price of the items should be 120. A little bit of Percentage change graphic thinking explained in the chapter of percentages, would easily give you that the marked price should be 200. Since, 10 toys are destroyed, it means that 1/6th of the toys are destroyed. Thus, the marked price of the toys on sale would be: 166.6666. To sell these at 120, we can find out what percent of 166.6666 is 120: Since: 120/166.666 = 360/500 = 0.72, this means that she should give a discount of 28%.

Alternately, you could also solve this question going through mathematical equations as follows – but this would take significantly more time:

Let the marked price of one toy be ₹X and the cost price be ₹Y.

According to the question:

$0.6X = 1.2Y$

$X = 2Y$

Cost price of 60 toys = 60Y

After destruction of 10 toys only 50 are remaining. (If 'p' is the offered discount), then:

Then, $X(1 - p) \times 50 = 72Y$

$1 - p = 0.72$ or $p = 28\%$.

## IIFT (2008-17)

1. The mean salary in ICM Ltd. was ₹1500, and the standard deviation was ₹400. A year later each employee got a ₹100 raise. After another year each employee's salary (including the above mentioned raise) was increased by 20%. The standard deviation of the current salary is: **(IIFT 2008)**
   (a) 460
   (b) 480
   (c) 580
   (d) None of the above

2. A boat goes 30 km upstream and 44 km downstream in 10 hours. In 13 hours, it can go 40 km upstream and 55 km downstream. The speed of the boat in still water is: **(IIFT 2008)**
   (a) 3 km/hour
   (b) 4 km/hour
   (c) 8 km/hour
   (d) None of the above

3. Fortuner, the latest SUV by Toyota Motors, consumes diesel at the rate of $\dfrac{1}{400}\left\{\left[\dfrac{1000}{x}\right] + x\right\}$ liters per km, when driven at the speed of x km per hour. If the cost of diesel is ₹35 per liter and the driver is paid at the rate of ₹125 per hour then find the approximate optimal speed (in km per hour) of Fortuner that will minimize the total cost of the round trip of 800 kms. **(IIFT 2009)**
   (a) 49
   (b) 55
   (c) 50
   (d) 53

4. Two motorists Anil and Sunil are practicing with two different sports cars: Ferrari and Mclaren, on the circular racing track, for the car racing tournament to be held next month. Both Anil and Sunil start from the same point on the circular track. Anil completes one round of the track in 1 minute and Sunil takes 2 minutes to complete a round. While Anil maintains same speed for all the rounds, Sunil halves his speed after the completion of each round. How many times Anil and Sunil will meet between the 6th round and 9th round of Sunil (6th and 9th round is excluded)? Assume that the speed of Sunil remains steady throughout each round and changes only after the completion of that round. **(IIFT 2009)**
   (a) 260
   (b) 347
   (c) 382
   (d) None of the above

5. Aditya, Vedus and Yuvraj alone can do a job in 6 weeks, 9 weeks and 12 weeks respectively. They work together for 2 weeks. Then Aditya leaves the job. Vedus leaves the job a week earlier to the completion of the work. The job would be completed in: **(IIFT 2009)**
   (a) 4 weeks
   (b) 5 weeks
   (c) 7 weeks
   (d) None of the above.

6. In 2006, Raveendra was allotted 650 shares of Sun Systems Ltd in the initial public offer, at the face value of ₹10 per share. In 2007, Sun Systems declared a bonus at the rate of 3:13. In 2008, the company again declared the bonus at the rate of 2:4. In 2009, the company declared a dividend of 12.5%. How much dividend does Raveendra get in 2009 as the percentage of his initial investment? **(IIFT 2009)**
   (a) 24.5%
   (b) 23.9%
   (c) 24.1%
   (d) 23%

7. Sukriti and Saloni are athletes. Sukriti covers a distance of 1 km in 5 minutes and 50 seconds, while Saloni covers the same distance in 6 minutes and 4 seconds. If both of them start together and run at uniform speed, by what distance will Sukriti win a 5 km mini marathon: **(IIFT 2009)**
   (a) 150 m
   (b) 192 m
   (c) 200 m
   (d) 225 m

8. A cylindrical overhead tank is filled by two pumps – P1 and P2. P1 can fill the tank in 8 hours while

P2 can fill the tank in 12 hours. There is a pipe P3 which can empty the tank in 8 hours. Both the pumps are opened simultaneously. The supervisor of the tank, before going out on a work, sets a timer to open P3 when the tank is half filled so that tank is exactly filled up by the time he is back. Due to technical fault P3 opens when the tank is one third filled. If the supervisor comes back as per the plan what percent of the tank is still empty?

**(IIFT 2009)**

(a) 25% tank      (b) 12% tank

(c) 10% tank      (d) None of the above

9. Bennett distribution company, a subsidiary of a major cosmetics manufacturer Bavlon, is forecasting the zonal sales for the next year. Zone I with current yearly sales of ₹193.8 lac is expected to achieve a sales growth of 7.25%; Zone II with current sales of ₹79.3 lac is expected to grow by 8.2%; and Zone III with sales of ₹57.5 lac is expected to increase sales by 7.15%. What is the Bennett's expected sales growth for the next year? **(IIFT 2009)**

(a) 7.46%      (b) 7.53%

(c) 7.88%      (d) 7.41%

10. A Techno company has 14 machines of equal efficiency in its factory. The annual manufacturing costs are ₹42,000 and establishment charges are ₹12,000. The annual output of the company is ₹70,000. The annual output and manufacturing costs are directly proportional to the number of machines. The share holders get 12.5% profit, which is directly proportional to the annual output of the company. If 7.14% machines remain closed throughout the year, then the percentage decrease in the amount of profit of the share holders would be: **(IIFT 2010)**

(a) 12%      (b) 12.5%

(c) 13.0%      (d) None of these

11. A Metro train from Mehrauli to Gurgaon has capacity to board 900 people. The fare charged (in ₹) is defined by the function $f = \left(54 - \dfrac{x}{32}\right)^2$ where 'x' is the number of the people per trip. How many people per trip will make the marginal revenue equal to zero? **(IIFT 2010)**

(a) 1728      (b) 576

(c) 484      (d) 364

12. Three Professors Dr. Gupta, Dr Sharma and Dr. Singh are evaluating answer scripts of a subject. Dr. Gupta is 40% more efficient than Dr. Sharma, who is 20% more efficient than Dr. Singh. Dr. Gupta takes 10 days less than Dr. Sharma to complete the evaluation work. Dr. Gupta starts the evaluation work and works for 10 days and then Dr. Sharma takes over. Dr. Sharma evaluates for next 15 days and then stops. In how many days, Dr. Singh can complete the remaining evaluation work. **(IIFT 2010)**

(a) 7.2 days      (b) 9.5 days

(c) 11.5 days      (d) None of these

13. Three pipes, A, B and C are connected to a tank. These pipes can fill the tank separately in 5 hrs, 10 hrs and 15 hrs respectively. When all the three pipes were opened simultaneously, it was observed that pipes A and B were supplying water at 3/4th of their normal rates for the first hour after which they supplied water at the normal rate. Pipe C supplied water at 2/3rd of its normal rate for first 2 hours, after which it supplied at its normal rate. In how much time, tank would be filled. **(IIFT 2010)**

(a) 1.05 Hrs      (b) 2.05 Hrs

(c) 3.05 Hrs      (d) None of these

14. To start a new enterprise, Mr. Yogesh has borroweda total of ₹60,000 from two money lenders with the interest being compounded annually, to berepaid at the end of two years. Mr. Yogesh repaid ₹38,800 more to the first money lender compared to the second money lender at the end of two years.The first money lender charged an interest rate,which was 10% more than what was charged by the second money lender. If Mr. Yogesh had instead borrowed ₹30,000 from each at their respective initial rates for two years, he would have paid ₹7,500 more to the first money lender compared to the second. Then money borrowed by Mr. Yogesh from the first money lender is? **(IIFT 2010)**

(a) 20,000      (b) 35,000

(c) 40,000      (d) 42,000

15. Mukesh, Suresh and Dinesh travel from Delhi toMathura to attend Janmasthmi Utsav. They have a bike, which can carry only two riders at a time as per traffic rules. Bike can be driven only by Mukesh. Mathura is 300 km from Delhi. All of them can walk at 15 Km/hr. All of them start their journey from Delhi simultaneously and are required to reach Mathura at the same time. If the speed of bike 60 Km/hr then what is the shortest possible time in which all three can reach Mathura at the same time. **(IIFT 2010)**

(a) $8\dfrac{2}{7}$ Hrs      (b) $9\dfrac{2}{7}$ Hrs

(c) 10 Hrs      (d) None of these

16. A small and medium enterprise imports two components A and B from Taiwan and China respectively and assembles them with other components for a toy. Component A contributes to 10% of production cost. Component B contributes to 20% of the production cost. Usually the company sells this toy at 20% above the production cost. Due to increase in the raw material and labour cost in both the countries, component A became 20% costlier and component B became 40% costlier. Owing to these reasons the

company increased its selling price by 15%. Considering that cost of other components does not change, what will be the profit percentage, if the toy is sold at the new price? **(IIFT 2010)**
(a) 15.5%   (b) 25.5%
(c) 35.5%   (d) 40%

17. Mandeep and Jagdeep had gone to visit Ranpur, which is a seaside town and also known for the presence of the historical ruins of an ancient kingdom. They stayed in a hotel, which is exactly 250 meters away from the railway station. At the hotel, Mandeep and Jagdeep learnt from a tourist information booklet that the distance between the sea-beach and the gate of the historical ruins is exactly 1 km. Next morning they visited the sea beach to witness sunrise and afterwards decided to have a race from the beach to the gate of the ruins. Jagdeep defeated Mandeep in the race by 60 meters or 12 seconds. The following morning they had another round of race from the railway station to the hotel. How long did Jagdeep take to cover the distance on the second day?
(a) 53 seconds   (b) 47 seconds
(c) 51 seconds   (d) 45 seconds

18. Sujoy, Mritunjoy and Paranjoy are three friends, who have worked in software firms *Z Solutions, G Software's and R Mindpower* respectively for a decade. The friends decided to float a new software firm named *XY Infotech* in January 2010. However, due to certain compulsions, Mritunjoy and Paranjoy were not able to immediately join the start-up in the appointed time. It was decided between friends that Sujoy will be running the venture as the full time director during 2010, and Mritunjoy and Paranjoy will be able to join the business only in January 2011. In order to compensate Sujoy for his efforts, it was decided that he will receive 10 percent of the profits and in the first year will invest lesser amount as compared to his friends. The remaining profit will be distributed among the friends in line with their contribution. Sujoy invested ₹35,000/- for 12 months, Mritunjoy invested ₹1,30,000/- for 6 months and Paranjoy invested ₹75,000/- for 8 months. If the total profit earned during 2010 was ₹4,50,000/-, then Paranjoy earned a profit of:
(a) ₹1,75,500   (b) ₹1,35,000
(c) ₹1,39,500   (d) None of the above

19. In Bilaspur village, 12 men and 18 boys completed construction of a primary health center in 60 days, by working for 7.5 hours a day. Subsequently the residents of the neighbouring Harigarh village also-decided to construct a primary health center in their locality, which would be twice the size of the facility built in Bilaspur. If a man is able to perform the work equal to the same done by 2 boys, then how many boys will be required to help 21 men to complete the work in Harigarh in 50 days, working 9 hours a day?
(a) 45 boys   (b) 48 boys
(c) 40 boys   (d) 42 boys

20. Aniket and Animesh are two colleagues working in *PQ Communications*, and each of them earned an investible surplus of ₹1,50,000/- during a certain period. While Animesh is a risk-averse person, Aniket prefers to go for higher return opportunities. Animesh uses his entire savings in Public Provident Fund (PPF) and National Saving Certificates (NSC). It is observed that one-third of the savings made by Animesh in PPF is equal to one-half of his savings in NSC. On the other hand, Aniket distributes his investible funds in share market, NSC and PPF. It is observed that his investments in share marketexceeds his savings in NSC and PPF by ₹20,000/- and ₹40,000/- respectively. The difference between the amount invested in NSC by Animesh and Aniket is:
(a) ₹25,000/-   (b) ₹15,000/-
(c) ₹20,000/-   (d) ₹10,000/-

21. In March 2011, *EF Public Library* purchased a total of 15 new books published in 2010 with a total expenditure of ₹4500. Of these books, 13 books were purchased from *MN Distributors*, while the remaining two were purchased from *UV Publishers*. It is observed that one-sixth of the average price of all the 15 books purchased is equal to one-fifth of the average price of the 13 books obtained from *MN Distributors*. Of the two books obtained from *UV Publishers*, if one-third of the price of one volume is equal to one-half of the price of the other, then the price of the two books are:
(a) ₹900/- and ₹600/-   (b) ₹600/- and ₹400/-
(c) ₹750/- and ₹500/-   (d) None of the above

22. 2 years ago, one-fifth of Amita's age was equal to one-fourth of the age of Sumita, and the average of their age was 27 years. If the age of Paramita is also considered, the average age of three of them declines to 24. What will be the average age of Sumita and Paramita 3 years from now?
(a) 25 years   (b) 26 years
(c) 27 years   (d) cannot be determined

23. A contract is to be completed in 56 days and 104 men are set to work, each working 8 hours a day. After 30 days, 2/5th of the work is finished. How many additional men may be employed so that work may be completed on time, each man now working 9 hours per day?
(a) 56 men   (b) 65 men
(c) 46 men   (d) None of the above

24. The ratio of number of male and female journalists in a newspaper office is 5 : 4. The newspaper has two sections, political and sports. If 30 percent of the male journalists and 40 percent of the female

journalists are covering political news, what percentage of the journalists (approx.) in the newspaper is currently involved in sports reporting?

(a) 65 percent      (b) 60 percent

(c) 70 percent      (d) None of the above

25. The ratio of 'metal 1' and 'metal 2' in Alloy 'A' is 3: 4. In Alloy 'B' same metals are mixed in the ratio 5: 8. If 26 kg of Alloy 'B' and 14kg of Alloy 'A' are mixed then find out the ratio of 'metal 1' and 'metal2' in the new Alloy.

(a) 3 : 2      (b) 2 : 5

(c) 2 : 3      (d) None of the above

26. The annual production in cement industry is subject to business cycles. The production increases for two consecutive years consistently by 18% and decreases by 12% in the third year. Again in the next two years, it increases by 18% each year and decreases by 12% in the third year. Taking 2008 as the base year, what will be the approximate effect on cement production in 2012?      **(IIFT 2012)**

(a) 24% increase      (b) 37% decrease

(c) 45% increase      (d) 60% decrease

27. Mr. Mishra invested ₹25,000 in two fixed deposits X and Y offering compound interest @ 6% per annum and 8% per annum respectively. If the total amount of interest accrued in two years through both fixed deposits is ₹3518, the amount invested in Scheme X is      **(IIFT 2012)**

(a) ₹12,000      (b) ₹13,500

(c) ₹15,000      (d) Cannot be determined

28. It takes 15 seconds for a train travelling at 60 km/hour to cross entirely another train half its length and travelling in opposite direction at 48 km/hour. It also passes a bridge in 51 seconds.

The length of the bridge is      **(IIFT 2012)**

(a) 550 m      (b) 450 m

(c) 500 m      (d) 600 m

29. 12 men can complete a work in ten days. 20 women can complete the same work in twelve days. 8 men and 4 women started working and after nine days 10 more women joined them. How many days will they now take to complete the remaining work?

     **(IIFT 2012)**

(a) 2 days      (b) 5 days

(c) 8 days      (d) 10 days

30. The Howrah-Puri express can move at 45 km/hour without its rake, and the speed is diminished by a value that varies as the square root of the number of wagons attached. If it is known that with 9 wagons, the speed is 30 km/hour, what is the greatest number of wagons with which the train can just move?

     **(IIFT 2012)**

(a) 63      (b) 64

(c) 80      (d) 81

31. Rohit bought 20 soaps and 12 toothpastes. He marked-up the soaps by 15% on the cost price of each, and the toothpastes by ₹20 on the cost price each. He sold 75% of the soaps and 8 toothpastes and made a profit of ₹385. If the cost of a toothpaste is 60% the cost of a soap and he got no return on unsold items, what was his overall profit or loss?

     **(IIFT 2012)**

(a) Loss of ₹355      (b) Loss of ₹210

(c) Loss of ₹250      (d) None of the above

32. A sum of ₹1400 is divided amongst A, B, C and D such that A's share : B's share = B's share : C's share = C's share: D's share = 3/4

How much is C's share?      **(IIFT 2012)**

(a) ₹72      (b) ₹288

(c) ₹216      (d) ₹384

33. If decreasing 70 by X percent yields the same result as increasing 60 by X percent, then X percent of 50 is      **(IIFT 2013)**

(a) 3.84

(b) 4.82

(c) 7.10

(d) The data is insufficient to answer the question

34. A mother along with her two sons is entrusted with the task of cooking Biryani for a family get together. It takes 30 minutes for all three of them cooking together to complete 50 percent of the task. The cooking can also be completed if the two sons start cooking together and the elder son leaves after 1 hour and the younger son cooks for further 3 hours. If the mother needs 1 hour less than the elder son to complete the cooking, how much cooking does the mother complete in an hour?      **(IIFT 2013)**

(a) 33.33%      (b) 50%

(c) 66.67%      (d) None of the above

35. It was a rainy morning in Delhi when Rohit drove his mother to a dentist in his Maruti Alto. They started at 8.30 AM from home and Rohit maintained the speed of the vehicle at 30 Km/hr. However, while returning from the doctor's chamber, rain intensified and the vehicle could not move due to severe water logging. With no other alternative, Rohit kept the vehicle outside the doctor's chamber and returned home along with his mother in a rickshaw at a speed of 12 Km/hr. They reached home at 1.30 PM. If they stayed at the doctor's chamber for the dental check-up for 48 minutes, the distance of the doctor's chamber from Rohit's house is      **(IIFT 2013)**

(a) 15 Km      (b) 30 Km

(c) 36 Km      (d) 45 Km

36. Two alloys of aluminium have different percentages of aluminium in them. The first one weighs 8 kg and the second one weighs 16 kg. One piece each of equal weight was cut off from both the alloys

and the first piece was alloyed with the second alloy and the second piece alloyed with the first one. As a result, the percentage of aluminium became the same in the resulting two new alloys. What was the weight of each cut-off piece?  **(IIFT 2013)**

(a) 3.33 kg                     (b) 4.67 kg

(c) 5.33 kg                     (d) None of the above

37. Three years ago, your close friend had won a lottery of ₹1 crore. He purchased a flat for ₹40 lacs, a car for ₹20 lacs and shares worth ₹10 lacs. He put the remaining money in a bank deposit that pays compound interest @ 12 percent per annum. If today, he sells off the flat, the car and the shares at certain percentage of their original value and withdraws his entire money from the bank, the total gain in his assets is 5%. The closest approximate percentage of the original value at which he sold off the three items is  **(IIFT 2013)**

(a) 60 percent                  (b) 75 percent

(c) 90 percent                  (d) 105 percent

38. The average of 7 consecutive numbers is P. If the next three numbers are also added, the average shall  **(IIFT 2013)**

(a) remain unchanged  (b) increase by 1

(c) increase by 1.5         (d) increase by 2

39. Capacity of tap Y is 60% more than that of X. If both the taps are opened simultaneously, they take 40 hours to fill the rank. The time taken by Y alone to fill the tank is  **(IIFT 2013)**

(a) 60 hours                    (b) 65 hours

(c) 70 hours                    (d) 75 hours

40. X and Y are the two alloys which were made by mixing Zinc and Copper in the ratio 6 : 9 and 7 : 11 respectively. If 40 grams of alloy X and 60 grams of alloy Y are melted and mixed to form another alloy Z, what is the ratio of Zinc and Copper in the new alloy Z?  **(IIFT 2014)**

(a) 6 : 9                        (b) 59 : 91

(c) 5 : 9                        (d) 59 : 90

41. A milk vendor sells 10 liters of milk from a can containing 40 liters of pure milk to the 1st customer. He then adds 10 liters of water to the milk can. He again sells 10 liters of mixture to the 2nd customer and then adds 10 liters of water to the can. Again he sells 10 liters of mixture to the 3rd customer and then adds 10 liters of water to the can and so on. What amount of pure milk will the 5th customer receive?  **(IIFT 2014)**

(a) 510/128 liters          (b) 505/128 liters

(c) 410/128 liters          (d) 405/128 liters

42. A ferry carries passengers to Rock of Vivekananda and back from Kanyakumari. The distance of Rock of Vivekananda from Kanyakumari is 100km. One day, the ferry started for Rock of Vivekananda with passengers on board, at a speed of 20 km per hour. After 90 minutes, the crew realized that there is a hole in the ferry and 15 gallons of sea water had already entered the ferry. Sea water is entering the ferry at the rate of 10 gallons per hour. It requires 60 gallons of water to sink the ferry. At what speed should the driver now drive the ferry so that it can reach the Rock of Vivekananda and return back to Kanyakumari just in time before the ferry sinks? (Current of the sea water from Rock of Vivekananda to Kanyakumari is 2 km per hour.)  **(IIFT 2014)**

(a) 40 km/hr towards the Rock & 39 km/hr while returning to Kanyakumari

(b) 41 km/hr towards the Rock & 38 km/hr while returning to Kanyakumari

(c) 42 km/hr towards the Rock & 36 km/hr while returning to Kanyakumari

(d) 35 km/hr towards the Rock & 39 km/hr while returning to Kanyakumari

43. The pre-paid recharge of Airtel gives 21% less talktime than the same price pre-paid recharge of Vodafone. The post-paid talktime of Airtel is 12% more than its pre-paid recharge, having the same price. Further, the post-paid talktime of same price of Vodafone is 15% less than its pre-paid recharge. How much percent less / more talktime can one get from the Airtel post-paid service compared to the post-paid service of Vodafone?  **(IIFT 2015)**

(a) 3.9% more                  (b) 4.7% less

(c) 4.7%more                   (d) 2.8% less

44. As a strategy towards retention of customers, the service centre of a split AC machine manufacturer offers discount as per the following rule: for the second service in a year, the customer can avail of a 10% discount; for the third and fourth servicing within a year, the customer can avail of 11% and 12% discounts respectively of the previous amount paid, Finally, if a customer gets more than four services within a year, he has to pay just 55% of the original servicing charges. If Rohan has availed 5 services from the same service centre in a given year, the total percentage discount availed by him is approximately:  **(IIFT 2015)**

(a) 16.52                        (b) 20.88

(c) 22.33                        (d) 24.08

45. A tank is connected with both inlet pipes and outlet pipes. Individually, an inlet pipe can fill the tank in 7 hours and an outlet pipe can empty it in 5 hours. If all the pipes are kept open, it takes exactly 7 hours for a completely filled-in tank to empty. If the total number of pipes connected to the tank is 11, how many of these are inlet pipes?  **(IIFT 2015)**

(a) 2                            (b) 4

(c) 5                            (d) 6

46. A firm is thinking of buying a printer for its office use for the next one year. The criterion for choosing is based on the least per-page printing cost. It can choose between an inkjet printer which costs ₹5000 and a laser printer which costs ₹8000. The per-page printing cost for an inkjet is ₹1.80 and that for a laser printer is ₹1.50. The firm should purchase the laser printer, if the minimum number of pages to be printed in the year exceeds **(IIFT 2015)**
    (a) 5000      (b) 10000
    (c) 15000      (d) 18000

47. A chartered bus carrying office employees travels everyday in two shifts- morning and evening. In the evening, the bus travels at an average speed, which is 50% greater than the morning average speed; but takes 50% more time than the amount of time it takes in the morning. The average speed of the chartered bus for the entire journey is greater/less than its average speed in the morning by: **(IIFT 2015)**
    (a) 18% less      (b) 30% greater
    (c) 37.5% greater      (d) 50% less

48. Sailesh is working as a sales executive with a reputed FMCG Company in Hyderabad. As per the Company's policy, Sailesh gets a commission of 6% on all sales upto ₹1,00,000 and 5% on all sales in excess of this amount. If Sailesh remits ₹2,65,000 to the FMCG company after deducting his commission, his total sales were worth: **(IIFT 2015)**
    (a) ₹1,20,000      (b) ₹2,90,526
    (c) ₹2,21,054      (d) ₹2,80,000

49. Three carpenters P, Q and R are entrusted with office furniture work. P can do a job in 42 days. If Q is 26% more efficient than P and R is 50% more efficient than Q, then Q and R together can finish the job in approximately: **(IIFT 2015)**
    (a) 11 days      (b) 13 days
    (c) 15 days      (d) 17 days

50. There are two alloys P and Q made up of silver, copper and aluminum. Alloy P contains 45% silver and rest aluminum. Alloy Q contains 30% silver, 35% copper and rest aluminum. Alloys P and Q are mixed in the ratio of 1 : 4.5. The approximate percentages of silver and copper in the newly formed alloy is: **(IIFT 2015)**
    (a) 33% and 29%      (b) 29% and 26%
    (c) 35% and 30%      (d) None of the above

51. Two farmers were cultivating wheat on their respective agricultural land in a village. Farmer A had an average production of 20 bushels from a hectare. Farmer B, who had 15 hectares of more land dedicated to wheat cultivation, had an output of 30 bushels of wheat from a hectare. If farmer B harvested 530 bushels of wheat more than farmer A, how many bushels of wheat did farmer A cultivate? **(IIFT 2016)**

(a) 50      (b) 80
(c) 160      (d) 200

52. In a local shop, as part of promotional measures, the shop owner sells three different varieties of soap, one at a loss of 13 percent, another at a profit of 23 percent and the third one at a loss of 26 percent. Assuming that the shop owner sells all three varieties of soap at the same price, the approximate percentage by which average cost price is lower or higher than the selling price is **(IIFT 2016)**
    (a) 10.5 higher      (b) 12.5 lower
    (c) 14.5 lower      (d) 8.5 higher

53. In the marketing management course of an MBA programme, you and your roommate can complete an assignment in 30 days. If you are twice as efficient as your roommate, the time required by each to complete the assignment individually is **(IIFT 2016)**
    (a) 45 days and 90 days
    (b) 30 days and 60 days
    (c) 40 days and 120 days
    (d) 45 days and 135 days

54. Swarn a SME enterprise borrowed a sum of money from a nationalized bank at 10% simple interest per annum and the same amount at 8% simple interest per annum from a microfinance firm for the same period. It cleared the first loan 6 months before the scheduled date of repayment and repaid the second loan just at the end of the scheduled period. If in each case it had to pay ₹62100 as amount then how much money and for what time period did it borrow? **(IIFT 2017)**
    (a) ₹55750, 2 years      (b) ₹52500, 2 years
    (c) ₹51750, 2.5 years      (d) ₹55750, 2.5 years

55. Somesh, Tarun and Nikhil can complete a work separately in 45, 60 and 75 days. They started the work together but Nikhil left after 5 days of start and Somesh left 2 days before the completion of the work. In how many days will the work be completed? **(IIFT 2017)**
    (a) 25 (1/7)      (b) 50(1/7)
    (c) 35 (5/7)      (d) 40(5/7)

56. A Pharmaceutical company produces two chemicals X and Y, such that X consists of 5% salt A and 10% salt B and Y consists of 10% salt A and 6% salt B. For producing the chemicals X and Y, the company requires at least 7 gm of Salt A and at least 7 gm of Salt B. If chemical X costs ₹10.50 per gm and chemical Y costs ₹7.80 per gm, what is the minimum cost at which the company can meet the requirement by using a combination of both types of chemicals? **(IIFT 2017)**
    (a) ₹810      (b) ₹850
    (c) ₹537      (d) None

57. Suntex Company plans to manufacture a new product line of Razor next year and sell it at a price of ₹12 per unit. The variable costs per unit in each production run is estimated to be 50% of the selling price, and the fixed costs for each production run is estimated to be ₹50,400. Based on their estimated costs how many units of the new product will company Suntex need to manufacture and sell in order for their revenue to be equal to their total costs for each production run? **(IIFT 2017)**
    (a) 5400      (b) 4200
    (c) 8400      (d) 2100

58. A mobile company that sells two models ACN-I and ACN-II of mobile, reported that revenues from ACN-I in 2016 were down 12% from 2015 and revenue from ACN-II sales in 2016 were up by 9% from 2015. If the total revenues from sales of both the mobile models ACN-I and ACN-II in 2016 were up by 3% from 2015, what is the ratio of revenue from ACN-I sales in 2015 to revenue from ACN-II sales in 2015? **(IIFT 2017)**
    (a) 5:2      (b) 2:5
    (c) 3:4      (d) None

59. Ramesh and Sohan start walking away from each other from a point P at an angle of 120°. Ramesh walks at a speed of 3 km/hour while Sohan walks at a speed of 4 km/hour. What is the distance between them after 90 minutes? **(IIFT 2017)**
    (a) 9.89 km      (b) 10.56 km
    (c) 9.12 km      (d) 12.42 km

60. The Drizzle Pvt. Ltd., a squash company has 2 cans of juice. The first contains 25% water and the rest is fruit pulp. The second contains 50% water and rest is fruit pulp. How much juice should be mixed from each of the containers so as to get 12 liters of juice such that the ratio of water to fruit pulp is 3:5? **(IIFT 2017)**
    (a) 6 liters, 6 liters      (b) 4 liters, 8 liters
    (c) 5 liters, 7 liters      (d) 9 liters, 3 liters

61. An overhead tank, which supplies water to a settlement, is filled by three bore wells. First two bore wells operating together fill the tank in the same time as taken by third bore well to fill it. The second bore well fills the tank 10 hours faster than the first one and 8 hours slower than the third one. The time required by the third bore well to fill the tank alone is: **(IIFT 2017)**
    (a) 9 hours      (b) 12 hours
    (c) 18 hours      (d) 20 hours

62. In 2011, Plasma—a pharmaceutical company—allocated ₹4.5 × 10⁷ for Research and Development. In 2012, the company allocated ₹60,000,000 for Research and Development. If each year the funds are evenly divided among $2 \times 10^2$ departments, how much more will each department receive this year than it did last year? **(IIFT 2012)**
    (a) ₹$2.0 \times 10^5$      (b) ₹$7.5 \times 10^5$
    (c) ₹$7.5 \times 10^4$      (d) ₹$2.5 \times 10^7$

63. At a reputed Engineering College in India, total expenses of a trimester are partly fixed and partly varying linearly with the number of students. The average expense per student is ₹400 when there are 20 students and ₹300 when there are 40 students. When there are 80 students, what is the average expense per student? **(IIFT 2012)**
    (a) ₹250      (b) ₹300
    (c) ₹330      (d) ₹350

64. A 10 liter cylinder contains a mixture of water and sugar, the volume of sugar being 15% of total volume. A few liters of the mixture is released and an equal amount of water is added. Then the same amount of the mixture as before is released and replaced with water for a second time. As a result, the sugar content becomes 10% of total volume. What is the approximate quantity of mixture released each time? **(IIFT 2012)**
    (a) 1 liters      (b) 1.2 liters
    (c) 1.5 liters      (d) 2 liters

65. Mrs. Sonia buys ₹249.00 worth of candies for the children of a school. For each girl she gets a strawberry flavoured candy priced at ₹3.30 per candy; each boy receives a chocolate flavoured candy priced at ₹2.90 per candy. How many candies of each type did she buy? **(IIFT 2013)**
    (a) 21, 57      (b) 57, 21
    (c) 37, 51      (d) 27, 51

66. The duration of the journey from your home to the college in the local train varies directly as the distance and inversely as the velocity. The velocity varies directly as the square root of the diesel used per km., and inversely as the number of carriages in the train. If, in a journey of 70 km. in 45 minutes with 15 carriages, 10 litres of diesel is required, then the diesel that will be consumed in a journey of 50 km in half an hour with 18 carriages is **(IIFT 2013)**
    (a) 2.9 litres      (b) 11.8 litres
    (c) 15.7 litres      (d) None of the above

67. Ravindra and Rekha got married 10 years ago, their ages were in the ratio of 5 : 4. Today Ravindra's age is one sixth more than Rekha's age. After marriage, they had 6 children including a triplet and twins. The age of the triplets, twins and the sixth child is in the ratio of 3: 2: 1. What is the largest possible value of the present total age of the family? **(IIFT 2014)**
    (a) 79      (b) 93
    (c) 101      (d) 107

68. Eight years after completion of your MBA degree, you start a business of your own. You invest INR 30,00,000 in the business that is expected to give you a return of 6%, compounded annually. If the expected number of years by which your investment shall double is 72/r, where r is the percent interest rate, the approximate expected total value of investment (in INR) from your business 48 years later is: **(IIFT 2014)**

   (a) 2,40,00,000        (b) 3,60,00,000
   (c) 4,80,00,000        (d) None of the above

69. The student fest in an Engineering College is to be held in one month's time and no sponsorship has yet been arranged by the students. Finally, the General Secretary (GS) of the student body took the initiative and decided to go alone for sponsorship collection. In fact, he is the only student doing the fund raising job on the first day. However, seeing his enthusiasm, other students also joined him as follows: on the second day, 2 more students join him; on the third day, 3 more students join the group of the previous day; and so on. In this manner, the sponsorship collection is completed in exactly 20 days. If an MBA student is twice as efficient as an Engineering student, the number of days which 11 MBA students would take to do the same activity, is: **(IIFT 2014)**

   (a) 70        (b) 80
   (c) 90        (d) 100

70. A pharmaceutical company manufactures 6000 strips of prescribed diabetic drugs for ₹80,000 every month. In July 2014, the company supplied 600 strips of free medicines to the doctors at various hospitals. Of the remaining medicines, it was able to sell 4/5th of the strips at 25 percent discount and the balance at the printed price of ₹25. Assuming vendor's discount at the rate of a uniform 30 percent of the total revenue, the approximate percentage profit/loss of the pharmaceutical company in July 2014 is: **(IIFT 2014)**

   (a) 5.5 percent (profit)  (b) 4 percent (loss)
   (c) 5.5 percent (loss)    (d) None of the above

## ANSWER KEY

| | | | |
|---|---|---|---|
| 1. (b) | 2. (c) | 3. (a) | 4. (c) |
| 5. (a) | 6. (d) | 7. (b) | 8. (c) |
| 9. (a) | 10. (b) | 11. (b) | 12. (a) |
| 13. (c) | 14. (c) | 15. (b) | 16. (b) |
| 17. (b) | 18. (b) | 19. (d) | 20. (d) |
| 21. (c) | 22. (b) | 23. (a) | 24. (a) |
| 25. (c) | 26. (c) | 27. (c) | 28. (a) |
| 29. (a) | 30. (c) | 31. (a) | 32. (d) |
| 33. (a) | 34. (b) | 35. (c) | 36. (c) |
| 37. (c) | 38. (c) | 39. (b) | 40. (b) |
| 41. (d) | 42. (c) | 43. (a) | 44. (b) |
| 45. (d) | 46. (b) | 47. (b) | 48. (d) |
| 49. (b) | 50. (a) | 51. (c) | 52. (a) |
| 53. (a) | 54. (c) | 55. (a) | 56. (a) |
| 57. (c) | 58. (b) | 59. (c) | 60. (a) |
| 61. (b) | 62. (c) | 63. (a) | 64. (d) |
| 65. (b) | 66. (b) | 67. (d) | 68. (c) |
| 69. (a) | 70. (c) | | |

### Solutions

1. One year later each employee got ₹100 raise it would not make any change in standard deviation. After another year each employee's salary was increased by 20% then the standard deviation = $1.2 \times 400 = ₹480$.

2. Let speed of boat in still water be X and speed of stream in still water be Y.

   Then according to the question,

   $$\frac{30}{X-Y} + \frac{44}{X+Y} = 10 \qquad \text{(i)}$$

   $$\frac{40}{X-Y} + \frac{55}{X+Y} = 13 \qquad \text{(ii)}$$

   Equation (i) × 4 – Equation (ii) × 3

   $$\frac{120}{X-Y} + \frac{176}{X+Y} - \frac{120}{X-Y} - \frac{165}{X+Y} = (40-39)$$

   $$\Rightarrow \frac{176}{X+Y} - \frac{165}{X+Y} = 1$$

   $$\Rightarrow X+Y = 11 \qquad \text{(iii)}$$

   Similarly, $(X-Y) = 5 \ldots\ldots$iv

   Solving equations iii and iv, we get X = 8 km/hr.

3. Total cost of the round trip of 800 kms =

   $$\frac{1}{400}\left\{\left[\frac{1000}{x}\right] + x\right\} \times 800 \times 35 + \frac{800 \times 125}{x} = y$$

   $$Y = \frac{70000}{x} + 70x + \frac{100000}{x}$$

   Now, differentiating both sides of the above equation with respect to x, we get

   $$\frac{dy}{dx} = -\frac{70000}{x^2} + 70 - \frac{100000}{x^2}$$

   For minimum total cost, $\frac{dy}{dx} = 0$.

   $$-\frac{70000}{x^2} + 70 - \frac{100000}{x^2} = 0$$

   $$x \approx 49 \text{ km/hr}$$

4. Sunil's time to cover a round is 2 min

   Till 6th round, Sunil's time to cover a round = 64 min

   During 7th and 8th round, time taken by Sunil will be 128 and 256 minutes

Since Anil maintains his speed and time as 1 minute, so total number of times both will meet between 6th and 9th round (both rounds excluded) = (128 + 256) − 2 = 382 times

5. Let the total work be 36

Efficiency of Aditya, Vedus and Yuvraj = $\frac{36}{6}, \frac{36}{9}, \frac{36}{12}$ or 6, 4, 3.

Work done for 2 weeks = 2 × 6 + 2 × 4 + 2 × 3 = 26

Now, Work left = 36 − 26 = 10

Let x weeks more is required to complete the job.

So we can write, 4(x − 1) + 3x = 10

⇒  x = 2 weeks

So the job would be completed in = 2 + 2 = 4 weeks.

6. Total investment = 650 × 10 = ₹6500.

Total number of share at the end of 2007 = 650 + 650

× $\frac{3}{13}$ = 800

Total number of share at the end of 2008 = 800 + 800

× $\frac{2}{4}$ = 1200

Similarly, for the year 2009, the total number of shares become 1200.

∴ Dividend in 2009 = $\frac{12.5}{100}$ × 10 × 1200

∴ Required percentage = $\dfrac{\dfrac{1}{8} \times 10 \times 1200}{6500}$ × 100

= $\frac{300}{13} \cong 23\%$

7. In one km race Sukriti beats Saloni by 364 − 350 = 14 seconds.

∴ in five km race Sukriti will beat Saloni by 5 × 14 = 70 seconds.

It means Saloni has to run 70 more seconds after Sukriti finishes the race.

∴ Sukriti wins the race by 70 × $\frac{1000}{350}$ = 200 m.

8. Let the capacity of tank be 24 liters. Efficiency of P1 = $\frac{24}{8}$ = 3, Efficiency of P2 = $\frac{24}{12}$ = 2, Efficiency of

P3 = $\frac{24}{8}$ = 3

P1 and P2 can fill the tank in $\frac{24}{2+3}$ = 4.8 hr

So timer is to start after 2.4 hrs.

So the supervisor will be back after = 2.4 + $\frac{12}{2+3-3}$ = 8.4 hours

But the P3 opens when the tank was 1/3rd full. i.e.

total water in tank is 8 Liters in $\frac{4.8}{3}$ = 1.6 h.

The tank is empty by 24 − (8 + (2 + 3 − 3)6.8) = 2.4 liters

Therefore, 10% of the tank is empty if the supervisor comes back as per the plan.

9. Expected sales growth

= $\dfrac{(193.8 \times 7.25) + (79.3 \times 8.2) + (57.5 \times 7.15)}{193.8 + 79.3 + 57.5}$

= 7.46%

10. Profit = 70000 − 54000 = ₹16,000

Now, 7.14 % out of 14 machines are not working it means 7.14% of 14 ≈ 1 out of 14 machines is not working.

Total cost = 42000 × $\frac{13}{14}$ + 12000 = ₹51,000

Annual output = $\frac{70000}{14}$ × 13 = ₹65,000

Profit = 65000 − 51000 = ₹14,000

Percentage decrease in profit = $\frac{2000}{16000}$ × 100 = 12.5%

11. Revenue r(x) = Total number of people × revenue per

people = $x\left(54 - \dfrac{x}{32}\right)^2$

= $x\left[54^2 - 2 \times 54 \times \dfrac{x}{32} + \left(\dfrac{x}{32}\right)^2\right]$

∴ $r'(x) = 54^2 - \dfrac{4 \times 54x}{32} + \dfrac{3x^2}{32^2}$

For zero marginal revenue

r'(x) = 0

On solving, we get

x = 576, 1728

Since x < 900, so x = 576

12. Let efficiency of Gupta, Sharma and Singh be a, b, c respectively.

a = 1.4b, b = 1.2c, a = 1.4 × 1.2 = 1.68c

$\dfrac{W}{b} - \dfrac{W}{1.4b}$ = 10 or $\dfrac{W}{b}$ = 35 = time taken by Sharma to

complete the task.

∴ Time taken by Gupta to complete the work = 35 − 10 = 25 days

∴ Time taken by Singh to complete the work = 35 × 1.2 = 42 days

Let Dr. Singh complete the rest of the work in 'x' days.

$\dfrac{W}{25} \times 10 + \dfrac{W}{35} \times 15 + \dfrac{W}{42} \times x = W$

$\dfrac{x}{42} = 1 - \left(\dfrac{2}{5} + \dfrac{3}{7}\right) = \dfrac{6}{35}$

⇒  x = $\dfrac{6}{35}$ × 42 = 7.2 days

Alternate solution: From the second statement we see that the work efficiency of Dr. Singh: Dr. Sharma: Dr. Gupta would be 1:1.2:1.68 = 10:12:16.8 = 50:60:84. Now, since we are given that Gupta takes 10 days less than Sharma to complete the work – we need to find out the work quantum. This is where LCM thinking sets in: The LCM of 60 and 84 would be 840. If the work amount was 840, Sharma would take 14 days (840/60) and Gupta would take 10 days (840/84) – a difference of only 4 days. But since the difference in time is 10 days, the work quantum needs to be multiplied by 2.5 to get total work = 840 × 2.5 = 2100. Thus, when Gupta works for 10 days and Sharma works for 15 days, the total work done would be: 84 × 10 + 60 × 15 = 1740. The work left would be 2100 − 1740 = 360, which would need to be done by Singh. Since, Singh works at the rate of 50 units per day, he would require 360/50 = 7.2 days.

13. Let the capacity of the tank be 30 liters and the efficiencies of 3 pipes be $A$, $B$ and $C$ respectively.

$$A = \frac{30}{5} = 6, B = \frac{30}{10} = 3, C = \frac{30}{15} = 2$$

Tank filled in the 1st hour = $\frac{3}{4}[6+3] + \frac{2}{3} \times 2 = \frac{97}{12}$

Tank filled in the 2nd hour = $6 + 3 + \frac{2}{3} \times 2 = 9 + \frac{4}{3} = \frac{31}{3}$

Tank filled in the 3rd hour = $6 + 3 + 2 = 11$

∴ Volume left = $30 - \left(\frac{97}{12} + \frac{31}{3} + 11\right) = \frac{7}{12} L$

It can be completed in another $\left(\frac{7}{12}\right) : 11 \approx 0.05$ hours

∴ Total time = $3 + 0.05 = 3.05$ hours.

14. Let the interest rates charged by the first money-lender and the second money lender be $(r + 10)\%$ and $r\%$ respectively.

As per the question,

$$30000\left(1 + \frac{r+10}{100}\right)^2 = 30000\left(1 + \frac{r}{100}\right)^2 + 7500$$

On solving we get r = 20%

Also, let ₹A be the amount borrowed from the first lender.

Then according to the question,

$$A\left(1 + \frac{30}{100}\right)^2 = (60000 - A)\left(1 + \frac{20}{100}\right)^2 + 38800$$

On checking the options, we get, A = ₹40,000.

15.

Delhi ├────Y────┬────X────┤ Mathura
       ←──── 300 kms ────→

Let Mukesh and Dinesh will start on bike and Suresh will start walking. Dinesh will get down at point X

and start walking towards Mathura, whereas Mukesh will come back on his bike to pick Suresh from Y and will turn back so that they all reach Mathura at the same time.

Suresh travelled 300 kms, partly on bike and partly walking, whereas Dinesh also travelled the same both of them taking the same time. Hence Delhi to Y = X to Mathura = A (say)

∴ Delhi to X + X to Y = 4A (speed of bike is 4 times walking speed).

∴ $X - Y = \frac{4A - A}{2} = 1.5A$

$A + 1.5A + A = 300$

∴ $3.5A = 300$ kms

∴ Required time

$= \frac{A}{15} + \frac{2.5A}{60} = \frac{300}{3.5 \times 15} + \frac{2.5 \times 300}{3.5 \times 60} = 9\frac{2}{7}$ hours.

16. Let the production cost be ₹100

Contribution of A = ₹10

Contribution of B = ₹20

Selling price = ₹120

Now, cost of A = 10 + 20% of 10 = ₹12 and cost of B = 20 + 40% of 20 = ₹28

New production cost = ₹110

New selling price = 1.15 × 120 = ₹138

∴ Profit percentage = $\frac{138 - 110}{110} \times 100 \cong 25.5\%$

17. In a 1 km race Mandeep was defeated by 60 m or 12 seconds.

Speed of Mandeep = 60/12 = 5 m/s

Mandeep took 250/5 = 50 seconds to travel from railway station to the hotel.

In 1 km race Jagdeep won by 12 seconds so in a 250 meters Jagdeep would win by 3 seconds.

Required time = 50 − 3 = 47 seconds.

18. Sujoy's, Mritunjoy's and Paranjoy's profit share are in the ratio = 35000 × 12 : 130000 × 6 : 75000 × 8 = 7 : 13 : 10

After giving 10% to Sujoy remaining amount = 0.9 × 450000 = 405000

∴ Paranjoy's share = $\frac{10}{7 + 13 + 10} \times 405000$

$= ₹135000$

Hence, option (b).

19. 12 men = 24 boys

12 men and 18 boys = 24 + 18 = 42 boys.

Total work = 42 × 60 × 7.5 boys-hours.

Harigarh work = 2 × 42 × 60 × 7.5 boys-hours.

21 men = 42 boys

Let total 'x' boys are needed to help 21 men.

$(42 + x) \times 9 \times 50 = 2 \times 42 \times 60 \times 7.5$

x = 42 boys.

20. Let Animesh invest ₹x in PPF and ₹y in NSC.

∴ $\dfrac{x}{3} = \dfrac{y}{2}$

Also, x + y = 150000

∴ $\dfrac{3y}{2} + y = 150000$ or y = ₹60,000.

If Aniket invests ₹z in PPF then, he invests ₹(z + 40000) in shares and ₹(z + 20000) in NSC.

z + z + 40000 + z + 20000 = 150000 or z = 30000

Aniket's investment in NSC = ₹50,000.

Animesh's investment in NSC = ₹60,000.

Difference = 60000 − 50000 = ₹10,000.

21. Let the average price of the 13 books purchased from MN distributors be x.

$\dfrac{\dfrac{4500}{15}}{6} = \dfrac{x}{5}$ or x = 250.

Total price of books purchased by 13 books = 13 x 250 = ₹3250

Price of books purchased from UV publications = ₹4500 − 3250 = ₹1250.

If the cost of the two books from UV publication be a and b respectively.

$\dfrac{a}{3} = \dfrac{b}{2}$

a + b = 1250

On solving the above two equations, we get: a = ₹750 and b = ₹500.

22. Let the ages of Amita, Sumita and Paramita be A, B and C respectively.

$\dfrac{A - 2}{5} = \dfrac{B - 2}{4}$  (1)

$\dfrac{A + B}{2} - 2 = 27$  (2)

On solving, we get A = 32 years, B = 26 years.

A − 2 + B − 2 + C − 2 = 72 or C = 20 years.

Required average = $\dfrac{B + 3 + C + 3}{2} = \dfrac{B + C}{2} + 3$

= 26 years.

23. After 30 days 60% of the work is left. Work done = $104 \times 30 \times 8 = 40\%$ of the work. Hence, work to be done in the remaining 26 days = 60% of the work = $1.5 \times 104 \times 30 \times 8$. To complete this in 26 days with

9 hours per day of working: $\dfrac{1.5 \times 104 \times 30 \times 8}{9 \times 26} = 160$

men would be required. Hence, we need 56 more men to be employed.

24. Percentage of the journalists involved in sports reporting = $\dfrac{5 \times 0.7 + 4 \times 0.6}{9} \times 100 \approx 65\%$

25. Ratio of metal 1 and metal 2 = $\left(14 \times \dfrac{3}{7} + 26 \times \dfrac{5}{13}\right) :$

$\left(14 \times \dfrac{4}{7} + 26 \times \dfrac{8}{13}\right) = 16 : 24 = 2 : 3$

26. Production in 2008 = 100, production in 2009 = 118, production in 2010 = 118 × 1.18 = 139.24, production in 2011 = 139.24 × 0.88 = 122.53, production in 2012 = 122.53 × 1.18 = 144.58. Option (c) is the closest answer and hence is the correct answer. Note: While doing these calculations, it might be a good idea to work with the percentage change graphic explained in the chapter on percentages.

27. Check the options option (c): Let the amount invested in scheme X is ₹15000.

Interest earned from scheme X (at 6% compound interest) = 15000 → 15000 + 6% of 15000 = 15000 + 900 → 15000 + 900 + 900 + 54 = 15000 + 1854

Interest earned from scheme Y (at 8% compound interest) = 10000 → 10000 + 800 → 10000 + 800 + 800 + 64 = 10000 + 1664

Total interest earned from both the schemes together = 1854 + 1664 = 3518, which is same as given in the question. Hence, this option is correct.

28. The relative speed of the two trains = 108 km/hour = 30 m/sec. Since, the two trains take 15 seconds to cross each other, the total length of the two trains would be 450 meters. If the length of the first train is d, the length of the second train would be 0.5d. Thus, 1.5d = 450 → d = 300 m.

While passing the bridge we will get: (300/18) × 51 = (length of bridge + 300)

Solving this we will get the length of the bridge as 550 m.

Option (a) is correct.

29. 12 men × 10 days = 20 women × 12 days → 120 man-days = 240 women days.

1 man-day = 2 women days.

Thus, 8 men and 4 women working for 9 days can be seen as 8 men & 2 men = 10 men working for 9 days. Hence, total work done before 10 more women joined them = 90 man-days. Work left = 120 − 90 = 30 man-days.

This work has to be done by 10 men + 10 women = 10 men + 5 men = 15 men. They would take 30 ÷ 15 = 2 days. Hence, Option (a) is correct

30. The equation for the speed of the train would be:

Speed = $45 - K\sqrt{N}$

When N = 9, speed is given as 30 km/hour. Hence, 30 = 45 – K $\sqrt{9}$ = 45 – 3K → K = 5.

Hence, the equation becomes:

Speed = 45 – 5 $\sqrt{N}$

The train would stop moving when N = 81. Hence, the train would just move when N = 80. Hence, Option (c) is correct.

31. Rohit has sold 15 soaps and 8 toothpastes. On each toothpaste, he makes a profit of ₹20, hence his profit on 8 toothpastes would be ₹160. Thus, his profit on 15 soaps would be ₹(385–160) = ₹225. Thus, his profit per soap = 225/15 = ₹15. Since, he has marked up his soap prices by 15%, it means that the cost of a soap = ₹100. Also, since the cost of a toothpaste = 60% the cost of a soap, the cost of a toothpaste = ₹60. According to the problem, he gets no return on unsold items. Hence, 5 soaps and 4 toothpastes would be a complete loss for him. The loss he would incur for these items = 5 × 100 + 4 × 60 = ₹740. But, he has already made a profit of ₹385. Hence, the overall loss would be = ₹(740– 385) = ₹355.

32. The ratio of A : B : C : D = 27: 36: 48:64.

Thus, C's share = (48/175) × 1400 = 384 Hence, option (d) is correct.

33. $\left(1 - \dfrac{x}{100}\right) \times 70 = \left(1 + \dfrac{x}{100}\right) \times 60$

∴  $10 = \dfrac{70x}{100} + \dfrac{60x}{100}$

∴  $x = \dfrac{100}{13}$

x% of 50 = $\dfrac{100}{13} \times \dfrac{1}{100} \times 50 = 3.84$

**Alternate Solution:**

Solve this one through options. One reading of the question sentence should tell you clearly that there would be a value of 'X' that would satisfy this—and hence Option (d) can be rejected. This leaves us to check the first three options. The following process would help you identify whether an option is correct or not.

For Option (c):

X % of 50 = 7.10 implies that the value of X must be 14.2%.

If we now visualise the equation

70 – 14.2% of 70 = 60 + 14.2% of 60, we can clearly realise that the LHS and the RHS of the above equation do not match. Hence, this option can be rejected.

For Option (b): X % of 50 = 4.82 implies that the value of X must be 9.64 %.

If we now visualise the equation 70 – 9.64 % of 70 = 60 + 9.64 % of 60, we can clearly realise that the LHS and the RHS of the above equation do not match.

Hence, this option can be rejected. Option (a) has to be correct and can be checked through the same thought.

34. Let the number of hours required to complete the work by mother, elder son and younger son be a, b and c hours respectively.

Therefore, the efficiencies of mother, elder son and younger son in one hour is 1/a, 1/b and 1/c respectively.

Mother takes one hour less than the elder son. So, a = b – 1.

According to the question:

$$\dfrac{1}{a} + \dfrac{1}{b} + \dfrac{1}{c} = 1 \qquad (1)$$

and

$$\dfrac{1}{b} + \dfrac{1}{c} + \dfrac{3}{c} = 1 \qquad (2)$$

$$1/c = (b – 1)/4b$$

As a = b – 1, by substituting the values of 1/a and 1/c in equation 1, we get:

$$\dfrac{1}{b-1} + \dfrac{1}{b} + \dfrac{b-1}{4b} = 1 \text{ or } b = 3$$

$$a = b – 1 = 3 – 1 = 2.$$

Percentage of work done by mother in 1 hour = $\dfrac{1}{2} \times 100 = 50\%$.

**Alternate Solution:**

The total work for them is 100% per hour. If we try to go through the options and try Option (b) which is the easiest to check – we get: The mother's work per hour = 50%. This would mean that the mother requires 2 hours to complete the task. Since it is given that the elder son takes one hour more than his mother to complete the task, it would imply that the elder son's time taken for the task = 3 hours → elder son's work per hour = 33.33%. Then the younger son's work per hour would be 100–50–33.33 = 16.66% per hour.

With these working rates, we need to confirm whether the last condition mentioned in the problem matches with these working rates for the two sons. The condition states that—"The cooking can also be completed if the two sons start cooking together and the elder son leaves after 1 hour and the younger son cooks for further 3 hours." If we go by this—we will get that the elder son would do 33.33% of the work in the first hour, while the younger son would cook for 4 hours and do 66.66% of the work—thus completing 100%

of the work together (since 33.333% + 66.666% = 100%). Thus, Option (b) is the correct option.

35. Time spent at the doctor's chamber = $\dfrac{48}{60} = \dfrac{4}{5}$

Total time spent during travelling = $5 - \dfrac{4}{5} = \dfrac{21}{5}$

Now let the distance between the doctor's clinic and Rohit's house be $d$ then

$$\dfrac{d}{20} + \dfrac{d}{12} + \dfrac{4}{5} = 5$$

∴  $d = 36$ km

Alternate Solution:

The equation that one needs to solve for this question is:

$d/30 + d/12 = 4.2$.

(4.2 here, means that the total time taken for the travel is 4 hours 12 minutes – since he comes home in exactly 5 hours, which includes the 48 minutes at the doctor's chamber.) The value of 'd' can then be checked from the options—the best option which fits the value of d = 36. Hence, Option (c) is correct.

36. Let percentage of Aluminium in 8 kg and 16 kg alloy be x and y respectively and weight of the pieces cut from both the alloys be w then according to the question:

∴  $\dfrac{(8-a)x + ay}{8 \times 100} = \dfrac{(16-a) + ax}{16 \times 100}$

∴  $16x - 2ax + 2ay = 16y - ay + ax$

∴  $16 - 2a = a$ or $3a = 16$

∴  $a = \dfrac{16}{3} = 5.33$ kg

**Alternate Solution:**

The main focus in this problem should be on understanding that the cut-off piece's weight should be such that the alloyed pieces that are created should have the same ratio weight-wise for each of the two alloys.

Thus, if the weight of the cut off pieces is 'w' each, then: (8–w)/w = w/(16–w).

Again to solve this, it is better to try to use the options given in the question to see which one fits the above equation. Using Option (c), we can see that if we take w = 5.33, we get: 2.66/5.33 = 5.33/10.66 = ½. Hence, Option (c) is correct

37. Total money deposited in the bank = 1,00,00,000 – (40,00,000 –20,00,000 – 10,00,000) = ₹30,00,000

Amount in bank after three years = 3000000 × (1.12)³ = ₹42,14,784

Total gain after 3 years is 5%.

Total value = 10000000 × 1.05 = ₹1,05,00,000

10500000 – 4214784 = 6285216

Clearly this value is closest to 90%.

**Alternate Solution:**

30 lac invested @ 12% per annum compounded, would approximately become 42 lac in three years. Since, he gets back 1.05 crore—his return on his remaining 70 lac would be equal to 1.05 crore – 42 lac = 63 lac—which is around 90% of the value of his investment of 70 lac.

Thus, Option (c) is the correct answer.

38. It can be experimentally verified by taking the values of the 7 integers as 1, 2, 3, 4, 5, 6 and 7 to get an average of 4, while the average of the group if the next three numbers are included would become 5.5 (the group of numbers would be 1, 2, 3, 4, 5, 6, 7, 8, 9 and 10). Thus, the average increases by 1.5. Hence, Option (c) is correct.

39. Let the work done by tap X in an hour be w. Then the work done by tap Y in an hour would be 1.6w. Together, they would do 2.6w work in an hour. Thus, the total work in 40 hours = 40 × 2.6w = 104w. This amount of work would be done by Y alone in $\dfrac{104w}{1.6w}$ hours = 65 hours.

Hence, Option (b) is correct.

40. Alloy X would contain 40% of zinc. Hence, 40 grams of alloy X contains 16 grams of zinc. Also, 60 grams of alloy Y would contain 60 × 7/18 = 23.33 grams of zinc. Thus in 100 grams of alloy Z we have 39.33 grams of zinc and 60.66 grams of copper. This works out to a ratio of 118:182 = 59:91. Option (b) is correct

41. Pure milk in the mixture after four replacements = $(40 - 10/40)^4 = (3/4)^4$

Pure milk in the final 10 litre mixture = $(3/4)^4 \times 10 = 405/128$.

Option (d)

**Alternate Solution:**

The first customer receives pure milk. The second receives 10 × 0.75 = 7.5 liters pure milk; In this fashion the fifth customer would receive:

10 × (3/4) × (3/4) × 3/4 × 3/4 = 405/128 liters of pure milk. Option (d) is the correct answer.

42. The ferry has exactly 4 hours and 30 minutes to complete the journey. The total distance it has to travel is 70 kms going towards the Rock and 100 kms coming back. For each of the given options, the total time can be calculated. We need to check for which of the options the total time is equal to 4 hours 30 minutes.

For Option (c): Time going towards the rock + Time coming back to Kanyakumari = 70/40 + 100/38 ≈ 262.9 minutes.

For the options (a) and (b), the time required is less than 262.9 minutes, while for the Option (d), the time required is more than 270 and hence is not possible. Since, the objective stated in the problem is to reach just in time, we would select the closest answer to 270 minutes and below 270 minutes.

Hence, Option (c) is correct.

43. Assume that for price x, Vodafone gives talk time of 100 seconds and Airtel gives talktime 79 seconds. For the same price in post-paid:

Talk time by Airtel = $1.12 \times 79 = 88.48$ seconds

Talktime by Vodafone = $100 \times 0.85 = 85$ seconds

Required percentage = $(88.48 - 85) \times 100/85 = 4.07\%$

Closest option is option (a).

44. Let the original service charge be ₹ 100

Rohan has paid 100, 90, $90 \times 0.89 = 80.1, 80.1 \times 0.88$ = 70.48 and 55 rupees for the five services

Total payment done by Rohan = $100 + 90 + 80.1 + 70.48 + 55 = ₹395.58$

Total discount availed by Rohan = $500 - 395.60 = ₹104.42$

Percentage discount = $104.42 \times 100/500 = 20.88\%$ (approx.)

45. Let the capacity of the Tank be 35 litres (LCM of 7 & 5).

Efficiency of inlet pipe = $35/7 = 5$ liters/min.

Efficiency of outlet pipe = $-35/5 = -7$ liters/min.

It takes 7 hours to empty the completely filled tank so the combined efficiency of all inlets and outlets is $-35/7 = -5$ litre/min. (–ve sign shows water is going out from the tank)

By checking the options, we get for option (d)

Net efficiency = $6 \times 5 + (11 - 6) \times (-7) = 30 - 35 = -5$ litres/min

Hence, this option is correct.

46. Let the minimum number of pages to be printed be n.

$5000 + 1.8x = 8000 + 1.5x$

$0.3x = 3000$

$x = 10,000.$

47. Let the speed of the bus in the morning be 'v' km/hr and it takes 't' hours in the morning.

Distance travelled by the bus in the morning = vt

Distance travelled by the bus in the evening = $1.5v \times 1.5t = 2.25$ vt

Average Speed = Total Distance/ Total time = $\dfrac{vt + 2.25\,vt}{t + 1.5\,t} = 1.3v$

Therefore, the average speed for the entire journey is 30% greater than it's average speed in the morning.

48. We can reject options (a) and (c) because these values are lower than ₹2,65,000. We are left with only two options (b) and (d).

Check option (d):

$280000 = 100000 + 180000$

$\qquad\qquad\downarrow\qquad\qquad\downarrow$

$\qquad\qquad 6\%\qquad\quad 5\%$

$\qquad\qquad 6000\qquad 9000$

Now, he will remit $2,80,000 - 6000 - 9000 = ₹2,65,000.$

So, this option is correct.

49. Let the efficiency of P be 'p'.

Efficiency of Q = 1.26 P

Efficiency of R = $1.26P + 1.26P \times (1.5) = 1.89P$

Combined efficiency of Q and R = $1.26P + 1.89P = 3.15P$

According to the question P takes 42 days to complete the work. So Q and R can finish the work in $42/3.15 = 13$ days.

50. 1kg P contains = 0.45 kgs Silver, 0.55 kg Aluminum

4.5 kg Q contains = 1.35 kg Silver, 1.575 kg Aluminum, 1.575 kg Copper.

Thus newly formed 5.5 kg of alloy contains 1.8 kg Silver & 1.575 kg copper.

Percentage of Silver = $1.8/5.5 \approx 33\%$

Percentage of Copper = $1.575 \times 100/5.5 \approx 29\%$

51. Let farmer A and farmer B have x hectares and x + 15 hectares land respectively.

According to the question:

$530 + 20x = 30(x + 15)$

By solving, we get x = 8

Former A cultivated $20 \times 8 = 160$ bushels.

52. Let the S.P. for each type of soap be ₹ 100

C.P of soap sold at 13% loss = $100/0.87 \approx ₹115$

C.P of soap sold at 23% profit = $100/1.23 \approx ₹81$

C.P of soap sold at 26% loss = $100/0.74 \approx ₹135$

Average C.P. = $(115 + 81 + 135)/3 \approx ₹110.3$

Required percentage = $(110.3 - 100) \times 100/100 = 10.3\%$

53. Check the options:

Option (a): 45 days and 90 days.

$$\dfrac{1}{\dfrac{1}{45} + \dfrac{1}{90}} = 30 \text{ days.}$$

Hence, option (a) is correct. Alternately, you can think through the options by using percentages. For option (a): Completing the work in 45 days means 2.22% work per day. Completing the work in 90 days means 1.11% work per day. Combined it would add up to 3.33% per day, which would mean 30 days. Hence, this option is correct.

54. Let, x be the amount, T is the time period, r is the interest rate.

According to the question:

$$10(T - 0.5) = 8(T)$$

T = 2.5 years. Checking options (c) and (d) we can see that only if the amount is 51750, would there be a final payment of 62100 (@8% Simple interest)

Hence, Option (c) is correct.

55. Let the total work is LCM of(45,60,75) = 900. Efficiencies of Somesh, Tarun and Nikhil are 20, 15, 12 units respectively.

$I^{st}$ 5 days work = $(20 + 15 + 12) \times 5 = 235$

Last 2 days work = $(15) \times 2 = 30$. So Somesh and Tarun would have to do 900-235-30 = 635 units of work. They would take 635/35 = 127/7 days. Hence, the required time = $5 + 2 + 127/7 = 176/7 = 25\frac{1}{7}$ days.

56. Let the quantity of chemical x &y be x gm and y gm respectively.

According to the question:

$$0.05x + 0.1y \geq 7$$
$$0.1x + 0.06y \geq 7$$

On solving the above two inequalities, we get

$$x \geq 40, \ y \geq 50$$

Minimum possible cost = $40 \times 10.5 + 50 \times 7.8 = ₹810$.

57. The margin per unit is ₹6. To cover the fixed costs of ₹50400, the company needs to sell 50400/6 = 8400 units.

58. Use alligation method explained in the chapter on alligations to solve this. The required ratio would be: 6:15 = 2:5

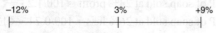

59. The figure for the given situation would look as follows:

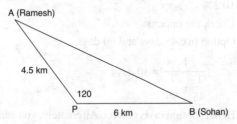

Distance between Ramesh and Sohan after 90 minutes

$$AB^2 = a^2 + b^2 - 2ab \cos 120$$
$$= 4.5^2 + 6^2 - 2 \times 4.5 \times 6 \times \cos 120^0$$
$$AB^2 = 83.25$$
$$AB = 9.12 \text{ km.}$$

60. The two juices contain 25% and 50% water respectively. The final mixture contains 37.5% of water. Hence, the mixing ratio should be 1:1 and we need 6 liters of each to make 12 liters of the mixture.

61. Let the $2^{nd}$ borewell takes 't' hours.

$I^{st}$ borewell takes t + 10 hours and $3^{rd}$ borewell takes 't – 8' hours.

First two borewells takes same time as the $3^{rd}$.

$$1/(t + 10) + 1/t = 1/(t - 8)$$

Now by checking the options or by solving the above equation we get t = 20 hours.

The $3^{rd}$ borewell will take = 20 – 8 = 12 hours.

Note: Alternately, you can also solve this using the options and fitting in the percentage values.

62. The extra amount per department would be $1.5 \times 10^7 \div 200 = ₹7.5 \times 10^4$. Hence, Option (c) is correct.

63. For 20 students, the total expenditure = $20 \times 400 = ₹8000$.

For 40 students, the total expenditure = $40 \times 300 = ₹12000$.

Thus, when we added 20 extra students, we added ₹4000 in cost. To go to the total cost of 80 students, we can simply add the additional variable cost of ₹8000 (for 40 students extra) to 12000 (the total cost of 40 students). Thus, for 80 students, the total cost would be ₹20000. Per student average cost would be 20000/80 = ₹250.

Hence, Option (a) is correct

64. Solving through options, we can check as follows:

Total sugar in 10 liters to start with = 1.5 liters. Total sugar to end within 10 liters = 1 liter. Hence, total sugar released = 1.5–1 = 0.5 liters.

Option (a)—If 1 liter is released each time:

First iteration, amount of reduction in sugar = 15% of 1 = 0.15 liters.

The mixture would now contain 8.65 water and 1.35 sugar.

Releasing 1 liter again would release less than 0.15 liters (and hence the total release cannot add up to 0.5 liters). Hence, we reject this option.

Option (d) is the easiest to check after Option (a).

Hence, we move to Option (d) next: Option (d)—If 2 liter is released each time: First iteration, amount of reduction in sugar = 15% of 2 = 0.3 liters. The mixture would now contain 8.8 water and 1.2 liters sugar.

Releasing 2 liter again would release 12% sugar = 0.24. Hence, total sugar released is 0.54—giving us approximately 10% sugar in the mixture. This is the closest option & hence option (d) is correct.

65. Solve this one through options. If you use Option (a) you get: $21 \times 3.3 + 57 \times 2.9 = 234.6 \neq 249$.

Option (b) gives us: $57 \times 3.3 + 21 \times 2.9 = 249$.

Hence, Option (b) is correct.

66. Let Distance of the journey = D, Diesel used per km = A and the number of carriages = N.

Then we have Time, $T = \dfrac{K \times D \times N}{\sqrt{A}}$

From the first set of values given in the question, we have T = 45, D = 70, N = 15 and A = 1/7. Putting these values in the equation we get: $K = 3/70\sqrt{7}$

The equation then becomes, $T = \dfrac{3 \times D \times N}{70\sqrt{7} \times \sqrt{A}}$

In the second case, D = 50 km, N = 18 and T = 30 minutes.

Solving for A, we get the value of A = 11.8. Hence, Option (b) is correct.

67. From the first two statements, it can be worked out that the ages of Ravindra and Rekha today are 35 and 30 respectively.

This is got by solving: $(5x + 10)/ (4x + 10) = 7/6$.

Since, they have been married for 10 years, the largest total age of the family would occur, if we put the triplets as 9 years olds each, the twins as 6 years old each and the single child as a 3-year old. The maximum possible total age of the family would work out to: $35 + 30 + 9 + 9 + 9 + 6 + 6 + 3 = 107$.

Option (d) is correct.

68. The investment is expected to double in 12 years. Thus, 30 lacs would double in 12 years, become 4 times in 24 years, 8 times in 36 years and 16 times in 48 years. Thus, the final value of the investment in 48 years would be 4,80,00,000. Option (c) is correct.

69. The total man-days of work (for engineering students) $= 1 + 3 + 6 + 10 + 15 + 21 + 28 + 36 + 45 + 55 + 66 + 78 + 91 + 105 + 120 + 136 + 153 + 171 + 190 + 210 = 1540$ man-days for engineering students.

Given that an MBA student is twice as efficient as an Engineering student, the number of man-days required for management students to complete the same task would be 1540/2 = 770 man-days. With 11 MBA students working at it, the number of days required to complete the job would be: 770/11 = 70 man-days. Hence, Option (a) is correct.

70. The total revenue the company would generate would be: $1080 \times 25 + 4320 \times 18.75 = 108000$.

From the 108000, there is a 30% vendors' discount. Hence, the total revenue is 75600. On a cost of ₹80000, this represents a 5.5% loss. Option (c) is correct.

# XAT (2008-17)

1. In a cricket match, TeamA scored 232 runs without losing a wicket. The score consisted of byes, wides and runs scored by the two opening batsmen: Ram and Shyam. The runs scored by the two batsmen are 26 times wides. There are 8 more byes than wides. If the ratio of the runs scored by Ram and Shyam is 6:7, then the runs scored by Ram is **(XAT 2008)**
   (a) 88  (b) 96
   (c) 102  (d) 112
   (e) None of the above

2. Mungeri Lal has two investment plans- A and B, to choose from, Plan A offers interest of 10% compounded annually while plan B offers interest of 12% per annum. Till how many years is plan B a better investment?  **(XAT 2009)**
   (a) 3  (b) 4
   (c) 5  (d) 6
   (e) 7

3. A salesman sells two kinds of trousers: cotton and woollen. A pair of cotton trousers is sold at 30% profit and a pair of woollen trousers is sold at 50% profit. The salesman has calculated that if he sells 100% more woollen trousers than cotton trousers, his overall profit will be 45%. However he ends up selling 50% more cotton trousers than woolen trousers. What will be his overall profit?  **(XAT 2009)**
   (a) 37.5%  (b) 40%
   (c) 41%  (d) 42.33%
   (e) None of the above

4. Rajesh walks to and fro to a shopping mall. He spends 30 minutes shopping. If he walks at a speed of 10 km an hour, he returns to home at 19.00 hours. If he walks at 15 km an hour, he returns to home at 18.30 hours. How fast must he walk in order to return at 18.15 hours?  **(XAT 2009)**
   (a) 17 km/hour  (b) 17.5 km/hour
   (c) 18 km/hour  (d) 19 km/hour
   (e) None of the above

**Directions for questions no. 5 to 7:** on the basis of the following information.

KK, an aspiring entrepreneur wanted to set up a pen drive manufacturing unit. Since technology was changing very fast, he wanted to carefully gauge the demand and the likely profits before investing. Market survey indicated that he would be able to sell 1 lac units before customers shifted to different gadgets. KK realized that he had to incur two kinds of costs – fixed costs (the costs which do not change, irrespective of number of units of pen drives produced) and variable costs ( = variable cost per unit multiplied by number of units). KK expected fixed cost to be ₹40 lac and variable cost to be ₹100 per unit. He expected each pen drive to be sold at ₹200.  **(XAT 2009)**

5. What would be the break-even point (defined as no profit, no loss situation) for KK's factory, in term of sales?
   (a) ₹80 lac      (b) ₹100 lac
   (c) ₹120 lac     (d) ₹140 lac
   (e) Cannot be found with the given data.

6. KK was skeptical that per unit variable cost might increase by 10% though the demand might remain same. What will be the expected changes in profit in such a case?
   (a) Profit would decrease by 10.33%
   (b) Profit will increase will by 15.75%
   (c) Profit would decrease by 15.75%
   (d) Profit will decrease by 16.67%
   (e) Profit will increase by 16.67%

7. He discussed his business plan with a chartered accountant. KK informed that he was contemplating a loan of ₹20 lac at simple interest of 10% per annum for starting the business. The chartered accountant informed him that in such a case KK has to pay interest, followed by 30% tax. By how much does KK's earning change with 20% growth in sales vis-à-vis the original sales volume, in both cases considering tax and interest on loan?
   (a) 20%        (b) 16.7%
   (c) 25.6%      (d) 33.3%
   (e) 34.5%

8. A manufacturer has 200 liters of acid solution, which has 15% acid content. How many liters of acid solution with 30% acid content may be added so that acid content in the resulting mixture will be more than 20% but less than 25%? **(XAT 2010)**
   (a) More than 100 liters but less than 300 liters
   (b) More than 120 liters but less than 400 liters
   (c) More than 100 liters but less than 400 liters
   (d) More than 120 liters but less than 300 liters
   (e) None of the above

9. A man borrows ₹6000 at 5% interest, on reducing balance, at the start of the year. If he repays ₹1200 at the end of each year, find the amount of loan outstanding, in Rupees, at the beginning of the third year.
   (a) 3162.75     (b) 4125.00
   (c) 4155.00     (d) 5100.00
   (e) 5355.00

**Answer question 10 and 11:** Based on the following information. **(XAT 2012)**
Ramya, based in Shanpur, took her car for a 400 km trip to Rampur. She maintained a log of the odometer readings and the amount of petrol she purchased at different petrol pumps at different prices (given below). Her car already had 10 Iitres of petrol at the start of the journey, and she first purchased petrol at the start of the journey, as given in table below, and she had 5 liters remaining at the end of the journey.

| | Odometer Reading (Km) | Petrol purchased (Liter) | Rate of Petrol (₹/liter) |
|---|---|---|---|
| Start of journey | 400 | 20 | 30 |
| | 600 | 15 | 35 |
| | 650 | 10 | 40 |
| End of journey | 800 | | |

10. What has been the mileage (in kilometers per liter) of her car over the entire trip?
    (a) 8.00       (b) 8.50
    (c) 9.00       (d) 9.50
    (e) None of the above

11. Her car's tank-capacity is 35 Iitres. Petrol costs ₹45/liter in Rampur. What is the minimum amount of money she would need for purchasing petrol for the return trip from Rampur to Shanpur, using the same route? Assume that the mileage of the car remains unchanged throughout the route, and she did not use her car to travel around in Rampur.
    (a) 1714      (b) 1724
    (c) 1734      (d) 1744
    (e) Data insufficient to answer.

12. City Bus Corporation runs two buses from terminus A to terminus B, each bus making 5 round trips in a day. There are no stops in between. These buses ply back and forth on the same route at different but uniform speeds. Each morning the buses start at 7 AM from the respective terminuses. They meet for the first time at a distance of 7 km from terminus A. Their next meeting is at a distance of 4 km from terminus B, while travelling in opposite directions. Assuming that the time taken by the buses at the terminuses is negligibly small, and the cost of running a bus is ₹20 per km, find the daily cost of running the buses (in ₹). **(XAT 2012)**
    (a) 3200      (b) 4000
    (c) 6400      (d) 6800
    (e) None of the above

13. Ram and Shyam form a partnership (with Shyam as working partner) and start a business by Investing ₹4000 and ₹6000 respectively. The conditions of partnership were as follows:
    - In case of profits till ₹200,000 per annum, profits would be shared in the ratio of the invested capital.
    - Profits from ₹200,001 till ₹400,000 Shyam would take 20% out of the profit, before the division of remaining profits, which will then be based on ratio of invested capital.
    - Profits in excess of ₹400,000, Shyam would take 35% out of the profits beyond Rs400,000, before the division of remaining profits, which will then be based on ratio of invested capital.

If Shyam's share in a particular year was ₹367000, which option indicates the total business profit (in ₹) for that year? **(XAT 2012)**

(a) 520,000      (b) 530,000

(c) 540,000      (d) 550,000

(e) None of the above

14. Prof. Mandal walks to the market and comes back in an auto. It takes him 90 minutes to make the round trip. If he takes an auto both ways it takes him 30 minutes. On Sunday, he decides to walk both ways. How long would it take him? **(XAT 2013)**

(a) 100 minutes      (b) 120 minutes

(c) 140 minutes      (d) 150 minutes

(e) None of the above

15. Mr. Mehra is planning for higher education expenses of his two sons aged 15 and 12. He plans to divide ₹15 lacs in two equal parts and invest in two different plans such that his sons may have access to ₹21 lacs each when they reach the age of 21. He is looking for plan that will give him a simple interest per annum. The rates of interest of the plans for his younger son and elder son should be **(XAT 2013)**

(a) 5% and 7.5% respectively

(b) 8% and 12% respectively

(c) 10% and 15% respectively

(d) 15% and 22.5% respectively

(e) 20% and 30% respectively

16. Albela, Bob and Chulbul have to read a document of seventy eight pages and make a presentation next day. They realize that the article is difficult to understand and they would require team work to finish the assignment. Albela can read a page in 2 minutes, Bob in 3 minutes, and Chulbul in 4 minutes. If they divide the article into 3 parts so that all three of them spend the equal amount of time on the article, the number of pages that Bob should read is

**(XAT 2013)**

(a) 24      (b) 25

(c) 26      (d) 27

(e) 28

17. Ramesh bought a total of 6 fruits (apples and oranges) from the market. He found that he required one orange less to extract the same quantity of juice as extracted from apples. If Ramesh had used the same number of apples and oranges to make the blend, then which of the following correctly represents the percentage of apple juice in the blend?

**(XAT 2013)**

(a) 25%      (b) 33.3%

(c) 60%      (d) 60.6%

(e) None of the above

18. The Maximum Retail Price (MRP) of a product is 55% above its manufacturing cost. The product is sold through a retailer, who earns 23% profit on his purchase price. What is the profit percentage (expressed in nearest integer) for the manufacturer who sells his product to the retailer? The retailer gives 10% discount on MRP. **(XAT 2015)**

(a) 31%      (b) 22%

(c) 15%      (d) 13%

(e) 11%

19. Product M is produced by mixing chemical X and chemical Y in the ratio of 5 : 4. Chemical X is prepared by mixing two raw materials, A and B, in the ratio of 1 : 3. Chemical Y is prepared by mixing raw materials, B and C, in the ratio of 2 : 1. Then the final mixture is prepared by mixing 864 units of product M with water. If the concentration of the raw material B in the final mixture is 50%, how much water had been added to product M? **(XAT 2015)**

(a) 328 units      (b) 368 units

(c) 392 units      (d) 616 units

(e) None of the above

20. The tax rates for various income slabs are given below. **(XAT 2015)**

| Income Slab (₹) | Tax rate |
| --- | --- |
| ≤500 | Nil |
| >500 to ≤2000 | 5% |
| >2000 to ≤5000 | 10% |
| >5000 to <10000 | 15% |

There are 15 persons working in an organization. Out of them, 3 to 5 persons are falling in each of the income slabs mentioned above. Which of the following is the correct tax range of the 15 persons? (E.g. If one is earning ₹2000, the tax would be: 500 × 0 + 1500 × 0.05)

(a) 1350 to 7350, both excluded

(b) 1350 to 9800, both included

(c) 2175 to 7350, both excluded

(d) 2175 to 9800, both included

(e) None of the above

21. In the beginning of the year 2004, a person invests some amount in a bank. In the beginning of 2007, the accumulated interest is ₹10,000 and in the beginning of 2010, the accumulated interest becomes ₹25,000. The interest rate is compounded annually and the annual interest rate is fixed. The principal amount is: **(XAT 2015)**

(a) ₹16,000      (b) ₹18,000

(c) ₹20,000      (d) ₹25,000

(e) None of the above

22. Rani bought more apples than oranges. She sells apples at ₹23 apiece and makes 15% profit. She sells oranges at ₹10 apiece and makes 25% profit. If she gets ₹653 after selling all the apples and oranges, find her profit percentage. **(XAT 2016)**

(a) 16.8%  (b 17.4%
(c) 17.9%  (d) 18.5%
(e) 19.1%

23. Pradeep could either walk or drive to office. The time taken to walk to the office is 8 times the driving time. One day, his wife took the car making him walk to office. After walking 1 km, he reached a temple when his wife called to say that he can now take the car. Pradeep figures out that continuing to walk to the office will take as long as walking back home and then driving to the office. Calculate the distance between the temple and the office.

**(XAT 2016)**

(a) 1  (b) 7/3
(c) 9/7  (d) 16/7
(e) 16/9

24. A water tank has M inlet pipes and N outlet pipes. An inlet pipe can fill the tank in 8 hours while an outlet pipe can empty the full tank in 12 hours. If all pipes are left open simultaneously, it takes 6 hours to fill the empty tank. What is the relationship between M and N?  **(XAT 2016)**

(a) M : N = 1 : 1  (b) M : N = 2 : 1
(c) M : N = 2 : 3  (d) M : N = 3 : 2
(e) None of the above

25. Company ABC starts an educational program in collaboration with Institute XYZ. As per the agreement, ABC and XYZ will share profit in 60:40 ratio. The initial investment of ₹100,000 on infrastructure is borne entirely by ABC whereas the running cost of ₹400 per student is borne by XYZ. If each student pays ₹2000 for the program find the minimum number of students required to make the program profitable, assuming ABC wants to recover its investment in the very first year and the program has no seat limits.  **(XAT 2016)**

(a) 63  (b) 84
(c) 105  (d) 157
(e) 167

26. Four two-way pipes A, B, C and D can either fill an empty tank or drain the full tank in 4, 10, 12 and 20 minutes respectively. All four pipes were opened simultaneously when the tank is empty. Under which of the following conditions the tank would be half filled after 30 minutes?  **(XAT 2017)**

(a) Pipe A filled and pipes B, C and D drained
(b) Pipe A drained and pipes B, C and D filled
(c) Pipes A and D drained and pipes B and C filled
(d) Pipes A and D filled and pipes B and C drained
(e) None of the above

27. A shop, which sold same marked price shirts, announced an offer - if one buys three shirts then the fourth shirt is sold at a discounted price of ₹100 only. Patel took the offer. He left the shop with 20 shirts after paying ₹20,000. What is the marked price of a shirt?  **(XAT 2017)**

(a) ₹1260  (b) ₹1300
(c) ₹1350  (d) ₹1400
(e) ₹1500

28. Arup and Swarup leave point A at 8 AM to point B. To reach B, they have to walk the first 2 km, then travel 4 km by boat and complete the final 20 km by car. Arup and Swarup walk at a constant speed of 4 km/hr and 5 km/hr respectively. Each rows his boat for 30 minutes. Arup drives his car at a constant speed of 50 km/hr while Swarup drives at 40 km/hr. If no time is wasted in transit, when will they meet again?  **(XAT 2017)**

(a) At 9.15 AM  (b) At 9.18 AM
(c) At 9.21 AM  (d) At 9.24 AM
(e) At 9.30 AM

29. The taxis plying in Wasseypur have the following fare structure: ₹20 for the first two kilometers, ₹5 for every km in excess of 2 km and up to 10 km, and ₹8 for every km in excess of 10 km. Bullock carts on the other hand charge ₹2 per km. Sardar Khan takes a taxi from the Wasseypur railway station to his home. On the way, at a distance of 14 km from the railway station, he meets Faizal Khan, and gets down from the taxi to talk to him. Later he takes a bullock cart to reach his home. He spends a total of ₹102 to reach his home from the railway station. How far is his home from the railway station?  **(XAT 2013)**

(a) 17  (b) 18
(c) 19  (d) 20
(e) 21

30. The mean of six positive integers is 15. The median is 18, and the only mode of the integers is less than 18. The maximum possible value of the largest of the six integers is  **(XAT 2013)**

(a) 26  (b) 28
(c) 30  (d) 32
(e) 34

31. Ram, Shyam and Hari went out for a 100 km journey. Ram and Hari started the journey in Ram's car at the rate of 25 kmph, while Shyam walked at 5 kmph. After sometime, Hari got off and started walking at the rate of 5 kmph and Ram went back to pick up Shyam. All three reached the destination simultaneously. The number of hours required for the trip was:  **(XAT 2013)**

(a) 8  (b) 7
(c) 6  (d) 5
(e) 4

32. Prof. Suman takes a number of quizzes for a course. All the quizzes are out of 100. A student can get an A grade in the course if the average of her scores is more than or equal to 90. Grade B is awarded to a student if the average of her scores is between 87 and 89 (both included). If the average is below

87, the student gets a C grade. Ramesh is preparing for the last quiz and he realises that he will need to score a minimum of 97 to get an A grade. After the quiz, he realises that he will score 70, and he will just manage a B. How many quizzes did Prof. Suman take? **(XAT 2014)**

(a) 6 (b) 7
(c) 8 (d) 9
(e) None of these

33. A teacher noticed a strange distribution of marks in the exam. There were only three distinct scores: 6, 8 and 20. The mode of the distribution was 8. The sum of the scores of all the students was 504. The number of students in the most populated category was equal to the sum of the number of students with lowest score and twice the number of students with the highest score. The total number of students in the class was: **(XAT 2017)**

(a) 50 (b) 51
(c) 53 (d) 56
(e) 57

34. Devanand's house is 50 km West of Pradeep's house. On Sunday morning, at 10 a.m., they leave their respective houses. Under which of the following scenarios, the minimum distance between the two would be 40 km?

Scenario I: Devanand walks East at a constant speed of 3 km per hour and Pradeep walks South at a constant speed of 4 km per hour.

Scenario II: Devanand walks South at a constant speed of 3 km per hour and Pradeep walks East at a constant speed of 4 km per hour.

Scenario III: Devanand walks West at a constant speed of 4 km per hour and Pradeep walks East at a constant speed of 3 km per hour. **(XAT 2015)**

(a) Scenario I only (b) Scenario II only
(c) Scenario III only (d) Scenario I and II
(e) None of the above

35. The median of 11 different positive integers is 15 and seven of those 11 integers are 8, 12, 20, 6, 14, 22, and 13. Statement I: The difference between the averages of four largest integers and four smallest integers is 13.25. Statement II: The average of all the 11 integers is 16. Which of the following statements would be sufficient to find the largest possible integer of these numbers? **(XAT 2015)**

(a) Statement I only.
(b) Statement II only.
(c) Both Statement I and Statement II are required.
(d) Neither Statement I nor Statement II is sufficient
(e) Either Statement I or Statement II is sufficient.

36. Three pipes are connected to an inverted cone, with its base at the top. Two inlet pipes, A and B, are connected to the top of the cone and can fill the empty cone in 8 hours and 12 hours, respectively. The outlet pipe C, connected to the bottom, can empty a filled cone in 4 hours. When the cone is completely filled with water, all three pipes are opened. Two of the three pipes remain open for 20 hours continuously and the third pipe remains open for a lesser time. As a result, the height of the water inside the cone comes down to 50%. Which of the following options would be possible? **(XAT 2015)**

(a) Pipe A was open for 19 hours.
(b) Pipe A was open for 19 hours 30 minutes.
(c) Pipe B was open for 19 hours 30 minutes.
(d) Pipe C was open for 19 hours 50 minutes.
(e) The situation is not possible.

## ANSWER KEY

| | | | |
|---|---|---|---|
| 1. (b) | 2. (b) | 3. (b) | 4. (e) |
| 5. (a) | 6. (e) | 7. (e) | 8. (c) |
| 9. (c) | 10. (a) | 11. (d) | 12. (d) |
| 13. (d) | 14. (d) | 15. (e) | 16. (a) |
| 17. (b) | 18. (d) | 19. (b) | 20. (a) |
| 21. (c) | 22. (b) | 23. (c) | 24. (e) |
| 25. (a) | 26. (a) | 27. (b) | 28. (d) |
| 29. (c) | 30. (d) | 31. (a) | 32. (d) |
| 33. (e) | 34. (a) | 35. (e) | 36. (c) |

**Solutions**

1. Let the total wides be w then runs scored by Ram and Shyam would be 26w and total byes would be w + 8

$$26w + w + w + 8 = 232 \text{ or } w = 8$$

So total runs scored by Ram and Shyam = $26 \times 8 = 208$

Ratio of runs scored by Ram and Shyam = 6: 7

∴ Runs scored by Ram = $208 \times \dfrac{6}{13} = 96$

2. Let Mr. Mungeri Lal invest an amount ₹P.

In plan A total amount after n years

$$A = P\left(1 + \frac{10}{100}\right)^n = P(1.1)^n$$

In plan B total amount after n years B = $P + \dfrac{P \times 12 \times n}{100} = P + P \times n \times 0.12$

Checking at different options of n = 3, 4, 5, A becomes greater than B when n = 5.

Hence, upto 4 years, plan B is better than plan A.

Alternative approach: Let the investment be ₹100.

Plan A: 100- → (100 + 10) = 110--(1ST Year) → 110 + 11 = 121-(2ND year) → 121 + 12.1 = 133.1(3rd year) → 133.1 + 13.31 = 146.41(4th year) → 146.41 + 14.64 ≈ 161 (5TH Year)

Plan B: 100- → 112--($1^{ST}$ Year) → 124-($2^{ND}$ year) → 136 ($3^{rd}$ year) → 148($4^{th}$ year) → 160($5^{TH}$ Year)

3. Let the cost price of 1 cotton trouser and 1 woollen trouser be 'x' and 'y' respectively.

   When number of woolen trousers sold is 100% more than cotton trousers

   $$\therefore \quad 1.3x + 1.5 \times 2 \times y = 1.45(x + 2y)$$
   $$\Rightarrow \quad 0.15x = 0.1y$$
   $$\Rightarrow \quad 3x = 2y$$

   When number of cotton trousers sold is 50% more than woollen trousers

   $$SP = 1.3x + \frac{1.5 \times 2y}{3}$$

   or $\quad SP = 1.3x + y = 2.8x$

   $$CP = x + \frac{2}{3}y = 2x$$

   $$Profit = \left(\frac{2.8x - 2x}{2x}\right) \times 100 = 40\%$$

4. If he increases his speed by 5 km/hr, then the travelling time is reduced by 30 minutes. It is possible when the distance between the home and mall is 15 km. (15/10 – 15/15) = 1.5 – 1 = 0.5 hour or 30 minutes)

   If he travels at a speed of v kmph then he'll reach home at 6: 15

   $$\therefore \quad \frac{15}{15} - \frac{15}{v} = 0.25$$

   By solving we get v = 20 kmph

5. Fix cost of 1 lac units = 40 lac

   Let the breakeven point be attained on the sale of 'x' units.

   Therefore, 40 lac + 100x = 200x

   or $\quad$ x = 40000·

   Hence the total sales = 40000 × 200 = ₹80 lac.

6. Total cost when variable cost increases by 10% then total cost = 40 lac + 100 × 1.1 lac = ₹150 lac

   Initial Profit = 200 lac – 140 lac = ₹60 lac

   New Profit = ₹200 lac – ₹150 lac = ₹50 lac

   % decrease in the profit = $\left(\frac{10}{60}\right) \times 100 = 16.67\%$

7. Initial profit = (200 lac – 140 lac) = ₹60 lac

   Interest paid by KK on 20 lac = 10% of 20 lac = ₹2 lac

   Profit after interest + taxes = 70% of (60 – 2) lac = ₹40.6 lac

   After 20% growth in sales, he sells 1.2 lac units

   New profit = (200 × 1.2) lac – (40 + 100 × 1.2) lac = ₹80 lac

   Interest paid = 10% of 20 lac = ₹2 lac

Profit after interest and taxes = 70% of (80 – 2) lac = ₹54.6 lac

$$\% \text{ change in earning} = \frac{54.6 - 40.6}{40.6} \times 100 = 34.5\%$$

8. Case 1: When the resultant acid solution be 20% concentration, then by using alligation method:

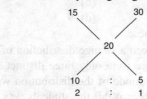

$$\therefore \text{ So the required solution} = \frac{200}{2} = 100 \text{ liters.}$$

Case 2: When the resultant acid solution is of 25% concentration, then:

So the required solution = 200 × 2 = 400 liters

Hence, we require more than 100 liters but less than 400 liters solution.

9. 6000 → 6000 + 300 – 1200 = 5100 → 5100 + 255 – 1200 = 4155 (at the start of the $3^{rd}$ year)

10. Mileage = total distance covered/total petrol consumed = (800 – 400)/(10 + 20 + 15 + 10 – 5) = 400/50 = 8 km/liter.

11. Before starting for Shanpur, Ramya's car has 5 liters of petrol. She can fill a maximum of 30 liters petrol. But to minimize the cost of petrol on the way is ₹40 per liter and ₹35 per liter.

    At first pump as well she will purchase enough petrol so that she can reach the second pump since the cost of petrol at the second pump is less.

    Minimum amount required

    $$= \frac{[150 - (5 \times 8)]}{8} \times 45 + \frac{50}{8} \times 40 + \frac{200}{8} \times 35 \approx ₹1744.$$

12. Let M be the point of first meeting and N be the point of second meeting. Let the distance MN = d km.

    A ← 7 km → | ← d km → | ← 4 km → B
    $\quad\quad\quad\quad$ M $\quad\quad\quad$ N

    Total distance covered by both the buses together before first meet = (11 + d) km.

    Total distance travelled by both the buses together from first to second meeting point = 2 × (11 + d) km.

    To cover this double distance each bus will take double the time and hence distance traveled by each bus from first to second meeting point will be double of what each of the buses travelled till first meeting. Bus from terminus A travels 7 km before first meeting and (d + 8) km between the first and second meeting. Hence d + 8 = 2 × 7 = 14

$$d = 6 \text{ km}$$

Hence, total distance between A and B = (7 + d + 4) km = (7 + 6 + 4) km = 17 km.

Hence, cost of running both the buses = 2 × (₹ 17 × 20 × 2 × 5) = ₹ 6,800

13. Let the profit (in ₹) for the year be ₹p. Then according to the question

$$\frac{3}{5} \times 200000 + \left(0.20 + \frac{3}{5} \times 0.8\right) \times 200000 +$$

$$\left(0.35 + \frac{3}{5} \times 0.65\right) \times (p - 400000) = 367000$$

$$256000 + 0.74 \times (p - 400000) = 367000$$

By solving the above equation we get p = ₹ 5,50,000.

14. From the starting sentence it is clear that since he takes 30 minutes in the auto going both ways, he must be taking 15 minutes each side. Thus, in his normal travels, walking to the market would take (90–15) = 75 minutes. Thus, if he were to walk both ways, he would take 150 minutes. Hence, option (d) is correct.

15. Let the interest rate for the 1st plan be x% per annum

then $7.5 + \dfrac{7.5 \times x \times (21 - 15)}{100} = 21$

On solving we get x = 20% so option (e) is correct.

Alternate Solution:

He has to invest ₹7.5 lacs in the name of each son. For the 15-year-old son, ₹7.5 lacs should convert to ₹21 lacs in 6 years time. This means that he should be getting simple interest of 13.5 lacs in 6 years (21-7.5). Thus, the simple interest per year should be 13.5/6 = ₹2.25 lacs. On an investment of 7.5 lacs, a simple interest of 2.25 lacs in a year works out to a 30% rate of interest.

Option (e) is correct.

Note: You do not need to work out the rate of interest of the younger child—as there is only one option with 30% rate of interest for the elder child. Even if you needed to work out the rate of interest for the younger child, you can easily see that 7.5 lacs should convert to 21 lacs in 9 years for the younger son. i.e. he should earn 13.5 lacs in 9 years—an annual interest of 1.5 lacs per year. On an investment of 7.5 lacs, an interest of 1.5 lacs means a rate of interest of 20%.

16. Solve this question using options. If we try using the first option, we get: If Bob reads 24 pages, he would take 72 minutes to read the same. Since, the time of reading per person should be equal, it means that Albela would read 72/2 = 36 pages and Chulbul would

read 72/4 = 18 pages. This gives us 78 as the total pages read. Hence, option (a) is correct.

17. Since the question tells us that the juice taken out of the apples is equal to the juice taken out by using 1 orange less than the number of apples, we should be able to see two scenarios here:

Case 1: Number of apples = 2 and number of oranges = 4.

In this case, the juice taken out of 2 apples = juice of 1 orange. Let us say that the quantity of juice in an apple is x, then the quantity of juice in 1 orange is 2x. So, if he uses the same number of apples and oranges, he would get: Total juice = juice from 2 apples + juice from two oranges = 2x + 4x = 6x. The percentage of apple juice in this blend would be: 33.33%.

Case 2: Number of apples bought = 3 and number of oranges bought = 3.

In this case, the juice taken out of 3 apples = juice of 2 oranges. Let us say that the quantity of juice in an apple is x, then the quantity of juice in 1 orange is 1.5x. So, if he uses the same number of apples and oranges, he would get:

Total juice = juice from 3 apples + juice from 3 oranges = 3x + 4.5x = 7.5x. The percentage of apple juice in this blend would be: 40%.

The value of 33.33% from Case I is the only possible value given in the options. Hence, option (b) is the correct answer.

18. Since the retailer sells the item at a 10% discount, if we assume that the cost of manufacturing was 100, the MRP would be 155 – we would get that the retailer sells at a 10% discount on 155. This means that the retailer would be selling the item at 0.9 × 155 = 139.5. Since the retailer sells at a 23% profit on his purchase price, his purchase price has to be such that if we add the effect of a 23% increase in the purchase price to the purchase price, we would get a selling price of 139.5 (approximately). Checking from the options, if we check the middle option of 15% - as the profit percentage for the manufacturer, we would get that the manufacturer sells at 115. However, adding 23% of 115 to 115, we would get 115 + 23% of 115 = 115 + 26.45 = 141.45. This is clearly above the required 139.5, and hence the manufacturer's profit would be below 15%. Checking Option (d) of 13% we get: Cost = 100, Manufacturer's selling price = retailer's purchase price = 113. Retailers' selling price = 113 + 23% of 113 ≈ 139.

This will clearly give us the closest answer to the question asked. Hence, Option (d) is correct

19. Since the final quantity of Product M used to prepare the final mixture is 864 units, the quantity of chemical X in the mixture would be 5/9 × 864 = 5 × 96 = 480.

Out of this 480 units, the amount of raw material B would be ¾ of 480 = 360 units.

Also, the quantity of chemical Y used in the final mixture would be 864 – 480 = 384. Out of this 2/3rd would be raw material B. Thus, total raw material B in the final mixture would be 360 + 256 = 616 units. This should be equal to half the final mixture. Thus, the final mixture prepared would be 2 × 616 = 1232. The amount of water in this mixture would be 1232 – 864 = 368 units. Option (b) is correct.

20. The maximum tax would be if the maximum possible numbers of people were earning the maximum possible amounts. This would happen under the following situation: 5 people earn 10000 (tax = 0 + 75 + 300 + 750 each), 4 people earn 5000 (tax = 0 + 75 + 300 each) and 3 people earn 2000 (tax = 0 + 75 each) and 3 people earn 500 (tax = 0). The total tax in this case would be: 1125 x 5 + 375 x 4 + 75 x 3 = 5625 + 1500 + 225 = 7350. However, we need to note here that the value would not include 7350, because the last tax slab is only till<10000

The minimum tax would be in the case that the maximum numbers of people are earning the least amounts. Thus, we get: 3 people earn just above 5000 (tax = 0 + 75 + 300 each), 3 people earn just above 2000 (tax = 0 + 75 each) and 4 people earn just above 500 (tax = 0 each) and 5 people earn under 500 (tax = 0). The total tax in this case would be: 375 × 3 + 75 × 3 = 1125 + 225 = 1350. However, we need to note here that the value would not include 1350, since we have calculated at the extreme values that are not included in the tax slabs. Hence, the minimum and maximum taxes possible are: 1350 and 7350 respectively (both excluded). Option (a) is correct.

21. Since compound interest is being used, the ratio of (Amount in the beginning of 2007)/(Amount in the beginning of 2004) = (Amount in the beginning of 2010)/(Amount in the beginning of 2007).

Checking the options, we see that Option (c) fits the situation perfectly, since: (20000 + 10000)/20000 = (20000 + 25000)/30000.

Both these ratios are equal to 3/2.

22. Cost price of an apple = ₹20

Cost price of an orange = ₹8

If she sells 'x' apples and 'y' oranges. Then, according to the question : 23x + 10y = 653 & x > y.

Possible value of (x, y) = (21, 17)

For (21, 17) the cost price = 21 × 20 + 17 × 8 = ₹556

% profit = $\frac{653 - 556}{556} \times 100 = 17.4\%$

23. Car's speed must be 8 times that of Pradeep's walkingspeed. Let the speeds of car and walking are 8v

and v respectively. If the distance between home and office is 'd' km. Then

$$d - 1/v = [1/8v + d/8v]$$
$$d - 1 = (1 + d)/8$$
$$8d - 8 = d + 1$$
$$7d = 9 \text{ or } d = 9/7 \text{ km.}$$

24. Let the capacity of the tank be 24 liters.

Efficiency of inlet pipe = 24/8 = 3

Efficiency of outlet pipe = 24/12 = 2. Since, the tank gets filled in 6 hours if all pipes are open, it follows that the net work per hour must be 24/6 = 4 units/hour. With M = 4 and N = 4, we get the requisite match for this situation. However, this can also be achieved using M = 2 and N = 1. Hence, the correct answer would be option (e).

25. If 'x' students enroll for the program, then to recover the cost: 100000 + 400x = 2000x

or    x = 62.5

So minimum 63 students must enroll to recover cost in the very first year.

26. Let the total capacity of the tank be 60 liters. Efficiencies of pipes A, B, C and D are 60/4, 60/10, 60/12, 60/20 or 15, 6, 5, 3 per minute respectively.

As tank would be half filled after 30 minutes. So, the combined efficiencies of all pipes must be 1 per minute. (30/30). Going by the options, we see that 1st option satisfies the given condition as 15 – (6 + 5 + 3) = 1. Hence, option (a) is correct.

27. If the marked price of the shirt is ₹x.

Then, according to the question:

$$(3x + 100) \times 5 = 20000$$
$$x = ₹1300$$

28. Total time taken by Arup to reach B from point A = (2/4) × 60 + 30 + (20/50) × 60 = 30 + 30 + 24 = 84 minutes.

Total time taken by Swarup to reach B from point A = (2/5) × 60 + 30 + (20/40) × 60 = 24 + 30 + 30 = 84 minutes.

Hence, they would be together at point B at 9.24 A.M.

29. The cost for the hire of the taxi for 14 kms would be given by: 20 + 8 × 5 + 4 × 8 = 92. Since, the total cost for his journey was ₹ 102, he would have spent ₹ 10 on the bullock cart – which means that he must have traveled 10/2 = 5 kms on the bullock cart. Hence, the total distance would be 14 + 5 = 19 kms.

30. For the largest of the six numbers to be the maximum possible value, the other five numbers should be the least possible. The sum of the six numbers = 6 × 15 = 90. Visualise this as __ + __ + __ + __ + __ + __ = 90 (putting the least number on the left and the maximum number on the right. Now we know that the

median of the numbers is 18—and since there are six numbers, the median would be the average of third and the fourth numbers in the list. Thus, the sum of the third and fourth numbers must be 36 (the numbers could be 17 + 19, 16 + 20, 15 + 21 etc.)

Now, the sum of the other four numbers (excluding the two numbers defining the median) would be 54. In order to make the largest number as big as possible, we would need to take the minimum possible values of the other three unknowns. This would occur under the following condition: 1 + 1 + 17 + 19 + 20 + _ = 90. Hence, the largest possible value for the highest number is 32. Hence, option (d) is correct.

31. From the information in the question, it can be concluded that the number of hours walked by Hari and the number of hours walked by Shyam should be equal. Consequently, the distances they have traveled walking should be equal. Also the distances they have traveled by car should be equal. The key judgment in this question is about how many kms would Ram have traveled with Hari initially.

Thinking in integers we get the following alternate numbers to represent the situation:

|  | Case 1 | Case 2 | Case 3 |
|---|---|---|---|
| Ram and Hari in car | 25 | 50 | 75 |
| Shyam in the same time | 5 | 10 | 15 |
|  | This case is rejected because Hari would have walked 75 km and Shyam < 25 | This case is rejected because Hari would have walked 50 km and Shyam < 50 | This case needs to be looked at further to see if it fits the description of the question |

If Ram and Hari went 75 kms—they would have traveled for 3 hours and in three hours Shyam would have covered 15 kms while walking. Since, Ram turns back to pick up Shyam, we can easily see using relative speed, that the point at which Ram would meet Shyam in this case is 25 km from the start. Thus, in this case, Hari would have a travel of 75 kms by car + 25 km walk while Shyam would have a travel of 25 km walk + 75 km by car. Both of them would reach the destination at the same time. Total time required = 25/5 + 75/25 = 5 + 3 = 8. Hence, Option (a) is correct.

32. The difference between just getting an A grade and just getting a B grade would be equal to (number of quizzes x 3). The difference between the required score to manage an A grade and the score achieved to just manage a B grade as given in the problem's information is equal to 97 – 70 = 27.

Thus, number of quizzes × 3 = 27.

Hence, number of quizzes is 9. Hence, Option (d) is correct.

33. Let the number of students scoring 6, 8 and 20 be a, b, and c respectively. So, 6a + 8b + 20c = 504

Also, since 'The number of students in the most populated category was equal to the sum of the number of students with lowest score and twice the number of students with the highest score' we get: a + 2c = b. Thus, 14a + 36c = 504.

By trying out values we get that: c = 7 and a = 18 which gives us b = 32. Therefore, total number of students = 18 + 32 + 7 = 57

Hence, Option (e) is the correct answer.

34. If we try to see what happens in the first scenario, we will get to see that the legs of the right triangle formed between Devanand and Pradeep after various time periods have elapsed would be given by:

| After time period of (in hours) | Distance of Devanand from Pradeep's house | Distance of Pradeep from his own house | Square of distance between Pradeep and Devanand |
|---|---|---|---|
| 1 | 47 | 4 | 2225 |
| 2 | 44 | 8 | 2000 |
| 3 | 41 | 12 | 1825 |
| 4 | 38 | 16 | 1700 |
| 5 | 35 | 20 | 1625 |
| 6 | 32 | 24 | 1600 |
| 7 | 29 | 28 | 1625 |

Thus, we can clearly see that the distance between them would reduce as the hours pass to a minimum of square root of 1600 ( = 40 kms) after 6 hours and then start increasing again. A similar analysis for scenario 2 would show that the minimum distance does not turn out to be 40 in this case. Scenario III is not worth considering since in that case they are moving towards each other and the minimum distance would be 0. Hence, Option (a) is correct.

35. In this case, we are given 8 of the 11 numbers, which can be placed in increasing order as: 6, 8, 12, 13, 14, Median 15, 20, 22

Clearly, three numbers above the median are missing. If we use only the statement I, we will get that the sum of the 4 largest numbers should be 53 more (logic 13.25 x 4) than the sum of the four smallest numbers. This means that the sum of the four largest numbers should be 92. (53 more than 6 + 8 + 12 + 13). In order to create the largest possible number in the list we would need to make sure that both 22 and 20 are part of the four largest numbers and also that two of the missing three numbers should be 16 each.

In such a case, the only missing number should be 92 – 22 – 20 – 16 – largest possible number = 34.

Thus, it is possible to find out the largest possible integer amongst these numbers using statement 1 alone.

Using Statement II alone, we get that the sum of the 11 numbers should be 176. We already know the sum of 8 of these numbers, while of the three missing numbers the scenario required to create the largest possible number would be that two of these numbers should be as small as possible. Since the median is 15, these two numbers should be 16 each. In this case the largest possible number can be found as: 176 – (6 + 8 + 12 + 13 + 14 + 15 + 16 + 16 + 20 + 22) = 34.

Thus, Statement I or Statement II is sufficient independently of each other.

Hence, Option (e) is the correct answer.

36. When the height of the water in the cone is halved, the volume of the water would go down to 12.5% of the original volume (a reduction of 87.5% of the total) – Logic of similarity of objects. Checking the options, this occurs for Option (c). Hence, Option (c) is correct.

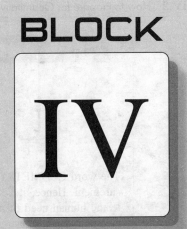

BLOCK

# IV

# Geometry

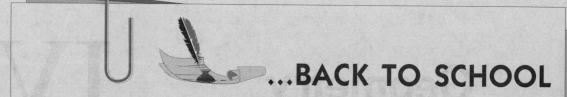

# ...BACK TO SCHOOL

The word GEOMETRY is derived from two words—GEO meaning earth and METRY meaning measurement. Hence, it is quite evident that geometry as a mathematical science developed mainly due to the human need of measuring land masses and distances. The major developments in the fields of Geometry and Mensuration are mainly credited to the ancient Egyptian and Greek civilisations. (In fact, this is one of the reasons why all formulae and theorems primarily carry Greek names.)

## Key Geometrical Concepts

**Point:** The point should be visualised as a singular dot. In physical terms, a point can be defined as a single dot that can be created on a plain paper by a very sharp pencil. It could also be visualised as a singular prick on a piece of paper by a very sharp nail or pin.

**Line:** Mathematically, lines are defined as a group of points which are straight one after another. All lines are supposed to extend infinitely in two directions.

## Segment of a Line

If a part of a line is cut out, we get a segment of a line.

Physically, the closest representations of a segment of a line would be a tight thread or the straight crease of a piece of paper.

**Plane:** The surface of a smooth wall or a table top is the closest representation of a portion of a plane.

## Some Geometrical Properties

**1. Lines Between Points:**  Let us take two distinct points in a plane. You can easily verify that an infinite number of lines can be drawn in the plane passing through any one of these two points. However, if you wanted to draw a line which passes through both the points, you will be able to draw only one line. This is an important result in Geometry.

**Property:**  Given any two distinct points in a plane, there exists one and only one line containing both the points. Alternately, we can state that two distinct points in a plane determine a unique line.

**2. Collinearity of Points:**  Collinear or non-collinear points are only defined in the context of three or more points.

Consider the situation of three points. There can only be two cases with respect to three points:

1. All the points lie on the same line. (Here, the points are said to be collinear).
2. All the three points do not lie on the same line (In this case the points are said to be non-collinear).

---

**Note:**  It is quite evident that we would discuss collinear or non-collinear points only if the number of points is more than two. Obviously, if there are only two points they would always lie on one line.

---

**3. Points in Common between Distinct Lines:**  In the case of distinct lines, there can only be two cases:

(a) There is one point in common: In such a case, the common point is called the point of intersection, and the two lines are called as intersecting lines.

(b) There is no point in common: In such a case, the two lines are non-intersecting and are also called as parallel lines.

The property can thus be stated as:

**Property:** Two distinct lines in a plane cannot have more than one point in common.

### 4. Lines and Points:

**Property:** Given a line and a point in the same plane, such that the point is not on the line, there is one and only one line which passes through the point and is parallel to the given line.

### 5. Lines:

**Property:** Two intersecting lines cannot be parallel to the same line.

### 6. Multiple Lines: There can be four distinct possibilities in such a case.

1. No two lines intersect each other
2. Some lines intersect
3. Every line intersects all other lines, but their respective points of intersection are different from each other.
4. Every pair of lines is intersecting and all the points of intersection coincide.

The reader is required to visualise the figures for each of these situations.

The remaining formulae and results for geometry have been given within the chapter. You are required to move to the respective formulae. However, an important note while you are doing this.

## Important Note

One of the least understood issues with respect to this block is:

How does a person move from:

**"Cannot Solve Geometry and Mensuration!" to "Can Solve Geometry and Mensuration!"**

**In fact, this transition should be your sole aim while studying and solving this block of chapters.**

As you are already aware, mere knowledge of formulae does not guarantee this movement. Then in that case what should a person do if he/she has to engineer this transition of abilities?

Well, the answer is really quite simple and for understanding the same you need to move out of conventional mathematical study processes. In your mind you need to create an awareness of how to think while solving a geometry/mensuration question. Here are a few tips that will help you through this transition:

### 1. Some Formulae are More Important than Others: For the CAT (and indeed all other MBA and aptitude examinations) your concentration should not be on memorising complex formulae. A close study of the past trends for questions from this block will show

you that the formulae themselves can be graded into the important and the not so important formulae. In fact, if you study over 200 questions from this block that have been asked in the CAT in the past decade or more, you will realise that over 98% of the questions are simply based on a small subset of geometrical formulae and results. This important set of formulae are listed below for your convenience:

**Lines:** Properties related to intersecting lines and angles formed.

**Polygons:** Basic properties of regular polygons.

**Triangles:** Pythagoras theorem, 30-60-90 triangle, 45-45-90 triangle, Sine rule, Properties of Exterior angles of a triangle, equilateral triangle, isosceles triangle.

**Quadrilaterals:** Areas, perimeters, diagonals and angles between diagonals for all standard quadrilaterals.

**Hexagon:** A Hexagon can be divided into six equal triangles.

### 2. Length/Area/Volume Measuring Formulae versus Angle Measuring Formulae: In your mind, divide the formulae into length/area/volume measuring formulae on the one hand and angle measuring formulae on the other hand. This will be very helpful, since most questions in this block can be clearly segregated as length or angle measuring questions. In such a scenario, in case you have a question requiring angle measurements, you will only require to think of angle measuring formulae.

---

**Note:** There are very few formulae that connect lengths with angles. (e.g. Sine rule and Cosine rule in the context of triangles).

---

### 3. The Use of Reverse Flowcharting for Solving Questions: All questions in geometry and mensuration ask you to find a particular value. Very often, it makes the question much more convenient to solve if instead of trying to find what is asked, you try to find a value which is related to the required value.

Thus, for example, if in a triangle $ABC$ angle $A$ is given to be 40° & angle $B$ is asked for and you are not getting a clear strategy for getting the value of angle $B$, then it might be wise to try to derive the value of angle $C$. If you can get $C$, then $B$ will be got by 140−$C$.

This process is called as reverse flowcharting and is an extremely crucial process for solving questions in geometry.

In other words, it can also be seen to be a deflection of the original question into a more convenient question.

---

**Note:** You are advised to concentrate on the special note for solving CAT questions provided prior to the LOD I Questions while studying this block.

## Pre-assessment Test

1. In the figure below, $AB=BC=CD=DE=EF=FG=GA$. Then, $\angle DAE$ is approximately:

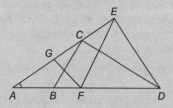

   (a) 15°          (b) 20°
   (c) 30°          (d) 25°

2. The figure below shows three circles, each of radius 25 and centres at $P$, $Q$ and $R$ respectively. Further $AB = 6, CD = 12$ and $EF = 15$. What is the perimeter of the triangle $PQR$?

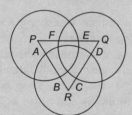

   (a) 117          (b) 116
   (c) 113          (d) 121

3. The figure shows a circle which has a diameter $AB$ and a radius 13. If chord $CA$ is 10 cm long, then find the area of $\triangle ABC$.

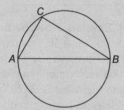

   (a) 240 sq.cm          (b) 120 sq.cm
   (c) 160 sq.cm          (d) None of these

4. The line $AB$ is 12 meters in length and is tangent to the inner one of the two concentric circles at point $C$. It is known that the radii of the two circles are integers. The radius of the inner circle is:

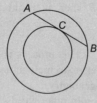

   (a) 5 meters          (b) 8 meters
   (c) 6 meters          (d) 3 meters

5. Four cities are connected by a road network as shown in the figure. In how many ways can you start from any city and come back to it without travelling on the same road more than once?

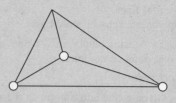

   (a) 14          (b) 12
   (c) 10          (d) 15

6. In the figure (not drawn to scale) given below, if $AL = LC = CT$, and $\angle TCD = 96°$. What is the value of the $\angle LTC$?

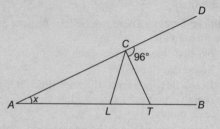

   (a) 32°          (b) 84°
   (c) 64°          (d) Cannot be determined

**Directions for Questions 7 to 9:** Answer the questions on the basis of the information given below.

Consider a cylinder of height $h$ cm and radius $r = 2/\pi$ cm as shown in the figure (not drawn to scale). A string of a certain length, when wound on its cylindrical surface, starting at point $A$ and ending at point $B$, gives a maximum of $n$ turns (in other words, the string's length is the minimum length required to wind $n$ turns).

7. What is the vertical spacing in cm between two consecutive turns?
   (a) $h/n$
   (b) $h/\sqrt{n}$
   (c) $h/n^2$
   (d) Cannot be determined with given information.

8. The same string, when wound on the four exterior four walls of a cube of side $n$ cm, starting at point $C$ and ending at point $D$, can give exactly one turn (as shown in the figure). The length of the string, in cm, is:

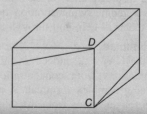

(a) $\sqrt{2}\ n$      (b) $\sqrt{17}\ n$

(c) $n$      (d) $\sqrt{13}\ n$

9. In the setup of the previous two questions, how is $h$ related to $n$?

  (a) $h = \sqrt{2}\ n$      (b) $h = \sqrt{17}\ n$

  (c) $h = n$      (d) $h = \sqrt{13}\ n$

10. Let *LMNOPQ* be a regular hexagon. What is the ratio of the area of the triangle *LNP* to that of the hexagon *LMNOPQ*?

  (a) 1/3      (b) 1/2

  (c) 2/3      (d) 5/6

11. In the figure below, a circle is inscribed inside a square. In the gap between the circle and the square (at the corner) a rectangle measuring 20 cm × 10 cm is drawn such that the corner *A* of the rectangle is also a point on the circumference of the circle. What is the radius of the circle in cm?

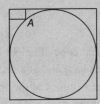

  (a) 30 cm      (b) 40 cm

  (c) 50 cm      (d) None of these

12. In the figure below *ABCDEF* is a regular hexagon. The $\angle AOF = 90°$ and *FO* is parallel to *ED*. What is the ratio of the area of the triangle *AOF* to that of the hexagon *ABCDEF*?

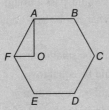

  (a) 1/12      (b) 1/8

  (c) 1/24      (d) 1/18

13. Sherry, a naughty boy, after a lot of convincing from his mother has agreed to mow the farm lawn, which is a 30 m by 40 m rectangle. The mower mows a 1 m wide strip. If Sherry starts at one corner and mows around the lawn towards the centre, about how many times would he go round before he has mowed half the lawn?

  (a) 4.3      (b) 4.5

  (c) 4.9      (d) 5.0

14. Two sides of a plot measure 32 meters and 24 meters and the angle between them is a perfect right angle. The other two sides measure 25 meters each and the other three angles are not right angles.

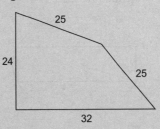

What is the area of the plot (in m²)?

  (a) 768      (b) 534

  (c) 696.5      (d) 684

15. Euclid has a triangle in mind. Its longest side has length 20 and another of its sides has length 10. Its area is 80 sq. cm. What is the exact length of its third side?

  (a) $\sqrt{260}$      (b) $\sqrt{250}$

  (c) $\sqrt{240}$      (d) $\sqrt{270}$

16. Consider a circle with unit radius. There are seven adjacent sectors, $S_1$, $S_2$, $S_3$,……., $S_7$, in the circle such that their total area is 1/16 of the area of the circle. Further, the area of $j$th sector is twice that of the $(j-1)$th sector, for $j = 2$……., 7. What is the angle, in radians, subtended by the arc of $S_1$ at the centre of the circle?

  (a) $\pi/508$      (b) $\pi/2040$

  (c) $\pi/1016$      (d) $\pi/2032$

17. The figure below shows a set of concentric squares. If the diagonal of the innermost square is 2 units, and if the distance between the corresponding corners of any two successive squares is 1 unit find the difference between the areas of the sixth and the seventh squares, counting from the innermost square.

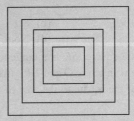

  (a) $\sqrt{2}$ sq. units      (b) 26 sq. units

  (c) 30 sq. units      (d) None of these

18. In the figure (not drawn to scale), rectangle *ABCD* is inscribed in the circle with center at *O*. The length of side *AB* is greater than that of side *BC*. The ratio of the area of the circle to the area of the rectangle *ABCD* is $\pi : \sqrt{3}$. The line segment

*DE* intersects *AB* at *E* such that ∠*ODC* = ∠*ADE*. What is the ratio *AE* : *AD*?

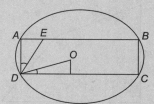

(a) 1 : √3      (b) 1 : √2
(c) √3 : 1      (d) 1 : 2

19. In Δ*ABC*, ∠*B* is a right angle, *AC* = 16 cm, and *D* is the mid-point of *AC*. The length of *BD* is:

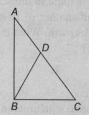

(a) 10 cm      (b) √15 cm
(c) 8 cm      (d) 7.5 cm

20. In triangle *DEF* shown below, points *A*, *B*, and *C* are taken on *DE*, *DF* and *EF* respectively such that *EC* = *AC* and *CF* = *BC*. If angle *D* = 50 degrees then what is angle *ACB* in degrees?

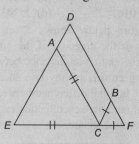

(a) 120      (b) 80
(c) 90      (d) None of these

21. *PQRS* is a square. *SR* is a tangent (at point *S*) to the circle with centre *O* and *TR* = *OS*. Then, the ratio of area of the square to the area of the circle is :

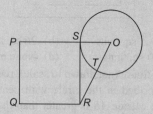

(a) π/3      (b) 11/7
(c) 3/π      (d) 7/11

22. In the adjoining figure, *AC* + *AB* = 5 *AD* and *AC* − *AD* = 8. Then, the area of the rectangle *ABCD* is:

(a) 45
(b) 50
(c) 60
(d) Cannot be answered

23. The figure shows the rectangle *ABCD* with a semicircle and a circle inscribed inside it as shown. What is the ratio of the area of the circle to that of the semicircle?

(a) (√2 −1)² : 1      (b) 2(√2 −1)² : 1
(c) (√2 −1)² : 2      (d) None of these

24. A right circular cone of height *h* is cut by a plane parallel to the base and at a distance *h*/3 from the base then the volumes of the frustum of the cone and the resulting cone are in the ratio:

(a) 1 : 3      (b) 8 : 19
(c) 19 : 8      (d) 7 : 1

25. Three identical cones with base radius *m* are placed on their bases so that each is touching the other two. There will be one and only one circle that would pass through each of the three vertices. What can be said about the radius of this circle?

(a) It would be smaller than *m*
(b) It would be equal to *m*
(c) It would be larger than *m*
(d) depends on the height of the cones

---

**ANSWER KEY**

| | | | |
|---|---|---|---|
| 1. (d) | 2. (a) | 3. (b) | 4. (b) |
| 5. (b) | 6. (c) | 7. (a) | 8. (b) |
| 9. (c) | 10. (b) | 11. (c) | 12. (a) |
| 13. (c) | 14. (d) | 15. (a) | 16. (c) |
| 17. (b) | 18. (a) | 19. (c) | 20. (b) |
| 21. (c) | 22. (c) | 23. (d) | 24. (c) |
| 25. (c) | | | |

---

# 11

# Geometry and Mensuration

The chapters on geometry and mensuration have their own share of questions in the CAT and other MBA entrance examinations. For doing well in questions based on this chapter, the student should familiarise himself/herself with the basic formulae and visualisations of the various shapes of solids and two-dimensional figures based on this chapter.

The following is a comprehensive collection of formulae based on two-dimensional and three-dimensional figures:

For the purpose of this chapter we have divided the theory in two parts:

- Part I consists of geometry and mensuration of two-dimensional figures
- Part II consists of mensuration of three-dimensional figures.

## PART I: GEOMETRY

## INTRODUCTION

Geometry and Mensuration are important areas in the CAT examination. In the Online CAT, the Quantitative Aptitude section has consisted of an average of 15–20% questions from these chapters. Besides, questions from these chapters appear prominently in all major aptitude based exams for MBAs, Bank POs, etc.

Hence, the student is advised to ensure that he/she studies this chapter completely and thoroughly. Skills to be developed while studying and practising this chapter will be based on the application of formula and visualisation of figures and solids.

The principal skill required for doing well in this chapter is the ability to apply the formulae and theorems.

The following is a comprehensive collection of formulae based on two-dimensional figures. The student is advised to remember the formulae in this chapter so that he is able to solve all the questions based on this chapter.

## THEORY

### Basic Conversions

| | |
|---|---|
| A. 1 m = 100 cm = 1000 mm<br>1 km = 1000 m<br>= 5/8 miles<br>1 inch = 2.54 cm | B. 1 m = 39.37 inches<br>1 mile = 1760 yd<br>= 5280 ft<br>1 nautical mile (knot)<br>= 6080 ft |
| C. 100 kg = 1 quintal<br>10 quintal = 1 tonne<br>= 1000 kg<br>1 kg = 2.2 pounds<br>(approx.) | D. 1 litre = 1000 cc<br>1 acre = 100 sq m<br><br>1 hectare = 10000 sq m |

## TYPES OF ANGLES

### Basic Definitions

*Acute angle:* An angle whose measure is less than 90 degrees. The following is an acute angle.

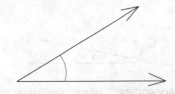

**Right angle:** An angle whose measure is 90 degrees. The following is a right angle.

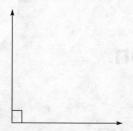

**Obtuse angle:** An angle whose measure is bigger than 90 degrees but less than 180 degrees. Thus, it is between 90 degrees and 180 degrees. The following is an obtuse angle.

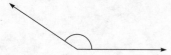

**Straight angle:** Is an angle whose measure is 180 degrees.

**Reflex angle:** An angle whose measure is more than 180 degrees but less than 360 degrees. The following is a reflex angle.

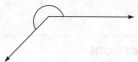

**Adjacent angles:** Angles with a common vertex and one common side. In the figure below, ∠1 and ∠2 are adjacent angles.

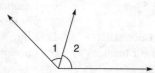

**Complementary angles:** Two angles whose measures add to 90 degrees ∠1 and ∠2 are complementary angles because together they form a right angle.

However, one thing that you should note is that, even though in the figure given here, the two angles are shown as adjacent, they need not be so to be called complementary. As long as two angles add up to 90 degrees, they would be called complementary (even if they are not adjacent to each other).

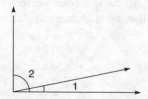

**Supplementary angles:** Two angles whose measures add up to 180 degrees. The following angles ∠1 and ∠2 are supplementary angles. However, supplementary angles do not need to be adjacent to be called supplementary (quite like complementary angles). The only condition for two angles to be called supplementary is if they are adding up to 180 degrees.

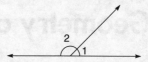

**Vertical angles:** Angles that have a common vertex and whose sides are formed by the same lines. The following(∠1 and ∠2) are vertical angles.

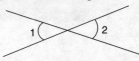

**Angles formed when two parallel lines, are crossed by a transversal:** When two parallel lines are crossed by a third line, (transversal), 8 angles are formed. Take a look at the following figure:

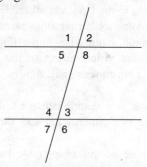

Angles 3,4,5,8 are interior angles.
Angles 1,2,6,7 are exterior angles.

**Alternate interior angles:** Pairs of interior angles on opposite sides of the transversal.

For instance, angle 3 and angle 5 are alternate interior angles. Angle 4 and angle 8 are also alternate interior angles. Both the angles in a pair of alternate interior angles are equal. Hence, in the figure we have: Angle 3 = Angle 5; Also Angle 4 = Angle 8.

**Alternate exterior angles:** Pairs of exterior angles on opposite sides of the transversal.

Angle 2 and angle 7 are alternate exterior angles. Angles 1 and 6 are also alternate exterior angles. Both the angles in a pair of alternate exterior angles are equal. Thus, in the figure Angle 2 = Angle 7 and Angle 1 = Angle 6.

**Co-interior angles:** When two lines are cut by a third line (transversal) co-interior angles are between the pair of lines on the same side of the transversal. If the lines that are being cut by the transversal are parallel to each other, the co-interior angles are supplementary (add up to 180 degrees). In the given figure, angles 3 and 8 are co-interior angles. Also, angles 4 and 5 are co-interior angles, since, the lines being cut are parallel in this case, ∠3 + ∠8 = 180. Also, ∠4 + ∠5 = 180.

**Corresponding angles:** Are pairs of angles that are in similar positions when two parallel lines are intersected by a transversal.

Angle 3 and angle 2 are corresponding angles. Similarly, the pairs of angles, 1 and 4; 5 and 7; 6 and 8 are corresponding angles. Corresponding angles are equal. Thus, in the figure- $\angle 1 = \angle 4$; $\angle 5 = \angle 7$; $\angle 2 = \angle 3$ & $\angle 6 = \angle 8$.

**Linear pair:** $\angle XOY$ and $\angle YOZ$ are linear pair angles. One side must be common (e.g. $OY$) and these two angles must be supplementary.

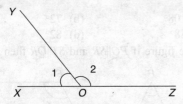

**Angles on the side of a line:** $\angle 1 + \angle 2 + \angle 3 = 180°$

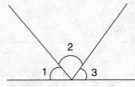

**Angles around the point:** $\angle 1 + \angle 2 + \angle 3 + \angle 4 + \angle 5 = 360°$

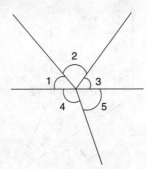

**Angle Bisector:** OY is the angle bisector for the $\angle XOZ$.

i.e., $\angle XOY = \angle ZOY = \dfrac{1}{2} \angle XOZ$

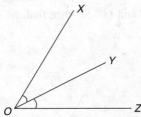

When a line segment divides an angle equally into two parts, then it is said to be the angle bisector ($OY$).

(Angle bisector is equidistant from the two sides of the angle.)

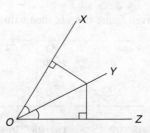

The disance between the lines $OX$ & $OY$ and the lines $OY$ & $OZ$ are equal to each other.

## PRACTICE EXERCISE

1. What is the value of x in the given figure?

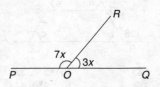

  (a) 18°          (b) 20°
  (c) 28°          (d) None of these

2. In the given figure, find the value of ($a + b$)

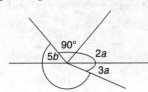

  (a) 50°          (b) 54°
  (c) 60°          (d) None of these

3. If $2a + 3$, $3a + 2$ are complementary, then $a = ?$
  (a) 17°          (b) 20°
  (c) 23°          (d) 26°

4. If $5x + 17°$ and $x + 13°$ are supplementary, then $x = ?$
  (a) 20°          (b) 25°
  (c) 30°          (d) None of these

5. An angle is exactly half of its complementary angle, then find the angle.
  (a) 30°          (b) 40°
  (c) 50°          (d) 60°

6. In the following figure, lines L1 and L2 are parallel to each other. Find the value of $q$.

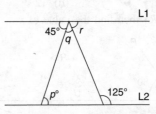

  (a) 60°          (b) 80°
  (c) 90°          (d) 85°

7. In the given figure if $L_1 \| L_2$ then values of $x$, $y$, $z$ are:

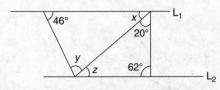

   (a) 98°, 98°, 36°    (b) 98°, 36°, 98°
   (c) 36°, 98°, 36°    (d) None of these

8. In the given diagram if $BC \| ED$ and $\angle BAC = 70°$, then find the value of d and c.

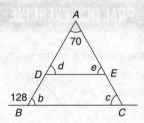

   (a) 52°, 58°    (b) 58°, 52°
   (c) 44°, 36°    (d) 36°, 44°

9. In the given diagram if $AB \| CD$ and $\angle ABO = 60°$ and $\angle BOC = 110°$, find $\angle OCD$

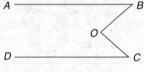

   (a) 40°    (b) 50°
   (c) 60°    (d) 70°

10. In the figure given, two parallel lines are intersected by a transversal. Then, find the value of $x$.

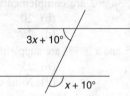

   (a) 40°    (b) 50°
   (c) 55°    (d) 65°

11. Maximum number of points of intersection of five lines on a plane is
   (a) 6    (b) 8
   (c) 10   (d) 12

12. If $PQ \| RS$ then find the value of $x$.

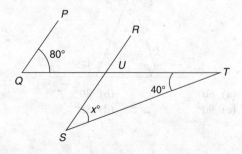

13. If $AB \| CD$ and $AF \| BE$ then the value of $x$ is:

   (a) 40°    (b) 60°
   (c) 70°    (d) 80°

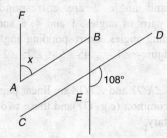

   (a) 108°    (b) 72°
   (c) 88°     (d) 82°

14. In the figure if $PQ \| SR$ and $ST \| QR$ then $x = ?$

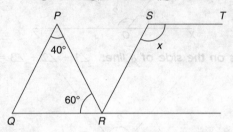

   (a) 70°    (b) 80°
   (c) 90°    (d) 100°

15. In the given figure, if $AB \| CD$ then the value of $x = ?$

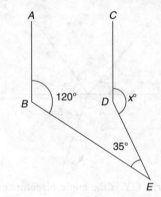

   (a) 135°    (b) 145°
   (c) 155°    (d) None of these

16. If $PQ \| RS$ and $QT \| SU$ then find the value of $x + y$

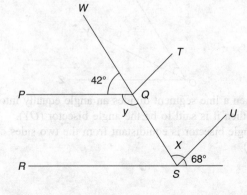

(a) 188°   (b) 202°
(c) 208°   (d) 212°

17. If $PQ\|RS$ and $AC$ is angle bisector of $\angle PAB$, $BC$ is angle bisector of $\angle RBA$. Then $\angle ACB = ?$

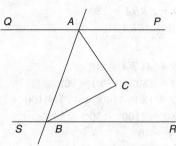

(a) 45°   (b) 75°
(c) 90°   (d) 110°

18. In the given figure if $AB\|CD$ then $x + y = ?$

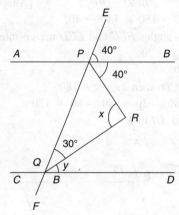

(a) 100°   (b) 110°
(c) 60°   (d) 125°

19. In the figure if $CD\|EF\|AB$ then, find the value of $x$.

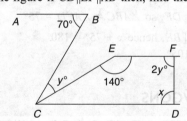

(a) 70°   (b) 90°
(c) 110°   (d) 120°

20. If in the given figure, $AB\|CD$ and $BC\|DE$, then $x =?$

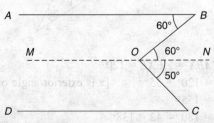

(a) 95°   (b) 105°
(c) 115°   (d) 125°

---

## ANSWER KEY

| | | | |
|---|---|---|---|
| 1 (a) | 2 (b) | 3 (a) | 4 (b) |
| 5 (a) | 6 (b) | 7 (b) | 8 (a) |
| 9 (b) | 10 (a) | 11 (c) | 12 (a) |
| 13 (b) | 14 (d) | 15 (c) | 16 (c) |
| 17 (c) | 18 (c) | 19 (d) | 20 (b) |

### Solutions

1. $7x + 3x = 180°$
   $10x = 180°$ or $x = 18°$.
   Option (a) is correct.

2. $90° + 2a + 3a + 5b = 360°$
   $5a + 5b = 270°$
   $a + b = 54°$

3. $2a + 3 + 3a + 2 = 90°$
   $5a + 5 = 90°$
   $a = \dfrac{85°}{5} = 17°$

4. $5x + 17° + x + 13° = 180°$
   $6x + 30° = 180°$
   $x = 25°$.
   Option b is correct.

5. We can solve this problem by checking the options.
   Option (a) = 30°, complementary angle of 30° is 60° and 30° is half of 60°.
   So option (a) is true. Alternately, we can also solve this using: $a + 2a = 90 \to a = 30°$.

6. $q + r = 180° – (45°) = 135°$
   $r + 125° = 180° \Rightarrow r = 55°$
   $q + 55° = 135°$
   $q = 80°$

7. $x + 20 + 62 = 180°$
   $x = 180° – 82° = 98°$
   $x = z$         [Alternate angles]
   $z = 98°$
   $x + y + 46° = 180°$
   $y = 180° – (46° + x) = 180° – (46° + 98°) = 36°$.

8. $\angle b = 180° – 128° = 52° = \angle d$ (Since they are corresponding angles).
   $\angle c = 180° – (70° + 52°) = 58°$

9. Draw line $MON\|AB\|CD$

   $\angle ABO = \angle BON$     [Alternate angles]

Hence, $\angle BON = 60°$

$\angle NOC = 110° - 60° = 50°$

Also, $\angle NOC = \angle OCD$      [Alternate angles]

$\angle OCD = 50°$

10. $3x + 10° + x + 10° = 180°$

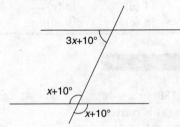

$4x = 160°$

$x = 40°$

11. $^5C_2 = \dfrac{5!}{2! \times 3!} = 10$

Option (c) is correct.

12. $\angle PQU = \angle SUQ = 80°$      [Alternate angles]

$\angle SUT = 180° - 80° = 100°$

$\angle UST = x = 40°$

13. If $AB \| CD$ then $\angle CEB + \angle ABE = 180°$

$\angle CEB = 108°$

$108° + \angle ABE = 180°$

$\angle ABE = 72°$

If $AB \| BD$ then $\angle ABE = x$      [Alternate angles]

$x = 72°$

14. $\angle QPR = \angle SRP = 40°$      [Alternative angles]

$x = \angle SRQ = \angle SRP + \angle PRQ$      [Alternative angles]

$x = 60° + 40° = 100°$

15. Extend $CD$ to $x$

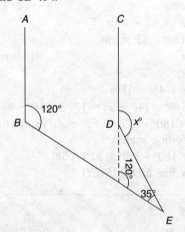

$\angle ABX = \angle CXE = 120°$

$x = 120° + 35°$      [$x$ is exterior angle of $\Delta DXE$]

$x = 155°$

16. $y = 180° - 42 = 138°$

$\angle PQW = \angle RSQ = 42°$

$42° + x + 68° = 180°$

$x = 70°$

$x + y = 70° + 138° = 208°$

17. $\angle ACB = 180° - (\angle CAB + \angle CBA)$

$\angle PAB + \angle RBA = 180°$

$\dfrac{\angle PAB}{2} + \dfrac{\angle RBA}{2} = 90°$

$\angle CAB + \angle CBA = 90°$

$\angle ACB = 180° - (90°) = 90°$

18. $\angle RPQ = 180° - (40° + 40°) = 100°$

$x = 180° - (100° + 30°) = 50°$

$30° + y = 40°$

     ($\angle BPQ$ and $\angle DQP$ are corresponding angles).

$y = 10°$

$x + y = 50° + 10° = 60°$

19. $\angle ABC = \angle BCD = 70°$      [Alternate angles]

$\angle ECD = 180° - 140° = 40°$

     [As angles $FEC$ and $ECD$ are co-interior angles]

$40° + y = 70°$

$y = 30°$

$EF \| CD$   then $2y + x = 180°$

$x = 180° - 2y = 180° - 60° = 120°$

20. Extend $AB$ to $E$

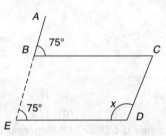

$BC \| DE$, so $\angle ABC = \angle AFD = 75°$

$CD \| BE$, hence $x + 75° = 180°$

$x = 105°$

## 🕰 POLYGONS

Polygons are plane figures formed by a closed series of rectilinear (straight) segments. The following are examples of polygons:

Triangle, Rectangle, Pentagon, Hexagon, Heptagon, Octagon, nonagon (9 sided), decagon, Undecagon or Hendecagon (11 sided), Dodecagon (12 sided), Triskaidecagon or Tridecagon (13 sided). Subsequent polygons are named as per the table below:

| Number of sides | Name of the Polygon |
| --- | --- |
| 14 | Tetradecagon, Terakaidecagon |
| 15 | Pentadecagon, Pentakaidecagon |
| 16 | Hexadecagon, Hexakaidecagon |

| No. of sides | Name of the polygon |
|---|---|
| 17 | Heptadecagon, Heptakaidecagon |
| 18 | Octadecagon, Octakaidecagon |
| 19 | Enneadecagon, Enneakaidecagon |
| 20 | Icosagon |
| 30 | Triacontagon |
| 40 | Tetracontagon |
| 50 | Pentacontagon |
| 60 | Hexacontagon |
| 70 | Heptacontagon |
| 80 | Ontacontagon |
| 90 | Enneacontagon |
| 100 | Hectogon, Hecatontagon |
| 1000 | Chiliagon |
| 10000 | Myriagon |
| | |

Polygons can broadly be divided into two types:

(a) *Regular polygons:* Polygons with all the sides and angles equal.

(b) *Irregular polygons:* Polygons in which all the sides or angles are not of the same measure.

Polygon can also be divided as *concave* or *convex* polygons.

Convex polygons are the polygons in which all the diagonals lie inside the figure otherwise it's a concave polygon

Polygons can also be divided on the basis of the number of sides they have.

| No. of sides | Name of the polygon | Sum of all the angles |
|---|---|---|
| 3 | Triangle | 180° |
| 4 | Quadrilateral | 360° |
| 5 | Pentagon | 540° |
| 6 | Hexagon | 720° |
| 7 | Heptagon | 500° |
| 8 | Octagon | 1080° |
| 9 | Nonagon | 1260° |
| 10 | Decagon | 1440° |

## Properties

1. Sum of all the angles of a polygon with $n$ sides = $(2n - 4)\pi/2$ or $(n - 2)\pi$ Radians = $(n - 2)$ 180° degrees

2. Sum of all exterior angles = 360°.
   i.e. In the figure below:
   $\theta_1 + \theta_2 + ... + \theta_6 = 360°$
   In general, $\theta_1 + \theta_2 + ... + \theta_n = 360°$

3. No. of sides = 360°/exterior angle.
   (Note: This property is true only for regular polygons)

4. Area = $(ns^2/4) \times \cot (180/n)$; where $s$ = length of side, $n$ = no. of sides.

(Note: This property is true only for regular polygons)

5. Perimeter = $n \times s$.
   (Note: This property is true only for regular polygons)

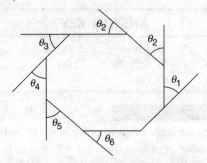

## PRACTICE EXERCISE

1. Each interior angle of a regular polygon is 140°. Then the number of sides is:
   (a) 6　　　　　　　　(b) 8
   (c) 9　　　　　　　　(d) 12

2. Each interior angle of a regular octagon is:
   (a) 90°　　　　　　　(b) 115°
   (c) 125°　　　　　　(d) 135°

3. The sum of the interior angles of a polygon is 1440°. The number of sides of the polygon is:
   (a) 8　　　　　　　　(b) 10
   (c) 12　　　　　　　(d) 14

4. Difference between interior and exterior angle of a polygon is 100°. Then the number of sides in the polygon is:
   (a) 8　　　　　　　　(b) 9
   (c) 10　　　　　　　(d) 11

5. If the ratio of interior and exterior angles of a regular polygon is 2:1, then find the number of sides of the polygon.
   (a) 6　　　　　　　　(b) 8
   (c) 10　　　　　　　(d) 12

6. The ratio of the measure of an angle of a regular octagon to the measure of its exterior angle is:
   (a) 2:1　　　　　　　(b) 1:3
   (c) 3:1　　　　　　　(d) 1:1

7. Ratio between, the number of sides of two regular polygons is 2:3 and the ratio between their interior angles is 3:4. The number of sides of these polygons respectively are:
   (a) 4,6　　　　　　　(b) 6,9
   (c) 8,12　　　　　　(d) None of these

8. Number of diagonals of a 6-sided polygon is
   (a) 6　　　　　　　　(b) 9
   (c) 12　　　　　　　(d) 15

9. Find the sum of all internal angles of a 5-point star.
   (a) 160°　　　　　　(b) 180°
   (c) 240°　　　　　　(d) 300°

10. If the length of each side of a hexagon is 6 cm, then the area of the hexagon is:
    (a)  54 cm²
    (b)  54√3 cm²
    (c)  68 cm²
    (d)  None of these

### ANSWER KEY

| | | | |
|---|---|---|---|
| 1. (c) | 2. (d) | 3. (b) | 4. (b) |
| 5. (a) | 6. (c) | 7. (a) | 8. (b) |
| 9. (b) | 10. (b) | | |

### Solutions

1. Exterior angle of given polygon = 180° – 140° = 40°
   Number of sides = 360°/40° = 9. [Since the sum of all exterior angles of a polygon is 360°)
   Option (c) is correct.

2. Total number of sides in octagon = 8
   Each interior angle = $\dfrac{(8-2) \times 180°}{8} = \dfrac{6 \times 180°}{8} = 135°$

3. Let the number of sides be $x$.
   Then according to the question
   $(x - 2) \times 180° = 1440°$
   $x - 2 = 8$
   $x = 10$.

4. Let the internal angle be $x$ and external angle be $y$, according to the question
   $x + y = 180°$    (i)
   $x - y = 100°$    (ii)
   $x = 140°, y = 40°$
   Number of sides = $\dfrac{360°}{40°} = 9$

5. If interior angle '$2x$' and exterior angle be $x$
   Then $2x + x = 180°$
   $3x = 180°$
   $x = 60°$
   Number of sides = 360°/60° = 6

6. Interior angle of a regular octagon = 135°
   Exterior angle of a regular octagon = 45°
   Required ratio = $\dfrac{135°}{45°}$ = 3:1

7. We can solve this problem by checking the options.
   Option (a) 4, 6
   Interior angle of a 4 sided polygon = 90°
   Interior angle of a 6-sided polygon = 120°
   So the ratio of interior angles = 90°:120° = 3:4
   Hence this option is correct.

8. Number of diagonals = $^6C_2 – 6$
   $= \dfrac{6!}{2!4!} - 6 \Rightarrow 15 - 6 = 9$

9. Sum of the angles of an $x$-pointed star = $(x - 4) \times \pi$
   So the required sum = $(5 - 4) \times \pi = 180°$

10. Required area = $6 \times \dfrac{\sqrt{3}}{4} \times 6^2$
    $= 54\sqrt{3}$ cm²

### TRIANGLES (Δ)

A triangle is a polygon having three sides. Sum of all the angles of a triangle = 180°.

**Types**
1. *Acute angle triangle:* Triangles with all three angles acute (less than 90°).
2. *Obtuse angle triangle:* Triangles with one of the angles obtuse (more than 90°).
   **Note:** We cannot have more than one obtuse angle in a triangle.
3. *Right angle triangle:* Triangle with one of the angles equal to 90°.
4. *Equilateral triangle:* Triangle with all sides equal. All the angles in such a triangle measure 60°.
5. *Isosceles triangle:* Triangle with two of its sides equal and consequently the angles opposite the equal sides are also equal.
6. *Scalene Triangle:* Triangle with none of the sides equal to any other side.

### Properties (General)

- Sum of the length of any two sides of a triangle has to be always greater than the third side.
- Difference between the lengths of any two sides of a triangle has to be always lesser than the third side.
- Side opposite to the greatest angle will be the greatest and the side opposite to the smallest angle the smallest.
- The sine rule: $a/\sin A = b/\sin B = c/\sin C = 2R$ (where $R$ = circum radius.)
- The cosine rule: $a^2 = b^2 + c^2 – 2bc \cos A$
  This is true for all sides and respective angles.

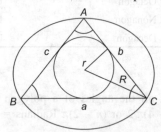

In case of a right triangle, the formula reduces to
$a^2 = b^2 + c^2$
Since cos 90° = 0

- The exterior angle is equal to the sum of two interior angles not adjacent to it.
  $$\angle ACD = \angle BCE = \angle A + \angle B$$

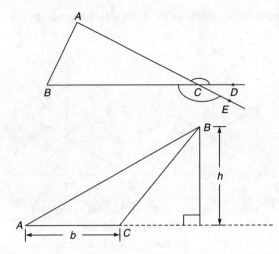

## Area

1. Area = 1/2 base × height or 1/2 *bh*.

   Height = Perpendicular distance between the base and vertex opposite to it

2. Area = $\sqrt{s(s-a)(s-b)(s-c)}$ (Heron's formula)

   where $s = \dfrac{a+b+c}{2}$      (a, b and c being the length of the sides)

3. Area = *rs* (where *r* is in radius)

4. Area = 1/2 × product of two sides × sine of the included angle

   = 1/2 *ac* sin B
   = 1/2 *ab* sin C
   = 1/2 *bc* sin A

4. Area = *abc*/4R

   where R = circum radius

**Congruency of Triangles**  Two triangles are congruent if all the sides of one are equal to the corresponding sides of another. It follows that all the angles of one are equal to the corresponding angles of another. The notation for congruency is $\left(\cong\right)$.

## Conditions for Congruency

1. *SAS congruency*: If two sides and an included angle of one triangle are equal to two sides and an included angle of another, the two triangles are congruent. (See figure below.)

   Here,      AB = PQ
                BC = QR

and      $\angle B = \angle Q$

So     $\Delta ABC \cong \Delta PQR$

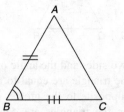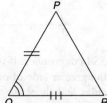

2. *ASA congruency*: If two angles and the included side of one triangle is equal to two angles and the included side of another, the triangles are congruent. (See figure below.)

   Here,      $\angle A = \angle P$
                 $\angle B = \angle Q$

   and      AB = PQ

   So     $\Delta ABC \cong \Delta PQR$

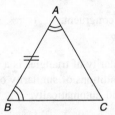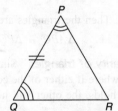

3. *AAS congruency*: If two angles and side opposite to one of the angles is equal to the corresponding angles and the side of another triangle, the triangles are congruent. In the figure below:

                 $\angle A = \angle P$
                 $\angle B = \angle Q$

   and      AC = PR

   So     $\Delta ABC \cong \Delta PQR$

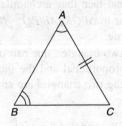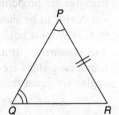

4. *SSS congruency*: If three sides of one triangle are equal to three sides of another triangle, the two triangles are congruent. In the figure below:

                 AB = PQ
                 BC = QR
                 AC = PR

   $\therefore$     $\Delta ABC \cong \Delta PQR$

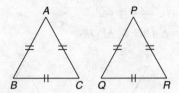

5. *SSA congruency*: If two sides and the angle opposite the greater side of one triangle are equal to the two sides and the angle opposite to the greater side of another triangle, then the triangles are congruent. The congruency doesn't hold if the equal angles lie opposite the shorter side. In the figure below, if

$$AB = PQ$$
$$AC = PR$$
$$\angle B = \angle Q$$

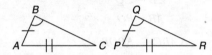

Then the triangles are congruent.

i.e.  $\triangle ABC \cong \triangle PQR$.

**Similarity of triangles**  Similarity of triangles is a special case where if either of the conditions of similarity of polygons holds, the other will hold automatically.

## Types of Similarity

1. *AAA similarity:*  If in two triangles, corresponding angles are equal, that is, the two triangles are equiangular then the triangles are similar.
   *Corollary (AA similarity):*  If two angles of one triangle are respectively equal to two angles of another triangle then the two triangles are similar. The reason being, the third angle becomes equal automatically.
2. *SSS similarity:*  If the corresponding sides of two triangles are proportional then they are similar.
   For $\triangle ABC$ to be similar to $\triangle PQR$, $AB/PQ = BC/QR = AC/PR$, must hold true.
3. *SAS similarity:*  If in two triangles, one pair of corresponding sides are proportional and the included angles are equal then the two triangles are similar.

   $$\triangle ABC \sim \triangle PQR$$

   If    $AB/BC = PQ/QR$   and   $\angle B = \angle Q$

**Note:**  In similar triangles; the following identity holds:

Ratio of medians = Ratio of heights = Ratio of circumradii = Ratio of inradii = Ratio of angle bisectors

## Properties of similar triangles

If the two triangles are similar, then for the proportional/

corresponding sides we have the following results.

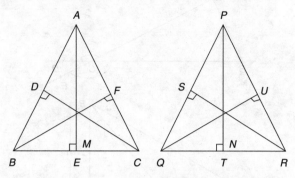

1. Ratio of sides = Ratio of heights (altitudes)
   = Ratio of medians
   = Ratio of angle bisectors
   = Ratio of inradii
   = Ratio of circumradii
2. Ratio of areas = Ratio of square of corresponding sides.

   *i.e.*, if $\triangle ABC \sim \triangle PQR$, then

   $$\frac{A(\triangle ABC)}{A(\triangle PQR)} = \frac{(AB)^2}{(PQ)^2} = \frac{(BC)^2}{(QR)^2} = \frac{(AC)^2}{(PR)^2}$$

While there are a lot of methods through which we see similarity of triangles, the one thing that all our Maths teachers forgot to tell us about similarity is the basic real life concept of similarity. i.e. **Two things are similar if they look similar!!**

If you have been to a toy shop lately, you would have come across models of cars or bikes which are made so that they look like the original—but are made in a different size from the original. Thus you might have seen a toy Maruti car which is built in a ratio of 1:25 of the original car. The result of this is that the toy car would look very much like the original car (of course if it is built well!!). Thus if you have ever seen a father and son looking exactly like each other, you have experienced similarity!!

You should use this principle to identify similar triangles. In a figure two triangles would be similar simply if they look like one another.

Thus, in the figure below if you were to draw the radii OB and O′A the two triangles MOB and MO′A will be similar to each other. Simply because they look similar. Of course, the option of using the different rules of similarity of triangles still remains with you.

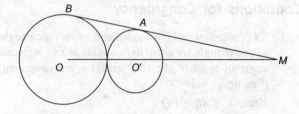

## Equilateral Triangles (of side $a$):

1. $(\because \sin 60 = \sqrt{3}/2 = h/\text{side})$

$$h = \frac{a\sqrt{3}}{2}$$

2. Area = $1/2$ (base) × (height) = $\frac{1}{2} \times a \times \frac{a\sqrt{3}}{2} = \frac{\sqrt{3}}{4} a^2$

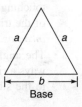

3. $R$ (circum radius) = $\frac{2h}{3} = \frac{a}{\sqrt{3}}$.

4. $r$ (in radius) = $\frac{h}{3} = \frac{a}{2\sqrt{3}}$.

## Properties

1. The incentre and circumcentre lies at a point that divides the height in the ratio $2:1$.
2. The circum radius is always twice the in radius. [$R = 2r$.]
3. Among all the triangles that can be formed with a given perimeter, the equilateral triangle will have the maximum area.
4. An equilateral triangle in a circle will have the maximum area compared to other triangles inside the same circle.

## Isosceles Triangle

Area = $\frac{b}{4}\sqrt{4a^2 - b^2}$

In an isosceles triangle, the angles opposite to the equal sides are equal.

## Right-Angled Triangle

**Pythagoras Theorem** In the case of a right angled triangle, the square of the hypotenuse is equal to the sum of the squares of the other two sides. In the figure below, for triangle $ABC$, $a^2 = b^2 + c^2$

Area = $1/2$ (product of perpendicular sides)

$R$(circumradius) = $\dfrac{\text{hypotenuse}}{2}$

Area = $rs$

(where $r$ = in radius and $s = (a + b + c)/2$ where $a$, $b$ and $c$ are sides of the triangle)

$\Rightarrow \quad 1/2\ bc = r(a + b + c)/2$

$\Rightarrow \quad r = (bc)/(a + b + c)$

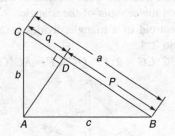

In the triangle $ABC$,

$$\Delta ABC \sim \Delta DBA \sim \Delta DAC$$

(*Note:* A lot of questions are based on this figure.)
Further, we find the following identities:

1. $\Delta ABC \sim \Delta DBA$
$\therefore \qquad AB/BC = DB/BA$
$\Rightarrow \qquad AB^2 = DB \times BC$
$\Rightarrow \qquad c^2 = pa$

2. $\Delta ABC \sim \Delta DAC$
$\qquad AC/BC = DC/AC$
$\Rightarrow \qquad AC^2 = DC \times BC$
$\Rightarrow \qquad b^2 = qa$

3. $\Delta DBA \sim \Delta DAC$
$\qquad DA/DB = DC/DA$
$\qquad DA^2 = DB \times DC$
$\Rightarrow \qquad AD^2 = pq$

## Basic Pythagorean Triplets

→ 3, 4, 5 → 5, 12, 13 → 7, 24, 25 → 8, 15, 17 → 9, 40, 41 → 11, 60, 61 → 12, 35, 37 → 16, 63, 65 → 20, 21, 29 → 28, 45, 53. These triplets are very important since a lot of questions are based on them.

Any triplet formed by either multiplying or dividing one of the basic triplets by any positive real number will be another Pythagorean triplet.

Thus, since 3, 4, 5 form a triplet so also will 6, 8 and 10 as also 3.3, 4.4 and 5.5.

**Similarity of Right Triangles** Two right triangles are similar if the hypotenuse and side of one is proportional to hypotenuse and side of another. (RHS–similarity–Right angle hypotenuse side).

## Important Terms with Respect to a Triangle

**1. Median** A line joining the mid-point of a side of a triangle to the opposite vertex is called a median. In the figure the three medians are $PG$, $QF$ and $RE$ where $G$, $E$ and $F$ are mid-points of their respective sides.

- A median divides a triangle into two parts of equal area.
- The point where the three medians of a triangle meet is called the *centroid* of the triangle.
- The centroid of a triangle divides each median in the ratio 2:1.
  i.e. $PC:CG = 2:1 = QC:CF = RC:CE$

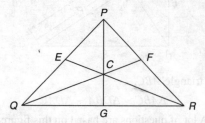

*Important formula with respect to a median*

→ $2 \times (\text{median})^2 + 2 \times (1/2 \text{ the third side})^2$

= Sum of the squares of other two sides

⇒ $2(PG)^2 + 2 \times \left(\dfrac{QR}{2}\right)^2$

= $(PQ)^2 + (PR)^2$

**2. Altitude/Height** A perpendicular drawn from any vertex to the opposite side is called the *altitude*. (In the figure, *AD*, *BF* and *CE* are the altitudes of the triangles).

- All the altitudes of a triangle meet at a point called the *orthocentre* of the triangle.
- The angle made by any side at the orthocentre and the vertical angle make a supplementary pair (i.e. they both add up to 180°). In the figure below:
  $$\angle A + \angle BOC = 180° = \angle C + \angle AOB$$

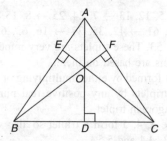

**3. Perpendicular Bisectors** A line that is a perpendicular to a side and bisects it is the perpendicular bisector of the side.

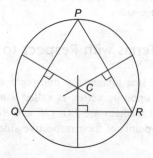

- The point at which the perpendicular bisectors of the sides meet is called the *circumcentre* of the triangle
- The circumcentre is the centre of the circle that circumscribes the triangle. There can be only one such circle.
- Angle formed by any side at the circumcentre is two times the vertical angle opposite to the side. This is the property of the circle whereby angles formed by an arc at the centre are twice that of the angle formed by the same arc in the opposite arc. Here we can view this as:
  $\angle QCR = 2\ \angle QPR$ (when we consider arc *QR* and it's opposite arc *QPR*)

### 4. Incenter

- The lines bisecting the interior angles of a triangle are the angle bisectors of that triangle.
- The angle bisectors meet at a point called the *incentre* of the triangle.
- The incentre is equidistant from all the sides of the triangle.

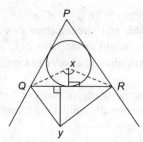

- From the incentre with a perpendicular drawn to any of the sides as the radius, a circle can be drawn touching all the three sides. This is called the *incircle* of the triangle. The radius of the incircle is known as *inradius*.
- The angle formed by any side at the incentre is always a right angle more than half the angle opposite to the side.
  This can be illustrated as $\angle QXR = 90 + \dfrac{1}{2}\ \angle P$
- If *QY* and *RY* are the angle bisectors of the exterior angles at Q and R, then:
  $\angle QYR = 90 - \dfrac{1}{2}\ \angle P$

## Mid-Point Theorem

The line segment joining the mid-points of two sides of a triangle is parallel to the third side and equal to half the third side.

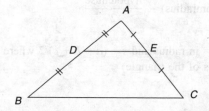

$$AD = BD \text{ and } AE = CE$$
$$DE \parallel BC$$

## Apollonius' theorem

"The sum of the squares of any two sides of any triangle equals twice the square on half the third side plus twice the square of the median bisecting the third side"

Specifically, in any triangle $ABC$, if $AD$ is a median, then

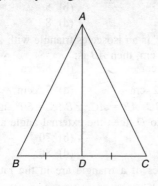

$$BD = CD$$
$AD$ is the median
$$AB^2 + AC^2 = 2(AD^2 + BD^2).$$

## Angle bisector theorem

In a triangle the angle bisector of an angle divides the opposite side to the angle in the ratio of the remaining two sides. i.e., $\dfrac{BD}{CD} = \dfrac{AB}{AC}$ and $BD \times AC - CD \times AB = AD^2$

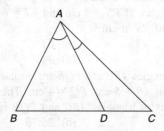

## Exterior angle bisector theorem

In a triangle the angle bisector (represented by CE in the figure) of any exterior angle of a triangle divides the side opposite to the external angle in the ratio of the remaining two sides i.e, $\dfrac{BE}{AE} \quad \dfrac{BC}{AC}$

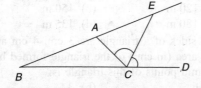

**Few important results:**

1. In a triangle $AE$, $CD$ and $BF$ are the medians then
$$3(AB^2 + BC^2 + AC^2) = 4(CD^2 + BF^2 + AE^2)$$

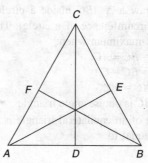

2. If the two triangles have the same base and lie between the same parallel lines (as shown in figure), then the area of two triangles will be equal.

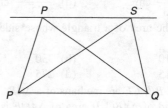

i.e. Area $(\Delta PQR) = $ Area$(\Delta PQS)$

## PRACTICE EXERCISE

1. Find the area of $\Delta PQR$

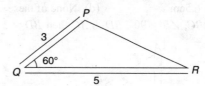

(a) $\dfrac{13\sqrt{3}}{4}$        (b) $\dfrac{15\sqrt{3}}{4}$

(c) $5\sqrt{3}$        (d) None of these

2. In $\Delta ABC$, $AB = AC = 5$ cm, $BC = 4$ cm, then find the area of $\Delta ABC$

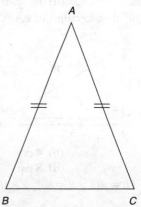

(a) $12\sqrt{3}$ cm²   (b) $2\sqrt{21}$ cm²

(c) $\sqrt{42}$ cm²   (d) None of these

3. If we draw a Δ ABC inside a circle (A, B, C are on the circumference of a circle). Then area of the ΔABC is maximum when:
(a) $AB = BC \neq AC$
(b) $AB = BC = CA$
(c) $\angle BAC = 90°$
(d) ΔABC is obtuse angle triangle

4. If height of an equilateral triangle is 10 cm, its area will be equal to:

(a) $100\sqrt{3}$ cm²   (b) $\dfrac{100}{3}\sqrt{3}$ cm²

(c) $\dfrac{100}{3}$ cm²   (d) $\dfrac{200\sqrt{3}}{3}$ cm²

5. Find the area of a triangle whose sides are 11, 60, 61
(a) 210   (b) 330
(c) 315   (d) 275

6. If AD, BE, CF are medians of a ΔABC and O is the centroid of ΔABC. If area of ΔAOF is 36 cm² then the area of ΔOFB + Area of ΔOEC = ?
(a) 36 cm²   (b) 54 cm²
(c) 72 cm²   (d) None of these

7. If three sides of a triangle are 5, 12, 13 then the circumradius of the triangle is:
(a) 6cm   (b) 2.5cm
(c) 6.5cm   (d) None of these

8. ΔABC, $\angle B = 90°$, $BD \perp AC$ then BD = ?

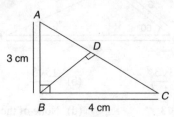

(a) 2.2 cm   (b) 2.4 cm
(c) 2.6 cm   (d) None of these

9. If $\angle A = 90°$ then in radius of ΔABC is:

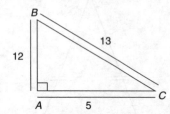

(a) 2 cm   (b) 4 cm
(c) 6 cm   (d) 8 cm

10. In ΔABC AB = AC, $\angle B = 80°$, $\angle BAD = 90°$, $\angle ADE$ = ?

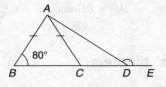

11. AD is the median of the triangle ABC and O is the centroid such that AO = 12 cm. The length of OD in cm is
(a) 4   (b) 5
(c) 6   (d) 8

12. If ΔABC is an isosceles triangle with $\angle C = 90°$ and AC = 7 cm, then AB is:
(a) 8.5 cm   (b) 8.2 cm
(c) $7\sqrt{2}$ cm   (d) 7.5 cm

13. In Δ ABC, AB = AC, $\angle BAC = 50°$, now CB is extended to D, then the external angle at $\angle DBA$ is:
(a) 90°   (b) 70°
(c) 115°   (d) 80°

14. The sides of a triangle are in the ratio 4:5:6. The triangle is:
(a) acute-angled
(b) right-angled
(c) obtuse-angled
(d) either acute-angled or right angled.

15. The sum of three altitudes of a triangle is
(a) equal to the sum of three sides
(b) less than the sum of sides
(c) $1/\sqrt{2}$ times of the sum of sides
(d) half the sum of sides

16. Two medians PS and RT of ΔPQR intersect at G at right angles. If PS = 9 cm and RT = 6 cm, then the length of RS in cm is
(a) 10   (b) 6
(c) 5   (d) 3

17. Two triangles ABC and PQR are similar to each other in which AB = 5 cm, PQ = 4 cm. Then the ratio of the areas of triangles ABC and PQR is
(a) 4:5   (b) 25:16
(c) 64:125   (d) 4:7

18. In ΔABC, the internal bisectors of $\angle ACB$ & $\angle ABC$ meet at X and $\angle BAC = 30°$. The measure of $\angle BXC$ is
(a) 95°   (b) 105°
(c) 125°   (d) 130°

19. The area of an equilateral triangle is $900\sqrt{3}$ sqm. Its perimeter is:
(a) 120 m   (b) 150 m
(c) 180 m   (d) 135 m

20. The sides of a triangle are 3 cm, 4 cm and 5 cm. The area (in cm²) of the triangle formed by joining the mid points of this triangle is:
(a) 6   (b) 3
(c) 3/2   (d) 3/4

## ANSWER KEY

| | | | |
|---|---|---|---|
| 1. (b) | 2. (b) | 3. (b) | 4. (b) |
| 5. (b) | 6. (c) | 7. (c) | 8. (b) |
| 9. (a) | 10. $170^0$ | 11. (c) | 12. (c) |
| 13. (c) | 14. (a) | 15. (b) | 16. (c) |
| 17. (b) | 18. (b) | 19. (c) | 20. (c) |

### Solutions

1. Area $= \dfrac{1}{2} \times 3 \times 5 \times \sin 60^o = \dfrac{15}{2} \times \dfrac{\sqrt{3}}{2} = \dfrac{15\sqrt{3}}{4}$

2. Area $= \dfrac{b}{4}\sqrt{4a^2 - b^2}$

   $= \dfrac{4}{4}\sqrt{4 \times 25 - 16} = \sqrt{84} = 2\sqrt{21}$ cm$^2$

3. An equilateral triangle will have the maximum are compared to other triangles inside the same circle. So $AB = BC = CA$.

4. $h = 10$ cm

   $h = \dfrac{a\sqrt{3}}{2} \Rightarrow a = \dfrac{10 \times 2}{\sqrt{3}} = \dfrac{20}{\sqrt{3}}$ cm

   Area $= \dfrac{1}{2} \times \dfrac{20}{\sqrt{3}} \times 10 = \dfrac{100}{\sqrt{3}}$ cm$^2$ or $\dfrac{100\sqrt{3}}{3}$ cm$^2$

5. 11, 60, 61 forms a Pythagoras triplet. Hence, the triangle is a right angled triangle.

   Area $= \dfrac{1}{2} \times 11 \times 60 = 330$

6. 'O' is the centroid of $\triangle ABC$

   Then area of $\triangle AOF =$ area $\triangle OFB =$ area of $\triangle OEC$

   Area $(\triangle OFB) +$ Area$(\triangle OEC) = 36 + 36 = 72$ cm$^2$

7. 5, 12, 13 forms a Pythagoras triplet.

   Circumradius $= 13/2 = 6.5$ cm

8. $\dfrac{1}{BD^2} = \dfrac{1}{4^2} + \dfrac{1}{3^2} = \dfrac{25}{144}$

   $BD = \left(\dfrac{144}{25}\right)^{\frac{1}{2}} = \dfrac{12}{5} = 2.4$ cm

9. In radius $= \dfrac{12 \times 5}{12 + 5 + 13} = \dfrac{60}{30} = 2$ cm

10. $\angle B = \angle ACB = 80°$

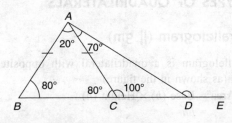

   $\angle BAC = 180° - (80° - 80°) = 20°$

$\angle ADE = \angle CAD + \angle ACD = 70° + 100° = 170°$

11. $D$, is the mid-point of side $BC$.

    Centroid 'O' divides $AD$ in the ratio 2:1

    $\therefore OD = \dfrac{12}{2} = 6$ cm.

12. $AC = BC = 7$ cm

    $\therefore AB = \sqrt{AC^2 + BC^2} = \sqrt{7^2 + 7^2} = \sqrt{98} = 7\sqrt{2}$ cm

13.

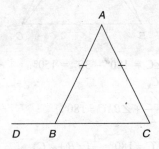

   $\angle ABC = \angle ACB$

   $\angle BAC = 50°$

   $\therefore \angle ABC + \angle ACB = 130°$

   $\angle ABC = 65°$

   $\therefore \angle ABD = 180° - 65° = 115°$

14. Let the sides of the triangle be $3x$, $4x$ and $6x$ units.

    Clearly, $(4x)^2 + (5x)^2 > (6x)^2$

    $\therefore$ The triangle will be acute angled.

15. For a triangle $PQR$, let the altitudes be $AP$, $BR$ and $CQ$ respectively. Then:

    $AP < PR$

    $BR < RQ$

    $CQ < PQ$

    $\therefore AP + BR + CQ < PQ + QR + PR$

16. $PS = 9$ cm

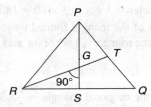

    $\Rightarrow GS = \dfrac{1}{3} \times 9 = 3$ cm

    $RT = 6$ cm

    $\Rightarrow RG = \dfrac{2}{3} \times 6 = 4$ cm

    $\therefore RS = \sqrt{3^2 + 4^2} = \sqrt{9 + 16} = 5$ cm

17. $\dfrac{\text{area of } \triangle ABC}{\text{area of } \triangle PQR} = \dfrac{AB^2}{PQ^2} = \dfrac{25}{16}$

18.

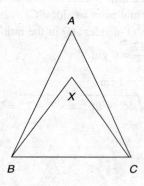

$\angle B + \angle C = 180° - 30° = 150°$

In $\triangle BXC$,

$$\frac{\angle B}{2} + \frac{\angle C}{2} + \angle BXC = 180°$$

$$\Rightarrow \angle BXC = 180° - \frac{1}{2}(\angle B + \angle C)$$

$$= 180° - \frac{150°}{2}$$

$$= 180° - 75° = 105°$$

19. Let the side of the equilateral triangle be $X$ cm. Area of equilateral triangle

$$= \frac{\sqrt{3}}{4} \times (X)^2$$

$$\Rightarrow \frac{\sqrt{3}}{4} \times (X)^2 = 900\sqrt{3}$$

$$\Rightarrow (X)^2 = \frac{900\sqrt{3} \times 4}{\sqrt{3}}$$

$$\therefore X = \sqrt{4 \times 900} = 60 \text{ meters}$$

$$\therefore \text{ Perimeter } = 3 \times X = 3 \times 60 = 180 \text{ meters}$$

20. The area of the triangle formed by joining the mid-point of the triangle is $1/4^{th}$ of the area of the original triangle.

Area of the origional triangle $= \frac{1}{2} \times 3 \times 4 = 6$ cm²

$$\therefore \text{ Required area } = \frac{1}{4} \times 6 = \frac{3}{2} \text{ cm}^2$$

## ⚙ QUADRILATERALS

## Area

(A) Area = 1/2 (product of diagonals) × (sine of the angle between, them)

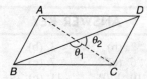

If $\theta_1$ and $\theta_2$ are the two angles made between themselves by the two diagonals, we have by the property of intersecting lines → $\theta_1 + \theta_2 = 180°$

Then, the area of the quadrilateral $= \frac{1}{2} d_1 d_2 \sin \theta_1$

$$= \frac{1}{2} d_1 d_2 \sin \theta_2.$$

(B) Area = 1/2 × diagonal × sum of the perpendiculars to it from opposite vertices $= \dfrac{d(h_1 + h_2)}{2}$.

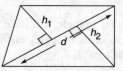

(C) Area of a circumscribed quadrilateral

$$A = \sqrt{(S-a)(S-b)(S-c)(S-d)}$$

Where $S = \dfrac{a+b+c+d}{2}$

(where $a$, $b$, $c$ and $d$ are the lengths of the sides.)

## Properties

1. In a convex quadrilateral inscribed in a circle, the product of the diagonals is equal to the sum of the products of the opposite sides. For example, in the figure below:

$(a \times c) + (b \times d) = AC \times BD$

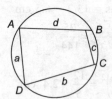

2. Sum of all the angles of a quadrilateral = 360°.

## ⚙ TYPES OF QUADRILATERALS

## 1. Parallelogram (|| gm)

A parallelogram is a quadrilateral with opposite sides parallel (as shown in the figure)

(A) Area = Base ($b$) × Height ($h$)
    $= bh$

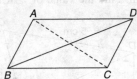

(B) Area = product of any two adjacent sides × sine of the included angle.

$$= ab \sin Q$$

(C) Perimeter = $2(a + b)$

where $a$ and $b$ are any two adjacent sides.

## Properties

(a) Diagonals of a parallelogram bisect each other.
(b) Bisectors of the angles of a parallelogram form a rectangle.
(c) A parallelogram inscribed in a circle is a rectangle.
(d) A parallelogram circumscribed about a circle is a rhombus.
(e) The opposite angles in a parallelogram are equal.
(f) The sum of the squares of the diagonals is equal to the sum of the squares of the four sides in the figure:

$$AC^2 + BD^2 = AB^2 + BC^2 + CD^2 + AD^2$$
$$= 2(AB^2 + BC^2)$$

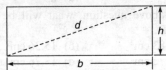

## 2. Rectangles

A rectangle is a parallelogram with all angles 90°

(a) Area = Base × Height = $b × h$

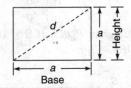

**Note:** Base and height are also referred to as the length and the breadth in a rectangle.

(b) Diagonal $(d) = \sqrt{b^2 + h^2}$ (by Pythagoras theorem)

## Properties of a Rectangle

(a) Diagonals are equal and bisect each other.
(b) Bisectors of the angles of a rectangle (a parallelogram) form another rectangle.
(c) All rectangles are parallelograms but the reverse is not true.

## 3. Rhombus

A parallelogram having all the sides equal is a rhombus.

(a) Area = 1/2 × product of diagonals × sine of the angle between them.

$= 1/2 × d_1 × d_2 \sin 90°$ (Diagonals in a rhombus intersect at right angles)

$= 1/2 × d_1 d_2$ (since $\sin 90° = 1$)

(b) Area = product of adjacent sides × sine of the angle between them.

## Properties

(a) Diagonals bisect each other at right angles.
(b) All rhombuses are parallelograms but the reverse is not true.
(c) A rhombus may or may not be a square but all squares are rhombuses.

## 4. Square

A square is a rectangle with adjacent sides equal or a rhombus with each angle 90°

(a) Area = base × height = $a^2$
(b) Area = 1/2 (diagonal)$^2$ = 1/2 $d^2$ (square is a rhombus too).
(c) Perimeter = $4a$ ($a$ = side of the square)
(d) Diagonal = $a\sqrt{2}$
(e) In radius = $\dfrac{a}{2}$

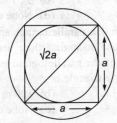

## Properties

(a) Diagonals are equal and bisect each other at right angles.
(b) Side is the diameter of the inscribed circle.
(c) Diagonal is the diameter of the circumscribing circle.

$\Rightarrow$ Diameter = $a\sqrt{2}$.

Circumradius = $a/\sqrt{2}$

## 5. Trapezium

A trapezium is a quadrilateral with only two sides parallel to each other.

(a) Area = 1/2 × sum of parallel sides × height = 1/2 (AB + DC) × h—For the figure below.

(b) Median = 1/2 × sum of the parallel sides (median is the line equidistant from the parallel sides)

For any line EF parallel to AB

$$EF = \frac{\{[P \times (AB)] + [Q \times (DC)]\}}{AD}$$

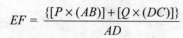
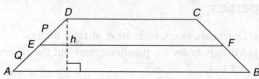

## Properties

(a) If the non-parallel sides are equal then diagonals will be equal too.

---

### PRACTICE EXERCISE

---

1. Find the smallest angle of a quadrilateral if the measure of it's interior angles are in the ratio of 1:2:3:4.
   (a) 18°　　　　　(b) 36°
   (c) 54°　　　　　(d) 72°

2. In a parallelogram PQRS if bisectors of P and Q meet at X, then the value of PXQ is
   (a) 45°　　　　　(b) 90°
   (c) 75°　　　　　(d) 60°

3. In a parallelogram PQRS, if S = 105° and PRQ = 25° then QPR = ?

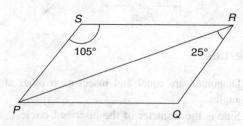

   (a) 40°　　　　　(b) 50°
   (c) 60°　　　　　(d) 55°

4. If one diagonal of a rhombus is equal to it's side, then the diagonals of the rhombus are in the ratio.
   (a) $\sqrt{3}:1$　　　　　(b) 3 : 1
   (c) 2 : 1　　　　　(d) None of these

5. A triangle and a parallelogram are constructed on the same base such that their areas are equal. If the altitude of the parallelogram is 100 m, then the altitude of the triangle is
   (a) 50 m　　　　　(b) 100 m
   (c) 200 m　　　　　(d) None of these

6. In a square PQRS, A is the mid point of PQ and B is the midpoint of QR, if area of $\triangle AQB$ is 100 m² then the area of the square PQRS = ?
   (a) 400 m²　　　　　(b) 250 m²
   (c) 600 m²　　　　　(d) 800 m²

7. In the previous question length of diagonal PR = ?
   (a) 20 m　　　　　(b) 30 m
   (c) 40 m　　　　　(d) $20\sqrt{2}$ m

8. If a triangle with area x, rectangle with area y, parallelogram with area z were all constructed on the same base and all have the same altitude, then which of the following options is true?
   (a) x = y = z　　　　　(b) x = y/2 = z
   (c) 2x = y = z　　　　　(d) 2x = 2y = z

9. □ABCD is a parallelogram, AC, BD are the diagonals & intersect at point O. X and Y are the centroids of $\triangle ADC$ and $\triangle ABC$ respectively. If BY = 6 cm, then OX = ?
   (a) 2 cm　　　　　(b) 3 cm
   (c) 4 cm　　　　　(d) 6 cm

10. If area of a rectangle with sides x and y is X and that of a parallelogram (which is strictly not a rectangle) with sides x and y is Y. Then:
    (a) X = Y　　　　　(b) X ≤ Y
    (c) X < Y　　　　　(d) X > Y

11. In □ABCD, A = 90°, BC = CD = 5 cm, AD = 3 cm, BA = 4 cm. Find the value of ∠BCD.

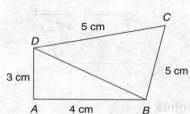

    (a) 45°　　　　　(b) 60°
    (c) 75°　　　　　(d) 85°

12. In the above question, what will be the area of □ABCD.
    (a) 16.83 cm²　　　　　(b) 15.36 cm²
    (c) 14.72 cm²　　　　　(d) 13.76 cm²

13. □PQRS is a parallelogram. 'O' is a point within it, and area of parallelogram PQRS is 50 cm². Find the sum of areas of $\triangle OPQ$ and $\triangle OSR$ (in cm²):
    (a) 15　　　　　(b) 20
    (c) 25　　　　　(d) 30

14. ABCD is a rhombus, such that AB = 5cm AC = 8 cm. Find the area of □ABCD

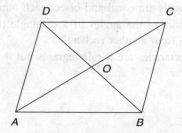

(a) 12 cm²        (b) 18 cm²
(c) 24 cm²        (d) 36 cm²

15. If *ABCD* is a trapezium then find the value of *x*.

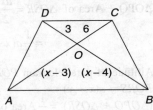

(a) 3            (b) 4
(c) 5            (d) 6

16. A square and a rhombus have the same base and the rhombus is inclined at 45° then what will be the ratio of area of the square to the area of the rhombus?
(a) 2:1          (b) $\sqrt{2}$:1
(c) 1:$\sqrt{2}$        (d) $\sqrt{3}$:1

17. *PQRS* is a quadrilateral and *PQ* || *RS*. *T* is the mid-point of *PQ*. *ST* || *RQ*. If area of the triangle $\Delta PST$ is 50 cm² then area of □*PQRS* is:

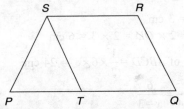

(a) 100 cm²       (b) 125 cm²
(c) 150 cm²       (d) 175 cm²

18. In □*ABCD*, *AB* = *BC*, *AD* = *CD*. *BD* and *AC* are diagonals of □*ABCD*. Such that *BD* = 10 cm, *AC* = 5 cm. Find area of □ABCD.

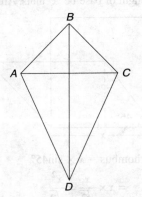

---

### ANSWER KEY

| | | | |
|---|---|---|---|
| 1. (b) | 2. (b) | 3. (b) | 4. (a) |
| 5. (c) | 6. (d) | 7. (c) | 8. (c) |
| 9. (b) | 10. (d) | 11. (b) | 12. (a) |
| 13. (c) | 14. (c) | 15. (c) | 16. (b) |
| 17. (c) | 18. 25 cm² | | |

---

### Solutions

1. Let the angles be *x*, 2*x*, 3*x*, 4*x* respectively
   According to the question:
   $x + 2x + 3x + 4x = 360°$
   $10x = 360°$
   $X = 36°$
   Smallest angle = 36°

2. $P + Q = 180°$
   $$\frac{\angle P}{2} + \frac{\angle Q}{2} = 90°$$
   $$\angle PXQ = 180° - \left[\frac{\angle P}{2} + \frac{\angle Q}{2}\right] = 180° - 90° = 90°$$

3. $PQR = PSR = 105°$
   $RPQ = 180° - (105° + 25°) = 50°$

4. Let *AB* = *BD* = *DC* = *a*, *AC* = *b*

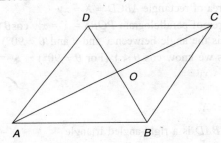

   In $\Delta COD$: $(CD)^2 = (OC)^2 + (OD)^2$
   $$a^2 = \left(\frac{b}{2}\right)^2 + \left(\frac{a}{2}\right)^2$$
   $$\frac{3a^2}{4} = \frac{b^2}{4}$$
   $$b = a\sqrt{3}$$
   $$\frac{b}{a} = \frac{\sqrt{3}}{1}$$

5. If '*b*' is the base and $h_1$, $h_2$ are altitudes of the triangle and parallelogram respectively.
   Then according to the question:
   $$\frac{1}{2} \times b \times h_1 = b \times h_2$$
   $$h_1 = 2h_2$$
   $$h_1 = 2 \times 100 = 200 \text{ m.}$$

6. Area of $\Delta AQB = \frac{1}{2} \times AQ \times BQ = 100 = 100$
   $$\frac{1}{2} \times \frac{PQ}{2} \times \frac{QR}{2} = 100$$
   $$PQ \times QR = 2 \times 2 \times 2 \times 100 = 800 \text{ cm}^2.$$

7. $PQ.QR = 800 \text{ cm}^2$
   $PQ = QR$ (□*PQRS* is a square)
   $(PQ)^2 = 800$

$PQ = 20\sqrt{2}$ cm

Length of the diagonal = $PQ\sqrt{2} = 20\sqrt{2} \times \sqrt{2} = 40$ m.

8. Area of triangle $= \dfrac{1}{2} \times$ *Area of Parallelogram*

$x = z/2$

Area of parallelogram = Area of rectangle.

$y = z$

$2x = y = z$

9. $\triangle ABC$ & $\triangle ADC$ are congruent to each other.

So $OD = OB$

$\dfrac{OD}{3} = \dfrac{OB}{3}$

$OX = OY$

$OX = \dfrac{BY}{2} = \dfrac{6}{2} = 3$ cm

10. Area of rectangle $ABCD = X = xy$

Area of parallelogram $PQRS = Y = x.y\cos\theta$ (where $\theta$ is the angle between $x$ and $y$ and $\theta \neq 90°$)

As we know $\cos\theta < 1$ (For $\theta \neq 90°$)

$Y < xy$

or

$Y < X$.

11. $\triangle BAD$ is a right-angled triangle

$BD = \sqrt{3^2 + 4^2} = \sqrt{25} = 5$ cm

In $\triangle BCD$ all the sides are equal to each other, so $\triangle BCD$ is an equilateral triangle

$\therefore BCD = 60°$

12. Area of $\square ABCD$ = Area of $\triangle ABC$ + Area of $\triangle BCD$

$= \dfrac{1}{2} \times 3 \times 4 + \dfrac{\sqrt{3}}{4}(5)^2$ cm$^2$

$= 6 + \dfrac{25\sqrt{3}}{4}$ cm$^2$

$= \left(6 + 6.25\sqrt{3}\right)$ cm$^2$

$= 16.83$ cm$^2$

13. Draw $OA \perp PQ$ and $OB \perp SR$.

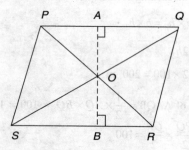

If $OA = x$, $OB = y$ and $PQ = SR = a$, $QR = PS = b$

Then area of $\triangle OPQ = \dfrac{1}{2} \times x \times a = \dfrac{ax}{2}$

Area of $\triangle OSR = \dfrac{1}{2} \times y \times a = \dfrac{ay}{2}$

Area of $\triangle OPQ$ + Area of $\triangle OSR = \dfrac{ax}{2} + \dfrac{ay}{2}$

$= \dfrac{1}{2}a(x + y)$

$x + y$ = Altitude of parallelogram $PQRS$

Area of $PQRS = a(x + y)$

Area of $(\triangle OPQ + \triangle OSR) = \dfrac{1}{2}$ Area of $\square PQRS$

$= \dfrac{1}{2} \times 50 = 25$ cm$^2$

14. $OC = \dfrac{AC}{2} = \dfrac{8}{2} = 4$ cm

$\because \angle DOC = 90°$

$\therefore OD^2 + OC^2 = CD^2$

$OD^2 + 4^2 = 5^2$

$OD^2 = 9$

$OD = 3$ cm

$BD = 2 \times OD = 2 \times 3 = 6$ cm

Area of $ABCD = \dfrac{1}{2} \times 6 \times 8 = 24$ cm$^2$

15. $\dfrac{3}{x-4} = \dfrac{6}{x-3}$

$3(x - 3) = 6(x - 4)$

$x - 3 = 2(x - 4)$

$x - 3 = 2x - 8$

$x = 5$

16. Let the length of base be '$x$' units. Area of square $= x^2$

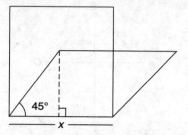

45°

$x$

Area of rhombus $= x \times x \times \sin 45°$

$= x \times \dfrac{x}{\sqrt{2}} = \dfrac{x^2}{\sqrt{2}}$

Required ratio $= x^2 : \dfrac{x^2}{\sqrt{2}}$

$= 1 : \dfrac{1}{\sqrt{2}}$

$= \sqrt{2} : 1$

17. $T$ is the midpoint of $PQ$

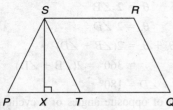

$PT = TQ$

Draw $SX \perp PQ$, if $SX = h$ and $PT = TQ = a$

Area of $\triangle PST = \dfrac{1}{2} \times a \times h = \dfrac{ah}{2}$

Area of $\square PQRS$ = Area of $\triangle PST$ + Area of $\square STQR$

$= \dfrac{ah}{2} + ah$

$= \dfrac{3ah}{2}$

$= 3[50] = 150$ cm$^2$

18. $\square ABCD$ has a kite like structure, so it's diagonals intersect each other perpendicularly

Area $= \dfrac{1}{2}$ (product of diagonals)

$= \dfrac{1}{2} \times 10 \times 5 = 25$ cm$^2$

## 🜚 REGULAR HEXAGON

(a) Area $= [(3\sqrt{3})/2]$ (side)$^2$

$= \dfrac{3\sqrt{3} \times a^2}{2}$

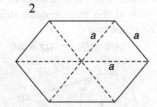

(b) A regular hexagon is actually a combination of 6 equilateral triangles all of side '$a$'.

Hence, the area is also given by: 6 × Area of an equilateral triangle having the same side as the side

of the hexagon $= 6 \times \dfrac{\sqrt{3}}{4} a^2$

(c) If you look at the figure closely it will not be difficult to realise that circumradius ($R$) = $a$; i.e the side of the hexagon is equal to the circumradius of the same.

## 🜚 CIRCLES

(a) Area $= \pi r^2$

(b) Circumference $= 2\pi r = (r = \text{radius})$

(c) Area $= 1/2 \times$ circumference $\times r$

**Arc:** It is a part of the circumference of the circle. The bigger one is called the *major arc* and the smaller one the *minor arc*.

(d) Length (Arc $XY$) $= \dfrac{\theta}{360} \times 2\pi r$

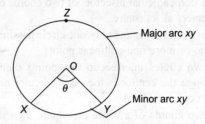

(e) **Sector of a circle** is a part of the area of a circle between two radii.

(f) Area of a sector $= \dfrac{\theta}{360} \times \pi r^2$

(where $\theta$ is the angle between two radii)

$= (1/2) r \times$ length (arc $xy$)

($\because \pi r\theta/180 = $ length arc $xy$)

$= \dfrac{1}{2} \times r \times \dfrac{\pi r\theta}{360}$

(g) **Segment:** A sector minus the triangle formed by the two radii is called the segment of the circle.

(h) Area = Area of the sector − Area $\triangle OAB$ =

$\dfrac{\theta}{360} \times \pi r^2 - \dfrac{1}{2} \times r^2 \sin\theta$

(i) Perimeter of segment = length of the arc + length of segment $AB$

$= \dfrac{\theta}{360} \times 2\pi r + 2r \sin\left(\dfrac{\theta}{2}\right)$

$= \dfrac{\pi r\theta}{180} + 2r \sin\left(\dfrac{\theta}{2}\right)$

(j) **Congruency:** Two circles can be congruent if and only if they have equal radii.

## Properties

(a) The perpendicular from the centre of a circle to a chord bisects the chord. The converse is also true.

(b) The perpendicular bisectors of two chords of a circle intersect at its centre.

(c) There can be one and only one circle passing through three or more non-collinear points.

(d) If two circles intersect in two points then the line through the centres is the perpendicular bisector of the common chord.

(e) If two chords of a circle are equal, then the centre of the circle lies on the perpendicular bisector of the two chords.

(f) Equal chords of a circle or congruent circles are equidistant from the centre.

(g) Equidistant chords from the centre of a circle are equal to each other in terms of their length.

(h) The degree measure of an arc of a circle is twice the angle subtended by it at any point on the alternate segment of the circle. This can be clearly seen in the following figure:

With respect to the arc $AB$, $\angle AOB = 2 \angle ACB$.

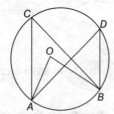

(i) Any two angles in the same segment are equal. Thus, $\angle ACB = \angle ADB$.

(j) The angle subtended by a semi-circle is a right angle. Conversely, the arc of a circle subtending a right angle at any point of the circle in its alternate segment is a semi-circle.

(k) Any angle subtended by a minor arc in the alternate segment is acute, and any angle subtended by a major arc in the alternate segment is obtuse.

In the figure below

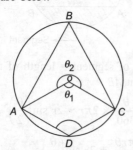

$\angle ABC$ is acute and

$\angle ADC$ = obtuse

Also     $\theta_1 = 2 \angle B$

And      $\theta_2 = 2 \angle D$

$\therefore$     $\theta_1 + \theta_2 = 2(\angle B + \angle D)$

$= 360° = 2(\angle B + \angle D)$

or $\angle B + \angle D = 180°$

or sum of opposite angles of a cyclic quadrilateral is $180°$.

(l) If a line segment joining two points subtends equal angles at two other points lying on the same side of the line, the four points are concyclic. Thus, in the following figure:

If,      $\theta_1 = \theta_2$

Then $ABCD$ are concyclic, that is, they lie on the same circle.

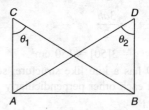

(m) Equal chords of a circle (or of congruent circles) subtend equal angles at the centre (at the corresponding centres.) The converse is also true.

(n) If the sum of the opposite angles of a quadrilateral is $180°$, then the quadrilateral is cyclic.

*Secant:*   A line that intersects a circle at two points.

*Tangent:*   A line that touches a circle at exactly one point.

(o) If a circle touches all the four sides of a quadrilateral then the sum of the two opposite sides is equal to the sum of other two

$$AB + DC = AD + BC$$

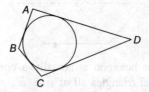

(p) In two concentric circles, the chord of the larger circle that is tangent to the smaller circle is bisected at the point of contact.

## Tangents

• Length of direct common tangents is

$$= \sqrt{(\text{Distance between their centres})^2 - (r_1 - r_2)^2}$$

where $r_1$ and $r_2$ are the radii of the circles

$$= \sqrt{(OO')^2 - (r_1 - r_2)^2}$$

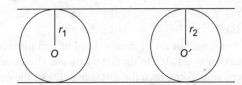

• Length of transverse common tangents is

$$= \sqrt{(\text{distance between their centres})^2 - (r_1 + r_2)^2}$$

$$= \sqrt{(OO')^2 - (r_1 + r_2)^2}$$

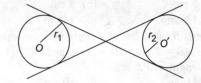

## 𝄌 ELLIPSE

• Perimeter $= \pi(a + b)$
• Area $= \pi ab$

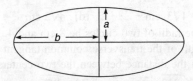

## PRACTICE EXERCISE

1. Find the area of a circle of radius 5cm.
   - (a) $25\pi$
   - (b) $20\pi$
   - (c) $22\pi$
   - (d) None of these

2. Find the circumference of the circle in the previous question:
   - (a) $10\pi$
   - (b) $5\pi$
   - (c) $7\pi$
   - (d) None of these

3. If $O$ is the center of the circle and $OC \perp AB$ and $AC = x + 6$, $BC = 2x - 4$, then $AB = ?$

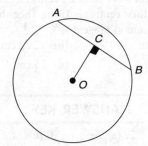

   - (a) 22
   - (b) 31
   - (c) 32
   - (d) 26

4. If $AB = CD$ and $AB = 12$ cm. '$O$' is the center of the circle, $OD = 8$ cm, $OE \perp CD$, Then length of $OE$ is

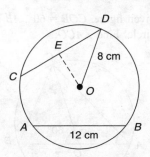

   - (a) 2 cm
   - (b) $2\sqrt{7}$ cm
   - (c) $2\sqrt{11}$ cm
   - (d) None of these

5. In the given figure, O is the centre of the circle. $ABO = 45°$. Find the value of $ACB$:

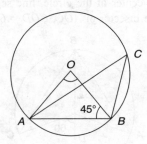

   - (a) 60°
   - (b) 75°
   - (c) 90°
   - (d) None of these

6. In the given figure, $AOC = 130°$, where $O$ is the center. Find $\angle CBE$:

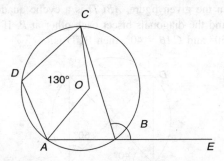

   - (a) 100°
   - (b) 70°
   - (c) 115°
   - (d) 130°

7. In the given figure, $\triangle ABC$ is an equilateral triangle. Find $\angle BEC$:

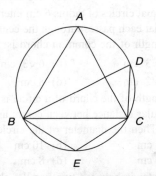

   - (a) 120°
   - (b) 60°
   - (c) 80°
   - (d) None of the above

8. In the given figure, $COB = 60°$, $AB$ is the diameter of the circle. Find $\angle ACO$:

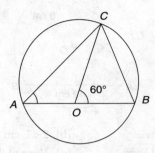

(a)  20°                     (b)  30°
(c)  35°                     (d)  40°

9. $O$ is the center of the circle, line segment $BOD$ is the angle bisector of $AOC$, $COD = 60°$. Find $ABC$:

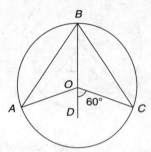

(a)  30°                     (b)  40°
(c)  50°                     (d)  60°

10. In the given figure, $ABCD$ is a cyclic quadrilateral and the diagonals bisect each other at $P$. If $CBD = 50°$ and $CAB = 40°$, then BCD is:

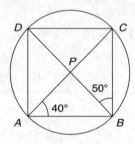

(a)  60°                     (b)  75°
(c)  90°                     (d)  105°

11. Two equal circles of radius 6 cm intersect each other such that each passes through the centre of the other. The length of the common chord is:

(a)  $2\sqrt{3}$ cm          (b)  $6\sqrt{3}$ cm
(c)  $2\sqrt{2}$ cm          (d)  8 cm

12. The length of the chord of a circle is 6 cm and perpendicular distance between centre and the chord is 4 cm. Then the diameter of the circle is equal to:

(a)  12 cm                   (b)  10 cm
(c)  16 cm                   (d)  8 cm

13. The distance between two parallel chords of length 6 cm each in a circle of diameter 10 cm is

(a)  8 cm                    (b)  7 cm
(c)  6 cm                    (d)  5.5 cm

14. The length of the common chord of two intersecting circles is 24. If the diameters of the circles are 30 cm and 26 cm, then the distance between the centers of the circles (in cm) is

(a)  13                      (b)  14
(c)  15                      (d)  16

15. If two equal circles whose centers are $O$ and $O'$, intersect each other at the points $A$ and $B$. $OO' = 6$ cm and $AB = 8$ cm, then the radius of the circles is

(a)  5 cm                    (b)  8 cm
(c)  12 cm                   (d)  14 cm

16. Chords $BA$ and $DC$ of a circle intersect externally at $P$. If $AB = 7$ cm, $CD = 5$ cm and $PC = 1$ cm, then the length of $PB$ is

(a)  11 cm                   (b)  10 cm
(c)  9 cm                    (d)  8 cm

17. Two circles touch each other internally. Their radii are 3 cm and 4 cm. The biggest chord of the greater circle which is outside the inner circle is of length:

(a)  $2\sqrt{3}$ cm          (b)  $3\sqrt{2}$ cm

(c)  $4\sqrt{3}$ cm          (d)  $4\sqrt{2}$ cm

18. If the radii of two circles be 8 cm and 4 cm and the length of the transverse common tangent be 13 cm, then the distance between the two centers is

(a)  $\sqrt{313}$ cm         (b)  $\sqrt{125}$ cm

(c)  $5\sqrt{2}$ cm          (d)  $\sqrt{135}$ cm

18. The distance between the centers of two equal circles, each of radius 6 cm, is 13 cm. the length of a transverse common tangent is

(a)  8 cm                    (b)  10 cm
(c)  5 cm                    (d)  6 cm

19. The radii of two circles are 9 cm and 4 cm, the distance between their centres is 13 cm. Then the length of the direct transverse common tangent is

(a)  12 cm                   (c)  $12\sqrt{2}$ cm
(c)  5 cm                    (d)  15 cm

20. The radii of two circles are 9cm and 4cm, the distance between their centres is 13cm. Then the length of the direct common tangent is

(a)  12 cm                   (b)  $12\sqrt{2}$ cm
(c)  5 cm                    (d)  15 cm

## ANSWER KEY

|       |       |       |       |
|-------|-------|-------|-------|
| 1. (a)  | 2. (a)  | 3. (c)  | 4. (b)  |
| 5. (d)  | 6. (c)  | 7. (a)  | 8. (b)  |
| 9. (d)  | 10. (c) | 11. (b) | 12. (b) |
| 13. (a) | 14. (b) | 15. (a) | 16. (b) |
| 17. (c) | 18. (a) | 19. (c) | 20. (a) |

## Solutions

1.  Area $= \pi r^2 = \pi \times 5^2 = 25\pi$

2.  Circumference $= 2\pi \times 5 = 10\pi$

3.  As $OC \perp AB$
    $AC = BC$
    $x + 6 = 2x - 4$
    $x = 10$
    $AB = x + 6 + 2x - 4 = 3x + 2 = 30 + 2 = 32$

4.  If $\overline{AB} = \overline{CD}$
    Then $AB = CD = 12$ cm
    If $CD = 12$, then $CE = DE = 6$cm
    $OE = \sqrt{8^2 - 6^2} = \sqrt{28} = 2\sqrt{7}$ cm

5.  $AO = BO$
    $ABO = BAO = 45°$
    $AOB = 180° - (45° + 45°) = 90°$
    $\angle ACB = \dfrac{\angle AOB}{2} = \dfrac{90°}{2} = 45°$
    $\angle ABC = \dfrac{130°}{2} = 65°$  $\angle CBE = 180° - 65° = 115°$

6.

7.  $BAC = 60°$
    $\angle BEC = 180° - \angle BAC = 180° - 60° = 120°$

8.  $\angle COB = 60°$
    $\angle AOC = 180° - 60° = 120°$
    $\angle CAO = \dfrac{60°}{2} = 30°$
    $\angle ACO = 180° - (120° + 30°) = 180° - 150° = 30°$

9.  $\angle COD = 60°$
    $\angle AOC = 2 \times 60° = 120°$
    $\angle ABC = \dfrac{120°}{2} = 60°$

10. $\angle CDB = \angle CAB = 40°$
    In $\triangle BDC = \angle BCD + 50° + 40° = 180°$
    $\angle BCD = 90°$

11. $OO' = 6$ cm
    $OC = 3$ cm
    $OA = 6$ cm
    $\therefore AC = \sqrt{6^2 - 3^2} = \sqrt{36 - 9} = \sqrt{27} = 3\sqrt{3}$ cm
    $\therefore AB = 6\sqrt{3}$ cm

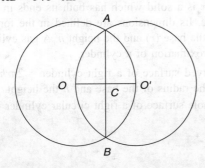

12. $AC = CB = 3$ cm
    $OC = 4$ cm
    $\therefore OA = \sqrt{OC^2 + CA^2}$
    $= \sqrt{4^2 + 3^2}$
    $= \sqrt{16 + 9} = \sqrt{25} = 5$ cm
    Diameter $= 10$ cm

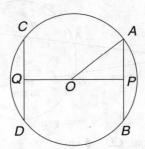

13.

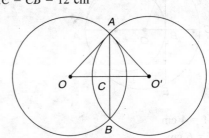

    $AB = CD$
    $OP = OQ$
    From $\triangle OAP$
    $OP = \sqrt{OA^2 - AP^2} = \sqrt{5^2 - 3^2} = \sqrt{25 - 9} = \sqrt{16} = 4$ cm
    $\therefore QP = 2 \times OP = 8$ cm

14.
    $AC = CB = 12$ cm

    $OC = \sqrt{15^2 - 12^2} = \sqrt{225 - 144} = \sqrt{81} = 9$ cm
    $O'C = \sqrt{13^2 - 12^2} = \sqrt{169 - 144} = \sqrt{25} = 5$ cm
    $\therefore OO' = 9 + 5 = 14$ cm

15.

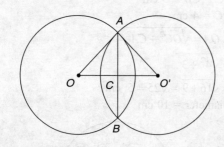

$AB = 8$ cm
$AC = BC = 4$ cm
$OC = CO' = 3$ cm

$\therefore OA = \sqrt{OC^2 + CA^2} = \sqrt{3^2 + 4^2} = \sqrt{9 + 16} = \sqrt{25} = 5$ cm

16.

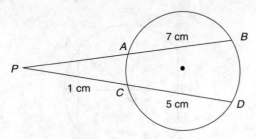

$AB = 7$ cm, $CD = 5$ cm
$PC = 1$ cm, $PA = x$ cm
$PA \times PB = PC \times PD$
$\Rightarrow x(x + 7) = 6 \times 5$

By solving we get $x = 3$ cm
$PB = 3 + 7 = 10$ cm

17.

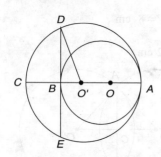

$O'A = 4$ cm
$AB = 6$ cm
$O'B = AB - O'A = 6 - 4 = 2$ cm
$BD = \sqrt{4^2 - 2^2} = 2\sqrt{3}$ cm
$DE = 4\sqrt{3}$ cm

18. Let the distance between the centers be $x$ cm.
$\Rightarrow 13 = \sqrt{x^2 - (8 + 4)^2}$
$\Rightarrow 169 = x^2 - 144$

$\Rightarrow x^2 = 169 + 144 = 313$
$\Rightarrow x = \sqrt{313}$ cm

19. Transverse common tangent
$= \sqrt{(\text{Distance between centres})^2 - (r_1 + r_2)^2}$
$= \sqrt{13^2 - 12^2} = \sqrt{25} = 5$ cm

20. Direct common tangent
$= \sqrt{(13)^2 - (9 - 4)^2} = \sqrt{169 - 25} = \sqrt{144} = 12$ cm

## STAR

Sum of angles of a star $= (2n - 8) \times \pi/2 = (n - 4)\pi$

---

# PART II: MENSURATION

---

The following formulae hold true in the area of mensuration:

## 1. Cuboid
A cuboid is a three dimensional box. It is defined by the virtue of it's length $l$, breadth $b$ and height $h$. It can be visualised as a room which has its length, breadth and height different from each other.

1. Total surface area of a cuboid $= 2(lb + bh + lh)$
2. Volume of the cuboid $= lbh$

## 2. Cube of side s
A cube is a cuboid which has all its edges equal i.e. length = breadth = height = $s$.

1. Total surface area of a cube $= 6s^2$.
2. Volume of the cube $= s^3$.

## 3. Prism
A prism is a solid which can have any polygon at both its ends. It's dimensions are defined by the dimensions of the polygon at it's ends and its height.

1. Lateral surface area of a right prism = Perimeter of base × height
2. Volume of a right prism = area of base × height
3. Whole surface of a right prism = Lateral surface of the prism + the area of the two plane ends.

## 4. Cylinder
A cylinder is a solid which has both its ends in the form of a circle. Its dimensions are defined in the form of the radius of the base ($r$) and the height $h$. A gas cylinder is a close approximation of a cylinder.

1. Curved surface of a right cylinder $= 2\pi rh$ where $r$ is the radius of the base and $h$ the height.
2. Whole surface of a right circular cylinder $= 2\pi rh + 2\pi r^2$

3. Volume of a right circular cylinder = $\pi r^2 h$

## 5. Pyramid

A pyramid is a solid which can have any polygon as its base and its edges converge to a single apex. Its dimensions are defined by the dimensions of the polygon at its base and the length of its lateral edges which lead to the apex. The Egyptian pyramids are examples of pyramids.

1. Slant surface of a pyramid = 1/2 × Perimeter of the base × slant height
2. Whole surface of a pyramid = Slant surface + area of the base
3. Volume of a pyramid = $\dfrac{\text{area of the base} \times}{3}$ height

## 6. Cone

A cone is a solid which has a circle at its base and a slanting lateral surface that converges at the apex. Its dimensions are defined by the radius of the base ($r$), the height ($h$) and the slant height ($l$). A structure similar to a cone is used in ice cream cones.

1. Curved surface of a cone = $\pi r l$ where $l$ is the slant height
2. Whole surface of a cone = $\pi r l + \pi r^2$
3. Volume of a cone = $\dfrac{\pi r^2 h}{3}$

## 7. Sphere

A sphere is a solid in the form of a ball with radius $r$.

1. Surface Area of a sphere = $4\pi r^2$
2. Volume of a sphere = $\dfrac{4}{3}\pi r^3$

## 8. Frustum of a pyramid

When a pyramid is cut the left over part is called the frustum of the pyramid.

1. Slant surface of the frustum of a pyramid = 1/2 * sum of perimeters of end * slant height.
2. Volume of the frustum of a pyramid = $\dfrac{k}{3}[E_1 + (E_1 \cdot E_2)^{1/2} + E_2]$ where $k$ is the thickness and $E_1$, $E_2$ the areas of the ends.

## 9. Frustum of a cone

When a cone is cut the left over part is called the frustum of the cone.

1. Slant surface of the frustum of a cone = $\pi(r_1 + r_2)l$ where $l$ is the slant height.
2. Volume of the frustum of a cone = $\dfrac{\pi}{3} k(r_1^2 + r_1 r_2 + r_2^2)$

*Space for Rough Work*

## 🎯 WORKED-OUT PROBLEMS

**Problem 11.1**  A right triangle with hypotenuse 10 inches and other two sides of variable length is rotated about its longest side thus giving rise to a solid. Find the maximum possible volume of such a solid.

    (a)  $(250/3)\pi \text{in}^3$        (b)  $(160/3)\pi \text{in}^3$

    (c)  $325/3\pi \text{in}^3$         (d)  None of these

**Solution**  Most of the questions like this that are asked in the CAT will not have figures accompanying them. Drawing a figure takes time, so it is always better to strengthen our imagination. The beginners can start off by trying to imagine the figure first and trying to solve the problem. They can draw the figure only when they don't arrive at the right answer and then find out where exactly they went wrong. The key is to spend as much time with the problem as possible trying to understand it fully and analysing the different aspects of the same without investing too much time on it.

Let's now look into this problem. The key here lies in how quickly you are able to visualise the figure and are able to see that

  (i)  the triangle has to be an isosceles triangle,

  (ii)  the solid thus formed is actually a combination of two cones,

  (iii)  the radius of the base has to be the altitude of the triangle to the hypotenuse.

After you have visualised this comes the calculation aspect of the problem. This is one aspect where you can score over others.

In this question the figure would be somewhat like this (as shown alongside) with triangles *ABC* and *ADC* representing the cones and *AC* being the hypotenuse around which the triangle *ABC* revolves. Now that the area has to be maximum with *AC* as the hypotenuse, we must realise that 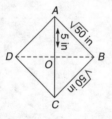 *ADB* has to be an isosceles triangle, which automatically makes *BCD* an isosceles triangle too. The next step is to calculate the radius of the base, which is essentially the height of the triangle *ABC*. To find that, we have to first find *AB*. We know

$$AC^2 = AB^2 + BC^2$$

For triangle to be one with the greatest possible area *AB* must be equal to *BC* that is, $AB = BC = \sqrt{50}$, since $AO = 1/2AC = 5$ inches.

Now take the right angle triangle *ABO*, *BO* being the altitude of triangle *AOC*. By Pythagoras theorem, $AB^2 = AO^2 + BO^2$, so $BO^2 = 25$ inches

The next step is to find the volume of the cone *ABD* and multiply it with two to get the volume of the whole solid.

Volume of the cone $ADB = \dfrac{\pi}{3} \times BO^2 \times AO = \dfrac{125\,\pi}{3}$

Therefore volume of the solid $ABCD = 2 \times \dfrac{250\,\pi}{3} = \dfrac{250\,\pi}{3}$

**Problem 11.2**  A right circular cylinder is to be made out of a metal sheet such that the sum of its height and radius does not exceed 9 cm can have a maximum volume of.

    (a)  54 p cm$^2$        (b)  108 p cm$^2$

    (c)  81 p cm$^2$        (d)  None of these

**Solution**  Solving this question requires the knowledge of ratio and proportion also. To solve this question, one must know that for $a^2b^3c^4$ to have the maximum value when $(a + b + c)$ is constant, $a$, $b$ and $c$ must be in the ratio $1:2:3$.

Now lets look at this problem.

Volume of a cylinder = $\pi r^2 h$.

If you analyse this formula closely, you will find that $r$ and $h$ are the only variable term. So for volume of the cylinder to be maximum, $r^2h$ has to be maximum under the condition that $r + h = 9$. By the information given above, this is possible only when $r:h = 2:1$, that is, $r = 6$, $h = 3$. So,

$$\text{Volume of the Cylinder} = \pi r^2 h$$
$$= \pi \times 6^2 \times 3$$
$$= \mathbf{108\pi}$$

**Problem 11.3**  There are five concentric squares. If the area of the circle inside the smallest square is 77 square units and the distance between the corresponding corners of consecutive squares is 1.5 units, find the difference in the areas of the outermost and innermost squares.

**Solution**  Here again the ability to visualise the diagram would be the key. Once you gain expertise in this aspect, you will be able to see that you will be able to see that the diameter of the circle is equal to the side of the innermost square that is

$$\pi r^2 = 77$$
or
$$r = 3.5\sqrt{2}$$
or
$$2r = 7\sqrt{2}$$

Then the diagonal of the square is 14 sq units.
Which means the diagonal of the fifth square would be 14 + 12 units = 26.

Which means the side of the fifth square would be $13\sqrt{2}$.

Therefore, the area of the fifth square = 338 sq units
Area of the first square = 98 sq units
Hence, the difference would be 240 sq. units.

**Problem 11.4** A spherical pear of radius 4 cm is to be divided into eight equal parts by cutting it in halves along the same axis. Find the surface area of each of the final piece.

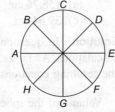

**Fig. (a)**

    (a) $20\ \pi$         (b) $25\ \pi$
    (c) $24\ \pi$         (d) $19\ \pi$

**Solution** The pear after being cut will have eight parts each of same volume and surface area. The figure will be somewhat like the above Figure (a) if seen from the top before cutting. After cutting it look something like the Figure (b).

Now the surface area of each piece = Area $ACBD$ + 2 (Area $CODB$).

The darkened surface is nothing but the arc $AB$ from side glance which means its surface area is one eighth the area of the sphere, that is, $1/8 \times 4\pi r^2 = (1/2)\pi r^2$.

Now $CODB$ can be seen as a semicircle with radius 4 cm.

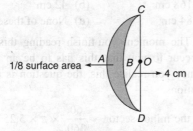

1/8 surface area

**Fig. (b)**

Therefore, 2 (Area $CODB$) = $2[(1/2)]\ \pi r^2 = \pi r^2$
$\Rightarrow$ surface area of each piece = $(1/2)\ \pi r^2 + \pi r^2$
$$= (3/2)\ \pi r^2$$
$$= 24\pi$$

**Problem 11.5** A solid metal sphere is melted and smaller spheres of equal radii are formed. 10% of the volume of the sphere is lost in the process. The smaller spheres have a radius, that is 1/9th the larger sphere. If 10 litres of paint were needed to paint the larger sphere, how many litres are needed to paint all the smaller spheres?

    (a) 90         (b) 81
    (c) 900       (d) 810

**Solution** Questions like this require, along with your knowledge of formulae, your ability to form equations. Stepwise, it will be something like this

*Step 1:* Assume values.

*Step 2:* Find out volume left.

*Step 3:* Find out the number of small spheres possible.

*Step 4:* Find out the total surface area of each small spheres as a ratio of the original sphere.

*Step 5:* Multiply it by 10.

**Step 1:** Let radius of the larger sphere be $R$ and that of smaller ones be $r$.

Then, volume = $\frac{4}{3}\pi R^3$ and $\frac{4}{3}\pi r^3 = \frac{4}{3}\pi (R/9)^3$ respectively for the larger and smaller spheres.

**Step 2:** Volume lost due to melting = $\frac{4}{3}\pi R^3 \times \frac{10}{100}$
$$= \frac{4\pi R^3}{30}$$

Volume left = $\frac{4}{3}\pi R^3 \times \frac{90}{100} = \frac{4\pi R^3 \times 0.9}{3}$

**Step 3:** Number of small spheres possible = Volume left/ Volume of the smaller sphere
$$= \frac{\frac{4}{3}\pi R^3 \times 0.9}{\frac{4}{3}\pi \times (R/9)^3} = 9^3 \times 0.9$$

**Step 4:** Surface area of larger sphere = $4\pi R^2$
Surface area of smaller sphere = $4\pi r^2 = 4\pi (R/9)^2$
$$= \frac{4\pi R^2}{81}$$

Surface area of all smaller spheres = Number of small spheres × Surface area of smaller sphere
$$= (9^3 \times .9) \times (4\pi R^2)/81$$
$$= 8.1 \times (4\pi R^2)$$

Therefore, ratio of the surface area is $\dfrac{\left[8.1 \times (4\pi R^2)\right]}{4\pi R^2} = 8.1$

**Step 5:**

    8.1 × number of litres = 8.1 × 10 = 81

**Problem 11.6** A solid wooden toy in the shape of a right circular cone is mounted on a hemisphere. If the radius of the hemisphere is 4.2 cm and the total height of the toy is 10.2 cm, find the volume of the wooden toy.

    (a) 104 cm³       (b) 162 cm³
    (c) 427 cm³       (d) 266 cm²

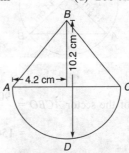

**Solution** Volume of the cone is given by $-1/3 \times \pi r^2 h$
Here, $r = 4.2$ cm; $h = 10.2 - r = 6$ cm
Therefore the volume of the cone = $1/3\ \pi \times (4.2)^2 \times 6$ cm
$$= 110.88\ \text{cm}^3$$

Volume of the hemisphere = $\frac{1}{2} \times \frac{4}{3}\pi r^3 = 155.23$
Total volume = 110.88 + 155.232 = 266.112

**Problem 11.7** A vessel is in the form of an inverted cone. Its depth is 8 cm and the diameter of its top, which is open, is 10 cm. It is filled with water up to the brim. When bullets, each of which is a sphere of radius 0.5 cm, are dropped into the vessel 1/4 of the water flows out. Find the number of bullets dropped in the vessel.

(a) 50  (b) 100  (c) 150  (d) 200

**Solution** In these type of questions it is just your calculation skills that is being tested. You just need to take care that while trying to be fast you don't end up making mistakes like taking the diameter to be the radius and so forth. The best way to avoid such mistakes is to proceed systematically. For example, in this problem we can proceed thus:

$$\text{Volume of the cone} = \frac{1}{3}\pi r^2 h = \frac{200}{3}\pi \text{ cm}^3$$

volme of all the lead shots = Volume of water that spilled out $= \frac{50}{3}\pi \text{ cm}^3$

$$\text{Volume of each lead shot} = \frac{4}{3}\pi r^3 = \frac{\pi}{6} \text{ cm}^3$$

Number of lead shots = (Volume of water that spilled out)/(Volume of each lead shot)

$$= \frac{\frac{50}{3}\pi}{\frac{\pi}{6}} = \frac{50}{3} \times 6 = 100$$

**Problem 11.8** *AB* is a chord of a circle of radius 14 cm. The chord subtends a right angle at the centre of the circle. Find the area of the minor segment.

(a) 98 sq cm  (b) 56 sq cm
(c) 112 sq cm  (d) None of these

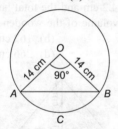

**Solution** Area of the sector $ACBO = \dfrac{90\pi \times 14^2}{360}$

$$= 154 \text{ sq cm}$$

$$\text{Area of the triangle } AOB = \frac{14 \times 14}{2}$$

$$= 98 \text{ sq cm}$$

Area of the segment *ACB* = Area sector *ACBO* – Area of the triangle *AOB* = **56 sq cm**

**Problem 11.9** A sphere of diameter 12.6 cm is melted and cast into a right circular cone of height 25.2 cm. Find the diameter of the base of the cone.

(a) 158.76 cm  (b) 79.38 cm
(c) 39.64 cm  (d) None of these

**Solution** In questions like this, do not go for complete calculations. As far as possible, try to cancel out values in the resulting equations.

$$\text{Volume of the sphere} = \frac{4}{3}\pi r^3 = \frac{4}{3}\pi(6.3)^3$$

$$\text{Volume of the cone} = \frac{1}{3}\pi r^2 h = \frac{\pi}{3}r^2(25.2)$$

Now, volume of the cone = volume of the sphere

Therefore, *r* (radius of the cone) = 39.69 cm

Hence the diameter = **79.38 cm**

**Problem 11.10** A chord *AB* of a circle of radius 5.25 cm makes an angle of 60° at the centre of the circle. Find the area of the major and minor segments. (Take $\pi = 3.14$)

(a) 168 cm²  (b) 42 cm²
(c) 84 cm²  (d) None of these

**Solution** The moment you finish reading this question, it should occur to you that this has to be an equilateral triangle. Once you realise this, the question is reduced to just calculations.

$$\text{Area of the minor sector} = \frac{60}{360} \times \pi \times 5.25^2$$

$$= 14.4375 \text{ cm}^2$$

$$\text{Area of the triangle} = \frac{\sqrt{3}}{4} \times 5.25^2 = 11.93 \text{ cm}^2$$

Area of the minor segment = Area of the minor sector – Area of the triangle = 2.5 cm²

Area of the major segment = Area of the circle – Area of the minor segment.

$$= 86.54 \text{ cm}^2 - 2.5 \text{ cm}^2 = \textbf{84 cm}^2$$

**Problem 11.11** A cone and a hemisphere have equal bases and equal volumes. Find the ratio of their heights.

(a) 1 : 2  (b) 2 : 1
(c) 3 : 1  (d) None of these

**Solution** Questions of this type should be solved without the use of pen and paper. A good authority over formulae will make things easier.

$$\text{Volume of the cone} = \frac{\pi r^2 h}{3} = \text{Volume of a hemisphere}$$

$$= \frac{2}{3}\pi r^3.$$

Height of a hemisphere = Radius of its base
So the question is effectively asking us to find out *h*/*r*
By the formula above we can easily see that *h*/*r* = **2/1**

# GEOMETRY

## LEVEL OF DIFFICULTY (I)

1. A vertical stick 20 m long casts a shadow 10 m long on the ground. At the same time, a tower casts the shadow 50 m long on the ground. Find the height of the tower.
   (a) 100 m
   (b) 120 m
   (c) 25 m
   (d) 200 m

2. In the figure, $\Delta ABC$ is similar to $\Delta EDC$.

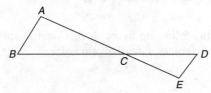

   If we have $AB = 4$ cm,
   $ED = 3$ cm, $CE = 4.2$ and
   $CD = 4.8$ cm, find the value of $CA$ and $CB$
   (a) 6 cm, 6.4 cm
   (b) 4.8 cm, 6.4 cm
   (c) 5.4 cm, 6.4 cm
   (d) 5.6 cm, 6.4 cm

3. The area of similar triangles, $ABC$ and $DEF$ are 144 cm² and 81 cm² respectively. If the longest side of larger $\Delta ABC$ be 36 cm, then the longest side of smaller $\Delta DEF$ is
   (a) 20 cm
   (b) 26 cm
   (c) 27 cm
   (d) 30 cm

4. Two isosceles $\Delta$s have equal angles and their areas are in the ratio 16:25. Find the ratio of their corresponding heights.
   (a) 4/5
   (b) 5/4
   (c) 3/2
   (d) 5/7

5. The areas of two similar $\Delta$s are respectively 9 cm² and 16 cm². Find the ratio of their corresponding sides.
   (a) 3:4
   (b) 4:3
   (c) 2:3
   (d) 4:5

6. Two poles of height 6 m and 11 m stand vertically upright on a plane ground. If the distance between their foot is 12 m, find the distance between their tops.
   (a) 12 m
   (b) 14 m
   (c) 13 m
   (d) 11 m

7. The radius of a circle is 9 cm and length of one of its chords is 14 cm. Find the distance of the chord from the centre.
   (a) 5.66 cm
   (b) 6.3 cm
   (c) 4 cm
   (d) 7 cm

8. Find the length of a chord that is at a distance of 12 cm from the centre of a circle of radius 13 cm.
   (a) 9 cm
   (b) 8 cm
   (c) 12 cm
   (d) 10 cm

9. If $O$ is the centre of circle, find $\angle x$

   (a) 35°
   (b) 30°
   (c) 39°
   (d) 40°

10. Find the value of $\angle x$ in the given figure.

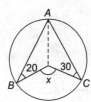

    (a) 120°
    (b) 130°
    (c) 110°
    (d) 100°

11. Find the value of $x$ in the figure, if it is given that $AC$ and $BD$ are diameters of the circle.

    (a) 60°
    (b) 45°
    (c) 15°
    (d) 30°

12. Find the value of $x$ in the given figure.

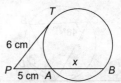

    (a) 2.2 cm
    (b) 1.6 cm
    (c) 3 cm
    (d) 2.6 cm

13. Find the value of $x$ in the given figure.

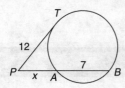

   (a) 16 cm         (b) 9 cm
   (c) 12 cm        (d) 7 cm

14. Find the value of $x$ in the given figure.

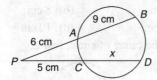

   (a) 13 cm        (b) 12 cm
   (c) 16 cm        (d) 15 cm

15. $ABC$ is a right angled triangle with $BC = 6$ cm and $AB = 8$ cm. A circle with centre $O$ and radius $x$ has been inscribed in $\triangle ABC$. What is the value of $x$?

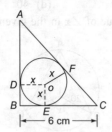

   (a) 2.4 cm       (b) 2 cm
   (c) 3.6 cm       (d) 4 cm

16. In the given figure $AB$ is the diameter of the circle and $\angle PAB = 25°$. Find $\angle TPA$.

   (a) 50°          (b) 65°
   (c) 70°          (d) 45°

17. In the given figure, find $\angle ADB$.

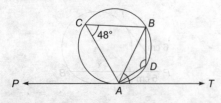

   (a) 132°        (b) 144°
   (c) 48°         (d) 96°

18. In the given figure, two straight lines $PQ$ and $RS$ intersect each other at $O$. If $\angle SOT = 75°$, find the value of $a$, $b$ and $c$.

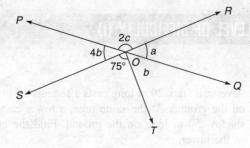

   (a) $a = 84°$, $b = 21°$, $c = 48°$
   (b) $a = 48°$, $b = 20°$, $c = 50°$
   (c) $a = 72°$, $b = 24°$, $c = 54°$
   (d) $a = 64°$, $b = 28°$, $c = 45°$

19. In the following figure $A$, $B$, $C$ and $D$ are the concyclic points. Find the value of $x$.

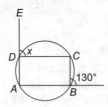

   (a) 130°        (b) 50°
   (c) 60°         (d) 30°

20. In the following figure, it is given that $O$ is the centre of the circle and $\angle AOC = 140°$. Find $\angle ABC$.

   (a) 110°        (b) 120°
   (c) 115°        (d) 130°

21. In the following figure, $O$ is the centre of the circle and $\angle ABO = 30°$, find $\angle ACB$.

   (a) 60°          (b) 120°
   (c) 75°          (d) 90°

22. In the following figure, find the value of $x$

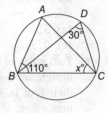

   (a) 40°          (b) 25°
   (c) 30°          (d) 45°

23. If $L_1 \parallel L_2$ in the figure below, what is the value of $x$.

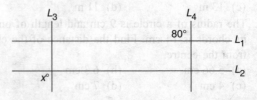

(a) 80°

(b) 100°

(c) 40°

(d) Cannot be determined

24. Find the perimeter of the given figure.

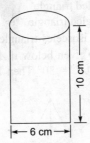

(a) $(32 + 3\pi)$ cm

(b) $(36 + 6\pi)$ cm

(c) $(46 + 3\pi)$ cm

(d) $(26 + 6\pi)$ cm

25. In the figure, $AB$ is parallel to $CD$ and $RD \parallel SL \parallel TM \parallel AN$, and $BR : RS : ST : TA = 3 : 5 : 2 : 7$. If it is known that $CN = 1.333\ BR$. Find the ratio of $BF : FG : GH : HI : IC$

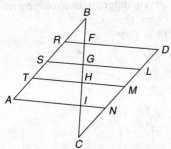

(a) $3 : 7 : 2 : 5 : 4$

(b) $3 : 5 : 2 : 7 : 4$

(c) $4 : 7 : 2 : 5 : 3$

(d) $4 : 5 : 2 : 7 : 3$

26. In $\triangle ABC$, if $\angle A = 60°$ and the angle bisectors of $\angle B$ and $\angle C$ meet at $X$ then $\angle BXC$ (in degrees) is = ?

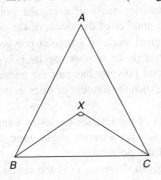

Directions for 27 and 28: $\triangle PQR$ is a right angled triangle and $\angle Q = 90°$, $PQ = 15$ cm, $QR = 20$ cm and $QS \perp PR$, then answer the following questions.

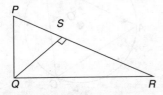

27. Find the length of $SR$ (in cm).

28. Find the length of $SQ$ (in cm).

29. In the given diagram $\triangle ABC$ is a right angled triangle, $\angle ABC = 90°$, $BD \perp AC$. If $AB : AC = 3 : 5$ and area of $\triangle ABD$ is 90 cm², then the area of $\triangle ABC$ (in cm²) is:

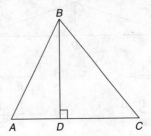

30. If the inradius of an equilateral triangle is $\sqrt{3}$ cm, then its area is:

(a) $7\sqrt{3}$ cm²

(b) $9\sqrt{3}$ cm²

(c) $10\sqrt{3}$ cm²

(d) $12\sqrt{3}$ cm²

31. If $\triangle ABC$ is a right angled triangle such that $\angle B = 90°$, $(AB + BC) - AC = 20$ cm and perimeter of $\triangle ABC = 60$ cm, then area of the triangle (in cm²) is.

32. Find the sum of the squares of the medians of a triangle whose sides are 6 cm, 7 cm, 8 cm.

33. In the diagram given below $RT \perp PQ$. $S$ is a point on $QR$ such that:

$\angle QPS = 40°$, $\angle TRQ = 30°$, then $\angle PSQ = $ ?

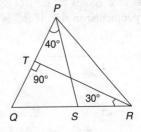

34. In the given diagram, $PQ$ touches the circle at $R$. $T$, $S$, $U$ are the points on the circle. If $\angle SRQ = 60°$ then $\angle SUR = $ ?

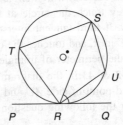

35. In a right angled triangle $\triangle PQR$, $\angle Q = 90°$, if A and B are points on the sides PQ and QR respectively then:

(a) $AR^2 + PB^2 = 2(PR^2 + AB^2)$

(b) $AR^2 + PB^2 = PR^2 + AB^2$

(c) $AR^2 + RB^2 = 0.5(PR^2 + AB^2)$

(d) None of these

36. In the given diagram if $AB\|CD\|EF$ then which of the given options is true.

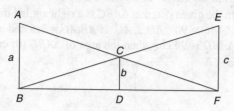

(a) $\dfrac{1}{a}-\dfrac{1}{c}=\dfrac{1}{b}$
(b) $\dfrac{1}{a}+\dfrac{1}{b}=\dfrac{1}{c}$
(c) $\dfrac{1}{b}-\dfrac{1}{a}=\dfrac{1}{c}$
(d) $\dfrac{1}{c}-\dfrac{1}{b}=\dfrac{1}{a}$

37. In the given figure $PR = QR = PS$, $\angle PSR = x$, $\angle TPS = 90°$ then $x = ?$

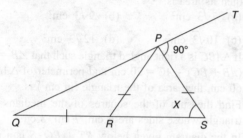

38. If the sides of a triangle measure 72, 75 and 21. What is the measure of its inradius?

39. $ABCD$ has area equals to 28. $BC$ is parallel to $AD$. $BA$ is perpendicular to $AD$. If $BC$ is 6 and $AD$ is 8, then what is $AB$?

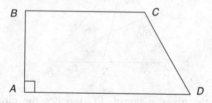

40. In the previous question, find $BC$.

41. Two tangents are drawn to a circle from an exterior point $A$; they touch the circle at points $B$ and $C$, respectively. A third tangent intersects segment $AB$ in $P$ and $AC$ in $R$, and touches the circle at $Q$. If $AB = 20$, then the perimeter of triangle $APR$ is:

**Question 42 & 43:** In the diagram given below, if $D$ is the mid-point of side $AC$ and $DB = AD = DC$ then answer the following questions:

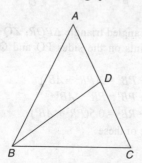

42. $\triangle ABC$ is a
(a) Right angled triangle
(b) Equilateral triangle
(c) Acute angled triangle
(d) Obtuse angled triangle

43. If $\triangle ABC$ is an isosceles triangle then $\angle BDC =$

44. In the diagram given below if $AB = AC$ and $\angle ADC = 2\angle ABD$, $\angle DAC = 30°$ Then $\angle BAD =$

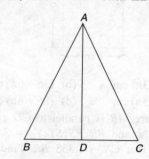

45. In the given diagram two concentric circles with center $O$ are shown.
If $\angle AOB = 120°$
Then $\angle OAP =$

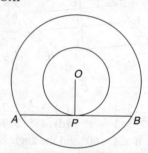

46. If the interior angle of a regular polygon is 120°, find the number of diagonals of the polygon ___.

47. The internal angle of a regular polygon exceeds the internal angle of another regular polygon by 18°. If the second polygon has half the number of sides as the first, then the number of sides in the first polygon is___.

48. The sum of the interior angles of a regular polygon is 40 times the exterior angle. Find the number of sides of the polygon.

49. In the given diagram, $O$ is the center of the circle. $\angle AOC = 140°$. If $AB = BC$ then find $\angle BCA =$ _____.

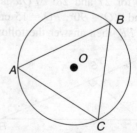

50. In the given diagram, if 'O' is the center of the circle, chord PR and SQ intersect each other at O, ∠POQ = 80°, then ∠QSR = ?

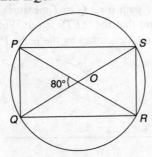

51. O is the center and AC is the tangent of the circle at B. In the diagram given below, if ∠OBE = 70°. Find ∠BOE:

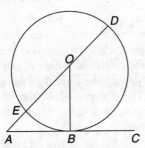

52. In the previous question find ∠BAO.

**Directions for question numbers 53 & 54:** Two circles having equal radius intersect each other at A and B as shown in the diagram below. The diameters AC and AD intersect at A. If C, B, D are collinear and ∠ACB = 30°, then answer the following questions:

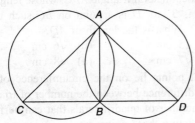

53. Find ∠CAD = _____
54. If BC = 2 cm, then AD (in cm) =
    (a) 4                      (b) 4/√2
    (c) 3                      (d) None of these
55. In the diagram O is the center of the circle. PS is the tangent of the circle at S. ∠OSQ = 50°. Find ∠SPR.

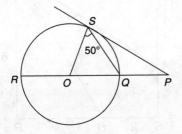

56. Lines joining midpoint of a quadrilateral form a_____
    (a) square                (b) parallelogram
    (c) rectangle             (d) None of these
57. In the given diagram □ABCD is a trapezium. If AB = 4 cm, CD = 6 cm and OB = 5 cm, then BD = _____ cm.

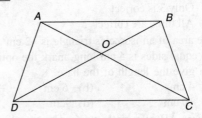

**Direction for question numbers 58 & 59:** In the given diagram PQRS is a trapezium and SR = 4√6 cm and ∠SQR = 60° ∠QSR = 45°. Answer the following questions:

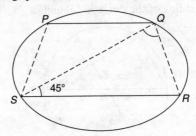

58. Length of QR is ____ cm
59. PS + QR = ____cm
60. ABCD is a rectangle with AD = 10. P is a point on BC such that ∠ APD = 90°. If DP = 8, then the length of BP is ____?
61. ABCD is a quadrilateral. The diagonals of ABCD intersect at the point P. The area of the triangles APD and BPC are 27 and 12, respectively. If the areas of the triangles APB and CPD are equal then the area of triangle APB is
    (a) 12                    (b) 15
    (c) 16                    (d) 18
62. In a right angle triangle BAC given below, AD is the altitude of the hypotenuse BC. The figure is followed by three possible inferences.

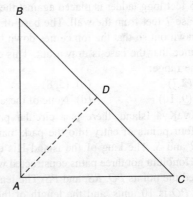

1. Triangle *ABD* and triangle *CAD* are similar.
2. Triangle *ADB* and triangle *CDA* are congruent.
3. Triangle *ADB* and triangle *CAB* are similar.

Mark the correct option

(a) 1 and 2 are correct

(b) 1 and 3 are correct

(c) Only 3 is correct

(d) All three are correct

63. The area of an isosceles triangle is 12 cm². If one of the equal sides is 5 cm long, mark the option which can give the length of the base.

(a) 4 cm    (b) 6 cm

(c) 10 cm    (d) 9cm

64. An arc AB of a circle subtends an angle '$x$' radian at the center O of the circle. If the area of the sector AOB is equal to the square of the length of the arc AB, then $x$ is:

65. What is the value of $c^2$ in the given figure, where the radius of the circle is '$a$' units?

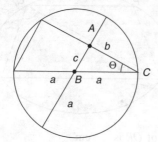

(a) $c^2 = a^2 + b^2 - 2\,ab\cos\theta$

(b) $c^2 = a^2 + b^2 - 2ab\sin\theta$

(c) $c^2 = a^2 - b^2 + 2ab\cos\theta$

(d) None of these.

66. In a circle, the height of an arc is 21 cm and the diameter is 84 cm. Find the chord of 'half of the arc'.

67. The perimeter of *a* right angled triangle measures 234 m and the hypotenuse measures 97 m. Then the other two sides of the triangle are measured as

(a) 100 m and 37 m    (b) 72 m and 65 m

(c) 80 m and 57 m    (d) None of these

68. A 25 feet long ladder is placed against the wall with its base 7 feet from the wall. The base of the ladder is drawn out so that the top comes down by half the distance that the base is drawn out. This distance is in the range:

(a) (2,7)    (b) (5, 8)

(c) (9, 10)    (d) None of these

69. In KyaKya Island, there is a circular park. There are four points of entry into the park, namely – *P*, *Q*, *R* and *S*. The king of the island His excellency Mr. Honolulu got three paths constructed which connected the points *PQ*, *RS*, and *PS*. The length of the path *PQ* is 10 units, and the length of the path *RS*

is 7 units. Later, the municipal corporation extended the paths *PQ* and *RS* past *Q* and *R* respectively, and they meet at a point *T* on the main road outside the park. The path from *Q* to *T* measures 8 units, and it was found that the $\angle PTS$ is 60°. Find the area (in square units) enclosed by the paths *PT*, *TS*, and *PS*.

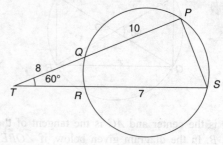

(a) $36\sqrt{3}$    (b) $54\sqrt{3}$

(c) $72\sqrt{3}$    (d) $90\sqrt{3}$

70. There are two circles $C_1$, and $C_2$ of radii 3 and 8 units respectively. The common internal tangent *T*, touches the circles at points *P* and *Q* respectively. The line joining the centers of the circles intersects *T* at *X*. The distance of *X* from the center of the smaller circle is 5 units. What is the length of the line segment *PQ*?

(a) $\leq 13$    (b) $>13$ and $\leq 14$

(c) $> 14$ and $< 15$    (d) $>15$ and $\leq 16$

71. In quadrilateral *PQRS*, *PQ* = 5 units, *QR* = 17 units, *RS* = 5 units, and *PS* = 9 units. The length of the diagonal *QS* can be:

(a) $> 10$ and $< 12$    (b) $> 12$ and $< 14$

(c) $> 14$ and $< 16$    (d) $>16$ and $<18$

72. In an equilateral triangle *ABC*, whose length of each side is 3 cm, *D* is a point on *BC* such that *BD* = *CD*/2. What is the length of *AD*?

(a) $\sqrt{5}$ cm    (b) $\sqrt{6}$ cm

(c) $\sqrt{7}$ cm    (d) $\sqrt{8}$ cm

73. Eight points lie on the circumference of a circle. The difference between the number of triangles and the number of quadrilaterals that can be formed by connecting these points is:

74. In a square *PQRS*, *A* and *B* are two points on *PS* and *SR* such that *PA* = 2*AS*, and *RB* = 2*BS*. If *PQ* = 6, the area of the triangle *ABQ* is

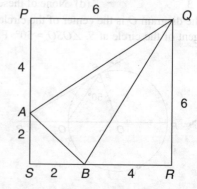

75. A pole has to be erected on the boundary of a circular park of diameter 13 meters in such a way that the difference of it's distances from two diametrically opposite fixed gates $A$ and $B$ on the boundary is 7 meters. The shortest distance of the pole from one of the gates is ____

*Space for Rough Work*

## LEVEL OF DIFFICULTY (II)

1. In a triangle *ABC*, point *D* is on side *AB* and point *E* is on side *AC*, such that *BCED* is a trapezium. *DE*:*BC* = 3:5. Calculate the ratio of the area of Δ*ADE* and the trapezium *BCED*.

   (a) 3:4  (b) 9:16
   (c) 3:5  (d) 9:25

2. *D*, *E*, *F* are the mid-points of the sides *BC*, *CA* and *AB* respectively of a Δ*ABC*. Determine the ratio of the area of triangles *DEF* and *ABC*.

   (a) 1:4  (b) 1:2
   (c) 2:3  (d) 4:5

3. In the adjoining figure, *ABCD* is a trapezium in which *AB* ∥ *DC* and *AB* = 3 *DC*. Determine the ratio of the areas of (Δ*AOB* and Δ*COD*).

   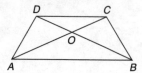

   (a) 9:1  (b) 1:9
   (c) 3:1  (d) 1:3

4. A ladder reaches a window that is 8 m above the ground on one side of the street. Keeping its foot on the same point, the ladder is twined to the other side of the street to reach a window 12 m high. Find the width of the street if the ladder is 13 m.

   (a) 15.2 m  (b) 14 m
   (c) 14.6 m  (d) 12 m

5. In the adjoining figure ∠*A* = 60° and ∠*ABC* = 80°, hence ∠*BQC* is

   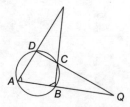

   (a) 40°  (b) 80°
   (c) 20°  (d) 30°

6. The diagram below represents three circular garbage cans, each of diameter 2 m. The three cans are touching as shown. Find, in meters, the perimeter of the rope encompassing the three cans.

   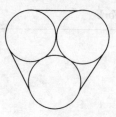

   (a) 2π + 6  (b) 3π + 4
   (c) 4π + 6  (d) 6π + 6

7. In the figure below, *PQ* = *QS*, *QR* = *RS* and angle *SRQ* = 100°. How many degrees is angle *QPS*?

   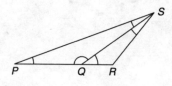

   (a) 20°  (b) 40°
   (c) 15°  (d) 30°

8. In the figure, *ABDC* is a cyclic quadrilateral with *O* as centre of the circle. If ∠*BOC* = 136°, find ∠*BDC*.

   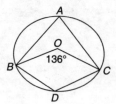

   (a) 110°  (b) 112°
   (c) 109°  (d) 115°

9. In the given figure, *AD* ∥ *BC*. Find the value of *x*, given that *AO* = 3; *OC* = *X* – 3; *BO* = 3*X* – 19; *OD* = *X* – 5.

   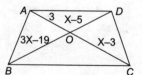

   (a) *x* = 8, 9  (b) *x* = 7, 8
   (c) *x* = 8, 10  (d) *x* = 7, 10

10. In the given figure $\dfrac{AO}{OC} = \dfrac{DO}{OB} = \dfrac{1}{2}$ and *AB* = 4 cm. Find the value of BC.

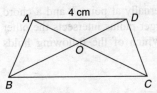

(a) 7 cm      (b) 8 cm
(c) 9 cm      (d) 10 cm

11. In the given figure, $AD$ is the bisector of $\angle BAC$, $AB$ = 6 cm, $AC$ = 5 cm and $BD$ = 3 cm. Find $DC$. It is given that $\angle ABD = \angle ACD$.

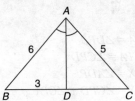

(a) 11.3 cm      (b) 2.5 cm
(c) 3.5 cm      (d) 4 cm

12. In a $\triangle ABC$, $AD$ is the bisector of $\angle BAC$, $AB$ = 8 cm, $BD$ = 6 cm and $DC$ = 3 cm. Find $AC$. (Given that $\angle ABC = \angle ACB$)

(a) 4 cm      (b) 6 cm
(c) 3 cm      (d) 5 cm

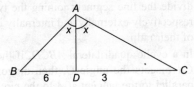

13. If $ABC$ is a quarter circle and a circle is inscribed in it and if $AB$ = 1 cm, find radius of smaller circle.

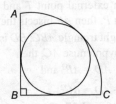

(a) $\sqrt{2} - 1$      (b) $(\sqrt{2} + 1)/2$
(c) $\sqrt{2} - 1/2$      (d) $1 - 2\sqrt{2}$

14. $ABC$ is an equilateral triangle. Point $D$ is on $AC$ and point $E$ is on $BC$, such that $AD = 2CD$ and $CE = EB$. If we draw perpendiculars from $D$ and $E$ to other two sides and find the sum of the length of two perpendiculars for each set, that is, for $D$ and $E$ individually and denote them as per ($D$) and per ($E$) respectively, then which of the following option will be correct.
(a) Per ($D$) > per ($E$)      (b) Per ($D$) < per ($E$)

(c) Per ($D$) = per ($E$)      (d) None of these

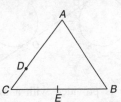

15. $ABCD$ is a trapezium in which $AB$ is parallel to $DC$, $AD = BC$, $AB$ = 6 cm, $AB = EF$ and $DF = EC$. If two lines $AF$ and $BE$ are drawn so that area of $ABEF$ is half of $ABCD$. Find $DF/CD$.

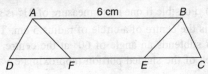

(a) 1/4      (b) 1/3
(c) 2/5      (d) 1/6

16. In the given figure, $\triangle ABC$ and $\triangle ACD$ are right angle triangles and $AB = x$ cm, $BC = y$ cm, $CD = z$ cm and $x \cdot y = z$ and $x$, $y$ and $z$ has minimum integral value. Find the area of $ABCD$
(a) 36 cm$^2$      (b) 64 cm$^2$
(c) 24 cm$^2$      (d) 25 cm$^2$

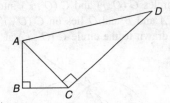

17. $OD$, $OE$ and $OF$ are perpendicular bisectors to the three sides of the triangle. What is the relationship between $m \angle BAC$ and $m \angle BOC$?

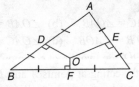

(a) $m\angle BAC = 180 - m\angle BOC$
(b) $m\angle BOC = 90 + 1/2\, m\angle BAC$
(c) $m\angle BAC = 90 + 1/2\, m\angle BOC$
(d) $m\angle BOC = 2m\angle BAC$

18. If two equal circles of radius 5 cm have two common tangent $AB$ and $CD$ which touch the circle on $A$, $C$ and $B$, $D$ respectively shown in the figure. If $CD$ = 24 cm, find the length of $AB$.
(a) 27 cm      (b) 25 cm
(c) 26 cm      (d) 30 cm

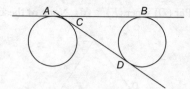

19. If a circle is provided with a measure of 19° on centre, is it possible to divide the circle into 360 equal parts?
    (a) Never
    (b) Possible when one more measure of 20° is given
    (c) Always
    (d) Possible if one more measure of 21° is given

20. $O$ is the centre of a circle of radius 5 cm. The chord $AB$ subtends an angle of 60° at the centre. Find the area of the shaded portion (approximate value).

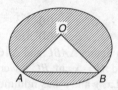

    (a) 50 cm²          (b) 62.78 cm²
    (c) 49.88 cm²       (d) 67.67 cm²

21. Two circles $C$ $(O, r)$ and $C$ $(O', r')$ intersect at two points $A$ and $B$ and $O$ lies on $C$ $(O', r')$. A tangent $CD$ is drawn to the circle $C$ $(O', r')$ at $A$. Then

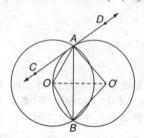

    (a) $\angle OAC = \angle OAB$   (b) $\angle OAB = \angle AO'O$
    (c) $\angle AO'B = \angle AOB$   (d) $\angle OAC = \angle AOB$

22. $PP'$ and $QQ'$ are two direct common tangents to two circles intersecting at points $A$ and $B$. The common chord on produced intersects $PP'$ at $R$ and $'QQ'$ at $S$. Which of the following is true?

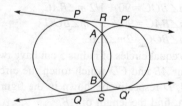

    (a) $RA^2 + BS^2 = AB^2$   (b) $RS^2 = PP'^2 + AB^2$
    (c) $RS^2 = PP'^2 + QQ'^2$  (d) $RS^2 = BS^2 + PP'^2$

23. Two circles touch internally at point $P$ and a chord $AB$ of the circle of larger radius intersects the other circle in $C$ and $D$. Which of the following holds good?

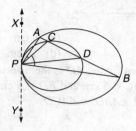

    (a) $\angle CPA = \angle DPB$
    (b) $2 \angle CPA = \angle CPD$
    (c) $\angle APX = \angle ADP$
    (d) $\angle BPY = \angle CPD + \angle CPA$

24. In a trapezium $ABCD$, $AB \parallel CD$ and $AD = BC$. If $P$ is point of intersection of diagonals $AC$ and $BD$, then all of the following is wrong except
    (a) $PA \cdot PB = PC \cdot PD$   (b) $PA \cdot PC = PB \cdot PD$
    (c) $PA \cdot AB = PD \cdot DC$   (d) $PA \cdot PD = AB \cdot DC$

25. All of the following is true except:
    (a) The points of intersection of direct common tangents and indirect common tangents of two circles divide the line segment joining the two centres respectively externally and internally in the ratio of their radii.
    (b) In a cyclic quadrilateral $ABCD$, if the diagonal $CA$ bisects the angle $C$, then diagonal $BD$ is parallel to the tangent at $A$ to the circle through $A, B, C, D$.
    (c) If $TA$, $TB$ are tangent segments to a circle $C(O, r)$ from an external point $T$ and $OT$ intersects the circle in $P$, then $AP$ bisects the angle $TAB$.
    (d) If in a right triangle $ABC$, $BD$ is the perpendicular on the hypotenuse $AC$, then
        (i) $AC \cdot AD = AB^2$ and
        (ii) $AC \cdot AD = BC^2$

**Directions 26 and 27:** Two cows are tethered at the mid-points of two adjacent sides of a square field. Each of them is tied with a rope in such a way that grazing area of each cow is a semicircular region of diameter equals to the side of square. If side of the square is 10 m, then answer the following questions.

26. What is the area of the grazing field that is grazed by both the cows (in m²)?
    (a) $12.5(\pi + 2)$          (b) $12.5(-2 + \pi)$
    (c) $25(2\pi + 1)$           (d) $25(2\pi - 1)$

27. For the given situation, the area of the non-grazed regions(in m²) is:
    (a) $75 + 12.5\pi$          (b) $75 - 12.5\pi$
    (c) $75 + 25\pi$            (d) $75 - 13\pi$

**Directions for 28 and 29:** In the rectangle PQRS, $M$ and N are two points on $SR$ and $PQ$ respectively such that $MN$ bisects $SQ$ perpendicularly at $O$. If $SR$ = 4 cm, $RQ$ = 3 cm.

28. What will be the value of $MO/SO$?
    (a) 0.8 　　　　　　 (b) 0.75
    (c) 0.65 　　　　　　 (d) None of these

29. Find the area of quadrilateral $SONP$.
    (a) 3.65 cm² 　　　　 (b) 4.66 cm²
    (c) 2.66 cm² 　　　　 (d) None of these

30. A rectangle $PQRS$ is inscribed in a semicircle of centre $O$ and diameter $MN$. $M$, $S$, $R$, $N$ are collinear. $RN = 2$ cm and $QR = 4$ cm, then what is the area of the semicircle not overlapped by the rectangle $PQRS$.
    (a) $(12.5\pi + 12)$ cm² 　 (b) $(12.5\pi - 12)$ cm²
    (c) $(12.5\pi + 24)$ cm² 　 (d) $(12.5\pi - 24)$ cm²

31. In the diagram given below, quadrilateral $PQRS$ is divided into six smaller triangles. The number inside the triangle mentionsit's area. If $SN/NR = 1.25$ then find the value of $a + b$.

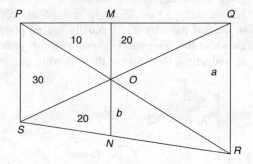

    (a) 42 　　　　　　 (b) 52
    (c) 54 　　　　　　 (d) 60

**Direction for 32 and 33:** In the figure given below: $QM$, $PN$, $RT$ are the altitudes of an isosceles triangle and $PQ = QR = 15$ cm and $PR = 18$ cm. Answer the following questions:

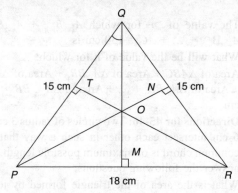

32. Find the ratio of $QT/QO = $ ?
    (a) 0.8 　　　　　　 (b) 0.6
    (c) 0.7 　　　　　　 (d) 0.9

33. The value of $OT$ is:

(a) 3.15 cm 　　　　 (b) 3.35 cm
(c) 3.05 cm 　　　　 (d) 3.55 cm

34. In the figure given below $\Delta PQR$ is a right angled triangle with $\angle P = 90°$. The center of the incircle of the given triangle is $O$. Circles with centers $O_1$ and $O_2$ touch the circle and two sides as shown in the figure. If the radius of the incircle of $\Delta PQR$ is 1 cm and $BR : BQ = 2:3$, then find the value of $r_1 : r_2$ (where $r_1$ is the radius of circle with center $O_1$ and $r_2$ is the radius of circle with center $O_2$).

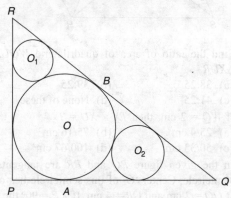

    (a) $(33 - 11\sqrt{5} - 6\sqrt{10} + 10\sqrt{2})/18$
    (b) $(33 + 11\sqrt{5} - 6\sqrt{10} - 10\sqrt{2})/18$
    (c) $(33 - 11\sqrt{5} + 6\sqrt{10} - 10\sqrt{2})/18$
    (d) $(33 + 11\sqrt{5} - 6\sqrt{10} - 10\sqrt{2})/18$

**Direction for 35 and 36:** A circle is inscribed in a triangle $PQR$. It touches side $PQ$ at point $X$. If $\angle P = 60°$ $PX = 3$ cm, $QX = 5$ cm, then answer the following questions.

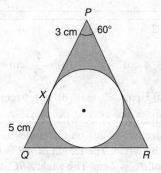

35. Find the radius of the circle.
    (a) $3\sqrt{\dfrac{5}{7}}$ 　　　　 (b) $\dfrac{5}{7}\sqrt{3}$
    (c) $3\sqrt{\dfrac{5}{17}}$ 　　　　 (d) None of these

36. Find the area of the shaded portion
    (a) $10\sqrt{3} - 3\pi$ cm² 　 (b) $10\sqrt{3} - 13\pi$ cm²
    (c) $10\sqrt{3} - 2\pi$ cm² 　 (d) None of these

**Direction 37 and 38:** In quadrilateral $PQRS$, $PQ\|SR$ and $PS\|QR$. $TU\|SR$ and $TU$ passes through the point of intersection of $PR$ & $WS$. If the ratio of the area of $\triangle POW$ to $\triangle SOR$ is 9:25, then answer the following questions:

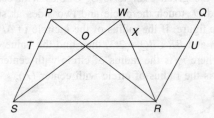

37. Find the ratio of area of quadrilateral $WQUX$ and $\triangle XUR$
    (a) 38:25          (b) 39:25
    (c) 41:25          (d) None of these

38. If $WQ = 2$ cm, then $TX \times XU = ?$
    (a) 25/4 cm²        (b) 75/16 cm²
    (c) 50/33 cm²       (d) 100/67 cm²

39. In the given figure $PQ$ and $PR$ are tangents of a semicircle. Center '$O$' of this semicircle lies on $QR$. If $QO = 2$ cm and $OR = 4$ cm. If $\angle P = 90°$ the radius of the semicircle is:

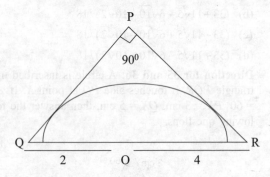

    (a) $\sqrt{5}/4$ cm          (b) $\dfrac{4}{\sqrt{5}}$ cm
    (c) $\sqrt{5}/3$ cm          (d) $\sqrt{5}/6$ cm

40. The radius of a circle with center $O$ is $\sqrt{50}$ cm . A and $C$ are two points on the circle, and $B$ is a point inside the circle. The length of $AB$ is 6 cm, and the length of $BC$ is 2 cm. The angle $ABC$ is a right angle. Find the square of the distance $OB$.
    (a) 26          (b) 25
    (c) 24          (d) 23

41. Triangle $ABC$ is a right angled triangle. $D$ and $E$ are mid points of $AB$ and $BC$ respectively. Read the following statements.
    I. $AE = 19$
    II. $CD = 22$
    III. Angle $B$ is a right angle.

Which of the following statements would be sufficient to determine the length of $AC$?
    (a) Statement I and Statement II.
    (b) Statement I and Statement III.
    (c) Statement II and III.
    (d) All three statements.

42. In $\triangle RPQ$, $\angle P = 120°$ angle bisector of $\angle P$ meets $RQ$ at $S$. $PQ = 9$ cm, $PS = 6$ cm. Then the value of $PR$ (in cm) is:

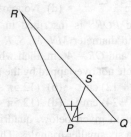

Direction for question 43 and 44: In the diagram given below in $\triangle ABC$ in which $AB = 5$ cm, $BC = 12$ cm, $AC = 13$ cm. Side $AB$ and $BC$ are divided in $n$-equal parts by $n - 1$ equally spaced points as shown in the diagram. $A_1$ joined to $B_1$, $A_2$ joined to $B_2$ and so on, then answer the following questions:

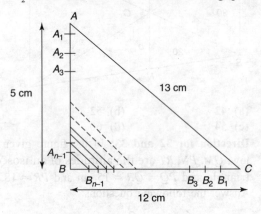

43. The value of '$n$' for which $A_{n-1}B_{n-1} + A_{n-2}B_{n-2} + A_{n-3}B_{n-3} + \ldots + AC = 130$ cm is __

44. What will be the value of n for which:
    Area of $\triangle ABC$ + Area of $\triangle A_1 BB_1$ + Area of $\triangle A_2 BB_2$ + Area of $\triangle A_3 BB_3$ + ... + Area of $\triangle A_{n-1} BB_{(n-1)} = 66$ cm²

**Directions for 45-46:** Two circles of radius 3 cm and 6 cm intersect each other in such a way that their common chord is of maximum possible length. Then answer the following questions:

45. What is the area of the triangle formed by joining the points of intersection of the two circles to the center of the bigger circle
    (a) $7\sqrt{3}$ cm²          (b) $9\sqrt{3}$ cm²
    (c) $10\sqrt{3}$ cm²         (d) $12\sqrt{3}$ cm²

46. What is the area of the region that is common to the two circles (in cm²)?

    (a) $\left[\dfrac{21}{2}\pi + 9\sqrt{3}\right]$　　(b) $\left[\dfrac{21}{2}\pi - 9\sqrt{3}\right]$

    (c) $\left[\dfrac{11}{2} + 9\sqrt{3}\right]$　　(d) $\left[\dfrac{11}{2} - 9\sqrt{3}\right]$

    **Direction for 47 and 48:** In the given diagram $PQR$ an isosceles right angle triangle with the center $O$ touches the side $QR$ at $W$, $PR$ at $X$ and $PQ$ at $Y$. If $PR = 3\sqrt{2}$ cm then answer the following questions:

    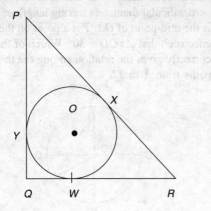

47. The ratio $PX:QW:PY$ is:

    (a) $1:(\sqrt{2}-1):1$　　(b) $1:\left(1-\dfrac{1}{\sqrt{2}}\right):1$

    (c) $1:\left(\sqrt{2}-\dfrac{1}{2}\right):1$　　(d) None of these

48. The area of quadrilateral $PYOX$:

    (a) $9(\sqrt{2}+1)$ cm²　　(b) $9(\sqrt{2}-1)$ cm²

    (c) $\dfrac{9}{2}(\sqrt{2}+1)$cm²　　(d) $\dfrac{9}{2}(\sqrt{2}-1)$cm²

49. In the given figure $\triangle ABC$ is an equilateral triangle. $BP \perp AC$ and $PR \perp AB$, $PQ \perp BC$. The ratio of area of $\triangle PRB$ and $\triangle PQC$ is

    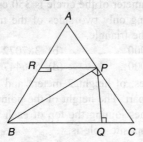

    (a) 4:1　　(b) 3:1
    (c) 2:1　　(d) None of these

50. In the previous question if length of side of equilateral triangle is 4 cm, then area of $\triangle RPQ$ is:

    (a) $\dfrac{3\sqrt{3}}{2}$ cm²　　(b) $\dfrac{3\sqrt{3}}{4}$ cm²

51. (c) $\dfrac{\sqrt{3}}{2}$ cm²　　(d) None of these

51. In isosceles triangle $PQR$ $PQ = PR$, $A$ and $B$ are points on $PR$ and $PQ$ respectively such that $AB \| QR$, $C$ and $D$ are the points on $QR$ such that $AC \| PD$. If $PQ = 10$ cm, $PA:AR = 2:3$ and $\angle APD = \angle BAC$, then find the length of $DC$ (in cm.)

52. In a $\triangle PQR$, $X$, $Y$, $Z$ are points on sides $PQ$, $QR$, $PR$ such that $PX:XQ = 1:1$, $PZ:ZR = 1:2$, $QY:YR = 2:3$. What is the ratio of the area of quadrilateral $XYRZ$ to that of $\triangle PXZ$?

    **Directions for 53 and 54:** In the diagram given below $ED$ is a tangent to the circle and line $AE$ intersects the circle at point $C$. $B$ is a point on $AC$ such that $DB$ is angle bisector of $\angle ADC$. If $\angle ADB = 30°$ and $\angle EDC : \angle ECD = 2 : 5$, then answer the following questions.

    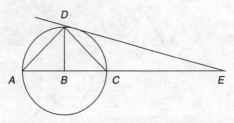

53. $\angle DEC$ (in degrees) is:

54. If $AB:AC = 1:3$ and $DC = 6$ cm. Then $AD$ (in cm) is

55. In a regular polygon, the number of sides is '$p$' times the number of diagonals. If the interior angle of the polygon is $x$, then $x = ?$

    (a) $\dfrac{2\pi(P+1)}{3P+2}$　　(b) $\dfrac{\pi(2+P)}{3P+2}$

    (c) $\dfrac{3\pi(P+2)}{3P+2}$　　(d) None of these

    **Direction for 56 and 57:** In the diagram given below, $\triangle PQR$, $\triangle QTR$ are right-angled triangles with $\angle PQR = \angle QTR = 90°$, $PR = 25$ cm, $PQ = 15$ cm, $QS = 12$ cm, $RT = 16$ cm. Then answer the following questions:

    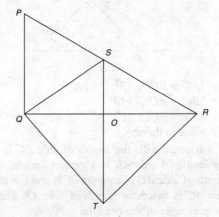

56. Find the ratio of $RO:OQ =$
    (a) 3:4
    (b) 5:4
    (c) 16:9
    (d) 25:16

57. If $ST = x$ cm then $x = ?$
    (a) 18.20
    (b) 18.60
    (c) 19.20
    (d) 19.60

58. In a triangle $ABC$, $AB = 3$, $BC = 4$ and $CA = 5$. Point $D$ is the midpoint of $AB$, point $E$ is on the segment $AC$ and point $F$ is on the segment $BC$. If $AE = 1.5$ and $BF = 0.5$ then $\angle DEF =$
    A. 30°
    B. 60°
    C. 45°
    D. 75°

59. In a $\Delta PQR$ three points $X$, $Y$, $Z$ lie on $PQ$, $QR$, $PR$ respectively and if $PX:QZ = 1:2$, $QX:QZ = 3:2$ and $PY:YR = 1:3$, then which of the following options is true.

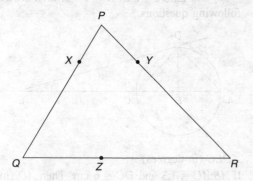

    (a) Area of $\Delta XYZ$ is maximum when $QZ:QR = 1:2$
    (b) Area of $\Delta XYZ$ is minimum when $QZ:QR = 2:3$
    (c) Area of $\Delta XYZ$ is maximum when $QZ:QR = 2:3$
    (d) Area of $\Delta XYZ$ will be same for any value of $QZ:QR$.

60. $ABCD$ is a square with sides of length 10 units. $OCD$ is an isosceles triangle with base $CD$. $OC$ cuts $AB$ at point $Q$ and $OD$ cuts $AB$ at point $P$. The area of trapezoid $PQCD$ is 80 square units. The altitude from $O$ of the triangle $OPQ$ is:

61. If $D$ is the midpoint of side $BC$ of a triangle $ABC$ and $AD$ is perpendicular to $AC$ then:

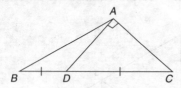

    (a) $3AC^2 = BC^2 - AB^2$
    (b) $3BC^2 = AC^2 - 3AB^2$
    (c) $5AB^2 = BC^2 + AC^2$
    (d) None of these.

62. In a triangle $ABC$ the length of side $BC$ is 295. If the length of side $AB$ is a perfect square, then length of side $AC$ is a power of 2, and the length of side $AC$ is twice the length of side $AB$. Determine the perimeter of the triangle.

63. There is a triangular building ($ABC$) located in the heart of Aurangabad, the city of Aurangzeb. The length of the one wall in the east ($BC$) direction is 397 feet. If the length of south wall ($AB$) is a perfect cube, the length of the southwest wall ($AC$) is a power of three, and the length of wall in southwest ($AC$) is thrice the length of side $AB$, determine the perimeter of this triangular building.
    (a) 3609 feet
    (b) 3813 feet
    (c) 3773 feet
    (d) 3313 feet

64. In a circular field, $AOB$ and $COD$ are two mutually perpendicular diameters having length of 4 meters. $X$ is the mid-point of $OA$. $Y$ is a point on the circumference such that $\angle YOD = 30°$. Which of the following correctly gives the relation among the three alternate paths from $X$ to $Y$?

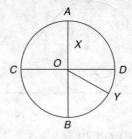

    (a) $XOBY : XODY : XADY :: 5.15 : 4.50 : 5.06$
    (b) $XADY : XODY : XOBY :: 6.25 : 5.34 : 4.24$
    (c) $XODY : XOBY : XADY :: 4.04 : 5.35 : 5.25$
    (d) $XADY : XOBY : XODY :: 5.19 : 5.09 : 4.04$

65. $ABCD$ is a parallelogram with $\angle ABC = 60°$. If the longer diagonal is of length 7 cm and the area of the parallelogram $ABCD$ is $15\frac{\sqrt{3}}{2}$ cm², then the perimeter of the parallelogram (in cm) is:

66. The center of a circle inside a triangle is at a distance of 625 cm, from each of the vertices of the triangle. If the diameter of the circle is 350 cm and the circle is touching only two sides of the triangle, find the area of the triangle.
    (a) 240000
    (b) 387072
    (c) 480000
    (d) 506447

67. Two poles, of height 2 meters and 3 meters, are 5 meters apart. The height of the point of intersection of the lines joining the top of each pole to the foot of the opposite pole is,
    (a) 1.2 meters
    (b) 1.0 meters
    (c) 5.0 meters
    (d) 3.0 meters

68. There are two squares $S_1$ and $S_2$ with areas 8 and 9 units, respectively. $S_1$ is inscribed within $S_2$, with one corner of $S_1$ on each side $S_2$. The corners of the smaller square divides the sides of the bigger square into two segments, one of length '$a$' and the other of length '$b$', where, $b > a$.
    A possible value of '$b/a$', is:

(a) ≥5 and <8

(b) ≥8 and <11

(c) ≥11 and <14

(d) ≥14 and <17

69. In $\triangle ABC$, $\dfrac{\angle A}{\angle B} = 1 - \dfrac{\angle C}{\angle B}$, then which of the following statement is true.

(a) $\triangle ABC$ is always an acute angled triangle

(b) $\angle > 90°$

(c) $AB^2 + BC^2 = AC^2$

(d) None of these

70. A city has a park shaped as a right angled triangle. The length of the longest side of this park is 80 m. The Mayor of the city wants to construct three paths from the corner point opposite to the longest side such that these three paths divide the longest side into four equal segments. Determine the sum of the squares of the lengths of the three paths (in m²)

71. In a rectangle *PQRS*, *PQ* = 14 cm, *X* is a point on *SR* such that *SX*:*XR* = 4:3 and *QX* = 10 cm. If ∠*PXQ* = *a*, ∠*XPQ* = *b*, ∠*XQP* = *c*, then which of the following is correct?

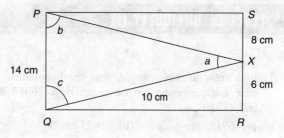

(a) $a > b > c$      (b) $b > c > a$

(c) $a > c > b$      (d) $c > b > a$

*Space for Rough Work*

# MENSURATION

**LEVEL OF DIFFICULTY (I)**

1. In a right angled triangle, find the hypotenuse if base and perpendicular are respectively 36015 cm and 48020 cm.

   (a) 69125 cm      (b) 60025 cm

   (c) 391025 cm     (d) 60125 cm

2. The perimeter of an equilateral triangle is $72\sqrt{3}$ m. Find its height.

   (a) 63 meters      (b) 24 meters

   (c) 18 meters      (d) 36 meters

3. The inner circumference of a circular track is 440 cm. The track is 14 cm wide. Find the diameter of the outer circle of the track.

   (a) 84 cm      (b) 168 cm

   (c) 336 cm      (d) 77 cm

4. A race track is in the form of a ring whose inner and outer circumference are 352 meter and 396 meter respectively. Find the width of the track.

   (a) 7 meters      (b) 14 meters

   (c) $14\pi$ meters    (d) $7\pi$ meters

5. The outer circumference of a circular track is 220 meter. The track is 7 meter wide everywhere. Calculate the cost of levelling the track at the rate of 50 paise per square meter.

   (a) ₹ 1556.5      (b) ₹ 3113

   (c) ₹ 593       (d) ₹ 693

6. Find the area of a quadrant of a circle whose circumference is 44 cm

   (a) 77 cm$^2$      (b) 38.5 cm$^2$

   (c) 19.25 cm$^2$    (d) $19.25\pi$ cm$^2$

7. A pit 7.5 meter long, 6 meter wide and 1.5 meter deep is dug in a field. Find the volume of soil removed in cubic meters.

   (a) 135 m$^3$      (b) 101.25 m$^3$

   (c) 50.625 m$^3$    (d) 67.5 m$^3$

8. Find the length of the longest pole that can be placed in an indoor stadium 24 meter long, 18 meter wide and 16 meter high.

   (a) 30 meters      (b) 25 meters

   (c) 34 meters      (d) $\sqrt{580}$ meters

9. The length, breadth and height of a room are in the ratio of 3:2:1. If its volume be 1296 m$^3$, find its breadth

   (a) 18 meters      (b) 18 meters

   (c) 16 meters      (d) 12 meters

10. The volume of a cube is 216 cm$^3$. Part of this cube is then melted to form a cylinder of length 8 cm. Find the volume of the cylinder.

    (a) 342 cm$^3$      (b) 216 cm$^3$

    (c) 36 cm$^3$      (d) Data inadequate

11. The whole surface of a rectangular block is 8788 square cm. If length, breadth and height are in the ratio of 4:3:2, find length.

    (a) 26 cm      (b) 52 cm

    (c) 104 cm      (d) 13 cm

12. Three metal cubes with edges 6 cm, 8 cm and 10 cm respectively are melted together and formed into a single cube. Find the side of the resulting cube.

    (a) 11 cm      (b) 12 cm

    (c) 13 cm      (d) 24 cm

13. Find curved and total surface area of a conical flask of radius 6 cm and height 8 cm.

    (a) $60\pi, 96\pi$      (b) $20\pi, 96\pi$

    (c) $60\pi, 48\pi$      (d) $30\pi, 48\pi$

14. The volume of a right circular cone is $100\pi$ cm$^3$ and its height is 12 cm. Find its curved surface area.

    (a) $130\,\pi$ cm$^2$      (b) $65\,\pi$ cm$^2$

    (c) $204\,\pi$ cm$^2$      (d) 65 cm$^2$

15. The diameters of two cones are equal. If their slant height be in the ratio 5:7, find the ratio of their curved surface areas.

    (a) 25:7      (b) 25:49

    (c) 5:49      (d) 5:7

16. The curved surface area of a cone is 2376 square cm and its slant height is 18 cm. Find the diameter.

    (a) 6 cm      (b) 18 cm

    (c) 84 cm      (d) 12 cm

17. The ratio of radii of a cylinder to a that of a cone is 1:2. If their heights are equal, find the ratio of their volumes?

    (a) 1:3      (b) 2:3

    (c) 3:4      (d) 3:1

18. A silver wire when bent in the form of a square, encloses an area of 484 cm$^2$. Now if the same wire is bent to form a circle, the area enclosed by it would be

(a) 308 cm²      (b) 196 cm²
(c) 616 cm²      (d) 88 cm²

19. The circumference of a circle exceeds its diameter by 16.8 cm. Find the circumference of the circle.

  (a) 12.32 cm      (b) 49.28 cm
  (c) 58.64 cm      (d) 24.64 cm

20. A bicycle wheel makes 5000 revolutions in moving 11 km. What is the radius of the wheel?

  (a) 70 cm      (b) 135 cm
  (c) 17.5 cm      (d) 35 cm

21. The volume of a right circular cone is $100\pi$ cm³ and its height is 12 cm. Find its slant height.

  (a) 13 cm      (b) 16 cm
  (c) 9 cm      (d) 26 cm

22. The short and the long hands of a clock are 4 cm and 6 cm long respectively. What will be sum of distances travelled by their tips in 4 days? (Take $\pi = 3.14$)

  (a) 954.56 cm      (b) 3818.24 cm
  (c) 2909.12 cm      (d) 2703.56 cm

23. The surface areas of two spheres are in the ratio of 1:4. Find the ratio of their volumes.

  (a) 1:2      (b) 1:8
  (c) 1:4      (d) 2:1

24. The outer and inner diameters of a spherical shell are 10 cm and 9 cm respectively. Find the volume of the metal contained in the shell. (Use $\pi = 22/7$)

  (a) 6956 cm³      (b) 141.95 cm³
  (c) 283.9 cm³      (d) 478.3 cm³

25. The radii of two spheres are in the ratio of 1:2. Find the ratio of their surface areas.

  (a) 1:3      (b) 2:3
  (c) 1:4      (d) 3:4

26. A sphere of radius $r$ has the same volume as that of a cone with a circular base of radius $r$. Find the height of cone.

  (a) $2r$      (b) $r/3$
  (c) $4r$      (d) $(2/3)r$

27. Find the number of bricks, each measuring 25 cm × 12.5 cm × 7.5 cm, required to construct a wall 12 m long, 5 m high and 0.25 m thick, while the sand and cement mixture occupies 5% of the total volume of wall.

  (a) 6080      (b) 3040
  (c) 1520      (d) 12160

28. A road that is 7 m wide surrounds a circular path whose circumference is 352 m. What will be the area of the road?

  (a) 2618 m²      (b) 654.5 m²
  (c) 1309 m²      (d) 5236 m²

29. In a shower, 10 cm of rain falls. What will be the volume of water that falls on 1 hectare area of ground?

  (a) 500 m³      (b) 650 m³
  (c) 1000 m³      (d) 750 m³

30. Seven equal cubes each of side 5 cm are joined end to end. Find the surface area of the resulting cuboid.

  (a) 750 cm²      (b) 1500 cm²
  (c) 2250 cm²      (d) 700 cm²

31. In a swimming pool measuring 90 m by 40 m, 150 men take a dip. If the average displacement of water by a man is 8 cubic meters, what will be the rise in the water level?

  (a) 30 cm      (b) 50 cm
  (c) 20 cm      (d) 33.33 cm

32. How many meters of cloth 5 m wide will be required to make a conical tent, the radius of whose base is 7 m and height is 24 m?

  (a) 55 m      (b) 330 m
  (c) 220 m      (d) 110 m

33. Two cones have their heights in the ratio 1:2 and the diameters of their bases are in the ratio 2:1. What will be the ratio of their volumes?

  (a) 4:1      (b) 2:1
  (c) 3:2      (d) 1:1

34. A conical tent is to accommodate 10 persons. Each person must have 6 m² space to sit and 30 m³ of air to breathe. What will be the height of the cone?

  (a) 37.5 m      (b) 150 m
  (c) 75 m      (d) None of these

35. A closed wooden box measures externally 10 cm long, 8 cm broad and 6 cm high. Thickness of wood is 0.5 cm. Find the volume of wood used.

  (a) 230 cubic cm      (b) 165 cubic cm
  (c) 330 cubic cm      (d) 300 cubic cm.

36. A cuboid of dimension 24 cm × 9 cm × 8 cm is melted and smaller cubes of side 3 cm are formed. Find how many such cubes can be formed.

  (a) 27      (b) 64
  (c) 54      (d) 32

37. Three cubes each of volume of 216 m³ are joined end to end. Find the surface area of the resulting figure.

  (a) 504 m²      (b) 216 m²
  (c) 432 m²      (d) 480 m²

38. A hollow spherical shell is made of a metal of density 4.9 g/cm³. If its internal and external radii are 10 cm and 12 cm respectively, find the weight of the shell. (Take $\pi = 3.1416$)

  (a) 5016 gm      (b) 1416.8 gm
  (c) 14942.28 gm      (d) 5667.1 gm

39. The largest cone is formed at the base of a cube of side measuring 7 cm. Find the ratio of volume of cone to cube.

    (a) 20:21           (b) 22:21
    (c) 21:22           (d) 11:42

40. A spherical cannon ball, 28 cm in diameter, is melted and cast into a right circular conical mould the base of which is 35 cm in diameter. Find the height of the cone correct up to two places of decimals.

    (a) 8.96 cm         (b) 35.84 cm
    (c) 5.97 cm         (d) 17.92 cm

41. Find the area of the circle circumscribed about a square each side of which is 10 cm.

    (a) 314.28 cm²      (b) 157.14 cm²
    (c) 150.38 cm²      (d) 78.57 cm²

42. Find the radius of the circle inscribed in a triangle whose sides are 8 cm, 15 cm and 17 cm.

    (a) 4 cm            (b) 5 cm
    (c) 3 cm            (d) $2\sqrt{2}$ cm

43. In the given diagram a rope is wound round the outside of a circular drum whose diameter is 70 cm and a bucket is tied to the other end of the rope. Find the number of revolutions made by the drum if the bucket is raised by 11 m.

    (a) 10              (b) 2.5
    (c) 5               (d) 5.5

44. A cube whose edge is 20 cm long has circles on each of its faces painted black. What is the total area of the unpainted surface of the cube if the circles are of the largest area possible?

    (a) 85.71 cm²       (b) 257.14 cm²
    (c) 514.28 cm²      (d) 331.33 cm²

45. The areas of three adjacent faces of a cuboid are x, y, z. If the volume is V, then V² will be equal to

    (a) xy/z            (b) yz/x²
    (c) x²y²/z²         (d) xyz

46. In the adjacent figure, find the area of the shaded region. (Use π = 22/7)

    (a) 15.28 cm²       (b) 61.14 cm²
    (c) 30.57 cm²       (d) 40.76 cm²

47. The diagram represents the area swept by the wiper of a car. With the dimensions given in the figure, calculate the shaded area swept by the wiper.

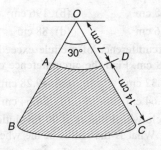

    (a) 102.67 cm       (b) 205.34 cm
    (c) 51.33 cm        (d) 208.16 cm

48. Find the area of the quadrilateral *ABCD*. (Given, $\sqrt{3}$ = 1.73)

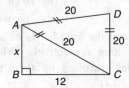

    (a) 452 sq units    (b) 269 sq units
    (c) 134.5 sq units  (d) 1445 g cm

49. The base of a pyramid is a rectangle of sides 18 m × 26 m and its slant height to the shorter side of the base is 24 m. Find its volume.

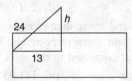

    (a) $156\sqrt{407}$    (b) $78\sqrt{407}$
    (c) $312\sqrt{407}$    (d) $234\sqrt{407}$

50. A wire is looped in the form of a circle of radius 28 cm. It is bent again into a square form. What will be the length of the diagonal of the largest square possible thus?

    (a) 44 cm           (b) $44\sqrt{2}$
    (c) $176/2\sqrt{2}$ (d) $88\sqrt{2}$

51. If *x* units are added to the length of the radius of a circle, what is the number of units by which the area of the circle is increased?

52. A man walked diagonally across a square lot. Approximately, what was the percentage reduction in the total distance that he walked vis-à-vis the distance he would have walked had he walked along the edges? (To the closest 1%)

53. The radius of circle is so increased that its circumference increased by 5%. The area of the circle then increases by                    **[SNAP 2009]**

    (a) 12.5%           (b) 10.25%
    (c) 10.5%           (d) 11.25%

54. The biggest possible cube is taken out of a right solid cylinder of radius 15 cm and height 20 cm respectively. What will be the volume of the cube?

55. How many cuboids of different dimensions can be assembled with 100 identical cubes?

56. What is the least number of square tiles required to pave the floor of a room 1517 cm long and 902 cm broad?

57. A wire, if bent into *a* square, encloses an *area* of 484 cm². This wire is cut into two pieces with the bigger piece having *a* length three-fourth of the original wire's length. Now, if *a* circle and *a* square are formed with the bigger and the smaller piece respectively, what would be the area enclosed by the two pieces?

58. A spiral staircase is made up of 13 successive semi-circles, with center alternately at *A* and *B*, starting with center at *A*. The radii of semicircles, thus developed, are 0.5 cm, 1.0 cm, 1.5 cm, and 2.0 cm and so on. The total length of the spiral is: Use $\pi = \dfrac{22}{7}$

59. A cylinder, a hemisphere and a cone stand on the same base and have the same heights. The ratio of the areas of their curved surface is:
    (a) $2:2:1$                      (b) $\sqrt{2}:\sqrt{2}:1$
    (c) $2:\sqrt{2}:1$               (d) None of these.

60. The radius of *a* spherical balloon, of radii 30 cm, increases at the rate of 2 cm per second. Then its curved surface area increases by:

61. A rectangular piece of paper is 22 cm long and 10 cm wide. A cylinder is formed by rolling the paper along its length. Find the volume of the cylinder.

62. Consider the volumes of the following objects and arrange them in **decreasing** order of their volumes:
    1. A parallelepiped of length 5 cm, breadth 3 cm and height 4 cm.
    2. A cube of each side 4 cm.
    3. A cylinder of radius 3 cm and length 3 cm.
    4. A sphere of radius 3 cm.
    (a) 4, 3, 2, 1                   (b) 4, 2, 3, 1
    (c) 4, 3, 1, 2                   (d) None of these.

63. A hemispherical bowl is filled with hot water to the brim. The contents of the bowl are transferred into a cylindrical vessel whose radius is 50% more than its height. If diameter of the bowl is the same as that of the vessel and the volume of the hot water in the cylindrical vessel is *x*% of the volume of the cylindrical vessel then *x* = ?

64. In a circular field, there is a rectangular tank of length 130 m and breadth 110 m. If the area of the land portion of the field is 20350 m² then the radius of the field is:

65. A tank internally measuring 150 cm × 120 cm × 100 cm has 1281600 cm³ water in it. Porous bricks are placed in the water until the tank is full up to its brim. Each brick absorbs one tenth of its volume of water. How many bricks, of 20 cm × 6 cm × 4 cm, can be put in the tank without spilling over the water?

66. A spherical metal ball of radius 10 cm is molten and made into 1000 smaller spheres of equal sizes. In this process the surface area of the metal is increased by *n* %. Then *n* =?

67. Suresh, who runs a bakery, uses a conical shaped equipment to write decorative labels (e.g., Happy Birthday etc.) using cream. The height of this equipment is 7 cm and the diameter of the base is 5 mm. A full charge of the equipment will write 330 words on an average. How many words can be written using two fifth of a litre of cream?

68. Your friend's cap is in the shape of a right circular cone of base radius 14 cm and height 26.5 cm. The approximate area of the sheet required to make 7 such caps is

69. In an engineering college there is a rectangular garden of dimensions 34 m by 21 m. Two mutually perpendicular walking corridors of 4 m width have been made in the central part and flowers have been grown in the rest of the garden. The area under the flowers is:

70. A right circular cone is enveloping a right circular cylinder that rests on the base of the cone.
    If the radius and the height of the cone is 4 cm and 10 cm respectively, and the radius of the cylinder is '*r*' cm, the largest possible curved surface area of the cylinder is '$a\pi r(b-r)$'.Then $a \times b = ?$

***Space for Rough Work***

## LEVEL OF DIFFICULTY (II)

1. The perimeter of a sector of a circle of radius 5.7 m is 27.2 m. Find the area of the sector.
   (a) 90.06 cm²
   (b) 135.09 cm²
   (c) 45 cm²
   (d) None of these

2. The dimensions of a field are 20 m by 9 m. A pit 10 m long, 4.5 m wide and 3 m deep is dug in one corner of the field and the earth removed has been evenly spread over the remaining area of the field. What will be the rise in the height of field as a result of this operation?
   (a) 1 m
   (b) 2 m
   (c) 3 m
   (d) 4 m

3. A vessel is in the form of a hollow cylinder mounted on a hemispherical bowl. The diameter of the sphere is 14 cm and the total height of the vessel is 13 cm. Find the capacity of the vessel.     (Take π = 22/7).

   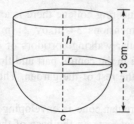

   (a) 321.33 cm
   (b) 1642.67 cm³
   (c) 1232 cm³
   (d) 1632.33 cm³

4. The sides of a triangle are 21, 20 and 13 cm. Find the area of the larger triangle into which the given triangle is divided by the perpendicular upon the longest side from the opposite vertex.
   (a) 72 cm²
   (b) 96 cm²
   (c) 168 cm²
   (d) 144 cm²

5. A circular tent is cylindrical to a height of 3 meters and conical above it. If its diameter is 105 m and the slant height of the conical portion is 53 m, calculate the length of the canvas 5 m wide to make the required tent.
   (a) 3894
   (b) 973.5
   (c) 1947 m
   (d) 1800 m

6. A steel sphere of radius 4 cm is drawn into a wire of diameter 4 mm. Find the length of wire.
   (a) 10,665 mm
   (b) 42,660 mm
   (c) 21,333 mm
   (d) 14,220 mm

7. A cylinder and a cone having equal diameter of their bases are placed in the Qutab Minar one on the other, with the cylinder placed in the bottom. If their curved surface area are in the ratio of 8 : 5, find the ratio of their heights. Assume the height of the cylinder to be equal to the radius of Qutab Minar. (Assume Qutab Minar to be having same radius throughout).
   (a) 1:4
   (b) 3:4
   (c) 4:3
   (d) 2:3

8. If the curved surface area of a cone is thrice that of another cone and slant height of the second cone is thrice that of the first, find the ratio of the area of their base.
   (a) 81:1
   (b) 9:1
   (c) 3:1
   (d) 27:1

9. A solid sphere of radius 6 cm is melted into a hollow cylinder of uniform thickness. If the external radius of the base of the cylinder is 5 cm and its height is 32 cm, find the uniform thickness of the cylinder.
   (a) 2 cm
   (b) 3 cm
   (c) 1 cm
   (d) 3.5 cm

10. A hollow sphere of external and internal diameters 6 cm and 4 cm respectively is melted into a cone of base diameter 8 cm. Find the height of the cone
    (a) 4.75 cm
    (b) 9.5 cm
    (c) 19 cm
    (d) 38 cm

11. Three equal cubes are placed adjacently in a row. Find the ratio of total surface area of the new cuboid to that of the sum of the surface areas of the three cubes.
    (a) 7:9
    (b) 49:81
    (c) 9:7
    (d) 27:23

12. If $V$ be the volume of a cuboid of dimension $x$, $y$, $z$ and $A$ is its surface, then $A/V$ will be equal to
    (a) $x^2y^2z^2$
    (b) $1/2\ (1/xy + 1/xz + 1/yz)$
    (c) $2\left(\dfrac{1}{x} + \dfrac{1}{y} + \dfrac{1}{z}\right)$
    (d) $1/xyz$

13. The minute hand of a clock is 10 cm long. Find the area of the face of the clock described by the minute hand between 9 a.m. and 9 : 35 a.m.
    (a) 183.3 cm²
    (b) 366.6 cm²
    (c) 244.4 cm²
    (d) 188.39 cm²

14. Two circles touch internally. The sum of their areas is 116π cm² and distance between their centres is 6 cm. Find the radii of the circles.
    (a) 10 cm, 4 cm
    (b) 11 cm, 4 cm
    (c) 9 cm, 5 cm
    (d) 10 cm, 5 cm

15. A toy is in the shape of a right circular cylinder with a hemisphere on one end and a cone on the other. The height and radius of the cylindrical part

are 13 cm and 5 cm respectively. The radii of the hemispherical and conical parts are the same as that of the cylindrical part. Calculate the surface area of the toy if the height of conical part is 12 cm.

(a) 1440 cm²      (b) 385 cm²

(c) 1580 cm²      (d) 770 cm²

16. A solid wooden toy is in the form of a cone mounted on a hemisphere. If the radii of the hemisphere is 4.2 cm and the total height of the toy is 10.2 cm, find the volume of wood used in the toy.

(a) 343.72 cm³      (b) 266.11 cm³

(c) 532.22 cm³      (d) 133.55 cm³

17. A cylindrical container whose diameter is 12 cm and height is 15 cm, is filled with ice cream. The whole ice-cream is distributed to 10 children in equal cones having hemispherical tops. If the height of the conical portion is twice the diameter of its base, find the diameter of the ice-cream cone.

(a) 6 cm      (b) 12 cm

(c) 3 cm      (d) 18 cm

18. A solid is in the form of a cylinder with hemispherical ends. The total height of the solid is 19 cm and the diameter of the cylinder is 7 cm. Find the total surface area of the solid.      (Use = 22/7).

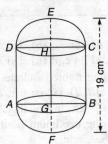

(a) 398.75 cm²      (b) 418 cm²

(c) 444 cm²      (d) 412 cm²

19. A cone, a hemisphere and a cylinder stand on equal bases and have the same height. What is the ratio of their volumes?

(a) 2 : 1 : 3      (b) 2.5 : 1 : 3

(c) 1 : 2 : 3      (d) 1.5 : 2 : 3

20. The internal and external diameters of a hollow hemispherical vessel are 24 cm and 25 cm respectively. The cost of painting 1 cm² of the surface is ₹ 0.05. Find the total cost of painting the vessel all over.      (Take $\pi$ = 22/7)

(a) ₹ 97.65      (b) ₹ 86.4

(c) ₹ 184      (d) ₹ 96.28

21. A solid is in the form of a right circular cylinder with a hemisphere at one end and a cone at the other end. Their common diameter is 3.5 cm and the heights of conical and cylindrical portion are respectively 6 cm and 10 cm. Find the volume of the solid.

(Use $\pi$ = 3.14)

(a) 117 cm²      (b) 234 cm²

(c) 58.5 cm²      (d) None of these

22. In the adjoining figure, *AOBCA* represents a quadrant of a circle of radius 3.5 cm with centre *O*. Calculate the area of the shaded portion.      (Use $\pi$ = 22/7)

(a) 35 cm²      (b) 7.875 cm²

(c) 9.625 cm²      (d) 6.125 cm²

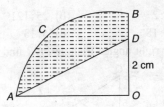

23. Find the area of the shaded region if the radius of each of the circles is 1 cm.

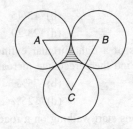

(a) $2 - \dfrac{\pi}{3}$      (b) $\sqrt{3} - \pi$

(c) $\sqrt{3} - \dfrac{\pi}{2}$      (d) $\sqrt{3} - \pi/4$

24. A right elliptical cylinder full of petrol has its widest elliptical side 2.4 m and the shortest 1.6 m. Its height is 7 m. Find the time required to empty half the tank through a hose of diameter 4 cm if the rate of flow of petrol is 120 m/min

(a) 60 min      (b) 90 min

(c) 75 min      (d) 70 min

25. Find the area of the trapezium *ABCD*.

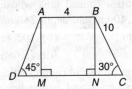

(a) $5/2(13 + 2\sqrt{3})$      (b) $\dfrac{5\sqrt{3}(13 + 5\sqrt{3})}{2}$

(c) $13(13 + 2\sqrt{3})$      (d) None of these

26. *PQRS* is the diameter of a circle of radius 6 cm. The lengths *PQ*, *QR* and *RS* are equal. Semi-circles are drawn with *PQ* and *QS* as diameters as shown in the figure alongside. Find the ratio of the area of the shaded region to that of the unshaded region.

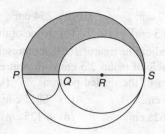

(a) 1:2        (b) 25:121

(c) 5:18        (d) 5:13

27. In the right angled triangle $PQR$ find $Rx$.

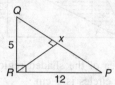

(a) 13/60       (b) 13/45

(c) 60/13       (d) 23/29

28. The radius of a right circular cylinder is increased by 50%. Find the percentage increase in volume

(a) 120%       (b) 75%

(c) 150%       (d) 125%

29. Two persons start walking on a road that diverge at an angle of 120°. If they walk at the rate of 3 km/h and 2 km/h repectively. Find the distance between them after 4 hours.

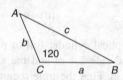

(a) $4\sqrt{19}$ km       (b) 5 km

(c) 7 km       (d) $8\sqrt{19}$ km

30. Water flows out at the rate of 10 m/min from a cylindrical pipe of diameter 5 mm. Find the time taken to fill a conical tank whose diameter at the surface is 40 cm and depth 24 cm.

(a) 50 min       (b) 102.4 min

(c) 51.2 min       (d) 25.6 min

31. The section of a solid right circular cone by a plane containing vertex and perpendicular to base is an equilateral triangle of side 12 cm. Find the volume of the cone.

(a) 72 cc       (b) 144 cc

(c) $72\sqrt{2}\,\pi$ cc       (d) $72\sqrt{3}\,\pi$ cc

32. Iron weighs 8 times the weight of oak. Find the diameter of an iron ball whose weight is equal to that of a ball of oak 18 cm in diameter.

(a) 4.5 cm       (b) 9 cm

(c) 12 cm       (d) 15 cm

33. In the figure, $ABC$ is a right angled triangle with $\angle B = 90°$, $BC = 21$ cm and $AB = 28$ cm. With $AC$ as diameter of a semicircle and with $BC$ as radius, a quarter circle is drawn. Find the area of the shaded portion correct to two decimal places

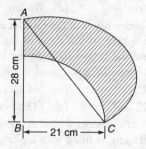

(a) 428.75 cm²       (b) 857.50 cm²

(c) 214.37 cm²       (d) 371.56

34. Find the perimeter and area of the shaded portion of the adjoining diagram:

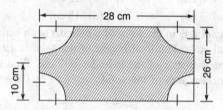

(a) 90.8 cm, 414 cm²       (b) 181.6 cm, 423.7 cm²

(c) 90.8 cm, 827.4 cm²       (d) 181.6 cm, 827.4 cm²

35. In the adjoining figure, a circle is inscribed in the quadrilateral $ABCD$. Given that $BC = 38$ cm, $AB = 27$ cm and $DC = 25$ cm, and that $AD$ is perpendicular to $DC$. Find the maximum limit of the radius and the area of the circle.

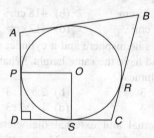

(a) 10 cm; 226 cm²       (b) 14 cm; 616 cm²

(c) 14 cm; 216 cm²       (d) 28 cm; 616 cm²

36. From a piece of cardboard, in the shape of a trapezium $ABCD$ and $AB \parallel DC$ and $\angle BCD = 90°$, a quarter circle ($BFEC$) with $C$ as its centre is removed. Given $AB = BC = 3.5$ cm and $DE = 2$ cm, calculate the area of the remaining piece of the cardboard.

(Take $\pi = 22/7$)

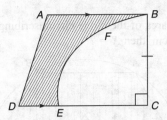

(a)  3.325 cm²              (b)  3.125 cm²
(c)  6.075 cm²              (d)  12.25 cm²

37. The inside perimeter of a practice running track with semi-circular ends and straight parallel sides is 312 m. The length of the straight portion of the track is 90 m. If the track has a uniform width of 2 m throughout, find its area.

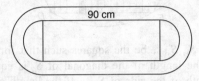

(a)  5166 m²               (b)  5802.57 m²
(c)  636.57 m²             (d)  1273.14 m²

38. Find the area of the triangle inscribed in a circle circumscribed by a square made by joining the mid-points of the adjacent sides of a square of side $a$.

(a)  $3a^2/16$             (b)  $\dfrac{3\sqrt{3}\,a^2}{16}$

(c)  $3/4\,a^2(\pi - 1/2)$   (d)  $\dfrac{3\sqrt{3}\,a^2}{32}$

39. Two goats are tethered to the diagonally opposite vertices of a square field formed by joining the mid points of the adjacent sides of another square field of side $20\sqrt{2}$ meters. The inner square field is fenced on all sides and the goats are allowed to graze only inside the inner field. If their grazing ropes are of a length of $10\sqrt{2}$ meters each, find the total area grazed by the two goats together.

(a)  $100\pi\,\text{m}^2$          (b)  $50\,(\sqrt{2}-1)\pi\,\text{m}^2$

(c)  $100\pi\,(3-2\sqrt{2})\,\text{m}^2$  (d)  $200\pi\,(2-\sqrt{2})\,\text{m}^2$

40. The area of the circle circumscribing three circles of unit radius touching each other is

(a)  $(\pi/3)\,(2+\sqrt{3})^2$     (b)  $6\pi\,(2+\sqrt{3})^2$

(c)  $3\pi\,(2+\sqrt{3})^2$        (d)  $\left(\dfrac{\pi}{6}\right)(2+\sqrt{3})^2$

41. Find the ratio of the diameter of the circles inscribed in and circumscribing an equilateral triangle to its height.
(a)  $1:2:1$               (b)  $2:4:3$
(c)  $1:3:4$               (d)  $3:2:1$

42. Find the sum of the areas of the shaded sectors given that $ABCDFE$ is any hexagon and all the circles are of same radius $r$ with different vertices of the hexagon as their centres as shown in the figure.

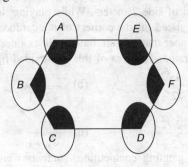

(a)  $\pi r^2$              (b)  $2\pi r^2$
(c)  $5\pi r^2/4$           (d)  $3\pi r^2/2$

43. Circles are drawn with four vertices as the centre and radius equal to the side of a square. If the square is formed by joining the mid-points of another square of side $2\sqrt{6}$, find the area common to all the four circles.

(a)  $[(\sqrt{3}-1)/2)]\,6\pi$   (b)  $4\pi - 3\sqrt{3}$

(c)  $1/2\,(\pi - 3\sqrt{3})$     (d)  $4\pi - 12(\sqrt{3}-1)$

44. $ABDC$ is a circle and circles are drawn with $AO$, $CO$, $DO$ and $OB$ as diameters. Areas $E$ and $F$ are shaded. $E/F$ is equal to

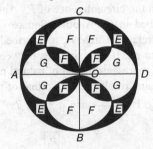

(a)  1                     (b)  1/2
(c)  1/2                   (d)  $\pi/4$

45. The diagram shows six equal circles inscribed in equilateral triangle $ABC$. The circles touch externally among themselves and also touch the sides of the triangle. If the radius of each circle is $R$, area of the triangle is

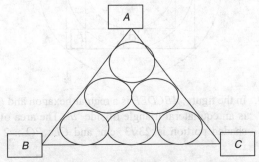

(a) $(6 + \pi\sqrt{3})R^1$       (b) $9R^2$

(c) $R^2(12 + 7\sqrt{3})$       (d) $R^2(9 + 6\sqrt{3})$

46. A boy Mithilesh was playing with a square cardboard of side 2 meters. While playing, he accidentally sliced off the corners of the cardboard in such a manner that a figure having all its sides equal was generated. The area of this eight sided figure is:

(a) $\dfrac{4\sqrt{2}}{\sqrt{2}+1}$       (b) $\dfrac{4}{\sqrt{2}+1}$

(c) $\dfrac{2\sqrt{2}}{\sqrt{2}+1}$       (d) $\dfrac{8}{\sqrt{2}+1}$

47. In a painting competition, students were asked to draw alternate squares and circles, circumscribing each other. The first student drew $A_1$ a square whose side is '$a$' meters. The second student drew Circle $C_1$ circumscribing the square $A_1$ such that all its vertices are on $C_1$. Subsequent students, drew square $A_2$ circumscribing $C_1$, Circle $C_2$ circumscribing $A_2$ and $A_3$ circumscribing $C_2$, and so on. If $D_N$ is the area between the square $A_N$ and the circle $C_N$, where $N$ is a natural number, then the ratio of the sum of all $D_N$ to $D_1$ for $N = 12$ is:

(a) 1       (b) $\dfrac{\pi}{2} - 1$

(c) $2^{12} - 1$       (d) $2^{11} - 1$

48. Let $P_1$ be the circle of radius $r$. A square $Q_1$ is inscribed in $P_1$ such that all the vertices of the square $Q_1$ lie on the circumference of $P_1$. Another circle $P_2$ is inscribed in $Q_1$. Another Square $Q_2$ is inscribed in the circle $P_2$. Circle $P_3$ is inscribed in the square $Q_2$ and so on. If $S_N$ is the area between $Q_N$ and $P_{N+1}$ where $N$ represents the set of natural numbers. If the ratio of sum of all such $S_N$ to that of the area of the square $Q_1$ is $\dfrac{a - \pi}{b}$ then $a + b = ?$

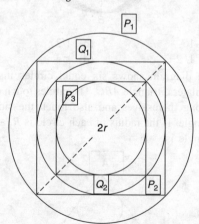

49. In the figure, $ABCDEF$ is a regular hexagon and $PQR$ is an equilateral triangle of side '$a$'. The area of the shaded portion is $23\sqrt{3}$ cm$^2$ and $CD : PQ :: 2 : 1$.

If the area of the circle circumscribing the hexagon is $X\pi$ cm$^2$ then $X = ?$

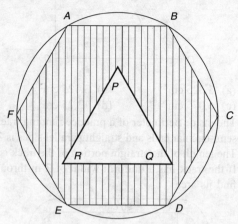

50. Let $S_1$, $S_2$, ....be the squares such that for each $n \geq 1$, the length of the diagonal of $S_n$ is equal to the length of the side of $S_{n+1}$. If the length of the side of $S_3$ is 4 cm. What is the area of the square $S_{11}$?

51. At the centre of a city's municipal park there is a large circular pool. A fish is released in the water at the edge of the pool. The fish swims north for 30 meters before it hits the edge of the pool. It then turns east and swims for 40 meters before it hits the edge of the pool. If the area of the pool is $X\pi$ m$^2$ then $X = ?$

(a) 625       (b) 125

(c) 250       (d) 500

52. The figure below has been obtained by folding a rectangle. The total area of the figure (as visible) is 144 square meters. Had the rectangle not been folded, the current overlapping part would have been a square. What would have been the total area of the original unfolded rectangle (in m$^2$)?

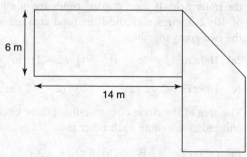

53. A solid metal cylinder of 10 cm height and 14 cm diameter is melted and re-cast into two cones in the proportion of 3 : 4 (volume), keeping the height 10 cm. What would be the percentage change in the flat surface area before and after?

(a) 9%       (b) 16%

(c) 25%       (d) 50%

54. A circular road is constructed outside a square field. The perimeter of the square field is 200 ft. If the width of the road is $7\sqrt{2}$ ft. and cost of construction is ₹100 per sq. ft. Find the lowest possible cost to construct 50% of the total road.
    (a) ₹70,400
    (b) ₹125,400
    (c) ₹140,800
    (d) ₹235,400

55. Diameter of the base of a water-filled inverted right circular cone is 26 cm. A cylindrical pipe, 5 mm in radius, is attached to the surface of the cone at a point. The perpendicular distance between the point and the base (the top) is 15 cm. The distance from the edge of the base to the point is 17 cm, along the surface. If water flows at the rate of 10 meters per minute through the pipe, how much time would elapse before water stops coming out of the pipe?
    (a) ≥ 5.2 minutes
    (b) ≥ 4.5 minutes but < 4.8 minutes
    (c) ≥ 4.8 minutes but < 5 minutes
    (d) ≥ 5 minutes but < 5.2 minutes

56. Consider a rectangle *ABCD* of area 90 units. The points *P* and *Q* trisect *AB*, and *R* bisects *CD*. The diagonal *AC* intersects the line segments *PR* and *QR* at *M* and *N* respectively. What is the area of the quadrilateral *PQNM*?
    (a) > 9.5 and ≤ 10
    (b) > 10 and ≤ 10.5
    (c) > 10.5 and ≤ 11
    (d) > 11 and ≤ 11.5

57. The central park of the city is 40 meters long and 30 meters wide. The mayor wants to construct two roads of equal width in the park such that the roads intersect each other at right angles and the diagonals of the park are also the diagonals of the small rectangle formed at the intersection of the two roads. Further, the mayor wants that the area of the two roads to be equal to the remaining area of the park. What should be the width of the roads?
    (a) 10 meters
    (b) 12.5 meters
    (c) 14 meters
    (d) 15 meters

58. A rectangular swimming pool is 48 m long and 20 m wide. The shallow edge of the pool is 1 m deep. For every 2.6 m that one walks up the inclined base of the swimming pool, one gains an elevation of 1 m. What is the volume of water (in cubic meters), in the swimming pool? Assume that the pool is filled up to the brim.
    (a) 528
    (b) 960
    (c) 6790
    (d) 10560

59. A thread is wound on a cylinder such that it makes exactly twenty-four complete turns around the cylinder. The two ends of thread touch the top and bottom of cylinder. If cylinder has a radius of 15 cm and its curved surface area is 2880 cm² then find the length of the string:

60. If the length of the minute hand and the hour of a clock are 4.2 cm and 2.1 cm. If the minute hand covers an area of 110.88 cm², then find the area covered by hour hand during the same period.
    [if π = 22/7]

61. Hiru has a rhombus shaped farm *ABCD*. This farm is surrounded, by a path of width 2 m, as shown in the diagram. If ∠*ADC* = 30°, *AD* = 10 m. Then the area of the path is:

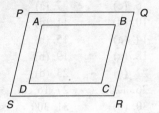

62. A series of infinite concentric squares are drawn as shown below. Starting with the first square *ABCD*, subsequent squares drawn are *PQRS*, *XYZW* and so on as shown in the diagram. If Areas of the squares *ABCD*, *PQRS*, *XYZW*, .... are 1, 3/2, 7/4, 15/8... and so on, then find the area of the diagram when the infinite number square is drawn.

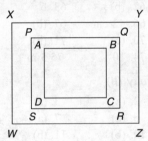

63. Three regular hexagons are drawn such that their diagonals cut each other at the same point and area $A_1:A_2:A_3$ = 1:2:3. Then the ratio of the length of the sides of the regular hexagons (from the smallest to the largest) is:
    (a) $1:\sqrt{2}:\sqrt{6}$
    (b) $1:\sqrt{2}:\sqrt{3}$
    (c) $1:\sqrt{3}:2\sqrt{2}$
    (d) $1:\sqrt{3}:\sqrt{6}$

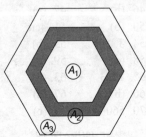

*Space for Rough Work*

# ANSWER KEY

## GEOMETRY

### Level of Difficulty (I)

| | | | |
|---|---|---|---|
| 1. (a) | 2. (d) | 3. (c) | 4. (a) |
| 5. (a) | 6. (c) | 7. (a) | 8. (d) |
| 9. (a) | 10. (d) | 11. (d) | 12. (a) |
| 13. (b) | 14. (a) | 15. (b) | 16. (b) |
| 17. (a) | 18. (a) | 19. (b) | 20. (a) |
| 21. (b) | 22. (a) | 23. (d) | 24. (d) |
| 25. (b) | 26. 120° | 27. 16 cm | 28. 12 cm |
| 29. 250 cm² | 30. (b) | 31. 300 | 32. 111.75 |
| 33. 80 | 34. 120 | 35. (b) | 36. (c) |
| 37. 60° | 38. 9 | 39. 4 cm | 40. √20cm |
| 41. 40 | 42. (a) | 43. 90° | 44. 50° |
| 45. 30° | 46. 9 | 47. 20 | 48. 10 |
| 49. 55° | 50. 50° | 51. 40° | 52. 50° |
| 53. 120° | 54. (d) | 55. 10° | 56. (b) |
| 57. 12.5cm | 58. 8cm | 59. 16cm | 60. 3.6 |
| 61. (d) | 62. (b) | 63. b | 64. 0.5 |
| 65. (a) | 66. 42 cm | 67. (b) | 68. (d) |
| 69. (c) | 70. (c) | 71. (b) | 72. (c) |
| 73. 14 | 74. 10 | 75 5 m | |

### Level of Difficulty (II)

| | | | |
|---|---|---|---|
| 1. (b) | 2. (a) | 3. (a) | 4. (a) |
| 5. (c) | 6. (a) | 7. (a) | 8. (b) |
| 9. (a) | 10. (b) | 11. (b) | 12. (a) |
| 13. (a) | 14. (c) | 15. (b) | 16. (a) |
| 17. (d) | 18. (c) | 19. (c) | 20. (d) |
| 21. (a) | 22. (b) | 23. (a) | 24. (b) |
| 25. (d) | 26. (b) | 27. (b) | 28. (b) |
| 29. (a) | 30. (d) | 31. (b) | 32. (a) |
| 33. (a) | 34. (c) | 35. (d) | 36. (a) |
| 37. (b) | 38. (b) | 39. (b) | 40. (a) |
| 41. (d) | 42. 18 | 43. 19 | 44. 5 |
| 45. (b) | 46. (b) | 47. (a) | 48. (d) |
| 49. (b) | 50. (b) | 51. 4cm | 52. 19:5 |
| 53. 40° | 54. 3 | 55. (b) | 56. 16:9 |
| 57. (c) | 58. (c) | 59. (d) | 60. 15 |
| 61. (a) | 62. 1063 | 63. (d) | 64. (d) |
| 65. 16 | 66. (b) | 67. (a) | 68. (d) |
| 69. (c) | 70. 5600 | 71. (c) | |

## MENSURATION

### Level of Difficulty (I)

| | | | |
|---|---|---|---|
| 1. (b) | 2. (d) | 3. (b) | 4. (a) |
| 5. (d) | 6. (b) | 7. (d) | 8. (c) |
| 9. (d) | 10. (d) | 11. (b) | 12. (b) |
| 13. (a) | 14. (b) | 15. (d) | 16. (c) |
| 17. (c) | 18. (c) | 19. (d) | 20. (d) |
| 21. (a) | 22. (b) | 23. (b) | 24. (b) |
| 25. (c) | 26. (c) | 27. (a) | 28. (a) |
| 29. (c) | 30. (a) | 31. (d) | 32. (d) |
| 33. (b) | 34. (d) | 35. (b) | 36. (b) |
| 37. (a) | 38. (c) | 39. (d) | 40. (b) |
| 41. (b) | 42. (c) | 43. (c) | 44. (c) |
| 45. (d) | 46. (c) | 47. (a) | 48. (b) |
| 49. (a) | 50. (b) | 51. $\pi x(2r + x)$ | 52. 29% |
| 53. (b) | 54. 800 | 55. 8 | 56. 814 |
| 57. 376.75 cm² | | 58. 143 cm | 59. (b) |
| 60. 480 π | 61. 385 cm³ | 62. (a) | 63. 100 |
| 64. 105 m | 65. 1200 | 66. 900 | |
| 67. 288000 | 68. 9240 cm² | 69. 510 sq. m. | 70. 20 |

### Level of Difficulty (II)

| | | | |
|---|---|---|---|
| 1. (d) | 2. (a) | 3. (b) | 4. (b) |
| 5. (c) | 6. (c) | 7. (b) | 8. (a) |
| 9. (c) | 10. (d) | 11. (a) | 12. (c) |
| 13. (a) | 14. (a) | 15. (d) | 16. (b) |
| 17. (a) | 18. (b) | 19. (c) | 20. (d) |
| 21. (d) | 22. (d) | 23. (c) | 24. (d) |
| 25. (d) | 26. (b) | 27. (c) | 28. (d) |
| 29. (a) | 30. (c) | 31. (d) | 32. (b) |
| 33. (a) | 34. (a) | 35. (d) | 36. (c) |
| 37. (c) | 38. (d) | 39. (a) | 40. (a) |
| 41. (b) | 42. (b) | 43. (d) | 44. (a) |
| 45. (c) | 46. (d) | 47. (c) | 48. 6 |
| 49. 16 | 50. 4096 cm² | 51. (a) | |
| 52. 162 m² | 53. (d) | 54. (b) | 55. (d) |
| 56. (d) | 57. (a) | 58. (d) | |
| 59. 408cm | 60. 2.31 | 61. 112m² | 62. 2 |
| 63. (d) | | | |

## Solutions and Shortcuts

### GEOMETRY

### Level of Difficulty (I)

1. (a)

When the length of stick = 20 m, then length of shadow = 10 m i.e. in this case length = 2 × shadow. With the same angle of inclination of the sun, the length of tower that casts a shadow of 50 m ⇒ 2 × 50 m = 100 m

i.e. height of tower = 100 m

2. (d)

$\Delta ABC \sim \Delta EDC$

Then $\dfrac{AC}{EC} = \dfrac{BC}{DC} = \dfrac{AB}{ED}$

Then $\dfrac{AC}{4.2} = \dfrac{4}{3} = AC = 5.6$ cm and

$$\frac{BC}{4.8} = \frac{4}{3} = BC = 6.4 \text{ cm}$$

3. (c)

For similar triangles $\Rightarrow$ (Ratio of sides)$^2$ = Ratio of areas

Then as per question $= \left(\frac{36}{x}\right)^2 = \frac{144}{81}$

{Let the longest side of $\Delta DEF = x$}

$\Rightarrow \frac{36}{x} = \frac{12}{9} \Rightarrow x = 27 \text{ cm}$

4. (a)

(Ratio of corresponding sides)$^2$ = Ratio of area of similar triangles

$\therefore$ Ratio of corresponding sides in this question

$$= \sqrt{\frac{16}{25}} = \frac{4}{5}$$

5. (a)

Ratio of corresponding sides $= \sqrt{\frac{9}{16}} = \frac{3}{4}$

6. (c)

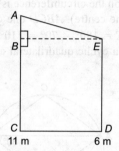

$BC = ED = 6 \text{ m}$

So $\quad AB = AC - BC = 11 - 6 = 5 \text{ m}$

$CD = BE = 12 \text{ m}$

Then by Pythagoras theorem:

$AE^2 = AB^2 + BE^2 \Rightarrow AE = 13 \text{ m}$

7. (a)

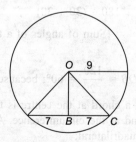

In the $\Delta OBC$; $BC = 7$ cm and $OC = 9$ cm, then using Pythagoras theorem.

$OB^2 = OC^2 - BC^2$

$OB = \sqrt{32} = 5.66 \text{ cm (approx)}$

8. (d)

In the $\Delta OBC$, $OB = 12$ cm, $OC = $ radius $= 13$ cm. Then using Pythagoras theorem;

$BC^2 = OC^2 - OB^2 = 25; BC = 5 \text{ cm}$

Length of the chord $= 2 \times BC = 2 \times 5 = 10 \text{ cm}$

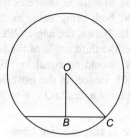

9. (a)

$\angle x = 35°$; because angles subtended by an arc, anywhere on the circumference are equal.

10. (d)

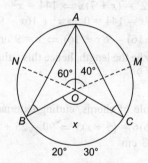

$\angle AOM = 2\angle ABM$ and

$\angle AON = 2\angle ACN$

because angle subtended by an arc at the centre of the circle is twice the angle subtended by it on the circumference on the same segment.

$\angle AON = 60°$ and $\angle AOM = 40°$

$\angle X = \angle AON + \angle AOM$

(∵ vertically opposite angles).

$\angle X = 100°$

Alternately, you could also solve this using the following process:

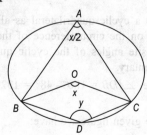

In the given figure, join the points $BD$ and $CD$. Then, in the cyclic quadrilateral ABDC, the sum of angles $x/2$ and y would be 180°. Hence, $y = 180 - x/2$. Also, the sum of the angles $OBD + OCD = 180 - 20 - 30$ = 130°. Therefore, $x + y = 230$ (as the sum of the angles of the quadrilateral OBDC is 360). Solving, the two equations, we get $x = 100$.

11. (d)

The triangle $BOC$ is an isosceles triangle with sides $OB$ and $OC$ both being equal as they are the radii of the circle. Hence, the angle $OBC$ = angle $OCB$ = 30°. Hence, the third angle of the triangle $BOC$ viz: Angle $BOC$ would be equal to 120°. Also, $BOC$ = $AOD$ = 120°. Hence, in the isosceles triangle $DOA$, Angle $ODA$ = Angle $DAO$ = $x$ = 30°.

12. (a)

By the rule of tangents, we know:

$6^2 = (5 + x)5 \Rightarrow 36 = 25 + 5x \Rightarrow 11 = 5x \Rightarrow x = 2.2$ cm

13. (b)

By the rule of tangents, we get

$12^2 = (x + 7)x \Rightarrow 144 = x^2 + 7x$
$\Rightarrow x^2 + 7x - 144 = 0 \Rightarrow x^2 + 16x - 9x - 144 = 0$
$\Rightarrow x(x + 16) - 9(x + 16) \Rightarrow x = 9$ or $-16$

−16 can't be the length, hence this value is discarded, thus, $x = 9$

14. (a)

By the rule of chords, cutting externally, we get

$\Rightarrow (9 + 6)6 = (5 + x)5 \Rightarrow 90 = 25 + 5x \Rightarrow 5x = 65$
$\Rightarrow x = 13$ cm

15. (b)

Use the formula: Inradius = Area/ Semi perimeter = 24/12 = 2 cm

16. (b)

$\angle APB$ = 90° (angle in a semicircle = 90°)
$\angle PBA$ = 180 − (90 + 25) = 65°
$\angle TPA$ = $\angle PBA$(the angle that a chord makes with the tangent, is subtended by the chord on the circumference in the alternate segment).
= 65°

Note: This is also called as the Alternate Segment Theorem.

17. (a)

$ADBC$ is a cyclic quadrilateral as all its four vertices are on the circumference of the circle. Also, the opposite angles of the cyclic quadrilateral are supplementary.

Therefore, $\angle ADB = 180 - 48° = 132°$

18. (a)

From the given figure we have:

$4b + 2c = 180$          (1)
$a + b = 105$          (2)
$4b = a$          (3)

Solving these equations, we get that $b = 21°$; $a = 84°$; $c = 48°$.

19. (b)

$\angle ABC = 180° - 130° = 50°$
        (∴ sum of angles on a line = 180°)
$\angle ADC = 180° - \angle ABC = 130°$
        (∵ opposite angles of a cyclic quadrilateral are supplementary).
$\angle x = 180° - 130° = 50°$
        (∴ sum of angles on a line = 180°)

20. (a)

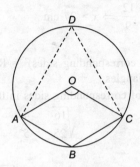

$\angle ADC = \dfrac{140}{2} = 70°$ (because the angle subtended by an arc on the circumference is half of what it subtends at the centre). $ABCD$ one cyclic quadrilateral So $\angle ABC = 180° - 70° = 110°$ (because opposite angles of a cyclic quadrilateral are supplementary).

21. (b)

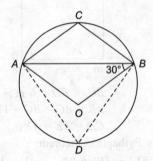

$OB$ = $OA$ = radius of the circle
$\angle AOB$ = 180 − (30 + 30)
        {Sum of angles of a triangle = 180°}
$\Rightarrow 120°$

Then $\angle ADB = \dfrac{120}{2} = 60°$; because the angle subtended by a chord at the centre is twice of what it can subtend at the circumference. Again, $ABCD$ is a cyclic quadrilateral;

So $\angle ACB = 180° - 60° = 120°$ (because opposite angles of cyclic quadrilateral are supplementary).

22. (a)

$\angle BAC = 30°$ (∵ angles subtended by an arc anywhere on the circumference in the same segment are equal).

In $\Delta BAC$; $\angle x = 180° - (110° + 30°) = 40°$

(∵ sum of angles of a triangle = 180°)

23. (d)

As $L_4$ and $L_3$ are not parallel lines, so there can't be any relation between 80° and x°.

Hence the answer cannot be determined.

24. (d)

Perimeter of the figure = $10 + 10 + 6 + 6\pi = 26 + 6\pi$

25. (b)

Since the lines AB and CD are parallel to each other, and the lines RD and AN are parallel, it means that the triangles RBF and NCI are similar to each other. Since the ratio of CN:BR = 1.333, if we take BR as 3, we will get CN as 4. This means that the ratio of BF:CI would also be 3:4. Also, the ratio of BR: RS:ST:TA = BF:FG:GH:HI = 3:5:2:7 (given). Hence, the correct answer is 3:5:2:7:4.

26 $\angle BXC = 90° + \frac{1}{2} \angle A$ (Using the logic that the angle bisectors of two angles of *a* triangle form an angle that is equal to $90^0$ + half the value of the third angle of the triangle).

$$= 90^o + \frac{1}{2} \times 60^o = 90^o + 30^o = 120^o$$

27. $PR = \sqrt{PQ^2 + QR^2}$ (Using Pythagoras Theorem)

$$= \sqrt{15^2 + 20^2} = \sqrt{625} = 25 \text{ cm}$$

$$SR = \frac{QR^2}{PR} = \frac{20^2}{25} = 16 \text{ cm}$$

(Property of a right-angled triangle)

28. $\frac{1}{SQ^2} = \frac{1}{PQ^2} + \frac{1}{QR^2}$ (Property of *a* right-angled triangle)

$$\frac{1}{SQ^2} = \frac{1}{15^2} + \frac{1}{20^2}$$

$$SQ^2 = \frac{20^2 \times 15^2}{20^2 + 15^2} \rightarrow SQ = \frac{20 \times 15}{25} = 12 \, cm$$

29. $\Delta ABD \sim \Delta ACB$

$$\frac{\text{area of } \Delta ABC}{\text{area of } \Delta ADB} = \frac{AC^2}{AB^2} = \left(\frac{5}{3}\right)^2 = \frac{25}{9}$$

(Using the property that in similar figures, area ratios are squared of the side ratios)

Area of $\Delta ABC = 90 \times \frac{25}{9} = 250 \text{ cm}^2$

30. Inradius of an equilateral triangle = $\frac{side}{2\sqrt{3}}$ (Formula for inradius)

Side = $2\sqrt{3} \times \sqrt{3} = 6cm$

Required area = $\frac{\sqrt{3}}{4} \times 6^2 = 9\sqrt{3} cm^2$ (Using the formula that the area of an equilateral triangle of side a is given by the formula: $\frac{\sqrt{3}}{4} \times a^2$.

31. Inradius of $\Delta ABC = \frac{(AB + BC) - AC}{2} = \frac{20}{2} = 10cm$

(Formula for inradius)

Semiperimeter = $s = \frac{60}{2} = 30cm$

$r = \frac{\text{Area}}{s}$

Area = $r \times s$ (Formula for area of any triangle using the semi-perimeter and inradius).

$= 10 \times 30 = 300 \text{ cm}^2$

32. 3 × (Sum of squares of the sides of a triangle) = 4 × (Sum of squares of the medians of the triangle).

$$\frac{3}{4}\left(6^2 + 7^2 + 8^2\right) = \text{Sum of square of medians}$$

$$= \frac{3}{4}[149] = 111.75 cm^2$$

33. In $\Delta QTR$: $\angle TOR = 180° - (90° + 30°) = 180° - 120° = 60°$ (Angles of a triangle add up to 180)

In $\Delta QPS$: $\angle PSQ = 180^o - (60^o + 40^o) = 80^o$

34. According to the Alternate Segment Theorem:

$\angle SRQ = = \angle STR = 60°$

☐ *TSUR* is a cyclic quadrilateral. Therefore $\angle STR + \angle SUR = 180°$

$\angle SUR = 180° - 60° = 120°$

35. $AR^2 = AQ^2 + RQ^2$ (Using Pythagoras Theorem)

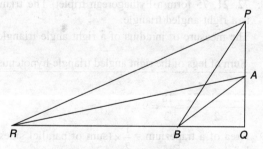

$PB^2 = PQ^2 + BQ^2$ (Pythagoras Theorem)

$AR^2 + PB^2 = (PQ^2 + RQ^2) + (AQ^2 + BQ^2)$

$= PR^2 + AB^2$

36. $AB \parallel CD$ therefore $\Delta ABF$ and $\Delta CDF$ are similar to each other

$$\frac{DF}{BF} = \frac{b}{a} \qquad \qquad \text{(i)}$$

Similarly $\Delta BCD$ and $\Delta BEF$ are similar each other:

$\dfrac{BD}{BF} = \dfrac{b}{c}$           (ii)

By adding (i) and (ii), we get

$\dfrac{BD}{BF} + \dfrac{DF}{BF} = \dfrac{b}{a} + \dfrac{b}{c}$

$\dfrac{BF}{BF} = \dfrac{b}{a} + \dfrac{b}{c} = 1$

$\dfrac{1}{b} = \dfrac{1}{a} + \dfrac{1}{c}$

$\dfrac{1}{b} - \dfrac{1}{a} = \dfrac{1}{c}$

37. $PR = PS$

$\angle PRS = \angle PSR$ (Angles opposite equal sides are equal in an isosceles triangle).

$\angle PRS = x$

Let $\angle RPQ = y$

$PR = QR$

$\angle RPQ = \angle PQR = y$(Angles opposite equal sides are equal in an isosceles triangle).

$\angle PRQ = 180° - 2y = 180° - x$

$x = 2y$ or $y = \dfrac{x}{2}$

$\angle RPS = 180° - 2x$

$\angle QPR + \angle RPS + 90° = 180°$

$\dfrac{x}{2} + 180° - 2x + 90° = 180°$

$90° = \dfrac{3x}{2}$

$x = 60°$

38. 72, 21, 75 form a Pythagorean triplet. The triangle is a right-angled triangle.

The measure of inradius of a right angle triangle =

$$\dfrac{\text{Sum of legs of the right angled triangle-hypotenuse}}{2}$$

$\dfrac{72 + 21 - 75}{2} = \dfrac{18}{2} = 9$

39. Area of a trapezium $= \dfrac{1}{2} \times$ (sum of parallel sides) $\times$ height

$28 = \dfrac{1}{2}(6 + 8)AB$

$AB = 4$ cm

40.

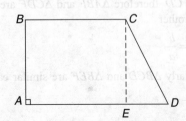

Draw $CE \perp AD$

$DE = 8 - 6 = 2$ cm

$CE = AB = 4$ cm

$CD = \sqrt{(4)^2 + (2)^2} = \sqrt{20}$ cm (Using Pythagoras theorem).

41. If $BP = x$, $CR = y$ then $PQ = BP = x$, $RC = QR = y($ The two tangents to a circle from an external point are equal in length)

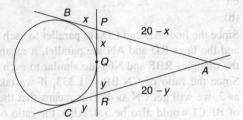

Perimeter of $\triangle APR = AP + PR + AR$

$= 20 - x + x + y + 20 - y$

$= 40$ units

42. $BD$ is the median of the triangle $ABC$ and $AD = DC = BD$ therefore $\triangle ABC$ is a right-angled triangle. Option ($a$) is correct.

43. $\triangle ABC$ is a right angled isosceles triangle

$\therefore AB = BC$ and $\angle A = \angle C = 45°$

$\therefore DB = DC$

$\therefore \angle DBC = \angle DCB$

$\angle DBC = 45°$

$\angle BDC = 180° - (45° + 45°) = 90°$

44. $\angle ADC = \angle ABD + \angle BAD$ (Using the property that the exterior angle is equal to opposite interior angles on the triangle $ABD$).

$2\angle ABD = \angle ABD + \angle BAD$

Hence, $\angle BAD = \angle ABD$

Let $\angle ABD = \angle BAD = \angle ACB = x$ (Note: $\angle ACB$ and $\angle ABC$ are equal as the triangle $ABC$ is an isosceles triangle).

Then in $\triangle ABC \Rightarrow 30° + x + x + x = 180°$

$3x = 150°$

$x = 50° = \angle BAD$

45. $\angle AOB = 120°$

$\angle AOP = \dfrac{120°}{2} = 60°$

In $\triangle AOP$: $\angle AOP + 90° + \angle OAP = 180°$

$\angle OAP = 180° - (90° + 60°) = 30°$

46. $\dfrac{(2n - 4)90°}{n} = 120°$ (Formula for interior angle of a regular polygon).

$\dfrac{n - 2}{n} = \dfrac{120°}{180°} = \dfrac{2}{3}$

$3n - 6 = 2n$

$n = 6$

Number of diagonals = $^6C_2 - 6 = 9$ (Number of diagonals of any $n$ sided polygon is given by the formula $^nC_2 - n$)

47. Let the number of sides of the polygons be $2n$ and $n$ respectively.

As per the question:

$18 = \dfrac{2n-2}{2n} \times 180° - \dfrac{n-2}{n} \times 180°$ (Formula for interior angle of a regular polygon applied to both the polygons).

$18 = \left[ \dfrac{n-1}{n} - \dfrac{n-2}{n} \right] 180°$

$18 = \dfrac{1}{n} \times 180°$

$\Rightarrow n = 10$ or $2n = 20$.

48. Let the number of sides in the polygon be n as per the question:

$(n-2)180° = 40\left( 180° - \left[ \dfrac{n-2}{n} \right] 180° \right)$

$(n-2)180° = 40\left\{ \dfrac{n-n+2}{n} \right\} 180°$

$\dfrac{2}{n} = \dfrac{(n-2)}{40}$

$n = 10$

49. $\angle ABC = \dfrac{\angle AOC}{2} = \dfrac{140°}{2} = 70°$ (Using the logic that the angle subtended by an arc at the center of a circle is twice the angle subtended by the same arc at any point on the circle).

$AB = BC$

$\angle BAC = \angle BCA$

$2\angle BCA + \angle ABC = 180°$

$2\angle BCA = 180° - \angle ABC = 180° - 70° = 110°$

$\angle BCA = \dfrac{110°}{2} = 55°$

50. $\angle QOR = 180° - \angle POQ = 180° - 80° = 100°$

$\angle QSR = \dfrac{\angle QOR}{2} = 50°$ (Using the logic that the angle subtended by an arc at the center of a circle is twice the angle subtended by the same arc at any point on the circle).

51. $OE = OB$ = radius of the circle.

$\angle OEB = \angle OBE$ (Angles opposite equal sides of an isosceles triangle are equal).

In $\triangle OEB: \angle OEB + \angle OBE + \angle BOE = 180°$

$2\angle OEB + \angle BOE = 180°$

$\angle BOE = 180° - 2\angle OEB = 180° - 2 \times 70°$

$= 40°$

52. In $\triangle OBA \Rightarrow \angle BAO + 90° + \angle AOB = 180°$

$\angle BAO = 180° - (90° + \angle AOB)$

$= 180° - (90° + 40°)$ (Since we have already found the angle $AOB$ as $40°$ in the previous question) $= 50°$

53. In $\triangle ACD : AC = AD$

$\angle ACD = \angle ADC = 30°$ (Angles opposite equal sides on an isosceles triangle are equal).

$\angle CAD = 180° - (\angle ACD + \angle ADC)$

$= 180° - (30° + 30°) = 120°$

54. In $\triangle ABC$ & $\triangle ABD$

$\angle ACB = \angle ADB$

$\angle ABC = \angle ABD = 90°$

$AC = AD$

$\triangle ABC \cong \triangle ABD$

$\therefore BC = BD$

$\therefore CD = 4$ cm

In $\triangle CAD = \dfrac{CD}{\sin 120°} = \dfrac{AD}{\sin 30°}$ (Using the Sine Rule and values of Sin 30 = 1/2 and value of Sin 120 = $\dfrac{\sqrt{3}}{2}$)

$AD = \dfrac{4}{\sqrt{3}} \times 2 \times \dfrac{1}{2} = \dfrac{4}{\sqrt{3}}\, cm$

55. $OS = OQ$

$\angle OSQ = \angle OQS = 50°$

$\angle SOQ = 180° - 100° = 80°$ (Angles of a triangle add up to 180)

In $\triangle OSP$:

$80° + 90° + \angle SPR = 180°$ (Angles of a triangle add up to 180)

$\angle SPR = 180° - (80° + 90°) = 10°$

56. Lines joining midpoint of a quadrilateral form a parallelogram.

57. Diagonals of trapezium intersect each other proportionally in the ratio of length of parallel sides. Therefore.

$\dfrac{AB}{CD} = \dfrac{OB}{OD}$

$OD = \dfrac{OB \times CD}{AB} = \dfrac{5 \times 6}{4} = 7.5 cm$

Length of diagonal $BD = 5 + 7.5 = 12.5$ cm

58. Using the Sine rule we get: $\dfrac{QR}{\sin 45°} = \dfrac{SR}{\sin 60°}$

$QR = 4\sqrt{6} \times \dfrac{1}{\sqrt{2}} \times \dfrac{2}{\sqrt{3}}$

$QR = 8$ cm

59. If a trapezium is inscribed in a circle then it is an isosceles trapezium with equal oblique sides.

$PS = QR = 8$ cm
$PS + QR = 8 + 8 = 16$ cm.

60.

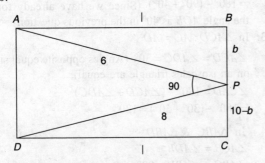

In $\triangle APD$: $AP = \sqrt{10^2 - 8^2} = \sqrt{36} = 6$

Let $AB = l$, $BP = b$

Now using the Pythagoras theorem on the triangles $ABP$ and $PCD$ we get two equations between $l$ and $b$ as follows:

In $\triangle ABP$: $l^2 + b^2 = 6^2$       (i)

In $\triangle PCD$: $l^2 + (10-b)^2 = 8^2$     (ii)

From equation (ii) - (i), we get

$-b^2 + (10-b)^2 = -6^2 + 8^2$

$100 - 20b = 28$

$b = 3.6$

61.

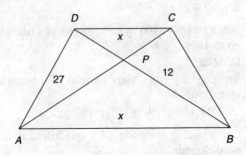

Let the area of $\triangle ABP$ and $\triangle DPC$ is $x$

$27 \times 12 = x \times x$

$x^2 = 27 \times 12$

$x = 18$.

62.

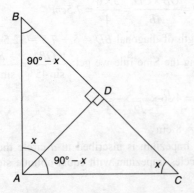

All the corresponding angles of $\triangle ABD$ and in $\triangle CAD$ are equal, so $\triangle ABD$ & $\triangle CAD$ are similar to each other.

So 1$^{st}$ statement is correct.

$\triangle ADB \sim \triangle CDA$. But it is not necessary that both triangles are congruent.

So statement (2) is incorrect.

In $\triangle ADB$ and $\triangle CAB$:

$\angle BAC = \angle ADB$

$\angle ABC = \angle ABD$

$\angle BCA = \angle BAD$

So $\triangle ADB \sim \triangle CAB$

So statement 3 is also correct. Hence option (b) is correct.

63.

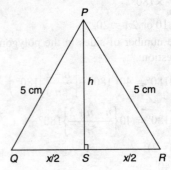

Area of $\triangle PQR = \frac{1}{2} \times x \times h = 12$ cm$^2$

$xh = 24 cm^2$

Also in the right angle $\triangle PQS$,

$(5)^2 = \left(\frac{x}{2}\right)^2 + h^2$

$x^2 + 4h^2 = 100$

$x^2 + 4\left(\frac{24}{x}\right)^2 = 100$

The above equation is satisfied only for $x = 6$. So option (b) is correct.

64. Let the radius of the circle be '$l$'.

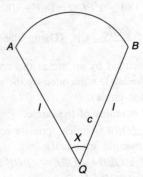

Length of arc = $\acute{l}x$

Area of the sector = $\frac{x}{2\pi} \times \pi l^2 = \frac{xl^2}{2}$

According to the question: $\frac{xl^2}{2} = (lx)^2$ or $x = 0.5$.

65. By applying cosine formula in $\triangle ABC$ we get:

$$cos\theta = \frac{a^2 + b^2 - c^2}{2ab} \text{ or } a^2 + b^2 - 2abcos\theta = c^2$$

66. Here $PQ$ is the chord. Height of chord = $RS$ = 21 cm

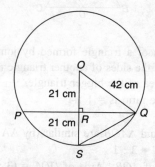

Here we need to find the length of chord $(QS)$ of half *arc QS*.

$RO = 42 - 21 = 21$ cm.

In $\triangle ORQ$ & $\triangle SRQ$ : $OR = RS$, $QR = QR$, $\angle ORQ = \angle SRQ = 90^0$

So both the triangles are congruent.

So $OQ = SQ = 42$ cm.

67. Let the other sides of the right angle triangle be $x$ and $y$ respectively.

Then according to the question: $\sqrt{x^2 + y^2} = 97$, $x + y = 234 - 97 = 137$

Now by checking the options we can see that only option $(b)$ satisfies both the equations.

So option $(b)$ is correct.

68. Let the base of the ladder is drawn out by $x$ feet.

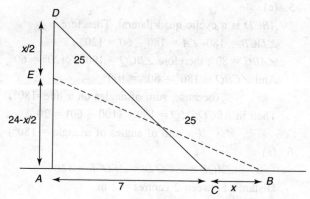

In $\triangle EAB : \left(24 - \frac{x}{2}\right)^2 + (7+x)^2 = 25^2$ (Using the Pythagoras theorem).

By solving the above quadratic equation we get $x = 0, 8$. So option $(d)$ is correct.

69. $TQ \times TP = TR \times TS$

$8 \times 18 = TR (TR + 7)$

$TR = 9$ units

Area of the $\triangle PTS = \frac{1}{2} \times 16 \times 18 \times sin 60^0 = 72\sqrt{3}$ sq. units

70.

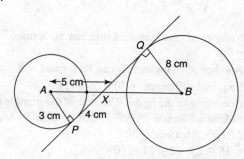

Let $A$ and $B$ are centers of circles. $PX = \sqrt{5^2 - 3^2} = 4$ cm

$\triangle APX$ and $\triangle BQX$ are similar to each other as their three angles are equal.

$$\frac{AP}{BQ} = \frac{PX}{QX}$$

$QX = 8 \times \frac{4}{3} = 10.66$ cm

$PQ = PX + XQ = 4 + 10.66 = 14.66$ cm

71. In $a$ triangle the sum of any two sides > 3$^{rd}$ side.

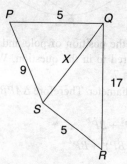

In $\triangle PQS$ $5 + 9 > x$ ; $x < 14$

In $\triangle RQS$ $x + 5 > 17$ ; $x > 12$

$14 > x > 12$

72.

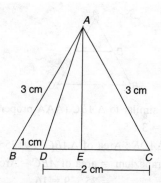

Draw $AE \perp BC$. Since $ABC$ is an equilateral triangle so $AE$ will bisect $BC$.

$DE = DC - EC = 2 - 3/2 = \frac{1}{2}$ cm

$AE = \sqrt{3^2 - 1.5^2} = \frac{3}{2}\sqrt{3}$ cm

$AD = \sqrt{\left(\frac{3}{2}\sqrt{3}\right)^2 + \left(\frac{1}{2}\right)^2} = \sqrt{7}$ cm

73. Number of quadrilaterals that can be formed = $^8C_4$ = 70
    Number of triangles that can be formed = $^8C_3$ = 56.
    Required difference = 70 − 56 = 14

74. According to the figure, The area of the triangle $QAB$ = Area of Square $PQRS$ − Area of $\triangle ABS$ − Area of $\triangle PAQ$ − Area of $\triangle QBR$
    = 36 − 2 − 12 − 12 = 10

75.

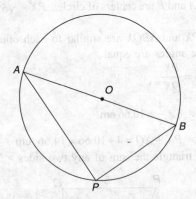

Let '$p$' be the position of pole and $A$ and $B$ are the gates referred to in the question. We are given that
$AP - BP = 7$
$AB$ is the diameter. Therefore $\triangle APB$ is a right angled triangle:
$AB^2 = AP^2 + BP^2$
$13^2 = (7 + BP)^2 + BP^2$

By solving we get $BP = 5$ m and $AP = 12$ m
Required shortest distance = 5 m.

**Level of Difficulty (II)**

1. (b)

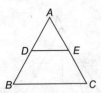

   $\triangle ADE$ is similar to $\triangle ABC$ (AAA property)
   $ED : BC = 3 : 5$
   Area of $\triangle ADE$ : Area of $\triangle ABC$ = 9 : 25
   Area of trapezium = area of $ABC$ − Area of $ADE$
   = 25 − 9 = 16

Thus,
Area of $\triangle ADE$ : Area of trapezium $EDBC$ = 9 : 16

2. (a)

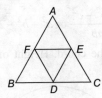

The area of a triangle formed by joining the mid-points of the sides of another triangle is always $1/4$th of the area of the bigger triangle.
   So, the ratio is = 1 : 4

3. (a)
   $\triangle DOC$ and $\triangle AOB$ are similar (by AAA property)
   $AB : DC = 3 : 1$
   So area of $AOB$ : Area of $DOC$ = $(3 : 1)^2 \Rightarrow 9 : 1$

4. (a)

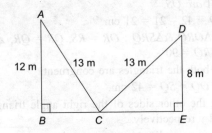

In $\triangle ABC$; $BC = \sqrt{13^2 - 12^2} = 5$

In $\triangle CDE$; $CE = \sqrt{13^2 - 8^2} = \sqrt{105} = 10.2$ approximately

Width of street = $BC + CE$ = 5 + 10.2 = 15.2 m

5. (c)
   $ABCD$ is a cyclic quadrilateral. Therefore
   $\angle DCB = 180 - \angle A = 180 - 60 = 120°$
   $\angle ABC = 80°$; therefore $\angle BCQ = 180° - 120° = 60°$
   And $\angle CBQ = 180° - 80° = 100°$
       (because, sum of angles on a line = 180°)
   Then in $\triangle BCQ$; $\angle Q = 180 - (100 + 60) = 20$
       (∵ sum of angles of triangle = 180°)

6. (a)
   $\angle AOB = \angle CO'D = \angle FO''E = 120°$
   Distance between 2 centres = 2 m
   ∴      $BC = DE = FA = 2$ m
   Perimeter of the figure = $BC + DE + FA$ + circumference of sectors $AOB$, $CO'B$ and $FO''E$.
       But three equal sectors of 120° = 1 full circle of same radius.

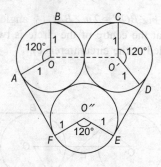

Therefore, perimeter of surface
$$= 2\pi r + BC + DE + FA = (2\pi + 6)\,m$$

**7. (a)**

In $\triangle QRS$; $QR = RS$, therefore $\angle RQS = \angle RSQ$
(because angles opposite to equal sides are equal).

Thus $\quad \angle RQS + \angle RSQ = 180° - 100° = 80°$

$\therefore \qquad \angle RQS = \angle RSQ = 40°$

$\qquad\qquad \angle PQS = 180° - 40° = 140°$

$\qquad$ (sum of angles on a line = 180°)

Then again $\angle QPS = \angle QSP$

$\qquad$ (∵ angles opposite to equal sides are equal)

Thus $\quad \angle QPS + \angle QSP = 180° - 140° = 40°$

And $\qquad \angle QPS = \angle QSP = 20°$

**8. (b)**

$\qquad\qquad \angle BOC = 136°$

$\angle BAC = \dfrac{136}{2} = 68°$ (because angle subtended by an arc anywhere on the circumference is half of the angle it subtends at the centre).

$\angle BDC = 180° - 68° = 112°$ (∵ $ABCD$ is a cyclic quadrilateral and its opposite angles are supplementary)

**9. (a)**

$\triangle DOA$ and $\triangle BOC$ are similar(AAA property)

Then $\dfrac{3}{x-3} = \dfrac{x-5}{3x-19}$

On solving this equation we get $x = 8$ or 9.

**10. (b)**

$\triangle AOD$ and $\triangle BOC$ are similar (AAA property)

$\dfrac{AO}{OC} = \dfrac{1}{2}$; therefore $\dfrac{AD}{BC} = \dfrac{1}{2} \Rightarrow \dfrac{4}{BC} = \dfrac{1}{2}$

$\Rightarrow \qquad BC = 8$ cm

**11. (b)**

$\triangle ABD$ and $\triangle ACD$ are similar(AAA property)

Then $\dfrac{AB}{BD} = \dfrac{AC}{CD} \rightarrow \dfrac{6}{3} = \dfrac{5}{CD} \rightarrow CD = 2.5$

On solving this equation we get $x = 8$ or 9.

**12. (a)**

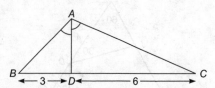

As $AD$ bisects $\angle CAB$, so $\triangle ABD$ is similar to $\triangle ACD$

Then $\dfrac{AB}{DB} = \dfrac{AC}{DC} \Rightarrow \dfrac{8}{6} = \dfrac{AC}{3} \Rightarrow AC = 4$ cm

**13. (a)**

Assume the radius of the inner smaller circle to be '$r$' and that of the outer quarter circle to be $R$. Then, we have from the solution figure, we know that $BO = R - r$ and $BD = OD = r$:

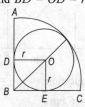

$(R-r)^2 = r^2 + r^2$ (Using Pythagoras theorem)

But we are given that R=1; hence we get:

$1 - 2r + r^2 = 2r^2$ or

$r^2 + 2r - 1 = 0$

Solving this quadratic equation, we get the solution for r = $(\sqrt{2}+1)$ or $(\sqrt{2}-1)$ cm

However, r cannot be greater than R and hence cannot exceed a value of 1 cm. Hence, we would reject the first value of $(\sqrt{2}+1)$ for r and select r = $(\sqrt{2}-1)$.

Option (a) is correct.

**14. (c)**

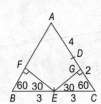

In the given figure, we can see that Per ($E$) would be the sum of $EF + EG$.

We have assumed the equilateral triangle to have a side of 6. Then, the triangles $EBF$ and $ECG$ are 30-60-90 triangles. Hence, if $EC = 3 = EB = 3$, then $EF = EG = 1.5\sqrt{3}$. Hence, the value of Per ($E$) = $3\sqrt{3}$. Similarly, if you draw the perpendiculars from the point $D$ to the sides $BC$ and $AB$, you would get the length of these perpendiculars as $DH + DJ = \sqrt{3} + 2\sqrt{3} = 3\sqrt{3}$. (Using 30-60-90 triangles). This can be seen from the given figure in triangles $JDA$ and $CHD$.

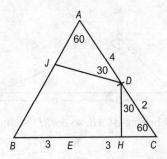

Hence, Per (D) = Per (E). Option (c) is correct.

15. (b)

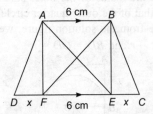

In the above question:

$$FE = AB = 6 \text{ cm}$$

$$\Delta ADF \cong \Delta BEC; \text{ so } DF = EC$$

Let $DF = EC = x$

Solving through options; e.g. option (b) 1/3; $x = 6$

Then by Pythagoras triplet $AF = 8$

Area of $ABEF = 8 \times 6 = 48 \text{ cm}^2$

Area of $\Delta AFD + \Delta BEC = 2 \times \dfrac{1}{2} \times 6 \times 8 \Rightarrow 48 \text{ cm}^2$

$\therefore$ Area of $ABCD = 48 + 48 = 96 \text{ cm}^2$. Hence the condition is proved.

16. (a)

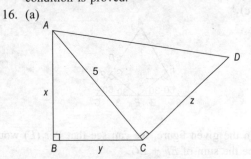

It is pretty obvious that the only values of x,y and z that satisfy the given situation are 3,4 and 12 respectively (Think in terms of Pythagoras triplets). The required area then is $A\Delta ABC + A\Delta ACD = 6 + 30 = 36 \text{ cm}^2$.

17. (d)

As the point 'O' is formed by the $\perp$ bisects to the three sides of the $\Delta$, so point 'O' is the circumcenter. This means that virtually, points A, B and C are on the circumference of the circumcircle.

Thus $m\angle BOC = 2m\angle BAC$ ($\because$ angle subtended by an arc at the centre of the circle is twice the angle subtended at the circumference).

18. (c)

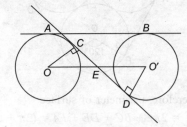

$$OC = O'D = 5 \text{ cm (radius)}$$

$$CD = 24 \text{ cm}$$

$\Delta COE$ and $\Delta EO'D$ are similar therefore $OE = O'E$ and $CE = ED = 12 \text{ cm}$

In $\Delta COE$; $OE^2 = CE^2 + OC^2$

$$= 12^2 + 5^2 = 169$$

$$OE = 13$$

$\therefore \quad OO' = OE + EO' = 13 + 13 = 26 \text{ cm}$

19. (c)

Since, we are given a measure of a 19° angle, if we use the measure 19 times, we would be able to measure 361° and hence, we can measure 361 – 360= 1°. Hence, it would be possible to divide the circle into 360 equal parts.

20. (d)

Area of the shaded portion = Area of circle – Area of triangle

$$\Rightarrow \text{ Area of circle} = \pi r^2 \Rightarrow \dfrac{22}{7} \times 5 \times 5 \Rightarrow \dfrac{22 \times 25}{7} \text{ cm}^2$$

$$= 78.57 \text{ cm}^2$$

Area of triangle $\Rightarrow \dfrac{1}{2} r^2 \sin\theta \Rightarrow \dfrac{1}{2} \times 25 \times \sin\theta$

$$\Rightarrow \dfrac{25\sqrt{3}}{4} \Rightarrow 6.25 \times 1.732 \Rightarrow 10.8$$

$\therefore$ Area of shaded portion = 78.57 – 10.8 = 67.77 cm²

21. (a)

$OB = OA = $ Radius of the circle

$\Rightarrow \quad \angle CAO = \angle OBA$

(angles in alternate segments are equal).

Now, if $\quad \angle CAO = \angle OBA$

$\therefore \qquad \angle CAO = \angle OAB$

$\therefore$ option (a) is correct.

22. (b)

23. (a)

Angle $XPA$ = angle $ABP$ = $x$

Angle $CPX$ = angle $CDP$ = $x + y$

Anlge $CDP$ is exterior angle of triangle $PDB$

So angle $CDP = DBP + DPB$

$$x + y = x + DPB$$

$$DPB = y$$

So angle $CPA = DPB$

24. (b)

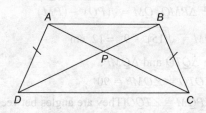

$$\Delta APD \sim \Delta CPB$$

$$\therefore \qquad \frac{PA}{PB} = \frac{PD}{PC}$$

i.e. $PA \cdot PC = PB \cdot PD$.

$\therefore$ option (b)

25. (d)

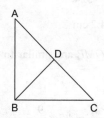

$$AC \cdot AD = AB^2$$

$$AC \cdot AD = BC^2$$

$$\Delta ABC \approx \Delta ADB$$

$$\therefore \quad \frac{AC}{AB} = \frac{AB}{AD}$$

(Corresponding sides of similar triangle are proportional)

$$AC \cdot AD = AB^2 \qquad \text{(i)}$$

Also, $\Delta ABC \, N \, \Delta BDC \Rightarrow \dfrac{AC}{BC} = \dfrac{BC}{CD}$

$$AC \cdot CD = BC^2 \qquad \text{(ii)}$$

Both conditions of option (d) are found, therefore (d) is the answer.

26.

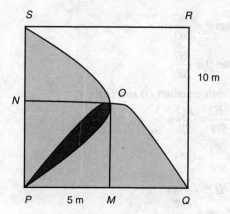

Let PQRS be the square grazing field and M, N are the points at which cows are tethered.

Area grazed by both cows = [Area of quadrant POM + Area of quadrant NOP] – [Area of square PMON]

$$= \frac{\pi}{4}(5)^2 \times 2 - 5 \times 5$$

$$= \frac{50}{4} \times \pi - 25$$

$$= \frac{25\pi}{2} - 25$$

$$= \frac{25\pi - 50}{2}$$

$$= \frac{25}{2}[\pi - 2] = 12.5(\pi - 2)\text{m}^2$$

27. Area of grazed region = Area of OMPN + Area of OMQ + Area of OSN

$$= 5^2 + \frac{\pi}{4}(5)^2 \times 2$$

$$= 25 + \frac{25\pi}{2} = \frac{25}{2}[\pi + 2] = 12.5(\pi + 2)$$

Area of non-grazed region = $10 \times 10 - 12.5\pi - 25$
$= 75 - 12.5\pi$ m²

28.

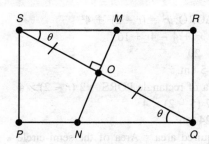

$$SQ = \sqrt{3^2 + 4^2} = \sqrt{25} = 5\text{cm}$$

$$SO = OQ = 2.5\text{cm}$$

If $\angle RSQ = \theta$

$\tan \theta = \dfrac{MO}{SO}$          (i)

$\tan \theta = \dfrac{RQ}{SR}$          (ii)

From equation (i) and (ii)

$\dfrac{MO}{SO} = \dfrac{RQ}{SR} = \dfrac{3}{4}$

$\dfrac{MO}{SO} = 0.75$

29. $OQ = 2.5$cm

$\tan \theta = \dfrac{ON}{OQ}$

$ON = OQ \tan\theta$

Area of $\Delta QNO = \dfrac{1}{2} \times OQ \times ON = \dfrac{1}{2} \times OQ \times OQ \tan\theta$

$= \dfrac{1}{2}(OQ)^2 \tan\theta$

$= \dfrac{1}{2} \times \left(\dfrac{5}{2}\right)^2 \times \dfrac{3}{4} = \dfrac{75}{32}$

Area of $\square$ SONP $= \dfrac{1}{2} \times 4 \times 3 - \dfrac{75}{32}$

$= 6 - \dfrac{75}{32}$

$= \dfrac{192 - 75}{32}$

$= \dfrac{117}{32} \text{ cm}^2 = 3.65 \text{ cm}^2$

30. Let 'r' be the radius of the semicircle.

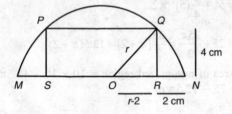

In $\Delta ORQ$: $r^2 = (r - 2)^2 + 4^2$

$r^2 = r^2 + 4 - 4r + 16$

$4r = 20$

$r = 5$ cm.

Area of rectangle PQRS $= 2 (r - 2) \times 4$

$= 2 (5 - 2) \times 4$

$= 24 \text{ cm}^2$

Required area = Area of the semi-circle − Area of

rectangle PQRS $= \dfrac{\pi}{2}(5)^2 - 24$

$= (12.5\pi - 24) \text{ cm}^2$

31. $\dfrac{\text{Area of } \Delta SNO}{\text{Area of } \Delta RNO} = \dfrac{20}{b} = \dfrac{SN}{NR} = 1.25$

$b = \dfrac{20}{1.25} = 16$

Area of $\Delta POS \times$ Area of $\Delta QOR =$ Area of $\Delta POQ \times$ Area of $\Delta SOR$ {Property of the diagonals of a quadrilateral]

$30 \times a = 30 \times 36$

$a = 36$

$a + b = 36 + 16 = 52$

32. In $\Delta PMQ : QM = \sqrt{(PQ)^2 - (PM)^2}$

$QM = \sqrt{(15)^2 - 9^2} = 12$ cm

In $\Delta QTO$ and $\Delta QMP$:

$\angle QTO = \angle QMP = 90°$

$\angle PQM = \angle TQO$[They are angles between the same lines]

Hence, $\Delta QTO \sim \Delta QMP$

$\dfrac{QT}{QO} = \dfrac{QM}{QP} = \dfrac{12}{15} = \dfrac{4}{5} = 0.8$

33. $TR^2 = QR^2 - QT^2 = PR^2 - PT^2$

$15^2 - QT^2 = 18^2 - (15 - QT)^2$

$15^2 - QT^2 = 18^2 - 15^2 - QT^2 + 30QT$

$30QT = 450 - 324$

$QT = \dfrac{126}{30} = 4.2$ cm

$\Delta QTO$ and $\Delta QMP$ are similar to each other then:

$\dfrac{QT}{OT} = \dfrac{QM}{PM}$

$OT = QT \times \dfrac{PM}{QM} = 4.2 \times \dfrac{9}{12}$

$= 3.15$ cm

34.

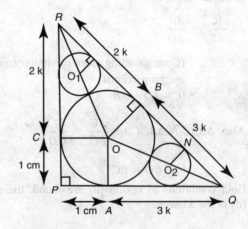

Let RB = RC = 2k

BQ = AQ = 3k

In $\Delta PQR$ $(2k + 1)^2 + (3k + 1)^2 = (2k + 3k)^2$

By solving we get k = 1

So $RB = RC = 2$ cm

$BQ = AQ = 3$ cm

$PQ = 1+3 = 4$ cm $PR = 1+2 = 3$ cm, $RQ = 2 + 3 = 5$ cm

$OQ = \sqrt{3^2 + 1^2} = \sqrt{10}$ cm

$OR = \sqrt{2^2 + 1^2} = \sqrt{5}$ cm

In the solution figure mark point M, where the perpendicular from $O_1$ cuts RB.

$O_1M \perp RB$, $O_2N \perp BQ$

In $\Delta OBR$ and $O_1MR$:

$$\frac{O_1M}{OB} = \frac{O_1R}{OR}$$

$$\frac{r_1}{1} = \frac{OR - (r_1 + 1)}{OR}$$

$$r_1 = \frac{\sqrt{5} - (r_1 + 1)}{\sqrt{5}}$$

By solving we get $r_1 = \frac{\sqrt{5} - 1}{\sqrt{5} + 1}$

Similarly $r_2 = \frac{\sqrt{10} - 1}{\sqrt{10} + 1}$

$$\frac{r_1}{r_2} = \frac{\sqrt{5} - 1}{\sqrt{5} + 1} \times \frac{\sqrt{10} + 1}{\sqrt{10} - 1} = \frac{(\sqrt{5} - 1)^2}{4} \times \frac{(\sqrt{10} + 1)^2}{9}$$

$$= (33 - 11\sqrt{5} + 6\sqrt{10} - 10\sqrt{2})/18$$

35.

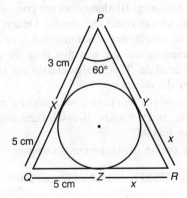

Let $ZR = x$ cm $= YR$

In $\Delta PQR$:

Using the Cosine rule, we get:

$$\cos 60^o = \frac{(3+5)^2 + (3+x)^2 - (5+x)^2}{2(3+5)(3+x)}$$

$8(3 + x) = 64 + 9 + x^2 + 6x - 25 - x^2 - 10x$

$24 + 8x = 64 - 16 - 4x$

$12x = 24$

$x = 2$ cm

Sides of the $\Delta PQR$: $PQ = 8$ cm

$RQ = 7$ cm

$PR = 5$ cm

Semi-perimeters $= \frac{8 + 7 + 5}{2} = 10$ cm

Area of $\Delta PQR = \sqrt{s(s-a)(s-b)(s-c)}$

$$= \sqrt{10(2)(3)(5)}$$

$= 10\sqrt{3}$ cm$^2$

Radius of incircle $= \frac{10\sqrt{3}}{10} = \sqrt{3}$ cm (Since area of a triangle is given by $s \times r$)

36. Area of the shaded portion =

$$10\sqrt{3} - \pi(\sqrt{3})^2 = 10\sqrt{3} - 3\pi \text{ cm}^2$$

37. $\Delta POW$ and $\Delta ROS$ are similar to each other:

$$\frac{PO}{OR} = \frac{OW}{OS} = \frac{PW}{SR} = \sqrt{\frac{\text{area of } (\Delta POW)}{\text{area of } (\Delta SOR)}} = \sqrt{\frac{9}{25}} = \frac{3}{5}$$

$PQ \parallel TU \parallel SR$. According to the basic proportionality theorem:

$$\frac{PT}{TS} = \frac{PO}{OR} = \frac{WO}{OS} = \frac{WX}{XR} = \frac{QU}{UR} = \frac{3}{5}$$

$\Delta WRQ$ and $\Delta XRU$ are similar and

$$\frac{XU}{WQ} = \frac{RX}{RW}$$

$$\frac{WX}{XR} = \frac{3}{5} \Rightarrow \frac{WX}{XR} + 1 = \frac{3}{5} + 1$$

$$\frac{WX + XR}{XR} = \frac{8}{5}$$

$$\frac{WR}{XR} = \frac{8}{5}$$

$$\frac{XR}{WR} = \frac{5}{8}$$

$$\frac{\text{Area of } (\Delta XRU)}{\text{Area of } (\Delta WRQ)} = \frac{5^2}{8^2} = \frac{25}{64}$$

$$\frac{\text{area of } \square WQUX}{\text{area of } \Delta XRU} = \frac{64 - 25}{25} = \frac{39}{25}$$

38. Let $SR = 5a$, then $PW = 3a$

$WQ = 5a - 3a = 2a$

But $WQ = 2$cm

$2a = 2$cm

$a = 1$cm

$$\frac{WQ}{XU} = \frac{WR}{XR} = \frac{3+5}{5} = \frac{8}{5}$$

$$XU = 2 \times \frac{5}{8} = \frac{5}{4} \text{cm}$$

$$TX = 5 - \frac{5}{4} = \frac{15}{4} \text{cm}$$

$$TX \times XU = \frac{15}{4} \times \frac{5}{4} = \frac{75}{16} \text{cm}^2$$

39.

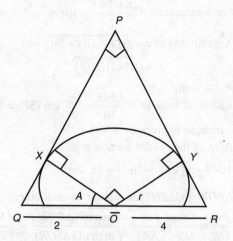

Let PQ and PR touches the semicircle at X and Y respectively.

$OX \perp PQ, \ OY \perp PR$

□ PXOY is a square, $\angle XOY = 90°$

Let the radius of the semicircle be r.

Let $\angle XOQ = A$, then in $\Delta OXQ$:

$$\cos A = \frac{r}{2} \qquad \text{(i)}$$

Similarly in $\Delta OYR$:

$$\cos(90° - A) = \frac{r}{4} \quad (\angle YOR = 180° - A - 90° - A)$$

$$\sin A = \frac{r}{4} \qquad \text{(ii)}$$

Squaring and adding equation (i) and (ii), we get

$$\cos^2 A + \sin^2 A = \left(\frac{r}{2}\right)^2 + \left(\frac{r}{4}\right)^2$$

$$1 = \frac{r^2}{4} + \frac{r^2}{16}$$

$$\frac{5r^2}{16} = 1$$

$$r^2 = 16/5$$

$$r = \frac{4}{\sqrt{5}} \ \text{cm}$$

40.

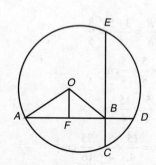

In this figure, our objective is to find the value of OB.

Obviously, the value of OB depends on the values of OF and FB. Hence, we would need to think of a way in which we can work out the values of OF and FB respectively.

If we were to take the values of BD as x and BE as y respectively, then using the intersecting chord theorem (for chords intersecting at right angles) we get:

$AB \times BD = BE \times BC$

$\rightarrow 6x = 2y \rightarrow y = 3x$

Now, $OF = \frac{3x-2}{2}$ and $AF = \frac{6+x}{2}$. Solving for x, using Pythagoras theorem, we get x as 4.

Then, in right angled triangle OFA, we have $OA^2 = OF^2 + AF^2$

$$OF^2 = 50 - \frac{(6+x)^2}{4} = 41 - 3x - \frac{x^2}{4}$$

Hence, OF = 5 and BF = AB − AF = 1.

Then in the right-angled triangle OFB, we get $OB^2 = OF^2 + FB^2 = 25 + 1 = 26$

Hence option (a) is correct.

41. First things first while solving this. If we do not include Statement III, we do not know which angle is a right angle and hence cannot uniquely calculate the value of the Side AC.

Also, Statement III alone does not gives us anything. Hence, we can reject Options (a). Option (b) and (c) gives us similar set of information – i.e., the value of 1 median and the fact that B is the right angle in the triangle. This is also clearly not sufficient to answer the question.

For option (d): We have 2 medians of a right-angled triangle, and we know B is the right angle. Hence, we can find AC.

Hence option (d) is the correct answer.

42.  area of $\Delta RPQ = \frac{1}{2} \times PR \times PQ \times \sin 120°$

area of $\Delta PSR = \frac{1}{2} \times PS \times PR \times \sin 60°$

area of $\Delta PSQ = \frac{1}{2} \times PS \times PQ \times \sin 60°$

$\frac{1}{2} \times PQ \times PR \times \sin 120° = \frac{1}{2} \times PS \times PR \times \sin 60°$

$\qquad\qquad\qquad\qquad + \frac{1}{2} \times PS \times PQ \times \sin 60°$

$\frac{9\sqrt{3}}{2} \times PR = 6 \times PR \times \frac{\sqrt{3}}{2} + 6 \times 9 \times \frac{\sqrt{3}}{2}$

$9PR = 6PR + 54$

$PR = \dfrac{54}{3} = 18$ cm

43.

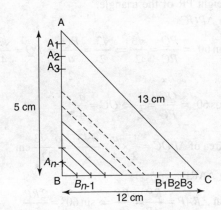

AB = 5cm

$A_{n-1}B = \dfrac{5}{n}$

$A_{n-2}B = \dfrac{10}{n}$, $A_{n-3}B = \dfrac{15}{n}$, ...

Similarly $BB_{n-1} = \dfrac{12}{n}, BB_{n-2} = \dfrac{24}{n}, BB_{n-3} = \dfrac{36}{n},...$

$A_{n-1}B_{n-1} = \sqrt{\left(\dfrac{5}{n}\right)^2 + \left(\dfrac{12}{n}\right)^2} = \dfrac{13}{n}$

$A_{n-2}B_{n-2} = \sqrt{\left(\dfrac{10}{n}\right)^2 + \left(\dfrac{24}{n}\right)^2} = \dfrac{26}{n}$

And so on...

$A_{n-1}B_{n-1} + A_{n-2}B_{n-2} + A_{n-3}B_{n-3} + ... +$

$AC = \dfrac{13}{n} + \dfrac{26}{n} + \dfrac{39}{n} + ...n$ terms =

$\dfrac{13}{n}[1 + 2 + 3 + ... + n] = 130$

$\dfrac{13}{n} \times \dfrac{n}{2}(n+1) = 130$

$(n+1) = 20$

$n = 19$

44. *Area of* $\Delta A_{n-1} BB_{n-1}$ *+ Area of* $\Delta A_{n-2} BB_{(n-2)}$ *+ Area of* $\Delta A_{n-3}BB_{(n-3)}$ *+ ... + Area of* $\Delta ABC = 66$ cm²
*Area of* $\Delta A_{n-1} BB_{n-1}$ *+ Area of* $\Delta A_{n-2} BB_{(n-2)}$ *+ Area of* $\Delta A_{n-3}BB_{(n-3)}$ *+ ... + Area of* $\Delta ABC = 66$ cm²

$\Rightarrow \dfrac{1}{2} \times \dfrac{5}{n} \times \dfrac{12}{n} + \dfrac{1}{2} \times \dfrac{10}{n} \times \dfrac{24}{n} + \dfrac{1}{2}$

$\times \dfrac{15}{n} \times \dfrac{36}{n} + ... + \dfrac{1}{2} \times 5 \times 12 = 66$

$\Rightarrow \dfrac{60}{2n^2}\left[1^2 + 2^2 + 3^2 + ... + n^2\right] = 66$

$\Rightarrow \dfrac{30}{n^2} \times \dfrac{n(n+1)(2n+1)}{6} = 66$

$\Rightarrow \dfrac{5}{n}(n+1)(2n+1) = 66$

$\Rightarrow n = 5$

45.

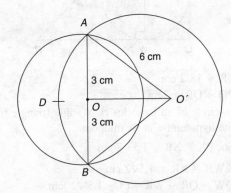

Let the center of the smaller and the bigger circle be O, O' respectively (as shown in the diagram above). And A, B are the points of intersection of the circles. The common chord will be of maximum length, if it is the diameter of the smaller circle. (note that you cannot make the common chord longer than the diameter of the smaller circle)

AB = 3 × 2 = 6 cm

O'A = O'B = 6cm

This means that the $\Delta ABO'$ is an equilateral triangle having side 6cm.

So area of $\Delta ABO' = \dfrac{\sqrt{3}}{4}(6)^2 = 9\sqrt{3}$ cm²

46. Area of intersection of the two circles =
Area of smaller circle/2 + Area of segment ABD

$= \dfrac{\pi(3)^2}{2} + (\text{area of segment } ADBO' - \text{area of } \Delta ABO')$

$= \dfrac{\pi}{2}(3)^2 + \left(\pi(6)^2 \times \dfrac{60^\circ}{360^\circ} - 9\sqrt{3}\right)$

$= \dfrac{9\pi}{2} + 6\pi - 9\sqrt{3}$

$= \left[\dfrac{21}{2}\pi - 9\sqrt{3}\right]$ cm²

47.

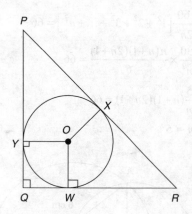

PR = 3 $\sqrt{2}$ cm

PQ = QR = 3cm

In-circle of an isosceles right angle triangle touches the hypotenuse at its midpoint.

So, PX = XR = 1.5 $\sqrt{2}$ cm

&WR = XR = 1.5$\sqrt{2}$ cm

QW = QR − WR = (3 − 1.5 $\sqrt{2}$ )cm

So the required ratio is:

1.5 $\sqrt{2}$ : 3 − 1.5 $\sqrt{2}$ : 1.5 $\sqrt{2}$

1 :( $\sqrt{2}$ − 1):1

48.   $\angle XOY = 180° − \angle YPX$

= 180° − 45° = 135°

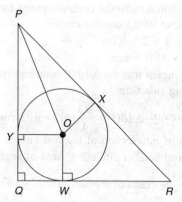

Radius of in-circle = OY = QW = $\left[ 3 - \dfrac{3}{2}\sqrt{2} \right]$ cm

Area of PYOX = *area of ΔPYO + area of PXO* = 2 (*area of ΔPYO*)

$= \dfrac{1}{2} \times \left[ 3 - \dfrac{3}{2}\sqrt{2} \right] \times \dfrac{3}{2}\sqrt{2} \times 2$

$= \dfrac{9}{2}\sqrt{2} - \dfrac{9}{4} \times 2 = \dfrac{9}{2}\sqrt{2} - \dfrac{9}{2} = \dfrac{9}{2}\left( \sqrt{2} - 1 \right)$ cm$^2$

49.   BP ⊥ AC, ΔABC is an equilateral triangle so AP = PC and if side of ΔABC is a. Then BP = $\dfrac{a\sqrt{3}}{2}$ (Altitude of an equilateral triangle). In order to find the area of ΔPQC we would need to find the base QC and the height PQ. Also, in order to find the area of the ΔPRB, we would need to find the base BR and the height PR of the triangle.

In ΔPQC:

$\sin 60° = \dfrac{PQ}{PC} = \dfrac{\sqrt{3}}{2} \Rightarrow \dfrac{\sqrt{3}}{2} = \dfrac{PQ}{\dfrac{a}{2}} \Rightarrow PQ = \dfrac{\sqrt{3}}{4}a$

$\cos 60° = \dfrac{QC}{PC} = \dfrac{1}{2} \Rightarrow QC = \dfrac{a}{4}$

Area of $\Delta PQC = \dfrac{1}{2} \times \dfrac{a}{4} \times \dfrac{a\sqrt{3}}{4} = \dfrac{a^2\sqrt{3}}{32}$ cm$^2$

In ΔARP

$\sin \angle RAP = \dfrac{RP}{AP} = \dfrac{RP}{\dfrac{a}{2}} \Rightarrow \sin 60° = \dfrac{2RP}{a}$

$RP = \dfrac{a\sqrt{3}}{4}$ cm

$\angle PBR = 30°$

$BR = PB \cos 30° = \dfrac{a\sqrt{3}}{2} \times \dfrac{\sqrt{3}}{2} = a \times \dfrac{3}{4}$

Area of $\Delta PRB = \dfrac{1}{2} \times RB \times PR = \dfrac{1}{2} \times \dfrac{3a}{4} \times \dfrac{a\sqrt{3}}{4}$

$= \dfrac{3a^2\sqrt{3}}{32}$

So the required ratio = $\dfrac{\dfrac{3a^2\sqrt{3}}{32}}{\dfrac{a^2\sqrt{3}}{32}} = 3:1$

50.

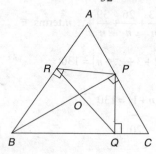

We have already seen AR = QC = a/4

⇒ RQ ∥ AC

⇒ΔBRQ ~ ΔBAC

$\dfrac{RQ}{AC} = \dfrac{BO}{BP} = \dfrac{BR}{AB} = \dfrac{AB - AR}{AB} = \dfrac{\dfrac{3a}{4}}{a} = \dfrac{3}{4}$

$\dfrac{RQ}{AC} = \dfrac{3}{4}$

$RQ = \dfrac{3a}{4}$ cm

$$BO = \frac{3}{4} \times \frac{a\sqrt{3}}{2} = \frac{3a\sqrt{3}}{8}$$

$$OP = BP - BO = \frac{a\sqrt{3}}{2} - \frac{3a\sqrt{3}}{8}$$

$$= \frac{a\sqrt{3}}{8} \text{ cm}$$

Area of $\Delta PRQ = \frac{1}{2} \times \frac{3a}{4} \times \frac{a\sqrt{3}}{8}$

$$= \frac{1}{2} \times \frac{3 \times 4}{4} \times \frac{4\sqrt{3}}{8}$$

$$= \frac{3\sqrt{3}}{4} \text{ cm}^2$$

**51.**

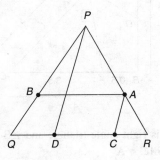

PQ = PR = 10cm.

PA: AR = 2:3

$$\Rightarrow PA = 10 \times \frac{2}{2+3} = 4 \text{ cm}, \ AR = 10 \times \frac{3}{2+3} = 6 \text{ cm}$$

In $\Delta PRD$ & $\Delta ACR$: AC ∥ PD

$$\Rightarrow \Delta ACR \sim \Delta PRD$$

$$\frac{PA}{AR} = \frac{DC}{CR} = \frac{2}{3} \qquad (1)$$

AB ∥ DC and AC ∥ PD

$$\Rightarrow \angle PDC = \angle BAC$$

$\angle APD = \angle BAC$ (given)

$$\Rightarrow \angle PDC = \angle APD \text{ or } PR = RD = 10\text{cm}.$$

$$\frac{DC}{CR} = \frac{2}{3} \quad \text{(From equation 1)}$$

$$DC = 10 \times \frac{2}{2+3} = 4 \text{ cm}$$

**52.**

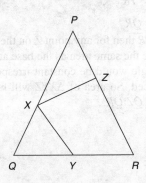

---

$$\frac{\text{Area of }\Delta PXZ}{\text{Area of }\Delta PQR} = \frac{\frac{1}{2} \times PX.PZ.\sin P}{\frac{1}{2} \times PQ.PR.\sin P}$$

$$= \left( \frac{PX}{PQ} \times \frac{PZ}{PR} \right) = \left( \frac{1}{2} \times \frac{1}{3} \right) = \frac{1}{6}$$

$$\frac{\text{Area of }\Delta QXY}{\text{Area of }\Delta PQR} = \frac{\frac{1}{2}QX.QY.\sin Q}{\frac{1}{2}.PQ.QR.\sin Q}$$

$$= \frac{QX}{PQ} \times \frac{QY}{QR} = \frac{1}{2} \times \frac{2}{5} = \frac{2}{10}$$

$$\frac{\text{Area of }\square XYRZ}{\text{Area of }\Delta PQR} = \frac{1 - \left( \frac{1}{6} + \frac{2}{10} \right)}{1} = \frac{19}{30}$$

$$\frac{\text{Area of }\square XYRZ}{\text{Area of }\Delta PXZ} = \frac{\frac{19}{30}}{\frac{1}{6}} = \frac{19}{5}$$

**53.**

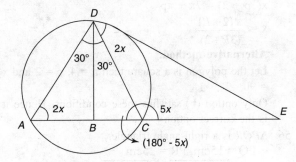

Let $\angle EDC = 2x$ and $\angle ECD = 5x$

According to alternate segment theorem:

$\angle EDC = \angle DAC$

$\angle DAC = 2x$

$\angle BCD = 180° - 5x$

$\angle ADB = \angle CDB = 30°$

In $\Delta ADC$ : $2x + (30° + 30°) + 180° - 5x = 180°$

$$x = \frac{60°}{3} = 20°$$

$\angle DEC = 180° - (40° + 100°) = 40°$

**54.** According to the internal angle bisector theorem:

$$\frac{AB}{BC} = \frac{AD}{DC}$$

$$\frac{AB}{AC} = \frac{1}{3} \Rightarrow \frac{AB}{BC} = \frac{1}{2}$$

$$\Rightarrow \frac{AD}{DC} = \frac{1}{2}$$

$AD = \dfrac{DC}{2} = \dfrac{6}{2} = 3\,\text{cm}$

55. In a n-sided regular polygon number of diagonals =
${}^{n}C_2 - n$

$= \dfrac{n(n-3)}{2}$

$p\left[\dfrac{n(n-3)}{2}\right] = n$

p(n − 3) = 2 $\Rightarrow \dfrac{2}{n-3} = p$

Internal angle x = $\dfrac{(n-2)\pi}{n}$. On transformation, we

get n = $\dfrac{2\pi}{\pi - x}$.

Hence P =

$\dfrac{2}{n-3} = \dfrac{2}{\left[\dfrac{2\pi}{\pi-x}\right] - 3} = \dfrac{2(\pi-x)}{2\pi - 3\pi + 3x} = \dfrac{2(\pi-x)}{3x-\pi}$

p = $\dfrac{2(\pi-x)}{3x-\pi}$

3xp − πp = 2π − 2x

x(3p + 2) = 2π + πp

x = $\dfrac{\pi(2+P)}{(3P+2)}$

**Alternative method:**

Let the polygon is a square then n = 4, p = 2 and x
= 90°

Only option (b) satisfies these conditions. Hence it
is the correct option.

56. $\Delta PQR$ is a right-angle triangle.
PQ = 15cm, PR = 25cm

$QR = \sqrt{PR^2 - PQ^2} = \sqrt{25^2 - 15^2} = \sqrt{400} = 20\,\text{cm}$

Since $PQ \times QR = 20 \times 15 = 300$ & $QS \times PR =$
$12 \times 25 = 300$, therefore $QS \perp PR$ (Note: This is
a property of right angled triangles that you should
know).

SR = $\sqrt{(20)^2 - 12^2} = 16\,\text{cm}$

In $\Delta QTR$ : QT = $\sqrt{QR^2 - RT^2} = \sqrt{20^2 - 16^2} = 12\,\text{cm}$

$\Delta QTR$ & $\Delta QSR$ are congruent to each other therefore
$\angle SOQ = \angle TOQ = 90°$

It is obvious that $ST \perp QR$.

Hence, $\Delta ROS \sim RQP$

$\dfrac{RO}{RQ} = \dfrac{RS}{RP} = \dfrac{16}{25}$

$\Rightarrow \dfrac{RO}{OQ} = \dfrac{16}{9}$

57. Area of quadrilateral $SQTR$ = Area of $\Delta$SQR + Area
of $\Delta$QTR. We know that the area of a quadrilateral is

given by Product of diagonals ÷ 2. Hence, we get:

$\dfrac{ST \times 20}{2} = \dfrac{1}{2} \times 12 \times 16 + \dfrac{1}{2} \times 12 \times 16$  (Using the

lengths of SQ, QR, QT & TR which we know from
the previous question and the given information)
Hence, ST = 19.20 cm

58.

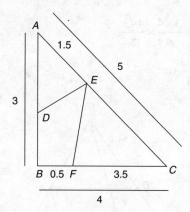

$\Delta ABC$ is right angle triangle and $\angle B = 90°$
Let $\angle BAC$ = A
$\Rightarrow \angle BCA = 90° - A$
In $\Delta ADE$: AD = AE = 1.5

$\Rightarrow \angle ADE = \angle AED = \dfrac{180° - A}{2} = 90° - \dfrac{A}{2}$

In $\Delta EFC$: EC = FC = 3.5 cm

$\angle CEF = \angle CFE = \dfrac{180° - (90° - A)}{2} = 45° + \dfrac{A}{2}$

$\angle AED + \angle DEF + \angle FEC = 180°$

$90° - \dfrac{A}{2} + \angle DEF + 45° + \dfrac{A}{2} = 180°$

$\angle DEF = 45°$

59. $\dfrac{PX}{QZ} = \dfrac{1}{2}$ and $\dfrac{QX}{QZ} = \dfrac{3}{2}$

$\therefore PX : XQ = 1 : 3$

$\Rightarrow \dfrac{PX}{XQ} = \dfrac{PY}{YR} = \dfrac{1}{3}$

$\therefore XY \parallel QR$

If $XY \parallel QR$ then for any point Z on the line QR, $\Delta XYZ$
will have the same area as the base and the height of
the triangle would be constant irrespective of where
Z is placed. So area of $\Delta XYZ$ will be same for any
value of $QZ:QR$.

60.

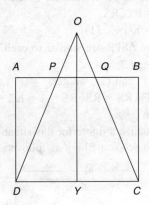

Let the altitude from O of $\Delta OPQ$ is $OX$ and OY $\perp$ DC

Area of $\square PQCD = \frac{1}{2}(PQ + DC)BC = 80$ sq units

$$\Rightarrow \frac{1}{2}(PQ + 10)10 = 80$$

$PQ = 6$ units

$\Delta OPQ$ and $\Delta ODC$ are similar triangles.

$$\frac{OX}{OY} = \frac{PQ}{DC} = \frac{6}{10}$$

$$\frac{OX}{OX + 10} = \frac{6}{10}$$

$10\, OX = 6\, OX + 60$

$OX = \dfrac{60}{4} = 15$ units

61. In $\Delta$ CAD : $AD^2 + CA^2 = CD^2$

Using Apollonius Theorem we get : $AB^2 + AC^2 = 2(AD^2 + CD^2)$

$AB^2 + AC^2 = 2AD^2 + BC^2/2$

$AB^2 + AC^2 = 2(CD^2 - AC^2) + BC^2/2$

$AB^2 + AC^2 = 2(BC^2/4 - AC^2) + BC^2/2$

$3AC^2 = BC^2 - AB^2$

Theory Note: **Apollonius' theorem** is a theorem relating the length of a median of a triangle to the lengths of its side. It states that "the sum of the squares of any two sides of any triangle equals twice the square on half the third side, together with twice the square on the median bisecting the third side" Specifically, in any triangle $ABC$, if $AD$ is a median, then

$AB^2 + AC^2 = 2(AD^2 + BD^2)$

62. Let $AC = 2^a$, where $a \in N$

$AB = AC/2 = \dfrac{2^a}{2} = 2^{a-1}$

According to the question AB is a perfect square. So $a - 1$ should be even or 'a' should be odd.

$AB + AC > BC$

---

$3AB > 295$

$AB > 98.33$

$2^{a-1} > 98.33$ .....(A)

$AC - AB < BC$

$2^a - 2^{a-1} < 295$ or $2^{a-1} < 295$ ....(B)

Only $a = 9$ satisfies equation A and B.

$\therefore AB = 2^8 = 256$, $AC = 2^9 = 512$

$\therefore$ Perimeter of the triangle $= 256 + 512 + 295 = 1063$

63. Let $AB = a^3$, $AC = 3^n$ according to the question : $3^n = 3.a^3$ or $a^3 = 3^{n-1}$

Perimeter $P = 397 + 3^n + 3^{n-1}$

$P - 397 = 3^{n-1}[3 + 1] = 4.3^{n-1}$

Thus P- 397 should be a multiple of both 3 and 4, only option (d) p = 3313 feet satisfies this condition, so option (d) is correct.

64.

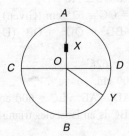

$XADY = 1 + 4\pi \times \dfrac{120°}{360°} = 1 + \dfrac{4\pi}{3} \approx 5.19$

$XOBY = 1 + 2 + 4\pi \times \dfrac{60°}{360°} = 3 + \dfrac{4\pi}{6} \approx 5.09$

$XODY = 1 + 2 + 4\pi \times \dfrac{30°}{360°} \approx 4.04$

$XADY : XOBY : XODY :: 5.19 : 5.09 : 4.04$

65.

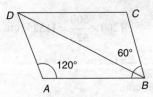

Let $AB = a$ and $AD = b$

Area of parallelogram $= ab \sin 60° = ab\dfrac{\sqrt{3}}{2} = 15\dfrac{\sqrt{3}}{2}$

$ab = 15$ .....(1)

By applying cosine rule in $\Delta$ ABD:

$\cos 120° = \dfrac{a^2 + b^2 - 49}{2ab} = -\dfrac{1}{2}$ or $a^2 + b^2 = 34$

$a^2 + \dfrac{225}{a^2} = 34$

By solving the above equation we get $a^2 = 9$ or $25$
$a = 3$ or $5$

ab = 15 so b = 5 or 3

Perimeter = 2(a + b) = 2(5 + 3) or 2(3 + 5) = 16 cm

66. Let ABC is the triangle and the circle touches AB, AC at D, E respectively as shown in the diagram.

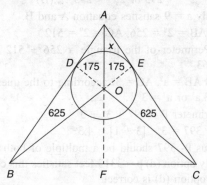

OD ⊥ AB & OE ⊥ AC

OA = OB = OC = 625 cm (Given)

In ΔODB, $BD^2 + OD^2 = OB^2$ (Using Pythagoras theorem)

$BD^2 + 175^2 = 625^2$

⇒ BD = 600 cm.

Similarly, AD = AE = EC = 600 cm

Hence, ΔABC is an isosceles triangle and AB = AC = 1200 cm

So, AF ⊥ BC

In ΔAEO and ΔAFC :

∠OAE = ∠CAF

∠AEO = ∠AFC = $90^0$

So, ΔAEO ~ ΔAFC

$$\frac{AE}{AF} = \frac{OE}{CF} = \frac{OA}{AC}$$

$$\frac{600}{AF} = \frac{175}{CF} = \frac{625}{1200}$$

So, AF = $1200 \times \frac{600}{625} = 1152$ cm and CF =

$1200 \times \frac{175}{625} = 336$ cm

CB = 672 cm

Area of Δ ABC = $\frac{1}{2} \times 672 \times 1152 = 387072$ cm²

67.

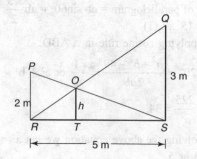

ΔROT and ΔRQS are similar to each other :

OT/QS = RT/ RS

RT/ RS = h/3 .....(1)

ΔSOT and ΔSPR are similar to each other :

ST/ SR = h/ 2 ......(2)

Adding (1) and (2), we get:

(RT + ST)/ RS = RS/ RS = 1 = h/2 + h/3

h = 1.2 m

68. If we visualize a figure for this situation, you would be able to see something as follows:

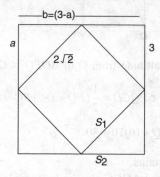

Solving through Pythagoras theorem, we will get a = 0.18 and b = 3 − 0.18 = 2.82.

Hence, the value of b/a = 2.82/0.18 = 15.666.

69. $\frac{\angle A}{\angle B} = 1 - \frac{\angle C}{\angle B}$

∠A = ∠B − ∠C

∠A + ∠C = ∠B

In ΔABC: ∠A + ∠B +C = 180°

2∠B = 180°

∠B = 90°

∴ $AB^2 + BC^2 = AC^2$

70.

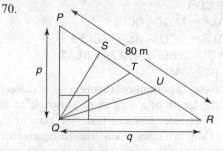

PR = 80 m, PS = ST = TU = UR = 20m

T is the midpoint of PR(hypotenuse) so PT = TR = QT = 40m

Applying Apollonius theorem in ΔPQT,

$p^2 + 40^2 = 2(QS^2 + 20^2)$ .....(1)

Again applying Apollonius theorem in ΔQRT,

$q^2 + 40^2 = 2(QU^2 + 20^2)$ .....(2)

By adding equation 1 and 2 we get :

$p^2 + q^2 + 2. \ 40^2 = 2 (QS^2 + QU^2) + 40^2$

$QS^2 + QU^2 = (p^2 + q^2 + 40^2)/2 = (80^2 + 40^2)/2 = 4000$ m²

$QS^2 + QU^2 + QT^2 = 4000 \ m^2 + 40^2 \ m^2 = 5600 \ m^2$

71. $PQ = SR = 14 cm$

$SX : XR = 4 : 3$

$SX = 8 cm, \ XR = 6 cm$

$QR = \sqrt{10^2 - 6^2} = 8 \ cm$

$PS = 8 cm$

$PX = \sqrt{8^2 + 8^2} = 8\sqrt{2} \ cm$

In $\triangle PXQ$: $PQ = 14 cm$, $PX = 8\sqrt{2} \ cm$, $QX = 10 cm$

$\therefore \ a > c > b$

## MENSURATION

### Level of Difficulty (I)

1. (b)

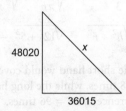

Let hypotenuse $= x$ cm

Then, by Pythagoras theorem:

$x^2 = (48020)^2 + (36015)^2$

$x \Rightarrow 60025 \ cm$

2. (d)

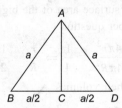

Let one side of the $\Delta$ be $= a$

Perimeter of equilateral triangle $= 3a$

$\therefore \qquad 3a = 72\sqrt{3} \rightarrow a = 24\sqrt{3} \ m$

Height $= AC$; by Pythagoras theorem

$AC^2 = a^2 - \left(\dfrac{a}{2}\right)^2$

$AC = 36 \ m$

3. (b)

Let inner radius $= r$; then $2\pi r = 440$ $\therefore \ r = 70$

Radius of outer circle $= 70 + 14 = 84 \ cm$

$\therefore$ Outer diameter $= 2 \times$ Radius $= 2 \times 84 = 168$

4. (a)

Let inner radius $= r$ and outer radius $= R$

Width $= R - r = \dfrac{396}{2\pi} - \dfrac{352}{2\pi}$

$\Rightarrow \ (R - r) = \dfrac{44}{2\pi} = 7 \ meters$

5. (d)

Let outer radius $= R$; then inner radius $= r = R - 7$

$2\pi R = 220 \Rightarrow R = 35 \ m;$

$r = 35 - 7 = 28 \ m$

Area of track $= \pi R^2 - \pi r^2 \Rightarrow \pi (R^2 - r^2) = 1386 \ m^2$

Cost of leveling it $= 1386 \times \dfrac{1}{2} = ₹ \ 693$

6. (b)

Circumference of circle $= 2\pi r = 44$

$= r = 7 \ cm$

Area of a quadrant $= \dfrac{\pi r^2}{4} = 38.5 \ cm^2$

7. (d)

Volume of soil removed $= l \times b \times h$

$= 7.5 \times 6 \times 1.5 = 67.5 \ m^3$

8. (c)

The longest pole can be placed diagonally (3-dimensional)

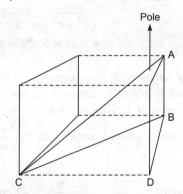

$BC = \sqrt{18^2 + 24^2} = 30$

$AC = \sqrt{30^2 + 16^2} = 34 \ m$

9. (d)

Let the common ratio be $= x$

Then; length $= 3x$, breadth $= 2x$ and height $= x$

Then; as per question $3x \cdot 2x \cdot x = 1296 \Rightarrow 6x^3 = 1296$

$\Rightarrow x = 6 \ m$

Breadth $= 2x = 12 \ m$

10. (d)

Data is inadequate as it's not mentioned that what part of the cube is melted to form cylinder.

11. (b)

Let the common ratio be $= x$

Then, length = $4x$, breadth = $3x$ and height = $2x$

As per question;

$2(4x \cdot 3x + 3x \cdot 2x + 2x \cdot 4x) = 8788$

$2(12x^2 + 6x^2 + 8x^2) = 8788 \Rightarrow 52x^2 = 8788$

$\Rightarrow \qquad x = 13$

Length = $4x = 52$ cm

12. **(b)**

The total volume will remain the same, let the side of the resulting cube be = $a$. Then,

$$6^3 + 8^3 + 10^3 = a^3 \Rightarrow a = \sqrt[3]{1728} = 12 \text{ cm}$$

13. **(a)**

Slant length = $l = \sqrt{6^2 + 8^2} = 10$ cm

Then curved surface area = $\pi rl = \pi \times 6 \times 10 \Rightarrow 60\pi$

And total surface area = $\pi rl + \pi r^2 \Rightarrow \pi((6 \times 10) + 6^2)$

$= 96\pi$ cm$^2$

14. **(b)**

$$\text{Volume of a cone} = \frac{\pi r^2 h}{3}$$

Then; $\qquad 100\pi = \frac{\pi r^2 \cdot 12}{3} \Rightarrow r = 5$ cm

Curved surface area = $\pi rl$

$$l = \sqrt{h^2 + r^2} \Rightarrow \sqrt{12^2 + 5^2} = 13$$

then, $\qquad \pi rl = \pi \times 13 \times 5 = 65\pi$ cm$^2$

15. **(d)**

Let the radius of the two cones be = $x$ cm

Let slant height of 1$^{st}$ cone = 5 cm and

Slant height of 2$^{nd}$ cone = 7 cm

Then ratio of covered surface area = $\dfrac{\pi \times 5}{\pi \times 7} = 5 : 7$

16. **(c)**

$$\text{Radius} = \frac{\pi rl}{\pi l} = \frac{2376}{3.14 \times 18} = 42 \text{ cm}$$

Diameter = $2 \times$ Radius = $2 \times 42 = 84$ cm

17. **(c)**

Let the radius of cylinder = 1$(r)$

Then the radius of cone be = 2$(R)$

Then as per question = $\dfrac{\pi r^2 h}{\dfrac{\pi R^2 h}{3}} \Rightarrow \dfrac{3\pi r^2 h}{\pi R^2 h}$

$\Rightarrow \dfrac{3r^2}{R^2} \Rightarrow 3 : 4$

18. **(c)**

The perimeter would remain the same in any case.

Let one side of a square be = $a$ cm

Then $a^2 = 484 \Rightarrow a = 22$ cm $\therefore$ perimeter = $4a = 88$ cm

Let the radius of the circle be = $r$ cm

Then $2\pi r = 88 \Rightarrow r = 14$ cm

Then area = $\pi r^2 = 616$ cm$^2$

19. **(d)**

Let the radius of the circle be = $\pi$

Then $\quad 2\pi r - 2r = 16.8 \Rightarrow r = 3.92$ cm

Then $\qquad\qquad 2\pi r = 24.64$ cm

20. **(d)**

Let the radius of the wheel be = $r$

Then $5000 \times 2\pi r = 1100000$ cm $\Rightarrow r = 35$ cm

21. **(a)**

Let the slant height be = $l$

Let radius = $r$

Then $v = \dfrac{\pi r^2 h}{3} \Rightarrow r = \sqrt{\dfrac{3v}{\pi h}} \Rightarrow \sqrt{\dfrac{3 \times 100\pi}{\pi \times 12}} = 5$ cm

$l = \sqrt{h^2 + r^2} = \sqrt{12^2 + 5^2} = 13$ cm

22. **(b)**

In 4 days the short hand would cover the circumference $4 \times 2 = 8$ times, while the long hand would cover its circumference $4 \times 24 = 96$ times.

Then, the total distance they would cover would be:

$(2 \times \pi \times 4)8 + (2 \times \pi \times 6)96 = 3818.24$ cm.

23. **(b)**

Let the radius of the smaller sphere = $r$

Then, the radius of the bigger sphere = $R$

Let the surface area of the smaller sphere = 1

Then, the surface area of the bigger sphere = 4

Then, as per question

$\Rightarrow \dfrac{4\pi r^2}{4\pi R^2} = \dfrac{1}{4} \Rightarrow \dfrac{r}{R} = \dfrac{1}{2} \Rightarrow R = 2r$

Ratio of their volumes

$= \dfrac{4\pi r^3}{3} \times \dfrac{3}{4\pi(2r)^3} \Rightarrow 1 : 8$

24. **(b)**

Inner radius$(\pi) = \dfrac{9}{2} = 4.5$ cm

Outer radius $(R) = \dfrac{10}{2} = 5$ cm

Volume of metal contained in the shell = $\dfrac{4\pi R^3 - 4\pi r^3}{3}$

$\Rightarrow \dfrac{4\pi}{3}(R^3 - r^3)$

$\Rightarrow 141.9$ cm$^3$

25. **(c)**

Let smaller radius $(r) = 1$

Then bigger radius $(R) = 2$

Then, as per question

$$\Rightarrow \frac{4\pi r^2}{4\pi R^2} = \left(\frac{r}{R}\right)^2 \Rightarrow \left(\frac{1}{2}\right)^2 = 1:4$$

26. (c)

As per question $\Rightarrow \dfrac{4\pi r^3}{3} = \dfrac{\pi r^2 h}{3} \Rightarrow h = 4r$

27. (a)

Volume of wall = $1200 \times 500 \times 25 = 15000000$ cm³

Volume of cement = 5% of 15000000 = 750000 cm³

Remaining volume = 15000000 – 750000

$= 14250000$ cm³

Volume of a brick = $25 \times 12.5 \times 7.5 = 2343.75$ cm³

Number of bricks used $= \dfrac{14250000}{2343.75} = 6080$

28. (a)

Let the inner radius = $r$

Then $2\pi r = 352$ m. Then $r = 56$

Then outer radius = $r + 7 = 63 = R$

Now, $\pi R^2 - \pi r^2 = $ Area of road

$\Rightarrow \quad \pi(R^2 - r^2) = 2618$ m²

29. (c)

1 hectare = 10000 m²

Height = 10 cm = $\dfrac{1}{10}$ m

Volume = $10000 \times \dfrac{1}{10} = 1000$ m³

30. (a)

Total surface area of 7 cubes $\Rightarrow 7 \times 6a^2 = 1050$

But on joining end to end, 12 sides will be covered.

So their area = $12 \times a^2 \Rightarrow 12 \times 25 = 300$

So the surface area of the resulting figure = 1050 – 300 = 750

31. (d)

Let the rise in height be = $h$

Then, as per the question, the volume of water should be equal in both the cases.

Now, $90 \times 40 \times h = 150 \times 8$

$h = \dfrac{150 \times 8}{90 \times 40} = \dfrac{1}{3}$ m $= \dfrac{100}{3}$ cm

$= 33.33$ cm

32. (d)

Slant height $(l) = \sqrt{7^2 + 24^2} = 25$ m

Area of cloth required = curved surface area of cone

$= \pi r l = \dfrac{22}{7} \times 7 \times 25 = 550$ m²

Amount of cloth required = $\dfrac{550}{5} = 110$ m

33. (b)

If the ratio of their diameters = 2 : 1, then the ratio of their radii will also be = 2 : 1

Let the radii of the broader cone = 2 and height be = 1

Then the radii of the smaller cone = 1 and height be = 2

Ratio of volumes = $\dfrac{\pi 2^2 \cdot 1}{3} \div \dfrac{\pi 1^2 \cdot 2}{3}$

$\dfrac{4\pi}{3} \times \dfrac{3}{2\pi} \Rightarrow 2:1$

34. (d)

Area of base = $6 \times 10 = 60$ m²

Volume of tent = $30 \times 10 = 300$ m³

Let the radius be = $r$, height = $h$, slant height = $l$

$\pi r^2 = 60 \Rightarrow r = \sqrt{\dfrac{60}{\pi}}$

$300 = \dfrac{\pi r^2 h}{3} \Rightarrow 900 = \pi \cdot \dfrac{60}{\pi} \cdot h \Rightarrow h = 15$ m

35. (b)

Volume of wood used = External Volume – Internal Volume

$\Rightarrow (10 \times 8 \times 6) - (10 - 1) \times (8 - 1) \times (6 - 1)$

$\Rightarrow 480 - (9 \times 7 \times 5) = 165$ cm²

36. (b)

Total volume in both the objects will be equal. Let the number of smaller cubes = $x$

$x \cdot 3^3 = 24 \times 9 \times 8 \Rightarrow x = \dfrac{24 \times 72}{27} = 64$

37. (a)

Let one side of the cube = $a$

Then $\quad\quad\quad a^3 = 216 \Rightarrow a = 6$ m

Area of the resultant figure

= Area of all 3 cubes – Area of covered figure

$\Rightarrow 216 \times 3 - (4 \times a^2) \Rightarrow 648 - 144 \Rightarrow 504$ m²

38. (c)

Volume of metal used = $\dfrac{4\pi R^3}{3} - \dfrac{4\pi r^3}{3}$

$= \dfrac{4\pi}{3}(12^3 - 10^3)$

$= 3047.89$ cm³

Weight = volume × density $\Rightarrow 4.9 \times 3047.89$

$\Rightarrow 14942.28$ gm

39. (d)

Volume of cube = $7^3 = 343$ cm³

Radius of cone = $\dfrac{7}{2} = 3.5$ cm

Height of cone = 7 cm

Ratio of volumes = $\dfrac{\dfrac{\pi r^2 h}{3}}{343} = \dfrac{22 \times 3.5 \times 3.5 \times 7}{7 \times 3 \times 343}$

$\Rightarrow 11:42$

40. (b)

The volume in both the cases will be equal. Let the height of cone be $= h$

$$4 \times \frac{22}{7} \times (14)^3 \times \frac{1}{3} = \frac{22}{7} \times \left(\frac{35}{2}\right)^2 \times \frac{h}{3}$$

$$\Rightarrow \qquad 4(14)^3 = h\left(\frac{35}{2}\right)^2 = h$$

$$= \frac{4 \times 14 \times 14 \times 14 \times 2 \times 2}{35 \times 35}$$

$$= h = 35.84 \text{ cm}$$

41. (b)

Diameter of circle $=$ diagonal of square

$$= \sqrt{10^2 + 10^2} = \sqrt{200} = 10\sqrt{2}$$

$$\therefore \text{ Radius } = \frac{10\sqrt{2}}{2} = 5\sqrt{2}$$

Area of circle $= \pi r^2 \Rightarrow 50\pi = 50 \times 3.14 = 157.14 \text{ cm}^3$

42. (c)

Area of triangle $= rS$; where $r =$ inradius

$$S = \frac{15 + 8 + 17}{2} = 20 \text{ cm}$$

$$\Delta = \sqrt{S(S-a)(S-b)(S-c)}$$

$$\Rightarrow \Delta \sqrt{20(20-15)(20-8)(20-17)}$$

$$\Delta = \sqrt{20 \times 5 \times 12 \times 3} = 60 \text{ cm}^2$$

$$r = \frac{\Delta}{S} = \frac{60}{20} = 3 \text{ cm}$$

43. (c)

Circumference of the circular face of the cylinder $= 2\pi r$

$$\Rightarrow 2 \times \frac{22}{7} \times \frac{35}{100} = 2.2 \text{ m}$$

Number of revolutions required to lift the bucket by

$$11 \text{ m} = \frac{11}{2.2} = 5$$

44. (c) Surface area of the cube $= 6a^2 = 6 \times (20)^2$

$$= 2400$$

Area of 6 circles of radius 10 cm $= 6\pi r^2$

$$= 6 \times \pi \times 100$$

$$= 1885.71$$

Remaining area $= 2400 - 1885.71 = 514.28$

45. (d)

$$x \cdot y \cdot z = lb \times bh \times lh = (lbh)^2$$

(V) Volume of a cuboid $= lbh$

So $\qquad V^2 = (lbh)^2 = xyz$

46. (c)

Diameter of the circle $=$ diagonal of rectangle

$$= \sqrt{8^2 + 6^2} = 10 \text{ cm}$$

Radius $= \dfrac{10}{2} = 5$ cm

Area of shaded portion $= \pi r^2 - lb$

$$= (22/7) \times 5^2 - 8 \times 6$$

$$= 30.57 \text{ cm}^2$$

47. (a)

Larger Radius $(R) = 14 + 7 = 21$ cm

Smaller Radius $(r) = 7$ cm

Area of shaded portion $\pi R^2 \dfrac{\theta}{360} - \dfrac{\pi r^2 \theta}{360}$

$$\Rightarrow \frac{\pi\theta}{360}(21^2 - 7^2) \Rightarrow 102.67 \text{ cm}$$

48. (b)

Area of quadrilateral $=$ Area of right angled triangle $+$ Area of equilateral triangle $x = \sqrt{20^2 - 12^2} = 16$

Area of quadrilateral $= \left(\dfrac{1}{2} \times 16 \times 12\right) + \dfrac{\sqrt{3}}{4} \times 20 \times 20$

$$= 269 \text{ units}^2$$

49. (a)

Height $= \sqrt{24^2 - 13^2} = \sqrt{407}$

Volume $= \dfrac{\text{Area of base} \times \text{height}}{3} \Rightarrow \dfrac{18 \times 26 \times \sqrt{407}}{3}$

$$\Rightarrow 156\sqrt{407}$$

50. (b)

The perimeter would remain the same in both cases.

Circumference of circle $= 2\pi r = 2 \times \dfrac{22}{7} \times 28 = 176$ cm

Perimeter of square $= 176$

Greatest side possible $= \dfrac{176}{4} = 44$ cm

Length of diagonal $= \sqrt{44^2 + 44^2}$

$$= \frac{88}{2} \cdot \sqrt{2} = 44\sqrt{2}$$

51. Let the initial radius of the circle $= r$

Area $= \pi r^2$

New radius $= (r + x)$

New area $= \pi(r + x)^2$

So the area increased by $\pi(r + x)^2 - r^2 = \pi x (2r + x)$

52. Let the side of square $PQRS$ be $x$ meters.

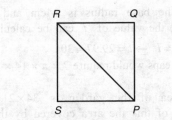

$PR = x\sqrt{2}$ meters or $1.414x$ meters

$PQ + QR = x + x = 2x$ m

Total saving $= 2x - 1.41x = 0.586\ x$ meters

% saving $= \dfrac{0.586x}{2x} \times 100 = 29.3\% \approx 29\%$

53. Two circles would be similar to each other. When you increase the length measures of a figure by a certain percentage, the effect is the multiplication of the length measure by a certain value. (Thus a 5% increase is the same as a multiplication of the original length by 1.05). In such a case the area measures, for a similar figure, get multiplied twice (by the same multiplier). Thus the New Area = Original Area $\times 1.05 \times 1.05 \rightarrow 10.25\%$ increase.

This can also be understood as below:

Circumference of a circle $= 2\pi r$, where $r$ is the radius.

Circumference $\alpha$ radius

As the circumference increases by 5%, the radius also increases by 5%

∴ New radius $= 1.05r$

∴ As area $\alpha\,(\text{radius})^2$

∴ New area $= (1.05)^2 \times$ old area $= 1.1025 \times$ old area

∴ Percentage increase in area $= 10.25\%$

54. Side of the biggest possible cube in given cylinder $= 20$ cm

Volume of cube $= (20)^3 = 800$

55. Only possible values are: $1 \times 1 \times 100$; $1 \times 2 \times 50$; $1 \times 4 \times 25$; $1 \times 5 \times 20$; $1 \times 10 \times 10$; $2 \times 2 \times 25$; $2 \times 5 \times 10$ & $4 \times 5 \times 5$.

Hence total possibilities are: 8

56. Length of largest tile $= H.C.F.$ of 1517 cm and 902 cm $= 41$ cm.

Area $= (41 \times 41)\,\text{cm}^2$

Required number of tiles $= \dfrac{1517 \times 902}{41 \times 41} = 814$

57. Side of square $= \sqrt{484} = 22$ cm

So length of the wire $= 4 \times 22 = 88$ cm

Longer part $= 88 \times \dfrac{3}{4} = 66$ cm. So the radius of the circle would be $\dfrac{66}{2\pi}$.

Shorter part $= 88 \times \dfrac{1}{4} = 22$ cm. So the length of the

side of the square would be $= \dfrac{11}{2}$.

Area of circle formed by longer part $=$

$\pi\left(\dfrac{66}{2\pi}\right)^2 = \dfrac{693}{2}\,cm^2\,(Using\,\pi = \dfrac{22}{7})$.

Area of square $= \left(\dfrac{11}{2}\right)^2 = \dfrac{121}{4}\,cm^2$

Therefore total area of both the pieces $=$

$\left(\dfrac{693}{2} + \dfrac{121}{4}\right) cm^2 = 376.75\,cm^2$

58. There are 13 successive semicircles with radii 0.5 cm, 1.0 cm, 1.5 cm, and so on.

Total length of the spiral $= \pi \times 0.5 + \pi \times 1.0 + ... + \pi \times 6.5 = \pi\,(0.5 + 1.0 + ... + 6.5) = 143$ cm

59. Let the three solids have base radius of $r$ units. Height of hemisphere $= r =$ height of cylinder $=$ Height of cone. The curved surface areas of the three solids are:

The curved surface area of the Cylinder $= 2\pi r \times r = 2\pi r^2$

The curved surface area of the Hemisphere: $2\pi r^2$

The curved surface area of the Cone $=$

$\pi\,r\sqrt{r^2 + r^2} = \sqrt{2}\pi r^2$

So the required ratio $= 2\pi r^2 : 2\pi r^2 : \sqrt{2}\pi r^2 = \sqrt{2} : \sqrt{2} : 1$

60. The curved surface area of sphere $S = 4\pi r^2$

The rate of change of the radius per unit time can be represented mathematically using:

$dr/dt = +\,2$ cm per second and $r = 30$ cm

The rate of change of the surface area $(s)$ would then be given by: $ds\,/dt = d(4\pi r^2)/dt = 4\pi \times 2r \times dr/dt = 8\,\pi \times 30 \times 2 = 480\,\pi$

61. Circumference of the base of the cylinder $= 22$

Let the radius of base of cylinder $r$.

$2\pi r = 22$ or $r = \dfrac{11}{\pi}$

Height of the cylinder $= 10$ cm

Volume of the cylinder $= \pi\left(\dfrac{11}{\pi}\right)^2 10 = 385\,cm^3$

62. Volume of parallelepiped $= 3 \times 4 \times 5 = 60$ cm$^3$

Volume of cube $= 4 \times 4 \times 4 = 64$ cm$^3$

Volume of the cylinder $= \pi\,(3)^2\,3 = 27\pi$ cm$^3$

Volume of sphere $= \dfrac{4}{3}\pi\,(3)^3 = 36\pi\,cm^3$

Therefore $4 > 3 > 2 > 1$

63. If radius of the hemispherical bowl is '$r$' then it's volume would be $\dfrac{2}{3}\pi r^3$

Radius of cylinder = $r$ and height = 2/3 $r$

Volume of cylinder = $\pi r^2 . \dfrac{2}{3} r = \dfrac{2}{3} \pi r^3$

It means that the volume of the hot water in the cylindrical vessel is 100% of the cylindrical vessel, therefore $x = 100$

64. Let the radius of the field be '$r$' meters. According to the question

$$\pi r^2 - (130 \times 110) = 20350$$

$$\pi r^2 = 20350 + 14300 = 34650$$

$$r^2 = 34650 \times \frac{7}{22} = 11025 \text{ or } r = 105 \text{ m}$$

65. Let $n$ bricks can be put in the tank without spilling over the water. According to the question the volume of the tank should be totally occupied by the available water and the bricks. Also, since the question tells us that each brick absorbs 10% of its' own volume of water, the additional volume added to the current water by each brick added to the tank would only by 90% of the brick's own volume. Let the number of bricks required by $n$. Then:

$$150 \times 120 \times 100 = n \times 20 \times 6 \times 4 \left(1 - \frac{10}{100}\right) + 1281600$$

$$150 \times 120 \times 100 - 1281600 = n \times 20 \times 6 \times 4 \times 0.9$$

$$n = \frac{518400}{20 \times 6 \times 4 \times 0.9} = 1200$$

66. Let radius of smaller sphere be '$r$ cm'.

$$\frac{4}{3} \times \pi \times (10)^3 = 1000 \times \frac{4}{3} \times \pi \times (r)^3$$

$$r = 1 \text{ cm}$$

Surface area of the larger sphere = $4\pi (10)^2 = 400\pi$

Total surface area of 1000 smaller spheres = $1000 \cdot 4\pi(1)^2 = 4000\pi$

Increase in the surface area = $4000\pi - 400\pi = 3600\pi$

Hence, surface area of the metal is increased by 900%. Therefore $n = 900$.

67. Volume of the conical writing equipment = $\dfrac{1}{3}\pi \left(2.5 \times 10^{-1}\right)^2 \times 7 = \dfrac{11}{24}$ cm$^3$

$11/24$ cm$^3$ cream can be used to write 330 words.

Number of words that can be written with 1 cm$^3$ cream = $330 \times \dfrac{24}{11} = 720$

Since 1 litre is 1000 cm$^3$, 2/5 litres = $\dfrac{2}{5} \times 1000 = 400$ cm$^3$.

Therefore, number of words that can be written with $\dfrac{2}{5}$ litre or 400 cm$^3$ = $400 \times 720 = 288000$

68. The surface area of the sheet required to make the cap would be equal to the lateral surface area of the cap, which is given by the formula $\pi \times r \times l$

Since the base radius is 14cm and height is 26.5cm, the value of '$l$' can be calculated using $r^2 + h^2 = l^2 \rightarrow l = 29.97 \approx 30$.

Thus, 7 caps would require $7 \times \pi \times 14 \times 30 = 9240$ cm$^2$

69. The area of the garden is $34 \times 21 = 714$ sq. m. Out of this the area covered by the paths = $4 \times 34 + 4 \times 21 - 4 \times 4 = 204$ sq. m. The remaining area being covered by flowers would be equal to: $714 - 204 = 510$ sq. m.

70. Surface area of the cylinder will be largest when the cylinder touches as shown in the diagram given below:

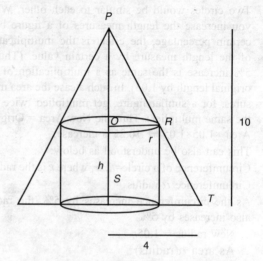

If $ST$ and $PS$ are the radius and height of the right circular cone respectively and $h$ is the height of the cylinder.

$\Delta POR$ and $\Delta PST$ are similar to each other.

$$\frac{PO}{PS} = \frac{OR}{ST}$$

$$\frac{10 - h}{10} = \frac{r}{4}$$

$$h = \frac{20 - 5r}{2}$$

*Curved surface area of the cylinder* = $2\pi rh$

$$2\pi r \left(\frac{20 - 5r}{2}\right)$$

$$5\pi r(4 - r)$$

By comparison we get $a = 5, b = 4$

$$a \times b = 5 \times 4 = 20$$

### Level of Difficulty (II)

1. (d)

Let the angle subtended by the sector at the centre be = $\theta$

Then,

$5.7 + 5.7 + (2\pi) \times 5.7 \times \dfrac{\theta}{360} = 27.2$

$11.4 + \dfrac{11.4 \times 3.14 \times \theta}{360} = 27.2$

$\Rightarrow \qquad \dfrac{\theta}{360} = 0.44$

Area of the sector $= \pi r^2 \dfrac{\theta}{360} \Rightarrow (22/7) \times (5.7)^2 \times 0.44$

$\qquad = 44.92$ approx.

2. (a)

Volume of mud dug out $= 10 \times 4.5 \times 3 = 135 \ m^3$

Let the remaining ground rise by $= h$ m

Then $\{(20 \times 9) - (10 \times 4.5)\}h = 135$

$\qquad\qquad 135h = 135 \Rightarrow h = 1$ m

3. (b)

Height of the cylinder $= 13 - 7 = 6$ cm

Radius of the cylinder and the hemisphere $= 7$ cm

Volume of the vessel = volume of cylinder + volume of hemisphere

$\Rightarrow \pi r^2 h + \dfrac{4\pi r^3}{3 \times 2} \Rightarrow 3.14 \times (7)^2 \times 6 + \dfrac{4 \times 3.14 \times (7)^3}{3 \times 2}$

$\Rightarrow 1642.6 \ cm^3$

4. (b)

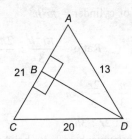

Let the original triangle be $= ACD$

Longest side $= AC = 21$cm

In the right angled $\triangle ABD$, by Pythagorean triplets, we get $AB = 5$ and $BD = 12$

Then, $BC = 21 - 5 = 16$

By Pythagoras theorem,

$\qquad BD^2 = CD^2 - BC^2 \Rightarrow BD = 12$ cm

Thus, our assumption is correct.

Area of the larger $\triangle BDC = \dfrac{1}{2} \times 16 \times 12 \Rightarrow 96 \ cm^2$

5. (c)

Radius $= 52.5$ m

Area of the entire canvas, used for the tent

= Surface area of cylinder + Surface area of cone

$= 2\pi rh + \pi rl$

$= 2 \times \dfrac{22}{7} \times 52.5 \times 3 + \dfrac{22}{7} \times 52.5 \times 53$

This surface area has to be equal to $5 \times w$.

Thus, we have $5w = 2 \times \dfrac{22}{7} \times 52.5 \times 3 + \dfrac{22}{7} \times 52.5 \times 53$

$\rightarrow w = 1947$

6. (c)

The volume in both the cases would be the same.

Therefore $= \dfrac{4\pi r^3}{3} = \pi r^2 h$

$\dfrac{4 \times 3.14 \times (4 \times 10)^3}{3} = 3.14 \times 2^2 \times h$

$\Rightarrow \qquad h = \dfrac{64000}{3} = 21333.33$ mm

7. (b)

As the cylinder and cone have equal diameters. So they have equal area. Let cone's height be $h_2$ and as per question, cylinder's height be $h_1$.

$\dfrac{2\pi r h_1}{\pi r \sqrt{h_2^2 + r^2}} = \dfrac{8}{5}$.

On solving we get the desired ratio as 4 : 3

8. (a)

Let the slant height of 1st cone $= L$

Then the slant height of 2nd cone $= 3L$

Let the radius of 1st cone $= r_1$

And let the radius of 2nd cone $= r_2$

Then, $\qquad \pi r_1 L = 3 \times \pi r_2 \times 3L$

$\Rightarrow \qquad \pi r_1 L = 9\pi r_2 L \Rightarrow r_1 = 9r_2$

Ratio of area of the base

$\dfrac{\pi r_1^2}{\pi r_2^2} \Rightarrow \left(\dfrac{r_1}{r_2}\right)^2 = \left(\dfrac{9}{1}\right)^2 \Rightarrow 81 : 1$

9. (c)

Let the internal radius of the cylinder $= r$

Then, the volume of sphere = Volume of cylinder

$\Rightarrow \qquad \dfrac{4\pi \cdot 6^3}{3} = \pi h(5^2 - r^2)$

$\Rightarrow \qquad \dfrac{864\pi}{3} = 32\pi(25 - r^2)$

$\Rightarrow \qquad r^2 = 16 \quad \Rightarrow \quad r = 4$ cm

So thickness of the cylinder $= 5 - 4 = 1$ cm

10. (d)

The volume in both the cases would be the same.

Let the height of the cone $= h$

Then, external radius $= 6$ cm

Internal radius $= 4$ cm

$$\Rightarrow \frac{4\pi(6^3 - 4^3)}{3} = \frac{\pi \cdot 4^2 \cdot h}{3}$$

$$\Rightarrow \quad h = \frac{6^3 - 4^3}{4} \Rightarrow h = \frac{216 - 64}{4} = 38 \text{ cm}$$

11. (a)

Let the side of the cube be $= a$ units

Total surface area of 3 cubes $= 3 \times 6a^2$
$$= 18a^2$$

Total surface area of cuboid $= 18a^2 - 4a^2 = 14a^2$

Ratio $= \dfrac{14a^2}{18a^2} = 7 : 9$

12. (c)

$$A = 2(xy + yz + zx)$$
$$V = xyz$$

$$A/V = \frac{2(xy + yz + zx)}{xyz} = \frac{2}{z} + \frac{2}{x} + \frac{2}{y}$$

$$\Rightarrow 2\left(\frac{1}{x} + \frac{1}{y} + \frac{1}{z}\right)$$

13. (a)

The entire dial of the clock $= 360^0$

In 35, minutes, the hand would traverse $210^0$ on the dial.

Hence, the required area $= \dfrac{210}{360} \times \pi \times 10 \times 10 = 183.33$ cm$^2$.

14. (a)

Let the radius of the bigger circle $= R$
Let the radius of the smaller circle $= r$
Then as per question; $R - r = 6$
Solving through options; only option (a) satisfies this condition.

15. (d)

Radius of cylinder, hemisphere and cone $= 5$ cm
Height of cylinder $= 13$ cm
Height of cone $= 12$ cm

Surface area of toy $= 2\pi rh + \dfrac{4\pi r^2}{2} + \pi rL$

$$L = \sqrt{h^2 + r^2} = \sqrt{12^2 + 5^2} = 13$$

Then $\Rightarrow (2 \times 3.14 \times 5 \times 13) + (2 \times 3.14 \times 25) + (3.14 \times 5 \times 13) \Rightarrow 770$ cm$^2$

16. (b)

Height of cone $= 10.2 - 4.2 = 6$ cm

Volume of wood $= \dfrac{\pi r^2 h}{3} + \dfrac{4\pi r^3}{3 \times 2}$

$$\Rightarrow \frac{3.14 \times (4.2)^2 \times 6}{3} + \frac{4 \times 3.14 \times (4.2)^3}{3 \times 2}$$

$$\Rightarrow 266 \text{ cm}^3$$

17. (a)

Volume of cylindrical container $= \pi(6)^2 15$

Volume of one cone $=$ volume of the cone + volume of hemispherical top $= \dfrac{1}{3}\pi r^2 4r + \dfrac{2}{3}\pi r^3 = 2\pi r^3$

(Where 'r' is the radius of the cone).

According to the question:

$10 \times 2\pi r^3 = \pi(6)^2 15$ or $r^3 = 27 \Rightarrow 2r = 2(27)^{\frac{1}{3}} = 6$ cm

Option (a) is true.

18. (b)

Radius of cylinder and hemispheres $= \dfrac{7}{2} = 3.5$ cm

Height of cylinder $= 19 - (3.5 \times 2) = 12$ cm

Total surface area of solid $= 2\pi rh + 4\pi r^2$

$$\Rightarrow 2 \times 3.14 \times 3.5 \times 12 + 4 \times 3.14 \times (3.5)^2$$

$$\Rightarrow 418 \text{ cm}^2$$

19. (c)

As they stand on the same base so their radius is also same.

Then; volume of cone $= \dfrac{\pi r^2 h}{3}$

Volume of hemisphere $= \dfrac{2\pi r^3}{3}$

Volume of cylinder $= \pi r^2 h$

$$\text{Ratio} = \frac{\pi r^2 h}{3} : \frac{2\pi r^3}{3} : \pi r^2 h$$

$$\Rightarrow \qquad \frac{h}{3} : \frac{2r}{3} : h$$

$$\Rightarrow \qquad h : 2r : 3h$$

Radius of a hemisphere $=$ Its height

So $\qquad h : 2h : 3h \Rightarrow 1 : 2 : 3$

20. (d)

Total cost of painting $=$ Total surface to be painted $\times 0.05 = \{$External Surface Area $+$ Internal Surface area $+$ Area of ring$\} \times 0.05$

$= \{2\pi R^2 + 2\pi r^2 + \pi(R^2 - r^2)\} \times 0.05 = ₹96.28$

21. (d)

Radius $= \dfrac{3.5}{2} = 1.75$ cm

Volume of solid $= \pi r^2 h + \dfrac{\pi r^2 h}{3} + \dfrac{2\pi r^3}{3}$

$$\Rightarrow \pi r^2 \left(h + \frac{h}{3} + \frac{r}{3}\right)$$

$$\Rightarrow 3.14 \times (1.75)^2 \times \left(10 + \frac{6}{3} + \frac{1.75}{3}\right)$$

$\Rightarrow 121 \text{ cm}^3$

22. (d)

Area of shaded portion = Area of quadrant – Area of triangle

$\Rightarrow \dfrac{\pi r^2}{4} - \dfrac{1}{2} \times 3.5 \times 2 = \dfrac{3.14 \times (3.5)^2}{4} - 3.5$

$\Rightarrow 6.125 \text{ cm}^2$

23. (c)

ABC is an equilateral triangle with sides = 2 cm

Area of shaded portion = Area of equilateral triangle –Area of 3 quadrant

$\Rightarrow$ i.e. $\dfrac{\sqrt{3}}{4} a^2 - 3\left(\pi r^2 \dfrac{\theta}{360}\right)$; $\theta = 60°$ (Since, $\Delta ABC$

is an equilateral triangle)

$\Rightarrow \dfrac{\sqrt{3}}{4} \times 2^2 - 3\left(3.14 \times 1 \times \dfrac{60}{360}\right)$

$\Rightarrow \sqrt{3} - \dfrac{3.14}{2} = \sqrt{3} - \dfrac{\pi}{2}$

24. (d)

Volume of elliptical cylinder=

$\pi\left(\dfrac{2.4}{2}\right)\left(\dfrac{1.6}{2}\right).7 = 21.12 \, m^3$

Amount of water emptied per minute=

$\pi\left(\dfrac{2}{100}\right)^2 120 \, m^3$

Time required to empty half the tank =

$\dfrac{\dfrac{21.12}{2}}{\pi\left(\dfrac{2}{100}\right)^2 120} = 70 \, min$

25. (d)

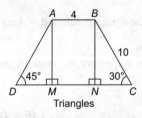
Triangles

AB and DC are the parallel sides

Height = $AM = BN$

$AB = MN = 4$

$\Delta BNC$ and $\Delta AMD$ are right angled triangles

In $\Delta BNC \Rightarrow \sin 30 = \dfrac{BN}{10} \Rightarrow BN = 5$

Using Pythagoras theorem $NC = \sqrt{10^2 - 5^2} = 5\sqrt{3}$

In$\Delta ADM$; $AM = 5$; $\tan 45 = \dfrac{AM}{DM} = 1 = \dfrac{5}{DM}$

$\Rightarrow \qquad DM = 5$

Area of trapezium $\Rightarrow \dfrac{1}{2}$ (Sum of Parallel sides) × height

$\Rightarrow \dfrac{1}{2}(4 + 4 + 5\sqrt{3} + 5) \times 5 = \dfrac{5(13 + 5\sqrt{3})}{2}$ (Answer)

26. (d)

$PQ = QR = RS = \dfrac{12}{3} = 4 \text{ cm}$

Area of unshaded region $\Rightarrow \dfrac{\pi 6^2}{2} + \dfrac{\pi 4^2}{2}$

$\Rightarrow 18\pi + 8\pi \Rightarrow 26\pi$

Area of shaded region $\Rightarrow \dfrac{\pi 6^2}{2} - \dfrac{\pi 4^2}{2}$

$\Rightarrow 18\pi - 8\pi = 10\pi$

Ratio = $\dfrac{10\pi}{26\pi} \Rightarrow \dfrac{5}{13} \Rightarrow 5 : 13$

27. (c)

$QP = \sqrt{5^2 + 12^2} = 13$

Area of the triangle = $\dfrac{1}{2} \times b \times h = 30$

$\Rightarrow$ As $Rx$ is $a \perp$ drawn to the hypotenuse

So $Rx = \dfrac{2 \times \text{Area}}{\text{Hypotenuse}} = \dfrac{60}{13}$

28. (d)

A 50% increase in the radius without increasing the height would mean a multiplication of the radius by 1.5. This would mean that the volume would get multiplied by 1.5 × 1.5 (since the volume formula is $\pi r^2 h$).

29. Distance after 4 hours = $AB = C$

$a = 3 \times 4 = 12; \, b = 2 \times 4 = 8$

and $\dfrac{a+b+c}{2} \Rightarrow \dfrac{12 + 8 + C}{2} \Rightarrow \left(10 + \dfrac{C}{2}\right)$

Area = $\sqrt{S(S-a)(S-b)(S-c)}$

Area = $\dfrac{1}{2} ab \sin 120°$

Area $\Rightarrow 48 \times \dfrac{\sqrt{3}}{2} = 24\sqrt{3}$

As per question:

$24\sqrt{3} = \sqrt{\left(10 + \dfrac{c}{2}\right)\left(\dfrac{c}{2} - 2\right)\left(2 + \dfrac{c}{2}\right)\left(10 - \dfrac{c}{2}\right)}$

On solving, we get $c = 4\sqrt{19}$ km

30. (c)

Volume of the cone =

$$\frac{\pi r^2 h}{3} = \frac{22 \times 20 \times 20 \times 24}{3 \times 7} = 10057.14 \text{ cm}^3$$

Diameter of the pipe = 5 mm = 0.5 cm.

Volume of water flowing out of the pipe per minute (in cm³) =

$1000 \times 0.25 \times 0.25 \times \pi = 196.42$ cm³

Hence, the time taken to fill the tank = $10057.14 \div 196.42 = 51.2$ minutes.

31. (d)

One side of the equilateral triangle = diameter of cone.

Therefore radius of cone = $\dfrac{12}{2} = 6$

Height of cone = Height of equilateral triangle

Height of cone = $6\sqrt{3}$

Volume of cone = $\dfrac{\pi r^2 h}{3}$

$$\Rightarrow \qquad \frac{\pi \times 6^2 \times 6\sqrt{3}}{3} = 72\sqrt{3}\pi \text{ cm}^3$$

32. (b)

Let the radius of the iron ball = $r_1$;

Let the radius of the oak ball = $r_0$;

Since, the weight of iron is eight times the weight of oak, the volume of the oak ball would need to be 8 times the volume of the iron ball for the same weight of the two balls.

Thus, we have:

$$\frac{4\pi r_0^3}{3} = \frac{8 \times 4\pi r_1^3}{3} \rightarrow r_0 = 2r_1$$

Hence, the diameter of the iron ball is half the diameter of the oak ball.

33. (a)

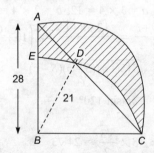

Area of shaded portion = Area of $ADC$ – Area of sector $DC$ + Area of $\triangle ADB$ – sector $BED$

$\Rightarrow$ Area of $ADC = \pi \times (17.5)^2 \times \dfrac{1}{2} = 481$ cm²

$\dfrac{\angle DBC}{\angle ABC} = \dfrac{21}{28} \Rightarrow \angle DBC = 67.5$ and $\angle DBA = 22.5$

$\Rightarrow$ Area of sector $DC = \left(\pi \times 21^2 \times \dfrac{67.5}{360}\right)$

$$-\left(\frac{1}{2} \times 21^2 \times Sin67.5\right) = 56 \text{ cm}^2$$

$\Rightarrow$ Area of $ADE = \left(\dfrac{1}{2} \times 28 \times 21\right)$

$$-\left(204 + \frac{1}{2} \times 21^2 \times \sin 22.5\right) = 5.6 \text{ cm}^2$$

Thus area of shaded portion = $480 - 56 + 5.6 = 429$ cm²

34. (a)

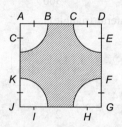

$KJ$ = radius of semicircles = 10 cm

4 Quadrants of equal radius = 1 circle of that radius

Area of shaded portion $\Rightarrow$ Area of rectangle – Area of circle

$\Rightarrow (28 \times 26) - (3.14 \times 10^2) \Rightarrow 414$ cm²

$BC = 28 - (10 + 10) = 8$ and $EF = 26 - (10 + 10) = 6$

Perimeter of shaded portion = $28$ cm + $2\pi r$

Answer $\Rightarrow 414$ cm² = Area and

Perimeter = 90.8 cm

35. (b)

Go through the option

Only option (b) is correct as its' area matches with the radius.

36. (c)

Area of remaining cardboard = Area of trapezium – Area of quadrant

$\Rightarrow$ Area of trapezium = $\dfrac{1}{2}$(sum of parallel sides)

$$\times \text{ height}$$

$$= \frac{1}{2} \times (AB + DC) \times BC$$

$$\Rightarrow \frac{1}{2} \times (3.5 + 5.5) \times 3.5$$

$$= 4.5 \times 3.5 = 15.75 \text{ cm}^2$$

Area of quadrant = $\dfrac{\pi r^2}{4} \Rightarrow \dfrac{3.14 \times 3.5 \times 3.5}{4} = 9.625$

$\Rightarrow$ Area of remaining cardboard = $15.7 - 9.6 = 6.075$ cm²

37. (c)

Circumference of the 2 semicircles = $312 - (90 + 90)$
$$= 132$$

2 semicircles = 1 circle with equal radius

So $2\pi r = 132 \Rightarrow 2r = \dfrac{132}{3.14} \Rightarrow 42$ m diameter

Area of track = Area within external border – Area within internal border

$\Rightarrow \pi(23^2 - 21^2) + 90 \times 46 - 90 \times 42$

$\Rightarrow 88\pi + 360 \Rightarrow 636.57$ m$^2$

38. (d)

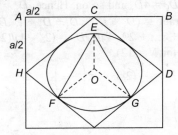

$AB$ = Side of the outermost square = $a$

$AC = CB = a/2$

$HC = \sqrt{\dfrac{a^2}{4} + \dfrac{a^2}{4}} = \dfrac{a}{\sqrt{2}}$

Diameter of circle = $\dfrac{a}{\sqrt{2}}$; radius = $\dfrac{a}{2\sqrt{2}}$

$O$ is the centre of the circle. Then $\angle EOF = 120°$

Then Area of $\Delta EOF = \dfrac{1}{2} EO \cdot OF \cdot \sin 120°$

$\Rightarrow \dfrac{1}{2} \times \dfrac{a^2}{8} \times \dfrac{\sqrt{3}}{2} = \dfrac{\sqrt{3}a^2}{32}$

Then area of $\Delta EFG = \dfrac{3\sqrt{3}a^2}{32}$

39. (a)

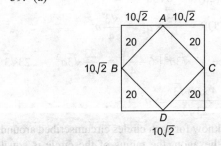

The length of rope of goat = $10\sqrt{2}$ m

Then the two goats will graze an area = Area of a semicircle with radius $10\sqrt{2}$ m.

So total area grazed = $\dfrac{\pi r^2}{2} \Rightarrow 100\pi$ m$^2$

40. (a)

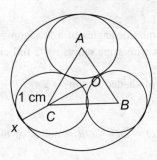

Let $A$, $B$, $C$ be centers of circles having radius 1 cm and $O$ is the center of the circle circumscribing these three circles.

$AC = AB = BC = 2$ cm

By using the formula of the circumradius we can calculate $OC$.

$OC = \dfrac{2 \times 2 \times 2}{4 \times \dfrac{\sqrt{3}}{4}(2)^2} = 2/\sqrt{3}$

$OX = OC + CX = \dfrac{2}{\sqrt{3}} + 1$cm

Required area = $\pi\left(\dfrac{2}{\sqrt{3}} + 1\right)^2 = \dfrac{\pi}{3}\left(2 + \sqrt{3}\right)^2$ cm$^2$.

41. (b)

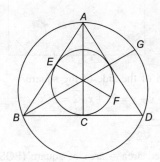

Let side of equilateral triangle = $a$

Then height = $\dfrac{a\sqrt{3}}{2}$

Area = $\dfrac{\sqrt{3}}{4}a^2$; $S = \dfrac{a+a+a}{2} = \dfrac{3a}{2}$

Diameter of inner circle = $\dfrac{2 \times \text{Area}}{S}$

$= \dfrac{\sqrt{3}}{2}a^2 \times \dfrac{2}{3a} = \dfrac{a}{\sqrt{3}}$

Diameter of outer circle = $\dfrac{a^3}{2 \times \text{Area}} = a^3 \times \dfrac{2}{\sqrt{3}a^2}$

$\Rightarrow \dfrac{2a}{\sqrt{3}}$

Ratio = $\dfrac{a}{\sqrt{3}} : \dfrac{2a}{\sqrt{3}} : \dfrac{a\sqrt{3}}{2} \Rightarrow$ Ratio = 2 : 4 : 3

42. (b)

Sum of interior angles of a hexagon = 720°

6 sectors with same radius $r = 2$ full circles of same radius

So area of shaded region $\Rightarrow 2\pi r^2$

43. (d)

44. (a)

$AO = CO = DO = OB$ = radius of bigger circle = $r$(let)

Then area of $(G + F) = \dfrac{\pi r^2}{2}$

Area of $2(G + F) = \pi r^2$. Also area of $2G + F + E = \pi r^2$

i.e. $2G + F + F = 2G + F + E \Rightarrow F = E$

So the ratio of areas $E$ and $F = 1 : 1$

45. (c)

46. If Mithilesh cut the cardboard as shown in the diagram below:

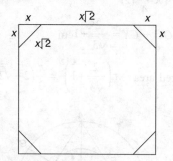

Length of the side of the square =

$x\sqrt{2} + x + x = 2x + x\sqrt{2} = 2$

$x = \dfrac{2}{2 + \sqrt{2}}$

Reduced area = area of square (PQSR) – (Sum of areas of four right angle triangles)

$= 4 - \left(4 \times \dfrac{1}{2} \times \dfrac{4}{\left(2 + \sqrt{2}\right)^2}\right) = \dfrac{8}{\sqrt{2} + 1}$ sq. units

47.

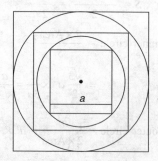

Let the radius of the circle be $x$ then according to the question:

$x^2 + x^2 = a^2$ or $x = \dfrac{a}{\sqrt{2}}$

$D_1 = \dfrac{\pi a^2}{2} - a^2$

For $A_2$ and $C_2$:

$C_2 = \pi a^2$ and $A_2 = 2a^2$

$D_2 = \pi a^2 - 2a^2 = 2\left(\dfrac{\pi}{2}a^2\right) = 2D_1$

Similarly $D_3 = 4D_1$ and so on. Hence, $D_N = 2^{N-1}D_1$

Required ratio = $(D_1 + D_2 + D_3 + D_4 + \dots D_N)/D_1$ = $(1 + 2 + 4 + \dots + 2^{(N-1)})D_1/D_1 = (2^N - 1)/(2 - 1) = (2^{12} - 1)$ (for $N = 12$).

48. $S_1 = Q_1 - P_2 = \dfrac{1}{2}(2r)^2 - \pi\left(\dfrac{r}{\sqrt{2}}\right)^2 = 2r^2 - \dfrac{\pi r^2}{2} = r^2\left(\dfrac{4 - \pi}{2}\right)$

$S_2 = Q_2 - P_3 = \dfrac{1}{2}(\sqrt{2}r)^2 - \dfrac{\pi r^2}{4} = r^2\left(\dfrac{4 - \pi}{4}\right)$

Required Sum $S_n = S_1 + S_2 + S_3\dots$

i.e. Sum of infinite GP having common ratio ½

$S_n = \left(\dfrac{r^2\dfrac{(4 - \pi)}{2}}{1 - \dfrac{1}{2}}\right) = 2r^2\left(\dfrac{4 - \pi}{2}\right) = r^2(4 - \pi)$

Required Ratio $= \dfrac{S_n}{Q_1} = \left(\dfrac{r^2(4 - \pi)}{2r^2}\right) = \dfrac{4 - \pi}{2}$

By comparing we get $a = 4$, $b = 2$, therefore $a + b = 4 + 2 = 6$

49. Area of Hexagon = Area of six equilateral triangles having their side equal to the side of the hexagon = $6 \times \dfrac{\sqrt{3}}{4} \times (2a)^2 = 6\sqrt{3}a^2$

Area of PQR = $\dfrac{\sqrt{3}}{4} \times a^2 = \dfrac{\sqrt{3}}{4}a^2$

Difference = $\sqrt{3}a^2\left(6 - \dfrac{1}{4}\right) = \dfrac{23}{4}\sqrt{3}a^2 = 23\sqrt{3}$

$\Rightarrow a^2 = \dfrac{4 \times 23\sqrt{3}}{23\sqrt{3}} \Rightarrow a^2 = 4$

Now, we know for such circles circumscribed around a regular hexagon, the radius of the circle is equal to the side of the hexagon. Hence, the radius of the circle is $2a$.

Area of circle $= \pi r^2 = \pi(2a)^2 = 4\pi a^2 = 4\pi \times 4 = 16\pi$ cm$^2$ $\because a^2 = 4$.

Therefore $X = 16$

50. Side of the square $S_3$ = Diagonal of the square $S_2$ = 4 cm

Side of a square is $\dfrac{1}{\sqrt{2}}$ times of its diagonal. So

side of square $S_2 = \dfrac{4}{\sqrt{2}}$ cm. = $2\sqrt{2}$ cm

Similarly side of square $S_1 = \dfrac{2\sqrt{2}}{\sqrt{2}} = 2$ cm. This means that the sides of the consecutive squares forms a Geometric Progression, with common ratio = $\sqrt{2}$ cm.

So side of $S_n = 2\left(\sqrt{2}\right)^{n-1} = 2^{\frac{n+1}{2}}$ cm

Side of $S_{11} = 2^{\frac{11+1}{2}} = 2^6 = 64$ cm

Area of the square = $64^2 = 4096$ cm²

51.

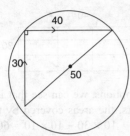

Radius of the circle = $\dfrac{1}{2}\left(\sqrt{(30^2 + 40^2)}\right) = 25$ m

Area of the pool = $\pi (25)^2 = 625\ \pi\text{m}^2 = X\pi$

Therefore $X = 625$

52.

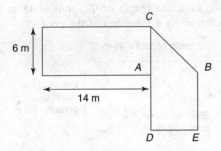

It can be seen from the diagram that actual area = folded area + area of triangular portion ($ABC$)

Area of triangular portion ($ABC$) = $\dfrac{1}{2} \times 6 \times 6 = 18$ m²

So, there is an increase of 18 m². Total area of the unfolded rectangle = 144 m² + 18 m² = 162 m².

53. Volume of cylinder= $\pi r^2 h = \pi \times 7^2 \times 10 = 1540$ cm³

Flat surface area of cylinder = $2\pi \times 7^2 = 308$ cm²

Cone 1: Volume= $(3/7) \times 1540 = 660$ cm³

Volume of cone = $(1/3)\ \pi r^2 h = 660$

$\Rightarrow (1/3)\pi r^2\ 10 = 660 \Rightarrow \pi r^2 = 66 \times 3 = 198$ cm²

Flat surface area= $\pi r^2 = 198$ cm²

Cone 2: Volume= $(4/7) \times 1540 = 880$ cm³

Volume of cone = $(1/3)\ \pi r^2 h = 880$

$\Rightarrow (1/3)\pi r^2\ 10 = 880 \Rightarrow \pi r^2 = 88 \times 3 = 264$ cm²

Final flat surface area = 198 + 264 cm² = 462 cm²

Increase in flat surface area = 462 − 308 = 154 cm²

Percentage increase = $(154/308) \times 100 = 50\%$

54. The following image explains the construction

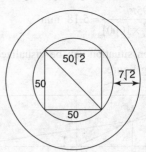

Radius of inner circle= $(1/2) \times 50\sqrt{2}$ ft. = $25\sqrt{2}$ ft.

Radius of outer circle = $32\sqrt{2}$ ft.

Area of the path = $\pi \times [(32\sqrt{2}\ \text{ft.})^2 - (25\sqrt{2}\ \text{ft.})^2]$ = 2508 ft²

Total cost = $2508 \times 100 = ₹250800$

50% of this = ₹125400

55. The following figure would exemplify the situation, with the pipe attached at a height of $h$ from the apex (bottom) of the cone.

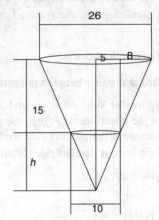

In the above figure the cones with height $h$ and the cone with height $h + 15$ are similar to each other. Hence using similarity we will get:

$\dfrac{10}{26} = \dfrac{h}{h+15}$

$\rightarrow 10h + 150 = 26h \rightarrow 16h = 150 \rightarrow h = 9.375$ cm

Based on this information we can then calculate the volume of water that would flow out from the pipe as: Total volume of the cone with height $(h + 15)$ − volume of cone of height $h$.

$= \dfrac{1}{3}\pi[(13^2 \times (15 + 9.375) - (5^2 \times 9.375)]$

Calculating this we get the volume of water that overflows = $1295\ \pi$ cm³

Further, the rate at which the water flows out of the hole per minute is given by:

$\pi \times (0.5^2 \times 1000)$ cm³

Hence, the required time can be given as,

$$\frac{1295\pi}{\pi \times \left(0.5^2 \times 1000\right)} = 5.18 \text{ min}$$

56. The given situation can be visualized based on the following figure:

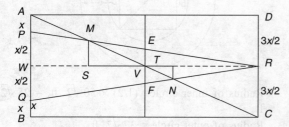

The area of the quadrilateral $PQNM$ = Area of $PQFE$ – Area Triangle $MVE$ + Area Triangle $VFN$.

So our focus to find the area of the required quadrilateral should shift to the area of the three individual components on the right hand side of the above equation.

Finding the area of quadrilateral $PQFE$:

Being a parallelogram, the required area would be given by:

$$\frac{1}{2} \times \text{sum of parallel sides} \times$$

perpendicular distance between the parallel sides.

In the figure, let side $AB = 3x$ and side $BC = y$. Then, for the quadrilateral $PQFE$, the perpendicular distance between the parallel side would be $y/2$.

Further, the sum of parallel sides would be equal to

$$PQ + EF = x + \frac{x}{2} = \frac{3x}{2}$$

Area of PQFE = $\frac{1}{2} \times \frac{3x}{2} \times \frac{y}{2}$

We know that the area of the rectangle is $3x \times y = 90$

Hence area of $PQFE = 90 \div 8 = 11.25$

Finding the area of the triangle $MEV$.

$$\frac{1}{2} \times \text{base} \times \text{height} = \frac{1}{2} \times EV \times \text{height}$$

Using similarity between $APM$ and $VEM$, we can see that since $AP = x$ and $EV = x/4$, the ratios of the lengths of $APM$ and $VEM$ would be 4:1.

Thus, if the height of $APM = 4h$, the height of $VEM = h$ and also $4h + h = y/2 \to h = $ height of $VEM$ with base $VE = y/10$

Hence, area triangle MEV = $\frac{1}{2} \times EV \times \text{height} = \frac{xy}{80}$ = 0.375

Similarly, the area of $\Delta VFN \approx 0.27$.

Thus, the required area = $11.25 - 0.375 + 0.27 \approx$ 11.145

57. Think of this question as follows:

The entire park is 1200 square meters. Out of this, the area of the road formed has to be 600 meters (based on the condition that 'the mayor wants that the area of the two roads to be equal to the remaining area of the park'). Also, the width of all the roads should be equal (since, the diagonals of the parks have to be diagonals of the small rectangle formed at the intersection of the two roads-it means that the rectangle formed at the intersection of the two roads should be a square). The figure would look as follows:

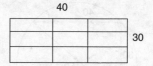

Using the options, we can see that if the road width is 10 meters, the areas covered by the roads would be $10 \times 40 + 10 \times 30 - 10 \times 10 = 600$, which would mean that exactly half the area of the park would be covered by roads.

Hence, option (a) is correct.

58. For every 2.6m that one walks along the slant part of the pool, there is a height of 1 m that is gained. Also, since the length of the pool is 48 m we get the following dimensions of the pool.

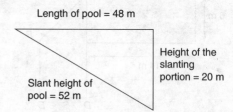

The pool would look as given in the figure below:

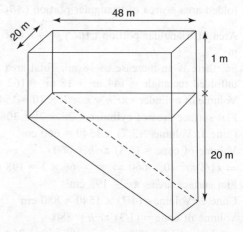

The volume of water in the pool = volume of the upper part + volume of the standard triangular vessel

$$= \left(\frac{1}{2} \times 48 \times 20\right) \times 20 + (48 \times 20 \times 1)$$

$\Rightarrow 48 \times 20 \times 11$

$\Rightarrow 10560 \ \text{m}^3$

Hence, option (d) is the correct answer.

59.

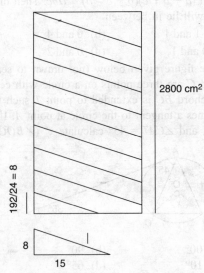

$h = \dfrac{2\pi rh}{2\pi r} = \dfrac{2880}{15} = 192 \ \text{cm}$

$I = \sqrt{8^2 + 15^2} = 17 \ \text{cm}$

Therefore length of one complete turn = 17 cm

Hence, total length of the thread = $17 \times 24 = 408$ cm

60. Let θ be the angle made by minute hand to cover an area of $110.88 \ \text{cm}^2$.

$\Rightarrow \dfrac{22}{7} \times (4.2)^2 \times \dfrac{\theta}{360°} = 110.88$

$\theta = \dfrac{110.88 \times 360° \times 7}{22 \times (4.2)^2}$

$\theta = 720°$

As we know that speed of hour hand is $\dfrac{1}{12}$ of the speed of minute hand therefore angle covered by hour hand during this period is $\dfrac{720°}{12} = 60°$

Area covered by hour hand = $\pi (2.1)^2 \times \dfrac{60°}{360°}$

$= \dfrac{22}{7} \times 2.1 \times 2.1 \times \dfrac{1}{6}$

$= 2.31 \ \text{cm}^2$

61.

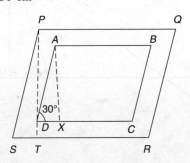

Draw $AX \perp DC$

$AX = 10 \ \sin 30° = 5 \ \text{m}$

If $PT \perp SR$

$PT = 5 + 2 + 2 = 9 \ \text{m}$

$PS = \dfrac{PT}{\sin 30°} = \dfrac{9}{1/2} = 18 \ \text{m}$

Area of the path = area of $PQRS$ – area of $ABCD$ (Using Area of rhombus = base × height)

$= 18 \times 9 - (10 \times 5)$

$= 162 - 50 = 112 \ \text{m}^2$

62. Area of $\square ABCD = 1$

Area of portion between $ABCD$ and $PQRS = \dfrac{3}{2} - 1$

$= \dfrac{1}{2}$

Area of the next portion (between $PQRS$ & $XYZW$)

$= \dfrac{7}{4} - \dfrac{3}{2} = \dfrac{1}{4}$

Area of the next portion $= \dfrac{15}{8} - \dfrac{7}{4} = \dfrac{1}{8}$

So the required area is the sum of the infinite Geometric Progression represented by: $1 + \dfrac{1}{2} + \dfrac{1}{4} + \dfrac{1}{8} + \ldots$

$= \dfrac{1}{1 - \dfrac{1}{2}} = 2$

63. If side of the smallest hexagon is '$a$' and the side of the second largest and largest hexagons are $b$ & $c$ respectively. Then according to the question:

$\dfrac{3\sqrt{3}}{2} a^2 = A_1$

$\dfrac{3\sqrt{3}}{2} b^2 = A_1 + A_2 = 3A_1$

$\dfrac{3\sqrt{3}}{2} c^2 = A_1 + A_2 + A_3 = 6A_1$

$a^2 : b^2 : c^2 = 1 : 3 : 6$

$a : b : c = 1 : \sqrt{3} : \sqrt{6}$

***Space for Rough Work***

# Extra Practice Exercise on Geometry and Mensuration

1. In the figure given what is the measure of $\angle ACD$

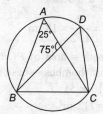

(a) 75°  (b) 80°
(c) 90°  (d) 105°

2. Two circles $C_1$ and $C_2$ of radius 2 and 3 respectively touch each other as shown in the figure. If $AD$ and $BD$ are tangents then the length of $BD$ is

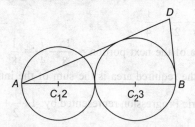

(a) $3\sqrt{6}$  (b) $5\sqrt{6}$
(c) $(3\sqrt{10})/2$  (d) 6

3. If the sides of a triangle measure 13, 14, 15 cm respectively, what is the height of the triangle for the base side 14.
(a) 10  (b) 12
(c) 14  (d) 13

4. A right angled triangle is drawn on a plane such that sides adjacent to right angle are 3 cm and 4 cm. Now three semi-circles are drawn taking all three sides of the triangle as diameters respectively (as shown in the figure). What is the area of the shaded regions $A_1 + A_2$

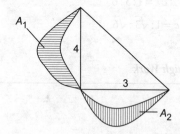

(a) $3\pi$  (b) $4\pi$
(c) $5\pi$  (d) None of these

5. A lateral side of an isosceles triangle is 15 cm and the altitude is 8 cm. What is the radius of the circumscribed circle

(a) 9.625  (b) 9.375
(c) 9.5  (d) 9.125

6. Let $a$, $b$, $c$ be the length of the sides of triangle $ABC$. Given $(a + b + c)(b + c - a) = \alpha bc$. Then the value of $\alpha$ will lie in between
(a) −1 and 1  (b) 0 and 4
(c) 0 and 1  (d) 0 and 2

7. In the figure given below (not drawn to scale). $A$, $B$ and $C$ are three points on a circle with centre $O$. The chord $BC$ is extended to point $T$ such that $AT$ becomes a tangent to the circle at point $A$. If $\angle CTA = 35°$ and $\angle CAT = 45°$ calculate $x°$ ($\angle BOC$)

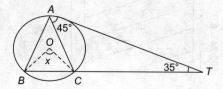

(a) 100°  (b) 90°
(c) 110°  (d) 65°

8. In the given figure

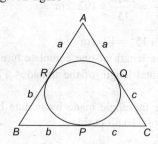

$AB = 20$
$BC = 15$
$CA = 19$

Calculate $a$, $b$, $c$
(a) $a = 12$, $b = 8$, $c = 7$
(b) $a = 8$, $b = 12$, $c = 7$
(c) $a = 9$, $b = 10$, $c = 15$
(d) $a = 10$, $b = 15$, $c = 9$

9. In the figure given below, $AB$ is perpendicular to $ED$. $\angle CED = 75°$ and $\angle ECF = 30°$. What is the measure of $\angle ABC$?

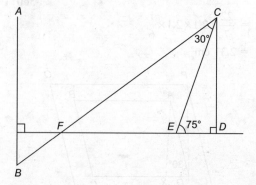

(a) 60°           (b) 45°
(c) 55°           (d) 30°

10. The angle between lines $L$ and $M$ measures 35° degrees. If line $M$ is rotated 45° degrees counter clockwise about point $P$ to line $M^1$ what is the angle in degrees between lines $L$ and $M^1$

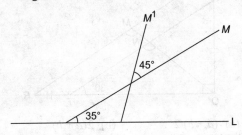

(a) 90°           (b) 80°
(c) 75°           (d) 60°

11. In the figure given below, $XYZ$ is a right angled triangle in which $\angle Y = 45°$ and $\angle X = 90°$. $ABCD$ is a square inscribed in it whose area is 64 cm². What is the area of triangle $XYZ$?

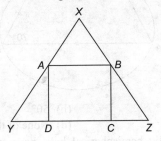

(a) 100           (b) 64
(c) 144           (d) 81

12. The area of circle circumscribed about a regular hexagon is $144\pi$. What is the area of hexagon?

(a) $300\sqrt{3}$      (b) $216\sqrt{3}$
(c) 256           (d) 225

13. Find the area of the shaded portion

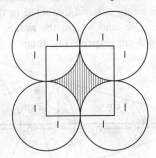

(a) $4 - \pi$         (b) $6 - \pi$
(c) $5 - \pi$         (d) $\pi$

14. The numerical value of the product of the three sides (which are integers when measured in cm) of a right angled triangle having a perimeter of 56 cm is 4200. Find the length of the hypotenuse.

(a) 24            (b) 25
(c) 15            (d) 30

15. In the figure $ABDC$ is a cyclic quadrilateral with $O$ as centre of the circle. Find $\angle BDC$.

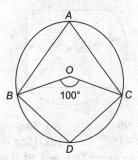

(a) 105°          (b) 120°
(c) 130°          (d) 95°

16. $B, O, P$ are centres of semicircles $AXC$, $AYB$ & $BZC$ respectively. $AC = 12$ cm. Find the area of the shaded region.

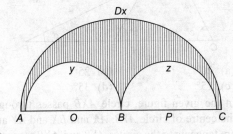

(a) $9\pi$           (b) $18\pi$
(c) $20\pi$          (d) $25\pi$

17. $O$ is the centre of the circle. $OP = 5$ and $OT = 4$, and $AB = 8$. The line $PT$ is a tangent to the circle. Find $PB$

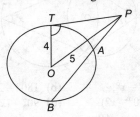

(a) 9 cm          (b) 10 cm
(c) 7 cm          (d) 8 cm

18. In the figure given below, $AB = 16$, $CD = 12$ and $OM = 6$. Calculate $ON$.

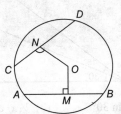

(a) 8             (b) 10
(c) 12            (d) 14

19. In the figure, $M$ is the centre of the circle. $1(QS) = 10\sqrt{2}$, $1(PR) = 1(RS)$ and $PR$ is parallel to $QS$. Find the area of the shaded region.

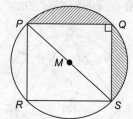

(a) $90\pi - 90$        (b) $50\pi - 100$
(c) $150\pi - 150$       (d) $125\pi - 125$

20. In the given figure $PBC$ and $PKH$ are straight lines. If $AH = AK$, $b = 70°$, $c = 40°$, the value of $d$ is

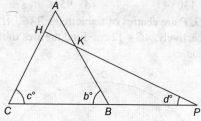

(a) $20°$        (b) $25°$
(c) $15°$        (d) $35°$

21. In the given figure, circle $AXB$ passes through '$O$' the centre of circle $AYB$. $AX$ and $BX$ and $AY$ and $BY$ are tangents to the circles $AYB$ and $AXB$ respectively. The value of $y°$ is

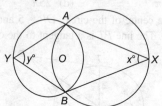

(a) $180° - x°$,        (b) $180° - 2x°$
(c) $\frac{1}{2}(90° - x°)$        (d) $90° - (x°/2)$

22. In the figure, $AB = x$
Calculate the area of triangle $ADC$ ($\angle B = 90°$)

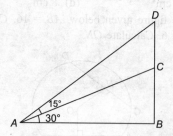

(a) $\frac{1}{2} x^2 \sin 30°$        (b) $\frac{1}{2} x^2 \cos 30°$
(c) $\frac{1}{2} x^2 \tan 30°$        (d) $\frac{1}{2} x^2(\tan 45° - \tan 30°)$

23. In the given figure $SQ = TR = a$, $QT = b$, $QM \perp PR$, $ST$ is parallel to $PR$.

$$m \angle STQ = 30°$$
$$m \angle SQT = 90°$$

Find $QM$.

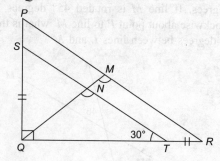

(a) $(a + b)/2$        (b) $2(a + b)$
(c) $(2a + b)/2$       (d) $(a + 2b)/2$

24. In the figure given, $AB$ is a diameter of the circle and $C$ and $D$ are on the circumference such that $\angle CAD = 40°$. Find the measure of the $\angle ACD$

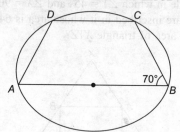

(a) $40°$        (b) $50°$
(c) $60°$        (d) None of these

25. Six solid hemispherical balls have to be arranged one upon the other vertically. Find the minimum total surface area of the cylinder in which the hemispherical balls can be arranged, if the radii of each hemispherical ball is 7 cm.

(a) 2056        (b) 2156
(c) 1232        (d) None of these

**Questions 26 and 27:**  In the following figure, there is a cone which is being cut and extracted in three segments having heights $h_1$, $h_2$ and $h_3$ and the radius of their bases 1 cm, 2 cm and 3 cm respectively, then

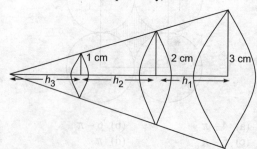

26. The ratio of the volumes of the smallest segment to that of the largest segment is

(a) $1 : 27$        (b) $27 : 1$
(c) $1 : 19$        (d) None of these

27. The ratio of the curved surface area of the second largest segment to that of the full cone is:
    (a) 1 : 3       (b) 4 : 9
    (c) Cannot be determined
    (d) None of these

28. On a semicircle with diameter $AD$, Chord $BC$ is parallel to the diameter. Further each of the chords $AB$ and $CD$ has Length 2 cm while $AD$ has length 8 cm. Find the length of $BC$.
    (a) 7.5 cm       (b) 7 cm
    (c) 7.75 cm       (d) Cannot be determined

29. In the given figure, $B$ and $C$ are points on the diameter $AD$ of the circle such that $AB = BC = CD$. Then find the ratio of area of the shaded portion to that of the whole circle.

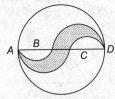

    (a) 1 : 3       (b) 2 : 3
    (c) 1 : 2       (d) None of these

30. In the given figure, $ABC$ is a triangle in which $AD$ and $DE$ are medians to $BC$ and $AB$ respectively, the ratio of the area of $\triangle BED$ to that of $\triangle ABC$ is

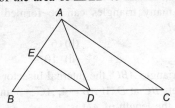

    (a) 1 : 4       (b) 1 : 16
    (c) Data inadequate       (d) None of these

31. Two identical circles intersect so that their centres, and the points at which they intersect, from a square of side 1 cm. The area in square cm of the portion that is common to the two circles is
    (a) $\pi/4$       (b) $\pi/2 - 1$
    (c) $\pi/5$       (d) $\sqrt{2} - 1$

32. If the height of a cone is trebled and its base diameter is doubled, then the ratio of the volume of the resultant cone to that of the original cone is
    (a) 9 : 1       (b) 9 : 2
    (c) 12 : 1       (d) 6 : 1

33. If two cylinders of equal volume have their heights in the ratio 2 : 3, then the ratio of their radii is
    (a) $\sqrt{3} : \sqrt{2}$       (b) 2 : 3
    (c) $\sqrt{5} : \sqrt{3}$       (d) $\sqrt{6} : \sqrt{3}$

34. Through three given non-collinear points, how many circles can pass.
    (a) 2       (b) 3
    (c) Both 1 and 2       (d) None of these

35. The area of the rectangle $ABCD$ is 2 and $BD = DE$. Find the area of the shaded region

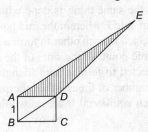

    (a) $\sqrt{5}$       (b) $2\sqrt{5}$
    (c) $\sqrt{(5/2)}$       (d) 1

36. In a right-angled triangle, the square of the hypotenuse is equal to twice the product of the other two sides. The acute angles of the triangle are
    (a) 30° and 30°       (b) 30° and 60°
    (c) 15° and 75°       (d) 45° and 45°

37. Find $\angle ALC$ if $AB \parallel CD$

    (a) 75       (b) 135
    (c) 110       (d) 145

38. If the sides of a triangle are in the ratio of $\frac{1}{2} : \frac{1}{3} : \frac{1}{4}$, the perimeter is 52 cm, then the length of the smallest side is
    (a) 12 cm       (b) 11 cm
    (c) 8 cm       (d) None of these

39. The number of distinct triangles with integral valued sides and perimeter as 14 is
    (a) 2       (b) 3
    (c) 4       (d) 5

40. A polygon has 65 diagonals. Then, what is the number of sides of the same polygon?
    (a) 11       (b) 12
    (c) 14       (d) None of these

41. $PQRS$ is a square drawn inside square $ABCD$ of side $2x$ units by joining the midpoints of the sides $AB$, $BC$, $CD$, $DA$. The square $TUVW$ is drawn inside $PQRS$, where $T$, $U$, $V$, $W$ are the midpoints of $SP$, $PQ$, $QR$ and $RS$ If the process is repeated an infinite number of times the sum of the areas of all the squares will be equal to:

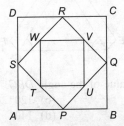

(a) $8x^2$      (b) $6x^2$
(c) $16x^2$      (d) $6x^2/2$

42. Suppose the same thing is done with an equilateral triangle of side $x$, wherein the mid points of the sides are connected to each other to form a second triangle and the mid points of the sides of the second triangle are connected to form a third triangle and so on an infinite number of times—then the sum of the areas of all such equilateral triangles would be:
(a) $3x^2$      (b) $6x^2$
(c) $12x^2$      (d) None of these

43. If in the figure given below $OP = PQ = 28$ cm and $OQ$, $PQ$ and $OP$ are all joined by semicircles, then the perimeter of the figure (shaded area) is equal to

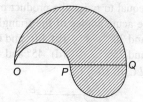

(a) 352 cm      (b) 264 cm
(c) 176 cm      (d) 88 cm

44. For the question above, what is the shaded area?
(a) 1352 sq. cm      (b) 1264 sq. cm
(c) 1232 sq. cm      (d) 1188 sq. cm

45. What is the area of the shaded portion? It is given that $ZV\|XY$, $WZ = ZX$, $ZV = 2a$ and $ZX = 2b$.

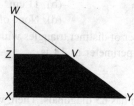

(a) $\dfrac{4ab}{2}$      (b) $\dfrac{8ab}{3}$

(c) $6ab$      (d) $3ab$

46. In the given figure there is an isosceles triangle $ABC$ with angle $A$ = angle $C$ = 50° $ABDE$ and $BCFG$ are two rectangles drawn on the sides $AB$ and $BC$ respectively, such that $BD = BG = AE = CF$.

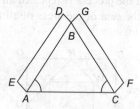

Find the value of the angle $DBG$.
(a) 80°      (b) 120°
(c) 100°      (d) 140°

47. In the figure, $ABE$, $DCE$, $BCF$ and $ADF$ are straight lines. $E = 50°$, $F = 56°$, find $\angle A$.

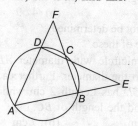

(a) 47°      (b) 37°
(c) 40°      (d) 42°

48. $ABC$ is an equilateral triangle. $PQRS$ is a square inscribed in it. Therefore
(a) $AR^2 = RC^2$      (b) $2AR^2 = RC^2$
(c) $3AR^2 = 4RC^2$      (d) $4AR^2 = 3RC^2$

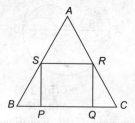

49. Consider the five points comprising the vertices of a square and the intersection point of its diagonals. How many triangles can be formed using these points?
(a) 4      (b) 6
(c) 8      (d) 10

50. In a triangle $ABC$, the internal bisector of the angle $A$ meets $BC$ at $D$. If $AB = 4$, $AC = 3$ and $\angle A = 60°$. Then, the length of $AD$ is:
(a) $2\sqrt{3}$      (b) $(12\sqrt{3})/7$
(c) $(15\sqrt{3})/8$      (d) $(6\sqrt{3})/7$

**Directions for Questions 51 and 52:** Answer the questions based on the following information.

A rectangle $PRSU$, is divided into two smaller rectangles $PQTU$ and $QRST$ by the line $QT$. $PQ = 40$ cm. $QR = 20$ cm, and $RS = 40$ cm. Points $A$, $B$, $F$ are within rectangle $PQTU$, and points $C$, $D$, $E$ are within the rectangle $QRST$. The closest pair of points among the pairs $(A, C)$, $(A, D)$, $(A, E)$, $(F, C)$, $(F, D)$, $(F, E)$, $(B, C)$, $(B, D)$, $(B, E)$ are 40 $\sqrt{3}$ cm apart.

51. Which of the following statements is necessarily true?
(a) The closest pair of points among the six given points cannot be $(F, C)$.
(b) Distance between $A$ and $B$ is greater than that between $F$ and $C$.
(c) The closest pair of points among the six given points is $(C, D)$, $(D, E)$ or $(C, E)$.
(d) None of the above.

52. $AB > AF > BF$; $CD > DE > CE$; and $BF = 24\sqrt{5}$ cm. Which is the closest pair of points among all the six given points?

    (a) $B, F$         (b) $C, D$

    (c) $A, B$         (d) None of these

53. If $ABCD$ is a square and $CDE$ is an equilateral triangle, what is the measure of $\angle DEB$?

    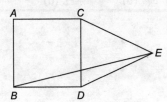

    (a) 15°         (b) 30°

    (c) 20°         (d) 45°

54. $AB \perp BC$, $BD \perp AC$ and $CE$ bisects $\angle C$, $\angle A = 30°$. Then, what is $\angle CED$?

    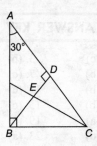

    (a) 30°         (b) 60°

    (c) 45°         (d) 65°

55. Instead of walking along two adjacent sides of a rectangular field, a boy took a short cut along the diagonal and saved a distance equal to half the longer side. Then, the ratio of the shorter side to the longer side is:

    (a) 1/2         (b) 2/3

    (c) 1/4         (d) 3/4

*Space for Rough Work*

## ANSWER KEY

| | | | |
|---|---|---|---|
| 1. (b) | 2. (c) | 3. (b) | 4. (d) |
| 5. (b) | 6. (b) | 7. (c) | 8. (a) |
| 9. (b) | 10. (b) | 11. (c) | 12. (b) |
| 13. (a) | 14. (b) | 15. (c) | 16. (a) |
| 17. (a) | 18. (a) | 19. (b) | 20. (c) |
| 21. d | 22. (d) | 23. (a) | 24. (d) |

| | | | |
|---|---|---|---|
| 25. (b) | 26. (c) | 27. (a) | 28. (b) |
| 29. (a) | 30. (a) | 31. (b) | 32. (c) |
| 33. (a) | 34. (d) | 35. (d) | 36. (d) |
| 37. (b) | 38. (a) | 39. (c) | 40. (d) |
| 41. (a) | 42. (d) | 43. (c) | 44. (c) |
| 45. (c) | 46. (c) | 47. (b) | 48. (d) |
| 49. (c) | 50. (b) | 51. (d) | 52. (d) |
| 53. (a) | 54. (b) | 55. (d) | |

# Coordinate Geometry

From the CAT point of view, Coordinate Geometry by itself is not a very significant chapter. Basically, applied questions are asked in the form of tabular representation or regarding the shape of the structure formed. However, it is advised to go through the basics and important formulae to have a feel-good effect as also to be prepared for surprises, if any, in the examination. Logical questions might be asked based on the formulae and concepts contained in this chapter. Besides, the student will have an improved understanding of the graphical representation of functions if he/she has gone through coordinate geometry.

The students who face any problems in this chapter can stop after solving LOD II and can skip LOD III.

## CARTESIAN COORDINATE SYSTEM

### Rectangular Coordinate Axes

Let $X'OX$ and $Y'OY$ be two mutually perpendicular lines through any point $O$ in the plane of the paper. Point $O$ is known as the origin. The line $X'OX$ is called the $x$-axis or axis of $x$; the line $Y'OY$ is known as the $y$-axis or axis of $y$; and the two lines taken together are called the coordinate axes or the axes of coordinates.

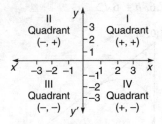

**Fig. 12.1**

Any point can be represented on the plane described by the coordinate axes by specifying its $x$ and $y$ coordinates.

The $x$ coordinate of the point is also known as the abscissa while the $y$ coordinate is also known as the ordinate.

**1. Distance Formula** If two points $P$ and $Q$ are such that they are represented by the points $(x_1, y_1)$ and $(x_2, y_2)$ on the $x$-$y$ plane (cartesian plane), then the distance between the points $P$ and $Q = \sqrt{(x_1 - x_2)^2 + (y_1 - y_2)^2}$ .

## Illustration

**Question 1:** Find the distance between the points $(5, 2)$ and $(3, 4)$.

**Answer:** Distance $= \sqrt{(5-3)^2 + (2-4)^2}$

$\left[ \text{Using the formula } \sqrt{(x_1 - x_2)^2 + (y_1 - y_2)^2} \right]$

$= 2\sqrt{2}$ units

**2. Section Formula** If any point $(x, y)$ divides the line segment joining the points $(x_1, y_1)$ and $(x_2, y_2)$ in the ratio $m:n$ internally,

then
$$x = (mx_2 + nx_1)/(m + n)$$
$$y = (my_2 + ny_1)/(m + n) \qquad \text{(See figure)}$$

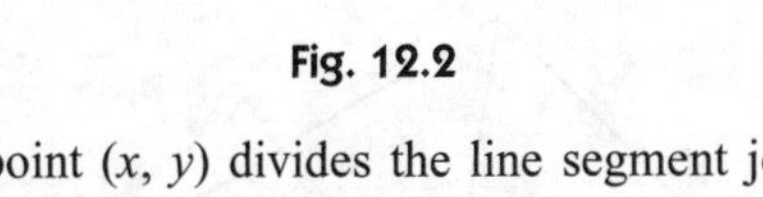

**Fig. 12.2**

If any point $(x, y)$ divides the line segment joining the points $(x_1, y_1)$ and $(x_2, y_2)$ in the ratio $m:n$ externally,

then
$$x = (mx_2 - nx_1)/(m - n)$$
$$y = (my_2 - ny_1)/(m - n)$$

## Illustration

**Question 2:** Find the point which divides the line segment joining (2, 5) and (1, 2) in the ratio 2:1 internally.

**Answers:** $X = (2.1 + 1.2)/(1 + 2) = 4/3$
$Y = (2.2 + 1.5)/(2 + 1) = 9/3 = 3$

**3. Area of a Triangle** The area of a triangle whose vertices are $A(x_1, y_1)$, $B(x_2, y_2)$ and $C(x_3, y_3)$ is given by

$$\left[\frac{\{x_1(y_2 - y_3) + x_2(y_3 - y_1) + x_3(y_1 - y_2)\}}{2}\right]$$

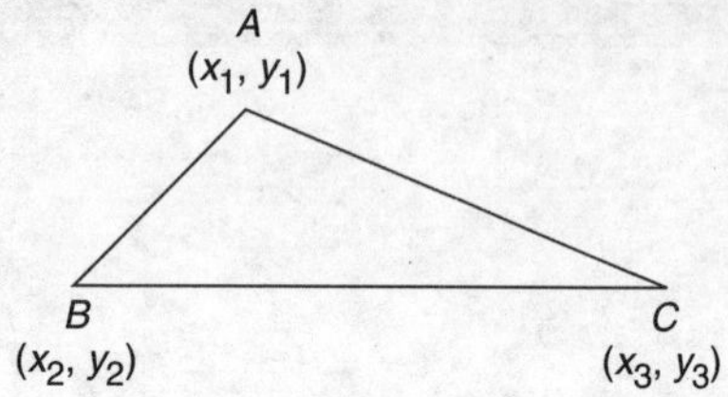

$A$
$(x_1, y_1)$

$B$
$(x_2, y_2)$
$C$
$(x_3, y_3)$

**Fig. 12.3**

[**Note:** Since the area cannot be negative, we have to take the modulus value given by the above equation.]

**Corollary:** If one of the vertices of the triangle is at the origin and the other two vertices are $A(x_1, y_1)$, $B(x_2, y_2)$, then the area of triangle is $\left|\dfrac{(x_1 y_2 - x_2 y_1)}{2}\right|$.

## Illustration

**Question 3:** Find the area of the triangle (0, 4), (3, 6) and (−8, −2).

**Answer:** Area of triangle $= |1/2 \{0 (6 - (-2)) + 3 ((-2) - 4) + (-8) (4-6)\}|$

$= |1/2 \{(0) + 3 (-6) + (-8) (-2)\}|$
$= |1/2 (-2)| = |-1| = 1$ square unit.

**4. Centre of Gravity or Centroid of a Triangle** The centroid of a triangle is the point of intersection of its medians (the line joining the vertex to the middle point of the opposite side). Centroid divides the medians in the ratio 2:1. In other words, the $CG$ or the centroid can be viewed as a point at which the whole weight of the triangle is concentrated.

**Formula:** If $A(x_1, y_1)$, $B(x_2, y_2)$ and $C(x_3, y_3)$ are the coordinates of the vertices of a triangle, then the coordinates of the centroid $G$ of that triangle are

$$x = (x_1 + x_2 + x_3)/3 \text{ and } y = (y_1 + y_2 + y_3)/3$$

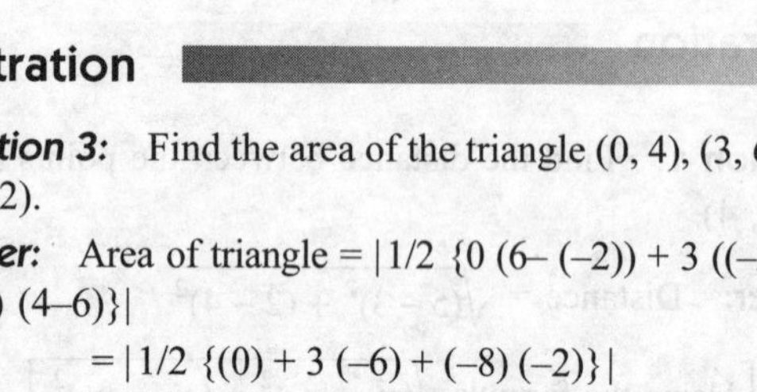

$A$

$G$

$B$
$C$

**Fig. 12.4**

## Illustration

**Question 4:** Find the centroid of the triangle whose vertices are (5, 3), (4, 6) and (8, 2).

**Answer:** $X$ coordinate $= (5 + 4 + 8)/3 = 17/3$

$Y$ coordinate $= (3 + 6 + 2)/3 = 11/3$

**5. In-centre of a Triangle** The centre of the circle that touches the sides of a triangle is called its In-centre. In other words, if the three sides of the triangle are tangential to the circle then the centre of that circle represents the in-centre of the triangle.

The in-centre is also the point of intersection of the internal bisectors of the angles of the triangle. The distance of the in-centre from the sides of the triangle is the same and this distance is called the in-radius of the triangle.

If $A(x_1, y_1)$, $B(x_2, y_2)$ and $C(x_3, y_3)$ are the coordinates of the vertices of a triangle, then the coordinates of its in-centre are

$$x = \frac{(ax_1 + bx_2 + cx_3)}{(a + b + c)} \quad \text{and} \quad y = \frac{(ay_1 + by_2 + cy_3)}{(a + b + c)}$$

where $BC = a$, $AB = c$ and $AC = b$.

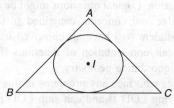

$A$

$\bullet I$

$B$
$C$

**Fig. 12.5**

## Illustration

**Question 5:** Find the in-centre of the right angled isosceles triangle having one vertex at the origin and having the other two vertices at (6, 0) and (0, 6).

**Answer:** Obviously, the length of the two sides $AB$ and $BC$ of the triangle is 6 units and the length of the third side is $(6^2 + 6^2)^{1/2}$.

Hence $a = c = 6$, $b = 6\sqrt{2}$

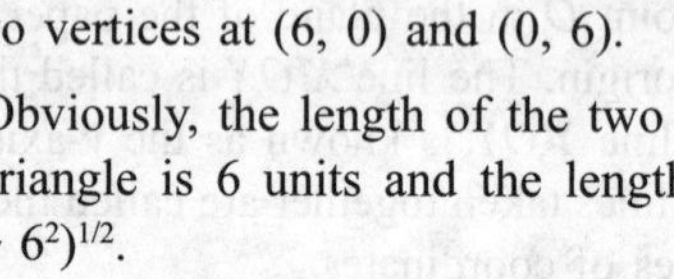

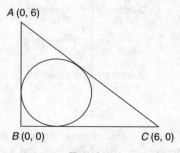

$A(0, 6)$

$B(0, 0)$
$C(6, 0)$

**Fig. 12.6**

In-centre will be at

$$\frac{(6.0 + 6\sqrt{2}.0 + 6.6)}{(6 + 6 + 6\sqrt{2})}, \frac{(6.6 + 6\sqrt{2}.0 + 6.0)}{(6 + 6 + 6\sqrt{2})}$$

$$= \frac{36}{12 + 6\sqrt{2}}, \frac{36}{12 + 6\sqrt{2}}$$

**6. Circumcentre of a Triangle**  The point of intersection of the perpendicular bisectors of the sides of a triangle is called its circumcentre. It is equidistant from the vertices of the triangle. It is also known as the centre of the circle which passes through the three vertices of a triangle (or the centre of the circle that circumscribes the triangle.)

Let $ABC$ be a triangle. If $O$ is the circumcentre of the triangle $ABC$, then $OA = OB = OC$ and each of these three represent the circum radius.

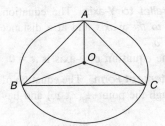

**Fig. 12.7**

## Illustration

**Question 6:**  What will be the circumcentre of a triangle whose sides are $3x - y + 3 = 0$, $3x + 4y + 3 = 0$ and $x + 3y + 11 = 0$?

**Answer:**  Let $ABC$ be the triangle whose sides $AB$, $BC$ and $CA$ have the equations $3x - y + 3 = 0$, $3x + 4y + 3 = 0$ and $x + 3y + 11 = 0$ respectively.

Solving the equations, we get the points $A$, $B$ and $C$ as $(-2, -3)$, $(-1, 0)$ and $(7, -6)$ respectively.

The equation of a line perpendicular to $BC$ is $4x - 3y + k = 0$.

[For students unaware of this formula, read the section on straight lines later in the chapter.]

This will pass through $(3, -3)$, the mid-point of $BC$, if $12 + 9 + k = 0 \Rightarrow k = -21$

Putting $k_1 = -21$ in $4x - 3y + k = 0$, we get $4x - 3y - 21 = 0$        (i)

as the equation of the perpendicular bisector of $BC$.

Again, the equation of a line perpendicular to $CA$ is $3x - y + k_1 = 0$.

This will pass through $(5/2, -9/2)$, the mid-point of $AC$ if

$$15/2 + 9/2 + k_1 = 0 \Rightarrow k_1 = -12$$

Putting $k_1 = -12$ in $3x - y + k_1 = 0$, we get $3x - y - 12 = 0$        (ii)

as the perpendicular bisector of $AC$.

Solving (i) and (ii), we get $x = 3$, $y = -3$.

Hence, the coordinates of the circumcentre of $\Delta ABC$ are $(3, -3)$.

**7. Orthocentre of a Triangle**  The orthocentre of a triangle is the point of intersection of the perpendiculars drawn from the vertices to the opposite sides of the triangle.

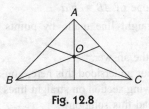

**Fig. 12.8**

## Illustration

**Question 7:**  Find the orthocentre of the triangle whose sides have the equations $y = 15$, $3x = 4y$, and $5x + 12y = 0$.

**Answer:**  Let $ABC$ be the triangle whose sides $BC$, $CA$ and $AB$ have the equations $y = 15$, $3x = 4y$, and $5x + 12y = 0$ respectively.

Solving these equations pairwise, we get coordinates of $A$, $B$ and $C$ as $(0, 0)$, $(-36, 15)$ and $(20, 15)$ respectively.

$AD$ is a line passing through $A$ $(0, 0)$ and perpendicular to $y = 15$.

So, equation of $AD$ is $x = 0$.

The equation of any line perpendicular to $3x - 4y = 0$ is represented by $4x + 3y + k = 0$.

This line will pass through $(-36, 15)$ if $-144 + 45 + k = 0 \Rightarrow k = 99$.

So the equation of $BE$ is $4x + 3y + 99 = 0$.

Solving the equations of $AD$ and $BE$ we get $x = 0$, $y = -33$.

Hence the coordinates of the orthocentre are $(0, -33)$.

**8. Collinearity of Three Points:**  Three given points $A$, $B$ and $C$ are said to be collinear, that is, lie on the same straight line, if any of the following conditions occur:

(i)  Area of triangle formed by these three points is zero.

(ii)  Slope of $AB$ = Slope of $AC$.

(iii)  Any one of the three points (say $C$) lies on the straight line joining the other two points (here $A$ and $B$).

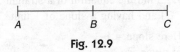

**Fig. 12.9**

## Illustration

**Question 8:**  Select the right option the points $(-a, -b)$, $(0, 0)$ and $(a, b)$ are

(a)  Collinear            (b)  Vertices of square

(c)  Vertices of a rectangle   (d)  None of these

**Answer:** We can use either of the three methods to check whether the points are collinear.

But the most convenient one is (ii) in this case.

Let $A$, $B$, $C$ are the points whose coordinates are $(-a, -b)$, $(0, 0)$ and $(a, b)$

Slope of $BC = b/a$

Slope of $AB = b/a$

So, the straight line made by points $A$, $B$ and $C$ is collinear.

Hence, (a) is the answer.

[If you have not understood this here, you are requested to read the following section on straight lines and their slopes and then re-read this solution]

*Alternative:* Draw the points on paper assuming the paper to be a graph paper. This will give you an indication regarding the nature of points. In the above question, point $(a, b)$ is in first quadrant for $a > 0$, $b > 0$ and point $(-a, -b)$ is directly opposite to the point $(a, b)$ in the third quadrant with the third point $(0, 0)$ in the middle of the straight line joining the points $A$ and $B$.

You can check this by assuming any value for '$a$' and '$b$'.

Also, you can use this method for solving any problem involving points and diagrams made by those points. However you should be fast enough to trace the points on paper. A little practice of tracing points might help you.

**9. Slope of a Line** The slope of a line joining two points $A$ $(x_1, y_1)$ and $B$ $(x_2, y_2)$ is denoted by $m$ and is given by $m = (y_2 - y_1)/(x_2 - x_1) = \tan \theta$, where $\theta$ is the angle that the line makes with the positive direction of $x$-axis. This angle $\theta$ is taken positive when it is measured in the anti-clockwise direction from the positive direction of the axis of $x$.

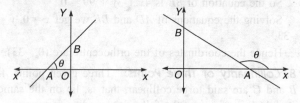

**Fig. 12.10**

## Illustration

**Question 9:** Find the equation of a straight line passing through $(2, -3)$ and having a slope of 1 unit.

**Answer:** Here slope = 1

And point given is $(2, -3)$.

So, we will use point-slope formula for finding the equation of straight line. This formula is given by:

$$(y - y_1) = m (x - x_1)$$

So, equation of the line will be $y - (-3) = 1 (x - 2)$

$\Rightarrow$ $\qquad\qquad y + 3 = x - 2$

$\Rightarrow$ $\qquad\qquad y - x + 5 = 0$

## 10. Different Forms of the Equations of a Straight Line

**(a) General Form** The general form of the equation of a straight line is $ax + by + c = 0$.

(First degree equation in $x$ and $y$). Where $a$, $b$ and $c$ are real constants and $a$, $b$ are not simultaneously equal to zero.

In this equation, slope of the line is given by $\dfrac{-a}{b}$.

The general form is also given by $y = mx + c$; where $m$ is the slope and $c$ is the intercept on $y$-axis.

In this equation, slope of the line is given by $m$.

**(b) Line Parallel to the X-axis** The equation of a straight line *parallel to the x-axis* and at a distance $b$ from it, is given by $y = b$.

Obviously, the **equation of the x-axis is $y = 0$**

**(c) Line Parallel to Y-axis** The equation of a straight line *parallel to the y-axis* and at a distance $a$ from it, is given by $x = a$.

Obviously, the **equation of y-axis is $x = 0$**

**(d) Slope Intercept Form** The equation of a straight line passing through the point $A$ $(x_1, y_1)$ and having a slope $m$ is given by

$$(y - y_1) = m (x - x_1)$$

**(e) Two Points Form** The equation of a straight line passing through two points $A$ $(x_1, y_1)$ and $B$ $(x_2, y_2)$ is given by

$$(y - y_1) = \frac{(y_2 - y_1)(x - x_1)}{(x_2 - x_1)}$$

Its slope $= \left( \dfrac{y_2 - y_1}{x_2 - x_1} \right)$

**(f) Intercept Form** The equation of a straight line making intercepts $a$ and $b$ on the axes of $x$ and $y$ respectively is given by

$$x/a + y/b = 1$$

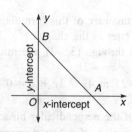

**Fig. 12.11**

If a straight line cuts $x$-axis at $A$ and the $y$-axis at $B$ then $OA$ and $OB$ are known as the intercepts of the line on $x$-axis and $y$-axis respectively.

## 11. Perpendicularity and Parallelism

*Condition for two lines to be parallel*: Two lines are said to be parallel if their slopes are equal.

For this to happen, ratio of coefficient of $x$ and $y$ in both the lines should be equal.

In a general form, this can be stated as: line parallel to $ax + by + c = 0$ is $ax + by + k = 0$ or $dx + ey + k = 0$ if $a/d = b/e$ where $k$ is a constant.

## Illustration

**Question 10:** Which of the lines represented by the following equations are parallel to each other?

1. $x + 2y = 5$
2. $2x - 4y = 6$
3. $x - 2y = 4$
4. $2x + 6y = 8$

(a) 1 and 2   (b) 2 and 4   (c) 2 and 3   (d) 1 and 4

**Answer:** Go through the options and check which of the two lines given will satisfy the criteria for two lines to be parallel. It will be obvious that option c is correct, that is, the line $2x - 4y = 6$ is parallel to the line $x - 2y = 4$.

**Question 11:** Find the equation of a straight line parallel to the straight line $3x + 4y = 7$ and passing through the point $(3, -3)$.

**Answer:** Equation of the line parallel to $3x + 4y = 7$ will be of the form $3x + 4y = k$.

This line passes through $(3, -3)$, so this point will satisfy the equation of straight line $3x + 4y = k$. So, $3.3 + 4.(-3) = k \Rightarrow k = -3$.

Hence, equation of the required straight line will be $3x + 4y + 3 = 0$.

*Condition for two lines to be perpendicular:* Two lines are said to be perpendicular if product of the slopes of the lines is equal to $-1$.

For this to happen, the product of the coefficients of $x$ + the product of the coefficients of $y$ should be equal to zero.

## Illustration

**Question 12:** Which of the following two lines are perpendicular?

1. $x + 2y = 5$
2. $2x - 4y = 6$
3. $2x + 3y = 4$
4. $2x - y = 4$

(a) 1 and 2   (b) 2 and 4   (c) 2 and 3   (d) 1 and 4

Check the equations to get option 4 as the correct answer.

**Question 13:** Find the equation of a straight line perpendicular to the straight line $3x + 4y = 7$ and passing through the point $(3, -3)$.

**Answer:** Equation of the line perpendicular to $3x + 4y = 7$ will be of the form $4x - 3y = K$.

This line passes through $(3, -3)$, so this point will satisfy the equation of straight line $4x - 3y = K$. So, $4.3 - 3.-3 \Rightarrow K = 21$.

Hence, equation of required straight line will be $4x - 3y = 21$.

**12. Length of Perpendicular or Distance of a Point from a Line** The length of perpendicular from a given point $(x_1, y_1)$ to a line $ax + by + c = 0$ is

$$\frac{|ax_1 + by_1 + c|}{\sqrt{a^2 + b^2}}$$

*Corollary:*

(a) Distance between two parallel lines.

   If two lines are parallel, the distance between them will always be the same.

   When two straight lines are parallel whose equations are $ax + by + c = 0$ and $ax + by + c_1 = 0$, then the distance between them is given by $\dfrac{|c - c_1|}{\sqrt{a^2 + b^2}}$.

(b) The length of the perpendicular from the origin to the line $ax + by + c = 0$ is given by $\dfrac{|c|}{\sqrt{a^2 + b^2}}$

## Illustration

**Question 14:** Two sides of a square lie on the lines $x + y = 2$ and $x + y = -2$. Find the area of the square formed in this way.

**Answer:** Obviously, the difference between the parallel lines will be the side of the square.

To convert it into the form of finding the distance of a point from a line, we will have to find out a point at which any one of these two lines cut the axes and then we will draw a perpendicular from that point to the other line, and this distance will be the side of the square.

To find the point at which the equation of the line $x + y = 2$ cut the axes, we will put once $x = 0$ and then again $y = 0$.

When $x = 0$, $y = 2$, so the coordinates of the point where it cuts $y$-axis is $(0, 2)$.

Now the point is $(0, 2)$, and the equation of line on which perpendicular is to be drawn is $x + y = -2$.

So, distance $= \dfrac{|1.0 + 1.2 + 2|}{\sqrt{1^2 + 1^2}} = \dfrac{4}{\sqrt{2}}$.

$\therefore$ Area $= \dfrac{16}{2} = 8$

*Alternatively:* Draw the points on the paper and you will get the length of diagonal as 4 units; so, length of side will be $2\sqrt{2}$ and, therefore, the area will be 8 sq units.

*Alternatively:* You can also use the formula for the distance between two parallel lines as

$$\frac{|2 + 2|}{\sqrt{1^2 + 1^2}} = \frac{4}{\sqrt{2}}$$

**13. Change of Axes**  If origin (0, 0) is shifted to (h, k) then the coordinates of the point (x, y) referred to the old axes and (X, Y) referred to the new axes can be related with the relation $x = X + h$ and $y = Y + k$.

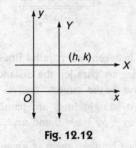

**Fig. 12.12**

## Illustration

**Question 15:**  If origin (0, 0) is shifted to (5, 2), what will be the coordinates of the point in the new axis which was represented by (1, 2) in the old axis?

*Space for Rough Work*

**Answer:**  Let (X, Y) be the coordinates of the point in the new axis.

Then,
$$1 = X + 5 \qquad \therefore \quad X = -4$$
$$2 = Y + 2 \qquad \therefore \quad Y = 0$$

So, the new coordinates of the point will be (–4, 0).

**14. Point of Intersection of Two Lines**  Point of intersection of two lines can be obtained by solving the equations as simultaneous equations.

### An Important Result

If all the three vertices of a triangle have integral coordinates, then that triangle cannot be an Equilateral triangle.

# LEVEL OF DIFFICULTY (I)

1. Find the distance between the points (3, 4) and (8, –6).

   (a) $\sqrt{5}$        (b) $5\sqrt{5}$

   (c) $2\sqrt{5}$       (d) $4\sqrt{5}$

2. Find the distance between the points (5, 2) and (0, 0).

   (a) $\sqrt{27}$       (b) $\sqrt{21}$

   (c) $\sqrt{29}$       (d) $\sqrt{31}$

3. Find the value of $p$ if the distance between the points (8, $p$) and (4, 3) is 5.

   (a) 6           (b) 0

   (c) Both (a) and (b)     (d) None of these

4. Find the value of $c$ if the distance between the point ($c$, 4) and the origin is 5 units.

   (a) 3           (b) –3

   (c) Both a and b      (d) None of these

5. Find the mid-point of the line segment made by joining the points (3, 2) and (6, 4).

   (a) $\left(\dfrac{9}{2}, 3\right)$       (b) $\left(\dfrac{-3}{2}, -1\right)$

   (c) $\left(\dfrac{9}{2}, -\dfrac{3}{2}\right)$       (d) $\left(\dfrac{3}{-1}\right)$

6. If the origin is the mid-point of the line segment joined by the points (2, 3) and ($x$, $y$), find the value of ($x$, $y$).

   (a) (2, 3)       (b) (–2, 3)

   (c) (–2, –3)     (d) (2, –3)

7. Find the points that divide the line segment joining (2, 5) and (–1, 2) in the ratio 2 : 1 internally.

   (a) (1, 2)       (b) (–3, 2)

   (c) (3, 1)       (d) (0, 3)

8. In what ratio does the $x$-axis divide the line segment joining the points (2, –3) and (5, 6)?

   (a) 2 : 1       (b) 1 : 2

   (c) 3 : 4       (d) 2 : 3

9. How many squares are possible if two of the vertices of a quadrilateral are (1, 0) and (2, 0)?

   (a) 1          (b) 2

   (c) 3          (d) 4

10. If the point $R$ (1, –2) divides externally the line segment joining $P$ (2, 5) and $Q$ in the ratio 3 : 4, what will be the coordinates of $Q$?

    (a) (–3, 6)       (b) (2, –4)

    (c) (7/3, 28/3)     (d) (1, 2)

11. Find the coordinates of the points that trisect the line segment joining (1, –2) and (–3, 4).

    (a) $\left(\dfrac{-1}{3}, 0\right)$       (b) $\left(\dfrac{-5}{3}, 2\right)$

    (c) Both (a) and (b)     (d) None of these

12. Find the coordinates of the point that divides the line segment joining the points (6, 3) and (–4, 5) in the ratio 3 : 2 internally.

    (a) $\left(0, \dfrac{-21}{5}\right)$       (b) $\left(0, \dfrac{21}{5}\right)$

    (c) $\left(\dfrac{11}{2}, \dfrac{14}{3}\right)$       (d) $\left(\dfrac{-11}{2}, \dfrac{-14}{3}\right)$

13. In Question 12 question, find the coordinates of the point if it divides the points externally.

    (a) (24, –9)       (b) (3, –5)

    (c) (–24, 9)       (d) (5, –3)

14. In what ratio is the line segment joining (–1, 3) and (4, –7) divided at the point (2, –3)?

    (a) 3 : 2       (b) 2 : 3

    (c) 3 : 5       (d) 5 : 3

15. In question 14, find the nature of division?

    (a) Internal       (b) External

    (c) Cannot be said

16. In what ratio is the line segment made by the points (7, 3) and (–4, 5) divided by the $y$-axis?

    (a) 2 : 3       (b) 4 : 7

    (c) 3 : 5       (d) 7 : 4

17. What is the nature of the division in the above question?

    (a) External       (b) Internal

    (c) Cannot be said

18. If the coordinates of the mid-point of the line segment joining the points (2, 1) and (1, –3) is ($x$, $y$) then the relation between $x$ and $y$ can be best described by

    (a) $3x + 2y = 5$       (b) $6x + y = 8$

    (c) $5x – 2y = 4$       (d) $2x – 5y = 4$

19. Points (6, 8), (3, 7), (–2, –2) and (1, –1) are joined to form a quadrilateral. What will be this structure?

    (a) Rhombus       (b) Parallelogram

    (c) Square        (d) Rectangle

20. Points (4, –1), (6, 0), (7, 2) and (5, 1) are joined to be a vertex of a quadrilateral. What will be the structure?

    (a) Rhombus       (b) Parallelogram

    (c) Square        (d) Rectangle

21. What will be the centroid of a triangle whose vertices are (2, 4), (6, 4) and (2, 0)?

    (a) $\left(\dfrac{7}{2}, \dfrac{5}{2}\right)$    (b) (3, 5)

    (c) $\left(\dfrac{10}{3}, \dfrac{8}{3}\right)$    (d) (1, 4)

22. The distance between the lines $4x + 3y = 11$ and $8x + 6y = 15$ is

    (a) 4    (b) $\dfrac{7}{10}$

    (c) $\dfrac{5}{7}$    (d) 26

23. If the mid-point of the line joining (3, 4) and (p, 7) is (x, y) and $2x + 2y + 1 = 0$, then what will be the value of p?

    (a) 15    (b) $\dfrac{-17}{2}$

    (c) –15    (d) $\dfrac{17}{2}$

24. Find the third vertex of the triangle whose two vertices are (–3, 1) and (0, –2) and the centroid is the origin.

    (a) (2, 3)    (b) $\left(\dfrac{-4}{3}, \dfrac{14}{3}\right)$

    (c) (3, 1)    (d) (6, 4)

25. Find the area of the triangle whose vertices are (1, 3), (–7, 6) and (5, –1).
    (a) 20    (b) 10
    (c) 18    (d) 24

26. Find the area of the triangle whose vertices are $(a, b + c)$, $(a, b - c)$ and $(- a, c)$.
    (a) $2ac$    (b) $2bc$
    (c) $b(a + c)$    (d) $c(a - b)$

27. The number of lines that are parallel to $2x + 6y + 7 = 0$ and have an intercept of length 10 between the coordinate axes is
    (a) 0    (b) 1
    (c) 2    (d) Infinite

28. Which of the following three points represent a straight line?

    (a) $\left(\dfrac{-1}{2}, 3\right)$, (–5, 6) and (– 8, 8)

    (b) $\left(\dfrac{-1}{2}, 3\right)$, (5, 6) and (– 8, 8)

    (c) $\left(\dfrac{1}{2}, 3\right)$, (–5, 6) and (– 8, 8)

    (d) $\left(\dfrac{-1}{2}, 3\right)$, $\left(\dfrac{5}{6}\right)$ and (8, 8)

29. Which of the following will be the equation of a straight line that is parallel to the y-axis at a distance 11 units from it?
    (a) $x = + 11, x = -11$    (b) $y = 11, y = -11$
    (c) $y = 0$    (d) None of these

30. Which of the following will be the equation of a straight line parallel to the y-axis at a distance of 9 units to the left?
    (a) $x = - 9$    (b) $x = 9$
    (c) $y = 9$    (d) $y = - 9$

31. What can be said about the equation of the straight line $x = 7$?
    (a) It is the equation of a straight line at a distance of 7 units towards the right of the y-axis.
    (b) It is the equation of a straight line at a distance of 7 units towards the left of the y-axis.
    (c) It is the equation of a straight line at a distance of 7 units below the x-axis.
    (d) It is the equation of a straight line at a distance of 7 units above the x-axis.

32. What can be said about the equation of the straight line $y = -8$?
    (a) It is the equation of a straight line at a distance of 8 units below the x-axis.
    (b) It is the equation of a straight line at a distance of 8 units above the x-axis.
    (c) It is the equation of a straight line at a distance of 8 units towards the right of the y-axis.
    (d) It is the equation of a straight line at a distance of 8 units towards the left of the y-axis.

33. Which of the following straight lines passes through the origin?
    (a) $x + y = 4$    (b) $x^2 + y^2 = - 6$
    (c) $x + y = 5$    (d) $x = 4y$

34. What will be the point of intersection of the equation of lines $2x + 5y = 6$ and $3x + 4y = 7$?

    (a) $\left(\dfrac{11}{7}, \dfrac{4}{7}\right)$    (b) $\left(\dfrac{-11}{7}, 4\right)$

    (c) $\left(3, \dfrac{-2}{7}\right)$    (d) $\left(4, \dfrac{-2}{5}\right)$

35. If $P$ (6, 7), $Q$ ( 2, 3) and $R$ (4, –2) be the vertices of a triangle, then which of the following is not a point contained in this triangle?
    (a) (4, 3)    (b) (3, 3)
    (c) (4, 2)    (d) (6, 1)

36. What will be the reflection of the point (4, 5) in the second quadrant?
    (a) (– 4, – 5)    (b) (– 4, 5)
    (c) (4, – 5)    (d) None of these

37. What will be the reflection of the point (4, 5) in the third quadrant?

(a) $(-4, -5)$      (b) $(-4, 5)$

(c) $(4, -5)$      (d) None of these

38. What will be the reflection of the point $(4, 5)$ in the fourth quadrant?

(a) $(-4, -5)$      (b) $(-4, 5)$

(c) $(4, -5)$      (d) None of these

39. If the origin gets shifted to $(2, 2)$, then what will be the new coordinates of the point $(4, -2)$?

(a) $(-2, 4)$      (b) $(2, 4)$

(c) $(4, 2)$      (d) $(2, -4)$

40. What will be the length of the perpendicular drawn from the point $(4, 5)$ upon the straight line $3x + 4y = 10$?

(a) $\dfrac{12}{5}$      (b) $\dfrac{32}{5}$

(c) $\dfrac{22}{5}$      (d) $\dfrac{42}{5}$

*Space for Rough Work*

## LEVEL OF DIFFICULTY (II)

1. Find the area of the quadrilateral the coordinates of whose angular points taken in order are (1, 1), (3, 4), (5, –2) and (4, –7).
   (a) 20.5　　　　　　　(b) 41
   (c) 82　　　　　　　　(d) 61.5

2. Find the area of the quadrilateral the coordinates of whose angular points taken in order are (–1, 6), (–3, –9), (5, –8) and (3, 9).
   (a) 48　　　　　　　　(b) 96
   (c) 192　　　　　　　(d) 72

3. Two vertices of a triangle are (5, –1) and (–2, 3). If the orthocenter of the triangle is the origin, what will be the coordinates of the third point?
   (a) (4, 7)　　　　　　(b) (–4, 7)
   (c) (–4, –7)　　　　　(d) (4, –7)

4. Find the equation of the straight line passing through the origin and the point of intersection of the lines $x/a + y/b = 1$ and $x/b + y/a = 1$.
   (a) $y = x$　　　　　　(b) $y = -x$
   (c) $y = 2x$　　　　　(d) $y = -2x$

5. One side of a rectangle lies along the line $4x + 7y + 5 = 0$. Two of its vertices are (–3, 1) and (1, 1). Which of the following may be an equation which represents any of the other three straight lines?
   (a) $7x - 4y = 3$　　　　(b) $7x - 4y + 3 = 0$
   (c) $y + 1 = 0$　　　　　(d) $4x + 7y = 3$

6. The points $(p{-}1, p + 2)$, $(p, p + 1)$, $(p + 1, p)$ are collinear for
   (a) $p = 0$　　　　　　(b) $p = 1$
   (c) $p = -1/2$　　　　(d) Any value of $p$

7. The straight line joining (1, 2) and (2, –2) is perpendicular to the line joining (8, 2) and (4, $p$). What will be the value of $p$?
   (a) –1　　　　　　　　(b) 1
   (c) 3　　　　　　　　(d) None of these

8. What will be the length of the perpendicular drawn from the point (–3, –4) to the straight line $12 (x + 6) = 5 (y - 2)$?
   (a) $5\left(\dfrac{4}{13}\right)$　　　　　(b) $5\left(\dfrac{1}{13}\right)$
   (c) $3\left(\dfrac{2}{13}\right)$　　　　　(d) $3\left(\dfrac{1}{13}\right)$

9. The area of the triangle with vertices at $(a, b + c)$, $(b, c + a)$ and $(c, a + b)$ is
   (a) 0　　　　　　　　(b) $a + b + c$
   (c) $a^2 + b^2 + c^2$　　　(d) 1

10. Find the distance between the two parallel straight lines $y = mx + c$ and $y = mx + d$? [Assume $c > d$]
    (a) $\left(\dfrac{(c - d)}{(1 + m^2)^{\frac{1}{2}}}\right)$　　　　(b) $\left(\dfrac{(d - c)}{(1 + m^2)^{\frac{1}{2}}}\right)$
    (c) $\left(\dfrac{d}{(1 + m^2)^{\frac{1}{2}}}\right)$　　　　(d) $\left(\dfrac{-d}{(1 + m)^{\frac{1}{2}}}\right)$

11. What will be the equation of the straight line that passes through the intersection of the straight lines $2x - 3y + 4 = 0$ and $3x + 4y - 5 = 0$ and is perpendicular to the straight line $3x - 4y = 5$?
    (a) $8x + 6y = \dfrac{32}{7}$　　　(b) $4x + 3y = \dfrac{84}{17}$
    (c) $4x + 3y = \dfrac{62}{17}$　　　(d) $8x + 6y = \dfrac{58}{17}$

12. In question 11, find the equation of the straight line if it is parallel to the straight line $3x + 4y = 5$?
    (a) $12x + 16y = \dfrac{58}{17}$　　(b) $3x + 4y = \dfrac{58}{17}$
    (c) $6x + 8y = \dfrac{58}{17}$　　　(d) None of these

13. The orthocenter of the triangle formed by the points (0, 0), (8, 0) and (4, 6) is
    (a) $\left(4, \dfrac{8}{3}\right)$　　　　　(b) (3, 4)
    (c) (4, 3)　　　　　　(d) $\left(3, \dfrac{5}{2}\right)$

14. The area of a triangle is 5 square units, two of its vertices are (2, 1) and (3, –2). The third vertex lies on $y = x + 3$. What will be the third vertex?
    (a) $\left(\dfrac{5}{3}, \dfrac{13}{3}\right)$　　　　(b) $\left(\dfrac{7}{2}, \dfrac{13}{2}\right)$
    (c) (3, 4)　　　　　　(d) (1, 2)

15. The equations of two equal sides $AB$ and $AC$ of an isosceles triangle $ABC$ are $x + y = 5$ and $7x - y = 3$ respectively. What will be the equation of the side $BC$ if area of triangle $ABC$ is 5 square units.
    (a) $x + 3y - 1 = 0$　　　(b) $x - 3y + 1 = 0$
    (c) $2x - y = 5$　　　　(d) $x + 2y = 5$

16. Three vertices of a rhombus, taken in order are (2, –1), (3, 4) and (–2, 3). Find the fourth vertex.
    (a) (3, 2)　　　　　　(b) (–3, –2)
    (c) (–3, 2)　　　　　(d) (3, –2)

17. Four vertices of a parallelogram taken in order are $(-3, -1)$, $(a, b)$, $(3, 3)$ and $(4, 3)$. What will be the ratio of $a$ to $b$?

    (a) $4 : 1$        (b) $1 : 2$

    (c) $1 : 3$        (d) $3 : 1$

18. What will be the new equation of straight line $3x + 4y = 6$ if the origin gets shifted to $(3, -4)$?

    (a) $3x + 4y = 5$        (b) $4x - 3y = 4$

    (c) $3x + 4y + 1 = 0$        (d) $3x + 4y - 13 = 0$

19. What will be the value of $p$ if the equation of straight line $2x + 5y = 4$ gets changed to $2x + 5y = p$ after shifting the origin at $(3, 3)$?

    (a) $16$        (b) $-17$

    (c) $12$        (d) $10$

20. A line passing through the points $(a, 2a)$ and $(-2, 3)$ is perpendicular to the line $4x + 3y + 5 = 0$. Find the value of $a$?

    (a) $-14/3$        (b) $18/5$

    (c) $14/3$        (d) $-18/5$

*Space for Rough Work*

## LEVEL OF DIFFICULTY (III)

1. The area of a triangle is 5 square units. Two of its vertices are (2, 1) and (3, –2). The third vertex lies on $y = x + 3$. What will be the third vertex?
   (a) (4, –7)          (b) (4, 7)
   (c) (–4, –7)          (d) (–4, 7)

2. One side of a rectangle lies along the line $4x + 7y + 5 = 0$. Two of its vertices are (–3, 1) and (1, 1). Which of the following is not an equation of the other three straight lines?
   (a) $14x – 8y = 6$          (b) $7x – 4y = –25$
   (c) $4x + 7y = 11$          (d) $14x – 8y = 20$

3. The area of triangle formed by the points $(p, 2–2p)$, $(1–p, 2p)$ and $(–4–p, 6–2p)$ is 70 units. How many integral values of $p$ are possible?
   (a) 2          (b) 3
   (c) 4          (d) None of these

4. What are the points on the axis of $x$ whose perpendicular distance from the straight line $x/p + y/q = 1$ is $p$?
   (a) $\dfrac{p}{q}\left[q + \sqrt{(p^2 + q^2)}\right], 0$
   (b) $\dfrac{p}{q}\left[q - \sqrt{(p^2 + q^2)}\right], 0$
   (c) Both (a) and (b)
   (d) None of these

5. If the medians $PT$ and $RS$ of a triangle with vertices $P$ (0, $b$), $Q$ (0, 0) and $R$ ($a$, 0) are perpendicular to each other, which of the following satisfies the relationship between $a$ and $b$?
   (a) $4b^2 = a^2$          (b) $2b^2 = a^2$
   (c) $a = –2b$          (d) $a^2 + b^2 = 0$

6. The point of intersection of the lines $x/a + y/b = 1$ and $x/b + y/b = 1$ lies on the line
   (a) $x + y = 1$          (b) $x + y = 0$
   (c) $x – y = 1$          (d) $x – y = 0$

7. $PQR$ is an isosceles triangle. If the coordinates of the base are $Q$ (1, 3) and $R$ (–2, 7), then the coordinates of the vertex $P$ can be
   (a) $\left(4, \dfrac{7}{2}\right)$          (b) (2, 5)
   (c) $\left(\dfrac{5}{6}, 6\right)$          (d) $\left(\dfrac{1}{3}, 2\right)$

8. The extremities of a diagonal of a parallelogram are the points (3, – 4) and (– 6, 5). If the third vertex is the point (–2, 1), the coordinate of the fourth vertex is
   (a) (1, 0)          (b) (–1, 0)
   (c) (–1, 1)          (d) (1, –1)

9. If the points $(a, 0)$, $(0, b)$ and $(1, 1)$ are collinear then which of the following is true?
   (a) $\dfrac{1}{a} + \dfrac{1}{b} = 2$          (b) $\dfrac{1}{a} - \dfrac{1}{b} = 1$
   (c) $\dfrac{1}{a} - \dfrac{1}{b} = 2$          (d) $\dfrac{1}{a} + \dfrac{1}{b} = 1$

10. If $P$ and $Q$ are two points on the line $3x + 4y = –15$, such that $OP = OQ = 9$ units, the area of the triangle $POQ$ will be
    (a) $18\sqrt{2}$ sq units          (b) $3\sqrt{2}$ sq units
    (c) $6\sqrt{2}$ sq units          (d) $15\sqrt{2}$ sq units

11. If the coordinates of the points $A$, $B$, $C$ and $D$ are (6, 3), (–3, –5), (4, –2) and ($a$, $3a$) respectively and if the ratio of the area of triangles $ABC$ and $DBC$ is 2 : 1, then the value of $a$ is
    (a) $\dfrac{-9}{2}$          (b) $\dfrac{9}{2}$
    (c) $\dfrac{-23}{36}$          (d) $\dfrac{23}{18}$

12. The equations of two equal sides $AB$ and $AC$ of an isosceles triangle $ABC$ are $x + y = 5$ and $7x – y = 3$ respectively. What will be the length of the intercept cut by the side $BC$ on the $y$-axis?
    (a) $\dfrac{9}{5}$          (b) 8
    (c) 1.5          (d) No unique solution

13. A line is represented by the equation $4x + 5y = 6$ in the coordinate system with the origin (0, 0). You are required to find the equation of the straight line perpendicular to this line that passes through the point (1, –2) [which is in the coordinate system where origin is at (–2, –2)].
    (a) $5x – 4y = 11$          (b) $5x – 4y = 13$
    (c) $5x – 4y = –3$          (d) $5x – 4y = 7$

14. $P$ (3, 1), $Q$ (6, 5) and $R$ ($x$, $y$) are three points such that the angle $PRQ$ is a right angle and the area of $\Delta\ PRQ$ is 7. The number of such points $R$ that are possible is
    (a) 1          (b) 2
    (c) 3          (d) 4

15. Two sides of a square lie on the lines $x + y = 1$ and $x + y + 2 = 0$. What is its area?
    (a) $\dfrac{11}{2}$          (b) $\dfrac{9}{2}$
    (c) 5          (d) 4

16. Find the value of $k$ if the straight line $2x + 3y + 4 + k(6x - y + 12) = 0$ is perpendicular to the line $7x + 5y = 4$.

    (a) $\dfrac{-33}{37}$

    (b) $\dfrac{-29}{37}$

    (c) $\dfrac{19}{37}$

    (d) None of these

17. If $p$ is the length of the perpendicular from the origin to the line $\dfrac{x}{a} + \dfrac{y}{b} = 1$, then which of the following is true?

    (a) $\dfrac{1}{p^2} = \dfrac{1}{b^2} - \dfrac{1}{a^2}$

    (b) $\dfrac{1}{p^2} = \dfrac{1}{a^2} - \dfrac{1}{b^2}$

    (c) $\dfrac{1}{p^2} = \dfrac{1}{a^2} + \dfrac{1}{b^2}$

    (d) None of these

18. How many points on $x + y = 4$ are there that lie at a unit distance from the line $4x + 3y = 10$?

    (a) 1

    (b) 2

    (c) 3

    (d) None of these

19. What will be the area of the rhombus $ax \pm by \pm c = 0$?

    (a) $\dfrac{3c^2}{ab}$

    (b) $\dfrac{4c^2}{ab}$

    (c) $\dfrac{2c^2}{ab}$

    (d) $\dfrac{c^2}{ab}$

20. The coordinates of the mid-points of the sides of a triangle are (4, 2), (3, 3) and (2, 2). What will be the coordinates of the centroid of the triangle?

    (a) $\left(3, \dfrac{7}{3}\right)$

    (b) $\left(-3, \dfrac{-7}{3}\right)$

    (c) $\left(3, \dfrac{-7}{3}\right)$

    (d) $\left(-3, \dfrac{7}{3}\right)$

**Space for Rough Work**

## ANSWER KEY

### Level of Difficulty (I)

| | | | |
|---|---|---|---|
| 1. (b) | 2. (c) | 3. (c) | 4. (c) |
| 5. (a) | 6. (c) | 7. (d) | 8. (b) |
| 9. (c) | 10. (c) | 11. (c) | 12. (b) |
| 13. (c) | 14. (a) | 15. (a) | 16. (d) |
| 17. (b) | 18. (b) | 19. (b) | 20. (a) |
| 21. (c) | 22. (b) | 23. (c) | 24. (c) |
| 25. (b) | 26. (a) | 27. (c) | 28. (a) |
| 29. (a) | 30. (a) | 31. (a) | 32. (a) |
| 33. (d) | 34. (a) | 35. (d) | 36. (b) |
| 37. (a) | 38. (c) | 39. (d) | 40. (c) |

### Level of Difficulty (II)

| | | | |
|---|---|---|---|
| 1. (a) | 2. (b) | 3. (c) | 4. (a) |
| 5. (a) | 6. (d) | 7. (b) | 8. (b) |
| 9. (a) | 10. (a) | 11. (c) | 12. (d) |
| 13. (a) | 14. (b) | 15. (d) | 16. (b) |
| 17. (a) | 18. (c) | 19. (b) | 20. (b) |

### Level of Difficulty (III)

| | | | |
|---|---|---|---|
| 1. (c) | 2. (d) | 3. (d) | 4. (c) |
| 5. (b) | 6. (d) | 7. (c) | 8. (b) |
| 9. (d) | 10. (a) | 11. (c) | 12. (b) |
| 13. (a) | 14. (b) | 15. (b) | 16. (b) |
| 17. (c) | 18. (b) | 19. (c) | 20. (a) |

### Hints

### Level of Difficulty (II)

1. Use the area of a triangle formula for the two parts of the quadrilateral separately and then add them.

4. Find the point of intersection of the lines by solving the simultaneous equations and then use the two-point formula of a straight line.

   *Alternative:* After finding out the point of intersection, use options to check.

6. For 3 points to be collinear,
   (i) Either the slope of any two of the 3 points should be equal to the slope of any other two points. OR
   (ii) The area of the triangle formed by the three points should be equal to zero.

   Solve using options.

7. Form the equation of the straight lines and then use the options.

10. Point of intersection of $y = mx + c$ with $x$-axis is $(-c/m, 0)$.

    Now use the formula for the distance of a point to a straight line.

11. Find the point of intersection of the lines and then put the coordinate of this point into the equation $4x + 3y = K$, which is perpendicular to the equation of straight line $3x - 4y = 5$, to find out $K$.

13. Orthocenter is the point of intersection of altitudes of a triangle and centroid divides the straight line

formed by joining circumcenter and the orthocenter in the ratio 2 : 1.

Let the vertices of the triangle be $O(0, 0)$, $A(8, 0)$ and $B(4, 6)$.

The equation of an altitude through $O$ and perpendicular to $AB$ is $y = 2/3x$ and similarly the equation of an altitude through A and perpendicular to $OB$ is $2x + 3y = 16$. Now find the point of intersection of these two straight lines.

14. Use the options.

    *Alternative:* Draw the points in the cartesian co-ordinate system and then use the simple geometry formula to calculate the point using the options.

15. Draw the points and then check with the options.

    *Alternative:* Find out the point of intersection with the help of options and then use the formula for area of ?.

17. Sum of $x$ and $y$ co-ordinates of opposite vertices in a parallelogram are same.

19. If the origin gets changed to $(h, k)$ from $(0, 0)$ then
    Old $x$ co-ordinate = New $x$ co-ordinate + $h$
    Old $y$ co-ordinate = New $y$ co-ordinate + $k$

20. Equation of any straight line perpendicular to the line $4x + 3y + 5 = 0$ will be of the form of $3x - 4y = k$, where $k$ is any constant.

    Now form the equation of the straight line with the given two points and then equate.

### Level of Difficulty (III)

1. First check the options to see that which of the points lie on the equation of straight line $y = x + 3$.

   And then again check the options, if needed, to confirm the second constraint regarding area of triangle.

2. Use the options.

3. Use the formula of area of a quadrilateral which will lead to a quadratic equation. Now solve the quadratic equation to see the number of integral solutions it can have.

4. Use the formula of distance of a point from the straight line using the options.

7. Use the options to find the length using the distance formula.

9. Make the slope of any two points equal to the slope of any other two points.

   Slope = Difference of $Y$ coordinates/Difference of $X$ coordinates.

14. Draw the points on cartesian coordinate system.

15. Length of the square can be find out using the method of finding out the distance between two parallel lines.

17. Use the formula (perpendicular distance of a point from a straight line.)

# TRAINING GROUND FOR BLOCK IV

## HOW TO THINK IN PROBLEMS ON BLOCK IV

In the back to school section of this block, I have already mentioned that there is very little use of complex and obscure formulae and results while solving questions on this block.

The following is a list of questions (with solutions) of what has been asked in previous years' CAT questions from this chapter. Hopefully you will realise through this exercise, what I am talking about when I say this. For each of the questions given below, try to solve on your own first, before looking at the solution provided.

1. A circle with radius 2 is placed against a right angle. As shown in the figure below, another smaller circle is placed in the gap between the circle and the right angle. What is the radius of the smaller circle?

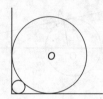

(a) $3 - 2\sqrt{2}$      (b) $4 - 2\sqrt{2}$

(c) $7 - 4\sqrt{2}$      (d) $6 - 4\sqrt{2}$

**Solution:** The solution of the above question is based on the following construction.

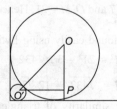

In the right triangle $OO'P$,

$OP = (2 - r)$, $O'P = (2 - r)$ and $OO' = 2 + r$

where $r$ is the radius of the smaller circle.
Using Pythagoras theorem:

$(2 + r)^2 = (2 - r)^2 + (2 - r)^2$

Solving, we get $r = 6 \pm 4\sqrt{2}$

$6 + 4\sqrt{2}$ cannot be correct since the value of $r$ should be less than 2.

**Note:** The key to solving this question is in the visualisation of the construction. If you try to use complex formulae while solving, your mind unnecessarily gets cluttered. The key to your thinking in this question is:

(1) Realise that you only have to use length measuring formulae. Hence, put all angle measurement formulae into the back seat.

(2) A quick mental search of the length measuring formulae available for this situation will narrow down your mind to the Pythagoras theorem.

(3) The key then becomes the construction of a triangle (right angled of course) where the only unknown is $r$.

---

2. ABCDEFGH is a cube. If the length of the diagonals $DF$, $AG$ & $CE$ are equal to the sides of a triangle, then the circumradius of that triangle would be

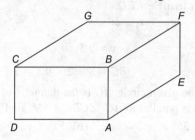

(a) Equal to the side of the cube

(b) $\sqrt{3}$ times the side of the cube

(c) $1/\sqrt{3}$ times the side of the cube

(d) Indeterminate

**Solution:** If we assume the side of the cube to be $a$ the triangle will be an equilateral triangle with side $a\sqrt{3}$. (we get this using Pythagoras theorem). Also, we know that the circumradius of an equilateral triangle is $1/\sqrt{3}$ times the side of the triangle.

Hence, in this case the circumradius would be $a$—equal to the side of the cube.

(Again the only formula used in this question would be the Pythagoras theorem.)

3. On a semicircle (diameter $AD$), chord $BC$ is parallel to the diameter $AD$. Also, $AB = CD = 2$, while $AD = 8$, what is the length of $BC$?

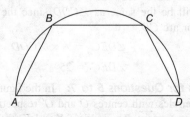

(a) 7.5      (b) 7

(c) 7.75      (d) None of these

**Solution:**   Think only of length measuring formulae (Pythagoras theorem is obvious in this case).

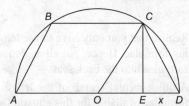

If we can find the value of $x$, we will get the answer for $BC$ as $AD - 2x$. Hence, we need to focus our energies in finding the value of $x$.

The construction above gives us two right angled triangles ($OEC$ and $DEC$).

In $\Delta\ OCE$, $OC = 4$ (radius) and $OE = (4 - x)$, Then: $(CE)^2 = 8x - x^2$. (Using Pythagoras Theorem)

Then in triangle $CED$:

$$(8x - x^2) + x^2 = 2^2$$

Hence,                              $x = 0.5$

Thus,                               $BC = 8 - 2 \times 0.5 = 7$

4. In the given circle, $AC$ is the diameter of the circle. $ED$ is parallel to $AC$. $\angle CBE = 65°$, find $\angle DEC$.

   (a)  35°                         (b)  55°
   (c)  45°                         (d)  25°

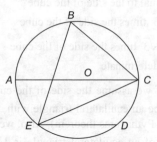

**Solution:**   Obviously this question has to be solved using only angle measuring tools. Further from the figure, it is obvious that we have to use angle measurement tools related to arcs of circles.

Reacting to the 65° information in the question above, you will get $\angle EOC = 130°$ (Since, the angle at the centre of the circle is twice the angle at any point of the circle).

Hence, $\angle AOE = 180 - 130 = 50°$

This, will be the same as $\angle COD$ since the minor arc $AE = $ minor arc $CD$.

Also,                 $\angle DEC\ = \frac{1}{2} \times \angle COD$

Hence,                $\angle DEC\ = 25°$

**Directions for Questions 5 to 7:**   In the figure below, $X$ and $Y$ are circles with centres $O$ and $O'$ respectively. $MAB$ is a common tangent. The radii of $X$ and $Y$ are in the ratio $4 : 3$ and $OM = 28$ cm.

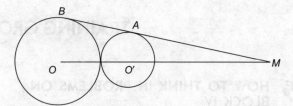

5. What is the ratio of the length of $OO'$ to that of $O'M$?

   (a)  1 : 4                       (b)  1 : 3
   (c)  3 : 8                       (d)  3 : 4

6. What is the radius of circle $X$?

   (a)  2 cm                        (b)  3 cm
   (c)  4 cm                        (d)  5 cm

7. The length of $AM$ is

   (a)  $8\sqrt{3}$ cm              (b)  $10\sqrt{3}$ cm
   (c)  $12\sqrt{3}$ cm             (d)  $14\sqrt{3}$ cm

**Solution:**   Construct $OB$ and $O'A$ as shown below.

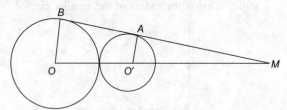

In this construction it is evident that the two right angled triangles formed are similar to each other. i.e. $\Delta OBM$ is similar to $\Delta O'AM$.

Hence, $OM : O'M = 4 : 3$ (since $OB : O'A = 4 : 3$)
Also, $OM = 28$ cm, $\therefore\ O'M = 21$ cm. $\rightarrow OO' = 7$ cm. Hence, the radius of circle $X$ is 4 cm (Answer to Q. 6).

5. Also: $OO' = 7$ and $O'M = 21$. Hence, required ratio $= 1 : 3$

7. $AM$ can be found easily using Pythagoras theorem.

$$AM^2 = 21^2 - 3^2 = 432$$

$$\therefore\ AM = \sqrt{432}\ = 12\sqrt{3}\ .$$

(Note: Only similarity of triangles and Pythagoras theorem was used here.)

8. In the figure, $ABCD$ is a rectangle inscribed inside a circle with center $O$. Side $AB > $ Side $BC$. The ratio of the area of the circle to the area of the rectangle is $\pi\ :\ \sqrt{3}$. Also, $\angle ODC = \angle ADE$. Find the ratio $AE : AD$.

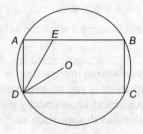

(a) $1 : \sqrt{3}$      (b) $1 : \sqrt{2}$

(c) $2\sqrt{3} : 1$      (d) $1 : 2$

**Solution:** In my experience, questions involving ratios of length typically involves the use of similar triangles. This question is no different.

Make the following construction:

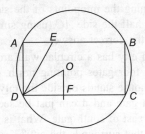

$\Delta OFD$ is similar to $\Delta AED$. Hence, the required ratio $AE : AD = OF/FD$

But $OF = \frac{1}{2}$ side $BC$ while $FD = \frac{1}{2}$ side $CD$.

Hence, we need the ratio of the side of the rectangle $BC : DC$ (This will give the required answer.)

From this point, you can get to the answer through a little bit of unconventional thinking.

The ratio of the area of the circle to that of the rectangle is given as $\pi : \sqrt{3}$. Hence, it is obvious that one of the sides has to have a $\sqrt{3}$ component in it. Hence, options 2 and 4 can be rejected. Also the required ratio has to be less than 1, hence, option (1) is correct.

**9.** Find $\angle BOA$.

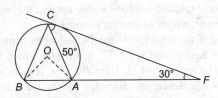

(a) $100°$      (b) $150°$

(c) $80°$      (d) Indeterminate

**Solution:** Obviously this question has to be solved using angle measurement tools.

In order to measure $\angle BOA$, you could either try to use theorems related to the angle subtended by arcs of a circle or solve using the isosceles $\Delta BOA$.

With this thought in mind start reacting to the information in the question.

$\angle CAF = 100°$. Hence $\angle BAC = 80°$

Also, $\angle OCA = (90 - ACF) = 90 - 50 = 40° = \angle OAC$ (Since the triangle $OCA$ is isosceles)

Hence $\angle OAB = 40°$

In isosceles $\Delta OAB$, $\angle OBA$ will also be $40°$

Hence $\angle BOA = 180 - 40 - 40 = 100°$

**10.** In the figure $AD = CD = BC$ and $\angle BCE = 96°$. How much is $\angle DBC$?

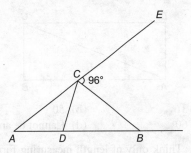

(a) $32°$      (b) $84°$

(c) $64°$      (d) Indeterminate

**Solution:** Get out your angle measuring formulae and start reacting to the information.

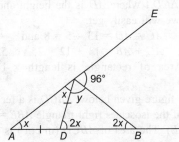

From the figure above, it is clear that

$$x + y = 180 - 96 = 84°$$

Also      $4x + y = 180°$

Solving we get $x = 32°$

Hence,      $\angle DBC = 2x = 64°$.

**11.** $PQRS$ is a square. $SR$ is a tangent (at point $S$) to the circle with centre $O$ and $TR = OS$. Then the ratio of area of the circle to the area of the square is

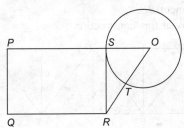

(a) $\pi/3$      (b) $11/7$

(c) $3/\pi$      (d) $7/11$

**Solution:** Looking at the options we can easily eliminate option (b) and (d), because in the ratio of the area of the circle to the area of the triangle we cannot eliminate $\pi$ and hence the answer should contain $\pi$.

Further the question is asking for the ratio $\dfrac{\text{Area of the circle}}{\text{Area of the square}}$ so, $\pi$ should be in the numerator.

Hence (a).

**12.** In the adjoining figure, $AC + AB = 5AD$ and $AC - AD = 8$. Then the area of the rectangle $ABCD$ is

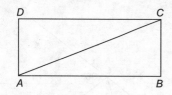

(a) 36                    (b) 50
(c) 60                    (d) Cannot be answered

**Solution:**   Think only of length measuring formulae (Pythagoras Theorem is obvious in this case).

There is no need of forming equations if you have the knowledge of some basic triplets like 3, 4, 5; 5, 12, 13 etc.

Now looking at the equations given in the question and considering $\Delta CDA$ where $AD$ is the height and $AC$ is the hypotenuse we will easily get,

$$AC - AD = 13 - 5 = 8 \text{ and}$$
$$AC + AB = 13 + 12 = 25 \text{ i.e. } 5AD$$

Hence, Area of rectangle is length × breadth i.e. $5 \times 12 = 60$

**13.** In the figure given below. $ABCD$ is a rectangle. The area of the isosceles right triangle $ABE = 7$ cm², $EC = 3(BE)$. The area of $ABCD$ (in cm²) is

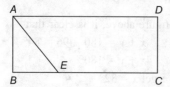

**Solution:**   The key to solve this question is in the visualisation of the construction and the equations.

It is given that $EC = 3 (BE)$ from this we can conclude that the whole side $BC$ can be divided in four equal parts of measurement $BE$.

Now look at this construction

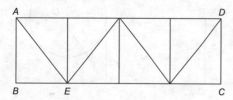

Each part is of equal area as 7 cm². Hence $7 \times 8 = 56$ cm²

**14.** In the given figure. $EADF$ is a rectangle and $ABC$ is a triangle whose vertices lie on the sides of $EADF$. $AE = 22$, $BE = 6$ $CF = 16$ and $BF = 2$. Find the length of the line joining the mid–points of the side $AB$ and $BC$

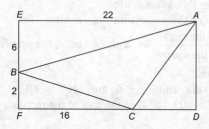

(a) $4\sqrt{2}$                    (b) 5
(c) 3.5                    (d) None of these

**Solution:**   Think only of length measuring formulae and triplets.

$EA = 22$ and $FC = 16$, So, $CD = 6$

$EF = 8$    So, $AD$ is also 8. Now using the triplet 6, 8, 10 based on basic triplet 3, 4, 5 we will get that $AC = 10$.

The line joining the midpoints of the sides $AB$ and $BC$ will be exactly half the side $AC$ (using similar triangles).

Hence, 5 is the correct answer.

**15.** A certain city has a circular wall around it and this wall has four gates pointing north, south, east and west. A house stands outside the city, 3 km north of the north gate and it can just be seen from a point nine km east of south gate. What is the diameter of the wall that surrounds the city?

**Solution:**   Make this construction

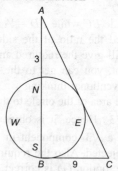

Given   $AN = 3$, $BC = 9$ and $\angle B$ is 90°. Now according to conventional method, we have to use tangent theorem to get to the answer, which will be very long.

Instead if we were to use the Pythagorean triplets again we would easily see the (9, 12, 15) triplet which is based on the basic triplet 3, 4, 5. Here $BC = 9$, Hence, $AC = 15$ and $AB = 12$. Hence, the diameter will be $12 - 3 = 9$ km.

**16.** Let $ABCDEF$ be a regular hexagon: What is the ratio of the area of the triangle $ACE$ to that of the hexagon $ABCDEF$?

**Solution:**   Make the following construction:

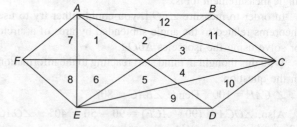

Now we have to find the ratio $\dfrac{\text{Area of } ACE}{\text{Area of } ABCDEF}$.

In order to do so we use the property of a regular hexagon (that it is a combination of 6 equilateral triangles).

We can easily see that we have divided all 6 equilateral triangles into two equal parts of the same area.

If we number all the equal areas as 1, 2, 3 ⋯ 12 as shown in the above construction we will get the answer as

$$\frac{\text{Sum of area of triangles } 1+2+3+4+5+6}{\text{Sum of area of triangle } 1+2+3\ldots+12}$$

Hence ½.

**17.** Euclid has a triangle in mind. Its longest side has length 20 and another of its side has length 10. Its area is 80. What is the exact length of its third side?

(a) $\sqrt{260}$       (b) $\sqrt{250}$

(c) $\sqrt{240}$       (d) $\sqrt{270}$

**Solution:** The solution of the above question is based on the following construction, where $AB = 20$ and $BD = 10$

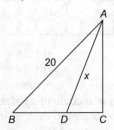

The question is asking for the exact length $AD$, of triangle $ABD$.

Think only of length measuring formulae (Pythagoras theorem is obvious in this case).

If we extend the side $BD$ upto a point $C$, the length $AC$ will give the Altitude or height of the $\triangle ABD$. Then we will get:

½ $b \times h \Rightarrow 80 \Rightarrow$ ½ $\times 10 \times h = 80 \Rightarrow h = 16$. i.e. $AC = 16$.

And now as $\triangle ABC$ is a right angled triangle, we can easily get the length of $DC$ as 2, based on the triplet 12, 16, 20.

Now, if $AC = 16$, $DC = 2$, we can easily get the exact length of $AD$ using Pythagoras theorem i.e. $AC = \sqrt{2^2 + 16^2}$ = $\sqrt{260}$

Hence (1).

(*Note:* In this solution we have only used Pythagorean triplet 12, 16, 20 to solve the question. The alternate method for solving this question is through the use of the semi perimeter of the triangle. This will lead to a very cumbersome and long solution to this question. For experimentation purposes you can try this solution for yourself.)

*Space for Rough Work*

## 🎯 BLOCK REVIEW TESTS

### REVIEW TEST 1

1. In the figure given below, if angle $ABC = 90$, and $BD$ is perpendicular to $AC$, & $BD = 4$ cm and $AD = 3$ cm, what will be the length of $BC$

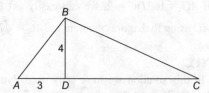

    (a) 13              (b) 20/3
    (c) 16/3           (d) 9

2. In the figure below, the measure of an angle formed by the bisectors of two angles in a triangle $ABC$ is 130 find the measure of an angle $B$.

    (a) 40              (b) 45
    (c) 50              (d) 80

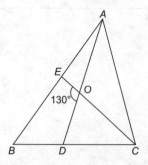

3. The perimeter of right triangle is 36 and the sum of the square of its sides is 450. The area of the right triangle is

    (a) 42              (b) 54
    (c) 62              (d) 100

4. The circles are tangent to one another and each circle is tangent to the sides of the right triangle $ABC$ with right angle $ABC$. If the larger circle has radius 12 and the smaller circle has radius 3, what is the area of the triangle?

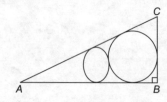

    (a) 420           (b) 620
    (c) 540           (d) 486

5. All the circles are tangent to one another / or the sides of the rectangle. All circles have radius 1. What is the area of the shaded region to the nearest whole unit, i.e. the region outside all the circles but inside the rectangle?

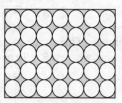

    (a) 27              (b) 28
    (c) 29              (d) 30

6. Given below are six congruent circles drawn internally tangent to a circle of a radius 21; each smaller circle is also tangent to each of its adjacent circles. Find the shaded area between the circle and the six smaller circles.

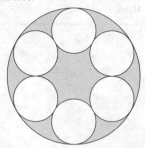

    (a) $136\pi$         (b) $196\pi$
    (c) $180\pi$         (d) $147\pi$

7. In the figure below, $O_1$ and $O_2$ are centers of the circles $O_1A$ is the circle centers at $O_2$.

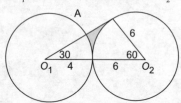

Find the area of the shaded region.

    (a) $22 - 7\pi$       (b) $24\sqrt{2} - 7\pi$
    (c) $18 - 9\pi$       (d) $24 - \pi22/3$

8. In the figure, which of the following is correct? Given: AB = BC

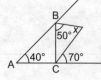

(a) $x = 60$      (b) $x = 70$
(c) $x = 10$      (d) $x = 120$

9. Triangle *PAB* is formed by three tangents to circle *O* and angle *APB* = 40; then the angle *BOA* equals

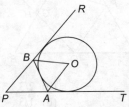

(a) 70      (b) 55
(c) 60      (d) 50

10. *PQRS* is a cyclic quadrilateral. The angle bisector of angle *P*, *Q*, *R* and *S* intersect at *A*, *B*, *C* and *D* as shown in the figure below. Then these four points form a quadrilateral *ABCD* is a:

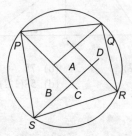

(a) Rectangle      (b) square
(c) rhombus      (d) cyclic quadrilateral

11. In the given figure, *O* is the center of the circle; angle *BOC* = $m°$, angle *BAC* = $n°$.then which of the following is correct?

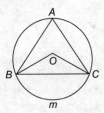

(a) $m + n = 90$      (b) $m + n = 180$
(c) $2m + n = 180$      (d) $m + 2n = 180$

12. Find the area of shaded portion given that the circles with centers *O* and *O'* are 6 cm and 18 cm in diameter respectively and *ACB* is a semi circle.

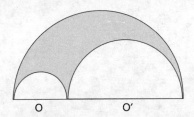

(a) $54\,\pi\,\text{cm}^2$      (b) $27\,\pi\,\text{cm}^2$
(c) $36\,\pi\,\text{cm}^2$      (d) $18\,\pi\,\text{cm}^2$

13. There are two spheres and one cube. The cube is inside the bigger sphere and the smaller sphere is inside the cube. Find the ratio of surface areas of the bigger sphere to the smaller sphere?

(a) $3 : 1$      (b) $2 : 1$
(c) $4 : 1$      (d) $2 : 1$

14. In the adjoining figure, a star is shown. What is the sum of the angles *P*, *Q*, *R*, *S* and *T*?

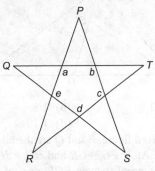

(a) 240      (b) 180
(c) 120      (d) Can't be determined

15. In the figure given below *PS* & *RT* are the medians each measuring 4 cm. triangle *PQR* is right angled at *Q*. what is the area of the triangle *PQR*?

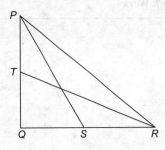

(a) 5.2      (b) 6.4
(d) 6.2      (d) 7.2

16. The area of the largest triangle that can be inscribed in a semi circle whose radius is

(a) $2R^2$      (b) $3R^2$
(c) $R^2$      (d) $3R^2/2$

17. *R* is *O* is the center of the circle having radius (*OP*) = *r*. *PQRSTU* is a regular hexagon and *PAQBRCS-DTEUFP* is a regular six pointed star.

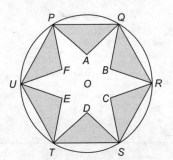

Find the perimeter of hexagon *PQRSTU*.

(a) 12*r*       (b) 9*r*

(c) 6*r*       (d) 8*r*

18. In the given figure *ABC* is a triangle in which *AD* = 3*CD* and *E* lies on *BD*, *DE* = 2*BE*. What is the ratio of area of triangle *ABE* and area of triangle *ABC*?

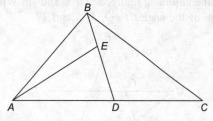

(a) 1/12       (b) 1/8

(c) 1/6       (d) 1/10

19. In the given figure, *P* and *Q* are the mid points of *AC* and *AB*. Also, *PG* = *GR* and *HQ* = *HR*. what is the ratio of area of triangle *PQR*: area of triangle *ABC*?

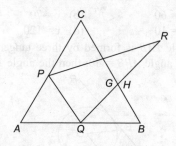

(a) 1/2       (b) 2/3

(c) 3/5       (d) 1/3

20. In the given figure, it is given that angle *C* = 90, *AD* = *DB*, *DE* is perpendicular to *AB* = 20, and *AC* = 12. The area of quadrilateral *ADEC* is:

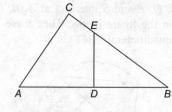

(a) 37(1/2)       (b) 75

(c) 48       (d) 58(1/2)

***Space for Rough Work***

# REVIEW TEST 2

1. Rectangle *PQRS* contains 4 congruent rectangles. If the smaller dimension of one of the small rectangles is 4 units, what is the area of rectangle *PQRS* in square units?

   (a) 144  (b) 172
   (c) 156  (d) 192

   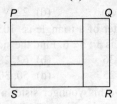

2. If the radii of the circles with centers *O* and *P*, as shown below are 4 and 2 units respectively. Find the area of triangle *ABC*.

   Given: angle *DOA* = angle *EPC* = 90

   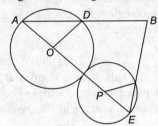

   (a) 36  (b) 62
   (c) 18  (d) 48

3. A cube of side 16 cm is painted red on all the faces and then cut into smaller cubes, each of side 4 cm. What is the total number of smaller cubes having none of their faces painted?

   (a) 16  (b) 8
   (c) 12  (d) 24

4. Identical regular pentagons are placed together side by side to form a ring in the manner shown. The diagram shows the first two pentagons. How many are needed to make a full ring?

   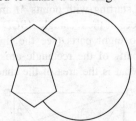

   (a) 9  (b) 10
   (c) 11  (d) 12

5. Find angle *EBC* + angle *ECB* from the given figure, given *ADE* is an equilateral triangle and angle *DCE* = 20°

   (a) 160  (b) 140
   (c) 100  (d) 120

6. *PQRS* is a square and *POQ* is an equilateral triangle. What is the value of angle *SOR*?

   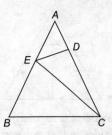

   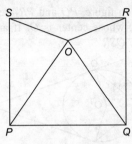

   (a) 150  (b) 120
   (c) 125  (d) 100

7. In the following figure *ABCD* is a square, angle *DAO* = 40 then find angle *BNO*.

   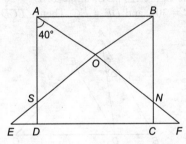

   (a) 50  (b) 60
   (c) 30  (d) 40

8. From an external point *P*, tangents *PA* and *PB* are drawn to a circle with center *O*. If *CO* is the tangent to the circle at a point *E* and *PA* = 14 cm, find the perimeter of △*CPD*.

   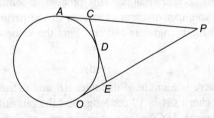

   (a) 21  (b) 28
   (c) 24  (d) 25

9. A circle is inscribed in an equilateral triangle; the radius of the circle is 2 cm. Find the area of triangle.

   (a) $12\sqrt{3}$  (b) $15\sqrt{3}$
   (c) $12\sqrt{2}$  (d) $18\sqrt{3}$

10. If interior angle of a regular polygon is 168°, then find no. of sides in that polygon.

    (a) 10        (b) 20
    (c) 30        (d) 25

11. In the given figure, $PQ$ and $PR$ are two tangents to the circle, whose center is $O$. If angle $QPR = 40°$, find angle $QSR$.

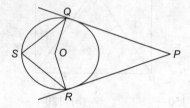

    (a) 60        (b) 70
    (c) 80        (d) 50

12. In the figure $AB \parallel DE$, angle $BAD = 20°$ and angle $DAE = 30°$, and $DE = EC$. Then $\angle ECD =$?

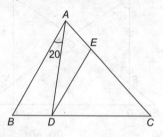

    (a) 60        (b) 65
    (c) 75        (d) 70

13. There is an equilateral triangle of side 32 cm. The mid-points of the sides are joined to form another triangle, whose mid-points are again joined to form still another triangle. This process is continued for '$n$' number of times. The sum of the perimeters of all the triangles is 180 cm. Find the value of $n$.

    (a) 4        (b) 5
    (c) 8        (d) 3

14. There is a circle of diameter $AB$ and radius 26 cm. If chord $CA$ is 10 cm long, find the ratio of area of triangle $ABC$ to the remaining area of circle.

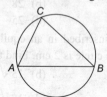

    (a) 0.60        (b) 0.30
    (c) 0.29        (d) 0.52

15. Ram Singh has a rectangular plot of land of dimensions 30 m * 40 m. He wants to construct a unique swimming pool which is in the shape of an equilateral triangle. Find the area of the largest swimming pool which he can have?

    (a) $300\sqrt{3}$ sq cm     (b) $225\sqrt{3}$ sq cm
    (c) $300$ sq cm       (d) $225\sqrt{}$ sq cm

16. The perimeter of a triangle is 105 cm. The ratio of its altitudes is 3 : 5 : 6. Find the sides of the triangle.

    (a) 72, 46, 36      (b) 62, 28, 41
    (c) 30, 60, 25      (d) 50, 30, 25

17. Rizwan gave his younger sister a rectangular sheet of paper. He halved it by folding it at the mid point of its longer side. The piece of paper again became a rectangle whose longer and shorter sides were in the same proportion as the longer and shorter sides of the original rectangle. If the shorter side of the original rectangle was 4 cm, find the diagonal of the smaller rectangle?

    (a) $3(3)^{1/2}$        (b) $5(3)^{1/2}$
    (c) $4(3)^{1/2}$        (d) $2(3)^{1/2}$

18. A rectangular hall, 50 m in length and 75 m in width has to be paved with square tiles of equal size. What is the minimum number of tiles required?

    (a) 4        (b) 5
    (c) 6        (d) 8

19. In triangle $ABC$ we have angle $A = 100$ degree and $B = C = 40$. The side $AB$ is produced to a point $D$ so that $B$ lies between $A$ and $D$ and $AD = BC$. Then $\angle BCD =$?

    (a) 20°        (b) 10°
    (c) 30°        (4) 40°

20. The sides of a cyclic quadrilateral are 9, 10, 12 and 16. If one of its diagonals is 14, then find the other diagonal?

    (a) 16        (b) 17
    (c) 18        (d) 19

21. Segments starting with points $M$ and $N$ and ending with vertices of the rectangle $ABCD$ divide the given figure into eight parts (see the figure). The areas of three parts of the rectangle are indicated in the picture. What is the area of the shaded region?

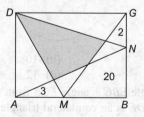

    (a) 25        (b) 40
    (c) 29        (d) 20

# ANSWER KEY

## Review Test 1

| 1. (b) | 2. (d) | 3. (b) | 4. (d) |
|--------|--------|--------|--------|
| 5. (d) | 6. (d) | 7. (d) | 8. (d) |
| 9. (a) | 10. (d) | 11. (a) | 12. (b) |
| 13. (a) | 14. (b) | 15. (b) | 16. (c) |
| 17. (c) | 18. (a) | 19. (a) | 20. (d) |

## Review Test 2

| 1. (d) | 2. (a) | 3. (b) | 4. (b) |
|--------|--------|--------|--------|
| 5. (c) | 6. (a) | 7. (d) | 8. (b) |
| 9. (a) | 10. (c) | 11. (b) | 12. (b) |
| 13. (a) | 14. (c) | 15. (a) | 16. (d) |
| 17. (c) | 18. (c) | 19. (b) | 20. (c) |
| 21. (a) | | | |

# TASTE OF THE EXAMS—BLOCK IV

## CAT (1999–2008, 2017)

1. The figure below shows two concentric circles with centre O. PQRS is a square inscribed in the outer circle. It also circumscribes the inner circle, touching it at points B, C, D and A. What is the ratio of the perimeter of the outer circle to that of polygon ABCD? **(CAT 1999)**

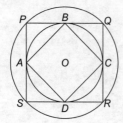

(a) $\dfrac{\pi}{4}$  (b) $\dfrac{3\pi}{2}$

(c) $\dfrac{\pi}{2}$  (d) $\pi$

2. There is a circle of radius 1 cm. Each member of a sequence of regular polygons $S_1(n)$, n = 4, 5, 6, …; where n is the number of sides of the polygon, is circumscribing the circle: and each member of the sequence of regular polygons $S_2(n)$, n = 4, 5, 6, … where n is the number of sides of the polygon, is inscribed in the circle. Let $L_1(n)$ and $L_2(n)$ denote the perimeters of the corresponding polygons of $S_1(n)$ and $S_2(n)$, then $\dfrac{\{L_1(13)+2\pi\}}{L_2(17)}$ is **(CAT 1999)**

(a) greater than $\dfrac{\pi}{4}$ and less than 1

(b) greater than 2

(c) greater than 1 and less than 2

(d) less than $\dfrac{\pi}{4}$

3. There is a square field of side 500 m length each. It has a compound wall along its perimeter. At one of its corners, a triangular area of the field is to be cordoned off by erecting a straight-line fence. The compound wall and the fence will form its borders. If the length of the fence is 100 m, what is the maximum area that can be cordoned off? **(CAT 1999)**

(a) 2,500 sq m  (b) 10,000 sq m
(c) 5,000 sq m  (d) 20,000 sq m

4. ABCD is a rhombus with the diagonals AC and BD intersecting at the origin on the x-y plane. The equation of the straight line AD is x + y = 1. What is the equation of BC? **(CAT 2000)**

(a) x + y = –1  (b) x – y = –1
(c) x + y = 1  (d) None of these

5. Consider a circle with unit radius. There are seven adjacent sectors, S1, S2, S3, ..., S7, in the circle such that their total area is 1/8 of the area of the circle. Further, the area of the jth sector is twice that of the (j – 1)th sector, for j = 2, ..., 7. What is the angle, in radians, subtended by the arc of S1 at the centre of the circle? **(CAT 2000)**

(a) $\pi/508$  (b) $\pi/2040$
(c) $\pi/1016$  (d) $\pi/1524$

6. If a, b and c are the sides of a triangle, and $a^2 + b^2 + c^2 = bc + ca + ab$, then the triangle is **(CAT 2000)**

(a) equilateral  (b) isosceles
(c) right-angled  (d) obtuse-angled

7. In the figure, AB = BC = CD = DE = EF = FG = GA. Then ∠DAE is approximately **(CAT 2000)**

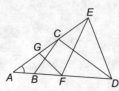

(a) 15°  (b) 20°
(c) 30°  (d) 25°

8. A square, whose side is 2 m, has its corners cut away so as to form an octagon with all sides equal. Then the length of each side of the octagon, in metres, is **(CAT 2001)**

(a) $\dfrac{\sqrt{2}}{\sqrt{2}+1}$  (b) $\dfrac{2}{\sqrt{2}+1}$

(c) $\dfrac{2}{\sqrt{2}-1}$  (d) $\dfrac{\sqrt{2}}{\sqrt{2}-1}$

9. In the diagram, ABCD is a rectangle with AE = EF = FB. What is the ratio of the areas of ΔCEF and that of the rectangle? **(CAT 2001)**

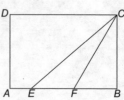

(a) 1/6  (b) 1/8
(c) 1/9  (d) None of these

10. Two sides of a plot measure 32 m and 24 m and the angle between them is a perfect right angle. The other two sides measure 25 m each and the other three angles are not right angles.

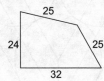

What is the area of the plot? **(CAT 2001)**
(a) 768 m²        (b) 534 m²
(c) 696.5 m²      (d) 684 m²

11. Euclid has a triangle in mind. Its longest side has length 20 and another of its sides has length 10. Its area is 80. What is the exact length of its third side? **(CAT 2001)**

(a) $\sqrt{260}$        (b) $\sqrt{250}$

(c) $\sqrt{240}$        (d) $\sqrt{270}$

12. In $\Delta DEF$ shown below, points A, B and C are taken on DE, DF and EF respectively such that EC = AC and CF = BC. If $\angle D = 40^0$, then $\angle ACB$ = **(CAT 2001)**

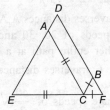

(a) 140°        (b) 70°
(c) 100°        (d) None of these

13. Based on the figure below, what is the value of x, if y = 10? **(CAT 2001)**

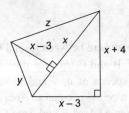

(a) 10        (b) 11
(c) 12        (d) None of these

14. A rectangular pool of 20 m wide and 60 m long is surrounded by a walkway of uniform width. If the total area of the walkway is 516 m², how wide, in metres, is the walkway? **(CAT 2001)**
(a) 4.3 m        (b) 3 m
(c) 5 m          (d) 3.5 m

15. In $\Delta ABC$, the internal bisector of $\angle A$ meets BC at D. If AB = 4, AC = 3 and $\angle A = 60^0$, then the length of AD is **(CAT 2002)**

(a) $2\sqrt{3}$        (b) $\dfrac{12\sqrt{3}}{7}$

(c) $\dfrac{15\sqrt{3}}{8}$        (d) $\dfrac{6\sqrt{3}}{7}$

16. The length of the common chord of two circles of radii 15 cm and 20 cm, whose centres are 25 cm apart, is **(CAT 2002)**
(a) 24 cm        (b) 25 cm
(c) 15 cm        (d) 20 cm

17. Four horses are tethered at four corners of a square plot of side 14 m so that the adjacent horses can just reach one another. There is a small circular pond of area 20 m² at the centre. Find the ungrazed area. **(CAT 2002)**
(a) 22 m²        (b) 42 m²
(c) 84 m²        (d) 168 m²

18. In the figure given below, ABCD is a rectangle. The area of the isosceles right triangle ABE = 7 cm²; EC = 3(BE). The area of ABCD (in cm²) is **(CAT 2002)**

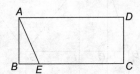

(a) 21 cm²        (b) 28 cm²
(c) 42 cm²        (d) 56 cm²

19. The area of the triangle whose vertices are (a, a), (a + 1, a + 1) and (a + 2, a) is **(CAT 2002)**
(a) $a^3$        (b) 1
(c) 2a           (d) $2^{1/2}$

20. Instead of walking along two adjacent sides of a rectangular field, a boy took a short cut along the diagonal and saved a distance equal to half the longer side. Then the ratio of the shorter side to the longer side is **(CAT 2002)**
(a) 1/2        (b) 2/3
(c) 1/4        (d) 3/4

21. Neeraj has agreed to mow a lawn, which is a 20 m × 40 m rectangle. He mows it with 1 m wide strip. If Neeraj starts at one corner and mows around the lawn toward the centre, about how many times would he go round before he has mowed half the lawn? **(CAT 2002)**
(a) 2.5        (b) 3.5
(c) 3.8        (d) 4

22. A piece of string is 40 cm long. It is cut into three pieces. The longest piece is three times as long as the middle-sized and the shortest piece is 23 cm shorter

than the longest piece. Find the length of the shortest piece. **(CAT 2002)**

(a) 27        (b) 5

(c) 4         (d) 9

23. In the figure, ACB is a right-angled triangle. CD is the altitude. Circles are inscribed within the ΔACD and ΔBCD. P and Q are the centers of the circles. The distance PQ is **(CAT 2002)**

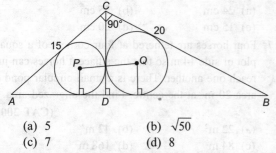

(a) 5        (b) $\sqrt{50}$

(c) 7        (d) 8

**Directions for Questions 24 and 25:** Answer the questions based on the following diagram.

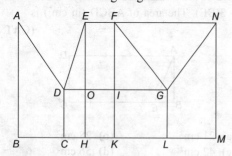

In the above diagram, $\angle ABC = 90° = \angle DCH = \angle DOE = \angle EHK = \angle FKL = \angle GLM = \angle LMN$

$AB = BC = 2CH = 2CD = EH = FK = 2HK = 4KL = 2LM = MN$ **(CAT 2002)**

24. The magnitude of $\angle FGO =$

(a) 30°        (b) 45°

(c) 60°        (d) None of these

25. What is the ratio of the areas of the two quadrilaterals ABCD to DEFG?

(a) 1 : 2        (b) 2 : 1

(c) 12 : 7        (d) None of these

**Directions for Questions 26 to 28:** Answer the questions on the basis of the information given below.

Consider three circular parks of equal size with centres at $A_1$, $A_2$, and $A_3$ respectively. The parks touch each other at the edge as shown in the figure (not drawn to scale). There are three paths formed by the triangles $A_1A_2A_3$, $B_1B_2B_3$, and $C_1C_2C_3$, as shown. Three sprinters A, B, and C begin running from points $A_1$, $B_1$ and $C_1$ respectively. Each sprinter traverses her respective triangular path clockwise and returns to her starting point.

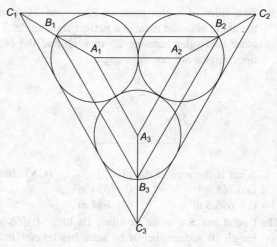

26. Let the radius of each circular park be r, and the distances to be traversed by the sprinters A, B and C be a, b and c respectively. Which of the following is true? **(CAT 2003)**

(a) $b - a = c - b = 3\sqrt{3}\ r$

(b) $b - a = c - b = \sqrt{3}r$

(c) $b = (a + c)/2 = 2(1 + \sqrt{3}\ )r$

(d) $c = 2b - a = (2 + \sqrt{3}\ )r$

27. Sprinter A traverses distances $A_1A_2$, $A_2A_3$, and $A_3A_1$ at average speeds of 20, 30 and 15 respectively. B traverses her entire path at a uniform speed of $(10\sqrt{3} + 20)$. C traverses distances $C_1C_2$, $C_2C_3$ and $C_3C_1$ at average speeds of $\dfrac{40}{3}(\sqrt{3} + 1), \dfrac{40}{3}(\sqrt{3} + 1)$ and 120 respectively. All speeds are in the same unit. Where would B and C be respectively, when A finishes her sprint? **(CAT 2003)**

(a) $B_1$, $C_1$

(b) $B_3$, $C_3$

(c) $B_1$, $C_3$

(d) $B_1$, Somewhere between $C_3$ and $C_1$

28. Sprinters A, B and C traverse their respective paths at uniform speeds of u, v and w respectively. It is known that $u^2 : v^2 : w^2$ is equal to Area A: Area B: Area C, where Area A, Area B and Area C are the areas of triangles $A_1A_2A_3$, $B_1B_2B_3$, and $C_1C_2C_3$ respectively. Where would A and C be when B reaches point $B_3$? **(CAT 2003)**

(a) $A_2$, $C_3$

(b) $A_3$, $C_3$

(c) $A_3$, $C_2$

(d) Somewhere between $A_2$ and $A_3$, Somewhere between $C_3$ and $C_1$

**Directions for Questions 29 to 31:** Answer the questions on the basis of the information given below.

Consider a cylinder of height $h$ cm and radius $r = 2/\pi$ cm as shown in the figure (not drawn to scale). A string of a certain length, when wound on its cylindrical surface, starting at point A and ending at point B, gives a maximum of n turns (in other words, the string's length is the minimum length required to wind n turns). **(CAT 2003)**

29. What is the vertical spacing between the two consecutive turns?

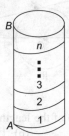

(a) $\dfrac{h}{n}$ cm      (b) $\dfrac{h}{\sqrt{n}}$ cm

(c) $\dfrac{h}{n^2}$ cm      (d) Cannot be determined

30. The same string, when wound on the exterior four walls of a cube of side n cm, starting at point C and ending at point D, can give exactly one turn (see figure, not drawn to scale). The length of the string is

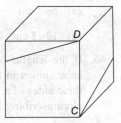

(a) $\sqrt{2}n$ cm      (b) $\sqrt{17}n$ cm

(c) $n$ cm      (d) $\sqrt{13}n$ cm

31. In the set-up of the previous two questions, how is $h$ related to $n$?

(a) $h = \sqrt{2}n$      (b) $h = \sqrt{17}n$

(c) $h = n$      (d) $h = \sqrt{13}n$

32. In the figure (not drawn to scale) given below, P is a point on AB such that AP : PB = 4 : 3. PQ is parallel to AC and QD is parallel to CP. In $\triangle$ARC, $\angle$ARC = $90°$, and in $\triangle$PQS, $\angle$PSQ = $90°$. The length of QS is 6 cm. What is the ratio of AP : PD? **(CAT 2003)**

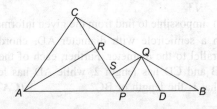

(a) 10:3      (b) 2:1

(c) 7:3      (d) 8:3

33. A car is being driven, in a straight line and at a uniform speed, towards the base of a vertical tower. The top of the tower is observed from the car and, in the process, it takes 10 min for the angle of elevation to change from $45°$ to $60°$. After how much more time will this car reach the base of the tower? **(CAT 2003)**

(a) $5(\sqrt{3}+1)$      (b) $6(\sqrt{3}+\sqrt{2})$

(c) $7(\sqrt{3}-1)$      (d) $8(\sqrt{3}-2)$

34. In the figure (not drawn to scale) given below, if AD = CD = BC and $\angle$BCE = $96°$, how much is the value of DBC? **(CAT 2003)**

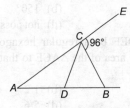

(a) $32°$      (b) $84°$

(c) $64°$      (d) Cannot be determined

35. Consider two different cloth-cutting processes. In the first one, n circular cloth pieces are cut from a square cloth piece of side $a$ in the following steps: the original square of side $a$ is divided into $n$ smaller squares, not necessarily of the same size, then a circle of maximum possible area is cut from each of the smaller squares. In the second process, only one circle of maximum possible area is cut from the square of side $a$ and the process ends there. The cloth pieces remaining after cutting the circles are scrapped in both the processes. The ratio of the total area of scrap cloth generated in the former to that in the latter is **(CAT 2003)**

(a) 1:1      (b) $\sqrt{2}$:1

(c) $\dfrac{n(4-\pi)}{4n-\pi}$      (d) $\dfrac{4n-\pi}{n(4-\pi)}$

36. Let $S_1$ be a square of side $a$. Another square $S_2$ is formed by joining the mid-points of the sides of $S_1$. The same process is applied to $S_2$ to form yet another square $S_3$, and so on. If $A_1, A_2, A_3, \ldots$ be the areas and $P_1, P_2, P_3, \ldots$ be the perimeters of $S_1, S_2, S_3, \ldots$, respectively, then the ratio $\dfrac{P_1 + P_2 + P_3 + \ldots}{A_1 + A_2 + A_3 + \ldots}$ equals **(CAT 2003)**

(a) $\dfrac{2(1+\sqrt{2})}{a}$      (b) $\dfrac{2(2-\sqrt{2})}{a}$

(c) $\dfrac{2(2+\sqrt{2})}{a}$      (d) $\dfrac{2(1+2\sqrt{2})}{a}$

37. In the figure given below (not drawn to scale), A, B and C are three points on a circle with centre O. The chord BA is extended to a point T such that CT becomes a tangent to the circle at point C. If ∠ATC = 30° and ∠ACT = 50°, then the angle ∠BOA is **(CAT 2003)**

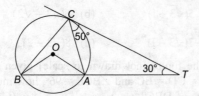

  (a) 100°        (b) 150°

  (c) 80°         (d) not possible to determine

38. Let ABCDEF be a regular hexagon. What is the ratio of the area of the ΔACE to that of the hexagon ABCDEF? **(CAT 2003)**

  (a) 1/3         (b) 1/2

  (c) 2/3         (d) 5/6

39. A piece of paper is in the shape of a right-angled triangle and is cut along a line that is parallel to the hypotenuse, leaving a smaller triangle. There was 35% reduction in the length of the hypotenuse of the triangle. If the area of the original triangle was 34 square inches before the cut, what is the area (in square inches) of the smaller triangle? **(CAT 2003)**

  (a) 16.665        (b) 16.565

  (c) 15.465        (d) 14.365

40. A square tin sheet of side 12 inches is converted into a box with open top in the following steps. The sheet is placed horizontally. Then, equal-sized squares, each of side x inches, are cut from the four corners of the sheet. Finally, the four resulting sides are bent vertically upwards in the shape of a box. If x is an integer, then what value of x maximizes the volume of the box? **(CAT 2003)**

  (a) 3         (b) 4

  (c) 1         (d) 2

41. A rectangular sheet of paper, when halved by folding it at the midpoint of its longer side, results in a rectangle, whose longer and shorter sides are in the same proportion as the longer and shorter sides of the original rectangle. If the shorter side of the original rectangle is 2, what is the area of the smaller rectangle? **(CAT 2004)**

  (a) $4\sqrt{2}$        (b) $2\sqrt{2}$

  (c) $\sqrt{2}$        (d) None of the above

**Directions for Questions 42 to 44:** Answer the questions on the basis of the information given below:

In the adjoining figure I and II, are circles with P and Q respectively. The two circles touch each other and have common tangent that touches them at points R and S respectively. This common tangent meets the line joining P and Q at O. The diameters of I and II are in the ratio 4 : 3. It is also known that the length of PO is 28 cm. **(CAT 2004)**

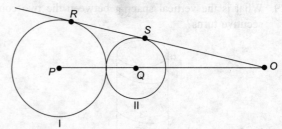

42. What is the ratio of the length of PQ to that of QO?

  (a) 1 : 4        (b) 1 : 3

  (c) 3 : 8        (d) 3 : 4

43. What is the radius of the circle II?

  (a) 2 cm        (b) 3 cm

  (c) 4 cm        (d) 5 cm

44. The length of SO is

  (a) $8\sqrt{3}$ cm        (b) $10\sqrt{3}$ cm

  (c) $12\sqrt{3}$ cm        (d) $14\sqrt{3}$ cm

45. If the lengths of diagonals DF, AG and CE of the cube shown in the adjoining figure are equal to the three sides of a triangle, then the radius of the circle circumscribing that triangle will be **(CAT 2004)**

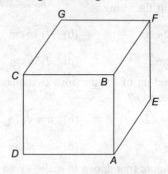

  (a) Equal to the side of cube

  (b) $\sqrt{3}$ times the side the cube

  (c) $\dfrac{1}{\sqrt{3}}$ times the side of the cube

  (d) impossible to find from the given information.

46. On a semicircle with diameter AD, chord BC is parallel to the diameter. Further, each of the chords AB and CD has length 2, while AD has length 8. What is the length of BC? **(CAT 2004)**

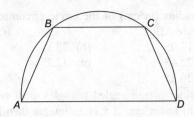

(a) 7.5             (b) 7
(c) 7.75          (d) None of the above

47. A circle with radius 2 is placed against a right angle. Another smaller circle is also placed as shown in the adjoining figure. What is the radius of the smaller circle? **(CAT 2004)**

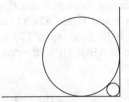

(a) $3 - 2\sqrt{2}$         (b) $4 - 2\sqrt{2}$

(c) $7 - 4\sqrt{2}$         (d) $6 - 4\sqrt{2}$

48. In the given figure, chord ED is parallel to the diameter AC of the circle. If ∠CBE = 65°, then what is the value of ∠DEC? **(CAT 2004)**

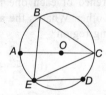

(a) 35°            (b) 55°
(c) 45°            (d) 25°

49. Two identical circles intersect so that their centers, and the points at which they intersect, form a square of side 1 cm. The area in sq. cm of the portion that is common to the two circles is
(a) $\pi/4$           (b) $(\pi/2) - 1$
(c) $\pi/5$           (d) $\sqrt{2} - 1$   **(CAT 2005)**

50. A jogging park has two identical circular tracks touching each other, and a rectangular track enclosing the two circles. The edges of the rectangles are tangential to the circles. Two friends, A and B, start jogging simultaneously from the point where one of the circular tracks touches the smaller side of the rectangular track. A jogs along the rectangular track, while B jogs along the two circular tracks in a figure of eight. Approximately, how much faster than A does B have to run, so that they take the same time to return to their starting point? **(CAT 2005)**
(a) 3.88%         (b) 4.22%
(c) 4.44%         (d) 4.72%

51. In the following figure, the diameter of the circle is 3 cm. AB and MN are two diameters such that MN is perpendicular to AB. In addition, CG is perpendicular to AB such that AE:EB = 1:2, and DF is perpendicular to MN such that NL:LM = 1:2. The length of DH in cm is **(CAT 2005)**

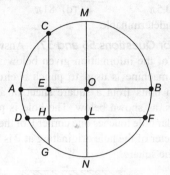

(a) $2\sqrt{2} - 1$         (b) $\dfrac{2\sqrt{2} - 1}{2}$

(c) $\dfrac{3\sqrt{2} - 1}{2}$         (d) $\dfrac{2\sqrt{2} - 1}{3}$

52. Consider the triangle ABC shown in the following figure where BC = 12 cm, DB = 9 cm, CD = 6 cm and ∠BCD = ∠BAC **(CAT 2005)**

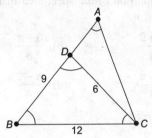

What is the ratio of the perimeter of ΔADC to that of the ΔBDC?
(a) 7/9          (b) 8/9
(c) 6/9          (d) 5/9

53. P, Q, S and R are points on the circumference of a circle of radius r, such that PQR is an equilateral triangle and PS is a diameter of the circle. What is the perimeter of the quadrilateral PQSR?

**(CAT 2005)**

(a) $2r(1 + \sqrt{3})$      (b) $2r(2 + \sqrt{3})$

(c) $r(1 + \sqrt{5})$        (d) $2r + \sqrt{3}$

54. A rectangular floor is fully covered with square tiles of identical size. The tiles on the edges are white and the tiles in the interior are red. The number of white tiles is the same as the number of red tiles. A possible value of the number of tiles along one edge of the floor is **(CAT 2005)**
(a) 10            (b) 12
(c) 14            (d) 16

55. A semi-circle is drawn with AB as its diameter. From C, a point on AB, a line perpendicular to AB is drawn meeting the circumference of the semi-circle at D. Given that AC = 2 cm and CD = 6 cm, the area of the semi-circle (in sq. cm) will be: **(CAT 2006)**
    (a) $32\pi$ (b) $50\pi$
    (c) $40.5\pi$ (d) $81\pi$
    (e) undeterminable

**Directions for Questions 56 and 57:** Answer questions on the basis of the information given below:

A punching machine is used to punch a circular hole of diameter two units from a square sheet of aluminium of width 2 units, as shown below. The hole is punched such that the circular hole touches one corner P of the square sheet and the diameter of the hole originating at P is in line with a diagonal of the square. **(CAT 2006)**

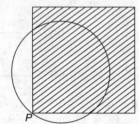

56. The proportion of the sheet area that remains after punching is:
    (a) $\dfrac{\pi + 2}{8}$ (b) $\dfrac{6 - \pi}{8}$
    (c) $\dfrac{4 - \pi}{4}$ (d) $\dfrac{\pi - 2}{4}$
    (e) $\dfrac{14 - 3\pi}{6}$

57. Find the area of the part of the circle (round punch) falling outside the square sheet.
    (a) $\dfrac{\pi}{4}$ (b) $\dfrac{\pi - 1}{2}$
    (c) $\dfrac{\pi - 1}{4}$ (d) $\dfrac{\pi - 2}{2}$
    (e) $\dfrac{\pi - 2}{4}$

58. An equilateral triangle BPC is drawn inside a square ABCD. What is the value of the angle APD in degrees? **(CAT 2006)**
    (a) 75 (b) 90
    (c) 120 (d) 135
    (e) 150

59. In a triangle ABC, the lengths of the sides AB and AC equal 17.5 cm and 9 cm respectively. Let D be a point on the line segment BC such that AD is perpendicular to BC. If AD = 3 cm, then what is

the radius (in cm) of the circle circumscribing the triangle ABC? **(CAT 2008)**
    (a) 17.05 (b) 27.85
    (c) 22.45 (d) 32.25
    (e) 26.25

60. Consider obtuse-angled triangles with sides 8 cm, 15 cm and x cm. If x is an integer then how many such triangles exist? **(CAT 2008)**
    (a) 5 (b) 21
    (c) 10 (d) 15
    (e) 14

61. Consider a square ABCD with midpoints E, F, G, H of AB, BC, CD and DA respectively. Let L denote the line passing through F and H. Consider points P and Q, on L and inside ABCD such that the angles APD and BQC both equal 120°. What is the ratio of the area of ABQCDP to the remaining area inside ABCD? **(CAT 2008)**
    (a) $\dfrac{4\sqrt{2}}{3}$ (b) $2 + \sqrt{3}$
    (c) $\dfrac{10 - 3\sqrt{3}}{9}$ (d) $1 + \dfrac{1}{\sqrt{3}}$
    (e) $2\sqrt{3} - 1$

62. Two circles, both of radii 1 cm, intersect such that the circumference of each one passes through the centre of the other. What is the area (in sq. cm.) of the intersecting region? **(CAT 2008)**
    (a) $\dfrac{\pi}{3} - \dfrac{\sqrt{3}}{4}$ (b) $\dfrac{2\pi}{3} + \dfrac{\sqrt{3}}{2}$
    (c) $\dfrac{4\pi}{3} - \dfrac{\sqrt{3}}{2}$ (d) $\dfrac{4\pi}{3} + \dfrac{\sqrt{3}}{2}$
    (e) $\dfrac{2\pi}{3} - \dfrac{\sqrt{3}}{2}$

63. Consider a right circular cone of base radius 4 cm and height 10 cm. A cylinder is to be placed inside the cone with one of the flat surfaces resting on the base of the cone. Find the largest possible total surface area (in sq. cm) of the cylinder. **(CAT 2008)**
    (a) $100\pi/3$ (b) $80\pi/3$
    (c) $120\pi/3$ (d) $130\pi/9$
    (e) $110\pi/7$

64. From a triangle ABC with sides of lengths 40 ft, 25 ft and 35 ft, a triangular portion GBC is cut off where G is the centroid of ABC. The area, in sq.ft, of the remaining portion of triangle ABC is **(CAT 2017)**
    (a) $225\sqrt{3}$ (b) $500/\sqrt{3}$
    (c) $275/\sqrt{3}$ (d) $250/\sqrt{3}$

65. Let ABC be a right-angled isosceles triangle with hypotenuse BC. Let BQC be a semi-circle, away from A, with diameter BC. Let BPC be an arc of a circle centered at A and lying between BC and BQC. If AB has length 6 cm then the area, in sq cm, of the region enclosed by BPC and BQC is **(CAT 2017)**
   (a) $9\pi - 18$  (b) 18
   (c) $9\pi$  (d) 9

66. A solid metallic cube is melted to form five solid cubes whose volumes are in the ratio 1:1:8:27:27. The percentage by which the sum of the surface areas of these five cubes exceeds the surface area of the original cube is nearest to **(CAT 2017)**
   (a) 10  (b) 50
   (c) 60  (d) 20

67. A ball of diameter 4 cm is kept on top of a hollow cylinder standing vertically. The height of the cylinder is 3 cm, while its volume is $9\pi$ cm³. Then the vertical distance, in cm, of the topmost point of the ball from the base of the cylinder is **(CAT 2017)**

68. Let ABC be a right-angled triangle with BC as the hypotenuse. Lengths of AB and AC are 15 km and 20 km, respectively. The minimum possible time, in minutes, required to reach the hypotenuse from A at a speed of 30 km per hour is **(CAT 2017)**

69. The shortest distance of the point $\left(\dfrac{1}{2}, 1\right)$ from the curve $y = |x - 1| + |x + 1|$ is **(CAT 2017)**
   (a) 1  (b) 0
   (c) $\sqrt{2}$  (d) $\sqrt{3}/2$

70. Let ABCDEF be a regular hexagon with each side of length 1 cm. The area (in sq cm) of a square with AC as one side is **(CAT 2017)**
   (a) $3\sqrt{2}$  (b) 3
   (c) 4  (d) $\sqrt{3}$

71. The base of a vertical pillar with uniform cross section is a trapezium whose parallel sides are of lengths 10 cm and 20 cm while the other two sides are of equal length. The perpendicular distance between the parallel sides of the trapezium is 12 cm. If the height of the pillar is 20 cm, then the total area, in square cm, of all six surfaces of the pillar is **(CAT 2017)**
   (a) 1300  (b) 1340
   (c) 1480  (d) 1520

72. If three sides of a rectangular park have a total length 400 ft, then the area of the park is maximum when the length (in ft) of its longer side is **(CAT 2017)**

73. ABCD is a quadrilateral inscribed in a circle with centre O. If ∠COD = 120 degrees and ∠BAC = 30 degrees, then the value of ∠BCD (in degrees) is **(CAT 2017)**

74. Let P be an interior point of a right-angled isosceles triangle ABC with hypotenuse AB. If the perpendicular distance of P from each of AB, BC, and CA is $4(\sqrt{2} - 1)$ cm, then the area, in sq cm, of the triangle ABC is **(CAT 2017)**

75. The points (2, 5) and (6, 3) are two end points of a diagonal of a rectangle. If the other diagonal has the equation $y = 3x + c$, then c is **(CAT 2017)**
   (a) −5  (b) −6
   (c) −7  (d) −8

## ANSWER KEY

| | | | |
|---|---|---|---|
| 1. (c) | 2. (b) | 3. (a) | 4. (a) |
| 5. (a) | 6. (a) | 7. (d) | 8. (b) |
| 9. (a) | 10. (d) | 11. (a) | 12. (c) |
| 13. (b) | 14. (b) | 15. (b) | 16. (a) |
| 17. (a) | 18. (d) | 19. (b) | 20. (a) |
| 21. (c) | 22. (c) | 23. (b) | 24. (d) |
| 25. (c) | 26. (a) | 27. (c) | 28. (b) |
| 29. (a) | 30. (b) | 31. (c) | 32. (c) |
| 33. (a) | 34. (c) | 35. (a) | 36. (c) |
| 37. (a) | 38. (b) | 39. (d) | 40. (d) |
| 41. (b) | 42. (b) | 43. (b) | 44. (c) |
| 45. (a) | 46. (b) | 47. (d) | 48. (d) |
| 49. (b) | 50. (d) | 51. (b) | 52. (a) |
| 53. (a) | 54. (b) | 55. (b) | 56. (b) |
| 57. (d) | 58. (e) | 59. (e) | 60. (c) |
| 61. (e) | 62. (e) | 63. (a) | 64. (b) |
| 65. (b) | 66. (b) | 67. 6 | 68. 24 |
| 69. (a) | 70. (b) | 71. (c) | 72. 200 |
| 73. 90 | 74. 16 | 75. (d) | |

### Solutions

1. Let the radius of the outer circle be r.

   ABCD is a square and length of its side would also be 'r'.

   Perimeter of ABCD = 4r

   Hence, the required ratio = $\dfrac{2\pi r}{4r} = \dfrac{\pi}{2}$

2. The perimeter of any polygon circumscribed about a circle is always greater than the circumference of the circle and the perimeter of any polygon inscribed in a circle is always less than the circumference of the circle.

   Hence, L1(13) > $2\pi \cdot 1$ and L2(17) < $2\pi$

   So {L1(13) + $2\pi$} > $4\pi$ and hence $\dfrac{\{L1(13) + 2\pi\}}{L2(17)}$ will be greater than 2.

3. In this case, the area of the triangle would be maximum when it is an isosceles triangle.

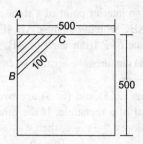

Length of AC = $\dfrac{100}{\sqrt{2}}$.

Area of the triangular region ABC

$$= \frac{1}{2} \times \frac{100}{\sqrt{2}} \times \frac{100}{\sqrt{2}} = 2{,}500 \text{ sq.m.}$$

4.

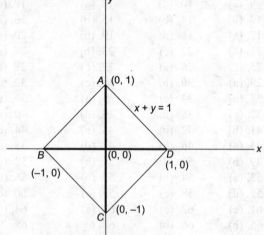

Equation of line BC is $\dfrac{X}{-1} + \dfrac{Y}{-1} = 1$ OR $x + y = -1$.

5. Let the area of sector $S_1$ be A units. Then the area of the corresponding sectors shall be 2A, 4A, 8A, 16A, 32A and 64A (since every successive sector has an angle that is twice the previous one). Hence, the total area then shall be 127A units. This is 1/8 of the total area of the circle. Hence, the total area of the circle will be 127A × 8 = 1016A units. Since, the total angle at the center of a circle is $2\pi$, the sector $S_1$ should account for $\dfrac{1}{1016}$ of this angle. Hence, angle of sector $S_1$ is $\dfrac{\pi}{508}$.

6. $a^2 + b^2 + c^2 = bc + ca + ab$

Now we can solve the problem by assuming values of a, b, c and substitute a = b = c = 1, we get that RHS = LHS. So option (a) is correct. Even by looking at the equation directly, we can easily make out that the only condition for the equation to be true would be when a = b = c.

7. In the figure in triangle ACB, let Angle AB = Angle BC = x; then Angle CBD = 2x (exterior angle). Then in triangle BCD angle CBD = angle CDB = 2x. Then Angle BCD = 180 – 4x and Angle DCE = 3x. (Because the three angles at the point C should add up to 180). In triangle CDE then, angle DCE = 3x = angle CED. Then angle CDE = 180 – 6x → Angle FDE = 180 – 4x.

Also, AGF = 180 – 2x (since angle AG = angle FG = x). Then angle FGE = 2x in triangle FGE, Angle FGE = Angle FEG = 2x.

Finally in triangle, DEF, Angle EFD = Angle FDE = 180 – 4x and the third angle of the triangle FED = x. Thus, 180 – 4x + 180 – 4x + x = 180 → 7x = 180 → x = 25° approximately.

8. Let the length of the edge cut at each corner be 'a' m. After cutting away the corners we'll find a regular octagon. Each side of the regular octagon was 2 – 2a.

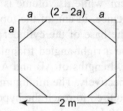

$\therefore \quad \sqrt{a^2 + a^2} = 2 - 2a \Rightarrow a\sqrt{2} = 2 - 2a$

$\Rightarrow \quad a\sqrt{2} \times (1 + \sqrt{2}) = 2 \Rightarrow a = \dfrac{\sqrt{2}}{\sqrt{2}+1}$. Then, side

of the octagon = 2 – 2a = $\dfrac{2}{\sqrt{2}+1}$. Option (b) is correct.

9. Let AB = p, BC = q

Area of $\Delta CEF = \dfrac{1}{2} \times \dfrac{p}{3} \times q = \dfrac{pq}{6}$

Area of ABCD = $pq$

Required ratio = $\dfrac{pq}{6} : pq = \dfrac{1}{6}$

10. $BD = \sqrt{32^2 + 24^2} = 40.$

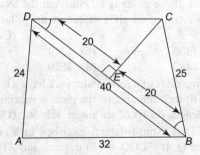

Draw CE ⊥ BD. As ∆BCD is isosceles triangle so DE = BE.

$CE = \sqrt{25^2 - 20^2} = 15$

So area of $\triangle ADB = \dfrac{1}{2} \times 32 \times 24 = 384$ sq.m

Area of $\triangle BCD = 2 \times \dfrac{1}{2} \times 15 \times 20 = 300$ sq.m

Hence, area of ABCD = 384 + 300 = 684 sq.m

11. Let's assume PQ be the longest side of 20 unit and another side AC is 10 unit. Hence RS $\perp$ PQ.

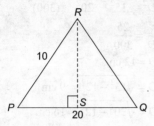

Since area of $\triangle PQR = 80 = \dfrac{1}{2} PQ \times RS$

So $RS = \dfrac{80 \times 2}{20} = 8$. In $\triangle PSR$; $PS = \sqrt{10^2 - 8^2} = 6$

Hence $SQ = 20 - 6 = 14$

So $QR = \sqrt{14^2 + 8^2} = \sqrt{196 + 64} = \sqrt{260}$ unit

12. Let $\angle CAE = \angle CEA = x$, $\angle CBF = \angle CFB = y$

$\angle ACE = 180 - 2x$, $\angle BCF = 180 - 2y$

In $\triangle DEF$: $x + y + 40° = 180°$

So $x + y = 140°$

So $\angle ACB + \angle ACE + \angle BCF = 180°$

$\angle ACB = 180° - \angle ACE - \angle BCF$

$= 180° - (180° - 2x) - (180° - 2y)$

$= 2(x + y) - 180° = 2 \times 140 - 180 = 100°$

13. We can solve this problem just by checking the options.

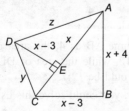

If we put $x = 11$, then in $\triangle ABC$ by applying Pythagoras theorem, we get AC = 17 cm. and CE = $17 - x = 17 - 11 = 6$ cm

$\triangle CED$ is a right angle triangle. For CE = 6 cm and DE = 8 cm, $y = 10$ cm

So for $x = 11$, all the conditions given in the question are satisfied.

14. Let width of the path be x meters.

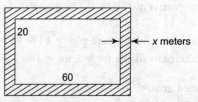

According to the question:
Area of the path = 516 m²
$\Rightarrow$ $(60 + 2x)(20 + 2x) - 60 \times 20 = 516$ m²
$\Rightarrow$ $1200 + 120x + 40x + 4x^2 - 1200 = 516$ m²
$\Rightarrow$ $4x^2 + 160x - 516 = 0 \Rightarrow x^2 + 40x - 129 = 0$
By solving we get x = 3.
Alternately, you could try to put the values of the width of the walkway from the options to check in which case do we get the value of the area of the walkway equaling 516.
For option (b) 3m we get total area = $60 \times 3 \times 2 + 20 \times 3 \times 2 + 3 \times 3 \times 4 = 516$ m².

15.

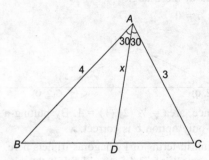

Let AD = x

Then Area of $\triangle ABC$ = Area of $\triangle ABD$ + Area of $\triangle ACD$

$\frac{1}{2} \times 4 \times 3 \times \sin 60 = \frac{1}{2} \times 4 \times x \times \sin 30 + \frac{1}{2} \times 3 \times x \times \sin 30$

$3\sqrt{3} = x + 3x/4$

Solving for x, we get $x = 12\sqrt{3}/7$

Option (b) is the correct answer.

16. Let the length of the chord be 'a' cm.

Area of $\triangle ABC = \dfrac{1}{2}(15 \times 20) = \dfrac{1}{2} \times 25 \times \dfrac{a}{2}$

$\Rightarrow$ $a = 24$ cm

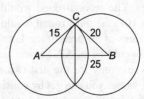

Alternately, you can think of this using Pythagoras theorem, by trying to split the length 25 of AB into two parts, through trial and error, you would arrive at a break up of 9 and 16, that would lead to two right triangles with sides: 15,12 and 9 & 12,16 and 20 respectively. Hence, the length of the chord would be $2 \times 12 = 24$.

17. Total area of the square plot = $14 \times 14 = 196$ m²
Total area available for grazing = $196 - 20 = 176$ m²

Grazed area = $\dfrac{\pi \times r^2}{4} \times 4 = \pi r^2 = 22 \times 7(r = 7) = 154$ m²

Ungrazed area = $176 - 154 = 22$ m²

18. Area of $\triangle ABE = 7$ cm²
Area of ABEF = $2 \times$ Area of $\triangle ABE = 14$ cm²
Area of $\square ABCD = 4 \times$ Area of ABEF $= 4 \times 14 = 56$ cm²

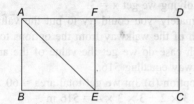

19. Area of the triangle =
Let $a = 0$

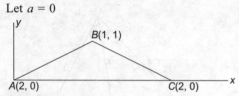

Hence, area = $\frac{1}{2}$ (2) (1) = 1. By putting $a = 0$, we get only option b is correct.

20. Think in terms of Pythagoras triplets here. The Pythagoras triple 3,4,5 would fulfill the given conditions of the problem, since if instead of walking along the adjacent sides (3 + 4), if he walks along the diagonal (5) he saves a distance (7 − 5 = 2) that is equal to half the length of the longer side.

21.

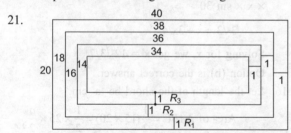

In the first round he would do $20 + 20 + 38 + 38 = 116$ meters. The second round would be $18 + 18 + 36 + 36 = 108$, the third round would be 100. (Note that the values of the area of the lawn mowed in every round would be an AP. So you need to calculate the total value only for the first two rounds and the remaining values you can get by considering the AP). Thus, in the fourth round he would do a total of 92 but to complete half the lawn he would need to do an additional of only 76 ($400 - 116 - 108 - 100$). This can be achieved in approximately 0.8 of the fourth round.

22. Let the middle sized piece = a
Largest piece = 3a
Shortest = 3a − 23,
$3a + a + (3a − 23) = 40$
$a = 9$
The shortest piece = 3a = 3(9) − 23 = 4.

23. $AB = \sqrt{(15)^2 + (20)^2} = 25$

$\dfrac{1}{CD^2} = \dfrac{1}{15^2} + \dfrac{1}{20^2} = \dfrac{625}{(300)^2}$

$\dfrac{1}{CD} = \dfrac{25}{300}$

$CD = 12$ cm.

$AD = \sqrt{15^2 - 12^2} = 9$ cm

$BD = \sqrt{20^2 - 12^2} = 16$ cm

Area of $\triangle ACD = \dfrac{1}{2} \times 12 \times 9 = 54$

$s = \dfrac{1}{2}(15 + 12 + 9) = 18$

$r_1 = \dfrac{\text{Area}}{s} \Rightarrow r_1 = 3$

Area of $\triangle BCD = \dfrac{1}{2} \times 16 \times 12 = 96$

$s = \dfrac{1}{2}(16 + 20 + 12) = 24$

$r_2 = \dfrac{\text{Area}}{s} \Rightarrow r_2 = 4$

In $\triangle PQS$, $PS = r_1 + r_2 = 7$ cm
$QS = r_2 - r_1 = 1$ cm
Hence, $PQ = \sqrt{50}$ cm

24. If $\tan \theta = \dfrac{FI}{IG} = \dfrac{\dfrac{AB}{2}}{\dfrac{AB}{4}} = 2$

Option (d) is correct.

25. If you assume AB as 4, the area of the trapezium ABCD = 12, while the area of DEFG = 7. Hence, the ratio would be 12:7.

Alternately, you could solve this using the formulae as follows:

Area of quadrilateral ABCD

$= \dfrac{1}{2} \times \dfrac{AB}{2} \times AB + \dfrac{AB}{2} \times AB = \dfrac{3AB^2}{4}$

Area of quadrilateral DEFG

$= \dfrac{1}{2} \times \dfrac{AB}{2} \times \dfrac{AB}{2} + \dfrac{AB}{2} \times \dfrac{AB}{2} + \dfrac{1}{2} \times \dfrac{AB}{4} \times \dfrac{AB}{2}$

$= \dfrac{7AB^2}{16}$

Hence, the required ratio $= \dfrac{3AB^2}{4}:\dfrac{7AB^2}{16} = 12:7$.

26. a, b and c are the perimeters of $\Delta A_1 A_2 A_3$, $\Delta B_1 B_2 B_3$ and $\Delta C_1 C_2 C_3$ respectively.

$A_1 A_2 = r + r = 2r$ or $a = 2r + 2r + 2r = 6r$.

$\angle A_1 B_1 B_2 = \angle A_2 B_2 B_1 = 30°$

$B_1 B_2 = A_1 A_2 + A_1 B_1 \cos 30° + A_2 B_2 \cos 30°$

$= 2r + r \cdot \sqrt{3}/2 + r \cdot \sqrt{3}/2 = 2r + r\sqrt{3}$

$b = (2r + r\sqrt{3}) \times 3$

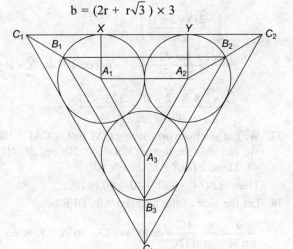

$\angle A_1 C_1 X = \angle A_2 C_2 Y = 30°$

$C_1 X = C_2 Y = A_1 X \cot 30° = r\sqrt{3}$

$C_1 C_2 = 2r + r\sqrt{3} + r\sqrt{3} = 2r + 2r\sqrt{3}$

$c = ((\sqrt{3}) + 1) \times 6r$

Hence, $b - a = c - b = 3 \times \sqrt{3} \times r$

Option (a) is correct.

27. Total time taken by A $= 2 \times \left(\left(\dfrac{1}{20}\right) + \left(\dfrac{1}{30}\right) + \left(\dfrac{1}{15}\right)\right) \times 10 = 3$

Distance travelled by B in first three hours $= 3 \times (10\sqrt{3} + 20)$. This is equal to the perimeter of $\Delta B_1 B_2 B_3$. So B will reach at $B_1$.

Time taken by C to be cover $C_1 C_2 = 1.5$ h

Time Taken by C to cover $C_2 C_3 = 1.5$ h

Hence C travels $2C/3$ in time t. So, B reaches $B_1$ and C reaches $C_3$ (Option c).

28. As per the question,

$$u = \dfrac{a}{2 \times \sqrt{3}}, v = \dfrac{b}{2 \times \sqrt{3}}, w = \dfrac{c}{2 \times \sqrt{3}}$$

Now, time taken by B $= \dfrac{4}{\sqrt{3}}$. So, Distance traveled by A $= 2 \times \dfrac{a}{3}$ and, Distance traveled by C $= 2 \times \dfrac{c}{3}$. Hence, they reach $A_3$, $C_3$ respectively.

Option (b) is correct.

29. The whole height of the cylinder is divided into 'n' equal parts.

So the vertical spacing between two consecutive turns $= \dfrac{h}{n}$.

30. If we unfold the lateral surfaces of the cube. It becomes a rectangle of sides 4n & n, and the string becomes the diagonal. Hence the required length $= \sqrt{(4n)^2 + n^2} = n\sqrt{17}$ cm.

31. If we unfold the lateral surfaces of the cylinder, it becomes a rectangle of sides – $2\pi r$ & h; and the length of the string equals to the diagonal. Diagonal $= 16(n)^2 + h^2 = 17(n^2)$ or $h = n$

32. In $\Delta BAC$, $AC \parallel PQ$

$\therefore \quad \dfrac{CQ}{QB} = \dfrac{AP}{PB} = \dfrac{4}{3}$

In $\Delta BPC$, $PC \parallel DQ$

$\therefore \quad \dfrac{PD}{DB} = \dfrac{CQ}{QB} = \dfrac{4}{3}$

If $\quad \dfrac{PD}{DB} = \dfrac{4}{3}$

$\therefore \quad PD = \dfrac{4}{7} PB$

$\dfrac{AP}{PD} = \dfrac{AP}{\dfrac{4}{7}PB} = \dfrac{7}{4} \times \dfrac{AP}{PB} = \dfrac{7}{4} \times \dfrac{4}{3} = 7/3$.

Option (c) is correct.

33. Let AB = H

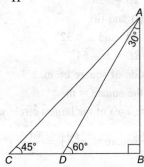

$\therefore \quad \tan 45° = \dfrac{AB}{BC} \rightarrow AB = BC$

$\therefore \quad \tan 60° = \dfrac{AB}{BD} \therefore \sqrt{3} = \dfrac{AB}{BD}, BD = \dfrac{AB}{\sqrt{3}}$

$\therefore \quad CD = BC - BD$

$= AB - \dfrac{AB}{\sqrt{3}}$

As time for traveling CD, i.e. $AB - \dfrac{AB}{\sqrt{3}}$ is 10 min.

$\therefore$ Time required for traveling $BD = \dfrac{\dfrac{AB}{\sqrt{3}}}{AB - \dfrac{AB}{\sqrt{3}}} \times 10$

$= \dfrac{1}{\sqrt{3}-1} \times 10$

$= \dfrac{10}{\sqrt{3}-1}$

$= \left(\dfrac{10}{\sqrt{3}-1} \times \dfrac{\sqrt{3}+1}{\sqrt{3}+1}\right)$

$= \dfrac{10(\sqrt{3}+1)}{2}$

$= 5(\sqrt{3}+1)$ minutes

34. $\angle ECB$ is exterior angle of $\triangle ACB$

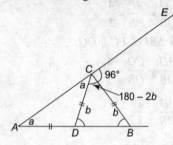

$\angle A + \angle B = \angle ECB = 96°$ (Sum of interior opposite angles).

i.e. $\quad a + b = 96°$ $\qquad\qquad$ (i)

Also $a + (180 - 2b) + 96° = 180°$

$\therefore \quad a - 2b + 96° = 0$

$\therefore \quad a - 2b = -96°$ $\qquad\qquad$ (ii)

Solving (i) and (ii)

$\quad b = 64°$ and $a = 32°$

$\therefore \quad \angle DBC = b = 64°$

35. Let the side of square be m.

Area of the square $= m^2$

Therefore, area of the largest circle which can be cut

from the square $= \pi\left(\dfrac{a}{2}\right)^2 = \dfrac{\pi a^2}{4}$

Area scrapped $= a^2 - \dfrac{\pi}{4}a^2 = a^2\left(1 - \dfrac{\pi}{4}\right)$

$\therefore \quad \dfrac{\text{Area scrapped}}{\text{Area of square}} = \dfrac{a^2\left(1-\dfrac{\pi}{4}\right)}{a^2} = 1 - \dfrac{\pi}{4}$

As this ratio does not depend on the value of the side of the square. Therefore, whether we cut a circle from smaller square or larger square, scrapped area will be a fixed percentage of square. Therefore, the required ratio will be 1:1.

36. Let $P_1 = P$ and $A_1 = A$. Then according to the question:

$\dfrac{P_1 + P_2 + P_3 + \cdots}{A_1 + A_2 + A_3 + \cdots} = \dfrac{P + \dfrac{P}{\sqrt{2}} + \cdots \infty}{A + \dfrac{A}{2} + \cdots \infty} = \dfrac{\dfrac{P}{1 - \dfrac{1}{\sqrt{2}}}}{2A}$

$= \dfrac{P\sqrt{2}}{\sqrt{2}-1} \times \dfrac{1}{2A}$

$= \left(\dfrac{\sqrt{2}P(\sqrt{2}+1)}{2A}\right)$

$= \dfrac{\sqrt{2} \times 4a(\sqrt{2}+1)}{2 \times a^2}$ $\quad$ (since, P = 4a, A = a$^2$)

$= \dfrac{\sqrt{2} \times 2(\sqrt{2}+1)}{a} = \dfrac{2(2+\sqrt{2})}{a}$

37. We can see from the triangle CAT that, $\angle CAT = 100$. We can also see that $\angle OCA = 40$. Hence, $\angle OAC = 40$. Thus, $\angle OAB = \angle OBA = 40°$.

Thus, $\angle BOA = 180 - 40 - 40 = 100$.

38. Let the side of the hexagon ABCDEF be 'a'

$\dfrac{a}{\sin 30°} = \dfrac{AC}{\sin 120°}$ or $AC = a\sqrt{3}$. So $\triangle ACE$ is equi-

lateral triangle with side $\sqrt{3}a$.

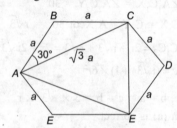

Area of hexagon $= \dfrac{\sqrt{3}}{4}a^2 \times 6$

Area as $\triangle ACE = \dfrac{\sqrt{3}}{4}(\sqrt{3}a)^2$

Therefore, the required ratio

$= \dfrac{\sqrt{3}}{4}(\sqrt{3}a)^2 : \dfrac{\sqrt{3}}{4}a^2 \times 6 = 1:2$

39.

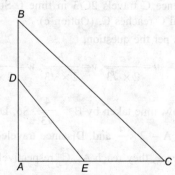

$\Delta DAE$ & $\Delta BAC$ are similar triangles and the ratio of the area of the similar triangles is the ratio of the square of the corresponding sides of the triangle.

Hence, the area of the smaller triangle = $34 \times 0.65 \times 0.65 = 14.365$

40. The length and breadth of the base would be $(12 - 2x)$ and $(12 - 2x)$ respectively. The height of the box would be 'x'. Thus, the total volume would be $(12 - 2x)(12 - 2x)x$. Checking the options, it can be seen that the volume is maximized for x = 2.

41. Let the length of the longer side be 'l' then according to the question:

$$\frac{l}{2} = \frac{2}{\frac{l}{2}} \Rightarrow \frac{l}{2} = \frac{4}{l} \text{ or } l = 2\sqrt{2}$$

Area of smaller rectangle = $\frac{l}{2} \times 2 = l = 2\sqrt{2}$ sq. units

42. In $\Delta PRO$, PR ∥ QS. Then,

$$\frac{OP}{OQ} = \frac{PR}{QS} = \frac{4}{3}$$

$$\frac{28}{OQ} = \frac{4}{3}$$

OQ = 21cm

PQ = OP − OQ = 28 − 21 = 7 cm

$$\frac{PQ}{OQ} = \frac{7}{21} = \frac{1}{3}$$

43. PQ = 7 = PR + QS

$$\frac{PR}{QS} = \frac{4}{3}$$

$\Rightarrow$  QS = 3 cm

44. $\Delta OSQ$ is a right angle triangle.

$$SO = \sqrt{OQ^2 - QS^2}$$
$$= \sqrt{21^2 - 3^2} = 12\sqrt{3} \text{ cm}$$

45. Let the length of the cube is 'a'.

Length of side of triangle = $a\sqrt{3}$

Radius of circumcircle of the triangle = $\frac{\text{side}}{\sqrt{3}} = a\sqrt{3}/\sqrt{3} = a$. Hence, option (a) is correct.

46.

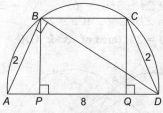

$$\frac{1}{2} \times AB \times BD = \frac{1}{2} \times AD \times BP$$

$$2\sqrt{8^2 - 2^2} = 8 \times BP$$

$$BP = \frac{\sqrt{15}}{2}$$

$$AP = DQ = \sqrt{2^2 - \left(\frac{\sqrt{15}}{2}\right)^2} = \sqrt{4 - \frac{15}{4}} = \frac{1}{2}$$

$$BC = PQ = 8 - \left(\frac{1}{2} + \frac{1}{2}\right) = 7$$

47. Let the radius of smaller circle ED = a. Let E be the center of the smaller circle.

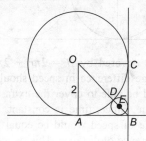

$\therefore$   EB = $a\sqrt{2}$

$\therefore$   OB = EB + ED + OD

$= a\sqrt{2} + a + 2$

Also OB = $2\sqrt{2}$

$\Rightarrow$   $a\sqrt{2} + a + 2 = 2\sqrt{2}$

$\Rightarrow$   $a = 6 - 4\sqrt{2}$

48.

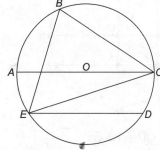

$\angle EAC = \angle CBE$ are the same (as they are in the same arc).

$\angle CEA = 90°$, (it is the angle subtended by the semicircle)

In $\triangle AEC$, $\angle ECA = 180° - 65° - 90° = 25°$. As $AC \parallel ED$ then $\angle DEC = \angle ACE = 25°$.

49. Common area = 2 × (area of sector ADC – area of $\triangle ADC$)

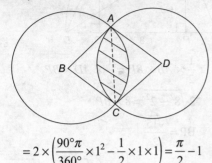

$$= 2 \times \left(\frac{90°\pi}{360°} \times 1^2 - \frac{1}{2} \times 1 \times 1\right) = \frac{\pi}{2} - 1$$

50. Distance covered by A = 2r + 2r + 4r + 4r = 12r

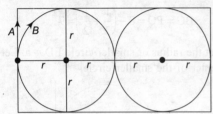

Distance covered by $B = 2\pi r + 2\pi r = 4\pi r$. The percentage difference in speed should be such that B should be able to cover the extra distance in the same time. Since, time is constant, the percentage difference of speed would be equal to the percentage difference of distance. This, would be given by:

$$\frac{4\pi r - 12r}{12r} \times 100 = 4.72\% \text{ approximately.}$$

51. In order to find DH, we can think of finding DL and subtracting HL from it.

As NL:LM = 1:2, NL = 1 cm, ML = 2 cm. Similarly AE = 1 cm, BE = 2 cm

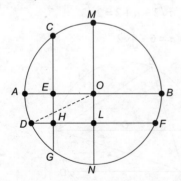

Construct OD, OD = 1.5 cm

OL = ON – LN = 1.5 – 1 = 0.5 cm

In $\triangle ODL$: DL = $\sqrt{OD^2 - OL^2} = \sqrt{1.5^2 - 0.5^2} = \sqrt{2}$ cm

$\Rightarrow DH = DL - HL = \sqrt{2} - \frac{1}{2} = \frac{2\sqrt{2}-1}{2}$. Option (b).

52. Ratio of perimeters of two similar triangles is the ratio of corresponding sides of the triangles.

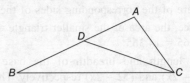

In $\triangle BDC$ and $\triangle BCA$, $\angle B$ is common and $\angle BCD = \angle BAC$. Therefore, $\triangle BDC \sim \triangle BCA$.

$$\frac{BD}{BC} = \frac{DC}{AC} = \frac{BC}{AB} \Rightarrow \frac{9}{12} = \frac{6}{AC} = \frac{12}{AB}$$

AC = 8 cm, AB = 16 cm.

DA = 16 – 9 = 7 cm

Perimeter of $\triangle DAC$: Perimeter of $\triangle BDC$ = (6 + 7 + 8): (9 + 6 + 12) = 21: 27 = 7: 9.

53.

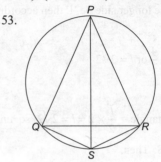

From the figure, it is clear that the triangle PRS is a 30-60-90 triangle with $\angle RPS$ as 30 and $\angle RSP$ as 60. Since PS = 2r, thus, SR = SQ = r and PR = PQ = r√3. Now apply Pythagoras to calculate all sides. Hence, correct option is option (a).

54. You would need to solve this using options. Suppose, there are 10 tiles along an edge of the rectangle – then all these edge tiles would be white. So, the number of white tiles would be 10 + 10 + x + x (where x is the number of unique tiles on the other edge of the rectangle).

With x = 1, the number of white tiles = 22, and the number of total tiles = 10 × 3 = 30. This cannot be the answer, as the number of red tiles would only be 8, which is less than required.

Next, take x as 2. In this case, White tiles = 24 and total tiles = 10 × 4 = 40. This cannot be the answer, as the number of red tiles would only be 16, which is less than required.

Next, take x as 3. In this case, White tiles = 26 and total tiles = 10 × 5 = 50. This cannot be the answer as the number of red tiles would only be 24, which is less than required.

Next, take x as 4. In this case, White tiles = 28 and total tiles = 10 × 6 = 60. This cannot be the answer, as the number of red tiles would be 32 which is more than required. Thus, we can reject 10 as the answer, as increasing x would only increase the number of red tiles further.

We, then check for option (b), whereby there could be 12 tiles on an edge of the rectangle.

Again, the number of white tiles would be 12 + 12 + x + x.

For x = 1, white tiles = 26 and total tiles = 12 × 3 = 36 tiles. This cannot be the answer, as the number of red tiles would be 10 only, which is less than required.

For x = 2, white tiles = 28 and total tiles 12 × 4 = 48 tiles. This cannot be the answer as the number of red tiles would be 20 only, which is less than required.

For x = 3, white tiles = 30 and total tiles 12 × 5 = 60 tiles. In this case, we see that the number of red tiles would also be equal to 30. Thus, 12 tiles along an edge is possible as an answer. Thus, the (b) option is correct.

55.

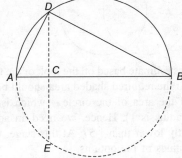

In the figure, we can see that the triangles ACD and ADB are similar to each other. Thus, the ratio of the legs of ADB would be 1:3 (since that is the ratio of the legs of ACD given to us). Also, using Pythagoras theorem, AD = $\sqrt{40}$, then AB = $3\sqrt{40}$. Again using the Pythagoras theorem of triangle ABD, we get that AB = 20 = diameter of the semi-circle. Hence, the area of the semi-circle = $\frac{1}{2} \times \pi \times r^2 = 50\pi$.

56.

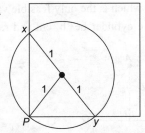

The sheet area that remains after punching is = 4 − (Area of semicircle + Area of ΔPXY) = $\left(4 - \left(\frac{\pi}{2} + \frac{1}{2} \times 1 \times 2\right)\right) = \frac{6 - \pi}{2}$

Required proportion = $\frac{6 - \pi}{2} : 4 = \frac{6 - \pi}{8}$

57. Area of the part of the circle (round punch) falling outside the square sheet = Area of the circle − (Area of semicircle + Area of ΔPXY) = $\pi(1)^2 - \left(\frac{\pi}{2} + 1\right)$

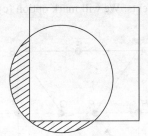

$= \pi - \frac{\pi}{2} - 1 = \frac{\pi - 2}{2}$

58.

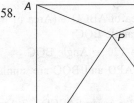

In the figure, ∠BPC = 60 (given) and also, BP = AB. Hence, if you were to look at the triangle ABP, it is isosceles. Also, Angle ABP = 30 and the angles APB and PAB are equal (as they are opposite equal sides of the isosceles triangle). This means, that in the central angle P, BPC = 60 and APB = 75 = CPD. Hence, the required angle APD = 360 − 60 − 75 − 75 = 150 (option e).

59. Radius of a circle circumscribing a triangle = circum radius of the triangle = $\frac{abc}{4 \times (\text{Area of the triangle})}$

$= \frac{a \times b \times c}{4 \times \left(\frac{1}{2} \times b \times AD\right)} = \frac{a \times c}{2 \times AD} = \frac{17.5 \times 9}{2 \times 3} = 26.25 \text{ cm}^2$

60. The set of all possible triangles is given by the set −{8, 15 −8, 9, 10, 11, 12, 13, 14, 15, 16, 17, 18, 19, 20, 21, 22}. But, we have to look for obtuse angled triangles only. In this context we could go through two alternate possibilities: If 15 is the largest side −in such a case, the third side should be √161 for a right angled triangle. In case, the side is greater than this value, then we will get an acute angled triangle.

Hence, for this case we will get the possible values as 8, 15, 8 to 8,15,12. After this value uptil 8,15,16, we will again get an acute angled triangle (8, 15, 17 being a Pythagoras triplet, the triangle with those dimensions would be right angled). After that, 8,15,18 to 8,15,22 would all be obtuse angled triangle. Thus, there would be 10 triangles which satisfy the given requirements. We will mark option (c) as the correct answer.

61.

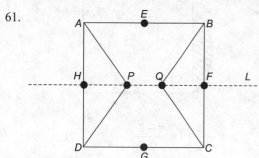

Area of ABQCDP = Area of ABCD – (Area of triangle APD + Area of triangle BQC)

Given that Angle APD = 120° = Angle BQC.

By symmetry triangles, APD and BQC are similar and have equal area.

Hence, Area of ABQCDP = Area of ABCD – 2(Area of triangle APD)

Now, area of triangle APD can be given as:

Let DH be 'x',

$\Rightarrow$  DH/HP = tan 60 = $\sqrt{3}$

$\Rightarrow$  HP = x/$\sqrt{3}$ cm

$\Rightarrow$  Area of triangle APD = $2 \times \frac{1}{2} \times \frac{x}{\sqrt{3}} = \frac{x^2}{\sqrt{3}}$ cm

$\Rightarrow$  Area of ABQCDP = Area of ABCD – 2(Area of triangle APD)

$\Rightarrow$  Area of ABQCDP

$= x^2 - \frac{x^2}{4\sqrt{3}} - \frac{x^2}{4\sqrt{3}} = x^2 \left(1 - \frac{1}{2\sqrt{3}}\right)$

Hence, required ratio can be given as =
Area of ABQCDP /(2(Area of triangle APD))

Required ratio = $x^2 \left(1 - \frac{1}{2\sqrt{3}}\right) : \frac{x^2}{2\sqrt{3}} = 2\sqrt{3} - 1$

Hence, option (e) is the correct option.

62. Both the circle have radii 1 cm then = AB = BC = CD = AC = 1 cm.

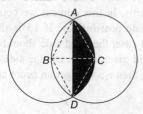

Therefore, $\Delta$ABC and $\Delta$DBC are equilateral triangle.
Hence, $\angle$ABD = $\angle$ABC + $\angle$DBC = 60° + 60° = 120°

Area of the shaded portion = Area of sector ACD –

Area of $\Delta$ABD = $\frac{120}{360} \times \pi 1^2 - \frac{1}{2} \cdot 1 \cdot 1 \cdot \sin 120°$ = $\frac{\pi}{3} - \frac{\sqrt{3}}{4}$

Required area = 2 · Area of the shaded portion =

$\left(\frac{\pi}{3} - \frac{\sqrt{3}}{4}\right)2 = \frac{2\pi}{3} - \frac{\sqrt{3}}{2}$ sq.cm

**Alternate Solution:**

Before thinking about this problem through mensuration based processes, try thinking of it this way:

Draw a rough sketch of this situation by drawing two intersecting circles as described (both with radii 1).

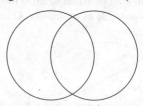

A close guess estimate based on the look of the figure tells you that the required shaded area should be less than half of the area of the circle – which is 3.14 (since the radius is 1). Hence, we need an answer that is slightly lower than 1.57. At this stage, try to check the values of the options.

See what happens when you do this,

Option (a) gives a value of 0.69 (approx) which is too small.

Option (b) gives a value of 2.95 (approx) which is too large.

Option (c) gives a value of 3.33 (approx) which is too large.

Option (d) gives a value of 5.05 (approx) which is too large again. This leaves us with only option (e), whose value is 1.24 which is the only feasible value.

63. Let the height of the cylinder be 'h' cm and radius be 'r' cm.

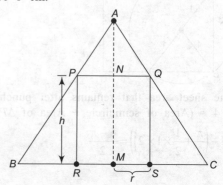

ΔANQ is similar to ΔQSC

$$\Rightarrow \quad \frac{AN}{NQ} = \frac{QS}{SC} \Rightarrow \frac{10-h}{r} = \frac{h}{4-r}$$

$$\Rightarrow \quad \frac{10}{h} - 1 = \frac{r}{4-r} \Rightarrow \frac{10}{h} = \frac{4}{4-r}$$

$$\therefore \quad h = \frac{5}{2}(4-r)$$

Surface area of the cylinder PQRS

$$= 2\pi[r^2 + hr] = 2\pi\left[r^2 + \frac{5r}{2}(4-r)\right]$$

$$= 2\pi\left[r^2 - \frac{5}{2}r^2 + 10r\right] = 2\pi\left[10r - \frac{3}{2}r^2\right]$$

$$= 2\pi\left[-\frac{3}{2}\left(r - \frac{10}{3}\right)^2 + \frac{50}{3}\right]$$

(Note: This is a key step in this problem to realize that

the expression $\left[10r - \frac{3}{2}r^2\right]$ can be written as a per-

fect square plus a constant as: $\left[-\frac{3}{2}\left(r - \frac{10}{3}\right)^2 + \frac{50}{3}\right]$.

Surface area will be maximum when $r - 10/3 = 0$
or $r = 10/3$. In this case, $h = 5/3$

So largest surface area

$$= 2\pi[r^2 + hr] = 2\pi\left[\frac{100}{9} + \frac{50}{9}\right] = 2\pi\left[\frac{50}{3}\right] = \frac{100\pi}{3}$$

64. Area of triangle ABC $= \sqrt{S(S-a)(S-b)(S-c)}$

where $S = \dfrac{40 + 25 + 35}{2} = 50$

$$= \sqrt{50(50-40)(50-35)(50-25)}$$

$$= \sqrt{50.10.15.25} = 250\sqrt{3}$$

Let E is the mid-point of BC.

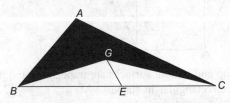

Area of ΔBGE = Area of ΔCGE = $\dfrac{1}{6}$ Area of ΔABC
Area of the remaining portion (after cutoff of triangle BGC)

$$= \frac{4}{6}(\text{Area of }\Delta ABC) = \frac{4}{6} \times 250\sqrt{3} = \frac{500}{\sqrt{3}} \text{ sq ft}$$

65.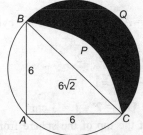

Area of arc BPC = Area of circular segment ABPC – Area of ΔABC

$$= \frac{1}{4}\pi(6)^2 - \frac{1}{2} \times 6 \times 6$$

$$= 9\pi - 18$$

Area of semicircle BQC $= \dfrac{\pi}{2} \times r^2 = \dfrac{\pi \times \overline{3\sqrt{2}}^2}{2} = 9\pi$

Area of shaded portion = Area of semi circle BQC – Area of arc BPC $= 9\pi - (9\pi - 18) = 18$ sq. cm

66. Let the side of five cubes are 1 cm, 1 cm, 2 cm, 3 cm, 3 cm respectively.

Sum of surface areas of the cubes $= 6[1^2 + 1^2 + 2^2 + 3^2 + 3^2] = 144$ sq. cm.

Volume of the five cubes $= 1^3 + 1^3 + 2^3 + 3^3 + 3^3 = 64$ cm³

Side length of the original cube $= (64)^{1/3} = 4$ cm.

Surface area of the original cube $= 6(4)^2 = 96$ sq. cm.

Required percentage increase from 96 to 144 sq. cm is 50%.

67. Let the radius of the cylinder is '$r$' cm

$\pi r^2 h = V = 9\pi$ (given). Since, $h = 3$ cm (given), $r = \sqrt{3}$.

As the radius of the cylinder is not equal to the radius of the sphere so the sphere would be at the top of the cylinder as shown in the following diagram.

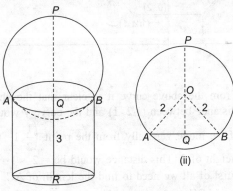

(ii)

Distance of the top of the sphere from bottom of the cylinder = PQ + QR = PQ + 3

In diagram II:

In $\Delta$ AOQ $\rightarrow$ AQ = AB/2 = Radius of the cylinder
= $\sqrt{3}$.

AO = Radius of the sphere = 2

$$OQ = \sqrt{AO^2 - OQ^2} = 1$$

Hence, PQ = PO + OQ = 2 + 1 = 3 cm

Thus, the height of the top of the sphere from the base of the cylinder = PQ + QR = 3 + 3 = 6 cm.

68.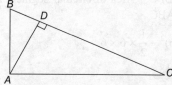

To reach at the hypotenuse BC in minimum time we have to follow the shortest possible path which is AD, where AD $\perp$ BC.

As we know that, $\dfrac{1}{AD^2} = \dfrac{1}{AB^2} + \dfrac{1}{AC^2} = \dfrac{1}{15^2} + \dfrac{1}{20^2}$

By solving the above equation we get, AD = 12 m.

Required time to reach at BC = $\dfrac{12}{30}$ h or $\dfrac{12}{30} \times 60$
= 24 min

69. y = |x − 1| + |x + 1|

For x < −1

    y = −(x − 1) − (x + 1) = −2x

for −1 < x < 1

    y = −x + 1 + x + 1 = 2

for x > 1

    y = x − 1 + x + 1 = 2x.

Thus, the graph of the function, y = |x − 1| + |x + 1| can be drawn as follows:

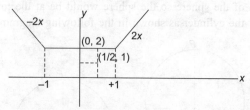

From the above curve it is clear that the shortest distance between (1/2, 1) and the curve y would be if we move vertically from the point $\left(\dfrac{1}{2}, 1\right)$ to the height of 2. This distance would be = 2 − 1 = 1.

70. First of all we need to find the length of AC.
In $\Delta$ABC:

$\angle BCA = \angle BAC = 120° − \angle CAF = 120° − 90°$
= 30°

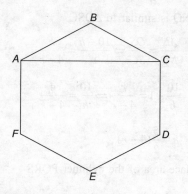

Apply sine rule in triangle ABC:

$$\frac{AB}{\sin 30°} = \frac{AC}{\sin 120°}$$

$$\frac{1}{\sin 30°} = \frac{AC}{\sin 120°}$$

$$AC = \frac{1}{\sin 30°} \cdot \sin 120° = \sqrt{3} \text{ cm}$$

$\left(\text{Using } \sin 30 = \dfrac{1}{2} \text{ and } \sin 120 = \dfrac{\sqrt{3}}{2}\right)$.

Area of the square with side AC = $\sqrt{3}^2$ = 3 sq. cm

71.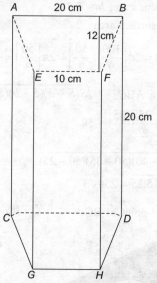

Top and bottom surfaces are trapeziums and the rest are rectangular in shape.

Sum of areas of top and the bottom surfaces = 2(Area of ABFE) = $2\left[\dfrac{10 + 20}{2} \cdot 12\right]$ = 360 square cm.

Note: Here we have used the formula for the area of a trapezium = $\dfrac{\text{Sum of parallel Sides}}{2} \times$ distance between the parallel sides.

The areas of the lateral sides of the pillar would be equal and both would be rectangles. To find the area of AEGC, we need the length of AE.

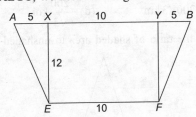

$$AE = \sqrt{12^2 + 5^2} = \sqrt{169} = 13 \text{ cm}$$

Sum of areas of AEGC and BFHD = 2(Area of AEGC) = 2(13 × 20) = 520 sq. cm.

Area of ABCD = 20 × 20 = 400 sq. cm.

Area of EFHG = 10 × 20 = 200 sq. cm.

Sum of all the six surfaces of the pillar = 360 + 520 + 400 + 200 = 1480 sq. cm.

72. Let the length and breadth of the rectangular park are L and B respectively.

Case I: If we are given the sum of the two lengths and one breadth of the rectangle: as 400:

We have: 2L + B = 400

B = 400 − 2L

Area = L × B = L × (400 − 2L) = 400L − 2L²

The area is maximum when the differentiation of this expression is 0:

Thus: d(area)/dL = 400 − 4L = 0

L = 100m → B = 200 m.

Case II: If we are given the sum of the two shorter sides and one longer side as 400:

We have: 2B + L = 400

L = 400 − 2B

Area = L × B = B × (400 − 2B) = 400B − 2B²

Differentiating, the area is maximum when: 400 − 4B = 0 → B = 100, which means that L = 200. (Since L + 2B = 400).

Hence longer side must be 200 m (in both the cases).

73.

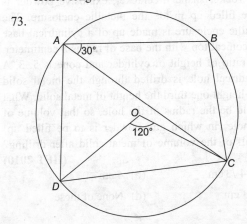

$$\angle CAD = \frac{\angle COD}{2} = \frac{120°}{2} = 60°$$

$$\angle BAD = \angle CAD + \angle BAC = 60° + 30° = 90°$$

Since, the Quadrilateral is a cyclic quadrilateral, the sum of the opposite angles would be 180. Hence, $\angle BCD = 90°$

74. As the distance of P from all the three sides AB, BC and CA are equal so it means 'P' is the in-centre of the triangle ABC.

Let AC = BC = a

$$\therefore \quad r = \frac{\Delta}{s} = \left( \frac{\dfrac{1}{2} \times a \times a}{\dfrac{a + a + a\sqrt{2}}{2}} \right)$$

$$= \frac{a}{\sqrt{2}}(\sqrt{2} - 1) = 4(\sqrt{2} - 1)$$

$$a = 4\sqrt{2} \text{ cm.}$$

Area of the triangle $= \dfrac{1}{2} \times 4\sqrt{2} \times 4\sqrt{2} = 16$ sq cm.

75. Diagonals of the rectangle bisects each other it means point $\left( \dfrac{2 + 6}{2}, \dfrac{3 + 5}{2} \right) = (4, 4)$ lies on the other diagonal y = 3x + c.

Therefore, 4 = 3.4 + c or c = 4 − 12 = −8.

## IIFT (2008-2017)

1. A spiral is made up of 13 successive semicircles, with center alternately at A and B, starting with center at A. The radii of semicircles, thus developed, are 0.5 cm, 1.0 cm, 1.5 cm, and 2.0 cm and so on. The total length of the spiral is:  **(IIFT 2008)**
   (a) 144 cm          (b) 143 cm
   (c) 147 cm          (d) None of these

2. The interior angles of a polygon are in Arithmetic Progression. If the smallest angle is 120° and common difference is 5°, then number of sides in the polygon is:  **(IIFT 2008)**
   (a) 7          (b) 8
   (c) 9          (d) None of these

3. A ladder 25 meters long is placed against a wall with its foot 7 meters away from the foot of the wall. How far should the foot be drawn out so that the top of the ladder may come down by half the distance by which the foot of the ladder is drawn out?  **(IIFT 2008)**
   (a) 6 meters          (b) 8 meters
   (c) 8.75 meters       (d) None of these

4. If D is the midpoint of side BC of a ∆ABC and AD is the perpendicular to AC then:  **(IIFT 2008)**

(a) $3AC^2 = BC^2 - AB^2$   (b) $3BC^2 = AC^2 - 3AB^2$
(c) $5AB^2 = BC^2 + AC^2$   (d) None of these

5. A cylinder, a hemisphere and a cone stand on the same base and have the same heights. The ratio of the areas of their curved surface is:   **(IIFT 2008)**

(a) 2: 2: 1                    (b) 2: $\sqrt{2}$ : 1

(c) $\sqrt{2}:\sqrt{2}:1$      (d) None of these

6. Radius of a spherical balloon, of radii 30 cm, increases at the rate of 2 cm per second. Then its curved surface area increases by:   **(IIFT 2009)**

(a) $120\pi$                   (b) $480\pi$
(c) $600\pi$                   (d) None of these

7. Mohan was playing with a square cardboard of side 2 metres. While playing, he sliced off the corners of the cardboard in such a manner that a figure having all its sides equal was generated. The area of this eight sided figure is:   **(IIFT 2009)**

(a) $\dfrac{4\sqrt{2}}{\sqrt{2}+1}$        (b) $\dfrac{4}{\sqrt{2}+1}$

(c) $\dfrac{2\sqrt{2}}{\sqrt{2}+1}$        (d) $\dfrac{8}{\sqrt{2}+1}$

8. Let $A_1$ be a square whose side is 'a' metres. Circle $C_1$ circumscribes the square $A_1$ such that all its vertices are on $C_1$. Another square $A_2$ circumscribes $C_1$. Circle $C_2$ circumscribes $A_2$ and $A_3$ circumscribes $C_2$, and so on. If $D_N$ is the area between the square $A_N$ and the circle $C_N$, where N is a natural number, then the ratio of the sum of all $D_N$ to $D_1$ is:   **(IIFT 2009)**

(a) 1                          (b) $\dfrac{\pi}{2} - 1$

(c) Infinity                   (d) None of these

**Directions for Questions 9 – 10:** Read the following information carefully and answer the questions:
A warship and a submarine (completely submerged in water) are moving horizontally in a straight line. The Captain of the warship observes that the submarine makes an angle of depression of 30°, and the distance between them from the point of observation is 50 km. After 30 minutes, the angle of depression becomes 60°.   **(IIFT 2009)**

9. Find the distance between them after 30 min from the initial point of reference.

(a) $\dfrac{50}{\sqrt{3}}$ km   (b) 25 km

(c) $\dfrac{25}{\sqrt{3}}$ km   (d) $25\sqrt{3}$ km

10. If both are moving in the same direction and the submarine is ahead of the warship in both the situations, then the speed of the warship, if the ratio of the speed of warship to that of the submarine is 2:1, is:

(a) $\dfrac{100}{\sqrt{3}}$ km   (b) $100\sqrt{3}$ km

(c) $200\sqrt{3}$ km            (d) $\dfrac{200}{\sqrt{3}}$ km

11. Find the ratio of shaded area to unshaded area.

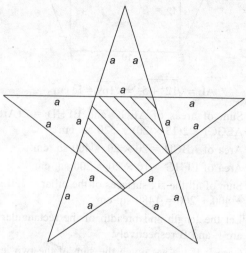

(a) $\dfrac{1}{5}(\sqrt{21} - 2)$        (b) $\dfrac{1}{5}(3\sqrt{7} - 2)$

(c) $\dfrac{1}{5}(3\sqrt{7} - 2\sqrt{3})$   (d) None of these

12. An arc AB of a circle subtends an angle 'x' radian at the center O of the circle. If the area of the sector AOB is equal to the square of the length of the arc AB, then x is:   **(IIFT 2009)**

(a) 0.5                         (b) 1.0
(c) 0.75                        (d) None of these

13. In a triangle ABC the length of side BC is 295. If the length of side AB is a perfect square, then the length of side AC is a power of 2, and the length of side AC is twice the length of side AB. Determine the perimeter of the triangle.   **(IIFT 2010)**

(a) 343                         (b) 487
(c) 1063                        (d) None of these

14. In a rocket shape firecracker, explosive powder is to be filled up inside the metallic enclosure. The metallic enclosure is made up of a cylindrical base and conical top with the base of radius 8 centimeter. The ratio of height of cylinder and cone is 5: 3. A cylindrical hole is drilled through the metal solid with height one third the height of metal solid. What should be the radius of the hole, so that volume of the hole (in which gun powder is to be filled up) is half of the volume of metal solid after drilling?   **(IIFT 2010)**

(a) $4\sqrt{3}$ cm             (b) 4 cm
(c) 3 cm                       (d) None of these

15. In a square of side 2 meters, isosceles triangles of equal area are cut from the corners to form a regular octagon. Find the perimeter and area of the regular octagon.

(a) $\dfrac{16}{2+\sqrt{2}}; \dfrac{4(1+\sqrt{2})}{3+2\sqrt{2}}$    (b) $\dfrac{8}{2+\sqrt{2}}; \dfrac{2(1+\sqrt{2})}{3+2\sqrt{2}}$

(c) $\dfrac{16}{1+\sqrt{2}}; \dfrac{3(1+\sqrt{2})}{3+2\sqrt{2}}$    (d) None of these

16. The area of a triangle is 6, two of its vertices are (1, 1) and (4, –1), the third vertex lies on y = x + 5. Find the third vertex

(a) $\left(\dfrac{2}{5}, \dfrac{27}{5}\right)$      (b) $\left(-\dfrac{3}{5}, \dfrac{22}{5}\right)$

(c) $\left(\dfrac{3}{5}, \dfrac{28}{3}\right)$      (d) None of these

17. What is the value of $c^2$ in the given figure, where the radius of the circle is 'a' unit. **(IIFT 2010)**

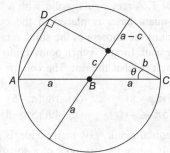

(a) $c^2 = a^2 + b^2 - 2ab \cos \theta$
(b) $c^2 = a^2 + b^2 - 2ab \sin \theta$
(c) $c^2 = a^2 - b^2 + 2ab \cos \theta$
(d) None of these

18. A rectangular piece of paper is 22 cm long and 10 cm wide. A cylinder is formed by rolling the paper along its length. Find the volume of the cylinder. **(IIFT 2011)**

(a) 175 cm³      (b) 180 cm³
(c) 185 cm³      (d) None of these

19. Consider the volumes of the following objects and arrange them in **decreasing** order:
   1. A parallelepiped of length 5 cm, breadth 3 cm and height 4 cm.
   2. A cube of each side 4 cm.
   3. A cylinder of radius 3 cm and length 3 cm.
   4. A sphere of radius 3 cm. **(IIFT 2011)**

(a) 4, 3, 2, 1      (b) 4, 2, 3, 1
(c) 4, 3, 1, 2      (d) None of these

20. In a circle, the height of an arc is 21 cm and the diameter is 84 cm. Find the chord of 'half of the arc'. **(IIFT 2011)**

(a) 45 cm      (b) 40 cm
(c) 42 cm      (d) None of these

21. A hemispherical bowl is filled with hot water to the brim. The contents of the bowl are transferred into a cylindrical vessel whose radius is 50% more than its height. If diameter of the bowl is the same as that of the vessel, the volume of the hot water in the cylindrical vessel is: **(IIFT 2012)**
(a) 60% of the cylindrical vessel
(b) 80% of the cylindrical vessel
(c) 100% of the cylindrical vessel
(d) None of the above

22. The perimeter of a right-angled triangle measures 234 m and the hypotenuse measures 97 m. Then the other two sides of the triangle are measured as **(IIFT 2012)**
(a) 100 m and 37 m    (b) 72 m and 65 m
(c) 80 m and 57 m    (d) None of these

23. In a circular field, there is a rectangular tank of length 130 m and breadth 110 m. If the area of the land portion of the field is 20350 m² then the radius of the field is **(IIFT 2012)**
(a) 85 m      (b) 95 m
(c) 105 m      (d) 115 m

24. There are two buildings, one on each bank of a river, opposite to each other. From the top of one building 60 m high, the angles of depression of the top and the foot of the other building are 30° and 60° respectively. What is the height of the other building? **(IIFT 2012)**
(a) 30 m      (b) 18 m
(c) 40 m      (d) 20 m

25. There is a triangular building (ABC) located in the heart of Jaipur, the Pink City. The length of the one wall in east (BC) direction is 397 feet. If the length of south wall (AB) is a perfect cube, the length of southwest wall (AC) is a power of three, and the length of the wall in the southwest (AC) is thrice the length of the side AB, determine the perimeter of this triangular building. **(IIFT 2013)**
(a) 3209 feet      (b) 3213 feet
(c) 3773 feet      (d) 3313 feet

26. Your friend's cap is in the shape of a right circular cone of base radius 14 cm and height 26.5 cm. The approximate area of the sheet required to make 7 such caps is **(IIFT 2013)**
(a) 6750 cm²      (b) 7280 cm²
(c) 8860 cm²      (d) 9240 cm²

27. Let $P_1$ be the circle of radius r. A square $Q_1$ is inscribed in $P_1$ such that all the vertices of the square $Q_1$ lie on the circumference of $P_1$. Another circle $P_2$ is inscribed in $Q_1$. Another Square $Q_2$ is inscribed in the circle $P_2$. Circle $P_3$ is inscribed in the square $Q_2$ and so on. If $S_N$ is the area between $Q_N$ and $P_{N+1}$ where N represents the set of natural numbers, then the ratio of sum of all such $S_N$ to that of the area of the square $Q_1$ is: **(IIFT 2014)**

(a) $\dfrac{4-\pi}{2}$     (b) $\dfrac{2\pi-4}{\pi}$

(c) $\dfrac{\pi-2}{2}$     (d) None of these

28. ABCDEF is a regular hexagon and PQR is an equilateral triangle of side a. The area of the shaded portion is X and CD : PQ : : 2 : 1. Find the area of the circle circumscribing the hexagon in terms of X. **(IIFT 2014)**

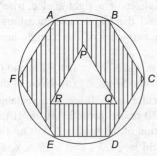

(a) $\dfrac{16\pi X}{23\sqrt{3}}$     (b) $\dfrac{42\pi X}{5\sqrt{3}}$

(c) $\dfrac{2\pi X}{3\sqrt{3}}$     (d) $2\sqrt{3}\pi X$

29. A right circular cylinder has a radius of 6 and a height of 24. A rectangular solid with a square base and a height of 20, is placed in the cylinder such that each of the corners of the solid is tangent to the cylinder wall. If water is then poured into the cylinder such that it reaches the rim, the volume of water is: **(IIFT 2014)**

(a) $288(\pi-5)$     (b) $288(2\pi-3)$

(c) $288(3\pi-5)$     (d) None of these

30. A ladder just reaches a window that is 8 metres high above the ground on one side of the street. Keeping one end of the ladder at the same place, the ladder is moved to the other side of the street so as to reach a 12 metre high window. If the ladder is 13 metres long, what is the width of the street? **(IIFT 2014)**

(a) 14.6 metres     (b) 15.8 metres

(c) 15.2 metres     (d) 15.5 metres

31. If in the figure below, angle XYZ = 90° and the length of the arc XZ = $10\pi$, then the area of the sector XYZ is: **(IIFR 2015)**

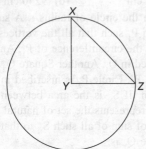

32. If a right circular cylinder of height 14 is inscribed in a sphere of radius 8, then the volume of the cylinder is: **(IIFT 2015)**

(a) 110     (b) 220

(c) 440     (d) 660

33. A ladder of 7.6 m long is standing against a wall and the difference between the wall and the base of the ladder is 6.4 m. If the top of the ladder now slips by 1.2 m, then the foot of the ladder shifts by approximately: **(IIFT 2015)**

(a) 0.4 m     (b) 0.6 m

(c) 0.8 m     (d) 1.2 m

34. Let PQRSTU be a regular hexagon. The ratio of the area of the triangle PRT to that of the hexagon PQRSTU is **(IIFT 2016)**

(a) 0.3     (b) 0.5

(c) 1     (d) None of the above

35. A right circular cylinder has a height of 15 and a radius of 7. A rectangular solid with a height of 12 and a square base, is placed in the cylinder such that each of the corners of the solid is tangent to the cylinder wall. Liquid is then poured into the cylinder such that it reaches the rim. The volume of the liquid is **(IIFT 2015)**

(a) $147(5\pi-8)$     (b) $180(\pi-5)$

(c) $49(5\pi-24)$     (d) $49(15\pi-8)$

36. A rectangular plank $\sqrt{10}$ metre wide, is placed symmetrically along the diagonal of a square of side 10 metres as shown in the figure. The area of the plank is: **(IIFT 2017)**

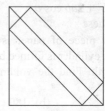

(a) $10(\sqrt{20}-1)$ sq. mt. (b) $10(\sqrt{5}-1)$ sq. mt.

(c) $10\sqrt{20}-1$ sq. mt.     (d) None

37. A flag pole on the top of a mall building is 75 m high. The height of the mall building is 325 m. To an observer at a height of 400 m, the mall building and the pole subtend equal angle $\theta$. If the horizontal distance of the observer from the pole is 'x' m then what is the value of x? **(IIFT 2017)**

(a) $20\sqrt{10}$ m     (b) $30\sqrt{10}$ m

(c) $25\sqrt{5}$ m     (d) None

38. A chord AB of length 24 cm is drawn in a circle of radius 13 cm. Find the area of the shaped portion APB. **(IIFT 2017)**

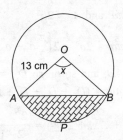

(a)  $13\pi x$ cm$^2$

(b)  $\dfrac{13\pi x}{180}$ cm$^2$

(c)  $\dfrac{169\pi x}{360} - 60$ cm$^2$

(d)  $\dfrac{169\pi x}{180} - 60$ cm$^2$

39. Two tangents are drawn from a point P on the circle with centre at O, touching the circle at point Q and T respectively. Another tangent AB touches the circle at point S. If angle QPT = 55°, find the angle AOB = ?  **(IIFT 2017)**

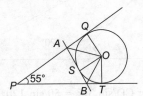

(a)  125°

(b)  62.5°

(c)  97.5°

(d)  95°

40. The coordinates of a triangle ABC are A(1, 5), B(–2, 3), and C(0, –4); find the equation of the median AD?  **(IIFT2017)**

(a)  $7x - 3y + 8 = 0$

(b)  $5x - 4y + 15 = 0$

(c)  $x + 3y - 16 = 0$

(d)  $11x - 4y + 9 = 0$

---

## ANSWER KEY

| | | | |
|---|---|---|---|
| 1. (b) | 2. (c) | 3. (b) | 4. (a) |
| 5. (d) | 6. (b) | 7. (d) | 8. (c) |
| 9. (a) | 10. (d) | 11. (d) | 12. (a) |
| 13. (c) | 14. (a) | 15. (d) | 16. (a) |
| 17. (a) | 18. (a) | 19. (a) | 20. (c) |
| 21. (c) | 22. (b) | 23. (c) | 24. (c) |
| 25. (d) | 26. (d) | 27. (a) | 28. (a) |
| 29. (c) | 30. (c) | 31. (c) | 32. (d) |
| 33. (b) | 34. (b) | 35. (a) | 36. (a) |
| 37. (b) | 38. (c) | 39. (b) | 40. (d) |

### Solutions

1. Total length of the spiral is equal to the sum of perimeter of all the semicircles.

Total length of the spiral = $\pi \times 0.5 + \pi \times 1.0 +$ ... $+ \pi \times 6.5 = \pi (0.5 + 1.0 + ... + 6.5) = 143$ cm.

$\left(\text{Using } \pi = \dfrac{22}{7}\right)$

2. Let the polygon have 'n' sides. Then the sum of interior angles

$$= \frac{n}{2}(2 \times 120 + (n-1)5) = \frac{n}{2}(235 + 5n)$$

We also know that for a polygon with n sides, the Sum of it's interior angles = $(n-2)\,180°$

Thus, we can equate: $\dfrac{n}{2}(235 + 5n) = (n-2)\,180°$

By solving or by putting the value of n from the given options, n = 9.

3. Let AB is the wall and AC and ED are the initial and final positions of the ladder.

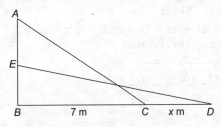

In $\triangle ABC$: AB = $\sqrt{(25)^2 - 7^2}$ = 24 m

If we move the ladder away 'x' meters from the wall. Then in $\triangle DBE$:

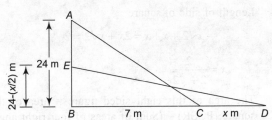

$$\left(24 - \frac{x}{2}\right)^2 + (7 + x)^2 = 25^2$$

$x = 8$ m.

4.

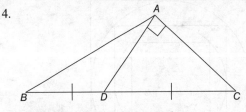

In $\triangle CAD$ : $AD^2 + CA^2 = CD^2$

$\quad AB^2 + AC^2 = 2(AD^2 + CD^2)$  (Using Apollonius Theorem)

$\quad AB^2 + AC^2 = 2AD^2 + BC^2/2$  (CD = BC/2)

$\quad AB^2 + AC^2 = 2(CD^2 - AC^2) + BC^2/2$

$\quad AB^2 + AC^2 = 2(BC^2/4 - AC^2) + BC^2/2$

$\quad 3AC^2 = BC^2 - AB^2$. Option (a) is correct.

5. Let the three solids have base radius 'r' and height of 'h' units. For the hemisphere h = r. Hence, for all

three solids, the value of h = r. The curved surface areas of the three solids are:

Cylinder = $2\pi r \times h = 2\pi rh = 2\pi r^2$

Hemisphere: $2\pi r^2$

$$\text{Cone} = \pi r\sqrt{r^2 + r^2} = \sqrt{2}\pi r^2$$

The required ratio = $2\pi r^2 : 2\pi r^2 : \sqrt{2}\pi r^2 = \sqrt{2} : \sqrt{2} : 1$
Option (c) is correct.

6. The curved surface area of sphere $S = 4\pi r^2$

$S = 4\pi r^2$

$dS/dt = 4\pi \cdot 2r \cdot dr/dt$

According to the question: dr/dt = 2 cm per second & r = 30 cm

$dS/dt = 4\pi \times 2r \times dr/dt = 8\pi \times 30 \times 2 = 480\pi$.
Option (b) is correct.

7.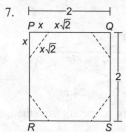

Length of side of square

$$= x\sqrt{2} + x + x = 2x + x\sqrt{2} = 2$$

$$x = \frac{2}{2 + \sqrt{2}}$$

The area of this eight sided figure = area of the square (PQSR) – (Sum of areas of four right angle triangles at the corner)

$$= 4 - \left(4 \times \frac{1}{2} \times \frac{4}{(2 + \sqrt{2})^2}\right) = \frac{8}{\sqrt{2} + 1} \text{ sq. units}$$

8.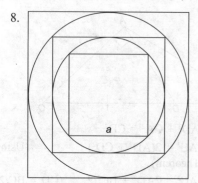

Let the radius of the inner circle be 'x' cm then according to the question:

$$x^2 + x^2 = a^2 \text{ or } x = \frac{a}{\sqrt{2}}$$

$$D_1 = \frac{\pi a^2}{2} - a^2$$

$C_2 = \pi a^2$ and $A_2 = 2a^2$

$$D_2 = \pi a^2 - 2a^2 = 2\left(\frac{\pi}{2}a^2 - a^2\right) = 2D_1$$

Also $D_3 = 4D_1$ and so on so $D_N = 2^{N-1}D_1$
Required ratio = $(D_1 + D_2 + D_3 + D_4 + \ldots D_N)/D_1 =$

$$(1 + 2 + 4 + \ldots + 2^{(N-1)}) = \frac{2^N - 1}{2 - 1} = 2^N - 1$$

Since, $N \to +\infty$, the required ratio is infinite.

9. Let A be the initial point of observation of the captain of warship and D and C be the initial and final positions of the submarine.

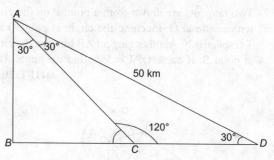

In $\triangle ACD$: CD/sin 30° = 50/sin 120°
       CD = $50/\sqrt{3}$ km

In triangle ACD, $\angle ADC = \angle CAD = 30°$ so, AC = CD = $50/\sqrt{3}$ km.

10.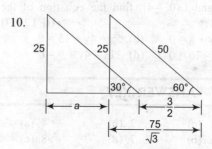

25 cot 60°= $75/\sqrt{3} - a/2$

$$\frac{25}{\sqrt{3}} = \frac{75}{\sqrt{3}} - \frac{a}{2}$$

$$a = \frac{100}{\sqrt{3}} \text{ km}.$$

So the required speed = $2 \cdot \frac{100}{\sqrt{3}} = \frac{200}{\sqrt{3}}$ km/hr

11. Unshaded area is equal of the area of the five equilateral triangles with side length 'a'.

Shaded area is equal to the area of regular pentagon of side length 'a'.

Unshaded area = $5 \cdot \frac{\sqrt{3}}{4}a^2$

Shaded area

$$= \frac{1}{2} \times 5 \times a^2 \times \sin\left(\frac{360}{5}\right) = \frac{5a^2}{2}\left(\frac{\sqrt{10 + 2\sqrt{5}}}{4}\right)$$

Required ratio

$$= \frac{5a^2}{2}\left(\frac{\sqrt{10 + 2\sqrt{5}}}{4}\right) : 5 \cdot \frac{\sqrt{3}}{4}a^2 = \frac{\sqrt{3}}{2}(\sqrt{10 + 2\sqrt{5}})).$$

Option (d) is correct.

12. Let the radius of the circle be 'l'.

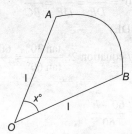

Area of the sector $= \frac{x}{2\pi} \times \pi l^2 = \frac{xl^2}{2}$

Square length of the arc $= (lx)^2$

According to the question: $\frac{xl^2}{2} = (lx)^2$ or x = 0.5

13. Let AC $= 2^a$, where 'a' is a natural number.

$$AC = 2AB \text{ or } AB = AC/2 = \frac{2^a}{2} = 2^{a-1}$$

According to the question AB is a perfect square. Therefore 'a – 1' is a multiple of 2 or 'a' must be an odd number.

AB + AC > BC

3AB > 295

AB > 98.33

$2^{a-1} > 98.33$　　　　　　　　　　(A)

Also, AC – AB < BC

$2^a - 2^{a-1} < 295$ or $2^{a-1}(2-1) < 295$　　(B)

The only satisfying value for equation A and B is a = 9

So AB $= 2^8 = 256$, AC $= 2^9 = 512$

So the perimeter of triangle = AB + AC + BC

= 256 + 512 + 295 = 1063

14. Let the height of cylinder and cone be 5x and 3x respectively. Then volume of the solid $= \pi(8)^2 5x +$

$\frac{\pi}{3}(8)^2 3x = 384\pi x$

Let the radius of drilled cylinder be r then it's volume

$$= \frac{\pi r^2 8}{3}x = \frac{1}{2}\left[384\pi x - \frac{\pi r^2 8}{3}x\right]$$

By solving we get, r $= 4\sqrt{3}$ cm.

15.

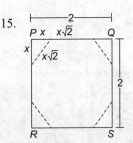

Length of side of square

$$= x\sqrt{2} + x + x = 2x + x\sqrt{2} = 2$$

$$x = \frac{2}{2 + \sqrt{2}}$$

Side of the regular octagon

$$= x\sqrt{2} = \frac{2}{2 + \sqrt{2}}\sqrt{2} = \frac{2}{1 + \sqrt{2}}$$

Perimeter of the regular octagon $= 8 \cdot \frac{2}{1 + \sqrt{2}} = \frac{16}{2 + \sqrt{2}}$

Area of the regular octagon

$$= 2(1 + \sqrt{2})x^2 = 2(1 + \sqrt{2})\left(\frac{2}{1 + \sqrt{2}}\right)^2 = \frac{8}{1 + \sqrt{2}}.$$

Option d.

16. Let the third vertex of the triangle be (x, x + 5). Then the area of the triangle $= \frac{1}{2}(1(-1 - x - 5) +$

$4(x + 5 - 1) + x(1 + 1)) = \frac{1}{2}(5x + 10) = 6$

$5x + 10 = \pm 12 \rightarrow x = 2/5$ or $-22/5$

(x, x + 5) = (2/5, 27/5) or (–22/5, 3/5). Option (a) matches the first value we got and hence is the correct answer.

17. In △ABC:

$$\cos\theta = \frac{a^2 + b^2 - c^2}{2ab} \text{ or } a^2 + b^2 - 2ab\cos\theta = c^2$$

18. Let the radius of base of cylinder r.

$$2\pi r = 10 \text{ or } r = \frac{5}{\pi}$$

Height of the cylinder = 22 cm

Volume of the cylinder $= \pi\left(\frac{5}{\pi}\right)^2 22 = 175$ cm³

19. Volume of parallelepiped $= 3 \times 4 \times 5 = 60$ cm³

Volume of cube $= 4 \times 4 \times 4 = 64$ cm³

Volume of the cylinder $= \pi(3)^2 3 = 27\pi$ cm³

Volume of sphere $= \frac{4}{3}\pi(3)^3 = 36\pi$ cm³

Therefore 4 > 3 > 2 > 1

20. In the diagram given below, PQ is the chord. Height of the arc = RS = 21cm

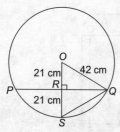

Here we need to find the length of chord (QS) of half arc QS.

RO = 42 – 21 = 21 cm.

In $\triangle ORQ$ & $\triangle SRQ$ : OR = RS, QR = QR, $\angle ORQ = \angle SRQ = 90°$

So both the triangle are congruent.

So OQ = SQ = 42 cm.

21. Volume of sphere = $\frac{2}{3}\pi r^3$

According to the question radius of cylinder = r and height = 2/3 r

So volume of cylinder = $\pi r^2 \cdot \frac{2}{3}r = \frac{2}{3}\pi r^3$

Therefore, the volume of the hot water in the cylindrical vessel is 100% of the cylindrical vessel. Option (c) is correct.

22. Let the other sides of the right angle triangle is x, y respectively.

Then according to the question: $\sqrt{x^2 + y^2} = 97$, $x + y = 234 - 97 = 137$

Now by checking the options we can see that only option (b) satisfies both the equations.

Hence, option (b) is correct.

23. Area of circle = area of land portion + area of rectangle = $20350 + (130 \times 110) = 34650$ m²

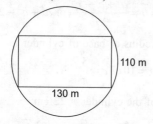

Let the radius of the circle be 'r' m.

$\pi r^2 = 34650$

By solving we get: r = 105 m.

24.

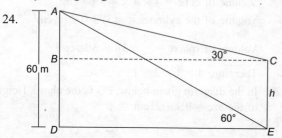

Let the height of the other building be 'h' and AD is the building of height 60 m. The 60 m high building makes an angle of depression 30° on top (C) and 60° at the bottom (E) of the other building.

In $\triangle ABC$:

$$\tan 30° = \frac{AB}{BC} = \frac{60-h}{BC} \tag{1}$$

In $\triangle ADE$:

$$\tan 60° = \frac{AD}{DE} = \frac{60}{DE} = \frac{60}{BC} \tag{2}$$

(As, BC = DE)

Equation 1/ equation 2: $\dfrac{\tan 30°}{\tan 60°} = \dfrac{60-h}{60}$

$$\frac{\frac{1}{\sqrt{3}}}{\sqrt{3}} = \frac{60-h}{60}$$

$$\frac{1}{3} = \frac{60-h}{60} \text{ or } 60 = 180 - 3h$$

$\therefore$ 3h = 120 or h = 40 m.

25. Let AB = $a^3$, AC = $3^n$

According to the question : $3^n = 3 \cdot a^3$ or $a^3 = 3^{n-1}$

Perimeter of the building = $397 + 3^n + 3^{n-1}$

For n = 7, perimeter = $397 + 3^7 + 3^6 = 3313$ feet

26. Surface area of the conical cap = $\pi \times r \times l =$

$\dfrac{22}{7} \times 14 \times \sqrt{(14)^2 + (26.5)^2} = 1320$ cm²

Total area to make 7 such caps = $7 \times 1320 = 9240$ cm²

27. Let the radius of $P_1$ be 'r'. Diameter of $P_1$ = Diagonal of $Q_1$ = 2r

Side of $Q_1 = \dfrac{2r}{\sqrt{2}} = r\sqrt{2}$

Side of $Q_1$ = Diameter of $P_2 = r\sqrt{2}$

Radius of $P_2 = \dfrac{r\sqrt{2}}{2} = r/\sqrt{2}$

Using similar approach we can see: the side length of the $Q_2 = r$ and the radius of the circle = r/2.

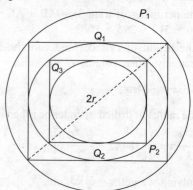

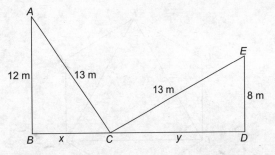

$S_1$ = area between $Q_1$ and $P_2$ = area of $Q_1$ – area of $P_2$

$$= (r\sqrt{2})^2 - \pi\left(\frac{r}{\sqrt{2}}\right)^2 = 2r^2 - \frac{(\pi r)^2}{2} = r^2\left(\frac{4-\pi}{2}\right)$$

$S_2$ = area between $Q_2$ and $P_3$ = $(r)^2 - \frac{\pi r^2}{4} = r^2\left(\frac{4-\pi}{4}\right)$

Similarly, $S_3 = r^2\left(\frac{4-\pi}{8}\right)$, $S_4 = r^2\left(\frac{4-\pi}{16}\right)$

Required Sum $S_n = S_1 + S_2 + S_3 \ldots$

$$= r^2\left(\frac{4-\pi}{2}\right) + r^2\left(\frac{4-\pi}{4}\right) + r^2\left(\frac{4-\pi}{8}\right) + \cdots.$$

On solving the above G.P. we get: $S_N = r^2(4-\pi)$

Required ratio = $S_N$/Area of $Q_1 = r^2(4-\pi) : 2r^2$

$$= \frac{4-\pi}{2}$$

28.

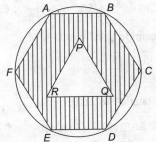

Side of the regular hexagon: Side of equilateral triangle = CD: PQ = 2: 1

If the side length of triangle is 'a' then the Side of the hexagon = 2a

Area of Hexagon = $6 \times \frac{\sqrt{3}}{4} \times (2a)^2 = 6\sqrt{3}a^2$

Area of PQR = $\frac{\sqrt{3}}{4} \times a^2 = \frac{\sqrt{3}}{4}a^2$

$$X = \sqrt{3}a^2\left(6 - \frac{1}{4}\right) = \frac{23}{4}\sqrt{3}a^2 \Rightarrow a^2 = \frac{4X}{23\sqrt{3}}$$

Area of circle

$$= \pi r^2 = \pi(2a)^2 = 4\pi a^2 = \frac{4\pi \times 4X}{23\sqrt{3}} = \frac{16\pi X}{23\sqrt{3}}$$

29. Volume of the cylinder = $\pi \times 6^2 \times 24 = 864\pi$

Diameter of the base = 12

Side of the Rectangular solid = $6\sqrt{2}$

Volume of rectangular solid = $(6\sqrt{2})^2 \times 20 = 1440$

Volume of water = $864\pi - 1440 = 288(3\pi - 5)$

30. Let the width of the road is 'x + y' m (as shown in the diagram).

$$x = \sqrt{13^2 - 12^2} = 5 \text{ m}$$

$$y = \sqrt{13^2 - 8^2} = 10.2 \text{ m}$$

Width of the road = x + y = 5 + 10.2 = 15.2 m

31. Since the length of arc XYZ is 10, it follows that the circumference of the circle would be $4 \times 10\pi = 40\pi$.

Naturally, r = 20. Area of the sector = $\frac{90}{360} \times \pi \times 20 \times 20 = 100\pi$.

32.

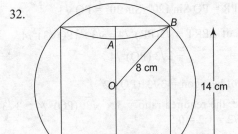

OB = 8 cm & OA = 7 cm.

$$AB = \sqrt{8^2 - 7^2} = \sqrt{15} \text{ cm}$$

Volume of the sphere = $\pi r^2 h = \pi \times \sqrt{15} \times \sqrt{15} \times 14$

$$= 660 \text{ cm}^3$$

33.

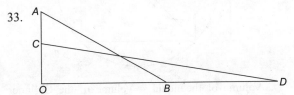

In the figure, AC = 1.2 m, OB = 6.4 m, AB = CD = 7.6 m. Let OC = x meters.

In $\triangle AOB$ :

$$(x + 1.2)^2 + (6.4)^2 = (7.6)^2$$

By solving we get: x = 2.9 meters

In $\triangle COD$: $x^2 + (6.4 + BD)^2 = (7.6)^2$

$$2.9^2 + (6.4 + BD)^2 = (7.6)^2$$

$$BD = 0.6 \text{ m}$$

34. $\triangle PRT$ is an equilateral triangle.

In $\triangle PQR$:

$$\angle PQR = 120°$$

$$\angle QPR = \angle QRP = 30°$$

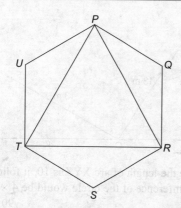

Apply Sine rule in $\Delta$PQR:

PR/Sin 120° = PQ/Sin 30°

PR = PQ Sin 120° /Sin 30° = PQ $\sqrt{3}$

Area of $\Delta$PRT = $\sqrt{3}$(PR)$^2$/4 = $\sqrt{3}$ × (PQ$\sqrt{3}$)$^2$/4

    = 3$\sqrt{3}$ (PQ)$^2$/4

Area of hexagon = 3$\sqrt{3}$ (PQ)$^2$/2

Hence, the required ratio = 3 × $\sqrt{3}$ (PQ)$^2$ /4 : 3$\sqrt{3}$ (PQ)$^2$/2 = 1:2 = 0.5

35. The top view of the rectangular solid inside the right circular cylinder is as shown in the diagram.

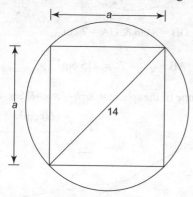

Volume of the liquid = Volume of the Cylinder − Volume of rectangular solid

Volume of the cylinder = $\pi$ (7)$^2$ × 15 = $\dfrac{22}{7}$ × 7$^2$ × 15 = 2310 cm$^3$

Let the side length of the square base of the rectangular solid be 'a' cm.

Then, according to the diagram:

    a$^2$ + a$^2$ = (14)$^2$

    a = 14/$\sqrt{2}$ = 7$\sqrt{2}$ cm.

Volume of the rectangular solid = 7$\sqrt{2}$ × 7$\sqrt{2}$ × 12 = 1176 cm$^3$

Volume of the liquid = 2310 − 1176 = 1134 cm$^3$

Now check the options: 147(5$\pi$ − 8) = 1134. Option (a) is correct.

36.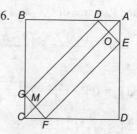

According to the question:

DE = $\sqrt{10}$

AD$^2$ + AE$^2$ = ($\sqrt{10}$)$^2$

2AD$^2$ = 10 (as AD = AE)

AD = $\sqrt{5}$ m

As $\angle$DAO = 45°

AO = AD Cos 45° = $\sqrt{5}$ × $\dfrac{1}{\sqrt{2}}$ = $\sqrt{\dfrac{5}{2}}$ = CM

Length of the rectangle = AC − AO − CM

= $10\sqrt{2} - \sqrt{\dfrac{5}{2}} - \sqrt{\dfrac{5}{2}}$

Length of the rectangle = $\sqrt{2}\,(10 - \sqrt{5})$

Area of the plank = $\sqrt{2}\,(10 - \sqrt{5}) \times \sqrt{10}$

= $\sqrt{2} \times \sqrt{5}(\sqrt{20} - 1) \times \sqrt{10}$

= $10(\sqrt{20} - 1)$

37. Let BC be the mall building of height 325 m and AB is the flag post of height 75 m. D is the observer at height of 400 m. Flag AB and building BC subtends an angle $\theta$ to the observer.

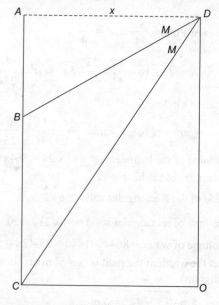

Let AD = x. AB = 75 m, BC = 325 m and OD = 400 m (given). In the figure:

$\angle ADB = M$, $\angle BDC = M$

AB = Height of the flag and BC = Height of the building

In $\triangle ABD$: $\tan M = 75/x$

In $\triangle ADC$: $\tan 2M = 400/x$

$2 \tan M/(1 - \tan^2 M) = 400/x$

$(2 \times 75/x)/1 - (75/x)^2 = 400/x \rightarrow 1 - (75/x)^2 = 150/400$

$\rightarrow (75/x)^2 = 1 - (150/400) = 250/400$

On solving this for x, we will get:

$x^2 = 9000$

$x = 30\sqrt{10}$ m.

38. Area of the sector OAPB = $\pi (13)^2 \times x/360$

Area of the $\triangle OAB$ = $\frac{1}{2} \times (13)^2 \sin x$

Area of the shaded portion APB = Area of the sector OAPB – Area of the $\triangle OAB$

$= \pi (13)^2 \times x/360 - \frac{1}{2} \times (13)^2 \times \sin x = 169\pi \times x/360 - (169 \sin x)/2$     (1)

Draw perpendicular OM on AB. As $\triangle AOB$ is isosceles triangle so, the perpendicular OM also bisects the angle AOB. $\angle AOM = \angle BOM = \dfrac{x}{2}$.

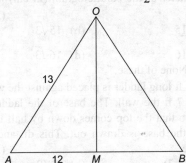

$OM = ((13^2 - (24/2)^2)^{1/2} = (13^2 - 12^2)^{1/2} = 5$ cm.

In $\triangle AMO$:

$\sin x/2 = AM/AO = 12/13$, $\cos x/2 = OM/AB = 5/13$

$\sin x = 2 \times \sin x/2 \times \cos x/2$

$= 2 \times \dfrac{12}{13} \times \dfrac{5}{13} = \dfrac{120}{13^2}$

On putting the value of Sinx in equation (1) we get:

Area of the shaded portion

$= 169\pi\, x/360 - \left(169 \times \dfrac{120}{(13)^2}\right)\Big/2$

$= 169\pi\dfrac{x}{360} - 60$

39. $\angle AOT = 180° - \angle APB$

$= 180° - 55° = 125°$

In $\triangle AQO$ and $\triangle ASO$:

$AQ = AS$   (AQ and AS are tangents on the circle from point A)

$OQ = OS$   (Radius of the circle)

$AO = AO$

$\therefore \quad \triangle AQO \cong \triangle ASO$

Therefore $\angle QOA = \angle AOS$     (1)

Similarly we can prove $\angle SOB = \angle BOT$     (2)

$\angle QOT = 125°$

$\angle QOA + \angle AOS + \angle SOB + \angle BOT = 125°$

From equation (1) and (2), we get:

$\angle AOS + \angle AOS + \angle SOB + \angle SOB = 125°$

$2(\angle AOS + \angle SOB) = 125°$

$\angle AOB = \dfrac{125°}{2} = 62.5°$

40.

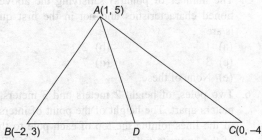

Co-ordinate of D = $((-2 + 0)/2, (3 - 4)/2) = (-1, -1/2)$

Equation of AD =

$(y - 5) = \dfrac{\left[\left(-\dfrac{1}{2}\right) - 5\right](x - 1)}{-1 - 1}$

$(y - 5) = + 11(x - 1)/4$

$11x - 11 = 4y - 20$

$11x - 4y = -9$ or $11x - 4y + 9 = 0$

Hence, Option (d) is correct.

## XAT (2009–2017)

1. ABCD is a square with sides of length 10 units. OCD is an isosceles triangle with base CD. OC cuts AB at point Q and OD cuts AB at point P. The area of trapezoid PQCD is 80 square units. The altitude from O of the triangle OPQ is:    **(XAT 2009)**

  (a) 12             (b) 13

  (c) 14             (d) 15

  (e) None of these.

2. How many differently shaped triangles exist in which no two sides are of the same length, each side is of integral unit length and the perimeter of the triangle is less than 14 units?    **(XAT 2009)**

  (a) 3              (b) 4

  (c) 5              (d) 6

  (e) None of these.

3. In a quadrilateral ABCD, BC = 10, CD = 14, AD = 12 and $\angle CBA = \angle BAD = 60°$. If AB = $a + \sqrt{b}$, where a and b are positive integers. Then a + b = **(XAT 2009)**

(a) 193
(b) 201
(c) 204
(d) 207
(e) None of these

**Directions for Questions 4–5:** Let $A_1, A_2, ...., A_n$ be the n points on the straight-line y = px + q. The coordinates of $A_k$ is $(x_k, y_k)$, where k = 1, 2, ...., n such that $x_1, x_2, ..., x_n$ are in arithmetic progression. The coordinates of $A_2$ is (2, –2) and $A_{24}$ is (68, 31). **(XAT 2010)**

4. The y-ordinate of $A_8$ is

(a) 13
(b) 10
(c) 7
(d) 5.5
(e) None of these.

5. The number of point(s) satisfying the above mentioned characteristics and not in the first quadrant is/are

(a) 1
(b) 2
(c) 3
(d) 7
(e) None of these.

6. Two poles, of height 2 meters and 3 meters, are 5 meters apart. The height of the point of intersection of the lines joining the top of each pole to the foot of the opposite pole is, **(XAT 2010)**

(a) 1.2 meters
(b) 1.0 meters
(c) 5.0 meters
(d) 3.0 meters
(e) None of these.

7. In an equilateral triangle ABC, whose length of each side is 3 cm, D is a point on BC such that BD = CD/2. What is the length of AD? **(XAT 2010)**

(a) $\sqrt{5}$ cm
(b) $\sqrt{6}$ cm
(c) $\sqrt{7}$ cm
(d) $\sqrt{8}$ cm
(e) None of these.

8. Let $S_1, S_2, ....$ be the squares such that for each n ≥ 1, the length of the diagonal of $S_n$ is equal to the length of the side of $S_{n+1}$. If the length of the side of $S_3$ is 4 cm, what is the length of the side of $S_n$? **(XAT 2010)**

(a) $2^{\frac{2n+1}{2}}$
(b) $2(n-1)$
(c) $2^{n-1}$
(d) $2^{\frac{n+1}{2}}$
(e) None of these.

9. A tank internally measuring 150 cm × 120 cm × 100 cm has 1281600 cm³ water in it. Porous bricks are placed in the water until the tank is full up to its brim. Each brick absorbs one tenth of its volume of water. How many bricks, of 20 cm × 6cm × 4 cm, can be put in the tank without spilling over the water? **(XAT 2010)**

(a) 1100
(b) 1200
(c) 1150
(d) 1250
(e) None of these.

10.

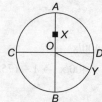

In a circular field, AOB and COD are two mutually perpendicular diameters having length of 4 meters. X is the mid-point of OA. Y is a point on the circumference such that $\angle YOD = 30°$. Which of the following correctly gives the relation among the three alternate paths from X to Y? **(XAT 2010)**

(a) XOBY : XODY : XADY :: 5.15 : 4.50 : 5.06
(b) XADY : XODY : XOBY :: 6.25 : 5.34 : 4.24
(c) XODY : XOBY : XADY :: 4.04 : 5.35 : 5.25
(d) XADY : XOBY : XODY :: 5.19 : 5.09 : 4.04
(e) XOBY : XADY : XODY :: 5.06 : 5.15 : 4.50

11. ABCD is a parallelogram with $\angle ABC = 60°$. If the longer diagonal is of length 7 cm and the area of the parallelogram ABCD is $15\dfrac{\sqrt{3}}{2}$ cm², then the perimeter of the parallelogram (in cm) is: **(XAT 2010)**

(a) 15
(b) $15\sqrt{3}$
(c) 16
(d) $16\sqrt{3}$
(e) None of these.

12. A 25 ft long ladder is placed against the wall with its base 7 ft the wall. The base of the ladder is drawn out so that the top comes down by half the distance that the base is drawn out. This distance is in the range: **(XAT 2011)**

(a) (2,7)
(b) (5, 8)
(c) (9, 10)
(d) (3, 7)
(e) None of these.

13. A straight line through point P of a triangle PQR intersects the side QR at the point S and circumcircle of the triangle PQR at the point T. If S is not the centre of the circumcircle, then which of the following is true? **(XAT 2011)**

(a) $\dfrac{1}{PS} + \dfrac{1}{ST} < \dfrac{2}{\sqrt{(QS)(QR)}}$

(b) $\dfrac{1}{PS} + \dfrac{1}{ST} < \dfrac{4}{QR}$

(c) $\dfrac{1}{PS} + \dfrac{1}{ST} > \dfrac{1}{\sqrt{(QS)(QR)}}$

(d) $\dfrac{1}{PS} + \dfrac{1}{ST} > \dfrac{4}{QR}$

(e) None of these.

**Directions for Questions 14–15:** A man standing on a boat south of a lighthouse, observes his shadow to be 24 meters long, as measured at the sea level. On sailing 300 meters eastwards, he finds his shadow as 30 meters long, measured in a similar manner. The height of the man is 6 meters above sea level.  **(XAT 2011)**

14. The height of the light house above the sea level is:
    (a) 90 m  (b) 94 m
    (c) 96 m  (d) 100 m
    (e) 106 m

15. What is the horizontal distance of the man from the light house in the second position?
    (a) 300 m  (b) 400 m
    (c) 500 m  (d) 600 m
    (e) None of these.

16. In a city, there is a circular park. There are four points of entry into the park, namely – P, Q, R and S. Three paths were constructed which connected the points PQ, RS, and PS. The length of the path PQ is 10 units, and the length of the path RS is 7 units. Later, the municipal corporation extended the paths PQ and RS past Q and R respectively, and they meet at a point T on the main road outside the park. The path from Q to T measures 8 units, and it was found that the angle PTS is 60°. Find the area (in square units) enclosed by the paths PT, TS, and PS.  **(XAT 2011)**

    (a) $36\sqrt{3}$  (b) $54\sqrt{3}$
    (c) $72\sqrt{3}$  (d) $90\sqrt{3}$
    (e) None of these.

17. Consider a square ABCD of side 60 cm. It contains arcs BD and AC drawn with centres at A and D respectively. A circle is drawn such that it is tangent to side AB, and the arcs BD and AC. What is the radius of the circle?  **(XAT 2011)**
    (a) 9 cm  (b) 10 cm
    (c) 12 cm  (d) 15 cm
    (e) None of these.

18. In a plane rectangular coordinate system, points L, M, N and O are represented by the coordinates (–5, 0), (1, –1), (0, 5), and (–1, 5) respectively. Consider a variable point P in the same plane. The minimum value of PL + PM + PN + PO is:  **(XAT 2011)**

    (a) $1 + \sqrt{37}$  (b) $5\sqrt{2} + 2\sqrt{10}$
    (c) $\sqrt{41} + \sqrt{37}$  (d) $\sqrt{41} + 1$
    (e) None of these.

19. A spherical metal of radius 10 cm is molten and made into 1000 smaller spheres of equal sizes. In this process the surface area of the metal is increased by:  **(XAT 2012)**
    (a) 1000 times  (b) 100 times
    (c) 10 times  (d) No change
    (e) None of these.

20. A city has a park shaped as a right angled triangle. The length of the longest side of this park is 80 m. The Mayor of the city wants to construct three paths from the corner point opposite to the longest side such that these three paths divide the longest side into four equal segments. Determine the sum of the squares of the lengths of the three paths.  **(XAT 2012)**

    (a) 4000 m  (b) 4800 m
    (c) 5600 m  (d) 6400 m
    (e) 7200 m

21. Carpenter Rajesh has a circular piece of plywood of diameter 30 feet. He has cut out two disks of diameter 20 feet and 10 feet. What is the diameter of the largest disk that can be cut out from the remaining portion of the plywood piece?  **(XAT 2012)**
    (a) > 8.00 feet and ≤ 8.20 feet
    (b) > 8.21 feet and ≤ 8.40 feet
    (c) > 8.41 feet and ≤ 8.60 feet
    (d) > 8.61 feet and ≤ 8.80 feet
    (e) > 8.81 feet and ≤ 9.00 feet

22. Suresh, who runs a bakery, uses a conical shaped equipment to write decorative labels (e.g., Happy Birthday etc.) using cream. The height of this equipment is 7 cm and the diameter of the base is 5 mm. A full charge of the equipment will write 330 words on an average. How many words can be written using three fifth of a litre of cream?  **(XAT 2012)**
    (a) 45090  (b) 45100
    (c) 46000  (d) 43200
    (e) None of these.

23. At the centre of a city's municipal park there is a large circular pool. A fish is released in the water at the edge of the pool. The fish swims north for 300 feet before it hits the edge of the pool. It then turns east and swims for 400 feet before hitting the edge again. What is the area of the pool?  **(XAT 2013)**
    (a) $62500\pi$  (b) $125000\pi$
    (c) $250000\pi$  (d) $500000\pi$
    (e) Cannot be answered from the given data

24. In a square PQRS, A and B are two points on PS and SR such that PA = 2AS, and RB = 2BS. If PQ = 6, the area of the triangle ABQ is  **(XAT 2013)**
    (a) 6  (b) 8
    (c) 10  (d) 12
    (e) 14

25. The radius of a circle with centre O is $\sqrt{50}$ cm. A and C two points on the circle, and B is a point inside the circle. The length of AB is 6 cm, and the length of BC is 2 cm. The angle ABC is a right angle. Find the square of the distance OB.  **(XAT 2013)**

(a) 26      (b) 25
(c) 24      (d) 23
(e) 22

26. In quadrilateral PQRS, PQ = 5 units, QR = 17 units, RS = 5 units, and PS = 9 units. The length of the diagonal QS can be: **(XAT 2014)**
(a) > 10 and < 12      (b) > 12 and < 14
(c) > 14 and < 16      (d) > 16 and < 18
(e) cannot be determined

27. There are two circles $C_1$, and $C_2$ of radii 3 and 8 units respectively. The common internal tangent T, touches the circles at points P and Q respectively. The line joining the centers of the circles intersects T at X. The distance of X from the center of the smaller circle is 5 units. What is the length of the line segment PQ? **(XAT 2014)**
(a) ≤ 13      (b) > 13 and ≤ 14
(c) > 14 and < 15      (d) > 15 and ≤ 16
(e) > 16

28. Triangle ABC is a right-angled triangle. D and E are midpoints of AB and BC respectively. Read the following statements. **(XAT 2014)**
 (i) AE = 19      (ii) CD = 22
(iii) Angle B is right angle.
Which of the following statements would be sufficient to determine the length of AC?
(a) Statement (i) and Statement (ii)
(b) Statement (i) and Statement (iii)
(c) Statement (ii) and (iii)
(d) Statement (iii) alone
(e) All three statements

29. There are two squares $S_1$ and $S_2$ with areas 8 and 9 units, respectively. $S_1$ is inscribed within $S_2$, with one corner of $S_1$ on each side $S_2$. The corners of the smaller square divides the sides of the bigger square into two segments, one of length 'a' and the other of length 'b', where, b > a.
A possible value of 'b/a', is: **(XAT 2014)**
(a) ≥ 5 and < 8      (b) ≥ 8 and < 11
(c) ≥ 11 and < 14      (d) ≥ 14 and < 17
(e) > 17

30. Diameter of the base of a water-filled inverted right circular cone is 26 cm. A cylindrical pipe, 5 mm is radius, is attached to the surface of the cone at a point. The perpendicular distance between the point and the base (the top) is 15 cm. The distance from the edge of the base to the point is 17 cm, along the surface. If water flows at the rate of 10 meters per minute through the pipe, how much time would elapse before water stops coming out of the pipe?
(a) < 4.5 minutes
(b) ≥ 4.5 minutes but < 4.8 minutes
(c) ≥ 4.8 minutes but < 5 minutes
(d) ≥ 5 minutes but < 5.2 minutes

(e) ≥ 5.2 minutes      **(XAT 2014)**

31. The figure below has been obtained by folding a rectangle. The total area of the figure (as visible) is 144 square meters. Had the rectangle not been folded, the current overlapping part would have been a square. What would have been the total area of the original unfolded rectangle? **(XAT 2015)**

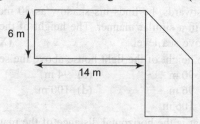

(a) 128 square meters      (b) 154 square meters
(c) 162 square meters      (d) 172 square meters
(e) None of the above

32. A solid metal cylinder of 10 cm height and 14 cm diameter is melted and re-cast into two cones in the proportion of 3: 4 (volume), keeping the height 10 cm. What would be the percentage change in the flat surface area before and after? **(XAT 2015)**
(a) 9%      (b) 16%
(c) 25%      (d) 50%
(e) None of the above

33. A circular road is constructed outside a square field. The perimeter of the square field is 200 ft. If the width of the road is $7 \times \sqrt{2}$ ft. and cost of construction is ₹ 100 per sq. ft. Find the lowest possible cost to construct 50% of the total road. **(XAT 2015)**
(a) ₹70,400      (b) ₹125,400
(c) ₹140,800      (d) ₹235,400
(e) None of the above

34. Two diagonals of a parallelogram intersect each other at coordinates (17.5, 23.5). Two adjacent points of the parallelogram are (5.5, 7.5) and (13.5, 16). Find the lengths of the diagonals. **(XAT 2015)**
(a) 15 and 30      (b) 15 and 40
(c) 17 and 30      (d) 17 and 40
(e) Multiple solutions are possible.

35. In the diagram below, CD = BF = 10 units and ∠CED = ∠BAF = 30°. What would be the area of triangle AED? (Note: Diagram below may not be proportional to scale.) **(XAT 2015)**

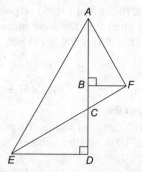

(a) $100 \times (\sqrt{2} + 3)$    (b) $\dfrac{100}{\sqrt{3} + 4}$

(c) $\dfrac{50}{\sqrt{3} + 4}$    (d) $50 \times (\sqrt{3} + 4)$

(e) None of these

36. The parallel sides of a trapezoid ABCD are in the ratio of 4: 5. ABCD is divided into an isosceles triangle ABP and a parallelogram PBCD (as shown below). ABCD has a perimeter equal to 1120 meters and PBCD has a perimeter equal to 1000 meters. Find Sin∠ABC, given 2∠DAB = ∠BCD. **(XAT 2015)**

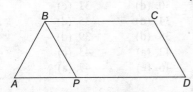

(a) 4/5    (b) 16/25
(c) 5/6    (d) 24/25
(e) A single solution is not possible

37. The centre of a circle inside a triangle is at a distance of 625 cm. from each of the vertices of the triangle. If the diameter of the circle is 350 cm. and the circle is touching only two sides of the triangle, find the area of the triangle. **(XAT 2015)**
(a) 240000    (b) 387072
(c) 480000    (d) 506447
(e) None of the above

38. A person is standing at a distance of 1800 meters facing a giant clock at the top of a tower. At 5.00 p.m., he can see the tip of the minute hand of the clock at 30 degree elevation from his eye-level. Immediately, the person starts walking towards the tower. At 5.10 pm., the person noticed that the tip of the minute hand made an angle of 60 degrees with respect to his eye-level. Using three-dimensional vision, find the speed at which the person is walking. The length of the minutes hand is $200\sqrt{3}$ meters ($\sqrt{3} = 1.732$). **(XAT 2015)**
(a) 7.2 km/hour    (b) 7.5 km/hour
(c) 7.8 km/hour    (d) 8.4 km/hour
(e) None of these

39. In the figure below, AB = AC = CD. If ADB = 20°, what is the value of BAD? **(XAT 2016)**

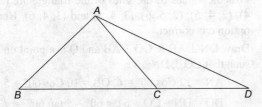

(a) 40°    (b) 60°
(c) 70°    (d) 120°
(e) 140°

40. ΔABC and ΔXYZ are equilateral triangles of 54 cm sides. All smaller triangles like ΔANM, ΔOCP, ΔQPX etc are also equilateral triangles. Find the area of the shape MNOPQRM. **(XAT 2016)**

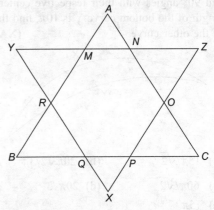

(a) $243\sqrt{3}$ sq. cm.    (b) $486\sqrt{3}$ sq. cm.
(c) $729\sqrt{3}$ sq. cm    (d) $4374\sqrt{3}$ sq. cm
(e) None of the above

41. A square piece of paper is folded three times along its diagonal to get an isosceles triangle whose equal sides are 10 cm. What is the area of the unfolded original piece of paper? **(XAT 2016)**
(a) 400 sq. cm.    (b) 800 sq. cm.
(c) $800\sqrt{2}$ sq. cm.    (d) 1600 sq. cm.
(e) Insufficient data to answer

42. The difference between the area of the circumscribed circle and the area of the inscribed circle of an equilateral triangle is 2156 sq. cm. What is the area of the equilateral triangle (in sq cm)? **(XAT 2016)**
(a) $686\sqrt{3}$    (b) 1000
(c) $961\sqrt{2}$    (d) $650\sqrt{3}$
(e) None of the above

43. Study the figure below and answer the question:

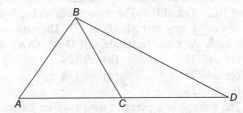

Four persons walk from point A to point D following different routes. The one following ABCD takes 70 minutes. Another person takes 45 minutes following ABD. The third person takes 30 minutes following route ACD. The last person takes 65 minutes

following route ACBD. If all were to walk at the same speed, how long will it take to go from point B to point C? **(XAT 2016)**
(a) 10 min.        (b) 20 min.
(c) 30 min.        (d) 40 min.
(e) Cannot be answered as the angles are unknown.

44. In the figure below, two circular curves create 60° and 90° angles with their respective centers. If the length of the bottom curve Y is $10\pi$, find the length of the other curve. **(XAT 2016)**

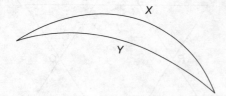

(a) $15\pi/\sqrt{2}$        (b) $20\pi\sqrt{2}/3$
(c) $60\pi/\sqrt{2}$        (d) $20\pi/3$
(e) $15\pi$

45. AB is a chord of a circle. The length of AB is 24 cm. P is (The midpoint of AB). Perpendiculars from P on either side of the chord meets the circle at M and N respectively. If PM < PN and PM = 8 cm, then what will be the length of PN? **(XAT 2017)**
(a) 17 cm        (b) 18 cm
(c) 19 cm        (d) 20 cm
(e) 21 cm

46. AB, CD and EF are three parallel lines, in that order. Let $d_1$ and $d_2$ be the distances from CD to AB and EF respectively. $d_1$ and $d_2$ are integers, where $d_1:d_2 = 2:1$, P is a point on AB, Q and S are points on CD and R is a point on F-F, If the area of the quadrilateral PQRS is 30 square units, what is the value of QR when value of SR is the least? **(XAT 2017)**
(a) slightly less than 10 units
(b) 10 units
(c) slightly greater than 10 units
(d) slightly less than 20 units
(e) slightly greater than 20 units

47. ABCD is a rectangle P, Q and R are the midpoint of BC, CD and DA. The point S lies on the line QR in such a way that SR:QS = 1:3. The ratio of the triangle APS and rectangle ABCD is **(XAT 2017)**
(a) 36/128        (b) 39/128
(c) 44/128        (d) 48/128
(e) 64/128

48. The volume of a pyramid with a square base is 200 cm³. The height of the pyramid is 13 cm. What will be the length of the slant edges (i.e. the distance between the apex and any other vertex), rounded to the nearest integer? **(XAT 2017)**

(a) 12 cm        (b) 13 cm
(c) 14 cm        (d) 15 cm
(e) 16 cm

---

## ANSWER KEY

| | | | |
|---|---|---|---|
| 1. (d) | 2. (c) | 3. (c) | 4. (c) |
| 5. (c) | 6. (a) | 7. (c) | 8. (d) |
| 9. (b) | 10. (d) | 11. (c) | 12. (e) |
| 13. (d) | 14. (e) | 15. (c) | 16. (c) |
| 17. (b) | 18. (b) | 19. (e) | 20. (c) |
| 21. (c) | 22. (d) | 23. (a) | 24. (c) |
| 25. (a) | 26. (b) | 27. (c) | 28. (e) |
| 29. (d) | 30. (d) | 31. (c) | 32. (d) |
| 33. (b) | 34. (d) | 35. (d) | 36. (a) |
| 37. (b) | 38. (d) | 39. (d) | 40. (b) |
| 41. (a) | 42. (a) | 43. (c) | 44. (a) |
| 45. (b) | 46. (e) | 47. (a) | 48. (c) |

### Solutions

1.

Area of trapezoid PQCD = $\frac{1}{2}(10 + PQ) \times 10 = 80$ or PQ = 6 cm.

PN = PQ/2 = 6/2 = 3 cm

AP = BQ = (AB – PQ)/2 = (AB – 2PN)/2
= (10 – 6)/2 = 2 cm.

ΔOPN and ΔDPA are similar to each other.

∴   ON/AD = PN/PA or ON/10 = 3/2 or ON = 15 cm.

2. Let the length of the three sides of the triangle be a, b and c.

a + b > c or a + b + c > c + c or a + b + c > 2c.

According to the question: 2c < 14 or c < 7 or any side of the triangle must be less than 7. Length of any side of the triangle must be greater than 1, otherwise one of the other sides would be greater or equal to 7, which is not possible. So the length of the side must be greater than 1 and less than 7.

Possible values of the sides of the triangle are (2, 3, 4), (2, 4, 5), (2, 5, 6), (3, 4, 5) and (3, 4, 6). Hence, option c is correct.

3. Draw DN ⊥ AB & CO ⊥ AB and Q is a point on DN such that CQ ⊥ DN.

AN = 12 Cos 60° = 6, OB = 10 Cos 60° = 5.

DQ = DN – CO = 6 tan 60° – 5 tan 60° = $\sqrt{3}$

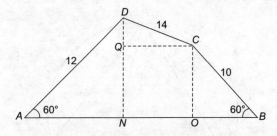

In $\Delta DQC : CQ = \sqrt{(14)^2 - 3} = \sqrt{193}$

Therefore AB = AN + NO + OB = 6 + 5 + $\sqrt{193} = a + \sqrt{b}$

Hence $a + b = 11 + 193 = 204$

4. If 'd' be the common difference. Then,

$A_{24} = A_2 + (23-1)d = 2 + (23-1)d = 68$ or $d = 3$.

(2, -2) & (68, 31) both lies on the line $px + q = y$

So, $2p - q = -2$      (1)

$68p + q = 31$      (2)

On solving equation (1) and (2) we get $p = \frac{1}{2}$, $q = -3$.

x co ordinate of $A_8 = 2 + (7-1)3 = 20$

y coordinate of $A_8 = p(\text{x co ordinate of } A_8) + q = \frac{1}{2} \times 20 - 3 = 7$

5. $A_1$ (−1, −7/2), $A_2$ (2, −2), $A_3$ (5, −1/2) are not in the first quadrant. Option (c).

6. Let PR and QS be the two poles. PR = 2 m and QS = 3 m. PS and QR cuts each other at point O and OT ⊥ RS.

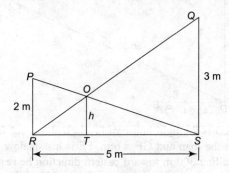

$\Delta$ROT and $\Delta$RQS are similar to each other:

OT/QS = RT/ RS

RT/ RS = h/3      (1)

Similarly, $\Delta$SOT and $\Delta$SPR are similar to each other:

ST/ SR = h/ 2      (2)

Adding (1) and (2), we get:

(RT + ST)/ RS = RS/ RS = 1 = h/2 + h/3

h = 1.2 m

7.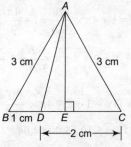

Draw AE ⊥ BC. Since ABC is an equilateral triangle so AE will bisect BC.

DE = DC − EC = 2 − 3/2 = ½ cm

$AE = \sqrt{3^2 - 1.5^2} = \frac{3}{2}\sqrt{3}$ cm

$AD = \sqrt{\left(\frac{3}{2}\sqrt{3}\right)^2 + \left(\frac{1}{2}\right)^2} = \sqrt{7}$ cm

8. Side of a square is $\frac{1}{\sqrt{2}}$ times of its diagonal. So the side of square $S_2 = \frac{4}{\sqrt{2}}$ cm. $= 2\sqrt{2}$ cm

Side length of square $S_1$ is $1/\sqrt{2}$ times of the side length of square $S_1$

∴   Side of square $S_1 = \frac{2\sqrt{2}}{\sqrt{2}} = 2$ cm

From the above analysis we can easily conclude that to get the side length of the next square we just need to multiply the side length of the previous square with $\sqrt{2}$.

So side of $S_n = 2(\sqrt{2})^{n-1} = 2^{\frac{n+1}{2}}$ cm

9. Let n bricks can be put in the tank without spilling over the water, these bricks take space equals to their volume but because of the presence of these bricks the volume of the water inside the tank would get reduced by 10% of the total volume of the bricks.

Free space in the tank = Total volume of 'n' porous bricks − Water soaked by these porous bricks. This free space has to be occupied with 'n' bricks with each brick only using 90% of its' volume. Thus, we can equate:

$150 \times 120 \times 100 - 1281600 = n \times 20 \times 6 \times 4\left(1 - \frac{10}{100}\right)$

On solving we get: $n = \dfrac{518400}{20 \times 6 \times 4 \times 0.9} = 1200$

10.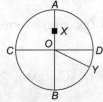

$$XADY = XA + ADY = 1 + 4\pi \times \frac{120}{360} = 1 + \frac{4\pi}{3} \approx 5.19$$

$$XOBY = XB + BY = 1 + 2 + 4\pi \times \frac{60}{360} = 3 + \frac{4\pi}{6} \approx 5.09$$

$$XODY = XO + OD + DY = 1 + 2 + 4\pi \times \frac{30}{360} \approx 4.04$$

$$XADY : XOBY : XODY :: 5.19 : 5.09 : 4.04$$

11.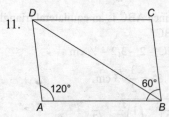

Let AB = a and AD = b

Area of parallelogram = $ab \sin 60^0 = ab\frac{\sqrt{3}}{2} = 15\frac{\sqrt{3}}{2}$

$ab = 15$        (1)

By applying cosine rule in $\Delta ABD$:

$$\cos 120° = \frac{a^2 + b^2 - 49}{2ab} = -\frac{1}{2} \text{ or } a^2 + b^2 = 34$$

$$a^2 + \frac{225}{a^2} = 34$$

By solving the above equation we get $a^2 = 9$ or $25$

a = 3 or 5

ab = 15 so b = 5 or 3

∴ Perimeter = 2(a + b) = 2(5 + 3) or 2(3 + 5) = 16 cm

12. Let AD be the wall and initial and the final position of the ladder are DC and EB respectively. Let the base of the ladder be drawn out by x m from C to B. The figure would look as shown:

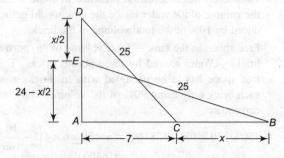

In $\Delta EAB$ : $\left(24 - \frac{x}{2}\right)^2 + (7 + x)^2 = 25^2$

On solving we get: x = 0, 8. Option (e) is correct.

13. $PS \times ST = QS \times SR$

$$\frac{PS + ST}{2} > \sqrt{PS \times ST} \quad (\text{A.M.} > \text{G.M.})$$

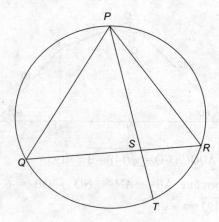

$$\frac{PS + ST}{2} > \sqrt{QS \times SR}$$

$$\frac{PS + ST}{2PS \cdot ST} > \frac{\sqrt{QS \times SR}}{QS \cdot QR}$$

$$\frac{1}{PS} + \frac{1}{ST} > \frac{2}{\sqrt{QS \times SR}} \quad (A)$$

$$\frac{QS + SR}{2} = \frac{QR}{2} > \sqrt{QS \times SR}$$

$$\frac{2}{\sqrt{QS \times SR}} > \frac{4}{QR} \quad (B)$$

From inequalities A and B we get:

$$\frac{1}{PS} + \frac{1}{ST} > \frac{4}{QR}$$

14.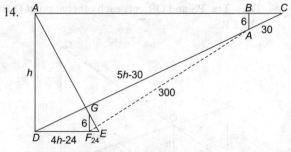

AD is the light house of height h above sea level. G is the man and GF = 6 m. FE is his shadow and on sailing 300 m toward eastern direction he reaches at H where he found that his shadow (HC) is 30 m long. Since $\Delta$ ADE and $\Delta$ GFE are similar,

$$\frac{AD}{GF} = \frac{DE}{EF}$$

$$\frac{h}{6} = \frac{DE}{24} \text{ or } DE = 4h$$

$$DF = 4h - 24$$

$$FH = 300m$$

Since $\Delta ACD$ and $\Delta BCH$ are similar,

$$\frac{h}{6} = \frac{DC}{30}$$

DC = 5h distance of the man from the

DH = 5h – 30

ΔDFH is right angle triangle so

$(4h - 24)^2 + (300)^2 = (5h - 30)^2$

On solving, we get h = 106 m

15. Horizontal distance of the man from the light house in the second position = 5h – 30 = 5 × 106 – 30 = 500 m

16.

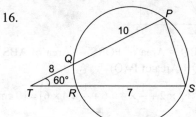

$PT \times QT = ST \times RT$

$8 \times 18 = TR (TR + 7)$

TR = 9

Area of the triangle PTS = $\frac{1}{2} \times 16 \times 18 \times \sin 60° =$ $72\sqrt{3}$ sq. units

17. Draw OQ ⊥ AD, OP ⊥ AB.

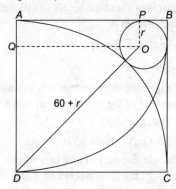

AO = 60 – r, DO = 60 + r and DQ = 60 – r

In ΔAOQ; $AP^2 = QO^2 = (60 - r)^2 - r^2$     (1)

In ΔDQO,

    $QO^2 = DO^2 - DQ^2$

⇒   $QO^2 = (60 + r)^2 - (60 - r)^2$ ...(ii)

⇒   $(60 - r)^2 + 3600 - 120r = (60 + r)^2$

On checking the options we get r = 10 cm.

18. If P lies on LN, then (PL + PN) will be minimum similarly if P lies on OM then PM + PO will be minimum.

PL + PM + PN + PO will be minimum if the point of intersection of the diagonals of quadrilateral LMNO and point P coincide.

$LN = \sqrt{(-5 - 0)^2 + (0 - 5)^2} = 5\sqrt{2}$

$MO = \sqrt{(1 - (-1))^2 + (-1 - 5)^2} = 2\sqrt{10}$

$PL + PM + PN + PO = 5\sqrt{2} + 2\sqrt{10}$

19. If the radius of a smaller sphere be 'r cm' then according to the question:

$$\frac{4}{3}\pi(10)^3 = 1000 \frac{4}{3}\pi(r)^3$$

$r = 1$ cm

Surface area of the larger sphere = $4\pi(10)^2 = 400\pi$

Total surface area of 1000 smaller spheres = 1000 $4\pi(1)^2 = 4000\pi$

Net increase in the surface area = $4000\pi - 400\pi = 3600\pi$

Hence, surface area of the metal is increased by 9 times. Option (e).

20. Let PQR is the park and $\angle Q = 90°$. The longest side is PR. Let points S, T and U divide the longest side in four equal parts. We need to get the value of $QS^2 + QT^2 + QU^2$

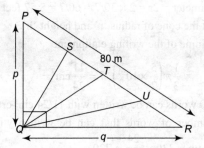

PR = 80 m, PS = ST = TU = UR = 20 m

T is the midpoint of PR(hypotenuse) so PT = TR = QT = 40 m

Applying Apollonius theorem in ΔPQT,

$p^2 + 40^2 = 2(QS^2 + 20^2)$     (1)

Applying Apollonius theorem in ΔQRT,

$q^2 + 40^2 = 2(QU^2 + 20^2)$     (2)

On adding equation 1 and 2, we get:

$p^2 + q^2 + 2. \, 40^2 = 2 (QS^2 + QU^2) + 40^2$

$QS^2 + QU^2 = (p^2 + q^2 + 40^2)/2 = (80^2 + 40^2)/2$
                = 4000 m

$QS^2 + QU^2 + QT^2 = 4000$ m $+ 40^2$ m = 5600 m

21. Let Rajesh cut down two circular pieces with center A and B and diameters 20 feet and 10 feet respectively. These two circles touch each other at point D. Let the largest disk that can be cut down from the circular disk has C as its center and its radius is equal to r feet.

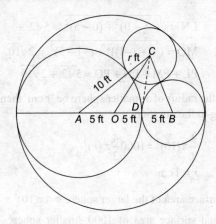

Applying Apollonius theorem in triangle ACD,

$$AC^2 + DC^2 = 2.(AO^2 + OC^2)$$
$$(10 + r)^2 + DC^2 = 2.(5^2 + (15 - r)^2)$$
$$DC^2 - r^2 + 80r = 400 \qquad (a)$$

Applying Apollonius theorem in triangle OCB:

$$(5 + r)^2 + (15 - r)^2 = 2(DC^2 + 5^2)$$
$$DC^2 - r^2 + 10r = 100 \qquad (b)$$

On subtracting (b) from (a), we get

$$70r = 300 \text{ or } r = 30/7 \text{ feet}$$

Diameter = $2r = 2 \times 30/7 = 60/7 = 8.57$ feet

22. Let the cone of radius 'r' and height 'h'.

Volume of the writing equipment

$$= \frac{1}{3}\pi\left(\frac{5}{2} \times 10^{-1}\right)^2 7 = \frac{11}{24}\text{cm}^3$$

330 words can be written with 11/24 cm³ cream.

Number of words that can be written with 1 cm³

$$\text{cream} = 330 \times \frac{24}{11} = 720$$

3/5 liters is equal to $\frac{3}{5} \times 1000 = 600$ cm³.

∴ Number of words that can be written with $\frac{3}{5}$ liter
(600 cm³) = 600 × 720 = 43200.

23.

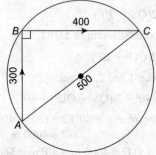

Let initially the fish was released at point A, then it swims toward north and reach at point B then it turns east and hits the pool at point C.

As $\angle ABC = 90°$, then AC must be the diameter of the circle.

Radius of the circle $= \frac{1}{2}(\sqrt{300^2 + 400^2}) = 250$ m

Area of the pool = $\pi(250)^2 = 62500\pi$ m²

24.

Area of ∆ABQ = Area of PQRS − (Area of ABS + Area of BRQ + Area of PAQ)

$$= 6 \times 6 - \left(\frac{1}{2} \times 2 \times 2 + \frac{1}{2} \times 4 \times 6 + \frac{1}{2} \times 4 \times 6\right) = 10 \text{ cm}^2$$

25.

To get an idea about the length of OB there is no need to consider point A.

$$OC = \sqrt{50} = 7.07$$
$$BC = 2$$

In a triangle, the difference of any two sides is always less than that of the 3rd side. So in ∆OBC:

$$OB > 7.07 - 2 > 5.07$$

$OB^2 > 25$. Only option (a) is correct.

26. In a triangle the sum of any two sides > 3rd side. Let the length of the diagonal QS be x cm.

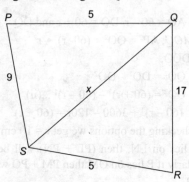

In ∆PQS  $5 + 9 > x$; $x < 14$

In ∆RQS  $x + 5 > 17$; $x > 12$

$$14 > x > 12$$

27. Let A and B are the centers of the circles $C_1$ and $C_2$ respectively.

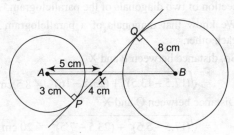

$$PX = \sqrt{5^2 - 3^2} = 4 \text{ cm}$$

$\Delta APX$ and $\Delta BQX$ are similar to each other.

$$\therefore \quad \frac{AP}{BQ} = \frac{PX}{QX}$$

$$QX = 8 \times \frac{4}{3} = 10.66 \text{ cm}$$

$$PQ = PX + XQ = 4 + 10.66 = 14.66 \text{ cm}$$

28. Without Statement (iii), we do not know which angle is a right angle and hence cannot uniquely calculate the value of the Side AC. Hence, we can reject Options (a).

Also Statement (iii) alone does not give us anything. Hence, we can reject option (d).

Options (b) and (c) give us the value of one median and the fact that B is the right angle in the triangle. This is also clearly not sufficient to answer the questions.

For option (e): two medians and angle B is the right angle triangle, we know B is the right angle, we can find AC. Option (e) is correct.

29. Side of the inner square = $\sqrt{8} = 2\sqrt{2}$

Side of the outer square = $\sqrt{9} = 3$

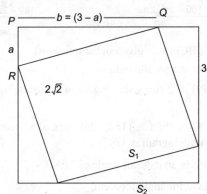

Let the inner square touches the outer square at Q and R and P is one of the four corners of the outer square. Apply Pythagoras theorem in $\Delta QPR$, $PQ^2 + PR^2 = RQ^2$

$$(3 - a)^2 + a^2 = 8$$

On solving we get, a = 0.18 and b = 3 – 0.18 = 2.82. Hence, the value of b/a = 2.82/0.18 = 15.666.

30. The following figure would exemplify the situation, with the pipe attached at a height of h from the apex (bottom) of the cone.

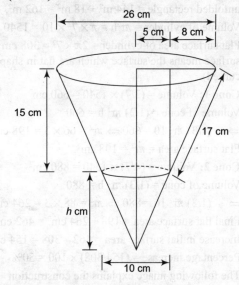

In the above figure the cones with height h and the cone with height h + 15 are similar to each other. Hence using similarity we will get:

$$\frac{10}{26} = \frac{h}{h+15}$$

$\rightarrow 10h + 150 = 26h \rightarrow 16h = 150 \rightarrow h = 9.375$ cm

Based on this information we can then calculate the volume of water that would flow out from the pipe as: Total volume of the cone with height (h + 15) – volume of cone height h.

$$= \frac{1}{3}\pi \left[(13^2 \times (15 + 9.375) - (5^2 \times 9.375)\right]$$

$$= 1295\pi \text{ cm}^3$$

The rate at which the water flows out of the hole per minute is given by:

$$\pi \times (0.5^2 \times 1000) \text{ cm}^3$$

Hence, the required time $= \dfrac{1295\pi}{\pi \times (0.5^2 \times 1000)}$

$$= 5.18 \text{ min}$$

31.

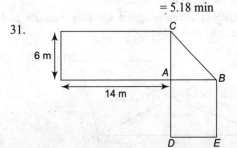

It can be seen from the diagram that actual area = folded area + area of triangular portion (ABC)

Area of triangular portion (ABC) = $\frac{1}{2} \times 6 \times 6 = 18$ m²

So, there is an increase of 18 m². Total area of the unfolded rectangle = 144 m² + 18 m² = 162 m².

32. Volume of cylinder = $\pi r^2 h = \pi \times 7^2 \times 10 = 1540$ cm³

Flat surface area of cylinder = $2\pi \times 7^2 = 308$ cm² (flat surface means the surface which are flat in shape not curved).

**Cone 1:** Volume = (3/7) × 1540 = 660 cm³

Volume of cone = (1/3) $\pi r^2 h$ = 660

⇒ (1/3) $\pi r^2$ 10 = 660 ⇒ $\pi r^2 = 66 \times 3 = 198$ cm²

Flat surface area = $\pi r^2 = 198$ cm²

**Cone 2:** Volume = (4/7) × 1540 = 880 cm³

Volume of cone = (1/3) $\pi r^2 h$ = 880

⇒ (1/3) $\pi r^2$ 10 = 880 ⇒ $\pi r^2 = 88 \times 3 = 264$ cm²

Final flat surface area = 198 + 264 cm² = 462 cm²

Increase in flat surface area = 462 − 308 = 154 cm²

Percentage increase = (154/308) × 100 = 50%

33. The following image explains the construction

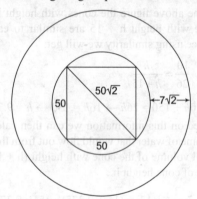

Radius of inner circle = (1/2) × $50\sqrt{2}$ ft. = $25\sqrt{2}$ ft.

Radius of outer circle = $25\sqrt{2} + 7\sqrt{2} = 32\sqrt{2}$ ft.

Area of the path = $\pi \times [(32\sqrt{2}$ ft.$)^2 - (25\sqrt{2}$ ft.$)^2]$
= 2508 ft²

Total cost = 2508 × 100 = ₹ 250800

50% of the total cost = ₹ 125400

34. Let PQRS is a parallelogram and diagonals PR and QS intersect each other at X.

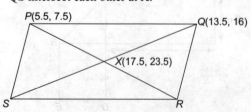

P(13.5, 16) and Q(5.5, 7.5) are adjacent points of the parallelogram and X(17.5, 23.5) is the point of intersection of two diagonals of the parallelogram.

We know that diagonals of a parallelogram bisect each other.

So, distance between P and X

$= \sqrt{(17.5 - 13.5)^2 + (23.5 - 16)^2} = 8.5$ cm

Distance between Q and X

$= \sqrt{(17.5 - 5.5)^2 + (23.5 - 7.5)^2} = 20$ cm

Lengths of diagonals = 8.5 × 2 = 17 cm, 20 × 2 = 40 cm

35. ECD = BCF = 60°

Also, AFB = 60°, BFC = 30°, AFC = 90°

In a 30° − 60° − 90° triangle, sides are in the ratio $1 : \sqrt{3} : 2$ (apply sine rule)

So, in ΔEDC, ED = $10\sqrt{3}$ units

Also, in ΔFBC, BF = 10 units

$FC = \frac{20}{\sqrt{3}}$ units and $BC = \frac{10}{\sqrt{3}}$

In ΔAFC, FC = $\frac{20}{\sqrt{3}}$ units. So, AC = $\frac{20}{\sqrt{3}}$ units

∴ $AD = \left(10 + \frac{40}{\sqrt{3}}\right)$ units

Area of ΔADE = $\frac{1}{2} \times 10\sqrt{3} \times \left(10 + \frac{40}{\sqrt{3}}\right)$ units

= $50(\sqrt{3} + 4)$ sq. units

36. Let us assume that ∠DAB = a, AB = c, AP = b.

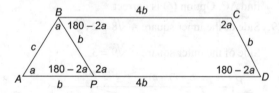

So, ∠BCD = 2 (given in the question)

PBCD is a parallelogram.

∠DPB = 2 (opposite angles of a parallelogram are equal)

∠PBC = ∠PDC = (180 − 2a) (sum of adjacent angles of parallelogram is 180°)

∠DPB is an exterior angle of ΔPAB.

By exterior angle theorem,

∠PBA + ∠PAB = ∠BPD

∠PBA + a = 2a ⇒ ∠PBA = a

Thus, in ΔPAB, PA = PB

∠ABC = a + (180 − 2a) = 180 − a

According to the given question,

Perimeter of ABCD = 10b + c = 1120 and Perimeter of BPDC = 10b = 1000

Solving the two equations, we get b = 100 and c = 120

$\sin(180 - a) = \sin a$

On applying sine rule to $\triangle PAB$,

$$\frac{100}{\sin a} = \frac{120}{\sin(180 - 2a)}$$

$$\Rightarrow \frac{100}{\sin a} = \frac{120}{\sin 2a}$$

$$\Rightarrow \frac{100}{\sin a} = \frac{120}{2 \sin a \cos a}$$

$\cos a = 3/5$

We know that, $1 - \cos^2 a = \sin^2 a$

Putting the value of cos a in this equation,

$$\Rightarrow 1 - (3/5)^2 = \sin^2 a$$

$$\Rightarrow \sin a = 4/5$$

37. Let ABC is the triangle and a circle with center O is inside this triangle in such a way that OA = OB = OC = 625 cm.

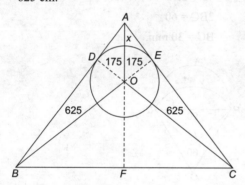

Draw OD ⊥ AB, OE ⊥ AC

In $\triangle$ODB, OD = 175 cm and OB = 625 cm

$$\Rightarrow BD^2 + OD^2 = OB^2$$

$$BD^2 + 175^2 = 625^2$$

$$\Rightarrow BD = 600 \text{ cm.}$$

Similarly, AD = AE = EC = 600 cm

Hence, $\triangle$ABC is an isosceles triangle and AB = AC = 600 + 600 = 1200 cm

So, AF will be perpendicular to BC

In $\triangle$AEO and $\triangle$AFC,

$$\angle OAE = \angle CAF$$

$$\angle AEO = \angle AFC$$

So, $\triangle$AEO ~ $\triangle$AFC

$$\frac{AE}{AF} = \frac{OE}{CF} = \frac{OA}{AC}$$

$$\frac{600}{AF} = \frac{175}{CF} = \frac{625}{1200}$$

So, AF = 1152 cm and CF = 336 cm

$$CB = 2 \times 336 = 672 \text{ cm}$$

Area of $\triangle ABC = \frac{1}{2} \times CB \times AF = \frac{1}{2} \times 672 \times 1152 = 387072 \text{cm}^2$

38.

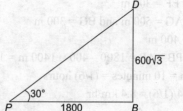

Let's assume at 5.00 p.m., the person is at point P. D is the tip of the minute hand which is 1800 m from P. So, PB = 1800, $\angle$DPB = 30°

$\tan DPB = DB/DP$ or DB = 1800 tan 30° = $600\sqrt{3}$

At 5.10 p.m. the minute hand of the clock moves by 60°and its new position is F. In 10 minutes the person moves from P to A and his new position is A now.

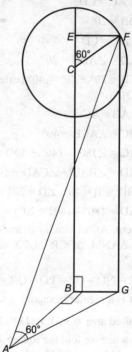

DC = CF = $200\sqrt{3}$ m (Given)

In $\triangle$FEC

$$\frac{FE}{\sin 60°} = \frac{200\sqrt{3}}{\sin 90°} = \frac{EC}{\sin 30°}$$

So, EC = $100\sqrt{3}$ m  and EF = 300 m

$$DE = DC - EC = 200\sqrt{3} - 100\sqrt{3} = 100\sqrt{3} \text{m}$$

$$FG = DB - DE = 600\sqrt{3} - 100\sqrt{3} = 500\sqrt{3} \text{m}$$

In $\triangle$ AFG, $\angle$FAG = 60° and FG = $500\sqrt{3}$ m

Similarly by applying Sine rule in triangle AFG, we get:

AG = 500 m

BG = EF = 300 m

In $\triangle$ABG, AG = 500 m and BG = 300 m

AB = 400 m

PA = PB – AB = 1800 – 400 = 1400 m = 1.4 km

Time taken = 10 minutes = (1/6) hours

Speed = 1.4/(1/6) = 8.4 km/hr

39.

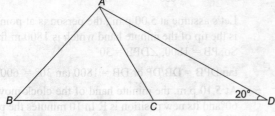

AB = AC = CD

$\angle$ADB = 20°

In $\triangle$ACD: AC = CD

$\angle$CAD = $\angle$ADC = 20°

$\angle$ACB = 20° + 20° = 40° (external angle of triangle ACD).

In $\triangle$ABC: AB = AC

$\angle$ABC = $\angle$ACB = 40°

$\angle$BAC = $\angle$180° – (40° + 40°) = 100°

$\angle$BAD = $\angle$BAC + $\angle$CAD = 100° + 20° = 120°

Or In $\triangle$ABD: $\angle$B = 40°, $\angle$D = 20°

$\angle$BAD = 180° – (40° + 20°) = 120°

40. AB = 54 cm. As all similar triangles are also equilateral so, $\triangle$ANM, $\triangle$OCP, $\triangle$QPX are equilateral triangles.

MN = MR = NO = OP = PQ = QR = 54/3 = 18 cm

MNOPQR is a regular hexagon.

Required area = $3\sqrt{3} \times (18)^2/2 = 486\sqrt{3}$ cm²

41. Each time when we fold the square along its diagonal its area would become half of the original area.

As square piece of paper is folded three times along its diagonal hence, area of the final triangle must be

$\dfrac{1}{2} \times \dfrac{1}{2} \times \dfrac{1}{2} = \dfrac{1}{8}$ of the area of square.

Area of final triangle = $\dfrac{1}{2} \times 10 \times 10 = 50$ cm²

Area of the square = 8 × 50 = 400 cm²

42. Let the length of the side of the triangle be 'a' cm.

Radius of incircle = $a/2\sqrt{3}$

Radius of circumcircle = $a/\sqrt{3}$

According to the question: $\pi[a/\sqrt{3}]^2 - \pi[a/2\sqrt{3}]^2 = 2156$

$a^2/3 - a^2/12 = 2156 \times 7/22 = 98 \times 7$

$3a^2/12 = 98 \times 7$

$a^2 = 4 \times 98 \times 7$

Area of the triangle = $\sqrt{3} \times a^2/4 = \sqrt{3} \times 4 \times 98 \times 7/4$

$= 686\sqrt{3}$ sq. cm.

43. According to the question:

AB + BC + CD = 70          (1)

AB + BD = 45          (2)

AC + CD = 30          (3)

AC + CB + BD = 65          (4)

Equation (1) + Equation (4) gives:

AB + BC + CD + AC + CB + BD = 70 + 65

(AB + BD) + 2BC + (AC + CD) = 135

From equation (3) and (4) we get:

45 + 2BC + 30 = 135

2BC = 60

BC = 30 min.

44.

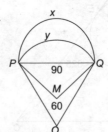

Here, curve X creates 90° and curve Y creates 60°.

Let the radius of curve X = x and radius of curve Y = y

For curve Y, $2\pi y \times 60/360 = 10\pi$ or y = 30.

In triangle POQ:

On applying sine rule in triangle POQ

PQ/sin 60° = PO/sin 60°

PQ = PO = 30 cm

In triangle PMQ: $\angle$PMQ = 90°, *PM = QM*

Hence, $\angle MPQ = \angle MQP$ = 45°

PQ/sin90° = PM/sin 45°

PM = x = $15\sqrt{2}$

Finally, length of curve X = $2\pi x/4 = 2 \times 15\sqrt{2}\pi/4 = 15\pi/\sqrt{2}$. Option (a) is the correct answer.

45.

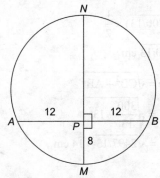

AP = PB = AB/2 = 24/2 = 12 cm.

AP × BP = PM × PN

12 × 12 = 8PN

PN = 18 cm.

46. Least possible value of SR = 1,
If SR = 1, PQ = 2.

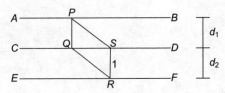

Area of the quadrilateral PQRS = area of triangle

PQS + area of triangle QSR = $\frac{1}{2} \times 2 \times QS + \frac{1}{2} \times 1 \times$
QS = 30

QS = 20

QR = $\sqrt{20^2 + 1^2} = \sqrt{401}$

So, QR is slightly greater than 20. Option (e).

47.

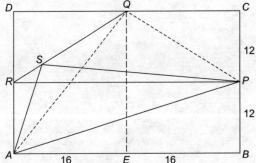

Meet points A and Q, Q and P and Q and E with dotted lines.

Area of ΔARQ = $\frac{1}{2} \times AR \times RQ \times \sin \angle ARQ$

Area of ΔARS = $\frac{1}{2} \times AR \times RS \times \sin \angle ARQ$

As SR : RQ = 1 : (1 + 3) = 1:4.

Area of ΔARS = $\frac{1}{4}$ Area of ΔARQ

Similarly we can prove: Area of ΔPQS = $\frac{3}{4}$ Area of ΔPQR

Area of ΔAPS = Area of ▭ABCD − Area of ΔAPB − Area of ΔRDQ − Area of ΔQCP − Area of ΔSQP − Area of ΔARS = Area of ▭ABCD − Area of ΔAPB − Area of ΔRDQ − Area of ΔQCP − $\frac{1}{4}$ Area of ΔARQ − ¾(Area of ΔPQR)

Let the length of side AB = a = CD.

and   BC = b = AD.

Area of ΔARQ = Area of rectangle ▭ADQE − Area of ΔDRQ − Area of ΔAQE

Area of ΔARQ = $\frac{ab}{2} - \frac{1}{2} \times \frac{a}{2} \times b - \frac{1}{2} \times \frac{a}{2} \times \frac{b}{2}$

$= \frac{ab}{2} - \frac{ab}{4} - \frac{ab}{8} = \frac{ab}{8}$

Area of ΔPQR = $\frac{1}{2} \times a \times \frac{b}{2} = \frac{ab}{4}$

Area of ΔAPS = $ab - \frac{1}{2} \times a \times \frac{b}{2} - \frac{1}{2} \times \frac{a}{2} \times \frac{b}{2} - \frac{1}{2}$

$\times \frac{a}{2} \times \frac{b}{2} - \frac{1}{4} \times \frac{ab}{8} - \frac{3}{4} \times \frac{ab}{4}$

= ab − ab/4 − ab/8 − ab/8 − ab/32 − 3ab/16

Required ratio = Area of ΔAPS/Area of ▭ABCD

= 9ab/32ab

= 9/32 = 36/128

Option (a) is correct.

48. Let point A be the apex of the pyramid. C and D are the opposite vertices of the square base. Draw AB ⊥ CD.

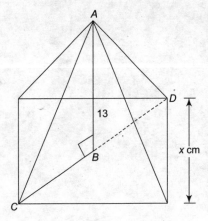

Volume of pyramid = $\frac{1}{3} \times$ area of base × height

Let the side of the square = x cm.

$$\frac{1}{3} \times x^2 \times 13 = 200$$

$$x^2 = 600/13 \Rightarrow x = \sqrt{600/13}$$

$$CD = x\sqrt{2} = \sqrt{600/13} \times \sqrt{2}$$

$$= \sqrt{1200/13}$$

CB = CD/2 (where B is the mid point of CD)

$$CB = (\sqrt{1200/13}) \times \frac{1}{2}$$

$$CB = \sqrt{300/13} \text{ cm}$$

Slant edge $= \sqrt{CB^2 + AB^2}$

$$= \sqrt{\frac{300}{13} + 13^2}$$

$$= \sqrt{2497/13} \approx 14 \text{ cm}$$

# Algebra

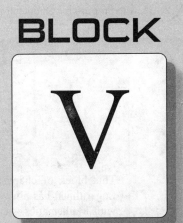

BLOCK

V

# ...BACK TO SCHOOL

This block of chapters (consisting of Functions, Inequalities, Quadratic and other Equations and Logarithms) has always been a source of discomfort for students who have had negative experiences with Mathematics. At the same time students who have had a positive experience with mathematics throughout their school, junior college and college years find these chapters extremely easy.

Throughout my experience in training students preparing for the CAT exam and other aptitude exams like CMAT, SNAP, IIFT, MAT, XAT, etc. I have always critically tried to understand the key mental representations that differentiate the two categories of students I have mentioned above—how is it that two students who are basically similarly talented with similar IQs be so different when it comes to Higher Maths?

The reason I am talking about this issue is that Block V consists of some of the most critical areas of the entire QA Section for the CAT exam. Besides the XLRI entrance test, XAT also has a very high focus on this block of chapters. Hence, this is one area where you simply cannot allow yourselves to remain in the *'I cannot solve Block V questions'* category if you want to seriously take a crack at the CAT Exam. However to enable students who are weak at Maths to move from the 'I cannot' to the 'I can' category in this block of chapters you will first have to believe that this can happen.

And the good news is that in my experience of having trained over 50000 students for aptitude examinations, I have seen a lot of mediocre students in Maths transit from being initially poor at the chapters of this block to becoming strong in the same.

If you belong to such a category of students what you first need to understand is that the reason for your inability in Higher Maths lies in the way you have approached it up to now. There is simply no reason that a better approach will not help you.

## WHAT APPROACH CHANGE DO YOU NEED?

To put it simply—rather than trying to study these Higher Maths chapters in so called Mathematical language, you need to study the same in plain logical language (with as little Maths as possible). The following write up is an attempt at the same. My attempt in the following part of this section is to give you in as simple language as possible some of the missing technology that makes you consider yourself weak at Maths (esp. this block of chapters).

The following is a list of startup issues you need to resolve in your mind in order to make yourself comfortable with this block of chapters.

ISSUE 1: The $X - Y$ Plot:
ISSUE 2: Locus of points
ISSUE 3: What is an equation?
ISSUE 4: Equations and Functions:
ISSUE 5:How Inequalities relate to Graphs of Functions?

## Let us Now Start to Look at these Issues One by One

***ISSUE 1: The X – Y Plot:***   The need for an $X - Y$ plot essentially arises out of the need to measure anything which cannot be measured in a single dimension.

*Contd*

For instance, any object that can be represented on a straight line (like a rope, a tape etc.) could be easily represented on the number line itself. However, when you are required to represent any two dimensional figures (like table top, a book etc.) simply unidimensional representations (which can be done on the number line only) are not sufficient.

You are required to be able to represent things in two dimensions.

For this purpose, a vertical line is drawn from point '0' of the number line. This line is perpendicular to the number line and is called the $Y$-axis (which in plain language terms can be understood as the axis which provides the vital second dimension of measurement which helps us describe plain figures better.)

In this situation, the horizontal line (which we know as the number line) is called the $X$-axis and the diagram which emerges represents what is known as the $X - Y$ plane and is also called as the $X - Y$ plot.

The number line (The $X$-axis) has a positive measurement direction on the right side of zero (and keeps going to a mathematically defined, in reality non-existent point called infinity.) On the left side of zero the $X$ axis shows negative measurements and keeps going to negative infinity.

In a similar manner, the $Y$-axis starts from 0 and moves upwards to positive infinity and moves downwards to negative infinity.

The following figures illustrate this point.

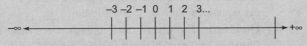

**Fig. 1**  The number line (Also the X axis)

As can be seen the $X - Y$ plot divides the plane into 4 parts (Quadrants). The origin is the point where both $X$ and $Y$ are zero.

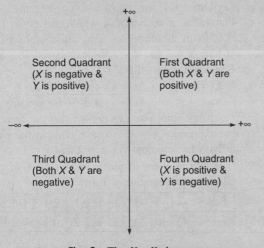

**Fig. 2**  The $X - Y$ plot

## Plotting a Point on the X – Y Plot

Suppose we have to plot the point (2, 3) on the $X - Y$ plot. In order to do so, we first need to understand what $x = 2$ means on the $X - Y$ chart. On the $X - Y$ plot if you start from the $x = 2$ point on the $X$-axis and draw a line parallel to the $Y$-axis you will get a set of points which represent a constant value of $x$ (=2). Similarly for $y = 3$, draw a line parallel to the $X$-axis from the $y = 3$ point on the $Y$-axis.

In this situation, the point of intersection between these two lines will be the point (2, 3).

I would encourage the reader to try to draw the figure as described above.

***ISSUE 2: Locus of Points***  In the above situation we have come across a set of points which represents $x = 2$. In mathematics lingo, a set of points is also referred to as a locus of points.

***ISSUE 3: What is an Equation?***  Consider the following:

    (a) $2x + 3 = 0$
    (b) $x^2 - 5x + 6 = 0$
    (c) $4x^3 - 3x^2 - 11x - 18 = 0$

In each of the above cases, we have a situation where there is an equality between what is written on the left side of the equality sign and the right side of the equality sign. i.e. LHS = RHS (Left Hand Side = Right Hand Side)

This is the basic definition of an equation.

## All Equations have solutions

Consider the first equation above:

Here you have: $2x + 3 = 0 \rightarrow 2x = -3 \rightarrow x = -3/2$
i.e. $x = -1.5$

This means that at the value $x = -1.5$, the condition of the equation (i.e. LHS = RHS) is satisfied. This value of $x$ is called the 'solution' or the 'root' of the equation.

---

**Note:**  The equation we have just seen had a highest power of '$x$' as 1. Such equations are called as linear equations. [We shall come to this issue of why they are called as linear equations shortly]. What you need to remember at this stage is that linear equations have only one solution. (or Root as mathematicians prefer to call it.)

---

***ISSUE 4: Equations and Functions:***  Before we move ahead into the second and third equations given above, let us first try to connect equations and functions.

If you remember we studied in school a chapter called as the equation of a straight line. For instance, parallel to the equation $2x + 3 = 0$ we have $y = 2x + 3$ (which was defined as the equation of a straight line – hence $2x + 3 = 0$ is called a linear equation).

In $y = 2x + 3$ we have a consistent relationship between the values of $x$ and the corresponding values of $y$ that we could get.

Thus for $y = 2x + 3$, we can create the following table giving us the specific points which satisfy the equation as below:

| $x$ | −3 | −2 | −1 | 0 | 1 | 2 |
|---|---|---|---|---|---|---|
| $y$ | −3 | −1 | +1 | 3 | 5 | 7 |

If you plot these points on the $X - Y$ plane, you will get the following figure.

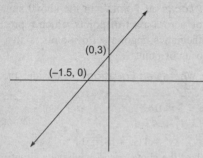

All the points in the table above will lie on this line. The locus of points which are commonly represented by $y = 2x + 3$ is represented by the line above.

In higher mathematics instead of calling expressions like $y = 2x + 3$ as linear equations, they are called as linear functions. (Perhaps the reason for this is that in higher maths, we are interested in identifying relationships and behaviors of interdependent variables especially how a change in one variable changes the other variables. Hence, while equations which are of the form $f(x) = 0$ deal with only one variable $x$, functions represent relationships between two or more variables. They are denoted in Maths as $y = f(x)$ [Reads as: $y$ is a function of $x$] or $y = f(a, b)$ [Read as: $y$ is function of $a$ and $b$].

In general whenever we have any expression in $x$ (denoted by $f(x)$) we can use it either as

$$y = f(x) \text{ [which is what a function is !!]}$$

$$f(x) = 0 \text{ [An equation]}$$

## Other Principles Related to Functions and Equations

(a) Every function of the form $y = f(x)$ can be plotted on the $X - Y$ plane.

For instance, consider what we did with the function $y = 2x + 3$. [This form of writing a function is called as its analytical representation, while the graph plotted is called as the graphical representation of the function.]

We first created a table where we started putting values of $x$ and getting the respective value for $y$. Thus, we got a locus of points (as shown in the table above) which represented the function $y = 2x + 3$. This representation of the function is called as the analytical representation of the function.

Further, the line representing $y = 2x + 3$ was plotted on the $X - Y$ plane. This is called as the graphical representation of the function.

(b) The point/points where the graph of the function $y = f(x)$ cuts the $x$-axis, represents the solution of the equation $f(x) = 0$.

Thus, if you noticed $y = 2x + 3$ cuts the $x$ axis at $x = -1.5$. At the same time the root or solution of the equation $2x + 3 = 0$ is $x = -1.5$.

This is not accidental but will happen in each and every case. Thus, in general you can state that the point where the graph of a function $y = f(x)$ cuts the $x$-axis is the solution of the equation $f(x) = 0$. [**Note:** This will be true for every expression in $x$-irrespective of the highest power of '$x$' in the expression.]

It is a consequence of this logic, that linear functions will cut the $x$-axis only once (since linear equations have only one solution.)

(c) **Quadratic Equations and Quadratic Functions:** Let us now pick up the equation: $x^2 - 5x + 6 = 0$.

If you solve this equation you will get the solution of this equation at two values of $x$. viz. at $x = 2$ as well as at $x = 3$.

[Remember, the root/solution of an equation is that value of the variable which makes the LHS = RHS in the equation. You can easily see that at both $x = 2$ and $x = 3$ the expression $x^2 - 5x + 6$ yields a value of 0.

At $x = 2$, $x^2 - 5x + 6 \rightarrow 2^2 - 5 \times 2 + 6 = 0$
At $x = 3$, $x^2 - 5x + 6 \rightarrow 3^2 - 5 \times 3 + 6 = 0$

At this point you can predict that the graph of the expression $y = x^2 - 5x + 6$ will cut the $x$ axis at both these points viz. $x = 2$ and $x = 3$.

If you now try to plot $y = x^2 - 5x + 6$, your tabular representation will be:

| $x$ | −5 | −4 | −3 | −2 | −1 | 0 | 1 | 2 | 3 | 4 | 5 |
|---|---|---|---|---|---|---|---|---|---|---|---|
| $y$ | 56 | 42 | 30 | 20 | 12 | 6 | 2 | 0 | 0 | 2 | 6 |

This locus of points will look like the figure below:

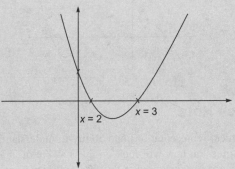

Naturally, the graph cuts the x axis at $x = 2$ and $x = 3$.

## Special Note on Quadratic Equations

Since all quadratic equations have two solutions, graph of the function for the same expression should cut the x-axis at two points.

However, this might not always be true.

For instance, look at the following graphs.

**Case 1:**

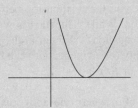

In this case the roots are said to be real and equal.

**Case 2:**

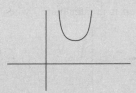

In this case the roots of the quadratic equation are imaginary with respect to the x-axis.

---

**Note:** You also need to know that quadratic functions can also look inverted as shown below. This occurs when the coefficient of $x^2$ is negative.

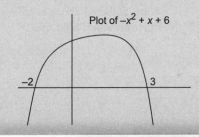

Plot of $-x^2 + x + 6$

In general, quadratic equations then can take any of six shapes (with respect to the x-axis):

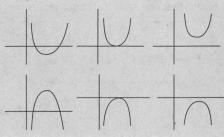

**(d)** How cubic functions look: Cubic functions have $x^3$ as their highest power of x. Cubic equations have three solutions and hence cubic functions will cut the x-axis thrice.

They can look like:

## CASE 1: When the Coefficient of $x^3$ is Positive

**(A)** Cubic functions with 3 distinct real roots (e.g.: $y = x^3 - 6x^2 + 11x - 6$)

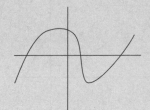

**(B)** Cubic function with three real and equal roots. e.g.: $y = (x - 1)^3$

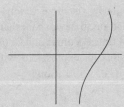

**(C)** Cubic function with one real and two imaginary roots

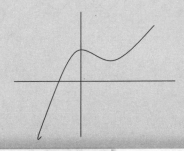

## CASE 2: When the Coefficient of $x^3$ is Negative

(A) Cubic function with 3 distinct real roots.

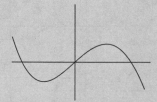

(B) Cubic function with three real and equal roots.

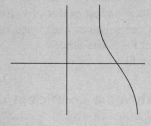

(C) Cubic function with one real and two imaginary roots.

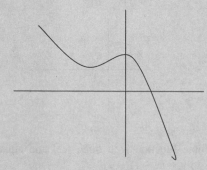

You can similarly visualize functions with highest power 4, 5 and so on to have shapes such that they can cut the $x$ – axis 4 times, 5 times and so on. The following are standard figures for expressions with

(a) Degree 4 (i.e. $x^4$) [4 roots]

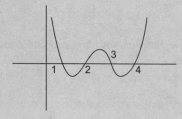

(b) Degree 5 [5 roots]

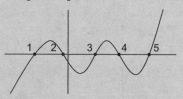

## A Key Note

Graphical representations and ability to understand how an expression in $x$ will look on the $X - Y$ plot is a very key factor in your moving towards proficiency and self dependence in this crucial block of chapters. Hence, I would encourage you to try to plot the graphs of as many $y = f(x)$ functions as you can imagine. To give you a target, I would recommend a minimum of 100 graphs to be plotted by you. Only then would you be able to move to a level of comfort in visualizing graphs.

## ISSUE 5: How Inequalities Relate to Graphs of Functions?

We have just seen the relationship between a function and an equation. While a function is written in the $y = f(x)$ form, an equation is written in the $f(x) = 0$ form.

An inequality (or an inequation) can be written in the form $f(x) > 0$ or $f(x) \geq 0$.

Thus, if we say $x^2 - 5x + 6 > 0$, we are looking for those values of $x$ where the above expression yields values above 0.

Going back to the graph for $x^2 - 5x + 6$, it is obvious that the function is greater than 0 when $x > 3$ or $x < 2$.

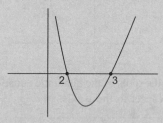

In such a case, the solution of the inequality $x^2 - 5x + 6 > 0$ becomes $x > 3$ or $x < 2$.

Understand here that when we are solving an inequality all we are bothered about is to see at what values of $x$ does the inequality hold true.

## Pre-assessment Test

***Directions for Questions 1 to 3:*** Answer the questions on the basis of the tables given below.

Two binary operations (+) and * are defined over the set $\{i, j, k, l, m\}$ as per the following tables:

| (+) | $i$ | $j$ | $k$ | $l$ | $m$ |
|-----|-----|-----|-----|-----|-----|
| $i$ | $i$ | $j$ | $k$ | $l$ | $m$ |
| $j$ | $j$ | $k$ | $l$ | $m$ | $i$ |
| $k$ | $k$ | $l$ | $m$ | $i$ | $j$ |
| $l$ | $l$ | $m$ | $i$ | $j$ | $k$ |
| $m$ | $m$ | $i$ | $j$ | $k$ | $l$ |

| * | $i$ | $j$ | $k$ | $l$ | $m$ |
|---|-----|-----|-----|-----|-----|
| $i$ | $i$ | $i$ | $i$ | $i$ | $i$ |
| $j$ | $i$ | $j$ | $k$ | $l$ | $m$ |
| $k$ | $i$ | $k$ | $m$ | $j$ | $l$ |
| $l$ | $i$ | $l$ | $j$ | $l$ | $k$ |
| $m$ | $i$ | $m$ | $l$ | $k$ | $j$ |

Thus according to the first table $k$ (+) $l = i$ while according to the second table $l * m = k$, and so on. Also, let $k^2 = k * k$, $l^3 = l * l * l$, and so on.

1. What is the smallest positive integer $n$ such that $k^n = l$?
   (a) 4       (b) 5
   (c) 2       (d) 3

2. Upon simplification $m$ (+) $[k * \{k$ (+) $(k * k)\}]$ equals
   (a) $j$       (b) $k$
   (c) $l$       (d) $m$

3. Upon simplification, $\{i^{10} * (k^{10}$ (+) $l^9)\}$ (+) $j^8$ equals
   (a) $j$       (b) $k$
   (c) $l$       (d) $m$

4. What is the sum of $n$ terms in the series: $\log m + \log (m^2/n) + \log (m^4/n^3) + \ldots\ldots$
   (a) $\log [n^{(n-1)}/m^{(n+1)}]^{n/2}$
   (b) $\log [m^m/n^n]^{n/2}$
   (c) $\log [m^{(1-n)}/n^{(1-m)}]^{n/2}$
   (d) $\log [m^{(n+1)}/n^{(n-1)}]^{n/2}$

5. If $n$ is such that $36 \le n \le 72$, then $x = (n^2 + 2\sqrt{n}(n+4) + 16)/(n + 4\sqrt{n} + 4)$ satisfies:
   (a) $20 < x < 54$       (b) $23 < x < 58$
   (c) $25 < x < 64$       (d) $28 < x < 60$

6. A real number $x$ is such that it satisfies the condition: $2 - 1/m < x \le 4 + 1/m$, for every positive integer $m$. Which of the following best describes the range of values that $x$ can take:

   (a) $1 < x < 5$       (b) $1 < x \le 4$
   (c) $1 < x \le 5$       (d) $1 \le x \le 4$

7. If $1/3 \log_3 M + 3 \log_3 N = 1 + \log_{0.008} 5$, then:
   (a) $M^9 = 9/N$       (b) $N^9 = 9/M$
   (c) $M^3 = 3/N$       (d) $N^9 = 3/M$

8. If $f(x) = \log \{(1 + x)/(1 - x)\}$, then $f(x) + f(y)$ is:
   (a) $f(x + y)$
   (b) $f\{(x + y)/(1 + xy)\}$
   (c) $(x + y) f\{1/(1 + xy)\}$
   (d) $f(x) + f(y)/(1 + xy)$

9. The nth element of a series is represented as:
   $X_n = (-2)^n X_{n-1}$
   If $X_0 = x$ and $x > 0$ then the following is always true.
   (a) $X_n$ is positive if $n$ is even
   (b) $X_n$ is positive if $n$ is odd
   (c) $X_n$ is negative if $n$ is even
   (d) None of these

10. The number of roots common between the two equations $x^3 + 3x^2 + 4x + 7 = 0$ and $x^3 + 2x^2 + 7x + 5 = 0$ is:
   (a) 0       (b) 1
   (c) 2       (d) 3

11. If $|y| \ge 1$ and $x = -|a|\, y$, then which one of the following is necessarily true?
   (a) $a - xy < 0$       (b) $a - xy \ge 0$
   (c) $a - xy > 0$       (d) $a - xy \le 0$

12. Consider the sets $T_n = \{n, n + 1, n + 2, n + 3, n + 4\}$, where $n = 1, 2, 3, \ldots\ldots, 96$. How many of these sets do not contain 6 or any integral multiple thereof (i.e., any one of the numbers 6, 12, 18, \ldots\ldots)?
   (a) 16       (b) 15
   (c) 14       (d) 13

13. If $13m + 1 < 2n$, and $n + 3 = 5y^2$, then:
   (a) $m$ is necessarily less than $n$
   (b) $m$ is necessarily greater than $n$
   (c) $m$ is necessarily equal to $n$
   (d) None of the above is necessarily true

14. If both $a$ and $b$ belong to the set $\{1, 2, 3, 4\}$, then the number of equations of the form $ax^2 + bx + 1 = 0$ having real roots is:
   (a) 10       (b) 7
   (c) 6       (d) 12

15. If three positive real numbers $x$, $y$ and $z$ satisfy $y - x = z - y$ and $xyz = 4$, then what is the minimum possible value of $y$?
   (a) $2^{1/3}$       (b) $2^{2/3}$
   (c) $2^{1/4}$       (d) $2^{3/4}$

16. There are 12 towns grouped into four zones with three towns per zone. It is intended to connect the

towns with telephone lines such that every two towns are connected with three direct lines if they belong to the same zone, and with only one direct line otherwise. How many direct telephone lines are required?

(a) 72      (b) 90
(c) 96      (d) 144

17. If $\log_{10} x + \log_{10} x = 2 \log_x 10$, then a possible value of $x$ is given by:

(a) 10      (b) 1/10
(c) 1/100      (d) None of these

18. Find the area enclosed by the region in sq. units described by $0 \leq x \leq 5$ and $0 \leq |y| \leq 8$.

(a) 40      (b) 80
(c) 160      (d) 120

19. The value of the expression $[(1/2) + (1/100)] + [(1/2) + (2/100)] + [(1/2) + (3/100)] + \ldots[(1/2) + (103/100)]$ is equal to

(a) 53      (b) 54
(c) 52      (d) None of these

20. The number of non-negative real roots of $2^x - x - 1 = 0$ equals:

(a) 0      (b) 1
(c) 2      (d) 3

21. Let $a, b, c$ and $d$ be four integers such that $a + b + c + d = 4m + 1$ where $m$ is a positive integer. Given $m$, which one of the following is necessarily true?

(a) The minimum possible value of $a^2 + b^2 + c^2 + d^2$ is $4m^2 - 2m + 1$
(b) The minimum possible value of $a^2 + b^2 + c^2 + d^2$ is $4m^2 + 2m + 1$
(c) The maximum possible value of $a^2 + b^2 + c^2 + d^2$ is $4m^2 - 2m + 1$

(d) The maximum possible value of $a^2 + b^2 + c^2 + d^2$ is $4m^2 + 2m + 1$

22. The 288th term of the series $a, b, b, c, c, c, d, d, d, d, e, e, e, e, e, f, f, f, f, f, f \ldots$ is

(a) $u$      (b) $v$
(c) $w$      (d) $x$

23. Find the area enclosed by the curve $|x| + |y| = 4$.

(a) 24      (b) 28
(c) 32      (d) 36

24. Let $y = \min \{(x + 8), (6 - x)\}$. If $x \, \varepsilon \, R$, what is the maximum value of $y$?

(a) 8      (b) 7
(c) 6      (d) 10

25. Let $S$ be the set of integers {3, 11, 19, 27, ...... 451, 459, 467} and $M$ be a subset of $S$ such that no two elements of $M$ add up to 470. The maximum possible number of elements in $M$ is:

(a) 32      (b) 28
(c) 29      (d) 30

## ANSWER KEY

| | | | |
|---|---|---|---|
| 1. (d) | 2. (a) | 3. (a) | 4. (d) |
| 5. (d) | 6. (c) | 7. (b) | 8. (b) |
| 9. (d) | 10. (a) | 11. (b) | 12. (a) |
| 13. (d) | 14. (b) | 15. (b) | 16. (b) |
| 17. (a) | 18. (b) | 19. (b) | 20. (c) |
| 21. (b) | 22. (d) | 23. (c) | 24. (b) |
| 25. (d) | | | |

# Functions

Quantities of various characters such as length, area, mass, temperature and volume either have constant values or they vary based on the values of other quantities. Such quantities are called constant and variable respectively.

Function is a concept of mathematics that studies the dependence between variable quantities in the process of their change. For instance, with a change in the side of a square, the area of the square also varies. The question of how the change in the side of the square affects the area is answered by a mathematical relationship between the area of the square and the side of the square.

Let the variable $x$ take on numerical values from the set $D$.

**A function is a rule that attributes to every number $x$ from $D$ one definite number $y$ where $y$ belongs to the set of real numbers.**

Here, $x$ is called the independent variable and $y$ is called the dependent variable.

The set $D$ is referred to as the *domain of definition* of the function and the set of all values attained by the variable $y$ is called the *range of the function*.

In other words, a variable $y$ is said to be the value of function of a variable $x$ in the domain of definition D if to each value of $x$ belonging to this domain there corresponds a definite value of the variable $y$.

This is symbolised as $y = f(x)$ where $f$ denotes the rule by which $y$ varies with $x$.

## 🎧 BASIC METHODS OF REPRESENTING FUNCTIONS

### Analytical Representation

This is essentially representation through a formula.

This representation could be a uniform formula in the entire domain, for example, $y = 3x^2$

or

by several formulae which are different for different parts of the domain.

**Example:**   $y = 3x^2$ if $x < 0$
and            $y = x^2$ if $x > 0$

In analytical representations, the domain of the function is generally understood as the set of values for which the equation makes sense.

For instance, if $y = x^2$ represents the area of a square then we get that the domain of the function is $x > 0$.

Problems based on the analytical representation of functions have been a favourite for the XLRI exam and have also become very common in the CAT over the past few years. Other exams are also moving towards asking questions based on this representation of functions.

### Tabular Representation of Functions

For representing functions through a table, we simply write down a sequence of values of the independent variable $x$ and then write down the corresponding values of the dependent variable $y$. Thus, we have tables of logarithms, trigonometric values and so forth, which are essentially tabular representations of functions.

The types of problems that appear based on tabular representation have been restricted to questions that give a table and then ask the student to trace the appropriate analytical representation or graph of the function based on the table.

### Graphical Representation of Functions

This is a very important way to represent functions. The process is: on the coordinate $xy$ plane for every value of $x$ from the domain $D$ of the function, a point $P(x, y)$ is constructed whose abscissa is $x$ and whose ordinate $y$ is got by putting the particular value of $x$ in the formula representing the function.

For example, for plotting the function $y = x^2$, we first decide on the values of $x$ for which we need to plot the graph.

Thus we can take $x = 0$ and get $y = 0$ (means the point $(0, 0)$ is on the graph).

Then for $x = 1$, $y = 1$; for $x = 2$, $y = 4$; for $x = 3$, $y = 9$ and for $x = -1$ $y = 1$; for $x = -2$, $y = 4$, and so on.

## EVEN AND ODD FUNCTIONS

### Even Functions

Let a function $y = f(x)$ be given in a certain interval. The function is said to be even if for any value of $x$

→
$$f(x) = f(-x)$$

Properties of even functions:

(a) The sum, difference, product and quotient of an even function is also an even function.

(b) The graph of an even function is symmetrical about the $y$-axis.

However, when $y$ is the independent variable, it is symmetrical about the $x$-axis. In other words, if $x = f(y)$ is an even function, then the graph of this function will be symmetrical about the $x$-axis. Example: $x = y^2$.

Examples of even functions: $y = x^2$, $y = x^4$, $y = -3x^8$, $y = x^2 + 3$, $y = x^4/5$, $y = |x|$ are all even functions.

The symmetry about the $y$-axis of an even function is illustrated below.

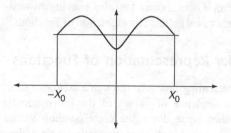

### Odd Functions

Let a function $y = f(x)$ be given in a certain interval. The function is said to be odd if for any value of $x$

$$f(x) = -f(-x)$$

Properties of odd functions.

(a) The sum and difference of an odd function is an odd function.

(b) The product and quotient of an odd function is an even function.

(c) The graph of an odd function is symmetrical about the origin.

The symmetry about the origin of an odd function is illustrated below.

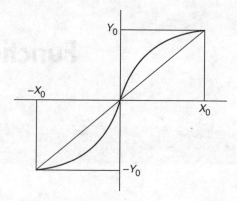

Examples of odd functions $y = x^3$, $y = x^5$, $y = x^3 + x$, $y = x/(x^2 + 1)$.

*Not all functions need be even or odd. However, every function can be represented as the sum of an even function and an odd function.*

### Inverse of a Function

Let there be a function $y = f(x)$, which is defined for the domain $D$ and has a range $R$.

Then, by definition, for every value of the independent variable $x$ in the domain $D$, there exists a certain value of the dependent variable $y$. In certain cases the same value of the dependent variable $y$ can be got for different values of $x$. For example, if $y = x^2$, then for $x = 2$ and $x = -2$ give the value of $y$ as 4.

In such a case, the inverse function of the function $y = f(x)$ *does not exist.*

However, if a function $y = f(x)$ is such that for every value of $y$ (from the range of the function $R$) there corresponds one and only one value of $x$ from the domain $D$, then the inverse function of $y = f(x)$ exists and is given by $x = g(y)$. Here it can be noticed that $x$ becomes the dependent variable and $y$ becomes the independent variable. Hence, this function has a domain $R$ and a range $D$.

Under the above situation, the graph of $y = f(x)$ and $x = g(y)$ are one and the same.

However, when denoting the inverse of the function, we normally denote the independent variable by $y$ and, hence, the inverse function of $y = f(x)$ is denoted by $y = g(x)$ and not by $x = g(y)$.

The graphs of two inverse functions when this change is used are symmetrical about the line $y = x$ (which is the bisector of the first and the third quadrants).

***Graphs of Some Simple Functions*** The student is advised to familiarise himself/herself with the following figures.

Graphs of $y = b$, $y = kx$, $y = kx + b$, $y = kx - b$.

Note the shifting of the line when a positive number $b$ is added and subtracted to the function's equation.

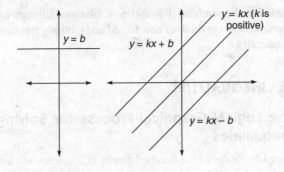

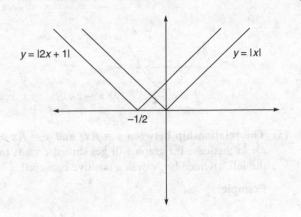

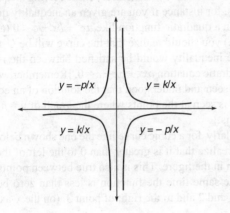

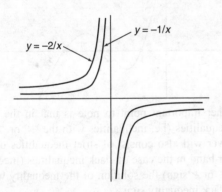

## SHIFTING OF GRAPHS

The ability to visualize how graphs shift when the basic analytical expression is changed is a very important skill. For instance if you knew how to visualize the graph of $(x + 2)^2 - 5$, it will definitely add a lot of value to your ability to solve questions of functions and all related chapters of block 5 graphically.

In order to be able to do so, you first need to understand the following points clearly:

**(1)** **The relationship between the graph of $y = f(x)$ and $y = f(x) + c$ (where $c$ represents a positive constant.):** The shape of the graph of $y = f(x) + c$ will be the same as that of the $y = f(x)$ graph. The only difference would be in terms of the fact that $f(x) + c$ is shifted $c$ units up on the $x - y$ plot.

The following figure will make it clear for you:

**Example:** Relationship between $y = x^2$ and $y = x^2 + 2$.

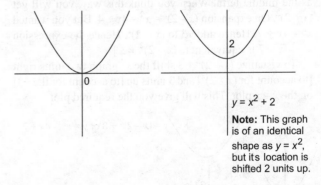

$y = x^2 + 2$

**Note:** This graph is of an identical shape as $y = x^2$, but its location is shifted 2 units up.

**(2)** **The relationship between $y = f(x)$ and $y = f(x) - c$:** In this case while the shape remains the same, the position of the graph gets shifted $c$ units down.

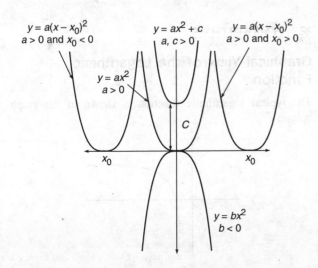

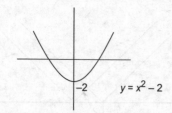

$y = x^2 - 2$

**(3) The relationship between $y = f(x)$ and $y = f(x + c)$:** In this case the graph will get shifted $c$ units to the left. (Remember, $c$ was a positive constant)

**Example:**

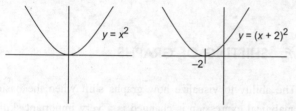

$y = x^2$      $y = (x + 2)^2$

**(4) The relationship between $y = f(x)$ and $y = f(x - c)$:** In this case the graph will get shifted $c$ units to the right on the $x - y$ plane.

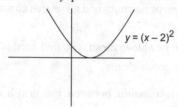

$y = (x - 2)^2$

## COMBINING MOVEMENTS

It is best understood through an example:

Visualizing a graph for a function like $x^2 - 4x + 7$.

First convert $x^2 - 4x + 7$ into $(x - 2)^2 + 3$

[**Note:** In order to do this conversion, the key point of your thinking should be on the $-4x$. Your first focus has to be to put down a bracket $(x - a)^2$ which on expansion gives $- 4x$ as the middle term. When you think this way, you will get $(x - 2)^2$. On expansion $(x - 2)^2 = x^2 - 4x + 4$. But you wanted $x^2 - 4x + 7$. Hence add +3 to $(x - 2)^2$. Hence the expression $x^2 - 4x + 7$ is equivalent to $(x - 2)^2 + 3$.]

To visualize $(x - 2)^2 + 3$ shift the $x^2$ graph two units right [to account for $(x - 2)^2$] and 3 units up [to account for the +3] on the $x - y$ plot. This will give you the required plot.

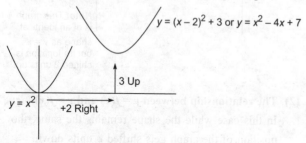

$y = (x - 2)^2 + 3$ or $y = x^2 - 4x + 7$

3 Up

$y = x^2$    +2 Right

**Task for the student:** I would now like to challenge and encourage you to think of how to add and multiply functions graphically.

## INEQUALITIES

### The Logical Graphical Process for Solving Inequalities

Your knowledge of the standard graphs of functions and how these shift can help you immensely while solving inequalities.

Thus, for instance if you are given an inequality question based on a quadratic function like $ax^2 + bx + c < 0$ (and $a$ is positive) you should realize that the curve will be $U$ shaped. And the inequality would be satisfied between the roots of the quadratic equation $ax^2 + bx + c = 0$. [Remember, we have already seen and understood that the solution of an equation $f(x) = 0$ is seen at the points where the graph of $y = f(x)$ cuts the $x$ axis.]

Similarly, for a cubic curve like the one shown below, you should realize that it is greater than 0 to the left of the point 1 shown in the figure. This is also true between points 2 and 3. At the same time the function is less than zero between points 1 and 2 and to the right of point 3. (on the x-axis.)

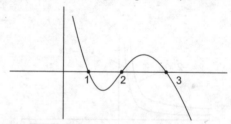

Another important point to note is that in the case of strict inequalities (i.e. inequalities with the '<' or '>' sign) the answer will also consist of strict inequalities only. On the other hand in the case of slack inequalities (inequalities having ≤ or ≥ sign) the solution of the inequality will also have a slack inequality sign.

## LOGARITHMS

### Graphical View of the Logarithmic Function

The typical logarithmic function is shown in the graph below:

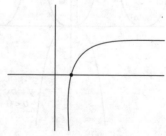

Note the following points about the logarithmic function $y = \log x$.

(1) It is only defined for positive values of $x$.

(2) For values of $x$ below 1, the logarithmic function is negative. At the same time for $x = 1$, the logarithmic function has a value of 0. (Irrespective of the base)

(3) The value of $\log x$ becomes 2, when the value of $x$ becomes equal to the square of the base.

(4) As we go further right on the $x$ axis, the graph keeps increasing. However, this increase becomes more and more gradual and hence the shape of the graph becomes increasingly flatter as we move further on the $x$ axis.

*Space for Notes*

## WORKED-OUT PROBLEMS

**Problem 13.1** Find the domain of the definition of the function $y = 1/(x^2 - 2x)^{1/2}$

(a) $(-\infty, -2)$      (b) $(-\infty, +\infty)$ except $[0, 2]$
(c) $(2, +\infty)$      (d) $(-\infty, 0)$

**Solution** For the function to be defined, the expression under the square root should be non-negative and the denominator should not be equal to zero.

So, $x^2 - 2x > 0$ and $(x^2 - 2x) \neq 0$
or, $x(x - 2) > 0$ or $(x^2 - 2x) \neq 0$

So, $x$ won't lie in between 0 and 2 and $x \neq 0$, $x \neq 2$.
So, $x$ will be $x (-\infty, +\infty)$ excluding the range $0 \leq x$ to $\leq 2$.

In exam situations, to solve the above problem, you should check the options as below.

**In fact, for solving all questions on functions, the student should explore the option-based approach.**

Often you will find that going through the option-based approach will help you save a significant amount of time. The student should try to improve his/her selection of values through practice so that he/she is able to eliminate the maximum number of options on the basis of every check. The student should develop a knack for disproving three options so that the fourth automatically becomes the answer. It should also be noted that if an option cannot be disproved, it means that it is the correct option.

What I am trying to say will be clear from the following solution process.

For this question, if we check at $x = 3$, the function is defined. However, $x = 3$ is outside the ambit of option $a$ and $d$. Hence, $a$ and $d$ are rejected on the basis of just one value check, and $b$ or $c$ has to be the answer.

Alternately, you can try to disprove each and every option one by one.

**Problem 13.2** Which of the following is an even function?

(a) $|x^2| - 5x$      (b) $x^4 + x^5$
(c) $e^{2x} + e^{-2x}$      (d) $|x|^2/x$

**Solution** Use options for solving.
If a function is even it should satisfy the equation $f(x) = f(-x)$.

We now check the four options to see which of them represents an even function.

Checking option (a) $f(x) = |x^2| - 5x$
Putting $-x$ in the place of $x$.

$$f(x) = |(-x)^2| - 5(-x)$$
$$= |x^2| + 5(x) \neq f(x)$$

Checking option (b) $f(x) = x^4 + x^5$.
Putting $(-x)$ at the place of $x$,

$$f(-x) = (-x)^4 + (-x)^5 = x^4 - x^5 \neq f(x)$$

Checking option (c), $f(x) = e^{2x} + e^{-2x}$
Putting $(-x)$ at the place of $x$.

$$f(-x) = e^{-2x} + e^{-(-2x)} = e^{-2x} + e^{2x} = f(x)$$

So (c) is the answer.

You do not need to go further to check for $d$. However, if you had checked, you would have been able to disprove it as follows:

Checking option (d), $f(x) = |x|^2/x$
Putting $f(-x)$ at the place of $x$,

$$f(-x) = |-x|^2/-x = |x|^2/-x \neq f(-x)$$

**Directions for Questions 13.3–13.6:**
Mark (a) if $f(-x) = f(x)$
Mark (b) if $f(-x) = -f(x)$
Mark (c) if neither (a) nor (b)

**Problem 13.3**

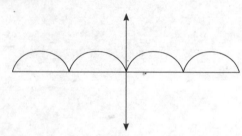

**Solution** The graph is symmetrical about the $y$-axis. This is the definition of an even function. So (a).

**Problem 13.4**

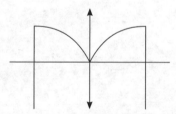

**Solution** The graph is symmetrical about the $y$-axis. This is the definition of an even function. So (a).

**Problem 13.5**

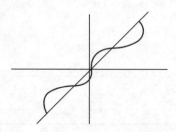

**Solution**  The graph is symmetrical about origin. This is the definition of an odd function. So (b).

**Problem 13.6**

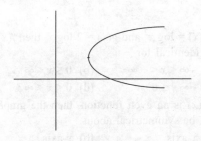

**Solution**  The graph is neither symmetrical about the y-axis nor about origin. So (c).

**Problem 13.7**  Which of the following two functions are identical?

   (a)  $f(x) = x^2/x$          (b)  $g(x) = (\sqrt{x})^2$
   (c)  $h(x) = x$
   (i)  (a) and (b)           (ii)  (b) and (c)
   (iii)  (a) and (c)          (iv)  None of these

**Solution**  For two functions to be identical, their domains should be equal.

Checking the domains of $f(x)$, $g(x)$ and $h(x)$,
$f(x) = x^2/x$, $x$ should not be equal to zero.
So, domain will be all real numbers except at $x = 0$.
$g(x) = (\sqrt{x})^2$, $x$ should be non-negative.
So, domain will be all positive real numbers.
$h(x) = x$, $x$ is defined every where.
So, we can see that none of them have the same domain. Hence, (*d*) is the correct option.

**Problem 13.8**  If $f(x) = 1/x$, $g(x) = 1/(1 - x)$ and $h(x) = x^2$, then find *fogoh* (2).

   (a)  –1                    (b)  1
   (c)  1/2                   (d)  None of these

**Solution**  *fogoh* (2) is the same as $f(g(h(2)))$

To solve this, open the innermost bracket first. This means that we first resolve the function $h(2)$. Since $h(2) = 4$ we will get

$f(g(h(2))) = f(g(4)) = f(-1/3) = -3$. Hence, the option (d) is the correct answer.

Read the instructions below and solve Problems 13.9 and 13.10.

$$A * B = A^3 - B^3$$
$$A + B = A - B$$
$$A - B = A/B$$

**Problem 13.9**  Find the value of (3 * 4) – (8 + 12).

   (a)  9                     (b)  9.25
   (c)  –9.25                 (d)  None of these

**Solution**  Such problems should be solved by the BODMAS rule for sequencing of operations.

Solving, thus, we get: (3 * 4) – (8 + 12)

   = –37 – (–4). [Note here that the '–' sign between –37 and –4 is the operation defined above.]
   = 37/4 = 9.25

**Problem 13.10**  Which of the following operation will give the sum of the reciprocals of $x$ and $y$ and unity?

   (a)  $(x + y) * (x - y)$
   (b)  $[(x * y) - x] - y$
   (c)  $(x + y) - (x - y)$
   (d)  None of these

For solving questions containing a function in the question as well as a function in the options (where values are absent), the safest process for students weak at math is to assume certain convenient values of the variables in the expression and checking for the correct option that gives us equality with the expression in the question. The advantages of this process of solution is that there is very little scope for making mistakes. Besides, if the expression is not simple and directly visible, this process takes far less time as compared to simplifying the expression from one form to another.

This process will be clear after perusing the following solution to the above problem.

**Solution**  The problem statement above defines the expression: $(1/x) + (1/y) + 1$ and asks us to find out which of the four options is equal to this expression. If we try to simplify, we can start from the problem expression and re-write it to get the correct option. However, in the above case this will become extremely complicated since the symbols are indirect. Hence, if we have to solve through simplifying, we should start from the options one by one and try to get the problem expression. However, this is easier said than done and for this particular problem, going through this approach will take you at least two minutes plus.

Hence, consider the following approach:

Take the values of $x$ and $y$ as 1 each. Then,

$$(1/x) + (1/y) + 1 = 3$$

Put the value of $x$ and $y$ as 1 each in each of the four options that we have to consider.

Option (a) will give a value of $-1 \neq 3$. Hence, option (a) is incorrect.

Opton (b) will give a value of 0. $0 \neq 3$. Hence, option (b) is incorrect.

Option (c) gives an answer of 0. $0 \neq 3$. Hence, option (c) is incorrect.

Now since options (a), (b) and (c) are incorrect and option (d) is the only possibility left, it has to be the answer.

## LEVEL OF DIFFICULTY (I)

1. Find the domain of the definition of the function $y = |x|$.
   (a) $0 \le x$
   (b) $-\infty < x < +\infty$
   (c) $x < +\infty$
   (d) $0 \le x < +\infty$

2. Find the domain of the definition of the function $y = \sqrt{x}$.
   (a) $-\infty < x < +\infty$
   (b) $x \le 0$
   (c) $x > 0$
   (d) $x \ge 0$

3. Find the domain of the definition of the function $y = \left| \sqrt{x} \right|$.
   (a) $x \ge 0$
   (b) $-\infty < x < +\infty$
   (c) $x > 0$
   (d) $x < +\infty$

4. Find the domain of the definition of the function $y = (x - 2)^{1/2} + (8 - x)^{1/2}$.
   (a) All the real values except $2 \le x \le 8$
   (b) $2 \le x$
   (c) $2 \le x \le 8$
   (d) $x \le 8$

5. Find the domain of the definition of the function $y = (9 - x^2)^{1/2}$.
   (a) $-3 \le x \le 3$
   (b) $(-\infty, -3] \cup [3, \infty)$
   (c) $-3 \le x$
   (d) $x \le 3$

6. Find the domain of the definition of the function $y = 1/(x^2 - 4x + 3)$.
   (a) $1 \le x \le 3$
   (b) $(-\infty, -3) \cup (3, \infty)$
   (c) $x = (1, 3)$
   (d) $-\infty < x < \infty$, excluding 1, 3

7. The values of $x$ for which the functions $f(x) = x$ and $g(x) = (\sqrt{x})^2$ are identical is
   (a) $-\infty < x < +\infty$
   (b) $x \ge 0$
   (c) $x > 0$
   (d) $x \le 0$

8. The values of $x$ for which the functions $f(x) = x$ and $g(x) = x^2/x$ are identical is
   (a) Set of real numbers excluding 0
   (b) Set of real numbers
   (c) $x \ge 0$
   (d) $x > 0$

9. If $f(x) = \sqrt{x^3}$, then $f(3x)$ will be equal to
   (a) $\sqrt{3x^3}$
   (b) $3\sqrt{x^3}$
   (c) $3\sqrt{(3x^3)}$
   (d) $3\sqrt{x^5}$

10. If $f(x) = e^x$, then the value of $7 f(x)$ will be equal to
    (a) $e^{7x}$
    (b) $7e^x$
    (c) $7 e^{7x}$
    (d) $e^x$

11. If $f(x) = \log x^2$ and $g(x) = 2 \log x$, then $f(x)$ and $g(x)$ are identical for
    (a) $-\infty < x < +\infty$
    (b) $0 \le x < \infty$
    (c) $-\infty x \le 0$
    (d) $0 < x < \infty$

12. If $f(x)$ is an even function, then the graph $y = f(x)$ will be symmetrical about
    (a) $x$-axis
    (b) $y$-axis
    (c) Both the axes
    (d) None of these

13. If $f(x)$ is an odd function, then the graph $y = f(x)$ will be symmetrical about
    (a) $x$-axis
    (b) $y$-axis
    (c) Both the axes
    (d) origin

14. Which of the following is an even function?
    (a) $x^{-8}$
    (b) $x^3$
    (c) $x^{-33}$
    (d) $x^{73}$

15. Which of the following is not an odd function?
    (a) $(x + 1)^3$
    (b) $x^{23}$
    (c) $x^{53}$
    (d) $x^{77}$

16. For what value of $x$, $x^2 + 10x + 11$ will give the minimum value?
    (a) 5
    (b) $+10$
    (c) $-5$
    (d) $-10$

17. In the above question, what will be the minimum value of the function?
    (a) $-14$
    (b) 11
    (c) 86
    (d) 0

18. Find the maximum value of the function $1/(x^2 - 3x + 2)$.
    (a) $11/4$
    (b) $1/4$
    (c) 0
    (d) None of these

19. Find the minimum value of the function $f(x) = \log_2 (x^2 - 2x + 5)$.
    (a) $-4$
    (b) 2
    (c) 4
    (d) $-2$

20. $f(x)$ is any function and $f^{-1}(x)$ is known as inverse of $f(x)$, then $f^{-1}(x)$ of $f(x) = \dfrac{1}{x} + 1$ is
    (a) $\dfrac{1}{x} - 1$
    (b) $x - 1$
    (c) $\dfrac{1}{(x-1)}$
    (d) $\dfrac{1}{x+1}$

**Directions for Questions 21 to 23:** Read the instructions below and solve.

$f(x) = f(x - 2) - f(x - 1)$, $x$ is a natural number
$f(1) = 0$, $f(2) = 1$

21. The value of $f(8)$ is
    (a) 0             (b) 13
    (c) −5          (d) −9

22. The value of $f(7) + f(4)$ is
    (a) 11           (b) −6
    (c) −12         (d) 12

23. What will be the value of $\displaystyle\sum_{n=1}^{9} f(n)$?
    (a) −12         (b) −15
    (c) −14         (d) −13

24. What will be the domain of the definition of the function $f(x) = {}^{8-x}C_{5-x}$ for positive values of $x$?
    (a) {1, 2, 3}         (b) {1, 2, 3, 4}
    (c) {1, 2, 3, 4, 5}    (d) {1, 2, 3, 4, 5, 6, 7, 8}

### Directions for Questions 25 to 38:

Mark $a$ if $f(-x) = f(x)$

Mark $b$ if $f(-x) = -f(x)$

Mark $c$ if neither $a$ nor $b$ is true

Mark $d$ if $f(x)$ does not exist at at least one point of the domain.

25.

26.

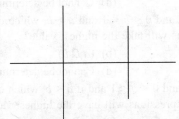

27.

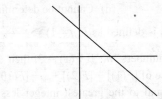

28.

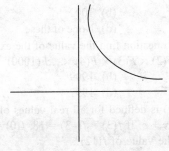

29.

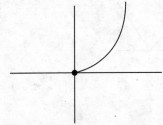

30.

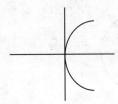

31.

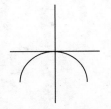

32.

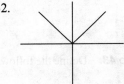

33.

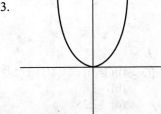

34.

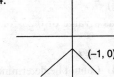

(−1, 0)

35.

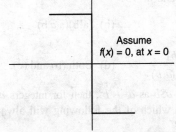

Assume
$f(x) = 0$, at $x = 0$

36.

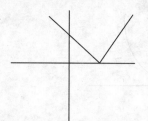

37.

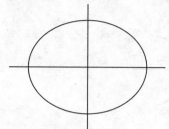

38.

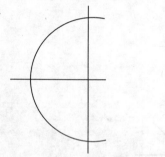

**Directions for Questions 39 to 43:** Define the following functions:

(i) $a @ b = \dfrac{a+b}{2}$

(ii) $a \# b = a^2 - b^2$

(iii) $(a\,!\,b) = \dfrac{a-b}{2}$

39. Find the value of $\{[(3@4)!(3\#2)] @ [(4!3)@(2\#3)]\}$.
   (a) −0.75      (b) −1
   (c) −1.5       (d) −2.25

40. Find the value of $(4\#3)@(2!3)$.
   (a) 3.25       (b) 3.5
   (c) 6.5        (d) 7

41. Which of the following has a value of 0.25 for $a = 0$ and $b = 0.5$?
   (a) $a @ b$    (b) $a \# b$
   (c) Either $a$ or $b$   (d) Cannot be determined

42. Which of the following expressions has a value of 4 for $a = 5$ and $b = 3$?
   (a) $\dfrac{(a!b)}{(a\#b)}$    (b) $(a!b)(a@b)$

   (c) $\dfrac{(a\#b)}{(a!b)(a@b)}$    (d) Both (b) and (c)

43. If we define $a\$b$ as $a^3 - b^3$, then for integers $a$, $b > 2$ and $a > b$ which of the following will always be true?

(a) $(a@b) > (a!b)$      (b) $(a@b) \geq (a!b)$
(c) $(a\#b) < (a\$b)$    (d) Both $a$ and $c$

**Directions for Questions 44 to 48:** Define the following functions:

(a) $(a\,M\,b) = a - b$      (b) $(a\,D\,b) = a + b$
(c) $(a\,H\,b) = (ab)$       (d) $(a\,P\,b) = a/b$

44. Which of the following functions will represent $a^2 - b^2$?
   (a) $(a\,M\,b)\,H\,(a\,D\,b)$   (b) $(a\,H\,b)\,M\,(a\,P\,b)$
   (c) $(a\,D\,b)/(a\,M\,b)$       (d) None of these

45. Which of the following represents $a^2$?
   (a) $(a\,M\,b)\,H\,(a\,D\,b) + b^2$
   (b) $(a\,H\,b)\,M\,(a\,P\,b) + b^2$
   (c) $\dfrac{(a\,M\,b)}{(a\,P\,b)}$
   (d) Both (a) and (c)

46. What is the value of $(3M4H2D4P8M2)$?
   (a) 6.5        (b) 6
   (c) −6.5       (d) None of these

47. Which of the four functions defined has the maximum value?
   (a) $(a\,M\,b)$     (b) $(a\,D\,b)$
   (c) $(a\,P\,b)$     (d) Cannot be determined

48. Which of the four functions defined has the minimum value?
   (a) $(a\,M\,b)$     (b) $(a\,D\,b)$
   (c) $(a\,H\,b)$     (d) Cannot be determined

49. If $0 < a < 1$ and $0 < b < 1$ and $a > b$, which of the 4 expressions will take the highest value?
   (a) $(a\,M\,b)$     (b) $(a\,D\,b)$
   (c) $(a\,P\,b)$     (d) Cannot be determined

50. If $0 < a < 1$ and $0 < b < 1$ and if $a < b$, which of the following expressions will have the highest value?
   (a) $(a\,M\,b)$     (b) $(a\,D\,b)$
   (c) $(a\,P\,b)$     (d) Cannot be determined

51. A function $F(n)$ is defined as $F(n-1) = \dfrac{1}{(2 - F(n))}$ for all natural numbers '$n$'. If $F(1) = 3$, then what is the value of $[F(1)] + [F(2)] + ... + [F(1000)]$? (Here, $[x]$ is equal to the greatest integer less than or equal to '$x$')
   (a) 1001       (b) 1002
   (c) 3003       (d) None of these

52. For the above question find the value of the expression: $F(1) \times F(2) \times F(3) \times F(4) \times .... F(1000)$
   (a) 2001       (b) 1999
   (c) 2004       (d) 1997

53. A function $f(x)$ is defined for all real values of $x$ as $f(x) = ax^2 + bx + c$. If $f(3) = f(-3) = 18, f(0) = 15$, then what is the value of $f(12)$?

(a) 63      (b) 159

(c) 102      (d) None of these

54. Two operations, for real numbers $x$ and $y$, are defined as given below.

   (i) $M(x \, \theta \, y) = (x + y)^2$

   (ii) $f(x \, \psi \, y) = (x - y)^2$

   If $M(x^2 \theta y^2) = 361$ and $M(x^2 \psi y^2) = 49$, then what is the value of the square root of $((x^2 y^2) + 3)$?

   (a) $\pm 81$      (b) $\pm 9$

   (c) $\pm 7$      (d) $\pm 11$

55. The function $\Psi(m) = [m]$, where $[m]$ represents the greatest integer less than or equal to $m$. Two real numbers $x$ and $y$ are such that $\Psi(4x + 5) = 5y + 3$ and $\Psi(3y+7) = x + 4$, then find the value of $x^2 \times y^2$.

   (a) 1      (b) 2

   (c) 4      (d) None of these

56. A certain function always obeys the rule: If $f(x.y) = f(x).f(y)$ where $x$ and $y$ are positive real numbers. A certain Mr. Mogambo found that the value of $f(128) = 4$, then find the value of the variable $M = f(0.5)$.

   $f(1).f(2).f(4).f(8).f(16).f(32).f(64).f(128).f(256)$

   (a) 128      (b) 256

   (c) 512      (d) 1024

57. $x$ and $y$ are non negative integers such that $4x + 6y = 20$, and $x^2 \le M/y^{2/3}$ for all values of $x$, $y$. What is the minimum value of $M$?

   (a) $2^{2/3}$      (b) $2^{1/3}$

   (c) $2^{8/3}$      (d) $4^{2/3}$

58. Let $\Psi(x) = \dfrac{x+3}{2}$ and $\theta(x) = 3x^2 + 2$. Find the value of $\theta(\Psi(-7))$.

   (a) 12      (b) 14

   (c) 50      (d) 42

59. If $F(a + b) = F(a). F(b) \div 2$, where $F(b) \ne 0$ and $F(a) \ne 0$, then what is the value of $F(12b)$?

   (a) $(F(b))^{12}$      (b) $F(b))^{12} \div 2$

   (c) $(F(b))^{12} \div 2^{12}$      (d) $(F(b))^{12} \div 2^{11}$

60. A function $a = \theta(b)$ is said to be reflexive if $b = \theta(a)$. Which of the following is/are reflexive functions?

   (i) $\dfrac{3b+5}{4b-3}$      (ii) $\dfrac{3b+5}{5b-2}$

   (iii) $\dfrac{2b+12}{12b-2}$

   (a) All of these are reflexive

   (b) Only (i) and (ii) are reflexive

   (c) Only (i) and (iii) are reflexive

   (d) None of these are reflexive.

61. $f(x) = \dfrac{1}{x}, g(x) = |3x - 2|$

   Then $f(g(x)) = ?$

(a) $\dfrac{1}{|3x-2|}$      (b) $\left| \dfrac{1}{3x} - 2 \right|$

(c) $\dfrac{1}{|3x|} - 2$      (d) None of these

**Directions for question numbers 62 to 66:**

$$f(x) = x^2 + \frac{1}{x^2}, \; g(x) = |x|, \; h(x) = x^3 - \frac{1}{x^3}, \; t(x),$$

$$= x^2 - \frac{1}{x^2} \text{ then answer the following questions:}$$

62. $f(g(x))$ is an:

   (a) Even function      (b) Odd function

   (c) Neither even nor odd

63. Which of the following options is true:

   (a) $f(x) = g(x) + (g(x))^2$

   (b) $f(x) = -f(g(x))$

   (c) $f(g(x)) = g(f(x))$

   (d) None of these

64. Out of $f(x)$, $g(x)$, $h(x)$, $t(x)$ how many are even functions.

65. Is $h(f(x))$ an even function or odd function? Type 1 if it is even, 2 if it is odd, 3 if it is neither even nor odd.

66. Is $h(t(x))$ an even function or an odd function or neither even nor odd. Type 1 if it is even, 2 if it is odd, 3 if it is neither even nor odd.

67. If $f(x) = \dfrac{x^2 + 1}{x - 1}$ then $f(f(f(2))) = 2$

**Directions for question numbers 68 and 69:**

   $S(x, y) = x + y$

   $P(x, y) = x \times y$

   $D(x, y) = x/y$

   $t(x, y) = |x - y|$

68. Find the value of $P(S(2,(D(3, 4)), 5) = ?$

69. $S(S(P(2,3), D(4,2)), t(1, 5)) = ?$

**Directions for question numbers 70 to 72:** Define the following functions as:

$$xPy = \begin{cases} |x - y|, \text{if } x < y \\ xQy, \text{otherwise} \end{cases}$$

$$xQy = \begin{cases} \dfrac{x}{y}, \text{if } x > y \\ xRy, \text{otherwise} \end{cases}$$

$$xRy = \begin{cases} x \times y, \text{if } x \le y \\ xSy, \text{otherwise} \end{cases}$$

$$xSy = \begin{cases} \dfrac{1}{xy}, \text{if } x > y \\ xPy, \text{otherwise} \end{cases}$$

Here $x$ & $y$ are real numbers. Solve the following questions based on these definitions of the above functions.

70. Find the value of $[(5P6)Q(4Q2)]S(3S1) =$ _____

71. Which of the following is true.
    (a) $(4P2) \neq (2P4)$      (b) $(4Q2) = (2R4)$
    (c) $(6Q3) = (2S(0.5))$   (d) None of these

72. If $(5P3)Q(4S2) = 20K1.5$. What is the correct operator to replace the '$K$'?

    Type 1 if your answer is '$P$'; Type 2 if your answer is '$Q$'; Type 3 if your answer is '$R$'; Type 4 if your answer is '$S$'

**Direction for question numbers 73 – 75:**

$[x]$ is defined as the greatest integer less than equals to $x$.

$\{x\}$ is defined as the least integer greater than or equal to $x$.

The functions $f$, $g$, $h$ and $i$ are defined as follows:

$f(a,b) = [a] + \{b\}$

$g(a,b) = [b] - \{a\}$

$h(a,b) = [a \div b]$

$i(a,b) = \{-a + b\}$

73. Find the value of $i(f(3,4)), g(3.5, 4.5)) =$
    (a) 2                  (b) 1
    (c) $-1$               (d) None of these

74. If $a^3 = 64, b^2 = 16$ and $8 + f(a,b) = -g(a,b)$ then $a - b = ?$

75. $f(1.2, -2.3) + g(-1.2, 2.3) = i(a, -1.3)$. Then which of the following values can $a$ take:
    (a) $-4.3$             (b) $-5.3$
    (c) $5.6$              (d) $-2.4$

**Directions of question numbers 76 & 77:**

Define the functions: $xPy = \dfrac{1}{1 + \dfrac{y}{x}}, xQy = 1 + \dfrac{x}{y}$

76. Which of the following equals to $\dfrac{x}{y}$?
    (a) $(xPy) + (xQy)$        (b) $(xPy) - (xQy)$
    (c) $(xPy) \times (xQy)$   (d) $(xPy) \div (xQy)$

77. If the functions $S(x, y) = (xPy)P(xQy)$ is defined, then find the value of $S(2, 3)$ (correct to two decimal points)?

**Directions for question numbers 78-80:**

Define the functions:

$aAb = |a - b|$

$aBb = [a \div b]$

$aCb = |a \times b|$

$$\min(x, y) = \begin{cases} y, \text{when } x > y \\ x, \text{when } y > x \\ 0, \text{when } x = y \end{cases}$$

$$\max(x, y) = \begin{cases} x^2, \text{when } x \geq y \\ y^2, \text{when } y \geq x \end{cases}$$

Here $a, b, x, y \in R$

78. Find the value of $(1 + \min(2A3, 1C2))B[\max(1A2, 1C1)] =$

79. The value of $\max(7A3, 16B2)$ would be equal to the value of which of the following options?
    (a) $(32B16)C(\max(4,8))$
    (b) $(32B2)C(\min(4,8))$
    (c) $(16B2)C((\min(4,8))$
    (d) None of these

80. $\max(3,4) \div \min(8, 4) = ?$
    (a) $8A2$             (b) $28B7$
    (c) $4C2$             (d) None of these

**Directions for question numbers 81 – 85:**

$f(a_1, a_2, a_3, \ldots, a_n) =$ minimum of $(a_1, a_2, \ldots a_n)$ and $g(a_1, a_2, a_3, \ldots a_n) =$ maximum of $(a_1, a_2, a_3 \ldots a_n)$
$h(x, y) = [x/y]$ where $[a]$ represents the greatest integer less than or equal to $a$.

$t(a_1, a_2, a_3, \ldots, a_n) = a_1 \times a_2 \times a_3 \times \ldots \times a_n$

$i(a_1, a_2, a_3, \ldots, a_n) = a_1 + a_2 + a_3 + \ldots + a_n$

81. If $f(1,3,5,7) + g(2,4,6,8) = h(aK, K)$
    Where $a, K$ are both positive integers, then the value of $a$ is:

82. The value of $f(t(1,2,3,4), i(1,2,3,4)) = ?$

83. The Value of $h(f(5,6,7,8), i(1,2,3,4)) = ?$

84. If $P = f(2,3,4,6)$, $Q = g(1,2,3,4)$, $R = h(8,4)$, $S = t(1,2,3,4)$, $T = i(4,5,6)$ then which of the following options is true?
    (a) $P < R = Q < S < T$   (b) $P = R < Q < S < T$
    (c) $P = R < Q < T < S$   (d) $P = R < Q = T < S$

85. $f(f(1,2,3), g(2,3,4), f(0,1,2), g(-3,-2) = ?$
    (a) $-3$              (b) $-2$
    (c) $1$               (d) $0$

86. Which of the following curves correctly represents $y = |x - 2|$?

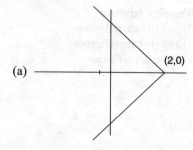

    (a)                                    (2,0)

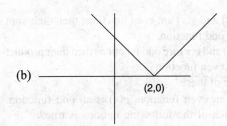

(b)

(2,0)

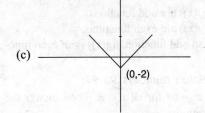

(c)

(0,-2)

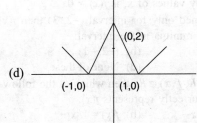

(0,2)

(d)

(-1,0)    (1,0)

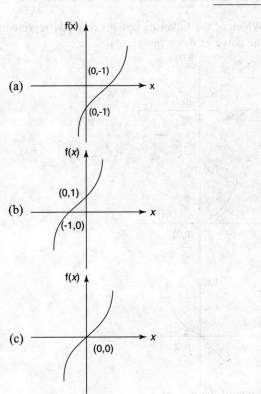

(a)

(0,-1)

(0,-1)

(b)

(0,1)

(-1,0)

(c)

(0,0)

(d) None of these

87. Which of the following represents the curve of
    $y = \log|x|$?

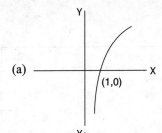

(a)

(1,0)

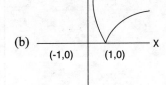

(b)

(-1,0)    (1,0)

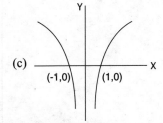

(c)

(-1,0)   (1,0)

(d) None of these

88. Which of the following options correctly represents
    the curve of $f(x) = (x - 1)^3$

89. Which of the following options correctly represents
    the curve $f(x) = \dfrac{e^{|x|}}{2}$

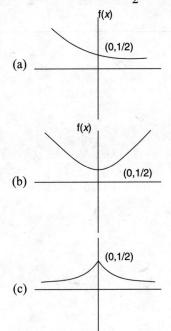

(a)

(0,1/2)

(b)

(0,1/2)

(c)

(0,1/2)

(d) None of these

90. Which of the following options correctly represents the curve of $f(x) = \max(x, x^2)$

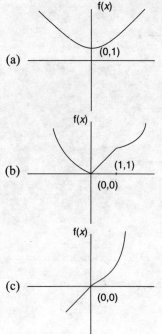

(a)

(b)

(c)

(d) None of these

91. Which of the following statements is true:
    (a) If $f(x)$ and $g(x)$ are odd functions then their sum is an even function.

(b) If $f(x)$ and $g(x)$ are even functions then their sum is an odd function.

(c) If $f(x)$ and $g(x)$ are odd functions then their product is an even function

(d) None of these

92. If $f(x)$ is an even function, $g(x)$ is an odd function. Then which of the following options is true?
    (a) $f(g(x))$ is an odd function, $g(f(x))$ is an even function.
    (b) $f(g(x))$, $g(f(x))$ are odd functions.
    (c) $f(g(x))$, $g(f(x))$ are even functions.
    (d) $g(f(x))$ is an odd function, $f(g(x))$ is an even function.

### Directions for question numbers 93-94:

If $f(x) = x^3 - x^2 - 6x$ for all $x \in R$. Then answer the following questions:

93. For how many values of x, is $f(x) = 0$

94. If $f(x)$ is defined only for interval $(-2, 3)$ then $f(x)$ will attain its minima in the interval:
    (a) $(-2, 0)$
    (b) $(-2, -1)$
    (c) $(0, 3)$
    (d) None of these

95. If for all $x \in R, f(x) \in R$, then which of the following options correctly represents $f(x)$:
    (a) $f(x) = \log x$
    (b) $f(x) = 1/|x|$
    (c) $f(x) = \log(x^4 + 7)$
    (d) $f(x) = 1/x$

***Space for Rough Work***

## LEVEL OF DIFFICULTY (II)

1. Find the domain of the definition of the function $y = 1/(4 - x^2)^{1/2}$.
   (a) $(-2, 2)$
   (b) $[-2, 2]$
   (c) $(-\infty, -2) \cup (2, \infty)$ excluding $-2$ and $2$
   (d) $(2, \infty)$

2. The domain of definition of the function
   $y = \dfrac{1}{\log_{10}(1 - x)} + (x + 2)^{1/2}$ is
   (a) $(-3, -2)$          (b) $[0, 1)$
   (c) $[-2, 1]$           (d) $[-2, 1)$ excluding 0

3. The domain of definition of $y = [\log_{10}\left(\dfrac{5x - x^2}{4}\right)]^{1/2}$ is
   (a) $[1, 4]$            (b) $[-4, -1]$
   (c) $[0, 5]$            (d) $[-1, 5]$

4. Which of the following functions is an odd function?
   (a) $2^{-x.x}$          (b) $2^{x-x.x.x}$
   (c) Both (a) and (b)    (d) Neither (a) nor (b)

5. The domain of definition of $y = [1 - |x|]^{1/2}$ is
   (a) $[-1, 0]$           (b) $[0, 1]$
   (c) $(-1, 1)$           (d) $[-1, 1]$

6. The domain of definition of $y = [3/(4 - x^2)] + \log_{10}(x^3 - x)$ is
   (a) $(-1, 0) \cup (1, \infty)$    (b) Not 2 or $-2$
   (c) (a) and (b) together  (d) None of these

7. If $f(t) = 2^t$, then $f(0), f(1), f(2)$ are in
   (a) AP                  (b) HP
   (c) GP                  (d) Cannot be said

8. Centre of a circle $x^2 + y^2 = 16$ is at $(0, 0)$. What will be the new centre of the circle if it gets shifted 3 units down and 2 units left?
   (a) $(2, 3)$            (b) $(-2, -3)$
   (c) $(-2, 3)$           (d) $(2, -3)$

9. If $u(t) = 4t - 5$, $v(t) = t^2$ and $f(t) = 1/t$, then the formula for $u(f(v(t)))$ is
   (a) $\dfrac{1}{(4t - 5)^2}$    (b) $\dfrac{4}{(t - 5)}$
   (c) $\dfrac{4}{t^2} - 5$       (d) None of these

10. If $f(t) = \sqrt{t}$, $g(t) = t/4$ and $h(t) = 4t - 8$, then the formula for $g(f(h(t)))$ will be
    (a) $\dfrac{\sqrt{t - 2}}{4}$    (b) $2\sqrt{t} - 8$
    (c) $\dfrac{\sqrt{(4t - 8)}}{4}$  (d) $\dfrac{\sqrt{(t - 8)}}{4}$

11. In the above question, find the value of $h(g(f(t)))$.
    (a) $\sqrt{t} - 8$      (b) $2\sqrt{t - 8}$
    (c) $\dfrac{\sqrt{t} + 8}{4}$    (d) None of these

12. In question number 10, find the formula of $f(h(g(t)))$.
    (a) $\sqrt{t} - 8$      (b) $\sqrt{(t - 8)}$
    (c) $2\sqrt{t} - 8$     (d) None of these

13. The values of $x$, for which the functions $f(x) = x$, $g(x) = (\sqrt{x})^2$ and $h(x) = x^2/x$ are identical, is
    (a) $0 \le x$           (b) $0 < x$
    (c) All real values     (d) All real values except 0

14. Which of the following is an even function?
    (a) $e^x$               (b) $e^{-x}$
    (c) $e^x + e^{-x}$      (d) $\dfrac{e^x + e^{-x}}{e^x - e^{-x}}$

15. The graph of $y = (x + 3)^3 + 1$ is the graph of $y = x^3$ shifted
    (a) 3 units to the right and 1 unit down
    (b) 3 units to the left and 1 unit down
    (c) 3 units to the left and 1 unit up
    (d) 3 units to the right and 1 unit up

16. If $f(x) = 5x^3$ and $g(x) = 3x^5$, then $f(x).g(x)$ will be
    (a) Even function       (b) Odd function
    (c) Both                (d) None of these

17. If $f(x) = x^2$ and $g(x) = \log_e x$, then $f(x) + g(x)$ will be
    (a) Even function       (b) Odd function
    (c) Both                (d) Neither (a) nor (b)

18. If $f(x) = x^3$ and $g(x) = x^2/5$, then $f(x) - g(x)$ will be
    (a) Odd function        (b) Even function
    (c) Neither (a) nor (b)  (d) Both

19. $f(x)$ is any function and $f^{-1}(x)$ is known as inverse of $f(x)$, then $f^{-1}(x)$ of $f(x) = 1/(x - 2)$ is
    (a) $\dfrac{1}{x} + 2$   (b) $\dfrac{1}{(x + 2)}$
    (c) $\dfrac{1}{x} + 0.5$  (d) None of these

20. $f(x)$ is any function and $f^{-1}(x)$ is known as inverse of $f(x)$, then $f^{-1}(x)$ of $f(x) = e^x$ is
    (a) $-e^x$              (b) $e^{-x}$
    (c) $\log_e x$          (d) None of these

21. $f(x)$ is any function and $f^{-1}(x)$ is known as inverse of $f(x)$, then $f^{-1}(x)$ of $f(x) = x/(x - 1)$, $x \ne 1$ is

(a) $x/(1 + x)$

(b) $\dfrac{x}{x^2 - 1}$

(c) $x/(x - 1)$

(d) $-x/(x + 1)$

22. Which of the following functions will have a minimum value at $x = -3$?

(a) $f(x) = 2x^3 - 4x + 3$

(b) $f(x) = 4x^4 - 3x + 5$

(c) $f(x) = x^6 - 2x - 6$

(d) None of these

**Directions for Questions 23 to 32:**

Mark (a) if $f(-x) = f(x)$

Mark (b) if $f(-x) = -f(x)$

Mark (c) if neither (a) nor (b) is true

Mark (d) if $f(x)$ does not exist at at least one point of the domain.

23.

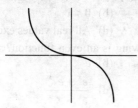

24.

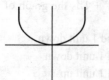

25.

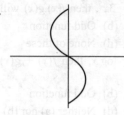

26.

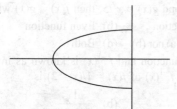

27.

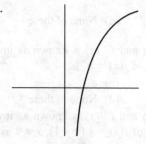

28.

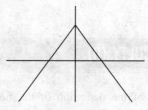

29.

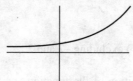

30.

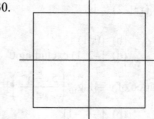

31.

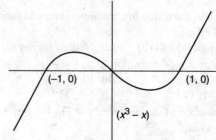

(−1, 0)    (1, 0)

$(x^3 - x)$

32.

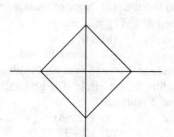

**Directions for Questions 33 to 36:** If $f(x)$ is represented by the graph below.

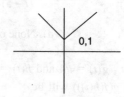

0,1

33. Which of the following will represent the function $-f(x)$?

34. Which of the following will represent the function $-f(x) + 1$?

35. Which of the following will represent the function $f(x) - 1$?

36. Which of the following will represent the function $f(x) + 1$?

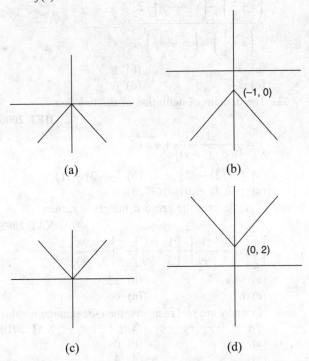

(a)            (b)

(c)            (d)

**Directions for Questions 37 to 40:** Define the following functions:

$$f(x, y, z) = xy + yz + zx$$
$$g(x, y, z) = x^2y + y^2z + z^2x \text{ and}$$
$$h(x, y, z) = 3\,xyz$$

Find the value of the following expressions:

37. $h[f(2, 3, 1), g(3, 4, 2), h(1/3, 1/3, 3)]$
    (a) 0             (b) 23760
    (c) 2640         (d) None of these

38. $g[f(1, 0, 0), g(0, 1, 0), h(1, 1, 1)]$
    (a) 0             (b) 9
    (c) 12           (d) None of these

39. $f[f(1, 1, 1), g(1, 1, 1), h(1, 1, 1)]$
    (a) 9             (b) 18
    (c) 27           (d) None of these

40. $f(1, 2, 3) - g(1, 2, 3) + h(1, 2, 3)$
    (a) −6           (b) 6
    (c) 12           (d) 8

41. If $f(x) = 1/\,g(x)$, then which of the following is correct?
    (a) $f(f(g(f(x)))) = f(g(g(f(f(x)))))$
    (b) $f(g(g(f(f(x))))) = f(f(g(g(g(x)))))$
    (c) $g(g(f(f(g(f(x)))))) = f(f(g(g(f(g(x))))))$
    (d) $f(g(g(g(f(x))))) = g(g(f(f(f(x)))))$

42. If $f(x) = 1/g(x)$, then the minimum value of $f(x) + g(x)$, $f(x) > 0$ and $g(x) > 0$, will be
    (a) 0
    (b) 2
    (c) Depends upon the value of $f(x)$ and $g(x)$
    (d) None of these

**Directions for Questions 43 to 45:**

If $R(a/b)$ = Remainder when $a$ is divided by $b$;
  $Q(a/b)$ = Quotient obtained when $a$ is divided by $b$;
  $SQ(a)$ = Smallest integer just bigger than square root of $a$.

43. If $a = 12$, $b = 5$, then find the value of $SQ[R\ \{(a + b)/b\}]$.
    (a) 0             (b) 1
    (c) 2             (d) 3

44. If $a = 9$, $b = 7$, then the value of $Q\ [[SQ(ab)+b]/a]$ will be
    (a) 0             (b) 1
    (c) 2             (d) None of these

45. If $a = 18$, $b = 2$ and $c = 7$, then find the value of $Q\ [\{SQ(ab) + R(a/c)\}/b]$.
    (a) 3             (b) 4
    (c) 5             (d) 6

**Directions for Questions 46 to 48:** Read the following passage and try to answer questions based on them.

$[x]$ = Greatest integer less than or equal to $x$
$\{x\}$ = Smallest integer greater than or equal to $x$.

46. If $x$ is not an integer, what is the value of $([x] - \{x\})$?
    (a) 0             (b) 1
    (c) −1           (d) 2

47. If $x$ is not an integer, then $(\{x\} + [x])$ is
    (a) An even number
    (b) An odd integer
    (c) $> 3x$
    (d) $< x$

48. What is the value of $x$ if $5 < x < 6$ and $\{x\} + [x] = 2x$?
    (a) 5.2          (b) 5.8
    (c) 5.5          (d) 5.76

49. If $f(t) = t^2 + 2$ and $g(t) = (1/t) + 2$, then for $t = 2$, $f[g(t)] - g[f(t)] = ?$
    (a) 1.2         (b) 2.6
    (c) 4.34       (d) None of these

50. Given $f(t) = kt + 1$ and $g(t) = 3t + 2$. If $fog = gof$, find $k$.
    (a) 2             (b) 3
    (c) 5             (d) 4

51. Let $F(x)$ be a function such that $F(x) F(x + 1) = - F(x - 1)F(x-2)F(x-3)F(x-4)$ for all $x \geq 0$. Given the values of If $F(83) = 81$ and $F(77) = 9$, then the value of $F(81)$ equals to
    (a) 27      (b) 54
    (c) 729      (d) Data Insufficient

52. Let $f(x) = 121 - x^2$, $g(x) = |x - 8| + |x + 8|$ and $h(x) = \min\{f(x), g(x)\}$. What is the number of integer values of $x$ for which $h(x)$ is equal to a positive integral value?
    (a) 17      (b) 19
    (c) 21      (d) 23

53. If the function $R(x) = \max(x^2 - 8, 3x, 8)$, then what is the max value of $R(x)$?
    (a) 4      (b) $\dfrac{1+\sqrt{5}}{2}$
    (c) $\infty$      (d) 0

54. If the function $R(x) = \min(x^2 - 8, 3x, 8)$, what is the max value of $R(x)$?
    (a) 4      (b) 8
    (c) $\infty$      (d) None of these

55. The minimum value of $ax^2 + bx + c$ is 7/8 at $x = 5/4$. Find the value of the expression at $x = 5$, if the value of the expression at $x = 1$ is 1.
    (a) 75      (b) 29
    (c) 121      (d) 129

56. Find the range of the function $f(x) = (x + 4)(5 - x)(x + 1)$.
    (a) $[-2, 3]$      (b) $(-\infty, 20]$
    (c) $(-\infty, +\infty)$      (d) $[-20, \infty)$

57. The function $f(x)$ is defined for positive integers and is defined as:
    $f(x) = 6^x - 3$, if $x$ is a number in the form $2n$.
    $= 6^x + 4$, if $x$ is a number in the form $2n + 1$.
    What is the remainder when $f(1) + f(2) + f(3) + ... + f(1001)$ is divided by 2?
    (a) 1      (b) 0
    (c) –1      (d) None of the above

58. $p$, $q$ and $r$ are three non-negative integers such that $p + q + r = 10$. The maximum value of $pq + qr + pr + pqr$ is
    (a) $\geq 40$ and $< 50$      (b) $\geq 50$ and $< 60$
    (c) $\geq 60$ and $< 70$      (d) $\geq 70$ and $< 80$

59. A function $\alpha(x)$ is defined for $x$ as $3\alpha(x) + 2\alpha(2 - x) = (x + 3)^2$. What is the value of $[\alpha(-5)]$ where $[x]$ represents the greatest integer less than or equal to $x$?
    (a) 37      (b) –38
    (c) –37      (d) Cannot be determined

60. For a positive integer $x$, $f(x + 2) = 3 + f(x)$, when $x$ is even and $f(x + 2) = x + f(x)$, when $x$ is odd. If $f(1) = 6$ and $f(2) = 4$, then find $f(f(f(f(1)))) \times f(f(f(f(2))))$.

61. If $x > 0$, the minimum value of      **XAT 2008**
    $$\dfrac{\left(x+\dfrac{1}{x}\right)^6 - \left(x^6 + \dfrac{1}{x^6}\right) - 2}{\left(x+\dfrac{1}{x}\right)^3 + \left(x^3 + \dfrac{1}{x^3}\right)} \text{ is } \_\_\_ ?$$
    (a) 3      (b) 1
    (c) 2      (d) 6

62. The domain of definition of the function      **IIFT 2006**
    $$y = \dfrac{1}{\{\log_{10}(3-x)\}} + \sqrt{x+7}$$
    (a) $[-7, 3) - \{2\}$      (b) $[-7, 3] - \{1\}$
    (c) $(-7, 3) - \{0\}$ (d) $(-7, 3)$

63. If $[x]$ denotes the greatest integer $\leq x$, then      **XAT 2008**
    $$\left[\dfrac{1}{3}\right] + \left[\dfrac{1}{3} + \dfrac{1}{99}\right] + \left[\dfrac{1}{3} + \dfrac{2}{99}\right] + ... \left[\dfrac{1}{3} + \dfrac{98}{99}\right] =$$
    (a) 98      (b) 33
    (c) 67      (d) 66

64. If $x$ and $y$ are real numbers, then the minimum value of $x^2 + 4xy + 6y^2 - 4y + 4$ is      **XAT 2010**
    (a) $-4$      (b) 0
    (c) 2      (d) 4

65. What is the maximum possible value of $(21 \sin X + 72 \cos X)$?      **XAT 2011**
    (a) 21      (b) 57
    (c) 63      (d) 75

66. The sum of the possible values of X in the equation $|x + 7| + |x - 8| = 16$ is:      **XAT 2014**
    (a) 0      (b) 1
    (c) 2      (d) 3

67. If $|3x+4| \leq 5$ and $a$ and $b$ are the minimum and maximum values of $x$ respectively, then $a + b =$

68. For how many positive integer values of $x$, is $x^3 - 16x + x^2 + 20 \leq 0$

69. $3f(x) + 2f\left(\dfrac{4x+5}{x-4}\right) = 7(x+3)$ where $x \in R$ and $x \neq$

    4. What is the value of $f(11)$?

**Directions for question number 70-71:** if $q = p \times [p]$ and '$q$' is an integer such that $7 < q < 17$. Then answer the following questions:

70. The number of positive real values of '$p$' is:

71. Find the product of all possible values of $p$.

72. If $f(1) = -1$, $f(2x) = 4f(x) + 9$, $f(x + 2) = f(x) + 8(x + 1)$. Find the value of $f(24) - f(7)$.

73. In the previous question, find the value of $f(1000)$

74. $f(x) = (x^2 + [x]^2 - 2x[x])^{1/2}$, where $x$ is real & $[x]$ denotes the greatest integer less than or equal to $x$. Find the value of $f(10.08) - f(100.08)$.

75. Find the sum of coefficients of the polynomial $(x - 4)^7 (x - 3)^4 (x - 5)^2$
    (a) $2^8 3^7$      (b) $-2^6.3^8$
    (c) $-2^8.3^7$      (d) $2^6.3^8$

76. A function $f(x)$ is defined as $f(x) = x - \dfrac{1}{9-3x} - 3$. If $x > 3$, then find the minimum possible value of $f(x)$.

    (a) $3 - \dfrac{1}{\sqrt{3}}$      (b) $\dfrac{1}{\sqrt{3}}$

    (c) $\sqrt{3} - \dfrac{1}{3}$      (d) $\sqrt{3} + \dfrac{1}{3}$

77. The graph of $h(x)$ and $g(x)$ are given below. Then which of the following defines the relation between $h(x)$ and $g(x)$?

    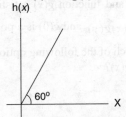 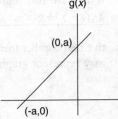

    (a) $\sqrt{3}g(x) - h(x) = a\sqrt{3}$

    (b) $\sqrt{3}g(x) + h(x) = a\sqrt{3}$

    (c) $g(x) + h(x)\sqrt{3} = \dfrac{a}{\sqrt{3}}$

    (d) None of these

78. Consider a function '$f$' is such that $\dfrac{f(xy)}{f(x+y)} = 1$ for all real values of $x$, $y$. If $f(6) = 7$ then the value of $f(-10) + f(10)$ is

79. A function $f(x)$ is defined such that
    $$f\left(\frac{x}{y}\right) = \frac{f(x)}{f(y)}.$$
    If $f(3) = 5$ then $f(81) = ?$

80. Find the sum of all the coefficients of the polynomial $(x - 4)^3 (x - 2)^{10} (x - 3)^3$

81. $f(x) = \begin{cases} 3^x \text{ when } x \text{ is an odd number.} \\ 3^x + 4 \text{ when } x \text{ is an even number.} \end{cases}$

    What is the value of
    $\dfrac{1}{4}[f(1) + f(2) + f(3) + f(4) + \ldots + f(n)]$ if $n = 72$.

    (a) $\dfrac{3}{8}(3^{72} - 1) + 36$    (b) $\dfrac{3}{8}(3^{72} + 1) + 36$

    (c) $\dfrac{3}{8}(3^{72}) + 36$    (d) None of these.

82. $f(x + y) = f(x.y)$ where $x$ and $y$ are real numbers and '$f$' is a real function.

If $f(10) = 12$ then $[f(7)]^{143} - [f(11)]^{143} + f(5) = ?$

83. Which of the following represents the curve of $|e^{-|x|}|$?

    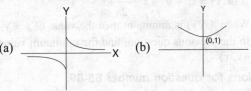

    (a)      (b)

    (c)      (d) None of these

84. Which of the following function correctly represents the curve of $|e^{-x} - 3|$:

    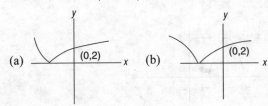

    (a)      (b)

    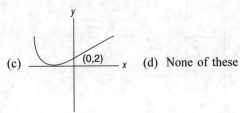

    (c)      (d) None of these

85. Which of the following represents the curve of $||\log|x - 3||$?

    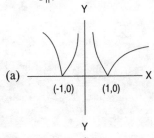

    (a)

    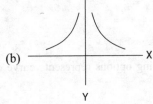

    (b)

    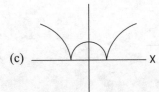

    (c)

(d) None of these.

86. $f(x, y) = x^2 + y^2 - x - \dfrac{3y}{2} + 1$

    When $f(x, y)$ is minimum then the value of $x + y = ?$

87. In the previous question, find the minimum value of $f(x, y)$

### Directions for question number 88-89:

88. If the graph given below represents $f(x + 5)$ then which of the given options would represent the graph of $f(-2 - x)$?

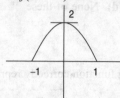

(a)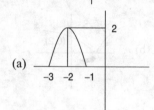

(b)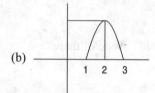

(c)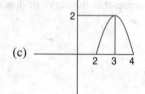

(d)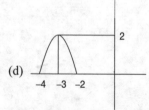

89. Which of the following options represents curve of $f(-2x)$?

(a)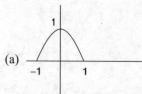

(b)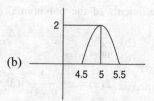

(c)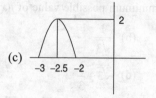

(d) None of these.

90. If $x, y$ are real numbers and function $g(x)$ satisfies $\dfrac{(g(x+y) + g(x-y))}{2} = g(x)g(y)$ and $g(0)$ is a positive real number then which of the following options may represent graph of $g(x)$?

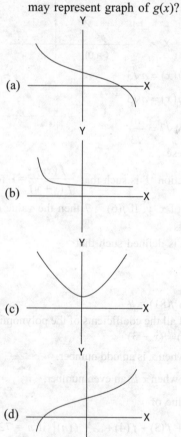

*Space for Rough Work*

## LEVEL OF DIFFICULTY (III)

1. Find the domain of the definition of the function $y = 1/(x - |x|)^{1/2}$.
   (a) $-\infty < x < \infty$    (b) $-\infty < x < 0$
   (c) $0 < x < \infty$    (d) No where

2. Find the domain of the definition of the function $y = (x - 1)^{1/2} + 2(1 - x)^{1/2} + (x^2 + 3)^{1/2}$.
   (a) $x = 0$    (b) $[1, \infty)$
   (c) $[-1, 1]$    (d) $x = 1$

3. Find the domain of the definition of the function $y = \log_{10} [(x - 5)/(x^2 - 10x + 24)] - (x + 4)^{1/2}$.
   (a) $x > 6$    (b) $4 < x < 5$
   (c) Both $a$ and $b$    (d) None of these

4. Find the domain of the definition of the function $y = [(x - 3)/(x + 3)]^{1/2} + [(1 - x)/(1 + x)]^{1/2}$.
   (a) $x > 3$    (b) $x < -3$
   (c) $-3 \leq x \leq 3$    (d) Nowhere

5. Find the domain of the definition of the function $y = (2x^2 + x + 1)^{-3/4}$.
   (a) $x \geq 0$    (b) All $x$ except $x = 0$
   (c) $-3 \leq x \leq 3$    (d) Everywhere

6. Find the domain of the definition of the function $y = (x^2 - 2x - 3)^{1/2} - 1/(-2 + 3x - x^2)^{1/2}$.
   (a) $x > 0$    (b) $-1 < x < 0$
   (c) $x^2$    (d) None of these

7. Find the domain of the definition of the function $y = \log_{10} [1 - \log_{10}(x^2 - 5x + 16)]$.
   (a) $(2, 3]$    (b) $[2, 3)$
   (c) $[2, 3]$    (d) None of these

8. If $f(t) = (t - 1)/(t + 1)$, then $f(f(t))$ will be equal to
   (a) $1/t$    (b) $-1/t$
   (c) $t$    (d) $-t$

9. If $f(x) = e^x$ and $g(x) = \log_e x$ then value of $fog$ will be
   (a) $x$    (b) $0$
   (c) $1$    (d) $e$

10. In the above question, find the value of $gof$.
    (a) $x$    (b) $0$
    (c) $1$    (d) $e$

11. The function $y = 1/x$ shifted 1 unit down and 1 unit right is given by
    (a) $y - 1 = 1/(x + 1)$    (b) $y - 1 = 1/(x - 1)$
    (c) $y + 1 = 1/(x - 1)$    (d) $y + 1 = 1/(x + 1)$

12. Which of the following functions is an even function?

13. Which of the following functions is not an odd function?
    (a) $f(t) = \log_2(t + \sqrt{t^2} + 1)$
    (b) $f(t) = (a^t + a^{-t})/(a^t - a^{-t})$
    (c) $f(t) = (a^t + 1)/(a^t - 1)$
    (d) All of these

   (a) $f(t) = (a^t + a^{-t})/(a^t - a^{-t})$
   (b) $f(t) = (a^t + 1)/(a^t - 1)$
   (c) $f(t) = t. (a^t - 1)/(a^t + 1)$
   (d) None of these

14. Find $fof$ if $f(t) = t/(1 + t^2)^{1/2}$.
    (a) $1/(1 + 2t^2)^{1/2}$    (b) $t/(1 + 2t^2)^{1/2}$
    (c) $(1 + 2t^2)$    (d) None of these

15. At what integral value of $x$ will the function $\frac{(x^2 + 3x + 1)}{(x^2 - 3x + 1)}$ attain its maximum value?
    (a) $3$    (b) $4$
    (c) $-3$    (d) None of these

16. Inverse of $f(t) = (10^t - 10^{-t})/(10^t + 10^{-t})$ is
    (a) $1/2 \log \{(1 - t)/(1 + t)\}$
    (b) $0.5 \log \{(t - 1)/(t + 1)\}$
    (c) $1/2 \log_{10} (2^t - 1)$
    (d) None of these

17. If $f(x) = |x - 2|$, then which of the following is always true?
    (a) $f(x) = (f(x))^2$    (b) $f(x) = f(-x)$
    (c) $f(x) = x - 2$    (d) None of these

**Directions for Questions 18 to 20:** Read the instructions below and solve:

$f(x) = f(x - 2) - f(x - 1)$, $x$ is a natural number
$f(1) = 0, f(2) = 1$

18. The value of $f(x)$ is negative for
    (a) All $x > 2$
    (b) All odd $x(x > 2)$
    (c) For all even $x(x > 0)$
    (d) $f(x)$ is always positive

19. The value of $f[f(6)]$ is
    (a) $5$    (b) $-1$
    (c) $-3$    (d) $-2$

20. The value of $f(6) - f(8)$ is
    (a) $f(4) + f(5)$    (b) $f(7)$
    (c) $-\{f(7) + f(5)\}$    (d) $-f(5)$

21. Which of the following is not an even function?
    (a) $f(x) = e^x + e^{-x}$     (b) $f(x) = e^x - e^{-x}$
    (c) $f(x) = e^{2x} + e^{-2x}$     (d) None of these

22. If $f(x)$ is a function satisfying $f(x) \cdot f(1/x) = f(x) + f(1/x)$ and $f(4) = 65$, what will be the value of $f(6)$?
    (a) 37     (b) 217
    (c) 64     (d) None of these

## Directions for Questions 23 to 34:

Mark (a) if $f(-x) = f(x)$,
Mark (b) if $f(-x) = -f(x)$
Mark (c) if neither (a) nor (b) is true
Mark (d) if $f(x)$ does not exist at at least one point of the domain.

23.

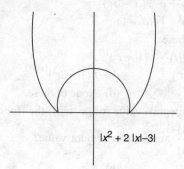

$|x^2 + 2 |x| - 3|$

24.

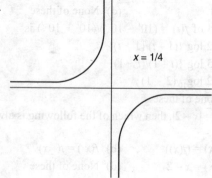

$x = 1/4$

25.

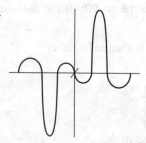

26.

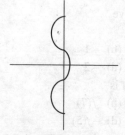

27.

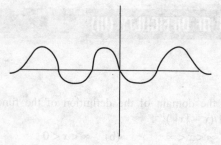

28.

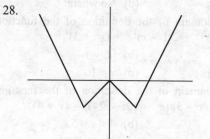

29.

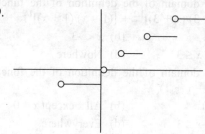

30.

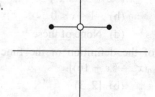

31.

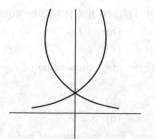

32.

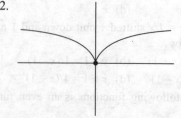

33.

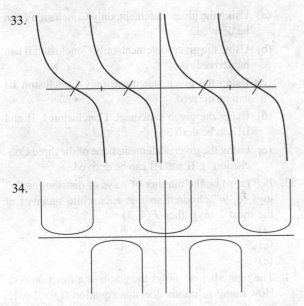

34.

**Directions for Questions 35 to 40:** Define the functions:

$A(x, y, z) = \text{Max} (\max (x, y), \min (y, z) \min (x, z))$
$B(x, y, z) = \text{Max} (\max (x, y), \min (y, z) \max (x, z))$
$C(x, y, z) = \text{Max} (\min (x, y), \min (y, z) \min (x, z))$
$D(x, y, z) = \text{Min} (\max (x, y), \max (y, z) \max (x, z))$
$\text{Max} (x, y, z) = \text{Maximum of } x, y \text{ and } z.$
$\text{Min} (x, y, z) = \text{Minimum of } x, y \text{ and } z.$
Assume that $x, y$ and $z$ are distinct integers.

35. For what condition will $A(x, y, z)$ be equal to Max $(x, y, z)$?
    (a) When $x$ is maximum (b) When $y$ is maximum
    (c) When $z$ is maximum (d) Either (a) or (b)

36. For what condition will $B(x, y, z)$ be equal to Min $(x, y, z)$?
    (a) When $y$ is minimum (b) When $z$ is minimum
    (c) Either (a) or (b) (d) Never

37. For what condition will $A(x, y, z)$ not be equal to $B(x, y, z)$?
    (a) $x > y > z$ (b) $y > z > x$
    (c) $z > y > x$ (d) None of these

38. Under what condition will $C(x, y, z)$ be equal to $B(x, y, z)$?
    (a) $x > y > z$ (b) $z > y > x$
    (c) Both $a$ and $b$ (d) Never

39. Which of the following will always be true?
    (I) $A(x, y, z)$ will always be greater than Min $(x, y, z)$
    (II) $B(x, y, z)$ will always be lower than Max $(x, y, z)$
    (III) $A(x, y, z)$ will never be greater than $B(x, y, z)$
    (a) I only (b) III only
    (c) Both $a$ and $b$ (d) All the three

40. The highest value amongst the following will be
    (a) Max/Min (b) $A/B$
    (c) $C/D$ (d) Cannot be determined

**Directions for Questions 41 to 49:** Suppose $x$ and $y$ are real numbers. Let $f(x, y) = |x + y|$ $F(f(x, y)) = -f(x, y)$ and $G(f(x, y)) = -F(f(x, y))$

41. Which one of the following is true?
    (a) $F(f(x, y)).G(f(x, y)) = -F(f(x, y)). G.(f(x, y))$
    (b) $F(f(x, y)).G(f(x, y)) \leq -F(f(x, y)). G.(f(x, y))$
    (c) $G(f(x, y)).f(x, y) = F(f(x, y)). (f(x, y))$
    (d) $G(f(x, y)).F(f(x, y)) = f(x, y). f(x, y)$

42. Which of the following has $a^2$ as the result?
    (a) $F(f(a, -a)).G(f(a, -a))$
    (b) $-F(f(a, a)).G(f(a, a))/4$
    (c) $F(f(a, a)).G(f(a, a))/2^2$
    (d) $f(a, a).f(a, a)$

43. Find the value of the expression.
    $$\frac{G(f(3, 2)) + F(f(-1, 2))}{f(2, -3) + G(f(1, 2))} \cdots$$
    (a) 3/2 (b) 2/3
    (c) 1 (d) 2

44. Which of the following is equal to
    $$\frac{G(f(32, 13)) + F(f(15, -5))}{f(2, 3) + G(f(1.5, 0.5))} ?$$
    (a) $\dfrac{2G(f(1, 2)) + (f(-3, 1))}{G(f(2, 6) + F(f(-8, 2))}$
    (b) $\dfrac{3.G(f(3, 4)) + F(f(1, 0))}{f(1, 1) + G(f(2, 0))}$
    (c) $\dfrac{(f(3, 4)) + F(f(1, 2))}{G(f(1, 1))}$
    (d) None of these

Now if $A(f(x, y)) = f(x, y)$
$B(f(x, y)) = -f(x, y)$
$C(f(x, y)) = f(x, y)$
$D(f(x, y)) = -f(x, y)$ and similarly
$Z(f(x, y)) = -f(x, y)$

Now, solve the following:

45. Find the value of $A(f(0, 1)) + B(f(1, 2)) + C(f(2, 3))$ $+ \ldots + Z(f(25, 26))$.
    (a) −50 (b) −52
    (c) −26 (d) None of these

46. Which of the following is true?
    (i) $A(f(0, 1)) < B(f(1, 2)) < C(f(2, 3))\ldots$
    (ii) $A(f(0, 1)). B(f(1, 2)) > B(f(1, 2)).C(f(2, 3)) > C(f(2, 3)). D(f(3, 4))$
    (iii) $A(f(0, 0)) = B(f(0, 0)) = C(f(0, 0)) = \ldots = Z(f(0, 0))$
    (a) only (i) and (ii) (b) only (ii) and (iii)
    (c) only (ii) (d) only (i)

47. If max $(x, y, z)$ = maximum of $x$, $y$ and $z$
    Min $(x, y, z)$ = minimum of $x$, $y$ and $z$
    $f(x, y) = |x + y|$
    $F(f(x, y)) = -f(x, y)$
    $G(f(x, y)) = -F(f(x, y))$
    Then find the value of the following expression:
    Min (max $[f(2, 3), F(f(3, 4)), G(f(4, 5))]$, min $[f(1, 2), F(f(-1, 2)), G(f(1, -2))]$, max $[f(-3\ -4), f(-5\ -1), G(f(-4, -6))])$
    (a) $-1$          (b) $-7$
    (c) $-6$          (d) $-10$

48. Which of the following is the value of
    Max. $[f(a, b), F(f(b, c)), G(f(c, d))]$
    for all $a > b > c > d$?
    (a) Anything but positive
    (b) Anything but negative
    (c) Negative or positive
    (d) Any real value

49. If another function is defined as $P(x, y) = \dfrac{F(f(x, y))}{(x.\ y)}$
    which of the following is second lowest in value?
    (a) Value of $P(x, y)$ for $x = 2$ and $y = 1$
    (b) Value of $P(x, y)$ for $x = 3$ and $y = 4$
    (c) Value of $P(x, y)$ for $x = 3$ and $y = 5$
    (d) Value of $P(x, y)$ for $x = 3$ and $y = 2$

50. If $f(s) = (b^s + b^{-s})/2$, where $b > 0$. Find $f(s + t) + f(s - t)$.
    (a) $f(s) - f(t)$          (b) $2 f(s).f(t)$
    (c) $4 f(s).f(t)$          (d) $f(s) + f(t)$

**Questions 51 to 60** are all actual questions from the XAT exam.

51. $A_0, A_1, A_2,...$ is a sequence of numbers with $A_0 = 1$, $A_1 = 3$, and $A_t = (t + 1)A_{(t - 1)} - tA_{(t-2)}$, where $t = 2,3,4...$
    Conclusion I. $A8 = 77$
    Conclusion II. $A10 = 121$
    Conclusion III. $A12 = 145$
    (a) Using the given statement, only Conclusion I can be derived.
    (b) Using the given statement, only Conclusion II can be derived.
    (c) Using the given statement, only Conclusion III can be derived.
    (d) Using the given statement, Conclusion I, II and III can be derived.
    (e) Using the given statement, none of the three Conclusions I, II and III can be derived.

52. A, B, C be real numbers satisfying $A < B < C$, $A + B + C = 6$ and $AB + BC + CA = 9$
    Conclusion I. $1 < B < 3$
    Conclusion II. $2 < A < 3$
    Conclusion III. $0 < C < 1$

(a) Using the given statement, only Conclusion I can be derived.
(b) Using the given statement, only Conclusion II can be derived.
(c) Using the given statement, only Conclusion III can be derived.
(d) Using the given statement, Conclusion I, II and III can be derived.
(e) Using the given statement, none of the three Conclusions I, II and III can be derived.

53. If $F(x, n)$ be the number of ways of distributing "$x$" toys to "$n$" children so that each child receives at the most 2 toys, then $F(4, 3) = $ ___?
    (a) 2          (b) 6
    (c) 3          (d) 4
    (e) 5

54. The figure below shows the graph of a function $f(x)$. How many solutions does the equation $f(f(x)) = 15$ have?
    (a) 5          (b) 6
    (c) 7          (d) 8
    (e) Cannot be determined from the given graph

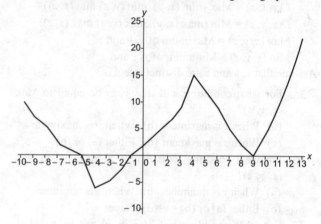

55. In the following question, a question is followed by two statements. Mark your answer as:
    (a) If the question can be answered by the first statement alone but cannot be answered by the second statement alone;
    (b) If the question can be answered by the second statement alone but cannot be answered by the first statement alone;
    (c) If the question can be answered by both the statements together but cannot be answered by any one of the statements alone;
    (d) If the question can be answered by the first statement alone as well as by the second statement alone;
    (e) If the question cannot be answered even by using both the statements together.

A sequence of positive integers is defined as $A_{n+1} = A_n^2 + 1$ for each $n \geq 1$. What is the value of the Greatest Common Divisor of $A_{900}$ and $A_{1000}$?

I. $A_0 = 1$          II. $A_1 = 2$

56. A manufacturer produces two types of products— A and B, which are subjected to two types of operations, viz., grinding and polishing. Each unit of product A takes 2 hours of grinding and 3 hours of polishing whereas product B takes 3 hours of grinding and 2 hours of polishing. The manufacturer has 10 grinders and 15 polishers. Each grinder operates for 12 hours/day and each polisher 10 hours/day. The profit margin per unit of A and B are ₹ 5/- and ₹ 7/- respectively. If the manufacturer utilises all his resources for producing these two types of items, what is the maximum profit that the manufacturer can earn?

(a) ₹ 280/-          (b) ₹ 294/-
(c) ₹ 515/-          (d) ₹ 550/-
(e) None of the above

57. Consider a function $f(x) = x^4 + x^3 + x^2 + x + 1$, where $x$ is a positive integer greater than 1. What will be the remainder if $f(x^5)$ is divided by $f(x)$?

(a) 1          (b) 4
(c) 5          (d) A monomial in $x$
(e) A polynomial in $x$

58. For all real numbers $x$, except $x = 0$ and $x = 1$, the function $F$ is defined by $F\left(\dfrac{x}{x-1}\right) = \dfrac{1}{x}$

If $0 < \alpha < 90°$ then $F((\operatorname{cosec} \alpha)^2) =$

(a) $(\sin \alpha)^2$          (b) $(\cos \alpha)^2$
(c) $(\tan \alpha)^2$          (d) $(\cot \alpha)^2$
(e) $(\sec \alpha)^2$

59. $F(x)$ is a fourth order polynomial with integer coefficients and with no common factor. The roots of $F(x)$ are $-2, -1, 1, 2$. If $p$ is a prime number greater than 97, then the largest integer that divides $F(p)$ for all values of $p$ is:

(a) 72          (b) 120
(c) 240          (d) 360
(e) None of the above.

60. If $x = (9 + 4\sqrt{5})^{48} = [x] + f$, where $[x]$ is defined as integral part of $x$ and $f$ is a fraction, then $x(1 - f)$ equals–

(a) 1
(b) Less than 1
(c) More than 1
(d) Between 1 and 2
(e) None of the above

61. If $3f(x+2) + 4f\left(\dfrac{1}{x+2}\right) = 4x$, $x \neq -2$, then $f(4) =$

(a) 7          (b) $-52/7$
(c) 8          (d) None of the above.

62. The figure below shows the graph of a function f(x). How many solutions does the equation $f(f(x)) = 15$ have for the span of the graph shown?

(a) 5          (b) 6
(c) 7          (d) 8

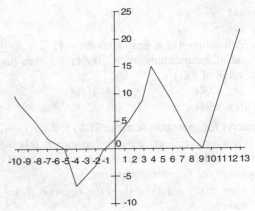

63. If $f(x) = (x-6), g(x) = \dfrac{(x-9)(x-1)}{(x-7)(x-3)}$

How many real values of $x$ satisfy the equation $[f(x)]^{g(x)} = 1$

64. A continuous function f(x) is defined for all real values of $x$, such that $f(x) = 0$, only for two distinct real values of x. Only for two distinct real values of $x$. It is also known that $f(4) + f(6) = 0$, $f(5).f(7) > 0$, $f(4).f(8) < 0$, $f(1) > 0$ & $f(2) < 0$

Which of the following statement must be true.

(a) $f(1)f(2)f(4) < 0$          (b) $f(5)f(6)f(7) < 0$
(c) $f(1)f(3)f(4) > 0$          (d) None of these

65. $f(x) = 7[x] + 4\{x\}$

where $[x]$ = Greatest integer less than or equals to $x$.

$\{x\} = x - [x]$

How many real values of $x$ satisfy the equation $f(x) = 12 + x$

(a) 0          (b) 1
(c) 2          (d) none of these

66. How many non-negative integer solutions $(x, y)$ are possible for the equation $x^2 - xy + y^2 = x + y$ such that $x \geq y$.

(a) 1          (b) 2
(c) 3          (d) 4

67. A function 'g' is defined for all natural numbers $n \geq 2$ as $\dfrac{g(n-1)}{g(n)} = \dfrac{n}{n-1}$

If $g(1) = 2$ then what is the value of

$$\dfrac{\left[\dfrac{1}{g(1)} \times \dfrac{1}{g(2)} \times \dfrac{1}{g(3)} \times \ldots \dfrac{1}{g(8)}\right]}{\left[\dfrac{1}{g(1)} + \dfrac{1}{g(2)} + \dfrac{1}{g(3)} + \ldots \dfrac{1}{g(8)}\right]}$$

(a) $8!/2^8$          (b) $8!/(2^8 . 18)$
(c) $8!/18.2^7$          (d) $8!/3^7.24$

68. f(x) is a polynomial of degree 77 which when divided by $(x - 1)$, $(x - 2)$, $(x - 3)$, $(x - 4)$,..., $(x - 77)$ it leaves $1, 2, 3, \ldots, 77$ respectively as the remainders. Find the value of $f(0) + f(78)$?

(a) 77

(b) 78

(c) −77

(d) 78!

69. A function $f(n)$ is defined as $f(n − 1) [2 − f(n)] = 1$ for all natural numbers '$n$'. If $f(1) = 3$, then find the value of $f(21)$

(a) 42/41

(b) 45/43

(c) 43/41

(d) 47/45

**Directions for question number 70&71:** If $f(x) = 10[x] + 22\{x\}$, where $[x]$ denotes the largest integer less than or equal to $x$ and $\{x\} = x − [x]$, (i.e. the fractional part of $x$) then answer the following questions.

70. How many solutions does the equation $f(x) = 250$ have?

(a) 0

(b) 1

(c) 2

(d) 3

71. Sum of all possible values of $x$ is

72. If $f(x + 1) = f(x) − f(x−1)$ and $f(5) = 6$ and $f(17) = 2f(16)$ then $f(17) = ?$

(a) 5

(b) 6

(c) 16

(d) 18

73. If $h(x)$ is a positive valued function and

$$\frac{h(x)}{h(x-1)} = \frac{h(x-2)}{h(x+1)} \text{ for all } x \geq 0$$

If $h(56) = 16$ and $h(52) = 4$ then $h(54) = ?$

74. $f(x) = 1 - \dfrac{2}{(x+1)}$

If $f^2(x) = f(f(x))$, $f^3(x) = f(f(f(x)))$, $f^4(x) = f(f(f(f(x))))$ and so on then find $f^{802}(x)$ at $x = −1/2$

**Directions for question number 75 – 76:** If $\log_3(x + y) + \log_3 (x − y) = 3$, where $x$ and $y$ are positive integers then answer the following questions:

75. If $y > 0$ then how many different pairs of $(x, y)$ are possible?

76. The Maximum value of $x + y =$ ____

**Direction for 77&78:**

$f(x) = |x + 2|$

$g(x) = x^2 − 7x + 10$

$h(x) = \min(f(x), g(x))$

77. For how many positive integer values of $x$, is $h(x) \leq 0$?

78. Find the sum of all integer values of $x$ for which $h(x) < 0$.

79. If $[x]$ denotes the greatest integer less than or equal to $x$. If $p$ and $q$ are two distinct real numbers and $[2p − 3] = q + 7$, $[3q + 1] = p + 6$ then the value of $p^2 \times q^2$ is:

80. If $f(a) = 3^a$ and $f(a + 1) = 3^{(a + 1)} + 4$, where '$a$' is an odd number, what is the value of:

$$\frac{1}{4}[f(1) + f(2) + f(3) + f(4) + \ldots + f(72)]$$

(a) $\dfrac{3}{8}(3^{72} − 1) + 36$

(b) $\dfrac{3}{8}(3^{72} − 1) − 36$

(c) $\dfrac{3}{8}(3^{72} + 1) + 36\dfrac{3}{8}(3^{72} + 1) + 36$

(d) None of these.

**Directions for question number 81 and 82:**

$f(x) = \dfrac{x^2}{4}$ and $g(x) = 2x^{[3x]} + 2$ where $[x]$ is the greatest integer less than or equal to '$x$'. Then answer the following questions:

81. Which of the following statement is true about $g(f(x))$?

(a) $g(f(x))$ is neither even nor odd.

(b) $g(f(x))$ is maximum for $x = 11$

(c) $g(f(x))$ will have its' minimum for a value of $x$ that obeys $\dfrac{3x^2}{4} \leq 1$

(d) None of these

82. Which of the following is the value of $g(f(x))$ at $x = 2$?

(a) 66

(b) 34

(c) 18

(d) 64

83. The area bounded between $|x + y| = 2$ and $|x − y| = 2$ is:

(a) 2

(b) 4

(c) 6

(d) 8

**Directions for question number 84 to 86:**

If $f(x) = |x| + |x + 4| + |x + 8| + |x + 12| + \ldots + |x + 4n|$, where $x$ is an integer and $n$ is a positive integer.

84. If $n = 8$, what is the minimum value of $f(x)$?

85. If $n = 7$, then for how many values of $x$, $f(x)$ is minimum.

86. For $n = 9$ which of the following statements is true?

(a) $f(x)$ will be minimum for a total 5 values of $x$.

(b) $f(−17) = f(−19)$

(c) Minimum value of $f(x)$ is 100

(d) All of these

87. Find the area enclosed by the graph $|x| + |y| = 3$

88. Find the area enclosed by curve $|x − 2| + |y − 3| = 3$

**Directions for question numbers 89 and 90:**

$8\{x\} = x + 2[x]$

$\{x\}$ denotes the fractional part of $x$.

$[x]$ denotes the greatest integer less than or equals to $x$.

89. For how many positive values of $x$, is the given equation true?

90. Find the difference of the greatest and the least value of $x$ for which the given equation is true? (till two digits after the decimal point)

**Directions for question numbers 91 and 92:**

If $f(x) = \dfrac{4^{x-1}}{4^{x-1}+1}$ and $g(x) = 2x$, then answer the following questions.

91. $fog\left(\dfrac{1}{4}\right) + fog\left(\dfrac{3}{4}\right) = ?$

92. $fog\left(\dfrac{1}{2}\right) + fog\left(\dfrac{1}{4}\right) + fog\left(\dfrac{1}{8}\right) + f\left(\dfrac{1}{16}\right)$

$\qquad + f\left(\dfrac{3}{4}\right) + fog\left(\dfrac{7}{8}\right) + fog\left(\dfrac{15}{16}\right) = ?$

**Directions for questions numbers 93 – 96:**

If for a positive integer $x$, $f(x + 2) = f(x) + 2(x + 1)$, when x is even and $f(x + 2) = f(x) + 1$, when $x$ is odd. If $f(1) = 1$ and $f(2) = 5$. Then answer the following questions.

93. $f(24) = ?$

94. $\left[\dfrac{f(14)}{f(11)}\right] = ?$, where [ ] denotes the greatest integer function

95. Which of the following statement is true?
   (a) For even value of $x$ value of $f(x)$ is also even
   (b) For odd value of $x$, value of $f(x)$ is odd.
   (c) For even value of $x$, value of $f(x)$ is odd.
   (d) None of these

96. Value of $f(f(f(f(3)))) + f(f(f(2))) = ?$

**Direction for question numbers 97 to 98:**

$F(x)$ is a 6$^{th}$ degree polynomial of $x$. It is given that $F(0) = 0$, $F(1) = 1$, $F(2) = 2$, $F(3) = 3$, $F(4) = 4$, $F(5) = 5$, $F(6) = 7 =$

97. Find the value of $F(8) =$

98. If $x$ is a negative integer then the minimum value of $F(x) = ?$

99. If $g(x + y) = g(x) \cdot g(y)$ and $g(1) = 5$, then find the value of $g(1) + g(2) + g(3) + g(4) + g(5)$.

100. In the previous question if

$$\sum_{p=1}^{n} g(q + p) = \dfrac{1}{4}\left(5^{p+3} - 125\right)$$

Where '$p$' is a positive integer then $q =$

**Space for Rough Work**

# ANSWER KEY

## Level of Difficulty (I)

| | | | |
|---|---|---|---|
| 1. (b) | 2. (d) | 3. (a) | 4. (c) |
| 5. (a) | 6. (d) | 7. (b) | 8. (a) |
| 9. (c) | 10. (b) | 11. (d) | 12. (b) |
| 13. (d) | 14. (a) | 15. (a) | 16. (c) |
| 17. (a) | 18. (d) | 19. (b) | 20. (c) |
| 21. (b) | 22. (b) | 23. (a) | 24. (c) |
| 25. (a) | 26. (d) | 27. (c) | 28. (c) |
| 29. (c) | 30. (d) | 31. (a) | 32. (a) |
| 33. (a) | 34. (a) | 35. (b) | 36. (c) |
| 37. (d) | 38. (d) | 39. (c) | 40. (a) |
| 41. (a) | 42. (d) | 43. (d) | 44. (a) |
| 45. (a) | 46. (c) | 47. (d) | 48. (d) |
| 49. (d) | 50. (d) | 51. (b) | 52. (a) |
| 53. (a) | 54. (b) | 55. (d) | 56. (d) |
| 57. (c) | 58. (b) | 59. (d) | 60. (c) |
| 61. (a) | 62. (a) | 63. (c) | 64. 3 |
| 65. 1 | 66. 1 | 67. 7.86 | 68. 13.75 |
| 69. 12 | 70. 1.5 | 71. (d) | 72. 2 |
| 73. (d) | 74. 8 | 75. (d) | 76. (c) |
| 77. 0.14 | 78. 2 | 79. (b) | 80. (b) |
| 81. 9 | 82. 10 | 83. 0 | 84. (c) |
| 85. −2 | 86. (b) | 87. (c) | 88. (a) |
| 89. (b) | 90. (b) | 91. (c) | 92. (c) |
| 93. 3 | 94. (c) | 95. (c) | |

## Level of Difficulty (II)

| | | | |
|---|---|---|---|
| 1. (a) | 2. (d) | 3. (a) | 4. (d) |
| 5. (d) | 6. (c) | 7. (c) | 8. (b) |
| 9. (c) | 10. (c) | 11. (a) | 12. (b) |
| 13. (b) | 14. (c) | 15. (c) | 16. (a) |
| 17. (d) | 18. (c) | 19. (a) | 20. (c) |
| 21. (c) | 22. (d) | 23. (b) | 24. (a) |
| 25. (d) | 26. (d) | 27. (c) | 28. (a) |
| 29. (c) | 30. (d) | 31. (b) | 32. (d) |
| 33. (b) | 34. (a) | 35. (c) | 36. (d) |
| 37. (c) | 38. (a) | 39. (c) | 40. (b) |
| 41. (c) | 42. (b) | 43. (c) | 44. (b) |
| 45. (c) | 46. (c) | 47. (b) | 48. (c) |
| 49. (d) | 50. (a) | 51. (a) | 52. (c) |
| 53. (c) | 54. (b) | 55. (b) | 56. (c) |
| 57. (b) | 58. (c) | 59. (c) | 60. (a) |
| 61. (d) | 62. (a) | 63. (b) | 64. (c) |
| 65. (d) | 66. (b) | 67. −8/3 | 68. 1 |
| 69. 30.8 | 70. 4 | 71. 440/3 | 72. 1054 |
| 73. 1999997 | 74. 0 | 75. (c) | 76. (b) |
| 77. (a) | 78. 14 | 79. 625 | 80. 216 |
| 81. (a) | 82. 12 | 83. (c) | 84. (a) |
| 85. (d) | 86. 1.25 | 87. 3/16 | 88. (d) |
| 89. (c) | 90. (c) | | |

## Level of Difficulty (III)

| | | | |
|---|---|---|---|
| 1. (d) | 2. (d) | 3. (c) | 4. (d) |
| 5. (d) | 6. (d) | 7. (d) | 8. (b) |
| 9. (a) | 10. (a) | 11. (c) | 12. (c) |
| 13. (a) | 14. (b) | 15. (a) | 16. (b) |
| 17. (d) | 18. (b) | 19. (c) | 20. (b) |
| 21. (b) | 22. (b) | 23. (a) | 24. (b) |
| 25. (b) | 26. (d) | 27. (b) | 28. (a) |
| 29. (c) | 30. (a) | 31. (d) | 32. (a) |
| 33. (d) | 34. (a) | 35. (d) | 36. (d) |
| 37. (c) | 38. (d) | 39. (c) | 40. (d) |
| 41. (b) | 42. (b) | 43. (c) | 44. (b) |
| 45. (c) | 46. (b) | 47. (a) | 48. (b) |
| 49. (b) | 50. (b) | 51. (e) | 52. (a) |
| 53. (b) | 54. (e) | 55. (d) | 56. (b) |
| 57. (c) | 58. (b) | 59. (d) | 60. (a) |
| 61. (b) | 62. (c) | 63. 3 | 64. (c) |
| 65. (b) | 66. (d) | 67. (b) | 68. (b) |
| 69. (c) | 70. (d) | 71. 73.36 | 72. (b) |
| 73. 8 | 74. 2 | 75. 2 | 76. 27 |
| 77. 4 | 78. 7 | 79. 784 | 80. (a) |
| 81. (c) | 82. (b) | 83. (d) | 84. 80 |
| 85. 5 | 86. (d) | 87. 18 | 88. 18 |
| 89. 2 | 90. 2.86 | 91. 1 | 92. 3.5 |
| 93. 291 | 94. 16 | 95. (c) | 96. 4 |
| 97. 36 | 98. 0 | 99. 3905 | 100. 2 |

## Solutions and Shortcuts

### Level of Difficulty (I)

1. $y = |x|$ will be defined for all values of $x$. From $= -\infty$ to $+\infty$

   Hence, option (b).

2. For $y = \sqrt{x}$ to be defined, $x$ should be non-negative. i.e. $x \geq 0$.

3. Since the function contains $a \sqrt{x}$ in it, $x \geq 0$ would be the domain.

4. For $(x - 2)^{1/2}$ to be defined $x \geq 2$.
   For $(8 - x)^{1/2}$ to be defined $x \leq 8$.
   Thus, $2 \leq x \leq 8$ would be the required domain.

5. $(9 - x^2) \geq 0 \Rightarrow -3 \leq x \leq 3$.

6. The function would be defined for all values of $x$ except where the denominator viz: $x^2 - 4x + 3$ becomes equal to zero.

   The roots of $x^2 - 4x + 3 = 0$ being 1, 3, it follows that the domain of definition of the function would be all values of $x$ except $x = 1$ and $x = 3$.

7. $f(x) = x$ and $g(x) = (\sqrt{x})^2$ would be identical if $\sqrt{x}$ is defined.

   Hence, $x \geq 0$ would be the answer.

8. $f(x) = x$ is defined for all values of $x$.

   $g(x) = x^2/x$ also returns the same values as $f(x)$ except at $x = 0$ where it is not defined.

Hence. option (a).

9. $f(x) = \sqrt{x^3} \Rightarrow f(3x) = \sqrt{(3x)^3} = 3\sqrt{3x^3}$ .
   Option (c) is correct.

10. $7 f(x) = 7 e^x$.

11. While $\log x^2$ is defined for $-\infty < x < \infty$ , $2 \log x$ is only defined for $0 < x < \infty$. Thus, the two functions are identical for $0 < x < \infty$.

12. $y$ – axis by definition.

13. Origin by definition.

14. $x^{-8}$ is even since $f(x) = f(-x)$ in this case.

15. $(x + 1)^3$ is not odd as $f(x) \neq -f(-x)$.

16. $dy/dx = 2x + 10 = 0 \Rightarrow x = -5$.

17. Required value $= (-5)^2 + 10(-5) + 11$
    $= 25 - 50 + 11 = -14$.

18. Since the denominator $x^2 - 3x + 2$ has real roots, the maximum value would be infinity.

19. The minimum value of the function would occur at the minimum value of $(x^2 - 2x + 5)$ as this quadratic function has imaginary roots.
    For $\quad y = x^2 - 2x + 5$
    $\quad\quad dy/dx = 2x - 2 = 0 \Rightarrow x = 1$
    $\Rightarrow \quad x^2 - 2x + 5 = 4$.
    Thus, minimum value of the argument of the log is 4. So minimum value of the function is $\log_2 4 = 2$.

20. $y = 1/x + 1$
    Hence, $\quad y - 1 = 1/x$
    $\Rightarrow \quad\quad x = 1/(y - 1)$
    Thus $\quad f^{-1}(x) = 1/(x - 1)$.

**21–23.**
$$f(1) = 0, f(2) = 1,$$
$$f(3) = f(1) - f(2) = -1$$
$$f(4) = f(2) - f(3) = 2$$
$$f(5) = f(3) - f(4) = -3$$
$$f(6) = f(4) - f(5) = 5$$
$$f(7) = f(5) - f(6) = -8$$
$$f(8) = f(6) - f(7) = 13$$
$$f(9) = f(7) - f(8) = -21$$

21. 13

22. $-8 + 2 = -6$

23. $0 + 1 - 1 + 2 - 3 + 5 - 8 + 13 - 21 = -12$.

24. For any $^nC_r$, $n$ should be positive and $r \geq 0$.
    Thus, for positive $x$, $5 - x \geq 0$
    $\Rightarrow x = 1, 2, 3, 4, 5$.

**Directions for Questions 25 to 38:** You essentially have to mark (a) if it is an even function, mark (b) if it is an odd function, mark (c) if the function is neither even nor odd.

Also, option (d) would occur if the function does not exist atleast one point of the domain. This means one of two things.

Either the function is returning two values for one value of $x$. (as in questions 26, 30, 37 and 38) or the function has a break in between (not seen in any of these questions).

We see even functions in: 25, 31, 32, 33 and 34, [Symmetry about the $y$ axis].

We see odd functions in question 35.

While the figures in Questions 27, 28, 29 and 36 are neither odd nor even.

39. $\{[(3@4)! (3 \#2)] @ [(4!3) @ (2 \# 3)]\}$
    $\{[(3.5) ! (5)] @ [ (0.5) @ (-5)]\}$
    $\{[-0.75] @ [-2.25]\} = -1.5$.

40. $(7) @ (-0.5) = 3.25$.

41. $0 @ 0.5 = 0.25$. Thus, $a$

42. $b = (1) (4) = 4$.
    $$C = \frac{(16)}{(1)(4)}$$
    $$16/4 = 4$$
    Hence, both (b) and (c).

43. (a) will always be true because $(a + b)/2$ would always be greater then $(a - b)/2$ for the given value range.
    Further, $a^2 - b^2$ would always be less than $a^3 - b^3$. Thus, option (d) is correct.

**44 – 48.**

44. Option $a = (a - b) (a + b) = a^2 - b^2$

45. Option $a = (a^2 - b^2) + b^2 = a^2$.

46. $3 - 4 \times 2 + 4/8 - 2 = 3 - 8 + 0.5 - 2 = -6.5$
    (using BODMAS rule)

47. The maximum would depend on the values of $a$ and $b$. Thus, cannot be determined.

48. The minimum would depend on the values of $a$ and $b$. Thus, cannot be determined.

49. Any of $(a + b)$ or $a/b$ could be greater and thus we cannot determine this.

50. Again $(a + b)$ or $a/b$ can both be greater than each other depending on the values we take for $a$ and $b$. E.g. for $a = 0.9$ and $b = 0.91$, $a + b > a/b$.
    For $a = 0.1$ and $b = 0.11$, $a + b < a/b$

51. Given that $F(n - 1) = \dfrac{1}{(2 - F(n))}$, we can rewrite the expression as $F(n) = (2F(n-1) -1)/((F(n-1))$.
    For $n = 2$: $F(2) = \dfrac{6-1}{3} \Rightarrow F(2) = \dfrac{5}{3}$.
    The value of $F(3)$ would come out as 7/5 and $F(4)$ comes out as 9/7 and so on. What we realise is that for each value of $n$, after and including $n = 2$, the value of $F(n) = \dfrac{2n+1}{2n-1}$.
    This means that the greatest integral value of $F(n)$ would always be 1 for $n = 2$ to $n = 1000$.

Thus, the value of the given expression would turn out to be:

$3 + 1 \times 999 = 1002$. Option (b) is the correct answer.

52. From the solution to the previous question, we already know how the value of the given functions at $n = 1, 2, 3$ and so on would behave.

Thus, we can try to see what happens when we write down the first few terms of the expression:

$F(1) \times F(2) \times F(3) \times F(4) \times \dots F(1000)$

$= 3 \times \dfrac{5}{3} \times \dfrac{7}{5} \times \dfrac{9}{7} \times \cdots \times \dfrac{2001}{1999} = 2001$.

53. Since $f(0) = 15$, we get $c = 15$.

Next, we have $f(3) = f(-3) = 18$. Using this information, we get:

$9a + 3b + c = 9a - 3b + c \rightarrow 3b = -3b$

$\therefore\quad 6b = 0 \rightarrow b = 0$.

Also, since

$f(3) = 9a + 3b + c = 18 \rightarrow$ we get: $9a + 15 = 18$ $\rightarrow a = 1/3$

The quadratic function becomes $f(x) = x^2/3 + 15$.

$f(12) = 144/3 + 15 = 63$.

54. What you need to understand about $M(x^2 \theta y^2)$ is that it is the square of the sum of two squares. Since $M(x^2 \theta\ y^2) = 361$, we get $(x^2 + y^2)^2 = 361$, which means that the sum of the sqaures of $x$ and $y$ viz. $x^2 + y^2 = 19$. (Note it cannot be $-19$ as we are talking about the sum of two squares, which cannot be negative under any circumstance).

Also, from $M(x^2 \psi y^2) = 49$, we get $(x^2 - y^2)^2 = 49$, $\rightarrow (x^2 - y^2) = \pm 7$

Based on these two values, we can solve for two distinct situations:

(a) When $x^2 + y^2 = 19$ and $x^2 - y^2 = 7$, we get $x^2 = 13$ and $y^2 = 6$

(b) When $x^2 + y^2 = 19$ and $x^2 - y^2 = -7$, we get $x^2 = 6$ and $y^2 = 13$

In both cases, we can see that the value of: $((x^2 y^2) + 3)$ would come out as $13 \times 6 + 3 = 81$ and the square root of its value would turn out to $\pm 9$. Option (b) is correct.

55. The first thing you need to understand while solving this question is that, since $[m]$ will always be integral, hence $\Psi(4x + 5)$ will also be integral. Since $\Psi(4x + 5) = 5y + 3$, naturally, the value of $5y + 3$ will also be integral. By a similar logic, the value of $x$ will also be an integer considering the second equation: $\Psi(3y + 7) = x + 4$.

Using, this logic we know that $\Psi(4x + 5) = 4x + 5$ (because, whenever $m$ is an integer the value of $[m] = m$).

This leads us to two linear equations as follows:

$4x + 5 = 5y + 3$ ...(i)

$3y + 7 = x + 4$ ...(ii)

Solving simultaneously, we will get: $x = -3$ and $y = -2$. Thus, $x^2 \times y^2 = 9 \times 4 = 36$.

56. Since $f(128) = 4$, we can see that the product of $f(256).f(0.5) = f(256 \times 0.5) = f(128) = 4$.

Similarly, the products $f(1).f(128) = f(2).f(64)$ $= f(4).f(32) = f(8).f(16) = 4$.

Thus, M $= 4 \times 4 \times 4 \times 4 \times 4 = 1024$.

Option (d) is the correct answer.

57. The only values of $x$ and $y$ that satisfy the equation $4x + 6y = 20$ are $x = 2$ and $y = 2$ (since, $x$, $y$ are non negative integers). This gives us: $4 \le M/2^{2/3}$. M has to be greater than $2^{8/3}$ for this expression to be satisfied. Option (c) is correct.

58. $\theta\ (\Psi(-7)) = \theta(-2) = 14$. Option (b) is correct.

59. $F(2b) = F(b + b) = F(b).F(b) \div 2 = (F(b))^2 \div 2$

Similarly, $F(3b) = F(b + b + b) = F(b + b).F(b) \div 2 = \{F(b)^2 \div 2\}.\{F(b)\} \div 2 = (F(b))^3 \div 2^2$

Similarly, $F(4b) = (F(b))^4 \div 2^3$.

Hence, $F(12b) = (F(b))^{12} \div 2^{11}$. Option (d) is correct.

60. To test for a reflexive function as defined in the problem use the following steps:

**Step 1:** To start with, assume a value of '$b$' and derive a value for 'a' using the given function.

**Step 2:** Then, insert the value you got for '$a$' in the first step into the value of '$b$' and get a new value of '$a$'. This value of '$a$' should be equal to the first value of '$b$' that you used in the first step. If this occurs the function would be reflexive. Else it is not reflexive.

Checking for the expression in (i) if we take $b = 1$, we get:

$a = 8/1 = 8$. Inserting, $b = 8$ in the function gives us $a = 29/29 = 1$. Hence, the function given in (i) is reflexive.

Similarly checking the other two functions, we get that the function in (ii) is not reflexive while the function in (iii) is reflexive.

Thus, Option (c) is the correct answer.

61. $f(g(x)) = f(|3x - 2|) = \dfrac{1}{|3x - 2|}$

Option (a) is correct.

62. $f(g(x)) = f(|x|) = |x|^2 + \dfrac{1}{|x|^2}$. This function would take the same values when you try to use a positive value or a negative value of $x$. For instance, if you were to put $x$ as 2 you would get the same answer as if you were to use $x$ as $-2$. Hence, $f(g(x))$ is an even function.

63. For this question, you would have to go through each of the options checking them for their correctness in order to identify the correct answer. Thus,

For option (a): $g(x) + (g(x))^2 = |x| + |x|^2$

$\Rightarrow f(x) \neq g(x) + (g(x))^2$. Hence, option (a) is not correct.

For option (b): $f(x) = x^2 + \dfrac{1}{x^2}, f(g(x)) = |x|^2 + \dfrac{1}{|x|^2}$

$f(x) \neq -f(g(x))$. Hence, option (b) is not correct.

For option (c): $g(f(x)) = \left| x^2 + \dfrac{1}{x^2} \right|$

$f(g(x)) = |x|^2 + \dfrac{1}{|x|^2}$ which is the same as $\left| x^2 + \dfrac{1}{x^2} \right|$.

Hence $f(g(x)) = g(f(x))$

∵ Hence option (c) is correct.

64. $f(x) = f(-x)$

$g(x) = g(-x)$

$h(x) = -h(-x)$

$t(x) = t(-x)$

Therefore 3 functions are even.

65. $f(x) = f(-x)$

$\Rightarrow h(f(x)) = h(f(-x))$

$\Rightarrow$ Hence, $h(f(x))$ is an even function. So the correct answer is 1.

66. $t(x) = t(-x)$

Hence, $h(t(x)) = h(t(-x))$

$\Rightarrow h(t(x))$ is an even function. Correct answer is 1.

67. $f(2) = \dfrac{2^2 + 1}{2 - 1} = 5$

$f(f(2)) = f(5) = \dfrac{5^2 + 1}{5 - 1} = \dfrac{26}{4}$

$f(f(f(2))) = f\left(\dfrac{26}{4}\right) = \dfrac{\left(\dfrac{26}{4}\right)^2 + 1}{\dfrac{26}{4} - 1} = \dfrac{\dfrac{676 + 16}{16}}{\dfrac{22}{4}}$

$= \dfrac{692}{16} \times \dfrac{4}{22} = 7.86$

68. $D(3, 4) = \dfrac{3}{4} = 0.75$

$S(2, D(3,4)) = S(2, 0.75) = 2.75$

$P(S(2, D(3,4)), 5) = P(2.75, 5) = 2.75 \times 5 = 13.75$

69. $P(2, 3) = 2 \times 3 = 6$

$D(4, 2) = 4 \div 2 = 2$

$S(P(2,3), D(4,2)) = S(6, 2) = 8$

$t(1, 5) = |1 - 5| = 4$

$S(8, 4) = 8 + 4 = 12$

**Solution for 70 to 72:**

70. $[(5\ P\ 6)Q(4\ Q\ 2)]S\ (3\ S\ 1)$

$= [(|5 - 6|)Q\ (4/2)]S\ (1/3)$

$= [1\ Q\ 2]S\left(\dfrac{1}{3}\right)$

$= [1\ R\ 2]S\left(\dfrac{1}{3}\right)$

$= [1 \times 2)S\left(\dfrac{1}{3}\right)$

$= 2\ S\ \dfrac{1}{3}$

$= \left(\dfrac{1}{2 \times \dfrac{1}{3}}\right) = \dfrac{3}{2} = 1.5$

71. For this question, we would need to check each option and select the one that is true.

Checking option (a) we can see that:

$(4P2) = (4Q2) = 4/2 = 2, (2P4) = |2 - 4| = 2$

So, option (a) is incorrect.

Checking option (b) we get:

$(4Q2) = 4/2 = 2, 2R4 = 2 \times 4 = 8$

Hence, Option (b) is incorrect.

Checking option (c) we get:

$(6Q3) = 6/3 = 2$

$2\ S\ (0.5) = 1/(2 \times 0.5) = 1$

Hence, Option (c) is incorrect.

Option (d) is correct.

72. $(5P3)Q(4S2) = (5\ Q\ 3)Q\left(\dfrac{1}{4.2}\right)$

$= \dfrac{5}{3}Q\dfrac{1}{8}$

$= \dfrac{40}{3}$

$20Q1.5 = 20 \div 1.5 = \dfrac{40}{3}$, therefore the operator $Q$ should replace 'K' in the equation.

**Solutions for 73 – 75**

73. $f(3, 4) = [3] + \{4\} = 3 + 4 = 7$

$g(3.5, 4.5) = [4.5] - \{3.5\} = 4 - 4 = 0$

$i(f(3,4), g(3.5, 4.5)) = i(7, 0) = -7$

Hence, option (d) is correct.

74. $a^3 = 64 \Rightarrow a = 4$

$b^2 = 16 \Rightarrow b = 4\ or\ -4$

When $a = 4, b = 4$

$f(4, 4) = [4] + \{4\} = 4 + 4 = 8$

$g(4, 4) = [4] - \{4\} = 4 - 4 = 0$

But these values do not satisfy the condition in the problem that $8 + f(a,b) = -g(a,b)$. Hence, we will try to use $a = 4$ and $b = -4$ to see whether that gives us the right set of values for the conditions to be matched.

When $a = 4$, $b = -4$

$$f(4,-4) = [4] + \{-4\} = 4 - 4 = 0$$

$$g(4,-4) = [-4] - \{4\} = -4 - 4 = -8$$

The given condition $8 + f(a,b) = -g(a,b)$ is satisfied here. Hence, $a = 4$ & $b = -4$. Therefore $a - b = 4 - (-4) = 8$

75. $f(1.2,-2.3) + g(-1.2,2.3)$

$$= [1.2] + \{-2.3\} + [2.3] - \{-1.2\}$$

$$= 1 - 2 + 2 + 1$$

$$= 2$$

$$= i(a,-1.3) = \{-a-1.3\}$$

For $a = -2.4 \Rightarrow i(-2.4,-1.3) = \{2.4-1.3\} = \{1.1\} = 2$

Hence, option (d) is correct.

### Solutions for 76 & 77:

76. Given: $xPy = \dfrac{1}{1+\dfrac{y}{x}} = \dfrac{x}{x+y}$ and $xQy = 1 + \dfrac{x}{y} = \dfrac{x+y}{y}$.

From this point you would need to read the options and check the one that gives you a value of $\dfrac{x}{y}$. It is easily evident here that:

$$(xPy) \times (xQy) = \frac{x}{x+y} \times \frac{x+y}{y} = \frac{x}{y}$$

Hence, Option (c) is correct.

77. $S(2,3) = (2P3)P(2Q3)$

$$= \left(\frac{2}{2+3}\right)P\left(\frac{2+3}{3}\right)$$

$$= \frac{2}{5}P\frac{5}{3} = \frac{\dfrac{2}{5}}{\dfrac{2}{5}+\dfrac{5}{3}} = 0.19$$

### Solutions for 78 – 80

78. $(1 + \min(2A3, 1C2))B(\max(1A2), 1C1)$

$$= [1 + \min(1, 2)]B\max(1, 1)$$

$$(1 + 1)B(1^2) = 2B1 = [2 \div 1] = 2$$

79. $\max(7A3, 16B2) = \max(4, 8) = 8^2 = 64$

Now by checking the options we get only option (b) that gives us the correct value.

$(32B2)C(\min(4, 8))$

$|[32 \div 2] \times 4| = |16 \times 4| = 64$

Hence option (b) is correct.

80. $\max(3, 4) \div \min(8, 4) = 4^2 \div 4 = 4$. Checking the options we see:

Option (a): $8A2 = |8 - 2| = 6$

Option (b): $28B7 = 28 \div 7 = 4$

Option (c): $4C2 = |4 \times 2| = 8$

Hence option (b) is correct.

### Solution for 81-85:

81. $f(1,3,5,7) + g(2,4,6,8) = 1 + 8 = 9$

$$h[aK, K] = \left[\frac{aK}{K}\right] = [a] = a, [a \in I]$$

$$\Rightarrow a = 9$$

82. $t(1,2,3,4) = 1 \times 2 \times 3 \times 4 = 24$

$i(1,2,3,4) = 1 + 2 + 3 + 4 = 10$

$f(t(1,2,3,4), i(1,2,3,4)) = f(24,10) = 10$

83. $f(5,6,7,8) = 5$, $i(1,2,3,4,) = 1 + 2 + 3 + 4 = 10$

$$h(5,10) = \left[\frac{5}{10}\right] = [0.5] = 0$$

84. $P = f(2,3,4,6) = 2$

$Q = g(1,2,3,4) = 4$

$$R = h(8,4) = \left[\frac{8}{4}\right] = 2$$

$S = t(1, 2, 3, 4) = 1 \times 2 \times 3 \times 4 = 24$

$T = i(4,5,6) = 4 + 5 + 6 = 15$

$\therefore P = R < Q < T < S.$

Option (c) is correct

85. $f(1,2,3) = 1, g(2,3,4) = 4, f(0,1,2)$

$$= 0, g(-3,-2) = -2$$

$f(1,4,0,-2) = -2.$

86. $|x|$

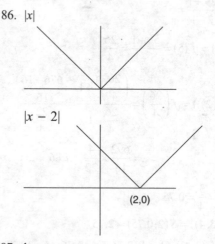

$|x - 2|$

(2,0)

87. $\log x$

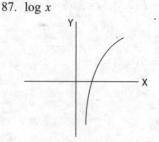

$f(x) \to f(|x|)$

Take mirror image about $y$-axis

$\log|x| \to$

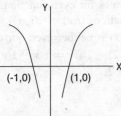

88. $x^3 \to$

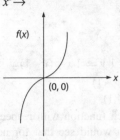

$(x - 1)^3 \to$

[Shift curve one unit right]

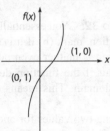

Hence option (a) is correct.

89. $e^x \to$

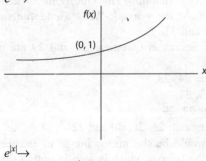

$e^{|x|} \to$

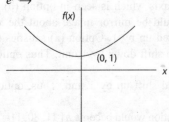

$\dfrac{e^{|x|}}{2} \to$

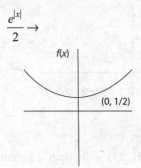

Option (b) is correct.

90. $\max(x, x^2) = \begin{cases} x^2, & \text{for } -\infty < x \le 0 \\ x, & \text{for } 0 \le x \le 1 \\ x^2, & \text{for } x > 1 \end{cases}$

$\Rightarrow f(x) = \max(x, x^2) \Rightarrow$

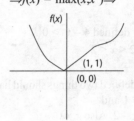

Option (b) is correct.

91. When $f(x)$ and $g(x)$ both are odd then $S(x) = f(x) + g(x)$

$S(-x) = f(-x) + g(-x) = -[f(x) + g(x)]$, $S(x)$ is an odd function. This conclusion rejects option (a).

Their product $P(x) = f(x).g(x)$

$P(-x) = f(-x).g(-x) = [-f(x)][-g(x)] = f(x)g(x)$. $P(x)$ is an even function. This is what is being said by the option (c). Hence, it is the correct answer.

If we check for option (b) we can see that: when $f(x)$ and $g(x)$ both are even then $S(x) = f(x) + g(x)$

$S(-x) = f(-x) + g(-x) = [f(x) + g(x)]$, $S(x)$ is an even function.

Hence only option (c) is true.

92. $f(g(-x)) = f(-g(x)) = f(g(x))$

∴ $f(g(x))$ is an even function.

$g(f(x)) = g(f(-x)) = g(f(x))$

∴ $g(f(x))$ is an even function.

Hence option (c) is true.

93. $f(x) = x^3 - x^2 - 6x$

$= (x + 2) x (x - 3)$

$\Rightarrow f(x) = 0$

$\Rightarrow (x + 2) x (x - 3) = 0$

$X = 0, 3, -2$. There are 3 such values.

94. Curve of $f(x)$ will look like this:

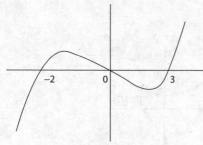

For interval $(-2, 3)$, $f(x)$ will attain it's minima in the interval $(0, 3)$.

95. Options (a), (b), (d) are undefined for $x = 0$
As $x^4 + 7$ is always positive for $x \in R$, therefore log $(x^4 + 7) \in R$ for all $x \in R$. Hence option (c) is true. Each of the other options have at least one value where $f(x)$ does not remain real.

## Level of Difficulty (II)

1. For the function to be defined $4 - x^2 > 0$
This happens when $-2 < x < 2$.
Option (a) is correct.

2. For the function to be defined two things should happen
(a) $(1 - x) > 0 \Rightarrow x < 1$ and
(b) $(x + 2) \geq 0 \Rightarrow x \geq -2$. Also $x \neq 0$
Thus, option (d) is correct.

3. $\dfrac{5x - x^2}{4} \geq 1 \Rightarrow 1 \leq x \leq 4$.

4. Neither $2^{-x \cdot x}$ nor $2^{x - x \cdot x \cdot x}$ is an odd function as for neither of them is $f(x) = -f(-x)$.

5. $1 - |x|$ should be non negative.
$[-1, 1]$ would satisfy this.

6. $4 - x^2 \neq 0$ and $(x^3 - x) > 0 \Rightarrow (-1, 0) \cup (1, \infty)$ but not 2 or $-2$.

7. $f(0) = 1, f(1) = 2$ and $f(2) = 4$
Hence, they are in G.P.

8. $x$ would become $-2$ and $y = -3$.

9. $u(f(v(t))) = u(f(t^2)) = u(1/t^2) = \left(\dfrac{4}{t^2}\right) - 5$.

10. $g(f(h(t))) = g(f(4t - 8)) = g\left(\sqrt{4t - 8}\right)$
$= \dfrac{\sqrt{4t - 8}}{4}$

11. $h(g(f(t))) = h(g(\sqrt{t})) = h(\sqrt{t}/4)$
$= \sqrt{t} - 8$

12. $f(h(g(t))) = f(h(t/4)) = f(t - 8) = \sqrt{t - 8}$.

13. All three functions would give the same values for $x > 0$. As $g(x)$ is not defined for negative $x$, and $h(x)$ is not defined for $x = 0$.

14. $e^x + e^{-x} = e^{-x} + e^x$
Hence, this is an even function.

15. $(x + 3)^3$ would be shifted 3 units to the left and hence $(x + 3)^3 + 1$ would shift 3 units to the left and 1 unit up. Option (c) is correct.

16. $f(x) \cdot g(x) = 15x^8$ which is an even function. Thus, option (a) is correct.

17. $(x^2 + \log_e x)$ would be neither odd nor even since it obeys neither of the rules for even function ($f(x) = f(-x)$) nor for odd functions ($f(x) = -f(-x)$).

18. $(x^3 - x^2/5) = f(x) - g(x)$ is neither even nor odd.

19. $y = 1/(x - 2) \Rightarrow (x - 2) = 1/y \Rightarrow x = 1/y + 2$.
Hence, $f^{-1}(x) = 1/x + 2$.

20. $y = e^x$
$\Rightarrow \log_e y = x$.
$\Rightarrow f^{-1}(x) = \log_e x$.

21. $y = x/(x - 1)$
$\Rightarrow (x - 1)/x = 1/y$
$\Rightarrow 1 - (1/x) = 1/y$
$\Rightarrow 1/x = 1 - 1/y \Rightarrow 1/x = (y - 1)/y$
$\Rightarrow x = y/(y - 1)$
Hence, $f^{-1}(x) = x/(x - 1)$.

22. If you differentiate each function with respect to $x$, and equate it to 0 you would see that for none of the three options will get you a value of $x = -3$ as its solution. Thus, option (d) viz. None of these is correct.

**Directions for Questions 23 to 32:** You essentially have to mark (a) if it is an even function, mark (b) if it is an odd function, mark (c) if the function is neither even nor odd.

Also, option (d) would occur if the function does not exist atleast one point of the domain. This means one of two things.

Either the function is returning two values for one value of $x$ or the function has a break in between. This is seen in Questions 25, 26, 30 and 32.

We see even functions in Questions 24 and 28. [Symmetry about the $y$ axis]. We see odd functions in Questions 23 and 31.

While the figures in Questions 27 and 29 are neither odd nor even.

Even $\Rightarrow$ 24, 28,
Odd 23, 31.
Neither 27, 29,
doesn't exist: 25, 26, 30 and 32.

33. $-f(x)$ would be the mirror image of the function, about the '$x$' axis which is seen in option (b).

34. $-f(x) + 1$ would be mirror image about the $x$ axis and then shifted up by 1. Option (a) satisfies this.

35. $f(x) - 1$ would shift down by 1 unit. Thus option (c) is correct.

36. $f(x) + 1$ would shift up by 1 unit. Thus, option (d) is correct.

37. The given function would become $h[11, 80, 1] = 2640$.

38. The given function would become $g[0, 0, 3] = 0$.

39. The given function would become $f[3, 3, 3] = 27$.

40. $f(1, 2, 3) - g(1, 2, 3) + h(1, 2, 3) = 11 - 23 + 18 = 6$.

41. The number of $g's$ and $f's$ should be equal on the LHS and RHS since both these functions are essentially inverse of each other.

Option (c) is correct.

42. The required minimum value would occur at $f(x) = g(x) = 1$.

43. $SQ\ [R[(a+b)/b]] = SQ\ [R[17/5]] \Rightarrow SQ\ [2] = 2$.

44. $Q\ [[SQ\ (63) + 7\ ]/9] = Q\ [[\ 8 + 7]/9] = Q\ [15/9] = 1$.

45. $Q\ [[SA\ (36) + R\ (18/7)]/2] = Q\ [(7 + 4)/2] = Q\ [11/2] = 5$.

46. $[x] - \{x\} = -1$.

47. $[x] + \{x\}$ will always be odd as the values are consecutive integers.

48. At $x = 5.5$, the given equation can be seen to be satisfied as: $6 + 5 = 2 \times 5.5 = 11$.

49. $f(g(t)) - g(f(t)) = f(2.5) - g(6) = 8.25 - 2.166 = 6.0833$.

50. $fog = f(3t + 2) = k(3t + 2) + 1$

    $gof = g\ (kt + 1) = 3(\ kt + 1) + 2$

    $k(\ 3t + 2) + 1 = 3\ (kt + 1) + 2$

    $\Rightarrow \qquad 2\ k + 1 = 5$

    $\Rightarrow \qquad k = 2$.

51. When the value of $x = 81$ and $82$ is substituted in the given expression, we get,

    $F(81)\ F(82) = -\ F(80)\ F(79)\ F(78)\ F(77)$ ...(i)

    $F(82)\ F(83) = -\ F(81)\ F(80)\ F(79)\ F(78)$ ...(ii)

    On dividing (i) by (ii), we get

    $\dfrac{F(81)}{F(83)} = \dfrac{F(77)}{F(81)} \Rightarrow F(81) \times F(81) = 81 \times 9$

    $\Rightarrow F(81) = 27$

    Option (a) is the correct answer.

52. In order to understand this question, you first need to develop your thought process about what the value of $h(x)$ is in various cases. A little bit of trial and error would show you that the value of $h(x)$ since it depends on the minimum of $f(x)$ and $g(x)$, would definitely be dependant on the value of $f(x)$ once $x$ becomes greater than 11 or less than –11. Also, the value of $g(x)$ is fixed as an integer at 16, whenever $x$ is between –8 to +8. Also, at $x = 9$, $x = 10$ and $x = -9$ and $x = -10$, the value of $h(x)$ would still be an integer.

    With this thought when you look at the expression of $f(x) = 121 - x^2$, you realise that the value of $x$ can be $-10, -9, -8, -7, ...0, 1, 2, 3, ....8, 9, 10$, i.e., 21 values of $x$ when $h(x) = g(x)$. When we use $x = 11$ or $x = -11$, the value of $f(x) = 0$ and is not a positive integral value.

    Hence, the correct answer is Option (c).

53. Since, $R(x)$ is the maximum amongst the three given functions, its value would always be equal to the highest amongst the three. It is easy to imagine that $x^2 - 8$ and $3x$ are increasing functions, therefore the value of the function is continuously increasing as you increase the value of $x$. Similarly $x^2 - 8$ would be increasing continuously as you go farther and farther down on the negative side of the $x$-axis. Hence, the maximum value of $R(x)$ would be infinity. Option (c) is the correct answer.

54. In this case, the value of the function, is the minimum of the three values. If you visualise the graphs of the three functions (viz: $y = x^2 - 8$, $y = 3x$ and $y = 8$) you realise that the function $y = 3x$ (being a straight line) will keep going to negative infinity as you move to the left of zero on the negative side of the $x$-axis.

    Hence, the minimum value of the function $R(x)$ after a certain point (when $x$ is negative) would get dictated by the value of $3x$. This point will be the intersection of the line $y = 3x$ and the function $y = x^2 - 8$ when $x$ is negative.

    The two intersection points of the line $(3x)$ and the quadratic curve $(x^2 - 8)$ would be got by equating $3x = x^2 - 8$. Solving this equation tells us that the intersection points are:

    $\dfrac{3 - \sqrt{41}}{2}$ and $\dfrac{3 + \sqrt{41}}{2}$.

    $R(x)$ would depend on the following structures based on the value of $x$:

    (i) When $x$ is smaller than $\dfrac{3 - \sqrt{41}}{2}$, the value of the function $R(x)$ would be given by the value of $3x$.

    (ii) When $x$ is between $\dfrac{3 - \sqrt{41}}{2}$ and 4 the value of the function $R(x)$ would be given by the value of $x^2 - 8$, since that would be the least amongst the three functions.

    (iii) After $x = 4$, on the positive side of the $x$-axis, the value of the function would be defined by the third function viz: $y = 8$.

    A close look at these three ranges would give you that amongst these three ranges, the third range would yield the highest value of $R(x)$. Hence, the maximum possible value of $R(x) = 8$. Option (b) is correct.

55. The expression is $2x^2 - 5x + 4$, and its value at $x = 5$ would be equal to $50 - 25 + 4 = 29$. Option (b) is correct.

56. At $x = 0$, the value of the function is 20 and this value rejects the first option. Taking some higher values of $x$, we realise that on the positive side, the value of the function will become negative when we take $x$ greater than 5 since the value of $(5 - x)$ would be negative. Also, the value of $f(x)$ would start tending to $-\infty$, as we take bigger values of $x$.

Similarly, on the negative side, when we take the value of $x$ lower than $-4$, $f(x)$ becomes positive and when we take it farther away from 0 on the negative side, the value of $f(x)$ would continue tending to $+\infty$. Hence, Option (c) is the correct answer.

57. The remainder when $6^x + 4$ is divided by 2 would be 0 in every case (when $x$ is odd)

Also, when $x$ is even, we would get $6^x - 3$ as an odd number. In every case the remainder would be 1 (when it is divided by 2.)

Between $f(2)$, $f(4)$, $f(6)$,...$f(1000)$ there are 500 instances when $x$ is even. In each of these instances the remainder would be 1 and hence the remainder would be 0 (in total). Option (b) is correct.

58. The product of $p$, $q$ and $r$ will be maximum if $p$, $q$ and $r$ are as symmetrical as possible. Therefore, the possible combination is (4, 3, 3).

Hence, maximum value of $pq + qr + pr + pqr = 4 \times 3 + 4 \times 3 + 3 \times 3 + 4 \times 3 \times 3 = 69$.

Hence, Option (c) is correct.

59. The equation given in the question is: $3\alpha(x) + 2\alpha(2-x) = (x + 3)^2$ ....(i)

Replacing $x$ by $(2-x)$ in the above equation, we get

$3\alpha(2-x) + 2\alpha(x) = (5-x)^2$

Solving the above pairs of equation, we get

$5\alpha(x) = 3(x + 3)^2 - 2(5 - x)^2 = 3(x^2 + 6x + 9) - 2(25 - 10x + x^2) = 3x^2 + 18x + 27 - 50 + 20x - 2x^2 = x^2 + 38x - 23$

Thus, $\alpha(x) = (x^2 + 38x - 23)/5$

Thus, $\alpha(-5) = -188/5 = -37.6$. The value of $[-37.6] = -38$. Hence, option (b) is the correct answer.

60. The first thing you do in this question is to create the chain of values of $f(x)$ for $x = 1, 2, 3$ and so on. The chain of values would look something like this:

| When x is odd | | | When x is even | | |
|---|---|---|---|---|---|
| $f(1)$ | Value is given | 6 | $f(2)$ | Value is given | 4 |
| $f(3)$ | $= 1 + f(1)$ | 7 | $f(4)$ | $= 3 + f(2)$ | 7 |
| $f(5)$ | $= 3 + f(3)$ | 10 | $f(6)$ | $= 3 + f(4)$ | 10 |
| $f(7)$ | $= 5 + f(5)$ | 15 | $f(8)$ | $= 3 + f(6)$ | 13 |
| $f(9)$ | $= 7 + f(7)$ | 22 | $f(10)$ | $= 3 + f(8)$ | 16 |
| $f(11)$ | $= 9 + f(9)$ | 31 | | | |

In order to evaluate the value of the embedded function represented by $(f(f(f(f(1)))))$, we can use the above values and think as follows:

$f(f(f(f(1)))) = f(f(f(6))) = f(f(10)) = f(16) = 25$

Also, $f(f(f(f(2)))) = f(f(f(4))) = f(f(7)) = f(15) = 55$

Hence, the product of the two values is $25 \times 55 = 1375$.

Option (a) is correct.

61. For $x > 0$, $x + \dfrac{1}{x}$ has a minimum value of 2, when $x$ is taken as 1. Why we would need to minimise $x + \dfrac{1}{x}$ is because it is raised to the power 6 in the numerator, so allowing $x + \dfrac{1}{x}$ to become greater than its' minimum would increase the value of the expression. Also, the value of any expression of the form $x^n + \dfrac{1}{x^n}$ would also give us a value of 2.

Hence, the value of the expression would be:

$$\frac{\left(x + \dfrac{1}{x}\right)^6 - \left(x^6 + \dfrac{1}{x^6}\right) - 2}{\left(x + \dfrac{1}{x}\right)^3 + \left(x^3 + \dfrac{1}{x^3}\right)} = \frac{2^6 - 2 - 2}{2^3 + 2} = 6$$

Hence, (d) is the correct choice.

62. The function would be defined when the term

$\dfrac{1}{\{\log_{10}(3 - x)\}}$ is real, which will occur when $x < 3$. However, if $x = 2$, then the denominator of the term becomes 0, which should not be allowed. The other limit of the function gets defined by the constraint defined by the term $\sqrt{x + 7}$. For $\sqrt{x + 7}$ to be real, $x \geq -7$ is the requirement. Hence, the required domain is:

Required domain $= -7 \leq x < 3$, $x \neq 2$

i.e., $x \in [-7, 3) - \{2\}$

Option (a) is correct.

63. $\left[\dfrac{1}{3}\right] + \left[\dfrac{1}{3} + \dfrac{1}{99}\right] + \left[\dfrac{1}{3} + \dfrac{2}{99}\right] + \left[\dfrac{1}{3} + \dfrac{65}{99}\right] = 0$

$\left[\dfrac{1}{3} + \dfrac{66}{99}\right] + \left[\dfrac{1}{3} + \dfrac{2}{99}\right] + ...\left[\dfrac{1}{3} + \dfrac{98}{99}\right] = 33$

$\left[\dfrac{1}{3}\right] + \left[\dfrac{1}{3} + \dfrac{1}{99}\right] + \left[\dfrac{1}{3} + \dfrac{2}{99}\right]$

$+ ...\left[\dfrac{1}{3} + \dfrac{98}{99}\right] = 0 + 33 = 33$

Option (b) is correct.

64. $x^2 + 4xy + 6y^2 - 4y + 4$

$= x^2 + 4y^2 + 4xy + 2y^2 - 4y + 2 + 2$

$= (x + 2y)^2 + 2(y^2 - 2y + 1) + 2$

The above expression is minimum for $y = 1$, $x = -2$

So minimum value of the given expression

$= 0 + 0 + 2 = 2$.

Option (c) is correct.

65. Let $f(X) = 21 \sin X + 72 \cos X$

$\Rightarrow f'(X) = 21 \cos X - 72 \sin X$

If $f'(X) = 0$, $21 \cos X = 72 \sin X$.

$\therefore \tan X = 21/72$ therefore $\sin X = 21/75$, $\cos X = 72/75$ (Since, from the value of $\tan X$ we can think of a right angled triangle with the legs as 21 and 72 respectively. This would give us the hypotenuse length of the triangle as 75 – using the Pythagoras theorem).

Since $f''(x) = -21 \sin X - 72 \cos X < 0$ therefore $f(X)$ has a maximum at $f'(X) = 0$. Thus, we can use the values of $\sin X = 21/75$ & $\cos X = 72/75$.

$\therefore$ Maximum value of

$$f(x) = \frac{21.21}{75} + \frac{72.72}{75} = \frac{75^2}{75} = 75$$

Option (d) is correct.

66. For $x < -7$

$|x + 7| + |x - 8| = -(x + 7) - (x - 8)$

$-(x + 7) - (x - 8) = 16$

$-2x + 1 = 16$

$x = -7.5$

For $-7 \le x \le 8$

$|x + 7| + |x - 8| = x + 7 - x + 8 = 15 \neq 16$

Therefore the given equation has no solution in this range.

For $x \ge 8$

$|x + 7| + |x - 8| = x + 7 + x - 8 = 2x - 1$

$2x - 1 = 16$

$\Rightarrow x = \frac{17}{2} = 8.5$

So the required sum $= -7.5 + 8.5 = 1$

Hence option (b) is correct.

67. $|3x + 4| \le 5$

$-5 \le 3x + 4 \le 5$

$-3 \le x \le 1/3$

$a = -3, b = 1/3$

$a + b = -3 + \frac{1}{3}$

$= -\frac{8}{3}$

68. $x^3 - 16x + x^2 + 20 \le 0 = (x + 5)(x - 2)^2 \le 0$

For any positive integer the given expression can never be less than 0. Therefore $x = 2$, is the only positive integer value of $x$ for which the given in-equality holds true. Alternately, you can also solve this question using trial and error, where you can start with $x = 1$ and then try to see the value of the expression at $x = 2$. At $x = 1$, the expression is positive, at $x = 2$ it is 0, while at $x = 3$ it again becomes positive. Once, $x$ crosses 3, the term $x^3$ by itself would become so large that it would not be possible to pull the value of the expression into the non-positive territory because the magnitude of the

negative term in the expression viz $16x$, would not be large enough to make the expression $\le 0$

69. Putting $x = 7$ in the given equation we get:

$3f(7) + 2f(11) = 70 \dots$ \hfill (1)

Similarly by putting $x = 11$ in the given equation we get:

$3f(11) + 2f(7) = 98 \dots$ \hfill (2)

Solving equation 1 and 2 we get

$$f(11) = \frac{154}{5} = 30.8$$

70. $q = p \times [p]$

When you start to think about the values of $q$ from 8 onwards to 16, the first solution is quite evident at $q = 9$ and $p = 3$. At $q = 10$, $p$ can be taken to be $10/3$ to give us the expression of $p \times [p]$ equal to 10. Similarly

For $q = 11$, $a = 3$, $p = 11/3$.

For $q = 16$, $a = 4$, $p = 4$

So the required number of positive real values of $p = 4$.

71. Required product is $= 3 \times \frac{10}{3} \times \frac{11}{3} \times 4 = \frac{440}{3}$

72. $f(3) = f(1) + 8(1 + 1)$

$= -1 + 16 = 15$

$f(5) = f(3) + 8(3 + 1)$

$= (15 + 32)$

$= 47$

$f(10) = 4.f(5) + 9$

$= 4 \times 47 + 9$

$= 197$

$f(20) = 4 \times 197 + 9$

$= 797$

$f(22) = f(20) + 8(20 + 1)$

$= 797 + 168$

$= 965$

$f(24) = 965 + 8(22 + 1) = 1149$

$f(7) = f(5) + 8(5 + 1) = 47 + 48 = 95$

Hence, $f(24) - f(7) = 1149 - 95 = 1054$

73. If we observe values of $f(x)$ for different values of $x$, then we can see that $f(x) = 2x^2 - 3$.

Hence, $f(1000) = 2(1000)^2 - 3$

$= 1999,997$

74. $f(x) = (x^2 + [x]^2 - 2x[x])^{1/2} = \left[(x - [x])^2\right]^{\frac{1}{2}} = x - [x]$

$f(x) = x - [x]$ represents the fractional part of $x$.

Hence $f(10.08) = 0.08$

$f(100.08) = 0.08$

$f(10.08) - f(100.08) = 0.08 - 0.08 = 0$

75. Let $f(x) = (x - 4)^7 (x - 3)^4 (x - 5)^2$

$f(1) = (1 - 4)^7 (1 - 3)^4 (1 - 5)^2$

$= (-3)^7 (-2)^4 (-4)^2$

$= -2^8 . 3^7$

Option (c) is correct.

76. $f(x) = x - \dfrac{1}{3(3-x)} - 3 = (x-3) + \dfrac{1}{3(x-3)} \geq$

$\left[(x-3) \times \dfrac{1}{3(x-3)}\right]^{\frac{1}{2}}$. Hence, $(x-3) + \dfrac{1}{3(x-3)} \geq \dfrac{1}{\sqrt{3}}$

Option (b) is correct.

77.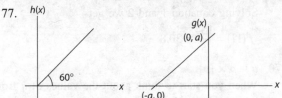

$h(x) = x \tan 60° = x\sqrt{3}$

$x = \dfrac{h(x)}{\sqrt{3}}$

$\dfrac{x}{-a} + \dfrac{g(x)}{a} = 1$

$g(x) = \left[1 + \dfrac{x}{a}\right] a = a + x = a + \dfrac{h(x)}{\sqrt{3}}$

$\sqrt{3}g(x) = a\sqrt{3} + h(x)$

$\sqrt{3}g(x) - h(x) = a\sqrt{3}$

Option (a) is correct.

Alternately, you can also solve this by looking at the values of the graphs. At $x = 0$, $h(x) = 0$ and $g(x) = a$. At $x = 1$, $h(x) = \sqrt{3}$ (This can be visualised, since the triangle that is formed by the graph of $h(x)$ with the x axis is a 30-60,90 triangle. Hence, if we take the side opposite the 30° angle as 1, the height (side opposite the 60° angle) would be $\sqrt{3}$. Also, the value of $g(x)$ would be $a + 1$ (since the gradient of the $g(x)$ slope is 45°). The first option satisfies both these pairs of values. Hence, it is the correct answer.

78. $\dfrac{f(xy)}{f(x+y)} = 1$ or $f(xy) = f(x + y)$

Put $x = 0$: $f(0.y) = f(0 + y) \Rightarrow f(y) = f(0)$
Put $y = 0$: $f(x.0) = f(x + 0) \Rightarrow f(x) = f(0)$
Therefore function '$f$' is a constant function. (This can also be interpreted since the function reads that the value of $f$ when you put an argument equal to the product of $x$ & $y$ is the same as the value of $f$ when you put the argument of the function as $x + y$).
$f(-10) = f(10) = f(6) = 7$
$f(-10) + f(10) = 7 + 7 = 14$

79. Putting $x = 9$, $y = 3$, in the above equation we get

$f\left(\dfrac{9}{3}\right) = \dfrac{f(9)}{f(3)}$

$f(3) = \dfrac{f(9)}{f(3)}$

$f(9) = [f(3)]^2 = 5^2 = 25$

Similarly $x = 81$, $y = 9$

$f\left(\dfrac{81}{9}\right) = \dfrac{f(81)}{f(9)}$

$f(9) = \dfrac{f(81)}{f(9)}$

$f(81) = [f(9)]^2 = 25^2 = 625$

80. We can find the sum of all coefficients of a polynomial by putting each of the variable equals to 1:
Therefore the required sum $= (1-4)^3 (1-2)^{10} (1-3)^3$
$= -3^3 \times 1 \times (-2)^3$
$= 27 \times 8$
$= 216$

81. $f(a) = 3^a$   (If $a$ is an odd number)
$f(a + 1) = 3^{a+1} + 4 = 3.3^a + 4$

$\dfrac{1}{4}[f(a) + f(a+1)] = \dfrac{3^a + 3.3^a + 4}{4}$

$= \dfrac{3^a.4 + 4}{4} = 3^a + 1$

$\Rightarrow \dfrac{1}{4}[f(1) + f(2)] + (f(3) + f(4))$

$+ \ldots + f(71) + f(72)]$

$= \dfrac{f(1) + f(2)}{4} + \dfrac{f(3) + f(4)}{4}$

$+ \ldots + \dfrac{f(71) + f(72)}{4}$

$= 3^1 + 1 + 3^3 + 1 + \ldots + 3^{71} + 1$
$= (3^1 + 3^3 + \ldots + 3^{71}) + 36$

$= \dfrac{3\left((3^2)^{36} - 1\right)}{3^2 - 1} + 36$

(using the formula for the sum of a geometric progression, since the series containing the powers of 3 is essentially a geometric progression).

$= \dfrac{3}{8}(3^{72} - 1) + 36$

82. Put $x = 0$ then $f(0 + y) = f(0) \rightarrow f(y) = p$
Put $y = 0$ then $f(x + 0) = f(0) \rightarrow f(x) = p$
Therefore '$f$' is a constant function
$f(7) = f(10) = f(5) = 12$
$[f(7)]^{143} - [f(11)]^{143} + f(5) = 12^{143} - 12^{143} + 12 = 12$

83. $e^{-x} \rightarrow$

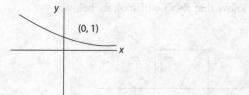

(0, 1)

$e^{-|x|} \rightarrow$

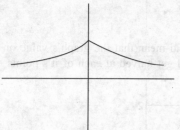

$|e^{-|x|}| \rightarrow$

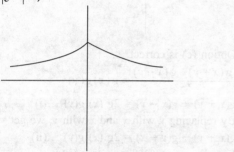

Hence option (c) is correct.

84. $e^{-x} \rightarrow$

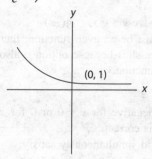

(0, 1)

$e^{-x} - 3 \rightarrow$

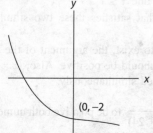

(0, −2

$|e^{-x} - 3| \rightarrow$

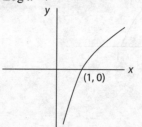

Hence option (a) is correct.

85. Log $x \rightarrow$

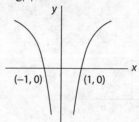

(1, 0)

$\log|x| \rightarrow$

(−1, 0)    (1, 0)

$\log|x-3| \rightarrow$

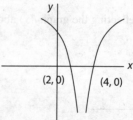

(2, 0)    (4, 0)

$|\log|x-3|| \rightarrow$

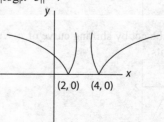

(2, 0)    (4, 0)

Option (d) is correct.

86. $f(x, y) = x^2 + y^2 - x - \dfrac{3y}{2} + 1$ can be split as:

$$= x^2 - x + \frac{1}{4} + y^2 - \frac{3y}{2} + \frac{9}{16} + \frac{3}{16}$$

$$= \left(x - \frac{1}{2}\right)^2 + \left(y - \frac{3}{4}\right)^2 + \frac{3}{16}$$

$f(x, y)$ will be minimum when $x = \frac{1}{2}$, $y = \frac{3}{4}$.

Therefore $x + y = \frac{1}{2} + \frac{3}{4} = \frac{5}{4} = 1.25$

87. $f(x, y)$ min $= 3/16$.

88. $f(x + 5)$

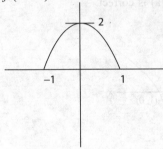

$f(x)$ can be obtained by shifting $f(x + 5)$ right by 5 units.

$f(x) \Rightarrow$

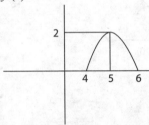

$f(-x)$ can be got by reflecting the graph $f(x)$ about the y – axis

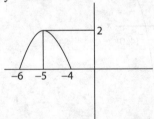

$f(-x - 2)$ can be got by shifting curve of $f(-x)$ to the right by 2 units

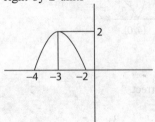

Option (d) is correct.

89. From our discussion of the previous question, we know that $f(-x)$ will look as below:

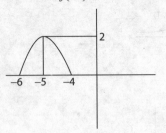

$f(-2x)$ would mean that the graph's value on the x-axis, would get halved at each of it's points

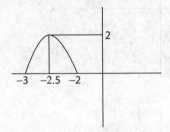

Option (c) is correct.

90. $\dfrac{g(x+y) + g(x-y)}{2} = g(x)g(y)$

$g(x + y) + g(x - y) = 2g(x)g(y)$ ...(i)

By replacing $y$ with $x$ and $x$ with $y$, we get

$g(x + y) + g(y - x) = 2g(x)g(y)$ ...(ii)

From equation (i) & equation (ii)

$g(x + y) + g(x - y) = g(x + y) + g(y - x)$

$g(x - y) = g(y - x)$

By putting $y = 0$, we get $g(x) = g(-x)$

Therefore $g(x)$ must be an even function: therefore only option (c) satisfies because option c also represents an even function.

### Level of Difficulty (III)

1. $x - |x|$ is either negative for $x < 0$ or 0 for $x \geq 0$. Thus, option (d) is correct.

2. The domain should simultaneously satisfy:

$$x - 1 \geq 0, (1 - x) \geq 0 \text{ and } (x^2 + 3) \geq 0.$$

Gives us: $x \geq 1$ and $x \leq 1$

The only value that satisfies these two simultaneously is $x = 1$.

3. For the function to exist, the argument of the logarithmic function should be positive. Also, $(x + 4) \geq 0$ should be obeyed simultaneously.

For $\dfrac{(x - 5)}{(x^2 - 10x + 24)}$ to be positive both numerator and denominator should have the same sign. Considering all this, we get:

$$4 < x < 5 \text{ and } x > 6.$$

Option (c) is correct.

4. Both the brackets should be non-negative and neither $(x + 3)$ nor $(1+ x)$ should be 0.

For $(x – 3)/(x + 3)$ to be non negative we have $x > 3$ or $x < – 3$.

Also for $(1– x)/(1+ x)$ to be non-negative $–1 < x < 1$. Since there is no interference in the two ranges, Option (d) would be correct.

8. $f(f(t)) = f((t–1)/(t+1))$

$$= \left[\left(\frac{t-1}{t+1}\right)-1\right]\Big/\left[\left(\frac{t-1}{t+1}\right)+1\right] = \frac{t-1-t-1}{t-1+t+1}$$

$= -2/2t = -1/t.$

9. $fog = f(\log_e x) = e^{\log_e x} = x.$

10. $gof = g(e^x) = \log_e e^x = x.$

11. Looking at the options, one unit right means $x$ is replaced by $(x – 1)$. Also, 1 unit down means $–1$ on the RHS.

Thus, $(y + 1) = 1/(x – 1)$.

12. For option (c) we can see that $f(t) = f(–t)$. Hence, option (c) is correct.

13. Option (b) is odd because:

$$\frac{a^{-t} + a^{t}}{a^{t} - a^{-t}} = -1 \times \left(\frac{a^{-t} + a^{t}}{a^{-t} - a^{t}}\right)$$

Similarly option (c) is also representing an odd function. The function in option (a) is not odd.

14. $f(f(t)) = f[t/(1+ t^2)^{1/2}] = t/(1 + 2t^2)^{1/2}.$

15. By trial and error it is clear that at $x = 3$, the value of the function is 19. At other values of '$x$' the value of the function is less than 19.

17. Take different values of $x$ to check each option. Each of Options (a), (b) and (c) can be ruled out. Hence, Option (d) is correct.

***Solutions to 18 to 20:***

$$f(1) = 0, f(2) = 1,$$
$$f(3) = f(1) - f(2) = -1$$
$$f(4) = f(2) - f(3) = 2$$
$$f(5) = f(3) - f(4) = -3$$
$$f(6) = f(4) - f(5) = 5$$
$$f(7) = f(5) - f(6) = -8$$
$$f(8) = f(6) - f(7) = 13$$

18. It can be seen that $f(x)$ is positive wherever $x$ is even and negative whenever $x$ is odd once $x$ is greater than 2.

19. $f(f(6)) = f(5) = -3.$

20. $f(6) – f(8) = 5 – 13 = -8 = f(7).$

21. Option (b) is not even since $e^x – e^{-x} \neq e^{-x} – e^x.$

22. We have $f(x) \cdot f(1/x) = f(x) + f(1/x)$

$\Rightarrow$   $f(1/x)[f(x) – 1] = f(x)$

For $x = 4$, we have $f(1/4) [f(4) – 1] = f(4)$

$\Rightarrow$   $f(1/4) [64] = 65$

$\Rightarrow$       $f(1/4) = 65/64 = 1/64 + 1$

This means $f(x) = x^3 + 1.$

For $f(6)$ we have $f(6) = 216 + 1 = 217.$

***Directions for Questions 23 to 34:*** You essentially have to mark (a) if it is an even function, mark (b) if it is an odd function, mark (c) if the function is neither even nor odd.

Also, Option (d) would occur if the function does not exist at, atleast one point of the domain. This means one of two things.

Either the function is returning two values for one value of $x$ or the function has a break in between (as in questions 26, 31 and 33).

We see even functions in Questions 23, 28, 30, 32 and 34 [Symmetry about the $y$ axis]. We see odd functions in Questions 24, 25 and 27.

While the figure in Question 29 is neither odd nor even.

***Solutions to 35–40:***

In order to solve this set of questions first analyse each of the functions:

$A(x, y, z)$ = will always return the value of the highest between $x$ and $y$.

$B(x, y, z)$ will return the value of the maximum amongst $x$, $y$ and $z$.

$C(x, y, z)$ and $D(x, y, z)$ would return the second highest values in all cases while max $(x, y, z)$ and min$(x, y, z)$ would return the maximum and minimum values amongst $x$, $y$, and $z$ respectively.

35. When either $x$ or $y$ is maximum.

36. This would never happen.

37. When $z$ is maximum, $A$ and $B$ would give different values. Thus, option (c) is correct.

38. Never.

39. I and III are always true.

40. We cannot determine this because it would depend on whether the integers $x$, $y$, and $z$ are positive or negative.

***Solutions to 41 to 49:***

$f(x, y)$ is always positive or zero

$F(f(x, y))$ is always negative or zero

$G(f(x, y))$ is always positive or zero

41. $F \times G$ would always be negative while $– F \times G$ would always be positive except when they are both equal to zero.

Hence, Option (b) $F \times G \leq – F \times G$ is correct.

42. Option (b) can be seen to give us $4a^2/4 = a^2.$

43. $(5 – 1)/(1+ 3) = 4/4 = 1.$

44. The given expression = $(45 – 10)/(5 + 2) = 35/7 = 5.$

Option (b) = $20/4 = 5.$

***Directions for Questions 45 to 49:*** Do the following analysis:

$A(f(x, y))$ is positive

$B$ ($f(x, y)$) is negative

$C$($f(x, y)$) is positive

$D$ ($f(x, y)$) is negative

$E$($f(x, y)$) is positive and so on.

45. $1 - 3 + 5 - 7 + 9 - 11 + \ldots - 51$

$= (1 + 5 + 9 + 13 + \ldots 49) - (3 + 7 + 11 \ldots + 51)$

$= -26$

46. Verify each statement to see that (ii) and (iii) are true.

47. The given expression becomes:

Min ( max [5, – 7, 9], min [3, – 1 , 1], max [7, 6, 10])

$= $ Min [ 9, – 1, 10]

$= -1$.

48. The given expression becomes:

Max $[|a + b|, -|b + c|, |c + d|]$

This would never be negative.

49. The respective values are:

$-3/2, -7/12, - 8/15$, and $-5/6$.

Option (b) is second lowest.

50. Let $s = 1, t = 2$ and $b = 3$

Then, $f(s + t) + f(s - t)$

$= f(3) + f(-1) = (3^3 + 3^{-3})/2 + (3^{-1} + 3^1)/2$

$= [(27 + (1/27)]/2 + [3 + (1/3)]/2$

$= 730/54 + 10/6$

$= 820/54 = 410/27$

Option (b) $2 f(s) \times f(t)$ gives the same value.

51. This question is based on the logic of a chain function. Given the relationship

$A_t = (t + 1)A_{(t - 1)} - tA_{(t - 2)}$

We can clearly see that the value of $A_2$ would depend on the values of $A_0$ and $A_1$. Putting $t = 2$ in the expression, we get:

$A_2 = 3A_1 - 2A_0 = 7; A_3 = 19; A_4 = 67$ and $A_5 = 307$. Clearly, A6 onwards will be larger than 307 and hence none of the three conclusions are true. Option (e) is the correct answer.

52. In order to solve this question, we would need to check each of the value ranges given in the conclusions: Checking whether Conclusion I is possible For B = 2, we get A + C = 4 (since A + B + C = 6). This transforms the second equation AB + BC + CA = 9 to:

$2(A + C) + CA = 9 \rightarrow CA = 1$.

Solving CA = 1 and A + C = 4 we get: $(4 - A)A = 1 \rightarrow A^2 - 4A + 1 = 0 \rightarrow A = 2 + 3^{1/2}$ and $C = 2 - 3^{1/2}$. Both these numbers are real and it satisfies A < B < C and hence, Conclusion I is true.

Checking Conclusion II: If we chose A = 2.5, the condition is not satisfied since we get the other two variables as $(3.5 + 11.25^{1/2}) \div 2 \approx 3.4$ and $(3.5 - 11.25^{1/2}) \div 2 \approx 0.1$. In this case, A is no longer the

least value and hence Conclusion II is rejected.

Checking Conclusion III we can see that 0 < C < 1 cannot be possible since C being the largest of the three values has to be greater than 3 (the largest amongst A, B, and C would be greater than the average of A, B, C).

Option (a) is correct.

53. The number of ways of distributing $n$ identical things to $r$ people such that any person can get any number of things including 0 is always given by $^{n+r-1}C_{r-1}$. In the case of $F(4,3)$, the value of $n = 4$ and $r = 3$ and hence the total number of ways without any constraints would be given by $^{4+3-1}C_{3-1} = {}^6C_2 = 15$. However, out of these 15 ways of distributing the toys, we cannot count any way in which more than 2 toys are given to any one child. Hence, we need to reduce as follows:

The distribution of 4 toys as (3, 1, 0) amongst three children A, B and C can be done in 3! = 6 ways.

Also, the distribution of 4 toys as (4, 0, 0) amongst three children A, B and C can be done in 3 ways.

Hence, the value of $F(4, 3) = 15 - 6 - 3 = 6$.

Option (b) is correct.

54. $f(f(x)) = 15$ when $f(x) = 4$ or $f(x) = 12$ in the given function. The graph given in the figure becomes equal to 4 at 4 points and it becomes equal to 12 at 3 points in the figure. This gives us 7 points in the given figure when $f(f(x)) = 15$. However, the given function is continuous beyond the part of it which is shown between –10 and +13 in the figure. Hence, we do not know how many more solutions to $f(f(x)) = 15$ would be there. Hence, Option (e) is the correct answer.

55. The given function is a chain function where the value of $A_{n+1}$ depends on the value $A_n$.

Thus for $n = 0$, $A_1 = A_0^2 + 1$.

For n = 1, $A_2 = A_1^2 + 1$ and so on.

In such functions, if you know the value of the function at any one point, the value of the function can be calculated for any value till infinity.

Hence, Statement I is sufficient by itself to find the value of the GCD of $A_{900}$ and $A_{1000}$.

So also, the Statement II is sufficient by itself to find the value of the GCD of $A_{900}$ and $A_{1000}$.

Hence, Option (d) is correct.

56. This question can be solved by first putting up the information in the form of a table as follows:

| | Product A | Product B | No of machines available | No of Hours/day per Machine. | Total Hrs. per day available for each activity |
|---|---|---|---|---|---|
| Grinding | 2 hr | 3 hr | 10 | 12 | 120 |
| Polishing | 3 hr | 2 hr | 15 | 10 | 150 |
| Profit | ₹ 5 | ₹ 7 | | | |

On the surface, the profit of Product B being higher, we can think about maximising the number of units of Product B. Grinding would be the constraint when we maximise Product B production and we can produce a maximum of $120 \div 3 = 40$ units of Product B to get a profit of ₹ 280. The clue that this is not the correct answer comes from the fact that there is a lot of 'polishing' time left in this situation. In order to try to increase the profit we can check that if we reduce production of Product B and try to increase the production of Product A, does the profit go up? When we reduce the production of Product B by 2 units, the production of Product A goes up by 3 units and the profit goes up by +1 ($-2 \times 7 + 3 \times 5$ gives a net effect of +1). In this case, the grinding time remains the same (as there is a reduction of 2 units $\times$ 3 hours/unit = 6 hours in grinding time due to the reduction in Product B's production, but there is also a simultaneous increase of 6 hours in the use of the grinders in producing 3 units of Product A). Given that a reduction in the production of Product B, with a simultaneous maximum possible increase in the production of Product A, results in an increase in the profit, we would like to do this as much as possible. To think about it from this point this situation can be tabulated as under for better understanding:

| | Product A Production (A) | Product B Production (B) | Grinding Machine Usage $= 3A + 2B$ | Polishing Machine Usage $= 2A + 3B$ | Time Left on Grinding Machine | Time Left on Polishing Machine | Profit $= 7A + 5B$ |
|---|---|---|---|---|---|---|---|
| Case 1 | 40 | 0 | 120 | 80 | 0 | 70 | 280 |
| Case 2 | 38 | 3 | 120 | 85 | 0 | 65 | 281 |
| Case 3 | 36 | 6 | 120 | 90 | 0 | 60 | 282 |

The limiting case would occur when we reduce the time left on the polishing machine to 0. That would happen in the following case:

| | | | | | | | |
|---|---|---|---|---|---|---|---|
| Optimal case | 12 | 42 | 120 | 150 | 0 | 0 | 294 |

Hence, the answer would be 294.

57. The value of $f(x)$ as given is: $f(x) = x^4 + x^3 + x^2 + x + 1 = 1 + x + x^2 + x^3 + x^4 + x^5$. This can be visualised as a geometric progression with 5 terms with the first term 1 and common ratio $x$. The sum of the GP $= f(x) = \dfrac{x^5 - 1}{x - 1}$

The value of $f(x^5) = x^{20} + x^{15} + x^{10} + x^5 + 1$ and this can be rewritten as:

$F(x^5) = (x^{20} - 1) + (x^{15} - 1) + (x^{10} - 1) + (x^5 - 1) + 5$. When this expression is divided by $f(x) = \dfrac{x^5 - 1}{x - 1}$ we get each of the first four terms of the expression would be divisible by it, i.e. $(x^{20} - 1)$ would be divisible by $f(x) = \dfrac{x^5 - 1}{x - 1}$ and would leave no remainder (because $x^{20} - 1$ can be rewritten in the form $(x^5 - 1) \times (x^{15} + x^{10} + x^5 + 1)$ and when you divide this expression by $\left(\dfrac{x^5 - 1}{x - 1}\right)$ we get the remainder as 0.)

A similar logic would also hold for the terms $(x^{15} - 1)$, $(x^{10} - 1)$ and $(x^5 - 1)$. The only term that would leave a

remainder would be 5 when it is divided by $\left(\dfrac{x^5 - 1}{x - 1}\right)$

Also, for $x \geq 2$ we can see the value of $\left(\dfrac{x^5 - 1}{x - 1}\right)$ would be more than 5. Hence, the remainder would always be 5 and Option (c) is the correct answer.

58. Start by putting $\dfrac{x}{x - 1} = (\text{cosec } \alpha)^2$ in the given expression

$F\left(\dfrac{x}{x - 1}\right) = \dfrac{1}{x}$

Now for $0 < \alpha < 90°$

$\dfrac{x}{x - 1} = (\text{cosec } \alpha)^2 \Rightarrow x = \dfrac{1}{1 - \sin^2 \alpha} \Rightarrow \dfrac{1}{x} = \cos^2 \alpha$

Hence, Option (b) is correct.

59. Given that the roots of the equation $F(x) = 0$ are $-2$, $-1$, 1 and 2 respectively and the $F(x)$ is a polynomial with the highest power of $x$ as $x^4$, we can create the value of

$F(x) = (x + 2)(x + 1)(x - 1)(x - 2)$

Hence, $F(p) = (P + 2)(P + 1)(P - 1)(P - 2)$

It is given to us that $P$ is a prime number greater than 97. Hence, $p$ would always be of the form $6n \pm 1$ where $n$ is a natural number greater than or equal to 17.

Thus, we get two cases for $F(p)$.

Case 1: If $p = 6n + 1$.

$F(6n + 1) = (6n + 3)(6n + 2)(6n)(6n - 1)$

$= 3(2n + 1) \cdot 2(3n + 1)(6n)(6n - 1)$

$= (36)(2n + 1)(3n + 1)(n)(6n - 1)$ ...(i)

If you try to look for divisibility of this expression by numbers given in the options for various values of $n \geq 17$, we see that the for $n = 17$ and $18$ both 360 divides the value of $F(p)$. However at $n = 19$, none of the values in the four options divides $36 \times 39 \times 58 \times 19 \times 113$. In this case however, at $n = 19$, $6n + 1$ is not a prime number hence, this case is not to be considered. Whenever we put a value of n as a value greater than 17, such that $6n+1$ becomes a prime number, we also see that the value of $F(p)$ is divisible by 360. This divisibility by 360 happens since the expression $(2n + 1)(3n + 1)(n)(6n - 1)$ ... is always divisible by 10 in all such cases. A similar logic can be worked out when we take $p = 6n-1$. Hence, the Option (d) is the correct answer.

60. In order to solve this question, we start from the value of $x = (9 + 4\sqrt{5})^{48}$.

Let the value of $x(1-f) = xy$. (We are assuming $(1-f) = y$, which means that $y$ is between 0 to 1).

The value of $x = (9 + 4\sqrt{5})^{48}$ can be rewritten as $[^{48}C_0\ 9^{48} + {}^{48}C_1\ 9^{47}(4\sqrt{5}) + {}^{48}C_2\ 9^{46}(4\sqrt{5})^2 + ... + {}^{48}C_{47}(9)(4\sqrt{5})^{47} + {}^{48}C_{48}\ (4\sqrt{5})^{48}]$ using the binary theorem.

In this value, it is going to be all the odd powers of the $(4\sqrt{5})$ which would account for the value of '$f$' in the value of $x$. Thus, for instance it can be seen that the terms ${}^{48}C_0\ 9^{48}, {}^{48}C_2\ 9^{46}(4\sqrt{5})^2, .... {}^{48}C_{48}\ (4\sqrt{5})^{48}$ would all be integers. It is only the terms: ${}^{48}C_1 9^{47}$ $(4\sqrt{5}), {}^{48}C_3\ 9^{45}(4\sqrt{5})^3, ... {}^{48}C_{47}\ (9)(4\sqrt{5})^{47}$ which would give us the value of '$f$' in the value of $x$. Hence, $x(1-f) = x [1 - {}^{48}C_1\ 9^{47}\ (4\sqrt{5}) - {}^{48}C_3\ 9^{45}$ $(4\sqrt{5})^3 - ... - {}^{48}C_{47}\ (9)(4\sqrt{5})^{47}]$

In order to think further from this point, you would need the following thought. Let $y = (9 - 4\sqrt{5})^{48}$.

Also, $x + y = \{{}^{48}C_0 9^{48} + {}^{48}C_1 9^{47}(4\sqrt{5}) + {}^{48}C_2 9^{46}(4\sqrt{5})^2 + ... + {}^{48}C_{47}\ (9)(4\sqrt{5})^{47} + {}^{48}C_{48}\ (4\sqrt{5})^{48}\} + \{{}^{48}C_0 9^{48} - {}^{48}C_1\ 9^{47}\ (4\sqrt{5}) + {}^{48}C_2\ 9^{46}\ (4\sqrt{5})^2 + ... - {}^{48}C_{47} (9)\ (4\sqrt{5})^{47} + {}^{48}C_{48}\ (4\sqrt{5})^{48}\} = 2\{{}^{48}C_0\ 9^{48} + {}^{48}C_2 9^{46}\ (4\sqrt{5})^2 + ... {}^{48}C_{48}\ (4\sqrt{5})^{48}\}$ – the bracket in this expression has only retained the even terms which are integral. Hence, the value of $x+y$ is an integer. Further, $x + y = [x] + f + y$ and hence, if $x+y$ is an integer, $[x] + f + y$ would also be an integer. This

automatically means that $f+y$ must be an integer (as $[x]$ is an integer).

Now, the value of $y$ is between 0 to 1 and hence when we add the fractional part of $x$ i.e. '$f$' to $y$, and we need to make it an integer, the only possible integer that $f + y$ can be equal to is 1.

Thus, if $f + y = 1 \rightarrow y = (1 - f)$.

In order to find the value of $x(1 - f)$ we can find the value of $x \times y$.

Then, $x(1 - f) = x \times y = (9 + 4\sqrt{5})^{48} \times (9 - 4\sqrt{5})^{48}$

$= (81 - 80)^{48} = 1$

$x(1 - f) = 1$

61. $3f(x + 2) + 4f\left(\dfrac{1}{x+2}\right) = 4x$

Let $x + 2 = t$

$3f(t) + 4f\left(\dfrac{1}{t}\right) = 4t - 8$ or $\dfrac{3}{4}f(t) + f\left(\dfrac{1}{t}\right)$

$= t - 2$ ...(1)

Now replacing t with $\dfrac{1}{t}$ in the above equation, we get

$3f\left(\dfrac{1}{t}\right) + 4f(t) = \dfrac{4}{t} - 8$ or $f\left(\dfrac{1}{t}\right) + \dfrac{4}{3}f(t)$

$= \dfrac{4}{3t} - \dfrac{8}{3}$ ....(2)

From (1) and (2)

$f(t) = \dfrac{12}{7}\left\{\dfrac{4}{3t} - \dfrac{8}{3} - t + 2\right\}$

$f(4) = \dfrac{12}{7}\left\{\dfrac{1}{3} - \dfrac{8}{3} - 4 + 2\right\} = \dfrac{-52}{7}$

62. According to the graph, $f(4) = 15$ and $f(12) = 15$. So $f(f(x)) = 15$ for $f(x) = 4, 12$.

According to the graph $f(x) = 4$ has four solutions. According to the graph $f(x) = 12$ has three solutions. Hence, the given equation has 7 solutions.

63. $[f(x)]^{g(x)} = 1$

Now three cases are possible:

Case I: $f(x) = 1$ and $g(x)$ may be anything.

$x - 6 = 1$ or $x = 7$

But for $x = 7, g(x)$ is not defined.

Case II: $f(x) = -1$ and $g(x)$ is an even exponent

$x - 6 = -1$

$x = 5$

For $x = 5$

$g(x) = \dfrac{(5-9)(5-1)}{(5-7)(5-3)} = \dfrac{-4 \times 4}{-2 \times 2} = 4$

So for $x = 5$, $g(x)$ is even, which satisfies the given equation.

Case III: $g(x) = 0$ and $f(x) \neq 0$

$\dfrac{(x-9)(x-1)}{(x-7)(x-3)} = 0$ for $x = 1, 9$

For $x = 1$ & $9$ $f(x) \neq 0$. So both of these values of $x$ satisfy the given equation.

So the given equation is satisfied for three values of $x$.

64. $f(4) + f(6) = 0$ implies that $f(4)$ & $f(6)$ are of opposite sign but same absolute value. Hence one root of the equation lies between 4 and 6.

$f(1) > 0$ & $f(2) < 0$ implies that another root lies between 1 and 2.

$f(5).f(7) > 0$ implies that $f(5)$ & $f(7)$ are of same sign, so $f(4)$ & $f(5)$ must be of opposite sign. So the second root of $f(x) = 0$ must lie between $x = 4$ & $x = 5$.

So $f(x)$ would look like:

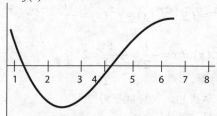

As $f(1) > 0$ & $f(2)$ & $f(4) < 0$

So $f(1) f(2) f(4) > 0$. Option (a) is incorrect.

As $f(5)$, $f(6)$ & $f(7)$ are greater than 0.

So $f(5) f(6) f(7) > 0$. So option (b) is wrong.

As $f(1) > 0$ & $f(3)$ & $f(4) < 0$. So $f(1) f(3) f(4) > 0$

So option (c) is true.

65. $f(x) = 12 + x$

$7[x] + 4\{x\} = 12 + x$

$3[x] + 4[[x] + \{x\}] = 12 + x$

$3[x] + 4x = 12 + x$

$3[x] + 3x = 12$

$[x] + x = 4$

Since 4 and $[x]$ are both integers, in the above equations $x$ must also be an integer. This means that the value of $[x] = x$. So:

$2x = 4$

$x = 2$

Therefore only one value of $x$ satisfies the given equation.

66. $x^2 - xy + y^2 = x + y$

Multiplying both sides by 2, we get:

$2x^2 - 2xy + 2y^2 = 2x + 2y$

$x^2 - 2xy + y^2 + x^2 - 2x + 1 + y^2 - 2y + 1 = 2$

$(x - y)^2 + (x - 1)^2 + (y - 1)^2 = 2$

In the question we are interested to find non-negative integer solutions therefore three cases are possible.

Case I: $x - y = 0$, $(x - 1)^2 = 1$, $(y - 1)^2 = 1$

Possible solutions $(0, 0)$ & $(2, 2)$

Case II: $(x - y)^2 = 1$, $(x - 1)^2 = 1$, $(y - 1)^2 = 0$

Possible solutions: $(2, 1)$, $(0, 1)$.

Case III: $(x - y)^2 = 1$, $(y - 1)^2 = 1$, $(x - 1)^2 = 0$

Possible solutions: $(1, 2)$ and $(1, 0)$

Possible solutions $(x, y)$ such that $x \geq y$ are $(0, 0)$, $(2, 2)$, $(1, 0)$, $(2, 1)$. There are 4 such solutions.

67. $g(n) = \dfrac{n-1}{n} g(n-1)$

$g(2) = \dfrac{1}{2} g(1)$

$g(3) = \dfrac{2}{3} g(2) = \dfrac{2}{3} \times \dfrac{1}{2} g(1) = \dfrac{1}{3} g(1)$.

Similarly:

$g(4) = \dfrac{1}{4} g(1); g(5) = \dfrac{1}{5} g(1);$

$g(6) = \dfrac{1}{6} g(1); g(7) = \dfrac{1}{7} g(1); g(8) = \dfrac{1}{8} g(1)$

Since $g(1) = 2$, the given expression would become:

$$\frac{\left[\dfrac{1}{2} \times \dfrac{2}{2} \times \dfrac{3}{2} \times \dots \dfrac{8}{2}\right]}{\left[\dfrac{1}{2} + \dfrac{2}{2} + \dfrac{3}{2} + \dots \dfrac{8}{2}\right]}$$

Required answer is $\dfrac{8!}{2^8} \times \dfrac{1}{18}$

68. Let $f(x) = a(x - 1)(x - 2)(x - 3)\dots(x - 77) + x$

Where '$a$' is any constant.

Now putting $x = 78$ in the above equation we get

$f(78) = a.77.76.75.74\dots1 + 78 = a.77! + 78$

Similarly $f(0) = a.(-1)(-2)(-3)\dots(-77) + 0$

$f(0) = a(-1)^{77}77! = -a.77!$

$f(78) + f(0) = a.77! + 78 - a.77! = 78$

69. $f(n - 1)(2 - f(n)) = 1$

$2 - f(n) = \dfrac{1}{f(n-1)}$

$f(n) = 2 - \dfrac{1}{f(n-1)}$

$f(2) = 2 - \dfrac{1}{f(1)} = 2 - \dfrac{1}{3} = \dfrac{5}{3}$

$f(3) = 2 - \dfrac{1}{f(2)} = 2 - \dfrac{3}{5} = \dfrac{7}{5}$

$f(4) = 2 - \dfrac{1}{f(3)} = 2 - \dfrac{5}{7} = \dfrac{9}{7}$

Observing this pattern, we can see that:

$f(n) = \dfrac{2n+1}{2n-1}$

$f(21) = \dfrac{2 \times 21 + 1}{2 \times 21 - 1} = \dfrac{43}{41}$

70. Since: $0 \leq \{x\} < 1$

The expression: $10[x] + 22\ \{x\} = 250$ gives us the inequality: $228 < 10\ [x] \le 250$

$$22.8 < [x] \le 25$$

Possible values of $[x]$ = 23, 24, 25

For $[x]$ = 23, $\{x\}$ = $\dfrac{250-230}{22} = \dfrac{20}{22} = \dfrac{10}{11}$

For $[x]$ = 24 $\{x\}$ = $\dfrac{250-240}{22} = \dfrac{10}{22} = \dfrac{5}{11}$

For $[x]$ = 25, $\{x\}$ = 0

So the possible values of $x$ are $23\dfrac{10}{11}, 24\dfrac{5}{11}, 25$.

So there are three possible values of $x$.

71. $23\dfrac{10}{11} + 24\dfrac{5}{11} + 25 = 73\dfrac{4}{11} \approx 73.36$

72. $f(x+1) = f(x) - f(x-1)$

$f(x) = f(x+1) + f(x-1)$

$f(17) = f(18) + f(16)$

$2f(16) = f(18) + f(16)$

$f(16) = f(18)$

Let $f(16) = f(18) = x$

$f(17) = 2x$

$f(16) = f(15) + f(17) \rightarrow f(15) = -x;$

$f(15) = f(14) + f(16) \rightarrow f(14) = -2x;$

$f(14) = f(13) + f(15) \rightarrow f(13) = -x;$

$f(13) = f(12) + f(14) \rightarrow f(12) = x$

$f(12) = f(11) + f(13) \rightarrow f(11) = 2x$

$f(11) = f(10) + f(12) \rightarrow f(10) = x$

$f(10) = f(9) + (f(11) \rightarrow f(9) = -x$

If we observe the above pattern of values that we are getting, we can observe that $f(18) = f(12)$; $f(17) = f(11)$; $f(16) = f(10)$ and $f(15) = f(9)$. Here we can easily observe that values repeat for every six terms. So $f(5) = f(11) = f(17) = 6$.

Option (b) is correct.

73. $\dfrac{h(x)}{h(x-1)} = \dfrac{h(x-2)}{h(x+1)}$

On putting $x = 54$ we get:

$\dfrac{h(54)}{h(53)} = \dfrac{h(52)}{h(55)}$ \hfill (i)

On putting $x = 55$, we get:

$\dfrac{h(55)}{h(54)} = \dfrac{h(53)}{h(56)}$ \hfill (ii)

Equation (i) ÷ Equation (ii)

$\dfrac{[h(54)]^2}{h(53) \times h(55)} = \dfrac{h(52) \times h(56)}{h(55) \times h(53)}$

$[h(54)]^2 = 4 \times 16$

$h(54) = 8$

74. $f(x) = 1 - \dfrac{2}{x+1} = \dfrac{x+1-2}{x+1} = \dfrac{x-1}{x+1}$

$f^2(x) = f(f(x)) = \dfrac{\dfrac{x-1}{x+1}-1}{\dfrac{x-1}{x+1}+1} = -\dfrac{1}{x}$

$f^3(x) = f(f(f)) = -\dfrac{x+1}{x-1}$

$f^4(x) = f(f(f(f(x)))) = x$

$f^5(x) = f(x) = \dfrac{x-1}{x+1}$

Here we can see that $f(x) = f^5(x)$ so the given function has a cyclicity of 4, therefore:

$f^n(x) = f^{n+4k}(x)$ where $k$ is a whole number

$f^{802} = f^{2+4\times200}(x) = f^2(x) = -\dfrac{1}{x}$

$f^{802}(x)\ at\ x = -\dfrac{1}{2} = -\dfrac{1}{-\dfrac{1}{2}} = 2$

75. $\log_3(x+y) + \log_3(x-y) = 3$

$\log_3(x^2 - y^2) = 3$

$x^2 - y^2 = 3^3 = 27$

$(x-y)(x+y) = 27$

Here both $(x+y)$ & $(x-y)$ are positive integers (since they have to be used as the arguments of the logarithmic functions. Hence, $(x-y) > 0$ or $x > y$. From this point, we need to think of factor pairs of 27, in order to find out the values that are possible for $x$ and $y$.

Case 1: $x + y = 9$, $x - y = 3$ or $x = 6$, $y = 3$

Case 2: when $x + y = 27$, $x - y = 1$ or $x = 14$, $y = 13$

Two pairs of $(x, y)$ are possible.

76. The maximum value of $x + y = 14 + 13 = 27$

77. In the following figure, the bold portion shows the graph of $h(x)$.

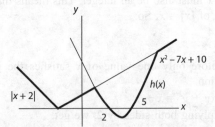

Therefore $h(x) \le 0$ for $x = 2, 3, 4, 5$. There are 4 such values.

78. We can observe from the graph that $h(x) < 0$ only for two integer values (3, 4) of $x$. So the required sum = 3 + 4 = 7.

79. $[2p - 3]$ is an integer. Hence, $q + 7$ is also an integer or $q$ must be an integer.

Similarly $p$ is also an integer (since $[3q + 1]$ is an integer, hence $p + 6$ should also be an integer.)

$\Rightarrow [2p - 3] = 2p - 3 = q + 7$

$2p - q = 10$               (i)

$\Rightarrow 3q + 1 = p + 6$

$3q - p = 5$               (ii)

By solving equations (i) and (ii) we get the values of $p$ and $q$ as:

$p = 7, q = 4$

The required answer is then given by $7^2 \times 4^2 = 784$.

80. $f(a) = 3^a$   (If $a$ is an odd number)

$f(a + 1) = 3^{(a + 1)} + 4 = 3.3^a + 4$

$\frac{1}{4}[f(a) + f(a+1)] = \frac{3^a + 3.3^a + 4}{4} = \frac{3^a.4 + 4}{4} = 3^a + 1$

$\Rightarrow \frac{1}{4}[f(1) + f(2) + (f(3) + f(4)) + ... + f(71) + f(72)]$

$= \frac{f(1) + f(2)}{4} + \frac{f(3) + f(4)}{4} + ... + \frac{f(71) + f(72)}{4}$

$= 3^1 + 1 + 3^3 + 1 + ... + 3^{71} + 1$

$= (3^1 + 3^3 + ... + 3^{71}) + 36$

$= \frac{3((3^2)^{36} - 1)}{3^2 - 1} + 36$

$= \frac{3}{8}(3^{72} - 1) + 36$

81. $g(f(x)) = 2.\dfrac{x^{2\left[\frac{3x^2}{4}\right]}}{4} + 2$

$= \dfrac{x^{2\left[\frac{3x^2}{4}\right]}}{2} + 2$

$g(f(x))$ is an even function, so option (a) is incorrect. As we increase the value of $x$, value of $g(f(x))$ will get increased. Therefore it will attain it's maxima at $\infty$. So option (b) is also incorrect.

$\dfrac{x^{2\left[\frac{3x^2}{4}\right]}}{2} + 2$ will attain it's minima when $0 \le \dfrac{3x^2}{4} \le 1$.

Since, the expression $\dfrac{3x^2}{4}$ is always going to be positive, hence we can say that the only constraint we need to match for the minima of the function is $\dfrac{3x^2}{4} \le 1$. Therefore, option(c) is true.

82. $\dfrac{x^{2\left[\frac{3x^2}{4}\right]}}{2} + 2 = 2^5 + 2 = 34$. Hence, option (b) is correct.

83.

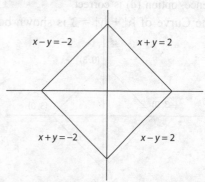

As shown in the above diagram the region bounded by $|x + y| = 2$ and $|x - y| = 2$ is a square of side $\sqrt{2^2 + 2^2} = 2\sqrt{2}$

Required area $= \left(2\sqrt{2}\right)^2 = 8$

84. For $n = 8$

$f(x) = |x| + |x + 4| + |x + 8| + ... + |x + 32|$

The minimum value of $f(x)$ will be when $x = -16$ when the middle term of this expression viz. $|x + 16|$ becomes 0. (i.e. it is minimized)

We have: $f(-16) = |-16| + |-12| + |-8| + |-4| + 0 + |4| + |8| + |12| + |16| = 80$

85. For $n = 7$, $f(x) = |x| + |x + 4| + |x + 8| + ... + |x + 28|$. In this case there would be two middle terms in the expression viz. $|x + 12|$ and $|x + 16|$. The value of the expression would be minimized when the value of the sum of the middle terms is minimized.

We can see that $|x + 12| + |x + 16|$ gets minimized at $-16 \le x \le -12$; Note that the values of the sum of the remaining 6 terms of the expression would remain constant whenever we take the values of $x$ between $-12$ and $-16$.

Thus, we have a total of 5 values at which the expression is minimised for $n = 7$.

86. For $n = 9$, $f(x) = |x| + |x + 4| + |x + 8| + ... + |x + 36|$. The middle terms of this expression are $|x + 16|$ and $|x + 20|$. Hence, this expression would attain its' minimum value when

$-20 \le x \le -16$

Therefore $f(x)$ is minimum for a total of 5 values of $x$.

Minimum value of $f(x)$ can be seen at $x = -16 \rightarrow$

$f(-16) = |-16| + |-16 + 4| + | + |-16 + 8| + |-16 + 12| + |-16 + 16| + |-16 + 20| + |-16 + 24| + |-16 + 28| + |-16 + 32| + |-16 + 36|$

$= 16 + 12 + 8 + 4 + 0 + 4 + 8 + 12 + 16 + 20$

$= 100$

For $n = 9$, $f(x)$ will be minimum for $x = -16$ to $-20$

$\therefore f(-17) = f(-19) = 100$ minimum value of $f(x)$

Hence, option (d) is correct.

87. The Curve of $|x| + |y| = 3$ is shown below

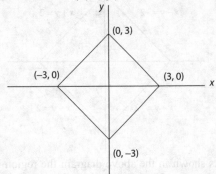

The curve is a square of side of length $3\sqrt{2}$ units.

Therefore required area $= \left(3\sqrt{2}\right)^2 = 18$ square units.

88. In the previous question we found the area of curve $|x| + |y| = 3$,

$|x - a| + |y - b| = 3$ also has the same graph with the same shape and size only it's center shifted to a new point $(a, b)$. (Previous center was $(0, 0)$).

Hence area enclosed by curve $|x - 2| + |y - 3| = 3$ is same as area enclosed by curve $|x| + |y| = 3 = 18$ square units

89. $8\{x\} = x + 2[x] \rightarrow 8\{x\} = [x] + \{x\} + 2[x] \rightarrow$

$7\{x\} = 3[x] \rightarrow [x] = \dfrac{7}{3}\{x\}$. This gives us the relationship between $[x]$ and $\{x\}$ and can also be expressed as $\{x\} = \dfrac{3}{7}[x]$.

Further, since $\{x\}$ is a fraction between 0 and 1 we get: $0 \le \dfrac{3}{7}[x] < 1 \rightarrow$

$0 \le 3[x] < 7 \rightarrow 0 \le [x] < \dfrac{7}{3}$

Thus, $[x] = 0, 1, 2$ (three possible values between the limits we got).

Then using the relationship between $\{x\}$ and $[x]$ we get the possible values of $\{x\} = 0, \dfrac{3}{7}, \dfrac{6}{7}$ when $[x]$ is 0,1 and 2 respectively.

Since $x = [x] + \{x\}$ we get $x = 0, \dfrac{10}{7}, \dfrac{20}{7}$

Therefore, there are two positive values of $x$ for which the given equation is true.

90. Difference between the greatest and least value of $x$

$= \dfrac{20}{7} - 0 = \dfrac{20}{7} = 2.85$

91. $f(x) = \dfrac{4^{x-1}}{4^{x-1}+1} = \dfrac{4^x}{4^x + 4}$

$fog(x) = \dfrac{4^{2x}}{4^{2x}+4}$

$fog(1-x) = \dfrac{4^{2(1-x)}}{4^{2(1-x)}+4}$

$= \dfrac{4^2 . 4^{-2x}}{4^2 . 4^{-2x}+4}$

$= \dfrac{4^2}{4^2 + 4.4^{2x}}$

$= \dfrac{4}{4 + 4^{2x}}$

$fog(x) + fog(1-x) = \dfrac{4^{2x}}{4^{2x}+4} + \dfrac{4}{4+4^{2x}}$

$= \dfrac{4^{2x}+4}{4^{2x}+4} = 1$

put $x = \dfrac{1}{4}$

we get $fog\left(\dfrac{1}{4}\right) + fog\left(1 - \dfrac{1}{4}\right) = fog\left(\dfrac{1}{4}\right) + fog\left(\dfrac{3}{4}\right) = 1$

$\Rightarrow fog\left(\dfrac{1}{4}\right) + fog\left(\dfrac{3}{4}\right) = 1$

92. put $x = \frac{1}{2}$

$fog\left(\dfrac{1}{2}\right) + fog\left(1 - \dfrac{1}{2}\right) = 1$

$2 fog\left(\dfrac{1}{2}\right) = 1 \Rightarrow fog\left(\dfrac{1}{2}\right) = \dfrac{1}{2}$

$fog\left(\dfrac{1}{2}\right) + fog\left(\dfrac{1}{4}\right) + fog\left(\dfrac{3}{4}\right) + fog\left(\dfrac{1}{8}\right)$

$+ fog\left(\dfrac{7}{8}\right) + fog\left(\dfrac{1}{16}\right) + fog\left(\dfrac{15}{16}\right)$

$= \dfrac{1}{2} + 1 + 1 + 1 = 3\dfrac{1}{2} = 3.5$

93. $f(x + 2) = f(x) + 2(x + 1)$ when $x$ is even.

$f(2) = 5$

$f(4) = f(2) + 2(2 + 1) = 5 + 6 = 11$

$f(6) = f(4) + 2(4 + 1) = 11 + 10 = 21$

Therefore for even values of $x$, $f(x) = \dfrac{x^2}{2} + 3$

$f(1) = 1$

$f(3) = 1 + 1 = 2$

$f(5) = 2 + 1 = 3$

$\Rightarrow$ For odd value of $x$, $f(x) = \dfrac{x+1}{2}$

$f(24) = \dfrac{(24)^2}{2} + 3$

$= 291$

94. $f(14) = \dfrac{(14)^2}{2} + 3 = 101$

$$f(11) = \frac{11+1}{2} = 6$$

$$\left[\frac{f(14)}{f(11)}\right] = \left[\frac{101}{6}\right] = [16.83] = 16$$

95. From the solution of question 93 it is clear that only option (c) is correct.

96. $f(f(f(f(3)))) + f(f(f(2)))$
$= f(f(f(2))) + f(f(5))$
$= f(f(5)) + f(3)$
$= f(3) + 2$
$= 2 + 2$
$= 4$

97. From the given information we can assume $F(x)$ as a sum of $P(x)$ and $x$, where
$P(x) = kx\,(x-1)\,(x-2)\,(x-3)\,(x-4)\,(x-5)$, $k$ is a constant.
$F(x) = kx\,(x-1)\,(x-2)\,(x-3)\,(x-4)\,(x-5) + x$
$F(6) = k \times 6 \times 5 \times 4 \times 3 \times 2 \times 1 + 6$
It is given $F(6) = 7$
$\therefore k \times 6! + 6 = 7$
$k \times 6! = 1$
Hence, $k = \dfrac{1}{6!}$

Thus, $F(x) = \dfrac{x(x-1)(x-2)(x-3)(x-4)(x-5)}{6!} + x$

$$F(8) = \frac{8 \times 7 \times 6 \times 5 \times 4 \times 3}{6!} + 8$$

$$= 28 + 8 = 36$$

98. By putting negative values of $x$, we can see that $F(x)$ is a decreasing function for negative integer values of $x$ therefore $F(x)$ will be minimum for $x = -1$

Minimum value of $f(x) = \dfrac{-1 \times -2 \times -3 \times -4 \times -5 \times -6}{6!} - 1$
$\Rightarrow 1 - 1 = 0$

99. $g(x + y) = g(x)\,g(y)$
$g(1 + 1) = g(1)\,.g(1) = g(1)^2 = 5^2 = 25$
$g(2) = 5^2$
Similarly, $g(3) = 5^3$, $g(4) = 5^4$, $g(5) = 5^5$
$g(1) + g(2) + g(3) + g(4) + g(5) = 5 + 25 + 125 + 625 + 3125 = 3905$

100. $g(x) = 5^x$
If we put $n = 1$ in the given summation then
$$g(q+1) = \frac{1}{4}(5^4 - 125) = \frac{500}{4} = 125$$
$5^{q+1} = 125 \Rightarrow q + 1 = 3$ or $q = 2$

# 14

# Inequalities

This chapter will seem to be highly mathematical to you when you read the theory contained in the chapter and look at the solved examples. For students weak in Math, there is no need to be disheartened about the seemingly high mathematical content. I would advise you to go through this chapter and internalise the concepts. However, keep in mind the fact that in an aptitude test, the questions will have options, and with options all you will need to do will be check the validity of the inequality for the different options.

In fact, the questions in this chapter have options on both the levels and with option-based solutions, all these questions will seem easy to you.

However, I would advise students aiming to score high marks in Quantitative Ability to try to mathematically solve all the questions on all three levels in this chapter (even though option-based solution will be much easier.)

Two real numbers or two algebraic expressions related by the symbol > ("Greater Than") or < ("Less Than") (and also by the signs $\geq$ or $\leq$ ) form an inequality.

$A < B, A > B$ (are plain inequalities)

$A \geq B, A \leq B$ (are called as inequations)

The inequality consists of two sides—the left hand side, $A$ and the right hand side, $B$. $A$ and $B$ can be algebraic expressions or they can be numbers.

An inequality with the < or > sign is called a *strict inequality* while an inequality having $\geq$ or $\leq$ sign is called a *slack inequality*. The expressions $A$ and $B$ have to be considered on the set where $A$ and $B$ have sense simultaneously. This set is called the set of permissible values of the inequality. If the terms on the LHS and the RHS are algebraic equations/identities, then the inequality may or may not hold true for a particular value of the variable/set of variables assumed.

The direction in which the inequality sign points is called *the sense of the inequality*. If two or several inequalities contain the same sign (< or >) then they are called *inequalities of the same sense*. Otherwise they are called *inequalities of the opposite sense*.

Now let us consider some basic *definitions* about inequalities.

For 2 real numbers $a$ and $b$

The inequality $a > b$ means that the difference $a - b$ is positive.

The inequality $a < b$ means that the difference $a - b$ is negative.

## PROPERTIES OF INEQUALITIES

For any two real numbers $a$ and $b$, only one of the following restrictions can hold true:

$$a = b, a > b \text{ or } a < b$$

**Definitions of Slack Inequalities**

The inequality $a \geq b$ means that $a > b$ or $a = b$, that is, $a$ is not less than $b$.

The inequality $a \leq b$ means that $a < b$ or $a = b$, that is, $a$ is not greater than $b$.

We can also have the following double inequalities for simultaneous situations:

$$a < b < c, a < b \leq c, a \leq b < c, a \leq b \leq c$$

---

### Properties of Inequalities

1. If $a > b$ then $b < a$ and vice versa.
2. If $a > b$ and $b > c$ then $a > c$.
3. If $a > b$ then for any $c, a + c > b + c$. In other words, an inequality remains true if the same number is added on both sides of the inequality.

---

*Contd*

## Properties of Inequalities (*Contd*)

4. Any number can be transposed from one side of an inequality to the other side of the inequality with the sign of the number reversed. This does not change the sense of the inequality.

5. If $a > b$ and $c > 0$ then $ac > bc$. Both sides of an inequality may be multiplied (or divided) by the same positive number without changing the sense of the inequality.

6. If $a > b$ and $c < 0$ then $ac < bc$. That is, both sides of an inequality may be multiplied (or divided) by the same negative number but then the sense of the inequality is reversed.

7. If $a > b$ and $c > d$ then $a + c > b + d$. (Two inequalities having the same sense may be added termwise.)

8. If $a > b$ and $c < d$ then $a - c > b - d$
   From one inequality it is possible to subtract termwise another inequality of the opposite sense, retaining the sense of the inequality from which the other was subtracted.

9. If $a, b, c, d$ are positive numbers such that $a > b$ and $c > d$ then $ac > bd$, that is, two inequalities of the same sense in which both sides are positive can be multiplied termwise, the resulting inequality having the same sense as the multiplied inequalities.

10. If $a$ and $b$ are positive numbers where $a > b$, then $a^n > b^n$ for any natural $n$.

11. If $a$ and $b$ are positive numbers where $a > b$ then $a^{1/n} > b^{1/n}$ for any natural $n \geq 2$.

12. Two inequalities are said to be equivalent if the correctness of one of them implies the correctness of the other, and vice versa.

   Students are advised to check these properties with values and form their own understanding and language of these rules.

## Certain Important Inequalities

1. $a^2 + b^2 \geq 2ab$ (Equality for $a = b$)

2. $|a + b| \leq |a| + |b|$ (Equality reached if both $a$ and $b$ are of the same sign or if one of them is zero.)
   This can be generalised as $|a_1 + a_2 + a_3 + \dots + a_n| \leq |a_1| + |a_2| + |a_3| + \dots |a_n|$

3. $|a - b| \geq |a| - |b|$

4. $ax^2 + bx + c \geq 0$ if $a > 0$ and $D = b^2 - 4ac \leq 0$. The equality is achieved only if $D = 0$ and $x = -b/2a$.

5. Arithmetic mean $\geq$ Geometric mean. That is,
   $$\frac{(a + b)}{2} \geq ab$$

6. $a/b + b/a \geq 2$ if $a > 0$ and $b > 0$ or if $a < 0$ and $b < 0$, that is, both $a$ and $b$ have the same sign.

## Certain Important Inequalities (*Contd*)

7. $a^3 + b^3 \geq ab(a + b)$ if $a > 0$ and $b > 0$, the equality being obtained only when $a = b$.

8. $a^2 + b^2 + c^2 \geq ab + ac + bc$

9. $(a + b)(b + c)(a + c) \geq 8\,abc$ if $a \geq 0$, $b \geq 0$ and $c \geq 0$, the equation being obtained when $a = b = c$

10. For any 4 numbers $x_1$, $x_2$, $y_1$, $y_2$ satisfying the conditions
    $$x_1^2 + x_2^2 = 1$$
    $$y_1^2 + y_2^2 = 1$$
    the inequality $|x_1 y_1 + x_2 y_2| \leq 1$ is true.

11. $\dfrac{a}{b^{1/2}} + \dfrac{b}{a^{1/2}} \geq a^{1/2} + b^{1/2}$ where $a \geq 0$ and $b \geq 0$

12. If $a + b = 2$, then $a^4 + b^4 \geq 2$

13. The inequality $|x| \leq a$, means that
    $$-a \leq x \leq a \text{ for } a > 0$$

14. $2^n > n^2$ for $n \geq 5$

## Some Important Results

■ If $a > b$, then it is evident that
   $$a + c > b + c$$
   $$a - c > b - c$$
   $$ac > bc$$
   $$a/c > b/c; \text{ that is,}$$
   *an inequality will still hold after each side has been increased, diminished, multiplied, or divided by the same positive quantity.*

   If $a - c > b$,
   By adding $c$ to each side,
   $a > b + c$; which shows that
   *in an inequality any term may be transposed from one side to the other if its sign is changed.*

■ If $a > b$, then evidently $b < a$; that is,
   *if the sides of an inequality be transposed, the sign of inequality must be reversed.*

■ If $a > b$, then $a - b$ is positive, and $b - a$ is negative; that is, $-a - (-b)$ is negative, and therefore $-a < -b$; hence,
   *if the signs of all the terms of an inequality be changed, the sign of inequality must be reversed.*

   Again, if $a > b$, then $-a < -b$ and, therefore, $-ac < -bc$; that is,
   *if the sides of an inequality be multiplied by the same negative quantity, the sign of inequality must be reversed.*

*Contd*

*Contd*

## Some Important Results (*Contd*)

If $a_1 > b_1, a_2 > b_2, a_3 > b_3, \ldots a_m > b_m$, it is clear that $a_1 + a_2 + a_3 + \ldots + a_m > b_1 + b_2 + b_3 + \ldots + b_m$; and $a_1 a_2 a_3 \ldots a_m > b_1 b_2 b_3 \ldots b_m$.

- If $a > b$, and if $p$, $q$ are positive integers, then or $a^{1/q} > b^{1/q}$ and, therefore, $a^{p/q} > b^{p/q}$; that is, $a^n > b^n$, where $n$ is any positive quantity. Further,

$$1/a^n < 1/b^n; \text{ that is } a^{-n} < b^{-n}$$

*The square of every real quantity is positive, and therefore greater than zero. Thus $(a-b)^2$ is positive.*

Let $a$ and $b$ be two positive quantities, $S$ their sum and $P$ their product. Then from the identity

$$4ab = (a+b)^2 - (a-b)^2$$

we have     $4P = S^2 - (a-b)^2$, and $S^2 = 4P + (a-b)^2$

Hence, if $S$ is given, $P$ is greatest when $a = b$; and if $P$ is given, $S$ is least when $a = b$;

That is, *if the sum of two positive quantities is given, their product is greatest when they are equal; and if the product of two positive quantities is given, their sum is least when they are equal.*

## To Find the Greatest Value of a Product, the Sum of Whose Factors is Constant

Let there be $n$ factors $a, b, c, \ldots n$, of a composite number and suppose that their sum is constant and equal to $S$.

Consider the product $abc \ldots n$, and suppose that $a$ and $b$ are any two unequal factors. If we replace the two unequal factors $a$ and $b$ by the two equal factors $(a+b)/2$, and $(a+b)/2$, the product is increased while the sum remains unaltered. Hence, so *long as the product contains two unequal factors it can be increased altering the sum of the factors; therefore, the product is greatest when all the factors are equal.* In this case the value of each of the $n$ factors is $S/n$, and the greatest value of the product is $(S/n)^n$, or $\{(a + b + c + \ldots + n/n\}^n$

This will be clearer through an example.

Let us define a number as $a \times b = c$ such that we restrict $a + b = 100$ (maximum).

Then, the maximum value of the product will be achieved if we take the value of $a$ and $b$ as 50 each.

Thus $50 \times 50 = 2500$ will be the highest number achieved for the restriction $a + b \le 100$.

Further, you can also say that $50 \times 50 > 51 \times 49 > 52 \times 48 > 53 \times 47 > 54 \times 46 > \ldots > 98 \times 2 > 99 \times 1$

Thus if we have a larger multiplication as $4 \times 6 \times 7 \times 8$ this will always be less than $5 \times 5 \times 7 \times 8$. [Holds true only for positive numbers.]

**Corollary** If $a$, $b$, $c \ldots k$, are unequal, $\{(a + b + c + \ldots + k)/n\}^n > abc \ldots k$;

that is, $(a + b + c + \ldots + k)/n > (abc \ldots k)^{1/n}$.

By an extension of the meaning of the arithmetic and geometric means this result is usually quoted as follows: *The arithmetic mean of any number of positive quantities is greater than the geometric mean.*

## Definition of Solution of an Inequality

The solution of an inequality is the value of an unknown for which this inequality reduces to a true numerical identity. That is, to solve an inequality means to find all the values of the variable for which the given inequality is true.

An inequality has no solution if there is no such value for which the given inequality is true.

**Equivalent Inequalities:** Two inequalities are said to be equivalent if any solution of one is also a solution of the other and vice versa.

If both inequalities have no solution, then they are also regarded to be equivalent.

To solve an inequality we use the basic properties of an inequality which have been illustrated above.

## Notation of Ranges

**1. Ranges Where the Ends are Excluded** If the value of $x$ is denoted as $(1, 2)$ it means $1 < x < 2$ i.e. $x$ is greater than 1 but smaller than 2.

Similarly, if we denote the range of values of $x$ as $-(7, -2)U(3, 21)$, this means that the value of $x$ can be denoted as $-7 < x < -2$ and $3 < x < 21$. This would mean that the inequality is satisfied between the two ranges and is not satisfied outside these two ranges.

**Based on this notation write the ranges of $x$ for the following representations:**

$$(1, +\infty) \, U \, (-\infty, -7)$$
$$(-\infty, 0) \, U \, (4, +\infty), (-\infty, 50) \, U \, (-50, +\infty)$$

**2. Ranges where the Ends are Included**

$$[2, 5] \text{ means } 2 \le x \le 5$$

**3. Mixed Ranges**

$$(3, 21] \text{ means } 3 < x \le 21$$

## Solving Linear Inequalities in one Unknown

A linear inequality is defined as an inequality of the form

$$ax + b \, I \, 0$$

where the symbol '*I*' represents any of the inequalities $<, >, \geq, \leq$.

For instance if $ax + b \leq 0$, then $ax \leq -b$

$\rightarrow x \leq -b/a$ if $a > 0$ and $x \geq -b/a$ if $a < 0$

**Example:** Solve the inequality $2(x - 3) - 1 > 3(x - 2) - 4(x + 1)$

$\rightarrow 2x - 7 > 3x - 6 - 4x - 4 \rightarrow 3x > -3$. Hence, $x > -1$

This can be represented in mathematical terms as $(-1, +\infty)$

**Example:** Solve the inequality $2(x - 1) + 1 > 3 - (1 - 2x)$

$\rightarrow 2x - 1 > 2 + 2x \rightarrow 0.x > 3 \rightarrow$ This can never happen. Hence, no solution.

**Example:** Solve the inequality $2(x - 1) + 1 < 3 - (1 - 2x)$

Gives: $0.x < 3$.

*This is true for all values of x*

**Example:** Solve the inequality $ax > a$.

This inequality has the parametre $a$ that needs to be investigated further.

If $a > 0$, then $x > 1$

If $a < 0$, then $x < 1$

## Solving Quadratic Inequalities

A quadratic inequality is defined as an inequality of the form:

$$ax^2 + bx + c \, I \, 0 \, (a \neq 0)$$

where the symbol $I$ represents any of the inequalities $<, >, \geq, \leq$.

For a quadratic expression of the form $ax^2 + bx + c$, $(b^2 - 4ac)$ is defined as the discriminant of the expression and is often denoted as $D$. i.e. $D = b^2 - 4ac$

The following cases are possible for the value of the quadratic expression:

### Case 1:  If $D < 0$

1. If $a < 0$ then $ax^2 + bx + c < 0$ for all $x$
2. If $a > 0$ then $ax^2 + bx + c > 0$ for all $x$.

In other words, we can say that if $D$ is negative then the values of the quadratic expression takes the same sign as the coefficient of $x^2$.

This can also be said as

If $D < 0$ then all real values of $x$ are solutions of the inequalities $ax^2 + bx + c > 0$ and $ax^2 + bx + c \geq 0$ for $a > 0$ and have no solution in case $a < 0$.

Also, for $D < 0$, all real values of $x$ are solutions of the inequalities $ax^2 + bx + c < 0$ and $ax^2 + bx + c \leq 0$ if $a < 0$ and these inequalities will not give any solution for $a > 0$.

### Case 2:  $D = 0$

If the discriminant of a quadratic expression is equal to zero, then the value of the quadratic expression takes the same sign as that of the coefficient of $x^2$ (except when

$x = -b/2a$ at which point the value of the quadratic expression becomes 0).

We can also say the following for $D = 0$:

1. The inequality $ax^2 + bx + c > 0$ has as a solution any $x \neq -(b/2a)$ if $a > 0$ and has no solution if $a < 0$.
2. The inequality $ax^2 + bx + c < 0$ has as a solution any $x \neq -(b/2a)$ if $a < 0$ and has no solution if $a > 0$.
3. The inequality $ax^2 + bx + c \geq 0$ has as a solution any $x$ if $a > 0$ and has a unique solution $x = -b/2a$ if $a < 0$.
4. The inequality $ax^2 + bx + c \leq 0$ has as a solution any $x$ if $a < 0$ and has a unique solution $x = -b/2a$ for $a > 0$.

### Case 3:  $D > 0$

If $x_1$ and $x_2$ are the roots of the quadratic expression then it can be said that:

1. For $a > 0$, $ax^2 + bx + c$ is positive for all values of $x$ outside the interval $[x_1, x_2]$ and is negative for all values of $x$ within the interval $(x_1, x_2)$. Besides for values of $x = x_1$ or $x = x_2$, the value of the quadratic expression becomes zero (By definition of the root).
2. For $a < 0$, $ax^2 + bx + c$ is negative for all values of $x$ outside the interval $[x_1, x_2]$ and is positive for all values of $x$ within the interval $(x_1, x_2)$. Besides for values of $x = x_1$ or $x = x_2$, the value of the quadratic expression becomes zero (By definition of the root).

Here are a few examples illustrating how quadratic inequalities are solved.

Solve the following inequalities.

**Example 1:**  $x^2 - 5x + 6 > 0$

**Solution:**  (a) The discriminant $D = 25 - 4 \times 6 > 0$ and $a$ is positive $(+1)$; the roots of the quadratic expression are real and distinct: $x_1 = 2$ and $x_2 = 3$.

By the property of quadratic inequalities, we get that the expression is positive outside the interval $[2, 3]$. Hence, the solution is $x < 2$ and $x > 3$.

We can also see it as $x^2 - 5x + 6 = (x - 2)(x - 3)$ and the given inequality takes the form $(x - 2)(x - 3) > 0$.

The solutions of the inequality are the numbers $x < 2$ (when both factors are negative and their product is positive) and also the numbers $x > 3$ (when both factors are positive and, hence, their product is also positive).

**Answer:**  $x < 2$ and $x > 3$.

**Example 2:**  $2x^2 + x + 1 \geq 0$

**Solution:**  The discriminant $D = 1 - 4 \cdot (-2) = 9 > 0$; the roots of the quadratic expression are real and distinct:

$$x_{1,2} = \frac{-1 \pm \sqrt{9}}{2 \cdot (-2)} = \frac{-1 \pm 3}{-4}$$

hence, $x_1 = -1/2$ and $x_2 = 1$, and consequently, $-2x^2 + x + 1 = -2(x + 1/2) \times (x - 1)$. We have

$$-2(x + 1/2)(x - 1) \geq 0 \text{ or } (x + 1/2)(x - 1) \leq 0$$

(When dividing both sides of an inequality by a negative number, the sense of the inequality is reversed). The inequality is satisfied by all numbers from the interval

$$[-1/2, 1]$$

Please note that this can also be concluded from the property of quadratic expressions when $D > 0$ and $a$ is negative.

**Answer:** $-1/2 \leq x \leq 1$.

**Example 3:** $2x^2 + x - 1 < 0$

**Solution:** $D = 1 - 4 \cdot (-2) \cdot (-1) < 0$, the coefficient of $x^2$ is negative. By the property of the quadratic expression when $D < 0$ and $a$ is negative $-2x^2 + x - 1$ attains only negative values.

**Answer:** $x$ can take any value.

**Example 4:** $3x^2 - 4x + 5 < 0$

**Solution:** $D = 16 - 4 \times 3 \times 5 < 0$, the coefficient of $x^2$ is positive. The quadratic expression $3x^2 - 4x + 5$ takes on only positive values.

**Answer:** There is no solution.

**Example 5:** $4x^2 + 4x + 1 > 0$.

**Solution:** $D = 16 - 4 \times 4 = 0$. The quadratic expression $4x^2 + 4x + 1$ is the square $(2x + 1)^2$, and the given inequality takes the form $(2x + 1)^2 > 0$. It follows that all real numbers $x$, except for $x = -1/2$, are solutions of the inequality.

**Answer:** $x \neq -1/2$.

**Example 6:** Solve the inequality $(a - 2)x^2 - x - 1 \geq 0$

Here, the value of the determinant $D = 1 - 4(-1)(a - 2)$ $= 1 + 4(a - 2) = 4a - 7$

There can then be three cases:

**Case 1:** $D < 0 \rightarrow a < 7/4$

Then the coefficient of $x^2 \rightarrow a - 2$ is negative.

Hence, the inequality has no solution.

**Case 2:** $D = 0$

$a = 7/4$. Put $a = 7/4$ in the expression and then the inequality becomes

$-(x - 2)^2 \geq 0$. This can only happen when $x = 2$.

**Case 3:** $D > 0$

Then $a > 7/4$ and $a \neq 2$, then we find the roots $x_1$ and $x_2$ of the quadratic expression:

$$x_1 = \frac{1 + \sqrt{4a - 7}}{2(a - 2)} \quad \text{and} \quad x_2 = \frac{1 - \sqrt{4a - 7}}{2(a - 2)}$$

Using the property of quadratic expression's values for $D > 0$ we get

If $a - 2 < 0$, the quadratic expression takes negative values outside the interval $[x_1, x_2]$. Hence, it will take positive values inside the interval $(x_1, x_2)$.

If $a - 2 > 0$, the quadratic expression takes positive values outside the interval $[x_1, x_2]$ and becomes zero for $x_1$ and $x_2$.

If $a - 2 = 0$, then we get a straight linear equation. $-x - 1 \geq 0 \rightarrow x \leq -1$.

## System of Inequalities in One Unknown

Let there be given several inequalities in one unknown. If it is required to find the number that will be the solution of all the given equalities, then the set of these inequalities is called a *system of inequalities*.

The solution of a system of inequalities in one unknown is defined as the value of the unknown for which all the inequalities of the system reduce to true numerical inequalities.

To solve a system of inequalities means to find all the solutions of the system or to establish that there is none.

Two systems of inequalities are said to be *equivalent* if any solution of one of them is a solution of the other, and vice versa. If both the systems of inequalities have no solution, then they are also regarded to be equivalent.

**Example 1:** Solve the system of inequalities:

$$3x - 4 < 8x + 6$$
$$2x - 1 > 5x - 4$$
$$11x - 9 \leq 15x + 3$$

**Solution:** We solve the first inequality:

$$3x - 4 < 8x + 6$$
$$-5x < 10$$
$$x > -2$$

It is fulfilled for $x > -2$.

Then we solve the second inequality

$$2x - 1 > 5x - 4$$
$$-3x > -3$$
$$x < 1$$

It is fulfilled for $x < 1$.

And, finally, we solve the third inequality:

$$11x - 9 \leq 15x + 3$$
$$-4x \leq 12$$
$$x \geq -3$$

It is fulfilled for $x \geq -3$. All the given inequalities are true for $-2 < x < 1$.

**Answer:** $-2 < x < 1$.

**Example 2:** Solve the inequality $\dfrac{2x - 1}{x + 1} < 1$

We have $\dfrac{2x - 1}{x + 1} - 1 < 0 \rightarrow \dfrac{x - 2}{x + 1} < 0$

This means that the fraction above has to be negative. A fraction is negative only when the numerator and the denominator have opposite signs.

Hence, the above inequality is equivalent to the following set of 2 inequalities:

$$x - 2 > 0 \quad \text{and} \quad x - 2 < 0$$
$$\text{and} \quad x + 1 < 0 \quad x + 1 > 0$$

From the first system of inequalities, we get $x > 2$ or $x < -1$. This cannot happen simultaneously since these are inconsistent.

From the second system of inequalities we get

$$x < 2 \text{ or } x > -1 \text{ i.e } -1 < x < 2$$

## Inequalities Containing a Modulus

Result:
$|x| \le a$, where $a > 0$ means the same as the double inequality

$$-a \le x \le a$$

This result is used in solving inequalities containing a modulus.

*Space for Notes*

**Example 1:** $|2x - 3| \le 5$

This is equivalent to $-5 \le 2x - 3 \le 5$

i.e. $\qquad 2x - 3 \ge -5 \quad \text{and} \quad 2x - 3 \le 5$
$$\qquad 2x \ge -2 \qquad\qquad x \le 4$$
$$\qquad x \ge -1$$

The solution is

$$-1 \le x \le 4$$

**Example 2:** $|1 - x| > 3$

$$|1 - x| = |x - 1|$$

Hence, $\qquad |x - 1| > 3 \rightarrow x - 1 > 3 \text{ i.e } x > 4$

or $\qquad x - 1 < -3 \text{ or } x < -2$

**Answer:** $x > 4$ or $x < -2$.

## ⊙ WORKED-OUT PROBLEMS

**Problem 14.1** Solve the inequality $\dfrac{1}{x} < 1$.

**Solution** $\dfrac{1}{x} < 1 \Leftrightarrow \dfrac{1}{x} - 1 < 0 \Leftrightarrow \dfrac{1-x}{x} < 0 \Leftrightarrow \dfrac{x-1}{x} > 0$.

This can happen only when both the numerator and denominator take the same sign (Why?)

**Case 1:** Both are positive: $x - 1 > 0$ and $x > 0$ i.e. $x > 1$.

**Case 2:** Both are negative: $x - 1 < 0$ and $x < 0$ i.e. $x < 0$.

**Answer:** $(-\infty, 0) \cup (1 + \infty)$

**Problem 14.2** Solve the inequality $\dfrac{x}{x+2} \leq \dfrac{1}{x}$.

**Solution** $\dfrac{x}{x+2} \leq \dfrac{1}{x} \Leftrightarrow \dfrac{x}{x+2} - \dfrac{1}{x} \leq 0 \Leftrightarrow \dfrac{x^2 - x - 2}{x(x+2)}$

$\leq 0 \Leftrightarrow \dfrac{(x-2)(x+1)}{x(x+2)} \leq 0$.

The function $f(x) = \dfrac{(x-2)(x+1)}{x(x+2)}$ becomes negative

when numerator and denominator are of opposite sign.

**Case 1:** Numerator positive and denominator negative: This occurs only between $-2 < x < -1$.

**Case 2:** Numerator negative and Denominator Positive: Numerator is negative when $(x - 2)$ and $(x + 1)$ take opposite signs. This can be got for:

*Case A:* $x - 2 < 0$ and $x + 1 > 0$ i.e. $x < 2$ and $x > -1$

*Case B:* $x - 2 > 0$ and $x + 1 < 0$ i.e. $x > 2$ and $x < -1$. Cannot happen.

Hence, the answer is $-2 < x \leq 2$.

**Problem 14.3** Solve the inequality $\dfrac{x}{x-3} \leq \dfrac{1}{x}$.

**Solution** $\dfrac{x}{x-3} \leq \dfrac{1}{x} \Leftrightarrow \dfrac{x}{x-3} - \dfrac{1}{x} \geq 0 \Leftrightarrow \dfrac{x^2 - x + 3}{x(x-3)}$

$\leq 0$. The function $f(x) = \dfrac{x^2 - x + 3}{x(x-3)}$

The numerator being a quadratic equation with $D < 0$ and $a > 0$, we can see that it will always be positive for all values of $x$. (From the property of quadratic inequalities).

Further, for the expression to be negative, the denominator should be negative.

That is, $x^2 - 3x < 0$. This will occur when $x < 3$ and $x$ is positive.

**Answer:** **(0, 3)**

Suppose $F(x) = (x - x_1)^{k1} (x - x_2)^{k2} \ldots (x_1 - x_n)^{kn}$, where $k_1$, $k_2 \ldots, k_n$ are integers. If $k_j$ is an even number, then the function $(x - x_j)^{kj}$ does not change sign when $x$ passes through the point $x_j$ and, consequently, the function $F(x)$ does not change sign. If $k_p$ is an odd number, then the function $(x - x_p)^{kp}$ changes sign when $x$ passes through the point $x_p$ and, consequently, the function $F(x)$ also changes sign.

**Problem 14.4** Solve the inequality $(x - 1)^2 (x + 1)^3 (x - 4) < 0$.

**Solution** The above inequality is valid for

**Case 1:** $x + 1 < 0$ and $x - 4 > 0$

That is, $x < -1$ and $x > 4$ simultaneously. This cannot happen together.

**Case 2:** $x + 1 > 0$ and $x - 4 < 0$

That is $x > -1$ or $x < 4$, i.e. $-1 < x < 4$ is the answer

**Problem 14.5** Solve the inequality $\dfrac{(x-1)^2(x+1)^3}{x^4(x-2)} \leq 0$

**Solution** The above expression becomes negative when the numerator and the denominator take opposite signs.

That means that the numerator is positive and the denominator is negative or vice versa.

**Case 1:** Numerator positive and denominator negative: The sign of the numerator is determined by the value of $x + 1$ and that of the denominator is determined by $x - 2$.

This condition happens when $x < 2$ and $x > -1$ simultaneously.

**Case 2:** Numerator negative and denominator positive: This happens when $x < -1$ and $x > 2$ simultaneously. This will never happen.

Hence, the answer is $-1 \leq x < 2$.

*Space for Rough Work*

## LEVEL OF DIFFICULTY (I)

*Solve the following inequalities:*

1. $3x^2 - 7x + 4 \leq 0$
   (a) $x > 0$
   (b) $x < 0$
   (c) All $x$
   (d) None of these

2. $3x^2 - 7x - 6 < 0$
   (a) $-0.66 < x < 3$
   (b) $x < -0.66$ or $x > 3$
   (c) $3 < x < 7$
   (d) $-2 < x < 2$

3. $3x^2 - 7x + 6 < 0$
   (a) $0.66 < x < 3$
   (b) $-0.66 < x < 3$
   (c) $-1 < x < 3$
   (d) None of these

4. $x^2 - 3x + 5 > 0$
   (a) $x > 0$
   (b) $x < 0$
   (c) Both (a) and (b)
   (d) $-\infty < x < \infty$

5. $x^2 - 14x - 15 > 0$
   (a) $x < -1$
   (b) $15 < x$
   (c) Both (a) and (b)
   (d) $-1 < x < 15$

6. $2 - x - x^2 \geq 0$
   (a) $-2 \leq x \leq 1$
   (b) $-2 < x < 1$
   (c) $x < -2$
   (d) $x > 1$

7. $|x^2 - 4x| < 5$
   (a) $-1 \leq x \leq 5$
   (b) $1 \leq x \leq 5$
   (c) $-1 \leq x \leq 1$
   (d) $-1 < x < 5$

8. $|x^2 + x| - 5 < 0$
   (a) $x < 0$
   (b) $x > 0$
   (c) All values of $x$
   (d) None of these

9. $|x^2 - 5x| < 6$
   (a) $-1 < x < 2$
   (b) $3 < x < 6$
   (c) Both (a) and (b)
   (d) $-1 < x < 6$

10. $|x^2 - 2x| < x$
    (a) $1 < x < 3$
    (b) $-1 < x < 3$
    (c) $0 < x < 4$
    (d) $x > 3$

11. $|x^2 - 2x - 3| < 3x - 3$
    (a) $1 < x < 3$
    (b) $-2 < x < 5$
    (c) $x > 5$
    (d) $2 < x < 5$

12. $|x^2 - 3x| + x - 2 < 0$
    (a) $(1 - \sqrt{3}) < x < (2 + \sqrt{2})$
    (b) $0 < x < 5$
    (c) $(1 - \sqrt{3}, 2 - \sqrt{2})$
    (d) $1 < x < 4$

13. $x^2 - 7x + 12 < |x - 4|$
    (a) $x < 2$
    (b) $x > 4$
    (c) $2 < x < 4$
    (d) $2 \leq x \leq 4$

14. $x^2 - |5x - 3| - x < 2$
    (a) $x > 3 + 2\sqrt{2}$
    (b) $x < 3 + 2\sqrt{2}$
    (c) $x > -5$
    (d) $-5 < x < 3 + 2\sqrt{2}$

15. $|x - 6| > x^2 - 5x + 9$
    (a) $1 \leq x < 3$
    (b) $1 < x < 3$
    (c) $2 < x < 5$
    (d) $-3 < x < 1$

16. $|x - 6| < x^2 - 5x + 9$
    (a) $x < 1$
    (b) $x > 3$
    (c) $1 < x < 3$
    (d) Both (a) and (b)

17. $|x - 2| \leq 2x^2 - 9x + 9$
    (a) $x > (4 - \sqrt{2})/2$
    (b) $x < (5 + \sqrt{3})/2$
    (c) Both (a) and (b)
    (d) None of these

18. $3x^2 - |x - 3| > 9x - 2$
    (a) $x < (4 - \sqrt{19})/3$
    (b) $x > (4 + \sqrt{19})/3$
    (c) Both (a) and (b)
    (d) $-2 < x < 2$

19. $x^2 - |5x + 8| > 0$
    (a) $x < (5 - \sqrt{57})/2$
    (b) $x < (5 + \sqrt{57})/2$
    (c) $x > (5 + \sqrt{57})/2$
    (d) Both (a) and (c)

20. $3|x - 1| + x^2 - 7 > 0$
    (a) $x > -1$
    (b) $x < -1$
    (c) $x > 2$
    (d) Both (b) and (c)

21. $|x - 6| > |x^2 - 5x + 9|$
    (a) $x < 1$
    (b) $x > 3$
    (c) $(1 < x < 3)$
    (d) both (a) and (b)

22. $(|x - 1| - 3)(|x + 2| - 5) < 0$
    (a) $-7 < x < -2$ and $3 < x < 4$
    (b) $x < -7$ and $x > 4$
    (c) $x < -2$ and $x > 3$
    (d) Any of these

23. $|x^2 - 2x - 8| > 2x$
    (a) $x < 2\sqrt{2}$
    (b) $x < 3 + 3\sqrt{5}$
    (c) $x > 2 + 2\sqrt{3}$
    (d) Both (a) and (c)

24. $(x - 1)\sqrt{x^2 - x - 2} \geq 0$
    (a) $x \leq 2$
    (b) $x \geq 2$
    (c) $x \leq -2$
    (d) $x \geq 0$

25. $(x^2 - 1)\sqrt{x^2 - x - 2} \geq 0$
    (a) $x \leq -1$
    (b) $x \geq -1$
    (c) $x \geq 2$
    (d) (a) and (c)

26. $\sqrt{\dfrac{x - 2}{1 - 2x}} > -1$
    (a) $0.5 > x$
    (b) $x > 2$
    (c) Both (a) and (b)
    (d) $0.5 < x \leq 2$

27. $\sqrt{\dfrac{3x-1}{2-x}} > 1$

    (a) $0 < x < 2$        (b) $0.75 < x < 4$

    (c) $0.75 < x < 2$    (d) $0 < x < 4$

28. $\sqrt{3x-10} > \sqrt{6-x}$

    (a) $4 < x \le 6$       (b) $x < 4$ or $x > 6$

    (c) $x < 4$          (d) $x > 8$

29. $\sqrt{x^2 - 2x - 3} < 1$

    (a) $(-1-\sqrt{5} < x < -3)$ (b) $1 \le x < (\sqrt{5}-1)$

    (c) $x > 1$         (d) None of these

30. $\sqrt{1 - \dfrac{x+2}{x^2}} < \dfrac{2}{3}$

    (a) $(-6/5) < x \le -1$ or $2 \le x < 3$

    (b) $(-6/5) \le x < -1$

    (c) $2 \le x < 3$

    (d) $(-6/5) \le x < 3$

31. $2\sqrt{x-1} < x$

    (a) $x > 1$        (b) $x \ge 1, x \ne 2$

    (c) $x < 1$        (d) $1 < x < 5$

32. $\sqrt{x+18} < 2 - x$

    (a) $x \le -18$     (b) $x < -2$

    (c) $x > -2$     (d) $-18 \le x < -2$

33. $x > \sqrt{24 + 5x}$

    (a) $x < 3$        (b) $3 < x \le 4.8$

    (c) $x \ge 24/5$     (d) $x > 8$

34. $\sqrt{9x-20} < x$

    (a) $4 < x < 5$     (b) $20/9 \le x < 4$

    (c) $x > 5$        (d) Both (b) and (c)

35. $\sqrt{x+7} < x$

    (a) $x > 2$        (b) $x > \sqrt{30}/2$

    (c) $x > (1+\sqrt{29})/2$  (d) $x > 1 + \sqrt{29}/2$

36. $\sqrt{2x-1} < x - 2$

    (a) $x < 5$        (b) $x > 5$

    (c) $x > 5$ or $x < -5$  (d) $5 < x < 15$

37. $\sqrt{x+78} < x + 6$

    (a) $x < 3$        (b) $x > 3$ or $x < 2$

    (c) $x > 3$        (d) $3 < x < 10$

38. $\sqrt{5-2x} < 6x - 1$

    (a) $0.5 < x$      (b) $x < 2.5$

    (c) $0.5 < x < 2.5$   (d) $x > 2.5$

39. $\sqrt{x+61} < x + 5$

    (a) $x < 3$        (b) $x > 3$ or $x < 1$

    (c) $x > 3$        (d) $3 < x < 15$

40. $x < \sqrt{2-x}$

    (a) $x > 1$        (b) $x < 1$

    (c) $-2 < x < 1$    (d) $-1 < x$

41. $x + 3 < \sqrt{x+33}$

    (a) $x > 3$        (b) $x < 3$

    (c) $-3 < x < 3$    (d) $-33 < x < 3$

42. $\sqrt{2x+14} > x + 3$

    (a) $x < -7$      (b) $-7 \le x < 1$

    (c) $x > 1$        (d) $-7 < x < 1$

43. $x - 3 < \sqrt{x-2}$

    (a) $2 \le x < (7+\sqrt{5})/2$ (b) $2 \le x$

    (c) $x < (7+\sqrt{5})/2$  (d) $x \le 2$

44. $x + 2 < \sqrt{x+14}$

    (a) $-14 \le x < 2$   (b) $x > -14$

    (c) $x < 2$       (d) $-11 < x < 2$

45. $x - 1 < \sqrt{7-x}$

    (a) $x > 3$        (b) $x < 3$

    (c) $-53 < x < 3$   (d) $-103 < x < 3$

46. $\sqrt{9x-20} > x$

    (a) $x < 4$        (b) $x > 5$

    (c) $x \le 4$ or $x \ge 5$  (d) $4 < x < 5$

47. $\sqrt{11-5x} > x - 1$

    (a) $x > 2, x < 5$   (b) $-3 < x < 2$

    (c) $-25 < x < 2$   (d) $x < 2$

48. $\sqrt{x+2} > x$

    (a) $-2 \le x < 2$    (b) $-2 \le x$

    (c) $x < 2$       (d) $x = -2$ or $x > 2$

**Directions for Questions 49 to 53:** Find the largest integral $x$ that satisfies the following inequalities.

49. $\dfrac{x-2}{x^2-9} < 0$

    (a) $x = -4$      (b) $x = -2$

    (c) $x = 3$       (d) None of these

50. $\dfrac{1}{x+1} - \dfrac{2}{x^2-x+1} < \dfrac{1-2x}{x^3+1}$

    (a) $x = 1$       (b) $x = 2$

    (c) $x = -1$     (d) None of these

51. $\dfrac{x+4}{x^2-9} - \dfrac{2}{x+3} < \dfrac{4x}{3x-x^2}$

    (a) $x = 1$       (b) $x = 2$

    (c) $x = -1$     (d) None of these

52. $\dfrac{4x+19}{x+5} < \dfrac{4x-17}{x-3}$

    (a) $x = 1$       (b) $x = 2$

    (c) $x = -1$     (d) None of these

53. $(x+1)(x-3)^2(x-5)(x-4)^2(x-2) < 0$

    (a) $x = 1$       (b) $x = -2$

    (c) $x = -1$     (d) None of these

**Directions for Questions 54 to 69:** Solve the following inequalities:

54. $(x-1)(3-x)(x-2)^2 > 0$
    (a) $1 < x < 3$
    (b) $1 < x < 3$ but $x \neq 2$
    (c) $0 < x < 2$
    (d) $-1 < x < 3$

55. $\dfrac{6x-5}{4x+1} < 0$
    (a) $-1/4 < x < 1$
    (b) $-1/2 < x < 1$
    (c) $-1 < x < 1$
    (d) $-1/4 < x < 5/6$

56. $\dfrac{2x-3}{3x-7} > 0$
    (a) $x < 3/2$ or $x > 7/3$
    (b) $3/2 < x < 7/3$
    (c) $x > 7/3$
    (d) None of these

57. $\dfrac{3}{x-2} < 1$
    (a) $2 < x < 5$
    (b) $x < 2$
    (c) $x > 5$
    (d) $x < 2$ or $x > 5$

58. $\dfrac{1}{x-1} \leq 2$
    (a) $x < 1$
    (b) $x \geq 1.5$
    (c) $-5 < x < 1$
    (d) Both (a) and (b)
    or $x \geq 1.5$

59. $\dfrac{4x+3}{2x-5} < 6$
    (a) $x < 2.5$
    (b) $x < 33/8$
    (c) $x \geq 2.5$
    (d) $x < 2.5$ or $x > 33/8$

60. $\dfrac{5x-6}{x+6} < 1$
    (a) $-6 < x < 6$
    (b) $-6 < x < 0$
    (c) $-6 < x < 3$
    (d) None of these

61. $\dfrac{5x+8}{4-x} < 2$
    (a) $x < 0$ or $x > 4$
    (b) $0 < x < 4$
    (c) $0 \leq x < 4$
    (d) $x > 4$

62. $\dfrac{x-1}{x+3} > 2$
    (a) $x < -7$
    (b) $x < -3$
    (c) $-7 < x < -3$
    (d) None of these

63. $\dfrac{7x-5}{8x+3} > 4$
    (a) $-17/25 < x < -3/8$
    (b) $x > -17/25$
    (c) $0 < x < 3/8$
    (d) $-17/25 < x < 0$

64. $\dfrac{x}{x-5} > \dfrac{1}{2}$
    (a) $-5 < x < 5$
    (b) $-5 < x < 0$
    (c) $-5 \leq x \leq 5$
    (d) $x < -5$ or $x > 5$

65. $x \leq \dfrac{6}{x-5}$
    (a) $x < -1$
    (b) $x > 5$
    (c) $x < 6$
    (d) $x \leq -1$ or $5 < x \leq 6$

66. $\dfrac{30x-9}{x-2} \geq 25(x+2)$

    (a) $x < -1.4$ or $x > 2$
    (b) $x < -1.4$ or $2 < x \leq 2.6$
    (c) $x \leq -1.4$ or $2 < x \leq 2.6$
    (d) None of these

67. $\dfrac{4}{x+2} > 3 - x$
    (a) $-2 < x < -1$ or $x > 2$
    (b) $-2 < x < 2$
    (c) $-2 < x < -1$
    (d) $0 < x < 3$

68. $x - 17 \geq \dfrac{60}{x}$
    (a) $x < -3$
    (b) $x < 20$
    (c) $-3 \leq x < 0$ or $x \geq 20$
    (d) $-3 < x \leq 0$ or $x \geq 20$

69. $\sqrt{x^2} < x + 1$
    (a) $x > 0.5$
    (b) $x > 0$
    (c) All $x$
    (d) $x > -0.5$

70. Find the smallest integral $x$ satisfying the inequality
    $$\dfrac{x-5}{x^2+5x-14} > 0$$
    (a) $x = -6$
    (b) $x = -3$
    (c) $x = -7$
    (d) None of these

71. Find the maximum value of $x$ for which $\dfrac{x+2}{x} \geq x$

**Directions for 72 and 73:** If $f(x) = |2x - 4|$ and $x$ is an integer. Then answer the following questions:

72. Find the maximum value of $x$ for which $f(x) \leq 5$.
73. Find minimum value of $x$ for which $f(x) \leq 5$.
74. For how many integer values of $x$, is the expression:
    $(x - 1)(4 - x)(x - 2)^2 > 0$

**Directions for Question numbers 75 and 76:**

If $\dfrac{x^2-5x+6}{|x|+5} \leq 0$

75. Find the minimum value of $x$, for which the above inequality is true.
76. For how many integer values of $x$, the above inequality is true.
77. Find the minimum value of $x$ for which $\dfrac{1}{x-0.5} < 2$ where $x \in I^+$

78. For how many integer values of $x$ is:
    $$\dfrac{x^2+6x-7}{x^2+1} > 2$$

79. Maximum value of $x$, for which $\dfrac{x^2-9}{x^2+x+1} \leq 0$

**Directions for Question numbers 80 and 81:**

$$\dfrac{x^2-7|x|+10}{x^2-8x+16} < 0$$

80. For how many negative integral values of $x$, is the above inequality true?

81. Find the sum of all integer values for which the above inequality is true.

**Direction for Question numbers 82 and 83:**

$$f(x) = \frac{x^2 - 4x + 5}{x^2 + 7x + 12}$$

82. For how many positive integer values of x is $f(x) \le 0$

83. For how many negative integer values of x is $f(x) \le 0$

84. If $f(x) = x^2 + 2|x| + 1$, then for how many real values of $x$ is: $f(x) \le 0$.

85. If $\dfrac{1}{|x| - 2} > \dfrac{1}{3}$ then the least positive integer value of $x$, for which this inequality is true?

*Space for Rough Work*

# LEVEL OF DIFFICULTY (II)

1. $x^2 - 5|x| + 6 < 0$
   - (a) $-3 < x < -2$
   - (b) $2 < x < 3$
   - (c) Both (a) and (b)
   - (d) $-3 < x < 3$

2. $x^2 - |x| - 2 \geq 0$
   - (a) $-2 < x < 2$
   - (b) $x \leq -2$ or $x \geq 2$
   - (c) $x < -2$ or $x > 1$
   - (d) $-2 < x < 1$

**Directions for Questions 3 to 16:** Solve the following polynomial inequalities

3. $(x - 1)(3 - x)(x - 2)^2 > 0$
   - (a) $1 < x < 2$
   - (b) $-1 < x < 3$
   - (c) $-3 < x < -1$
   - (d) $1 < x < 3, x \neq 2$

4. $\dfrac{0.5}{x - x^2 - 1} < 0$
   - (a) $x > 0$
   - (b) $x \leq 0$
   - (c) $x \geq 0$
   - (d) For all real $x$

5. $\dfrac{x^2 - 5x + 6}{x^2 + x + 1} < 0$
   - (a) $x < 2$
   - (b) $x > 3$
   - (c) $2 < x < 3$
   - (d) $x < 2$ or $x > 3$

6. $\dfrac{x^2 + 2x - 3}{x^2 + 1} < 0$
   - (a) $x < -3$
   - (b) $-7 < x < -3$
   - (c) $-3 < x < 1$
   - (d) $-7 < x < 1$

7. $\dfrac{(x - 1)(x + 2)^2}{-1 - x} < 0$
   - (a) $x < -1$
   - (b) $x < -1$ or $x > 1$
   - (c) $x < -1$ and $x \neq 2$
   - (d) $x < -1$ or $x > 1$ and $x \neq -2$

8. $\dfrac{x^2 + 4x + 4}{2x^2 - x - 1} > 0$
   - (a) $x < -2$
   - (b) $x > 1$
   - (c) $x \neq 2$
   - (d) None of these

9. $x^4 - 5x^2 + 4 < 0$
   - (a) $-2 < x < 1$
   - (b) $-2 < x < 2$
   - (c) $-2 < x < -1$ or $1 < x < 2$
   - (d) $1 < x < 2$

10. $x^4 - 2x^2 - 63 \leq 0$
    - (a) $x \leq -3$ or $x \geq 3$
    - (b) $-3 \leq x \leq 0$
    - (c) $0 \leq x \leq 3$
    - (d) $-3 \leq x \leq 3$

**Directions for Questions 11 to 67:** Solve the following polynomial and quadratic inequalities

11. $\dfrac{5x - 1}{x^2 + 3} < 1$
    - (a) $x < 4$
    - (b) $1 < x < 4$
    - (c) $x < 1$ or $x > 4$
    - (d) $1 < x < 3$

12. $\dfrac{x - 2}{x^2 + 1} < -\dfrac{1}{2}$
    - (a) $-3 < x < 3$
    - (b) $x < -3$
    - (c) $-3 < x < 6$
    - (d) $-3 < x < 1$

13. $\dfrac{x + 1}{(x - 1)^2} < 1$
    - (a) $x > 3$ or $x$ is negative
    - (b) $x > 3$
    - (c) $x > 3$ or $-23 < x < 0$
    - (d) $x$ is negative and $x > 2$

14. $\dfrac{x^2 - 7x + 12}{2x^2 + 4x + 5} > 0$
    - (a) $x < 3$ or $x > 4$
    - (b) $3 < x < 4$
    - (c) $4 < x < 24$
    - (d) $0 < x < 3$

15. $\dfrac{x^2 + 6x - 7}{x^2 + 1} \leq 2$
    - (a) $x$ is negative
    - (b) $x \geq 0$
    - (c) $x > 0$ or $x < 0$
    - (d) Always

16. $\dfrac{x^4 + x^2 + 1}{x^2 - 4x - 5} < 0$
    - (a) $x < -1$ or $x > 5$
    - (b) $-1 < x < 5$
    - (c) $x > 5$
    - (d) $-5 < x < -1$

17. $\dfrac{1 + 3x^2}{2x^2 - 21x + 40} < 0$
    - (a) $0 < x < 8$
    - (b) $2.5 < x < 8$
    - (c) $-8 < x < 8$
    - (d) $3 < x < 8$

18. $\dfrac{1 + x^2}{x^2 - 5x + 6} < 0$
    - (a) $x < 2$
    - (b) $x > 3$
    - (c) Both $a$ and $b$
    - (d) $2 < x < 3$

19. $\dfrac{x^4 + x^2 + 1}{x^2 - 4x - 5} > 0$
    - (a) $-1 < x < 5$
    - (b) $x < -1$ or $x > 5$
    - (c) $x \leq -1$ or $x > 5$
    - (d) $-1 < x < 1$

20. $\dfrac{1 - 2x - 3x^2}{3x - x^2 - 5} > 0$

(a) $x < -1$ or $x > 1/3$    (b) $x < -1$ or $x = 1/3$

(c) $-1 < x < 1/3$    (d) $x < 1/3$

21. $\dfrac{x^2 - 5x + 7}{-2x^2 + 3x + 2} > 0$

(a) $x > 0.5$    (b) $x > -0.5$

(c) $-0.5 < x < 5$    (d) $-0.5 < x < 2$

22. $\dfrac{2x^2 - 3x - 459}{x^2 + 1} > 1$

(a) $x > -20$    (b) $x < 0$

(c) $x < -20$    (d) $-20 < x < 20$

23. $\dfrac{x^2 - 1}{x^2 + x + 1} < 1$

(a) $x > -2$    (b) $x > 2$

(c) $-2 < x < 2$    (d) $x < 2$

24. $\dfrac{1 - 2x - 3x^2}{3x - x^2 - 5} > 0$

(a) $1 < x < 3$    (b) $1 < x < 7$

(c) $-3 < x < 3$    (d) None of these

25. $\dfrac{x}{x^2 - 3x - 4} > 0$

(a) $-1 < x < 0$    (b) $4 < x$

(c) both (a) and (b)    (d) $-1 < x < 4$

26. $\dfrac{x^2 + 7x + 10}{x + 2/3} > 0$

(a) $-5 < x < -2$ or $\dfrac{-2}{3} < x < \infty$

(b) $-5 < x < 8$

(c) $x < -2$

(d) $x > -2$

27. $\dfrac{3x^2 - 4x - 6}{2x - 5} < 0$

(a) $x < (2 - \sqrt{22})/3$

(b) $x > (2 + \sqrt{22})/3$

(c) $(2 - \sqrt{22})/3 < x < (2 + \sqrt{22})/3$

(d) None of these

28. $\dfrac{17 - 15x - 2x^2}{x + 3} < 0$

(a) $-8.5 < x \le -3$

(b) $-17 < x < -3$

(c) $-8.5 < x < -3$ or $x > 1$

(d) $-8.5 < x < 1$

29. $\dfrac{x^2 - 9}{3x - x^2 - 24} < 0$

(a) $-3 < x < 3$    (b) $x < -3$ or $x > 3$

(c) $x < -5$ or $x > 5$    (d) $x < -7$ or $x > 7$

30. $\dfrac{x + 7}{x - 5} + \dfrac{3x + 1}{2} \ge 0$

(a) $1 < x < 5$    (b) $-1 < x < 5$

(c) $1 \le x \le 3$ or $x > 5$    (d) $-1 < x < 3$

31. $2x^2 + \dfrac{1}{x} > 0$

(a) $x > 0$    (b) $x < -1/2$

(c) Both (a) and (b)    (d) None of these

32. $\dfrac{x^2 - x - 6}{x^2 + 6x} \ge 0$

(a) $x < -6$    (b) $-2 \le x < 0$

(c) $x > 3$    (d) All of these

33. $\dfrac{x^2 - 5x + 6}{x^2 - 11x + 30} < 0$

(a) $x < 3$ or $x > 5$

(b) $2 < x < 4$ or $5 < x < 7$

(c) $2 < x < 3$ or $5 < x < 6$

(d) $2 < x < 3$ or $5 < x < 7$

34. $\dfrac{x^2 - 8x + 7}{4x^2 - 4x + 1} < 0$

(a) $x < 1$ or $x > 7$    (b) $1 < x < 7$

(c) $-7 < x < 1$    (d) $-7 < x < 7$

35. $\dfrac{x^2 - 36}{x^2 - 9x + 18} < 0$

(a) $-6 < x < 3$    (b) $-6 < x < 6$

(c) $x < -6$ or $x > 3$    (d) $-3 < x < 3$

36. $\dfrac{x^2 - 6x + 9}{5 - 4x - x^2} \ge 0$

(a) $-5 < x < 1$ or $x = 3$    (b) $-5 \le x < 1$ or $x = 3$

(c) $-5 < x \le 1$ or $x = 3$    (d) $-5 \le x \le -1$

37. $\dfrac{x - 1}{x + 1} < x$

(a) $x < -1$    (b) $x > -1$

(c) $-1 < x < 1$    (d) For all real values of $x$

38. $\dfrac{1}{x + 2} < \dfrac{3}{x - 3}$

(a) $-4.5 < x < -2$    (b) $-4.5 < x < -2$ or $3 < x$

(c) $-4.5 < x < -2, x > 3$    (d) (b) or (c)

39. $\dfrac{14x}{x + 1} - \dfrac{9x - 30}{x - 4} < 0$

(a) $-1 < x < 1$ or $4 < x < 6$

(b) $-1 < x < 4, 5 < x < 7$

(c) $1 < x < 4$ or $5 < x < 7$

(d) $-1 < x < 1$ or $5 < x < 7$

40. $\dfrac{5x^2 - 2}{4x^2 - x + 3} < 1$

(a) $x < 1$

(b) $-2 < x < 2$

(c) $-2.7 < x < 1.75$

(d) $(-(1 + \sqrt{21})/2 < x < (\sqrt{21} - 1)/2$

41. $\dfrac{x^2 - 5x + 12}{x^2 - 4x + 5} > 3$

(a) $x > 0.5$    (b) $1/2 < x < 3$

(c) $x < 0.5, x > 3$    (d) $1 < x < 3$

42. $\dfrac{x^2 - 3x + 24}{x^2 - 3x + 3} < 4$

(a) $x < -1$    (b) $4 < x < 8$

(c) $x < 4$ or $x > 8$    (d) None of these

43. $\dfrac{x^2 - 1}{2x + 5} < 3$

(a) $x < -2.5$ or $-2 < x < 8$

(b) $-2.5 < x < -2$

(c) $-2.5 < x < 8$

(d) Both (a) and (b)

44. $\dfrac{x^2 + 1}{4x - 3} > 2$

(a) $x > 7$    (b) $x > 7, x < 87$

(c) $0.75 < x < 1, x > 7$    (d) $0.25 < x < 1, x > 7$

45. $\dfrac{x^2 + 2}{x^2 - 1} < -2$

(a) $-1 < x < 2$

(b) $-1 < x < 1,$

(c) $-1 < x < 0, 0 < x < 1$

(d) $-2 < x < 2$

46. $\dfrac{3x - 5}{x^2 + 4x - 5} > \dfrac{1}{2}$

(a) $x < -5$    (b) $x > 1$

(c) $-5 < x < 1$    (d) $-5 < x < 5$

47. $\dfrac{2x + 3}{x^2 + x - 12} \le \dfrac{1}{2}$

(a) $-4 < x < -3, 3 < x < 6$

(b) $-4 < x < -3, 0 < x < 6$

(c) $x < -4, -3 \le x < 3, x > 6$

(d) $x < -4, x > 6$

48. $\dfrac{5 - 2x}{3x^2 - 2x - 16} < 1$

(a) $x < -\sqrt{7}$    (b) $-2 < x < \sqrt{7}$

(c) $8/3 \le x$    (d) All of these

49. $\dfrac{15 - 4x}{x^2 - x - 12} < 4$

(a) $x < -\sqrt{63}/2, -3 < x < \sqrt{63}/2$

(b) $x > 4$

(c) Both (a) and (b)

(d) $x > 4, x < -63/2$

(e) None of these

50. $\dfrac{1}{x^2 - 5x + 6} > 1/2$

(a) $1 < x < 2, 3 < x < 4$    (b) $1 < x < 4$

(c) $x < 1, x > 3$    (d) None of these

51. $\dfrac{5 - 4x}{3x^2 - x - 4} < 4$

(a) $x < -\dfrac{\sqrt{7}}{2}$    (b) $-1 < x < \dfrac{\sqrt{7}}{2}$

(c) $x > 4/3$    (d) All of these

52. $\dfrac{(x + 2)(x^2 - 2x + 1)}{4 + 3x - x^2} \ge 0$

(a) $x < -2$ or $-1 < x < 4$

(b) $-2 < x < 4$ or $x > 6$

(c) $-2 < x < -1$ or $x > 4$

(d) None of these

53. $\dfrac{4}{1 + x} + \dfrac{2}{1 - x} < 1$

(a) $-1 < x < 1$    (b) $x < -1$

(c) $x > 1$    (d) both (b) and (c)

54. $2 + 3/(x + 1) > 2/x$

(a) $x < -2$    (b) $-1 < x < 0$

(c) $1/2 < x$    (d) All of these

55. $1 + \dfrac{2}{x - 1} > \dfrac{6}{x}$

(a) $0 \le x \le 1$    (b) $2 \le x \le 3$

(c) $-\infty < x < 1$    (d) Always except (a) and (b)

56. $\dfrac{x^4 - 3x^3 + 2x^2}{x^2 - x - 30} > 0$

(a) $x < -5$    (b) $1 < x < 2$

(c) $x > 6$    (d) Both (b) and (c)

57. $\dfrac{x - 1}{x} - \dfrac{x + 1}{x - 1} < 2$

(a) $-1 \le x \le 0$    (b) $1/2 \le x \le 1$

(c) $0 < x < 1/2$    (d) Always except (a) and (b)

58. $\dfrac{2(x - 3)}{x(x - 6)} \le \dfrac{1}{x - 1}$

(a) $x < 0$    (b) $1 < x < 6$

(c) Both (a) and (b)    (d) Always except (a) and (b)

59. $\dfrac{2(x - 4)}{(x - 1)(x - 7)} \ge \dfrac{1}{x - 2}$

(a) $1 < x < 2$ or $7 < x$    (b) $2 < x$

(c) $2 < x < 7$    (d) Both (a) and (c)

60. $\dfrac{2x}{x^2-9} \le \dfrac{1}{x+2}$

    (a) $x < -3$        (b) $-2 < x < 3$
    (c) All except (a) and (b)    (d) Both (a) and (b)

61. $\dfrac{1}{x-2} + \dfrac{1}{x-1} > \dfrac{1}{x}$

    (a) $-\sqrt{2} < x < 0$ or $2 < x$
    (b) $\sqrt{2} < x$
    (c) $1 < x < \sqrt{2}$
    (d) Both (a) and (c)

62. $\dfrac{7}{(x-2)(x-3)} + \dfrac{9}{x-3} + 1 < 0$

    (a) $-5 < x < 4$
    (b) $-5 < x < 1$ and $1 < x < 3$ and $x$ is not 2
    (c) $-5 < x < 1$ and $2 < x < 3$
    (d) $x < 1$

63. $\dfrac{20}{(x-3)(x-4)} + \dfrac{10}{x-4} + 1 > 0$

    (a) $x < -2$       (b) $-1 < x < 3$ and $4 < x$
    (c) All except (a) and (b)    (d) Both (a) and (b)

64. $\dfrac{(x-2)(x-4)(x-7)}{(x+2)(x+4)(x+7)} > 1$

    (a) $x < -7$       (b) $x < -7$ and $-4 < x < -2$
    (c) $-4 < x < 2$      (d) None of these

65. $\dfrac{(x-1)(x-2)(x-3)}{(x+1)(x+2)(x+3)} > 1$

    (a) $-3 \le x \le -2$     (b) $x < -3$
    (c) $-2 < x < -1$      (d) None of these

66. $(x^2 + 3x + 1)(x^2 + 3x - 3) \ge 5$

    (a) $x < -4$ or $-2 < x$
    (b) $-2 < x < -1$ or $1 < x$
    (c) $x \le -4$; $-2 \le x \le -1$; $1 \le x$
    (d) $x < -4$ or $1 < x$

67. $(x^2 - x - 1)(x^2 - x - 7) < -5$

    (a) $-2 < x$
    (b) $-2 < x < -1$ and $1 < x < 4$
    (c) $-2 < x < -1$ and $2 < x < 3$
    (d) $-2 < x < 0$ and $2 < x < 3$

**Directions for Questions 68 to 92:** Solve inequalities based on modulus

68. $|x^3 - 1| \ge 1 - x$

    (a) $-1 < x < 0$      (b) $x < -1$
    (c) $0 < x$           (d) Always except (a)

69. $\dfrac{x^2 - 5x + 6}{|x| + 7} < 0$

    (a) $2 \le x \le 3$      (b) $2 < x$
    (c) $1 < x < 3$       (d) $2 < x < 3$

70. $\dfrac{x^2 + 6x - 7}{|x + 4|} < 0$

    (a) $-7 < x < -5$ and $-4 < x < 1$
    (b) $-7 < x < -5$ and $-4 < x < 0$
    (c) $-7 < x < -4$ and $-4 < x < 1$
    (d) None of these

71. $\dfrac{|x-2|}{x-2} > 0$

    (a) $2 < x < 10$      (b) $3 \le x$
    (c) $2 \le x$         (d) $2 < x$

72. $\left|\dfrac{2}{x-4}\right| > 1$

    (a) $2 < x < 4$; $4 \le x \le 5$   (b) $2 < x \le 4$; $4 \le x \le 5$
    (c) $2 < x < 4$; $4 < x < 6$   (d) $2 < x < 4$; $4 \le x \le 6$

73. $\left|\dfrac{2x-1}{x-1}\right| > 2$

    (a) $2 < x$        (b) $1 < x$
    (c) $3/4 < x < 1$     (d) Both (b) and (c)

74. $\left|\dfrac{x^2 - 3x - 1}{x^2 + x + 1}\right| < 3$

    (a) $x < -2$       (b) $-1 < x$
    (c) Always except (b)   (d) Both (a) and (b)

75. $\dfrac{x^2 - 7|x| + 10}{x^2 - 6x + 9} < 0$

    (a) $-5 \le x \le -2$; $2 < x < 5$
    (b) $-5 < x < -2$; $2 < x < 5$
    (c) $-5 < x < -2$; $2 < x < 3$; $3 < x < 5$
    (d) $-5 < x < -2$; $3 < x < 5$

76. $\dfrac{|x+3| + x}{x+2} > 1$

    (a) $-5 < x \le -2$     (b) $-2 \le x \le -1$
    (c) $-1 < x$        (d) Always except (b)

77. $\dfrac{|x-1|}{x+2} < 1$

    (a) $-8 < x \le -3$
    (b) $-3 < x \le -2$
    (c) Always except $x = -2$
    (d) Both (a) and (b)

78. $\dfrac{|x+2| - x}{x} < 2$

    (a) $-5 \le x < 0$      (b) $0 \le x \le 1$
    (c) Both (a) and (b)     (d) Always except (b)

79. $\dfrac{1}{|x| - 3} < \dfrac{1}{2}$

    (a) $x < -5$ and $-3 < x < 3$
    (b) $3 \le x \le 5$

(c) $-5 \leq x \leq -3$

(d) Always except (b) and (c)

80. $\left| \dfrac{3x}{x^2 - 4} \right| \leq 1$

(a) $x \leq -4$ and $-1 \leq x \leq 1$

(b) $4 \leq x$

(c) Both of these

(d) None of these

81. $\left| \dfrac{x^2 - 5x + 4}{x^2 - 4} \right| \leq 1$

(a) $[0 < x < 8/5] \ U \ [5/2 < x < +\infty]$

(b) $[0, 5/2] \ U \ [16/5, +\infty]$

(c) $[0, 8/5] \ U \ [5/2, +\infty]$

(d) $[0, 8/5] \ U \ [5/2, +\infty]$

82. $\dfrac{|x - 3|}{x^2 - 5x + 6} \geq 2$

(a) $[3/2, 1]$　　　(b) $[1, 2]$

(c) $[1.5, 2]$　　　(d) None of these

83. $\dfrac{x^2 - |x| - 12}{x - 3} \geq 2x$

(a) $-101 < x < 25$　　　(b) $[-\infty, 3]$

(c) $x \leq 3$　　　(d) $x < 3$

84. $|x| < \dfrac{9}{x}$

(a) $x < -1$　　　(b) $0 < x < 3$

(c) $1 < x < 3; x < -1$　　　(d) $-\infty < x < 3$

85. $1 + \dfrac{12}{x^2} < \dfrac{7}{x}$

(a) $x < -2; 2 < x < 3$　　　(b) $3 \leq x < 4$

(c) Both (a) and (b)　　　(d) None of these

86. $\dfrac{(x^2 - 4x + 5)}{(x^2 + 5x + 6)} \geq 0$

(a) $-\infty < x < \infty$　　　(b) $x < -3$

(c) $x > -2$　　　(d) Both (b) and (c)

87. $\dfrac{x + 1}{x - 1} \geq \dfrac{x + 5}{x + 1}$

(a) $x < -1$　　　(b) $0 < x < 3$

(c) $1 < x \leq 3, x < -1$　　　(d) $-\infty < x < 3$

88. $\dfrac{x - 1}{x^2 - x - 12} \leq 0$

(a) $x < -3; 2 < x < 3$　　　(b) $3 \leq x < 4$

(c) Both (a) and (b)　　　(d) None of these

89. $1 < (3x^2 - 7x + 8)/(x^2 + 1) \leq 2$

(a) $1 < x < 6$　　　(b) $1 \leq x < 6$

(c) $1 < x \leq 6$　　　(d) $1 \leq x \leq 6$

90. If $f'(x) \geq g(x)$, where $f(x) = 5 - 3x + \dfrac{5}{2}x^2 - \dfrac{x^3}{3}$, $g(x) = 3x - 7$

(a) $[2, 3]$　　　(b) $[2, 4]$

(c) $x = 2.5$　　　(d) None of these

91. $f'(x) \geq g'(x)$, if $f(x) = 10x^3 - 13x^2 + 7x$, $g(x) = 11x^3 - 15x^2 - 3$

(a) $[-1, 7/3]$　　　(b) $[-1, 3.5]$

(c) $[-1, 9/3]$　　　(d) $[1, 7/3]$

92. $\dfrac{1}{x - 2} - \dfrac{1}{x} \leq \dfrac{2}{x + 2}$

(a) $(-2, -1) \ U \ (2, +\infty)$　(b) $-2 < x < 1$

(c) Both (a) and (b)　　　(d) None of these

**Directions for Questions 93 to 95:**  Solve the following irrational inequalities.

93. $(x - 1)\sqrt{x^2 - x - 2} \geq 0$

(a) $x < 2$　　　(b) $3 \leq x < \infty$

(c) Always except (a)　(d) Both (a) and (b)

94. $(x^2 - 1)\sqrt{x^2 - x - 2} \geq 0$

(a) $x < -1$　　　(b) $2 \leq x$

(c) Both (a) and (b)　　　(d) None of these

95. $\dfrac{\sqrt{x - 3}}{x - 2} > 0$

(a) $0 \leq x < 2$　　　(b) $x > 3$

(c) $0 < x < 1$　　　(d) Both (b) and (c)

96. If $x$ satisfies the inequality $|x - 1| + |x - 2| + |x - 3| \geq 6$, then: **IIFT 2010**

(a) $0 \leq x \leq 4$　　　(b) $x \leq 0$ or $x \geq 4$

(c) $x \leq -2$ or $x \geq 3$　　　(d) $x \geq 3$

**Direction 97 and 98: If $f(x) = |x + 4| - |x - 4|$ and $|f(x)| < 8$, then answer the following questions:**

97. How many integer values of $x$ satisfies the above inequality?

(a) 6　　　(b) 7

(c) 8　　　(d) 9

98. What is the sum of all positive integer values of $x$ satisfying the above inequality?

(a) 5　　　(b) 6

(c) 8　　　(d) 10

**Directions for question number 99-100**: If $x > -6$ and $\dfrac{1}{x - 5} + \dfrac{1}{x + 3} < 0$, then answer the following questions:

99. Find the number of positive integer values of $x$, which satisfy the given inequality.

100. Find the sum of all positive integer values of $x$ which satisfy the given inequality.

**Direction for question 101-102:**

$|4x - 3| \leq 8$ and $|3y + 4| \leq 17$ then answer the following questions:

101. Minimum value of $|x|+|y| =$

102. Maximum value of $|x| - |y| =$

103. If $f(x) = \dfrac{x}{2x^2 + 5x + 8}$ for all $x > 0$ what is the greatest value of $f(x)$?
     (a) 1/4  (b) 1/8
     (c) 1/13  (d) 1/5

104. The Shaded portion of which of the following options represents $y \geq x^2$, $y \leq 3$

     (a)
     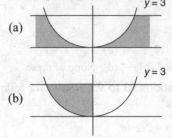

     (b)

(c)

$x = -\sqrt{3}$     $x = \sqrt{3}$

(d) None of these

105. Find the range of values of $x$ for which $x^4 + 8x < 8x^3 + x^2$
     (a) $(-1,0) \cup (1,8)$  (b) $(0,1) \cup (8,\infty)$
     (c) $(-\infty,-8) \cup (1, 8)$  (d) $(-1, 0) \cup (8, \infty)$

106. If $\dfrac{45}{25x^{14} - 8x^7 + 1} \leq p$
     Then minimum value of $p =$

107. If $0 \leq x \leq 13$ for how many integer values of $x$, $7^{x-1} + 11^{x-1} > 170$

108. If $f(x) = \min(3x + 4, 6 - 2x)$ and $f(x) < p$ where $p$ is an integer then the minimum possible value of $p = ?$

109. For how many non-negative integer values of '$x$' is $||||||x - 1| - 2| - 3| - 4|-5|-6|-7| < 9$
     (a) 35  (b) 36
     (c) 37  (d) 38

*Space for Rough Work*

## ANSWER KEY

### Level of Difficulty (I)

| | | | |
|---|---|---|---|
| 1. (d) | 2. (a) | 3. (d) | 4. (d) |
| 5. (c) | 6. (a) | 7. (d) | 8. (d) |
| 9. (c) | 10. (a) | 11. (d) | 12. (c) |
| 13. (c) | 14. (d) | 15. (b) | 16. (d) |
| 17. (d) | 18. (c) | 19. (d) | 20. (d) |
| 21. (c) | 22. (a) | 23. (d) | 24. (b) |
| 25. (d) | 26. (d) | 27. (c) | 28. (a) |
| 29. (d) | 30. (a) | 31. (b) | 32. (d) |
| 33. (d) | 34. (d) | 35. (c) | 36. (b) |
| 37. (c) | 38. (c) | 39. (c) | 40. (b) |
| 41. (d) | 42. (b) | 43. (a) | 44. (a) |
| 45. (b) | 46. (d) | 47. (d) | 48. (a) |
| 49. (a) | 50. (a) | 51. (b) | 52. (b) |
| 53. (b) | 54. (b) | 55. (d) | 56. (a) |
| 57. (d) | 58. (d) | 59. (d) | 60. (c) |
| 61. (a) | 62. (c) | 63. (a) | 64. (d) |
| 65. (d) | 66. (c) | 67. (a) | 68. (c) |
| 69. (b) | 70. (a) | 71. 2 | 72. 4 |
| 73. 0 | 74. 1 | 75. 2 | 76. 2 |
| 77. 2 | 78. 0 | 79. 3 | 80. 2 |
| 81. −4 | 82. 5 | 83. 1 | 84. 0 |
| 85. 3 | | | |

### Level of Difficulty (II)

| | | | |
|---|---|---|---|
| 1. (c) | 2. (b) | 3. (d) | 4. (d) |
| 5. (c) | 6. (c) | 7. (d) | 8. (d) |
| 9. (c) | 10. (d) | 11. (c) | 12. (d) |
| 13. (a) | 14. (a) | 15. (d) | 16. (b) |
| 17. (b) | 18. (d) | 19. (b) | 20. (a) |
| 21. (d) | 22. (c) | 23. (a) | 24. (d) |
| 25. (c) | 26. (a) | 27. (d) | 28. (c) |
| 29. (b) | 30. (c) | 31. (d) | 32. (d) |
| 33. (c) | 34. (b) | 35. (a) | 36. (a) |
| 37. (b) | 38. (b) | 39. (a) | 40. (d) |
| 41. (b) | 42. (d) | 43. (a) | 44. (c) |
| 45. (c) | 46. (c) | 47. (c) | 48. (d) |
| 49. (c) | 50. (a) | 51. (d) | 52. (a) |
| 53. (d) | 54. (d) | 55. (d) | 56. (d) |
| 57. (d) | 58. (c) | 59. (a) | 60. (d) |
| 61. (d) | 62. (b) | 63. (d) | 64. (b) |
| 65. (d) | 66. (c) | 67. (c) | 68. (d) |
| 69. (d) | 70. (c) | 71. (d) | 72. (c) |
| 73. (d) | 74. (d) | 75. (c) | 76. (d) |
| 77. (c) | 78. (d) | 79. (d) | 80. (c) |
| 81. (a) | 82. (d) | 83. (d) | 84. (b) |
| 85. (d) | 86. (d) | 87. (c) | 88. (d) |
| 89. (d) | 90. (d) | 91. (a) | 92. (d) |
| 93. (c) | 94. (c) | 95. (b) | 96 (b) |
| 97 (b) | 98 (b) | 99 (3) | 100 9 |
| 101 0 | 102 2.75 | 103 (c) | 104 (c) |
| 105 (a) | 106 125 | 107 10 | 108 6 |
| 109 (c) | | | |

## Solutions and Shortcuts

While practically solving inequalities remember the following:

1. The answer to an inequality question is always in the form of a range and represents the range of values where the inequality is satisfied.

2. In the cases of all continuous functions, the point at which the range of the correct answer will start, will always be a solution of the same function if written as an equation.

   This rule is only broken for non-continuous functions.

   Hence, if you judge that a function is continuous always check the options for LHS = RHS at the starting point of the option.

3. The correct range has to have two essential properties if it has to be the correct answer:
   (a) The inequality should be satisfied for each and every value of the range.
   (b) There should be no value satisfying the inequality outside the range of the correct option.

Questions on inequalities are always solved using options and based on (3) (a) and (3) (b) above we would reject an option as the correct answer if:

(i) we find even a single value not satisfying the inequality within the range of a single option.

(ii) we can reject given option, even if we find a single value satisfying the inequality but not lying within the range of the option under check.

I will now show you certain solved questions on this pattern of thinking.

### Level of Difficulty (I)

1. At $x = 0$, inequality is not satisfied. Thus, option (c) is rejected. Also $x = 0$ is not a solution of the equation. Since, this is a continuous function, the solution cannot start from 0. Thus options (a) and (b) are not right. Further, we see that the given function is quadratic with real roots. Hence, option (d) is also rejected.

2. At $x = 0$, inequality is satisfied. Hence, options (b) and (c) are rejected. $x = 3$ gives LHS = RHS. and $x = -0.66$ also does the same. Hence. roots of the equation are 3 and − 0.66.

   Thus, option (a) is correct.

3. At $x = 0$, inequality is not satisfied.

   Hence, options (b), (c) are rejected. At $x = 2$, inequality is not satisfied. Hence, option (a) is rejected.

   Thus, option (d) is correct.

4. The given quadratic equation has imaginary roots and is hence always positive.

   Thus, option (d) is correct

5. At $x = 0$ inequality is not satisfied. Thus option (d) is rejected.

$x = -1$ and $x = 15$ are the roots of the quadratic equation. Thus, option (c) is correct.

6. At $x = 0$, inequality is satisfied.

Thus, options, (c) and (d) are rejected.

At $x = 1$, inequality is satisfied

Hence, we choose option (a).

7. At $x = 0$ inequality is satisfied, option (b) is rejected.

At $x = 2$, inequality is satisfied, option (c) is rejected.

At $x = 5$, LHS = RHS.

At $x = -1$, LHS = RHS.

Thus, option (d) is correct.

8. At $x = 0$ inequality is satisfied.

Thus, options (a), (b), are rejected. Option (c) is obviously not true, as there will be values of $x$ at which the inequality would not be satisfied.

Option (d) is correct.

10. At $x = 1$ and $x = 3$ LHS = RHS.

At $x = 2$ inequality is satisfied.

At $x = 0.1$ inequality is not satisfied.

At $x = 2.9$ inequality is satisfied.

At $x = 3.1$ inequality is not satisfied.

Thus, option (a) is correct.

12. The options need to be converted to approximate values before you judge the answer. At $x = 0$, inequality is satisfied.

Thus, option (b) and (d) are rejected.

Option (c) is correct.

13. At $x = 0$, inequality is not satisfied, option (a) is rejected.

At $x = 5$, inequality is not satisfied, option (b) is rejected.

At $x = 2$ inequality is not satisfied.

Option (d) is rejected.

Option (c) is correct.

14. At $x = 0$, inequality is satisfied, option (a) rejected.

At $x = 10$, inequality is not satisfied, option (c) rejected.

At $x = -5$, LHS = RHS.

Also at $x = 5$, inequality is satisfied and at $x = 6$, inequality is not satisfied.

Thus, option (d) is correct.

15. At $x = 2$, inequality is satisfied.

At $x = 0$, inequality is not satisfied.

At $x = 1$, inequality is not satisfied but LHS = RHS.

At $x = 3$, inequality is not satisfied but LHS = RHS.

Thus, option (b) is correct.

Solve other questions of LOD I and LOD II in the same fashion.

71. $\dfrac{x+2}{x} - x \geq 0$

$\dfrac{x+2-x^2}{x} \geq 0$

$\dfrac{x^2 - x - 2}{x} \leq 0$

$\dfrac{(x-2)(x+1)}{x} \leq 0$

Case 1: $(x - 2)(x + 1) \geq 0$ and $x < 0$

This occurs only for $x \leq -1$

Case 2: $(x - 2)(x + 1) \leq 0$ and $x$ positive.

This occurs when $0 < x \leq 2$

Therefore maximum value of $x$ which satisfies the condition is at $x = 2$.

**Solution for 72 & 73:**

$x$ is an integer.

$|2x - 4| \leq 5$

$-5 \leq 2x - 4 \leq 5$

$-1 \leq 2x \leq 9$

$-\dfrac{1}{2} < x \leq \dfrac{9}{2}$.

72. Maximum value of $x = 4$.

73. Minimum value of $x = 0$.

74. $(x - 1)(4 - x)(x - 2)^2 > 0$

As $(x - 2)^2$ is always non-negative

This means that the product of the first two brackets would be positive. This also means that $(x - 1)(x - 4) < 0$

$\Rightarrow 1 < x < 4$

$x$ has two integer values 2 and 3 between 1 and 4.

But for $x = 2$, $(x - 1)(4 - x)(x - 2)^2 = 0$

$\Rightarrow$ Therefore the given inequality is true only for one integer value of $x$.

**Solution for 75 and 76:**

$\dfrac{x^2 - 5x + 6}{|x| + 5} \leq 0$

$\dfrac{(x-2)(x-3)}{|x| + 5} \leq 0$

Case I: $x > 0$

In this case the expression would become:

$\Rightarrow \dfrac{(x-2)(x-3)}{x+5} \leq 0$

$\Rightarrow 2 \leq x \leq 3$

Case II: $x < 0$

In this case the expression would become:

$\dfrac{(x-2)(x-3)}{-x+5} \leq 0$

$\dfrac{(x-2)(x-3)}{x-5} \geq 0$

The above inequality is not satisfied for any negative value of $x$.

Therefore solution of the above inequality $\rightarrow 2 \le x \le 3$

75. Minimum value of $x = 2$

76. The above inequality is true for two integral values of $x$.

77. $x \in I^+$ means $x$ is a positive integer.

Now we can check the above inequality by putting positive integer values of $x$.

For $x = 1, \dfrac{1}{1-0.5} = 2$, so $x = 1$ is not a solution.

For $x = 2, \dfrac{1}{2-0.5} = \dfrac{1}{1.5} < 2$, therefore $x = 2$ is a solution.

The correct answer is $x = 2$.

78. $\dfrac{x^2+6x-7}{x^2+1} - 2 > 0$

$\dfrac{-x^2+6x-9}{x^2+1} > 0$

$\dfrac{(x-3)^2}{x^2+1} < 0$

$(x-3)^2 > 0, x^2 + 1 > 0$

So the above inequality is not true for any real value of $x$.

79. $x^2 + x + 1 > 0$ (It is a quadratic equation with negative discriminant)

Hence, for the expression to be non-positive, the numerator has to be non-positive. *i.e.* $x^2 - 9 \le 0$

$(x-3)(x+3) \le 0$

$\Rightarrow -3 \le x \le 3$

Required maximum value of $x = 3$

## Solution for 80 and 81

$\dfrac{(|x|)^2 - 7|x| + 10}{x^2 - 2 \times 4 \times x + 4^2} < 0$

$\dfrac{(|x|-5)(|x|-2)}{(x-4)^2} < 0$

$\Rightarrow 2 < |x| < 5$, but $x \ne 4$

The upper limit defines the range of $x$ as: $-5 < x < 5$

The lower limit defines the range of $x$ as: $x < -2, x > 2$

To obey both the limits we will get: $-5 < x < -2$, $2 < x < 5$ & $x \ne 4$.

80. The above inequality is true for $x = -4, -3$.

Therefore for two negative integral values of $x$ the given inequality is true.

81. Required Sum $= -4 - 3 + 3 = -4$

## Solution 82 – 83:

82. $\dfrac{x^2 - 4x + 5}{x^2 + 7x + 12} \le 0$

$\dfrac{(x-5)(x+1)}{(x+4)(x+3)} \le 0$

$-4 < x < -3$ and $-1 \le x \le 5$

Therefore $f(x) \le 0$ is true for a total of 5 positive integer values of $x$. (1, 2, 3, 4 and 5)

83. $f(x) \le 0$ is true for only one negative integer value of $x$. (at $x = -1$)

84. $x^2 + 2|x| + 1 \le 0$

$|x|^2 + 2|x| + 1 \le 0$

$(|x| + 1)^2 \le 0$

This is not possible for any real value of $x$.

85. $\dfrac{1}{|x|-2} - \dfrac{1}{3} > 0$

$\dfrac{(3-|x|+2)}{3(|x|-2)} > 0$

$\dfrac{5-|x|}{|x|-2} > 0$

$x \in (-5, -2) \cup (2, 5)$

Therefore the least positive integer value of $x = 3$

## Level of Difficulty (II)

96. If we put $x = 3$,

Then $|3 - 1| + |3 - 2| + |3 - 3| = 3 \le 6$

Therefore option (*a*), (*c*), (*d*) are not correct.

Hence only option (*b*) is correct.

97. $|f(x)| < 8$

$||x+4| - |x-4|| < 8$

$-8 < |x+4| - |x-4| < 8$

Case I : when $x \le -4$

$\Rightarrow |x+4| - |x-4| = -x - 4 + x - 4 = -8$, therefore the above inequality is not true for any $x \le -4$

Case II when $x \ge 4$:

$|x+4| - |x-4| = x + 4 - x + 4 = 8$, therefore the above inequality is not true for any $x \ge 4$

Case III: when $-4 < x < 4$

$|x+4| - |x-4| = x + 4 + x - 4 = 2x$

$\Rightarrow x = \{-3, -2, -1, 0, +1, +2, +3\}$

So the inequality $|f(x)| < 8$ is true for seven integer values of $x$.

98. Required sum $= 1 + 2 + 3 = 6$

99. $\dfrac{1}{x-5} + \dfrac{1}{x+3} < 0$

$\dfrac{x+3+x-5}{(x+3)(x-5)} < 0$

$\dfrac{2x-2}{(x+3)(x-5)} < 0$

$\dfrac{x-1}{(x+3)(x-5)} < 0$

$\dfrac{(x-1)^2}{(x-1)(x+3)(x-5)} < 0$. The numerator of this expression would always be positive.

Hence we need: $(x-1)(x+3)(x-5) < 0$

$x < -3$ or $1 < x < 5$, therefore the given inequality is true for three positive integer values of $x$ i.e $x = 2, 3$ or $4$.

100. Required sum $= 2 + 3 + 4 = 9$

101. $-8 \le 4x - 3 \le 8$      $|3y + 4| \le 17$

$-5 \le 4x \le 11$      $-17 \le 3y + 4 \le 17$

$-\dfrac{5}{4} \le x \le \dfrac{11}{4}$      $-7 \le y \le \dfrac{13}{3}$

$x$ and $y$ both can be zero, therefore minimum value of $|x| + |y| = 0 + 0 = 0$

102. $|x| - |y|$ will be maximum when $|x|$ is maximum and $|y|$ is minimum

$(|x| - |y|)_{max} = |x|_{max} - |y|_{min}$

$= \dfrac{11}{4} - 0$

$= \dfrac{11}{4} = 2.75$

103. $f(x) = \dfrac{x}{2x^2 + 5x + 8} = \dfrac{1}{2x + \dfrac{8}{x} + 5}$

$f(x)$ is maximum where denominator is minimum

$\dfrac{\left(2x + \dfrac{8}{x}\right)}{2} \ge \sqrt{2x \times \dfrac{8}{x}}$

$2x + \dfrac{8}{x} \ge 4$

$\left(2x + \dfrac{8}{x}\right)_{min} = 8$

$(f(x))_{max} = \dfrac{1}{8 + 5} = \dfrac{1}{13}$

104. Solution: $y \ge x^2$

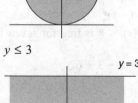

$y \le 3$

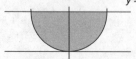

By combining the above graphs we get

$y = 3$

Hence option (c) is correct.

105. $x^4 - 8x^3 - x^2 + 8x < 0$

$x^3(x - 8) - x(x - 8) < 0$

$(x^3 - x)(x - 8) < 0$

$x(x - 1)(x + 1)(x - 8) < 0$.

This expression would be alternately positive and negative in various ranges of $x$ as shown below:

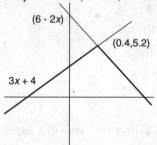

$x \in (-1, 0) \cup (1, 8)$

Hence option (a) is correct.

106. $(5x^7)^2 - 2 \times 5x^7 \times \dfrac{4}{5} + \dfrac{16}{25} - \dfrac{16}{25} + 1$

$\dfrac{45}{\phantom{x}} = \dfrac{45}{\left(5x^7 - \dfrac{4}{5}\right)^2 + \dfrac{9}{25}}$

Minimum value of $p$ is the maximum value of

$\dfrac{45}{25x^{14} - 8x^7 + 1}$

Minimum value of $\left(5x^7 - \dfrac{4}{5}\right)^2 = 0$

$(p)_{min} = \dfrac{45}{\dfrac{9}{25}} = 5 \times 25 = 125$

107. For $x = 3$, $7^{3-1} + 11^{3-1} = 7^2 + 11^2 = 170$

$7^{x-1} + 11^{x-1}$ is an increasing function so for $x > 3$, $7^{x-1} + 11^{x-1} > 170$

$\therefore 7^{x-1} + 11^{x-1} > 170$ for a total $13 - 3 = 10$ values of $x$.

108. $3x + 4$ is an increasing while $6 - 2x$ is a decreasing function.

Graph of min $(3x + 4, 6 - 2x)$

From the graph it is clear that maximum value of $f(x) = 5.2$, which occurs at $x = 0.4$

$f(x) < p$ (where $p$ is an integer)

Least value of $p$ must be 6.

109. For maximum possible values of $x$ which satisfy the above inequality all the modulus open with a positive sign i.e.

$|x - 1| > 0$, $||x - 1| - 2| > 0$, $|||x - 1| - 2| - 3| > 0$ etc.

Hence for $x = x_{max}$ the given inequality will be

$x - 1 - 2 - 3 - 4 - 5 - 6 - 7 < 9$

$x_{max} < 37$

Hence a total for 37 non-negative integers (0 to 36) are possible. Option (c) is correct.

# 15

# Quadratic and Other Equations

We have already seen in the *Back to School* part of this block the key interrelationship between functions, equations and inequalities. In this chapter we are specifically looking at questions based on equations—with an emphasis on quadratic equations. Questions based on equations are an important component of the CAT and XAT exam and hence your ability to formulate and solve equations is a key skill in the development of your thought process for QA.

As you go through with this chapter, focus on understanding the core concepts and also look to create a framework in your mind which would account for the typical processes that are used for solving questions based on equations.

## THEORY OF EQUATIONS

### Equations in one variable

An equation is any expression in the form $f(x) = 0$; the type of equation we are talking about depends on the expression that is represented by $f(x)$. The expression $f(x)$ can be linear, quadratic, cubic or might have a higher power and accordingly the equation can be referred to as linear equations, quadratic equations, cubic equations, etc. Let us look at each of these cases one by one.

### Linear Equations

**$2x + 4 = 0$; we have the expression for $f(x)$ as a linear expression in $x$.** Consequently, the equation $2x+4 = 0$ would be charaterised as a linear equation. This equation has exactly 1 root (solution) and can be seen by solving $2x+4 = 0 \rightarrow x = -2$ which is the root of the equation. Note that the root or solution of the equation is the value of '$x$' which would make the LHS of the equation equal the RHS of the equation. In other words, the equation is

satisfied when the value of $x$ becomes equal to the root of the equation.

The linear function $f(x)$ when drawn would give us a straight line and this line would be intersecting with the $x$-axis at the point where the value of $x$ equals the root (solution) of the equation.

### Quadratic Equations

**An equation of the form: $2x^2 - 5x + 4 = 0$; we have the expression for $f(x)$ as a quadratic expression in $x$.** Consequently, the equation $2x^2 - 5x + 4 = 0$ would be charaterised as a quadratic equation. This equation has exactly 2 roots (solutions) and leads to the following cases with respect to whether these roots are real/imaginary or equal/unequal.

Case 1: Both the roots are real and equal;
Case 2: Both the roots are real and unequal;
Case 3: Both the roots are imaginary.

A detailed discussion of quadratic equations and the analytical formula based approach to identify which of the above three cases prevails follows later in this chapter.

The graph of a quadratic function is always U shaped and would just touch the $X$-Axis in the first case above, would cut the $X$-Axis twice in the second case above and would not touch the $X$-Axis at all in the third case above.

Note that the roots or solutions of the equation are the values of '$x$' which would make the LHS of the equation equal the RHS of the equation. In other words, the equation is satisfied when the value of $x$ becomes equal to the root of the equation.

### Cubic Equations

**An equation of the form: $x^3 + 2x^2 - 5x + 4 = 0$ where the expression $f(x)$ is a cubic expression in $x$.** Consequently, the expression would have three roots or solutions.

Depending on whether the roots are real or imaginary we can have the following two cases in this situation:

**Case 1:** All three roots are real; (Graph might touch/cut the x-axis once, twice or thrice.)

In this case depending on the equality or inequality of the roots we might have the following cases:

**Case (i)** All three roots are equal; (The graph of the function would intersect the X-axis only once as all the three roots of the equation coincide.)

**Case (ii)** Two roots are equal and one root is distinct; (In this case the graph cuts the X-axis at one point and touches the X-Axis at another point where the other two roots coincide.)

**Case (iii)** All three roots are distinct from each other. (In this case the graph of the function cuts the x-axis at three distinct points.)

**Case 2:** One root is real and two roots are imaginary. (Graph would cut the X-axis only once.)

The shapes of the graph that a cubic function can take has already been discussed as a part of the discussion on the *Back to School* write up of this block.

**Note:** For a cubic equation $ax^3 + bx^2 + cx + d = 0$ with roots as $l$, $m$ and $n$:

The product of its three roots viz: $l \times m \times n = -d/a$;

The sum of its three roots viz: $l + m + n = -b/a$

The pairwise sum of its roots taken two at a time viz: $lm + ln + mn = c/a$.

## 🎓 THEORY OF QUADRATIC EQUATIONS

An equation of the form

$$ax^2 + bx + c = 0 \tag{1}$$

where $a$, $b$ and $c$ are all real and $a$ is not equal to 0, is a quadratic equation. Then,

$D = (b^2 - 4ac)$ is the discriminant of the quadratic equation.

If $D < 0$ (i.e. the discriminant is negative) then the equation has no real roots.

If $D > 0$, (i.e. the discriminant is positive) then the equation has two distinct roots, namely,

$x_1 = (-b + \sqrt{D})/2a$, and $x_2 = (-b - \sqrt{D})/2a$
and then $ax^2 + bx + c = a(x - x_1)(x - x_2)$ (2)

If $D = 0$, then the quadratic equation has equal roots given by

$$x_1 = x_2 = -b/2a$$
and then $ax^2 + bx + c = a(x - x_1)^2$ (3)

To represent the quadratic $ax^2 + bx + c$ in form (2) or (3) is to expand it into linear factors.

## Properties of Quadratic Equations and Their Roots

(i) If $D$ is a *perfect square* then the roots are *rational* and in case it is not a perfect square then the roots are *irrational*.

(ii) In the case of imaginary roots ($D < 0$) and if $p + iq$ is one root of the quadratic equation, then the other must be the conjugate $p - iq$ and vice versa (where $p$ and $q$ are real and $i = \sqrt{-1}$)

(iii) If $p + \sqrt{q}$ is one root of a quadratic equation, then the other must be the conjugate $p - \sqrt{q}$ and vice versa. (where $p$ is rational and $\sqrt{q}$ is a surd).

(iv) If $a = 1$, $b$, $c \in I$ and the roots are rational numbers, then the root must be an integer.

## The Sign of a Quadratic Expression

Let $f(x) = y = ax^2 + bx + c$ where $a$, $b$, $c$ are real and $a \neq 0$, then $y = f(x)$ represents a parabola whose axis is parallel to $y$-axis. For some values of $x$, $f(x)$ may be positive, negative or zero. Also, if $a > 0$, the parabola opens upwards and for $a < 0$, the parabola opens downwards. This gives the following cases:

(i) $a > 0$ and $D < 0$ (The roots are imaginary)

The function $f(x)$ will always be positive for all real values of $x$. So $f(x) > 0 \ \forall \ x \in R$. Naturally the graph as shown in the figure does not cut the X-Axis.

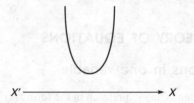

(ii) When $a > 0$ and $D = 0$ (The roots are real and identical.)

$f(x)$ will be positive for all values of $x$ except at the vertex where $f(x) = 0$.

So $f(x) \geq 0 \ \forall \ x \in R$. Naturally, the graph touches the X-Axis once.

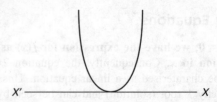

(iii) When $a > 0$ and $D > 0$ (The roots are real and distinct)

Let $f(x) = 0$ have two real roots $\alpha$ and $\beta$ ($\alpha < \beta$) then $f(x)$ will be positive for all real values of $x$ which are lower than $\alpha$ or higher than $\beta$; $f(x)$ will be equal to zero when $x$ is equal to either of $\alpha$ or $\beta$.

When $x$ lies between $\alpha$ and $\beta$ then $f(x)$ will be negative. Mathematically, this can be represented as

$f(x) > 0 \ \forall \ x \in (-\infty, \alpha) \cup (\beta, \infty)$

and $f(x) < 0 \ \forall \ x \in (\alpha, \beta)$ (Naturally the graph cuts the $X$ axis twice)

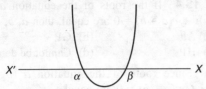

(iv) When $a < 0$ and $D < 0$ (Roots are imaginary)

$f(x)$ is negative for all values of $x$. Mathematically, we can write $f(x) < 0 \ \forall \ x \in R$. (The graph will not cut or touch the $X$ axis.)

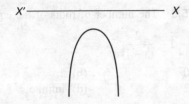

(v) When $a < 0$ and $D = 0$ (Roots are real and equal)

$f(x)$ is negative for all values of $x$ except at the vertex where $f(x) = 0$. i.e. $f(x) \leq 0 \ \forall \ x \in R$ (The graph touches the $X$ axis once.)

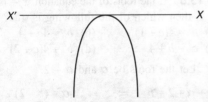

(vi) When $a < 0$ and $D > 0$

Let $f(x) = 0$ have two roots $\alpha$ and $\beta$ ($\alpha < \beta$) then $f(x)$ will be negative for all real values of $x$ that are lower than $\alpha$ or higher than $\beta$. $f(x)$ will be equal to zero when $x$ is equal to either of $\alpha$ or $\beta$. The graph cuts the $X$ axis twice.

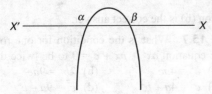

When $x$ lies between $\alpha$ and $\beta$ then $f(x)$ will be positive. Mathematically, this can be written as

$f(x) < 0 \ \forall \ x \in (-\infty, \alpha) \cup (\beta, \infty)$ and $f(x) > 0 \ \forall \ x \in (\alpha, \beta)$.

Sum of the roots of a quadratic

Equation $= -b/a$.

Product of the roots of a quadratic equation $= c/a$

## Equations in more than one Variable

Sometimes, an equation might contain not just one variable but more than one variable. In the context of an aptitude examination like the CAT, multiple variable equations may be limited to two or three variables. Consider this question from an old CAT examination which required the student to understand the interrelationship between the values of $x$ and $y$.

The question went as follows:

$4x - 17y = 1$ where $x$ and $y$ are integers with $x, y > 0$ and $x, y < 1000$. How many pairs of values of $(x, y)$ exist such that the equation is satisfied?

In order to solve this equation, you need to consider the fact that $4x$ in this equation should be looked upon as a multiple of 4 while $17y$ should be looked upon as a multiple of 17. A scan of values which exist such that a multiple of 4 is 1 more than a multiple of 17 starts from $52 - 51 = 1$, in which case the value of $x = 13$ and $y = 3$. This represents the first set of values for $(x, y)$ that satisfies the equation.

The next pair of values in this case would happen if you increase $x$ from 13 to 30 (increase by 17 which is the coefficient of $y$); at the same time increase $y$ from 3 to 7 (increase by 4 which is the coefficient of $x$). The effect this has on $4x$ is to increase it by 68 while $17y$ would also increase by 68 keeping the value of $4x$ exactly 1 more than $17y$. In other words, at $x = 30$ and $y = 7$ the equation would give us $120 - 119 = 1$. Going further, you should realise that the same increases need to be repeated to again identify the pair of $x, y$ values. ($x = 47$ and $y = 11$ gives us $188 - 187 = 1$)

Once, you realise this, the next part of the visualisation in solving this question has to be on creating the series of values which would give us our desired outcomes everytime.

This series can be viewed as

(13,3); (30,7); (47,11); (64,15)....and the series would basically be two arithmetic progressions running parallel to each other (viz: 13, 30, 47, 64, 81,....) and (3, 7, 11, 15, 19,...) and obviously the number of such pairs would depend on the number of terms in the first of these arithmetic progressions (since that AP would cross the upper limit of 1000 first).

You would need to identify the last term of the series below 1000. The series can be visualised as 13, 30, 47, 64,... 999 and the number of terms in this series is $986/17 + 1 = 59$ terms. [Refer to the chapter on arithmetic Progressions for developing the thinking that helps us do these last two steps.]

## 🎯 WORKED-OUT PROBLEMS

**Problem 15.1**  Find the value of $\sqrt{6+\sqrt{6+\sqrt{6+...}}}$

(a) 4

(b) 3

(c) 3.5

(d) 2.5

**Solution**  Let $y = \sqrt{6+\sqrt{6+\sqrt{6+...}}}$

Then, $y = \sqrt{6+y}$ $\Rightarrow$ or $y^2 - y - 6 = 0$

or, $(y+2)(y-3) = 0$ $\Rightarrow$ $y = -2, 3$

$y = -2$ is not admissible

Hence $y = 3$

*Alternative:* Going through options:

Option (a): For 4 to be the solution, value of the whole expression should be equal to 16. Looking into the expression, it cannot be equal to 16. So, option (a) cannot be the answer. Option (b): For 3 to be the solution, the value of the expression should be 9.

So, the expression is $= \sqrt{6+\sqrt{6+\sqrt{6+...}}}$

But $\sqrt{6} \approx 2.4$, hence $= \sqrt{6+\sqrt{8.4}} \cong \sqrt{8.9+...} \cong 3$

(Since, the remaining part is negligible in value)

**Problem 15.2**  One of the two students, while solving a quadratic equation in $x$, copied the constant term incorrectly and got the roots 3 and 2. The other copied the constant term and coefficient of $x^2$ correctly and got his roots as $-6$ and 1 respectively. The correct roots are

(a) 3, $-2$

(b) $-3, 2$

(c) $-6, -1$

(d) 6, $-1$

**Solution**  Let $\alpha$, $\beta$ be the roots of the equation. Then $\alpha + \beta = 5$ and $\alpha\beta = -6$. So, a possible equation is $x^2 - 5x - 6 = 0$. The roots of the equation are 6 and $-1$.

**Problem 15.3**  If $p$ and $q$ are the roots of the equation $x^2 + px + q = 0$

(a) $p = 1$

(b) $p = 1$ or $0$ or $-\dfrac{1}{2}$

(c) $p = -2$

(d) $p = -2$ or $0$

**Solution**  Since $p$ and $q$ are roots of the equation $x^2 + px + q = 0$,

$p^2 + p^2 + q = 0$ and $q^2 + pq + q = 0$

$\Rightarrow$ $2p^2 + q = 0$ and $q(q + p + 1) = 0$

$\Rightarrow$ $2p^2 + q = 0$ and $q = 0$ or $q = -p - 1$

When we use, $q = 0$ and $2p^2 + q = 0$

we get $p = 0$.

or when we use $q = -p - 1$ and $2p^2 + q = 0$

we get $2p^2 - p - 1 = 0 \rightarrow$ which gives us

$p = 1$ or $p = -1/2$

Hence, there can be three values for $p$

i.e. $p = 1$, $p = 0$, or $p = -\dfrac{1}{2}$

**Problem 15.4**  If the roots of the equation $a(b - c)x^2 + b(c - a)x + c(a - b) = 0$ are equal, then $a$, $b$, $c$ are in

(a) AP

(b) GP

(c) HP

(d) Cannot be determined

**Solution**  Since roots of the equation $a(b-c)x^2 + b(c-a)x + c(a-b) = 0$ are equal

$\Rightarrow$ $b^2(c-a)^2 - 4ac(b-c)(a-b) = 0$

$\Rightarrow$ $b^2(c+a)^2 - 4abc(a+c) + 4a^2c^2 = 0$

$\Rightarrow$ $[b(c+a) - 2ac]^2 = 0$ $\Rightarrow$ $b(c+a) - 2ac = 0$

$\Rightarrow$ $b = (2ac)/(a+c)$ $\Rightarrow$ $a, b, c$, are in HP

**Problem 15.5**  The number of roots of the equation

$x - \dfrac{2}{(x-1)} = 1 - \dfrac{2}{(x-1)}$ is

(a) 0

(b) 1

(c) 2

(d) infinite

**Solution**  The equation gives $x = 1$.

But $x = 1$ is not admissible because it gives $x - 1 = 0$ which, in turn, makes the whole expression like this: $x - 2/0 = 1 - 2/0$. But $2/0$ is not defined. Hence, no solution is possible.

**Problem 15.6**  If the roots of the equation $x^2 - bx + c = 0$ differ by 2, then which of the following is true?

(a) $c^2 = 4(c + 1)$

(b) $b^2 = 4c + 4$

(c) $c^2 = b + 4$

(d) $b^2 = 4(c + 2)$

**Solution**  Let the roots be $\alpha$ and $\alpha + 2$.

Then $\alpha + \alpha + 2 = b$ $\Rightarrow$ $\alpha = (b-2)/2$ (1)

and $\alpha(\alpha + 2) = c$ $\Rightarrow$ $\alpha^2 + 2\alpha = c$ (2)

Putting the value of $\alpha$ from (1) in (2).

$((b-2)/2)^2 + 2((b-2)/2) = c$

$\Rightarrow$ $(b^2 + 4 - 4b)/4 + b - 2 = c$

$\Rightarrow$ $b^2 + 4 - 8 = 4c$

$\Rightarrow$ $b^2 = 4c + 4$

$\therefore$ Option (b) is the correct answer.

**Problem 15.7**  What is the condition for one root of the quadratic equation $ax^2 + bx + c = 0$ to be twice the other?

(a) $b^2 = 4ac$

(b) $2b^2 = 9ac$

(c) $c^2 = 4a + b^2$

(d) $c^2 = 9a - b^2$

**Solution**

$\therefore$ $\alpha + 2\alpha = -(b/a)$ and $\alpha \times 2\alpha = c/a$

$\Rightarrow$ $3\alpha = -(b/a)$ $\Rightarrow$ $\alpha = -b/3a$

and $2\alpha^2 = c/a$ $\Rightarrow$ $2(-b/3a)^2 = c/a$

$\Rightarrow \quad 2b^2/9a^2 = c/a \qquad \Rightarrow \qquad 2b^2 = 9ac$

Hence the required condition is $2b^2 = 9ac$.

*Alternative*: Assume any equation having two roots as 2 and 4 or any equation having two roots one of which is twice the other.

When roots are 2 and 4, then equation will be $(x - 2)(x - 4) = x^2 - 6x + 8 = 0$.

Now, check the options one by one and you will find only **(b)** as a suitable option.

**Problem 15.8** Solve the system of equations

$$\begin{cases} 1/x + 1/y = 3/2, \\ 1/x^2 + 1/y^2 = 5/4 \end{cases}$$

**Solution** Let $1/x = u$ and $1/y = v$. We then obtain

$$\begin{cases} u + v = 3/2, \\ u^2 + v^2 = 5/4 \end{cases}$$

From the first equation, we find $v = (3/2) - u$ and substitute this expression into the second equation

$$u^2 + ((3/2) - u)^2 = 5/4 \text{ or } 2u^2 - 3u + 1 = 0$$

when $u_1 = 1$ and $u_2 = 1/2$; consequently, $v_1 = 1/2$ and $v_2 = 1$. Therefore, $x_1 = 1$,

$$y_1 = 2 \quad \text{and} \quad x_2 = 2, y_2 = 1$$

Answer: (1, 2) and (2, 1).

**Problem 15.9** The product of the roots of the equation $mx^2 + 6x + (2m - 1) = 0$ is $-1$. Then $m$ is

    (a) 1                 (b) 1/3

    (c) −1              (d) −1/3

**Solution** We have $(2m - 1)/m = -1 \Rightarrow m = 1/3$

**Problem 15.10** If $13x + 17y = 643$, where $x$ and $y$ are natural numbers, what is the value of two times the product of $x$ and $y$?

    (a) 744            (b) 844

    (c) 924            (d) 884

**Solution** The solution of this question depends on your visualisation of the multiples of 13 and 17 which would satisfy this equation. (Note: your reaction to $13x$ should be to look at it as a multiple of 13 while $17y$ should be looked at as a multiple of 17). A scan of multiples of 13 and 17 gives us the solution at $286 + 357$ which would mean $13 \times 22$ and $17 \times 21$ giving us $x$ as 22 and $y$ as 21. The value of $2xy$ would be $2 \times 22 \times 21 = 2 \times 462 = 924$.

**Problem 15.11** If $[x]$ denotes the greatest integer $\leq x$, then

$$\left[\frac{1}{3}\right] + \left[\frac{1}{3} + \frac{1}{99}\right] + \left[\frac{1}{3} + \frac{2}{99}\right] + \cdots \left[\frac{1}{3} + \frac{198}{99}\right] =$$

    (a) 99             (b) 66

    (c) 132           (d) 167

**Solution** When the value of the sum of the terms inside the function is less than 1, the value of its greatest integer function would be 0. In the above sequence of values, the value inside the bracket would become equal to 1 or more from the value $\left[\frac{1}{3} + \frac{66}{99}\right]$.

Further, this value would remain between 1 to 2 till the term $\left[\frac{1}{3} + \frac{164}{99}\right]$.

There would be 99 terms each with a value of 1 between 66/99 to 164/99. Hence, this part of the expression would each yield a value of 1 giving us:

$$\left[\frac{1}{3} + \frac{66}{99}\right] + \left[\frac{1}{3} + \frac{67}{99}\right] + \cdots \left[\frac{1}{3} + \frac{164}{99}\right] = 99$$

Further, from $\left[\frac{1}{3} + \frac{165}{99}\right] + \left[\frac{1}{3} + \frac{167}{99}\right] + \cdots \left[\frac{1}{3} + \frac{198}{99}\right]$

$$= 2 \times 34 = 68$$

This gives us a total value of $99 + 68 = 167$ which means that Option (d) is the correct answer.

*Space for Rough Work*

## LEVEL OF DIFFICULTY (I)

1. Find the maximum value of the expression

$$\frac{1}{x^2 + 5x + 10}$$

   (a) $\frac{15}{2}$

   (b) 1

   (c) $\frac{4}{15}$

   (d) $\frac{1}{3}$

2. Find the maximum value of the expression $(x^2 + 8x + 20)$.

   (a) 4

   (b) 2

   (c) 29

   (d) None of these

3. Find the minimum value of the expression $(p + 1/p)$; $p > 0$.

   (a) 1

   (b) 0

   (c) 2

   (d) Depends upon the value of $p$

4. If the product of roots of the equation $x^2 - 3(2a + 4)$ $x + a^2 + 18a + 81 = 0$ is unity, then $a$ can take the values as

   (a) 3, – 6

   (b) 10, – 8

   (c) –10, –8

   (d) –10, – 6

5. For the equation $2^{a+3} = 4^{a+2} - 48$, the value of $a$ will be

   (a) $\frac{-3}{2}$

   (b) –3

   (c) –2

   (d) 1

6. The expression $a^2 + ab + b^2$ is _____ for $a < 0$, $b < 0$.

   (a) $\neq 0$

   (b) $< 0$

   (c) $> 0$

   (d) $= 0$

7. If the roots of equation $x^2 + bx + c = 0$ differ by 2, then which of the following is true?

   (a) $a^2c^2 = 4(1 + c)$

   (b) $4b + c = 1$

   (c) $c^2 = 4 + b$

   (d) $b^2 = 4(c + 1)$

8. If $f(x) = (x + 2)$ and $g(x) = (4x + 5)$, and $h(x)$ is defined as $h(x) = f(x) \cdot g(x)$, then sum of roots of $h(x)$ will be

   (a) $\frac{3}{4}$

   (b) $\frac{13}{4}$

   (c) $\frac{-13}{4}$

   (d) $\frac{-3}{4}$

9. If equation $x^2 + bx + 12 = 0$ gives 2 as its one of the roots and $x^2 + bx + q = 0$ gives equal roots then the value of $b$ is

   (a) $\frac{49}{4}$

   (b) – 8

   (c) 4

   (d) $\frac{25}{2}$

10. If the roots of the equation $(a^2 + b^2)x^2 - 2(ac + bd)x + (c^2 + d^2) = 0$ are equal then which of the following is true?

   (a) $ab = cd$

   (b) $ad = bc$

   (c) $ad = \sqrt{bc}$

   (d) $ab = \sqrt{cd}$

11. For what value of $c$ the quadratic equation $x^2 - (c + 6)x + 2(2c - 1) = 0$ has sum of the roots as half of their product?

   (a) 5

   (b) – 4

   (c) 7

   (d) 3

12. Two numbers a and b are such that the quadratic equation $ax^2 + 3x + 2b = 0$ has – 6 as the sum and the product of the roots. Find $a + b$.

   (a) 2

   (b) –1

   (c) 1

   (d) –2

13. If $\alpha$ and $\beta$ are the roots of the Quadratic equation $5y^2 - 7y + 1 = 0$ then find the value of $\frac{1}{\alpha} + \frac{1}{\beta}$.

   (a) $\frac{7}{25}$

   (b) –7

   (c) $\frac{-7}{25}$

   (d) 7

14. Find the value of the expression

$$\left( \sqrt{x + (\sqrt{x + (\sqrt{x \cdots +})})} \right)$$

   (a) $\frac{1}{2}\left[ 2\sqrt{(2x - 1)} + 1 \right]$ (b) $\frac{1}{2}\left[ \sqrt{(4x + 1)} + 1 \right]$

   (c) $\frac{1}{2}\left[ 2\sqrt{(2x - 1)} - 1 \right]$ (d) $\frac{1}{2}\left[ \sqrt{(4x - 1)} - 1 \right]$

15. If $a = \sqrt{(7 + 4\sqrt{3})}$, what will be the value of $\left( a + \frac{1}{a} \right)$?

   (a) 7

   (b) 4

   (c) 3

   (d) 2

16. If the roots of the equation $(a^2 + b^2)x^2 - 2b(a + c)x + (b^2 + c^2) = 0$ are equal then $a$, $b$, $c$, are in

   (a) AP

   (b) GP

   (c) HP

   (d) Cannot be said

17. If $\alpha$ and $\beta$ are the roots of the equation $ax^2 + bx + c = 0$ then the equation whose roots are $\alpha + \frac{1}{\beta}$ and $\beta + \frac{1}{\alpha}$ is

(a) $abx^2 + b(c + a)x + (c + a)^2 = 0$

(b) $(c + a)x^2 + b(c + a)x + ac = 0$

(c) $cax^2 + b(c + a)x + (c + a)^2 = 0$

(d) $cax^2 + b(c + a)x + c(c + a)^2 = 0$

18. If $x^2 + ax + b$ leaves the same remainder 5 when divided by $x - 1$ or $x + 1$ then the values of $a$ and $b$ are respectively

(a) 0 and 4  (b) 3 and 0

(c) 0 and 3  (d) 4 and 0

19. Find all the values of $b$ for which the equation $x^2 - bx + 1 = 0$ does not possess real roots.

(a) $-1 < b < 1$  (b) $0 < b < 2$

(c) $-2 < b < 2$  (d) $-1.9 < b < 1.9$

**Directions for Questions 20 to 24:**  Read the data given below and it solve the questions based on.

If $\alpha$ and $\beta$ are roots of the equation $x^2 + x - 7 = 0$ then.

20. Find $\alpha^2 + \beta^2$

(a) 10  (b) 15

(c) 5  (d) 18

21. Find $\alpha^3 + \beta^3$

(a) 22  (b) −22

(c) 44  (d) 36

22. For what values of $c$ in the equation $2x^2 - (c^3 + 8c - 1)x + c^2 - 4c = 0$ the roots of the equation would be opposite in signs?

(a) $c \in (0, 4)$  (b) $c \in (-4, 0)$

(c) $c \in (0, 3)$  (d) $c \in (-4, 4)$

23. The set of real values of $x$ for which the expression $x^2 - 9x + 20$ is negative is represented by

(a) $-4 < x < 4$  (b) $4 < x < 5$

(c) $x < 4$ or $x > 5$  (d) $-4 < x < 5$

24. The expression $x^2 + kx + 9$ becomes positive for what values of $k$ (given that $x$ is real)?

(a) $k < 6$  (b) $k > 6$

(c) $|k| < 6$  (d) $|k| \le 6$

25. If $9^{a-2} \div 3^{a+4} = 81^{a-11}$, then find the value of $3^{a-8} + 3^{a-6}$.

(a) 972  (b) 2916

(c) 810  (d) 2268

26. Find the number of solutions of $a^3 + 2^{a+1} = a^4$, given that $n$ is a natural number less than 100.

(a) 0  (b) 1

(c) 2  (d) 3

27. The number of positive integral values of $x$ that satisfy $x^3 - 32x - 5x^2 + 64 \le 0$ is/are

(a) 4  (b) 5

(c) 6  (d) More than 6

28. Find the positive integral value of $x$ that satisfies the equation $x^3 - 32x - 5x^2 + 64 = 0$.

(a) 5  (b) 6

(c) 7  (d) 8

29. If $a$, $b$, $c$ are positive integers, such that $\dfrac{1}{a} + \dfrac{1}{b} + \dfrac{1}{c} = \dfrac{29}{72}$, how many sets of $(a, b, c)$ exist?

(a) 3  (b) 4

(c) 5  (d) 6

30. The variables $p$, $q$, $r$ and $s$ are correlated with each other with the following relationship: $s^{0.5}/p = q/r^2$. The ranges of values for $p$, $q$ and $r$ are respectively: $-0.04 \le p \le -0.03$, $-0.25 \le q \le -0.09$, $1 \le r \le 7$ Determine the difference between the maximum and minimum value of $s$?

(a) $-0.2$  (b) $0.02$

(c) $0.1$  (d) None of these

**Directions for questions number 31 to 34:**  If graph of $y = f(x)$ is shown in the diagram below, then answer the following questions

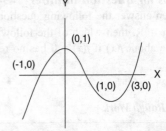

31. If $f(x) = 0$ has '$n$' real roots then $n =$

32. Sum of all roots of $f(x) = 0$ is:

33. Total number of roots of $f(x) = 2$ is:

34. Total number of roots of $f(|x|) = 0$ is:

35. If m, n are the roots of $px^2 + qx + r = 0$ and $m + k$, $n + k$ are the roots of the equation $ax^2 + bx + c = 0$ then $k = ?$

(a) $\dfrac{1}{2}\left[\dfrac{b}{a} - \dfrac{q}{p}\right]$  (b) $\dfrac{1}{2}\left[\dfrac{q}{p} - \dfrac{b}{a}\right]$

(c) $\dfrac{1}{2}\left[\dfrac{q}{p} + \dfrac{b}{a}\right]$  (d) None of these

36. If $m$, $n$ are the roots of the equation $px^2 + qx + r = 0$ and $km$, $kn$ are the roots of the equation $ax^2 + bx + c = 0$, then $k =$

(a) $\sqrt{\dfrac{cp}{ar}}$  (b) $\sqrt{\dfrac{cr}{ap}}$

(c) $\sqrt{\dfrac{ap}{cr}}$  (d) None of these

37. For how many real values of $x$, is $x^2 = |x|$

38. For how many different values of $p$, does the equation $16x^2 + px + 9 = 0$ have equal roots.

39. If $m$, $n$ are the roots of the equation $x^2 - 6x + 3 = 0$, then the equation whose roots are $m^2$, $n^2$ could be:

(a) $x^2 - 36x + 9 = 0$  (b) $x^2 - 18x + 6 = 0$

(c) $x^2 - 42x + 9 = 0$  (d) None of these

40. If $m$, $n$ are the roots of the equation $x^2 + ax + b = 0$ and $m$, $n$, $a$, $b$ all are real numbers then which of the following options can never be a value for $(a, b)$:
    (a) $(1, 1)$      (b) $(3, 2)$
    (c) $(4, 4)$      (d) $(7, 3)$

41. If $a$ and $b$ are roots of the equation $x^2 + ax + b = 0$ then:
    (a) $a = 1, b = -2$      (b) $a = 0, b = -2$
    (c) $a = 1, b = 0$      (d) None of these

42. Find the numbers of real roots of the equation $x^2 + 3|x| + 2 = 0$

43. The number of real roots of the equation
    $x^2 + (x + 1)^2 + (x - 2)^2 = 0$

44. The numbers of real solutions of the equation
    $3^{2x^2 + 3x + 1} = 0$

**Directions for question number 45-46:** $f(x) = -x^2 + x - 4$, then answer the following questions.

45. If $x \in R$, then which of the following statements is true about $f(x)$ if $f(x) = 0$ has no real root.

(a) The Graph of $f(x) = -x^2 + x - 4$ opens upward & $f(x) = 0$ has no real root.
(b) Graph of $f(x) = -x^2 + x - 4$ opens downward & $f(x) = 0$ has 2 real roots that are equal.
(c) Graph of $f(x) = -x^2 + x - 4$ opens downward & $f(x) = 0$ has no real root.
(d) None of these

46. If $a$, $b$ are two positive integers and both $a$ and $b$ are greater than 1000 then $f(a).f(b)$ is
    (a) $> 0$      (b) $< 0$
    (c) $= 0$      (d) $\leq 0$

47. Find the number of real roots of the equation $|x|^2 - 2|x| - 3 = 0$.

48. For how many real values of $x$ is $3^{x^2 - 2x - 1} = 9$

49. For how many values of $k$, the absolute value of the difference between the roots of the equation $x^2 + kx + 15 = 0$ is 2

50. If $f(x) = x^2 - 8x + 12$, then for how many integer values of $x$ is $f(x) \leq 0$.

51. In the above question for what value of $x$, does $f(x)$ attain it's minimum value.

*Space for Rough Work*

## LEVEL OF DIFFICULTY (II)

1. In the Maths Olympiad of 2020 at Animal Planet, two representatives from the donkey's side, while solving a quadratic equation, committed the following mistakes:

   (i) One of them made a mistake in the constant term and got the roots as 5 and 9.

   (ii) Another one committed an error in the coefficient of $x$ and he got the roots as 12 and 4.

   But in the meantime, they realised that they are wrong and they managed to get it right jointly. Which of the following could be the quadratic equation?

   (a) $x^2 + 4x + 14 = 0$    (b) $2x^2 + 7x - 24 = 0$

   (c) $x^2 - 14x + 48 = 0$    (d) $3x^2 - 17x + 52 = 0$

2. If the roots of the equation $a_1x^2 + a_2x + a_3 = 0$ are in the ratio $r_1 : r_2$ then

   (a) $r_1 \cdot r_2 \cdot a_1^2 = (r_1 + r_2) a_3^2$

   (b) $r_1 \cdot r_2 \cdot a_2^2 = (r_1 + r_2)^2 a_1 \cdot a_3$

   (c) $r_1 \cdot r_2 \cdot a_2 = (r_1 + a_2)^2 a_1 \cdot a_2$

   (d) $r_1 \cdot r_2 \cdot a_1^2 = (r_1 + r_2)^2 a_3 \cdot a_2$

3. For what value of $a$ do the roots of the equation $2x^2 + 6x + a = 0$, satisfy the conditions $\left(\dfrac{\alpha}{\beta}\right) + \left(\dfrac{\beta}{\alpha}\right) < 2$.

   (a) $a < 0$ or $a > \dfrac{9}{2}$    (b) $a > 0$

   (c) $-1 < a < 0$    (d) $-1 < a < 1$

4. For what value of $b$ and $c$ would the equation $x^2 + bx + c = 0$ have roots equal to $b$ and $c$.

   (a) $(0, 0)$    (b) $(1, -2)$

   (c) $(1, 2)$    (d) Both (a) and (b)

5. The sum of a fraction and its reciprocal equals 85/18. Find the fraction.

   (a) $\dfrac{2}{6}$    (b) $\dfrac{2}{3}$

   (c) $\dfrac{2}{9}$    (d) $\dfrac{4}{9}$

6. A journey between Mumbai and Pune (192 km apart) takes two hours less by a car than by a truck. Determine the average speed of the car if the average speed of the truck is 16 km/h less than the car.

   (a) 48 km/h    (b) 64 km/h

   (c) 16 km/h    (d) 24 km/h

7. If both the roots of the quadratic equation $ax^2 + bx + c = 0$ lie in the interval $(0, 3)$ then $a$ lies in

   (a) $(1, 3)$    (b) $(-1, -3)$

   (c) $(-\sqrt{121}/91, -\sqrt{8})$    (d) None of these

8. If the common factor of $(ax^2 + bx + c)$ and $(bx^2 + ax + c)$ is $(x + 2)$ then

   (a) $a = b$, or $a + b + c = 0$

   (b) $a = c$, or $a + b + c = 0$

   (c) $a = b = c$

   (d) $b = c$, $a + b + c = 0$

9. If $P = 2^{2/3} + 2^{1/3}$ then which of the following is true?

   (a) $p^3 - 6p - 6 = 0$    (b) $p^3 - 6p + 6 = 0$

   (c) $p^3 + 6p - 6 = 0$    (d) $p^3 + 6p + 6 = 0$

10. If $f(x) = x^2 + 2x - 5$ and $g(x) = 5x + 30$, then the roots of the quadratic equation $g[f(x)]$ will be

    (a) $-1, -1$    (b) $2, -1$

    (c) $-1 + \sqrt{2}, -1 - \sqrt{2}$    (d) $1, 2$

11. If one root of the quadratic equation $ax^2 + bx + c = 0$ is three times the other, find the relationship between $a$, $b$ and $c$.

    (a) $3b^2 = 16\,ac$    (b) $b^2 = 4ac$

    (c) $(a + c)^2 = 4b$    (d) $(a^2 + c^2)/ac = \dfrac{b}{2}$

12. If $x^2 - 3x + 2$ is a factor of $x^4 - ax^2 + b = 0$ then the values of $a$ and $b$ are

    (a) $-5, -4$    (b) $5, 4$

    (c) $-5, 4$    (d) $5, -4$

13. Value of the expression $(x^2 - x + 1)/(x - 1)$ cannot lie between

    (a) $1, 3$    (b) $-1, -3$

    (c) $1, -3$    (d) $-1, 2$

14. The value of $p$ satisfying $\log_3 (p^2 + 4p + 12) = 2$ are

    (a) $1, -3$    (b) $-1, -3$

    (c) $-4, 2$    (d) $-4, -2$

15. If $q, r > 0$ then roots of the equation $x^2 + qx - r = 0$ are

    (a) Both negative    (b) Both positive

    (c) Of opposite sign but equal magnitude

    (d) Of opposite sign

16. If two quadratic equations $ax^2 + ax + 3 = 0$ and $x^2 + x + b = 0$ have a common root $x = 1$ then which of the following statements hold true?

    (a) $a + b = -3.5$    (b) $ab = 3$

    (c) $\dfrac{a}{b} = \dfrac{3}{4}$    (d) $a - b = -0.5$

    (a) $A, B, C$    (b) $B, C, D$

    (c) $A, C, D$    (d) $A, B, D$

17. If the expression $ax^2 + bx + c$ is equal to 4 when $x = 0$ leaves a remainder 4 when divided by $x + 1$ and a remainder 6 when divided by $x + 2$, then the values of $a$, $b$ and $c$ are respectively
    (a) 1, 1, 4          (b) 2, 2, 4
    (c) 3, 3, 4          (d) 4, 4, 4

18. If $p$ and $q$ are the roots of the equation $x^2 - px + q = 0$, then
    (a) $p = 1, q = -2$      (b) $p = 0, q = 1$
    (c) $p = -2, q = 0$      (d) $p = -2, q = 1$

19. Sum of the real roots of the equation $x^2 + 5|x| + 6 = 0$
    (a) Equals to 5          (b) Equals to 10
    (c) Equals to –5         (d) None of these

20. The value of $p$ for which the sum of the square of the roots of $2x^2 - 2(p - 2)x - p - 1 = 0$ is least is
    (a) 1                (b) $\dfrac{3}{2}$
    (c) 2                (d) –1

21. For what values of $p$ would the equation $x^2 + 2(p - 1)x + p + 5 = 0$ possess at least one positive root?
    (a) $P \in (-\infty, -5)$      (b) $P \in (-\infty, -1]$
    (c) $P \in (1, \infty)$        (d) $P \in (-5, 1)$

22. If $a, b \in \{1, 2, 3, 4\}$, then the number of the equations of the form $ax^2 + bx + 1 = 0$ having real roots is
    (a) 10               (b) 7
    (c) 6                (d) 12

23. If $a^2 + b^2 + c^2 = 1$, then which of the following cannot be a value of $(ab + bc + ca)$?
    (a) 0                (b) 1/2
    (c) $\dfrac{-1}{4}$          (d) –1

24. If one root of the equation $(I - m)x^2 + Ix + 1 = 0$ is double of the other and is real, find the greatest value of $m$.
    (a) $\dfrac{9}{8}$           (b) $\dfrac{8}{7}$
    (c) $\dfrac{8}{6}$           (d) $\dfrac{7}{5}$

25. The set of values of $p$ for which the roots of the equation $3x^2 + 2x + p(p - 1) = 0$ are of opposite sign is
    (a) $(-\infty, 0)$        (b) $(0, 1)$
    (c) $(1, \infty)$         (d) $(0, \infty)$

26. One day each of Neha's friends consumed some cold drink and some orange squash. Though the quantities of cold drink and orange squash varied for the friends, the total consumption of the two liquids was exactly 9 litres for each friend. If Neha had one-ninth of the total cold drink consumed and one-eleventh of the total orange squash consumed. Find the ratio of the quantity of cold drink to that of orange squash consumed by Neha on that day?
    (a) 3 : 2             (b) 5:4
    (c) 2 : 1            (d) 1:1

27. $Q_1(x)$ and $Q_2(x)$ are quadratic functions such that $Q_1(10) = Q_2(8) = 0$. If the corresponding equations $Q_1(x) = 0$ and $Q_2(x) = 0$ have a common root and $Q_1(4) \times Q_2(5) = 36$, what is the value of the common root?
    (a) 10               (b) 6
    (c) Either 9 or 6        (d) Cannot be determined

28. For the above question if it is known that the coefficient of $x^2$ for $Q_1(x) = 0$ is 1/15 and that of $Q_2(x) = 0$ is 1, then which of the following options is a possible value of the sum of the roots of $Q_2(x) = 0$?
    (a) 18               (b) 36
    (c) 25               (d) 11

29. Which of the following could be a possible value of '$x$' for which, each of the fractions is in its simplest form, where $[x]$ stands for the greatest integer less than or equal to '$x$'?
$$\frac{[x]+7}{10}, \frac{[x]+18}{11}, \frac{[x]+31}{12}, \frac{[x]+46}{13}, \cdots, \frac{[x]+1489}{39} \text{ and}$$
$$\frac{[x]+1567}{40}$$
    (a) 95.71            (b) 93.71
    (c) 94.71            (d) 92.71

30. $x - y = 8$ and $P = 7x^2 - 12y^2$, where $x, y > 0$. What is the maximum possible value of $P$?
    (a) Infinite             (b) 352.8
    (c) 957.6            (d) 604.8

31. If the equations $5x + 9y + 17z = a$, $4x + 8y + 12z = b$ and $2x + 3y + 8z = c$ have at least one solution for $x$, $y$ and $z$ and $a$, $b$, and $c \neq 0$, then which of the following is true?
    (a) $4a - 3b - 3c = 0$      (b) $3a - 4b - 3c = 0$
    (c) $4a - 3b - 4c = 0$      (d) Nothing can be said

32. If the roots of the equation $x^3 - ax^2 + bx - 1080 = 0$ are in the ratio $2 : 4 : 5$, find the value of the coefficient of $x^2$.
    (a) 33               (b) 66
    (c) –33              (d) 99

33. If the roots of the equation $px^3 - 20x^2 + 4x - 5 = 0$, where $p \neq 0$, are $l$, $m$ and $n$, then what is the value of $\dfrac{1}{lm} + \dfrac{1}{mn} + \dfrac{1}{ln}$?
    (a) 5                (b) –4
    (c) 4                (d) 8

34. The cost of 10 pears, 8 grapes and 6 mangoes is ₹ 44. The cost of 5 pears, 4 grapes and 3 mangoes is ₹ 22. Find the cost of 4 mangoes and 3 grapes, if the cost of each of the items, in rupees, is a natural number and the cost of no two items is the same.

(a) ₹ 17      (b) ₹18

(c) ₹ 14      (d) Cannot be determined

35. The number of positive integral solutions to the system of equations $a_1 + a_2 + a_3 + a_4 + a_5 = 47$ and $a_1 + a_2 = 37$ is

(a) 2376      (b) 2246

(c) 2024      (d) 1296

36. If $f(x)$ is a quadratic polynomial, such that $f(5) = 75$ and $f(-5) = 55$, and $f(p) = f(q) = 0$, then find $p \times q$, given that the value of the constant term in the polynomial is 10.

(a) 2      (b) −3

(c) 5      (d) Cannot be determined

37. If $|a| + a + b = 75$ and $a + |b| - b = 150$, then what is the value of $|a| + |b|$?

(a) 105      (b) 60

(c) 90      (d) Cannot be determined

38. If $[x]$ represents the greatest integer less than or equal to $x$, then the value of $\left\lfloor 315^{\frac{1}{3}} \right\rfloor + \left\lfloor 316^{\frac{1}{3}} \right\rfloor + \left\lfloor 317^{\frac{1}{3}} \right\rfloor + ... + \left\lfloor 515^{\frac{1}{3}} \right\rfloor$ is

(a) 1383      (b) 1379

(c) 1183      (d) 1351

39. $a, b, c, d$ and $e$ are five consecutive integers $a < b < c < d < e$ and $a^2 + b^2 + c^2 = d^2 + e^2$. What is/are the possible value(s) of $d$?

(a) −2 and 10      (b) −1 and 11

(c) 0 and 12      (d) None of these

40. The 9 to 9 supermarket purchases $x$ litres of fruit juice from the Fruit Garden Inc for a total price of $\$ 4x^2$ and sells the entire $x$ litres at a total price of $\$ 10 \times (15 + 16x)$. Find the minimum amount of profit that the 9 to 9 supermarket makes in the process.

(a) 1700      (b) 1,000

(c) 1,750      (d) 1,300

41. If $\alpha, \beta$ are the roots of the quadratic equation $x^2 + mx + 1 = 0$ and $\gamma, \delta$ are the roots of the equation $x^2 + nx + 1 = 0$, then the value of $(\alpha - \gamma)(\beta - \gamma)(\alpha + \delta)(\beta + \delta)$ is equal to    **IIFT 2006**

(a) $n^2 - m^2$.      (b) $m^2 - n^2$.

(c) $2m^2 - n^2$.      (d) None of the above

42. Find the roots of the quadratic equation $bx^2 - 2ax + a = 0$      **IIFT 2010**

(a) $\dfrac{\sqrt{b}}{\sqrt{b} \pm \sqrt{a-b}}$      (b) $\dfrac{\sqrt{a}}{\sqrt{b} \pm \sqrt{a-b}}$

(c) $\dfrac{\sqrt{a}}{\sqrt{a} \pm \sqrt{a-b}}$      (d) $\dfrac{\sqrt{a}}{\sqrt{a} \pm \sqrt{a+b}}$

43. If $x^2 + 3x - 10$ is a factor of $3x^4 + 2x^3 - ax^2 + bx - a + b - 4$, then the closest approximate values of $a$ and $b$ are      **IIFT 2013**

(a) 25, 43      (b) 52, 43

(c) 52, 67      (d) None of the above

44. If $x$ is real, the smallest value of the expression $3x^2 - 4x + 7$ is:      **IIFT 2013**

(a) 2/3      (b) ¾

(c) 7/9      (d) None of the above

45. If $0 < p < 1$ then the roots of the equation $(1 - p) x^2 + 4x + p = 0$ are ___?      **XAT 2008**

(a) Real and of opposite sign.

(b) Real and both negative

(c) Imaginary

(d) Real and both positive

46. The number of possible real solution(s) of y in the equation $y^2 - 2y \cos x + 1 = 0$ is ___?   **XAT 2008**

(a) 0      (b) 1

(c) 2      (d) 3

47. A polynomial $ax^3 + bx^2 + cx + d$ intersects the $x-$axis at 1 and −1, and $y$-axis at 2. The value of $b$ is:      **XAT 2014**

(a) − 2      (b) 0

(c) 1      (d) 2

48. If $x^3 - mx^2 + nx - p = 0$ has three roots $\alpha, \beta, \gamma$. If we add 3 in each of the roots of $x^3 - mx^2 + nx - p = 0$ then we get the roots of the equation $x^3 - ax^2 + bx - 27 = 0$. What is the value of $p + 9m + 3n$.

(a) 0      (b) 1

(c) −54      (d) 54

49. If the roots of the equation $x^3 + qx^2 + rx + s = 0$ are in $GP$, then which of the following is true:

(a) $r^2 = q^2 s$      (b) $r^3 = q^3 s$

(c) $r = qs^2$      (d) $r = qs^3$

50. The graph of $ax^2 + bx + c$ is shown below. Then which of the following is true?

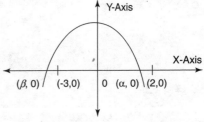

(a) $a < 0, b < 0, c > 0$      (b) $a < 0, b < 0, c < 0$

(c) $a < 0, b > 0, c > 0$      (d) $a < 0, b > 0, c < 0$

51. If '$x$' is $a$ real number then what is the number of solutions for the equation: $(x^8 + 12)^{1/2} = x^4 - 2$

(a) 0      (b) 1

(c) 2      (d) Cannot be determined

52.. How many integer values of '$p$' are there such that the inequality $x^2 + 4px + (p + 3) > 0$ is true for all values of $x$?

53. If $g(x) = x^3 - px^2 - \dfrac{qx}{2} - r$ can be factorized as $(x - p)(x - q)(x - r)$, then $f(4) = ?$

54. The roots of $x^3 - px^2 + qx - r = 0$ are $a, b, c$ while the roots of $x^3 + wx^2 + yz - 47 = 0$ are $a + 2, b + 2, c + 2$,
Then the value of $4p + 2q + r =$?

**Directions for question number 55-56: One of the roots of the equation $x^2 + bx + 3b = 0$ ($b \in R$) is thrice the other root, then answer the following questions.**

55. What is the value of $3b$.

56. Which of the following options correctly represents roots of the equation $x^2 - 33x + 17b = 0$
    (a) $b, b + 1$           (b) $b - 1, b$
    (c) $b - 1, b + 1$       (d) None of these

57. The roots of $x^2 + 5x + a = 0$ are $p$ and $q$ while the roots of $x^2 + 23x + b = 0$ are $q$ and $r$. If $p, q, r$ are in anArithmetic Progression then the value of $|a \times b| = $?

58. $f(x) = (x - 2)(x^2 + 2x + 5)$
If $a, b, c$ are the roots of $f(x) = 0$, then the value of $a^3 + b^3 + c^3$ would be equal to?

59. If $f(x) = px^2 + qx + r$ and $f(x)$ is exactly divisible by $(x + 2)$ and $(x + 3)$ but leaves remainder of 7 when divided by $(x - 1)$, find the approximate value of $q$?

60. If $f(x) = 4x - 7\sqrt{x}$, which of the following statements is true about the roots of the equation $f(x) = 2$.
    (a) It has only one real root which is not an integer.
    (b) It has no real root

(c) It has one real root which is a positive integer.
(d) It has two real roots.

61. If the equation $ax^2 + bx + a = 0(a > 0)$ has real and positive roots then which of the following is always true?
    (a) $b < 2a$           (b) $b < 0$
    (c) $b \le -2a$        (d) All the options are true.

62. If $p, q, r$ are real and $(x - p)(x - q) + (x - q)(x - r) + (x - r)(x - p) = 0$ if $p \ne q \ne r$ then which of the following options is true?
    (a) Roots of the given equations are imaginary.
    (b) Roots of the given equation are real.
    (c) Roots of the given equation are equal.
    (d) None of these

63. If $f(x) = px^2 + qx + r$ and $g(x) = rx^2 + qx + p$. If one root of $f(x) = 0$ is 2 and one root of $g(x) = 0$ is ¼, then find the sum of the roots of $f(x)$ and $g(x)$.

64. The number of distinct points at which the curve $y^3 - 4y^2 + x^2 - 5x + 3y = 0$ intersects either the y-axis or the x-axis is.

65. If the sum of the roots of the quadratic equation $px^2 + qx + r = 0$ is equal to the sum of the square of their reciprocals, mark all the correct statements.

**IIFT 2006**

(a) $r/p, p/q$ and $q/r$ are in $A. P.$
(b) $p/ r, q/p$ and $r/q$ are in $G. P.$
(c) $p/r, q/p$ and $r/q$ are in $H. P.$
(d) Option ($a$) and ($c$) both.

**Space for Rough Work**

## LEVEL OF DIFFICULTY (III)

1. $f(x) = ax^2 + bx + c$ & $a < 0$.

   The equation $f(x) = 0$ has two distinct roots which is from the set $\{-2, -1, 0, 1, 2\}$. How many different pairs of roots of $f(x)$ are possible such that $f(0)$ is greater than or equals to 0?.
   - (a) 4
   - (b) 6
   - (c) 8
   - (d) 10

2. $px^2 + qx + r = 0$ has one root greater than 3 and other root less than 1. Which of the following is necessarily true?
   - (a) $p(4p + 2q + r) < 0$
   - (b) $p(4p + 2q + r) > 0$
   - (c) $p(4p - 2q + r) < 0$
   - (d) $p(9p - 3q + r) < 0$

3. If $f(x, y) = 4^{x^y} + x^{4^y}$ then what is the total number of solutions for the equation $f(x, y) = 5$.
   - (a) 0
   - (b) 1
   - (c) 2
   - (d) More than 2.

**Directions for question number 4 & 5::** If 'd' is a root of the equation $ax^2 + bx + c = 0$ and 'c' is a root of the equation $ax^2 + bx + d = 0$ and if $c \neq d$ then answer the following questions:

4. Find the value of $c + d$:
   - (a) $a(b - 1)$
   - (b) $\dfrac{b-1}{a}$
   - (c) $\dfrac{1-b}{a}$
   - (d) None of these

5. Which of the following equations has roots $-c, -d$.
   - (a) $ax^2 + a(b - 1)x + b - 1 = 0$
   - (b) $ax^2 - a(1 - b)x + 1 - b = 0$
   - (c) $ax^2 + a(1 - b)x + 1 - b = 0$
   - (d) None of these

6. The values of a quadratic function $f(x)$ is a positive for all values of $x$, except for $x = 4$. If $f(0) = 10$. Find the value of $f(-4)$.

7. Find all values of '$a$', such that 4 lies somewhere between the roots of the equation $3x^2 + 4ax + (a + 3) = 0$ for all values of $x$.
   - (a) $a < -3$
   - (b) $a < -2$
   - (c) $a > 3$
   - (d) $a > 2$

8. $f(x) = x^3 - (5 + k)x^2 + (6 + 5k)x - 6k$, where '$k$' is an odd prime number and $k > 3$. What is the range of values of $x$ for which $f(x) < 0$.
   - (a) $2 < x < 3$ or $x > k$
   - (b) $x < 2, 3 < x < k$
   - (c) $x < 3, x > k$
   - (d) none of these

9. $f(x, p) = a(x - p)^2 + b(x - p) + c$, where $a$, $b$, $c$ are constants and $a < 0$ and '$p$' is a natural number. It is given that the roots of the equation $ax^2 + bx + c = 0$ are 3, 4. Then, the value of $x$ at which $f(x, 5)$ attains its maximum value is:
   - (a) 9
   - (b) 8.5

   - (c) 7.5
   - (d) 5.5

10. $f(x) = [x]^2 - 11[x] + 30$, where $[x]$ represents the largest integer less than or equal to $x$, then what is the sum of all integer solutions of the equation $f(x) = 0$

11. If all the three roots of the equation $x^3 - 12x^2 + px - 42 = 0$ are unequal and prime. Then $p =$

**Directions for question number 12&13:**
   If $f(x) = x^3 - px^2 - 2qx + r$ and
   $g(x) = (x - p)(x - q)(x - r)$
   Answer the following questions.

12. The value of $p + q$ for which $f(x) = g(x)$ is:

13. The value of $f(4)$ if $f(x) = g(x)$ is:

14. If $f(x) = (b - 1)x^2 + (c + d)x + e$ and $a:b = 1:2$, $b:c = 2:3$, $c:d = 3:4$, $d:e = 4:5$. Then find the square of difference of the roots of the equation $f(x) = 0$.

15. $\log_3 x \times \log_3 y + \log_3 z \times \log_3 xy = 11$, where $x, y, z$ all are real numbers.
   If $(\log_3 x)^2 + (\log_3 y)^2 = 14 - (\log_3 z)^2$
   and $xyz = k_1^2 = k_2^3$ then $k_1 + k_2 =$

**Direction for 16 and 18:** $f(x) = ax^2 - 150x + 5b$ where $a$ and $b$ are two positive integers. Then answer the following questions

16. For how many ordered pairs $(a, b)$ will $(x - 3)$ be a factor of $f(x)$.

17. Maximum possible value of $a + b$ for which $(x - 3)$ is a factor of $f(x)$

18. If $a$ & $b$ are integers then for how many ordered pairs $(a, b)$ will $(x - 3)$ be a factor of $f(x)$
   - (a) 9
   - (b) 18
   - (c) 180
   - (d) None of these

**Directions for question number 19 & 20:** if $f(x) = x^3 - 12x^2 + 47x - 60$ then answer the following questions:

19. How many quadratic equations of the form $x^2 + bx + c = 0$, can be formed such that both the roots of the quadratic equation are common with the roots of $f(x) = 0$?
   - (a) 3
   - (b) 5
   - (c) 6
   - (d) None of these

20. If the product of all the roots of the quadratic equations of the form $x^2 + bx + c = 0$, that can be formed such that both roots of the quadratic equation are common with the roots of $f(x) = 0$ is $p$ then $p^{1/4} = ?$
   - (a) 30
   - (b) 40
   - (c) 50
   - (d) 60

**Direction for 21 and 22:** If all the roots of $(x - k)^3 (x - 7) - 27 = 0$ are integers then answer the following questions:

21. How many integer values can $k$ have?
22. Difference between the maximum and minimum possible values of $k$ is
23. The Value of $p$ for which the sum of the square of the roots of the equation $x^2 - (p - 3)x + (p - 4) = 0$ is minimum is.
24. If $f(x) = x^2, g(x) = x^3 - 2^x$, where $x$ is a positive integer then for how many values of $x$, is $f(x) = g(x)$

**Directions for question number 25-26:** If $h(x)$ is a quadratic function which attains it's maximum value of 10 at $x = 4$. If $t(x)$ is a function such that $3h(x) + 5t(x) = 0$ then answer the following questions:

25. Which of the following option is true?
    (a) $h(x)$ and $t(x)$ have roots of opposite sign.
    (b) Sum of roots of $h(x)$ and $t(x)$ is 0.
    (c) Sum of roots of $h(x)$ is equal to the sum of roots of $t(x)$
    (d) None of these
26. Minimum value of $t(x)$ is_
27. The curve shown below can possibly represent which of the following equation (Assume the curve does not exist at $x = 0$)

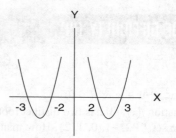

(a) $\dfrac{6}{|x|} = 5 + |x|$     (b) $-\dfrac{6}{|x|} = 5 - |x|$

(c) $\dfrac{6}{|x|} = 5 - |x|$     (d) None of these

28. If $f(x) = max(|x^2 - 4|, 2x + 4)$ then find the number of solutions of the equation $f(x) = \dfrac{5}{2}$

29. Find the number of real solutions of the equation $||x| - 1| = e^x$

30. Find the number of real solutions of equation $|||x| - 1| - 2| = \left(\dfrac{1}{2}\right)^x$

*Space for Rough Work*

## ANSWER KEY

### Level of Difficulty (I)

| | | | |
|---|---|---|---|
| 1. (c) | 2. (d) | 3. (c) | 4. (c) |
| 5. (d) | 6. (c) | 7. (d) | 8. (c) |
| 9. (b) | 10. (b) | 11. (c) | 12. (b) |
| 13. (d) | 14. (b) | 15. (b) | 16. (b) |
| 17. (c) | 18. (a) | 19. (c) | 20. (b) |
| 21. (b) | 22. (a) | 23. (b) | 24. (c) |
| 25. (c) | 26. (b) | 27. (d) | 28. (d) |
| 29. (d) | 30. (b) | 31  3 | 32  3 |
| 33  1 | 34  4 | 35. (b) | 36. (a) |
| 37  3 | 38  2 | 39. (c) | 40. (a) |
| 41 (a) | 42  0 | 43  0 | 44  0 |
| 45 (c) | 46 (a) | 47  2 | 48  2 |
| 49  2 | 50  5 | 51  4 | |

### Level of Difficulty (II)

| | | | |
|---|---|---|---|
| 1. (c) | 2. (b) | 3. (d) | 4. (d) |
| 5. (c) | 6. (a) | 7. (d) | 8. (a) |
| 9. (a) | 10. (a) | 11. (a) | 12. (b) |
| 13. (d) | 14. (b) | 15. (d) | 16. (a) |
| 17. (a) | 18. (c) | 19. (d) | 20. (b) |
| 21. (b) | 22. (b) | 23. (d) | 24. (a) |
| 25. (b) | 26. (d) | 27. (d) | 28. (a) |
| 29. (c) | 30. (d) | 31. (c) | 32. (c) |
| 33. (c) | 34. (b) | 35. (d) | 36. (c) |
| 37. (a) | 38. (a) | 39. (d) | 40. (c) |
| 41 (a) | 42 (c) | 43 (c) | 44 (d) |
| 45 (b) | 46 (c) | 47 (a) | 48 (a) |
| 49 (b) | 50 (a) | 51 (a) | 52  1 |
| 53  31.5 | 54  39 | 55  48 | 56 (a) |
| 57  1568 | 58  30 | 59  2.92 | 60 (c) |
| 61 (d) | 62 (b) | 63  6.75 | 64  5 |
| 65 (d) | | | |

### Level of Difficulty (III)

| | | | |
|---|---|---|---|
| 1. (c) | 2. (a) | 3. (d) | 4. (c) |
| 5. (c) | 6. 40 | 7. (a) | 8. (b) |
| 9. (b) | 10. 11 | 11. 41 | 12. 3/2 |
| 13. 54 | 14. 29 | 15. 36 | 16. 9 |
| 17. 86 | 18. (d) | 19. (c) | 20. (d) |
| 21. 4 | 22. 52 | 23. 4 | 24. 1 |
| 25. (c) | 26. -6 | 27. c | 28. 2 |
| 29. 3 | 30. 5 | | |

### Solutions and Shortcuts

### Level of Difficulty (I)

1. For the given expression to be a maximum, the denominator should be minimized. (Since, the function in the denominator has imaginary roots and is always positive). $x^2 + 5x + 10$ will be minimized at $x = -2.5$ and its minimum values at $x = -2.5$ is 3.75.
   Hence, required answer = $1/3.75 = 4/15$.

2. Has no maximum.

3. The minimum value of $(p + 1/p)$ is at $p = 1$. The value is 2.

4. The product of the roots is given by: $(a^2 + 18a + 81)/1$.
   Since product is unity we get: $a^2 + 18a + 81 = 1$
   Thus, $a^2 + 18a + 80 = 0$
   Solving, we get: $a = -10$ and $a = -8$.

5. Solve through options. LHS = RHS for $a = 1$.

6. For $a$, $b$ negative the given expression will always be positive since, $a^2$, $b^2$ and $ab$ are all positive.

7. To solve this take any expression whose roots differ by 2.
   Thus,    $(x - 3)(x - 5) = 0$
   $\Rightarrow$            $x^2 - 8x + 15 = 0$
   In this case, $a = 1$, $b = -8$ and $c = 15$.
   We can see that $b^2 = 4(c + 1)$.

8. $h(x) = 4x^2 + 13x + 10$.
   Sum of roots $- 13/4$.

9. $x^2 + bx + 12 = 0$ has 2 as a root.
   Thus, $b = -8$.

10. Solve this by assuming each option to be true and then check whether the given expression has equal roots for the option under check.
    Thus, if we check for option (b).
    $ad = bc$.
       We assume $a = 6$, $d = 4$ $b = 12$ $c = 2$ (any set of values that satisfies $ad = bc$).
    Then   $(a^2 + b^2)x^2 - 2(ac + bc)x + (c^2 + d^2) = 0$
    $180 x^2 - 120 x + 20 = 0$.
    We can see that this has equal roots. Thus, option (b) is a possible answer. The same way if we check for $a$, $c$ and $d$ we see that none of them gives us equal roots and can be rejected.

11. $(c + 6) = 1/2 \times 2(2c - 1) \Rightarrow c + 6 = 2c - 1 \Rightarrow c = 7$

12. $-3/a = -6 \Rightarrow a = \frac{1}{2}$,
    $2b/a = -6$ and $a = \frac{1}{2}$
    Gives us    $b = -1.5$.
    $a + b = -1$.

13. $1/\alpha + 1/\beta = (\alpha + \beta)/\alpha\beta$
    $= (7/5)/(1/5) = 7$.

14. $y = \sqrt{x + \sqrt{x + \sqrt{x + \cdots}}}$
    $\Rightarrow y = \sqrt{x + y}$
    $\Rightarrow y^2 = x + y$
    $y^2 - y - x = 0$
    Solving quadratically, we have option (b) as the root of this equation.

15. The approximate value of $a = \sqrt{13.92} = 3.6$ (approx).
    $a + 1/a = 3.6 + 1/3.6$ is closest to 4.

16. Solve by assuming values of $a$, $b$, and $c$ in AP, GP and HP to check which satisfies the condition.

17. Assume any equation:
    Say $x^2 - 5x + 6 = 0$
    The roots are 2, 3.
    We are now looking for the equation, whose roots are:
    $(2 + 1/3) = 2.33$ and $(3 + 1/2) = 3.5$.
    Also $a = 1$, $b = -5$ and $c = 6$.

    Put these values in each option to see which gives 2.33 and 3.5 as its roots.

18. Remainder when $x^2 + ax + b$ is divided by $x - 1$ is got by putting $x = 1$ in the expression. Thus, we get.
    $a + b + 1 = 5$ and
    $b - a + 1 = 5$
    $\Rightarrow$ $b = 4$ and $a = 0$

19. $b^2 - 4 < 0 \Rightarrow -2 < b < 2$

20. $(\alpha^2 + \beta^2) = (\alpha + \beta)^2 - 2\alpha\beta$
    $= (-1)^2 - 2 \times (-7) = 15$.

21. $(\alpha^3 + \beta^3) = (\alpha + \beta)^3 - 3\alpha\beta(\alpha + \beta)$
    $= (-1)^3 - 3 \times (-7)(-1)$
    $= -1 - 21 = -22$

22. For the roots to be opposite in sign, the product should be negative.
    $(c^2 - 4c)/2 < 0 \Rightarrow 0 < c < 4$.

23. The roots of the equation $x^2 - 9x + 20 = 0$ are 4 and 5. The expression would be negative for $4 < x < 5$.

24. The roots should be imaginary for the expression to be positive
    i.e. $k^2 - 36 < 0$
    thus $-6 < k < 6$ or $|k| < 6$.

25. Simplifying the equation $9^{a-2} \, 3^{a+4} = 81^{a-11}$ we will get: $3^{2a-4} \div 3^{a+4} = 3^{4a-44}$. This gives us:
    $2a-4 - a - 4 = 4a-44 \to a-8 = 4a-44 \to 3a = 36 \to a = 12$.
    Hence, we have to evaluate the value of $3^4 + 3^6 = 81 + 729 = 810$. Option (c) is correct.

26. In order to think of this situation, you need to think of the fact that "the cube of a number + a power of two" (LHS of the equation) should add up to the fourth power of the same number.
    The only in which situation this happens is for $8 + 8 = 16$ where $a = 2$ giving us $2^3 + 2^3 = 2^4$.
    Hence, Option (b) is the correct answer.

27. The values of $x$, where the above expression turns out to be negative or 0 are $x = 2, 3, 4, 5, 6, 7$ or 8. Hence, Option (d) is correct.

28. The value of the LHS would become $512 - 256 - 320 + 64 = 0$ when $x = 8$.

29. The above equation gets satisfied at $a = 9$, $b = 8$ and $c = 6$. (In order to visualise this, look for sets of 3 numbers with an LCM of 72). All different arrangements of (9, 8, 6) will be possible values of $(a, b, c)$.

Possible arrangements of $(a, b, c)$ are (9, 8, 6), (8, 9, 6), (6, 8, 9), (8, 6, 9), (6, 9, 8), (9, 6, 8). Thus, there are a total of 6 such sets possible. So option (d) is correct.

30. The equation can be rewritten as $s^{0.5} = \dfrac{pq}{r^2}$ or $s = \dfrac{(pq)^2}{r^4}$

    The maximum value of $s$ will happen when $pq$ is maximum and $r$ is minimum. $pq$ is maximum when $p = -0.04$ and $q = -0.25$ and $r = 1$ similarly $s$ will be minimum when $p = -0.03$ and $q = -0.09$ and $r = 7$.

    $$s_{max} = \frac{(-0.04 \times -0.25)^2}{1} \quad s_{min} = \frac{(-0.03 \times -0.09)^2}{7^4}$$

    $$s_{max} - s_{min} = \frac{(-0.04 \times -0.25)^2}{1} - \frac{(-0.03 \times -0.09)^2}{7^4}$$

    $\approx 0.0001$

31. Graph of $f(x) = 0$ cuts x-axis at three distinct points. Therefore $f(x) = 0$ has three roots.

32. Sum of roots of $f(x) = 0$ is $-1 + 1 + 3 = 3$.

33.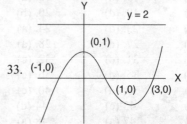

The $y = 2$ line intersects the curve $y = f(x)$ at only one point, hence total number of roots of $f(x) = 2$ is 1.

34. Process to draw graph $f(|x|)$ if graph of $f(x)$ is given: First erase the negative $x$ portion of $f(x)$ then take a mirror image of positive $X$ portion. Curve of $y = f(|x|)$ is shown below

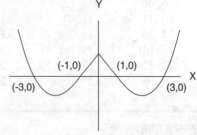

Here we can see that the curve of $y = f(|x|)$ cuts the x-axis at four distinct points, hence $y = f(|x|)$ has four real roots.

35. $m + n = -\dfrac{q}{p}$         (i)

    $(m + k) + (n + k) = -\dfrac{b}{a}$

$$m + n + 2k = -\frac{b}{a} \qquad \text{(ii)}$$

Subtract equation (i) from equation (ii):

$$2k = -\frac{b}{a} + \frac{q}{p}$$

$$k = \frac{1}{2}\left[\frac{q}{p} - \frac{b}{a}\right]$$

Option (b) is correct.

36. $mn = \dfrac{r}{p}$      (i)

$$(mk)(nk) = mnk^2 = \frac{c}{a} \qquad \text{(ii)}$$

Equation (ii) ÷ equation (i)

$$k^2 = \frac{c}{a} \times \frac{p}{r}$$

$$k = \sqrt{\frac{cp}{ar}}$$

Option (a) is correct.

37. For $x \geq 0 : x^2 = x$
$\Rightarrow x^2 - x = 0$
$\Rightarrow x(x - 1) = 0$
$\Rightarrow x = 0, 1$
For $x < 0 : x^2 = -x$
$\Rightarrow x^2 + x = 0$
$\Rightarrow x(x + 1) = 0$
$\Rightarrow x = 0, -1$
Therefore for three real values of $x$, we will get $x^2 = |x|$

38. $16x^2 + px + 9 = 0$
For equal roots, the discriminant of the above equation must be zero.
$p^2 - 4 \times 16 \times 9 = 0$
$p^2 = 4 \times 16 \times 9$
$p = \pm(2 \times 4 \times 3) = \pm 24$
Therefore for two different values of $p$, $16x^2 + px + 9 = 0$, has equal roots.

39. $m + n = 6$, $mn = -3$
$(m + n)^2 = m^2 + n^2 + 2mn$
$36 = m^2 + n^2 - 6$
$m^2 + n^2 = 42$ (Sum of roots of the required equation)
Also, since $mn = -3$, the value of $m^2n^2 = 9$ (product of roots of the required equation)
Therefore the equation must be $x^2 - 42x + 9 = 0$..
Option (c) is correct.

40. Checking from the options, if we put $a = 1$ & $b = 1$ (from option (a)) then we get the equation, $x^2 + x + 1 = 0$, and this equation does not have any real roots. So, this option is correct.

41. $a + b = -a$, $ab = b$

$\Rightarrow ab = b$
$\Rightarrow ab - b = 0$
$\Rightarrow (a - 1)b = 0$
This gives us two possibilities: $b = 0$ or $a = 1$
For $b = 0$, $a + 0 = -a$, $\Rightarrow a = 0$
For $a = 1$, $1 + b = -1 \Rightarrow b = -2$
Option (a) is correct.

42. For $x > 0$
$\Rightarrow x^2 + 3x + 2 = 0$
$\Rightarrow x^2 + 2x + x + 2 = 0$
$\Rightarrow (x + 2)(x + 1) = 0$
$\Rightarrow x = -1$ or $-2$
But here $x > 0$, so these values of $x$ are not possible in this case.
For $x < 0$
$\Rightarrow x^2 - 3x + 2 = 0$
$\Rightarrow (x - 2)(x - 1) = 0$
$\Rightarrow x = 1$ or $2$
But here $x < 0$, so these values of $x$ are not possible in this case.
Therefore the given equation has no real root.

43. $x^2 + (x + 1)^2 + (x - 2)^2 = 0$
It is possible when $x = 0$, $x + 1 = 0$, $x - 2 = 0$ (Since each of the terms within the brackets in the given expression is non-negative).
Thus we get the required values of $x = 0$, $x = -1$, $x = 2$ all at the same time. It is not possible that a variable would have the same. Therefore the given equation has no real root.

44. $a^x$ can never be equal to 0 for any real value of $x$. Therefore $3^{2x^2 + 3x + 1}$ can never be equal to 0 for any real value of $x$. So the given equation has no real solution.

45. $f(x) = -x^2 + x - 4$
The discriminant of the equation $f(x) = 0$ is less than zero. Therefore $f(x) = 0$ has no real root and the coefficient of $x^2$ is less than 0. Therefore $f(x) = -x^2 + x - 4$ opens downward. Hence option (c) is correct.

46. $f(x)$ is less than 0 for all real values of $x$ (As $D < 0$, $a < 0$).
Therefore $f(a) < 0$, $f(b) < 0$
$f(a) . f(b) > 0$
Hence option (a) is correct.

47. $|x|^2 - 2|x| - 3 = 0$
$\Rightarrow (|x| - 3)(|x| + 1) = 0$
$\Rightarrow |x| = 3, -1$
$|x| = -1$ is not possible
$\Rightarrow |x| = 3$
$\Rightarrow x = \pm 3$
Therefore for the given equation only two real roots are possible.

48. $3^{x^2 - 2x - 1} = 9 = 3^2$

$\Rightarrow x^2 - 2x - 1 = 2$

$\Rightarrow x^2 - 2x - 3 = 0$

$\Rightarrow (x - 3)(x + 1) = 0$

$\Rightarrow x = 3, -1$

The given equation has two solutions. Hence, there are two values of $x$ at which the equation is satisfied.

49. Let the roots of the equation $x^2 + kx + 15 = 0$ be $m$, $n$.

$m + n = -k$, $mn = 15$, $m - n = 2$

$(m + n)^2 - 4mn = (m - n)^2$

$k^2 - 60 = 4$

$k^2 = 64$

$k = +8, -8$

The Correct answer is 2.

50. $f(x) = x^2 - 8x + 12 = (x - 2)(x - 6)$

$\therefore f(x) \leq 0$ for $x = 2, 3, 4, 5$ and 6

$\therefore$ Correct answer is 5.

51. $f(x) = 0$ has two roots 2, 6 and curve of $f(x)$ opens upwards. So $f(x)$ is minimum for $f'(x) = 0$. This gives us $2x - 8 = 0$. Thus, the function would attain it's minimum at $x = 4$

Therefore $f(x)$ is minimum for $x = 4$.

### Level of Difficulty (II)

1. From (i) we have sum of roots = 14 and from (ii) we have product of roots = 48. Option (c) is correct.

2. Assume the equation to be $(x - 1)(x - 2) = 0$ which gives $a_1 = 1$, $a_2 = -3$ and $a_3 = 2$ and $r_1 = 1$, $r_2 = 2$. With this information check the options.

3. $\dfrac{\alpha}{b} + \dfrac{\beta}{\alpha} < 2 \rightarrow \dfrac{\alpha^2 + \beta^2}{\alpha\beta} < 2$

$\rightarrow \dfrac{(\alpha + \beta)^2 - 2\alpha^2\beta^2}{\alpha\beta} < 2$

Use the formulae for sum of the roots and product of the roots.

4. Solve using options. It can be seen that at $b = 0$ and $c = 0$ the condition is satisfied. It is also satisfied at $b = 1$ and $c = -2$.

5. $2/9 + 9/2 = 85/18$.

6. Solve using options, If the car's speed is 48 kmph, the truck's speed would be 32 kmph. The car would take 4 hours and the bus 6 hours.

7. For each of the given options it can be seen that the roots do not lie in the given interval. Thus, option (d) is correct.

8. Using $x = -2$, we get $4a - 2b + c = 4b - 2a + c = 0$.

Thus, $a = b$ and $a + b + c = 0$.

9. Use an approximation of the value of $p$ to get the correct option. Such questions are generally not worth solving through mathematical approaches under the constraint of time in the examination.

10. $g(f(x)) = 5x^2 + 10x + 5$

Roots are $-1$ and $-1$.

11. Solve using options.

For option a, $3b^2 = 16\ ac$

We can assume $b = 4$, $a = 1$ and $c = 3$.

Then the equation $ax^2 + bx + c = 0$ becomes:

$x^2 + 4x + 3 = 0 \Rightarrow x = -3$ or $x = -1$

which satisfies the given conditions.

12. $x^2 - 3x + 2 = 0$ gives its roots as $x = 1, 2$.

Put these values in the equation and then use the options.

13. Trial and error gives us value as $-1$ at $x = 0$. If you try more values, you will see that you cannot get a value between $-1$ and 2 for this expression.

14. $p^2 + 4p + 12 = 9$

$\Rightarrow p^2 + 4p + 3 = 0$

$p = -3$ and $-1$.

15. The roots would be of opposite sign as the product of roots is negative.

16. Use the value of $x = 1$ in each of the two quadratic equations to get the value of $a$ and $b$ respectively. With these values check the options for their validity.

17. We get $c = 4$ (by putting $x = 0$)

Then, at $x = -1$, $a - b + 4 = 4$. So $a - b = 0$.

At $x = -2$, $4a - 2b + 4 = 6 \Rightarrow 4a - 2b = 2 \Rightarrow 2a = 2 \Rightarrow a = 1$, Thus, option (a) is correct.

18. Solve by checking each option for the condition given. Option c gives: $x^2 + 2x = 0$ whose roots are $-2$ and 0.

19. The following cases will arise

**Case 1: $x > 0$**

$x^2 + 5x + 6 = 0$

On solving we get $x = -2, -3$ which is not possible as $x > 0$.

**Case 2: $x < 0$**

$x^2 - 5x + 6 = 0$

On solving we get $x = 2, 3$ which is not possible as $x < 0$.

So no real root is possible. Option (d) is correct.

20. We have to minimize : $R_1^2 + R_2^2$ or $(R_1 + R_2)^2 - 2R_1R_2$

$\Rightarrow (p - 2)^2 - 2 \times (-(p + 1)/2) = p^2 - 4p + 4 + p + 1$

$= p^2 - 3p + 5$.

This is minimized at $p = 1.5$. or $3/2$.

21. Go through trial and error. At $p = 2$, both roots are imaginary. So, option (c) is rejected.

At $p = 0$, roots are imaginary. So option (d) is rejected.

At $p = -1$, we have both roots positive and equal.
At $p > -1$, roots are imaginary Thus, option (b) is correct.

22. $b^2 - 4a \geq 0$ for real roots.
   If $b = 1$, no value possible for $a$.
   If $b = 2$, $a = 1$ is possible.
   If $b = 3$, $a$ can be either 1 or 2 and if $b = 4$, $a$ can be 1, 2, 3 or 4.
   Thus, we have 7 possibilities overall.

23. $(a + b + c)^2 = a^2 + b^2 + c^2 + 2(ab + bc + ca)$
   $\Rightarrow 1 + 2(ab + bc + ca)$.
   Since, $(a + b + c)^2 = \geq 0 \Rightarrow ab + bc + ca \geq -1/2$
   Option (d) is not in this range and is hence not possible.

25. $p(p - 1)/3 < 0$ (Product of roots should be negative).
   $\Rightarrow p(p - 1) < 0$
   $p^2 - p < 0$.
   This happens for $0 < p < 1$.
   Option (b) is correct.

26. Let there be '$n$' friends of Neha which would mean that the amount of total liquids consumed by the group would be $9n$. Further let the total amount (in litres) of cold drink consumed by Neha and her friends be '$x$' litres. Then, the amount of orange squash consumed by the friends will be $9n–x$. As per the given information, we know that Neha has consumed one-ninth of the total cold drink (i.e. $x/9$) and also that she has consumed one-eleventh of the total orange squash $(9n–x)/11$. Also, since Neha has consumed a total of 9 litres of the liquids we will get:
   $$\frac{x}{9} + \frac{(9n - x)}{11} = 9$$
   $\Rightarrow 11x + 81n - 9x = 891$
   $\rightarrow 2x + 81n = 891 \rightarrow x = (891 - 81n) \div 2$.
   In this equation, $n$ is an integer and $x$ should be less than $9n$. This gives rise to the inequality:
   $0 < x < 9n \rightarrow 0 < (891–81n)/2 < 9n \rightarrow 0 < 891 - 81n < 18n$.
   The only value of n that satisfies this inequality is at $n = 10$.
   This means that there were 10 friends in the group and the amount of liquids consumed in total would have been 90 litres (9 litres each). Putting this value in the equation, we get: $2x + 810 = 891 \rightarrow x = 40.5$. This would mean that Neha consumes $40.5/9 = 4.5$ litres of cold drink and hence she would consume 4.5 litres of orange squash. The required ratio would be 1:1.

27. Let the common root be '$m$'. Since we know that $Q_1(10) = 0$, it means that 10 would be one of the roots of $Q_1$. By the same logic it is given to us that 8 is one of the roots of $Q_2$. Using this information we have:

$Q_1 = c_1 \times (x - 10) \times (x - m)$
and $Q_2 = c_2 \times (x - 8) \times (x - m)$. Note: $c_1$ and $c_2$ are constants (each not equal to 0).

The only information we have beyond this is that the product $Q_1(4) \times Q_2(5) = 36$. However, it is evident that by replacing $x = 4$ and $x = 5$ in the expressions for $Q_1$ and $Q_2$ respectively, we would not get any conclusive value for $m$ since the value of $m$ would depend on the values of $c_1$ and $c_2$. You can see this happening here:
$c_1 \times -6 \times (4 - m) \times c_2 \times -3 \times (5 - m) = 36$
$c_1 \times c_2 \times (20 - 9m + m^2) = 2$
In this equation it can be clearly seen that the value of the common root '$m$' would be dependent on the values of $c_1$ and $c_2$ and hence we cannot determine the answer to the question. Option (d) becomes the correct answer.

28. Since we got: $c_1 \times c_2 \times (20 - 9m + m^2) = 2$ as the equation in the previous solution, we can see that if we insert $c_1 = 1/15$ and $c_2 = 1$ in this equation we will get:
$m^2 - 9m + 20 = 30 \rightarrow m^2 - 9m - 10 = 0 \rightarrow (m–10)(m+1) = 0 \rightarrow m = 10$ or $m = -1$. i.e., the common roots for the two equations could either be 10 or -1 giving rise to two cases for the quadratic equation $Q_2 = 0$:

**Case 1:** When the common root is 10; $Q_2$ would become $\rightarrow (x - 8)(x - 10) = x_2 - 18x + 80$. The sum of roots for $Q_2(x) = 0$ in this case would be 18.

**Case 2:** When the common root is -1; $Q_2$ would become $\rightarrow (x - 8)(x + 1) = x_2 - 7x - 8$. The sum of roots for $Q_1(x) = 0$ in this case would be 7.

Option (a) gives us a possible sum of roots as 18 and hence is the correct answer.

29. In order to solve this question, the first thing we need to do is to identify the pattern of the numbers in the expression. The series 7, 18, 31, 46 etc can be identified as 7, $7 + 11 \times 1$; $7 + 12 \times 2$; $7 + 13 \times 3$ and so on. Thus, the logic of the term when 39 is in the denominator is $7 + 39 \times 38 = 1489$ and the last term is $7 + 40 \times 39 = 1567$.
The series can be rewritten as:

$$\frac{[x]+7}{10}, 1+\frac{[x]+8}{11}, 2+\frac{[x]+7}{12}, 3+\frac{[x]+7}{13} \cdots 29+\frac{[x]+7}{39}$$

and $30 + \dfrac{[x]+7}{40}$

For each of these to be in their simplest forms, the value of $[x]$ should be such that $[x] + 7$ is co-prime to each of the 31 denominators (from 10 to 40). From amongst the options, Option (c) gives us a value such that $[x] + 7 = 101$ which is a prime number and would automatically be co-prime with the other values.

30. $x - y = 6$ $x = 6 + y$. Substituting this value of $x$ in the expression for the value of $P$ we get:

$P = 7(6 + y)^2 - 12y^2$

$P = 252 + 7y^2 + 84y - 12y^2 = 84y - 5y^2 + 252$

Differentiating $P$ with respect to $y$ and equating to zero we get:

$84 - 10y = 0 \rightarrow y = 8.4$

The maximum value of $P$ would be got by inserting $y = 8.4$ in the expression. It gives us:

$84 \times 8.4 - 5 \times 8.4^2 + 252 = 705.6 - 5 \times 70.56 + 252 = 957.6 - 352.8 = 604.8$.

31. Only in the case of Option (c) do we get the LHS of the equation $4a - 3b - 4c = 0$ such that all the $x$, $y$ and $z$ cancel each other out. Hence, Option (c) is the sole correct answer.

32. The equation can be thought of as $(x - 2m)$ $(x - 4m)$ $(x - 5m) = 0$. The value of the constant term would be given by $(-2m) \times (-4m) \times (-5m)$ which would give us an outcome of $-40m^3$ which is equal to $-1080$. Solving $-40m^3 = -1080 \rightarrow m = 3$. Hence, the roots of the equation being $2m$, $4m$ and $5m$ would be 6,12 and 15 respectively. Hence, the equation would become $(x - 6)$ $(x - 12)(x - 15) = 0$. The coefficient of $x^2$ would be $(-15x^2 - 6x^2 - 12x^2) = -33x^2$. Hence, the value of '$a$' would be $+33$. Option (c) would be the correct answer.

33. The value of the expression $\dfrac{1}{lm} + \dfrac{1}{mn} + \dfrac{1}{ln} = \dfrac{l m n}{}$ $(l + m + n)/l^2 m^2 n^2 = (l + m + n)/l m n$. For any cubic equation of the form $ax^3 + bx^2 + cx + d = 0$, the sum of the roots is given by $-b/a$; while the product of the roots is given by $-d/a$. The ratio $(l + m + n)/l m n = b/d = -20/-5 = 4$.

Option (c) is correct.

34. When you look at this question it seems that there are two equations with three unknowns. However a closer look of the second equation shows us that the second equation is the same as the first equation-i.e. $10p + 8g + 6m = 44$ and $5p + 4g + 3m = 22$ are nothing but one and the same equation. Hence you have only one equation with three unknowns. However, before you jump to the 'cannot be determined' answer consider this thought process.

The cost of 10 pears would be a multiple of 10 (since all costs are natural numbers). Similarly, the cost of 8 grapes would be a multiple of 8 while the cost of 6 mangoes would be a multiple of 6.

Thus, the first equation can be numerically thought of as follows :

By fixing the cost of 10 pears as a multiple of 10 and the cost of 8 grapes as a multiple of 8, we can see whether the cost of mangoes turns out to be a multiple of 6.

| Total cost | Total cost of 10 pears | Total cost of 8 grapes | Total cost of 6 mangoes | |
|---|---|---|---|---|
| 44 | 10 | 16 | 18 | Possible |
| 44 | 10 | 24 | 10 | Not possible |
| 44 | 10 | 32 | 2 | Not possible |
| 44 | 20 | 8 | 16 | Not possible |
| 44 | 20 | 24 | 0 | Not possible |
| 44 | 30 | 8 | 6 | Not possible since both the cost of mangoes and grapes turns out to be ₹ 1 per unit. (They have to be distinct.) |

Thus, there is only one possibility that fits into the situation. The cost per pear = ₹ 1. The cost per grape = ₹ 2 per unit and the cost per mango = ₹ 3 per unit. Hence, the total cost of 4 mangoes + 3 grapes = 12 + 6 = ₹ 18. Option (b) is correct.

35. There are 36 ways of distributing the sum of 37 between $a_1$ and $a_2$ such that both $a_1$ and $a_2$ are positive and integral. (From 1,36; 2,35; 3,34; 4,33...; 36,1) Similarly, there are $^9C_2$ (= 36) ways of distributing the residual value of 10 amongst $a_3$, $a_4$ and $a_5$. Thus, there are a total of $36 \times 36 = 1296$ ways of distributing the values amongst the five variables such that each of them is positive and integral. Option (d) is the correct answer.

36. Let the polynomial be $f(x) = ax^2 + bx + 10$.

The value of $f(5)$ in this case would be:

$f(5) = 25a + 5b + 10 = 75$

$f(-5) = 25a - 5b + 10 = 45$

$f(5) - f(-5) = 10b = 30 \rightarrow b = 3$. The polynomial expression is: $ax^2 + 3x + 10$.

Further, if we put the value of $b = 3$ in the equation for $f(5)$ we would get: $25a + 15 + 10 = 75 \rightarrow 25a = 50 \rightarrow a = 2$.

Since $f(p)$ and $f(q)$ are both equal to zero it means that $p$ and $q$ are the roots of the equation $2x^2 + 3x + 10 = 0$. Finding $p \times q$ would mean that we have to find the product of the roots of the equation. The

product of the roots would be equal to $10/2 = 5$.
Option (c) is the correct answer.

37. The various possibilities for the values of $a$ and $b$ (in terms of their being positive or negative) would be as follows:

Possibility 1: $a$ positive and $b$ positive;

Possibility 2: $a$ positive and $b$ negative;

Possibility 3: $a$ negative and $b$ positive;

Possibility 4: $a$ negative and $b$ negative.

Let us look at each of these possibilities one by one and check out which one of them is possible.

Possibility 1: If $a$ and $b$ are both positive the second equation becomes $a = 150$ (since the value of $|b| - b$ would be equal to zero if $b$ is positive). However, this value of '$a$' does not fit the first equation since the value of the LHS would easily exceed 75 if we use $a = 150$ in the first equation. Hence, the possibility of both $a$ and $b$ being positive is not feasible and can be rejected.

Through similar thinking the possibilities 3 and 4 are also rejected. Consider this:

For possibility 3: $a$ negative and $b$ positive the second equation would give us $a = 150$ which contradicts the presupposition that $a$ is negative. Hence, this possibility can be eliminated.

For possibility 4: $a$ negative and $b$ negative- the first equation would give us $b = 75$ (since the value of $|a| + a$ would be equal to zero if $a$ is negative) which contradicts the presupposition that $b$ is negative. Hence, this possibility can be eliminated.

The only possibility that remains is Possibility 2: $a$ positive and $b$ negative. In this case, the equations would transform as follows:

$|a| + a + b = 75$ would become $2a + b = 75$;

$a + |b| - b = 150$ would become $a - 2b = 150$.

Solving the two equations simultaneously we will get the value of $a = 60$ and $b = -45$.

The sum of $|a| + |b| = 60 + 45 = 105$

Option (a) is the correct answer.

38. The value of the expression would be dependent on the individual values of each of the terms in the expression. $[315^{1/3}]$ would give us a value of 6 and so would all the terms upto $[342^{1/3}]$. (as $6^3 = 216$ and $7^3 = 343$) Hence, the value of the expression from $[315^{1/3}] + [316^{1/3}] + ... + [342^{1/3}] = 28 \times 6 = 168$

Similarly, the value of the expression from $[343^{1/3}] + [344^{1/3}] + ... + [511^{1/3}] = 169 \times 7 = 1183$.

Also, the value of the expression from $[512^{1/3}] + [513^{1/3}] + ... + [515^{1/3}] = 4 \times 8 = 32$.

Thus, the answer $= 168 + 1183 + 32 = 1383$. Option (a) is correct.

39. The five consecutive integers can be represented by:

$(c - 2)$; $(c - 1)$; $c$; $(c + 1)$ and $(c + 2)$.
Then we have $a^2 + b^2 + c^2 = d^2 + e^2$ giving us:
$(c - 2)^2 + (c - 1)^2 + c^2 = (c + 1)^2 + (c + 2)^2 \rightarrow$
$3c^2 - 6c + 5 = 2c^2 + 6c + 5 \rightarrow$
$c^2 - 12c = 0 \rightarrow$
$c = 0$ or $c = 12$.
Hence, the possible values of $d = c + 1$ would be 1 or 13.
Option (d) is correct.

40. The profit of the 9 to 9 supermarket would be:
Total Sales Price $-$ Total cost price
$= 10 \times (15 + 16x) - 4x^2$
$= -4x^2 + 160x + 150$
The maximum value of this function can be traced by differentiating it with respect to $x$ and equating to 0. We get:
$-8x + 160 = 0 \rightarrow x = 20$. The maximum value of Profit would occur at $x = 20$.
The maximum profit would be $= -4 \times 20^2 + 160 \times 20 + 150 = -1600 + 3200 + 150 = 1750$.
Option (c) is the correct answer.

41. $\alpha + \beta = -m$ and $\alpha\beta = 1$
$\Rightarrow \gamma + \delta = -n$ and $\gamma\delta = 1$
$(\alpha - \gamma)(\beta - \gamma)(\alpha + \delta)(\beta + \delta) = (\alpha - \gamma)(\beta + \delta)(\beta - \gamma)(\alpha + \delta)$
$= [\alpha\beta + \alpha\delta - \gamma\beta - \gamma\delta][\alpha\beta + \beta\delta - \alpha\gamma - \gamma\delta]$
$= [1 + \alpha\delta - \gamma\beta - 1][1 + \beta\delta - \gamma\alpha - 1]$
$= (\alpha\delta - \gamma\beta)(\beta\delta - \gamma\alpha)$
$= 1.\delta^2 - \alpha^2.1 - \beta^2.1 + \gamma^2.1 = (\delta^2 + \gamma^2) - (\alpha^2 + \beta^2)$
$= [(\delta + \gamma)^2 - 2\delta\gamma] - [(\alpha + \beta)^2 - 2\alpha\beta]$
$= [(-n)^2 - 2.1] - [(-m)^2 - 2.1] = n^2 - m^2$
Option (a) is correct.

42. Roots of the given equation $= \dfrac{2a \pm \sqrt{4a^2 - 4ab}}{2b}$

$= \dfrac{a \pm \sqrt{a^2 - ab}}{b}$

$= \dfrac{\sqrt{a}\left(\sqrt{a} \pm \sqrt{a-b}\right)}{b} \times \dfrac{\sqrt{a} \mp \sqrt{a-b}}{\sqrt{a} \mp \sqrt{a-b}} = \dfrac{\sqrt{a}}{\sqrt{a} \pm \sqrt{a-b}}$.

Option (c) is correct.

43. $(x^2 + 3x - 10) = 0$
$(x - 2)(x + 5) = 0$ or $x = 2, -5$
Therefore for $x = +2$ and $x = -5$
$3x^4 + 2x^3 - ax^2 + bx - a + b - 4 = 0$
For $x = 2 \rightarrow 3(2)^4 + 2(2)^3 - 4a + 2b - a + b - 4 = 0$
$48 + 16 - 4a + 2b - a + b - 4 = 0$
$5a - 3b = 60$ ...(i)
For $x = -5$,
$3 \times (-5)^4 + 2 \times (-5)^3 - a \times (-5)^2 + b \times (-5) - a + b - 4 = 0$

$1875 - 250 - 25a - 5b - a + b - 4 = 0$

$26a + 4b = 1621$ ...(ii)

By solving equation (i) and (ii) we get:

$a \approx 52, b \approx 67$

44. Let $f(x) = 3x^2 - 4x + 7$

$f'(x) = 6x - 4 = 0$ or $x = 2/3$

The minimum value of $f(x)$ would then be given by:

$3(2/3)^2 - 4(2/3) + 7 = 17/3$

45. Discriminant of the given equation is $16 - 4(1 - p)$ $p$ or $16 - 4p(1 - p) > 0$ for $0 < p < 1$.

Sum of roots $\left(\dfrac{-4}{(1-p)}\right) < 0$ for $0 < p < 1$

Product of roots $\left(\dfrac{p}{1-p}\right) > 0$ for $0 < p < 1$.

Therefore, roots of the given equation are real and negative.

46. $y^2 - 2y \cos x + 1 = 0$ ... (i)

For real $y$ $D \geq 0$ we get that $4 \cos^2 x \geq 4$

This will be true when $\cos x \geq 1$ & $\cos x \leq -1$

As $-1 \leq \cos x \leq 1$: Hence, the only possible value of $\cos x$ for which $4(\cos^2 x - 1) \geq 0$ are 1 and $-1$.

Hence, number of possible real solutions are 2.

∴ Option (c) is the correct choice.

47. We are given that the expression $ax^3 + bx^2 + cx + d$ intersects the x-axis at 1 & $-1$. It means that at $x = 1$ and $-1$ the value of the given polynomial is equal to 0.

∴ $a + b + c + d = 0$ & $-a + b - c + d = 0$

∴ $2(b + d) = 0$

∴ $b + d = 0$          (1)

We are also given that, $ax^3 + bx^2 + cx + d$ intersects the y – axis at 2. This means that at $x = 0$, the value of the given polynomial is equal to 2.

$0 + d = 2$

∴ $d = 2$          (2)

From equations (1) & (2), $b = -2$

48. $(\alpha + 3)(\beta + 3)(\gamma + 3) = 27$

$\alpha\beta\gamma + 9(\alpha + \beta + \gamma) + 3(\alpha\beta + \beta\gamma + \gamma\alpha) + 27 = 27$

$P + 9m + 3n = 0$ (Note the product of the roots of the equation $x^3 - mx^2 + nx - p = 0$ would be equal to $p$, the sum of the roots would be equal to $m$, the pair-wise product of the roots would be equal to $n$.

49. Using mathematical induction, let us assume the roots to be 1, 2, 4.

The sum of the roots $= 1 + 2 + 4 = -q \rightarrow q = -7$

The product of the roots $= 1.2.4 = -s \rightarrow s = -8$

The pair-wise product of the roots $r = 1 \times 2 + 2 \times 4 + 4 \times 1 \Rightarrow r = 14$

Only option (b) satisfies for $r = 14$, $q = -7$, $s = -8$

So option (b) is correct.

50. Graph opens downward, so $a < 0$

As we can see that $\alpha < 2$, $\beta < -3$.

So sum of roots of $ax^2 + bx + c$ is less than 0 or

$-\dfrac{b}{a} < 0$

$or \dfrac{b}{a} > 0$

As $a < 0$, so $b < 0$

Product of the roots is also less than 0.

$\alpha\beta = \dfrac{c}{a} < 0$

As $a < 0$, so $c > 0$

Hence option (a) is correct.

51. $x^8 + 12$ is always greater than $x^8$.

So $(x^8 + 12)^{1/2}$ will always be greater than $(x^8)^{1/2} = x^4$

$x^4$ will always be greater than $x^4 - 2$

so $(x^8 - 12)^{1/2}$ will always be greater than $x^4 - 2$.

Hence, the LHS and the RHS of the given equation can never be equal to each other. This means that there are no solutions for the given equation. Hence, option (a) is correct.

52. For the inequality to be true for all values of $x$, the quadratic expression $x^2 + 4px + (p + 3)$ should have imaginary roots. Using the Discriminant $< 0$, we get:

$16p^2 - 4(p + 3) < 0$

$16p^2 - 4p - 12 < 0$

$4p^2 - p - 3 < 0$

$4p^2 - 4p + 3p - 3 < 0$

$4p(p - 1) + 3(p - 1) < 0$

$(4p + 3)(p - 1) < 0$

$p \in (-3/4, 1)$

Only possible integer value of $p$ in this range would be at $p = 0$.

Hence, there is only one integer value of $p$ that satisfies the condition.

53. $g(x) = x^3 - px^2 - \dfrac{q}{2}x - r = (x - p)(x - q)(x - r)$

$p + q + r = p$

$q + r = 0$          (i)

$pq + qr + pr = -\dfrac{q}{2} \Rightarrow p(q + r) + qr = -\dfrac{q}{2} \Rightarrow r = -\dfrac{1}{2}$

$q = \dfrac{1}{2}$

$pqr = r$

$pq = 1$

$p = 2$

$g(4) = (4)^3 - 2(4)^2 - \dfrac{1}{4}(4) + \dfrac{1}{2}$

$= 64 - 32 - 1 + \dfrac{1}{2}$

$= 31.5$

54. $(a + 2)(b + 2)(c + 2) = 47$

$abc + 4(a + b + c) + 2(ab + bc + ca) + 8 = 47$

$4p + 2q + r=39$

55. Let the roots of $x^2 + bx + 3b = 0$ are $a$ and $3a$.

$a + 3a = -b \Rightarrow 4a = -b$      (i)

$3a^2 = 3b \Rightarrow a^2 = b$      (ii)

By solving equation (i) and (ii), we get

$a = -4, b = 16$

Value of $3b = 3 \times 16 = 48$

56. The given equation is $x^2 - 33x + 17 \times 16 = 0$

$x^2 - 33x - 272 = 0$

Roots of the equation are 16, 17 or $b, b + 1$. Hence, Option (a) is correct.

57. $p + q = -5$

$q + r = -23$

$p + 2q + r = -28$ or $(p + r) + 2q = -28$---(i).

Since, $p$, $q$ and $r$ are in Arithmetic Progression, the value of $(p + r) = 2q$. Using this in equation (i), we get:

$4q = -28$ or $q = -7$. Using the logic of the Arithmetic Progression, we can get the values of $p$ and $r$ respectively as:

$p = 2, r = -16$

$|a \times b| = |pq \times qr| = pq^2r| = |2 \times -7^2 \times -16| = 1568$

58. $f(x) = (x - 2)(x^2 + 2x + 5) = x^3 - 2x^2 + 2x^2 + 5x - 4x - 10$

$= x^3 + x - 10$

$a + b + c = 0$      $abc = 10$

If $a + b + c = 0$ then

$a^3 + b^3 + c^3 = 3abc = 3 \times (10) = 30$

59. $f(x)$ is exactly divisible by $(x + 2)$, $(x + 3)$

Therefore $f(-2) = f(-3) = 0$

$4p - 2q + r = 0$      (i)

$9p - 3q + r = 0$      (ii)

Also, since the remainder of $f(x)$ when divided by $(x - 1)$ is 7, we can use $f(1) = 7$, which in turn gives us that:

$p + q + r = 7$      (iii)

By solving equations (i), (ii), (iii) we get $q \approx 2.92$

60. $f(x) = 4x - 7\sqrt{x} = 2$

Let $t = \sqrt{x}$

$\Rightarrow 4t^2 - 7t = 2$

$\Rightarrow 4t^2 - 7t - 2 = 0$

$\Rightarrow 4t(t - 2) + 1(t - 2) = 0$

$\Rightarrow t = -\dfrac{1}{4}, 2$

$\Rightarrow \sqrt{x} = -\dfrac{1}{4}$ or $2$.  (However, the value of $\sqrt{x} = -\dfrac{1}{4}$

is not possible)

$\sqrt{x} = 2 \rightarrow x = 4$

Only option (c) is correct.

61. $b^2 - 4a^2 \geq 0$ (roots are real)

$(b - 2a)(b + 2a) \geq 0$

Both the roots are positive therefore the sum of the roots must be greater than 0.

$-\dfrac{b}{a} > 0$

But $a > 0$ so $b$ must be less than 0.

$\therefore b - 2a < 0$ or $b < 2a$ & $b + 2a \leq 0$ or $b \leq -2a$.

Therefore all the options are true.

62. $(x - p)(x - q) + (x - q)(x - r) + (x - r)(x - p) = 0$

$\Rightarrow x^2 - (p + q)x + pq + x^2 - (q + r)x + qr + x^2 - (p + r)x + pr = 0$

$3x^2 - 2(p + q + r)\, x + pq + qr + pr = 0$

Discriminant of the above equation $= 4(p + q + r)^2 - 12(pq + qr + pr)$

$= 4[p^2 + q^2 + r^2 + 2pq + 2pr + 2qr - 3pq - 3pr - 3qr]$

$= 4[p^2 + q^2 + r^2 - pr - qr - pr]$

$= \dfrac{4}{2}\left[(p-q)^2 + (q-r)^2 + (p-r)^2\right]$

$= 2[(p - q)^2 + (q - r)^2 + (p - r)^2]$

As $p$, $q$, $r$ are not equal to each other, so the discriminant of the given equation is always greater than 0, therefore the roots are real.

Option (b) is true.

63. $f\left(\dfrac{1}{x}\right) = p\left(\dfrac{1}{x}\right)^2 + q\left(\dfrac{1}{x}\right) + r$

$= rx^2 + qx + p$

$= g(x)$

Therefore, the roots of $g(x)$ and $f(x)$ are the inverse of each other.

$\therefore$ The roots of $f(x) = 0$ are 2 and 4

The Roots of $g(x) = 0$ are $\dfrac{1}{2}, \dfrac{1}{4}$

Required sum $= 2 + 4 + \dfrac{1}{2} + \dfrac{1}{4} = 6.75$

64. When the curve intersects the x – axis, then $y = 0$

$\Rightarrow x^2 - 5x = 0$

$\Rightarrow (x)(x - 5) = 0$ or $x = 0, 5$

When the curve intersects the y – axis then $x = 0$

$y^3 - 4y^2 + 3y = 0$

$y(y^2 - 4y + 3) = 0$

$y(y - 3)(y - 1) = 0$

$y = 0, 1, 3$

Therefore number of required points are 5.

65. Let $x$ and $y$ be the roots of the given equation. Then,

$x + y = \dfrac{-q}{p}$ and $x \times y = \dfrac{r}{p}$

Now, $\dfrac{1}{x^2} + \dfrac{1}{y^2} = \dfrac{x^2 + y^2}{(xy)^2} = \dfrac{(x+y)^2 - 2xy}{(xy)^2}$

$$= \frac{\left(\frac{-q}{p}\right)^2 - 2\left(\frac{r}{p}\right)}{\left(\frac{r}{p}\right)^2}$$

As per the question:

$$\frac{-q}{p} = \frac{\left(\frac{-q}{p}\right)^2 - 2\left(\frac{r}{p}\right)}{\left(\frac{r}{p}\right)^2}$$

$$\Rightarrow 2p^2r = pq^2 + qr^2$$

$$\Rightarrow \frac{p^2r}{pqr} = \frac{pq^2}{pqr} + \frac{qr^2}{pqr} \qquad \text{(dividing by } pqr\text{)}$$

$$\Rightarrow \frac{2p}{q} = \frac{q}{r} + \frac{r}{p} \qquad (1)$$

From equation 1 it is clear that $\frac{r}{p}$, $\frac{p}{q}$ and $\frac{q}{r}$ are in arithmetic progression so option (a) is correct.

As $\frac{q^2}{p^2} \neq \frac{p}{r} \times \frac{r}{q} = \frac{p}{q}$, so option (b) is incorrect.

Option (c): As $\frac{r}{p}$, $\frac{p}{q}$ and $\frac{q}{r}$ are in arithmetic progression, their reciprocals are in harmonic progression. Therefore this option is also correct.

Hence option (d) is correct.

### Level of Difficulty (III)

1. $f(0)$ is greater than or equals to 0 means that the value of $c \geq 0$. Also, since '$a$' is negative as given in the question, the product of the roots given by $\frac{c}{a}$ would be negative or zero. So the roots of $f(x) = 0$ are of opposite sign or their product is zero.

   So the possibilities for the two roots from the given values are: (0, 2), (0, 1), (1, –2), (0, –1), (0, –2), (–1, 2), ( –2, 2), ( –1, 1). Therefore a total of 8 different sets are possible for the roots of $f(x) = 0$.

   Option (c) is correct.

2. Let $f(x) = px^2 + qx + r$

   $px^2 + qx + r = 0$. Here two cases are possible:

   **Case I:** $p > 0$

   When $p > 0$ then $px^2 + qx + r$ will open upward and $p \times f(2) < 0$ will give us that $p(4p + 2q + r) < 0$. This is the same value as option (a). Hence, option (a) is correct. Option (b) is automatically rejected since it is the opposite of option (a).

   Note: Option (c) is rejected because In this case whether $p \times f(-2)$ [Which will give us $p(4p - 2q$

+ r] is greater than or less than zero depends upon the location of the other root which is less than 1. Similarly, Option (d) is rejected as it is asking you to commit about the value of $p \times f(-3) < 0$. Whether this value is greater than or less than zero depends upon the location of the other root of $f(x) = 0$ (which is less than 1)

So option (b), (c), (d) are not necessarily be true.

**Case II:** $p < 0$

When $p < 0$ then $p f(2) < 0$ [because $f(x)$ will open downward].

In this case whether $p f(-2)$, $p f(-3)$ will be greater than or less than zero depends upon the location of the other root of $f(x) = 0$. So only option (a) is correct in this case too.

3. $f(x, y) = 5$

   $4^{x^y} + x^{4^y} = 5$

   If $x = 1$, then the above equation satisfies for any integral value of $y$. So option (d) is correct.

4. $d$ is $a$ root of the equation $ax^2 + bx + c = 0$

   $\therefore ad^2 + bd + c = 0 \qquad (i)$

   $c$ is $a$ root of the equation $ax^2 + bx + d = 0$

   $\therefore ac^2 + bc + d = 0 \qquad (ii)$

   Equation (ii) – equation (i):

   $a(c^2 - d^2) + b(c - d) + (d - c) = 0$

   $a(c - d)(c + d) + b(c - d) - (c - d) = 0$

   $(c - d)[a(c + d) + b - 1] = 0$. In this expression, the value of $[a(c + d) + b - 1]$ has to be zero because it is given that $c \neq d$.

   Solving: $[a(c+d)+b-1] = 0$, we get $(c + d) = \frac{1-b}{a}$

   Option (c) is correct.

5. $-(c+d) = \frac{b-1}{a}$ (iii) (From the solution of the previous question) Note: This gives us the sum of the roots of the required equation, whose roots are $-c$ and $-d$.

   Next in order to get the product of the roots of the required equation: Divide equation (i) by $d$ and equation (ii) by $c$ and then by equating we get:

   $$\frac{ad^2 + bd + c}{d} = \frac{ac^2 + bc + d}{c}$$

   $$\left(ad + b + \frac{c}{d}\right) = ac + b + \frac{d}{c}$$

   $$a(c - d) = \frac{c}{d} - \frac{d}{c} = \frac{(c-d)(c+d)}{cd}$$

   $$cd = \frac{c+d}{a} = \frac{1-b}{a^2} \qquad \text{(iv) (product of roots of the required equation)}$$

Equation whose roots are $-c, -d$ is

$x^2 - (sum\ of\ roots)x + product\ of\ roots = 0$

$x^2 - \dfrac{b-1}{a}x + \dfrac{1-b}{a^2} = 0$

$ax^2 + a(1-b)x + 1 - b = 0$

Option $(c)$ is correct.

6. Let $f(x) = ax^2 + bx + c$

$f(4) = 16a + 4b + c = 0$    [At $x = 4$ $f(x) = 0$].

$f(0) = c = 10$

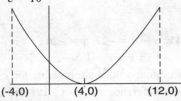

$(-4,0)$     $(4,0)$     $(12,0)$

$f(x)$ is symmetric about $x = 4$.

$f(3) = f(5)$

$9a + 3b + c = 25a + 5b + c$

$16a + 2b = 0$

$8a + b = 0$

$b = -8a$

$f(4) = 0$

$16a + 4b + 10 = 0$

$16a - 32a + 10 = 0$

$a = \dfrac{10}{16} = \dfrac{5}{8}$

$f(-4) = 16a - 4b + 10$

$= 16 \times \dfrac{5}{8} - 4 \times (-8) \times \dfrac{5}{8} + 10$

$= 10 + 20 + 10 = 40$

Alternative method: the minimum value of $f(x)$ must be 0 and this minima occur at $x = 4$.

Let $f(x) = a(x-4)^2$

$f(0) = 16a = 10$

$a = \dfrac{5}{8}$

Hence $f(x) = \dfrac{5}{8}(x-4)^2$

$f(-4) = \dfrac{5}{8} \times (-8)^2 = 40$

7. 4 lies in between roots of the equations so:

$3(4)^2 + 4a\,(4) + a + 3 < 0$

$48 + 16a + a + 3 < 0$

$17a + 51 < 0$

$a < -3$

Option $(a)$ is correct.

8. $f(x) = x^3 - (5+k)x^2 + (6 + 5k)x - 6k$

Let $k = 5$

$f(x) = x^3 - 10x^2 + 31x - 30$

By factorization we get:

$f(x) = (x-2)(x-3)(x-5)$

$f(x) < 0$ for $x < 2,\ 3 < x < 5$.

Similarly we can put few other values of $x$ and confirm that $f(x) < 0$ for $x < 2$ and for $3 < x < k$

9. $f(x, 5) = a(x-5)^2 + b(x-5) + c$

$ax^2 + bx + c$ has roots 3, 4. Then roots of $f(x, 5)$ are

$5 + 3, 5 + 4 = 8, 9$.

$f(x, 5)$ attains it's maximum value at $\dfrac{8}{2}\dfrac{9}{2} = \dfrac{17}{2} = 8.5$

Option $(b)$ is correct.

10. $[x]^2 - 11[x] + 30 = 0$

$[x]^2 - 5[x] - 6[x] + 30 = 0$

$([x] - 5)([x] - 6) = 0$

$[x] = 5, 6$

The integer solutions of $x$ are at $x = 5$ and 6

So the required $sum = 5 + 6 = 11$

11. If the three roots are $x, y, z$

$\Rightarrow x + y + z = 12$

Only one combination of $(x, y, z) = (2, 3, 7)$ is possible.

Product of the roots $= 2 \times 3 \times 7 = 42$.

So the chosen values are correct.

$p = 2 \times 3 + 3 \times 7 + 2 \times 7 = 6 + 21 + 14 = 41$

12. $f(x) = g(x)$

$x^3 - px^2 - 2qx + r = (x-p)(x-q)(x-r)$

$p + q + r = p \Rightarrow q + r = 0$  \hfill (1)

$pq + qr + pr = -2q$

$p(q + r) + qr = -2q$

As $q + r = 0$ from equation 1 therefore $qr = -2q$

$r = -2$

$q = +2$

$pqr = -r$

$pq = -1$

$p = -1/2$

So the required value of $p + q = -\dfrac{1}{2} + 2 = \dfrac{3}{2}$

13. $f(x) = g(x)$

$f(x) = g(x) = (x-p)(x-q)(x-r)$

$f(4) = \left(4 + \dfrac{1}{2}\right)(4-2)(4+2)$

$= \dfrac{9}{2} \times 2 \times 6$

$= 54$

14. $a:b:c:d:e = 1:2:3:4:5$

$f(x) = x^2 + 7x + 5$

Let the roots of $f(x) = 0$ be $A$ and $B$

$(A - B)^2 = (A + B)^2 - 4AB = (-7)^2 - 4 \times 5 = 29$

15. $\log_3 x \times \log_3 y + \log_3 z \times \log_3 xy = 11$

$\log_3 x \times \log_3 y + \log_3 z\, [\log_3 x + \log_3 y] = 11$

Let $\log_3 x = A, \log_3 y = B, \log_3 z = C$

$AB + C[A + B] = 11$

$AB + BC + AC = 11$

$\& \ A^2 + B^2 = 14 - C^2$

$A^2 + B^2 + C^2 = 14$

This clearly identifies the values of $A$, $B$ and $C$ as 1,2, and 3. Thus, we get $x$, $y$ and $z$ as 3, 9 and 27 in no particular order. Also

$xyz = 3^6 = (3^2)^3 = (3^3)^2$

*Therefore* $k_1 = 3^3 \& \ k_2 = 3^2$

$k_1 + k_2 = 3^3 + 3^2 = 27 + 9 = 36$

16. $(x - 3)$ is a factor of $f(x)$ then $f(3) = 0$

$9a - 150 \times 3 + 5b = 0$

$9a - 450 + 5b = 0$

$a = 50 - \dfrac{5}{9}b$

$a \ \& \ b$ are positive integers, therefore $b$ must be a multiple of 9.

For $b = 9$, $a = 45$

$b = 18$, $a = 40$

$b = 27$, $a = 35$

$b = 36$, $a = 30$

$b = 45$, $a = 25$

$b = 54$, $a = 20$

$b = 63$, $a = 15$

$b = 72$, $a = 10$

$b = 81$, $a = 5$

Therefore total possible ordered pairs of $(a, b)$ is 9

17. Maximum possible value of $a + b = 81 + 5 = 86$

18. If $a \ \& \ b$ are integers then $a \ \& \ b$ both can be negative then there are infinite pairs of $(a, b)$ for which $(x - 3)$ is a factor of $f(x)$.

Hence, option $(d)$ is correct.

19. $f(x) = x^3 - 12x^2 + 47x - 60 = (x - 3)(x - 4)(x - 5)$

The possible equations are:

$(x - 3)^2, (x - 4)^2, (x - 5)^2, (x - 3)(x - 4), (x - 4)(x - 5), (x - 3)(x - 5)$. We get a total of 6 such equations. Hence, option (c) is correct.

20. Required product $= 3^2 \times 4^2 \times 5^2 \times 4 \times 5 \times 3 \times 5 \times 3 \times 4$

$p = 3^4 \times 4^4 \times 5^4$

$p^{1/4} = 3 \times 4 \times 5 = 60$

Option $(d)$ is correct.

21. $(x - k)^3 (x - 7) - 27 = 0$

$(x - k)^3 (x - 7) = 27$

Roots of the equations are integers, which means that $x$ is an integer. Now the following four cases are possible:

**Case I:** $(x - k)^3 = 27$, $x - 7 = 1$

**Case II:** $(x - k)^3 = 1$, $x - 7 = 27$

**Case III:** $(x - k)^3 = -27$, $x - 7 = -1$

**Case IV:** $(x - k)^3 = -1$, $x - 7 = -27$

**Case I:** $x - 7 = 1 \Rightarrow x = 8$

$(8 - k)^3 = 27$

$8 - k = 3$

$k = 5$

**Case II:** $(x - 7) = 27 \Rightarrow x = 34$

$(x - k)^3 = 1 \Rightarrow 34 - k = 1$

$k = 33$

**Case III:** $(x - k)^3 = -27$, $x - 7 = -1$

Therefore, $x = 6$

$x - k = -3$

$k = 9$

**Case IV:** $x - 7 = -27$, $x = -20$

$x - k = -1$ or $k = x + 1 = -20 + 1 = -19$

Therefore four values are possible for $k$.

22. Required difference $= 33 - (-19) = 52$.

23. Let the roots of the quadratic equation be $a$, $b$

$a + b = (p - 3)$

$ab = (p - 4)$

$a^2 + b^2 = (p - 3)^2 - 2(p - 4)$

$= (p - 3)^2 - 2(p - 4)$

$= (p - 3)^2 - 2(p - 3) + 1 + 1$

$= (p - 3 - 1)^2 + 1$

$= (p - 4)^2 + 1$

$(a^2 + b^2)$ is minimum for $p = 4$.

24. $f(x) = g(x)$

$x^2 = x^3 - 2^x$

$x^3 - x^2 = 2^x$

$x^2(x - 1) = 2^x$

for $x = 2$; $x^2(x - 1) = 2^x$

For $x > 2$, either $x^2$ or $(x - 1)$ is odd and hence $x^2(x - 1)$ cannot be equal to $2^x$. Therefore $f(x) = g(x)$ only for one value of $x$.

25. $3h(x) + 5t(x) = 0$

$t(x) = -\dfrac{3}{5}h(x)$

If $h(x) = -(x - p)(x - q)$ then $t(x) = \dfrac{3}{5}(x - p)(x - q)$

Therefore roots of $t(x)$ and $h(x)$ are same, so their sums are also equal. Option (c) is correct.

26. if $h(x)$ is maximum at $x = 4$ then $t(x)$ will be minimum at $t = 4$ and it's minimum value will be $-\dfrac{3}{5}$ times of the maximum value of $h(x)$.

$t(x)|_{\min} = -\dfrac{3}{5}h(x)|_{\max} = -\dfrac{3}{5} \times 10 = -6$

27. If we see the graph carefully, then we get:

For $x < 0$ $f(x) = (x - (-3))(x - (-2)) = (x + 2)(x + 3)$

For $x > 0$ $f(x) = (x - 2)(x - 3)$

$\Rightarrow f(x) = (|x| - 2)(|x| - 3)$

$|x|^2 - 5|x| + 6 = 0$

$$\frac{6}{|x|} = 5 - |x|$$

∴ Option (c) is correct.

Alternately, you can try to put the values of x as −2, −3, 2 and 3 in the options to see which of the given options satisfies the conditions of the problem.

28. $f(x) = max(|x^2 - 4|, 2x + 4)$

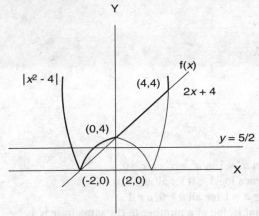

As we can see in the diagram shown above that $y = \frac{5}{2}$ intercepts $f(x)$ at two different points therefore the given equation has two solutions.

29. $||x| - 1| = e^x$

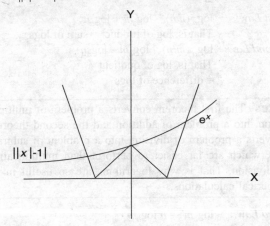

The Curve of $e^x$ cuts the curve of $||x| - 1|$ at three points. Therefore, the given equation has three solutions.

30. $||x| - 1|$ would look like the figure shown below:

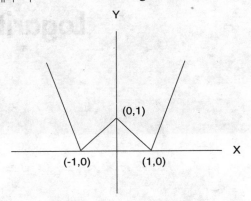

$||x| - 1| - 2$ would look like the figure shown below:

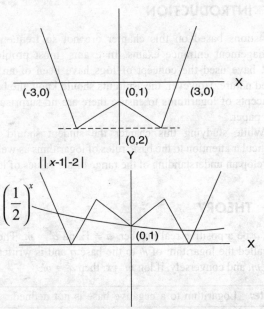

The graph of $(1/2)^x$ cuts the graph of $||x - 1| - 2|$ at five distinct points. Therefore the given equation has five solutions.

# 16

# Logarithms

## INTRODUCTION

Questions based on this chapter are not so frequent in management entrance exams. In exams, most problems that have used the concept of logs have been of an applied nature. However, the aspirants should know the basic concepts of logarithms to ensure there are no surprises in the paper.

While studying this chapter the student should pay particular attention to the basic rules of logarithms as well as develop an understanding of the range of the values of logs.

## THEORY

Let $a$ be a positive real number, $a \neq 1$ and $a^x = m$. Then $x$ is called the logarithm of $m$ to the base $a$ and is written as $\log_a m$, and conversely, if $\log_a m = x$, then $a^x = m$.

**Note:** Logarithm to a negative base is not defined.

Also, logarithm of a negative number is not defined. Hence, in the above logarithmic equation, $\log_a m = x$, and we can say that $m > 0$ and $a > 0$.

Thus $a^x = m \Rightarrow x = \log_a m$ and $\log_a m = x \Rightarrow a^x = m$

**In short, $a^x = m \Rightarrow x = \log_a m$.**

$x = \log_a m$ **is called the logarithmic form and $a^x = m$ is called the exponential form of the equation connecting $a$, $x$ and $m$.**

## Two Properties of Logarithms

1. $\log_a 1 = 0$ **for all $a > 0$, $a \neq 1$**
   **That is, log 1 to any base is zero**
   Let $\log_a 1 = x$. Then by definition, $a^x = 1$

But $a^0 = 1$ ∴ $a^x = a^0 \Leftrightarrow x = 0$.
Hence $\log_a 1 = 0$ for all $a > 0$, $a \neq 1$

2. $\log_a a = 1$ **for all $a > 0$, $a \neq 1$**
   **That is, log of a number to the same base is 1**
   Let $\log_a a = x$. Then by definition, $a^x = a$.
   But $a^1 = a$ ∴ $a^x = a^1 \Rightarrow x = 1$.
   Hence $\log_a a = 1$ for all $a > 0$, $a \neq 1$.

## Laws of Logarithms

*First Law:*    $\log_a(mn) = \log_a m + \log_a n$
               That is, log of product = sum of logs
*Second Law:* $\log_a(m/n) = \log_a m - \log_a n$
               That is, log of quotient
               = difference of logs

**Note:** The first theorem converts a problem of multiplication into a problem of addition and the second theorem converts a problem of division into a problem of subtraction, which are far easier to perform than multiplication or division. That is why logarithms are so useful in all numerical calculations.

*Third Law:*    $\log_a m^n = n \log_a m$

## Generalisation

1. $\log(mnp) = \log m + \log n + \log p$
2. $\log(a_1 a_2 a_3 \dots a_k) = \log a_1 + \log a_2 + \dots + \log a_k$

**Note:** *Common logarithms*: We shall assume that the base $a = 10$ whenever it is not indicated. Therefore, we shall denote $\log_{10} m$ by $\log m$ only. The logarithm calculated to base 10 are called common logarithms.

## The Characteristic and Mantissa of a Logarithm

The logarithm of a number consists of two parts: the *integral* part and the *decimal* part. The integral part is known as the *characteristic* and the decimal part is called the *mantissa*.

For example,

In log 3257 = 3.5128, the integral part is 3 and the decimal part is .5128; therefore, characteristic = 3 and mantissa = .5128.

*It should be remembered that the mantissa is always written as positive.*

*Rule:* To make the mantissa positive (in case the value of the logarithm of a number is negative), subtract 1 from the integral part and add 1 to the decimal part.

Thus,  $-3.4328 = -(3 + .4328) = -3 - 0.4328$
$$= (-3 - 1) + (1 - 0.4328)$$
$$= -4 + .5672.$$

so the mantissa is = .5672.

**Note:** The characteristic may be positive or negative. When the characteristic is negative, it is represented by putting a bar on the number.

Thus instead of $-4$, we write $\bar{4}$.

Hence we may write $-4 + .5672$ as $\bar{4}.5672$.

## Base Change Rule

Till now all rules and theorems you have studied in Logarithms have been related to operations on logs with the same basis. However, there are a lot of situations in Logarithm problems where you have to operate on logs having different basis. The base change rule is used in such situations.

This rule states that

(i)  $\log_a (b) = \log_c (b)/\log_c (a)$

It is one of the most important rules for solving logarithms.

(ii)  $\log_b (a) = \log_c (a)/\log_b (c)$
A corollary of this rule is

(iii)  $\log_a (b) = 1/\log_b (a)$

(iv)  log $c$ to the base $a^b$ is equal to $\dfrac{\log a^c}{b}$.

## Results on Logarithmic Inequalities

(a) If $a > 1$ and $\log_a x_1 > \log_a x_2$ then $x_1 > x_2$
(b) If $a < 1$ and $\log_a x_1 > \log_a x_2$ then $x_1 < x_2$

*Applied conclusions for logarithms*

1. The characteristic of common logarithms of any positive number less than 1 is negative.
2. The characteristic of common logarithm of any number greater than 1 is positive.
3. If the logarithm to any base $a$ gives the characteristic $n$, then we can say that the number of integers possible is given by $a^{n+1} - a^n$.

**Example:** $\log_{10} x = 2.bcde...$, then the number of integral values that $x$ can take is given by: $10^{2+1} - 10^2 = 900$. This can be physically verified as follows. Log to the base 10 gives a characteristic of 2 for all 3 digit numbers with the lowest being 100 and the highest being 999. Hence, there are 900 integral values possible for $x$.

4. If $-n$ is the characteristic of $\log_{10} y$, then the number of zeros between the decimal and the first significant number after the decimal is $n - 1$.

Thus if the log of a number has a characteristic of $-3$ then the first two decimal places after the decimal point will be zeros.

Thus, the value will be $-3.00ab...$

*Space for Notes*

## 🎯 WORKED-OUT PROBLEMS

**Problem 16.1** Find the value of $x$ in $3^{|3x-4|} = 9^{2x-2}$

    (a) 8/7             (b) 7/8

    (c) 7/4             (d) 16/7

**Solution** Take the log of both sides, then we get,

$$|3x-4| \log 3 = (2x-2) \log 9$$
$$= (2x-2) \log 3^2$$
$$= (4x-4) \log 3$$

Dividing both sides by log 3, we get

$$|3x-4| = (4x-4) \tag{1}$$

Now,      $|3x-4| = 3x-4$ if $x > 4/3$

so if         $x > 4/3$

$$3x-4 = 4x-4$$

or           $3x = 4x$

or           $3 = 4$

But this is not possible.

Let's take the case of $x < 4/3$

Then       $|3x-4| = 4-3x$

Therefore, $4-3x = 4x-4$ from     (1)

or           $7x = 8$

or           $x = 8/7$

**Problem 16.2** Solve for $x$.

$$\log_{10} x - \log_{10} \sqrt{x} = 2 \log_x 10$$

**Solution** Now, $\log_{10} \sqrt{x} = \frac{1}{2} \times \log_{10} x$

Therefore, the equation becomes

$$\log_{10} x - \frac{1}{2} \log_{10} x = 2 \log_x 10$$

or      $\frac{1}{2} \log_{10} x = 2 \log_x 10 \tag{2}$

Using base change rule ($\log_b a = 1/\log_a b$)

Therefore, equation (2) becomes

$$\frac{1}{2} \log_{10} x = 2/\log_{10} x$$

$\Rightarrow$       $(\log_{10} x)^2 = 4$

or        $\log_{10} x = 2$

Therefore,     $x = 100$

**Problem 16.3** If $7^{x+1} - 7^{x-1} = 48$, find $x$.

**Solution** Take $7^{x-1}$ as the common term. The equation then reduces to

$$7^{x-1}(7^2 - 1) = 48$$
or          $7^{x-1} = 1$
or      $x-1 = 0$ or $x = 1$

**Problem 16.4** Calculate: $\log_2(2/3) + \log_4(9/4)$

$$= \log_2(2/3) + (\log_2(9/4)/\log_2 4)$$
$$= \log_2(2/3) + 1/2 \log_2(9/4)$$
$$= \log_2(2/3) + 1/2 (2 \log_2 3/2)$$
$$= \log_2 2/3 + \log_2 3/2 = \log_2 1 = 0$$

**Problem 16.5** Find the value of the expression

$1/\log_3 2 + 2/\log_9 4 - 3/\log_{27} 8$

Passing to base 2

we get

$$\log_2 3 + 2\log_2 9 - 3\log_2 27$$

$$= \log_2 3 + \frac{4 \log_2 3}{2} - \frac{9 \log_2 3}{3}$$

$$= 3\log_2 3 - 3\log_2 3$$

$$= 0$$

**Problem 16.6** Solve the inequality.

(a)        $\log_2(x+3) < 2$

$\Rightarrow$          $2^2 > x+3$

$\Rightarrow$          $4 > x+3$

              $1 > x$

or              $x < 1$

But log of negative number is not possible.

Therefore,    $x+3 \geq 0$

That is,       $x \geq -3$

Therefore,    $-3 \leq x < 1$

(b)    $\log_2(x^2 - 5x + 5) > 0$

$$= x^2 - 5x + 5 > 1$$
$$\rightarrow x^2 - 5x + 4 > 0$$
$$\rightarrow (x-4)(x-1) > 0$$

Therefore, the value of $x$ will lie outside 1 and 4.

That is, $x > 4$ or $x < 1$.

*Space for Rough Work*

## LEVEL OF DIFFICULTY (I)

1. log 32700 = ?
   (a) log 3.27 + 4        (b) log 3.27 + 2
   (c) 2 log 327           (d) 100 × log 327

2. log . 0867 = ?
   (a) log 8.67 + 2        (b) log 8.67 − 2
   (c) $\dfrac{\log 867}{1000}$        (d) −2 log 8.67

3. If $\log_{10} 2$ = .301 find $\log_{10} 125$.
   (a) 2.097               (b) 2.301
   (c) 2.10                (d) 2.087

4. $\log_{32} 8$ = ?
   (a) 2/5                 (b) 5/3
   (c) 3/5                 (d) 4/5

*Find the value of x in equations 5–6.*

5. $\log_{0.5} x = 25$
   (a) $2^{-25}$          (b) $2^{25}$
   (c) $2^{-24}$          (d) $2^{24}$

6. $\log_3 x = \dfrac{1}{2}$
   (a) 3                   (b) $\sqrt{3}$
   (c) $\dfrac{3}{2}$     (d) $\dfrac{2}{3}$

7. $\log_{15} 3375 \times \log_4 1024$ = ?
   (a) 16                  (b) 18
   (c) 12                  (d) 15

8. $\log_a 4 + \log_a 16 + \log_a 64 + \log_a 256 = 10$. Then $a$ = ?
   (a) 4                   (b) 2
   (c) 8                   (d) 5

9. $\log_{625} \sqrt{5}$ = ?
   (a) 4                   (b) 8
   (c) 1/8                 (d) 1/4

10. If log x + log (x + 3) = 1 then the value(s) of x will be, the solution of the equation
    (a) x + x + 3 = 1      (b) x + x + 3 = 10
    (c) x (x + 3) = 10     (d) x (x + 3) = 1

11. If $\log_{10} a = b$, find the value of $10^{3b}$ in terms of $a$.
    (a) $a^3$             (b) 3a
    (c) a × 1000          (d) a × 100

12. 3 log 5 + 2 log 4 − log 2 = ?
    (a) 4                  (b) 3
    (c) 200                (d) 1000

*Solve equations 13–25 for the value of x.*

13. log (3x − 2) = 1
    (a) 3                  (b) 2
    (c) 4                  (d) 6

14. log (2x − 3) = 2
    (a) 103                (b) 51.5
    (c) 25.75              (d) 26

15. log (12 − x) = −1
    (a) 11.6               (b) 12.1
    (c) 11                 (d) 11.9

16. log ($x^2$ − 6x + 6) = 0
    (a) 5                  (b) 1
    (c) Both (a) and (b)   (d) 3 and 2

17. log $2^x$ = 3
    (a) 9.87               (b) 3 log 2
    (c) 3/log 2            (d) 9.31

18. $3^x = 7$
    (a) $1/\log_7 3$      (b) $\log_7 3$
    (c) $1/\log_3 7$      (d) $\log_3 7$

19. $5^x = 10$
    (a) log 5              (b) log 10/log 2
    (c) log 2              (d) 1/log 5

20. Find x, if $0.01^x = 2$
    (a) log 2/2            (b) 2/log 2
    (c) −2/log 2           (d) −log 2/2

21. Find x if log x = log 7.2 − log 2.4
    (a) 1                  (b) 2
    (c) 3                  (d) 4

22. Find x if log x = log 1.5 + log 12
    (a) 12                 (b) 8
    (c) 18                 (d) 15

23. Find x if log x = 2 log 5 + 3 log 2
    (a) 50                 (b) 100
    (c) 150                (d) 200

24. log (x − 13) + 3 log 2 = log (3x + 1)
    (a) 20                 (b) 21
    (c) 22                 (d) 24

25. log (2x − 2) − log (11.66 − x) = 1 + log 3
    (a) 452/32             (b) 350/32
    (c) 11                 (d) 11.33

*Space for Rough Work*

## LEVEL OF DIFFICULTY (II)

1. Express $\log \dfrac{\sqrt[3]{a^2}}{b^5\sqrt{c}}$ or $\dfrac{a^{2/3}}{b^5\sqrt{c}}$ in terms of $\log a$, $\log b$ and $\log c$.

   (a) $\dfrac{3}{2}\log a + 5\log b - 2\log c$

   (b) $\dfrac{2}{3}\log a - 5\log b - \dfrac{1}{2}\log c$

   (c) $\dfrac{2}{3}\log a - 5\log b + \dfrac{1}{2}\log c$

   (d) $\dfrac{3}{2}\log a + 5\log b - \dfrac{1}{2}\log c$

2. If $\log 3 = .4771$, find $\log(.81)^2 \times \log\left(\dfrac{27}{10}\right)^{\frac{2}{3}} \div \log 9$.

   (a) 2.689            (b) $-0.0552$
   (c) 2.2402         (d) 2.702

3. If $\log 2 = .301$, $\log 3 = .477$, find the number of digits in $(108)^{10}$.
   (a) 21             (b) 27
   (c) 20             (d) 18

4. If $\log 2 = .301$, find the number of digits in $(125)^{25}$.
   (a) 53             (b) 50
   (c) 25             (d) 63

5. Which of the following options represents the value of $\log\sqrt{128}$ to the base .625?

   (a) $\dfrac{2+\log_8 2}{\log_8 5 - 1}$      (b) $\dfrac{\log_8 128}{2\log_8 0.625}$

   (c) $\dfrac{2+\log_8 2}{2(\log_8 5 - 1)}$      (d) Both (b) and (c)

6-8. Solve for $x$:

   $\log\dfrac{75}{35} + 2\log\dfrac{7}{5} - \log\dfrac{105}{x} - \log\dfrac{13}{25} = 0.$

   (a) 90             (b) 65
   (c) 13             (d) 45

7. $2\log\dfrac{4}{3} - \log\dfrac{x}{10} + \log\dfrac{63}{160} = 0$

   (a) 7              (b) 14
   (c) 9              (d) 3

8. $\log\dfrac{12}{13} - \log\dfrac{7}{25} + \log\dfrac{91}{3} = x$

   (a) 0              (b) 1
   (c) 2              (d) 3

**Questions 9 to 11:** Which one of the following is true

9. (a) $\log_{17}275 = \log_{19}375$ (b) $\log_{17}275 < \log_{19}375$
   (c) $\log_{17}275 > \log_{19}375$ (d) Cannot be determined

10. (a) $\log_{11}1650 > \log_{13}1950$
    (b) $\log_{11}1650 < \log_{13}1950$
    (c) $\log_{11}1650 = \log_{13}1950$
    (d) None of these

11. (a) $\dfrac{\log_2 4096}{3} = \log_8 4096$

    (b) $\dfrac{\log_2 4096}{3} < \log_8 4096$

    (c) $\dfrac{\log_2 4096}{3} > \log_8 4096$

    (d) Cannot be determined

12. $\log\dfrac{16}{15} + 5\log\dfrac{25}{24} + 3\log\dfrac{81}{80} = \log x$, $x = ?$

    (a) 2            (b) 3
    (c) 0            (d) None of these

If $\log 2 = 0.301$ and $\log 3 = .4771$ then find the number of digits in the following.

13. $60^{12}$
    (a) 25            (b) 22
    (c) 23            (d) 24

14. $72^9$
    (a) 17            (b) 20
    (c) 18            (d) 15

15. $27^{25}$
    (a) 38            (b) 37
    (c) 36            (d) 35

**Questions 16 to 18:** Find the value of the logarithmic expression in the questions below.

16. $\dfrac{\log\sqrt{27} + \log 8 - \log\sqrt{1000}}{\log 1.2}$

    where, $\log_{10} 2 = 0.30103$, $\log_{10} 3 = 0.4771213$
    (a) 1.77         (b) 1.37
    (c) 2.33         (d) 1.49

17. $\dfrac{1}{\log_{xy}(xyz)} + \dfrac{1}{\log_{yz}(xyz)} + \dfrac{1}{\log_{zx}(xyz)} =$

    (a) 1            (b) 2
    (c) 3            (d) 4

18. $\log a^n/b^n + \log b^n/c^n + \log c^n/a^n$
    (a) 1            (b) $n$
    (c) 0            (d) 2

19. $\log_{10} x - \log_{10} \sqrt{x} = 2 \log_x 10$ then $x = ?$
    (a) 50
    (b) 100
    (c) 150
    (d) 200

20. $\left(\dfrac{21}{10}\right)^x = 2$. Then $x = ?$

    (a) $\dfrac{\log 2}{\log 3 + \log 7 - 1}$
    (b) $\dfrac{\log 2}{\log 3 + \log 7 + 1}$

    (c) $\dfrac{\log 3}{\log 2 + \log 7 - 1}$
    (d) $\dfrac{\log 2}{\log 3 - \log 7 + 1}$

21. $\log (x^3 + 5) = 3 \log (x + 2)$ then $x = ?$
    (a) $\dfrac{-2 + \sqrt{2}}{2}$
    (b) $\dfrac{-2 - \sqrt{2}}{2}$

    (c) Both (a) and (b)
    (d) None of these

22. $(a^4 - 2a^2 b^2 + b^4)^{x-1} = (a - b)^{-2} (a + b)^{-2}$ then $x = ?$
    (a) 1
    (b) 0
    (c) None of these
    (d) 2

23. If $\log_{10} 242 = a$, $\log_{10} 80 = b$ and $\log_{10} 45 = c$, express $\log_{10} 36$ in terms of $a$, $b$ and $c$.

    (a) $\dfrac{(c-1)(3c+b-4)}{2}$
    (b) $\dfrac{(c-1)(3c+b-4)}{3}$

    (c) $\dfrac{(c-1)(3c-b-4)}{2}$
    (d) None of these

24. For the above problem, express $\log_{10} 66$ in terms of $a$, $b$ and $c$.

    (a) $\dfrac{(c-1)(3c+b-4)}{8}$
    (b) $\dfrac{3(a+c)+(2b+-5)}{6}$

    (c) $\dfrac{3(a+c)+(2b-5)}{6}$
    (d) $\dfrac{3(c-1)(3c+b-4)}{6}$

25. $\log_2 (9 - 2^x) = 10^{\log (3-x)}$. Solve for $x$.
    (a) 0
    (b) 3
    (c) Both (a) and (b)
    (d) 0 and 6

26. If $\dfrac{\log x}{b-c} = \dfrac{\log y}{c-a} = \dfrac{\log z}{a-b}$. Mark all the correct options.    **IIFT 2006**
    (a) $xyz = 1$
    (b) $x^a y^b z^c = 1$
    (c) $x^{b+c} y^{c+a} z^{a+b} = 1$
    (d) All the options are correct.

27. What will be the value of $x$ if it is given that:
    $\log_x \left[\dfrac{1}{5} + \dfrac{1}{12} + \dfrac{1}{21} + \dfrac{1}{32} + \dfrac{1}{45} + \dots + \infty \text{ terms}\right]^2 = 2$

28. $(\log_4 x^2)(x \log_{27} 8)(\log_x 243)$ is equal to:
    (a) $2x$
    (b) $5x$
    (c) $3x$
    (d) 1

29. For how many real values of $x$ will the equation $\log_3 \log_6 (x^3 - 18x^2 + 108x) = \log_2 \log_4 16$ be satisfied?

30. If $n = 12\sqrt{3}$

    $\dfrac{1}{\log_2 n} + \dfrac{1}{\log_3 n} + \dfrac{1}{\log_4 n}$

    $+ \dfrac{1}{\log_6 n} + \dfrac{1}{\log_8 n}$

    $+ \dfrac{1}{\log_9 n} + \dfrac{1}{\log_{18} n} = ?$

31. $(\log_2 x)^2 + 2 \log_2 x - 8 = 0$, Where x is a natural number. If $x^p = 64$, then what is the value of $x + p$.

    **Directions for 41 and 42:** $A = \sum_{i=2}^{a} \log_3 (i)$, $B = \sum_{j=2}^{b} \log_3 (j)$ & $C = \sum_{k=2}^{(a-b)} \log_3 \log_3 k$, where $a \geq b$. If $D = A - B - C$. Then answer the following questions.

32. If $a = 10$ then for what value of $b$, D is minimum

33. For $a = 6$, D is maximum for $b =$

34. If '$p$' and '$q$' are integers and $\log_p (-q^2 + 6q - 8) + \log_q (-2p^2 + 20p - 48) = 0$ then $p \times q = ?$

*Space for Rough Work*

## ANSWER KEY

### Level of Difficulty (I)

| | | | |
|---|---|---|---|
| 1. (a) | 2. (b) | 3. (a) | 4. (c) |
| 5. (a) | 6. (b) | 7. (d) | 8. (a) |
| 9. (c) | 10. (c) | 11. (a) | 12. (b) |
| 13. (c) | 14. (b) | 15. (d) | 16. (c) |
| 17. (c) | 18. (a) | 19. (d) | 20. (d) |
| 21. (c) | 22. (c) | 23. (d) | 24. (b) |
| 25. (c) | | | |

### Level of Difficulty (II)

| | | | |
|---|---|---|---|
| 1. (b) | 2. (b) | 3. (a) | 4. (a) |
| 5. (d) | 6. (c) | 7. (a) | 8. (c) |
| 9. (b) | 10. (a) | 11. (a) | 12. (d) |
| 13. (b) | 14. (a) | 15. (c) | 16. (d) |
| 17. (b) | 18. (c) | 19. (b) | 20. (a) |
| 21. (c) | 22. (b) | 23. (d) | 24. (c) |
| 25. (a) | 26. (d) | 27. 25/48 | 28. (b) |
| 29. 1 | 30. 4 | 31. 7 | 32. 10 |
| 33. 3 | 34. 15 | | |

## Solutions and Shortcuts

### Level of Difficulty (I)

1. $\text{Log } 32700 = \log 3.27 + \log 10000 = \log 3.27 + 4$

2. $\text{Log } 0.0867 = \log (8.67/100) = \log 8.67 - \log 100$
   $\text{Log } 8.67 - 2$

3. $\log_{10} 125 = \log_{10}(1000/8) = \log 1000 - 3\log 2$
   $= 3 - 3 \times 0.301 = 2.097$

4. $\log_{32} 8 = \log 8/\log 32$ (By base change rule)
   $= 3 \log 2/5\log 2 = 3/5.$

5. $\log_{0.5} x = 25 \Rightarrow x = 0.5^{25} = (½)^{25} = 2^{-25}$

6. $x = 3^{1/2} = \sqrt{3}.$

7. $\log_{15} 3375 \times \text{Log}_4 1024$
   $= 3 \log_{15} 15 \times 5 \log_4 4 = 3 \times 5 = 15.$

8. The given expression is:
   $\text{Log}_a (4 \times 16 \times 64 \times 256) = 10$
   i.e. $\log_a 4^{10} = 10$
   Thus, $a = 4.$

9. $1/2 \log_{625} 5 = [1/(2 \times 4)] \log_5 5 = 1/8.$

10. $\log x (x + 3) = 1 \Rightarrow 10^1 = x^2 + 3x.$
    or $x(x + 3) = 10.$

11. $\log_{10} a = b \Rightarrow 10^b = a \Rightarrow$ By definition of logs.
    Thus $10^{3b} = (10^b)^3 = a^3.$

12. $3 \log 5 + 2 \log 4 - \log 2$
    $= \log 125 + \log 16 - \log 2$
    $= \log (125 \times 16)/2 = \log 1000 = 3.$

13. $10^1 = 3x - 2 \Rightarrow x = 4.$

14. $10^2 = 2x - 3 \Rightarrow x = 51.5$

15. $1/10 = 12 - x \Rightarrow x = 11.9$

16. $x^2 - 6x + 6 = 10^0 \Rightarrow x^2 - 6x + 6 = 1$
    $\Rightarrow x^2 - 6x + 5 = 0$
    Solving gives us $x = 5$ and $1.$

17. $x \log 2 = 3$
    $\log 2 = 3/x.$
    Therefore, $x = 3/\log 2$

18. $3^x = 7 \Rightarrow \log_3 7 = x$
    Hence $x = 1/\log_7 3$

19. $x = \log_5 10 = 1/\log_{10} 5 = 1/\log 5.$

20. $x = \log_{0.01} 2 = -\log 2/2.$

21. $\log x = \log (7.2/2.4) = \log 3 \Rightarrow x = 3$

22. $\log x = \log 18 \Rightarrow x = 18$

23. $\log x = \log 25 + \log 8 = \log (25 \times 8 ) = \log 200.$

24. $\log (x - 13) + \log 8 = \log [3x + 1]$
    $\Rightarrow \log (8x - 104) = \log (3x + 1)$
    $\Rightarrow 8x - 104 = 3x + 1$
    $5x = 105 \Rightarrow x = 21$

25. $\log (2x - 2)/(11.66 - x) = \log 30$
    $\Rightarrow (2x - 2)/(11.66 - x) = 30$
    $2x - 2 = 350 - 30x$
    Hence, $32x = 352 \Rightarrow x = 11.$

### Level of Difficulty (II)

1. $2/3 \log a - 5 \log b - 1/2 \log c.$

2. $2 \text{ Log } (81/100) \times 2/3 \log (27/10) \div \log 9$
   $= 2 [\log 3^4 - \log 100] \times 2/3 [(\log 3^3 - \log 10)] \div 2 \log 3$
   $= 2 [\log 3^4 - \log 100] \times 2/3 [(3\log 3 - 1)] \div 2 \log 3$
   Substitute $\log 3 = 0.4771 \Rightarrow - 0.0552.$

3. Let the number be $y$.
   $$y = 108^{10}.$$
   $\Rightarrow \log y = 10 \log 108$
   $\text{Log } y = 10 \log (27 \times 4)$
   $\text{Log } y = 10 [3\log 3 + 2 \log 2]$
   $\text{Log } y = 10 [ 1.43 + 0.602]$
   Hence $\log y = 10[2.03] = 20.3$
   Thus, $y$ has 21 digits.

4. $\log y = 25 \log 125$
   $= 25 [\log 1000 - 3 \log 2] = 25 \times (2.097)$
   $= 52 +$
   Hence 53 digits.

5. $0.5 \log_{0.625} 128$
   $= 0.5 [\log_8 128/\log_8 0.625]$
   $= 1/2 [ \log_8 128/\log_8 0.625]$
   $$\frac{\text{Log}_8 128}{2(\log_8 5 - \log_8 8 )} = \frac{\text{Log}_8 128}{2[\log_8 5 - 1]} = \frac{2 + \log_8 2}{2(\log_8 5 - 1)}$$

6. $(75/35) \times (49/25) \times (x/105) \times (25/13) = 1$
   $\Rightarrow x = 13$

7. $(16/9) \times (10/x) \times (63/160) = 1$
   $\Rightarrow x = 7$

8. Solve in similar fashion.

9. $\log_{17} 275 < \log_{19} 375$

   Because the value of $\log_{17} 275$ is less than 2 while $\log_{19} 375$ is greater then 2.

10. $\log_{11} 1650 > 3$

    $\log_{13} 1950 < 3$

    Hence, $\log_{11} 1650 > \log_{13} 1950$

11. $\dfrac{\log_2 4096}{3} = \log_8 4096$

12. $x = (16/15) \times (25^5/24^5) \times (81^3/80^3)$

    None of these is correct.

13 – 15.

Solve similarly as 3 and 4.

18. $\log\left(a^n b^n c^n / a^n b^n c^n\right) = \log 1 = 0$

19. $(1/2) \log x = 2\log_x 10$

    $\Rightarrow \quad \log x = 4 \log_x 10$

    $\Rightarrow \quad \log x = 4/\log_{10} x \Rightarrow (\log x)^2 = 4$

    So $\log x = 2$ and $x = 100$.

20. $x = \log_{(21/10)} 2$

    $= \dfrac{\log 2}{\log 21 - \log 10} = \dfrac{\log 2}{[\log 3 + \log 7 - 1]}$

21. $6x^2 + 12x + 3 = 0 \quad$ or $\quad 2x^2 + 4x + 1 = 0$

    Solving we get both the options (a) and (b) as correct. Hence, option (c) is the correct answer.

25. For $x = 0$, we have LHS

    $\log_2 8 = 3$.

    RHS: $10^{\log 3} = 3$.

    We do not get LHS = RHS for either $x = 3$ or $x = 6$. Thus, option (a) is correct.

26. $\dfrac{\log x}{b-c} = \dfrac{\log y}{c-a} = \dfrac{\log z}{a-b} = k$

    $\Rightarrow x = 10^{k(b-c)}, y = 10^{k(c-a)}, z = 10^{k(a-b)}$

    $\therefore xyz = 10^{k(b-c+c-a+a-b)} = 10^0 = 1$

    Therefore option (a) is correct.

    $x^a y^b z^c = 10^{k[a(b-c) + b(c-a) + c(a-b)]}$

    $= 10^{k(ab - ac + bc - ab + ca - bc)}$

    $= 10^{K.0} = 1$

    Therefore option (b) is correct.

    $x^{b+c} y^{c+a} z^{a+b} = 10^{k[(b+c)(b-c) + (c+a)(c-a) + (a+b)(a-b)]}$

    $= 10^{k.0} = 1$

    Therefore option (c) is also correct.

    Since all the first three options are correct, we choose option (d) as the correct answer.

27. $\log_x \left[\dfrac{1}{5} + \dfrac{1}{12} + \dfrac{1}{21} + \dfrac{1}{32} + \dfrac{1}{45} + \dots + \infty \text{ terms}\right]^2$

    $= 2\log_x \left(\dfrac{1}{5} + \dfrac{1}{12} + \dfrac{1}{21} + \dfrac{1}{32} + \dfrac{1}{45} + \dots + \infty \text{ terms}\right)$

Let $\dfrac{1}{5} + \dfrac{1}{12} + \dfrac{1}{21} + \dfrac{1}{32} + \dfrac{1}{45} + \dots + \infty \text{ terms} = P$

$P = \dfrac{1}{4}\left[\dfrac{4}{1\times 5} + \dfrac{4}{2\times 6} + \dfrac{4}{3\times 7} + \dfrac{4}{4\times 8} + \dfrac{4}{5\times 9} + \dots \infty\right]$

$4P = \left[1 - \dfrac{1}{5} + \dfrac{1}{2} - \dfrac{1}{6} + \dfrac{1}{3} - \dfrac{1}{7} + \dfrac{1}{4} - \dfrac{1}{8} + \dfrac{1}{5} - \dfrac{1}{9}\right]$

$4P = \left[1 + \dfrac{1}{2} + \dfrac{1}{3} + \dfrac{1}{4}\right]$

$4P = \dfrac{25}{12}$

$P = \dfrac{25}{48}$

$\log_x \dfrac{25}{48} = 1$ or $x = 25/48$

28. $\log_4 x^2 . x\log_{27} 8 . \log_x 243 = \dfrac{2\log x}{\log 4} . \dfrac{x\log 8}{\log 27} . \dfrac{\log 243}{\log x}$

    $= \dfrac{\log x}{\log 2} . \dfrac{3x\log 2}{3\log 3} . \dfrac{5\log 3}{\log x} = 5x$

29. $\log_2(\log_4 16) = \log_2 \log_4 4^2 = \log_2 2 = 1$

    $\log_3 \log_6 (x^3 - 18x^2 + 108x) = 1$

    $\log_6(x^3 - 18x^2 + 108x) = 3$

    $x^3 - 18x^2 + 108x = 6^3$

    $x^3 - 18x^2 + 108x - 216 = 0$

    $(x - 6)^3 = 0$

    $x = 6$ is the only value for which the above equation is true.

30. $n = 12\sqrt{3} = 2^2 \times 3^{1.5}$

    $\dfrac{1}{\log_2 n} + \dfrac{1}{\log_3 n} + \dfrac{1}{\log_4 n} + \dfrac{1}{\log_6 n}$

    $+ \dfrac{1}{\log_8 n} + \dfrac{1}{\log_9 n} + \dfrac{1}{\log_{18} n}$

    $= \log_n 2 + \log_n 3 + \log_n 4 + \log_n 6 + \log_n 8 + \log_n 9 + \log_n 18$

    $= \log_n (2 \times 3 \times 4 \times 6 \times 8 \times 9 \times 18)$

    $= \log_n (2^8 \times 3^6)$

    $= \log_n (2^2 \times 3^{1.5})^4$

    $= 4 \log_n (2^2 \times 3^{1.5})$

    $= 4\log_{2^2 \times 3^{1.5}} (2^2 \times 3^{1.5}) = 4$

31. $(\log_2 x)^2 + 2\log_2 x - 8 = 0$

    $(\log_2 x)^2 + 4\log_2 x - 2\log_2 x - 8 = 0$

    $\log_2 x [\log_2 x + 4] - 2 [\log_2 x + 4] = 0$

    $[\log_2 x - 2] [\log_2 x + 4] = 0$

    Since, $x$ is a natural number hence $[\log_2 x + 4]$ cannot be zero. Hence, $\log_2 x - 2 = 0$

    $\log_2 x = 2$

    $x = 2^2 = 4$

    We are given that: $x^p = 64$. Since $x$ is 4, this means

that:

$4^p = 64$

$p = 3$

Hence, the value of $(x + p) = 4 + 3 = 7$

32. $A = \sum_{i=1}^{a} \log_3 i = \log_3 1 + \log_3 2 + \log_3 4 + \ldots + \log_3 a$

$= \log_3 (2.3.4 \ldots a) = \log_3 (a!)$

Similarly $B = \log_3 (b!), C = \log_3 (a - b)!$

$D = \log_3 a! - \log_3 b! - \log_3 (a - b)!$

$= \log_3 \dfrac{a!}{b!(a-b)!}$

$= \log_3 (^aC_b)$

If $a = 10$, then D will be minimum when $b = 10$, since the smallest value of $^nC_r$ occurs when $n = r$.

33. If $a = 6$, then D will be maximum for $b = 3$ (Since the value of $^nC_r$ attains its' maximum when the value of $r$ is half the value of $n$)

34. Both $p$, $q$ must be greater than 0 as logarithms are not defined to negative bases. Now looking at the two parts of the expression we see that both:

$-q^2 + 6q - 8 > 0$ and $-2p^2 + 20p - 48 > 0$.

This leads us to the following conclusions:

$q^2 - 6q + 8 < 0$. Hence, $(q - 2)(q - 4) < 0$. The only integer value of $q$ that satisfies this is $q = 3$.

Likewise, $2p^2 - 20p + 48 < 0$ means $2(p - 4)(p - 6) < 0$

Only integer value of p which satisfies the above In equality is $p = 5$.

$\therefore p \times q = 3 \times 5 = 15$

*Space for Rough Work*

# TRAINING GROUND FOR BLOCK V

## HOW TO THINK IN PROBLEMS ON BLOCK V

1. Let $x_1, x_2, \ldots, x_{100}$ be positive integers such that $x_! + x_{!-1} + 1 = k$ for all !, where k is a constant. If $x_{10} = 1$, then the value of $x_1$ is

(a) $k$  (b) $k - 2$
(c) $k + 1$  (d) $1$

**Solution:** Using the information in the expression which defines the function, we realise that if we use $x_{10}$ as $x_!$, the expression gives us:

$x_{10} + x_9 + 1 = k \rightarrow x_9 = k - 2$; Further, using the value of $x_9$ to get the value of $x_8$ as follows:

$x_9 + x_8 + 1 = k \rightarrow k - 2 + x_8 + 1 = k \rightarrow x_8 = 1$;

Next: $x_8 + x_7 + 1 = k \rightarrow x_7 = k - 2$.

In this fashion, we can clearly see that $x_6$ would again be 1 and $x_5$ be $k$–2; $x_4 = 1$ and $x_3 = k$–2; $x_2 = 1$ and $x_1 = k$–2. Option (b) is correct.

2. If $a_0 = 1$, $a_1 = 1$ and $a_n = a_{n-2} a_{n-1} + 3$ for $n > 1$, which of the following options would be true?

(a) $a_{450}$ is odd and $a_{451}$ is even
(b) $a_{450}$ is odd and $a_{451}$ is odd
(c) $a_{450}$ is even and $a_{451}$ is even
(d) $a_{450}$ is even and $a_{451}$ is odd

**Solution:** In order to solve this question, you need to think about how the initial values of $a_x$ would behave in terms of being even and odd.

The value of $a_2 = 1 \times 1 + 3 = 4$ (This is necessarily even since we have the construct as follows: Odd × Odd + Odd = Odd + Odd = Even.)

The value of $a_3 = 1 \times 4 + 3 = 7$ (This is necessarily odd since we have the construct as follows: Odd × Even + Odd = Even + Odd = Odd.)

The value of $a_4 = 4 \times 7 + 3 = 31$ (This is necessarily odd since we have the construct as follows: Odd × Even + Odd = Even + Odd = Odd.)

The value of $a_5 = 7 \times 31 + 3 = 220$ (This is necessarily even since we have the construct as follows: Odd × Odd + Odd = Odd + Odd = Even.)

The next two in the series values viz: $a_6$ and $a_7$ would be odd again since they would take the construct of Odd × Even + Odd = Even + Odd = Odd. Also, once $a_6$ and $a_7$ turn out to be odd, it is clear that $a_8$ would be even and $a_9$ $a_{10}$ would be odd again. Thus, we can understand that the terms $a_2$, $a_5$, $a_8$, $a_{11}$, $a_{14}$ are even while all other terms in the series are odd. Thus, the even terms occur when we take a term whose number answers the description of $a_{3n+2}$. If you look at the options, all the four options in this question are asking about the value of $a_{450}$ and $a_{451}$. Since, neither of these terms is in the series of $a_{3n+2}$, we can say that both of these are necessarily odd and hence, Option (b) would be the correct answer.

3. If $\dfrac{a+b}{b+c} = \dfrac{c+d}{d+a}$, then

(a) $a = c$
(b) either $a = c$ or $a + b + c + d = 0$
(c) $a + b + c + d = 0$
(d) $a = c$ and $b = d$

**Solution:** Such problems should be solved using values and also by doing a brief logical analysis of the algebraic equation. In this case, it is clear that if $a = c = k$ (say), the LHS of the expression would become equal to the RHS of the expression (and both would be equal to 1). Once we realise that the expression is satisfied for LHS = RHS, we have to choose between Options $a$, $b$ and $d$. However, a closer look at Option (d) shows us that since it says $a = c$ and $b = d$ it is telling us that both of these (i.e., $a = c$ as well as $b = d$) get satisfied and we have already seen that even if only $a = c$ is true, the expression gets satisfied. Thus, there is no need to have $b = d$ as simultaneously true with $a = c$ as true. Based on this logic we can reject Option (d). To check for Option (b) we need to see whether $a + b + c + d = 0$ would necessarily be satisfied if the expression is true. In order to check this, we can take a set of values for $a$, $b$, $c$ and $d$ such that their sum is equal to 0 and check whether the equation is satisfied. Taking, $a$, $b$, $c$ and $d$ as 1, 2, 3 and –6 respectively we get the LHS of the expression as $3/(-1) = -3$; the RHS of the expression would be $(-3)/(-5) = 3/5$ which is not equal to the LHS. Thus, we can understand that $a + b + c + d = 0$ would not necessarily satisfy the equation. Hence, Option (a) is the correct answer.

4. If $a$, $b$, $c$ and $d$ satisfy the equations

$a + 7b + 3c + 5d = 0$
$8a + 4b + 6c + 2d = -32$
$2a + 6b + 4c + 8d = 32$
$5a + 3b + 7c + d = -32$

Then $(a + d)(b + c)$ equals

(a) 64  (b) –64
(c) 0  (d) None of the above

**Solution:** Adding each of the four equations in the expression we get: $16(a + d) + 20(b + c) = -32$.

Also, by adding the second and the third equations we get: $a + b + c + d = 0$, which means that $(a + d) = -(b + c)$.

Then from: $16(a + d) + 20(b + c) = -32$, we have: $-16(b + c) + 20(b + c) = -32 \rightarrow 4(b + c) = -32$. Hence, $(b + c) = -8$ and $(a + d) = 8$. Hence, the multiplication of $(a + d)(b + c) = -64$

5. For any real number $x$, the function $I(x)$ denotes the integer part of $x$ – i.e., the largest integer less than or equal to $x$. At the same time the function $D(x)$

denotes the fractional part of $x$. For arbitrary real numbers $x$, $y$ and $z$, only one of the following statements is correct. Which one is it?

(a) $I(x + y) = I(x) + I(y)$

(b) $I(x + y + z) = I(x + y) + I(z) = I(x) + I(y + z) = I(x + z) + I(y)$

(c) $I(x + y + z) = I(x + y) + I(z + D(y + x))$

(d) $D(x + y + z) = y + z - I(y + z) + D(x)$

**Solution:** There are three principle themes you need to understand in order to answer such questions.

1. **Thinking in language**. The above question is garnished with a plethora of mathematical symbols. Unless you are able to convert each of the situations given in the options into clear logical language, your mind cannot make sense of what is written in the options. The best mathematical brains work this way. Absolutely nobody has the mathematical vision to solve such problems by simply reading the notations in the problem and/or the options.

2. While thinking in language terms in the case of a question such as this, in order to understand and grasp the mathematical situation confronting us, the best thing to do is to put values into the situation. This is very critical in such problems because as you can yourself see – if you are thinking about say $I(x + y + z)$ and you keep the same notation to think through the problem, you would need to carry $I(x + y + z)$ throughout the thinking inside the problem. On the other hand if you replace the $I(x + y + z)$ situation by replacing values for $x$, $y$ and $z$, the expression would change to a single number. Thus, if you take $I(4.3 + 2.8 + 5.3) = I(12.4) = 12$. Obviously thinking further in the next steps with 12, as the handle, would be much easier than trying to think with $I(x + y + z)$.

3. Since the question here is asking us to identify the correct option which always gives us LHS = RHS, we can proceed further in the problem using the options given to us. While doing this, when you are testing an option, the approach has to be to try to think of values for the variables such that the option is rejected, i.e., we need to think of values such that LHS ≠ RHS. In this fashion, the idea is to eliminate 3 options and identify the one option that cannot be eliminated because it cannot be disproved.

Keeping these principles in mind, if we try to look at the options in this problem we have to look for the one correct statement.

Let us check Option (a) to begin with:

The LHS can be interpreted as: $I(x + y)$ means the integer part of $x + y$. Suppose we use $x$ as 4.3 and $y$ as 4.2 we would get $I(x + y) = I(4.3 + 4.2) = I(8.5) = 8$.

The RHS in this case would be $I(4.3) + I(4.2) = 4 + 4 = 8$. This gives us LHS = RHS.

However, if you use $x = 4.3$ and $y = 4.8$ you would see that LHS = $I(4.3 + 4.8) = I(9.1) = 9$, while the RHS would

be $I(4.3) + I(4.8) = 4 + 4 = 8$. This would clearly gives us LHS ≠ RHS and hence this option is incorrect.

The point to note here is that whenever you are solving a function based question through the rejection of the options route, the vision about what kind of numbers would reject the case becomes critical. My advise to you is that as you start solving questions through this route, you would need to improve your vision of what values to assume while rejecting an option. This is one key skill that differentiates the minds and the capacities of the top people from the average aspirants. Hence, if you want to compete against the best you should develop this numerical vision. To illustrate what I mean by numerical vision, think of a situation where you are faced with the expression $(a + b) > (a \times b)$. Normally this does not happen, except when you are multiplying with numbers between 0 and 1.)

Moving on with our problem. Let us look at Option (b).

$I(x + y + z) = I(x + y) + I(z) = I(x) + I(y + z) = I(x + z) + I(y)]$

In order to reject this option, the following values would be used:

$x = 4.3$, $y = 5.1$, and $z = 6.7$

LHS = $I(4.3 + 5.1 + 6.7) = I(16.1) = 16$

When we try to see whether the first expression on the RHS satisfies this we can clearly see it does not because:

$I(x + y) + I(z)$ would give us $I(4.3 + 5.1) + I(6.7) = I(9.4) + I(6.7) = 9 + 6 = 15$ in this case.

Thus, $I(x + y + z) = I(x + y) + I(z)$ is disproved and this option can be rejected at this point.

We thus move onto Option (c), which states:

$I(x + y + z) = I(x + y) + I(z + D(y + x))$

Let us try this in the case of the values we previously took, i.e., $x = 4.3$, $y = 5.1$, and $z = 6.7$

We get:

$I(4.3 + 5.1 + 6.7) = I(4.3 + 5.1) + I(6.7 + D(4.3 + 5.1))$

$\rightarrow I(16.1) = I(9.4) + I(6.7 + D(9.4))$

$\rightarrow I(16.1) = I(9.4) + I(6.7 + 0.4)$

$\rightarrow I(16.1) = I(9.4) + I(7.1)$

$\rightarrow 16 = 9 + 7.$

Suppose we try 4.3, 4.9 and 5.9 we get:

$I(4.3 + 4.9 + 5.9) = I(4.3 + 4.9) + I(5.9 + D(4.3 + 4.9))$

$\rightarrow I(15.1) = I(9.2) + I(5.9 + D(9.2))$

$\rightarrow I(15.1) = I(9.4) + I(5.9 + 0.2)$

$\rightarrow I(15.1) = I(9.4) + I(6.1)$

$\rightarrow 15 = 9 + 6.$

We can see that this option is proving to be difficult to shake off as a possible answer. However, this logic is not enough to select this as the correct answer. In order to make sure that you never err when you solve a question this way, you would need to either do one of two things at this point in the problem solving approach.

Approach 1: Try to understand and explain to yourself the mathematical reason as to why this option should be correct.

Approach 2: Try to eliminate the remaining option/s at this point of time.

Amongst these, my recommendation would be to go for Approach 2 because that is likely to be easier than Approach 1. Approach 1 is only to be used in case you have seen and understood during your checking of the option as to why the particular option is always guaranteed to be true. In case, you have not seen the mathematical logic for the same during your checking of the option, you typically should not try to search for the logic while trying to solve the problem. The quicker way to the correct answer would be to eliminate the remaining option/s.

(Of course, once you are done with solving the question, during your review of the question, you should ideally try to explain to yourself as to why one particular option worked – because that might become critical mathematical logic inside your mind for the next time you face a similar mathematical situation.)

In this case, let us try to do both. To freeze Option (c) as the correct answer, you would need to look at Option (d) and try to reject it.

Option (d) says:

$D(x + y + z) = y + z - I(y + z) + D(x)$

Say we take $x = 4.3$, $y = 5.1$, and $z = 6.7$ we can see that:

$D(4.3 + 5.1 + 6.7) = 4.3 + 5.1 - I(4.3 + 5.1) + D(4.3) \rightarrow$

$D(16.1) = 9.4 - I(9.4) + D(4.3) \rightarrow$

$0.1 = 9.4 - 9 + 0.3 \rightarrow$

$0.1 = 0.7$, which is clearly incorrect.

Hence, Option (c) is the correct answer.

If we were to look at the mathematical logic for Option (c) (for our future reference) we can think of why Option (c) would always be true as follows:

One of the problems in these greatest integer problems is what can be described as the loss of value due to the greatest integer function.

Thus $I(4.3 + 4.8) > I(4.3) + I(4.8)$ since the LHS is 9 and the RHS is only 8. What happens here is that the LHS gains by 1 unit because the .3 and the .8 in the two numbers add up to 1.1 and help the sum of the two numbers to cross 9. On the other hand if you were to look at the RHS in this situation, you would realise that the decimal values of 4.3 and 4.8 are individually both lost.

In this context, when you look at the LHS of the equation given in Option (c), you see that the value of the LHS would retain the integer values of $x$, $y$ and $z$ while the sum of the decimal values of $x$, $y$ and $z$ would get aggregated and combined into 1 number. This gives us three cases:

Case 1: When the addition of the decimal values of $x$, $y$ and $z$ is less than 1;

Case 2: When the addition of the decimal values of $x$, $y$ and $z$ is more than 1 but less than 2;

Case 3: When the addition of the decimal values of $x$, $y$ and $z$ is more than 2 but less than 3.

Each of these three cases would be further having a two way fork – viz:

Case A: When the addition of the decimal values of $x$ and $y$ add up to less than 1;

Case B: When the addition of the decimal values of $x$ and $y$ add up to more than 1 but less than 2.

I would encourage the reader to take this case from this point and move it to a point where you can explore each of these six situations and see that for all these situations, the value of the LHS of the expression is equal to the value of the RHS of the equation.

6. During the reign of the great government in the country of Riposta, the government forms committees of ministers whenever it is faced with a problem. One particular year, there are $x$ ministers in the government and they are organised into 4 committees such that:

 (i) Each minister belongs to exactly two committees.

 (ii) Each pair of committees has exactly one minister in common.

 Then

 (a) $x = 4$

 (b) $x = 6$

 (c) $x = 8$

 (d) $x$ cannot be determined from the given information

**Solution:** In order to think about this situation, you need to think of the number of unique people you would need in order to make up the committees as defined in the problem. However, before you start to do this, a problem you need to solve is—how many members do you put in each committee?

Given the options for $x$, when we look at the options, it is clear that the number is unlikely to be larger than 4. Hence, suppose we try to think of committees with 4 members, we will get the following thought process:

First, we create the first two committees with exactly 1 member common between the two committees. We would get the following table at this point of time:

| Committee 1 | Committee 2 | Committee 3 | Committee 4 |
| --- | --- | --- | --- |
| 1 | 4 | | |
| 2 | 5 | | |
| 3 | 6 | | |
| 4 | 7 | | |

Here we have taken the individual members of the committees as 1, 2, 3, 4, 5, 6 and 7. We have obeyed the second rule for committee formation (i.e. each pair of committees has exactly one member in common) by taking only the member 4 as the common member.

From this point in the table, we need to try to fill in the remaining committees obeying the twin rules given in the problem.

So, each member should belong to exactly two committees and each pair of committees should have only 1 member in common.

When we try to do that in this table we reach the following point.

| Committee 1 | Committee 2 | Committee 3 | Committee 4 |
|---|---|---|---|
| 1 | 4 | 7 | |
| 2 | 5 | 1 | |
| 3 | 6 | 8 | |
| 4 | 7 | 9 | |

Here we have taken 7 common between the Committees 2 and 3, while 1 is common between Committees 1 and 3. This point freezes the individuals 1, 4 and 7 as they have been used twice (as required). However, this leaves us with 2, 3, 5, 6, 8 and 9 to be used once more and only Committee 4 left to fill in into the table. This is obviously impossible to do and hence, we are sure that each committee would not have had 4 members.

Obviously, if 4 members are too many, we cannot move to trying 5 members per committee. Thus, we should move trying to form committees with 3 members each.

When we do so, the following thought process unfolds:

We first fill in the first two committees by keeping exactly one person common between these committees. By taking the person '3' as a common member between Committees 1 and 2, we reach the following table:

| Committee 1 | Committee 2 | Committee 3 | Committee 4 |
|---|---|---|---|
| 1 | 3 | | |
| 2 | 4 | | |
| 3 | 5 | | |

We now need to fill in Committee 3 with exactly 1 member from Committee 1 and exactly 1 member from Committee 2. Also, we cannot use the member number '3' as he has already been used twice. Thus, by repeating '5' from Committee 2 and '1' from Committee 1 we can reach the following table.

| Committee 1 | Committee 2 | Committee 3 | Committee 4 |
|---|---|---|---|
| 1 | 3 | 5 | |
| 2 | 4 | 1 | |
| 3 | 5 | | |

Since the remaining person in Committee 3 would have to be unique from members of Committees 1 and 2, we would need to introduce a new member (say 6) in order to complete Committee 3. Thus, our table evolves to the following situation.

| Committee 1 | Committee 2 | Committee 3 | Committee 4 |
|---|---|---|---|
| 1 | 3 | 5 | |
| 2 | 4 | 1 | |
| 3 | 5 | 6 | |

At this point, the members 2, 4 and 6 have not been used a second time. Also, the committee 4 has to have its 3 members filled such that it has exactly 1 member common with committees 1, 2 and 3 respectively.

This is easily achieved using the following structure.

| Committee 1 | Committee 2 | Committee 3 | Committee 4 |
|---|---|---|---|
| 1 | 3 | 5 | 2 |
| 2 | 4 | 1 | 4 |
| 3 | 5 | 6 | 6 |

Hence, we can clearly see that the value of $x$ is 6, i.e., the government had 6 ministers.

7. During the IPL Season 14, the Mumbai Indians captained by a certain Sachin Tendulkar who emerged out of retirement, played 60 games in the season. The team never lost three games consecutively and never won five games consecutively in that season. If N is the number of games the team won in that season, then N satisfies
   (a) $24 \leq N \leq 48$      (b) $20 \leq N \leq 48$
   (c) $12 \leq N \leq 48$      (d) $20 \leq N \leq 42$

**Solution:** In order to solve this question, we need to see the limit of the minimum and maximum number of matches that the team could have won. Let us first think about the maximum number of matches the team could have won. Since the team 'never won five games consecutively' during that season, we would get the value for the maximum number of wins by trying to make the team win 4 games consecutively—as many times as we can. This can be thought of as follows:

WWWWLWWWWLWWWWL... and so on.

From the above sequence, we can clearly see that with 4 wins consecutively, we are forming a block of 5 matches in which the team has won 4 and lost 1. Since, there are a total of 60 matches in all, there would be 12 such blocks of 5 matches each. The total number of wins in this case would amount to $12 \times 4 = 48$ (this is the highest number possible).

This eliminates Option 4 as the possible answer.

If we think about the minimum number of wins, we would need to maximise the number of losses. In order to do so, we get the following thought process:

Since the team never lost three games consecutively, for the maximum number of losses the pattern followed would be—

LLWLLWLLWLLW... and so on

Thus, there are two losses and 1 win in every block of 3 matches. Since, there would be a total of 20 such blocks, it would mean that there would be a total of $20 \times 1 = 20$ wins. This number would represent the minimum possible number of wins for the team.

Thus, N has to be between 20 and 48. Thus, Option (b) is correct.

8. If the roots of the equation $x^3 - ax^2 + bx - c = 0$ are three consecutive integers, then what is the smallest possible value of $b$?
   (a) $-1/\sqrt{3}$      (b) $-1$
   (c) $0$      (d) $1$
   (e) $1/\sqrt{3}$

**Solution:** Since the question represents a cubic expression, and we want the smallest possible value of b—keeping the constraint of their roots being three consecutive values—a little bit of guesstimation would lead you to think of –1, 0 and 1 as the three roots for minimising the value of b.

Thus, the expression would be $(x + 1)(x)(x – 1) = (x^2 + x)(x – 1) = x^3 – x$. This gives us the value of b as –1.

It can be seen that changing the values of the roots from –1, 0 and 1 would result in increasing the coefficient of x—which is not what we want. Hence, the correct answer should be that the minimum value of b would be –1.

**Note:** that for trial purposes if you were to take the values of the three roots as 0, 1, and 2, the expressions would become $x(x – 1)(x – 2) = (x^2 – x)(x – 2)$ which would lead to the coefficient of x being 2. This would obviously increase the value of the coefficient of x above –1.

You could also go for changing the three consecutive integral roots in the other direction to –2, –1 and 0. In such a case the expression would become: $x(x + 2)(x + 1) = (x2 + 2x)(x + 1)$ → which would again give us the coefficient of x as + 2.

The total solving time for this question would be 30 seconds if you were to hit on the right logic for taking the roots as –1, 0 and 1. In case you had to check for the value of b in different situations by altering the values of the roots (as explained above) the time would still be under 2 minutes.

9. A shop stores x kg of rice. The first customer buys half this amount plus half a kg of rice. The second customer buys half the remaining amount plus half a kg of rice. Then the third customer buys half the remaining amount plus half a kg of rice. Thereafter, no rice is left in the shop. Which of the following best describes the value of x?

(a) $2 \leq x \leq 6$      (b) $5 \leq x \leq 8$
(c) $9 \leq x \leq 12$      (d) $11 \leq x \leq 14$
(e) $13 \leq x \leq 18$

**Solution:** This question is based on odd numbers as only with an odd value of x would you keep getting integers if you halved the value of rice and took out another half a kg from the shop store.

From the options, let us start from the second option. (**Note:** In such questions, one should make it a rule to start from one of the middle options only as the normal realisation we would get from checking one option would have been that more than one option gets removed if we have not picked up the correct option—as we would normally know whether the correct answer needs to be increased from the value we just checked or should be decreased.)

Thus trying for x = 7 according to the second option, you would get

$7 \rightarrow 3 \rightarrow 1 \rightarrow 0$ (after three customers).

This means that $5 \leq x \leq 8$ is a valid option for this question. Also, since the question is definitive about the correct range,

there cannot be two ranges. Hence, we can conclude that Option 2 is correct.

**Note:** The total solving time for this question should not be more than 30 seconds. Even if you are not such an experienced solver through options, and you had to check 2–3 options in order to reach the correct option, you would still need a maximum of 90 seconds.

**Directions for Questions 10 and 11:** Let $f(x) = ax^2 + bx + c$, where a, b and c are certain constants and $a \neq 0$. it is known that $f(5) = -3 f(2)$ and that 3 is a root of $f(x) = 0$.

10. What is the other root of $f(x) = 0$?
    (a) –7      (b) –4
    (c) 2      (d) 6
    (e) Can not be determined

11. What is the value of $a + b + c$?
    (a) 9      (b) 14
    (c) 13      (d) 37
    (e) Can not be determined

**Solution:** Since, 3 is a root of the equation, we have $9a + 3b + c = 0$ (**Theory point**—A root of any equation $f(x) = 0$ has the property that if it is used to replace 'x' in every part of the equation, then the equation $f(x) = 0$ should be satisfied.)

Also $f(5) = -3f(2)$ gives us that $25a + 5b + c = -3(4a + 2b + c) \rightarrow 37a + 11b + 4c = 0$

Combining both equations we can see that $37a + 11b + 4c = 4(9a + 3b + c) \rightarrow a - b = 0$. i.e., $a = b$

Now, we know that the sum of roots of a quadratic equation is given by $-b/a$. Hence, the sum of roots has to be equal to –1. Since one of the roots is 3, the other must be –4.

The answer to Question 10 would be Option (2).

For Question 11 we need the sum of $a + b + c$. We know that $a + b = 0$. Also, product of roots is –12. One of the possible equations could be $(x – 3)(x + 4) = 0 \rightarrow x^2 + x – 12 = 0$, which gives us the value of $a + b + c$ as –10. However, –10 is not in the options. This should make us realise that there is a possibility of another equation as: $(2x – 6)(2x + 8) = 0 \rightarrow 4x^2 + 4x – 48 = 0$ in which case the value of $a + b + c$ changes. Hence, the correct answer is 'cannot be determined'.

12. Suppose, the seed of any positive integer n is defined as follows:

    Seed(n) $= n$, if $n < 10$

           $= $ seed$(s(n))$, otherwise,

    Where $s(n)$ indicates the sum of digits of n. For example, Seed(7) = 7, seed (248) = seed(2 + 4 + 8) = seed (14) = seed (1 + 4) = seed (5) = 5 etc. How many positive integers n, such that $n < 500$, will have seed (n) = 9?
    (a) 39      (b) 72
    (c) 81      (d) 108
    (e) 55

**Solution:** The first number to have a seed of 9 would be the number 9 itself.

The next number whose seed would be 9 would be 18, then 27 and you should recognise that we are talking about numbers which are multiples of 9. Hence, the number of such numbers would be the number of numbers in the Arithmetic Progression:

9, 18, 27, 36, 45, ....495 = [(495 – 9)/9] + 1 = 55 such numbers.

13. Find the sum of $\sqrt{1+\dfrac{1}{1^2}+\dfrac{1}{2^2}}+\sqrt{1+\dfrac{1}{2^2}+\dfrac{1}{3^2}}+\dots$

$+\sqrt{1+\dfrac{1}{2007^2}+\dfrac{1}{2008^2}}$

(a) $2008-\dfrac{1}{2008}$ (b) $2007-\dfrac{1}{2007}$

(c) $2007-\dfrac{1}{2008}$ (d) $2008-\dfrac{1}{2007}$

(e) $2008-\dfrac{1}{2009}$

**Solution:** Such questions are again solved through logical processes. If you were to try this problem by going through mathematical processes you would end up with a messy solution which is not going to yield any answer in any reasonable time frame.

Instead, look at the following process.

The first thing you should notice is that the value in the answer has got something to do with the number 2008. Suppose we were to look at only the first term of the expression, by analogy the value of the sum should have something to do with the number 2. Accordingly by looking at the value obtained we can decide on which of the options fits the given answer.

So, for the first term, we see that the value is equal to the square root of 2.25 = 1.5

By analogy that in this case the value of 2008 is 2, the value of 2007 would be 1 and 2009 would be 3. Replacing these values the options become:

(a) $2-\dfrac{1}{2}$ (b) $1-\dfrac{1}{1}$

(c) $1-\dfrac{1}{2}$ (d) $2-\dfrac{1}{1}$

(e) $2-\dfrac{1}{3}$

It can be easily verified that only Option (a) gives a value of 1.5. Hence, that is the only possible answer as all other values are different. In case you need greater confirmation and surety, you can solve this for the first two terms too.

14. A function $f(x)$ satisfies $f(1) = 3600$, and $f(1) + f(2) + \dots + f(n) = n^2 f(n)$, for all positive integers $n > 1$. What is the value of $f(9)$?

(a) 80 (b) 240
(c) 200 (d) 100
(e) 120

**Solution:** This question is based on chain functions where the value of the function at a particular point depends on the previous values.

$f(1) + f(2) = 4 f(2) \to f(1) = 3 f(2) \to f(2) = 1200$

Similarly, for $f(3)$ we have the following expression:

$f(1) + f(2) + f(3) = 9 f(3) \to f(3) = 4800/8 = 600$

Further $f(1) + f(2) + f(3) = 15 f(4) \to f(4) = 5400/15 = 360$

Further $f(1) + f(2) + f(3) + f(4) = 24 f(5) \to 5760/24 = f(5) = 240$

If you were to pause a while at this point and try to look at the pattern of the numerical outcomes in the series we are getting we get:

3600, 1200, 600, 360, 240, 1200/7

A little bit of perceptive analysis about the fractions used as multipliers to convert $f(1)$ to $f(2)$ and $f(2)$ to $f(3)$ and so on will tell us that the respective multipliers themselves are following a pattern viz:

$f(1) \times 1/3 = f(2)$;
$f(2) \times 2/4 = f(3)$;
$f(3) \times 3/5 = f(4)$ and $f(4) \times 4/6 = f(5)$

Using this logic string we can move onto the next values as follows:

$f(6) = 240 \times 5/7 = 1200/7$;
$f(7) = 1200/7 \times 6/8 = 900/7$;
$f(8) = 900/7 \times 7/9 = 100$ and
$f(9) = 100 \times 8/10 = 80$.

Thus, Option (a) is the correct answer.

**Directions for Questions 15 and 16:** Let $S$ be the set of all pairs $(i, j)$ where $1 \le i < j \le n$, and $n \ge 4$. Any two distinct members of $S$ are called "friends" if they have one constituent of the pairs in common and "enemies" otherwise. For example, if $n = 4$, then $S = \{(1, 2), (1, 3), (1, 4), (2, 3), (2, 4), (3, 4)\}$. Here, $(1, 2)$ and $(1, 3)$ are friends, $(1, 2)$ and $(2, 3)$ are also friends, but $(1, 4)$ and $(2, 3)$ are enemies.

15. For general $n$, how many enemies will each member of $S$ have?

(a) $n-3$ (b) $(n^2-3n-2)/2$
(c) $2n-7$ (d) $(n^2-5n+6)/2$
(e) $(n^2-7n+14)/2$

**Solution:** Solve by putting values: Suppose we have $n = 5$; The members would be $\{(1,2), (1,3), (1,4), (1,5), (2,3), (2,4), (2,5), (3,4), (3,5), (4,5)\}$

In this case any member can be found to have 3 enemies.

Thus the answer to the above question should give us a value of 3 with $n = 5$.

Option (a): $n-3 = 5-3 = 2$. Hence, cannot be the answer.
Option (b): $8/2 = 4$. Hence, cannot be the answer.

Option (c): $10 - 7 = 3$. To be considered.

Option (d): $6/2 = 3$. To be considered.

Option (e): $4/2 = 2$. Hence, cannot be the answer.

We still need to choose one answer between Options (c) and (d).

It can be seen that for $n = 6$, the values of Options (c) and (d) will differ. Hence, we need to visualise how many enemies each member would have for $n = 6$.

The members would be {(1,2), (1,3), (1,4), (1,5), (1,6), (2,3),(2,4), (2,5), (2,6), (3,4), (3,5), (3,6), (4,5), (4,6), (5,6)}. It can be clearly seen that the member (1,2) will have 6 enemies. Option (c) gives us a value of 5 and hence can be eliminated while Option (d) gives us a value of 6 leaving it as the only possible answer.

16. For general $n$, consider any two members of $S$ that are friends. How many other members of $S$ will be common friends of both these members?

    (a) $(n^2 - 5n + 8)/2$    (b) $2n - 6$

    (c) $n(n-3)/2$    (d) $n - 2$

    (e) $(n^2 - 7n + 16)/2$

**Solution:** Again for this question consider the following situation where $n = 6$.

The members would be {(1,2), (1,3), (1,4), (1,5), (1,6), (2,3),(2,4), (2,5), (2,6), (3,4), (3,5), (3,6), (4,5), (4,6), (5,6)}.

**Suppose we consider the pair (1,2) and (1,3). Their common friends would be (1,4), (1,5), (1,6) and (2,3).**

**Thus there are 4 common friends for any pair of friendly members. (You can verify this by taking any other pair of friend members.)**

**Thus for $n = 6$, the answer should be 4.**

Checking the options it is clear that only option 4 gives us a value of 4.

**Maximum Solving time: 60 – 90 seconds**

17. In a tournament, there are $n$ teams $T_1, T_2, ..., T_n$, with $n > 5$. Each team consists of $k$ players, $k > 3$. The following pairs of teams have one players in common:

    $T_1$ & $T_2$, $T_2$ & $T_3$, ..., $T_{n-1}$ & $T_n$, and $T_n$ & $T_1$.

    No other pair of teams has any player in common. How many players are participating in the tournament, considering all the $n$ teams together?

    (a) $n(k-2)$    (b) $k(n-2)$

    (b) $(n-1)(k-1)$    (d) $n(k-1)$

    (e) $k(n-1)$

**Thought process:**

If we take 6 teams and 4 players per team, we would get 4 players in $T_1$ (each one of them unique), 3 more players in $T_2$ (since 1 player of $T_2$ would be shared with $T_1$), 3 more players in $T_3$ (since 1 player of $T_3$ would be shared with $T_2$), 3 more players in $T_4$ (since 1 player of $T_4$ would be shared with $T_3$), 3 more players in $T_5$ (since 1 player of $T_5$ would be shared with $T_4$) and 2 more players in $T_6$ (since 1 player of

$T_6$ would be shared with $T_5$ and one with $T_1$). Hence, there would be a total of 18 ($4 + 3 + 3 + 3 + 3 + 2$) players with $n = 6$ and $k = 4$. Checking from the options we see that only Option (d) gives us 18 as the solution.

**Maximum solution time: 60 seconds.**

18. Consider four digit numbers for which the first two digits are equal and the last two digits are also equal. How many such numbers are perfect squares?

    (a) 4    (b) 0

    (b) 1    (d) 3

    (e) 2

**Thought process:**

A lot of CAT takers got stuck on this question for over 5–7 minutes in the exam, since they tried to find out the squares of all two digit numbers starting from 32. However, if you are aware of the logic of finding squares of two digit numbers, you would realise that only three two-digit numbers after 32 have the last two digits in their squares equal (38, 62 and 88). Hence, you do not need to check any other number apart from these three. Checking these you would get the square of 88 as 7744. And hence, there is only one such number.

*Note:* Of course, you would ignore the values of squares with the last two digits as '00'.

19. A confused bank teller transposed the rupees and paise when he cashed a cheque for Shailaja, giving her rupees instead of paise and paise instead of rupees. After buying a toffee for 50 paise, Shailaja noticed that she was left with exactly three times as much as the amount on the cheque. Which of the following is a valid statement about the cheque amount?

    (a) Over Rupees 22 but less than Rupees 23

    (b) Over Rupees 18 but less than Rupees 19

    (c) Over Rupees 4 but less than Rupees 5

    (d) Over Rupees 13 but less than Rupees 14

    (e) Over Rupees 7 but less than Rupees 8

**Thought Process:**

**Deduction 1:** Question Interpretation: The solution language for this question requires you to think about what possible amount could be such that when its rupees and paise value are interchanged, the resultant value is 50 paise more than thrice the original amount.

**Dedcution 2: Option checking process:**

Armed with this logic, suppose we were to check for Option (a) i.e., the value is above ₹ 22 but below ₹ 23. This essentially means that the amount must be approximately between ₹ 22.66 and ₹ 22.69. (We get the paise amount to be between 66 and 69 based on the fact that the relationship between the Actual Amount, $x$ and the transposed amount $y$ is: $y - 50$ paise $= 3x$.

Hence, values below 22.66 and values above 22.70 are not possible.

→ From this point onwards we just have to check whether this relationship is satisfied by any of the values between ₹ 22.66 and ₹ 22.69.

→ Also, realise the fact that in each of these cases the paise value in the value of the transposed amount $y$ would be 22. Thus, $3x$ should give us the paise value as 72 (since we have to subtract 50 paise from the value of '$y$' in order to get the value of $3x$).

→ This also means that the unit digit of the paise value of $3x$ should be 2.

→ It can be clearly seen that none of the numbers 66, 67, 68 or 69 when being multiplied by 3 give us a units digit of 2. Hence, this is not a possible answer.

Checking for Option (b) in the same fashion:

You should realise that the outer limit for the range of values when the amount is between 18 and 19 is: 18.54 to 18.57. Also, the number of paise in the value of the transposed sum '$y$' would be 18. Hence, the value of $3x$ should give us a paise value as 68 paise. Again, using the units digit principle, it is clear that the only value where the units digit would be 8 would be for a value of 18.56.

Hence, we check for the check amount to be 18.56. Transposition of the rupee and paise value would give us 56.18. When you subtract 50 paise from this you would get 55.68 which also happens to be thrice 18.56. Hence, the correct answer is Option (b).

Notice here that if you can work out this logic in your reactions, the time required to check each option would be not more than 30 seconds. Hence, the net problem solving time to get the second option as correct would not be more than 1 minute. Add the reading time and this problem should still not require more than 2 minutes.

20. How many pairs of positive integers $m$, $n$ satisfy $1/m + 4/n = 1/12$ where $n$ is an odd integer less than 60?

   (a) 7          (b) 5
   (c) 3          (d) 6
   (e) 4

**Thought Process:**

**Deduction 1:** Since two positive fractions on the LHS equals 1/12 on the right hand side, the value of both these fractions must be less than 1/12. Hence, $n$ can take only the values 49, 51, 53, 55, 57 and 59.

**Deduction 2:** We now need to check which of the possible values of $n$ would give us an integral value of $m$.

The equation can be transformed to: $1/12 - 4/n = 1/m$

→ $(n - 48)/12n = 1/m$. On reading this equation you should realise that for $m$ to be an integer the LHS must be able to give you a ratio in the form of $1/x$. It can be easily seen that this occurs for $n = 49$, $n = 51$ and $n = 57$. Hence, there are only 3 pairs.

21. The price of Darjeeling tea (in rupees per kilogram) is $100 + 0.1 n$, on the $n^{th}$ day of 2007 ($n = 1, 2, ..., 100$), and then remains constant. On the other hand, the price of Ooty tea (in rupees per kilogram) is $89 + 0.15n$, on the $n^{th}$ day of 2007 ($n = 1, 2, ..., 365$). On which date in 2007 will the prices of these two varieties of tea be equal?

   (a) May 21          (b) April 11
   (c) May 20          (d) April 10
   (e) June 30

The gap between the two prices initially is of ₹11 or 1100 paise. The rate at which the gap closes down is 5 paise per day for the first hundred days. (The gap covered would be 500 paise which would leave a residual gap of 600 paise.) Then the price of Darjeeling tea stops rising and that of Ooty tea rises at 15 paise per day. Hence, the gap of 600 paise would get closed out in another 40 days. Hence, the prices of the two varieties would become equal on the $140^{th}$ day of the year. $31 + 28 + 31 + 30 + 20 = 140$, means May $20^{th}$ is the answer.

22. Let $a$, $b$, $m$, $n$ be positive real numbers, which satisfy the two conditions that
   (i) If $a > b$ then $m > n$; and
   (ii) If $a > m$ then $b < n$
   Then one of the statements given below is a valid conclusion. Which one is it?
   (a) If $a < b$ then $m < n$     (b) If $a < m$ then $b > n$
   (c) If $a > b + m$ then $m < b$
   (d) If $a > b + m$ then $m > b$

The best way to think about this kind of a question is to try to work out a possibility matrix of the different possibilities that exist with respect to which of the values is at what position relative to each other. While making this kind of a figure for yourself, use the convention of keeping the higher number on top and the lower number below.

If we look at Condition (i) as stated in the problem, it states that: if $a > b$ then $m > n$

This gives us multiple possibilities for the placing of the four variables in relative order of magnitude. These relative positions of the variables can be visualised as follows for the case that $a > b$:

|                          | Possibility 1 | Possibility 2 | Possibility 3 |
|--------------------------|---------------|---------------|---------------|
| Largest number           | a             | a             | a             |
| 2nd largest number       | b             | m             | m             |
| 3rd largest number       | m             | b             | n             |
| Smallest number          | n             | n             | b             |

Looking at the options, Option (a) can be rejected because, when we use the condition If $X$ then necessarily $Y$, it does not mean that If Not $X$, then not $Y$.

For instance, if I make a statement like – "If the Jan Lokpal Bill is passed, corruption will be eradicated from the country; this does not mean that if the Jan Lokpal Bill is not passed then corruption would not be eradicated from the country."

**Note:** For this kind of reverse truth to exist the existing starting conditionality has to be of the form, only if X, then Y. In such a case the conclusion, if not X, then not Y is valid.

For instance, if I make a statement like – "Only if the Jan Lokpal Bill is passed, will corruption be eradicated from the country; this necessarily means the reverse – i.e. if the Jan Lokpal Bill is not passed then corruption would not be eradicated from the country."

This exact logic helps us eliminate the first option – which says that if $a < b$ then m should be less than $n$ (this would obviously not happen just because if $a > b$, then $m$ is greater than $n$ – we would need the only if condition in order for this to work in the reverse fashion.)

Option (b) has the same structure based on the Condition (ii) in the problem – it tries to reverse a "If X, then Y conditionality" into a "If not X, then not Y" conclusion – which would only have been valid in the case of 'Only if X' as explained above.

This leaves us with Options (c) and (d) to check. If you go through these options, you realise that they are basically opposite to each other.

The following thought process would help you identify which of these is the correct answer.

When we say that $a > b + m$ where $a$, $b$ and $m$ are all positive it obviously means that a must be greater than both $b$ and $m$. Thus, in this situation we have $a > b$ as well as $a > m$. In this case both the Conditions (i) and (ii) would activate themselves. It is at this point that the possibility matrix for the case of $a > b$ would become usable.

The possibility matrix that exists currently for $a > b$ is built using the following thought chain:

First think of the various positions in which '$a$' and '$b$' can be put, with '$a$' greater than '$b$' given that we have to fix up 4 numbers in decreasing order. The following possibilities emerge when we do this.

|  | Possibility 1 | Possibility 2 | Possibility 3 | Possibility 4 | Possibility 5 | Possibility 6 |
|---|---|---|---|---|---|---|
| Largest number | a | a | a |  |  |  |
| 2nd largest number | b | a |  | a | a |  |
| 3rd largest number |  | b |  |  | b | a |
| Smallest number |  |  | b | b |  | b |

When we add the fact that when $a > b$, then m is also greater than n to this picture, the complete possibility matrix emerges as below:

|  | Possibility 1 | Possibility 2 | Possibility 3 | Possibility 4 | Possibility 5 | Possibility 6 |
|---|---|---|---|---|---|---|
| Largest number | a | a | a | m | m | m |
| 2nd largest number | b | m | m | a | a | n |
| 3rd largest number | m | b | n | n | b | a |
| Smallest number | n | n | b | b | n | b |

Now, for Options (c) and (d) we know that the condition to be checked for is $a > b + m$ which means that $a > b$ and $a > m$ simultaneously. We have drawn above the possibility matrix for $a > b$. We also know from Condition (ii) in the problem above, that when $a > m$, then b should be less than $n$. Looking at the possibility matrix we need to search for cases where simultaneously each of the following is occurring- (i) $a > b$; (ii) $a > m$ and $b < n$. We can see that the possibilities 1, 2 and 5 will get rejected because in each of these cases b is not less than $n$. Similarly, Possibilities 4 and 6 both do not have $a > m$ and hence can be rejected. Only Possibility 3 remains and in that case, we can see than $m > b$.

Hence, Option (d) is correct.

23. A quadratic function $f(x)$ attains a maximum of 3 at $x = 1$. The value of the function at $x = 0$ is 1.
   What is the value of $f(x)$ at $x = 10$?
   (a) –119          (b) –159
   (c) –110          (d) –180
   (e) –105

Let the equation be $ax^2 + bx + c = 0$. If it gains the maximum at $x = 1$ it means that '$a$' is negative.
   Also $2ax + b = 0 \rightarrow x = -b/2a$. So $-b/2a$ should be 1. So the expression has to be chosen from:
   $-X^2 + 2x + c$
   $-2X^2 + 4x + c$

$-3X^2 + 6x + c$ ....and so on (since we have to keep the ratio of $-b/2a$ constant at 1).

Also, it is given that the value of the function at $x = 0$ is 1. This means that $c = 1$. Putting this value of c in the possible expressions we can see that at $x = 1$, the value of the function is equal to 3 in the case:

$-2X^2 + 4x + 1$

So the expression is $- 2X^2 + 4x + 1$

At $x = 10$, the value would be $-200 + 40 + 1 = -159$.

**Directions for Questions 24 and 25:** Let $a_1 = p$ and $b_1 = q$, where $p$ and $q$ are positive quantities. Define

$$a_n = pb_{n-1}, \qquad b_n = qb_{n-1}, \text{ for even } n > 1,$$
$$\text{and} \qquad a_n = pa_{n-1}, \qquad b_n = qa_{n-1}, \text{ for odd } n > 1.$$

**24.** Which of the following best describes $a_n + b_n$ for even $n$?

(a) $q(pq)^{(n/2-1)}(p+q)$    (b) $(pq)^{(n/2-1)}(p+q)$

(c) $q^{(1/2)n}(p+q)$    (d) $q^{(1/2)n}(p+q)^{(1/2)n}$

(e) $q(pq)^{(n/2)-1}(p+q)^{(1/2)n}$

Again to solve this question, we need to use values. Let $a_1 = p = 5$ and $b_1 = q = 7$ (any random values.)

In such a case,

$a_2 = 5 \times 7 = 35$ and $b_2 = 7 \times 7 = 49$. So the sum of $a_2 + b_2 = 84$.

Checking the values we get:

Option a: $7 \times 1 \times (12) = 84$

Option b: $1 \times (12)$

Option c: $7 \times (12)$

Option d: $7 \times (12)$

Option e: $7 \times (12)$

Obviously apart from Option 2 all other options have to be considered. So it is obvious that the question setter wants us to go at least till the value of n as 4 to move ahead.

$a_3 = 5 \times 35 = 175$, $b_3 = 7 \times 35 = 245$

$a_4 = 5 \times 245 = 1225$, $b_4 = 7 \times 245 = 1715$

Sum of $a_4 + b_4 = 2940$.

Option a: $7 \times 35 \times 12 = 2940$,

Option c: $7 \times 7 \times 12$ eliminated

Option d: $7 \times 7 \times 12 \times 12$ eliminated

Option e: $7 \times 35 \times 12 \times 12$ eliminated

Hence, only Option (a) gives us a value of 2940 for $n = 4$. Thus it has to be correct.

**25.** If $p = 1/3$ and $q = 2/3$, then what is the smallest odd $n$ such that $a_n + b_n < 0.01$ ?

(a) 7      (b) 13

(c) 11      (d) 9

(e) 15

According to the question $a_1 = p = 1/3$ and $b_1 = q = 2/3$.

$a_2 = 1/3 \times 2/3 = 2/9$, $b_2 = 2/3 \times 2/3 = 4/9$

$a_3 = 1/3 \times 2/9 = 2/27$, $b_3 = 2/3 \times 2/9 = 4/27$

$a_4 = 1/3 \times 4/27 = 4/81$, $b_3 = 2/3 \times 4/27 = 8/81$

In this way, you can continue to get to the value of $n$ at

which the required sum goes below 0.01. (It would happen at $n = 9$). However, if you are already comfortably placed in the paper, you can skip this process as it would be time consuming and also there is a high possibility of silly errors being induced under pressure.

**26.** The number of ordered pairs of integers $(x, y)$ satisfying the equation $x^2 + 6x + 2y^2 = 4 + y^2$ is

(a) 12      (b) 8

(c) 10      (d) 14

These kinds of questions and thinking are very common in examinations and hence you need to understand how to solve such questions.

In order to think of such questions, you need to first 'read' the equation given. What do I mean by 'reading' the equation? Let me illustrate:

The first thing we do is to simplify the equation by putting all the variables on the LHS. This would give us the equation $x^2 + 6x + y^2$. When we have an equation like $x^2 + 6x + y^2 = 4$, we should realise that the value on the RHS is fixed at 4. Also, if we take a look at the LHS of the equation we realise that the terms $x^2$ and $y^2$ would always be positive integers or 0 (given that $x$ and $y$ are integers). $6x$ on the other hand could be positive, zero or negative depending on the value of $x$ (if $x$ is positive $6x$ is also positive, if $x$ is negative $6x$ would be negative and if $x$ is 0, $6x$ would also be zero.)

Thus, we can think of the following structures to build a value of 4 on the LHS for the equation to get satisfied:

| | Value of $x^2$ | Value of $6x$ | Value of $y^2$ |
|---|---|---|---|
| Case 1 | 0 | 0 | + |
| Case 2 | + | + | + |
| Case 3 | + | − | + |
| Case 4 | + | − | 0 |

Once you have these basic structures in place, you can think of the cases one by one. Thinking in this structured fashion makes sure that you do not miss out on any possible solutions — and that, as you should realise, is critical for any situation where you have to count the number of solutions. You simply cannot get these questions correct without identifying each possible situation. Trying to do such questions without first structuring your thought process this way would lead to disastrous results in such questions!! Hence, this thinking is very critical for your development of quantitative thinking.

Let us look at **Case 1:** In Case 1, since the value of the first two components on the LHS are 0, it must mean that we are talking about the case of $x = 0$. Obviously, in this case the entire value of 4 for the LHS has to be created by using the term $y^2$.

Thus to make $y^2 = 4$, we can take $y = +2$ or $y = -2$. This gives us two possible solutions $(0, 2)$ and $(0, -2)$

**Case 2:** The minimum positive value for $6x$ would be when $x = 1$. This value for $6x$ turns out to be $6-$ which has already made the LHS larger than 4. To this if we were to add two more positive integers for the values of $x^2$ and $y^2$ it would simply take the LHS further up from $+6$. Hence, in Case 2 there are no solutions.

**Case 3:** In this case the value of $x$ has to be negative and $y$ can be either positive or negative. Possible negative values of $x$ as $-1, -2, -3, -4, -5$ etc. give us values for $6x$ as $-6, -12, -18, -24, -30$, etc.

We then need to fill in values of $x^2$ and $y^2$ and see whether it is possible to add an exact value to any of these and get $+4$ as the final value of the LHS.

This thinking would go the following way:

If $6x = -6$: $x$ must be $-1$ and hence $x^2 = 1$. Thus, $x^2 + 6x = -5$, which means for $x^2 + 6x + y^2 = 4$ we would need $-5 + y^2 = 4 \rightarrow y^2 = 9 \rightarrow y = +3$ and $y = -3$

Thus we have identified two more solutions as $(-1, 3)$ and $(-1, -3)$.

If $6x = -12$: $x$ must be $-2$ and hence $x^2 = 4$. Thus, $x^2 + 6x = -8$, which means for $x^2 + 6x + y^2 = 4$ we would need $-8 + y^2 = 4 \rightarrow y^2 = 12 \rightarrow y$ is not an integer in this case and hence we get no new solutions for this case.

If $6x = -18$: $x$ must be $-3$ and hence $x^2 = 9$. Thus, $x^2 + 6x = -9$, which means for $x^2 + 6x + y^2 = 4$ we would need $-9 + y^2 = 4 \rightarrow y^2 = 13 \rightarrow y$ is not an integer in this case and hence we get no new solutions for this case.

If $6x = -24$: $x$ must be $-4$ and hence $x^2 = 16$. Thus, $x^2 + 6x = -8$, which means for $x^2 + 6x + y^2 = 4$ we would need $-8 + y^2 = 4 \rightarrow y^2 = 12 \rightarrow y$ is not an integer in this case and hence we get no new solutions for this case.

If $6x = -30$: $x$ must be $-5$ and hence $x^2 = 25$. Thus, $x^2 + 6x = -5$, which means for $x^2 + 6x + y^2 = 4$ we would need $-5 + y^2 = 4 \rightarrow y^2 = 9 \rightarrow y = +3$ and $y = -3$

Thus we have identified two more solutions as $(-5, 3)$ and $(-5, -3)$.

If $6x = -36$: $x$ must be $-6$ and hence $x^2 = 36$. Thus, $x^2 + 6x = 0$, which means for $x^2 + 6x + y^2 = 4$ we would need $0 + y^2 = 4 \rightarrow y^2 = 4 \rightarrow y = +2$ and $y = -2$

Thus we have identified two more solutions as $(-6, 2)$ and $(-6, -2)$.

If $6x = -42$: $x$ must be $-7$ and hence $x^2 = 49$. Thus, $x^2 + 6x = 7$, which means that $x^2 + 6x$ itself is crossing the value of 4 for the LHS. There is no scope to add any value of $y^2$ as a positive integer to get the LHS of the equation equal to 4. Thus, we can stop at this point.

Notice that we did not need to check for the Case 4 because if there were a solution for Case 4, we would have been able to identify it while checking for Case 3 itself.

Thus, the equation has 8 solutions.

27. The number of ordered pairs of integral solutions $(m, n)$ which satisfy the equation $m \times n - 6(m + n) = 0$ with $m \le n$ is:

(a) 5          (b) 10
(c) 12         (d) 9

In order to solve a question of this nature, you again first need to 'read' the equation:

The equation $m \times n - 6(m + n) = 0$ can be restructured as: $m \times n = 6(m + n)$

When we read an equation of this form, we should be able to read this as:

The LHS is the product of two numbers, while the RHS is always going to be a multiple of 6. Further, we also know that the value of $m \times n$ would normally always be higher than the value of $m + n$. Thus, we are trying to look for situations where the product of two integers is six times their sum.

While looking for such solutions, we need to look for situations where either:

The RHS is non negative – hence = 0, 6, 12, 18, 24, 30, 36…

The RHS is negative – hence = $-6, -12, -18$…

We would now need to use individual values of $m + n$ in order to check for whether $m \times n = 6(m + n)$

For $m + n = 0$; $6(m + n) = 0$. If we use m and $n$ both as 0, we would get $0 = 0$ in the two sides of the equation. So this is obviously one solution to this equation.

For the RHS = $-6$, we can visualise the product of $m \times n$ as $-6$, if we use m as $-3$ and n as 2 or vice versa. Thus, we will get two solutions as $(2, -3)$ and $(-3, 2)$

For the RHS = $-12$, $m + n = -2$, which means that $m$ and $n$ would take values like $(-4, 2)$; $(-5, 3)$; $(-6, 4)$. If you look inside the factor pairs of $-12$, there is no factor pair which has an addition of $-2$.

For RHS = $-18$, $m + n = -3$. Looking into the factor pairs of 18 (viz: $1 \times 18$, $2 \times 9$, $3 \times 6$) we can easily see $-6$ and 3 as a pair of factors of $-18$ which would add up to $-3$ as required. Thus, we get two ordered solutions for (m,n) viz: $(-6, 3)$; $(3, -6)$

For RHS = $-24$, $m + n = -4$. If we look for factors of $-24$, which would give us a difference of $-4$, we can easily see that within the factor pairs of 24 (viz: $1 \times 24$, $2 \times 12$, $3 \times 8$ and $4 \times 6$) there is no opportunity to create a sum of $m + n = -4$.

For RHS = $-30$, $m + n = -5 \rightarrow$ factors of 30 are $2 \times 15$, $5 \times 6$; there is no opportunity to create a $m + n = -5$ and $m \times n = -30$ simultaneously. Hence, there are no solutions in this case.

For RHS = $-36$, $m + n = -6 \rightarrow$ factors of 36 are $2 \times 18$, $3 \times 12$, $4 \times 9$ and we can stop looking further; there is no opportunity to create $m + n = -6$ and $m \times n = -36$ simultaneously. Hence, there are no solutions in this case.

For RHS = $-42$, $m + n = -7 \rightarrow$ factors of 42 are $2 \times 21$, $3 \times 14$, $6 \times 7$ and we can stop looking further; there is no opportunity to create $m + n = -42$ and $m \times n = -7$ simultaneously. Hence, there are no solutions in this case.

For RHS = $-48$, $m + n = -8 \rightarrow$ factors of 48 are $2 \times 24$, $3 \times 16$, $4 \times 12$… $4 \times 12$ gives us the opportunity to create $m + n = -8$ and $m \times n = -48$ simultaneously. Hence, there are two solutions in this case viz: $(4, -12)$ and $(-12, 4)$

**Note:** While this process seems to be extremely long and excruciating, it is important to note that there are a lot of refinements you can make in order to do this fast. The 'searching inside the factors' shown above is itself a hugely effective short cut in this case. Further, when you are looking for pairs of factors for any number, you need not look at the first few pairs because their difference would be very large. This point is illustrated below:

For RHS = −54, $m + n = −9 \rightarrow$ factors of 54 are $3 \times 18$, $6 \times 9$ and we can stop looking further; (Notice here that we did not need to start with $1 \times 54$ and $2 \times 27$ because they are what can be called as 'too far apart' from each other). There is no opportunity to create $m + n = −6$ and $m \times n = −36$ simultaneously. Hence, there are no solutions in this case.

For RHS = −60, $m + n = −10 \rightarrow$ relevant factor search for 60 are $4 \times 15$, $5 \times 12$ and we can stop looking further; there is no opportunity to create $m + n = −10$ and $m \times n = −60$ simultaneously. Hence, there are no solutions in this case.

For RHS = −66, $m + n = −11 \rightarrow$ relevant factor search for 66 is $6 \times 11$ and we can stop looking further; there is no opportunity to create $m + n = −11$ and $m \times n = −66$ simultaneously. Hence, there are no solutions in this case.

**Note:** While solving through this route each value check should take not more than 5 seconds at the maximum. The question that starts coming into one's mind is, how far does one need to go in order to check for values?? Luckily, the answer is not too far.

As you move to the next values beyond −66, −72 (needs $m + n = −12$, while the factors of 72 do not present this opportunity), −78 (needs $m + n = −13$, which does not happen again).

To move further you need to start working out the logic when $6(m + n)$ is positive. In such a case, the value of $m$ and $n$ would both need to be positive for $m \times n$ also to be positive. If $m + n = 1$, we cannot get two positive values of $m$ and $n$ such that their product is 6. If $m + n = 2$, $m \times n = 12$ would not happen.

A little bit of logical thought would give you that the first point at which this situation would get satisfied. That would be when $6(m + n) = 144$ which means that $m + n = 24$ and for $m \times n$ to be equal to 144, the value of each of $m$ and $n$ would be 12 each.

(A brief note about why it is not possible to get a value before this:

If we try $6(m + n) = 132$ (for instance), we would realise that $m + n = 22$. The highest product $m \times n$ with a limit of $m + n = 22$ would occur when each of $m$ and $n$ is equal and hence individually equal to 11 each. However, the value of 11 for $m$ and $n$ gives us a product of 121 only, which is lower than the required product of 132. This would happen in all cases where $6(m + n)$ is smaller than 144.)

Checking subsequent values of $6(m + n)$ we would get the following additional solutions to this situation:

| $6(m + n)$ | $(m + n)$ | Relevant Factor pairs for the value of $6(m + n)$ | Solutions |
|---|---|---|---|
| 150 | 25 | 10,15 | 10,15; 15,10 |
| 156 | 26 | None | None |
| 162 | 27 | 9,18 | 9,18; 18,9 |
| 168,174 | 28,29 | None | None |
| 180,186 | 30,31 | None | None |
| 192 | 32 | 8,24 | 8,24; 24,8 |
| 198,204 | 33,34 | None | None |
| 210,216 | 35,36 | | |

Break-down of the above thought process:

Note that while checking the factor pairs for a number like 216, if you were to list the entire set of factors along with the sum of the individual factors within the pairs, you would get a list as follows:

Factor Pairs for 216:

| Pair | Sum of Factors in the Pair |
|---|---|
| $1 \times 216$ | 217 |
| $2 \times 108$ | 110 |
| $3 \times 72$ | 75 |
| $4 \times 54$ | 58 |
| $6 \times 36$ | 42 |
| $8 \times 27$ | 35 |
| $9 \times 24$ | 33 |
| $12 \times 18$ | 30 |

However, a little bit of introspection in the correct direction would show you that this entire exercise was not required in order to do what we were doing in this question – i.e., trying to solve for $m + n = 36$ and $m \times n = 216$.

The first five pairs where the larger number itself was greater than or equal to 36 were irrelevant as far as searching for the correct pair of factors is concerned for this question. When we saw the sixth pair of $8 \times 27$, we should have realised that since the sum of $8 + 27 = 35$, which is $< 36$, the subsequent pairs would also have a sum smaller than 36. Hence, you can stop looking for more factors for 216.

Thus, effectively to check whether a solution exists for $6(m + n) = 216$, in this question, all we needed to identify was the $8 \times 27 = 216$ pair and we can reject this value for $6(m + n)$ giving us an integral solution in this case.

This entire exercise can be completed in one '5 second thought' as follows:

If $6(m + n) = 216 \rightarrow m + n = 36$ then one factor pair is $6 \times 36$ itself whose sum obviously is more than 36. So, looking for the next factor pair where the smaller number is $> 6$, we see that $8 \times 27$ gives us a factor pair sum of $8 + 27 = 35 < 36$ and hence we reject this possibility.

Also, you should realise that we do not need to look further than 216 – as for values after 216, when we go to the next factor pair after $6 \times (m + n)$, we would realise that the sum of the factor pair would be lower than the required value for the immediately next factor pair.

Hence, the following solutions exist for this question: 0,0; 2,–3; –3,2; 3,–6; –6,3; 4,–12; –12,4; 12,12; 15,10; 10,15; 9,18; 18,9; 8,24; 24,8

A total of 14 solutions

---

**Author's note:** Doubtless this question is very long, but if you are able to understand the thought process to adopt in such situations, you would do yourself a big favor in the commonly asked questions of finding number of integral solutions.

---

**28.** How many positive integral solutions exist for the expression $a^2 - b^2 = 666$?

In order to solve this question, we need to think of the expression $(a - b)(a + b) = 666$ Obviously, the question is based on factor pairs of 666. If we look at the list of factor pairs of 666 we get:

| | |
|---|---|
| 1 | 666 |
| 2 | 333 |
| 3 | 222 |
| 6 | 111 |
| 9 | 74 |
| 18 | 37 |

Since, 37 is a prime number, we will get no more factor pairs.

Now, if we look at trying to fit in the expression $(a - b)(a + b)$ for any of these values, we see the following occurring:

**Example:** $(a - b) = 9$ and $(a + b) = 74$. If we try to solve for $a$ and $b$ we get: $2a = 83$ (by adding the equations) and '$a$' would not be an integer. Consequently, $b$ would also not be an integer and we can reject this possibility as giving us a solution of $a^2 - b^2 = 666$.

Armed with this logic if we were to go back to each of the factor pairs in the table above, we realise that the sum of the two factors within a factor pair is always odd and hence none of these factor pairs would give us a solution for the equation.

Thus, the correct answer would be 0.

**29.** How many positive integral solutions exist for the expression $a^2 - b^2 = 672$?

In order to solve this question, we need to think of the expression $(a - b)(a + b) = 672$ Obviously, the question is based on factor pairs of 672. If we look at the list of factor pairs of 672 we get:

| | | Sum of factors |
|---|---|---|
| 1 | 672 | Odd |
| 2 | 336 | Even |
| 3 | 224 | Odd |
| 4 | 168 | Even |
| 6 | 112 | Even |
| 8 | 84 | Even |
| 12 | 56 | Even |
| 16 | 42 | Even |
| 21 | 32 | Odd |
| 24 | 28 | Even |

Based on our understanding of the logic in the previous question, we should realise that this works for all situations where the sum of factors is even. Hence, there are 7 positive integral solutions to the equation $a^2 - b^2 = 672$.

**30.** The function $a_n$ is defined as $a_n - a_{n-1} = 2n$ for all $n \geq 2$. $a_1 = 2$.

Find the value of $a_1 + a_2 + a_3 + \ldots a_{12}$

In order to solve such questions, the key is to be able to identify the pattern of the series. A little bit of thought would give you the following structure:

$$a_1 = 2$$
$$a_2 - a_1 = 4 \rightarrow a_2 = 6$$
$$a_3 - a_2 = 6 \rightarrow a_3 = 12$$
$$a_4 - a_3 = 8 \rightarrow a_4 = 20$$
$$a_5 - a_4 = 10 \rightarrow a_5 = 30$$

If we look for the pattern in these numbers we should be able to see the following:
$$2 + 6 + 12 + 20 + 30 \ldots$$
$$= 2(1 + 3 + 6 + 10 + 15 + \ldots)$$

Looking at it this way shows us that the numbers in the brackets are consecutive triangular numbers.

Hence, for the sum till $a_{12}$ we can do the following:
$$2(1 + 3 + 6 + 10 + 15 + 21 + 28 + 36 + 45 + 55 + 66 + 78) = 728.$$

**31.** The brothers Binnu and Kinnu have been challenged by their father to solve a mathematical puzzle before they are allowed to go out to play. Their father has asked them "Imagine two integers $a$ and $b$ such that $1 \leq b \leq a \leq 10$. Can you correctly find out the value of the expression $\sum ab$?" Can you help them identify the correct value of the foregoing expression?

(a) 1155          (b) 1050
(c) 1705          (d) None of these

This question is again based on a pattern recognition principle. The best way to approach the search of the pattern is to start by working out a few values of the given expression. The following pattern would start emerging:

| Value of a | Possible values of b | Value of the sum of the possible products 'a × b' | Explanation |
|---|---|---|---|
| 1 | 1 | 1 | With 'a' as 1, the only value for b is 1 itself. |
| 2 | 1, 2 | $2 \times 1 + 2 \times 2 = 2 \times 3$ | With 'a' as 2, b can take the values of 1 and 2 – and $2 \times 1 + 2 \times 2$ can be written as $2 \times 3$ |
| 3 | 1, 2, 3 | $3 \times 1 + 3 \times 2 + 3 \times 3 = 3 \times 6$ | With 'a' as 3, b can take the values of 1, 2 and 3 – and $3 \times 1 + 3 \times 2 + 3 \times 3$ can be written as $3 \times 6$ |
| 4 | 1, 2, 3, 4 | $4 \times 1 + 4 \times 2 + 4 \times 3 + 4 \times 4 = 4 \times 10$ | |

At this point you should realise that the values are following a certain pattern – the series of values for 'a' are multiplied by a series of consecutive triangular numbers (1, 3, 6, 10 and so on.) Thus, we can expect the subsequent numbers to be got by multiplying 5 × 15, 6 × 21, 7 × 28, 8 × 36, 9 × 45 and 10 × 55.

Hence, the answer can be got by:

$1 \times 1 + 2 \times 3 + 3 \times 6 + 4 \times 10 + 5 \times 15 + 6 \times 21 + 7 \times 28 + 8 \times 36 + 9 \times 45 + 10 \times 55 =$
$1 + 6 + 18 + 40 + 75 + 126 + 196 + 288 + 405 + 550 = 1705$

**32.** For the above question, what would be the answer in case the inequality is expressed as: $1 \le b < a \le 10$?

In this case the solution would change as follows:

| Value of a | Possible values of b | Value of the sum of the possible products 'a × b' | Explanation |
|---|---|---|---|
| 1 | No possible values for 'b', since b has to be greater than or equal to 1 but less than 'a' at the same time | 0 | With 'a' as 1, b has no possible values that it can take. |
| 2 | 1 | $2 \times 1$ | With 'a' as 2, b can only take the value of 1. |
| 3 | 1, 2 | $3 \times 1 + 3 \times 2 = 3 \times 3$ | With 'a' as 3, b can take the values of 1 and 2 – and $3 \times 1 + 3 \times 2$ can be written as $3 \times 3$ |
| 4 | 1, 2, 3 | $4 \times 1 + 4 \times 2 + 4 \times 3 = 4 \times 6$ | With 'a' as 4, b can take the values of 1,2 and 3 – and $4 \times 1 + 4 \times 2 + 4 \times 3$ can be written as $4 \times 6$ |

At this point you should realise that the values are following a certain pattern (just like in the previous question) – the series of values for 'a' are multiplied by a series of consecutive triangular numbers (1, 3, 6, 10 and so on). The only difference in this case is that the multiplication is what can be described as 'one removed', i.e., it starts from the value of 'a' as 2. Thus, we can expect the subsequent numbers to be got by multiplying 5 × 10, 6 × 15, 7 × 21, 8 × 28 and 9 × 36 and 10 × 45. Notice here that the values of 'a' can go all the way till 10 in this case as the inequality on the rightmost side of the expression is $a \le 10$.

Hence, the answer can be got by:

$1 \times 0 + 2 \times 1 + 3 \times 3 + 4 \times 6 + 5 \times 10 + 6 \times 15 + 7 \times 21 + 8 \times 28 + 9 \times 36 + 10 \times 45 =$
$0 + 2 + 9 + 24 + 50 + 90 + 147 + 224 + 324 + 450 = 1320.$

**33.** Consider the equation of the form $x^2 + bx + c = 0$. The number of such equations that have real roots and have coefficients b and c in the set {1, 2, 3, 4, 5, 6, 7), is
(a) 20  (b) 25
(c) 27  (d) 29

We know that in order to have the roots of an equation to be real, we should have the values of the discriminant of the quadratic equation (defined as the value $b^2 - 4ac$ for a standard quadratic equation $ax^2 + bx + c = 0$) to be non-negative.

In the context of the given equation in this problem, since the value of the coefficient of $x^2$ is 1, it means that we need to have $b^2 - 4c$ to be positive or 0.

The only thing to be done from this point is to look for possible values of a and b which fit this requirement. In order to do this, assume a value for 'b' from the set {1, 2, 3, 4, 5, 6, 7} and try to see which values of b and c satisfy $b^2 - 4c \ge 0$.

When b = 1, c can take none of the values between 1 and 6, since "$b^2 - 4c$" would end up being negative
When b = 2, c can be 1;
When b = 3, c can be 1 or 2;
When b = 4, c can be 1 or 2 or 3 or 4;

When $b = 5$, $c$ can take any value between 1 and 6;

When $b = 6$, $c$ can take any value between 1 and 7;

When $b = 7$, $c$ can take any value between 1 and 7

Thus, there are a total of 27 such equations with real roots.

**34.** The number of polynomials of the form $x^3 + ax^2 + bx + c$ which are divisible by $x^2 + 1$ and where $a$, $b$ and $c$ belong to $\{1, 2, ...., 8\}$, is

(a) 1            (b) 8

(c) 9            (d) 10

For a polynomial $P(x)$ to be divisible by another polynomial $D(x)$, there needs to be a third polynomial $Q(x)$ which would represent the quotient of the expression $P(x)/D(x)$. In other words, this also means that the product of the polynomials $D(x) \times Q(x)$ should equal the polynomial $P(x)$.

In simpler words, we are looking for polynomials that would multiply $(x^2 + 1)$ and give us a polynomial in the form of $x^3 + ax^2 + bx + c$. The key point in this situation is that the expression that would multiply $(x^2 + 1)$ to give an expression of the form $x^3 + ....$ Would necessarily be of the form $(x + \text{constant})$. It is only in such a case that we would get an expanded polynomial starting with $x^3$. Further, the value of the constant has to be such that the product of $1 \times$ constant would give a value for 'c' that would belong to the set $\{1, 2, 3, 4, 5, 6, 7, \text{ or } 8\}$. Clearly, there are only 8 such values possible for the constant – viz $1, 2, 3,...8$ and hence the required polynomials that would be divisible by $x^2 + 1$ would be got by the expansion of the following expressions: $(x^2 + 1)(x + 1)$; $(x^2 + 1)(x + 2)$; $(x^2 + 1)(x + 3)$;...; $(x^2 + 1)(x + 8)$. Thus, there would be a total of eight such expressions which would be divisible by $x^2 + 1$. Hence, Option (b) is the correct answer.

**35.** A point $P$ with coordinates $(x, y)$ is such that the product of the coordinates $xy = 144$. How many possible points exist on the $X$–$Y$ plane such that both $x$ and $y$ are integers?

(a) 15          (b) 16

(c) 30          (d) 32

The number of values for $(x, y)$ such that both are integers and their product is equal to 144 is dependent on the number of factors of 144. Every factor pair would gives us 4 possible solutions for the ordered pair $(x, y)$. For instance, if we were to consider $1 \times 144$ as one ordered pair, the possible values for $(x, y)$ would be $(1,144)$; $(144,1)$; $(-1,-144)$; $(-144,-1)$. This would be true for all factor pairs except the factor pair $12 \times 12$. In this case, the possible pairs of $(x, y)$ would be $(12,12)$ and $(-12,-12)$.

If we find out the factor pairs of 144 we will get the following list:

| Factor Pair | Number of solutions for (x, y) |
| --- | --- |
| 1 × 144 | 4 solutions – as explained above |
| 2 × 72 | 4 solutions |
| 3 × 48 | 4 solutions |

| Factor Pair | Number of solutions for (x, y) |
| --- | --- |
| 4 × 36 | 4 solutions |
| 6 × 24 | 4 solutions |
| 8 × 18 | 4 solutions |
| 9 × 16 | 4 solutions |
| 12 × 12 | 2 solutions |

Thus, there are a total of 30 solutions in this case.

**36.** Let $x_1, x_2, ......, x_{40}$ be forty nonzero numbers such that $x_i + x_{i+1} = k$ for all $i$, $1 \le i \le \infty$. If $x_{14} = a$, $x_{27} = b$, then $x_{30} + x_{39}$ equals

(a) $3(a + b) - 2k$

(b) $k + a$

(c) $k + b$

(d) None of the foregoing expressions

Since, $x_{14} = a$, $x_{15}$ would equal $(k - a)$ [we get this by equating $x_{14} + x_{15} = k \to a + x_{15} = k \to x_{15} = (k - a)$]. By using the same logic on the equation $x_{15} + x_{16} = k$, we would get $x_{16} = a$. Consequently $x_{17} = k - a$, $x_{18} = a$, $x_{19} = k - a$, $x_{20} = a$. Thus, we see that every odd term is equal to '$k - a$' and every even term is equal to '$a$'. Further, we can develop a similar logic for $x_i$ in the context of '$b$'. Since, $x_{27} = b$, $x_{28} = k - b$, $x_{29} = b$ and so on. This series also follows a similar logic with $x_i$ being equal to $b$ when '$i$' is odd and being equal to $k - b$ when '$i$' is even.

Thus, for every value of $x_i$, we have two ways of looking at its value—viz either in terms of $a$ or in terms of $b$. Thus, for any $x_{\text{even}}$, we have for instance $x_{20} = a = k - b$.

Solving $a = k - b$ we get $a + b = k$.

Further, when we look at trying to solve for the specific value of what the question has asked us, i.e., the value of $x_{30} + x_{39}$ we realise that we can either solve it in terms of '$a$' or in terms of '$b$'. If we try to solve it in terms of '$a$' we would see the following happening:

$X_{30} + x_{39} = a + k - a = k$

Similarly, in terms of '$b$' $x_{30} + x_{39} = k - b + b = k$. Since we know that $k = a + b$ (deduced above), we can conclude $x_{30} + x_{39} = a + b$. However, if we look at the options, none of the options is directly saying that.

Options (b) and (c) can be rejected because their values are not equal to $a + b$. A closer inspection of Option (a), gives us an expression: $3(a + b) - 2k$. This expression can be expressed as $3(a + b) - 2(a + b) = (a + b)$ and hence this is the correct answer.

**37.** The great mathematician Ramanujam, once was asked a puzzle in order to test his mathematical prowess. He was given two sets of numbers as follows:

Set $X$ is the set of all numbers of the form: $4^n - 3n - 1$, where $n = 1, 2, 3, .....$

Set Y is the set of all numbers of the form $9n$, where $n = 0, 1, 2, 3, .........$

Based on these two definitions of the set, can you help Ramanujam identify the correct statement from amongst the following options:

(a) Each number in $Y$ is also in $X$
(b) Each number in $X$ is also in $Y$
(c) Every number in $X$ is in $Y$ and every number in $Y$ is in $X$.
(d) There are numbers in $X$ that are not in $Y$ and vice versa.

In order to solve such questions conveniently, you would need to first create a language representation for yourself with respect to the two sets.

Set $X$ can be mentally thought of as:

A positive integral power of 4 – a multiple of 3 (with the multiplier being equal to the power of 4 used) – a constant value '1'.

Thus, the set of values in $X$ can be calculated as (0, 9, 54, 243 and so on)

Similarly, Set $Y$ can be thought of as multiples of 9, starting from $9 \times 0 = 0$.

The numbers that would belong to the set $Y$ would be: (0, 9, 18, 27, 36 and pretty much all multiples of 9)

It can be clearly seen that while all values in $X$ are also in $Y$, the reverse is not true. Hence, the statement in Option (b) is correct.

**38.** The number of real roots of the equation

$$\log_{2x}\left(\frac{2}{x}\right)(\log_2(x))^2 + (\log_2(x))^4 = 1,$$ for values

of $x > 1$, is

(a) 0        (b) 1
(c) 2        (d) 27

The only way to handle such questions is to try to get a 'feel' of the equation by inserting a few values for $x$ and trying to see the behaviour of the various terms in the equation.

Towards this end, let us start by trying to insert values for $x$ in the given equation.

Because the problem tells us that $x > 1$, the first value of $x$ which comes to mind is $x = 2$. At $x = 2$, the value of the LHS would become equal to 1. This can be thought of as follows:

LHS $= \log_{2x}(1)(\log_2(2))^2 + (\log_2(2))^4 = 0 + 1 = 1$.

As we try to take higher values of $x$ as 3, 4, 5 and so on we realise first that for values like 3, 5 we will get terms like

$\log_6 (2/3)(\log_2 (3))^2 + (\log_2 (3))^4$ which is clearly not going to be an integral value, because terms like $\log_2 3$, $\log_6 2$ and $\log_6 3$ would have irrational decimal values by themselves. In fact, we can see that for numbers of $x$ that are not powers of 2, we would never get an integral value to the LHS of the expression.

Thus, we need to see the behaviour of the expression only for values of $x$ like 4, 8 and so on before we can conclude about the number of real roots of the equation.

At $x = 4$, the expression becomes:

$\log_8 (2/4)(\log_2(4))^2 + (\log_2(4))^4$

By thinking about this expression it is again clear that there are going to be decimals in the first part of the expression—although they are going to be rational numbers and not irrational—and hence we cannot summarily rule out the possibility of an integral value of this expression—without doing a couple of more calculations. However, there is another thought which can help us confirm that the equation will not get satisfied in this case because the LHS is much bigger than the RHS.

This thought goes as follows:

The LHS has two parts: The first part is $\log_8 (2/4)$ $(\log_2(4))^2$ while the second part is $(\log_2(4))^4$; The value of the second part is 16 while the value of the first part (though it is negative) is much smaller than the required –15 which will make the LHS = 1.

Hence, we can reject this value.

**39.** The number of points at which the curve $y = x^6 + x^3 - 2$ cuts the $x$-axis is

(a) 1        (b) 2
(c) 4        (d) 6

By replacing $x^3 = m$, the equation given in the question, can be written in the form:

$y = m^2 + m - 2 \rightarrow$
$y = (m + 2)(m - 1) \rightarrow m = -2$ and $m = 1$.

This gives $x^3 = -2$ and $x^3 = 1$. This gives us two clear values of $x$ (these would be the roots of the equation) and hence $x$, the curve would cut the '$x$' axis at two points exactly.

**40.** Number of real roots of the equation $8x^3 - 6x + 1 = 0$ lying between $-1$ and 1, is

(a) 0        (b) 1
(c) 2        (d) 3

In order to trace the number of real roots for any equation (cubic or larger) the only feasible way to look at it is to try to visualise how many times the graph of the parallel function (in this case: $8x^3 - 6x + 1$) cuts the $X$-axis.

The following thought process would help you do this:

Since the question is asking us to find out the number of real roots of $8x^3 - 6x + 1 = 0$ between the range $-1$ and $+1$, we will need to investigate only the behaviour of the curve for the function $y = 8x^3 - 6x + 1$ between the values $-1$ and $+1$

The first thing we do is to look at the values of the function at $-1$, 0 and $+1$.

At $x = -1$; the value of the function is $-8 + 6 + 1 = -1$.

At $x = 0$; the value of the function is 1.

At $x = 1$: the value of the function is 3.

If plotted on a graph, we can visualise the three points as given here.

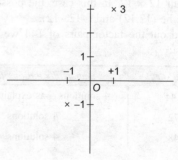

From this visualisation it is clear that the value of the function is –1 at $x = -1$ and $+1$ at $x = 0$ and $+3$ at $x = 1$. It is clear that somewhere between –1 and $+1$, the function would cut the $x$-axis at least once as it transits from a negative value to a positive value. Hence, the equation would necessarily have at least one root between –1 to 0. What we need to investigate in order to solve this question is specifically— does the function cut the $x$-axis more than once during this range of values on the $x$-axis? Also, we should realise that in case the graph will cut the $X$–axis more than once, it would cut it thrice—since if it goes from negative to positive once, and comes back from positive to negative, it would need to become positive again to go above the $x$-axis.

This can be visualised as the following possible shapes:

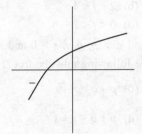 

If the graph cuts the $x$-axis once (and it has one real root in this range)

If the graph cuts the $x$-axis thrice (and it has three real roots in this range)

Of course the graph can technically also cut the $x$-Axis twice between the values of $x = 0$ and $x = 1$. In such a case, the graph would look something like below:

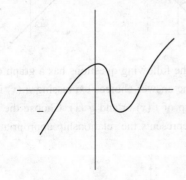

Which of these graphs would be followed would depend on our analysis of the behaviour of the values of $8x^3 - 6x + 1$ between the values of $x$ between –1 and 0 first and then between 0 and 1.

Between –1 and 0:

The value of $8x^3$ would remain negative, while $-6x$ would be positive and $+1$ would always remain constant. If we look that the values of $8x^3$ as we increase the value of $x$ from –1 to $-0.9$ to $-0.8$ to $-0.7$ to … $-0.1$, the negative impact of $8x^3$ reduces as its magnitude reduces. (Please understand the difference between magnitude and value when we are talking about a negative number. For instance when we talk about increasing a negative number its magnitude is decreased).

At the same time the positive magnitude of $-6x$ also reduces but the rapidity with which the value of $-6x$ would decrease will be smaller than the rapidity with which the value of $8x^3$ would decrease. Hence, the positive parts of the expression would become 'more powerful' than the negative part of the expression – and hence the graph would not cut the $x$-axis more than once between –1 and 0.

The last part of our investigation, then would focus on the behaviour of the graph between the values of $x = 0$ and $x = 1$. When $x$ moves into the positive direction (i.e., when we take $x > 0$) we realise that of the three terms $8x^3$ and $+1$ would be positive, while the value of $-6x$ would be negative.

It can be easily visualised that at $x = 1/4$, the value of the expression on the LHS of the equation becomes: $8/64 - 6/4 + 1$, which is clearly negative. Thus, after $x = 0$, when we move to the positive values of $x$, the value of the expression $8x^3 - 6x + 1$ becomes negative once more. Thus the correct graph would look as below:

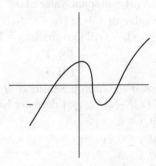

Thus, the equation has three real roots between –1 and $+1$.

## BLOCK REVIEW TESTS

### REVIEW TEST 1

**Directions for Questions 1 to 3:** These are based on the functions defined below

$Q(a, b)$ = Quotient when $a$ is divided by $b$

$R^2(a, b)$ = Remainder when $a$ is divided by $b$

$R(a, b) = a^2/b^2$

$SQ(a, b) = \sqrt{(a-1)/(b-1)}$

1. $SQ(5, 10) - ? > 0$
   (a) $(8/3) R(5, 10)$
   (b) $R^2(5, 10) + Q(5, 10)$
   (c) $R^2(5, 10)/2$
   (d) $\frac{1}{2}\{R(2,3) + SQ(17,26)\}$

2. $SQ(a, b)$ is same as
   (a) $bQ(a, b) + R^2(a)$
   (b) $\sqrt{R(a,b) - 1}$
   (c) $[R\{(a-1), (b-1)\}$
   (d) $\sqrt{R(a,1) - 1}/\sqrt{R(b,1)}$

3. Which of the following relations cannot be false?
   (a) $R(a, b) = R^2(a, b) \cdot Q(a, b)$
   (b) $a^2 \cdot Q(a, b) = b^2 \cdot R^2(a, b)$
   (c) $a = R^2(a, b) + y \cdot Q(a, b)$
   (d) $SQ(a, b) = R(a, b) \cdot R^2(a, b)$

**Directions for Questions 4 to 7:** *Answer the questions based on the following information:*

$W(a, b)$ = least of $a$ and $b$

$M(a, b)$ = greatest of $a$ and $b$

$N(a)$ = absolute value of $a$

4. Find the value of $1 + M[y + N\{-W(x, y)\}, N\{y + W(M(x, y), N(y))\}]$ given that $x = 2$ and $y = -3$.
   (a) 0
   (b) 1
   (c) 2
   (d) 3

5. Given that $a > b$, then the relation $M\{N(x), W(x, y)\} = W[x, N\{M(x, y)\}]$ does not hold if
   (a) $x > 0, y < 0, |x| > |y|$
   (b) $x > 0, y < 0, |y| > |x|$
   (c) $x > 0, y > 0$
   (d) $x < 0, y < 0$

6. Which of the following must be correct for $x, y < 0$
   (a) $N(W(x, y)) \le W(N(x), N(y))$
   (b) $N(M(x, y)) > W(N(x), N(y))$
   (c) $N(M(x, y)) = W(N(x), N(y))$
   (d) $N(M(x, y)) < M(N(x), N(y))$

7. For what value of $x$ is $W(x^2 + 2x, x + 2) < 0$?
   (a) $-2 < x < 2$
   (b) $-2 < x < 0$
   (c) $x < -2$
   (d) Both (2) and (3)

8. It is given that, $(a^{n-3} + a^{n-5} b^2 + \ldots + b^{n-3}) pq = 0$, where $p$ and $q \ne 0$ and $n$ is odd then $\dfrac{(a^n - b^n)(a+b)}{(a^n + b^n)(a-b)}$ =?
   (a) 1
   (b) $-1$
   (c) 3/2
   (d) 0

9. If $f = \dfrac{1}{\log_2 \pi} + \dfrac{1}{\log_{4.5} \pi}$, which of the following is true?
   (a) $f > 4$
   (b) $2 < f < 4$
   (c) $1 < f < 2$
   (d) $0 < f < 1$

10. If $px + qy > rx + sy$, and $y, x, p, q, r, s > 0$ and if $x < y$, then which of the following must be true?
    (a) $\dfrac{p}{q} > \dfrac{q}{r}$
    (b) $p - q > r - s$
    (c) $p + q > r + s$
    (d) $p + q < r + s$

**Directions for Questions 11 to 13:** $f(x)$ *and* $g(x)$ *are defined by the graphs shown below:*

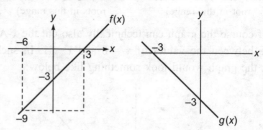

Each of the following questions has a graph of function $h(x)$ with the answer choices expressing $h(x)$ in terms of a relationship of $f(x)$ or/and $g(x)$. Choose the alternative that could represents the relationship appropriately.

11.

(a) $6f(x) + 6g(x)$
(b) $-1.5f(x) + 1.5g(x)$
(c) $1.5f(x) + 1.5g(x)$
(d) None of these

12.

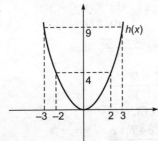

(a) $9 - f(x)\, g(x)$
(b) $[f(x) + g(x) + 4]^2 + [f(x) - 2]^2 + [g(x)]$
(c) $[f(x) - g(x) + 4]^2 - 2$
(d) $f(x)g(x) - 9$

13.

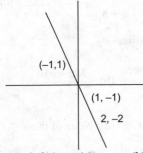

(a) $2f(x) + g(x)$     (b) $f(x) + 2g(x) - 9$
(c) $\dfrac{3}{2}\, f(x) + \dfrac{g(x)}{2}$     (d) None of these

14. If $p^a = q^b = r^c$ and $\dfrac{p}{q} = \dfrac{q}{r}$, $\left(\dfrac{1}{a} + \dfrac{1}{c}\right) b = ?$

(a) 1              (b) 1/2
(c) 3/4            (d) 2

15. What could be the equation of the following curve?

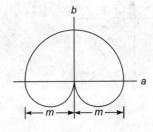

(a) $(a^2 + b^2)^2 = m^2(a^2 + b^2)$
(b) $(a^2 + b^2 - mb)^2 = m^2(a^2 + b^2)$
(c) $a^2 + b^2 - mb = m^2(a^2 + b^2)$
(d) None of these

**Directions for Questions 16 to 18:** It is given that $f(x) = p^x$, $g(x) = (-p)^x$; $h(x) = (1/p)^x$, $k(x) = (-1/p)^x$

16. Think of a situation where a function is odd or even, if the function is odd it is given a weightage of 1; otherwise, it is given a weightage of 0. What is the result if the weightages of four functions are added?

(a) 2              (b) 0
(c) 1              (d) –1

17. If '$p$' and '$x$' are both whole numbers other than 0 and 1, which of the functions must have the highest value?

(a) $g(x)$ only          (b) $f(x)$ only
(c) $g(x)$ and $h(x)$ both  (d) $h(x)$ and $k(x)$ both

18. Which of the following is true if '$p$' is a positive number and $x$ is a real number?

(a) $\{f(x) - h(x)\} / \{g(x) - k(x)\}$ is always positive
(b) $f(x)\cdot g(x)$ is always negative
(c) $f(x)\cdot h(x)$ is always greater than one
(d) $g(x)\cdot h(x)$ could exist outside the real domain

19. If $x$, and $y \geq 1$ and belong to set of integers then which of the following is true about the function $(xy)^n$?

(a) The function is odd if '$x$' is even and '$y$' is odd.
(b) The function is odd if '$x$' is odd and '$y$' is even.
(c) The function is odd if '$x$' and '$y$' both are odd.
(d) The function is even if '$x$' and '$y$' both are odd.

20. If $f(a,b)$ = remainder left upon division of $b$ by $a$, then the maximum value for $f(f(a, b), f(a + 1, b + 1)) \times f(f(a, b), 0)$ is ..... ($b$ and $a$ are co-primes)

(a) $a - 1$          (b) $a$
(c) 0              (d) 1

**Space for Rough Work**

# REVIEW TEST 2

1. The number of solutions of $\dfrac{\log 5 + \log(y^2 + 1)}{\log(y - 2)} = 2$ is:

    (a) 3
    (b) 2
    (c) 1
    (d) None of these

**Information for Questions 2 and 3:** Given below are two graphs labeled $F(x)$ and $G(x)$. Compare the graphs and give the answer in accordance to the options given below:

    (a) $F(-x) = G(x) + x/3$
    (b) $F(-x) = -G(x) - x/2$
    (c) $F(-x) = -G(x) + x/2$
    (d) None of these

2.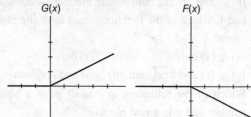

3.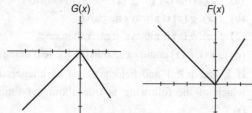

4. If $a$ is a natural number which of the following statements is always true?
    (a) $(a + 1)(a^2 + 1)$ is odd
    (b) $9a^2 + 6a + 6$ is even
    (c) $a^2 - 2a$ is even
    (d) $a^2(a^2 + a) + 1$ is odd

5. In the figure below, equation of the line $PQ$ is

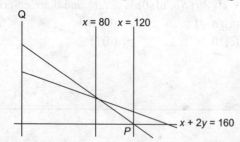

    (a) $x + y = 120$
    (b) $2x + y = 120$
    (c) $x + 2y = 120$
    (d) $2x + y = 180$

6. For which of the following functions is $\dfrac{f(a) - f(b)}{a - b}$ constant for all the numbers '$a$' and '$b$', where $a \neq b$?

    (a) $f(y) = 4y + 7$
    (b) $f(y) = y + y^2$
    (c) $f(y) = \cos y$
    (d) $f(y) = \log_e y$

7. Given that $f(a, b, c) = \dfrac{a + b + c}{3}$ then

    (a) $f(a, b, c) \geq \dfrac{|a| + |b| + |c|}{3}$

    (b) $f(a, b, c) \geq \max(a, b, c)$

    (c) $|f(a, b, c)| \geq \dfrac{|a + b + c|}{3}$

    (d) $|f(a, b, c)| \leq \dfrac{|a| + |b| + |c|}{3}$

8. We are given two variables $x$ and $y$. The values of the variables are $x = \dfrac{1}{a + b}$ and $y = \dfrac{3}{c + x}$. Find the value of the expression $\dfrac{7y}{x}$

    (a) $\dfrac{21(a + b)^2}{ca + cb + 1}$
    (b) $\dfrac{3(a + b)}{7ab + ac}$

    (c) $\dfrac{7}{3(ca + cb + 1)}$
    (d) None of these

9. If $p = \dfrac{12 - |x - 3|}{12 + |x - 3|}$ the maximum value that '$p$' can attain is:

    (a) 1
    (b) 2
    (c) 21
    (d) 12

10.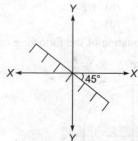

    Refer to the graph. What does the shaded portion represent?
    (a) $x + y \leq 0$
    (b) $x \geq y$
    (c) $x + 1 \geq y + 1$
    (d) $x + y \geq 0$

11. If $a, b, c$ are positive numbers and it is known that $a^2 + b^2 + c^2 = 8$ then:

    (a) $a^3 + b^3 + c^3 \leq 16\sqrt{\dfrac{2}{3}}$

    (b) $a^3 + b^3 + c^3 \geq 64$

    (c) $a^3 + b^3 + c^3 \geq 16\sqrt{\dfrac{2}{3}}$

    (d) $a^3 + b^3 + c^3 \leq 64$

12. Find the value of the expression given in terms of variables '$x$' and '$y$'.

$$\frac{(x^2 + (a-c)x - ac)(x^2 - ax - bx + ab)(x+c)}{(x^2 - a^2)(x^2 - bx^2 - c^2 x + bc^2)}$$

(a) $\dfrac{(x-b)(x-c)}{(x-a)}$

(b) $\dfrac{(x+a)(x+c)}{(x-b)}$

(c) $\dfrac{(x+a)(x-b)}{(x-c)}$

(d) None of these

**Directions for Questions 13 and 14:** These questions are based on the relation given below:

$f^a(y) = f^{a-1}(y-1)$ where $a > 1$ (integer values only) and $f^1(y) = 2/y$ if '$y$' is positive or $f^1(y) = 1/(y^2 + 1)$ otherwise.

13. What is $f^a(a-1)$?

(a) 0          (b) 1

(c) 2          (d) Indeterminate.

14. What is the value of $f^a(a+1)$?

(a) 1          (b) a

(c) 2a         (d) 2

15. Raman derived an equation to denote distance of a Haley's comet ($x$) in the form of a quadratic equation. Distance is given by solution of quadratic $x^2 + Bx + c = 0$. To determine constants of the above equation for Haley's Comet, two separate series of experiments were conducted by Raman. Based on the data of first series, value of $x$ obtained is (1, 8) and based on the second series of data, value of $x$ obtained is (2, 10). Later on it is discovered that first series of data gave incorrect value of constant $C$ while second series of data gave incorrect value of constant $B$. What is the set of actual distance of Haley's Comet found by Raman?

(a) (11, 3)          (b) (6, 3)

(c) (4, 5)           (d) (3,11)

16. '$a$', '$b$' and '$c$' are three real numbers. Which of the following statements is/are always true?

(A) $(a-1)(b-1)(c-1) < abc$.

(B) $(a^2 + b^2 + c^2)/2 \geq ca + cb - ab$

(C) $a^2 b \sqrt{c}$ is a real number

(a) Only $A$ is true      (b) Only $B$ and $C$ are true

(c) Only $B$ is true      (d) None is true

17. If we have $f[g(y)] = g[f(y)]$, then which of the following is true?

(a) $[f[f[g[g[g[g(y)]]]]]] = [f[g[g[f[f[g(y)]]]]]]$

(b) $[f[f[f[g[f[g(y)]]]]]] = f[f[g[g[g[f(y)]]]]]$

(c) $[g[f[g[g[g[f(y)]]]]]] = [f[g[g[f[f[f(y)]]]]]]$

(d) $[g[f[g[g[f[g[f(y)]]]]]]] = [f[g[g[g[g[g[f(y)]]]]]]]$

18. $f(a) = \dfrac{a^8 - 1}{a^2 + 1}$ and $g(a) = \dfrac{a^4 - 3}{(a+1)^2}$, what is $f\left(\dfrac{1}{g(2)}\right)$?

(a) 0.652          (b) $\dfrac{1468}{2250}$

(c) $-\dfrac{734}{1625}$          (d) None of these

19. Dev was solving a question from his mathematics book when he encountered the expression $\dfrac{\log a}{b-c} = \dfrac{\log b}{c-a} = \dfrac{\log c}{a-b}$ then $a^a \, b^b \, c^c$ is

(a) –1          (b) 1

(c) 0.5          (d) 2

20. The number of integral solutions of $\dfrac{\log 5 + \log(a^2 + 1)}{\log(a-2)}$ = is:

(a) 3          (b) 2

(c) 1          (d) None of these

**Space for Rough Work**

# REVIEW TEST 3

**Directions for the Questions 1 to 3:** Refer to the data given below and answer the questions.

Given $\dfrac{a}{b} = \dfrac{1}{2}$, $\dfrac{c}{d} = \dfrac{1}{3}$ and $z = \dfrac{a+c}{b+d}$, answer the questions below on limits of $z$.

1. If $y \geq 0$ and $p \geq 0$ then the limits of '$z$' are:
   - (a) $z \leq 0$ or $z \geq 1$
   - (b) $\dfrac{1}{3} \leq z \leq \dfrac{1}{2}$
   - (c) $z \geq \dfrac{1}{2}$ or $z \leq \dfrac{1}{3}$
   - (d) $0 \leq z \leq 1$

2. $c \leq 0$ and $1/3 \leq z \leq 1/2$ only if:
   - (a) $a > 1.5c$
   - (b) $c > -1$
   - (c) $a \leq 0$
   - (d) $a > -1.5c$

3. If $a = -31$, which of the following value of '$d$' gives the highest value of '$z$'?
   - (a) $d = 72$
   - (b) $d = 721$
   - (c) $d = -31$
   - (d) $d = 0$

4. Find the integral solution of: $5y - 1 < (y + 1)^2 < (7y - 3)$
   - (a) 2
   - (b) $2 < y < 4$
   - (c) $1 < y < 4$
   - (d) 3

5. If $f(a) = \dfrac{a-1}{a+1}$, $x \geq 0$ and if $y = f\left(\dfrac{1}{a}\right)$ then
   - (a) As '$a$' decreases, '$y$' decreases
   - (b) As '$a$' increases, '$y$' decreases
   - (c) As '$x$' increases, '$y$' increases
   - (d) As '$x$' increases, '$y$' remains unchanged

6. If $f$ and $g$ are real functions defined by $f(a) = a + 2$ and $g(a) = 2a^2 + 5$, then fog is equal to
   - (a) $2a^2 + 7$
   - (b) $2a^2 + 5$
   - (c) $2(a+2)^2 + 5$
   - (d) $2a + 5$

7. If '$p$' and '$q$' are the roots of the equation $x^2 - 10x + 16 = 0$, the value of $(1 - p)(1 - q)$ is
   - (a) $-7$
   - (b) 7
   - (c) 16
   - (d) $-16$

8. Given that '$a$' and '$b$' are positive real numbers such that $a + b = 1$, then what is the minimum value of $\sqrt{12 + \dfrac{1}{a^2}} + \sqrt{12 + \dfrac{1}{b^2}}$ ?
   - (a) 8
   - (b) 16
   - (c) 24
   - (d) 4

9. Let $p$, $q$ and $r$ be distinct positive integers satisfying $p < q < r$ and $p + q + r = k$. What is the smallest value of $k$ that does *not* determine $p$, $q$, $r$ uniquely?
   - (a) 9
   - (b) 6
   - (c) 7
   - (d) 8

10. Given odd positive integers $p$, $q$ and $r$ which of the following is not necessarily true?
    - (a) $p^2 q^2 r^2$ is odd
    - (b) $3(p^2 + q^3)r^2$ is even
    - (c) $5p + q + r^4$ is odd
    - (d) $r^2 (p^4 + q^4)/2$ is even

11. $f(a) = (a^2 + 1)(a^2 - 1)$ where $a = 1, 2, 3 \ldots$ which of the following statement is not correct about $f(a)$?
    - (a) $f(a)$ is always divisible by 5
    - (b) $f(a)$ is always divisible by 3
    - (c) $f(a)$ is always divisible by 30
    - (d) None of these

**Directions for Questions 12 and 13:** The following questions are based on the graph of parabola plotted on $x - y$ axes. Answer the questions according to given conditions if applicable and deductions from the graph.

12.

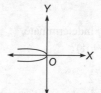

The above graph represent the equations
   - (a) $y^2 = kx$, $k > 0$
   - (b) $y^2 = kx$, $k < 0$
   - (c) $x^2 = ky - 1$, $k < 0$
   - (d) $x^2 = ky - 1$, $k > 0$

13.

The above graph represents the equation
   - (a) $x^2 = ky$, $k < 0$
   - (b) $y^2 = kx + 1$, $k > 0$
   - (c) $y^2 = kx + 1$, $k < 0$
   - (d) None of these

14. Mala while teaching her class on functions gives her students a question.

    According to the question the functions are $f(x) = -x$, $g(x) = x$. She also provides her students with following functions also.

    $$f(x, y) = x - y \text{ and } g(x, y) = x + y$$

    Since she wants to test the grasp of her students on functions she asks them a simple question "which of the following is not true?" and provides her students with the following options. None of her students were able to answer the question in single attempt. Can you answer her question?
    - (a) $f[f(g(x, y))] = g(x, y)$
    - (b) $g[f[g[f(x, y)]]] = f(x, y)$
    - (c) $f(x) + g(x) + f(x, y) + g(x, y) = g(x) - f(x)$
    - (d) None of these

**Directions for Questions 15 and 16:** We are given that $f(x) = f(y)$ and $f(x, y) = x + y$, if $x, y > 0$

$f(x, y) = xy$, if $x, y = 0$

$f(x, y) = x - y$, if $x, y < 0$

$f(x, y) = 0$, otherwise

15. Find the value of the following function: $f[f(2, 0),$ $f(-3, 2)] + f[f(-6, -3), f(2, 3)]$.

   (a) 0                    (b) 2

   (c) –8                   (d) None of these

16. Find the value of the following function:

   $\{ f[f(1, 2), f(2, 3)] \} \times \{ f[f(1.6, 2.9), f(-1, -3)] \}$

   (a) 12                   (b) 36

   (c) 48                   (d) 52

17. Given that $f(a) = a(a + 1)(a + 2)$ where $a = 1, 2,$ 3, …. Then find $S = f(1) + f(2) + f(3) + \ldots\ldots +$ $f(10)$?

   (a) 4200                 (b) 4290

   (c) 4400                 (d) None of these

18. We have three inequalities as:

   (i) $2^a > a$           (ii) $2^a > 2a + 1$

   (iii) $2^a > a^2$

For what natural numbers $n$ are all the three inequalities satisfied?

   (a) $a \geq 3$          (b) $a \geq 4$

   (c) $a \geq 5$          (d) $a \geq 6$

19. For the curve $x^3 - 3xy + 2 = 0$, the set A of points on the curve at which the tangent to the curve is horizontal and the set $B$ of points on the curve at which the tangent to the curve is vertical are respectively:

   (a) $(1, 1)$ and $(0, 0)$      (b) $(0, 0)$ and $(1, 1)$

   (c) $(1, 1)$ and null set      (d) None of these

20. If $f(a) = a^2 - \dfrac{1}{a^2}$ and $g(a) = \dfrac{1}{\sqrt{f(a) - 4}}$, then the real domain for all values of '$a$' such that $f(a)$ and $g(a)$ are both real and defined is represented by the inequality:

   (a) $a^2 - a - 1 > 0$          (b) $a^4 - 4a^2 - 1 > 0$

   (c) $a^2 - 4a - 1 > 0$         (d) None of these

*Space for Rough Work*

# ANSWER KEY

## Review Test 1

| | | | |
|---|---|---|---|
| 1. (d) | 2. (c) | 3. (c) | 4. (c) |
| 5. (d) | 6. (c) | 7. (d) | 8. (a) |
| 9. (c) | 10. (c) | 11. (c) | 12. (a) |
| 13. (d) | 14. (d) | 15. (b) | 16. (b) |
| 17. (b) | 18. (d) | 19. (b) | 20. (c) |

## Review Test 2

| | | | |
|---|---|---|---|
| 1. (d) | 2. (d) | 3. (d) | 4. (d) |
| 5. (a) | 6. (a) | 7. (d) | 8. (a) |

| | | | |
|---|---|---|---|
| 9. (a) | 10. (a) | 11. (c) | 12. (d) |
| 13. (b) | 14. (a) | 15. (c) | 16. (c) |
| 17. (c) | 18. (d) | 19. (b) | 20. (d) |

## Review Test 3

| | | | |
|---|---|---|---|
| 1. (b) | 2. (c) | 3. (d) | 4. (b) |
| 5. (b) | 6. (a) | 7. (d) | 8. (a) |
| 9. (d) | 10. (d) | 11. (d) | 12. (b) |
| 13. (d) | 14. (b) | 15. (a) | 16. (d) |
| 17. (b) | 18. (c) | 19. (c) | 20. (b) |

# TASTE OF THE EXAMS—BLOCK V

## CAT (1999-2008, 2017)

**Directions for questions 1 to 4:** Answer the questions based on the following information.

In each of the following questions, a pair of graphs F(x) and F1(x) is given. These are composed of straight line segments, shown as solid lines, in the domain x ∈ (−2, 2). **(CAT 1999)**

Choose the answer as

  a. if $F1(x) = -F(x)$

  b. if $F1(x) = F(-x)$

  c. if $F1(x) = -F(-x)$

  d. if none of the above is true

1.

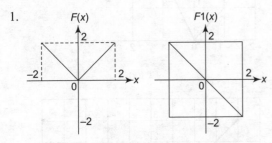

  (a) a           (b) b

  (c) c           (d) d

2.

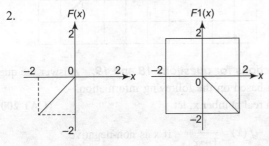

  (a) a           (b) b

  (c) c           (d) d

3.

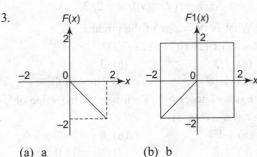

  (a) a           (b) b

  (c) c           (d) d

4.

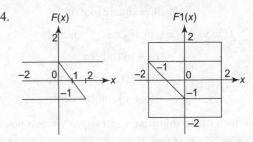

  (a) a           (b) b

  (c) c           (d) d

**Directions for question 5 to 7:** These questions are based on the situation given below.

Let x and y be real numbers and let **(CAT 1999)**

$$f(x, y) = |x + y|, F(f(x, y)) = -f(x, y) \text{ and } G(f(x, y)) = -F(f(x, y))$$

5. Which of the following statements is true?

  (a) $F(f(x, y)) \times G(f(x, y)) = -F(f(x, y)) \times G(f(x, y))$

  (b) $F(f(x, y)) \times G(f(x, y)) > -F(f(x, y)) \times G(f(x, y))$

  (c) $F(f(x, y)) \times G(f(x, y)) \neq G(f(x, y)) \times F(f(x, y))$

  (d) $F(f(x, y)) \times G(f(x, y)) \leq G(f(x, y)) \times f(-x, -y)$

6. What is the value of $f(G(f(1, 0)), f(F(f(1, 2)), G(f(1, 2))))$?

  (a) 3           (b) 2

  (c) 1           (d) 0

7. Which of the following expressions yields $x^2$ as its result?

  (a) $F(f(x, -x))) \times G(f(x, -x))$

  (b) $F(f(x, x)) \times G(f(x, x)) \times 4$

  (c) $-F(f(x, x) \times G(f(x, x)) \div \log_2 16$

  (d) $f(x, x) \times f(x, x)$

**Directions for questions 8 and 9:** Answer the questions based on the following information. **(CAT 2000)**

A, B and C are three numbers. Let

  @ (A, B) = Average of A and B,

  / (A, B) = Product of A and B, and

  × (A, B) = The result of dividing A by B.

8. The sum of A and B is given by

  (a) / (@ (A, B), 2)     (b) × (@ (A, B), 2)

  (c) @ (/ A, B), 2)      (d) @ (× (A, B), 2)

9. Average of A, B and C is given by

  (a) @ (/ (@ (/ (B, A), 2), C), 3)

  (b) × (@ (/ (@ (B, A), 3), C), 2)

  (c) / (×(× (@ (B, A), 2), C), 3)

  (d) / (× (@ (/ (@ (B, A) 2), C), 3), 2)

**Directions for questions 10 and 11:** Answer the questions based on the following information.
For real numbers x and y, let **(CAT 2000)**

$$f(x, y) = \begin{cases} \text{Positive square root of} \\ (x + y), \text{ if } (x + y)^{0.5} \text{ is real} \\ (x + y)^2 \text{ otherwise} \end{cases}$$

$$g(x, y) = \begin{cases} (x + y)^2, \text{ if } (x + y)^{0.5} \text{ is real} \\ -(x + y), \text{ otherwise} \end{cases}$$

10. Which of the following expressions yields a positive value for every pair of non-zero real numbers (x, y)?
    (a) f(x, y) – g(x, y)  (b) (f(x, y) – (g(x, y))²
    (c) g(x, y) – (f(x, y))²  (d) f(x, y) + g(x, y)

11. Under which of the following conditions is f(x, y) necessarily greater than g(x, y)?
    (a) Both x and y are less than –1
    (b) Both x and y are positive
    (c) Both x and y are negative
    (d) y > x

**Directions for questions 12 to 14:** Answer the questions based on the following information.
For three distinct real numbers x, y and z, let **(CAT 2000)**
    f(x, y, z) = Min(Max(x, y), Max(y, z), Max(z, x))
    g(x, y, z) = Max(Min(x, y), Min(y, z), Min(z, x))
    h(x, y, z) = Max(Max(x, y), Max(y, z), Max(z, x))
    j(x, y, z) = Min(Min(x, y), Min(y, z), Min(z, x))
    m(x, y, z) = Max(x, y, z)
    n(x, y, z) = Min(x, y, z)

12. Which of the following is necessarily greater than 1?
    (a) [h(x, y, z) – f(x, y, z)] / j(x, y, z)
    (b) j(x, y, z) / h(x, y, z)
    (c) f(x, y, z) / g(x, y, z)
    (d) [f(x, y, z) + h(x, y, z) – g(x, y, z)] / j(x, y, z)

13. Which of the following expressions is necessarily equal to 1?
    (a) [f(x, y, z) – m(x, y, z)] / [g(x, y, z) – h(x, y, z)]
    (b) [m(x, y, z) – f(x, y, z)] / [g(x, y, z) – n(x, y, z)]
    (c) [j(x, y, z) – g(x, y, z)] / h(x, y, z)
    (d) [f(x, y, z) – h(x, y ,z)] / f(x, y, z)

14. Which of the following expressions is indeterminate?
    (a) [f(x, y, z) – h(x, y, z)] / [g(x, y, z) – j(x, y, z)]
    (b) [f(x, y, z) + h(x, y, z) + g(x, y, z) + j(x, y, z)] / [j(x, y, z) + h(x, y, z) – m(x, y, z) – n(x, y, z)]
    (c) [g(x, y, z) – j(x, y, z)] / [f(x, y, z) – h(x, y, z)]
    (d) [h(x, y, z) – f(x, y, z)] / [n(x, y, z) – g(x, y, z)]

**Directions for questions 15 to 17:** Given below are three graphs made up of straight line segments shown as thick lines. In each case choose the answer as
**(CAT 2000)**
    (a) if f(x) = 3 f(–x)
    (b) if f(x) = –f(–x)
    (c) if f(x) = f(–x)
    (d) if 3f(x) = 6 f(–x), for x ≥ 0

15.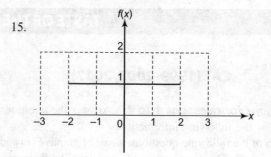

16.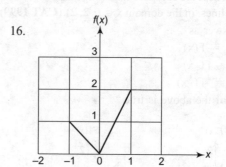

17.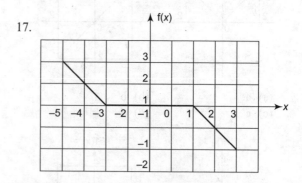

**Directions for questions 18 and 19:** Answer the questions based on the following information.
For a real number x, let **(CAT 2000)**

$$f(x) = \frac{1}{1 + x} \quad \text{if x is non-negative}$$

$$= 1 + x \quad \text{if x is negative}$$

$$f^n(x) = f(f^{n-1}(x)), \; n = 2, 3, \ldots$$

18. What is the value of the product
    f(2) f²(2) f³(2) f⁴(2) f⁵(2)?
    (a) 1/3  (b) 3
    (c) 1/18  (d) None of these

19. r is an integer ≥ 2. Then what is the value of
    f^{r-1}(–r)+f^r(–r)+f^{r+1}(–r)?
    (a) –1  (b) 0
    (c) 1  (d) None of these

20. If the equation x³ – ax² + bx – a = 0 has three real roots, then it must be the case that **(CAT 2000)**
    (a) b = 1  (b) b ≠ 1
    (c) a = 1  (d) a ≠ 1

21. The set of all positive integers is the union of two disjoint subsets: **(CAT 2000)**
    {f(1), f(2), ..., f(n), ...} and {g(1), g(2), ..., g(n), ...},
    where
    f(1) < f(2) < ... < f(n) ..., and g(1) < g(2) < ... < g(n) ..., and
    g(n) = f(f(n)) + 1 for all n ≥ 1.
    What is the value of g(1)?
    (a) 0
    (b) 2
    (c) 1
    (d) Cannot be determined

22. For all non-negative integers x and y, f(x, y) is defined as below. **(CAT 2000)**
    f(0, y) = y + 1
    f(x + 1, 0) = f(x, 1)
    f(x + 1, y + 1) = f(x, f(x + 1, y))
    Then what is the value of f(1, 2)?
    (a) 2
    (b) 4
    (c) 3
    (d) Cannot be determined

23. x and y are real numbers satisfying the conditions 2 < x < 3 and –7 < y < –1. Which of the following expressions will have the least value? **(CAT 2001)**
    (a) $x^2y$
    (b) $xy^2$
    (c) 5xy
    (d) None of these

24. 'm' is the largest positive integer such that n > m. Also, it is known that $n^3 - 7n^2 + 11n - 5$ is positive. Then, the largest possible value for m is: **(CAT 2001)**
    (a) 4
    (b) 5
    (c) 8
    (d) None of these

25. Let x, y be two positive numbers such that x + y = 1. Then, the minimum value of $(x+1/x)^2+(y+1/y)^2$ is... **(CAT 2001)**
    (a) 12
    (b) 20
    (c) 12.5
    (d) 13.3

26. The number of real roots of the equation $\dfrac{A^2}{x}+\dfrac{B^2}{x^{-1}}=1$ where A and B are real numbers not equal to zero simultaneously, is **(CAT 2002)**
    (a) None
    (b) 1
    (c) 2
    (d) 1 or 2

27. Suppose for any real number x, [x] denotes the greatest integer less than or equal to x. Let L(x, y) = [x] + [y] + [x + y] and R(x, y) = [2x] + [2y]. Then it is impossible to find any two positive real numbers x and y for which **(CAT 2002)**
    (a) L(x, y) = R(x, y)
    (b) L(x, y) ≠ R(x, y)
    (c) L(x, y) < R(x, y)
    (d) L(x, y) > R(x, y)

28. If $f(x)=\log\left(\dfrac{1+x}{1-x}\right)$, then f(x) + f(y) is: **(CAT 2002)**
    (a) f(x+y)
    (b) f{(x+y)/(1+xy)}
    (c) (x+y)f{1/(1+xy)}
    (d) f(x)+f(y)/(1+xy)

29. If both a and b belong to the set {1, 2, 3, 4}, then the number of equations of the form $ax^2 + bx + 1 = 0$ having real roots is **(CAT 2002)**
    (a) 10
    (b) 7
    (c) 6
    (d) 12

30. What is the sum of 'n' terms in the series $\log m + \log\left(\dfrac{m^2}{n}\right) + \log\left(\dfrac{m^3}{n^2}\right) + \log\left(\dfrac{m^4}{n^3}\right)+\cdots?$ **(CAT 2002)**
    (a) $\log\left[\dfrac{n^{n-1}}{m^{n+1}}\right]^{n/2}$
    (b) $\log\left[\dfrac{m^m}{n^n}\right]^{n/2}$
    (c) $\log\left[\dfrac{m^{1-n}}{n^{1-m}}\right]^{n/2}$
    (d) $\log\left[\dfrac{m^{n+1}}{n^{n-1}}\right]^{\frac{n}{2}}$

31. The number of roots common between the two equations $x^3 + 3x^2 + 4x + 5 = 0$ and $x^3 + 2x^2 + 7x + 3 = 0$ is **(CAT 2003)**
    (a) 0
    (b) 1
    (c) 2
    (d) 3

32. A real number x satisfying $1-\dfrac{1}{n}<x\le3+\dfrac{1}{n}$, for every positive integer n, is best described by **(CAT 2003)**
    (a) 1< x < 4
    (b) 1 < x ≤ 3
    (c) 0 < x ≤ 4
    (d) 1 ≤ x ≤ 3

**Directions for questions 33 to 35:** Answer the questions on the basis of the tables given below.
Two binary operations ⊕ and * are defined over the set {a, e, f, g, h} as per the following tables:

| ⊕ | a | e | f | g | h |
|---|---|---|---|---|---|
| a | a | e | f | g | h |
| e | e | f | g | h | a |
| f | f | g | h | a | e |
| g | g | h | a | e | f |
| h | h | a | e | f | g |

| * | a | e | f | g | h |
|---|---|---|---|---|---|
| a | a | a | a | a | a |
| e | a | e | f | g | h |
| f | a | f | h | e | g |
| g | a | g | e | h | f |
| h | a | h | g | f | e |

Thus, according to the first table f ⊕ g = a, while according to the second table g*h = f, and so on. Also, let $f^2 = f * f$, $g^3 = g*g*g$, and so on. **(CAT 2003)**

33. What is the smallest positive integer n such that $g^n$ = e?
    (a) 4
    (b) 5
    (c) 2
    (d) 3

34. Upon simplification, f ⊕[f * {f ⊕(f * f )}] equals
    (a) e
    (b) f
    (c) g
    (d) h

35. Upon simplification, {a¹⁰*(f¹⁰⊕ g⁹)} ⊕ e⁸ equals
    (a) e
    (b) f
    (c) g
    (d) h

36. If n is such that $36 \leq n \leq 72$, then

    $x = \dfrac{n^2 + 2\sqrt{n}\,(n+4) + 16}{n + 4\sqrt{n} + 4}$   satisfies   (CAT 2003)

    (a)  $20 < x < 54$   (b)  $23 < x < 58$
    (c)  $25 < x < 64$   (d)  $28 < x < 60$

37. If $|b| \geq 1$ and $x = -|a|b$, then which one of the following is necessarily true?   (CAT 2003)
    (a)  $a - xb < 0$   (b)  $a - xb \geq 0$
    (c)  $a - xb > 0$   (d)  $a - xb \leq 0$

38. If $\dfrac{1}{3} \log_3 M + 3 \log_3 N = 1 + \log_{0.008} 5$, then:   (CAT 2003)
    (a)  $M^9 = 9/N$   (b)  $N^9 = 9/M$
    (c)  $M^3 = 3/N$   (d)  $N^9 = 3/M$

39. Let $f(x) = ax^2 - b\,|x|$, where a and b are constants. Then at $x \neq 0$, $f(x)$ is   (CAT 2003)
    (a)  maximized whenever $a > 0$, $b > 0$
    (b)  maximized whenever $a > 0$, $b < 0$
    (c)  minimized whenever $a > 0$, $b > 0$
    (d)  minimized whenever $a > 0$, $b < 0$

40. The number of non-negative real roots of $2^x - x - 1 = 0$ equals   (CAT 2003 L)
    (a)  0   (b)  1
    (c)  2   (d)  3

41. When the curves $y = \log_{10} x$ and $y = x^{-1}$ are drawn in the x-y plane, how many times do they intersect for values $x \geq 1$?   (CAT 2003)
    (a)  Never   (b)  Once
    (c)  Twice   (d)  More than twice.

42. Let $g(x) = \max(5 - x, x + 2)$. The smallest possible value of $g(x)$ is:   (CAT 2003)
    (a)  4.0   (b)  4.5
    (c)  1.5   (d)  None of the above

43. The function $f(x) = |x - 2| + |2.5 - x| + |3.6 - x|$, where x is a real number, attains a minimum at:   (CAT 2003)
    (a)  $x = 2.3$   (b)  $x = 2.5$
    (c)  $x = 2.7$   (d)  None of the above

44. Let p and q be the roots of the quadratic equation $x^2 - (a - 2) x - (a + 1) = 0$. What is the minimum possible value of $p^2 + q^2$?   (CAT 2003)
    (a)  0   (b)  3
    (c)  4   (d)  5

45. If $\log_3 2$, $\log_3 (2^x - 5)$, $\log_3 (2^x - 7/2)$ are in arithmetic progression, then the value of x is equal to:
    (a)  5   (b)  4
    (c)  2   (d)  3   (CAT 2003)

46. Consider the following two curves in the x-y plane; $y = x^3 + x^2 + 5$ and $y = x^2 + x + 5$ which of the following statements is true for $-2 \leq x \leq 2$?   (CAT 2003)

    (a)  The two curves intersect once.
    (b)  The two curves intersect twice.
    (c)  The two curves do not intersect.
    (d)  The two curves intersect thrice.

47. If $f(x) = x^3 - 4x + p$, and f(0) and f(1) are of opposite signs, then which of the following is necessarily true   (CAT 2004)
    (a)  $-1 < p < 2$   (b)  $0 < p < 3$
    (c)  $-2 < p < 1$   (d)  $p > 3$ or $p < 0$

**Directions for questions 48 and 49:**   Answer the questions on the basis of the information given below.

   $f_1(x) = x$        $0 \leq x \leq 1$
           $= 1$        $x \geq 1$
           $= 0$        Otherwise
   $f_2(x) = f_1(-x)$   for all x
   $f_3(x) = -f_2(x)$   for all x
   $f_4(x) = f_3(-x)$   for all x   (CAT 2004)

48. How many of the following products are necessarily zero for every x.

    $f_1(x)f_2(x)$, $f_2(x)f_3(x)$, $f_2(x)f_4(x)$?
    (a)  0   (b)  1
    (c)  2   (d)  3

49. Which of the following is necessarily true?
    (a)  $f_4(x) = f_1(x)$ for all x
    (b)  $f_1(x) = -f_3(-x)$ for all x
    (c)  $f_2(-x) = f_4(x)$ for all x
    (d)  $f_1(x) = f_3(x) = 0$ for all x

50. Let $u = (\log_2 x)^2 - 6\log_2 x + 12$ where x is a real number. Then the equation $x^u = 256$, has.   (CAT 2004)

    (a)  no solution for x
    (b)  exactly one solution for x
    (c)  exactly two distinct solutions for x
    (d)  exactly three distinct solutions for x

51. For which value of k does the following pair of equations yield a unique solution of x such that the solution is positive?   (CAT 2005)
    $x^2 - y^2 = 0$
    $(x - k)^2 + y^2 = 1$
    (a)  2   (b)  0
    (c)  $\sqrt{2}$   (d)  $-\sqrt{2}$

52. Let g(x) be a function such that $g(x + 1) + g(x - 1) = g(x)$ for every real x. Then for what value of p is the relation $g(x+p) = g(x)$ necessarily true for every real x?   (CAT 2005)
    (a)  5   (b)  3
    (c)  2   (d)  6

53. The graph of $y - x$ against $y + x$ is as shown below. (All graphs in this question are drawn to scale and the same scale has been used on each axis.)   (CAT 2006)

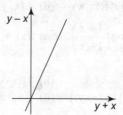

Which of the following shows the graph of y against x?

(a)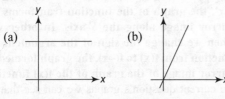

(b)

(c)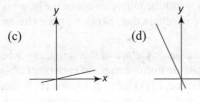

(d)

(e)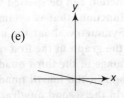

54. What values of x satisfy $x^{\frac{2}{3}} + x^{\frac{1}{3}} - 2 \leq 0$ ('x' is a real number)? **(CAT 2006)**
   (a) $-8 \leq x \leq 1$
   (b) $-1 \leq x \leq 8$
   (c) $1 < x < 8$
   (d) $1 < x \leq 8$
   (e) $-8 \leq x \leq 8$

55. Let $f(x) = \max(2x + 1, 3 - 4x)$, where x is any real number. Then the minimum possible value of $f(x)$ is: **(CAT 2006)**
   (a) 1/3
   (b) 1/2
   (c) 2/3
   (d) 4/3
   (e) 5/3

56. If $\log_Y x = (a . \log_Z y) = (b . \log_X z) = ab$, then which of the following pairs of values for (a, b) is not possible? **(CAT 2006)**
   (a) $(-2, 1/2)$
   (b) $(1,1)$
   (c) $(0.4, 2.5)$
   (d) $(a, 1/a)$
   (e) $(2,2)$

57. A function $f(x)$ satisfies $f(1) = 3600$ and $f(1) + f(2) + ... + f(n) = n^2 f(n)$, for all positive integers n > 1. What is the value of $f(9)$? **(CAT 2007)**
   (a) 80
   (b) 240
   (c) 200
   (d) 100
   (e) 120

58. A quadratic function $f(x)$ attains a maximum of 3 at x = 1. The value of the function at x = 0 is 1. What is the value $f(x)$ at x = 10? **(CAT 2007)**
   (a) $-119$
   (b) $-159$
   (c) $-110$
   (d) $-180$
   (e) $-105$

**Directions for Questions 59 and 60:** Let $f(x) = ax^2 + bx + c$, where a, b and c are certain constants and $a \neq 0$. It is known that $f(5) = -3f(2)$, and that 3 is a root of $f(x) = 0$. **(CAT 2008)**

59. What is the other root of $f(x) = 0$?
   (a) $-7$
   (b) $-4$
   (c) 2
   (d) 6
   (e) cannot be determined

60. What is the value of a + b + c?
   (a) 9
   (b) 14
   (c) 13
   (d) 37
   (e) cannot be determined

61. Let $f(x)$ be a function satisfying $f(x)f(y) = f(xy)$ for all real x, y. If $f(2) = 4$, then what is the value of $f(1/2)$? **(CAT 2008)**
   (a) 0
   (b) 1/4
   (c) 1/2
   (d) 1
   (e) cannot be determined

62. If the roots of the equation $x^3 - ax^2 + bx - c = 0$ are three consecutive integers, then what is the smallest possible value of b? **(CAT 2008)**
   (a) $-1/\sqrt{3}$
   (b) $-1$
   (c) 0
   (d) 1
   (e) $1/\sqrt{3}$

63. If x is real number such that $\log_3 5 = \log_5(2 + x)$, then which of the following is true? **(CAT 2017)**
   (a) $0 < x < 3$
   (b) $23 < x < 30$
   (c) $x > 30$
   (d) $3 < x < 23$

64. Let $f(x) = x^2$ and $g(x) = 2^x$, for all real x. Then the value of $f(f(g(x)) + g(f(x)))$ at x = 1 is **(CAT 2017)**
   (a) 16
   (b) 18
   (c) 36
   (d) 40

65. The minimum possible value of the sum of the squares of the roots of the equation **(CAT 2017)** $x^2 + (a + 3)x - (a + 5) = 0$ is
   (a) 1
   (b) 2
   (c) 3
   (d) 4

66. If $9^{x-1/2} - 2^{2x-2} = 4^x - 3^{2x-3}$, then x is **(CAT 2017)**
   (a) 3/2
   (b) 2/5
   (c) 3/4
   (d) 4/9

67. If $\log(2^a *3^b *5^c)$ is the arithmetic mean of $\log(2^2 *3^3 *5)$, $\log(2^6 *3 *5^7)$, and $\log(2 *3^2 *5^4)$, then a equals **(CAT 2017)**

68. If $f(ab) = f(a)f(b)$ for all positive integers a and b, then the largest possible value of f(1) is **(CAT 2017)**

69. Let $f(x) = 2x - 5$ and $g(x) = 7 - 2x$. Then $|f(x) + g(x)| = |f(x)| + |g(x)|$ if and only if
   (a) $5/2 < x < 7/2$
   (b) $x \leq 5/2$ or $x \geq 7/2$
   (c) $x < 5/2$ or $x \geq 7/2$
   (d) $5/2 \leq x \leq 7/2$ **(CAT 2017)**

70. The area of the closed region bounded by the equation $|x| + |y| = 2$ in the two-dimensional plane is
   (a) $4\pi$
   (b) 4
   (c) 8
   (d) $2\pi$ **(CAT 2017)**

71. Suppose, $\log_3 x = \log_{12} y = a$, where x, y are positive numbers. If G is the geometric mean of x and y, then $\log_6 G$ is equal to **(CAT 2017)**
(a) $\sqrt{a}$      (b) 2a
(c) a/2      (d) a

72. If $x +1 = x^2$ and $x > 0$, then $2x^4$ is **(CAT 2017)**
(a) $6 + 4\sqrt{5}$      (b) $3 + 5\sqrt{5}$
(c) $5 + 3\sqrt{5}$      (d) $7 + 3\sqrt{5}$

73. The value of $\log_{0.008}\sqrt{5} + \log_{\sqrt{3}}81 - 7$ is equal to **(CAT 2017)**
(a) 1/3      (b) 2/3
(c) 5/6      (d) 7/6

74. If $9^{2x-1} - 81^{x-1} = 1944$, then x is? **(CAT 2017)**
(a) 3      (b) 9/4
(c) 4/9      (d) 1/3

75. If $f_1(x) = x^2 + 11x + n$ and $f_2(x) = x$, then the largest positive integer n for which the equation $f_1(x) = f_2(x)$ has two distinct real roots, is **(CAT 2017)**

76. If $f(x) = (5x + 2)/(3x - 5)$ and $g(x) = x^2 - 2x - 1$, then the value of $g(f(f(3)))$ is **(CAT 2017)**
(a) 2      (b) 1/3
(c) 6      (d) 2/3

## ANSWER KEY

| | | | |
|---|---|---|---|
| 1. (d) | 2. (b) | 3. (b) | 4. (c) |
| 5. (d) | 6. (c) | 7. (c) | 8. (a) |
| 9. (d) | 10. (d) | 11. (a) | 12. (d) |
| 13. (a) | 14. (b) | 15. (c) | 16. (d) |
| 17. (b) | 18. (c) | 19. (b) | 20. (b) |
| 21. (b) | 22. (b) | 23. (c) | 24. (b) |
| 25. (c) | 26. (d) | 27. (d) | 28. (b) |
| 29. (b) | 30. (d) | 31. (a) | 32. (c) |
| 33. (a) | 34. (d) | 35. (a) | 36. (d) |
| 37. (b) | 38. (b) | 39. (b) | 40. (c) |
| 41. (b) | 42. (d) | 43. (b) | 44. (d) |
| 45. (d) | 46. (d) | 47. (b) | 48. (c) |
| 49. (b) | 50. (b) | 51. (c) | 52. (d) |
| 53. (d) | 54. (a) | 55. (e) | 56. (e) |
| 57. (a) | 58. (b) | 59. (b) | 60. (e) |
| 61. (b) | 62. (b) | 63. (d) | 64. (c) |
| 65. (c) | 66. (a) | 67. 3 | 68. 1 |
| 69. (d) | 70. (c) | 71. (d) | 72. (d) |
| 73. (c) | 74. (b) | 75. 24 | 76. (a) |

**Solutions**

1. If you look at the graph closely, you can observe that as you move along the X-axis, from 0 towards the left, both the graphs of F(x) and F1(x) are the same. Thus, we can conclude that: For x < 0, F1(x) = F(x)

When x > 0, the value of F1(x) is opposite in sign to the value of F(x). Hence, for x > 0, we can conclude F1(x) = –F(x). Hence, Option (d) is correct.

2. **Theory tip: In a function f(x) when we change the sign of the argument of the function from 'x' to '–x', the graph of the function transforms to it's mirror image along the Y-axis. In other words, when we change the sign of the argument of the function from f(x) to f(–x), the graph formed is the mirror image of the graph of the f(x) function.** In the current question's graphs we can see that graph of F1(x) is just the mirror image of the graph of F(x). Thus, we conclude that, F1(x) = F(–x). Option (b) is correct.

3. We see the same picture in this question - where the two graphs are mirror images of each other around the Y-axis. Hence, F1(x) = F(–x). Option (b) is correct.

4. **Theory tip: An odd function can be spotted when we see a graph of a function, that is symmetrical about the origin. Symmetry about the origin means that a point of the graph in the first quadrant, would have it's image in the third quadrant and a point of the graph in the fourth quadrant would have it's image in the second quadrant. In other words, suppose you move from the origin to the right by a certain distance along the X-axis. You observe the value of the graph at that point - if the graph is in the first quadrant, then on moving left from the origin by a equal distance on the X-axis, the graph should have a corresponding point in the third quadrant. Also, the absolute value of the Y coordinate of the graph in the first quadrant, should be equal to the value of the Y-coordinate of the graph in the third quadrant for the corresponding values of x. For example, if we consider the graph of $y = x^3$. For x = 2, the function's value would be 8 and lie in the first quadrant. For x = –2, the function's value would be –8 and lie in the third quadrant.**

In the figures for F(x) and F1(x), we see that points in the first quadrant in F(x) are mirrored in the third quadrant in F1(x) and likewise points in the fourth quadrant in F(x) are mirrored in the second quadrant of F1(x). So, we can conclude that F1(x) = –F(–x) and hence option (c) is correct.

**Solution to Questions 5 to 7:**
**Special Tip: In such questions, normally students try to solve by taking values for the given variables and then try to match the answers from the options. A better way to solve such questions is to first read the functions in logical language before you proceed. In this question, for instance, f(x,y) is a function with two arguments, namely x and y and it returns a value of the modulus of the sum of x and y. This means that f(x,y) would always be a positive function. Then F(f(x,y)) is a function that would always give us a negative value - since it is simply given by –f(x,y). In effect this means that F(f(x,y)) is a function that simply changes the sign of the value returned by**

the function f(x,y) and hence f(x,y) and F(f(x,y)) would have the same magnitude, but would be opposite in sign. Armed with this information, if you look at G(f(x,y)), you realise that this function is again a sign change function from F(f(x,y)). This means, that the value of G(f(x,y)) after two sign changes would become the same as the value of f(x,y). With this analysis of the functions, you can move onto the questions.

5. **If you read the options in your mind as:** Option (a) F(f) × G(f) = –F(f) × G(f), you realise that the two sides of this equation would not be the same, as they would have different signs. Hence, option (a) can be rejected. Option (b): F(f) × G(f) > –F(f) × G(f). On analysing this option, we realise that the Left Hand side of the option's inequality would be a negative value, while the right hand side would always be necessarily positive. Hence, option (b) can actually be seen to be always false. Option (c): F(f) × G(f) ≠ G(f) × F(f), has no reason to be true, since the value of a product is always same and doesn't depend on the order in which the multiplication is done. Moving onto option (d) we see that in Option (d) F(f(x, y)) × G(f(x, y)) ≤ G(f(x, y)) × f(–x, –y), the left hand side would always be negative since in essence it is just F(f) × G(f). For analysing the right hand side, we need to think as follows: On the right hand side, there is no effect of changing the arguments of 'f' from x,y to –x, –y, since the value the function f(x,y) would return would always be the modulus of the sum of the arguments. Thus, for instance, if we try to calculate the values of f(2,3) and f(–2,3), we would see the function has the same value. Hence, you can simply read the RHS as: G(f(x, y)) × f(x,y). It is self evident, based on our discussion above, that the values of G(f(x,y)) and f(x,y) would always have the same sign. Hence, the product G(f(x, y)) × f(–x, –y) would always be positive. Hence, the RHS of option (d) would always be greater than or equal to the value of the LHS. Hence, option (d) is correct.

6. f(G(f(1, 0)), f(F(f(1, 2)), G(f(1, 2)))) = f(G(f(1, 0)), f(3, –3)) = f(G(f(1, 0)), 0) = f(1, 0) = 1. Hence, option (c) is correct.

7. Check the options: Option (c): –F(f(x, x)).G(f(x, x)) ÷ log₂ 16 =

   –F(f(x, x) × f(x, x)) ÷ log₂2⁴ = (2x × 2x) ÷ log₂16

   $= \dfrac{4x^2}{\log_2 2^4} = x^2$

8. When you check the first option, you see that: @ (A, B) = (A + B)/2. Then:

   $/ \{@ (A, B), 2\} = / \dfrac{(A+B)}{2}, 2 = \dfrac{A+B}{2} \times 2 = A + B.$

9. By putting some values of A, B, C and checking the options, we get option (d) is correct. **Special Tip: In these situations, while taking the values of** A,B,C assume values that are outside the first set of values that come to your mind. This is necessary because the question setter also knows that test takers would solve these questions using values. Hence, he would often try to set traps for test takers by creating confusing options to the question. In this process, the way the question setter thinks is that he tries to guess the set of values that test takers would assume - and then set incorrect options that would mislead them by giving the required numerical answer. Thus, for questions such as these, if you take values of A,B and C as 1,2,3 or 2,2,2 or 0,1,2 and such values, you expose yourself to the danger of falling into the question setter's trap options. Thus my advise is to avoid the first set of values that come to your mind - because the question setter can also guess those as the values that most test takers would take. To avoid, these traps, it is then best to take values that are outside the normal range that most people would take. Thus, something like 4,8 and 9 would be a good set of values to take. (I would avoid taking something like 6,8 and 10 - think why? Because the answer of the average of A, B and C would coincide with the value of B in such a case.)

The solution would go as follows, with A = 4, B = 8 and C = 9, we are looking for the option that gives us a value of 7 as its' answer.

Option (a) @ (/ (@ (/ (B, A), 2), C), 3) would be: @ (/ (@ (/ (8, 4), 2), 9), 3) =

@ (/ (@ (32, 2), 9), 3) = @ (/ (15, 9), 3) =@ (135, 3) = 69 ≠ 7. Hence, we reject this option.

Checking for option (d) we see that: / (× (@ (/ (@ (B, A) 2), C), 3), 2) =

/ (× (@ (/ (@ (8, 4) 2), 9), 3), 2) = / (× (@ (/ (6, 2), 9), 3), 2) = / (× (@ (12, 9), 3), 2) =

/ (× (10.5, 3), 2) = / (3.5, 2) =7. Thus, option (d) becomes the correct answer. (Note: in this approach, since we have not solved the question through algebraic solving - but just by taking values, we need to make sure that when we select an option as the answer it should be the only option satisfying the requirement of the question. Hence, in this question, we select option (d) not just because it is giving us the required value of 7, but because it is the only option giving us that value).

**Solutions to questions 10 and 11:**
**When you read the functions logically, in this case we see the following:**

f(x, y) is always non-negative – since it returns the value of the positive square root of (x + y) is x + y ≥ 0 and if x + y < 0, then it would return the square of the value of (x + y). Likewise, g(x, y) would also always be positive - since if x + y is negative, then we take the value of g(x, y) as – (x + y) → which would always give a positive value.

10. With this analysis, if we look at the options, it is clear that the value in option (d) f(x, y) + g(x, y) would always be positive. Hence, we can directly mark option (d) as the correct answer. If you do not spot that in this question, you would have to solve the question by checking the options by putting different values of x,y. You would be able to get that options (a), (b) and (c) could be both negative as well as positive, depending on the values of x and y. But option (d) would always be positive. However, needless to say, this approach would end up taking much longer time than the approach that directly spots the answer.

11. Let's check the options one by one.

    Option (a): Both x and y are less than –1.

    Then, f(x, y) = (x + y)² and g(x, y) = –(x + y).

    Substituting any value of x, y < –1, we get f(x, y) always greater than g(x, y).

    We do not need to check the further options once we get that. (Note: Logically also you can see that f(x, y) being the square of (x + y) would increase the value of (x + y) by squaring it – when x, y are both less than –1, while g(x, y) would just give you a positive value by changing the sign of (x + y) from negative to positive – without raising the value of the number. Hence, for x, y < –1, f(x, y) would always be greater than g(x, y).

**Solutions to questions 12 to 14:**
A closer reading of the given functions tells us that the function:

f(x, y, z) = Min(Max(x, y), Max(y, z), Max(z, x)) gives us the second highest value of the three numbers x, y, z;

g(x, y, z) = Max(Min(x, y), Min(y, z), Min(z, x)) gives us the second highest value of the three numbers x, y, z;

h(x, y, z) = Max(Max(x, y), Max(y, z), Max(z, x)) gives us the highest value of the three numbers x, y, z;

j(x, y, z) = Min(Min(x, y), Min(y, z), Min(z, x)) gives us the minimum value of the three numbers x, y, z;

m(x, y, z) = Max(x, y, z) gives us the highest value of the three numbers x, y, z;

n(x, y, z) = Min(x, y, z) gives us the minimum value of the three numbers x, y, z;

Thus, we have: f(x, y, z) = g(x, y, z); h(x, y, z) = m(x, y, z) and j(x, y, z) = n(x, y, z).

With this starting understanding if we move into the questions, the solving of the questions would be much easier than by blindly substituting values in the options and checking to see which answer is correct.

12. Since we are looking at a value 'necessarily greater than 1' it means we are looking for the numerator to be greater than the denominator. When we look at the first option, we see that: (h – f)/j = (highest - second highest)/lowest → Can be more than or less than one depending on the values we choose for x, y and z;

    Option (b) j/h = minimum/maximum would necessarily be less than 1;

Option (c) f/g = (second highest)/(second highest) = 1;

Option (d) [f + h – g]/j = h/j (since f and g are same) = maximum/minimum → necessarily greater than 1.

13. Option (a) is [second highest - highest]/[second highest - highest] = 1. Hence, option (a) is correct.

14. For an indeterminate expression, we need the denominator to be zero. This would occur only when the components of the denominator cancel out. Checking the options, the first option has a denominator of g – h = second highest - highest ≠ 0. Hence, option (a) is not indeterminate. In option (b), we see that the denominator is j + h – m – n = minimum + maximum – maximum – minimum = 0. Hence, the denominator is 0 and hence option (b) is indeterminate.

15. f(x)= f(–x), so option (c) is correct.

16. 3f(x) = 6f(–x), option (d) is correct.

17. f(x) = –f(–x), option b is correct

18. $f(2) = \dfrac{1}{1+2} = \dfrac{1}{3}$, $f^2(2) = f\left(\dfrac{1}{3}\right) = \dfrac{1}{1+\dfrac{1}{3}} = \dfrac{3}{4}$,

    $f^3(2) = f\left(\dfrac{3}{4}\right) = \dfrac{4}{7}$, $f^4(2) = f\left(\dfrac{4}{7}\right) = \dfrac{7}{11}$,

    $f^5(2) = f\left(\dfrac{7}{11}\right) = \dfrac{11}{18}$

    $f(2)\, f^2(2)\, f^3(2)\, f^4(2)\, f^5(2) = \dfrac{1}{3} \times \dfrac{3}{4} \times \dfrac{4}{7} \times \dfrac{7}{11} \times \dfrac{11}{18} = \dfrac{1}{18}$

19. Let r = 2

    f(–2) = 1 – 2 = –1

    $f^2(–2) = f(–1) = 1 – 1 = 0$

    $f^3(–2) = 1/1 + 0 = 1$

    $f^{r-1}(–r) + f^r(–r) + f^{r+1}(–r) = –1 + 0 + 1 = 0$

20. If b = 1, then the factors are (x – a)(x² + 1). This yields 2 imaginary roots. So, option b (b ≠ 1) is the required answer.

21. In the question, f(n) represents the series of all odd numbers 1,3,5,7,9… and g(n) represents the series of all even numbers 2,4,6,8,10,.. Hence, g(1)=2.

22. f(0, 1) = 1 + 1 = 2

    f(x + 1, 0) = f(x, 1)

    put x = 0, f(0 +1, 0) = f(1, 0) = f(0, 1) = 2

    f(x + 1, y + 1) = f(x, f(x + 1, y))

    put x = 0, y = 0 in the above equation we get:

    f(1, 1)= f(0, f(1, 0))= f(0, 2) = 2 + 1= 3.

    Now put x = 0, y = 1 in f(x + 1, y + 1) = f(x, f(x + 1, y)), we get:

    f(1, 2)= f(0, f(1, 1))= f(0, 3) = 3 + 1= 4.

23. x²y and 5xy both have negative value. For 2 < x < 3 and –7 < y < –1, 5xy will be the smaller than x²y. Hence, option (c) is correct.

24. n³ – 7n² + 11n – 5 = (n – 1)²(n – 5) > 0 for n > 5. Hence, the largest possible value of m is 5.

25. The required minimum value would occur when both x and y are taken as 1/2. Then the required sum

$$= \left(\frac{1}{2^2} + 2^2\right) + \left(\frac{1}{2^2} + 2^2\right) = 6.25 + 6.25 = 12.5$$

26. The given would have only one real root if either A or B is equal to 0 (as both can never be zero simultaneously).

When both A and B are nonzero then, it would be a quadratic equation so in this case there would be two real roots.

So option (d) is correct.

27. We can solve this problem just by inserting values for x and y in the given expressions. Put x = 2.2 and y = 1.7

L(x, y) = 6 & R(x, y) = 7 so we can eliminate option b, c.

Now put x = y = 1 then L(x, y)= R(x, y). So we can eliminate option (a).

So option (d) is the correct option.

28. The best and the quickest way to solve this problem is to put x = y and check the options.

$$f(x)+ f(y)= f(x)+ f(x)= 2f(x) = 2\log\left(\frac{1+x}{1-x}\right)$$

Now check the options. Option (b) gives us:

$$F\{(x + y)/(1 + xy)\}= f\{(x + x)/(1 + x.x)\}$$

$$= f\left(\frac{2x}{1+x^2}\right) = \log\left(\frac{1+\frac{2x}{1+x^2}}{1-\frac{2x}{1+x^2}}\right)$$

$$= \log\left(\frac{1 + 2x + x^2}{1 + x^2 - 2x}\right)$$

$$= \log\left(\frac{1+x}{1-x}\right)^2 = 2\log\left(\frac{1+x}{1-x}\right)$$

Hence, this is the correct answer.

Alternately, you could also solve this question by taking x = y = 0.5. (Note: Since, there are no constraints on the values of x and y, you are free to take any value that is convenient). At x = y = 0.5: we get: f(x) + f(y) = 2 log 3 = log 9. Only, option (b) gives us log 9 as its' outcome if we insert x = y = 0.5 in it. Hence, this option would be correct.

29. $ax^2 + bx + 1 = 0$

For real roots

$b^2 - 4ac \geq 0$

$\therefore\quad b^2 - 4a(1) \geq 0$

$\therefore\quad b^2 \geq 4a$

For a = 1, possible values of b are 2, 3, 4.

a = 2, 4a = 8, possible values of b are 3, 4.

a = 3, 4a = 12, possible value of b is 4.

a = 4, 4a = 16, possible value of b is 4.

∴ Number of equations possible = 7.

30. $\log m + \log\left(\frac{m^2}{n}\right) + \log\left(\frac{m^3}{n^2}\right) + \cdots n$ terms

$$\log\frac{m \cdot m^2 \cdot m^3 \dots m^n}{1 \cdot n \cdot n^2 \cdot n^3 \dots n^{n-1}} = \log m^{1+2+\dots n}/n^{1.2\dots n-1}$$

$$= \log\frac{m^{\frac{n(n+1)}{2}}}{n^{\frac{n(n-1)}{2}}} = \log\left[\frac{m^{n+1}}{n^{n-1}}\right]^{\frac{n}{2}}$$

31. The intersection points between two functions, are got by equating, the two functions. Thus, we have x³ + 3x² + 4x + 5 = x³ + 2x² + 7x + 3 → x = 1,2. However, we can see that none of these two intersection points is the root of either of the equations: x³ + 3x² + 4x + 5 = 0 or x³ + 2x² + 7x + 3 = 0

32. $1 - \frac{1}{n} < x \leq 3 + \frac{1}{n}$

By putting n = 1, we get

∴ $0 < x \leq 4$. Hence option (b) is correct.

33. g² = g * g = h

g³ = g² * g = h * g = f

g⁴ = g³ * g = f * g = e

∴    n = 4

34. f ⊕ [f * {f ⊕ (f * f)}]

= f ⊕ [f * {f ⊕ h}]]

= f ⊕ [f * e}]

= f ⊕ [f]]

= h

35. e⁸ = e² * e² * e² * e²

= e * e * e * e= e

∴  $a^{10} = (a^2)^5 = (a * a)^5 = a^5 = a * (a * a)^2 = a * a = a$

g⁴ = e or g⁸ = g⁴ * g⁴ = e * e = e

g⁹ = g⁸ * g = g * e = g

Similarly we can prove that $f^{10} = f$

∴  {a¹⁰ * (f¹⁰⊕g⁹ )} ⊕e⁸ = {a * (f⊕g )} ⊕e

= a*a ⊕e

= a ⊕e = e

36. $x = \dfrac{n^2 + 2\sqrt{n}\,(n + 4) + 16}{n + 4\sqrt{n} + 4}$

Put x = 36

∴    $x = \dfrac{(36)^2 + 2 \times 6 \times 40 + 16}{36 + 24 + 4}$

$= \dfrac{(36)^2 + 2 \times 6 \times 40 + 16}{64}$

$= \dfrac{81 + 30 + 1}{4} = \dfrac{112}{4} = 28$

The least value of x = 28, option (d) is correct.

37. Put a = 0 and b = 1

We get: x = –|a| b = 0

a – xb = 0 – 0 = 0. By putting a = 1 and b = 1 we get x= –1 and a – xb = 2

Hence, a – xb ≥ 0.

38. We can solve this problem by checking the options.

$$1 + \log_{0.008} 5 = 1 + \frac{\log_{10} 5}{\log_{10} 0.008}$$

$$= 1 + \frac{\log 10 - \log 2}{3(\log 2 - 1)} = 1 - \frac{1}{3} = \frac{2}{3}$$

Option (b): $N^9 = 9/M$

$$\frac{1}{3}\log_3 M + 3\log_3 N$$

$$= \frac{1}{3}\log_3 \left(\frac{9}{N^9}\right) + 3\log_3 N = \frac{2}{3}\log_3 3 = \frac{2}{3}$$

So option (b) is correct.

39. $x^2$ and |x| are always positive for any value of x. For a > 0 and b < 0 the given expression will always be positive and attain its maximum value.

40. $2^x - x - 1 = 0$

$2^x = x + 1$

For x = 0 and 1, the LHS and the RHS of the above equation are equal. So, x = 0 is a solution of the above equation.

For $x = 2, 3, 4, \ldots 2^x > x + 1$. So the given equation has 2 solutions. Option (c) is correct.

41. This question can be conveniently handled if you know the graphs of the two functions for x > 0. The following picture shows quite clearly that they would intersect only once. Hence, option (b) is correct.

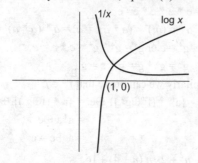

42. The bold portion of the curve given below is max(5 – x, x + 2).

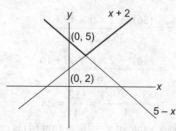

g(x) attains its minimum value at a point where 5 – x = 2 + x

5 – x = x+ 2

x = 1.5

At x = 1.5, g(x) = 5 – 1.5 = 3.5. Option (d) is correct.

43. **Theory tip: Any function of the type |x – 3| + |5 – x| would attain its' least value when x is between 3 to 5. Also that least value would be 5 – 3 = 2. Thus, at x = 2, |x – 3| + |5 – x| at x = 3 = 0 + 2; at x = 3.1 = 0.1 + 1.9; at x = 3.5 = 0.5 + 1.5 at x = 5 = 2 + 0. It can be seen to be equal to 2 for all values of x between 3 to 5. After 5 and before 3 on the x axis, the value of the function would start increasing from it's minimum value. Task for student: See how |x – 2| + |3.6 – x| behaves as you alter the value of x between 2 to 3.6. Also, see the rate at which the function changes its' value when you go beyond 3.6 and when you go below 2 for the value of x.**

When you look at this function, you can easily realise that the value of the function |x – 2| + |3.6 – x| would be equal to 1.6 whenever we take the value of x between 2 to 3.6. Naturally, then the function would attain its' minimum value when |2.5 – x| is minimised. This would happen at x = 2.5.

So at x = 2.5, f(x) attains its minimum value.

44. $(p^2 + q^2) = (p + q)^2 - 2pq = (a - 2)^2 + 2(a + 1) = a^2 - 2a + 6 = a^2 - 2a + 1 + 5 = (a - 1)^2 + 5$. This expression can be minimised at a – 1 = 0 and its minimum value is 5.

45. Put the values of x from the options to check which option works to solve this question. We get for x = 3, the three values are: $\log_3 2$, $\log_3 3$, and $\log_3 4.5$, which is equal to the series: $\log_3 2$; $\log_3 2 + \log_3 1.5$; $\log_3 2 + \log_3 1.5 + \log_3 1.5$ - three terms of an AP. Hence, option (d) is correct.

46. In order to find the number of intersection points of the curves between –2 ≤ x ≤ 2, we need to equate the two equations and look for the values of x at which the two are equal. Thus, $x^3 + x^2 + 5 = x^2 + x + 5$

→ $x^3 = x$ (We know that $x^3$ and x would be equal at three values viz: 0,1 and –1)

∴ x = 0, –1, 1

So the two curves intersect thrice for –2 ≤ x ≤ 2.

47. Theory tip: The reaction to two values of a function being of opposite sign is that their product would be negative. Thus we have: f(0) × f(1) < 0.

Also we realise that for x = 0, the value of the function would be p; while for x = 1, its' value would be p – 3. Hence,

p × (p – 3) < 0

p × (3 – p) > 0

Only option (b) satisfies the above inequality.

**Solution for Questions 48 and 49:**

The best method to solve this problem is the graphical approach

$$f_1(x) = x \qquad 0 \le x \le 1$$
$$\qquad = 1 \qquad x \ge 1$$
$$\qquad = 0 \qquad \text{Otherwise}$$
$$f_2(x) = f_1(-x) \quad \text{for all } x$$
$$f_3(x) = -f_2(x) \quad \text{for all } x$$
$$f_4(x) = f_3(-x) \quad \text{for all } x$$

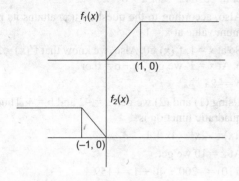

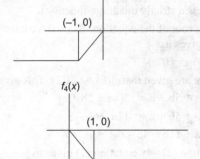

48. From the above graphs it can be seen that $f_1(x)f_2(x) = 0$ and $f_2(x)f_4(x) = 0$ for all values of x. Hence, option (c) is the correct answer.

49. From the graphs it can be seen that option (b) is correct.

50. Since $2^8 = 256 = 4^4 = 16^2 = x^u$, the possible sets of values which would satisfy the given equation are $2^8$, $4^4$ or $16^2$.

    Possible values of (x, u) are (2, 8), (4, 4), (16, 2).

    Now by putting these values one by one in the given equation we get only (4, 4) satisfies the given equation. Hence, option (b) is correct.

51. $(x - k)^2 + y^2 = 1$

    $x^2 + k^2 - 2kx + y^2 = 1$

    As $x^2 = y^2, x^2 + k^2 - 2kx + x^2 = 1$

    $2x^2 - 2kx + k^2 - 1 = 0$

    This is a quadratic equation and the question says that the solution is unique and positive so D = 0, which gives us: $4k^2 - 8(k^2 - 1) = 0$

    Or $k = \sqrt{2}$

For $k = \sqrt{2}$ the sum and the product of the roots of the given equation are positive.

So $k = \sqrt{2}$ is the required answer.

52. We are given a starting relationship for the function g(x), that says that:

    $g(x + 1) + g(x - 1) = g(x)$

    Now, in this expression, if we put x = x +1 we get g(x + 2) + g(x)= g(x + 1). From these two relationships, we see that:

    $g(x) - g(x - 1) = g(x + 2) + g(x) \rightarrow g(x + 2) = -g(x - 1)$. Again by putting x = x + 1 we get: $g(x + 3) = -g(x)$.

    By putting x = x + 3 we get $g(x + 6)= -g(x + 3) = g(x)$. Thus, we realise that $g(x) = g(x + 6)$. Hence, p = 6.

    Note: This can be solved much simpler by taking a starting value of x and proceeding as follows: If x = 1 we get:

    $g(1) = g(2) + g(0) \rightarrow g(0) = g(1) - g(2)$. Also, if x = 2 we get: $g(2) = g(1) + g(3) \rightarrow g(3) = g(2) - g(1)$. It can be seen that $g(0) = -g(3)$. By the same logic $g(6) = -g(3)$. This essentially means that $g(6) = g(0)$. Hence, if p = 6, we get $g(x + p) = g(x)$. Option (d) is the correct answer.

53. From the original graph it can be seen that when y + x = 0, y - x = 0. So, obviously if we take the value of x as 0, the value of y will also be 0 in the correct X-Y graph. So, the correct graph has to pass through the origin. Hence, option (a) is rejected. Further looking at the original graph, we can see that y-x grows faster than y + x when we move right on the y + x axis. When y + x = 1, y - x = 2 (we can see this since the question says that all the graphs are drawn to scale). Thus, we need a point on the correct graph where, if y = 1.5, x = -0.5. Only the graph in option (d) satisfies this and hence option (d) is the correct answer.

54. Put x = 8 in the given inequality, we get:

    $\rightarrow (8)^{2/3} + (8)^{1/3} - 2$

    $\rightarrow 4 + 2 - 2 = 4$

    So, x = 8 does not satisfy the given inequality.

    Hence option (b), (c), (d) &(e) are wrong.

    So only option (a) is correct.

55. $f(x) = \max(2x +1, 3 - 4x) \rightarrow$ The following graph would depict the correct picture for the function (f(x)).

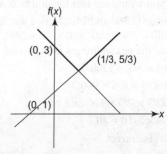

The intersection point of the two straight lines would be got by equating the two lines:

Thus, we have: $2x + 1 = 3 - 4x$

$\rightarrow 6x = 2$

Hence, $x = 1/3$

$f(x)_{\text{at } x = 1/3} = 2.(1/3) + 1 = 5/3$. This is the minimum value of the function.

From the above curve it is clear that $f(x)$ (which is shown by the dark line) attains its minimum value at $x = 1/3$ and it's value is $5/3$ at $x = 1/3$. Hence, the correct option is option (e).

56. $\text{Log}_z y = b$ or $y = z^b$

$\text{Log}_x z = a$ or $z = x^a$

And $x = y^{ab}$

Substituting options in these expressions:

For Option (a): $x = y^{-1}$ – (a), $y = z^{1/2}$ – (b) and $z = x^{-2}$ – (c). Putting (c) in (b), we get that $y = x^{-1}$ which confirms the original expression. Hence, option (a) is possible and hence cannot be the answer.

For Option (b): $x = y$, $y = z$ and $z = x$. Again all relationships are maintained. Hence, option (b) is possible and hence cannot be the answer.

For Option (c): $x = y$, $y = z^{2.5}$ and $z = x^{0.4}$. Substituting the value of $z$ from the third expression into the second, we again get $y = x$, which is consistent with the first expression viz: $x = y$. Hence, option (c) is possible and hence cannot be the answer.

For Option (d) we get: $x = y$, $y = z^{1/a}$ and $z = x^a$. Substituting the value of $z$ from the third expression into the second, we again get $y = x$, which is consistent with the first expression viz: $x = y$. Hence, option (d) is possible and hence cannot be the answer. For Option (e) we get: $x = y^4$, $y = z^2$ and $z = x^2$. Substituting the value of $z$ from the third expression into the second, we get $y = x^4$, which is not consistent with the first expression viz: $x = y^4$. Hence, option (e) is not a possible set of values for (a, b) and hence is the correct answer.

57. $f(1) + f(2) = 4f(2) \rightarrow f(1) = 3f(2) \rightarrow f(2) = 1200$

$f(1) + f(2) + f(3) = 9 f(3) \rightarrow f(3) = 4800/8 = 600$.

$f(1) + f(2) + f(3) = 15f(4) \rightarrow f(4) = 5400/15 = 360$

$f(1) + f(2) + f(3) + f(4) = 24f(5) \rightarrow 5760/24 = f(5)$
$= 240$

At this stage, if you look at the chain of values you've created, you would see that the numbers are:

$3600, 1200, 600, 360$ and $240$. Notice that $3600 \times 1/3 = 1200$; $1200 \times 2/4 = 600$; $600 \times 3/5 = 360$; $360 \times 4/6 = 240$. Thus, the next numbers in the series would be:

$f(6) = 240 \times 5/7 = 1200/7$

$f(7) = 1200/7 \times 6/8 = 900/7$

$f(8) = 900/7 \times 7/9 = 100$ and

$f(9) = 100 \times 8/10 = 80$.

Option (a) is correct.

58. There are three things given in the question. Since $f(x)$ is a quadratic function, we can start with let $f(x) = ax^2 + bx + c$;

At $x = 0$, $f(x) = 1$ can be interpreted as: $f(0) = 1$. But $f(0)$ for $ax^2 + bx + c$ would be equal to c. Hence, $c = 1$. Thus, the function becomes $f(x) = ax^2 + bx + 1$

Next, we are given that $f(1) = 3$. Thus, $f(1) = 3 = a + b + c$

or $a + b + 1 = 3$ or $a + b = 2$      (1)

Also, according to the question $f(x)$ attains its maximum value at $x = 1$

So at $x = 1$, $f'(x) = 0$. Also, we know that $f'(x) = 2ax + b$. At $x = 1$, we get $2a + b = 0$ or

$b = -2a$      (2)

Using (1) and (2) we get: $a = -2$ and $b = 4$. Thus, the quadratic function is:

$f(x) = -2x^2 + 4x + 1$

At $x = 10$ we get:

$f(10) = -200 + 40 + 1 = -159$

Option (b) is correct.

59. $f(x) = ax^2 + bx + c$ where a is not equal to 0 (means that this is a strictly quadratic function).

As 3 is a root of the equation, $f(x) = 0$ we have $f(3) = 0$. This gives us:

$9a + 3b + c = 0$      (1)

Next, we are given that: $f(5) = -3f(2)$. This gives us:

$\quad 25a + 5b + c = -3[4a + 2b + c]$

$\quad 25a + 5b + c = -12a - 6b - 3c$

$\quad 37a + 11b + 4c = 0$      (2)

$\rightarrow$ equation (2) $-4x$ equation (1) gives us

$\rightarrow a - b = 0$ or $a = b$

Sum of roots of $f(x) = -b/a = -b/b = -1$

Since, one root is given as 3, the other root must be $-4$. (Since, $3 + $ other root $= -1$)

60. This question is asking us to find the value of $a + b + c$. This is indeterminate - as there are infinite quadratic equations having roots as 3 and $-4$. This can be thought of mathematically as follows:

$\quad f(x) = a(x - 3)(x + 4)$

$\quad\quad = a(x^2 + x - 12) = ax^2 + ax - 12a$

$\quad b = a, c = -12a$

$\quad a + b + c = a + a - 12a = -10a$

As we can see, the value of $a + b + c$ depends on the value of 'a' which is not known. So the value of 'a + b + c' cannot be determined.

Option (e) is correct.

61. $f(x). f(y) = f(xy)$

Put $x = 2$, $y = 1$

$f(2). f(1) = f(2)$

$f(1) = 1$

Now put x = 2, y = 1/2

we get f(2).f(1/2) =f(2. 1/2) = f(1)

f(1/2) = f(1)/f(2) =1/4

Option (b)

62. Let the roots of the equations are $\alpha - 1$, $\alpha$, $\alpha + 1$. For a cubic equation of the form:

x³– ax² + bx– c = 0, the sum of the pair wise product of the roots would be given by b.

Thus, $b = \alpha(\alpha - 1) + (\alpha - 1)(\alpha + 1) + \alpha(\alpha + 1)$

$b = \alpha^2 + \alpha^2 - 1 + \alpha^2 = 3\alpha^2 - 1$

$b = 3\alpha^2 - 1$

$3\alpha^2 > 0$. To minimize the value of b we need to minimize the value of $3\alpha^2$ and minimum possible value of $3\alpha^2 = 0$

$b_{min} = -1$. Hence, option (b) is correct.

**Alternate Solution:**

Since the question represents a cubic expression, and we want the smallest possible value of b, keeping the constraint of their roots being three consecutive values—a little bit of guess estimation would lead you to think of –1, 0 and 1 as the three roots for minimising the value of b.

Thus, the expression would be (x + 1)(x)(x – 1) = (x² + x)(x – 1) = x³ – x. This gives us the value of b as –1.

It can be seen that changing the values of the roots from –1, 0 and 1 would result in increasing the coefficient of x—which is not what we want. Hence, the correct answer should be –1 (option (b)).

[Note: for trial purposes if you were to take the values of the three roots as 0, 1 and 2, the expressions would become x(x – 1)(x – 2) = (x² – x)(x – 2) which would lead to the coefficient of x being 2. This would obviously increase the value of the coefficient of x above –1.

You could also go for changing the three consecutive integral roots in the other direction to –2, –1 and 0. In such a case the expression would become: x(x + 2)(x + 1) = (x² + 2x)(x + 1) which would again give us the coefficient of x as +2.]

The total solving time for this question would be 30 seconds if you were to hit on the right logic for taking the roots as –1, 0 and 1. In case, you had to check for the value of b in different situations by altering the values of the roots (as explained above), the time would still be under 2 minutes.

63. No need to solve this question mathematically, we can solve it just by estimating the value ranges of log₃ 5 and then matching them with the value range of $\log_5(2 + x)$ by picking up values of x from the options.

The first thing we realise is that: $\log_3 9 > \log_3 5 > \log_3 3$

$2 > \log_3 5 > 1$. Hence, we want $\log_5(2 + x)$ to lie between 1 to 2. The only option that gives us the value of $\log_5(2 + x)$ between 1 to 2 would be the fourth one.

Going through the other options (a to c) we can reject them as follows:

⇒ Option (a): When $0 < x < 3$ then $\log_5(2 + x)$ will always less than 1 because 2 + x = 2 + 3 = 5 and $\log_5(2 + 3) = \log_5 5 = 1$. This option is not correct.

⇒ Option (b): When $23 < x < 29$, then minimum value of $\log_5(2 + x) = \log_5(2 + 23) = \log_5 25 = 2$. So this option is also not correct. Similarly option (c) is also not correct.

Hence, option (d) is correct.

64. $f(x) = x^2$, $g(x) = 2^x$

$$f(f(g(x))) + g(f(x)) = (2^{2x} + 2^{x^2})^2$$

At x = 1, $f(f(g(x))) + g(f(x)) = (2^{2x} + 2^{x^2})^2 = (2^{2 \times 1} + 2^{1^2})^2 = (4 + 2)^2 = 36$. Hence, option (c) is correct.

65. Let the values of roots of the equation be p and q.

$p^2 + q^2 = (p + q)^2 - 2pq = (a + 3)^2 + 2(a + 5) = a^2 + 9 + 6a + 2a + 10$

$= a^2 + 8a + 16 + 3 = (a + 4)^2 + 3$

Minimum possible value of $(a + 4)^2 + 3$ is 3 (when we take a = –4). Hence, option (c) is correct.

66. By checking the options we can see that for x = 3/2 the LHS and RHS of the above equation are equal to each other. So option (a) is correct.

67. Arithmetic mean = $[\log (2^2 \times 3^3 \times 5) + \log(2^6 \times 3 \times 5^7)$

$+ \log (2 \times 3^2 \times 5^4)]/3 = \log (2^9 \times 3^6 \times 5^{12})^{\frac{1}{3}} = \log(2^3 \times 3^2 \times 5^4) = \log(2^a \times 3^b \times 5^c)$

By comparing we get $a = 3$.

68. f(ab) = f(a)f(b)

Put a = 1, b = 0

f(0) = f(1)f(0)

→ f(1)=1.

69. $|f(x) + g(x)| = |f(x)| + |g(x)|$

$f(x) = 2x - 5$, $g(x) = 7 - 2x$

$|2x - 5 + 7 - 2x| = |2x - 5| + |7 - 2x|$

$2 = |2x - 5| + |7 - 2x|$

By checking the options, we get that the above equation satisfies for any value of x which lies in between 5/2 and 7/2 (including both the values). So, option (d) is correct.

70. Curve of $|x| + |y| = 2$ is as shown below:

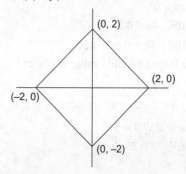

There are four triangles with base 2 and height 2 in this figure. The area of each triangle is 2. Hence, the area of the enclosed region is $2 \times 4 = 8$

71. $\log_3 x = \log_{12} y = a$

Or $x = 3^a$, $y = 12^a$

$$G = \sqrt{xy} = \sqrt{3^a \cdot 12^a} = \sqrt{6^{2a}} = 6^a$$

$$\log_6 G = \log_6 6^a = a$$

72. $x + 1 = x^2$

$$x^2 - x - 1 = 0$$

$$x = \frac{1 \pm \sqrt{5}}{2}$$

According to the question, $x > 0$, hence, $x = \dfrac{1 + \sqrt{5}}{2}$

$$2x^4 = 2\left[\frac{1 \pm \sqrt{5}}{2}\right]^4 = \frac{2}{16}[1 + 5 + 2\sqrt{5}]^2 = \frac{1}{8}[6 + 2\sqrt{5}]^2$$

$$= \frac{1}{8}[36 + 20 + 24\sqrt{5}] = \frac{1}{8}[56 + 24\sqrt{5}] = 7 + 3\sqrt{5}$$

Option (d) is correct.

Alternately, from the point where we got the value of $x = \dfrac{1 + \sqrt{5}}{2}$, we can use the value of the square root of 5 as 2.23 and check with the options to get the correct answer.

73. $\log_{0.008} \sqrt{5} = \frac{1}{2} \log_{0.008} 5 = \frac{1}{6} \log_{0.2} 5 = 1/(6\log_5 0.2)$

$= 1/(6\log_5 1/5) = -1/6$

$$\log_{\sqrt{3}} 81 = 2\log_3 3^4 = 8.$$

Required answer $= -\dfrac{1}{6} + 8 - 7 = \dfrac{5}{6}$

74. $9^{2x-1} - 81^{x-1} = 9^{2x-1} - 9^{2x-2} = 9^{2x-2}(9-1) = 1944$

$$9^{2x-2} = 243$$

$$3^{4x-4} = 3^5 \text{ or } 4x - 4 = 5 \text{ or } x = 9/4$$

75. $f_1(x) = x^2 + 11x + n$ and $f_2(x) = x$

$$x^2 + 11x + n = x$$

$$x^2 + 10x + n = 0$$

If the above equation has two distinct real roots then $b^2 - 4ac > 0$

$$10^2 - 4n > 0$$

$$100 - 4n > 0 \text{ or } n < 25$$

So the largest possible value of n is 24.

76. $f(3) = \dfrac{5 \times 3 + 2}{3 \times 2 - 5} = \dfrac{17}{4}$

Similarly $f(17/4) = 3$.

$g(3) = 3^2 - 3 \times 2 - 1 = 2$

# XAT (2008–2017)

1. Let X = {a, b, c} and Y = {1, m}.  **(XAT 2008)**

Consider the following four subsets of X × Y.

$F_1$ = {(a, 1), (a, m), (b, 1), (c, m)}
$F_2$ = {(a, 1), (b, 1), (c, 1)}
$F_3$ = {(a, 1), (b, m), (c, m)}
$F_4$ = {(a, 1), (b, m)}

Which one, amongst the choices given below, is a representation of functions from X to Y?

(a) $F_2$ and $F_3$  
(b) $F_1$, $F_2$ and $F_3$  
(c) $F_2$, $F_3$ and $F_4$  
(d) $F_3$ and $F_4$  
(e) None of the above

2. If $0 < p < 1$ then roots of the equation $(1 - p)x^2 + 4x + p = 0$ are ___?  **(XAT 2008)**

(a) Both 0  
(b) Real and both negative  
(c) Imaginary  
(d) Real and both positive  
(e) Real and of opposite sign.

3. If $x > 0$, the minimum value of  **(XAT 2008)**

$$\frac{\left(x + \frac{1}{x}\right)^6 - \left(x^6 + \frac{1}{x^6}\right) - 2}{\left(x + \frac{1}{x}\right)^3 + \left(x^3 + \frac{1}{x^3}\right)} \text{ is } \underline{\quad}?$$

(a) 0  
(b) 1  
(c) 2  
(d) 3  
(e) None of the above.

4. The number of possible real solution(s) of y in equation $y^2 - 2y \cos x + 1 = 0$ is ___?  **(XAT 2008)**

(a) 0  
(b) 1  
(c) 2  
(d) 3  
(e) None of the above.

5. If $3f(x+2) + 4f\left(\dfrac{1}{x+2}\right) = 4x$, $x \neq -2$, then f(4) =  **(XAT 2008)**

(a) 7  
(b) 52/7  
(c) 8  
(d) 56/7  
(e) None of the above.

6. If [x] denotes the greatest integer $< = x$, then  **(XAT 2008)**

$$\left[\frac{1}{3}\right] + \left[\frac{1}{3} + \frac{1}{99}\right] + \left[\frac{1}{3} + \frac{2}{99}\right] + \cdots \left[\frac{1}{3} + \frac{98}{99}\right] =$$

(a) 98  
(b) 33  
(c) 67  
(d) 66  
(e) 34

7. Let a and b be the roots of the quadratic equation  **(XAT 2009)**

$x^2 + 3x - 1 = 0$ if

$P_n = a^n + b^n$ for $n \geq 0$, then, for $n \geq 2$, $P_n =$

(a) $-3P_{n-1} + P_{n-2}$  
(b) $3P_{n-1} - P_{n-2}$  
(c) $-P_{n-1} + 3P_{n-2}$  
(d) $P_{n-1} + 3P_{n-2}$  
(e) None of the above.

8. If x and y are real numbers, then the minimum value of $x^2 + 4xy + 6y^2 - 4y + 4$ is   **(XAT 2010)**
   (a) −4
   (b) 0
   (c) 2
   (d) 4
   (e) None of the above.

9. The operation (x) is defined by (i) (1) = 2 (ii) (x + y) = (x).(y) for all positive integers x and y. If $\sum_{x=1}^{n}(x) = 1022$, then n = ?   **(XAT 2010)**
   (a) 8
   (b) 9
   (c) 10
   (d) 11
   (e) None of the above

10. The domain of the function $f(x) = \log_7\{\log_3(\log_5(20x - x^2 - 91))\}$ is:   **(XAT 2011)**
    (a) (7, 13)
    (b) (8, 12)
    (c) (7, 12)
    (d) (12, 13)
    (e) None of the above

11. What is the maximum possible value of $(21 \sin X + 72 \cos X)$?   **(XAT 2011)**
    (a) 21
    (b) 57
    (c) 63
    (d) 75
    (e) None of the above

12. Consider a function $f(x) = x^4 + x^3 + x^2 + x + 1$, where x is a positive integer greater than 1. What will be the remainder if $f(x^5)$ is divided by $f(x)$?   **(XAT 2013)**
    (a) 1
    (b) 4
    (c) 5
    (d) a monomial in x
    (e) a polynomial in x

13. A polynomial $ax^3 + bx^2 + cx + d$ intersects x-axis at 1 and −1, and y-axis at 2. The value of b is:   **(XAT 2014)**
    (a) −2
    (b) 0
    (c) 1
    (d) 2
    (e) Cannot be determined

14. The sum of the possible values of X in the equation $|X + 7| + |X - 8| = 16$ is:   **(XAT 2014)**
    (a) 0
    (b) 1
    (c) 2
    (d) 3
    (e) None of the above

15. The value of the expression:   **(XAT 2014)**
    $\sum_{i=2}^{100} \frac{1}{\log_i 100!}$ is:
    (a) 0.01
    (b) 0.1
    (c) 1
    (d) 10
    (e) 100

16. If $f(x^2 - 1) = x^4 - 7x^2 + k_1$ and $f(x^3 - 2) = x^6 - 9x^3 + k_2$ then the value of $(k_2 - k_1)$ is   **(XAT 2015)**
    (a) 6
    (b) 7
    (c) 8
    (d) 9
    (e) None of the above

17. For a positive integer x, define f(x) such that $f(x + a) = f(a \times x)$, where a is an integer and f(1) = 4. If the value of f(1003) = k, then the value of 'k' will be:   **(XAT 2015)**

(a) 1003
(b) 1004
(c) 1005
(d) 1006
(e) None of the above

18. f is a function for which f(1) = 1 and f(x) = 2x + f(x − 1) for each natural number x ≥ 2. Find f(31).   **(XAT 2016)**
    (a) 869
    (b) 929
    (c) 951
    (d) 991
    (e) None of the above

19. If x and y are real numbers, the least possible value of the expression.   **(XAT 2017)**
    $4(x - 2)^2 + 4(y - 3)^2 - 2(x - 3)^2$ is:
    (a) −8
    (b) −4
    (c) −2
    (d) 0
    (e) 2

20. If f(x) = ax + b, a and b are positive real numbers and if f(f(x)) = 9x + 8, then the value of a + b is:   **(XAT 2017)**
    (a) 3
    (b) 4
    (c) 5
    (d) 6
    (e) None of the above

## ANSWER KEY

| | | | |
|---|---|---|---|
| 1. (a) | 2. (b) | 3. (e) | 4. (c) |
| 5. (e) | 6. (b) | 7. (a) | 8. (c) |
| 9. (b) | 10. (b) | 11. (d) | 12. (c) |
| 13. (a) | 14. (b) | 15. (c) | 16. (c) |
| 17. (e) | 18. (d) | 19. (b) | 20. (c) |

**Solutions**

1. For sets X and Y, a function from X to Y is a set of ordered pairs F of members of these sets such that for every x in X there is a unique y in Y for which the pairs (x, y) is in F. In other simpler words, for one value from X, there should be only one unique value in Y. Only F2 and F3 satisfy this. Hence, option (a) is the correct answer.

2. $D = 16 - 4(1 - p)p$ or $16 - 4p(1 - p) > 0$ for $0 < p < 1$.

   Sum of roots $= \left(\frac{-4}{(1-p)}\right) < 0$ because $0 < p < 1$ and

   Product of roots $= \left(\frac{p}{1-p}\right) > 0$ for $0 < p < 1$.

   Therefore, roots of the given equation are real and negative. Option (b) is correct.

3. Since $x + \frac{1}{x}$ has a minimum value of 2 for x > 0.

   $$\frac{\left(x + \frac{1}{x}\right)^6 + \left(x^6 + \frac{1}{x^6}\right) - 2}{\left(x + \frac{1}{x}\right)^3 + \left(x^3 + \frac{1}{x^3}\right)} = \frac{2^6 - 2 - 2}{2^3 + 2} = 6$$

   Hence, option (e) is the correct answer.

4. For real y, D ≥ 0 or $4\cos^2 x \geq 4$.

Or: $4(\cos^2 x - 1) \geq 0$. This would occur only when $\cos x \geq 1$ and $\cos x \leq -1$. As the value of cos x lies between −1 to +1, it means that the expression we derived would only be ≥ 0 when cos x is 1 or −1. Hence, the number of possible real solutions are 2.

∴ Option (c) is the correct answer.

5. Since the target value for us is to find f(4), we can first put a value of x = 2 in the equation $3f(x+2) + 4f\left(\dfrac{1}{x+2}\right)$ to get: $3f(4) + 4f(1/4) = 8$ …..(1)

Next, putting x = −1.75, we get: $3f(1/4) + 4f(4) = -7$. Equation (1) × 3 - equation (2) × 4 gives:

−7 f(4) = 52. Hence, f(4) = −52/7. Option (e) is the correct answer.

6. $\left[\dfrac{1}{3}\right] + \left[\dfrac{1}{3} + \dfrac{1}{99}\right] + \left[\dfrac{1}{3} + \dfrac{2}{99}\right] + \cdots + \left[\dfrac{1}{3} + \dfrac{65}{99}\right] = 0$

$\left[\dfrac{1}{3} + \dfrac{66}{99}\right] + \left[\dfrac{1}{3} + \dfrac{67}{99}\right] + \cdots + \left[\dfrac{1}{3} + \dfrac{98}{99}\right] = 33$

$\left[\dfrac{1}{3}\right] + \left[\dfrac{1}{3} + \dfrac{1}{99}\right] + \left[\dfrac{1}{3} + \dfrac{2}{99}\right]$

$+ \cdots \left[\dfrac{1}{3} + \dfrac{98}{99}\right] = 0 + 33 = 33.$

Option (b) is the correct answer.

7. Given that $x^2 + 3x - 1 = 0$, we know that the sum of the roots is -3 and the product of the roots is -1. Assume the roots to be a and b. We have:

a + b = −3, ab = −1

$P_2 = a^2 + b^2 = (a+b)^2 - 2ab = 11$

$P_1 = a^1 + b^1 = -3$

$P_0 = a^0 + b^0 = 2$. We can see that: $P_2 = -3P_1 + P_0$. Matching this equation with the options, we see that the option (a) $P_n = -3P_{n-1} + P_{n-2}$ gives us the required relationship. Hence, Option (a) is correct.

8. $x^2 + 4xy + 6y^2 - 4y + 4$

$= x^2 + 4y^2 + 4xy + 2y^2 - 4y + 2 + 2$

$= (x + 2y)^2 + 2(y^2 - 2y + 1) + 2$

$= (x + 2y)^2 + 2(y - 1)^2 + 2$

The above expression is minimum when y = 1, x = −2. So minimum value is = 0 + 0 + 2 = 2.

9. It can be seen from the defined functions that: $(1 + 1) = (2) = (1)(1) = 2^2$

$(2 + 1) = (2)(1) = 2^2 \cdot 2 = 2^3$

Thus, we can conclude that the function: $(n + 1) = 2^n$

$\sum_{x=1}^{n} (x) = (1) + (2) + (3) + (4) + \cdots (n) = 1022$

$2 + 2^2 + 2^3 + \ldots + 2^n = 1022.$

The above equation satisfies for n = 9. Option (b) is the correct answer.

10. $f(x) = \{\log_7\{\log_3(\log_5(20x - x^2 - 91))$. This function would be defined if:

$\log_3(\log_5(20x - x^2 - 91)) > 0$

This gives us that: $\log_5(20x - x^2 - 91)) > 1$

Using the definition of logs we get: $20x - x^2 - 91 > 5$

⇒ $x^2 - 20x + 96 < 0$

Or x ∈ (8, 12). Option (b) is correct.

11. Let f(X) = 21 sin X + 72 cos X

$-\sqrt{a^2 + b^2} \leq a\sin x + b\cos x \leq \sqrt{a^2 + b^2}$

$-\sqrt{21^2 + 72^2} \leq 21\sin x + 72\cos x \leq \sqrt{21^2 + 72^2}$

$\rightarrow -75 \leq 21\sin x + 72\cos x \leq 75$

12. $f(x) = x^4 + x^3 + x^2 + x + 1 = \dfrac{x^5 - 1}{x - 1}$ Using the formula for the sum of the terms of a geometric progression.

$f(x^5) = x^{20} + x^{15} + x^{10} + x^5 + 1$

$\therefore \mathrm{Rem}\left(\dfrac{f(x^5)}{f(x)}\right) = \mathrm{Rem}\left(\dfrac{\begin{array}{c}x^{20} - 1 + x^{15} - 1 \\ + x^{10} - 1 + x^5 - 1 + 5\end{array}}{\dfrac{x^5 - 1}{x - 1}}\right)$

$= (x - 1)\mathrm{Rem}\left(\dfrac{x^{20} - 1}{x^5 - 1} + \dfrac{x^{15} - 1}{x^5 - 1} + \dfrac{x^{10} - 1}{x^5 - 1} + \dfrac{x^5 - 1}{x^5 - 1}\right)$

$+ \mathrm{Rem}\left(\dfrac{5}{x^5 - 1}\right)$

Required remainder = (x − 1) × 0 + 5 = 5

13. When a polynomial intersects the x-axis, the value of y = 0. When a polynomial intersects the y-axis, the value of x = 0. If we take the polynomial as $y = ax^3 + bx^2 + cx + d$, we get:

Intersects x-axis at x = 1 implies: a + b + c + d = 0;
Intersects x-axis at x = −1 implies: −a + b − c + d = 0; Hence, 2(b + d) = 0 or simply put (b + d) = 0.
Intersects y-axis at y = 2 implies: 0 + d = 2 → d = 2. Hence, b = −2. Hence, Option (a) is correct.

14. You need to consider the value of the expression for three ranges of values of X. If X ≥8, |X + 7| and |X − 8| are both non-negative.

If −7 ≤ X < 8, |X + 7| is positive and |X − 8| is negative. & If X < −7, |X + 7| and |X − 8| are both negative. For the first case:

If X ≥ 8, |X + 7| and |X − 8| are both non-negative. |X + 7| = X + 7 and |X − 8| = X − 8. Hence, |X + 7| + |X − 8| = 16; Implies X + 7 + X − 8 = 16 → 2X − 1 = 16 Therefore x = 8.5.

**For the second case:**

If $-7 \leq X < 8$, $|X + 7|$ is positive and $|X - 8|$ is negative. $|X + 7| = X + 7$ and $|X - 8| = 8 - X$. Hence, $X + 7 + 8 - X = 16$. This leads to the ridiculous outcome $15 = 16$. Of course this is not possible and hence we can rule out this range - i.e. there would be no value of X between $-7 \leq x < 8$ that would satisfy this equation.

**For the third case:**

If $x < -7$, $|x + 7|$ and $|x - 8|$ are both negative.

$|x + 7| = -7 - x$ and $|x - 8| = 8 - x$. Thus, we get:

$-7 - x + 8 - x = 16 \rightarrow 2x = -15 \rightarrow x = -7.5$.

Thus, we have two possible values of x: i.e. 8.5 and $-7.5$ and their sum $= 8.5 - 7.5 = 1$.

Hence option (b) is correct.

15. The given expression would be equal to:

$\log_{100!}2 + \log_{100!}3 + \log_{100!}4 + \dots + \log_{100!}100 = \log_{100!}100! = 1$.

16. We are given that: $f(x^2 - 1) = x^4 - 7x^2 + k_1$

Putting $x = 0$, we will get: $f(-1) = k_1$     (1)

Similarly for: $f(x^3 - 2) = x^6 - 9x^3 + k_2$

put $x = 1$ : $f(-1) = -8 + k_2$     (2)

Equation (1) - Equation (2) will give us:

$0 = k_1 + 8 - k_2$

$k_2 - k_1 = 8$.

Option (c) is correct.

17. $f(a + x) = f(ax)$. If we use $a = 1$ and $x = 1$, we get: $f(2) = f(1)$ by using the definition of the function. Hence, $f(1) = f(2) = 4$. Next, by using $a = 2$ and $x = 1$, we get $f(2 + 1) = f(3) = f(2.1) = f(2) = 4$. By following the same pattern we get $f(1003) = 4$. Hence, the value of $k = 4$ and option (e) is the correct answer.

18. We are given that: $f(x) = 2x + f(x - 1)$ for $x \geq 2$. Using this definition of the function continuously, we get:

$f(2) = 2.2 + f(1) = 4 + 1 = 5 = 2^2 + 1$

$f(3) = 2.3 + f(2) = 6 + 5 = 11 = 3^2 + 2$

$f(4) = 2.4 + f(3) = 8 + 11 = 19 = 4^2 + 3$

By following similar pattern, we get $f(31) = 31^2 + 30 = 961 + 30 = 991$

Option (d) is correct.

19. To minimize the value of the given expression we need to maximize the value of the negative quantities and minimize the value of the positive quantities.

$4(y - 3)^2$ will be minimum at $y = 3$. After putting $y = 3$, we are left with

$4(x - 2)^2 - 2(x - 3)^2 = 4[x^2 - 4x + 4] - 2[x^2 - 6x + 9]$

$= 2x^2 - 4x - 2$

$= 2[x^2 - 2x - 1]$

$= 2[x^2 - 2x + 1 - 1 - 1]$

$= 2[(x - 1)^2 - 2]$

$= 2(x - 1)^2 - 4$

The above expression will be minimum at $x = 1$ and it's minimum value $= -4$

20. $f(x) = ax + b$

$f(f(x)) = a(ax + b) + b$

$= a^2x + ab + b$.

But the question says that $f(f(x)) = 9x + 8$. Hence,

$a^2 = 9 \rightarrow a = 3$.

and $ab + b = 8 \rightarrow$

$3b + b = 8 \rightarrow b = 2$

Hence, $a + b = 3 + 2 = 5$

## IIFT (2008-2017)

1. If three positive real numbers a, b and c ($c > a$) are in Harmonic Progression, then $\log (a + c) + \log (a - 2b + c)$ is equal to: **(IIFT 2008)**
   (a) $2 \log (c - b)$    (b) $2 \log (c - c)$
   (c) $2 \log (c - a)$    (d) $\log a + \log b + \log c$

2. If $\log_2 x \cdot \log_{x/64} 2 = \log_{x/16} 2$. Then x is **(IIFT 2008)**
   (a) 2    (b) 4
   (c) 16    (d) 12

3. Find the root of the quadratic equation $bx^2 - 2ax + a = 0$ **(IIFT 2010)**
   (a) $\dfrac{\sqrt{b}}{\sqrt{b \pm \sqrt{a - b}}}$    (b) $\dfrac{\sqrt{a}}{\sqrt{b \pm \sqrt{a - b}}}$
   (c) $\dfrac{\sqrt{a}}{\sqrt{a \pm \sqrt{a - b}}}$    (d) $\dfrac{\sqrt{a}}{\sqrt{a \pm \sqrt{a + b}}}$

4. If [x] is the greatest integer less than or equal to 'x' then find the value of the following series: $\sqrt{1} + \sqrt{2} + \sqrt{3} + \sqrt{4} + \dots + \sqrt{361}$ **(IIFT 2010)**
   (a) 4408    (b) 4839
   (c) 3498    (d) 3489

5. What is the value of $\sqrt{\dfrac{a}{b}}$, if $\log_4 \log_4 4^{a-b} = 2\log_4 (\sqrt{a} - \sqrt{b}) + 1$ **(IIFT 2010)**
   (a) $-5/3$    (b) 2
   (c) $5/3$    (d) 1

6. $\log_5 2$ is **(IIFT 2010)**
   (a) An integer    (b) A rational number
   (c) A prime number    (d) An irrational number

7. Find the value of x from the following equation: $\log_{10} 3 + \log_{10}(4x + 1) = \log_{10}(x + 1) + 1$ **(IIFT 2010)**
   (a) 2/7    (b) 7/2
   (c) 9/2    (d) None of the above

8. If x satisfies the inequality $|x - 1| + |x - 2| + |x - 3| \geq 6$, then: **(IIFT 2010)**
   (a) $0 \leq x \leq 4$    (b) $x \leq 0$ or $x \geq 4$
   (c) $x \leq -2$ or $x \geq 3$    (d) None of the above

9. The equation $7^{x-1} + 11^{x-1} = 170$ has **(IIFT 2012)**
   (a) no solution    (b) one solution
   (c) two solutions    (d) three solutions

10. If log 3, log($3^x - 2$) and log($3^x + 4$) are in arithmetic progression, then x is equal to **(IIFT 2012)**
    (a) 8/3
    (b) $\log_3 8$
    (c) $\log_2 3$
    (d) 4

11. If $x^2 + 3x - 10$ is a factor of $3x^4 + 2x^3 - ax^2 + bx - a + b - 4$, then the closest approximate values of a and b are **(IIFT 2013)**
    (a) 25, 43
    (b) 52, 43
    (c) 52, 67
    (d) None of the above

12. If $\log_{10}x - \log_{10}\sqrt[3]{x} = 6\log_x 10$ then the value of x is **(IIFT 2013)**
    (a) 10
    (b) 30
    (c) 100
    (d) 1000

13. If $\log_{13}\log_{21}\{\sqrt{x+21} + \sqrt{x}\} = 0$, then the value of x is **(IIFT 2013)**
    (a) 21
    (b) 13
    (c) 81
    (d) None of the above

14. If x is real, the smallest value of the expression $3x^2 - 4x + 7$ is: **(IIFT 2013)**
    (a) 2/3
    (b) ¾
    (c) 7/9
    (d) None of the above

15. The value of $\log_7\log_7 \sqrt{7\sqrt{7\sqrt{7}}}$ is equal to: **(IIFT 2014)**
    (a) 7
    (b) $\log_7 2$
    (c) $1 - 3\log_2 7$
    (d) $1 - 3\log_7 2$

16. The value of x for which the equation $\sqrt{4x+9} + \sqrt{4x-9} = 5 + \sqrt{7}$ will be satisfied, is: **(IIFT 2015)**
    (a) 1
    (b) 2
    (c) 3
    (d) 4

17. If $\log_{25}5 = a$ and $\log_{25}15 = b$, then the value of $\log_{25}27$ is: **(IIFT 2015)**
    (a) $3(b + a)$
    (b) $3(1 - b - a)$
    (c) $3(a + b - 1)$
    (d) $3(1 - b + a)$

18. The smallest integer x for which the inequality $(x - 7)/(x^2 + 5x - 36) > 0$ is given by **(IIFT 2016)**
    (a) −12
    (b) 9
    (c) −9
    (d) −8

19. Find the value of x which satisfies the following equation **(IIFT 2016)**
    $4\log_7(x - 8) = \log_3 81$
    (a) 8
    (b) 18
    (c) 20
    (d) None of the above

20. $(1 + 5)\log_e 3 + (1 + 5^2)(\log_e 3)^2 /2! + (1 + 5^3)(\log_e 3)^3 /3! + \ldots$ **(IIFT 2017)**
    (a) 12
    (b) 244
    (c) 243
    (d) 245

21. If $f(x) = 1/(1 + x)$, then find the value of $f[f\{f(x)\}]$, at x = 5 **(IIFT 2017)**
    (a) 7/9
    (b) 7/13
    (c) 5/13
    (d) None of these

## ANSWER KEY

| | | | |
|---|---|---|---|
| 1. (c) | 2. (b) | 3. (c) | 4. (a) |
| 5. (c) | 6. (d) | 7. (b) | 8. (b) |
| 9. (b) | 10. (b) | 11. (c) | 12. (d) |
| 13. (d) | 14. (d) | 15. (d) | 16. (d) |
| 17. (c) | 18. (d) | 19. (d) | 20. (b) |
| 21. (b) | | | |

### Solutions

1. If a, b and c are in harmonic progression, then
$$b = \frac{2ac}{a + c}$$
As per the question,
$$\log(a + c) + \log(a + c - 2b) = \log[(a + c)(a + c - 2b)]$$
$$= \log[(a + c)(a + c - 4ac/(a + c))]$$
$$= \log\left[(a+c) \times \frac{(a + c)^2 - 4ac}{(a + c)}\right]$$
$$= \log[(c - a)]^2$$
Since a < c, therefore $\log[(c - a)^2]$ should be expressed as $\log[(c - a)^2] = 2\log(c - a)$. Option (c) is correct.

2. Given $\log_2 x \cdot \log_{x/64}2 = \log_{x/16}2$
We can solve this problem just by checking the options.
If we put x = 4 in LHS we have
$$(2\log_2 2)\left(\log_{\frac{1}{16}}2\right) = \frac{2\log_2 2}{(-4)\log_2 2} = -\frac{1}{2}$$
Similarly, in RHS $= \log_{\frac{1}{4}}2 = -\frac{1}{2}$. Since, LHS = RHS, this would be the correct answer.

3. Roots of the given equation
$$= \frac{2a \pm \sqrt{4a^2 - 4ab}}{2b} = \frac{a \pm \sqrt{a^2 - ab}}{b}$$
$$= \frac{\sqrt{a}(\sqrt{a} \pm \sqrt{a-b})}{b} \times \frac{\sqrt{a} \mp \sqrt{a-b}}{\sqrt{a} \mp \sqrt{a-b}} = \frac{\sqrt{a}}{\sqrt{a} \pm \sqrt{a-b}}$$

4. $\sqrt{1} + \sqrt{2} + \sqrt{3} = 1 \times 3$.
$\sqrt{4} + \sqrt{5} + \cdots + \sqrt{8} = 2 \times 5$
$\sqrt{9} + \sqrt{10} + \cdots + \sqrt{15} = 3 \times 7$
The series would continue till: $4 \times 9$; $5 \times 11$; $6 \times 13$; $7 \times 15$; $8 \times 17$; $9 \times 19$; $10 \times 21$; $11 \times 23$; $12 \times 25$; $13 \times 27$; $14 \times 29$; $15 \times 31$; $16 \times 33$; $17 \times 35$ and $18 \times 37$. The $k^{th}$ term of this series is $k \times (2k + 1) = 2k^2 + k$ and $S_k = 2\Sigma k^2 + \Sigma k = 2 \times k(k + 1)(2k + 1)/6 + k(k + 1)/2$
Since, k = 18 we get
$S_{18} = 4389$
Also the value of $[\sqrt{361}] = 19$
Hence, the total sum would be $= 4389 + 19 = 4408$. Option (a) is correct.

5. $\log_4\log_4 4^{a-b} = \log_4(\sqrt{a}-\sqrt{b})^2 + 1$

$\log_4\log_4 4^{a-b} = \log_4(\sqrt{a}-\sqrt{b})^2 + \log_4 4$

$+ \log_4(a-b) = \log_4 4(a+b-2\sqrt{ab})$

$(a-b) = 4(a+b-2\sqrt{ab})$ & $a-b \neq$ or $a \neq b$

$3a + 5b - 8\sqrt{ab} = 0$

$3\left(\sqrt{\dfrac{a}{b}}\right)^2 - 8\sqrt{\dfrac{a}{b}} + 5 = 0$

Now put the options in place of $\sqrt{\dfrac{a}{b}}$, and check the options, we get only option c that satisfies the above equation. So this is the correct answer.

6. $\log_s 2 = p \Rightarrow 2 = 5^p$

This is possible only if p is irrational.

7. $\log_{10} 3 + \log_{10}(4x+1) = \log_{10}(x+1) + \log_{10} 10$

$\log_{10} 3(4x+1) = \log_{10}(x+1)10$

$3 \times (4x+1) = (x+1) \times 10$

$2x = 7$ or $x = 7/2$

8. Case (a): $x < 1$

$\Rightarrow \quad 1-x+2-x+3-x \geq 6$ or $x \leq 0$.

Hence, this case is possible.

Case (b): $1 \leq x < 2$

$\Rightarrow \quad x-1+2-x+3-x \geq 6$ or $x \leq -2$

Hence, this case is not possible.

Case (c): $2 \leq x < 3$

$\Rightarrow \quad x-1+x-2+3-x \geq 6$ or $x \geq 6$

Hence, this case is not possible.

Case (d): $x \geq 3$

$\Rightarrow \quad x-1+x-2+x-3 \geq 6$ or $x \geq 4$

Hence, this case is possible.

Therefore, required solution set is $x \leq 0$ and $x \geq 4$.

**Alternative method:** Check the options.

At $x = 0$ and 4, the given expression is equal to 6 and for all values of $x < 0$ and $x > 4$ the value of the given expression is greater than 6. At $x = 1$ and $x = 3$ the value of given expression is 3. Hence, option (b) is correct. Obviously, this method would prove much simpler to do and also much faster.

9. The equation is in the form: Power of 7 + Power of 11 = 170. A little bit of introspection shows us that this can only happen at 49 + 121 = 170. For this, we need $7^2 + 11^2 = 170$. The value of x = 3, satisfies this equation. Hence, the equation has only 1 solution. Option (b) is correct.

10. Since, the three terms are in an Arithmetic Progression it means:

$\log(3^x - 2) - \log 3 = \log(3^x + 4) - \log(3^x - 2)$

Assume $3^x = n$, we will get:

$\log(n-2)/(3) = \log(n+4)/(n-2) \rightarrow n^2 - 4n + 4 = 3n + 12$. Hence, $n^2 - 7n - 8 = 0$.

Hence, $(n-8)(n+1) = 0$. This gives us: n = 8 or n = −1. However, since $n = 3^x$, we know that $3^x$ cannot be negative. Thus, we have $3^x = 8 \rightarrow x = \log_3 8$

Hence, Option (b) is correct.

11. The equation $x^2 + 3x - 10$ has two factors 2 and −5. Putting x = 2 in the expression $3x^4 + 2x^3 - ax^2 + bx - a + b - 4$, we get: $48 + 16 - 4a + 2b - a + b - 4 = 0 \rightarrow 5a - 3b = 60$ ...(i)

We also have: x = −5. Putting x = −5 in the expression $3x^4 + 2x^3 - ax^2 + bx - a + b - 4$, we get: $26a + 4b = 1621$

Solving (i) and (ii) simultaneously we get a = 52 and b = 67. Option (c) is correct.

*Note:* These are the closest answers, as asked by the question.

12. $\log_{10} x - \log_{10} \sqrt[3]{x} = \dfrac{6}{\log_{10} x}$

$\therefore \qquad \log_{10} x - \dfrac{1}{3}\log_{10} x = \dfrac{6}{\log_{10} x}$

Put $\log_{10} x = t$

$\therefore \qquad t^2 - \dfrac{1}{3}t^2 = 6$

$\therefore \qquad t^2 = 9$

$\therefore \qquad t = \pm 3$

For t = +3, x = 1000 and for t = −3, x = 0.001 − which can be rejected as it is not there in the options.

$\therefore \qquad x = 1000$

13. $\log_{13}\log_{21}\{\sqrt{x+21} + \sqrt{x}\} = 0$ implies:

$\log_{21}\{\sqrt{x+21} + \sqrt{x}\} = 13^0 = 1$ implies:

$\{\sqrt{x+21} + \sqrt{x}\} = 21^1$. The value of x can be visualised to be 100 because at x = 100, LHS = RHS.

Hence, option (d) is correct.

14. $3x^2 - 4x + 7 = 3\left(x^2 - \dfrac{4}{3}x + \dfrac{7}{3}\right) = 3\left(\left(x-\dfrac{2}{3}\right)^2 + \dfrac{17}{9}\right)$

The above expression will be minimum when x = 2/3 in that case the value of the above expression = $3 \times 17/9 = 17/3$

**Alternate Solution:** The given expression would have its minima at the value of x got by differentiating the quadratic expression with respect to x and equating the resultant linear expression to 0. We get $6x - 4 = 0$, which means that the minima would occur at x = 2/3. The minimum value would be got by putting x = 2/3 in the given expression. We get, minimum value = 12/9 − 8/3 + 7 = 17/3. Hence, option (d) is correct.

15. $\sqrt{7\sqrt{7\sqrt{7}}} = \sqrt{7\sqrt{7^{\frac{3}{2}}}} = \sqrt{7 \times 7^{\frac{3}{4}}} = 7^{\frac{7}{8}}$

$\log_7\log_7 7^{\frac{7}{8}} = \log_7(7/8) = \log_7 7 - \log_7 8 = 1 - \log_7 8 = 1 - 3\log_7 2$. Option (d) is correct.

16. Check the options we get that only x = 4 satisfies the given equation.

17. We have $\log_{25}27 = 3\log_{25}3$.

    Also, $b = \log_{25}15 = \log_{25}5 + \log_{25}3$

    Thus, we get: $\log_{25}27 = 3(b - a)$. But $a = \log_{25}5 = \dfrac{1}{2}$

    $\log_5 5 = \dfrac{1}{2}$.

    Thus: $\log_{25}27 = 3\left(b - \dfrac{1}{2}\right) = 3\left(b + \dfrac{1}{2} - \dfrac{1}{2} - \dfrac{1}{2}\right)$

    $\qquad\qquad = 3(b + a - 1)$.

18. $(x - 7)/(x^2 + 5x - 36) > 0 \rightarrow (x - 7)/(x + 9)(x - 4) > 0$.
    For this inequality to not be satisfied – there should be either 3 negative values or one negative value in the three brackets.

    Checking the options we can see that at x = –8 and 9 the LHS of the above inequality is greater than 0.

Hence, we get the lowest value at x = –8. Hence option (d) is correct.

19. $4\log_7(x - 8) = \log_3 81 = \log_3 3^4 = 4$

    $4\log_7(x - 8) = 4$. This gives us that x = 15, since $\log_7(x - 8)$ should be 1.

20. The given expression can be written in the form:

    $= [1 + 5\log_e 3 + 5^2(\log_e 3)^2/2! + \ldots -1] + [1 + \log_e 3 + (\log_e 3)^2/2! + (\log_e 3)^2/3! + (\log_e 3)^2/4! + \ldots -1]$

    $= e^{5\log_e 3} - 1 + [e^{\log_e 3} - 1]$

    $= e^{\log_e 243} + e^{\log_e 3} - 2$

    $= 243 + 3 - 2 = 244$.

21. $f(x) = 1/(1 + x)$. So: $f(5) = 1/(1 + 5) = 1/6$

    $\qquad f(1/6) = 1/(1 + 1/6) = 6/7$

    $f(6/7) = 1/(1 + 6/7) = 7/13$. Hence, option (b) is correct.

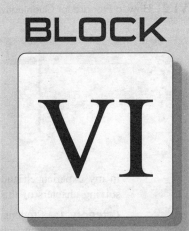

# BLOCK VI

# Counting

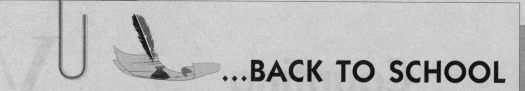

# ...BACK TO SCHOOL

In my experience, students can be divided into two broad categories on the basis of their ability in solving chapters of this block.

*Category 1:* Students who are comfortable in solving questions of this block, since they understand the underlying concepts well.

*Category 2:* Students who are not able to tackle questions of this block of chapters since they are not conversant with the counting tools and methods in this block.

If you belong to the second category of students, the main thing you would need to do is to familiarise yourself with the counting methods and techniques of Permutations and Combinations. Once you are through with the same, you would find yourself relatively comfortable at both Permutations & Combinations (P&C) and Probability—the chapters in this block which create the maximum problems for students. Set Theory being a relatively easier chapter, the Back to School section of this block concentrates mostly on P & C and Probability. However, before we start looking at these counting methods, right at the outset, I would want you to remove any negative experiences you might have had while trying to study P& C and Probability. So if you belong to the second category of students, you are advised to read on:

Look at the following table:

|  |  |  |  |  |
|---|---|---|---|---|
|  |  |  |  |  |
|  |  |  |  |  |
|  |  |  |  |  |
|  |  |  |  |  |

Suppose, I were to ask you to count the number of cells in the table above, how would you do it??

$$5 \times 5 = 25!!$$

I guess, all of you realise the fact that the number of cells in this table is given by the product of the number of rows and columns. However, if you ask a 5 year old child to count the same, he would be counting the number of cells physically. In fact, when you were 5 years old, you would also have required to do a physical count of the number of cells in the table. However, there must have come a point where you must have understood that in all such situations (no. of cells in a table, no. of students in a class, etc.) the total count is got by simply multiplying the number of rows and the number of columns. What I am interested in pointing out to you, is that the discovery of this process for this specific counting situation surely made your counting easier!! What used to take you much longer started taking you shorter times. Not only that, in situations where the count was too large (e.g. 100 rows × 48 columns) an infeasible count became extremely easy. So why am I telling you this??

Simply because just as the rows into columns tool for counting had the effect of making your count easier, so also the tools for counting which P& C describe will also have the effect of making counting easier for you in the specific situations of counting that you will encounter. My experience of training students shows that the only reason students have problems in this block is because it has not been explained properly to them in their +2 classes.

*Contd*

If you try to approach these chapters with the approach that it is not meant to complicate your life but to simplify it, you might end up finding out that there is nothing much to fear in this chapter.

## ✒ THE TOOL BOX APPROACH TO P&C

While studying P&C, your primary objective should be to familiarise yourself with each and every counting situation. You also need to realise that there are a limited number of counting situations which you need to tackle. You can look at this as the process of the creation of what can be described as a counting tool box.

Once this tool box is created, you would be able to understand the basic situations for counting. Then solving tough questions becomes a matter of simplifying the language of the question into the language of the answer—a matter I would come back to later.

Let us now proceed to list out the specific counting situations which you need to get a hold on. You need to know and understand the following twelve situations of counting and the tools that are used in these situations. Please take note that these tools are explained in detail in various parts of the text on the Permutations and Combinations chapter. You are required to keep these in mind along with the specific situations in which these apply. Look at these as a kind of comprehensive list of situations in which you should know how to count using mathematical tools for your convenience.

## The Twelve Counting Situations and Their Tools

**Tool No. 1:** The $^nC_r$ **tool**—This tool is used for the specific situation of counting the number of ways of selecting r things out of n **distinct** things.

**Example:** Selecting a team of 11 cricketers out of a team of 16 distinct players will be $^{16}C_{11}$.

**Tool No. 2:** The tool for counting the number of selections of r things out of n **identical** things. (Always 1)

**Example:** The number of ways of selecting 3 letters out of five A's. Note that in such cases there will only be one way of selecting them.

**Tool No. 3:** The $2^n$ **tool**—The tool for selecting any number (including 0) of things from n **distinct** things ($^nC_0 + {}^nC_1 + {}^nC_2 \ldots + {}^nC_n = 2^n$). Example the number of ways you can or cannot eat sweets at a party if there are ten sweets and you have the option of eating one piece of as many sweets as you like or even of not eating any sweet. Will be given by $2^{10}$.

**Corollary:** The $2^n - 1$ **tool**—Used when zero selections are not allowed. For instance in the above situation if you are asked to eat at least one sweet and rejecting all sweets is not an option.

**Tool No. 4:** The $n + 1$ **tool**—The tool for selecting any number (including 0) of things from n **identical** things. For instance, if you have to select any number of letters from A, A, A, A and A then you can do it in six ways.

**Tool No. 5:** The $^{n+r-1}C_{r-1}$ **tool**—The tool for distributing n identical things amongst r people/groups such that any person/group might get any number (including 0). For instance, if you have to distribute 7 identical gifts amongst 5 children in a party then it can be done in $^{(7+5-1)}C_{(5-1)}$ ways. i.e. $^{11}C_4$ ways.

**Tool No. 6:** The $^{n-1}C_{r-1}$ **tool**—The tool for distributing n identical things amongst r people/groups such that any person/group might get any number (except 0).

Suppose in the above case you have to give at least one gift to each child it can be done in: $^6C_4$ ways.

**Tool No. 7:** The mnp rule tool—The tool for counting the number of ways of doing three things when each of them has to be done and there are m ways of doing the first thing, $n$ ways of doing the second thing and p ways of doing the last thing. Suppose you have to go from Lucknow to Varanasi to Patna to Ranchi to Jamshedpur and there are 5 trains from Lucknow to Varanasi & there are 4 trains from Varanasi to Patna, six from Patna to Ranchi and 3 from Ranchi to Jamshedpur, then the number of ways of going from Lucknow to Jamshedpur through Varanasi, Patna & Ranchi is $5 \times 4 \times 6 \times 3 = 360$.

Note that this tool is extremely crucial and is used to form numbers and words.

For example how many 4 digit numbers can you form using the digits 0, 1, 2, 3, 4, 5 & 6 only without repeating any digits. In this situation the work outline is to choose a digit for the first place (=6, any one out of 1, 2, 3, 4, 5 & 6 as zero cannot be used there), then choosing a digit for the second place (=6, select any one out of 5 remaining digits plus 0), then a digit for the third place (5 ways) and a digit for the fourth place (4 ways).

**Tool No 8:** The r! tool for arrangement—This tool is used for counting the number of ways in which you can arrange r things in r places. Notice that this can be derived out of the mnp rule tool.

**Tool No 9:** The AND rule tool—Whenever you describe the counting situation and connect two different parts of the count by using the conjunction 'AND', you will always replace the 'AND' with a multiplication sign between the two parts of the count. This is also used for solving Probability questions. For instance, suppose you have to choose a vowel 'AND' a consonant from the letters of the word PERMIT, you can do it in $^4C_1 \times {}^2C_1$ ways.

**Tool No 10:** **The OR rule tool**—Whenever you describe the counting situation and connect two different parts of the count by using the conjunction 'OR, you will always replace the 'OR' with an Addition sign between the two parts of the count. This is also used for solving Probability questions. For instance, suppose you have to select either 2 vowels or a consonant from the letters of the word PERMIT, you can do it in $^4C_2 + {}^2C_1$ ways.

**Tool No 11:** **The Circular Permutation Tool [($n$ – 1)! Tool]**—This gives the number of ways in which $n$ distinct things can be placed around a circle. The need to reduce the value of the factorial by 1 is due to the fact that in a circle there is no defined starting point.

**Tool No 12:** **The Circular Permutation Tool when there is no distinction between clockwise and anti clockwise arrangements [($n$ – 1)!/2 Tool]**—This gives the number of ways in which $n$ distinct things can be placed around a circle when there is no distinction between clockwise and anti clockwise arrangements. In such a case the number of circular permutations are just divided by 2.

## Two More Issues

**(1) What about the $^nP_r$ tool?** The $^nP_r$ tool is used to arrange $r$ things amongst $n$. However, my experience shows that the introduction of this tool just adds to the confusion for most students. A little bit of smart thinking gets rid of all the problems that the $^nP_r$ tool creates in your mind. For this let us consider the difference between the $^nP_r$ and the $^nC_r$ tools.

$$^nC_r = n!/[r! \times (n-r)!] \text{ while } {}^nP_r = n!/[(n-r)!].$$

A closer look would reveal that the relationship between the $^nP_r$ and the $^nC_r$ tools can be summarised as:

$$^nP_r = {}^nC_r \times r!$$

**Read this as:** If you have to arrange $r$ things amongst $n$ things, then simply select $r$ things amongst $n$ things and use the $r!$ tool for the arrangement of the selected $r$

items amongst themselves. This will result in the same answer as the $^nP_r$ tool.

In fact, for all questions involving arrangements always solve the question in two parts—First finish the selection within the question and then arrange the selected items amongst themselves. This will remove a lot of confusions in questions of this chapter.

**(2) Treat Both Permutations and Combinations and Probability as English language chapters rather than Maths chapters:** One of the key discoveries in getting stronger at this block is that after knowing the basic twelve counting situations and their tools (as explained above) you need to stop treating the questions in this chapter as questions in Mathematics and rather treat them as questions in English. Thus, while solving a question in these chapters your main concentration and effort should be on converting the question language into the answer language.

## What do I mean by this?

Consider this:

**Question Language:** What is the number of ways of forming 4 letter words from 5 vowels and 6 consonants such that the word contains one vowel and three consonants?

To solve this question, first create the answer language in your mind:

**Answer Language:** Select one vowel out of 5 **AND** select three consonants out of 6 **AND** arrange the four selected letters amongst themselves.

Once you have this language the remaining part of the answer is just a matter of using the correct tools. Thus, the answer is $^5C_1 \times {}^6C_3 \times 4!$

As you can see, the main issue in getting the solution to this question was working out the language by connecting the various parts of the solution using the conjunction AND (In this case, the conjunction OR was not required.). Once, you had the language all you had to do was use the correct tools to count.

The most difficult of questions are solved this way. This is why I advise you to treat this chapter as a language chapter and not as a chapter in Mathematics!!

## Pre-assessment Test

1. How many words of 11 letters could be formed with all the vowels present in even places, using all the letters of the alphabet? (without repetitions)
   (a) $^{21}P_6.5!$       (b) $21!$
   (c) $^{21}P_5(5!)$       (d) $^{26}P_s$

2. A candidate is required to answer 6 out of 10 questions, which are divided into two groups each containing 5 questions, and he is not permitted to attempt more than 4 from each group. In how many ways can he make up his choice?
   (a) 300       (b) 200
   (c) 400       (d) 100

3. $m$ men and $n$ women are to be seated in a row so that no two women sit together. If $m > n$, then find the number of ways in which they can be seated.
   (a) $m! \times ^{m+1}P_n$       (b) $m! \times ^{m+1}C_n$
   (c) $m! \times ^mP_n$       (d) $m! \times ^mC_n$

4. How many different 4-digit numbers can be made from the first 4 whole numbers, using each digit only once?
   (a) 20       (b) 18
   (c) 24       (d) 20

5. How many different 4-digit numbers can be made from the first 4 natural numbers, if repetition is allowed?
   (a) 128       (b) 512
   (c) 256       (d) None of these

6. How many six-lettered words starting with the letter $T$ can be made from all the letters of the word TRAVEL?
   (a) 5       (b) 5!
   (c) 124       (d) None of these

7. In the question above, how many words can be made with $T$ and $L$ at the end positions?
   (a) 24       (b) 5!
   (c) 6!       (d) None of these

8. If the letters of the word ATTEMPT are written down at random, find the probability that all the T's are together.
   (a) 2/7       (b) 1/7
   (c) 4/7       (d) 3/7

9. A bag contains 3 white and 2 red balls. One by one, two balls are drawn without replacing them. Find the probability that the second ball is red.
   (a) 2/5       (b) 1/10
   (c) 2/10       (d) 3/5

10. Three different numbers are selected from the set $X = \{1,2,3,4,\ldots,10\}$. What is the probability that the product of two of the numbers is equal to the third?
    (a) 3/10       (b) 1/40
    (c) 1/20       (d) 4/5

**Directions for Questions 11 and 12:**   Read the passage below and solve the questions based on it.

India plays two matches each with New Zealand and South Africa. In any match, the probability of different outcomes for India is given below:

| Outcome | Win | Loss | Draw |
| --- | --- | --- | --- |
| Probability | 0.5 | 0.45 | 0.05 |
| Points | 2 | 0 | 1 |

Outcome of all the matches are independent of each other.

11. What is the probability of India getting at least 7 points in the contest? Assume South Africa & New Zealand Play 2 matches.
    (a) 0.025       (b) 0.0875
    (c) 0.0625       (d) 0.975

12. What is the probability of South Africa getting at least 4 points? Assume South Africa and New Zealand play 2 matches.
    (a) 0.2025       (b) 0.0625
    (c) 0.0425       (d) Can't be determined

13. If $^nC_4 = 126$, then $^np_4 = ?$
    (a) 126       (b) 126 * 2!
    (c) 126 * 4!       (d) None of these

14. The number of ways, in which a student can choose 5 courses out of 9 courses, if 2 courses are compulsory, is
    (a) 53       (b) 35
    (c) 34       (d) 32

15. What is the value of $^{18}C_{16}$?
    (a) 5!       (b) 6!
    (c) 153       (d) Can't be determined

16. How many triangles can be drawn from $N$ given points on a circle?
    (a) N!       (b) 3!
    (c) N! / 3!       (d) $(N-1)N(N-2)/6$

17. Following are the alphabets for which the alphabet and its mirror image are same. A, H, I, M, O, T, U, V, W, Y, X. These alphabets are called as symmetrical. Other are called as unsymmetrical. A password containing 4 alphabets (without repetitions) is to be formed using symmetrical alphabets. How many such passwords can be formed?
    (a) 720       (b) 330
    (c) 7920       (d) Can't be determined

18. How many 5 letter words can be formed out of 10 consonants and 4 vowels, such that each contains

3 consonants and 2 vowels?

(a) $^{10}P_3 \times {}^4P_2 \times 5!$    (b) $^{10}C_3 \times {}^4C_2 \times 5!$

(c) $^{10}P_3 \times {}^4C_2 \times 5!$    (d) $^{10}C_2 \times {}^4P_2 \times 5!$

19. A question paper consists of two sections $A$ and $B$ having respectively 3 and 4 questions. Four questions are to be solved to qualify in that paper. It is compulsory to solve at least one question from Section A and two questions from Section B. In how many ways can a candidate select the questions to qualify in that paper?

(a) 30    (b) 18

(c) 48    (d) 60

20. A student is allowed to select at most $n$ books from a collection of $(2n + 1)$ books. If the total number of ways in which he can select at least one book is 63, find the value of $n$.

(a) 4    (b) 3

(c) 5    (d) 6

21. A man and a woman appear in an interview for two vacancies for the same post. The probability of a man's selection is 1/4 and that of a woman's selection is 1/3. What is the probability that both of them will be selected?

(a) 1/12    (b) 1/3

(c) 2/5    (d) 3/7

22. In Question 21, what will be the probability that only one of them will be selected?

(a) 11/12    (b) 1/2

(c) 7/12    (d) 5/12

23. In Question 21, what will be the probability that none of them will be selected?

(a) 1/2    (b) 1/3

(c) 2/5    (d) 3/7

24. How many different signals can be made by hoisting 5 different coloured flags one above the other, when any number of them may be hoisted a time?

(a) $2^5$    (b) $^5P_5$

(c) 325    (d) None of these

25. Find the number of ways in which the letters of the word MACHINE can be arranged so that the vowels may occupy only odd positions.

(a) $4! \times 4!$    (b) $^7P_3 \times 4!$

(c) $^7P_4 \times 3!$    (d) None of these

## ANSWER KEY

| | | | |
|---|---|---|---|
| 1. (a) | 2. (b) | 3. (a) | 4. (b) |
| 5. (c) | 6. (b) | 7. (d) | 8. (b) |
| 9. (a) | 10. (b) | 11. (b) | 12. (d) |
| 13. (c) | 14. (b) | 15. (c) | 16. (d) |
| 17. (c) | 18. (b) | 19. (a) | 20. (b) |
| 21. (a) | 22. (d) | 23. (a) | 24. (c) |
| 25. (a) | | | |

# Permutations and Combinations

## STANDARD THEORY

Factorial Notation! Or $\lfloor$

$$\lfloor n = n(n-1)(n-2)\ldots 3.2.1$$

$$n! = \underline{n}(n-1)(n-2)\ldots 3.2.1$$

= Product of $n$ consecutive integers starting from 1.

1. $0! = 1$

2. Factorials of only Natural numbers are defined.

$n!$ is defined only for $n \geq 0$

$n!$ is not defined for $n < 0$

4. $^nC_r = 1$ when $n = r$.

5. Combinations (represented by $^nC_r$) can be defined as the number of ways in which $r$ things at a time can be **SELECTED** from amongst $n$ things available for selection.

The key word here is **SELECTION**. Please understand here that the order in which the $r$ things are selected has no importance in the counting of combinations.

$^nC_r$ = Number of combinations (selections) of $n$ things taken $r$ at a time.

$^nC_r = n!/[r!(n-r)!]$; where $n \geq r$ ($n$ is greater than or equal to $r$).

Some typical situations where selection/combination is used:

(a) Selection of people for a team, a party, a job, an office etc. (e.g. Selection of a cricket team of 11 from 16 members)

(b) Selection of a set of objects (like letters, hats, points pants, shirts, etc) from amongst another set available for selection.

In other words any selection in which the order of selection holds no importance is counted by using combinations.

6. Permutations (represented by $^nP_r$) can be defined as the number of ways in which $r$ things at a time can be **SELECTED & ARRANGED** at a time from amongst $n$ things.

The key word here is **ARRANGEMENT**. Hence please understand here that the order in which the $r$ things are arranged has critical importance in the counting of permutations.

In other words permutations can also be referred to as an **ORDERED SELECTION**.

$^nP_r$ = number of permutations (arrangements) of $n$ things taken $r$ at a time.

$^nP_r = n!/(n-r)!$; $n \geq r$

Some typical situations where **ordered selection/permutations** are used:

(a) Making words and numbers from a set of available letters and digits respectively

(b) Filling posts with people

(c) Selection of batting order of a cricket team of 11 from 16 members

(d) Putting distinct objects/people in distinct places, e.g. making people sit, putting letters in envelopes, finishing order in horse race, etc.)

The exact difference between selection and arrangement can be seen through the illustration below:

## Selection

Suppose we have three men A, B and C out of which 2 men have to be selected to two posts.

This can be done in the following ways: AB, AC or BC (These three represent the basic selections of 2 people out of three which are possible. Physically they can be counted as 3 distinct selections. This value can also be got by using $3C_2$.)

Note here that we are counting AB and BA as one single selection. So also AC and CA and BC and CB are considered to be the same instances of selection since the order of selection is not important.

## Arrangement

Suppose we have three men A, B and C out of which 2 men have to be selected to the post of captain and vice captain of a team.

In this case we have to take AB and BA as two different instances since the order of the arrangement makes a difference in who is the captain and who is the vice captain.

Similarly, we have BC and CB and AC and CA as 4 more instances. Thus in all there could be 6 arrangements of 2 things out of three.

This is given by $^3P_2 = 6$.

7. **The Relationship Between Permutation & Combination:**

    When we look at the formulae for Permutations and Combinations and compare the two we see that,

    $$^nP_r = r! \times {}^nC_r$$

    $$= {}^nC_r \times {}^rP_r$$

    This in words can be said as:

    The permutation or arrangement of $r$ things out of $n$ is nothing but the selection of $r$ things out of $n$ followed by the arrangement of the $r$ selected things amongst themselves.

8. **MNP Rule:** If there are three things to do and there are M ways of doing the first thing, N ways of doing the second thing and P ways of doing the third thing then there will be **M × N × P** ways of doing all the three things together. The works are mutually inclusive.

    This is used to for situations like:

    The numbers 1, 2, 3, 4 and 5 are to be used for forming 3 digit numbers without repetition. In how many ways can this be done?

    Using the MNP rule you can visualise this as: There are three things to do→ The first digit can be selected in 5 distinct ways, the second can be selected in 4 ways and the third can be selected in 3 different ways. Hence, the total number of 3 digit numbers that can be formed are $5 \times 4 \times 3 = 60$

9. When the pieces of work are mutually exclusive, there are M+N+P ways of doing the complete work.

### Important Results

The following results are important as they help in problem solving.

1. Number of permutations (or arrangements) of $n$ different things taken all at a time = $n!$

2. Number of permutations of $n$ things out of which $P_1$ are alike and are of one type, $P_2$ are alike and are of a second type and $P_3$ are alike and are of a third type and the rest are all different = $n! / P_1! P_2! P_3!$

    **Illustration:** The number of words formed with the letters of the word Allahabad.

    **Solution:** Total number of Letters = 9 of which $A$ occurs four times, $L$ occurs twice and the rest are all different.

    Total number of words formed = $9! / (4! \, 2! \, 1!)$

3. Number of permutations of $n$ different things taken $r$ times when repetition is allowed = $n \times n \times n \times \ldots$ ($r$ times) = $n^r$.

    **Illustration:** In how many ways can 4 rings be worn in the index, ring finger and middle finger if there is no restriction of the number of rings to be worn on any finger?

    **Solution:** Each of the 4 rings could be worn in 3 ways either on the index, ring or middle finger. So, four rings could be worn in $3 \times 3 \times 3 \times 3 = 3^4$ ways.

4. Number of selections of $r$ things out of $n$ identical things = 1

    **Illustration:** In how many ways 5 marbles can be chosen out of 100 identical marbles?

    **Solution:** Since, all the 100 marbles are identical Hence, Number of ways to select 5 marbles = 1

5. Total number of selections of zero or more things out of $k$ identical things = $k + 1$.

    This includes the case when zero articles are selected.

6. Total number of selections of zero or more things out of n different things =
    $^nC_o + {}^nC_1 + {}^nC_2 + \ldots + {}^nC_n$
    $^nC_o + {}^nC_1 + {}^nC_2 + \ldots + {}^nC_n = 2^n$

    Corollary: The number of selections of 1 or more things out of $n$ different things = $^nC_1 + {}^nC_2 + \ldots + {}^nC_n = 2^n - 1$

7. Number of ways of distributing $n$ identical things among $r$ persons when each person may get any number of things = $^{n+r-1}C_{r-1}$

    Imagine a situation where 27 marbles have to be distributed amongst 4 people such that each one of them can get any number of marbles (including zero marbles). Then for this situation we have, $n = 27$(no. of identical objects), $r = 4$ (no. of people) and the answer of the number of ways this can be achieved is given by:

    $^{n+r-1}C_{r-1} = {}^{30}C_3$.

8. Corollary: No. of ways of dividing $n$ non distinct things to $r$ distinct groups are:

    $^{n-1}C_{r-1} \rightarrow$ For non-empty groups only

Also, the number of ways in which $n$ distinct things can be distributed to $r$ different persons:
$$= r^n$$

9. Number of ways of dividing $m + n$ different things in two groups containing $m$ and $n$ things respectively =
$$^{m+n}C_n \times {}^mC_m =$$
$$= (m + n)! \, / m! \; n!$$
Or, $^{m+n}C_m \times {}^nC_n = (m + n)! \, / \, n! \; m!$

10. Number of ways of dividing $2n$ different things in two groups containing $n$ things $= 2n! \, / \, n! \; n! \; 2!$

11. $^nC_r + {}^nC_{r-1} = {}^{n+1}C_r$

12. $^nC_x = {}^nC_y \Rightarrow x = y$ or $x + y = n$

13. $^nC_r = {}^nC_{n-r}$

14. $r \cdot {}^nC_r = n \cdot {}^{n-1}C_{r-1}$

15. $^nC_r \, / \, (r + 1) = {}^{n+1}C_{r+1} \, / ( \, n + 1)$

16. For $^nC_r$ to be greatest,
    (a) if $n$ is even, $r = n/2$
    (b) if $n$ is odd, $r = (n + 1)/2$ or $(n - 1)/2$

17. Number of selections of $r$ things out of $n$ different things
    (a) When $k$ particular things are always included
    $$= {}^{n-k}C_{r-k}$$
    (b) When $k$ particular things are excluded $= {}^{n-k}C_r$
    (c) When all the $k$ particular things are not together in any selection
    $$= {}^nC_r - {}^{n-k}C_{r-k}$$
    No. of ways of doing a work with given restriction = total no. of ways of doing it — no. of ways of doing the same work with opposite restriction.

18. The total number of ways in which 0 to $n$ things can be selected out of $n$ things such that $p$ are of one type, $q$ are of another type and the balance $r$ of different types is given by: $(p + 1)(q + 1)(2^r - 1)$.

19. Total number of ways of taking some or all out of $p + q + r$ things such that $p$ are of one type and $q$ are of another type and $r$ of a third type
    $$= (p + 1)(q + 1)(r + 1) - 1$$
    [Only non-empty sets]

20. $\dfrac{^nC_r}{^nC_{r-1}} = \dfrac{n - r + 1}{r}$

21. Number of selections of $k$ consecutive things out of $n$ things in a row $= n - k + 1$

## Circular Permutations

Consider two situations:
There are three $A$, $B$ and $C$. In the first case, they are arranged linearly and in the other, around a circular table –

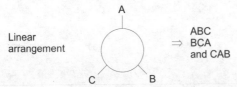

For the linear arrangement, each arrangement is a totally new way. For circular arrangements, three linear arrangements are represented by one and the same circular arrangement.

So, for six linear arrangements, there correspond only 2 circular arrangements. This happens because there is no concept of a starting point on a circular arrangement. (i.e., the starting point is not defined.)

Generalising the whole process, for $n!$, there corresponds to be $(1/n) \; n!$ ways.

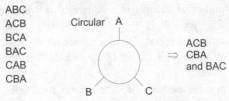

### Important Results

1. Number of ways of arranging $n$ people on a circular track (circular arrangement) $= (n - 1)!$

2. When clockwise and anti-clockwise observation are not different then number of circular arrangements of $n$ different things $= (n - 1)! \, /2$
   e.g. the case of a necklace with different beads, the same arrangement when looked at from the opposite side becomes anti-clockwise.

3. Number of selections of $k$ consecutive things out of $n$ things in a circle
   $= n$ when $k < n$
   $= 1$ when $k = n$

### Some More Results

1. Number of terms in $(a_1 + a_2 + \dots + a_n)^m$ is $^{m+n-1}C_{n-1}$

   **Illustration:** Find the number of terms in $(a + b + c)^2$.

   **Solution:** $n = 3$, $m = 2$
   $^{m+n-1}C_{n-1} = {}^4C_2 = 6$
   Corollary: Number of terms in
   $(1 + x + x^2 + \dots x^n)^m$ is $mn + 1$

2. Number of zeroes ending the number represented by
   $n! = [n \, /5] + [n \, /5^2] + [n \, /5^3] + \dots [n \, /5^x]$
   [ ] Shows greatest integer function where $5^x \le n$

   **Illustration:** Find the number of zeroes at the end of 1000!

   **Solution:** $[1000/5] + [1000/5^2] + [1000/5^3] + [1000/5^4]$
   $200 + 40 + 8 + 1 = 249$
   Corollary: Exponent of 3 in $n! = [n!/3] + [n!/32] + [n!/3^3] + \dots [n!/3^x]$ where $3^x \le n$
   [ ] Shows greatest integer $fn$.

   **Illustration:** Find how many exponents of 3 will be there in 24!.

   **Solution:** $[24/3] + [24/3^2] = 8 + 2 = 10$

3. Number of squares in a square of $n \times n$ side $= 1^2 + 2^2 + 3^2 + 4^2 + \ldots n^2$

Number of rectangles in a square of $n \times n$ side $= 1^3 + 2^3 + 3^3 + 4^3 + \ldots n^3$. (This includes the number of squares.)

Thus the number of squares and rectangles in the following figure are given by:

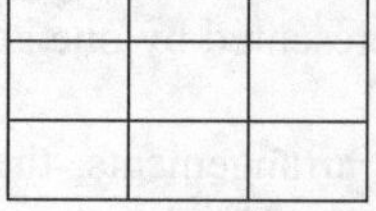

Number of squares $= 1^2 + 2^2 + 3^2 = 14 = \in n^2$

Number of rectangles $= 1^3 + 2^3 + 3^3 = 36 \ (\in n)^2 = \in n^3$ for the rectangle.

A rectangle having $m$ rows and $n$ columns:

The number of squares is given by: $m.n + (m - 1)(n - 1) + (m - 2)(n - 2) + \ldots$ until any of $(m - x)$ or $(n - x)$ comes to 1.

The number of rectangles is given by: $(1 + 2 + \ldots + m)(1 + 2 + \ldots + n)$

**Space for Notes**

## 🎯 WORKED-OUT PROBLEMS

In the following examples the solution is given upto the point of writing down the formula that will apply for the particular question. The student is expected to calculate the values after understanding the solution.

**Problem 17.1**  Find the number of permutations of 6 things taken 4 at a time.

**Solution**  The answer will be given by $^6P_4$.

**Problem 17.2**  How many 3-digit numbers can be formed out of the digits 1, 2, 3, 4 and 5?

**Solution**  Forming numbers requires an ordered selection. Hence, the answer will be $^5P_3$.

**Problem 17.3**  In how many ways can the 7 letters $M$, $N$, $O$, $P$, $Q$, $R$, $S$ be arranged so that $P$ and $Q$ occupy continuous positions?

**Solution**  For arranging the 7 letters keeping $P$ and $Q$ always together we have to view $P$ and $Q$ as one letter. Let this be denoted by $\underline{PQ}$.

Then, we have to arrange the letters $M$, $N$, $O$, $\underline{PQ}$, $R$ and $S$ in a linear arrangement. Here, it is like arranging 6 letters in 6 places (since 2 letters are counted as one). This can be done in 6! ways.

However, the solution is not complete at this point of time since in the count of 6! the internal arrangement between $P$ and $Q$ is neglected. This can be done in 2! ways. Hence, the required answer is 6! × 2!.

**Task for the student:** What would happen if the letters $P$, $Q$ and $R$ are to be together? (Ans: 5! × 3!)

What if $P$ and $Q$ are never together? (Answer will be given by the formula: Total number of ways – Number of ways they are always together)

**Problem 17.4**  Of the different words that can be formed from the letters of the words BEGINS how many begin with $B$ and end with $S$?

**Solution**  $B$ & $S$ are fixed at the start and the end positions. Hence, we have to arrange $E$, $G$, $I$ and $N$ amongst themselves. This can be done in 4! ways.

**Task for the student:** What will be the number of words that can be formed with the letters of the word BEGINS which have $B$ and $S$ at the extreme positions? (Ans: 4! × 2!)

**Problem 17.5**  In how many ways can the letters of the word VALEDICTORY be arranged, so that all the vowels are adjacent to each other?

**Solution**  There are 4 vowels and 7 consonants in Valedictory. If these vowels have to be kept together, we have to consider AEIO as one letter. Then the problem transforms itself into arranging 8 letters amongst themselves (8! ways). Besides, we have to look at the internal arrangement of the 4 vowels amongst themselves. (4! ways)

Hence Answer = 8! × 4!.

**Problem 17.6**  If there are two kinds of hats, red and blue and at least 5 of each kind, in how many ways can the hats be put in each of 5 different boxes?

**Solution**  The significance of at least 5 hats of each kind is that while putting a hat in each box, we have the option of putting either a red or a blue hat. (If this was not given, there would have been an uncertainty in the number of possibilities of putting a hat in a box.)

Thus in this question for every task of putting a hat in a box we have the possibility of either putting a red hat or a blue hat. The solution can then be looked at as: there are 5 tasks each of which can be done in 2 ways. Through the MNP rule we have the total number of ways = $2^5$ (Answer).

**Problem 17.7**  In how many ways can 4 Indians and 4 Nepalese people be seated around a round table so that no two Indians are in adjacent positions?

**Solution**  If we first put 4 Indians around the round table, we can do this in 3! ways.

Once the 4 Indians are placed around the round table, we have to place the four Nepalese around the same round table. Now, since the Indians are already placed we can do this in 4! ways (as the starting point is defined when we put the Indians. Try to visualize this around a circle for placing 2 Indians and 2 Nepalese.)

Hence, Answer = 3! × 4!

**Problem 17.8**  How many numbers greater than a million can be formed from the digits 1, 2, 3, 0, 4, 2, 3?

**Solution**  In order to form a number greater than a million we should have a 7 digit number. Since we have only seven digits with us we cannot take 0 in the starting position. View this as 7 positions to fill:

_ _ _ _ _ _ _

To solve this question we first assume that the digits are all different. Then the first position can be filled in 6 ways (0 cannot be taken), the second in 6 ways (one of the 6 digits available for the first position was selected. Hence, we have 5 of those 6 digits available. Besides, we also have the zero as an additional digit), the third in 5 ways (6 available for the 2nd position – 1 taken for the second position.) and so on. Mathematically this can be written as:

$$6 \times 6 \times 5 \times 4 \times 3 \times 2 \times 1 = 6 \times 6!$$

This would have been the answer had all the digits been distinct. But in this particular example we have two 2's and two 3's which are identical to each other. This complication is resolved as follows to get the answer:

$$\frac{6 \times 6}{2! \times 2!}$$

**Problem 17.9** If there are 11 players to be selected from a team of 16, in how many ways can this be done?

**Solution** $^{16}C_{11}$.

**Problem 17.10** In how many ways can 18 identical white and 16 identical black balls be arranged in a row so that no two black balls are together?

**Solution** When 18 identical white balls are put in a straight line, there will be 19 spaces created. Thus 16 black balls will have 19 places to fill in. This will give an answer of: $^{19}C_{16}$. (Since, the balls are identical the arrangement is not important.)

**Problem 17.11** A mother with 7 children takes three at a time to a cinema. She goes with every group of three that she can form. How many times can she go to the cinema with distinct groups of three children?

**Solution** She will be able to do this as many times as she can form a set of three distinct children from amongst the seven children. This essentially means that the answer is the number of selections of 3 people out of 7 that can be done.

Hence, Answer = $^{7}C_{3}$.

**Problem 17.12** For the above question, how many times will an individual child go to the cinema with her before a group is repeated?

**Solution** This can be viewed as: The child for whom we are trying to calculate the number of ways is already selected. Then, we have to select 2 more children from amongst the remaining 6 to complete the group. This can be done in $^{6}C_{2}$ ways.

**Problem 17.13** How many different sums can be formed with the following coins:

5 rupee, 1 rupee, 50 paisa, 25 paisa, 10 paisa and 1 paisa?

**Solution** A distinct sum will be formed by selecting either 1 or 2 or 3 or 4 or 5 or all 6 coins.

But from the formula we have the answer to this as : $2^6 - 1$.

[Task for the student: How many different sums can be formed with the following coins:

5 rupee, 1 rupee, 50 paisa, 25 paisa, 10 paisa, 3 paisa, 2 paisa and 1 paisa?

Hint: You will have to subtract some values for double counted sums.]

**Problem 17.14** A train is going from Mumbai to Pune and makes 5 stops on the way. 3 persons enter the train during the journey with 3 different tickets. How many different sets of tickets may they have had?

**Solution** Since the 3 persons are entering during the journey they could have entered at the:

1$^{st}$ station (from where they could have bought tickets for the 2$^{nd}$, 3$^{rd}$, 4$^{th}$ or 5$^{th}$ stations or for Pune → total of 5 tickets.)

2$^{nd}$ station (from where they could have bought tickets for the 3$^{rd}$, 4$^{th}$ or 5$^{th}$ stations or for Pune → total of 4 tickets.)

3$^{rd}$ station (from where they could have bought tickets for the 4th or 5th stations or for Pune → total of 3 tickets.)

4$^{th}$ station (from where they could have bought tickets for the 5$^{th}$ station or for Pune → total of 2 tickets.)

5$^{th}$ station (from where they could have bought a ticket for Pune → total of 1 ticket.)

Thus, we can see that there are a total of $5 + 4 + 3 + 2 + 1 = 15$ tickets available out of which 3 tickets were selected. This can be done in $^{15}C_{3}$ ways (Answer).

**Problem 17.15** Find the number of diagonals and triangles formed in a decagon.

**Solution** A decagon has 10 vertices. A line is formed by selecting any two of the ten vertices. This can be done in $^{10}C_{2}$ ways. However, these $^{10}C_{2}$ lines also count the sides of the decagon.

Thus, the number of diagonals in a decagon is given by: $^{10}C_{2} - 10$ (Answer)

Triangles are formed by selecting any three of the ten vertices of the decagon. This can be done in $^{10}C_{3}$ ways (Answer).

**Problem 17.16** Out of 18 points in a plane, no three are in a straight line except 5 which are collinear. How many straight lines can be formed?

**Solution** If all 18 points were non-collinear then the answer would have been $^{18}C_{2}$. However, in this case $^{18}C_{2}$ has double counting since the 5 collinear points are also amongst the 18. These would have been counted as $^{5}C_{2}$ whereas they should have been counted as 1. Thus, to remove the double counting and get the correct answer we need to adjust by reducing the count by $(^{5}C_{2} - 1)$.

Hence, Answer = $^{18}C_{2} - (^{5}C_{2} - 1) = ^{18}C_{2} - ^{5}C_{2} + 1$

**Problem 17.17** For the above situation, how many triangles can be formed?

**Solution** The triangles will be given by $^{18}C_{3} - ^{5}C_{3}$.

**Problem 17.18** A question paper had ten questions. Each question could only be answered as True (T) or False (F). Each candidate answered all the questions. Yet, no two candidates wrote the answers in an identical sequence. How many different sequences of answers are possible?

(a) 20　　　　　　　(b) 40
(c) 512　　　　　　(d) 1024

**Solution** $2^{10} = 1024$ unique sequences are possible. Option (d) is correct.

**Problem 17.19** When ten persons shake hands with one another, in how many ways is it possible?

(a) 20     (b) 25
(c) 40     (d) 45

**Solution** For $n$ people there are always $^nC_2$ shake hands. Thus, for 10 people shaking hands with each other the number of ways would be $^{10}C_2 = 45$.

**Problem 17.20** In how many ways can four children be made to stand in a line such that two of them, $A$ and $B$ are always together?

(a) 6     (b) 12
(c) 18     (d) 24

**Solution** If the children are $A$, $B$, $C$, $D$ we have to consider $A$ & $B$ as one child. This, would give us 3! ways of arranging $AB$, $C$ and $D$. However, for every arrangement with $AB$, there would be a parallel arrangement with $BA$. Thus, the correct answer would be $3! \times 2! = 12$ ways. Option (b) is correct.

**Problem 17.21** Each person's performance compared with all other persons is to be done to rank them subjectively. How many comparisons are needed to total, if there are 11 persons?

(a) 66     (b) 55
(c) 54     (d) 45

**Solution** There would be $^{11}C_2$ combinations of 2 people taken 2 at a time for comparison. $^{11}C_2 = 55$.

**Problem 17.22** A person X has four notes of Rupee 1, 2, 5 and 10 denomination. The number of different sums of money she can form from them is

(a) 16     (b) 15
(c) 12     (d) 8

**Solution** $2^4 - 1 = 15$ sums of money can be formed. Option (b) is correct.

**Problem 17.23** A person has 4 coins each of different denomination. What is the number of different sums of money the person can form (using one or more coins at a time)?

(a) 16     (b) 15
(c) 12     (d) 11

**Solution** $2^4 - 1 = 15$. Hence, option (b) is correct.

**Problem 17.24** How many three-digit numbers can be generated from 1, 2, 3, 4, 5, 6, 7, 8, 9, such that the digits are in ascending order?

(a) 80     (b) 81
(c) 83     (d) 84

**Solution** Numbers starting with 12 – 7 numbers

Numbers starting with 13 – 6 numbers; 14 – 5, 15 – 4, 16 – 3, 17 – 2, 18 – 1. Thus total number of numbers starting from 1 is given by the sum of 1 to 7 = 28.

Number of numbers starting from 2- would be given by the sum of 1 to 6 = 21

Number of numbers starting from 3- sum of 1 to 5 = 15

Number of numbers starting from 4 – sum of 1 to 4 = 10

Number of numbers starting from 5 – sum of 1 to 3 = 6

Number of numbers starting from 6 = 1 + 2 = 3

Number of numbers starting from 7 = 1

Thus a total of: $28 + 21 + 15 + 10 + 6 + 3 + 1 = 84$ such numbers. Option (d) is correct.

**Problem 17.25** In a carrom board game competition, $m$ boys $n$ girls ($m > n > 1$) of a school participate in which every student has to play exactly one game with every other student. Out of the total games played, it was found that in 221 games one player was a boy and the other player was a girl.

Consider the following statements:

I. The total number of students that participated in the competition is 30.

II. The number of games in which both players were girls is 78.

Which of the statements given above is/are correct?

(a) I only     (b) II only
(c) Both I and II     (d) Neither I nor II.

**Solution** The given condition can get achieved if we were to use 17 boys and 13 girls. In such a case both statement I and II are correct. Hence, option (c) is correct.

**Problem 17.26**

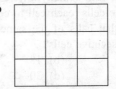

In how many different ways can all of 5 identical balls be placed in the cells shown above such that each row contains at least 1 ball?

(a) 64     (b) 81
(c) 84     (d) 108

**Solution** The placement of balls can be 3, 1, 1 and 2, 2, 1. For 3, 1, 1- If we place 3 balls in the top row, there would be $^3C_1$ ways of choosing a place for the ball in the second row and $^3C_1$ ways of choosing a place for the ball in the third row. Thus, $^3C_1 \times ^3C_1 = 9$ ways. Similarly there would be 9 ways each if we were to place 3 balls in the second row and 3 balls in the third row. Thus, with the 3, 1, 1 distribution of 5 balls we would get $9 + 9 + 9 = 27$ ways of placing the balls.

We now need to look at the 2, 2, 1 arrangement of balls. If we place 1 ball in the first row, we would need to place 2 balls each in the second and the third rows. In such a case, the number of ways of arranging the balls would be $^3C_1 \times ^3C_2 \times ^3C_2 = 27$ ways. (choosing 1 place out of 3 in the first row, 2 places out of 3 in the second row and 2 places out of 3 in the third row).

Similarly if we were to place 1 ball in the second row and 2 balls each in the first and third rows we would get 27 ways of placing the balls and another 27 ways of placing the balls if we place 1 ball in the third row and 2 balls each in the other two rows.

Thus with a 2, 2, 1 distribution of the 5 balls we would get $27 + 27 + 27 = 81$ ways of placing the balls.

Hence, total number of ways = Number of ways of placing the balls with a 3,1,1 distribution of balls + number of ways of placing the balls with a 2, 2, 1 distribution of balls = $27 + 81 = 108$.

Hence, option (d) is correct.

**Problem 17.27** There are 6 different letter and 6 correspondingly addressed envelopes. If the letters are randomly put in the envelopes, what is the probability that exactly 5 letters go into the correctly addressed envelopes?

(a) Zero          (b) 1/6
(c) 1/2           (d) 5/6

**Solution** If 5 letters go into the correct envelopes the sixth would automatically go into it's correct envelope. Thus, there is no possibility when exactly 5 letters are correct and 1 is wrong. Hence, option (a) is correct.

**Problem 17.28**

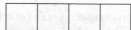

There are two identical red, two identical black and two identical white balls. In how many different ways can the balls be placed in the cells (each cell to contain one ball) shown above such that balls of the same colour do not occupy any two consecutive cells?

(a) 15          (b) 18
(c) 24          (d) 30

**Solution** In the first cell, we have 3 options of placing a ball. Suppose we were to place a red ball in the first cell- then the second cell can only be filled with either black or white – so 2 ways. Subsequently there would be 2 ways each of filling each of the cells (because we cannot put the colour we have already used in the previous cell).

Thus, the required number of ways would be $3 \times 2 \times 2 \times 2 = 24$ ways.

Hence, option (c) is correct.

**Problem 17.29**

How many different triangles are there in the figure shown above?

(a) 28          (b) 24
(c) 20          (d) 16

**Solution** Look for the smallest triangles first—there are 12 of them.

Then, look for the triangles which are equal to half the rectangle—there are 12 of them.

Besides, there are 4 bigger triangles (spanning across 2 rectangles).

Thus a total of 28 triangles can be seen in the figure.

Hence, option (a) is correct.

**Problem 17.30** A teacher has to choose the maximum different groups of three students from a total of six stu-

dents. Of these groups, in how many groups there will be included a particular student?

(a) 6          (b) 8
(c) 10         (d) 12

**Solution** If the students are $A$, $B$, $C$, $D$, $E$ and $F$- we can have $^6C_3$ groups in all. However, if we have to count groups in which a particular student (say $A$) is always selected- we would get $^5C_2 = 10$ ways of doing it. Hence, option (c) is correct.

**Problem 17.31** Three dice (each having six faces with each face having one number from 1 to 6) are rolled. What is the number of possible outcomes such that at least one dice shows the number 2?

(a) 36          (b) 81
(c) 91          (d) 116

**Solution** **All 3 dice have twos** – 1 case.

**Two dice have twos:**

This can principally occur in 3 ways which can be broken into:

If the first two dice have 2- the third dice can have 1, 3, 4, 5 or 6 = 5 ways.

Similarly, if the first and third dice have 2, the second dice can have 5 outcomes → 5 ways and if the second and third dice have a 2, there would be another 5 ways. Thus a total of 15 outcomes if 2 dice have a 2.

**With only 1 dice having a two-** If the first dice has 2, the other two can have $5 \times 5 = 25$ outcomes.

Similarly 25 outcomes if the second dice has 2 and 25 outcomes if the third dice has 2. A total of 75 outcomes. Thus, a total of $1 + 15 + 75 = 91$ possible outcomes with at least.

Hence, option (c) is correct.

**Problem 17.32** All the six letters of the name SACHIN are arranged to form different words without repeating any letter in any one word. The words so formed are then arranged as in a dictionary. What will be the position of the word SACHIN in that sequence?

(a) 436          (b) 590
(c) 601          (d) 751

**Solution** All words staring with $A$, $C$, $H$, $I$ and $N$ would be before words starting with S. So we would have 5! Words (= 120 words) each starting with $A$, $C$, $H$, $I$ and $N$. Thus, a total of 600 words would get completed before we start off with $S$. SACHIN would be the first word starting with $S$, because $A$, $C$, $H$, $I$, $N$ in that order is the correct alphabetical sequence. Hence, Sachin would be the 601st word. Hence, option (c) is correct.

**Problem 17.33** Five balls of different colours are to be placed in three different boxes such that any box contains at least one 1 ball. What is the maximum number of different ways in which this can be done?

(a) 90          (b) 120
(c) 150         (d) 180

**Solution** The arrangements can be [3 & 1 & 1 or 1 & 3 & 1 or 1 & 1 & 3] or 2 & 2 & 1 or 2 & 1 & 2 or 1 & 2 and 2.

Total number of ways = $3 \times {}^5C_3 \times {}^2C_1 \times {}^1C_1 + 3 \times {}^5C_2 \times {}^3C_2 \times {}^1C_1 = 60 + 90 = 150$ ways

Hence, option (c) is correct.

**Problem 17.34** Amit has five friends: 3 girls and 2 boys. Amit's wife also has 5 friends : 3 boys and 2 girls. In how many maximum number of different ways can they invite 2 boys and 2 girls such that two of them are Amit's friends and two are his wife's?

(a) 24　　　　　　　(b) 38
(c) 46　　　　　　　(d) 58

**Solution** The selection can be done in the following ways:

2 boys from Amit's friends and 2 girls from his wife's friends OR 1 boy & 1 girl from Amit's friends and 1 boy and 1 girl from his wife's friends OR 2 girls from Amit's friends and 2 boys from his wife's friends.

The number of ways would be:

$${}^2C_2 \times {}^2C_2 + {}^3C_1 \times {}^2C_1 \times {}^3C_1 \times {}^2C_1 + {}^3C_2 \times {}^3C_2 = 1 + 36 + 9 = 46 \text{ ways.}$$

**Problem 17.35**

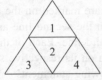

In the given figure, what is the maximum number of different ways in which 8 identical balls can be placed in the small triangles 1, 2, 3 and 4 such that each triangle contains at least one ball?

(a) 32　　　　　　　(b) 35
(c) 44　　　　　　　(d) 56

**Solution** The ways of placing the balls would be 5, 1, 1, 1 (4!/3! = 4 ways); 4, 2, 1 & 1 (4!/2! = 12 ways); 3, 3, 1, 1 (4!/2! × 2! = 6 ways); 3, 2, 2, 1 (4!/2! = 12 ways) and 2, 2, 2, 2 (1 way). Total number of ways = 4 + 12 + 6 + 12 + 1 = 35 ways. Hence, option (b) is correct.

**Problem 17.36** 6 equidistant vertical lines are drawn on a board. 6 equidistant horizontal lines are also drawn on the board cutting the 6 vertical lines, and the distance between any two consecutive horizontal lines is equal to that between any two consecutive vertical lines. What is the maximum number of squares thus formed?

(a) 37　　　　　　　(b) 55
(c) 91　　　　　　　(d) 225

**Solution** The number of squares would be $1^2 + 2^2 + 3^2 + 4^2 + 5^2 = 55$. Hence, option (b) is correct.

**Problem 1.37** Groups each containing 3 boys are to be formed out of 5 boys—A, B, C, D and E such that no group contains both C and D together. What is the maximum number of such different groups?

(a) 5　　　　　　　(b) 6
(c) 7　　　　　　　(d) 8

**Solution** All groups – groups with C and D together = ${}^5C_3 - {}^3C_1 = 10 - 3 = 7$

**Problem 17.38**

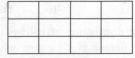

In how many maximum different ways can 3 identical balls be placed in the 12 squares (each ball to be placed in the exact centre of the squares and only one ball is to be placed in one square) shown in the figure given above such that they do not lie along the same straight line?

(a) 144　　　　　　(b) 200
(c) 204　　　　　　(d) 216

**Solution** The thought process for this question would be:

All arrangements (${}^{12}C_3$) – Arrangements where all 3 balls are in the same row ($3 \times {}^4C_3$)– arrangements where all 3 balls are in the same straight line diagonally (4 arrangements) – arrangements where all 3 balls are in the same column (4 arrangements) = ${}^{12}C_3 - 3 \times {}^4C_3 - 4 - 4 = 220 - 12 - 4 - 4 = 200$ ways.

Hence, option (b) is correct.

**Problem 17.39** How many numbers are there in all from 6000 to 6999 (Both 6000 and 6999 included) having at least one of their digits repeated?

(a) 216　　　　　　(b) 356
(c) 496　　　　　　(d) 504

**Solution** All numbers – numbers having no numbers repeated = $1000 - 9 \times 8 \times 7 = 1000 - 504 = 496$ numbers. Hence, option (c) is correct.

**Problem 17.40** Each of two women and three men is to occupy one chair out of eight chairs, each of which is numbered from one to eight. First, women are to occupy any two chairs from\those numbered one to four; and then the three men would occupy any three chairs out of the remaining six chairs. What is the maximum number of different ways in which this can be done?

(a) 40　　　　　　　(b) 132
(c) 1440　　　　　　(d) 3660

**Solution** ${}^4C_2 \times 2! \times {}^6C_3 \times 3! = 6 \times 2 \times 20 \times 6 = 1440$. Hence, option (c) is correct.

**Problem 17.41** A box contains five set of balls while there are three balls in each set. Each set of balls has one ball, whose colour is different from every other ball in that set and also from every other ball in any other set. What is the least number of balls that must be removed from the box in order to claim with certainty that a pair of balls of the same colour has been removed?

(a) 6　　　　　　　(b) 7
(c) 9　　　　　　　(d) 11

**Solution** Let $C1, C2, C3, C4$ and $C5$ be the 5 distinct colours which have no repetition. For being definitely sure that we have picked up 2 balls of the same colour we need to consider the worst case situation.

Consider the following scenario:

| Set 1 | Set 2 | Set 3 | Set 4 | Set 5 |
|-------|-------|-------|-------|-------|
| C1    | C2    | C3    | C4    | C5    |
| C6    | C8    | C7    | C9    | C9    |
| C7    | C6    | C10   | C10   | C8    |

In the above distribution of balls each set has exactly 1 ball which is unique in it's colour while the colours of the other two balls are shared at least once in one of the other sets. In such a case, the worst scenario would be if we pick up the first 10 balls and they all turn out to be of different colours. The 11th ball has to be of a colour which has already been taken. Thus, if we were to pick out 11 balls we would be sure of having at least 2 balls of the same colour. Hence, option (d) is correct.

**Problem 17.42** In a question paper, there are four multiple-choice questions. Each question has five choices with only one choice as the correct answer. What is the total number of ways in which a candidate will not get all the four answers correct?

(a) 19        (b) 120

(c) 624       (d) 1024

**Solution** $5^4$ would be the total number of ways in which the questions can be answered. Out of these there would be only 1 way of getting all 4 correct. Thus, there would be 624 ways of not getting all answers correct.

**Problem 17.43**

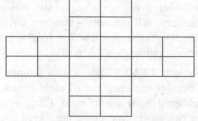

Each of 8 identical balls is to be placed in the squares shown in the figure given in a horizontal direction such that one horizontal row contains 6 balls and the other horizontal row contains 2 balls. In how many maximum different ways can this be done?

(a) 38        (b) 28

(c) 16        (d) 14

**Solution** The 6 balls must be on either of the middle rows. This can be done in 2 ways. Once, we put the 6 balls in their single horizontal row- it becomes evident that for placing the 2 remaining balls on a straight line there are 2 principal options:

1. Placing the two balls in one of the four rows with two squares. In this case the number of ways of placing the balls in any particular row would be 1 way (since once you were to choose one of the 4 rows, the balls would automatically get placed as there are only two squares in each row.) Thus the total number of ways would be $2 \times 4 \times 1 = 8$ ways.

2. Placing the two balls in the other row with six squares. In this case the number of ways of placing the 2 balls in that row would be $^6C_2$. This would give us $^2C_1 \times 1 \times ^6C_2 = 30$ ways. Total is $30 + 8 = 38$ ways.

Hence, option (a) is correct.

**Problem 17.44** In a tournament each of the participants was to play one match against each of the other participants. 3 players fell ill after each of them had played three matches and had to leave the tournament. What was the total number of participants at the beginning, if the total number of matches played was 75?

(a) 8        (b) 10

(c) 12       (d) 15

**Solution** The number of players at the start of the tournament cannot be 8, 10 or 12 because in each of these cases the total number of matches would be less than 75 (as $^8C_2$, $^{10}C_2$ and $^{12}C_2$ are all less than 75.) This only leaves 15 participants in the tournament as the only possibility.

Hence, option (d) is correct.

**Problem 17.45** There are three parallel straight lines. Two points $A$ and $B$ are marked on the first line, points $C$ and $D$ are marked on the second line and points $E$ and $F$ are marked on the third line. Each of these six points can move to any position on its respective straight line.

Consider the following statements:

I. The maximum number of triangles that can be drawn by joining these points is 18.

II. The minimum number of triangles that can be drawn by joining these points is zero.

Which of the statements given above is/are correct?

(a) I only       (b) II only

(c) Both I and II     (d) Neither I nor II

**Solution** The maximum triangles would be in case all these 6 points are non-collinear. In such a case the number of triangles is $^6C_3 = 20$. Statement I is incorrect.

Statement II is correct because if we take the position that $A$ and $B$ coincide on the first line, $C$ & $D$ coincide on the second line, $E$ & $F$ coincide on the third line and all these coincidences happen at 3 points which are on the same straight line- in such a case there would be 0 triangles formed. Hence, option (b) is correct.

**Problem 17.46** A mixed doubles tennis game is to be played between two teams (each team consists of one male and one female). There are four married couples. No team is to consist of a husband and his wife. What is the maximum number of games that can be played?

(a) 12       (b) 21

(c) 36       (d) 42

**Solution** First select the two men. This can be done in $^4C_2$ ways. Let us say the men are $A$, $B$, $C$ and $D$ and their respective wives are $a$, $b$, $c$ and $d$.

If we select $A$ and $B$ as the two men then while selecting the women there would be two cases as seen below:

**Case 1:**

| $A$ | If $b$ is selected to partner $A$ |
|---|---|
| $B$ | There will be 3 choices for choosing $B$'s partner – viz $a$, $c$ and $d$ |

Thus, total number of ways in this case = $^4C_2 \times 1 \times {^3C_1}$ = 18 ways.

*Space for Rough Work*

**Case 2:**

| $A$ | If either $c$ or $d$ is selected to partner $A$ |
|---|---|
| $B$ | There will be 2 choices for choosing $B$'s partner – viz $a$ and any one of $c$ and $d$ |

Total number of ways of doing this = $^4C_2 \times 2 \times {^2C_1}$ = 24 ways.

Hence, the required answer is $18 + 24 = 42$ ways.

Hence, option (d) is correct.

## LEVEL OF DIFFICULTY (I)

1. How many numbers of 3-digits can be formed with the digits 1, 2, 3, 4, 5 (repetition of digits not allowed)?
   - (a) 125
   - (b) 120
   - (c) 60
   - (d) 150

2. How many numbers between 2000 and 3000 can be formed with the digits 0, 1, 2, 3, 4, 5, 6, 7 (repetition of digits not allowed?
   - (a) 42
   - (b) 210
   - (c) 336
   - (d) 440

3. In how many ways can a person send invitation cards to 6 of his friends if he has four servants to distribute the cards?
   - (a) $6^4$
   - (b) $4^6$
   - (c) 24
   - (d) 120

4. In how many ways can 5 prizes be distributed to 8 students if each student can get any number of prizes?
   - (a) 40
   - (b) $5^8$
   - (c) $8^5$
   - (d) 120

5. In how many ways can 7 Indians, 5 Pakistanis and 6 Dutch be seated in a row so that all persons of the same nationality sit together?
   - (a) 3!
   - (b) 7!5!6!
   - (c) 3!.7!.5!.6!
   - (d) 182

6. There are 5 routes to go from Allahabad to Patna & 4 ways to go from Patna to Kolkata, then how many ways are possible for going from Allahabad to Kolkata via Patna?
   - (a) 20
   - (b) $5^4$
   - (c) $4^5$
   - (d) $5^4 + 4^5$

7. There are 4 qualifying examinations to enter into Oxford University: RAT, BAT, SAT, and PAT. An Engineer cannot go to Oxford University through BAT or SAT. A CA on the other hand can go to the Oxford University through the RAT, BAT & PAT but not through SAT. Further there are 3 ways to become a CA(viz., Foundation, Inter & Final). Find the ratio of number of ways in which an Engineer can make it to Oxford University to the number of ways a CA can make it to Oxford University.
   - (a) 3:2
   - (b) 2:3
   - (c) 2:9
   - (d) 9:2

8. How many straight lines can be formed from 8 non-collinear points on the X-Y plane?
   - (a) 28
   - (b) 56
   - (c) 18
   - (d) 19860

9. If $^nC_3 = {}^nC_8$, find $n$.
   - (a) 11
   - (b) 12
   - (c) 14
   - (d) 10

10. In how many ways can the letters of the word DELHI be arranged?
    - (a) 119
    - (b) 120
    - (c) 60
    - (d) 24

11. In how many ways can the letters of the word PATNA be rearranged?
    - (a) 60
    - (b) 120
    - (c) 119
    - (d) 59

12. For the arrangements of the letters of the word PATNA, how many words would start with the letter P?
    - (a) 24
    - (b) 12
    - (c) 60
    - (d) 120

13. In Question no.11, how many words will start with P and end with T?
    - (a) 3
    - (b) 6
    - (c) 11
    - (d) 12

14. If $^nC_4 = 70$, find $n$.
    - (a) 5
    - (b) 8
    - (c) 4
    - (d) 7

15. If $^{10}P_r = 720$, find $r$.
    - (a) 4
    - (b) 5
    - (c) 3
    - (d) 6

16. How many numbers of four digits can be formed with the digits 0, 1, 2, 3 (repetition of digits is not allowed?
    - (a) 18
    - (b) 24
    - (c) 64
    - (d) 192

17. How many numbers of four digits can be formed with the digits 0, 1, 2, 3 (repetition of digits being allowed?
    - (a) 12
    - (b) 108
    - (c) 256
    - (d) 192

18. How many numbers between 200 and 1200 can be formed with the digits 0, 1, 2, 3 (repetition of digits not allowed?
    - (a) 6
    - (b) 6
    - (c) 2
    - (d) 14

19. For the above question, how many numbers can be formed with the same digits if repetition of digits is allowed?
    - (a) 48
    - (b) 63
    - (c) 32
    - (d) 14

20. If $(2n + 1)P_{(n-1)} : (2n - 1)P_n = 7:10$ find $n$
    (a) 4       (b) 6
    (c) 3       (d) 7

21. If $(^{28}C_{2r} : {}^{24}C_{2r-4}) = 225:11$ Find the value of $r$.
    (a) 10      (b) 11
    (c) 7       (d) 9

22. Arjit being a party animal wants to hold as many parties as possible amongst his 20 friends. However, his father has warned him that he will be financing his parties under the following conditions only:
    (a) The invitees have to be amongst his 20 best friends.
    (b) He cannot call the same set of friends to a party more than once.
    (c) The number of invitees to every party have to be the same.
      Given these constraints Arjit wants to hold the maximum number of parties. How many friends should he invite to each party?
    (a) 11      (b) 8
    (c) 10      (d) 12

23. In how many ways can 10 identical presents be distributed among 6 children so that each child gets at least one present?
    (a) $^{15}C_5$      (b) $^{16}C_6$
    (c) $^9C_5$      (d) $6^{10}$

24. How many four digit numbers are possible, criteria being that all the four digits are odd?
    (a) 125     (b) 625
    (c) 45      (d) none of these

25. A captain and a vice-captain are to be chosen out of a team having eleven players. How many ways are there to achieve this?
    (a) 10.9     (b) $^{11}C_2$
    (c) 110     (d) 10.9!

26. There are five types of envelopes and four types of stamps in a post office. How many ways are there to buy an envelope and a stamp?
    (a) 20      (b) 45
    (c) 54      (d) 9

27. In how many ways can Ram choose a vowel and a consonant from the letters of the word ALLAHABAD?
    (a) 4       (b) 6
    (c) 9       (d) 5

28. There are three rooms in a motel: one single, one double and one for four persons. How many ways are there to house seven persons in these rooms?
    (a) 7!/1!2!4!     (b) 7!
    (c) 7!/3       (d) 7!/3!

29. How many ways are there to choose four cards of different suits and different values from a deck of 52 cards?

(a) 13.12.11.10     (b) $^{52}C_4$
(c) 134        (d) 52.36.22.10

30. How many new words are possible from the letters of the word PERMUTATION?
    (a) 11!/2!       (b) (11!/2!) – 1
    (c) 11! – 1      (d) None of these

31. A set of 15 different words are given. In how many ways is it possible to choose a subset of not more than 5 words?
    (a) 4944      (b) $4^{15}$
    (c) $15^4$       (d) 4943

32. In how many ways can 12 papers be arranged if the best and the worst paper never come together?
    (a) 12!/2!       (b) 12! – 11!
    (c) (12! – 11!)/2    (d) 12! – 2.11!

33. In how many ways can the letters of the word 'EQUATION' be arranged so that all the vowels come together?
    (a) $^9C_4 \cdot {}^9C_5$      (b) 4!.5!
    (c) 9!/5!        (d) 9! – 4!5!

34. A man has 3 shirts, 4 trousers and 6 ties. What are the number of ways in which he can dress himself with a combination of all the three?
    (a) 13          (b) 72
    (c) 13!/3!.4!.6!   (d) 3!.4!.6!

35. How many motor vehicle registration number of 4 digits can be formed with the digits 0, 1, 2, 3, 4, 5? (No digit being repeated.)
    (a) 1080      (b) 120
    (c) 300       (d) 360

36. How many motor vehicle registration number plates can be formed with the digits 1, 2, 3, 4, 5 (No digits being repeated) if it is given that registration number can have 1 to 5 digits?
    (a) 100       (b) 120
    (c) 325       (d) 205

**Directions for Question 37 to 39:** There are 25 points on a plane of which 7 are collinear. Now solve the following:

37. How many straight lines can be formed?
    (a) 7        (b) 300
    (c) 280     (d) none of these

38. How many triangles can be formed from these points?
    (a) 453      (b) 2265
    (c) 755      (d) none of these

39. How many quadrilaterals can be formed from these points?
    (a) 5206     (b) 2603
    (c) 13015    (d) None of these

40. There are ten subjects in the school day at St. Vincent's High School but the sixth standard students have only 5 periods in a day. In how many ways can we form a time table for the day for the sixth standard students if no subject is repeated?
    (a) 510
    (b) 105
    (c) 252
    (d) 30240

41. There are 8 consonants and 5 vowels in a word jumble. In how many ways can we form 5-letter words having three consonants and 2 vowels?
    (a) 67200
    (b) 8540
    (c) 720
    (d) None of these

42. How many batting orders are possible for the Indian cricket team if there is a squad of 15 to choose from such that Sachin Tendulkar is always chosen?
    (a) 1001.11!
    (b) 364.11!
    (c) 11!
    (d) 15.11!

43. There are 5 blue socks, 4 red socks and 3 green socks, all different in Debu's wardrobe. He has to select 4 socks from this set. In how many ways can he do so?
    (a) 245
    (b) 120
    (c) 495
    (d) 60

44. A class prefect goes to meet the principal every week. His class has 30 people apart from him. If he has to take groups of three every time he goes to the principal, in how many weeks will he be able to go to the principal without repeating the group of same three which accompanies him?
    (a) $^{30}P_3$
    (b) $^{30}C_3$
    (c) 30!/3
    (d) None of these

45. For the above question if on the very first visit the principal appoints one of the boys accompanying him as the head boy of the school and lays down the condition that the class prefect has to be accompanied by the head boy every time he comes then for a maximum of how many weeks (including the first week) can the class prefect ensure that the principal sees a fresh group of three accompanying him?
    (a) $^{30}C_2$
    (b) $^{29}C_2$
    (c) $^{29}C_3$
    (d) None of these

46. How many distinct words can be formed out of the word PROWLING which start with R & end with W?
    (a) 8!/2!
    (b) 6!2!
    (c) 6!
    (d) None of these

47. How many 7-digit numbers are there having the digit 3 three times & the digit 5 four times?
    (a) 7!/(3!)(5!)
    (b) $3^3 \times 5^5$
    (c) 77
    (d) 35

48. How many 7-digit numbers are there having the digit 3 three times & the digit 0 four times?
    (a) 15
    (b) $3^3 \times 4^4$

49. From a set of three capital consonants, five small consonants and 4 small vowels how many words can be made each starting with a capital consonant and containing 3 small consonants and two small vowels.
    (a) 3600
    (b) 7200
    (c) 21600
    (d) 28800

50. Several teams take part in a competition, each of which must play one game with all the other teams. How many teams took part in the competition if they played 45 games in all?
    (a) 5
    (b) 10
    (c) 15
    (d) 20

51. In how many ways a selection can be made of at least one fruit out of 5 bananas, 4 mangoes and 4 almonds?
    (a) 129
    (b) 149
    (c) 139
    (d) 109

52. There are 5 different Jeffrey Archer books, 3 different Sidney Sheldon books and 6 different John Grisham books. The number of ways in which at least one book can be given away is
    (a) $2^{10} - 1$
    (b) $2^{11} - 1$
    (c) $2^{12} - 1$
    (d) $2^{14} - 1$

53. In the above problem, find the number of ways in which at least one book of each author can be given.
    (a) $(2^5 - 1)(2^3 - 1)(2^8 - 1)$
    (b) $(2^5 - 1)(2^3 - 1)(2^3 - 1)$
    (c) $(2^5 - 1)(2^3 - 1)(2^3 - 1)$
    (d) $(2^5 - 1)(2^3 - 1)(2^6 - 1)$

54. There is a question paper consisting of 15 questions. Each question has an internal choice of 2 options. In how many ways can a student attempt one or more questions of the given fifteen questions in the paper?
    (a) $3^7$
    (b) $3^8$
    (c) $3^{15}$
    (d) $3^{15} - 1$

55. How many numbers can be formed with the digits 1, 6, 7, 8, 7, 6, 1 so that the odd digits always occupy the odd places?
    (a) 15
    (b) 12
    (c) 18
    (d) 20

56. There are five boys of McGraw-Hill Mindworkzz and three girls of I.I.M Lucknow who are sitting together to discuss a management problem at a round table. In how many ways can they sit around the table so that no two girls are together?
    (a) 1220
    (b) 1400
    (c) 1420
    (d) 1440

57. Amita has three library cards and seven books of her interest in the library of Mindworkzz. Of these books she would not like to borrow the D.I. book,

unless the Quants book is also borrowed. In how many ways can she take the three books to be borrowed?

(a) 15       (b) 20

(c) 25       (d) 30

58. From a group of 12 dancers, five have to be taken for a stage show. Among them Radha and Mohan decide either both of them would join or none of them would join. In how many ways can the 5 dancers be chosen?

(a) 190       (b) 210

(c) 278       (d) 372

59. Find the number of 6-digit numbers that can be formed using the digits 1, 2, 3, 4, 5, 6 once such that the 6-digit number is divisible by its unit digit. (The unit digit is not 1.)

(a) 620       (b) 456

(c) 520       (d) 528

60. An urn contains 5 boxes. Each box contains 5 balls of different colours red, yellow, white, blue and black. Rangeela wants to pick up 5 balls of different colours, a different coloured ball from each box. If from the first box in the first draw, he has drawn a red ball and from the second box he has drawn a black ball, find the maximum number of trials that are needed to be made by Rangeela to accomplish his task if a ball picked is not replaced.

(a) 12       (b) 11

(c) 20       (d) 60

61. How many rounds of matches does a knock-out tennis tournament have if it starts with 64 players and every player needs to win 1 match to move at the next round?

(a) 5       (b) 6

(c) 7       (d) 64

62. There are $N$ men sitting around a circular table at $N$ distinct points. Every possible pair of men except the ones sitting adjacent to each other sings a 2 minute song one pair after other. If the total time taken is 88 minutes, then what is the value of $N$?

(a) 8       (b) 9

(c) 10       (d) 11

63. In a class with boys and girls a chess competition was played wherein every student had to play 1 game with every other student. It was observed that in 36 matches both the players were boys and in 66 matches both were girls. What is the number of matches in which 1 boy and 1 girl play against each other?

(a) 108       (b) 189

(c) 210       (d) 54

64. Zada has to distribute 15 chocolates among 5 of her children Sana, Ada, Jiya, Amir and Farhan. She has to make sure that Sana gets at least 3 and at most 6

chocolates. In how many ways can this be done if each child gets at least one chocolate?

(a) 495       (b) 77

(c) 417       (d) 425

65. Mr Shah has to divide his assets worth ₹ 30 crores in 3 parts to be given to three of his sons Ajay, Vijay and Arun ensuring that every son gets assets atleast worth ₹ 5 crores. In how many ways can this be done if it is given that the three sons should get their shares in multiples of ₹ 1 crore?

(a) 136       (b) 152

(c) 176       (d) 98

66. Three variables $x$, $y$, $z$ have a sum of 30. All three of them are non-negative integers. If any two variables don't have the same value and exactly one variable has a value less than or equal to three, then find the number of possible solutions for the variables.

(a) 98       (b) 285

(c) 68       (d) 252

67. The letters of the word ALLAHABAD are rearranged to form new words and put in a dictionary. If the dictionary has only these words and one word on every page in alphabetical order then what is the page number on which the word LABADALAH comes?

(a) 6269       (b) 6268

(c) 6087       (d) 6086

68. If $x$, $y$ and $z$ can only take the values 1, 2, 3, 4, 5, 6, 7 then find the number of solutions of the equation $x + y + z = 12$.

(a) 36       (b) 37

(c) 38       (d) 31

69. There are nine points in a plane such that no three are collinear. Find the number of triangles that can be formed using these points as vertices.

(a) 81       (b) 90

(c) 9       (d) 84

70. There are nine points in a plane such that exactly three points out of them are collinear. Find the number of triangles that can be formed using these points as vertices.

(a) 81       (b) 90

(c) 9       (d) 83

71. If $xy$ is a 2-digit number and $u$, $v$, $x$, $y$ are digits, then find the number of solutions of the equation: $(xy)^2 = u! + v$

(a) 2       (b) 3

(c) 0       (d) 5

72. Ten points are marked on a straight line and eleven points are marked on another straight line. How many triangles can be constructed with vertices from among the above points?

(a) 495      (b) 550

(c) 1045      (d) 2475

73. For a scholarship, at the most $n$ candidates out of $2n + 1$ can be selected. If the number of different ways of selection of at least one candidate is 63, the maximum number of candidates that can be selected for the scholarship is

(a) 3      (b) 4

(c) 2      (d) 5

74. One red flag, three white flags and two blue flags are arranged in a line such that,

(a) no two adjacent flags are of the same colour

(b) the flags at the two ends of the line are of different colours.

In how many different ways can the flags be arranged?

(a) 6      (b) 4

(c) 10      (d) 2

75. Sam has forgotten his friend's seven-digit telephone number. He remembers the following: the first three digits are either 635 or 674, the number is odd, and the number nine appears once. If Sam were to use a trial and error process to reach his friend, what is the minimum number of trials he has to make before he can be certain to succeed?

(a) 1000      (b) 2430

(c) 3402      (d) 3006

76. There are three cities $A$, $B$ and $C$. Each of these cities is connected with the other two cities by at least one direct road. If a traveler wants to go from one city (origin) to another city (destination), she can do so either by traversing a road connecting the two cities directly, or by traversing two roads, the first connecting the origin to the third city and the second connecting the third city to the destination. In all there are 33 routes from $A$ to $B$ (including those via $C$). Similarly there are 23 routes from $B$ to $C$ (including those via $A$). How many roads are there from $A$ to $C$ directly?

(a) 6      (b) 3

(c) 5      (d) 10

77. Let $n$ be the number of different 5-digit numbers, divisible by 4 that can be formed with the digits 1, 2, 3, 4, 5 and 6, with no digit being repeated. What is the value of $n$?

(a) 144      (b) 168

(c) 192      (d) none of these

78. How many numbers greater than 0 and less than a million can be formed with the digits 0, 7 and 8?

(a) 486      (b) 1086

(c) 728      (d) none of these

79. In how many ways is it possible to choose a white square and a black square on a chess board so that the squares must not lie in the same row or column?

(a) 56      (b) 896

(c) 60      (d) 768

***Directions for Questions 80 and 81:*** Answer these questions based on the information given below.

Each of the 11 letters $A$, $H$, $I$, $M$, $O$, $T$, $U$, $V$, $W$, $X$ and $Z$ appear same when looked at in a mirror. They are called symmetric letters. Other letters in the alphabet are asymmetric letters.

80. How many four-letter computer passwords can be formed using only the symmetric letters (no repetition allowed)?

(a) 7920      (b) 330

(c) 14640      (d) 419430

81. How many three-letter computer passwords can be formed (no repetition allowed) with at least one symmetric letter?

(a) 990      (b) 2730

(c) 12870      (d) 15600

82. Twenty seven persons attend a party. Which one of the following statements can never be true?

(a) There is a person in the party who is acquainted with all the twenty six others.

(b) Each person in the party has a different number of acquaintances.

(c) There is a person in the party who has an odd number of acquaintances.

(d) In the party, there is no set of three mutual acquaintances.

83. There are 6 boxes numbered 1, 2, ....6. Each box is to be filled up either with a red or a green ball in such a way that at least 1 box contains a green ball and the boxes containing green balls are consecutively numbered. The total number of ways in which this can be done is

(a) 5      (b) 21

(c) 33      (d) 60

84. How many numbers can be formed with odd digits 1, 3, 5, 7, 9 without repetition?

(a) 275      (b) 325

(c) 375      (d) 235

85. In how many ways five chocolates can be chosen from an unlimited number of Cadbury, Five-star, and Perk chocolates?

(a) 81      (b) 243

(c) 21      (d) 31

***Directions for Questions 86 and 87:*** In a chess tournament there were two women participating and every participant played two games with the other participants. The number of games that the men played among themselves exceeded the number of games that the men played with the women by 66.

86. The number of participants in the tournament were?
    - (a)  12
    - (b)  13
    - (c)  15
    - (d)  11

87. The total number of games played in the tournament were?
    - (a)  132
    - (b)  110
    - (c)  156
    - (d)  210

**Space for Rough Work**

## LEVEL OF DIFFICULTY (II)

1. How many even numbers of four digits can be formed with the digits 1, 2, 3, 4, 5, 6 (repetitions of digits are allowed)?
   - (a) 648
   - (b) 180
   - (c) 1296
   - (d) 600

2. How many 4 digit numbers divisible by 5 can be formed with the digits 0, 1, 2, 3, 4, 5, 6 and 6?
   - (a) 220
   - (b) 249
   - (c) 432
   - (d) 288

3. There are 6 pups and 4 cats. In how many ways can they be seated in a row so that no cats sit together?
   - (a) $6^4$
   - (b) $10!/(4!).(6!)$
   - (c) $6! \times {}^7P_4$
   - (d) None of these

4. How many new words can be formed with the word MANAGEMENT all ending in $G$?
   - (a) $10!/(2!)^4 - 1$
   - (b) $9!/(2!)^4$
   - (c) $10!/(2!)^4$
   - (d) None of these

5. Find the total numbers of 9-digit numbers that can be formed all having different digits.
   - (a) ${}^{10}P_9$
   - (b) $9!$
   - (c) $10! - 9!$
   - (d) $9.9!$

6. There are $V$ lines parallel to the $x$-axis and '$W$' lines parallel to $y$-axis. How many rectangles can be formed with the intersection of these lines?
   - (a) ${}^vP_2.{}^wP_2$
   - (b) ${}^vC_2.{}^wC_2$
   - (c) ${}^{v-2}C_2.{}^{w-2}C_2$
   - (d) None of these

7. From 4 gentlemen and 4 ladies a committee of 5 is to be formed. Find the number of ways of doing so if the committee consists of a president, a vice-president and three secretaries?
   - (a) ${}^8P_5$
   - (b) 1120
   - (c) ${}^4C_2 \times {}^4C_3$
   - (d) None of these

8. In the above question, what will be the number of ways of selecting the committee with at least 3 women such that at least one woman holds the post of either a president or a vice-president?
   - (a) 420
   - (b) 610
   - (c) 256
   - (d) None of these

9. Find the number of ways of selecting the committee with a maximum of 2 women and having at the maximum one woman holding one of the two posts on the committee.
   - (a) 16
   - (b) 512
   - (c) 608
   - (d) 324

10. The crew of an 8 member rowing team is to be chosen from 12 men, of which 3 must row on one side only and 2 must row on the other side only. Find the number of ways of arranging the crew with 4 members on each side.
    - (a) 40,320
    - (b) 30,240
    - (c) 60,480
    - (d) None of these

11. In how many ways 5 MBA students and 6 Law students can be arranged together so that no two MBA students are side by side?
    - (a) $\dfrac{7!6!}{2!}$
    - (b) $6!.6!$
    - (c) $5!.6!$
    - (d) ${}^{11}C_5$

12. The latest registration number issued by the Delhi Motor Vehicle Registration Authority is DL-5S 2234. If all the numbers and alphabets before this have been used up, then find how many vehicles have a registration number starting with DL-5?
    - (a) 1,92,234
    - (b) 1,92,225
    - (c) 1,72,227
    - (d) None of these

13. There are 100 balls numbered $n_1, n_2, n_3, n_4, \ldots n_{100}$. They are arranged in all possible ways. How many arrangements would be there in which $n_{28}$ ball will always be before $n_{29}$ ball and the two of them will be adjacent to each other?
    - (a) $99!/2!$
    - (b) $99!.2!$
    - (c) $99!$
    - (d) None of these

14. Find the sum of the number of sides and number of diagonals of a hexagon.
    - (a) 210
    - (b) 15
    - (c) 6
    - (d) 9

15. A tea party is arranged for $2M$ people along two sides of a long table with $M$ chairs on each side. $R$ men wish to sit on one particular side and $S$ on the other. In how many ways can they be seated (provided $R, S \le M$)
    - (a) ${}^MP_R.{}^MP_S$
    - (b) ${}^MP_R.{}^MP_S({}^{2M-R-S}P_{2M-R-S})$
    - (c) ${}^{2M}P_R.{}^{2M-R}P_S$
    - (d) None of these

16. In how many ways can '$mn$' things be distributed equally among $n$ groups?
    - (a) ${}^{mn}P_m.{}^{mn}P_n$
    - (b) ${}^{mn}C_m.{}^{mn}C_n$
    - (c) $(mn)!/(m!)(.n!)$
    - (d) None of these

17. In how many ways can a selection be made of 5 letters out of 5As, 4Bs, 3Cs, 2Ds and 1E?
    - (a) 70
    - (b) 71
    - (c) ${}^{15}C_5$
    - (d) None of these

18. Find the number of ways of selecting 'n' articles out of $3n + 1$, out of which $n$ are identical.
    (a) $2^{2n-1}$
    (b) $^{3n+1}C_n/n!$
    (c) $^{3n+1}P_n/n!$
    (d) None of these

19. The number of positive numbers of not more than 10 digits formed by using 0, 1, 2, 3 is
    (a) $4^{10} - 1$
    (b) $4^{10}$
    (c) $4^9 - 1$
    (d) None of these

20. There is a number lock with four rings with each ring having digits 0 to 9. How many attempts at the maximum would have to be made before getting the right number?
    (a) $10^4$
    (b) 255
    (c) $10^4 - 1$
    (d) None of these

21. Find the number of numbers that can be formed using all the digits 1, 2, 3, 4, 3, 2, 1 only once so that the odd digits occupy odd places only.
    (a) $4!/(2!)^2$
    (b) $7!/(2!)^3$
    (c) $1!.3!.5!.7!$
    (d) None of these

22. There is a 7-digit telephone number with all different digits. If the digit at extreme right and extreme left are 5 and 6 respectively, find how many such telephone numbers are possible.
    (a) 120
    (b) 1,00,000
    (c) 6720
    (d) None of these

23. If a team of four persons is to be selected from 8 males and 8 females, then in how many ways can the selections be made to include at least one male.
    (a) 3500
    (b) 875
    (c) 1200
    (d) None of these

24. In the above question, in how many ways can the selections be made if it has to contain at the maximum three women?
    (a) 1750
    (b) 1200
    (c) 875
    (d) None of thes

25. How many figures are required to number a book containing 150 pages?
    (a) 450
    (b) 360
    (c) 262
    (d) None of these

26. There are 8 orators A, B, C, D, E, F, G and H. In how many ways can the arrangements be made so that A always comes before B and B always comes before C.
    (a) $8!/3!$
    (b) $8!/6!$
    (c) $5!.3!$
    (d) $8!/(5!.3!)$

27. There are 4 letters and 4 envelopes. In how many ways can wrong choices be made?
    (a) $4^3$
    (b) $4! - 1$
    (c) 16
    (d) $4^4 - 1$

28. In the question above, find the number of ways in which only one letter goes in the wrong envelope?
    (a) $4^3$
    (b) $^4C_1 + {}^4C_2 + {}^4C_3 + {}^4C_4$

29. In question 27, find the number of ways in which only two letters go in the wrong envelopes?
    (a) 4
    (b) 5
    (c) 6
    (d) 3

30. A train is running between Patna to Howrah. Seven people enter the train somewhere between Patna and Howrah. It is given that nine stops are there in between Patna and Howrah. In how many ways can the tickets be purchased if no restriction is there with respect to the number of tickets at any station? 2 people do not buy the same ticket.
    (a) $^{45}C_7$
    (b) $^{63}C_7$
    (c) $^{56}C_7$
    (d) $^{52}C_7$

31. There are seven pairs of black shoes and five pairs of white shoes. They all are put into a box and shoes are drawn one at a time. To ensure that at least one pair of black shoes are taken out, what is the number of shoes required to be drawn out?
    (a) 12
    (b) 13
    (c) 7
    (d) 18

32. In the above question, what is the minimum number of shoes required to be drawn out to get at least 1 pair of correct shoes (either white or black)?
    (a) 12
    (b) 7
    (c) 13
    (d) 18

33. In how many ways one white and one black rook can be placed on a chessboard so that they are never in an attacking position?
    (a) $64 \times 50$
    (b) $64 \times 49$
    (c) $63 \times 49$
    (d) None of these

34. How many 6-digit numbers have all their digits either all odd or all even?
    (a) 31,250
    (b) 28,125
    (c) 15,625
    (d) None of these

35. How many 6-digit numbers have at least 1 even digit?
    (a) 884375
    (b) 3600
    (c) 880775
    (d) 15624

36. How many 10-digit numbers have at least 2 equal digits?
    (a) $9 \times {}^{10}C_2 \times 8!$
    (b) $9.10^9 - 9.9!$
    (c) $9 \times 9!$
    (d) None of these

37. On a triangle ABC, on the side AB, 5 points are marked, 6 points are marked on the side BC and 3 points are marked on the side AC (none of the points being the vertex of the triangle). How many triangles can be made by using these points?
    (a) 90
    (b) 333
    (c) 328
    (d) None of these

38. If we have to make 7 boys sit with 7 girls around a round table, then the number of different relative arrangements of boys and girls that we can make so that there are no two boys nor any two girls sitting next to each other is
   (a) $2 \times (7!)^2$
   (b) $7! \times 6!$
   (c) $7! \times 7!$
   (d) None of these

39. If we have to make 7 boys sit alternately with 7 girls around a round table which is numbered, then the number of ways in which this can be done is
   (a) $2 \times (7!)^2$
   (b) $7! \times 6!$
   (c) $7! \times 7!$
   (d) None of these

40. In the Suniti Building in Mumbai there are 12 floors plus the ground floor. 9 people get into the lift of the building on the ground floor. The lift does not stop on the first floor. If 2, 3 and 4 people alight from the lift on its upward journey, then in how many ways can they do so? (Assume they alight on different floors.)
   (a) $^{11}C_3 \times ^3P_3$
   (b) $^{11}P_3 \times ^9C_4 \times ^5C_3$
   (c) $^{10}P_3 \times ^9C_4 \times ^5C_3$
   (d) $^{12}C_3$

**Directions for Questions 41 and 42.** There are 40 doctors in the surgical department of the AIIMS. In how many ways can they be arranged to form a team with:

41. 1 surgeon and an assistant
   (a) 1260
   (b) 1320
   (c) 1440
   (d) 1560

42. 1 surgeon and 4 assistants
   (a) $40 \times ^{39}C_4$
   (b) $41 \times ^{39}C_4$
   (c) $41 \times ^{40}C_4$
   (d) None of these

43. In how many ways can 10 identical marbles be distributed among 6 children so that each child gets at least 1 marble?
   (a) $^{15}C_5$
   (b) $^{15}C_9$
   (c) $^{10}C_5$
   (d) $^9C_5$

*Space for Rough Work*

44. Seven different objects must be divided among three people. In how many ways can this be done if one or two of them can get no objects?
   (a) 15120
   (b) 2187
   (c) 3003
   (d) 792

45. How many 6-digit even numbers can be formed from the digits 1, 2, 3, 4, 5, 6 and 7 so that the digits should not repeat?
   (a) 720
   (b) 1440
   (c) 2160
   (d) 6480

46. How many 6-digit even numbers can be formed from the digits 1, 2, 3, 4, 5, 6 and 7 so that the digits should not repeat and the second last digit is even?
   (a) 720
   (b) 320
   (c) 2160
   (d) 1440

47. How many 5-digit numbers that do not contain identical digits can be written by means of the digits 1, 2, 3, 4, 5, 6, 7, 8 and 9?
   (a) 6048
   (b) 7560
   (c) 5040
   (d) 15,120

48. How many different 4-digit numbers are there which have the digits 1, 2, 3, 4, 5, 6, 7 and 8 such that the digit 1 appears exactly once.
   (a) $7 . ^8P_4$
   (b) $^8P_4$
   (c) $4.7^3$
   (d) $7^3$

49. How many different 7-digit numbers can be written using only three digits 1, 2 and 3 such that the digit 3 occurs twice in each number?
   (a) $^7C_2 . 2^5$
   (b) $7!/(2!)$
   (c) $7!/(2!)^3$
   (d) None of these

50. How many different 4-digit numbers can be written using the digits 1, 2, 3, 4, 5, 6, 7 and 8 only once such that the number 2 is contained once.
   (a) 360
   (b) 840
   (c) 760
   (d) 1260

# LEVEL OF DIFFICULTY (III)

1. The number of ways in which four particular persons $A, B, C, D$ and six more persons can stand in a queue so that $A$ always stands before $B$, $B$ always before $C$ and $C$ always before $D$ is
   (a) $10!/4!$
   (b) $^{10}P_4$
   (c) $^{10}C_4$
   (d) None of these

2. The number of circles that can be drawn out of 10 points of which 7 are collinear is
   (a) 130
   (b) 85
   (c) 45
   (d) Cannot be determined

3. How many different 9-digit numbers can be formed from the number 223355888 by rearranging its digits so that the odd digits occupy even positions?
   (a) 120
   (b) $9!/(2!)^3.3!$
   (c) $(4!)(2!)^3.3!$
   (d) None of these

4. How many diagonals are there in an $n$-sided polygon $(n > 3)$?
   (a) $(^nC_2 - n)$
   (b) $^nC_2$
   (c) $n(n-1)/2$
   (d) None of these

5. A polygon has 54 diagonals. Find the number of sides.
   (a) 10
   (b) 14
   (c) 12
   (d) 9

6. The number of natural numbers of two or more than two digits in which digits from left to right are in increasing order is
   (a) 127
   (b) 128
   (c) 502
   (d) 512

7. In how many ways a cricketer can score 200 runs with fours and sixes only?
   (a) 13
   (b) 17
   (c) 19
   (d) 16

8. A dices is rolled six times. One, two, three, four, five and six appears on consecutive throws of dices. How many ways are possible of having 1 before 6?
   (a) 120
   (b) 360
   (c) 240
   (d) 280

9. The number of permutations of the letters $a, b, c, d, e, f, g$ such that neither the pattern '*beg*' nor '*acd*' occurs is
   (a) 4806
   (b) 420
   (c) 2408
   (d) None of these

10. In how many ways can the letters of the English alphabet be arranged so that there are seven letters between the letters $A$ and $B$?
    (a) $31!.2!$
    (b) $^{24}P_7.18!.2$
    (c) $36.24!$
    (d) None of these

11. There are 20 people among whom two are sisters. Find the number of ways in which we can arrange them around a circle so that there is exactly one person between the two sisters?
    (a) $18!$
    (b) $2!.19!$
    (c) $19!$
    (d) None of these

12. There are 10 points on a straight line $AB$ and 8 on another straight line, $AC$ none of them being $A$. How many triangles can be formed with these points as vertices?
    (a) 720
    (b) 640
    (c) 816
    (d) None of these

13. In an examination, the maximum marks for each of the three papers is 50 each. The maximum marks for the fourth paper is 100. Find the number of ways with which a student can score 60% marks in aggregate.
    (a) 3,30,850
    (b) 2,33,551
    (c) 1,10,551
    (d) None of these

14. How many rectangles can be formed out of a chessboard?
    (a) 204
    (b) 1230
    (c) 1740
    (d) None of these

15. On a board having 18 rows and 16 columns, find the number of squares.
    (a) $^{18}C_2.\ ^{16}C_2$
    (b) $^{18}P_2.\ ^{16}P_2$
    (c) $18.16 + 17.15 + 16.14 + 15.13 + 14.12 + \ldots\ldots + 4.2 + 3.1$
    (d) None of these

16. In the above question, find the number of rectangles.
    (a) $^{18}C_2.\ ^{16}C_2$
    (b) $^{18}P_2.\ ^{16}P_2$
    (c) 171.136
    (d) None of these

**Directions for Questions 17 and 18:** Read the passage below and answer the questions.

In the famous program *Kaun Banega Crorepati*, the host shakes hand with each participant once, while he shakes hands with each qualifier (amongst participant) twice more. Besides, the participants are required to shake hands once with each other, while the winner and the host each shake hands with all the guests once.

17. How many handshakes are there if there are 10 participants in all, 3 finalists and 60 spectators?
    (a) 118
    (b) 178
    (c) 181
    (d) 122

18. In the above question, what is the ratio of the number of handshakes involving the host to the number of handshakes not involving the host?

(a) 43 : 75      (b) 76 : 105

(c) 46 : 75      (d) None of these

19. What is the percentage increase in the total number of handshakes if all the guests are required to shake hands with each other once?

(a) 82.2%      (b) 822%

(c) 97.7%      (d) None of these

20. Two variants of the CAT paper are to be given to twelve students. In how many ways can the students be placed in two rows of six each so that there should be no identical variants side by side and that the students sitting one behind the other should have the same variant?

(a) $2 \times {}^{12}C_6 \times (6!)^2$      (b) $6! \times 6!$

(c) $7! \times 7!$      (d) None of these

21. For the above question, if there are now three variants of the test to be given to the twelve students (so that each variant is used for four students) and there should be no identical variants side by side and that the students sitting one behind the other should have the same variant. Find the number of ways this can be done.

(a) $6!^2$      (b) $6 \times 6! \times 6!$

(c) $6!^3$      (d) None of these

22. Five boys and three girls are sitting in a row of eight seats. In how many ways can they be seated so that not all girls sit side by side?

(a) 36,000      (b) 45,000

(c) 24,000      (d) None of these

23. How many natural numbers are there that are smaller than $10^4$ and whose decimal notation consists only of the digits 0, 1, 2, 3 and 5, which are not repeated in any of these numbers?

(a) 32      (b) 164

(c) 31      (d) 212

24. Seven different objects must be divided among three people. In how many ways can this be done if one or two of them must get no objects?

(a) 381      (b) 36

(c) 84      (d) 180

25. Seven different objects must be divided among three people. In how many ways can this be done if at least one of them gets exactly 1 object?

(a) 2484      (b) 1218

(c) 729      (d) None of these

26. How many 4-digit numbers that are divisible by 4 can be formed from the digits 1, 2, 3, 4 and 5?

(a) 36      (b) 72

(c) 24      (d) None of these

27. How many natural numbers smaller than 10,000 are there in the decimal notation of which all the digits are different?

(a) 2682      (b) 4474

(c) 5274      (d) 1448

28. How many 4-digit numbers are there whose decimal notation contains not more than two distinct digits?

(a) 672      (b) 576

(c) 360      (d) 448

29. How many different 7-digit numbers are there the sum of whose digits are odd?

(a) $45.10^5$      (b) $24.10^5$

(c) 224320      (d) None of these

30. How many 6-digit numbers contain exactly 4 different digits?

(a) 4536      (b) 2,94,840

(c) 1,91,520      (d) None of these

31. How many numbers smaller than $2.10^8$ and are divisible by 3 can be written by means of the digits 0, 1 and 2 (exclude single digit and double digit numbers)?

(a) 4369      (b) 4353

(c) 4373      (d) 4351

32. Six white and six black balls of the same size are distributed among ten urns so that there is at least one ball in each urn. What is the number of different distributions of the balls?

(a) 25,000      (b) 26,250

(c) 28,250      (d) 13,125

33. A bouquet has to be formed from 18 different flowers so that it should contain not less than three flowers. How many ways are there of doing this in?

(a) 5,24,288      (b) 2,62,144

(c) 2,61,972      (d) None of these

34. How many different numbers which are smaller than $2.10^8$ can be formed using the digits 1 and 2 only?

(a) 766      (b) 94

(c) 92      (d) 126

35. How many distinct 6-digit numbers are there having 3 odd and 3 even digits?

(a) 55      (b) $(5.6)^3.(4.6)^3.3$

(c) 281250      (d) None of these

36. How many 8-digit numbers are there the sum of whose digits is even?

(a) 14400      (b) $4.5^5$

(c) $45.10^6$      (d) None of these

**Directions for Questions 37 and 38:** In a chess tournament there were two women participating and every participant played two games with the other participants. The number of games that the men played among themselves exceeded the number of games that the men played with the women by 66.

37. The number of participants in the tournament were:

(a) 12      (b) 13

(c) 15      (d) 11

38. The total number of games played in the tournament were:

(a) 132      (b) 110

(c) 156      (d) 210

39. There are 5 bottles of sherry and each have their respective caps. If you are asked to put the correct cap to the correct bottle then how many ways are there so that not a single cap is on the correct bottle?

(a) 44      (b) $5^5 - 1$

(c) $5^5$      (d) None of these

40. Amartya Banerjee has forgotten the telephone number of his best friend Abhijit Roy. All he remembers is that the number had 8-digits and ended with an odd number and had exactly one 9. How many possible numbers does Amartya have to try to be sure that he gets the correct number?

(a) $104.9^5$      (b) $113.9^5$

(c) $300.9^5$      (d) $764.9^5.6!$

41. In Question 40, if Amartya is reminded by his friend Sharma that apart from what he remembered there was the additional fact that the last digit of the number was not repeated under any circumstance then how many possible numbers does Amartya have to try to be sure that he gets the correct number?

(a) $200.8^5 + 72.9^5$      (b) $8.96$

(c) $36.8^5 + 7.96$      (d) $36.8^5 + 8.9^6$

42. How many natural numbers not more than 4300 can be formed with the digits 0,1, 2, 3, 4 (if repetitions are allowed)?

(a) 574      (b) 570

(c) 575      (d) 569

43. How many natural numbers less than 4300 can be formed with the digits 0, 1, 2, 3, 4 (if repetitions are not allowed)?

(a) 113      (b) 158

(c) 154      (d) 119

44. How many even natural numbers divisible by 5 can be formed with the digits 0, 1, 2, 3, 4, 5, 6 (if repetitions of digits not allowed)?

(a) 1957      (b) 1956

(c) 1236      (d) 1235

45. There are 100 articles numbered $n_1, n_2, n_3, n_4, \ldots n_{100}$. They are arranged in all possible ways. How many arrangements would be there in which $n_{28}$ will always be before $n_{29}$.

(a) $5050 \times 99!$      (b) $5050 \times 98!$

(c) $4950 \times 98!$      (d) $4950 \times 99!$

46. The letters of the word PASTE are written in all possible orders and these words are written out as in a dictionary. Then the rank of the word SPATE is

(a) 432      (b) 86

(c) 59      (d) 446

47. The straight lines $S_1, S_2, S_3$ are in a parallel and lie in the same plane. A total number of $A$ points on $S_1$; $B$ points on $S_2$ and $C$ points on $S_3$ are used to produce triangles. What is the maximum number of triangles formed?

(a) $^{A+B+C}C_3 - {}^A C_3 - {}^B C_3 - {}^C C_3 + 1$

(b) $^{A+B+C}C_3$

(c) $^{A+B+C}C_3 + 1$

(d) $\left( {}^{A+B+C}C_3 - {}^A C_3 - {}^B C_3 - {}^C C_3 \right)$

48. The sides $AB$, $BC$, $CA$ of a triangle $ABC$ have 3, 4 and 5 interior points respectively on them. The total number of triangles that can be constructed by using these points as vertices are

(a) 212      (b) 210

(c) 205      (d) 190

49. A library has 20 copies of CAGE; 12 copies each of RAGE Part1 and Part 2; 5 copies of PAGE Part 1, Part 2 and Part 3 and single copy of SAGE, DAGE and MAGE. In how many ways can these books be distributed?

(a) $62!/(20!)(12!)(5!)$      (b) $62!$

(c) $62!/(37)^3$      (d) $62!/(20!)(12!)^2(5!)^3$

50. The AMS MOCK CAT test CATALYST 19 consists of four sections. Each section has a maximum of 45 marks. Find the number of ways in which a student can qualify in the AMS MOCK CAT if the qualifying marks is 90.

(a) 36,546      (b) 6296

(c) 64906      (d) None of these

**Space for Rough Work**

## ANSWER KEY

### Level of Difficulty (I)

| | | | |
|---|---|---|---|
| 1. (c) | 2. (b) | 3. (b) | 4. (c) |
| 5. (c) | 6. (a) | 7. (b) | 8. (a) |
| 9. (a) | 10. (b) | 11. (d) | 12. (b) |
| 13. (a) | 14. (b) | 15. (c) | 16. (a) |
| 17. (d) | 18. (d) | 19. (b) | 20. (c) |
| 21. (c) | 22. (c) | 23. (c) | 24. (b) |
| 25. (c) | 26. (a) | 27. (a) | 28. (a) |
| 29. (a) | 30. (b) | 31. (a) | 32. (d) |
| 33. (b) | 34. (b) | 35. (d) | 36. (c) |
| 37. (c) | 38. (b) | 39. (d) | 40. (d) |
| 41. (a) | 42. (a) | 43. (c) | 44. (b) |
| 45. (b) | 46. (c) | 47. (d) | 48. (a) |
| 49. (c) | 50. (b) | 51. (b) | 52. (d) |
| 53. (d) | 54. (d) | 55. (c) | 56. (d) |
| 57. (c) | 58. (d) | 59. (d) | 60. (a) |
| 61. (b) | 62. (d) | 63. (a) | 64. (d) |
| 65. (a) | 66. (d) | 67. (a) | 68. (b) |
| 69. (d) | 70. (d) | 71. (b) | 72. (c) |
| 73. (a) | 74. (a) | 75. (c) | 76. (a) |
| 77. (c) | 78. (c) | 79. (d) | 80. (a) |
| 81. (c) | 82. (b) | 83. (b) | 84. (b) |
| 85. (b) | 86. (b) | 87. (c) | |

### Level of Difficulty (II)

| | | | |
|---|---|---|---|
| 1. (a) | 2. (b) | 3. (c) | 4. (b) |
| 5. (d) | 6. (b) | 7. (b) | 8. (d) |
| 9. (b) | 10. (c) | 11. (a) | 12. (d) |
| 13. (c) | 14. (b) | 15. (b) | 16. (d) |
| 17. (b) | 18. (d) | 19. (a) | 20. (c) |
| 21. (d) | 22. (c) | 23. (d) | 24. (a) |
| 25. (d) | 26. (a) | 27. (b) | 28. (d) |
| 29. (c) | 30. (a) | 31. (d) | 32. (c) |
| 33. (b) | 34. (b) | 35. (a) | 36. (b) |
| 37. (b) | 38. (b) | 39. (a) | 40. (b) |
| 41. (d) | 42. (a) | 43. (d) | 44. (b) |
| 45. (c) | 46. (a) | 47. (d) | 48. (c) |
| 49. (a) | 50. (b) | | |

### Level of Difficulty (III)

| | | | |
|---|---|---|---|
| 1. (a) | 2. (b) | 3. (d) | 4. (a) |
| 5. (c) | 6. (c) | 7. (b) | 8. (b) |
| 9. (a) | 10. (c) | 11. (d) | 12. (b) |
| 13. (c) | 14. (d) | 15. (c) | 16. (c) |
| 17. (c) | 18. (b) | 19. (d) | 20. (a) |
| 21. (d) | 22. (a) | 23. (b) | 24. (a) |
| 25. (b) | 26. (c) | 27. (c) | 28. (b) |
| 29. (a) | 30. (b) | 31. (c) | 32. (b) |
| 33. (c) | 34. (a) | 35. (c) | 36. (c) |
| 37. (b) | 38. (c) | 39. (a) | 40. (c) |
| 41. (a) | 42. (c) | 43. (b) | 44. (b) |
| 45. (c) | 46. (b) | 47. (d) | 48. (c) |
| 49. (d) | 50. (c) | | |

**Hints**

### Level of Difficulty (III)

1. $^{10}C_4 \times 6! = 10!/4!$

2. For drawing a circle we need 3 non collinear points. This can be done in:

   $$^3C_3 + {}^3C_2 \times {}^7C_1 + {}^3C_1 \times {}^7C_2 = 1 + 21 + 63 = 85$$

3. The odd digits have to occupy even positions. This can be done in $\dfrac{4!}{2!2!} = 6$ ways.

   The other digits have to occupy the other positions.

   This can be done in $\dfrac{5!}{3!2!} = 10$ ways.

   Hence total number of rearrangements possible = 6 × 10 = 60.

4. The number of straight lines is $^nC_2$ out of which there are $n$ sides. Hence, the number of diagonals is $^nC_2 - n$.

5. $^nC_2 - n = 54$.

6. We cannot take '0' since the smallest digit must be placed at the left most place. We have only 9 digits from which to select the numbers. First select any number of digits. Then for any selection there is only one possible arrangement where the required condition is met. This can be done in $^9C_1 + {}^9C_2 + {}^9C_3 + ... + {}^9C_9$ ways = $2^9 - 1 = 511$ ways.

   But we can't take numbers which have only one digit, hence the required answer is 511 – 9.

7. 200 runs can be scored by scoring only fours or through a combination of fours and sixes.

   Possibilities are 50 × 4, 47 × 4 + 2 × 6, 44 × 4 + 4 × 6 … A total of 17 ways.

8. Of the total arrangements possible (6!) exactly half would have 1 before 6. Thus, 6!/2 = 360.

9. Total number of permutations without any restrictions – Number of permutations having the '*acd*' pattern – Number of permutations having the '*beg*' pattern + Number of permutations having both the '*beg*' and '*acd*' patterns.

10. *A* and *B* can occupy the first and the ninth places, the second and the tenth places, the third and the eleventh place and so on… This can be done in 18 ways.

    *A* and *B* can be arranged in 2 ways.

    All the other 24 alphabets can be arranged in 24! ways.

    Hence the required answer = 2 × 18 × 24!

11. First arrange the two sisters around a circle in such a way that there will be one seat vacant between them. [This can be done in 2! ways since the arrangement of the sisters is not circular.]

    Then, the other 18 people can be arranged on 18 seats in 18! ways.

12. $^{10}C_2 \times {}^8C_1 + {}^{10}C_1 \times {}^8C_2 = 360 + 280 = 640$

14. A chess board consists 9 parallel lines × 9 parallel lines. For a rectangle we need to select 2 parallel lines and two other parallel lines that are perpendicular to the first set. Hence, $^9C_2 \times {}^9C_2$

15-16. Based on direct formulae.

15. This is a direct result based question. Option (c) is correct. Refer to result no. 6 in Important Results 2.

16. $(1 + 2 + 3 + \ldots + 18) (1 + 2 + 3 + \ldots + 16)$

17-19. Based on simple counting according to the conditions given in the passage

17. $^{10}C_1 + 3 \times 2 + {}^{10}C_2 + 60 + 60 = 181$

18. Handshakes involving host = 76
Hence, the required ratio is 76: 105.

19. The guests (Spectators) would shake hands $^{60}C_2$ times = 1770.
Required percentage increase = 977.9%.

20. First select six people out of 12 for the first row. The other six automatically get selected for the second row. Arrange the two rows of people amongst themselves. Besides, the papers can be given in the pattern of 121212 or 212121. Hence the answer is $2 \times ({}^{12}C_6 \times 6! \times 6!)$.

21. The difference in this question from the previous question is the number of ways in which the papers can be distributed. This can be done by either distributing three different variants in the first three places of each row or by repeating the same variant in the first and the third places.

22. Required permutations = Total permutations with no condition – permutations with the conditions which we do not have to count.

23. We have to count natural numbers which have a maximum of 4 digits. The required answer will be given by:
Number of single digit numbers + Number of two digit numbers + Number of three digit numbers + Number of four digit numbers.

24. Let the three people be *A*, *B* and *C*.
If 1 person gets no objects, the 7 objects must be distributed such that each of the other two get 1 object at least.
This can be done as 6 & 1, 5 & 2, 4 & 3 and their rearrangements.
The answer would be
$$({}^7C_6 + {}^7C_5 + {}^7C_4) \times 3! = 378$$
Also, two people getting no objects can be done in 3 ways.
Thus, the answer is 378 + 3 = 381

25. If only one gets 1 object
The remaining can be distributed as: (6,0), (4, 2), (3, 3).

$(^7C_1 \times {}^6C_6 \times 3! + {}^7C_1 \times {}^6C_4 \times 3! + {}^7C_1 \times {}^6C_3 \times 3!/2!)$
$$= 42 + 630 + 420 + 1092.$$
If 2 people get 1 object each:
$$^7C_1 \times {}^6C_1 \times {}^5C_5 \times 3!/2! = 126.$$
Thus, a total of 1218.

26. Natural numbers which consist of the digits 1, 2, 3, 4. and 5 and are divisible by 4 must have either 12, 24, 32 or 52 in the last two places. For the other two places we have to arrange three digits in two places.

27. No. of 1 digit nos = 9
No. of 2 digit nos = 81
No. of 3 digit nos = $9 \times 9 \times 8 = 648$
No. of 4 digit nos = $9 \times 9 \times 8 \times 7 = 4536$
Total nos = 9 + 81 + 648 + 4536 = 5274

28. If the two digits are *a* and *b* then 4 digit numbers can be formed in the following patterns.
*aabb*; *aaab* or *aaaa*.
You will have to take two situations in each of the cases- first when the two digits are non zero digits and second when the two digits are zero.

29. For the total of the digits to be odd one of the following has to be true:
The number should contain 1 odd + 6 even or 3 odd + 4 even or 5 odd + 2 even or 7 odd digits. Count each case separately.

33. $^{18}C_4 + {}^{18}C_5 + {}^{18}C_6 + \ldots + {}^{18}C_{17} + {}^{18}C_{18}$
$= [{}^{18}C_0 + {}^{18}C_4 + \ldots + {}^{18}C_{18}] - [{}^{18}C_0 + {}^{18}C_1 + {}^{18}C_2 + {}^{18}C_3]$
$= 2^{18} - [1 + 18 + 153 + 816]$
$= 261158$

35. Total number of 6 digit numbers having 3 odd and 3 even digits (including zero in the left most place) $= 5^3 \times 5^3$.
From this subtract the number of 5 digit numbers with 2 even digits and 3 odd digits (to take care of the extra counting due to zero)

36. There will be 5 types of numbers, viz. numbers which have
All eight digits even or six even and two odd digits or four even and four odd digits or two even and six odd digits or all eight odd digits. This will be further solved as below:
Eight even digits $\rightarrow 5^8 - 5^7 = 4 \times 5^7$
Six even and two odd digits $\rightarrow$
when the left most digit is even $\rightarrow 4 \times {}^7C_5 \times 5^5 \times 5^5$
when the left most digit is odd $\rightarrow 5 \times {}^7C_6 \times 5^6 \times 5^1$
Four even and four odd digits $\rightarrow$
when the left most digit is even $\rightarrow 4 \times {}^7C_5 \times 5^5 \times 5^4$
when the left most digit is odd $\rightarrow 5 \times {}^7C_4 \times 5^4 \times 5^3$
Two even and six odd digits $\rightarrow$
when the left most digit is even $\rightarrow 4 \times {}^7C_1 \times 5 \times 5^6$

when the left most digit is odd → $5 \times {}^7C_2 \times 5^2 \times 5^5$

Eight odd digits → 58

37–38. Solve through options.

39. This question is based on a formula: The condition is that '$n$' things (each thing belonging to a particular place) have to be distributed in '$n$' places such that no particular thing is arranged in its correct place.

$$n! - \frac{n!}{1!} + \frac{n!}{2!} - \frac{n!}{3!}$$ sign of the terms will be alternate

and the last term will be $\frac{n!}{n!}$.

However, this can also be solved through logic.

40. The possible cases for counting are:

Number of numbers when the units digit is nine + the number of numbers when neither the units digit nor the left most is nine + number of numbers when the left most digit is nine.

42. The condition is that we have to count the number of natural numbers not more than 4300.

The total possible numbers with the given digits = $5 \times 5 \times 5 \times 5 = 625 - 1 = 624$.

Subtract form this the number of natural number greater than 4300 which can be formed from the given digits = $1 \times 2 \times 5 \times 5 - 1 = 49$.

Hence, the required number of numbers = $624 - 49 = 575$.

43. The required answer will be given by

The number of one digit natural number + number of two digit natural numbers + the number of three digit natural numbers + the number of four digit natural number starting with 1, 2, or 3 + the number of four digit natural numbers starting with 4.

46. The following words will appear before SPATE. All words starting with $A$ + All words starting with $E$ + All words starting with $P$ + All words starting with $SA$ + All words starting with $SE$ + SPAET

47. For the maximum possibility assume that no three points other than given in the question are in a straight line.

Hence, the total number of $\Delta$'s = ${}^{A+B+C}C_3 - {}^AC_3 - {}^BC_3 - {}^CC_3$

48. Use the formula $\dfrac{n!}{p!q!r!}$.

$n(E) = 7 \times 6 \times 5 \times 4 \times 3 \times 2 \times {}^7C_2$

$n(S) = 7^7$

$n(E) = 8 \times 7 + 8 \times 7 = 112$

$n(S) = 64C_2 = \dfrac{2 \times 8 \times 7 \times 2}{64 \times 63} = \dfrac{1}{18}$

49. Use the formula $\dfrac{n!}{p!q!r!}$

---

**Solutions and Shortcuts**

*Level of Difficulty (I)*

1. The number of numbers formed would be given by $5 \times 4 \times 3$ (given that the first digit can be filled in 5 ways, the second in 4 ways and the third in 3 ways – MNP rule).

2. The first digit can only be 2 (1 way), the second digit can be filled in 7 ways, the third in 6 ways and the fourth in 5 ways. A total of $1 \times 7 \times 6 \times 5 = 210$ ways.

3. Each invitation card can be sent in 4 ways. Thus, $4 \times 4 \times 4 \times 4 \times 4 \times 4 = 4^6$.

4. In this case since nothing is mentioned about whether the prizes are identical or distinct we can take the prizes to be distinct (the most logical thought given the situation). Thus, each prize can be given in 8 ways — thus a total of $8^5$ ways.

5. We need to assume that the 7 Indians are 1 person, so also for the 6 Dutch and the 5 Pakistanis. These 3 groups of people can be arranged amongst themselves in 3! ways. Also, within themselves the 7 Indians the 6 Dutch and the 5 Pakistanis can be arranged in 7!, 6! And 5! ways respectively. Thus, the answer is $3! \times 7! \times 6! \times 5!$.

6. Use the MNP rule to get the answer as $5 \times 4 = 20$.

7. An engineer can make it through in 2 ways, while a CA can make it through in 3 ways. Required ratio is 2:3. Option (b) is correct.

8. For a straight line we just need to select 2 points out of the 8 points available. ${}^8C_2$ would be the number of ways of doing this.

9. Use the property ${}^nC_r = {}^nC_{n-r}$ to see that the two values would be equal at $n = 11$ since ${}^{11}C_3 = {}^{11}C_8$.

10. There would be 5! ways of arranging the 5 letters. Thus, $5! = 120$ ways.

11. Rearrangements do not count the original arrangements. Thus, $5!/2! - 1 = 59$ ways of rearranging the letters of PATNA.

12. We need to count words starting with P. These words would be represented by P _ _ _ _.

The letters ATNA can be arranged in $4!/2!$ ways in the 4 places. A total of 12 ways.

13. P _ _ _ T. Missing letters have to be filled with A,N,A. $3!/2! = 3$ ways.

14. Trial and error would give us ${}^8C_4$ as the answer. ${}^8C_4 = 8 \times 7 \times 6 \times 5/4 \times 3 \times 2 \times 1 = 70$.

15. ${}^{10}P_3$ would satisfy the value given as ${}^{10}P_3 = 10 \times 9 \times 8 = 720$.

16. $3 \times 3 \times 2 \times 1 = 18$.

17. $3 \times 4 \times 4 \times 4 = 192$

18. Divide the numbers into three-digit numbers and 4-digit numbers—Number of 3 digit numbers = $2 \times$

$3 \times 2 = 12$. Number of 4-digit numbers starting with $10 = 2 \times 1 = 2$. Total = 14 numbers.

19. 3-digit numbers = $2 \times 4 \times 4 - 1 = 31$ (−1 is because the number 200 cannot be counted); 4-digit numbers starting with $10 = 4 \times 4 = 16$, Number of 4 digit numbers starting with $11 = 4 \times 4 = 16$. Total numbers = $31 + 16 + 16 = 63$.

20. At $n = 3$, the values convert to $^7P_2$ and $^5P_3$ whose values respectively are 42 & 60 giving us the required ratio.

21. At $r = 7$, the value becomes $(28!/14! \times 14!)/(24!/10! \times 14!) \rightarrow 225:11$.

22. The maximum value of $^nC_r$ for a given value of $n$, happens when $r$ is equal to the half of $n$. So if he wants to maximise the number of parties given that he has 20 friends, he should invite 10 to each party.

23. This is a typical case for the use of the formula $^{n-1}C_{r-1}$ with $n = 10$ and $r = 6$. So the answer would be given $^9C_5$.

24. For each digit there would be 5 options (viz 1, 3, 5, 7, 9). Hence, the total number of numbers would be $5 \times 5 \times 5 \times 5 = 625$.

25. $^{11}C_1 \times ^{10}C_1 = 110$. Alternately, $^{11}C_2 \times 2!$

26. $5 \times 4 = 20$.

27. In the letters of the word ALLAHABAD there is only 1 vowel available for selection (A). Note that the fact that A is available 4 times has no impact on this fact. Also, there are 4 consonants available — viz: L, H, B and D. Thus, the number of ways of selecting a vowel and a consonant would be $1 \times ^4C_1 = 4$.

28. Choose 1 person for the single room & from the remaining choose 2 people for the double room & from the remaining choose 4 people for the 4 persons room $\rightarrow ^7C_1 \times ^6C_2 \times ^4C_4$.

29. From the first suit there would be 13 options of selecting a card. From the second suite there would be 12 options, from the third suite there would be 11 options and from the fourth suite there would be 10 options for selecting a card. Thus, $13 \times 12 \times 11 \times 10$.

30. Number of 11 letter words formed from the letters P, E, R, M, U, T, A, T, I, O, N = $11!/2!$.
Number of new words formed = total words −1 = $11!/2! - 1$.

31. $^{15}C_0 + ^{15}C_1 + ^{15}C_2 + ^{15}C_3 + ^{15}C_4 + ^{15}C_5 = 1 + 15 + 105 + 455 + 1365 + 3003 = 4944$

32. All arrangements – Arrangements with best and worst paper together = $12! - 2! \times 11!$.

33. The vowels EUAIO need to be considered as 1 letter to solve this. Thus, there would be 4! ways of arranging Q, T and N and the 5 vowels taken together. Also, there would be 5! ways of arranging the vowels amongst themselves. Thus, we have $4! \times 5!$.

34. $^3C_1 \times ^4C_1 \times ^6C_1 = 72$.

35. 4-digit Motor vehicle registration numbers can have 0 in the first digit. Thus, we have $6 \times 5 \times 4 \times 3 = 360$ ways.

36. Single digit numbers = 5
Two digit numbers = $5 \times 4 = 20$
Three digit numbers = $5 \times 4 \times 3 = 60$
Four digit numbers = $5 \times 4 \times 3 \times 2 = 120$
Five digit numbers = $5 \times 4 \times 3 \times 2 \times 1 = 120$
Total = $5 + 20 + 60 + 120 + 120 = 325$

37. $^{25}C_2 - ^7C_2 + 1 = 280$

38. $^{25}C_3 - ^7C_3 = 2265$

39. $^{25}C_4 - ^7C_4 - ^7C_3 \times ^{18}C_1 = 11985$

40. $^{10}C_5 \times 5! = 30240$

41. $^8C_3 \times ^5C_2 \times 5! = 67200$

42. The selection of the 11 player team can be done in $^{14}C_{10}$ ways. This results in the team of 11 players being completely chosen. The arrangements of these 11 players can be done in 11!.
Total batting orders = $^{14}C_{10} \times 11! = 1001 \times 11!$
(**Note:** Arrangement is required here because we are talking about forming batting orders).

43. $^{12}C_4 = 495$

44. $^{30}C_3$

45. $^{29}C_2$

46. R _ _ _ _ _ _ W. The letters to go into the spaces are P, O, L, I, N, G. Since all these letters are distinct the number of ways of arranging them would be 6!.

47. $7!/3! \times 4! = 35$

48. The number has to start with a 3 and then in the remaining 6 digits it should have two 3's and four 0's. This can be done in $6!/2! \times 4! = 15$ ways.

49. $^3C_1 \times ^5C_3 \times ^4C_2 \times 5! = 21600$

50. If the number of teams is $n$, then $^nC_2$ should be equal to 45. Trial and error gives us the value of $n$ as 10.

51. From 5 bananas we have 6 choices available (0, 1, 2, 3, 4 or 5). Similarly 4 mangoes and 4 almonds can be chosen in 5 ways each.
So total ways = $6 \times 5 \times 5 = 150$ possible selections.
But in this 150, there is one selection where no fruit is chosen.
So required no. of ways = $150 - 1 = 149$
Hence Option (b) is correct.

52. For each book we have two options, give or not give. Thus, we have a total of $2^{14}$ ways in which the 14 books can be decided upon. Out of this, there would be 1 way in which no book would be given. Thus, the number of ways is $2^{14} - 1$.
Hence, Option (d) is correct.

53. The number of ways in which at least 1 Archer book is given is $(2^5 - 1)$. Similarly, for Sheldon and Grisham we have $(2^3 - 1)$ and $(2^6 - 1)$. Thus required answer would be the multiplication of the three. Hence, Option (d) is the correct answer.

54. For each question we have 3 choices of answering the question (2 internal choices + 1 non-attempt). Thus, there are a total of $3^{15}$ ways of answering the question paper. Out of this there is exactly one way in which the student does not answer any question. Thus there are a total of $3^{15} - 1$ ways in which at least one question is answered.

    Hence, Option (d) is correct.

55. The digits are 1, 6, 7, 8, 7, 6, 1. In this seven-digit no. there are four odd places and three even places—OEOEOEO. The four odd digits 1, 7, 7, 1 can be arranged in four odd places in $[4!/2! \times 2] = 6$ ways [as 1 and 7 are both occurring twice].

    The even digits 6, 8, 6 can be arranged in three even places in $3!/2! = 3$ ways.

    Total no. of ways = $6 \times 3 = 18$.

    Hence, Option (c) is correct.

56. We have no girls together, let us first arrange the 5 boys and after that we can arrange the girls in the spaces between the boys.

    Number of ways of arranging the boys around a circle = $[5 - 1]! = 24$.

    Number of ways of arranging the girls would be by placing them in the 5 spaces that are formed between the boys. This can be done in $^5P_3$ ways = 60 ways.

    Total arrangements = $24 \times 60 = 1440$.

    Hence, Option (d) is correct.

57. Books of interest = 7, books to be borrowed = 3

    Case 1— Quants book is taken. Then D.I book can also be taken.

    So Amita is to take 2 more books out of 6 which she can do in $^6C_2 = 15$ ways.

    Case 2— If Quants book has not been taken, the D.I book would also not be taken.

    So Amita will take three books out of 5 books. This can be done in $^5C_3 = 10$ ways.

    So total ways = $15 + 10 = 25$ ways.

    Hence Option (c) is correct.

58. We have to select 5 out of 12.

    If Radha and Mohan join- then we have to select only $5 - 2 = 3$ dancers out of $12 - 2 = 10$ which can be done in $^{10}C_3 = 120$ ways.

    If Radha and Mohan do not join, then we have to select 5 out of $12 - 2 = 10$-> $^{10}C_5 = 252$ ways.

    Total number of ways = $120 + 252 = 372$.

    Hence, Option (d) is correct.

59. The unit digit can either be 2, 3, 4, 5 or 6.

    When the unit digit is 2, the number would be even and hence will be divisible by 2. Hence all numbers with unit digit 2 will be included which is equal to 5! Or 120.

    When the unit digit is 3, then in every case the sum of the digits of the number would be 21 which is a multiple of 3. Hence all numbers with unit digit 3 will be divisible by 3 and hence will be included. Total number of such numbers is 5! or 120.

    Similarly for unit digit 5 and 6, the number of required numbers is 120 each.

    When the unit digit is 4, then the number would be divisible by 4 only if the ten's digit is 2 or 6. Total number of such numbers is $2 \times 4!$ or 48.

    Hence total number of required numbers is $(4 \times 120) + 48 = 528$.

    Hence, Option (d) is the answer.

60. As we need to find the maximum number of trials, so we have to assume that the required ball in every box is picked as late as possible. So in the third box, first two balls will be red and black. Hence third trial will give him the required ball. Similarly, in fourth box, he will get the required ball in fourth trial and in the fifth box, he will get the required ball in fifth trial. Hence maximum total number of trials required is $3 + 4 + 5 = 12$.

    Hence, Option (a) is the answer.

61. Since every player needs to win only 1 match to move to the next round, therefore the 1$^{st}$ round would have 32 matches between 64 players out of which 32 will be knocked out of the tournament and 32 will be moved to the next round. Similarly in 2$^{nd}$ round 16 matches will be played, in the 3$^{rd}$ round 8 matches will be played, in 4$^{th}$ round 4 matches, in 5$^{th}$ round 2 matches and the 6$^{th}$ round will be the final match. Hence total number of rounds will be 6 $(2^6 = 64)$.

    Hence, option (b) is the answer.

62. Total number of pairs of men that can be selected if the adjacent ones are also selected is $^NC_2$. Total number of pairs of men selected if only the adjacent ones are selected is N. Hence total number of pairs of men selected if the adjacent ones are not selected is $^NC_2 - N$.

    Since the total time taken is 88 min, hence the number of pairs is 44.

    Hence, $^NC_2 - N = 44 \rightarrow N = 11$.

    Hence, Option (d) is the answer.

63. Let the number of boys be $B$. Then $^BC_3 = 36 \rightarrow B = 9$

    Let the number of girls be $G$. Then $^GC_2 = 66 \rightarrow G = 12$

    Therefore total number of students in the class = $12 + 9 = 21$. Hence total number of matches = $^{21}C_2 = 210$. Hence, number of matches between 1 boy and 1 girl = $210 - (36 + 66) = 108$.

    Hence, Option (a) is the answer.

64. With 3 chocolates to Sana, the remaining 12 chocolates, would then get divided among 4 children, with each child getting minimum 1 chocolate in $^{11}C_3$ ways.

    With 4 chocolates to Sana, the remaining 11 chocolates, would then get divided among 4 children, with each child getting minimum 1 chocolate in $^{10}C_3$ ways. With 5 chocolates to Sana, the remaining 10 chocolates, would then get divided among 4 children, with each child getting minimum 1 chocolate in $^9C_3$ ways. With 6 chocolates to Sana, the remaining 9 chocolates, would then get divided among 4 children, with each child getting minimum 1 chocolate in $^8C_3$ ways. The total number of distributions = 165 + 120 + 84 + 56 = 425. Hence, option (d) is correct.

65. Firstly we will give 5 crores each to the three sons. That will cover 15 crores out of 30 crores leaving behind 15 crores. Now 15 crores can be distributed in three people in 17!15!2! ways or 136 ways.
Hence, Option (a) is the answer.

66. Let $x = 3$. Then $y + z = 27$. For the conditions given in the question, no. of solutions is 20.
Similarly for $x = 2$ there will be 20 solutions, for $x = 1$ there will be 22 solutions and for $x = 0$, there will be 22 solutions. Therefore total 84 solutions are possible.
Similarly for $y = 3$ to 0, there will be 84 solutions and for $z = 3$ to 0, there will be 84 solutions.
Hence there will be total of 252 solutions. Hence, Option (d) is the answer.

67. No. of words starting with A = 8!/ 2!3! = 3360.
No. of words starting with B = 8!/ 2!4! = 840
No. of words starting with D = 8!/2!4! = 840
No. of words starting with H = 8!/2!4! = 840
Now words with L start.
No. of words starting with LAA = 6!/2! = 360
Now LAB starts and first word starts with LABA.
No. of words starting with LABAA = 4! = 24
After this the next words will be LABADAAHL, LABADAALH, LABADAHAL, LABADAHLA and hence, Option (a) is the answer.

68. We will consider $x = 7$ to $x = 1$.
For $x = 7$, $y + z = 5$. No. of solutions = 4
For $x = 6$, $y + z = 6$. No. of solution = 5
For $x = 5$, $y + z = 7$. No. of solutions = 6
For $x = 4$, $y + z = 8$. No. of solutions = 7
For $x = 3$, $y + z = 9$. No. of solutions = 6
For $x = 2$, $y + z = 10$. No. of solutions = 5
For $x = 1$, $y + z = 11$. No. of solutions = 4
Hence number of solutions = 37
Hence, Option (b) is the answer.

69. As no three points are collinear, therefore every combination of 3 points out of the nine points will give us a triangle. Hence, the answer is $^9C_3$ or 84.
Hence, Option (d) is correct.

70. The number of combinations of three points picked from the nine given points is $^9C_3$ or 84. All these combinations will result in a triangle except the com-

bination of the three collinear points. Hence number of triangles formed will be 84 − 1 = 83.
Hence, Option (d) is the answer.

71. $(xy)^2 = u! + v$
Here xy is a two-digit number and maximum value of its square is 9801. 8! is a five-digit number => $u$ is less than 8 and 4! is 24 which when added to a single digit will never give the square of a two-digit number. Hence $u$ is greater than 4. So, possible values of $u$ can be 5, 6 and 7.
If $u = 5$, $u! = 120$ => $(xy)^2 = u! + v$ => $(xy)^2 = 120 + v = 120 + 1 = 121 = 11^2$
If $u = 6$, $u! = 720$ => $(xy)^2 = u! + v$ => $(xy)^2 = 720 + v = 720 + 9 = 729 = 27^2$
If $u = 7$, $u! = 5040$ => $(xy)^2 = u! + v$ => $(xy)^2 = 5040 + v = 5040 + 1 = 5041 = 71^2$
So there are three cases possible. Hence, 3 solutions exist for the given equation.
Hence, Option (b) is the correct answer.

72. In order to form triangles from the given points, we can either select 2 points from the first line and 1 point from the second OR select one point from the first line and 2 from the second.
This can be done in:
$^{10}C_2 \times {}^{11}C_1 + {}^{10}C_1 \times {}^{11}C_2 = 495 + 550 = 1045$

73. If we have '$n$' candidates who can be selected at the maximum, naturally, the answer to the question would also represent '$n$'.
Hence we check for the first option. If $n = 3$, then $2n + 1 = 7$ and it means that there are 7 candidates to be chosen from. Since it is given that the number of ways of selection of at least 1 candidate is 63, we should try to see, whether selecting 1, 2 or 3 candidates from 7 indeed adds up to 63 ways. If it does this would be the correct answer.
$^7C_1 + {}^7C_2 + {}^7C_3 = 7 + 21 + 35 = 63$. Thus, the first Option fits the situation and is hence correct.

74. This problem can be approached by putting the white flags in their possible positions. There are essentially 4 possibilities for placing the 3 white flags based on the condition that two flags of the same color cannot be together:
1, 3, 5; 1, 3, 6; 1, 4, 6 and 2, 4, 6.
Out of these 4 possible arrangements for the 3 white flags we cannot use 1, 3, 6 and 1, 4, 6 as these have the same color of flag at both ends- something which is not allowed according to the question. Thus there are only 2 possible ways of placing the white flags— 1, 3, 5 OR 2, 4, 6. In each of these 2 ways, there are a further 3 ways of placing the 1 red flag and the 2 blue flags. Thus we get a total of 6 ways.
Option (a) is correct.

75. The possible numbers are:

| 635 _ _ _ 9 | 9 in the units place | $9 \times 9 \times 9 = 729$ numbers |
|---|---|---|
| 635 _ _ _ _ | 9 used before the units place | $3 \times 9 \times 9 \times 4 = 972$ numbers |
| 674 _ _ _ 9 | 9 in the units place | $9 \times 9 \times 9 = 729$ numbers |
| 674 _ _ _ _ | 9 used before the units place | $3 \times 9 \times 9 \times 4 = 972$ numbers |
| Total | | 3402 numbers |

76. We need to go through the options and use the MNP rule tool relating to Permutations and Combinations. We can draw up the following possibilities table for the number of routes between each of the three towns. If the first option is true, i.e., there are 6 routes between *A* to *C*:

| A-C | Possibilities for C-B | Possibilities for total routes A-C-B (Say X) | Possibilities for Total routes A–B (Y) |
|---|---|---|---|
| 6 | 5, 4, 3, 2, 1 | 30, 24, 18, 12, 6 | 3, 9, 15, 21, 27 |
| | | | Note: these values are derived based on the logic that X + Y = 33 |

We further know that there are 23 routes between *B* to *C*.

From the above combinations the possibilities for the routes between *B* to *C* are:

| B–A (Y in the table above) | A–C | B–A–C | B–C | Total |
|---|---|---|---|---|
| 3 | 6 | 18 | 5 | 23 |
| 9 | 6 | 54 not possible | 4 | |
| 15 | 6 | 90 not possible | 3 | |
| 21 | 6 | 126 not possible | 2 | |
| 27 | 6 | 162 not possible | 1 | |

It is obvious that the first possibility in the table above satisfies all conditions of the given situation. Option (a) is correct.

77. With the digits 1, 2, 3, 4, 5 and 6 the numbers divisible by 4 that can be formed are numbers ending in: 12, 16, 24, 32, 36, 52, 56 and 64.

Number of numbers ending in 12 are: $4 \times 3 \times 2 = 24$

Thus the number of numbers is $24 \times 8 = 192$

Option (c) is correct.

78. A million is 1000000 (i.e. the first seven digit number). So we need to find how many numbers of less than 7 digits can be formed using the digits 0,7 and 8.

Number of 1 digit numbers = 2

Number of 2 digit numbers = $2 \times 3 = 6$

Number of 3 digit numbers = $2 \times 3 \times 3 = 18$

Number of 4 digit numbers = $2 \times 3 \times 3 \times 3 = 54$

Number of 5 digit numbers = $2 \times 3 \times 3 \times 3 \times 3 = 162$

Number of 6 digit numbers = $2 \times 3 \times 3 \times 3 \times 3 \times 3 = 486$

Total number of numbers = 728. Option (c) is correct.

79. The white square can be selected in 32 ways and once the white square is selected 8 black squares become ineligible for selection. Hence, the black square can be selected in 24 ways. $32 \times 24 = 768$. Option (d) is correct.

80. Since there are 11 symmetric letters, the number of passwords that can be formed would be $11 \times 10 \times 9 \times 8 = 7920$. Option (a) is correct.

81. This would be given by the number of passwords having:

1 symmetric and 2 asymmetric letters + 2 symmetric and 1 asymmetric letter + 3 symmetric and 0 asymmetric letters

$^{11}C_1 \times ^{15}C_2 \times 3! + ^{11}C_2 \times ^{15}C_1 \times 3! + ^{11}C_3 \times 3! = 11 \times 105 \times 6 + 55 \times 15 \times 6 + 11 \times 10 \times 9 = 6930 + 4950 + 990 = 12870$. Option (c) is correct.

82. Each of the first, third and fourth options can be obviously seen to be true— no mathematics needed there. Only the second option can never be true.

In order to think about this mathematically and numerically— think of a party of 3 persons say *A*, *B* and *C*. In order for the second condition to be possible, each person must know a different number of persons. In a party with 3 persons this is possible only if the numbers are 0, 1 and 2. If *A* knows both *B* and *C* (2), *B* and *C* both would know at least 1 person— hence it would not be possible to create the person knowing 0 people. The same can be verified with a group of 4 persons i.e., the minute you were to make 1 person know 3 persons it would not be possible for anyone in the group to know 0 persons and hence you would not be able to meet the condition that every person knows a different number of persons. Option (b) is correct.

83. With one green ball there would be six ways of doing this. With 2 green balls 5 ways, with 3 green balls 4 ways, with 4 green balls 3 ways, with 5 green balls 2 ways and with 6 green balls 1 way. So a total of $1 + 2 + 3 + 4 + 5 + 6 = 21$ ways. Option (b) is correct.

84. One digit no. = 5; Two digit nos = $5 \times 4 = 20$; Three digit no = $5 \times 4 \times 3 = 60$; four digit no = $5 \times 4 \times 3 \times 2 = 120$; Five digit no.= $5 \times 4 \times 3 \times 2 \times 1 = 120$ Total number of nos = 325. Hence Option (b) is correct.

85. For each selection there are 3 ways of doing it. Thus, there are a total of $3 \times 3 \times 3 \times 3 \times 3 = 243$. Hence, Option (b) is correct.

86. Solve this one through options. If you pick up option (a) it gives you 12 participants in the tournament.

This means that there are 10 men and 2 women. In this case there would be $2 \times {}^{10}C_2 = 90$ matches amongst the men and $2 \times {}^{10}C_1 \times {}^2C_1 = 40$ matches between 1 man and 1 woman. The difference between number of matches where both participants are men and the number of matches where 1 participant is a man and one is a woman is $90 - 40 = 50$ – which is not what is given in the problem.

With 13 participants → 11 men and 2 women. In this case there would be $2 \times {}^{11}C_2 = 110$ matches amongst the men and $2 \times {}^{11}C_1 \times {}^2C_1 = 44$ matches between 1 man and 1 woman. The difference between number of matches where both participants are men and the number of matches where 1 participant is a man and one is a woman is $110 - 44 = 66$ – which is the required value as given in the problem. Thus, option (b) is correct.

87. Based on the above thinking we get that since there are 13 players and each player plays each of the others twice, the number of games would be $2 \times {}^{13}C_2 = 2 \times 78 = 156$.

## Level of Difficulty (II)

1. Number of even numbers = $6 \times 6 \times 6 \times 3$

2. We need to think of this as: Number with two sixes or numbers with one six or number with no six.

   0, 1, 2, 3, 4, 5, 6 and 6

   Numbers with 2 sixes:

   Numbers ending in zero    ${}^5C_1 \times 3!/2! = 15$

   Numbers Ending in 5 and

   (a) Starting with 6      ${}^5C_1 \times 2! = 10$

   (b) Not starting with 6   ${}^4C_1$ (as zero is not allowed) = 4

   Number with 1 six or no sixes.

   Numbers ending in 0     ${}^6C_3 \times 3! = 120$

   Numbers ending in 5     ${}^5C_1 \times {}^5C_2 \times 2! = 100$

   Thus a total of 249 numbers.

3. First arrange 6 pups in 6 places in 6! ways.

   This will leave us with 7 places for 4 cats. Answer = $6! \times {}^7p_4$.

4. Arrangement of M, A, N, A, E, M, E, N, T is

   $$\frac{9!}{2! \times 2! \times 2! \times 2!}.$$

5. For nine places we have following number of arrangements.

   $9 \times 9 \times 8 \times 7 \times 6 \times 5 \times 4 \times 3 \times 2$

6. For a rectangle, we need two pair of parallel lines which are perpendicular to each other. We need to select two parallel lines from '$v$' lines and 2 parallel lines from '$w$' lines. Hence required number of parallel lines is ${}^vC_2 \times {}^wC_2$.

7. From 8 people we have to *arrange* a group of 5 in which three are similar $\dfrac{8P_5}{3!}$ or $\dfrac{8C_5 \times 5!}{3!}$.

8. $\dfrac{4C_4 \times 4C_1 \times 5!}{3!} + \dfrac{4C_2 \times 4C_3 \times 5!}{3!} - 4C_2 \times 4C_3 \times 2C_2 \times 2!$

9. Since the number of men and women in the question is the same, there is no difference in solving this question and solving the previous one (question number 8) as committees having a maximum of 2 women would mean committees having a minimum of 3 men and committees having at maximum one woman holding the post of either president or vice president would mean at least 1 man holding one of the two posts.

   Thus, the answer would be:

   Number of committees with 4 men and 1 woman (including all arrangements of the committees) + Number of committees with 3 men and 2 women (including all arrangements of the committees)–Number of committees with 3 men and 2 women where both the women are occupying the two posts.

   $= ({}^4C_4 \times {}^4C_1 \times 5!)/3! + ({}^4C_3 \times {}^4C_2 \times 5!)/3! - ({}^4C_3 \times {}^4C_2 \times {}^2C_2 \times 2!) = 80 + 480 - 48 = 512$

10. ${}^7C_1 \times {}^6C_2 \times 4! \times 4! = 60480$

11. First make the six law students sit in a row. This can be done in 6! Ways. Then, there would be 7 places for the MBA students. We need to select 5 of these 7 places for 5 MBA students and then arrange these 5 students in those 5 places. This can be done in ${}^7C_5 \times 5!$ Ways.

    Thus, the answer is:

    $6! \times {}^7C_5 \times 5! = 7! \times 6!/2!$

12. The required answer will be given by counting the total number of registration numbers starting with DL-5A to DL-5R and the number of registration numbers starting with DL-5S that have to be counted.

13. Out of 100 balls arrange 99 balls (except $n_{28}$) amongst themselves. Now put $n_{28}$ just before $n_{29}$ in the above arrangement.

14. ${}^6C_2 = 15$.

15. We need to arrange $R$ people on $M$ chairs, $S$ people on another set of $M$ chairs and the remaining people on the remaining chairs. ${}^MP_R \times {}^MP_S \times {}^{2M-R-S}P_{2M-R-S}$.

16. Each group will consists of m things. This can be done in: ${}^{mn}C_m \cdot {}^{mn-m}C_m \cdot {}^{mn-2m}C_m \cdots {}^mC_m$

    $= \dfrac{mn!}{(mn-m)!m!} \cdot \dfrac{(mn-m)!}{(mn-2m)!m!} \cdots \dfrac{m!}{0!m!} = \dfrac{mn!}{(m!)^n}$

    Divide this by $n!$ since arrangements of the n groups amongst themselves is not required.

    Required number of ways $= \dfrac{mn!}{(m!)^n \cdot n!}$

17. Number of ways of selecting 5 different letters = ${}^5C_5 = 1$

Number of ways of selecting 2 similar and 3 different letters = $^4C_1 \times {}^4C_3 = 16$

Number of ways of selecting 2 similar letters + 2 more similar letters and 1 different letter = $^4C_2 \times {}^3C_1 = 18$

Number of ways of selecting 3 similar letters and 2 different letters = $^3C_1 \times {}^4C_2 = 18$

Number of ways of selecting 3 similar letters and another 2 other similar letters = $^3C_1 \times {}^3C_1 = 9$

Number of ways of selecting 4 similar letters and 1 different letter = $^2C_1 \times {}^4C_1 = 8$

Number of ways of selecting 5 similar letters = $^1C_1 = 1$

Total number of ways = $1 + 16 + 18 + 18 + 9 + 8 + 1 = 71$.

18. Divide $3n + 1$ articles in two groups.
    (i) $n$ identical articles and the remaining
    (ii) $2n + 1$ non-identical articles
    We will select articles in two steps. Some from the first group and the rest from the second group.

| Number of articles from first group | Number of articles from second group | Number of ways. |
|---|---|---|
| 0 | $n$ | $1 \times {}^{2n+1}C_n$ |
| 1 | $n - 1$ | $1 \times {}^{2n+1}C_{n-1}$ |
| 2 | $n - 2$ | $1 \times {}^{2n+1}C_{n-2}$ |
| 3 | $n - 3$ | $1 \times {}^{2n+1}C_{n-3}$ |
| .. | .. | ............... |
| $n - 1$ | 1 | $1 \times {}^{2n+1}C_1$ |
| $n$ | 0 | $1 \times {}^{2n+1}C_0$ |

Total number of ways = $^{2n+1}C_n + {}^{2n+1}C_{n-1} + {}^{2n+1}C_{n-2}$
$+ ....^{2n+1}C_1 + {}^{2n+1}C_0 = \dfrac{2^{2n+1}}{2} = 2^{2n}$.

19. We have four options for every place including the left most.
    So the total number of numbers = $4 \times 4 \times 4 \times ... = 4^{10}$.
    We have to consider only positive numbers, so we don't consider one number in which all ten digits are zeroes.

20. Total number of attempts = $10^4$ out of which one is correct.

21. For odd places, the number of arrangements = $\dfrac{4!}{2!2!}$
    For even places, the number of arrangements = $\dfrac{3!}{2!}$
    Hence the total number of arrangements = $\dfrac{4! \times 3!}{2! \times 2! \times 2!}$

22. The number would be of the form $\underline{6} \underline{\phantom{xxxx}} \underline{5}$
    The 5 missing digits have to be formed using the digits 0, 1, 2, 3, 4, 7, 8, 9 without repetition.
    Thus, $^8C_5 \times 5! = 6720$

23. $1m + 3f = {}^8C_1 \times {}^8C_3 = 8 \times 56 = 448$
    $2m + 2f = {}^8C_2 \times {}^8C_2 = 28 \times 28 = 784$
    $3m + 1f \; ^8C_3 \times {}^8C_1 = 56 \times 8 = 448$
    $4m + 0f = {}^8C_4 \times {}^8C_0 = 70 \times 1 = 70$
    Total = 1750

24. Solve this by dividing the solution into,
    3 women and 1 man or
    2 women and 2 men or
    1 woman and 3 men or
    0 woman and 4 men.
    This will give us:
    $^8C_3 \times {}^8C_1 + {}^8C_2 \times {}^8C_2 + {}^8C_1 \times {}^8C_3 + {}^8C_0 \times {}^8C_4$
    $= 448 + 784 + 448 + 70 = 1750$

25. For 1 to 9 we require 9 digits
    For 10 to 99 we require $90 \times 2$ digits
    For 100 to 150 we require $51 \times 3$ digits

26. Select any three places for $A$, $B$ and $C$. They need no arrangement amongst themselves as A would always come before $B$ and $B$ would come before $C$.
    The remaining 5 people have to be arranged in 5 places.
    Thus, $^8C_3 \times 5! = 56 \times 120 = 6720$ OR $8!/3!$

27. Total number of choices = 4! out of which only one will be right.

28. At least two letters have to interchange their places for a wrong choice.

29. Select any two letters and interchange them ($^4C_2$).

30. $^{45}C_7$ ( refer to solved example 16.14).

31. For one pair of black shoes we require one left black and one right black. Consider the worst case situation:
    $7LB + 5LW + 5RW + 1RB$ or
    $7RB + 5LW + 5RW + 1LB = 18$ shoes

32. For one pair of correct shoes one of the possible combinations is $7LB + 5LW + 1R$ ($B$ or $W$) = 13
    Some other cases are also possible with at least 13 shoes.

33. The first rook can be placed in any of the 64 squares and the second rook will then have only 49 places so that they are not attacking each other.

34. When all digits are odd.
    $5 \times 5 \times 5 \times 5 \times 5 \times 5 = 5^6$
    When all digits are even
    $4 \times 5 \times 5 \times 5 \times 5 \times 5 = 4 \times 5^5$
    $5^6 + 4 \times 5^5 = 28125$

35. All six digit numbers – Six digit numbers with only odd digits.
    $= 900000 - 5 \times 5 \times 5 \times 5 \times 5 \times 5 = 884375$.

36. "Total number of all 10-digits numbers – Total number of all 10-digits numbers with no digit repeated"

will give the required answer.
$$= 9 \times 10^9 - 9 \times {}^9P_8$$

37. There will be two types of triangles

    The first type will have its vertices on the three sides of the $\triangle ABC$.

    The second type will have two of it's vertices on the same side and the third vertex on any of the other two sides.

    Hence, the required number of triangles
    $$= 6 \times 5 \times 3 + {}^6C_2 \times 8 + {}^5C_2 \times 9 + {}^3C_2 \times 11$$
    $$= 90 + 120 + 90 + 33$$
    $$= 333$$

38. First step – arrange 7 boys around the table according to the circular permutations rule. i.e. in 6! ways.

    Second step – now we have 7 places and have to arrange 7 girls on these places. This can be done in ${}^7P_7$ ways. Hence, the total number of ways = 6! × 7!

39. 2 × 7! × 7! (Note: we do not need to use circular arrangements here because the seats are numbered.)

40. We just need to select the floors and the people who get down at each floor.

    The floors selection can be done in ${}^{11}C_3$ ways.

    The people selection is ${}^9C_4 \times {}^5C_3$.

    Also, the floors need to be arranged using 3!

    Thus, ${}^{11}C_3 \times {}^9C_4 \times {}^5C_3 \times 3!$  or  ${}^{11}P_3 \times {}^9C_4 \times {}^5C_3$

41. To arrange a surgeon and an assistant we have ${}^{40}P_2$ ways.

42. To arrange a surgeon and 4 assistants we have  or $40 \times {}^{39}C_4$ ways.

43. Give one marble to each of the six children. Then, the remaining 4 identical marbles can be distributed amongst the six children in ${}^{(4+6-1)}C_{(6-1)}$ ways.

44. Since it is possible to give no objects to one or two of them we would have 3 choices for giving each item. Thus, $3 \times 3 \times 3 \times 3 \times 3 \times 3 = 2187$.

45. For an even number the units digit should be either 2, 4 or 6. For the other five places we have six digits. Hence, the number of six digit numbers $= {}^6P_5 \times 3 = 2160$.

46. Visualize the number as:

    – – – – –

    This number has to have the last two digits even. Thus, ${}^3C_2 \times 2!$ will fill the last 2 digits.

    For the remaining places : ${}^5C_4 \times 4!$

    Thus, we have ${}^5C_4 \times 4! \times {}^3C_2 \times 2! = 720$

47. ${}^9C_5 \times 5! = 15120$

48. ${}^4C_1 \times 7 \times 7 \times 7 = {}^4C_1 \times 7^3$

49. Select the two positions for the two 3's. After that the remaining 5 places have to be filled using either 1 or 2.

    Thus, ${}^7C_2 \times 2^5$

50. ${}^4C_1 \times {}^7C_3 \times 3! = 840$

# 18

# Probability

## CONCEPT AND IMPORTANCE OF PROBABILITY

Probability is one of the most important mathematical concepts that we use/come across in our day-to-day life. Particularly important in business and economic situations, probability is also used by us in our personal lives. For a lot of students who are not in touch with Mathematics after their Xth/XIIth classes, this chapter, along with permutations and combinations, is seen as an indication that XIIth standard Mathematics appear in the MBA entrance exams. This leads to students taking negative approach while tacking/preparing for the Mathematics section. Students are advised to remember that the Math asked in MBA entrance is mainly logical while studying the chapter.

As I set out to explain the basics of this chapter, I intend to improve your concepts of probability to such an extent that you feel in total control of this topic.

For those who are reasonably strong, my advice would be to use this chapter both for revisiting the basic concepts as well as for extensive practice.

Probability means the chance of the occurrence of an event. In layman terms, we can say that it is the likelihood that something—that is defined as the event—will or will not occur. Thus probabilities can be estimated for each of the following events in our personal lives:

(a) the probability that an individual student of B.Com will clear the CAT,

(b) The chance that a candidate chosen at random will clear an interview,

(c) The chance that you will win a game of flush in cards if you have a trio of twos in a game where four people are playing,

(d) The likelihood of India's winning the football World Cup in 2014.

(e) The probability that a bulb will fuse in it's first day of operation, and so on.

The knowledge of these estimations helps individuals decide on the course of action they will take in their day-to-day life. For instance, your estimation/ judgement of the probability of your chances of winning the card game in Event *c* above will influence your decision about the amount of money you will be ready to invest in the stakes for the particular game. The application of probability to personal life helps in improving our decision making.

However, the use of probability is much more varied and has far reaching influence on the world of economics and business. Some instances of these are:

(a) the estimation of the probability of the success of a business project,

(b) the estimation of the probability of the success of an advertising campaign in boosting the profits of a company,

(c) the estimation of the probability of the death of a 25-year old man in the next 10 years and that of the death of a 55-year old man in the next 10 years leading to the calculation of the premiums for life insurance,

(d) the estimation of the probability of the increase in the market price of the share of a company, and so on.

## UNDERLYING FACTORS FOR REAL-LIFE ESTIMATION OF PROBABILITY

The factors underlying an event often affect the probability of that event's occurrence. For instance, if we estimate the probability of India winning the 2015 World Cup as 0.14 based on certain expectations of outcomes, then this probability will definitely improve if we know that Sachin Tendulkar will score 800 runs in that particular World Cup.

As we now move towards the mathematical aspects of the chapter, one underlying factor that recurs in every question of probability is that whenever one is asked the question, what is the probability? the immediate question that arises/should arise in one's mind is the probability of what?

The answer to this question is the probability of the EVENT.

The EVENT is the cornerstone or the bottomline of probability. Hence, the first objective while trying to solve any question in probability is to define the event.

The event whose probability is to be found out is described in the question and the task of the student in trying to solve the problem is to define it.

In general, the student can either define the event narrowly or broadly. Narrow definitions of events are the building blocks of any probability problem and whenever there is a doubt about a problem, the student is advised to get into the narrowest form of the event definition.

The *difference* between the narrow and broad definition of event can be explained through an example:

**Example:**  What is the probability of getting a number greater than 2, in a throw of a normal unbiased dice having 6 faces?

The broad definition of the event here is getting a number greater than 2 and this probability is given by 4/6. However, this event can also be broken down into its more basic definitions as:

The event is defined as getting 3 or 4 or 5 or 6. The individual probabilities of each of these are 1/6,1/6,1/6 and 1/6 respectively.

Hence, the required probability is 1/6 + 1/6 + 1/6 + 1/6 = 4/6 = 2/3.

Although in this example it seems highly trivial, the narrow event-definition approach is very effective in solving difficult problems on probability.

In general, event definition means breaking up the event to the most basic building blocks, which have to be connected together through the two English conjunctions— AND and OR.

## The Use of the Conjunction AND (Tool No. 9)

Refer *Back to school* section. Whenever we use AND as the natural conjunction joining two separate parts of the event definition, we replace the AND by the multiplication sign.

Thus, if $A$ AND $B$ have to occur, and if the probability of their occurrence are $P(A)$ and $P(B)$ respectively, then the probability that $A$ AND $B$ occur is got by connecting $P(A)$ AND $P(B)$. Replacing the AND by multiplication sign we get the required probability as:

$$P(A) \times P(B)$$

**Example:**  If we have the probability of $A$ hitting a target as 1/3 and that of $B$ hitting the target as 1/2, then the probability that both hit the target if one shot is taken by both of them is got by

**Event Definition:** $A$ hits the target AND $B$ hits the target.

$$\rightarrow P(A) \times P(B) = 1/3 \times 1/2 = 1/6$$

(Note that since we use the conjunction AND in the definition of the event here, we multiply the individual probabilities that are connected through the conjunction AND.)

## The Use of the Conjunction OR (Tool No. 10)

Refer Back to school section. Whenever we use OR as the natural conjunction joining two separate parts of the event definition, we replace the OR by the addition sign.

Thus, if $A$ OR $B$ have to occur, and if the probability of their occurrence are $P(A)$ and $P(B)$ respectively, then the probability that $A$ OR $B$ occur is got by connecting $P(A)$ OR $P(B)$. Replacing the OR by addition sign, we get the required probability as

$$P(A) + P(B)$$

**Example:**  If we have the probability of $A$ winning a race as 1/3 and that of $B$ winning the race as 1/2, then the probability that either $A$ or $B$ win a race is got by

**Event Definition:** $A$ wins OR $B$ wins.

$$\rightarrow P(A) + P(B) = 1/3 + 1/2 = 5/6$$

(Note that since we use the conjunction OR in the definition of the event here, we add the individual probabilities that are connected through the conjunction OR.)

## Combination of AND and OR

If two dice are thrown, what is the chance that the sum of the numbers is not less than 10.

**Event Definition:** The sum of the numbers is not less than 10 if it is either 10 OR 11 OR 12.

Which can be done by
(6 AND 4) OR (4 AND 6) OR (5 AND 5) OR (6 AND 5) OR (5 AND 6) OR (6 AND 6)
that is, $1/6 \times 1/6 + 1/6 \times 1/6 + 1/6 \times 1/6 + 1/6 \times 1/6 + 1/6 \times 1/6 + 1/6 \times 1/6 = 6/36 = 1/6$

The bottomline is that no matter how complicated the problem on probability is, it can be broken up into its narrower parts, which can be connected by ANDs and ORs to get the event definition.

Once the event is defined, the probability of each narrow event within the broad event is calculated and all the narrow events are connected by Multiplication (for AND) or by Addition (for OR) to get the final solution.

**Example:** In a four game match between Kasporov and Anand, the probability that Anand wins a particular game is 2/5 and that of Kasporov winning a game is 3/5. Assuming that there is no probability of a draw in an individual game, what is the chance that the match is drawn (Score is 2–2).

For the match to be drawn, 2 games have to be won by each of the players. If 'A' represents the event that Anand won a game and K represents the event that Kasporov won a game, the event definition for the match to end in a draw can be described as: [The student is advised to look at the use of narrow event definition.]

(A&A&K&K) OR (A&K&A&K) OR (A&K&K&A)
OR (K&K&A&A) OR (K&A&K&A) OR
(K&A&A&K)

This further translates into

$(2/5)^2(3/5)^2 + (2/5)^2(3/5)^2 + (2/5)^2(3/5)^2 + (2/5)^2(3/5)^2$

$+ (2/5)^2(3/5)^2 + (2/5)^2(3/5)^2$

$= (36/625) \times 6 = 216/625$

After a little bit of practice, you can also think about this directly as:

$^4C_2 \times (2/5)^2 \times {}^2C_2 \times (3/5)^2 = 6 \times 1 \times 36/625 = 216/625$

Where, $4C_2$ gives us the number of ways in which Anand can win two games and $2C_2$ gives us the number of ways in which Kasporov can win the remaining 2 games (obviously, only one).

## BASIC FACTS ABOUT PROBABILITY

For every event that can be defined, there is a corresponding non-event, which is the opposite of the event. The relationship between the event and the non-event is that they are mutually exclusive, that is, if the event occurs then the non-event does not occur and vice versa.

The event is denoted by $E$; the number of ways in which the event can occur is defined as $n(E)$ and the probability of the occurrence of the event is $P(E)$.

The non-event is denoted by $E'$; the number of ways in which the non-event can occur is defined as $n(E')$ while the probability of the occurrence of the event is $P(E')$.

The following relationships hold true with respect to the event and the non-event.

$n(E) + n(E')$ = sample space representing all the possible events that can occur related to the activity.

$$P(E) + P(E') = 1$$

This means that if the event does not occur, then the non-event occurs.

$$\rightarrow P(E) = 1 - P(E')$$

This is often very useful for the calculation of probabilities of events where it is easier to describe and count the non-event rather than the event.

## Illustration

The probability that you get a total more than 3 in a throw of 2 dice.

Here, the event definition will be a long and tedious task, which will involve long counting. Hence, it would be more convenient to define the non-event and count the same.

Therefore, here the non-event will be defined as

A total not more than 3 → 2 or 3 → (1&1) OR (1&2) OR (2&1) = 1/36 + 1/36 + 1/36 = 3/36 = 1/12. However, a word of caution especially for students not comfortable at mathematics: Take care while defining the non-event. Beware of a trap like → event definition: Total > 10 in two throws of a dice does not translate into a non-event of < 10 but instead into the non-event of ≤ 10.

## SOME IMPORTANT CONSIDERATIONS WHILE DEFINING EVENT

**Random Experiment** An experiment whose outcome has to be among a set of events that are completely known but whose exact outcome is unknown is a random experiment (e.g. Throwing of a dice, tossing of a coin). Most questions on probability are based on random experiments.

**Sample Space** This is defined in the context of a random experiment and denotes the set representing all the possible outcomes of the random experiment. [e.g. Sample space when a coin is tossed is (Head, Tail). Sample space when a dice is thrown is (1, 2, 3, 4, 5, 6).]

**Event** The set representing the desired outcome of a random experiment is called the event. Note that the event is a subset of the sample space.

**Non-event** The outcome that is opposite the desired outcome is the non-event. Note that if the event occurs, the non-event does not occur and vice versa.

**Impossible Event** An event that can never occur is an impossible event. The probability of an impossible event is 0. e.g. (Probability of the occurrence of 7 when a dice with 6 faces numbered 1–6 is thrown).

**Mutually Exclusive Events** A set of events is mutually exclusive when the occurrence of any one of them means that the other events cannot occur. (If head appears on a coin, tail will not appear and vice versa.)

**Equally Likely Events** If two events have the same probability or chance of occurrence they are called equally likely events. (In a throw of a dice, the chance of 1 showing on the dice is equal to 2 is equal to 3 is equal to 4 is equal to 5 is equal to 6 appearing on the dice.)

**Exhaustive Set of Events** A set of events that includes all the possibilities of the sample space is said to be an exhaustive set of events. (e.g. In a throw of a dice the number is less than three or more than or equal to three.)

**Independent Events** An event is described as such if the occurrence of an event has no effect on the probability of the occurrence of another event. (If the first child of a couple is a boy, there is no effect on the chances of the second child being a boy.)

**Conditional Probability** It is the probability of the occurrence of an event $A$ given that the event $B$ has already occurred. This is denoted by $P(A|B)$. (E.g. The probability that in two throws of a dices we get a total of 7 or more, given that in the first throw of the dices the number 5 had occurred.)

## The Concept of Odds For and Odds Against

Sometimes, probability is also viewed in terms of *odds* for and *odds against* an event.

Odds in favour of an event $E$ is defined as: $\dfrac{P(E)}{P(E)'}$

Odds against an event is defined as: $\dfrac{P(E)'}{P(E)}$

**Expectation:** The expectation of an individual is defined as Probability of winning × Reward of winning

**Illustration:** A man holds 20 out of the 500 tickets to a lottery. If the reward for the winning ticket is ₹ 1000, find the expectation of the man.

*Space for Notes*

*Solution:* Expectation = Probability of winning × Reward of winning = $\dfrac{20}{500} \times 1000 = ₹\ 40$.

## ANOTHER APPROACH TO LOOK AT THE PROBABILITY PROBLEMS

The probability of an event is defined as

$$\frac{\text{Number of ways in which the event occurs}}{\text{Total number of outcomes possible}}$$

This means that the probability of any event can be got by counting the numerator and the denominator independently.

Hence, from this approach, the concentration shifts to counting the numerator and the denominator.

Thus for the example used above, the probability of a number > 2 appearing on a dice is:

$$\frac{\text{Number of ways in which the event occurs}}{\text{Total number of outcomes possible}} = \frac{4}{6}$$

The counting is done through any of

(a) The physical counting as illustrated above,

(b) The use of the concept of permutations,

(c) The use of the concept of combinations,

(d) The use of the MNP rule.

[*Refer to the chapter on Permutations and Combinations to understand b, c and d above.*]

## WORKED-OUT PROBLEMS

**Problem 18.1** In a throw of two dice, find the probability of getting one prime and one composite number.

**Solution** The probability of getting a prime number when a dices is thrown is 3/6 = 1/2. (This occurs when we get 2, 3 or 5 out of a possibility of getting 1, 2, 3, 4, 5 or 6.)

Similarly, in a throw of a dice, there are only 2 possibilities of getting composite numbers viz : 4 or 6 and this gives a probability of 1/3 for getting a composite number.

Now, let us look at defining the event. The event is—getting one prime and one composite number.

This can be got as:

The first number is prime and the second is composite OR the first number is composite and the second is prime.

$$= (1/2) \times (1/3) + (1/3) \times (1/2) = 1/3$$

**Problem 18.2** Find the probability that a leap year chosen at random will have 53 Sundays.

**Solution** A leap year has 366 days. 52 complete weeks will have 364 days. The 365th day can be a Sunday (Probability = 1/7) OR the 366th day can be a Sunday (Probability = 1/7). Answer = 1/7 + 1/7 = 2/7.

Alternatively, you can think of this as: The favourable events will occur when we have Saturday and Sunday or Sunday and Monday as the 365th and 366th days respectively. (i.e. 2 possibilities of the event occurring). Besides, the total number of ways that can happen are Sunday and Monday OR Monday and Tuesday ... OR Friday and Saturday OR Saturday and Sunday.

**Problem 18.3** There are two bags containing white and black balls. In the first bag, there are 8 white and 6 black balls and in the second bag, there are 4 white and 7 black balls. One ball is drawn at random from any of these two bags. Find the probability of this ball being black.

**Solution** The event definition here is: 1st bag and black ball OR 2nd Bag and Black Ball. The chances of picking up either the 1st OR the 2nd Bag are 1/2 each.

Besides, the chance of picking up a black ball from the first bag is 6/14 and the chance of picking up a black ball from the second bag is 7/11.

Thus, using these values and the ANDs and ORs we get:

$$(1/2) \times (6/14) + (1/2) \times (7/11) = (3/14) + (7/22) = (66 + 98)/(308) = 164/308 = 41/77$$

**Problem 18.4** The letters of the word LUCKNOW are arranged among themselves. Find the probability of always having NOW in the word.

**Solution** The required probability will be given by the equation

= No. of words having NOW/Total no. of words

= 5!/7! = 1/42 [See the chapter of Permutations and Combinations to understand the logic behind these values.]

**Problem 18.5** A person has 3 children with at least one boy. Find the probability of having at least 2 boys among the children.

**Solution** The event is occurring under the following situations:

(a) Second is a boy and third is a girl OR

(b) Second is a girl and third is a boy OR

(c) Second is a boy and third is a boy

This will be represented by: $(1/2) \times (1/2) + (1/2) \times (1/2) + (1/2) \times (1/2) = 3/4$

**Problem 18.6** Out of 13 applicants for a job, there are 5 women and 8 men. Two persons are to be selected for the job. The probability that at least one of the selected persons will be a woman is:

**Solution** The required probability will be given by

First is a woman and Second is a man   OR

First is a man and Second is a woman   OR

First is a woman and Second is a woman

i.e. $(5/13) \times (8/12) + (8/13) \times (5/12) + (5/13) \times (4/12)$
$$= 100/156 = 25/39$$

Alternatively, we can define the non-event as: There are two men and no women. Then, probability of the non-event is

$$(8/13) \times (7/12) = 56/156$$

Hence,        $P(E) = (1 - 56/156) = 100/156 = 25/39$

[*Note:* This is a case of probability calculation where repetition is not allowed.]

**Problem 18.7** The probability that $A$ can solve the problem is 2/3 and $B$ can solve it is 3/4. If both of them attempt the problem, then what is the probability that the problem gets solved.

**Solution** The event is defined as:

$A$ solves the problem   AND   $B$ does not solve the problem

OR

$A$ doesn't solve the problem   AND $B$ solves the problem

OR

$A$ solves the problem   AND   $B$ solves the problem.

Numerically, this is equivalent to:

$$(2/3) \times (1/4) + (1/3) \times (3/4) + (2/3) \times (3/4)$$
$$= (2/12) + (3/12) + (6/12) = 11/12$$

**Problem 18.8** Six positive numbers are taken at random and are multiplied together. Then what is the probability that the product ends in an odd digit other than 5.

**Solution** The event will occurs when all the numbers selected are ending in 1, 3, 7 or 9.

If we take numbers between 1 to 10 (both inclusive), we will have a positive occurrence if each of the six numbers selected are either 1, 3, 7 or 9.

The probability of any number selected being either of these 4 is 4/10 (4 positive events out of 10 possibilities) [*Note:* If we try to take numbers between 1 to 20, we will have a probability of 8/20 = 4/10. Hence, we can extrapolate up to infinity and say that the probability of any number selected ending in 1, 3, 7 or 9 so as to fulfill the requirement is 4/10.]

Hence, answer = $(0.4)^6$

**Problem 18.9** The probability that Arjit will solve a problem is 1/5. What is the probability that he solves at least one problem out of ten problems?

**Solution** The non-event is defined as:

He solves no problems i.e. he doesn't solve the first problem and he doesn't solve the second problem ... and he doesn't solve the tenth problem.

Probability of non-event = $(4/5)^{10}$

Hence, probability of the event is $1-(4/5)^{10}$

**Problem 18.10** A carton contains 25 bulbs, 8 of which are defective. What is the probability that if a sample of 4 bulbs is chosen, exactly 2 of them will be defective?

**Solution** The probability that exactly two balls are defective and exactly two are not defective will be given by $(4C_2) \times (8/25) \times (7/24) \times (17/23) \times (16/22)$

**Problem 18.11** Out of 40 consecutive integers, two are chosen at random. Find the probability that their sum is odd.

**Solution** Forty consecutive integers will have 20 odd and 20 even integers. The sum of 2 chosen integers will be odd, only if

(a) First is even and Second is odd OR

(b) First is odd and Second is even

Mathematically, the probability will be given by:

$P$(First is even) $\times$ $P$(Second is odd) + $P$(First is odd) $\times$ $P$(second is even)

$= (20/40) \times (20/39) + (20/40) \times (20/39)$

$= (2 \times 20^2/40 \times 39) = 20/39$

**Problem 18.12** An integer is chosen at random from the first 100 integers. What is the probability that this number will not be divisible by 5 or 8?

**Solution** For a number from 1 to 100 not be divisible by 5 or 8, we need to remove all the numbers that are divisible by 5 or 8.

Thus, we remove 5, 8, 10, 15, 16, 20, 24, 25, 30, 32, 35, 40, 45, 48, 50, 55, 56, 60, 64, 65, 70, 72, 75, 80, 85, 88, 90, 95, 96, and 100.

i.e. 30 numbers from the 100 are removed.

Hence, answer is 70/100 = 7/10 (required probability)

Alternatively, we could have counted the numbers as number of numbers divisible by 5 + number of numbers divisible by 8 – number of numbers divisible by both 5 or 8.

$$= 20 + 12 - 2 = 30$$

**Problem 18.13** From a bag containing 8 green and 5 red balls, three are drawn one after the other. Find the probability of all three balls being green if

(a) the balls drawn are replaced before the next ball is picked

(b) the balls drawn are not replaced.

**Solution**

(a) When the balls drawn are replaced, we can see that the number of balls available for drawing out will be the same for every draw. This means that the probability of a green ball appearing in the first draw and a green ball appearing in the second draw as well as one appearing in the third draw are equal to each other.

Hence answer to the question above will be:

Required probability $= \dfrac{8}{13} \times \dfrac{8}{13} \times \dfrac{8}{13} = (8^3/13^3)$

(b) When the balls are not replaced, the probability of drawing any color of ball for every fresh draw changes. Hence, the answer here will be:

Required probability $= \dfrac{8}{13} \times \dfrac{7}{12} \times \dfrac{6}{11}$

*Space for Rough Work*

# LEVEL OF DIFFICULTY (I)

1. In throwing a fair dice, what is the probability of getting the number '3'?

   (a) $\dfrac{1}{3}$   (b) $\dfrac{1}{6}$

   (c) $\dfrac{1}{9}$   (d) $\dfrac{1}{12}$

2. What is the chance of throwing a number greater than 4 with an ordinary dice whose faces are numbered from 1 to 6?

   (a) $\dfrac{1}{3}$   (b) $\dfrac{1}{6}$

   (c) $\dfrac{1}{9}$   (d) $\dfrac{1}{8}$

3. Find the chance of throwing at least one ace in a simple throw with two dice.

   (a) $\dfrac{1}{12}$   (b) $\dfrac{1}{3}$

   (c) $\dfrac{1}{4}$   (d) $\dfrac{11}{36}$

4. Find the chance of drawing 2 blue balls in succession from a bag containing 5 red and 7 blue balls, if the balls are not being replaced.

   (a) $\dfrac{3}{13}$   (b) $\dfrac{21}{64}$

   (c) $\dfrac{7}{22}$   (d) $\dfrac{21}{61}$

5. From a pack of 52 cards, two are drawn at random. Find the chance that one is a knave and the other a queen.

   (a) $\dfrac{8}{663}$   (b) $\dfrac{1}{6}$

   (c) $\dfrac{1}{9}$   (d) $\dfrac{1}{12}$

6. If a card is picked up at random from a pack of 52 cards. Find the probability that it is
   (i)  a spade.

   (a) $\dfrac{1}{9}$   (b) $\dfrac{1}{6}$

   (c) $\dfrac{1}{4}$   (d) $\dfrac{1}{4}$

   (ii)  a king or queen.

   (a) $\dfrac{3}{13}$   (b) $\dfrac{2}{13}$

   (c) $\dfrac{7}{52}$   (d) $\dfrac{1}{169}$

   (iii)  'a spade' or 'a king' or 'a queen'

   (a) $\dfrac{21}{52}$   (b) $\dfrac{5}{13}$

   (c) $\dfrac{19}{52}$   (d) $\dfrac{15}{52}$

7. Three coins are tossed. What is the probability of getting
   (i)  2 Tails and 1 Head

   (a) $\dfrac{1}{4}$   (b) $\dfrac{3}{8}$

   (c) $\dfrac{2}{3}$   (d) $\dfrac{1}{8}$

   (ii)  1 Tail and 2 Heads

   (a) $\dfrac{3}{8}$   (b) $1$

   (c) $\dfrac{2}{3}$   (d) $\dfrac{3}{4}$

8. Three coins are tossed. What is the probability of getting
   (i)  neither 3 Heads nor 3 Tails?

   (a) $\dfrac{1}{2}$   (b) $\dfrac{1}{3}$

   (c) $\dfrac{2}{3}$   (d) $\dfrac{3}{4}$

   (ii)  three heads

   (a) $\dfrac{1}{8}$   (b) $\dfrac{1}{4}$

   (c) $\dfrac{1}{2}$   (d) $\dfrac{2}{3}$

9. For the above question, the probability that there is at least one tail is:

   (a) $\dfrac{2}{3}$   (b) $\dfrac{7}{8}$

   (c) $\dfrac{3}{8}$   (d) $\dfrac{1}{2}$

10. Two fair dice are thrown. Find the probability of getting

(i)  a number divisible by 2 or 4.

(a) $\dfrac{1}{2}$         (b) $\dfrac{3}{4}$

(c) $\dfrac{1}{3}$         (d) $\dfrac{2}{3}$

(ii)  a number divisible by 2 and 4.

(a) $\dfrac{1}{3}$         (b) $\dfrac{1}{4}$

(c) $\dfrac{3}{4}$         (d) $\dfrac{5}{7}$

(iii)  a prime number less than 8.

(a) $\dfrac{11}{13}$         (b) $\dfrac{1}{13}$

(c) $\dfrac{1}{4}$         (d) $\dfrac{13}{36}$

11.  A bag contains 3 green and 7 white balls. Two balls are drawn from the bag in succession without re-placement. What is the probability that
(i)  both are white?

(a) $\dfrac{1}{7}$         (b) $\dfrac{5}{11}$

(c) $\dfrac{7}{11}$         (d) $\dfrac{7}{15}$

(ii)  they are of different colour?

(a) $\dfrac{7}{15}$         (b) $\dfrac{7}{9}$

(c) $\dfrac{5}{11}$         (d) $\dfrac{7}{11}$

12.  100 students appeared for two examinations. 60 passed the first, 50 passed the second and 30 passed both. Find the probability that a student selected at random has failed in both the examinations?

(a) $\dfrac{1}{5}$         (b) $\dfrac{1}{7}$

(c) $\dfrac{5}{7}$         (d) $\dfrac{5}{6}$

13.  What is the probability of throwing a number greater than 2 with a fair dice?

(a) $\dfrac{2}{3}$         (b) $\dfrac{2}{5}$

(c)  1         (d) $\dfrac{3}{5}$

14.  Three cards numbered 2, 4 and 8 are put into a box. If a card is drawn at random, what is the probability that the card drawn is

(i)  a prime number?

(a)  1         (b) $\dfrac{1}{3}$

(c) $\dfrac{4}{5}$         (d) $\dfrac{5}{7}$

(ii)  an even number?

(a)  1         (b) $\dfrac{2}{3}$

(c) $\dfrac{1}{2}$         (d) $\dfrac{3}{5}$

(iii)  an odd number?

(a)  1         (b)  0

(c) $\dfrac{1}{3}$         (d) $\dfrac{2}{3}$

15.  Two fair coins are tossed. Find the probability of obtaining
(i)  2 Heads

(a)  1         (b) $\dfrac{2}{3}$

(c) $\dfrac{1}{2}$         (d) $\dfrac{1}{4}$

(ii)  1 Head and 1 Tail

(a) $\dfrac{1}{2}$         (b)  1

(c) $\dfrac{1}{3}$         (d) $\dfrac{2}{3}$

(iii)  2 Tails

(a)  1         (b) $\dfrac{1}{4}$

(c) $\dfrac{2}{3}$         (d) $\dfrac{1}{2}$

16.  In rolling two dices, find the probability that
(i)  there is at least one '6'

(a) $\dfrac{11}{36}$         (b) $\dfrac{22}{36}$

(c) $\dfrac{15}{36}$         (d) $\dfrac{29}{36}$

(ii)  the sum is 5

(a) $\dfrac{1}{4}$         (b) $\dfrac{1}{9}$

(c) $\dfrac{1}{2}$         (d) $\dfrac{1}{6}$

17.  From a bag containing 4 white and 5 black balls a man draws 3 at random. What are the odds against these being all black?

(a) $\dfrac{5}{37}$  (b) $\dfrac{37}{5}$

(c) $\dfrac{11}{13}$  (d) $\dfrac{13}{37}$

18. Amit throws three dice in a special game of Ludo. If it is known that he needs 15 or higher in this throw to win then find the chance of his winning the game.

(a) $\dfrac{5}{54}$  (b) $\dfrac{17}{216}$

(c) $\dfrac{13}{216}$  (d) $\dfrac{15}{216}$

19. Find out the probability of forming 187 or 215 with the digits 1, 2, 3, 4, 5, 6, 7, 8, 9 when only numbers of three digits are formed and when
 (i) repetitions are not allowed

(a) $\dfrac{12}{504}$  (b) $\dfrac{18}{504}$

(c) $\dfrac{2}{504}$  (d) $\dfrac{24}{504}$

 (ii) repetitions are allowed

(a) $\dfrac{2}{729}$  (b) $\dfrac{6}{729}$

(c) $\dfrac{11}{729}$  (d) $\dfrac{4}{729}$

20. In a horse race there were 18 horses numbered 1–18. The probability that horse 1 would win is 1/6, that 2 would win is 1/10 and that 3 would win is 1/8. Assuming that a tie is impossible, find the chance that one of the three will win.

(a) $\dfrac{47}{120}$  (b) $\dfrac{119}{120}$

(c) $\dfrac{11}{129}$  (d) $\dfrac{1}{5}$

21. Two balls are to be drawn from a bag containing 8 grey and 3 blue balls. Find the chance that they will both be blue.

(a) $\dfrac{1}{5}$  (b) $\dfrac{3}{55}$

(c) $\dfrac{11}{15}$  (d) $\dfrac{14}{45}$

22. Two fair dice are thrown. What is the probability of
 (i) throwing a double?

(a) $\dfrac{1}{6}$  (b) 1

(c) $\dfrac{2}{3}$  (d) $\dfrac{1}{2}$

 (ii) the sum is greater than 10

(a) $\dfrac{2}{3}$  (b) $\dfrac{2}{5}$

(c) $\dfrac{1}{6}$  (d) $\dfrac{1}{12}$

 (iii) the sum is less than 10?

(a) $\dfrac{5}{6}$  (b) $\dfrac{2}{5}$

(c) $\dfrac{3}{5}$  (d) $\dfrac{2}{3}$

23. In a certain lottery the prize is ₹ 1 crore and 5000 tickets have been sold. What is the expectation of a man who holds 10 tickets?
(a) ₹ 20,000  (b) ₹ 25,000
(c) ₹ 30,000  (d) ₹ 15,000

24. Two letters are randomly chosen from the word LIME. Find the probability that the letters are *L* and *M*.

(a) $\dfrac{1}{2}$  (b) $\dfrac{1}{4}$

(c) $\dfrac{1}{3}$  (d) $\dfrac{1}{6}$

**Directions for Questions 25 to 27:**  Read the following passage and answer the questions based on it.
 The Bangalore office of Infosys has 1200 executives. Of these, 880 subscribe to the *Time* magazine and 650 subscribe to the *Economist*. Each executive may subscribe to either the *Time* or the *Economist* or both. If an executive is picked at random, answer questions 25–27.

25. What is the probability that
 (i) he has subscribed to the *Time* magazine.

(a) $\dfrac{11}{15}$  (b) $\dfrac{11}{12}$

(c) $\dfrac{7}{15}$  (d) $\dfrac{7}{11}$

 (ii) he has subscribed to the *Economist*.

(a) $\dfrac{13}{21}$  (b) $\dfrac{13}{20}$

(c) $\dfrac{13}{24}$  (d) $\dfrac{12}{30}$

26. He has subscribed to both magazines.

(a) $\dfrac{22}{40}$  (b) $\dfrac{11}{40}$

(c) $\dfrac{12}{20}$  (d) $\dfrac{4}{20}$

27. If among the executives who have subscribed to the *Time* magazine, an executive is picked at random.

What is the probability that he has also subscribed to the *Economist*?

(a) $\dfrac{3}{8}$      (b) $\dfrac{5}{8}$

(c) $\dfrac{2}{3}$      (d) $\dfrac{1}{8}$

28. A bag contains four black and five red balls. If three balls from the bag are chosen at random, what is the chance that they are all black?

(a) $\dfrac{1}{21}$      (b) $\dfrac{1}{20}$

(c) $\dfrac{2}{23}$      (d) $\dfrac{1}{9}$

29. If a number of two digits is formed with the digits 2, 3, 5, 7, 9 without repetition of digits, what is the probability that the number formed is 35?

(a) $\dfrac{1}{10}$      (b) $\dfrac{1}{20}$

(c) $\dfrac{2}{11}$      (d) $\dfrac{1}{11}$

30. From a pack of 52 playing cards, three cards are drawn at random. Find the probability of drawing a king, a queen and jack.

(a) $\dfrac{16}{5525}$      (b) $\dfrac{1}{13^3}$

(c) $\dfrac{1}{14^3}$      (d) $\dfrac{1}{15^3}$

31. A bag contains 20 balls marked 1 to 20. One ball is drawn at random. Find the probability that it is marked with a number multiple of 5 or 7.

(a) $\dfrac{3}{10}$      (b) $\dfrac{7}{10}$

(c) $\dfrac{1}{11}$      (d) $\dfrac{2}{3}$

32. A group of investigators took a fair sample of 1972 children from the general population and found that there are 1000 boys and 972 girls. If the investigators claim that their research is so accurate that the sex of a new born child can be predicted based on the ratio of the sample of the population, then what is the expectation in terms of the probability that a new child born will be a girl?

(a) $\dfrac{243}{250}$      (b) $\dfrac{250}{257}$

(c) $\dfrac{9}{10}$      (d) $\dfrac{243}{493}$

33. A bag contains 3 red, 6 white and 7 black balls. Two balls are drawn at random. What is the probability that both are black?

(a) $\dfrac{1}{8}$      (b) $\dfrac{7}{40}$

(c) $\dfrac{12}{40}$      (d) $\dfrac{13}{40}$

34. A bag contains 6 red, 4 white and 8 blue balls. If three balls are drawn at random, find the probability that

(i) all the three balls are of the same colour.

(a) $\dfrac{17}{240}$      (b) $\dfrac{5}{51}$

(c) $\dfrac{31}{204}$      (d) None of these

(ii) all the three balls are blue.

(a) $\dfrac{8}{51}$      (b) $\dfrac{50}{51}$

(c) $\dfrac{7}{102}$      (d) $\dfrac{13}{51}$

35. If $P(A) = 1/3$, $P(B) = 1/2$, $P(A \cap B) = 1/4$ then find $P(A' \cup B')$

(a) $\dfrac{1}{3}$      (b) $\dfrac{2}{5}$

(c) $\dfrac{2}{3}$      (d) $\dfrac{3}{4}$

36. *A* and *B* are two candidates seeking admission to the IIMs. The probability that *A* is selected is 0.5 and the probability that both *A* and *B* are selected is at most 0.3. Is it possible that the probability of *B* getting selected is 0.9.

(a) No      (b) Yes

(c) Either (a) or (b)      (d) Can't say

37. The probability that a student will pass in Mathematics is 3/5 and the probability that he will pass in English is 1/3. If the probability that he will pass in both Mathematics and English is 1/8, what is the probability that he will pass in at least one subject?

(a) $\dfrac{97}{120}$      (b) $\dfrac{87}{120}$

(c) $\dfrac{53}{120}$      (d) $\dfrac{120}{297}$

38. The odds in favour of standing first of three students Amit, Vikas and Vivek appearing at an examination are 1 : 2. 2 : 5 and 1 : 7 respectively. What is the probability that either of them will stand first (assume that a tie for the first place is not possible).

(a) $\dfrac{168}{178}$    (b) $\dfrac{122}{168}$

(c) $\dfrac{5}{168}$    (d) $\dfrac{125}{168}$

39. $A$, $B$, $C$ are three mutually exclusive and exhaustive events associated with a random experiment. Find $P(A)$ if it is given that $P(B) = 3/2 \, P(A)$ and $P(C) = 1/2 \, P(B)$.

(a) $\dfrac{4}{13}$    (b) $\dfrac{2}{3}$

(c) $\dfrac{12}{13}$    (d) $\dfrac{1}{13}$

40. $A$ and $B$ are two mutually exclusive events of an experiment. If $P(A') = 0.65$, $P(A \cup B) = 0.65$ and $P(B) = p$, find the value of $p$.
   (a) 0.25    (b) 0.3
   (c) 0.1    (d) 0.2

41. A bag contains 4 white and 2 black balls. Another contains 3 white and 5 black balls. If one ball is drawn from each bag, find the probability that
   (i) both are white.

(a) $\dfrac{1}{3}$    (b) $\dfrac{2}{3}$

(c) $\dfrac{1}{4}$    (d) $\dfrac{3}{4}$

   (ii) both are black.

(a) $\dfrac{3}{24}$    (b) $\dfrac{1}{24}$

(c) $\dfrac{3}{12}$    (d) $\dfrac{5}{24}$

   (iii) one is white and one is black.

(a) $\dfrac{13}{24}$    (b) $\dfrac{15}{24}$

(c) $\dfrac{11}{21}$    (d) $\dfrac{1}{2}$

42. The odds against an event is 5 : 3 and the odds in favour of another independent event is 7 : 5. Find the probability that at least one of the two events will occur.

(a) $\dfrac{52}{96}$    (b) $\dfrac{69}{96}$

(c) $\dfrac{71}{96}$    (d) $\dfrac{13}{96}$

43. Kamal and Monica appeared for an interview for two vacancies. The probability of Kamal's selection is 1/3 and that of Monica's selection is 1/5. Find the probability that only one of them will be selected.

(a) $\dfrac{2}{5}$    (b) $\dfrac{1}{5}$

(c) $\dfrac{5}{9}$    (d) $\dfrac{2}{3}$

44. A husband and a wife appear in an interview for two vacancies for the same post. The probability of husband's selection is $(1/7)$ and that of the wife's selection is 1/5. What is the probability that
   (i) both of them will be selected?

(a) $\dfrac{1}{35}$    (b) $\dfrac{2}{35}$

(c) $\dfrac{3}{35}$    (d) $\dfrac{1}{7}$

   (ii) one of them will be selected?

(a) $\dfrac{1}{7}$    (b) $\dfrac{3}{7}$

(c) $\dfrac{2}{7}$    (d) $\dfrac{5}{7}$

   (iii) none of them will be selected?

(a) $\dfrac{24}{35}$    (b) $\dfrac{20}{35}$

(c) $\dfrac{21}{35}$    (d) $\dfrac{2}{7}$

   (iv) at least one of them will be selected?

(a) $\dfrac{12}{35}$    (b) $\dfrac{11}{35}$

(c) $\dfrac{16}{35}$    (d) $\dfrac{1}{5}$

***Space for Rough Work***

## LEVEL OF DIFFICULTY (II)

1. Two fair dices are thrown. Given that the sum of the dice is less than or equal to 4, find the probability that only one dice shows two.

   (a) $\dfrac{1}{4}$      (b) $\dfrac{1}{2}$

   (c) $\dfrac{2}{3}$      (d) $\dfrac{1}{3}$

2. *A* can hit the target 3 times in 6 shots, *B* 2 times in 6 shots and *C* 4 times in 6 shots. They fire a volley. What is the probability that at least 2 shots hit?

   (a) $\dfrac{1}{2}$      (b) $\dfrac{1}{3}$

   (c) $\dfrac{2}{3}$      (d) $\dfrac{3}{4}$

3. There are two bags, one of them contains 5 red and 7 white balls and the other 3 red and 12 white balls, and a ball is to be drawn from one or the other of the two bags. Find the chance of drawing a red ball.

   (a) $\dfrac{37}{120}$      (b) $\dfrac{30}{120}$

   (c) $\dfrac{11}{120}$      (d) None of these

4. In two bags there are to be put altogether 5 red and 12 white balls, neither bag being empty. How must the balls be divided so as to give a person who draws one ball from either bag

   (i) the least chance of drawing a red ball?

   (a) $\dfrac{3}{35}$      (b) $\dfrac{5}{32}$

   (c) $\dfrac{7}{32}$      (d) $\dfrac{1}{16}$

   (ii) the greatest chance of drawing a red ball?

   (a) $\dfrac{3}{4}$      (b) $\dfrac{2}{3}$

   (c) $\dfrac{5}{8}$      (d) $\dfrac{5}{7}$

5. If 8 coins are tossed, what is the chance that one and only one will turn up Head?

   (a) $\dfrac{1}{16}$      (b) $\dfrac{3}{35}$

   (c) $\dfrac{3}{32}$      (d) $\dfrac{1}{32}$

6. What is the chance that a leap year, selected at random, will contain 53 Sundays?

   (a) $\dfrac{2}{7}$      (b) $\dfrac{3}{7}$

   (c) $\dfrac{1}{7}$      (d) $\dfrac{5}{7}$

7. Out of all the 2-digit integers between 1 to 200, a 2-digit number has to be selected at random. What is the probability that the selected number is not divisible by 7?

   (a) $\dfrac{11}{90}$      (b) $\dfrac{33}{90}$

   (c) $\dfrac{55}{90}$      (d) $\dfrac{77}{90}$

8. A child is asked to pick up 2 balloons from a box containing 10 blue and 15 red balloons. What is the probability of the child picking, at random, 2 balloons of different colours?

   (a) $\dfrac{1}{2}$      (b) $\dfrac{2}{3}$

   (c) $\dfrac{1}{3}$      (d) $\dfrac{3}{5}$

9. Tom and Dick are running in the same race; the probability of their winning are 1/5 and 1/2 respectively. Find the probability that

   (i) either of them will win the race.

   (a) $\dfrac{7}{10}$      (b) $\dfrac{3}{10}$

   (c) $\dfrac{1}{5}$      (d) $\dfrac{7}{9}$

   (ii) neither of them will win the race.

   (a) $\dfrac{7}{10}$      (b) $\dfrac{3}{10}$

   (c) $\dfrac{2}{5}$      (d) $\dfrac{4}{5}$

10. Two dice are thrown. If the total on the faces of the two dices are 6, find the probability that there are two odd numbers on the faces?

    (a) $\dfrac{2}{5}$      (b) $\dfrac{1}{5}$

    (c) $\dfrac{5}{9}$      (d) $\dfrac{3}{5}$

11. Amarnath appears in an exam that has 4 subjects. The chance he passes an individual subject's test is 0.8. What is the probability that he will

    (i) pass in all the subjects?

    (a) $0.8^4$      (b) $0.3^4$

    (c) $0.7^3$      (d) None of these

(ii) fail in all the subjects?
(a) $0.4^2$      (b) $0.2^4$
(c) $0.3^4$      (d) None of these
(iii) pass in at least one of the subjects?
(a) 0.99984      (b) 0.9984
(c) 0.0016      (d) None of these

12. A box contains 2 tennis, 3 cricket and 4 squash balls. Three balls are drawn in succession with replacement. Find the probability that
(i) all are cricket balls.
(a) $\dfrac{1}{27}$      (b) $\dfrac{2}{27}$

(c) $\dfrac{25}{27}$      (d) $\dfrac{1}{8}$

(ii) the first is a tennis ball, the second is a cricket ball, the third is a squash ball.
(a) $\dfrac{8}{243}$      (b) $\dfrac{5}{243}$

(c) $\dfrac{4}{243}$      (d) $\dfrac{11}{243}$

(iii) all three are of the same type.
(a) $\dfrac{11}{81}$      (b) $\dfrac{1}{9}$

(c) $\dfrac{13}{81}$      (d) $\dfrac{17}{81}$

13. With the data in the above question, answer the questions when the balls are drawn in succession without replacement.
(i)
(a) $\dfrac{3}{84}$      (b) $\dfrac{1}{84}$

(c) $\dfrac{5}{84}$      (d) None of these

(ii)
(a) $\dfrac{2}{21}$      (b) $\dfrac{4}{21}$

(c) $\dfrac{1}{21}$      (d) $\dfrac{1}{9}$

(iii)
(a) $\dfrac{3}{84}$      (b) $\dfrac{1}{84}$

(c) $\dfrac{5}{84}$      (d) $\dfrac{11}{84}$

14. In the Mindworkzz library, there are 8 books by Stephen Covey and 1 book by Vinay Singh in shelf A. At the same time, there are 5 books by Stephen Covey in shelf B. One book is moved from shelf A to shelf B. A student picks up a book from shelf B. Find the probability that the book by Vinay Singh.

(i) is still in shelf A.
(a) $\dfrac{1}{3}$      (b) $\dfrac{8}{9}$

(c) $\dfrac{3}{4}$      (d) None of these

(ii) is in shelf B.
(a) $\dfrac{3}{54}$      (b) $\dfrac{4}{54}$

(c) $\dfrac{5}{54}$      (d) None of these

(iii) is taken by the student.
(a) $\dfrac{3}{54}$      (b) $\dfrac{1}{54}$

(c) $\dfrac{2}{27}$      (d) None of these

15. The ratio of number of officers and ladies in the Scorpion Squadron and in the Gunners Squadron are 3 : 1 and 2 : 5 respectively. An individual is selected to be the chairperson of their association. The chance that this individual is selected from the Scorpions is 2/3. Find the probability that the chairperson will be an officer.
(a) $\dfrac{25}{42}$      (b) $\dfrac{13}{43}$

(c) $\dfrac{11}{43}$      (d) $\dfrac{7}{42}$

16. A batch of 50 transistors contains 3 defective ones. Two transistors are selected at random from the batch and put into a radio set. What is the probability that
(i) both the transistors selected are defective?
(a) $\dfrac{4}{1225}$      (b) $\dfrac{3}{1225}$

(c) $\dfrac{124}{1224}$      (d) None of these

(ii) only one is defective?
(a) $\dfrac{141}{1225}$      (b) $\dfrac{121}{1225}$

(c) $\dfrac{123}{1224}$      (d) None of these

(iii) neither is defective?
(a) $\dfrac{1082}{1224}$      (b) $\dfrac{1081}{1225}$

(c) $\dfrac{1081}{1224}$      (d) None of these

17. The probability that a man will be alive in 35 years is $\dfrac{3}{5}$ and the probability that his wife will be alive is $\dfrac{3}{7}$. Find the probability that after 35 years.

(i) both will be alive.

(a) $\dfrac{2}{35}$      (b) $\dfrac{9}{35}$

(c) $\dfrac{6}{35}$      (d) $\dfrac{3}{35}$

(ii) only the man will be alive.

(a) $\dfrac{12}{35}$      (b) $\dfrac{11}{35}$

(c) $\dfrac{13}{35}$      (d) $\dfrac{8}{35}$

(iii) only the wife will be alive.

(a) $\dfrac{2}{35}$      (b) $\dfrac{3}{35}$

(c) $\dfrac{6}{35}$      (d) $\dfrac{11}{35}$

(iv) at least one will be alive.

(a) $\dfrac{27}{35}$      (b) $\dfrac{12}{35}$

(c) $\dfrac{11}{35}$      (d) $\dfrac{7}{35}$

18. *A* speaks the truth 3 out of 4 times, and *B* 5 out of 6 times. What is the probability that they will contradict each other in stating the same fact?

(a) $\dfrac{2}{3}$      (b) $\dfrac{1}{3}$

(c) $\dfrac{5}{6}$      (d) None of these

19. A party of *n* persons sit at a round table. Find the odds against two specified persons sitting next to each other.

(a) $\dfrac{n+1}{2}$      (b) $\dfrac{n-3}{2}$

(c) $\dfrac{n+3}{2}$      (d) None of these

20. If 4 whole numbers are taken at random and multiplied together, what is the chance that the last digit in the product is 1, 3, 7 or 9?

(a) $\dfrac{15}{653}$      (b) $\dfrac{12}{542}$

(c) $\dfrac{16}{625}$      (d) $\dfrac{17}{625}$

21. In four throws with a pair of dices what is the chance of throwing a double twice?

(a) $\dfrac{11}{216}$      (b) $\dfrac{25}{216}$

(c) $\dfrac{35}{126}$      (d) $\dfrac{41}{216}$

22. A life insurance company insured 25,000 young boys, 14,000 young girls and 16,000 young adults. The probability of death within 10 years of a young boy, young girl and a young adult are 0.02, 0.03 and 0.15 respectively. One of the insured persons dies. What is the probability that the dead person is a young boy?

(a) $\dfrac{36}{165}$      (b) $\dfrac{25}{166}$

(c) $\dfrac{26}{165}$      (d) $\dfrac{32}{165}$

23. Three groups of children contain 3 girls and 1 boy, 2 girls and 2 boys, and 1 girl and 2 boys respectively. One child is selected at random from each group. The probability that the three selected consist of 1 girl and 2 boys is

(a) $\dfrac{3}{8}$      (b) $\dfrac{1}{5}$

(c) $\dfrac{5}{8}$      (d) $\dfrac{3}{5}$

24. A locker at the world famous WTC building can be opened by dialing a fixed three-digit code (between 000 and 999). Don, a terrorist, only knows that the number is a three-digit number and has only one six. Using this information he tries to open the locker by dialing three digits at random. The probability that he succeeds in his endeavour is

(a) $\dfrac{1}{243}$      (b) $\dfrac{1}{900}$

(c) $\dfrac{1}{1000}$      (d) $\dfrac{3}{216}$

25. In a bag there are 12 black and 6 white balls. Two balls are chosen at random and the first one is found to be black. The probability that the second one is also black is:

(a) $\dfrac{11}{17}$      (b) $\dfrac{12}{17}$

(c) $\dfrac{13}{18}$      (d) None of these

26. In the above question, what is the probability that the second one is white?

(a) $\dfrac{3}{17}$      (b) $\dfrac{6}{17}$

(c) $\dfrac{5}{17}$      (d) $\dfrac{1}{17}$

27. A fair dice is tossed six times. Find the probability of getting a third six on the sixth throw.

(a) $\dfrac{{}^5C_2\,5^2}{6^2}$      (b) $\dfrac{{}^5C_2\,5^3}{6^6}$

(c) $\dfrac{{}^5C_3\,5^2}{6^3}$      (d) $\dfrac{{}^5C_3\,5^2}{6^6}$

28. In shuffling a pack of cards, four are accidentally dropped. Find the chance that the dropped cards should be one from each suit.

(a) $\dfrac{13^4}{{}^{52}C_4}$      (b) $\dfrac{12^4}{{}^{52}C_2}$

(c) $\dfrac{13^2}{{}^{34}C_2}$      (d) $\dfrac{12^2}{{}^{22}C_3}$

29. Three of the six vertices of a regular hexagon are chosen at random. The probability that the triangle with these vertices is equilateral is

    (a) $\dfrac{1}{10}$      (b) $\dfrac{3}{10}$

    (c) $\dfrac{1}{5}$      (d) $\dfrac{4}{10}$

30. There are 5 red shoes and 4 black shoes in a sale. They have got all mixed up with each other. What is the probability of getting a matched shoe if two shoes are drawn at random?

    (a) $\dfrac{6}{9}$      (b) $\dfrac{4}{9}$

    (c) $\dfrac{2}{9}$      (d) $\dfrac{5}{9}$

31. A person draws a card from a pack of 52, replaces it and shuffles it. He continues doing it until he draws a heart. What is the probability that he has to make 3 trials?

    (a) $\dfrac{9}{64}$      (b) $\dfrac{3}{64}$

    (c) $\dfrac{5}{64}$      (d) $\dfrac{1}{64}$

32. For the above problem, what is the probability if he does not replace the cards?

    (a) $\dfrac{274}{1700}$      (b) $\dfrac{123}{1720}$

    (c) $\dfrac{247}{1700}$      (d) $\dfrac{234}{1500}$

33. An event $X$ can happen with probability $P$, and event $Y$ can happen with probability $P'$. What is the probability that exactly one of them happens?
    (a) $P + P' - 2PP'$      (b) $2PP' - P' + P$
    (c) $P - P' + 2PP'$      (d) $2P'P - P' + P$

34. In the above question, what is the probability that at least one of them happens?
    (a) $P + P' + PP'$      (b) $P + P' - PP'$
    (c) $2PP' - P' - P$      (d) $P + P' - 2PP'$

35. Find the probability that a year chosen at random has 53 Mondays.

    (a) $\dfrac{2}{7}$      (b) $\dfrac{5}{28}$

    (c) $\dfrac{1}{28}$      (d) $\dfrac{3}{28}$

36. There are four machines and it is known that exactly two of them are faulty. They are tested one by one in a random order till both the faulty machines are

identified. Then the probability that only two tests are needed is

    (a) $\dfrac{2}{3}$      (b) $\dfrac{1}{6}$

    (c) $\dfrac{1}{3}$      (d) $\dfrac{5}{6}$

37. For the above question, the probability that exactly 3 tests will be required to identify the 2 faulty machines is

    (a) $\dfrac{1}{2}$      (b) $1$

    (c) $\dfrac{1}{3}$      (d) $\dfrac{2}{3}$

38. Seven white balls and three black balls are randomly placed in a row. Find the probability that no two black balls are placed adjacent to each other.

    (a) $\dfrac{7}{15}$      (b) $\dfrac{2}{15}$

    (c) $\dfrac{3}{7}$      (d) $\dfrac{2}{7}$

39. A fair coin is tossed repeatedly. If Head appears on the first four tosses then the probability of appearance of tail on the fifth toss is

    (a) $\dfrac{1}{7}$      (b) $\dfrac{1}{2}$

    (c) $\dfrac{3}{7}$      (d) $\dfrac{2}{3}$

40. The letters of the word 'article' are arranged at random. Find the probability that the vowels may occupy the even places.

    (a) $\dfrac{2}{35}$      (b) $\dfrac{1}{35}$

    (c) $\dfrac{3}{36}$      (d) $\dfrac{2}{34}$

41. What is the probability that four Ss come consecutively in the word MISSISSIPPI?

    (a) $\dfrac{4}{165}$      (b) $\dfrac{2}{165}$

    (c) $\dfrac{3}{165}$      (d) $\dfrac{1}{165}$

42. Eleven books, consisting of five Engineering books, four Mathematics books and two Physics books, are arranged in a shelf at random. What is the probability that the books of each kind are all together?

    (a) $\dfrac{5}{1155}$      (b) $\dfrac{2}{1155}$

    (c) $\dfrac{3}{1155}$      (d) $\dfrac{1}{1155}$

43. Three students appear at an examination of Mathematics. The probability of their success are 1/3, 1/4,

1/5 respectively. Find the probability of success of at least two.

(a) $\frac{1}{6}$

(b) $\frac{2}{5}$

(c) $\frac{3}{4}$

(d) $\frac{3}{5}$

44. A bag contains 8 white and 4 red balls. Five balls are drawn at random. What is the probability that two of them are red and 3 are white?

(a) $\frac{12}{44}$

(b) $\frac{14}{33}$

(c) $\frac{14}{34}$

(d) $\frac{15}{34}$

45. A team of 4 is to be constituted out of 5 girls and 6 boys. Find the probability that the team may have 3 girls.

(a) $\frac{4}{11}$

(b) $\frac{3}{11}$

(c) $\frac{5}{11}$

(d) $\frac{2}{11}$

46. 12 persons are seated around a round table. What is the probability that two particular persons sit together?

(a) $\frac{2}{11}$

(b) $\frac{1}{6}$

(c) $\frac{3}{11}$

(d) $\frac{3}{15}$

47. Six boys and six girls sit in a row randomly. Find the probability that all the six girls sit together.

**Space for Rough Work**

(a) $\frac{3}{22}$

(b) $\frac{1}{132}$

(c) $\frac{1}{1584}$

(d) $\frac{1}{66}$

48. From a group of 7 men and 4 women a committee of 6 persons is formed. What is the probability that the committee will consist of exactly 2 women?

(a) $\frac{5}{11}$

(b) $\frac{3}{11}$

(c) $\frac{4}{11}$

(d) $\frac{2}{11}$

49. A bag contains 5 red, 4 green and 3 black balls. If three balls are drawn out of it at random, find the probability of drawing exactly 2 red balls.

(a) $\frac{7}{22}$

(b) $\frac{10}{33}$

(c) $\frac{7}{12}$

(d) $\frac{7}{11}$

50. A bag contains 100 tickets numbered 1, 2, 3, …, 100. If a ticket is drawn out of it at random, what is the probability that the ticket drawn has the digit 2 appearing on it?

(a) $\frac{19}{100}$

(b) $\frac{21}{100}$

(c) $\frac{32}{100}$

(d) $\frac{23}{100}$

## LEVEL OF DIFFICULTY (III)

1. Out of a pack of 52 cards one is lost; from the remainder of the pack, two cards are drawn and are found to be spades. Find the chance that the missing card is a spade.
   (a) $\dfrac{11}{50}$      (b) $\dfrac{11}{49}$
   (c) $\dfrac{10}{49}$      (d) $\dfrac{10}{50}$

2. $A$ and $B$ throw one dice for a stake of ₹ 11, which is to be won by the player who first throws a six. The game ends when the stake is won by $A$ or $B$. If $A$ has the first throw, what are their respective expectations?
   (a) 5 and 6      (b) 6 and 5
   (c) 11 and 0      (d) 9 and 2

3. Counters marked 1, 2, 3 are placed in a bag and one of them is withdrawn and replaced. The operation being repeated three times, what is the chance of obtaining a total of 6 in these three operations?
   (a) $\dfrac{11}{27}$      (b) $\dfrac{7}{27}$
   (c) $\dfrac{1}{27}$      (d) $\dfrac{5}{14}$

4. A speaks the truth 3 times out of 4, B 7 times out of 10. They both assert that a white ball is drawn from a bag containing 6 balls, all of different colours. Find the probability of the truth of the assertion.
   (a) $\dfrac{12}{49}$      (b) $\dfrac{3}{10}$
   (c) $\dfrac{21}{40}$      (d) None of these

5. In a shirt factory, processes $A$, $B$ and $C$ respectively manufacture 25%, 35% and 40% of the total shirts. Of their respective productions, 5%, 4% and 2% of the shirts are defective. A shirt is selected at random from the production of a particular day. If it is found to be defective, what is the probability that it is manufactured by the process $C$?
   (a) $\dfrac{16}{69}$      (b) $\dfrac{25}{69}$
   (c) $\dfrac{28}{69}$      (d) $\dfrac{27}{44}$

6. A pair of fair dice are rolled together till a sum of either 5 or 7 is obtained. The probability that 5 comes before 7 is
   (a) 0.45      (b) 0.4
   (c) 0.5      (d) 0.7

7. For the above problem, the probability of 7 coming before 5 is:
   (a) $\dfrac{3}{5}$      (b) 0.55
   (c) 0.4      (d) 0.7

8. For the above problem, the probability of 4 coming before either 5 or 7 is:
   (a) $\dfrac{3}{13}$      (b) $\dfrac{7}{13}$
   (c) $\dfrac{11}{13}$      (d) $\dfrac{10}{13}$

9. The probability of a bomb hitting a bridge is 1/2 and two direct hits are needed to destroy it. The least number of bombs required so that the probability of the bridge being destroyed is greater than 0.9 is:
   (a) 7 bombs      (b) 3 bombs
   (c) 8 bombs      (d) 9 bombs

10. What is the probability of the destruction of the bridge if only 5 bombs are dropped?
    (a) 62.32%      (b) 81.25%
    (c) 45.23%      (d) 31.32%

11. Sanjay writes a letter to his friend from IIT, Kanpur. It is known that one out of '$n$' letters that are posted does not reach its destination. If Sanjay does not receive the reply to his letter, then what is the probability that Kesari did not receive Sanjay's letter? It is certain that Kesari will definitely reply to Sanjay's letter if he receives it.
    (a) $\dfrac{n}{(2n-1)}$      (b) $\dfrac{n-1}{n}$
    (c) $\dfrac{1}{n}$      (d) None of these

12. A word of 6 letters is formed from a set of 16 different letters of the English alphabet (with replacement). Find out the probability that exactly 2 letters are repeated.
    (a) $\dfrac{225 \times 224 \times 156}{16^6}$      (b) $\dfrac{18080}{16^6}$
    (c) $\dfrac{15 \times 224 \times 156}{16^6}$      (d) None of these

13. A number is chosen at random from the numbers 10 to 99. By seeing the number, a man will sing if the product of the digits is 12. If he chooses three numbers with replacement, then the probability that he will sing at least once is:
    (a) $1 - \left(\dfrac{43}{45}\right)^3$      (b) $\left(\dfrac{43}{45}\right)^3$

(c) $1 - \dfrac{48 \times 86}{90^3}$  (d) None of these

14. In a bag, there are ten black, eight white and five red balls. Three balls are chosen at random and one is found to be black. The probability that the rest two are white. Find the probability that the remaining two balls are white.

(a) $\dfrac{8}{23}$  (b) $\dfrac{4}{33}$

(c) $\dfrac{10 \times 8 \times 7}{23 \times 22 \times 21}$  (d) $\dfrac{5}{23}$

15. In the above question, find the probability that the remaining two balls are red.

(a) $\dfrac{10}{231}$  (b) $\dfrac{12}{231}$

(c) $\dfrac{12}{363}$  (d) None of these

16. Ten tickets are numbered 1, 2, 3..., 10. Six tickets are selected at random one at a time with replacement. The probability that the largest number appearing on the selected ticket is 7 is:

(a) $\dfrac{(7^6 - 1)}{10^6}$  (b) $\dfrac{7^6 - 6^6}{10^6}$

(c) $\dfrac{6^6}{10^6}$  (d) None of these

17. A bag contains 15 tickets numbered 1 to 15. A ticket is drawn and replaced. Then one more ticket is drawn and replaced. The probability that first number drawn is even and second is odd is

(a) $\dfrac{56}{225}$  (b) $\dfrac{26}{578}$

(c) $\dfrac{57}{289}$  (d) None of these

18. Six blue balls are put in three boxes. The probability of putting balls in the boxes in equal numbers is

(a) $\dfrac{1}{21}$  (b) $\dfrac{1}{8}$

(c) $\dfrac{1}{28}$  (d) $\dfrac{1}{7}$

19. AMS employs 8 professors on their staff. Their respective probability of remaining in employment for 10 years are 0.2, 0.3, 0.4, 0.5, 0.6, 0.7, 0.8, 0.9. The probability that after 10 years at least 6 of them still work in AMS is

(a) 0.19  (b) 1.22
(c) 0.1  (d) None of these

20. A person draws a card from a pack of 52, replaces it and shuffles it. He continues doing so until he draws a heart. What is the probability that he has to make at least 3 trials?

(a) $\dfrac{3}{17}$  (b) $\dfrac{8}{19}$

(c) $\dfrac{2}{17}$  (d) $\dfrac{11}{16}$

21. Hilips, the largest white goods producer in India, uses a quality check scheme on produced items before they are sent into the market. The plan is as follows: A set of 20 articles is readied and 4 of them are chosen at random. If any one of them is found to be defective then the whole set is put under 100% screening again. If no defectives are found, the whole set is sent into the market. Find the probability that a box containing 4 defective articles will be sent into the market.

(a) $\dfrac{364}{969}$  (b) $\dfrac{364}{963}$

(c) $\dfrac{96}{969}$  (d) $\dfrac{343}{969}$

22. In the above question, what is the probability that a box containing only one defective will be sent back for screening?

(a) $\dfrac{2}{3}$  (b) $\dfrac{1}{5}$

(c) $\dfrac{2}{5}$  (d) $\dfrac{4}{5}$

23. If the integers $m$ and $n$ are chosen at random from 1 to 100, then the probability that a number of the form $7^m + 7^n$ is divisible by 5 is

(a) $\dfrac{1}{4}$  (b) $\dfrac{1}{2}$

(c) $\dfrac{1}{16}$  (d) $\dfrac{1}{6}$

24. Three numbers are chosen at random without replacement from (1, 2, 3 ..., 10). The probability that the minimum number is 3 or the maximum number is 7 is

(a) $\dfrac{12}{37}$  (b) $\dfrac{11}{40}$

(c) $\dfrac{13}{35}$  (d) $\dfrac{14}{35}$

25. An unbiased dice with face values 1, 2, 3, 4, 5 and 6 is rolled four times. Out of the 4 face values obtained, find the probability that the minimum face value is not less than 2 and the maximum face value is not greater than 5.

(a) $\dfrac{16}{81}$  (b) $\dfrac{14}{6^4}$

(c) $\dfrac{16}{80}$  (d) None of these

26. Three faces of a dice are yellow, two faces are red and one face is blue. The dice is tossed three times.

Find the probability that the colours yellow, red and blue appear in the first, second and the third toss respectively.

(a) $\dfrac{1}{18}$

(b) $\dfrac{1}{12}$

(c) $\dfrac{1}{9}$

(d) $\dfrac{1}{36}$

27. If from each of three boxes containing 3 white and 1 black, 2 white and 2 black, 1 white and 3 black balls, one ball is drawn at random, then the probability that 2 white and 1 black ball will be drawn is

(a) $\dfrac{13}{32}$

(b) $\dfrac{12}{14}$

(c) $\dfrac{12}{25}$

(d) $\dfrac{3}{13}$

28. Probabilities that Rajesh passes in Math, Physics and Chemistry are $m$, $p$ and $c$ respectively. Of these subjects, Rajesh has a 75% chance of passing in at least one, 50% chance of passing in at least two and 40% chance of passing in exactly two. Find which of the following is true.

(a) $p + m + c = \dfrac{19}{20}$

(b) $p + m + c = \dfrac{27}{20}$

c) $pmc = \dfrac{1}{20}$

(d) $pmc = \dfrac{1}{8}$

29. There are 5 envelopes corresponding to 5 letters. If the letters are placed in the envelopes at random, what is the probability that all the letters are not placed in the right envelopes?

(a) $\dfrac{119}{120}$

(b) $\dfrac{59}{60}$

(c) $\dfrac{23}{24}$

(d) $\dfrac{4^5}{5^5}$

30. For the above question what is the probability that no single letter is placed in the right envelope.

(a) $\dfrac{12}{35}$

(b) $\dfrac{11}{30}$

(c) $\dfrac{12}{25}$

(d) $\dfrac{3}{12}$

31. An urn contains four tickets having numbers 112, 121, 211, 222 written on them. If one ticket is drawn at random and $Ai$ ($i = 1, 2, 3$) be the event that the $i$th digit from left of the number on ticket drawn is 1, which of these can be said about the events $A_1$, $A_2$ and $A_3$?

(a) They are mutually exclusive

(b) $A_1$ and $A_3$ are not mutually exclusive to $A_2$

(c) $A_1$ and $A_3$ are mutually exclusive

(d) Both $b$ and $c$

32. The probability that a contractor will get a plumbing contract is 2/3 and the probability that he will get an electric contract is 5/9. If the probability of getting at least one contract is 4/5, what is the probability that he will get both the contracts?

(a) $\dfrac{19}{45}$

(b) $\dfrac{13}{45}$

(c) $\dfrac{12}{35}$

(d) $\dfrac{11}{23}$

33. If $P(A) = 3/7$, $P(B) = 1/2$ and $P(A' \cap B') = 1/14$, then are $A$ and $B$ are mutually exclusive events?

(a) No

(b) Yes

(c) Either yes or no

(d) Cannot be determined

34. Six boys and six girls sit in a row at random. Find the probability that the boys and girls sit alternately.

(a) $\dfrac{1}{132}$

(b) $\dfrac{1}{462}$

(c) $\dfrac{1}{623}$

(d) $\dfrac{1}{231}$

35. A problem on mathematics is given to three students whose chances of solving it are 1/2, 1/3 and 1/4 respectively. What is the chance that the problem will be solved?

(a) $\dfrac{2}{3}$

(b) $\dfrac{3}{4}$

(c) $\dfrac{1}{3}$

(d) $\dfrac{1}{2}$

36. $A$ and $B$ throw a pair of dice alternately. $A$ wins if he throws 6 before $B$ throws 5 and $B$ wins if he throws 5 before $A$ throws 6. Find $B$'s chance of winning if $A$ makes the first throw.

(a) $\dfrac{1}{2}$

(b) $\dfrac{5}{12}$

(c) $\dfrac{1}{3}$

(d) $\dfrac{5}{11}$

37. Two persons $A$ and $B$ toss a coin alternately till one of them gets Head and wins the game. Find $B$'s chance of winning if $A$ tosses the coin first.

(a) $\dfrac{1}{3}$

(b) $\dfrac{2}{3}$

(c) $\dfrac{1}{2}$

(d) None of these

38. A bag contains 3 red and 4 white balls and another bag contains 4 red and 3 white balls. A dice is cast and if the face 1 or 3 turns up, a ball is taken from the first bag and if any other face turns up, a ball is taken from the second bag. Find the probability of drawing a red ball.

(a) $\dfrac{11}{20}$

(b) $\dfrac{12}{21}$

(c) $\dfrac{2}{11}$

(d) $\dfrac{11}{21}$

39. Three groups of children contain respectively 3 girls and 1 boy, 2 girls and 2 boys, and 1 girl and 3 boys. One child is selected at random from each group.

The probability that the three selected consists of 1 girl and 2 boys is:

(a) $\dfrac{13}{32}$

(b) $\dfrac{12}{32}$

(c) $\dfrac{15}{32}$

(d) $\dfrac{11}{32}$

40. The probabilities of A, B and C solving a problem are $\dfrac{1}{3}, \dfrac{2}{7}$ and $\dfrac{3}{8}$ respectively. If all the three try to solve the problem simultaneously, find the probability that exactly one of them will solve it.

(a) $\dfrac{26}{65}$

(b) $\dfrac{25}{56}$

(c) $\dfrac{52}{65}$

(d) $\dfrac{25}{52}$

41. A bag contains 5 black and 3 red balls. A ball is taken out of the bag and is not returned to it. If this process is repeated three times, then what is the probability of drawing a black ball in the next draw of a ball?

(a) 0.7

(b) 0.625

(c) 0.1

(d) None of these

42. For question 41, what is the probability of drawing a red ball?

(a) 0.375

(b) 0.9

(c) 0.3

(d) 0.79

43. One bag contains 5 white and 4 black balls. Another bag contains 7 white and 9 black balls. A ball is transferred from the first bag to the second and then a ball is drawn from the second bag. Find the probability that the ball drawn is white.

(a) $\dfrac{7}{18}$

(b) $\dfrac{5}{9}$

(c) $\dfrac{4}{9}$

(d) $\dfrac{11}{18}$

44. V Anand and Gary Kasparov play a series of 5 chess games. The probability that V Anand wins a game is 2/5 and the probability of Kasparov winning a game is 3/5. There is no probability of a draw. The series will be won by the person who wins 3 matches. Find the probability that Anand wins the series. (The series ends the moment when any of the two wins 3 matches.)

(a) $\dfrac{992}{3125}$

(b) $\dfrac{273}{625}$

(c) $\dfrac{1021}{3125}$

(d) $\dfrac{1081}{3125}$

45. There are 10 pairs of socks in a cupboard from which 4 individual socks are picked at random. The probability that there is at least one pair is.

(a) $\dfrac{195}{323}$

(b) $\dfrac{99}{323}$

(c) $\dfrac{198}{323}$

(d) $\dfrac{185}{323}$

46. A fair coin is tossed 10 times. Find the probability that two Heads do not occur consecutively.

(a) $\dfrac{1}{2^4}$

(b) $\dfrac{1}{2^3}$

(c) $\dfrac{1}{2^5}$

(d) None of these

47. In a room there are 7 persons. The chance that two of them were born on the same day of the week is

(a) $\dfrac{1080}{7^5}$

(b) $\dfrac{2160}{7^5}$

(c) $\dfrac{540}{7^4}$

(d) None of these

48. In a hand at a game of bridge what is the chance that the 4 kings are held by a specified player?

(a) $\dfrac{10}{4165}$

(b) $\dfrac{11}{4165}$

(c) $\dfrac{110}{4165}$

(d) None of these

49. One hundred identical coins each with probability P of showing up Heads are tossed once. If $0 < P < 1$ and the probability of Heads showing on 50 coins is equal to that of Heads showing on 51 coins, then value of P is

(a) $\dfrac{1}{21}$

(b) $\dfrac{49}{101}$

(c) $\dfrac{50}{101}$

(d) $\dfrac{51}{101}$

50. Two small squares on a chess board are chosen at random. Find the probability that they have a common side:

(a) $\dfrac{1}{12}$

(b) $\dfrac{1}{18}$

(c) $\dfrac{2}{15}$

(d) $\dfrac{3}{14}$

*Space for Rough Work*

# ANSWER KEY

## Level of Difficulty (I)

| | | | |
|---|---|---|---|
| 1. (b) | 2. (a) | 3. (d) | 4. (c) |
| 5. (a) | 6(i). (c) | 6(ii). (b) | 6(iii). (c) |
| 7(i). (b) | 7(ii). (a) | 8(i). (d) | 8(ii). (a) |
| 9. (b) | 10(i). (a) | 10(ii). (b) | 10(iii). (d) |
| 11(i). (d) | 11(ii). (a) | 12. (a) | 13. (a) |
| 14(i). (b) | 14(ii). (a) | 14(iii). (b) | 15(i). (d) |
| 15(ii). (a) | 15(iii). (b) | 16(i). (a) | 16(ii). (b) |
| 17. (b) | 18. (a) | 19(i). (c) | 19(ii). (a) |
| 20. (a) | 21. (b) | 22(i). (a) | 22(ii). (d) |
| 22(iii). (a) | 23. (a) | 24. (d) | 25(i). (a) |
| 25(ii). (c) | 26. (b) | 27. (a) | 28. (a) |
| 29. (b) | 30. (a) | 31. (a) | 32. (d) |
| 33. (b) | 34(i). (b) | 34(ii). (c) | 35. (d) |
| 36. (a) | 37. (a) | 38. (d) | 39. (a) |
| 40. (b) | 41(i). (c) | 41(ii). (d) | 41(iii). (a) |
| 42. (c) | 43. (a) | 44(i). (a) | 44(ii). (c) |
| 44(iii). (a) | 44(iv). (b) | | |

## Level of Difficulty (II)

| | | | |
|---|---|---|---|
| 1. (d) | 2. (a) | 3. (a) | 4(i) (b) |
| 4(ii) (c) | 5. (d) | 6. (a) | 7. (d) |
| 8. (a) | 9(i) (a) | 9(ii) (b) | 10. (d) |
| 11(i) (a) | 11(ii) (b) | 11(iii) (b) | 12(i) (a) |
| 12(ii) (a) | 12(iii) (a) | 13(i) (b) | 13(ii) (c) |
| 13(iii) (c) | 14(i) (b) | 14(ii) (c) | 14(iii) (b) |
| 15. (a) | 16(i) (b) | 16(ii) (a) | 16(iii) (b) |
| 17(i) (b) | 17(ii) (a) | 17(iii) (c) | 17(iv) (a) |
| 18. (b) | 19. (b) | 20. (c) | 21. (b) |
| 22. (b) | 23. (a) | 24. (a) | 25. (a) |
| 26. (b) | 27. (b) | 28. (a) | 29. (a) |
| 30. (b) | 31. (a) | 32. (c) | 33. (a) |
| 34. (b) | 35. (a) | 36. (b) | 37. (c) |
| 38. (a) | 39. (b) | 40. (b) | 41. (a) |
| 42. (d) | 43. (a) | 44. (b) | 45. (d) |
| 46. (a) | 47. (b) | 48. (a) | 49. (a) |
| 50. (a) | | | |

## Level of Difficulty (III)

| | | | |
|---|---|---|---|
| 1. (a) | 2. (b) | 3. (b) | 4. (c) |
| 5. (a) | 6. (b) | 7. (a) | 8. (a) |
| 9. (a) | 10. (b) | 11. (a) | 12. (a) |
| 13. (a) | 14. (b) | 15. (a) | 16. (b) |
| 17. (a) | 18. (c) | 19. (a) | 20. (d) |
| 21. (a) | 22. (b) | 23. (a) | 24. (b) |
| 25. (a) | 26. (d) | 27. (a) | 28. (b) |
| 29. (a) | 30. (b) | 31. (b) | 32. (a) |
| 33. (b) | 34. (b) | 35. (b) | 36. (d) |
| 37. (a) | 38. (d) | 39. (b) | 40. (b) |
| 41. (a) | 42. (a) | 43. (c) | 44. (a) |
| 45. (b) | 46. (b) | 47. (b) | 48. (b) |
| 49. (d) | 50. (b) | | |

## Solutions and Shortcuts

### Level of Difficulty (I)

1. Out of a total of 6 occurrences, 3 is one possibility = 1/6.

2. 5 or 6 out of a sample space of
   1, 2, 3, 4, 5   or   6 = 2/6 = 1/3

3. Event definition is:
   (1 and 1) or (1 and 2) or (1 and 3) or (1 and 4) or
   (1 and 5) or (1 and 6) or (2 and 1) or (3 and 1) or
   (4 and 1) or (5 and 1) or (6 and 1)
   Total 11 out of 36 possibilities = 11/36

4. Event definition: First is blue and second is blue
   = $7/12 \times 6/11 = 7/22$.

5. Knave and queen or Queen and Knave →
   $4/52 \times 4/51 + 4/52 \times 4/51 = 8/663$

6. (i) 13/52 = 1/4
   (ii) 4 kings and 4 queens out of 52 cards.
   Thus, 8/52 = 2/13.
   (iii) 13 spades + 3 kings + 3 queens → 19/52.

7. (i) Event definition is: $T$ and $T$ and $H$ or $T$ and $H$
   and $T$ or $H$ and $T$ and $T = 3 \times 1/8 = 3/8$.
   (ii) Same as above = 3/8.

8. (i) Probability of 3 heads = 1/8
   Also, Probability of 3 tails = 1/8.
   Required probability $= 1 - (1/8 + 1/8) = 6/8$
   = 3/4.
   (ii) $H$ and $H$ and $H = 1/8$.

9. At least one tail is the non-event for all heads.
   Thus, $P$ (at least 1 tail) = 1 − P(all heads)
   = 1 − 1/8 = 7/8.

10. (i) Positive outcomes are 2(1 way), 4(3 ways),
    6(5 ways) 8(5 ways), 10 (3 ways), 12 (1way).
    Thus, 18/36 = 1/2
    (ii) Positive outcomes are: 4, 8 and 12
    4 (3 ways), 8(5 ways) and 12(1 way)
    Gives us 9/36 = 1/4.
    (iii) Positive outcomes are 2(1 way), 3(2 ways),
    5(4 ways), 7(6 ways). Total of 13 positive out-
    comes out of 36.
    Thus, 13/36.

11. (i) First is white and second is white $7/10 \times 6/9 = 7/15$.
    (ii) White and Green or Green and White
    $7/10 \times 3/9 + 3/10 \times 7/9$
    $42/90 = 7/15$.

12.

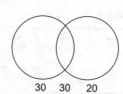

30    30    20

From the figure it is evident that 80 students passed at least 1 exam. Thus, 20 failed both and the required probability is 20/100 = 1/5.

13. 3 or 4 or 5 or 6 = 4/6 = 2/3

14. (i) Since 2 is the only prime number out of the three numbers, the answer would be 1/3
    (ii) Since all the numbers are even, it is sure that the number drawn out is an even number. Hence, the required probability is 1.
    (iii) Since there are no odd numbers amongst 2, 4 and 8, the required probability is 0.

15. (i) The event would be Head and Head → ½ × ½ = ¼
    (ii) The event would be Head and Tail OR Tail and Head → = ½ × ½ + ½ × ½ = 1/2
    (iii) The event would be Tail and Tail → ½ × ½ = ¼

16. (i) With a six on the first dice, there are 6 possibilities of outcomes that can appear on the other dice (viz. 6 & 1, 6 & 2, 6 & 3, 6 & 4, 6 & 5 and 6 & 6). At the same time with 6 on the second dice there are 5 more possibilities for outcomes on the first dice: (1 & 6, 2 & 6, 3 & 6, 4 & 6, 5 & 6)
    Also, the total outcomes are 36. Hence, the required probability is 11/36.
    (ii) Out of 36 outcomes, 5 can come in the following ways – 1 + 4; 2 + 3; 3 + 2 or 4 + 1 → 4/36 = 1/9.

17. Odds against an event = $\dfrac{p(E')}{p(E)}$

    In this case, the event is: All black, i.e., First is black and second is black and third is black.
    $P(E) = 5/9 × 4/8 × 3/7 = 60/504 = 5/42.$
    Odds against the event = 37/5.

18. Event definition is: 15 or 16 or 17 or 18.
    15 can be got as: 5 and 5 and 5 (one way)
    Or
    6 and 5 and 4 (Six ways)
    Or
    6 and 6 and 3 (3 ways)
    Total 10 ways.
    16 can be got as: 6 and 6 and 4 (3 ways)
    Or
    6 and 5 and 5 (3 ways)
    Total 6 ways.
    17 has 3 ways and 18 has 1 way of appearing.
    Thus, the required probability is: (10 + 6 + 3 + 1)/216 = 20/216 = 5/54.

19. (i) Positive outcomes = 2 (187 or 215)
    Total outcomes = 9 × 8 × 7
    Required probability = 2/504 = 1/252
    (ii) = 2/729.

20. 1/6 + 1/10 + 1/8 = 47/120

21. The event definition would be given by:

22. (i) There are six doubles (1, 1; 2 & 2; 3 & 3; 4 & 4; 5 & 5; 6 & 6) out of a total of 36 outcomes → 6/36 = 1/6
    (ii) Sum greater than 10 means 11 or 12 → 3/36 = 1/12
    (iii) Sum less than 10 is the non event for the case sum is 10 or 11 or 12. There are 3 ways of getting 10, 2 ways of getting 11 and 1 way of getting a sum of 12 in the throw of two dice. Thus, the required probability would be 1 – 6/36 = 5/6.

23. Expectation = Probability of winning × Reward of winning = (10/5000) × 1 crore = (1 crore/500) = 20000.

24. $1/{}^4C_2$ = 1/6.

25.

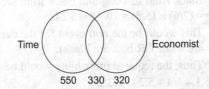

Time        Economist
550   330   320

    (i) 880/1200 = 11/15
    (ii) 650/1200 = 13/24

26. 330/1200 = 11/40

27. 330/880 = 3/8

28. Black and Black and Black = 4/9 × 3/8 × 2/7 = 24/504 = 1/21.

29. $1/{}^5P_2$ = 1/20.

30. 6 × (4/52) × (4/51) × (4/50) = 16/5525.

31. Positive Outcomes are: 5, 7, 10, 14, 15 or 20
    Thus, 6/20 = 3/10.

32. 972/1972 = 243/493.

33. Black and black = (7/16) × 6/15 = 7/40

34. (i) The required probability would be given by:
    All are Red OR All are white OR All are Blue
    = (6/18)×(5/17)×(4/16) + (4/18)×(3/17)×(2/16) + (8/18)×(7/17)×(6/16)
    = 480/(18 × 17 × 16)
    (ii) All blue = (8 × 7 × 6)/(18 × 17 × 16) = 7/102

35. The required value of the union of the two non events (of A and B) would be 1 – 1/4 = ¾

36. P (Both are selected) = P(A) × P(B)
    Since P(A) = 0.5, we get
    0.3 = 0.5 × 0.6.
    The maximum value of P(B) = 0.6.
    Thus P(B) = 0.9 is not possible.

37.

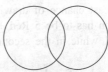

19/40   1/8   5/24

We have: 19/40 + 1/8 + 5/24 = 97/120

38. P (Amit) = 1/3

    P (Vikas) = 2/7

    P (Vivek) = 1/8.

    Required Probability = 1/3 + 2/7 + 1/8 = 125/168.

39. $P(A) + P(B) + P(C) = 1 \rightarrow 2P(B)/3 + P(B) + P(B)/2 = 1 \rightarrow 13P(B)/6 = 1 \rightarrow P(B) = 6/13$. Hence, $P(A) = 4/13$

40. $P(A) = 1 - 0.65 = 0.35$.

    Hence, $P(B) = 0.65 - 0.35 = 0.3$

41. (i) The required probability would be given by the event:

    White from first bag and white from second bag = $(4/6) \times (3/8) = \frac{1}{4}$

    (ii) The required probability would be given by the event:

    Black from first bag and black from second bag = $(2/6) \times (5/8) = 10/48 = 5/24$

    (iii) This would be the non event for the event [both are white OR both are black).

    Thus, the required probability would be:

    $1 - 1/4 - 5/24 = 13/24$.

42. $P(E_1)$ 3/8

    $P(E_2) = 7/12$.

    Event definition is: $E_1$ occurs and $E_2$ does not occur or $E_1$ occurs and $E_2$ occurs or $E_2$ occurs and $E_1$ does not occur.

    $(3/8) \times (5/12) + (3/8) \times (7/12) + (5/8) \times (7/12) = 71/96$.

43. Kamal is selected and Monica is not selected or Kamal is not selected and Monica is selected $\rightarrow (1/3) \times (4/5) + (2/3) \times (1/5) = (6/15) = (2/5)$.

44. (i) $1/5 \times 1/7 = 1/35$

    (ii) $(1/5) \times (6/7) + (4/5) \times (1/7) = 10/35 = 2/7$.

    (iii) $(4/5) \times (6/7) = 24/35$

    (iv) Both selected or 1 selected = $1/35 + 2/7 = 11/35$.

## Level of Difficulty (II)

1. The possible outcomes are:

    (1, 1); (1, 2); (2, 1), (2, 2), (3, 1); (1, 3).

    Out of six cases, in two cases there is exactly one '2'

    Thus, the correct answer is 2/6 = 1/3.

2. Event definition is A hits, B hits and C hits OR any two of the three hits.

3. The event can be defined as:

    First bag is selected and red ball is drawn.

    or second bag is selected and red ball is drawn.

    $1/2 \times 5/12 + \frac{1}{2} \times 3/15 = (5/24) + (3/30) = 37/120$

4. (a) For the least chance of drawing a red ball the distribution has to be 5 Red + 11 white in one bag and 1 white in the second bag. This gives us

    $$\frac{1}{2} \times \frac{5}{16} + \frac{1}{2} \times 0 = \frac{5}{32}$$

    (b) For the greatest chance of drawing a red ball the distribution has to be 1 Red in the first bag and 4 red + 12 white balls in the second bag. This gives us

    $$\frac{1}{2} \times 1 + \frac{1}{2} \times \frac{4}{16} = \frac{5}{8}$$

5. One head and seven tails would have eight positions where the head can come.

    Thus, $8 \times (1/2)^8 = (1/32)$

6. A leap year has 366 days – which means 52 completed weeks and 2 more days. The last two days can be (Sunday, Monday) or (Monday, Tuesday) or ....... (Saturday, Sunday).

    2 scenarios out of 7 have a 53rd Sunday.

    Thus, 2/7 is the required answer.

7. The count of the event will be given by:

    The number of all 2 digit integers – the number of all 2 digit integers divisible by 7

8. Blue and Red or Red and Blue

    = $(10/25) \times (15/24) + (15/25) \times (10/24) = (1/2)$.

9. (i) 1/5 + ½ = 7/10.

    (ii) 1 – (7/10) = (3/10)

10. A total of six can be made in any of the following ways (1 + 5, 2 + 4, 3 + 3, 4 + 2, 5 + 1)

11. The event definitions are:

    (a) Passes the first AND Passes the second AND Passes the third AND Passes the fourth

    (b) Fails the first AND Fails the second AND Fails the third AND Fails the fourth

    (c) Fails all is the non-event.

12. (i) First is cricket and second is cricket and third is cricket $\rightarrow (3/9) \times (3/9) \times (3/9) = (1/27)$

    (ii) $(2/9) \times (3/9) \times (4/9) = (8/243)$

    (iii) All are cricket or all are tennis or all are squash. $(3/9)^3 + (2/9)^3 + (4/9)^3 = (99/729) = (11/81)$

13. (i) $(3/9) \times (2/8) \times (1/7) = (1/84)$

    (ii) $(2/9) \times (3/8) \times (4/7) = (1/21)$

    (iii) $(3/9) \times (2/8) \times (1/7) + 0 + (4/9) \times (3/8) \times (2/7)$

    30/504 = 5/84

14. The event definitions are

    (i) The book transferred is by Stephen Covey

    (ii) The book transferred is by Vinay Singh AND The book picked up is by Stephen Covey

    (iii) The book transferred is by Stephen Covey AND The book picked up is by Vinay Singh.

15. $(2/3) \times (3/4) + (1/3) \times (2/7) = (1/2) + (2/21) = (25/42)$

16. (i) $(3/50) \times (2/49) = (3/1225)$

    (ii) $(3/50) \times (47/49) + 47/50 \times (3/49) = (141/1225)$

    (iii) $(47/50) \times (46/49) = (1081/1225)$

17. (i) $(3/5) \times (3/7) = (9/35)$

    (ii) $(3/5) \times 4/7) = (12/35)$

(iii) $(2/5) \times (3/7) = (6/35)$

(iv) $(3/5) \times (4/7) + (2/5) \times (3/7) + (3/5) \times (3/7) = 27/35$

18. They will contradict each other if: $A$ is true and $B$ is false or $A$ is false and $B$ is true.

$$(3/4) \times (1/6) + (1/4) \times (5/6) = 1/3.$$

19. For the counting of the number of events, think of it as a circular arrangement with $n - 1$ people (by considering the two specified persons as one). This will give you $n(E) = (n - 2)! \times (2)!$

20. The whole numbers selected can only be 1, 3, 7 or 9 and cannot contain 2, 4, 6, 8, 0 or 5.

21. $^4C_2 \times (6/36)^2 \times (30/36)^2 = 6 \times (1/36) \times (25/36) = 25/216.$

22. The required probability will be given by the expression:

$$\frac{\text{The number of young boys who will die}}{\text{The total number of people who will die}}$$

23. Girl and Boy and Boy or Boy and Girl and Boy

Or

Boy and Boy and Girl

$= (3/4) \times (2/4) \times (2/3) + (1/4) \times (2/4) \times (2/3)$
$\qquad + (1/4) \times (2/4) \times (1/3) = 18/48 = 3/8.$

24. $n(E) = 1$

$n(S) = {}^3C_1 \times 9 \times 9 = 243$

25. 11/17 (if the first one is black, there will be 11 black balls left out of 17)

26. 6/17

27. There must have been two sixes in the first five throws. Thus, the answer is given by:

$$^5C_2 \times \frac{1}{6} \times \frac{1}{6} \times \frac{1}{6} \times \frac{5}{6} \times \frac{5}{6} \times \frac{5}{6}$$

28. $\dfrac{^{13}C_1 \times {}^{13}C_1 \times {}^{13}C_1 \times {}^{13}C_1}{^{52}C_4}$

29. There will be $^6C_3$ triangles formed overall. Out of these visualise the number of equilateral triangles.

30. $(5/9) \times (4/8) + (4/9) \times (3/8) = 32/72 = 4/9$

As matched shoes means both red or both black.

31. The event definition here is that first is not a heart and second is not a heart and third is a heart $= (3/4) \times (3/4) \times (1/4) = 9/64.$

32. $(39/52) \times (38/51) \times (13/50) = 247/1700.$

33. The event definition will be: Event $X$ happens and $Y$ doesn't happen Or $Y$ happens and $X$ does not happen.

34. $X$ happens and $Y$ does not happen or $X$ doesn't happen and $Y$ happens or $X$ happens and $Y$ happens

$$P \times (1 - P-) + (1 - P) \times P' + P \times P' = P + P' - PP'$$

35. Same logic as question 6.

36. $(2/4) \times (1/3) = 1/6.$ ( Faulty and faulty)

37. Faulty and not Faulty and Faulty or Not Faulty and Faulty and Faulty $= (2/4) \times (2/3) \times (1/2) + (2/4) \times (2/3) \times (1/2) = 1/3.$

38. When you put the 7 balls with a gap between them in a row, you will have 8 spaces.

39. The appearance of head or tail on a toss is independent of previous occurrences.

Hence, 1/2.

40. $\dfrac{3! \times 4!}{7!} = 1/35.$

41. $P = \dfrac{\text{No. of arrangements with four S together}}{\text{Total No. of arrangements}}$

$$= \frac{[8!(4! \times 2!)]}{[11!/(4! \times 4! \times 2!)]}$$

$$= 8! \times 4!/11! = 24/990 = 4/165.$$

42. $\dfrac{(5! \times 4! \times 2! \times 3!)}{11!} = \dfrac{24 \times 2 \times 6}{11 \times 10 \times 9 \times 8 \times 7 \times 6} = 1/1155.$

43. $(1/3) \times (1/4) \times (4/5) + (1/3) \times (3/4) \times (1/5) + (2/3) \times (1/4) \times (1/5) + (1/3) \times (1/4) \times (1/5)$
$= 10/60 = 1/6.$

44. $^5C_3 \times [ (8/12) \times (7/11) \times (6/10) \times (4/9) \times (3/8)] = 14/33.$

45. $^5C_3 \times {}^6C_1/{}^{11}C_4 = 2/11$

46.
$$P = \frac{\text{Total no of ways in which two people sit together}}{\text{Total No. of ways}}$$

$$= (10! \times 2!)/11!$$

47. Consider the 6 girls to be one person. Then the number of arrangements satisfying the condition is given by $n(E) = 7! \times 6!$

48. $^6C_2 \times [ (7/11) \times (6/10) \times (5/9) \times (4/8) \times (4/7) \times (3/6)]$
$\qquad = 5/11.$

49. The event definition is Red AND Red AND Not Red OR Red AND Not Red AND Red OR Not Red AND Red AND Red.

50. The numbers having 2 in them are: 2, 12, 22, 32....92 and 21, 23, 24, 25....29. Hence, $n(E) = 19.$

## Level of Difficulty (III)

1. This problem has to be treated as if we are selecting the third card out of the 50 remaining cards.

11 of these are spades.

Hence, 11/50.

2.

| | Chance that A will win | Chance that B will win |
|---|---|---|
| First throw | $\dfrac{1}{6}$ | $\dfrac{5}{6} \times \dfrac{1}{6}$ |
| Second throw | $\dfrac{5}{6} \times \dfrac{5}{6} \times \dfrac{1}{6}$ | $\dfrac{5}{6} \times \dfrac{5}{6} \times \dfrac{5}{6} \times \dfrac{1}{6}$ |
| Third throw | $\dfrac{5}{6} \times \dfrac{5}{6} \times \dfrac{5}{6} \times \dfrac{5}{6} \times \dfrac{1}{6}$ | $\dfrac{5}{6} \times \dfrac{5}{6} \times \dfrac{5}{6} \times \dfrac{5}{6} \times \dfrac{5}{6} \times \dfrac{1}{6}$ |

The chance that $A$ will win is an infinite GP with a $= \dfrac{1}{6}$ and $r = \dfrac{25}{36}$.

Similarly, the chance that $B$ will win is an infinite GP with $a = \dfrac{5}{36}$ and $r = \dfrac{25}{36}$.

3. A total of 6 can be obtained by either $(1 + 2 + 3)$ or by $(2 + 2 + 2)$.

4. $A$ is true and $B$ is true $= (3/4) \times (7/10) = (21/40)$.

5. The required probability will be given by:

$$\dfrac{\text{Percentage of defective from } C}{\text{Percentage of defectives from } A, B \text{ and } C}$$

6. and 7.

We do not have to consider any sum other than 5 or 7 occurring.

A sum of 5 can be obtained by any of $[4 + 1, 3 + 2, 2 + 3, 1 + 4]$

Similarly a sum of 7 can be obtained by any of $[6 + 1, 5 + 2, 4 + 3, 3 + 4, 2 + 5, 1 + 6]$

For 6:    $n(E) = 4$, $n(S) = 6 + 4$

         $P = 0.4$

For 7:    $n(E) = 6$

         $n(S) = 6 + 4$     $P = 0.6$

8. The number of ways for a sum of 4 = 3 i.e. $[3 + 1, 2 + 2, 1 + 3]$

9. Try to find the number of ways in which 0 or 1 bomb hits the bridge if $n$ bombs are thrown.

The required value of the number of bombs will be such that the probability of 0 or 1 bomb hitting the bridge should be less than 0.1.

10. The required probability will be given by: $1 - [^nC_0 + {}^nC_1] \left(\dfrac{1}{2}\right)^n$ for $n = 5$.

11. The required answer will be given by:

$$\dfrac{\text{P (Kesari does not receive the letter)}}{\begin{array}{c}\text{P (Kesari does not receive the letter)} + \\ \text{P (Kesari replied and Sanjay did not} \\ \text{receive the reply)}\end{array}}$$

12. $n(E) = {}^6C_2 \times 16 \times 15 \times 14 \times 13 \times 12$

    $n(S) = 16^6$

13. The number of events for the condition that he will sing = 4. [34, 43, 26, 62]

The number of events in the sample = 90.

Probability that he will sing at least once

= 1 − Probability that he will not sing.

14. The required probability would be given by the event definition:

First is white and second is white = $8/22 \times 7/21 = 4/33$

15. The required probability would be given by the event definition:

First is red and second is red = $5/22 \times 4/21 = 10/231$

16. The number of ways in which 6 tickets can be selected from 10 tickets is $10^6$.

The number of ways in which the selection can be done so that the condition is satisfied = $7^6 - 6^6$.

17. In the first draw, we have 7 even tickets out of 15 and in the second we have 8 odd tickets out of 15.

Thus, $(7/15) \times (8/15) = 56/225$.

18. The total number of ways in which the 6 identical balls can be distributed amongst the three boxes such that each box can get 0, 1, 2, 3, 4, 5 or 6 balls is given by the formula: $^{n+r-1}C_r$ where $n$ is the number of identical balls and $r$ is the number of boxes. This will give the sample space.

19. Event definition:

Any six of them work AND four leave OR any seven work AND three leave OR any eight work AND two leave OR any nine work AND one leaves OR All ten work.

20. "To make at least 3 trials to draw a heart" implies that he didn't get a heart in the first two trials.

21. A box containing 4 defectives would get sent to the market if all the 4 articles selected are not defective.

Thus, $^{16}C_4/^{20}C_4 = 364/969$

22. If the box contains only 1 defective, it would be sent back if the defective is one amongst the 4 selected for testing.

To ensure one of the 4 is selected, the no. of ways is $^{19}C_3$, while the total no. of selections of 4 out of 20 is $^{20}C_4$.

Thus, $^{19}C_3/^{20}C_4 = 1/5$.

23. For divisibility by 5 we need the units digit to be either 0 or 5.

The units digit in the powers of 7 follow the pattern − 7, 9, 3, 1, 7, 9, 3, 1, 7, 9.......

Hence, divide 1 to 100 into four groups of 25 elements each as follows.

       $A = 1, 5, 9, ------ \rightarrow 25$ elements

       $B = 2, 6, 10, ------ \rightarrow 25$ elements

       $C = 3, 7, 11, ------ \rightarrow 25$ elements

       $D = 4, 8, 12, ------ \rightarrow 25$ elements

Check the combination values of $m$ and $n$ so that $7^m + 7^n$ is divisible by 5.

24. $P(\text{minimum 3})$ or $P(\text{maximum 7})$

$P(\text{minimum 3}) = {}^7C_2/{}^{10}C_3 = 21/120$

$P(\text{max 7}) = {}^6C_2/{}^{10}C_2 = 15/120$

---

**Note:** The logic for this can be explained for minimum 3 conditions as: Since the minimum value has to be 3, the remaining 2 numbers have to be selected from 4 to 10. This can be done in ${}^7C_2$ ways.

---

25. For the event to occur, the dice should show values from 2, 3, 4 or 5. This is similar to selection with repetition.

26. Yellow and Red and Blue $= (3/6) \times (2/6) \times (1/6)$
$= (6/216) = 1/36$.

27. Two white and one black can be obtained only through the following three sequences:

Ball drawn from $A$ and $B$ are white and the ball drawn from $C$ is Black.     or

Ball drawn from $A$ and $C$ are white and the ball drawn from $B$ is Black.     or

Ball drawn from $B$ and $C$ are white and the ball drawn from $A$ is Black.

28. At least one means (exactly one + exactly two + exactly three)

At least two means (exactly two + exactly three)

The problem gives the probabilities for passing in at least one, at least two and exactly two.

29. All four are not in the correct envelopes means that at least one of them is in a wrong envelope. A little consideration will show that one letter being placed in a wrong envelope is not possible, since it will have to be interchanged with some other letter.

Since, there is only one way to put all the letters in the correct envelopes, we can say that the event of not all four letters going into the correct envelopes will be given by

$5! - 1 = 119$

30. $n(E) = 44$

$n(S) = 120$

31. $A_1 = (112 \text{ or } 121)$

$A_2 = (112 \text{ or } 211)$

$A_3 = (121 \text{ or } 211)$

Option (b) is correct.

32.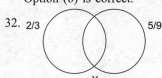
2/3          5/9

X

From the venn diagram we get:

$(2/3) + (5/9) - x = 4/5 \rightarrow x = (2/3) + (5/9) - (4/5)$
$= 19/45$

33.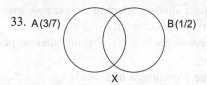
A (3/7)          B (1/2)

X

Also $P(A \cup B) = 1 - P(A' \cap B')$

$(3/7) + (1/2) - x = 13/14 \rightarrow x = 0$

Thus, there is no interference between $A$ and $B$ as $P(A \cap B) = x = 0$. Hence, $A$ and $B$ are mutually exclusive.

34. The required probability will be given by $\dfrac{2 \times 6! \times 6!}{12!}$.

35. The non-event in this case is that the problem is not solved.

36-37. Are similar to Question No. 2 of LOD III.

38. The event definition will be:

The first bag is selected AND a red ball is selected. OR

The second bag is selected AND a red ball is selected.

39. The event definition is:

A girl is selected from the first group and one boy each are selected from the second and third groups. OR A girl is selected from the second group and one boy each are selected from the first and third groups. OR A girl is selected from the third group and one boy each are selected from the first and second groups.

40. The event definition will be:

A solves the problem and $B$ and $C$ do not solve the problem. OR $B$ solves the problem and $A$ and $C$ do not solve the problem. OR $C$ solves the problem and $A$ and $B$ do not solve the problem.

41. The three balls that are taken out can be either 3 black balls or 2 black and 1 red ball or 1 black and 2 red ball or 3 red balls.

Each of these will give their own probabilities of drawing a black ball.

42. 3 Blacks and 4th is Red or 2 Blacks and 1 Red and 4th is Red or 1 Black and 2 Reds and 4th is Red

$= (5/8) \times (4/7) \times (3/6) \times (3/5) + {}^3C_1 \times (5/8) \times (4/7)$
$\times (3/6) \times (2/5) + {}^3C_1 \times (5/8) \times (3/7) \times (2/6) \times (1/5)$

$= \dfrac{180 + 360 + 90}{1680} = 630/1680 = 3/8 = 0.375$

43. The event definition would be: Ball transferred is white and white ball drawn

Or

Ball transferred is black and white ball is drawn.

The answer will be given by:

$(5/9) \times (8/17) + (4/9) \times (7/17) = 68/153 = 4/9$

44. Solve this on a similar pattern to the example given in the theory of this chapter.

45. Required probability = 1 − probability that no pair is selected

46. We can have a maximum of 5 heads.

    For 0 heads → $P(E) = (1/2^{10}) \times 1$

    For 1 heads → $P(E) = (1/2^{10}) \times 1$

    For 2 heads and for them not to occur consecutively we will need to see the possible distribution of 8 tails and 2 heads.

    Since the 2 heads do not need to occur consecutively, this would be given by (All − 2heads together)

    → $({}^{10}C_8 - 9)$

    $$P(E) = \frac{({}^{10}C_8 - 9)}{2^{10}}$$

    Solving in this fashion, we would get $1/2^3$.

47. This can be got by taking the number of ways in which exactly two people are born on the same day divided by the total number of ways in which 7 people can be born in 7 days of a week. For the first part select two people from 7 in ${}^7C_2$ ways & select a day from the week on which they have to be born in ${}^7C_1$ ways & for the remaining 5 people select 5 days out of the remaining six days of the week & then the number of arrangements of these 5 people in 5 days-thus a total of ${}^7C_2 \times {}^7C_1 \times {}^6C_5 \times 5!$ ways. Also, the number of ways in which seven people can be born on 7 days would be given by $7^7$. Hence, the answer is given by: $({}^7C_2 \times {}^7C_1 \times {}^6C_5 \, 5!/7^7) = 21 \times 7 \times 6 \times 120/7^7 = 3 \times 6 \times 120/7^5 = 2160/7^5$.

48. This can be got by defining the number of ways in which the player can get a deal of 13 cards if he gets all four kings divided by the number of ways in which the player can get a deal of 13 cards without any constraints from 52 cards:

    The requisite value would be given by: ${}^{48}C_9/{}^{52}C_{13} = [48!/39! \times 9!] \times [13! \times 39!/52!] = (48! \times 13! \times 39!)/(39! \times 9! \times 52!) = 13 \times 12 \times 11 \times 10/52 \times 51 \times 50 \times 49 = 1 \times 11/17 \times 17 \times 5 \times 49 = 11/4165$

49. $P$ of heads showing on 50 coins $= {}^{100}C_{50} \times P^{50}(1 - p)^{50}$

    $P$ of heads showing on 51 coins $= {}^{100}C_{51} \times P^{51}(1 - p)^{49}$

    Both are equal

    $${}^{100}C_{50} \times P^{50}(1 - P)^{50} = {}^{100}C_{51} \times P^{51}(1 - P)^{49}$$

    or $\dfrac{100 \times 49 \times \ldots \times 52 \times 51}{1 \times 2 \times \ldots \times 49 \times 50} \times (1 - P)$

    $= \dfrac{100 \times 99 \times \ldots \times 53 \times 52}{1 \times 2 \times \ldots \times 48 \times 49} \times P$

    or $\dfrac{51}{50} \times (1 - P) = P$

    or $51 \times (1 - P) = 50 \, P$

    or $51 - 51 \, P = 50 \, P$

    or $51 = 101 \, P$

    $\therefore P = \dfrac{51}{101}$

50. The common side could be horizontal or vertical. Accordingly, the number of ways the event can occur is.

    $n(E) = 8 \times 7 + 8 \times 7 = 112$

    $n(S) = 64C_2$

    $= \dfrac{2 \times 8 \times 7 \times 2}{64 \times 63} = \dfrac{1}{18}$

# 19

# Set Theory

Set Theory is an important concept of mathematics which is often asked in aptitude exams. There are two types of questions in this chapter:

(i) Numerical questions on set theory based on venn diagrams

(ii) Logical questions based on set theory

**Let us first take a look at some standard theoretical inputs related to set theory.**

## ⬤ SET THEORY

**Look at the following diagrams:**

**Figure 1:** Refers to the situation where there are two attributes $A$ and $B$. (Let's say $A$ refers to people who passed in Physics and $B$ refers to people who passed in Chemistry.) Then the shaded area shows the people who passed both in Physics and Chemistry.

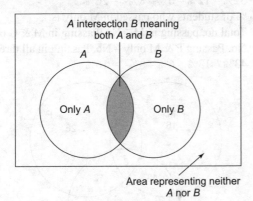

In mathematical terms, the situation is represented as:
Total number of people who passed at least 1 subject = $A + B - A \cap B$

**Figure 2:** Refers to the situation where there are three attributes being measured. In the figure below, we are talking about people who passed Physics, Chemistry and/or Mathematics.

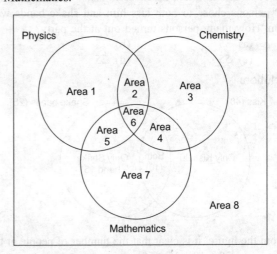

**In the above figure, the following explain the respective areas:**

**Area 1:** People who passed in Physics only

**Area 2:** People who passed in Physics and Chemistry only (in other words—people who passed Physics and Chemistry but not Mathematics)

**Area 3:** People who passed Chemistry only

**Area 4:** People who passed Chemistry and Mathematics only (also, can be described as people who passed Chemistry and Mathematics but not Physics)

**Area 5:** People who passed Physics and Mathematics only (also, can be described as people who passed Physics and Mathematics but not Chemistry)

**Area 6:** People who passed Physics, Chemistry and Mathematics

**Area 7:** People who passed Mathematics only

**Area 8:** People who passed in no subjects

Also take note of the following language which there is normally confusion about:

People passing Physics and Chemistry—Represented by the sum of areas 2 and 6

People passing Physics and Maths—Represented by the sum of areas 5 and 6

People passing Chemistry and Maths—Represented by the sum of areas 4 and 6

People passing Physics—Represented by the sum of the areas 1, 2, 5 and 6

**In mathematical terms, this means:**

Total number of people who passed at least 1 subject = $P + C + M - P \cap C - P \cap M - C \cap M + P \cap C \cap M$

**Let us consider the following questions and see how these figures work in terms of real time problem solving:**

## Illustration 1

At the birthday party of Sherry, a baby boy, 40 persons chose to kiss him and 25 chose to shake hands with him. 10 persons chose to both kiss him and shake hands with him. How many persons turned out at the party?

    (a) 35                  (b) 75

    (c) 55                  (d) 25

**Solution:**

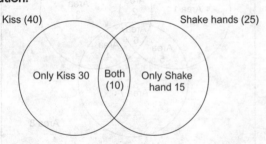

Kiss (40)                         Shake hands (25)

Only Kiss 30   Both (10)   Only Shake hand 15

From the figure, it is clear that the number of people at the party were $30 + 10 + 15 = 55$.

We can of course solve this mathematically as below:

Let $n(A)$ = No. of persons who kissed Sherry = 40

$n(B)$ = No. of persons who shake hands with Sherry = 25

and $n(A \cap B)$ = No. of persons who shook hands with Sherry and kissed him both = 10

Then using the formula, $n(A \cup B) = n(A) + n(B) - n(A \cap B)$

$n(A \cup B) = 40 + 25 - 10 = 55$

## Illustration 2

**Directions for Questions 1 to 4:** Refer to the data below and answer the questions that follow:

In an examination 43% passed in Math, 52% passed in Physics and 52% passed in Chemistry. Only 8% students passed in all the three. 14% passed in Math and Physics

and 21% passed in Math and Chemistry and 20% passed in Physics and Chemistry. Number of students who took the exam is 200.

Let Set P, Set C and Set M denotes the students who passed in Physics, Chemistry and Math respectively. Then

1. How many students passed in Math only?
    (a) 16                  (b) 32
    (c) 48                  (d) 80

2. Find the ratio of students passing in Math only to the students passing in Chemistry only?
    (a) 16:37            (b) 29:32
    (c) 16:19            (d) 31:49

3. What is the ratio of the number of students passing in Physics only to the students passing in either Physics or Chemistry or both?
    (a) 34/46           (b) 26/84
    (c) 49/32           (d) None of these

4. A student is declared pass in the exam only if he/she clears at least two subjects. The number of students who were declared passed in this exam is?
    (a) 33                  (b) 66
    (c) 39                  (d) 78

**Sol.** Let P denote Physics, C denote Chemistry and M denote Maths.

% of students who passed in P and C only is given by % of students who passed in P and C - % of students who passed all three = 20% – 8% = 12%

% of students who passed in P and M only is given by % of students who passed in P and M - % of students who passed all three = 14% – 8% = 6%

% of students who passed in M and C only is:

% of students who passed in C and M - % of students who passed all three = 21% – 8% = 13%

So, % of students who passed in P only is given by:

Total no. passing in P – No. Passing in P & C only – No. Passing P & M only – No. Passing in all three→

52% – 12% – 6% – 8%- = 26%

% of students who passed in M only is:

Total no. passing in M – No. Passing in M & C only – No. Passing P & M only – No. Passing in all three→

43% – 13% – 6% – 8%- = 16%

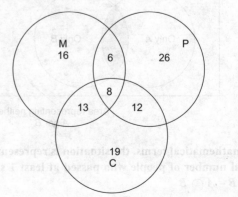

M 16       6       P 26

8

13       12

19 C

% of students who passed in Chemistry only is
Total no. passing in C – No. Passing in P & C only – No.
Passing C & M only – No. Passing in all three →
52% – 12% – 13% – 8%– = 19%

The answers are:

1.  Only Math =16% = 32 people. Option (b) is correct.
2.  Ratio of Only Math to Only Chemistry = 16:19. Option (c) is correct.
3.  26:84 is the required ratio. Option (b) is correct.
4.  39 % or 78 people. Option (d) is correct.

## Illustration 3

In the Mindworkzz club all the members participate either in the Tambola or the Fete. 320 participate in the Fete, 350 participate in the Tambola and 220 participate in both. How many members does the club have?

(a)  410
(b)  550
(c)  440
(d)  None of these

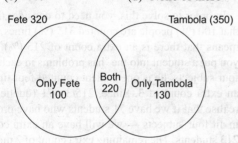

Fete 320    Tambola (350)

Only Fete 100    Both 220    Only Tambola 130

The total number of people = 100 + 220 + 130 = 450
Option (d) is correct.

## Illustration 4

There are 20000 people living in Defence Colony, Gurgaon. Out of them 9000 subscribe to Star TV Network and 12000 to Zee TV Network. If 4000 subscribe to both, how many do not subscribe to any of the two?

(a)  3000
(b)  2000
(c)  1000
(d)  4000

Star TV (9000)    Zee TV (12000)

Only Star TV =
9000 – 4000
= 5000
Both
4000
Only Zee TV =
12000 – 4000
= 8000

The required answer would be 20000 – 5000 – 4000 – 8000 = 3000.

## Illustration 5

***Directions for Questions 1 to 3:*** Refer to the data below and answer the questions that follow.

Last year, there were 3 sections in the Catalyst, a mock CAT paper. Out of them 33 students cleared the cut-off in Section 1, 34 students cleared the cut-off in Section 2 and 32 cleared the cut-off in Section 3. 10 students cleared the cut-off in Section 1 and Section 2, 9 cleared the cut-off in Section 2 and Section 3, 8 cleared the cut-off in Section 1 and Section 3. The number of people who cleared each section alone was equal and was 21 for each section.

1.  How many cleared all the three sections?
    (a)  3
    (b)  6
    (c)  5
    (d)  7
2.  How many cleared only one of the three sections?
    (a)  21
    (b)  63
    (c)  42
    (d)  52
3.  The ratio of the number of students clearing the cut-off in one or more of the sections to the number of students clearing the cutoff in Section 1 alone is?
    (a)  78/21
    (b)  3
    (c)  73/21
    (d)  None of these

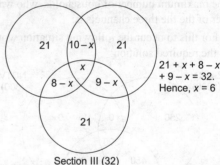

Section I (33)    Section II (34)

21    $10 - x$    21

$x$

$8 - x$    $9 - x$

$21 + x + 8 - x$
$+ 9 - x = 32.$
Hence, $x = 6$

21

Section III (32)

**Since, $x = 6$, the figure becomes:**

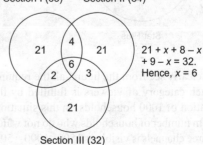

Section I (33)    Section II (34)

21    4    21

6

2    3

$21 + x + 8 - x$
$+ 9 - x = 32.$
Hence, $x = 6$

21

Section III (32)

The answers would be:

1.  6. Option (b) is correct.
2.  21+21+21=63. Option (b) is correct.
3.  (21+21+21+6+4+3+2)/21 = 78/21. Option (a) is correct.

## Illustration 6

In a locality having 1500 households, 1000 watch Zee TV, 300 watch NDTV and 750 watch Star Plus. Based on this information answer the questions that follow:

1. The minimum number of households watching Zee TV and Star Plus is:

   **Logic:** If we try to consider each of the households watching Zee TV and Star Plus as independent of each other, we would get a total of 1000 + 750 = 1750 households. However, we have a total of only 1500 households in the locality and hence, there has to be a minimum interference of at least 250 households who would be watching both Zee TV and Star Plus. Hence, the answer to this question is 250.

2. The minimum number of households watching both Zee TV and NDTV is:

   In this case, the number of households watching Zee TV and NDTV can be separate from each other since there is no interference required between the households watching Zee TV and the households watching NDTV as their individual sum (1000 + 300) is smaller than the 1500 available households in the locality. Hence, the answer in this question is 0.

3. The maximum number of households who watch neither of the the three channels is:

   For this to occur the following situation would give us the required solution:

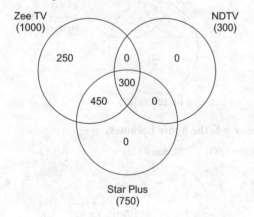

Zee TV
(1000)

NDTV
(300)

250　　0　　0

300

450　　0

0

Star Plus
(750)

As you can clearly see from the figure, all the requirements of each category of viewers is fulfilled by the given allocation of 1000 households. In this situation, the maximum number of households who do not watch any of the three channels is visible as 1500 – 1000 = 500.

## Illustration 7

1. In a school, 90% of the students faced problems in Mathematics, 80% of the students faced problems in Computers, 75% of the students faced problems in Sciences, and 70% of the students faced problems in Social Sciences. Find the minimum percent of the students who faced problems in all four subjects.

   **Solution:** In order to think about the minimum number of students who faced problems in all four subjects you would need to think of keeping the students who did not face a problem in any of the subjects separate from each other. We know that 30% of the students did not face problems in Social Sciences, 25% of the students did not face problems in Sciences, 20% students did not face problems in computers and 10% students did not face problems in Mathematics. If each of these were separate from each other, we would have 30+25+20+10=85% people who did not face a problem in one of the four subjects. Naturally, the remaining 15% would be students who faced problems in all four subjects. This represents the minimum percentage of students who faced problems in all the four subjects.

2. For the above question, find the maximum possible percentage of students who could have problems in all 4 subjects.

   In order to solve this, you need to consider the fact that 100 (%) people are counted 315 (%) times, which means that there is an extra count of 215 (%). When you put a student into the 'has problems in each of the four subjects' he is one student counted four times — an extra count of 3. Since, 215/3= 71 (quotient) we realise that if we have 71 students who have problems in all four subjects — we will have an extra count of 213 students. The remaining extra count of 2 more can be matched by putting 1 student in 'has problems in 3 subjects' or by putting 2 students in 'has problems in 2 subjects'. Thus, from the extra count angle, we have a limit of 71% students in the 'have problems in all four categories.'

   However, in this problem there is a constraint from another angle — i.e. there are only 70% students who have a problem in Social Sciences — and hence it is not possible for 71% students to have problems in all the four subjects. Hence, the maximum possible percentage of people who have a problem in all four subjects would be 70%.

3. In the above question if it is known that 10% of the students faced none of the above mentioned four problems, what would have been the minimum number of students who would have a problem in all four subjects?

   If there are 10% students who face none of the four problems, we realise that these 10% would be common to students who face no problems in Mathematics, students who face no problems in Sciences, students who face no problems in Computers and students who face no problems in Social Sciences.

   Now, we also know that overall there are 10% students who did not face a problem in Mathematics; 20%

students who did not face a problem in computers; 25% students who did not face a problem in Sciences and 30% students who did not face a problem in Social Sciences. The 10% students who did not face a problem in any of the subjects would be common to each of these 4 counts. Out of the remaining 90% students, if we want to identify the minimum number of students who had a problem in all four subjects we will take the same approach as we took in the first question of this set — i.e. we try to keep the students having problems in the individual subjects separate from each other. This would result in: ·0% additional students having no problem in Mathematics; 10% additional students having no problem in Computers; 15% additional students having no problem in Sciences and 20% additional students having no problem in Social Sciences. Thus, we would get a total of 45% (0+10+15+20=45) students who would have no problem in one of the four subjects. Thus, the minimum percentage of students who had a problem in all four subjects would be 90 – 45 = 45%.

# Illustration 8

In a class of 80 students, each of them studies at least one language—English, Hindi and Sanskrit. It was found that 65 studied English, 60 studied Hindi and 55 studied Sanskrit.

1. Find the maximum number of people who study all three languages.

   This question again has to be dealt with from the perspective of extra counting. In this question, 80 students in the class are counted 65 + 60 + 55 = 180 times — an extra count of 100. If we put 50 people in the all three categories as shown below, we would get the maximum number of students who study all three languages.

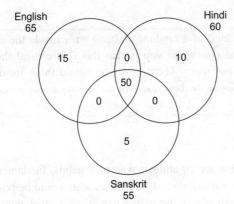

2. Find the minimum number of people who study all three languages.

   In order to think about how many students are necessarily in the 'study all three languages' area of the figure (this thinking would lead us to the answer to

the minimum number of people who study all three languages) we need to think about how many people we can shift out of the 'study all three category' for the previous question. When we try to do that, the following thought process emerges:

**Step 1:** Let's take a random value for the all three categories (less than 50 of course) and see whether the numbers can be achieved. For this purpose we try to start with the value as 40 and see what happens. Before we move on, realise the basic situation in the question remains the same — 80 students have been counted 180 times — which means that there is an extra count of 100 students & also realise that when you put an individual student in the all three categories, you get an extra count of 2, while at the same time when you put an individual student into the 'exactly two languages category', he/she is counted twice — hence an extra count of 1. The starting figure we get looks something like this:

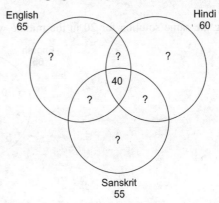

At this point, since we have placed 40 people in the all three categories, we have taken care of an extra count of $40 \times 2 = 80$. This leaves us with an extra count of 20 more to manage and as we can see in the above figure we have a lot of what can be described as 'slack' to achieve the required numbers. For instance, one solution we can think of from this point is as below:

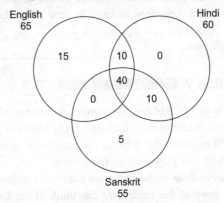

One look at this figure should tell you that the solution can be further optimised by reducing the middle value in the figure since there is still a lot of 'slack' in the figure — in the form of the number of students in the 'exactly one language category'. Also, you can easily see that there are many ways in which this solution could have been achieved with 40 in the middle. Hence, we go in search of a lower value in the middle.

So, we try to take an arbitrary value of 30 to see whether this is still achievable.

In this case we see the following as one of the possible ways to achieve this (again there is a lot of slack in this solution as the 'only Hindi' or the 'only Sanskrit' areas can be reallocated):

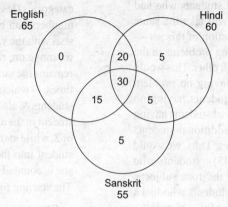

Trying the same solution for 20 in the middle we get the optimum solution:

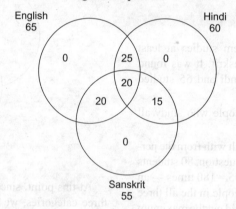

We realise that this is the optimum solution since there is no 'slack' in this solution and hence, there is no scope for re-allocating numbers from one area to another.

***Author's note:***  You might be justifiably thinking how do you do this kind of a random trial and error inside the exam? That's not the point of this question at this place. What I am trying to convey to you is that this is a critical thought structure which you need to have in your mind. Learn it here and do not worry about how you would think inside the exam — remember you would need to check only the four options to choose the best one. We are talking about a multiple choice test here.

## Illustration 9

In a group of 120 athletes, the number of athletes who can play Tennis, Badminton, Squash and Table Tennis is 70, 50, 60 and 30 respectively. What is the maximum number of athletes who can play none of the games?

In order to think of the maximum number of athletes who can play none of the games, we can think of the fact that

since there are 70 athletes who play tennis, fundamentally there are a maximum of 50 athletes who would be possibly in the 'can play none of the games'. No other constraint in the problem necessitates a reduction of this number and hence the answer to this question is 50.

## LEVEL OF DIFFICULTY (I)

**Directions for Questions 1 and 2:** Refer to the data below and answer the questions that follow:

In the Indian athletic squad sent to the Olympics, 21 athletes were in the triathlon team; 26 were in the pentathlon team; and 29 were in the marathon team. 14 athletes can take part in triathlon and pentathlon; 12 can take part in marathon and triathlon; 15 can take part in pentathlon and marathon; and 8 can take part in all the three games.

1. How many players are there in all?
   - (a) 35
   - (b) 43
   - (c) 49
   - (d) none of these

2. How many were in the marathon team only?
   - (a) 10
   - (b) 14
   - (c) 18
   - (d) 15

**Directions for Questions 3 and 4:** Refer to the data below and answer the questions that follow.

In a test in which 120 students appeared, 90 passed in History, 65 passed in Sociology and 75 passed in Political Science. 30 students passed in only one subject and 55 students in only two. 5 students passed no subjects.

3. How many students passed in all the three subjects?
   - (a) 25
   - (b) 30
   - (c) 35
   - (d) Data insufficient

4. Find the number of students who passed in at least two subjects.
   - (a) 85
   - (b) 95
   - (c) 90
   - (d) Data insufficient

**Directions for Questions 5 to 8:** Refer to the data below and answer the questions that follow.

5% of the passengers who boarded Guwahati- New Delhi Rajdhani Express on 20th February, 2002 do not like coffee, tea and ice cream and 10% like all the three. 20% like coffee and tea, 25% like ice cream and coffee and 25% like ice cream and tea. 55% like coffee, 50% like tea and 50 % like ice cream.

5. The number of passengers who like only coffee is greater than the passengers who like only ice cream by
   - (a) 50%
   - (b) 100%
   - (c) 25%
   - (d) 0

6. The percentage of passengers who like both tea and ice cream but not coffee is
   - (a) 15
   - (b) 5
   - (c) 10
   - (d) 25

7. The percentage of passengers who like at least 2 of the 3 products is
   - (a) 40
   - (b) 45
   - (c) 50
   - (d) 60

8. If the number of passengers is 180, then the number of passengers who like ice cream only is

   - (a) 10
   - (b) 18
   - (c) 27
   - (d) 36

**Directions for Questions 9 to 15:** Refer to the data below and answer the questions that follow.

In a survey among students at all the IIMs, it was found that 48% preferred coffee, 54% liked tea and 64% smoked. Of the total, 28% liked coffee and tea, 32% smoked and drank tea and 30% smoked and drank coffee. Only 6% did none of these. If the total number of students is 2000 then find

9. The ratio of the number of students who like only coffee to the number who like only tea is
   - (a) 5:3
   - (b) 8:9
   - (c) 2:3
   - (d) 3:2

10. Number of students who like coffee and smoking but not tea is
    - (a) 600
    - (b) 240
    - (c) 280
    - (d) 360

11. The percentage of those who like coffee or tea but not smoking among those who like at least one of these is
    - (a) more than 30
    - (b) less than 30
    - (c) less than 25
    - (d) None of these

12. The percentage of those who like at least one of these is
    - (a) 100
    - (b) 90
    - (c) Nil
    - (d) 94

13. The two items having the ratio 1:2 are
    - (a) Tea only and tea and smoking only.
    - (b) Coffee and smoking only and tea only.
    - (c) Coffee and tea but not smoking and smoking but not coffee and tea.
    - (d) None of these

14. The number of persons who like coffee and smoking only and the number who like tea only bear a ratio
    - (a) 1:2
    - (b) 1:1
    - (c) 5:1
    - (d) 2:1

15. Percentage of those who like tea and smoking but not coffee is
    - (a) 14
    - (b) 14.9
    - (c) less than 14
    - (d) more than 15

16. 30 monkeys went to a picnic. 25 monkeys chose to irritate cows while 20 chose to irritate buffaloes. How many chose to irritate both buffaloes and cows?
    - (a) 10
    - (b) 15
    - (c) 5
    - (d) 20

**Directions for Questions 17 to 20:** Refer to the data below and answer the questions that follow.

In the CBSE Board Exams last year, 53% passed in Biology, 61% passed in English, 60% in Social Studies, 24% in Biology & English, 35% in English & Social

Studies, 27% in Biology and Social Studies and 5% in none.

17. Percentage of passes in all subjects is
    (a) Nil
    (b) 12
    (c) 7
    (d) 10

18. If the number of students in the class is 200, how many passed in only one subject?
    (a) 48
    (b) 46
    (c) more than 50
    (d) less than 40

19. If the number of students in the class is 300, what will be the % change in the number of passes in only two subjects, if the original number of students is 200?
    (a) more than 50%
    (b) less than 50%
    (c) 50%
    (d) None of these

20. What is the ratio of percentage of passes in Biology and Social Studies but not English in relation to the percentage of passes in Social Studies and English but not Biology?
    (a) 5:7
    (b) 7:5
    (c) 4:5
    (d) None of these

**Directions for Questions 21 to 25:** Refer to the data below and answer the questions that follow.

In the McGraw-Hill Mindworkzz Quiz held last year, participants were free to choose their respective areas from which they were asked questions. Out of 880 participants, 224 chose Mythology, 240 chose Science and 336 chose Sports, 64 chose both Sports and Science, 80 chose Mythology and Sports, 40 chose Mythology and Science and 24 chose all the three areas.

21. The percentage of participants who did not choose any area is
    (a) 23.59%
    (b) 30.25%
    (c) 37.46%
    (d) 27.27%

22. Of those participating, the percentage who choose only one area is
    (a) 60%
    (b) more than 60%
    (c) less than 60%
    (d) more than 75%

23. Number of participants who chose at least two areas is
    (a) 112
    (b) 24
    (c) 136
    (d) None of these

24. Which of the following areas shows a ratio of 1:8?
    (a) Mythology & Science but not Sports: Mythology only
    (b) Mythology & Sports but not Science: Science only
    (c) Science: Sports
    (d) None of these

25. The ratio of students choosing Sports & Science but not Mythology to Science but not Mythology & Sports is
    (a) 2:5
    (b) 1:4
    (c) 1:5
    (d) 1:2

**Directions for Questions 26 to 30:** Refer to the data below and answer the questions that follow.

The table here gives the distribution of students according to professional courses.

| Courses | STUDENTS | | | |
| | English | | Maths | |
| | MALES | FEMALES | MALES | FEMALES |
| --- | --- | --- | --- | --- |
| Part-time MBA | 30 | 10 | 50 | 10 |
| Full-time MBA only | 150 | 8 | 16 | 6 |
| CA only | 90 | 10 | 37 | 3 |
| Full time MBA & CA | 70 | 2 | 7 | 1 |

26. What is the percentage of Math students over English students?
    (a) 50.4
    (b) 61.4
    (c) 49.4
    (d) None of these

27. The average number of females in all the courses is (count people doing full-time MBA and CA as a separate course)
    (a) less than 12
    (b) greater than 12
    (c) 12
    (d) None of these

28. The ratio of the number of girls to the number of boys is
    (a) 5:36
    (b) 1:9
    (c) 1:7.2
    (d) None of these

29. The percentage increase in students of full-time MBA only over CA only is
    (a) less than 20
    (b) less than 25
    (c) less than 30
    (d) more than 30

30. The number of students doing full-time MBA or CA is
    (a) 320
    (b) 80
    (c) 160
    (d) None of these.

**Directions for Questions 31 to 34:** Refer to the data below and answer the questions that follow:

A newspaper agent sells The TOI, HT and IN in equal numbers to 302 persons. Seven get HT & IN, twelve get The TOI & IN, nine get The TOI & HT and three get all the three newspapers. The details are given in the Venn diagram:

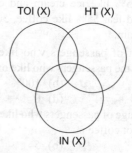

31. How many get only one paper?
    (a) 280
    (b) 327
    (c) 109
    (d) None of these

32. What percent get The TOI or The HT or both (but not The IN)?
    (a) more than 65%
    (b) less than 60%
    (c) ≅ 64%
    (d) None of these.

33. The number of persons buying The TOI and The HT only, The TOI and The IN only and The HT and The IN only are in the ratio of
    - (a) 6:4:9
    - (b) 6:9:4
    - (c) 4:9:6
    - (d) None of these

34. The difference between the number reading The HT and The IN only and HT only is
    - (a) 77
    - (b) 78
    - (c) 83
    - (d) None of these.

35. A group of 78 people watch Zee TV, Star Plus or Sony. Of these, 36 watch Zee TV, 48 watch Star Plus and 32 watch Sony. If 14 people watch both Zee TV and Star Plus, 20 people watch both Star Plus and Sony, and 12 people watch both Sony and Zee TV find the ratio of the number of people who watch only Zee TV to the number of people who watch only Sony.
    - (a) 9:4
    - (b) 3:2
    - (c) 5:3
    - (d) 7:4

**Directions for Questions 36 and 37:** Answer the questions based on the following information.

The following data was observed from a study of car complaints received from 180 respondents at Colonel Verma's car care workshop, viz., engine problem, transmission problem or mileage problem. Of those surveyed, there was no one who faced exactly two of these problems. There were 90 respondents who faced engine problems, 120 who faced transmission problems and 150 who faced mileage problems.

36. How many of them faced all the three problems?
    - (a) 45
    - (b) 60
    - (c) 90
    - (d) 20

37. How many of them faced either transmission problems or engine problems?

*Space for Rough Work*

- (a) 30
- (b) 60
- (c) 90
- (d) 40

**Directions for Questions 38 to 42:** given below are five diagrams one of which describes the relationship among the three classes given in each of the five questions that follow. You have to decide which of the diagrams is the most suitable for a particular set of classes.

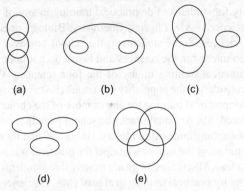

38. Elephants, tigers, animals
39. Administrators, Doctors, Authors
40. Platinum, Copper, Gold
41. Gold, Platinum, Ornaments
42. Television, Radio, Mediums of Entertainment
43. Seventy percent of the employees in a multinational corporation have VCD players, 75 percent have microwave ovens, 80 percent have ACs and 85 percent have washing machines. At least what percentage of employees has all four gadgets?
    - (a) 15
    - (b) 5
    - (c) 10
    - (d) Cannot be determined

## LEVEL OF DIFFICULTY (II)

1. At the Rosary Public School, there are 870 students in the senior secondary classes. The school is widely known for its science education and there is the facility for students to do practical training in any of the 4 sciences – viz: Physics, Chemistry, Biology or Social Sciences. Some students in the school however have no interest in the sciences and hence do not undertake practical training in any of the four sciences. While considering the popularity of various choices for opting for practical training for one or more of the choices offered, Mr. Arvindaksham, the school principal noticed something quite extraordinary. He noticed that for every student in the school who opts for practical training in at least M sciences, there are exactly three students who opt for practical training in at least (M – 1) sciences, for M = 2, 3 and 4. He also found that the number of students who opt for all four sciences was half the number of students who opt for none. Can you help him with the answer to "How many students in the school opt for exactly three sciences?"
   - (a) 30
   - (b) 60
   - (c) 90
   - (d) None of these

2. A bakery sells three kinds of pastries—pineapppple, chocolate and black forest. On a particular day, the bakery owner sold the following number of pastries: 90 pineapple, 120 chocolate and 150 black forest. If none of the customers bought more than two pastries of each type, what is the minimum number of customers that must have visited the bakery that day?
   - (a) 80
   - (b) 75
   - (c) 60
   - (d) 90

3. Gauri Apartment housing society organised annual games, consisting of three games – viz: snooker, badminton and tennis. In all, 510 people were members in the apartments' society and they were invited to participate in the games — each person participating in as many games as he/she feels like. While viewing the statistics of the performance. Mr Capoor realised the following facts. The number of people who participated in at least two games was 52% more than those who participated in exactly one game. The number of people participating in 1, 2 or 3 games respectively was at least equal to 1. Being a numerically inclined person, he further noticed an interesting thing — the number of people who did not participate in any of the three games was the minimum possible integral value with these conditions. What was the maximum number of people who participated in exactly three games?
   - (a) 298
   - (b) 300
   - (c) 303
   - (d) 304

4. A school has 180 students in its senior section where foreign languages are offered to students as part of their syllabus. The foreign languages offered are: French, German and Chinese and the numbers of people studying each of these subjects are 80, 90 and 100 respectively. The number of students who study more than one of the three subjects is 50% more than the number of students who study all the three subjects. There are no students in the school who study none of the three subjects. Then how many students study all three foreign languages?
   - (a) 18
   - (b) 24
   - (c) 36
   - (d) 40

**Directions for Questions 5 and 6:** Answer the questions on the basis of the information given below.

In the second year, the Hampard Business School students are offered a choice of the specialisations they wish to study from amongst only three specialisations —Marketing, Finance and HR. The number of students who have specialised in only Marketing, only Finance and only HR are all numbers in an Arithmetic Progression—in no particular order. Similarly, the number of students specialising in exactly two of the three types of subjects are also numbers that form an Arithmetic Progression.

The number of students specialising in all three subjects is one-twentieth of the number of students specialising in only Finance which in turn is half of the number of students studying only HR. The number of students studying both Marketing and Finance is 15, whereas the number of students studying both Finance and HR is 19. The number of students studying HR is 120, which is more than the number of students studying Marketing (which is a 2 digit number above 50). It is known that there are exactly 4 students who opt for none of these specialisations and opt only for general subjects.

5. What is the total number of students in the batch?
   - (a) 223
   - (b) 233
   - (c) 237
   - (d) Cannot be determined

6. What is the number of students specialising in both Marketing and HR?
   - (a) 11
   - (b) 21
   - (c) 23
   - (d) Cannot be determined

**Directions for Questions 7 to 9:** In the Stafford Public School, students had an option to study none or one or more of three foreign languages viz: French, Spanish and German. The total student strength in the school was 2116 students out of which 1320 students studied French and 408 students studied both French and Spanish. The number of people who studied German was found to be 180 higher than the number of students who studied Spanish. It was also observed that 108 students studied all three subjects.

7. What is the maximum possible number of students who did not study any of the three languages?

    (a) 890           (b) 796

    (c) 720           (d) None of these

8. What is the minimum possible number of students who did not study any of the three languages?

    (a) 316           (b) 0

    (c) 158           (d) None of these

9. If the number of students who used to speak only French was 1 more than the number of people who used to speak only German, then what could be the maximum number of people who used to speak only Spanish?

    (a) 413           (b) 398

    (c) 403           (d) 431

**Directions for Questions 10 to 13:** In the Vijayant-khand sports stadium, athletes choose from four different racquet games (apart from athletics which is compulsory for all). These are Tennis, Table Tennis, Squash and Badminton. It is known that 20% of the athletes practising there are not choosing any of the racquet sports. The four games given here are played by 460, 360, 360 and 440 students respectively. The number of athletes playing exactly 2 racquet games for any combination of two racquet games is 40. There are 60 athletes who play all the four games but in a strange coincidence, it was noticed that the number of people playing exactly 3 games was also equal to 20 for each combination of 3 games.

10. What is the number of athletes in the stadium?

    (a) 1140         (b) 1040

    (c) 1200         (d) 1300

11. What is the number of athletes in the stadium who play either only squash or only Tennis?

    (a) 120           (b) 220

    (c) 340           (d) 440

12. How many athletes in the stadium participate in only athletics?

    (a) 160           (b) 1040

    (c) 260           (d) 220

13. If all the athletes were compulsorily asked to add one game to their existing list (except those who were already playing all the four games) — then what will be the number of athletes who would be playing all 4 games after this change?

    (a) 80           (b) 100

    (c) 120           (d) 140

**Directions for Questions 14 and 15:** Answer the questions on the basis of the following information.

In the Pattabhiraman family, a clan of 192 individuals, each person has at least one of the three Pattabhiraman characteristics—Blue eyes, Blonde hair, and sharp mind. It is also known that:

  (i) The number of family members who have only blue eyes is equal to the number of family members who have only sharp minds and this number is also equal to twice the number of family members who have blue eyes and sharp minds but not blonde hair.

 (ii) The number of family members who have exactly two of the three features is 50.

(iii) The number of family members who have blonde hair is 62.

(iv) Among those who have blonde hair, 26 family members have at least two of the three characteristics.

14. If the number of family members who have blue eyes is the maximum amongst the three characteristics, then what is the maximum possible number of family members who have both sharp minds and blonde hair but do not have blue eyes?

    (a) 11           (b) 10

    (c) 12           (d) Cannot be determined

15. Which additional piece of information is required to find the exact number of family members who have blonde hair and blue eyes but not sharp minds?

    (a) The number of family members who have exactly one of the three characterisitcs is 140.

    (b) Only two family members have all three characteristics.

    (c) The number of family members who have sharp minds is 89.

    (d) The number of family members who have only sharp minds is 52.

16. In a class of 97 students, each student plays at least one of the three games – Hockey, Cricket and Football. If 47 play Hockey, 53 play Cricket, 72 play Football and 15 play all the three games, what is the number of students who play exactly two games?

    (a) 38           (b) 40

    (c) 42           (d) 45

**Directions for Questions 17 to 19:** Answer the questions on the basis of the information given below.

In the ancient towns of Mohenjo Daro, a survey found that students were fond of three kinds of cold drinks (Pep, Cok and Thum). It was also found that there were three kinds of beverages that they liked (Tea, Cof and ColdCof).

The popluation of these towns was found to be 400000 people in all—and the survey was conducted on 10% of the population. Mr. Yadav, a data analyst observed the following things about the survey:

  (i) The number of people in the survey who like exactly two cold drinks is five times the number of people who like all the three cold drinks.

(ii) The sum of the number of people in the survey who like Pep and 42% of those who like Cok but not Pep is equal to the number of people who like Tea.

(iii) The number of people in the survey who like Cof is equal to the sum of 3/8$^{th}$ of those who like Cok and ½ of those who like Thum. This number is also equal to the number who like ColdCof.

(iv) 18500 people surveyed like Pep;

(v) 15000 like all the beverages and 3500 like all the cold drinks;

(vi) 14000 do not like Pep but like Thum;

(vii) 11000 like Pep and exactly one more cold drink;

(viii) 6000 like only Cok and the same number of people like Pep and Thum but not Cok.

17. The number of people in the survey who do like at least one of the three cold drinks?

(a) 38500        (b) 31500
(c) 32500        (d) 39500

18. What is the maximum number of people in the survey who like none of the three beverages?

(a) 24000        (b) 16000
(c) 12000        (d) Cannot be determined

19. What is the maximum number of people in the survey who like at least one of the three beverages?

(a) 7000         (b) 32,000
(c) 33000        (d) Cannot be determined

20. In a certain class of students, the number of students who drink only tea, only coffee, both tea and coffee and neither tea nor coffee are $x$, $2x$, $\dfrac{57}{x}$ and $\dfrac{57}{3x}$ respectively. The number of people who drink coffee can be

(a) 41           (b) 40
(c) 59           (d) Both a and c.

*Space for Rough Work*

# ANSWER KEY

## Level of Difficulty (I)

| | | | |
|---|---|---|---|
| 1. (b) | 2. (a) | 3. (b) | 4. (a) |
| 5. (b) | 6. (a) | 7. (c) | 8. (b) |
| 9. (c) | 10. (b) | 11. (a) | 12. (d) |
| 13. (c) | 14. (b) | 15. (a) | 16. (b) |
| 17. (c) | 18. (b) | 19. (c) | 20. (a) |
| 21. (d) | 22. (c) | 23. (c) | 24. (a) |
| 25. (b) | 26. (d) | 27. (b) | 28. (b) |
| 29. (c) | 30. (a) | 31. (a) | 32. (c) |
| 33. (b) | 34. (d) | 35. (a) | 36. (c) |
| 37. (b) | 38. (b) | 39. (e) | 40. (d) |
| 41. (a) | 42. (b) | 43. (c) | |

## Level of Difficulty (II)

| | | | |
|---|---|---|---|
| 1. (b) | 2. (b) | 3. (c) | 4. (c) |
| 5. (c) | 6. (c) | 7. (b) | 8. (b) |
| 9. (d) | 10. (d) | 11. (c) | 12. (c) |
| 13. (d) | 14. (a) | 15. (c) | 16. (d) |
| 17. (a) | 18. (b) | 19. (c) | 20. (d) |

## Solutions and Shortcuts

### Level of Difficulty (I)

**Solutions for Questions 1 and 2:** Since there are 14 players who are in triathlon and pentathlon, and there are 8 who take part in all three games, there will be 6 who take part in only triathlon and pentathlon. Similarly,

Only triathlon and marathon = 12 – 8=4 & Only Pentathlon and Marathon = 15 – 8 = 7.

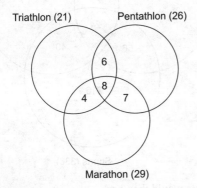

Triathlon (21)          Pentathlon (26)

Marathon (29)

The figure above can be completed with values for each sport (only) plugged in:

The answers would be:

3 + 6 + 8 + 4 + 5 + 7 + 10 = 43. Option (b) is correct.

Option (a) is correct.

### Solutions for Questions 3 and 4:

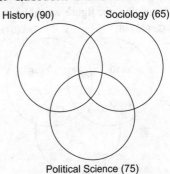

History (90)          Sociology (65)

Political Science (75)

The given situation can be read as follows:

115 students are being counted 75+65+90= 230 times.

This means that there is an extra count of 115. This extra count of 115 can be created in 2 ways.

A.  By putting people in the 'passed exactly two subjects' category. In such a case each person would get counted 2 times (double counted), i.e., an extra count of 1.

B.  By putting people in the 'all three' category, each person put there would be triple counted. 1 person counted 3 times – meaning an extra count of 2 per person.

The problem tells us that there are 55 students who passed exactly two subjects. This means an extra count of 55 would be accounted for. This would leave an extra count of 115 – 55 = 60 more to be accounted for by 'passed all three' category. This can be done by using 30 people in the 'all 3' category.

Hence, the answers are:

3.  Option (b)

4.  Option (a)

**Solutions for Questions 5 to 8:** Based on the information provided we would get the following figure:

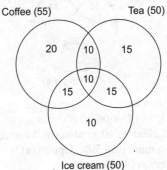

Coffee (55)          Tea (50)

Ice cream (50)

The answers could be read off the figure as:

5.  [(20 – 10)/10] * 100 = 100%. Option (b) is correct.

6.  15% (from the figure). Option (a) is correct.

7.  10+10+15+15=50%. Option (c) is correct.

8.  Only ice cream is 10% of the total. Hence, 10% of 180 =18. Option (b) is correct.

**Solutions for Questions 9 to 15:** If you try to draw a figure for this question, the figure would be something like:

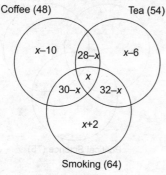

We can then solve this as:

$x - 10 + 28 - x + x + 30 - x + x + 2 + 32 - x + x - 6 = 94 \rightarrow$
$x + 76 = 94 \rightarrow x = 18.$

**Note:** In this question, since all the values for the use of the set theory formula are given, we can find the missing value of students who liked all three as follows:

$94 = 48 + 54 + 64 - 28 - 32 - 30 + \text{All three} \rightarrow \text{All three} = 18$

As you can see this is a much more convenient way of solving this question, and the learning you take away for the 3 circle situation is that whenever you have all the values known and the only unknown value is the center value – it is wiser and more efficient to solve for the unknown using the formula rather than trying to solve through a venn diagram.

Based on this value of $x$ we get the diagram completed as:

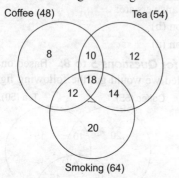

The answers then are:
9. $8:12 = 2:3 \rightarrow$ Option (c) is correct.
10. 12 % of 2000 = 240. Option (b) is correct.
11. $30/94 \rightarrow$ more than 30%. Option (a) is correct.
12. 94%. Option (d) is correct.
13. Option (c) is correct as the ratio turns out to be 10:20 in that case.
14. $12:12 = 1:1 \rightarrow$ Option (b) is correct.
15. 14%. Option (a) is correct.
16. $30 = 25 + 20 - x \rightarrow x = 15.$ Option (b) is correct.

**Solutions for Questions 17 to 20:**
Let people who passed all three be $x$. Then:
$53 + 61 + 60 - 24 - 35 - 27 + x = 95$
$\rightarrow x = 7.$

The venn diagram in this case would become:

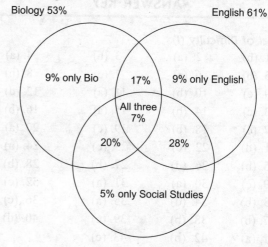

17. Option (c) is correct.
18. 23% of 200 = 46. Option (b) is correct.
19. If the number of students is increased by 50%, the number of students in each category would also be increased by 50%. Option (c) is correct.
20. $20:28 = 5:7.$ Option (a) is correct.

**Solutions for Questions 21 to 25:** The following figure would emerge on using all the information in the question:

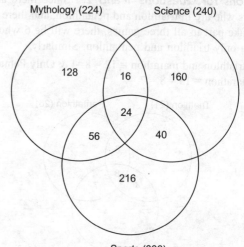

The answers would then be:
21. $240/880 = 27.27\%.$ Option (d) is correct.
22. $504/880 = 57.27\%.$ Hence, less than 60. Option (c) is correct.
23. $40 + 16 + 56 + 24 = 136.$ Option (c) is correct.
24. Option a gives us $16:128 = 1:8.$ Option (a) is hence correct.
25. $40:160 \rightarrow 1:4.$ Option (b) is correct.

**Solutions for Questions 26 to 30:** The following Venn diagrams would emerge:

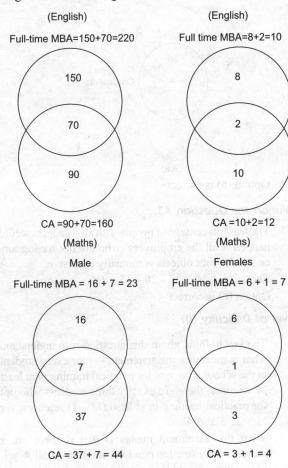

(English)

Full-time MBA=150+70=220

150

70

90

CA =90+70=160

(Maths)

(English)

Full time MBA=8+2=10

8

2

10

CA =10+2=12

(Maths)

Male

Full-time MBA = 16 + 7 = 23

16

7

37

CA = 37 + 7 = 44

Females

Full-time MBA = 6 + 1 = 7

6

1

3

CA = 3 + 1 = 4

26. Math Students = 130. English Students =370
    130/370 = 35.13%. Option (d) is correct.

27. Number of Female Students = 10 + 8 + 10 + 2 + 10 + 6 + 3 + 1 = 50. Average number of females per course = 50/3 = 16.66. Option (b) is correct.

28. 50:450 = 1:9. Option (b) is correct.

29. 40/140 → 28.57%. Option (c) is correct.

30. From the figures, this value would be 150+8+ 90 + 10 + 16+6+37+3= 320. Option (a) is correct.

**Solutions for Questions 31 to 34:** The following figure would emerge-

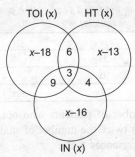

TOI (x)    HT (x)

$x-18$   6   $x-13$

9   3   4

$x-16$

IN (x)

Based on this figure we have:

$x + x - 13 + 4 + x - 16 = 302 \rightarrow 3x - 25 = 302 \rightarrow x = 327$. Hence, $x = 109$.

Consequently the figure becomes:

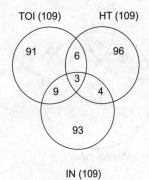

TOI (109)    HT (109)

91   6   96

3

9   4

93

IN (109)

The answers are:

31. 91 + 93 + 96 = 280. Option (a) is correct.

32. 193/302 ≅ 64%

33. 6:9:4 is the required ratio. Option (b) is correct.

34. 96 – 4 = 92. Options (d) is correct.

35. $78 = 36 + 48 + 32 - 14 - 20 - 12 + x \rightarrow x = 8$.

The figure for this question would become:

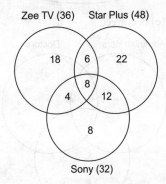

Zee TV (36)    Star Plus (48)

18   6   22

8

4   12

8

Sony (32)

Required ratio is 18:8 → 9:4. Option (a) is correct.

36. Option (c)

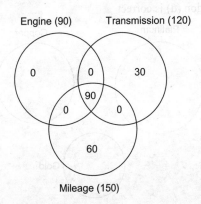

Engine (90)    Transmission (120)

0   0   30

90

0   0

60

Mileage (150)

37. There are 30 such people. Option (b) is correct.

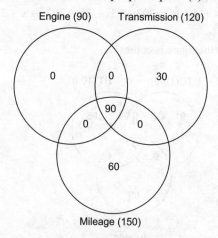

Engine (90)    Transmission (120)

0        0        30

90

0        0

60

Mileage (150)

### Solutions for Questions 38 to 42:

38. Option (b) is correct

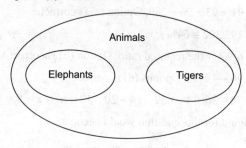

Animals

Elephants        Tigers

39. Option (e) is correct.

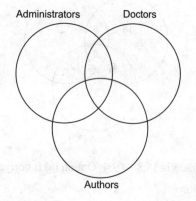

Administrators    Doctors

Authors

40. Option (d) is correct.

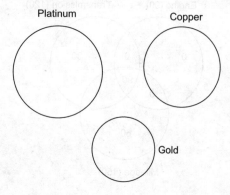

Platinum        Copper

Gold

41. Option (a) is correct.

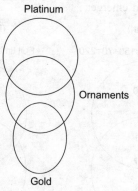

Platinum

Ornaments

Gold

42. Option (b) is correct

### Solution for Question 43:

43. The least percentage of people with all 4 gadgets would happen if all the employees who are not having any one of the four objects is mutually exclusive.

Thus, $100 - 30 - 25 - 20 - 15 = 10$

Option (c) is correct

### Level of Difficulty (II)

1. The key to think about this question is to understand what is meant by the statement —"for every student in the school who opts for practical training in at least M sciences, there are exactly three students who opt for practical training in at least $(M - 1)$ sciences, for M = 2, 3 and 4"

What this statement means is that if there are $x$ students who opt for practical training in all 4 sciences, there would be $3x$ students who would opt for practical training in at least 3 sciences. Since opting for at least 3 sciences includes those who opted for exactly 3 sciences and those who opted for exactly 4 sciences—we can conclude from this that:

The number of students who opted for exactly 3 sciences = Number of students who opted for at least 3 sciences – Number of students who opted for all 4 sciences = $3x - x = 2x$

Thus, the number of students who opted for various number of science practicals can be summarised as below:

| | Number of students who opted for at least n subjects | Number of students who opted for exactly n subjects |
|---|---|---|
| n = 4 | x | x |
| n = 3 | 3x | 2x |
| n = 2 | 9x | 6x |
| n = 1 | 27x | 18x . |

Also, number of students who opt for none of the sciences = twice the number of students who opt for exactly 4 sciences = $2x$.

Based on these deductions we can clearly identify that the number of students in the school would be: $x + 2x + 6x + 18x + 2x = 29x = 870 \rightarrow x = 30$.

Hence, number of students who opted for exactly three sciences = $2x = 60$

2. (b) In order to estimate the minimum number of customers we need to assume that each customer must have bought the maximum number of pastries possible for him to purchase.

Since, the maximum number of pastries an individual could purchase is constrained by the information that no one bought more than two pastries of any one kind—this would occur under the following situation—First 45 people would buy 2 pastries of all three kinds, which would completely exhaust the 90 pineapple pastries and leave the bakery with 30 chocolate and 60 black forest pastries. The next 15 people would buy 2 pastries each of the available kinds and after this we would be left with 30 black forest pastries. 15 people would buy these pastries, each person buying 2 pastries each.

Thus, the total number of people (minimum) would be: 45 + 15 + 15 = 75.

3. (c) Let the number of people who participated in 0, 1, 2 and 3 games be A, B, C, D respectively. Then from the information we have:

C+D = 1.52 × B (Number of people who participate in at least 2 games is 52% higher than the number of people who participate in exactly one game)

A + B + C + D = 510 (Number of people invited to participate in the games is 510)

This gives us: $A + 2.52B = 510 \rightarrow B = \dfrac{25}{63}(510 - A)$

For A to be minimum, $510 - A$ should give us the largest multiple of 63. Since, $63 \times 8 = 504$ we have A = 6.

Also, 2.52B = 504, so B = 200 and C+D = 1.52B = 304.

For number of people participating in exactly 3 games to be maximum, the number of people participating in exactly 2 games has to be minimised and made equal to 1. Thus, the required answer = 304 – 1 = 303.

4. (c) In order to think about this question, the best way is to use the process of slack thinking. In this question, we have 180 students counted 270 times. This means that there is an extra count of 90 students. In a three circle venn diagram, extra counting can occur only due to exactly two regions (where 1 individual student would be counted in two subjects leading to an extra count of 1) and the exactly three region (where 1 individual student would be counted in 3 subjects leading to an extra count of 2).

This can be visualised in the figure below:

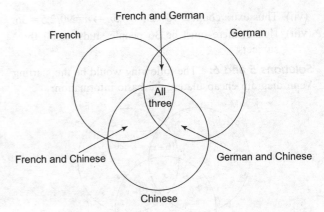

A student placed in the all three area will be counted three times when you count the number of students studying French, the number of students studying German and the number of students studying Chinese independently. Hence, HE/SHE would be counted three times—leading to an extra count of 2 for each individual places here.

A person placed in any of the three 'Exactly two' areas would be counted two times when we count the number of students studying French, the number of students studying German and the number of students studying Chinese independently. Hence, HE/SHE would be counted two times—leading to an extra count of 1 for each individual placed in any of these three areas.

The thought chain leading to the solution would go as follows:

(i) 180 students are counted 80 + 90 + 100 = 270 times.

(ii) This means that there is an extra count of 90 students.

(iii) Extra counts can fundamentally occur only from the 'exaclty two' areas or the all three area in the figure.

(iv) We also know that 'The number of students who study more than one of the three subjects is 50% more than the number of students who study all the three subjects' hence we know that if there are a total of '$n$' students studying all three subjects, there would be $1.5n$ students studying more than one subject. This in turn means that there must be $0.5n$ students who study two subjects.

(Since, number of students studying more than 1 subject = number of students studying two subjects + number of students studying three subjects.

i.e. $1.5n = n +$ number of students studying 2 subjects $\rightarrow$ number of students studying 2 subjects = $1.5n - n = 0.5n$)

(v) The extra counts from the $n$ students studying 3 subjects would amount to $n \times 2 = 2n$ – since each student is counted twice extra when he/she studies all three subjects.

(vi) The extra counts from the $0.5n$ students who study exactly two subjects would be equal to $0.5n \times 1 = 0.5n$.

(vii) Thus extra count = $90 = 2n + 0.5n \rightarrow n = 90/2.5 = 36$.

(viii) Hence, there must be 36 people studying all three subjects.

**Solutions 5 and 6:** The following would be the starting Venn diagram encapsulating the basic information:

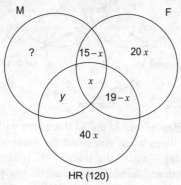

From this figure we get the following equation:
$40x + (19 - x) + x + y = 120$. This gives us $40x + y = 101$

Thinking about this equation, we can see that the value of $x$ can be either 1 or 2. In case we put $x$ as 1, we get $y = 61$ and then we have to also meet the additional condition that $15-x$, $19-x$ and $y$ should form an AP which is obviously not possible (since it is not possible practically to build an AP having two positive terms below 19 and the third term being 61. Hence, this option is rejected.

Moving forward, the other possible value of $x$ from the equation is $x = 2$ in which case we get, $y = 21$ and $15 - x = 13$ and $19 - x = 17$. Thus, we get the AP 13, 17, 21 which satisfies the given conditions. Putting $x = 2$ and $y = 21$ in the figure, the venn diagram evolves to:

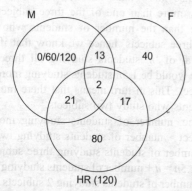

In this figure the value that only Marketing takes can either be 0, 60 or 120 (to satisfy the AP condition). However, since the total number of students in Marketing is a two digit number above 50, the number of people studying only marketing would be narrowed down to the only possibility which remains – viz 60.

Thus, the number of students studying in the batch
$= 120 + 40 + 60 + 13 + 4 = 237$.
The number of students specialising in both Marketing and HR is $21 + 2 = 23$

5. (d) The total number of students is 237.

6. (c) The number of students studying both Marketing and HR is 23.

**Solutions 7 to 9:**

7 & 8: In order to think about the possibility of the maximum and/or the minimum number of people who could be studying none of the three languages, you need to first think of the basic information in the question. The basic information in the question can be encapsulated by the following Venn diagram:

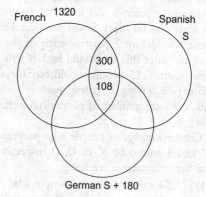

At this point we have the flexibility to try to put the remaining numbers into this Venn diagram while maintaining the constraints the question has placed on the relative numbers in the figure. In order to do this, we need to think of the objective with which we have to fill in the remaining numbers in the figure. At this stage you have to keep two constraints in mind while filling the remaining numbers:

(a) The remaining part of the French circle has to total $1320 - 408 = 912$;

(b) The German circle has to be 180 more than the Spanish circle.

When we try to fill in the figure for making the number of students who did not study any of the three subjects maximum:

You can think of first filling the French circle by trying to think of how you would want to distribute the remaining 912 in that circle. When we want to maximise the number of students who study none of the three, we would need to use the minimum number of people inside the three circles—while making sure that all the constraints are met.

Since we have to forcefully fit in 912 into the remaining areas of the French circle, we need to see whether while doing the same we can also meet the second constraint.

This thinking would lead you to see the following solution possibility:

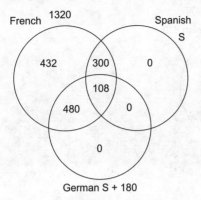

In this case we have ensured that the German total is 180 more than the Spanish total (as required) and at the same time the French circle has also reached the desired 1320. Hence, the number of students who study none of the three can be 2116–1320 = 796 (at maximum).

When minimising the number of students who have studied none of the three subjects, the objective would be to use the maximum number of students who can be used in order to meet the basic constraints. The answer in this case can be taken to as low as zero in the following case:

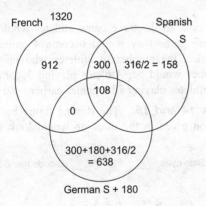

**Note:** While thinking about the numbers in this case, we first use the 912 in the 'only French' area. At this point we have 796 students left to be allocated. We first make the German circle 180 more than the Spanish circle (by taking the only German as 300 +180 to start with, this is accomplished). At this point, we are left with 316 more students, who can be allocated equally as 316 ÷ 2 for both the 'only German' and the 'only Spanish' areas.

Thus, the minimum number of students who study none of the three is 0.

**Solution 9:**
In order to think about this question, let us first see the situation we had in order to maintain all constraints.

If we try to fit in the remaining constraints in this situation we would get:

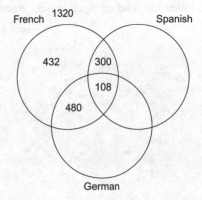

This leaves us with a slack of 796 people which would need to be divided equally since we cannot disturb the equilibrium of German being exactly 180 more than Spanish.

This gives us the following figure:

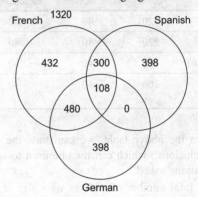

When you think about this situation, you realise that it is quite possible to increase Spanish if we reduce the only French area and reallocate the reduction into the 'only French' and German area. A reduction of 10 from the 'only French' area can be visualised as follows:

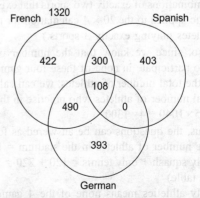

In this case, as you can see from the figure above, the number of students who study only Spanish has gone up by 5 (which is half of 10).

Since, there is still some gap between the 'only German' and the 'only French' areas in the figure, we should close that gap by reducing the 'only French' area as much as possible.

The following solution figure would emerge when we think that way:

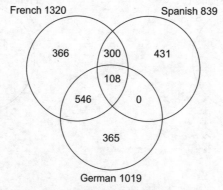

Hence, the maximum possible for the only Spanish area is 431.

**Solutions 10 to 13:** The information given in the question can be encapsulated in the following way:

| Game | Only that game | 2 games combination 1 | 2 games combination 2 | 2 games combination 3 | 3 games combination 1 | 3 games combination 2 | 3 games combination 3 | All 4 games |
|---|---|---|---|---|---|---|---|---|
| Tennis (460) | 220 | 40 | 40 | 40 | 20 | 20 | 20 | 60 |
| TT (360) | 120 | 40 | 40 | 40 | 20 | 20 | 20 | 60 |
| Squash (360) | 120 | 40 | 40 | 40 | 20 | 20 | 20 | 60 |
| Badminton (440) | 200 | 40 | 40 | 40 | 20 | 20 | 20 | 60 |

From the above table, we can draw the following conclusions,, which can then be used to answer the questions asked.

The total number of athletes who play at least one of the four games = 220 + 120 + 120 + 200 + 40×6 + 20×4 + 60 = 1040

(Note : that in doing this calculation, we have used 40 × 6 for calculating how many unique people would be playing exactly two games—where 40 for each combination is given and there are $^4C_2$= 6 combinations of exactly two sports that exist. Similar logic applies to the 20 × 4 calculation for number of athletes playing exactly 3 sports.)

Also, since we know that the number of athletes who participate in none of these four games is 20% of the total number of athletes, we can calculate the total number of athletes who practise in the stadium as 5×1040 ÷ 4 = 1300.

Thus, the questions can be answered as follows:

10. The number of athletes in the stadium = 1300.
11. Only squash + only tennis = 120 + 220 = 340 (from the table)
12. Only athletics means none of the 4 games = total number of athletes − number of athletes who play at least one game = 1300 − 1040 = 260.

13. In case all the three game athletes would add one more game they would become 4 game athletes. Hence, the number of athletes who play all four games would be: Athletes playing 3 games earlier + athletes playing all 4 games earlier = 80+60=140

**Solutions 14 and 15:** The starting figure based on the information given in the question would look something as below:

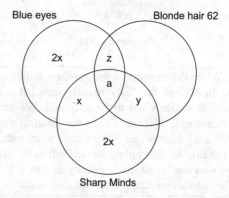

From this figure we see a few equations:
$x + y + z = 50$; $a + y + z = 26 \rightarrow x - 24 = a$.
Also, since, $5x + 62 = 192$, we get the value of $x$ as 26. The figure would evolve as follows.

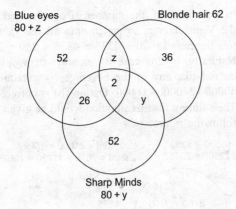

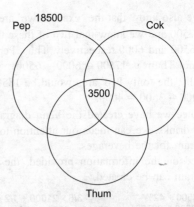

Based on this we can deduce the answer to the two questions as:

14. For the number of family members with blue eyes to be maximum, the family members with both sharp minds and blonde hair, but not blue eyes (represented by '$y$' in the figure), would be at maximum 11 because we would need to keep $z > y$. Hence, Option (a) is the correct answer.

15. If we are given the information in Option (c) we know the value of $y$ would be 9 and hence, the value of $z$ would be determined as 15. Hence, Option (c) provides us the information to determine the exact number of family members who have blonde hair and blue eyes but not sharp minds. Notice here that the information in each of the other options is already known to us.

16. Solve this again using slack thinking by using the following thought process:

97 students are counted $47 + 53 + 72 = 172$ times—which means that there is an extra count of 75 students ($172 - 97 = 75$). Now, since there are 15 students who are playing all the three games, they would be counted 45 times—hence they take care of an extra count of $15 \times 2 = 30$. (**Note:** in a 3 circle venn diagram situation, any person placed in the all three areas is counted thrice—hence he/she is counted two extra times).

This leaves us with an extra count of 45 to be managed—and the only way to do so is to place people in the exactly two areas. A person placed in the 'exactly two games area' would be counted once extra. Hence, with each student who goes into the 'exactly two games' areas it would be counted once extra. Thus, to manage an extra count of 45, we need to put 45 people in the 'exactly two' area. Option (d) is correct.

**Solutions 17 to 19:** When you draw a Venn diagram for the three cold drinks, you realise as given here.

Once you fill in the basic information into the Venn diagram, you reach the following position:

At this point we know that since the 'all three area' is 3500, the value of the 'exactly two areas' would be $5 \times 3500 = 17500$. Also, we know that "11000 like Pep and exactly one more cold drink" which means that the area for Cok and Thum but not Pep is equal to $17500 - 11000 = 6500$. Further, when you start adding the information: "6000 like only Cok and the same number of people like Pep and Thum but not Cok," the Venn Diagram transforms to the following:

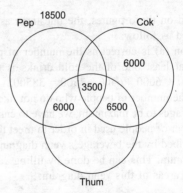

Filling in the remaining gaps in the picture we get:

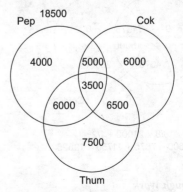

Note, we have used the following info here:
Thum but not Pep is 14000 and since we already know that Thum and Cok but not Pep is 6500, the value of 'only Thum' would be $14000 - 6500 = 7500$.

We also know that the 'exactly two' areas add up to 17500 and we know that two of these three areas are 6500 and 6000 respectively. Thus, Pep and Cok but not Thum is 17500 – 6000 – 6500 = 5000. Finally, the 'only Pep' area would be 18500 – 5000 – 6000 – 3500 = 4000.

Once we have created the Venn diagram for the cold drinks, we can focus our attention to the Venn diagram for the beverages.

Based on the information provided, the following diagram can be created.

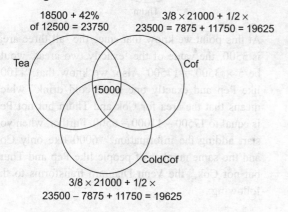

18500 + 42% of 12500 = 23750

3/8 × 21000 + 1/2 × 23500 = 7875 + 11750 = 19625

Tea

15000

Cof

ColdCof

3/8 × 21000 + 1/2 × 23500 – 7875 + 11750 = 19625

Based on these figures, the questions asked can be solved as follows:

17. Option (a) is correct as the number of people who like at least one of the cold drinks is the sum of 18500 + 6000 + 6500 + 7500 = 38500.

18. For the number of people who do not like any of the beverages to be maximum, we have to ensure that the number of people used in order to meet the situation described by the beverage's venn diagram should be minimum. This can be done by filling values in the inner areas of this venn diagram:

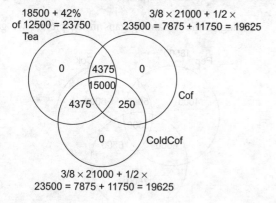

18500 + 42% of 12500 = 23750
Tea

3/8 × 21000 + 1/2 × 23500 = 7875 + 11750 = 19625

0    4375    0
15000
4375    250
Cof
0    ColdCof

3/8 × 21000 + 1/2 × 23500 = 7875 + 11750 = 19625

In this situation, the number of people used inside the Venn diagram to match upto all the values for this figure = 15000 + 4375 + 4375 + 250 = 24000. Naturally, in this case the number of people who do not like any of the beverages is maximised at 40000 – 24000 = 16000. Option (b) is correct.

19. The solution for this situation would be given by the following figure:

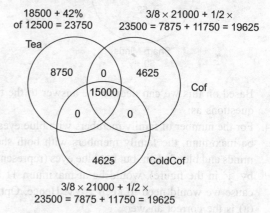

18500 + 42% of 12500 = 23750

3/8 × 21000 + 1/2 × 23500 = 7875 + 11750 = 19625

Tea

8750    0    4625
15000
0    0
Cof

4625    ColdCof

3/8 × 21000 + 1/2 × 23500 = 7875 + 11750 = 19625

The number of people who like at least one of the three beverages is:
15000 + 8750 + 4625 + 4625 = 33000. Option (c) is correct.

20. The number of people cannot be a fraction in any situation. We can deduce that the values of $x$ and $3x$ have to be factors of 57. This gives us that the values of $x$ can only be either 1 or 19 (for both $x$ and $3x$ to be a factor of 57).

So, the number of people who drink coffee is equal to $2x + 57/x$ which can be 59 (if $x = 1$) or 41 (if $x = 19$).

Hence, Option (d) is correct.

# TRAINING GROUND FOR BLOCK VI

## 🎧 HOW TO THINK IN PROBLEMS ON BLOCK VI

1. The probability that a randomly chosen positive divisor of $10^{29}$ is an integer multiple of $10^{23}$ is : $a2/b2$, then '$b - a$' would be: **(XAT 2014)**
   (a) 8
   (b) 15
   (c) 21
   (d) 23
   (e) 45

**Solution:** This question appeared in the XAT 2014 exam. The number $10^{29} = 2^{29} \times 5^{29}$.

Factors or divisors of such a number would be of the form: $2^a \times 5^b$ where the values of $a$ and $b$ can be represented as $0 \leq a, b \leq 29$, i.e., there are $30 \times 30 = 900$ possibilities when we talk about randomly selecting a positive divisor of $10^{29}$.

Next, we need to think of numbers which are integral multiples of $10^{23}$. Such numbers would be of the form $2^x \times 5^y$ such that $x, y \geq 23$.

Hence, the number of values possible when the chosen divisor would also be an integer multiple of $10^{23}$ would be when $23 \leq x, y \leq 29$. There would be $7 \times 7 = 49$ such combinations.

Thus, the required probability is $49 \div 900$. In the context of $a^2 \div b^2$, the values of $a$ and $b$ would come out as 7 and 30 respectively. The required difference between $a$ and $b$ is 23. Hence, Option (d) is correct.

2. Aditya has a total of 18 red and blue marbles in two bags (each bag has marbles of both colors). A marble is randomly drawn from the first bag followed by another randomly drawn from the second bag, the probability of both being red is 5/16. What is the probability of both marbles being blue?
   **(XAT 2014)**
   (a) 1/16
   (b) 2/16
   (c) 3/16
   (d) 4/16
   (e) None of the above

**Solution:** This problem has again appeared in XAT 2014. The problem most students face in such situations is to understand how to place how many balls of each colour in each bag. Since there is no directive given in the question that tells us how many balls are there and/or how many balls are placed in any bag the next thing that a mathematically oriented mind would do would be to try to assume some variables to represent the number of balls in each bag. However, if you try to do so on your own you would realise that that would be the wrong way to solve this quesiton as it would lead to extreme complexity while solving the problem. So how can we think alternately? Is there a smarter way to think about this question?

Yes indeed there is. Let me explain it to you here. In order to think about this problem, you would need to first think about how a fraction like 5/16 would emerge. The value of $5/16 = 10/32 = 15/48 = 20/64 = 25/80 = 30/96$ and so on. Next, you need to understand that there are a total of 18 balls and this 18 has to be broken into two parts such that their product is one of the above denominators. Scanning the denominators we see the opportunity that the number $80 = 10 \times 8$ and hence we realise that the probability of both balls being red would happen in a situation where the structure of the calculation would look something like: $(r_1/10) \times (r_2/8)$. Next, to get 25 as the corresponding numerator with 80 as the denominator the values of $r_1$ and $r_2$ should both be 5. This means that there are 5 red balls out of ten in the first bag and 5 red balls out of 8 in the second bag. This further means that the number of blue balls would be 5 out of 8 and 3 out of 8. Thus, the correct answer would be: $(5/10) \times (3/8) = 25/80 = 5/16$. Hence, Option (c) is the correct answer.

3. The scheduling officer for a local police department is trying to schedule additional patrol units in each of two neighbourhoods – southern and northern. She knows that on any given day, the probabilities of major crimes and minor crimes being committed in the northern neighbourhood were 0.418 and 0.612, respectively, and that the corresponding probabilities in the southern neighbourhood were 0.355 and 0.520. Assuming that all crimes occur independent of each other and likewise that crime in the two neighbourhoods are independent of each other, what is the probability that no crime of either type is committed in either neighbourhood on any given day?
   **(XAT 2011)**
   (a) 0.069
   (b) 0.225
   (c) 0.690
   (d) 0.775
   (e) None of the above

**Solution:** This question appeared in XAT 2011, and the key to solving this correctly is to look at the event definition. A major crime not occurring in the northern neighbourhood is the non-event for a major crime occurring in the nothern neighbourhood on any given day. Its probability would be $(1-0.418) = 0.582$.

The values of minor crime not occurring in the northern neighbourhood and a major crime not occurring in the southern neighbourhood and a minor crime not occurring in the northern neighbourhood would be $(1-0.612)$; $(1-0.355)$ and $(1-0.520)$ respectively. The value of the required probability would be the probability of the event:

Major crime does not occur in the northern neighbourhood and minor crime does not occur in the northern neighbourhood and major crime does not occur in the southern neighbourhood and minor crime does not occur in the northern neighbourhood =

$(1-0.418) \times (1-0.612) \times (1-0.355) \times (1-0.520)$. Option (a) is the closest answer.

4. There are four machines in a factory. At exactly 8 pm, when the mechanic is about to leave the factory, he is informed that two of the four machines are not working properly. The mechanic is in a hurry, and decides that he will identify the two faulty machines before going home, and repair them next morning. It takes him twenty minutes to walk to the bus stop. The last bus leaves at 8 :32 pm. If it takes six minutes to identify whether a machine is defective or not, and if he decides to check the machines at random, what is the probability that the mechanic will be able to catch the last bus?

(a) 0      (b) 1/6
(c) 1/4      (d) 1/3
(e) 1

**Solution:** The first thing you look for in this question, is that obviously the mechanic has only 12 minutes to check the machines before he leaves to catch the bus. In 12 minutes, he can at best check two machines. He will be able to identify the two faulty machines under the following cases:
(The first machine checked is faulty AND the second machine checked is also faulty) OR (The first machine checked is working fine AND the second machine checked is also working fine)

Required probability = $\frac{2}{4}\times\frac{1}{3}+\frac{2}{4}\times\frac{1}{3}=\frac{1}{3}$

5. Little Pika who is five and half years old has just learnt addition. However, he does not know how to carry. For example, he can add 14 and 5, but he does not know how to add 14 and 7. How many pairs of consecutive integers between 1000 and 2000 (both 1000 and 2000 included) can Little Pika add?

(a) 150      (b) 155
(c) 156      (d) 258
(e) None of the above

**Solution:** This question again appeared in the XAT 2011 exam. If you try to observe the situations under which the addition of two consecutive four-digit numbers between 1000 and 2000 would come through without having a carry over value in the answer you would be able to identify the following situations – each of which differs from the other due to the way it is structured with respect to the values of the individual digits:

**Category 1:** 1000 + 1001; 1004 +1005, 1104 + 1105 and so on. A little bit of introspection should show you that in this case, the two numbers are 1abc and 1abd where $d = c + 1$. Also, for the sum to come out without any carry-overs, the values of $a$, $b$ and $c$ should be between 0 and 4 (including both). Thus, each of $a$, $b$ and $c$ gives us 5 values each – giving us a total of $5 \times 5 \times 5 = $ **125 such situations.**

**Category 2:** 1009 + 1010; 1019 + 1020; 1029 + 1030; 1409 + 1410. The general form of the first number here would be 1ab 9 with the values of $a$ and $b$ being between 0 and 4 (including both). Thus, each of $a$, $b$ and $c$ gives us 5 values each – giving us a total of $5 \times 5 = $ **25 such situations**.

**Category 3:** 1099 + 1100; 1199 + 1200; 1299 + 1300; 1399 + 1400 and 1499 + 1500. There are only **5 such pairs.** Note that 1599 + 1600 would not work in this case as the addition of the hundreds' digit would become more than 10 and lead to a carry-over.

**Category 4:** 1999 + 2000 is the only other situation where the addition would not lead to a carry-over calculation. Hence, **1 more situation.**

The required answer = 125 + 25 + 5 + 1 = 156. Option (c) is the correct answer.

6. In the country of Twenty, there are exactly twenty cities, and there is exactly one direct road between any two cities. No two direct roads have an overlapping road segment. After the election dates are announced, candidates from their respective cities start visiting the other cities. The following are the rules that the election commission has laid down for the candidates:
- Each candidate must visit each of the other cities exactly once.
- Each candidate must use only the direct roads between two cities for going from one city to another.
- The candidate must return to his own city at the end of the campaign.
- No direct road between two cities would be used by more than one candidate.

The maximum possible number of candidates is
(a) 5      (b) 6
(c) 7      (d) 8
(e) 9

**Solution:** Again an XAT 2011 question. Although this question carried a very high weightage (it had 5 marks where 'normal questions' had 1 to 3 marks) it is not so difficult once you understand the logic of the question. The key to understanding this question is from two points.

(a) Since there is exactly one direct road between any pair of two cities – there would be a toal of $20C_2$ roads = 190 roads.

(b) The other key condition in this question is the one which talks about each candidate must visit each of the other cities exactly once and 'No direct road between two cities would be used by more than one candidate.' This means two things. i) Since each candidate visits each city exactly once, if there are '$c$' candidates, there would be a total of 20c roads used and since no road is repeated it means that the 20 roads Candidate A uses will be different from the 20 roads Candidate B uses and so on. Thus, the value of $20c \leq$ 190 should be an inequality that must be satisfied.This gives us a maximum possible value of $c$ as 9. Hence, Option (e) is correct.

7. In a bank the account numbers are all 8 digit numbers, and they all start with the digit 2. So, an account number can be represented as $2x_1x_2x_3x_4x_5x_6x_7$. An

account number is considered to be a 'magic' number if $x_1x_2x_3$ is exactly the same as $x_4x_5x_6$ or $x_5x_6x_7$ or both, $x_i$ can take values from 0 to 9, but 2 followed by seven 0s is not a valid account number. What is the maximum possible number of customers having a 'magic' account number?

(a) 9989          (b) 19980

(c) 19989         (d) 19999

(e) 19990

**Solution:** This question appeared in XAT 2011. In order to solve this question, we need to think of the kinds of numbers which would qualify as magic numbers. Given the definition of a magic number in the question, a number of form 2mnpmnpq would be a magic number while at the same time a number of the form 2mnpqmnp would also qualify as a magic number. In this situation, each of m,n and p can take any of the ten digit values from 0 to 9. Also, q would also have ten different possibilities from 0 to 9. Thus, the total number of numbers of the form 2mnpmnpq would be $10^4 = 10000$. Similarly, the total number of numbers of the form 2mnpqmnp would also be $10^4 = 10000$. This gives us a total of 20000 numbers. However, in this count the numbers like 21111111, 22222222, 23333333, 24444444 etc have been counted under both the categories. Hence we need to remove these numbers once each (a total of 9 reductions). Also, the number 20000000 is not a valid number according to the question. This number needs to be removed from both the counts.

Hence, the final answer = $20000 - 9 - 2 = 19989$.

8. If all letters of the word "CHCJL" be arranged in an English dictionary, what will be the 50th word?

(a) HCCLJ        (b) LCCHJ

(c) LCCJH        (d) JHCLC

(e) None of the above

**Solution:** A Xat 2010 question. In the English dictionary the ordering of the words would be in alphabetical order. Thus, words starting with C would be followed by words starting with H, followed by words starting with J and finally words starting with L. Words starting with C = 4! = 24; Words starting with H = 4! ÷ 2! = 12 words. Words starting with J = 4! ÷ 2! = 12 words. This gives us a total of 48 words. The 49th and the 50th words would start with L. The 49th word would be the first word starting with L (=LCCHJ) and the 50th word would be the 2nd word starting with L – which would be LCCJH. Option (c) is correct.

9. The supervisor of a packaging unit of a milk plant is being pressurised to finish the job closer to the distribution time, thus giving the production staff more leeway to cater to last minute demand. He has the option of running the unit at normal speed or at 110% of normal – "fast speed". He estimates that he will be able to run at the higher speed 60% of time. The packet is twice as likely to be damaged at the higher speed which would mean temporarily stop-

ping the process. If a packet on a randomly selected packaging runs has probability of 0.112 of damage, what is the probability that the packet will not be damaged at normal speed?

(a) 0.81          (b) 0.93

(c) 0.75          (d) 0.60

(e) None of the above

**Solution:** Again a XAT 2013 question. Let the probability of the package being damaged at normal speed be '$p$'. This means that the probability of the damage of a package when the unit is running at a fast speed is '$2p$'. Since, he is under pressure to complete the production quickly, we would need to assume that he runs the unit at fast speed for the maximum possible time (60% of the time).

Then, we have

Probability of damaged packet in all packaging runs

$= 0.6 \times 2p + 0.4 \times p = 0.112$.

$\Rightarrow p = 0.07$

Probability of non damaged packets at normal speed

$= 1 - p = 1 - 0.07 = 0.93$. Option (b) is correct.

10. Let X be a four-digit positive integer such that the unit digit of X is prime and the product of all digits of X is also prime. How many such integers are possible?

(a) 4          (b) 8

(b) 12         (d) 24

(e) None of these

**Solution:** This one is an easy question as all you need to do is understand that given the unit digit is a prime number, it would mean that the number can only be of the form $abc2$; $abc3$ or $abc5$ or $abc7$. Further, for each of these, the product of the four digits $a \times b \times c \times$ units digit has to be prime. This can occur only if $a = b = c = 1$. Thus, there are only 4 such numbers viz: 1112, 1113, 1115 and 1117. Hence, Option (a) is correct.

11. The chance of India winning a cricket match against Australia is 1/6. What is the minimum number of matches India should play against Australia so that there is a fair chance of winning at least one match?

(a) 3          (b) 4

(c) 5          (d) 6

(e) None of the above

**Solution:** This is another question from the XAT 2009 test paper. A fair chance is defined when the probability of an event goes to above 0.5. If India plays 3 matches, the probability of at least one win will be given by the non-event of losing all matches. This would be:

$1 - (5/6)^3 = 1 - 125/216 = 91/216$ which is less than 0.5. Hence, Option (a) is rejected.

For four matches, the probability of winning at least 1 match would be:

$1 - (5/6)^4 = 1 - 625/1296 = 671/216$ which is more than 0.5. Hence, Option (b) is correct.

12. Two teams *Arrogant* and *Overconfident* are participating in a cricket tournament. The odds that team *Arrogant* will be champion is 5 to 3, and the odds that team *Overconfident* will be the champion is 1 to 4. What are the odds that either *Arrogant* or team *Overconfident* will become the champion?
    (a) 3 to 2          (b) 5 to 2
    (c) 6 to 1          (d) 7 to 1
    (e) 33 to 7

**Solution:** You need to be clear about what odds for an event mean in order to solve this. Odds for team *Arrogant* to be champion being 5 to 3 means that the probability of team *Arrogant* being champion is 5/8. Similarly, the probability of team *Overconfident* being champion is 1/5 (based on odds of team *Overconfident* being champion being 1 to 4). Thus, the probability that either of the teams would be the champion would be

$$= \frac{5}{8} + \frac{1}{5} = \frac{33}{40}$$

This means that in 40 times, 33 times the event of one of the teams being champion would occur. Hence, the odds for one of the two given teams to be the chamion would be 33 to 7.

So required odds will be 33 to 7. Option (e) is correct.

13. Let X be a four-digit number with exactly three consecutive digits being same and is a multiple of 9. How many such X's are possible?
    (a) 12          (b) 16
    (c) 19          (d) 21
    (e) None of the above

**Solution:** Since the number has to be a multiple of 9, the sum of the digits would be either 9 or 18 or 27. Also, the number would either be in the form aaab or baaa. For the sum of the digits to be 9, we would have the following cases:

$a = 1$ and $b = 6$ for the numbers 1116 and 6111;
$a = 2$ and $b = 3$ for the numbers 2223 and 3222;
$a = 3$ and $b = 0$ for the number 3330 and
$b = 9$ and $a = 0$ for the number 9000. We get a total of 6 such numbers.

Similarly for the sum of the digits to be 18 we will get:
3339, 9333; 4446, 6444; 5553, 3555; 6660. We get a total of 7 such numbers.

For the sum of the digits to be 27 we will get the numbers: 6669, 9666; 7776, 6777; 8883, 3888 and 9990. Thus, we get a total of 7 such numbers. Hence, the total number of numbers is 20. Option (e) is correct.

14. A shop sells two kinds of rolls—egg roll and mutton roll. Onion, tomato, carrot, chilli sauce and tomato sauce are the additional ingredients. You can have any combination of additional ingredients, or have standard rolls without any additional ingredients subject to the following constraints:

    (a) You can have tomato sauce if you have an egg roll, but not if you have a mutton roll.
    (b) If you have onion or tomato or both you can have chilli sauce, but not otherwise.

    How many different rolls can be ordered according to these rules?
    (a) 21          (b) 33
    (c) 40          (d) 42
    (e) None of the above.

**Solution:** Let the 5 additional ingredients onion, tomato, carrot, chilli sauce and tomato sauce are denoted by O, T, C, CS, TS respectively.

**Number of ways of ordering the egg roll:**

For the egg roll there are a total of 32 possibilities (with each ingredient being either present or not present – there being 5 ingredients the total number of possibilities of the combinations of the egg rolls would be equal to $2 \times 2 \times 2 \times 2 \times 2 = 32$ ways).

However, out of these 32 instances, the following combinations are not possible due to the constraint given in Statement (b) which tells us that to have CS in the roll either of onion or tomato must be present (or both should be present). The combinations which are not possible are:

(CS) (CS, TS) (CS, C) (CS, C, TS)

Total number of ways egg roll can be ordered $= 32 - 4 = 28.$

**Number of ways of ordering the mutton roll:**

Total number of cases for mutton roll without any constraints $= 2 \times 2 \times 2 \times 2 = 16$ ways. Cases rejected due to constraint given in statement (b): (CS); (CS,C) $\rightarrow 16 - 2 = 14$ cases.

Total number of ways or ordering a roll $= 28 + 14 = 42$. Option (d) is correct.

15. Steel Express stops at six stations between Howrah and Jamshedpur. Five passengers board at Howrah. Each passenger can get down at any station till Jamshedpur. The probability that all five persons will get down at different stations is:

    (a) $\dfrac{^6P_5}{6^5}$          (b) $\dfrac{^6C_5}{6^5}$

    (c) $\dfrac{^7P_5}{7^5}$          (d) $\dfrac{^6C_5}{7^5}$

    (e) None of the above.

**Solution:** The required probability would be given by:

$$\frac{\left(\begin{array}{c}\text{Total number of ways in which 5 people can get down} \\ \text{at 5 different stations from amongst 7 stations}\end{array}\right)}{\left(\begin{array}{c}\text{Total number of ways in which 5 people can get down} \\ \text{at 7 stations}\end{array}\right)}$$

The value of the numerator would be $^7P_5$, while the value of the denominator would be $7^5$. The correct answer would be Option (c).

**16.** In how many ways can 53 identical chocolates be distributed amongst 3 children– $C_1$, $C_2$ and $C_3$ – such that $C_1$ gets more chocolates than $C_2$ and $C_2$ gets more chocolates than $C_3$?

(a) 468        (b) 344
(c) 1404       (d) 234

**Solution:** 53 identical chocolates can be distributed amongst 3 children in $^{55}C_2$ ways =1485 ways ($^{n+r-1}C_{r-1}$ formula). Out of these ways of distributing 53 chocolates, the following distributions methods are not possible as they would have two values equal to each other– (0, 0, 53); (1, 1, 51); (2, 2, 49)....(26, 26, 1).

There are 27 such distributions, but when allocated to $C_1$, $C_2$ and $C_3$ respectively, each of these distributions can be allocated in 3 ways amongst them. Thus, $C_1$= 0, $C_2$ = 0 and $C_3$= 53 is counted differently from $C_1$ = 0, $C_2$ = 53 and $C_3$ = 0 and also from $C_1$ = 53, $C_2$ = 0 and $C_3$ = 0. This will remove $27 \times 3 = 81$ distributions from 1485, leaving us with 1404 distributions. These 1404 distributions are those where all three numbers are different from each other. However, whenever we have three different values allocated to three children, there can be 3! = 6 ways of allocating the three different values amongst the three people. For instance, the distribution of 10, 15 and 48 can be seen as follows:

| $C_1$ | $C_2$ | $C_3$ | |
|------|------|------|---|
| 48 | 15 | 10 | Only case which meets the problems' requirement. |
| 48 | 10 | 15 | |
| 15 | 48 | 10 | |
| 15 | 10 | 48 | |
| 10 | 15 | 48 | |
| 10 | 48 | 15 | |

Hence, out of every six distributions counted in the 1404 distributions we currently have, we need to count only one. The answer can be arrived at by dividing $1404 \div 6 = 234$. Option (d) is correct.

**17.** In a chess tournament at the ancient Olympic Games of Reposia, it was found that the number of European participants was twice the number of non-European participants. In a round robin format, each player played every other player exactly once. The tournament rules were such that no match ended in a draw – any conventional draws in chess were resolved in favour of the player who had used up the lower time. While analysing the results of the tournament, K.Gopal the tournament referee observed that the number of matches won by the non-European players was equal to the number of matches won by the European players. Which of the following can be the total number of matches in which a European player defeated a non-European player?

(a) 57        (b) 58
(c) 59        (d) 60

**Solution:** If we assume the number of non-European players to be n, the number of European players would be 2n. Then there would be three kinds of matches played –

Matches between two Europan players – a total of $^{2n}C_2$ matches – which would yield a European winner.

Matches between two non-European players – a total of $^nC_2$ matches, – which would yield a non-European winner.

Matches, between a European and a non-European player $= 2n^2$. These matches would have some European wins and some non-European wins. Let the number of European wins amongst these matches be $x$, then the number of non-European wins $= 2n^2 - x$.

Now, the problem clearly states that the number of European wins = Number of non-European wins

$$\Rightarrow \quad \frac{2n(2n-1)}{2} + x = \frac{n(n-1)}{2} + 2n^2 - x$$

$$\Rightarrow \quad n(n+1) = 4x$$

This means that the value of 4 times the number of wins for a European player over a non-European player should be a product of two consecutive natural numbers (since n has to be a natural number).

Among the options, $n = 60$ is the only possible value as the value of $4 \times 60 = 15 \times 16$.

Hence, Option (d) is correct.

**18.** A man, starting from a point M in a park, takes exactly eight equal steps. Each step is in one of the four directions – East, West, North and South. What is the total number of ways in which the man ends up at point M after the eight steps?

(a) 4200       (b) 2520
(c) 4900       (d) 5120

**Solution:** For the man to reach back to his original point, the number of steps North should be equal to the number of steps South. Similarly, the number of steps East should be equal to the number of steps West.

The following cases would exist:

4 steps north and 4 steps south = $8!/(4! \times 4!) = 70$ ways;

3 steps north, 3 steps south, 1 step east and 1 step west = $8!/(3! \times 3!) = 1120$ ways;

2 steps north, 2 steps south, 2 steps east and 2 steps west = $8!/(2! \times 2! \times 2! \times 2!) = 2520$ ways;

1 step north, 1 step south, 3 steps east and 3 steps west = $8!/(3! \times 3!) = 1120$ ways;

4 Steps east and 4 steps west =$8!/(4! \times 4!) = 70$ ways;

Thus, the total number of ways = $70 \times 2 + 1120 \times 2 + 2520 = 140 + 2240 + 2520 = 4900$ ways.

Option (c) is correct.

## REVIEW TEST 1

1. 18 guests have to be seated, half on each side of a long table. 4 particular guests desire to sit on one particular side and 3 others on the other side. Determine the number of ways in which the sitting arrangements can be made
   (a) $^{11}P_n \times (9!)^2$    (b) $^{11}C_5 \times (9!)^2$
   (c) $^{11}P_6 \times (9!)^2$    (d) None of these

2. If $m$ parallel lines in a plane are intersected by a family of $n$ parallel lines, find the number of parallelograms that can be formed.
   (a) $m^2 \times n^2$    (b) $m^{(m+1)}n^{(n+1)}/4$
   (c) $^mC_2 \times {}^nC_2$    (d) None of these

3. A father with eight children takes three at a time to the zoological garden, as often as he can without taking the same three children together more than once. How often will he go and how often will each child go?
   (a) $^8C_3, {}^7C_3$    (b) $^8C_3, {}^7C_2$
   (c) $^8P_3, {}^7C_3$    (d) $^8P_3, {}^7C_2$

4. A candidate is required to answer 7 questions out of 2 questions which are divided into two groups, each containing 6 questions. He is not permitted to attempt more than 5 questions from either group. In how many different ways can he choose the 7 questions?
   (a) 390    (b) 520
   (c) 780    (d) None of these

5. Find the sum of all 5 digit numbers formed by the digits 1, 3, 5, 7, 9 when no digit is being repeated.
   (a) 4444400    (b) 8888800
   (c) 13333200    (d) 6666600

6. Consider a polygon of n sides. Find the number of triangles, none of whose sides is the side of the polygon.
   (a) $nC_3 - n - n \times (n-4)C_1$
   (b) $n(n-4)(n-5)/3$
   (c) $n(n-4)(n-5)/6$
   (d) $n(n-1l(n-2)/3$

7. The number of 4 digit numbers that can be formed using the digits 0, 2, 3, 5 without repetition is
   (a) 18    (b) 20
   (c) 24    (d) 20

8. Find the total number of words that can be made by using all the letters from the word MACHINE, using them only once.
   (a) 7!    (b) 5020
   (c) 6040    (d) 7!/2

9. What is the total number of words that can be made by using all the letters of the word REKHA, using each letter only once?
   (a) 240    (b) 4!
   (c) 124    (d) 5!

10. How many different 5-digit numbers can be made from the first 5 natural numbers, using each digit only once?
    (a) 240    (b) 4!
    (c) 124    (d) 5!

11. There are 7 seats in a row. Three persons take seats at random. What is the probability that the middle seat is always occupied and no two persons are sitting on consecutive seats?
    (a) 7/70    (b) 14/35
    (c) 8/70    (d) 4/35

12. Let N = $33^x$. where $x$ is any natural no. What is the probability that the unit digit of $N$ is 3?
    (a) 1/4    (b) 1/3
    (c) 1/5    (d) 1/2

13. Find the probability of drawing one ace in a single draw of one card out of 52 cards.
    (a) $1/(52 \times 4)$    (b) 1/4
    (c) 1/52    (d) 1/13

14. In how many ways can a committee of 4 persons be made from a group of 10 people?
    (a) 10! / 4!    (b) 210
    (c) 10! / 6!    (d) None of these

15. In Question 14, what is the number of ways of forming the committee, if a particular member must be there in the committee?
    (a) 12    (b) 84
    (c) 9!/ 3!    (d) None of these

16. A polygon has 54 diagonals. The numbers of sides of this polygon are
    (a) 12    (b) 84
    (c) 3. 3!    (d) 4. 4!

17. An anti-aircraft gun can take a maximum of 4 shots at an enemy plane moving away from it, the probabilities of hitting the plane at first, second, third and fourth shots are 0.4, 0.3, 0.2 and 0.1 respectively. What is the probability that the gun hits the plane?
    (a) 0.7654    (b) 0.6976
    (c) 0.3024    (d) 0.2346

18. 7 white balls and 3 black balls are placed in a row at random. Find the probability that no two black balls are adjacent.
    (a) 2/15    (b) 7/15
    (c) 8/15    (d) 4/15

19. The probability that A can solve a problem is 3/10 and that B can solve is 5/7. If both of them attempt to solve the problem, what is the probability that the problem can be solved?
   (a) 3/5           (b) 1/4
   (c) 2/3           (d) 4/5

20. The sides *AB*, *BC*, *CA* of a triangle *ABC* have 3, 4 and 5 interior points respectively on them. Find the number of triangles that can be constructed using these points as vertices.
   (a) 180         (b) 105
   (c) 205         (d) 280

21. From 6 gentlemen and 4 ladies, a committee of 5 is to be formed. In how many ways can this be done if there is no restriction in its formation?
   (a) 256         (b) 246
   (c) 252         (d) 260

22. From 4 officers and 8 jawans in how many ways can 6 be chosen to include exactly one officer?

(a) $^{12}C_6$         (b) 1296
(c) 1344         (d) 224

23. From 4 officers and 8 jawans in how many ways can 6 be chosen to include atleast one officer?
   (a) 868         (b) 924
   (c) 896         (d) none of these

24. Two cards are drawn one after another from a pack of 52 ordinary cards. Find the probability that the first card is an ace and the second drawn is an honour card if the first card is not replaced while drawing the second.
   (a) 12/13         (b) 12/51
   (c) 1/663         (d) None of these

25. The probability that Andrews will be alive 15 years from now is 7/15 and that Bill will be alive 15 years from now is 7/10. What is the probability that both Andrews and Bill will be dead 15 years from now?
   (a) 12/150         (b) 24/150
   (c) 49/150         (d) 74/150

*Space for Rough Work*

## REVIEW TEST 2

1. A group consists of 100 people; 25 of them are women and 75 men; 20 of them are rich and the remaining poor; 40 of them are employed. The probability of selecting an employed rich woman is:
   (a) 0.05                    (b) 0.04
   (c) 0.02                    (d) 0.08

2. Out of 13 job applicants, there are 5 boys and 8 men. It is desired to choose 2 applicants for the job. The probability that at least one of the selected applicant will be a boy is:
   (a) 5/13                    (b) 14/39
   (c) 25/39                   (d) 10/13

3. Fours dogs and three pups stand in a queue. The probability that they will stand in alternate positions is:
   (a) 1/34                    (b) 1/35
   (c) 1/17                    (d) 1/68

4. Asha and Vinay play a number game where each is asked to select a number from 1 to 5. If the two numbers match, both of them win a prize. The probability that they will not win a prize in a single trial is:
   (a) 1/25                    (b) 24/25
   (c) 2/25                    (d) None of these

5. The number of ways in which 6 British and 5 French can dine at a round table if no two French are to sit together is given by:
   (a) $6! \times 5!$          (b) $5! \times 4!$
   (c) 30                      (d) $7! \times 5!$

6. A cricket team of 11 players is to be formed from 20 players including 6 bowlers and 3 wicketkeepers. Find the number of ways in which a team can be formed having exactly 4 bowlers and 2 wicketkeepers:
   (a) 20790                   (b) 6930
   (c) 10790                   (d) 360

7. Three boys and three girls are to be seated around a circular table. Among them one particular boy Rohit does not want any girl neighbour and one particular girl Shaivya does not want any boy neighbour. How many such arrangements are possible?
   (a) 5                       (b) 6
   (c) 4                       (d) 2

8. Words with five letters are formed from ten different letters of an alphabet. Then the number of words which have at least one letter repeated is
   (a) 19670                   (b) 39758
   (c) 69760                   (d) 99748

9. Sunil and Kapil toss a coin alternatively till one of them gets a head and wins the game. If Sunil starts the game, the probability that he (Sunil) will win is:

10. The number of pallelograms that can be formed if 7 parallel horizontal lines intersect 6 parallel vertical lines, is:
    (a) 42                     (b) 294
    (c) 315                    (d) None of these

11. $1.3.5...(2n - 1)/2.4.6...(2n)$ is equal to:
    (a) $(2n)! \div 2^n (n!))^2$     (b) $(2n)! \div n!$
    (c) $(2n - 1) \div ) n - 1)!$    (d) $2^n$

12. How many four-digit numbers, each divisible by 4 can be formed using the digits 1, 2, 3, 4 and 5 (repetitions allowed)?
    (a) 100                    (b) 150
    (c) 125                    (d) 75

13. A student is to answer 10 out of 13 questions in a test such that he/she must choose at least 4 from the first five questions. The number of choices available to him is:
    (a) 140                    (b) 280
    (c) 196                    (d) 346

14. The number of ways in which a committee of 3 ladies and 4 gentlemen can be appointed from a meeting consisting of 8 ladies and 7 gentlemen, if Mrs. Pushkar refuses to serve in a committee if Mr.Modi is its member, is
    (a) 1960                   (b) 3240
    (c) 1540                   (d) None of these

15. A room has 3 lamps. From a collection of 10 light bulbs of which 6 are not good, a person selects 3 at random and puts them in a socket. The probability that he will have light, is:
    (a) 5/6                    (b) 1/2
    (c) 1/6                    (d) None of these

16. Two different series of a question booklet for an aptitude test are to be given to twelve students. In how many ways can the students be placed in two rows of six each so that there should be no identical series side by side and that the students sitting one behind the other should have the same series?
    (a) $2 \times {}^{12}C_6 \times (6!)^2$     (b) $6! \times 6!$
    (c) $7! \times 7 \times$                    (d) None of these

17. The letters of the word PROMISE are arranged so that no two of the vowels should come together. The total number of arrangements is:
    (a) 49                     (b) 1440
    (c) 7                      (d) 1898

18. Find the remainder left after dividing $1! + 2! + 3! + ... + 1000!$ by 7.
    (a) 0                      (b) 5
    (c) 21                     (d) 14

19. In the McGraw-Hill Mindworkzz mock test paper, there are two sections, each containing 4 questions. A candidate is required to attempt 5 questions but

not more than 3 questions from any section. In how many ways can 5 questions be selected?

(a) 24            (b) 48

(c) 72            (d) 96

20. A bag contains 10 balls out of which 3 are pink and rest are orange. In how many ways can a random sample of 6 balls be drawn from the bag so that at the most 2 pink balls are included in the sample and no sample has all the 6 balls of the same colour?

(a) 105           (b) 168

(c) 189           (d) 120

*Space for Rough Work*

# ANSWER KEY

## Review Test 1

| | | | |
|---|---|---|---|
| 1. (b) | 2. (c) | 3. (b) | 4. (c) |
| 5. (d) | 6. (a) | 7. (a) | 8. (a) |
| 9. (d) | 10. (d) | 11. (d) | 12. (a) |
| 13. (d) | 14. (b) | 15. (b) | 16. (a) |
| 17. (b) | 18. (b) | 19. (d) | 20. (c) |
| 21. (c) | 22. (d) | 23. (c) | 24. (d) |
| 25. (b) | | | |

## Review Test 2

| | | | |
|---|---|---|---|
| 1. (c) | 2. (c) | 3. (b) | 4. (b) |
| 5. (b) | 6. (a) | 7. (c) | 8. (c) |
| 9. (c) | 10. (c) | 11. (a) | 12. (c) |
| 13. (a) | 14. (d) | 15. (d) | 16. (b) |
| 17. (b) | 18. (b) | 19. (b) | 20. (b) |

# TASTE OF THE EXAMS—BLOCK VI

## CAT QUESTIONS (1999-2008, 2017)

1. Ten points are marked on a straight-line and 11 points are marked on another straight-line. How many triangles can be constructed with vertices from among the above points? **(CAT 1999)**
   (a) 495      (b) 550
   (c) 1045      (d) 2475

2. For a scholarship, at the most n candidates out of $2n + 1$ can be selected. If the number of different ways of selection of at least one candidate is 63, the maximum number of candidates that can be selected for the scholarship is **(CAT 1999)**
   (a) 3      (b) 4
   (c) 6      (d) 5

3. In a survey of political preferences, 78% of those asked were in favour of at least one of the proposals: I, II and III. 50% of those asked favoured proposal I, 30% favoured proposal II and 20% favoured proposal III. If 5% of those asked favoured all three of the proposals, what percentage of those asked favoured more than one of the three proposals? **(CAT 1999)**
   (a) 10      (b) 12
   (c) 17      (d) 22

4. Sam has forgotten his friend's seven-digit telephone number. He remembers the following: the first three digits are either 635 or 674, the number is odd, and the number 9 appears once. If Sam were to use a trial and error process to reach his friend, what is the minimum number of trials he has to make before he can be certain to succeed? **(CAT 2000)**
   (a) 10,000      (b) 2,430
   (c) 3,402      (d) 3,006

5. There are three cities: A, B and C. Each of these cities is connected with the other two cities by at least one direct road. If a traveller wants to go from one city (origin) to another city (destination), she can do so either by traversing a road connecting the two cities directly, or by traversing two roads, the first connecting the origin to the third city and the second connecting the third city to the destination. In all there are 33 routes from A to B (including those via C). Similarly, there are 23 routes from B to C (including those via A). How many roads are there from A to C directly? **(CAT 2000)**
   (a) 6      (b) 3
   (c) 5      (d) 10

6. One red flag, three white flags and two blue flags are arranged in a line such that: **(CAT 2000)**

I. No two adjacent flags are of the same colour.
II. The flags at the two ends of the line are of different colours.
In how many different ways can the flags be arranged?
   (a) 6      (b) 4
   (c) 10      (d) 2

7. The figure below shows the network connecting cities A, B, C, D, E and F. The arrows indicate permissible direction of travel. What is the number of distinct paths from A to F?

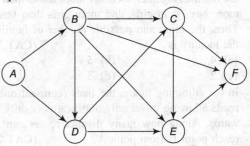

   (a) 9      (b) 10
   (c) 11      (d) None of these

8. Let n be the number of different five-digit numbers, divisible by 4 with the digits 1, 2, 3, 4, 5 and 6, no digit being repeated in the numbers. What is the value of n? **(CAT 2001)**
   (a) 144      (b) 168
   (c) 192      (d) None of these

**Directions for questions 9 and 10:** Answer the questions based on the following information. Each of the 11 letters A, H, I, M, O, T, U, V, W, X and Z appears same when looked at in a mirror. They are called symmetric letters. Other letters in the alphabet are asymmetric letters. **(CAT 2002)**

9. How many four-letter computer passwords can be formed using only the symmetric letters (no repetition allowed)?
   (a) 7,920      (b) 330
   (c) 14,640      (d) 4,19,430

10. How many three-letter computer passwords can be formed (no repetition allowed) with at least one symmetric letter?
   (a) 990      (b) 2,730
   (c) 12,870      (d) 15,600

11. In how many ways is it possible to choose a white square and a black square on a chessboard so that the squares must not lie in the same row or column? **(CAT 2002)**
   (a) 56      (b) 896
   (c) 60      (d) 768

12. How many numbers greater than 0 and less than a million can be formed with the digits 0, 7 and 8? **(CAT 2002)**
    (a) 486
    (b) 1,084
    (c) 728
    (d) None of these

13. Ten straight lines, no two of which are parallel and no three of which pass through any common point, are drawn on a plane. The total number of regions (including finite and infinite regions) into which the plane would be divided by the lines is **(CAT 2002)**
    (a) 56
    (b) 255
    (c) 1024
    (d) not unique

14. Each family in a locality has at most two adults, and no family has fewer than 3 children. Considering all the families together, there are more adults than boys, more boys than girls, and more girls than families. Then, the minimum possible number of families in the locality is **(CAT 2004)**
    (a) 4
    (b) 5
    (c) 2
    (d) 3

15. In the adjoining figure, the lines represent one-way roads allowing travel only northwards or only westwards. Along how many distinct routes can a car reach point B from point A? **(CAT 2004)**

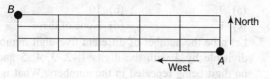

    (a) 15
    (b) 56
    (c) 120
    (d) 336

16. Three Englishmen and three Frenchmen work for the same company. Each of them knows a secret not known to others. They need to exchange these secrets over person-to-person phone calls so that eventually each person knows all six secrets. None of the Frenchmen knows English, and only one Englishman knows French. What is the minimum number of phone calls needed for the above purpose? **(CAT 2005)**
    (a) 5
    (b) 10
    (c) 9
    (d) 15

17. In a chess competition involving some boys and girls of a school, every student had to play exactly one game with every other student. It was found that in 45 games both the players were girls, and in 190 games both were boys. The number of games in which one player was a boy and the other was a girl is **(CAT 2005)**
    (a) 200
    (b) 216
    (c) 235
    (d) 256

18. Let S be the set of five-digit numbers formed by digits 1, 2, 3, 4 and 5, using each digit exactly once such that exactly two odd positions are occupied by odd digits. What is the sum of the digits in the rightmost position of the numbers in S? **(CAT 2005)**
    (a) 228
    (b) 216
    (c) 294
    (d) 192

19. There are 6 tasks and 6 persons. Task 1 cannot be assigned either to person 1 or to person 2; task 2 must be assigned to either person 3 or person 4. Every person is to be assigned one task. In how many ways can the assignment be done? **(CAT 2006)**
    (a) 144
    (b) 180
    (c) 192
    (d) 360
    (e) 716

20. A survey was conducted of 100 people to find out whether they had read recent issues of Golmal, a monthly magazine. The summarized information regarding readership in 3 months is given below:
    Only September: 18;  September but not August: 23;
    September and July: 8;  September: 28;  July: 48;
    July and August: 10;  None of the three months: 24.
    What is the number of surveyed people who have read exactly two consecutive issues (out of the three)? **(CAT 2006)**
    (a) 7
    (b) 9
    (c) 12
    (d) 14
    (e) 17

21. How many integers, greater than 999 but not greater than 4000, can be formed with the digits 0, 1, 2, 3 and 4, if repetition of digits is allowed? **(CAT 2008)**
    (a) 499
    (b) 500
    (c) 375
    (d) 376
    (e) 501

**Directions for questions 22 and 23:** The figure below shows the plan of a town. The streets are at right angles to each other. A rectangular park (P) is situated inside the town with a diagonal road running through it. There is also a prohibited region (D) in the town. **(CAT 2008)**

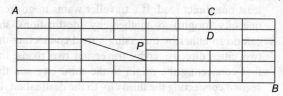

22. Neelam rides her bicycle from her house at A to her office at B, taking the shortest path. Then the number of possible shortest paths that she can choose is
    (a) 60
    (b) 75
    (c) 45
    (d) 90
    (e) 72

23. Neelam rides her bicycle from her house at A to her club at C, via B taking the shortest path. Then the

number of possible shortest paths that she can choose is

(a) 1170  (b) 630
(c) 792  (d) 1200
(e) 936

24. In how many ways can 8 identical pens be distributed among Amal, Bimal and Kamal so that Amal gets atleast 1 pen, Bimal gets atleast two pens and Kamal gets atleast 3 pens? **(CAT 2017)**

25. In how many ways can 7 identical erasers be distributed among 4 kids in such a ways that each kid gets atleast one eraser and no kid gets more than 3 erasers? **(CAT 2017)**

26. There are 12 towns grouped into four zones with three towns per zone. It is intended to connect the towns with telephone lines such that every two towns are connected with three direct lines if they belong to the same zone, and with only one direct line otherwise. How many direct telephone lines are required?

(a) 72  (b) 90
(c) 96  (d) 144

27. A survey on a sample of 25 new cars being sold at a local auto-dealer was conducted to see which of the three popular options (air conditioning, ratio and power windows) were already installed. The survey found:

- 15 had air conditioning
- 2 had air conditioning and power windows but no radios
- 12 had radio
- 6 had air conditioning and radio but no power windows
- 11 had power windows
- 4 had radio and power windows
- 3 had all three options.

What is the number of cars that had none of the options? **(CAT 2003)**

(a) 4  (b) 3
(c) 1  (d) 2

**Directions for questions 28 and 29:** Answer the questions on the basis of information given below.

A string of three English letters is formed as per the following rules:

(a) The first letter is any vowel.
(b) The second letter is m, n or p.
(c) If the second letter is m, then the third letter is any vowel which is different from the first letter.
(d) If the second letter is n, then the third letter is e or u.
(e) If the second letter is p, then the third letter is the same as the first letter.

28. How many strings of letters can possibly be formed using the above rules? **(CAT 2003)**

29. How many strings of letters can possibly be formed using the above rules such that the third letter of the string is e? **(CAT 2003)**

(a) 8  (b) 9
(c) 10  (d) 11

30. 70 percent of the employees in a multi-national corporation have VCD players, 75 percent have microwave ovens, 80 percent have ACs and 85 percent have washing machines. At least what percentage of employees have all the four gadgets? **(CAT 2003)**

(a) 15  (b) 5
(c) 10  (d) Cannot be determined

31. N persons stand on the circumference of a circle at distinct points. Each possible pair of persons, not standing next to each other, sings a two-minute song, one pair after the other. If the total time taken for singing is 28 minutes, what is N? **(CAT 2004)**

(a) 5  (b) 7
(c) 9  (d) None of the above

32. A new flag is to be designed with six vertical stripes using some or all of the colours yellow, green, blue and red. Then, the number of ways this can be done such that no two adjacent stripes have the same colour is: **(CAT 2004)**

(a) $12 \times 81$  (b) $16 \times 192$
(c) $20 \times 125$  (d) $24 \times 216$

33. What is the number of distinct terms in the expansion of $(a + b + c)^{20}$? **(CAT 2008)**

(a) 231  (b) 253
(c) 242  (d) 210
(e) 228

**Directions for questions 34 and 35:** Answer the questions on the basis of the information given below.

New Age Consultants has three consultants—Gyani, Medha and Buddhi. The sum of the number of projects handled by Gyani and Buddhi individually is equal to the number of projects in which Medha is involved. All three consultants are involved together in six projects. Gyani works with Medha in 14 projects. Buddhi has two projects with Medha but without Gyani, and three projects with Gyani but without Medha. The total number of projects for New Age Consultants is one less than twice the number of projects in which more than one consultant is involved.

34. What is the number of projects in which Gyani alone is involved? **(CAT 2003 LEAKED)**

(a) Uniquely equal to zero
(b) Uniquely equal to 1
(c) Uniquely equal to 4
(d) Cannot be determined uniquely

35. What is the number of projects in which Medha alone is involved? **(CAT 2003 LEAKED)**
    (a) Uniquely equal to zero
    (b) Uniquely equal to 1
    (c) Uniquely equal to 4
    (d) Cannot be determined

## ANSWER KEY

| | | | |
|---|---|---|---|
| 1. (b) | 2. (a) | 3. (c) | 4. (c) |
| 5. (a) | 6. (a) | 7. (b) | 8. (c) |
| 9. (a) | 10. (c) | 11. (d) | 12. (c) |
| 13. (a) | 14. (d) | 15. (b) | 16. (c) |
| 17. (a) | 18. (b) | 19. (a) | 20. (b) |
| 21. (d) | 22. (d) | 23. (a) | 24. 6 |
| 25. 16 | 26. (b) | 27. (d) | 28. (d) |
| 29. (c) | 30. (c) | 31. (d) | 32. (a) |
| 33. (a) | 34. (d) | 35. (b) | |

### Solutions

1. A triangle can be formed when we take two points from any of the lines and meet those points from any point of the second line. Number of triangles = ${}^{10}C_2 \times 11 + {}^{11}C_2 \times 10 = 45 \times 11 + 55 \times 10 = 1045$.

2. If we have n candidates who can be selected at the maximum, naturally, the answer to the question would also represent n. Also, we see that the options are also giving us values for n.

   Hence, we check for the first option. If n = 3, then $2n + 1 = 7$ and it means that there are 7 candidates to be chosen from. Since it is given that the number of ways of selection of at least 1 candidate is 63, we should try to see, whether selecting 1, 2 or 3 candidates from 7 indeed adds up to 63 ways. If it does this would be the correct answer.

   ${}^7C_1 + {}^7C_2 + {}^7C_3 = 7 + 21 + 35 = 63$. Thus, the first option fits the situation and is correct.

3. 78% favoured at least one. Also, the count of the three values given for favouring I, favouring II and favouring III is 100. Thus, we have an extra count of 22 – i.e. 78 people are counted 100 times, so 22 people are extra because they would be counted twice or thrice (People who favoured 2 proposals would be counted twice – so once extra; people who favoured three proposals would be counted thrice – so twice extra).

   We are also given that 5% people are counted thrice (Those who favour all three proposals). Hence, they would account for 10 extra counts ($5 \times 2$). Naturally, the remaining 12 extra counts should happen due to the people who favoured 2 proposals. Thus, we can see that 12% people were counted twice. The percentage who favoured more than one of the proposals would be $12 + 5 = 17$.

**Alternate solution:** Formula is - Favouring I + Favouring II + Favouring III - (favoured exactly 2 proposals) – 2(favoured exactly 3 proposals) = 78

$50 + 30 + 20 - (F) - 2 \times 5 = 100$

By solving we get, F = 12

People who favoured more than one of the three proposals = People who favoured two proposals + People who favoured three proposals = $12 + 5 = 17\%$

4. There are two possible cases.

   Case 1: The number 9 comes at the end.

   Case 2: 9 comes at position 4, 5, or 6.

   In both these cases, the blanks can be occupied by any of the available 9 digits (0, 1, 2, ..., 8).

   For the first case, the number 9 can occupy the last position

   Thus, total possible numbers would be $2 \times (9 \times 9 \times 9) = 1458$.

   For the second case, the number 9 can occupy any of the given position 4, 5, or 6, and there shall be an odd number at position 7. Thus, the total number of ways shall be $2 \times [3 \times (9 \times 9 \times 4)] = 1944$.

   Hence, total ways = 1458 + 1944 = 3402

5. We need to go through the options and use the MNP rule tool relating to Permutations and Combinations.

   If the first option is true—i.e. there are 6 routes between A to C:

   Then, the number of routes between C to B and consequently the number of routes between A to B would be given by the following possibilities:

| Routes Between A-C | C to B (possibilities) | Routes from A-C-B | Direct routes from A to B | Total routes from A to B |
|---|---|---|---|---|
| 6 | 5 | 30 | 3 | 33 |
| | 4 | 24 | 9 | 33 |
| | 3 | 18 | 15 | 33 |
| | 2 | 12 | 21 | 33 |
| | 1 | 6 | 27 | 33 |

   We also know that there are 23 routes between B to C. If the given numbers in the first possibility of the table are true, we see that B-A-C we would have $3 \times 6 = 18$ routes and from B to C we would have 5 routes – a total of 18 + 5 as required. Hence, this option fits the situation perfectly. Option (a) is correct.

6. This problem can be approached by putting the white flags in their possible positions. There are essentially 4 possibilities for placing the 3 white flags based on the condition that two flags of the same color cannot be together:

   1, 3, 5; 1,3,6; 1,4,6 and 2,4,6.

Out of these 4 possible arrangements for the 3 white flags we cannot use 1, 3, 6 and 1, 4, 6 as these have the same colored flag at both ends – something, which is not allowed according to the question. Thus there are only 2 possible ways of placing the white flags – 1, 3, 5 or 2, 4, 6. In each of these 2 ways, there are a further 3 ways of placing the 1 red flag and the 2 blue flags. Thus, we get a total of 6 combinations.

7. Ten ways can be counted in this case: 7 through AB – (CF, CEF, BF, EF, DCF, DCEF, DEF) and three through AD (EF, CF and CEF).

8. Three cases are possible

**Case 1: When the unit's digit is 2**

Total possible numbers = $\underline{2} \times \underline{3} \times \underline{4} \times \underline{3} \times \underline{1} = 72$

**Case 2: When the unit's digit is 4**

Total possible numbers = $\underline{2} \times \underline{3} \times \underline{4} \times \underline{2} \times \underline{1} = 48$

**Case 3: When the unit's digit is 6**

Total possible numbers = $\underline{2} \times \underline{3} \times \underline{4} \times \underline{3} \times \underline{1} = 72$

Total possible numbers = $72 + 72 + 48 = 192$

9. Total four-letter computer passwords that can be formed using only the symmetric letters (no repetition allowed) = $11 \times 10 \times 9 \times 8 = 7920$

10. Total possible numbers = Total number of passwords using all letters – Total number of passwords using no symmetric letters= $(26 \times 25 \times 24) - (15 \times 14 \times 13) = 12870$

11. A white square can be selected in 32 ways and once the white square is selected, 8 black squares become ineligible for selection (4 in the same row and 4 in the same column). So the number of black squares available = 24.

Hence the required number of ways = $32 \times 24 = 768$

12. Total numbers = 1 digit numbers + 2 digit numbers + 3 digit numbers + 4 digit numbers + 5 digit numbers + 6 digit numbers = $2 + 2 \times 3 + 2 \times 3^2 + 2 \times 3^3 + 2 \times 3^4 + 2 \times 3^5$

$= 2 (1 + 3 + 3^2 + 3^3 + 3^4 + 3^5) = 728$

13. Let the number of lines be 'x'.

The number of regions would be given by =

$\dfrac{x(x+1)}{2} + 1,$

Now put x = 10 in the above equation, we get number

of regions = $\dfrac{10 \times 11}{2} + 1 = 56$

14. Two families together have at most $2 \times 2 = 4$ adults and at least 6 children.

Number of adults (4) > Number of boys > Number of girls > 2 (Not possible).

Three families together have at most $2 \times 3 = 6$ adults and at least 9 children.

Number of families (3) < Number of girls (4) < Number of boys (5) < Number of adults (6)

With three families all conditions are satisfied. Hence, option (d) is correct.

15. From A to B, there are 8 one-way roads. Out of these 8 roads, 3 roads are in Northwards and 5 roads are westwards. The required number of routes would be given by $^8C_3$

Therefore the required number of distinct routes =

$\dfrac{8!}{3!5!} = 56$

16. Let the Englishmen be A, B and C. Out of these, let C know French. Also, the French can be assumed to be D, E and F. First of all, let A and B call C so that C knows all the three secrets with the Englishmen. Also, then let D and E call F, so that F knows all the three secrets with the French. Then, let C call F to exchange all secrets. At this point C and F would know all 6 secrets. They then need to transmit it to A, B and D, E respectively. So, C must call A and B. Also, F must call D and E. Thus, there will be a total of 2+2+1+2+2=9 calls (option c).

17. Let there be 'x' boys and 'y' girls

$^yC_2 = 45 \Rightarrow \dfrac{y(y-1)}{2} = 45 \Rightarrow y(y-1) = 90 \Rightarrow y = 10$

$^xC_2 = 190 \Rightarrow \dfrac{x(x-1)}{2} = 190 \Rightarrow x(x-1) = 380 \Rightarrow x = 20$

Number of games between one boy and one girl= $^{20}C_1 \times ^{10}C_1 = 10 \times 20 = 200$.

18. The number of numbers formed with 5 as the ending digit would be $2C_1 * 2C_1 * 2! * 2! = 16$. Similarly, the number of numbers formed with 1 and 3 in the units digit would be 16 and 16 respectively. Also, the number of numbers formed with 2 and 4 in the units place respectively, would be given by $^3C_2 \times 2! \times 2! = 12$ each.

Thus, the sum of the rightmost digits would be $16 \times 5 + 16 \times 3 + 16 \times 1 + 12 \times 2 + 12 \times 4 = 216$. Option (b) is correct.

19. Task 2 can be assigned in 2 ways and Task 1 can be assigned in 3 ways and Tasks 3 to 6 can be assigned in 4! ways. Thus, the required answer would be: $2 \times 3 \times 4! = 2 \times 3 \times 4 \times 3 \times 2 \times 1 = 144$ ways.

20. Total people reading the newspaper in consecutive months (July and August and August and September) is $2 + 7 = 9$ people.

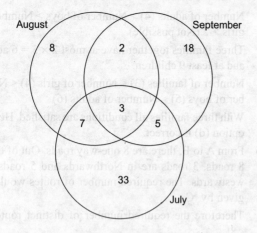

21. The integers can be identified as follows:

    4-digit numbers starting with 1: $5 \times 5 \times 5 = 125$

    4-digit numbers starting with 2: $5 \times 5 \times 5 = 125$

    4-digit numbers starting with 3: $5 \times 5 \times 5 = 125 +$ the number 4000.

    Hence, the answer would be $125 + 125 + 125 + 1 = 376$ (option (d)).

22. Neelam has to take the diagonal of the rectangular park compulsorily if she wants to take the shortest route. Hence, the key becomes to get her from vertex A to the start of the diagonal of the rectangular field and from the end of the diagonal vertex B.

    The solution to this question would be given by the algorithm $^4C_2 \times {}^6C_2 = 6 \times 15 = 90$

    (option (d)).

    **Note:** This algorithm is again one of the "either you know it or you are dead" algorithms that the CAT paper regularly presents. What I mean to say by this is that if you do not know this algorithm before-hand then it is highly unlikely that you would be able to do this question derive this logic especially under the pressure situation of the CAT.

    **Theory Point:**

    To understand this logic let us look at the following examples where we are required to find the number of ways of going from one corner of a grid to the opposite corner by traversing along the lines of the sides of the rectangles:

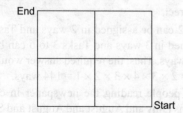

In this case the total number of ways is 6. You are welcome to verify the number by physically counting

the number of ways. (Note that 6 can also be given by $^4C_2!$)

Consider a few more examples before we conclude about an algorithm for the same.

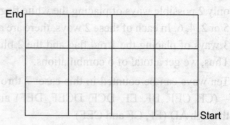

In the above figure the number of ways of traversing the grid would be given by $^7C_3 = 35$.

In order to explain the logic, it is simply given by the formula:

$^{(\text{NUMBER OF ROWS} + \text{NUMBER OF COLUMNS})}C_{(\text{NUMBER OF ROWS})}$

This formula will always work.

**Note:** If you know this algorithm, you would do this question in less than 30 seconds. If not, you would require at least 3-4 minutes to get a wrong answer — wrong because it is unlikely that you would be able to count correctly under the CAT pressure.

23. The answer to this question has to be a multiple of 90 (answer to the previous question). Hence, there are only two possible answers. The correct answer would be given by:

    $90 \times$ number of ways in which Neelam can go from B to point C.

    It can be easily verified that the number of ways of going from B to C is greater than 7. Hence, the option 630 would be rejected and you can go ahead and mark 1170 as the correct answer option. Thus, we will mark option (a).

24. After distributing 1, 2 and 3 pens to Amal, Bimal and Kamal we are left with only 2 pens.

    Now we can distribute 2 (n) pens among 3 (r) persons in $^{n+r-1}C_{r-1}$ ways. Hence, we have $^4C_2$ ways = 6 ways.

25. After distributing one eraser to each of the four kids we are left only with 3 erasers.

    We can distribute these 3 erasers in the following ways:

    **Case 1:** When one kid gets 2 erasers and one kid gets 1 eraser. We can do this in 12 ways.

    **Case 2:** When three kids get 1 eraser each. We can do this in 4 ways.

    Hence the required number of ways = $12 + 4 = 16$.

26. There will be 9 lines within each zone giving a total of 36 intra zonal lines. Also let us say that the towns are (A,B,C); (D,E,F); (G,H,I) and (J,K and L). Then, each of A, B and C would have 9 inter-zonal lines (total 27) D, E, F would have 6 each for a total of 18

and G, H, I would have 3 each for a total of 9 lines. Adding all these up, we would get: 36 + 27 + 18 + 9 = 90.

27.

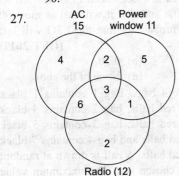

AC 15    Power window 11

4   2   5

3

6   1

2

Radio (12)

From the figure, it is clear that option (d) is the correct answer.

**Solutions for 28 and 29:**
First of all make a structure of what are the possible combinations:

With m as the middle letter – (vowel) – m – (another vowel)

With n as the middle letter – (vowel) – n – (e or u)

With p as the middle letter – (vowel) – p – (same vowel)

28. The number of possible letter strings are—
With m: $5 \times 4 = 20$, with n = $5 \times 2 = 10$, with p: $5 \times 1 = 5$

Thus, a total of 35 possible strings can possibly be formed (option d).

29. With m: 4, with n: 5, with p: 1. Thus a total of 10 stings can be formed with e as the third letter (option c).

30. The least percentage of people with all the four gadgets would happen if all the employees who are not having any one of the four objects is mutually exclusive.

Thus, $100 - 30 - 25 - 20 - 15 = 10$ (Option c).

31. You would have to do this problem through trial and error. For N = 7, the possible pairs are: 1-3, 1-4, 1-5, 1-6, 2-4, 2-5, 2-6, 2-7, 3-5, 3-6, 3-7, 4-6, 4-7, 5-7 — a total of 14 pairs which would make 28 minutes. Hence, we will mark option (b).

32. This can be solved using the mnp rule. For the first vertical stripe we can use any of 4 colours, for the second we would have only 3 options, same for the third to the sixth stripe. Hence, the required answer would be $4 \times 3 \times 3 \times 3 \times 3 \times 3 = 12 \times 81$ (option a).

33. The question is representative of $(a + b + c) (a + b + c) \dots (a + b + c)$—twenty times. What you should realise at the outset while solving this question is that for each term, the sum of all powers of a, b and c would be 20. Hence, with this insight when you start solving the problem, you would make the following realisations:

The first term would be $a^{20} b^0 c^0$

For the next series of terms, you would get with $a^{19}$ two ways in which you could distribute the remaining power as $a^{19} b^1 c^0$ or $a^{19} b^0 c^1$.

When you go for $a^{18}$, the remaining two power values can be distributed in three ways: viz: $a^{18} b^2 c^0$ or $a^{18} b^1 c^1$ or $a^{18} b^0 c^2$.

So, where is this leading you to? A little bit of thought and previous experience with triangular numbers (incidentally one of the favourite logics for CAT paper setters) will make you realise at this point that all we are doing in this question is adding the first 21 natural numbers. i.e., $1 + 2 + 3 + 4 + \dots 21 = 231$.

Hence, we will mark option (a).

**Solutions to 34 and 35:**
If we consider the number of projects for Gyani alone as 'g' and Buddhi alone as 'b', we will get the equation: $g + b = 17$. Hence, we cannot determine uniquely the value of g or b.

However, for question 35, we know that $g + b + m = 18$. Since $g + b = 17$, $m = 1$. Hence, the answers are:

34. Option (d)
35. Option (b)

## IIFT QUESTIONS (2008-2017)

1. In the MBA Programme of a B-School, there are two sections A and B. 1/4th of the students in section A and 4/9th of the students in section B are girls. If two students are chosen at random, one each from section A and section B as class representative, the probability that exactly one of the students chosen is a girl, is: **(IIFT 2014)**
   (a) 23/72     (b) 11/36
   (c) 5/12     (d) 17/36

2. The total number of eight-digit landline telephone numbers that can be formed having at least one of their digits repeated is: **(IIFT 2014)**
   (a) 98185600     (b) 97428800
   (c) 100000000     (d) None of the above

3. In an Engineering college in Pune, 8 males and 7 females have appeared for Student Cultural Committee selection process. 3 males and 4 females are to be selected. The total number of ways in which the committee can be formed, given that Mr. Raj is not to be included in the committee if Ms. Rani is selected, is: **(IIFT 2014)**
   (a) 1960     (b) 2840
   (c) 1540     (d) None of the above

4. A bag contains 8 red and 6 blue balls. If 5 balls are drawn at random, what is the probability that 3 of them are red and 2 are blue? **(IIFT 2011)**

(a) 80/143        (b) 50/143
(c) 75/143        (d) None of the above

5. In how many ways can four letters of the word 'SERIES' be arranged?        **(IIFT 2010)**
(a) 24        (b) 42
(c) 84        (d) 102

6. The number of distinct terms in the expansion of $(X + Y + Z + W)^{30}$ are:        **(IIFT 2009)**
(a) 4060        (b) 5456
(c) 27405        (d) 46376

7. A card is drawn at random from a well shuffled pack of 52 cards.

P(X): Probability that the card drawn is black or a king

P(Y): Probability that the card drawn is a club or a heart or a jack.

P(Z): Probability that the card drawn is an ace or a diamond or a queen.

Then which of the following is correct?

**(IIFT 2009)**
(a) P(X) > P(Y) > P(Z)
(b) P(X) ≥ P(Y) = P(Z)
(c) P(X) = P(Y) > P(Z)
(d) P(X) = P(Y) = P(Z)

8. The game of "chuck-a-luck" is played at carnivals in some parts of Europe. Its rules are as follows: you pick a number from 1 to 6 and the operator rolls three dice. If the number you picked comes up on all three dice, the operator pays you 3; if it comes up on two dice, you are paid 2; and if it comes up on just one die, you are paid 1. Only if the number you picked does not come up at all, you pay the operator 1. The probability that you will win money playing in this game is:        **(IIFT 2008)**
(a) 0.52        (b) 0.753
(c) 0.42        (d) None of the above

9. If $^{n+2}C_8 : {}^{n-2}P_4 = 57 : 16$, then n =        **(IIFT 2008)**
(a) 20        (b) 22
(c) 15        (d) None of the above

10. Ashish is studying late into the night and is hungry. He opens his mother's snack cupboard without switching on the lights, knowing that his mother has kept 10 packets of chips and biscuits in the cupboard. He pulls out 3 packets from the cupboard, and all of them turn out to be chips. What is the probability that the snack cupboard contains 1 packet of biscuits and 9 packets of chips?        **(IIFT 2012)**
(a) 6/55        (b) 12/73
(c) 14/55        (d) 7/50

11. A student is required to answer 6 out of 10 questions in an examination. The questions are divided into two groups, each containing 5 questions. She is not allowed to attempt more than 4 questions from each group. The number of different ways in which the student can choose the 6 questions is        **(IIFT 2012)**

(a) 100        (b) 160
(c) 200        (d) 280

12. The probability that in a household LPG will last 60 days or more is 0.8 and that it will last at most 90 days is 0.6. The probability that the LPG will last 60 to 90 days is        **(IIFT 2012)**
(a) 0.40        (b) 0.30
(c) 0.75        (d) None of the above

13. Suppose there are 4 bags. Bag 1 contains 1 black and $a^2 - 6a + 9$ red balls, bag 2 contains 3 black and $a^2 - 6a + 7$ red balls, bag 3 contains 5 black and $a^2 - 6a + 5$ red balls and bag 4 contains 7 black and $a^2 - 6a + 3$ red balls. A ball is drawn at random from a randomly chosen bag. The maximum value of probability that the selected ball is black, is

**(IIFT 2013)**
(a) $16/(a^2 - 6a + 10)$        (b) $20/(a^2 - 6a + 10)$
(c) 1/16        (d) None of the above

14. Out of 8 consonants and 5 vowels, how many words can be made, each containing 4 consonants and 3 vowels?        **(IIFT 2013)**
(a) 700        (b) 504000
(c) 3528000        (d) 7056000

15. Witrex Brown, an E-commerce company gives home delivery of its valuable products after receiving final order on their website by different modes of transportation like bike, scooter, tempo and truck. The probabilities of using bike, scooter, tempo and truck are respectively 2/9, 1/9, 4/9 and 2/9. The probabilities of delivering the product late to the destination by using these modes of transport are 3/5, 2/5, 1/5 and 4/5. If the product reached to the destination in time, find the probability that a scooter was used to deliver the product.        **(IIFT 2017)**
(a) 1/10        (b) 4/25
(c) 3/25        (d) None

16. A premier B-school, which is in process of getting an AACSB accreditation, has 360 second year students. To incorporate sustainability into their curriculum, it has offered 3 new elective subject in the second year namely Green Supply Chain, Global Climate Change & Business and Corporate Governance. Twelve students have taken all the three electives, and 120 students have taken Green Supply Chain. There are twice as many students who study Green Supply Chain and Corporate Governance but not Global Climate Change & Business, as those who study both Green Supply Chain and Global Climate Change & Business but not the Corporate Governance, and 4 times as many who Study all the three, 124 students study Corporate Governance. There are 72 students who could not muster up the courage to take up any of these subject. The group of students who study both Green Supply Chain and Corporate Governance but not Global Climate Change & Business is exactly

the same as the group made up of the students who study both Global Climate Change & Business and Corporate Governance. How many students study Global Climate Change & Business only?

**(IIFT 2017)**

(a) 176　　　　　　　(b) 104
(c) 152　　　　　　　(d) 188

17. The internal evaluation for Economic course in an Engineering programme is based on the score of four quizzes. Rahul has secured 70, 80 and 90 marks in the first three quizzes. The fourth quiz has ten True-false type questions carrying 10 marks. What is the probability that Rahul's average internal marks for the Economic course is more than 80, given that he decides to guess randomly on the final quiz?

(a) 12/1024　　　　　(b) 11/1024
(c) 11/256　　　　　 (d) 12/256　　**(IIFT 2015)**

18. During the essay writing stage of MBA admission process in a reputed B-school, each group consists of 10 students. In one such group, two students are batchmates from the same IIT department. Assuming that the students are sitting in a row, the number of ways in which the students can sit so that the two batchmates are not sitting next to each other, is:

**IIFT 2015**

(a) 3540340　　　　　(b) 2874590
(c) 2903040　　　　　(d) None of the above

19. In a certain village, 22% of the families own agricultural land, 18% own a mobile phone and 1600 families own both agricultural land and a mobile phone. If 68% of the families neither own agriculture land nor a mobile phone, then the total number of families living in the village is:　**(IIFT 2015)**

(a) 20000　　　　　　(b) 10000
(c) 8000　　　　　　 (d) 5000

20. In the board meeting of a FMCG Company, everybody present in the meeting shakes hand with everybody else. If the total number of handshakes is 78, the number of members who attended the board meeting is:　　　　　　**(IIFT 2015)**

(a) 7　　　　　　　　(b) 9
(c) 11　　　　　　　 (d) 13

21. The answer sheets of 5 engineering students can be checked by any one of nine professors. What is the probability that all the 5 answer sheets are checked by exactly 2 professors?　　**(IIFT 2012)**

(a) 20/2187　　　　　(b) 40/2187
(c) 40/729　　　　　 (d) None of the above

22. In a sports meet for senior citizens organised by the Rotary Club in Kolkata, 9 married couples participated in the table tennis mixed double event. The number of ways in which the mixed double team can be made, so that no husband and wife play in the same set, is　　　　　**(IIFT 2013)**

(a) 1512　　　　　　 (b) 1240
(c) 960　　　　　　　(d) 640

23. Two trains P and Q are scheduled to reach New Delhi railway station at 10.00 AM. The probability that train P and train Q will be late is 7/9 and 11/27 respectively. The probability that train Q will be late, given that train P is late, is 8/9. Then the probability that neither train will be late on a particular day is

**(IIFT 2013)**

(a) 40/81　　　　　　(b) 41/81
(c) 77/81　　　　　　(d) 77/243

24. A survey was conducted to test relative aptitudes in quantitative and logical reasoning of MBA applicants. It is perceived (prior to the survey) that 80 percent of MBA applicants are extremely good in logical reasoning, while only 20 percent are extremely good in quantitative aptitude. Further, it is believed that those with strong quantitative knowledge are also sound in data interpretation, with conditional probability as high as 0.87. However, some MBA applicants who are extremely good in logical reasoning can be also good in data interpretation, with conditional probability 0.15. An applicant surveyed is found to be strong in data interpretation. The probability that the applicant is also strong in quantitative aptitude is　　　**(IIFT 2013)**

(a) 0.4　　　　　　　(b) 0.6
(c) 0.8　　　　　　　(d) 0.9

25. The business consulting division of TCS has overseas operations in 3 locations: Singapore, New York and London. The Company has 22 analysts covering Singapore, 28 covering New York and 24 covering London. 6 analysts cover Singapore and New York but not London, 4 analysts cover Singapore and London but not New York, and 8 analysts cover New York and London but not Singapore. If TCS has a total of 42 business analysts covering at least one of the three locations: Singapore, New York and London, then the number of analysts covering New York alone is:　　　　　**(IIFT 2014)**

(a) 14　　　　　　　 (b) 28
(c) 5　　　　　　　　(d) 7

## ANSWER KEY

| | | | |
|---|---|---|---|
| 1. (d) | 2. (d) | 3. (c) | 4. (d) |
| 5. (d) | 6. (b) | 7. (c) | 8. (c) |
| 9. (d) | 10. (c) | 11. (c) | 12. (a) |
| 13. (d) | 14. (c) | 15. (c) | 16. (b) |
| 17. (b) | 18. (c) | 19. (a) | 20. (d) |
| 21. (b) | 22. (a) | 23. (b) | 24. (b) |
| 25. (d) | | | |

**Solutions**

1. Let there be 4 students in section A(1 girl, 3 boys).

   Let there be 9 students in section B(4 girls, 5 boys).

   **Case 1:** A girl is chosen from section A and a boy is chosen from section B

   Probability = $(1/4) \times (5/9) = 5/36$

   **Case 2:** A boy is chosen from section A and a girl is chosen from section B

   Probability = $(3/4) \times (4/9) = 12/36$

   Required probability = $(5/36) + (12/36) = 17/36$

2. Total possible numbers = (Total 8 Digit numbers) – (Total 8 Digit numbers with no digit repetition)

   $= 90000000 - 9 \times 9 \times 8 \times 7 \times 6 \times 5 \times 4 \times 3 = 88367040$

3. Required number of ways to form the committee = Total number of ways to select 3 males and 4 females from 8 males and 7 females – total number of ways to form the committee when Raj and Rani both are in the committee = ${}^8C_3 \times {}^7C_4 - {}^7C_2 \times {}^6C_3 = 1540$

4. Number of ways of selecting 3 red balls and 2 blue balls = ${}^8C_3 \times {}^6C_2$

   Number of ways of selecting 5 balls = ${}^{14}C_5$

   Required probability $= {}^8C_3 \times {}^6C_2 / {}^{14}C_5 = \dfrac{15 \times 56}{14 \times 143} = \dfrac{60}{143}$

5. **Case A:** When all alphabets are different

   Then the number of ways = $4! = 24$

   **Case B:** 2 letters are same and remaining 2 are different

   Number of ways = ${}^2C_1 \times {}^3C_2 \times \dfrac{4!}{2!} = 72$

   **Case 3:** 2 letters are same and remaining 2 are also same.

   Number of ways = $\dfrac{4!}{2!2!} = 6$

   Total cases = $24 + 72 + 6 = 102$.

6. Number of distinct terms in the expansion of $(X + Y + Z + W)^{30}$ are $= {}^{(30+4-1)}C_{(4-1)} = {}^{33}C_3 = 5456$

7. There are total 26 blacks and out of which 2 are kings. We have 2 cards which are kings but not black so the value of $P(X) = \dfrac{26+2}{52} = \dfrac{28}{52}$

   Similarly: $P(Y) = \dfrac{13+13+2}{52} = \dfrac{28}{52}$

   $P(Z) = \dfrac{3+13+3}{52} = \dfrac{19}{52}$.

   $P(X) = P(Y) > P(Z)$. Option (c) is correct.

8. Probability of winning the game = 1 – probability of losing the game

   He/she will lose money when none of the three dice shows the picked number on the top surface.

   Probability of winning the game =1 – probability of losing the game = $1 - \dfrac{5}{6} \times \dfrac{5}{6} \times \dfrac{5}{6} = 1 - \dfrac{125}{216} = \dfrac{91}{216}$

9. $\dfrac{n + 2_{C_8}}{n - 2_{P_4}} = \dfrac{57}{16}$

   Now put the options and check. We get n = 19.

10. Since we know that there are at least 3 packets of chips, it means that the actual situation could involve any of the following break-ups between chip packets and biscuit packets.

    (3,7); (4,6); (5,5); (6,4); (7,3); (8,2); (9,1) or (10,0).

    We are looking for the probability of the actual situation being (9,1).

    The number of ways of selecting 3 packets of chips from the given possibilities above would be given by ${}^3C_3 + {}^4C_3 + {}^5C_3 + {}^6C_3 + {}^7C_3 + {}^8C_3 + {}^9C_3$ to ${}^{10}C_3 = 330$. Out of these, the total number of ways in which 3 chip packets could come out from the (9,1) situation would be $= {}^9C_3 = 84$. The required probability would be given by $84/330 = 14/55$. Hence, Option (c) is correct.

11. 3 cases are possible here:

    Case a: 3 questions from section 1 and 3 questions from section 2 = ${}^5C_3 \times {}^5C_3 = 100$

    Case b: Number of ways to choose 4 questions from section 1 and 2 questions from section 2 = ${}^5C_4 \times {}^5C_2 = 50$

    Case c: Number of ways to choose 2 questions from section 1 and 4 questions from section 2 = ${}^5C_2 \times {}^5C_3 = 50$

    Total possible ways = $100 + 50 + 50 = 200$

12. The probability that the LPG lasts 60 days or more = 0.8. This means that the probability that the LPG would last less than 60 days = $1 - 0.8 = 0.2$.

    The probability that the LPG would last less than or equal to 90 days = 0.6.

    Thus, the required probability that the LPG would last between 60 to 90 days = Probability that the LPG would last less than 90 days – Probability that the LPG would last less than 60 days = $0.6 - 0.2 = 0.4$.

13. Probability to select a black ball =

    $\dfrac{1}{4} \left[ \dfrac{1}{a^2 - 6a + 9 + 1} + \dfrac{3}{a^2 - 6a + 7 + 3} + \dfrac{5}{a^2 - 6a + 5 + 5} + \dfrac{7}{a^2 - 6a + 3 + 7} \right] = \dfrac{4}{a^2 - 6a + 10}$

    The probability will be maximum when $a^2 - 6a + 10$ is minimum.

    However, the probability of an event cannot be greater than 1. We also know that 'a' must be a natural number. At a = 3, the denominator is minimised, but the value of the probability comes out as 4, which is not possible. At a = 4, required probability = 4/2 = 2 - not possible. At a = 5, required probability = 4/5. This would be the maximum possible value. Hence, option (d) is correct.

14. 3 vowels can be selected in = $^5C_3$ = 10 ways

    4 consonants can be selected from 8 in $^8C_4$ = 70 ways

    Required number of words = $^5C_3 \times ^8C_4 \times 7!$ = 70 × 10 × (7!) = 3528000

15. Probability of delivery product on time by all means = 2/9 × 2/5 + 1/9 × 3/5 + 4/9 × 4/5 + 2/9 × 1/5 = 25/45

    Probability of delivery of product on time by scooter = 1/9 × 3/5 = 3/45

    Required probability = (3/45)/(25/45) = 3/25

16. Based on the information provided, we can make the following Venn diagram:

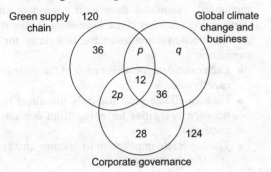

    p = 24, 2p = 48

    36 + 24 + q + 48 + 12 + 36 + 28 = 288 → q = 104. Hence, option (b) is correct.

17. Average marks for the Economic course would be more than 80 when he scores more than 80 marks in the final quiz. It is possible if he attempts 9 or 10 questions correctly.

    Number of ways to attempt 9 or 10 questions correctly = $^{10}C_9 + 1$ = 11

    Number of ways to attempt 10 questions = $2^{10}$ = 1024

    Required probability = 11/1024

18. Required number of seating arrangements = total number of possible arrangements – total number of arrangements in which the two IITians sit together = 10! – 9! × 2! = 10.9! – 9! × 2 = 8 × 9! = 2903040.

19. If 68% of the families neither own agriculture land nor a mobile phone then 32% owns either agriculture land or mobile phone or both.

    Percentage of population own both agricultural land and a mobile phone = 22 + 18 – 32 = 8%.

    8% of population = 1600

    Total population = (1600 × 100)/8 = 20000. Option (a) is correct.

20. Let 'n' people attended the board meeting, then total number of handshakes = $^nC_2$ = 78

    By solving or by checking the options we get n = 13.

21. The required probability would be given by:

    The number of ways in which the papers are checked by exactly two professors/The number of ways in which the papers can be checked overall

    The denominator of the above expression would simply be 9 × 9 × 9 × 9 × 9 = $9^5$ (since each paper can be checked by any of the nine professors).

    Now for the 5 papers to be checked by exactly two professors, the number of ways would be given by the following logic:

    There are $^9C_2$ ways of selecting the two professors and once the professors are selected each of the five papers can be checked in 2 ways.

    Thus, the value should be $^9C_2 \times 2^5$. However, once the two professors are selected, in these $2^5$ ways of checking the 5 papers, there would be exactly 2 ways in which all the papers are checked only by one of the two professors.

    Hence, the required value would be given by $^9C_2 \times (2^5 - 2)$.

    The required probability would then be given by:

    $(^9C_2 \times 30)/9^5 = 40/2187$

    Hence, Option (b) is correct.

22. The number of ways of selecting 2 men and 2 women (such that there would be no husband wife pair in the same set) would be $^9C_2 * ^7C_2$. Further, there are two ways in which we can form the two teams for the same set of players. Thus, the correct answer would be: $^9C_2 \times ^7C_2 \times 2$ = 36 × 21 × 2 = 1512. Hence, Option (a) is correct.

23. Let the probability of P coming late = P(P); the probability of Q coming late = P(Q).

    Then: $P(P \cup Q) = P(P) + P(Q) - P(P \cap Q)$

    Where $P(P \cup Q)$ means the situation where at least one of the two trains P and Q is late and $P(P \cap Q)$ means the situation where both the trains P and Q are late. The value of $P(P \cap Q)$ = 7/9 × 8/9 = 56/81. This gives us:

    $P(P \cup Q)$ = 7/9 + 11/27 – 56/81 = (63 + 33 – 56)/81 = 40/81.

    Thus, the probability that none of the two trains is late = 1 – Probability that at least 1 train is late.

    The required answer = 1 – 40/81 = 41/81.

    Hence, Option (b) is correct.

24. Out of every 100 applicants, 80 are extremely good at Logical Reasoning while 20 are extremely good at Quantitative Aptitude. Further, since the probability of someone who is extremely good at Quantitative Aptitude also being strong at Data Interpretation is

0.87, we can expect $20 \times 0.87 = 17.4$ people out of 20 to be strong at DI.

Also, since the related probability for someone being strong at DI if he/she is strong at LR is 0.15, we get $80 \times 0.15 = 12$ people who would be expected to be strong at DI (from the 80 who are strong at LR). Thus, we get a total of 29.4 people in every 100 who would be strong at DI. Naturally, if we find someone who is strong at DI, the probability he/she would also be strong at QA = $17.4/29.4 \approx 0.6$.

Hence, Option (b) is correct.

25. The following figure represents the situation given to us:

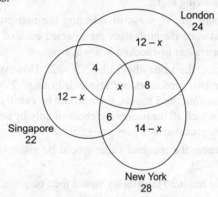

From the figure and from the information in the question, it is clear that:

$(12 - x) + 6 + 4 + x + (14 - x) + 8 + (12 - x) = 42$

Hence, $56 - 2x = 42 \rightarrow x = 7$.

New York alone = $14 - x = 14 - 7 = 7$.

Hence, option (d) is correct.

## XAT QUESTIONS (2009-2017)

1. The probability that a randomly chosen positive divisor of $10^{29}$ is an integer multiple of $10^{23}$ is $a^2/b^2$, then '$b - a$' would be: **(XAT 2014)**
   (a) 8                     (b) 15
   (c) 21                    (d) 23
   (e) 45

2. Aditya has a total of 18 red and blue marbles in two bags (each bag has marbles of both colours). A marble is randomly drawn from the first bag followed by another randomly drawn from the second bag, the probability of both being red is 5/16. What is the probability of both marbles being blue?
   **(XAT 2014)**
   (a) 1/16                  (b) 2/16
   (c) 3/16                  (d) 4/16
   (e) None of these

3. 70% of the students who joined XLRI last year play football. 75% play cricket 80% play basketball and

85% play carom. The minimum percentage of students who play all four games is:     **(XAT 2013)**
   (a) 5%                    (b) 10%
   (c) 15%                   (d) 20%
   (e) None of the above

4. Six playing cards are lying face down on a table, two of them are kings. Two cards are drawn at random. Let $a$ denote the probability that at least one of the cards drawn is a king and $b$ denote the probability of not drawing a king. The ratio $a/b$ is
   **(XAT 2013)**
   (a) $\geq 0.25$ and $\leq 0.5$    (b) $\geq 0.5$ and $\leq 0.75$
   (c) $\geq 0.75$ and $\leq 1.0$    (d) $\geq 1.0$ and $\leq 1.25$
   (e) $\geq 1.25$

5. In the country of Twenty, there are exactly twenty cities, and there is exactly one direct road between any two cities. No two direct roads have an overlapping road segment. After the election dates are announced, candidates from their respective cities start visiting the other cities. Following are the rules that the election commission has laid down for the candidates:
   - Each candidate must visit each of the other cities exactly once.
   - Each candidate must use only the direct roads between two cities for going from one city to another.
   - The candidate must return to his own city at the end of the campaign.
   - No direct road between two cities would be used by more than one candidate. The maximum possible number of candidates is     **XAT 2011**
   (a) 5                     (b) 6
   (c) 7                     (d) 8
   (e) 9

6. There are 240 second year students in a B-School. The Finance area offers 3 electives in the second year. These are Financial Derivatives, Behavioural Finance, and Security Analysis. Four students have taken all the three electives, and 48 students have taken Financial Derivatives. There are twice as many students who study Financial Derivatives (48) and Security Analysis (124) but not Behavioural Finance (53), as those who study both Financial Derivatives and Behavioural Finance but not Security Analysis, and 4 times as many who study all the three. 124 students study Security Analysis. There are 59 students who could not muster courage to take up any of these subjects. The group of students who study both Financial Derivatives and Security Analysis but not Behavioural Finance, is exactly the same as the group made up of students who study both Behavioural Finance and Security Analysis. How many students study Behavioural Finance only?
   **(XAT 2011)**

7. ...

bers, ...
number ca... 30
account number...
if $x_1x_2x_3$ is exactly...
both, $x_i$ can take values...8 digit num-
by seven 0s is not a valid ac... an account
the maximum possible number of $x_7$. An
a 'magic' account number? ...mber
(a) 9989
(c) 19989    (b) 19980
(e) 19990    (d) 19999

8. Let X be a four-digit positive integer such that the
unit digit of X is prime and the product of all digits
of X is also prime. How many such integers are
possible?
(a) 4
(c) 12    (b) 8    **(XAT 2010)**
(e) None of these    (d) 24

9. Let X be a four-digit number with exactly three
consecutive digits being same and is a multiple of
9. How many such X's are possible? **(XAT 2009)**
(a) 12
(c) 19    (b) 16
(e) None of the above    (d) 21

10. If F(x, n) be the number of ways of distributing "x"
toys to "n" children so that each child receives at
the most 2 toys, then F(4, 3) = _____?**(XAT 2008)**
(a) 2
(c) 3    (b) 6
(e) 5    (d) 4

11. Ramesh plans to order a birthday gift for his friend
from an online retailer. However, the birthday coincides with the festival season during which there is
a huge demand for buying online goods and hence
deliveries are often delayed. He estimates that the
probability of receiving the gift, in time, from the
retailers A, B, C and D would be 0.6, 0.8, 0.9 and
0.5 respectively. Playing safe, he orders from all
four retailers simultaneously. What would be the
probability that his friend would receive the gift in
time?
(a) 0.004
(c) 0.216    (2) 0.006    **(XAT 2015)**
(e) 0.996    (d) 0.994

12. In an amusement park along with the entry pass a
visitor gets two of the three available rides (A, B and
C) free. On a particular day 77 opted for ride A, 55
opted for B and 50 opted for C; 25 visitors opted
for both A and C, 22 opted for both A and B, while
no visitor opted for both B and C. 40 visitors did

not opt for ride A or B, or both. How many visited
with the entry pass on that day?
(a) 102    (b) 115
(c) 130    (d) 135
(e) 150

     **(XAT 2016)**

13. A dice is rolled twice. What is the probability that
the number in the second roll will be higher than
that in the first?    **(XAT 2017)**
(a) 5/36    (b) 8/36
(c) 15/36    (d) 21/36
(e) None of the above

class of 60, along with English as a common
...students can opt to major in Mathematics,
in bo...ology or a combination of any two. 6
the average... in both Mathematics and Physics, 15
Mathematics ...ics and Biology, but no one majors
Biology is 60. However... and Biology. In an English test,
in English, of students of... by students majoring in
What is the maximum possible... of students majoring in
who major ONLY in Physics?...bined average mark
(a) 30      ...majors, is 50.
(c) 20    (b) 25
(e) None of the above.    (d) 15   **...T 2017)**

---

### ANSWER KEY

| | | | |
|---|---|---|---|
| 1. (d) | 2. (c) | | |
| 5. (e) | 6. (a) | 3. (b) | |
| 9. (e) | 10. (b) | 7. (c) | 4. (e) |
| 13. (c) | 14. (d) | 11. (e) | 8. (a) |
| | | | 12. (e) |

### Solutions

1. $10^{29} = 2^{29} \times 5^{29}$

Total number of divisors of $10^{29} = (29 + 1) \times (29 + 1)$
= 900

$10^{29}/10^{23} = 10^6 = 2^6 \times 5^6$

Number of divisors of $10^{29}$ which are integral multiples of $10^{23} = (6 + 1) \times (6 + 1) = 49$.

Probability that a randomly chosen positive divisor of

$10^{29}$ is an integral multiple of $10^{23} = \dfrac{a^2}{b^2} = \dfrac{49}{900}$

$\dfrac{a^2}{b^2} = \dfrac{49}{900} \Rightarrow \dfrac{a}{b} = \dfrac{7}{30} \Rightarrow b - a = 23$

2. Probability

Let there be 'r' red marbles in the first bag and 'R' red
marbles in the second bag.

Also, let there be 'b' blue marbles in the first bag and
'B' blue marbles in the second bag.

Then $(r + b) + (R + B) = 18$. The number of ways of selecting 1 marble from the first bag and one marble from the second bag $= (r + b) \times (R + B)$.

Also, the number of ways of selecting a red marble from the first bag and a red marble from the second bag $= r \times R$. Hence, the probability of selecting two red marbles would be given by:

$r \times R/(r + b) \times (R + B) = 5/16$.

This equation shows us that the value of $(r + b + B)$ must be a multiple of 16 while the va~~l~~~~u~~n must be a multiple of 5.

We now know that $(r + b) + (R + B)$ ~~multiple~~ $\times (R + B)$ = a multiple of 16. If ~~we~~ 18 into two parts, such that th~~e~~ $8 = 80$. of 16, we get two cases:

Case I: $16 \times 2 = 32$ an~~d~~ ~~the~~n $r \times R = 10$ (in order to Analysing Case I: ~~/~~16 between the two).

If $(r + b) \times (R +$ ~~16~~ balls in one bag and 2 balls in the maintain the There w~~e~~ sec~~ond~~ bag must contain 1 red and 1 blue ball. T~~h~~~~e~~, $R = 1$ and $B = 1$ i.e., Since $r \times R = 10$ we get $r = 10$ and $b = 6$. The probability of both balls being blue in this case would turn out as:

$1/2 \times 6/16 = 3/16$

If we try to solve the other case in the same way, we get $r = 5$, $R = 5$ and $b = 3$ and $B = 5$ and the probability of both balls being blue becomes $1/2 \times 3/8 = 3/16$

We get the same answer in both the cases. Hence, option (c) is correct.

3. This can be interpreted as: The maximum percentage of people in the all 4 categories would occur when the students comprising the percentage of people not playing any one of the four games is unique for each game.

Since, 70% of the students play football, 30% of the students would not play football. Hence we 'lose' 30% students from the all four categories.

Similarly, percentage of students not playing cricket = 25%, percentage of students not playing basketball = 20% and percentage of students not playing carom = 15%. The minimum percentage of people playing all four would be got when we take each of these categories as distinct from each other. Thus, required answer = $100 - 30 - 25 - 20 - 15 = 100 - 90 = 10$.

4. b = The probability that neither of the cards is a king is given by:

First is not a king and second is not a king = $4/6 \times 3/5$

= $12/30 = 2/5 = 0.4$

---

~~ing~~ through the options, only ~~th~~e situation i.e. $a/b \geq 1.25$. Hence, a = ~~the~~ correct answer.

k~~e~~ $^{20}C_2 = 190$

~~Th~~e maximum number of candidates be 'n'. Since ~~ea~~ch candidate must visit 20 cities during his campaign, these n candidates will use 20n roads.

Thus, $20n < 190$ or $n < 9.5$

So the maximum possible value of $n = 9$.

6. The following deductions can be made based on the information provided:

(a) Number of students who study Financial Derivatives and Security Analysis but not Behavioural Finance = $4 \times 4 = 16$

(b) Number of students who study both Financial Derivatives and Behavioural Finance but not Security Analysis= 16/2= 8

(c) Total students who study at least one of the given three subjects= 240 − 59 = 181.

Now we can draw the Venn diagram as follows:

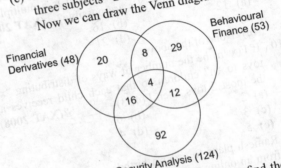

From the above Venn diagram we can find there are a total of 29 students who study Behavioral Finance only.

7. $x_1x_2x_3x_4x_5x_6x_7$ can be of the form PQRSPQR or PQRS.PQR can be chosen in $10 \times 10 \times 10 = 1000$ ways.

S can be chosen in 10 ways.

$x_1x_2x_3x_4x_5x_6x_7$ can be formed in $2 \times 1000 \times 10 = 20000$ ways. However, we would need to modify this answer, as there is some extra counting in this. There are essentially two things you need to take care of: (i) The number 20000000 has been counted twice, whereas it should not be counted at all, since it is not a valid number. Hence, we would need to reduce the count by 2.

(ii) The numbers 21111111, 22222222, 23333333, ..., 29999999 have each been counted twice, while they should be counted only once each. Thus, we would need to reduce the count by 9.

(a) 29 (b) 30
(c) 32 (d) 35
(e) None of the above options

7. In a bank the account numbers are all 8 digit numbers, and they all start with the digit 2. So, an account number can be represented as $2x_1x_2x_3x_4x_5x_6x_7$. An account number is considered to be a 'magic' number if $x_1x_2x_3$ is exactly the same as $x_4x_5x_6$ or $x_5x_6x_7$ or both, $x_i$ can take values from 0 to 9, but 2 followed by seven 0s is not a valid account number. What is the maximum possible number of customers having a 'magic' account number? **(XAT 2011)**
(a) 9989 (b) 19980
(c) 19989 (d) 19999
(e) 19990

8. Let X be a four-digit positive integer such that the unit digit of X is prime and the product of all digits of X is also prime. How many such integers are possible? **(XAT 2010)**
(a) 4 (b) 8
(c) 12 (d) 24
(e) None of these

9. Let X be a four-digit number with exactly three consecutive digits being same and is a multiple of 9. How many such X's are possible? **(XAT 2009)**
(a) 12 (b) 16
(c) 19 (d) 21
(e) None of the above

10. If F(x, n) be the number of ways of distributing "x" toys to "n" children so that each child receives at the most 2 toys, then F(4, 3) = _____?**(XAT 2008)**
(a) 2 (b) 6
(c) 3 (d) 4
(e) 5

11. Ramesh plans to order a birthday gift for his friend from an online retailer. However, the birthday coincides with the festival season during which there is a huge demand for buying online goods and hence deliveries are often delayed. He estimates that the probability of receiving the gift, in time, from the retailers A, B, C and D would be 0.6, 0.8, 0.9 and 0.5 respectively. Playing safe, he orders from all four retailers simultaneously. What would be the probability that his friend would receive the gift in time? **(XAT 2015)**
(a) 0.004 (2) 0.006
(c) 0.216 (d) 0.994
(e) 0.996

12. In an amusement park along with the entry pass a visitor gets two of the three available rides (A, B and C) free. On a particular day 77 opted for ride A, 55 opted for B and 50 opted for C; 25 visitors opted for both A and C, 22 opted for both A and B, while no visitor opted for both B and C. 40 visitors did

not opt for ride A or B, or both. How many visited with the entry pass on that day?
(a) 102 (b) 115
(c) 130 (d) 135
(e) 150
**(XAT 2016)**

13. A dice is rolled twice. What is the probability that the number in the second roll will be higher than that in the first? **(XAT 2017)**
(a) 5/36 (b) 8/36
(c) 15/36 (d) 21/36
(e) None of the above

14. In a class of 60, along with English as a common subject, students can opt to major in Mathematics, Physics, Biology or a combination of any two. 6 Students major in both Mathematics and Physics, 15 major in both Physics and Biology, but no one majors in both Mathematics and Biology. In an English test, the average mark scored by students majoring in Mathematics is 45 and that of students majoring in Biology is 60. However, the combined average mark in English, of students of these two majors, is 50. What is the maximum possible number of student who major ONLY in Physics? **(XAT 2017)**
(a) 30 (b) 25
(c) 20 (d) 15
(e) None of the above.

## ANSWER KEY

1. (d) 2. (c) 3. (b) 4. (e)
5. (e) 6. (a) 7. (c) 8. (a)
9. (e) 10. (b) 11. (e) 12. (e)
13. (c) 14. (d)

**Solutions**

1. $10^{29} = 2^{29} \times 5^{29}$
Total number of divisors of $10^{29} = (29 + 1) \times (29 + 1) = 900$
$10^{29}/10^{23} = 10^6 = 2^6 \times 5^6$
Number of divisors of $10^{29}$ which are integral multiples of $10^{23} = (6 + 1) \times (6 + 1) = 49$.
Probability that a randomly chosen positive divisor of
$10^{29}$ is an integral multiple of $10^{23} = \dfrac{a^2}{b^2} = \dfrac{49}{900}$
$\dfrac{a^2}{b^2} = \dfrac{49}{900} \Rightarrow \dfrac{a}{b} = \dfrac{7}{30} \Rightarrow b - a = 23$

2. Probability
Let there be 'r' red marbles in the first bag and 'R' red marbles in the second bag.
Also, let there be 'b' blue marbles in the first bag and 'B' blue marbles in the second bag.

Then $(r + b) + (R + B) = 18$. The number of ways of selecting 1 marble from the first bag and one marble from the second bag $= (r + b) \times (R + B)$.

Also, the number of ways of selecting a red marble from the first bag and a red marble from the second bag $= r \times R$. Hence, the probability of selecting two red marbles would be given by:

$r \times R/(r + b) \times (R + B) = 5/16$.

This equation shows us that the value of $(r + b) \times (R + B)$ must be a multiple of 16 while the value of $r \times R$ must be a multiple of 5.

We now know that $(r + b) + (R + B) = 18$ and $(r + b) \times (R + B) =$ a multiple of 16. If we try to break down 18 into two parts, such that their product is a multiple of 16, we get two cases:

Case I: $16 \times 2 = 32$ and Case II: $10 \times 8 = 80$.

Analysing Case I:

If $(r + b) \times (R + B) = 32$, then $r \times R = 10$ (in order to maintain the ratio of 5/16 between the two).

There would be 16 balls in one bag and 2 balls in the second bag.

The second bag must contain 1 red and 1 blue ball. i.e., $R = 1$ and $B = 1$

Since $r \times R = 10$ we get $r = 10$ and $b = 6$. The probability of both balls being blue in this case would turn out as:

$1/2 \times 6/16 = 3/16$

If we try to solve the other case in the same way, we get $r = 5$, $R = 5$ and $b = 3$ and $B = 5$ and the probability of both balls being blue becomes $1/2 \times 3/8 = 3/16$

We get the same answer in both the cases. Hence, option (c) is correct.

3. This can be interpreted as: The maximum percentage of people in the all 4 categories would occur when the students comprising the percentage of people not playing any one of the four games is unique for each game.

Since, 70% of the students play football, 30% of the students would not play football. Hence we 'lose' 30% students from the all four categories.

Similarly, percentage of students not playing cricket = 25%, percentage of students not playing basketball = 20% and percentage of students not playing carom = 15%. The minimum percentage of people playing all four would be got when we take each of these categories as distinct from each other. Thus, required answer $= 100 - 30 - 25 - 20 - 15 = 100 - 90 = 10$.

4. $b$ = The probability that neither of the cards is a king is given by:

First is not a king and second is not a king $= 4/6 \times 3/5 = 12/30 = 2/5 = 0.4$

$a$ = The probability that at least one card drawn is a king = the non-event of both are not kings $= 1 - 0.4 = 0.6$

$a/b = 0.6/0.4 = 1.5$. Looking through the options, only the Option (e) fits the situation i.e. $a/b \geq 1.25$. Hence, Option (e) is the correct answer.

5. Total paths $= {}^{20}C_2 = 190$

Let the maximum number of candidates be '$n$'. Since each candidate must visit 20 cities during his campaign, these $n$ candidates will use $20n$ roads.

Thus, $20n < 190$ or $n < 9.5$

So the maximum possible value of $n = 9$.

6. The following deductions can be made based on the information provided:

(a) Number of students who study Financial Derivatives and Security Analysis but not Behavioural Finance $= 4 \times$ those who study all three $= 4 \times 4 = 16$

(b) Number of students who study both Financial Derivatives and Behavioural Finance but not Security Analysis $= 16/2 = 8$

(c) Total students who study at least one of the given three subjects $= 240 - 59 = 181$.

Now we can draw the Venn diagram as follows:

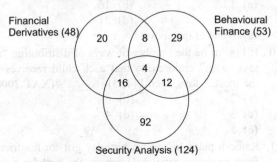

From the above Venn diagram we can find there are a total of 29 students who study Behavioral Finance only.

7. $x_1 x_2 x_3 x_4 x_5 x_6 x_7$ can be of the form PQRSPQR or PQRPQRS. PQR can be chosen in $10 \times 10 \times 10 = 1000$ ways.

S can be chosen in 10 ways.

$x_1 x_2 x_3 x_4 x_5 x_6 x_7$ can be formed in $2 \times 1000 \times 10 = 20000$ ways. However, we would need to modify this answer, as there is some extra counting in this. There are essentially two things you need to take care of: (i) The number 20000000 has been counted twice, whereas it should not be counted at all, since it is not a valid number. Hence, we would need to reduce the count by 2.

(ii) The numbers 21111111, 22222222, 23333333, ..., 29999999 have each been counted twice, while they should be counted only once each. Thus, we would need to reduce the count by 9.

Hence, the correct answer would be: 20000 − 2 − 9 = 19989.

8. The unit digit is a prime number so it can only be either 2, 3, 5 or 7.

   Now if the product of all four digit is prime, then rest of the three digits other than the unit's digit has to be 1.

   Only 4 numbers 1112, 1113, 1115, 1117 are possible.

9. Let the four digit number be 'AAAB' or 'BAAA'

   Since the number has to be a multiple of 9, therefore, $3A + B$ should either be 9, 18 or 27.

   **Case a:** $3A + B = 9$

   Possible numbers: (1116, 6111, 2223, 3222, 3330, 9000)

   **Case b:** $3A + B = 18$

   Possible number: (3339, 9333, 4446, 6444, 5553, 3555, 6660)

   **Case 3:** $3A + B = 27$

   Possible number: (6669, 9666, 8883, 3888, 7776, 6777, 9990)

   Hence, 20 numbers are possible.

10. $F(4, 3)$ is the number of ways of distributing 4 toys among 3 children. Each child can get either 0 or 1 or 2 toys. The 4 toys can be distributed among three children in 6 ways (1,1,2; 1,2,1; 2,1,1; 0,2,2; 2,0,2; 2,2,0)

11. Probability that Ramesh doesn't receive the gift from A on time = 1 − 0.6 = 0.4

    Probability that Ramesh doesn't receive the gift from B on time = 1 − 0.8 = 0.2

    Probability that Ramesh doesn't receive the gift from C on time = 1 − 0.9 = 0.1

    Probability that Ramesh doesn't receive the gift from D on time = 1 − 0.5 = 0.5

    Probability that Ramesh doesn't receive the gift on time from any of the four retailers = 0.4 × 0.2 × 0.1 × 0.5 = 0.004

    Probability that Ramesh's friend would receive the gift in time = 1 − 0.004 = 0.996

12. We can start by thinking of this problem using the following Venn diagram:

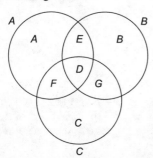

Based on the clues given to us in the problem, we can make the following deductions in the same order:

(a) $D + G = 0$ OR $D = G = 0$
(b) $F + D = 25$ OR $F = 25$
(c) $E + D = 22$ OR $E = 22$
(d) $A + E + D + F = 77$ OR $A = 30$
(e) $B + E + D + G = 55$ OR $B = 33$
    $C + F + D + G = 50$ OR $C = 25$

According to the question 40 did not opt for A and B or both that means 40 did not opt for any ride or opt ride for C. Required Sum = $A + B + C + D + E + F + G = 30 + 33 + 40 + 0 + 25 + 22 + 0 = 150$.

13. Total possible cases = 36

    Total favourable cases = 5 (when the first number rolled is 1) + 4(when the first number rolled is 2) + 3(when the first number rolled is 3) + 2(when the first number rolled is 4) + 1(when the first number rolled is 5) = 15

    Required probability = 15/36. Option (c).

14.

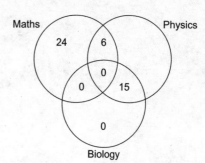

From the information about the average score in English for students majoring in Mathematics and Biology, we can deduce that the number of students in Mathematics and Biology must be in the ratio 2:1 (Using Alligation). Then, in order to maximize the number of people who would major Only in Physics, we would need to minimize all the other areas of the Venn diagram.

Thus, we put Only Biology as 0 and Only Maths as 24 (so that Math: Biology = 30:15 = 2:1).

In this case, we get the maximum possible number of students who major only in Physics = 60 − 30 − 15 = 15.